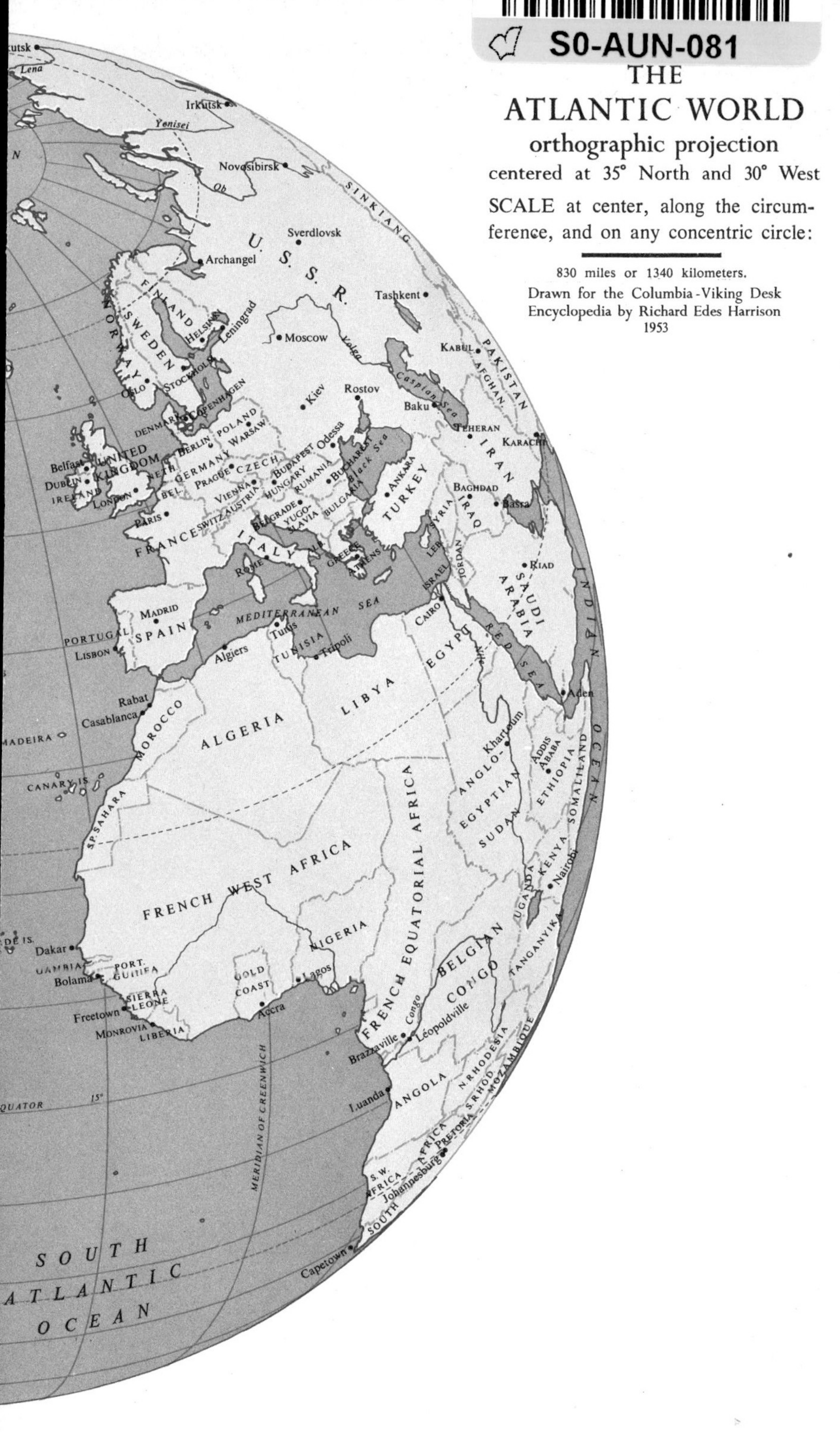
THE
ATLANTIC WORLD
orthographic projection
centered at 35° North and 30° West
SCALE at center, along the circumference, and on any concentric circle:
830 miles or 1340 kilometers.
Drawn for the Columbia-Viking Desk Encyclopedia by Richard Edes Harrison
1953
Lena
Irkutsk
Yenisei
Novosibirsk
Ob
SINKIANG
Sverdlovsk
U. S. S. R.
Archangel
Tashkent
FINLAND
SWEDEN
NORWAY
Helsinki
Leningrad
Moscow
Volga
Kabul
PAKISTAN
AFGHAN.
Caspian Sea
Oslo
Stockholm
Copenhagen
Kiev
Rostov
Baku
Teheran
Karachi
DENMARK
POLAND
Warsaw
Odessa
IRAN
Belfast
UNITED KINGDOM
Dublin
IRELAND
London
Berlin
GERMANY
NETH.
BEL.
Prague
CZECH.
Budapest
HUNGARY
RUMANIA
Bucharest
Black Sea
Ankara
TURKEY
Baghdad
IRAQ
Basra
Paris
Vienna
AUSTRIA
SWITZ.
Belgrade
YUGOSLAVIA
BULGARIA
FRANCE
ITALY
Rome
GREECE
Athens
SYRIA
LEB.
JORDAN
ISRAEL
Riad
SAUDI ARABIA
INDIAN OCEAN
Madrid
SPAIN
PORTUGAL
Lisbon
MEDITERRANEAN SEA
Algiers
Tunis
TUNISIA
Tripoli
Cairo
EGYPT
Nile
RED SEA
Aden
Rabat
Casablanca
MOROCCO
ALGERIA
LIBYA
MADEIRA
CANARY IS.
Khartoum
ANGLO-EGYPTIAN SUDAN
Addis Ababa
ETHIOPIA
SOMALILAND
SP. SAHARA
FRENCH WEST AFRICA
FRENCH EQUATORIAL AFRICA
KENYA
Nairobi
UGANDA
NIGERIA
Dakar
GAMBIA
PORT. GUINEA
Bolama
GOLD COAST
Lagos
SIERRA LEONE
Freetown
Monrovia
LIBERIA
Accra
BELGIAN CONGO
TANGANYIKA
Congo
Léopoldville
Brazzaville
MERIDIAN OF GREENWICH
N. RHODESIA
MOZAMBIQUE
S. RHOD.
ANGOLA
Luanda
EQUATOR
15°
PRETORIA
S. W. AFRICA
Johannesburg
SOUTH AFRICA
SOUTH ATLANTIC OCEAN
Capetown

THE COLUMBIA-VIKING DESK ENCYCLOPEDIA

L – Z

VOLUME TWO

THE COLUMBIA-VIKING DESK ENCYCLOPEDIA

Compiled and edited at Columbia University
by the staff of The Columbia Encyclopedia
WILLIAM BRIDGWATER, Editor-in-chief

L – Z

VOLUME TWO

PUBLISHED BY THE VIKING PRESS
NEW YORK

PUBLISHED IN OCTOBER 1953 BY THE VIKING PRESS, INC.
18 EAST 48 STREET, NEW YORK, N. Y.

PRINTED IN THE UNITED STATES OF AMERICA

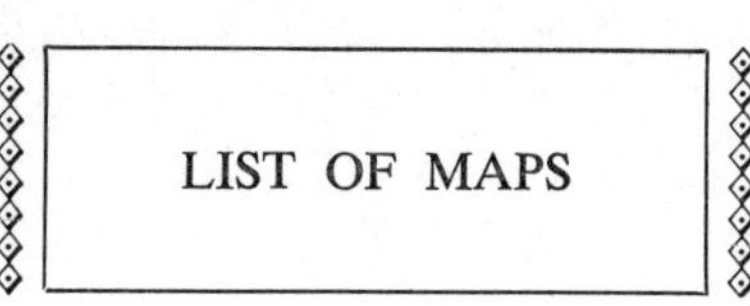

LIST OF MAPS

MAPS

As a rule the articles on places do not give cross references to maps; but countries, principal cities, large rivers, and many other geographic features may be located on the maps of their respective continents

WORLD MAPS

CONTINENT MAPS

LIST OF ILLUSTRATIONS

Grouped under subject headings for convenient comparison of related material. A number of subjects have been included in the illustrations, though not in the text, when it was felt that a picture served the purpose better than words

List of Illustrations

TABLES AND LISTS

TABLES

The following data are arranged in tabular form

LISTS

Some of the ready-reference material in the text is located as follows

PRONUNCIATION KEY

PRONUNCIATION KEY

NOTES

The purpose of the pronunciation symbols is to give at least one serviceable way in which the word in question may be pronounced when used by careful speakers of English.

In this work a pronunciation is ordinarily indicated for words printed in boldface when this pronunciation is not obvious to the English-speaking reader. Of two or more words or names in succession spelled and pronounced alike, a pronunciation is frequently indicated for the first occurrence only.

For names of localities in English-speaking areas the local pronunciation is preferred, provided it is acceptable to careful speakers.

For foreign words and names the speaker of English desires to use a pronunciation that will be acceptable to other speakers of English (unless he is speaking in a foreign language). In many cases (e.g., Paris) there is a traditional pronunciation that resembles little the current native pronunciation, and attempts to introduce into English conversation an approximation of the native form (something like pärē′) are regarded as an affectation. It is customary with foreign names that have no conventional English form to pronounce them with English sounds approximating the foreign ones. Such an approximation is indicated in this work, whenever there is no established usage to follow.

Actual good foreign-language pronunciations can be acquired only through imitation and study. Nevertheless, Englishmen and Americans have for many years made a practice of imitating roughly five French sounds: ã, ẽ, õ, ũ, and ü. A speaker of English can attain ã by saying äng without the closure at the back of the mouth necessary to make ng, breathing through nose and mouth as well; ẽ is similarly like the beginning of ăng, õ like that of ōng, and ũ like that of ûng. To approximate ü say o͞o with vigor, then, keeping the lips rounded, change the sound quickly to ē.

For Latin words the venerable English tradition is followed [e.g., Caesar (sē′zůr)], except where some other pronunciation is well established, as in ecclesiastical names [e.g., Salve Regina (säl′vā rājē′nů)]. The so-called classical pronunciation, which approximates the pronunciation Caesar used [e.g., Caesar (kī′sär)], is not given, as being not usual in English conversation.

Pronunciation Key

- ā — f*a*te (fāt), f*ai*l (fāl), v*a*cation (vākā′shu̇n)
- â — c*a*re (kâr), M*a*ry (mâ′rē)
- ă — b*a*t (băt), *a*dd (ăd), m*a*rry (mă′rē)
- ä — f*a*ther (fä′dhu̇r), m*a*rble (mär′bu̇l)
- ã — French t*an*t (tã), Rou*en* (ro͞oã′), and similar sounds in some other languages
- b — *b*ack (băk), ca*b* (kăb)
- ch — *ch*ap (chăp)
- d — *d*ock (dŏk), co*d* (kŏd)
- dh — fa*th*er (fä′dhu̇r), *th*en (dhĕn). Compare with th.
- ē — *e*ven (ē′vu̇n), cl*ea*ring (klēr′ĭng), obv*i*ous (ŏb′vēu̇s)
- ĕ — *e*nd (ĕnd), m*e*t (mĕt), m*e*rry (mĕ′rē)
- ẽ — French v*in* (vẽ), bi*en* (byẽ), and similar sounds in some other languages
- f — *f*at (făt), *Ph*ilip (fĭ′lĭp)
- g — *g*et (gĕt), ta*g* (tăg)
- h — *h*at (hăt). See also ch, dh, kh, sh, th, zh, and hw
- hw — *wh*ere (hwâr), *wh*at (hwŏt)
- ī — f*i*ne (fīn), b*uy*er (bī′u̇r)
- ĭ — p*i*n (pĭn), p*i*t (pĭt), sp*i*r*i*t (spĭrĭt), fat*e*d (fā′tĭd)
- j — *j*am (jăm), e*dg*e (ĕj), *g*inger (jĭn′ju̇r)
- k — coo*k* (ko͝ok), ta*ck*le (tă′ku̇l)
- kh — lo*ch* (lŏkh), German Aa*ch*en (ä′khu̇n), Li*ch*t (lĭkht), and similar sounds in some other languages
- l — pea*l* (pēl), pu*ll* (po͝ol)
- m — ha*mm*er (hă′mu̇r)
- n — di*nn*er (dĭ′nu̇r)
- ng — si*ngi*ng (sĭng′ĭng), fi*ng*er (fĭng′gu̇r), sa*ng* (săng), sa*n*k (săngk)
- ō — h*o*pe (hōp), potat*o* (pu̇tā′tō)
- ô — *o*rbit (ôr′bĭt), f*a*ll (fôl)
- ŏ — h*o*t (hŏt), t*o*ddy (tŏ′dē), b*o*rrow (bŏ′rō)
- õ — French d*on*t (dõ), chans*on* (shãsõ′), and similar sounds in some other languages
- oi — bo*i*l (boil), r*oy*al (roi′u̇l)
- o͞o — b*oo*t (bo͞ot), l*o*se (lo͞oz)
- o͝o — f*oo*t (fo͝ot), p*u*rely (pyo͝or′lē), manip*u*late (mu̇nĭ′pyo͝olāt)
- ou — sc*ou*t (skout), cr*ow*d (kroud)
- p — *p*i*p*e (pīp), ha*pp*y (hă′pē)
- r — *r*oad (rōd), appea*r*ed (u̇pērd′), ca*r*pente*r* (kär′pu̇ntu̇r)
- s — *s*aw (sô), ca*s*e (kās)
- sh — *sh*all (shăl), na*ti*on (nā′shu̇n)
- t — *t*igh*t* (tīt), ra*t*ing (rā′tĭng)
- th — *th*in (thĭn), my*th* (mĭth). Compare with dh.
- ū — f*u*me (fūm), *eu*phemism (ū′fu̇mĭzm)
- û — c*u*rl (kûrl), Hamb*u*rg (hăm′bûrg), French *œu*vre (û′vru̇), p*eu* (pû), German sch*ö*n (shûn), G*oe*the (gû′tu̇), and similar sounds in some other languages
- ŭ — b*u*tter (bŭ′tu̇r), s*u*ds (sŭdz), h*u*rry (hŭ′rē)
- u̇ — *a*ffair (u̇fâr′), sof*a* (sō′fu̇), contr*a*vene (kŏntru̇vēn′), m*o*nop*o*ly (mu̇nŏ′pu̇lē), s*u*burb*a*n (su̇bûr′bu̇n), call*ou*s (kă′lu̇s), rath*e*r (ră′dhu̇r)
- ü — French Cl*u*ny (klünē′) German L*ü*beck (lü′bĕk), and similar sounds in some other languages
- ũ — French Mel*un* (mu̇lũ′), Chambr*un* (shãbrũ′), and similar sounds in some other languages
- v — *v*est (vĕst), tri*v*ial (trĭ′vēu̇l)
- w — *w*ax (wăks)
- y — *y*ou (yo͞o), bun*io*n (bŭ′nyu̇n)
- z — *z*ipper (zĭ′pu̇r), ea*s*e (ēz), tread*s* (trĕdz)
- zh — plea*s*ure (plĕ′zhu̇r), rou*g*e (ro͞ozh)

- ′ — main accent, written after accented vowel or syllable: Nebraska (nu̇bră′sku̇), James Buchanan (jāmz′ būkă′nu̇n)
- ″ — secondary accent: Mississippi (mĭ″su̇sĭ′pē)
- – — dash, replacing obvious portion of pronunciation: hegemony (hĭjĕ′mu̇nē, hē–, hĕ′ju̇mō″nē, hĕ′gu̇–)
- - — hyphen, to prevent ambiguity: Erlanger (ûr′lăng-u̇r), dishearten (dĭs-här′tu̇n)

Note

The List of Maps, List of Illustrations, Tables and Lists found in the front of Volume I and the Pronunciation Key and Notes from pages xiv and xv in Volume I have been duplicated in the front of this volume for easy reference.

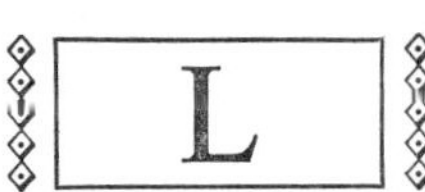

La. For names beginning thus and not listed here, see second element; e.g., for La Guaira, see GUAIRA, LA.

La, chemical symbol of the element LANTHANUM.

Laaland or **Lolland** (both: lô'län), low island (479 sq. mi.; pop. 87,150), Denmark, in Baltic Sea, S of Zealand. Sugar beets are main crop. Nakskov and Maribo are chief cities.

Labadie, Jean de, or **Jean de la Badie** (zhã' dü lä bädē'), 1610–74, French mystic. A Catholic priest, he became a Protestant minister (c.1650). In Holland he estab. the Labadists, a religious community dedicated to simple living, holding goods and children in common. Movement was dead by 1732.

Laban (lā'–), father of Leah and Rachel, uncle of Jacob. Gen. 24.29–60; 29–31.

Labé, Louise (lwēz' läbā'), c.1520–1566, French poet. Her sonnets and elegies are outstanding love poems.

Labiche, Eugène (ûzhĕn' läbēsh'), 1815–88, French playwright. His best-known comedy is the farcical *Le Voyage de M. Perrichon* (with Édouard Martin, 1860).

La Boétie, Étienne de (ātyĕn' dü lä bôäsē'), 1530–63, French judge, remembered for his friendship with Montaigne and as author of a fiery and original attack on despotism, *Discours sur la servitude volontaire; ou, Contr'un* (Eng. tr., *Anti-Dictator,* 1942).

labor, term used both for the effort of performing a task and for the social group doing the work. In the ancient world the status of labor was low, since most physical work was done by slaves. During the feudal period, skilled artisans were influential citizens. With the introduction of machinery, status of labor was again depressed. Since 19th cent., labor has become organized (see UNION, LABOR) so as to bargain collectively with employers and to place pressure on governments. See STRIKE, CHILD LABOR, MIGRATORY LABOR, SLAVERY.

labor, in medicine: see BIRTH.

labor, hours of. Until the Industrial Revolution, the work day varied from 11 to 14 hr. With the growth of capitalism and the introduction of machinery, longer hours began to prevail. The great competition for work forced workers to accept whatever conditions employers imposed. A day of 16 hr. was not uncommon, with 14 to 15 hr. the accepted working day. First law on the length of a working day was passed (1833) in England, limiting miners to 12 hr. and children under 13 to 8 hr. The 10-hr. day was legally established in 1848, and shorter hours at the same pay were achieved gradually thereafter. In the U.S., the 8-hr. day was generally accepted by 1912. The WAGES AND HOURS ACT of 1938 recognizes 40 hrs. as the maximum ordinary work week.

Labor, United States Department of, organized in 1913 under Secretary of Labor by act of U.S. Congress. Began in 1884 as Bureau of Labor in U.S. Dept. of Interior. Department includes following major units: Bureau of Labor Statistics; Women's Bureau; U.S. Employment Service; Bureau of Labor Standards; Bureau of Apprenticeship; Wage and Hour and Public Contracts Divisions; Bureau of Veterans' Reemployment Rights.

Labor Day, holiday celebrated in U.S. and Canada on first Monday in Sept. to honor the workingman.

labor law, legislation dealing with workers. The earliest English factory law dealt (1802) with the health, safety, and morals of child textile workers. Labor unions were legalized in 1825, but agreements among their members to seek better hours and wages were punishable as conspiracy until 1871. In the U.S., the Norris-LaGuardia act (1932) outlawed the use of injunctions in labor disputes, the Wagner Act (establishing the NATIONAL LABOR RELATIONS BOARD; 1935) required employers to accept collective bargaining, and the WAGES AND HOURS ACT (1938) set up minimum standards of hours and wages in basic industries; the TAFT-HARTLEY LABOR ACT (1947) sharply modified the acts of 1932 and 1935 and introduced an 80-day injunction procedure in labor disputes affecting the national welfare.

Labor Relations Act: see NATIONAL LABOR RELATIONS BOARD; TAFT-HARTLEY LABOR ACT.

labor union: see UNION, LABOR.

La Bourdonnais, Bertrand François Mahé de (bĕrtrã' frãswä' mäā' dü lä bōōrdônā'), 1699–1753, French naval officer in service of

French India Co. Captured Madras (1746). After a quarrel with Dupleix he was recalled, tried for treason, and acquitted.

Labour party, British political party. Founded in 1900 as result of long history of trade-union activity that became effective after Reform Act (1867) enfranchised the urban workers. Aided by Fabian Society (founded 1883). Until 1918 it was a federation of trade unions and socialist groups, with no individual members. Split in World War I over British participation in the war. Ramsay MACDONALD became first Labour prime minister in 1924. After domestic reforms, recognition of USSR, and peace efforts in the Ruhr, he was overthrown over a forged letter supposedly written by Grigori Zinoviev. Labour was returned to power in 1929. Hampered by deepening economic crisis, MacDonald formed (1931) a coalition ministry and was read from the party. Moving to the left, party advocated nationalization of industries and opposition to any foreign war. By 1937 new leaders were Herbert Morrison, Ernest BEVIN and Clement ATTLEE. Intellectual leaders were Hugh Dalton and Harold Laski. Labour entered coalition government in World War II. Won 1945 elections; Attlee became prime minister. Passed national health bill, nationalized important industries, and estab. the dominions of India and Pakistan (1947). The 1951 election restored Conservatives to power. Left wing of party, headed by Aneurin Bevan, has been challenging moderate leadership of Attlee.

Labrador (lă'brŭdôr″), dependency of NEWFOUNDLAND, E Canada (c.110,000 sq. mi.; pop. 7,890), at mouth of Gulf of St. Lawrence; cap. Battle Harbour. Population (largely Algonquin Indians and Eskimo) scattered along Atlantic coast with a few white settlers in fishing villages and missions (e.g., Carteret, Battle Harbour, Rigolet, Hopedale, Nain). Icy Labrador Current and lack of transportation facilities discourage settlement and development of mineral and hydroelectric resources. Probably explored by Vikings c.1000, and later by Cabot (1498), Corte Real (1500), and Cartier (1534). Became British after Treaty of Paris (1763), with jurisdiction given to N.F. 1763–64 and again in 1809. Moravian missions, estab. in 1760s, shared fur trade with Hudson's Bay Co., which virtually controlled peninsula until 1870. Claims to NE peninsula (called Ungava) settled 1927 by British Privy Council.

Labrador Current: see OCEAN CURRENTS.

labradorite (lă'brŭdôrīt″), variety of FELDSPAR, usually gray, brown, or green. Some varieties showing color play of red, yellow, blue, green (labradorescence) are used for decorative purposes.

La Brea (lŭ brā'ŭ), area in Los Angeles, S Calif. Tar pits here yielded prehistoric remains.

La Bruyère, Jean de (zhã' dŭ lä brüyĕr'), 1645–96, French writer; tutor at the house of the prince de Condé. His great work is *Les Caractères* (1688), in small part translations of THEOPHRASTUS, but mainly a series of brilliant character sketches, maxims, and short essays. Though he applied his strong moral views to the contemporary scene, he was a detached observer, rather than a reformer.

Labuan (lŭbōō'ŭn), island (35 sq. mi.; pop. 8,500), off NW Borneo, attached to British colony of North Borneo since 1946.

laburnum (lŭbûr'nŭm), small ornamental tree (*Laburnum anagyroides*), native to Europe, widely grown in U.S. It has sprays of yellow flowers in spring.

lac (lăk), resinous exudate from bodies of female scale insects from which SHELLAC is prepared. Insects feed on sap of trees, which form resinous secretion around bodies of female and young. Crude material is sticklac. When purified and red coloring is removed, it is seed-lac from which shellac is made. Red coloring is sometimes used as dye and pigment.

Lacaille, Nicolas Louis de (nēkôlä' lwē dŭ läkä'yŭ), 1713–62, French astronomer, noted for calculations. Recorded positions of many stars of S Hemisphere.

Laccadive Islands (lă'kŭdīv), group of coral atolls (10 sq. mi.; pop. 18,355), in Arabian Sea, off Malabar Coast of India; part of Madras state.

lace, patterned openwork fabric made by hand or by machine. General types of handmade laces include needlepoint, bobbin lace, tatting, and crochet work. Needlepoint, the most costly, is worked with a needle in variations of the buttonhole stitch; Venetian point or *punto in aria* developed in Italy from reticella cutwork. From the early laces patterned in France after Venetian point, developed *point de France;* among later French laces are Alençon, Argentan, and Valenciennes. Brussels is a name used for either needlepoint or bobbin lace of a certain style. Pillow, bone, or bobbin lace, woven with bobbins, includes *point d'Angleterre* (similar to Flemish point), Valenciennes (fine, diamond-meshed), Mechlin (very filmy), torchon (simple and loose), Honiton (English lace with net foundation and appliqués of delicate braid), duchesse (exquisite patterns, with much raised work), Maltese (coarse), and Chantilly (delicate mesh, ornate patterns). Crocheted lace reached its finest development in Ireland. There are also knitted laces and those made by knotting (e.g., tatting, macramé). Machine-made lace dates from late 18th cent.

Lacedaemon (lăsŭdē'mŭn), in Greek mythology, ruler of LACONIA or Lacedaemon; son of Zeus. He gave his capital the name of his wife, Sparta.

La Chaise, François d'Aix de (frãswä' dāks' dŭ lä shĕz'), 1624–1709, French Jesuit, confessor of Louis XIV. Held considerable influence. Père-Lachaise cemetery in Paris is named for him.

Lachaise, Gaston (läshāz'), 1882–1935, American sculptor, b. Paris. Famous for his female nudes.

Lachesis, one of the FATES.

Lachine (lŭshēn'), city (pop. 27,773), S Que., Canada, on Montreal Isl., at E end of L. St. Louis; settled 1675. Iron and steel founding and mfg. of tires, wires, and tiles. Is SW terminus of **Lachine Canal** connecting L. St. Louis and St. Lawrence R. at Montreal (opened 1825).

Lachish (lā'kĭsh), anc. Amorite city, S Palestine. Captured by Joshua; later besieged by Sennacherib.

Lachute (lùshōōt'), town (pop. 6,179), SW Que., Canada, on North R. and W of Montreal. Woolen and paper mills, lumbering, and dairying.

Lackawanna (lăkùwä'nù), city (pop. 27,658), W N.Y., on L. Erie S of Buffalo. Iron and steel. Has Our Lady of Victory basilica, charitable institutions.

Lackawanna, river rising in NE Pa. and flowing 50 mi. SSW through anthracite region to Susquehanna R. near Pittston.

Laclede, Pierre (pyĕr' läklĕd'), c.1724–1778, French pioneer in U.S. As fur trader with René Auguste CHOUTEAU, helped found St. Louis (1763–64).

Laclos, (Pierre) Choderlos de (pyĕr' shôdĕrlō' dù läklō'), 1741–1803, French author and general. His savage novel of manners, *Les Liaisons dangereuses* (1782; Eng. tr., *Dangerous Acquaintances,* 1924), had great influence.

Lac Mégantic, Que.: see MÉGANTIC.

Lacombe (lùkōm'), town (pop. 2,277), S central Alta., Canada, S of Edmonton. A dominion government experimental farm is here.

Laconia (lùkō'nēù) or **Lacedaemon** (lăsùdē'mùn), anc. region, S Peloponnesus, Greece. On the Eurotas, the main river, stood SPARTA, the cap.

Laconia, city (pop. 14,745), central N.H., N of Concord. Resort center. Hosiery, textile machinery, and wood products. Holds annual international dog-sled derby. To N are Lakeport, hq. of U.S. mail boat on L. Winnipesaukee, and The Weirs, resort.

Lacordaire, Jean Baptiste Henri (zhã' bätēst' ãrē' läcôrdĕr'), 1802–61, French Roman Catholic preacher. A liberal, he was a collaborator of LAMENNAIS, but after the pope condemned the liberal program, he submitted. Later he was a famed preacher at Notre Dame in Paris; joined the Dominicans (1840). Favored the Revolution of 1848 and went into exile after coup d'état of Napoleon III.

Lacoste, René (rùnā' läkôst'), 1905–, French tennis player. Member French team that won Davis Cup, 1927.

La Crosse (lù krôs), city (pop. 47,535), W Wis., on the Mississippi (bridged) at confluence of Black and La Crosse rivers, in dairy area. Site of late 18th cent. fur-trading post. Mfg. of farm equipment, air-conditioning systems, and rubber footwear. Park has U.S. fish hatchery.

lacrosse (lùkrôs'), national sport of Canada since 1867. Played by two teams of 10 players on grass-covered playing field 60 to 70 yd. wide by 110 yd. long. Lacrosse gained following in U.S. after 1880s, particularly in North Atlantic states. Women's lacrosse team has 12 players.

La Cruz, Ramón de: see CRUZ, RAMÓN DE LA.

Lactantius (lăktăn'shùs), c.260–340, Christian apologist, b. Africa. Converted to Christianity, he became a member of Constantine's household. His writings on Christian doctrine and Christian history show his wide knowledge of pagan rhetoric and literature.

lactic acid, colorless organic acid, present in sour milk and formed in animals as result of muscle contraction. Usually prepared commercially by bacterial fermentation of glucose. Used in tanning and dyeing and in medicine.

lactose (lăk'tōs) or **milk sugar,** white crystalline carbohydrate with 12 carbon, 22 hydrogen, 11 oxygen atoms. It has the same formula as sucrose and maltose but differs in structure. Found in mammalian milk and cells of mammary gland, it is important in diet of young mammals. When hydrolyzed (by acid or enzyme) it yields glucose and galactose.

La Cueva, Juan de: see CUEVA, JUAN DE LA.

Ladd, William, 1778–1841, American peace advocate. He proposed (1840) plan for a world congress and court of nations.

Ladies' Peace: see CAMBRAI, TREATY OF.

Ladislas. For rulers thus named, see LADISLAUS; LANCELOT; ULADISLAUS.

Ladislaus, Hung. *László,* kings of Hungary. **Ladislaus I** (Saint Ladislaus), 1040–95, reigned 1077–95. Conquered Croatia 1091; compelled CUMANS to accept Christianity and allowed them to settle in certain parts of Hungary; reformed law code. Was noted for his valor and chivalry. **Ladislaus V** (Ladislaus Posthumus), 1440–57; posthumous son of the German king, Albert II. Duke of Austria by birth, he was claimed as king by the Bohemian diet and in 1444 was also elected king of Hungary, but his guardian, Emperor Frederick III, refused to let him leave his court until 1452. In 1453 he was crowned king of Bohemia and entered Hungary, but actual rule was exercised by GEORGE OF PODEBRAD in Bohemia and by John HUNYADI in Hungary.

Ladislaus, king of Naples: see LANCELOT.

Ladislaus, Pol. *Władysław,* kings of Poland. **Ladislaus I** (the Short), 1260–1333, crowned king 1320, restored unified Polish kingdom after 82 years of division. **Ladislaus II** or **Ladislaus Jagiello** (yägyĕ'lō), 1350?–1434, grand duke of Lithuania (1377–86), acceded to the Polish throne in 1386 by marrying Queen JADWIGA. He was baptized and converted Lithuania to Christianity. Though Lithuania was ruled by other members of the JAGIELLO dynasty (see WITOWT), Ladislaus' marriage was the basis of the eventual union of the Polish and Lithuanian nations. The victory over the Teutonic Knights at Tannenberg (1410) and the First Peace of TORUN (1411) were the main events of his reign. His son **Ladislaus III,** 1424–44, succeeded him in Poland and as Uladislaus I was elected king of Hungary (1440). He led two crusades against the Turks and was defeated and slain at Varna. The name also appears as Wladislaw, Wladyslav, and Wladislas.

Ladoga, Lake (lä'dōgù), largest lake in Europe, area c.7,000 sq. mi., S Karelo-Finnish SSR and NW European RSFSR, NE of Leningrad. Max. depth 732 ft. The Svir (from L. Onega), Vuoksi (from Saima lake system of Finland), and Volkhov (from L. Ilmen) are the main feeders; Neva R. is main outlet. Because of difficult navigation the S shore of L. Ladoga is paralleled by the Ladoga Canals, 100 mi. long, connecting Svir and Neva rivers. N shore belonged to Finland until its cession to USSR in 1940 (confirmed 1947). Valaam isl., in N part of lake, has famous Russian monastery dating from 12th cent.

ladybird or **ladybug,** beetle of the family Coccinellidae. It is oval, reddish, or yellow spotted with black or black spotted with red or yellow; most species eat aphids and other harmful insects. Australian ladybird was imported by U.S. to eat cottony-cushion scale which is destructive to citrus fruit. Injurious herbivorous species are the Mexican bean beetle and the squash beetle.

Lady Margaret Hall: see OXFORD UNIVERSITY.

Lady of the Lake: see ARTHURIAN LEGEND.

Ladysmith, town (pop. 14,221), W Natal, South Africa. Named for wife of Sir Harry Smith, governor of Cape Colony. British forces were besieged here, 1899–1900, during Boer War. Cotton milling.

lady's-slipper or **moccasin flower,** wild flower of genus *Cypripedium* of orchid family, native to north temperate zone. There are white-, yellow-, and pink-flowered species in North America.

Lae (lä'ĕ), town, on E New Guinea, Territory of New Guinea, on Huon Gulf. Serves air transport lines into near-by gold fields. Occupied 1942 by Japanese, regained 1943 by Allied forces.

Laënnec, René Théophile Hyacinthe (rùnā' tāôfēl' yäsĕt läänĕk'), 1781–1826, French physician. He invented the stethoscope and used it in diagnosis.

Laertes (lāûr'tēz), in Greek mythology, king of Ithaca; father of Odysseus. He joined the Calydonian hunt and was one of the Argonaut heroes.

La Farge, John (lù färzh'), 1835–1910, American artist, writer, and worker in stained glass. A man of wide culture, he did much to create a tradition of the fine arts in America. His grandson, **Oliver La Farge,** 1901–, writer and anthropologist, is best known for his novel, *Laughing Boy* (1929).

Lafayette or **La Fayette, Marie Joseph Paul Yves Roch Gilbert du Motier, marquis de** (märē' zhôzĕf' pôl' ēv' rôk zhĕlbĕr' dù môtyā' märkē' dù läfäyĕt'), 1757–1834, French general and statesman. Despite opposition by his government, he sailed for America in 1777 to join Washington's army. Was made major general by Congress; was wounded at Brandywine (1777) and was at Valley Forge. After a trip to France (1779–80), where he negotiated for French aid, he played a vital part in the YORKTOWN CAMPAIGN. Active in the French Revolution, he became commander of the National Guard (July 15, 1789) and in 1792 commanded an army. A moderate, he sought to save the monarchy but in his irresolution missed his opportunity, deserted his army, and was imprisoned in Austria (1792–97). His triumphal tour of the U.S. in 1824–25 has passed into legend. He also took part in the July Revolution.

La Fayette, Marie Madeleine Pioche de la Vergne, comtesse de (märē' mädùlĕn' pyôsh' dù lä vĕr'nyù, kōtĕs'), 1634–92, French novelist. Mme de La Fayette's classic masterpiece, *La Princesse de Clèves* (1678), was the first French psychological novel.

Lafayette (lă"fēĕt'). **1** City (pop. 35,568), W Ind., on Wabash R. and NW of Indianapolis; settled 1825. Agr. grain and livestock center. Mfg. of rubber, paper, and metal products. Battle of TIPPECANOE fought near by, Nov., 1811. Seat of PURDUE UNIVERSITY. **2** City (pop. 33,541), S La., on Vermilion R. N of Vermilion Bay; laid out c.1824 by Acadians. Shipping and commercial center for agr. and mineral area, it has sugar refineries, cotton and cottonseed-oil processing plants, machine and railroad shops, and creameries. Seat of Southwestern Louisiana Inst. (coed.; 1898).

Lafayette, Mount: see FRANCONIA MOUNTAINS.

Lafayette College: see EASTON, Pa.

Lafayette Escadrille (ĕskùdrĭl'), group of American volunteer aviators in World War I in French air service. In Jan., 1918, outfit was reorganized in U.S. army as 103d Pursuit squadron.

Laffite or **Lafitte, Jean** (both: zhã' läfēt'), c.1780–c.1825, leader of a band of privateersmen and smugglers. Preyed on Spanish commerce off La. and Texas. Aided U.S. in battle of New Orleans.

La Follette, Robert M(arion) (lùfŏ'lĭt), 1855–1925, American statesman. Under his governorship of Wis. reform legislation known as Wisconsin Idea was instituted. As U.S. Senator (1906–25) he took courageous, independent stands; supported reform, opposed both war measures and international peace bodies. As PROGRESSIVE PARTY presidential candidate in 1924 he polled 5,000,000 votes. Known as "Fighting Bob" La Follette. His wife, **Belle Case La Follette,** 1859–1931, was an ardent feminist and able adviser to her husband. Their older son, **Robert M(arion) La Follette, Jr.,** 1895–1953, U.S. Senator (1925–47), generally backed New Deal legislation. Another son, **Philip (Fox) La Follette,** 1897–, was governor of Wis. (1931–33, 1935–39).

La Follette (lù fŏl'ĭt), city (pop. 5,797), E Tenn., on Norris L. and NNW of Knoxville at E base of Cumberland Plateau. Coal-mining center.

La Fontaine, Henri (ãrē' läfōtĕn'), 1854–1943, Belgian jurist. Headed Internatl. Peace Bureau from 1907; was awarded 1913 Nobel Peace Prize.

La Fontaine, Jean de (zhã' dù), 1621–95, French poet, author of the famous *Fables choisies* (1668–94), 12 books of c.230 fables. Their material is largely based on Aesop, Phaedrus, and other classics (see FABLE), but La Fontaine's subtle originality, exquisite charm, and perfection of verse place him beside Molière and Racine. As a poet of nature, he stands unique in 17th-cent. French literature. Though popular with children, his fables are essentially satires, sometimes bitter and cynical, always sophisticated; their appeal is universal. Other works include *Contes et nouvelles en vers* (1664), imitations in verse of Boccaccio and Ariosto.

LaFontaine, Sir Louis Hippolyte, 1807–64, Canadian statesman. Formed the Baldwin-LaFontaine ministry (1842–43) with Robert Baldwin. Second Baldwin-LaFontaine ministry (1848–51) was notable for its reforms and achievement of responsible government.

Laforgue, Jules (zhül' läfôrg'), 1860–87, French poet, one of the SYMBOLISTS.

Lafourche, Bayou (bī'ō läfōōsh', bī'ōō), SE La., flowing to Gulf of Mexico. Former Mississippi R. outlet, now dammed at Donaldsonville.

Lagan (lă'gŭn), river of N. Ireland, rising in Co. Down and flowing 45 mi. to Belfast Lough at Belfast.

Lagash (lā'găsh) or **Shirpurla** (shĭrpōōr'lŭ), anc. city of SUMER, S Babylonia. Flourished c.3000 B.C., rivaled Kish and Umma until it was destroyed, and rose to new supremacy under Gudea (c.2450 B.C.).

Lagerkvist, Par (Fabian) (pâr' fä'bēän lä'gŭrkvĭst), 1891–, Swedish poet, dramatist, and novelist. His writings reflect his interest in political and social problems; his verse has had a marked influence on Swedish poetry. Among his novels are *The Dwarf* (1944) and *Barabbas* (1950). Awarded the 1951 Nobel Prize in Literature.

Lagerlof, Selma, Swed. *Lagerlöf* (lä'gŭrlûv), 1858–1940, Swedish novelist. Winner of 1909 Nobel Prize in Literature, she was also the first woman to be elected (1914) to the Swedish academy. Popular stories (many laid in Varmland prov.) are *The Story of Gosta Berling* (1894), *The Ring of the Lowenskolds* (1931), and *The Wonderful Adventures of Nils* (1906).

Lagos (lä'gōs), city (pop. 90,193), cap. of Nigeria, port on lagoon just off Gulf of Guinea. Comprises Lagos and Iddo isls. and a mainland section. Notorious slave market from 18th to mid-19th cent. Ceded 1861 to British. In 1886 Lagos and surrounding area became self-governing colony and protectorate, which in 1906 was combined with protectorate of Southern Nigeria. Exports include palm oil and cacao.

Lagos (lä'gōōsh), city (pop. 6,938), SW Portugal, in Algarve, on the Atlantic. It was the starting point of Portuguese explorers at the time of Henry the Navigator and now harbors important sardine and tuna fishing fleets.

La Grande (lä grănd'), city (pop. 8,635), NE Oregon, E of Blue Mts. and SE of Pendleton. Processes and ships fruit, livestock, lumber; rail shops.

Lagrange, Joseph Louis, Comte (zhôzĕf' lwē' kōt lägrãzh'), 1736–1813, French mathematician and astronomer, b. Turin. Calculus of variations is in part based on his method of solving isoperimetrical problems; he also made notable contributions in application of differential calculus to theory of probabilities and in solution of equations. He made studies on the libration of the moon and on satellites of Jupiter and made calculations of the motions of the planets.

La Grange (lŭ grānj'). **1** City (pop. 25,025), W Ga., SW of Atlanta near Chattahoochee R. Textile center, with sawmills. La Grange Col. is here. City was a center of state-wide textile strike, 1934. **2** Residential village (pop. 12,002), NE Ill., W suburb of Chicago; settled in 1830s. Aluminum products.

LaGuardia, Fiorello H(enry) (fēūrĕ'lō lŭgwär'dēŭ), 1882–1947, U.S. Congressman (1917–19, 1923–33) and Fusion mayor of New York city (1934–45). Fought for labor reforms in Congress. Executed vast program of municipal improvement. Because of his first name jocularly called "the Little Flower."

LaGuardia Field: see QUEENS, New York city borough.

Laguna (lŭgōō'nŭ), Indian pueblo village (1948 pop. 2,932), W central N.Mex., W of Albuquerque. Most recent of N.Mex. pueblos; founded 1699. Western Keresan language. Annual feast to San José.

Laguna Beach (lŭgōō'nŭ), residential and resort city (pop. 6,661), S Calif., SE of Los Angeles. Artists' colony.

Laguna District [Span.,= lake, so called from shallow lakes on plain], irrigated area (c.900,000 acres), E Durango and W Coahuila, Mexico. Land was redistributed (1936) on *ejido* system by Lázaro Cárdenas.

La Halle, Adam de: see ADAM DE LA HALLE.

La Hire (lä ēr'), c.1390–c.1443, French commander in Hundred Years War; real name Étienne de Vignolles. Helped Joan of Arc in victory of Patay (1429).

La Hire or **La Hyre, Laurent de** (both: lä ēr'), 1606–56, French portrait and historical painter.

Lahontan, Louis Armand, baron de (läōtã'), 1666–c.1713, French explorer in America. His admiration of Indian life influenced European thought.

Lahontan, Lake (lŭhŏn'tŭn, läōtã'), extinct lake of enormous size in W Nev. and NE Calif. Brought into existence by glacial age, it vanished soon after Pleistocene epoch; several lakes in Nev. are remnants. Area rich in fossils.

Lahore (lŭhôr'), city (pop. 849,000), cap. of Punjab prov., W Pakistan. Flourished under Mogul rule, 16th–17th cent. Was Sikh cap. in 19th cent. Notable remains of Moslem art are palace of Jahangir and Shalimar gardens (1667). Punjab Univ. and famed museum of Indian antiquities are here. Mfg. and financial center.

Lahti (lä'tē, läkh'tē), city (pop. 45,190), central Finland. Center of Finnish furniture industry.

La Hyre, Laurent de: see LA HIRE, LAURENT DE.

Laibach (lī'bäkh), German name of LJUBLJANA, Yugoslavia. At the **Congress of Laibach,** 1821, widening of the breach between Great Britain and the powers of the Holy Alliance became apparent. The congress countenanced the suppression by Austrian forces of the insurrection in Naples.

laissez faire (lĕ"sā fâr'), doctrine that an economic system functions best without governmental interference. Historically, it was a reaction against MERCANTILISM, wherein governments imposed controls on industry and trade in order to strengthen the state. The French PHYSIOCRATS first formulated the doctrine, and it was developed by Adam SMITH, who maintained that competition, motivated by self-interest, would regulate economic life more effectively than would the state. This originally radical individualistic doctrine came to be a principle of classical economics and political conservatism. Theoretically, the theory of laissez faire is still insisted on by private enterprise as an antidote to socialism, but the tendency of business combinations to evolve into monopolies has led to a shift in emphasis from individualism to the importance of private profit as an incentive to progress.

Laius, father of OEDIPUS.

La Jolla (lü hoi'yü), resort and residential part of San Diego, S Calif. Sea beaches, caves, and cliffs attract visitors. Scripps Inst. of Oceanography of Univ. of California is here.

La Junta (lü ho͞on'tü, hŭn'tü), city (pop. 7,712), SE Colo., on Arkansas R. below Pueblo. Trade and rail center in sugar-beet, grain region. Has museum commemorating BENT'S FORT.

Lake, Simon, 1866–1945, American designer of submarines. His type was at first disregarded by the U.S. navy, but it was used by Germans in World War I and was later adopted by the Allies.

lake, body of standing water surrounded by land. Most lakes originate in glacial action by excavation and filling in of depressions or by damming of rivers by ice or moraine. Lakes are also caused by interference in river courses, by filling in of extinct volcanic craters, by volcanic separation of parts of ocean. Lakes disappear because of detrital deposits and lowering of affluent streams in humid climate, or (in arid regions) because of greater evaporation than precipitation. World's largest lakes are Caspian Sea, L. Superior, Victoria Nyanza, Aral Sea, L. Michigan, L. Huron. World's highest lake is L. Titicaca, 12,500 ft. above sea level; lowest, the Dead Sea, 1,292 ft. below sea level.

lake, in dyeing, insoluble compound formed in the material by action between organic dye and MORDANT.

Lake Bluff, village (pop. 2,000), NE Ill., on L. Michigan N of Chicago. Great Lakes Naval Training Station is just N.

Lake Charles, city (pop. 41,272), SW La., on L. Charles, port on deepwater channel from Gulf of Mexico; settled 1852. Shipping center for rice, oil, lumber, and cotton area with mfg. of turpentine, fertilizer, and chemicals. Has rice and lumber mills, refineries, cotton gins.

Lake City. 1 City (pop. 7,571), N Fla., W of Jacksonville near Suwannee R.; founded in 1830s. Tobacco and lumber products. Has U.S. veterans' hospital. **2** Town (pop. 5,112), E central S.C., S of Florence, in truck and tobacco area. **3** Town (pop. 1,827), E Tenn., NNW of Knoxville, near Norris Dam.

Lake District, region (c.30 mi. in diameter) of mountains and lakes in Cumberland, Westmorland, and Lancashire, England. Has 15 lakes and some of England's highest peaks. Area a favorite resort of artists and writers. Wordsworth, Coleridge, and Southey called Lake poets; Keats, Shelley, and other poets have also lived here.

lake dwelling, habitation built over shallow waters of lake or marsh, supported by piles or artificial mounds. Prehistoric lake dwellers lived in Africa, Asia, and New World; most famous were the Neolithic inhabitants of European Alpine region.

Lake Forest, residential city (pop. 7,819), NE Ill., on L. Michigan N of Chicago. Seat of Lake Forest Col.

Lake Geneva, resort city (pop. 4,300), SE Wis., on L. Geneva and SW of Milwaukee.

Lake George, N.Y.: see GEORGE, LAKE.

Lakehurst, borough (pop. 1,518), E N.J., SW of Lakewood. Site of U.S. naval air station with facilities for dirigibles. First used by the *Shenandoah* 1923. U.S. terminal for transatlantic airships from 1924 until the *Hindenburg* burned here, 1937.

Lakeland, city (pop. 30,851), central Fla., E of Tampa in lake region. Settled in 1870s, it developed after railroad came in 1884. Processing and shipping center for citrus fruits. Mfg. of machinery and boats. Seat of Florida Southern Col. (Methodist; coed.; 1886). Has Hindu temple.

Lake of the Woods, c.70 mi. long, N Minn., SE Man., and W Ont. Fed by Rainy R. and drained by Winnipeg R. Separates Northwest Angle, northernmost land of continental U.S., from rest of Minn. Resort center with fish and game.

Lake Placid, resort village (pop. 2,999), NE N.Y., in the Adirondacks, surrounding Mirror L. and at S end of L. Placid (4 mi. long, 1–2 mi. wide). Noted eastern sports center. Scene of 1932 Olympic winter games. Near are famous bobsled run (opened 1930), farm and grave of John Brown.

Lake Success, village (pop. 1,264), SE N.Y., on NW Long Isl. Temporary hq. of the UN 1946–51.

Lakeville, Conn.: see SALISBURY.

Lake Wales, resort city (pop. 6,821), central Fla., W of L. Kissimmee and E of Tampa. Processes and ships fruit. Shrine of Ste Anne des Lacs (scene of annual R.C. pilgrimage) is near.

Lakewood. 1 See SKOWHEGAN, Maine. **2** Inland resort township (pop. 9,970), E N.J., SSE of Freehold. Former Rockefeller estate, now a state reserve, is near. **3** City (pop. 68,071), NE Ohio, on L. Erie, W suburb of Cleveland. Mfg. of metal products.

Lake Worth, resort city (pop. 11,777), SE Fla., on Atlantic coast just S of Palm Beach.

Lalande, Joseph Jérôme de (zhôzĕf' zhārōm' dü lälãd'), 1732–1807, French astronomer, influential teacher and author, and establisher of annual Lalande Prize (1802) in astronomy.

Lalique, René (rünā' lälēk'), 1860–1945, French designer of jewelry and glass.

Lally, Thomas Arthur, baron de Tollendal, comte de (tômä' ärtür' bärõ' dü tôlãdäl' kõt' dü lälē'), 1702–66, French general of Irish parentage; governor of French India (1758–61). His surrender to the English at Pondichéry ended the French empire in India. After a highly irregular trial in France he was executed for treason. His son, with Voltaire's aid, secured his posthumous rehabilitation (1778).

Lalo, Édouard (ādwär' lälō'), 1823–92, French composer. His works include an opera, *Le Roi d'Ys* (1888), and *Symphonie espagnole* for violin and orchestra.

Lamaism, BUDDHISM of Tibet and Mongolia; in doctrine differing but slightly from Mahayana (Indian) Buddhism from which it was derived. Tradition says the religion was imported by Indian and Chinese wives of a 7th-cent. king. A later king invited an Indian monk to found monastery near Lhasa (749), beginning Red Hat sect which still exists. Another Indian monk, Atisa, in 11th cent. reformed Lamaism and tried to eliminate elements of Bon (native religion). Translation of Sanskrit writings into *Kanjur* and *Tanjur*, Lamaist scriptures, was begun. The Saskya monastery was after the conversion of Kublai Khan given temporal rule of W Tibet. Under lama [priest] Tsong-kha-pa, Atisa's sect was reformed (15th cent.) as celibate Yellow Hat order, and in 1640 its 5th Ta-lai or Dalai Lama was given temporal rule of all Tibet by Mongol prince. Hierarchical priesthood developed; palace monastery was built near Lhasa. Dalai Lama is considered divine and is believed to be reincarnated immediately on death, perpetuating succession (14th installed 1940). Second to him is the abbot Panchen Lama (or Tashi). Saints, gods, spirits, and genii are worshipped.

Lamar (lůmär'), **Lucius Quintus Cincinnatus,** 1825–93, American statesman. U.S. Representative from Miss. (1857–60, 1873–77); U.S. Senator (1877–85). U.S. Secretary of the Interior (1885–88); Associate Justice of U.S. Supreme Court (1888–93).

Lamar, Mirabeau Buonaparte, 1798–1859, Texas statesman, b. Ga. As president of Texas (1838–41) he secured recognition of Texas independence by European countries; carried out vigorous Indian policy; laid foundations of present Texas public education system; founded capital at Austin.

Lamar (lůmär'), city (pop. 6,829), SE Colo., on Arkansas R. and E of Pueblo. Farm processing center.

Lamarck, Jean Baptiste Pierre Antoine de Monet, chevalier de (zhã bäptēst' pyĕr' ãtwän' dů mônā' shůvälyā' dů lämärk'), 1744–1829, French naturalist. Noted as introducer of evolutionary theories, of term *Invertebrata,* and for classification of invertebrates. Regarded founder of invertebrate paleontology. His skill as a botanist was first shown in his *Flore français* (1778). **Lamarck's theory of evolution** is based on belief that organism passes to offspring characteristics developed because of need created by its environment. This is known as the theory of inheritance of acquired characteristics, which is no longer accepted by Western scientists.

Lamarque (lůmärk'), village (pop. 7,359), S Texas, NW of Galveston. In agr. (strawberries, truck), oil area.

Lamartine, Alphonse de (älfõs' dů lämärtēn'), 1790–1869, French poet, novelist, and statesman. Author of *Les Méditations poétiques* (1820; including well-known "Le Lac") and of *Harmonies* (1829), in which he expressed his personal lyricism in musical verse. His religious orthodoxy turned to pantheism in *Jocelyn* (1836) and *La Chute d'un ange* (1838). He wrote *Histoire des Girondins* (1847) in praise of the Girondists. After the FEBRUARY REVOLUTION of 1848, he headed the provisional government. Politically idealistic, democratic, and pacific, his moderation eventually caused his supporters to desert him. Later works include the novel *Graziella* (1849).

Lamb, Lady Caroline: see MELBOURNE, WILLIAM LAMB, 2D VISCOUNT.

Lamb, Charles, 1775–1834, English essayist. A friend from boyhood of Coleridge, he worked as a clerk at India House (1792–1825). Collaborated with his sister Mary in *Tales from Shakespear* (1807). His *Specimens of English Dramatic Poets* (1808) estab. his reputation as a critic, and his famous *Essays of Elia* (collected 1823, 1833) marked him as the great master of the familiar literary style. Despite personal and family handicaps, he was able to give to his essays the warm, humorous quality of his personality.

Lamb, William: see MELBOURNE, WILLIAM LAMB, 2D VISCOUNT.

lamb: see MUTTON; SHEEP.

Lambeth, metropolitan borough (pop. 230,105), S London, England, S of the Thames. Site of Lambeth Palace (chief residence of Archbishop of Canterbury and scene of Lambeth conferences), St. Thomas's Hospital (9th cent.), and Doulton ware potteries.

lamb's quarters, European annual weed (*Chenopodium album*) of goosefoot family, naturalized in North America. It has small green flowers and whitish leaves used for greens when young.

Lambton, John George: see DURHAM, JOHN GEORGE LAMBTON, 1ST EARL OF.

Lamennais or **La Mennais, Felicité Robert de** (fālēsētā' rōbĕr' dů lämůnā'), 1782–1854, French Roman Catholic apologist. Leader of a liberal group, he was aided by MONTALEMBERT and LACORDAIRE in founding (1830) the journal *Avenir,* which forwarded ultramontanism, opposed Gallicanism, and maintained that the Church could not be free under royal government. In clash with the royalist clergy, he appealed to Pope Gregory XVI, who condemned liberal doctrines in encyclical *Mirari vos.* Lamennais retired for two years, emerged as a non-Christian, and died outside the Church. Ironically he probably did more than any other man to end Gallicanism and forward papal power. His *Paroles d'un croyant* (1834) expressed liberal humanitarianism.

Lamentations, book of Old Testament, ascribed to Jeremiah, a series of poems mourning the fallen Jerusalem. Chapters 1–4 are each divided into equal groups of lines; initial letters of the groups form an alphabetical acrostic in Hebrew.

La Mesa (lů mā'sů), city (pop. 10,946), S Calif., near San Diego, in citrus, truck, and poultry area.

Lamesa (lůmē'sů), city (pop. 10,704), NW Texas, S of Lubbock on S Llano Estacado; settled 1903. Center of agr. and cattle area with cotton gins and cottonseed oil mills.

La Mettrie, Julien Offray de (lä mĕtrē'), 1709–51, French physician and materialist philosopher. Explained man's mind and all his actions on a mechanical basis. Wrote *Man, the Machine* (1748).

Lamia (lā'mēů), in Greek mythology, grief-crazed woman whose name was used to frighten children. Her own children were killed by Hera, jealous of Zeus' love for her, and thereafter Lamia, envious of happy mothers, stole and killed their children.

Lamia (Gr. lämē'ä), city (pop. 25,843), E central Greece. Founded c.5th cent. B.C. as chief city of Malis; became an ally of Athens. Gave its name to Lamian War (323–322 B.C.) waged by the united Greeks against Antipater, who was besieged here.

Lammermuir Hills (lămůrmūr', lă'můrmūr) or

Lammermoor Hills (-mo͝or'), broad range of hills, East Lothian and Berwickshire, Scotland.

Lamont, Thomas W(illiam), 1870–1948, American banker. A partner of J. P. Morgan & Co. after 1910. Served abroad as U.S. financial adviser in 1920s and 1930s. Benefactor of Harvard.

La Motte-Fouqué: see FOUQUÉ.

lamp, lighting device, originally a vessel for holding oil burned through a wick. Used since Paleolithic period. Forms include float-wick lamp (wick was supported above oil), primitive open-cruse type, and spouted saucer type, e.g., Betty lamp of American colonists. Circular wick with open center eliminated smokiness; it was invented 18th cent. by Aimé Argand who also introduced glass lamp chimney. In mid-19th cent. kerosene superseded other oils for lamps. For the electric lamp, see LIGHTING.

lampblack: see SOOT.

Lampedusa (lämpādo͞o'zä), Mediterranean island (77 sq. mi.; pop. 3,821), between Malta and Tunis, belonging to Italy. Sponge and sardine fishing.

Lampman, Archibald, 1861–99, Canadian nature poet, author of *Among the Millet* (1888).

Lamy, Jean Baptiste (zhã' bätēst' lämē'), 1814–88, Roman Catholic archbishop in U.S. Southwest, b. France. Willa Cather's *Death Comes for the Archbishop* (1927) is based on his career.

Lanai (lùnī'), island (141 sq. mi.; pop. 3,136), one of Hawaiian Isls., W of Maui. Formerly used only for cattle grazing; after 1922 developed as pineapple-growing center.

Lanarkshire (lă'nùrkshĭr, lă'närk–) or **Lanark,** county (892 sq. mi.; pop. 1,614,125), S central Scotland. In Clyde R. valley, it has level plain in N and mountains in S. Extensive mfg. and rich mineral deposits in and near Glasgow. Central agr. region has cattle, sheep, and dairying. County town is **Lanark,** burgh (pop. 6,219), on Clyde R. New Lanark, just S, scene of social experiments by Robert Owen.

Lancashire (lăng'kùshĭr, –shùr), **Lancaster** (lăng'kùstùr), or **Lancs** (lăngks), county (1,878 sq. mi.; pop. 5,116,013), NW England, on Irish Sea. E and N parts in Lake District; W and S are lowlands with rich coal and iron deposits. FURNESS separated from rest of county by Morecombe Bay. Most populous county of England with one of world's great industrial regions centered around MANCHESTER and LIVERPOOL. Has textiles (notably cotton), much mfg., and large shipyards. County also a duchy, vested in the sovereign. County town is **Lancaster,** municipal borough (pop. 51,650), on Lune R. Has textile and other mfg. and flour mills.

Lancaster, earls and dukes of: see LANCASTER, HOUSE OF; JOHN OF GAUNT.

Lancaster, John of: see JOHN OF LANCASTER.

Lancaster, Joseph, 1778–1838, English Quaker educator. In 1801 he founded a free elementary school using a type of MONITORIAL SYSTEM. Later, he came to America to lecture and promote his ideas.

Lancaster, England: see LANCASHIRE.

Lancaster. 1 City (pop. 2,402), central Ky., S of Lexington. Site of Kennedy House, said to have been used in *Uncle Tom's Cabin,* is near by. **2** Town (pop. 3,601), central Mass., NE of Wachusett Reservoir. Has one of Bulfinch's finest churches (1817). Birthplace of Burbank. **3** Village (pop. 8,665), W N.Y., E of Buffalo; settled 1810. Steel, wood, and glass products. **4** City (pop. 24,180), S central Ohio, SE of Columbus and on Hocking R.; founded 1800. Mfg. of flint glass and farm machinery. Birthplace of W. T. Sherman. **5** City (pop. 63,774), SE Pa., on Conestoga R. and W of Philadelphia; settled c.1721. Center of Pa. Dutch region and one of richest agr. areas in nation, it has large stockyard and mfg. of tobacco, linoleum, and watches. Seat of Franklin and Marshall Col. (Evangelical-Reformed; for men; formed 1853 by merger of Franklin Col. and Marshall Col.). Munitions center in Revolution. Continental Congress met here briefly in 1777. State cap. 1799–1812. Was W terminus of Lancaster Turnpike. Birthplace of Robert Fulton. Pres. Buchanan is buried here and his near-by home is historic memorial. **6** Town (pop. 7,159), N S.C., NNE of Columbia near N.C. line. Textile mills and farms.

Lancaster, house of (lăng'kùstùr), royal family of England. Title began in 1267 when Henry III gave it to his second son, **Edmund, earl of Lancaster,** 1245–96, called Edmund Crouchback from a cross he wore on crusade. He had been made titular king of Sicily in 1254 but the title lapsed. His son, **Thomas, earl of Lancaster,** 1277?–1322, opposed Piers Gaveston and the Despensers under Edward II, led the baronial party, and was executed for treason. His brother, **Henry, earl of Lancaster,** 1281?–1355, was chief adviser to Edward III in his seizure of power from his mother. His son, **Henry, duke of Lancaster,** 1299?–1361, was made duke for victories in the Hundred Years War. He died without male issue and the title passed to JOHN OF GAUNT, fourth son of Edward III, who married Henry's daughter, Blanche. His son became the first Lancastrian king as HENRY IV. Others were HENRY V and HENRY VI. Struggle with the rival house of YORK led to Wars of the ROSES.

Lancelot or **Ladislaus,** c.1376–1414, king of Naples (1386–1414); son of Charles III. His reign was consumed by his struggle with the rival claimant, Louis II of Naples, and with the antipope John XXIII. He had Rome sacked in 1413.

Lancelot, Sir: see ARTHURIAN LEGEND.

Lancret, Nicolas (nēkôlä' lãkrā'), 1690–1743, French painter, whose style is suggestive of Watteau. Painted balls, fairs, and other festivities.

Lancs, county, England: see LANCASHIRE.

Lander, city (pop. 3,349), W central Wyo., on Popo Agie R. Tourist center in dude-ranch area near Fort Washakie, Wind River Indian Reservation hq.

Landes (lãd'), region of Gascony, SW France; a sandy, marshy area stretching for c.100 mi. along Atlantic coast. Sheep grazing. Part has been reclaimed through drainage and forestation. It occupies part of Gironde dept. and most of **Landes** dept. (3,614 sq. mi.; pop. 248,395; cap. Mont-de-Marsan).

land-grant colleges and universities, institutions benefiting from Morrill Act of 1862. These now number 69. Hatch Act (1887) provided for research and experiment stations, Smith-Lever Act (1914) for extension work in agriculture and home economics.

Landis, Kenesaw Mountain, 1866–1944, American jurist, commissioner of baseball (1921–44). He did much to restore public faith in baseball after 1920 "Black Sox" scandal.

Landon, Alf(red) M(ossman), 1887–, governor of Kansas (1933–37) and unsuccessful Republican candidate for President (1936).

Landon, Letitia Elizabeth, pseud. **L.E.L.,** 1802–38, English poet and novelist, whose contributions in verse to the *Literary Gazette* had wide appeal.

Landor, Walter Savage, 1775–1864, English author, best known for *Pericles and Aspasia* (1836) and especially for prose dialogues, *Imaginary Conversations* (1824–53). His verse is of wide range.

Landowska, Wanda (ländôf'skä), 1877–, Polish-French harpsichordist, pianist, and teacher. Made her American debut in 1923. She has done much to revive interest in the harpsichord and its music.

Landsberg an der Warthe (länts'bĕrk än dĕr vär'tů), Pol. *Gorzów Wielkopolski,* town (1939 pop. 48,053; 1946 pop. 19,796), E. Brandenburg, on Warthe R.; transferred to Polish administration 1945. Trade and transportation center.

Landseer, Sir Edwin Henry (lăn'sēr), 1802–73, English animal painter, extremely popular in his day.

Lands End, promontory, Cornwall; SW extremity of England. Has granite cliffs 100 ft. high.

Landskrona (länskrōō'nä), seaport city (pop. 25,089), Malmohus co., S Sweden, on the Oresund; founded 1413. It has shipyards, flour mills, sugar refineries, and metalworks. Town was burned 1428 by Hansa merchants and devastated in 16th- and 17th-cent. wars. Its citadel was built 1540. Swedes defeated Danes in naval battle here, 1677.

landslide, slipping of a mass of rock and earth down a slope. Main cause is saturation with water, which increases weight, lessens friction. Caused also by earthquakes. Landslides dam streams and destroy forests, farm land, habitations, life, and cause floods.

Landsmaal: see NORWEGIAN LANGUAGE.

Landsteiner, Karl (kärl länt'shtīnûr), 1868–1943, American medical research worker, b. Vienna. For discovery of human blood groups, he won 1930 Nobel Prize in Physiology and Medicine. With A. S. Wiener, he identified Rh blood factor (1940).

Lane, James Henry, 1814–66, American politician, called "Liberator of Kansas." Encouraged antislavery men to emigrate to Kansas; secured Free State control of legislature. U.S. Senator (1861–66).

Lane, Joseph, 1801–81, American general in Mexican War, territorial governor of Oregon (1848–50). Also superintendent of Indian affairs there.

Lane, Sir Ralph, c.1530–1603, leader of first attempted English settlement in America, on ROANOKE ISLAND, N.C. (1585).

Lane, Ralph Norman Anell: see ANGELL, SIR NORMAN.

Lanett (lůnĕt'), cotton-milling city (pop. 7,434), E Ala., on Chattahoochee R. and ENE of Montgomery.

Lanfranc (lăn'frăngk), d. 1089, Italian churchman, archbishop of Canterbury. A theologian and scholar trained in France under BERENGAR OF TOURS, he founded the famous school at Bec and wrote (against Berengar) a widely popular treatise on transubstantiation. He was a friend of William the Conqueror, and after the Norman Conquest reluctantly became archbishop of Canterbury. A strong reformer, he did much to root out abuses in the English church and came into conflict with King William II.

Lang, Andrew, 1844–1912, Scottish scholar and man of letters. He wrote graceful poetry in French forms, as in *Ballades in Blue China* (1880, 1881). His anthropological theory of myth appears in *Myths, Literature, and Religion* (2 vols., 1887). Lang is best known, however, for prose translations of the *Odyssey* (1879, with S. H. Butcher), the *Iliad* (1883, with Walter Leaf and Ernest Myers), and *Aucassin and Nicolete* (1887).

Lang, Cosmo Gordon, 1864–1945, English churchman, archbishop of York (1908–28), archbishop of Canterbury (1928–42). He exercised some influence in the abdication of Edward VIII.

Langdell, Christopher Columbus (lăng'důl), 1826–1906, American teacher of law. As dean of Harvard Law School after 1875, he introduced (with J. B. Ames) the "case method" of law study, which was then at Columbia and later almost universally accepted.

Langdon, John, 1741–1819, American statesman. Largely responsible for N.H. ratifying Constitution as ninth state, thus making instrument effective. U.S. Senator (1789–1801).

Lange, Christian Louis (krĭs'tyän lōō'ē läng'ů), 1869–1938, Norwegian pacifist and Nobel Prize winner (1921).

Langeland (läng'ůlăn), island (110 sq. mi.; pop. 20,354), Denmark, in Baltic Sea, between Fyn and Laaland. Produces grain. Langeland Belt, strait, joins Great Belt and Baltic Sea.

Langensalza (läng"unzäl'tsä), town (pop. 16,013), Thuringia, central Germany. Has kept part of medieval walls and castle. Scene of victory of Emperor Henry IV over rebellious Saxons and Thuringians (1075); of Prussians over Hanoverians (1866). Bad Langensalza, near by, has sulphur springs.

Langerhans, islands of, in medicine: see PANCREAS.

Langlade, Augustin (ōgüstē' lãgläd'), c.1695–c.1771, French Canadian fur trader. Estab. fur trade at Green Bay, Wis. His son, **Charles Michel de Langlade,** 1729–1800, aided in fur trading and was a leader in French and Indian Wars.

Langland, William, c.1332–c.1400, supposed author of PIERS PLOWMAN, b. probably Ledbury, near Welsh Marches; lived in London. Took minor orders, but because of marriage never became priest.

Langley, Samuel Pierpont, 1834–1906, American scientist. A pioneer in mechanics-of-flight studies and heavier-than-air flight experiments. Flew models successfully (1896), but full-scale aircraft, financed by War Dept., in 1903 could not be launched. Reconstructed in 1914, it flew. Invented bolometer (instrument for recording variations in heat radiation); pioneered in studies of infrared radiation. Helped to popularize astronomy. Secretary of Smithsonian Institute from 1887.

Langmuir, Irving (lăng'mūr), 1881–, American chemist. He contributed to development of radio vacuum tube, introduced atomic-hydrogen welding. Won 1932 Nobel Prize for work in surface chemistry—development of new technique for molecule study, which has applications in research on immunology.

Langres (lã'grů), town (pop. 5,624), Haute-Marne dept., NE France, surrounded by wooded Langres Plateau. Medieval fortifications. Cutlery industry. Birthplace of Diderot.

Langston University: see GUTHRIE, Okla.

Langtry, Lillie, 1852–1929, English actress, called the Jersey Lily. A noted beauty, she was painted by Millais and Burne-Jones. *Lady Windermere's Fan* was written by Wilde as a vehicle for her.

Langtry [for Lillie Langtry], village, W Texas, on Rio Grande near mouth of the Pecos. Near old town of Langtry where "law west of Pecos," Judge Roy Bean, meted out whisky and justice at his saloon.

language, systematic human vocal communication. It is a distinctive, exclusive, and universal mark of the human species, but its origin is unknown. When languages resemble each other in a systematic way they are held to be genetically related. Though scientifically estab., such relationships have always been on the basis of sounds of the languages and the way the sounds are grouped in systematic patterns; no certainty has been attained in comparing the fundamental grammatical structures of languages. Maximal groups of related languages are called families and stocks. For a survey of the important languages by families, see tables on pp. 687–89. In the tables asterisks indicate extinct languages and locations are general.

Languedoc (lãgdôk'), region and former province, S France; historic cap. Toulouse. It consists of Lower Languedoc, along Mediterranean coast, with cities of Nîmes, Montpellier, and Narbonne; of the fertile Garonne plains, with Toulouse as center (agr., wine growing); and of part of the Massif Central (incl. the Cévennes, Vivarais, and Velay). Languedoc corresponds roughly to Narbonensis prov. of Roman Gaul, the later Septimania. Its history before its incorporation into the French royal domain (1271) is largely that of the county of TOULOUSE.

langue d'oc and langue d'oïl (lãg dôk', dôēl', dô'yů), names of the two principal groups of medieval French dialects, *oc* and *oïl* being their respective words for *yes. Langue d'oc* was spoken S of a line running roughly from Bordeaux to Grenoble. The *langue d'oïl* dialect of the Paris region gradually developed into modern French. Both *langue d'oïl* and *langue d'oc* (e.g., Provençal) dialects (*patois*) persisted, however, in some rural regions.

Lanier, Sidney (lůnēr'), 1842–81, American poet, b. Ga. A Confederate soldier, he was imprisoned and lost his health. Lanier was a musician (flutist with Peabody Orchestra, Baltimore) and devoted much attention to the relationship of music and poetry—the subject of his *Science of English Verse* (1880). His own poems show the use of musical principles as in "The Symphony" and "The Marshes of Glynn." Some of his shorter poems, notably "The Song of the Chattahoochee" and "A Ballad of Trees and the Master" have lasting popularity.

Lanka: see CEYLON.

Lannes, Jean (zhã' län'), 1769–1809, marshal of France; one of Napoleon's chief lieutenants. Fell at Essling.

lanolin (lă'nůlĭn), greasy yellow substance from wool. It is used as ointment base, in finishing and preserving leather, in some varnishes and paints.

Lansbury, George, 1859–1940, British Labour party leader. Founded (1912) and edited the *Daily Herald,* the voice of British labor. Pacifist and reformer, he headed Labour party in Parliament 1931–35.

Lansdale, borough (pop. 9,762), SE Pa., N of Philadelphia. Mfg. of clothing and metal products.

Lansdowne, Henry Charles Keith Petty Fitzmaurice, 5th **marquess of** (lănz'doun), 1845–1927, British statesman. As foreign secretary tried to end England's diplomatic aloofness by alliances.

Lansdowne, borough (pop. 12,169), SE Pa., SW residential suburb of Philadelphia. Metal products.

Lansford, borough (pop. 7,487), E Pa., S of Hazleton. Anthracite mining and mfg. of clothing.

Lansing, Robert, 1864–1928, U.S. Secretary of State (1915–20). Authority on international law. Advocated U.S. joining in World War I with Allies. Disapproved Covenant of League of Nations as part of peace treaty.

Lansing. 1 Village (pop. 8,682), NE Ill., S suburb of Chicago near Ind. line. **2** City (pop. 92,129), state cap. (since 1847), S Mich., at junction of Grand and Cedar rivers; settled 1837. Development came with railroads (1870s) and automobile industry (1901). Mfg. of automobiles, buses, trucks, automotive equipment, metal products, chemicals, and paints.

Lanston, Tolbert, 1844–1913, American inventor of a typesetting machine, MONOTYPE (patented 1887).

lantana (lăntā'nů), tropical shrubs of genus *Lantana. Lantana camara,* grown as bedding or greenhouse plant, has clusters of red or yellow flowers.

lanthanum (lăn'thůnům), relatively common metallic element of rare earths (symbol = La; see also ELEMENT, table). It is gray-white, ductile, malleable.

Laoag (läwäg'), municipality (pop. 44,406), on NW Luzon, Philippines. Trade center for rice area.

Laocoön (lāŏk'ōōn), in Greek legend, priest of Apollo who warned the Trojans not to touch wooden horse made by the Greeks in Trojan War. Two sea serpents, sent (according to different versions) by Athena, Poseidon, or Zeus, killed Laocoön and his two sons. Struggle is represented by Greek statue now in the Vatican. Pliny names Agesander,

The Indo-European Languages

SUBFAMILY	GROUP		PRINCIPAL LANGUAGES
Germanic	W	High	Bavarian, Swiss Alemannic, Pennsylvania Dutch, Alsatian—Swabian Franconian—Old* and Middle* High German, German—Yiddish
		Low	Old Saxon*, Plattdeutsch (Modern Low German) Lower Franconian*, Dutch, Flemish, Afrikaans
			Anglo-Frisian 1. Frisian 2. Old English*, Middle English*—Middle Scots* English: British, American, Colonial, etc., each with standard and dialect variations—Scottish
	N		Old Norse*, Icelandic—Norwegian, incl. Landsmaal Old Swedish*, Swedish—Danish, Dano-Norwegian—Faroese
	E		Gothic*
Celtic	Continental		Gaulish*
	Brythonic		Middle Welsh*, Welsh—Cornish*—Breton
	Goidelic		Old*, Middle*, and Modern Irish, Scottish Gaelic, Manx
Italic			Umbrian*
	Latin and Romanic (Romance)		Old: Old Latin*, Classic Latin*, Medieval Latin*
			Middle: Vulgar Latin*—Old Italian*, Old French*
			Italian, standard (Tuscan) and dialects Sardinian—Dalmatian*—Rumanian Rhaeto-Romanic: Romansh, Ladin or Frioul French, Canadian F., Louisiana F.—dialects of N France Provençal, dialects of S France—Catalan Spanish, American S., Philippine S.—Judeo-Spanish Portuguese, Brazilian Portuguese—Galician
			Oscan*
Albanian			Albanian
Hellenic or Greek			Ionian*, Homeric G.*—Classical Attic*, Hellenistic G.*, Koine*, Biblical G.* (OT, NT), Byzantine G.*—Modern G.
			Doric*, Choral Doric*, Corinthian*—Aeolic*—Cyprian*
Slavic or Slavonic	E		Russian—Ukrainian, Ruthenian—White Russian
	S		Slovene, Serbo-Croat, Bulgarian—Old Church Slavonic*
	W		Polish—Sorbian or Wendish—Czech, Slovak
Baltic			Old Prussian*, Lithuanian, Lettish
Indo-Iranian	Iranian		Western: Avestan*, Old Persian*—Pahlavi*, Sogdian* Persian—Caspian dialects—Kurdish
			Eastern: Baluchi, Afghan or Pushtu, Pamir dialects
			Northern: Ossetian
	Indic or Indo-Aryan		Old: Vedic*, Sanskrit*
			Middle: Prakrit* (several languages), Pali*
			Northwestern languages, Kashmiri, et al.—Romany Lahnda, Sindhi, Gujarati, Marathi—Bhili, Rajasthani Panjabi, Pahari, W. Hindi—standard Hindustani and Urdu—E. Hindi, Bihari Bengali, Oriya, Assamese Singhalese or Sinhalese
Tokharian*			Tokharian A* (of Turfan), Tokharian B* (Kuchean)
Armenian			Classical Armenian*, Armenian
Anatolian*			Hittite* (Kanesian), Hieroglyphic Hittite* Luwian*, Lycian*, Lydian*

The Mongolic or Mongolian Languages

Eastern	Literary Mongolian, Mongolian proper or Halha, incl. new standard language of Urga South Mongolian, incl. Harachin, Chahar, Ordos Buryat, incl. new standard, Selenga, et al.
Western	Oirat, incl. Kalmuck, Kobdo Oirat Afghanistan Mongol

The Finno-Ugric Family

Finno-Permian Group
1. Finnish incl. Estonian Lappish Mordvinian Cheremiss 2. Permian Zyrian (or Komi) Udmurt (Votyak)
Ugric Group
Obi Ugric Vogul, Ostyak Hungarian or Magyar

The Malayo-Polynesian Languages

Indonesian Group			
W	Malagassy		
	N	Formosan	
		Philippine Tagalog Bisayan Ilocano Igorot Magindanao	
		Eastern Chamorro Palau NE Celebes	
	S	W	Malay Sumatran Nias, et al. Maduran, Bugi Balinese, Macassar
		E	Javanese Sundanese Borneo Dyak Sumba, et al.
E: Aru, Savu, et al.			
Micronesian Group			
	Caroline Yap Ponape Gilbertese Marshallese Nauru Marianas		
Melanesian Group			
	S Melanesian Central Melanesian Fijian C Solomons N Melanesian Santa Cruz		
Polynesian Group			
W	Vaitupu (Ellices) Samoan, Tongan, et al.		
E	Maori Rarotonga Tahitian Society Tuamotu Marquesan Hawaiian Rapanui (Easter Isl.)		

An asterisk (*) indicates a dead language.

LINGUISTIC FAMILIES (continued)

The Semitic and Related Groups

GROUP	LANGUAGE
Akkadian	Babylonian*, Assyrian* Nuzi Akkadian*
Canaanite	Old Canaanite* Moabite* Phoenician*, Punic* Hebrew*, New Hebrew Ugaritic*
Aramaic	W Aramaic: Biblical*, Palestinian*, Modern Syriac* Mandean* Neo Syriac
Arabic	Classical Arabic Arabian Arabic Iraqi Arabic Syrian Arabic Egyptian Arabic Western Arabic, incl. Maltese, Andalusian Arabic*
	Himyaritic*—Soqotri

GROUP	LANGUAGE
Ethiopic	Geez* Tigrigna Tigré Amharic Gafat Harari Gurагé
Hamito-Semitic	Egyptian* Coptic*
Hamitic	Old Libyan*
	Modern Berber: 1. Tuareg, Kabyle, et al. 2. Riff, Algerian, et al.
	Guanche* (Canaries)
Cushitic	Beja Afar and Saho Somali Galla Agaw—Bilin Sidama—Gonga

The Turkic Languages

East Turkic	Oirat Altai, North Altai, Abakan, Kizil, Baraba, Uigur, et al.
West Turkic	Kirghiz, Irtysh, Bashkir, Volga Kirghiz, et al.
Tatar or Central Turkic	Kashgar, Yarkand, Sart, Taranchi, Uzbek, et al.
South Turkic	Turkmen, Azerbaijanian and Caucasian Turkic Standard Turkish and related (Anatolian or Ottoman) dialects Crimean Turkish
Yakut	
Chuvash	

The Sino-Tibetan or Indo-Chinese Languages

Tibeto-Burman	Standard Tibetan, Tibeto-Himalayan, North Assamese Bodo, Kachin, Naga (all in S Assam)
Burman	Standard Burmese, Burmese dialects Karen language and others
Chinese	Standard Written Chinese, Ancient* and Modern North Chinese Central Coastal Chinese Kiangsi dialects Cantonese and Hakka
Tai or Thai	Standard Siamese, Southeastern Tai, incl. Laos Eastern Tai, incl. Lakya of Hainan Northern Tai, incl. Shan

The Dravidian Family

Tamil (Coromandel Coast) Malayalam (S Malabar)
Kanarese (Malabar Coast) Kulu Kota Toda
Telugu (N Coromandel Coast)
Central Dravidian Gondhi Kurukh, Malto Bhil Kolami Naiki
Brahui (Baluchistan)

The Siouan Stock

GROUP	LANGUAGE
Eastern	Catawba
Ohio	Ofo*, Biloxi*, Tutelo*
Missouri	Hidatsa, Crow
Mississippi or Chiwere	Iowa, Oto, Missouri* Winnebago
Dhegiha	Omaha, Ponca, Quapaw, Osage, Kansa*
Mandan	
Dakota	Sioux Assiniboin

Native Linguistic Families of the U.S. and Canada

FAMILY	SUGGESTED KINSHIP	FORMER LOCATION
Eskimo-Aleut		Arctic America Aleutians, Alaska
Eyak		Copper R. delta
Athapascan		separate table
Tlingit	Athapascan	SE Alaska, NW B.C.
Haida	Athapascan	Queen Charlotte Isl.
Tsimshian	Penutian	Prince Rupert region
Wakashan	Algonquian	Coastal B.C., Wash.
Salishan	Algonquian	separate table
Kootenai	Algonquian	SE B.C. and vicinity
Chimakuan	Algonquian	Cape Flattery, Wash.
Chinook	Penutian	Lowest Columbia R.
Shahaptin incl. Yakima, Nez Percé	Waiilatpuan Lutuamian Penutian	S Washington N and central Oregon E central Idaho
Waiilatpuan incl. Cayuse	Shahaptin Penutian	N Oregon
Kalapuya	Penutian	Upper Willamette R.
Siuslaw—Yakonan, incl. Lower Umpqua	Penutian	Middle coast of Oregon
Coos	Penutian	Coos R., SW Oregon
Lutuamian incl. Klamath and Modoc	Shahaptin Waiilatpuan Penutian	S Oregon
Takelma	Penutian	Rogue R., SW Oregon
Karok	Hokan	Extreme NW Calif.
Yurok—Wiyot	Algonquian	Klamath R., NW Calif.
Chimariko	Hokan	NW California
Shasta—Achomawi	Hokan	N and NE California
Penutian	Tsimshian et al.	Central California
Yana*	Hokan	NE California
Washo	Hokan	Lake Tahoe region
Yuki	Hokan	Round Valley, Calif.
Pomo	Hokan	Calif. coast N of S.F.
Esselen*	Hokan	Coast S of San Francisco
Salinan*	Hokan	San Luis Obispo coast
Chumashan*	Hokan	Santa Barbara coast
Uto-Aztecan		separate table
Yuman	Hokan	separate table
Zuñi		Zuñi, N.Mex.
Keresan	Hokan	N.Mex.; see PUEBLO INDIANS
Tanoan	Uto-Aztecan	separate table
Kiowa	Tanoan Uto-Aztecan	NW Okla. and neighboring Kan., Texas
Algonquian		separate table
Siouan	Hokan	separate table
Tonkawa*	Hokan	Austin region, Texas
Karankawa*	Hokan	Middle Texas coast
Caddoan	Hokan	separate table
Atacapa*	Tunica	SW La., SE Texas
Natchez-Muskogean	Hokan	separate table
Yuchi	Siouan	E Tenn., E Ga.
Iroquoian	Caddoan Hokan	1. N.Y. state and vic. 2. Va. and Carolinas

An asterisk (*) indicates a dead language.

LINGUISTIC FAMILIES OF THE AMERICAS (concluded)

The Athapascan Stock

GROUP	LANGUAGE
Northern (in Alaska, NW Canada)	Kutchin
	Sarsi, Beaver, Sekani
	Chipewyan, Yellowknife, Slave
Northwestern	Hoopa, (Upper) Umpqua*, et al.
Apachean	Navaho, Apache, Lipan, Kiowa Apache

The Salishan Stock

Inland	Okanogan
	Flathead
	Coeur D'Alene
	Shuswap
Coastal	Bella Coola
	Clallam
	Nisqualli
	Puyallup
	Tillamook

The Algonquian Stock

Central and Eastern	1. Cree, Montagnais, Naskapi
	Menominee
	Fox, Sauk, Kickapoo
	Shawnee
	Miami*, Illinois*
	Potawatami
	Ojibwa, Ottawa, Algonquin
	Delaware
	Powhatan*
	2. Natick*, Narragansett*
	Mohegan*, Pequot*
	Penobscot, Abnaki
	Passamaquoddy, Malecite
	Micmac
Blackfoot	Blackfoot, Piegan, Blood
Cheyenne	
Arapaho	Arapaho, Atsina, Nawathinehena

The Natchez-Muskogean Stock

Natchez	
Muskogean	W: Choctaw, incl. Chickasaw
	E: Alibamu, Creek, incl. Seminole

The Tanoan Stock

Tiwa	Taos, Picuris
	Sandia, Isleta, Isleta del Sur
Towa	Jemez, Pecos*
Tewa	San Juan, S. Clara, San Ildefonso, Nambé, Pojoaque*, Tesuque, Hano

The Caddoan Stock

Pawnee	Pawnee proper, Skiri Pawnee, Arikara
	Kitsai or Kichai
	Wichita (two languages)
Caddo	Caddo proper
	Haina

The Yuman Stock

NW—Arizona	Yavapaí, Walapai, Havasupai
Colorado—Gila	Mohave, Halchidhoma, Kavelchadom, Maricopa, Yuma
Colorado Delta	Cocopa, Halyikwamai, Kahwan
S Calif.—Lower Calif.	Diegueño, Kamia, Akwa'ala, Kiliwa

The Uto-Aztecan Stock

GROUP	LANGUAGE	LOCATION
Southern-Californian	Cahuilla, Luiseño, et al.	S Calif.
Hopian	Hopi, Bannock, et al.	NE Ariz., S Idaho, to E Calif.
Utan	Ute, Paiute, et al.	W Colo. to SE Calif.
Shoshonean	Shoshone, Comanche	SW Wyo. to Calif., Central Texas
Taracahitian	Tarahumara, Yaqui, et al.	Chihuahua, Sonora, Sinaloa
	Cora, Huichol	Jalisco, Nayarit
Aztecoidan	Nahuatlan, et al.	Middle America
Piman	Pima—Papago, Tepehuan, et al.	Gila R. to Nayarit

The Mayan Stock

Huastec		Tampico area
Yucatec	Maya	Yucatán
Quichoid	Cakchiquel, Quiché, et al.	Chiapas and Central America
Mamoid	Mam, Aguacatec, Jacaltec	
Chiapan	Tzeltal, Tzotzil, Tabasco Chontal	Chiapas, Tabasco, Guatemala

Native Stocks of Latin America

STOCK	LOCATION
Seri (Hokan kinship?)	Sonora coast
Tarascan	Michoacán
Otomí	Hidalgo, Mexico state
Matlatzinca	Mexico state
Totonac	Vera Cruz, Puebla
Subtiaba-Tlapanec (Hokan kinship?)	1. Nicaragua 2. Guerrero
Puebla Popoloca—Mazatec	Puebla, Oaxaca
Zapotec	Oaxaca
Mixtec	Oaxaca, Guerrero
Huave (Penutian kin?)	Oaxaca
Mixe-Zoque (Penutian?)	Vera Cruz, Oaxaca
Chinantec	Oaxaca
Oaxaca Chontal	Oaxaca
Xinca	SE Guatemala
Miskito—Suma—Matagalpa or Misumalpa	Honduras, Salvador Mosquito Coast
Chorotega	Nicaragua, Costa Rica
Cariban	West Indies, Caribbean coasts
Arawakan	Amazonia
Chibchan	Costa Rica to Colombia
Kechua	Bolivia, Peru plateau
Aymar	Titicaca region
Tupí-Guaraní	Coastal, central Brazil, Paraguay
Gê	Maranhão and vicinity
Araucanian	Chile

An asterisk (*) indicates a dead language.

Athenodorus, and Polydorus, Greek sculptors of 1st cent. B.C., as creators of the work.

Laodicea (lāŏ″dĭsē′ů), anc. city of Asia Minor; under Rome a Christian center and seat of one of the Seven Churches.

Laoighis (lā′ĭsh) or **Leix** (lā′ĭsh, lāks), inland county (664 sq. mi.; pop. 49,697), S central Ireland, in Leinster; co. town Port Laoghise. Formerly Queen's Co. Mostly level, it has Slieve Bloom Mts. in N. Agr. and dairying are main occupations.

Laon (läõ′), city (pop. 14,868), Aisne dept., N France. Its famous Church of Notre Dame (12th–13th cent.; a cathedral until French Revolution) dominates the plain from a rocky height.

Laos (lä′ōs), kingdom (91,400 sq. mi.; pop. 1,169,000), NW INDO-CHINA; cap. Vientiane. Bounded on N by China, E by Viet Nam, S by Cambodia, and W by Burma and Thailand. Drained by Mekong R. Mainly a rugged plateau cut by deep valleys. Chief exports include coffee, benzoin, and opium. Under Siamese control from early 19th cent. to 1893, when sovereignty was shifted to France. Monarchy estab. 1947. Joined French Union as associated state in 1950. In April, 1953, the French suffered a setback in the Indo-Chinese war when Viet Minh troops invaded Laos from Viet Nam.

Lao-tze or **Lao-tzu** (both lou′dzŭ), b. c.604 B.C., Chinese philosopher, legendary founder of TAOISM.

La Paz (lä päs′), city (pop. 319,600), W Bolivia, *de facto* cap. and largest city of Bolivia (Sucre is *de jure* cap.); founded 1548. In a narrow valley (alt. c.12,000 ft.), it lacks fuel and power and has little mfg. Chief tourist attractions are near-by Illimani and L. Titicaca.

La Paz, city (pop. 10,401), cap. of S territory, Lower California, Mexico; pearl fishing center.

Lapeer (lůpēr′), city (pop. 6,143), S Mich., E of Flint and on South Bend of Flint R., in grain and dairy area. Mfg. of metal products.

La Pérouse, Jean François de Galaup, comte de (dů gälō′ kōt′ dů lä pārōōz′), 1741–c.1788, French navigator. Led French government expedition in 1785 to explore Pacific, seeking Northwest Passage. He discovered (1787) **La Pérouse Strait,** a channel, 25 mi. wide, separating Hokkaido, Japan, from Sakhalin, USSR. Sometimes called Soya Strait.

lapis lazuli (lă′pĭs lăz′yōōlī, –lē), a gem, deep blue, violet, or greenish blue, usually flecked with yellow iron pyrites. Found in Afghanistan, Chile, Siberia, Burma, U.S. Formerly made into vases, bowls; used also for beads, small ornaments.

Laplace, Pierre Simon, marquis de (pyĕr′ sēmō′ märkē′ dů läpläs′), 1749–1827, French astronomer and mathematician, evolver of scientific form of NEBULAR HYPOTHESIS. His research on motions of heavenly bodies was published in his *Mécanique céleste* (1799–1825). His notable work in mathematics includes development of theory of probabilities.

Lapland, Finnish *Lappi,* Nor. *Lapland,* Swed. *Lappland,* vast region of N Europe, largely within Arctic Circle. It includes Finnmark, Troms, and part of Nordland counties (Norway); historic Lappland prov., now comprising Norrbotten and Vasterbotten counties (Sweden); N Finland; and Kola peninsula (RSFSR). Region is mountainous in N, rising to 6,965 ft. in the KEBNEKAISE (Sweden), and consists largely of tundra in NE. It has extensive forests and many lakes and rivers. Its rich mineral resources include highgrade iron ore (esp. at KIRUNA, Sweden), copper (Sulitelma, Norway), nickel (Pechenga, RSFSR), and apatite (Kirovsk, RSFSR). Narvik and Murmansk are important ports. **Lapps** or **Laplanders,** the indigenous population (c.30,000) are concentrated mainly in Norway, where they are called Finns. Largely nomadic, they follow their reindeer herds, fish, and hunt. They are believed to have come from central Asia and to have been pushed N by other migrations. Though nominally conquered by Sweden and Norway in Middle Ages, their Christianization was not completed until 18th cent. Finno-Ugric language.

La Plata (lä plä′tä), city (pop. 302,073), cap. of Buenos Aires prov., E Argentina, SE of Buenos Aires. Founded 1882 as cap. of prov. after Buenos Aires had been federalized. Has large meat-packing plants. Renamed Eva Perón (1952).

La Plata, Río de: see PLATA, RÍO DE LA.

La Pointe (lů point′), town, on Madeline Isl. (largest of APOSTLE ISLANDS), N Wis. French fortified trading post here 1693–98, 1718–59. American Fur. Co. had post here early 19th cent.

Laporte, Roland (rōlā′ läpôrt′), 1675–1704, French leader of the CAMISARDS, known as Roland. Betrayed, he fell defending himself.

La Porte (lů pôrt′), city (1951 special census pop. 20,414), NW Ind., E of Gary; settled 1830. Produces road-building material, machinery, and furniture. Resort with many lakes.

Lapps: see LAPLAND.

Laptev Sea (läp′tyĭf), section of Arctic Ocean, bounded by E Siberia (S), Severnaya Zemlya and Taimyr Peninsula (W), and New Siberian Isls. (E). Navigable in Aug. and Sept.

lapwing, crested plover of Old World, also called green plover or pewit. It has a deep, iridescent green back, greenish-black crown and crest, black throat and upper breast, white under parts, and fawn tail coverts.

Larache (läräsh′), Arabic *El Araish,* city (pop. 41,286), W Spanish Morocco; port on the Atlantic. Near site of Phoenician settlement, which was later a Roman colony. Held by Spain 1610–89. Exports include grain, skins, and fruit.

Laramie (lă′růmē), city (pop. 15,581; alt. 7,145 ft.), SE Wyo., on Laramie R. and WNW of Cheyenne; settled 1868. Transportation, trade, and industrial center for cattle and sheep region; mfg. of building materials. Seat of Univ. of Wyoming (land-grant, state supported; coed.; chartered 1886, opened 1887). Near by is site of Fort Sanders, estab. 1866 to protect Overland Trail and railroad workers.

Laramie, river rising in N Colo. in S Medicine Bow Mts. Flows 216 mi. NE to North Platte R. in Wyo.

Laramie, Fort, Wyo.: see NATIONAL PARKS AND MONUMENTS (table).

Laramie Mountains: see FRONT RANGE.

larceny, unlawful taking and carrying away of the property of another with intent to deprive the owner of its use or to appropriate it to the use of the perpetrator or of someone else. Usually distinguished from EMBEZZLEMENT and from false pretenses, larceny is in some U.S. states defined to include them. Grand larceny, usually a felony, differs from petty larceny, usually a misdemeanor, as to the value of the property stolen.

larch or **tamarack** (tă'mùrăk), tree of genus *Larix*. Larches are conifers of the pine family but are not evergreen. Widely distributed in N Hemisphere, they are grown for ornament and lumber. American larch or hackmatack is *Larix laricina*. Timber of *L. occidentalis* of W U.S. used in construction.

Larchmont, suburban village (pop. 6,330), SE N.Y., on Long Isl. Sound between New Rochelle and Mamaroneck. Yachting center.

Larcom, Lucy (lär'kùm), 1824–93, American poet. A worker in the Lowell, Mass., cotton mills, she attracted the interest of Whittier by her sweet and idealistic poems.

Lardner, Ring(gold Wilmer), 1885–1933, American short-story writer. A sports reporter, he turned to fiction and gained fame with vigorous stories in *You Know Me Al* (1916), *How to Write Short Stories* (1924), and other volumes. Pungent idiom of the sports world and the street made him a much-imitated master of tough and sardonic humor.

Laredo (lùrā'dō), city (pop. 51,910), SW Texas, on Rio Grande (bridged) opposite Nuevo Laredo, Mexico. Founded by Spanish in 1750s, it grew as post on road to other Texas cities. Mexican after Texas Revolution, city went to U.S. after Mexican War. Border city and port of entry, it developed through ranching and farming and discovery of oil and gas. Has antimony smelter, foundries, refineries, hat factory, and meat-packing plants.

La Reine, Fort (lä rĕn'), S Man., on Assiniboine R., near the present Portage la Prairie. Built 1738 by Vérendrye.

lares and penates (lâ'rēz, pùnā'tēz), in Roman religion, household gods. Each household had one lar and two penates. The lar was a youth bearing cup and drinking horn; penates were dancing youths, also with drinking horns. The three images stood together in a niche, and offerings were made to them before meals and on festive occasions.

Largillière, Nicolas de (lärzhēlyār'), 1656–1746, French portrait painter. Influenced by Rubens.

Largo Caballero, Francisco (fränthē'skō lär'gō käbälyā'rō), 1869–1946, Spanish Socialist leader. Led in overthrow of monarchy (1931). Premier of Loyalist government 1936–37. Died in Paris.

Larissa (lùrĭ'sù, Gr. lä'rēsä), city (pop. 41,163), N Greece, on the Peneus; cap. of Thessaly. Was annexed by Macedon 4th cent. B.C.; became a Roman ally 196 B.C. Partly destroyed in World War II.

lark, member of large family of perching birds, chiefly of Old World and best known through SKYLARK. Horned larks belong to the only American species. MEADOW LARK belongs to blackbird family.

Larkspur, residential town (pop. 2,905), W Calif., N of San Francisco and near Mt. Tamalpais. Larkspur Canyon near by has redwood grove.

larkspur or **delphinium,** annual or perennial plant of genus *Delphinium* with handsome spires of flowers. Annual kinds are commonly called larkspur and are white, pink, red, or purple; perennials, known as delphinium, are usually white or blue.

Larksville, borough (pop. 6,360), NE Pa., near Wilkes-Barre. Anthracite mining.

La Rochefoucauld, François, duc de (frãswä' dük dù lä rôshfōōkō'), 1613–80, French author. He described his part in the FRONDE (he was wounded at the Faubourg Saint-Antoine) in his remarkable memoirs, but his great work is *Réflexions ou sentences et maximes morales* (1665), in which he viewed selfishness (*amour-propre*) as mainspring of human behavior. His style, peerless in its hard brilliance and incisive clarity, made the maxim a major genre in French literature.

La Rochejaquelein, Henri du Vergier, comte de (ãrē' dü vĕrzhyā' kōt dù lä rôshzhäkùlē'), 1772–94, French commander of counterrevolutionary army in the VENDÉE. Fell in battle.

Lars Porsena or **Lars Porsenna** (lärz' pôr'sùnù, pôrsĕ'nù), semilegendary king of Clusium, Etruria. Conquered Rome and reinstated TARQUIN family (c.500? B.C.), though legend says that heroism of the Romans caused him to abandon the conquest.

larva (lär'vù), term for stage between egg and pupa in life of insects with complete metamorphosis, and for nymph stage of insects with incomplete metamorphosis. It is sometimes used also for immature stages of other animals (e.g., mollusks, crustaceans, fish, amphibia). Grubs are larvae of beetle, bee, and some related insects; maggots are larvae of certain flies; mosquito larvae are wrigglers or wigglers. Larvae usually eat ravenously; many do great damage to crops, foods, etc.

larvae (lär'vē), in Roman religion, ghosts of the dead. To keep them from returning to frighten the living, rites, the Lemuria, were celebrated silently at night in May. See MANES.

larynx (lă'rĭngks), voice organ lying above windpipe. Composed of cartilages, membranes, and two elastic vocal cords extending from front to back wall.

Las. For names beginning thus and not listed here, see second element; e.g., for **Las** Palmas, see PALMAS, LAS.

La Salle, Jean Baptiste de: see JOHN BAPTIST DE LA SALLE, SAINT.

La Salle, Robert Cavelier, sieur de (rōbĕr' kävùlyā' syûr' dù lä säl'), 1643–87, French explorer in North America. Commanded Fort Frontenac, developed trade, built forts. Descended the Mississippi to mouth (1682), claiming entire valley for France. Murdered by own men in futile attempt to reach mouth of the Mississippi by sea.

Lasalle (lùsăl') or **Ville Lasalle,** residential town (pop. 11,633), S Que., Canada, SW of Montreal and on St. Lawrence R.

La Salle (lù săl'), city (pop. 12,083), N Ill., on Illinois R. adjoining Peru, in agr. and mining area; laid out 1837. Mfg. of meat, glass, metal, and zinc products and cement. Near by is Starved Rock.

Las Animas (läs ä'nēmäs), city (pop. 3,223), SE Colo., E of Pueblo. Kit Carson Mus. and site of Bent's Fort are near.

Lascaris, Constantine (kŏn'stŭntēn lă'skŭrĭs), d. 1501?, Greek grammarian. After fall of Constantinople he came to Italy. His Greek grammar (1476) was first book printed in Greek characters.

Las Casas, Bartolomé de (bärtōlōmā' dā läs kä'säs), 1474–1566, Spanish missionary and historian, called Apostle to the Indies. Ordained a priest in Hispaniola 1510, he worked most of his life (in Hispaniola, Peru, Guatemala) for abolition of Indian slavery and for bettering the lot of all Indians. Largely through his efforts the New Laws (1542) were adopted to protect Indians in colonies. Wrote monumental *Historia de las Indias*.

Las Cruces (läs kroō'sĭs), town (pop. 12,325), SW N.Mex., on Rio Grande and NNW of El Paso, Texas, in irrigated farm (cotton, grain, sugar beets, fruit, vegetables) and dairy area; founded 1848. Near by are Tortugas, Indian village, and New Mexico Col. of Agr. and Mechanic Arts (land-grant; coed.; 1889).

Lashio (lăsh'yō), town (pop. 4,638), cap. of Shan State, E Upper Burma; head of Burma Road.

Lashkar (lŭsh'kŭr), city (pop. 113,718), winter cap. of Madhya Bharat, India; commercial and rail center. Palace of maharaja of Gwalior is here.

Lasker, Emanuel (āmä'noōĕl), 1868–1941, German chess player. Won (1894) world's championship by defeating Steinitz, lost (1921) title to Capablanca.

Laski, Harold J(oseph) (lă'skē), 1893–1950, English political scientist, economist, and writer, chairman (1945–46) of the British Labour party, grad. Oxford. He was a member of the executive committee of the Fabian Society and a professor at London School of Economics and Univ. of London. His numerous books include *Reflections on the Revolution of Our Time* (1943) and *The American Democracy* (1948). He taught and lectured much in the U.S.

Lassalle, Ferdinand (fĕr'dēnänt läsäl'), 1825–64, German socialist. In contrast to Marx, he emphasized the role of the state and favored a state system of workers' cooperatives. He greatly influenced the German politics of his day and helped establish the first German workers' political party.

Lassen Peak (lă'sŭn, lä'–), 10,453 ft. high, in Cascade Range, N Calif., is only active volcano in U.S. Included in **Lassen Volcanic National Park:** see NATIONAL PARKS AND MONUMENTS (table).

Last Supper, of Jesus and His disciples at the time of the Pasch just before His crucifixion (Mat. 26.17–30; Mark 14.12–26; Luke 22.7–39; John 13–17; 1 Cor. 11.23–29). For the sacrament, see EUCHARIST and LORD'S SUPPER. It has been a favorite subject of painting; best known is that of Leonardo da Vinci.

Las Vegas (läs vā'gŭs). **1** City (pop. 24,624), S Nev., near Colorado R.; settled 1855 by Mormons and abandoned 1857. U.S. army built Fort Baker here, 1864. In ranching and mining area, city grew after railroad arrived in 1905. Now a resort, famed for gambling and divorces. Atomic Energy Commission installations are near. **2** City (pop. 7,494; alt 6,398 ft.), sometimes called East Las Vegas, N N.Mex., ESE of Santa Fe. Forms one community with Las Vegas town (pop. 6,269; settled c.1835), sometimes called West Las Vegas. Mountain and health resort with dude ranches near by. Shipping center in agr. sheep, and cattle area. Seat of New Mexico Highlands Univ.

Latakia (lătŭkē'ŭ), city (pop. c.35,000), W Syria, port on Mediterranean opposite Cyprus. Was ancient Phoenician city and the Roman Laodicea ad Mare. Incorporated into Syria 1942. Now known for special type of tobacco.

La Tène (lä tĕn'), anc. Celtic settlement, L. Neuchâtel, Switzerland. Tenian culture of second Iron Age, spanning period from 6th cent. B.C. to end of 1st cent. B.C., was so named for antiquities found here.

Lateran (lă'tŭrŭn), name of group of buildings of SE Rome facing the Piazza San Giovanni. Occupies land once belonging to the Laterani and given to the Church by Constantine. The basilica, known as St. John Lateran, is cathedral of Rome, the pope's church, and first-ranking church in Roman Catholic world. Original basilica, built perhaps before 311, was restored 5th–10th cent.; rebuilt and altered 14th–18th cent. Original Lateran palace was replaced in 16th cent. by present palace.

Lateran Councils, 9th–12th and 18th ecumenical councils of the Roman Catholic Church. **1** 1123, summoned by CALIXTUS II. Confirmed Concordat of Worms (1122) ending the INVESTITURE controversy. Forbade clerical marriage or concubinage. **2** 1139, convened by Innocent II to heal the wounds left by schism of antipope Anacletus II (d. 1138). **3** 1179, convened by ALEXANDER III after the Peace of Venice (1178) had reconciled Emperor Frederick I. Most important canon gave papal election exclusively to the cardinals. **4** 1215, convened by INNOCENT III as pinnacle of his pontificate. Its decrees included a statement of faith, definition of transubstantiation, laws for trials of clergy, arrangements for a new crusade. Made annual confession and communion at Easter time minimal requirements for church membership. **5** 1512–17, convened by JULIUS II, continued by LEO X, called to counter an attempt (1510) by Louis XII of France to revive the conciliar theory (see SCHISM, GREAT). The council ratified a papal agreement with France, the Concordat of 1516. It also republished the bull of Julius (1503) declaring that simony invalidated a papal election.

Lateran Treaty, concordat between the Holy See and Italy, signed in 1929 in the Lateran Palace by Cardinal GASPARRI for PIUS XI and by MUSSOLINI for Victor Emmanuel III. Unification of Italy (completed 1871) brought confiscation by the state of all papal possessions except a few buildings. The pope was then granted an annual indemnity, but subsequent popes refused indemnity and looked upon themselves as prisoners. These problems, called the Roman Question, were solved by the treaty, which provided for a sovereign and independent new state called Vatican City and a guarantee of the pope's inviolability by the Italian government.

Lateur, Frank: see STREUVELS, STIJN.

latex: see RUBBER.

lathe (lādh), machine tool to hold and turn wood or metal while it is cut into form desired. The term is also used for loom frame carrying the reed which parts the warp and beats up the weft and for a type of potter's wheel.

Lathrop, Rose Hawthorne, 1850–1926, American Roman Catholic nun; daughter of Nathaniel Hawthorne. She and her husband (the author George Parsons Lathrop) were converted to Catholicism in 1891. She worked much in and near New York city for the care of the poor afflicted with incurable cancer. After her husband's death (1898), she became a nun, and as Mother (Mary) Alphonsa founded a community of Dominican nuns.

Latimer, Hugh (lă'tĭmůr), c.1485–1555, English bishop and martyr. Refused to recant Protestantism at his trial after accession of Catholic Mary I; was burned at the stake with Nicholas RIDLEY.

Latin America, Spanish-speaking, Portuguese-speaking, and French-speaking countries of North America (S of the U.S.), South America, Central America, and West Indies. The 20 republics are Argentina, Bolivia, Brazil, Chile, Colombia, Costa Rica, Cuba, Dominican Republic, Ecuador, El Salvador, Guatemala, Haiti, Honduras, Mexico, Nicaragua, Panama, Paraguay, Peru, Uruguay, and Venezuela. Term also used to include Puerto Rico, French West Indies, and other islands of West Indies where Romance languages are spoken.

Latin Empire of Constantinople: see CONSTANTINOPLE, LATIN EMPIRE OF.

Latini, Brunetto (brōōnĕt'tō lätē'nē), d. 1294?, Italian scholar. Teacher of Dante, he is immortalized in *The Divine Comedy*.

Latin Kingdom of Jerusalem: see JERUSALEM, LATIN KINGDOM OF.

Latin language, Italic language of anc. Rome, standard tongue of most of the Roman Empire. It continued in Romance languages. Schoolbook Latin is that of Cicero and Caesar. The Latin of the Christian Fathers is still official language of Roman liturgy in Roman Catholic Church.

Latins, in anc. times, inhabitants of Latium. Their many small settlements united against Etruscans and Samnites, came under dominance of Rome (338 B.C.). All Latins were granted Roman citizenship after the SOCIAL WAR of 90 B.C.

Latin Way: see ROMAN ROADS.

Latium (lā'shēům), Ital. *Lazio,* region (6,634 sq. mi.; pop. 2,654,924), central Italy, between the Apennines and the Tyrrhenian Sea; cap. Rome. It includes the CAMPAGNA DI ROMA and the former PONTINE MARSHES. The Tiber is the chief river. Region produces wine, olive oil, cereals, vegetables. Inhabited by the LATINS in ancient times, Latium later shared the history of the PAPAL STATES until its annexation by Italy (1870).

La Tour, Georges de (zhôrzh' dů lä tōōr'), 1593–1652, French painter. Used bold nocturnal light effects and simplified, solid forms, as in *Education of the Virgin* (Frick Coll., N.Y.).

La Tour, Maurice Quentin de (mōrēs' kãtẽ' dů lä tōōr'), 1704–88, French portraitist in pastel.

La Tour d'Auvergne, Théophile Corret de (tāôfēl' kôrā' dů lä tōōr' dōvĕr'nyů), 1743–1800, French officer, celebrated for his bravery. Though a nobleman, he fought for the French Revolution and fell in battle. He refused promotion above grade of captain, was officially called "first grenadier of France."

La Trappe: see TRAPPISTS.

La Trémoille or **La Trimouille, Georges de** (zhôrzh' dů lä trāmoi'yů or trēmōō'yů), c.1385–1446, French nobleman, favorite of Charles VII from 1427 to 1433. Probably in Burgundian pay, he favored negotiated peace, opposed Joan of Arc.

Latrobe, Benjamin Henry (lůtrōb'), 1766–1820, American architect, b. England. Came to U.S. in 1796, became surveyor of public buildings in 1803. Introduced Greek forms, important in classic revival; his Bank of the U.S. (now the old Philadelphia Custom House) was based on the Parthenon. Built first American cathedral, the Roman Catholic cathedral in Baltimore (1805–18). Designed Sedgely (1800), a residence near Philadelphia, an early example of Gothic revival in America. A son, **Benjamin Henry Latrobe,** 1806–78, was an eminent engineer. Another son, **John Hazlehurst Boneval Latrobe,** 1803–91, was a lawyer and philanthropist, who supported African colonization of Liberia.

Latrobe, borough (pop. 11,811), SW Pa., ESE of Pittsburgh. Coal mining and mfg. of metal products. Seat of St. Vincent Col.

Latter-Day Saints, Church of Jesus Christ of, religious sect founded (1830) in N.Y. by Joseph SMITH. Its members are called MORMONS, and hq. are in Salt Lake City. Beliefs are based on Bible, Book of Mormon, revelations to Smith (in *Doctrines and Covenants*), and *The Pearl of Great Price* (sayings ascribed to Moses and Abraham). Church is organized with Twelve Apostles. It is marked by importance of revelation and by stress on the interdependence of spiritual and temporal life.

Latter Day Saints, Reorganized Church of Jesus Christ of, separatist group from Mormon Church. Estab. 1852. Hq. since 1904 at Independence, Mo.

Lattimore, Owen, 1900– , American author and educator. Author of books on Far East, and editor of *Pacific Affairs* (1934–41). Director (from 1938) of School of Internatl. Affairs at Johns Hopkins. Adviser (1941–42) to Chiang Kai-shek, and economic adviser (1945–46) Japanese Reparations Commission. Cleared 1950 of espionage charges. Indicted (Dec., 1952) on charges of perjury growing out of hearings before congressional committee.

La Tuque (lä tük'), town (pop. 9,538), S Que., Canada, on St. Maurice R. and NW of Quebec. Pulp-milling center with hydroelectric station.

Latvia (lăt'vēů), Lettish *Latvija,* republic (24,900 sq. mi.; 1935 pop. 1,950,502), NE Europe, bordering on Baltic Sea (W), Estonia

(N), RSFSR (E), and Lithuania (S); cap. RIGA. Its incorporation in 1940 into the USSR as a constituent republic has not been recognized by U.S. (as of 1953). Latvia is a generally hilly, agr. plain (dairying, stock raising, timber). Industries produce fine and heavy machinery. Population is largely Lutheran, except in Roman Catholic Latgale region, in the NE. The regions of Kurzeme and Zemgale, S of Western Dvina R., share the history of COURLAND, of which they were part; Latgale and Vidzeme, N of the Dvina, were part of LIVONIA. With the third Polish partition (1795), all Latvia was in Russian hands, but the German "Baltic barons," settled since the times of the Livonian Knights, remained the dominating class. Devastated in World War I, Latvia was proclaimed independent in 1918 but was invaded in 1919 by Soviet troops. Peace was restored in 1920. In 1934 the parliamentary regime was replaced by a rightist dictatorship under Karlis Ulmanis. USSR secured military bases in 1939, and in 1940 occupied Latvia and made it a constituent Soviet republic. Occupied by Germans 1941–44.

Laud, William, 1573–1645, English churchman, archbishop of Canterbury. Worked with Charles I to oust all Puritans from church positions. Parliamentarians opposed his persecution of nonconformists by tyrannical courts. By decreeing Anglican prayer book compulsory in Scotland he precipitated Bishops' Wars. Condemned by House of Commons through bill of attainder, he was executed.

laudanum: see OPIUM.

Lauderdale, James Maitland, 8th **earl of** (mātʹlůnd, lôʹdůrdāl), 1759–1839, Scottish statesman and author. Long an ardent Whig, he finally became a Tory. Wrote many tracts (e.g., *Inquiry into the Nature and Origin of Public Wealth,* 1804).

Lauderdale, John Maitland, duke of (lôʹdůrdāl), 1616–82, Scottish politician. Imprisoned (1651–60) for support of Charles II. An unpopular member of the CABAL, he was powerful in Scotland.

Laudon or **Loudon, Gideon Ernst, Freiherr von** (both: gēʹdāôn ĕrnstʹ frīʹhĕr fŭn louʹdôn), 1717–90, Austrian field marshal. Defeated Frederick II at Kunersdorf (1759); captured Belgrade from Turks (1789).

Laudonnière, René Goulaine de (růnāʹ gōōlĕnʹ dů lōdônyĕrʹ), fl. 1562–82, French colonizer in Fla. Estab. Fort Caroline near mouth of St. Johns R. (1564). Escaped massacre of settlement by Pedro MENÉNDEZ DE AVILÉS.

Laue, Max von (mäks fŭn louʹů), 1879–, German physicist. Won 1914 Nobel Prize for method of measuring wave lengths of X rays by using a crystal.

Lauenburg (louʹůnbōōrk), former duchy, N Germany, on the lower Elbe; chief city Lauenburg an der Elbe (pop. 11,137). Duchy of Saxe-Lauenburg was held from 1181 by a branch of the Ascanian house of Saxony, upon whose extinction in 1689 it passed to Hanover. Transferred to Danish crown in 1815 (but as member of German Confederation), it was seized by Prussia in Danish War of 1864 and incorporated into Schleswig-Holstein in 1865. Bismarck was created duke of Lauenburg (1890) but never used the title.

laughing gas, colorless gas with sweet taste and odor. It is a compound of nitrogen and oxygen, nitrous oxide. Widely used as dental anesthetic; laughing hysteria is common aftereffect.

Launcelot of the Lake, Sir: see ARTHURIAN LEGEND.

Launceston (lônʹsĕstůn, lŏnʹ–), city (pop. 37,717), on N Tasmania, Australia; port at junction of the North Esk and South Esk; founded 1805. Second largest city of state. Exports dairy products, flour, lumber.

Laura, beloved lady of Petrarch, thought to have been Laura de Noves (1308?–1348), wife of Hugo de Sade.

Laurel. 1 Town (pop. 4,482), W central Md., NE of Washington, D.C. Has large race track. **2** City (pop. 25,038), SE Miss., SE of Jackson on Tallahala Creek; founded 1881. Processes lumber and farm products. Near U.S. Indian school and reservation.

laurel of history and classical literature is an evergreen tree, *Laurus nobilis,* native to Mediterranean region, and called also bay and sweet bay. To the ancients it symbolized victory and merit. Its leaves, sold as bay leaves, are used as flavoring for meats and soups. See also CALIFORNIA LAUREL; MOUNTAIN LAUREL.

Laurencin, Marie (märēʹ lōrāsēʹ), 1885–, French painter. Her work usually has a young girl as the subject, done in pastel colors with a flat surface.

Laurens, Henry (lôʹrůnz), 1724–92, American Revolutionary statesman. Promoted colonial opposition to Britain. President of Second Continental Congress (1777–78). His son, **John Laurens,** 1754–82, patriot officer in American Revolution, drew up terms for surrender of Cornwallis.

Laurens, city (pop. 8,658), NW S.C., NW of Columbia. Mfg. of textiles and glass.

Laurent, Robert (lôʹrůnt), 1890–, American sculptor. Known for sensitive interpretations of the figure.

Laurentian Mountains, range in S Que., Canada, N of St. Lawrence and Ottawa rivers. Resort area.

Laurentian Plateau (lôrĕnʹshůn, lů–), roughly shield-shaped region of rock (also called Canadian shield), the first part of the North American continent permanently elevated above sea level. It is the earth's greatest area of exposed Archaean rocks—largely of granite, gneiss, and schist. During the Pleistocene epoch ice sheets gouged out numerous lake basins, taking away much of the soil. The region is rich in natural resources, including minerals, forests, fur.

Lauria, Roger of: see ROGER OF LORIA.

Laurier, Sir Wilfrid (lôʹrēā), 1841–1919, Canadian statesman, prime minister (1896–1911). Sought to develop dominion within framework of empire.

Laurinburg, town (pop. 7,134), S N.C., near S.C. line, SW of Fayetteville. Mfg. of cotton products and textiles.

Lausanne (lōzänʹ), city (pop. 107,225, incl. Ouchy, its port on L. of Geneva), cap. of Vaud canton, SW Switzerland. Watchmaking; printing; tourism. Seat of Swiss federal tribunal. Was ruled by its bishops till 1536, when it was conquered by Bern and accepted the Reformation. School of theology, a famous center of Calvinism, was founded 1537, was made a university 1890. Bernese rule ended 1798, when Lausanne became cap. of liberated Vaud.

Lausanne, Conference of, 1922–23, peace conference held to write a new peace treaty with Turkey, whose new government under Kemal Pasha (see ATATURK) did not recognize the earlier Treaty of SÈVRES. The treaty, signed 1923, restored E Thrace, the Straits Zone, the Smyrna dist., and other territories to full Turkish sovereignty; abolished foreign zones of influence and capitulations; demanded no reparations. The Straits were to remain demilitarized and subject to an international convention (see DARDANELLES). A separate agreement between Turkey and Greece provided for compulsory exchange of minorities.

Lausitz and **Lausitzer Neisse:** see LUSATIA; NEISSE.

Lautrec, Henri de Toulouse: see TOULOUSE-LAUTREC.

Lauzon (lōzō′), town (pop. 9,643), S Que., Canada, on St. Lawrence R. and NE of Lévis. Has large dry dock. Shipbuilding and lumbering.

Lauzun, Antonin Nompar de Caumont, duc de (ãtônē′ nōpär′ dü kōmō′ dük dü lōzū′), 1633–1723, marshal of France. Despite Louis XIV's opposition, he seems to have secretly married Mlle de Montpensier (c.1681), with whom he quarreled and separated 1684. He brought James II's family to safety from England to France (1688) and in 1689–90 commanded the Irish expedition which ended in defeat at the Boyne.

lava (lä′vü), igneous rock erupted by a volcano on the earth's surface or the ocean floor or from a fissure. The term is applied both to liquid and hardened rock. Lavas are composed chiefly of silica and metallic oxides, varying in color and texture. Before it is exposed to the air lava is called magma. Conflicting theories have been proposed to explain the heat and liquidity of magma, its source, and the cause of its rise in the earth.

Lava Beds National Monument: see NATIONAL PARKS AND MONUMENTS (table).

Lavaca Bay: see MATAGORDA BAY.

Laval, François Xavier de (läväl′), 1623?–1708, French prelate in Canada, first bishop of Quebec (1674–88). Under his strong leadership Quebec church became vital force of colonial life. Founded a seminary, later nucleus of Laval Univ. Fought bitterly with governors. Appears as a character in Willa Cather's novel *Shadows on the Rock.*

Laval, Pierre (pyĕr′), 1883–1945, French politician. At first a socialist, later a conservative, he was twice premier (1931–32, 1935–36). Publication of the Hoare-Laval plan, which proposed to appease Italy by giving it a large part of Ethiopia, caused his fall in 1936. An advocate of Franco-German cooperation, he reached new prominence after the fall of France (1940). In 1940 Marshal Pétain made him foreign minister but soon dismissed him as an intriguer. Reinstated, with full dictatorial powers, in 1942, Laval to all appearances acted as a tool of Germany (see VICHY GOVERNMENT). In 1945, after a much-criticized trial for treason, he was executed.

Laval, town (pop. 28,171), cap. of Mayenne dept., NW France, on Mayenne R. Linen mfg.

Lavalleja, Juan Antonio (hwän′ äntō′nyō läväyä′hä), c.1786–1853, Uruguayan revolutionist. Led the Thirty-three Immortals in declaration of independence from Brazil in 1825. After Uruguay became independent (1827), Lavalleja and Fructuoso Rivera both sought presidency. Rivera won, but Lavalleja led revolts. One of a triumvirate chosen (1852) to govern Uruguay, he died before serving.

La Vallière, Louise de (lwēz′ dü lä välyĕr′), 1644–1710, French noblewoman. Became Louis XIV's mistress in 1661; bore him four children. He made her a duchess (1667) but left her for Mme de Montespan.

Laval University: see QUEBEC, Que.

Lavater, Johann Kaspar (yō′hän käs′pär lä′vätür), 1741–1801, Swiss preacher and theological writer. Remembered for his work on physiognomy.

lavender, aromatic shrubby herb (*Lavendula officinalis*) native to Mediterranean region. It has gray foliage and spikes of small purple flowers. Its flowers are valued for scenting linens, and oil of lavender is used in toiletries and perfumery.

Laveran, (Charles Louis) Alphonse (älfōs′ lävürã′), 1845–1922, French physician. Won 1907 Nobel Prize in Physiology and Medicine for work on protozoa in disease causation. Found cause of malaria (1880).

La Vérendrye, Pierre Gaultier de Varennes, sieur de: see VÉRENDRYE.

Lavery, Sir John (lā′vürē), 1856–1941, British painter, leader of Glasgow school of painting.

Lavisse, Ernest (ĕrnĕst′ lävēs′), 1842–1922, French historian, professor at Sorbonne. Noted for brilliant editorship of several collectively written histories of France, in which he wrote some of best volumes.

Lavoisier, Antoine Laurent (ãtwän′ lōrã′ lävwäzyā′), 1743–94, French chemist, physicist, a founder of modern chemistry. He was one of the first to introduce quantitative chemical methods. He determined the nature of combustion and the role of oxygen in respiration. His classification was the basis of distinction between elements and compounds and of the system of chemical nomenclature. As one of the farmers general he was guillotined during the Reign of Terror.

La Voisin, French poisoner: see POISON AFFAIR.

Lavongai (lävông′ī), volcanic island (c.460 sq. mi.; pop. c.5,000), SW Pacific, in BISMARCK ARCHIPELAGO and part of Territory of New Guinea.

Law, Andrew Bonar (bŏ′nür), 1858–1923, British Conservative statesman. In 1916 he became chancellor of exchequer under Lloyd George. Led revolt from wartime coalition government (1922) and became prime minister. Soon resigned because of ill-health.

Law, John, 1671–1729, Scottish financier in France. Set up (1716) Banque générale, with paper currency issue guaranteed by the state. Acquired commercial monopoly in Louisiana (1717) and set up huge stock company. This was merged (1720) with the bank. Frenzied speculation led to wholesale ruin (see Mississippi Scheme).

Law, William, 1686–1761, English clergyman, nonjuror, noted for controversial, devotional, and mystical writings, which wielded great influence. He was a chief figure in the Bangorian Controversy.

Law, the, in Judaism: see Torah.

Lawes, Sir John Bennet, 1814–1900, English agriculturist. He founded experimental farm at Rothamsted and developed superphosphate which marked beginning of chemical fertilizer industry.

Lawes, Lewis E(dward), 1883–1947, American penologist, warden (1920–41) at Sing Sing Prison, N.Y.

law merchant: see commercial law.

lawn, grass turf or greensward in private grounds or public park. Requires good soil, frequent watering and mowing, occasional rolling and fertilizing. Grasses often used in N U.S. are redtop and other bent types, bluegrass (esp. Kentucky bluegrass), fescue grass, and white clover. In S U.S. lawns are often of Bermuda grass, St. Augustine grass, carpet grass, Korean lawn grass. Lawn may be started with seed, runners or stolons (if creeping bents, Bermuda, or carpet grass is used), or blocks of sod.

Lawnside, borough (1,566), SW N.J., SE of Camden. Site bought by abolitionists for Negroes, 1840. Almost all inhabitants are Negroes.

Lawrence, Saint, d. 258, Roman martyr, supposed to have been roasted to death on a gridiron. Feast: Aug. 10.

Lawrence, Abbott, 1792–1855, American textile manufacturer and statesman. A founder of Lawrence, Mass. While U.S. minister to Great Britain (1849–52) he helped relieve tension over proposed isthmian canal and status of Mosquito Coast. His nephew, **Amos Adams Lawrence,** 1814–86, was a colonizer and philanthropist. He backed Emigrant Aid Company in settlement of Kansas. Aided founding of Univ. of Kansas and Lawrence Col. at Appleton, Wis.

Lawrence, Charles, 1709–60, governor of Nova Scotia, b. England. Mainly by his orders the Acadians were deported (see Acadia).

Lawrence, D(avid) H(erbert), 1885–1930, English author. He wrote of primitive and natural passions, trying to show instinctive forces in man that might bring happiness. Novels include *Sons and Lovers* (1913), *The Rainbow* (1915), *Women in Love* (1920), *The Plumed Serpent* (1926), and *Lady Chatterley's Lover* (1928). He also wrote stories, essays, and other works (e.g., *Mornings in Mexico,* 1927). Traveled in search of health, spending some time in N.Mex.

Lawrence, Ernest Orlando, 1901–, American physicist. Won 1939 Nobel Prize for invention of cyclotron and research in atomic structure.

Lawrence, James, 1781–1813, American naval hero. Commanded *Chesapeake* in battle with British frigate *Shannon* (1813). His dying command, "Don't give up the ship!" became popular naval battle cry.

Lawrence, Sir Thomas, 1769–1830, English portrait painter. Succeeded Reynolds as painter in ordinary to the king (1792) and was knighted in 1815. The fashionable portrai painter of his day, he was perhaps most suc cessful in studies of children, notably *Th Calmady Children* (Metropolitan Mus.) an *Pinkie* (Huntington Gall.). Another well known portrait is that of Mrs. Siddons (Nat Gall., London).

Lawrence, T(homas) E(dward), 1888–193 British adventurer, soldier, and schola Joined revolt of Feisal I in World War I an helped defeat the Turks. Feeling that th Arabs had been betrayed in British action after the war, he joined RAF under an as sumed name. "Lawrence of Arabia" attracte much popular attention by his exotic caree Wrote *The Seven Pillars of Wisdom* (193 abridged version, *Revolt in the Desert,* 1927 and translated the *Odyssey.*

Lawrence, William, 1850–1941, American Epis copal bishop of Mass. (1893). Founde Church pension system. His son, **Willia Appleton Lawrence,** 1889–, became bisho of Western Mass. in 1937.

Lawrence. 1 City (pop. 23,351), NE Kansa on Kansas R. and WSW of Kansas City Founded 1854 for New England Emigran Aid Co. by Charles Robinson, it was name for A. A. Lawrence. Had first church (1854 of Kansas settlers. Political center of the Fre Staters, it was actual, though not legal, cap for a time after 1857. Proslavery raid (1856 led to Pottawatamie killings by John Brown Town sacked 1863 by W. C. Quantrill Processing and shipping center for grain growing and truck-farming area. Seat o Univ. of Kansas and Haskell Inst. (1884) largest Indian school in U.S. **2** Industrial cit (pop. 80,536), NE Mass., on Merrimack R (water power) and NE of Lowell. Settle 1655; laid out 1845 as industrial town b Boston capitalists, who built dam, mills workers' dwellings. Became a world cente for woolens. Mfg. also of cotton goods shoes; paper, rubber, plastic products; radi equipment, machinery. Scene of labor strif (I.W.W.) in 1912.

Lawrenceburg. 1 City (pop. 4,806), SE Ind., o the Ohio and W of Cincinnati, in agr. area **2** City (pop. 5,442), S Tenn., SSW of Nash ville, in dairy, livestock, and cotton area.

Lawrence College of Wisconsin: see Appleton

Lawrenceville. 1 City (pop. 6,328), SE Ill. WNW of Vincennes, Ind., in agr. area. Re fines oil; mfg. of oil-well and telephone equip ment. **2** Village (pop. 1,056), W N.J., nea Trenton. Has transoceanic radiotelephon transmitting station and Lawrenceville Schoo for boys (prep.; nonsectarian; estab. 1810)

Lawrie, Lee (lô'rē), 1877–, American sculpto His *Prometheus* at Rockefeller Center, Ne York.

Lawson, Ernest, 1873–1939, American land scape painter, one of The Eight. Painted i impressionistic style.

lawsuit: see procedure.

Lawton, city (pop. 34,757), SW Okla., nea Wichita Mts.; founded 1901. Commercial an industrial center of agr. area (esp. cotton) Oil, asphalt, and granite deposits near. U.S Fort Sill, Fort Sill Indian school, and Med icine Park close by.

laxative, substance used to stimulate elimination

of wastes from intestines. Various kinds act by irritating intestines to increased muscular action, by increasing bulk in tract, or by lubricating tract. Their use may inhibit normal intestinal action, prevent absorption of essential food elements, or cause rupturing of appendix.

Laxness, Halldor (Kiljan) (häl'dōr kĭl'yän läkhs'nĕs), 1902–, Icelandic novelist. Early works had religious, later had Communist, tinge. In novel cycles *Salka Valka* (1931–32) and *Independent People* (1934–35) he created a new modern style in Icelandic literature.

Layamon (lā'ŭmŭn, -mŏn, lī'-, lä'mŭn), fl. c.1200, first prominent Middle English poet, author of *Brut,* chronicle of early history of Britain.

Layard, Sir Austen Henry (lā'ŭrd), 1817–94, English archaeologist and diplomat. Excavated in Mesopotamia and Babylon (1842–51). Minister to Spain (1869–77). Ambassador to Constantinople (1877–80).

Lazarillo de Tormes (läthärē'lyō dā tôr'mās), Spanish picaresque novel published before 1554. Formerly ascribed to Hurtado de Mendoza.

Lazarus (lă'-). **1** Brother of Mary and Martha, raised from the dead by Jesus. John 11.1–44; 12.1–5. **2** Beggar-hero of parable told by Jesus. Luke 16.19–25.

Lazarus, Emma, 1849–87, American poet, b. N.Y. city, best known for *Songs of a Semite* (1882); *Poems* (1889). Her Statue of Liberty poem (1886) is carved inside the pedestal of the statue.

Le. For names beginning thus and not listed here, see second element; e.g., for Le Havre, see HAVRE, LE.

Leacock, Stephen (Butler), 1869–1944, Canadian economist and humorist, b. England. Head of department of political science and economics at McGill Univ. (1908–36). Best known for his many volumes of humorous essays and stories, including many parodies.

Lead, city (pop. 6,422), W S.Dak., in the Black Hills near Wyo. line; laid out 1876 after discovery of gold here. Site of Homestake Mine, largest gold mine in the U.S.

lead, heavy metallic element (symbol = Pb; see also ELEMENT, table), one of the oldest metals used by man. Light silver when freshly cut, it darkens on exposure to air. It is soft, malleable, of low tensile strength, and a poor conductor. It is a component of many alloys. Used for covering cables, as lining for laboratory sinks, in electrolytic cells, in chambers for making sulphuric acid, in storage battery plates. Compounds (all poisons) are used in paints, glass, gasoline, in thickening oils, in construction.

lead poisoning, industrial disease (also called plumbism and painter's colic) caused by absorption of lead through respiratory or digestive tracts. It may result from drinking from receptacles containing lead. Supervision of working conditions in industries using lead has reduced incidence of disease.

Leadville, mining city (pop. 4,081; alt. c.10,200 ft.), central Colo., near headwaters of Arkansas R. SW of Denver. Area had brief gold boom, c.1860. Lead with high silver content caused new boom, 1877. One of world's great silver camps by 1880 (c.40,000 pop.), it declined with repeal of Sherman Silver Act in 1893, but soon revived with new gold boom. Fortunes made fast, often lost fast. History of H. A. W. TABOR symbolizes Leadville's story. Some mining and smelting still carried on (near-by Climax has large molybdenum output). Tourism.

Leaf, river of N Que., Canada, issuing from L. Minto, and flowing c.300 mi. NE to Ungava Bay.

leaf, one of the chief vegetative organs of a plant. Green color is caused by pigment CHLOROPHYLL, necessary for PHOTOSYNTHESIS, the process by which carbohydrates (sugar and starch) are formed. Thus leaves are ultimate basis of most animal life. Autumn coloration of leaves is caused by low temperatures and other factors which destroy chlorophyll and make visible other pigments. Combinations of these pigments are present in variegated leaves; white leaves, often produced by blanching, result from lack of pigments. See *ill.*, p. 999.

leafhopper, any of numerous species of small leaping insects of family Cicadellidae, order Homoptera. Found over most of world; nearly all plants are damaged by some species.

leaf insect, leaf-eating, usually arboreal insect, order Phasmatida (formerly included in Orthoptera). Walking leaf is winged tropical species resembling leaf; WALKING STICK resembles a twig.

League or **Holy League,** 1576–98, organization of French Catholics, aimed at suppression of Protestantism during Wars of RELIGION; founded by Henri, 3d duc de GUISE. King HENRY III, fearing Guise's ambition, proclaimed himself its head and dissolved it in 1577, but in 1585 the League was revived to prevent the succession of Henry of Navarre (see HENRY IV), who ultimately defeated it in spite of the support it received from Spain.

League of Nations, former international organization, predecessor of UNITED NATIONS, which had as aims maintenance of peace, arbitration of international disputes, and promotion of international cooperation. It was product of World War I and ideas of General SMUTS, Léon BOURGEOIS, and Lord Robert Cecil. Pres. Woodrow WILSON incorporated proposal into FOURTEEN POINTS and was chief figure in founding of League at Paris Peace Conference in 1919. Basis of League was Covenant, included in Treaty of VERSAILLES. Geneva was hq. League consisted of assembly composed of all members; council composed of Great Powers (England, France, Italy, and Japan, later also Germany and USSR); and several allied bodies, e.g., WORLD COURT and INTERNATIONAL LABOR ORGANIZATION. Covenant had 26 articles concerning organization, need for disarmament, guarantees of territorial status quo against aggression, provision for arbitration and conciliation with SANCTION against aggressors. It provided for treaties, MANDATE system of colonial administration, international cooperation in labor and humanitarian enterprises. League suffered severe handicap in refusal of

U.S. to join and in insistence of all members upon their national sovereignty. A general DISARMAMENT CONFERENCE was called, but was unsuccessful. League failed, moreover, because powerful nations could not be coerced into mutual compromise or acceptance of its decisions. However, among problems settled by League were Swedish-Finnish dispute over ALAND ISLANDS (1920); status of N SCHLESWIG and Upper SILESIA, settled by plebiscites (1920, 1921); population exchanges of Greece, Turkey, and Bulgaria after Treaty of Lausanne of 1923; and Yugoslav-Hungarian dispute after assassination (1934) of King ALEXANDER of Yugoslavia. League extended much aid to refugees, especially Armenians; helped suppress white slave and opium traffic; pioneered in health surveys; extended aid to needy states, e.g., Austria; and furthered international cooperation in many fields. Early failures were Polish refusal to accept League decision in VILNA dispute; shelving of Geneva Protocol because of British opposition; and split of France and LITTLE ENTENTE with Great Britain. League's decay began with Second CHINO-JAPANESE WAR in 1931 and withdrawal of Japan from League. League was unable to stop war of Bolivia and Uruguay over Chaco (1932–35). Adolf Hitler began to rearm, withdrew Germany from League 1933, remilitarized Rhineland 1936, denounced Treaty of Versailles 1936, and seized Austria 1938. Italy under Mussolini attacked ETHIOPIA 1935, disregarding economic sanction by League. Japan resumed war with China 1937, and appeasement policy of dominant League members—Great Britain and France—reached apex in MUNICH PACT 1938, which virtually discarded League as international instrument. League dissolved itself, April, 1946, and transferred its services and real estate to UN.

League of Women Voters, organized in Chicago in Feb., 1920. Purposes are to educate women in use of vote and through educational and research campaigns to improve the general political, economic, and social structure.

Leah, Jacob's unloved first wife; mother of Reuben, Simeon, Levi, Judah, Issachar, Zebulun. Gen. 29–30.

Leahy, Frank (William) (lā'hē), 1908–, American football coach. Head coach Boston College 1939–41; athletic director and head coach Notre Dame 1941–43, 1946–. In four complete seasons through 1949, Notre Dame played 38 straight games without defeat (though with two ties).

Leamington, town (pop. 6,950), S Ont., Canada, on L. Erie and SE of Windsor. Port, resort, and agr. center with canneries.

Leamington (lĕ'mĭngtŭn), officially Royal Leamington Spa, municipal borough (pop. 36,345), Warwickshire, England; health resort with mineral springs.

Leander, lover of HERO.

Lear (lēr), legendary English king, turned out by two elder daughters, then welcomed by third, whom he had disinherited. Subject of Shakspere's great tragedy.

Lear, Edward, 1812–88, English artist and humorist, known for illustrated limericks and poems (as in *A Book of Nonsense,* 1846).

Leaside, NE suburb of Toronto (pop. 16,233), S Ont., Canada. Mfg. of trucks.

leather, skin or hide of mammals, reptiles, or birds tanned to prevent decay and to impart flexibility and toughness. Pelts usually are dehaired, submitted to TANNING process, made pliable with fats, and desired finish is produced by process such as glazing, coloring, lacquering, suèding, or embossing. The pelt or leather is split by machine into flesh and grain (hair-side) layers to achieve required thickness. Artificial leather has fabric base usually coated with synthetic substance.

Leavenworth (lĕ'vŭnwûrth), city (pop. 20,579), NE Kansas, on the Missouri and NW of Kansas City. Oldest city in Kansas, it was settled 1854 by proslavery Missourians. Had state's first newspaper (1854). Was supply point for westbound travelers. Trade center for agr. and coal area, it has flour milling, meat packing, metalworking, and mfg. of furniture.

Leavenworth, Fort, U.S. military post, on Missouri R. and near Leavenworth, Kansas. Built 1827 to protect traffic of old Santa Fe Trail. At present it includes a command and general staff school and a Federal penitentiary.

Lebanon (lĕ'bŭnŭn), republic (3,927 sq. mi.; pop. 1,165,208), SW Asia; cap. Beirut. Bordered on W by the Mediterranean, on N and E by Syria, and on S by Israel. Valley of El Bika (which produces grain and fruit) lies between coastal Lebanon Mts. and Anti-Lebanon range (on E border). In ancient times the region was dominated by Hittites and Aramaeans; it later became center of PHOENICIAN CIVILIZATION. With Syria the area came under Roman dominion and was included in Byzantine Empire until part of it fell to Arabs in 7th cent. Despite enmity of the DRUSES, the MARONITES remained strong enough to keep the region predominantly Christian. After the Crusades, area was under Ottoman control until World War I, after which Levant States (Syria and Lebanon) were put under French mandate. Lebanon became a republic under the mandate in 1926; treaty of 1936 (not ratified by France) provided for freedom after three-year transition period. In World War II, Vichy control overthrown by British and Free French forces, June–July, 1941. Lebanon became free on Jan. 1, 1944. Joined Arab League in 1945.

Lebanon. 1 City (pop. 7,631), central Ind., NW of Indianapolis, in dairying region. Metal products. **2** City (pop. 4,640), central Ky., SE of Louisville. A national cemetery is near. **3** City (pop. 6,808), S central Mo., NE of Springfield, in an Ozark timber and farm area. Has garment factory and food-processing plants. **4** Town (pop. 8,495), W N.H., S of Hanover and near Connecticut R. Wood products and woolens. **5** City (pop. 5,873), NW Oregon, SSE of Salem, in fruit (esp. strawberries) and grain region. Paper and lumber mills. **6** City (pop. 28,156), E Pa., ENE of Harrisburg; settled c.1720. Center of rich agr. area with mfg. of iron and steel products and textiles. **7** Town (pop.

7,913), central Tenn., E of Nashville in timber and farm area. The HERMITAGE is near. Mfg. of wood and cloth products.

Lebanon, anc. *Libanus,* mountain range, Lebanon, paralleling Mediterranean coast. Rises to 10,131 ft. Famed in ancient times for its huge cedars.

Leblanc, Nicholas, 1742–1806, French chemist. He developed the **Leblanc process** for commercial preparation of soda from common salt. Salt is treated with sulphuric acid to yield sodium sulphate; this is reduced by carbon to give sodium sulphide. Sodium carbonate (soda) is formed by reaction between this and limestone. This process was largely displaced by the Solvay process.

Lebrun, Albert (älbĕr′ lůbrŭ′), 1871–1950, last president of Third Republic of France. Elected 1932 and reelected 1939, he was deprived of all authority by Marshal Pétain in 1940. In 1944 he recognized Charles de Gaulle as provisional president of France.

Le Brun, Charles (shärl′ lů brŭ′), 1619–90, French artist. In 1648 he founded Royal Academy to replace guilds. As painter to Louis XIV he directed decorative works at Versailles and Chateau de Vaux.

Lebrun, Élisabeth Vigée-: see VIGÉE-LEBRUN.

Lecce (lĕt′chā), city (pop. 42,622), S Apulia, S Italy. Was a semi-independent county, 1053–1463. Has many baroque churches and palaces.

Lech (lĕkh), river, c.175 mi. long, rising in Vorarlberg, Austria, and flowing NE through Bavaria, past Augsburg, into the Danube. In 1632 Gustavus II of Sweden defeated Tilly, who was mortally wounded, on the Lech near its confluence with the Danube. On the **Lechfeld,** a plain near Augsburg, Otto I decisively defeated the Magyars in 955.

Lecky, William Edward Hartpole, 1838–1903, British historian. His major work, *History of England in the Eighteenth Century* (8 vols., 1878–90), ranks him as literary historian very near to Gibbon.

Leclerc, Charles Victor Emmanuel (shärl′ vēktôr′ ĕmänüĕl′ lůklĕr′), 1772–1802, French general; first husband of Pauline Bonaparte. In 1801 he led the expedition against TOUSSAINT L'OUVERTURE in Haiti. His treacherous arrest of Toussaint led to a native revolt under DESSALINES, who expelled the French. Leclerc died of yellow fever on Tortuga.

Leclerc, Jacques Philippe (zhäk′ fēlēp′), 1902–47, French general. His real name was Philippe, comte de Hauteclocque. In World War II he led Free French forces in epic march from Lake Chad to Tripoli (Dec., 1942–Jan., 1943); took part in Tunisian campaign (1943) and in liberation of Paris (1944).

Lecompton (lůkŏmp′tůn), city (pop. 263), NE Kansas, on Kansas R. and E of Topeka. Territorial cap. 1855–58. Here was formulated proslavery **Lecompton Constitution.** Slavery clause was approved in Dec., 1857, as Free State men declined to vote. Pres. Buchanan urged Congress to admit Kansas under this constitution, but bill could not pass the House. Submitted to popular vote, constitution was decisively rejected in Aug., 1858.

Leconte de Lisle, Charles (shärl′ lůkōt′ dů lēl′), 1818–94, French poet, the leading Parnassian. A pessimist, he saw death as only reality and drew inspiration from antiquity, as in *Poèmes antiques* (1852), *Poésies barbares* (1862), and *Poèmes tragiques* (1884).

Le Corbusier (lů kôrbüzyā′), pseud. of Charles Édouard Jeanneret, 1887–, Swiss architect. His first experimental studies (1915) showed a new and radical attitude toward technical and aesthetic problems of building. His famous "Citrohan" model for dwellings (1921) expressed new construction methods. Exerted wide influence on modern architecture by his writings. A prize winner in competition (1927) for Geneva palace of League of Nations, he was chosen in 1946 as one of group of architects to design UN headquarters in New York.

Lecouvreur, Adrienne (ädrēĕn′ lůkōōvrûr′), 1692–1730, French actress. After her debut in 1717, she was the idol of the public until her mysterious death. Her romance with Maurice de Saxe was tragic.

Leda (lē′dů), in Greek mythology, wife of Tyndareus, king of Sparta, and by him mother of Clytemnestra. In one legend, Zeus visited Leda as swan, and she bore two eggs; from one issued Helen and from the other came Castor and Pollux.

Ledo Road: see BURMA ROAD.

Ledru-Rollin, Alexandre Auguste (älĕksã′drů ōgüst′ lůdrü′-rôlē′), 1807–74, French politician. An active promoter of the FEBRUARY REVOLUTION of 1848, he was minister of the interior in Lamartine's government and introduced universal suffrage. Passing to the opposition after the JUNE DAYS, he formed the Social Democratic party but was soon after forced to flee to England (1849).

Ledyard, John (lĕd′yůrd), 1751–89, American adventurer. Failed to secure funds in U.S. or France for expedition to find Northwest Passage. Attempted to walk across Europe and through Siberia; arrested at Yakutsk and sent back.

Lee, Virginia family, of which Robert E. LEE was most distinguished member. **Richard Lee,** d. 1664, American colonist, b. England, was the founder of the Lee family of Va. **Arthur Lee,** 1740–92, was an American Revolutionary diplomat, agent of Continental Congress to secure French aid. Recalled after quarrel with Silas Deane. His brother, **Francis Lightfoot Lee,** 1734–97, served in Continental Congress (1775–80) and signed Declaration of Independence. Another brother, **Richard Henry Lee,** 1732–94, also served in Continental Congress (1774–80, 1784–87) and signed Declaration of Independence. U.S. Senator (1789–92). A fourth brother, **William Lee,** 1739–95, diplomatic agent of Continental Congress, was unable to obtain support from Austria or Prussia. Unofficial U.S.-Dutch treaty he helped draft became cause of war between Great Britain and the Netherlands. **Henry Lee,** 1756–1818, American Revolutionary cavalry general, usually known as Light-Horse Harry Lee, was a cousin of these four brothers and father of Robert E. Lee.

Lee, Ann, 1736–84, religious visionary, founder of SHAKERS in America, b. England. She formed (1776) first Shaker settlement at present Watervliet, N.Y.

Lee, Arthur: see LEE, family.

Lee, Charles, 1731–82, American Revolutionary general, b. England. Settled in Va. (1773). Traitorously aided British when captured in 1776. Later exchanged, but court-martialed for disobedience at battle of Monmouth (1778). Criticism of Washington led to dismissal (1780).

Lee, Fitzhugh: see LEE, ROBERT E.

Lee, Francis Lightfoot: see LEE, family.

Lee, George Washington Custis: see LEE, ROBERT E.

Lee, Henry: see LEE, family.

Lee, Jason, 1803–45, American pioneer in Oregon, a Methodist missionary. Missions founded by him and his associates were centers of settlement.

Lee, John Doyle, 1812–77, American Mormon leader. Executed for leading massacre (1857) at MOUNTAIN MEADOWS.

Lee, Light-Horse Harry: see LEE, family.

Lee, Nathaniel, 1653?–1692, English dramatist. He wrote poetic tragedies with classical backgrounds, notably *The Rival Queens* (1677).

Lee, Richard, and **Richard Henry Lee:** see LEE, family.

Lee, Robert E(dward), 1807–70, general in chief of Confederate armies in Civil War; son of Henry Lee. Superintendent of West Point (1852–55). Though he loved the Union and the army, he was loyal to Va. when it seceded. Became military adviser to Jefferson Davis and, from June 1, 1862, commander of Army of Northern Virginia. He checked G. B. McClellan's threat to Richmond in SEVEN DAYS BATTLES (June 26–July 2), and defeated John Pope in second battle of Bull Run (Aug. 29–30). McClellan, however, checked his first Northern invasion, ANTIETAM CAMPAIGN (Sept.). He defeated A. E. Burnside at Fredericksburg (Dec. 13, 1862), and Joseph Hooker at CHANCELLORSVILLE (May 2–4, 1863). Assumed full blame for failure of GETTYSBURG CAMPAIGN. In 1864 he repulsed U. S. Grant's attacks in WILDERNESS CAMPAIGN, but could not prevent long siege of Petersburg. Appointed general in chief, Feb., 1865. Surrendered to Grant at Appomattox Courthouse, April 9, 1865. After war he was president of Washington Col. (now Washington and Lee Univ.). A great commander, a man of exalted character, Lee was idolized by South and has become an American hero. His son, **George Washington Custis Lee,** 1832–1913, was a Confederate general. Succeeded his father as president of Washington and Lee Univ. (1871–97). Another son, **William Henry Fitzhugh Lee,** known as **Rooney Lee,** 1837–91, was a Confederate cavalry general. Served creditably under J. E. B. Stuart. **Fitzhugh Lee,** 1835–1905, Confederate cavalry general, was a nephew of R. E. Lee. Brilliantly covered retreat from Antietam campaign.

Lee, Sir Sidney, 1859–1926, English editor of *Dictionary of National Biography*.

Lee, William: see LEE, family.

Lee, William Henry Fitzhugh: see LEE, ROBERT E.

Leech, John, 1817–64, English caricaturist and illustrator, associated mainly with *Punch* magazine.

leech, annelid worm, round or slightly flattened, with segments externally divided by secondary rings, and a suction disk at each end of the body. Leeches live chiefly in fresh water (a few on land and in sea) in temperate and tropical regions. Most are bloodsuckers. Leech of genus *Hirudo* was formerly much used by physicians to bleed patients.

leechee: see LITCHI.

Leech Lake, large lake, N central Minn., SE of Bemidji and lying mainly within Leech Lake Indian Reservation. Used as reservoir.

Leeds, county borough (pop. 504,954) and city, W. Riding of Yorkshire, England; center of industrial district (to W and S) and important transportation junction. Has mfg. of woolen and metal goods, chemicals, and glass. Yorkshire Col. (1874) became Univ. of Leeds in 1904. Triennial music festivals are held. Near-by Kirkstall Abbey founded 1152.

leek, hardy garden vegetable (*Allium porrum*), closely related to onion. Leafstalk and basal leaves, which have a mild onion flavor, are blanched and served like asparagus, or used in soups and stews. Its leaves are worn by the Welsh on St. David's day.

Lee Mansion National Memorial, N. Va., across Potomac R. from Washington, D.C., in Arlington Natl. Cemetery. As Arlington House was home of R. E. Lee, inherited by his wife. Abandoned by Lees in Civil War; was used as field hospital after first battle of Bull Run. Made memorial 1925.

Leesburg, city (pop. 7,395), N central Fla., between Harris and Griffin lakes. Head of navigation on Oklawaha R. system. Processes and ships fruit and truck.

Leeuwarden (lā'vär"důn), Frisian *Lieuwert*, municipality (pop. 72,008), cap. of Friesland prov., N Netherlands; chartered 1435. An agr. and dairying center, it is important cattle market. Has mfg. of clothing and artificial silk. It was gold- and silver-working center, 16th–18th cent.

Leeuwenhoek, Antony van (än'tōnē vän lā'vůnho͝ok"), 1632–1723, Dutch student of natural history. He made powerful lenses and simple microscopes and, using them, was first to see protozoa and bacteria; he gave first complete description of red blood cells.

Leeward Islands (lo͞o'ůrd, lū'ůrd, lē'ůrd), N group of Lesser Antilles in West Indies, extending SE from Puerto Rico to Windward Isls. Principal islands are VIRGIN ISLANDS of the U.S., GUADELOUPE (French), St. Eustatius and Saba (Dutch), SAINT MARTIN (jointly owned by Dutch and French) and British Leeward Isls. colony (ANTIGUA, SAINT KITTS, Nevis, Montserrat, and British Virgin Isls.). Discovered by Columbus (1493). A long contest between England, France, and Spain for possession was finally resolved at end of Napoleonic Wars (1815).

Le Fanu, (Joseph) Sheridan (lĕ'fůnū), 1814–73, Irish novelist and journalist, known for tales of mystery and terror, notably *Uncle Silas* (1864).

Lefebvre, Jules Joseph (zhül' lůfĕ'vrů), 1836–1912, French figure painter, a popular teacher.

Lefkosha, Turkish name of NICOSIA, Cyprus.

Le Gallienne, Richard (lůgăl'yůn), 1866–1947, English literary critic, man of letters; a contributor to *Yellow Book*. Lived long in U.S.

His daughter, **Eva Le Gallienne,** 1899–, American actress, producer, played in dramas by Molnar, Ibsen and others. Founded (1926) Civic Repertory Theatre and (1946, with Margaret Webster) American Repertory Theatre.

Legal Tender cases, lawsuits before U.S. Supreme Court testing Legal Tender Act of 1862. Passed to meet wartime currency needs, act authorized issue of greenbacks without any reserve or specie basis. Declared unconstitutional in 1870, act was held valid in 1871 and 1884.

Legaré, Hugh Swinton (lŭgrē′), 1797–1843, American statesman. U.S. Attorney General (1841–43). A founder of *Southern Review;* its editor 1828–32.

Legaspi (lŭgä′spē), town (pop. 15,780), on SE Luzon, Philippines; port on Albay Gulf.

Legendre, Adrien Marie (ädrēē′ märē′ lŭzhã′drŭ), 1752–1833, French mathematician. He is noted for work on theory of numbers and elliptical integrals, and for the invention (independently of Gauss) of method of least squares. Collaborated in drawing up centesimal trigonometric tables. Wrote influential mathematical works.

Léger, Alexis Saint-Léger (älĕksēs′ sē-lāzhā′ lāzhā′), pseud. **Saint-Jean Perse,** 1887–, French poet, statesman. He was Briand's aide and in 1933 became general secretary of ministry of foreign affairs. He is considered by many as greatest French poet of his age. His poetry includes *Éloges* (1910), *Anabase* (1924; Eng. tr. by T. S. Eliot, 1930), *Exil* (1942).

Léger, Fernand (fĕrnã′ lāzhā′), 1881–, French painter. A modified cubist, he depicts the machine in dynamic style. Created two abstract designs for auditorium of UN General Assembly building, New York.

Leghorn (lĕg′hôrn), Ital. *Livorno,* city (pop. 109,067), Tuscany, central Italy; third largest port on Italian W coast. Seat of naval academy. Was developed in 16th cent. by the Medici; in 1590 Ferdinand I made it a free port and opened it to religious and political refugees. Damage in World War II includes cathedral and 16th-cent. synagogue.

legion, large unit of the Roman army. Varied in number (from 3,000 to 6,000 men in Caesar's time); divided into cohorts (in turn, divided into centuries). Primarily heavy infantry, the soldiers carried armor, weapons, provisions, and camping equipment. They accomplished the Roman conquests, but were finally vulnerable to highly mobile cavalry and guerrilla warfare of their enemies.

Legion of Honor: see DECORATIONS, CIVIL AND MILITARY.

legitimation, the act of giving a child born out of wedlock the status of legitimacy. Subsequent marriage of the parents is the general form in the U.S., though some states require special proceedings, and in others one or both parents may adopt the child.

Legnano (lānyä′nō), city (pop. 31,959), N Italy, NW of Milan. Scene of defeat of Emperor Frederick I by Lombard League (1176).

Legros, Alphonse (älfõs′ lŭgrō′), 1837–1911, French painter of religious subjects, portraits, and peasant scenes. Taught in London.

Leguía, Augusto Bernardino (ougōōs′tō bĕrnärdē′nō lāgē′ä), 1863–1932, president of Peru (1908–12, 1919–30). His acceptance of Jacna-Arica compromise coupled with economic depression, his financial dealings, and his dictatorial rule caused his overthrow.

legume (lĕ′gūm), common name for pulse or pea family (Leguminosae) which contains plants of ornamental and economic value, e.g., peas, beans, clover, acacia, wisteria, lupine. Some legumes are used as green manure to increase nitrogen of the soil.

Lehar, Franz (lā′här), 1870–1948, composer of operettas, b. Komarno (then in Hungary); after 1889 he lived in Vienna. *The Merry Widow* (1905) was his outstanding success.

Lehi (lē′hī), place, SW Palestine, where Samson slew Philistines with jawbone of an ass. Judges 15.9–20.

Lehigh, river rising in NE Pa. and flowing 103 mi. S and W through coal and mfg. region to Delaware R. at Easton.

Lehighton, borough (pop. 6,565), E Pa., on Lehigh R. and NNW of Allentown. Textile mills.

Lehigh University, at Bethlehem, Pa.; nonsectarian, mainly for men; chartered and opened 1866.

Lehman, Herbert H(enry) (lē′mŭn), 1878–, American statesman. Notable Democratic governor of N.Y. (1932–42). U.S. Senator (1949–).

Lehman Caves National Monument: see NATIONAL PARKS AND MONUMENTS (table).

Lehmann, Lilli (lā′män), 1848–1929, German operatic soprano. Sang in the first Bayreuth Festival, 1876. Appeared at the Metropolitan Opera, New York, 1885–90. She was also a great lieder singer and a noted teacher.

Lehmann, Lotte, 1888–, German-American soprano. Made her American debut in Chicago as Sieglinde in *Die Walküre* in 1930. Appeared at the Metropolitan Opera, New York, 1934–46. As a concert artist, she was known for her singing of lieder.

Lehmbruck, Wilhelm (vĭl′hĕlm lām′brŏŏk), 1881–1919, German sculptor. His female nudes have a Gothic elongation.

Leibl, Wilhelm (vĭl′hĕlm lī′bŭl), 1844–1900, German genre and portrait painter. Lived most of his life as a Bavarian peasant. Intensely realistic style.

Leibniz or **Leibnitz, Gottfried Wilhelm, Baron von** (līp′nĭts), 1646–1716, German philosopher and mathematician, who was also learned in science, history, and law. Served as a diplomat in service of archbishop of Mainz and was long in Paris. He developed the infinitesimal calculus (1675–76) without knowing of Newton's work in the field. Later he served the duke of Brunswick and became first president of the Prussian academy of science (he had suggested its founding). His philosophy—expressed in such works as *Monadology* (1714) and *Principles of Nature and Grace* (1714) and many letters and essays—rests fundamentally on the conception of the universe as made up of an infinite number of units of spiritual force or matter, which he called monads. These, being substance, cannot interact, but each reflects the universe in itself (thus making perception possible). There is a hierarchy of monads rising up to God, the supreme monad, who allows freedom of the will but still shapes the world as the best of all possible worlds.

Leicester, Robert Dudley, earl of (lĕ'stûr), 1532?–1588, English courtier and favorite of Queen ELIZABETH. Involved in plot to place Lady Jane Grey upon throne, he was later pardoned. Elizabeth for a time thought of marrying him. Leader at court (from c.1564) of Puritan party which desired war with Spain, he commanded (1585–87) an unsuccessful expedition to the Low Countries.

Leicester, England: see LEICESTERSHIRE.

Leicester of Holkham, Thomas William Coke, earl of (kŏŏk, hōl'kûm), 1752–1842, English politician and agriculturist. For over 50 years he represented Norfolk in Parliament. His improvement of breeds of livestock and development of his estate led to more scientific farming.

Leicestershire (lĕ'stûrshĭr) or **Leicester** (lĕs'-tûr), inland county (832 sq. mi.; pop. 630,893), central England. Primarily agr. and pastoral county, it makes well-known Stilton cheese. Has famous fox-hunting centers. Defeat of Richard III by Henry VII at Bosworth (1485) ended Wars of the Roses. County town is **Leicester,** county borough (pop. 285,061), an ancient town with Roman and Norman remains. Richard III was buried here. Has ruins of abbey where Wolsey died. Long an industrial city; manufactures include shoes and hosiery.

Leiden or **Leyden** (both: lī'dûn), municipality (pop. 86,914), South Holland prov., W Netherlands, on Old Rhine R., NE of The Hague. Though mfg. of textiles (since Middle Ages) and machinery are important, it is famed chiefly for its university (founded 1575), oldest in the Netherlands. Univ. of Leiden was center of Protestant theological learning and of science and medicine in 17th and 18th cent. LEYDEN JAR was invented here. ELZEVIR family made Leiden a printing center after 1580. Leiden dates from Roman times. In 1574 it was saved from surrender to the Spanish when William the Silent ordered dikes cut to flood surrounding land, thus enabling GUEUX fleet to sail to its relief. Home of many of the Pilgrims before 1620. Birthplace of Rembrandt and Jan Steen. Landmarks include the Hoglandsche Kerk (15th cent.) and the Pieterskerk (14th cent.).

Leif Ericsson (lēf'), fl. 1000, Norse discoverer of America, b. probably in Iceland; son of ERIC THE RED. One old Norse saga (the more widely accepted) says discovery was accidental, but another says he voyaged W from Greenland intentionally, then wintered at VINLAND.

Leighton, Clare (lā'tûn), 1899–, English print maker and illustrator. Known for woodcuts and engravings.

Leighton, Frederick Leighton, Baron, 1830–96, English painter. His popular pictures generally depicted subjects taken from antiquity.

Leighton, Robert, 1611–84, Scottish prelate. A noted Presbyterian preacher, he signed Covenant (1643). He accepted (1661) bishopric of Dunblane and sought a basis for union of Presbyterianism and episcopacy.

Leinster (lĕn'stûr, lĭn'–), province (7,580 sq. mi.; pop. 1,281,117), Ireland, comprising counties of Carlow, Dublin, Kildare, Kilkenny, Laoighis, Longford, Louth, Meath, Offaly, Westmeath, Wexford, and Wicklow. Most populous and fertile of provinces, it constitutes most of central Irish plain.

Leipzig (līp'sĭg, Ger. līp'tsĭkh), city (pop. 607,655), largest city of Saxony, E Germany, on Pleisse R., in Russian zone of occupation. A major commercial, industrial, and cultural center, it was until World War II the center of German book and music publishing and of the European fur trade. It has mfg. of textiles, steel, machinery, and chemicals and two great yearly industrial fairs. Its famous university was founded 1409. Chartered 1174, Leipzig soon rose to commercial importance. Leibniz and Richard Wagner were born at Leipzig; J. S. Bach was cantor of the Church of St. Thomas, 1723–50; Mendelssohn made the Gewandhaus concerts (begun 1743 in a former guildhouse) internationally famous; the Leipzig conservatory of music achieved world fame. City was heavily damaged in World War II. Among damaged buildings are the Church of St. Thomas and the former supreme court of Germany. Other landmarks include 13th-cent. Pauline church; Auerbach's Keller, an inn made famous by Goethe's *Faust;* the stock exchange (1682); the 17th-cent. Church of St. John (with Bach's tomb); and Wagner's house of birth. The **battle of Leipzig,** Oct. 16–19, 1813, also called Battle of the Nations, was a decisive allied victory over Napoleon I. During the battle most of Napoleon's German auxiliary forces went over to the allies. A large monument commemorates the battle, which cost c.120,000 casualties.

Leiria (lärē'ů), city (pop. 7,208), SW Portugal, in Estremadura. It played a prominent part in history of medieval Portugal. Its castle, built 12th cent., dominates city from a cliff.

Leisler, Jacob (lī'slûr), 1640–91, leader of insurrection in colonial N.Y. (1689–91), b. Germany. A Protestant champion, he seized control of colony until captured by English forces and hanged.

Leith (lēth), former burgh (part of Edinburgh since 1920), Midlothian, Scotland, on S shore of Firth of Forth; Scotland's second largest seaport. Has fishing, fish curing, and varied mfg.

Leitha (lī'tä), Hung. *Lajta,* river, 112 mi. long, formed in E Austria by two headstreams and flowing NE and E to an arm of the Danube in NW Hungary. Historic boundary between Austria (Cisleithania) and Hungary (Transleithania).

Leitrim (lē'trĭm), county (589 sq. mi.; pop. 44,591), NW Ireland, in Connaught; Co. town Carrick-on-Shannon. Area is mountainous in N and level S of Lough Allen. Grazing and agr. are chief occupations, but soil and climate are poor.

Leix, county, Ireland: see LAOIGHIS.

Leixões (lākshō'ĕsh), seaport of OPORTO, Portugal.

Lek (lĕk), navigable river, 40 mi. long, central Netherlands. It flows W from the Lower RHINE to the New Maas (see MEUSE). Crossed by Merwede Canal.

Lekain (lůkẽ′), 1728–78, French actor, whose real name was Henri Louis Cain. Protégé of Voltaire, he was one of the great tragic actors of his time. Used natural diction and costuming.

L. E. L.: see LANDON, LETITIA ELIZABETH.

Leland, Charles Godfrey: see BREITMANN, HANS.

Lely, Sir Peter (lē′lē), 1618–80, Dutch portrait painter. Real name was Pieter van der Faes. Succeeded Van Dyck as painter to the English court.

Leman, Lake: see GENEVA, Switzerland.

Le Mars (lů märz′), city (pop. 5,844), NW Iowa, on Floyd R. and NE of Sioux City. Agr. trade and mfg.

Lemberg, Ukraine: see LVOV.

Lemercier, Jacques (lůměrsyā′), c.1585–1654, French architect of the Renaissance. Designed many churches for the Jesuits. Built Richelieu's Paris residence (later transformed into Palais-Royal) and entire town of Richelieu in W central France.

lemming, rodent related to mouse. Common or brown lemming (genus *Lemmus*) of arctic and antarctic regions has long, brownish, grayish, or black fur. In periods of overpopulation and food scarcity lemmings, especially in Scandinavia, swarm overland, through water, despite obstacles, eating vegetation on way; if they reach sea before urge subsides they swim until drowned. Collared lemming (*Dicrostonyx*) of circumpolar range turns white in winter. Lemming mouse (*Synaptomys*) of North America is related form; species called bog lemming found S to NE U.S.

Lemnos (lěm′nŏs), Aegean island (186 sq. mi.; pop. 23,842), Greece. Fishing, livestock, agr. Kastron is chief town and port. Sacred to Hephaestus in antiquity. After the fall of Constantinople (1204) during the Fourth Crusade, Lemnos became a Latin principate; belonged to Venice (1464–79), to Turkey (1479–1912).

lemon, citrus tree and its fruit (*Citrus limonia*) probably native to India. Unknown to Greeks and Romans, it was introduced in 12th or 13th cent. by Arabs into Spain; from there it reached Mediterranean basin and then spread into most tropical and subtropical regions. Lemons are an important crop in Calif. They are high in vitamins and are main source of commercial citric acid. Lemon oil is extracted from the skin.

lemon balm, perennial Eurasian herb (*Melissa officinalis*), naturalized in North America. Its lemon-flavored leaves are used as seasoning. It is sometimes called bee balm.

Lemonnier, Pierre Charles (pyĕr′ shärl′ lůmônyā′), 1715–99, French astronomer. He is especially noted for studies of moon, terrestrial magnetism, and atmospheric electricity.

Lemoyne, residential borough (pop. 4,605), SE Pa., on Susquehanna R. opposite Harrisburg. Northernmost point of Confederate advance, 1863.

lemur (lē′mûr), primitive Old World arboreal primate with a foxlike muzzle and huge eyes. Tails, if present, are frequently long and bushy. Usually lemurs are gregarious and many are chiefly nocturnal. They eat insects, fruits, small birds, eggs, lizards. True lemur is confined to Madagascar and neighboring islands. Related animals are galagos ("bush baby") of S Africa, African potto, Oriental slow loris and slender loris, indri or endrina, sifaka, mouse lemur, and aye-aye of Madagascar. The tarsier is usually considered intermediate between lemur and New World monkey.

Lena (lē′nů), river in RSFSR, the easternmost and longest (2,648 mi.) of Siberia. Rising near L. Baikal, it flows NE, then NW to empty through 150-mile-wide delta into Laptev Sea. Navigable for 2,135 mi. Coal, oil, and gold are found along its course.

Le Nain (lů nẽ′), family of French painters consisting of three brothers: **Antoine Le Nain** (ãtwän′), 1588?–1648, **Louis Le Nain** (lwē), 1593?–1648, and **Mathieu Le Nain** (mätyû′), 1607–77. They came to Paris from Laon c.1629. Collaborated in much of their work, which portrayed humble people in everyday settings, as in *Mendicants* (Metropolitan Mus.).

Lenape: see DELAWARE INDIANS.

Lenard, Philipp Eduard Anton (fē′lĭp ā′dōōärt än′tōn lā′närt), 1862–1947, German physicist. Won 1905 Nobel Prize for research on cathode rays.

Lenau, Nikolaus (nē′kōlous lā′nou), pseud. of Nikolaus Niembsch von Strehlenau, 1802–50, German romantic poet, b. near Timisoara (then in Hungary). His lyrics, imbued with melancholy and pessimism, and his epic *Faust* (1836) are his best-known works. He became insane in 1844.

Lenbach, Franz von (fränts′ fŭn lān′bäkh), 1836–1904, German portrait painter, eminent in his day.

Lenclos, Ninon de (nēnõ′ dů lãklō′), b. 1620?, d. 1705 or 1706, French beauty and wit. Her salon at Paris gathered many famous figures of her time. The Great Condé, La Rochefoucauld, and Saint-Évremont were among her many lovers.

lend-lease. Lend-Lease Act, passed by U.S. Congress (1941), gave President power to sell, transfer, lend, or lease necessary war supplies to nations whose defense was vital to U.S. in World War II. By end of war most of United Nations had been declared eligible for lend-lease aid, though not all demanded or received it. Certain countries (e.g., Great Britain, Belgium) provided "reverse lend-lease" to American forces overseas. End of lend-lease aid was announced Aug. 31, 1945. Total aid given exceeded $50,600,000,000.

L'Enfant, Pierre Charles (pyĕr′ shärl′ lãfã′), 1754–1825, American architect, b. France. Volunteered as a private in American Revolution. His plans for capital at Washington were rejected in 1792, but in 1901 were used as basis for city's development.

Lenglen, Suzanne (süzän′ lãglĕn′), 1899–1938, French tennis player. French women's singles champion (1920–23; 1925–26); British women's singles champion (1919–23; 1925).

Lenin, Vladimir Ilyich (lĕ′nĭn, Rus. vlŭdyē′mĭr ĭl′yēch lyĕ′nĭn), 1870–1924, Russian revolutionist, founder of Soviet Russia; b. Simbirsk (now Ulyanovsk) as V. I. Ulyanov, the son of a school official. Studied law at Kazan and St. Petersburg but gave up legal practice to turn to the study of Marx and to revolutionary activities; was twice exiled to Siberia. He left Russia in 1900; in 1903, at London, he brought about split of Russian Social Democratic party into BOLSHEVISM AND MENSHEVISM. Back in Russia in 1905–7, he was responsible for the participation of the Bolsheviks in the imperial Duma. In Switzerland during World War I, Lenin, denouncing imperialism as the last stage of capitalism, called on the proletariat to oppose the imperialist war by a world-wide struggle against all capitalism. After the outbreak of the RUSSIAN REVOLUTION (Feb., 1917) the German government helped Lenin to return to Russia, in the correct assumption that he would disrupt the Russian war effort. In Nov., 1917, Lenin overthrew the Kerensky government, became chairman of the Council of People's Commissars, and estab. the "dictatorship of the proletariat." He saw the revolution through to victory in the civil war of 1918–20; the UNION OF SOVIET SOCIALIST REPUBLICS was founded. In 1921 he introduced the NEW ECONOMIC POLICY as an expedient to raise Russia from economic ruin. The COMINTERN (founded 1919) was largely his creation. As chairman of the Communist party and of the Council of People's Commissars, he ruled as virtual dictator. His death opened a contest for his succession from which Stalin emerged victorious. His mausoleum in the Red Square at Moscow is a Communist shrine. His elaboration of Marxism, called Leninism, has as its main features his analysis of imperialism; his insistence on the necessity of a strongly organized and disciplined Communist party to prepare and guide the proletarian revolution; his uncompromising atheism; and his willingness to resort to opportunism (though he remained dogmatically opposed to gradualist compromise or to any revision of Marxist doctrine). Regarded by Stalinists and Trotskyites alike as the liberator of the proletariat, he is considered by other Socialists as a despot who betrayed and enslaved the working class. His writings and speeches have been translated into English.

Leningrad (lĕ'nĭngrăd), second largest city (pop. 3,191,304) of USSR, in RSFSR, at S end of Karelian Isthmus; former cap. of Russia. Named St. Petersburg until 1914, Petrograd 1914–24. Its founder, Peter the Great, ordered (1703) his new capital, "a window looking on Europe," built on newly conquered delta through which the NEVA enters Gulf of Finland. Italian and French architects planned a spacious city of classical beauty, which became a brilliant international, cultural, and social center. It also had become the chief industrial center of Russia, with large armament plants, when St. Petersburg workers precipitated the 1905 revolution and carried out Russian Revolution of 1917. Moscow replaced it as cap. in 1918. In the course of World War II Leningrad, protected by KRONSTADT, withstood a two-year German siege (1941–43). Principal thoroughfare of the city is Nevsky Prospekt, where points of interest include Winter Palace, HERMITAGE mus., and Falconet's equestrian statue of Peter the Great. Among other notable sites are the university (founded 1819), and fortress of SS. Peter and Paul (city's oldest building). Leningrad is the principal port and foremost machine- and electrical-goods mfg. center of USSR. Suburbs include PUSHKIN, with the Summer Palace, and former imperial residences of PETERHOF and GATCHINA.

Lenin Peak, 23,382 ft. high, Tadzhik SSR, in Trans-Alai range in central Asia; second-highest point in USSR. Formerly called Kaufmann Peak.

Lenni-Lenape: see DELAWARE INDIANS.

Lennox, Matthew Stuart or **Stewart,** 4th **earl of,** 1516–71, Scottish nobleman. Leader of the Catholic nobles, he married his son, Lord DARNLEY, to Mary Queen of Scots. Became regent (1570), but queen's party declared war against him and he was killed.

Lennox, Fort: see ÎLE-AUX-NOIX, FORT.

Lennoxville, town (pop. 2,895), SE Que., Canada, on St. Francis and Massawippi rivers and E of Sherbrooke. Seat of Univ. of Bishop's Col. (Anglican; coed.; 1843).

Lenoir (lŭnôr'), town (pop. 7,888), W N.C., in Blue Ridge foothills. Resort with furniture mfg.

Lenoir City, industrial city (pop. 5,159), E Tenn., SW of Knoxville and on Tennessee R., in timber and farm area. Fort Loudon Dam near.

Lenoir Rhyne College: see HICKORY, N.C.

Lenôtre or **Le Nôtre, André** (ãdrā' lŭnō'trů), 1613–1700, French landscape architect. His designs for formal gardens at Versailles and Fontainebleau exerted wide influence.

Lenox, James, 1800–1880, American bibliophile and philanthropist. His fine collection of paintings and books in Lenox Library (now part of New York Public Library).

Lenox, resort town (pop. 3,627), W Mass., in the Berkshires S of Pittsfield. Scene of annual BERKSHIRE SYMPHONIC FESTIVAL at "Tanglewood," former estate, mainly in adjoining Stockbridge town; estate has Hawthorne's cottage (burned 1890; rebuilt, dedicated as shrine 1948).

Lens (lãs), town (pop. 34,134), Pas-de-Calais dept., N France. Industrial center in coal dist. French victory over imperials at Lens (1648) was last important battle of Thirty Years War.

lens, circular piece of glass with two curved surfaces or with one curved and the other plane. All light rays passing through lens are bent (by REFRACTION) except those that pass through optical center. Converging lenses bend emerging light rays inward and toward each other; such lenses (e.g. double convex and plano-convex) are thicker at the center than at edges. Diverging lens causes rays to be bent outward and away from each other; such lenses (e.g., double concave or plano-concave) are thicker at the edges than at the center. Each curved surface of lens is considered part of the surface of a sphere; the center of that sphere is called center of curvature. Line through optical center connecting centers of curvature is principal axis. The distance from the principal focus to optical center is called focal length. Aberration is the phenomenon of an inexact focus. IMAGE formed by lens varies according to curvature of the surfaces. Devices in which lenses are used include CAMERA, MICROSCOPE, SEARCHLIGHT, SPECTACLES, STEREOSCOPE, TELESCOPE.

Lent [Old Eng.,= spring], Latin *Quadragesima,* Christian period of fasting and penitence preparatory to Easter. In the West, penitential season begins with Septuagesima, ninth Sunday before Easter. Lent begins on Ash Wednesday, 40th weekday prior to Easter, and ends at noon on Holy Saturday, the day before Easter. The last week of Lent is Holy Week.

lentil, leguminous Old World annual plant (*Lens esculenta*) grown for its beanlike seeds, also called lentils. It has long been a staple food.

Lenz, Jakob (yä'kôp lĕnts'), 1751–92, German author of the STURM UND DRANG period. He befriended Goethe at Strasbourg but later lampooned him; died in poverty and insanity. Wrote plays of social criticism (*Der Hofmeister,* 1774; *Die Soldaten,* 1776) and poetry which suggests his inner conflict.

Leo I, Saint (the Great), c.400–461, pope (440–61), Doctor of the Church; one of greatest early pontiffs. With aid of Valentinian III fought Manichaeism in Italy. Subduing St. Hilary of Arles, he confirmed the authority of pope over bishops. In Nestorian-Monophysite controversy he wrote the celebrated *Tome of Leo* on natures of Christ, later adopted at Council of CHALCEDON. Persuaded ATTILA (452) and his Huns not to sack Rome. Feast: April 11.

Leo III, Saint, d. 816, pope (795–816). He was attacked by family of his predecessor, ADRIAN I, who hoped to render him unfit for the papacy. He recovered and fled to Charlemagne, who came to Rome, where he was crowned. Leo worked to unite East and West and did much to beautify Rome.

Leo IX, Saint, 1002–54, pope (1049–54). A relative of Emperor Conrad II, educated and made bishop (1027) at Toul. Initiated reform of clergy in which chief figure was Hildebrand (later GREGORY VII). The heresy of BERENGAR OF TOURS also occupied the pope. Leo was defeated at Civitella (1053) by the Normans of S Italy. Michael Cerularius, patriarch of Constantinople, attacked the pope (1042), and Leo excommunicated him (1054)—an act that began the formal schism of East and West.

Leo X, 1475–1521, pope (1513–21) (Giovanni de' Medici). Son of Lorenzo de' MEDICI, he was made a cardinal in boyhood and was head of the family before he was 30. His chief fame rests on his patronage of RAPHAEL, continuation of St. Peter's by Bramante, and on his literary circle. Fifth LATERAN COUNCIL failed to effect desired reforms and the Protestant REFORMATION began when Martin LUTHER posted his theses (1517). Leo excommunicated the reformers (1520) but did not give the crisis much attention.

Leo XIII, 1810–1903, pope (1878–1903), an Italian named Gioacchino Pecci. He devoted himself to forming Catholic attitudes appropriate to the modern world and issued several encyclicals to that end. *Immortale Dei* (1885) charted the course for Catholics as responsible citizens in modern democratic states. *Rerum novarum* (1891), one of the most important of all encyclicals, outlined Catholic social ideals, pointing to the abuses of capitalism and the deficiencies of Marxism. To meet intellectual attacks on the Church he declared the philosophy of St. Thomas Aquinas official and founded the Inst. of Thomistic Philosophy at Louvain. In his reign the KULTURKAMPF was ended in Germany with a victory for the Church (1887).

Leo, Byzantine emperors. **Leo I** (the Great or the Thracian), d. 474, reigned 457–74. Broke the power of the Germans in the Roman army but failed in a naval expedition against Vandals (468). **Leo III** (the Isaurian), c.680–740, reigned 717–40. He checked the Arabs (717–18) and reorganized the empire. His civil code, the *Ecloga,* is characterized by Christian feeling. Popes Gregory II and Gregory III opposed his ICONOCLASM and defied his expeditions against Rome. **Leo V** (the Armenian), d. 820, reigned 813–20. Reviving iconoclasm, he deposed the patriarch Nicephorus (815) and persecuted Theodore of Studium. He was murdered. **Leo VI** (the Wise or the Philosopher), 862?–912, reigned 886–912. His accession forced the resignation of PHOTIUS. His *Basilica,* a modernization of the law of Justinian I, was published 887–93 and was intended to supersede the *Ecloga* of Leo III.

Leo (lē'ō) [Latin,= lion], fifth sign of ZODIAC.

Leo Africanus, early 16th cent., Moorish traveler in Africa and near East. Wrote description of African journeys, long only known source on Sudan.

Leoben (lāō'bůn), city (pop. 35,785), Styria, S central Austria, on Mur R. Industrial center of coal-mining area. Armistice preliminary to Treaty of CAMPO FORMIO was signed here 1797.

Leochares (lēŏ'kůrēz), 4th cent. B.C., Greek sculptor. Possibly the creator of *Apollo Belvedere* (Vatican).

Leominster (lĕ'mĭnstůr), city (pop. 24,075), N Mass., N of Worcester. Plastics and machinery.

León, Juan Ponce de: see PONCE DE LEÓN, JUAN.

León, Luis Ponce de (lwēs' pōn'thā dā lāōn'), 1527?–1591, Spanish lyric poet, monk and mystic. He translated the Song of Songs, wrote notable odes and some prose works.

León (lāōn'), city (pop. 74,155), Guanajuato, central Mexico; founded 1576. Once the second largest city in Mexico, it is still an agr. and mining center, with some mfg. (leather goods, fabrics).

León (lāōn'), city (pop. 31,008), NW Nicaragua, second largest city of republic; founded 1524 on L. Managua; moved (1610) after earthquake. Stronghold of liberal forces after independence from Spain (1821), it was the rival of Granada. Now trade center of agr. area.

Leon (lē'ŏn), Span. *León,* region and former kingdom (20,594 sq. mi.; pop. 1,732,082), NW Spain, bordering on Portugal. Chief cities: Leon, Palencia, Salamanca, Valladolid, Zamora. Mostly a dry plateau crossed by the Duero. Cantabrian Mts. in N have coal mines, forests, minerals. Conquered from the Moors by the kings of Asturias (8th–9th cent.), the region became the kingdom of Leon and Asturias. It was twice united with the neighboring kingdom of Castile (1037–65, under Ferdinand I of Castile; 1072–1157, under Alfonso VI, Urraca, and Alfonso VII) before a permanent union was effected by Ferdinand III (1230). Its historic cap., **Leon** (pop. 43,260), is an agr. and commercial center dating from Roman times. Conquered from Moors 882, it replaced Oviedo as cap. in 10th cent.; declined when Valladolid became favorite royal residence. Among its many ancient buildings is the Gothic cathedral (13th–14th cent.).

Leonardo da Pisa: see FIBONACCI, LEONARDO.

Leonardo da Vinci (lēōnär'dō dä vēn'chē), 1452–1519, Italian artist and scientist, the supreme example of Renaissance genius, b. Vinci. The natural son of a Florentine notary and a peasant girl, he was apprenticed in 1466 to Verrocchio in Florence. The unfinished *Adoration of the Magi* (Uffizi), painted in 1481, shows his early mastery of dramatic chiaroscuro. Went to Milan c.1482, became court artist to Lodovico Sforza. While in Milan he wrote his *Trattato della pittura*, began his notebooks (dealing with problems of hydraulics, mechanics, anatomy, geology, and botany), and with the help of his pupil Ambrogio de Predis painted the *Madonna of the Rocks* (2 versions: Louvre and Natl. Gall., London). Also of this period is the *Last Supper* fresco (Milan). Returned to Florence 1500 and served Cesare Borgia as military engineer, and painted the *Mona Lisa* (Louvre). Back in Milan (1506–13) he served the French king Louis XII as architect and engineer, while continuing his activities as painter, sculptor, and teacher; here he did *St. Anne, Mary and the Child* (Louvre). From 1513 to c.1515 he worked for Pope Leo X in Rome, where he did the young *St. John the Baptist* (Louvre). Invited by Francis I, he went to France, where for the rest of his life he was left free to conduct research.

Leoncavallo, Ruggiero (rōōd-jā'rō lā"ōn-käväl'lō), 1858–1919, Italian composer. He wrote several operas and songs (e.g., *Mattinata*), but his opera *Pagliacci* (1892) was his one outstanding success.

Leonia (lēō'nyů), borough (pop. 7,378), NE N.J., near W approach to George Washington Bridge.

Leonidas (lēŏ'nĭdůs), d. 480 B.C., king of Sparta. When the Persians invaded Greece under Xerxes (480), he and his men held the pass at THERMOPYLAE and were all killed.

Leonov, Leonid (lyäůnyēt' lyäô'nŭf), 1899–, Russian novelist of psychological and social realism. Among his novels in praise of Soviet policies are *The Thief* (1927), *Sot* (1930), *The Road to the Ocean* (1935), and *Chariot of Wrath* (1944).

leopard, mammal of cat family (genus *Panthera*, or, in some classifications, *Felis*) found in Africa and Asia. It is also called panther or pard. It has thick fur, the ground color yellow-buff, rusty, or gray, patterned with black rosettes. Black leopard often occurs in litter of normal color. Snow leopard, irbis, or ounce lives at high altitudes in Tibet and Himalayas. Leopards prey on monkeys, dogs, other mammals, and birds and reptiles.

Leopardi, Giacomo, Conte (jä'kōmō kōn'tā läōpär'dē), 1798–1837, Italian poet. He wrote lyric poetry that ranks with Petrarch's and prose unequaled in Italian for simplicity and purity. His lyrics express agnosticism and pessimism. His prose works show tender wit and irony.

Leopold, emperors (also kings of Bohemia and Hungary). **Leopold I,** 1640–1705. The salient events of his reign (1658–75) were his wars with Louis XIV of France; the rebellion of THOKOLY (1678); the Turkish siege of VIENNA (1683); and the victorious Treaty of KARLOWITZ with Turkey (1699). He was fortunate in having such able generals as Montecucculi, Charles V of Lorraine, and Eugene of Savoy. **Leopold II,** 1747–92, as Leopold I grand duke of Tuscany (1765–90), succeeded his brother JOSEPH II as emperor in 1790. Though he had proved himself an able reformer in Tuscany, he was obliged to revoke most of his brother's reforms to pacify his Hungarian, Bohemian, and Belgian subjects. He was the last crowned king of Bohemia. In 1791, to aid his brother-in-law, Louis XVI of France, he instigated the Declaration of Pillnitz, which helped precipitate the FRENCH REVOLUTIONARY WARS a few weeks after his death.

Leopold, kings of the Belgians. **Leopold I,** 1790–1865, third son of Francis Frederick, duke of Saxe-Coburg-Saalfeld, was elected king of newly formed Belgium in 1831. Called "Uncle of Europe," he was the husband of Princess Charlotte (daughter of George IV of England); brought about marriage of his niece, Queen Victoria, with his nephew, Prince Albert. **Leopold II,** 1835–1909. His reign (1865–1909) was one of industrial and colonial expansion (see BELGIAN CONGO). Notorious for his ruthless greed and his dissolute private life. **Leopold III,** 1901–, succeeded his father Albert I in 1934. Lost his wife, Queen Astrid (a Swedish princess) in an automobile accident (1935). In 1936 he announced that Belgium would remain neutral in any armed conflict. In World War II, after Germany invaded Belgium (May, 1940), he led Belgian resistance but on May 28 he surrendered his armies to Germany, despite the opposition of his ministers. He was held a prisoner of war by the Germans, first at his castle at Laken, after 1944 in Germany. Accusations of treason and collaboration with Germany prevented his return to Belgium until 1950 and embittered Belgian postwar politics. In 1951 he abdicated in favor of his son Baudouin. In 1941 he had married a commoner, whom he later created princess of Réthy.

Leopold I, 1676–1747, prince of Anhalt-Dessau (1693–1747). As field marshal in the Prussian army he organized infantry under Frederick William I and distinguished himself under Frederick II.

Leopoldville, city (pop. c.137,000), cap. of Belgian Congo, on Congo R. Founded 1887 by Henry Stanley, named for Belgian king, Leopold II. Main base of navigation on the Congo.

Leovigild (lēŏ'vĭgĭld"), d. 586, Visigothic king

of Spain (568–86). Made notable additions to Visigothic laws.

Lepage, Jules Bastien-: see BASTIEN-LEPAGE, JULES.

Lepanto, battle of (lĭpăn'tō), Oct. 7, 1571, naval battle fought off Lepanto (see NAUPAKTOS), Greece, between fleet of the Holy League, commanded by John of Austria, and Turkish fleet, commanded by Ochiali Pasha. Allies (mostly Spanish, Venetian, and papal ships) virtually destroyed Turkish fleet, captured or killed c.15,000 Turks, liberated c.10,000 Christian galley slaves. Among allied wounded was Cervantes. Allied victory ended threat of Turkish naval supremacy in Mediterranean.

lepidodendron (lĕ"pĭdōdĕn'drŭn), extinct tree, genus *Lepidodendron,* many species of which flourished in the Carboniferous period. They grew to heights of 50–100 ft., with diameter of 4–6 ft.

Lepidus (lĕ'pĭdŭs), family of anc. Rom. **Marcus Aemilius Lepidus** (ēmĭ'lēŭs), d. 77 B.C., raised an army to challenge the senatorial leader, CATULUS, but was defeated. His son, **Marcus Aemilius Lepidus,** d. 13 B.C., was consul with Caesar (46 B.C.). With ANTONY and Octavian (AUGUSTUS) formed the Second Triumvirate. After victory at Philippi he governed Africa and conquered Sicily, but Augustus later deprived him of his offices.

leprosy, infectious disease caused by a bacterium. Lepromatous or cutaneous form is marked by hard, nodular swellings in skin and mucous membranes of throat, nose, eyes. In the neural type, less acute, germs accumulate in nerves and cause partial loss of sensation. It is transmitted chiefly by close contact with patient for months or years. Incubation period commonly is 5–20 years. Most prevalent in tropics and subtropics; endemic in parts of Fla., Texas, La. In U.S. patients are treated at National Leprosarium, Carville, La. Disease is ancient; segregation laws date from c.7th cent.

Lerdo de Tejada, Miguel (mēgĕl' lĕr'dhō dā tāhä'dhä), d. 1861, Mexican liberal statesman, a leader of the Revolution of Ayutla. Initiated Ley Lerdo (1856), which provided for forced sale of all real property of Catholic Church. His younger brother, **Sebastián Lerdo de Tejada** (sāvästyän'), 1820?–1889, was also an important liberal in Revolution of Ayutla. After the death of Júarez, he served as provisional president (1872–76) and was driven from office by Porfirio Diaz.

Lérida (lā'rēdhä), city (pop. 35,061), cap. of Lérida prov., NE Spain, in Catalonia, on Segre R. Center of fertile agr. region. Ancient Ilerda, it was scene of Caesar's victory over Pompey's generals (49 B.C.). Held by Moors A.D. 714–1149. Seat of a university c.1300–1717. A key defense point for Barcelona in civil war of 1936–39, it fell to Insurgents 1938. Has medieval castle, Romanesque cathedral.

Lerma, Francisco Gómez de Sandoval y Rojas, duque de (fränthēs'kō gō'mĕth dā sändōväl' ē rō'häs dōō'kā dā lĕr'mä), 1552?–1625, chief minister of Philip III of Spain from 1598 to 1618. His corruption led to his downfall. Was later compelled to give up part of wealth he had appropriated in connection with expulsion of Moriscos (1609).

Lermontov, Mikhail Yurevich (mēkhŭyēl' yōōr'yĭvĭch lyĕr'mŭntŭf), 1814–41, Russian author. His masterpiece is *The Demon* (1829–41; Eng. tr., 1930), an autobiographical poem laid in the Caucasus, where he spent much of his life. His novel *A Hero of Our Time* (1840; Eng. tr., 1928) foreshadows Gogol in its realism and its characteristic theme of frustration. Second only to Pushkin as a lyricist, he died, like Pushkin, in a duel.

Lerwick (lûr'wĭk, lĕ'rĭk), burgh (pop. 5,538), Mainland Isl., co. town of Shetland Isls., Scotland; most northerly town of British Isles.

Le Sage, Alain René (älē' rŭnā' lŭ säzh'), 1668–1747, French author. *Turcaret* (1709), a comedy of character, satirizes the new plutocracy. His masterpiece is the classic *Gil Blas de Santillane* (1715–35; Eng. tr. by Tobias Smollett, 1749), a picaresque novel distinguished for its wit and realism.

Lesbos (lĕz'bŏs), Aegean island (632 sq. mi.; pop. 134,054), Greece, off W Turkey, also called Mytilene; chief city Mytilene. Center of civilization in 7th cent. B.C.; home of poets Sappho and Alcaeus. Joined Delian League and revolted unsuccessfully against Athens (428 B.C.). Aristotle and Epicurus lived here.

Lescarbot, Marc (lĕskärbō'), fl. 1599–1619, lawyer, poet, and historian of New France, b. France.

Lescaze, William (lĕskäz'), 1896–, American architect, born and trained in Switzerland.

Les Cheneaux Islands (lā shĕn'ō), group of 35 small islands, S of E Upper Peninsula, N Mich., in L. Huron NE of Straits of Mackinac. Annual regatta.

Leschetizky, Theodor (lĕshŭtĭts'kē), 1830–1915, Polish pianist and teacher; pupil of Czerny. Among his pupils were Paderewski and Gabrilowitsch.

Lescot, Pierre (lĕskō'), c.1510–1578, French architect of early Renaissance. Beginning in 1546 he built earliest parts of the palace that later became the Louvre. All his known works have sculptural decoration by Jean Goujon.

lese majesty or **leze majesty** (both: lēz' mă'jĭstē) [Latin *laesae maiestatis (crimen)* = (crime of) violating majesty], offense against the dignity of the sovereign or of a state. First appeared in Rome as offense against the state and, later, against the person of the emperor. Since the disappearance of absolute monarchy, the crime has tended to decline, although acts of TREASON are still criminal. In the U.S., attacks on public officials are protected by the right of free speech if not attended by threats of violence.

Lesina, Yugoslavia: see HVAR.

Leslie, Frank, 1821–80, American engraver and publisher of family periodicals, b. England. Real name was Henry Carter. Illustrations made by his artists on the battlefield in Civil War now have historical value. His second wife, **Miriam Florence (Folline) Leslie,** c.1836–1914, ably managed the business after his death. An ardent feminist, she wrote several books.

lespedeza, plant of genus *Lespedeza,* also called

bush clover. Common lespedeza or Japanese clover (*Lespedeza striata*), an annual, is forage crop in S U.S. and a means of enriching soil and checking erosion. It grows to c.18 in., has branched stems, three-parted leaves, small pink or purplish flowers.

Lespinasse, Julie de (zhülē' dü lĕspēnäs'), 1732–76, French woman of letters; niece of Mme DU DEFFAND. In 1764 she treacherously left her aunt's house to found her own literary salon, taking her friend D'Alembert and other lights along with her. Her letters to the comte de Guibert remain a classic chronicle of unhappy love (written 1773–76; Eng. trs., 1901, 1929).

Lesseps, Ferdinand Marie, vicomte de (fĕrdēnā' märē' vēkōt' dü lĕsĕps'), 1805–94, French diplomat and engineer who planned and supervised Suez Canal and attempted Panama Canal.

Lesser Slave Lake, 60 mi. long and 3–10 mi. wide, central Alta., Canada, NNW of Edmonton. Drains E into Athabaska R. by Lesser Slave R.

Lessing, Gotthold Ephraim (gôt'hôlt ā'frāĭm), 1729–81, German author, chief figure of the ENLIGHTENMENT in Germany. His dramatic criticism (*Hamburgische Dramaturgie,* 1767–69) attacked the imitators of French classicism and held Shakspere up as a model for German playwrights; his *Laokoon* (1766) is a classic of modern aesthetics. His own dramatic works include the tragedies *Miss Sara Sampson* (1755) and *Emilia Galotti* (1779); the comedy *Minna von Barnhelm* (1767), a very successful piece; and the noble drama of ideas, *Nathan der Weise* (1779), a plea for peaceful coexistence of religious faiths. His friend Moses MENDELSSOHN is said to have been the model for Nathan. Lessing was drawn into interminable polemics on theological, aesthetic, and antiquarian subjects. All these are characterized by his sharp wit and erudition. In his *Die Erziehung des Menschengeschlechts* (1780) [the education of mankind] he sketched the evolution of mankind, through progressive stages of revealed religion, toward a divinely ordained society.

Le Sueur, Eustache (ûstäsh' lü süûr'), 1617–55, French religious painter. Best works in Louvre.

Le Tellier, Michel (mēshĕl' lü tĕlyā'), 1603–85, French statesman, chancellor of France under Louis XIV. Father of Louvois.

Lethbridge, city (pop. 22,947), S Alta., Canada, on Oldman R. and SE of Calgary. Center of coal-mining, ranching, and agr. area. Has grain elevators, food processing plants, and clothing mills. Hq. of Royal Canadian Mounted Police in Alta.

Lethe (lē'thē) [Gr.,= oblivion], in Greek mythology, river of forgetfulness in Hades. Its waters were partaken of both by arriving dead and by departing souls being reincarnated into world of the living.

Lethington, William Maitland of: see MAITLAND, WILLIAM.

Leticia (lātē'sēä), town, SE Colombia, on upper Amazon. Border dispute in region between Colombia and Peru was decided by League of Nations (1934)—first instance of action by an international body in an area covered by Monroe Doctrine.

Leto (lē'tō), in Greek religion, mother by Zeus of Apollo and Artemis. Hera, in jealousy, caused her to wander, but Zeus chained floating island of Delos to bottom of the sea; here she bore the twins. They took tragic revenge on NIOBE for insulting Leto.

Lettish, Baltic language of Latvia. It belongs to the Indo-European family. See LANGUAGE (table).

lettre de cachet (lĕ'trü dü käshā'), in French law under the *ancien régime,* a private, sealed document sent as an official communication from the king to an individual or a group. It was much used in the 16th and 17th cent. to give notice of imprisonment or exile, and the victim had no recourse. It was used by the revolutionists as a symbol of tyranny.

lettuce, annual garden plant (*Lactuca sativa*), cultivated from antiquity. Varieties include head or cabbage lettuce, the leaf or loose type, and Cos lettuce or romaine which forms long, upright leaves. It is grown on large scale in U.S.; much of winter crop comes from Fla. and Calif.

Leucas or **Leukas,** one of IONIAN ISLANDS.

Leucippus (lūsĭ'pùs), 5th cent. B.C., Greek philosopher, reputed founder of atomic theory and teacher of DEMOCRITUS.

leucocyte: see WHITE CORPUSCLE.

Leuctra (lo͝ok'trü), village of anc. Greece, in Boeotia, 7 mi. SW of Thebes. Here the Thebans under Epaminondas defeated Sparta (371 B.C.).

Leukas or **Leucas,** one of IONIAN ISLANDS.

leukemia lo͞okē'mēü), serious malady marked by abnormal increase of white blood cells (leucocytes) or their precursors. It is thought to be a malignant disease of bone marrow which spreads by way of blood. Usually it is attended by anemia.

Leuna (loi'nä), town (pop. 9,918), Saxony-Anhalt. Center of German synthetic chemical industry.

Leuthen (loi'tün), village near Breslau, Lower Silesia. Scene of brilliant victory of Frederick II of Prussia over Austrians (1757).

Leutze, Emanuel (loit'sü), 1816–68, American historical painter, b. Germany. Works include mural on staircase of Capitol, Washington, D.C., and *Washington Crossing the Delaware* (Metropolitan Mus.).

Levant (lüvănt') [Ital.,= east], region of the E shore of the Mediterranean from Egypt to, and including, Turkey. Syria and Lebanon are sometimes called the Levant States.

Le Vau, Louis (lü vō'), 1612–70, French architect, who designed the nucleus of palace of Versailles.

levee (lĕ'vē), embankment along a river to keep high waters from flooding adjacent plain. Levees are built by piling earth on cleared, leveled surface. Broad at the base, they narrow to a level crown on which temporary embankments or sacks of soil can be placed as protection from unusually high waters. Since intensity of flood discharge increases in channel leveed on both banks and since silt deposits raise level of river beds, levee-system planning and use of auxiliary measures are vital. In U.S., levee systems are along Mississippi and Sacramento rivers; in Europe, dikes of Holland are form of levee, and embankments are used along Danube, Vistula, and Po.

Levelers, extremist English Puritan sect active (1647–49) during Puritan Revolution. Leader was John LILBURNE. Aims were religious and social equality. Movement was crushed by Cromwell.

leveling: see SURVEYING.

Levelland (lĕ'vŭlănd″), town (pop. 8,264), NW Texas, W of Lubbock on Llano Estacado. Center of agr. (cotton, grains) and oil area.

Leven, Loch (lŏkh lē'vŭn). **1** Lake, between Inverness-shire and Argyllshire, Scotland. **2** Lake, Kinross-shire, Scotland. Leven R. flows from lake E through Fifeshire to Firth of Forth.

Lever, Charles James (lē'vûr), 1806–72, Irish novelist, author of *Charles O'Malley* (1841), *Arthur O'Leary* (1844) and *Tom Burke of "Ours"* (1844).

lever, simple machine consisting of bar or rod either attached or supported at some point (fulcrum) along its length. A force applied anywhere along bar or rod tends to rotate it about the fulcrum. A small force properly distant from fulcrum will overcome larger force closer to fulcrum. This principle is basic to its many practical applications, e.g., in forceps, scissors, pliers, spades, wheelbarrow, beam balance, and other devices. See *ill.*, p. 793.

Leverrier, Urbain Jean Joseph (ürbē' zhā' zhôzĕf' lùvĕryā'), 1811–77, French astronomer. He discovered, independently of J. C. Adams, planet Neptune. He completed revision of planetary theories 1875.

Levi (lē'vī), son of Jacob, ancestor of the LEVITES. Tribe did not have its own allotment in Canaan. Gen. 29.34; 34; 46.11; 49.5–7.

Levi, Carlo (kär'lō lā'vē), 1902–, Italian writer, painter, and anti-Fascist leader, a physician. His powerful novel, *Christ Stopped at Eboli* (1945), is based on his experiences as an exile in Lucania.

leviathan (lēvī'–), in Bible, huge beast, possibly the crocodile. Job 41; Pss. 74.14; 104.26; Isa. 27.1.

Levi ben Gershon: see GERSONIDES.

Levi-Civita, Tullio (tōōl'lyō lā'vē-chē'vētä), 1873–1942, Italian mathematician, known for researches in pure geometry, hydrodynamics, and absolute differential calculus (on which Einstein in part depended).

levirate marriage: see MARRIAGE.

Lévis (lē'vĭs, Fr. lāvē'), city (pop. 13,162), S Que., Canada, on St. Lawrence R. opposite Quebec; settled 1647. Base for Wolfe's siege of Quebec 1759. Port with shipbuilding, woodworking, and mfg. of trucks and chemicals.

Levites (lē'–), among anc. Hebrews, a religious caste, descendants of Levi, son of Jacob. Not counted as one of the 12 tribes of Israel; held no portion of land in Canaan. Instead certain cities were given a quota of Levites to support. Levites were Temple servants at Jerusalem; later were teachers of the Law. Ex. 6.16; 32.26–28; 38.21; Num. 1; 3–5; 8; Deut. 18; Joshua 21; 1 Chron. 6; 9; 15; 23; 2 Chron. 17.8,9; 19.8–11; 20.19–21; 23; Ezra 7.24; 8.20.

Leviticus (lēvĭ'tĭkŭs), book of Old Testament, third of books of Law (the Pentateuch or Torah), named for the Levites. Book contains: general liturgical laws governing worship, sacrifice, and purification; specific rules regarding individual conduct.

Levkosia, Greek name of NICOSIA, Cyprus.

levulose: see FRUCTOSE.

Lévy-Bruhl, Lucien (lüsyē' lāvü-brül'), 1857–1939, French philosopher, sociologist, and ethnologist, known for research and writings on primitive mentality.

Lewes, George Henry (lōō'ĭs), 1817–78, English author. As editor of *Fortnightly Review* (1865–66) he won fame as a critic. Most noted work is *Life of Goethe* (1855). He guided, lived with, and finally married George ELIOT.

Lewes (lōō'ĭs, –ĭz, lū'–), municipal borough (pop. 13,104), co. town of Sussex East, England; farm center. Scene of victory by Simon de Montfort over Henry III (1264). Has archaeological museum.

Lewes (lōō'ĭs), resort town (pop. 2,904), SE Del., at mouth of Delaware Bay NW of Rehoboth Beach. Harbor protected by Delaware Breakwater. Deep-sea fishing. Site of first European settlement on the Delaware; settled 1631 by Dutch.

Lewes (lōō'ĭs), river, upper course of Yukon R., rising in N B.C. and Yukon territory, Canada, and flowing c.300 mi. NW to Pelly R. at Fort Selkirk.

Lewis. For rulers thus named, see LOUIS.

Lewis, Cecil Day: see DAY LEWIS, CECIL.

Lewis, C(live) S(taples), 1898–, British writer, noted for advocacy of Christianity in such books as *The Screw-tape Letters* (1942).

Lewis, John L(lewellyn), 1880–, American labor leader. Head of UNITED MINE WORKERS OF AMERICA (1920–); built up union, won power for himself. Taking his union from the American Federation of Labor, he helped form and headed (1935–40) the CONGRESS OF INDUSTRIAL ORGANIZATIONS, which he left in 1940. His aggressive strike tactics have led to conflicts with courts and government but greatly benefited the union.

Lewis, Matthew Gregory, 1775–1818, English author of "Gothic" horror tales; known as "Monk" Lewis from his extravagant thriller *The Monk* (1796).

Lewis, Meriwether, 1774–1809, American explorer, leader of LEWIS AND CLARK EXPEDITION.

Lewis, Morgan, 1754–1844, American general, governor of N.Y. (1804–7). In War of 1812 he captured Fort George, commanded at battle of Sackets Harbor.

Lewis, Sinclair, 1885–1951, American novelist. Important among many realistic and satirical novels are *Main Street* (1920), *Babbitt* (1922), *Arrowsmith* (1925), *Elmer Gantry* (1927), *It Can't Happen Here* (1935). Awarded Nobel Prize for 1930.

Lewis, (Percy) Wyndham, 1886–, English writer and painter. A leader in artistic movement called vorticism, he won more fame with more conventional paintings. His novels and essays are satirical.

Lewis, Hebrides, Scotland: see LEWIS WITH HARRIS.

Lewis. 1 Early name of SNAKE R. **2** River rising

in Cascade Range, SW Wash., and flowing c.95 mi. SW to the Columbia NW of Vancouver. Furnishes power.

Lewis and Clark Cavern National Monument: see MORRISON CAVE STATE PARK.

Lewis and Clark expedition, 1803–6, military exploring expedition across the North American continent. Headed by Pres. Jefferson's private secretary, Meriwether Lewis, aided by William Clark. Purpose was to search out route to the Pacific and to gather information about Indians and Far West. Following a winter of training, the members set out in 1804 from St. Louis up the Missouri. Their Indian woman guide, SACAJAWEA, aided them in crossing the Rockies. After wintering on the coast, they began their return journey, splitting temporarily to follow separate routes along the Marias and the Yellowstone, and arrived in St. Louis, Sept. 23, 1806. Their expedition, of which many records were kept, opened vast new territories to knowledge.

Lewisburg. 1 Borough (pop. 5,268), central Pa., on W branch of Susquehanna R. and NW of Sunbury. Mfg. of textiles and lumber products. Seat of Bucknell Univ. (Baptist; coed.; 1846). **2** Town (pop. 5,164), central Tenn., S of Nashville. Livestock, dairy, and timber center. Mfg. of shoes and stoves.

lewisite: see POISON GAS.

Lewisohn, Ludwig (lo͞o'ĭzōn), 1882–, American writer of criticism, novels (e.g., *The Island Within,* 1928), autobiography (*Up Stream,* 1922; *Mid-Channel,* 1929; *Haven,* 1940), and works on Jews and Zionism. Also translated German literature.

Lewiston. 1 City (pop. 12,985), NW Idaho, at junction of Snake and Clearwater rivers and at Wash. line. Site visited by Lewis and Clark, 1805. Founded 1861 after gold was found on Clearwater R. First cap. of Idaho Territory (1863–64). Had Idaho's first newspaper (1862). Lumber, fruit, livestock center. **2** Industrial city (pop. 40,974), SW Maine, at falls (power) of Androscoggin R. (bridged here) opposite Auburn; settled 1770. Second largest city in Maine. Mfg. of textiles (since early 19th cent.), shoes, wood and metal products, and brick. Seat of Bates Col. (coed.; 1863).

Lewistown. 1 City (pop. 2,630), central Ill., SW of Peoria. Source of *Spoon River Anthology* by E. L. Masters, whose home it was. Indian mounds are near. **2** City (pop. 6,573), central Mont., SE of Great Falls; laid out 1882. Scene of gold rush in 1880s. Trade center of agr. (grain), stock-raising, and mining region. Mfg. of building materials and oil refining. **3** Borough (pop. 13,894), central Pa., on Juniata R. and NW of Harrisburg; settled as trading post 1754. Mfg. of metal products and rayon.

Lewis with Harris, island (825 sq. mi.; pop. 28,042), off NW Scotland, mostly northerly of Outer Hebrides. Lewis, N part, in Ross and Cromarty co.; Harris, in Inverness-shire. Little cultivated, it has fishing and stock raising. Harris tweeds made here.

Lexington. 1 City (pop. 55,534), N central Ky., SE of Frankfort in bluegrass region; founded 1779. Thoroughbred horse-raising center and tobacco market, it processes tobacco and liquor and has railroad shops. Seat of Univ. of KENTUCKY and Transylvania Col. (Disciples of Christ; coed., chartered 1780 and 1783, opened at Danville 1785, moved 1789). Called Kentucky Univ. for some years after affiliation with that school; pioneer medical and law schools closed 1915. Alumni include Jefferson Davis and J. C. Breckenridge. Here are homes of J. H. Morgan, Henry Clay, and Mary T. Lincoln, U.S. hospital for drug addicts, veterans' hospital, and national cemetery. **2** Residential town (pop. 17,335), E Mass., NW of Boston; settled c. 1640. Monument on the green marks site of first battle of the Revolution (April 19, 1775) (see LEXINGTON AND CONCORD, BATTLES OF). **3** City (pop. 5,074), W Mo., on the Missouri and E of Kansas City, in a coal and farm area. Besieged and captured (Sept., 1861) by Missouri militia under Gen. Sterling Price in Civil War. **4** City (pop. 5,068), S Nebr., on Platte R. and SE of North Platte, in grain region. Center of irrigation and power project. **5** City (pop. 13,571), central N.C., S of Winston-Salem in Yadkin valley; settled 1775. Has flour, lumber, and cotton mills. **6** Town (pop. 5,976), western Va., in Shenandoah Valley NNW of Lynchburg; laid out 1777. Partially burned in Civil War. R. E. Lee and Stonewall Jackson buried here. Seat of WASHINGTON AND LEE UNIVERSITY, and Virginia Military Inst. (state supported; for men; opened 1839; called West Point of the South).

Lexington and Concord, battles of, opening engagements of American Revolution, April 19, 1775. A British infantry column, sent to capture colonial military stores at Concord, encountered armed resistance at Lexington, fought another engagement at Concord, and withdrew to Boston.

Leyden, Lucas van: see LUCAS VAN LEYDEN.

Leyden, Netherlands: see LEIDEN.

Leyden jar, early form of electrical CONDENSER. Modern form is a glass jar partially coated, inside and out, with tin foil and closed by a nonconducting stopper with brass rod knobbed at one end, connected to foil at other.

Leysin (lāzē'), village, Vaud canton, Switzerland, with sanatoriums for tubercular diseases.

Leyte (lā'tā), island (2,785 sq. mi.; pop. 835,532), one of Visayan Isls., Philippines, just SW of Samar. Produces sugar cane, rice, hemp, and corn. U.S. forces defeated the Japanese in decisive battle of Leyte Gulf (Oct., 1944).

leze majesty: see LESE MAJESTY.

Lhasa (lä'sŏŏ), city (pop. c.20,000; alt. 12,087 ft.), cap. of Tibet. Center of Lamaism. Near by are Potala (main palace of Dalai Lama) and three great monasteries. Holiest temple in city is Jokang, which contains jeweled image of Buddha. Traditional hostility of Tibetan clergy to foreigners has led Lhasa to be called Forbidden City.

L'Hôpital or **L'Hospital, Michel de** (both: mēshĕl' dü l'ōpētäl'), c.1505–1573, chancellor of France under Catherine de' Medici. Favored religious toleration. Was forced out of office by the Guises (1567).

Li, chemical symbol of the element LITHIUM.

Liaosi, province: see MANCHURIA.

Liaotung (lyou'dŏŏng'), province (40,000 sq. mi.; pop. 11,000,000), S Manchuria; cap. Antung. Bounded SE by Korea along Yalu R.; occupies peninsula jutting into Yellow Sea. Tip of Liaotung peninsula leased 1898 by the Russians from China as Kwantung Territory (including Dairen and PORT ARTHUR); after Russo-Japanese War lease taken over by Japan 1905. After World War II most of Kwantung Territory included 1945 in Port Arthur naval-base district under joint Sino-Soviet control. Liaotung is Manchuria's chief industrial area; produces iron and coal.

Liaquat Ali Khan (lēä'kŭt ä'lē kän'), 1895–1951, political leader of Pakistan, educated in India and at Oxford. Headed Moslem League, 1946–47. With creation of Pakistan (1947) he became its prime minister. Shot fatally on Oct. 16, 1951, by fanatic Afghan who wanted autonomy for Pathan tribes.

Liard (lē'ärd"), river of W Canada, 570 mi. long, rising in SE Yukon and flowing ESE into B.C., then N to Mackenzie R. in Mackenzie dist. Navigable to Fort Liard, 165 mi. from its mouth.

Libanus: see LEBANON, mountain range.

Libau, Latvia: see LIEPAJA.

Libby Prison, Richmond, Va., used for captured Union officers in Civil War, formerly tobacco warehouse. Living conditions were notoriously bad, causing death of thousands.

libel and **slander,** two forms of defamation (exposure to hatred, contempt, ridicule, or pecuniary loss). Libel requires some permanent form (e.g., a writing or picture), whereas slander is committed orally, by gesture, or the like. In both cases the defamation must affect a living person (thus attacking a large group such as doctors or lawyers is unactionable). Truth is generally a defense; however, sometimes even a false statement is excusable, if based on a normally reliable source such as a reputable credit-rating agency. Some abusive terms are libelous or slanderous per se, regardless of the character of the person attacked. Broader protection under the law is granted by rights of privacy, which may not be invaded.

Liber (lī'bûr) [Latin,= free], in Roman religion, god of fertility and wine. Identified with Bacchus. His consort **Libera** (lī'bûrŭ) was identified with Persephone or Ariadne. Liberalia was their festival.

Liberal, city (pop. 7,134), SW Kansas, near Okla. line. Grazing, agr., gas fields.

liberal arts, term originally used to mean studies suited to freemen. In the Middle Ages included the trivium (grammar, logic, rhetoric) and the quadrivium (arithmetic, geometry, astronomy, music). In modern times the liberal arts have been considered to be studies based primarily on the humanities as opposed to specialized, vocational, or purely scientific training.

Liberal party, in British history, organization that grew out of Whig party. Lord John RUSSELL is credited with the party's name. Its policies were free trade, religious liberty, abolition of slavery, and extension of franchise. W. E. GLADSTONE sponsored great reforms (e.g., REFORM BILLS). First Irish Home Rule Bill (1886) split the two-party system on greater class basis. Great Whig landowners joined Conservatives. In the 1890s an imperialist group dominated the party. An external threat was the new Labour party. Sir Henry Campbell-Bannerman's reorganization led to Liberal victory in 1906. David LLOYD GEORGE headed World War I coalition (1916–22). Party has declined and is now negligible.

Liberal party, in U.S. history, organized 1944 in New York city by AMERICAN LABOR PARTY dissenters favoring New Deal policies and opposing spread of totalitarianism. Its platform called for a strong UN, greater national development program, extension of civil liberties.

Liberal Republican party, in U.S. history, organization formed in 1872 by Republicans discontented at political corruption and policies of Grant's first administration. Leaders included Carl Schurz, Horace GREELEY. Party urged civil service reform and an end to Reconstruction program of radical Republicans. U. S. Grant, however, was reelected.

Liberec (lē'bĕrĕts), Ger. *Reichenberg,* city (pop. 29,690), N Bohemia, Czechoslovakia, on the Lausitzer Neisse. Textile mfg. (wool, cotton, linen, silk).

Liberia (lībē'rēŭ), republic (c.43,000 sq. mi.; est. pop. 1,600,000), W Africa, on the Atlantic, between British Sierra Leone and French Ivory Coast; cap. Monrovia. Founded 1822 by American Colonization Society as colony of freed slaves from U.S. Became a free republic in 1847, with its government modeled on that of U.S. To further economic progress a 99-year lease to c.1,000,000 acres was granted to Firestone Co. for development of rubber plantations. In World War II the U.S. developed defense bases in Liberia, building a large air field and modernizing Monrovia harbor. By agreement with the government a group of American businessmen began far-reaching program in 1949 to further country's economic and social development. Railroad was built to link Monrovia with iron mines in interior; cacao growing and use of lumber resources were encouraged.

Liberius (lībĕr'ēŭs), pope (352–66). Urged Emperor Constantius to call the Council of Arles (353), where, however, papal legates, subdued by imperial favor toward ARIANISM, voted against St. ATHANASIUS. Liberius, refusing to be coerced, was banished; an antipope, Felix, was set up. In 358 Liberius was allowed to return as pope, and after the death of Constantius he openly avowed his orthodoxy and reasserted the primacy of Rome.

Liberty, vacation and health resort village (pop. 4,658), SE N.Y., in the Catskills.

liberty, general term for the sum of specific liberties or freedoms, such as religious liberty, political liberty, and freedom of speech. Fundamental is personal liberty, the physical freedom to come and go as one pleases. Freedom of worship and of private religious judgment were greatly restricted before the Protestant Reformation, and political liberties, such as the right to vote, were little known before the 19th cent. Anarchism, individualism, socialism, and nationalism all represent different ways of seeking human liberty. Stages in the process of acquiring liberties are exemplified by the struggle for the MAGNA CARTA in 1215, the Habeas Corpus Act (1679), the feminist movement in the 19th and 20th cent., and the demands of ethnic minorities and colonies for political rights. Such philosophers as Locke, Rousseau, and Jefferson popularized the notion that the individual possesses certain natural rights or liberties. Since the French Revolution, liberty has become closely connected with equality of opportunity: the freedom to develop one's potentialities.

Liberty, Statue of, colossal statue, on Bedloe's Isl. in New York harbor, commanding entrance to New York city. Designed by F. A. Bartholdi, it commemorates French and American revolutions. Statue (152 ft. high and made of copper sheets) is in form of woman with uplifted arm holding a torch; its base is 11-pointed star, and the c.150-ft.-high pedestal is of concrete faced with granite. Presented in 1884 to U.S. by Franco-American Union, became national monument in 1924.

Liberty Bell, historic relic now exhibited in Independence Hall, Philadelphia. Hung in steeple of Hall 1753; rung July, 1776, to proclaim Declaration of Independence; hidden in Allentown (1777–78) during British occupation of Philadelphia; moved to tower 1781. Bell was cracked in 1835.

Liberty party, in U.S. history, antislavery political organization founded in 1840 by those abolitionists, under James G. BIRNEY, who repudiated W. L. Garrison's nonpolitical stand. Vote given Birney in 1844 threw presidency to J. K. Polk. In 1848 party united with antislavery Whigs and Democrats to form FREE-SOIL PARTY.

Libertyville, village (pop. 5,425), NE Ill., NNW of Chicago; center of farm area.

Libon (lī'bŏn), 5th cent. B.C., Greek architect. Built the Doric temple to Zeus at Olympia.

Libra (lī'brů) [Latin,= the balance], seventh sign of ZODIAC.

library. Earliest known library was a collection of clay tablets in Babylonia in 21st cent. B.C. There were ancient Egyptian temple libraries, and the library of Assur-bani-pal (d. 626? B.C.) in Nineveh was the most noted before Greek times. The temple at Jerusalem contained a sacred library. In Greece private book collections date from 6th cent. B.C., first public library from 330 B.C. Most famous libraries of antiquity were those of ALEXANDRIA and PERGAMUM. First Roman libraries were brought from Greece, Asia Minor, and Syria. Continental and English libraries are successors of the monastic libraries that preserved learning for centuries. The Arabs collected (9th to 15th cent.) many libraries. In 15th cent. the Vatican Library, oldest public library in Europe, was formed. Sorbonne library at Paris was founded in 1257. Many other great university libraries were opened in the 14th cent. Among the chief modern libraries are the BIBLIOTHÈQUE NATIONALE, Paris; the BRITISH MUSEUM, London; the BODLEIAN LIBRARY, Oxford; the VATICAN LIBRARY, Rome; the AMBROSIAN LIBRARY, Milan; the Laurentian, Florence; the Lenin Library, Moscow; the LIBRARY OF CONGRESS, Washington, D.C.; the NEW YORK PUBLIC LIBRARY; the libraries at Harvard. A public library had been opened in Boston in 1653. First circulating library in U.S. chartered in Philadelphia in 1732. Late 19th cent. brought free access to books, and Andrew Carnegie funds helped create many new libraries. Three widely used book-classification systems are those of Melvil DEWEY, Charles Ammi CUTTER, and Library of Congress.

Library of Congress, U.S. national library, at Washington, D.C., estab. 1800. An act of 1870 provided that copies of all books copyrighted in U.S. must go to Library of Congress. Now open to the public as a reference library. Mainly supported by congressional appropriations.

library school. Since Melvil Dewey estab. (1887) at Columbia Univ. a school for training library workers, over 30 of these schools have come into operation in U.S. and Canada (e.g., at Univ. of Illinois, Pratt Institute, Los Angeles Public Library). Univ. of Chicago was first graduate school to confer doctoral degree in library science. There are now library schools in Europe and South America.

libretto [Ital.,= little book], the text of an opera or an oratorio. Outstanding librettists have been Pietro Metastasio, Philippe Quinault, Lorenzo Da Ponte, W. S. Gilbert, and Hugo von Hofmannsthal. Wagner tried to achieve a perfect union of text and music by writing his own librettos.

Libreville (lēbrůvēl'), town (pop. 9,900), SW French Equatorial Africa, port on Gulf of Guinea. Hardwoods are exported.

Libya (lĭ'bēů), kingdom (c.680,000 sq. mi.; est. pop. 1,168,000), N Africa, fronting on the Mediterranean; winter cap. Tripoli, summer cap. Bengasi. Comprises Tripolitania, Cyrenaica, and Fezzan. Much of Libya is desert. Dates, olives, and oranges are grown in coastal oases. Area was successively ruled by Carthage, Rome, and the Vandals. Vying for control over it in Middle Ages were Arabia, Morocco, and Egypt. Spain and Knights of Malta briefly held dominion in 16th cent. Was under Ottoman rule from 1551 to 1911, when seized by Italy. Its development as Italian colony began only in 1930s, when c.20,000 colonists were brought from home country. Libya was important battleground in World War II (see NORTH AFRICA, CAMPAIGNS IN). In accordance with UN decision of 1949, Libya became independent on Dec. 24, 1951, with Idris I (former titular king of Cyrenaica) as ruler.

Licata (lēkä'tä), anc. *Phintias,* city (pop. 30,641), S Sicily, Italy. It is a seaport shipping sulphur, asphalt, cheese. Founded 3d cent. B.C., it was refuge of people of Gela after Gela's destruction. Off near-by Cape Ecnomus Romans won in 256 B.C. a decisive battle in the Punic Wars. Licata was an Allied landing point in invasion of Sicily (1943).

lichen (lī'kůn), slow-growing simple plant form, usually gray, but often red, rust, or brown, found on rocks or tree stumps from arctic to tropics. A lichen is composed of algae and fungi living together. When growing on rocks, lichens by their acids start the long process of weathering by which rocks are changed into soil.

Lichfield, municipal borough (pop. 10,624),

Staffordshire, England. Market town, famous for its three-spired cathedral (13th–14th cent.) and associations with Dr. Johnson, who was born and lived here.

Lichnowsky, Karl Max, Fürst (lĭkhnôf'skē), 1860–1928, German diplomat; ambassador to London 1912–14. In a privately printed pamphlet (1916) he accused his government of failing to support him in his efforts to avert World War I; its publication in the U.S. (1917) caused his expulsion from the Prussian house of lords.

Licinius (līsĭn'ēus), d. 325, Roman emperor. Coemperor with Galerius, he later allied himself with CONSTANTINE I and defeated Maximin in 313, becoming sole ruler in the East. Later defeated twice and put to death by Constantine.

Licinius Calvus Stolo, Caius (kā'yŭs, kăl'vŭs stō'lō), fl. 375 B.C., tribune to whom are attributed the Licinian Rogations. These laws limited the amount of public land held by one person, regulated debts, and ordained that one consul must be plebeian.

Licking, river rising in E Ky., SE of Salyersville, and flowing 320 mi. NW to Ohio R. opposite Cincinnati. G. R. Clark's group met here 1780 for march up the Little Miami. Battle of Blue Licks (1782) occurred in Licking valley. Partly navigable, it is a busy trade route.

licorice (lĭk'ŭrĭs), Old World perennial plant (*Glycyrrhiza glabra*) and the sweet substance obtained from its roots, used medicinally and in confectionery.

Lidice (lĭ'dĭsē, Czech lĭ'dyĭtsĕ), village (former pop. 446), central Bohemia, Czechoslovakia, near Kladno. In reprisal for assassination of Reinhard Heydrich, Nazi "protector" (i.e., governor) of Bohemia and Moravia, the Germans razed Lidice, killed all men, deported women and children (1942).

Lido di Venezia (lē'dō dē vānā'tsyä), beach resort near Venice, Italy.

Lie, Jonas (lē), 1880–1940, American landscape marine painter, b. Norway.

Lie, Jonas Lauritz Idemil (yō'näs lou'rĭts ē'dŭmēl lē'), 1833–1908, Norwegian novelist. His stories of ordinary family life (e.g., *The Pilot and His Wife,* 1874) were the first modern Norwegian novels.

Lie, Marius Sophus (mä'rēōōs sō'fōōs lē'), 1842–99, Norwegian mathematician, noted for studies of differential equations and for continuous transformation groups.

Lie, Trygve (Halvdan) (trüg'vŭ hälv'dän lē'), 1896–, Norwegian statesman. Foreign minister of Norway from 1941, he was chosen in 1946 first secretary general of the United Nations. Pursued conciliatory policy. His resignation took effect 1953. Dag Hammarskjold was chosen to succeed him.

Lieber, Thomas: see ERASTUS, THOMAS.

Lieberman, Max, 1847–1935, German genre painter, who depicted life of workers and peasants.

Liebig, Justus, Baron von (yōōs'tōōs bärōn' fŭn lē'bĭkh), 1803–73, German chemist. In almost 50 years of teaching he profoundly influenced the training of leading chemists. He improved organic analysis and made valuable contributions to agricultural chemistry including the development of artificial fertilizers.

Liebknecht, Wilhelm (vĭl'hĕlm lēp'kŭnĕkht), 1826–1900, German Socialist leader. Influenced by Karl Marx, he founded with his disciple Bebel the German Social Democratic party (1869). Was imprisoned for two years under Bismarck's anti-Socialist laws. Served in Reichstag 1874–1900. His son, **Karl Liebknecht,** 1871–1919, served in Reichstag as member of radical wing of Social Democrats from 1912. Refused to support government in World War I; founded SPARTACUS PARTY. After failure of Spartacist revolt of 1919 he and Rosa LUXEMBURG were arrested and killed while being carried to prison.

Liebler, Thomas: see ERASTUS, THOMAS.

Liechtenstein (lĭkh'tŭnshtīn"), sovereign principality (62 sq. mi.; pop. 11,218), in the Alps between Austria and Switzerland; cap. Vaduz. The Rhine forms its W boundary. Pastures, agr. Much revenue is derived from moderate taxes on internatl. holding companies with hq. at Vaduz. Ruling prince is Francis Joseph II (acceded 1938). Elected diet has 15 members. There is no army. Population is Roman Catholic and German-speaking. Principality was created 1718 as immediate fief of Holy Roman Empire by uniting county of Vaduz and barony of Schellenberg, acquired by the old Austrian family of Lichtenstein. A member of German Confederation from 1815, it sided with Austria in Austro-Prussian War of 1866 but was overlooked in peace treaty, thus remaining technically at war with Prussia. Liechtenstein family was prominent under the Hapsburg empire, but after World War I the principality became oriented toward Switzerland, whose currency it accepted in 1921. It entered a custom union with Switzerland in 1924 and is represented abroad by the Swiss government.

lied and lieder: see SONG.

lie detector, any scientific instrument recording bodily changes (e.g., in respiration, pulse rate, blood pressure) caused by telling of lies. W. M. Marston (1914–15), John A. Larson (1921), Leonarde Keeler (1926) were noted for such devices. W. G. Summers's psychogalvanometer (1936) measures electrical changes on skin. Usually lie detector evidence is legally inacceptable because of similarity of physical changes caused by emotional factors (such as feelings of guilt) to those caused by lies.

Liége (lyāzh), Flemish *Luik,* province (1,526 sq. mi.; pop. 973,911), E Belgium, in industrial Meuse valley and agr. Ardennes plateau. Chief cities: Liége, Verviers, Spa, Seraing. Coal mining, metallurgy, wool mfg. Population is largely French-speaking (see WALLOONS); EUPEN and MALMÉDY dists. are German-speaking. Province shared history of prince-bishopric of Liége, of which it was a part. The cap., **Liége** (pop. 432,471, incl. suburbs), on the Meuse and at the head of the Albert Canal, is a commercial, industrial, and transportation center as well as the cultural cap. of French-speaking Belgium. Mfg. of arms (at Herstal), machinery, beer, flour. Episcopal see. Seat of university (founded 1817). A trading center from the 10th cent., Liége became the cap. of a prince-bishopric which comprised most of modern Liége prov. and parts of Limburg and Namur provs. The rising guilds took part in city government, and in 1373 the bishop's officials were placed under supervision of a tribunal of 22 persons; this Peace of the Twenty-Two remained in force (with interruptions) till 1792. In 1467 Charles the Bold of Burgundy, who had imposed his protectorate on Liége, punished the rebellious citizens by abolishing communal liberties. The citizens, encouraged by Louis XI of France, rose against Charles, but Charles forced Louis to assist him in repressing the revolution and sacked Liége (1468). Though still a sovereign member of the Holy Roman Empire, the bishopric was in practice dependent on Spain and Austria from 16th cent. to 1792 (see NETHERLANDS, AUSTRIAN AND SPANISH). Despite its strong fortifications it fell to the Germans in 1914 and 1940. Liberated by U.S. troops (1944), it was bombarded by rocket weapons during Battle of the Bulge (1944–45), but the principal buildings and thoroughfares of the handsome city suffered little damage.

Liegnitz (lēg'nĭts), Pol. *Legnica,* city (pop. 24,357), Lower Silesia; transferred to Polish administration 1945. Textile mfg. It was the seat of a principality ruled by a branch of the PIAST dynasty from 1248 till 1675, when it passed to Austria; ceded to Prussia 1742. At near-by Wahlstatt the Mongols defeated the Germans and Poles (1241), and the Prussians under Blücher defeated the French (1813).

Liepaja (lēĕ'päyä), Ger. *Libau,* city (pop. (57,098), SW Latvia; an ice-free port on Baltic Sea. Steel mills, paper mills, shipyards. First mentioned 1263, it passed with Courland to Russia in 1795 and was an important commercial center in late 19th and early 20th cent.

Liestal (lēs'täl), town (pop. 7,211), cap. of half-canton of Basel-Land, NW Switzerland. Textiles.

Lieven, Dorothea, Princess (lē'vůn), 1785–1857, Russian noblewoman; wife of the Russian ambassador to London (1812–34). A brilliant personality, she was a friend of Metternich, Wellington, and Guizot; her Paris salon (after 1834) was noted, as was her witty correspondence (*The Private Letters of Princess Lieven,* 1938).

life insurance: see INSURANCE.

Liffey (lĭ'fē), river of Ireland, flowing 50 mi. from Co. Wicklow through Dublin to Dublin Bay.

lift: see ELEVATOR; LOCK, CANAL.

ligan: see FLOTSAM, JETSAM, AND LIGAN.

light, form of energy not yet adequately explained by any one theory. Corpuscular (or emission) theory of Newton said light consists of minute particles (corpuscles) emitted from luminous bodies and traveling through space. This was superseded by wave theory of Christiaan Huygens. This states that light consists of waves traveling in luminiferous ether at high velocity with transverse vibration at right angles to direction of wave and proceeding in straight lines. Electromagnetic theory of J. C. Maxwell classes visible light as form of electromagnetic radiation occurring in waves shorter than infrared but longer than ultraviolet. QUANTUM THEORY says light is form of radiant energy given off from luminous bodies in tiny quantities called photons. Light is often described in termsof effect on eye (see VISION). As such, it is limited to radiations of wave length between infrared and ultraviolet; neither infrared nor ultraviolet rays can be "seen" by man. Light is said to be energy that makes visible the bodies producing it and those reflecting it. PHOTOMETRY deals with measurement of relative intensity of light source and illumination. Transparent objects let light pass through them; translucent objects let light through but scatter rays; opaque objects do not permit light passage. Light travels in straight lines through uniform transparent substance; its velocity in air is c.186,000 mi. per second. Explanation of REFRACTION is based on differences in velocity in different media. When light rays strike bodies through which they cannot pass, some are absorbed, some undergo reflection. Color of light depends on wave length. White light is all colors combined; its composition is determined by its dispersion. Light is involved in PHOTOSYNTHESIS. Studies of light can be traced from the early Greeks, through the discoveries of optical instruments (e.g., microscope, telescope) and the work of many investigators including Snell, Descartes, Thomas Young, Fresnel, Malus, Fizeau, Foucault, Helmholtz, Michelson, and Morley.

lighthouse, structure equipped to give optical or radio-electrical guidance to ships and airplanes. In 1789 U.S. Congress took over lighthouses formerly privately operated. Lighthouse Board appointed in 1852 was superseded in 1910 by Lighthouse Service, which was transferred to U.S. coast guard (1939) from Dept. of Commerce. From 1934, so-called remote-control stations began to replace lighthouses; these have radio apparatus to operate lamps, fog signals, radio beacon.

lighting. Earliest methods of lighting, by open fire, firebrands, and torches, were followed by development of LAMP, CANDLE, and lantern. All still survive in various civilizations and for various uses. The lantern, enclosed in glass or equipped wtih a chimney, is to some extent superseded by the flashlight. Use of gas for lighting was stimulated by invention of Bunsen burner and Welsbach mantle. Illuminating gases include coal gas, air gas, acetylene, water gas, and producer gas. First development in electric lighting was arc lamp evolved from carbon arc. Carbon-arc street lamps appeared in Cleveland in 1879 and came into wide use. Mercury-arc lamp was developed in 1903. Arc lights are used in floodlights, some searchlights, spotlights, and projectors. In 1879 Edison patented the first commercially practical incandescent lamp (one in which current passes through filament offering high resistance and enclosed in a vacuum). Neon lamp was invented in 1911 by Georges Claude. Fluorescent lamp consists of tube containing argon and trace of mercury and with inner walls coated with fluorescent powder; electric current causes mercury vapor to emit ultraviolet radiation which causes power to fluoresce. Sodium vapor lamps are among those used experimentally for highway lighting.

lightning: see THUNDERSTORM.

light-year, unit of distance (c.5.87 million million mi.) based on speed of light (186,000 mi. per sec.), used for measurements in space. An object is one light-year distant when its light takes one year to reach observer.

Ligne, Charles Joseph, prince de (shärl' zhôzĕf' prēs' dù lēnyù), 1735–1814, Austrian courtier and field marshal, of an ancient family of Hainaut. His remark on the Congress of Vienna (*Le congrès danse, mais ne marche pas*—the congress dances but takes no steps) has remained famous. His memoirs and correspondence (Eng. tr. of selections, 1927) mirror his charm, gaiety, and metropolitanism.

lignite (lĭg'nīt) or **brown coal,** a carbonaceous fuel intermediate between PEAT and COAL, brown or yellowish in color and woody in texture. Its flame is smoky and heating power low.

lignum vitae (lĭg'nùm vī'tē), tropical American evergreen tree (*Guaiacum,* or *Guajacum, officinale*). Valued for its hard resinous wood and gum resin used in certain drugs.

Ligny (lēnyē'), village, Namur prov., central Belgium, NE of Charleroi and near Fleurus. Here Napoleon defeated Prussians early in WATERLOO CAMPAIGN (1815).

Liguori, Alfonso Maria de': see ALPHONSUS LIGUORI.

Liguria (lĭgōō'rēù), region (2,098 sq. mi.; pop. 1,466,810), NW Italy, extending along Mediterranean (called here the Ligurian Sea) from the French border to La Spezia; cap. GENOA. Coastal strip forms Italian RIVIERA; inland rise the Ligurian Alps (W) and Ligurian Apennines (E). Fishing, gardening, wine growing, agr. are main occupations. Ancient Ligurii occupied Mediterranean coast from Rhone to Arno, but Celtic migrations and Phoenician, Greek, and Carthaginian colonists displaced them in 4th cent. B.C. Region was subdued by Romans in 2d cent. B.C. During later Middle Ages Genoa gradually gained control of most of Liguria, which shared the history of its cap. from the 16th cent. until its annexation to Sardinia (1815).

lilac, flowering shrub of genus *Syringa,* native to Europe and Asia, and widely grown in America since colonial times. The fragrant purple, white, or rosy-pink flowers are usually borne in cone-shaped clusters in late spring. The term French lilac refers to modern double-flowered hybrids.

Lilburne, John, 1614?–1657, English political leader and pamphleteer for the LEVELERS. Spent much of his life in prison or exile for agitation.

Liliencron, Detlev, Freiherr von (dĕt'lĕf frī'hĕr fŭn lē'lyùnkrōn), 1844–1909, German lyric poet.

Lilienthal, David E(li) (lĭ'lyùnthôl), 1899–, American public official. Appointed a director of TVA in 1933; its chairman 1941–46. As chairman of U.S. Atomic Energy Commission (1947–49) he pioneered in civilian control of U.S. atomic-energy program.

Lilienthal, Otto (ô'tō lē'lyùntäl), 1848–96, German aeronautical engineer and pioneer experimenter with heavier-than-air flight. Improved gliders. His brother, **Gustav Lilienthal** (gōōs'täf), 1849–1933, was associate in experiments.

Lilith (lĭ'lĭth), in Talmudic tradition, a female demon; in legend, Adam's first wife.

Liliuokalani (lēlēōō"ōkälä'nē), 1838–1917, last reigning queen of Hawaiian Isls. (1891–93). Dethroned in 1893, formally renounced royal claims in 1895. Lived much in U.S. thereafter. Wrote many songs (e.g., *Aloha Oe* or *Farewell to Thee*).

Lille (lēl), city (pop. 179,778), cap. of Nord dept., N France. Textile mfg. center (gave its name to lisle). Seat of a university (founded 1887) and of an important art museum. Was chief city of county of Flanders; after 1668 cap. of French Flanders prov. Its huge citadel was built by Vauban. Other landmarks include old stock exchange (17th cent.) and unfinished cathedral (begun 1854).

Lillehammer (lĭ'lùhämùr), town (pop. 6,565), co. seat of Opland co., SE Norway, N of Oslo and on N end of L. Mjosa; founded 1827. It is commercial and tourist center for the fertile Gudbransdal. Its folk museum exhibits old buildings of the region.

Lillie, Beatrice, 1898–, English comedienne, b. Canada. Made her debut in 1914. Won an international reputation for sophisticated wit in such shows as *Charlot's Revue* (1922, 1924), *Seven Lively Arts* (1945), *An Evening with Beatrice Lille* (1952).

Lillo, George, 1693–1739, English playwright. In *The London Merchant; or, The History of George Barnwell* (1731) he created first modern melodrama.

Lilly, John: see LYLY, JOHN.

Lilly, William (c.1468–1522): see LILY, WILLIAM.

Lilly, William, 1602–81, English astrologer. Somewhat popular as a prophet and caster of horoscopes, he issued an annual almanac and foretold events. His best-known work is *Christian Astrology* (1647).

Lily, William, c.1468–1522, English scholar, first headmaster of St. Paul's School, and coauthor of the Eton Latin grammar. Also Lilly, Lyly.

lily, ornamental perennial plant of genus *Lilium,* with scaly bulb. The flowers, often fragrant, are of great diversity in form and color. Widely cultivated are the Madonna lily of Europe, the Easter lily, the golden-rayed lily of Japan, and the regal and tiger lilies of China. Others, including the meadow lily and Turk's cap lily, are native to North America. In religion and art the lily symbolizes purity.

Lilybaeum (lĭlĭbē'ùm), anc. city of Sicily (modern Marsala); founded by Carthage 396 B.C. Withstood long Roman siege (250–242 B.C.).

lily of the valley, perennial spring-blooming plant (*Convallaria majalis*), native to Europe, Asia, and mountains of SE U.S. Its dainty, white, bell-shaped, fragrant flowers are borne on a stalk which rises between two shiny leaves. It thrives in shade.

Lima (lē'mä), city (pop. 533,645), W Peru, cap. and largest city of Peru; founded 1535 by Francisco Pizarro. Its port is Callao. Its cultural supremacy on continent was contested in colonial times only by Bogotá and in magnificence and political prestige its only peer in Spanish America was Mexico city. Univ. of San Marcos, founded here in 1551, is one of finest in South America.

Lima (lī'mů), city (pop. 50,246), NW Ohio, N of Dayton; laid out in 1831. Mfg. of railroad equipment, machinery, and electrical goods. Has limestone quarries.

Liman von Sanders, Otto (ô'tō lē'män fŭn zän'dŭrs), 1855–1929, German general. Reorganized Turkish army (1913); commanded Turks in GALLIPOLI CAMPAIGN (1915–16).

Limassol (lēmäsôl'), city (pop. 22,799), S Cyprus, a Mediterranean port. Has a large wine trade.

Limburg, Fr. *Limbourg,* province (930 sq. mi.; pop. 475,716), NE Belgium, bordering on the Netherlands; cap. Hasselt. Crossed by Meuse R. and Albert Canal. Agr.; coal mining. Population is largely Flemish. Most of province was included in prince-bishopric of Liége until 1792 and formed part of Dutch province of Limburg, 1815–39.

Limburg, province (840 sq. mi.; pop. 684,105), SE Netherlands, bordering on Belgium and Germany; cap. MAASTRICHT. Contains chief coal deposits of Netherlands. Population is mostly Roman Catholic. Former duchy of Limburg comprised S part of the modern Dutch province and E portion of modern Liége prov., Belgium. Limbourg, a small town E of Liége, was the cap. Duchy was divided between United Netherlands and Spanish Netherlands 1648; united (with altered boundaries) in 1815 under kingdom of the Netherlands. Dutch-Belgian treaty of 1839 divided it into Dutch and Belgian provinces of Limburg.

lime, small citrus tree (*Citrus aurantifolia*) and its green fruit, similar to the lemon. Native to SE Asia, it is susceptible to frost injury and is cultivated in U.S. only in S Fla. Limes are high in vitamins and yield citric acid.

lime or **quicklime,** calcium oxide, a common, white amorphous solid. It is made by heating LIMESTONE in kiln. Used to make porcelain, glass, alkalies; in sugar purification; in treating soils; as insecticide. A basic anhydride, it reacts with water to form calcium hydroxide. This process is slaking, product is **slaked lime,** a white bulky powder. It is used in mortar, plaster, whitewash; to counteract soil acidity; in refining beet sugar. In solution it forms limewater. **Lime-sulphur,** a mixture of calcium sulphides, is an insecticide.

Limehouse, district of docks, warehouses, and factories of London, England, on the Thames. Noted as the Chinese district of London.

Limerick (lī'mŭrĭk), county (1,037 sq. mi.; pop. 142,559), S Ireland, in Munster. An agr. plain, dairy farming and salmon fishing are chief occupations. Has hydroelectric plant on Shannon R. County town is **Limerick,** county borough (pop. 42,970), a seaport at head of Shannon estuary and only town of any size in county. Cap. of Munster under Brian Boru. Last stronghold of James II, it has stone on which treaty was signed (1691) giving Irish and Catholics certain rights. Has Protestant (12th cent.) and Catholic cathedrals and Norman castle.

limestone, sedimentary rock composed wholly or in part of calcium carbonate (calcite). Ordinarily it is white, but impurities (carbon, iron oxide) give it variety of colors. Formed by consolidation of marine invertebrate skeletons or from chemical precipitation. Important uses: flux in smelting iron ore, source of lime, ingredient of Portland cement, building stone. Varieties include chalk, dolomite, and marble.

lime-sulphur: see LIME.

limewater, solution of calcium hydroxide (or slaked lime). Used to test for carbon dioxide, in treating acid burns, and as an antacid.

Lim Fjord (lēm' fyôrd"), strait, c.110 mi. long, cutting across N Jutland, Denmark, and connecting North Sea with the Kattegat. It broke through to the North Sea in 1825. Aalborg is chief port on it.

liming (lī'mĭng), application to soil of calcium in various forms, e.g., marl, chalk, limestone, shells, or hydrated lime. It neutralizes soil, improves texture, increases activity of soil bacteria. Oversupply may be injurious to plants.

Limoges (lēmôzh'), city (pop. 99,535), cap. of Haute-Vienne dept., S central France, on Vienne R.; historic cap. of LIMOUSIN. It was burned and its people were massacred by Edward the Black Prince (1371) and it was devastated again in the Wars of Religion (16th cent.). The famous Limoges enamel industry, fully developed by the 13th cent. reached its peak with Léonard LIMOUSIN. Turgot, as intendant of Limoges (1761–74) introduced its celebrated china manufactures. Limoges has a cathedral (13th–16th cent.), a notable ceramics museum, and an art gallery. Birthplace of Renoir.

limonite (lī'mŭnīt), **brown hematite,** or **bog iron,** yellow to dark brown hydrated iron oxide, used as pigment and iron ore.

Limousin or **Limosin, Léonard** (lāônär' lēmōōzē', lēmōzē'), c.1505–c.1577, French painter, member of family of Limoges enamel artists.

Limousin (lēmōōzē'), region and former province, S central France, in Corrèze and Haute-Vienne depts.; historic cap. LIMOGES. Hilly region with fertile agr. lowlands. The viscounty of Limoges (part of Aquitaine) passed under English rule in 1152; was annexed to France by Philip II in 1204; ceded back to England by Louis IX in 1259; ravaged by Edward the Black Prince in Hundred Years War; and recovered for France by Du Guesclin. A fief of the Bourbon-Vendôme family, it became part of the royal domain after the accession of Henry IV (1589).

Limpopo (lĭmpō'pō), river, c.1,000 mi. long, rising in Transvaal prov., South Africa. Flows through Mozambique to empty into Indian Ocean. Also called Crocodile R.

Linacre or **Lynaker, Thomas** (both: lĭ'nŭkŭr), 1460?–1524, English humanist and physician. He wrote a Latin grammar (c. 1523), translated many of Aristotle's and Galen's works into Latin, and founded Royal Col. of Physicians and readerships in medicine at Oxford and Cambridge. Erasmus and Sir Thomas More were among his pupils.

Linares (lēnä'rēs), city (pop. 31,720), S Spain, in Andalusia. Silver and lead mines near by.

Lincoln, Abraham, 1809–65, 16th President of the United States. Born in log cabin in Hardin co., Ky. (now in Larue co.), the son of Thomas Lincoln and of Nancy Hanks, he grew up on the frontier as family moved forward. Mostly self-schooled. Story of early love affair with Ann RUTLEDGE is now discredited. Moving to Springfield, Ill., in 1837, he practiced law there. U.S. Representative (1847–49). As Republican candidate for U.S. Senate in 1858, Lincoln made his mark in debates with Stephen A. DOUGLAS. He was not an abolitionist, but he regarded slavery as an "injustice" and an evil; opposed its extension. Elected President in 1860. His wise control after CIVIL WAR began practically amounted to dictatorship. Cabinet was rent by internal jealousies and hatred; radical abolitionists condemned him as too mild; conservatives were gloomy over war's progress. He was in constant trouble with the generals. EMANCIPATION PROCLAMATION and Gettysburg Address express high moral tone he sought to give Northern cause. His second inaugural address included memorable phrase, "With malice toward none; with charity for all"; presaged a peace without conquest, RECONSTRUCTION without destruction. Assassinated by John Wilkes BOOTH in 1865. Became object of adultation and symbol of American democracy. His wife, **Mary Todd Lincoln,** 1818–82, met and married Lincoln in 1842. Many unkind comments have been made about her, especially by W. H. Herndon. Of the four sons she bore, only **Robert Todd Lincoln,** 1843–1926, lived to manhood. He was a lawyer and a public official. Papers of his father which he owned he left to Library of Congress; in 1947 these papers were opened to the public.

Lincoln, Benjamin, 1733–1810, American Revolutionary general. Served in Saratoga campaign (1777). Failed to take Savannah (1779); surrendered at Charleston (1780). Helped suppress Shays's Rebellion in Mass. (1787).

Lincoln, Mary Todd and **Robert Todd:** see LINCOLN, ABRAHAM.

Lincoln, England: see LINCOLNSHIRE.

Lincoln. 1 City (pop. 14,362), central Ill., NNE of Springfield, center of a farming area; settled in 1830s. Platted and promoted (1853) with aid of Abraham Lincoln, who practiced law here 1847–59. Light mfg. (esp. china). **2** City (pop. 98,884), state cap. (since 1867), SE Nebr., W of the Missouri, in prairie region; founded 1864. Second largest city and educational center of state, it is rail, trade, and industrial center for extensive grain and livestock area. Food processing, oil refining, and mfg. of bricks and farm, printing, and office equipment. Modern capitol completed 1934. Seat of Univ. of NEBRASKA, Union Col. (Seventh-Day Adventist; coed.; 1891), and Nebraska Wesleyan Univ. (coed.; 1887). W. J. Bryan lived here, 1887–1916. **3** Town (pop. 11,270), NE R.I., on Blackstone R. and N of Providence. Limestone quarrying since colonial times. Textiles.

Lincoln, Mount: see PARK RANGE.

Lincoln City, settlement, SW Ind., NE of Evansville; laid out 1872 on site of Thomas Lincoln's farm. Park near by has Nancy Hanks Lincoln Memorial (with her grave) and site of Lincoln cabin, built 1816.

Lincoln College: see OXFORD UNIVERSITY.

Lincoln Heights, suburban city (pop. 5,531), SW Ohio, N of Cincinnati.

Lincoln Memorial, monument in Potomac Park, Washington, D.C., designed by Henry Bacon; dedicated 1922. Has heroic statue of Lincoln by Daniel Chester French and murals by Jules Guérin.

Lincoln Park, city (pop. 29,310), SE Mich., residential suburb SW of Detroit.

Lincolnshire or **Lincoln,** maritime county (2,665 sq. mi.; pop. 706,574), E England. Has three administrative districts—Parts of Holland in SE, Parts of Kesteven in SW, and Parts of Lindsey. Low, flat, and marshy region, it has many dikes and canals. Agr. and fishing are main occupations; there is some shipbuilding and mfg. Has many medieval churches and remains. County town is **Lincoln,** county borough (pop. 69,412), in Parts of Lindsey; a transportation center. An ancient British fort, it was important under Romans and Danes. Cathedral (built 1075–1501) has famous bell "Great Tom of Lincoln" in 271-ft. tower. Lincoln Castle, many times besieged, was begun in 1068 by William I.

Lincoln's Inn: see INNS OF COURT.

Lincolnton, textile-mill town (pop. 5,423), W central N.C., NW of Charlotte.

Lincoln University: see JEFFERSON CITY, Mo.

Lind, Jenny, 1820–87, Swedish soprano. Made her debut in 1838 as Agathe in Weber's *Der Freischütz.* In 1841 studied with Manuel García. Under the management of P. T. Barnum she toured (1850–52) the U.S. Called "the Swedish nightingale," she was the greatest coloratura soprano of her time.

Lindau (lĭn′dou), town (pop. 19,768), Württemberg-Hohenzollern, SW Germany, on an island in L. of Constance. With its district (120 sq. mi.; pop. 57,970) it belonged to Bavaria until in 1945 it was incorporated into French occupation zone.

Lindbergh, Charles A(ugustus), 1902–, American aviator. Nonstop, solo New York–to–Paris transatlantic flight in 1927 brought sudden fame. Kidnaping and death of his son in 1932 caused family to move to England in 1935. With Alexis Carrel invented (1936) a "mechanical heart." Resigned army reserve commission following criticism of his antiwar speeches. Served U.S. in Europe and Pacific as civilian consultant in World War II. His wife, **Anne (Spencer) Morrow Lindbergh,** 1907–, daughter of Dwight W. Morrow, accompanied and aided her husband on long flights and wrote several books.

Linden, city (pop. 30,644), NE N.J., SSW of Elizabeth; site bought from Indians 1664. Oil refinery; mfg. of pharmaceuticals, motors, and chemicals.

linden or **basswood,** ornamental deciduous tree of genus *Tilia* of N Hemisphere. Fragrant flowers are attractive to bees. Wood is valued for Venetian blinds, inexpensive furniture, and other articles.

Lindenhurst, village (pop. 8,644), SE N.Y., on S shore of Long Isl. near Babylon. Mfg. of machinery, aircraft and marine instruments, and cabinets.

Lindesnes (lĭn′dŭsnĕs) or **the Naze** (nāz), cape, extreme S Norway, on North Sea at entrance of the Skagerrak. Its beacon was first (1650) in Norway.

Lindisfarne (lĭn'dĭsfärn) or **Holy Island,** small island off Northumberland coast, England. Celtic Christianity first estab. in England here in 635. St. Cuthbert was famous bishop. Lindisfarne Gospels or Book of Durham, illuminated Latin manuscript now in British Mus., was written here before 700.

Lindsay, or **Lyndsay, Sir David,** c.1490–c.1555, Scottish Protestant poet. Wrote several satires against Catholic Church (e.g., *The Testament and Complaynt of Our Soverane Lordis Papyngo,* 1530) and long morality play of religious and political criticism, *Ane Pleasant Satyre of the Three Estaitis* (1540).

Lindsay, (Nicholas) Vachel (vā'chŭl), 1879–1931, American poet, b. Ill. He lived as a prairie troubadour, selling his rhymes for bread. Among his works are *The Congo* (1914), *The Chinese Nightingale* (1917), *Johnny Appleseed* (1928).

Lindsay, town (pop. 9,603), S Ont., Canada, NE of Toronto, in lake district. Woolen, flour, lumber mills.

Lindsay, town (pop. 5,060), S central Calif., SE of Fresno. Processes and ships oranges and olives.

Lindsey, Ben(jamin Barr), 1869–1943, American judge and reformer. He pioneered in establishing juvenile courts. Advocated trial marriages.

Lindsey, Parts of: see LINCOLNSHIRE, England.

Línea, La (lä lē'nāä), fortified city (pop. 35,-101), S Spain, on Strait of Gibraltar. Its position at border of neutral zone which separates it from the British colony gives it strategic importance.

Line Islands, group of 10 islands (including Palmyra and Christmas Isl.) in central and S Pacific, S of Hawaiian Isls. and extending N-S. Roughly separated into two groups by the equator.

linen, fabric or yarn made from the fiber of flax. Probably the earliest vegetable fiber in use, linen has been found in Egyptian tombs more than 3,500 years old. It was the principal European textile of the Middle Ages; Flanders has been famed for it since the 11th cent. Today, Ireland is chief producer of fabric; the greatest quantity of flax fiber is grown in Russia, the finest in Belgium. The amount of handwork involved until recently in processing linen restricted the development of the industry in the U.S.

Linfield College: see MCMINNVILLE, Oregon.

lingua franca (lĭng'gwŭ frăng'kŭ) [language of the Franks], spoken language, usually hybrid, used for limited communication among peoples of mutually unintelligible languages. The original lingua franca was used for commerce in the Mediterranean after the Crusades. Similar polyglot tongues include pidgin English, Chinook jargon, and Swahili. Occasionally term is applied to a formal language (e.g., French as language of diplomacy).

linguistics, scientific study of language. Its central aspect is descriptive study of a given language. Comparative or historical linguistics, study of relation of languages to each other, was developed especially in 19th-cent. Germany. The descriptive field developed notably in U.S. Linguistics, an anthropological science, has contacts with other sciences, e.g. with physics through PHONETICS. Some parts of language study are not apparently amenable to attack by scientific methods and are not, therefore, fields of linguistics at all. See PHILOLOGY.

Liniers, Jacques de (Span. lēnēärz'; Fr. lēnyā'), 1753–1810, French officer in Spanish service, viceroy of Río de la Plata. Was twice successful in recapturing Buenos Aires from British invaders (1806, 1807).

Linkoping, Swed. *Linköping* (lĭn'chû"pĭng), industrial city (pop. 54,552), co. seat of Ostergotland co., SE Sweden, on Gota Canal. It has rail shops, ironworks, sugar refineries and textile mills. It has been an episcopal see since 1120. Its cathedral was begun 1230.

Linlithgow (lĭnlĭth'gō), burgh (pop. 3,929), co. town of West Lothian, Scotland. Linlithgow Palace, former residence of Scottish kings, was birthplace of James V and Mary Queen of Scots.

Linlithgowshire, Scotland: see WEST LOTHIAN.

Linnaeus (lĭnē'ŭs), 1707–78, Swedish botanist. His name was originally Karl von Linné. A founder of modern systematic botany, he established the binomial method of designating plants and animals. The 1758 edition of his *Systema naturae* (1735) is used as basis of Linnaean nomenclature.

Linnhe, Loch (lŏkh lĭ'nē), inlet, Argyllshire, Scotland, extending 20 mi. NE from Firth of Lorne.

linoleum (lĭnō'lēŭm), resilient floor or wall covering of jute or burlap surfaced with mixture of powdered cork, oxidized linseed oil, gums or other ingredients, and coloring matter. Patented 1863 by English rubber manufacturer, Frederick Walton.

linotype, trade name of machine that makes slugs, each doing the work of a line of handset type. Patented by Ottmar Mergenthaler (1884), it was first used at the N.Y. *Tribune* (1886). Operated by a keyboard, it assembles brass matrices into a line, casts the slug, distributes the matrices.

linseed, seed of flax plant from which **linseed oil,** an amber fatty oil, is made. Used as DRYING OIL in paint and varnish, in making linoleum, oilcloth, and ink, and in medicine. **Linseed cake,** made by pressing flaxseed (after removing most of the oil) into cakes, is a concentrated livestock feed.

Linton, William James, 1812–97, Anglo-American wood engraver and political reformer. Edited and wrote for several radical periodicals in England. In 1867 he moved to U.S., where he helped to revive art of wood engraving.

Linton, city (pop. 5,973), SW Ind., SSE of Terre Haute. Coal mining.

Linyü, China: see SHANHAIKWAN.

Lin Yutang (lĭn' yü'täng'), 1895–, Chinese-American writer; in U.S. since c.1928. His books have been written largely in English. They include *My Country and My People* (1935), *The Importance of Living* (1937), and *Chinatown Family* (1948, a novel).

Linz (lĭnts), city (pop. 185,177), cap. of Upper Austria, on the Danube. River port; mfg. center (iron and steel works, machinery, textiles, chemicals). Dates from Roman times. Episcopal see.

lion, mammal (*Felis leo* or genus *Panthera*) of cat family, found in Africa, SW Asia, W India. It is extinct in Europe, much of Asia, Asia Minor. Lions are yellow to brown, short-haired, and the tail is tipped by a dark tuft. Usually the male has black or tawny mane. Male (with tail) is 9–10 ft. long, up to 500 lb. Lions hunt antelope, zebra, other animals, and also eat carrion. Usually only old or weak lions attack man.

Lion, Gulf of, Fr. *Golfe du Lion,* bay of the Mediterranean, S France, from Spanish border to Toulon.

Lions International, organization of business and professional men, founded 1914 by Melvin Jones. Furthers community projects.

Lipari Islands (lĭ'pûrē) or **Aeolian Islands** (ēō'lēŭn), volcanic group (44 sq. mi.; pop. 17,697), Italy, N of Sicily, in Tyrrhenian Sea. In ancient mythology, the residence of the wind god Aeolus. The chief islands are Lipari; Vulcano (mythical site of fire god's workshop), with a volcano emitting sulphur vapors; and Stromboli, with an active volcano 3,040 ft. high. The islands have long been a place of political exile. Pumice stone, wine, and currants are the chief exports.

Lipchitz, Jacques (zhäk' lēpshēts'), 1891–, French sculptor, b. Lithuania. Was allied with cubists. Known for skeletal constructions and transparents (made by melted-wax technique).

Li Po (lē' pō', bō) or **Li Tai Po** (tī'), c.700–762, Chinese poet of T'ang dynasty. Largely traditional in theme, his poems describe grief of separated lovers, beauty of nature, and the solace found in wine. He conveys exquisitely his sense of mystery in the universe. The 2,000 extant poems are said to comprise only a tenth of his output.

Lippe (lĭ'pù), former state (469 sq. mi.; 1939 pop. 187,220), NW Germany, between Teutoburg Forest and Weser R.; cap. Detmold. Was incorporated in 1946 with North Rhine-Westphalia. Region is mainly agr. It is crossed by Lippe R., a tributary of the Rhine. A lordship from 12th cent. and a county from 16th cent., it was subdivided several times after 1613. Two counties (after 1720, principalities) emerged—Lippe or Lippe-Detmold and SCHAUMBURG-LIPPE. Lippe joined German Confederation 1815; German Empire 1871; Weimar Republic 1919. In 1897 the contested succession to Lippe was awarded to Count Ernest of Lippe-Biesterfeld. His son, Prince Leopold, abdicated 1918; his nephew, Bernhard zu Lippe-Biesterfeld (b. 1911), married (1937) Juliana who became queen of the Netherlands.

Lippi (lĭp'pē), name of two Florentine painters of 15th cent. **Fra Filippo Lippi** (frä' fēlĭp'pō), c.1406–1469, also called Lippo Lippi, was a Carmelite. Master of color and graceful line (as shown by *Coronation of the Virgin*), he taught Botticelli, Benozzo Gozzoli, and Il Pesellino. Enjoyed patronage of the Medici. His son, **Filippino Lippi** (fēlēppē'nō), c.1457–1504, studied under Botticelli. Finished Masaccio's frescoes in Brancacci Chapel, Florence.

Lippmann, Gabriel (gäbrēēl' lēpmän'), 1845–1921, French physicist. Won 1908 Nobel Prize for discovery of method for photographic reproduction of colors through use of interference process.

Lippmann, Walter (lĭp'mŭn), 1889–, American essayist, an editor on *New Republic* and N.Y. *World*. After 1931 wrote syndicated column on world affairs for N.Y. *Herald Tribune.*

Lipsius, Justus (lĭp'sēŭs), 1547–1606, Flemish scholar, authority on Roman literature, history, and antiquities. His edition of Tacitus is famous.

Lipton, Sir Thomas (Johnstone), 1850–1931, British merchant and yachting enthusiast. Opened (1876) a grocery store which he expanded into a large chain of stores. Made five unsuccessful attempts to win the *America's* Cup yachting trophy.

liquefaction, in physics, change of substance from solid or gaseous state to liquid. It is held to be a change in kinetic energy of molecules. Change from solid to liquid or liquid to gas requires heat; change from gas to liquid or liquid to solid requires taking away heat. Liquefaction of gas can be effected by subjecting gas to high pressure and cooling it below its critical temperature.

liqueur (lĭkŭr'), strong alcoholic beverage made by distilling spirits flavored with herbs, fruits, or other substances and usually sweetened. Liqueurs contain from c.27% to 80% alcohol.

liquid, one of three states of matter in which substance has definite volume but no definite shape. Since liquids flow into shape of containing vessel they are classed with gases as fluids. Liquid changes to gas at its boiling point, to solid at its freezing or melting point. By fractional distillation liquids in a mixture can be separated from each other because they vaporize at their own distinct boiling points. Cohesion between molecules of liquid is not sufficient to prevent those at free surface from bounding off at ordinary temperatures (see EVAPORATION). Liquids exhibit SURFACE TENSION and CAPILLARITY. DIFFUSION can occur between two liquids. In general, liquids expand when heated, contract when cooled; they exert pressure on sides of a container and on any body immersed in them; pressure is transmitted undiminished in all directions. Liquids exert a buoyant force on immersed body (see ARCHIMEDES' PRINCIPLE; SPECIFIC GRAVITY).

liquid air, air that has been liquefied by compression and cooling to very low temperatures. It must be kept in Dewar flask since at ordinary temperatures it absorbs heat rapidly and reverts to gaseous state. Used for freezing other substances and as a source of nitrogen, oxygen, argon (and other inert gases).

liquor laws, legislation restricting or controlling the manufacture and sale of alcoholic beverages. Intent is often to prevent immoderate use of intoxicants as well as to raise revenue. Licensing and direct taxation are the favorite methods of control. In Sweden was inaugurated (1865) the Goteborg licensing system, which eliminated private profit from sale of spirits. National PROHIBITION was attempted in the U.S. 1919–33. Local option to prohibit sale of liquor is retained by some states and cities.

Liri (lē'rē), river of S central Italy, rising in Apennines and flowing into Tyrrhenian Sea near Gaeta. Below its junction with the Rapido it is called Garigliano (combined length of Liri and Garigliano, 98 mi.). Hydroelectric stations. In World War II, Allies gained access to Rome through Liri valley after long and bitter fighting, notably at Cassino (1943–44).

Lisa, Manuel (lē'sŭ), 1772–1820, American fur trader. Led expeditions in upper Missouri R. region. Helped form Missouri Fur Co.

Lisbon (lĭz'bŭn), Port. *Lisboa,* city (pop. 783-919), cap. of Portugal and of Estremadura prov., on mouth of Tagus R. A thriving Atlantic port, it is also an important center of transoceanic air transport. See of an archbishop (titular patriarch). University was founded 1910. Built on seven hills, Lisbon is dominated by the old Castel São Jorge. Lisbon's importance dates from its conquest from the Moors by Alfonso I (1147). Though largely rebuilt after the great earthquake of 1755, it has preserved several medieval buildings, especially the old Alfama quarter around the cathedral. The Renaissance Monastery of São Vicente contains the tombs of the Braganza kings. At Belén, on N shore of the Tagus near the sea, is the magnificent monastery built by Manuel I to commemorate Vasco da Gama's discovery of the route to India. Camões was born in Lisbon.

Lisburn (lĭz'bûrn, lĭs'–), urban district (pop. 14,778), Co. Antrim, N. Ireland. Main industry, linen mfg., introduced by Huguenots in 1594. Episcopal seat of a Catholic and a Protestant diocese.

Lisieux (lēzyû'), town (pop. 11,569), Calvados dept., N France, one of oldest towns of Normandy. The shrine of St. Theresa of the Child Jesus is a major place of pilgrimage.

Lismore (lĭsmôr', lĭz–), market town (pop. 1,174), Co. Waterford, Ireland. In 7th cent., town had an abbey and a great school. Lismore Castle has medieval Irish manuscript, the Book of Lismore.

Lismore (lĭz'môr, lĭzmôr'), island, c.10 mi. long and 1½ mi. wide, Argyllshire, Scotland, in Loch Linnhe. Has several old castles. Book of the Dean of Lismore (16th cent.) is one of the oldest and most valuable of Gaelic collections.

Lissoy, Co. Westmeath, Ireland: see AUBURN.

List, Friedrich (lĭst), 1789–1846, German economist. Forced to emigrate (1825) to U.S. for advocating reforms. Returned (1832) as U.S. consul at Leipzig. Favored commercial association of German states. Many of his ideas were adopted.

Lister, Joseph Lister, 1st Baron (lĭ'stŭr), 1827–1912, English surgeon, founder of antiseptic surgery. He proved the value of use of carbolic acid as ANTISEPTIC and of heat sterilization of instruments in decreasing postoperative infections (1865). Introduced absorbable ligature, drainage tube, and other operative techniques.

Liszt, Franz (lĭst), 1811–86, Hungarian pianist and composer. He was regarded as the greatest pianist of his age, and all the principal artistic figures of the time were among his friends. He lived with Mme d'Agoult, 1833–44, and their daughter Cosima was the wife of Hans von Bülow and later of Wagner. His colorful life was as romantic as his music. He developed the tone poem (e.g., *Les Préludes*) which influenced Wagner and Richard Strauss. His *Années de pélerinage,* his Hungarian Rhapsodies, his etudes and concertos for piano, and his Dante and Faust symphonies are his chief works.

Li Tai Po: see LI PO.

Litchfield. 1 Town (pop. 4,964), W Conn., SW of Torrington. Includes part of Bantam L. Here, Judge Tapping Reeve started first school in U.S. for law only (1784–1833). Birthplace of Ethan Allen, Henry Ward Beecher, and Harriet Beecher Stowe. **2** City (pop. 7,208), S Central Ill., S of Springfield, in coal and farm area. Mfg. of radiators and shoes.

litchi or **leechee,** small Chinese tree (*Litchi chinensis*), with nutlike fruit in a thin rough shell. The Chinese use fruit fresh, dried, or preserved; for commerce it is dried. Now grown in S Fla. and Calif.

litharge (lĭ'thärj), yellow monoxide of lead made by heating lead in air. It is used in making paints, glass, etc., and in treating rubber.

lithium (lĭ'thēŭm), silvery-white metallic element (symbol = Li; see also ELEMENT table). It is an alkali metal, very soft, and the lightest of metals. Its compounds color a flame bright red and are used in pyrotechnics. It is alloyed with aluminum, lead, beryllium; certain lithium salts are used to increase capacity of storage cells, others are used in medicine.

lithography (lĭthŏ'grŭfē), type of surface printing, used both as an art process and as a commercial printing process. A lithograph is printed from a stone except in commercial lithography, which uses grained metal plates. The drawing is usually made in reverse directly on a slab of stone with a lithographic crayon or ink that contains soap or grease. The fatty acid of this material forms an insoluble soap on the surface, which will accept the greasy printing ink and reject water. Next, the design is fixed against spreading by treatment with a gum arabic and nitric acid solution. The drawing is washed off with turpentine and water and is then ready to be inked with a roller and printed. The process was invented c.1796 by Aloys Senefelder in Germany. He used limestone, which is still considered the best material for lithography as an art process.

lithopone (lĭ'thŭpōn), white pigment, a mixture of barium sulphate and zinc sulphide. It is used in interior paints and cheaper enamels.

Lithuania (lĭthōōā'nēŭ), Lithuanian *Lietuva,* republic (c.25,000 sq. mi.; pop. c.3,000,000), NE Europe, on the Baltic Sea; cap. Vilna. Its incorporation in 1940 into the USSR as a constituent republic has not been recognized by the U.S. (as of 1953). A flatland drained by the Niemen, Lithuania is largely agr. (dairying, stock raising). The population is largely Roman Catholic. In the 13th cent. the Liths or Lithuanians, who were then still pagans, formed a unified state to defend themselves against the LIVONIAN KNIGHTS and TEUTONIC KNIGHTS. Under the grand dukes Gedimin and Olgerd (14th cent.)

Lithuania acquired all Belorussia, much of the Ukraine, and sections of Great Russia, becoming one of the largest states of medieval Europe. In 1386 Grand Duke Jagiello became king of Poland as LADISLAUS II and was baptized. The union of Poland and Lithuania under the JAGIELLO dynasty was at first a close alliance of two independent nations. Under WITOWT (reigned 1392–1430) Lithuania reached its greatest power, but it declined under the pressure of the expanding grand duchy of Moscow. In 1569 Lithuania and Poland united as a single state. The upper classes became thoroughly polonized. Russia annexed all Lithuania in the Polish partitions of 1772–95. In 1918 Lithuania proclaimed its independence. It successfully resisted attacks by Bolshevik troops but became involved in lengthy international disputes after the Polish seizure of VILNA (1920) and the Lithuanian seizure of the MEMEL TERRITORY (1923). Kaunas was the cap. until the recovery of Vilna in 1940. The virtual dictatorship of Augustine Voldemaras (1926–29) was succeeded by that of Antanas Smetona (1929–39); a constitution along corporative (fascist) lines became law in 1938. Lithuania was forced in 1939 to grant military bases to the USSR. In 1940 it was occupied by Soviet troops and inc. into the USSR. During German occupation (1941–44) in World War II, its Jewish minority (c.7%) was largely exterminated.

Lithuanian, Baltic language of Lithuania. It belongs to Indo-European family. See LANGUAGE (table).

Lititz (lĭ'tĭts), borough (pop. 5,568), SE Pa., N of Lancaster. Mfg. of chocolate, pretzels, shoes, and textiles.

litmus, organic dye that turns blue in alkalies and red in acids, therefore classed as indicator. It is used in form of treated paper and is prepared chiefly in Netherlands from certain lichens.

Little, Lou, 1893–, American football coach. Head coach at Columbia since 1930.

Little America, Antarctic exploration base, on Ross Shelf Ice, S of Bay of Whales. Estab. 1929 by Richard E. Byrd and used subsequently by him and other explorers.

Little Belt: see BELT, GREAT.

Little Bighorn, river rising in N Wyo., in Bighorn Mts. and flowing N to enter S Mont. and join Bighorn R. at Hardin. Scene, June 25, 1876, of defeat and death, at hands of the Sioux, of G. A. CUSTER. Battlefield is now national monument.

Little Colorado, river, rising in W N.Mex. near Ariz. line and flowing NW 315 mi. across Ariz. to Colorado R. in the Grand Canyon.

Little Compton, town (pop. 1,556), SE R.I., between Sakonnet R. and Mass. line. R.I. Red fowl originated here. John and Priscilla Alden's daughter Elizabeth buried here. Includes Sakonnet resort.

Little Entente (äntänt', ãtãt'), defensive alliance formed after World War I by Czechoslovakia, Rumania, and Yugoslavia and supported by France. Purpose was to preserve territorial status quo estab. by treaties of Versailles, Saint-Germain, Trianon, and Neuilly and to prevent union between Germany and Austria. It was effectively ended when Czechoslovakia was dismembered by Munich Pact (1938).

Little Falls. 1 City (pop. 6,717), central Minn., on the Mississippi and NNW of St. Cloud. Farm trade center with mfg. of food and wood products. **2** Township (pop. 6,405), NE N.J., SW of Paterson. Laundry plant. **3** City (pop. 9,541), E central N.Y., SE of Utica, on Mohawk R. (water power) and the Barge Canal. Mfg. of clothing and footwear.

Littlefield, city (pop. 6,540), NW Texas, NW of Lubbock on Llano Estacado. Processes cotton, grains, poultry, and dairy products.

Little Flower of Jesus: see THERESA, SAINT (Theresa of the Child Jesus).

Little Masters, term applied to a group of 16th-cent. German engravers, mostly followers of Dürer. Group includes Albrecht Altdorfer, Heinrich Aldegrever, the Beham brothers, and Georg Pencz.

Little Minch, Scotland: see MINCH.

Little Missouri, river rising in NE Wyo. and flowing 560 mi. NE and E to the Missouri in W N.Dak.

Little Rock, city (pop. 102,213), state cap., central Ark., on Arkansas R. and in Ouachita foothills; laid out 1820. Rail focus and state's largest city and commercial center, it is in diversified-farming, mining (bauxite, coal, clay), timber, oil, and natural-gas region. Has large cotton trade. Mfg. of cottonseed and wood products and chemicals. Seat of Univ. of Arkansas medical school. Old capital (1836) is now war memorial. Birthplace of Gen. Douglas MacArthur. NORTH LITTLE ROCK is across the river.

Little Russia: see UKRAINE.

Little Sioux (sōō), river rising in SW Minn. near Iowa line and flowing SW 221 mi. across NW Iowa to the Missouri S of Sioux City. Tributaries include Maple R., West Fork, and Elliott Creek. Included in flood-control and soil-conservation program (1947) affecting large areas in NW Iowa.

Little Tennessee, river rising in Blue Ridge, NE Ga., and flowing N into N.C., then WNW around the Smokies into Tenn. to Tennessee R. Has Fontana and Cheoah dams in N.C., and Calderwood Dam in Tenn.

Littleton, Sir Thomas, 1422–81, English jurist, author of a short work on the types of estates in land in England (*Tenures*).

Litvinov, Maxim Maximovich (mŭksyēm' mŭksyē'mŭvĭch lyĭtvē'nŭf), 1876–1952, Russian foreign commissar (1930–39) whose real name was Wallach. Advocated cooperation with Western powers, firm stand against Axis. Replaced by Molotov shortly before German-Soviet pact. Ambassador to U.S. 1941–43.

Liutprand (lēōōt'pränd), d. 744, Lombard king of Italy (712–44). Favored Roman law; created a centralized state by curbing powers of local dukes and bishops; expanded his domain N into Bavaria; died at Ravenna in campaign against Byzantine exarchs.

Livadiya (lyĭvä'dyēŭ), Black Sea resort near Yalta, RSFSR, in S Crimea. Its former imperial palace (built 1910–11), now a sanatorium, was F. D. Roosevelt's residence during Yalta Conference (1945).

Live Oak, city (pop. 4,064), N Fla., E of Tallahassee. Chief bright-leaf-tobacco market of Fla.

liver, large, reddish-brown gland. In man, it lies below diaphragm chiefly on right side; it is divided into four unequal lobes. Functions include secretion of bile; conversion of glucose into a starch (glycogen), which is reconverted when need arises; storage of antianemic principle; conversion of protein wastes; destruction of worn-out red corpuscles. See *ill.*, p. 763.

liver fluke: see FLUKE.

Liverpool, seaport (pop. 789,532), Lancashire, England, on Mersey R. Greatest port in W Britain and one of world's leading trade centers, it has docks over 7 mi. long. Europe's leading cotton market, its importance has declined since World War II. Connected by tunnel with Birkenhead. Cathedral, when finished, will be England's largest. Univ. of Liverpool chartered 1903. Heavily bombed 1940–41.

liverwort, small flowerless plant usually growing in moist places and considered intermediate between aquatic algae and terrestrial mosses and ferns. Among the genera are *Marchantia* and *Riccia*.

livery companies, name for English GUILDS in city of London. Chartered largely by Edward III in 14th cent. For ceremonies, they assumed distinctive livery or costume and distinctive badge, and thus attired have formed colorful part of municipal pageants and royal coronations down to present time. Attained political power under Edward III, having right to elect common council of city of London. They were incorporated, held lands and other wealth, and administered schools, e.g., St. Paul's and Merchant Taylors'. Their character has changed with rise of capitalism and competitive system, but there are still some 75 livery companies today, 12 of them known as the great companies.

Livia Drusilla (lĭv′ēŭ drōōsĭl′ŭ), c.55 B.C.–A.D. 29, mother of Roman emperor TIBERIUS and of Drusus Germanicus. In 38 B.C. Augustus forced her to be divorced and marry him. After Tiberius' accession she tried to control government.

Livingston, family of American statesmen, diplomats, and jurists. **Robert Livingston,** 1654–1728, b. Scotland, acquired wealth and lands in N.Y. and exerted control in the provincial assembly. His grandson, **Robert R. Livingston,** 1718–75, was a Whig political leader in N.Y. His son, the younger **Robert R. Livingston,** 1746–1813, a famous lawyer, negotiated the Louisiana Purchase as minister to France. His brother, **Edward Livingston,** 1764–1836, jurist and statesman, was Secretary of State (1831–33) under Andrew Jackson and also minister to France (1833–35). Another grandson of Robert Livingston (1654–1728) was **Peter Van Brugh Livingston,** 1710–92. A Whig supporter preceding American Revolution, he was president of first provincial congress (1775). His brother, **Philip Livingston,** 1716–78, signed the Declaration of Independence and was an original promoter of King's Col. (now Columbia Univ.). Another brother, **William Livingston,** 1723–90, was first governor of N.J. under state constitution of 1777. William's son, **Henry Brockholst Livingston,** 1757–1823, was a justice of U.S. Supreme Court (1806–23).

Livingston. 1 City (pop. 7,683), S Mont., o Yellowstone R. and N of Yellowstone Nat Park. Rail, tourist, and trade center in agr and mining area. **2** Township (pop. 9,932) NE N.J., near Passaic R. and NW of Newark

Livingstone, David (lĭ′vĭngstŭn), 1813–73 Scottish missionary and explorer in Africa Missionary in Bechuanaland (1841–52). Dis covered Victoria Falls (1855). When he ha been long unheard from, H. M. STANLEY wa sent in search of him and found him (1871)

Livingstone, town (pop. 7,899), S Norther Rhodesia, near Victoria Falls; tourist cente Named for the explorer David Livingstone Was cap. of Northern Rhodesia, 1911–35.

Livius Andronicus (lĭ′vēŭs ăndrŭnī′kŭs), fl. 3 cent. B.C., Roman poet who introduce Greek literature into Rome. Founded Lati comedy.

Livonia (lĭvō′nēŭ) or **Livland,** region of N Europe, on the Baltic Sea, comprising presen ESTONIA and N LATVIA. It is named for th Livs, a Finnic people, who were conquere by the LIVONIAN KNIGHTS (13th cent.). Re ducing the Livs to serfdom, the knight formed a powerful state which also com prised S Latvia. Its chief cities—Riga, Tartu Tallinn—were German in culture and wer members of the Hanseatic League. The dis solution of the Livonian Order (1561) wa followed by a contest for its domains amon Poland, Russia, and Sweden. COURLAND (i.e. S Latvia) became a duchy under Polish over lordship. Latgale (NE Latvia) passed to Po land and, in 1771, to Russia. Estonia passe to Sweden; Vidzeme (NW Latvia) passe first to Poland, then (1629) to Sweden; both Vidzeme and Estonia were conquered b Peter I in 1710 and formally ceded to Russi in 1721. Livonia was a Russian provinc (government) 1783–1918.

Livonian Knights, German military religiou order, founded c.1202 by the bishop of Riga to Christianize the Baltic countries; als called the Brothers of the Sword and Knight Swordbearers. Habit: white robe with re cross and sword. They conquered COURLAN and LIVONIA but were routed by the Lithu anians at Siauliai (1236) and as a resul formed a union with the TEUTONIC KNIGHTS until 1525. Weakened by the Reformatio and by Russian attacks, they disbanded i 1561 but kept their vast estates. The "Baltic barons," who dominated the Baltic provs until World War I, were largely descende from the knights.

Livorno, Italy: see LEGHORN.

Livy (Titus Livius) (lĭ′vē), 59 B.C.–A.D. 17 Roman historian. His life work was the *History of Rome,* 35 of the original 142 books surviving; there are fragments of others, and all but two are known through epitomes. Noted for his freedom of expression and masterly style.

Lizard, the, promontory, Cornwall, England. S extremity is southernmost point of Grea Britain.

lizard, reptile of tropical and temperate regions. The body is scaly, most species have four limbs, and usually eyelids and ear openings are present. Tail in many forms is easily broken off and regenerated. The tongue may be short and wide or long and forked. Many lizards can undergo color changes. Most are insectivorous; few are herbivorous or omnivorous. Some lay eggs; some bear live young. Size ranges from few inches to 8–12 ft. in komodo or dragon lizard. Flying lizards, which glide from tree to tree, live in Malay Archipelago; frilled lizards in N Australia. See also CHAMELEON; GILA MONSTER; GLASS SNAKE; HORNED TOAD; IGUANA.

Ljubljana (lyōō'blyänä), Ger. *Laibach,* city (pop. 120,994), cap. of Slovenia, NW Yugoslavia, on Sava R. It is a trade center with varied mfg. and a Roman Catholic archiepiscopal see. University was founded 1919. Until 1918 it was cap. CARNIOLA, part of Austria. Scene of Congress of LAIBACH (1821).

llama (lä'mù), South American domesticated hoofed mammal (*Lama*) of camel family, believed to be descended from guanaco. Smaller than camel, it has no hump and somewhat resembles a sheep. Llamas are brown, white, black, or piebald. They live in herds up to snow line in Andes.

Llandudno (lăndŭd'nō, –dĭd'nō), urban district (pop. 16,712), Caernarvonshire, Wales, on a point of land jutting into the Irish Sea; a popular resort.

Llanelly (lănĕ'lē, –ĕ'thlē), municipal borough (pop. 34,329), Caermarthenshire, Wales. Has important coal exports and metal works.

Llano Estacado (lä'nō ĕstùkä'dō) [Span.= staked plain], S grasslands of Great Plains plateau, E N.Mex. and W Texas. On S is Cap Rock escarpment, which runs across Texas Panhandle SW almost to SE N.Mex. High N plains around Amarillo are distinguished from the somewhat lower South Plains, centered around Lubbock. All are wind-swept grasslands, formerly cattle country, now dotted by farms (irrigated and dry) and by oil and gas fields.

llanos (yä'nōs), Spanish American term for prairies, specifically those of Orinoco basin in Venezuela and part of E Colombia. Despite the bad climate, in colonial and early republican times *llaneros* (comparable to gauchos of Argentine pampa) herded several million head of cattle here.

Llewelyn ap Gruffydd (lōōē'lĭn äp grōō'fĭdh, thlōōē'lĭn, grĭ'fĭdh), d. 1282, first prince of Wales (1267). Had great power in N Wales but English invasions brought total disaster. He was one of the last fighters for Welsh liberties.

Lloyd George, David, 1st **Earl Lloyd-George of Dwyfor** (dōōē'vôr), 1863–1945, British statesman. Liberal anti-imperialist member of Parliament for 54 years from 1890. Opposed South African War. Chancellor of exchequer under Herbert Asquith, he ended veto power of House of Lords by taking social insurance issue to the people in 1910 election. Prime minister in coalition cabinet (1916–22). One of the "Big Four" at Paris Peace Conference in 1919. Opposed appeasement policy before World War II.

Lloyd's, London insurance underwriting corporation of some 300 individual syndicates. Founded late 17th cent., it is now international in scope. Deals mainly with marine insurance, but insures against many kinds of risk.

loam, soil composed of clay, sand, and silt, with particles of many sizes rather evenly mixed. Loams are gritty, plastic when moist, and retain more water and contain more nutriment than sandy soil.

Loanda, Angola: see LUANDA.

Lobachevsky, Nikolai Ivanovich (nyĭkùlī' ēvä'-nùvĭch lŭbŭchĕf'skē), 1793–1856, Russian mathematician. He pioneered in non-Euclidean geometry and originated a system of geometry which challenged Euclid's fifth postulate.

lobbying, practice of influencing legislation or government officials by agents who serve special interests. The pressure may be exerted through data, publicity, threat of political reprisals, or pledges of support. Lobbyists are required by law to register, but lobbying is nevertheless frequently condemned as an abuse of representational government.

lobelia (lōbē'lyù), annual or perennial plant (genus *Lobelia*) with tubular flowers. Annuals for window boxes or gardens are compact or trailing forms of blue or white S African *Lobelia erinus.* The scarlet cardinal flower (*L. cardinalis*) is a choice North American wild flower.

Lobito (lōbē'tō), town (pop. 13,592), Angola; port on the Atlantic. Terminus of railroad to rich copper-mining area of Katanga, Belgian Congo.

Lob Nor or **Lop Nor** (both: lôp'nôr'), marshy salt-lake depression, E Sinkiang prov., China.

Lobos Islands (lō'bōs) or **Seal Islands,** off coast of NW Peru; valuable for deposits of guano.

lobster, marine crustacean, with five pairs of jointed legs, the first pair having pincerlike claws. An outer skeleton, usually greenish brown, covers the body and appendages. Lobsters move slowly on land and rapidly in water, on ocean bottom. Female with eggs is called "berried lobster." Common American lobster is *Homarus americanus.* Chief U.S. fisheries are in Maine and Mass.

Locarno (lōkär'nō), town (pop. 7,747), Ticino canton, S Switzerland. Tourist resort. Here in 1925 was signed the **Locarno Pact,** a series of treaties of mutual guarantee and arbitration entered into by England, France, Germany, Italy, Belgium, Czechoslovakia, and Poland. The major treaty guaranteed the W boundaries of Germany as fixed by the Treaty of Versailles of 1919. Germany also agreed to demilitarize a strip of the Rhineland and was guaranteed entry into the League of Nations. A serious flaw of the treaties, which were intended as the foundation of European security, was the absence of a guarantee of Germany's E frontier. Briand, Stresemann, and Austin Chamberlain were the chief framers of the pact.

locative (lŏk'–), in grammar of certain languages (e.g., Sanskrit), CASE referring to location.

Loch (lŏkh, lŏk). For names of Scottish lakes and inlets beginning thus, see second part of name: e.g., for Loch Long, see LONG, LOCH. See also LAKE.

Lochner, Stephan (shtĕ'fän lôkh'nùr), d. 1451, German painter, main representative of Cologne school.

lock, canal, enclosed water area for raising or lowering a vessel from one water level to another, used in rivers and canals where course is not level and at dock entrances. To pass to higher level, water in lock is lowered to level of floating vessel, gate is opened, ship moves in, and gate is closed. Water enters lock from higher level until water level in two is the same. Procedure is reversed when vessel goes from higher to lower level.

lock and key. Lock usually consists of sliding, pivoted, or rotary bolt guarded by an obstacle either fixed (warded) as in most padlocks or movable (tumbler) and controlled by a key with a flat, pipe, or pin shank. In the time lock, used since c.1875, a clock mechanism prevents opening until time set.

Locke, David Ross: see NASBY, PETROLEUM V.

Locke, John, 1632–1704, English philosopher, founder of British empiricism. In political exile in Holland (1683–89) he completed his famous *Essay concerning Human Understanding.* A practical psychology, it held that the mind at birth is a blank upon which human experience inscribes all knowledge. After the Glorious Revolution (1688) he returned to England. In *Two Treatises on Government* (1689) he justified constitutional monarchy. He contradicted Hobbes by asserting the original state of nature was good, and men equal and independent. The state, he held, was formed by social contract and should be guided by belief in natural rights. This was in essence a plea for democracy, which bore fruit in the U.S. Constitution. His empiricism was expanded by Berkeley and Hume, and the men of the Enlightenment regarded him as the prophet of reason.

Lockhart, John Gibson, 1794–1854, Scottish lawyer and literary critic; son-in-law of Sir Walter Scott. His biography of Scott (7 vols., 1837–38) is a classic. He was editor of *Quarterly Review* 1825–53.

Lockhart, city (pop. 5,573), S central Texas, SSE of Austin. Center of agr., dairying, and oil area. Texans defeated Comanches (1840) at battle of Plum Creek to NE.

Lock Haven, city (pop. 11,381), N Pa. on W branch of Susquehanna R. and SW of Williamsport; settled 1769. Mfg. of aircraft and building materials.

lockjaw: see TETANUS.

Lockland, city (pop. 5,736), SW Ohio, near Cincinnati. Mfg. of aircraft, building materials.

lockout, dismissal and prevention of reemployment, adopted by employers to resist labor demands or to break a strike by importing new workers. Lockouts have generally been considered legal when not in violation of the terms of a joint agreement.

Lockport. 1 City (pop. 4,955), NE Ill., N of Joliet, at locks connecting Chicago Sanitary and Ship Canal with Des Plaines R. Also has locks of old Illinois and Michigan Canal. **2** City (pop. 25,133), W N.Y., on the Barge Canal and NE of Buffalo; settled 1816 around locks of old Erie canal. Steel, paper, food products.

Lockyer, Sir (Joseph) Norman (lŏk′yůr), 1836–1920, English astronomer, pioneer in spectroscopic examination of stars. Authority on solar physics and chemistry.

Locofocos (lō″kōfō′kōz), name given in derision to members of faction that split off from Democratic party in N.Y. Name arose when members worked by light of candles and "locofoco" matches at Tammany Hall meeting on Oct. 29, 1835. As Friends of Equal Rights or Equal Rights party, the group, anti-bank and reformist, urged a vague but fervid leveling program. United with Workingman's party, group for several years disturbed and revitalized regular parties. After adoption of ideas by Van Buren Democrats in 1837, Equal Rights men returned to Democratic party.

locomotive, a railroad engine. Pioneer locomotive builders include Richard TREVITHICK, George STEPHENSON, who demonstrated practicability of steam engine in 1829 with famous *Rocket;* John Stevens, who built c.1825 the first U.S. locomotive; Peter Cooper, whose *Tom Thumb* (1830) was first practical American locomotive; Mathias Baldwin, constructor in 1832 of *Old Ironsides;* and J. B. Jervis, who introduced in 1832 swivel truck at forward end which increased safe passage around corners. Modern reciprocating engine consists essentially of steam engine and boiler; superheated steam admitted to cylinders causes pressure on pistons which is transmitted to driving wheels connected by side rods. Electric locomotives, introduced c.1895, are used chiefly on steep grades and on runs of high traffic density. Diesel-electric locomotives, introduced in U.S. c.1924, are used as switching engines and on many runs.

locomotor ataxia (lōkůmō′tůr ůtăk′sēů) or **tabes dorsalis** (tā′bēz dôrsā′lĭs), chronic progressive disease of nervous system. Impairment of the senses determining position and vibrations results in muscular incoordination accompanied by uncertainty in walking. Occurs in syphilitic individuals.

locoweed, leguminous plant of W U.S. which when eaten by cattle causes in them a nervous disorder. Common kinds are species of *Astragalus* and *Oxytropus.*

Locris (lō′krĭs), region of anc. Greece, in three regions (separated chiefly by Phocis), N of Boeotia. Locrians, long settled, rivaled Phocians. They founded a colony in S Italy.

locust, name used both for any grasshopper with antennae shorter than body and for those short-horned forms that migrate in swarms. The 17-year locust is a CICADA.

locust, leguminous deciduous tree or shrub (genus *Robinia*) native to U.S. and Mexico. The common locust is black, or yellow locust (*Robinia pseudoacacia*) sometimes called acacia or false acacia. It has clusters of fragrant flowers similar to sweet peas. The wood is durable. It is attacked by locust borer.

Lodge, Henry Cabot, 1850–1924, U.S. Senator from Mass. (1893–1924). A conservative, party-line Republican, he bitterly opposed Pres. Wilson's peace policy and led the attack on Treaty of Versailles and League of Nations. His grandson, **Henry Cabot Lodge, Jr.,** 1902–, U.S. Senator from Mass. (1937–44, 1947–53), became head of the U.S. mission to the UN in 1953.

Lodge, Sir Oliver (Joseph), 1851–1940, English

physicist. He contributed to wireless telegraphy; studied electrons, the ether, lightning. He was interested in reconciling science and religion and in psychical research.

Lodge, Thomas, 1558?–1625, English writer. Prose tales interspersed with poems most important (e.g., *Rosalynde,* 1590). Also wrote poem *Scillaes Metamorphosis* (1589) and tuneful sonnet-cycle *Phillis* (1593).

Lodi (lō'dē), city (pop. 23,305), Lombardy, N Italy, on Adda R. Here Bonaparte defeated the Austrians on May 10, 1796.

Lodi (lō'dī). **1** City (pop. 13,798), central Calif., N of Stockton. Produces wine and olive oil. **2** Borough (pop. 15,392), NE N.J., NE of Passaic. Dye works; mfg. of machinery.

Lodomeria: see VLADIMIR-VOLYNSKI, USSR.

Lodore (lōdôr'), waterfalls, Cumberland, England; celebrated in Southey's "The Cataract of Lodore."

Lodz (lōdz, lo͞oj, Pol. wo͞oj), Pol. *Łódź,* industrial city (pop. c.622,500), Poland, SW of Warsaw. Incorporated in 15th cent., it passed to Prussia 1793, to Russia 1815; reverted to Poland 1919. From 1820 to 1900 it developed into cap. of Polish industry, producing chiefly textiles and clothing.

Loeb, Jacques (lōb), 1859–1924, American physiologist, b. Germany. Known for tropism theory and for experiments in inducing parthenogenesis and regeneration by chemical stimulus.

Loeb, Solomon, 1828–1903, American banker, b. Germany. A founder of banking house of Kuhn, Loeb and Co. in New York city. His son, **James Loeb,** 1867–1933, was a banker and philanthropist. Founded and endowed Loeb Classical Library; helped found part of present JUILLIARD SCHOOL OF MUSIC.

Loeffler, Charles Martin (lĕf'lůr), 1861–1935, American composer, b. Alsace. His works include the *Pagan Poem* (1909) for orchestra, *Canticle of the Sun* (1925) for solo voice and orchestra, *Evocations* (1931) for women's chorus and orchestra, and chamber works.

loess (lō'ĭs), unstratified yellowish clay soil, believed to have been carried by wind. Extensive deposits occur along the Mississippi and in NW U.S., where it is largely of glacial origin, and in China, where it is of desert origin. Loess is rich in organic matter and very fertile, but easily eroded.

Loewi, Otto (lō'ē), 1873–, German pharmacologist and physiologist. Shared 1936 Nobel Prize in Physiology and Medicine for study of chemical transmission of nerve impulses. He came to U.S. in 1940.

Loewy, Raymond Fernand (lō'ē), 1895–, American industrial designer, b. France.

Löffler, Friedrich (frē'drĭkh lûf'lůr), 1852–1915, German bacteriologist. He related diphtheria to causative organism now known as Klebs-Löffler bacillus.

Lofoten (lō'fōtůn) and **Vesteralen** (vĕ'stůrôlůn; Nor. *Vesterålen*), two contiguous island groups (c.2,000 sq. mi.; pop. c.80,000), off NW Norway, in Norwegian Sea, 1–50 mi. off mainland. Entirely within Arctic Circle, they extend c.150 mi. NE–SW. Climate is tempered by North Atlantic Drift. The MAELSTROM is S of Moskenes isl. Vesteralen group, S of Lofoten group, includes Hinnoy, largest island of Norway. Herring and cod fisheries of Lofoten and Vesteralen isls. are among world's largest. Vesteralen is also spelled Vesteraalen.

Lofting, Hugh, 1886–1947, American writer of juvenile stories, b. England. Author and illustrator of "Dr. Doolittle" stories.

Logan, James, 1674–1751, American colonial statesman and scholar, b. Ireland, of Scottish parents. Adviser to William Penn, he supported proprietary rights in Pa. Acting governor of province (1736–38). Engaged in botanical research.

Logan, John Alexander, 1826–86, American politician, Union general in Civil War. Fought in Vicksburg and Atlanta campaigns. U.S. Congressman (1867–71); U.S. Senator (1871–77, 1879–86). Inaugurated MEMORIAL DAY (1868).

Logan, Sir William Edmond, 1798–1875, Canadian geologist. Head of Geological Survey of Canada (1843–69); constructed maps and sections. Work summarized in *The Geology of Canada* (1863).

Logan. 1 City (pop. 5,972), S central Ohio, on Hocking R. and SE of Columbus. Mfg. of shoes, foundry products, pottery, and tools. **2** City (pop. 16,832), N Utah, N of Ogden and on Logan R.; founded 1859 by Mormons. Processing center for irrigated farm, dairy area. Here are Mormon temple and tabernacle and UTAH STATE AGRICULTURAL COLLEGE. Near by are Logan Canyon and Logan Peak. **3** City (pop. 5,079), S W.Va., on Guyandot R. and SSW of Charleston, in mine and farm area.

Logan, Mount, 19,850 ft. high, extreme SW Yukon, just E of Alaska; highest peak in Canada and second highest in North America.

loganberry, blackberrylike plant of genus *Rubus,* grown on Pacific coast for its large red-purple fruit.

Logansport, city (pop. 21,031), N Ind., at junction of Wabash and Eel rivers NE of Lafayette; settled c.1826. Farm produce shipping center with mfg. of fire apparatus, radiators, farm equipment.

logarithm (lŏ'gůrĭdhm). Each positive number has logarithm, which is power to which third number (called base) must be raised to obtain that positive number. Logarithms of numbers using 10 as the base are called common logarithms; if base is *e* (approximately 2.718) they are natural logarithms. Since logarithms are exponents, they satisfy rules of exponents and hence simplify calculations.

Log College: see TENNENT, WILLIAM.

Logos (lō'gŏs) [Gr.,= Word], concept of Greek and Hebrew metaphysics. The central idea is that Logos links God and man. HERACLITUS held the Logos was fire, ordering and animating the world. The Stoics called God as the active law guiding the world the Logos. The Old Testament idea of Wisdom of God active in the world was merged with ancient Hebrew concept of active Word of God. NEOPLATONISM adapted the idea of the Logos into the system of emanations. PHILO taught that God, remote from the world, acts in it through mediation of the Logos (Divine Reason). Gospel of St. John states that the

Logos, eternal God, took flesh and became man in time; the Logos is Jesus.

logwood, leguminous tree (*Haematoxylon campechianum*), native to Central America and grown in parts of N South America and West Indies. Its brown-red heartwood yields haematoxylin dye.

Lohengrin (lō′ŭn-grĭn), in medieval German story, a knight of the Grail, son of Parzifal. Led by a swan to rescue Princess Elsa of Brabant, he then marries her. When she asks his name, in violation of a pledge, he must return to the castle of the Grail, and the swan, now revealed as Elsa's brother, reappears. Its fullest form is in German epic (c.1285–90) ascribed to Wolfram von Eschenbach. Story was used by Wagner.

Loir (lwär), river, 193 mi. long, N central France, rising S of Chartres and flowing generally SW to the Sarthe N of Angers.

Loire (lwär), department (1,853 sq. mi.; pop. 631,591), E central France, in Lyonnais; cap. Saint-Étienne. The **Loire river,** 625 mi. long, is the longest of France. Rising in Cévennes mts., it flows NW to Orléans, then swings SW to the Atlantic at Saint-Nazaire. Nevers, Blois, Tours, Angers, and Nantes are also on or near its course. The Allier, Cher, Vienne, and Maine are its chief tributaries. The Loire valley, a region of rich fields, gardens, and vineyards, has fostered traditions of civilized living which have become the heritage of all France. The châteaux of the Loire—notably Blois, Amboise, Chambord, Chenonceaux, and Chinon—are synonymous with French history and civilization.

Loire-Inférieure (lwär″-ēfāryûr′), department (2,693 sq. mi.; pop. 665,064), NW France, in S Brittany; cap. Nantes.

Loiret (lwärā′), department (2,630 sq. mi.; pop. 346,918), N central France; cap. Orléans.

Loir-et-Cher (lwär-ā-shĕr′), department (2,479 sq. mi.; pop. 242,419), N central France; cap. Blois.

Lois (lō′ĭs), grandmother of Timothy. 2 Tim. 1.5.

Loisy, Alfred (Firmin) (älfrĕd′ lwäzē′), 1857–1940, French biblical critic. Ordained a Roman Catholic priest (1879), he later became the leader of Catholic MODERNISM. His teachings were condemned by the Holy See, and he was excommunicated (1908).

Loki (lō′kē), in Norse myth, personification of the evil principle. He caused trouble for the other gods.

Lolland, Denmark: see LAALAND.

Lollardry (lŏ′lûrdrē) or **Lollardy,** 14th-cent. English movement for religious reform led by John WYCLIF and his "poor priests." Abuses in the Church, the great wealth of high churchmen, the appalling poverty of the poor—these contributed to making Lollardry popular. The chief teachings of the Lollards (mostly expressed in a memorial to Parliament in 1395) were that the clergy should be rigidly poor; that the doctrines of the sacraments (especially transubstantiation) were false; that the ordinary believer could arrive at true doctrine solely by reading the Bible for himself; and that celibacy of priests and nuns was unnatural and wrong. The movement gained much momentum by 1400, and the high clergy and the government feared the Lollards. In 1401 a parliamentar statute was passed against them. The Lollarc grew fanatic and even entered on a sma rebellion under Sir John Oldcastle. This wa easily put down (1414), and the movemer went underground. Just how much influenc it had on the later Reformation is a matte of dispute. Many Lollard doctrines were re flected by the Hussites.

Lombard, Peter: see PETER LOMBARD.

Lombard, residential village (pop. 9,817), N Ill., W suburb of Chicago.

Lombard League. When in 1158 Emperor Fred erick I at the Diet of Roncaglia asserted th imperial authority over all Lombard com munes, the rival towns of Lombardy unite against him and in 1167 formed a sing league, backed by Pope Alexander III. Th League defeated Frederick at Legnan (1176) and in the Peace of Constance (1183 received confirmation of the freedom of th communes. Revived in 1226 against Fred erick II, the League was defeated at Co tenuova (1237) and split into Guelph an Ghibelline cities.

Lombardo (lōmbär′dō), Italian family of sculp tors and architects. Emigrants from Lom bardy c.1450, they were leaders in architec tural Renaissance in Venice. The mos distinguished of them were **Pietro Lombardo** c.1435–1515, who worked on court façade c the doge's palace, and his sons, **Antonio Lom bardo,** c.1458–1516?, and **Tullio Lombardo** c.1455–1532.

Lombards (lŏm′bûrdz, –bärdz), Latin *Lango bardi,* anc. Germanic people. In 568 they in vaded N Italy under ALBOIN and estab. kingdom with Pavia as cap. Their conquest spread to most of Italy save Byzantine an papal holdings of Ravenna, Pentapolis, Rome and along coast. Kingdom soon split int duchies (notably Spoleto and Benevento) but in 584 Authari restored Lombard king dom, which reached its flower under LIUT PRAND (d. 744). Arians at first, Lombard later accepted Catholicism and assimilate Latin culture. Their attacks on Rome brough forth Frankish intervention under PEPIN TH SHORT (751) and CHARLEMAGNE (772), wh after his victory over DESIDERIUS wa crowned with iron crown of Lombard kings This crown, also used for coronations of late emperors, is now kept at MONZA. Duchy o Benevento survived until Norman conques (11th cent.). Lombards gave their name t Lombardy.

Lombard Street, London. Street of banks an financial houses named for Lombard money lenders who settled here in 12th cent.

Lombardy (lŏm′bûrdē), Ital. *Lombardia,* re gion (9,189 sq. mi.; pop. 5,836,479), N Italy bordering on Switzerland, in the S Alps an the Po valley; cap. MILAN. Other cities in clude BERGAMO, BRESCIA, COMO, CREMONA MANTUA, PAVIA. The Po valley, irrigated sinc Roman times, is a rich grain region. The mulberry is extensively cultivated for silk production. Lombardy is the chief industria region of Italy. Conquered from its Gallic inhabitants by the Romans (3d cent. B.C.) the region became the Roman province o Cisalpine Gaul. In A.D. 569 it became the center of the kingdom of the LOMBARDS, and in 774 it was added by Charlemagne to his empire. In 11th cent. power gradually passed from feudal lords to autonomous communes. These united against imperial pretensions as the LOMBARD LEAGUE (1167) but fell apart in 13th cent. Lombard merchants and bankers had a major share in revival of European economy. Rivalry among cities favored the rise of two families who shared Lombardy between themselves—the VISCONTI dukes of Milan (succeeded by the SFORZA) and the GONZAGA of Mantua. Parts of Lombardy passed to Venice (e.g., Bergamo) and to the Swiss (e.g., the Ticino). After the ITALIAN WARS of the 16th cent., Lombardy was ruled by Spain (1535–1713), Austria (1713–96), France (1796–1814), and Austria (as Lombardo-Venetian kingdom, in union with Venetia, 1815–59). Annexed to Sardinia 1859.

Lombok, island (1,825 sq. mi.; pop. 701,290), Indonesia, one of Lesser Sundas. Products include coffee, sugar, cotton, and indigo. Noted by the naturalist A. R. Wallace as being part of dividing line between fauna of Asia and that of Australia.

Lombroso, Cesare (chā'zärā lōmbrō'zō), 1835–1909, Italian criminologist. Maintained (1876) theory (now outmoded) that the criminal is an atavistic type marked by distinct physical and psychological traits.

Loménie de Brienne, Étienne Charles (ātyĕn' shärl' lōmānē' dù brēĕn'), 1727–94, French statesman; archbishop of Toulouse (1763–88) and of Sens (1788–91). Succeeded Calonne in control of finances (1787); exiled the Parlement of Paris to Troyes because of its opposition to his proposed fiscal reforms; left office in popular disfavor (1788). He was made a cardinal in 1788. Died in prison during Terror.

Lomond, Loch (lŏkh lō'mŭnd, -mŭn), lake, between Dumbartonshire and Stirlingshire, Scotland. Largest (23 mi. long and 5 to less than 1 mi. wide) and one of most beautiful of Scottish lakes, it has Ben Lomond (3,192 ft. high) overlooking N end.

Lomonosov, Mikhail Vasilyevich (mēkhŭyēl' vŭsē'lyŭvĭch lŭmŭnô'sŭf), 1711–65, Russian scientist and writer. His experiments anticipated mechanical nature of heat and kinetic theory of gases. A founder of modern Russian literature, he reformed Russian literary language and altered character of Russian prosody by adopting principle of tonic rather than syllabic versification.

Lomonosov, formerly **Oranienbaum** (ōrä'nyŭnboum), city (pop. over 10,000), RSFSR, on Gulf of Finland near Leningrad. Site of a palace built 1714 by Peter I and of Catherine II's "Chinese Palace" (built 1768). Was renamed 1948.

Lompoc (lŏm'pōk), city (pop. 5,520), S Calif., NW of Santa Barbara. Produces flowers and seeds. Near by are kieselguhr quarries and oil fields.

London, Jack (John Griffith London), 1876–1916, American novelist and short-story writer. A sailor, a gold seeker in the Klondike, and a newspaperman, he wrote adventure tales romantic in effect though rawly realistic in setting and character (e.g., *The Call of the Wild,* 1903; *The Sea-Wolf,* 1904; *White Fang,* 1905). Championed the socialistic I.W.W. and wrote socialist novels (e.g., *Martin Eden,* 1909) and tracts.

London, city (pop. 95,343), S Ont., Canada, on Thames R. and SW of Toronto. Trade and mfg. center of agr. region. Seat of Univ. of Western Ontario (coed.; 1878) and affiliated Huron and Ursuline colleges. Site selected as future capital of Upper Canada 1752, but the city not actually founded until 1826.

London, cap. of United Kingdom and chief city of the British Empire, on both sides of the Thames. Greater London (c.693 sq. mi.; pop. 8,346,137), includes parts of the counties of Essex, Kent, Hertfordshire, Middlesex, and Surrey. Administrative county of London (117 sq. mi.; pop. 3,348,336) includes 28 metropolitan boroughs, each with own mayor and council, responsible to London Co. Council. Present form of municipal government began in 12th cent. Core of London is the City (1 sq. mi.; pop. 5,268). London lost its importance when Romans left in 5th cent.; emerged again (886) under Alfred. Nucleus of TOWER OF LONDON was built by William I. THE LIVERY COMPANIES became important in 13th–14th cent. Medieval London saw beginnings of INNS OF COURT, SAINT PAUL'S CATHEDRAL, and WESTMINSTER ABBEY. In 1665 the great plague took c.75,000 lives, and in 1666 great fire destroyed most of city. Rebuilt by Christopher Wren. Galleries and museums include British Mus., Victoria and Albert Mus., Tate Gallery, Natl. Gallery, and Wallace Coll. Univ. of LONDON is in Bloomsbury. Among famous streets are Fleet St., the STRAND, PICCADILLY, WHITEHALL, PALL MALL, Downing St., Lombard St., Bond St., and Regent St. In World War II many historic buildings and many ancient churches were destroyed or damaged.

London, village (pop. 5,222), central Ohio, WSW of Columbus. Mfg. of metal products.

London, Declaration of, international code of maritime law, especially as related to war, proposed in 1909 by leading European naval powers, U.S., and Japan, after meeting in conference at London, England, in 1908. Dealing with many controverted points (e.g., blockade, contraband, prize), it largely restated existing law but showed greater regard for rights of neutrals. Declaration was ratified by U.S. senate but not by many other powers; thus it never went into effect officially.

London, University of, founded in London, England, in 1836 to give examinations and degrees. Teaching functions were added in 1898. Now has many affiliated colleges, institutions, and schools (e.g., London School of Economics and Political Science).

London Bridge, granite, five-arched bridge over the Thames, in central London. 928 ft. long, present structure was built 1824–31. First bridge built in 963. Only bridge over the Thames until 18th cent.

London Company, corporation granted charter (1606) by James I to locate colonies in America. Given tract of land fronting 100 mi. on the sea and extending 100 mi. inland somewhere between lat. 34° and 41° N. Company expedition founded Jamestown (1607). Charter of 1609 replaced local council with absolute governor. Third charter (1612) made company self-governing, but disagreement over policies created dissension. Company dissolved in 1624 following unfavorable investigation.

London Conference, name of several international meetings held at London, England, the most important of which are listed below. At the **London Conference of 1830–31** the chief powers of Europe agreed to estab. Greece as independent principality, with boundaries fixed by London Protocol of 1829. The conference also considered the revolt of the Belgians against William I of the Netherlands. Mediation was unsuccessful, but late in 1831 joint French and British intervention compelled William to evacuate Belgium. The **London Conference of 1838–39,** which prepared the final Dutch-Belgian separation treaty, divided disputed Luxembourg and Limburg between Dutch and Belgian crowns. For the **London Conference of 1852,** see SCHLESWIG-HOLSTEIN; for the **London Conference of 1908,** see LONDON, DECLARATION OF.

Londonderry or **Derry,** maritime county (804 sq. mi.; pop. 155,520), N. Ireland, in Ulster. Largely mountainous area whose damp, cold climate allows little agr. Chief occupations are linen making, distilling, and fishing. *Londonderry Air* probably from region originally. County town is **Londonderry** or **Derry,** county borough (pop. 50,099), on Foyle R., a major Irish seaport. Chief export is cattle. Varied industries include linen weaving and distilling. Given to City of London corporation in 1608 and name changed to Londonderry. City withstood siege of James II's forces for 105 days in 1689. U.S. naval base in World War II.

Long, Crawford Williamson, 1815–78, American physician, pioneer in use of ether anesthesia (1842).

Long, Huey P(ierce), 1893–1935, American political leader in La. As governor (1928–31) and U.S. Senator (1931–35) he promoted a "Share-the-Wealth" program by ruthless and demagogic means. Assassinated at Baton Rouge.

Long, Perrin Hamilton, 1899–, American physician, known for research on sulfa drugs.

Long, Stephen Harriman, 1784–1864, American explorer. In 1817 he explored the upper Mississippi region; in 1819–20, the Rocky Mts.

Long, Loch (lŏkh), inlet, c.20 mi. long, between Argyllshire and Dumbartonshire, Scotland.

Long Beach. 1 City (pop. 250,767), S Calif., on harbor on San Pedro Bay and S of Los Angeles; laid out 1882. Year-round resort. Mfg. of aircraft, soap, and tires. Has shipyards and canneries. Refines and ships oil from wells of Signal Hill, independent city (pop. 4,040) within Long Beach. **2** Resort city (pop. 15,586), SE N.Y., on S shore of Long Isl., S of Rockville Centre; inc. as a city 1922.

Long Branch, SW residential suburb of Toronto (pop. 8,727), S Ont., Canada, on L. Ontario.

Long Branch, city (pop. 23,090), E N.J., N of Asbury Park; settled 1740. Presidents Grant and Garfield had homes here. Noted resort since early 19th cent.

Longchamp, William of (lông′shămp), d. 1197, chancellor of England (1190–91), bishop of Ely. Joined (1189) Richard I against Henry II. Upon Richard's accession, William rose rapidly to become acting head of both church and state. Rebellion of John and the barons drove him from England in 1191.

Longchamp (lõshã′), famous racecourse of Paris, France, in the Bois de Boulogne.

Longfellow, Henry Wadsworth, 1807–82, American poet, b. Portland, Maine; long a professor of modern languages and belles lettres. His poetry was highly popular in his time, and his kindly figure loomed large on the literary horizon. Many of his short sentimental and "inspirational" verses are still familiar to every American schoolchild (e.g., "A Psalm of Life," "Excelsior," "The Village Blacksmith"), as are some of his longer tales in verse (e.g., *Evangeline,* 1847, based on the expulsion of the Acadians; *The Song of Hiawatha,* 1855, a sentimental treatment of Indian legends; *The Courtship of Miles Standish,* 1858; "Paul Revere's Ride" in *Tales of a Wayside Inn,* 1863). He helped introduce much foreign literature to the U.S., using the meter of the Finnish *Kalevala* for *Hiawatha,* translating Dante, and modeling some verse on Spanish forms. He also wrote an early travel book, *Outre-Mer* (1833–34), and the prose romance *Hyperion* (1839).

Longford (lông′fürd), inland county (403 sq. mi.; pop. 36,218), Ireland, in Leinster; co. town Longford. Level area with many lakes, bogs, and marshes. Dairy farming is chief occupation.

Longhi, Pietro (pyā′trō lông′gē), 1702–85, Venetian genre painter. His son, **Alessandro Longhi,** 1733–1813, was a portrait painter and engraver.

Longinus (Dionysius Cassius Longinus) (lŏnjī′nŭs), c.213–273, Greek rhetorician, philosopher. Only slight fragments of his work survive, and his fame rests on a classic treatise of literary criticism incorrectly attributed to him, *On the Sublime,* or *Longinus on the Sublime,* which treats what would be called now "loftiness of style."

Long Island, 118 mi. long and 12–20 mi. wide (pop. 5,237,909), SE N.Y., extending ENE from Hudson R. mouth and separated from Staten Isl. by the Narrows of New York Bay, from Manhattan and the Bronx by East R., from Conn. by Long Isl. Sound. Along c.75 mi. of its S shore is a barrier beach sheltering large bays from the Atlantic. E end terminates in 2 flukes, the longer in Montauk Point (mŏn′tôk″), easternmost point in N.Y. state. Counties (E–W) are Kings (Brooklyn borough) and Queens (parts of New York city), Nassau, Suffolk. Has many resorts and parks (e.g., Jones Beach), fine estates, commuters' suburbs (W portion), farms (potatoes, truck) and fishing villages. Settled 1636; both Dutch and English estab. colonies here before English gained control in 1664. Extensive settlement occurred after development of New York city and building of railroads and highway system.

Long Island, battle of, in American Revolution, Aug. 27–30, 1776. To protect New York city and lower Hudson valley from British, George Washington sent force to defend

Brooklyn Heights on Long Isl. British, under Sir William Howe, laid siege. Washington evacuated army and retreated N, fighting delaying actions.

ong Island City: see QUEENS, New York city borough.

ong Island Sound, Atlantic arm, c.90 mi. long and 3–20 mi. wide, separating Long Isl. from N.Y. and Conn. mainland. Extends from Block Isl. Sound to East R. (connection to New York Bay). Coastal shipping route; pleasure boating, fisheries.

ong Island University: see BROOKLYN, N.Y.

ongmeadow, suburb town (pop. 6,508), SW Mass., on Connecticut R. just S of Springfield.

ongmont, city (pop. 8,099), N Colo., N of Denver, in rich farm area, with coal mines.

ong Parliament: see PARLIAMENT.

ongs Peak: see FRONT RANGE.

ongstreet, Augustus Baldwin, 1790–1870, American humorist; author of *Georgia Scenes* (1835), realistic sketches filled with frontier humor.

ongstreet, James, 1821–1904, Confederate general. Fought at Bull Run, in Peninsular campaign, at Fredericksburg. At Gettysburg his delay in offensive may have cost Lee the battle. Distinguished himself in Wilderness campaign. Considered poor strategist but excellent tactician. Career still disputed.

ongueuil (lõgû'yù), residential city (pop. 11,103), SW Que., Canada, on St. Lawrence R. opposite Montreal.

ongueville, Anne Geneviève, duchesse de (än' zhùnùvyĕv' düshĕs' dù lõgvēl'), 1619–79, French beauty and politician, a leader of the FRONDE; sister of Louis II de Condé. Made her peace with court 1653.

ongview. 1 City (pop. 24,502), E Texas, W of Shreveport, La. and near Sabine R. Boomed after 1930 discovery of East Texas oil fields. **2** Inland port city (pop. 20,339), SW Wash., at junction of Cowlitz and Columbia rivers (latter bridged to Oregon); founded 1923. Lumber mills and food-processing and aluminum plants.

ongworth, Nicholas, 1869–1931, U.S. Representative (1903–13, 1915–31). Speaker of House (1925–31). Married Alice Lee Roosevelt, daughter of Pres. Theodore Roosevelt, at White House (1906).

ongwy (lõwē'), town (pop. 12,064), Meurthe-et-Moselle dept., NE France. It is an industrial center of Lorraine iron-mining dist.

önnrot, Elias (ĕlē'äs lûn'rōōt), 1802–84, Finnish philologist, compiler of the KALEVALA, Finnish national epic. From 1828 he traveled through Finland, Lapland, and NW Russia, collecting fragments of the epic (pub. 1835, 1849).

ookout, Cape, E N.C., headland at meeting of Core and Shackelford banks, SW of Cape Hatteras; has lighthouse.

ookout Mountain, town (pop. 1,675), E Tenn., near Chattanooga. On Lookout Mt. (2,126 ft. high, extending into Ga., Ala.), scene of Civil War battle in CHATTANOOGA CAMPAIGN; partly in Chickamauga and Chattanooga Natl. Military Park. Limestone caves, cable railway, observatory, and museum are here.

oom, frame or machine used for weaving. Has a beam, on which warp threads are wound; heddles (rods or cords), each with an eye through which a warp thread is drawn; the harness, a frame which operates to form a shed for insertion of weft threads between warp threads; the reed, which pushes each new weft row against the finished cloth; and a beam to hold the roll of finished fabric. Hand looms operated by foot treadles were forerunners of the power loom patented 1785 by Edmund Cartwright. The Jacquard loom, invented by J. M. Jacquard and perfected by 1804, made it possible to weave any design.

loon, migratory aquatic bird of colder parts of N Hemisphere, found in fresh and salt water. It is a swift flier and a strong swimmer and adept diver. Common North American loon or great northern diver is black and white bird (c.32 in. long).

Loos, Adolf (ä'dôlf lōs'), 1870–1933, Austrian architect. Influenced development of functional style.

Loos (lô-ôs'), town (pop. 3,170), Pas-de-Calais dept., N France. In World War I it was recaptured by British forces from the Germans with tremendous losses (Oct., 1915).

Lope de Rueda (lō'pā dā rōōā'dhä), 1510?–1565, Spanish dramatist, author of comedies, farces, and *pasos* (a dramatic form created by him), precursor of the Golden Age of Spanish literature.

Lope de Vega (Carpio), Felix (fā'lēks lō'pā dā vā'gä), 1562–1635, Spanish dramatic poet, a chief figure of the Golden Age of Spanish literature. His many plays range from tragedy to farce and are notable for warmth of feeling, wit, highly dramatic effects, and character portrayal. His disregard of the classic unities freed the drama and had much influence on other writers. He also wrote epics, lyric poetry, and tales.

López, Francisco Solano (fränsē'skō sōlä'nō lō'pās), 1826?–1870, president of Paraguay (1862–70). Succeeded his father, Carlos Antonio López (president, 1844–62). Ambitious and arrogant, Francisco brought on a war with Argentina, Brazil, and Uruguay (see TRIPLE ALLIANCE, WAR OF THE), in which he was killed. Considered by some Latin Americans as champion of rights of small nations against aggression of more powerful neighbors.

López, Narciso (närsē'sō), 1798?–1851, Spanish American soldier, b. Venezuela. When his plan for a Cuban revolution against Spain was discovered, he fled to U.S. (1848). Captured and executed in later filibustering expedition to Cuba.

López de Legaspi, Miguel (mēgĕl' lō'pāth dā lāgä'spē), d. 1572, Spanish navigator. Led expedition which conquered Philippines (1563–70). His conquest was accomplished largely by peaceful means. Founded modern Manila (1571).

López de Mendoza, Iñigo, marqués de Santillana: see SANTILLANA.

López y Fuentes, Gregorio (grāgō'rēō lō'pās ē fwān'tās), 1895–, Mexican novelist, poet, and journalist, known for realistic novels on centuries-long oppression of Indians, e.g., *El Indio* (1935).

Lop Nor: see LOB NOR.

loquat (lō'kwŏt), small ornamental evergreen

tree (*Eriobotrya japonica*), native to China. It is grown in S U.S. for its small fragrant white flowers and pear-shaped fruits eaten fresh or used in preserves.

Lorain, city (pop. 51,202), W Ohio, on L. Erie at mouth of Black R. and W of Cleveland; settled 1807. Ore-shipping port with shipbuilding; mfg. of iron and steel, chemicals, and clothing; commercial fisheries and sandstone quarries.

Loras College: see DUBUQUE, Iowa.

Lorca, Federico García: see GARCÍA LORCA.

Lords, House of: see PARLIAMENT.

Lord's Prayer or **Our Father,** the principal Christian prayer, taught by Jesus to his disciples. Mat. 6.9–13; Luke 11.2–4. English versions vary. Roman Catholics do not add the doxology ("For thine is the kingdom," etc.) which is used by most Protestants. Prayer is called, in Latin, Pater or Pater Noster.

Lord's Supper, Protestant sacrament of the EUCHARIST. REFORMATION leaders rejected transubstantiation but retained belief in the sacrament as mystically uniting believers and Christ. Lutherans held that there is a change by which the body and blood of Christ become really present in the bread and wine; the extreme view of ZWINGLI was that communion was purely symbolic. Calvanists imputed a spiritual meaning only to the words of institution; this has been the prevailing Protestant view. The communion service, usually short, varies widely among Protestants. It always involves both bread and wine; this was a crucial point with the Hussites. Quakers reject the sacrament altogether.

Lorelei (lô'rŭlī), cliff, 433 ft. high, W Germany, overlooking dangerous narrows of the Rhine, about midway between Coblenz and Bingen. Heine's poem *Die Lorelei* tells legend of a fairy who lived here and lured sailors to their death by her singing. Another legend places the Nibelungs' hoard here.

Lorentz, Hendrick Antoon (hĕn'drŭck än'tōn lō'rĕnts), 1853–1928, Dutch physicist, pioneer in formulating relations between electricity, magnetism, light. One of first to postulate concept of electrons. Shared 1902 Nobel Prize for explanation of Zeeman effect (change in spectrum lines in magnetic field).

Lorentz, Pare (pâr' lôrĕnts'), 1905–, American film director. Director of U.S. Film Service (1938–40), he produced such documentary films as *The Plow That Broke the Plains* (1936), *The River* (1937).

Lorenzetti (lōrāntsĕt'tē), two Sienese painters, brothers, who introduced naturalism into Sienese art. They were **Pietro Lorenzetti** (pyā'trō), c.1280–1348, and **Ambrogio Lorenzetti** (ämbrō'jō), d. 1348?. Both were influenced by Giovanni Pisano. Many of their religious paintings are in churches in Siena.

Lorenzini, Carlo: see COLLODI, CARLO.

Lorenzo, Fiorenzo di: see FIORENZO DI LORENZO.

Lorenzo di Credi (lōrān'tsō dē krā'dē), 1459–1537, Florentine painter and sculptor, who was greatly influenced by Leonardo da Vinci.

Lorenzo di Pietro (dē pyā'trō), c.1412–1480, Sienese painter and sculptor, called Il Vecchietta.

Lorenzo Monaco (mō'näkō), c.1370–1425?, Florentine painter, a Camaldolite mon[k]. Real name was Piero di Giovanni. His wor[k] has features of Sienese school and of Giott[o].

Loreto (lŭrĕ'tō), small town, central Italy. Ha[s] shrine of Holy House of the Virgin in Naza[reth], said to have been brought here throug[h] the air by angels in 13th cent. A church bui[lt] around the house is rich in works of art.

Loretto Heights College: see DENVER, Colo.

Loria, Roger of: see ROGER OF LORIA.

Lorient (lôryā'), town (pop. 10,764; 1936 pop. 40,753), Morbihan dept., NW France; po[rt] and naval station on the Atlantic. Founde[d] 1664. A German submarine base in Worl[d] War II, it was heavily bombed by Allies bu[t] held out until end of European war.

Loris-Melikov, Mikhail Tarielovich (mĕ khŭyĕl' tŭryĕl'ŭvĭch lô'rĭs-mĕ'lyĭkŭf), 1825–88, Russian general and statesman, of Armenian descent. Was created a count for hi[s] services in Russo-Turkish War of 1877–78. As minister of the interior (1880–84) he promoted liberal reforms, which were voide[d] after Alexander II's assassination.

Lorme, Marion de: see DELORME, MARION.

Lorrain, Claude: see CLAUDE LORRAIN.

Lorraine (lŭrān', lô–, Fr. lôrĕn'), Ger. *Lothringen,* region and former province, [E] France, in Moselle, Meurthe-et-Moselle, Meuse, and Vosges depts.; historic ca[p]. Nancy. Crossed by Meuse and Moselle river[s] and by Vosges mts., it is a generally hilly, agr., and pastoral region. Its iron fields, among the largest in Europe, depend largel[y] on German Ruhr coal. Except in Mosell[e] dept. (cap. METZ), where German is largel[y] spoken, Lorraine is predominantly French speaking. A remnant of the kingdom o[f] LOTHARINGIA, Lorraine after 10th cent. became a duchy of the Holy Roman Empire. The independent bishoprics of Metz, Toul, and Verdun were annexed to France 1552. The duchy itself was united with Bar (see BAR-LE-DUC) in 1431 through the accessio[n] of RENÉ of Anjou as duke. Charles the Bol[d] of Burgundy seized Lorraine but was defeated and slain at Nancy by Duke René I[I] and his Swiss allies. In the 16th cent. th[e] GUISE family, a branch of the house of Lorraine, gained great influence in France. Occupied by France in the Thirty Years War, Lorraine was recovered in 1697 by Leopold I. His heir Francis married Maria-Theresa o[f] Austria and as Emperor Francis I founde[d] the house of HAPSBURG-LORRAINE. By an arrangement (1735) with Louis XV of France he exchanged Lorraine for Tuscany; Lorraine was given to Louis's father-in-law STANISLAUS I of Poland, upon whose death i[t] was to pass to France. Stanislaus died i[n] 1766, and Lorraine became French. In 187[1] Moselle dept. was ceded to Germany, as a result of the Franco-Prussian War, and unite[d] with ALSACE to form the imperial territory o[f] Alsace-Lorraine. It was restored to France i[n] 1918 but was again briefly annexed to Germany in World War II. Lorraine suffere[d] heavily in both world wars: Verdun was a center of fighting in 1916–18; Metz and th[e] Vosges in 1944.

Lorris, Guillaume de: see GUILLAUME DE LORRIS.

Los Alamos (lŏs ăl'ŭmōs), community (pop

9,934; alt. 7,500 ft.), N. N.Mex., near Rio Grande and NW of Sante Fe. First atomic bomb was made here and tested (July 16, 1945) at Alamogordo air base.

Los Angeles (lŏs ăng'gŭlŭs, ăn'jŭlŭs, –lēz), city (pop. 1,970,358), S Calif., on Pacific coast; founded 1781. Site visited 1769 by Gaspar de Portolá. Several times cap. of Alta California, it was cattle ranching center under Spanish and Mexicans. Taken by U.S. forces 1846. Expanded with railroads (1876, 1885), discovery of oil (1890s), motion pictures (early 20th cent.), and aircraft mfg. (early 1920s). A major port, rail, and air center, it is tourist mecca and motion picture cap. of world. Also a radio and television center, it has other industries including mfg. of aircraft and food (esp. citrus fruits), metal, wood, and chemical products. Oil fields are near. Large increase in pop. since World War II. It has absorbed HOLLYWOOD, Encino, Tujunga, Venice, Van Nuys, and other towns. Incorporated cities in metropolitan area (with over 29,000 pop.) are Alhambra, Beverly Hills, Burbank, Glendale, Huntington Park, Inglewood, Long Beach, Pasadena, Pomona, Santa Ana, Santa Monica, and South Gate. International airport at Culver City. Seat of Univ. of SOUTHERN CALIFORNIA, Univ. of CALIFORNIA at Los Angeles, Occidental Col. (coed.; 1887), Loyola Univ. of Los Angeles (R.C.; mainly for men; 1865), and George Pepperdine Col. (coed.; 1937). Water comes from Colorado and Owens rivers and Mono Basin, and Hoover Dam supplies power.

Lossing, Benson John (lŏ'sĭng), 1813–91, American historian and wood engraver, known for illustrated books on American Revolution and Civil War.

Lost Battalion, popular name given to eight American units of 77th Division, numbering c.600 men, which were cut off by German forces in World War I after the launching of an American attack in Argonne Forest in early Oct., 1918. Some 400 men perished before units were rescued.

Lost Dauphin (dô'fĭn). The obscure circumstances of the death of LOUIS XVII of France made it possible for impostors to claim that they were the "Lost Dauphin"—i.e., Louis XVII. In the U.S., Eleazer WILLIAMS was the most important claimant. There were even rumors that J. J. Audubon was the Lost Dauphin.

Lost tribes, 10 Jewish tribes transported to Assyria after the conquest of Israel. Conjecture has linked them with, among other groups, the Hindus, the English, and American Indians.

Lot, nephew of Abraham. A good man, he was warned by an angel to leave the doomed Sodom. His wife looked back and was turned into pillar of salt. Gen. 11–14; 19.

Lot (lôt), department (2,018 sq. mi.; pop. 154,-897), SW France, in Quercy; cap. Cahors. The **Lot** river, 300 mi. long, rising in the Cévennes mts., flows W through Quercy and joins the Garonne near Agen.

Lot-et-Garonne (lôt"-ā-gärôn'), department (2,079 sq. mi.; pop. 265,449), SW France; cap. Agen.

Lothair (lōthâr'), emperors and German kings. **Lothair I,** 795–855, was associated in power with his father, LOUIS I, from 817 and succeeded him as emperor in 840, with the E part of the Carolingian empire as his share. His attempt to gain sole rule over the empire was checked by his brothers Charles (later Emperor CHARLES II) and LOUIS THE GERMAN, who defeated him at Fontenoy (841) and in 843 forced on him the Treaty of VERDUN. His remaining lands were divided on his death among his sons, the main shares falling to Emperor Louis II and to Lothair, king of Lotharingia. **Lothair II** (the Saxon), 1075–1137, duke of Saxony from 1106, was elected German king to succeed Henry V (1125). With the help of his son-in-law, HENRY THE PROUD, he defeated the antiking Frederick of Hohenstaufen and Frederick's brother Conrad (who was to succeed him as Conrad III). He was crowned emperor at Rome in 1133. Lothair was active in the conversion of NE Germany to Christianity.

Lothair, 941–86, French king (954–86). Tried unsuccessfully to take Lorraine from Emperor Otto II.

Lothair, d. 869, king of LOTHARINGIA (855–69).

Lotharingia (lŏthŭrĭn'jŭ). The Treaty of VERDUN (843) divided the Carolingian empire into three parts, the central portion falling to Emperor Lothair I. Of that portion, the N part was inherited in 855 by Lothair's second son, also named Lothair, whose kingdom was named Lotharingia. It comprised, roughly, the modern Netherlands, Belgium, Luxembourg, NW Germany, Alsace, and Lorraine (the name *Lorraine* is derived from Lotharingia). This was in turn divided by the Treaty of MERSEN (870) between the E Frankish and W Frankish kingdoms (i.e., Germany and France). Emperor Henry I gained control over all Lotharingia; Otto I in 959 divided it into the duchies of Lower Lorraine (in the N) and Upper Lorraine (S). In Upper Lorraine the ducal title continued until 1766 in what came to be known simply as the duchy of LORRAINE, a relatively small area. In Lower Lorraine, the ducal title soon disappeared, and many fiefs emerged, notably Brabant, Bouillon, Limburg, Jülich, Cleves, Berg, Hainaut, and the bishopric of Liége.

Lothians, the (lō'dhēŭnz), division of Scotland, including East Lothian, West Lothian, and Midlothian. Ancient Lothian was part of Northumbria.

Loti, Pierre (pyĕr' lôtē'), pseud. of Julien Viaud, 1850–1923, French author, a navy officer. His novels *Pêcheur d'Islande* (1886, Eng. tr., *An Iceland Fisherman*) and *Ramuntcho* (1897; Eng. tr., 1897) and his travel book *Vers Ispahan* (1904) are among his best-known works, noted for accurate exotic settings, sobriety of style, and romantic pessimism.

Lotophagi: see LOTUS-EATERS.

Lötschberg Railway (lûch'bĕrk), Swiss electrical railroad crossing Bernese Alps from Thun to Brig. **Lötschberg Tunnel** (9 mi. long; max. alt. 4,078 ft.) carries it under Lötschen Pass.

Lotto, Lorenzo (lōrān'tsō lôt'tō), c.1480–1556, Venetian painter, known for sensitive portraits.

lotus, name for certain water plants. The true Egyptian lotus (*Nymphaea*) is a blue or white WATER LILY and a national emblem of Egypt. The Indian lotus or sacred bean (*Nelumbo nucifera*) is an aquatic plant with large pink flowers; its seed pods resemble a sprinkling-can nozzle. The blossom is symbolic in the religion and art of India. American lotus (*Nelumbo lutea*) has yellow flowers.

lotus-eaters or **Lotophagi** (lōtŏ'fŭjī), people on N coast of Africa who lived on lotus, which caused forgetfulness and indolence. Some of Odysseus' men ate lotus and had to be dragged back to ships.

Lotze, Rudolph Hermann (lō'tsŭ), 1817–81, German philosopher. Conceding that the physical world is governed by mechanical laws, he explained relation and development in the universe as functions of a world mind. His medical studies were pioneer efforts in modern scientific psychology.

Loubet, Émile (āmĕl' lo͞obā'), 1838–1929, president of France (1899–1906). Granted pardon to Dreyfus. During his term Franco-British Entente Cordiale began.

Loudon, Gideon Ernst, Freiherr von: see LAUDON.

Loudon (lou'dŭn), town (pop. 3,567), E Tenn., SW of Knoxville near Fort Loudon Dam, at junction of Tennessee and Little Tennessee rivers. Site of Fort Loudon (1756, fell to Cherokee 1760) near.

loudspeaker or **speaker,** device translating audiofrequency electric currents into audible sound. A diaphragm (a stiff paper cone or metal disk) which reproduces sound by molecular disturbance is attached to small coil movable in response to current of driving amplifier. One type with great power has no diaphragm but includes compressor for supplying air to horn through valve which modifies air stream.

Louis, Saint: see LOUIS IX, king of France.

Louis, emperors. **Louis I** or **Louis the Pious,** Fr. *Louis le Débonnaire,* 778–840, son of Charlemagne. Became king of Aquitaine 781; coemperor with his father 813; sole emperor 814. In 817 he took his son LOTHAIR I as coemperor and gave Aquitaine and Bavaria to his sons PEPIN I and LOUIS THE GERMAN. His attempts at creating a kingdom for Charles, his son by second marriage (later Emperor CHARLES II), led to rebellions by his other sons, notably in 829–30 and 833. Abandoned by his troops, he was defeated near Colmar (833; battle of the "Field of Lies," Ger. *Lügenfeld*). However, the sons fell out among themselves and Louis was restored to power. He died while trying to uphold a new division of the empire, between Lothair and Charles. The raids of the Norsemen were intensified during his weak reign. **Louis II,** d. 875, was the son of Lothair I, who made him king of Italy (844) and whom he succeeded as emperor (855). His power in Italy was curbed by the independent Lombard dukes and by the Arab invasion. After the death of his brother LOTHAIR (869), he claimed Lotharingia, but the Treaty of MERSEN (870) divided it between his uncles Charles the Bald (who later succeeded him as Charles II) and Louis the German. **Louis IV** or **Louis the Bavarian,** 1287?–1347, duke of Upper Bavaria, was elected German king in 1314 to succeed Henry VII. A minority faction elected Frederick the Fair of Hapsburg, whom Louis defeated and captured at Mühldorf (1322). From 1324 to his death Louis struggled against the papacy. On the theory evolved by MARSILIUS OF PADUA, that princes owed their rule to the will of the people, he had himself crowned emperor by the "representatives of the Roman people" (1328) and in 1338 claimed that the imperial title could be conferred by the electors without papal confirmation. By marriage and investiture he sought to add Brandenburg, Tyrol, and Holland to the Wittelsbach family possessions, but none of these acquisitions proved permanent. In 1346 Pope Clement VII declared him deposed and secured the election of Charles IV. Louis was successfully resisting his rival when he died in a hunting accident.

Louis, kings of Bavaria. **Louis I,** 1786–1868, son of Maximilian I, reigned 1825–48. A lavish patron, he made Munich a center of the arts. He was at first a liberal, but his later turn toward reaction and his scandalous liaison with Lola MONTEZ led to his enforced abdication in favor of his son Maximilian II. **Louis II,** 1845–86, son of Maximilian II, reigned 1864–86. Handsome, gifted, liberal, romantic, he also displayed a prodigality and eccentricity which eventually turned into incurable insanity. He spent a fortune on his friend Richard Wagner, who held great influence over him. Confined after 1866 at his fantastic château on L. Starnberg, he drowned himself, forcing his physician to share his death. His brother Otto I, who succeeded him, was also insane. **Louis III,** 1845–1921, succeeded his father Luitpold as regent for Otto I (1912); proclaimed himself king 1913; was forced to abdicate 1918.

Louis, Frankish kings and kings of France. *Carolingian dynasty.* **Louis I:** see LOUIS I, emperor. **Louis II** (the Stammerer), 846–79, son of Emperor Charles II, reigned in France 877–79. His succession was shared by his sons Carloman and **Louis III,** c.863–882, who routed the Normans at Saucourt (881). **Louis IV** (Louis d'Outre-Mer), 921–54, son of Charles III (the Simple), spent his youth in exile in England; was recalled and made king in 936 by the nobles under the leadership of Hugh the Great. His energy and independence displeased Hugh, who made war on him but was forced to submit in 950. **Louis V** (the Sluggard), c.967–987, last Carolingian, reigned 986–87; was succeeded by Hugh Capet.

Capetian dynasty, direct line. **Louis VI** (the Fat), 1081–1137, reigned 1108–37. Laid groundwork for unified monarchy by increasing royal domain, destroying castles of robber barons, favoring Church and burgher class. Was chronically at war with Henry I of England, whose inroads from Normandy he checked. His son **Louis VII** (the Young), c.1120–1180 (reigned 1137–80), continued centralizing policy and took part in Second Crusade (1147–49). His divorce from ELEANOR OF AQUITAINE (1152) and her marriage to Henry II of England gave English a foothold in SW France and led to recurrent warfare. His grandson **Louis VIII,** 1187–1226 (reigned 1223–26), invaded England

(1216) but was defeated at Lincoln (1217). Resuming the Albigensian Crusade (1226), he conquered Languedoc. His son **Louis IX** or **Saint Louis,** 1214–70, began his reign in 1226 under the regency of his mother, BLANCHE OF CASTILE. In 1241–43 he secured submission of Poitou, repulsed an English invasion, and defeated RAYMOND VII of Toulouse. He led the Seventh Crusade to Egypt (1248), was defeated and captured at El Mansura (1250), and, after being ransomed, remained in the Holy Land until 1254. Another crusade, against Tunis, ended with his death of the plague soon after his landing. His reign was for France a period of peace, prosperity, and progress. He stamped out private warfare, simplified administration, improved the distribution of taxes, and extended the right of appealing to the crown to all cases. The great Gothic cathedrals were largely built during his reign, as was SAINTE-CHAPELLE in Paris. Embodying the ideals of a Christian monarch, he was canonized in 1297. Feast: Aug. 25. **Louis X,** Fr. *Louis le Hutin* [the quarrelsome], 1289–1316 (reigned 1314–16), was dominated by his uncle, Charles of Valois.

Valois dynasty. **Louis XI,** 1423–83, reigned 1461–83. As dauphin he joined several conspiracies against his father, Charles VII, but after his accession he devoted himself to creating a new, national state, based on the central power of the crown. This goal he achieved, despite the military superiority of his enemies the great nobles, by dint of stubbornness, skillful and unscrupulous diplomacy, and bribery. The League of the Public Weal, formed 1465 and headed by CHARLES THE BOLD of Burgundy and FRANCIS II of Brittany, forced him to grant concessions which he violated soon afterward. A new coalition was formed against him in 1467. Louis forced the Peace of Ancenis on Francis of Brittany (1468) but was outfoxed for once by Charles the Bold, who lured him to Péronne for an interview and then refused to let him go until Louis had helped him suppress the revolt of Liége, which Louis himself had stirred up. After Charles's death (1477) Louis seized part of the inheritance of MARY OF BURGUNDY—Burgundy, Picardy, Artois, and Franche-Comté. Louis tended toward autocratic rule and chose his advisers among men of humble origin. Though he revoked the PRAGMATIC SANCTION OF BOURGES and practiced a superstitious brand of piety that bordered on mania, he intervened freely in church matters. He dreaded assassination and died in virtual self-imprisonment at the castle of Plessis-les-Tours. **Louis XII,** 1462–1515, called "father of the people," son of Charles d'ORLÉANS, succeeded his cousin Charles VIII in 1498 and married Charles's widow, ANNE OF BRITTANY. He resumed the ITALIAN WARS (1499) but was expelled from Italy by the HOLY LEAGUE (1513).

Bourbon dynasty. **Louis XIII,** 1601–43, son of Henry IV, began his reign in 1610 under the regency of his mother, MARIE DE' MEDICI. He married ANNE OF AUSTRIA (1615). In 1617 he procured the murder of CONCINI and exiled his mother, but in 1622 he was reconciled with her and in 1624 he entrusted the government to her protégé, Cardinal RICHELIEU. The Cardinal and his successor, MAZARIN, dominated the rest of his reign. His son, **Louis XIV,** 1638–1715, called "Roi Soleil" (Sun King) and "the Great," brought the monarchy to its zenith. His long reign (1643–1715) began under the regency of his mother, Anne of Austria, and was dominated by MAZARIN until 1661. Chief events of that period were the French victory in the THIRTY YEARS WAR, the FRONDE, and the Peace of the PYRENEES with Spain (1659), which resulted in Louis's marriage with Marie Thérèse of Austria. The period 1661–83 was one of administrative and economic reform, in which COLBERT played the leading part. France became an absolute monarchy, epitomized by Louis's apocryphal remark, *L'état, c'est moi* [I am the state]. The administration passed from the nobles into the hands of loyal civil servants. Commerce, industry, naval power, and colonies were expanded along the principles of MERCANTILISM. Louis's quest for supremacy in Europe began with the War of DEVOLUTION and the third of the DUTCH WARS, which netted him Franche-Comté and part of Flanders. In the following 10 years he seized, on various pretexts, several border cities, notably Strasbourg (1681). Colbert's death (1683) gave LOUVOIS increased influence, but after 1691 Louis ceased to take advice from his ministers. The period 1683–1715 was marked by large-scale foreign wars, caused chiefly by European fears of Louis's aggressive designs (see GRAND ALLIANCE, WAR OF THE; SPANISH SUCCESSION, WAR OF THE). These wars brought France no gains but exhausted its resources. The persecution of the HUGUENOTS after the revocation of the Edict of NANTES (1685) depopulated entire provinces. Louis's GALLICANISM caused a violent quarrel with the papacy (1673–93); Louis had to give in. He ruthlessly suppressed JANSENISM. Among his mistresses, Mlle de LA VALLIÈRE and Mme de MONTESPAN were the most influential; in 1684 he secretly married Mme de MAINTENON. The cent. of Louis XIV is the great classical age of French culture; Pascal, Corneille, Molière, Racine were among the foremost names of his reign. Louis himself was a generous and discerning patron. The pomp and etiquette surrounding his life at VERSAILLES symbolized the almost divine dignity to which he had raised the office of king. His great-grandson, **Louis XV,** 1710–74, succeeded him under the regency of Philippe II d'ORLÉANS. Cardinal FLEURY guided his policies after 1726, and his mistress, Mme de POMPADOUR, from 1743 to her death (1764). His queen, MARIE LESZCZYNSKA, and his last mistress, Mme DU BARRY, held no political influence. Louis's participation in the War of the POLISH SUCCESSION, the War of the AUSTRIAN SUCCESSION, and the SEVEN YEARS WAR cost France its colonial empire. The extravagance, corruption, immorality, and inefficiency of his court ruined the treasury and prepared the French Revolution while the philosophers of the ENLIGHTENMENT helped to undermine the established order. The saying, *Après moi le déluge* [after me, the flood], though wrongly attributed to Louis XV, aptly sums up his irresponsible rule. His grandson and successor, **Louis XVI,** 1754–93, was ill equipped to deal with the problems he inherited. Shy, well-intentioned, stupid, and phlegmatic, he preferred hunting and his locksmith's workshop to his royal duties. What popularity he had was offset by the unpopularity of his pleasure-loving queen, MARIE ANTOINETTE. The intrigues of the queen, of the chief minister, Maurepas, and of the court faction led to the dismissal of his ablest ministers—TURGOT (1776) and NECKER (1781). French intervention in the American Revolution brought the treasury to the brink of bankruptcy; in 1788 Louis recalled Necker, in 1789 he opened the STATES-GENERAL: the FRENCH REVOLUTION entered its first phase. Swayed alternately by his horror of violence and the rash advice of his queen and courtiers, he ended by letting events take their course. In June, 1791, he and his family attempted to flee abroad in disguise but were stopped at Varennes and brought back to Paris. Louis made a sincere attempt at fulfilling the few duties left him under the constitution of 1791, but the suspicion of treason hung over the royal couple, and when France suffered reverses early in the French Revolutionary Wars, this suspicion was naturally increased. The royal family was imprisoned in the Temple (Aug., 1792) and the monarchy was abolished. Tried for treason by the Convention, the king was sentenced to death by a vote of 387 to 334. He was guillotined Jan. 21, 1793, facing death with steadfast courage. His son, **Louis XVII,** 1785–1795?, was imprisoned from 1792 to his death but was proclaimed king in 1793 by the French royalists in exile. The brutality of his jailer, Antoine Simon, hastened the death of the delicate child. The rumor that he actually was rescued and that another child was substituted for him, though impossible to disprove, deserves extreme skepticism; it inspired several impostors to exploit the legend of a LOST DAUPHIN. **Louis XVIII,** 1755–1824, brother of Louis XVI, was known as count of Provence until his proclamation as king by the émigrés (1795). He had fled abroad in 1791, was hunted through Europe by Napoleon I, but was placed on the French throne in 1814 by the victorious allies with the help of TALLEYRAND. He sought to conciliate the former revolutionists and granted a liberal constitutional charter. Forced to flee during the HUNDRED DAYS, he returned after Napoleon's defeat at Waterloo (1815). After the assassination of his nephew, the duc de Berry (1820), the ultraroyalists, led by his brother (later CHARLES X), triumphed over the moderate policy of Louis and his minister Decazes. The new and ultrareactionary VILLÈLE ministry curtailed the franchise and curbed civil liberties and continued this course under Charles X.

Louis, kings of Hungary. **Louis I** (the Great), 1326–82, succeeded his father Charles I in Hungary (1342) and his uncle Casimir III as king of Poland (1370). He conquered Dalmatia from Venice; was recognized as overlord by the princes of Serbia, Walachia, Moldavia, and Bulgaria; campaigned successfully against the Turks; and brought the power of Hungary to its greatest height. Two expeditions to avenge the murder of his brother Andrew at the court of JOANNA I of Naples ended in a truce with Joanna (1352). Louis fostered art and learning and introduced the Italian Renaissance into Hungary. He provided for his succession by marrying his daughter Mary to Sigismund of Luxemburg (later Emperor SIGISMUND) and his daughter JADWIGA to Ladislaus Jagiello of Lithuania (later LADISLAUS II of Poland). **Louis II,** 1506–26, succeeded his father Uladislaus II as king of Hungary and Bohemia (1516). He was slain and his army was destroyed by the Turks in the battle of MOHACS. The crowns of Hungary and Bohemia passed to Louis's brother-in-law, Ferdinand of Austria (later Emperor Ferdinand I).

Louis, titular kings of Naples, dukes of Anjou and counts of Provence (see ANGEVIN dynasty). **Louis I,** 1339–84, second son of John II of France, was a great-great-grandson of Charles II of Naples. In 1380 JOANNA I of Naples adopted him as heir, repudiating her first choice, Charles of Durazzo. Charles, however, conquered Naples and was crowned king as CHARLES III (1381). Louis died while trying to expel his rival. Backed by the papacy and France, his heirs sought to make good their claim, but without lasting effect. His son, **Louis II,** 1377–1417, warred against Charles III and LANCELOT. **Louis III,** 1403–34, son of Louis II, invaded Naples in 1420. Queen JOANNA II called Alfonso V of Aragon to her aid and made him her heir, but after quarreling with Alfonso she adopted Louis instead (1423). Louis had conquered most of the kingdom when he died, leaving his claim to his brother RENÉ.

Louis I, 1838–89, king of Portugal (1861–89).

Louis, Joe (Joseph Louis Barrow) (lo͞o′ĭs), 1914–, American boxer. Won (1937) heavyweight championship by knocking out James J. Braddock. When he first retired (1949) from ring, he had defended his title 24 times, scoring 21 knockouts. Attempted to regain crown, but was defeated (1950) by Ezzard Charles, knocked out (1951) by Rocky Marciano.

Louis, Pierre Charles Alexandre (pyĕr′ shärl älĕksã′drů lwē′), 1787–1872, French physician. Introduced use of statistics in medicine. Noted for research on tuberculosis and typhoid fever.

Louisburg (lo͞o′ĭsbûrg), town (pop. 1,120), E Cape Breton Isl., N.S., Canada, SE of Sydney. Just SW was site of French fort Louisbourg, built 1720–40, guarding entrance to Gulf of St. Lawrence. Port became naval and fishing base. Captured by force of New Englanders 1745, but returned to France 1748. Taken by British 1758, it became Wolfe's base for operations against Quebec (1759). Razed by British 1760. Site now Louisbourg Natl. Historic Park (340 acres; 1928).

Louise, 1776–1810, queen of Prussia, consort of Frederick William III; a princess of Mecklenburg-Strelitz. Her patriotic bearing in the Napoleonic Wars won her great popularity. In 1807 she humiliated herself in vain at Tilsit before Napoleon, begging him to lighten the peace terms for Prussia.

Louise, Lake, 1½ mi. long, alt. 5,680 ft., SW Alta., Canada, in Banff Natl. Park. Resort noted for mountain peaks and snow fields. Discovered 1880.

Louise of Savoy, 1476–1531, mother of Francis I of France, during whose absences she acted as regent. Negotiated Treaty of Cambrai (1529).

Louisiade Archipelago (lo͞oē″zēăd′), comprising c.10 volcanic islands and numerous coral reefs, SW Pacific, part of Territory of Papua. Battle of Coral Sea (1942) was fought near by.

Louisiana, state (50,820 sq. mi.; pop. 2,683,516), S U.S.; admitted 1812 as 18th state (slaveholding); cap. Baton Rouge. Bordered on S by Gulf of Mexico, partly on E by Mississippi R. Low country on Gulf coastal plains and Mississippi alluvial plain; low hills in N. Major cities are New Orleans, Shreveport, Monroe, Alexandria, Lake Charles. Waterways include Red River, Ouachita, Atchafalaya, Calcasieu rivers; Teche, Macon, Lafourche bayous. Pontchartrain is largest lake. Intracoastal Waterway traverses marshes. Produces rice, sugar cane, furs, oil, natural gas, sulphur, salt, cotton, truck, potatoes, livestock, fish. Main industries based on processing these products. Visited by Spanish 1541–42; claimed for France by La Salle in 1682. Natchitoches oldest town (1714). Mississippi Scheme of John Law brought large settlement. La. W of Mississippi R. ceded to Spain (1762), E of river to England (1763). French settlers arrived from Acadia. Spanish La. retroceded to France 1800; went to U.S. in Louisiana Purchase (1803). Settlement of West Florida Controversy extended area. Andrew Jackson defeated British at battle of New Orleans (1815). Progress came from cotton gin, new sugar-refining methods, steamboat. Joined Confederacy 1861. Adm. Farragut captured New Orleans (1862); Grant's Vicksburg campaign left only W La. to South. Suffered much in Reconstruction. Politics colorful (esp. governorship of Huey P. Long). Economy has changed through fall of plantations, rise of farm tenancy, discovery of oil and gas.

Louisiana, city (pop. 4,389), NE Mo., on the Mississippi below Hannibal. Ammonia plant was converted to study and produce synthetic fuels.

Louisiana Purchase. Pres. Jefferson, fearing the results of French occupation of New Orleans, instructed Robert R. Livingston, U.S. minister to France, to attempt to purchase New Orleans and West Florida from France. Napoleon, to whom Louisiana was of diminishing importance, permitted his ministers to open negotiations for sale of all of Louisiana. Purchase, in which James Monroe participated, was accomplished at a price of about $15,000,000; made effective by a treaty dated April 30, 1803, and ratified by U.S. on Oct. 21, 1803. Boundaries were not settled for several years (see West Florida Controversy). From Louisiana Purchase, which more than doubled size of U.S., were carved all or part of 13 states.

Louisiana State University and Agricultural and Mechanical College, at Baton Rouge; land-grant, state supported, coed.; chartered 1853, opened 1860, moved 1869, became university 1870, and absorbed Agricultural and Mechanical Col. 1877. W. T. Sherman was first head. Has medical center in New Orleans, and Audubon Sugar School. Greatly expanded during Huey Long's regime.

Louis Napoleon: see Napoleon III.

Louis period styles, 1610–1793, a series of modes of interior decoration in France. Louis XIII period (1610–43) was transition from the baroque to classical dignity of Louis XIV style (1643–1715), marked by extensive use of colorful tapestries, rich hangings, murals, and large mirrors. Furniture was made of ebony or covered with silver, gilt, or lacquer, and was scaled to huge proportions of rooms. Regence style (1715–23) was transition to intimate gaiety of Louis XV style (1723–74) with its free curves, smaller rooms, and use of chinoiserie and rococo ornament. Classical revival of Louis XVI style (1774–93) brought return of straight lines, symmetry, and proportions in wall treatment and furniture. See *ill.*, p. 456.

Louis Philippe (lwē′ fēlēp′), 1773–1850, king of the French (1830–48); son of Philippe Égalité (see Orléans, Louis Philippe Joseph, duc d'). Deserted French army 1793; lived in England and U.S. until Bourbon Restoration. As duke of Orléans, he was prominent in liberal opposition to Charles X, after whose overthrow (see July Revolution) he was chosen "king of the French." As king, he affected bourgeois manners, symbolized by his eternal umbrella, and became known as the "citizen king." His reign, the "July Monarchy," gave business its fullest opportunities and was marked by colonial expansion (the conquest of Algeria) and the effects of the Industrial Revolution. It was an era of peace and uninhibited money making. The constitutional charter of 1814 was liberalized but continued to exclude the nonpropertied from the polls. The growth of the industrial proletariat and its inhuman living conditions led to the rise of radical doctrines (e.g., of Karl Marx and Louis Blanc). In the arts, romanticism reacted against the dull conventionality of the era. Against growing opposition, the king and his successive cabinets resorted to reactionary measures. Guizot was the leading political figure after 1840; Thiers passed to the liberal opposition. A systematic campaign for electoral reform helped to precipitate the February Revolution of 1848. Louis Philippe abdicated and went to England. His supporters and those of his descendants were called Orléanists (see Orléans, family), as opposed to legitimists (adherents of the senior branch of the Bourbon dynasty).

Louis the Bavarian: see Louis IV, emperor.

Louis the Child, 893–911, German king (899–911), son of Emperor Arnulf and last of German line of Carolingians.

Louis the German, c.804–876, East Frankish king; son of Emperor Louis I, who gave him Bavaria in 817. In the conflict between his brother Lothair I and his father, Louis sided now with the one, now with the other. After his father's death (840), he joined forces with his half-brother Charles the Bald (later

Emperor CHARLES II) against Lothair, whom they defeated at Fontenoy (841) and forced to accept the Treaty of VERDUN (843), which made Germany and France separate kingdoms. Louis later campaigned against Charles (858–59, 875), but the two agreed on partitioning Lotharingia in the Treaty of MERSEN (870). Louis's succession was divided among his sons Louis the Younger, Charles the Fat (later Emperor Charles III), and Carloman.

Louis the Pious: see LOUIS I, emperor.

Louis the Stammerer: see LOUIS II, king of France.

Louis the Younger, d. 882, German king, ruler (876–82) over Saxony, Franconia, and Thuringia; son of LOUIS THE GERMAN. Shared succession with his brothers CARLOMAN (d. 880) and Charles the Fat (later Emperor CHARLES III).

Louisville. **1** (lo͞o'ĭsvĭl) City (pop. 2,231), E Ga., SW of Augusta and on Ogeechee R. Laid out 1786 as prospective cap. of Ga. State buildings completed 1795. Seat of government until 1804. **2** (lo͞o'ēvĭl) City (pop. 369,129), N Ky., SW of Cincinnati at Falls of the Ohio (power); laid out 1773 and settled after G. R. Clark built fort 1778. Fort Nelson built by Clark 1782. Union base in Civil War, it grew as river, then as rail shipping point. State's largest city, it is port and industrial, financial, and market center. Has railroad shops, distilleries, and meat, tobacco, oil, and food processing plants. Seat of Univ. of Louisville (city supported; coed.; opened as medical institute 1837, chartered as university 1846) with Speed Scientific School and Louisville Municipal Col. for Negroes; and Nazareth Col. (R.C.; for women; 1920). Here are Churchill Downs (Kentucky Derby race track), grave of G. R. Clark, and (near by) home and tomb of Zachary Taylor. **3** (lo͞o'ĭsvĭl) City (pop. 5,282), E central Miss., SW of Columbus, in timber and farm area.

Louisville, University of: see LOUISVILLE, Ky.

Loup, river formed in E central Nebr. by junction of North Loup R., 212 mi. long, and Middle Loup R., 221 mi. long. Flows 68 mi. E to Platte R. at Columbus. Used in power project.

Lourdes (lo͝ord, lo͝ordz, Fr. lo͝ord), town (pop. 12,421), Hautes-Pyrénées dept., SW France. Near-by grotto, where Our Lady of Lourdes appeared to St. BERNADETTE in 1858, is visited by up to a million pilgrims a year seeking miraculous cures.

Lourenço Marques (lôrĕn'sō mär'kĕs), city (pop. 93,516), cap. of Mozambique; port on Delagoa Bay. Named for Lourenço Marques, Portuguese trader who explored area in 1544. Chief exports include coal and livestock products from South Africa.

louse, name both for a bloodsucking and for a chewing or biting insect. Both groups are small wingless insects. Bloodsuckers have piercing, sucking mouth parts, are external parasites of man and other mammals. The biting or chewing lice attack birds, including poultry, some mammals; they feed on epidermal scales, hairs, feathers, dried blood; usually associated with uncleanliness. See *ill.*, p. 601.

Louth (louth, loudh), maritime county (317 sq. mi.; pop. 66,194), Ireland, in Leinster; co. town Dundalk. Smallest Irish county, i chief occupations are dairying and fishin Has some linen mfg.

Louvain (lo͞ovān', Fr. lo͞ovē'), Flemish *Leuve* city (pop. 37,188), Brabant prov., centr Belgium, on Dyle R. Brewing industry. Wa cap. of Brabant until 15th cent. Louvain an episcopal see and has one of world's lead ing Catholic universities (founded 1426) The university library, with unique colle tions, was destroyed in World War I, rebui with funds from U.S., and destroyed agai in World War II. The Gothic city hall (1447 63) was also damaged.

L'Ouverture, Toussaint: see TOUSSAIN L'OUVERTURE.

Louvois, Michel Le Tellier, marquis de (mēshĕ lů tĕlyā' märkē' dů lo͞ovwä'), 1639–91 French minister of war under Louis XIV Introduced completely modernized militar system which made French army the strong est in Europe and long served as universa model. Gaining much influence after deat of Colbert (1683), he was largely responsibl for the ruthless execution of the revocatio of the Edict of Nantes (1685) and for th devastation of the Palatinate (1689).

Louvre (lo͞o'vûr), art museum, Paris. Buil 1204 by Philip II as fortress-palace, recon structed after 1541, and converted into na tional museum by Napoleon. Among it treasures are Leonardo's *Mona Lisa* and th sculpture *Victory of Samothrace*.

Louÿs, Pierre (pyĕr' lwē'), 1870–1925, Frenc novelist and poet. Noted for novel *Aphrodit* (1896) and poems *Chansons de Biliti* (1894).

love bird: see PARAKEET.

love-in-a-mist, annual plant (*Nigella dama scena*) with wispy blue or white flowers an finely cut foliage. Seeds of *N. sativa,* calle black cumin, have been used in the Ol World for seasoning.

Lovejoy, Elijah Parish, 1802–37, America abolitionist. Edited *Observer* at Alton, Ill Killed defending press against mob, Nov. 7 1837. His martyrdom advanced abolitionis cause. His brother, **Owen Lovejoy,** 1811–64 witness of killing, took up cause and becam leader of Ill. abolitionists.

Lovejoy, Ill.: see BROOKLYN.

Lovelace, Richard, 1618–57, English poet, one of CAVALIER POETS. A royalist, he was imprisoned by Commonwealth in 1648. His first and chief work, *Lucasta: Epodes, Odes, Sonnets, Songs, &c.* (1649), includes well-known lyrics "To Althea from Prison" and "To Lucasta, Going to the Wars."

Lovelock, city (pop. 1,604), W Nev., on Humboldt R. Center of Humboldt project (1935–36).

Low, David (lō), 1891–, British political cartoonist, b. New Zealand. Comments perceptively on national and international affairs. Created "Colonel Blimp," symbolizing the British ultraconservative.

Low, Seth, 1850–1916, American political reformer, president of Columbia Univ. (1889–1901). Mayor of New York city (1901–3); reformed police and education departments, reorganized city finances.

Low, W(ill) H(icok), 1853–1932, American

painter, an early exponent of the plein-air school.

Low Archipelago: see TUAMOTU ISLANDS.

Low Church: see ENGLAND, CHURCH OF.

Low Countries, region of NW Europe comprising the NETHERLANDS, BELGIUM, and the grand duchy of LUXEMBOURG. The name is a political and historic rather than a geographic concept. See also FLANDERS; BRABANT; HOLLAND; NETHERLANDS, AUSTRIAN and SPANISH.

Lowell, distinguished American family of Mass. **Francis Cabot Lowell,** 1775–1817, a pioneer in textile manufacture, was the chief mover in building at Waltham, Mass., the first U.S. factory to perform all operations needed to convert raw cotton into cloth. Lowell, Mass., was named for him. His nephew, **James Russell Lowell,** 1819–91, was an outstanding poet of the 19th cent. His poetry ranges from the didactic (e.g., *The Vision of Sir Launfal,* 1848) to the satiric (notably in the *Biglow Papers,* in Yankee dialect, collected as books 1848, 1867) and acutely critical (*A Fable for Critics,* 1848). He was professor of French and Spanish at Harvard (1856–86), editor of several periodicals (notably the *Atlantic Monthly,* 1857–61; the *North American Review,* 1864–72), and an essayist. He served also as minister at Madrid (1877–80) and London (1880–85) and did much to gain European respect for American letters and customs. Of a later generation of the family two brothers and a sister were especially well known. **Percival Lowell,** 1855–1916, was an astronomer, an authority on the planet Mars, and founder (1894) of Lowell Observatory, Flagstaff, Ariz. **Abbott Lawrence Lowell,** 1856–1943, was professor of political science and later (1909–33), president of Harvard. There he modified the elective system, set up general examinations in their major fields for B.A. candidates, and instituted the tutorial system—all with a view to increasing general education and decreasing specialization for undergraduates. **Amy Lowell,** 1874–1925, was a poet. After writing conventional poetry in *A Dome of Many-coloured Glass* (1912), she joined the IMAGISTS and attracted much interest with her free verse and polyphonic prose (as in *Sword Blades and Poppy Seed,* 1914; *Can Grande's Castle,* 1918; *What's o'Clock,* 1925). She wrote a life of Keats (1925).

Lowell, city (pop. 97,249), NE Mass., on Merrimack R. at junction with Concord R. and NNW of Boston; settled 1653. Became great textile center after mills were built 1822; mfg. also of electrical and leather products. Has Lowell Textile Inst. (coed.; 1895). Whistler's birthplace preserved.

Lower Austria, Ger. *Niederösterreich,* province (7,097 sq. mi.; pop. 1,249,610), NE Austria. Though outside its boundaries, Vienna is provincial cap. Over half of Austrian industry centers in Vienna and Wiener Neustadt basins; there is oil near Zistersdorf. Most of province is hilly and agr. area. History is that of Austria.

Lower Avon: see AVON **1,** river, England.

Lower California, Span. *Baja California,* peninsula, c.760 mi. long, and 30–150 mi. wide, NW Mexico, separating Gulf of California from Pacific. Politically divided into N territory (27,655 sq. mi.; pop. 226,871; cap. Mexicali) and S territory (27,979 sq. mi.; pop. 60,495; cap. La Paz). Most of land is semiarid and undeveloped but there is copper, silver, and gold mining and some pearl fishing. Agua Caliente and Tijuana are resorts in N territory.

Lower Canada: see QUEBEC, province.

Lower Saxony, Ger. *Niedersachsen,* German state (18,231 sq. mi.; pop. 6,795,128), NW Germany; cap. Hanover. Formed 1946 in British zone of occupation, it includes former Prussian prov. of HANOVER and former states of BRUNSWICK, OLDENBURG, and SCHAUMBURG-LIPPE. Area has had no historic unity since 1180, when Emperor Frederick I broke up duchy of Henry the Lion of Saxony. Name continued as geographic expression and designated (16th cent.–1806) an imperial circle of Holy Roman Empire. Lower Saxony joined Federal Republic of [West] Germany in 1949.

Lowestoft (lō'stôft, –stŭf), municipal borough (pop. 42,837), Suffolk East, England; fishing port, yachting center, and resort. Lighthouse marks most easterly point of England. Lowestoft ware, fine bone china, was made here 1757–1802.

Lowie, Robert Harry, 1883–, American anthropologist, b. Vienna. An authority on North American Indians, he contributed much to anthropological theory.

Loyalists, in American Revolution, colonials who adhered to British cause. Most numerous among propertied class, clergy, and officeholders under crown. Strongest in far southern and Middle Atlantic colonies. Fighting sometimes led to civil war with raids and reprisals. Many fled to British-held lands. Patriots confiscated many Loyalist estates.

Loyalty Islands, coral group (800 sq. mi.; pop. 11,854), S Pacific, 60 mi. E of NEW CALEDONIA, of which they are a dependency. Chief export is copra.

Loyang (lō'yäng'), city (pop. 77,159), NW Honan prov., China. Agr. and stock-raising center. Was cap. of Chou dynasty (770–255 B.C.) and Eastern Han dynasty (c.100 A.D.). Continued intermittently to be imperial residence until 13th cent. Nationalist government briefly moved here from Nanking in 1932. Called Honan until 1913.

Loyola, Ignatius of: see IGNATIUS OF LOYOLA, SAINT.

Loyola University (loiō'lu). **1** Mainly at Chicago; Jesuit, partly coed.; chartered and opened 1870 as St. Ignatius Col., renamed 1909. Includes a liberal-arts college at West Baden Springs, Ind. Has large collection of writings on the Jesuits. **2** See NEW ORLEANS, La. **3 Loyola University of Los Angeles:** see Los ANGELES, Calif.

Lozère (lôzĕr'), department (2,000 sq. mi.; pop. 90,523), S France, in Languedoc; cap. Mende.

Lu, chemical symbol of the element LUTETIUM.

Lualaba: see CONGO, river.

Luanda (lōōän'dŭ), city (pop. 66,932), cap. of Angola; port on the Atlantic; founded 1575. Center of slave traffic to Brazil, 17th–18th cent. Formerly called Loanda.

Lubbock, city (pop. 71,747), NW Texas, S of

Amarillo on Llano Estacado; founded 1891. Processes and ships cotton, grain, poultry, dairy products, cattle, and oil. Seat of Texas Technological Col. (coed.; 1923).

Lubec (lo͞o'bĕk), resort and fishing town (pop. 2,973), SE Maine, on PASSAMAQUODDY BAY S of Eastport. WEST QUODDY HEAD is SE.

Lübeck (lo͞o'bĕk, Ger. lü'bĕk), city (pop. 237,860), Schleswig-Holstein, N Germany; a major Baltic seaport on mouth of Trave R. Produces machinery, textiles, marzipan. Its third city charter, granted 1158 by Henry the Lion, was copied by many N German cities. A free imperial city from 1226, Lübeck under its merchant aristocracy rose to leadership of the HANSEATIC LEAGUE, whose diets met here until 1630. Occupied by the French 1806–13, it joined in 1815 the German Confederation as a free Hanseatic city, a status it retained until 1937, when it was inc. into Schleswig-Holstein prov. of Prussia. Despite damage received in World War II, the inner city remains a monument of medieval N German architecture. There are several fine Gothic churches (13th and 14th cent.), old patrician residences, and the Holstentor, a famous city gate flanked by two towers (15th cent.). Thomas Mann, born in Lübeck, describes the city in his *Buddenbrooks.* The city was not part of the former bishopric of Lübeck, whose rulers resided from c.1300 at near-by Eutin. Territorial princes of the Holy Roman Empire, the bishops accepted the Reformation (16th cent.). The prince-bishopric passed to a branch of the Danish house of Holstein-Gottorp, which in 1773 also acquired the duchy of Oldenburg. Secularized in 1803, it became a district of Oldenburg but was transferred to Schleswig-Holstein in 1937.

Lubitsch, Ernst (ĕrnst' lo͞o'bĭch), 1892–1947, German film director; in U.S. after 1922. Noted for such films as *Design for Living* and *Ninotchka.*

Lublin (lo͞o'blēn), city (pop. c.111,000), E Poland. Trade and mfg. center. One of oldest Polish towns, it was the scene of the diet which united Poland with Lithuania (1569). It passed to Austria 1795, to Russia 1815. Seat of temporary Polish Socialist government (1918) and of provisional Polish government after liberation by Soviet forces in 1944. The latter was broadened by Yalta Conference (Feb., 1945) to include members of London cabinet of Polish government in exile and recognized by Potsdam Conference (Aug., 1945) as sole Polish authority. Catholic university of Lublin was founded 1918.

lubrication, introduction of a substance (lubricant) between contact surfaces of moving parts to reduce friction. Unlubricated surfaces produce dry or solid friction, resulting in injury by abrasion and in generation of heat causing one part to "seize" the other because of unequal expansion, or to develop (in metals) "hot points" which may cause welding of metals. Lubrication aims to produce thin-film or (better) fluid-film friction. In thin-film friction, boundary layers of the lubricant tend to be absorbed by contact surfaces thus producing slipperiness and separation which prevent intermolecular attraction between surfaces. Thin-film friction usually occurs with heavy loads, slow speeds, or intermittent action. In fluid or thick-film friction, moving surfaces form separative pressure film which carries load. Excessively thick fluid film increases internal friction in fluid causing power loss. Lubricants, usually a fat or oil, grease, or slippery solid, are obtained largely from petroleum or shale oil. Machinery requires controllable, varied lubricators, ranging from drop-feed and wick-feed types to collar devices and bath-oiling and splash-oiling arrangements.

Lucan (Marcus Annaeus Lucanus) (lū'kŭn), A.D. 39–A.D. 65, Latin poet. Forced to kill himself for plotting against Nero. Ten books of his epic *Pharsalia* (on civil war between Caesar and Pompey) survive.

Lucania (lūkā'nēŭ), anc. region of S Italy between Gulf of Taranto and Tyrrhenian Sea; now in Campania and Basilicata. Italic tribes and Greek colonists were subjected by Rome (3d cent. B.C.). Chief cities were Heraclea and Paestum.

Lucas van Leyden (lü'käs vän lī'dŭn), 1494–1533, Dutch painter and engraver, whose real name was Lucas Jacobsz. His realistic and dramatic pictures represent the beginning of Dutch genre painting. Also depicted biblical scenes.

Lucca (lo͝ok'kä), city (pop. 32,896), Tuscany, central Italy, near Tyrrhenian Sea. Trade center for olive oil and wine; tobacco mfg. A Roman town, it became (6th cent.) cap. of a Lombard duchy and (12th cent.) seat of a free commune, later a prosperous republic. It was a major medieval banking center and famous for its velvets and damasks. Save for short periods under tyrants, notably CASTRACANI, and foreign rule, republic was independent until Napoleon I made it a principality in 1805. It became part of duchy of Parma in 1817, of grand duchy of Tuscany in 1847. Annexed by Sardinia 1860. Height of economic and artistic flower came 12th–15th cent., when the cathedral and churches of San Frediano and San Michele were built.

Lucerne (lo͞osûrn'), Ger. *Luzern,* canton (576 sq. mi.; pop. 223,409), central Switzerland. Agr., pastoral, and forested. Population is mainly German-speaking and Catholic. One of FOUR FOREST CANTONS, its history is that of its cap., **Lucerne** (pop. 60,365), which grew up around an 8th-cent. monastery. It became a Hapsburg possession in 1291 but joined Swiss Confederation 1332 and gained full freedom 1386. Chief town of the SONDERBUND 1845–47. Thorvaldsen's Lion of Lucerne monument (1820–21) memorializes SWISS GUARDS. City has 14th–15th-cent. covered bridges and 8th-cent. church (Hofkirche). There are machine and printing industries. A summer resort, Lucerne is on **Lake of Lucerne,** Ger. *Vierwaldstättersee* (area 44 sq. mi.), noted for scenery. Lake borders cantons of Lucerne, Uri, Schwyz, and Unterwalden. Reuss R. flows through it.

lucerne: see ALFALFA.

Lucian, fl. 2d cent., Greek prose writer. Wrote nearly 80 works, known for their wit and vigorous satire. Most outstanding are his dialogues (*Dialogues of the Gods, Dialogues of the Dead,* etc.) satirizing ancient mythology and contemporary philosophy. *The True History* parodied incredible adventure stories.

Lucifer (lū'sĭfůr) [Latin,= light-bearing], the planet Venus as the morning star. In Isaiah 14.12, Lucifer refers to king of Babylon, but was misunderstood to mean the fallen angel. Hence term became a name for SATAN. Name in Greek was Phosphorus.

Lucilius, Caius (kā'ůs lūsĭ'lēůs), c.180–102? B.C., Latin poet. Founder of Latin satire.

Lucioni, Luigi (lwē'jē lōōchō'nē), 1900–, American painter, b. Italy. Paints still life, landscapes, and portraits in polished style, accurate drawing, clear color.

Luck, Ukraine: see LUTSK.

Luckner, Felix, Graf von (fā'lĭks gräf' fůn lōōk'nůr), 1886–, German naval hero of World War I. In command of the commerce raider *Seeadler* he destroyed $25,000,000 worth of Allied shipping before his capture (1918). Was nicknamed "Sea Devil."

Lucknow (lŭk'nou), city (pop. 387,177) SW Uttar Pradesh, India, on Gumti R. Was cap. of nawabs of Oudh, 1775–1856. During Sepoy Rebellion, British garrison and colony were besieged here, July–Nov., 1857. City retaken 1858 by Sir Colin Campbell. Seat of Lucknow Univ. Rail and industrial center.

Lucrece (lūkrēs') or **Lucretia** (lūkrē'shů), in Roman legend, virtuous matron. Victim of rape by Sextus, son of Tarquinius Superbus, she begged her husband to avenge her and stabbed herself. The ensuing revolt drove the TARQUINS from Rome.

Lucretius (Titus Lucretius Carus) (lūkrē'shůs), c.99 B.C.–c.55 B.C., Roman poet. His one celebrated work, *De rerum natura* [*On the Nature of Things*], in beautiful hexameter verse, sets forth arguments founded upon Epicurean philosophy. It urges man not to fear the gods or death, since "man is lord of himself." His proof, based on an atomic theory (not the same as modern atomic theory), states that the universe came into being through the workings of natural laws in the combining of atoms.

Lucullus (Lucius Licinius Lucullus Ponticus) (lūkŭ'lůs), c.110–56 B.C., Roman general. A faithful follower of Sulla in the Social War, he was given offices and became successful commander against MITHRIDATES VI of Pontus. Attempts to reform Roman administration in Asia made him unpopular, and he was replaced by Pompey. In retirement Lucullus was known for showy elegance of life.

Ludendorff, Erich (ā'rĭkh lōō'důndôrf), 1865–1937, German general. As chief of staff to HINDENBURG during World War I he was largely responsible for the victories credited to his superior. He later took part in ultranationalist movements, notably in Munich "beer-hall putsch" of HITLER (1923). With his second wife, Dr. Mathilde Ludendorff, he founded an "Aryan" cult, wrote cranky pamphlets.

Ludington, city (pop. 9,506), N Mich., harbor on L. Michigan at mouth of Pere Marquette R. Resort with fishing and some mfg. Monument marks Father Marquette's first burial place.

Ludlow, Roger, fl. 1590–1664, one of founders of Conn., b. England. Founded Fairfield in 1639. Completed first codification of Conn. laws (1650).

Ludlow (lŭd'lō), municipal borough (pop. 6,455), Shropshire, England. Has old houses and ruins of 11th-cent. castle. Butler wrote *Hudibras* here.

Ludlow. 1 City (pop. 6,374), N Ky., on Ohio R. Suburb of Covington and Cincinnati. Rail center with mfg. of furniture and machinery. **2** Town (pop. 8,660), S Mass., NE of Springfield; settled c.1750. Jute and flax products.

Ludwig. For German rulers thus named, see LOUIS.

Ludwig, Emil (ā'mēl lōōt'vĭkh), 1881–1948, German author. Among his translated popular humanized biographies are *Goethe* (1920), *Napoleon* (1924), *Bismarck* (1926), and *The Son of Man* (1928; a life of Jesus).

Ludwig, Karl (kärl'), 1816–95, German physiologist, famous as professor and head of physiological institute at Univ. of Leipzig.

Ludwigshafen (lōōt"vĭkhs-hä'fůn), city (pop. 122,329), Rhineland-Palatinate, W Germany, on the Rhine. An important transshipment point, it has a large chemical industry and mfg. of machinery and automobiles. Heavily damaged in World War II.

Lufkin, city (pop. 15,135), E Texas, ENE of Houston; founded 1882. Center for lumbering, newsprint mfg. (from native pine), woodworking. Also has farm products, foundries, and livestock.

Lugano (lōōgä'nō), town (pop. 17,718), Ticino canton, S Switzerland. A scenic summer resort, it is on **Lake of Lugano,** Ital. *Lago di Lugano* or *Ceresio* (area c.19 sq. mi.), which lies both in Switzerland and in Italy.

Lugansk, Ukraine: see VOROSHILOVGRAD.

Lugo (lōō'gō), city (pop. 21,115), cap. of Lugo prov., NW Spain, in Galicia, on Miño R. Agr. center. Has Roman walls and 12th-cent. cathedral.

Luini, Bernardino (bārnärdē'nō lōōē'nē), c.1480–1532, Italian painter, influenced by Leonardo; known for graceful female figures.

Luitpold (lōō'ĭtpôlt), 1821–1912, regent of Bavaria (1886–1912). Ruled for his insane nephews LOUIS II and OTTO I.

Luke, Saint, Gentile physician, friend and companion of St. Paul and St. Mark. Since 2d cent. regarded as author of the Gospel according to St. Luke and the Acts of the Apostles. Acts 20; 21; Col. 4.14; 2 Tim. 4.11. His symbol: an ox. Feast: Oct. 28.

Luke, Gospel according to Saint, book of New Testament. It gives a unique account of Jesus' birth, tells of His ministry, and ends with the passion and resurrection. Verses 9.51–18.14 mainly unparalleled in other Gospels; contain many favorite passages. See also SYNOPTIC GOSPELS.

Lukeman, (Henry) Augustus, 1871–1935, American sculptor of historical monuments. Completed the gigantic sculptures on Stone Mt., Ga., started by Gutzon Borglum.

Luks, George (lōōks), 1867–1933, American portrait and genre painter. A member of The Eight.

Lule (lü'lů), Swed. *Lule älv,* river rising in N Sweden and flowing 280 mi. from Lapland mts. to the Baltic at Lulea. Its potential power, partly utilized at PORJUS, exceeds 2,000,000 hp.

Lulea (lü'lůō"), Swed. *Luleå,* city (pop. 22,514), co. seat of Norrbotten co., N

Sweden, port (ice-bound in winter) on Gulf of Bothnia at mouth of Lule R. Exports include Lapland iron ore, timber, and reindeer hides. There are iron smelting and pulp milling.

Lull, Ramon (rämōn' lo͞ol'), or **Raymond Lully,** c.1236–1315, Catalan philosopher. Turning to religion in 1266, he became a Franciscan and longed to convert Islam. His study of Arabic and Moslem culture enriched his teaching (in France and Majorca), and he went to Africa and the East. His works (notably *Ars major*) argue that all articles of faith can be demonstrated by logic; set forth an elaborate system of symbols; and express profound mysticism. Later generations supposed him a magician.

Lull, Richard Swann, 1867–, American paleontologist. He taught at Yale (1906–36) and was director of Peabody Museum (1922–36). He was editor of the *American Journal of Science* (1933–49) and author of *Organic Evolution* (1917; rev. ed. 1948).

Lully, Jean Baptiste (zhã' bäptēst' lülē'), 1632–87, French composer, b. Italy. In 1653 he became chamber composer and conductor to Louis XIV. He composed many ballets to plays of Molière and others but is best known for his operas. Among them are *Alceste* (1674), *Cadmus et Hermione* (1673), *Amadis* (1684), and *Armide* (1686). He created a style which held the French operatic stage until the advent of Gluck.

Lully, Raymond: see LULL, RAMON.

lumber, name used in U.S. and Canada for timber which has been cut into boards. In U.S. it was one of first industries; Maine was the leading early producer but later Oregon, Wash., and Calif. assumed the lead and southern states became increasingly important. Logging (felling and preparation of timber for shipment to sawmills) was a frontier industry. Stories and legends of feats of the lumberjack are a colorful chapter in American folklore.

Lumberton, town (pop. 9,186), S N.C., on Lumber R., and S of Fayetteville. Processes tobacco, textiles, and lumber.

Lumière, Louis Jean (lümyĕr'), 1864–1948, and **Auguste Marie Louis Nicholas Lumière,** 1862–, French inventors, brothers. Invented (1895) the cinematograph, first mechanism to project moving pictures on a screen where they could be seen by an audience.

luminescence: see FLUORESCENCE; PHOSPHORESCENCE.

Luna, Alvaro de (älvä'rō dā lo͞o'nä), 1388?–1453, constable of Castile. As favorite of John II he virtually ruled kingdom until the queen's enmity led to his execution.

Luna, Pedro de, 1328–1423, Spanish cardinal, antipope as Benedict XIII (1394–1417; see SCHISM, GREAT). He was a supporter of ROBERT OF GENEVA and was elected to succeed him. As France shifted allegiance from and to the Avignon papacy, Benedict's position shifted. He was finally deposed at the Council of CONSTANCE (1417), but refused to accept the election of MARTIN V.

Lunacharsky, Anatoli Vasilyevich (ŭnŭtô'lyē vŭsē'lyŭvĭch lo͞onŭchär'skē), 1875–1933, Russian revolutionist, dramatist, and poet. As commissar of education (1917–29) he greatly encouraged the Soviet theater. Three of his plays are available in English (*Three Plays*, 1923).

lunacy: see INSANITY.

lunar caustic: see SILVER.

Lund (lŭnd), city (pop. 33,954), Malmohus co., S Sweden, NE of Malmo. It is a university town and publishing center. University was founded 1666 by Charles XI. City was mentioned c.920 in the sagas. It became an archbishop's see in 11th cent. and a Lutheran bishopric in 1536. In 1658 it passed from Denmark to Sweden. There is a 10th-cent. cathedral.

Lundy's Lane, locality just W of Niagara Falls, scene of stubborn engagement of War of 1812, fought July 25, 1814. American forces pushing into Canada encountered British troops. After night-long fight against superior numbers, Americans withdrew to Fort Erie. Both sides had heavy casualties.

Lüneburg (lü'nŭbo͝ork), city (pop. 58,269), Lower Saxony, NW Germany, on Ilmenau R. Salt- and chemical works. It was long cap. of dukes of Brunswick-Lüneburg (see HANOVER). Important member of Hanseatic League. Late Gothic in character as exemplified in huge city hall (12th–18th cent.) and gabled houses. Has salt springs and mud baths. **Lüneburger Heide** (lü'nŭbo͝orgŭr hī'dŭ), a vast heath, lies between Elbe and Aller rivers; sheep raising.

Lunéville (lünāvēl'), town (pop. 19,065), Meurthe-et-Moselle dept., NE France, on Meurthe R. Faïence industry. Treaty signed here 1801 between France and Austria substantially renewed terms of Treaty of CAMPO FORMIO. Palace (18th-cent.), damaged in World War II, was residence of STANISLAUS I.

lungs, respiratory organs of air-breathing vertebrates. In humans two lungs invested with membranes (pleura) lie in chest cavity. Carbon dioxide and oxygen are interchanged in air cells. See *ill.*, p. 763.

Lunt, Alfred, 1893–, American actor; husband of Lynn FONTANNE with whom he has acted since 1924.

lupine or **lupin,** annual or perennial leguminous plant, of genus *Lupinus,* sometimes grown for forage and cover crop, but mostly for ornament in North America. Varieties of *Lupinus perennis* bear spikes of richly colored bonnet-shaped blooms. Others include tree lupine (*L. arborescens*) and BLUEBONNET.

Luray (lo͞orā'), tourist town (pop. 2,731), N Va., in Shenandoah Valley SW of Front Royal. Hq. of Shenandoah Natl. Park. Here are **Luray Caverns,** limestone caves known for beauty of formations.

Luria, Isaac ben Solomon (lo͞o'rēŭ), 1534–72, Jewish cabalist, called Ari, b. Jerusalem; leader of a large circle of mystics. Also spelled Loria.

Lusatia (lo͞osā'shŭ), Ger. *Lausitz,* Pol. *Łużyce,* region (pop. c.1,000,000), E Germany, bounded by Lusatian Mts. in S and by Oder R. in E. Chief towns: Bautzen, Görlitz, Sagan, Zittau. Region consists of Upper Lusatia, in NE Saxony, and Lower Lusatia, in S Brandenburg and Lower Silesia. Lusatian Neisse R. separates Russian-occupied and

Polish-administered parts of E Germany. Agr. and heavily forested, Lusatia also produces textiles and lignite. Lusatians (also called Sorbs) are descended from Slavic WENDS; some, as in SPREE FOREST, still speak Wendish. Region was colonized by Germans in 10th cent., frequently changed masters. Saxon from 1635 to 1815, when larger part went to Prussia.

Lüshun, China: see PORT ARTHUR.

Lusiads, The: see CAMÕES, LUÍS DE.

Lusignan (lüzēnyã'), French noble family. It was prominent in the Crusades and ruled Cyprus 1192–1489. Its ancestral castle, in Poitou, was built according to legend by the fair MELUSINE. Guy of Lusignan (d. 1194) married Sibylla, sister of Baldwin IV of Jerusalem, and was chosen king of Jerusalem on the death of Baldwin V (1186). Defeated and captured at Hattin by Saladin in 1187, he was released in 1188 and began the siege of Acre, which was taken in 1191 with the help of Richard I of England and Philip II of France (Third Crusade). After Sibylla's death (1190), Guy's right to the throne was contested by CONRAD of Montferrat, who had Philip II's support. Guy abdicated 1192 but was invested as king of Cyprus by Richard I. Cyprus continued under Guy's brother AMALRIC II and his descendants. A branch of the family also ruled Lesser Armenia (Cilicia) 1342–75, and the family listed the kingships of Jerusalem and Armenia among its sonorous but largely empty titles. Cyprus flourished under Lusignan rule and was a center of French medieval culture, but it declined after 1370, becoming dependent on Venice, Genoa, and Egypt. The rule of Caterina CORNARO ended with outright annexation by Venice (1489).

Lusin (lōō'sĭn'), 1881–1936, Chinese author. Known primarily for his brilliant political essays, although he first won fame for his short stories. Complete works are translated into English.

Lusitania (lūsĭtā'nēŭ), Roman province in Iberian peninsula, including modern central Portugal and much of W Spain. It was inhabited by the Lusitani, tribes subdued by Rome only after death of their leader, Viriatus, in 139 B.C. Old identification of ancestors of the Portuguese with the Lusitanians is now largely ignored.

Lusitania, liner under British registration sunk without warning off Irish coast by German submarine on May 7, 1915. Of more than 1,000 lost, 114 were American citizens. Incident had much to do with preparing way for U.S. entry into World War I.

lusterware: see POTTERY.

lute: see STRINGED INSTRUMENTS.

Lutetia, Roman name of PARIS, France.

lutetium (lōōtē'shēŭm), rare element (symbol = Lu; see also ELEMENT, table); metal of rare earths.

Luther, Hans (häns' lōō'tŭr), 1879–, German statesman. As finance minister (1923–24) he helped Schacht stabilize currency. Later was chancellor (1925–26), president of Reichsbank (1930–33), German ambassador to U.S. (1933–37).

Luther, Martin, 1483–1546, German leader of Protestant Reformation. By 1505 he had completed master's examination at Univ. of Erfurt and began study of law. Instead, he entered monastery of Augustine friars, was ordained priest in 1507, and was assigned to the Univ. of Wittenberg. Through his study and thought he became convinced that sinner's hope lay entirely in grace of God and redemption by Christ, accepted through faith. In 1510, on mission to Rome, he was shocked by spiritual laxity in high church circles. Returning to Wittenberg, he formulated plans for reformation of church doctrine and practices. In 1517 he protested dispensation of INDULGENCE then being granted by Johann TETZEL. In challenge he posted his historic 95 theses on door of castle church. These aroused ire of church authorities. At Augsburg in 1518 Luther refused to recant and stood openly against certain doctrines. He further stirred ire of Roman Church in supporting new nationalism with German state control of German church. When a papal bull of condemnation came, Luther burned it publicly. In 1521 formal excommunication was pronounced, and he was summoned before Diet of Worms. When an edict demanded his seizure, he took refuge in the Wartburg. There he translated New Testament into German and began the translation of entire Bible that was to be a great force in molding the German language. He returned to Wittenberg and there remained for rest of his life. His opposition to the Peasants' War (1524–25) cost him some popularity, but he was generally revered. In 1525 he married a former nun, Katharina von Bora, who bore him six children. Under his sanction Philipp Melanchthon wrote and presented Augsburg Confession at Diet of Augsburg (1530). Luther had many controversies, esp. with Zwingli and later with Calvin over LORD'S SUPPER, which divided Protestants into the Lutheran Church and Reformed Churches. He was active in building up competent education system and wrote widely on church matters. The religious faith based on his teachings is **Lutheranism.** Luther had conservative attitude, as distinguished from views of Reformed (Calvinistic) communions. The principal statements of faith were collected in the BOOK OF CONCORD (1580), fundamental doctrine being justification by faith. Baptism was counted necessary but no form was specified, and no uniform liturgy was required. In general a synodical form of organization was set up, but unity of the church is unity of doctrine rather than of structure. In Germany, Lutheranism has always been in close association with political life. Lutheran Church is estab. church of Denmark, Iceland, Sweden, Norway, and Finland. In North America, Lutherans formed first congregation in 1638 at Fort Christina (Wilmington, Del.); second on Manhattan in 1648. In 18th cent. exiles from Palatinate estab. German Lutheran churches in N.Y., Pa., Del., Md., and South. In 1748 Heinrich Melchior MÜHLENBERG formed in Pa. the first synod.

Luther College: see DECORAH, Iowa.

Luton (lōō'tŭn), municipal borough (pop. 110,370), Bedfordshire, England. Center of straw-plaiting industry, estab. here in time of James I.

Lutsk (lo͝otsk), Pol. *Łuck,* city (1931 pop. 35,700), W Ukraine, on Styr R. Agr. market center. The seat of the princes of VOLHYNIA in Middle Ages, it passed to Russia 1795, reverted to Poland 1921, was ceded to Russia 1945.

Lutter am Barenberge (lo͞o'tůr äm bä'rŭn-bĕrgů), town (pop. 2,547), central Germany, near Brunswick. Here in 1626 Tilly defeated Christian IV of Denmark in the Thirty Years War.

Lutyens, Sir Edward Landseer (lŭ'chůnz, lŭ't-yůnz), 1869–1944, English architect. Planned New Delhi, India; designed Cenotaph in London.

Lützelburger, Hans (häns' lü'tsůlbo͝orgůr), d. 1526, German wood engraver, also called Hans Franck. Executed *Dance of Death* designs of Holbein, the younger.

Lützen (lüt'sůn), town (pop. 5,739), Saxony-Anhalt, E Germany, SW of Leipzig. In Thirty Years War Gustavus II of Sweden defeated Wallenstein here in 1632, but fell in the battle. In 1813 Napoleon I defeated Russian and Prussian forces at near-by Grossgörschen.

Luxembourg, François Henri, duc de (frãswä' ãrē' dük dů lüksãbo͞or'), 1628–95, marshal of France. He distinguished himself in all the wars of Louis XIV, especially in the War of the Grand Alliance (victorious at Fleurus, 1690; Steenkerke, 1692; Neerwinden, 1693).

Luxembourg or **Luxemburg** (both: lŭk'sůmbûrg), grand duchy (999 sq. mi.; pop. 290,992), W Europe, bordering on Belgium, Germany, and France; cap. Luxembourg. It includes the S Ardennes mts. and part of the Luxembourg-Lorraine iron-mining basin. Luxembourg ranks sixth among the steel-producing countries of Europe (not counting USSR). It formed a customs union with Belgium in 1922 and joined the BENELUX bloc in 1947. A constitutional monarchy, it has a bicameral legislature. Catholicism is the prevailing religion. French is the official, German the literary language, but a Low German dialect is widely spoken. The county of Luxembourg (originally Lützelburg) emerged (10th cent.) as one of the largest fiefs of the Holy Roman Empire, but it was gradually whittled down by its neighbors to its present size. Its counts also ruled the Holy Roman Empire and Bohemia 1308–1437. Raised to a duchy by Emperor Charles IV, Luxembourg continued under a cadet line. (A distant collateral line also played a prominent role in French history.) Conquered by Philip the Good of Burgundy in 1443, the duchy passed after 1482 to the Hapsburgs and became part of the Spanish, after 1714 Austrian, Netherlands (see NETHERLANDS, AUSTRIAN AND SPANISH). The Congress of Vienna (1814–15) made it a grand duchy, member of the German Confederation but in personal union with the Netherlands. Luxembourg shared in the Belgian revolt of 1830. After much wrangling, Belgium in 1839 received the larger part of the grand duchy—i.e., the present LUXEMBOURG prov. of Belgium. The rest continued as member of the German Confederation until 1866 and under the kings of the Netherlands until 1890, when Wilhelmina acceded in the Netherlands and Duke Adolf of NASSAU became grand duke of Luxembourg. His successors were his daughters Marie Adelaide (abdicated 1919) and Charlotte (married Prince Felix of Bourbon-Parma). Neutral Luxembourg was occupied by the Germans in World War I (1914–18) and in World War II (1940–44), when Grand Duchess Charlotte fled with her government to London. Luxembourg joined in the Five-Power Pact with England, France, Belgium, and the Netherlands (1948) and in the North Atlantic Treaty (1949).

Luxembourg, province (1,706 sq. mi.; pop. 213,917), SE Belgium, in the Ardennes; cap. Arlon. Cattle raising. Steel mfg. in S. Population is mostly French-speaking but includes large German minority. Province was detached from grand duchy of LUXEMBOURG in 1839.

Luxembourg or **Luxemburg,** city (pop. 61,996), cap. of grand duchy of Luxembourg, on Alzette R. Has picturesque houses, 16th-cent. grand ducal palace. Was strongly fortified until 1867. Became hq. of European Coal and Steel Community (see SCHUMAN PLAN) 1952.

Luxembourg Palace, in Paris, France, was built 1615–20 in Renaissance style for Marie de' Medici by Salomon de Brosse. Houses French council of the Republic (formerly senate). Was used for the peace conference of 1946. Luxembourg gardens are famous.

Luxemburg, Rosa (rō'zä lo͝ok'sůmbo͝ork), 1870?–1919, German revolutionist, b. Russian Poland. A brilliant writer and orator, she rose to leading position in Social Democratic party and, with Karl LIEBKNECHT, founded SPARTACUS PARTY in World War I. After her release from protective custody in 1918 she helped to transform Spartacists into German Communist party. Arrested in the Spartacist uprising of 1919, she and Liebknecht were murdered by soldiers who were taking them to prison.

Luxemburg, grand duchy and city: see LUXEMBOURG.

Luxeuil (lüksû'yů), former abbey, at Luxeuil-les-Bains, Haute-Saône dept., E France. Founded 590 by St. Columban (whose rule was soon replaced by St. Benedict's), it became a major center of early medieval learning. Its abbots came to rank as princes of Holy Roman Empire. Abolished in French Revolution.

Luxor (lo͝ok'sôr), town (pop. 24,118), central Egypt, on the Nile. Near Karnak, it occupies part of site of THEBES. Chief ruin is temple of Luxor, built in reign of Amenhotep III as temple to Amon.

Luynes, Charles d'Albert, duc de (shärl' dälbĕr' dük' dů lüēn'), 1578–1621, constable of France, favorite of Louis XIII. With Louis's collaboration he planned assassination of CONCINI (1617), exiled Marie de' Medici, and became chief minister, with great power.

Luzán, Ignacio de (ēgnä'thyō dā lo͞othän'), 1702–54, Spanish scholar and critic, author of *La poética* (1737), statement of the rules of neoclassical poetry.

Luzern, Switzerland: see LUCERNE.

Luzerne (lo͞ozûrn'), borough (pop. 6,176), NE Pa., near Wilkes-Barre. Anthracite mining.

Luzon (lo͞ozŏn'), island (40,420 sq. mi.; pop. 7,374,798), largest and most important of Philippine Isls. Manila, cap. of republic, is on SW coast. Paralleling part of E coast is the mountain range Sierra Madre. Mt. Mayon and Mt. Taal in S are active volcanoes. Produces sugar cane, rice, cotton, hemp, and tobacco. Limited mining of gold, iron, copper, and manganese. Inhabited mainly by Ilocanos and Tagalogs. Invaded Dec. 10, 1941, by the Japanese; Allied forces made last stand on BATAAN and CORREGIDOR. U.S. and guerrilla forces regained the island early in 1945.

Luzzatto, Moses Hayyim (hä'yēm lo͞ot-tsät'tō), 1707–47, Hebrew poet and playwright, a leader in the renaissance of Hebrew literature. Wrote allegorical *Glory to the Righteous.*

Lvov, Prince Georgi Yevgenyevich (gēôr'gē yĭvgā'nyŭvĭch lyŭvôf'), 1861–1925, Russian liberal statesman. After abdication of Nicholas II (Feb., 1917) he headed provisional government. Resigned July, 1917; succeeded by Kerensky.

Lvov (lyŭvôf'), Ger. *Lemberg,* Pol. *Lwów,* city (1931 pop. 316,177), W Ukraine, in N foothills of Carpathians. Transportation and industrial center (machinery, textiles, chemicals, oil refining). Seat of a university (founded 1658). Founded c.1250 by a prince of Galicia, Lvov soon grew to commercial importance on Vienna-Kiev route and was a major Polish stronghold against attacks from E. After first Polish partition (1772), Lvov became cap. of Austrian Galicia. Lost and retaken by Austria in World War I (1914, 1915), it was taken by Poland in 1919 and confirmed in Polish possession by Treaty of Riga (1921). It was annexed to USSR in 1939 and formally ceded by Poland in 1945. During German occupation in World War II (1941–44) most of its 100,000 Jewish inhabitants were exterminated. Among historic buildings are a 16th-cent. palace and three cathedrals (two dating from 14th cent.).

Lyautey, Louis Hubert Gonzalve (lwē' übĕr' gōzälv' lyōtā'), 1854–1934, marshal of France. As French resident general in Morocco (1912–16, 1917–25), he proved an extremely able colonial administrator and may be said to have created modern Morocco.

lycanthropy (līkăn'thrŭpē) [from Gr.,= wolf-man]. Belief that person can by witchcraft or magic take on form and nature of animal is widespread in time and space. Most common is belief in the werewolf, person who changes into a wolf and eats human flesh, then returns to human form. The morbid desire to eat human flesh, characteristic of certain psychoses, is also called lycanthropy.

lyceum, association providing lectures and entertainments. The first organization of Josiah HOLBROOK grew into Natl. American Lyceum, for 40 years a powerful force in adult education, social discussion, and political reform. Movement waned after Civil War, but was succeeded by CHAUTAUQUA MOVEMENT.

Lycomedes (līkō'mŭdēz), in Greek legend, king of Skyros, who killed Theseus.

Lycurgus (līkûr'gŭs), legendary reformer of Spartan constitution (said to be of 7th cent. B.C.).

Lydda (lĭ'dŭ), Arabic *Ludd,* city (pop. over 10,000), central Israel, SE of Tel Aviv; just N is Israel's chief international airport. City mentioned in Old Testament as Lod. Lydda was the scene of Peter's healing of the paralytic (Acts 9.32). It was occupied by Crusaders in 1099, destroyed by Saladin in 1191, and rebuilt by Richard Cœur de Lion. City is the traditional birthplace of St. George.

lyddite: see PICRIC ACID.

Lydgate, John (lĭd'gāt), c.1370–c.1450, prolific English poet, a monk. He was a pedestrian imitator of Chaucer (as in *The Fall of Princes,* c.1430).

Lydia, Christian convert at whose home in Philippi Paul stayed. Acts 16.14–40.

Lydia, anc. country, W Asia Minor; cap. Sardis. Flourished from time of King Gyges (seized power 687 B.C.) to that of King CROESUS (defeated by Persians before 540 B.C.). Its wealth was proverbial.

lye, name for several substances strongly alkaline in solution. In U.S. it commonly indicates sodium hydroxide, which is used in making hard soaps, in textile manufacture, canning industry, leather tanning, petroleum refining. It causes destruction of animal tissues.

Lyell, Sir Charles (lī'ŭl), 1797–1875, English geologist. He did much to popularize the theory of UNIFORMISM, first proposed by James Hutton, and was author of many works on geology.

Lyly or **Lilly, John** (lĭl'ē), 1554?–1606, English prose writer and dramatist. He is remembered chiefly for *Euphues* (published as *Euphues; or the Anatomy of Wit,* 1578, and *Euphues and His England,* 1580), a popular didactic novel written in highly ornamented euphuistic style, stressing alliteration, learned allusion, and antithesis.

lymphatic system (lĭmfă'tĭk), system of vessels and nodes through which lymph is conveyed in the body. Lymph, derived chiefly from blood plasma, filters through capillary walls and serves as exchange medium between blood and body cells. Small lymph vessels unite into two main channels emptying into veins. Trapping of bacteria in lymph nodes prevents their passage into blood.

Lynaker, Thomas: see LINACRE, THOMAS.

Lynbrook, residential village (pop. 17,314), SE N.Y., on SW Long Isl., settled before Revolution. Mfg. of sportswear, machinery, metal products.

Lynch, Charles, 1736–96, American Revolutionary soldier. Term "lynch law" may be derived from his name. Presided over extralegal court in Bedford co., Va., which summarily punished Loyalists.

Lynch, village (pop. 440), N Nebr., between Missouri and Niobrara rivers. Excavation of near-by prehistoric settlements was begun in 1936.

Lynchburg, city (pop. 47,727), S Va., on James R., in Blue Ridge foothills; settled 1757. Trade center and tobacco market, it has mfg. of shoes, textiles, and clothing. Confederate supply base in Civil War; resisted Union assault 1864. Seat of RANDOLPH-MACON WOM-

AN'S COLLEGE and Lynchburg Col. Near by is Sweet Briar Col. (nonsectarian; for women; opened 1906) which stresses individualized education and honors work; in 1948 began sponsoring junior-year-in-France plan.

lynching, extralegal infliction of capital punishment by a self-constituted group. Though origin of the word is unknown, there are various explanations, one of the most popular being that it is derived from the extralegal court (1780) of Col. Charles Lynch, a Revolutionary soldier. American pioneers, in settlements where law had not yet been established, tended to punish by lynching such crimes as horse stealing and rape. In the South during the reconstruction, there was considerable resort to lynching, particularly by the Ku Klux Klan, when Negroes were accused of serious crimes against whites. Lynching today is very rare, although Southern legislators still block antilynching bills on the grounds of Federal interference in state matters.

Lynd, Robert Staughton, 1892–, American sociologist, b. New Albany, Ind. With his wife, Helen Merrell Lynd, he made a noted sociological study of Muncie, Ind., published (1929) as *Middletown: a Study in Contemporary American Culture.*

Lyndhurst. 1 Township (pop. 19,980), NE N.J., near Rutherford. Machinery, metal products, clothing. **2** City (pop. 7,359), NE Ohio, E suburb of Cleveland.

Lyndsay, Sir David: see LINDSAY, SIR DAVID.

Lynn, Norfolk, England: see KING'S LYNN.

Lynn, city (pop. 99,738), E Mass., on Massachusetts Bay arm and NE of Boston; settled 1629. Mfg. of shoes, electrical appliances, and machinery.

Lynn Canal, N arm of Chatham Strait and Stephens Passage, 90 mi. long, SE Alaska, extending to Skagway. Navigable throughout. Thrusts N between mountains to inlets of Chilkoot and Chilkat rivers. Provides sea lane to Haines, Chilkoot, and Skagway.

Lynn Regis, Norfolk, England: see KING'S LYNN.

Lynwood, city (pop. 25,823), S Calif., adjacent to Los Angeles. Metal products and chemicals.

lynx (lĭngks), short-tailed mammal (*Lynx* or *Felis*) with soft, thick black-marked beige to gray fur and tufted ears. Common or northern lynx of Europe found in Alps, Scandinavia, N Russia; some races in Asia. American species are BOBCAT and Canada lynx.

Lyon, Mary, 1797–1849, American educator. In 1837 she founded what is now Mt. Holyoke Col. at SOUTH HADLEY, Mass.

Lyon, Matthew, 1750–1822, American politician and pioneer, b. Ireland. Founded Fair Haven, Vt. (1783). Able exponent of frontier views as Congressman from Vt. (1797–1801) and Ky. (1803–11).

Lyonesse (lī'ūnĕs"), region W of Cornwall, now sunk 40 fathoms under sea. In Celtic legend, home of Tristram and of the Lady of Lyones.

Lyons, Joseph Aloysius, 1879–1939, Australian prime minister (1932–39). Helped form United Australia coalition party. Restored solvency in depression.

Lyons (lī'ünz), Fr. *Lyon* (lyõ), city (pop. 439,861), cap. of Rhône dept., E central France; a port at confluence of Rhone and Saône rivers. A leading silk and rayon center of Europe, it also has chemical, electrical, and metallurgical industries. Seat of a stock exchange (founded 1506, oldest in France) and of a university (founded 1808). Founded 43 B.C. as Roman colony (Lugdunum), it became chief city of Gaul and a cradle of Christianity. Its archbishops exercized temporal rule until c.1307, when Philip IV inc. Lyonnais region and its cap., Lyons, into royal domain. WALDENSES emerged here in 12th cent. Lyons was devastated 1793 in reprisal for a counterrevolutionary insurrection. Invention of Jacquard loom helped to restore prosperity. Generally modern, city has preserved old quarter around Cathedral of St. John (12th–14th cent.). Birthplace of emperors Claudius and Caracalla, St. Ambrose, Ampère.

Lyons, Councils of, 13th and 14th ecumenical councils of the Roman Catholic Church. **1** 1245, convened by INNOCENT IV. Deposed Emperor FREDERICK II, who paid no heed. **2** 1274, summoned by Gregory X to discuss the Holy Land, remove schism of East and West, and reform the Church. Reunion of Constantinople and Rome, previously proposed by Emperor Michael VIII, was proclaimed and then ignored. Among the clerical reforms was establishment of the conclave.

lyre: see STRINGED INSTRUMENTS.

lyre bird, Australian bird; the tail plumage of the male when spread out resembles a lyre. The lyre is fully developed in fourth year. Both sexes have brown plumage. They are poor fliers.

lyric, in ancient Greece, a short poem accompanied by a musical instrument, usually a lyre. Word often refers to songlike quality of poetry; as opposed to narrative or dramatic poetry it refers to any short poem (sonnet, ode, song, elegy) expressing a personal emotion. Sappho, Alcaeus, and Pindar wrote Greek lyrics. Latin lyrics of Catullus and Horace were followed by Christian hymns, folk songs, and troubadour songs of Middle Ages. Lyric has been a major form of poets in English literature.

Lys (lēs), Flemish *Leie,* river, 135 mi. long, NE France and Belgium, flowing NE past Armentières and Courtrai into Scheldt at Ghent. Scene of heavy fighting in World War I.

Lysander (līsăn'dûr), d. 395 B.C., Spartan naval commander, diplomat, credited with capture of Athenian fleet (405 B.C.) and with submission of Athens (404 B.C.) that ended the PELOPONNESIAN WAR.

Lysenko, Trofim Denisovich (lĭsĕng'kō, Rus. trŭfēm' dyĭnyē'sŭvĭch lĭsyĕn'kŭ), 1898–, Russian agronomist, leader of Soviet school of genetics opposing theories accepted by most geneticists. He supports doctrine of inheritance of characteristics acquired through environmental influence.

Lysias (lĭ'sēŭs), c.459–c.380 B.C., Greek orator. One of the best Greek prose writers. His oration against Eratosthenes is a model of Greek oratory.

Lysimachus (līsĭ'mŭkŭs), c.355 B.C.–281 B.C.,

general of Alexander the Great. After Alexander's death, he took Thrace and fought vigorously in the wars of the DIADOCHI, gaining W Asia Minor after the defeat of ANTIGONUS I (314 B.C.). Lysimachus was defeated and killed at Magnesia ad Sipylum, ending his war with Seleucus.

Lysippus (līsĭ'pŭs), 4th cent. B.C., Greek sculptor, head of Sicyon school. Largely originated Hellenistic style of sculpture. He modified proportions of the human figure set by the canon of Polyctetus. Copies of his bronzes include the APOXYOMENUS (Vatican). Said to have produced 1,500 works.

Lytton, Baron, and **earl of:** see BULWER-LYTTON.

M

M'. Names beginning thus are entered as if spelled Mac–. See the article MAC.

Maas, Nicolaas: see MAES, NICOLAAS.

Maas, Dutch and Flemish name for MEUSE river.

Maastricht (mäs'trĭkht″), municipality (pop. 74,449), cap. of Limburg prov., SE Netherlands, on the Meuse and the Albert Canal system; formerly spelled Maestricht. Transportation center; mfg. of textiles, ceramics, glass, chemicals. Dating from Roman times, it belonged to domain of early Frankish kings, later passed to dukes of LIMBURG. The Spanish under Farnese captured it from the Dutch rebels in 1579 and massacred many inhabitants, but the Dutch recovered it in 1632 and were confirmed in its possession in 1648. A strategic fortress, it repeatedly fell into French hands, notably in 1673 and 1794. Cathedral of St. Servatius, founded 6th cent., is oldest church in Netherlands.

Mabillon, Jean (zhã' mäbēyō'), 1632–1707, French scholar. His *De re diplomatica* (1681, 1704) first used critical method in authenticating documents.

Mabinogion (măbĭnō'gēŭn) [Welsh plural of *Mabinogi* = youthful career], collection of medieval Welsh stories from manuscripts called the *White Book of Rhydderch* and the *Red Book of Hergest.* First four tales are *The Four Branches of the Mabinogi.* Other tales show Welsh verisons of tales that were to become part of Arthurian legend. A famous English translation was made by Lady Charlotte Guest.

Mabuse, Jan de (yän' dŭ mäbüz'), c.1478–c.1533, Flemish painter. Real name was Jan Gossaert or Gossart. Influenced by work of Italian masters.

Mac, Mc, or **M'** [Irish,= son], element in names derived from Irish and Scottish Gaelic patronymics. In most such names second element was a forename; others included titles or epithets. It is untrue that some forms of the prefix are more typically Scottish or Irish. In this book all names beginning with any of the three forms are alphabeted as Mac–.

macadam road, constructed of compacted layers of small stones. Introduced c.1815, it superseded dirt roads in Europe and U.S. and revolutionized road transportation. Earlier water-bound macadam (small compacted stones sprinkled with stone dust and water, then rolled) largely replaced by bituminous macadam (bituminous surface is spread over macadam, often not sprinkled).

McAdoo, William Gibbs (mă'kŭdōō), 1863–1941, American political leader, U.S. Secretary of the Treasury (1913–18). Prominent Democratic contender for presidency in 1920 and 1924. U.S. Senator from Calif. (1933–39). His second wife was a daughter of Woodrow Wilson.

McAfee, Mildred Helen (mă'kŭfē), 1900–, American educator. She was president of Wellesley Col., 1936–48, and director of the WAVES, 1942–46.

McAlester (mŭkăl'ĭstŭr), city (pop. 17,878), SE Okla., ESE of Oklahoma City; settled c.1870. Trade center for agr. area with cotton gins and food processing plants. Coal mines, oil wells. Former Choctaw cap.

Macalester College: see SAINT PAUL, Minn.

McAllen, city (pop. 20,067), S Texas, WNW of Brownsville; settled 1904. Has food-processing and chemical plants and oil refineries. Winter resort.

McAllister, (Samuel) Ward, 1827–95, American social leader. Designated the Four Hundred members of "true" N.Y. society (1892).

Macao or **Macau** (mŭkou'), Portuguese colony (6 sq. mi.; pop. 374,737), SE China, on estuary of Canton R. Portuguese settlement was begun 1557; present holdings confirmed by treaty with China 1887. Colony consists of **Macao** city (pop. 312,717), on Macao isl., and 3 offshore islets. City was leading port for China's foreign trade until rise of Hong Kong in 19th cent. Now derives much revenue from smuggling and gambling interests.

macaque: see MONKEY.

macaroni, generic name for shaped and dried doughs prepared from flour (usually semolina, a durum wheat flour) and water. Similar pastes probably originated in Asia and reached Europe in 13th cent. Varieties include tubes, ribbons, elbows, cords (spaghetti), fine strands (vermicelli). Noodles, usually flat ribbons, contain eggs. All may be stored dry and are prepared for eating by boiling.

MacArthur, Arthur, 1845–1912, American general. Served in Civil War and Spanish-American War. Military governor of Philippines (1900–1901). His son, **Douglas MacArthur,** 1880–, is also a general. Fought in France during World War I. Chief of Staff 1930–35. Commanded U.S. armed forces in Far East during World War II. Promoted general of the army ("five-star general") in 1944. Directed Allied occupation of Japan after war. Dismissed by Pres. Truman in 1951 in dispute over China policy. Became chairman of Remington Rand, Inc. in 1952.

Macassar or **Makassar** (both: mŭkă'sŭr), town (pop. 84,855), E Indonesia, on SW Celebes isl. Exports coffee, teak, spices, and copra. In World War II, in Macassar Strait (between Borneo and Celebes) the Japanese were defeated in a naval battle.

Macau, China: see MACAO.

Macaulay, Thomas Babington, 1800–1859, English historian and author. Had a distinguished career in Parliament and in India (1834–38). In 1857 made Baron Macaulay of Rothley. His major work was *The History of England from the Accession of James the Second* (5 vols., 1849–61), noted for colorful and dramatic presentation of facts and events from a Whig point of view. His poetry, in *Lays of Ancient Rome* (1842), was very popular.

macaw (mŭkô'), name of several species of parrot family, native to Central and South America. They are large and colorful and have long tails and large hooked beaks.

Macbeth, d. 1057, king of Scotland (1040–57). A commander for Duncan I, he defeated and slew Duncan and took his kingdom. Was defeated and killed by Malcolm III. Subject of Shakspere's *Macbeth.*

Maccabees (măk'ŭbēz), also called Hasmoneans or Asmoneans, Jewish family of the 2d and 1st cent. B.C. which led in opposition to Syrian dominance and Hellenizing tendencies and in the restoration of Jewish political and religious life. Resisting desecration of the Temple, Mattathias, a priest, killed a Syrian officer; he fled with his five sons and began a guerrilla warfare. On his death (166 B.C.) the leadership passed to his son Judas Maccabeus, from whose surname the family name is derived. Judas resisted a Syrian army and renewed Jewish religious life by rededicating the Temple; the feast of Hannukah celebrates this event. Judas was killed in 161 B.C. opposing the conquering army of Bacchides; his brother and successor Jonathan was slain in 143 B.C. Under the last brother, Simon, recognized as civil ruler and high priest, Palestine enjoyed peace. Simon was murdered by his son-in-law (135 B.C.); Simon's son John Hyrcanus gained the leadership in the ensuing strife, and ruled until his death (105? B.C.). John's grandson, John Hyrcanus II, a high priest, acquired temporal rule upon the death of his mother, Salome Alexandra; his brother Aristobulus II revolted, and a civil war followed. Rome intervened and captured Jerusalem (63 B.C.). With the execution of Hyrcanus II for treason (30 B.C.), the family ceased to exist. Their influence continued, however, in opposition to Romanization. Best sources for the family history are **Maccabees,** in Western Canon, last two books of Old Testament; placed in Apocrypha in AV. 1 Maccabees begins with the rebellion of Mattathias and ends with murder of Simon. 2 Maccabees emphasizes religious rather than historical issues with accounts of martyrdom of Jews resisting Hellenization. It is composed in self-deprecatory, witty style (e.g., 2.23–32; 4.40; 5.21). There are other books of Maccabees among the PSEUDEPIGRAPHA.

Maccabees, Feast of the: see HANUKKAH.

McCarthy, Joseph R(aymond), 1909–, U.S. Senator from Wis. (1947–), a Republican. Known for vigorous attacks on many as Communists and subversives.

M'Carthy, Justin, 1830–1912, British historian, novelist, and journalist. Works include *Dear Lady Disdain* (1875) and *A History of Our Own Times* (1879–1905). His son, **Justin Huntly M'Carthy,** 1860–1936, wrote the novel *If I Were King* (1901), on which the musical *The Vagabond King* was based.

McClellan, George Brinton, 1826–85, Union general in Civil War. Commander, Dept. of the Ohio (1861); cleared western Va. of Confederate troops. Briefly commander in chief. Commanded Army of the Potomac (1862); he failed in PENINSULA CAMPAIGN but checked R. E. Lee in ANTIETAM CAMPAIGN. Relieved of command in Nov., 1862. He was a leader in criticizing Lincoln as Democratic nominee for President in 1864.

McClernand, John Alexander, 1812–1900, Union general in Civil War. Commanded river expedition in Vicksburg campaign (1863); later led 13th Corps in Grant's successful advance on Vicksburg.

Macclesfield (măk'ŭlzfēld), municipal borough (pop. 35,981), Cheshire, England. Silk mfg. center of England, it also has tanning and papermaking.

McClintock, Sir Francis Leopold, 1819–1907, British arctic explorer. Participated in several expeditions seeking lost Franklin party. Discovered and mapped Prince Patrick Isl. Commanded Lady Franklin's expedition (1857–59); found records disclosing Franklin's fate.

McCloskey, John, 1810–85, American cardinal, archbishop of New York after 1864, principal builder of St. Patrick's Cathedral.

McClure, Alexander Kelly, 1828–1909, American journalist and political leader. Early Republican, supported Lincoln; a leader of Liberal Republican party in 1872. Founded Philadelphia *Times* in 1875.

McClure, Sir Robert John Le Mesurier, 1807–73, British arctic explorer. Commanded one of two ships seeking Franklin party in W Arctic Archipelago (1850–53). Discovered McClure Strait. First proved existence of Northwest Passage.

McClure, S(amuel) S(idney), 1857–1949, American editor, publisher, b. Ireland; emigrated to U.S. as a boy. Founded (1893) and edited *McClure's Magazine,* notable for "muckraking" attacks on the evils of big business and economic and political corruption.

McComb, city (pop. 10,401), SW Miss., SSW of Jackson near La. line; founded c.1857. Mfg. and trade center for cotton and truck area. Railroad shops.

McConnelsville, village (pop. 1,941), NE Ohio on Muskingum R. and SE of Zanesville. Council Rock, with Indian pictographs, near by.

McCook, Alexander McDowell, 1831–1903, Union general in Civil War. Fought ably at Perryville (1862). Routed at Murfreesboro and Chickamauga; relieved of command in Oct., 1863, later exonerated.

McCook, city (pop. 7,678), S Nebr., on Republican R. near Kansas line. Trade and processing center in grain and livestock area. Has railroad shops.

McCormack, John, 1884–1945, Irish-American tenor. He sang principally in concert and for phonograph records and became widely beloved, especially for the singing of simple sentimental songs.

McCormick, Cyrus Hall, 1809–84, inventor of the reaper, first demonstrated in 1831 and patented in 1834. The Chicago factory was built in 1847; by 1851 McCormick's reaper was known in England and soon after throughout Europe. Although other reapers were introduced, McCormick, through his unusual business ability, kept his in the running. His nephew, **Robert Sanderson McCormick,** 1849–1919, was first American ambassador to Austria-Hungary (1902). Married daughter of Joseph MEDILL. His son, **Joseph Medill McCormick,** 1877–1925, managed Chicago *Tribune* after 1907, was U.S. Representative (1917–19) and U.S. Senator (1919–25). His wife, **Ruth Hanna McCormick,** 1880–1945, daughter of Mark Hanna, served in U.S. Congress (1929–31). Another son of R. S. McCormick was **Robert R(utherford) McCormick,** 1880–, who gained sole ownership of Chicago *Tribune.* He attracted attention by attacks on U.S. participation in world affairs.

McCoy, Isaac, 1784–1846, American missionary among the Indians. As a Federal agent after 1830, he supervised removal of Wabash Valley tribes to places chosen by him in Kansas and Okla.

MacCracken, Henry Mitchell, 1840–1918, American educator. After 1884 he was vice chancellor of what is now New York Univ. and chancellor there 1891–1910. The University Heights campus was acquired and the medical school merged with Bellevue Hospital Medical Col. during his administration. One of his sons, **Henry Noble MacCracken,** 1880–, was president of Vassar Col. 1915–46.

McCrae, John, 1872–1918, Canadian poet. His famous poem, "In Flanders Fields," was written under fire in World War I.

McCullers, Carson, 1917–, American novelist, b. Ga., author of evocative psychological studies, principally set in the South (e.g., *The Heart Is a Lonely Hunter,* 1940; *The Member of the Wedding,* 1946).

McCulloch, Hugh (mŭk'ŭlŭ), 1808–95, U.S. Secretary of the Treasury (1865–69, 1884–85). Favored severe deflation in Pres. Johnson's administration.

McCulloch vs. Maryland, case, decided 1819 by U.S. Supreme Court. Involved control of currency. Md. opposed U.S. branch bank in Baltimore. Decision upheld supremacy of Federal government over states.

Macdhui, Ben, Scotland: see BEN MACDHUI.

Macdonald, Alexandre, 1765–1840, marshal of France, of Scottish descent. Fought in French Revolutionary and Napoleonic wars; was created duke of Taranto for his distinguished conduct at Wagram (1809).

Macdonald, Flora, 1722–90, Scottish Jacobite heroine. Aided Charles Edward Stuart to escape to the Continent after his defeat (1746) at Culloden Moor. Commemorated in Highland legend and poetry.

Macdonald, George, 1824–1905, Scottish novelist and poet, known for tales of rural Scotland (e.g., *Robert Falconer,* 1867), narrative poem *Within and Without* (1855), and especially his juvenile classic *At the Back of the North Wind* (1871).

Macdonald, Sir John Alexander, 1815–91, Canadian statesman, first premier of Dominion of Canada, b. Glasgow. Became premier in 1847. Dominant figure in promoting union of provinces. Forced to resign when PACIFIC SCANDAL broke (1873). Returned as premier in 1878.

MacDonald, (James) Ramsay, 1866–1937, British statesman. A founder of Labour party, he was its leader in House of Commons (1911–14) until discredited for pacifist stand. First Labour prime minister (1924), he was defeated for supposed pro-Communism on issue of Zinoviev letter. Premier of second Labour cabinet (1929), he accepted post of prime minister in Conservative dominated National government (1931). This act and his policy of economic nationalism caused him to be repudiated by Labour party.

McDonald, Ranald, 1824–94, American adventurer. Reared in Pacific Northwest. Reached Japan in 1848; imprisoned and subjected to ordeals, but because of his courage he was released in 1849.

Macdonough, Thomas (mŭkdŏ'nŭ), 1783–1825, American naval officer. Commanded L. Champlain fleet in War of 1812. His flagship, *Saratoga,* defeated the *Confiance* in significant naval battle (1814).

McDougall, Alexander, 1731–86, American Revolutionary patriot and general, b. Scotland. Helped form Sons of Liberty in N.Y. Served through Revolution.

McDougall, William, 1871–1938, American psychologist, b. England. He pioneered in physiological and social psychology and was noted for biological approach to problems of psychology.

MacDowell, Edward A(lexander), 1861–1908, American composer. His chief works are four piano sonatas, the *Indian Suite* for orchestra, two piano concertos, and numerous smaller works, including the popular *Woodland Sketches* (including "To a Wild Rose," "To a Water Lily") for piano. His widow, Marian Nevins MacDowell, founded the MacDowell Colony for composers, artists, and writers at Peterborough, N.H.

McDowell, Ephraim, 1771–1830, American pioneer surgeon. In 1809 he made surgical history by performing the first ovariotomy (removal of an ovary). Known also for skill in lithotomy.

McDowell, Irvin, 1818–85, Union general in Civil War. Commanded at first battle of BULL RUN and led Pope's 3d Corps in second battle (1862). Shared blame for defeat; removed from command.

mace: see NUTMEG.

Macedon (mă'sůdŏn), anc. country of the Balkan Peninsula, roughly equivalent at its height to modern Macedonia. In the 7th cent. B.C. a state under Greek rulers began to develop. This PHILIP II with well-trained armies and well-organized administration made the master state of Greece after victory at Chaeronea (338 B.C.). His brilliant son, ALEXANDER THE GREAT, carried victory even to the limits of the known world and incidentally, with it, HELLENISTIC CIVILIZATION. After his death (323 B.C.) his successors (the DIADOCHI) broke up the empire by incessant wars, in which Macedon suffered. The drain of manpower for armies and the ruinous battles weakened the country, which was frequently under control of Epirus. ANTIGONUS II restored Macedon, but PHILIP V was defeated by Rome in the Macedonian Wars (215–205 B.C., 200–194 B.C.), and matters went worse under Perseus, who lost the Third Macedonian War (171–168 B.C.). After a pretender, Andriscus, tried to assert independence, Macedon became the first Roman province, Macedonia (146 B.C.).

Macedonia (măsůdō'nēů), region of SE Europe, in the Balkan Peninsula, extending N from the Aegean Sea between Epirus and Thrace. Roughly corresponding to ancient MACEDON, it is predominantly mountainous, pastoral, and agr. Tobacco is an important crop. Politically, the region is divided into Greek Macedonia (13,380 sq. mi.; pop. 1,754,092; cap. Salonica), the Yugoslav autonomous republic of Macedonia (10,229 sq. mi.; pop. 1,152,054; cap. Skoplje), and Bulgarian Macedonia (pop. 252,258). In the Middle Ages, the Byzantine emperors had an uneasy hold over Macedonia, which repeatedly was the prey of invaders, notably the Bulgars. It was conquered by Stephen Dushan of Serbia in the 14th cent. and, after his death, by the Ottoman Turks. Macedonia became a patchwork of religions and nationalities—Christians, Moslems, Jews; Serbs, Bulgars, Greeks, Turks. When the Ottoman Empire began to break up in the 19th cent., Macedonia was claimed by Greece, Serbia, and Bulgaria. The Treaty of SAN STEFANO gave the major share (incl. the coast) to Bulgaria, but the Congress of BERLIN restored direct Turkish rule (1878). Secret terrorist organizations (*komitadjis*), working to free Macedonia from the Turks, were supported by Bulgaria, which gained a large share of Macedonia in the First Balkan War (1912–13). In the Second Balkan War (1913), Greece and Serbia defeated Bulgaria and obtained approximately the present boundaries. Population exchanges after 1923 resulted in the replacement of most of the Bulgarian and Turkish elements in Greek Macedonia by Greek refugees from Asia Minor. Nevertheless, Bulgaria continued to agitate for a greater share of Macedonia. Border incidents, terrorism, and mutual accusations of violations of minority rights created an explosive situation. In World War II all Macedonia was briefly held by Bulgaria (1941–44), but the peace treaty of 1947 restored the former boundaries.

Maceió (mäsäô'), city (pop. 102,301), NE Brazil, cap. of Alagoas state; an Atlantic port. Area produces cotton and sugar; city has some factories.

MacEwen, Sir William (můkū'ůn), 1848–1924, Scottish surgeon, especially noted for surgery of brain and spinal cord.

McFee, Henry Lee, 1886–1953, American painter. Early work was influenced by cubism and expressionism; later style was naturalistic.

McFee, William, 1881–, Anglo-American author, a marine engineer, b. London; in U.S. after 1911. Wrote novels and sketches of nautical life (e.g., *Casuals of the Sea*, 1916).

Macgillicuddy's Reeks (můgĭ'lůkŭ"dēz rēks'), mountains of Co. Kerry, Ireland, near Lakes of Killarney. They include Carrantuohill (3,414 ft.), the highest peak in Ireland, and other peaks over 3,000 ft. high.

McGillivray, Alexander (můgĭ'lĭvrā), 1759–93, Indian chief. Son of a Scots trader and his French-Creek wife. Allied Creeks with the Spanish in 1784; attacked American frontier settlements. Signed treaty with U.S. (1790), but later repudiated it.

McGill University: see MONTREAL, Que.

McGrath, J(ames) Howard (můgrath'), 1903–, U.S. Attorney General (1949–52). Resigned during controversy over investigation of Justice Dept.

McGraw, John J(oseph), 1873–1934, American baseball manager. Led N.Y. Giants to 10 pennants (1904–5, 1911–13, 1917, 1921–24) and three world series victories (1905, 1921–22).

MacGregor, Robert: see ROB ROY.

McGregor, town (pop. 1,138), NE Iowa, on the Mississippi almost opposite mouth of Wisconsin R. Annual American School of Wild Life Protection sessions. Effigy Mounds Natl. Monument is near by.

McGuffey, William Holmes (můgŭ'fē), 1800–1873, American educator. He compiled the six McGuffey Eclectic Readers (1836–57), used for nearly two generations, with estimated sales of 122,000,000 copies.

Machado, Antonio (mächä'dhō), 1875–1939, Spanish lyric poet, author of *Soledades* (1903; brooding and evocative poems on nature and man) and other volumes, collaborator with his brother, Manuel Machado (1874–1947), in plays, both original and translated.

Machado, Gerardo (hārär'dō mächä'dhō), 1871–1939, president of Cuba (1925–33). Began his regime with interest in material and social reform. Became dictatorial and instituted bloody terrorism of secret police. U.S. finally intervened, and Machado was forced to flee. Died in Miami Beach, Fla.

Machado de Assis, Joaquim Maria (zhwäkēm' můrē'ů můshä'dō dů äsēzh'), 1839–1908, Brazilian realist novelist. Pictures of Brazilian social conditions in *Iaiá Garcia* (1878), *Memórias postumas de Braz Cubas* (1881), *Quincas Barba* (1891), and *Dom Casmurro* (1900) show psychological insight and are highlighted by ironic humor. Considered by many Brazil's greatest writer.

Machen, Arthur (mă'kŭn), 1863–1947, British author of bizarre romances (e.g., *The Great God Pan,* 1894; *The Three Impostors,* 1895; *The Hill of Dreams,* 1907) and essays, all notable for exquisite style.

McHenry, James, 1753–1816, American statesman. In Continental Congress (1783–86). U.S. Secretary of War (1797–1800); followed leadership of Alexander Hamilton. Fort McHenry named for him.

McHenry, Fort, former U.S. military post in Baltimore, Md., now a national monument and historic shrine (estab. 1939). Fort's defense against British bombardment (Sept. 13–14, 1814) inspired Francis Scott Key to compose the STAR-SPANGLED BANNER.

Machias (mŭchī'ŭs), town (pop. 2,063), SE Maine, on Machias R.; settled 1763. Burnham Tavern (1770), historical museum, has mementos of "first naval battle of the Revolution." This was the capture of a British ship in June, 1775, off **Machiasport** town (pop. 781), at head of Machias Bay and E of Machias.

Machiavelli, Niccolò (nēk-kōlō' mäkyävĕl'lē), 1469–1527, Italian author and statesman, an outstanding figure of the Renaissance; b. Florence. Playing a leading role under the Florentine republic (1492–1512), he was sent on diplomatic missions to France, to the pope, and to the emperor. As secretary of the republican council from 1506 he organized an efficient citizens' militia. The restoration of the Medici in 1512 forced his retirement to his country estate, where he wrote his chief works. His most famous book, *The Prince,* has made his name a symbol of political unscrupulousness. Actually, it is neither moral nor immoral, but is instead the first objective, scientific analysis of the methods by which political power is obtained and kept. Its complete detachment lends the book an air of cynicism but contributes to its lucid brilliance. Its influence even to most recent times is incalculable. Machiavelli's personal preference seems to have been for the republican form of government. He also was an ardent champion of Italian unity. In his *Discourses on the First Ten Books of Livy* he expounded the first modern general theory of politics; his *History of Florence* with its scientific approach opened a new era in history writing. He also wrote poems and plays, notably the ribald comedy *Mandragola.*

machine. Term commonly used for complicated assembly of parts operating together to do work. It is applied technically to any device increasing intensity of applied force, changing direction of force, or changing one form of motion or energy into another. Thus the lever, pulley, inclined plane, screw, and wheel and axle are simple machines. Mechanical advantage of a machine is ratio between the resistance or load and the force applied to overcome it. Since some force is required to overcome friction this ratio does not hold exactly, so mechanical advantage is calculated as ratio between the distance the force applied moves and the distance the resistance moves. Efficiency of a machine is degree in percentage to which machine accomplishes the work it is capable theoretically of doing if there were no friction. Complex machines are complicated combinations of the simple machines. Certain machines used to transform some other form of energy (e.g., heat) into mechanical energy are known as engines. See also HYDRAULIC MACHINE; *ill.,* p. 793.

machine gun, firearm discharging rifle bullets with great rapidity, utilizing for firing either the power of recoil or the explosion gases as the gun is fired. Developed almost exclusively by American inventors (including R. J. Gatling and J. M. Browning). First used in the Franco-Prussian War, it was employed extensively in World War I.

Machpelah (măkpē'lŭ), cave bought by Abraham for family tomb. Gen. 23; 25.9,10; 49.29–32; 50.13.

Machu Picchu (mä'chōō pēk'chōō), fortress city of anc. Incas, Peru, c.50 mi. NW of Cuzco. May have been home of the Inca prior to migration to Cuzco, as well as last stronghold after Spanish conquest.

McIntosh, Millicent Carey, 1898–, American educator, dean of Barnard College after 1947 and president after 1952.

McIntyre, James Francis Aloysius, 1886–, American cardinal. Roman Catholic auxiliary bishop of New York (1940–48) and archbishop of Los Angeles (after 1948), he was made cardinal 1953.

Macip or **Masip, Vicente Juan** (vēthān'tā hwän' mäthēp', mäsēp'), c.1500–1579, Spanish painter, who was strongly influenced by Italian art. Also called Juan de Juanes and Vicente Joanes.

MacIver, Robert M(orrison) (mŭkē'vŭr), 1882–, Scottish sociologist, at Columbia Univ. after 1927. His works include *Society: Its Structure and Changes* (1931) and *The Web of Government* (1947).

Mack, Connie (Cornelius McGillicuddy), 1862–, American baseball manager. Managed Philadelphia Athletics (1901–1950) to nine pennants (1902, 1905, 1910–11, 1913–14, 1929–31) and five world series (1910–11, 1913, 1929–30).

McKay, Claude (mŭkā'), 1890–1948, American Negro author, b. Jamaica, British West Indies. His works include poetry (e.g., *Harlem Shadows,* 1922), novels (e.g., *Home to Harlem,* 1927), and an autobiography (*A Long Way from Home,* 1937).

McKay, Donald, 1810–80, American shipbuilder, b. Nova Scotia. From his Boston shipyard came sleek, swift clippers, some of the most beautiful ships ever upon the sea. Among them were the *Flying Cloud,* the *Sovereign of the Seas,* the *Great Republic,* and the *Glory of the Seas.*

McKay, Douglas, 1893–, U.S. Secretary of the Interior (1953–). Governor of Oregon (1949–52).

Mackay, John William (mă'kē), 1831–1902, American financier, b. Ireland. Made fortune in Nev. silver mines. Formed the Postal Telegraph Cable Co. (1886).

MacKaye, Percy (mŭkī′), 1875–, American author, b. New York city. Wrote long poems, and collected Ky. mountain folklore.

McKeesport, city (pop. 51,502), SW Pa., on Monongahela R. at mouth of Youghiogheny R. and SE of Pittsburgh; settled 1755. Mfg. of iron and steel products and tin plate. Braddock's camp and crossing are marked with tablets. Was armament center in World War II.

McKees Rocks, borough (pop. 16,241), SW Pa., NW of Pittsburgh; settled c.1764. Mfg. of steel products and chemicals; bituminous coal mining.

Mackensen, August von (ou′gōōst fŭn mä′-kŭnzŭn), 1849–1945, German field marshal. In World War I he defeated the Russians in the battle of the MASURIAN LAKES (1915); occupied Rumania (1917). Later was active as a monarchist leader.

Mackenzie, Sir Alexander, 1764?–1820, Canadian fur trader and explorer, b. Scotland. Supervised Athabaska fur district. Followed then unknown Mackenzie R. to Arctic Ocean (1789). Completed first overland journey across North America N of Mexico (1793).

Mackenzie, Alexander, 1822–92, Canadian statesman, b. Scotland. First Liberal prime minister of dominion (1873–78).

Mackenzie, Henry, 1745–1831, Scottish novelist, best known for *The Man of Feeling* (1771).

Mackenzie, Sir William, 1849–1923, Canadian railroad builder and financier. Helped organize and build Canadian Northern Railway.

Mackenzie, William Lyon, 1795–1861, Canadian journalist and insurgent leader, b. Scotland. As publisher of *Colonial Advocate* (1824–34) he attacked Family Compact. Founded the *Constitution* as a Reform party organ (1836). Enraged by policies of Sir F. B. Head and by defeat of Reform party, Mackenzie and a group of insurgents attempted to seize Toronto (1837), but rebellion was quickly put down. He escaped to U.S., set up provisional government on Navy Isl. in Niagara R. Later imprisoned for 18 months by U.S. for violating neutrality laws (see CAROLINE AFFAIR). Returned to Canada 1849.

Mackenzie, provisional district: see NORTHWEST TERRITORIES, Canada.

Mackenzie, river of NW Canada, with its basin between the Rockies (W) and the Laurentian Plateau (E), flowing N and NNW to the Arctic Ocean. The Mackenzie proper is 1,120 mi. long, flowing between Great Slave L. and the Arctic Ocean. Mackenzie R. system includes Great Slave R. (between Great Slave L. and L. Athabaska), and Peace and Athabaska rivers, chief headstreams. Together they form a continuous stream 2,514 mi. long (second longest in North America), navigable for c.2,000 mi. with only one portage. Delta at mouth is 80–100 mi. wide. Long important in fur trading. Recently oil fields and mineral resources have been developed. Valley has regular air service. Named for Sir Alexander Mackenzie, who explored it 1789.

Mackenzie King, William Lyon: see KING, WILLIAM LYON MACKENZIE.

mackerel, spiny-finned fish related to tuna and bluefish. It is spindle shaped, has a deeply forked tail and a series of small, spiny finlets on dorsal and ventral sides between dorsal and ventral fins and tail. Common mackerel (*Scomber scombrus*), c.12 in. long, travels in schools. It spawns in deep waters, swims to coastal waters in spring, and returns to deep waters in autumn. Spanish mackerel and frigate mackerel are related forms.

McKim, Charles Follen, 1847–1909, American architect, who belonged to firm of McKim, Mead, and White, which handled many important commissions. Favored classic architecture and its Renaissance derivatives. A founder and first president of American Academy in Rome.

Mackinac (mă′kĭnô″), strait between peninsula of Upper Mich. and Lower Mich., separating L. Huron and L. Michigan. Name is shortening of Michilimackinac. Early used as gathering place for nomadic Indians. Important trading center and military post in New France. Passed into British control 1761. Garrison massacred by Indians 1763. Treaty of Ghent gave it permanently to U.S. ownership. Long the chief center of operations for American Fur Co. Lost importance in 1840s as fur trade declined.

Mackinaw City, resort village (pop. 970), N Mich., on S shore of Straits of Mackinac. Rebuilt stockade of French Fort Michilimackinac is here.

McKinley, William, 1843–1901, 24th President of the United States (1897–1901). A Republican U.S. Representative from Ohio (1877–91), he sponsored highly protective McKinley Tariff Act. Governor of Ohio (1892–96). The skill of M. A. HANNA and a gold-standard party platform elected him President in 1896. Trouble with Spain ended in the SPANISH-AMERICAN WAR, McKinley asking Congress for the declaration though Spain had hinted at concessions to avoid war. After victory, he demanded Philippine Isls. for U.S. Signed bill to annex Hawaii; supported Open Door policy in China. Advanced interests of American commerce. Currency Act of 1900 consolidated gold-standard policy. Reelected in 1900, he was shot down at Buffalo, N.Y., on Sept. 6, 1901, by Leon Czolgosz; died on Sept. 14.

McKinley, Mount (20,270 ft.), S central Alaska, in Alaska range, in Mount McKinley Natl. Park. Highest peak in North America. First climbed by Hudson Stuck 1913.

McKinney, city (pop. 10,560), N Texas, NNE of Dallas; founded 1842. Handles cotton, grains (esp. corn), pecans, truck, and textiles.

Maclaurin, Colin, 1698–1746, Scottish mathematician, philosopher, authority on fluxional calculus.

MacLeish, Archibald (mŭklēsh′), 1892–, American poet, notable for technical innovation and proficiency. His early poems were highly personal; his later work speaks of social responsibility. Among his volumes are *Conquistador* (1932) and *The Fall of the City* (1937; radio verse drama). He was the head of the Library of Congress 1939–44.

MacLennan, Hugh, 1907–, Canadian novelist,

author of *Two Solitudes* (1945), *The Precipice* (1948).

Macleod, Fiona: see SHARP, WILLIAM.

Macleod, John James Rickard (mŭkloud′), 1876–1935, Scottish physiologist. He shared 1923 Nobel Prize in Physiology and Medicine for work on use of insulin in treating diabetes.

Maclise, Daniel (mŭklēs′), 1806–70, British portrait and historical painter, b. Ireland.

McLoughlin, John (mŭklŏk′lĭn), 1784–1857, fur trader in Oregon, b. Canada. Hudson's Bay Co. man in Columbia R. country (1824–46). Controlled Indians, expanded trade, aided settlers.

Maclure, William, 1763–1840, American geologist, b. Scotland. In his early business career in London he made a fortune. He visited America in 1782 and 1796 and on his third visit undertook an extensive survey. His *Observations on the Geology of the United States* (1809; 2d ed., 1817) and the accompanying geologic map marked an epoch in American geological history.

MacMahon, Marie Edmé Patrice de (märē′ ĕdmā′ pätrēs′ dů mäkmäō′), 1808–93, marshal of France, president of France (1873–79), duke of Magenta; of Irish ancestry. Fought in Crimean War; defeated Austrians at Magenta (1859); held a command in Franco-Prussian War; aided in suppression of Commune of Paris (1871). Chosen president of France by the royalist majority of the National Assembly, he sought to restore the Bourbons but failed. In 1875 France received a republican constitution. MacMahon's persistent habit of appointing royalist cabinets despite the clear republican majority in parliament eventually forced his resignation. Jules Grévy succeeded him.

McMaster, John Bach, 1852–1932, American historian. Known for *History of the People of the United States* (8 vols., 1883–1913; Vol. IX, 1927).

McMaster University: see HAMILTON, Ont.

MacMillan, Donald B(axter), 1874–, American arctic explorer. Made ethnological studies of Labrador Eskimo (1911, 1912). Led Greenland expedition (1913–17) and subsequent arctic expeditions, collecting varied scientific data and specimens. Made extensive air surveys (1944).

McMillan, Edwin Mattison, 1907–, American physicist. Shared 1951 Nobel Prize in Chemistry for discoveries in chemistry of elements having atomic number greater than that of uranium. He is codiscoverer of neptunium (element 93) and plutonium (element 94); known also for work on microwave radar and on sonar. Associated with Univ. of California from 1932.

McMinnville. 1 City (pop. 6,635), NW Oregon, SW of Portland. Trade center in lumber, wheat, dairy area. Seat of Linfield Col. (Baptist; coed.; 1857). **2** Town (pop. 7,577), central Tenn., ESE of Nashville. Mfg. of wood, marble products, shoes, and hosiery. Here are tree nurseries.

MacMonnies, Frederick William (mŭkmŏ′nēz), 1863–1937, American sculptor of monuments. His *Civic Virtue* (formerly in City Hall Park, New York) was the subject of much controversy.

McMurrough, Dermot: see DERMOT MCMURROUGH.

McNaughton, Andrew George Latta (mŭknô′tŭn), 1887–, Canadian engineer and army officer. Became president of Canadian Natl. Research Council in 1935. During World War II he commanded Canadian forces in Great Britain. Delegate to Security Council of UN (1948–49).

MacNeice, Louis (mŭknēs′), 1907–, British poet. He joined "Oxford revolt" against formal language, and his three volumes of collections (1940, 1945, 1948) show his connection with Auden, Spender, and T. S. Eliot. Among his translations are *Agamemnon* (1936) and *Faust* (1951).

MacNeil, Hermon Atkins, 1866–1947, American sculptor, best known for his Indians and pioneers.

Macomb (mŭkōm′), city (pop. 10,592), W Ill., SSW of Galesburg; laid out 1831. Trade and industrial center in farm and coal area. Mfg. of clay and metal products.

Macon, Nathaniel (mā′kŭn), 1758–1837, American statesman. U.S. Representative (1791–1815; speaker of the House 1801–7) and Senator (1815–28) from N.C. A staunch Jeffersonian.

Mâcon (mäkõ′), town (pop. 18,221), cap. of Saône-et-Loire dept., E central France, on Saône R. Famous for red Burgundy wine. Birthplace of Lamartine.

Macon (mā′kŭn), city (pop. 70,252), central Ga., at head of navigation on Ocmulgee R. and SE of Atlanta. Fort Hawkins settled on E bank of river 1806; Macon, laid out 1823 on W bank, annexed Newtown (Fort Hawkins) 1829. Industrial and shipping center for extensive farm area (cotton, truck, livestock), it has textile and lumber mills. Clay products are made, and foods processed. Seat of Wesleyan Col. (for women; 1836) and Mercer Univ. (Baptist; coed.; 1833). Sidney Lanier's birthplace is preserved. Ocmulgee Natl. Monument is near.

Macon, Bayou (bī′ō mā′kŭn, bī′ōō), rising in SE Ark. and flowing S to Tensas R. in NE La. Was haunt of the James brothers.

Macpherson, James, 1736–96, Scottish poet. His epics *Fingal* (1761) and *Temora* (1763), purportedly translations from Irish bard Ossian, were widely translated in Europe and influenced romantic movement. Later investigation proved them to be based on Gaelic myths but written by Macpherson himself.

McPherson, city (pop. 8,689), central Kansas, NNE of Hutchinson and on old Santa Fe trail. Refines and ships oil and mills flour.

Macready, William Charles (mŭkrē′dē), 1793–1873, English actor and manager. Won fame as Richard III (1819). Managed Covent Garden (1837–39) and Drury Lane (1841–43). Appeared in U.S. in 1826, 1843 and 1847 when the Astor Place riot (instigated by Edwin FORREST supporters) occurred.

McReynolds, James Clark (mŭkrĕ′nŭldz), 1862–1946, U.S. Attorney General (1913–14), Associate Justice of U.S. Supreme Court (1914–41). Strict constructionist; a key figure in F. D. Roosevelt's unsuccessful attack on Supreme Court.

Macrobius (mŭkrō′bēŭs), fl. c.400, Latin writer, philosopher. His seven-book dialogue,

Saturnalia, is a source of quotations from early writers.

Macy, Anne Sullivan, 1866–1936, American educator, teacher and companion of Helen KELLER after 1887. As a child she learned manual alphabet at Perkins Inst., where she was sent because of eye trouble.

Madagascar (mădŭgă'skŭr), island (227,602 sq. mi.; pop. c.4,153,000), in Indian Ocean, separated from Africa by Mozambique Channel; overseas territory of French Union. Coffee (chief export) is grown in uplands between fertile coastal plain and forested mountains in interior. Main ports are Tamatave, linked by rail with Tananarive (chief town), and Majunga. Natives are Malagasy (a Malay stock). Discovered 1500 by Portuguese explorers. Brought under French control, 1885–1905. In World War II, island was under Vichy government until 1942, when it was occupied by British troops. A former colony, it became an overseas territory in 1946, with representation in French parliament.

Madariaga, Salvador de (sälvädhōr' dā mädhryä'gä), 1886– Spanish essayist and internationalist. He held posts in the League of Nations and the diplomatic service, but is best known for historical studies (e.g., of Columbus and Cortés) and essays on national psychologies (e.g., *The Genius of Spain,* 1928, originally in English; *Ingleses, franceses, españoles,* 1928).

Madawaska, river, S Ont., Canada, rising in Algonquin Provincial Park and flowing 250 mi. E to Ottawa R. W of Ottawa.

madder, Old World dye plant (*Rubia tinctorum*) with whorled leaves and small yellow flowers. Alizarin, the source of such pigments as madder purple and madder orange, was obtained from its fleshy roots from ancient times; it is now made synthetically.

Madeira (mŭdā'rŭ), river, formed by junction of Beni and Mamoré on Bolivian-Brazilian border. With Mamoré it forms greatest tributary of Amazon.

Madeira Islands (mŭdēr'ŭ, mŭdâ'rŭ), archipelago (c.300 sq. mi.; pop. 269,179), far off Moroccan coast in the Atlantic, forming Funchal dist. of Portugal; cap. Funchal. Though they were known as early as the 14th cent., their discovery is traditionally credited to explorers under orders of Prince Henry the Navigator, 1418–19. They comprise the uninhabited Desert and Savage island groups, Porto Santo Isl., and **Madeira,** largest of the archipelago. Madeira is noted for its beautiful mountains and valleys; its mild climate, which makes it a favorite health resort; its wine; and its embroidery industry.

Madera (mŭdâ'rŭ), city (pop. 10,497), central Calif., NW of Fresno in San Joaquin Valley; laid out 1876. Produces wood, wine, canned foods, cotton. Served by Madera Canal of CENTRAL VALLEY project.

Madero, Francisco Indalecio (fränsē'skō ēndälā'syō mädhā'rō), 1873–1913, Mexican statesman, president of Mexico (1911–13). A champion of democracy and social reform, he was the leader of the great revolution against Díaz (1910), but in his own administration he could not control the various revolutionary forces which had been unleashed. Overthrown by Huerta, Madero was arrested and shot, allegedly in an attempt to escape.

Madhya Bharat (mäd'yŭ bŭ'rŭt), state (46,710 sq. mi.; pop. 7,941,642), W central India; winter cap. Lashkar, summer cap. Indore. Includes former princely states of Indore and Gwalior.

Madhya Pradesh (mäd'yŭ prä'dĭsh), state (130,323 sq. mi.; pop. 21,327,898), central India; cap. Nagpur. Formerly called Central Provs. and Berar. Rich agr. area, with dense forests and large deposits of manganese and coal. Cotton-textile mfg.

Madison, James, 1751–1836, 4th President of the United States (1809–17), b. Va. Member of Continental Congress (1780–83, 1787–88). Worked successfully to have FEDERAL CONSTITUTIONAL CONVENTION called in 1787, and was chief drafter of the Constitution. Fought for its adoption by contributing to FEDERALIST PAPERS. As U.S. Congressman from Va. (1789–97) he strongly advocated first ten amendments to Constitution, steadfastly supported Thomas Jefferson. Prepared Virginia resolutions (see KENTUCKY AND VIRGINIA RESOLUTIONS) protesting Alien and Sedition Acts. U.S. Secretary of State (1801–9). Jefferson's choice as his successor. WAR OF 1812, chief event of Madison's administration, proved difficult. New Englanders at Hartford Convention resisted "Mr. Madison's War"; British burned the White House in Sept., 1814. After the war Madison encouraged the new nationalism. In retirement he lived quietly with his wife, **Dolly Madison,** 1768–1849, who had been official hostess for Jefferson and her husband and who was noted for the magnficence of her entertaining as well as for charm, tact, and grace.

Madison. 1 Village (pop. 7,963), SW Ill., on the Mississippi and adjoining Granite City. Railroad yards. Mfg. of steel products. **2** City (pop. 7,506), SE Ind., on Ohio R. and NE of Louisville, Ky. Tobacco market; mfg. of textiles. **3** Residential borough (pop. 10,417), NE N.J., SE of Morristown; settled 1685. Rose-growing center. Sayre House (1745) was Wayne's hq. Seat of Drew Univ. (Methodist; mainly for men; opened 1867); includes Brothers Col. (since 1928). **4** City (pop. 5,153), SE S.Dak., NW of Sioux Falls. Farm trade center and resort near lakes. **5** City (pop. 96,056), state cap., S Wis., on isthmus between lakes Monona and Mendota, in Four Lakes group; founded 1836. Chosen territorial cap. before settlement. State's second largest city and trade, mfg. (machinery, electrical equipment), and cultural center of dairy region. City of many parks. Seat of Univ. of WISCONSIN.

Madison, river rising in Yellowstone Natl. Park, NW Wyo., and flowing 183 mi. N through Mont. to Jefferson and Gallatin rivers, forming the Missouri.

Madison, Mount: see PRESIDENTIAL RANGE.

Madisonville, city (pop. 11,132), W Ky., ENE of Paducah, in farm, timber, and oil area; settled 1807. Tobacco market.

Madoc or **Madog,** fl. 1170?, quasi-historical Welsh prince; discoverer of America in Welsh legend.

Madoera, Indonesia: see MADURA.

Madras (mŭdrăs'), state (127,768 sq. mi.; pop. 56,952,232), S India, including Laccadive Isls. Coromandel and Malabar coasts are its most fertile areas. Textile mfg. is important. Colonies were estab. here by the Portuguese in 16th cent., and by the Dutch, French, and British in 17th cent. By 1801 the British had become supreme in the area. **Madras,** city (pop. 777,481), on Coromandel Coast, is state cap. and main port; founded 1639 by the British. Textile and mfg. center. Seat of Madras Univ. Near by is Mt. St. Thomas, traditional site of martyrdom (A.D. 68) of Thomas the apostle.

Madrazo (mädrä'thō), family of Spanish painters, leaders of the academic school. Eminent members included **José de Madrazo y Agudo,** 1781–1859, and his grandson **Raimundo de Madrazo y Garreta,** 1841–1920.

Madre de Dios (mädrā' dā dyōs'), river, c.700 mi. long, rising in Andes of SE Peru and flowing NE through Bolivia to Beni R. Forests of the Madre de Dios valley formerly exploited for rubber.

Madrid (mŭdrĭd', Span. mädhrēdh'), city (pop. 1,088,647), cap. of Spain, in New Castile, on the Manzanares. Chief communications center of Spain; rivaled only by Barcelona in commercial and industrial importance. Archiepiscopal see; seat of university (transferred from ALCALÁ DE HENARES 1836). Originally a Moorish fortress, Madrid fell to Castile in 1083 but became the Spanish cap. only in 1561. It expanded under the Bourbons in the 18th cent., when the royal palace, the world-famous PRADO Mus., and other fine buildings were erected. In May, 1808, a popular uprising against French occupation was bloodily suppressed. In the civil war of 1936–39, Madrid under the command of Gen. José Miaja resisted 29 months of siege by the Insurgents but surrendered in March, 1939. Madrid is essentially a modern city. Its W suburbs, particularly the modern Ciudad Universitaria [university city], were heavily damaged during the siege.

madrigal. The Italian madrigal of the 14th cent. was a poetic form consisting of from one to four stanzas of three iambic pentameters each, followed by two rhymed lines in a contrasting meter. Subject matter was usually pastoral or amatory. Composers of the period made contrapuntal two- and three-voice settings of the madrigal. The number of voices was later increased to four or five. Brought into England in the late 16th cent., the madrigal came to mean an unaccompanied part song. Outstanding English madrigalists were William Byrd, Thomas Morley, and Orlando Gibbons.

madroña (mŭdrōn'yŭ), broad-leaved evergreen tree or shrub (*Arbutus menziesi*) native to W coast of U.S. It has white flowers followed by showy red berries.

Madura or **Madoera** (both: mädōō'rä), island (1,762 sq. mi.; pop. 1,858,183), Indonesia, near Java. Has chalky soil. Chief products are salt and fish.

Maecenas (Caius Cilnius Maecenas) (mĭsē'nŭs, mē–), d. 8 B.C., Roman statesman and patron of letters under Augustus. His famous literary circle included Horace, Vergil, Propertius. His name is the symbol of the wealthy benefactor of the arts.

Maelstrom (māl'strŭm), Nor. *Malstrøm,* narrow sound in Lofoten isls., NW Norway, just S of Moskenes isl. Its powerful tidal currents create a dangerous whirlpool, and its name is used for all fatal whirlpools.

Maerlant, Jacob van (mär'länt), c.1235–c.1300, Flemish poet, earliest important figure of Dutch literature. Wrote lyric poems, chivalric verse romances, and long didactic poems.

Maes or **Maas, Nicolaas** (nē'kōläs mäs'), 1632–93, Dutch genre and portrait painter. Was influenced first by Rembrandt, later by Van Dyck.

Maestricht, Netherlands: see MAASTRICHT.

Maeterlinck, Maurice (mōrēs' mätĕrlĕk'), 1862–1949, Belgian author who wrote in French. He was considered the representative dramatist of the SYMBOLISTS. His works, mystical and metaphysical, include critical essays, the zoological study *The Life of the Bee* (1901), and the famous dramas *Pelléas et Mélisande* (1892), *Monna Vanna* (1902), and *The Blue Bird* (1909). He won the 1911 Nobel Prize in Literature and was created a count by King Albert.

Mafeking (mă'fĭkĭng), town (pop. 5,864), N Cape Prov., South Africa; extraterritorial cap. of Bechuanaland protectorate. In South African War British forces under Lord Baden-Powell were besieged here by Boer forces, Oct. 12, 1899–May 17, 1900.

Mafia (mä'fēä), name of organized bands of Sicilian brigands in 19th and 20th cent. They lacked the hierarchic organization of the CAMORRA; each band operated on its own. As an institution, the Mafia dates from feudal times, when lords hired brigands to guard their estates and in exchange afforded them protection from the royal authority. Political corruption gave the Mafia tremendous influence until its suppression by Mussolini. Emigrants brought it to the U.S. (esp. to La.).

Magallanes, Chile: see PUNTA ARENAS.

magazine: see PERIODICAL.

Magazine, Mount: see OUACHITA MOUNTAINS.

Magdala (măg'dŭlŭ), place on shore of Sea of Galilee. Mat. 15.39; sometimes given as Magadan; traditional home of Mary Magdalen. Identified with Mejdel, a hamlet on W shore.

Magdalen: see MARY MAGDALEN.

Magdalena (mägdhälā'nä), river, over 1,000 mi. long, rising in SW Colombia and flowing N to Caribbean near Barranquilla. Discovered (1501) by Bastidas, it is republic's natural avenue of communication, but navigation is difficult because of rapids and sand bars. Explored by Jiménez de Quesada (1536).

Magdalen College: see OXFORD UNIVERSITY.

Magdalene College: see CAMBRIDGE UNIVERSITY.

Magdalen Islands (măg'dŭlŭn), group of nine main islands and numerous islets (102 sq. mi.; pop. 9,999), in Gulf of St. Lawrence, E Que., Canada, N of Prince Edward Isl. Discovered 1534 by Cartier. Fishing and sealing.

Magdeburg (mäk'dŭbōōrk), city (1939 pop. 336,838; 1946 pop. 236,326), Saxony-Anhalt, E central Germany, on the Elbe. Inland port; mfg. center (machinery, paper, textiles, beet sugar). Became archiepiscopal see 968. The archbishops later ruled a vast territory as princes of the Holy Roman Empire and granted the city a charter (1188) which gave it self-rule and exempted it from all duties save rent payments; this "Magdeburg Law" was copied by hundreds of Central European towns. Magdeburg prospered as a member of the Hanseatic League, accepted the Reformation 1524, and became a stronghold of Lutheranism. In 1561–63 the archbishop, a prince of the house of Brandenburg, also went over to Protestantism; members of his family continued (with dubious legality) to rule the archbishopric as administrators. In the Thirty Years War the imperials under Tilly stormed Magdeburg after a long siege (1630–31). In the ensuing sack, which Tilly vainly sought to halt, the city burned down and c.20,000 people (half the pop.) perished. The Peace of Westphalia (1648) provided for the transfer of the former archbishopric to Brandenburg. Magdeburg became an important Prussian fortress and (1816) the cap. of the former Saxony prov. of Prussia. More than half the city was destroyed in World War II. Birthplace of GUERICKE, inventor of the Magdeburg hemispheres, and of Baron von Steuben.

Magellan, Ferdinand (mŭjĕ'lŭn), c.1480–1521, Portuguese navigator. Received Spanish support in proposal to reach the Moluccas by W route. Sailed (1519) with five vessels; crossed from Atlantic to Pacific by strait named for him. Killed by Philippine natives. Only one ship completed first voyage around world (1522). Voyage proved roundness of earth, revolutionized ideas of relative proportion of land and water, revealed Americas as new world, distinct from Asia.

Magellan, Strait of, c.350 mi. long and 2½–15 mi. wide, separating South America from Tierra del Fuego. But for a few miles at W end which pass through Argentina, straits are in Chile. Discovered by Magellan (1520). Were important to sailing ships before Panama Canal was built. Open city on strait is Punta Arenas.

Magendie, François (frãswä' mäzhãdē'), 1783–1855, French physician, pioneer in experimental physiology.

Magenta (mäjăn'tä), town (pop. 10,470), Lombardy, N Italy, near Milan. Here in 1859 the French and Sardinians defeated the Austrians. MacMahon, who commanded the French, was created duke of Magenta.

magenta: see FUCHSINE.

Maggiore, Lago (lä'gō mäd-jō'rā), or **Verbano** (vĕrbä'nō), lake, area 82 sq. mi., c.40 mi. long, in the Alpine foothills of N Italy and S Switzerland. It is formed by the Ticino R. Stresa (Italy) and Locarno (Switzerland) are among its many resorts. The Borromean Isls., near Stresa, include Isola Bella, with the Borromeo Palace (now museum) and gardens.

Magi (mā'jī), priestly caste of anc. Persia, reputedly possessed of "magic" powers. After Zoroaster's death Magian priests headed Zoroastrianism; the greatest was Saena. See WISE MEN OF THE EAST.

magic [from Persian priests, *Magi*], practice of manipulating course of nature by supernatural means. Its aim (use and changing of nature) approximates that of science, an outgrowth of magic. It is allied to religion, but whereas religion reverences and worships supernatural beings, magic seeks to control supernatural forces to a desired end. This is done by means of verbal or written pronouncements, wearing of an amulet, or by imitative acts (e.g., agr. fertility rites based on analogy between plant and human generation). Almost all ancient peoples practiced magic. Christian Church has always combated black (i.e., malevolent) magic. Those who practiced it were considered sorcerers and witches. Many present-day superstitions are remnants of pagan magic, and belief in its powers is still extant. See YOGA.

magic lantern: see STEREOPTICON.

magic square, square divided into parts with letters or numbers inscribed therein which, whether read horizontally, vertically, or diagonally, spells same word or gives same sum. Such squares in ancient times were thought to have magic powers.

Maginot Line (mă'zhĭnō), system of fortifications along E frontier of France, extending from the Swiss to the Belgian border. Started by André Maginot (1877–1932), French war minister in 1929–30. It proved useless as the Germans flanked it in 1940.

Magliabechi, Antonio (mälyäbā'kē), 1633–1714, Italian librarian and scholar. Appointed (1673) court librarian by Cosimo III de' Medici, grand duke of Tuscany, to whom he bequeathed his library, which now forms part of National Library of Florence.

Magna Carta or **Magna Charta,** the most important instrument of English constitutional history, issued by King John at Runnymede, under compulsion by the barons, in 1215. Purpose of original charter was to insure feudal rights and guarantee that king could not encroach on baronial privileges. Provisions also guaranteed freedom of church and customs of towns; protection of rights of subjects and communities (which king could be compelled to observe); and words later to be interpreted as guarantees of trial by jury and habeas corpus. John repudiated charter as a grant made under coercion, was released from its observance by pope, and civil war broke out. Later reissues of charter had significant omissions; remaining clauses came to be known as Great Charter or Charter of Liberties. Later it became symbol of supremacy of constitution over king.

Magna Graecia (măg'nŭ grē'shŭ) [Latin,= great Greece], collective term for Greek colonies in S Italy, founded mostly in 8th cent. B.C., on both coasts S of Bay of Naples and Gulf of Taranto. These city-states did not thrive as did those of closely related Greek Sicily and declined badly after 500 B.C. Cumae, Tarentum, Heraclea, and Crotona were among them. They early brought Romans in contact with Greek culture.

magnalium (măgnā'lēŭm), alloy of aluminum and magnesium (c.5%). Lighter and more workable than aluminum, it is used in making metal mirrors and scientific instruments.

Magnesia, two anc. towns of Lydia, now W Turkey, so called because settled by Magnetes of E Thessaly. Magnesia ad Maeandrum (SE of Smyrna) was later colonized by Ionians and given by the Persian king to Themistocles, who died there. Magnesia ad Sipylum was on the Hermus R. at the foot of Mt. Sipylus, NE of Smyrna; scene of Roman victory over Antiochus III (190 B.C.).

magnesia (măgnē'zhů), magnesium oxide. Because of high melting point and low heat conductivity it is used to line electric furnaces, make firebricks, cover hot pipes, etc. Suspension in water is milk of magnesia, an antacid and laxative.

magnesite (măg'nůsīt), a magnesium carbonate mineral, white, yellow, or gray. It is mixed with magnesium chloride to make oxychloride cement; also used in making firebrick, Epsom salts, face powder.

magnesium (măgnē'sēům), active metallic element (symbol = Mg; see also ELEMENT, table), silver white, ductile, malleable. Sometimes included as metal of alkaline earths. Forms many compounds. It burns brilliantly in air and is used in making signal lights and fireworks. It also is used in medicine, in photography, and in alloys with aluminum. It is present in some glass, in soil (as salts), in chlorophyll. A strip of the metal is used as a fuse in thermite process.

magnet: see MAGNETISM.

magnetic poles. The earth, like any magnet (see MAGNETISM), has two magnetic poles—surface points where magnetic force is vertically downwards (dipping needle stands at 90°) and where horizontal compass is useless. North magnetic pole was placed (1948) at lat. 73° N, long. 100° W; south magnetic pole is at present near lat. 70° S, long. 148° E.

magnetism, property of attracting iron, probably first observed in a form of magnetite called lodestone which is called a natural magnet. Artificial magnets are substances that acquire magnetism after special treatment, e.g., by rubbing or stroking a bar of iron or steel with a strong magnet or by laying the piece of metal parallel to a magnet and tapping it gently (this is magnetic induction). An ELECTROMAGNET can be made by winding around a soft iron bar or core a coil of insulated wire carrying an electric current. When a suspended steel bar magnet can move freely it comes to rest in a general N–S direction, because of the magnetic effect of the earth; end of the bar pointing in northerly direction is N-seeking pole and opposite end is S-seeking pole. Like poles (i.e., N and N or S and S) repel each other while unlike attract. Magnetism of a magnet is concentrated in region of its poles, a condition termed polarity. Area in which magnetism is active is called magnetic field of force. Theoretically, the flow of magnetic force is through a continuous path (closed circuit), the direction of flow being from N-seeking pole outward through lines of force (lines through which magnetism appears to act) to S-seeking pole and from there through body of magnet to N-seeking pole. Strength of magnetic field is measured according to number of lines of force crossing unit area (e.g., 1 sq. cm.). One theory of nature of magnetism holds that it is a property of molecules and depends on their arrangement in body of magnet; another states that magnetism is caused by movement of electrons in the atom. Contributors to knowledge of magnetism include William Gilbert, C. A. de Coulomb, C. F. Gauss, A. M. Ampère, Oersted, Michael Faraday, Joseph Henry, Harold Pender, J. C. Maxwell, and J. J. Thomson. The study of **terrestrial magnetism** is based on assumption that earth is a gigantic magnet. Compass needles do not point directly to N and S geographical poles of earth because magnetic and geographical poles do not coincide. Deviation of compass needle from geographic N–S direction is called declination. Magnetic poles are not fixed so declination at given point varies. Isogonic lines drawn on map indicate points on earth's surface where declination is same. If magnetic needle is mounted so it is free to move it does not remain horizontal at all points on earth's surface; this deviation is called dip or inclination. At magnetic poles needle is vertical, at magnetic equator no dip is observable. Among those who contributed to study of terrestial magnetism are William Gilbert, Alexander von Humboldt, Gauss, Johann von Lamont, and L. A. Bauer.

magnetite (măg'nůtīt), lustrous black magnetic iron oxide, an important iron ore, occurring in crystals, masses, and loose sand. A variety known as lodestone shows magnetic polarity.

magnifying glass: see MICROSCOPE.

Magnitogorsk (mŭgnyē"tůgôrsk'), city (pop. c.200,000), RSFSR, on Ural R. Planned 1929, it grew rapidly into the chief metallurgical center of the USSR. Industries are based on high-grade magnetite mined in Magnitaya Mt. (on which city is built), iron ore and alloys from Urals, coal from Karaganda and Kuznetsk Basin.

magnitude, in astronomy, term denoting brightness of celestial object. Ptolemy's scale of six gradations, in which first magnitude was assigned to brightest stars, was later systematized and extended by estab. of ratio of brightness (2.51) between any two successive magnitudes. A star c.2.51 times as bright as standard first magnitude star is of zero magnitude; still greater brightness is expressed by negative numbers.

Magnolia, city (pop. 6,918), SW Ark., near La. line. Processes oil, cotton, and lumber.

magnolia, handsome deciduous or evergreen tree or shrub (*Magnolia*) native to North and Central America and Asia. The southern magnolia or bull bay (*Magnolia grandiflora*) has huge white flowers. The lily or saucer magnolia (*M. liliflora* or *M. purpurea*), with rose flowers in early spring, is hardy in U.S. Other magnolias include the sweet bay (*M. virginiana*) and the cucumber tree (*M. acuminata*).

Magnus, Norwegian kings. **Magnus I** (the Good), 1024–47, son of St. Olaf, succeeded the deposed Sweyn as king of Norway in 1035; in 1042 he succeeded HARTHACANUTE in Denmark. A rebellion in Denmark kept him from asserting his claim to England. After 1046 he was forced to share his throne with his uncle and successor, Harold III. **Magnus VI** (the Law Mender), 1238–80, king of Norway (1263–80), made peace with

Scotland by ceding the Hebrides and Isle of Man (1266). He revised the law code (1274), introducing the concept that crime is an offense against the state rather than against the individual and making the throne the source of justice. He also gave increased freedom to the cities; fixed the royal succession; created a new royal council and nobility; made a concordat with the Church. **Magnus VII,** 1316–73, king of Norway (1319–43, by succession) and of Sweden (1319–64, by election). Neglecting Norway in favor of Sweden, he was forced in 1343 to abdicate as king of Norway in favor of his son Haakon VI but exercised a nominal regency until 1355. In Sweden he was forced from the throne (1356–59) by his rebellious son Eric (d. 1359) and in 1361 had to accept Haakon as joint king. Magnus and Haakon in 1363 concluded an alliance with Waldemar IV of Denmark against the Hanseatic League; Haakon married Waldemar's daughter MARGARET. This Danish alliance was unpopular with the Swedes, who in 1364 deposed both Magnus and Haakon and chose Albert of Mecklenburg as king. Magnus was imprisoned 1365–71 and spent his last years in Norway.

Magog, in Bible: see GOG.

Magog (mā'gŏg), town (pop. 12,423), S Que., Canada, SW of Sherbrooke and on L. Memphremagog; founded by Loyalists after 1776. Resort and trade center with textile mills, woodworking, and dairying.

magpie, bird of crow family, c.20 in. long. American or black-billed magpie has black, iridescent plumage except for white abdomen and wing patches. It makes huge, domed nests in trees.

Magruder, John Bankhead, 1810–71, Confederate general. Successfully held off McClellan at Yorktown (1862). Recaptured Galveston, Texas (1863).

Magyars (mŏd'yärz, măg'yärz), the people of Hungary. They belong to the Finno-Ugric language family. Originally nomadic, they migrated c.460 from the Urals to N Caucasia, where they came in close contact with Turkic peoples; from them they learned agr. and borrowed their political and military organization. In the 9th cent. the PETCHENEGS forced them W; led by ARPAD, the Magyars settled in Hungary c.895. Ferocious mounted warriors, they conquered Moravia and penetrated deep into Germany but were checked by Emperor Otto I at the Lechfeld (955). With St. STEPHEN, who introduced Christianity, the history of Hungary begins.

Mahabharata (mŭhä'bä'rŭtŭ), great Sanskrit epic of India, composed 200 B.C.–A.D. 200 by bardic poets and later revised by philosophical writers. Its 110,000 couplets of 16-syllable lines tell of a fabulous dynastic struggle in kingdom of Hastinapur. Contains BHAGAVAD-GITA.

Mahan, Alfred Thayer (mŭhăn'), 1840–1914, American writer on naval affairs. His books, such as *The Influence of Sea Power upon History* (1890), had wide influence. Related naval affairs to international politics and economics.

Mahanoy City (mähŭnoi'), borough (pop. 10,934), E Pa., NE of Pottsville; settled 1859. Anthracite mining; mfg. of textiles and beer.

Mahdi [Arabic = divine guide] (mä'dē), in Islam, title of the IMAN, the man who will arise at end of the world as leader of faithful. Despite canonical saying and Sunnite belief that "There is no Mahdi but Jesus," Shiism periodically gives rise to men claiming to be the Mahdi. Perhaps most prominent of these was **Mohammed Ahmed,** 1848–85, in Anglo-Egyptian Sudan. He led a rebellion in 1881 against Egyptian rule, but died soon after capturing Khartoum. His followers, the **Mahdists,** were decisively defeated in 1898 by Anglo-Egyptian army under Lord Kitchener.

Mahican Indians (mŭhē'kŭn), confederacy of North American tribes of Algonquian linguistic stock, occupying the banks of the upper Hudson in 17th cent. They warred with the Mohawk, who with the aid of Dutch arms subdued them. Most of them were driven to join the Deleware Indians or seek protection of the Iroquois Confederacy. One remnant became the Christianized Stockbridge Indians. The name Mohican is applied to the whole group and to the E branch of the group, the MOHEGAN INDIANS.

Mahler, Gustav (mä'lŭr), 1860–1911, Austrian composer, conductor of the Imperial Opera, Vienna, 1897–1907. From 1908 to 1911 he conducted both the Metropolitan Opera, New York, and the Philharmonic Symphony. His works include nine symphonies (some with chorus) and the song cycle *Das Lied von der Erde* (for solo voices, chorus, and orchestra).

Mahmud II (mämōōd', mä'mōōd), 1784–1839, Ottoman sultan (1808–39). A vigorous reformer, he destroyed the JANIZARIES (1826); began "westernization" of Turkey. He could not prevent the loss of GREECE and fought unsuccessfully against MOHAMMED ALI of Egypt. His son Abdu-l-Mejid succeeded him.

mahogany, valuable hardwood obtained chiefly from the West Indian or Spanish mahogany tree (*Swietenia mahogani*) native to the West Indies and S Fla. The wood, golden brown to dark, rich, red brown, is hard and close-grained, and valued for furniture. African mahogany is obtained from *Khaya ivorensis.*

Mahone, William (mŭhōn'), 1826–95, Confederate general and Va. politician. Fought chiefly in campaigns in N Va. U.S. Senator (1881–87). He controlled Va. politics for several years.

Mahoning (mŭhō'nĭng), river rising in NE Ohio near Alliance and flowing c.90 mi. N then SE past Youngstown into Pa. to Shenango R., forming Beaver R. Berlin Dam (1943) is for flood control and power.

Mahrattas or **Marathas** (both: mŭrä'tŭz), Marathi-speaking people of W central India. Led by Sivaji, they conquered much territory in 17th cent. and by mid-18th cent. had displaced Mogul empire as leading power in India. Subdued 1818 by the British. Mahratta cap. was Poona.

Mährisch Ostrau, Czechoslovakia: see MORAVSKA OSTRAVA.

Mai, Angelo (än'jālō mī'), 1782–1854, Italian philologist, cardinal (from 1838) of the

Roman Church. He discovered manuscript of Cicero's *De republica.*

Maia (mā'ŭ, mī'ŭ). **1** In Greek religion, one of Pleiades; daughter of Atlas and nymph Pleione and mother of Hermes by Zeus. **2** In Roman religion, goddess of spring and fertility (month of May named for her).

Maiden Castle, anc. fortress, Dorsetshire, England. Finest earthwork in British Isles, c.115 acres in area. Excavations show occupation c.2000 B.C.

maidenhair fern, delicate fern (*Adiantum*) mostly native to tropics and grown as a pot plant. *Adiantum pedatum* is native to the North American woodlands.

Maidstone (mād'stŭn), municipal borough (pop. 54,026), co. seat of Kent, England. Has hospital (founded 1260 for pilgrims to Canterbury) and archbishops' palace. Birthplace of William Hazlitt.

Maidu Indians (mī'dōō), North American tribes of Penutian linguistic stock, located in early 19th cent. on E tributaries of Sacramento river. Their culture was typical of California area with brush shelters, acorn gathering, and a spirit cult.

Maikop (mīkôp'), city (pop. 67,302), Krasnodar Territory, RSFSR, at N foot of Greater Caucasus. Maikop oil fields are SW, connected by pipe line with refineries at Krasnodar and Black Sea port of Tuapse. Occupied 1942–43 by Germans in World War II.

mail: see POSTAL SERVICE.

Maillol, Aristide (ärēstēd' mäyôl'), 1861–1944, French sculptor. A neoclassicist, he is best known for his simple, massive figures of women.

Maimonides (mīmŏ'nĭdēz), called Rambam, 1135–1204, rabbi, physician, philosopher, b. Córdoba, Spain; d. Cairo. He attempted to codify the Jewish oral law in the Mishna Torah [copy of the Law]. Foremost among his many other writings is the *Moreh Nebukim* (Eng. tr., *Guide for the Perplexed,* 1919), in which he elucidated baffling religious and metaphysical problems; it has profoundly influenced Jewish and Christian religious thinkers.

Main (mān, Ger. mīn), river, 307 mi. long, central and W Germany, formed in N Bavaria by two affluents (Red and White Main) and flowing W past Bamberg, Schweinfurt, Würzburg, and Frankfurt into the Rhine opposite Mainz. Navigable from Bamberg; connected by canal with the Danube.

Maine, Sir Henry James Sumner, 1822–88, English jurist and historian. Known for work on history of laws as history of civilization. Books include *Ancient Law* (1861; new ed., 1931).

Maine (mān, Fr. mĕn), region and former province, NW France, in Sarthe and Mayenne depts.; historic cap. Le Mans. Watered by Mayenne, Loir, and Sarthe rivers, it is largely agr. Stock raising (horses) in Perche hills. A county from the 10th cent., later a duchy, it shared the history of ANJOU after 1110, was inc. into royal domain 1481. Several later royal princes were titular dukes of Maine.

Maine, state (33,215 sq. mi.; pop. 913,774), NE U.S.; admitted 1820 as 23d state (free); cap. AUGUSTA. PORTLAND, LEWISTON, BANGOR other important cities. Bounded S by the Atlantic; Saint John and Saint Croix rivers form part of boundary with New Brunswick. Many rivers (e.g., PENOBSCOT, KENNEBEC, ANDROSCOGGIN, Saco), lakes (MOOSEHEAD LAKE is largest), mountains (KATAHDIN is highest), islands (MOUNT DESERT ISLAND is largest). Mfg. of wood products, textiles, shoes; farming (potatoes quite important, grains, fruits, dairy, and poultry); lumbering; fishing; mining; tourism. Champlain estab. short-lived colony at mouth of the St. Croix (1604–5). Further French development prevented by Sir Samuel Argall (1613). Settlements attempted by Sir Ferdinando GORGES. Later came under control of Mass. (1659). Strength of troublesome Indians broken in Queen Anne's War. Set up as admiralty district of Mass. in 1775. Turned from commerce to industry through disturbances of Embargo Act of 1807 and War of 1812. Admitted as state through MISSOURI COMPROMISE. NORTHEAST BOUNDARY DISPUTE ended by WEBSTER-ASHBURTON TREATY of 1842. Mainly Republican state since Civil War. First state to have prohibition law (1851–1934). Hydro-electric power developed in 20th cent. but restricted to state. The trend toward industrialization and urbanization has been strong in recent times.

Maine, short river, W France, formed just N of Angers by the confluence of the Sarthe and Mayenne rivers and flowing S into the Loire.

Maine, U.S. battleship, center of a serious international incident in 1898. In Havana harbor on Feb. 15 a mysterious explosion occurred, and the *Maine* sank with a loss of 260 men. Separate U.S. and Spanish inquiries reached differing conclusions as to cause of explosion; neither inquiry fixed responsibility. "Remember the Maine" became an American catchword in SPANISH-AMERICAN WAR.

Maine, University of: see ORONO.

Maine-et-Loire (mĕn"-ā-lwär'), department (2,787 sq. mi.; pop. 496,068), NW France, in Anjou; cap. Angers.

Mainland. 1 Island, Orkney Isls., Scotland: see POMONA. **2** Island (pop. 15,172), 55 mi. long and 20 mi. wide, off N Scotland, largest of Shetland Isls. Has Lerwick, county town of the Shetlands.

Maintenon, Françoise d'Aubigné, marquise de (frãswäz' dōbēnyā' märkēz' dŭ mētŭnõ'), 1635–1719, second wife of Louis XIV of France; granddaughter of T. A. d'AUBIGNÉ. Born in France and baptized a Catholic, she spent her childhood in Martinique and was brought up a Protestant. After her father's death she and her mother returned to France, where they lived in great poverty. She was converted to Catholicism and became very devout. At 16 she married the poet SCARRON (d. 1660), through whom she entered Parisian society, and after his death she was appointed governess for the children of Mme de MONTESPAN, whom she gradually replaced in the king's affections. Louis XIV created her a marquise, but in all likelihood she resisted his advances until a year after the queen's death, when the king married her in a secret morganatic ceremony (1684). Her influence was largely responsible for the austere and somewhat hypocritical tone of the court, but she probably had little weight in political matters. In her later years she gave much attention to the school of Saint-Cyr (see SAINT-CYR-L'ÉCOLE).

Mainz (mīnts), city (pop. 87,046), cap. of Rhineland-Palatinate, W Germany, on the Rhine opposite mouth of the Main. Its French name, Mayence, is sometimes also used in English. River port; trade center (Rhine wines); mfg. (chemicals, machinery). University (1477–1816; reconstituted 1946 as Johannes Gutenberg Univ.). The Roman Maguntiacum, Mainz became (8th cent.) an archiepiscopal see under St. BONIFACE. Later archbishops acquired territories on both sides of the Rhine and Main. They ranked first among the ELECTORS, crowned the German kings, and were archchancellors of the Holy Roman Empire. Under their rule Mainz flourished commercially and culturally. GUTENBERG made it the first printing center. Mainz was occupied by the French in 1792 and ceded to them in 1797; the archbishopric was secularized and reduced to a diocese in 1803. The Congress of Vienna in 1815 gave Mainz along with Rhenish HESSE to the grand duchy of Hesse-Darmstadt. More than half destroyed in World War II, Mainz was assigned in 1945 to the French zone of occupation, but the suburbs E of the Rhine passed to Hesse (U.S. zone). The Romanesque cathedral (consecrated 1009), the Renaissance electoral palace, and other historic buildings were heavily damaged.

Maipú (mīpo͞o'), battlefield, central Chile, a few mi. S of Santiago. Victory of San Martín here (1818) assured Chilean independence from Spain and made possible the liberating expedition to Peru.

Maisonneuve, Paul de Chomedey, sieur de (shômdā' syûr' dů māzõnûv'), c.1612–1676, founder (1642) and first governor of Montreal, Canada, b. France.

Maistre, Joseph de (zhôzĕf' dů mĕ'strů), 1754?–1821, French writer, b. Savoy. Was Sardinian ambassador to St. Petersburg 1803–17. Detesting 18th-cent. rationalism, he developed with great logical skill his idea that the world should be one, under the absolute spiritual rule of the pope (*Du pape*, 1819; *Les Soirées de Saint-Pétersbourg*, 1821). His brother **Xavier de Maistre** (zävyā'), 1763–1852, served in the Russian army. He wrote *Voyage autour de ma chambre* (1794), a witty peregrination from object to object in his room, allowing each to call up recollections. *Le Lépreux de la cité d'Aoste* [the leper of Aosta] (1811) is a remarkable portrayal of Christian resignation.

Maitland, Frederic William, 1850–1906, English legal historian. Major work is *The History of English Law before the Time of Edward I* (2 vols., 1895), written with Sir Frederick Pollock.

Maitland, John: see LAUDERDALE, JOHN MAITLAND, DUKE OF.

Maitland, William (Maitland of Lethington), 1528?–1573, Scottish statesman. Secretary of State to Mary Queen of Scots, he sought to effect union of Scotland and England. Abandoned Mary after her marriage to Bothwell, but later became leader of her party.

maize: see CORN.

Majano, Benedetto da: see BENEDETTO DA MAJANO.

Majdanek (mīdä'nĕk), extermination camp (see CONCENTRATION CAMP), Poland, near Lublin, estab. and operated by the Germans in World War II. About 1,500,000 persons (mostly Jews) were killed in its gas chambers.

majolica: see POTTERY.

Majorca (můjôr'ků), Span. *Mallorca*, Mediterranean island (1,405 sq. mi.; pop. 327,102), Spain, largest of BALEARIC ISLANDS; cap. Palma. Its scenery and mild climate make it a popular resort. Agr., hog and sheep raising, fruit growing; mining (lead, marble, copper). Majorca became a kingdom in 1276 under a branch of the house of Aragon. It comprised the Balearic Isls., Roussillon, and several fiefs in S France; its cap. was Perpignan. In 1343 Peter IV of Aragon reunited the kingdom with Aragon. In the Spanish civil war of 1936–39 Majorca early passed to the Insurgent side.

Majorian (můjô'rēůn), d. 461, West Roman emperor (457–61). RICIMER raised him to power but, finding him too vigorous and independent, slew him in battle. Majorian's expedition against Gaiseric (460) was unsuccessful. He enacted laws to protect the people from excessive taxes.

Majuba Hill (můjo͞o'bů), NW Natal, South Africa, in Drakensberg range. Here in 1881 a British force was routed by Boer troops under Joubert.

Makassar, Indonesia: see MACASSAR.

Makemie, Francis (můkĕ'mē), 1658–1708, American clergyman, called founder of Presbyterianism in America, b. Ireland. As missionary he organized churches (c.1682) in Md. and first presbytery (1706) in Pa.

Makeyevka (mŭkyā'ŭfkŭ), city (pop. 240,145), SE Ukraine, in Donets Basin. Major metallurgical and coal-mining center.

Makhachkala (můkhäch"kŭlä'), city (pop. 86,847), cap. of Dagestan ASSR, SE European RSFSR; a Caspian seaport. Its oil refineries are linked by pipe line with the Grozny fields. Formerly called Petrovsk.

Makin: see GILBERT ISLANDS.

Malabar Coast (mă'lůbär), SW coast of India from Goa to S tip of peninsula at Cape Comorin. Bounded inland by Western Ghats. Fertile area.

Malacca (můlă'ků), city (pop. 54,507), cap. of Settlement of Malacca (633 sq. mi.; pop. 258,508), Malaya, on SW coast of Malay Peninsula. On Strait of Malacca, which links Indian Ocean with South China Sea. Founded c.1400, it became a rich trade center of SE Asia. In 15th cent., kings of Malacca extended their power over much of Malay Peninsula and Sumatra and introduced Islam into Malay world. Seized 1511 by Portuguese under Afonso de Albuquerque. Held by Dutch from 1641 to 1824, when it was ceded to Britain. Declined with rise of Singapore.

Malachi (mă'lůkī), **Malachias** (–kī'ůs), or **Malachy** (mă'lůkē), last book of Old Testament in AV. Author is otherwise unknown.

Book is chiefly concerned with the neglect of the Law and foreign marriages among the people, ending with prediction of a messiah.

malachite (mă'lůkīt), green mineral, carbonate of copper, occurring as crystals or in masses. An important copper ore, it is used also as a gem, for various ornaments, and is ground to make pigment. Found in U.S., Cuba, Chile, Russia, Rhodesia, Australia.

Malachy, Saint (mă'lůkē), 1095–1148, Irish churchman, successively abbot of Bangor, bishop of Connor, archbishop of Armagh, and bishop of Down. Reformed the Irish church, making it conform to the plan of the Church on the Continent. Friend of Bernard of Clairvaux. Feast: Nov. 23.

Maladetta Mountains (mälädĕ'tä), Span. *Montes Malditos,* massif of central Pyrenees, Spain, near French border. Pyrenees reach highest point here in Pico de ANETO.

Málaga (mä'lägä), city (pop. 208,344), cap. of Málaga prov., S Spain, in Andalusia; a Mediterranean port and winter resort. Exports sweet Malaga wine, fruit, fish, olive oil. Was founded by Phoenicians. Taken by the Moors in 711, it flourished later as chief port of the Moorish kingdom of Granada until its fall (1487) to Ferdinand and Isabella. Has cathedral (begun 16th cent.), ruins of Moorish alcazar, and an imposing cathedral, the Gibralfaro.

Malakhov (mŭlä'khŭf), hill just E of Sevastopol, RSFSR, S Crimea. Stronghold during Crimean War; stormed by French (1855) after long siege.

Malan, Daniel F(rançois) (mălän'), 1874–, prime minister of Union of South Africa (1948–), leader of Nationalist party. A determined advocate of *apartheid* (racial segregation) and of white supremacy. Returned to power by 1953 elections.

Malaparte, Curzio (mäläpär'tā), pseud. of **Curzio Suckert,** 1898–, Italian writer. He both defended and criticized Fascism. His works include *Kaputt* (Eng. tr., 1946) and *The Skin* (Eng. tr., 1952).

Malaren (mĕ'lärůn) or **Malar,** Swed. *Mälaren,* lake, area 440 sq. mi., E Sweden. Extends c.70 mi. W from Stockholm, which is on strait connecting it with Baltic Sea. On its shores and islands are resorts and castles, e.g., Skokloster and Gripsholm.

malaria, infectious febrile disease caused by certain protozoa (genus *Plasmodium*), transmitted by anopheles mosquito. Three main types are benign and malignant tertian, in which chills occur every 48 hr.; and quartan, with chills every 72 hr. Shaking chills coincide with release of microorganisms from red blood cells. Drugs specific against malaria include quinine and atabrine. See *ill.,* p. 813.

Malartic (mälärtēk'), town (pop. 5,983), W Que., Canada, W of Val d'Or, in Rouyn mining area.

Malaspina (mălůspē'nů), glacier, 1,500 sq. mi., SE Alaska, on Gulf of Alaska and S of Mt. St. Elias.

Malaspina, volcano: see CANLAON, MOUNT.

Malatesta (mälätĕs'tä), Italian family which ruled RIMINI 13th–15th cent. Most famous were Giovanni Malatesta, husband of FRANCESCA DA RIMINI, and Sigismondo Pandolfo Malatesta (1417–68), a typical Renaissance ruler, who built the Malatesta temple in Rimini.

Malatya (mälätē'ä), anc. *Melitene,* city (pop. 49,077), E central Turkey, in Armenia, at E foot of Taurus mts. Cotton milling; agr. trade center. Was an important city of ancient Cappadocia.

Malay: see MALAYAN.

Malaya (můlā'ů), federation (50,600 sq. mi.; pop. 5,226,549), in S part of Malay Peninsula; cap. Kuala Lumpur. Comprises two British settlements (PENANG and MALACCA) and nine British-protected states. European influence in Malaya dates from 1511, when Malacca fell to the Portuguese. The Dutch followed in 1641 and controlled Malacca area until Napoleonic Wars, after which the British became dominant in the area. In 1895 Perak, Selangor, Negri Sembilan, and Pahang were formed into Federated Malay States. In 1909 Siam lost Kedah, Kelantan, Perlis, and Trengganu to the British, who combined Johore with these areas to form Unfederated Malay States. Malaya was occupied by the Japanese throughout most of World War II. In 1946 the British estab. Malayan Union, comprising all Malaya except Singapore, and dissolved STRAITS SETTLEMENTS. In 1948 union was reorganized as Federation of Malaya, under British high commissioner. Political unrest led to war (begun 1948) between Malayan guerrillas and British troops.

Malayalam (mä″lůyä'lům), language of the Dravidian family. See LANGUAGE (table).

Malayan (můlā'ůn) or **Malay** (mā'lā), one of a population of some 100,000,000 inhabitants of SE Asia and adjacent islands. Term *Indonesian* is used both synonymously with Malayan and for people of interior districts. Physical appearance is generally Mongoloid; the many languages or dialects form a group of the Malayo-Polynesian languages.

Malay Archipelago or **Malaysia,** great island group, SE of Asia, in Indian and Pacific oceans, comprising Indonesia and the Philippines.

Malay language, one of the chief languages of the Malayo-Polynesian family. See LANGUAGE (table).

Malay Peninsula (můlā'), southern extremity of continent of Asia, between Indian Ocean and Strait of Malacca on W and South China Sea on E. Stretches south for c.400 mi. from Isthmus of Kra (its narrowest point) to Singapore. N part forms part of Thailand; S part is occupied by Federation of Malaya. Mountain range (rising to c.7,000 ft.) forms backbone of peninsula. Largely jungle. Area is one of world's leading producers of tin and rubber.

Malaysia: see MALAY ARCHIPELAGO.

Malazgirt, Turkey: see MANZIKERT.

Malbaie, La: see MURRAY BAY.

Malbork, former East Prussia: see MARIENBURG.

Malcolm III (Malcolm Canmore), d. 1093, king of Scotland (1054–93), son of Duncan I and successor of MACBETH. His frequent wars with England insured independence of his kingdom and made possible church reforms of his wife, St. MARGARET OF SCOTLAND.

Malden, residential and industrial city (pop. 59,804), E Mass., N suburb of Boston; settled 1640. Metal products, rubber footwear, and chemicals.

Malditos, Montes: see MALADETTA MOUNTAINS.

Maldive Islands (măl'dīv), republic (c.115 sq. mi.; pop. 82,068), comprising a group of atolls in Indian Ocean, SW of Ceylon; under British protection. Inhabitants are mainly Moslem. Formerly a sultanate, the islands became a republic on Jan. 1, 1953.

Maldon (môl'-), municipal borough (pop. 9,721), Essex, England. Leader of East Saxons, Byrhtnoth, killed here (991) in battle celebrated in one of last Anglo-Saxon heroic poems.

Mâle, Émile (āmēl' mäl'), 1862–, French art historian, authority on medieval sculpture.

Malebranche, Nicolas (mälbrăsh'), 1638–1715, French Cartesian philosopher. Laid greater stress on dualism of mind and matter in doctrine of occasionalism, maintaining that interaction between the two is impossible.

Malenkov, Georgi Maksimilianovich (gēôr'gē mäksēmĭlyä'nůvĭch mälyĕnkôf'), 1901–, Russian premier (1953–). A favorite of Stalin, he rose to secretary of the central committee of the Communist party; directed war production in World War II; became deputy premier 1946; became premier after Stalin's death in 1953.

Malesherbes, Chrétien Guillaume de Lamoignon de (krātyĕ' gēyōm' dů lämwänyō̃' dů mälzĕrb'), 1721–94, French magistrate and statesman, twice minister under Louis XVI (1774–76, 1787–88). Undertook Louis XVI's defense in king's trial (1792). Was guillotined as a royalist.

Malherbe, François de (frãswä' dů mälĕrb'), c.1558–1628, French poet and critic. His poetry was cold and official, but his insistence on objectivity, clarity, and perfection of form influenced the classical ideal in French literature.

Malheur (můlŏŏr'), river, E Oregon, rising in Blue Mts. and flowing c.165 mi. NE to Snake R. at Ontario. Used in Vale irrigation project.

Malibran, Maria (mälēbrã'), 1808–36, operatic contralto, b. Paris; pupil of her father, Manuel GARCÍA. One of the most popular singers of her day.

Malibu Beach (măl'ĭbōō), beach resort, S Calif., W of Los Angeles. Has many film stars' homes.

malice, in law, intent to violate the law of crimes or torts to injure another. It need not involve malignancy but may be simply inferred from reckless or wanton acts. Malice aforethought (i.e., deliberate intent) is a technical element of murder.

Malines (můlēn', můlēnz', Fr. mälēn'), Flemish *Mechelen,* city (pop. 60,740), Antwerp prov., N Belgium, on Dyle R. In English it is also known as Mechlin. Famous for exquisite lace formerly made here; now has textile mills. Archiepiscopal see since 1561, it is seat of primate of Belgium. Cathedral of St. Rombaut (13th cent.) has famous carillon and contains Van Dyck's *Crucifixion.* Other landmarks are archiepiscopal palace and city hall (14th cent.). Birthplace of Frans Hals.

Malinowski, Bronislaw (brŏnē'slŏf mălĭnŏf'skē), 1884–1942, Polish-English anthropologist. One of founders of functionalist school in social anthropology. He made intensive studies of Trobriand primitives.

Malipiero, Gian Francesco (jän' fränchā'skō mälēpyā'rō), 1882–, Italian composer, editor of works of Monteverdi, and researcher in early Italian music. His own works include songs, choral and orchestral works, and operas (e.g., *Giulio Cesare,* 1936).

Mallarmé, Stéphane (stāfän' mälärmā'), 1842–98, French poet, leader of the SYMBOLISTS. He held that poetry should express the transcendental and correspond most closely to music. He disregarded syntax and was often hermetic. Though hardly popular (he earned a meager living by teaching English), he was the center of a brilliant literary group, gathered every Tuesday evening at his flat, and he influenced all modern French writing.

malleability, property of metal describing extent to which it can be hammered, beaten, pressed, or rolled into thin sheets. Metals vary in this respect; gold is most malleable metal. Temperature and impurities affect malleability.

Mallorca, Balearic island: see MAJORCA.

mallow, white- or pink-flowered annual or perennial plants of genus *Malva.* The pink-flowered marsh mallow (*Althaea officinalis*) is found in swamps of E U.S. The rose mallow is hibiscus.

Malmaison (mälmāzō̃'), château at Rueil-Malmaison, a W suburb of Paris, France. Was residence of Bonaparte 1800–1803 and of Empress Josephine 1809–14. Napoleonic museum.

Malmédy (mälmādē'), town (pop. 5,569), Liége prov., SE Belgium, near German border. Treaty of Versailles transferred it from Prussia to Belgium (see EUPEN).

Malmesbury (mämz'bůrē), municipal borough (pop. 2,509), Wiltshire, England. Site of magnificent abbey founded in 7th cent.

Malmo (măl'mō), Swed. *Malmö,* maritime industrial city (pop. 192,498), co. seat of Malmohus co., SE Sweden, on the Oresund opposite Copenhagen. It has shipyards, machine shops, textile mills, sugar refineries, and tobacco, rubber, and chemical plants. Founded 12th cent., it was major herring port during Hanseatic period. Until annexed by Sweden as part of SKANE in 1658, it was under Denmark. Bothwell was a prisoner in Malmo castle (built 1537).

Maloja (mälō'yä), pass, Grisons canton, Switzerland, leading from Engadine Valley to Italy.

Malolos (mälō'lōs), municipality (pop. 33,384), on SW Luzon, Philippines, NW of Manila. Short-lived revolutionary capital was set up here in 1898 under Emilio Aguinaldo.

Malone, Dumas (dōōmä' můlōn'), 1892–, American historian and editor, professor of history at Columbia Univ. (1945–). Editor in chief of *Dictionary of American Biography* (1931–36). Undertook later a four-volume work on Jefferson.

Malone, Edmund, 1741–1812, Irish Shaksperian scholar, noted as exposer of Shaksperian forgeries of William IRELAND (1796). He published editions of Shakspere (1790) and Dryden (1800).

Malone (mŭlōn'), village (pop. 9,501), N N.Y., on Salmon R. near Quebec line. Mfg. of metal powders, clothing, paper, and furniture. FENIAN MOVEMENT members gathered here (1866, 1870) to attack Canada.

Malory, Sir Thomas, d. 1471, English author of *Morte d'Arthur,* last medieval English treatment of ARTHURIAN LEGEND. The long romance is notable for heroic tone and vigorous prose style.

Malpighi, Marcello (märchĕl'lō mälpē'gē) 1628–94, Italian anatomist, pioneer microscopist. His observation of blood in capillaries completed proof of circulation theory.

Malplaquet (mälpläkā'), village, Nord dept., N France. Here in 1709 Marlborough and Eugene of Savoy defeated the French.

Malraux, Andé (ãdrā' mälrō'), 1895–, French author. Profoundly concerned with the problems of freedom and revolution, he took an active part in the Chinese civil war (1925–27), on the side of the Kuomintang, and in the Spanish civil war of 1936–39, on the Loyalist side. From these experiences came two of the most powerful social novels of his time—*La Condition Humaine* (1933; Eng. tr., *Man's Fate*) and *L'Espoir* (1938; Eng. tr., *Man's Hope*). His *Psychology of Art* (1947; Eng. tr., 2 vols., 1949) has an entirely novel approach to esthetics. Malraux, though early associated with Communism, in 1947 became Gen. Charles de Gaulle's propaganda chief.

malt, a partly germinated grain (usually barley) dried and cured for use in brewing. Rich in carbohydrates and protein, it has nutritional value.

Malta (môl'tŭ), British colony (total area 122 sq. mi.; total pop. 305,991) in the Mediterranean S of Sicily, comprising islands of Malta (95 sq. mi.), Gozo, and Comino; cap. Valletta. Group sometimes called the Maltese Isls. Has belonged to Phoenicians, Greeks, Carthaginians, Romans, and Saracens. Given (1530) to KNIGHTS HOSPITALERS who held it until surrender to Napoleon in 1798. Annexed by British in 1814. Valletta is chief British Mediterranean naval and military base. Malta suffered over 2,000 air raids in World War II; entire pop. awarded decoration for bravery by George VI in 1942. The 1947 constitution gave limited self-government. British naval dockyards chief source of employment. St. Paul shipwrecked here.

Malta, city (pop. 2,095), N Mont., on Milk R. and E of Havre. Chief town of Milk R. project.

Malta, Knights of: see KNIGHTS HOSPITALERS.

Malta fever: see BRUCELLOSIS.

Maltese Islands: see MALTA.

Malthus, Thomas Robert (măl'thŭs), 1766–1834, English economist, pioneer in modern population study. In *An Essay on the Principle of Population* (1798; rev. ed., 1803), he contended that poverty is unavoidable because population increases by geometrical ratio and the means of subsistence by arithmetical ratio. He believed that the only preventive checks to growth of population were war, famine, disease, and "moral restraint" (see BIRTH CONTROL). Subsequent POPULATION trends have outmoded much of his analysis.

maltose (môl'tōs) or **malt sugar,** carbohydrate with same chemical formula as sucrose; results from action of an enzyme on starch.

Malvern (môl'vŭrn, mô'–), urban district (pop. 21,681), Worcestershire, England. Medicinal springs make it a favorite watering place. Annual dramatic festival begun in 1928 as tribute to G. B. Shaw.

Malvern, city (pop. 8,072), S central Ark., SE of Hot Springs. Mfg. of wood products, brick, chemicals, shoes, and cotton. Aluminum plant near.

Malverne, residential village (pop. 8,086), SE N.Y., on SW Long Isl. ESE of Jamaica.

Malvern Hill: see SEVEN DAYS BATTLES.

Malvern Hills, range of hills, c.9 mi. long, on the Worcestershire-Herefordshire border, England.

Mamaroneck (mŭmă'rŭnĕk), residential village (pop. 15,016), SE N.Y., on Long Isl. Sound near New Rochelle; settled 1661. Food, wood, metal products.

Mamelukes (mă'mŭlo͞oks) [Arabic,= slaves], originally slaves brought to Egypt by Fatimite caliphs in 10th cent. and by later Ayyubite sultans and trained as soldiers. Many were freed and rose to high rank. In 1250 the Mameluke emir Eibek killed last Ayyubite ruler and proclaimed himself sultan. For c.250 years Egypt was ruled by Mamelukes, who at one time controlled much of Asia Minor. Their two dynasties were Bahrites (1250–1382), chiefly Turks and Mongols, and Burjites (1382–1517), chiefly Circassians. They retained high posts even after Turkish conquest of Egypt (1517). Their rebellion against the Turks was put down by Napoleon in 1798, and in 1811 their power was totally destroyed by Mohammed Ali.

Mamison or **Mamisson** (both: mŭmēsôn'), pass, 9,550 ft. high, USSR, in Greater Caucasus, on border between Georgian SSR and RSFSR. Crossed by Ossetian Military Road; links Ardon and Rion river valleys.

mammal, warm-blooded animal of highest vertebrate class, Mammalia. Female has glands that secrete milk to nourish young. In most, the body is hairy. The heart is four-chambered and a diaphragm separates thorax from abdomen. Young of higher mammals are fed prenatally through placenta and are born alive except among egg-laying monotremes. Orders include Carnivora (flesh-eaters); Cetacea (e.g., whale); Rodentia (see RODENT); Perissodactyla and Artiodactyla (both hoofed mammals); and primate order (incl. man).

mammon, Aramaic term meaning riches, retained in New Testament Greek. Mat. 6.24; Luke 16.9,11,13.

mammoth, extinct elephant which ranged over parts of Eurasia and North America during Pleistocene epoch. Shoulder height of imperial mammoth was c.13½ ft.; of woolly variety 9 ft. Whole specimens have been found preserved by freezing in Siberia.

Mammoth Cave National Park: see NATIONAL PARKS AND MONUMENTS (table).

Mammoth Hot Springs, Wyo., hq. of Yellowstone Natl. Park (see NATIONAL PARKS AND MONUMENTS, table).

Mamoré (mämōrā'), river, c.600 mi. long, Bolivia, formed by tributaries in Andes and plains of central Bolivia. Flows N to Brazil forming small section of Brazil-Bolivia border. Joins Beni to form Madeira.

Mamun (mämōōn'), 786–833, 7th ABBASID caliph (813–33), son of HARUN-AL-RASHID. Belonged to a rationalistic sect of Islam. Arts and sciences flourished under his reign.

man: see ANTHROPOLOGY; MAN, PRIMITIVE; ANATOMY; PHYSIOLOGY. See *ill.*, p. 763.

Man, Isle of, island (221 sq. mi.; pop. 55,213), Great Britain, in Irish Sea; cap. Douglas. Scenery and mild climate make it a resort. Has varied agr., dairying, fishing, and quarrying. Formerly held by Norway, Scotland, and earls of Derby, it has been under British crown since 1827. Manx language is now little spoken.

man, primitive, or **early man.** Millions of human beings of forms transitional between the apelike and the contemporary lived in the Pleistocene period. There arose then roughly three types. The most primitive men, *Pithecanthropus* (Java ape man) and *Sinanthropus* (Peking man), both probably variants of *Homo erectus,* showed modern and archaic physical features. They were capable of speech, used fire, and lived in bands. Neanderthaloid man (*Homo neanderthalensis*) was found in association with Mousterian culture and ranged from Europe to Africa and central Asia. Among the earliest confirmed representatives of *Homo sapiens* is Cro-Magnon man, although many believe that *Homo sapiens* existed before the disappearance of Neanderthal man. Evidence from Mt. Carmel suggests that modern man may be a mixture of Neanderthal and other types, such as Cro-Magnon. An even more complicated mixture of traits has been found in fossils such as those of the Solo man of Java, which present a mosaic of traits of *Pithecanthropus,* Neanderthal, and *Homo sapiens.* Whatever the origin of *Homo sapiens,* many hold it probable that he is in part the result of crossing with other types, which took place whenever early men in their wanderings came in contact.

Managua (mänä'gwä), city (pop. 104,444), W Nicaragua; cap. and largest city of Nicaragua, on S shore of L. Managua. Made permanent cap. (1855) as compromise to end feud between Granada and Leon. U.S. marines stationed here, 1912–25, 1926–33.

Manáos, Brazil: see MANAUS.

Manasquan (măn'ŭskwän), Atlantic resort borough (pop. 3,178), E N.J., SSW of Asbury Park.

Manassas, town (pop. 1,804), N Va., WSW of Alexandria. Civil war battles of BULL RUN, fought near by, sometimes called battles of Manassas.

Manasseh (mŭnă'sē) or **Manasses** (–sŭs). **1** Son of Joseph and ancestor of one of the 12 tribes of Israel. Tribe settled both E and W of Jordan R. Gen. 41.51; Num. 26.28–34; Deut. 3.13; Joshua 17; 2 Kings 10.33; 1 Chron. 2.21–23; 5.25–26; 7.14–19; Rev. 7.6. **2** Died c.643 B.C., king of Judah (c.698–c.643 B.C.). Denounced in Bible as one of Judah's worst kings, he later reformed. 2 Kings 21; 2 Chron. 33; Mat. 1.10. The Prayer of Manasses, one of the PSEUDEPIGRAPHA, placed in Apocrypha in AV, is a penitential psalm ascribed to the repentant king.

manatee (mănŭtē'), herbivorous aquatic mammal (*Trichechus*) allied to dugong. Its oil, flesh, and hide are used by man.

Manaus (mŭnä'ŭs, Port. mŭnoush'), city (pop. 110,678), cap. of Amazonas state, NW Brazil, on left bank of Rio Negro near junction with Amazon. Though more than 900 mi. inland, Manaus is large port for ocean-going vessels. Founded in late 17th cent., it thrived during wild rubber boom, is now metropolis of all upper Amazon. Formerly Manáos.

Mancha, La (lä män'chä), region of central Spain, in New Castile; a high, barren plateau. Made famous by DON QUIXOTE, whose home was in a village of La Mancha.

Manche (mãsh) [Fr. name for English Channel], department (2,295 sq. mi.; pop. 435,432), NW France, in Normandy; cap. Saint-Lô. Includes COTENTIN peninsula, Cherbourg, Mont-Saint-Michel.

Manchester (măn'chŭstŭr), city (pop. 703,175), Lancashire, England, on Irwell, Medlock, Irk and Tib rivers; center of England's most densely populated area and world's foremost cotton city. MANCHESTER SHIP CANAL makes city a seaport. Artificial-silk industry balanced losses in cotton after World War I. Relics have been found of Roman city. Mentioned in Domesday Book. Has long led in liberal reform movements. Scene of PETERLOO MASSACRE in 1819. Manchester *Guardian* dates from 1821. Site of Victoria Univ. (1846), Cooperative Col. (1919), two art galleries and libraries. Home of Hallé Orchestra. Suffered heavy bomb damage in World War II.

Manchester. 1 Town (pop. 34,116), central Conn., E of Hartford; settled c.1672. Textiles, metal goods. **2** City (pop. 82,732), S N.H., on Merrimack R. between Concord and Nashua; settled 1722. First (1846) and largest city in state. Great Amoskeag (ăm'ŭskĕg) cotton textile mills (power from Amoskeag Falls) closed Sept., 1935. Amoskeag Industries, Inc. (citizens' organization) bought the property in Sept., 1936, and sold or leased its parts to various concerns. Textiles, shoes, machinery, building materials, and luggage. Seat of St. Anselm's Col. Grenier Air Force Base was built 1941. **3** Resort town (pop. 2,425), SW Vt., N of Bennington and E of Mt. Equinox.

Manchester school, group of English economists of the 19th cent., led by Richard Cobden and John Bright. Chief tenets were FREE TRADE and LAISSEZ FAIRE.

Manchester Ship Canal, 35½ mi. long; connecting Manchester, England, with the Mersey estuary above Birkenhead. Opened in 1894.

Manchester terrier: see TERRIER.

Manchu: see CH'ING, dynasty.

Manchukuo (mănchōō'kwō), former state

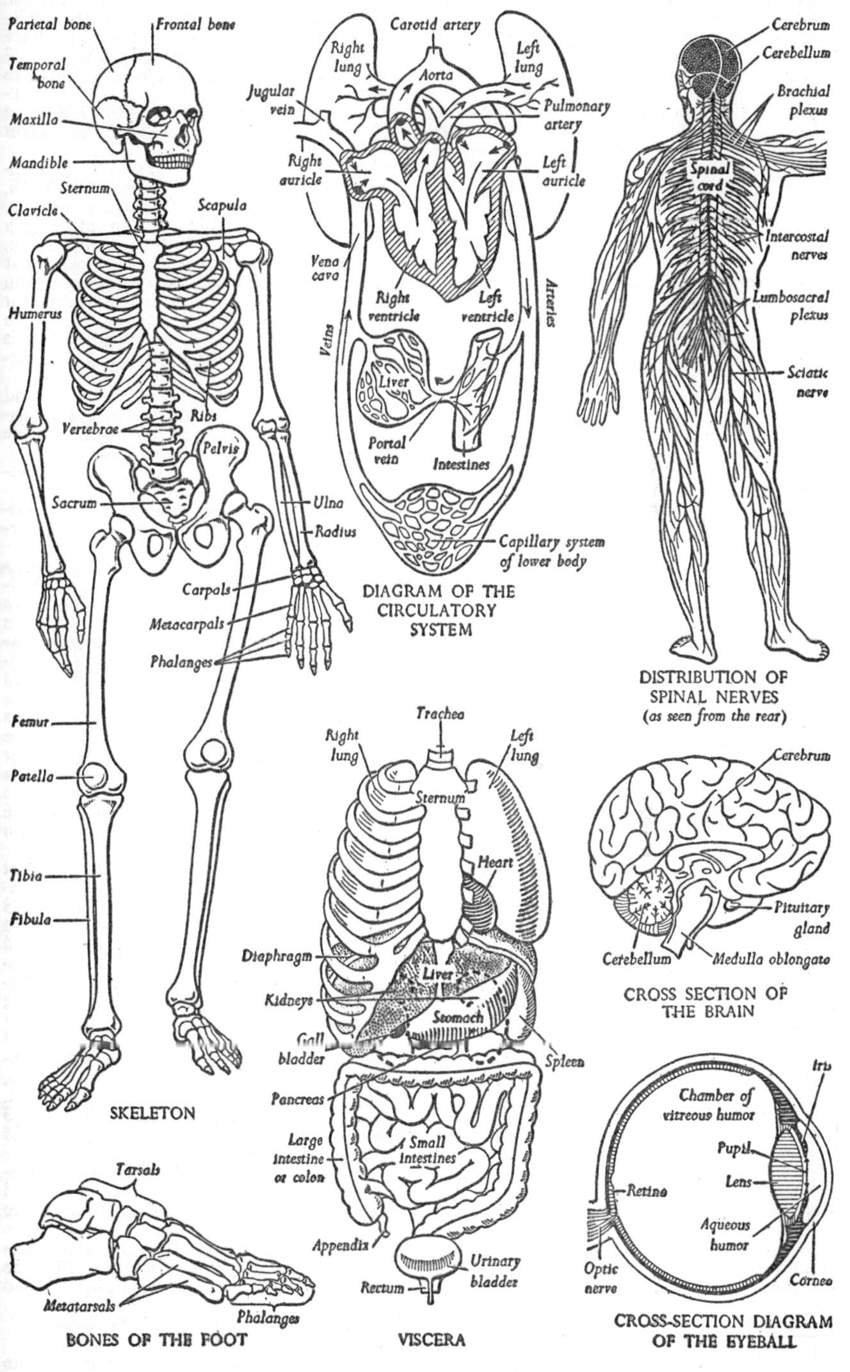
Parietal bone
Frontal bone
Temporal bone
Maxilla
Mandible
Sternum
Clavicle
Scapula
Humerus
Ribs
Vertebrae
Pelvis
Sacrum
Ulna
Radius
Carpals
Metacarpals
Phalanges
Femur
Patella
Tibia
Fibula
SKELETON
Carotid artery
Right lung
Left lung
Aorta
Jugular vein
Pulmonary artery
Right auricle
Left auricle
Vena cava
Right ventricle
Left ventricle
Veins
Arteries
Liver
Portal vein
Intestines
Capillary system of lower body
DIAGRAM OF THE CIRCULATORY SYSTEM
Cerebrum
Cerebellum
Brachial plexus
Spinal cord
Intercostal nerves
Lumbosacral plexus
Sciatic nerve
DISTRIBUTION OF SPINAL NERVES (as seen from the rear)
Trachea
Right lung
Left lung
Sternum
Heart
Diaphragm
Liver
Kidneys
Stomach
Gall bladder
Spleen
Pancreas
Large intestine or colon
Small intestines
Appendix
Urinary bladder
Rectum
VISCERA
Cerebrum
Pituitary gland
Cerebellum
Medulla oblongata
CROSS SECTION OF THE BRAIN
Tarsals
Metatarsals
Phalanges
BONES OF THE FOOT
Iris
Chamber of vitreous humor
Pupil
Lens
Retina
Aqueous humor
Optic nerve
Cornea
CROSS-SECTION DIAGRAM OF THE EYEBALL

(512,766 sq. mi.; pop. 43,233,954), comprising Manchuria and Jehol prov.; cap. Hsinking (Changchun). A Japanese-controlled puppet state, it was nominally ruled by Henry Pu Yi. Restored to China after World War II.

Manchuria (mănchŏŏ′rēŭ), region (585,000 sq. mi.; pop. 44,000,000), NE China. Separated from USSR largely by Amur, Argun, and Ussuri rivers and from Korea by Yalu and Tumen rivers. Its great central plain, surrounded by mountains, is drained by Liao and Sungari rivers. Agr. (soybeans, kaoliang, grain), lumbering; major mines (mostly iron and coal) in SW. Russian penetration of Manchuria began c.1900. After Russo-Japanese War (1904–5) Japan replaced Russia as dominant foreign power in region (see LIAOTUNG). After 1911 Manchuria was ruled by war lords, notably Chang Tso-lin. Occupying entire area in 1931 Japan set up puppet state of MANCHUKUO (expired 1945). After World War II Manchuria came under Communist rule; divided into 6 provinces (Heilungkiang, JEHOL, Kirin, Liaosi, LIAOTUNG, Sungkiang) and Inner Mongolian Autonomous Region (see MONGOLIA).

Mancini (mänchē′nē), family name of five sisters, nieces of Cardinal Mazarin. Born in Rome, they were called to France by their uncle. Laure (1636–57) married a grandson of Henry IV and was the mother of Louis Joseph, duc de Vendôme. Olympe (1639?–1708) married the count of Soissons, of the house of Savoy-Carignan, and was the mother of Eugene of Savoy. Implicated in the POISON AFFAIR (1680), she fled to the Low Countries. Marie (c.1640–c.1715) was loved by Louis XIV, but Mazarin broke up the liaison and married her to a Prince Colonna. Hortense (1646–99), Mazarin's favorite and most beautiful niece, married Armand Charles de la Porte, who was made duke of Mazarin. She left him and became a favorite at the English court. Marie Anne (1649?–1714), duchess of Bouillon, was the center of a literary circle and a patroness of La Fontaine. Also implicated in the Poison Affair, she was banished from court (1680).

Manco Capac (mäng′kō käpäk′). **1** Legendary founder of Inca dynasty of Peru. **2** Died 1544, last of Inca rulers; son of Huayna Capac.

Mandaeans (măndē′ŭnz), small religious sect in Iran and Iraq, also known as Christians of St. John (i.e., St. John the Baptist), Nasoreans, Sabaeans, and Subbi. Their rite preserves ancient beliefs: an astrology similar to the Babylonian; an emanation system and dualism like GNOSTICISM, but, unlike Gnostics, stressing fertility rather than asceticism. Their chief rite is frequent baptism, and they hold that living water is the principle of life. The *Ginza Rba* is their holy book.

Mandalay (măn″dŭlā′), town (pop. 163,527), Upper Burma, on Irrawaddy R. Was cap. of Burmese kingdom, 1860–85. Royal palace and famous pagodas suffered severe damage in World War II. Terminus of rail line from Rangoon.

mandamus, writ ordering the performance of a ministerial act (i.e., an act which a person or body is obligated by law to perform, without discretion or choice). It is an extraordinary remedy, not used unless usual legal remedies have failed. One sample of use is order by a superior court compelling a lower court to accept a suit which it had illegally refused.

Mandan (măn′dăn), city (pop. 7,298), S N.Dak., on Heart and Missouri rivers opposite Bismarck. Railroad division point; distribution center for grain, dairy area. Lewis and Clark wintered here 1804–5.

Mandan Indians, North American tribe of Siouan linguistic stock, living in historic times on the Missouri R. Sedentary "village" Indians, they lived from agr. and were culturally associated with the Arikara and the Hidatsa. Virtually wiped out by smallpox in 18th and 19th cent.

mandarin (măn′dŭrĭn) [from Port. *mandar* = to govern], an official under the Ch'ing dynasty of China. The nine grades in the civil service were shown by a different colored button worn on the dress cap. Mandarin Chinese is the language spoken throughout China except in the W and parts of the S. The Peking dialect of Mandarin is the official national speech.

mandates, system of trusteeship estab. by Article 22 of Covenant of League of Nations for former Turkish territories and German colonies. Areas in three classes: A, Turkish territories, with provisional independence; B, German African colonies, with commercial equality; C, other German colonies, as part of mandatories' empires. League administered system through 11-member Mandates Commission. See also TRUSTEESHIP, TERRITORIAL.

Mandeville, Bernard, 1670–1733, English satirical writer on ethical subjects, known especially for *The Fable of the Bees; or, Private Vices, Public Benefits* (1714), an attack on social restraint of individuals.

Mandeville, Sir John, pseudonym of 14th-cent. author of *The Voiage and Travaile of Sir John Mandeville.* The writer calls himself Englishman. Work first composed probably in Liége in French (c.1371), soon translated into many languages. Purporting to be record of author's travels through Jerusalem and rest of Orient, the book is compilation of authentic travels of others, interspersed with fantastic lore.

mandolin: see STRINGED INSTRUMENTS.

mandrake, European perennial (*Mandragora officinarum*) often mentioned in literature and the subject of many legends and superstitions. Its root, the source of a narcotic used during the Middle Ages as a pain killer, crudely resembles the human form. MAY APPLE is also called mandrake.

mandrill, mainly arboreal W African baboon (*Mandrillus*) with short tail, red and blue rump patches.

manes (mā′nēz), in Roman religion, spirits of the dead taken collectively, also called euphemistically *di manes* [good gods]. They were placated with offerings at graves of the dead. Later identified with *di parentes* [family ancestors], they watched over family along with lares and penates. See LARVAE.

Manet, Édouard (ādwär′ mänā′), 1832–83, French impressionist painter. Throughout his lifetime his works (notably the *Olympia*) were violently attacked by the critics. But he had a strong following among his fellow painters and a friend in Zola, who lost his position on a newspaper for defending him. Usually considered the greatest protagonist of impressionism and of plein-air painting, which he helped to originate. Achieved dramatic and vigorous paintings with the utmost economy of means. Greatly influenced his contemporaries.

Manfred, c.1232–1266, last Hohenstaufen king of Sicily (1258–66); natural son of Emperor Frederick II. Was regent in Sicily after 1250 for his brother CONRAD IV and his nephew CONRADIN. In 1254 he was obliged to restore Sicily to the papacy, retaining only Taranto as a fief held from the pope, but he soon rebelled, conquered S Italy and Sicily, assumed leadership of all Italian Ghibellines, and in 1258 had himself crowned at Palermo. Pope Urban IV retorted by investing Charles of Anjou with Sicily as CHARLES I. Manfred was defeated by Charles at Benevento and fell in the battle. His son-in-law, Peter III of Aragon, became king of Sicily after the Sicilian Vespers (1282).

manganese (măng'gŭnēs), metallic element (symbol = Mn; see also ELEMENT, table), gray tinged with pink, not malleable, harder than iron. Chemically active, it forms many compounds. Does not occur free but compounds are widely distributed. Used in alloys to increase hardness; it is present in steel. Compounds are used in paints, dry cells, as oxidizing agents, antiseptics, disinfectants.

Mangareva: see GAMBIER ISLANDS.

mange (mānj), skin disease of domestic animals and sometimes man, usually caused by mites. The resulting itching may lead to bacterial infections. Known also as scab or scabies, the disease may be treated with various chemicals.

Mangin, Charles (shärl' mãzhē), 1866–1925, French general. Served in Sudan and North Africa; was prominent in defense of Verdun.

mango, evergreen tree (*Mangifera indica*) native to Asia and long grown in the tropics for its large, delicious fruit which has yellow-red skin and golden flesh. It is now cultivated in Fla. and Calif.

mangrove (măng'grōv), tropical evergreen tree which produces stiltlike aerial roots from the trunk. The American mangrove (*Rhizophora mangle*) is abundant along shores and in brackish marshes in S Fla., Mexico, West Indies, Central and South America.

Manhasset (mănhăs'ĭt), suburban village (1940 pop. 5,099), on N shore of Long Isl., SE N.Y., near the head of Manhasset Bay and E of Great Neck.

Manhattan. 1 City (pop. 19,056), NE Kansas, WNW of Topeka near junction of Big Blue and Kansas rivers; founded 1854. Trade and processing center of agr. and grazing area. Seat of KANSAS STATE COLLEGE OF AGRICULTURE AND APPLIED SCIENCE. **2** Borough (land area 22 sq. mi.; pop. 1,960,101) of NEW YORK city, SE N.Y., coextensive with New York co. Composed chiefly of Manhattan isl. (c.12 mi. long and 2 mi. wide at greatest width), but also including islands in East R. and in New York Bay (GOVERNORS ISLAND; ELLIS ISLAND; Bedloe's Isl., with Statue of Liberty); bounded on W by Hudson R., NE and N by Harlem R. and Spuyten Duyvil Creek. Many bridges, tunnels, ferries link it to the other boroughs and to N.J. DUTCH WEST INDIA COMPANY bought Manhattan from Manhattan Indians in 1626 for trinkets worth $24; first known as NEW AMSTERDAM, it became New York under the English 1664; its boundaries were those of New York city until 1874, when several Westchester co. communities were inc. into city; became a New York city borough 1898. Commercial, cultural, financial heart of the city, with extensive and diversified mfg., tremendous wholesale and retail trade, major distributing facilities (rail, ship, truck), banking and finance establishments. Here are METROPOLITAN MUSEUM OF ART, AMERICAN MUSEUM OF NATURAL HISTORY, MUSEUM OF MODERN ART; hq. of NEW YORK PUBLIC LIBRARY; numerous theaters (theatrical center of the country) and institutions of music, COLUMBIA UNIVERSITY, parts of College of the City of NEW YORK and of NEW YORK UNIVERSITY, NEW SCHOOL FOR SOCIAL RESEARCH, JUILLIARD SCHOOL OF MUSIC, theological seminaries and medical schools, COOPER UNION; Trinity Church (chartered 1697), SAINT PATRICK'S CATHEDRAL, Cathedral of SAINT JOHN THE DIVINE, Riverside Church, Temple Emanu-El. Famous areas: HARLEM, GREENWICH VILLAGE, the BOWERY; streets: BROADWAY, FIFTH AVENUE, WALL STREET; parks: the BATTERY, CENTRAL PARK, Fort Tryon Park (with the Cloisters). Some of the much-visited buildings are: Empire State Building, Rockefeller Center, Jumel Mansion, and UN hq.

Manhattan Beach, resort and residential city (pop. 17,330), S Calif., SW of Los Angeles.

Manhattan College: see BRONX, THE, N.Y.

Manhattan Indians, North American tribe of Algonquian linguistic stock, occupying in early 17th cent. N Manhattan isl. and near-by areas. The Dutch bought the island from them in 1626 and then practically destroyed them in wars of 1640–45.

Manheim, borough (pop. 4,246), SE Pa., NW of Lancaster. Munitions center in Revolution. Here H. W. Steigel produced first flint glass in U.S.

manic-depressive psychosis, functional disorder involving mania or depression or fluctuation between the two. Manic patient is exalted, extravagant, distracted, tends toward moral laxness, antisocial behavior. Depressive patient has pathological melancholia, ideas of unworthiness, sin, suicide. Recovery is likely but danger of recurrence always remains. Shock therapy may shorten depressive phase. Predisposition may be hereditary.

Manichaeism (mă'nĭkēĭzŭm) or **Manichaeanism** (mănĭkē'ŭnĭzŭm), religion founded by a 3d-cent. Persian named Mani, who announced himself a prophet in 242, was driven into exile under Zoroastrian pressure, and finally after his return was flayed to death. His religion, however, spread over the Roman Empire and Asia. The influence of Buddhism and Gnosticism was strong, and Manichaeism took the dualism of ZOROASTRIANISM, spiritualizing the struggle between light and dark into warfare between good and evil. The teaching was strongly ascetic, and the "elect" or "perfect" practiced strict celibacy and austerity; they were assured of immediate happiness after death. The lower "auditors" or "hearers," laymen, could marry once but were called on to restrict sensual pleasures; they might hope to be reborn among the elect. This widespread religion was successfully opposed by Christianity and died out as a dynamic faith c.500, though it was later revived among Paulicians, Bogomils, Cathari, and Albigenses.

Manich Depression, RSFSR: see MANYCH DEPRESSION.

Manicouagan (mănĭkwä'gŭn), river, rising in E central Que., Canada, and flowing S c.310 mi. to St. Lawrence R. SW of Baie Comeau.

Manihiki (mänĭhē'kē), atoll (pop. 435), S Pacific, E of Samoa. Discovered 1822 by Americans; placed under New Zealand Cook Isls. administration, 1901.

Manila (mŭnĭ'lŭ), city (pop. 983,906), cap. and chief port of Philippines, on SW Luzon, on Manila Bay. Divided into two sections by navigable Pasig R. Here are Malacañan Palace (presidential mansion), Univ. of Santo Tomás, Univ. of the Philippines, Natl. Univ., and Philippine Women's Univ. In 1571 a Spanish colony was estab. here by López de Legaspi. Early in World War II, city was heavily bombed by the Japanese; Intramuros (old walled city) was destroyed.

Manila Bay, inlet of South China Sea, in SW Luzon, Philippines. At entrance is Corregidor isl. In Spanish-American War, Spanish fleet was destroyed here by Adm. George Dewey.

Manila hemp, important cordage fiber obtained from the abacá or Manila hemp plant (*Musa textilis*), a close relative of the banana. Leafstalks yield the strong fibers, the finer being used in fabrics, the coarse in ropes, matting twine, and paper.

Manin, Daniele (dänyä'lā mänēn'), 1804–57, Italian patriot. Became head of Venetian republic when Venice rebelled against Austrian rule (1848) and organized resistance to a long siege by the Austrians. After the Venetian surrender (Aug., 1849), he went into exile at Paris.

Manipur (mŭnĭpŏŏr'), state (8,620 sq. mi.; pop. 512,069), NE India; cap. Imphal. Lies in heavily forested Manipur Hills. Invaded 1944 by Japan.

Manistee (mănĭstē'), city (pop. 8,642), N Mich., on L. Michigan at mouth of Manistee R. and W of Cadillac, in fruit region. Resort, shipping, and industrial center with salt plants.

Manistique (mănĭstēk'), resort city (pop. 5,086), E Upper Peninsula, N Mich., on L. Michigan at mouth of Manistique R. Shipping and fishing center with lumbering and mfg. of wood products.

manito (mă'nĭtō), name used among Indians of Algonquian linguistic stock to describe supernatural power permeating all things, equated by some missionaries and romanticists with the Christian God.

Manitoba (mănĭtō'bŭ), province (219,723 sq. mi., with water surface 246,512 sq. mi.; pop. 776,541) W central Canada; cap. WINNIPEG. Easternmost of the Prairie Provs., it has large uninhabited tundra in N, wooded lake area in central part (largest lakes are WINNIPEG, Manitoba, WINNIPEGOSIS), and broad farmlands in S. Other large cities are SAINT BONIFACE and BRANDON. Major rivers are Red, Assiniboine, Churchill, and Nelson. Agr. (wheat, other grains, potatoes) main occupation, supplemented by lumbering, mining (copper, gold, zinc, silver, cadmium), and fur farming. Area chartered to Hudson's Bay Co. 1670 as part of Rupert's Land. Competition from French fur traders died out after 1763. Agr. settlement made in Red R. valley by Lord SELKIRK 1812. Dominion bought land between Ont. and B.C. from Hudson's Bay Co. 1869. Purchase unsuccessfully resisted in Red River insurrection led by Louis RIEL. Province created 1870 embracing small area S of L. Winnipeg, enlarged 1881, and extended to Hudson Bay 1912. Outlet to grain markets through Great Lakes achieved when railroads reached Winnipeg, now a major world grain center. Railroad to CHURCHILL on Hudson Bay, completed 1929, opened short sea route eastward. Winnipeg district suffered disastrous floods 1950.

Manitoba, University of: see WINNIPEG, Man.

Manitoulin Islands (mănŭtōō'lĭn), archipelago made up of three large and several smaller islands, separating N part of L. Huron from North Channel and from NW Georgian Bay. Manitoulin Isl. (80 mi. long, 2–32 mi. wide), largest lake island in world, encloses over 100 lakes and has rugged coast. Drummond Isl. (c.20 mi. long, 11 mi. wide) belongs to Mich., the rest to Ontario. Resorts and fishing.

Manitou Springs, Colo.: see COLORADO SPRINGS.

Manitowoc (mă"nĭtŭwŏk'), city (pop. 27,598), E Wis., on L. Michigan at mouth of Manitowoc R. and N of Sheboygan. North West Co. estab. trading post here 1795; permanently settled 1837. Fishing industry gave way to shipbuilding in 1860s. Metal goods.

Maniu, Iuliu (yōō'lyōō mänyōō'), 1873–1951?, Rumanian politician, leader of Peasant party. Premier 1928–30, 1932–33. A liberal, he was tried for treason in 1947 by the Communist regime and sentenced to life imprisonment.

Manizales (mänēsä'lēs), city (pop. 51,025), W central Colombia in Andes; founded c.1846; commercial and agr. center, especially of coffee.

Mankato (măn-kā'tō), city (pop. 18,809), S Minn., on Minnesota R. and SW of Minneapolis; platted 1852. Center of dairy, farm, and quarry area, with mfg. of agr. equipment and food products. Sibley Park was site of Camp Lincoln, where over 300 Sioux were held after 1862 uprising.

Manley, Mary de la Rivière, 1663–1724, English author. Among her works, often scurrilous, most famous is the prose romance *New Atlantis* (1709–10).

Manlius Capitolinus, Marcus (kă"pĭtŭlī'nŭs), d. 384? B.C., Roman consul (392 B.C.). Took refuge in the Capitol when Rome was taken by the Gauls (c.389 B.C.); aroused by cackling geese at night, he repulsed the Gauls from the hill. Later impeached for treason and thrown from the Tarpeian Rock. His kinsman **Titus Manlius Imperiosus Torquatus,** 4th cent. B.C., fought the Gauls (361 B.C.), killing one of their leaders in single combat and taking his torque (hence name Torquatus). He subjugated the Latins (340 B.C.) and killed his own son for engaging the enemy against his orders.

Mann (män), family of German writers. **Heinrich Mann** (hīn'rĭkh), 1871–1950, wrote the novels *Professor Unrat* (Eng. trs., *The Blue Angel,* 1932, *Small Town Tyrant,* 1944); *The Little Town* (1909); the trilogy *Das Kaiserreich* (1917–25; Eng. tr., *The Patrioteer,* 1921, *The Poor,* 1917, and *The Chief,* 1925); and a biography of Henry IV of France (1935–38). He wrote with romantic passion and fierce satire. His brother, **Thomas Mann** (tō'mäs), 1875–, is one of the outstanding literary figures of the 20th cent. His first novel, *Buddenbrooks* (1900; Eng. tr., 1924), brought him fame. His shorter works were collected in *Stories of Three Decades* (1936). These reflected his preoccupation with the proximity of art to neurosis, the artist's longing for death, the affinity of genius to disease, and the problem of the artist's position in a bourgeois society—themes which appear, too, in the novel *The Magic Mountain* (1924; Eng. tr., 1927), perhaps his masterpiece. In his tetralogy on the biblical story of Joseph (1933–43), however, the gloomy turbulence of his early work is replaced by a somewhat idyllic but profound study of the mythological and psychological. In 1948 appeared *Dr. Faustus,* in 1951 *The Holy Sinner.* Thomas Mann's political essays denouncing fascism are published in *Order of the Day* (1942); his literary essays are collected as *Essays of Three Decades* (1947). He left Germany in 1933 and later (1936) came to the U.S., returning to Europe in 1952. He received the 1929 Nobel Prize in Literature. His son, **Klaus Mann** (klous), 1906–49, was a novelist, essayist, and playwright. His works include *Alexander: a Novel of Utopia* (1929; Eng. tr., 1930); *Pathetic Symphony* (1936; Eng. tr., 1948); and *Turning Point* (1942).

Mann, Horace (măn), 1796–1859, American educator. Became a member of Mass. legislature in 1827 and secretary of state board of education in 1837. He won much note for his reforms in reorganizing the school system, with improvement in buildings and equipment as well as in quality of instruction and in the training and salaries of teachers.

Mann, James Robert, 1856–1922, U.S. Representative from Ill. (1897–1922). Author (1910) of **Mann Act,** also known as White Slave Act, which forbade, under heavy penalties, transportation of women from one state to another for immoral purposes.

Mann, Thomas and **Klaus Mann:** see MANN, family.

manna, in Bible, flaky, white edible substance provided by God for the Hebrews in the wilderness. It fell on the ground, was baked or stewed, and had a sweet taste. Ex. 16; Num. 11.7,8; Joshua 5.12. Many botanical definitions of manna have been proposed. Christians have compared the symbol to the body of Christ in the sacrament of communion.

Mann Act: see MANN, JAMES ROBERT.

Mannerheim, Baron Carl Gustav Emil (kärl' gŭ'stäv ā'mĭl mä'nûrhām), 1867–1951, Finnish field marshal. Rose to rank of general in tsarist army. A hero of Finland's liberation, he was regent of the new republic in 1919. He commanded Finnish forces in the Finnish-Russian War of 1939–40 and again 1941–44. President of Finland 1944–46. The **Mannerheim Line,** a fortified line of defense across the Karelian Isthmus, was planned by him. It was taken by the Russians in 1940 and was dismantled.

Mannheim, Karl (kärl' män'hīm), 1893–1947, Austro-Hungarian sociologist. Taught in Germany and at Univ. of London. His *Ideology and Utopia* (1929) treats of social beliefs and thought.

Mannheim (män'hīm), city (pop. 244,000), Württemberg-Baden, W Germany, on the Rhine opposite Ludwigshafen and at mouth of the Neckar. Inland port; industrial center (machinery, precision instruments, chemicals). Chartered 1606; became residence of electors palatine (see PALATINATE) 1720. The famous Mannheim orchestra ranked first among European orchestras in 18th cent. and greatly influenced symphonic writing (notably Mozart's). Schiller began his career at the Mannheim theater (1782–83). Mannheim passed to Baden in 1803. It was largely destroyed in World War II. The electoral palace and the regularly laid out baroque buildings of the inner city were heavily damaged or destroyed.

Manning, Henry Edward, 1808–92, English cardinal. Educated at Oxford, he became an Anglican pastor, but under the influence of the OXFORD MOVEMENT he followed J. H. NEWMAN and W. G. WARD into the Roman Catholic Church (1851), in which he was later ordained. He strongly advocated social reforms, tried to improve prison conditions, and fought for the rights of workingmen. After he had succeeded Wiseman as archbishop of Westminster (1865) he was influential in the labor movement, and in 1889 he supported the London dock strike, then single-handedly settled it. He opposed Catholic participation in Anglican universities, thus coming in conflict with Newman, with whom he later disagreed violently on the enunciation of papal infallibility, which Manning favored.

Manning, William Thomas, 1866–1949, American Episcopal bishop of N.Y. (1921–46). He greatly forwarded work on Cathedral of St. John the Divine.

Manoel, name of Portuguese rulers: see MANUEL.

manorial system or **seignorial system** (sēnyô'rēŭl), economic-social system in which peasants of medieval Europe held lands they tilled. Fundamental basis was holding of lands from lord (Fr. *seigneur*) of estate in return for fixed dues in kind, money, and services. System was allied with FEUDALISM, but was not feudal as it had no connection with fief. It flourished 11th to 15th cent. and declined with wide growth of towns and of capitalistic commerce which broke down small unit, the manor, and built up larger units. System was based on division of land into self-sufficient estates—great domains.

Such domain was held by a lord, who might be king, ecclesiastical lord, baron, or any lesser noble. Land was in his holding, not given to man who tilled it but only loaned in return for dues and services. Peasant was either a SERF, who was bound to lord, or VILLEIN, who was not personally bound but held land by fixed payment. Domain was divided into arable land, meadow, woodland, and waste. Arable land was held by peasant, meadow in common, and woodland by lord. Manor was also administrative and political unit, with manorial courts, and unit for raising of taxes and for public improvements.

Man o' War, 1917–47, American race horse by Fair Play out of Mahubah, owned by Samuel Riddle after 1918. "Big Red" raced only as two-year-old and three-year-old, won 20 of 21 races, set five world records. Only loss was to horse named Upset at Saratoga, 1919. Became leading sire of all time.

Manresa (mänrā'sä), city (pop. 34,075), NE Spain, in Catalonia. Cotton and silk mfg. The grotto where St. Ignatius used to pray during his stay at Manresa (1522–23) is now a place of pilgrimage.

Mans, Le (lů mã'), city (pop. 90,693), cap. of Sarthe dept., NW France, on the Sarthe; historic cap. of Maine. Metallurgy. Dates from pre-Roman times. Its cathedral (11th–13th cent.), partly Romanesque, partly Gothic, is noted for its daring system of flying buttresses and contains the tomb of Queen Berengaria of England.

Mansart or **Mansard, François** (both: frãswä' mäsär'), 1598–1666, French architect, whose works are fine examples of French classical design. His Church of Val-de-Grâce, Paris, may have influenced Wren's design of St. Paul's Cathedral, London. His pupil and grandnephew, **Jules Hardouin Mansart** (zhül' ärdwẽ'), c.1646–1708, designed Grand Trianon (Versailles), Place Vendôme (Paris), and Dôme des Invalides. The family name is applied to a type of roof (*ill.*, p. 573).

Mansfeld, Peter Ernst, Graf von (pā'tůr ĕrnst' gräf' fŭn mäns'fĕlt), 1580?–1626, German nobleman, commander of a mercenary force in the Thirty Years War. He fought, with varying success, on the Protestant side in the service of Frederick the Winter King and, later, in Dutch and English pay. Wallenstein routed him at Dessau (1626).

Mansfield, Katherine, 1888–1923, British short-story writer, whose real name was Kathleen Beauchamp; wife of John Middleton MURRY. Her stories (as in *The Garden Party,* 1922) show techniques that strongly influenced later writers.

Mansfield, Richard, 1854–1907, American actor. A success in *Beau Brummel* (1890), *Cyrano de Bergerac* (1898), he was also among first to do Shaw in U.S.

Mansfield. 1 Town (pop. 10,008), NE Conn., N of Willimantic; settled c.1692. Includes Storrs village, main seat of Univ. of Connecticut (land-grant; state supported; coed.); chartered and opened 1881 as Storrs Agricultural School, it became a college 1893, Connecticut Agricultural Col. 1899, a university 1939. **2** Town (pop. 4,440), NW La., S of Shreveport. Confederate victory at Sabine Crossroads (Apr. 8, 1864) commemorated by near-by park. **3** Town (pop. 7,184), SE Mass., SSW of Boston. Machine parts. **4** City (pop. 43,564), N central Ohio, WSW of Akron; laid out 1808. Mfg. of electrical appliances and steel and brass products.

Mansfield, Mount: see GREEN MOUNTAINS.

Manship, Paul, 1885–, American sculptor. Often inspired by classical mythology for his subjects.

manslaughter, homicide without justification or excuse, distinguished from murder by absence of malice aforethought. The crime is usually by statute divided into degrees (e.g., voluntary manslaughter, an intentional killing committed in the heat of passion provoked by the victim; involuntary manslaughter, an unintentional killing resulting from a minor crime such as rioting or reckless driving).

Mansur (mänsŏŏr') or **Al Mansur,** d. 775, 2d ABBASID caliph (754–75); brother and successor of Abu-l-Abbas. Founded Baghdad in 762.

Mansur or **Al-Mansur,** 914–1002, Moslem regent of Córdoba, known in Spanish as Almanzor. Acting in name of Hisham II, he extended power of Omayyad caliphs throughout Moslem Spain. Gave up premiership in 991, but held actual power until his death.

Mansura, El (ĕl mänsŏŏ'rů), town (pop. 102,519), N Egypt, on the Nile. Here in 1250 the Crusaders led by Louis IX were defeated by the Mamelukes.

Mantegna, Andrea (ändrā'ä mäntā'nyä), 1431–1506, Italian painter of Paduan school. Married the daughter of Jacopo Bellini. Worked under patronage of the Gonzagas of Mantua. Strongly influenced by the antique, he was a master of anatomy and perspective. Works include *Holy Family* (Metropolitan Mus.), *Parnassus,* and *Triumph of Virtue* (both in Louvre).

Mantell, Robert Bruce (măn"tĕl'), 1854–1928, British-American actor. Made debut 1876, formed company 1905. Excelled in Shakspere and melodrama.

Mantinea (măn"tĭnē'ů), city of anc. Arcadia, Greece. Here Thebes defeated Sparta and Epaminondas was killed (362 B.C.).

mantis (măn'tĭs), member of insect group usually considered a family (Mantidae) of order Orthoptera, found in most warm countries. Body is elongated and bears two pairs of wings. Mantis holds forelegs as though praying. Female often eats its smaller mate. Young hatch as wingless nymphs. See *ill.*, p. 601.

Mantua (măn'chŏŏů, –tŏŏů), Ital. *Mantova,* city (pop. 36,489), Lombardy, N Italy, on the Mincio R. An Etruscan and later a Roman city, it became a free commune (12th cent.). The GONZAGA family gained power in 1328 and made Mantua a flourishing center of Renaissance culture. A duchy from 1530, it was contested after 1627 between the Nevers branch of the Gonzaga family (backed by France) and the Guastalla branch (backed by Spain). The Nevers branch won and held Mantua until its extinction (1708), when the duchy was annexed by Austria. After a period of French control (1797–1814), the strategic fortress reverted to Austria, which ceded it to Italy in 1866. Among the architectural treasures of Mantua are the Gonzaga palace (13th–18th cent.), with frescoes by Mantegna; the Palazzo del Te, created by Giulio Romano; the Church of Sant' Andrea, designed by Alberti; and the city hall (begun 1250). Vergil was born near Mantua.

Manu (mă'nōō), in Hindu legend, a divinely inspired lawgiver. The Laws of Manu, compiled (probably between 200 B.C. and A.D. 200) from diverse ancient sources, govern Brahman ritual and daily life.

Manua (mänōō'ä), district (pop. 2,597), American Samoa, comprising Tau, Ofu, and Olosega islands; annexed 1899 by U.S. Cradle of their race, according to Samoan tradition.

Manuel, Byzantine emperors. **Manuel I** (Manuel Comnenus), c.1120–1180, succeeded his father John II in 1143. When the Second Crusade (1147–49) devastated his territories, he made a truce with the Seljuk Turks, thus leaving them free to defeat the Crusaders. His later diplomacy supported Pope Alexander III against Emperor Frederick I and aimed at the reunion of the Eastern and Western empires and churches. His crushing defeat by the Turks at Myriocephalon put an end to his ambitions (1176). He favored foreigners at his court and encouraged the settlement of Genoese, Pisan, and Venetian colonies at Constantinople. **Manuel II** (Manuel Palaeologus), 1348?–1425. During his reign (1391–1425) the Turks reduced the empire to Constantinople and its environs. Tamerlane's victory over Bajazet (1402) saved Constantinople from Turkish capture.

Manuel, kings of Portugal. **Manuel I,** 1469–1521, reigned 1495–1521. Under him Portugal reached the zenith of its colonial and commercial power, owing to such explorers as Vasco da GAMA and CABRAL and such commanders as Francisco de ALMEIDA and Afonso de ALBUQUERQUE. Manuel reluctantly undertook measures for forcible conversion of the Jews (1496–97), causing many to emigrate, and he set a trend toward royal absolutism. **Manuel II,** 1889–1932, succeeded his father Charles I in 1908. In 1910 he was dethroned and a republic was estab. He spent his exile in England.

manure, any material used as fertilizer, especially barnyard manure. Green manure is a crop plowed under to improve soils.

manuscript, a handwritten work as distinguished from printing or typescript. Oldest manuscripts were on PAPYRUS; earliest extant dates probably to c.3500 B.C. Later PARCHMENT was much used (important parchment scrolls of Old Testament books written in 2d and 3d cent. B.C. were found in 1947 in Palestine). The science of dealing with old manuscripts, paleography, is highly technical; manuscripts are carefully compared to determine their age, history, and relationship to other manuscripts. Those of the Middle Ages were often illuminated in colors on vellum, a variety of parchment. PAPER was invented in China in 2d cent. A.D., but not known in Europe until 12th cent. Printed book dates from 15th cent. After that point manuscripts are of more importance for literary criticism than for other knowledge. See BOOK.

Manutius, Aldus: see ALDUS MANUTIUS.

Manville, borough (pop. 8,597), N central N.J., SW of Bound Brook. Asbestos products, textiles.

Manx (măngks), language of the Celtic subfamily of Indo-European languages. See LANGUAGE (table).

Manych Depression (mä'nĭch), lowland, SE European RSFSR, between the Lower Don and the Caspian Sea. It is drained by the Western Manych R., c.200 mi. long, a tributary of the Don, and by the Eastern Manych R., which flows c.100 mi. E to a system of salt lakes and marches c.75 mi. W of the Caspian Sea. A canal linking the Don and the Caspian has been projected. Also spelled Manich.

Manzala, Egypt: see MENZALEH.

Manzanares (mänthänä'rĕs), river, c.55 mi. long, central Spain. Flows S past Madrid to the Jarama, a tributary of the Tagus.

Manzikert (măn'zĭkûrt), Turkish *Malazgirt,* village of E Turkey. Here in 1071 the Seljuk Turks under Alp Arslan routed and captured Emperor ROMANUS IV, thus gaining control of most of Asia Minor.

Manzoni, Alessandro (älĕs-sän'drō mändzō'nē), 1785–1873, Italian author. The famous romantic novel *I promessi sposi* (1825–26; Eng. tr., *The Betrothed,* 1828), established him as a chief figure in Italian literature. He also wrote plays, notable religious poetry in *Inni sacri* (1812–22), and an ode, *Cinque Maggio* (1821), inspired by Napoleon's death.

Maori: see NEW ZEALAND.

Mao Tse-tung (mou' dzŭ-dōōng'), 1893–, leader and a founder of Chinese Communist party. Chairman of central government council of Chinese People's Republic (estab. 1949).

Map, Walter, c.1140–c.1210, British writer and churchman, author of *De nugis curialium* (1181?–1193?), a Latin prose collection of legends, anecdotes, and court gossip told with wit and satire. Name also Mapes.

map, conventionalized picture of earth's surface pattern drawn on flat surface. Physical features, political or cultural features, or both, may be emphasized. Each point on map corresponds to geographic position in terms of a definite SCALE and PROJECTION. Cartography (i.e., map making) antedates art of writing. Present system was estab. by Greeks, especially Ptolemy, whose underestimation of earth's size was uncorrected until Mercator's age. Arabs carried on work, especially Idrisi (12th cent.). Rediscovery of Ptolemy's *Geographia,* invention of printing and engraving, and great voyages of discovery caused renaissance of cartography (c.1500). After 1750 many European governments undertook systematic mapping of their countries. In U.S. the Geological Survey (estab. 1879) has mapped much of the country. At Internatl. Geographical Congress meetings (1890, 1909, 1913) Albrecht Penck presented plans for a world map at uniform scale; work is only partly completed. Aerial photography is a valuable aid in map making.

maple, ornamental and useful tree of genus *Acer,* native to the N Hemisphere. Maples have deeply cut or lobed leaves. Sugar maple

(*Acer saccharum*) furnishes bird's-eye and curly maple prized by cabinetmakers. Other North American species include red or swamp maple (*A. rubrum*), with red or orange foliage in autumn, and the fast-growing silver maple (*A. saccharinum*). The Norway maple (*A. platanoides*) is a European native while the small kinds with purple or red leaves are native to Japan. **Maple syrup** is the sap obtained chiefly from the sugar and black maple in early spring. Once a staple sweetening, its use is now mainly for confectionery and flavoring.

Maplewood. 1 Suburban city (pop. 13,416), E Mo., W of St. Louis; settled c.1865. **2** Suburban township (pop. 25,201), NE N.J., W of Newark. Map publishing.

map projection: see PROJECTION.

maquis (mäkē'), the brush country of Corsica; hence, the robber bands who hid out in the brush and, in World War II, the underground resistance in France under German occupation. Supplied with weapons parachuted by Allied planes, the *maquis* was organized into the FFI (French Forces of the Interior), which helped in the liberation of France (1944).

Mar, earls of. John Erskine, 1st **earl of Mar,** d. 1572, was regent of Scotland and had custody of young king James VI. His son, **John Erskine,** 2d **earl of Mar,** 1556–1634, seized control of James VI in 1578. Later negotiated question of James's succession to English throne. **John Erskine,** 6th **earl of Mar,** 1675–1732, was Scottish leader of Jacobites. Played a leading part in promoting union of Scotland with England. His rebellion (1715) on behalf of Old Pretender failed and he fled to France.

marabou, large African bird of stork family. It has long legs, and a huge bill, is 4–5 ft. tall, with a 10-ft. wing spread. Adjutant bird of India is of same genus; their names are sometimes interchanged. Its elongated tail feathers were once popular as trimming in ladies' clothing.

Marabouts (mă'rŭbōōts) [Arabic,= devotee hermit], Berber Moslem sect which spread from NW Africa to Spain (11th–12th cent.). Venerated as saints, prophets, the Marabouts live in monasteries or attached to mosques.

Maracaibo (märäkī'bō), port (pop. 233,488), NW Venezuela, second largest city of Venezuela, at outlet of L. Maracaibo. Founded 1571, it was sacked five times by buccaneers in 17th cent. Foreign interests (British, Dutch, U.S.) in exploiting vast oil resources have brought about improvement in health conditions of city. Besides oil, exports include coffee, cacao, sugar, hardwoods.

Maracaibo, Lake, area c.5,000 sq. mi., NW Venezuela; discovered 1499 by Vespucci. Surrounding area is largely unexploited agriculturally, but since 1918 production of petroleum has been a vital activity here. Lake is major artery of communication for products, but the channel connecting it with Gulf of Venezuela is in places only 11 ft. deep, and goods must be transshipped at Maracaibo.

Marajó (märŭzhô'), island (c.150 mi. long and c.100 mi. wide; pop. 124,312), N Brazil, in mouth of Amazon, dividing river into Amazon proper and Pará R.

Maranhão (märänyã'õ), state (129,270 sq. mi.; pop. 1,600,396), NE Brazil; cap. SÃO LUIS. Fronts on Atlantic in N and has low, hot coastal plain where most of population lives. Babassu nuts (processed for vegetable oil) are important product. In S, in fertile valleys, cotton, sugar, rice, and tobacco are grown. French settled here in 1612 but were displaced by Portuguese (1615).

Marañón (märänyōn'), river, a headstream of the Amazon, rising in central Peru, flowing NNE through Andes almost to Ecuador, then NE and E to Ucayali R. Often considered part of Amazon proper. Descended by Ursúa (1560).

maraschino (mă"rŭskē'nō), liqueur prepared from a sour cherry of Dalmatia. **Maraschino cherry** is the name given to cherries preserved in Maraschino or in imitation syrup.

Marat, Jean Paul (zhã' pôl' märä'), 1743–93, French revolutionist, b. Switzerland. A physician and scientist, he turned toward politics in 1789, founding the journal *L'Ami du peuple* [the friend of the people], in which he attacked everybody in power with vicious virulence. After its suppression, he published the paper secretly. His articles were instrumental in the overthrow of the monarchy (Sept., 1792). Elected to the Convention, he was a leader of the extremist CORDELIERS and waged deadly war on the GIRONDISTS. A skin disease forced him to spend much of his time in a warm bath. He was in his bath when Charlotte CORDAY stabbed him to death.

Marathas: see MAHRATTAS.

Marathi (mŭrä'tē), language of the Indic group of the Indo-Iranian subfamily of Indo-European languages. See LANGUAGE (table).

Marathon (măr'ŭthŏn), village and plain, anc. Greece, NE of Athens. Here the Athenians defeated the Persians in 490 B.C. (see PERSIAN WARS). A runner was sent to bear news of the victory to Athens, and from his run is derived the name of the **marathon race,** a long-distance run standardized (1908) as 26 mi. and 385 yd. It was first included in the Olympic games in 1896.

Marble, Alice, 1913–, American tennis player. U.S. women's singles champion (1936, 1938–40).

marble, limestone composed of calcite or dolomite crystals, this structure resulting from extreme metamorphism. Sometimes is snow white, but color varies widely because of impurities, which add greatly to beauty of stone when polished. Used for statuary, monuments, public buildings. Found in British Isles, Belgium, France, Germany, Italy, Greece, U.S. Finest U.S. marble comes from Vt., though other states are important producers.

Marblehead, town (pop. 13,765), NE Mass., on the coast NE of Boston; settled 1629. Longtime fishing port; resort since 19th cent.; yachting center. Has Revolutionary Fort Sewall and graves of many Revolutionary soldiers.

marbling, process of coloring sides, edges, or end papers of books to suggest marble patterns. Colors are arranged on a liquid surface to which book surfaces are applied. In tree marbling, in which the effect suggests a tree trunk and branches, liquid colors are run over a surface bent to form a trough.

Marburg (mär'bŏŏrk) or **Marburg an der Lahn** (än dĕr län'), city (pop. 39,256), Hesse, W Germany, in former Electoral Hesse, on the Lahn R. Its medieval castle, which dominates the picturesque city, was the residence of the landgraves of Hesse 13th–17th cent. Philip of Hesse founded (1527) its famous Protestant university. In 1529 LUTHER and ZWINGLI met at the castle in the Marburg Colloquy, sponsored by Philip, but reached no agreement. St. Elizabeth of Hungary is buried in the fine Gothic church dedicated to her; in 1946 she came into profane company when the bodies of Hindenburg and of Frederick William I and Frederick II of Prussia were transferred here.

Marburg, Yugoslavia: see MARIBOR.

Marbury vs. Madison, case, decided 1803 by U.S. Supreme Court. Involved one of Pres. John Adams's "midnight appointments" which new administration failed to carry through. The opinion, written by Chief Justice John Marshall, was first Supreme Court decision authorizing all courts to review constitutionality of legislation.

Marc, Franz (fränts' märk'), 1880–1916, German post-impressionist painter. Evolved a style dominated by colorful crystallike patterns.

Marc Antony, Roman general: see ANTONY.

Marcel, Étienne (ātyĕn' märsĕl'), d. 1358, French popular leader; merchants' provost of Paris. He won from the dauphin (later Charles V) enormous concessions to the States-General (*Grande Ordonnance,* 1357). Charles soon revoked his concessions; Marcel, in alliance with Charles II of Navarre, was preparing Paris for resistance to the dauphin when he was assassinated.

Marcellus, Marcus Claudius (märsĕl'ŭs), c.268–208 B.C., Roman consul. In the Second Punic War he besieged Syracuse and captured it (212 B.C.); he also took Capua from the Carthaginians (211). Plutarch wrote his biography.

March, earls of: see MORTIMER, family.

March, river, Czechoslovakia: see MORAVIA.

March: see MONTH.

Marche (märsh), region and former province, central France, in Creuse and Haute-Vienne depts.; part of the Massif Central. Towns: Guéret, Aubusson. Agr., sheep raising. A border fief (march) of old Aquitaine, it passed to Lusignan family in 13th cent. and later to the house of Bourbon. Was annexed to royal domain 1527.

Marches, the, Ital. *Marche,* region (3,744 sq. mi.; pop. 1,278,071), central Italy, between Apennines and Mediterranean; cap. Ancona. Agr., vineyards. Region was included in Pepin's donation to the popes, but after the 10th cent. the emperors granted fiefs in the area (the marches of Ancona, Fermo, and Camerino), while several cities (e.g., Urbino, Pesaro) were ruled by local dynasties. Reconquest by the popes was completed 16th–17th cent.; Marches formed part of Papal States until their annexation (1860) by Sardinia.

Marchfeld (märkh'fĕlt"), strategic plain, Lower Austria, NE of Vienna, between Danube and Morava (Ger. *March*) rivers. Here OTTOCAR II of Bohemia defeated Bela IV of Hungary (1260); Rudolf I defeated Ottocar II (1278); and Archduke Charles of Austria defeated Napoleon I (battle of Aspern, 1809, followed by Napoleon's victory at Wagram).

Marcian (mär'shŭn), c.390–457, East Roman emperor (450–57). Convoked Council of CHALCEDON (451). Refused to pay tribute to ATTILA.

Marcion (mär'shŭn), fl. 144, founder of Marcionites, first great heresy to rival Catholicism. Taught a dualism like that of GNOSTICISM and rejected the God of the Old Testament entirely. Stressed ascetic practices and influenced Manichaeism, which finally absorbed Marcionism.

Marconi, Guglielmo, Marchese (gōōlyĕl'mō märkā'zā märkō'nē), 1874–1937, Italian physicist. Shared 1909 Nobel Prize in Physics for development of wireless telegraphy. His achievement based on earlier work on electromagnetic waves. Transmitted long-wave signals in 1895, transatlantic signals in 1901.

Marco Polo: see POLO, MARCO.

Marcos de Niza (mär'kōs dā nē'sä), c.1495–1558, missionary explorer in Spanish North America; a Franciscan friar who served in Peru, Guatemala, and Mexico. Headed expedition (1539) into territory N of present Sonora in search of rich Indian cities about which Cabeza de Vaca reported to Viceroy Antonio de Mendoza. The friar's stories of fabulous Seven Cities of Cibola confirmed Cabeza de Vaca's stories, but were proved wrong by the expedition of Coronado (1540).

Marcus Aurelius (mär'kŭs ôrē'lēŭs), 121–180, Roman emperor (161–180) and Stoic philosopher; nephew of Faustina, wife of Antoninus Pius, who adopted him; husband of Faustina, daughter of Antoninus. Succeeded with Lucius Verus in 161, became sole emperor 169. Devoted himself to defending the empire and was successful. He is, however, best remembered for his philosophic *Meditations,* notable for epigrammatic, classic expression.

Marcus Hook, borough (pop. 3,843), SE Pa., on Delaware R. and SW of Philadelphia. Oil refining. Was rendezvous of Blackbeard and other pirates.

Marcus Island, volcanic island, area 1 sq. mi., W Pacific, 700 nautical mi. E of Bonin Isls. Discovered 1896 by Japanese; annexed 1899 by Japan. Had naval and air bases in World War II. Under U.S. military rule since end of war.

Marcy, William Learned, 1786–1857, American statesman. U.S. Senator from N.Y. (1831–32). Term "spoils system" supposedly originated from speech of his defending practice. U.S. Secretary of War (1845–49); U.S. Secretary of State (1853–57).

Marcy, Mount: see ADIRONDACK MOUNTAINS.

Mar del Plata (mär' dhĕl plä'tä), city (pop. 114,729), Buenos Aires prov., Argentina; fashionable Atlantic coast resort.

Mardi Gras (mär'dē grä'), French name for Shrove Tuesday. As last day before Lent, it was occasion for merrymaking in Middle Ages. Many cities (e.g., New Orleans, Rio de Janeiro, Nice, and Cologne) preserve the custom and now hold elaborate carnivals for several days before Mardi Gras itself.

Marduk: see BABYLONIAN RELIGION.

Maree, Loch (lŏkh mürē′), lake (13½ mi. long and 2 mi. wide), Ross and Cromarty co., Scotland.

Mare Island: see VALLEJO, Calif.

Marengo (mürĕng′gō), village, Piedmont, NW Italy. Scene of famous victory of French under Bonaparte over Austrians under Melas (June 14, 1800).

Margaret, 1353–1412, queen of Denmark, Norway, and Sweden; daughter of Waldemar IV of Denmark. Married to Haakon VI of Norway in 1363, she ruled as regent for her son Olaf (in Denmark from 1375; in Norway after Haakon's death, 1380). After Olaf's death (1387), she defeated the Swedish king, Albert of Mecklenburg (1389) and persuaded the Danish, Norwegian, and Swedish diets to accept her grandnephew, Eric of Pomerania, as king. He was crowned at Kalmar, and the KALMAR UNION of the three kingdoms was drawn up (1397). Eric was actually a puppet king; Margaret remained the real ruler. She governed autocratically and sought to consolidate and centralize her vast empire.

Margaret (Rose), 1930–, British princess, daughter of George VI and only sister of Elizabeth II.

Margaret Maid of Norway, 1283–90, queen of Scotland (1286–90), daughter of Eric II of Norway and granddaughter of Alexander III of Scotland. Her death led to great civil war of Scotland over succession.

Margaret Mary, Saint, 1647–90, French nun, promoter of the cult of the Sacred Heart in the Roman Catholic Church. Her family name was Alacoque. Canonized 1920. Feast: Oct. 17.

Margaret Maultasch (moul′täsh) [Ger.,= pocket mouth], 1318–69, countess of Tyrol (1335–63). After a turbulent reign, in the course of which she divorced one husband and buried another, she abdicated and left Tyrol to the Hapsburgs. In popular legend she is known as the Ugly Duchess, a woman of great evil power. Her portrait was Tenniel's model for the "duchess" in *Alice in Wonderland*.

Margaret of Angoulême: see MARGARET OF NAVARRE.

Margaret of Anjou (ăn′jōō), 1430?–1482, queen consort of HENRY VI of England. Became highly unpopular by her autocratic rule through the feeble king. Struggle between followers of Richard, duke of York, and king's supporters grew into Wars of the ROSES (1455). Eventually captured (1471), she returned to France and died in poverty.

Margaret of Austria, 1480–1530, daughter of Emperor Maximilian I and Mary of Burgundy. She was regent of the Netherlands and guardian of her nephew, the later Emperor Charles V, 1507–15. After 1518 she again governed the Netherlands for Charles and was one of his most influential advisers. She ruled with wisdom and moderation. In 1529 she negotiated the Treaty of CAMBRAI.

Margaret of Navarre or **Margaret of Angoulême** (ãgōōlām′), 1492–1549, queen of Navarre; sister of Francis I of France. Her second husband was Henri d'Albret, titular king of Navarre. She was a patron of Marot and Rabelais and wrote the *Heptameron* (72 stories in Boccaccio's manner), a classic of French Renaissance literature.

Margaret of Parma, 1522–86, natural daughter of Emperor Charles V. She became duchess of Parma by marriage to Ottavio Farnese (1538) and governed the Netherlands 1559–67 for her half-brother, Philip II of Spain. Following a conciliatory policy, she secured the recall of the unpopular Cardinal GRANVELLE (1564) but was firm toward the Flemish national party and its leaders, Count Egmont and William the Silent. In 1567 ALBA arrived at Brussels to put down opposition by force. Margaret, opposing Alba's harsh policy, resigned.

Margaret of Scotland, Saint, d. 1093, queen of Scotland; wife of MALCOLM III and sister of Edgar Atheling. Promoted church reform and founded new monasteries, creating a pro-English trend in Scotland.

Margaret of Valois (välwä′), 1553–1615, queen of France and Navarre, daughter of Henry II; called Queen Margot. Married Henry of Navarre (later HENRY IV of France) 1572; the wedding was the prelude to the massacre of SAINT BARTHOLOMEW'S DAY. Her intrigues and notorious immorality caused her banishment from Paris (1583) and, after she attempted an armed rebellion, her confinement at the castle of Usson (1587–1605). Her marriage was annulled 1599, and she later was permitted to return to Paris. At Usson she assembled a prominent literary circle. Her memoirs, letters, and other writings show considerable talent.

Margaret Tudor, 1489–1541, queen of James IV of Scotland, daughter of Henry VII and sister of Henry VIII of England. After James's death she married Archibald Douglas, 6th earl of Angus. Played large part in Scottish politics, her affiliations varying with her personal interest.

margarine (mär′jürēn), artificial butter, an emulsified blend of edible vegetable oils or animal fats. In U.S., most margarine is made from refined cottonseed and soybean oils, churned, usually with milk, salted, and sometimes colored yellow. Commonly fortified with vitamin A, it is similar to butter in composition and in nutritional qualities. Oleomargarine is its legal designation in U.S.

Margarita (märgärē′tä), island (43 mi. long, 22 mi. wide), off coast of N Venezuela. Discovered (1498) by Columbus, was important pearl fishing center. With surrounding islands forms state of Nueva Esparta, of which La Asunción (pop. 4,502), is cap.

Margate (mär′gĭt), municipal borough (pop. 42,487), Isle of Thanet, Kent, England; seaport and resort.

Margelan (mŭrgyĭlän′), city (pop. 44,327), Uzbek SSR, in Fergana Valley. Silk mfg. since 10th cent.

Marggraf, Andreas Sigismund (ändrā′äs zē′gĭsmōōnt märk′gräf), 1709–82, German pioneer in analytical chemistry. He isolated zinc, improved method of producing phosphorus, discovered beet sugar.

margin, an amount of cash placed with a broker for speculation in securities. It forms a percentage of the money involved, the broker supplying the balance. By the Securities Exchange Act (1934) the Federal Reserve Board can control speculation by fixing the percentage of the margin.

marginal unit, in economics, the last unit of a given commodity that an owner will sell and a purchaser will buy. It is said to have marginal utility. Marginal land is land that barely repays the cost of labor and capital applied to its cultivation.

marguerite, daisylike perennial (*Chrysanthemum frutescens*) of Canary Isls. It is grown in pots by florists. Paris daisy is another name.

Maria (mürē'ü), queens of Portugal. **Maria I,** 1734–1816, daughter of Joseph I, was married to her uncle, who became joint ruler with her as Peter III (1777). They began their reign with the dismissal of POMBAL. After Peter's death (1786) she ruled alone, but by 1792 she had become insane, and her son (later John VI) assumed the regency. **Maria II** (Maria da Gloria), 1819–53, became queen in 1826, when her father abdicated the Portuguese throne to become emperor of Brazil as PEDRO I. She was betrothed to her uncle, Dom MIGUEL, who deposed her in 1828. Maria was taken to England but regained her throne in 1834, after the victory of the liberal forces, led by her father and assisted by England. The rest of her reign was marked by chronic revolutions. Her second husband, Ferdinand of Saxe-Coburg, ruled jointly with her as Ferdinand II after 1837; her son Louis I succeeded her.

Maria Christina, 1806–78, queen of Spain, fourth consort of Ferdinand VII. Her regency (1833–40) for her daughter ISABELLA II was troubled by the revolt of the CARLISTS and was overthrown by ESPARTERO. She later regained much influence at her daughter's court.

Maria Christina, 1858–1929, queen of Spain, consort of Alfonso XII. During her regency (1885–1902) for her son Alfonso XIII, Spain lost the Spanish-American War.

María Luisa (lwē'sä), 1751–1819, queen of Spain, consort of CHARLES IV. Dissolute and domineering, she, with her lover GODOY, controlled the government. She shared her husband's internment (1808–14).

Mariamne (mârēăm'nē), d. 29 B.C., one of Herod the Great's 10 wives, greatly loved by him. After false accusations by Herod's sister, Herod had her murdered.

Mariana, Juan de (hwän' dā märyä'nä), 1536?–1623?, Spanish historian, political philosopher. Known for *Historiae de rebus Hispaniae* and *De rege et regis institutione,* which condoned tyrannicide.

Marianao (märyänä'ō), city (pop. 120,163), NW Cuba; practically a suburb of Havana.

Marianas Islands (märēä'näs), island group (370 sq. mi.; pop. c.29,700), W Pacific, 1,500 mi. E of Philippines, extending in 500-mi. chain from N to S. Chief islands are GUAM, Saipan, and Tinian. Sugar cane, coffee, and coconuts are produced. Inhabited by Japanese, Chamorros, and Micronesians. Discovered 1521 by Magellan, group was named the Marianas by Spanish Jesuits arriving in 1668. A Spanish possession, 1668–1898, group was sold to Germany in 1899, except Guam, which became U.S. possession. Japan occupied German islands 1914, received mandate 1922, claimed them as possession 1935. Captured 1944 by U.S. forces. In 1947, group (exclusive of Guam) was included in U.S. Trust Territory of the Pacific Isls. under UN trusteeship.

Marianna, city (pop. 5,845), NW Fla., NW of Tallahassee. Lumber mills and limestone quarries.

Marianske Lazne, Czechoslovakia: see MARIENBAD.

Maria Theresa, Ger. *Maria Theresia,* 1717–80, empress as consort of FRANCIS I (reigned 1745–65), queen of Bohemia and Hungary (1740–80); daughter of Emperor Charles VI. She succeeded to the Hapsburg lands under the PRAGMATIC SANCTION but had to defend her rights in the War of the AUSTRIAN SUCCESSION (1740–48) and the SEVEN YEARS WAR (1756–63). She lost most of Silesia to Prussia but won S Poland in the Polish partition of 1772, which she signed with tears while helping herself generously. With her chancellor, KAUNITZ, she governed ably and shrewdly; her reign was an era of prosperity. Though conservative and devoutly Catholic, she cooperated in agrarian and other reforms with her son, JOSEPH II, with whom she shared her power after he became emperor in 1765. A model wife and mother (of 16 children) and a kindhearted ruler, she was very popular. During her reign Vienna became, with Gluck and MOZART, the foremost musical center of Europe.

Mari Autonomous Soviet Socialist Republic (mä'rē), administrative division (8,900 sq. mi.; pop. 579,456), E central European RSFSR, in middle Volga valley; cap. Ioshkar-Ola. Forests; agr. The Mari (over half of pop.) formerly called Cheremiss, are a Finnic people. The rest of the inhabitants are mostly Russians. Dominated by the Eastern Bulgars 9th–12th cent., later by the Golden Horde, the region was conquered by Ivan IV in 1552.

Maribor (mä'rĭbôr), Ger. *Marburg,* city (pop. 66,498), Slovenia, N Yugoslavia, on Drava R. Mfg. center (cars, textiles, leather, chemicals). Belonged to Styria (Austria) until 1919. Has Gothic cathedral (R.C.), Renaissance city hall.

Marie, 1875–1938, queen of Rumania, consort of Ferdinand I; daughter of Alfred, duke of Edinburgh and of Saxe-Coburg-Gotha (a son of Victoria of England). She helped to bring Rumania into the Allied camp in World War I; served as Red Cross nurse. She traveled widely, visiting U.S. in 1926. Wrote novels and autobiography (in English).

Marie Antoinette (ăntünĕt, ãtwänĕt'), 1755–93, queen of France, consort of LOUIS XVI; daughter of Emperor Francis I and Maria Theresa. Distrusted because of her Austrian origin and finding in Louis a most inadequate husband, the beautiful young queen threw herself into a life of pleasure and careless extravagance. She probably had no share in the Affair of the DIAMOND NECKLACE, but this and other scandals, as well as the greed of her favorites, increased her unpopularity. She contributed to the dismissal of Turgot (1776), was hostile to Necker's economy measures, and showed little understanding of the problems of her time. The famous solution to the bread famine—"Let them eat cake"—is, however, unjustly attributed to her. After the birth of her first son she became more sedate and responsible. She probably had little influence on the king's policy during the first two years of the FRENCH REVOLUTION. After 1791, when the royal couple had failed in its attempted flight, the king's apathy forced her to conduct negotiations with MIRABEAU and BARNAVE. At the same time, she secretly urged Austrian intervention, and it is generally held that she betrayed the French campaign plans for 1792 to the enemy. She was imprisoned in the Temple and, after Louis's execution, in the Conciergerie. Convicted of treason, she was guillotined Oct. 16. The brutality to which she was subjected during her last months (particularly the sadistic pleasure her jailers took in informing her of the mistreatment of her child, LOUIS XVII) and the unfairness of her trial dwarf any of the faults she thus expiated. She faced her martyrdom with noble and heroic firmness.

Marie Byrd Land, Antarctic area, E of Ross Shelf Ice and Ross Sea and S of Amundsen Sea. Discovered and claimed for U.S. by Richard E. Byrd 1929.

Marie Caroline, 1752–1814, queen of the Two Sicilies, consort of Ferdinand I; daughter of Empress Maria Theresa. With her favorites, Sir John ACTON and Emma, Lady HAMILTON, she was a center of intrigues.

Marie de France (dů frãs′), fl. 1185, French poet who lived in England. She wrote a dozen lais, based on Celtic sources, with love as main theme.

Marie de' Medici (mĕd′ĭchē), 1573–1642, queen of France; daughter of Francesco de' Medici, grand duke of Tuscany. Became second wife of Henry IV in 1600 and was regent for her son Louis XIII after Henry's assassination (1610). With her favorite CONCINI she dissipated the treasury and adopted a pro-Hapsburg policy. Though banished after Concini's murder (1617), she was reconciled to her son in 1622. In 1630 her former favorite, Cardinal RICHELIEU, had her exiled from court; in 1631 she fled to the Netherlands, never to return. She was the mother of Queen Henrietta Maria of England.

Marie Leszczynska (lĕshchĭn′sků), 1703–68, queen of France; daughter of STANISLAUS I of Poland. Married Louis XV 1725; bore him 10 children.

Marie Louise, 1791–1847, empress of the French; daughter of Emperor Francis I of Austria. She was married to NAPOLEON I in 1810, bore him a son (see NAPOLEON II), and abandoned him in 1814. The Congress of Vienna made her duchess of Parma, Piacenza, and Guastalla, which she ruled ineptly from 1816 till her death. In 1821 she married, morganatically, her lover Count Neipperg. After his death she married another Austrian count, Bombelles.

Marienbad (märē′ůnbät), Czech *Mariánské Lázně,* spa (pop. 6,027), NW Bohemia, Czechoslovakia. Has noted mineral springs and baths.

Marienburg (märē′ůnbo͝ork), Pol. *Malbork,* town (pop. 10,017), former East Prussia; transferred to Polish administration 1945. Founded 1274 by Teutonic Knights; became seat of their grand master 1309; was sold to Poland 1457; passed to Prussia 1772. Its Gothic castle (14th cent.; restored 19th cent.) is a magnificent example of German secular medieval architecture.

Marie Thérèse of Austria (märē′ tārĕz′), 1638–83, queen of France, consort of Louis XIV; daughter of Philip IV of Spain. Her marriage (1660) had been stipulated in the Peace of the Pyrenees. Louis neglected her for a series of mistresses.

Marietta (mârēĕt′ů). **1** City (pop. 20,687), NW Ga., NW of Atlanta. Mfg. of hosiery, furniture, prefabricated houses, and aircraft. A national cemetery is here. Just W is Kennesaw Mt. Natl. Battlefield Park, commemorating a Union defeat 1864. **2** City (pop. 16,006), SE Ohio, at junction of Muskingum and Ohio rivers. First permanent settlement in Old Northwest, founded 1788 among mound builders' earthworks by Ohio Company of Associates. Grew as shipbuilding and shipping center for agr. area. Now has mfg. of metal products and chemicals. Seat of Marietta Col. (coed.; 1835). Intercollegiate regatta held here 1950 and 1951. Preserved are Gen. Putnam's house (in Campus Martius Memorial State Mus.) and land office.

Mariette, Auguste Édouard (märyĕt′), 1821–81, French Egyptologist. Directed excavations in pyramid fields.

Marignano, battle of (märēnyä′nō), 1515, victory of Francis I of France and his Venetian allies over the Swiss. One of the bloodiest engagements of the Italian Wars, it was fought near Marignano (now Melegnano), a town SE of Milan. As a result, Massimiliano Sforza lost Milan to the French and the Swiss gave up further military ventures.

marigold, widely grown annual (*Tagetes*) with colorful yellow, orange, or maroon and gold flowers. The large-flowered African and smaller French types are derived from native Mexican species. Marsh marigold and pot marigold (*Calendula*) are unrelated.

marihuana: see MARIJUANA.

Mariinsk System (mŭrē′ĭnsk), inland navigation route, NW European RSFSR, linking the Neva R. with the Volga at Shcherbakov by way of several lesser rivers and several canals. It makes possible uninterrupted navigation from the Baltic to the Caspian Sea and is also connected with the Northern Dvina and thus with the White Sea.

marijuana or **marihuana** (both: märůwä′nů, -hwä′nů, mă-), habit-forming drug obtained from HEMP plant. Effects combine excitation and depression. Sale illicit.

Marin, John (mă′rĭn), 1870–, American landscape painter, best known as a water-colorist.

marine biology, study of plants and animals of the sea and their relationship to each other and their environment. Marine organisms may be grouped by mode of life as nekton (swimming, freely migrating animals), plankton (floating, drifting plants or animals), and benthos (plants or animals living on sea bottom, including sessile forms, creeping organisms, burrowing animals). Distribution depends on chemical and physical properties, circulation, and light penetration of sea water; plants exist only to c.300 ft. See also OCEANOGRAPHY.

marine engine has heavier construction than engine for land use. So-called reduction gearing, enabling high-speed engine operation (for economy) and low propeller speed (for efficiency), developed with the steam turbine. Also used are reciprocating steam engine, Diesel engine, and gasoline engine. See *ill.*, p. 389.

marine insurance: see INSURANCE.

marines, troops usually having ranks comparable to those of the army and serving on board warships or in conjunction with naval operations. The Continental Marines, established in 1775, fought in the American Revolution. The present U.S. Marine Corps was created by Congress in 1798. It was incorporated into the Navy in 1947 as a complete operating unit.

Marinette (mărĭnĕt′), city (pop. 14,178), NE Wis., on Green Bay at mouth of Menominee R. (bridged to Menominee, Mich.). Fisheries, dairy plants, and paper mills.

Marinetti, Filippo Tommaso (fēlēp′pō tōmmä′zō märēnĕt′tē), 1876–1944, Italian author, founder of futurism, a movement to glorify the dynamic character of the 20th-cent. machine age, together with war and danger; an early advocate of Fascism.

Marino, Giovanni Battista (jōvän′nē bät-tē′stä märē′nō), 1569–1625, Italian poet, noted for elaborately florid style, called *marinismo*, which influenced literature of several countries.

Marion, Francis, c.1732–1795, American partisan leader in Revolution. Organized cavalry troop (1780) which conducted guerrilla warfare against British in S.C. Known as the Swamp Fox.

Marion. 1 City (pop. 10,459), S Ill., NNE of Cairo. Mining and shipping center in agr. (fruit, grain) and coal area. **2** City (pop. 30,081), E central Ind., NNW of Muncie; settled 1826. Farm trade center near gas and oil fields. Mfg. of glass and metal products and paper. **3** City (pop. 5,916), E central Iowa, just NE of Cedar Rapids. Railroad division point. **4** City (pop. 33,817), central Ohio, N of Columbus; laid out 1821. Rail and agr. trade center with mfg. of steam shovels, farm and road-construction machinery, and metal products. Home of W. G. Harding now a museum. **5** Town (pop. 6,834), E S.C., E of Florence. Lumbering, farming, and cotton processing. **6** Town (pop. 6,982), SW Va., in Holston R. valley. Lumber, grain, and textile milling, and limestone quarrying. Near by are White Top Mt. (with annual music festival) and Mt. Rogers.

Marion, Fort: see SAINT AUGUSTINE, Fla.

marionette: see PUPPET.

Mariposa (mă″rĭpō′zů), town, central Calif. A boom town of the Mother Lode in the gold rush, it is today a gateway to Yosemite Natl. Park.

Mariposa lily, bulbous plant of genus *Calochortus* with tuliplike flowers in spring. It is native to the U.S. and is also called butterfly tulip.

Maris (mä′rĭs), three Dutch painters, who were brothers. **Jacob** or **Jakob Maris,** 1837–99, the most famous, produced some of finest landscape paintings of The Hague school. **Matthew** or **Matthijs Maris,** 1839–1917, and **William** or **Willem Maris,** 1844–1910, are also best known for their landscapes.

Maritain, Jacques (märĕtē′), 1882–, French neo-Thomist philosopher. Converted to Catholicism in 1916, he broadened the teachings of St. Thomas Aquinas and applied them to various fields of modern life, as in *An Introduction to Philosophy* (1923–30), *True Humanism* (1938), and *Christianity and Democracy* (1944).

Maritime Commission, United States, estab. 1936 by Congress. Replaced U.S. Shipping Board. Designed to develop a merchant fleet capable of serving as a naval and military auxiliary in time of war or national emergency, and to provide essential shipping service at all times.

maritime law, system of law concerning navigation and overseas commerce. Agreements between states on shipping began in ancient days and created a body of customs and usages which in the late Middle Ages was incorporated under influence of Roman laws into such collections as the *Consolato del Mare, The Law of Oléron* and the English *Black Book of the Admiralty*. In England admiralty courts grew up but were more and more restricted until abolished in 1873. In the U.S. maritime cases (except for collision at sea) are under Federal jurisdiction.

Maritime Provinces, the Atlantic seaboard provinces of NOVA SCOTIA, NEW BRUNSWICK, and PRINCE EDWARD ISLAND in E CANADA. As part of New France this region was called ACADIA. Before Canadian confederation (1867) these provinces were politically distinct from Canada proper.

Maritime Territory, Rus. *Primorski Krai,* administrative division (64,900 sq. mi.; pop. c.1,475,000), RSFSR, between Manchuria and Sea of Japan; cap. Vladivostok. Has densely wooded coastal range rich in minerals (lead, zinc, tin, molybdenum). Coal mines in S. Important fisheries on coast. Population is Russian and Ukrainian with Korean, Chinese, and Mongol minorities. For history, see FAR EASTERN TERRITORY.

Maritsa (märē′tsä), river, c.300 mi. long, rising in Bulgaria and flowing SE and S, partly along Greek-Turkish border, into the Aegean Sea. Plovdiv and Adrianople lie on its course.

Maritzburg, South Africa: see PIETERMARITZBURG.

Mariupol, Ukraine: see ZHDANOV.

Marius, Caius, c.155 B.C.–86 B.C., Roman general, a plebeian. He was seven times consul and won a reputation in wars against Jugurtha (under Quintus Metellus and then as sole commander) and against the Germans.

The rival of SULLA, he was reputed to be the friend of the people. When Sulla got the command against Mithridates VI, Marius fled, but returned to seize Rome with the help of CINNA, and butchered his opponents. Civil war followed, and Sulla triumphed with much bloodshed. Julius Caesar, nephew of Marius' wife, was much influenced by him.

Marivaux, Pierre de (pyĕr' dů märēvō'), 1688–1763, French dramatist. His love comedies—e.g., *Le Jeu de l'amour et du hasard* (1730), *Le Legs* (1736), *Les Fausses Confidences* (1737)—are remarkable for extreme psychological refinement and for a lightness and simplicity bordering on artificiality.

marjoram: see SWEET MARJORAM.

Mark, Saint, friend and companion of St. Peter, St. Paul, and St. Luke; since 2d cent. regarded as author of the Gospel according to St. Mark. His full name was John Mark. His mother is thought to have owned house where Last Supper was held. Acts 12.12,25; 13.5; 15.37–39; Col. 4.10,11; Philemon 24; 2 Tim. 4.11; 1 Peter 5.13. He is the patron of Venice. His symbol is a lion. Feast: April 25.

Mark, Gospel according to Saint, book of New Testament, shortest and simplest of the Gospels. Only Gospel to have no passage unparalleled in another Gospel; many critics hold that it was the first composed. It narrates the life of Jesus from his baptism by John the Baptist to the passion and resurrection. See also SYNOPTIC GOSPELS.

Markham, Sir Clements Robert, 1830–1916, English geographer and writer. Directed India Office geographical work (1867–77). Authority on Inca civilization. Wrote biographies, books of his travels.

Markham, Edwin, 1852–1940, American poet, noted for "The Man with a Hoe" (1899).

Markiewicz, Con(stance Georgine Gore-Booth), Countess (märkyā'vĭts), 1884?–1927, Irish patriot. Sentenced to death for her part in the 1916 rebellion, she was later released. Served in the Sinn Fein parliament (1918–22) and also in the Dáil Éireann (1923–27).

Markova, Alicia (märkō'vů, mär'kůvů), 1910–, English ballet dancer, whose real name is Lilian Alicia Marks. She combines ethereal quality with strong technique; her most famous role is Giselle.

marl, a clay soil mixed with carbonate of lime, sometimes shells of minute invertebrates. Valued as dressing and fertilizer, for correcting soil acidity and making it lighter.

Marlboro, city (pop. 15,756), E Mass., W of Boston. Mfg. of shoes, lamps, paper, metal products.

Marlborough, John Churchill, 1st duke of (märl'bůrů), 1650–1722, English general and statesman, one of greatest military commanders of history. Under James II he crushed the rebellion of the duke of Monmouth. Supported William III against James II; later gave secret aid to Jacobites. Won countless victories in War of SPANISH SUCCESSION. His wife, Sarah Jennings (1660–1744), was influential friend of Queen ANNE (in whose reign his power was greatest). With GODOLPHIN he turned to the Whigs who favored the war. The Whigs fell in 1711, and he and his wife were dismissed. On accession of George I in 1714 he again commanded the army.

Marlborough, municipal borough (pop. 4,556), Wiltshire, England. Marlborough Col. (built 1843) has grounds said to contain body of Merlin, of Arthurian Legend.

Marlborough House, in London, on Pall Mall. Built 1710 by Wren for duchess of Marlborough. Residence of dowager Queen Mary.

Marlin, city (pop. 7,099), E central Texas, SE of Waco and near Brazos R. Resort with mineral springs (ships mineral crystals) and hospitals.

Marlowe, Christopher, 1564–93, English dramatist and poet. Leader of a "radical" group, he was accused of atheism and blasphemy and possibly a plot led to his being stabbed to death by a drinking companion. For dramatic power and development of blank verse into most expressive English meter, he is regarded as greatest Elizabethan playwright next to Shakspere. Among his powerful poetic dramas are *Tamburlaine* (c.1587), *Dr. Faustus* (c.1588), *The Jew of Malta* (c.1589), and *Edward II* (c.1592).

Marlowe, Julia, 1865?–1950, American actress, b. England, whose real name was Sarah Frances Frost. Played Shaksperian roles (e.g., Juliet) opposite her second husband, E. H. SOTHERN.

marmalade (mär'můlād), a thick, tart preserve of fruit pulp (often citrus) similar to jam.

Marmara or **Marmora, Sea of,** anc. *Propontis*, area c.4,300 sq. mi., between Europe and Asia; connected with the Black Sea through the BOSPORUS and with the Mediterranean through the DARDANELLES. Its shores belong entirely to Turkey.

Mármol, José (hōsā' mär'mōl), 1817–71, Argentine romantic writer. He was exiled to Montevideo because of opposition to Rosas. His novel *Amalia* (1851–55) depicts the tyranny of Rosas.

Marmont, Auguste Frédéric Louis Viesse de (ōgüst' frādārēk' lwē'vyĕs' dů märmō'), 1774–1852, marshal of France. For his part in the battle of Wagram (1809) Napoleon made him duke of Ragusa and governor of Illyria. Succeeding Masséna in the Peninsula War, he was defeated at Salamanca (1812). In 1814 he made a convention with the allies which made Napoleon's military position hopeless. He supported the Bourbon restoration.

Marmora, Sea of: see MARMARA, SEA OF.

marmoset (mär'můzĕt), small arboreal monkey (*Callithrix*) of Central and South America. It is squirrel-size and has a long, hairy tail and clawed feet.

marmot (mär'můt), rodent (*Marmota*) allied to squirrel. It has a stout body, rounded ears, strong digging claws, and coarse fur, chiefly brown (often white-tipped). Lives in burrows and hibernates. Chiefly Old World marmot skins used in fur trade. See also WOODCHUCK.

Marmousets (märmōōzā'), [Fr.,= little fellows], ministers of Charles V of France, so called by the royal princess because of their humble origin. CLISSON was the most prominent. They again held power under Charles VI, 1388–92.

Marne (märn), department (3,168 sq. mi.; pop. 386,926), NE France, in Champagne; cap. Châlons-sur-Marne. Rheims is the chief city. Named for the **Marne** river, 325 mi. long, which rises in the Langres Plateau and flows W past Châlons, Épernay, and Château-Thierry to join the Seine near Paris. The two **battles of the Marne** in World War I were both crucial. In the first (Sept. 6–9, 1914), the German advance on Paris seemed assured when, for reasons that are still debated, William II called it off. A notable incident of this battle was the dispatch of the French "taxicab" army by Gen. GALLIENI. In the second battle (July, 1918), the last great German offensive was decisively repulsed; U.S. troops took a prominent part.

Marne, Haute: see HAUTE-MARNE.

Marnix, Philip van (fē'lĭp vän mär'nĭks), 1540–98, Flemish patriot, lord of Sainte-Aldegonde. A Calvinist, he was leader in the struggle for independence from Spain and a supporter of William the Silent. Wrote *Wilhelmus van Nassauwe,* national anthem of the Netherlands.

Maronites (mă'rŭnīts), Arabic-speaking Christian community in Lebanon (like Melchites and Syrian Catholics) in communion with the pope. Their liturgy (in Syriac) is of Antiochene type with Latin imitations. Head is called patriarch of Antioch. Priests are allowed to marry. In 19th cent. massacres of Maronites by Druses brought intervention of France, which obtained modern hold on Syria.

Maros, river, Rumania: see MURES.

Maros Vasarhely, Rumania: see TARGUL-MURES.

Marot, Clément (klāmā' märō'), 1496?–1544, French court poet, author of graceful rondeaux, ballades, epigrams. Translated Psalms into French verse.

Marprelate controversy (mär'prĕ"lĭt), 16th-cent. English religious argument. Under pseudonym of Martin Marprelate seven Puritan pamphlets appeared (1588–89), satirizing Church of England authoritarianism and starting flood of literature from both factions.

Marquand, J(ohn) P(hillips) (märkwänd'), 1893–, American novelist. Spent his boyhood in Newburyport, Mass. Among his many novels are *The Late George Apley* (1937), *H. M. Pulham, Esq.* (1941), *Point of No Return* (1949), "Mr. Moto" adventure stories.

Marquesas Islands (märkā'säs), volcanic group of 11 islands, S Pacific, c.740 mi. NE of Tahiti. Included in FRENCH ESTABLISHMENTS IN OCEANIA. Chief islands are Nuku Hiva and Hiva Oa. Islands are fertile and mountainous. Exports include copra, tobacco, and vanilla. S cluster of islands was discovered 1595 by a Spaniard; N cluster in 1791 by an American. Commodore David Porter persuaded natives to agree to annexation to U.S. in 1813, but Congress took no action. Ceded 1842 to France. Of all Polynesian peoples, Marquesans suffered greatest decline from European diseases. Grave of Gauguin on Hiva Oa.

Marquette, Jacques (zhäk' märkĕt'), 1637–75, French missionary and explorer in North America, a Jesuit priest. With Louis JOLLIET he estab. existence of waterway from the St. Lawrence to Gulf of Mexico in voyage down the Mississippi.

Marquette (märkĕt'), city (pop. 17,202), W Upper Peninsula, N Mich., on L. Superior. Iron ore shipping point and center of mining, lumbering, farming, and resort area, it has mfg. of foundry and wood products and chemicals.

Marquette University: see MILWAUKEE, Wis.

Marquis, Don(ald Robert Perry) (mär'kwĭs), 1878–1937, American columnist, whose mild and hilarious social satire is expressed through his characters "The Old Soak," "archy," a cockroach, and "mehitabel," a cat.

Marrakesh (märä'kĕsh), commercial city (pop. 238,237), French Morocco. Founded 1062 by Yusuf ibn Tashufin as cap. of Almoravides. Noted landmark is 220-ft. tower of Koutoubya mosque (completed 1195). City was formerly starting point for trans-Saharan caravans. Renowned for fine leather goods.

marram grass: see BEACH GRASS.

marriage, union of persons of opposite sex as husband and wife, forming new family, sanctioned by custom and religion. Marriage is generally initiated by rite combining words and symbolic acts, dramatizing and making public the new relationship. Where group is divided into clans, the individual is required to marry outside his clan, a practice known as exogamy. At same time, he must marry within his tribe, a practice known as endogamy; in small tribes, this results in inbreeding. Monogamy is dominant form of marriage in all groups, even where polygamy is permitted. Of variant forms of marriage, polygyny, or marriage of one man to more than one wife, is more frequent than polyandry, the marriage of one woman to more than one husband. In polygynous unions, usually one chief wife ranks above the others. The custom of levirate marriage, practiced by the ancient Hebrews, required that a man marry his deceased brother's wife. Throughout history and in many lands today the parents of the bride and groom customarily negotiate marriage, often binding it with property exchange. In Christian countries, the Church exercises close supervision over marriage, but civil marriage is now permitted in most countries.

Marryat, Frederick (măr'ēăt) 1792–1848, English novelist. Long naval service gave Captain Marryat material for tales of sea adventure (e.g., *Frank Mildmay,* 1829; *Mr. Midshipman Easy,* 1836). *Masterman Ready* (1841–42) is a story for children.

Mars (märz), in Roman religion, god of war. The father of Romulus, he occupied, next to Jupiter, the highest place in Roman religion. In early times he was probably god of fertility. He had many temples in Rome. Festivals to him were held in March (named for him). Identified with Greek Ares.

Mars, in astronomy, PLANET revolving (with its two satellites) around sun in orbit next outside that of earth. Mean distance from sun is c.141,540,000 mi.; period of revolution c.1.88 years; mean diameter c.4,216 mi. Surface is dull red or orange; greenish areas near equator are believed to be vegetation. Tilt of axis (24°50′) results in seasons nearly twice as long as on earth; polar white spots increase and diminish with seasonal regularity. Network of dark lines called canals, reported 1877 by Schiaparelli, are regarded by some astronomers as work of intelligent beings. Temperatures believed to range from 80°F. to −130°F. See *ill.*, p. 1187.

Marsala (märsä′lä), seaport (pop. 24,650), Sicily, Italy, on Cape Boeo, westernmost point of the island; anc. LILYBAEUM. Noted for sweet wine. Here in 1860 Garibaldi began conquest of Two Sicilies.

Marseillaise (märsůlāz′), French national anthem, written and composed by ROUGET DE LISLE; originally called *Chant de guerre de l'armée du Rhin*. Became known as the *Marseillaise* because it was sung by soldiers from Marseilles as they marched on the Tuileries (Aug. 10, 1792).

Marseilles (märsālz′), Fr. *Marseille* (märsā′-yů), city (pop. 551,640), cap. of Bouches-du-Rhône dept., SE France; second largest city and chief Mediterranean port of France. Its port is connected with the Rhone by the Rove Tunnel, a 4½ mi. underground canal (opened 1927). Mfg. of soap, chemicals, machinery; shipbuilding. Settled by Greeks c.600 B.C., ancient Massilia later became an ally of Rome, which annexed it 49 B.C. Sharing the history of Provence, it passed to the French crown 1486. The 19th cent. brought great commercial expansion. A gleaming white city rising in a semicircle from the sea, Marseilles is famous for its beauty. The slums of the port section, long famous for its vice, crime, and exotic mixture of races, were razed by the Germans in World War II. Much of the waterfront was gutted by Allied guns in the landing of Aug., 1944. Part of Aix-en-Provence Univ. is now at Marseilles.

Marsh, Othniel Charles, 1831–99, American paleontologist, first professor of paleontology at Yale, also curator of the Peabody Museum. Served with U.S. Geological Survey on many expeditions to West, and made large collection of fossil vertebrates, now at Yale and National Museum. His discoveries influenced teaching of evolution.

Marsh, Reginald, 1898–, American painter, b. Paris. Often depicts Manhattan street life.

marsh: see SWAMP.

Marshal, William: see PEMBROKE, WILLIAM MARSHAL, 1ST EARL OF.

Marshall, Alfred, 1842–1924, English economist. His systemization of classical economic theories laid foundation of neoclassical school of economics. Developed theory of marginal utility. Principal work: *Principles of Economics* (1890).

Marshall, George C(atlett), 1880–, American army officer and statesman, chief of staff (1939–45) and Secretary of State (1947–49). Became general of the army ("five-star general") in 1944. Integrated EUROPEAN RECOVERY PROGRAM (called Marshall plan).

Marshall, James Wilson, 1810–85, American pioneer, discoverer of gold in Calif. Discovery launched famous gold rush of 1849.

Marshall, John, 1755–1835, fourth Chief Justice of U.S. Supreme Court (1801–35). Raised prestige and power of Supreme Court and molded Constitution by breadth and wisdom of his interpretations—achievement made despite bitter quarrels with Jefferson and later Presidents. Made indisputable the right of Supreme Court to review Federal and state laws and pronounce final judgment on their constitutionality. Viewed the Constitution both as a precise document setting forth specific powers and as a living instrument which should be broadly interpreted to give Federal government means to act effectively within its limited sphere. In general he opposed states' rights doctrines, and there were many criticisms advanced against him.

Marshall. 1 City (pop. 5,777), S Mich., on Kalamazoo R. and near Battle Creek. Mfg. of metal products. **2** City (pop. 5,923), SW Minn., WNW of Mankato. Farm and dairy trade center. **3** City (pop. 8,850), N central Mo., N of Sedalia, in farm area. Mfg. of shoes. **4** City (pop. 22,327), E Texas, WNW of Shreveport, La.; settled 1838. Processes and ships truck, cotton, oil, lumber, bricks, dairy products, carbon, and cottonseed oil.

Marshall College: see HUNTINGTON, W.Va.

Marshall Islands, archipelago (70 sq. mi.; pop. 10,223), central Pacific, 2,595 nautical mi. N of Auckland, New Zealand. Comprises 34 atolls and coral islands, of which KWAJALEIN is the most important. Inhabited by Micronesians, who produce copra for export. Discovered 1526 by the Spanish; visited 1788 by Captains Gilbert and Marshall. Was German protectorate, 1885–1914. Occupied in 1914 by Japan, who received mandate 1922 and claimed sovereignty over group in 1935. Captured 1944 by U.S. forces. Included in 1947 in U.S. Trust Territory of the Pacific Isls. under UN trusteeship. Bikini atoll was site of atom-bomb test in 1946.

Marshall Plan: see EUROPEAN RECOVERY PROGRAM.

Marshalltown, city (pop. 19,821), central Iowa, on Iowa R. and NE of Des Moines; settled 1851. Industrial, trade, and rail center with meat packing and mfg. of metal products.

Marshalsea (mär′shůlsē), former prison in London, closed in 1842. Setting of Dickens' *Little Dorrit*.

Marshfield. 1 City, Oregon: see COOS BAY. **2** City (pop. 12,394), central Wis., SE of Eau Claire; settled 1868. Dairy products.

marsh gas: see METHANE.

marsh mallow: see MALLOW.

marsh marigold, spring-blooming perennial (*Caltha*) of north temperate zone, found in wet places. Common marsh marigold (*Caltha palustris*) or cowslip has rounded glossy leaves and shining yellow flowers similar to buttercups.

Marsh's test, chemical test for arsenic and antimony discovered by James Marsh (1789–1846), English chemist. The unknown is treated with zinc, which combines with arsenic to form arsine; this is burned in air and deposits on a cold plate an "arsenic mirror" that is soluble in sodium hypochlorite. In test for antimony, stibine is formed and "mirror" is insoluble in sodium hypochlorite.

Marsilius of Padua (märsĭ′lēůs, pă′dūů), d. c.1342, Italian political theorist, supporter of

Emperor LOUIS IV, for whom he wrote his great work, the *Defensor Pacis.* This work holds that the power of the state and the power of the church derive equally from the people. The church should be limited solely to worship, and governing powers of the pope Marsilius held to be self-arrogated. These views caused great scandal at the time.

Marston, John, 1576–1634, English satirist and dramatist. Wrote tragedies *Antonio and Mellida* and *Antonio's Revenge* (both 1602), *The Malcontent* (1604; with John Webster), and *Eastward Ho!* (1605; with Ben Jonson and George Chapman).

Marston Moor, W. Riding of Yorkshire, England. Battle fought here (July 2, 1644) gave parliamentarians a decisive victory over royalists.

marsupial (märsōō'pēul, –sū'–), member of order of pouched mammals, found chiefly in Australia. In most, the female lacks a true placenta. Young are born in undeveloped state. The kangaroo and the opossum are marsupials.

Marsyas (mär'sēŭs), in Greek mythology, Phrygian satyr. Skilled in use of Athena's flute, he challenged lyre-playing Apollo to a contest. The Muses favored Apollo, who flayed Marsyas. A river, called for him the Marsyas, sprang from his blood or from tears of his mourners.

marten, carnivorous, largely arboreal mammal (*Martes*) of weasel family, found in North America, Europe, central Asia. Well known are the American marten (or pine marten), FISHER, Siberian SABLE.

Martens, Frederick (mär'tĕns), Rus. *Feodor Feodorovich Martens,* 1845–1909, Russian authority on international law, professor at Univ. of St. Petersburg (1871–1905). Influenced Russian diplomacy; laid base for Hague Conferences; hoped for a world community based on common standard of civilization.

Martens, Georg Friedrich von, 1756–1821, German authority on international law, professor at Göttingen (1784–89), state councilor of Westphalia (1808–13), representative of Hanover at the Frankfurt diet (1816–21). Wrote a monumental comparative study of modern law and commenced an enormous collection of treaties.

Martha, friend of Jesus, sister of Mary and Lazarus of Bethany. Luke 10.38–42; John 11.1–46; 12.1–9. Concerned mainly with her duties, she is the symbol of the active, as against the contemplative, life.

Martha's Vineyard, island in the Atlantic, off SE Mass.; 20 mi. long and 10 mi. wide; separated from Elizabeth Isls. and Cape Cod by Vineyard Sound. Gosnold visited here 1602; settled 1642. Includes towns of EDGARTOWN, GAY HEAD, OAK BLUFFS, Tisbury (including VINEYARD HAVEN village). Whaling and fishing were important, but island is now mainly resort. Boat and air connections with mainland.

Martí, José (hōsā' märtē'), 1853–95, Cuban writer and leader of movement for independence; outstanding poet and one of greatest prose writers of Hispanic America. Exiled at age of 16 because of revolutionary activities, he continued his efforts for independence in Spain, Mexico, Guatemala, Venezuela, New York. Supported himself by contributing articles to New York *Sun* and Buenos Aires *Nacion.* Returned to Cuba in 1895 and died at battle of Dos Ríos.

Martial (Marcus Valerius Martialis) (mär'shŭl), A.D. c.40–c.104, Roman writer. His witty, original verse became the model for the modern epigram.

Martianus, Capella: see CAPELLA, MARTIANUS.

Martignac, Jean Baptiste Gay, vicomte de (zhã' bäptēst' gā' vēkōt' dů märtēnyäk'), 1778–1832, French statesman under Charles X. His ministry (1827–29) proposed liberal reforms but was overthrown by the ultraroyalists. Polignac succeeded him.

Martin, Saint, c.316–397?, bishop of Tours. While yet a heathen, he gave his cloak to a beggar. After conversion he went (c.360) to St. Hilary of Poitiers and built himself a hermitage. Acclaimed bishop against his will (371). Feast: Nov. 11. St. Martin's summer (mid-Nov.) named for him.

Martin I, Saint, d. 655, pope (649–55). Defying Emperor Constans II, he summoned a council that condemned MONOTHELETISM. The emperor had him imprisoned, then banished to the Crimea. Feast: Nov. 12.

Martin IV, d. 1285, pope (1281–85), a Frenchman. He supported the efforts of Charles of Anjou to restore the Latin Kingdom of Constantinople, thus alienating the Eastern Church. After the SICILIAN VESPERS, he turned all his power against Aragon.

Martin V, 1368–1431, pope (1417–31), a Roman named Oddone Colonna. The conclave of the Council of CONSTANCE chose him as pope to end the Great SCHISM. He rehabilitated Rome and papal power, restoring Church unity. He rejected the conciliar theory popular at Constance, but did follow the wishes of that council in calling a new one at Pavia (1423). This was ineffective and Martin summoned another to meet at Basel in 1431. He was opposed by Antipope Benedict XIII (Pedro de LUNA) and later by Antipope Clement VIII (Gil Sánchez Múñoz). Martin prevailed.

Martin, Archer John Porter, 1910–, English biochemist. Shared 1952 Nobel Prize in Chemistry for discovery of partition chromatography, a new method for separating compounds in chemical analysis.

Martin, Homer Dodge, 1836–97, American landscape painter. Influenced by Barbizon school.

martin, name used chiefly for certain swallows —European martin, bank swallow or sand martin of Europe and North America, American purple martin (destroys insects and chases crows).

Martin du Gard, Roger (rôzhā' märtē' dů gär'), 1881–, French novelist, author of *Les Thibault* (8 vols., 1922–40; Eng. tr., *The World of the Thibaults*), in which he dissects the conflicting strata and beliefs of modern French society. Was awarded 1937 Nobel Prize in Literature.

Martineau, Harriet (mär'tĭnō), 1802–76, English writer. Interested in reform, she advocated, in turn, Unitarianism, abolition, mesmerism, and positivism. Among her many works are *Illustrations of Political Economy*

(9 vols., 1832–34); *Society in America* (1837), written after a tour of the U.S.; and a free translation (1853) of Comte's *Cours de philosophie positive.*

Martinelli, Giovanni (jōvän'nē märtĕnĕl'lē), 1885–, Italian-American operatic tenor. Appeared at the Metropolitan Opera, New York, 1913–46.

Martinez (märtē'nŭs), city (pop. 8,268), W Calif., on Suisun Bay and NNE of Oakland. Oil refining, copper smelting, wine making, and fishing. Reservoir here is end of Contra Costa Canal.

Martínez de Campos, Arsenio (ärsān'yō märtē'nĕth dā käm'pōs), 1831–1900, Spanish general. Brought Carlist Wars and Cuban Ten Years War to an end; was premier 1879. Sent to Cuba in 1895, he was criticized for leniency toward the insurgents and was replaced by Weyler.

Martínez de la Rosa, Francisco (fränthē'skō märtēnāth dā lä rō'sä), 1787–1862, Spanish romantic dramatist, poet, novelist, historian.

Martínez Ruiz, José (hōsā' märtē'nāth rōōēth'), 1873–, pseud. Azorín (äsōrēn'), Spanish essayist, novelist, and dramatist of the Generation of 1898, noted for descriptive and psychological essays and penetrating literary criticism.

Martínez Sierra, Gregorio (grāgō'rēō märtē'nāth syĕ'rä), 1881–1947, Spanish dramatist, novelist, poet, widely known for drama *The Cradle Song* (1911).

Martini, Simone (sēmō'nā märtē'nē), or **Simone di Martino,** c.1283–1344, a leader of Sienese school of painting; master of delicate, sinuous line.

Martinique (märtĭnēk'), overseas dept. of the French Republic (427 sq. mi.; pop. 261,595), in Windward Isls., West Indies; cap. FORT-DU-FRANCE. Discovered by Columbus, 1502, it was colonized by French under Esnambuc from 1635. Sugar cane, introduced from Brazil in 1654, is principal crop. Rum is a major export. Island is subject to tidal waves, earthquakes, volcanic eruptions (most disastrous of which was that of Pelée, 1902).

Martino, Simone di: see MARTINI, SIMONE.

Martinsburg, city (pop. 15,621), in E Panhandle of W.Va., SW of Hagerstown; chartered 1778. Mfg. of textiles, hosiery, and wood products. Belle Boyd, Confederate spy, lived and was imprisoned here. Near-by Bunker Hill, settled c.1729, is oldest recorded settlement in W.Va.

Martins Ferry, city (pop. 13,220), E Ohio, on Ohio R. opposite Wheeling, W.Va.; settled 1785 as Norristown. Has coal mining and mfg. of steel. Birthplace of W. D. Howells.

Martinsville. 1 City (pop. 5,991), S central Ind., on White R. and SW of Indianapolis. Health resort with artesian springs. **2** City (pop. 17,251), SW Va., WNW of Danville in Blue Ridge foothills; founded 1793. Center of agr. area. Mfg. of furniture and textiles.

Martinu, Bohuslav (bô'hōōsläf mär'tĭnōō), 1890–, Czech composer; came to the U.S. in 1941. He has written symphonies, operas, a Concerto Grosso, and *Memorial to Lidice* (1943) for orchestra.

Martiny, Philip (märtē'nē), 1858–1927, American sculptor, b. Alsace. Decorations for public buildings.

Marvel, Ik, pseud. of **Donald Grant Mitchell,** 1822–1908, American author. Sentimental essays in *Reveries of a Bachelor* (1850) and *Dream Life* (1851) were long popular.

Marvell, Andrew, 1621–78, English poet, best known for lyrics, such as "The Garden," "To His Coy Mistress," and for his "Horatian Ode" to Cromwell.

Marwar, India: see JODHPUR.

Marx, Karl, 1818–83, German social philosopher and radical leader, the chief theorist of modern socialism. Took (1842) a Ph.D. degree at Jena. In Paris (1843) he began his lifelong association with Friedrich ENGELS, with whom, in 1848, he published the *Communist Manifesto,* a basic formulation of MARXISM. From 1850 until his death he lived in London. Here he founded (1864) the International Workingmen's Association (see INTERNATIONAL, FIRST) and wrote his monumental work *Das Kapital* (Vol. I, 1867; Vols. II and III, posthumously ed. by Engels, 1885–94), a book which has exerted an incalculable influence on modern world. Most modern forms of SOCIALISM and COMMUNISM are derived from his dynamic theory of social change. He adapted Hegel's dialectical method to his own materialistic position to produce theory of DIALECTICAL MATERIALISM.

Marx, Wilhelm (vĭl'hĕlm), 1863–1946, chancellor of Germany (1923–24, 1926–28); head of Catholic Center party. Accepted Dawes Plan (1924). Was defeated by Hindenburg in presidential elections (1925).

Marx Brothers, a team of American comedians. They are Julius (1895–), called Groucho; Arthur (1893–), called Harpo; and Leonard (1891–), called Chico. Originally in vaudeville and on the stage, they have been popular in moving pictures since 1929.

Marxism, economic-political system named for Karl MARX. It is also known as economic or materialistic determinism, scientific (as opposed to utopian) socialism, and DIALECTICAL MATERIALISM. Virtually all modern socialist and communist thought is directly based on Marxism. Marx and Friedrich ENGELS published in 1848 the *Communist Manifesto,* in which the fundamental assumptions of the system were set forth. It was asserted that "the history of all hitherto existing society is the history of class struggles." Every social order based on class division contains the germs of its own destruction, until the emergence of a classless society. The modern social struggle is between the bourgeoisie (i.e., the capitalist class) and the nonpropertied proletariat. In *Das Kapital,* Marx developed his theory that the value of the commodities consumed by a worker is less than the value of the commodities he produces; the difference, called surplus value, represents the profit of the capitalist. Marx prophesied that the proletariat would become the ruling class and centralize production in the hands of the state, which would, in its turn, "wither away." To hurry along this inevitable process, revolution was to be used if necessary.

Mary, the Virgin, mother of Jesus, the principal saint, called Our Lady. Her name in Hebrew is Miriam. The New Testament tells much of her, though the principal stress is upon the annunciation to her by Gabriel that she was to bear the Savior and upon the actual birth of Jesus. She was married to Joseph, a carpenter of Nazareth, and she was a cousin of Elizabeth, mother of John the Baptist. She played some part in Jesus' public life, notably in the miracle at Cana, and she stood at the foot of the Cross when her Son was crucified. She was honored from early days in Christianity, and tradition has supplied other details of her life: that her parents were St. Joachim and St. Anne; that she was presented and dedicated at the Temple as a virgin; that she was later protected chastely by St. Joseph; and that after the death of Jesus she was cared for by St. John the Divine. Mary is the object of the highest veneration in the Orthodox and the Roman Catholic Church because of her unique position doctrinally defined as Mother of God; expressly, however, she is not the object of worship, which is restricted to God alone. The Roman Catholic Church has other important dogmas concerning the Virgin, among them that she was born without original sin (doctrine of the Immaculate Conception); that she remained a virgin throughout her life (the "brethren of the Lord" in the Bible being construed to mean only kinsmen); that she was "assumed" directly into heaven in the body (doctrine of the Assumption). Most Catholics express their veneration and love for her by daily recitation of the Ave Maria and frequent saying of the rosary, and there are many other prayers and hymns in her honor. Besides these ordinary attentions she is also specially venerated under various aspects—some derived from titles (as Our Lady Queen of Heaven; Our Lady Star of the Sea or Stella Maris), some from events of her life (as Our Lady of the Immaculate Conception; Our Lady of Sorrows), some from miraculous events or visions associated with her (see CZESTOCHOWA; GUADALUPE HIDALGO; LOURDES; FÁTIMA). Every Saturday and the month of May are devoted to her, and she has many special feasts, among them: Dec. 8, the Immaculate Conception (important in U.S., because Our Lady in her Immaculate Conception is patron of U.S.); Feb. 2, the Purification of Our Lady (Candlemas); March 25, the Annunciation (Lady Day); Aug. 15, the Assumption (principal of her feasts); Sept. 8, the Birthday of Our Lady. Though Protestant churches generally discarded veneration of Mary, she is revered especially by "high-church" groups in the Anglican and Episcopal churches, respected (particularly at Christmas) in nonevangelical churches, and disregarded in extreme evangelical churches. Stories concerning her rejected in all Western churches appear in the PSEUDEPIGRAPHA.

Mary, queens of England. **Mary I,** 1516–58, queen 1553–58, was the daughter of HENRY VIII and KATHARINE OF ARAGON. After her parents' divorce Mary was forced to acknowledge herself as illegitimate and to repudiate Catholic Church. Pope absolved her from these statements, and she remained loyal to her faith. Succeeded her brother, Edward VI, after an unsuccessful attempt was made to put Lady Jane Grey on the throne. Her marriage in 1554 to PHILIP II of Spain and consequent Spanish alliance were unpopular. Papal authority was reestab. in 1554. Religious persecutions and loss of Calais increased popular hatred of "Bloody Mary." **Mary II,** 1662–94, queen 1689–94, was the daughter of James II and Anne Hyde. Reared as Protestant, she married William of Orange in 1677. Was joint sovereign with him (see WILLIAM III) after Glorious Revolution of 1688, but ruled only during his absences.

Mary, 1867–1953, queen consort of George V and mother of Edward VIII and George VI of England.

Mary, in Bible. **1** Mary, the Virgin. **2** MARY MAGDALEN. **3** One of those to stand at foot of the Cross. Possibly the mother of James the Less; also identified as sister of Mary, the Virgin. Mat. 27.56, 61; Mark 15.40,47; 16.1; Luke 24.10; John 19.25. **4** Sister of Lazarus and Martha of Bethany. Her greatest happiness was to sit at Jesus' feet and listen to his teachings. Luke 10.38–42; John 11.1–46; 12.1–9. Some identify her with Mary Magdalen.

Mary, Turkmen SSR: see MERV.

Mary Baldwin College: see STAUNTON, Va.

Maryknoll (mâ'rĕnōl), place, SE N.Y., near Ossining, hq. of Catholic Foreign Mission Society of America; estab. 1911. Here priests ("Maryknoll Fathers") are trained for foreign missions.

Maryland, state (10,577 sq. mi.; pop. 2,343,001), E U.S.; one of Thirteen Colonies; cap. ANNAPOLIS; metropolis BALTIMORE. Bordered largely by POTOMAC R. on W and SW; partly by the Atlantic on E. CHESAPEAKE BAY separates E shore from main part of state. Farming (poultry, tobacco, truck, dairy products, cattle, fine horses); fishing; processing of produce and sea food. Mfg. of steel, ships, transportation equipment, chemicals, textiles; refines oil, sugar. William Claiborne set up trading post on Kent Isl. 1631. Territory under proprietorship of the Calverts 1632–89. Attempt to achieve religious freedom (esp. for Catholics) was opposed by encroaching Puritans. Supported American Revolution. Remained in Union during Civil War, though torn between two loyalties. Industry prospered after war. Remains true border state (reflected in differences between tidewater and upland Md.).

Maryland, University of, at College Park and Baltimore (with Maryland State Col. at PRINCESS ANNE); land-grant and state supported, coed.; chartered and opened 1807 as Col. of Medicine of Maryland, became university 1812. Has absorbed Maryland Agricultural Col., Baltimore Dental Col. (1840; first U.S. dental school), and several law and pharmacy schools.

Marlebone, Saint (sŭnt mâ'rēlŭbōn'), metropolitan borough (pop. 75,764) of NW London, England. Includes zoological and botanical gardens, B.B.C. studios, Mme Tussaud's waxworks, Harley St. (a center of medical practice), and London's chief shopping district.

Mary Magdalen or **Mary Magdalene** (both: măg'dŭlŭn; formerly môd'lŭn, hence *maudlin,* i.e., tearful), woman cured of madness by Jesus; one of those who waited at the Cross and among the first to see the risen Jesus. Mat. 27.56,61; 28; Mark 15.47; 16; Luke 8.2; 24; John 19.25; 20. Traditionally identified with the reformed prostitute who anointed Jesus' feet (Luke 2.36–50), she has become the symbol of the penitent, hence the word *Magdalen*. Also identified with Mary of Bethany. Widely venerated among Christians. Feast: July 22.

Marymount College: see TARRYTOWN, N.Y.

Mary of Burgundy, 1457–82, daughter of CHARLES THE BOLD, whose death in 1477 left her the richest heiress in Europe. Louis XI of France immediately attacked her inheritance, seizing Burgundy and Picardy and threatening the Low Countries and Franche-Comté. To win her subjects' support, Mary issued, at Ghent, the Great Privilege, which restored the former liberties of Flanders, Brabant, Hainaut, and Holland. In the same year (1477) she married her ally, Maximilian of Austria (later Emperor MAXIMILIAN I), who defeated the French at Guinegate (1479). Mary's untimely death in a riding accident left her son Philip (later PHILIP I of Castile) as heir and thus transferred the Low Countries to Hapsburg control. Troubles in the Netherlands forced Maximilian to ratify (1483) the Treaty of ARRAS, which gave Franche-Comté and Artois to France (ceded back by France 1493).

Mary of England (Mary Tudor), 1496–1533, queen consort of Louis XII of France, daughter of Henry VII of England. After death of Louis (1515) she married Charles Brandon, duke of Suffolk.

Mary of Guise (gēz), 1515–60, queen of Scotland, wife of James V and mother of Mary Queen of Scots. After James's death (1542) she sought to bring France and Scotland together. As regent (after 1554), she married her daughter to the French dauphin and brought in French troops to oppose the Protestant and pro-English party.

Mary of Modena (mŏ'dĭnů), 1658–1718, queen of James II of England. As a devout Catholic she was unpopular in England. Birth of her son (a Catholic heir) was a cause of revolution of 1688.

Mary Queen of Scots (Mary Stuart), 1542–87, only child of James V of Scotland and MARY OF GUISE. She was sent by her mother to France, where she grew up and married (1558) Francis II. After his death in 1560, she returned to Scotland as queen in 1561. Despite harsh attacks from John Knox, she refused to abandon her Catholicism and her charm and intelligence won many over. To reinforce her claim to succeed ELIZABETH on the English throne, she married (1565) her English cousin Lord DARNLEY. Soon despised by Mary, he joined a conspiracy of Protestant nobles who murdered her trusted counselor, David RIZZIO. Mary, however, talked Darnley over and escaped to loyal nobles. Her son, James I, was born soon after. At this period she fell in love with earl of BOTHWELL. Darnley, disliked by everyone, was murdered in 1567. Bothwell, widely suspected of the murder, was acquitted and married Mary. Outraged Scots flew to arms. Mary surrendered at Carberry Hill, abdicated, and named earl of Murray as regent. She escaped (1586) and gathered a large force, but was defeated by Murray and fled to England. Although welcomed by Elizabeth, she became a prisoner. In prison she became involved in several ill-starred plots with English Catholics, the Spanish, the French, and others. Finally confirmed her son's kingship (1583) but was denied liberty. In 1586 a plot to murder Elizabeth was reported. Charged with being an accomplice, Mary was tried and beheaded in 1587. Deeply religious in her later years, Mary's conduct at trial and execution gained much admiration. A clear-cut decision about her guilt is made difficult by web of intrigue surrounding both the murder of Darnley and the plot against Elizabeth.

Marysville, city (pop. 7,826), N central Calif., at confluence of Yuba and Feather rivers, N of Sacramento. Fruitgrowing center.

Maryville. 1 City (pop. 6,834), NW Mo., N of St. Joseph, in livestock (esp. hogs) area. **2** City (pop. 7,742), E Tenn., S of Knoxville, in fruitgrowing area. Lumbering and textile mfg. Has log cabin where Sam Houston taught.

Mary Washington College: see VIRGINIA, UNIVERSITY OF.

Masaccio (mäzät'chō), 1401–1428?, Florentine painter, pioneer of Italian Renaissance. Real name was Tommaso Guidi. His frescoes (esp. those in Brancacci Chapel of Church of Santa Maria del Carmine, Florence) were studied by such painters as Michelangelo and Raphael. Began new era of painting by expert use of perspective and by naturalistic treatment of figures and landscape.

Masaniello (mäzänyĕl'lō), 1620–1647, Neapolitan revolutionist, whose original name was Tommaso Aniello; a fisherman. He led a rebellion against increased taxation (1647) but came to terms with the viceroy, who promised reforms and made him captain general. The title went to Masaniello's head; he was killed by his own supporters.

Masaryk, Thomas Garrigue (gùrēg' mä'sărĭk), 1850–1937, chief founder and first president (1919–35) of Czechoslovakia, b. Moravia. Taught philosophy at Prague Univ.; married Charlotte Garrigue, an American. Leading the Czech independence party from 1907, he headed (with BENES) the Czechoslovak national council at Paris during World War I and was acclaimed president of the new republic in Nov., 1918 (reelected 1920, 1927, 1934). He resigned because of his age in 1935 and was succeeded by Benes. An ardent liberal and democrat, he was revered by the great majority of the people but was attacked by extremists of all sorts. Among his writings translated into English are *Spirit of Russia* (1919), *The Making of a State* (1927), *Ideals of Humanity* (1938), *Modern Man and Religion* (1938). His son **Jan Masaryk** (yän), 1886–1948, became (1940) foreign minister of the Czechoslovak government in exile at London during World War II. He kept that post after his government's return to Prague (1945) until his death, shortly after the Communist coup d'état of Feb., 1948. He was a liberal but advocated cooperation with Russia. According to the official account of his death, he committed suicide by leaping from a window, but the exact circumstances remain subject to speculation.

Mascagni, Pietro (pyă'trō mäskä'nyē), 1863–1945, Italian composer of operas (e.g., *L'amico Fritz, Iris,* and the popular *Cavalleria rusticana*).

Mascara (mă'skûrù), city (pop. 26,086), NW Algeria, SE of Oran. Became headquarters of Abdu-l-Kadir in 1832; occupied by the French in 1841. A market center, noted for its white wine.

Mascarene Islands (măskûrēn'), in Indian Ocean, E of Madagascar. Include MAURITIUS, RÉUNION, and RODRIGUEZ.

Masefield, John, 1878–, English poet laureate (after 1930). A boyhood spent at sea was basis for first poems, *Salt-Water Ballads* (1902), containing "Sea Fever" and "Cargoes." First long narrative poem, *The Everlasting Mercy* (1911), won him fame. Of later poetry best known are *The Widow in the Bye Street* (1912) and *Dauber* (1913). Author also of novels (e.g., *Sard Harker,* 1924), plays, books for boys, and sketches.

Masereel, Frans (fräns' mäsārāl'), 1889–, Belgian painter and illustrator of books. Famous for woodcuts expressing miseries of men.

Masham, Abigail, Lady, d. 1734, favorite of Queen Anne of England. Power behind the throne, she gave influence to her kinsman, Robert Harley, until they quarreled in 1714; then to Henry St. John.

Masinissa (măsĭnĭ'sù), c.238–149 B.C., king of Numidia. Joined Romans (206 B.C.) in the Second Punic War and led cavalry in victory at Zama. When Carthage began to revive, he attacked Carthaginian territory and brought on the Third Punic War. Also Massinissa.

mask, artificial face or head covering used as disguise or protection, fashioned of many kinds of materials. Medicinal, religious, protective masks have been used by many primitive peoples. Theatrical masks have appeared in Japanese *no* dramas, Chinese temple dramas, in Greek and Roman theaters, Italian commedia dell'arte, medieval miracle plays, in modern German expressionist drama, and in Eugene O'Neill's work. Death masks date from ancient times. See also MASQUE.

Maskat, Arabia: see MUSCAT.

Maskelyne, Nevil (nĕ'vùl mă'skùlĭn), 1732–1811, English astronomer. Estab. *Nautical Almanac* (1766). He was astronomer royal from 1765.

Masolino da Panicale (mäzōlē'nō dä pänē-kä'lā), 1383–c.1447, Florentine painter, whose real name was Tommaso di Christoforo Fini. Works represent transition between tradition estab. by Giotto and later techniques involving perspective and chiaroscuro. His frescoes in Brancacci chapel were continued by his pupil Masaccio, completed by Filippino Lippi.

Mason, George, 1725–92, American statesman. Drew up Virginia Declaration of Rights. Member of Federal Constitutional Convention (1787). A Bill of Rights he forwarded formed basis for first ten amendments to U.S. Constitution. His grandson, **James Murray Mason,** 1798–1871, was U.S. Senator from Va. (1847–61) and Confederate diplomat. Appointed Confederate commissioner to England (1861), he was seized en route and interned at Boston (see TRENT AFFAIR).

Mason, John, 1586–1635, founder of New Hampshire, b. England. Received land grant 1629. Claims to land by heirs led to litigation and favorable settlement. Rights sold in 1746 to 12 Portsmouth men, Masonian Proprietors, who issued permits to settle.

Mason and Slidell Affair: see TRENT AFFAIR.

Mason City, city (pop. 27,980), N central Iowa, NW of Waterloo; settled 1853 by Masons. Rail, trade, and industrial center of agr. area with mfg. of food and clay products.

Mason-Dixon line, boundary between Pa. and Md. (lat. 39° 43′ 26.3″ N), surveyed by English astronomers Charles Mason and Jeremiah Dixon in 1763–67 to settle boundary dispute. Term popularly used to distinguish South from North.

Masonian Proprietors: see MASON, JOHN.

Masonic orders: see FREEMASONRY.

Masora (mùsō'rù) [Heb.,= traditional], collection of critical annotations made by Hebrew scholars called Masoretes to establish the text of the Old Testament. Since the Hebrew alphabet has no vowels, the Masoretes had to formulate rules for an accurate reading of each verse. They evolved two systems of vowels: the Tiberian (now in use), consisting of curves, dots, and dashes, which can be traced to the 7th cent., and the Babylonian, a more complicated system of earlier origin. The language of the Masora is mostly Aramaic; many scholars contributed to the work, which ceased c.1425.

Masovia (mùsō'vēù), Pol. *Mazowsze,* historic region, central Poland; cap. Warsaw. Became duchy under one of four branches of PIAST dynasty in 1138; was annexed by Polish crown 1526.

Maspero, Gaston (gästō' mäspùrō'), 1846–1916, French Egyptologist. Founded French School of Oriental Archaeology at Cairo, did valuable work at Luxor and Karnak, and wrote several well-known works on ancient history.

Masquat, Arabia: see MUSCAT.

masque or **mask** (both: măsk), form of dramatic entertainment, usually mythological or allegorical in form, popular in early 17th-cent. England. Popularity at court resulted in masques becoming elaborate spectacles emphasizing costumes, scenery, dancing, and music. Ben Jonson wrote many masques.

masquerade. Now usually a fancy dress or costume ball in which guests wear half-face masks, masquerades originally accompanied religious festivals such as Greek Bacchanalia, Roman Saturnalia, and Purim feast of the Jews. Masquerade balls were introduced into England from France in 16th cent.

Mass [Latin,= dismissal], in the Roman Catholic Church and also among Anglo-Catholics, the primary religious service, a performance of the sacrament of the EUCHARIST. In most, but not all, Roman Catholic churches the Mass is said in Latin according to the liturgy of the city of Rome. The service is the same all over the world, though minor variant "uses" are permitted to certain groups (e.g., the Dominican order). Some parts of the text of the Mass are invariable; these make up the "ordinary." Other parts change with the occasion and the day; these prayers are "proper" to the occasion. The Mass may be merely read by the priest (Low Mass) or it may be an elaborate ritual, a solemn, or High, Mass, with a priest, deacon, and subdeacon (usually also priests) and choir. In a sung Mass, some portions are chanted solo at the altar with choral response, some portions are merely read, and nine hymns are sung by the choir. Of these nine, four are "proper": the introit, the anthem after the epistle, the offertory, and the communion; their texts are rendered in plain song. The other five are "ordinary"—*Kyrie eleison, Gloria in excelsis* (omitted in penitential seasons), creed, *Sanctus,* and *Agnus Dei*—and are the portions for which musical settings have been written by many composers (including Palestrina, Bach, Mozart, Beethoven, and Verdi). The central portion of the Mass is the eucharistic prayer, the canon, which is read rapidly and inaudibly. Some of the other prayers are read audibly, some silently.

mass, in physics, quantity of matter in a body without regard to volume or pull of gravity. "Weight" is measurement of force of gravity and depends on where measurement is made; mass is constant and this is sometimes called standard weight. Local weight divided by local acceleration of gravity multiplied by standard acceleration of gravity equals mass. According to theory of relativity, mass is not constant; both inertia and mass are held to increase as velocity approaches that of light.

Massa (mäs′sä), city (pop. 12,508), Tuscany, central Italy, near Tyrrhenian Sea. Marble quarries. From 15th to 19th cent., it was the cap. of the small principality (later duchy) of Massa and Carrara, ruled by the Malaspina and Cybo-Malaspina families. In 1829 the duchy passed, through marriage, to the house of Austria-Este (dukes of Modena); in 1859 it was united with Sardinia. Has 15th-cent. castle and cathedral.

Massachusetts, state (8,257 sq. mi.; pop. 4,690,-514), NE U.S.; one of Thirteen Colonies; cap. Boston. Other cities are Worcester, Springfield, Fall River, Cambridge, New Bedford, Somerville, Lowell, Lynn. Bounded E and S by the Atlantic. To E is coastal plain (with Cape Cod); W are uplands and Berkshire Hills, split by Connecticut R. valley. Mfg. of electrical supplies, textiles, shoes, ships, metal and rubber products; also food processing, printing, and publishing. Farming yields corn, potatoes, cranberries, poultry, truck, dairy products. Fishing important. Mayflower brought Pilgrims to Plymouth 1620. Plymouth Colony developed under William Bradford. Salem (1626) became center for Puritan Massachusetts Bay Company. John Winthrop brought over large Puritan group, founded Boston (1630). Colony became a theocracy. Education emphasized early. Member of New England Confederation. Difficulties with England (Navigation Acts, Stamp Act, Townshend Acts) preceded Boston Massacre and Boston Tea Party and precipitated American Revolution (see Lexington and Concord, battles of, and Bunker Hill, battle of). Postwar depres sion caused violence in Shays's Rebellio (1786). Dissatisfaction with Embargo Ac of 1807 and War of 1812 led to Hartfor Convention. Decline of shipping cause rise of industry. Leaders of thought aros (see Unitarianism, transcendentalism) Union vigorously supported in Civil Wa Increased industrialism brought struggle c labor unions for recognition. Two worl wars expanded industries.

Massachusetts, University of: see Amherst.

Massachusetts Bay, inlet of the Atlantic, wher Mass. coast curves inward. Extends fror Cape Ann to Cape Cod. Boston Bay an Cape Cod Bay are arms of it.

Massachusetts Bay Company, English char tered company, organized (1628) with gran of land between Charles and Merrima rivers, extending W to "the South Sea. Puritan leaders estab. colony at present sit of Boston as religious and political refuge Attempts by Sir Ferdinando Gorges t annul claims were unsuccessful. Compan and colony were synonymous until compan ceased to exist in 1684.

Massachusetts Institute of Technology, at Cam bridge; nonsectarian, land-grant, mainly fo men; chartered 1861, opened 1865 by W B. Rogers in Boston, moved to Cambridg 1916. Leading technical school of universit grade with first school of architecture i U.S. Pioneered in various forms of engineer ing. Conducts combination course wit group of liberal arts colleges. Has nautica museums and important technical library.

Massachusetts State Teachers College: se Framingham.

Massasoit (măsŭsoit′), c.1580–1661, chief o the Wampanoag Indians. Signed treaty wit Pilgrims (1621) which he faithfully ob served. His son, Metacomet, became famou as King Philip.

Massawa (mŭsä′wŭ), city (pop. c.25,000) Eritrea; port on Red Sea; market for pearls Was cap. of Eritrea 1885–97. Allied base i World War II.

Masséna, André (ãdrā′ mäsānä′), 1758–1817 marshal of France under Napoleon I, wh created him duke of Rivoli (1808) an prince of Essling (1810). Helped win battl of Rivoli (1797); defeated Korsakov a Zurich (1799); took part in victories o Essling and Wagram (1809). His failure i the Peninsular War has been blamed on hi colleagues' lack of cooperation. He sup ported Louis XVIII in 1814; remained neu tral during Hundred Days (1815).

Massena (mŭsē′nŭ), village (pop. 13,137), N N.Y., near St. Lawrence R. and NE o Ogdensburg, in dairy area; settled 1790 Large aluminum plant. Near by is Roosevel Internatl. Bridge (1934).

Massenet, Jules (zhül′ mäsŭnĕ′), 1842–1912 French composer. He wrote oratorios, songs and orchestral suites, but is best known fo his operas (e.g., *Le Cid, Manon, Hérodiade* and *Werther*).

Massif Central (mäsēf′ sãträl′), great moun tainous plateau (average alt. c.2,650 ft. covering most of central France. Its core i the volcanic mass of the Auvergne mts (Puy de Sancy, 6,187 ft. high), and it com prises the *causses* of QUERCY and ROUERGUE and the CÉVENNES mts. Sheep raising, dairying, cattle raising; agr. in valleys. Coal mines. Clermont-Ferrand, Le Creusot, Saint-Étienne are industrial centers.

Massilia, anc. city in Gaul: see MARSEILLES.

Massillon, city (pop. 29,594), NE Ohio, on Tuscarawas R. and W of Canton; settled 1812. Coal shipping point with mfg. of steel and aluminum products and clothing. Has a state mental hospital.

Massine, Léonide (lāônēd' mäsēn'), 1896–, Russian ballet dancer and choreographer. Works include *Gaité parisienne* and *The Three-cornered Hat.*

Massinger, Philip, 1583–1640, English dramatist. Wrote tragedy *Duke of Milan* (1618) and satirical comedies *A New Way to Pay Old Debts* (1625) and *The City Madam* (1632). Collaborated with John Fletcher, Dekker, and possibly with Shakspere (in *King Henry VIII*).

Massive, Mount: see SAWATCH MOUNTAINS.

Massys, Matsys, Messys, or **Metsys, Quentin** (kvĕn'tĭn masīs', mätsīs', mĕ–, mĕt–), c.1466–1530, Flemish painter. Though influenced by Italian Renaissance, he retained intimacy and color of earlier Flemish art. His sons, **Jan Massys,** c.1509–1575, and **Cornelis Massys,** d. c.1580, were also painters.

Masters, Edgar Lee, 1879–1950, American poet, known for *Spoon River Anthology* (1915), a volume of free-verse "epitaphs," picturing the secret lives of people in the small-town Midwest. Also wrote a caustic biography of Lincoln.

mastodon (măs'tůdŏn"), extinct mammal from which elephants probably developed. Earliest known forms associated with Oligocene epoch in Africa were c.4½ ft. in height. Their descendants, the size of large elephants, spread over Eurasia and North America, persisting into the Pleistocene epoch.

mastoid (mă'stoid) or **mastoid process,** cone-shaped portion of temporal bone behind ear. Infection of mastoid cells (mastoiditis) is serious since brain and large blood vessels of neck may become involved.

Masudi (mäsōō'dē), d. 956, Arabian historian, geographer, and philosopher, b. Baghdad. His *Muruj adh-Dhahab* is a history of the universe from creation to A.D. 947. Traveled in many lands.

Masulipatam (můsōō"lůpŭ'tům) or **Bandar** (bŭn'důr), city (pop. 59,146), NE Madras, India; port on Bay of Bengal. First major British trading post in India was founded here in 1611. Cloth mfg.

Masuria (můzōō'rēů), Pol. *Mazury,* S region of former East Prussia, transferred to Polish administration 1945; chief city Lyck. Lakes, forests. The **Masurian Lakes** were the scene of heavy fighting in World War I. After Samsonov's defeat at TANNENBERG, the Russians under Rennenkampf were driven by the Germans under Mackensen into the lake country and lost 125,000 men. A second Russian drive into East Prussia was repulsed in Feb., 1915.

masurium: *see* TECHNETIUM.

Matabele (mătůbē'lē), Bantu-speaking tribe of W Southern Rhodesia. Founded 1823 when a Zulu general fled with some followers into what is now Transvaal and began attacking surrounding tribes and white settlers. Suppressed 1896 by the British.

Matagorda Bay (mătůgôr'dů), Gulf of Mexico inlet, S Texas, protected by Matagorda Peninsula. Probably visited 1685 by LaSalle. Lavaca Bay is arm. Has small ports. Matagorda Isl. is sand bar at entrance of San Antonio Bay.

Mata Hari (mä'tů hä'rē), 1876–1917, Dutch-Indonesian dancer and spy in German service during World War I. Her real name was Margaretha Geertruida Zelle. In 1917 she was executed by the French.

Matamoros, Mariano (märyä'nō mätämō'rōs), d. 1814, Mexican revolutionist in war against Spain, a priest.

Matamoros (mätämō'rōs), city (pop. 7,961), Tamaulipas, NE Mexico, on Rio Grande, near mouth, opposite Brownsville, Texas.

Matane (můtăn), town (pop. 6,345), E Que., Canada, on St. Lawrence R., NW Gaspé Peninsula, ENE of Rimouski. Lumbering center and pulpwood port.

Matanuska Valley (mătůnōō'sků), region, S Alaska, W of Chugach Mts. and crossed by Matanuska R. Agr. area with coal deposits and timber stands. U.S. government resettled farmers from Middle Western drought area here 1935.

Matanzas (mätän'säs), port (pop. 54,844), W Cuba, E of Havana. Has sugar refineries, tanneries, fertilizer plants. Once a pirate haven.

Matanzas, Fort: see SAINT AUGUSTINE, Fla.

Matapan, Cape (mă'tůpăn"), anc. *Taenarum* or *Tainaron,* S extremity of Greek mainland and of the Peloponnesus, projecting into Ionian Sea. British won naval victory (1941) off cape over Italians in World War II.

Matapedia, Lake (mătůpē'dēů), E Que., Canada, 14 mi. long, 2 mi. wide, at base of Gaspé Peninsula.

match. Friction match devised 1827 in England. Phosphorus match invented 1831 in France. Nontoxic chemicals are used in modern match. In safety match, invented 1855 in Sweden, oxidizing agent on tip is ignited by striking on special material on matchbox.

mate (mä'tā), **yerba mate** (yĕr'bä), or **Paraguay tea,** evergreen tree (*Ilex paraguariensis*) and the tea brewed from its leaves since ancient times by South American Indians. The tea, high in caffeine, is popular in much of South America. The gourd cups in which it is made are also called mate.

materialism, any philosophical system maintaining that the final reality of the universe is matter; opposed to idealism. Notable materialists in the ancient world were DEMOCRITUS, the Stoics, and the Epicureans. Materialism again became prominent in the 17th cent. with GASSENDI and Thomas HOBBES and in the 18th cent. with the philosophers of the Enlightenment. Various types of materialist philosophy gained wide following in the 19th and 20th cent. In common use, materialism means devotion to money and worldly things, to the exclusion of spiritual and intellectual values.

materials, strength of: see STRENGTH OF MATERIALS.

mathematics, study of numerical quantities and their relationships, of spatial quantities and their relationships, and of various abstractions of such relationships. The chief branches studied in school and college are ARITHMETIC (numerical quantities); ALGEBRA and theory of numbers (whole numbers only), which are arithmetical abstractions; GEOMETRY (spatial quantities); TRIGONOMETRY; and CALCULUS. All mathematical method is closely founded on logic, and mathematics has from ancient times been related to philosophy and to science (calculus is fundamental in important aspects of modern physics).

Mather, Richard (mă'dhûr), 1596–1669, British Puritan clergyman in North America. His son, **Increase Mather,** 1639–1723, was a Puritan pastor in Boston (1664–1723). A conservative upholder of Puritan theocracy, he opposed Sir Edmund Andros and supported Sir William PHIPS. His son, **Cotton Mather,** 1663–1728, clergyman and writer, assisted his father and succeeded him as pastor. His religious writings had wide influence. Remembered for his part in Salem witch trials of 1692. A promoter of learning, he was also a power in the state.

Mathew, Theobald, 1790–1856, Irish social worker, a Capuchin priest called "the apostle of temperance." He took and persuaded others to take a pledge of total abstinence. Worked for social welfare.

Mathews, Shailer, 1863–1941, American theologian, educator, and author. Taught history and theology at Univ. of Chicago (1894–1933) where he was dean (1908–33) of divinity school.

Mathewson, Christopher (Christy Mathewson), 1880–1925, American baseball pitcher. A right-hander, he won 373 major-league games. Won 30 or more games each of three consecutive seasons (1903–05); pitched three shutout victories in 1905 world series; won 37 games in 1908.

Mathura, India: see MUTTRA.

Matilda, Saint: see HENRY I, German king.

Matilda or **Maud,** 1102–67, queen of England, daughter of Henry I. First married to Emperor Henry V, after his death (1125) she married Geoffrey IV. At her father's death (1135) her cousin STEPHEN took the throne. In 1139 Matilda and her half-brother Robert, earl of Gloucester, challenged Stephen. She was made "lady of the English" in 1141 but soon dethroned. Withdrew (1148) in favor of her son, Henry II.

Matilda, 1046–1115, countess of Tuscany. Ruled larger part of central Italy. At her castle at CANOSSA Henry IV humiliated himself before Gregory VII (1077). She made a will bequeathing her alodial lands to the Holy See, but there are indications that she later changed it in favor of Emperor Henry V. Henry, at any rate, seized her lands in 1116. The dispute over her lands continued under later emperors and popes, while the Tuscan cities themselves achieved independence.

Matisse, Henri (ārē' mätēs'), 1869–, French painter and sculptor, the outstanding representative of FAUVISM. Renounced academic style, developing instead along a postimpressionistic line of brighter, simpler design. His travels in Morocco inspired decorative canvases in which bold patterns of lines and flowers serve as background for odalisques. Other works include still lifes and interiors. Uses large surfaces of pure color and reduces aerial perspective to a minimum. Designed the chapel Ste Marie du Rosaire at Vence, near Nice, France.

Mato Grosso (mä'tō grô'sŏŏ), state (487,47[illegible] sq. mi.; pop. 528,451), central and W Brazil; cap. CUIABÁ. Other chief city is Corumbá. Borders Bolivia on W, Paraguay on SW and S. Drained to N by tributaries of Amazon and to S by the Paraguay and Paraná. Cattle raising is principal occupation, but farms are being opened. First explored and settled by gold seekers but mineral resources are still largely undeveloped.

matriarchy (mā'trēär"kē), society (or aspect of a society) having its social base in the mother, rather than the father. In many societies lineage is traced only through the mother, and the mother determines the place of residence and rules family conduct. Sometimes the mother's brother has more authority over the family than the father. Opposite is patriarchy.

Matsuoka, Yosuke (yō'skĕ mätsŏŏ'ōkŏŏ), 1880–1946, Japanese statesman. Graduate of Univ. of Oregon law school. In 1932 he led Japanese delegation out of League of Nations. Foreign minister in Konoye cabinet, 1940–41. After World War II indicted as war criminal but death prevented trial.

Matsys, Quentin: see MASSYS, QUENTIN.

Mattagami Lake (mŏŏtă'gŏŏmē), 88 sq. mi., W Que., Canada, N of Val d'Or.

Mattathias, father of the MACCABEES. 1 Mac. 2.

Matteawan: see BEACON, N.Y.

Matteotti, Giacomo (jä'kōmō mät-tāôt'tē), 1885–1924, Italian Socialist leader, outstanding opponent of the early Fascist regime. His murder by Fascist hirelings marked the actual beginning of Mussolini's complete dictatorship.

matter, anything that occupies space, has weight and mass, and exhibits such properties as INERTIA, ELASTICITY, impenetrability. Law of conservation of matter states it can neither be created nor destroyed. Kinetic molecular theory holds that matter is composed of many minute particles (see MOLECULE) in constant vibratory motion. Change from any of three states of matter (gas, liquid, solid) to another is physical change and does not alter molecule. Atomic theory is concerned with nature and internal structure of molecules. CHEMICAL REACTION is change in which matter is broken down into atoms, then recombined into molecules. Recent work has shown that TRANSMUTATION OF ELEMENTS is possible. Matter is divided into living and nonliving.

Matterhorn (mä'tûrhôrn), Fr. *Mont Cervin*, Ital. *Monte Cervino,* peak, 14,701 ft. high, on Swiss-Italian border, SW of Zermatt. First scaled 1865 by Edward Whymper. Near-by **Matterjoch** (mä'tûryôkh) or Théodule is a pass linking Italy with Switzerland.

Matthew, Saint, one of the Twelve Apostles, [illegible]

publican of Capernaum. Also called Levi. Mat. 9.9–13; 10.3; Mark 2.14; Luke 5.27,29. Since 2d cent. regarded as author of the Gospel according to St. Matthew. His symbol: a young man or an angel. Feast: Sept. 21.

Matthew, Gospel according to Saint, first book of New Testament, traditionally ascribed to Matthew the Apostle. It gives unique account of Jesus' birth, tells of His ministry, and ends with the Passion and Resurrection. See also SYNOPTIC GOSPELS.

Matthew of Paris or **Matthew Paris,** d. 1259, English historian, monk of St. Albans and historiographer of the convent. His *Chronica majora,* a history of the world, is valuable source book.

Matthew of Westminster, imaginary author of English chronicle in Latin, *Flores historium,* written by several monks, including Matthew of Paris.

Matthew Paris: see MATTHEW OF PARIS.

Matthews, (James) Brander, 1852–1929, American authority on the drama. Taught at Columbia 1891–1924.

Matthias, Saint, apostle chosen by lot to replace Judas Iscariot. Acts 1.23–26: Feast: Feb. 24.

Matthias, 1557–1619, German emperor (1612–19). After negotiating the Peace of Vienna (1606) with BOCSKAY, he had himself proclaimed head of the house of Hapsburg, in view of the incapacity of his brother, Emperor RUDOLF II. He forced Rudolf to yield him the rule of Hungary, Austria, and Moravia in 1608 and that of Bohemia in 1611; in 1612 he succeeded him as emperor. Influenced by Melchoir, Cardinal Klesl (or Khlesl), he sought a compromise between Catholics and Protestants. Matthias had his son FERDINAND II crowned king of Bohemia in 1617 and of Hungary in 1618. His lack of resolution in the face of the Bohemian rising of 1618 caused Germany to drift into the THIRTY YEARS WAR.

Matthias Corvinus (kôrvī'nŭs), 1443?–1490, king of Hungary (1458–90); son of John HUNYADI and successor of Ladislaus V. He fought successfully against the Turks and, with papal blessing, made war on his father-in-law, GEORGE OF PODEBRAD, king of Bohemia. He conquered Moravia, Silesia, and Lusatia and in 1469 took the title king of Bohemia. The struggle continued until 1478, when Ladislaus II of Bohemia (later also ULADISLAUS II of Hungary) made a compromise peace that allowed Matthias to retain his title and conquests during his lifetime. In 1482 Matthias attacked Emperor Frederick III, from whom he conquered most of Austria (incl. Vienna, 1485); all his conquests reverted to their former rulers after his death. A true Renaissance despot, Matthias was warlike, harsh, and grasping but a generous patron of art and learning. He founded the famous Corvina library at Buda.

Mattoon (măt"tōōn'), city (pop. 17,547), E central Ill., SE of Decatur. Trade, industrial, rail center of agr. (corn, soybeans, broomcorn) area. Mfg. of wood products and Diesel engines.

Mattson, Henry Elis, 1887–, American landscape painter, b. Sweden.

matzoth (mät'sŭ, mät'sōth) [Heb.,= unleavened], bread made without leaven. Eaten by Jews during PASSOVER.

Mauclerc, Pierre: see PETER I, duke of Brittany.

Maud: see MATILDA, queen of England.

Maugham, W(illiam) Somerset (môm), 1874–, English novelist, playwright, and short-story writer. His most famous novel is *Of Human Bondage* (1915). Other well-known works are novel *The Moon and Sixpence* (1919); short story "Miss Thompson," dramatized as *Rain;* satire *Cakes and Ale* (1930); novel *The Razor's Edge* (1944); and play *The Constant Wife* (1927).

Maui (mou'ē), island (728 sq. mi.; pop. 40,-103), second largest of Hawaiian Isls. Consists of two mountain masses, constituting E and W peninsulas, connected by an isthmus. HALEAKALA is highest peak. Has cattle ranches and sugar and pineapple plantations. Chief port is Lahaina.

Maumee (mômē'), city (pop. 5,548), NW Ohio, on Maumee R. and SW of Toledo. Fort Miami, last of several military or trading posts on this site, was surrendered by British after War of 1812.

Maumee, river formed at Fort Wayne, NE Ind., by St. Joseph and St. Marys rivers. Flows c.130 mi. NE past Toledo, Ohio, to L. Erie.

Mauna Kea (mou'nŭ kā'ŭ), mountain, 13,784 ft. high, on Hawaii, T.H.; world's highest island mountain.

Mauna Loa (mou'nŭ lō'ŭ), mountain, 13,675 ft. high, on Hawaii, T.H. Its many craters include KILAUEA and MOKUAWEOWEO.

Maupassant, Guy de (gē' dŭ mōpäsā'), 1850–93, French author. He wrote some 300 short stories, some of which are unsurpassed in style, craftsmanship, and psychological realism. Among them are "Boule de Suif" ("Tallow Ball"), "La Ficelle," ("The Piece of String"), and "Miss Harriet." "The Necklace," his most popular story, is hardly representative of his best work. Among his novels are *Une Vie* (1883; Eng. tr., *A Life*) and *Bel Ami* (1885). Maupassant, greatly influenced by Flaubert, in turn influenced modern short-story writing. He went mad in 1891.

Maupeou, René Nicolas de (rŭnā' nēkôlä' dŭ mōpōō'), 1714–92, chancellor of France 1768–74). Dissolved PARLEMENT of Paris and provincial parlements; substituted a new parlement and a system of superior courts (1771). Strove to abolish sale of offices. His high-handed methods made him unpopular. Louis XVI dismissed him, restored parlements (1774).

Maupertuis, Pierre Louis Moreau de (pyĕr' lwē' môrō' dŭ mōpĕrtüē'), 1698–1758, French mathematician, astronomer, and author of works on astronomy, cosmology, and biology. His work on Newton's theory won him membership in Royal Society of London (1728); he headed expedition to Lapland (1736–37) where he confirmed Newton's theory of flattening of earth at poles.

Maurepas, Jean Frédéric Phélippeaux, comte de (zhā' frēdārēk' fālēpō' kōt' dŭ môrŭpä'),

1701–81, French statesman. His hostility to Mme de Pompadour caused his dismissal from the ministry in 1749. Appointed minister of state (1774), he caused the dismissal of Turgot (1776) and of Necker (1781); supported alliance with American colonies.

Mauretania (môrĭtā'nyů), region in N Africa in Roman times, vaguely W of Numidia. In 2d cent. B.C. Bocchus, father-in-law of Jugurtha of Numidia, built the kingdom of Mauretania (in present N Morocco and W Algeria). Augustus put Juba II on the throne (25 B.C.). Later revolts caused Claudius to make the region two Roman provinces, but native chiefs were never wholly subdued.

Mauriac, François (frãswä' mōryäk'), 1885–, French novelist, author of *The Desert of Love* (1925; Eng. tr., 1929), *Thérèse Desqueyroux* (1927; Eng. tr., 1928), *Vipers' Tangle* (1932; Eng., 1933), and other novels which place him among the foremost Catholic writers of his time. Received 1952 Nobel Prize in Literature.

Maurice (mô'rĭs), c.539–602, Byzantine emperor (582–602). Restored KHOSRU II in Persia (591). Was murdered by the usurper Phocas.

Maurice, 1521–53, duke (1541–47) and elector (1547–53) of Saxony. He joined, then abandoned, the SCHMALKALDIC LEAGUE and was rewarded (1547) by Emperor Charles V with the rank of elector and with Electoral Saxony (both taken from his cousin, John Frederick I). He then formed a league against Charles, secured French aid, and negotiated the Treaty of PASSAU (1552), whereupon he turned about once more and made war on his ex-ally, Albert Alcibiades of Brandenburg-Kulmbach. He fell in battle.

Maurice of Nassau, 1567–1625, prince of Orange (1618–25), stadholder of Holland and Zeeland (1584–1625) and of Utrecht, Gelderland and Overijssel (1589–1625). He succeeded his father, William the Silent, as leader of the United Provs. in the struggle for independence from Spain. From his elder brother, Philip William, he inherited the principality of Orange. After a successful campaign on land and sea he concluded (1609) a 12-year truce with Spain, thus virtually establishing Dutch independence. To his chief adviser, OLDENBARNEVELDT, was due the great expansion of Dutch trade in the East. In the struggle between strict Calvinists and REMONSTRANTS, Maurice sided with the Calvinists and countenanced Oldenbarneveldt's execution. His brother Frederick Henry succeeded him.

Maurice of Saxony: see MAURICE (1521–53) and SAXE, MAURICE, COMTE DE (1696–1750).

Mauritania (môrĭtā'nēů), French overseas territory (c.449,800 sq. mi.; pop. 497,000), NW French West Africa, on the Atlantic. Its cap., Saint-Louis, is in Senegal. Mainly desert. Became a French protectorate in 1903 and an overseas territory in 1946.

Mauritius (môrĭ'shēůs), island (720 sq mi.; pop. 419,185), in Indian Ocean, one of Mascarene Isls. With Rodriguez and outlying dependencies it forms a British colony; Cap. Port Louis. Sugar is main crop and export. Discovered 1507 by the Portuguese, occupied 1638–1710 by the Dutch, and settled 1721 by the French, who named it Île de France La Bourdonnais was governor, 1735–46. Island was captured 1810 by the British. Abolition of slavery in British Empire (1834 caused influx of laborers from India, wh now outnumber the native Negroes.

Maurocordatos, Alexander: see MAVROCORDATOS.

Maurois, André (ãdrā' mōrwä'), 1885–, French author. Noted for novel *The Silence of Colonel Bramble* (1918; Eng. tr., 1920) and fo biographies of Shelley (*Ariel*, 1923), Byron Disraeli, Chateaubriand, Washington, an others.

Maurras, Charles (shärl' môräs'), 1868–1952 French author and critic. Edited the royalis daily *Action française*. Sentenced (1945) t life imprisonment for collaboration wit Germans in World War II, he was release shortly before his death.

Maury, Matthew Fontaine (mô'rē), 1806–73 American hydrographer, a naval office Made valuable charts of the Atlantic. H *Physical Geography of the Sea* (1885) wa first classic of modern oceanography.

Maurya (mou'ůryů), Indian dynasty, 325–18 B.C., founded by SANDRACOTTUS (Chandra gupta). ASOKA, his grandson, united nearl all India and Afghanistan. Substituted Bud dhism for Hinduism and began a golden ag of arts and public works.

mausoleum (môsůlē'ům), a tomb, especiall one of some size and elaborateness, so calle from sepulcher of that name at Halicarnas sus, Asia Minor, erected c.352 B.C. for Mau solus of Caria. One of seven wonders o the ancient world, it was a white marbl structure, richly decorated by Scopas an other sculptors, probably including Praxite les. A famous Roman mausoleum is that o Hadrian, now called CASTEL SANT' ANGELO Most celebrated of mausoleums built unde Mogul emperors of India is TAJ MAHAL.

Mausolus (môsō'lůs), d. 353 B.C., Persian sa trap, ruler of Caria and Rhodes. After h death, his wife erected the mausoleum a Halicarnassus.

maverick (măv'rĭck), in cowboy terminolog an unbranded yearling calf or any older an mal not bearing the owner's mark. Formerl such an animal became the property of th first person to brand it.

Mavrocordatos or **Maurocordatos, Alexande** (both: mäv"rôkôr-dhä'tôs), 1791–1865, Gree statesman. Drafted declaration of Greek in dependence (1821). Later, as president o national assembly, he opposed pro-Russia policy of Demetrios Ypsilanti and Cap d'Istria. Was premier under King Otto afte 1831.

Maxen (mäk'sůn), village, Saxony, E Ge many, S of Dresden. Here, in Seven Yea War, a Prussian army surrendered to Dau 1759.

Maxentius (măksĕn'shůs), d. 312, Roman em peror in Italy and Africa; son of MAXIMIAN After CONSTANTIUS I died (306) he wa aided by his father in making his claim t the throne good, opposing Severus, Galeriu and CONSTANTINE I. Ultimately Constantin defeated him in the decisive battle of Milvia Bridge (312).

Maxim, family of inventors and munitic

makers. **Sir Hiram Stevens Maxim,** 1840–1916, b. Sangerville, Maine, moved to England, where he invented (1884) the Maxim machine gun. His other inventions include explosives and a heavier-than-air airplane. His brother, **Hudson Maxim,** 1853–1927, b. Orneville, Maine, remained in the U.S. He was a chemist and developed a number of explosives. **Hiram Percy Maxim,** 1869–1936, b. Brooklyn, N.Y., was the son of Sir Hiram. He, too, remained in the U.S. He invented an automobile and a silencer for explosive weapons. Perhaps more useful inventions of his were silencers for gasoline engines.

Maximian (măksĭ'mēŭn), d. 310, Roman emperor. Was made subemperor in 285 and ruled jointly with Diocletian (286–305). Both emperors abdicated in 305 in favor of Constantius I and Galerius, but the death of Constantius (306) caused a complicated struggle for power. Maximian at first aided his son Maxentius, defeating Severus in Italy and gaining the support of Constantine I (who married his daughter Fausta). Later he fell out with Maxentius and fled to Constantine. He revolted in 310 and was forced to commit suicide.

Maximilian, emperors and German kings. **Maximilian I,** 1459–1519. His father, Emperor Frederick III, secured his election as king in 1486 and delegated most of his powers to him. Sole ruler after Frederick's death (1493), he was never crowned emperor by the pope but in 1508 took the title emperor-elect, which was also assumed by his successors (see Holy Roman Empire). His marriage to Mary of Burgundy (1477) brought the Low Countries and Franche-Comté to the house of Austria but involved him in war with France, as did his marriage by proxy to Anne of Brittany (1490). The Treaty of Senlis (1493) restored Artois and Franche-Comté, which he had lost to France in the Treaty of Arras of 1482, to his family possessions. In the same year he married a niece of Ludovico Sforza, who paid him a huge dowry and whom he invested as duke of Milan. This third marriage, and his difficulties with Venice, involved him in the Italian Wars, which drained his funds and made him dependent on loans from the Fugger family. He gained nothing in Italy and was equally unsuccessful in his favorite project of a crusade against the Turks. His reign was marked by attempts at constitutional reforms of the Holy Roman Empire; by the ascendency of the towns (notably the Swabian League, which he favored) and of the merchant classes; by the flowering of German art and humanism (he was a patron of Dürer and Ulrich von Hutten); and by the beginning of the Reformation. His dynastic policy secured for his grandsons Charles V and Ferdinand I one of the largest successions in history—the Low Countries, the Spanish empire, Austria, Bohemia, and Hungary. Maximilian, because of his chivalrous and slightly quixotic disposition, has been called the last of the knights. **Maximilian II,** 1527–76, son of Ferdinand I, was crowned German king and king of Bohemia in 1562 and king of Hungary in 1563; in 1564 he succeeded his father as emperor-elect. He probably sympathized with Lutheranism and granted considerable religious freedom, while at the same time encouraging the Catholic Reform. In 1568 he made a truce with Turkey by which he agreed to pay tribute to the sultan for his share of Hungary. He died while preparing to invade Poland, where he had been elected king by a minority of the nobles, the majority having chosen Stephen Bathory.

Maximilian, 1832–67, emperor of Mexico (1864–67); brother of Austrian Emperor Francis Joseph. When Mexican conservatives sought aid of Napoleon III in founding a Mexican empire, Maximilian was persuaded to accept the crown. When he and his wife, Carlotta, arrived in Mexico (1864), they found most of Mexico hostile to them and loyal to Benito Juárez. Maximilian's tenure rested solely on French soldiers, and when Napoleon III was compelled to withdraw these (1866–67), the flimsy fabric of Mexico's empire dissolved. Carlotta went to Europe to seek aid. Maximilian took personal command of his forces, was captured, and was shot (1867). Carlotta went mad but survived Maximilian 60 years.

Maximilian, electors and kings of Bavaria. **Maximilian I,** 1573–1651, duke of Bavaria from 1597, founded the Catholic League (1609) and headed it in the Thirty Years War. He was rewarded by Emperor Ferdinand II for his aid against Frederick the Winter King with the rank of elector (see electors) and with the Upper Palatinate (1623). He secured Wallenstein's dismissal in 1630. **Maximilian I,** 1756–1825, king of Bavaria (1806–25), acceded in 1795 as duke of Palatinate-Zweibrücken and in 1799 as elector of Bavaria. His alliance with Napoleon I earned him vast territorial increases (1805), the royal title (1806), and leadership over the Confederation of the Rhine. He passed over to the allies just before the battle of Leipzig (1813). With his minister Montgelas he carried out important social reforms and granted a liberal constitution (1818). His grandson, King **Maximilian II,** 1811–64, succeeded his father Louis I in 1848. He was a liberal and a patron of art and learning. His son Louis II succeeded him.

Maximilian, prince of Baden (Max of Baden), 1867–1929, chancellor of Germany (Oct.–Nov., 1918). Began to negotiate for an armistice with the Allies of World War I; surrendered government to Friedrich Ebert after Emperor William II's flight.

Maximin (măk'sĭmĭn), name of two Roman emperors. **1** Died 238, ruled 235–38. A Thracian soldier of great physical strength, he was chosen emperor at Mainz by rebels against Alexander Severus. He warred successfully against the Germans, but was overthrown by Gordian I. **2** Died 313, proclaimed himself emperor 308 in opposition to Licinius and was powerful after the death of Galerius (310), but allied himself with Maxentius, was defeated by Licinius, and was superseded by Constantine I. Called also Maximin Daia.

Maximus, d. 388, Roman emperor of the West

(383–88), after murdering GRATIAN to get the throne. Defeated Valentinian II in Italy (387), but was beaten and put to death by Theodosius.

Max-Müller, Friedrich: see MÜLLER, MAX.

Max of Baden: *see* MAXIMILIAN, PRINCE OF BADEN.

Maxwell, James Clerk (klärk), 1831–79, Scottish physicist. Developed theory of electromagnetic field on mathematical basis; said electricity and magnetic energy travel in transverse waves and light waves are of this nature. Studied heat, kinetic theory of gases, color and color blindness. Unit of magnetic flux, the maxwell, is named for him.

May, Thomas, 1595–1650, English translator and poet. Known for translations of *Virgil's Georgics* (1628), and *Selected Epigrams of Martial* (1629).

May: see MONTH.

May, Cape: see CAPE MAY.

Maya (mä'yä, mī'ů), American Indians, mostly in Yucatan peninsula and Chiapas in Mexico, in Guatemala, and in W Honduras. Mayan languages (see LANGUAGE, table) are spoken in this area and in a few isolated spots elsewhere. Theirs was one of the greatest of pre-Columbian civilizations; although archaeologists have learned much about it from early Spanish writings and 20th-cent. excavations, much remains to be discovered. Sylvanus G. Morley divides their early history into three periods—Pre-Maya (2500 B.C.?–A.D. 317). Old Empire (317–987). and New Empire (987–1697)—*empire* being merely a convenient term, since government was by city-states. In the late Pre-Maya came invention of the calendar, hieroglyphic writing, and beginning of stone architecture. The Old Empire saw territorial and cultural consolidation and flowering of architecture in cities (Copán, Quiriguá, Palenque). For reasons still unknown these cities were abandoned, and the New Empire was based on new cities founded after migration (CHICHÉN ITZÁ, Mayapán, Uxmal). Mexican influence was strong because of migration or invasion. The last part of this period was dominated by civil wars and the Spanish conquest under the elder and younger Francisco de MONTEJO. In the city-states the hereditary chieftain, the priests, and the nobility held power. Outstanding achievements of the Maya were their highly accurate calendar; their massive architecture, notable for harmony and rich decoration; their knowledge of mathematics; and their development of writing.

Mayagüez (mīägwās'), city (pop. 87,307), W Puerto Rico; a port on Mona Passage; center of fertile agr. region. Colleges of agr. and mechanical arts of Univ. of Puerto Rico are here.

Mayakovsky, Vladimir (vlŭdyē'mĭr mī'ŭkôf'skē), 1893–1930, Russian poet. Leader of the futuristic school, he became the chief spokesman in verse of the revolution. Died by suicide.

May apple, North American woodland perennial (*Podophyllum peltatum*) with large lobed leaves and solitary white flowers in spring, followed by an an edible berry. The roots yield a drug. It is also called mandrake.

May beetle: see JUNE BEETLE.

May Day, first day of May. Celebration proba bly originated in spring festivals of goddesse of fertility of India and Egypt. In mediev England the chief feature of the celebratio was dancing around Maypole. This custor survives for exhibition purposes in Englan and U.S. In 1889 Second Socialist Inte national designated May Day as holiday fo radical labor, and it is very important da in USSR.

Mayence, Germany: see MAINZ.

Mayenne, Charles de Lorraine, duc de (shär dů lôrĕn' dük' dů mäyĕn'), 1554–161 French Catholic general. Succeeded h brother Henri, 3d duc de Guise, as head o LEAGUE. In 1596 he broke with his Spanis allies; made peace with King Henry IV.

Mayenne (mäyĕn'), department (2,012 sq. mi pop. 256,317), NW France, in Maine; cap Laval.

Mayer, Tobias (tōbē'äs mī'ůr), 1723–62, Ge man astronomer and mathematician, note for his lunar tables (1752) and zodiacal sta catalogue.

Mayerling (mī'ůrlĭng), village, Lower Austri SW of Vienna. Here, in a hunting lodg Archduke RUDOLF and Maria Vetsera m their death (1889).

Mayfair, fashionable residential area of W London, England. Includes Berkeley an Grosvenor Squares.

Mayfield, city (pop. 8,990), SW Ky., S o Paducah in farm, clay, and timber are Tobacco and mule market and trade, an industrial center of agr. area. Cemetery ha curious Woolridge monuments.

Mayfield Heights, residential city (pop. 5,807 NE Ohio, E of Cleveland.

Mayflower: see TRAILING ARBUTUS.

Mayflower, ship which in 1620 brought Pi grims from England to New England. Aft two-month voyage land was sighted in Nov and settlement was estab. at Plymouth, Mas Group signed agreeemnt for government o colony known as **Mayflower Compact.** So ciety of Mayflower Descendants (estab 1894) is for proved descendants of *Ma flower* passengers.

Maynard (mā'nůrd), town (pop. 6,978), Mass., near Concord.

Maynooth (mā'nōōth, mānōōth'), town (po 572), Co. Kildare, Ireland. Seat of St. Pa rick's Col., chief Irish institution for trai ing Catholic clergy.

Mayo, Charles Horace (mā'ō), 1865–193 American surgeon, specialist in goiter an cataract. With his brother, **William Jame Mayo,** 1861–1939, specialist in abdomin surgery, he developed **Mayo Clinic** fro small clinic opened 1889 by their father i Rochester, Minn. They estab. 1915 May Foundation for Medical Education and Re search at Univ. of Minnesota.

Mayo (mā'ō), county (2,084 sq. mi.; pop. 148 120), W Ireland, in Connaught; co. tow Castlebar. Mountainous in W, it has man lakes and deeply indented coastline. Oa and potatoes are grown and livestock raised. Population is dwindling.

maypop: see PASSIONFLOWER.

Maysville, city (pop. 8,632), N Ky., on Ohi R. (bridged) and SE of Covington. Tran portation, trade and industrial center wi distilleries and tobacco and metal-products plants. Here Daniel Boone had tavern and U. S. Grant went to school. Site of Simon Kenton's trading post near by.

Maywood. 1 Residential and industrial city (pop. 13,292), S Calif., SSE of Los Angeles; founded 1920. Auto-assembling, steel, food-processing plants. **2** Residential village (pop. 27,473), NE Ill., W suburb of Chicago and on Des Plaines R., in industrial area. **3** Residential borough (pop. 8,667), NE N.J., near Hackensack, inc. 1894.

Mazarin, Jules (zhül' mäzärē'), 1602–61, Italian cardinal, chief minister of Louis XIII and Louis XIV of France. His original name was Giulio Mazarini. Served in papal army; was papal nuncio to France 1634–36; entered French service as protégé of Cardinal Richelieu, whom he succeeded 1642. Though never ordained a priest, he was made cardinal in 1641. He completely dominated the regent, ANNE OF AUSTRIA, to whom he may have been secretely married. Though he won excellent terms for France in the Peace of WESTPHALIA (1648), his financial abuses and dictatorial, centralizing policy provoked the troubles of the FRONDE. His victory over the Fronde (1653) and the Peace of the PYRENEES with Spain (1659) marked the triumph of his diplomacy.

Mazarin Bible (mă'zŭrĭn), probably the first book printed by Gutenberg and from movable types at Mainz, 1456. Its folio pages of two columns of 42 lines each were in gothic type and hand-illuminated. A copy was first rediscovered in Cardinal Mazarin's library. One of the finest printed books, it is also called the Gutenberg or 42-line Bible.

Mazatlán (mäsätlän'), city (pop. 32,117), Sinaloa, NW Mexico; a port on the Pacific. Spanish colonial trade with Philippines began development of port.

Mazeppa (mŭzĕ'pŭ), 1644?–1709, hetman of Cossacks in Ukraine. Joined Charles XII of Sweden against Peter I of Russia, died a refugee in Turkey. Byron's poem *Mazeppa* relates how the husband of young Mazeppa's Polish mistress tied him naked to a horse, which was driven into the steppes.

Mazo, Juan Bautista Martínez del (hwän' boutēs'tä märtē'nĕth dĕl mä'thō), c.1612–1667, Spanish landscape and portrait painter. Was son-in-law of Velázquez, with whom he often collaborated.

Mazzini, Giuseppe (jōōzĕp'pā mät-sē'nē), 1805–72, Italian patriot and revolutionist, a key figure of the RISORGIMENTO. After 1831 he spent most of his life in exile, chiefly in London. In books and periodicals he expounded his revolutionary doctrine, advocating a unified Italian republic as his aim and direct popular action as the means. His writings, imbued with highest idealism, are also distinguished for style. Mazzini took direct part in the revolution of Milan (1848), in the Roman republic of 1849, and in other ventures. His ideas clashed with those of CAVOUR, who eventually won out.

Mc–. Names beginning thus are entered as if spelled Mac–. See the article MAC.

Mdina, Malta: see CITTÀ VECCHIA.

Mead, George Herbert (mēd), 1863–1931, American philosopher, proponent of "social behaviorism."

Mead, Margaret, 1901–, American anthropologist. She contributed toward enlarging scope of anthropology through work on relation of culture to personality. Perhaps the most widely known of her works is *Coming of Age in Samoa* (1928).

Mead, William Rutherford, 1846–1928, American architect; partner in firm of McKim, Mead, and White.

mead, alcoholic beverage fermented of honey and water, sometimes spiced. Known in ancient times.

Mead, Lake: see HOOVER DAM.

Meade, George Gordon, 1815–72, Union general in Civil War. Distinguished in Seven Days battles, at Antietam, Fredericksburg, Chancellorsville. Commanded Army of Potomac from 1863; at Gettysburg he won greatest battle of war. His sound generalship in Wilderness campaign aided final victory.

meadow beauty, rose-flowered perennial (*Rhexia virginica*) native to moist fields in E North America.

meadow lark, North American bird of blackbird family, with black-and-brown streaked coat, yellow breast with black crescent. It nests in grass.

meadow saffron, hardy Old World crocuslike plant of genus *Colchicum* most species of which bloom in autumn. Corms and seeds of *Colchicum autumnale* yield COLCHICINE.

meadowsweet, hardy perennial of genus *Filipendula* with large clusters of small flowers. Common species in North America are the native pink-flowered queen of the prairie and the Eurasian white queen of the meadow.

Meadville, city (pop. 18,972), NW Pa., S of Erie; settled c.1788. Trade center in agr. area with mfg. of zippers, rayon, and metal products. Seat of Allegheny Col. (coed.; 1816).

Meagher, Thomas Francis (mär), 1823–67, Irish revolutionist and Union general in Civil War, b. Ireland. Aided Irish rebellion of 1848; escaped to New York city in 1852. Organized and led "Irish Brigade" that fought with Army of Potomac through Chancellorsville in the Civil War.

mean, in statistics, a type of average. Arithmetic mean of a group of numbers equals their sum divided by their number; geometric mean is square root of product of the quantities.

Meany, George, 1894–, American labor leader, president of American Federation of Labor (1952–). A.F. of L. secretary-treasurer 1940–52.

Meares, John (mērz), 1756?–1809, British naval officer, explorer, and trader. Explored coast of Alaska. Built trading post on NOOTKA SOUND (1788).

measles (rubeola), contagious epidemic disease caused by virus. Incubation period c.10 days. Attended by fever and by rash beginning on face and neck. Attack usually gives lifelong immunity. German measles (rubella) is similar but milder. Incubation period 10–21 days. Attack does not give immunity. Reported as harmful to embryo when contracted by mother in early pregnancy.

measures: see WEIGHTS AND MEASURES.

meat, the flesh of animals, especially of cattle,

sheep, lambs, and swine, intended for food. Although sometimes used in distinction from game, poultry, and fish, the term may also apply to all animal flesh. Meat contains chiefly water, protein, and fat, with some minerals; it is almost entirely utilized by the body. Lean and fat flesh of a carcass and certain glands and organs (heart, liver, kidneys, tongue, tripe, brains, sweetbreads) are edible. Cooking softens tissue, coagulates blood and albumen, destroys undesirable organisms in meat, and imparts flavor.

Meath (mēth, mēdh), county (903 sq. mi.; pop. 66,232), E Ireland, in Leinster; co. town Trim. Farming and cattle raising are important. Long considered a fifth province of Ireland. TARA was seat of the high kings of Ireland.

meat packing, one of the largest modern industries, in its present form dates from the introduction of refrigeration, first used for a railroad shipment in 1870. It includes the operation of large central plants (such as those for which Chicago is known) for buying, inspecting, slaughtering, and preparing animals for food; utilization of by-products for many purposes; and the distribution of meat by means of refrigerated warehouses, railroad cars, and steamships. Federal laws prescribe examination of animals slaughtered for interstate trade or export.

Meaux (mō), city (pop. 13,030), Seine-et-Marne dept., N France, on Marne R.; chief city of Brie. Has cathedral (12th–16th cent.) with tomb of Bossuet, who was bishop of Meaux.

Mecca (mĕ'kŭ), city (pop. 90,000), cap. of Hejaz, Saudi Arabia, c.50 mi. from its port, Jidda. Birthplace of MOHAMMED the Prophet; holiest city of Islam. Called Macoraba by Ptolemy, city was ancient center of commerce and a holy place of Arab sects before rise of Islam. Mohammed's flight (the hegira) from Mecca in 622 is beginning of Moslem era. City was captured by Mohammed in 630. Sacked in 930 by the Karmathians, captured in 1517 by Ottoman Turks, and held 1803–13 by the Wahabis. In 1916 it became cap. of Husein ibn Ali, who overthrew Turkish rule and made himself king of the Hejaz; he was ousted by Ibn Saud in 1924. Here is the great mosque, the Haram, enclosing the KAABA (chief goal of Moslem pilgrimages), near which is the holy well, the Zemzen. Trade depends almost wholly on pilgrims. Though then banned to unbelievers, city was visited in 19th cent. by Richard Burton and other non-Moslems in disguise.

mechanical advantage: see MACHINE.

mechanics, branch of physics concerned with action of forces upon bodies (solids, liquids, or gases). Science of mechanics treats primarily of motion, of effects of forces applied to bodies in motion (kinetics) and motion alone (kinematics) without considering causes, such as mass and force. Kinetics and kinematics are sometimes classed together under dynamics; statics is a branch treating of bodies in equilibrium and of the forces holding them in that state. Mechanics of liquids deals with hydrostatics (bodies of liquids in equilibrium), hydrodynamics (motion of liquids and principles involved), and hydraulics (application of these principles t machines). Mechanics of gases (pneumatics is concerned largely with pressure exerted b atmosphere and with physical properties o gases in general. See *ills.*, pp. 389, 793.

Mechanicsburg, borough (pop. 6,786), S Pa. WSW of Harrisburg. Mfg. of clothing an metal products.

Mechanicsville: see SEVEN DAYS BATTLES.

Mechanicville, city (pop. 7,385), E N.Y., N o Albany, on the Hudson and on the Barg Canal. Railroad shops. Clothing, knit goods food, paper products.

mechanized warfare, in the broadest sense modern mobile attack and defense depend ing upon machines, particularly those pow ered by gasoline engines. Such warfare cen ters around use of the tank and the armore vehicle, with support and supply from motor ized columns and airplanes. The tank and th automobile, already used in World War I presaged the full potential of mechanize warfare as displayed by the Germans i World War II. The Allies quickly countere by building up mechanized units of their ow and evolving an effective defense techniqu based on the use of artillery and aircraft.

Mechelen or **Mechlin,** Belgium: see MALINES

Mechnikov, Ilya Ilyich: see METCHNIKOFF ÉLIE.

Mecklenburg (Ger. mĕ'klŭnbŏŏrk), state (8, 856 sq. mi.; pop. 2,139,640), [East] Germa Democratic Republic. on Baltic Sea; cap Schwerin. Has fertile agr. plain, forests lakes. Cities of Rostock, Wismar, Stralsun were long important as Hanseatic ports. Set tled by Slavic Wends in 6th cent., regio was Christianized and colonized by Ger mans in 12th cent. Its Wendish princes wer raised to dukes of Holy Roman Empire i 1348. In 1628 Mecklenburg was awarded t Wallenstein, its conqueror, but in 1632 it re verted to its old dynasty. In 1701 began th division of the territory into two duchie (after 1815, grand duchies)—Mecklenburg Schwerin and Mecklenburg-Strelitz. Bot sided with Prussia in Austro-Prussian Wa (1866) and joined the German Empire i 1871. Grand dukes were deposed 1918. I 1934 both Mecklenburgs were united as single state, and after 1945, when Mecklen burg came under Russian occupation, th state was enlarged by the addition of Hithe Pomerania (minus Stettin).

Mecklenburg Declaration of Independence, al legedly proclaimed at Charlotte, N.C., b citizens of Mecklenburg co., May 20, 1775 Widely regarded as spurious document. Anti British resolutions actually adopted May 31 1775, do not mention independence.

Medea (mēdē'ŭ), in Greek mythology, princes of Colchis, famous for her knowledge o sorcery. She aided Jason, against will of he father, Aeëtes, to gain Golden Fleece, an fled with him, killing her brother to detai her father. When Jason later wished to marr Creusa, Medea sent her a magic weddin gown which burned her to death. Medea the killed her own children by Jason and went t Athens where she married Aegeus.

Medellín (mādhāyēn'), city. (pop. 143,952; al c.5,000 ft.), W central Colombia; founde

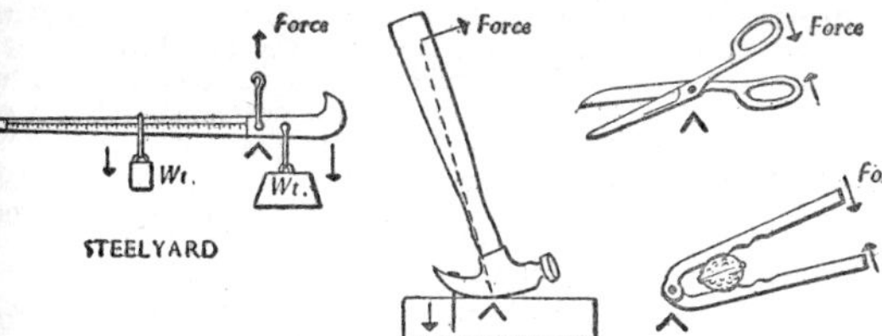

STEELYARD

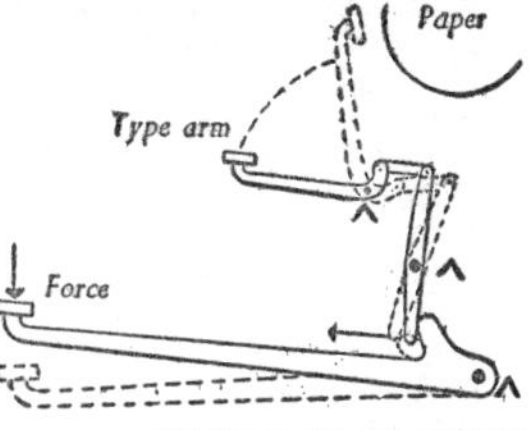

DIAGRAM OF OPERATION OF A TYPEWRITER KEY

.EVER The moments (= force x distance) around the fulcrum, ∧, are equal.

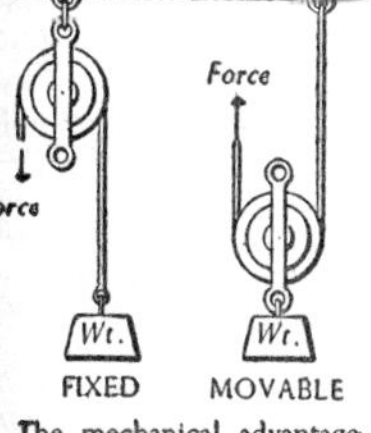

FIXED MOVABLE

The mechanical advantage of the movable pulley pictured above is twice that of the fixed.

ULLEY

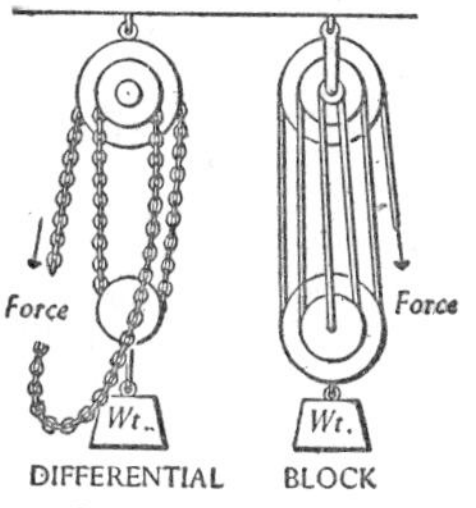

DIFFERENTIAL PULLEY

BLOCK AND TACKLE

Systems of pulleys give even greater mechanical advantage.

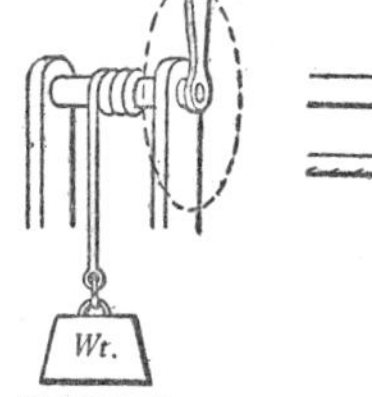

WINDLASS

CAPSTAN

WHEEL AND AXLE

The amount of force required is proportional to the radii of wheel and axle.

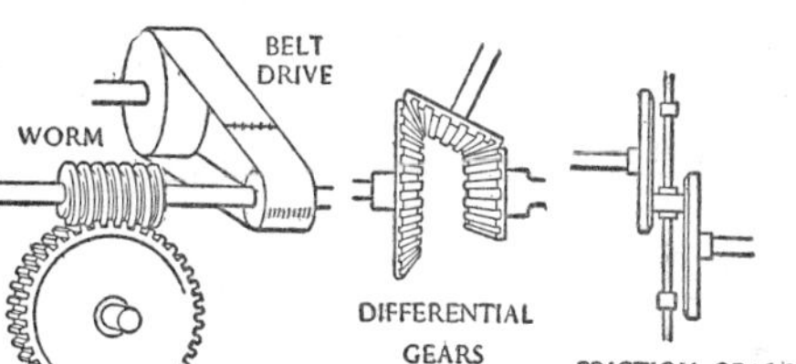

DIFFERENTIAL GEARS

FRICTION GEARS

·EARS

·ears are derived from the wheel-and-axle principle. They are used to change the direc-·on of applied force, to change one kind of motion into another, or to alter ratios and ·ence power.

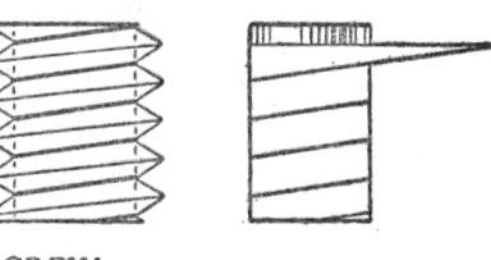

SCREW

A screw is essentially an inclined plane wrapped around a cylinder.

·NCLINED PLANE

·he mechanical advantage is ·etermined by the height and ·ngth of the incline.

WEDGE

A wedge is a double inclined plane.

JACK

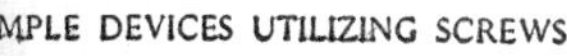

MECHANIC'S VISE

ARCHIMEDES' SCREW

An early device for lifting water.

SIMPLE CRANE

This is essentially a combination of levers, pulleys, and gears.

·MPLE DEVICES UTILIZING SCREWS

1675. The leading industrial center of republic, Medellín also exports coffee (introduced after 1918).

Medes, anc. people of Asia Minor: see MEDIA.

Medford. 1 City (pop. 66,113), E Mass., N suburb of Boston, on Mystic R.; settled 1630. Paper boxes, metal products, chemicals. Main seat of Tufts Col. (non-sectarian; for men and women; chartered 1852, opened 1855 by Universalists); cooperates with Harvard in Crane (theology) and Fletcher (law, diplomacy) schools, and with other colleges; has some divisions at Boston. **2** City (pop. 17,305), SW Oregon, W of Klamath Falls; founded 1883. Processing and shipping center in agr. (dairy, fruit, truck) and lumbering region. Fishing and hunting area, Crater Lake Natl. Park, Oregon Caves Natl. Monument are near.

Media (mē'dēù), anc. country of W Asia, in region now in W Iran and S Azerbaijan SSR; cap. Ecbatana. It is said that a dynasty founded by Arbaces ruled until Cyrus the Great forcibly annexed it to Persia. The inhabitants were the Medes, who were supposed to be learned in astronomy and the magic arts.

Media, borough (pop. 5,726), SE Pa., W of Philadelphia. Near-by Providence Meetinghouse (1664) has graves of many William Penn followers.

median (mē'dēùn), in statistics, a type of average. In a group of numbers, as many of the numbers are larger than the median as are smaller.

Medici (mĕ'dĭchē, Ital. mā'dēchē), Italian family which directed the destinies of FLORENCE (and, after 1569, of TUSCANY) from the 15th cent. to 1737. Their rise from obscurity to immense wealth as merchants and bankers marked the triumph of the capitalist class over guild merchants and artisans. Until 1532 the democratic constitution of Florence was outwardly upheld, but the Medici exerted actual control over the government (except when exiled, 1494–1512, 1527–30) without holding any permanent official position. They are perhaps best remembered as patrons of the RENAISSANCE. Under their usually tolerant rule Florence rivaled ancient Athens. The first important member and common ancestor of the senior and junior lines of the family was Giovanni di Bicci de' Medici (1360–1429). Below follows an account of the principal members of both lines, in chronological order.

Senior line. **Cosimo de' Medici** (kō'zēmō), 1389–1464, son of Giovanni di Bicci, was first of his family to rule Florence. Banished 1433, he returned 1434 and with support of the people became the acknowledged leading citizen of the republic. He vastly expanded the family's banking business and, despite lavish charities and patronage, doubled his fortune. In Florence, he made his power as little felt as possible; in foreign policy, he sought a balance of power among Italian states. Founded Medici Library and academy for Greek studies (headed by Ficino); protected major artists of his time. His son, **Piero de' Medici** (pyā'rō), 1416–69, nicknamed Il Gottoso [the gouty], succeeded as head of family. He put down a plot against his life but allowed conspirators to go free (1466). His son and successor, **Lorenzo de' Medici** (lōrän'tsō), 1449–92, called Lorenzo il Magnifico, was a towering figure of the Renaissance. An astute politician, generous patron, and able scholar and poet, he showed little success as a business man; lavish public entertainments made him popular but drained his funds. In 1478 took place the PAZZI CONSPIRACY, in which Lorenzo's brother Giuliano de' Medici was killed; Lorenzo was merely wounded and the plot collapsed. Resulting warfare with Pope Sixtus IV ended in 1481. Lorenzo allowed his enemy SAVONAROLA to preach freely. His second son, **Giovanni de' Medici** (jōvän'nē), became pope (see LEO X); his oldest son and successor, **Piero de' Medici,** 1471–1503, was expelled from Florence in 1494 by the republicans, led by Savonarola, during the invasion of Italy by Charles VIII of France. In 1512 Piero's youngest brother, **Giuliano de' Medici** (jōōlyä'nō), 1479–1516, reentered Florence with the help of the Holy League. He became duke of Nemours by marriage (1515). After his death, control over Florence was exercised by Leo X through Piero's son **Lorenzo de' Medici,** 1492–1519, whom Leo also made duke of Urbino (1516). Giuliano's and Lorenzo's statues by Michelangelo adorn their tombs in the Church of San Lorenzo, Florence. Lorenzo's daughter was CATHERINE DE' MEDICI, queen of France. After Lorenzo's death his cousin **Giulio de' Medici** (see Pope CLEMENT VII) took control of Florence. Elected pope (1523), he continued to rule through Giuliano's illegitimate son, **Ippolito de' Medici** (ēp-pô'lētō), 1509–35, whom he made a cardinal in 1531, and through **Alessandro de' Medici** (älĕs-sän'drō), 1511–37, who probably was an illegitimate son of Lorenzo de' Medici, duke of Urbino. The Medici were expelled from Florence in 1527 as a result of the invasion of Italy by the army of Emperor Charles V, but in 1530 Clement restored them to power. Clement favored Alessandro, who was made head of the republic (1531) and hereditary duke of Florence (1532) by Charles V, and who married Charles's daughter Margaret (later known as Margaret of Parma). His tyranny was resented by the Florentines, who in 1535 sent Ippolito to lay their grievances before Charles V. Ippolito died on his way, probably poisoned on Alessandro's orders. He had been a lavish patron of literature. Two years later Alessandro was murdered by Lorenzino de' Medici (1515–47), a member of the younger line and his former boon companion. The republican uprising Lorenzino had anticipated did not materialize, and the succession fell to Cosimo I. Lorenzino was assassinated in Venice on Cosimo's orders.

Younger line and grand dukes of Tuscany. This line is descended from **Lorenzo de' Medici,** d. 1440, younger son of Giovanni di Bicci. His great-grandson **Giovanni de' Medici,** 1498–1526, called Giovanni delle Bande Nere [of the black bands], was a famous condottiere. He fought in the service of Leo X, on whose death he acquired his nickname because of the black stripes of mourning on his banners. He continued in papal service, except in 1525, when he fought and was wounded on the side of Francis I of France. His older son, **Cosimo I de' Medici,** 1519–74, succeeded Alessandro as duke of Florence (1537), assumed absolute authority, acquired Siena (1555), and in 1569 was raised to grand duke by Pope Pius V. Under his able, though ruthless, rule Florence reached its highest political and material power. His son **Francesco de' Medici** (frän-chä'skō), 1541–87, reigned 1574–87. He allowed the Hapsburgs to establish a virtual protectorate over his grand duchy. His daughter MARIE DE' MEDICI became queen of France. His second wife was Bianca CAPELLO. His brother **Ferdinand I de' Medici,** 1549–1609, succeeded him as grand duke after resigning his cardinalate. He built the famous Villa Medici at Rome and founded LEGHORN. His son and successor, **Cosimo II de' Medici,** 1590–1620, was a patron of Galileo. His son **Ferdinand II de' Medici,** 1610–70 (reigned 1620–70), founded the Accademia del Cimento, first European academy of natural sciences (1657). His son **Cosimo III de' Medici,** 1642–1723, reigned 1670–1723. His government was one of bigoted and corrupt despotism. His son and successor, **Gian Gastone de' Medici** (jän' gästō'nā), 1671–1737, was the last male member of the family. His succession was settled in 1735 on Francis of Lorraine (later Emperor FRANCIS I).

medicine, art and science of treatment and prevention of disease. Because origin of disease was unknown, for centuries its treatment was coupled with magic and superstition. More scientific practice of medicine began in ancient Asiatic civilizations including those of Mesopotamia. Israel later formulated hygienic laws and Arabs contributed to knowledge of drugs. In Europe, progress can be traced through Greek school of ASCLEPIADES OF BITHYNIA and HIPPOCRATES. GALEN contributed original experimental work and encouraged dissection. Remnants of early learning were preserved during Middle Ages by Christian Church and Arab physicians. Medical school estab. 9th cent. at Salerno was prototype of others. Work of VESALIUS stimulated more accurate anatomical studies. Valuable contributions made later by William HARVEY, Edward JENNER, John HUNTER, and many others. Medical progress was hampered for centuries by refusal of physicians to perform SURGERY. Bloodletting was common practice from ancient times until late 18th cent. Development of HOMEOPATHY influenced revolt against prescription of large doses of drugs. Mortality declined sharply during 19th cent. after formulation by PASTEUR of germ theory of disease and introduction of antiseptic methods by LISTER. Work of Robert KOCH and others in bacteriology led to identification of specific disease-causing agents and to development of methods of producing IMMUNITY. Of inestimable value was discovery of INSULIN and other hormones, radium, SULFA DRUGS, and ANTIBIOTIC SUBSTANCES. With growth of medicine has come trend toward specialization and stringent educational requirements for physicians. See also ANESTHESIA; OBSTETRICS; PSYCHOSOMATIC MEDICINE; TROPICAL MEDICINE.

Medicine Bow Mountains, outlying E range of Rocky Mts. extending S from town of Medicine Bow, Wyo., NW of Laramie, to Cameron Pass, Colo. Medicine Bow Peak is 12,005 ft. high.

Medicine Hat, city (pop. 16,364), SE Alta., Canada, on South Saskatchewan R. and SE of Edmonton. Center of natural-gas, coal, ranching, and dry farming area. Has railroad shops, foundries, and grain mills. Made Northwest Mounted Police post 1882.

Medicine Lodge, city (pop. 2,288), S Kansas, WSW of Wichita. Peace treaty made near here with Plains Indians in 1867 is commemorated by pageant every five years (since 1927). Carry Nation, a resident, began her antisaloon crusade here, 1899.

Medill, Joseph (mùdĭl'), 1823–99, American journalist, b. Canada. Controlled Chicago *Tribune* 1874–99. Helped found Republican party.

Medina, José Toribio (hōsā' tōrē'byō mādhē'nä), 1852–1930, Chilean scholar. His numerous works cover vast range of learning: history, biography, bibliography, archaeology, journalism.

Medina (mĭdē'nù), city (pop. 12,000), Hejaz, Saudi Arabia; sacred city of Islam, second only to Mecca. Situated in an oasis. Before the HEGIRA (622), it was called Yathrib. Became Mohammed's base for converting and conquering Arabia. Was center of Islamic state until 662, when the Omayyads shifted the cap. to Damascus. Held by Ottoman Turks, 1517–1916, it was briefly occupied by the Wahabis, 1804–12. In World War I it was captured by Husein ibn Ali, who was ousted 1924 by Ibn Saud. Chief building is the great mosque, containing tombs of Mohammed, Fatima, and the caliphs Abu Bakr and Oman.

Medina (mùdī'nù). **1** Village (pop. 6,179), W N.Y., on the Barge Canal and E of Lockport. Mfg. of textiles, canned foods, furniture, and iron products. **2** City (pop. 5,097), N Ohio, NW of Akron. Mfg. of apiary supplies and toys.

Medina Sidonia, Alonso Pérez de Guzmán, duque de (mādhē'nä sēdhō'nyä), 1550–1615, commander of Spanish ARMADA.

Mediterranean Sea, largest inland sea, surrounded by Europe, Asia, Africa. Area is c.1,145,000 sq. mi.; max. length, c.2,300 mi.; max. width, c.1,200 mi.; greatest depth, c.14,435 ft., off Cape Matapan. It connects with the Atlantic by the Strait of Gibraltar; with the Black Sea by the Dardanelles, Sea of Marmara, Bosporus; with the Red Sea by the Suez Canal. Of higher salinity than the Atlantic, it has little tidal variation. Its shores are chiefly mountainous. Suez Canal (1869) reestab. its ancient commercial and strategic military importance. European civilization was born on the shores of the Mediterranean, which encompassed the civilized world in ancient and medieval times.

medlar, small, deciduous tree (*Mespilus germanica*) of the rose family, with white or pink flowers. Native to Europe and Asia, it has long been grown in Europe for its apple-shaped fruit.

Médoc (mādôk'), district of Bordeaux wine

region, on W bank of Gironde R.; chief town Pauillac. Vineyards include Château Lafite, Château Margaux.

Medusa (mĭdū'zŭ), in Greek mythology, most famous of the three GORGON monsters. Once beautiful, she offended Athena, who made her so hideous that all who looked on her were turned to stone. Perseus slew her and gave her head to Athena. It still kept its petrifying power, and Athena used it on her aegis.

Medway, river of SE England, flowing 70 mi. from two headstreams in Sussex and Surrey to the Thames.

meerschaum (mēr'shôm) [Ger.,= sea foam], a mineral, hydrous magnesium silicate, resembling white clay, chiefly used for making tobacco pipes. Soft and easily carved before drying. Tobacco smoke stains it a rich brown. Main source Asia Minor.

Meerut (mē'rŭt), city (pop. 169,290), NW Uttar Pradesh, India; trade center. Scene of one of first major outbreaks of Sepoy Rebellion (1857).

megalithic monuments (mĕgŭlĭ'thĭk), huge, simple stone structures, found especially along coast of W Europe. Earliest date from 2d millennium B.C.

Mégantic (mŭgăn'tĭk, Fr. māgātĕk') or **Lac Mégantic,** town (pop. 6,164), SE Que., Canada, on L. Mégantic, ENE of Sherbrooke. Rail center.

Megara (mĕ'gŭrŭ, mĕ'gärä), town (pop. 13,360), central Greece, on site of anc. town of Megara, cap. of small dist. of Megaris. Dorians made it wealthy by maritime trade. After Persian Wars Athenian aid was summoned against the Corinthians (459 B.C.), but later expulsion of Athenians helped to provoke the Peloponnesian War.

megatherium (mĕgŭthēr'ēŭm), extinct ground sloth widely distributed in North and South America during the Pleistocene. It attained a length of 18 ft. and had massive hind legs and tail.

Megiddo, anc. city, Palestine, on S edge of plain of Esdraelon. Archaeological remains found here date back to c.2000 B.C. Many important battles were fought at Megiddo; here Deborah defeated Sisera, and Josiah was killed. Plain called Megiddon in Zech. 12.11. See also ARMAGEDDON.

Mehemet. For persons thus named, see MOHAMMED.

Meiggs, Henry (mĕgz), 1811–77, American promoter and railroad contractor. One of most spectacular railroad builders in South America.

Meigs, Fort, founded (Feb., 1813) in War of 1812 by Gen. W. H. Harrison on Maumee R., near present Perrysburg, Ohio, across river from British Fort Miami. British attacks (esp. in May and July, 1813) failed to take this "Gibraltar of the West."

Meiji (mā'jē), reign name of Emperor MUTSUHITO of Japan. Meiji restoration (1868) was revolution in Japanese government won by overthrowing Tokugawa Shogunate and returning full power to emperor. Revolt was precipitated by shogun's submission to foreign demands (1854), enmity of powerful clans, and general discontent. Shogun surrendered 1868 to emperor after brief civil war. Crushing of Satsuma rebellion (1877) against new government ensured supremacy of imperial government led by reform groups favoring Westernization. Feudalism abolished; land held by great clans nationalized; new constitution adopted 1889.

Meiklejohn, Alexander (mĭ'kŭlŏn), 1872–, American educator, president of Amherst Col. 1912–24, professor of philosophy at Univ. of Wisconsin (1926–38) and chairman of Experimental Col. (1927–32).

Meiningen (mī'nĭng-ŭn), city (pop. 23,700), Thuringia, central Germany, on Werra R. Cap. of duchy of Saxe-Meiningen 1680–1918. Ducal theater and orchestra enjoyed world reputation in late 19th cent.

Meinong, Alexius (mī'nŏng), 1853–1920, Austrian philosopher and psychologist; pupil of BRENTANO and a founder of first psychological laboratory in Austria.

Meissen (mī'sŭn), city (pop. 48,348), Saxony, E Germany, on the Elbe. Famous since 1710 for porcelain ware, known as "Dresden" china in English. Became 965 seat of margraviate of Meissen, where WETTIN dynasty of SAXONY originated.

Meissonier, Jean Louis Ernest (zhã' lwē' ĕrnĕst' māsônyā'), 1815–91, French painter of genre and battle scenes having much accurate detail.

Meissonier, Juste Aurèle (zhüst' ōrĕl'), 1693?–1750, French goldsmith and decorator to Louis XV. He is generally considered to be originator of ROCOCO style.

meistersinger (mī'stŭr–) [Ger.,= mastersinger], member of one of the musical and poetic guilds which flourished in Germany from 14th to 16th cent., succeeding the MINNESINGER. Wagner's *Die Meistersinger von Nürnberg* faithfully represents the guild practices. Hans SACHS was the greatest meistersinger.

Meitner, Lise (lē'zŭ mīt'nŭr), 1878–, Austrian-Swedish physicist, mathematician, codiscover of protactinium. She made studies of disintegration products of radium, thorium, and actinium, and of action of beta rays. Her work on bombardment of uranium nucleus contributed to atomic bomb.

Meknès (mĕknĕs'), (pop. 159,811), French Morocco; trade center on fertile plateau. Founded in 11th cent. as Almohade fort. Near by is palace built in 17th cent. by Sultan Ismail.

Mekong (mākŏng'), river of SE Asia, c.2,600 mi. long. Rises in Tibet and flows SE through Yünnan prov., China, and Indo-China to South China Sea. Forms vast delta (great rice-growing area) in Cochin China.

Melanchthon, 1497–1560, German scholar and humanist and after Luther chief figure of Lutheran Reformation; original name Philipp Schwarzerd. His *Loci communes* (1521) presented and explained principles of Reformation, and he was liaison between Luther and the humanists, often representing him at conferences. He wrote the Augsburg Confession (1530).

Melanesia (mĕlŭnē'zhŭ), one of three main divisions of Pacific islands, in S and SW Pacific, S of equator. Includes the Solomons, New Hebrides, New Caledonia, Bismarck Archipelago, and Admiralty and Fiji isls. People are largely of Negroid stock; their languages are Malayo-Polynesian (see LANGUAGE, table).

Melba, Dame Nellie, 1861?–1931, Australian soprano, whose original name was Helen Porter Mitchell. She sang at Covent Garden, 1888–1926, and at the Metropolitan Opera, New York, 1893–1910.

Melbourne, William Lamb, 2d **Viscount** (mĕl'bûrn), 1779–1848, English Whig statesman. Prime minister (1834, 1835–41), he taught statecraft to young Queen Victoria. Did not promote the many reforms made during his administration. His wife, **Caroline Lamb, Viscountess Melbourne,** 1785–1828, is better remembered for her love affair with Lord Byron than for the minor novels she wrote.

Melbourne (mĕl'bûrn), city (pop. 99,861; metropolitan pop. 1,226,409), cap. of Victoria, Australia, port on Yarra R. near its mouth on Hobson's Bay (N arm of Port Phillip Bay). Was first commonwealth cap. (1901–27). Known as Dootigala when settled in 1835; renamed in 1837 for the British prime minister. Commercial center with mfg. of textiles and machinery. Exports wheat, meat, and wool. Seat of Univ. of Melbourne (1854), Conservatorium of Music (1910), and Natl. Art Gall. (1904). Royal mint is here. Many suburbs are seaside resorts.

Melchers, Gari (gâ'rē mĕl'chûrz), 1860–1932, American figure, genre, and portrait painter.

Melchior: see WISE MEN OF THE EAST.

Melchior, Lauritz (lou'rĭts mĕl'kēôr), 1890–, Danish heroic tenor. Sang at the Bayreuth Festivals, 1925–31; at the Metropolitan Opera, New York, 1926–50.

Melchites (mĕl'kīts) [royalists, from Syriac,= king], Christian community of Syria, Jordan, Palestine, Egypt, and America. In communion with the pope, they have a Byzantine rite (in Arabic), and their head is called patriarch of Antioch. They are distinct from Maronites and Syrian Catholics. Also Melkites.

Melchizedek or **Melchisedec** (both mĕlkĭ'–), king of Salem and "priest of the most high God" who blessed Abraham. Gen. 14.18–20. Later regarded as typifying priesthood of the Messiah. Ps. 110.4; Heb. 5–7.

Melcombe Regis: see WEYMOUTH AND MELCOMBE REGIS.

Meleager (mĕlēā'jûr), hero in Greek mythology. At his birth it was prophesied that he would die when a certain log in the fire burned, so his mother hid that log. He was an Argonaut and later led CALYDONIAN HUNT. To Atalanta, whom he loved, he gave the Calydonian boar's skin. When his brothers objected, he slew them. Then his mother threw the hidden log on the fire, and Meleager died when it was burned.

Melfi (mĕl'fē), city (pop. 14,190), Basilicata, S Italy. Noted for its wine. Cap. of Norman county of Apulia in 11th cent. Emperor Frederick II promulgated here his code, the Constitutions of Melfi or the Liber Augustalis.

Melilla (mālē'lyä), city (pop. 94,319), on Mediterranean coast of Spanish Morocco. Held by Spain since 1497, it is governed as part of Spanish province of Málaga. A port, with exports of iron ore.

Melitene, Turkey: see MALATYA.

Melitopol (mälyĕtô'pŭl), city (pop. 75,735), S Ukraine. Heavy machinery, food products. Was recovered 1943 from the Germans after bloody battle.

Melk or **Mölk** (both: mĕlk), town (pop. 3,139), Lower Austria, on the Danube. Earliest residence of Austrian rulers. Its splendid Benedictine abbey, founded 1089, has a library containing a rich collection of ancient manuscripts and incunabula.

Mellon, Andrew (William), 1855–1937, American financier, industrialist, and public official. President of Mellon Natl. Bank, Pittsburgh. Held large interests in many key American industries (notably aluminum). U.S. Secretary of the Treasury (1921–31); reduced national debt. NATIONAL GALLERY OF ART resulted from his benefactions.

melodrama, originally a spoken text with musical background, as in Greek drama. Popular in 18th cent. (e.g., works of Pietro Metastasio). Action was generally romantic, violent; virtue usually triumphed. Term later used for plays having overdrawn characters, smashing climaxes, and great appeal to sentiment, with or without music.

melon, trailing annual vine (*Cucumis melo*), native to Asia, and its fruit, an important market crop in the U.S. where growing seasons are long. Varieties include muskmelons, which have soft rind and netted surface and are often called cantaloupe (although true cantaloupe is a hard-shelled Mediterranean variety), and the winter types—casaba, honeydew, and Persian. See also WATERMELON.

Melos (mē'lŏs), Aegean island (61 sq. mi.; pop. 6,045), Greece, in the Cyclades; also known as Milo. Flourished as center of Aegean civilization (Early Minoan period, after 3000 B.C.). Resistance to Athenian imperialism led to massacre of population (416 B.C.). Famous Venus of Milo (now in Louvre, Paris), was discovered here in 1820.

Melozzo da Forlì (mālôt'tsō dä fōrlē'), 1438–94, Umbrian painter, a pioneer in bold foreshortening.

Melpomene, Muse of tragedy: see MUSES.

Melrose, burgh (pop. 2,146), Roxburghshire, Scotland. Site of one of Scotland's finest ruins—Melrose Abbey, founded in 1136 and now owned by the nation. Abbey, described in Scott's *Lay of the Last Minstrel,* contains the heart of Robert the Bruce.

Melrose, city (pop. 26,988), E Mass., N of Boston; settled c.1629. Home furnishings.

Melrose Park, residential village (pop. 13,366), NE Ill., W suburb of Chicago, in industrial area.

melting point, temperature at which substance changes from solid to liquid; under standard pressure, each solid has specific melting point. When heat is applied, temperature rises until liquefaction begins and no further rise occurs until substance is entirely liquefied. Heat needed to change one gram of substance from solid to liquid at melting point is latent heat of fusion. Usually melting and freezing points of substance are the same.

Melton Mowbray (mōb'rē), urban district (pop. 14,052), Leicestershire, England.

Known for pork pies and Stilton cheese, it is also known as a fox-hunting center.

Melun (mùlũ'), town (pop. 15,128), cap. of Seine-et-Marne dept., N France. Was an early Capetian residence. Near by is Château of Vaux, built for Nicolas Fouquet.

Mélusine (mālüzēn') or **Melusina** (mĕlyo͞osē'nä), in French legend, water sprite who married a mortal. She built fairy castle from which Lusignan is said to be derived. At times she was a mermaid, and when her husband discovered this, she left him.

Melville, Andrew, 1545–1622, Scottish religious reformer. As rector (after 1590) of St. Andrews, he reorganized Scottish universities. Successor to John Knox, he molded Scottish church, introducing presbyterian system, and fought for its independence.

Melville, George Wallace, 1841–1912, American naval engineer and arctic explorer. Led only surviving boat of De Long expedition (1879). Noted for role in modernization of U.S. navy.

Melville, Herman, 1819–91, American author. Experience aboard the whaler *Acushnet,* and ashore in the Marquesas (among the cannibalistic Typees) and in Tahiti gave him the background of the sea and far places for his novels such as *Typee: a Peep at Polynesian Life* (1846), *Omoo: a Narrative of Adventures in the South Seas* (1847), and *Mardi and a Voyage Thither* (1849). His masterpiece is generally considered to be *Moby-Dick;* or, *The Whale* (1851), a powerful and symbolic work of idealistic but bitter philosophy. Among his other works are *Pierre* (1852); *Piazza Tales* (short stories, 1856); poems, notably *Clarel* (1876); and another novel, *Billy Budd, Foretopman* (first published 1924). Melville died an obscure customs official and achieved a major position long after his death.

Melville, Lake, 120 mi. long, up to 25 mi. wide, SE Labrador. Receives Hamilton R. in Goose Bay and reaches the Atlantic through Hamilton Inlet.

Melville Bay, broad indentation of W coast of Greenland, opening SW into Baffin Bay.

Melville Island, 200 mi. long, 30–130 mi. wide, W Franklin dist., Northwest Territories, Canada, in Arctic Ocean. Largest (c.16,503 sq. mi.) of Parry Isls., separated from Victoria Isl. by Viscount Melville Sound. Discovered 1819 by Sir W. E. Parry.

Melville Island, area 2,400 sq. mi., in Timor Sea, off N coast of Australia; aboriginal reservation. Here was made first British settlement in the Northern Territory (1824–28).

Melville Sound: see VISCOUNT MELVILLE SOUND.

Melvindale, residential city (pop. 9,483), SE Mich., SW suburb of Detroit.

Memel (mā'mùl), Lithuanian *Klaipeda,* Rus. *Klaypeda,* city (pop. 41,297), W Lithuania; a Baltic port on the Kurisches Haff. Founded 1252 by the Teutonic Knights, it belonged to Prussia until 1919, when the Treaty of Versailles placed Memel and surrounding territory (1,026 sq. mi.; 1941 pop. 134,034) under French administration. The territory was forcibly occupied by Lithuania 1923; became an autonomous region of Lithuania 1924; was returned to Germany (under threat of war) 1939; reverted to Lithuania 1945. For **Memel** river, see NIEMEN.

Memling or **Memlinc, Hans** (häns' mĕm'lĭng, –lĭngk), c.1430–1494, Flemish religious painter; follower of the Van Eycks and of Van der Weyden. Name is sometimes spelled Hemling.

Memnon (mĕm'nŏn), in Greek mythology, king of Ethiopia; son of Tithonus and Eos. He fought for Troy against the Greeks, and, though killed by Achilles, was made immortal by Zeus to please Eos.

Memorial Day or **Decoration Day.** In U.S., now the day for decorating graves of all American soldiers; inaugurated 1868 to honor Civil War veterans. Celebrated in the North on May 30, in the South on April 26, May 10, or June 3.

memory, term indicating ability to retain and to recall images of objects or situations of past experience. Memories affecting personality often can be recalled only through hypnosis or psychoanalysis. Learning ability also affects memory. Experiments show that rate of forgetting is highest at first; rapid learners retain better than slow learners; things consistent with intellectual bias and emotional needs are best remembered. Attempts to establish a physical basis for memory have been hypothetical and subject to question.

Memphis (mĕm'fĭs), cap. of the Old Kingdom of anc. Egypt (c.3400–c.2445 B.C.), at apex of Nile delta near Cairo; founded by MENES. Across the Nile are the pyramids, extending to Gizeh.

Memphis, city (pop. 396,000), SW Tenn., on bluffs above the Mississippi at Wolf R. mouth; planned 1819. De Soto may have crossed river here; La Salle's Fort Prudhomme may have been here. Site disputed by British, French, Spanish in 18th cent. U.S. built fort here 1797. Fell to Union navy under elder C. H. Davis, June 6, 1862; served as Federal base for rest of Civil War. River port and rail center (with shops), it is a cotton, lumber, and livestock market. Mfg. of cottonseed products, feeds, wire, rubber, and chemicals. Has TVA power. Seat of Southwestern at Memphis (Presbyterian; coed.; 1875) and Univ. of TENNESSEE divisions. Has museums, art gallery, parks, and holds annual cotton carnival. Beale St. made famous by W. C. HANDY.

Memphremagog, Lake (mĕm"frùmā'gŏg), 30 mi. long and up to 4 mi. wide, mainly in S Que., partly in N Vt. Newport, Vt., and Magog, Que., are on lake.

Menahem (mĕ'nùhĕm), d. c.737 B.C., king of Israel (c.749–c.737 B.C.). A general of the army, he murdered Shallum for the throne. Gave tribute to the Assyrians. 2 Kings 15.13–22.

Menai Strait (mĕ'nī), channel of Irish Sea, between Anglesey Isl. and Caernarvonshire, N Wales.

Menander (mĭnăn'dùr), 342?–291? B.C., Greek poet of the New Comedy. Only fragments remain of his plays, which were imitated by Plautus and Terence and through them influenced 17th-cent. comedy.

Menasha (mùnă'shù), city (pop. 12,385), E

Wis., on L. Winnebago opposite Neenah and on Fox R.; settled before 1850. Mfg. of paper and wood products. Region visited by early French explorers.

Mencius (mĕn′shŭs), Mandarin *Meng-tse,* 371?–288? B.C., Chinese sage. He believed man was innately good, not selfish, but man will be free to do good only if he has the peace of mind which follows from material well-being. Rulers must ensure such security or be deposed. *The Book of Mencius* is a classic commentary on doctrines of CONFUCIUS.

Mencken, H(enry) L(ouis), 1880–, American editor, author, and critic. A journalist in Baltimore (notably on *Sun* papers) after 1906, he later with George Jean Nathan edited *Smart Set* (1914–23). As founder (1924) and editor of *American Mercury* (1925–33), Mencken attacked American complacency and bourgeois customs. He also wrote on American speech in *The American Language* (1919; 4th ed., 1936; later supplements).

Mendel, Gregor Johann (grā′gôr yō′hän mĕn′-dŭl), 1822–84, Austrian scientist and Roman Catholic priest. In his experiments, chiefly with garden peas, he carried on systematic cross-breeding and kept records of many offspring over several generations, on the basis of which he formulated principles of heredity. **Mendelism** is system of heredity based on his conclusions (Mendel's laws) which state that separate characters are inherited independently of one another; each reproductive cell receives only one of pair of alternative factors existing in other body cells; and some factors are dominant over others. See also GENETICS; HEREDITY.

Mendelejeff, Dmitri Ivanovich (mĕndŭlā′ŭf, Rus. dŭmē′trē ēvä′nŭvĭch myĭndyĭlyā′ŭf), 1834–1907, Russian chemist. He developed concept of PERIODIC LAW of classification of elements; predicted properties of elements then unknown; studied nature of solutions and expansion of liquids.

Mendele mocher sforim (mĕn′dŭlŭ môkh′ŭr sfô′rĭm), pseud. of **Sholem (or Solomon) Yakob Abramovich,** 1836–1917, Yiddish novelist, b. Russia. His style greatly influenced later writers.

Mendelism: see MENDEL, GREGOR JOHANN.

Mendelsohn, Erich (ā′rĭkh mĕn′dŭlzōn), 1887–, German architect, an exponent of German expressionism. His Potsdam observatory (1927) was highly original structure suggestive of sculpture. Has worked in England and Palestine; moved to U.S. in 1941.

Mendelssohn, (Jakob Ludwig) Felix (mĕn′-dŭlsŭn), 1809–47, German composer. He conducted in Düsseldorf, Leipzig, and London. His compositions include the Overture to *A Midsummer Night's Dream* (written when he was 17); five symphonies, of which the Scotch, Italian, and Reformation symphonies are best known; the E Minor violin concerto; *The Hebrides,* concert overture; and two oratorios, *St. Paul* and *Elijah.* His father changed the family name to Mendelssohn-Bartholdy, a form seldom used.

Mendelssohn, Moses, 1729–86. German-Jewish philosopher, a leader in the movement for cultural assimilation. His philosophical writings, which anticipated the aesthetics of Kant and J. C. F. von Schiller, include *Philosophische Gesprache* (1755) and *Phädon* (1767).

Mendès, Catulle (kätül′ mēdĕs′), 1841–1909, French poet, critic, and novelist; one of the PARNASSIANS.

Mendip Hills, range of hills, c.23 mi. long and 6 mi. wide, Somerset, England. They contain many caves and beautiful gorges, notably near Cheddar.

Mendocino, Cape (mĕndŭsē′nō), promontory, westernmost point of Calif., N of San Francisco.

Mendota (mĕndō′tŭ). **1** City (pop. 5,129), N Ill., N of La Salle. Processing, shipping center in agr. area. Mfg. of tools and machinery. **2** Village, SE Minn., just S of St. Paul at junction of Minnesota R. with the Mississippi. First permanent white settlement in state, it was known before 1819, but settlement dates from 1834. Some old houses restored.

Mendoza, Antonio de (äntō′nyō dā′ mändō′-thä), 1490?–1552, Spanish conquistador, first viceroy of New Spain (1535–40) and viceroy of Peru (1551–52). He alleviated the misery of the Indians, encouraged education, brought first printing press to America, quelled numerous revolts, pushed exploration into N. Was called "the good viceroy."

Mendoza, Diego Hurtado de: see HURTADO DE MENDOZA, DIEGO.

Mendoza, Íñigo López de: see SANTILLANA, ÍÑIGO LÓPEZ DE MENDOZA, MARQUÉS DE.

Mendoza, Pedro de (pā′dhrō), b. 1501 or 1502, d. 1537, Spanish conquistador, first *adelantado* of Río de la Plata (present Argentina). Founded Buenos Aires (1536), but attacks by Indians made place untenable. Mendoza, returning to Spain, died at sea.

Mendoza (mĕndō′sä), city (pop. 97,496), cap. of Mendoza prov., metropolis of W Argentina, in an oasis irrigated by Mendoza R.; founded (1561) by Pedro del Castillo. The wine industry is controlled by large Italian population. Oil exploitation is increasing.

Menelaus (mĕnŭlā′ŭs), in Greek mythology, king of Sparta; husband of Helen, father of Hermione, and younger brother of Agamemnon. When Paris abducted Helen to Troy, the other Greeks joined Menelaus in Trojan War. Afterward Helen rejoined him in Sparta.

Menelik II (mĕ′nulĭk), 1844–1913, emperor of Ethiopia after 1889. After the death of Emperor Theodore II (1868) he conquered most of the country with Italy's aid and seized the throne. Signed a treaty (1889) with Italy which made Ethiopia a protectorate. His denunciation of the Treaty provoked Italian invasion (1895–96). Ousting the invaders he forced Italy's recognition of Ethiopia's freedom. Made efforts to centralize and modernize his country.

Mene, Mene, Tekel, Upharsin (mē′nē, tē′–, ūfär′–), in Bible, riddle written on wall by mysterious hand at Belshazzar's feast. Daniel translated it as "to number, to number, to weigh, to divide" and interpreted it to mean the fall of Babylon. Dan. 5.5–29.

Menéndez de Avilés, Pedro (pā′dhrō mānĕn′-

děth dā ävēlěs′), 1519–74, Spanish naval officer and colonizer. Massacred French settlement of Fort Caroline under René de LAUDONNIÈRE; also killed group under Jean RIBAUT. Founded St. Augustine, Fla., in 1565.

Menéndez y Pelayo, Marcelino (märthālē′nō mānĕn′dĕth ē pälä′yō), 1856–1912, Spanish literary historian and critic.

Menes (mē′nēz), fl. 3400? B.C., first ruler of the Old Kingdom, anc. EGYPT; reputed to have united N and S kingdoms and to have founded Memphis.

Menger, Karl (mĕng′ûr), 1840–1921, Austrian economist, a founder of the Austrian school of economics. Taught at Univ. of Vienna 1873–1903. He advanced the theory of marginal utility.

Mengs, Anton Raphael (än′tōn rä′fäĕl mĕngs′), 1728–79, German historical and portrait painter, b. Bohemia. Did some of best work in Spain.

Meng-tse: see MENCIUS.

menhaden (mĕnhā′dûn), fish related to shad and herring, found from Nova Scotia to Brazil. It is a source of oil, poultry feed, and fertilizer.

meningitis (mĕnĭnjī′tĭs), inflammation of meninges (membranes of brain and spinal cord). Commonly results from infection by any of several organisms. Called cerebrospinal meningitis when both brain and spinal cord are affected. See *ill.*, p. 813.

Menken, Adah Isaacs, 1835–68, American actress, whose real name was Dolores Adios Fuertes. Noted for unconventionality, she caused a sensation in *Mazeppa*.

Menkure (mĕnkōō′rā), fl. 2800? B.C., king of anc. Egypt, successor of Khafre, IV dynasty. Built third pyramid at Gizeh.

Menlo Park. 1 Residential city (pop. 13,587), W Calif., S of San Francisco. **2** Village, NE N.J., NE of New Brunswick. Memorial tower commemorates T. A. Edison, whose workshops were here 1876–87.

Menninger, Karl A(ugustus) (mĕ′nĭnjûr), 1893–, and **William C(laire) Menninger,** 1899–, American psychiatrists, brothers. Karl and his father founded the Menninger Clinic, Topeka, Kansas (1920), and were joined by William (1926). The Menninger Foundation (1941) is a psychiatric center. After World War II, Karl helped found the Winter Veterans' Administration Hospital, center of world's largest psychiatric training program. He wrote *The Human Mind* (1930).

Mennonites, Protestant sect arising among Swiss Anabaptists; first called Swiss Brethren, renamed for Menno Simons. In Zurich, group seceded (1523–25) from state church, rejecting its authority and also infant baptism. They were nonresistants, and refused to take oaths; took Bible as sole rule of faith and retained only two sacraments, baptism and Lord's Supper. Sect spread to Russia, France, and Holland, where Dordrecht Confession was issued in 1632. In America, Mennonites settled (1683) at Germantown, Pa., and are found mainly in Pa., Ohio, and Middle West. The Amish are among the numerous Mennonite bodies.

Menno Simons (mĕ′nō sē′mōns), 1496?–1561, Dutch religious reformer, leader in Holland and Germany of moderate Anabaptists, later called Mennonites.

Menominee (mûnŏm′ûnē), city (pop. 11,151), W Upper Peninsula, N Mich., on Green Bay at mouth of Menominee R. (bridged to Marinette, Wis.); settled c.1840. Fishing port with mfg. of paper and wood products and machinery. Resort.

Menominee, river formed by union of Brule and Michigamme rivers above Iron Mountain, W Upper Peninsula, N Mich. Flows S c.118 mi. into Green Bay at Menominee, forming part of Wis.-Mich. line. Hydroelectric power.

Menominee Indians, North American tribe of Algonquian linguistic stock, in 17th–19th cent., a sedentary people of Eastern Woodlands area, inhabiting Wis. and Mich. They depended on wild rice for subsistence and fought bitter wars for control of rice areas. In 1854 settled on reservation in Wis.

Menomonie (mûnŏm′ûnē), city (pop. 8,245), W Wis., NW of Eau Claire and on Red Cedar R. Mfg. and trade center of dairy area.

menopause (mĕ′nûpôz), period of normal cessation of menstruation, also called change of life and climacteric. Results from gradual slowing of ovarian activity. Commonly occurs between ages of 45–50.

Menorca, Spain: see MINORCA.

Menotti, Gian-Carlo (jän′-kär′lō mānôt′tē), 1911–, American composer, b. Italy. His outstanding works are the operas *Amelia Goes to the Ball* (1937); *The Old Maid and the Thief* (1939); *The Medium* (1946); *The Telephone* (1947); *The Consul* (1950); and *Amahl and the Night Visitors* (1951).

Menshevism: see BOLSHEVISM AND MENSHEVISM.

Menshikov, Aleksandr Danilovich (ŭlyĭksän′-dûr dŭnyē′lûvĭch mĕn′shĭkûf), 1672–1729, Russian field marshal and statesman. Of lowly origin, he was Peter the Great's boon companion, later became his chief adviser, and was made a prince. He ably carried out Peter's reforms. On Peter's death, he helped place Catherine I on the throne and was the chief power during her reign.

menstruation, flow of blood from uterus, occurring in women from puberty to menopause usually in 28-day cycles. Controlled by hormones secreted by certain endocrine glands; associated with release of ovum from ovary, after which cells lining uterus increase. Unless conception occurs, egg and sloughed cells are discharged with flow of blood.

mental age: see INTELLIGENCE.

mental hygiene, science of promoting mental health and preventing mental disease through psychiatry and psychology. Reformers in 19th cent. roused periodic waves of interest in problems of the insane, but mental hygiene movement as such resulted directly from Clifford W. Beers's *A Mind That Found Itself* (1908), describing his experiences in asylums. The Natl. Committee for Mental Hygiene was founded 1909. The mental hygiene movement, supported by noted individuals, was spread through U.S. by state organizations. An Internatl. Committee was formed 1930. In U.S. the movement won wide reforms in institutional care, estab. child-guidance clinics, spread information through publications, e.g., *Mental Hygiene,* published quarterly from 1917.

mental tests, standard tests for studying psychological traits or special abilities (as opposed to INTELLIGENCE TESTS). Schools use aptitude and achievement tests to compare ability and actual accomplishment; business administrators use tests for special talents and motor skills to learn potential capacities of applicants. Psychoanalysis gave rise to "projective" tests based on individual's tendency to project unconscious attitudes into ambiguous situations. Hermann Rorschach used 10 standardized inkblots, had patient tell what he saw. Henry A. Murray's Thematic Apperception Test uses a standard series of pictures about which stories must be told. Lipot Szondi used photographs of 48 mentally disturbed or sexually perverted people; a given number of those liked and those disliked must be chosen. Other projective tests are word-association, finger painting, and draw-a-man tests.

Mentana (māntä'nä), village NE of Rome, Italy, where GARIBALDI was defeated by French and papal troops (1867).

Menton (mãtõn'), town (pop. 11,079), Alpes-Maritimes dept., SE France, at Italian border; resort on the Riviera. A plebiscite transferred it from Sardinia to France in 1860.

Mentor (mĕn'tůr, –tôr"), in Greek mythology, friend of Odysseus and tutor of Telemachus. His name is proverbial for a faithful and wise adviser.

Mentor, village (pop. 2,383), NE Ohio, near L. Erie and NE of Cleveland. Garfield was living here when he was elected President.

Menuhin, Yehudi (yůhōō'dē mĕn'ūĭn), 1916–, American violinist, b. U.S., of Russian parents. Made his debut at seven; later studied with Adolph Busch and Enesco. He returned to the concert stage a mature artist and in the first rank of violinists.

Menzaleh or **Manzala** (both: mĕnzä'lů), lagoon, area 660 sq. mi., Egypt, partly separated from the Mediterranean by narrow spit (site of Port Said).

Menzel, Adolph Friedrich Erdmann von (mĕn'tsůl), 1815–1905, German historical painter.

Menzies, Robert Gordon, 1894–, Australian statesman; prime minister 1939–41, 1949–.

Mephibosheth (mĕ"fĭbō'–), Jonathan's lame son, to whom King David restored Saul's lands. David thus fulfilled his vow of friendship made with Jonathan that was to include each other's children. 2 Sam. 4.4; 9; 16.1,4; 19.24. Also Merib-baal.

Mephistopheles (mĕfĭstŏf'ůlēz), in the German FAUST legend, the personification of the devil.

Merab, daughter of Saul promised to David but married to another man instead. 1 Sam. 18.17–19. Called MICHAL (probably by textual error) at 2 Sam. 21.8.

Merano (mārä'nō), Ger. *Meran,* city (pop. 22,575), Trentino-Alto Adige, N Italy; Alpine resort.

mercantilism (mûr'kůntĭlĭzům), important economic policy in Western Europe from 1500 until the Industrial Revolution and the advent of laissez-faire ideas. Mercantilist nations, identifying money with wealth, sought to obtain bullion by increased manufactures and exports, taxation of imports, and state colonial exploitation. State control was a vital part of the process. British mercantilism flourished under Henry VIII, Elizabeth, and Cromwell. Chief French exponent was Jean COLBERT.

Mercator, Gerardus (jůrär'důs mûrkā'tůr, mûr–), Latin form of real name, **Gerhard Kremer** (gā'rärt krā'můr), 1512–94, Flemish geographer, mathematician, cartographer. His first map using PROJECTION named for him appeared 1569.

Merced (můrsĕd'), city (pop. 15,278), central Calif., NW of Fresno. Tourist and farm center in San Joaquin Valley. Yosemite Natl. Park is NE.

Mercedes (mûrsā'dēz), city (pop. 10,081), S Texas, WNW of Brownsville; founded 1907. Packing and processing of citrus fruits and vegetables; some meat packing.

mercerizing, process of treating cotton textiles with sodium hydroxide and drying under tension to produce greater strength and luster. Developed by John Mercer, English chemist, in mid-19th cent.

Mercer University: see MACON, Ga.

Merchants Adventurers, English trading company in Low Countries and German free cities in 16th and 17th cent. Derived from GUILD system and forerunner of CHARTERED COMPANIES, it operated in cloth market of Netherlands and greatly influenced English foreign trade. Dissolved in Napoleonic Wars.

Mercia, kingdom of (mûr'shů), in Anglo-Saxon England, consisting generally of the region of the Midlands. Settled by Angles c.500. Overlordship extended over all S England by Penda and Wulfhere. After death of Offa (796), it gradually was taken over by Wessex. Part of it was later included in the Danelaw (886).

Mercier, Désiré Joseph (dāzĕrā' zhōzĕf' mârsēā'), 1851–1926, Belgian cardinal. As professor of philosophy at Louvain, he became a leader in 20th-cent. revival of Thomistic scholasticism. Made Roman Catholic archbishop of Malines (1906) and cardinal (1907), he did much to promote social welfare. In World War I, Mercier was the fearless spokesman of the Belgians when the country was under German conquest.

Mercury, Roman equivalent of HERMES.

Mercury, in astronomy, PLANET revolving in orbit nearest sun. Its mean distance from sun is c.35,960,000 mi. Period of revolution c.88 days, probably same as period of rotation on axis. Same side believed always toward sun; probably has no atmosphere. Passes through phases similar to moon's. Transits across sun's disk occur at intervals of 7–13 years in November and 13–46 years in May. See *ill.,* p. 1187.

mercury or **quicksilver,** silvery, liquid metallic element (symbol = Hg [Lat. *hydroargyrus*]; see also ELEMENT, table). It forms mercurous and mercuric compounds. Forms special alloy (AMALGAM) with other metals. Used in barometer because of great weight and in thermometer because of equal expansion per degree rise in temperature. Occurs free to limited extent. Chief ore is cinnabar. Mercury-arc lamp is fused quartz tube with confined mercury; when current is passed through, metal vaporizes, giving greenish-blue luminescence.

Mer de Glace (mĕr″ dů gläs′) [Fr.,= sea of ice] glacier, 3½ mi. long, E France, on N slope of Mont Blanc, near Chamonix.

Meredith, George, 1828–1909, English novelist and poet. First gaining notice with *The Ordeal of Richard Feverel* (1859), he wrote a series of novels notable for psychological insight and close inspection of the relationship of the individual and social events; among them are *Evan Harrington* (1860), *Rhoda Fleming* (1865), *The Egoist* (1879), *The Tragic Comedians* (1880), *Diana of the Crossways* (1885), and *Lord Ormont and His Aminta* (1894). His poetry, dealing with the same themes, includes a well-known sequence "Modern Love" and individual poems such as "Love in the Valley" and "Lucifer in Starlight." His critical essay, "On . . . the Comic Spirit," has been much admired.

Meredith, Owen: see BULWER-LYTTON, EDWARD R.

Merezhkovsky, Dmitri Sergeyevich (důmē′trē sĭrgā′ůvĭch mârĭshkôf′skē), 1865–1941, Russian author and religious philosopher. Parts of his trilogy *Christ and Antichrist* (1896–1905) were very popular in English—*Julian the Apostle, The Death of the Gods, The Romance of Leonardo da Vinci.* He went into exile in 1918.

Mergenthaler, Ottmar (ôt′mär mĕr′gůntä″lůr), 1854–99, American inventor of the LINOTYPE, b. Germany.

Merian, Matthäus (mätĕ′o͞os mä′rēän), the elder, 1593–1650, Swiss engraver. Settled c.1623 in Frankfurt-am-Main. Etchings include *Dance of Death* and Bible illustrations. His son, **Matthäus Merian,** the younger, 1621–87, was a portrait and historical painter, his daughter, **Maria Sibylla Merian,** 1647–1717, was a naturalist and painter of insects and flowers.

Mérida (mä′rēdhä), city (pop. 96,852), cap. of Yucatan, SE Mexico, in NW part of Yucatan peninsula; founded 1542 on site of ruined Mayan city. Tourist attractions are near-by Chichén Itzá and Uxmal.

Mérida (mä′rēdhä), city (pop. 22,440), SW Spain, in Estremadura, on Guadiana R. A Roman colony, it became cap. of Lusitania. Roman remains (e.g., bridge, triumphal arch) are among most important in Spain. Prospered under Moors, 713–1228.

Meriden (mĕ′rĭdůn), city (pop. 44,088), S central Conn., SW of Hartford; settled 1661. Mfg. of silverware (since 18th cent.), electrical equipment, and precision goods.

Meridian. 1 Village (pop. 1,810), SW Idaho, W of Boise, in Boise project. **2** City (pop. 41,893), E Miss., E of Jackson near Ala. line; founded c.1854. Trade, shipping, and industrial center for farm, livestock and lumber area. Temporary cap. 1863. Destroyed by Sherman, Feb. 1864.

meridian, imaginary line drawn on earth's surface from pole to pole, cutting equator and all parallels at a right angle. International agreement (1884) designated the Greenwich meridian as zero or prime meridian; other meridians are measured E and W to 180 longitude.

Mérimée, Prosper (prôspĕr′ märēmā′), 1803-70, French author. He is best known for his short novels *Colomba* (1840) and *Carmen* (1845; basis of Bizet's opera), in which he treats his romantic themes in concise, lucid style and with psychological realism.

Merino sheep: see SHEEP.

Merionethshire (mĕrēŏ′nůthshĭr) or **Merioneth,** county (660 sq. mi.; pop. 41,456), N Wales; co. seat Dolgelley. Mountainous region with poor soil, it draws wealth from manganese, slate, and limestone deposits. Beautiful scenery attracts tourists. One of the last areas to submit to English influence a large percentage of population speak Welsh.

Meriwether Lewis National Monument: see NATIONAL PARKS AND MONUMENTS (table).

Merlin: see ARTHURIAN LEGEND.

Mermaid Tavern, in Elizabethan London where Shakspere, Ben Johnson, and their friends often met.

Merneptah (mĕrnĕp′tä), d. c.1215 B.C., king of anc. Egypt. Succeeded his father, RAMSES II, in 1225. His reign started decline of dynasty XIX.

Merodach (mĕ′rōdăk), biblical form of the god Marduk of Babylon. Jer. 50.2.

Merodach-baladan (–bă′lůdăn) [Assyrian,= Marduk has given a son], fl. 721 B.C., Chaldaean prince. Sargon of Assyria drove him from Babylon (c.710). In 705 B.C., on Sargon's death, he returned.

Merom, Waters of: see BAHR EL-HULEH.

Merope (mĕ′růpē), in Greek mythology. **1** One of the Pleiades; daughter of Atlas and nymph Pleione. One legend calls her the lost Pleiad. **2** Daughter of Oenopion. She was loved by ORION.

Merovingians (mĕr″ōvĭn′jůnz), dynasty of Frankish kings, descended from the semilegendary Meroveus, chief of the Salian FRANKS, whose grandson CLOVIS I founded the Frankish monarchy (481). Clovis's kingdom was divided among his descendants into kingdom of AUSTRASIA, NEUSTRIA, AQUITAINE, BURGUNDY, Paris, and Orléans; these were often combined and at times reunited under a sole ruler (under Clotaire I, 558–61; Clotaire II, 613–c.622; Dagobert I, 630–33). Before Dagobert, chronic warfare among the kingdoms was the rule; Dagobert's successors, the "idle kings," left government to mayors of the palace, the CAROLINGIANS. In 751 Pepin the Short deposed Childeric III, the last Merovingian, and became king.

Merrill, city (pop. 8,951), central Wis., at junction of Wisconsin and Prairie rivers and N of Wausau. Mfg. of paper and furniture. Near by are Grandfather Falls of Wisconsin R.

Merrimac: see MONITOR AND MERRIMAC.

Merrimack, river formed in S central N.H., at Franklin, by junction of Pemigewasset and Winnipesaukee rivers. Flows S into NE Mass., then NE to the Atlantic below Newburyport; c.110 mi. long. Furnishes power to mfg. centers.

Merritt Island, c.30 mi. long and up to 7 mi. wide, E Fla. Separated from mainland on W by Indian R. and from Cape Canaveral by Banana R. Citrus fruit.

Merry Mount: see MORTON, THOMAS.

Merseburg (mĕr'zŭbŏŏrk), city (pop. 33,978), Saxony-Anhalt, E central Germany, on the Saale. Lignite mining; industries (steel, paper, machinery, chemicals). Bishopric of Merseburg, founded 968, was secularized 1561 and passed to Saxony. City was seat of dukes of Saxe-Merseburg 1656–1738; passed to Prussia 1815. Its many ancient buildings were largely destroyed in World War II.

Mersen, Treaty of, 870, signed by CHARLES II (the Bald) of the W Franks (i.e., France) and LOUIS THE GERMAN, at Mersen (Dutch *Meersen*), now in Netherlands. It divided LOTHARINGIA between France (which received, roughly, the Low Countries and Lorraine) and Germany (which received Alsace and left bank of Lower Rhine).

Mersey (mûr'zē), river of England, flowing 70 mi. between Lancashire and Cheshire, from Stackport to Irish Sea NW of Liverpool. Estuary, 16 mi. long and 2 mi. wide, is navigable for ocean-going liners. River is of great commercial importance.

Merthyr Tydfil (mûr'thŭr tĭd'vĭl), county borough (pop. 61,093), Glamorganshire, Wales. In center of great coal field, it has iron and steel works.

Merton, Thomas (mûr'tŭn), 1915–, American religious writer and poet, b. France, a Trappist monk since 1941. His works include poetry (e.g., *Figures for an Apocalypse,* 1947), devotional books (e.g., *Seeds of Contemplation,* 1949), and well-known autobiographical volumes (e.g., *The Seven Storey Mountain,* 1948).

Merton, Walter de, d. 1277, English bishop, founder of Merton Col., Oxford. In 1264 he obtained charter of incorporation and estab. at Malden, Surrey, a "House of Scholars," later transferred to Oxford. This marks beginning of collegiate system of education. Merton became model for other colleges.

Merton College: see OXFORD UNIVERSITY.

Merv (myĕrf), anc. city in large oasis of Kara Kum dessert, Turkmen SSR, on Murgab R. As Margiana it was cap. of a N province of ancient Persia. A center of medieval Islamic culture, it was conquered from Uzbeks by Russia in 1884. Near old Merv (now called Bairam-Ali) there grew a new Merv (pop. 37,100), renamed Mary in 1937. Textile mfg.

Merwede, river, Netherlands: see MEUSE.

Meryon, Charles (shärl' mĕryō'), 1821–68, French etcher, known for poetic series of etchings of old sections of Paris.

Mesa (mā'sŭ), city (pop. 16,790), S central Ariz., in SALT RIVER VALLEY; founded 1878 by Mormons. Univ. of Arizona experimental farm is here.

mesa (mā'sŭ) [Span.,= table], name given in SW U.S. to a small, isolated tableland or a flat-topped hill, with at least two steep, often perpendicular, sides. Picturesque; often deep red or yellow. Less precipitous, smaller formations are buttes.

Mesabi (mŭsä'bē), range of low hills, NE Minn., known as iron range. Richest of three iron ranges: Vermilion (NE Minn., between Vermilion L. and Ely; first ore shipped 1884), Mesabi (between Grand Rapids and Aurora; Hibbing and Virginia are centers; first ore shipped 1892), and Cuyuna (central Minn., between Brainerd and Aitkin; first ore shipped 1911). Leonidas Merritt, with brothers, discovered Mesabi iron 1887, estab. claims to area, organized company to exploit ore 1890. John D. Rockefeller took over 1893. Mesabi ore in horizontal layers mined by open-pit method. Ores of other ranges in vertical strata, less accessible. Most of ore shipped from Duluth.

Mesa Verde Natonal Park: see NATIONAL PARKS AND MONUMENTS (table).

mescal (mĕskăl'), Mexican spirituous liquor, usually obtained by distilling a liquid made from leaves, juicy stalk, and roots of certain species of agave (maguey). Name is sometimes given to liquor distilled from agave sap which, fermented, is pulque and also to drug obtained from peyote.

Mesdag, Hendrik Willem (hĕn'drĭk vĭ'lŭm mĕs'däkh), 1831–1915, Dutch marine painter. Mesdag Mus., The Hague, is his gift to the nation.

Mesha (mē'–), king of Moab, contemporary of Ahab. 2 Kings 3. Composed inscription on Moabite Stone.

Meshach (mē'–), one of the THREE HOLY CHILDREN.

Meshed (mĕsh'hĕd), city (pop. 167,471), NE Iran; a leading center of Shiite pilgrimage. Site of 9th-cent. shrine of the Imam Riza. Located near the USSR and Afghanistan frontiers, it assumed strategic importance after late 19th cent.

Mesilla (māsē'yä), historic village (pop. 1,264), SW N.Mex., on Rio Grande and S of Las Cruces; settled c.1850. It was a central station on overland mail route. Changed hands several times in Civil War; proclaimed cap. of new Confederate territory. Mesilla Valley came to U.S. under Gadsden Purchase (1853).

Mesmer, Friedrich (or **Franz) Anton** (mĕz'mŭr), 1733?–1815, German physician. He developed a system of treatment through hypnotism known as mesmerism.

mesmerism: see HYPNOTISM.

Mesolonghi, Greece: see MISSOLONGHI.

meson (mĕ'zŏn) or **mesotron** (mĕ'zŭtrŏn), nuclear particle intermediate in mass between electron and proton. Positive, negative, and neutral mesons are identified. Most have life span of few millionths of second; yield energy on disintegration.

Mesopotamia (mĕ"sŭpŭtā'mēŭ) [Gr.,= between rivers], region of W Asia, around the lower Tigris and the lower Euphrates, now in Iraq. The heart of it was a plain, rendered fertile in ancient times by canals. This "cradle of civilization" saw the rise of city-states older than Egypt—Eridu, Ur, Lagash, Akkad, Babylon. Civilization as early as the 4th millennium B.C. flowered into the empires of BABYLONIA and ASSYRIA. It declined later but was still important in the Byzantine Empire. Hulagu Khan and his Mongols laid the area waste in A.D. 1298, and it is today largely arid and barren, but enriched by oil wells.

mesotron: see MESON.

Mesozoic era (mĕsůzō'ĭk), one of the grand divisions of geologic time (the fourth if Archeozoic and Proterozoic are considered separately, i.e., not combined as pre-Cambrian). In North America, the land, especially the Appalachian region, was in general elevated and subject to erosion; much of the West was often submerged as geosynclines (enormous downfolds) were formed. Mesozoic life was dominated by reptiles. Dinosaurs were numerous in the TRIASSIC, were more abundant during the JURASSIC and CRETACEOUS, but most forms became extinct when violent disturbances brought the era to an end. See also GEOLOGY, table.

mesquite (mĭskēt'), leguminous spiny shrub (*Prosopis glandulosa*). It is native to arid and chaparral regions of SW U.S. Fruit pods have edible pulp. Other species are in South America, Asia, Africa.

Messalina (Valeria Messalina) (mĕsůlī'nů), d. A.D. 48, corrupt Roman empress, wife of CLAUDIUS I, who had her killed after a serious scandal.

Messenia (mĕsē'nēů), anc. region of Peloponnesus, SW Greece. A Messenian city, Pylos, an early center of Mycenaean culture. Held subject by Sparta after c.700 B.C., Messenia revolted several times and was freed from Spartan control when Thebes defeated Sparta at Leuctra (371 B.C.).

Messiaen, Olivier (ôlēvyā' mĕsyē'), 1908–, French organist, composer of religious music, and teacher. Some of his works are based on scale formulas of his own invention. His compositions include *L'Ascension,* for orchestra; a symphony, *Turangalia; Le Banquet céleste,* for organ; and Masses and songs.

Messiah (můsī'ů) or **Messias** (můsī'ůs) [Heb.,= anointed], in Judaism, a righteous man who will be sent by God to restore Israel. The idea developed among the Jews in their adversity. Jesus Christ considered himself and is considered by Christians to be the promised Messiah to whom the Old Testament pointed. The Christian ideal of the Messiah is fundamentally different from the Jewish conception in the aspect of suffering; the common idea of Jesus' time was that the Messiah should reign in glory on earth.

Messina (măsē'nä), Mediterranean port (pop. 192,051), NE Sicily, Italy; one of the large commercial centers of the island. Founded (8th cent. B.C.) by Greeks as Zancle, it later was called Messana. Roman intervention to protect Messina from Syracuse brought on (264 B.C.) the Punic Wars. Messina was later a wealthy city under the Roman Empire and throughout the Middle Ages, but declined somewhat later. It was conquered (1860) by Garabaldi in his Sicilian campaign. The city suffered a severe earthquake in 1908 and was rebuilt. It is on the **Strait of Messina,** c.20 mi. long, 2–10 mi. wide, which separates the Italian peninsula from Sicily and connects the Ionian and Tyrrhenian seas. Its currents and whirlpools gave rise to legends on dangers to sailors (see SCYLLA).

Messys, Quentin: see MASSYS, QUENTIN.

mestizo (mĕstē'sō) [Span.,= mixture], person of mixed race. In Latin American countries, descendants of Spanish or Portuguese and Indians.

Mestrovic, Ivan (ē'vän mĕsh'trōvĭch), 1883–, Yugoslav sculptor. His style is a modern adaptation of archaic Greek sculpture and Byzantine tradition. Often treats religious subjects.

metabolism (můtă'bůlĭzům), sum of chemical processes resulting in growth, production of body heat and energy, and maintenance of vital functions. Basal metabolism represents minimum energy needed to maintain normal temperature of body at rest.

metal, chemical ELEMENT with characteristic metallic luster, ability to conduct heat and electricity, capacity to form positive ION. About two thirds of known elements are metallic. They differ in hardness, ductility, malleability, tensile strength, density, melting point; definite line between metals and nonmetals cannot be drawn. Chromium is hardest metal; softest is cesium. Silver is best electric conductor; copper, gold, aluminum follow. All metals are relatively good heat conductors. They can be arranged in order of activity in electromotive or replacement series. In general, any metal will replace in compounds any other metal, or hydrogen, which it precedes in the series and will be replaced by any which it follows. Metals fall into groups according to PERIODIC LAW; certain similar elements fall into families, e.g., alkali metals, alkaline earth metals, RARE EARTHS. Metals differ from nonmetals chemically in forming positive ions, basic oxides, and hydroxides. Many metals corrode on exposure to moist air, i.e., enter into chemical reaction which results in formation of new compound. Metals are combined with nonmetals in salts. When mixed in definite amount, metals form alloys. Some metals occur uncombined, most are combined in ores. For uses of specific metals and their compounds, see separate articles.

metallurgy (mĕ'tůlûr"jē), branch of chemistry concerned with extraction of metals from their ores. Processes used depend upon chemical nature of ore to be treated and properties of metal to be extracted. If metal occurs uncombined chemically in sand or rock, mechanical methods alone sometimes produce relatively pure metal. Finely divided waste material is washed away or separated by gravity; rock is crushed and heated until metal fuses and separates. Other processes involve use of a flux—material that will combine with waste when heat is applied—to form a lighter mass called slag which floats and can be skimmed off. Gold and silver are sometimes treated with mercury in which they dissolve, forming an amalgam. CYANIDE PROCESS is also used for extraction of gold and silver. Generally chemical rather than mechanical processes must be used since most metals occur in nature in chemical compounds. Treatment of ore by heat is smelting. Oxides are heated with reducing agent, e.g., carbon in the form of coke or coal; waste, called gangue, mixed with ore is removed by a flux. Sulphide ore is commonly roasted (heated in air) to form metal oxide, which is then reduced. Carbonate ore is heated, oxide of metal formed and then reduced with carbon. Some active metals, e.g., aluminum, barium, calcium, magnesium, potassium, and sodium, are prepared by electrolysis. Flotation process can be used for many ores; it involves adding a chemical to pulverized ore, forming a froth when air is added to mixture, brushing off wet ore which rises to surface, and filtering out mineral.

metamorphic rocks: see ROCK.

metamorphism (mĕ″tŭmôr′fĭzŭm), in geology, processes bring about profound changes in rock. Causes include heat, infiltration of liquids or gases, thrust or pull of earth movements, weight of overlying rocks, or (most commonly) the combination of two or more of these. Schist, gneiss, marble, and slate are common metamorphic rocks.

metaphor (mĕ′tŭfŭr, –fôr) [Gr.,= transfer] and **simile** (sĭ′mŭlē) [Latin,= likeness], in rhetoric, two figures of speech. In metaphor, an object belonging to one class of things is referred to as if it belonged to another class, either explicitly ("All the world's a dream") or by implication (referring to a beloved woman as "a rose without a thorn"). In simile, an object is explicitly compared to another object ("My love is like a red, red rose").

metaphysical poets, group of English poets of the 17th cent. Their primary subject was the relation of God and man; their poetry was marked by unusual figures—blending passion and logic—termed metaphysical conceits. The poems show intellectual wit and subtle argument. Chief metaphysical poets were Donne, Traherne, George Herbert, Crashaw, and Henry Vaughan.

Metastasio, Pietro (pyā′trō mātästä′zēō), pseud. of Pietro Bonaventura Trapassi, 1698–1782, Italian author of melodramas, used as librettos for operas by many composers, including Hasse, Handel, Haydn, Mozart, and Gluck. Long court poet at Vienna, Metastasio exercised much influence on 18th-cent. opera.

Metaurus (mĭtô′rŭs), river of central Italy, flowing into the Adriatic. On its banks Romans defeated Carthaginians under Hasdrubal 207 B.C.

Metaxas, John (mā′täksäs″), 1871–1941, Greek general and royalist politician. As premier (1936–41) he governed dictatorially. He successfully directed Greek resistance against Italy after 1940.

Metcalf, Willard Leroy (mĕt′kăf), 1858–1925, American landscape painter. Taught at Cooper Union and Art Students League, New York.

Metcalfe, Charles Theophilus Metcalfe, 1st **Baron,** 1785–1846, British colonial administrator, b. India. After a long career in the Indian civil service he was governor general of Canada 1843–45.

Metchnikoff, Élie (mĕch′nĭkôf), Rus. *Ilya Ilyich Mechnikov,* 1845–1916, Russian biologist. Developed theory that certain white corpuscles (phagocytes) ingest and destroy bacteria. Shared 1908 Nobel Prize in Physiology and Medicine for work on immunity. Associated with Pasteur Inst., Paris.

Metellus (mētĕ′lŭs), distinguished anc. Roman family. **Quintus Caecilius Metellus Macedonicus** (măsĭdō′nĭkŭs), d. 115 B.C., conquered Macedonia (148 B.C.) and pacified Greece (146). His nephew **Quintus Caecilius Metellus Numidicus** (nūmĭ′dĭkŭs), d. 91? B.C., led the senatorial party. As consul (109 B.C.) he conducted the Numidian War against Jugurtha. Fought against MARIUS Saturninus and was exiled (100). His son, **Quintus Caecilius Metellus Pius** (pī′ūs), d. c.63 B.C., continued his father's opposition to Marius. In 89 B.C. he fought in the Social War; in the civil war he defended Rome against Marius and CINNA. Joining SULLA in 83, he defeated the Marians and became consul (80 B.C.). In Spain he warred against Sertorius. For his adoptive son, **Quintus Caecilius Metellus Pius Scipio,** see SCIPIO.

meteor (mē′tēŭr), one of the small bodies entering earth's atmosphere from space and becoming incandescent partly because of collisions of emitted atoms and air molecules. Estimated to become visible at height of 60–90 mi. and to move at average velocity of c.26 mi. per second. Called shooting or falling star if no brighter than zero-magnitude star; fireball or bolide if very large or brighter. If it reaches earth, it is called a METEORITE. Meteor showers are common at certain times of year at intervals coinciding with comet periods; appear to proceed from certain constellations.

Meteor Crater: see WINSLOW, Ariz.

meteorite (mē′tēŭrīt), METEOR that reaches earth's surface. Those called siderites are composed of metal; aerolities, of stone; siderolites, of metal and stone. Their surface, liquefied by heat and pressure resulting from rapid passage through atmosphere, forms crust as friction finally reduces velocity. Velocity of giant meteorites is so great that impact with earth results in penetration beneath ground, accompanied by compression, heating, vaporization, and expansion of gases which may cause explosion shattering meteorite and carving crater in ground. Meteorites have been discovered in most parts of world.

meteorology (mē″tēŭrŏl′ŭjē), science of atmosphere with its associated phenomena, WEATHER. Dates from 5th cent. B.C. Progress as a science began with development of physics and basic instruments (wind vane, 1500; thermometer, c.1593; mercurial barometer, 1643).

methane (mĕ′thān), commonly called marsh gas, a colorless, odorless gas. Burns in air, explosive when mixed with air. Formed by decomposition of organic matter in swamps and marshes, it is chief component of natural gas and fire damp. It is used as a fuel and illuminant and in treating steel. It consists of one carbon atom and four hydrogens, and is the first member of saturated hydrocarbon series, **methane** or **paraffin series.** Other members have same relation between number of carbons and hydrogens. They are common compounds occurring in benzine, gasoline, kerosene, paraffin. Substances considered derivatives include chloroform, methyl alcohol, ethyl alcohol, formaldehyde, acetic acid.

methanol: see METHYL ALCOHOL.

Methodism, doctrine, polity, and worship of Protestant denominations originating in England under John WESLEY. He and his brother Charles, George WHITEFIELD, and others formed group at Oxford in 1729. Their resolve to conduct lives and study by "rule and method" won them name Methodists. Followers preached in houses, barns, and open fields. Lay preachers were trained and given "circuits," and a system of itinerancy began. First annual conference in 1744 adopted Articles of Religion, based largely on Thirty-nine Articles though stress was put on repentance, faith, sanctification, and full, free salvation. Whitefield could not agree to this doctrine and became leader of Calvinistic Methodists. Main body adopted constitution 1784, formally separated from Church of England 1791, and organized Wesleyan Methodist Church. In America real beginning of Methodism was in N.Y. under preaching of Philip Embury (c.1766). In 1771 Francis ASBURY brought about rapid spread of Methodism, with first conference in 1773. In 1784 Methodist Episcopal Church was formed, with Asbury and Thomas Coke as bishops. As in England the church divided into many branches. Issue of slavery separated Methodist Episcopal Church South (1845) from main body. But in 1939 these two, with Methodist Protestant Church, united as Methodist Church.

Methodius, Saint: see CYRIL AND METHODIUS, SAINTS.

Methuen, (mĭthōō'ŭn), town (pop. 24,477), NE Mass., near N.H. line NW of Lawrence; settled c.1642. Mfg. of worsteds, yarn, and wooden heels.

Methuselah (mēthū'–), son of Enoch, known for the length of his life: according to Bible, he lived 969 years. Gen. 5.21. Mathusala: Luke 3.37.

methyl (mĕ'thĭl), organic radical with one carbon, three hydrogen atoms; name derived from methane. Has never been isolated but is in many compounds.

methyl alcohol, methanol (mĕ'thŭnōl), or **wood alcohol,** colorless, poisonous, liquid alcohol, inflammable, miscible with water. Used as organic solvent, in making formaldehyde, as denaturant. Prepared by destructive distillation of wood or by synthetic process with combination of carbon monoxide and hydrogen.

methylbenzene: see TOLUENE.

metric system, system of weights and measurements worked out in France and adopted by many nations. Based on meter (theoretically 1/10,000,000 of distance from equator to pole, measured on earth's surface; legally, the length of platinum bar kept in Paris). Surface unit is the are (100 sq. meters); volume unit, the liter (cube of 1/10 meter); weight unit, the gram (theoretical weight of distilled water filling cube with edges of 1/100 meter). Weights or measures larger or smaller than meter are related to these units by a decimal system (e.g., kilometer equals 1,000 meters, etc.). For equivalents of metric denominations, see WEIGHTS AND MEASURES (table).

Metropolis (mĭtrŏ'pŭlĭs), city (pop. 6,093), S Ill., on Ohio R. and E of Cairo, in farm and timber area. State park here has site of Fort Ascension (later Fort Massac) estab. by French 1757; later held by British and Americans. Clark landed here 1778 at start of his Illinois campaign. Kincaid Indian mounds are in the general area.

Metropolitan Museum of Art, New York city founded 1870. Opened 1880 on present site in Central Park facing Fifth Ave. Building owned by city, which provides upkeep; supported mainly by private endowment and membership dues. Admission is free. Outstanding features include European paintings, medieval art (part of which is in the CLOISTERS), Egyptian and American wings, and Costume Inst. (containing costumes from all over the world).

Metropolitan Opera Company, term used in referring collectively to organizations which have produced opera at the Metropolitan Opera House, New York. The house was built by members of New York society who could not be accommodated with boxes at the Acad. of Music. The first presentation, on Oct. 22, 1883, was Gounod's *Faust*. Devastated by fire in 1892, the opera house was rebuilt and taken over by the Metropolitan Opera and Real Estate Co. The management became known as the Metropolitan Opera Co. for the first time in 1908. The gradual transference from private to public ownership, with performances underwritten by public subscription, was completed when the Metropolitan Opera Association, Inc. (formed 1932 to replace the Metropolitan Opera Co.) bought the opera house (1940) from the Metropolitan Opera and Real Estate Co. Among the Metropolitan's directors have been Leopold Damrosch, Maurice Grau, Heinrich Conrad, Gatti-Casazza, Edward Johnson, and Rudolph Bing. The world's greatest singers and conductors have contributed to its rich traditions and glamorous legend.

Metsu or **Metzu, Gabriel** (both: gä'brēĕl mĕt'sü), 1630?–1667, Dutch genre painter, b. Leiden. Worked mainly in Amsterdam.

Metsys, Quentin: see MASSYS, QUENTIN.

Meternich, Clemens, Fürst von (klē'mĕns fürst' fŭn mĕ'tŭrnĭkh), 1773–1859, Austrian statesman, b. Coblenz, Germany. As the minister of foreign affairs from 1809, he negotiated the marriage of MARIE LOUISE to Napoleon I (1810) and an alliance with France (1812), but in 1813, after attempting to mediate between Napoleon and the Allies, he joined the Allied camp. At the Congress of Vienna (1814–15) he sought a general balance of power, opposed Russian and Prussian expansion in Poland and Saxony, and secured a dominant place for Austria in the GERMAN CONFEDERATION. A dominating figure of the HOLY ALLIANCE, Metternich based his extreme conservatism on the theory that peace and order could be secured by an immutable maintenance of the *status quo*. Espionage, censorship, and armed repression of liberal movements were essential features of his policy, and the era 1815–48 has been called the Age of Metternich. Ousted by the Revolution of 1848, he returned to Vienna in 1851. He was created a prince in 1818.

Metuchen (mŭtŭ'chŭn), borough (pop. 9,879), NE N.J.; NE of New Brunswick. Auto assembly plant; mfg. of chemicals and insulation products.

Metz (mĕts, Fr. mĕs), city (pop. 65,472), cap. of Moselle dept., NE France, on the Moselle; a cultural and commercial center of LORRAINE. An early episcopal see, it became the cap. of AUSTRASIA (6th cent.). Bishops ruled considerable territory as fief of Holy Roman Empire, but the city itself became a free imperial city in 12th cent. Metz was annexed to France in 1552 after a sort of plebiscite. In the Franco-Prussian War, Marshal Bazaine capitulated with 180,000 men after a two-month siege (1870). Annexed to Germany 1871–1918, Metz was a center of pro-French sentiment. In World War II it was liberated from German occupation by U.S. troops after heavy fighting for its outer fortifications (1944). The city retains many medieval buildings, notably its Gothic cathedral.

Metzu, Gabriel: see METSU, GABRIEL.

Meudon (mûdõ'), town (pop. 20,106), Seine-et-Oise, dept., N France. Astrophysics dept. of Paris Observatory is in a pavilion of 17th-cent. château. Rabelais was curate of Meudon.

Meun, Jean de: see JEAN DE MEUN.

Meunier, Constantin (kõstätĕ' mûnyä'), 1831–1905, Belgian sculptor and painter. Chiefly concerned with expressing dignity of the worker. Masterpiece is unfinished *Monument to Labor* (Brussels).

Meurthe (mûrt), river, 105 mi. long, E France, in Lorraine. Rises in the Vosges and flows NW to the Moselle just N of Nancy.

Meurthe-et-Moselle (mûr'tämôzĕl'), department (2,039 sq. mi.; pop. 528,805), NE France, in Lorraine; cap. Nancy.

Meuse (mûz), department (2,410 sq. mi.; pop. 188,786), NE France, in Lorraine; cap. Bar-le-Duc.

Meuse (mūz, Fr. mûz), Dutch and Flemish *Maas,* river, c.560 mi. long, traversing NE France, S Belgium, and the Netherlands. It flows N from Langres Plateau, winds E through an industrial and mining region centered on Liège (Belgium), turns N into the Netherlands at Maastricht, swings W, and branches out to form a common delta with the Rhine. Bergsche Maas branch flows into a North Sea inlet S of Dordrecht. Maas branch flows NW to join the WAAL in forming the Merwede, which bifurcates into the Lower Merwede and the New Merwede. Latter forms the Hollandschdiep, a North Sea estuary. A branch of the Lower Merwede is the Old Meuse. The New Meuse is a continuation of the LEK. The Meuse is linked with Antwerp by ALBERT CANAL, with Dutch ports by intricate system of waterways. A strategic line of defense, valley has often been a battleground.

Mewar, India: see UDAIPUR.

Mexia (mùhä'ù), city (pop. 6,627), E central Texas, ENE of Waco. Processing center of oil and cotton area.

Mexicali (mĕksĭkä'lē), city (pop. 18,775), cap. of N district of Lower California, Mexico; farm center in IMPERIAL VALLEY.

Mexican art. The massive classic art of ancient Mayan and Aztec civilizations has influenced later artistic developments of Mexico. Highly developed arts are also identified with the pre-Aztec civilization of the Toltec. Unique medium of early Mexican art was feather painting (feathers gummed against a background to make a picture). European art (esp. painting) was introduced after Spanish conquest of Mexico. In 17th and 18th cent. natives became adept at religious oil painting and wax modeling, adding mellowness and richness of color to Spanish styles. Baltásar de Echave, the elder, who is considered the first great Mexican artist, founded the first native school (1609). Notable 18th-cent. artists included José Ibarra and Miguel Cabrera; outstanding in late 19th and early 20th cent. were José María Velasco and José Guadalupe. Since the 1910 revolution, mural painting to express social themes has become important, with Diego Rivera, José Orozco, and David Alfaro Siqueiros among its chief exponents. A noted abstract painter is Rufino Tamayo. Wood sculpture and folk arts (e.g., weaving, pottery making, silverwork) have long flourished. For Mexican architecture, see SPANISH COLONIAL ARCHITECTURE.

Mexican hairless dog: see TOY DOG.

Mexican War, 1846–48, fought by U.S. and Mexico. While immediate cause was annexation of Texas (Dec., 1845), other factors disturbed peaceful relations. American citizens had long-standing clams against Mexico; many wished acquisition of Calif. After admission of Texas into Union, Pres. Polk sent John Slidell to offer assumption of American claims by his government in return for boundary adjustment and to purchase Calif. and N.Mex. Mexico declined to negotiate. War was supported by imperialists and by those who wished to see slaveholding territory extended. In March, 1846, Gen. Zachary TAYLOR occupied Point Isabel, at mouth of the Rio Grande. To the Mexicans, who claimed the Nueces as the boundary, this was an act of aggression. After Mexican crossing of the Rio Grande and shelling of Fort Brown (then Fort Taylor), U.S. declared war, May 12, 1846. Santa Fe was taken by S. W. KEARNY; Calif. exchanged Mexican for American rule. American victories preceded drawn battle with forces under SANTA ANNA at Buena Vista, Feb., 1847. Supported by naval task force, Winfield SCOTT took Veracruz, then began drive on Mexico city. Following the storming of Chapultepec, American troops entered Mexico city, Sept. 14, 1847, remaining until peace was restored. Treaty of GUADALUPE HIDALGO was ratified by U.S. Senate on March 10, 1848.

Mexico (mĕk'sĭkō), Span. *México* or *Méjico* (both: mĕ'hēkō), republic (760,373 sq. mi.; pop. 25,581,250), North America, between U.S. and Central America; cap. Mexico city. Administratively divided into 28 states, 3 territories, and Federal District. States are (see individual articles): Aguascalientes, Campeche, Chiapas, Chihuahua, Coahuila, Colima, Durango, Guanajuato, Guerrero, Hidalgo, Jalisco, Mexico, Michoacán, Morelos, Nayarit, Nuevo León, Oaxaca, Puebla, Querétaro, San Luis Potosí, Sinaloa, Sonora, Tabasco, Tamaulipas, Tlaxcala, Veracruz, Yucatan, Zacatecas. Territories are Lower California (two) and Quintana Roo. Much of Mexico is mountainous (see SIERRA

MADRE) with narrow, hot coastal plains and high central plateau transversed by E–W range with lofty volcanoes (e.g., Popocatepetl, Ixtacihuatl, Orizaba, Paricutín). Acapulco and Mazatlán are harbors on the Pacific; Tampico and Veracruz on the Gulf of Mexico. The Laguna District, an irrigated area in N, is agriculturally productive, but most of N is desert and semiarid with stock-raising the principal occupation. Population is mostly on central plateau with principal cities located there—MEXICO city, GUADALAJARA, MONTERREY, PUEBLA; in them are most industries, except for oil industry on E coast, mining in the mountains, and many home crafts (pottery, baskets, weaving). Climate varies with altitude; although Mexico lies mostly in tropical zone, it has hot, temperate, and cool areas. Agr. products vary with the climate, (tropical fruits, rubber, chicle, sugar cane, cacao, corn, wheat, tobacco, cotton). The country was the seat of highly developed ancient Indian civilizations; MAYA, TOLTEC, AZTEC, Mixtec, and Zapotec. Early visits to coast had been made by Fernández de Córdoba, 1517, and Grijalva, 1518, and soon Spanish conquest was accomplished under Cortés after 1519. In 1528 the first *audiencia* was set up, and the viceroyalty of New Spain under Antonio de Mendoza was estab. in 1535. Most of present Mexico and former Spanish holdings in present U.S. (from Ga. and Fla. to Calif.) were occupied in 16th and 17th cent. Population developed slowly into three groups—white, mestizo, Indian—who did not coalesce easily in spite of efforts of some able administrators and churchmen (e.g., ZUMÁRRAGA; the two Luis de VELASCO). Friction between these groups, plus dissatisfaction with the political power of the Church and with the Spanish mercantilist system which drained Mexico of its mineral wealth all helped bring about the rebellion against Spain led by the priest Hidalgo y Costilla, who issued the *grito de Dolores* on Sept. 16, 1811. Independence was finally achieved in 1821, with the establishment of a short-lived empire under Agustín de Iturbide. A period of selfish strife among leaders (notably SANTA ANNA) brought a series of presidents for the next several decades, with land problems and other social evils going unsolved. In 1836, Texas successfully revolted against Mexico, and in 1845, when the U.S. accepted Texas as a state, the Mexican War ensued. A democratic reform movement was led by Benito Juárez and resulted in the constitution of 1857. The conservatives sought aid abroad, and with the help of French soldiers were able to make Maximilian emperor of Mexico (1864–67). Juárez opposed the empire and at its fall again ruled Mexico but was unable to put his reforms into effect. Porfirio Díaz became president in 1876 and continued as dictator of Mexico until 1910. His regime was marked by material development, increase in foreign investments, and growth of national wealth but social conditions steadily worsened and education stagnated. A revolution, led by Francisco I. Madero in 1910, succeeded. Madero, however, proved incapable of accomplishing reforms, and another period of civil war followed under such leaders as Huerta, Carranza, Zapata, Villa (whose troubles with the U.S. brought on a U.S. expedition into Mexico, 1916), Obregon, and De la Huerta. A reform constitution was adopted in 1917, still the basic constitution of Mexico. Under it mineral wealth was expropriated from foreign owners. Politically CALLES was long dominant. With the inauguration of Lázaro Cardenas (1934) a vigorous program of social, educational, and industrial reforms was instituted which has continued to the present. The building of the Inter-American Highway greatly increased the number of U.S. tourists. Mexico declared war on the Axis powers in 1942; in 1945, the Inter-American Conference on the Problems of War and Peace met in Mexico city and drew up the Act of Chapultepec (see PAN-AMERICANISM). Later presidents are: Manuel Ávila Camacho (1940–46), Miguel Alemán (1946–52), Adolfo Ruiz Cortines (1952–).

Mexico, state (8,268 sq. mi.; pop. 1,317,303), central Mexico; cap. TOLUCA. State encircles the Federal District except on the S. A range of high mountains (N–S) lies between Toluca and Mexico city, but most of the state lies in the flat Valley of Mexico. Mining, agr., and stock raising are chief activities; mfg. includes processing of agr. and dairy products, making of textiles, baskets, glassware, pottery, bricks.

Mexico, city (pop. 1,448,422; alt. 7,800 ft.), central Mexico, cap. and largest city of Mexico, in SW part of Valley of Mexico near S end of plateau of Anáhuac on site of former L. Texcoco. The volcanoes of Popocatepetl and Ixtacihuatl are near by. The climate is cool, dry (with rainy season late May–early Sept.), and healthful. The city fans out from a central plaza (called the Zócalo) where the cathedral and Natl. Palace are located to the sprawling suburbs (called *colonias*). Near-by places of interest include Xochimilco, Guadalupe Hidalgo, and pyramids of Teotihuacán. Architecturally the city is a mixture of buildings of various styles—Spanish colonial, 19th-cent. French, starkly modern. The Natl. Univ. (founded in 16th cent.), which until Nov., 1952, was scattered throughout the city, has been consolidated in a completely modern University City in a suburb. Many of the public buildings have murals by Diego Rivera, Orozco, and Siqueiros. The city's chief problems have from its beginning been its drainage system and a potable water supply. Many of its finest buildings (notably the Palace of Fine Arts) are sinking as a result of the drying of the old lake bed. The completion in 1951 of a $26,000,000 project bringing water from L. Lerma has solved the water-supply problem. From the time that Cortés built a city where the Aztec capital, TENOCHTITLÁN, had stood throughout the Spanish regime, the brief empires of Iturbide and Maximilian, and the republic of Mexico, it has been not only the political capital but the financial and cultural center of the nation. Recent industrial developments plus a tourist trade mounting since completion of the Inter-American highway has brought increasing prosperity.

Mexico, city (pop. 11,623), central Mo., NE of Columbia, in farm area; laid out 1836. Raises saddle horses. Has mfg. of firebrick and shoes.

Mexico, Gulf of, arm of Atlantic Ocean, 700,000 sq. mi., 1,000 mi. E–W, 800 mi. N–S; bordered N by U.S., SW by Mexico; opens to Atlantic through Florida Straits (Gulf Stream exit) N of Cuba, to Caribbean through Yucatan Channel S of Cuba. Deepest part (Sigsbee Deep) 12,714 ft. Shore line mostly low, sandy, marshy. Main ports are Tampico and Veracruz in Mexico; Corpus Christi, Galveston, Houston, Mobile, New Orleans, and Pensacola in U.S.; and Havana in Cuba. Receives Mississippi, Sabine, Brazos, Colorado (of Texas), and Rio Grande rivers. Has oil deposits.

Meyer, Adolf (ä'dôlf mī'ůr), 1866–1950, American psychiatrist, b. Switzerland. He suggested term "mental hygiene" and was active in the movement in U.S. His system, psychobiology, considered each patient's problem in light of his total personality.

Meyer, Conrad Ferdinand (kôn'rät fĕr'dēnänt mī'ůr), 1825–98, Swiss poet and novelist, one of the foremost stylists in modern German literature. His short novels are usually laid in the Renaissance period.

Meyer, Lothar (lōtär' mī'ůr), 1830–95, German chemist. Contributed to development of PERIODIC LAW; evolved atomic volume curve.

Meyerbeer, Giacomo (jäkō'mō mī'yůrbâr), 1791–1864, German composer, of Jewish ancestry, whose real name was Jakob Liebmann Beer. He wrote in many forms, but his greatest success was in opera—*Robert le Diable, Les Huguenots, Le Prophète, L'Africaine,* and *Dinorah.*

Meyerhof, Otto (ô'tō mī'ůrhōf), 1884–1951, German physiologist. Shared 1922 Nobel Prize in Physiology and Medicine for work on cellular oxidation and transformation of lactic acid in muscles.

Meynell, Alice (Thompson) (mĕ'nůl), 1847–1922, English poet and essayist on Roman Catholic themes. Her poems, variously published, were collected in 1923.

Mézières (māzyĕr'), town (pop. 7,898), cap. of Ardennes dept., NE France, on the Meuse opposite Charleville, its twin city. Its capture (1918) by the Allies marked last major battle of World War I.

Mg, chemical symbol of the element MAGNESIUM.

Miami. 1 Town (pop. 4,329), E Ariz., near GLOBE, in mining area; copper-smelting center. **2** City (pop. 249,276), SE Fla., on Biscayne Bay at mouth of Miami R. Largest city in state and one of leading resorts (esp. in winter) of E U.S., with extensive recreational facilities. Air transportation center, with a number of air bases (private and governmental) and important connections with Latin America. Handles coastal and foreign shipping. Greater Miami includes Miami, MIAMI BEACH, CORAL GABLES, and HIALEAH. Settled in 1870s near site of a Seminole War post, Fort Dallas. H. M. Flagler made it a rail terminus in 1896, dredged the harbor, and began city's development as a resort. Greatest growth came during land boom of 1920s. A Seminole Indian village is at Musa Isle. **3** City (pop. 11,801), NE Okla., on Neosho R. Center for lead, zinc, cattle, and farm area.

Miami, Fort: see FORT WAYNE, Ind.; SAINT JOSEPH, Mich.; MAUMEE, Ohio.

Miami, Great and **Little,** rivers: see GREAT MIAMI.

Miami, University of: see CORAL GABLES, Fla.

Miami Beach, city (pop. 46,282), SE Fla., part of Greater Miami, on island between Biscayne Bay (crossed by causeways) and the Atlantic. Developed slowly until 1920s. Popular resort.

Miamisburg, city (pop. 6,329), SW Ohio, on Great Miami R. and SW of Dayton, in state's leading tobacco area. Near by is large Indian mound.

Miami Shores. 1 Village (pop. 5,086), SE Fla. Separated 1932 from Miami. **2** Former name of NORTH MIAMI, Fla.

Miami Springs, town (pop. 5,108), SE Fla., NW suburb of Miami.

Miami University: see OXFORD, Ohio.

Miaskovsky, Nikolai (Yakovlevich) (nyĭkůlī' myŭskôf'skē), 1881–1950, Russian composer of symphonies and chamber, piano, and vocal music.

mica (mī'ků), name for group of minerals, silicates of aluminum and potassium. Mica splits into thin, elastic sheets; occurs in granites, gneiss, schist. Common varieties are muscovite (usually colorless) and biotite (black). Sheet mica is used in many ways, e.g., as insulating material, to make diaphragms for phonographs, loud-speakers, etc.; it is ground for use in fancy paints and for various ornamental purposes. Chief sources are India and Brazil.

Micah or **Micheas** (mīkē'–), book of Old Testament. The prophet Micah, a contemporary of Isaiah (fl. 710 B.C.), foretold doom of Judah and Israel. Messianic prophecy in 5.2–6 is famous. Mat. 2.6; John 7.42.

Michael [Heb.,= Who is like God?], archangel, who appears in Bible as prince or warrior. Dan. 10.13,21; 12.1; Jude 9; Rev. 12.7. In Christian tradition he is the conqueror of Satan and carries a sword and has appeared at various times to humans (e.g., to Joan of Arc). His chief feast, called Michaelmas, is Sept. 29.

Michael, Byzantine emperors. **Michael I** (Michael Rhangabe), d. c.845, reigned 811–13. Recalled Theodore of Studium from exile. Was deposed after being routed by Bulgars. **Michael II** (the Stammerer), d. 829, a Phrygian, helped Leo V to power after Michael I's deposition. He became emperor in 820 after his supporters had murdered Leo. The controversy over ICONOCLASM, which he favored over orthodoxy, was ended during the minority of his grandson, **Michael III** (the Drunkard), 839–67, who reigned 842–67. The iconoclasts were overthrown, the PAULICIANS persecuted. Addicted to drink and debauches, Michael left the government to his uncle, the Caesar Bardas, whose able administration was marked by the missions of SS. CYRIL AND METHODIUS. Michael's boon companion Basil had Bardas murdered in 866, murdered Michael in 867, and became emperor as BASIL I. **Michael VIII,** 1224–82, first of the Palaeologus dynasty, became emperor of Nicaea in 1259 by first sharing, then usurping, the throne of John IV, whom he had blinded and imprisoned. In 1261 he recovered Constantinople by an ingenious stratagem (his soldiers entered at night through an unused aqueduct). Thus the Latin Empire fell and the Byzantine Empire was restored. The rest of his life was spent in struggle with the Seljuk Turks and with CHARLES I of Naples. To win papal support against Charles he negotiated for union of the Eastern and Western Churches (see LYONS, SECOND COUNCIL OF), but eventually failed. He helped to prepare the SICILIAN VESPERS, which broke Charles's power. An able scholar, he left an interesting autobiography.

Michael (Michael Romanov), 1596–1645, tsar of Russia (1613–45), founder of ROMANOV dynasty. His election ended Time of Troubles (see DMITRI).

Michael, 1921–, king of Rumania. His father, Prince Carol (later CAROL II), having renounced the succession, he became king in 1927 under a regency. In 1930 Carol returned to be recognized as king, but on Carol's abdication in 1940 Michael became king again. He overthrew the dictatorship of ANTONESCU in 1944 and made an armistice with the Allies. In 1947 his Communist-dominated government forced him to abdicate. In exile, he married Princess Anne of Bourbon-Parma.

Michael (Michael Obrenovich), 1823–68, prince of Serbia. Succeeded his brother Milan 1839. His attempts at reform led to his deposition in 1842. Alexander Karageorgevich became prince, but in 1858 Michael's father MILOSH was restored. On Milosh's death (1860) Michael became prince again. He modernized his country and prepared its complete liberation from Turkish vassalage. He was murdered by members of the Karageorgevich faction.

Michaelmas: see MICHAEL, archangel.

Michaelmas daisy: see ASTER.

Michael the Brave, d. 1601, prince of Walachia (1593–1601). After ordering a general massacre of the Turks in Walachia, he forced the sultan to grant him virtual independence (1596) and conquered Transylvania (1599) and Moldavia (1600). His dealings with the imperial court of Vienna were marked by duplicity on both sides and ended with his assassination by an imperial agent. His empire fell apart on his death.

Michal (mī'kůl), daughter of Saul, wife of David. 1 Sam. 18.20; 19.12; 2 Sam. 6.16. See MERAB.

Micheas (mīkē'ůs), variant of MICAH.

Michelangelo (Buonarroti) (mīkůlăn'jůlō, Ital. mēkälän'jälō bwônär-rō'tē), 1475–1564, Italian artist, one of the greatest figures of Italian Renaissance and of world art history, b. Caprese, Tuscany. Studied in Florence with Domenico Ghirlandaio and at art school held in Medici gardens. Lived two years of his youth in palace of Lorenzo de' Medici, where he met the humanists Pico della Mirandola and Politian. Worked in Rome (1496–1501) and carved *Bacchus* (Bargello, Florence) and *Pietà* (St. Peter's, Rome). Returning to Florence (1501), he was commissioned by the city to execute the giant *David* (Academy, Florence). Called to Rome in 1505 to execute tomb for Pope Julius II, but major interruptions, such as work on ceiling of SISTINE CHAPEL (1508–12), kept the project uncompleted for c.30 years; most significant work on it includes colossal *Moses* (San Pietro in Vincoli, Rome). Worked 1520–34 on Medici chapel (Florence), in which he achieved unity of sculpture and architecture. In 1529 he assisted as engineer in defense of Florence. After suppression of Florentine freedom he again went to Rome. Sonnets written in this period were inspired by the young nobleman Tommaso Cavalieri and the poetess Vittoria Colonna. Painted the *Last Judgment* (Sistine Chapel) 1534–41 and executed frescoes for Pauline Chapel (Vatican) 1541–50. In 1546 he became chief architect of St. Peter's. *Pietà* in Florence cathedral shows tendency toward the spiritual in his old age.

Michelet, Jules (zhül' mēshůlā'), 1798–1874, French writer, greatest historian of romantic school. Major work *Histoire de France* (many vols., 1833–67).

Michelozzi, Michelozzo (mēkälôt'tsō mēkälôt'-tsē), 1396–1472, Italian architect and sculptor. With Brunelleschi he shared leadership in establishing Renaissance style. Built Riccardi Palace and Medici Chapel in Santa Croce (both in Florence).

Michelson, Albert Abraham (mī'kůlsůn), 1852–1931, American physicist. He won 1907 Nobel Prize and is known especially for his determination of velocity of light and experimental studies of ether drift which contributed to theory of relativity.

Michener, James A(lbert), 1907–, American author. His works include *Tales of the South Pacific* (1947; later made into the musical play *South Pacific*), *The Fires of Spring* (1949), *Return to Paradise* (1951), and *The Voice of Asia* (1951).

Michigan, state (57,022 sq. mi.; pop. 6,371,-766), N U.S., in Great Lakes region; admitted 1837 as 26th state (free); cap. LANSING. Other cities are DETROIT, GRAND RAPIDS, FLINT, DEARBORN, PONTIAC. In two parts, Upper Peninsula and Lower Peninsula, separated by Straits of Mackinac. Farming (dairying, grains, fruits, potatoes, livestock); mining (iron, copper, oil, salt); fishing; lumbering. Mfg. of motor vehicles and parts, steel, machinery, food products, airplanes, furniture, paper; printing and publishing. First explored and settled by French; important fur-trading center. Taken by English in French and Indian Wars. Passed to U.S. after American Revolution. In British hands in War of 1812 until W. H. Harrison in battle of the Thames and O. H. Perry in battle of L. Erie restored American prestige. Period of economic expansion preceded Civil War; Mich. supported Union. Farmer discontent in late 19th cent. brought legislation for agrarian improvement. 20th cent. has seen rise of automobile industry (esp. under Henry FORD). Labor unions gained not without conflicts, in 1930s–40s. World War II saw great industrial expansion.

Michigan, Lake, 22,400 sq. mi., 307 mi. long, 118 mi. wide, 923 ft. deep; third largest of

Great Lakes, 579.79 ft. above sea level. Mich. is E and N, Ill. and Wis. W, and Ind. S. Empties NE into L. Huron. Linked with Mississippi R. by Illinois Waterway. Ports to N are icebound four months a year. Much shipping is done despite abrupt, fierce storms. Shore cities include Michigan City and Gary, Ind.; Chicago, Evanston, and Waukegan, Ill.; Kenosha, Racine, Milwaukee, Manitowoc, and Two Rivers, Wis.; Escanaba, Manistee, Ludington, Muskegon, Grand Haven, and Benton Harbor, Mich. Green Bay is largest arm. Discovered 1634 by Jean Nicolet.

Michigan, University of, at Ann Arbor, state supported, coed. Chartered 1817 as Catholepistemiad (or University) of Michigania, rechartered 1821 and 1837; opened as school in Detroit 1817, reopened as college in Ann Arbor 1841. Has noted library and museums and observatories in Ann Arbor, in South Africa, and near Detroit.

Michigan City, city (pop. 28,395), NW Ind., on L. Michigan ENE of Gary; settled 1830. Summer resort. Mfg. of furniture, Pullman cars.

Michigan State College of Agriculture and Applied Science, at East Lansing; with land-grant support, coed; chartered 1855, opened 1857 as first state agricultural college, renamed 1925. Has courses in police administration.

Michilimackinac: see MACKINAC.

Michoacán (mēchōäkän'), state (23,202 sq. mi.; pop. 1,412,830), W Mexico; cap. MORELIA. Extends from the Pacific to the central plateau, with wide variation in topography, climate, and soil. Mining is chief occupation in mountains (Sierra Madre Occidental and E-W volcanic chain). Fine cabinet wood and dyewoods come from forests. Agr. dominates state; sugar cane, coffee, vanilla, tobacco, cereals. Of interest to tourists are L. PÁTZCUARO, L. CHAPALA, PARICUTÍN (volcano), TARASCAN INDIANS.

Michurin, Ivan Vladimirovich (ēvän' vlŭdyē'mĭrŭvĭch mēchōō'rĭn), 1855–1935, Russian horticulturist. His theory that hereditary changes can be induced by grafting and that acquired characters are inherited was elaborated by T. D. Lysenko and his followers and was officially supported (1948) by Soviet Central Committee.

Mickiewicz, Adam (mētskyĕ'vĭch), 1798–1855, greatest romantic poet of Poland. Arrested (1823) for activities in secret patriotic societies, he was deported to Russia, whence he fled (1829). He taught literature in Paris after 1840 and died in Constantinople, where he was organizing a Polish legion against Russia. His chief works (all tr. into English) are the epic poems *Pan Tadeusz* (1834) and *Konrad Wallenrod* (1825–28) and the dramatic poem *Forefather's Eve* (1823).

Micon (mī'kŏn), fl. c.460 B.C., Greek painter and sculptor. Collaborated with Polygnotus in painting the *Battle of Marathon* in Stoa Poecile, Athens.

microbiology: see BIOLOGY.

Micronesia (mīkrōnē'zhŭ), one of three main divisions of Pacific islands, in W Pacific, N of equator. Includes the Carolines, Marshalls, Marianas, and Gilbert Isls. Inhabitants stem from Negroid and Mongoloid stock and speak Malayo-Polynesian languages (see LANGUAGE, table).

microphone (mī'krŭfōn), device converting acoustic energy of sound waves into electrical energy waves, used to record, broadcast, and amplify sound. Early types based on fact of resistance varying inversely with pressure holding electrical contacts together. Other common types generate audio voltages responding to pressure of sound; crystal type uses piezoelectric effect of Rochelle salt crystals. Ribbon or velocity type and moving coil or dynamic type both use Faraday electromagnetic induction principle.

microscope, optical instrument used to increase apparent size of object. Magnifying glass, a double convex LENS, is simple microscope. When object is placed within focal length of double convex lens, a virtual IMAGE is produced which is erect and larger than object; magnification is expressed in diameters. Compound microscope is two or more such lenses fixed in hollow metal tube; tube can be raised or lowered. Object is magnified by lower lens, image of object by upper. It is used to examine unicellular organisms, cells, and tissues. Ultramicroscope consists of compound microscope with arrangement by which object to be viewed is illuminated by point of light at right angles to plane of objective (lower lens) and focused beneath it; used in studying colloids. Electron microscope permits greater magnification and depth of focus; uses instead of light rays a stream of electrons controlled by electric or magnetic fields. Image may be thrown on fluorescent screen or photographed. Invention of compound microscope ascribed to Zacharias Janssen c.1590 and to Galileo 1609 or 1610.

Midas (mī'dŭs), in Greek legend, king of Phrygia. Because he befriended Silenus, Dionysus granted him the power of turning everything into gold by touch. Tired of his gift when even food became gold, he washed away the power in Pactolus R. A historical King Midas of Phrygia lived in 8th cent. B.C.

Middelburg, municipality (pop. 20,605), cap. of Zeeland prov., SW Netherlands, on Walcheren isl., NNE of Flushing. It flourished commercially in Middle Ages and belonged to Hanseatic League. Now a trade and mfg. center, it produces wood, metal, and food products. It was captured 1574 as last Spanish fortress in Zeeland. Flooded in World War II and taken 1944 by British troops, but 15th-cent. city hall and 12th-cent. abbey remain.

Middle Ages, period in W European history, also called Dark Ages. Exact dates are misleading, but period began roughly with fall of Western Roman Empire in 476, and ended with discovery of America by Columbus in 1492. End of period also marked by REFORMATION, change in scholarship and fine arts known as RENAISSANCE, and invention of printing. Christianity was a struggling religion early in the period but became the binding force of medieval culture. Through religious leaders like St. THOMAS AQUINAS and St. FRANCIS of Assisi unity of Europe was in faith, doctrine, and institutions of Christianity. Empires of CHARLEMAGNE and HOLY ROMAN EMPIRE were ambitious but insecure. A secular institution allied with Christianity was chivalry. Conspicuous military adventures included CRUSADES. GOTHIC ARCHITECTURE was originated and carried to highest development. In literature, masters were DANTE and CHAUCER. Secular organizations were typically local (see FEUDALISM), artisans banded in GUILDS.

Middleboro, town (pop. 10,164), including Middleboro village (pop. 5,889), SE Mass., between Plymouth and Taunton; settled 1660. Mfg. of shoes.

Middlebury, town (pop. 4,778), W Vt., S of Burlington; permanently settled 1783. Sheldon Art Mus. (1829) has colonial collections. Seat of **Middlebury College** (nonsectarian; coed.; 1800); holds noted conference for writers and foreign-language summer schools at near-by Bread Loaf.

middle class: see BOURGEOISIE.

Middle English literature, 1100–1500, literature in transitional dialects between Anglo-Saxon and modern English. Much writing in England at the time was in Latin and in Anglo-Norman (French). Until c.1250 English works were mostly religious (e.g., in prose, ANCREN RIWLE; in verse, *An Orison of Our Lady*), but there also appeared some secular works (e.g., *Brut* of LAYAMON; OWL AND THE NIGHTINGALE; SUMER IS ICUMEN IN, rhymed lyric for a love song). Writing in Anglo-Norman, the language of the upper classes, produced more sophisticated works such as lais by Marie de France and the *Tristan* romance by Thomas of Britain. As English became the ascendant language (1250–1350), many works were composed, both religious (e.g., *The Debate of the Body and Soul;* writings of mystic Richard Rolle) and secular, mainly romances—some adapted from French such as those of the ARTHURIAN LEGEND, others from English tradition such as HAVELOK THE DANE. The last half of the 14th cent. saw the apex of Middle English in the works of the anonymous poet of The PEARL and SIR GAWAIN AND THE GREEN KNIGHT; William LANGLAND, supposed author of PIERS PLOWMAN; and Geoffrey CHAUCER, the outstanding Middle English artist and one of greatest figures of English literature. A lesser contemporary was John GOWER. In the 15th cent., numerous English imitators of Chaucer appeared, such as John LYDGATE, King JAMES I and Robert HENRYSON. Also in the 15th cent. appeared some excellent anonymous poetry in the carol and BALLAD, and English medieval drama reached a peak in the Wakefield mystery cycle (see MIRACLE PLAY) and the morality *Everyman*. Expressive, flexible English prose developed in the translation of the Bible by John PURVEY, in popular translations like the *Voiage* of Sir John MANDEVILLE, and in the vigorous narrative of the *Morte d'Arthur* of Sir Thomas MALORY.

Middlesboro, city (pop. 14,482), S Ky., in the Cumberlands at point where Ky., Tenn., and Va. meet; founded 1889. Resort and center of mining and agr. area, has metal and wood products. Cumberland Gap, Pinnacle Mt., and Cudjo's Cave are near by.

Middlesbrough (–brù), county borough (pop. 147,336), N. Riding of Yorkshire, England, on Tees R. estuary. Has great iron and steel plants and metallurgical schools, libraries, and museums.

Middlesex, inland county (232 sq. mi.; pop. 2,268,776), S central England, within Greater London area. Residential suburb traversed by main traffic routes. Towns include Brentford, Harrow, Tottenham, Uxbridge, Hampton, Hounslow, and Staines.

Middlesex, borough (pop. 5,943), N central N.J., near Bound Brook. Paint, tiles, metal products.

Middle Temple: see INNS OF COURT.

Middleton, Conyers, 1683–1750, English clergyman, rationalistic theologian and controversialist; librarian (after 1721) at Cambridge Univ. He had celebrated arguments with Richard Bentley, and his *Letter from Rome, Showing an Exact Conformity between Popery and Paganism* (1729) roused a storm of protest.

Middleton, Thomas, 1570?–1627, English dramatist and pamphleteer. Wrote realistic comedies, such as *A Trick to Catch the Old One* (1608), *The Honest Whore* (1604; with Dekker), and a tragicomedy, *The Witch* (1617). His most powerful tragedies were *The Changeling* and *Women Beware Women* (both c.1623). His pamphlets show intimacy with London's underworld.

Middletown. 1 City (pop. 29,711), central Conn., on Connecticut R. (bridged here 1938) below Hartford; settled 1650. Textiles, metal goods, chemicals. Seat of Wesleyan Univ. (liberal arts college; nonsectarian; for men); opened 1831 by Methodists. **2** City (pop. 22,586), SE N.Y. SW of Newburgh. Farm trade center with railroad shops, foundries; clothing, textiles, chemicals, leather goods. **3** City (pop. 33,695), SW Ohio, on Great Miami R. and near Hamilton; laid out 1802. Trade center in agr. area with steel-rolling and paper mills; mfg. of clothing, textiles, and machinery. **4** Borough (pop. 9,184), SE Pa., on Susquehanna R. and SE of Harrisburg. Mfg. of stoves, clothing, and shoes. **5** Resort town (pop. 7,382), SE R.I., between Newport and Portsmouth on Rhode Isl.

Middletown: see LYND, ROBERT STAUGHTON.

Middle West or **Midwest,** part of U.S. about Great Lakes and upper Mississippi valley. This vague term is sometimes applied to all of N U.S. between the Alleghenies and the Rockies, but more often to only Ohio, Ind., Ill., Mich., Wis., Minn., Iowa, Mo., Kansas, and Nebr. The Dakotas may be included, and even Prairie Provs. of Canada. Some of world's richest farm land, it is known for corn and hogs and wheat. Has huge industries, such as mfg. of cars and tires. Popularly conservative, isolationist, Protestant, "American," the region actually has a variety of creeds and peoples. The region has a distinctive dialect of English.

Midgard [Norse,= middle court], in Norse mythology, the earth.

Midhat Pasha (mĭd-hät′ pä′shä), 1822–84, Turkish statesman. Leader of the reforming

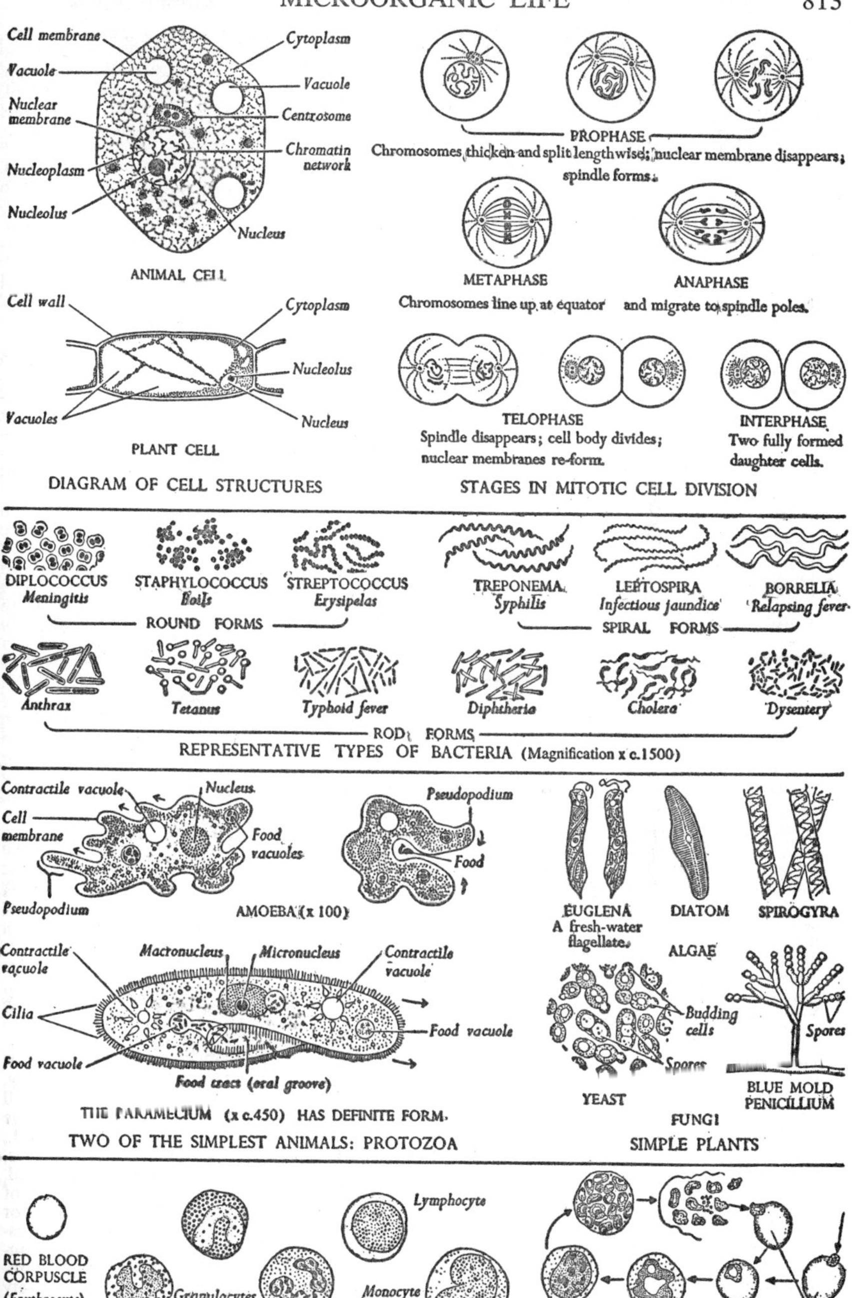
Cell membrane
Cytoplasm
Vacuole
Vacuole
Nuclear membrane
Centrosome
Chromatin network
Nucleoplasm
Nucleolus
Nucleus
ANIMAL CELL
Cell wall
Cytoplasm
Nucleolus
Vacuoles
Nucleus
PLANT CELL
DIAGRAM OF CELL STRUCTURES
PROPHASE
Chromosomes thicken and split lengthwise; nuclear membrane disappears; spindle forms.
METAPHASE
Chromosomes line up at equator
ANAPHASE
and migrate to spindle poles.
TELOPHASE
Spindle disappears; cell body divides; nuclear membranes re-form.
INTERPHASE
Two fully formed daughter cells.
STAGES IN MITOTIC CELL DIVISION
DIPLOCOCCUS
Meningitis
STAPHYLOCOCCUS
Boils
STREPTOCOCCUS
Erysipelas
ROUND FORMS
TREPONEMA
Syphilis
LEPTOSPIRA
Infectious jaundice
BORRELIA
Relapsing fever
SPIRAL FORMS
Anthrax
Tetanus
Typhoid fever
Diphtheria
Cholera
Dysentery
ROD FORMS
REPRESENTATIVE TYPES OF BACTERIA (Magnification x c.1500)
Contractile vacuole
Nucleus
Cell membrane
Food vacuoles
Pseudopodium
Pseudopodium
Food
AMOEBA (x 100)
EUGLENA
A fresh-water flagellate.
DIATOM
SPIROGYRA
ALGAE
Contractile vacuole
Macronucleus
Micronucleus
Contractile vacuole
Cilia
Food vacuole
Food vacuole
Food tract (oral groove)
THE PARAMECIUM (x c.450) HAS DEFINITE FORM.
TWO OF THE SIMPLEST ANIMALS: PROTOZOA
Budding cells
Spores
Spores
YEAST
BLUE MOLD
PENICILLIUM
FUNGI
SIMPLE PLANTS
RED BLOOD CORPUSCLE
(Erythrocyte)
(x 1000)
Lymphocyte
Granulocytes
Monocyte
WHITE BLOOD CORPUSCLES, (Leucocytes) (x 900)
BLOOD CELLS These do not divide, but are formed by body organs.
Erythrocytes
Series showing erythrocyte being invaded by malaria parasite.

party that deposed Abdu-l-Aziz (1876), he framed the first Turkish constitution but was soon dismissed by Abdu-l-Hamid II and was later strangled.

Midi, Pic du, France: see PIC DU MIDI.

Midianites (mĭ'dēŭn–), enemies of the Hebrews who were defeated by Gideon. Gen. 25.2; 37.28,36; Ex. 3.1; Num. 31.1–9; Judges 6–8.

Midland, town (pop. 7,206), S Ont., Canada, on E Georgian Bay and W of Toronto. Port with government coal dock, textile mills, and mfg. of machinery. Near by is shrine to Jesuit martyrs.

Midland. 1 City (pop. 14,285), S Mich., at junction of Pine, Chippewa, and Tittabawassee rivers W of Bay City. Early lumber town, developed after 1890 by Dow Chemical Co. Oil, coal, and salt in area. **2** Borough (pop. 6,491), W Pa., on Ohio R and NW of Pittsburgh. Mfg. of steel, machinery, and coke. Has shipyard and railroad shops. **3** City (pop. 21,713), W Texas, on S border of Llano Estacado, WNW of San Angelo; settled 1885. Oil company offices and plants (fields at Odessa). Cattle shipping and cotton ginning.

Midland Park, borough (pop. 5,164), NE N.J., N of Paterson. Textiles.

Midlands, region of central England. Includes the counties of Bedford, Buckingham, Derby, Leicester, Northampton, Nottingham, Rutland, and Warwick.

Midlothian (mĭdlō'dhēŭn), formerly **Edinburghshire,** county (366 sq. mi.; pop. 565,-746), E central Scotland. County town is EDINBURGH, cap. of Scotland. Mainly agr. region (market gardening, stock raising, and dairying), it also has fishing and mfg. (paper, whisky, and ironware). Leith and Granton are shipbuilding centers.

Midrash (mĭd'răsh) [Heb.,= investigation], a homiletical interpretation of the Scriptures by Jewish rabbis since A.D. c.200. It is incorporated in the Mishna of the TALMUD, and, like the Gemara, contains elements of both HALAKAH and haggada. Midrashim were compiled for many books of the Bible.

midsummer day, feast of the nativity of St. John the Baptist, June 24. The preceding night is **midsummer night** or St. John's Eve, and because it comes near the solstice, it is in many parts of Europe connected with magic. Great bonfires are built and there is merrymaking. Emphasis on love and lovers on this night undoubtedly reflects old fertility rites.

Midway, group (2 sq. mi.; pop. 473) comprising Sand and Eastern islands with surrounding atoll, central Pacific, c.1,150 mi. NW of Honolulu. U.S. discovery (1859); annexed 1867. Cable station (1903), and civil (1935) and military (1941) air base. Scene (June 5–6, 1942) of **battle of Midway,** a decisive U.S. victory in World War II. Fought entirely with aircraft, it caused destruction of a Japanese battle fleet, crippling of Japanese navy, and end of Pacific invasion threat.

Midwest: see MIDDLE WEST.

Midwest City, residential town (pop. 10,166), central Okla., Oklahoma City suburb.

midwifery: see OBSTETRICS.

Mieris (mē'rĭs), family of Dutch genre and portrait painters of Leiden. **Frans van Mieris,** 1635–81, the most important, excelled in faithful rendering of texture. His sons and pupils were **Jan van Mieris,** 1660–90, and **Willem van Mieris,** 1662–1747.

Miës van der Rohe, Ludwig (lo͞ot'vĭkh mē'ĕs vän dĕr rō'ŭ), 1886–, German-American architect. Headed the BAUHAUS, 1932–33. In 1938 became director of Armour Inst. (now Illinois Inst. of Technology).

Mifflin, Thomas, 1744–1800, American Revolutionary general and politician. Rose to be quartermaster general. President of Continental Congress (1783–84). Governor of Pa. (1790–99).

Mignard, Pierre (pyĕr' mēnyär'), 1610–95, French painter. Lived many years in Italy and did portraits of two popes. In France he served Louis XIV.

mignonette (mĭnyŭnĕt'), Old World annual (*Reseda odorata*) with small sweetly fragrant flowers of white, yellowish, or greenish.

migraine (mī'grān, mĭgrān'), intense headache usually recurring periodically. Pain, commonly arising in one temple, results from expansion of arteries in neck and brain and is often attended by visual disturbances, vertigo, and nausea.

migration, movement of people into new and usually distant areas. Migrations, which played an important part in the peopling of the world, have been due to physical changes (e.g., glaciers) or economic, political, or religious pressure. Internal migration is exemplified by population shift from country to city. See IMMIGRATION; MIGRATORY LABOR.

migration of animals, movements of animals in large numbers from one place to another. Sporadic migrations are made by the LEMMING, the locust or migratory grasshopper, and the army worm. Many butterflies undertake seasonal migrations. SALMON migrate from salt water to fresh water to breed, and the freshwater EEL breeds in the Atlantic Ocean SE of Bermuda. Sea turtles return to land to lay eggs. In Africa, game animals migrate to avoid drought. Regular seasonal migrations are best exemplified by birds, but the causes of these flights are not fully understood. Various theories attribute migration to climatic changes and glacial movements in geologic time, to failure of food supply and temperature changes, and to need for avoiding overcrowding at breeding season. Many agree, however, that migration probably results from an environmental stimulus and an allied physiological one. Experiments made by William Rowan with juncos and other birds support the theory that the chief external stimulus is variation in day length (with resulting variation in amount of activity) causing enlargement of reproductive organs, and the internal stimulus is the production of a hormone by the reproductive organs. Especially long migrations are made by the arctic TERN and golden PLOVER.

migratory labor (mī'grŭtô"rē), workers such as those who follow crops from place to place, or urban dwellers who seek seasonal employment on the land. In the 1930s, many farmers of the plains states—perhaps as many as 3,000,000 in all—became migrants because of drought. In wartime, migratory workers travel about to jobs in war plants.

Miguel (mēgĕl′), 1802–66, Portuguese prince; younger brother of PEDRO I of Brazil. In 1826 he became guardian of Pedro's daughter MARIA II, to whom he was betrothed, but in 1828 he accepted the crown for himself from the Cortes. Supported by the reactionary factions, he fought against the liberal forces commanded by Pedro I, who had English support (1832–34). Defeated, he left Portugal. Miguelist uprisings against Maria II all failed.

Mikhailovich, Draja or **Dragoliub** (drä′zhä mēhī′lôvĭch, drä′gôlyōōb″), 1893?–1946, Yugoslav soldier. In World War II he led Serbian guerrilla forces (*chetniks*) in successful operations against the Axis armies; was promoted to general and appointed war minister by Yugoslav government in exile. He soon clashed with the partisans of Marshal TITO, who accused him of collaborating with the Axis. In 1944 his dwindling forces lost Allied support, and he was reluctantly dismissed by his king. He was captured, tried for treason at Belgrade, and executed despite world-wide protests against the irregularity of his conviction.

Mikulov, Czechoslovakia: see NIKOLSBURG.

Milan (Milan Obrenovich) (mĭ′län), 1854–1901, prince (1868–82) and king (1882–89) of Serbia. Declared war on Turkey (1876; see RUSSO-TURKISH WARS); secured recognition of full independence of Serbia at Congress of Berlin (1878); took title king (1882). After proclaiming a liberal constitution (1889), he abdicated in favor of his son Alexander.

Milan (mĭlăn′, mĭ′lŭn), Ital. *Milano,* city (pop. 1,068,079), cap. of Lombardy, N Italy. Chief industrial and commercial city of Italy; produces textiles, machinery, chemicals; leading European silk market; publishing center (esp. of music). Has a Catholic university (founded 1921), a state university (founded 1924); world-famous opera house (Teatro alla Scala); art gallery (Brera palace). Of Celtic origin, Milan (Latin *Mediolanum*) served as cap. of the late Western Empire. Twice destroyed in barbarian invasions (c.450, 539), it became a free commune in 12th cent. and, despite its destruction by Emperor Frederick I (1163), emerged as leading city of the LOMBARD LEAGUE. In the 13th cent. Milan lost its republican liberties. The VISCONTI family took control in 1277 and was succeeded in 1450 by the SFORZA. Made a duchy in 1395, Milan became one of the chief Italian states (comprising most of LOMBARDY) and a brilliant center of the Renaissance. The duchy repeatedly changed hands in the ITALIAN WARS and passed to Spain in 1535, to Austria in 1713. Bonaparte took Milan in 1796 and made it the cap. of the Cisalpine Republic (1797) and of the kingdom of Italy (1805–14). Restored to Austria in 1815, Milan briefly expelled its foreign masters in 1848. It was ceded to Sardinia in 1859. Heavily damaged in World War II, it was rebuilt along modern lines. Its best-known building is the Gothic cathedral (begun 1386, finished 1813), with its elaborate lacework in stone. Among other landmarks are a Romanesque church, founded 386 and dedicated to St. AMBROSE, the great bishop of Milan; Santa Maria delle Grazie, with a refectory containing Leonardo da Vinci's *Last Supper;* and the imposing Sforza castle, designed by Leonardo and Bramante.

Milan (mī′lŭn), village (pop. 846), N Ohio, SE of Sandusky. Birthplace of T. A. Edison.

Milan Decree, 1807, issued by Napoleon I to enforce CONTINENTAL SYSTEM. Authorized French warships and privateers to capture neutral vessels sailing from British-held territory.

mildew, fungus disease of plants which dwarfs and distorts growth. Powdery mildew, which grows on the leaf surfaces of many plants, forms a gray or white coating. Dusting with sulphur is a control. Other mildews attack leather, fabrics, and paper.

Miles, Nelson Appleton, 1839–1925, American army officer. Served in Civil War and later in Indian campaigns. Commanded troops in Pullman strike (1894). Commander in chief of army (1895–1903).

Miles City, city (pop. 9,243), SE Mont., on Yellowstone R. Grew up around Fort Keogh (1877). Makes saddles and leather goods. Ships wool and livestock.

Miletus (mīlē′tŭs), anc. seaport, W Asia Minor, in Caria, near Samos. Occupied by the Greeks in settlement of the Aegean (c.1000 B.C.), it became a principal city of Ionia. Led in colonization and took the lead in revolt against Persia (499 B.C.).

milfoil: see YARROW.

Milford. 1 Town (pop. 26,870), SW Conn., at mouth of Housatonic R. on Long Isl. Sound E of Bridgeport; settled 1639. Has resorts and yacht harbor. Produces oysters, truck, dairy products, and metal goods. **2** City (pop. 5,179), S central Del., S of Frederica. Trade center for truck farms. **3** Town (pop. 15,442), including Milford village (pop. 14,396), S Mass., SE of Worcester; settled 1662. Mfg. of shoes and metal products.

Milford Haven, urban district (pop. 11,717), Pembrokeshire, Wales, on N side of Milford Haven Bay; one of Britain's chief fishing ports.

Milhaud, Darius (däryüs′ mēyō′), 1892–, French composer, now teaching in the U.S. He often combines simple diatonic melodies in polytonal counterpoint, producing a highly dissonant effect. His compositions include operas (e.g., *Christophe Colombe;* ballets (e.g., *Le Bœuf sur le toit; or, The Nothing Doing Bar*); concertos; orchestral works (e.g., *Suite Française*); and chamber music.

Military Academy, United States; see UNITED STATES MILITARY ACADEMY.

militia, military force of volunteers, formed on permanent basis for use only in emergencies. An early example was Anglo-Saxon *fyrd.* In the 19th cent. various states of the United States had their militias, which participated in all the wars of that cent. They were superseded, in 1903, by the National Guard. Militia troops in U.S. lost importance when conscription was introduced in World War I.

Miliukov, Pavel Nikolayevich: see MILYUKOV.

Milk, river, 729 mi. long, rising in NW Mont. and flowing N into Alberta, E and S into Mont., then SE to the Missouri below Fort Peck Dam. Milk R. project irrigates c.140,000 acres, also using St. Mary R. Fresno Dam is 111 ft. high, 2,070 ft. long.

milk, glandular secretion from breast or udders of animals that suckle their young. In addition to cow's milk, man has used milk from the mare, goat, ewe, camel, ass, zebra, reindeer, and llama. Milk, the best source of calcium, contains most of the vitamins, especially vitamin A, and is a nearly complete food for infants and valuable in the diet of adults. Milk of Jersey and Guernsey cows is especially rich in fat. Skim milk, fat free, is low in vitamin A. Milk may be partially evaporated (canned milk) or dried as a powder; sweetened evaporated milk is known as condensed milk. Malted milk is a dried mixture of milk and mash of barley malt and wheat flour. DAIRYING is subject to Federal, state, and local laws. PASTEURIZATION checks bacterial growth.

milk snake: see KING SNAKE.

milk sugar: see LACTOSE.

milkweed, tall New World perennial plant of genus *Asclepias* found in swamps and open fields. The plants usually have milky sap and clusters of small flowers, purple in the common milkweed (*Asclepias syriaca*); the fruit pods enclose the many seeds, each of which bears a tuft of silk.

Milky Way system or **Galaxy** (gă'lŭksē), system of stars and nebulae. Comprises c.30 thousand million stars in the form of a disk; greatest diameter is c.100,000 light-years; thickness c.10–16 thousand light-years. Solar system is c.30,000 light-years from center. Position of earth permits observation of numerous stars appearing to form white pathway commonly called Milky Way.

Mill, James, 1773–1836, British philosopher, b. Scotland. In London he wrote and edited periodicals. His *History of India* (1817) won him a position at India House. Became an associate of Bentham and one of the leaders in utilitarian thought. His son, **John Stuart Mill,** 1806–73, developed the theories of utilitarianism, tempering them with humanitarianism, and even reflected some agreement with socialism. He insisted upon the method of empiricism as the source of all knowledge. His *Essay on Liberty* (1859) is one of the most celebrated documents of political economy. He stressed that pleasure (considered as the basic motivating force by utilitarians) should be measured by quality as well as quantity. He pushed many political and social reforms and had direct influence on events as well as a profound, indirect influence on subsequent economists and philosophers. Among his works are *System of Logic* (1843), *Principles of Political Economy* (1848), *Utilitarianism* (1863), *Auguste Comte and Positivism* (1865), and a famous autobiography (1873).

Millais, Sir John Everett (mĭlā'), 1829–96, English painter, a leading member of PRE-RAPHAELITES. Was a close friend of Ruskin.

Millay, Edna St. Vincent, 1892–1950, American lyric poet. She first attracted notice with "Renascence" (1912), and later gained a large audience with her volumes—*A Few Figs from Thistles* (1920), *Second April* (1921), *The Ballad of the Harp Weaver* (1922; later in *The Harp-Weaver and Other Poems,* 1923). She also wrote dramatic verse, as in *Aria da Capo* (1920); *The King's Henchman* (1927; libretto for opera); *The Murder of Lidice* (1942; for radio). Her sonnets (in various vols. and in *Fatal Interview,* 1931) are much admired.

Millburn, residential township (pop. 14,560), NE N.J., W of Newark; settled c.1725. Includes Short Hills.

Millbury, town (pop. 8,347), S Mass., S of Worcester. Mfg. of textiles and metal products.

Milledgeville, city (pop. 8,835), central Ga., on Oconee R. and NE of Macon. Laid out 1803 as site of state cap., it was seat of government 1804–67. Processing center for cotton and clay area. Here are Georgia State Col. for Women (1889) and many fine old classic revival houses.

Mille Lacs Lake (mĭl" lăk'), 18 mi. long, 14 mi. wide, E central Minn., N of Minneapolis. Visited 1679 by Sieur Duluth. Hennepin and companions Indian captives here 1680. Tourist and sport center.

millepede: see MILLIPEDE.

Miller, Arthur, 1915–, American dramatist, author of *All My Sons* (1947), *Death of a Salesman* (1949).

Miller, Cincinnatus Heine (or **Hiner**)**:** see MILLER, JOAQUIN.

Miller, Henry, 1860–1926, American actor-manager, b. London. Appeared with Modjeska and the Boucicault troupe. Became a star (1897) in his own play *Heartsease* and thereafter was his own manager.

Miller, Joaquin (wäkēn'), pseud. of **Cincinnatus Heine** (or **Hiner**) **Miller,** 1839?–1913. American poet, who lived on the Pacific Northwest frontier. His best-known volume is *Songs of the Sierras* (1871), and his best-known poem is "Columbus."

Miller, Joe, 1684–1738, English popular comedian. He did not actually write the collection of puns and trite witticisms called *Joe Miller's Jests,* but the publisher John Mottley put his name on it.

Miller, Kenneth Hayes, 1876–1952, American painter and teacher, associated with New York School of Art and Art Students League.

Miller, Samuel Freeman, 1816–90, Associate Justice of U.S. Supreme Court (1862–90). Concerned with general welfare, practical application of law.

Miller, William, 1782–1849, American founder (1845) of Second ADVENTISTS, often called Millerites. From 1831 he prophesied second coming of Christ in 1843, then set date in 1844.

Millerand, Alexandre (älĕksã'drù mēlrã'), 1859–1943, French politician. At first a Socialist, after World War I an ardent nationalist and rightist, he was premier in 1920 and president of France 1920–24.

Milles, Carl (mĭ'lŭs), 1875–, Swedish sculptor, a follower of Rodin. His work consists mainly of large linear human figures (e.g., statues in Rockefeller Center, New York).

Millet, Jean François (zhã' frãswä' mēlā'),

1814–75, French painter, an outstanding member of Barbizon school. His *Gleaners* and *Angelus* are in the Louvre.

millet (mĭ'lŭt), popular name for certain grasses and cereals including the common or hog millet (*Panicum miliaceum*) and foxtail millet (*Setaria italica*). Hog millet has been grown since ancient times for human food and forage. In North America the foxtail millet is a fodder plant.

Milligan, ex parte, case decided by the U.S. Supreme Court in 1866 in which the suspension (1863) of habeas corpus by Lincoln in the military arrest and trial of a civilian was voided, the court ruling that civilians might be tried by military tribunal only if because of invasion or disorder the civil courts cannot function to give them justice.

Millikan, Robert Andrews (mĭ'lĭkŭn), 1868–, American physicist and educator. Won 1923 Nobel Prize for measurement of charge on electron and work on photoelectric effect. Made important studies of cosmic rays, X rays, physical and electrical constants. He was associated with Univ. of Chicago (1896–1921) and California Inst. of Technology (1921–45).

milling. Wheat and other grains were originally ground into flour by pounding between two stones. This led to the mortar and pestle, superseded by the quern, in which grain placed on one millstone was ground by revolving an upper stone. This device was adapted to animal, wind, or water power. Windmills became widespread in Europe after the Crusades. Steam power and improvements in machinery came with the Industrial Revolution. Modern grinding processes involve about 180 operations. Processing centers for grains and other materials are called mills.

Millinocket, town (pop. 5,890), central Maine, on a branch of Penobscot R. SE of Millinocket L. Paper mills (built 1899–1900).

millipede or **millepede** (both: mĭ'lŭpēd), wormlike segmented arthropod, somewhat similar to centipede but body is more cylindrical and legs more numerous. Feeds on plants (some injure crops) and decaying vegetation.

Mills, Ogden L(ivingston), 1884–1937, American political leader. U.S. Congressman from N.Y. (1921–27); noted as fiscal expert. Secretary of the Treasury (Feb., 1932–March, 1933).

Mills, Robert, 1781–1855, American architect of the classic revival period. As official architect of public buildings in Washington, D.C., he designed the Washington Monument (1836), which was executed without the base originally intended for it.

Mills College: see OAKLAND, Calif.

Millspaugh, A(rthur) C(hester) (mĭlz'pô), 1883–, American political scientist. Served as financial adviser to Iran (1922–27, 1943–45) and Haiti (1927–29). Staff member of Brookings Inst. (1929–42, 1946–48). Author of works on political science.

Millvale, borough (pop. 7,287), SW Pa., on Allegheny R. opposite Pittsburgh. Mfg. of metal products and boxes; meat packing.

Mill Valley, residential town (pop. 7,331), W Calif., N of San Francisco and at foot of Mt. Tamalpais. Near by is Muir Woods Natl. Monument.

Millville, city (pop. 16,041), S N.J., E of Bridgeton; settled 1756. Farm trade center (poultry, truck, fruit). River fisheries. Mfg. of glass, textiles, and cast iron.

Milmore, Martin, 1844–83, American sculptor, b. Ireland. Known for monumental sculpture and for portrait busts.

Milne, A(lan) A(lexander) (mĭln), 1882–, English dramatist and humorous writer for children; assistant editor of *Punch* (1906 14). His novel, *The Red House Mystery* (1921), is a classic of its genre. His books of verse for children include *When We Were Very Young* (1924) and *Now We Are Six* (1927), and children's stories are in *Winnie-the-Pooh* (1926). Among his successful comedies are *Mr. Pim Passes By* (1919) and *The Dover Road* (1922).

Milnes, Richard Monckton: see HOUGHTON, RICHARD MONCKTON MILNES, 1st BARON.

Milo (mī'lō) or **Milon** (mī'lŏn), fl. 500 B.C., athlete of anc. Greece. Many times a victor in wrestling at Olympic and Pythian games.

Milo (Titus Annius Papianus Milo), 95 B.C.–47 B.C., Roman partisan leader. As tribune (57), he recalled Cicero from exile. A gang hired by him fought the gang of P. CLODIUS and kept Rome in an uproar. POMPEY was appointed sole consul to restore order, and Milo was exiled. Joining a revolt, he was defeated and killed.

Milo (mī'lō), town (pop. 2,898), central Maine, NNW of Bangor, serving Schoodic, Seboois, Sebec lakes.

Milosh (Milosh Obrenovich) (mĭ'lôsh), 1780–1860, prince of Serbia (1817–39, 1858–60), founder of OBRENOVICH dynasty. An illiterate shepherd, he fought the Turks under KARAGEORGE, later his rival. In 1815 he led a successful rebellion; in 1817, after killing Karageorge, he took the title prince of Serbia (confirmed 1830 by the sultan, who remained his sovereign) and ruled tyrannically. Forced to abdicate in 1839, he was recalled in 1858.

Miltiades (mĭltī'ŭdēz), d. 489 B.C., Athenian general in the PERSIAN WARS. In 490 he defeated the Persians at Marathon, then forcemarched 20 mi. to Athens and successfully defended the city from attack by sea.

Milton, John, 1608–74, English poet. Educated at St. Paul's School and Christ's College, Cambridge, he early prepared to be a poet His early work includes "On the Morning of Christ's Nativity" (1629), "L'Allegro," "Il Penseroso," the masque *Comus* (1634), and the elegy "Lycidas" (1638). He traveled on Continent (1638–40), chiefly in Italy. Growing trouble in England drew him home to support the Puritan cause. He wrote prose pamphlets on church government (e.g., *Of Reformation in England,* 1641) and later issued tracts defending the imprisonment and execution of Charles I (notably, *The Tenure of Kings and Magistrates,* 1649). In 1643 he had married Mary Powell, who soon left him, but later returned. He wrote four tracts on divorce. In 1644 appeared his *Areopagitica,* an eminent defense of freedom of the press. He was Latin secretary in Cromwell's government and its chief defender in several notable tracts. His arduous duties brought on complete blindness—the best known of his distinguished sonnets is the poignant "On His Blindness." At the Restoration (1660) Milton was fined and driven into retirement. It was then that he dictated his epics *Paradise Lost* (1667) and *Paradise Regained* (1671). In the first he recounts the story of Satan's rebellion against God and of Adam and Eve with the stated intention to "justify the ways of God to men." In the second he tells the story of Christ's temptation. *Paradise Lost* is one of the world's greatest epics. Its sonorous blank verse is unsurpassed in English. Among other works written at the close of his life is *Samson Agonistes* (1671), a distinguished drama on the classic Greek model. While much of Milton's work is representative of the Puritan age, it is also supremely universal and timeless.

Milton. 1 Village (pop. 8,232), SW Ill. 2 Town (pop. 22,395), E Mass., S of Boston; settled 1636. Food products. Here is Harvard's Blue Hill meteorological observatory. 3 Borough (pop. 8,578), E Pa., on West Branch of Susquehanna R. and S of Williamsport. Mfg. of metal products and clothing.

Milvian Bridge, over the Tiber, near Rome. Here Constantine I saw the cross in the sky presaging victory; defeated Maxentius to become sole ruler of the West (312). Also Mulvian Bridge.

Milwaukee (mĭlwô'kē), city (pop. 637,932), SE Wis., N of Chicago and at point where Milwaukee, Menomonee, and Kinnickinnic rivers join to enter L. Michigan. Largest city in Wis. and shipping center with good harbor, it is famous for brewing and meat packing. Missionaries here in late 17th cent.; North West Co. estab. trading post 1795; and Solomon JUNEAU came 1818. Several settlements in area merged after 1835 as Milwaukee village. After 1848 German refugees, including Carl SCHURZ, spurred growth. Socialists influential here. Seat of Milwaukee-Downer Col. (nonsectarian; for women; opened 1848, chartered 1851) and Marquette Univ. (R.C.; coed.; chartered 1864, opened 1881, became university 1907).

Milwaukie, city (pop. 5,253), NW Oregon, on Willamette R. just S of Portland. Trees from Iowa started state's cherry industry here in 1847.

Milyukov or **Miliukov, Pavel Nikolayevich** (pä'vĭl nyĭkŏlī'ŭvĭch mēlyōōkôf'), 1859–1943, Russian statesman and historian. As foreign minister (Feb.–May, 1917) he made himself unpopular by insisting on carrying out obligations to Russia's World War I allies. Author of *Outlines of Russian Culture* (Eng. tr., 3 vols., 1942).

Mimico (mĭ'mĭkō), SW suburb of Toronto (pop. 11,342), S Ont., Canada, on L. Ontario.

mimicry, in biology, an organism's advantageous resemblance to another of different species or to feature of environment (this is usually called PROTECTIVE COLORATION). Mimicry is often observed among insects. In theory of H. W. Bates, through natural selection an edible insect (for example) acquires deceptive resemblance to inedible insect, thus escaping aggressor; this occurs only if no radical changes in structure required. Animals may also mimic prey or an animal feared by others.

mimosa, leguminous woody or herbaceous plant of genus *Mimosa,* native to tropical America, with feathery foliage and rounded flower clusters, similar to acacia. The sensitive plant (*Mimosa pudica*) has leaves which fold up when touched.

minaret (mĭnŭrĕt'), small tower used in Moslem architecture. A part of most mosques, it has one or more projecting balconies, from which the muezzin chants his summons to prayer. Early minarets (7th–12th cent.) are square with little adornment; those after 12th cent. are slender and richly decorated.

Minas de Ríotinto, Spain: see RÍO TINTO.

Minas Gerais (mē'nŭs zhŭrīsh') [Port.,= various mines], state (224,701 sq. mi.; pop. 7,839,792), E Brazil; cap., BELO HORIZONTE. Inland state on central plateau cut off from coast by mountain escarpment, has largest known iron reserves in world; also deposits of manganese, diamonds, gold, and semiprecious stones. Gold was first discovered 1698. Old cap., Ouro Prêto, was important colonial city. Late in 18th cent. Minas was center of literary group and here in 1788 Tiradentes led an abortive revolt against Portuguese government. Today Minas is second most populous state in Brazil. Besides mining, agr. and cattle breeding are important.

Minch or **North Minch,** strait, 25 to 35 mi. wide, separating Lewis with Harris Isl., Outer Hebrides, from mainland of Scotland. Little Minch separates Skye from neighboring Outer Hebrides.

Mincio (mēn'chō), river of Lombardy, N Italy. Called Sarca R. before entering L. Garda; from there the Mincio flows c.40 mi., past Mantua, to the Po. Sarca-Garda-Mincio line, marking natural border between Lombardy and Venetia, was long of strategic importance.

mind: see PSYCHOLOGY.

Mindanao (mĭndŭnä'ō), island (36,536 sq. mi.; pop. 1,828,071), second largest of Philippine Isls.; NE of Borneo. Off its NE coast in Philippine Sea is Mindanao Deep (35,400 ft.). Mainly mountainous, rising to 9,690 ft. at Mt. Apo. Has large W peninsula (site of Zamboanga). The navigable Mindanao, 200 mi. long, is largest river. Products include hemp, rice, corn, and coffee. Many of the natives are Moros, whose religion is Islam.

Minden (mĭn'dŭn), city (pop. 40,811), North Rhine-Westphalia, NW Germany; a port at junction of Ems-Weser and Weser-Elbe canals. An episcopal see from c.800, it joined the Hanseatic League (13th cent.) and accepted the Reformation (1530). The secularized bishopric passed to Brandenburg in 1648. Scene of English-Hanoverian victory over French (1759). Cathedral (11th–13th cent.) and city hall (13th–17th cent.) were destroyed in World War II.

Minden, city (pop. 9,787), NW La., NE of Shreveport. Trade center of agr. area with cotton gins and cottonseed mills. Oil wells near.

Mindoro (mĭndô'rō), island (3,758 sq. mi.; pop. 116,988), Philippines, SW of Luzon.

Coal is mined, and rice and coconuts are grown.

mind reading: see TELEPATHY.

Mindszenty, Joseph (mĭnd′sĕntē), 1892–, Hungarian cardinal, archbishop of Esztergom, Catholic primate of Hungary. Imprisoned for his anti-German attitude in World War II, he later opposed the Communist regime and was arrested on charges of treason in 1948. At his sensational trial he pleaded guilty to fantastic charges and was sentenced to life imprisonment. It is widely held in the free world that his confessions were extorted either by drugs or by extreme moral pressure.

mine, in warfare, explosive weapon used in land and sea operations. The submarine mine is used against ships; it consists of a watertight case enclosing an explosive charge, and its use dates back to the 16th cent. There are controlled mines (connected by electric cable to a shore station and detonated from there) and contact mines (detonated electrically or mechanically upon contact with an outside body). Land mines were sown over wide areas (mine fields) in World War I and World War II by defenders as well as attackers.

Mineola (mĭnēō′lŭ), village (pop. 14,831), SE N.Y., on W Long Isl. Commercial center with repair and service shops for near-by U.S. Mitchel Air Force Base.

mineral, inorganic substance occurring in nature, having definite chemical composition and physical properties, and often a typical crystalline form. (Some organic substances are included.) A few minerals are elements (e.g., carbon, gold, mercury), but most are compounds. Rocks are usually mixtures of minerals, lacking the definite chemical formula which characterizes their mineral constituents.

mineral water, water flowing from hot or cold springs, containing dissolved mineral salts and often charged with gases. Many people believe in the curative powers of such waters.

Mineral Wells, city (pop. 7,801), N Texas, near Brazos R. and W of Fort Worth. Health resort. Has sericulture and mfg. of mineral crystals and hosiery. Near are Camp Wolters and L. Mineral Wells reservoir in Trinity R. system.

Minersville, borough (pop. 7,783), E Pa., NNW of Pottsville. Coal mining and mfg. of clothing.

Minerva, in Roman religion, goddess of learning and handicrafts. Identified with Greek ATHENA.

Ming (mĭng), dynasty of China, 1368–1644. Founded by Chu Yüan-chang, a former Buddhist monk, who expelled the Mongols from China. Empire at its height extended from Burma to Korea. Despite Ming opposition to foreign trade, European settlements were made at Macao and Canton. Era marked by literary achievements and renowned for fine porcelain.

Mingan Islands (mĭng′gŭn), group of 15 small islands and many islets, E Que., Canada, N of Anticosti Isl., in Mingan Passage of St. Lawrence R. Discovered by Cartier 1535.

Mingrelia (mĭn-grē′lēŭ), region, W Georgian SSR, a lowland bordering on Black Sea; main port Poti. Produces tea and grapes. The COLCHIS of the ancients, later a vassal principality of Ottoman Empire, it was annexed by Russia 1803.

Minho (mē′nyō), Span. *Miño,* river rising in NW Spain and flowing c.210 mi. S and SW to the Atlantic. Forms Spanish-Portuguese border. It gives its name to the northernmost province (1,868 sq. mi.; pop. 741,510) of Portugal; cap. Braga.

Minidoka project, S Idaho, in Snake R. valley, for irrigation. Minidoka Dam (built 1909; forms L. Walcott near Rupert) and AMERICAN FALLS Dam (built 1927; collects water for privately irrigated lands) impound Snake R. Project serves an area around Minidoka and Burley and another near Gooding and Shoshone. Jackson L., Wyo., stores water.

minimum wage, lowest wage permitted in an industry, government, or other organization, introduced first in New Zealand in 1894. Aim is to assure wage earners a minimally decent standard of living. First held unconstitutional in U.S., the minimum wage was established by 1938 Fair Labor Standards Act. In 1949 the minimum wage was set at $.75 an hour.

mining, the extraction of ores or other mineral resources from the earth. Deposits are worked from the surface or from underground. Placer mining involves no excavating; gold and diamonds which accumulate in stream beds are washed out by panning, sluicing, hydraulic nozzles, dredging. In open-pit mining, ore is dug at the surface. Deep mines require vertical shafts with horizontal tunnels.

minister, in diplomacy: see DIPLOMATIC SERVICE and EXTERRITORIALITY.

Minitari Indians: see HIDATSA INDIANS.

mink, semiaquatic mammal (*Mustela*) of weasel family, found in N Hemisphere. American mink has slender, arched body, bushy tail. Valued for rich brown fur. Secretes acrid musk.

Minkowski, Hermann (hĕr′män mĭn-kôfskē), 1864–1909, Russian mathematician. He contributed to development of theory of numbers and evolved a four-dimensional geometry credited with influencing formulation of geometrical expression of general theory of relativity.

Minneapolis (mĭ″nēă′pŭlĭs). **1** City (pop. 1,801), N central Kansas, N of Salina. Rock City, area of curious eroded geological formations, is near. **2** City (pop. 521,718), E Minn., largest city in state, on both sides of the Mississippi at Falls of St. Anthony and adjoining its Twin City, St. Paul; settled c.1847 on site of Fort SNELLING (1819). Twin Cities are financial, industrial, and commercial center of large agr. area. Minneapolis has flour mills, dairy products plants, and mfg. (machinery, agr. equipment, clothing). Here are many lakes and parks, and Univ. of MINNESOTA.

Minneapolis Symphony Orchestra, founded 1903. Among its conductors have been Eugene Ormandy (1931–36), Dimitri Mitropoulous (1936–49), and Antal Dorati.

Minnehaha Falls (mĭ″nēhä′hä″) [traditionally Indian,= laughing water], over 50 ft. high, in SE Minneapolis, in Minnehaha Creek, which flows from L. Minnetonka to the Mississippi. Included in public park. Name immortalized in Longfellow's *Hiawatha.*

minnesinger (mĭ'nēsĭng"ŭr), in German literature, a singer of *Minne* (romantic love), corresponding to the TROUBADOUR of S France. Minnesingers flourished in the 12th and 13th cent. Greatest were Walther von der Vogelweide and Wolfram von Eschenbach.

Minnesota, state (84,068 sq. mi.; pop. 2,982,-483), N U.S., in Great Lakes region; admitted 1858 as 32d state (free); cap. SAINT PAUL. Other cities are MINNEAPOLIS, DULUTH. Bounded E by L. Superior, St. Croix R. and Mississippi R., NW by Red R. Watershed for three river systems: Hudson Bay, Great Lakes–St. Lawrence, Mississippi-Missouri. State of lakes, prairies (esp. S), some highlands. Farming (grains, livestock, dairying, truck); mining (iron, granite, limestone); lumbering. Food, meat processing; mfg. of machinery, paper, chemicals; printing and publishing. French and British fur traders gave way to American Fur Co. E part included in NORTHWEST TERRITORY, W part joined by Louisiana Purchase. Became territory in 1849. Lumbering was major industry. Big Soo Canal opened waterway to E. Sioux uprising during and after Civil War. Farmer discontent in late 19th cent. expressed in GRANGER MOVEMENT. State is leader in use of cooperatives. Mfg. stimulated by World War II.

Minnesota, river, 332 mi. long, rising in Big Stone L. at W boundary of Minnesota and flowing SE to Mankato, then NE to the Mississippi at Mendota. As St. Peter or St. Pierre R. was explorers' and fur traders' route. Follows valley of prehistoric River Warren, outlet of L. Agassiz.

Minnesota, University of, mainly at Minneapolis; landgrant, state supported, coed.; chartered 1851 and 1868, opened as university 1869. Has two-year General Col. Includes school of medicine (for affiliated foundation, see MAYO, CHARLES H.) and branches at St. Paul and Duluth. Library has Scandinavian collection. In General Col., through extension work, effort has been made to raise general cultural level.

Minnetonka, Lake (mĭ"nĭtŏng'kŭ), 10 mi. long, E Minn., just W of Minneapolis. Outlet is Minnehaha Creek. Resorts on shore.

minnow, name for certain fish of carp family. In Europe, refers chiefly to small form, *Phoxinus phoxinus;* in America, chiefly to many small minnows of same family. Squawfish or Sacramento pike (c.3 ft.) is largest in U.S.

Miño, river: see MINHO.

Minoan civilization, period of anc. culture in AEGEAN CIVILIZATION. Named for King Minos of Crete and covered Bronze Age (3000–1200 B.C.). Our archaeological knowledge, derived from palace at CNOSSUS, shows it developed from simple culture with pictographic writing into high culture with linear writing. It declined in last period as cultural center passed to Troy and Greek mainland.

Mino da Fiesole (mē'nō dä fyā'zōlā) or **Mino di Giovanni** (dē jōvän'nē), 1431–84, Florentine sculptor of the early Renaissance. Produced many tombs.

Minorca (mĭnôr'kŭ), Span. *Menorca,* island (271 sq. mi.; pop. 43,025),Spain, in W Mediterranean, second largest of BALEARIC ISLANDS; chief city Port Mahon. Products include cereals, wine, olive oil, and flax. Stock raising. Has many megalithic monuments. Minorca shared history of Balearic Isls. until 1708; frequently changed hands in 18th cent. (British, 1708–56; French, 1756–63; British, 1763–82; occupied by French and Spanish, 1782; recovered by England, 1798; definitely awarded to Spain, 1802). Was held by Loyalists in Spanish civil war until 1939.

minority, in international law, population group with a characteristic culture and a sense of identity living in a state where another culture group is dominant. Religious minorities were known from earliest times, but it was only with the rise of nationalism at the beginning of the 19th cent. that the question of ethnic minorities became a burning one in Europe. Nationalist aspirations frequently led to suppression of minorities, and the situation led to many international clashes when a minority group was supported by, or stirred up by, their fellows in another state (as the Slavs in Austria-Hungary before World War I, the Sudeten Germans in Czechoslovakia in the 1930s). Minorities may, however, face problems that are social rather than political (e.g., Negroes in the U.S.), or they may be linked with similar minorities in other states largely by resistance to oppression (e.g., Jewish minorities facing the forces of anti-Semitism in various states of the Western world).

Minos (mī'nŏs, –nŭs), in Greek myth, king of Crete; son of Zeus and Europa and father of Ariadne and Phaedra. His wife also bore the MINOTAUR. There was presumably a historical King Minos of Crete, after whom is named archaic MINOAN CIVILIZATION.

Minot, George Richards (mī'nŭt), 1885–1950, American physician and pathologist. Shared 1934 Nobel Prize in Physiology and Medicine for research on value of liver in treating pernicious anemia.

Minot (mī'nŭt), city (pop. 22,032), NW N. Dak., on Souris R. and NNW of Bismarck; settled 1886. Rail, trade, and distribution center for agr. (esp. wheat) area; food processing; lignite mining.

Minotaur (mĭ'nŭtôr), monstrous offspring of Pasiphaë and a bull, with head of bull and body of man. Minos, husband of Pasiphaë, had Daedalus build Labyrinth to keep the monster. Theseus killed him.

Minseito (mēn"sā'tō), Japanese political party. First formed in 1881 by Okuma as the Kaishinto. Chief rival of SEIYUKAI from 1927 to 1932. Was loosely tied to Mitsubishi interests.

Minsk (Rus. mēnsk), city (pop. 238,772), cap. of Belorussia. Industrial center (cars, tractors, textiles, wood products). Was cap. of principality conquered 1326 by Lithuania. Passed to Russia 1793. In Middle Ages, Minsk became one of largest Jewish centers of Eastern Europe. Virtually destroyed in World War II by Germans, who held it 1941–44. Jews were exterminated.

minstrel, professional secular musician of the

Middle Ages, especially one of unusual talent who was attached to a court to play or sing the songs of the TROUBADOR or TROUVÈRE. Term indicated a higher social class than the jongleur. In the 19th and early 20th cent., NEGRO MINSTREL shows were very popular in the U.S.

mint, name for a plant family, Labiatae, a group characterized by square stems, aromatic foliage, and often showy flowers. Among the members of the family are catnip, thyme, bee balm, and lavender. The name is used more specifically for plants of the genus *Mentha* of the same family, e.g., PEPPERMINT and SPEARMINT.

mint julep: see JULEP.

Minton, English family of potters. **Thomas Minton,** 1765–1836, founded a small pottery at Stoke-on-Trent and created the famous WILLOW-PATTERN WARE. His son **Herbert Minton,** 1793–1858, developed the firm and made it famous.

Minturnae (mĭntûr'nē), anc. town, Latium, Italy; near modern Minturno. Founded by the Aurunci or Ausones, it became a flourishing Roman colony (295 B.C.). It guarded the Appian Way bridge over the Liris R.

minuet (mĭnūet'), French dance in 3–4 meter, introduced (1650) at Louis XIV's court. Popular during 17th–18th cent. Left a definite imprint on the era's music (e.g., works of Haydn and Mozart).

Minuit, Peter (mĭn'ūĭt), c.1580–1638, first director general of New Netherland (1626–31). Purchased Manhattan from Indians. Helped found NEW SWEDEN (1638).

Minya Konka (mĭn'yŏŏ kŏng'kŏŏ), peak, 24,900 ft. high, Sikang prov., China, in Tahsüeh Mts. Climbed 1932 by American expedition.

Miocene epoch (mī'ùsēn), third epoch of the Tertiary period of geologic time. The Atlantic and Gulf coasts and the Great Valley of Calif. were extensively submerged. Mid-Miocene saw uplift of Cascades and Coast Ranges, with accompanying volcanic activity. Cool climate increased grass areas at expense of forests. Mammalian life was marked by further development of the horse. Mastodons, weasels, camels, cats, and others appeared. See also GEOLOGY, table.

Miquelon (mĭ'kùlŏn, Fr. mēkùlõ'), two islands (area 83 sq. mi.), and adjacent island group of St. Pierre (10 sq. mi.), consituting territory of the French Union, S of N.F., Canada; pop. c.4,354; cap. St. Pierre. Nearness to Grand Banks makes islands important fishing base. Settled by French c.1660, taken several times by British. In French possession since early 19th cent.

Mirabeau, Victor Riquetti, marquis de (vēktôr' rēkĕtē' märkē' dù mērābō'), 1715–89, French leader of the PHYSIOCRATS, father of the statesman and revolutionist. **Honoré Gabriel Riquetti, comte de Mirabeau** (ōnôrā' gäbrēĕl', kõt'), 1749–91. The younger Mirabeau's life before 1789 was a series of wild excesses. He was repeatedly jailed on request of his father, with whom he carried on a long public quarrel. Though noble, he was elected a delegate of the third estate for the STATES GENERAL of 1789, where his formidable eloquence made him a leading figure. His aim was to create a constitutional monarchy; when events took a radical turn late in 1789, Mirabeau came to a secret understanding with the king and queen in order to save the monarchy. His moderate policy was attacked by the Jacobins, but he died just before his dealings with the court were discovered.

miracle, departure from the usual course of nature attributed to supernatural interposition. Adherents of the principal monotheistic religions—Judaism, Christianity, and Islam—have generally agreed in explaining miracles by the omnipotence of one God, the Creator, alone able to interrupt the operation of nature or to allow miracles to be wrought through man by delegating that power to a particular person. The miracle of the Resurrection has always been considered the central fact of Christianity, and the Virgin Birth is usually called a miracle. Among the many miracles of Jesus recorded in the Gospels were raising the dead, casting out demons, healing of the blind, lame, and sick, and performing awesome acts such as stilling the storm, walking on the water, feeding the multitude with a few loaves and fishes, and turning water into wine. The New Testament also records miracles done by apostles. Every age of Christianity has had miracles supposedly performed. They are especially associated with saints' bodies and relics and with shrines. The Roman Catholic Church requires rigid attestation of miracles before canonization, but does not officially require belief in miracles other than those in the Bible and those officially incorporated into dogma. Protestants generally reject miracles except those in the Bible. There are also several instances of miracles in the Old Testament (e.g., Elijah being fed by the ravens).

miracle play or **mystery play,** medieval form of drama, developed (10th–16th cent.) from small scenes added to mass at Christmas and Easter. Simple, dramatic presentation of religious stories originally in Latin, miracle plays later were done in French, English, or German. As plays lengthened and audiences grew they were performed outside churches. This increased realism, humor, and secularism. Moralities (e.g., *Everyman*) were 15th cent. offshoots. The PASSION PLAY is the chief modern example of the miracle play.

mirage (mĭrāzh'), optical illusion that causes person to see what appears to be a real object where none is. Can be explained by facts that light rays undergo REFRACTION when passing from medium of one density into another of different density and combined surfaces of two such media act like mirror under certain conditions and cause REFLECTION of light rays. Since density of air varies at different temperatures, mirage is formed when light rays pass through layers of air of different densities and when they are reflected as they strike line of adjacent surfaces at extremely oblique angles. Fata morgana (fä'tä môrgä'nä) is a form of mirage, especially evident at Strait of Messina, in which images of objects are seen suspended over object or in water.

Miranda, Francisco de (fränsē'skō dā mērän'dä), 1750–1816, Venezuelan revolutionist, b. Caracas. Imbued with ideas gained in American Revolution and French Revolutionary wars, he became apostle of Venezuelan liberty. Led in preliminary stages of struggle for independence but when he surrendered to Spanish (1812), Bolivar imprisoned him. Later Spanish seized him and kept him imprisoned for rest of his life.

Miranda, Francisco de Sá de: see SÁ DE MIRANDA, FRANCISCO DE.

Mirandola, Giovanni Pico della: see PICO.

Miriam, sister of Moses and Aaron, who watched over the baby Moses in the bulrushes and led the women in song by the Red Sea. Later stricken with leprosy for defying Moses. Ex. 2.4–8; 15.20,21; Num. 12. Miriam and Mary are forms of the same original name.

Miró, Joan (hwän' mērō'), 1893–, Catalan surrealist painter; early went to Paris. He uses brilliant color, free forms with geometric lines.

mirror. REFLECTION of light is such that clear-cut reproductions of objects are formed when light rays from object fall on certain surfaces; such a surface is called a mirror and IMAGE of object is a reproduction. Mirrors usually are plate glass with one surface coated to serve as reflecting surface. Junction of reflecting surface and glass is mirror line. Plane mirror is one with flat surface; image is almost exactly like object, illusion of perspective is created. Image appears to be behind mirror, but is at mirror line. Image is virtual and same size as object and appears to be same distance behind mirror as object is in front of it. Exactness of image depends on quality and condition of mirror. In concave mirror center of reflecting surface is farther from object than are edges. Center of imaginary sphere of which it is part is center of curvature. Line through center of curvature and mid-point of mirror is principal axis; principal focus is point halfway between center of curvature and vertex. Size, nature, and position of image depend on position of object in relation to principal focus and center of curvature. In convex mirror image is always smaller than object, erect, and virtual. Mirrors are used in interior decoration, in microscopes to reflect light, in astronomical telescope.

Mirzapur (mēr'zäpo͝or"), city (pop. 70,944), SE Uttar Pradesh, India, on Ganges R. Has noted temple to Kali, consort of Siva. Trade center.

Misael (mĭ'sāůl), one of the THREE HOLY CHILDREN.

miscarriage: see ABORTION.

miscegenation (mĭ"sĭjĭnā'shůn), the interbreeding of persons of different racial types. It is now believed that only ill effects are those resulting from social disapproval of mixed unions.

misdemeanor, a minor crime, distinguished from a felony. In the U.S., a misdemeanor is usually punishable summarily by fine and imprisonment for less than a year. Conviction for a misdemeanor does not cancel citizenship or subject an alien to deportation.

Miseno, Cape (mēzä'nō), S Italy, at NW end of Bay of Naples. Was site of Roman naval station founded by Augustus.

Miserere (mĭzůrĕr'ē), the 51st (or 50th) Psalm, beginning, "Miserere mei, Deus (Have mercy upon me, O God)"; one of the penitential psalms. Palestrina and Allegri are among those who have written music for it.

Mishael (mĭ'shāůl), one of the THREE HOLY CHILDREN.

Mishawaka (mĭshůwô'ků), city (pop. 32,913), N Ind., on St. Joseph R. and near South Bend; settled c.1830. Mfg. of clothing, rubber, plastic goods, and metal products.

Mishna: see MIDRASH; TALMUD.

Miskolc (mĭsh'kôlts), city (pop. 77,362), NE Hungary, on Sajo R. Has large iron and steel mills.

Mission, city (pop. 10,765), S Texas, WNW of Brownsville, founded 1908 near extant Spanish chapel (1824). Packs and cans citrus fruits (esp. grapefruit) and vegetables. Annual Citrus Fiesta.

Missionary Ridge: see CHATTANOOGA CAMPAIGN.

missions, name of organizations that extend religious teaching, at home or abroad, and of efforts to disseminate Christian religion. History of church from beginning has been history of missions, which spread Christianity through Asia Minor into Europe by way of Greece and Rome. The following centuries saw notable missionary labors in Scotland, Ireland, Central Europe, and among Northmen, reaching into Iceland and Greenland. St. PATRICK, St. AUGUSTINE, and St. BONIFACE are great names of the large era. In 16th cent. missionaries took part in exploration and colonization of America, especially the Jesuits and the Franciscans. In colonial days Roger WILLIAMS and John ELIOT did notable work among Indians, as did Moravian Church. In the 19th cent. missionary work was intense in Africa and Asia and continues so today; it has been graced by such diverse figures as David LIVINGSTONE and Albert SCHWEITZER.

Mississippi, state (47,420 sq. mi.; pop. 2,178,914), S U.S.; admitted 1817 as 20th state (slaveholding); cap. JACKSON. Other cities are MERIDIAN, VICKSBURG, HATTIESBURG, GREENVILLE, LAUREL, BILOXI, NATCHEZ, GULFPORT. Bordered W mostly by MISSISSIPPI R., partly by Pearl R.; S by Gulf of Mexico (with MISSISSIPPI SOUND). Mostly in Gulf coastal plain. Between Mississippi R. and Yazoo R., from Memphis to Vicksburg, is Yazoo Basin or the Delta. Farming (cotton, grains, tung nuts, dairying, livestock, sugar cane, truck); mfg. of wood products, textiles; food processing. Mining (oil, natural gas, clay); lumbering; fishing; coast resorts. Settled by French 1699. Area disputed in WEST FLORIDA CONTROVERSY. High price for cotton and land boom brought settlers. Seceded from Union 1861; saw Civil War action at battle of SHILOH and in VICKSBURG CAMPAIGN. Suffered in Reconstruction. Sharecropping system rose after war. Plagued with race problem. Illiteracy problem has largely declined. Recent industrial growth helped by TVA, community subsidization.

Mississippi, river, c.2,350 mi. long, principal river of U.S., "main stem" of system draining area of 1,244,000 sq. mi. in 31 states and two Canadian provinces. Rises in N Minn near L. Itasca and flows S across Minn., past Wis., Ill., Iowa, Ky., Mo., Tenn., Ark., and La. to Gulf of Mexico. Navigable S of Falls of St. Anthony at Minneapolis. Sediment deposits from delta crossed by river's several mouths. Chief tributaries include Ohio, Missouri, Arkansas, and Red rivers. St. Louis, Mo., is largest river city. Levee building against floods began at New Orleans under the French 1717; flood control act of 1928, following flood of 1927, brought great engineering program to the river and its tributaries. Indians made much use of river. La Salle traveled it to mouth and claimed region for France 1682. Spanish followed French control of river 1762. Louisiana Purchase (1803) ended international wrangling and schemes for new nations. Thereafter valley began democratic settlement; river and ports became centers for westward migration. Steamboats, especially after 1830s, marked zenith of river life. Civil War victories (as at Island No. 10 and in Vicksburg campaign) led to Union gaining control of river and cutting off Confederacy from supply bases W. Following war and with coming of railroads, ports deteriorated. River traffic still heavy, but no longer vital.

Mississippi, University of: see Oxford.

Mississippian period: see Carboniferous period.

Mississippi Scheme, plan formulated by John Law for colonization and commercial exploitation of Mississippi valley for French. Overspeculation and haste brought collapse of plan, but number of settlers was increased.

Mississippi Sound, arm of Gulf of Mexico, c.80 mi. long, 7–15 mi. wide, separated from the Gulf by islands and sand bars. Extends from L. Borgne (La.) on W, E to Mobile Bay. Washes Miss. and parts of Ala. and La. Bay St. Louis, Pass Christian, Gulfport, Biloxi, Pascagoula, Miss., on Sound.

Mississippi State College: see Starkville.

Mississippi State College for Women: see Columbus.

Missolonghi (mĭsùlông'gē) or **Mesolonghi** (mĕsù–), Gr. *Mesolongion,* town (pop. 10,565), W central Greece; a port on an inlet of Gulf of Patras. Major stronghold of Greek insurgents in Greek War of Independence, it was besieged by the Turks in 1822 and 1825–26. Lord Byron died here in 1824.

Missoula (mĭzōō'lù), city (pop. 22,485), W Mont., on Clark Fork (here called the Missoula) near mouth of Bitterroot R. Estab. 1865 at present site. Growth aided by railroads. Commercial and industrial point in mining and agr. region. Food-processing plants. Seat of Montana State Univ. (see Univ. of Montana). Fort Missoula (1877) is near.

Missouri, state (69,270 sq. mi.; pop. 3,954,653), central U.S.; admitted 1821 as 24th state (slaveholding) under Missouri Compromise; cap. Jefferson City. Cities are Saint Louis, Kansas City, Springfield, Saint Joseph. Bounded E by Mississippi R., partly NW by Missouri R. Prairie land to N; S are Ozark Mountains; part of Great Plains are in SW; Mississippi flood plains in SE. Mfg. of shoes, food and grain products, beer, chemicals; meat packing; printing and publishing. Farming (corn, livestock, grains, potatoes, fruit, cotton); mining (lead, zinc, coal, limestone, granite, marble, fire clay, glass sand). French worked lead deposits, estab. fur trade; founded Sainte Genevieve 1732, St. Louis 1764. Went to U.S. in Louisiana Purchase (1803). Territory estab. 1812. Stayed with Union in Civil War. Some fighting in Mo., notably guerrilla warfare (esp. under W. C. Quantrill). Postwar confusion marked by some violence (e.g., Jesse James). Steamboat traffic declined as railroads grew. Industry developed. Political position enhanced by election of H. S. Truman, native son, to presidency. It is hoped that eventually the Missouri river basin project will help agr.

Missouri, river, 2,714 mi. long, longest river of U.S. and chief tributary of the Mississippi, formed where Gallatin, Madison, and Red Rock–Jefferson (main headstream of the Missouri) rivers join in SW Mont. at Three Forks. Flows SE across N.Dak. and S.Dak., past E Nebr. and parts of E Kansas and W Iowa, through Mo. to the Mississippi c.17 mi. above St. Louis. Tributaries include Milk, Yellowstone, and Platte rivers. Largest river city is Kansas City. U.S. Missouri river basin project is planned. River a trade artery for Indians; lower river familiar to fur traders after 1762. Lewis and Clark opened up mountain country 1804–6 and area became well known with fur trade of mountain men in 1820s and 1830s. Steamboats became important. In 1840s and 1850s, the Missouri and the Platte were part of route to Oregon and Calif.; Mormon route to Utah. Before and after Civil War river traffic boomed, but railroads caused decline. River now important for power and irrigation.

Missouri, University of, mainly at Columbia; land-grant, state supported, coed.; chartered 1839, opened 1841; oldest state university W of the Mississippi. Includes schools of journalism (1908; oldest in world) and, at Rolla, mines and metallurgy.

Missouri Compromise, 1820–21, measures passed by U.S. Congress to end first of a series of crises concerning extension of slavery into national territory. Provided that Maine would enter Union as free state, Mo. as slave state; prohibited slavery elsewhere in Louisiana Purchase N of 36°30′, a proviso which held until 1854, when Kansas-Nebraska Bill repealed Missouri Compromise.

Missouri river basin project, plan advanced 1944 for coordinated development and control of the Missouri and its basin lands. States chiefly involved are Mont., Colo., Wyo., N.Dak., S.Dak., Nebr., Kansas, and Mo. For the plan Flood Control Act of 1944 authorized over 100 dams, reservoirs, and levees intended to irrigate c.5,500,000 acres, control floods, improve navigation, restore surface and ground water, and develop hydroelectric power. Project will also conserve wildlife and abate stream pollution. Committee of federal and state representatives estab. 1945 to help advance the scheme, which will ultimately include existing projects such as those of North Platte and South Platte rivers, and control other tributaries. Kanopolis Dam on Smoky Hill

R. was first unit of the project completed (1948).

Mistassini (mĭstŭsē'nē), river, central Que., Canada, flowing c.200 mi. S, then SE to L. St. John. W is **Lake Mistassini** which drains W to James Bay.

Misti, El (ĕl mē'stē), volcano, 19,166 ft. high, S Peru, near Arequipa. With a perfect, snow-capped cone, it is apparently significant in Inca religion and has figured in many Peruvian legends and poems.

mistletoe, evergreen plant with white berries, parasitic on many trees and shrubs. The European mistletoe of literature, sacred to the druids, is *Viscum album*. The mistletoe of American holiday markets is of the genus *Phoradendron*.

Mistral, Frédéric (frādārĕk' mēsträl'), 1830–1914, French Provençal poet, leader of the Felibrige movement promoting Provençal as a literary language. His best-known work is the verse romance *Mirèio* (1859; Eng. tr., 1857). Shared 1904 Nobel Prize in Literature with Echegaray.

Mistral, Gabriela (gäbrēā'lä mēsträl), 1889–, Chilean poet, whose real name is Lucila Godoy Alcayaga. An educator of note, she also served in diplomatic posts and in League of Nations. Her poems are simple and fluently lyrical. She was awarded the 1943 Nobel Prize in Literature.

Mitau, Latvia: see JELGAVA.

Mitchell, Donald Grant: see MARVEL, IK.

Mitchell, Margaret, 1900?–1949, American novelist. Her one novel, *Gone with the Wind* (1936), dealt with the Civil War and Reconstruction periods. Both the book and the motion picture version (1939) were enormously popular.

Mitchell, S(ilas) Weir, 1829–1914, American physician and author. Pioneered in applying psychology to medicine. Also wrote historical romances (*Hugh Wynne, Free Quaker*, 1896) and psychological studies (*Constance Trescot*, 1905).

Mitchell, Wesley C(lair), 1874–1948, American economist, author of *Business Cycles*. With evidence from behaviorist psychology, attacked orthodox economics.

Mitchell, William Lendrum, 1879–1936, American general, advocate of large, independent air force. "Billy" Mitchell's criticisms led to court-martial in 1926.

Mitchell. 1 City (pop. 3,245), SW Ind., S of Bedford. Near-by state park has caves and a restored pioneer village. **2** City (pop. 12,123), SE S.Dak., near James R. and L. Mitchell, WNW of Sioux Falls; platted 1879. Trade and processing center for agr., dairy, and livestock area. Seat of Dakota Wesleyan Univ. (Methodist; coed.; 1885). Holds annual agr. festival in Corn Palace.

Mitchell, Mount, peak, 6,684 ft., W N.C., in Black Mts. NE of Asheville; highest peak of E U.S.

Mitchill, Samuel Latham, 1764–1831, American scientist. An educator of note, he taught at Columbia (1792–1801) and College of Physicians and Surgeons (1807–26) and in 1826 helped found Rutgers Medical Col. (no longer in existence). He introduced chemical nomenclature of Lavoisier and was a pioneer in research in mineralogy, geology, and zoology. Served in N.Y. state assembly (1791, 1798, 1810), in U.S. House of Representatives (1801–4, 1810–13), and U.S. Senate (1804–9).

mite, small, often microscopic, arachnid of tick order, of world-wide distribution. Itch mite burrows into skin of humans and other mammals. Other mites attack vegetation and infest stored foods.

Mitford, Mary Russell, 1787–1855, English writer, noted for rural sketches in *Our Village* (1824–32).

Mithra (mĭ'thrŭ) [Old Persian,= friend], anc. cultic god of Iran and India. Originally a minor figure of Zoroastrianism, he became in 5th cent. B.C. chief Persian god. Extension of his cult into Mesopotamia and Armenia made it a world-wide religion, **Mithraism** (mĭ'thrŭĭzŭm). It was one of great religions of Roman Empire, more general in 2d cent A.D. than Christianity. Its central myth was story of Mithra's slaying of a sacred bull in a grotto. Its ethics were rigorous, loyalty was inculcated, and fasting and continence were prescribed. A mystery-faith, it had sacramental forms, e.g., baptism, and the sacred banquet. Mithraism was long in dying out.

Mithridates VI or **Mithradates VI** (Eupator) (mĭthrĭdā'tēz; ū'pŭtôr), c.131 B.C.–63 B.C. king of anc. Pontus, called Mithridates the Great. Rival expansion of territories brought him into war with Rome. In the First Mithridatic War (88–84 B.C.) he conquered all Asia Minor and defied SULLA in Greece. In 85 he was defeated in both spheres. In the Second War (83–81 B.C.) he defeated the Romans. In the Third War (74–63 B.C.) Lucullus defeated Mithridates, and POMPEY drove the king into the Crimea, where he had himself killed by a slave.

Mitilini, Greece: see MYTILENE.

Mitla (mēt'lä) [Nahuatl,= abode of the dead], religious center of the Zapotec, near Oaxaca, SW Mexico.

mitosis (mĭtō'sĭs), in growth of plants and animals, method of division of the nucleus of a cell, characteristic of body (somatic) cells as distinguished from sex cells (gametes). Process varies, but generally may be divided into four or five stages that are continuous. In prophase chromatin material in the nucleus of the cell thickens and forms chromosomes, which split lengthwise; the nuclear membrane disappears, and a spindle-shaped structure forms (this forming is sometimes considered a separate phase, the prometaphase). In metaphase the chromosomes move to the equator of the spindle. During anaphase, the two halves of each chromosome separate, and all draw into two groups around poles of the spindle. In telophase, nuclear membrane forms around each group, and thus two nuclei are complete, each with same number of chromosomes as original nucleus. Usually the cell then splits into two, one for each nucleus. In sex cells of animals and plants that reproduce by union of two cells, a further process, called meiosis, occurs as the sex cells mature. Complex changes take place in stages similar to those of mitosis, but in meiosis the number of chromosomes is reduced by half (reduction division); when egg and sperm nucl unite in fertilization the normal number of chromosomes for the species is restored. The new individual develops by mitotic divisions of the fertilized egg. See *ill.*, p. 813.

Mitre, Bartolomé (bär"tōlōmā' mē'trā), 1821–1906, Argentine statesman, general, and author, president of Argentina (1862–68). Forced into exile by Rosas, he had colorful career as journalist and soldier in Uruguay, Bolivia, Peru, and Chile. Aided Urquiza in overthrow of Rosas (1852), then warred with Urquiza. National political unity was achieved and reforms were initated during his presidency. Founded newspaper *La Nación* (Buenos Aires) and wrote works on history.

Mitropoulos, Dimitri (dēmēt'rē mētrô'pōōlôs), 1896?–, American conductor, b. Greece. Conductor of the Minneapolis Symphony Orchestra (1937–46), he became in 1949 associate conductor of the New York Philharmonic and permanent conductor in 1950. He is known as a champion of contemporary music.

Mitscherlich, Eilhard (īl'härt mĭ'chûrlĭkh), 1794–1863, German chemist. Discovered principle of ISOMORPHISM, worked on compounds of phosphorus and arsenic, discovered nitrobenzene and some acids.

Mitsubishi: see ZAIBATSU.

Mitsui: see ZAIBATSU.

Mitylene, Greece: see MYTILENE.

Miya-jima, Japan: see ITSUKU-SHIMA.

Mizpah or **Mizpeh** (mĭz'pŭ) [Heb.,= watch tower]. **1** See GALEED. **2** Meeting place of anc. Hebrews on important occasions. Judges 20.1; 21.1,5,8; 1 Sam. 7.5.

Mjosa (myû'sä), Nor. *Mjøsa,* lake, area 141 sq. mi., depth 1,453 ft., SE Norway; largest in Norway. It is drained by a tributary of the Glomma. Lillehammer, Gjovik, and Hamar are on its shores.

Mn, chemical symbol of the element MANGANESE.

Mnemosyne (nēmŏ'sĭnē, –zĭnē) [Gr.,= memory], Greek personification of memory; daughter of Uranus and Gaea and mother of the nine MUSES by Zeus.

Mnesicles (nĕ'sĭklēz), 5th cent. B.C., Greek architect. Designed the PROPYLAEA and possibly the ERECHTHEUM on the Acropolis at Athens.

Mo, chemical symbol of the element MOLYBDENUM.

moa (mō'ŭ), extinct flightless New Zealand bird, related to kiwi, emu, cassowary, and ostrich.

Moab (mō'ăb), anc. nation in hilly region E of Dead Sea, sporadically at war with the Hebrews. Moabites traditionally descended from Lot; language on MOABITE STONE almost the same as biblical Hebrew. Gen. 19.37; Num. 22–24; Judges 3; 2 Kings 3; Isa. 15–16; Jer. 48; Ezek. 25; Amos 2; Zeph. 2.

Moab, town (pop. 1,274), E Utah, on Colorado R. Near by are Arches Natl. Monument and vanadium and uranium mines.

Moabite stone, erected by Mesha of Moab, who composed the inscription (850 B.C.) on it to commemorate a victory in his revolt against Israel. Discovered 1868 at Dibon; fragments are in the Louvre.

Moallakat: see MUALLAQAT.

mob, in psychology, a group of people, strongly interacting, their conduct dominated by suggestion and emotion, not reason. Crowds, lacking intense mob emotionality, may become mobs in stress or danger. Fervent or hysterical leaders can drive crowds to mob heroism or extreme brutality. In mobs, individuals are in heightened, almost hypnotic state of suggestibility and lose normally controlling inhibitions. See also SOCIAL PSYCHOLOGY.

Moberg, Vilhelm (vĭl'hĕlm mōō'bĕryŭ), 1898–, Swedish novelist and dramatist. His novels (e.g., *Ride This Night!* 1941; *The Emigrants,* 1950) often deal with lives of small farmers.

Moberly (mō'bûrlē), city (pop. 13,115), N central Mo., NNW of Columbia; laid out 1866. In area of coal and fire-clay deposits, it has rail shops and light mfg.

Mobile (mōbēl'), city (pop. 129,009), SW Ala., at mouth of Mobile R. (crossed by Bankhead Tunnel, 1941) on MOBILE BAY. Only seaport in state; has large South American trade. Processes and ships food, lumber, cotton, naval stores, paper; ships iron, steel products. Shipbuilding; mfg. of asbestos, chemicals. Founded 1710 by sieur de Bienville; cap. of La. 1710–19. Ceded to Britain 1763, taken by Spain 1780, by U.S. 1813. Rebel ships ran Federal blockade from here in Civil War, until Adm. Farragut's victory (1864). Captured by Gen. CANBY, 1865. In 1937, second free port in U.S. estab. here. Has cathedral (R.C.), ante-bellum homes, U.S. marine hospital. Spring Hill Col. (Jesuit; for men; 1831) is near. Annual Mardi Gras (from 1704), Azalea Trail Festival (from 1929).

Mobile, river in SW Ala. formed by junction of Alabama and Tombigbee rivers. Flows c.45 mi. S to Mobile. Here it enters **Mobile Bay,** a Gulf of Mexico arm, c.35 mi. long from the Gulf to mouth of river and 8–18 mi. wide. Ship channel enters Gulf between Mobile Point and Dauphin Isl. Battle won here on Aug. 5, 1864, by Adm. FARRAGUT.

moccasin flower: see LADY'S-SLIPPER.

Mocha (mō'kŭ), town (pop. 600), Yemen, SW Arabia; a port on Red Sea. Formerly noted for coffee export. Declined in 19th cent. with rise of Aden.

mockingbird, North American songbird of catbird and brown thrasher family, allied to thrushes and wrens. Noted for melodious song and as mimic.

mock orange or **syringa,** deciduous shrub of genus *Philadelphus,* native to Eurasia and North America. Their fragrant white flowers blooming in late spring are similar to orange blossoms. *Syringa* is the generic name for the unrelated lilac.

Moctezuma: see MONTEZUMA.

mode, in grammar: see MOOD.

mode, in music, any pattern of arrangement of the tones and half-tones of a scale. Modes are not scales; they vary in patterns of tones and half-tones. This can best be understood by considering the white keys of the piano. One mode can be represented by the series of white keys from D to D, whereas another would be from F to F, and so on. The pattern of whole and half-tones from D to D would thus be 1, ½, 1, 1, 1, ½, 1; from F to F it would be 1, 1, 1, ½, 1, 1, ½. A melody composed within one mode, if transferred to another, would be completely changed. The use of modes evolved from the highly developed modal system of ancient Greece. In medieval plain song, there were eight modes, four called authentic, four plagal, each authentic mode having a corresponding plagal one (later, after 1547, there were 12). The difference between an authentic mode and its plagal is in range. For example, the authentic mode (D–D) has as its plagal A–A, but there is an authentic mode A–A that has as its plagal E–E. If, in a piece of music written in the D mode, the melody fell between D and D, the mode would be authentic; if between A and A, the mode would be plagal.

mode, in statistics, an infrequently used type of average. In a group of numbers, the mode is the number occurring most frequently.

Model Parliament: see PARLIAMENT.

Modena (mô'dänä), city (pop. 50,451), Emilia-Romagna, N central Italy, on Aemilian Way. Agr. center. Free commune from 12th cent. Passed to ESTE family 1288; became a duchy 1452. Has 12th-cent. Romanesque cathedral and fine art collections.

modern art: see ABSTRACT ART; CUBISM; DADA; FAUVISM; FUTURISM; IMPRESSIONISM; POST-IMPRESSIONISM.

modernism, in religion, movement to reconcile developments of 19th-cent. science and philosophy with historic Christianity. It arose from evident disparity between Darwin's theory of evolution and old literal interpretation of Genesis and was influenced by attempts to read Darwinian principles into history of civilization. Its general trait was to reject belief in supernatural, and to consider Church as only a human society. Ideas were opposed by fundamentalists in 1920s and by Anglican groups. In the Roman Catholic Church a similar movement headed by Loisy was declared heretical by the pope (1907).

modernismo (mōdhĕrnē'smō), movement in Spanish literature, beginning in Latin America in late 19th cent. with poetry of José Martí. It was marked by conscious artistry in choosing images, portraying color, and creating subtle word music. The subject matter of modernist poetry is exotic, remote, and escapist (swans, princesses, Japanese landscape). The best-known modernist in both poetry and prose was Rubén DARÍO.

Modestinus, Herennius (hůrē'nēůs mŏdůstī'-nůs), fl. c.250 B.C., Roman jurist, much cited in the Corpus Juris Civilis.

Modesto (mōdĕ'stō), city (pop. 17,389), central Calif., SE of Stockton and on Tuolumne R.; founded 1870. Processing and trade center for fruit, poultry, and dairy products of San Joaquin Valley.

Modigliani, Amedeo (ämādā'ō mōdēlyä'nē), 1884–1920, Italian painter. Studied in Florence but early went to Paris, where his sculptures were influenced by cubism and Negro art. In paintings he used distortion for emotional effect. Recognized only by leading artists during short life; died in poverty.

Modjeska, Helena (můjĕ'sků), 1844–1909, Polish actress; in U.S. after 1877. Considered among greatest tragic actresses of her time in *Adrienne Lecouvreur, Doll's House,* and plays of Shakspere.

Modoc Indians (mō'dŏk), North American tribe of Lutuamian linguistic stock, in early 19th cent. in SW Oregon and N Calif. Their culture was almost identical with that of KLAMATH INDIANS, their kinsmen. Trouble between the Modoc and early American settlers ended when a group of Modoc under Captain Jack left the reservation in 1870, defended themselves in lava beds of N Calif., murdered Gen. Edward R. S. Canby and another U.S. mediator, and were finally defeated. The tribe was dispersed.

Modred, Sir: see ARTHURIAN LEGEND.

modulation, in music, changing from one key to another in a composition. Among devices used to make this transition smooth to the ear is using a chord common to both the old and new keys as a pivot. If there is no common chord between the two keys, a passage may have to move through several keys before the desired modulation has been effected smoothly. In enharmonic modulation, a chord of the old key is simply changed in notation (e.g., A sharp becomes B flat) and is then considered a chord of the new key.

Moe, Jorgen Engebretsen, Nor. *Jørgen Engebretsen Moe* (yûr'gůn ĕng'ůbrĕtsůn mō'ů), 1813–82, Norwegian folklorist and poet, bishop of Kristiansand.

Moesia (mē'shů), anc. region SE Europe. Organized as Roman prov. (A.D. 44) including, roughly, modern Serbia (Upper Moesia) and Bulgaria (Lower Moesia).

Mofaddaliyat (mōfä"dälēät') or **Mufaddaliyat** (mōō–), great Arabic anthology compiled by Al Mufaddal of Kufa (d. c.775). Contains 126 poems by 67 authors of Golden Age of Arabic poetry (500–650).

Moffat Tunnel: see FRONT RANGE.

Mogilev (mŭgēlyôf'), city (pop. 99,440), E Belorussia. It is an industrial and transportation center on the Dnieper.

Mogollon Plateau (mōgōyōn'), tableland c.7,000–8,000 ft. high, E central Ariz., S of Winslow. Mogollon Rim, its rugged S escarpment, is sometimes called Mogollon Mts. Not directly linked to Mogollon Mts. of W N.Mex.

Mogul (mō'gŭl) or **Mughal** (mōōgŭl'), Moslem empire of India, 1526–1817. Founded by BABER, who claimed descent from the Mongol conqueror Jenghiz Khan. Its greatest rulers were AKBAR, SHAH JEHAN, and AURANGZEB. Disintegrated in 18th cent. under blows of Sikhs and Mahrattas, but the British maintained puppet emperor until 1857. Empire's lasting achievements were in art (see MOSLEM ART AND ARCHITECTURE).

Mohacs, Hung. *Mohács* (mô'häch), city (pop. 18,355), S Hungary, on the Danube. Here on Aug. 29, 1526, Louis II of Hungary was disastrously defeated by Suleiman I of Turkey. The king and nearly the entire Hungarian army were killed. Louis's defeat, which laid Hungary open to Turkish domination, was partly caused by the probably deliberate failure of John Zapolya to join Louis with his Transylvanian contingent. I

1687 Charles V of Lorraine routed the Turks on the same battlefield.

mohair, hair of the Angora goat or a fabric made from it alone or combined with other fibers.

Mohammed (mōhŏ'mĭd, mōhă'mĭd) [Arabic,= praised], 570?–632, the Prophet of ISLAM, founder of one of the world's great religions, b. Mecca. Born into the tribe of Koreish, which ruled Mecca, he married Khadija, a wealthy widow, After he was 40 he had visions that were to be collected and recorded in the KORAN; these were the basis of the new religion, which made little headway in Mecca, though he converted Ali, who married Mohammed's daughter Fatima, and Abu Bakr. A plot to murder him led to his flight (the HEGIRA) in 622 to Yathrib (now Medina). From this event Islam counts its dates. At Medina he built a theocratic state, from which the great Mohammedan empire was to grow. He fought with Mecca, but in 630 it fell to him without a fight. His sayings are the law of Islam, together with the Koran. In later life he had many wives, notably Ayesha. Name also Mahomet, Muhammad, and other forms (e.g., Mehemet).

Mohammed, Ottoman sultans. **Mohammed II** (the Conqueror), 1429–81, reigned 1451–81. He completed the conquest of the Byzantine Empire by storming Constantinople after a 50-day siege (1453). He also conquered most of the Balkan Peninsula but was checked at Belgrade by Hunyadi, in Albania by Scanderbeg, and in Rhodes by the Knights Hospitalers. In Asia, he conquered Karamania and Trebizond. He captured Otranto, in Italy (1480), but the expedition had no results. The true founder of the Ottoman Empire, he was outstanding as a commander, an administrator, and a scholar. **Mohammed IV,** 1641–92, reigned 1648–87. His army, driven back from the siege of Vienna (1683), was routed at Mohacs (1687), and he was deposed. **Mohammed V,** 1844–1918, succeeded to the throne in 1909, the Young Turk revolution having deposed his brother, Abdu-l-Hamid II. ENVER PASHA held the actual control. His reign was a series of disasters: the loss of Tripoli to Italy (1911–12); the BALKAN WARS (1912–13); and the defeat of Turkey in World War I. Turkey capitulated to the Allies soon after the accession of his brother, **Mohammed VI,** 1861–1926, who accepted the Treaty of SÈVRES and ruled as a puppet of the Allies. He was overthrown and exiled in 1922 by Kemal ATATURK. His cousin Abdu-l-Mejid succeeded him as caliph, but in 1924 the caliphate was abolished, and all Ottoman princes were exiled.

Mohammed Ahmed: see MAHDI.

Mohammed Ali, 1769–1849, pasha (governor) of Egypt after 1805. In 1811 he dealt final blow to power of the MAMELUKES. With his son IBRAHIM PASHA, he defended the Turkish sultan (his nominal overlord) in campaigns in Arabia and in Greece, where he scored successes until his defeat in battle of NAVARINO. When the sultan denied him the governorship of Syria, he turned against him and marched into Syria (1833). His revolt, begun 1839 in Asia Minor, was checked by opposition of European powers. By way of compromise, Abdu-l-Mejid, the sultan, made governorship hereditary in Mohammed's line. Present royal family of Egypt is descended from him.

Mohammedan and **Mohammedanism:** see ISLAM.

Mohammed ibn Tumart (ĭ'bŭn to͞omärt'), c.1080–1128?, Berber Moslem leader, founder of the ALMOHADES.

Mohammed Reza Shah Pahlevi (rēzä' shä' pä'lŭvē), 1919–, shah of Iran. In 1941 he succeeded his father, Reza Shah Pahlevi. Visited the U.S. in 1949. Launched liberal Seven-Year Plan for economic development of country. His reign has seen rise of leftist Tudeh party and nationalization of oil industry. He clashed with Premier Mossadegh in 1953.

Mohave, river and desert: see MOJAVE.

Mohave Indians (mōhä'vē), North American tribe of Yuman linguistic stock, formerly on Ariz. and Calif. banks of Colorado R. Practiced semisedentary agr.

Mohawk, river, largest tributary of the Hudson, rising in central N.Y. and flowing c.140 mi. S and SE, past Rome, Utica, Amsterdam, Schenectady, to the Hudson at Cohoes. Paralleled by the Barge Canal from Rome to its mouth. ERIE CANAL (1825) also followed it. Beautiful, fertile valley was scene of many battles in French and Indian War and in Revolution; important route in western migration.

Mohawk Indians: see IROQUOIS CONFEDERACY.

Mohawk Trail. 1 Old road in N.Y. following Mohawk R., important as route for settlers emigrating W. **2** Motor highway across N Mass. from Greenfield to North Adams.

Mohegan Indians, North American tribe, also called Mohican, the E branch of the MAHICAN INDIANS. In SW Conn. in the 17th cent. they joined with the Pequot, but later Uncas rebelled against Pequot rule and formed a band generally known as the Mohegan. This band in alliance with the English became very powerful, but as white settlement increased the Indians declined and died out on a reservation in Conn.

Mohenjo-Daro (mōhĕn'jō-dä'rō), archaeological site in Sind, W Pakistan, near Indus R. Gave its name to **Mohenjo-Daro civilization** or **Indus civilization,** revealed by finds here and at Harappa, 400 mi. NE, in S Punjab near Ravi R. It was an urban culture resembling that of Sumer, which existed at same time (3d millennium B.C.). Cotton textiles and burnt modern-type brick were used. Quasi-pictographic writing, as yet undeciphered, is apparently related to that of Sumer, to Brahmi alphabet of India and to South Arabian alphabet. Shift of river course caused decline of Mohenjo-Daro.

Mohican Indians: see MAHICAN INDIANS; MOHEGAN INDIANS.

Mohl, Hugo von (ho͞o'gō fŭn mōl'), 1805–72, German botanist. An expert on microscopy, he is noted for research on nature of protoplasm and chlorophyll and on physiology of higher plants; laid foundation for later work on structure of palms and cycads.

Moholy-Nagy, Laszlo (lä'slō môhoi-nŏ'dyŭ), 1895–1946, Hungarian painter and designer.

A founder of constructivism. Taught at BAUHAUS in Germany and later at its offshoot, the Chicago Inst. of Design.

Moisie (mwäzē′), river of E Que., Canada, rising near Labrador border and flowing 210 mi. S to St. Lawrence R. Near mouth is Moisie village.

Moissan, Henri (ārē′ mwäsā′), 1852–1907, French chemist. Won 1906 Nobel Prize for isolating fluorine and inventing an electric-arc furnace.

Moivre, Abraham de (äbrä-äm′ dů mwä′vrů), 1667–1754, French-English mathematician. He assisted Royal Society in deciding between Newton and Leibniz as prior inventor of differential calculus. Contributed to trigonometry and law of probabilities.

Mojave (mōhä′vē), river of S Calif. rising in San Bernardino Mts. and flowing c.100 mi. N and NE, mostly underground, to disappear in Mojave Desert. Also spelled Mohave.

Mojave Desert, c.15,000 sq. mi. of barren mountains and flat desert valleys in S Calif., S of the Sierra Nevada and N of the San Gabriel and San Bernardino Mts. Supports mining (silver, gold, tungsten, iron), granite quarrying, and chemical extraction (borax, potash, salt). Its lakes are usually dry. Mojave R is in S part. Death Valley is to N.

Moji (mō′jē), industrial city (pop. 109,567), N Kyushu, Japan; port on Shimonoseki Strait. Tunnel connects it with Shimonoseki on Honshu.

Moki Indians: see HOPI INDIANS.

Mokuaweoweo (mōko͞o′ůwā′ōwā′ō), active volcano, on Hawaii, T.H., on summit of Mauna Loa. Crater is 3.7 mi. long, 1.7 mi. wide, and 800 ft. deep.

molasses, viscid residue separated from cane sugar during crystallization process. The least-refined grade, blackstrap, used in stock feed, alcohol manufacture, and for human food. Greater refining produces lighter grades with more sugar; they are used as food and to make rum.

Molay, Jacques de (zhäk′ dů mōlā′), 1243?–1314, last grand master of the KNIGHTS TEMPLARS. Summoned to France in 1306, he was tried for heresy by an inquisitorial court, confessed under torture, and was burned when he recanted.

mold, name for certain multicellular fungi, generally saprophytic. One of the commonest is the black bread mold (*Rhizopus nigricans*). Species of *Penicillium* are useful in the preparation of certain cheeses. PENICILLIN and other antibiotics are obtained from certain molds. Some molds cause mildew, ringworm, and other diseases. See *ill.*, p. 813.

Moldau (môl′dou), Czech *Vltava,* longest river in Czechoslovakia, rising in Bohemian Forest, and flowing 267 mi. N past Prague into the Elbe.

Moldavia (mŏldā′vēů), historic province (c.14,700 sq. mi.; pop. 2,598,258), E Rumania, between the Carpathians (W) and the Pruth R. (E); cap. Jassy. Galati, on the Danube, is the chief port. A fertile plain drained by Sereth R., it is the granary of Rumania. Region formed part of Roman Dacia. After many foreign invasions, Moldavia became a principality under native rulers (14th cent.); it then also included BUKOVINA and BESSARABIA. The princes ruled despotically; the boyars (great landowners) reduced rural population to serfdom. Moldavia reached its height under Stephen the Great, but after his death (1504) became tributary to Turkey. Early in 18th cent. the native princes were replaced by governors (hospodars) mostly Greek PHANARIOTS, appointed by the sultans. Their rule ended 1822 after the Greek insurrection instigated by Alexander YPSILANTI, and native hospodars were appointed. The Treaty of ADRIANOPLE (1829) made Moldavia a virtual Russian protectorate, but in 1856 the Congress of Paris guaranteed the independence—under nominal Turkish overlordship—of the two Danubian Principalities (Walachia and Moldavia). With the accession (1859) of Alexander John Cuza as prince of both principalities, the history of modern Rumania began.

Moldavian Soviet Socialist Republic, constituent republic (c.13,000 sq. mi.; pop. c.2,660,000) of the USSR, in SE Europe, separated from Rumania by the Pruth R.; cap. Kishinev. Population is mostly Moldavian (i.e., Rumanian-speaking), with Russian, Jewish, Ukrainian, and Bulgarian minorities. The republic, which corresponds to the larger part of BESSARABIA, was estab. 1940, after Rumania had ceded Bessarabia back to Russia.

Molde Fjord (môl′dů, mô′lů), inlet (60 mi. long) of North Sea, W Norway. Town of Molde (pop. 3,774), tourist center, is on N bank overlooking the Dovrefjell. Famous Romsdal Fjord is an arm.

mole, in chemistry: see MOLECULAR WEIGHT.

mole, in zoology, small insectivorous burrowing mammal belonging to various genera found in Europe, Asia, North America. Moles have soft, thick, gray or brown fur; pointed muzzle; small, weak eyes; no external ears; strong forelimbs, digging claws.

Molech or **Moloch** (both mō′lůk), Canaanitish god of fire, to whom children were offered in sacrifice. Shrine was at Tophet in valley of Hinnom. Solomon and Ahaz are said to have introduced this worship. Lev. 18.21; 20.2; 1 Kings 11.7; 2 Kings 23.10; Jer. 32.35.

molecular weight (můlĕ′kyo͞olůr), relative weight of MOLECULE of substance compared with a standard. Can be calculated from FORMULA by adding relative weights (ATOMIC WEIGHT) of atoms in molecule. Molecular weights can be determined by various methods in laboratory; are important in chemical analysis. Gram-molecular weight (or mole) of substance is often used, i.e., weight in grams equal numerically to molecular weight of substance.

molecule (mŏl′ůkūl), smallest particle into which substance can be divided without changing properties. Molecules are in constant, vibratory motion; state or form in which matter appears (liquid, solid, or gas) depends on velocity of molecules and distance between them. In general, when heat is applied to substance, molecules vibrate faster and move farther apart; at constant pressure this causes expansion. When heat is withdrawn contraction occurs. If heat is added continuously, the velocity of molecules becomes so great that change of state occurs. Pressure also affects molecular state of substance. Molecules are made up of atoms either of same kind or of two or more kinds; substances differ according to structure and composition of their molecules. Molecules of different substances differ in size, weight, structure. Molecular structure is affected in chemical action.

Molière, Jean Baptiste Poquelin (zhã bäptēst′ pôkůlē′ môlyĕr′), 1622–73, French dramatist and actor, one of the world's greatest comic authors. Originally named Poquelin and son of a prosperous merchant in Paris, he early joined the BÉJART company of actors. After touring the provinces, the company was estab. in Paris (1658); in 1665 it became the King's Troupe and in 1680 the COMÉDIE FRANÇAISE. In Louis XIV, Molière found a generous patron and a protector against his many enemies. The genius of Molière is equally apparent in his broad farces (such as *Le Médecin malgré lui,* 1666; *Les Fourberies de Scapin,* 1671) and in his great comedies of character, in which he ridicules a vice or a type of excess by caricaturing a person incarnating it. Among these timeless satires are *L'Avare* (1668)—the miser; *Le Bourgeois gentilhomme* (1670)—the parvenu; *Les Femmes savantes* (1672)—bluestockings; *Le Malade imaginaire* (1673)—the hypochondriac; and *Tartuffe* (1664)—the religious hypocrite. In *Le Misanthrope* (1666), perhaps his greatest play, the chief character is psychologically more complex, the plot less conventional, as is also the case in *L'École des femmes* (1663). Both these plays probably caricature Molière himself. *Amphytrion* (1668) is Molière's most poetic and one of his funniest works. There are many English translations.

Molina, Luis (lwēs′ mōlē′nä), 1535–1600, Spanish Jesuit. His *Concordia* (1589) set forth a doctrine since called Molinism in an attempt to reconcile the dogma of God's grace and that of man's free will. The theology of Francisco SUÁREZ was an effort at compromise between Thomism and Molinism.

Molina, Tirso de: see TIRSO DE MOLINA.

Moline (mōlēn′), city (pop. 37,397), NW Ill., on the Mississippi (bridged); platted 1843. Forms, with ROCK ISLAND, EAST MOLINE, and DAVENPORT, Iowa, an economic unit called Quad Cities. Transportation, trade, and industrial center; coal fields near by. Mfg. of farm equipment and machinery, wood and metal products. John DEERE moved here 1847.

Molinos, Miguel de (mēgĕl′ dā mōlē′nōs), 1640–97, Spanish mystic, founder of QUIETISM. His *Guida spirituale* (1675) detailed perfection as complete contemplative passivity of soul. He was condemned by the Inquisition (1687) and died in prison.

Molise, region of Italy: see ABRUZZI E MOLISE.

Mölk, Austria: see MELK.

mollusk (mŏ′lůsk), chiefly aquatic, invertebrate animal of phylum Mollusca. It has a soft, unsegmented body with the under part usually forming a muscular foot. Many forms have an external shell, some have an internal one, a few have no shell. Classes include gastropods, e.g., snail, slug; cephalopods, e.g., squid; and bivalves, e.g., clam, oyster, mussel.

Mollwitz (môl′vĭts), village near Breslau, Lower Silesia, where Frederick II of Prussia defeated Austrians in 1741. Battle proved superiority of modern infantry over cavalry.

Molly Maguires (můgwī′ůrz), secret organization of Irishmen in coal districts of Scranton, Pa., c.1865–75. An attempt to combat oppressive industrial and living conditions, it often resorted to murdering the police, who were controlled by the mine owners. A strike was organized in 1875, but the organization's power was finally broken by the spying activity of the Pinkerton agency on behalf of the industrialists. Twenty miners were hanged.

Molnar, Ferenc (fĕ′rĕnts môl′när), 1878–1952, Hungarian dramatist and novelist. His plays, very successful in the U.S., include *Liliom, The Swan, The Guardsman,* and *The Play's the Thing.*

Moloch, in Bible: see MOLECH.

Molokai (mō′lōkī), island (259 sq. mi.; pop. 5,280), one of Hawaiian Isls. Cattle, pineapples. On N coast is Kalaupapa Settlement (leper colony, estab. 1860), where Father DAMIEN worked and died.

Molotov, Vyacheslav Mikhailovich (vyĕ″chĭsläf′ mēkhī′lůvĭch mô′lůtůf), 1890–, Russian statesman whose real name is Skriabin. Chairman of council of people's commissars (i.e., premier) 1930–41; vice premier from 1941; foreign minister (1939–49, 1953–). Negotiated Russo-German nonaggression pact (1939). Was outstanding Russian spokesman in world affairs during World War II and postwar years.

Molotov, city (pop. c.450,000), RSFSR, on Kama R., in W foothills of the Urals; named Perm until 1940. Major inland port and transportation center; produces pig iron, machinery, chemicals, wood products. Has numerous cultural institutions.

molting, periodic shedding and renewal of outer skin or skeleton, fur, or feathers of animal. In birds, the number and completeness of molts varies; loss and replacement of feathers is usually gradual, in sequence. Invertebrates, e.g., insects and crabs, with outer skeletons shed them periodically to permit growth. Snakes shed skins; mammals change from heavy winter to light summer coat, and some change color.

Moltke, Helmuth, Graf von (hĕl′mōōt gräf′ fŭn môlt′ků), 1800–1891, Prussian field marshal. Served in Danish army before 1822, in Turkish army 1835–39. As chief of the general staff from 1858 he shaped the modern Prussian army and was the chief architect of the Prussian victories in the Danish, Austro-Prussian, and Franco-Prussian wars. Resigned 1888. His nephew **Helmuth von Moltke,** 1848–1916, succeeded SCHLIEFFEN as chief of staff in 1906. Shortly before the outbreak of World War I he modified and weakened Schlieffen's famous plan.

Moluccas (můlŭ′kůz) or **Spice Islands,** island group (c.32,300 sq. mi.; pop. 560,000), Indonesia, between Celebes and New Guinea. Includes HALMAHERA, CERAM, AMBOINA, and TERNATE. Discovered in early 16th cent. by the Portuguese; taken in 17th cent. by the Dutch, who monopolized clove trade.

molybdenite (mŭlĭb'dŭnīt), a mineral, molybdenum disulphide, blue gray, with metallic luster and greasy feel. An important ore of molybdenum, found in Saxony, Bohemia, England, Australia, U.S.

molybdenum (mŭlĭb'dŭnŭm), rare, silvery metallic element (symbol = Mo; see also ELEMENT, table). Has luster, can be drawn into wires and thin sheets. Combines with various substances. Does not occur uncombined; ores are widely but sparingly distributed. Used to make alloy steel, in radio-tube grids and filaments, and in electrodes.

Mombasa (mŏmbä'sŭ), city (pop. 84,746), Kenya, port on Indian Ocean, on Mombasa Isl. and near-by mainland area. An early center of Arab trade, it was visited 1498 by Vasco da Gama. Held by Portuguese until 1698, when it was recaptured by Arabs. Later became part of Zanzibar sultanate and passed to Great Britain c.1880. Ships coffee, cotton, and tin (from Uganda).

momentum (mōmĕn'tŭm), term commonly used to indicate force or power that moving body exerts to maintain its motion. In mechanics it is defined as the quantity of motion of the body, specifically the product of its mass and velocity. An external force acting on a body or system of bodies causes change in momentum of the body. Impulse of a force (i.e., product of force and time in which it acts) upon a body is measured by change in momentum. If no external force acts on body in motion or a system of bodies there is no change in momentum, even though there is, in some cases, internal disturbance of the system; this conclusion is known as principle of conservation of momentum.

Mommsen, Theodor (tā'ōdōr môm'sŭn), 1817–1903, German historian. Major work *History of Rome* (vols. I-III, 1854–56; Vol. V, 1885). Received 1902 Nobel Prize in Literature.

Momus or **Momos** (both: mō'mŭs), in Greek myth, personification of mockery and rebuke; son of Night.

Monaca (mŏn'ŭkŭ), borough (pop. 7,415), W Pa., on Ohio R. and NW of Pittsburgh. Mfg. of glass and metal products.

Monaco, Lorenzo: see LORENZO MONACO.

Monaco (mŭnä'kō, mŏ'nŭkō), principality (c.370 acres; pop. c.20,000), on the Mediterranean, an enclave within SE France. Consists of three adjoining sections: Monaco (cap.), La Condamine (business dist.), and MONTE CARLO. Its beautiful situation and its famous gambling casino make it one of the most fashionable Riviera resorts. Reigning prince: Rainier III. Casino, privately managed as concession, supplies most of state revenue. Only c.2,000 inhabitants are Monegasque subjects; these are barred from gambling. Principality has customs union with France; its currency is interchangeable with French. Monaco was ruled by Genoese Grimaldi family from 13th cent.; in 1731 the French Matignon family succeeded to principality by marriage; it adopted the name Grimaldi. Monaco was under Spanish protection from 1524, under French protection from 1641, under Sardinian protection 1815–61. By treaty of 1918, succession to the throne must be approved by the French government.

monad: see BRUNO, GIORDANO; LEIBNIZ, G. W.

Monadhliath Mountains (mō'nŭlē'ŭ), Inverness-shire, Scotland, between the Spey valley and Loch Ness.

Monadnock (mŭnăd'nŏk), isolated peak, 3,165 ft. high, SW N.H., NW of Jaffrey.

Monaghan (mŏ'nŭgŭn), inland county (498 sq. mi.; pop. 57,215), Ireland, in Ulster; co. town Monaghan. Primarily an agr. area. Much livestock is raised.

Monahans (mŏn'ŭhănz), city (pop. 6,311), W Texas, N of Pecos R. Processes oil, gasoline, carbon black, and cottonseed products. Chemical plant near by.

monarchianism (mōnär'kēŭnĭzŭm) [Gr.,= belief in the rule of one], concept of God, holding his sole authority even over Christ and the Holy Spirit. Its characteristic tenet, that God the Father and Jesus Christ are one person, was developed as ADOPTIONISM and as philosophy of SABELLIUS.

monasticism, organized life in common in a retreat from worldly life for religious purposes. Men who belong to these communities are monks and their establishments are monasteries; communities of women are commonly called convents and their inhabitants nuns. The monastic life is known to most great religions—Buddhism (incl. Lamaism), Jainism, and Islam, as well as Christianity. In Christianity it arose from movement to seek voluntary seclusion of a hermit's life. In the Eastern Orthodox Church monks still have cenobitic (i.e., hermitlike but lived in common) practices. The usual rules are those of St. Basil the Great (see BASILIAN MONKS). In the West communal life has been the usual form of monasticism since the time of St. Benedict. The Benedictine abbeys under his rule were the preservers of Roman civilization in the period of chaos from the 6th to the 10th cent. and were the source of later learning. In the Roman Catholic Church there are many orders of monks and nuns, including the friars—FRANCISCANS, DOMINICANS, and CARMELITES. Some are entirely secluded (enclosed) but most are devoted to teaching, charity, or missionary work. The Jesuits (see JESUS, SOCIETY OF) and the Christian Brothers are typical of modern monastic effort. In the Reformation many monasteries were destroyed, and in general Protestantism has not fostered the ascetic ideal of monasticism.

Monastir, Yugoslavia: see BITOLJ.

monazite (mō'nŭzīt), one of the rare earths and the chief source of thorium and cerium. Brown or reddish with resinous luster, translucent to opaque. Occurs with granites and gneisses but more commonly in river and beach sands derived from monazite-bearing rocks.

Moncenisio, Italian name for Mont CENIS.

Monck, Charles Stanley, 4th **Viscount,** 1819–94, governor general of Canada (1861–68).

Monck or **Monk, George,** 1st **duke of Albemarle,** 1608–70, English soldier and politician. Lieutenant-general under Cromwell, he subdued the Scots in 1651. In 1660 he supported the Stuarts, raised an army, and persuaded Parliament to dissolve itself. On his advice Charles II issued Declaration of Breda and the Restoration was effected.

Moncks Corner, town (pop. 1,818), SE S.C., N of Charleston, on Cooper R. near Santee-Cooper hydro-electric and navigation project.

Monckton Milnes, Richard: see HOUGHTON, RICHARD MONCKTON MILNES, 1ST BARON.

Moncton, city (pop. 27,334), SE N.B., on Petitcodiac R. and NE of St. John. Industrial and transportation center in lumbering and farming area. Settled by French, who were followed (1763) by Germans from Pennsylvania.

Monday: see WEEK.

Mondrian, Piet (pēt' môn'drēän), 1872–1944, Dutch painter. Influenced by cubists, he developed a geometric, nonobjective style called neoplasticism. Influenced Bauhaus movement. Generally used only primary colors; typical compositions have only vertical and horizontal lines at 90° angles.

monel metal (mōnĕl'), silver white alloy of copper and nickel (c.⅓ copper, ⅔ nickel) with small amount of other metals. It is strong, resists acid corrosion, holds bright finish.

Monessen (mu̇nĕs'u̇n), city (pop. 17,896), SW Pa., on Monongahela R. and S of Pittsburgh; laid out 1897. Steel and iron works.

Monet, Claude (klōd' mônā'), 1840–1926, French impressionist landscape painter. With Sisley and Berthe Morisot he organized the exhibition of 1875, which the critics derisively called impressionist, after the title of one of his pictures, *Impression: soleil levant*. Lived in extreme poverty until 1883 when he gained some recognition. A leader in plein-air painting, he eliminated black and brown and achieved light effects by means of broken color.

Moneta, Ernesto Teodoro (mōnā'tä), 1833–1918, Italian pacifist, president (1906) of the International Peace Congress in Milan. Awarded 1907 Nobel Peace Prize.

monetary union, agreement among nations to unify currency values, stabilizing currencies or arriving at a common currency. Best-known monetary unions are the Latin Monetary Union (formed 1865) and the Scandinavian union (1873). The Bretton Woods agreements of 1944 planned the International Monetary Fund.

money, term involving two concepts—the abstract units of value and the means of payment. Many ancient communities took cattle as their standard of value but made payments with manageable objects. Similarly the Code of Hammurabi indicated that silver was used for both purposes. A great variety of objects have served as money, e.g., shells, tobacco, and dried fish. Precious metals, because of their durability, convenience, and high intrinsic value, are preferred. However, the intrinsic value of the object being used as money is no longer important. (State coinage, said to have originated in Lydia in 7th cent. B.C., enabled governments to issue coins whose nominal value exceeded their value as metals.) Paper currency, much in use for the past 300 years, is usually backed by some standard commodity of intrinsic value into which it may be converted upon demand. U.S. currency was based on BIMETALLISM during most of the 19th cent., and on a full gold standard from 1900 to 1933. Since the 1934 Gold Reserve Act, the U.S. has been on a modified gold standard of value, but gold is no longer used as a medium of exchange. Today the favored means of payment is the bank check, rather than coin or currency.

Monferrato, Italy: see MONTFERRAT.

Monge, Gaspard, comte de Péluse (gäspär' mōzh' kōt' du̇ pālüz'), 1746–1818, French mathematician and physicist. His geometrical researches laid foundations of modern descriptive geometry.

Mongolia (mŏn-gō'lēu̇), Asiatic region (1,000,000 sq. mi.; pop. 3,500,000), lying roughly between Sinkiang prov., China, on W and Manchuria on E, between Siberia on N and Great Wall of China on S. Comprises Mongolian People's Republic (Outer Mongolia) and Inner Mongolia (Chahar, Suiyuan, Ningsia provs., China). Mainly a high plateau with Gobi desert in central part. Exports include wool, cloth, and hides. Jenghiz Khan conquered Mongolia c.1205 and led Mongols in creating a great empire. China took Inner Mongolia c.1635. In late 17th cent. she subjugated Outer Mongolia; it broke away in 1921 to become in 1924 **Mongolian People's Republic** (615,000 sq. mi.; pop. 1,000,000). Closely allied to USSR, the republic (comprising over half of Mongolia) remained unrecognized by China until 1945. In 1949 Chinese Communists joined most of N Inner Mongolia to parts of Manchuria to form **Inner Mongolian Autonomous Region** (230,000 sq. mi.; pop. 2,000,000).

Mongolian languages: see LANGUAGE (table).

Mongolian People's Republic: see MONGOLIA.

Mongolism: see FEEBLE-MINDEDNESS.

Mongols (mŏng'gu̇lz), Asiatic people, numbering c.3,000,000 and distributed mainly in Mongolia, N and W Manchuria, and Buryat-Mongol ASSR in USSR. Group includes KALMUCKS. Mainly a pastoral people adhering to Lamaism. Mongol hordes, especially those which conquered Russia and penetrated Europe, included large elements of Turkic and other peoples; these became known collectively as TATARS. Mongols established YÜAN dynasty in China, khanate of GOLDEN HORDE in Russia, and other khanates in Turkistan and Persia.

mongoose (mŏn'gōōs), small carnivorous mammal related to civet, found chiefly in India, SE Asia, Africa. Indian mongoose (*Herpestes*) is agile and slender, has brownish-gray fur, and is c.30 in. long, including tail. It kills venomous snakes and rats.

Monhegan (mŏnhē'gĭn), resort island, 10 mi. off coast of S Maine near Bristol. Battle between *Boxer* and *Enterprise* fought offshore, 1813.

monitor, type of warship used in Civil War; named from *Monitor,* built by John Ericsson for Union navy, launched 1862. Characterized by revolving turret carrying two 11-in. guns. Deck was only 18 in. above water. Heavily sheathed in iron. This vessel was involved in the famous drawn battle of **Monitor and Merrimac.** The *Merrimac* was a frigate, scuttled by the Union, raised by the *Con-*

federates and made into an ironclad, the *Virginia.* The battle between the two ironclads in Hampton Roads, March 9, 1862, altered naval warfare.

monitorial system, method of elementary education devised by Joseph Lancaster and Andrew Bell to make maximum use of limited facilities to furnish schooling to the poor. Sometimes called Lancasterian system. All pupils met in one room; there the teacher instructed the monitors, the older and better students, and these taught the other pupils.

Moniz, Egas (ā'gùsh mō'nēsh), 1874–, Portuguese physician. Shared 1949 Nobel Prize in Physiology and Medicine for developing prefrontal lobotomy (brain operation used in treating certain mental disorders). Author of many medical works.

Monk, George: see MONCK, GEORGE, 1ST DUKE OF ALBEMARLE.

monk: see MONASTICISM.

monkey, mammal of primate order. Old World monkeys include the family of true monkeys (e.g., macaque, baboon, and langur) and the APE family. Man is often classed in a third family. In these the nasal septum is narrow; nostrils are directed down; there are 32 teeth. New World monkeys and marmosets are arboreal; the nose is flat; nostrils are directed sidewise; usually there are 36 teeth.

Mon-Khmer languages (mōn'-kùmâr'), group of Austro-Asiatic languages scattered over SE Asia. They include Mon or Talaing (Burma), Khmer or Cambodian (Thailand and S Indo-China), and Cham (Indo-China).

monkshood: see ACONITE.

Monmouth, James Scott, duke of (mŏn'mùth), 1649–85, claimant to English throne, natural son of Charles II. After Popish Plot agitation (1678) supporters of Protestant succession championed him as King's heir. After accession of James II (1685) he landed in England and raised a small force. Was defeated, captured, and beheaded.

Monmouth, England: see MONMOUTHSHIRE.

Monmouth, city (pop. 10,193), W Ill., W of Galesburg; laid out 1831. Center for livestock, farm, and clay area. Mfg. of clay and metal products. Seat of Monmouth Col.

Monmouth, battle of, in American Revolution, June 28, 1778, near Monmouth Courthouse (now Freehold, N.J.). Attack on British suddenly turned into retreat by Charles LEE. Arrival of Washington and Steuben prevented American rout; British escaped.

Monmouthshire (mŏn'mùth-shĭr) or **Monmouth,** border county (546 sq. mi.; pop. 424,647), W England. Low, fertile land in Wye valley, rising to hills in N and NW. Has grazing, farming, and fruit growing, but large coal and iron deposits are area's main importance. Sometimes considered as part of Wales. Many inhabitants speak Welsh. County town is **Monmouth,** municipal borough (pop. 5,432), a market town.

Monnier, Henry (ãrē' mônyā'), 1799–1877, French lithographer and writer of satiric sketches and plays, creator of characters pillorying the French bourgeoisie, notably with Mme Gibou and M. Joseph Prudhomme.

Monocacy (mùnŏ'kùsē), river rising in S Pa. and crossing Md. to join the Potomac S of Frederick, Md. Just E of Frederick was fought Civil War battle, July 9, 1864. Although defeated, Gen. Lew Wallace delayed Confederate move on Washington.

Monongahela (mùnŏng"gùhē'lù), city (pop. 8,922), SW Pa., on Monongahela R. and S of Pittsburgh. Mfg. of metal products and chemicals. Center in Whisky Rebellion.

Monongahela, river formed in N W.Va. Flows 128 mi. N into SW Pa. and joins Allegheny R. at Pittsburgh to form Ohio R.

Monophysitism (mùnŏ'fĭsĭ"tĭzùm), heresy of 5th and 6th cent. continuing the principles of EUTYCHES, opposing NESTORIANISM. It challenged the orthodox creed of Chalcedon by saying that Jesus Christ had only one nature. In the East, the emperor invalidated (c.476) the Council of CHALCEDON and after several attempts at compromise which satisfied neither side, the pope excommunicated the East. By the 6th cent. Monophysitism dominated Syria, Egypt, and Armenia, and after alternate periods of imperial favor and suppression, a permanent schism set in (by 600) and the COPTIC, JACOBITE, and ARMENIAN churches were estab. See also MONOTHELETISM.

monopoly (mùnŏ'pùlē), virtually complete control of the supply of a product, forcing consumers to purchase at whatever price the owner fixes. Government monopolies, such as the postal system, are often operated in the public interest, and socialism advocates the extension of this principle to all basic industries. Monopolies may be constructed by controlling the entire production and marketing of a product (see CARTEL), or by forming corporation mergers or agreements to restrain competition (see TRUST). In the U.S. antitrust laws act to curb private monopolies.

Monotheletism or **Monothelitism** (mùnŏ'thĭlĭtĭ"zùm), 7th-cent. heresy condemned by Third Council of CONSTANTINOPLE (680). It declared that Christ had two natures but operated with one will and was adopted by HERACLIUS I as imperial compromise between MONOPHYSITISM and orthodoxy. Vehemently opposed by Rome, it died out after 680 except among Syrian MARONITES.

monotype (mŏ'nùtīp) [Greek *mono* = one], a machine invented by Tolbert Lanston (patented 1887) for casting and setting type for printing. Monotype makes each character separately, assembling as in hand composition. Keyboard unit punches holes in a roll of paper, which is used in casting unit to govern casting and assembling of type.

Monreale (mōnrāā'lā), town (pop. 14,340), NW Sicily, Italy, near Palermo. Has famous cathedral (founded 1174) with Byzantine mosaics.

Monro, Harold, 1879–1932, English poet. Founded periodicals *Poetry Review* (1911) and *Chapbook* (1919–25), which influenced the poetry of his day. His *Collected Poems* appeared in 1933.

Monroe, Harriet, 1860–1936, American editor, critic, poet, founder (1912) and long editor of influential *Poetry: a Magazine of Verse* in Chicago.

Monroe, James, 1758–1831, 5th President of the United States (1817–25), b. Va. Foundation of his political career was friendship that resulted from his studying law (1780–83) under Thomas Jefferson. As U.S. Senator (1790–94) he violently assailed Federalists. Served on diplomatic missions to France, Spain, and England. U.S. Secretary of State (1811–17), Secretary of War (1814–15). His two administrations as President have been known as the "era of good feeling." Florida question and boundary question with Canada were resolved; the settlement of Liberia took place with his approval; struggle over slavery question was met by MISSOURI COMPROMISE; MONROE DOCTRINE was announced.

Monroe. 1 City (pop. 38,572), N La., on Ouachita R., in agr. and natural gas area; settled c.1785 as Fort Miro. Mfg. of carbon black, chemicals, and lumber, paper, meat, cotton, and cottonseed products. **2** City (pop. 21,467), SE Mich., on L. Erie at mouth of Raisin R. and SW of Detroit; settled c.1780. Shipping point for agr. area with nurseries and mfg. of paper and metal products. Limestone quarries near. Scene of Raisin R. massacre (1813), and "Toledo War" (see TOLEDO, Ohio). Home of G. A. Custer. **3** City (pop. 10,140), S N.C., SE of Charlotte. settled area. **4** City (pop. 7,037), S Wis., SW of Madison, in dairy region. Population largely of Swiss descent. Cheese center with annual cheese fair.

Monroe, Fort, at Old Point Comfort, Va., commanding entrance to Chesapeake Bay and Hampton Roads. Held by Union in Civil War; prison (1865–67) of Jefferson Davis. Hq. U.S. army field forces 1946.

Monroe, Mount: see PRESIDENTIAL RANGE.

Monroe Doctrine, dual principle of American foreign policy enunciated in Pres. Monroe's message to Congress, 1823. Doctrine grew out of two diplomatic problems: minor clash with Russia concerning NW coast of North America, and fear that European governments commonly called Holy Alliance would seek to regain Latin American states that had recently revolted from Spain. The British foreign minister, Canning, wanted to send a joint Anglo-American note to powers of the Holy Alliance, but J. Q. Adams insisted on U.S. acting alone and drafted the doctrine. Two main points: no new colonization in the Americas, no European interference in American nations. Though never recognized in international law, it was several times invoked with success. As imperialistic tendencies appeared in U.S., doctrine came to be viewed with suspicion by Latin American countries as protecting U.S. hegemony, a suspicion heightened by the "corollary" of Theodore Roosevelt saying that fear of European intervention in an ill-conducted Latin American country would justify U.S. intervention. Feeling against the doctrine decreased in the 1920s and disappeared with Roosevelt's "good neighbor" policy.

Monrovia (mŭnrō'vēŭ) [for Pres. James Monroe], city (pop. c.12,000), cap. of Liberia; port on the Atlantic. Founded 1822 by American Colonization Society as haven for ex-slaves from U.S. In World War II its harbor was vastly improved by U.S.

Monrovia, city (pop. 20,186), S Calif., NE of Los Angeles; laid out 1886. Growing and packing of citrus fruit.

Mons (mŏnz, Fr. mõs), Flemish *Bergen,* city (pop. 25,684), cap. of Hainaut prov., SW Belgium, at junction of Condé-Mons Canal and Canal du Centre, it is processing and shipping center for Borinage coal-mining dist. Became seat of counts of Hainaut in 9th cent. It was repeatedly attacked in wars of 16th, 17th, and 18th cent., and in World War I was scene of first British-German battle (1914). Among the buildings preserved are a 12th-cent. castle chapel and a 15th-cent. town hall.

Monsalvat or **Monserrat,** Spain: see MONTSERRAT.

Monson, town (pop. 6,125), S Mass., E of Springfield. Here are granite quarries and textile mills.

monsoon (mŏnso͞on'), a wind changing direction with season. Monsoons are most notable in India, where they bring heavy rains, but they appear also in Iberian peninsula, Africa, Australia, and China.

Mont, (Karel Maria) Pol(ydoor) de (mõ'), 1857–1931, Flemish poet and critic. Curator (1904–19) of the museum of fine arts in Antwerp, he defended modern tendencies in art, and forwarded the Flemish literary revival. Author of lyrics and short stories.

Montagna, Bartolomeo (bärtōlōmā'ō mōntä'nyä), c.1450–1523, Italian religious painter, founder of school of Vicenza.

Montagnards: see MOUNTAIN, THE.

Montagu, Charles: see HALIFAX, CHARLES MONTAGU, EARL OF.

Montagu, John: see SANDWICH, JOHN MONTAGU, 4TH EARL OF.

Montagu, Lady Mary Wortley, 1689–1762, English wit and letter writer. Her letters, notably a series from Turkey, where her husband was ambassador 1716–18, were witty and informative. Pope, once her friend, later bitterly satirized her.

Montague, town (pop. 7,812), N Mass., SE of Greenfield. Has large hydroelectric plant. Includes Turners Falls village (pop. 5,179), site of first dam across Connecticut R.

Montaigne, Michel Eyquem, seigneur de (mŏntān', Fr. mēshĕl' ākĕm' sānyûr' dù mōtĕn'yù), 1533–92, French author. He was a magistrate until 1570 and mayor of Bordeaux (1581–85), but after 1571 he lived mostly in a rural retreat, aloof from the religious and political troubles of his time. His *Essais* (1st ed., 1580; 1st complete ed., 1595) are considered the finest examples of the essay ever written; their influence on European literature is incalculable. In them, Montaigne reveals himself intimately and fully, digressing on a wide variety of subjects, in a style unsurpassed in wisdom, directness, expressive imagery, vigor, charm, and ironic humor. The "Apologie de Raimond Sebond," longest of the essays, states most fully his philosophy of skepticism.

Montale, Eugenio (āo͞ojā'nyō mōntä'lā), 1896–, Italian modernist poet, author of volumes *Ossi de seppia* (1925) and *Le occasioni* (1940); often compared to T. S. Eliot.

Montalembert, Charles Forbes René de Tryon, comte de (mõtälābĕr'), 1810–70, French orator and writer. A collaborator with Lacordaire and Lamennais in the Catholic liberal movement and in editing *L'Avenir,* he submitted to papal condemnation of the journal. He used his oratorical powers to oppose Napoleon III in the early years of the empire. He accepted the dogma of papal infallibility, which he had contested earlier. His *Monks of the West* (7 vols., 1860–77) is still a standard (though incomplete) work.

Montana, state (146,316 sq. mi.; pop. 591,024), NW U.S.; admitted 1889 as 41st state; cap. HELENA. Other cities are BUTTE, GREAT FALLS, BILLINGS. BITTERROOT RANGE to W, Great Plains in E. YELLOWSTONE main river. Mining (copper, silver, gold, zinc, lead, manganese, sapphires, natural gas, oil, coal). Farming (wheat, potatoes, corn, livestock, fruits, sugar beets). Mfg. based on processing of resources. Tourism (e.g., Glacier Natl. Park). Area opened after Louisiana Purchase. Fur trade estab. Discovery of gold (1860s), silver (1875), and copper (c.1880), as well as growth of ranching, brought settlers. G. A. CUSTER wiped out by Sioux at Little Bighorn R. in 1876. Anaconda controls state's copper. Drought in 20th cent. brought irrigation, Federal water power projects. World War II put large demands on copper industry.

Montana, University of, state system of higher education constituted 1913, with hq. at Helena. Its six units include Montana State Univ. (coed.; chartered 1893) at Missoula, Montana State Col. (1893) at Bozeman, Montana School of Mines (1893) at Butte.

Montañes, Juan Martínez (mōntän'yĕs), c.1568–1649, Spanish sculptor, famous for polychrome figures in wood. Work is best seen in Seville.

Montanism (mŏn'tùnĭzùm), enthusiastic Christian movement in 2d cent., led by Montanus and two prophetesses of Phrygia. It stressed ecstatic prophecy and severe asceticism in immediate expectation of Judgment Day. Montanists believed that a Christian fallen from grace could not be redeemed. By c.220 Montanism had died as a sect.

Montargis (mõtärzhē'), town (pop. 13,529), Loiret dept., N central France. Agr. market. Has kept medieval aspect. The celebrated legend of the dog of Montargis, which may have some basis in fact, tells of the murder, near Montargis, of Aubry de Montdidier, a courtier of Charles V, by one Macaire (c.1371). Aubry's dog showed such animosity toward Macaire that the king ordered a trial by combat between the dog and Macaire, armed with a cudgel. The dog won; Macaire confessed and was hanged.

Montauban (mõtōbã'), city (pop. 23,016), cap. of Tarnet-Garonne dept., S France, on Tarn R. Textile mills. Was a stronghold of Albigenses in 13th cent., of Huguenots in 16th cent. Birthplace of Ingres, whose work is richly represented in cathedral and museum.

Montauk Point, N.Y.; see LONG ISLAND.

Mont Blanc (mõ blã'), Alpine massif on Franco-Italian border. It rises to 15,781 ft. (in France), highest point of the Alps. Mer de Glace, largest of its numerous glaciers, flows into Chamonix valley. First ascended 1786.

Montcalm, Louis Joseph de (mŏntkäm'), 1712–59, French general. Sent (1756) to defend Canada in French and Indian War. Captured Fort Ontario (1756), Fort William Henry (1757), and withstood strong attack on Ticonderoga (1758). Defended Quebec against a siege by Gen. James Wolfe until British strategy effected an open engagement on Plains of Abraham. English won (Sept. 13, 1759), but both Montcalm and Wolfe were killed.

Montclair, residential town (pop. 43,927), NE N.J., NNW of Newark; settled 1669. Has art museum containing works of Inness, who lived here.

Mont-Dore (mõ-dôr'), town (pop. 2,165), Puy-de-Dôme dept., central France. Thermal station and winter sports center. It lies at foot of the Puy de Sancy, highest peak of Mont-Dore mountain group of Auvergne (6,187 ft.).

Monte Albán (mōn'tā älbän'), anc. city of the Zapotec in Oaxaca, SW Mexico; seat of advanced culture c.200 B.C.–A.D. 1521. Excavation begun in 1931 revealed vast treasure of jewelry and elaborate carvings.

Montebello (mŏntĭbĕ'lō), city (pop. 21,735), S Calif., SE of Los Angeles. Oil wells; truck and flower farms.

Monte Carlo (mŏn"tē kär'lō), town (pop. 7,967), principality of Monaco, on the Riviera. It is one of the world's most famous gambling resorts.

Monte Cassino (mōn'tā käs-sē'nō), famous monastery on a hill, 1,702 ft. high, overlooking town of CASSINO, Latium, central Italy. Abbey, founded c.529 by St. BENEDICT of Nursia, was a great center of Christian learning and piety; its influence on European civilization is immeasurable. It was destroyed by the Lombards in 581; by the Arabs in 883; by earthquake in 1349; by Allied aerial bombardment in 1944, the German garrison having used the abbey as fortress. Most of valuable manuscripts of library had been removed to safety.

Montecatini (mōn"tākätē'nē), town (pop. 8,292), Tuscany, central Italy. Health resort.

Monte Cristo (mŏn"tē krĭ'stō), small Italian island in Tyrrhenian Sea, made famous by Dumas père's novel, *The Count of Monte Cristo.*

Montecucculi or **Montecuccoli, Raimondo, conte di** (rīmōn'dō kōn'tā dē mōn'tākŏŏk'-kŏŏlē, -kōlē), 1609–81, Italian field marshal in imperial service. Fought in Thirty Years War; defeated Turks at Szent-Gotthard Hungary (1664).

Montefiore, Sir Moses Haim (mŏn"tĭfēô'rē), 1784–1885, British-Jewish philanthropist, b. Leghorn. He worked to alleviate discriminatory practices against Jews and was influential in preparing the way for political Zionism.

Montego Bay (mŏntē'gō), port (pop. 11,547) on NW Jamaica, British West Indies; winter resort.

Montejo, Francisco de (fränthē'skō dā mōntā'-hō), b. c.1473 or c.1479, d. c.1548, Spanish conquistador. Commissioned to conquer the Maya of Yucatán, he made two unsuccessful attempts, one from the E (1527–28), and one from W (1531–35). His son of the same name finally subdued the Maya (1546).

Montemayor, Jorge de (hôr'hā dā mōn"-tāmäyôr'), c.1520–1561, Spanish poet and novelist, author of pastoral novel *Diana* (1559?).

Montemezzi, Italo (ēˈtälō mōntāmĕtˈtsē), 1875–1952, Italian composer of operas (e.g., *L'amore dei tre re,* 1913, and *La nave,* 1918).

Montenegro (mŏnʺtŭnēˈgrō), Serbo-Croatian *Crna Gora,* autonomous republic (5,343 sq. mi.; pop. 376,573), SW Yugoslavia, bordering on Adriatic and on Albania; cap. TITOGRAD. Mountainous, difficult of access, it has forests and pastures (sheep and goat raising) and some agr. in the Zeta R. valley and near L. of Scutari. The Montenegrin people are Serbs, mostly of Eastern Orthodox faith. The region formed the semi-independent principality of Zeta in 14th-cent. Serbia. After the Serbian defeat at Kossovo (1389), Montenegro for five centuries resisted all Turkish attempts at subjugation. The Turks did, however, control part of the present republic, and Venice held the coast, including Kotor. From 1516 to 1851 Montenegro was ruled by the prince-bishops (called *vladikas*) of Cetinje. DANILO I (reigned 1696–1735) made the episcopal succession hereditary from uncle to nephew (the bishops being barred from marrying) and initiated (1715) the traditional alliance with Russia. DANILO II (reigned 1851–60) secularized the principality, transferring his spiritual functions to an archbishop; his successor NICHOLAS I secured recognition of Montenegrin independence (1878) and proclaimed himself king (1910). Montenegro gained some territory in the Balkan Wars (1912–13); in World War I it invaded Albania and declared war on Austria but was occupied by Austro-German forces 1915–18. In Nov., 1918, the king having been deposed, Montenegro was united with Serbia. It gained autonomy and some additional coastal territory under the 1946 constitution of Yugoslavia.

Monterey (mŏntůrāˈ), city (pop. 16,205), W Calif., on Monterey Bay and S of San Francisco. Resort and home of artists and authors. Bay named 1602 by Sebastián Vizcaino. In 1770 Gaspar de Portolá estab. a presidio (now U.S. army post) and Junípero Serra, a mission. Intermittent cap. of Alta Calif. 1775–1846. Taken by U.S. navy 1846. State constitutional convention met here 1849. State's first theater (1844) and first brick building (1847) stand. Sardine fisheries and canneries. Fruit and vegetable canneries.

Monterey Park, residential city (pop. 20,395), S Calif., E of Los Angeles, founded 1910.

Monterrey (mōntĕrāˈ), city (pop. 186,092), cap. of Nuevo León, NE Mexico; third largest city of Mexico (after Mexico city and Guadalajara); founded 16th cent. Except for Mexico city, the most important industrial city in country (and a popular resort on Inter-American Highway), it has mfg. of beer, paper, flour, cotton goods, iron and steel, furniture, textiles, cigars, bricks, and glass and metal goods. City is regarded as evidence of Mexico's potential ability to develop a balanced economy.

Montespan, Françoise Athénaïs, marquise de (frãswäzˈ ätänäēsˈ märkēzˈ dů mōtůspäˈ), 1641–1707, mistress of Louis XIV of France. Succeeded Mlle de la Vallière and was followed by Mme de Maintenon in king's favor.

Montesquieu, Charles de Secondat, baron de la Brède et de (shärlˈ dů sůkōdäˈ bärōˈ dů lä brĕdˈ ā dů mōtůskyûˈ), 1689–1755, French political philosopher; a high magistrate at Bordeaux. His *Persian Letters* (1721; Eng. tr., 1730), a satire of European society, is one of the world's masterpieces of irony. *Reflections on the Causes of the Grandeur and Declension of the Romans* (1734; Eng. tr., 1734) presents, in a few lapidary and luminous pages, a philosophy of history akin to that of VICO. His most influential work was *The Spirit of the Laws* (1748; Eng. tr., 1750), a scientific study of comparative government. Its theory of checks and balances found its way into the U.S. Constitution. Its analysis of geographic and economic factors in the origin of laws, its wise emphasis on the complexity of the subject, and its caution against ready-made utopias have influenced several later schools of political thought.

Montessori, Maria (märēˈä mōntĕs-sōˈrē), 1870–1952, Italian educator and physician; first woman to receive medical degree in Italy (1894). Her method for education of preschool children features development of initiative through individual freedom of action, improvement of sense perception, and development of coordination.

Monteux, Pierre (pyĕrˈ mōtûˈ), 1875–, French-American conductor. As conductor (1911–14) of Diaghilev's Ballet Russe, he conducted premières of ballets of Stravinsky, Ravel, and Debussy. He conducted various U.S. orchestras including the Boston Symphony (1919–24), and the San Francisco (1935–51).

Montevallo (mŏntĭvăˈlō), town (pop. 2,150), central Ala., S of Birmingham. Seat of Alabama Col. (state: for women; 1893).

Monteverdi, Claudio (klouˈdyō mōntāvĕrˈdē), 1567–1643, Italian composer, first great name in operatic history. His bold experiments in instrumentation contributed to the development of the modern orchestra. His best-known operas are *Orfeo* and *L'incoronazione de Poppea.* He also wrote religious music and madrigals.

Montevideo (mŏntůvĭˈdēō), city (pop. 5,459), W Minn., on Minnesota R. and NW of Granite Falls, in agr. area. Near-by Camp Release State Park commemorates release in 1862 of 269 white captives of Sioux.

Montevideo (mōntāvēdhäˈō), city (pop. 750,000), Uruguay, cap. and largest city of Uruguay. On the Río de la Plata, it is one of major ports of South America. Founded (1726) because of rival colonial expansion of Portuguese and Spanish, it has seen much strife and in 19th cent. was besieged many times by warring factions. Today it is a beautiful modern city, governmental, financial, and commercial focus of nation. The national university is here.

Monte Vista (mŏnʺtĭ vĭsˈtů), city (pop. 3,272; alt. c.7,500 ft.), S Colo., in San Luis Valley on Rio Grande. Near by are Picture Rocks (with pictographs), dude ranches, potato farms, gold and silver mines.

Montez, Lola (mŏnˈtĕz, mŏntĕzˈ), 1818?–1861, Irish dancer and adventuress whose real name was Gilbert. Her sensational success was due to beauty rather than artistry. She became official mistress of LOUIS I of Bavaria, who made her a countess, and virtually ruled Bavaria until her banishment in 1848. She died in poverty in the U.S.

Montezuma (mŏntŭzo͞o'mŭ) or **Moctezuma** (mŏktäso͞o'mä), 1480?–1520, Aztec ruler (1502–20). Reign was marked by incessant warfare and unrest among subject peoples, facilitating conquest by Hernán Cortés. Montezuma vacillated in his policy towards Spanish and was killed in later fighting between Spanish and Aztecs.

Montezuma Castle National Monument: see NATIONAL PARKS AND MONUMENTS (table).

Montferrat (mŏntfŭrăt' -rät'), Ital. *Monferrato,* historic region of Piedmont, NW Italy, S of the Po. Has noted vineyards. A marquisate after 10th cent., with Casale as cap. after 1435, it passed to GONZAGA family of Mantua in 1536. Savoy invaded Montferrat in 1612, and in 1631 part of the marquisate was assigned to Savoy, the remainder in 1713.

Montfort, Simon de (mŏnt'fŭrt, Fr. mõfôr'), c.1160–1218, French nobleman, leader of the crusade against the ALBIGENSES. Combining religious fanaticism with ruthless ambition, he laid waste S France. After his victory at MURET he was proclaimed (1215) lord of Toulouse and Montauban. In 1217 Raymond VI of Toulouse recovered some of his lands, and Simon fell fighting him. Through his mother, Simon claimed the earldom of Leicester. He was the father of **Simon de Montfort,** c.1208–1265, earl of Leicester, leader of revolt against HENRY III of England. In 1258 he was active in forcing king to accept the PROVISION OF OXFORD. In 1260 he broke with Henry. He assumed leadership in BARONS' WAR. In 1264 fierce civil war broke out. After victory at Lewes Montfort became master of England. The Great Parliament he summoned in 1265 was one of most important in history of Parliament in that he called representatives from boroughs and towns, as well as knights from each shire. The wars were resumed and Montfort was defeated and killed at Evesham.

Montgolfier, Joseph Michel (zhôzĕf' mēshĕl' mõgôlfyā'), 1740–1810, and **Jacques Étienne Montgolfier** (zhäk ātyĕn'), 1745–99, French inventors (brothers) of first practical balloon, demonstrated 1783.

Montgomery, Bernard Law, 1st **Viscount Montgomery of Alamein,** 1887–, British field marshal. Became idol of British public in World War II after victory at ALAMEIN (1942). Field commander of all ground forces in invasion of Normandy. Headed British occupation forces in Germany 1945–46. Chief of imperial general staff 1946–49. In 1951 he was made deputy supreme commander of NATO.

Montgomery, Lucy Maud, 1874–1942, Canadian novelist. Her first novel, *Anne of Green Gables* (1908), and its sequels have been popular stories for girls.

Montgomery, Richard, 1738?–1775, American Revolutionary general, b. Ireland. Commanded Montreal expedition in QUEBEC CAMPAIGN. Killed in assault on Quebec.

Montgomery, county, Wales: see MONTGOMERYSHIRE.

Montgomery, city (pop. 106,525), state cap. (since 1846), SE central Ala., on Alabama R. (navigable here), in Black Belt; settled 1817. Rail center; cotton, livestock, dairy market; mfg. of textiles, fertilizer, cottonseed and lumber products; food (esp. meat) packing. First cap. of CONFEDERACY (1861). Fell to Union troops, 1865. Seat of Huntingdon Col. (Methodist; for women; 1854). Has "First White House of the Confederacy." Maxwell and Gunter air force bases are near.

Montgomeryshire (mŭntgŭ'mŭrēshĭr) or **Montgomery,** border county (797 sq. mi.; pop. 45,989), Wales; co. town Montgomery. Hilly region, devoted mostly to pasturage and farming. Important in medieval times as fortified border district.

month, period of passage of MOON through its phases, usually reckoned at c.29 or 30 days. Months of the CALENDAR are roughly equated to phases of the moon. Some calendars (e.g., the Moslem) are based on this calculation, and feast days change seasons. Names in West and birthstones are: *January* [from Janus], garnet; *February* [from Latin,= expiatory, because of rites in February], amethyst; *March* [from Mars], aquamarine and bloodstone; *April,* diamond; *May,* emerald; *June* [from gens (clan) *Junius*], pearl, alexandrite, moonstone; *July* [from Julius Caesar], ruby; *August* [from Augustus], peridot and sardonyx; *September* [from Latin,= seven], sapphire; *October* [eight], opal and tourmaline; *November* [nine], topaz; *December* [ten] turquoise and zircon.

Montherlant, Henry de (ãrē' dŭ mõtĕrlã'), 1896–, French author. His novels, glorifying force and the masculine ego, include *Les Bestiaires* (1926; Eng. tr., *The Bullfighters,* 1927) and the tetralogy *Les Jeunes Filles* (1936–40; Eng. tr., 2 vols., 1937–40).

Monti, Vincenzo (vēnchän'tsō mōn'tē), 1754–1828, Italian poet, known chiefly for his epic *Bassvilliana* (1793) and for translations of Homer.

Monticelli, Adolphe (ädôlf' mõtēsĕlē'), 1824–86, French painter. Represented in Lille and Marseilles.

Monticello (mŏntĭsĕl'ō), resort village (pop. 4,223), SE N.Y., in hills NW of Middletown.

Monticello, estate, central Va., SE of Charlottesville, home (for 56 yrs.) and burial place of Thomas Jefferson, who designed mansion. Building materials prepared on estate and construction done largely by Jefferson's slaves. Mansion begun 1770, occupied 1772. Early example of American classic revival, it is owned by Thomas Jefferson Memorial Foundation. Near by is "Ash Lawn," Monroe's home.

Montluçon (mõlüsõ'), town (pop. 45,535), Allier dept., central France, on Cher R. Metallurgical center. Has 15th–16th cent. houses, castle of dukes of Bourbon.

Montmagny (mõmänyē'), town (pop. 5,844), SE Que., Canada, on St. Lawrence R. and ENE of Quebec. Silk and rayon mills and woodworking.

Montmartre (mõmär'trŭ), hill in Paris, France, topped by Church of SACRÉ-CŒUR, on right bank of the Seine; highest point of Paris

Ancient quarter was long a favorite residence of bohemian world and is famous for its night life.

Montmorency (mŏnt″mŭrĕn′sē, Fr. mõmôrãsē′), French noble family. Most notable members were: **Mathieu, baron de Montmorency** (mätyû′ bärõ′ dů), d. 1230, constable of France, called the Great Constable. Took part in battle of Bouvines (1214); fought Albigenses (1226). **Anne, duc de Montmorency** (än′ dük′ dů), 1493?–1567, constable of France. Captured with Francis I at Pavia (1525), he helpd negotiate Francis's release and received governorship of Languedoc, which remained in his family until 1632. He took Metz from the Spanish (1552); was captured at Saint-Quentin (1557); sided with Guises in Wars of Religion; was killed in siege of Paris. His son, **Henri, duc de Montmorency** (ãrē′), 1534–1614, marshal and constable of France, was known as count of Damville before 1579. Though a zealous Catholic, he was led by the murder of his relative COLIGNY to advocate a conciliatory policy toward the Huguenots. He adhered to Henry of Navarre in 1589.

Montmorency (mŏnt″mŭrĕn′sē), village (pop. 5,817), S Que., Canada, on St. Lawrence R. and NE of Quebec. Power for Quebec and area is furnished by plant here at Montmorency Falls on Montmorency R. which flows from the Laurentian Mts. to the St. Lawrence R.

Montparnasse (mõpärnäs′), quarter of Paris, France, on left bank of the Seine. Its noted cafés are centers of Parisian artistic and intellectual life.

Mont Pelée: see PELÉE.

Montpelier (mŏntpēl′yŭr), city (pop. 8,599), state cap. (since 1805), central Vt. on Winooski R. and NW of Barre; settled 1787. Produces granite, textiles, wood products, and machinery. Has supreme court with Vermont Historical Society Coll.

Montpelier, estate, central Va., NNW of Richmond; home of James Madison, built c.1760, now privately owned. Madison and his wife buried near by.

Montpellier (mõpĕlyā′), city (pop. 80,673), cap. of Hérault dept., S France, near the Mediterranean; trade center for wines and brandy. A fief under counts of Toulouse after 8th cent., it passed in 13th cent. to kings of Majorca, from whom Philip VI of France bought it in 1349. It was a Huguenot center taken by Louis XIII in 1622. Its university was founded 1289. Famous faculty of medicine is traced to 10th cent.

Montpensier, Louise d'Orléans, duchesse de (lwēz′ dôrlāã düshĕs′ dů mõpãsyā′), 1627–93, French princess, called La Grande Mademoiselle; daughter of Gaston d'Orléans. A leader of the FRONDE, she relieved Orléans at the head of her troops and opened the gates of Paris to Condé's retreating soldiers (1652). Her love affair and secret marriage with LAUZUN ended in separation.

Montreal (mŏntrēôl′), city (pop. 1,021,520), S Que., Canada, on Montreal Isl. in St. Lawrence R. at foot of Mt. Royal. Largest city in Canada and its commercial, financial, and industrial center, it has excellent harbor at head of navigation on St. Lawrence R. and direct connections to Great Lakes via Lachine Canal. Major transshipment point with large grain elevators and cold-storage warehouses and mfg. of steel products, railroad equipment, machinery, paper, pulp, leather, and clothing. Visitors are attracted by its foreign air and many old buildings. Seat of McGill Univ. (nonsectarian, coed.; opened 1829), noted for graduate work in the physical sciences; and the **University of Montreal** (French language; R.C., pontifical; coed.). Site visited by Cartier (1535) and Champlain (1603). Settled 1642, it became a fur trade center. Fortified 1725, taken by British 1760, and briefly held by American forces 1775. Cap. of Upper Canada 1844–49. Population remains largely French.

Montreal North, N suburb of Montreal (pop. 14,081), S Que., Canada, on Montreal Isl.

Montreux (mõtrû′), name of the adjacent communes of Montreux-Châtelard, Planches, and Veytaux (combined pop. 17,424), Vaud canton, SW Switzerland, on NE bank of L. of Geneva. Resort; chocolate mfg.

Montreux Convention, 1936, international agreement permitting Turkey to refortify DARDANELLES. Ratified by all signers of Treaty of Lausanne of 1923 except Italy.

Montrose, James Graham, 5th **earl and** 1st **marquess of,** 1612–50, Scottish nobleman, soldier. Leader in Bishops' Wars, he then supported Charles I from fear of a Presbyterian oligarchy. With highland troops he defeated Presbyterian army six times 1644–45. After king's defeat at Naseby he was unable to unite Scottish royalists and was finally hanged.

Montrose, city (pop. 4,964), SW Colo., on Uncompahgre R. and SE of Grand Junction. Near by are carnotite deposits (source of radium, uranium) and Black Canyon of the Gunnison Natl. Monument.

Monts, Pierre du Guast, comte de (pyĕr′ dü gwäst′ kõt′ dů mõ′), c.1560–c.1630, French colonizer in North America, called the sieur de Monts. Patron of Samuel de Champlain. Planted first French colony in Canada at Port Royal (present Annapolis Royal) in 1605.

Mont-Saint-Michel (mõ-sã-mēshĕl′), rocky isle (pop. 149) in English Channel, NW France, 1 mi. off Norman coats; accessible by land at low tide and connected with mainland by causeway. The cone-shaped rock is girt by medieval walls and towers; above rise the clustered buildings of the village and the celebrated Benedictine abbey, crowned by the abbey church. Abbey was founded 708 by Aubert, bishop of Auvranches, according to directions received from Archangel Michael in a vision. The six abbatial buildings facing the sea form unit called La Merveille (built 1203–28), one of the great treasures of Gothic architecture. In the Hundred Years War the abbey was successful in repulsing all English attempts to capture it.

Montserrat (mŏntsŭrăt′), island (c.37 sq. mi.; pop. 14,333), British West Indies; a presidency of Leeward Isls. colony; discovered by Columbus 1493.

Montserrat or **Monserrat** (both: mŏn″sŭrăt′, mŏnt″–), mountain of NE Spain, NW of Barcelona, rising abruptly to 4,054 ft. from a plain. Half-way up is a celebrated Benedictine monastery, a major shrine of pilgrimage. Only ruins are left of old monastery (11th cent.); new monastery dates from 19th cent. The Renaissance church contains black wooden image of the Virgin, carved, according to tradition, by St. Luke. In the Middle Ages the mountain, also called Monsalvat, was thought to have been the site of the castle of the Holy GRAIL. At Montserrat, St. Ignatius of Loyola vowed himself to the religious life.

Monza (mōn'tsä), city (pop. 58,503), Lombardy, N Italy. Textile and machinery mfg. Has automobile races. Its cathedral (founded 6th cent.) contains iron crown of Lombardy, said to have been made from nails of Christ's cross. Charlemagne, Charles V, Napoleon I, and other emperors were crowned with it as kings of Italy.

mood or **mode,** in Latin INFLECTION, one of four major sets of forms of verbs. Three of them cross with the category of person and are subdivided by tenses: indicative (used normally), imperative (in commands), and subjunctive (in certain kinds of subordinated constructions). Fourth set, the infinitive, is nonpersonal. These names of moods are often used for similar categories in other languages.

Moodus, village in East Haddam town, S Conn., SE of Middletown. "Moodus noises," underground rumblings, are thought to be caused by minor earthquakes.

Moody, Dwight L(yman), 1837–99, American evangelist; associated after 1870 with Ira D. Sankey in evangelistic tours in U.S. and Great Britain. Founded Northfield Seminary (1879), Mt. Hermon School (1881), mission school (1889), now Moody Bible Inst.

Moody, Helen Wills: see WILLS, HELEN NEWINGTON.

Moody, William Vaughn, 1869–1910, American lyric poet and dramatist. Vigorous liberal and philosophic verse in *The Masque of Judgment* (1900) and *Poems* (1901). Best-known prose play is *The Great Divide* (1909; originally, *A Sabine Woman* 1906).

moon, earth's only SATELLITE (diameter c.2,160 mi.). Earth-moon system revolves about sun in orbit of center of combined mass (c.2,900 mi. from earth's center). Moon revolves about earth in elliptical orbit; mean distance between their centers is 238,857 mi. Because moon's periods of rotation on axis and revolution about earth are equal, same side of moon is always toward earth but about 59% of its surface comes into view in a month owing to librations (rocking movements) of the moon. On the surface appear plains, mountains, craters. Apparent changes of shape result from variation in amount of visible surface as position changes relative to earth and sun. New moon phase occurs when moon is between earth and sun; full moon, when earth is between sun and moon. Month is measured by moon's revolution. Sidereal month, interval between recurrence of conjunction with any given star, averages c.27⅓ days. Synodic month, time required to bring moon again into same position relative to sun (e.g., interval from one new moon to next), averages c.29½ days. Difference results from earth's rotation, which brings earth forward in path around sun, making moon appear to move westward. Its revolution about earth makes moon seem to move eastward relative to constellations; because this apparent eastward movement is more rapid than that of sun, moon rises on an average 50½ min. later each night. See also ECLIPSE. See *ill.*, p. 1187.

Moon, Mountains of the: see RUWENZORI.

Mooney, Thomas J., 1883–1942, American labor agitator. Convicted of a bomb killing in 1916, he was sentenced to death. His case aroused international interest because of a wide belief in his innocence. In 1918 his sentence was commuted to life imprisonment, and in 1939 he was pardoned.

moonflower, tropical American night-blooming vine (*Calonyction aculeatum*) with white, fragrant flowers, similar to the morning-glory.

moonstone, variety of feldspar used as a gem. It has a milky bluish sheen.

Moore, Clement Clarke, 1779–1863, American poet, grad. Columbia, 1798. He is remembered for his "Visit from St. Nicholas" (1823), beginning "'Twas the night before Christmas." A biblical scholar, he compiled Greek and Hebrew lexicon (1809).

Moore, George, 1852–1933, Irish novelist, noted for his brilliant style. His poetry and novels (e.g., *Esther Waters,* 1894) have been much admired, as have *Brook Kerith* (1916; on the life of Christ), *Héloïse and Abélard* (1921), and autobiographical works.

Moore, George Edward, 1873–, English philosopher; a neorealist opponent of idealism.

Moore, Henry, 1898–, English sculptor. His works are notable for balancing of mass with vacant spaces that emphasize three-dimensionality. Commissioned by British government in 1940 to make series of drawings in underground bomb shelters.

Moore, Sir John, 1761–1809, British general. Noted for brilliant retreat and victory (in which he was killed) at Coruña, Spain, in Peninsular War.

Moore, John Bassett, 1860–1947, American authority on international law. Was Assistant Secretary of State (1898) and represented the U.S. in various international affairs. Compiled many documents in international law.

Moore, Marianne, 1887–, American poet, acting editor of *Dial* (1925–29). Her precise, witty verse is distinguished by impeccably crisp style. Among her volumes are *Poems* (1921) and *Selected Poems* (1935).

Moore, Thomas, 1779–1852, Irish poet, best known for *Irish Melodies,* songs published 1808–34, including such favorites as "Believe Me if All Those Endearing Young Charms" and "Oft in the Stilly Night." His poetic romance *Lalla Rookh* (1817) was popular. He was Byron's close friend and biographer.

Moores Creek Natonal Military Park: see NATIONAL PARKS AND MONUMENTS (table).

Moorestown, residential township (pop. 9,123), SW N.J., E of Camden. Has several 18th-cent. houses.

Mooresville, textile-mill town (pop. 7,121), W central N.C., N of Charlotte.

Moorhead, city (pop. 14,870), NW Minn., on Red R. opposite Fargo, N.Dak. Ships grain, potatoes, and dairy products. Seat of Concordia Col. (Evangelical Lutheran; coed.; 1891).

Moorish art and architecture: see MOSLEM ART AND ARCHITECTURE.

Moors, nomadic people of N Africa, once inhabitants of Mauretania. Converted to Islam in 8th cent., and became fanatic Moslems. Crossed into Spain in 711 and easily overran crumbling Visigothic kingdom of RODERICK. Spreading beyond Pyrenees into France, they were turned back at Tours by CHARLES MARTEL 732. Moors made TOLEDO, CÓRDOBA, and SEVILLE centers of learning and culture, but never had a strong central government. Christian reconquest of Spain began with recovery of Toledo (1085) by Alfonso VI, king of Leon and Castile, and ended with recovery of Granada by Ferdinand and Isabella in 1492. Moors were driven from Spain, leaving contributions to W Europe in art, architecture, medicine, science, and learning well-nigh incalculable.

moose, largest of deer family (*Alce*), found in Canada, Alaska, N U.S. Two species: the American and the larger Alaska or Kenai moose. The moose has a heavy brown body, lighter-colored legs, and flattened, usually palmately branched antlers. Old World species is called ELK.

Moose Factory, trading post, NE Ont., Canada, on island in Moose R. near James Bay. Estab. 1671, destroyed c.1696, rebuilt 1730.

Moosehead Lake, 35 mi. long and 10 mi. wide, area 120 sq. mi., W Maine, N of Augusta. Largest lake in Maine. Center of resort region. Steamers link shore points. Source of Kennebec R.

Moose Jaw, city (pop. 24,355), S Sask., Canada, W of Regina. Railroad and trade center with oil refineries, grain elevators, stockyards, and flour, lumber, and woolen mills.

moraine (mŭrān′, mō–), rock waste carried and deposited by a glacier. The great ice sheets of the Pleistocene left terminal moraines extending across North America and Europe.

Morales, Luis de (lwēs′ dā mōrä′lĕs), c.1509–1586, Spanish painter of intense and melancholy religious works. Lived and worked in Badajoz.

morality play: see MIRACLE PLAY.

morals: see ETHICS.

Moran, Edward, 1829–1901, American painter of marine and historical subjects, b. England. Settled in U.S. in 1844. His brothers **Thomas Moran,** 1837–1926, and **Peter Moran,** 1841–1914, both painted landscapes; his sons **Edward Percy Moran,** 1862–1935, and **John Léon Moran,** 1864–1941, were genre painters.

Morat (môrä′), Ger. *Murten,* town (pop. 2,405), Fribourg canton, W Switzerland, on L. Morat. Swiss defeated CHARLES THE BOLD here 1476.

Moratín, Leandro Fernández de: see FERNÁNDEZ DE MORATÍN, LEANDRO.

Morava (mô′rävä), Ger. *March,* river, 227 mi. long, Czechoslovakia and Austria, rising in Sudetes and flowing generally S past Olmütz into the Danube near Bratislava. See also MARCHFELD.

Moravia, Alberto (älbĕr′tō mōrä′vyä), 1907–, Italian novelist, whose real name is Alberto Pincherle. Of his grimly realistic novels, best known is *The Woman of Rome* (1947).

Moravia (mŭrā′vēŭ, mō–), Czech *Morava,* Ger. *Mähren,* region, central Czechoslovakia. Chief cities: BRNO, OLMÜTZ, MORAVSKA, OSTRAVA, ZLIN. With Czech SILESIA, it formed until 1949 a single province (10,350 sq. mi.; pop. 3,134,614), now united with BOHEMIA. Drained by the Morava R., it is a hilly, fertile agr. region and has important industries (textiles, machinery, coal, metallurgy, shoes). The Moravians, a branch of W Slavs, settled here c.6th cent. By the 9th cent. their dukes ruled an empire including Bohemia, Silesia, S Poland, and N Hungary; Christianity was introduced 863 by SS CYRIL AND METHODIUS. The empire broke up in the 10th cent. and fell to the Magyars. After Emperor Otto I's victory over the Magyars (955), Moravia became a march of the Holy Roman Empire. From the 11th cent. it was in effect a crownland of the kingdom of Bohemia, with which it passed under Hapsburg rule in 1526 and became part of Czechoslovakia in 1918. The Moravian towns were largely Germanized after the 13th cent., while the rural population remained Czech. As a result of the Munich Pact (1938), Germany annexed Czech Silesia and part of Moravia. From 1939 to 1945 Bohemia and Moravia were a German "protectorate," but after World War II the pre-1938 boundaries were restored and most of the German-speaking population was expelled.

Moravia, resort village (pop. 1,480), W central N.Y., near Owasco L. and SW of Syracuse. Millard Fillmore was born near here.

Moravian Church, Renewed Church of the Brethren, or **Unitas Fratrum,** evangelical communion; the adherents are called United Brethren or Herrnhuters. Arose (1457) among followers of John Huss as Church of the Brotherhood. Consecration of a bishop (1467) caused break with Church of Rome. Persecution drove the Brethren from Bohemia. In 1722 a group took refuge in Saxony, at Herrnhut on estate of Graf von ZINZENDORF. Missionary effort carried movement to West Indies, North and South America, Asia, and Africa. In Pa., Bethlehem, Nazareth, and Lititz were founded c.1740 and became center of faith in America. Church has modified episcopacy and simple ritual.

Moravian College and **Moravian College for Women:** see BETHLEHEM, Pa.

Moravska Ostrava (mô′räfskä ô′strävä), Ger. *Mährisch Ostrau,* city (pop. 116,25), NE Moravia, Czechoslovakia; industrial center of coal-mining region. With several other adjacent communities, it forms Greater Ostrava (pop. c.180,000). Has iron and steel mills and produces rolling stock, machinery, ship and bridge parts, chemicals.

Moray, Scottish name: see MURRAY.

Moray Firth (mŭ′rē, –rā), inlet of North Sea, NE Scotland. Extends from Kinnairds Head,

Aberdeenshire, to Duncansbay Head, Caithness.

Morayshire (mŭ'rēshĭr) or **Elginshire** (ĕl'gĭnshĭr), maritime county (477 sq. mi.; pop. 48,211), NE Scotland; co. town Elgin. Interior hills devoted to grazing; coastal plain is heavily cultivated. Region saw much strife among early Picts.

Morbihan (môrbēā'), department (2,739 sq. mi.; pop. 506,884), NW France, in Brittany; cap. Vannes.

mordant (môr'dunt), substance used to make fast certain dyes on cloth. Either the mordant or colloid produced by it adheres to fiber, attracts and fixes an oppositely charged colloidal dye, forming an insoluble precipitate (a lake). Acid mordants are used with basic dyes and vice versa. Certain dyes not requiring mordant are made more vivid with it.

Mordecai (môr"dēkā'ī), guardian and uncle of ESTHER.

Mordred, Sir: see ARTHURIAN LEGEND.

Mordvinian Autonomous Soviet Socialist Republic (môrdvĭ'nēun), autonomous republic (10,080 sq. mi.; pop. 1,188,598), central European RSFSR, in uplands W of the Middle Volga; cap. Saransk. Primarily agr., it also has mineral resources (oil shale, peat, phosphorite). Population is 55% Russian, 40% Mordvinian, a Finnic people which adopted Russian culture and Greek Orthodox religion from Russian colonies estab. here in 16th cent.

More, Sir Anthony: see MORO, ANTONIO.

More, Hannah, 1745–1833, English author, a noted bluestocking. A founder of Religious Tract Society (1799). Her novel *Coelebs in Search of a Wife* (1808) was very popular in her day.

More, Paul Elmer, 1864–1937, American editor, essayist, and critic, a leader of "new humanists" and an authority on Greek philosophy. Edited the *Nation.* Chief works are *Shelburne Essays* (11 vols., 1904–21) and *The Greek Tradition* (5 vols., 1921–31).

More, Sir Thomas (St. Thomas More), 1478–1535, author of UTOPIA, English statesman and humanist, saint and martyr in the Roman Catholic Church. Rose in the favor of Henry VIII to become lord chancellor 1529, but he disapproved the king's divorce from Katharine of Aragon and retired in 1532. He was cleared of charges connected with Elizabeth BARTON, but he refused to subscribe to Act of Supremacy. He was imprisoned and finally beheaded on charge of treason. Canonized 1935. Feast: July 6.

Morea, Greece: see PELOPONNESUS.

Moréas, Jean (zhã' môrāäs'), 1856–1910, French poet, b. Athens. His name was originally Papadiamantopoulos. First a symbolist (*Les Syrtes,* 1884), he gradually turned to classic style, as in *Stances* (1899–1901) and in the drama *Iphigénie* (1903).

Moreau, Gustave (güstäv' môrō'), 1826–98, French painter, known for his pictures of the weird and mystical. His house in Paris is now a state-owned museum of art.

Moreau, Jean Victor (zhã' vēktôr'), 1763–1813, French general in FRENCH REVOLUTIONARY WARS. Won decisive victory over Austrians at Hohenlinden (1800). Opposed Napoleon, who exiled him. In 1813 he served with allies against Napoleon, was killed in battle.

Moreau (murō'), river rising in NW S.Dak. and flowing 289 mi. E to the Missouri. Used in Missouri R. basin project.

Morehead City, resort and fishing town (pop. 5,144), E N.C., on Newport R. opposite Beaufort.

Morelia (mōrā'lyä), city (pop. 44,304; alt. 6,187 ft.), cap. of Michoacán, W Mexico; founded as Valladolid (1541) by Viceroy Antonio de Mendoza. Chief manufactures are shawls, hats, flour, cotton goods, soap, beer, cigars, cigarettes, wine. Iturbide and Morelos y Pavón were born here.

Morelos (y Pavón), José María (hōsā' märē'ä mōrā'lōs ē pävōn'), 1765–1815, Mexican leader in the revolution against Spain, national hero. A liberal priest, he joined the revolution (1810), conducted a brilliant campaign in S, was elected generalissimo with chief executive's powers (1813). Captured by Iturbide's forces, he was shot.

Morelos (mōrā'lōs), state (1,917 sq. mi.; pop. 268,863), central Mexico; cap. and chief city CUERNAVACA. Mountainous, with broad semiarid valleys opening to the S, state is chiefly agr. State named in honor of Morelos y Pavón. Depredations of Zapata and regime of Carranza caused almost irreparable damage to sugar industry and agr. productivity.

Morenci (murĕn'sē), town (pop. 6,541), E Ariz., near N. Mex. line, on hillside around copper mines.

Moretto, Il (ēl mōrĕt'tō), c.1498–1554, Italian painter of portraits and religious subjects, whose real name was Alessandro Bonvicino. Leading painter of Brescian school, teacher of Moroni. Influenced by the Venetians but developed own style, marked by cool and luminous coloring.

Morgagni, Giovanni Battista (jōvän'nē bättē'stä mōrgä'nyē), 1682–1771, Italian anatomist, noted for studies of effect of disease on body.

Morgan, American family of financiers and philanthropists. **Junius Spencer Morgan,** 1813–90, headed international banking enterprise which handled most of British funds invested in U.S. His son **J(ohn) Pierpont Morgan,** 1837–1913, built family fortunes into colossal financial and industrial empire. Increased his railroad holdings. Formed in 1901 U.S. Steel Corp., first billion-dollar corporation in world. Subject to much criticism and held as popular symbol of wealth. He dispensed numerous philanthropies and was a renowned art collector. **J(ohn) Pierpont Morgan,** 1867–1943, became active head of house of Morgan when his father died in 1913. Helped finance World War I. Like his father, he disliked publicity; continued philanthropies. His sister, **Anne Morgan,** 1873–1952, a leading feminist, was devoted to philanthropic and civic organizations.

Morgan, Daniel, 1736–1802, American Revolutionary general. Captured in attack on Quebec. Exchanged 1776. Took part in Saratoga campaign. Defeated British at Cowpens, S.C. (1780).

Morgan, Sir Henry, 1635?–1688, British buccaneer. Led Barbados pirates c.1666, but was later given British authority for his exploits.

Knighted as a hero (1674). Made lieutenant governor of Jamaica.

Morgan, John Hunt, 1825–64, Confederate general. Noted for daring raids in Civil War; most famous one in 1863 through Ky., Ind., and Ohio.

Morgan, J(ohn) Pierpont, and **Junius Spencer Morgan:** see MORGAN, family.

Morgan, Justin: see JUSTIN MORGAN.

Morgan, Lewis H(enry), 1818–81, American anthropologist. Originally a lawyer, he became interested in N.Y. Indians and wrote notable report on Iroquois League. His concern with social organization and social evolution was shown in his *Ancient Society* (1877) and other works.

Morgan, Thomas Hunt, 1866–1945, American zoologist. Won 1933 Nobel Prize in Physiology and Medicine for theory that hereditary unit characters are dependent upon certain factors, or genes, in the chromosome, the behavior of which he studied and mapped.

Morgan, resort city (pop. 1,064), N Utah, on Weber R. and SE of Ogden. Trade center in Weber R. project. Also Morgan City.

Morgan City, city (pop. 9,759), S La., port on Atchafalaya R. at Berwick Bay. Handles oil, sulphur, chemicals, and shells, and has shipyards and sea food processing and shipping.

Morgan le Fay: see ARTHURIAN LEGEND.

Morgan Library: see PIERPONT MORGAN LIBRARY.

Morganton, town (pop. 8,311), W N.C., ENE of Asheville. Mfg. of textiles, hosiery, furniture, and leather products.

Morgantown, city (pop. 25,525), N W.Va., on Monongahela R. and S of Pittsburgh; settled 1767. Coal-mining center with mfg. of glass and chemicals. Seat of West Virginia Univ. (land-grant; state supported; coed.; opened 1867).

Morgarten (mōr'gärtůn), mountain slope, central Switzerland, c.5 mi. N of Schwyz. Here in 1315 a small Swiss force decisively defeated the Austrians, thus paving the way for Swiss independence.

Morgenstern, Christian (krĭs'tyän môr'gůnshtĕrn), 1871–1914, German poet-philosopher. Though influenced by mysticism and theosophy, he is best known for his whimsical humor. *Galgenlieder* (1905) and *Palmström* (1910) are volumes of grotesque verse. *Ich und du* (1911) contains love lyrics.

Morgenthau, Henry (môr'gůnthô), 1856–1946, American banker, diplomat, and philanthropist, b. Germany. Ambassador to Turkey (1913–16). Raised funds for Near East relief (1919–21); later directed resettlement of Greek refugees. An incorporator of Red Cross in U.S. His son, **Henry Morgenthau, Jr.,** 1891–, was Secretary of the Treasury (1934–45). Supervised huge sale of government bonds, advocated international monetary stabilization. Authored famous plan for reconverting German industries to agr. and the service trades.

Moriah (mōrī'ů), place where Abraham was to sacrifice Isaac. Gen. 22.2. May be same as Mt. Moriah.

Moriah, Mount, biblical name of hill of E Jerusalem; site of Solomon's Temple. 2 Chron. 3.1.

Moriscos (môrĭ'skōz), Spanish Moors converted to Christianity after Christian reconquest of Spain. Moslems were generally tolerated before 1492, but later faced the choice of conversion or expulsion. Many converts secretly continued to practice Islam. Growing intolerance led to Moorish uprisings, which were severely suppressed (1500–1502, 1568–71). In 1609 all Moriscos were expelled from Spain. This inhuman measure also had evil consequences for Spain's economy.

Morison, Samuel Eliot, 1887–, American historian. Works include *Admiral of the Ocean Sea* (1942), biography of Christopher Columbus which won Pulitzer Prize 1943; official *Tercentennial History of Harvard College and University* (3 vols., 1930–36); and, by U.S. appointment, official *History of United States Naval Operations in World War II* (5 of 14 projected vols., 1947–).

Morison, Stanley, 1889–, English typographer and journalist; typographical consultant to Cambridge Univ. Press, English Monotype Corp., and the London *Times* (1929–44). He became editor of *The Times Literary Supplement* in 1945.

Morisot, Berthe (bĕrt' môrēzō'), 1841–95, French impressionist painter. She was influenced by Manet, then Monet. Typical is *La Toilette* (Art Inst., Chicago).

Morland, George, 1763–1804, English genre and landscape painter; pupil of his father, Henry Morland (c.1730–1797), a portrait painter. Produced over 4,000 pictures. His masterpiece, *Interior of a Stable,* is in Natl. Gall., London.

Morley, Christopher, 1890–, American novelist and familiar essayist, a founder and editor (1924–40) of the *Saturday Review of Literature.* His novels and studies, usually in a light vein, include *Parnassus on Wheels* (1917), *Where the Blue Begins* (1922), and *Kitty Foyle* (1939).

Morley, John, 1838–1923, English statesman and man of letters. Edited *Fortnightly Review* 1867–83. Secretary of state for India 1905–10; lord president of the council 1910–14. Author of a number of fine biographies.

Morley, Sylvanus Griswold, 1883–1948, American archaeologist. Specialist in Middle American archaeology and in Maya hieroglyphics.

Morley, Thomas, b. 1557 or 1558, d. 1603, English composer, noted mainly for his madrigals and settings of Shakspere's songs. He also wrote anthems, services, Latin motets, and a treatise on theory.

Mormons, popular name of members of Church of Jesus Christ of LATTER-DAY SAINTS, founded by Joseph SMITH after golden tablets of Book of Mormon had been revealed to him at Palmyra, N.Y. He gathered followers rapidly and in 1831 estab. group at Kirtland, Ohio. Conflict with "Gentile" neighbors in Mo. caused them to move to a new Zion at Nauvoo, Ill., but again hostility arose, culminating in mob murder in 1846 of Smith and his brother Hyrum. Mormons went W and settled (1847) in valley of Great Salt Lake. After many hardships they, under Brigham Young's brilliant guidance, created a self-sustaining economy and weathered trouble with neighbors as well as with U.S. government. Young's announcement of doctrine of plural marriage caused Congress to pass anti-polygamy laws and prevented admission of Utah as state until 1896, after Pres. Wilford Woodruff in 1890 accepted laws as binding in secular life.

Mornay, Philippe de, seigneur du Plessis-Marly (fēlēp′ dů môrnā′ sānyûr′ dü plĕsē′-märlē′), 1549–1623, French Protestant leader and apologist in the Wars of Religion.

morning-glory, annual or perennial plant, usually climbing, of genus *Ipomoea.* Its funnel-shaped flowers (variously colored) open in the morning.

Morny, Charles, duc de (shärl′ dük′ dů môrnē′), 1811–65, French statesman; natural son of Hortense de Beauharnais and Joseph, comte de Flahaut (a natural son of Talleyrand). Helped place his half-brother Napoleon III on throne; played important role in Second Empire.

Moro [Span.,= Moor], one of a group of Moslem natives of Mindanao and Sulu Archipelago in Philippines and of Borneo, who were converted in great missionary extension of Islam from India in 15th and 16th cent. Not ethnically or linguistically units, they are of largely Malayan stock. Have long maintained enmity toward Christian Filipinos. Chief occupation is agriculture; industries are cloth weaving, pottery making, boatbuilding, metal crafts.

Moro, Antonio (äntō′nyō mô′rō), c.1512–c.1575, Flemish portraitist, court painter to the Hapsburgs; also called Sir Anthony More. Visited Spain, Portugal, and England (where he painted Mary Tudor).

Morocco (mŭrŏ′kō), sultanate (c.160,000 sq. mi.; pop. 9,850,000), N Africa, on the Mediterranean and the Atlantic. Bordered by Spanish Sahara (S) and by Algeria (S and E). Nominally ruled by the sultan, who is mainly important as religious leader of the Moslems. Politically divided into three parts: French Morocco (c.151,000 sq. mi.; pop. 8,617,387), a protectorate and since 1946 an associated state of the French Union, with cap. at RABAT; Spanish Morocco (c.7,600 sq. mi.; pop. 1,082,009), a protectorate (roughly coextensive with the RIF), with cap. at TETUÁN; and the international zone of TANGIER. Coastal enclaves directly governed by Spain are CEUTA, MELILLA, and IFNI. Population is concentrated on coastal plains, where grains, citrus fruit, olives, and grapes are grown. Atlas Mts. occupy central Morocco and contain valuable mineral resources (esp. phosphates, shipped mainly from CASABLANCA). The area was roughly coextensive with ancient Roman district of MAURETANIA. Islam was brought by the Arabs, who first invaded Morocco in 683. Independent state was first estab. 788; Moroccan power reached its height under the great Berber dynastics of the ALMORAVIDES and the ALMOHADES. European encroachments began 1415 with Portuguese capture of Ceuta and subsequent seizure of most of the main ports. Decline of Portuguese influence began with their defeat by the Moors at the battle of ALCAZARQUIVIR (1578). The Alouites, the present ruling house, came to power in 1660, succeeding the Saadian or first Sherifian dynasty. Like the other BARBARY STATES, Morocco was a pirate base 17th–19th cent. In 19th cent. its strategic and economic importance excited the interest of European powers, and an explosive situation was soon created by intense rivalry. A temporary settlement was reached by Algeciras Conference (1906), which assured protection of German investments and gave France and Spain authority to police Morocco. But peace was soon broken by several clashes, notably the AGADIR incident. In 1911 Germany agreed to a French protectorate in Morocco in exchange for French territory in Africa. French and Spanish protectorates were estab. 1912. In World War II, French Morocco remained loyal to the Vichy regime after fall of France (1940). Allied forces landed at major ports on Nov. 8, 1942, and on Nov. 11 all resistance ended. After the war an independence movement won the active support of Sultan Sidi Mohammed, but it was firmly opposed by France and Spain.

Morone (mōrō′nā), name of two Italian religious painters of Veronese school. **Domenico Morone,** b. c.1442, d. after 1517, and his son, **Francesco Morone,** 1471–1529, were both influenced by Mantegna.

Moroni, Giovanni Battista (jōvän′nē bät-tē′stä mōrō′nē), c.1525–1578, portrait painter of Brescian school; pupil of Il Moretto. Works have much force.

moronity: see FEEBLE-MINDEDNESS.

Moronobu (Moronobu Hishigawa) (mōrō′-nōbōō), fl. 1659–95, Japanese genre artist; pioneer in use of wood block for book illustration and popular sheet prints. Illustrated book of etiquette and feminine hygiene.

Morpheus (môr′fēůs, môr′fūs) [Gr.,= shaper], in Greek and Roman mythology, god of dreams; son of Sleep. He brought dreams of human forms.

morphine, derivative of OPIUM.

Morphy, Paul Charles (môr′fē), 1837–84, American chess player. At 21 he was acknowledged the greatest player in world. After 1859 mental instability ended his chess play.

morrice dance: see MORRIS DANCE.

Morrill, Justin Smith (mŏ′růl), 1810–98, U.S. Representative (1855–67) and Senator (1867–98) from Vt. Best known for Morrill Act (1862), which provided for granting of public lands for establishment of educational institutions.

Morrilton, city (pop. 5,483), W central Ark., on Arkansas R., in livestock and cotton area. Has cotton mill, sawmill, and meat-packing plant.

Morris, family of American landowners and statesmen. **Richard Morris,** d. 1672, purchased land from Dutch in what became N.Y. His son, **Lewis Morris,** 1671–1746, first governor of N.J. (1738–46) after its separation from N.Y., became first lord of N.Y. family manor, called Morrisania, in 1697. His namesake and grandson, **Lewis Morris,** 1726–98, signer of the Declaration of Independence, was prominent in N.Y. affairs before and after American Revolution. His half brother, **Gouverneur Morris** (gŭvůrnēr′, –nōōr′), 1752–1816, aided the patriot cause in American Revolution, assisted in handling finances of new government (1781–85), and helped write the Constitution.

Morris, Robert, 1734–1806, American banker, "financier of American Revolution," signer of Declaration of Independence, b. England. Superintendent of finance (1781–84). Founded national bank.

Morris, William, 1834–96, English artist, writer, printer, and socialist. Studied painting with D. G. Rossetti and was influenced by Ruskin and Burne-Jones. In 1861 he estab. Morris and Company, whose furnishings and art objects refreshed Victorian taste. He indirectly sponsored the arts and crafts movement by using medieval craft techniques in his factory. Study of the medieval also influenced his verse tales—*The Earthly Paradise* (3 vols., 1868–70) and the epic poem *Sigurd the Volsung* (1876). He spent his last 20 years working for socialism, writing *A Dream of John Ball* (1888), *News from Nowhere* (1891), and *Socialism: Its Growth and Outcome* (1893). His last artistic venture was the improvement of printing through the Kelmscott Press.

Morris, city (pop. 6,926), NE Ill., on Illinois R. and SW of Chicago, in coal and clay area. Shipping center with paper and leather products.

Morris Brown College: see ATLANTA, Ga.

morris dance or **morrice dance,** rustic dance of N England, derived from country festivals (e.g., May Day) as early as 15th cent. Main dancers were Robin Hood, Maid Marian, hobbyhorse, and fool.

Morris Island: see CHARLESTON, S.C.

Morris Jesup, Cape, northernmost land point in the world, N Greenland, in Peary Land. At lat. 83°39′N, it is 440 mi. from North Pole.

Morrison, Herbert Stanley, 1888–, British statesman. Home secretary and minister of home security 1940–45. In Labour government he was lord president of privy council and leader in House of Commons (1945–51) and foreign secretary (1951).

Morrison Cave State Park, SW Mont., on Jefferson R. and SE of Butte. Large limestone cave was in former Lewis and Clark Cavern Natl. Monument.

Morristown. 1 Residential town (pop. 17,124), N N.J., WNW of Newark; settled c.1710. Mfg. of electrical and metal products, clothing, and paving materials; greenhouses. Washington made Morristown his winter hq. (1776–77, 1779–80) during the Revolution. Morristown Natl. Historical Park (see NATIONAL PARKS AND MONUMENTS, table) is here. Town's old buildings include Jabez Campfield House where Alexander Hamilton courted Elizabeth Schuyler 1779–80. S. F. B. Morse and Alfred Vail worked here. Near by is Seeing Eye establishment for training dogs. **2** Town (pop. 13,019), E Tenn., ENE of Knoxville, settled 1783. Dairy, poultry, and tobacco center. Cherokee Dam on Holston R. and Douglas Dam on French Broad R. are near by.

Morrisville, borough (pop. 6,787), SE Pa., on Delaware R. opposite Trenton, N.J. Washington had hq. here, Dec. 8–14, 1776. Near by is Pennsbury, William Penn's manor (reconstructed 1946). Here is one of largest steel plants in nation.

Morro Castle (mô′rō), three forts in West Indies: (1) at entrance of harbor of Havana, Cuba, erected 1589; (2) at entrance of harbor of Santiago de Cuba, taken by American forces in Spanish-American War, 1898; (3) on harbor of San Juan, Puerto Rico.

Morrow, Dwight W(hitney), 1873–1931, American diplomat. Ambassador to Mexico (1927–30).

Morse, Jedidiah, 1761–1826, American Congregational clergyman. Opposed Unitarianism. Wrote series of geography textbooks that were widely used. His son, **Samuel Finley Breese Morse,** 1791–1872, was an inventor and artist. In portrait painting especially he gained considerable reputation and was a founder of the National Academy of Design (1825). He invented the electric telegraph, devised MORSE CODE, and experimented with submarine cable telegraphy. His brother, **Sidney Edwards Morse,** 1794–1871, was a journalist, inventor, and geographer. With a brother, R. C. Morse, he founded (1823) the *New-York Observer*. Coinventor (c.1839) of cerography, method of making stereotype plates; perfected the bathometer (1866). Edited and wrote geography textbooks.

Morse code [for S. F. B. Morse], an arbitrary set of signals used on TELEGRAPH. International code is a simplified form used in radio telegraphy. American Morse differs from international in 11 letters, in all numerals except numeral 4, and in punctuation. Unit of code is *dot,* representing a very brief depression of telegraph key; *dash* is three times as long. Message is translated through combination of dots and dashes representing letters, numbers, punctuation, and pauses between letters and words.

mortar, in warfare, field piece which fires projectiles at a high trajectory; mostly used by infantry because of ease of handling and emplacement.

Mortimer, English noble family. **Roger de Mortimer,** 1st **earl of March,** 1287?–1330, opposed EDWARD II and the Despensers in wars of 1321–22. Escaped to France where Queen ISABELLA became his mistress. They invaded England and forced Edward II to abdicate (1326). Virtually ruled England until EDWARD III had him seized, tried, and executed. His great-grandson, **Edmund de Mortimer,** 3d **earl of March** and 1st **earl of Ulster,** 1351–81, married Philippa, granddaughter of Edward III. This marriage led to claim to throne by house of YORK. His son, **Roger de Mortimer,** 4th **earl of March** and 2d **earl of Ulster,** 1374–98, was proclaimed heir presumptive by Richard II in 1385. He was killed fighting in Ireland. His son, **Edward de Mortimer,** 5th **earl of March** and 3d **earl of Ulster,** 1391–1425, succeeded his father as heir presumptive to the throne. Imprisoned (1399) after the revolution of Henry IV, he was released by Henry V (1413) and served in the French Wars. His death ended the male line. He refused to aid plots to put him on the throne, including those of his uncle, **Sir Edmund de Mortimer,** 1376–1409?. Allied himself with Owen Glendower and the Percy family against Henry IV.

mortmain [Fr.,= dead hand] (môrt′mān″),

ownership of land by religious, charitable, or business corporation. As imperishable legal entity such body can hold and increase property to detriment of state in taxes and other dues. In 13th cent. Church holdings led to conflict between Church and state; by 19th cent. rights were greatly restricted. Business corporations have generally been freed from restrictions.

Morton, James Douglas, 4th **earl of,** d. 1581, regent of Scotland (1572–78). A principal in murder of David Rizzio, he was later convicted and beheaded for his part in the murder of Lord Darnley.

Morton, Sarah Wentworth, 1759–1846, American poet, long reputed the author of the first American novel, *The Power of Sympathy* (1789), now generally credited to William Hill BROWN.

Morton, Thomas, fl. 1622–47, British trader and adventurer. Pilgrims, disliking him for his "scandalous" revelry at Merry Mount and his rival trade with the Indians, arrested him and sent him to England.

Morton, William Thomas Green, 1819–68, American dentist and physician. Demonstrated ether anesthesia (1846) at Massachusetts General Hospital.

mosaic (mōzā'ĭk), art of producing surface ornament by inlaying colored pieces of marble, glass, tile, or other material. In Italy and the Roman colonies floor patterns were produced both by large slabs of marble in contrasting colors and by small marble tesserae or cubes. Tessera floors varied from simple geometrical patterns in black and white to huge designs of figures or animals. Glass mosaics were used to decorate walls of ancient basilicas. The craft reached perfection in 6th cent. at Byzantium (Constantinople), where gold mosaics were extensively used to decorate Hagia Sophia. In the West, Ravenna became the center of Byzantine mosaic, 5th–6th cent. Revival of the art in Italy, 11th–13th cent., produced such beautiful mural works as those of St. Mark's Church, Venice. Rise of fresco decoration in early 14th cent. in Italy caused decline of mosaic. Modern workers use ancient system (setting each piece by hand in the damp cement mortar) as well as a new method of fastening the tesserae with glue on a paper cartoon drawn in reverse and then transferring to the mortar.

Mosby, John Singleton (môz'bē), 1833–1916, Confederate partisan leader. His Partisan Rangers raided Union cavalry, communications, and supplies. Famous feat was capture of E. H. Stoughton at Fairfax Courthouse in 1863.

Moscow (mŏ'skou, mŏ'skō), Rus. *Moskva,* city (125 sq. mi.; pop. c.5,100,000), cap. of USSR and of RSFSR, in central European Russia and on the Moskva R. It is the largest city and the largest industrial concentration of the USSR, producing 15% of the total Soviet output (steel, machinery, automobiles, aircraft, rolling stock, chemicals, textiles); a major transportation and communications center; hq. of the Communist party. Has Lomonosov Univ. (founded 1755); Soviet Acad. of Sciences; numerous technical schools; several famous theaters, notably the Moscow Art Theatre and the Bolshoi Theater (opera and ballet); Tretyakov art gallery and other museums. See of the patriarch of the Russian Orthodox Church. First mentioned 1147, Moscow was made c.1271 the seat of a principality under Daniel, son of Grand Duke Alexander Nevsky of Vladimir-Suzdal. Moscow rose to commercial importance. In the 14th cent. the grand dukes of Vladimir made it their cap. and took the title grand dukes of Moscow or Muscovy. IVAN III and VASILY III enlarged the state, which under them became identical with Great RUSSIA. Moscow was twice burned by the Tatars (1381, 1572), was briefly held by the Poles in the Time of Troubles (liberated by a volunteer army under Prince Pozharski, 1612), and was occupied by Napoleon I in Sept., 1812. A few days later, a fire broke out, burned the entire city except its few stone buildings, and forced the French to begin their disastrous retreat. It probably was started accidentally by French looters. From 1713 to 1918 St. Petersburg superseded Moscow as cap. of Russia. Moscow doubled its population between World Wars I and II and underwent considerable modernization. A subway system was opened 1935; huge housing projects were undertaken. Construction of the Palace of the Soviets (planned to reach 1,300 ft. in height) was interrupted by World War II, when Moscow nearly was captured by a two-pronged German drive (Dec., 1941). The heart of Moscow is Red Square, which contains the 16th-cent. Cathedral of St. Basil, one of the most imposing and exuberant examples of Russian architecture, and the mausoleum of Lenin and Stalin. Red Square abuts on one side on the KREMLIN, the nerve center of the Soviet Union, and on the other side on the old Kitaigorod [Chinatown] dist., once the merchant quarter and now the site of many public buildings. Moscow is surrounded by a belt of large parks and of suburbs.

Moscow (mŏs'kō), city (pop. 10,593), NW Idaho, at Wash. line N of Lewiston; founded 1871. Shipping and processing center for wheat area. Seat of Univ. of Idaho (land-grant, state supported; coed.; opened 1892); pioneered in student-cooperative living.

Moscow Art Theatre, world-famous Russian repertory theater founded (1898) by STANISLAVSKY and Nemirovich-Danchenko. Greatly influenced theaters throughout the world (esp. by Chekhov productions).

Moscow Conferences, four meetings (1941–45) at Moscow. At first (Sept.–Oct., 1941) Great Britain and U.S. planned lend-lease aid to Russia. At second (Oct., 1943) Britain, U.S., and USSR pledged formation of UN. At third (Oct., 1944) Churchill and Stalin made agreements respecting Poland, Bulgaria, and Yugoslavia. For fourth conference (Dec., 1945), see FOREIGN MINISTERS, COUNCIL OF.

Moseley, Henry Gwyn Jeffreys (mōz'lē), 1887–1915, English physicist. His brilliant research led to his arrangement of chemical elements according to atomic numbers; this resolved the few discrepancies inherent in Mendelejeff's system (see PERIODIC LAW). Moseley was killed at Gallipoli in World War I.

Moselle (mōzĕl'), department (2,405 sq. mi.;

pop. 622,145), NE France, in LORRAINE; cap. Metz.

Moselle (mōzĕl′), Ger. *Mosel,* river, 320 mi. long, E France and W Germany, rising in Vosges mts. and flowing N past Épinal, Toul, and Metz, then along German-Luxembourg frontier, past Trier, and into the Rhine at Coblenz. German section of valley has many old castles and celebrated vineyards.

Moses (mō′–), lawgiver of Israel, the prophet who led his people out of bondage in Egypt to edge of Canaan, the Promised Land. Through Moses, God gave the Ten Commandments, the criminal code, and liturgical law to the people; these are called Mosaic Law. Moses' story, including his dramatic rescue from the bulrushes and his divine calling at the burning bush, is told in the books of Exodus, Leviticus, Numbers, and Deuteronomy. Authorship of these and Genesis (collectively the Pentateuch) ascribed to him. Moses mentioned throughout Bible. Among the PSEUDEPIGRAPHA is the Assumption of Moses.

Moses, Anna Mary Robertson, 1860–, American painter known as Grandma Moses. A farmer's wife, she began painting in her 70's; her so-called American primitives depict scenes of farm life.

Moskva (mŭskvä′), river, 315 mi. long, central European RSFSR, flowing E, past Moscow, into Oka R. Connected with the Volga by Moscow Canal (80 mi. long), below which it is navigable (April–Nov.).

Moslem: see ISLAM.

Moslem art and architecture. The art which the nomadic Moslems brought to the lands around the Mediterranean in the 7th cent. was purely ornamental and lacked a definite building style. Local styles, mainly Christian (i.e., Syrian, Byzantine, or Coptic), were used as a basis on which to display surface decorations, chiefly of geometrical design. In 7th and 8th cent. great mosques were built, including those at Cairo, Damascus, and Córdoba. In 11th and 12th cent. Egypt became the center of architectural activity; here a distinctive tomb mosque was developed and elaborate minarets were built. The same period saw flowering of Moorish style in Spain, chief examples of which are the GIRALDA tower and palace of ALHAMBRA. Spanish art subsequent to expulsion (1492) of Moors continued to reflect Moorish influence (see MUDEJAR). Persian art evolved a distinctive MOSQUE type (e.g., Blue Mosque at Tabriz, 1437–68) and dominated native traditions in India to produce such structures as the TAJ MAHAL. The Turks added Moslem surface adornment to Byzantine architecture; their greatest architect in the style was SINAN. In all Moslem styles the arch (see *ill.,* p. 61) occurs in many variations: pointed, multifoil, ogee, and horseshoe; interior ornamentation includes ceramic wainscots and stucco wall carvings. In minor arts (e.g., metalwork, pottery making, rug weaving), as in architecture, the emphasis is on ornament, which is based on the arabesque, intertwined bands, and the flowing Arabic script.

Moslem League, political organization of India, founded 1906. Led by JINNAH after 1934. In 1940 it demanded creation of PAKISTAN, opposed by INDIAN NATIONAL CONGRESS. Won most of the Moslem vote in 1946 elections and forced the acceptance of separate Moslem state in 1947.

Mosley, Sir Oswald (Ernald), 1896–, British fascist leader. Organized (1932) the British Union of Fascists. Interned 1940–43. After World War II he attempted to revive the movement.

mosque (mŏsk), building for worship used by the Moslem faith. Certain mosques, called madrasahs, also serve as theological schools. Essential elements of mosque design are the *maksoura* (prayer hall with the *mihrab* or prayer niche, which indicates direction of Mecca); the *dikka* (platform for services) near which is the mimbar or pulpit; and a large court with minarets at its corners, a central fountain, and arcaded porticoes. First domical mosque was that of Omar at Jerusalem, built 687, but such mosques were not commonly built until about 13th cent. Moorish school produced the huge mosque at Córdoba, Spain (built 8th–10th cent.). Persian mosques are characterized by pointed bulbous domes and gorgeous tile decoration. Turkish school converted Byzantine architecture to Islamic uses, making a notable model of HAGIA SOPHIA; another superb monument achieved at Constantinople was mosque of Suleiman, built 1550–57 by the architect Sinan. Indian school retained bulbous domes and round minarets of Persian school but used stone and marble for exteriors rather than traditional Persian tile sheathing. Under the Moguls were built such magnificent mosques as Pearl Mosque at Agra.

mosquito (mŭskē′tō), insect of fly family, of almost world-wide distribution. Female pierces skin, injects own salivary fluid, sucks blood of humans and many animals. Usually lays eggs in stagnant water. Yellow fever, malaria, and other diseases are transmitted by bite of certain species. See *ill.,* p. 601.

Mosquito Coast, Span., *Mosquitia* (mōskētē′ä), region, never exactly delimited, c.40 mi. wide extending from San Juan R. in Nicaragua N along coast into NE Honduras. Name is derived from Mosquito Indians in area over whom Great Britain estab. protective kingdom at Bluefields (1678). British seized San Juan del Norte in 1848, causing Nicaraguan and U.S. protest, and expansion was checked by Clayton-Bulwer Treaty. In 1860 autonomy of Mosquito Kingdom was secured by a treaty between Nicaragua and Great Britain, but in 1894 it was forcibly incorporated into Nicaragua. N part is still claimed by Honduras.

Moss (môs), city (pop. 17,415), co. seat of Ostfold co., SE Norway, on E shore of Oslo Fjord. Shipyards, sawmills, foundries; seaside resort. Personal union of Sweden and Norway was signed here Aug. 14, 1814.

moss, small primitive plant of class Musci of world-wide distribution. Usually characterized by tufted growth, mosses are often evergreen and some are creeping, others erect. One moss, SPHAGNUM, is a source of peat. Club moss, reindeer moss, Spanish moss, and flowering moss or pyxie are unrelated.

Mossadegh, Mohammed (mōsädĕkh′), 1880–,

Iranian statesman, leader of National Front party; premier (1951–). His nationalizing of the British-owned oil industry in 1951 led to a break in diplomatic relations with Great Britain and international repercussions. Received dictatorial powers from the Majlis, 1952–53. In trying to do away with the limited power of the shah he was opposed by the powerful Moslem leader, speaker of the Majlis, Ayatollah Kashani.

Mostar (mô'stär), city (pop. 23,239), Yugoslavia; chief city of Hercegovina.

most-favored-nation clause, provision in commercial treaties that the signatory will enjoy benefits equal to those accorded to any other state. Clauses may be unilateral (i.e., only one of the signatories receives favored treatment) or bilateral. Many Asiatic countries were bound to Western nations by unilateral clauses, but in recent years such clauses have usually been bilateral.

Mosul (mō'sŭl, mōsōōl'), city (pop. 203,273), N Iraq, on Tigris R., opposite ruins of Nineveh and S of Tepe Gawra. After c.750 it was chief center of N Mesopotamia. Occupied by British in 1918, formally renounced by Turkey in 1926. Inhabited mainly by Arabs. Once known for fine cotton goods called muslins from its name. Near by are large oil fields.

motet, name given to an important musical form of the 13th cent. and to a different form which originated in the Renaissance. The medieval motet was usually a three-voice composition arranged in a brief reiterated rhythmic pattern. Each part had a separate text; sometimes both French and Latin, and sacred and secular subject matter were mingled in one motet. The second voice was called *motetus* [from Fr. *mot* = word], hence the term motet. The Renaissance motet had a single Latin text, with four to six voices, and was free from 13th-cent. rhythmic rigidity. The peak of this form is reached in the six motets of Bach. Since his time, the term motet has been applied to almost any kind of sacred choral polyphony but usually refers to the unaccompanied Latin motets used in the Roman Catholic Church.

moth, any of insect group comprising with BUTTERFLY group the order Lepidoptera. See also CLOTHES MOTH; CODLING MOTH; CUTWORM; GYPSY MOTH; SILKWORM.

Mother Lode, belt of gold-bearing quartz, central Calif., E of Sacramento and San Joaquin rivers and W of the Sierra Nevada. Sometimes limited to strip c.70 mi. long and 1–6½ mi. wide, running NW from Mariposa. Discovery of placer gold on South Fork of American R. led to 1848 rush.

mother-of-pearl or **nacre** (nā'kŭr), iridescent substance secreted by mantle and lining shells of some mollusks, e.g., pearl oyster, pearl mussel, abalone.

Motherwell and Wishaw (wĭ'shô), burgh (pop. 68,137), Lanarkshire, Scotland. In coal and iron region, it has important steel industry and other mfg.

motion. A body in act of changing its position relative to another body is said to be in motion relative to that body. Thus passenger in moving car, though at rest in relation to car, is in motion relative to earth; bodies in motion on earth are also in motion relative to ether through which earth is moving (if ether is considered stationary or moving at velocity other than that of earth). Newton's **laws of motion:** (1) a body remains in a state of rest or of uniform motion in a straight line unless compelled by some external force acting upon it to change that state; (2) a change in momentum is proportional to the force causing the change and takes place in the direction in which the force is acting, or the increase or decrease in velocity is proportional to the force; and (3) to every action there is an equal and opposite reaction. These laws and that of universal gravitation continued to serve as basic principles of dynamics, maintaining their importance through times of discovery and hypothesis which led to Einstein's theory of relativity.

motion pictures: see MOVING PICTURES.

Motley, John Lothrop, 1814–77, American historian and diplomat. Known for *The Rise of the Dutch Republic* (3 vols., 1856) and *The Life and Death of John of Barneveld* (1874). Served as minister to Austria (1861–67) and to Great Britain (1869–70).

Moton, Robert Russa (mō'tŭn), 1867–1940, American Negro educator. He was commandant (1890–1915) of Hampton Inst. and afterwards principal of Tuskegee Inst., from which he retired as president in 1935. He received Harmon (1930) and Spingarn (1932) awards.

motor, electric, machine which transforms electrical energy into mechanical energy. Its function reverses that of generator, but is based on same general principle. Usually it consists of a fixed cylindrical frame with copper conductors wound through iron parts to produce a magnetic field of force (see MAGNETISM) inside, where the ARMATURE revolves about a shaft held by the frame and connects with driving gear. Interaction between magnetic poles (the fields of force) makes armature rotate and turn gear. Electric motors are classified according to type of electric current by which they are driven as direct-current (DC) or alternating-current (AC) motors. The universal motor can be used with either direct or alternating current and is used to drive small portable machines.

Mott, John Raleigh, 1865–, American official of Y.M.C.A. Shared Nobel Peace Prize with Emily Balch in 1946.

Mott, Lucretia (Coffin), 1793–1880, American feminist and reformer. Organized Female Anti-Slavery Society, and her home was a station on Underground Railroad. Refusal of London antislavery convention (1840) to admit women led her and Elizabeth Cady Stanton to organize (1848) first woman's rights convention.

Mott, Valentine, 1785–1865, American surgeon, especially noted for skill in ligating arteries and for bone surgery.

Moulins (mōōlē'), city (pop. 20,832), cap. of Allier dept., central France, on Allier R.; historic cap. of Bourbonnais. Ironworks; tanneries. Among its historic and artistic treasures are a famous 15th-cent. tryptich, in the cathedral; the former convent of the Order of Visitation, founded 1616 by St. Jane Frances de Chantal (who died here);

the ruined castle of the dukes of Bourbon; and the Renaissance pavilion of Anne de Beaujeu.

Moulmein (mo͞olmān'), town (pop. 65,506), S Lower Burma; port on Salween R. mouth. Was chief town of British Burma, 1826–52. Exports rice and teak.

Moultrie, William (mo͞ol'trē), 1731–1805, American Revolutionary general. Defense of fort on Sullivans Isl. (later named Fort Moultrie) prevented fall of Charleston in 1776.

Moultrie (mōl'trē), city (pop. 11,639), SW Ga., on Ochlockonee R. and SE of Albany. Tobacco market. Mfg. of cotton goods, meat packing, food canning.

Moultrie, Fort, on Sullivans Isl., at harbor of Charleston, S.C. Figured in action that started Civil War (see SUMTER, FORT). Held by Confederates till evacuation of Charleston in Feb., 1865.

Mound, village (pop. 2,061), E Minn., on L. Minnetonka and W of Minneapolis. Resort in farm area.

Mound Bayou, town (pop. 1,328), NW Miss., NNE of Greenville in farm area; founded 1887. All-Negro self-governing community.

mound builders, in American archaeology, peoples who built mounds in area from Wis. to Gulf of Mexico and from Mississippi R. to Appalachian Mts. All were sedentary farmers in villages, but were unconnected politically. Mounds vary in size (some being more than 100 acres) and purpose (tumuli; foundations for buildings; fortresses; temples). Mound builders supposed to be ancestors of Indians.

Mound City, city (pop. 2,167), S Ill., on the Ohio and near Cairo. Important Union naval base during Civil War; Civil War shipyard still used. National cemetery near by.

Mound City Group National Monument: see NATIONAL PARKS AND MONUMENTS (table); MOUND BUILDERS.

Moundsville, city (pop. 14,772), in N Panhandle of W.Va., on Ohio R. and S of Wheeling; organized 1865. Mfg. of glass and enamel ware; coal mining.

Moundville, town (pop. 901), W Ala., SW of Birmingham and on Black Warrior R., near state monument noted for numerous large Indian mounds.

Mount, William Sidney, 1807–68, American painter, noted for humorous scenes of country life.

Mountain, the, in the French Revolution, deputies of extreme left, who sat on the raised seats in the National Convention. Among the *Montagnards* were the JACOBINS and CORDELIERS; they ruled France during REIGN OF TERROR (1793–94). See also PLAIN, THE.

mountain, a high land mass with little level ground at its summit. Some mountains are isolated but usually they occur in a group or range—either a single complex ridge or a series of related ridges. Mountain system is a group of ranges closely related in form and origin; chain is a group of systems occupying same general region; cordillera, zone, or belt is complex of ranges, systems, and chains occupying a whole area of a continent. Some mountains are remains of plateaus dissected by erosion; others are either volcanic cones or intrusions of igneous rock forming domes. Fault-block mountains are formed by raising huge blocks of earth's surface relative to neighboring blocks. All great mountain chains are either fold mountains or complex structures in the forming of which folding, faulting, and igneous activity have been involved; most have been uplifted vertically after folding occurred. Ultimate causes of earth movements resulting in mountain building are not definitely known. Some doubt has been cast on long-accepted idea that earth movements are adjustments of crust to shrinking interior. More recent is hypothesis that earth movements are isostatic, i.e., adjustments which keep weights of sections of earth's crust approximately equal.

Mountainair, village (pop. 1,418; alt. c.6,550 ft.), central N.Mex., SSE of Albuquerque. Pueblo ruins, Gran Quivira natl. and state monuments are near.

mountain ash, name for hardy ornamental trees and shrubs of genus *Sorbus,* native to the N Hemisphere. They have showy clusters of red berrylike fruits. The European species (*Sorbus aucuparia*) is also called rowan tree.

Mountain-Badakhshan (–bŭdŭkhshän'), Rus. *Gorno-Badakhshan,* autonomous *oblast* or region (23,600 sq. mi.; pop. c.50,000), SE Tadzhik SSR, in the PAMIR; cap. Khorog. Borders E on China, S and W on Afghanistan, and is separated from Pakistan by narrow Afghan strip. Livestock raising, wheat growing. Population is mainly Tadzhik with some Kirghiz tribes. Despite Afghan claims and British opposition, Russia annexed the region in late 19th cent.

Mountain Brook, town (pop. 8,359), N central Ala., S suburb of Birmingham.

mountain goat: see ROCKY MOUNTAIN GOAT.

Mountain-Karabakh (–kŭrŭbäkh'), Rus. *Nagorno-Karabakh,* autonomous *oblast* or region (1,700 sq. mi.; pop. c.130,000), SW Azerbaijan SSR, on E slopes of the Lesser Caucasus; cap. Stepanakert. Forest and agr.; produces cotton and silk. Population is largely Armenian.

mountain laurel, ornamental evergreen shrub (*Kalmia latifolia*) native to E North America. It is not a true laurel. In spring it bears lovely clusters of pink or white flowers. It requires an acid soil.

mountain lion: see PUMA.

Mountain Meadows, small valley, c.3 mi. long and c.¼ mi. wide, extreme SW Utah, c.300 mi. SSW of Salt Lake City. In Sept., 1857, some 140 emigrants bound for Calif. were massacred here by a group under the fanatical Mormon, J. D. Lee, at a time when Mormons bitterly resented coming of U.S. troops. Lee was later executed.

mountain men, trappers and traders who made the area of Rocky Mts. in U.S. familiar to the public. Tough and self-reliant, they were members of loose companies. Guided expeditions, also led wagon trains of settlers to Oregon.

mountain sheep: see BIGHORN.

Mountains of the Moon: see RUWENZORI.

Mountain View, village (pop. 2,880), S Alaska, just E of Anchorage.

Mountain View, city (pop. 6,563), W Calif.,

SE of San Francisco. Fruit canning and packing.

Mount Airy, town (pop. 7,192), N N.C., NW of Winston-Salem in Blue Ridge foothills. Produces granite, textiles, and furniture.

Mount Allison University: see SACKVILLE, N.B.

Mountbatten, family: see also BATTENBERG.

Mountbatten, Louis (Francis Albert Victor Nicholas), 1st **Earl Mountbatten of Burma** (mountbă'tŭn), 1900–, British admiral, great-grandson of Queen Victoria. In World War II he directed Commando raids on Norway and France and Allied operations against the Japanese in Burma in 1943. Last British viceroy of India (1947). Became NATO naval commander in the Mediterranean in 1952.

Mountbatten, Philip: see EDINBURGH, PHILIP MOUNTBATTEN, DUKE OF.

Mount Carmel. 1 City (pop. 8,732), SE Ill., on Wabash R. below Vincennes, Ind. Trade and industrial center in agr. area. Mfg. of electronic and sports equipment. **2** Borough (pop. 14,222), E Pa., E of Sunbury; laid out 1835. Anthracite mining.

Mount Clemens, city (pop. 17,027), SE Mich., NE of Detroit and on Clinton R. near its mouth on L. St. Clair; settled c.1798. Health resort with mineral springs and mfg. of metal products and pottery. Has Selfridge Field, U.S. air base.

Mount Desert Island (dĭzûrt'), off coast of S Maine, in Frenchman Bay SE of Bangor; almost divided by Somes Sound into E and W halves (each c.10 mi. long, 5 mi. wide). Champlain landed here and named island, 1604. Jesuit mission estab. 1613. French claims were relinquished 1713. First settlement made c.1762. Area is mountainous and wooded, with lakes, trout streams, and beaches. Resort development began mid-19th cent. On island are Mt. Desert town (pop. 1,776), including Northeast Harbor and Seal Harbor villages, and BAR HARBOR. Marine biological laboratory near Bar Harbor. E half of island includes most of Acadia Natl. Park (see NATIONAL PARKS AND MONUMENTS, table).

Mount Edgecumbe, village (pop. 1,147), SE Alaska, on S Kruzof Isl., at foot of Mt. Edgecumbe.

Mount Healthy, city (pop. 5,533), SW Ohio, N suburb of Cincinnati. Mfg. of clothing.

Mount Holly, village (pop. 8,206), W N.J., E of Camden. Farm trade center; textiles. Has Friends' meetinghouse (1775), courthouse (1796), firehouse (1752), Stephen Girard's home (1777), and John Woolman Memorial Bldg. (1771).

Mount Holyoke College: see SOUTH HADLEY, Mass.

Mount Kisco, residential village (pop. 5,907), SE N.Y., N of White Plains.

Mount McKinley National Park: see NATIONAL PARKS AND MONUMENTS (table).

Mount of Olives: see OLIVES, MOUNT OF.

Mount Pleasant. 1 City (pop. 5,843), SE Iowa, NW of Burlington. Limestone quarries near by. **2** City (pop. 11,393), S Mich., W of Bay City and on Chippewa R.; settled before 1860. Processes oil, sugar, and dairy products. **3** Borough (pop. 5,883), SW Pa., SE of Pittsburgh. Mfg. of glass and coke; coal mining. **4** Town (pop. 2,931), central Tenn., SSW of Nashville. Meriwether Lewis Natl. Monument is near by. **5** City (pop. 6,342), E Texas, SE of Paris. City has cottonseed milling, woodworking, oil refining, and lumbering. **6** City (pop. 2,030), central Utah, S of Provo, in Sanpete project (sheep, alfalfa).

Mount Rainier (rā'nûr), town (pop. 10,989), W central Md., suburb NE of Washington, D.C.

Mount Rainier National Park: see NATIONAL PARKS AND MONUMENTS (table).

Mount Robson Provincial Park, 803 sq. mi., E B.C., Canada, in Rocky Mts., W of Jasper, Alta. In the park is Mt. Robson (12,972 ft. high), highest peak in the Canadian Rockies.

Mount Rushmore National Memorial: see RUSHMORE, MOUNT.

Mount Stephen, George Stephen, 1st **Baron,** 1829–1921, Canadian financier and railroad builder, b. Scotland. Became president of bank of Montreal in 1876. Helped to construct Canadian Pacific Railway; its president 1881–88.

Mount Sterling, city (pop. 5,294), N central Ky., E of Lexington in bluegrass region. Trade center of livestock and farm area. Sacked by Gen. J. H. Morgan in Civil War. Indian mounds near by.

Mount Union College: see ALLIANCE, Ohio.

Mount Vernon. 1 City (pop. 15,600), S Ill., SE of Centralia. Trade and rail center for farm, coal, and oil area. Mfg. of freight cars and apparel. **2** City (pop. 6,150), SW Ind., on Ohio R. near junction with Wabash R. and W of Evansville. Trade center for farm area. Prehistoric remains found near by. **3** Town (pop. 2,320), E Iowa, ESE of Cedar Rapids. Seat of Cornell Col. (Methodist; coed.; 1853). **4** Town (pop. 1,106), central Ky., S of Lexington and on old Wilderness Road. Langford House (1790) served as Indian fort. Great Saltpeter Caves near by were Civil War mines. **5** City (pop. 71,899), SE N.Y., just N of the Bronx; settled 1664, separated from Eastchester 1892. Oil-distributing center with mfg. of dies, machinery, silverware, electrical equipment, chemicals, and rubber and food products. Here is St. Paul's Church Natl. Historic Site. **6** City (pop. 12,185), central Ohio, NE of Columbus; laid out 1805. Farm trade center with mfg. of engines and paperboard products. **7** City (pop. 5,230), NW Wash., on Skagit R. Processes farm and dairy products.

Mount Vernon, national shrine, N Va., overlooking Potomac R. near Alexandria; home of George Washington from 1747 to his death. Land patented 1674, house built 1743, Washington inherited estate 1754. Mansion (restored after Washington's notes) is wood structure with Georgian design and with columned portico. Has fine gardens and outbuildings. Tomb (built 1831–37) holds remains of George and Martha Washington.

Mourne Mountains (môrn), in S part of Co. Down, N. Ireland. Highest peak is Slieve Donard, 2,796 ft.

mouse, name for various small rodents of all continents. House mouse (*Mus musculus*) is believed to have evolved from wild mice of central Asia. It damages grains and other food, leather, and other materials. Sometimes produces 5–8 litters per year.

Moussorgsky, Modest (Petrovich) (mŭdyĕst' mōōsôrg'skē), 1839–81, Russian composer. His masterpiece, the opera *Boris Godunov,* was later revised by Rimsky-Korsakov. Outstanding are his piano suite, *Pictures at an Exhibition* (later orchestrated by Ravel) and *Night on Bald Mountain,* for orchestra.

mouth, oral cavity forming beginning of digestive tract. It is divided by teeth and gums into outer vestibule and mouth cavity proper. Roof is formed by hard and soft palates; tongue rests on floor. Teeth prepare food for digestion which begins in mouth by action of SALIVA.

mouth organ: see HARMONICA 1.

moving pictures, motion pictures, or **cinema** (sĭ'nůmů), a series of pictures produced by projecting on a screen the images in a film. These images are photographs of objects at successive instants of motion projected so rapidly that the eye perceives them as in continuous motion. Work on such serial photographs began in the 1870s and was furthered by inventions of Thomas A. Edison and the Lumière brothers. Projection on screens replaced penny arcade peep-shows. As the novelty decreased, longer pictures were gradually made. Improved techniques and subjects were introduced (esp. by Georges Méliés and Edwin S. Porter). D. W. GRIFFITH set the general structure of the form as it is known today. Hollywood, Calif., became the center of the industry. Early anonymity of actors gave way (largely because of such personalities as Mary Pickford and Charles Chaplin) to the star system in which actors dwarfed producers. In 1926 sound effects and music were successfully used; dialogue was introduced in Al Jolson's *Jazz Singer* (1927). Color films were successful after the development (c.1932) of the Technicolor process. Besides dramatic films there are such special types as the ANIMATED CARTOON, the newsreel (dating from 1909, one of the earliest film types), and the documentary film. The making of so-called three-dimensional films, using either the principle of the stereoscope with special glasses or projection upon a large curved screen, was begun on a wide scale in 1952.

Mowbray, Thomas: see NORFOLK, THOMAS MOWBRAY, 1ST DUKE OF.

Mozambique (mō"zůmbēk') or **Portuguese East Africa,** Portuguese colony (297,731 sq. mi.; pop. 5,732,767), SE Africa, on Indian Ocean; cap. Lourenço Marques. Lowlands are in coastal areas, savanna highlands in interior. Coal, gold, and mica are mined. Exports include copra, sugar, cashew nuts, and sisal. Settling in early 16th cent., the Portuguese carried on a flourishing slave trade until slavery was abolished here in 1878. Ruled by an appointed governor.

Mozarabs (mōză'růbz), community of independent Christians under the rule of the Moors in medieval Spain; under a local ruler (count) responsible to Moslem caliph. Maintained their own hierarchy under the archbishop of Toledo; used Visigothic, not Moslem, canon law. Their liturgy, called the Mozarabic rite, was like that of ancient Gaul. Chief centers: Toledo, Seville, Córdoba.

Mozart, Wolfgang Amadeus (vôl'gäng ämädā'-ōōs mō'tsärt), 1756–91, Austrian composer, b. Salzburg. Under the tutelage of his father, Leopold Mozart (court musician to the archbishop of Salzburg), the boy became a child prodigy at the harpsichord, violin, and organ, and appeared at court and in aristocratic circles throughout Europe. He tried long to secure a suitable position and finally was appointed to succeed Gluck as imperial chamber musician and court composer in 1787; nevertheless he died in poverty. He wrote in all forms—Masses and other church music (he was feverishly trying to finish his Requiem Mass when he died); vocal music; instrumental pieces (e.g., the popular *Eine kleine Nachtmusik*); chamber music (his string quartets rank with the greatest); sonatas; and concertos (25 for piano; others for violin, flute, horn, and other instruments). Opera was perhaps his greatest interest. Among his operas are *Idomeneo* (1781); *The Marriage of Figaro* (1786); *Don Giovanni* (1787); *Così fan tutte* (1790); and *Die Zauberflöte* (The Magic Flute, 1791). He wrote many symphonies; the last three, generally considered his best—No. 39 in E flat, No. 40 in G minor, and No. 41 (called the Jupiter) in C—were written in 1788 in the space of three months. A catalogue of Mozart's works was made by Ludwig von Köchel (pub. 1862; revised by Alfred Einstein, 1937). Works are usually identified by their numbers in this list.

Mtskhet (můtskhyĕt') or **Mtskheta** (můtskhyĕ'-tů), town (pop. over 2,000), Georgian SSR, NW of Tiflis and on Kura R. Cap. of Georgia to 5th cent. Has 15th-cent. cathedral, with tombs of Georgian rulers.

Muallaqat (mōōä"läkät') or **Moallakat** (mō–), Arabic anthology compiled by Hammad al Rawiya (d. c.775). Its seven odes, some written by greatest Arabic poets, reflect pre-Islamic Bedouin life.

Muawiya (mōōä'wēä), d. 680, first OMAYYAD caliph, b. Mecca. Became secretary to Mohammed the Prophet. Served Omar as governor of Syria. Opposed ALI and helped depose HASAN, Ali's son. As caliph he unified the Moslem empire by his statesmanship.

mucilage (mū'sůlĭj), thick glutinous fluid related to natural gums. It is secreted by certain plants, e.g., marsh mallow, flax, some seaweeds (agar contains mucilage). Functions of mucilage in plant include checking loss of water, aiding seed dispersal, serving as food reserve. Used in medicine as emollient and demulcent. Is used also as adhesive.

Mudania or **Mudanya** (both: mōōdä'nyä), town (pop. 5,624), NW Turkey, on Asiatic shore of Sea of Marmara; port for near-by Bursa.

Mudd, Samuel Alexander, 1833–83, Confederate sympathizer, physician in Md., who on April 15, 1865, set broken leg of Lincoln's assassin, J. W. Booth. Sentenced to life imprisonment; pardoned 1869.

Mudejar (mōō-dhä'här), name given to the Moors in Spain converted to Christianity and to style of Spanish architecture and decoration, strongly influenced by Moorish taste, which developed after Christian reconquest. Elements of Mohammedan art were used in architecture, and ornamental work was marked by Oriental emphasis on geometrical effect.

Mueller, Paul Herman (poul hĕr'män mü'lûr), 1899–, Swiss research chemist. Won 1948 Nobel Prize in Physiology and Medicine for discovery of insecticidal powers of DDT (1939).

Mufaddaliyat: see MOFADDALIYAT.

mufti (mŭf'tē), in Moslem law, attorney who writes opinions (*futwas*) on legal subjects. The *futwas* were binding only in fields of marriage, divorce, and inheritance. The Grand Mufti of Constantinople was (until 1924) head of Moslem religious administration in Turkey. For the mufti of Jerusalem, see HUSSEINI. The term mufti, meaning civilian dress of military or naval man, is derived from the apparel of the attorney.

Mughal: see MOGUL, empire of India.

mugwumps (mŭg'wŭmps"), in U.S. history, slang term applied to Republicans who in 1884 deserted their party nominee, J. G. Blaine, to vote for Grover Cleveland, Democratic nominee.

Muhammad: see MOHAMMED.

Mühlberg (mül'bĕrk), town (pop. 4,466), Saxony-Anhalt, E Germany, where Emperor Charles V defeated the SCHMALKALDIC LEAGUE (1547).

Mühlenberg, Heinrich Melchior (hīn'rĭkh mĕl'khēôr mü'lûnbĕrk), 1711–87, American Lutheran clergyman, b. Germany; came to Pa. 1742. He became leader of all Lutherans in colonies, and formed first synod (1748). His eldest son, **John Peter Gabriel Muhlenberg** (mū'lûnbûrg), 1746–1807, was Lutheran clergyman, Revolutionary officer, and legislator, serving three terms in the House of Representatives. **Frederick Augustus Conrad Muhlenberg,** 1750–1801, second son of Heinrich, was pastor of churches in Pa. and of Christ Church, New York city (1773–76). He was a delegate (1779–80) to the Continental Congress and member (1789–97) of the House of Representatives, twice as speaker. Heinrich's great-grandson, **William Augustus Muhlenberg,** 1796–1877, was an Episcopal clergyman, hymn writer, and philanthropist; rector of the Church of Holy Communion, New York city; and founder (1858) of St. Luke's Hospital. Among his hymns is *I Would Not Live Alway.*

Muhlenberg College: see ALLENTOWN, Pa.

Mühlhausen (mülhou'zûn), city (pop. 48,013), Thuringia, central Germany, on Unstrut R. Mfg. center of electrical equipment and sewing machines. It was dominated during Peasants' War by Thomas MÜNZER, executed here 1525. Free imperial city 1251–1803. Awarded to Prussia 1815. Transferred to Thuringia after 1945.

Muich-Dhui, Ben, Scotland: see BEN MACDHUI.

Muir, Alexander, 1830–1906, Canadian song writer, b. Scotland. Wrote *The Maple Leaf Forever* (1867), regarded by many as national hymn of Canada.

Muir, John, 1838–1914, American naturalist, b. Scotland. Came to U.S. in 1849 and settled in Calif. in 1868. Muir Woods National Monument was named for him in recognition of his efforts as conservationist and crusader for national parks. He wrote a number of books on his travels in the U.S. He discovered Muir glacier (Alaska) and journeyed also to Russia, India, Australia.

Muir Glacier, area 350 sq. mi., SE Alaska, in Glacier Bay Natl. Monument, SW of Skagway. Explored 1880 by John Muir.

Muir Woods National Monument: see NATIONAL PARKS AND MONUMENTS (table).

Mukachevo (mŏŏ'kăchĕvô), Czech *Mukačevo,* Hung. *Munkács,* city (pop. 26,123), W Ukraine, in Ruthenia. Trade center.

Mukden (mŏŏk'dûn, mŏŏk'dûn), Chinese *Shenyang,* city (pop. 1,120,918), cap. Manchuria, in, but independent of, Liaotung prov. Political and economic center of Manchuria. Aircraft plants, textile mills. Cap. of Manchu emperors, 1625–44. Russia began development of Mukden in c.1900; her interests were taken over by Japan after Russo-Japanese War. During early phase of Chinese republic, city was seat of war lords, notably Chang Tso-lin.

mulberry, deciduous tree of genus *Morus,* native to N Hemisphere, with blackberrylike fruit. White mulberry (*Morus alba*) has been grown in China since early times for the leaves, used to feed silkworms. Other plants called mulberry include French mulberry (*Callicarpa americana*) with violet berries, and the paper mulberry (*Broussonetia papyrifera*).

mule, the sterile hybrid of jackass and mare. The hybrid of stallion and jennet is sometimes called mule but more often hinny. Mules, generally larger and more spirited than asses, are tough, sure-footed and are favored over horses as pack animals.

Mulhacén (mŏŏläthān'), highest peak (11,411 ft.) of Spain, in the Sierra Nevada.

Mülhausen, France: see MULHOUSE.

Mülheim (mül'hīm) or **Mülheim an der Ruhr** (än dĕr rŏŏr'), city (pop. 148,606), North Rhine-Westphalia, NW Germany, adjoining Essen; an industrial center of RUHR dist.

Mulholland, John, 1898–, American magician. Gifted as a boy, he has become one of most celebrated of stage performers of magic. He also has written on magic and on spiritism.

Mulhouse (mülŏŏz'), Ger. *Mülhausen,* city (pop. 85,956), Haut-Rhin dept., E France, in Alsace, on Ill R. and Rhone-Rhine Canal. Textile mills, chemical (esp. potash) plants, and metalworks. Free imperial city from 13th cent. and an allied member of Swiss Confederation from 1515. Voted union with France in 1798. Damaged in World War II.

Mull, island (224,324 acres; pop. 2,903) of Inner Hebrides, off W Scotland, in Argyllshire. Mountainous, it has a deeply indented and picturesque coastline. Chief occupation is grazing.

Mullan, John, 1830–1909, American army officer, pioneer road builder. Built military road from Fort Benton, Mont., to Walla Walla, Wash. (1858–62); helped open up country to miners and settlers.

mullein, Old World herbaceous plant (*Verbascum*), chiefly biennial. Common mullein (*Verbascum thapsus*), with woolly leaves and a tall spike of yellow blooms, grows along roadsides and in fields in North America. Moth mullein (*V. blattaria*) is smaller and has cream-colored flowers.

Müller, Hermann (hĕr′män mü′lůr), 1876–1931, chancellor of Germany (1920, 1928–30), a Social Democrat. As foreign minister in 1919 he signed the Treaty of Versailles.

Muller, Hermann Joseph (mŭ′lůr), 1890–, American geneticist and educator. Won 1946 Nobel Prize in Physiology and Medicine for discoveries regarding hereditary changes or mutations produced by X rays.

Müller, Johannes: see REGIOMONTANUS.

Müller, Johannes Peter (yōhä′nus pā′tůr mü′lůr), 1801–58, German physiologist and anatomist. Famed as teacher, researcher, and author of work on human physiology (1833–40).

Müller, Wilhelm (vĭl′hĕlm), 1794–1827, German lyric poet. The song cycles *Die schöne Müllerin* (1823) and *Winterreise* (1827) by Franz SCHUBERT are set to his lyrics. He was the father of **Max Müller** (Friedrich Maximilian Müller or Friedrich Max-Müller), 1823–1900, German philologist and Orientalist. He popularized philology and mythology. His greatest work was *Sacred Books of the East* (51 vols.; begun 1875), translations of Oriental religious writings.

Mull of Galloway (gă′lůwā), headland, Wigtownshire, Scotland; southernmost point of Scotland.

Mulock, Dinah Maria (mū′lŏk), later **Mrs. Craik,** 1826–87, English didactic novelist, known for her *John Halifax, Gentleman* (1856) and a children's classic *The Little Lame Prince* (1875).

Mulroy Bay, inlet of the Atlantic, 12 mi. long, indenting N coast of Ireland, in Co. Donegal.

Multan (mōōltän′), city (pop. 190,000), S Punjab, W Pakistan. Dates from time of Alexander the Great. Mfg. of steel products.

multiplication, a basic process in arithmetic and algebra, in which a number or numerical quantity is increased by taking it a certain number of times. Multiplicand is the number acted upon; multiplier, the number showing the times the multiplicand is to be taken; product is result. The symbol of the operation is × or · and, in algebra, simple juxtaposition (e.g., xy means x × y).

Multscher, Hans (mōōl′chůr), fl. 1427–67, noted German sculptor and painter of Swabian school of Ulm.

Mumford, Lewis, 1895–, American author and critic. His major views are set forth in a trilogy *Technics and Civilization* (1934), *The Culture of Cities* (1938), and *The Condition of Man* (1944). Other works include *Herman Melville* (1929), *Conduct of Life* (1951), and *Art and Technics* (1952). He edited *Roots of Contemporary American Architecture* (1952).

mummy, corpse preserved by embalming. Mummification seems related to belief in life after death, the body being preserved so that soul may return to it.

mumps, epidemic disease caused by virus. Marked by swelling and pain in parotid and other salivary glands. Incubation period 12–26 days. Attack usually gives lifelong immunity.

Mun, Albert, comte de (älbĕr′ kōt′ dů mū′), 1841–1914, French Catholic leader. Advocated social reform and organized Catholic workers' associations.

Münch, Charles (münsh′), 1891–, French conductor; conductor of the Paris Conservatoire orchestra, 1938–46. In 1949 he succeeded Koussevitsky as conductor of the Boston symphony orchestra.

Munch, Edvard (ĕd′värt mōōngk′), 1863–1944, Norwegian painter. Studied in Paris under Bonnat. His work, which shows influence of neo-impressionism, is highly original in color and design and full of psychological suggestion.

Munchausen, Baron (mŭnchô′zůn, –chou′zůn), Ger. *Karl Friedrich Hieronymus, Baron von Münchhausen,* 1720–97, German cavalry officer whose tales of his incredible adventures in Russia became classics. Written and published (1785) in English by Rudolf Erich Raspe, they were put into German by G. A. Bürger.

München, Bavaria: see MUNICH.

München Gladbach (mün′khůn glät′bäkh), city (pop. 122,388), North Rhine-Westphalia, NW Germany. Center of Rhenish cotton textile industry.

Münchhausen: see MUNCHAUSEN, BARON.

Muncie, city (pop. 58,470), E Ind., on White R and NE of Indianapolis; platted 1827. Rail and trade center of agr. area with mfg. of glass and metal products, dairying, and meat packing. Original of "Middletown" in sociological research of R. S. and Helen M. Lynd.

Mundelein, George William (mŭn′důlīn), 1872–1939, Roman Catholic archbishop of Chicago (after 1915); made cardinal (1924). He criticized Nazism severely. Mundelein was active in social work.

Munhall, borough (pop. 16,437), SW Pa., on Monongahela R. and ESE of Pittsburgh. Has large steel works; scene of Homestead strike.

Munich (mū′nĭk), Ger. *München,* city (pop. 831,017), cap. of Bavaria and of Upper Bavaria, on Isar R. and at foot of Bavarian Alps. A commercial, industrial, and cultural center, it produces machinery, chemicals, precision instruments. Brewing and printing also are important industries. Archiepiscopal see. University, founded 1472 at INGOLSTADT, was transferred to Munich 1826. Academy of fine arts has long been of international importance. Chartered 1158 and cap. of Bavaria from 1255, Munich did not expand until 19th cent., when the art-loving kings of Bavaria built it up as a "modern Athens." It was the scene of Hitler's "beer-hall putsch" of 1923 and later became his party hq. Nearly half of the handsome city was destroyed in World War II, including the Glyptothek and the Old and New Pinakothek, which were among the world's foremost art museums (most of their contents were saved). The 15th-cent. Liebfrauenkirche [Church of Our Lady], chief landmark of Munich, and the royal palace were heavily damaged. Undamaged were the Propyläen, a monumental gate on the palace square, and St. Michael's Church, one of the finest German baroque churches. Near

Munich is the famous château of NYMPHENBURG.

Munich Pact, Sept. 29–30, 1938, agreement signed at Munich, Bavaria, by Hitler for Germany, Mussolini for Italy, Neville Chamberlain for Great Britain, Édouard Daladier for France, and their respective foreign ministers. It permitted the immediate occupation by Germany of large parts of CZECHOSLOVAKIA. Czechoslovakia itself was not consulted in the negotiations, nor was the USSR, although it had promised to assist Czechoslovakia if France did likewise. The events leading up to the pact began in the summer, when Hitler openly began to support the agitation of German nationalists in Czechoslovakia, particularly in the SUDETES, for self-rule. The Czech government offered a compromise, but Hitler kept increasing his demands; by Sept., war seemed imminent. At this point Prime Minister Chamberlain, meeting Hitler at Berchtesgaden, yielded to Hitler's demand for annexation of some border areas. France, though pledged by treaty to support Czechoslovakia, followed suit, and Czechoslovakia accepted. At a second meeting, at Bad Godesberg, Hitler vastly increased his demands, and Chamberlain rejected them. War seemed certain, when Mussolini proposed a meeting at Munich. There, within a few hours, France and England yielded to Hitler. Czechoslovakia gave in; Pres. Benes resigned; and Chamberlain, back in London, announced that he had won "peace in our time." The plebiscites stipulated by the pact never took place. On the basis of a provision for Polish and Hungarian minorities, Poland and Hungary seized, respectively, the TESCHEN dist. and S Slovakia. Finally, in March, 1939, Czecho-Slovakia, as the truncated state was called, was dissolved by Hitler. The Munich Pact, which marked the height of Western appeasement policy toward Hitler, is believed by some to have delayed World War II by a year, while others believe that a firmer stand in 1938 might have forestalled war.

municipal government: see CITY GOVERNMENT.

municipal home rule: see HOME RULE, MUNICIPAL.

municipal ownership: see PUBLIC OWNERSHIP.

Munising (mū'nĭsĭng), city (pop. 4,339), N Upper Peninsula, N Mich., on Munising Bay of L. Superior and SE of Marquette. Scenic resort center touched by lake steamers.

Munk, Kaj (kī' mŏŏngk'), 1898–1944, Danish playwright, a clergyman. His dramas, all with a strong ethical slant, include *The Word* (1932) and *Niels Ebbesen* (1943). An opponent of the Nazi invaders, he was murdered by Germans or Danish Nazi sympathizers.

Munkacs, Ukraine: see MUKACHEVO.

Munkacsy, Michael (mŏŏn'kächĭ), 1844–1900, Hungarian genre and historical painter, whose real name was Michael Lieb. His *Christ before Pilate* has been widely reproduced.

Munn vs. Illinois, case decided by U.S. Supreme Court in 1876. Munn had been found guilty in 1872 of violating Ill. state laws providing for fixing of max. charges for storage of grain. Court upheld constitutionality of Granger laws (see GRANGER MOVEMENT), maintaining that regulation of business devoted to public use was a matter of public interest.

Múñoz Marín, Luis (lwēs' mōō'nyōs märēn'), 1898–, Puerto Rican liberal leader and journalist. Organized (1938) and headed Popular Democratic party, whose slogan "Bread, Land, and Liberty" won large peasant following. In 1948 won first election for governorship of Puerto Rico.

Munro, Dana Carlton, 1866–1933, American educator and historian. Professor (1915–33) of medieval history at Princeton. An authority on Crusades, he worked wholly from contemporary sources, wrote and edited many books on medieval civilization.

Munro, Hector Hugh, pseud. **Saki** (sä'kē), 1870–1916, British author, b. Burma of Scottish parents; killed in World War I. A journalist, he gained immortality by his short stories, notable for dryly brilliant style, sharp wit, and sparkling imagination. He also wrote novels (e.g., *The Unbearable Bassington,* 1912) and letters.

Munsey, Frank Andrew, 1854–1925, American publisher. In 1882 he began publishing career with magazine *Argosy, Munsey's Magazine* (1889), and others. In 1891 he entered newspaper field, buying and selling papers, and after 1916 he controlled such papers as New York *Press, Sun, Herald, Tribune, Mail,* and *Evening Telegram.*

Münster, Sebastian (mün'stûr), 1489–1552, German scholar and geographer. His geography, *Cosmographia universalis* (1544), was standard for over a century.

Munster (mŭn'stûr), province (9,317 sq. mi.; pop. 917,306), SW Ireland, largest of the four provinces. Includes Clare, Cork, Kerry, Limerick, Tipperary, and Waterford counties. Was an ancient kingdom.

Münster (mün'stûr), city (pop. 119,788), North Rhine-Westphalia, NW Germany; a port on Dortmund-Ems Canal. Machinery and hardware mfg. Founded as episcopal see c.800, Münster was the scene of the theocratic experiment of JOHN OF LEIDEN in 1533–35 and of the signing of the Treaty of Münster (1648; see WESTPHALIA, PEACE OF). The prince-bishopric of Münster, which included a large part of Westphalia, was secularized in 1803. Münster was famous for its many fine medieval buildings until its virtual destruction in World War II. University was chartered 1773, restored 1902.

Muntenia, Rumania: see WALACHIA.

Munthe, Axel (mŭn'tù), 1857–1949, Swedish physician and writer; lived for many years on Capri. Wrote (in English) *The Story of San Michele* (1929).

Münzer, Thomas (tō'mäs mün'tsûr), c.1489–1525, German Anabaptist, leader in Reformation. An associate of Luther in 1519, he diverged as his political and social beliefs grew more radical. He advocated simple, godly, communistic society, which was realized briefly in communistic theocracy at Mülhausen.

Muonio, river: see TORNE.

Murad or **Amurath,** Ottoman sultans. **Murad I,** 1326?–1389, reigned 1362?–1389. Took Adrianople (1361) and forced Byzantine Empire to pay tribute (1373). Was killed just before victory at Kossovo. **Murad II,** 1403–51, reigned 1421–51. Seized Salonica from the Venetians (1430); defeated Christian army at Varna (1444). Basically of peaceful disposition, he was a patron of poetry and learning. **Murad IV,** 1612?–1640, last of the warrior-sultans, reigned 1623–40. Recovered Baghdad from Persia (1638); ordered death of his brother Bajazet (subject of Racine's tragedy, *Bajazet*). His strength and severity were prodigious. **Murad V,** 1840–1904, who was insane, reigned briefly in 1876. Was dominated by Midhat Pasha.

Murano (mo͝orä'nō), town (pop. 6,368), Venetia, NE Italy, on small islands in Venetian lagoon. Center of Venetian glass industry since 13th cent. Has a Venetian-Byzantine church (7th–12th cent.).

Murasaki Shikibu (mo͝orä'sä"kē shkē'bo͞o), b. c.978, Japanese novelist. Lady Murasaki is celebrated for *Genji-Monogatari* [tale of Genji].

Murat, Joachim (zhôäshē' mürä'), 1767–1815, marshal of France, king of Naples. Helped Bonaparte in coup d'état of 18 Brumaire; married Caroline BONAPARTE (1800); became grand duke of Berg 1806; succeeded Joseph Bonaparte as king of Naples 1808. A brilliant cavalry leader, he played a major part in all Napoleonic campaigns. In 1813 he saved his throne by an agreement with Austria, but he lost it in 1815 by rejoining Napoleon during Hundred Days. Was captured and shot in attempt to regain Naples. His son, **Achille Murat** (äshēl'), 1801–47, American author, came to U.S. in 1823 and settled in Fla. Wrote works praising U.S. democracy.

Muratori, Ludovico Antonio (lo͞odōvē'kō äntō'nyō mo͞orätō'rē), 1672–1750, Italian scholar, a priest. Edited collections of historical documents, the *Rerum Italicarum scriptores* (1723–38) and *Antiquitates Italicae medii aevi* (1738–42), and discovered early list of New Testament books.

Murchison, Sir Roderick Impey (mûr'kĭsŭn), 1792–1871, British geologist. He investigated unclassified strata below Old Red Sandstone and as a result established the Silurian system. Later, with Adam Sedgwick, he established the Devonian.

Murcia (mûr'shŭ, mo͞or–, Span. mo͞or'thyä), region (10,108 sq. mi.; pop. 1,094,173), SE Spain, on the Mediterranean. Dry and hot, but irrigated garden areas and Segura R. valley yield fruits and vegetables. Hemp, esparto, and minerals (lead-silver ore, iron, zinc) are exported. Silk culture is traditional occupation. Carthaginians founded here Cartago Nova (now Cartagena) in 3d cent. B.C. Taken in 8th cent. by Moors, who made it independent kingdom of Murcia in 11th cent. Became 1243 a vassal of Castile, which in 1266 annexed it outright. Cap. of the Moorish kingdom was **Murcia** city (pop. 60,113), on Segura R. Has silk mills and food-processing plants. Gothic cathedral (14th–15th cent.), with rococo façade, and episcopal palace are landmarks. University was founded 1915.

murder, criminal HOMICIDE, distinguished usually from MANSLAUGHTER in having the element of MALICE aforethought. Likewise a killing incidentally committed in the course of a felony (e.g., rape or robbery) is murder. Some statutes set different degrees of murder; in these murder in the first degree generally is a calculated act of slaying receiving the severest penalty (normally capital punishment).

Mures (mo͞o'rĕsh), Hung. *Maros,* river, 550 mi. long, rising in Carpathians in Rumania and flowing W into Hungary to join the Theiss at Szeged.

Muret (mürā'), small town of S France, near Toulouse. Here in 1213 Simon de Montfort decisively defeated RAYMOND VI of Toulouse and PETER II of Aragon in the Albigensian Crusade.

Murfree, Mary Noailles: see CRADDOCK, CHARLES EGBERT.

Murfreesboro. 1 Town, SW Ark., near Little Missouri R. and near only U.S. diamond mine (now closed). **2** City (pop. 13,052), central Tenn., on Stones R. and SE of Nashville. Shipping, processing, and trade center of dairy, grain, and timber area. State cap. 1819–25. Andrew Jackson and T. H. Benton practiced here. Scene of Civil War battle of Murfreesboro (or Stones River) fought Dec. 31–Jan. 2, 1863. This Union victory marked by Stones River Natl. Military Park.

Murger, Henri (ãrē' mürzhĕr'), 1822–61, French author of *Scènes de la vie de bohème* (serially, 1845–49), basis of Puccini's opera *La Bohème.*

muriatic acid: see HYDROCHLORIC ACID.

Murillo, Bartolomé Estéban (myo͞orĭ'lō), 1617?–1682, Spanish painter, b. Seville. Famous for religious pictures of a sweet charm and for paintings of street urchins. Early in his career he visited Madrid (1642–45), where he was befriended by Velázquez. Born a poor orphan but ended his days as favorite painter of Seville. His paintings of the *Assumption* are among his most renowned work.

Murmansk (mo͞or'mŭnsk), city (pop. 117,054), N European RSFSR, on NW Kola Peninsula; an ice-free port on Kola Gulf of Barents Sea. Largest city within Arctic Circle. Founded 1915 and connected with Leningrad by railroad in 1916, it was strategically important in both world wars for supplies to Russia from Western Allies. During civil war it was occupied (1918–20) by Allied interventionist forces.

Murom (mo͞o'rŭm), city (1926 pop. 22,607), central European RSFSR, on Oka R.; machinery mfg. One of oldest Russian cities (founded 864).

Murphy, Frank, 1893–1949, Associate Justice of U.S. Supreme Court (1940–49). Known for liberal opinions.

Murphy, John Benjamin, 1857–1916, American surgeon. Contributed new techniques especially in surgery of blood vessels, digestive system, and chest.

Murphy, William Parry, 1892–, American physician. Shared 1934 Nobel Prize in Physiology and Medicine for work on liver treatment of pernicious anemia.

Murphy, town (pop. 2,433), W N.C., in Nantahala Natl. Forest near Ga. line.

Murphysboro, city (pop. 9,241), S Ill., on Big

Muddy R. and N of Cairo. Center for dairy and coal area. Mfg. of clothing, food and metal products. Has memorial to J. A. Logan, born here.

Murray, (George) Gilbert (Aimé), 1866–, British classical scholar, best known as a translator of Greek drama.

Murray, James, 1722–94, British general, first civil governor of Canada (1764–68), b. Scotland. His efforts to protect French Canadians paved way for Quebec Act (1774) and earned him enmity of many of the English.

Murray, Sir James Augustus Henry, 1837–1915, English lexicographer, editor (from 1879) of the *New English Dictionary* (the *Oxford English Dictionary*).

Murray or **Moray, James Stuart,** 1st **earl of** (both: mŭ'rē), 1531?–1570, natural son of James V and half brother of MARY QUEEN OF SCOTS. An adviser of Mary, he became regent after her abdication. Largely responsible for success of Scottish Reformation.

Murray, John, 1741–1815, founder of Universalist church in America, b. England; emigrated 1770. He was pastor (after 1779) of the Independent Church of Christ, Gloucester, Mass., and (after 1793) of the Universalist Society of Boston.

Murray, Sir John, 1841–1914, British oceanographer and marine naturalist, noted for his deep-sea observations, b. Canada.

Murray, Nicholas, 1803–61, Presbyterian clergyman, b. Ireland; after 1834 pastor at Elizabeth, N.J. Nicholas Murray Butler was his grandson.

Murray, Philip, 1886–1952, American labor leader, b. Scotland. Headed C.I.O. steel workers' organizing campaign (1936). President of C.I.O. (1940–52) and of United Steel Workers of America (1942–52).

Murray. 1 City (pop. 6,035), SW Ky., SE of Paducah and near Tenn. line, in tobacco and livestock area. **2** City (pop. 9,006), N central Utah, S of Salt Lake City, in irrigated farm area. Lead smelter.

Murray, principal river of Australia, rising in SE New South Wales in Australian Alps and flowing W to Encounter Bay in South Australia. Forms 1,200 mi. of Victoria–New South Wales border. Total length, including the DARLING (main tributary), is 2,310 mi. Important primarily for irrigation; has Hume Reservoir (70 sq. mi.), largest in Australia.

Murray Bay, village (pop. 2,324), S Que., resort on N shore of the St. Lawrence at mouth of Murray (or Malbaie) R., NE of Quebec. Called also La Malbaie.

Murrieta, Joaquín (hwäkēn' mo͞oryā'tä), 1829?–1853, Calif. bandit, b. Mexico.

Murry, J(ohn) Middleton, 1889–, English author and critic. His works include *Fyodor Dostoevsky* (1916), *Keats and Shakespeare* (1925), and *William Blake* (1933). He wrote a valuable biography of his wife, Katherine Mansfield (1933), and edited her work. Also wrote a biography of his friend, D. H. Lawrence (1931).

Murten, Switzerland: see MORAT.

Musa Dag or **Musa Dagh** (both: mo͞o'sü däg'), peak, 4,445 ft. high, S Turkey, rising from the Mediterranean W of Antioch. Heroic stand of Armenians against Turks here in World War I is immortalized in Werfel's *Forty Days of Musa Dagh.*

Muscat, Maskat, or **Masqat** (all: mŭ'skăt), city (pop. 4,200), cap. of Oman, SE Arabia; port on Gulf of Oman. Held by Portugal from 1508 to 1648, when it fell to Persian princes. Became cap. of Oman 1741.

Muscatine (mŭskùtēn'), city (pop. 19,041), SE Iowa, on the Mississippi below Davenport; settled 1833. Mfg. of pearl buttons and metal and food products. Near-by Muscatine Isl. noted for fine melons.

muscle, contractile body tissue. Skeletal (striated) muscles controlled by will, constitute red flesh. Plain (unstriated) muscles (in alimentary canal and vessel walls) and heart muscles are controlled by autonomic nervous system.

Muscle Shoals, town (pop. 1,937), NW Ala., on Tennessee R. opposite Florence. Here, rapids (Muscle Shoals) formerly extended 37 mi. upstream, had 134-ft. drop, were unnavigable. Canalized in 1830s (unsuccessfully) by Ala. and in 1890 by army engineers. Finally submerged by Wilson and Wheeler dams, units of the TENNESSEE VALLEY AUTHORITY, which bought unused U.S. nitrate works (1916) in 1933. TVA made Muscle Shoals the center of experimental development of phosphate and nitrate fertilizers, animal foods. Various products (e.g., synthetic rubber) made in chemical works.

muscovite: see MICA.

Muscovy: see MOSCOW.

Muscovy Company (mŭ'skùvē) or **Russia Company,** first major English joint-stock trading company, chartered 1555. Sent out trading and exploring expeditions to Russia and Asia. Its ventures ended in 1615.

Muses [Gr., whence also *music*], nine Greek goddesses, patrons of arts and sciences; daughters of Zeus and Mnemosyne. Calliope (kùlī'ōpē) was Muse of epic poetry and eloquence; Euterpe (ūtûr'pē), of music or of lyric poetry; Erato (ĕr'ùtō), of the poetry of love; Polyhymnia (pŏlēhĭm'nēù), of oratory and sacred poetry; Clio (klī'ō), of history; Melpomene (mĕlpŏm'ĭnē), of tragedy; Thalia (thùlī'ù), of comedy; Terpsichore (tûrpsĭk'ùrē), of choral song and dance; Urania, of astronomy. Apollo was their leader. Their worship originated among the Thracians, and they are connected with the Pierian spring, fountain of AGANIPPE, and Mt. Ida.

Museum of Fine Arts, Boston, chartered and inc. 1870, after a decision by Boston Athenaeum, Harvard Univ., and Massachusetts Inst. of Technology to combine their separate collections. First building was opened 1876, the present one in 1909. Supported by private endowments and contributions. Most notable of its collections is that of Chinese and Japanese art. Egyptian wing and collection of John Singer Sargent's paintings are also important.

Museum of Modern Art, New York city, estab. 1929. Its founders included Mrs. John D. Rockefeller and Lillie P. Bliss. Permanent building was erected 1939 on ground donated by the Rockefellers. Among its facilities are a reference library and film library. Privately supported.

mushroom, fleshy fungus with dome-shaped

cap which has spore-bearing gills on its under surface. Mushrooms, especially inedible and poisonous ones, are often called toadstools. One of the most poisonous is the deadly amanita or death angel (*Amanita phalloides*). The common edible meadow mushroom (*Agaricus campestris*) is raised commercially from spawn (prepared material containing the rootlike mycelium of the mushroom). For subterranean mushrooms, see TRUFFLE.

musical glasses: see HARMONICA 2.

musical notation, the visual symbols used to indicate musical sounds. Early Western music was written in neumes (probably derived from grammatical accent marks) which indicated only the outline of a melody and reminded the singer of a melody previously learned by ear. By the end of the 12th cent., the staff, perfected by Guido d'Arezzo, was in use. Guido placed letters on certain lines to indicate their pitch and thereby also the pitch of the remaining lines and spaces. These letters evolved into the clef signs used today. Differences in coloring (with red and black ink) and in shape (square or diamond) were used to indicate the time-value of a note. Stems and flags were added, and time signatures eventually replaced coloration in indicating note value. In 15th cent., the shape of notes became round, as it is today. Key signatures developed early, sharps and flats assuming their present shapes by the end of the 17th cent. The five-line staff became standard in the 16th cent., and ledger lines were used to indicate pitches outside the compass of the staff. Expression signs and Italian phrases to indicate tempo and dynamics came into use in the 17th cent. See also TABLATURE.

musk, secretion of abdominal gland of adult male MUSK DEER. One of most valuable perfume fixatives. Chief constituent is muscone. Synthetic forms are now marketed. Musklike substance is obtainable from American muskrat.

musk deer, small deer (*Moschus moschiferus*) found at high altitudes in Siberia, Tibet, Himalayas, Korea, Sakhalin. It has coarse hair, usually brown, and is c.20–24 in. high at shoulder. Its numbers are depleted by destruction for musk.

Muskegon (mŭskē'gŭn), city (pop. 48,429), S Mich., on S shore of Muskegon L.; port of L. Michigan; settled c.1810. Early fur trade center, later was lumbering center 1837–c.1890. Shipping center and port for resort, farm, and fruit-growing region, with oil wells, refineries, and mfg. of metal products.

Muskegon, river rising in Houghton L. in N Mich. and flowing 227 mi. SW to L. Michigan. At mouth widens into **Muskegon Lake** (c.2½ mi. wide, c.5½ mi. long), on which is Muskegon city.

Muskegon Heights, city (pop. 18,828), S Mich., S suburb of Muskegon. Mfg. of machinery.

muskellunge (mŭ'skŭlŭnj), large, carnivorous North American fresh-water game fish of pike family.

Muskhogean: see NATCHEZ-MUSKOGEAN.

Muskingum, river formed in E Ohio by union of Walholding and Tuscarawas rivers, and flowing c.111 mi. S then SE to Ohio R. at Marietta.

Muskingum College: see NEW CONCORD, OHIO.

Muskogean: see NATCHEZ-MUSKOGEAN.

Muskogee (mŭskō'gē), city (pop. 37,289), E Okla., near Arkansas R. and SE of Tulsa; settled 1872. Rail and trade center of agr. and oil area. Processes oil, meat, and flour; mfg. of feed, glass, iron, and brick. Made U.S. Indian agency 1874. VA hospital, memorial park near by.

Muskogian: see NATCHEZ-MUSKOGEAN.

Muskoka Lakes (mŭskō'kŭ), group of lakes in S Ont., Canada, E of Georgian Bay, in resort region.

musk ox, hoofed, herbivorous mammal (*Ovibos moschatus*) of arctic America and Greenland. It is oxlike, c.4–5 ft. high at shoulder and has broad, flattened horns. Valued for flesh, milk, and wool.

muskrat, North American aquatic rodent, also called musquash. Common muskat (*Ondatra*) has gray underfur with black, brown, or rust hairs; is 17–25 in. long including the tail; and has partially webbed hind feet. Valued for fur, flesh, and musk.

muslin, an inclusive name for a group of white cotton fabrics. Originally signifying the gauzy cottons of ancient India, name came to be applied to many grades and sorts of fabric, plain (as in some sheetings) or dotted, figured, or tamboured, as in Swiss muslins.

mussel, bivalve mollusk. Sea mussel, common on N Atlantic coasts, is used for food. Fresh-water mussel yields pearl and mother-of-pearl.

Musselburgh (mŭ'sŭlbŭrŭ), burgh (pop. 17,012), Midlothian, Scotland, suburb of Edinburgh. Golf links and racecourse here are famous.

Musset, Alfred de (älfrĕd' dŭ müsā'), 1810–57, French poet. His exquisite love lyrics (e.g., "La Nuit de mai") and narrative poems (e.g., "Rollo"), imbued with melancholy, irony, and sensuousness, place him among the greatest romantic poets. He also wrote short novels and prose plays—including such gems as the comedies *Fantasio* (1833) and *Le Chandelier* (1835) and the tragedy *Lorenzaccio* (1833). *On ne badine pas avec l'amour* (1836), a comedy with a tragic ending, echoes his disillusionment after his tragic love affair with George Sand.

Mussolini, Benito (bānē'tō mōōs-sōlē'nē), 1883–1945, Italian dictator, founder and leader (Ital. *Duce*) of FASCISM. A Socialist in his youth, he edited *Avanti*, a Milan daily, but broke with Socialism in World War I and founded his own paper, *Popolo d'Italia*. He served in the army (1915–17) and was seriously wounded. After the war he organized his followers, mostly war veterans, into the aggressively nationalist Fascist party. Strikes and general unrest gave him a pretext for ordering the Fascists to march on Rome (Oct. 28, 1922). King VICTOR EMMANUEL III called on him to form a cabinet. By degrees, Mussolini transformed his government into a ruthless dictatorship, particularly after the murder of MATTEOTTI (1924). Parliamentary government was suspended 1928 and replaced by the Fascist CORPORATIVE STATE. Among Mussolini's positive achievements were the LATERAN TREATY with the papacy (1929) and great public projects, such as the draining of the Pontine Marshes. His imperialist and belligerent policy led to the conquest of ETHIOPIA (1935–36), intervention in the Spanish civil war (1936–39), and the annexation of Albania (1939). The Ethiopian adventure isolated Italy from the W democracies, and Mussolini turned to Hitler as an ally. In the AXIS partnership, Mussolini gradually became a mere puppet of Hitler. He allowed the German annexation of Austria (1938) and in 1940 entered World War II. His increasing dependency on Germany and the failure of his military ventures resulted in his overthrow and arrest (July, 1943). Badoglio became premier, but Mussolini, freed by a daring German rescue party, estab. a puppet government in N Italy. After the collapse of German arms, he was captured near Como by Italian partisans, who shot him and Clara Petacci, his mistress. Their bodies were hanged in a public square at Milan. His megalomaniac attempt to restore the Augustan empire thus ended in ruin.

Mussorgsky, Modest: see MOUSSORGSKY, MODEST.

Mustafa Kemal: see ATATURK, KEMAL.

Mustafa Nahas: see NAHAS PASHA.

mustang (mŭ'stăng), small, swift, hardy semiwild horse of W U.S., Texas, Mexico. Descended from Spanish explorers' Arabian horses, which escaped and founded herds of wild horses gradually captured by Indians. This changed Great Plains culture; Plains Indians became more numerous and powerful. Untamed mustang is called a bronco.

mustard, Old World annual plant of cabbage genus (*Brassica*) with yellow flowers. The seeds of black mustard (*Brassica nigra*) and white mustard (*B. hirta*) are used in the condiment mustard. Indian mustard (*B. juncea*) is usually grown for greens. All are naturalized in U.S.

mustard gas, substance used as POISON GAS, so called because of odor and blistering properties. It is light, colorless, oily liquid compound of carbon, hydrogen, chlorine, sulphur. Vapor attacks mucous membranes of respiratory tract, destroys lung tissue, blisters skin, produces conjunctivitis.

mutation (mūtā'shŭn), in biology, a change in a GENE resulting in the appearance in the offspring (of plant or animal) of a character not present in parents but potentially transmissible by offspring. In broader sense, mutation includes also variations resulting from chromosome aberrations. Mutation may occur either in somatic (body) tissue or in germinal (sex-cell) tissue; if it occurs in somatic tissue of animal it is not passed on to offspring but in plants it can be transmitted by vegetative reproduction, e.g., by grafting. Cause of mutation is not known but occurrence is more frequent in offspring of parents treated with X rays, radium, ultraviolet radiation, heat rays, and certain chemicals. Mutation is believed to be a chief agent in evolution, since by such changes new species are believed to evolve; inability to mutate in changing environment may lead to extinction of a species.

Mutsuhito (mōō"tsōōhē'tō), 1852–1912, emperor of Japan (1867–1912). Reign name was MEIJI.

mutton, flesh of sheep prepared as food; it is deep red with firm white fat. If animal is young (generally six weeks to three months old), it is known as lamb; this flesh is preferred in U.S.

Muttra or **Mathura** (both: mŭ'trů), city (pop. 80,532), W Uttar Pradesh, India, on Jumna R. Traditional birthplace of Krishna, it attracts Hindu pilgrims. Rich in archaeological remains.

Mutual Security Program. Mutual Security Act of 1951, passed by U.S. Congress, estab. Mutual Security Agency to replace ECA as administrator of economic aid to foreign countries and to coordinate economic, military, and technical aid programs. In 1953 Harold E. Stassen succeeded W. Averell Harriman as director of program.

Muybridge, Eadweard (ēd'wůrd mī'brĭj), 1830–1904, English photographer and student of animal locomotion. After experimentation (1872) in photographing moving objects for U.S. government he was engaged by Leland Stanford to record, with succession of cameras, the movements of a horse. Invented (1881) zoopraxiscope, which projected animated pictures on a screen, a forerunner of moving picture.

MVD: see SECRET POLICE.

Mycenae (mīsē'nē), anc. city, Argolis, Greece; significant as center of Mycenaean civilization.

Mycenaean civilization (mīsēnē'ŭn), type of anc. AEGEAN CIVILIZATION known from excavations at Mycenae. Undertaken by Heinrich Schliemann and others after 1876, these helped rewrite history of Greece. Locale was inhabited 3000 B.C., but not by Greeks. In period of city's greatness (c.1600 B.C.) people were Achaeans, an offshoot of Greek family. Architecture of fortress-palace and tombs was massive. People had close relations with Crete, and early culture paralleled Minoan civilization except that Mycenaeans were illiterate. After c.1300 B.C., invasion of Greeks from North led to decline and end of civilization by 900 B.C. Excavations have given new value to *Illiad* and *Odyssey* as sources of information on a phase of Mycenaean civilization.

My Country, 'Tis of Thee: see AMERICA, hymn.

Myers, Gustavus, 1872–1942, American historian. In muckraking era of American literature, wrote exposés such as *History of Tammany Hall* (1901) and *History of the Great American Fortunes* (3 vols., 1910).

Myitkyina (myĭt'chĭnä), town (pop. 7,328), cap. of Kachin state, N Upper Burma, on Irrawaddy R. Trade center on Ledo Road. In World War II it fell to Allies in Aug., 1944, after 78-day siege.

Mylae (mī'lē), anc. port, N Sicily, now Milazzo. Here in 260 B.C. the Romans won a naval victory over Carthage in First Punic War. Here also Agrippa defeated Sextus Pompeius, the pirate ruler (36 B.C.).

myopia: see NEARSIGHTEDNESS.

Myrdal, Gunnar (gŭ'när mēr'däl), 1898–, Swedish economist, sociologist, and public official. Adviser to Swedish government on economic and social policy 1933–38. Madc

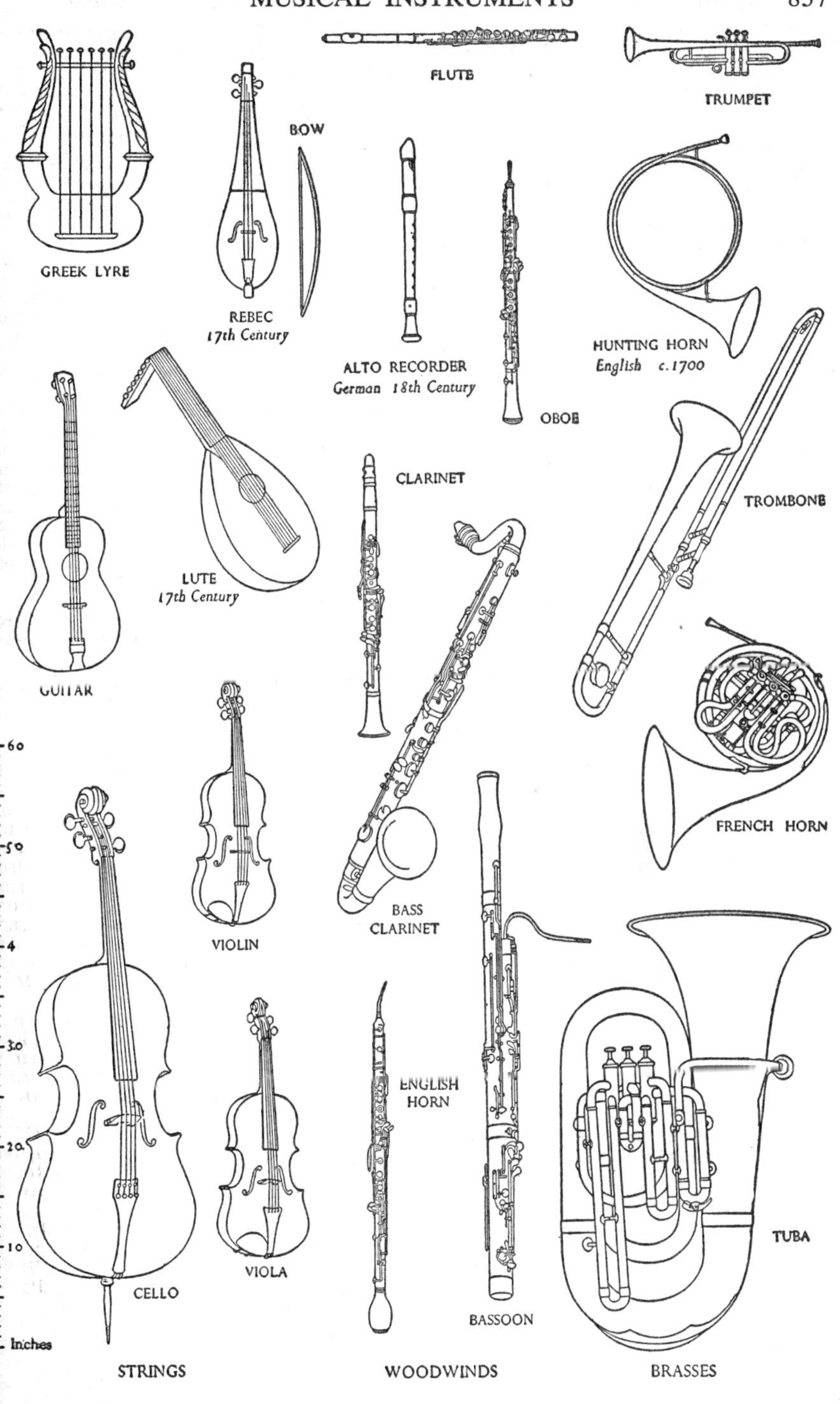

STRINGS WOODWINDS BRASSES

a study (1938–42) for the Carnegie Corp. of the American Negro problem; wrote *The American Dilemma* (1944). Secretary of Commerce of Sweden 1945–47. Executive secretary of UN Economic Commission for Europe (1947–).

Myrmidons (mûr'mĭdŭnz, –dŏnz"), anc. Greek tribe of Thessaly; in Homer, the warriors of Achilles, descendants of ants changed into men by Zeus to serve his son Aeacus.

Myron (mī'rŭn), 5th cent. B.C., Greek sculptor, reputedly a pupil of Ageladas. His works have perished, but two of them are known by copies, the DISCOBOLUS and *Athena and Marsyas* (Rome).

myrrh (mŭr), name for small thorny tree of genus *Commiphora* of E Africa and Arabia, and the gum resins yielded by various species. Bitter or herabol myrrh, used medicinally, is obtained from *Commiphora myrrha.* In the Bible (Mat. 2.11) myrrh is associated with frankincense. A European herb, sweet cicely, is also called myrrh.

myrtle. The classic myrtle is a shrub (*Myrtus communis*), native to Mediterranean regions. It has small, shiny, aromatic leaves, white or rosy flowers, blackish berries. Periwinkle is also called myrtle.

Myrtle Beach, beach-resort town (pop. 3,345), E S.C., on coast SE of Conway.

Mysore (mīsôr'), state (29,458 sq. mi.; pop. 9,071,678), S India; cap. Bangalore. Formerly a princely state. Its large tea, coffee, rubber, and spice plantations are mainly in W Ghats. Produces nearly all India's gold; iron ore and manganese are also mined. Steel and textile mills, aircraft plants. Old Mysore dynasty, overthrown 1761 by Hyder Ali, was restored in 1799, when his son, Tippoo Sahib, was defeated by the British. Joined free state of India in 1947. **Mysore,** city (pop. 150,-540), is seat of the maharaja and a mfg. center. Wide streets and many parks make it a "garden city." Maharaja's throne is said to rival Peacock Throne of Delhi. Part of Univ. of Mysore is here.

mysteries, in Greek religion, term used for certain secret cults. Conventional religions of Greece and Rome were mainly for state and family and only secondarily for the individual, who therefore sought an emotional religion that would fulfill his desire for salvation and immortality. This the mysteries supplied. Though they were highly secret, we know the four stages through which the initiate passed—purification rites, teaching of mystic knowledge, sacred drama (core of mystery), and garlanding of the initiate to signify his union with deity. Since mystery deities, e.g., Demeter, Persephone, and Dionysus, were fertility gods, origin of mysteries may have been FERTILITY RITES. Most important Greek cults were Eleusinian and Orphic mysteries. All Roman mysteries were importations—e.g., Isis cult, which came from Egypt as fertility cult but became ascetic religion glorifying continence and chastity.

mystery play: see MIRACLE PLAY.

mystery story: see DETECTIVE STORY.

Mystic, Conn.: see STONINGTON.

mysticism, in its proper meaning, practice of uniting oneself with the Deity or other unifying principle of life, linked with religion; in a more popular sense any sort of nonrational belief. It is a term much used to refer to the religious in India, who are, technically, quietists. The aim of Christian mysticism is union with God, and in the literature of mysticism several stages have been distinguished. Visions may or may not accompany mystical practices. Some of the great Christian mystics have been St. Augustine, St. Gregory I, St. Hildegard of Bingen, Hugh of Saint Victor, Jacopone da Todi, St. Thomas Aquinas, Ramon Lull, Nicholas of Cusa, St. Catherine of Siena, St. John of the Cross, St. Theresa of Ávila, and St. Theresa of Lisieux. Among Protestants the Society of Friends (the Quakers) have been vigorous in promoting mysticism. In Judaism the CABALA has been important, and the modern Hasidim are mystics. In Islam, Sufism was the most important mystic expression.

myth [Gr.], in its usual sense, traditional story concerning supernatural events and gods. It differs from legends or sagas, which record human doings, and from fairy tales or fables, invented to amuse or to teach. Association of myth and religion is close, and religious rites often rehearse events of a myth. Myths combine religious purpose with an explanatory one (i.e., mythmaker tries to interpret nature by personification). In 4th cent. B.C. Euhemerus called myths exaggerated adventures of real people. Modern investigation of myths began with Max MÜLLER, who considered them linguistic corruptions. The allegorical interpretation is that myths were invented to point out truth but later were taken literally; the theological, that they are foreshadowings of Scriptures or corruptions of them. Sir James Frazier, in *The Golden Bough,* stated that all myths originally were linked with idea of fertility in nature. Most anthropologists now do not believe in one general theory for all myths, but in specific explanation for myths of a single people. Myths have been widely used in literature—both those that are borrowed from old religions and those reshaped for the writer's own purpose.

Mytilene (mĭtĭlē'nē), chief city (pop. 27,125) on Lesbos isl., Greece; a port on Aegean Sea opposite Asia Minor. Sometimes spelled Mitylene or Mitilini. The name is also occasionally applied to whole island of Lesbos.

Mzab (mŭzäb'), group of Saharan oases in central Algeria. Settled in 11th cent. by members of a heretic Moslem sect. Mzabites are still a closely-knit cultural group. Chief center is Ghardaïa.

N

N, chemical symbol of the element NITROGEN.
Na, chemical symbol of the element SODIUM.
Naaman (nā'ŭmŭn), Syrian captain whom Elisha cured of leprosy. 2 Kings 5.
Nabal (nā'bŭl) [Heb.,= fool], man who resisted David's attempts at extortion. David's anger was appeased by the charm of ABIGAIL, Nabal's wife. 1 Sam. 25.
Nablus (näblōōs'), town (est. pop. 24,660), Palestine, N of Jerusalem. Here was the Hebrew city SHECHEM, rebuilt by Hadrian and called Neapolis. Near by are reputed sites of Joseph's tomb and Jacob's well. Long the cap. of Samaria, it still has a small colony of SAMARITANS. Populated mainly by Moslems, city is now in territory claimed by Jordan.
Nabonidus (năbŭnī'dŭs), d. 538? B.C., last king of the Chaldaean dynasty of Babylon. Not of Nebuchadnezzar's family, he may have usurped the throne. His kingdom fell to Cyrus of Persia c.538 B.C. Bible calls last king of Babylonia BELSHAZZAR.
Naboth (nā'–), man who refused to sell his vineyard to Ahab and was put to death. Elijah cursed Ahab for this action. 1 Kings 21; 2 Kings 9.21–37.
Nabuco, Joaquim (zhwäkēm' nŭbōō'kŭ), 1849–1910, Brazilian writer and statesman, strongest single force in abolition of slavery in Brazil.
Nacogdoches (nă"kŭdō'chĭs), city (pop. 12,-327), E Texas, NE of Houston. Spanish mission founded here 1716; settled 1779. Eastern bastion of Spanish against French. Twice seized (1812, 1819) by U.S. filibusters after Louisiana Purchase. Aided rebels in Texas Revolution 1835–36. Long-time cotton center with sawmills and food and oil processing. Has Old Stone Fort (replica of Spanish colonial presidio) at S. F. Austin State Col.
Nadab (nā'–), **1** Aaron's son, a priest, died with Abihu for offering "strange fire"; exact nature of crime not clear. Ex. 6.23; 24; 28; Lev. 10; Num. 3.1–4; 26.61; 1 Chron. 6.3; 24.1–2. **2** Died c.909 B.C., king of Israel (c.910–c.909 B.C.), succeeded Jeroboam I. Murdered by Baasha. 1 Kings 15.25–31.
Nadelman, Elie, 1882–1946, Polish-American sculptor, b. Warsaw. Worked in wood and metal.
Nadir Shah or **Nader Shah** (both: nä'dēr shä'), 1688–1747, shah of Iran (1736–47), founder of Afshar dynasty. Won power under Safavid dynasty by his victories over the Afghans and the Turks. Became shah when Safavid line came to an end. Successfully invaded India in 1739, carrying off vast treasure, notably Koh-i-noor diamond and Peacock Throne. His conquests restored limits of Iran to what they had been under the Sassanidae.
Näfels (nā'fŭls), village of Glarus canton, E Switzerland. Scene of Swiss victory over Austrians (1388).
Nagasaki (nägä'säkē), city (pop. 198,642), W Kyushu, Japan; port on Nagasaki Bay. Shipyards, fisheries. Was early Christian center. First Japanese port to receive Western trade, it was opened 1560 to Holland, 1854 to U.S., and 1858 to other Western powers. In World War II it was target (Aug. 9, 1945) of second atomic bomb.
Nagorno-Karabakh, Azerbaijan SSR: see MOUNTAIN-KARABAKH.
Nagoya (nä"gō'yä), industrial city (pop. 853,-085), central Honshu, Japan; port on Ise Bay. Engineering works, chemical plants, textile mills. Seat of Nagoya Imperial Univ. and a Shinto shrine founded in 2d cent. Castle here was built 1612 by Ieyasu.
Nagpur (näg'pŏŏr), city (pop. 301,957), cap. of Madhya Pradesh, India. Was cap. of Mahratta kingdom of Nagpur, 1743–1817. Rail and textile mfg. center. Seat of Nagpur Univ.
Naguib, Mohammed (nägēb'), 1901–, Egyptian general. Led the coup which deposed Farouk in 1952 and assumed direct control as premier. With the long-range dictatorial powers granted him by the cabinet he began land reform and a purge of corruption in government. Settled the problem of ANGLO-EGYPTIAN SUDAN by treaty with Great Britain 1953.
Nagyszeben, Rumania: see SIBIU.
Nagyszombat, Czechoslovakia: see TRNAVA.
Nagyvarad, Rumania: see ORADEA.
Naha (nä'hä), port town (pop. 44,779), on Okinawa isl., in Ryukyu Isls.; headquarters of U.S. military governor of the Ryukyus since Aug., 1945.
Nahas Pasha (Mustafa Nahas) (nähäs' päshä'), 1876–, Egyptian political leader. Succeeded Zaghlul Pasha as head of WAFD party and was chief negotiator of Anglo-Egyptian treaty (1936) which set Egypt free. Lost his enormous power after Gen. Naguib took control of the government in Sept., 1952.
Nahuatlan (nä'wŏt"lŭn), group of languages of Uto-Aztecan linguistic stock. See LANGUAGE, table.
Nahum (nā'ŭm), book of Old Testament. Written in poetry, it is a prophecy of doom against Nineveh, which fell in 612 B.C. Identity of prophet unknown.
Naidu, Sarojini (sŭrō'jĭnē nī'dōō), 1879–1949, Indian poet and political leader. Became first woman president of Indian Natl. Congress in 1925. Her poetry, written in English, deals romantically with Indian themes.
Nain (nā'ĭn), village SE of Nazareth where Jesus raised a widow's son from the dead. Luke 7.11.

Nairnshire (nârn'shĭr, –shůr), or **Nairn,** county (163 sq. mi.; pop. 8,719), N Scotland; co. town Nairn. Land, rising inland from coast, is used mostly for cattle grazing. Cawdor Castle, traditional scene of Duncan's murder by Macbeth, is here.

Nairobi (nīrō'bē), town (pop. 118,976; alt. c.5,450 ft.), cap. of Kenya; founded 1899. Rebuilt c.1920 on modern town plan. Ships coffee and sisal by rail to Mombasa, its port.

Naismith, James (nā'smĭth), 1861–1939, American athletic director. Originated (1891), with help of Luther H. Gulick, basketball as gymnasium sport.

Najaf, Iraq: see NEJEF.

Nájera (nä'hārä), city (pop. 2,994), NW Spain, in New Castile. Here Peter the Cruel and Edward the Black Prince defeated Henry of Trastamara and Du Guesclin (1367).

Nakhichevan Autonomous Soviet Socialist Republic (nŭkhēchĭvän'yů), autonomous republic (2,100 sq. mi.; pop. c.130,000), Azerbaijan SSR, bordering S on Iran. Irrigated lowlands produce cotton, tobacco, rice, wheat. Winegrowing and sericulture in foothills. Population is 80% Azerbaijani Turks and 15% Armenians. The cap. is **Nakhichevan** (1926 pop. 10,296), near Aras R. An Armenian trade center in 15th cent., it was ceded to Russia by Persia in 1828. Has Greek, Roman, and medieval ruins.

Nalchik (näl'chĭk), city (pop. 47,993), cap. of Kabardian ASSR, RSFSR, on N slope of the Greater Caucasus. Health and tourist resort.

Namaqualand (nůmä'kwůlănd), coastal region of SW Africa. Inhabited by Namaquas, a Hottentot tribe numbering c.25,000.

Nampa (năm'pů), city (pop. 16,185), SW Idaho, W of Boise; estab. 1885. Processing and shipping center of rich farm and dairy area in BOISE PROJECT.

Namur (nůmŏŏr', Fr. nämür'), province (1,413 sq. mi.; pop. 357,774), S Belgium, crossed by Meuse R. and Ardennes plateau. Has stone quarries, coal and iron ore, glass and cutlery mfg. Population is mostly French-speaking (see WALLOONS). Province was formed by combining former county of Namur with parts of Hainaut and of former bishopric of Liége. The cap. is **Namur** (pop. 31,637), at confluence of the Meuse and the Sambre. Produces leather and metal goods. Episcopal see. County of Namur was bought by Philip the Good of Burgundy in 1421; later shared history of Austrian and Spanish Netherlands. A strategic fortress, city was taken by French 1692, retaken by Dutch 1695, garrisoned by Dutch under Barrier Treaties of 1709, 1713, and 1715. Annexed to France 1792–1814. New citadel dates from 19th cent. City was heavily bombed in World War II.

Nanaimo (nůnī'mō), city (pop. 7,196), on the Strait of Georgia, Vancouver Isl., SW B.C., Canada, NNW of Victoria. Coal port with herring fleet, and center of farm and lumbering region.

Nana Sahib (nä'nä sä'hĭb), b. c.1821, a leader of Sepoy Rebellion; adopted son of last peshwa (hereditary chief) of the Mahrattas. Responsible for massacre of British colony at Cawnpore.

Nanchang (nän'jäng'), commercial city (pop. 266,651), cap. Kiangsi prov., China; port on Kan R. delta on Poyang L. Has university and medical college.

Nancy (Fr. nãsē'), city (pop. 108,131), cap. of Meurthe-et-Moselle dept., NE France, on Meurthe R. and Marne-Rhine Canal; historic cap. and cultural and commercial center of LORRAINE. Charles the Bold of Burgundy was defeated and killed here in 1477 by René II of Lorraine and his Swiss allies. A model of 18th-cent. urban planning, the center of modern Nancy was largely built up under STANISLAUS I. Particularly noteworthy are Place Stanislas, Place de la Carrière, the cathedral (1703–42), and the ducal palace (1502–44). University was founded 1854.

Nanda Devi (nŭn'dů dā'vē), mountain, c.25,-650 ft. high, N Uttar Pradesh, India, in Himalayas. Climbed 1936 by Anglo-American expedition.

Nanga Parbat (nŭng'gů pŭr'bůt), peak, 26,660 ft. high, W Kashmir, in Himalayas. Several attempts to climb it have ended in disaster.

Nanking (năn'kĭng', nän'jĭng'), city (pop. 1,084,995), in, but independent of, Kiangsu prov., China, on Yangtze R. Political and literary center; seat of several universities. Site of Sun Yat-sen memorial. Has textile mfg. Was cap. of Ming dynasty from 1368 to 1421. Treaty signed here 1842 ended Opium War and opened China to foreign trade. In Taiping Rebellion it was held by rebels 1853–64. Served briefly as seat of Sun Yat-sen's provisional presidency (1912). Was cap. of Nationalist government from 1928 to 1937 (when government moved temporarily to Chungking), and from 1945 to 1949, when it fell to Communists. Japanese surrender was signed here Sept., 1945.

Nansen, Fridtjof (frĭt'yôf), 1861–1930, Norwegian arctic explorer, scientist, statesman, and humanitarian. Planned to reach North Pole by drifting with ice in special crush-resistant ship, *Fram*. Never reached pole, but gained much valuable new arctic information and international fame. First Norwegian minister to Great Britain (1906–8). Directed international commission for sea study; made several scientific voyages (1910–14). Noted for service in Russian famine and work in war prisoner repatriation. Awarded Nobel Peace Prize 1922.

Nantes (nănts, Fr. nãt), city (pop. 187,259), cap. of Loire-Inférieure dept., W France; a shipping center on Loire R. and largest city of Brittany. Its ocean port is at SAINT-NAZAIRE. Shipbuilding; metallurgy; rail yards. Has castle of dukes of Brittany and 15th-cent. cathedral, with ducal tombs. Was severely bombed in World War II. In 1793 some 3,000–5,000 royalist troops of the VENDÉE were massacred at Nantes, largely by drowning, by the French revolutionists (*noyades*).

Nantes, Edict of, 1598, issued by Henry IV of France at end of Wars of Religion to define the rights of French Protestants (see HUGUENOTS). It granted liberty of conscience and the right of private worship to all; liberty of public worship wherever it had been previously granted; royal subsidies to Protestant schools; and the right for Protestants to fortify and garrison c.200 cities. The last provision, intended to serve as guarantee of the other rights, created a state within the state—a condition incompatible with the policies of Richelieu, Mazarin, and Louis XIV. The fall of La Rochelle (1628) ended the Protestants' political privileges. Louis XIV's anti-Protestant measures culminated in the revocation of the edict (1685). His promise to respect private worship was not kept. Though the edict of revocation forbade Protestants to leave France, many thousands fled to escape persecution, leaving several provinces almost depopulated. Louis's measure contributed to the political isolation and economic decline of France.

Nanticoke (năn'tĭkōk), city (pop. 20,160), NE Pa., on Susquehanna R. below Wilkes-Barre. Mfg. of rayon and nylon yarn and cigars; anthracite mining.

Nantucket (năntŭ'kĭt), island in the Atlantic, 14 mi. long and 3½ mi. wide, c.25 mi. S of Cape Cod, Mass., across Nantucket Sound; separated on W from Martha's Vineyard by Muskeget Channel. Visited 1602 by Gosnold; settled after 1659. Nantucket and small adjacent islands comprise Nantucket town (pop. 3,484). One of the chief whaling towns until c.1850; became summer resort and artists' colony. Has whaling museum in old sperm-candle factory. Nantucket village (pop. 2,901), trade center with fine harbor, is on N coast. Siasconset or Sconset (both: skŏn'sĭt) is summer resort on the Atlantic (E). First U.S. lightship station (1856) is off Nantucket.

Nanty Glo (năn'tē glō), borough (pop. 5,425), SE Pa., NE of Johnstown. Bituminous coal mining.

Nanuet (nănūĕt'), village (1940 pop. 2,057), SE N.Y., W of Nyack. Has Internatl. Shrine of St. Anthony.

Naomi (nāō'mē), Ruth's mother-in-law. Ruth 1.19,20.

Napa (nă'pụ), city (pop. 13,579), W Calif., on Napa R. and N of Oakland; settled 1840. Ships fruit, dairy products, and poultry. Produces wine, clothing, and leather goods, and processes fruit.

Naperville (nā'pụrvĭl), city (pop. 7,013), NE Ill., E of Aurora, in farm area. Mfg. of cheese and furniture. Seat of North Central Col.

Naphtali (năf'tụlī), son of Jacob, ancestor of one of the 12 tribes of Israel. Tribe settled NW of Sea of Galilee. Gen. 30.7; 46.24; 49.21. Nephthalim: Mat. 4.13,15; Rev. 7.6.

naphtha (năf'thụ, năp'–), colorless, volatile, inflammable liquid mixture of hydrocarbons obtained from fractional distillation of petroleum, wood, and coal tar. Used as organic solvent, in making varnish and soap, as cleaning fluid.

naphthalene (năf'thụlēn, năp'–), colorless, crystalline solid with pungent odor. A coal-tar derivative, it is used in dyes, insecticides, solvents.

naphthol (năf'thōl, năp'–), either of two crystalline derivatives of naphthalene with same chemical formula but differing in atomic arrangement. They show antiseptic properties and are used also to make some dyes.

Napier, John (nā'pēr, nụpēr'), 1550–1617, Scottish mathematician. Invented logarithm and wrote an original work containing the first logarithmic table and first use of the word *logarithm*. He invented various methods of abbreviating arithmetical calculations, including Napier's rods or bones (a sort of abacus) based on multiples of numbers. He introduced the decimal point in writing numbers.

Naples, Ital. *Napoli*, city (pop. 739,349; with suburbs 865,913), cap. of Campania, S Italy. Italy's second largest port, it lies at base and on slopes of hills rising from Bay of Naples (dominated by Mt. Vesuvius), and occupies one of most beautiful sites of Europe. Mfg. of food, metal, and leather products; also textiles and chemicals. Famed for its songs and festivals. Old Santa Lucia quarter is characteristic of the once rampant slums. An ancient Greek colony mentioned as Parthenope and Neapolis, Naples was conquered 4th cent. B.C. by Romans, by Byzantines in 6th cent. A.D. It was an independent duchy from 8th cent. until Roger II added it to kingdom of Sicily in 1139. After Sicilian Vespers (1282) Italian peninsula S of the Papal States became kingdom of Naples (see separate article), annexed to Sardinia in 1860. City suffered tremendous damage in World War II from both Allies and Germans. Among innumerable churches (most of them restored in baroque style in 17th and 18th cent.) is Cathedral of St. Januarius, where are two vials of the saint's blood, said to liquefy miraculously twice a year. Other landmarks include several medieval castles, the national museum (Farnese collection and objects excavated at Pompeii and Herculaneum), the San Carlo Opera (opened 1737), the university (founded 1224), and a fine aquarium.

Naples, kingdom of, former state, S Italy, comprising present ABRUZZI E MOLISE, APULIA, BASILICATA, CALABRIA, and CAMPANIA; cap. Naples. Conquered by the Normans under ROBERT GUISCARD and his successors (11th–12th cent.), it became part of the kingdom of SICILY, which passed to the ANGEVIN dynasty in 1266. The SICILIAN VESPERS (1282) resulted in the expulsion of the Angevins from Sicily proper; the Angevin possessions on the mainland, which they held in fief from the pope, became known as the kingdom of Naples. The 14th and 15th cent. were marked by recurrent warfare between the Neapolitan Angevins and the Aragonese kings of Sicily. After 1380, a long struggle for the succession in Naples broke out between two rival branches of the Angevin dynasty (see CHARLES, kings of Naples; JOANNA, queens of Naples; LANCELOT; LOUIS, kings of Naples; RENÉ). In 1442 Alfonso V of Aragon conquered Naples, and in 1443 the pope invested him as king. After Alfonso's death, Naples continued under a branch of the Aragonese dynasty, while the Angevin claim was inherited by Charles VIII of France. Charles's brief occupation of Naples (1495) started off the ITALIAN WARS, which in 1504–5 resulted in the union of Naples with the crown of Aragon. Under the Spanish viceroys the kingdom sank into misery and backwardness, with ruthless exploitation by the crown and the great landowners. The effects of these conditions are still acutely felt,

S Italy remaining one of the poorest regions of Europe. Naples was transferred to Austria by the Peace of Utrecht (1713) but was reconquered by the Spanish in the War of POLISH SUCCESSION. From 1759 Naples and Sicily were ruled as separate kingdoms by a branch of the Spanish Bourbons (see BOURBON-SICILY). The Bourbons were briefly expelled in 1799 (see PARTHENOPEAN REPUBLIC) and again in 1806–15, when Napoleon I gave the kingdom first to his brother Joseph BONAPARTE (1806–8), then to his marshal Joachim MURAT. After the Bourbon restoration Naples and Sicily were united into the single kingdom of the Two SICILIES, which in 1860 fell to Sardinia as Italy was being unified.

Napo (nä'pō), river, more than 550 mi. long, rising in N Ecuador and flowing SE into Peru, where it joins Amazon. First explored by Orellana (1540) and later by Teixeira (1638).

Napoleon I, 1769–1821, emperor of the French, b. Ajaccio, Corsica; son of Carlo and Letizia BONAPARTE. Attended military schools in Brienne and Paris. In 1793 the Bonaparte family, who had supported French interests against PAOLI, fled Corsica. Having attracted notice at the capture of Toulon (1793), Napoleon was promoted brigadier general. In 1795 his determined action in the VENDÉMIAIRE uprising made him the man of the hour. In command of the Italian campaign of 1796–97 (see FRENCH REVOLUTIONARY WARS) he transformed his demoralized, starving troops into an invincible army and, after the victories of Lodi, Arcole, and Rivoli, negotiated the Treaty of CAMPO FORMIO with Austria. His plan to strike at England through India led to his expedition to EGYPT (1798), where he won the battle of the PYRAMIDS but lost his fleet at ABOUKIR. News of French reverses in Italy and political instability in France determined him to return to France, leaving KLÉBER in charge at Cairo. The coup d'état of 18 BRUMAIRE (1799), engineered by SIEYÈS, overthrew the Directory and estab. the CONSULATE, with Napoleon as First Consul. By a series of energetic measures Napoleon halted inflation, made peace with the Church (see CONCORDAT OF 1801), began a new legal code (see CODE NAPOLÉON), and, after crossing the Saint Bernard, defeated the Austrians at Marengo (1800). The treaties of LUNÉVILLE (1801) and AMIENS (1802) brought brief peace; in 1803 England again declared war on France. Elected consul for life in 1802, Napoleon had himself proclaimed emperor of the French in 1804 and king of Italy in 1805. He was crowned at Notre Dame cathedral by Pope PIUS VII (Dec. 2, 1804). The new constitution was soon curtailed. In 1805, the Third Coalition (England, Austria, Russia, and Sweden, joined 1806 by Prussia) was formed. Napoleon defeated Austria at AUSTERLITZ (1805); Prussia at JENA (1806); Russia at Friedland (1806); the Peace of TILSIT (1807) left Napoleon master of the Continent. Peace with Sweden (1808) left only England in the field. Defeated at sea at TRAFALGAR (1805), Napoleon resolved upon economic warfare against England (see CONTINENTAL SYSTEM). The map of Europe was remade, with Napoleon controlling a much-enlarged France and Italy as emperor-king; Germany, as protector of the CONFEDERATION OF THE RHINE; Switzerland, as "Mediator"; Holland, through his brother Jérôme BONAPARTE; Naples, through his brother Joseph BONAPARTE and, after 1808 (when he made Joseph king of Spain), through his brother-in-law Joachim MURAT. Austria's attempt to renew warfare was crushed at WAGRAM (1809), and in 1810, after annulling his marriage with JOSEPHINE, he married Archduchess MARIE LOUISE of Austria. Meanwhile, the PENINSULAR WAR in Spain (1808–14) and the Continental System showed up the weaknesses of his empire. In 1812, at the head of the *Grande Armée* (500,000 French and auxiliary troops), Napoleon attacked Russia, his only remaining rival on the Continent. He entered Moscow (Sept. 14), but after the Moscow fire was forced to order a retreat by his lack of supplies and winter quarters (Oct. 19). The Russians, who until then had avoided battles and practiced a scorched-earth policy, now began to harry his army. After the passage of the BEREZINA, the retreat became a rout; the *Grande Armée* was annihilated. Napoleon hastened to Paris to raise a new army. A new coalition (Russia, Prussia, England, Sweden, and—after Aug., 1813—Austria) came into existence, defeated Napoleon at LEIPZIG, and pursued him into France. On April 12, 1814, Napoleon abdicated. He was exiled to Elba, which the allies gave him as sovereign principality. His victors were still deliberating at the Congress of Vienna when Napoleon, with a handful of followers, landed in France (March 1, 1815). Once more France rallied to him; LOUIS XVIII fled. Napoleon's rule of the Hundred Days ended disastrously in the WATERLOO CAMPAIGN. After his second abdication he surrendered to a British warship, hoping to find asylum in England, but was taken to SAINT HELENA, where he spent his dreary exile dictating memoirs. He died of cancer. His body, brought back to France in 1840, is entombed under the dome of the Invalides, Paris. Napoleon's personality and achievements remain subject to extreme controversy, but of his exceptional genius and tremendous impact on modern history there is no doubt. For the peace settlements following the Napoleonic Wars, see PARIS, TREATY OF, 1814 and 1815; VIENNA, CONGRESS OF.

Napoleon II, 1811–32, son of Napoleon I and of Marie Louise. Held titles king of Rome (1811–14), prince of Parma (1814–18), and duke of Reichstadt (1818–32). Napoleon I abdicated in his favor in 1815, but he never ruled, spending his life as virtual prisoner in Vienna, where he died of tuberculosis. The pitiful life of the "Eaglet" is the subject of Rostand's drama *L'Aiglon.*

Napoleon III (Louis Napoleon Bonaparte), 1808–73, emperor of the French (1852–70); son of Louis BONAPARTE, king of Holland, and of Hortense de BEAUHARNAIS; nephew of Napoleon I. His youth was spent in Switzerland, Germany, and England. Two early attempts (1836, 1840) at having himself proclaimed emperor in France failed dismally. He was sentenced to life imprisonment (1840), escaped to England (1846), returned to France after the Revolution of 1848, and, posing as champion of law, order, and democracy, was elected president of the republic (Dec., 1848). Increasingly dictatorial, he dissolved the legislative assembly by a coup d'état (Dec. 2, 1851), brutally suppressed a workers' uprising, and gained dictatorial power under the constitution of Jan., 1852. In Nov., 1852, a plebiscite confirmed his new title, emperor of the French. The internal history of the "Second Empire" falls into three periods. Until 1860 Napoleon ruled as absolute dictator; in 1860–67 he sought to regain some of his popularity by lifting restrictions on civil liberties and widening the powers of the legislative assembly; the years 1867–70 are known as the Liberal Empire, in which the opposition gained great power under such leaders as Jules Favre, Émile Ollivier, and Adolphe THIERS. The entire period was one of material progress, industrial expansion, and imperialistic ventures (e.g., acquisition of Cochin China, construction of Suez Canal, intervention in MEXICO). French participation (1854–56) in the CRIMEAN WAR restored French military prestige. In Italian affairs, Napoleon intervened decisively. In 1849 French forces restored Pope Pius IX on his throne; in 1859, following up the PLOMBIÈRES agreement, he joined Sardinia in making war on Austria. After his Pyrrhic victory of SOLFERINO, Napoleon concluded the separate peace of VILLAFRANCA DI VERONA, which considerably antagonized the Italians. His virtual protectorate over the Papal States delayed their incorporation into Italy until 1870. Napoleon's ill-advised confidence in his military strength contributed to the outbreak (1870) of the FRANCO-PRUSSIAN WAR. He took the field in person and was captured at Sedan. A bloodless revolution in Paris declared him deposed; in 1871 he went into exile in England. His wife, Empress EUGÉNIE, bore him a son, who fell in British service.

Napoleon, city (pop. 5,335), NW Ohio, on Maumee R. and SW of Toledo, in agr. area.

Napoleonic Wars, 1803–15: see NAPOLEON I.

Nara (nä'rä), city (pop. 82,399), S Honshu, Japan; anc. cultural and religious center. Was first permanent cap. (710–84) of Japan. Here is 7th-cent. Buddhist temple, Horyu ji, oldest in Japan. Imperial Mus. has art treasures of Nara period.

Narbada (nůrbŭ'dů), river, c.775 mi. long, central India. Sacred to Hindus.

Narbonne (närbôn'), city (pop. 26,301), Aude dept., S France, near the Mediterranean. The first Roman colony (estab. 118 B.C.) in Transalpine Gaul, it became the cap. of Narbonensis prov. and an early archiepiscopal see. It reached great prosperity and independence in the Middle Ages, but the silting up of its port and the expulsion (13th cent.) of its large Jewish population caused its decline. Has a splendid cathedral and 13th-cent. archiepiscopal palace (now city hall).

Narcissus (närsĭ'sůs), in Greek myth, beautiful youth who refused all love, even that of Echo. He fell in love with his own image in a pool and, pining away, died for love of himself.

narcissus, spring-blooming, bulbous plant of Old World genus *Narcissus*. Some species are also called daffodils, especially the yellow trumpet-shaped types. The common daffodil is *Narcissus pseudo-narcissus*. Poet's narcissus (*N. poeticus*) has fragrant white flowers with a red crown. The jonquil (*N. jonquilla*) has fragrant yellow flowers. The Chinese sacred lily and paper white narcissus (varieties of *N. tazetta*) are not hardy in cold regions.

narcotics (närkŏ'tĭks), substances producing stupor that eventually becomes coma and may be fatal. They are used in medicine to relieve pain (anodynes) or produce sleep (hypnotics). Chief narcotics are opium and its derivatives. Illicit traffic is fought by U.S. Bureau of Narcotics and United Nations commission estab. 1946.

Narew (nä'rĕf), Rus. *Narev,* river, 245 mi. long, rising in Byelorussian SSR and flowing W into the Vistula near Warsaw, Poland. Navigable in part.

Nariño, Antonio (äntō'nyō närē'nyō), 1767–1823, Colombian revolutionist. A liberal intellectual, he was one of first South Americans to foment revolution against Spain and argue for independence. Imprisoned for translating and distributing copies of *The Declaration of the Rights of Man* (1795), he escaped to Europe. Later he returned to South America to help in revolution.

Naroda, peak, RSFSR: see URALS.

Narragansett (nărůgăn'sĕt), town (pop. 2,288), S R.I., on W shore of Narragansett Bay. Includes Point Judith promontory and resort, and Narragansett Pier resort (pop. 1,247), near 18th-cent. pier.

Narragansett Bay, arm of the Atlantic, 30 mi. long and 3–12 mi. wide, deeply indenting R.I. state. Its many inlets provided harbors advantageous to colonial trade, later to resort development. Providence is on arm at head of bay, RHODE ISLAND at entrance; also contains Conanicut and Prudence isls.

Narragansett Indians, North American tribe of Algonquian linguistic stock, occuping most of R.I. in the 17th cent. Their chief, Canonicus, sold land to Roger Williams. They sided with the settlers in the Pequot War but in King Philip's War were decimated by the whites in the Swamp Fight (1675).

Narragansett Pier, R.I.: see NARRAGANSETT.

Narrows, the: see NEW YORK BAY.

Narses (när'sēz), c.478–c.573, Roman general under Justinian I. The rival and successor of BELISARIUS in Italy, he became exarch at Ravenna after defeating (552) the Ostrogoth TOTILA.

Narva (när'vů), city (pop. 23,512), NE Estonia, on Narva R. Textile and machinery mfg.; sawmills. Founded by Danes 1223; passed to Livonian Knights 1346; was member of Hanseatic League. After dissolution of Livonian Order (1581) it was contested between Russia and Sweden. In 1700 Charles XII of Sweden, with inferior forces, routed Peter I of Russia at Narva, but in 1704 Peter took the city, which remained Russian to 1919. The **Narva,** river, 47 mi. long, flows from L. Peipus into the Gulf of Finland, forming border between RSFSR and Estonia. Furnishes power to Narva city.

Narváez, Pánfilo de (pän'fēlō dā närvä'ĕth), c.1470–1528, Spanish conquistador. After an unsuccessful attempt in Mexico to make Cortés submit to the authority of the governor of Cuba, he was commissioned to conquer and settle Florida. In 1528 he reached Florida, sent his ships on to Mexico, and led his men inland in search of gold. Disappointed and harassed by Indians, they returned to coast, built crude vessels, and set out for Mexico. All save Cabeza de Vaca and three companions were lost.

Narváez, Ramón María (rämōn' märē'ä närvä'ĕth), 1800–1868, Spanish soldier and statesman; created duque de Valencia 1845. He helped to overthrow Espartero (1843) and was several times premier under Isabella II. His policy was reactionary.

Narvik (när'vĭk), town (pop. 10,281), Nordland co., NW Norway, port on Ofoten Fjord opposite Lofoten isls. Founded 1887 as Atlantic port (ice-free) for KIRUNA (Sweden) iron ore. German-held 1940–45, except for brief Allied occupation, May 28–June 9, 1940.

Naryn, river, USSR: see SYR DARYA.

Nasby, Petroleum V., pseud. of **David Ross Locke**, 1833–88, American journalist. In the Civil War, Locke aided the Union cause with satiric letters in his newspapers, supposed to be by a stupid, prejudiced, pro-slavery man, the Rev. Petroleum Vesuvius Nasby.

Naseby (nāz'bē), village, Northamptonshire, England. Parliamentarians defeated royalists in a decisive battle near here in 1645.

Nash, John, 1752–1835, English architect, who initiated neoclassic Regency style. Famous for achievements in town planning, notably his design for Regent St. in London with its graceful Quadrant.

Nash, Ogden, 1902–, American humorous poet, noted especially for skilled versification and cleverly outrageous rhymes.

Nash, Richard (Beau Nash), 1674–1762, English dandy; master of ceremonies and society leader at Bath.

Nashe or **Nash, Thomas**, 1567–1601, English satirist and pamphleteer. Wrote moralizing satire, violently attacked the Puritans in the Marprelate controversy, and then engaged triumphantly in a scurrilous pamphlet battle with Richard and Gabriel Harvey. His whole life was stormy. He is best remembered for a novel foreshadowing Defoe's work—*The Unfortunate Traveler; or, The Life of Jack Wilton* (1594). With Marlowe he wrote a tragedy, *Dido, Queen of Carthage.*

Nashoba (năshō'bù), former community, SW Tenn., on Wolf R. and near Memphis. Founded 1825 by Frances WRIGHT and others as place to educate Negro slaves for freedom. Plan unsuccessful due to poor management, sickness, and hostility of outsiders. Abandoned 1829–30.

Nashua, city (pop. 34,669), S N.H., at junction of Nashua and Merrimack rivers near Mass. line; settled c.1655. Threatened closing in 1948 of largest textile mill resulted in its sale to citizens' group, which arranged immediate partial operation and eventual full use of the plants. Mfg. of textiles, shoes, wood products, tools, hardware, and machinery.

Nashville. 1 Town (pop. 526), S central Ind., E of Bloomington. Beautiful scenery attracts tourists. Has art gallery and several resident painters. **2** City (pop. 174,307), state cap. (since 1843), central Tenn., on Cumberland R.; founded 1780 at N end of NATCHEZ TRACE. Grew as cotton center, river port, and rail focus. Abandoned in Civil War to Federals under D. C. Buell after fall of Fort DONELSON, Feb. 16, 1862. J. B. HOOD beaten by Union Gen. G. H. Thomas here, Dec. 15–16, 1864. Port, shipping, industrial, and educational center. Mfg. of food and tobacco products, shoes, rayon, aircraft, and cellophane; printing and publishing houses, railroad shops. Seat of VANDERBILT UNIVERSITY, FISK UNIVERSITY, and Meharry Medical Col. (Negro; coed.; 1876). Points of interest include capitol, J. K. Polk tomb, war memorial building, and old churches and houses. Near the HERMITAGE.

Nasik (nä'sĭk), city (pop. 55,524), N Bombay, India. Linked with legend of Rama, it is a holy place of Hindu pilgrimage.

Nassau (nă'sô, Ger. nä'sou), former duchy, W Germany, N and E of Main and Rhine rivers, since 1945 comprised in Hesse; historic cap. Wiesbaden. Agr. and forested region, famous for Rhine wines (Rüdesheim, Johannisberg) and spas (Bad Homburg, Bad Ems). Duchy takes name from small town of Nassau, on Lahn R., where a count of Laurenburg, ancestor of counts of Nassau, built his castle in 12th cent. In 1255 the dynasty split into two main lines. (1) Walramian line, founded by Count Walram II, ruled Nassau (raised to a duchy 1806) until 1866, when it was annexed by Prussia as a result of Austro-Prussian War. With former Electoral Hesse, Nassau formed Hesse-Nassau prov. of Prussia 1866–1945. In 1890 Duke Adolf of Nassau succeeded to grand duchy of Luxembourg, which continues under Nassau dynasty. (2) The Ottonian line, descended from Walram's younger brother Otto, acquired lordship of Breda, Netherlands, in 15th cent. and rose to prominence with WILLIAM THE SILENT, who inherited principality of ORANGE in S France and became stadholder of Netherlands. His great-grandson, William III of Orange, became king of England; at his death (1702), the title prince of Orange passed to collateral branch of Nassau-Dietz, which, as house of Orange, has ruled the NETHERLANDS from 1747.

Nassau (nă'sô), city (pop. 29,391), cap. of Bahama Isls.; port on New Providence. Rendezvous for pirates, notably Blackbeard in 18th cent., it is now the commercial and social center of colony and a tourist resort.

Nast, Thomas, 1840–1902, American political cartoonist, b. Germany. His work exerted great influence on politics of New York city. Created the tiger, elephant, and donkey as symbols of Tammany Hall, Republican party, and Democratic party.

nasturtium (nùstûr'shùm), dwarf or climbing plant (*Tropaeolum majus*), native to tropical America, widely used as U.S. garden plant, with spurred single or double flowers in shades of red, yellow, and orange. Sometimes the seeds are pickled and used as capers, and leaves and flowers are added to salads.

Natal (nŭtäl′), province (35,284 sq. mi.; pop. 2,202,392), E South Africa, on Indian Ocean; cap. Pietermaritzburg; chief town Durban. Sugar and tobacco are grown along the coast, and much coal is mined in interior highlands. The Boers on their trek reached Natal in 1837 and after defeating the Zulus founded republic of Natal (1838). In 1843 the British annexed Natal, which became crown colony in 1856 and absorbed Zululand in 1897. Became province of South Africa in 1910.

Natal (nŭtäl′), city (pop. 97,736), cap. of Rio Grande do Norte state, NE Brazil; port just above mouth of Potengi R. Far out on NE bulge of Brazil and only 2,000 mi. from towns in Africa, it was important as an airport in World War II.

Natchez (nă′chĭz), city (pop. 22,740), SW Miss., on bluffs above Mississippi R. Trade, shipping and processing center for cotton and livestock area. Founded 1716 by Bienville as Fort Rosalie; wiped out by Natchez Indians 1729. Passed to England (1763), Spain (1779), U.S. (1798). Cap. of Territory of Miss. 1798–1802. Location on Natchez Trace and Mississippi R. brought prosperity. Taken by Federals 1863. Fine colonial and ante-bellum homes shown during annual spring festival.

Natchez Indians, North American tribe of Natchez-Muskogean linguistic stock, living in SW Miss. in the 17th cent. They warred on the French settlers and massacred many at Fort Rosalie (1729). The French retaliated and scattered the tribe.

Natchez-Muskogean (mŭskō′gēŭn), linguistic family of North American Indians. Among the languages it included were Natchez, Alibamu, Choctaw, Chickasaw, and Creek. Muskogean also appears as Muskhogean and Muskogian.

Natchez Trace, road from Natchez, Miss., to Nashville, Tenn., very important from 1780s to 1830s. Grew from Indian trails. First used only northward (flatboats used only southward); used both ways with U.S. expansion SW. Made post road 1800, improved by army. Jackson used it to New Orleans in War of 1812 and in Indian campaigns. Declined with rise of steamboat. Natchez Trace Parkway (estab. 1934, 450 mi.) commemorates, generally follows it.

Natchitoches (nă′kĭtŏsh), city (pop. 9,914), NW La., near Red R. and N of Shreveport. Oldest city in La., founded 1715 by French as military and trading post. Produces, processes, and ships cotton.

Nathan (nā′–), prophet in time of David and Solomon. He denounced David for marrying Bathsheba. Later his advice saved the kingdom for Solomon. 2 Sam 7; 12; 1 Kings 1; 1 Chron. 29.29; 2 Chron. 9.29.

Nathan, George Jean, 1882–, American editor and critic. He was an editor with H. L. Mencken on *Smart Set* (1914–23) and the *American Mercury* (1924–30), but is chiefly noted for the exacting standards and violent expression in his criticism of the drama.

Nathanael (nŭthă′–), one of the Twelve Apostles. John 1.45–51; 21.2. Identified with BARTHOLOMEW.

Natick (nā′tĭk), town (pop. 19,838), E Mass., W of Boston. Shoes. Founded in 1651 as a "praying Indian" village by John ELIOT.

Nation, Carry, 1846–1911, American temperance agitator. Convinced of divine appointment, she began breaking up saloons with a hatchet in 1900.

National Academy of Design, society of American painters, sculptors, and engravers, with hq. on upper Fifth Ave., New York city; estab. 1825, inc. 1828. Founders included S. F. B. Morse, Asher B. Durand, and Daniel Huntington. Operates tuition-free school.

National Archives, estab. 1934 by U.S. Congress for preservation of Federal government records.

national bank, in the U.S., bank of a class estab. by Congress in 1863–64. These banks were required to invest in U.S. bonds and were then authorized to issue their notes as currency, up to 90% of the value of their bonds. All national banks are now members of the FEDERAL RESERVE SYSTEM, whose notes gradually replaced those of the national banks after 1913.

National City, residential and industrial city (pop. 26,832), S Calif., on San Diego Bay SW of San Diego. Produces refined oil and citrus fruit by-products.

National Council of the Churches of Christ in the United States of America, interdenominational organization composed of some 25 Protestant and 4 Eastern Orthodox bodies, founded 1950. It is not a governing body, but promotes general spiritual welfare through various activities.

national debt: see DEBT, PUBLIC.

national forests in 42 states of U.S., Alaska, and Puerto Rico now total over 220,000,000 acres. Federal government also owns c.4,500,000 acres of forest lands in national parks and monuments, over 8,000,000 in Indian reservations. Administered by Forest Service of Dept. of Agriculture, which does research on forest fires, tree diseases and pests, lumber products, land drainage, correct harvesting.

National Gallery, London, one of permanent art collections of Great Britain. Its building in Trafalgar Square was built 1832–38. Especially rich in Italian paintings of 15th and 16th cent.

National Gallery of Art, Washington, D.C., a bureau of the Smithsonian Inst., estab. 1937 by act of Congress. Funds for the building (designed by John Russell Pope and opened in 1941) and his own collection were given by Andrew W. Mellon. Other art donors included Samuel H. Kress and Joseph E. Widener. Rich in Italian and French painting.

nationalism, political and social philosophy in which good of nation is paramount. Word used loosely and mostly in derogatory sense implying excessive zeal for national welfare and advancement. Though exact definition is impossible, nationalism is characterized by patriotism, and by faith in political and cultural values of a nation and in its destiny. Extreme nationalism arose in 19th cent. and has led to many clashes within and between countries. Many see nationalism as a divisive force in the world; others point to its invigorating effect on peoples.

National Labor Relations Board (NLRB), set up under the National Labor Relations Act of 1935 (also known as the Wagner Act) which affirms labor's right to organize and bargain collectively. Its principal function is to investigate charges of (and to render decisions on) unfair labor practices by employers, but with the passage (1947) of the Taft-Hartley Act, the NLRB's field was extended to cover complaints filed by employers against unions.

national parks and monuments. The Natl. Park Service, a bureau of U.S. Dept., of Interior, was estab. 1916 to correlate administration of national parks and monuments then under the charge of the department. In 1933 its trusteeship was extended to include certain areas hitherto under the jurisdiction of other government departments; by 1950 it was administering some 182 areas. In addition to those listed in NATIONAL PARKS AND MONUMENTS table (see pp. 868–71), the Natl. Park Service has charge of certain national cemeteries, parkways, and capital parks and also has responsibilities toward certain national recreational areas and historic sites not owned by the government. National parks may be estab. only by Congress; the President may designate national monuments.

National Recovery Administration, 1933–36, U.S. administrative bureau estab. under Natl. Industrial Recovery Act, designed to encourage industrial recovery and combat widespread unemployment. NRA head was H. S. Johnson; emblem was Blue Eagle. Over 500 compulsory fair-practice codes were adopted for various industries. U.S. Supreme Court decision of May, 1935, voided code system, made NRA ineffective. Many of its labor provisions were reenacted in later legislation (e.g., WAGES AND HOURS ACT).

National Republican party, in U.S. history, short-lived political organization opposed to Andrew Jackson. Formed after Jackson victory in 1828 by wealthier classes and others fearing his radical ideas. Nominated Henry Clay in 1831. By 1836 party had united with other groups to form WHIG PARTY.

National Road, authorized by Congress 1806, begun 1815. Great highway of Western migration. First section (Cumberland road), from Cumberland to Wheeling, opened in 1818. Turned over to states, which collected tolls for maintenance, road eventually ran to St. Louis. Present U.S. Highway 40 follows its route closely.

National Socialism, ideology of the National Socialist German Workers' party (abbreviated in German as NSDAP) in GERMANY. It became the program of the totalitarian dictatorship of Adolf HITLER, 1933–45. (The term *Nazi* was a derisive abbreviation of National Socialist.) The program, formulated by Hitler in *Mein Kampf* (1923) and based in part on the pseudoscientific speculations of Alfred ROSENBERG, drew on such diverse sources as Gobineau's and H. S. Chamberlain's racial theories; Lassallean socialism; Italian FASCISM; GEOPOLITICS; and some of Nietzsche's ideas. It appealed to the masses of defeated Germany through hysterical nationalism and ANTI-SEMITISM, resentment of the Treaty of Versailles, and certain anticapitalist features; it also found support among capitalists and industrialists, who hoped to use it as a tool against German Social Democracy and as a bulwark against Communism. The basic principles of its ideology were the superiority of the Nordic or Aryan "master race," which was to be led by a supreme, infallible *Führer* [leader] to victory over its internal and external enemies—notably the Jews and Communists, who were credited with a plot to enslave the world. All German-speaking peoples were to be united in a single empire (the "Third Reich"), which was to last 1,000 years, and to rule the inferior races. The emotional appeal of these theories was immense and received impetus from skillful propaganda, mass meetings, and uniformed militias—the brown-shirted SA (*Sturmabteilung,* or storm troops) and the black SS (*Schutzstaffel,* or security echelon; originally Hitler's bodyguard). The party symbol was the swastika. After Hitler took power, the NSDAP became the sole legal party and the chief instrument of his policy. Its rule of brutality and terror led, after the outbreak of World War II, to the slaughter of millions (see CONCENTRATION CAMP; WAR CRIMES), and it eventually fell under the complete control of its own SECRET POLICE. The NSDAP had affiliates in other countries (esp. Austria and Czechoslovakia).

National Trust, British association to preserve for the nation places of natural beauty or buildings of architectural or historic interest; founded 1894. May either acquire land inalienably or protect private property by special covenant.

National University, at Manila; founded 1900 as Colegio Filipino, inc. 1921 under present name. First nonsectarian university in the Philippines.

National Youth Administration, 1935–44, estab. by U.S. Congress. At first purpose was to find part-time work for unemployed youths; emphasis later shifted to training youths for war work.

NATO: see NORTH ATLANTIC TREATY.

Nattier, Jean Marc (zhã' märk' nätyā'), 1685–1766, fashionable French portrait painter at court of Louis XV.

Natural Bridge, village, western Va., SW of Lexington. Natural Bridge over Cedar Creek (arch 215 ft. high, span 90 ft.) is W. Once owned by Thomas Jefferson.

Natural Bridges National Monument: see NATIONAL PARKS AND MONUMENTS (table).

natural gas, mixture of gases obtained from the earth and widely used as fuel. Composition varies, but is chiefly methane. It is commonly associated with production of petroleum, but also occurs far from oil fields. Pipe lines, some more than 1,000 mi. long, carry the fuel to industrial centers. The largest U.S. producers are Texas, Okla., Calif., La., W.Va. Some gasoline is obtained from natural gas.

natural resources, conservation of: see CONSERVATION OF NATURAL RESOURCES.

natural rights, theory holding that man is born with inalienable rights; known to Greeks, developed by Rousseau and Jefferson.

Naugatuck (nô'gŭtŭk"), borough (pop. 17,455), SW Conn., on Naugatuck R. below Waterbury; settled 1702. Rubber center (Goodyear estab. plant here, 1843). Metal and plastic products and chemicals.

Naugatuck, river rising in NW Conn., flowing c.65 mi. S, past mfg. centers, to Housatonic R. at Derby.

Nauheim, Germany: see BAD NAUHEIM.

Naumburg (noum'bo͝ork), city (pop. 41,379), Saxony-Anhalt, E central Germany, on Saale R. It is famed for its cathedral (13th–14th cent.), which has fine German Gothic sculptures.

Naupaktos (nôpăk'tŭs), Ital. *Lepanto,* town (pop. 5,494), W central Greece; a port on Gulf of Corinth. Important Athenian naval base in Peloponnesian War. It passed to Venice 1407, to Turkey 1499, and was again held by Venice 1687–99. Naval battle of LEPANTO took place here (1571).

Nauplia (nô'plēŭ), Gr. *Nauplion,* port town (pop. 7,960), S Greece, on E coast of Peloponnesus. First cap. of independent Greece, 1830–34 (succeeded by Athens).

Nauru (näo͞o'ro͞o), atoll (8 sq. mi.; pop. 2,855), central Pacific. Discovered 1798 by the British. Annexed 1888 by Germany, it was occupied in World War I by Australians, who won mandate over it in 1920. Came under UN trusteeship in 1947, held jointly by Great Britain, Australia, New Zealand. Occupied throughout World War II by Japanese. Important for rich phosphate deposits.

Naushon, island, Mass.: see ELIZABETH ISLANDS.

Nausicaä (nôsĭ'kāŭ), in the *Odyssey,* princess of Phaeacia, who led shipwrecked Odysseus to her father's court and helped entertain him.

nautilus (nô'tŭlŭs), either of two types of mollusk. One genus (*Nautilus*) is represented by pearly or chambered nautilus of S Pacific; habit of secreting shell in successive "chambers" is celebrated in poem by O. W. Holmes. Paper nautilus or argonaut (*Argonauta*) is found in most warm waters.

Nauvoo (nôvo͞o'), city (pop. 1,242), W Ill., on the Mississippi and N of Keokuk, Iowa; settled shortly after 1830 as Commerce, occupied and renamed 1839 by MORMONS under Joseph SMITH. Pop. reached c.20,000 under Mormons. After Smith's death, 1844, group left for Utah (1846). French communist colony (the Icarians) under Étienne CABET was here 1849–56. Smith's house still stands.

Navaho Indians or **Navajo Indians** (both: nä'vŭhō), North American tribe of Athapascan linguistic stock. A nomadic tribe of the Southwest, they lived in earth-covered lodges in winter, brush shelters in summer. Sheep were introduced in the early 17th cent. and the Navaho became primarily sheep raisers. Warlike, they raided the Pueblo Indians, and they resisted the whites until Kit Carson subdued them by killing their sheep (1863–64). Many Navaho were imprisoned until 1868, when they were given a reservation in NE Ariz., NW N.Mex., and SE Utah. Their turquoise and silver jewelry and their textiles (esp. blankets) are popular among whites.

Navajo National Monument: see NATIONAL PARKS AND MONUMENTS (table).

Naval Academy, United States: see UNITED STATES NAVAL ACADEMY.

naval conferences, international assemblies to consider rules of naval warfare, limitation of armaments, and related topics. *London Naval Conference* (1908–9), with delegates of 10 naval powers, convened to reach agreement on establishment of International Prize Court. Adopted Declaration of London, which, though unratified, influenced international law. Pres. Harding called *Washington Conference* (1921–22) to consider naval matters in Pacific. Attended by Great Britain, Japan, Italy, France, U.S., China, Netherlands, Portugal, and Belgium. Several treaties resulted. A Five-Power Treaty—Britain, U.S., Japan, France, Italy—estab. tonnage ratio, especially in capital ships and aircraft carriers. Another five-power treaty governed submarines. In Four-Power Pact France, Japan, Britain, and U.S. agreed to respect one another's rights in Pacific. Treaties were to stand until Dec. 31, 1936. Two Nine-Power treaties guaranteed independence and integrity of China. *Geneva Conference* of 1927 and *London Conference* of 1930 failed to limit armaments, though a new ratio was estab. In 1934 Japan declared intention to terminate Washington Conference treaty, and withdrew from *London Conference* of 1935. All attempts of other powers to limit armaments failed in part. With outbreak of war in 1939, treaties were completely abandoned.

Navarino, battle of (nävärē'nō), 1827, naval battle in Greek War of Independence, resulting from Turkey's refusal to accept an armistice demanded by England, France, and Russia. Egyptian fleet of MOHAMMED ALI, anchored at Pylos (then called Navarino), was defenseless against allied attack; its destruction influenced Egypt's withdrawal from Greek war in 1828.

Navarre (nŭvär'), Span. *Navarra,* province (4,024 sq. mi.; pop. 369,618), N Spain, bordering on France, between W Pyrenees and Ebro R.; cap. Pamplona. Pastures, vineyards, cattle raising. Sparsely populated. Population is largely of Basque stock (see BASQUES). The Basque kingdom of Navarre (founded 824 as kingdom of Pamplona) expanded quickly and reached its zenith under SANCHO III, who ruled over nearly all Christian Spain (1000–1035). On his death, Navarre went to his son García. The kingdom then also comprised the Basque Provs. and, N of the Pyrenees, the district of Lower Navarre (now in France). The crown passed, by inheritance and marriage, to the counts of Champagne (1234), the kings of France (1305), the counts of Évreux (1349), JOHN II of Aragon (1425), the counts of FOIX (1479), and the lords of ALBRET (1494), from whom it devolved upon HENRY IV of France and his Bourbon successors until Louis XVI. In fact, however, Ferdinand V of Aragon seized all but Lower Navarre in 1512 and thus brought it to Spain. The Spanish kings carried the title kings of Navarre

NATIONAL PARKS

Name	Location	Date Estab.	Area (acres)	Special Characteristics
Acadia	S Maine	1919	28,545.62	Mountain and coast scenery. See MOUNT DESERT ISLAND.
Big Bend	W Texas	1944	692,304.70	Canyons and desert plain.
Bryce Canyon	SW Utah	1928	36,010.38	Box canyon with fantastic and beautifully colored walls.
Carlsbad Caverns	SE N.Mex.	1930	45,526.59	Great limestone caverns.
Crater Lake	SW Oregon	1902	160,290.33	Very blue lake in crater.
Everglades	S Fla.	1947	1,100,173.00	Saw-grass prairies and mangrove forests. See EVERGLADES.
Glacier	NW Mont.	1910	998,415.93	Rocky Mt. region of glaciers, forests, and lakes.
Grand Canyon	NW Ariz.	1919	645,295.91	Tremendous gorge of the Colorado river, remarkable for formations and coloring.
Grand Teton	NW Wyo.	1929	95,360.46	Most scenic portion of the Teton Range.
Great Smoky Mountains	W N.C., E Tenn.	1930	505,173.79	Wild, beautiful area. See GREAT SMOKY MOUNTAINS.
Hawaii	T.H.	1916	176,456.60	Volcanic region, with two active volcanoes.
Hot Springs	SW central Ark.	1921	1,019.13	Mineral hot springs.
Isle Royale	N Mich.	1940	133,838.51	Forested island, the largest in Lake Superior, with moose herd.
Kings Canyon	E Calif.	1940	453,064.82	Beautiful Kings river canyons; sequoias.
Lassen Volcanic	N Calif.	1916	103,429.28	Mt. Lassen, only active volcano in United States proper.
Mammoth Cave	S Ky.	1936	50,695.73	Underground passages with beautiful limestone formations.
Mesa Verde	SW Colo.	1906	51,017.87	Well-preserved prehistoric cliff dwellings.
Mount McKinley	Central Alaska	1917	1,939,319.04	Highest peak in North America, 20,300 ft. high; glaciers.
Mount Rainier	SW central Wash.	1899	241,571.09	Some 26 active glaciers.
Olympic	NW Wash.	1938	840,838.69	Rain forests and glaciers. See OLYMPIC MOUNTAINS.
Platt	S Okla.	1906	911.97	Sulphur and other cold mineral springs.
Rocky Mountain	N central Colo.	1915	253,131.45	Many snow-capped peaks over 10,000 ft. high.
Sequoia	Central Calif.	1890	385,099.79	Groves of giant sequoias; Mt. Whitney; Kern river canyon.
Shenandoah	N Va.	1935	193,472.98	Forested mountains of the Blue Ridge; Skyline Drive.
Wind Cave	SW S.Dak.	1903	26,576.15	Limestone caverns in the Black Hills.
Yellowstone	Wyo., Mont., Idaho	1872	2,213,206.55	Geysers, Yellowstone canyon, falls, great wildlife sanctuary.
Yosemite	Central Calif.	1890	757,000.62	Beautiful mountain region with Yosemite Valley.
Zion	SW Utah	1919	94,241.06	Multicolored gorge in desert and canyon region.

NATIONAL HISTORICAL PARKS

Name	Location	Date Estab.	Area (acres)	Special Characteristics
Abraham Lincoln	Central Ky. near Hodgenville	1939	116.50	Traditional birthplace cabin on site of Lincoln's birthplace.
Chalmette	SE La.	1939	69.61	Part of scene of battle of New Orleans in War of 1812.
Colonial	SE Va.	1936	7,134.60	Historic Yorktown, Jamestown, Williamsburg, and Cape Henry.
Morristown	N N.J.	1933	958.37	Washington's headquarters. See MORRISTOWN.
Saratoga	E N.Y.	1948	2,113.59	Scene of American victory over British in American Revolution. See SARATOGA CAMPAIGN.

NATIONAL MONUMENTS

Name	Location	Date Estab.	Area (acres)	Special Characteristics
Ackia Battleground	NE Miss.	1938	49.15	See TUPELO.
Andrew Johnson	NE Tenn. in Greenville	1942	17.08	President Johnson's home, tailor shop, and grave.
Appomattox Court House	Central Va.	1940	968.25	Scene of Lee's surrender to Grant. See APPOMATTOX.
Arches	E Utah near Moab	1929	33,929.94	Giant arches formed by erosion.
Aztec Ruins	NW N.Mex. near Farmington	1923	27.14	Ruins of 12th-century Indian town.

NATIONAL MONUMENTS (continued)

Name	*Location*	*Date Estab.*	*Area (acres)*	*Special Characteristics*
Badlands	SW S.Dak.	1939	123,052.46	See BADLANDS.
Bandelier	N N.Mex. near Santa Fe	1916	27,048.89	Ruins of prehistoric Indian homes.
Big Hole Battlefield	SW Mont.	1910	200.00	Scene of attack by U.S. soldiers on Chief JOSEPH.
Black Canyon of the Gunnison	SW Colo. near Montrose	1933	13,176.02	Deep, narrow canyon of the Gunnison river.
Cabrillo	S Calif. on San Diego Bay	1913	0.50	Memorial to Juan Rodríguez Cabrillo.
Canyon de Chelly	NE Ariz.	1931	83,840.00	Red sandstone canyons with many cliff dwellings.
Capitol Reef	S Utah	1937	33,068.74	20-mile-long sandstone cliff.
Capulin Mountain	NE N.Mex. E of Raton	1916	680.42	Huge cinder cone of recently extinct volcano.
Casa Grande	S Ariz. E of Casa Grande	1918	472.50	Casa Grande [big house] in ruins of prehistoric villages.
Castillo de San Marcos	NE Fla.	1924	18.51	Old masonry fort. See SAINT AUGUSTINE.
Castle Pinckney	SE S.C.	1924	3.50	Part of the early defenses of Charleston harbor.
Cedar Breaks	SW Utah near Cedar City	1933	6,172.20	Amphitheater (2,000 ft. deep) formed by erosion.
Chaco Canyon	NW N.Mex. S of Farmington	1907	21,239.95	Important Indian ruins.
Channel Islands	Off S Calif.	1938	26,819.26 (land and water area)	Including Santa Barbara and Anacapa islands; fossils; sea lions.
Chiricahua	SE Ariz.	1924	10,529.80	Curious rock formations—pillars, balanced rocks, fantastic figures.
Colorado	W Colo. near Grand Junction	1911	18,120.55	Huge monoliths, curious products of erosion.
Craters of the Moon	S Idaho	1924	47,210.67	Volcanic cones, craters, fissure lava flows.
Custer Battlefield	S Mont. near Hardin	1946	765.34	Site of Custer massacre. See LITTLE BIGHORN, river.
Death Valley	SE Calif., S Nev.	1933	1,860,138.31	Lowest land area in North America with distinctive desert vegetation.
Devil Postpile	Central Calif., SE of Yosemite	1911	798.46	Basaltic columns, some 60 ft. high.
Devils Tower	NE Wyo.	1906	1,193.91	Volcanic rock tower, rising c.1,280 ft. from Belle Fourche river bed.
Dinosaur	NE Utah, NW Colo., near Vernal, Utah	1915	190,798.49	Rich fossil quarries in fine condition; area of great scientific interest.
Effigy Mounds	NE Iowa	1949	1,000.00	Indian mounds in bird and animal shapes.
El Morro	W N.Mex.	1906	240.00	Sandstone monolith, with inscriptions of Spanish explorers and early American emigrants.
Fort Frederica	Off SE Ga.	1945	74.53	Ruins of fort built by James Oglethorpe. See SEA ISLANDS.
Fort Jefferson	Off S Fla.	1935	86.82	Building of this fort began in 1846. See DRY TORTUGAS.
Fort Laramie	E Wyo. SE of Casper	1938	214.41	Buildings of old fort on the Oregon Trail.
Fort McHenry	N Md.	1939	47.64	Birthplace of the *Star-spangled Banner*. See MCHENRY, FORT.
Fort Marion				See SAINT AUGUSTINE.
Fort Matanzas	NE Fla.	1924	227.76	Spanish fort. See SAINT AUGUSTINE.
Fort Pulaski	SE Ga.	1924	5,427.39	Fort on Cockspur Island. See PULASKI, FORT.
Fort Sumter	SE S.C. at Charleston	1948	2.40	Scene of engagement which opened the Civil War. See SUMTER, FORT.
Fossil Cycad	SW S.Dak. near Hot Springs	1922	320.00	Area in Black Hills containing fossilized plants.
George Washington Birthplace	E Va. near Fredericksburg	1930	393.68	Estate and reconstructed mansion. See WAKEFIELD.
Gila Cliff Dwellings	SW N.Mex. near Silver City	1907	160.00	Well-preserved cliff dwellings in 150-foot cliff.
Glacier Bay	SE Alaska	1925	2,297,734.10	Tidewater glaciers.

NATIONAL MONUMENTS (continued)

Name	*Location*	*Date Estab.*	*Area (acres)*	*Special Characteristics*
Grand Canyon	NW Ariz.	1932	196,051.00	Part of Grand Canyon including Torowcap Point.
Gran Quivira	Central N.Mex. near Mountainair	1909	450.94	Ruins of Spanish mission and Indian pueblos.
Great Sand Dunes	S Colo. SW of Alamosa	1932	35,908.19	Large, high sand dunes in Sangre de Cristo Mts.
Holy Cross	W central Colo.	1929	1,392.00	Snow-filled crevasses, forming a cross.
Homestead	SE Nebr. near Beatrice	1939	162.73	Site of first farm claimed under Homestead Act of 1862.
Hovenweep	SE Utah, SW Colo. near Blanding, Utah	1923	299.34	Four groups of prehistoric pueblos and cliff dwellings.
Jewel Cave	SW S.Dak. near Hot Springs	1908	1,274.56	Limestone caves, chambers connected by narrow galleries, in Black Hills.
Joshua Tree	SE Calif. near Indio	1936	695,221.64	Stand of the rare Joshua trees, a species of yucca.
Katmai	S Alaska	1918	2,697,590.00	Volcanic area, with the Valley of Ten Thousand Smokes.
Lava Beds	N Calif. NE of Mt. Shasta	1925	46,027.56	Examples of volcanic activity; scene of Modoc Indian war.
Lehman Caves	E Nev. near Ely	1922	640.00	Gray and white limestone caves; stalactites.
Meriwether Lewis	Central Tenn. near Hohenwald	1925	300.00	Grave of the leader of the Lewis and Clark expedition.
Montezuma Castle	Central Ariz. S of Flagstaff	1906	738.09	Well-preserved cliff dwellings.
Mound City Group	S central Ohio near Chillicothe	1923	57.00	Prehistoric Indian mounds.
Muir Woods	W Calif. near Mill Valley	1908	424.56	Grove of redwoods.
Natural Bridges	SE Utah near Blanding	1908	2,649.70	Three sandstone bridges, one 222 ft. high, with 261-foot span.
Navajo	NE Ariz.	1909	360.00	Ruins of several large cliff dwellings.
Ocmulgee	Central Ga. near Macon	1936	683.48	Remains of mounds and prehistoric towns.
Old Kasaan	SE Alaska	1916	38.00	Site of abandoned Haida Indian village.
Oregon Caves	SW Oregon S of Grants Pass	1909	480.00	Limestone caverns of beauty and variety.
Organ Pipe Cactus	S Ariz. W of Tucson	1937	328,161.73	Organ pipe cactus and other desert growth unique to the region.
Perry's Victory Memorial	N Ohio NW of Sandusky	1936	14.25	Site of Oliver H. Perry's victory in War of 1812 at Put in Bay.
Petrified Forest	E Ariz. E of Holbrook	1906	85,303.63	Petrified logs from Triassic period; part of the Painted Desert.
Pinnacles	S Calif. S of Hollister	1908	12,817.77	Rock spires 500–1,200 ft. high; caves.
Pipe Spring	NW Ariz. near the Grand Canyon	1923	40.00	Spring first visited by Mormons; old fort; in Kaibab Indian Reservation.
Pipestone	SW Minn. near Pipestone	1937	115.60	Quarry here was source for Indian peace pipes.
Rainbow Bridge	S Utah	1910	160.00	Pink sandstone arch, 309 ft. high.
Saguaro	SE Ariz. near Tucson	1933	53,669.24	Saguaro, other cacti, and varied desert growth.
Scotts Bluff	W Nebr. near Scottsbluff	1919	2,196.44	Landmark on the Oregon Trail.
Shoshone Cavern	NW Wyo. near Cody	1909	212.37	Big cave with encrustations of crystals.
Sitka	SE Alaska near Sitka	1910	57.00	Site of an Indian defeat by the Russian settlers.
Statue of Liberty	SE N.Y.	1924	10.38	See LIBERTY, STATUE OF.
Sunset Crater	N Ariz. near Flagstaff	1930	3,040.00	Red, yellow, and orange volcanic crater; ice caves; lava flows.

NATIONAL MONUMENTS (continued)

Name	Location	Date Estab.	Area (acres)	Special Characteristics
Timpanogos Cave	N central Utah near Salt Lake City	1922	250.00	Limestone cavern on Mt. Timpanogos.
Tonto	S central Ariz. near Roosevelt Dam	1907	1,120.00	Two well-preserved cliff dwellings at junction of Tonto Creek and Salt river.
Tumacacori	S Ariz. N of Nogales	1908	10.00	Mission founded by Eusebio F. KINO, rebuilt by Franciscans.
Tuzigoot	Central Ariz. near Clarksdale	1939	42.67	Excavated Indian ruins.
Verendrye	NW N.Dak.	1917	253.04	Commemorates Vérendrye's explorations.
Walnut Canyon	N Ariz. near Flagstaff	1915	1,641.62	Cliff dwellings.
Wheeler	SW Colo.	1908	300.00	Pinnacles and gorges, carved by volcanic action and erosion.
White Sands	S central N.Mex. near Alamogordo	1933	140,247.04	Wind-drifted gypsum sands; dunes 10–60 ft. high.
Whitman	SE Wash. near Walla Walla	1940	45.84	Site of mission of Marcus WHITMAN.
Wupatki	N Ariz. N of Flagstaff	1924	35,013.03	Several prehistoric pueblos.
Yucca House	SW Colo. near Cortez	1919	9.60	Remains of prehistoric Indian village.
Zion	SW Utah	1937	33,920.75	Examples of geologic phenomena; Hurricane Fault and colorful Kolob Canyon.

NATIONAL MILITARY PARKS

Name	Location	Date Estab.	Area (acres)	Special Characteristics
Chickamauga and Chattanooga	NW Ga., E Tenn.	1890	8,127.16	See CHATTANOOGA.
Fort Donelson	N Tenn.	1928	102.54	See DONELSON, FORT.
Fredericksburg and Spotsylvania County Battlefields Memorial	N Va.	1927	2,420.71	See FREDERICKSBURG, Va.
Gettysburg	S Pa.	1895	2,534.11	See GETTYSBURG, Pa.
Guilford Courthouse	Central N.C. near Greensboro	1917	148.83	Battle in Carolina campaign of American Revolution.
Kings Mountain	N S.C.	1931	4,012.00	See KINGS MOUNTAIN.
Moores Creek	SE N.C. near Wilmington	1926	30.00	Battlefield in the American Revolution.
Petersburg	SE Va.	1926	1,531.02	See PETERSBURG, Va.
Shiloh	S Tenn.	1894	3,729.26	See SAVANNAH, Tenn.
Stones River	Central Tenn.	1927	323.86	See MURFREESBORO, Tenn.
Vicksburg	W Miss.	1899	1,323.56	See VICKSBURG, Miss.

NATIONAL MEMORIAL PARK

Name	Location	Date Estab.	Area (acres)	Special Characteristics
Theodore Roosevelt	SW N.Dak.	1947	58,341.26	Part of Roosevelt's Elkhorn ranch; Badlands along Little Missouri river.

NATIONAL BATTLEFIELD PARKS

Name	Location	Date Estab.	Area (acres)	Special Characteristics
Kennesaw Mountain	NW Ga. near Marietta	1947	3,094.21	Union defeat in Atlanta campaign.
Richmond	E Va.	1944	684.44	See RICHMOND, Va.

until 1833, when Navarre sided with the Carlists.

Navarrete, Juan Fernández (nävärā'tā), 1526–79, Spanish religious painter, court painter to Philip II. Influenced by the Venetians.

Navarro, Madame de: see ANDERSON, MARY A.

Navas de Tolosa (nä'väs dā tōlō'sä), town (pop. 1,134), S Spain, in Andalusia. Here in 1212 Alfonso VIII of Castile routed the Moors.

Navasota (nă'vůsō'tů), city (pop. 5,188), E central Texas, near confluence of Navasota and Brazos rivers and NW of Houston. Shipping and processing center for cotton and lumber area. Has statue of LaSalle, allegedly killed near by.

Navigation Acts, in British colonial history, name given to parliamentary Acts of Trade. An outgrowth of MERCANTILISM, they were caused by threat to English navigators of rise of Dutch carrying trade. First Navigation Act (1660) aimed to bar foreigners from English trade; to regulate plantation trade; to give England the monopoly of certain colonial produce. In 1663 shipment from English ports was required of all foreign goods for American plantations. Last important act was the Act to Prevent Frauds and Abuses of 1696. Contention that the American revolution partly derives from the Acts is questionable. More adverse effects were felt in Ireland, Scotland, and the Channel Isls. Acts were repealed in 1849.

Navigators' Islands: see SAMOA.

Navy, United States Department of the, estab. 1798 by act of Congress as a separate department headed by Secretary of the Navy. Functioned as separate department until 1947, when it was incorporated in Natl. Military Establishment; in 1949 became a division of U.S. Dept. of Defense.

Navy Island, S Canada, in Niagara R., just above Niagara Falls. Here W. L. MACKENZIE estab. hq. in rebellion of 1837.

Naxos (năk'sŏs, Gr. näk'sôs), island (169 sq. mi.; pop. 20,132), off S Greece, in Aegean Sea, largest and most important of the CYCLADES. Exports a noted white wine and other agr. products. In legend Theseus abandoned ARIADNE here.

Nayarit (näyärēt'), state (10,547 sq. mi.; pop. 292,343), W Mexico, on the Pacific; cap., TEPIC. Volcanic soil, heavy rains, and variation in altitude cause variety of agr. produce. Forest and mineral wealth on mainland and on Las TRES MARÍAS isls. are almost unexploited. Separated from Jalisco as territory 1884, it became a state 1917.

Nazarenes (nă'zůrēnz), group of German artists of early 19th cent. who worked in Rome and tried to revive Christian art. Exerted much influence in Germany. Inspired by early Italian painters, they worked from imagination and not from nature. Members included J. F. Overbeck, Philipp Veit, and Peter von Cornelius. Were at one time called Pre-Raphaelites, but little of their work links them to later English group.

Nazareth (nă'–), town (pop. over 20,000), N Israel. Here Jesus lived before beginning his ministry. It is a pilgrimage center with many shrines and churches.

Nazareth, borough (pop. 5,830), E Pa., NW of Easton. Mfg. of clothing and cement.

Nazareth College: see LOUISVILLE, Ky.; ROCHESTER, N.Y.

Nazarite, in Bible, man dedicated to the service of Jehovah by various vows, either his own or those of his parents, (e.g., to abstain from wine, not to cut his hair). Samson was a Nazarite. Num. 6.1–21; Judges 13.4,5.

Naze, the, Norway: see LINDESNES.

Nazi: see NATIONAL SOCIALISM.

Nazimova, Alla (nůzĭ'můvů), 1879–1945, Russian-American actress. Studied with Stanislavsky. In U.S. after 1905, she was memorable in Ibsen roles and in *Mourning Becomes Electra* (1931–32).

Nb, chemical symbol of the element NIOBIUM.

Nd, chemical symbol of the element NEODYMIUM.

Ne, chemical symbol of the element NEON.

Neagh, Lough (lŏkh nā), lake, 18 mi. long and 11 mi. wide, N. Ireland, in Counties Armagh, Tyrone, Londonderry, Antrim, and Down. Largest fresh-water body in British Isles, it has fine fisheries.

Neanderthal (nēăn'dûrtäl"), small valley, W Germany, E of Düsseldorf. Here in 1856 skeletal remains of the so-called Neanderthal man were discovered (see MAN, PRIMITIVE).

Neapolis (nēă'půlĭs) [Gr.,= new city], name of many anc. Greek and Roman cities (e.g., Naples, Italy).

Nearchus (nēär'kůs), fl. 324 B.C., Macedonian general. Commanded Alexander's fleet in voyage from India up Persian coast to Susa (325–324 B.C.).

Near Islands: see ALEUTIAN ISLANDS.

nearsightedness or **myopia** (mīō'pēů), sight defect resulting when light rays focus in front of retina. It is caused by abnormal length of eyeball from front to back or by distortion of lens.

neat's-foot oil, yellow, almost odorless oil obtained by boiling feet of cattle. It is used as a lubricant and in leather dressing.

Nebo, Mount, summit of Pisgah ridge from which Moses viewed Canaan, the Promised Land. Deut. 34.1.

Nebraska, state (76,653 sq. mi.; pop. 1,325,-510), central U.S., in GREAT PLAINS; admitted 1867 as 37th state; cap. LINCOLN. OMAHA largest city. Bounded NE and E by MISSOURI R. PLATTE R. important. Plains rise to tableland in W. Agr. of grains (esp. wheat, corn), sugar beets; raising of livestock. Industries based on these products. Part of Louisiana Purchase (1803). Scene of fur-trading activities. First permanent settlement BELLEVUE (c.1823). Made territory under KANSAS-NEBRASKA BILL (1854). Land boom in 1860s. Ranchers opposed the coming of homesteaders who opened farms despite severe winter and droughts. Hard times caused farmers to support the GRANGER MOVEMENT and POPULIST PARTY in late 19th cent. Depression of 1930s was severe, but food demands of World War II, soil conservation, agr. experimentation have revived agr.

Nebraska, University of, mainly at Lincoln; land-grant, state supported; coed.; chartered 1869, opened 1871.

Nebraska City, city (pop. 6,872), SE Nebr., on

Missouri R. and E of Lincoln. Processes livestock, grain, truck, and dairy products.

Nebraska Wesleyan University: see LINCOLN.

Nebuchadnezzar (nĕ″byủkủdnĕ′zủr; nĕ″bủ–), d. 562 B.C., king of Babylonia (c.605–562 B.C.); son of Nabopolassar. In his father's reign he defeated the Egyptians under NECHO (605). In 597 B.C. he quelled revolt of Judah and set Zedekiah on throne. Putting down a new revolt, he took king and nobles captive, thus beginning the Captivity. Under Nebuchadnezzar Babylonia flourished and Babylon became magnificent. Also Nebuchadrezzar, Nebuchodonosor.

nebula (nĕ′byŏŏlủ), in astronomy, a cloudlike mass, usually luminous. Within our Galaxy exist planetary nebulae, each a central star with shell of gaseous material; bright diffuse nebulae; and dark diffuse nebulae (masses of opaque particles). Luminosity of galactic nebulae attributed to reflection from, and radiation excited by, associated stars. Extragalactic nebulae are star systems (most of them spiral) similar to our Galaxy. Their apparent recession from earth supports expanding universe theory.

nebular hypothesis, theory of origin of solar system to which Laplace gave scientific form. Postulates that solar system was once a vast rotating mass of hot nebulous matter contracting as it cooled and increasing its speed of rotation; that centrifugal force caused successive rings to be detached, the smaller revolving more rapidly; that from each ring evolved a planet. Theory now held untenable because each ring would tend to form many small bodies rather than planets and momentum of planetary rotation is too great relative to that of sun.

Necessity, Fort, entrenched camp at Great Meadows (near present Uniontown, Pa.), site of defeat of George Washington and Va. militia by French in 1754. Grave of Gen. Braddock is near Fort Necessity Natl. Battlefield Site.

Necho (nē′kō), reigned 609–593 B.C., king of anc. Egypt, of XXVI dynasty; son of PSAMTIK. After fall of Nineveh (612) he took Palestine and Syria after battle of Megiddo. His empire fell when Nebuchadnezzar came W. Necho met him at Carchemish, was beaten (605) and returned to Egypt.

Neckar (nĕ′kär), river, 228 mi. long, SW Germany, rising in Black Forest and flowing N and W through Württemberg and Baden, past Tübingen, Esslingen, Stuttgart, Heilbronn, and Heidelberg, to join the Rhine at Mannheim. Navigable from Stuttgart. Celebrated for its scenic charm.

Necker, Jacques (zhäk′ nĕkĕr′), 1732–1804, French banker and financial expert, b. Geneva, Switzerland. After the fall of TURGOT, whose free-trade policy he had criticized, he became director of the treasury (1776) and director general of finances (1777). He sought to limit the growing national debt by stringent economies, which made him unpopular with the court. He resigned in 1781, after making public the financial situation in his *Compte rendu,* and retired to Coppet, his Swiss estate. In 1788, when France was on the verge of bankruptcy, Louis XVI recalled him and made him minister of state. Necker gained immense popularity by recommending the calling of the STATES-GENERAL. When the court party secured his dismissal, the populace stormed the Bastille (July 14, 1789) and forced his reinstatement. He resigned in 1790 and retired to Coppet. His wife, **Suzanne (Curchod) Necker,** 1739–94, wrote on various subjects, notably *Réflexions sur le divorce* (1794). Her salon was very influential. Their daughter was Mme de Staël.

nectarine: see PEACH.

Needham (nē′dủm), residential town (pop. 16,313), E Mass., WSW of Boston; settled 1680. Mfg. of knit goods, elastic goods and surgical, dental instruments.

Needles, city (pop. 4,051), SE Calif., on Colorado R. near Hoover Dam. Mojave Indian trade center.

Neenah (nē′nủ), city (pop. 12,437), E Wis., on L. Winnebago opposite MENASHA; settled 1835. Wood and metal products are made.

Neer, Aert van der (ärt′ vän dĕr nār′), 1603–77, Dutch landscape painter. Excelled in painting light effects (e.g., moonlight scenes and sunsets). His son, **Eglan Hendrik van der Neer,** c.1635–1703, is noted for his paintings of luxurious interiors, hunting scenes, and biblical subjects.

Neerwinden (nārvĭn′dủn), village SE of Louvain, Belgium. Here in 1693 the French under Luxembourg defeated William III of England, and in 1793 the Austrians defeated the French under Dumouriez.

negative, in PHOTOGRAPHY, a film after developing and fixing. It is so named because light and dark areas of image are reversed. Developing is done in darkness; fixing process stops further reduction of silver salts. Metallic silver and gelatin form the image. A positive is produced from negative by printing, i.e., placing negative between light source and sensitive paper. After exposure to light the sensitive paper is treated chemically and "print" is washed and dried.

Negaunee, (nĭgô′nē), city (pop. 6,472), W Upper Peninsula, N Mich., on Marquette iron range near Ishpeming. Resort. Iron discovered here 1844.

Negev (nĕ′gĕv) or **Negeb** (–gĕb), semidesert region (c.4,700 sq. mi.), S Israel, between the Mediterranean and Gulf of Aqaba. Borders on Egypt (W) and on Jordan (E). Today its only town is Beersheba, but in ancient times it had several prosperous cities. Comprises over a third of Israeli territory. Plans have been made to open it up to agr. and settlement. Scene of fighting between Egyptian and Israeli forces, 1948.

Negoiul (nĕgoi′ŏŏl) or **Negoi** (nĕgoi′), peak, 8,361 ft. high, Rumania; highest of Transylvanian Alps.

Negri, Ada (ä′dä nā′grē), 1870–1945, Italian writer, known for her love lyrics and an autobiographical novel, *Morning Star* (1921).

Negri Sembilan: see MALAYA.

Negro, member of any of several groups of peoples, characterized physically by black or dark brown skin, wooly hair, broad flat nose, prominent eyes with yellowish cornea, thick lips, and prognathous jaw. Term most properly applied to tribes of central and W Africa. Negroid peoples include Negrillo and

Negrito (see PYGMY). Negroes in Africa generally have crude form of agr. and simple handicrafts; religion is generally form of ANIMISM. Negroes once invaded Egypt, and various Negro kingdoms flourished in N Africa. Begun in 15th cent., slave trade from Africa was profitable European enterprise by 17th cent. Negroes entered the Americas by 1501. First Negroes in present U.S. came to Va. in 1619. Tobacco planting increased Negro slavery in South. Although Northern colonies also had slaves, after American Revolution slavery there gradually declined. Large-scale production of cotton in South, spurred by invention of cotton gin in 1793, greatly increased slavery. Life of slaves on cotton plantations was often harsh. Slavery became important political issue in MISSOURI COMPROMISE (1820) and KANSAS-NEBRASKA BILL (1854). EMANCIPATION PROCLAMATION technically freed slaves of Confederacy. Difficult problem of adjustment after Civil War met by FREEDMEN'S BUREAU and Republican RECONSTRUCTION program, countered by KU KLUX KLAN organization of Southerners. Share-cropping system left Negro in economically poor position, and Southern states maintained "white supremacy" through enactment of segregation and poll tax laws. Wide Negro migration to North sometimes resulted in race riots. Negroes fought in both World Wars, made cultural contributions to American life, and widened scope of activities in public life, but questions of economic and political discrimination still pose a problem in U.S.

Negro, Rio (rē'ō nā'grō), river of N Brazil, one of chief tributaries of Amazon and a primary commercial channel. Originates as Guainía in Colombia. A natural canal connects it with Orinoco. There are many other rivers named Rio Negro (Span., Río Negro).

Negro minstrel, white entertainer in Negro make-up. T. D. Rice gave first blackface performance (song-and-dance act *Jim Crow*) c.1828. After 1846 Christy's minstrels (see CHRISTY, E. P.) set minstrel show pattern with interlocutor and two end men telling jokes as well as chorus and soloists to sing. After 1870, vaudeville, films, and radio eclipsed minstrel shows.

Negropont, Greece: see CHALCIS; EUBOEA.

Negros (nā'grōs), island (4,905 sq. mi.; pop. 1,218,710), one of Visayan Isls., in Philippines. Mainly mountainous. Products include sugar cane, rice, and hemp. Silliman Univ. (1901) is at Dumaguete on SE coast. Negritos inhabit interior.

Nehemiah (nē"ůmī'ů), central figure of book of **Nehemiah:** see EZRA.

Nehru, Jawaharlal (jůwähůrläl' ně'rōō),1889–, Indian statesman, b. Allahabad, educated at Harrow and Cambridge. Admitted to the bar in 1912. After massacre of Amritsar (1919) he joined in struggle for India's freedom. Headed Indian Natl. Congress several times after 1929. His advocacy of industrialization and socialization was opposed by Gandhi, whose ideal was an agrarian society. Spent most of the period 1930–36 in jail for conducting civil disobedience campaigns. In World War II he was again imprisoned for opposing aid to the British, who refused to free India immediately. With creation of new state of India in 1947 he became its prime minister and continued to hold that office after elections of 1952. Wrote several books, including *Glimpses of World History* (1936) and the autobiography, *Toward Freedom.*

Neilson, William Allan (nēl'sůn), 1869–1946, American educator, a Shaksperian scholar. He was president of Smith Col., 1917–39, and editor in chief of second edition (1934) of *Webster's New International Dictionary.*

Neisse (nī'sů), two rivers of Silesia; tributaries of the Oder. The **Glatzer Neisse** (glä'tsůr), 120 mi. long, rises in the Sudetes and winds NE past Glatz. The **Lausitzer Neisse** (lou'zĭ"tsůr) or **Lusatian Neisse** (lōōsā'shůn), Czech *Lužická Nisa,* 140 mi. long, is farther W. Rising in Czechoslovakia, it flows N across the Sudetes and Lusatia, past Gorlitz, and forms the border between the [East] German Democratic Republic and Polish-administered Germany.

Nejd (nějd), former emirate, N central Arabia, now forming a province of SAUDI ARABIA. It is mainly a plateau with oasis in E part; RIAD is chief city. The WAHABI leader, Ibn Saud, conquered the Nejd from Turkey, 1900–1912.

Nejef (ně'jěf) or **Najaf** (nä'jäf), town, central Iraq; pilgrimage center for Shiite Moslems. Tomb of Ali, son-in-law of Mohammed, is here.

Nekhtnebf (někt"ně'bůf), Gr. *Nectanebos,* name of two kings of anc. Egypt. **Nekhtnebf I** (reigned 379–361 B.C.) founded the XXIX dynasty. Resisted a Persian invasion successfully. Built splendid temples. **Nekhtnebf II** (reigned 359–343 B.C.) was the son of a viceroy. He overthrew the son of Nekhtnebf I. He also was a builder. Beat off one Persian invasion but was defeated in another.

Nekrasov, Nikolai Alekseyevich (nyĭkůlī' ŭlyĭksyā'ĭvĭch nyĭkrä'sůf), 1821–77, Russian poet and publicist. The driving force of his life was to improve social conditions—especially the lot of the peasant—in Russia. This theme permeates his literary journal, *Contemporary* (1846–66), as well as his lyrics and narrative poems. *Who Is Happy in Russia?* (1873) is a satirical portrait of Russia under serfdom.

Nelson, (John) Byron (Jr.), 1912–, American golfer. Won U.S. Natl. Open title 1939, P.G.A. title 1940.

Nelson, Horatio Nelson, Viscount, 1758–1805, English naval hero. Won fame in FRENCH REVOLUTIONARY WARS. His destruction of French fleet at Aboukir (1798) ended Napoleon I's plan of conquest in the East. While assisting king of Sicily, he prolonged his stay in Naples because of the presence there of his mistress, Lady HAMILTON. Defeated the Danes at Copenhagen (1801). Destroyed combined French and Spanish fleets off Cape TRAFALGAR (1805), but was killed in action.

Nelson, William Rockhill, 1841–1915, American journalist. Launched Kansas City *Evening Star* in 1880. His editorship gained national attention.

Nelson, city (pop. 6,772), SE B.C., Canada, on Kootenay R. and N of Spokane, Wash. Railroad and mining center.

Nelson, river, N Man., Canada, rising at N end

of L. Winnipeg and flowing 400 mi. NE to Hudson Bay at Port Nelson. Mouth discovered by Sir Thomas Button 1612. Was fur trade route.

Nemacolin's Path (nĕ'mŭkō"lĭnz), Indian trail between Potomac and Monongahela rivers, going from site of present Cumberland, Md., to mouth of Redstone Creek (where Brownsville, Pa., now stands). Route of George Washington's first Western expedition and of Gen. Braddock's expedition. National Road was built on same route.

Neman, Russian name of NIEMEN, river.

Nemea (nē'mēŭ), anc. city, N Argolis, Greece. At the temple of Zeus were held the Nemean games (begun 573 B.C.), one of four Panhellenic festivals.

Nemean lion (nĭmē'ŭn, nē'mēŭn), beast of Nemea, invulnerable to weapons. HERCULES strangled it.

Nemesis (nĕm'ĭsĭs), Greek personification of law and order as avenging itself on the violator.

Nemi, Lake (nā'mē), small crater lake, Latium, central Italy. Here are the sacred wood and ruins of a famous temple of Diana. Two pleasure ships of Emperor Caligula, at lake's bottom for almost 2,000 years, were raised 1930–31.

Nemours (nŭmōōr'), town (pop. 5,336), Seine-et-Marne dept., N France. Was cap. of a duchy held in fief by house of Armagnac until 16th cent. and later given in appanage to various princely houses. Du Pont family of Delaware originated here.

Nemunas, Lithuanian name of NIEMEN, river.

Nenets National Okrug (nyĕ'nyĭts), administrative division (67,300 sq. mi.; pop. c.30,000), NE European RSFSR. Inhabitants are chiefly Nentsy—formerly and still generally known as SAMOYEDES.

Nennius, fl. 796, Welsh writer, to whom is ascribed the *Historia Britonum,* important because it records early British legends, especially about King Arthur.

neoclassicism. In English literature, Restoration and 18th-cent. period is often called Age of Neoclassicism or Age of Reason: classical learning, ancient literary "rules," reason, and common sense were preferred to enthusiasm and uncontrolled imagination. In architecture, see CLASSIC REVIVAL.

neodymium (nē"ōdĭ'mēŭm), rare metallic element of rare earths (symbol = Nd; see also ELEMENT, table). Used in some yellow-green glassware and goggles.

Neolithic period (nēŭlĭ'thĭk, nēō–) or **New Stone Age,** period of industrial development following the Paleolithic period or Old Stone Age, and characterized by new sources of food supply and use of polished stone tools. Pottery making, carpentry, and weaving emerged. Domestic animals and agr. appeared, and no new important species of animals have since been added to those domesticated in this period.

neon, rare gaseous element (symbol = Ne; see also ELEMENT, table), colorless, odorless, tasteless, chemically inert. Produces reddish orange glow when confined in glass tube through which electric current passes; used in electric advertising signs and airplane beacons.

Neoplatonism (nē"ōplā'tŭnĭzŭm), last of the great Greco-Roman pagan philosophies, so called because it was to some extent a return to Platonic doctrines with rejection of Stoic and Epicurean teachings. Though it was foreshadowed by many, notably Philo, Neoplatonism was founded by PLOTINUS in the 3d cent. The system was antimaterialistic and mystical. Neoplatonists believed that there is an utterly transcendent One or Unity (the great Cause and Principle), from whom everything in the universe proceeds by a process of emanations: the divine Mind emanates from the One, the world soul from the divine Mind; below that in scale come particular souls and finally material things. The fundamental idea of the connection of the individual soul with the One was to be paralleled in Christian mysticism. Plotinus' chief followers were Porphyry, Iamblichus, Proclus, and Hypatia. Emperor Julian was Neoplatonic. Justinian in 529 banned pagan schools, and Neoplatonism itself soon disappeared, but its influence continued through the Middle Ages.

Neoptolemus (nē"ŏptŏ'lĭmŭs), in Greek legend, son of Achilles and Deidamia; husband of Hermione (daughter of Menelaus and Helen). Brave but cruel, he killed Priam at the altar of Zeus in the Trojan War. After the war Andromache and Helenus were his slaves. Also called Pyrrhus.

Neo-Pythagoreanism (nē'ō-pĭthă"gŭrē'ŭnĭzŭm), philosophical and religious movement of 2d cent. and 1st cent. B.C., centering at Alexandria and based on revival of mystical doctrines derived from teachings of Pythagoras. Neo-Pythagoreans stressed sacrifices and miracles and held certain rarefied beliefs (objective reality of numbers, transmigration of souls, oneness of all in Divinity) without a well-developed mysticism. The movement lost out in rivalry with Neoplatonism. Its chief leader was Apollonius of Tyana.

Neosho (nēō'shō), city (pop. 5,790), SW Mo., SSE of Joplin, in an Ozark farm and resort area. Pro-Confederate convention passed ineffective ordinance of secession here in 1862.

Neosho, river, c.460 mi. long, rising in E central Kansas and flowing SE into Okla., where it is chiefly known as Grand R., then S to the Arkansas near Muskogee. In Okla., GRAND RIVER DAM is SE of Vinita, and Fort Gibson Dam is NNE of FORT GIBSON.

NEP: see NEW ECONOMIC POLICY.

Nepal (nŭpôl'), kingdom (c.56,000 sq. mi.; pop. 6,283,649), S central Asia, between India and Tibet; cap. Katmandu. In N is main section of Himalayas, including Mt. Everest. Nepal Valley (where rice, wheat, and fruits are produced) is the only densely populated area. Trades almost exclusively with India and Tibet. The Nepalese are mainly Hindus, with Buddhists forming a minority; they speak Tibeto-Burman languages. Since 18th cent. Nepal has been dominated by the GURKHA. In 1792 it first entered into treaty relations with the British, who recognized its full sovereignty in treaty of 1923. Ruled by premier belonging to Rana family until 1951, when successful revolts gave power to the king, who had formerly been a mere figurehead.

Nepos, Cornelius (nē′pŏs), c.100 B.C.–c.25 B.C., Roman historian, known for his biographies.

Neptune, in Roman religion, anc. god of water. Probably an indigenous god of fertility, he was later identified with Greek POSEIDON, god of sea.

Neptune, N.J.: see OCEAN GROVE.

Neptune, in astronomy, eighth PLANET in order from sun. With atmosphere and two satellites, it revolves about sun in c.164.8 years at mean distance of c.2,793,400,000 mi. Mean diameter c.31,000 mi., rotation period c.15.8 hr. Discovery (1846) resulted from independent computations by J. C. Adams and U. J. J. Leverrier. See *ill.*, p. 1187.

neptunium, chemical element (symbol = Np; atomic no. = 93), discovered in 1940 by E. M. McMillan and P. H. Abelson by means of the cyclotron at Univ. of California.

Nerchinsk (nyĕr′chĭnsk), city (pop. c.15,300), RSFSR, in SE Siberia, on Trans-Siberian RR. Formerly a place of exile. By Treaty of Nerchinsk (1689) Russia conceded Far Eastern Siberia to China.

Nernst, Walther (väl′tůr nĕrnst′), 1864–1941, German physicist and chemist. Worked on osmotic pressure, ionization, electroacoustics, astrophysics. Won 1920 Nobel Prize for work in thermodynamics and behavior of matter at temperatures approaching absolute zero.

Nero (Claudius Caesar) (nē′rō), A.D. 37–A.D. 68, Roman emperor (A.D. 54–A.D. 68), son of AGRIPPINA II, who persuaded CLAUDIUS I to adopt Nero. When Claudius died, Nero succeeded; when his mother, losing control of her son, intrigued in favor of Claudius' son Britannicus, Britannicus died, probably poisoned at Nero's order. The brutal behavior that has made the emperor's name a byword came, however, after he was under the influence of POPPAEA SABINA, whom he later married. He murdered his mother and later his wife (Octavia). Rumor blamed him for the great fire of Rome (A.D. 64), but he accused the Christians of setting it and began the first persecution. A plot against him the next year caused him to begin a bloody series of violent deaths (including those of Seneca and Poppaea), which bred new revolts. When one was proving successful he committed suicide. He greatly fancied himself as a poet and an artist and said when he was dying, "What an artist the world is losing in me!"

Neruda, Jan (yän′ nĕ′ro͝odä), 1834–91, Czech essayist and poet. Noted for a collection of tales, *Stories from Mala Strama* (1878), and lyric poetry which has been compared to Heine's for its clarity and simplicity. Of his dramas, *Francesca da Rimini* (1860) is best known.

Neruda, Pablo (pä′blō närо͞o′dhä), pseud. of Naftali Ricardo Reyes, 1904–, Chilean surrealist poet, notable for bold experiments in verse.

Nerva (Marcus Cocceius Nerva) (nûr′vů), A.D. c.30–98, Roman emperor (A.D. 96–98), chosen by the senate on the death of DOMITIAN. Unassuming and mild, he aided the poor and tolerated the Christians. Unable to manage the Praetorian guard, he adopted TRAJAN and turned over rule to him.

Nerval, Gérard de (zhārär′ dů nĕrväl′), pseud. of Gérard Labrunie, 1808–55, French author. He translated Goethe's *Faust* (1828), wrote fantastic short stories, travel sketches, and poems. His life ended in madness and suicide.

Nervo, Amado (ämä′dhō nĕr′vō), 1870–1919, Mexican poet, a leader of *modernismo*. Most of his verses deal with his inward world where he sought peace from torments without.

nervous system, system comprising nerves and nerve tissue of animal body and concerned with coordination and control of other systems and organs. In human it consists of central nervous system (BRAIN and SPINAL CORD); peripheral nervous system (nerve fibers connecting receptors, or sense organs, with effectors, or muscles and glands); and autonomic nervous system (nerves and ganglia, or groups of nerve cells, regulating actions, not under control of will, of the smooth muscle tissue of digestive and circulatory systems and the secretory action of glands). Portions of autonomic system, usually functioning antagonistically, are parasympathetic system (including fibers arising in midbrain and sacral region) and sympathetic system (including fibers arising in thoracic and lumbar region of spinal cord, a chain of ganglia on either side of cord, and plexuses composed of ganglia and fibers). Unit of structure is neuron, or nerve cell, typically a nucleated cell body with one or more branching processes (dendrons or dendrites) and a single sheathed process (axon). Sensory, or afferent, fibers carry impulse from receptor to central system; motor, or efferent, fibers transmit impulse to effector. A nerve consists of fibers, either of one type or mixed, bound together with connective tissue. Human body has 12 pairs of cranial nerves, 31 pairs of spinal nerves. Reflex arc is pathway from receptor over sensory fibers to central system and thence over motor fibers to effector. Reflex action, not under voluntary control, results from stimulation of a sensory nerve. Conditioned reflex, acquired through association of particular stimulus with specific result, is basis of habit formation and learning. See *ill.*, p. 763.

Nesiotes: see CRITIUS AND NESIOTES.

Ness, Loch (lŏkh), lake (c.24 mi. long; c.1 mi. wide), Inverness-shire, Scotland, part of Caledonian Canal along Great Glen. Very deep, it is overhung by mountains. A "monster," 40–50 ft. long, has supposedly been seen in the loch.

Nesselrode, Karl Robert, Count (nĕ′sůlrōd), 1780–1862, Russian statesman of German descent. b. Lisbon. Guided Russian foreign policy 1816–56.

Nessus (nĕ′sůs), in Greek legend, centaur who carried travelers across the river Evenus. He tried to abduct Deianira, but Hercules shot him with a poisoned arrow. Dying, he gave his bloody robe to Deianira, telling her to give it to her husband, Hercules, when his love waned. She did, and the poisoned robe ("the shirt of Nessus") killed Hercules.

nest, refuge in which animal lays eggs or gives birth to young and where young pass their helpless period. Many birds and certain insects, fish, reptiles, and mammals build nests. Among birds, male selects territory and female usually selects site and does most of construction of nest; factors in choice of site are access to food, protection from elements, and concealment from enemies. Among some birds, the male assists the female with incubation. Many birds lay eggs on ground and build no nest. See *ill.*, p. 135.

Nestor (nĕ'stûr), in Greek mythology, wise king of Pylos; husband of Eurydice and father of Antilochus. He took part in Argonaut expedition and Calydonian hunt and, when very old, in the Trojan War.

Nestorianism, heresy advanced by Nestorius, 5th-cent. patriarch of Constantinople. Its chief point was objection to calling the Virgin Mary the Mother of God, saying that she bore him as a man. Cyril of Alexandria opposed this view, and the Councils of Ephesus (431), Chalcedon (451), and Constantinople (553) clarified the orthodox position that the two natures of Jesus Christ (divine and human) are inseparably joined in one person and partake of one divine substance. The clergy of Antioch briefly stayed out of communion with Alexandria, but only the Persian church upheld Nestorius to the end. It became a separate Christian community, the **Nestorian Church,** which now has some members in Iraq, Iran, and Malabar, India (as well as a few in the U.S.). The liturgy (in Syriac) is probably Antiochene; the rite is called Chaldean or East Syrian, and the Church is sometimes called the Assyrian Church. They uphold Nestorius' teaching on the title of the Virgin, but otherwise their doctrines have little connection with Nestorius. The Church was spread across the East from the 7th to the 10th cent. Also using the Chaldean rite are the Chaldean Catholics, who have been separated from the Nestorian Church since the 16th cent. and are in communion with the pope. The Nestorians were subject to persecution by Chinese, Hindus, and Moslems, and in the 19th and early 20th cent. were the object of massacres by Kurds and Turks.

Nestroy, Johann Nepomuk (yō'hän nä'pōmo͝ok nĕs'troi), 1801–62, Austrian dramatist and actor. Known for his farce *Lumpacivagabundus* (1833) and for his parodies of the romantic drama.

Netcong, resort borough (pop. 2,284), NW N.J., near L. Musconetcong. It has a transoceanic radiotelephone station.

Netherlands, Dutch *Nederland* or *Nederlanden,* kingdom (12,868 sq. mi.; with water surface, incl. IJSSELMEER, 15,765 sq. mi.; pop. 9,625,499), NW Europe, on the North Sea, bordering on Belgium (S) and Germany (E). It is also known in unofficial usage as Holland. Chief cities: AMSTERDAM (constitutional cap.), The HAGUE (*de facto* cap.), ROTTERDAM, UTRECHT, HAARLEM. There are 11 provinces, with considerable self-governing power. The coastal provinces, largely won from the sea by centuries of toil, are NORTH HOLLAND, SOUTH HOLLAND, ZEELAND, UTRECHT, GELDERLAND, OVERIJSSEL, FRIESLAND, GRONINGEN. The inland provinces are NORTH BRABANT, LIMBURG, DRENTHE. The country's wealth is derived from commerce (world's fourth largest merchant marine), industry (textiles, machinery, processed foods, electrical equipment, chemicals), dairying (esp. cheese), cattle raising, truck gardening, flower growing, and fishing. There are coal mines, and Dutch interests control much of the world's petroleum and tin production (in the former Dutch colonies in INDONESIA). Colonies: see WEST INDIES; GUIANA, DUTCH. Transit trade owes its volume to canal system which interconnects the main rivers (Scheldt, Meuse, Waal, Rhine) and links them with the waterways of Germany and Belgium. The Netherlands is a hereditary monarchy with a bicameral legislature (States-General). Succession is settled on house of Orange (see NASSAU). Protestants outnumber Catholics by c.500,000; all religions receive state subsidies. In Roman times the region was settled by Germanic Batavi (W of Rhine) and Frisians (E of Rhine). It passed under Frankish rule (5th–8th cent.) and later to the Holy Roman Empire. The counts of HOLLAND were the most powerful lords of the region, which in the 15th cent. passed to the dukes of BURGUNDY and after 1482 to the house of Hapsburg. Emperor Charles V in 1555 made all the Low COUNTRIES (incl. modern Netherlands) over to his son, Philip II of Spain. Philip's attempt to introduce the Spanish Inquisition and to abolish self-government led to a general uprising, led by WILLIAM THE SILENT, prince of Orange. Spain recovered the S provinces (i.e., modern Belgium; see NETHERLANDS, AUSTRIAN AND SPANISH), but Holland and the other six N provinces drew together in 1579 (Union of Utrecht) and declared their independence (1581). The struggle with Spain continued, except for a 12-year truce (1609–21) and became part of the Thirty Years War. In 1648 the independence of the United Provs. was formally recognized. The 17th cent. was the golden age of the Netherlands. Through the Dutch EAST INDIA COMPANY and DUTCH WEST INDIA COMPANY the Dutch gained a vast colonial empire and captured most of the world's carrying trade. Jewish and Huguenot refugees contributed to the prosperity and cultural life. The rule of the house of Orange (through the office of stadholder) was repeatedly interrupted by the republican party until 1747, when the stadholderate was made hereditary. After the DUTCH WARS against England and France and the wars of the GRAND ALLIANCE and the SPANISH SUCCESSION, the Netherlands emerged as strong as ever, but in the 18th cent. it lost its trade supremacy to England. Occupied by the French revolutionary armies in 1794, the Netherlands became the BATAVIAN REPUBLIC (1795), was made a kindgom under Louis BONAPARTE (1806), and was annexed to France (1810). The Congress of Vienna (1814–15) united the former United Provs. with the former Austrian Netherlands (i.e., Belgium) as a single kingdom. BELGIUM seceded 1830. Neutral in World War I, the Netherlands was invaded, without warning, by German forces in World War II. During the German occupation (1940–45) the Netherlands suffered heavily. Nearly all of its 112,000 Jews were exterminated. The Dutch government fled abroad, and Dutch forces continued to fight alongside the Allies against Germany and Japan. Postwar recovery was speedy, but early in 1953 the country suffered one of the worst disasters in its history when a North Sea storm flooded one third of its area. A charter member of the UN, the Netherlands joined the BENELUX union and the European Recovery Program (1947) as well as the North Atlantic Treaty (1949). Kings and ruling queens of the Netherlands from 1815: WILLIAM I; WILLIAM II; WILLIAM III; WILHELMINA; JULIANA.

Netherlands, Austrian and Spanish, that part of the LOW COUNTRIES which remained in possession of the house of Austria after the secession of the United Provs. (1581). The death of MARY OF BURGUNDY (1482) brought Flanders, Brabant, Artois, Hainaut, Luxembourg, Limburg, Holland, and Zeeland to the Hapsburgs; Emperor Charles V added Utrecht, Gelderland, Overijssel, Friesland, and Drenthe. His successor, PHILIP II of Spain, attempted to stamp out Protestantism and to curtail the powers of the provincial estates (assemblies). The cruel measures of the duke of ALBA provoked a general uprising, led by WILLIAM THE SILENT of Orange. By 1585 Alessandro FARNESE had reconquered the S provinces (i.e., roughly, modern Belgium and Luxembourg) for Spain, but the seven N provinces were definitely lost (see NETHERLANDS). Protestantism was extirpated in the Spanish Netherlands. In the wars of the 17th cent., Spain lost several border areas to the United Provs. and to France. The remainder passed to the Austrian branch of the Hapsburgs by the Peace of Utrecht (1714). The reforms introduced by Emperor Joseph II met Catholic and conservative resistance and led to a declaration of independence (1789). Austrian control was peaceably restored in 1790, but in 1794 the country was conquered by the French revolutionary armies. It was formally ceded to France 1797 and incorporated with the kingdom of the Netherlands 1815. For later history, see BELGIUM; LUXEMBOURG.

Netherlands East Indies: see INDONESIA.

Netherlands New Guinea: see NEW GUINEA.

Netherlands West Indies: see CURAÇAO.

Nethersole, Dame Olga (nĕ'dhûrsōl), 1870–1951, English actress. Won fame in England and U.S. in *Camille, Sapho,* and *The Second Mrs. Tanqueray.*

Néthou, Pic de: see ANETO, PICO DE.

Netley, village, Hampshire, England; site of one of chief military hospitals in England.

nettle, weedy annual or perennial plant of genus *Urtica,* native to the Old World, with stinging hairs which sometimes cause a rash. In some places nettles have been used medicinally and for food and fiber. Horse nettle is a nightshade.

Neuber, (Friederike) Karoline (kärōlē'nů noi'bůr), 1697–1760, German actress-manager. With her husband, Johann Neuber, she managed a company (after 1727) and was its leading actress in Racine, Corneille, Molière dramas (translated by J. C. Gottsched) presented for the first time in Germany.

Neuchâtel (nûshätĕl'), Ger. *Neuenburg,* canton (309 sq. mi; pop. 127,205), W Switzerland, in Jura mts. Cattle raising, dairying, wine growing. Watchmaking (notably at Le Locle and La Chaux-de-Fonds). Population is mainly French-speaking and Protestant. A county of the Holy Roman Empire, Neuchâtel was allied with the Swiss Confederation from the 15th cent. It became an independent principality in 1648. In 1707 the kings of Prussia succeeded the house of Orléans-Longueville as princes of Neuchâtel. Their rule was interrupted 1806–13 by that of Marshal Berthier. Neuchâtel, though still a principality, became a Swiss canton in 1815. The monarchy was overthrown in 1848; in 1857, after some complications, the king of Prussia renounced his claim to the principality. The cap., **Neuchâtel** (pop. 23,799), has a cathedral, an old castle, and a university. It lies on the **Lake of Neuchâtel,** 24 mi. long, 4–5 mi. wide, which is surrounded by fine vineyards.

Neuilly-sur-Seine (nûyē'-sür-sĕn'), residential suburb (pop. 58,658) of Paris, France, near Bois de Boulogne. Here in 1919 was signed the **Treaty of Neuilly,** between Bulgaria and the Allies of World War I. Bulgaria ceded part of W Thrace to Greece and some border areas to Yugoslavia. S Dobruja was confirmed in Rumanian possession.

neuralgia (nŏŏrăl'jů, nyŏŏ–), paroxysmal pain along course of peripheral sensory nerve or its branches. Varieties are distinguished according to part affected (e.g., facial, intercostal) or according to cause (e.g., syphilitic neuralgia).

neuritis (nŏŏrī'tĭs, nyŏŏ–), degenerative change in nerve fibers. Causes include deficiency in vitamins (esp. B_1 and B_2), injury, disease, toxic substances, and pressure.

neurosis, functional mental disorder whose symptoms result from compromise between gratification of and defense against libidinal impulses. Neurosis causes persistent fatigue, intellectual constriction, feelings of alienation, reactions disproportionate to stimuli, somatic disorders (see PSYCHOSOMATIC MEDICINE). Normality, neurosis, and PSYCHOSIS differ only quantitatively. FREUD attributed psychoneurosis (neurosis of mental origin) to frustration of infantile sexual drives (e.g., OEDIPUS COMPLEX) in first six years when ego is weak, fears censure; unsolved infantile conflicts appear under later stress as neurotic symptoms. Alfred ADLER, JUNG, Karen HORNEY, H. S. SULLIVAN, deviated from Freud. Social anthropologists have shown that behavior neurotic in one culture is normal in others.

Neusatz, Yugoslavia: see NOVI SAD.

Neuse (nūs), river rising N N.C. in piedmont near Va. line and flowing SE c.300 mi. to Pamlico Bay.

Neusiedler Lake (noi'zēdlůn), Ger. *Neusiedlersee,* Hung. *Fertö tó,* E Austria and W Hungary; c.20 mi. long. Château of ESTERHAZY family is at S end.

Neustrelitz (noi"shtrā'lĭts), town (pop. 24,692), Mecklenburg, N Germany. Founded 1733 as cap. of Mecklenburg-Strelitz. Damaged in World War II.

Neustria (nūs'trēů), Frankish kingdom (6th–

8th cent.), in France N of the Loire; cap. Soissons. For history, see MEROVINGIANS.

neutrality, in international law, status of a nation refraining from entry into war between other states and holding impartial attitude. At start of conflict nonbelligerent state issues proclamation of neutrality to explain its position. This serves also to warn own nationals it will not protect them if they commit unneutral acts. Proclamation commits nation to strict impartiality in relations with warring states, and obligates belligerents to respect neutral territory and territorial waters.

Neutrality Act, passed by U.S. Congress in 1935. Designed to keep U.S. out of possible European war by banning shipment of war materials to belligerents at the discretion of the President. Later revisions and the LEND-LEASE policy made act practically inoperative even before Pearl Harbor.

neutralization, chemical process which involves mixing and reacting of acid and basic solutions. Commonly refers to reaction between active acid and active base to form salt and water. Hydrogen (H) ion of acid and hydroxyl (OH) ion of base come together to form water (HOH). The salt is made of metallic element of base and element or radical (other than H) of acid. Heat produced is heat of neutralization. Process is important in determining concentration of acids in solution, in industrial processes, in removing excess acids.

Neutral Nation, group of North American Indians of Iroquoian linguistic stock, living in the 17th cent. on N shore of L. Erie; so called because they were at first neutral in Iroquois-Huron wars. When remnants of the Huron joined the Neutral Nation (1649) the Iroquois virtually wiped out the group.

neutron (nū'trŏn), nuclear particle of matter of minute size, with no charge. Some believe it consists of a proton and an electron held together. Bombardment of some elements with neutrons produces nuclear changes. See also ATOMIC ENERGY. See *ill.*, p. 989.

Neva (nē'vů), river, 46 mi. long, RSFSR, connecting L. Ladoga with Gulf of Finland at LENINGRAD. Linked by canal with Volga R. and White Sea.

Nevada (nůvă'dů, nůvä'dů), state (109,802 sq. mi.; pop. 160,083), W U.S.; admitted 1864 as 36th state; cap. CARSON CITY. Main cities are RENO, LAS VEGAS. Lies in GREAT BASIN, with the Sierra Nevada on W border. Most rivers (including HUMBOLDT) have no sea outlet. Mining main industry (silver, gold, copper, zinc, tungsten, mercury); also ranching, farming. Tourist trade important (esp. gambling and divorce centers of Reno and Las Vegas). Area not well known until explorations of J. C. FRÉMONT (1843–45). Part of Utah Territory (1850); estab. separately (1861) after Mormon difficulties with government, gold and silver strikes (see COMSTOCK LODE). Statehood rushed to aid passage of Thirteenth Amendment. Mining dominates state, but changes in price of minerals often shake economy. Atomic-weapons testing ground, U.S. Air Force bombing range NW of Las Vegas.

Nevada (nůvā'dů), city (pop. 8,009), SW Mo., W of Joplin. Shipping center for farm, oil, asphalt, coal area.

Nevada, University of: see RENO.

Nevers (nůvěr'), city (pop. 32,246), cap. of Nièvre dept., central France, on the Loire at mouth of the Nièvre. Pottery and china mfg. Has ducal palace (15th–16th cent.), Romanesque Church of St. Étienne (11th cent.), and cathedral (13th–16th cent.). The county of Nevers was inherited in 1384 by the house of Burgundy, was raised to a duchy in 1539, and later passed to a cadet line of the GONZAGA family. Annexed to the royal domain in 1669, the duchy became the Nivernais prov. of France, an agr., stock-raising region. The ducal title, purchased by Cardinal Mazarin 1659, remained in his family.

Neville (nĕ'vĭl), English noble family. One of the most powerful in country, they shared control of N with the Percy family. **Ralph Neville,** 1st **earl of Westmorland,** 1364–1425, was married to half-sister of Henry IV. Supported Henry against Richard II and helped put down Percy revolts in 1403 and 1405. His daughter Cicely was mother of Edward IV and Richard III. His grandson, **Richard Neville, earl of Warwick,** 1428–71, was chief baronial figure in Wars of the ROSES. By marriage he inherited huge Beauchamp estates. Fought for Yorkists and was principal man in early reign of EDWARD IV. After king's marriage (1464) to Elizabeth Woodville, Warwick began to intrigue with duke of Clarence and fled to France. Invaded England (1470) and restored Henry VI. Edward secured aid from Burgundy and Warwick was defeated and slain in battle of Barnet.

Nevin, Ethelbert (Woodbridge), 1862–1901, American composer and pianist. He wrote popular songs, notably *My Rosary,* and composed a setting of Eugene Field's *Little Boy Blue.* Of his piano works, perhaps *Narcissus* is best known.

Nevins, Allan, 1890–, American historian. Author and editor of many works on American scene. Twice won Pulitzer Prize for biography: with *Grover Cleveland* (1932) and *Hamilton Fish* (1936). *Ordeal of the Union* (2 vols., 1947) and *The Emergence of Lincoln* (2 vols., 1950) comprise history of years 1847–61.

Nevis, Ben, Scotland: see BEN NEVIS.

New Albany, city (pop. 29,346), SE Ind., on Ohio R. opposite Louisville, Ky., settled c.1800. Mfg. of wood products and auto parts.

New Alesund: see SPITSBERGEN.

New Amsterdam, early name of NEW YORK city, Dutch colony (1625–64), cap. of NEW NETHERLAND.

New Archangel, Alaska: see SITKA.

Newark, Ont.: see NIAGARA-ON-THE-LAKE.

Newark. 1 (nōō'ärk", nū'–) Town (pop. 6,713), NW Del., SW of Marshallton; settled before 1700. Vulcanized fiber and packaged food. Seat of Univ. of Delaware (land-grant, state supported; coed.), which dates from a Pa. Presbyterian school, founded 1743 and moved to Newark 1765. Chartered 1769 by the Penns as Newark Acad., it became a college 1833 and was called Delaware Col. 1843–1921. **2** (nōō'ůrk, nū'–) City (pop. 438,776), NE N.J., on Passaic R. and Newark Bay, and W of lower Manhattan; settled from Conn. by Treat and others 1666. Largest city in N.J.; important industrial, transshipping, and commercial metropolis. Port Newark and Newark Airport (1929) are administered by Port of New York Authority. Rapid industrial growth of 19th cent. spurred by improved rail and water transportation. Jewelry industry began 1801 and insurance 1810; celluloid first made here 1872 by J. W. Hyatt. Diverse mfg. (electrical equipment, machinery, wire and metal products, paper and leather goods, chemicals, paint, fountain pens) and meat packing. Seat of Newark Colleges of RUTGERS UNIVERSITY, Newark Col. of Engineering (state, city supported; mainly for men; opened 1919). Has Plume House (c.1710; probably city's oldest house); Trinity Cathedral (1810); Sacred Heart Cathedral (begun 1898); First Presbyterian Church (1791); Newark Public Library (1888), developed mainly by J. C. DANA, who founded Newark Mus. 1909; statue of Lincoln (in front of courthouse) and *Wars of America* (1926; in Military Park), both by Borglum. Birthplace of Aaron Burr and Stephen Crane. **3** Village (pop. 10,295), W central N.Y., on the Barge Canal and SE of Rochester. Nurseries; mfg. of paper, chemicals, and metal products. **4** City (pop. 34,275), central Ohio, on Licking R. and E of Columbus; plotted 1801. Trade center for agr. area. Mfg. of wire and cables and electrical equipment. Has many Indian mounds.

New Bedford, city (pop. 109,189), SE Mass., on harbor at mouth of Acushnet R. on Buzzards Bay; settled 1640. Nearly destroyed by British in Revolution. World's greatest whaling port (first whaler fitted out 1755) until mid-19th cent. Then cotton mfg. grew; mfg. also of electrical equipment, tools, rubber goods, glass, and machinery. Has Jonathan Bourne whaling museum. Seamen's Bethel (1832) is a scene in Melville's *Moby Dick.*

New Bern, city (pop. 15,812), E N.C., port and trading center at junction of Neuse and Trent rivers; settled (1710) by Swiss. Early colonial cap., seat of first provincial convention 1774. Has Tyrone Palace, capitol, and governor's mansion. Taken by Union troops, March, 1862.

Newberry, Walter Loomis, 1804–68, American merchant and banker. His numerous philanthropies include the **Newberry Library** in Chicago, an internationally known free reference library, specializing in history, literature, music, philology.

Newberry. 1 Village (pop. 2,802), E Upper Peninsula, N Mich., between Sault Ste Marie and Munising. Resort hq. for Tahquamenon Falls. **2** Town (pop. 7,546), N central S.C., NW of Columbia, in farm and dairy area. Mfg. of cotton goods and mattresses.

Newberry Library: see NEWBERRY, WALTER LOOMIS.

Newbery, John, 1713–67, English author and first publisher of children's books. Possibly wrote *The History of Little Goody Two-Shoes* (1765). Newbery medal (for children's book) estab. in his honor in 1922.

New Braunfels (broun'fŭlz), city (pop. 12,210), S central Texas, on Guadalupe R. and NE of San Antonio; settled 1845 by Germans. Beauty of Comal R. makes city a resort. It has power plants and mfg. of clothing, textiles, furniture, and flour. Near by is Landa Park.

New Brighton, borough (pop. 9,535), W Pa., NW of Pittsburgh. Mfg. of clay and metal products and machinery. Merrick library and museum is here.

New Britain, industrial city (pop. 73,726), central Conn., SW of Hartford; settled 1686–90. Metalworking (esp. tin, brass) center since early 18th cent., it is known as the Hardware City.

New Britain, volcanic island (14,600 sq. mi.; pop. c.80,000), SW Pacific, largest of BISMARCK ARCHIPELAGO. Mountainous, with active volcanoes and hot springs. In NE is Rabaul, which was key Japanese naval base, 1942–44.

New Brunswick, province (27,473 sq. mi.; with water surface 27,985 sq. mi.; pop. 515,697), E Canada; cap. FREDERICTON. A Maritime Prov., its coastline on the Gulf of St. Lawrence (E) and the Bay of Fundy (S) provides excellent fishing and shipping facilities. The rolling countryside is marked by ridges, lakes, and navigable rivers (St. John, St. Croix, Miramichi). Lumbering, paper milling, and allied industries (operated largely by hydroelectric power) are main activities. Fuel resources include much untapped water power, coal, gas, and oil. Fertile river valleys and reclaimed marshlands support dairying and agr. (grains, potatoes, berries, fruit). Abundant fish and game exist. Seaside towns and islands (e.g., GRAND MANAN and CAMPOBELLO) are summer resorts. Trade flows through ports of SAINT JOHN and MONCTON, implemented by railroad connections throughout the province, E to N.S., and W to Que. Province visited by Cabots 1497. First settlement made at mouth of the St. Croix by de Monts and Champlain 1604. During the early period when both France and England claimed the area, all of N.S. and N.B. was called ACADIA by the French and Nova Scotia by the English. British control gained by the Peace of Utrecht (1713–14) and Acadians forcibly expelled. New Brunswick became separate colony 1784 after United Empire Loyalists sought haven here. Responsible government granted 1849. Accepted confederation with other provinces to form dominion of Canada 1867.

New Brunswick, city (pop. 38,811), E N.J. on Raritan R. at E terminus of old Delaware and Raritan Canal and SW of Newark; settled 1681. Grew as commercial and grain-shipping center. British troops quartered here in Revolution; Washington stopped here 1776. Industry (rubber, chemicals, textiles) began in 19th cent.; medical- and surgical-supply factory opened 1886; mfg. also of machinery and motor vehicles. Seat of RUTGERS UNIVERSITY and affiliated New Jersey Col. for Women and New Jersey State Col. of Agriculture. U.S. Camp Kilmer is near. Joyce Kilmer's birthplace and several pre-Revolutionary houses are preserved.

New Brunswick, University of: see FREDERICTON.

Newburgh, city (pop. 31,956), SE N.Y., on W bank of the Hudson opposite Beacon; settled 1709 by Palatines, resettled 1752 by English and Scotch. Mfg. of textiles, rugs, and machinery. Former whaling town, now deep-water port. Hasbrouck House was Washington's hq., April, 1782–Aug., 1783. Continental Army was disbanded here.

Newburyport, city (pop. 14,111), NE Mass., on Merrimack R. just above its mouth; settled 1635. Former shipping, whaling, and shipbuilding center. Mfg. of shoes, silverware, and electrical supplies. Birthplace of W. L. Garrison.

New Caledonia, volcanic island (8,548 sq. mi.; pop. c.48,000), SW Pacific, on California–New Zealand air route. Has important mining industry (esp. nickel and chrome). Coffee is chief crop. Natives are blend of Melanesian and Polynesian; indentured laborers are Javanese and Tonkinese. Discovered 1774 by Capt. Cook. Claimed 1835 by the French, who used it 1864–94 as penal colony. In World War II island was Free French; occupied 1942 by U.S. forces to prevent Japanese invasion. Chief town, Nouméa, is cap. of French overseas territory of **New Caledonia** (9,401 sq. mi.; pop. c.60,000), which comprises New Caledonia isl., Loyalty Isls., and several small islands.

New Canaan, residential town (pop. 8,001), SW Conn., NE of Stamford; settled c.1700.

New Castile, Spain: see CASTILE.

Newcastle, Thomas Pelham-Holles, duke of, 1693–1768, English politician. Prime minister 1754–56, his weak policy in Seven Years War caused his fall. Nominal head of Pitt-Newcastle administration 1757–62.

Newcastle, William Cavendish, duke of, 1592–1676, English soldier and politician. Gave financial aid (nearly £1,000,000 in all) and military aid to royalist cause in Puritan Revolution.

Newcastle, city (pop. 127,138), New South Wales, Australia, on Port Hunter (Newcastle Harbour); center of largest coal-mining area in Australia. Founded 1797. Exports coal, wheat, and wool.

New Castle. 1 City (pop. 5,396), NE Del., on Delaware R. and S of Wilmington. Rayon, steel, aircraft. Stuyvesant built Fort Casimir near here, 1651. Successively held by Swedes, Dutch, English. Cap. of Three Lower Counties-on-the-Delaware, 1704–77. **2** City (pop. 18,271), E Ind., on Big Blue R. and S of Muncie, founded c.1820. Trade and distribution center in farm area. Mfg. of metal products. Birthplace of Wilbur Wright near by. **3** Town (pop. 583), SE N.H., on island in Portsmouth harbor (bridged to mainland). Has ruins of Fort Constitution, seized by colonists 1774. **4** City (pop. 48,834), W Pa., on Shenango R. and NNW of Pittsburgh; settled 1798. Mfg. of tin plates, metal products, and pottery. Near by is Cascade Park, summer amusement center.

Newcastle, city (pop. 3,395), NE Wyo., SW of Black Hills, in region of caves, canyons, and lakes. Ships livestock, lumber, oil products, and bentonite.

Newcastle-on-Tyne or **Newcastle-upon-Tyne,** county borough (pop. 291,723), co. seat of Northumberland, England, on Tyne R. Called Monkchester until the Conquest because of its many monastic settlements. Renamed for castle, built in 1080. Has Col. of Medicine and Armstrong Col. of Science, both affiliated with Univ. of Durham. Has great coal-shipping industry and is one of England's chief shipbuilding centers. Suffered severe depression in 1920s.

Newcastle-under-Lyme, municipal borough (pop. 70,028), Staffordshire, England, in the Potteries area. Has coal mines, potteries, and other industries.

New Church: see NEW JERUSALEM, CHURCH OF THE.

New College: see OXFORD UNIVERSITY.

Newcomb, Simon, 1835–1909, American astronomer, an authority on moon's motion. He constructed standard planetary system tables. He was known also as mathematician.

Newcomb College: see TULANE UNIVERSITY.

Newcomen, Thomas (nūkŭ'mŭn), 1663–1729, English inventor of early atmospheric steam engine similar to that patented (1698) by Thomas Savery. In partnership with Savery he later developed improved steam engine used to pump water.

New Concord, village (pop. 1,797), central Ohio, E of Zanesville. Seat of Muskingum Col. (Presbyterian; coed.; 1836).

New Cumberland, borough (pop. 6,204), S Pa., on Susquehanna R. opposite Harrisburg. Mfg. of textiles, hosiery, and tobacco products.

New Deal, expression commonly adopted to describe reform legislation enacted under F. D. Roosevelt's administration. U.S. Congress in special session (1933) enacted laws designed to combat the economic depression and to institute long-range social and economic reforms; set up many emergency organizations (e.g., NATIONAL RECOVERY ADMINISTRATION), some long-term organizations (e.g., TENNESSEE VALLEY AUTHORITY). Later Democratic Congresses expanded and modified these laws (e.g., SOCIAL SECURITY). Following adverse Supreme Court decisions, the President tried unsuccessfully to reorganize the Court (1937). New Deal, which had been especially supported by agrarian, liberal, and labor groups, was increasingly criticized, but most New Deal legislation was still intact after World War II.

New Delhi, India: see DELHI.

New Economic Policy (NEP), program for economic reconstruction of war-torn Russia, adopted by Lenin 1921. A temporary measure, it enlisted aid of non-Communists by restoring a limited system of private enterprise. Having accomplished its purpose, it was replaced in 1928 by the Five Year Plan.

New England, name applied to region comprising six states of NE U.S.—Maine, N.H., Vt., Mass., R.I., Conn. Region was so named in 17th cent. because of its resemblance to English coast. Partly cut off from rest of U.S. by Appalachian Mts. on W; land slopes gradually toward Atlantic Ocean and Long Isl. Sound. Connecticut R. is only large river. Generally rather barren soil encouraged development of commerce and fisheries along deeply indented coast line. Great shipbuilding center during era of wooden ships. Chief center of events leading to American Revolution; scene of Revolution's opening engagements. Threatened secession in War of 1812. Growth of mfg. (esp. cotton textiles) was rapid thereafter; region is now highly industrialized. It has long led in literary and educational activities. Geographic and early political conditions developed type known as Yankee—resourceful, thrifty, generous, self-governing.

New England Confederation, union for "mutual safety and welfare" formed in 1643 by colonies of Mass. Bay, Plymouth, Conn., and New Haven. Weakened by rivalry of colonies and advisory nature of league. Confederation declined after 1664 except for activity in King Philip's War.

New England Conservatory of Music: see BOSTON.

New England Primer, American schoolbook, first published before 1690; compiled by Benjamin Harris. Some 2,000,000 were sold during 18th cent.

New Forest, anc. royal hunting ground, Hampshire, England. Made a forest under William I. Since 1877 it has been a national park of 92,400 acres.

Newfoundland (nū″fŭndlănd′, nū′fŭndlănd″), island and easternmost province with LABRADOR as a dependency (excluding Lab., 42,734 sq. mi.; pop. 353,526), E Canada, in Atlantic Ocean at mouth of Gulf of St. Lawrence; cap. SAINT JOHN'S. Steep rocky cliffs edge a thousand inlets, with many islands offshore. The wooded plateau of the interior is broken by lakes and marshes where fur-bearing animals, waterfowl, and fish are abundant. Hydroelectric power is used for mfg. (paper, pulpwood) and mining (copper, gypsum, iron, zinc). Agr. is limited and much food must be imported. Fishing, particularly at the GRAND BANKS, dominates the economy. Population, concentrated on Avalon Peninsula, is predominantly of Irish and British extraction. N.F. is Britain's senior colony, discovered by Cabot 1497 and formally claimed 1583 by Sir Humphrey Gilbert. France contested this claim until the Peace of Utrecht (1713–14) gave sovereignty to England, with France maintaining special fishing rights to 1904. N.F. was awarded jurisdiction over Lab. 1763–64 and again in 1809. Representative government estab. 1832 and responsible government 1855. Islanders rejected entry into Canada in 1869 and were refused it in 1890s because of their precarious financial position. In World War I the island over-extended its economy and sought aid from a commission from the United Kingdom. The Amulree Report was issued, responsible government was suspended (1934), and a commission appointed to administer the government. During World War II N.F. became an important Canadian and U.S. air and radio base. The Atlantic Charter was signed in Newfoundland waters 1941. Voted for union with Canada 1948.

Newfoundland dog: see SHEEP DOGS.

New France: see CANADA.

Newgate (nū′gĭt), former London prison, dating from 12th cent. Scene of efforts to improve prison conditions. Outside executions held here until 1868. Torn down in 1902.

New Georgia: see SOLOMON ISLANDS.

New Glasgow, town (pop. 9,933), N N.S., Canada, port on East R. and NE of Halifax, in coal region. Mfg. of steel products, boilers, and bricks.

New Goa, Portuguese India: see GOA.

New Granada (grŭnä′dŭ), former Spanish colony, N South America, which included at its greatest extent modern Colombia, Ecuador, Panama, and Venezuela. It was for a time (18th–early 19th cent.) a viceroyalty.

New Guinea (gĭ′nē) or **Papua** (pă′pūŭ, pä′po͞oä), island (c.304,200 sq. mi.; pop. 1,500,000), except for Greenland largest in world, separated from N Australia by Torres Strait and Arafura Sea. Separated into Netherlands (or Dutch) New Guinea (W), Territory of Papua (SE), and Territory of New Guinea (NE). Island is c.1,500 mi. long and 400 mi. wide. Largely tropical jungle with vast mountain ranges rising to more than 16,000 ft. Inhabited by Melanesians, Negritos, and Papuans. Fauna is like that of Australia and consists mainly of marsupials and monotremes. Chief product is copra. Gold is mined in E area. Visited early 16th cent. by Spanish and Portuguese explorers, who were followed 17th–18th cent. by the Dutch, English, and Germans. In World War II island was invaded 1942 by Japan and gallantly defended by small Allied force based at Port Moresby. Wholly regained by Allies July, 1944.

New Guinea, Territory of (93,000 sq. mi.; pop. c.725,000), SW Pacific. Includes NE New Guinea, BISMARCK ARCHIPELAGO, and two of Solomon Isls. (Buka and Bougainville). Territory belonged to Germany from 1884 to 1914, when it was occupied by Australian forces. Mandated 1920 to Australia, which won UN trusteeship over it in 1947.

New Hampshire, state (9,304 sq. mi., pop. 533,242), NE U.S.; one of Thirteen Colonies; cap. CONCORD. MANCHESTER is largest city. Hilly, wooded section with lakes except for rolling seaboard in SE. Connecticut R. forms W boundary. Mfg. of shoes, paper and wood products, cotton and woolen goods, machinery; farming (poultry, dairying, potatoes, apples); lumbering; fishing; mining (granite, feldspar, mica); resorts. To N are WHITE MOUNTAINS, PRESIDENTIAL RANGE. In S are isolated peaks ("monadnocks"). MERRIMACK R. much used for power. Patent for region given to John MASON in 1620s. After boundary disputes, royal colony estab. 1679. Further difficulties arose over NEW HAMPSHIRE GRANTS. Cast ninth, and deciding, vote in ratification of U.S. Constitution. DARTMOUTH COLLEGE CASE argued successfully by famous native son, Daniel WEBSTER. Pres. Franklin Pierce was born here. Republican party came into power after Civil War, has usually stayed there since. Conservation measures, water-power projects added in 20th cent. Trend away from one-industry towns, toward broader economy since depression of 1930s.

New Hampshire, University of: see DURHAM.

New Hampshire Grants, early name for present Vt., given because most early settlers came in under land grants from Benning Wentworth, governor of N.H. Conflict over boundary with N.Y. led to organizing of GREEN MOUNTAIN BOYS and to violence.

New Harmony, town (pop. 1,360), SW Ind., on Wabash R. and WNW of Evansville; founded 1815. Settled by HARMONY SOCIETY under George Rapp; holdings sold 1825 to Robert OWEN, who estab. communistic colony. Colony existed until 1828. Many Rappite buildings remain.

New Haven, city (pop. 164,443), S Conn., on harbor on Long Isl. Sound. Founded 1637–38 as strict Puritan theocracy, it joined Conn. colony in 1664 and was joint cap. with Hartford 1701–1875. Raided by British in Revolution, blockaded in War of 1812. Was important sealing port in late 18th and early 19th cent. Now second largest Conn. city and an industrial center, it has mfg. of firearms, clocks, locks, toys, sewing machines, tools, and elevators; railroad shops. Seat of YALE UNIVERSITY. City centers on the old green, with three graceful early 19th-cent. churches. Has sandstone cliffs—West Rock, with Judges' Cave in which 2 regicides hid, and East Rock.

New Hebrides (hĕ'brĭdēz), island group (c.5,700 sq. mi.; pop. 44,750), S Pacific. Principal islands are Espiritu Santo (largest) and Efate (site of Vila, cap. of condominium). Mountainous and in malarial area. Natives are Melanesians. Products include copra, coffee, and mother-of-pearl. Discovered 1606 by the Portuguese. Governed jointly by Great Britain and France since 1887. In World War II, group supported the Free French.

New Hope, borough (pop. 1,066), SE Pa., on Delaware R. and NW of Trenton. Artist colony with old stone farmhouses.

New Hyde Park, residential village (pop. 7,349), on NW Long Isl., SE N.Y., near Mineola.

New Iberia (ībēr'ēů), city (pop. 16,467), S La., on Bayou Teche; settled c.1779 by Spanish. Processes sugar cane, rice, vegetables, and sea food. Oil fields and salt mines (Avery Isl.) are near. Has fine plantation house.

Newington, town (pop. 9,110), central Conn., near Hartford; settled in late 17th cent.

New Ireland, volcanic island (3,340 sq. mi.; pop. c.19,000), SW Pacific, in BISMARCK ARCHIPELAGO. Formerly called New Mecklenburg.

New Jersey, state (7,522 sq. mi.; pop. 4,835,-329), E U.S.; one of Thirteen Colonies; cap. TRENTON. Other main cities are NEWARK, JERSEY CITY, CAMDEN, PATERSON, ELIZABETH. Bounded S and W by Delaware R. and Delaware Bay; E by Hudson R., New York Bay, Atlantic Ocean. Industry concentrated mainly in Triassic lowlands region; coastal plains in S have farms, ocean resorts. Highly developed transportation system. Mfg. of chemicals, food products, textiles, machinery, rubber and leather goods, plastics; also dyeing, shipbuilding, printing and publishing. Has refineries, copper smelting plants. Farming (truck, poultry, dairying); mining (zinc, marl, clay). Resort center. First settled by Dutch and Swedes. Area seized by English in 1664. W N.J. granted to Lord John Berkeley, E N.J. to Sir George CARTERET. Period marked by confusion over land claims; rule reverted to crown in 1702. Important center in American Revolution (e.g., battles of Trenton, PRINCETON, and MONMOUTH). Third state to ratify Constitution. Next 50 years brought enormous expansion, change from agr. to industry. Woodrow Wilson sponsored reform movement as governor 1910–12). Production soared during World War II. Adopted new constitution in 1947.

New Jersey College for Women: see RUTGERS UNIVERSITY.

New Jersey Turnpike, part of N.J. highway system extending 115 mi. NE from Deepwater on Delaware R. to Ridgefield Park, near the Hudson; toll road.

New Jerusalem, Church of the, or **New Church,** religious body estab. by followers of SWEDENBORG. First congregation founded in London (1788), general conference in 1789. In U.S. teachings were introduced (1784) by James Glen. New Church society formed (1792) in Baltimore with general convention in 1817. In 1890 separatists estab. group named (1897) General Church of the New Jerusalem. Polity is modified episcopacy, with much freedom in local societies.

New Kensington, city (pop. 25,146), SW Pa., on Allegheny R. and NNE of Pittsburgh; laid out 1891. Has large aluminum plant and mfg. of magnesium sheets and glass products.

New Lanark, Scotland: see LANARK.

Newlands, Francis Griffith, 1848–1917, U.S. Representative from Nev. (1893–1903); U.S. Senator (1903–17). Wrote Reclamation Act of 1902 and Newlands Act of 1913 concerning labor problems.

Newlands project, irrigation and power development, W. Nev.; estab. 1903–8. Includes two dams on the Carson (Carson River, 1905; Lahontan, 1915) and two on the Truckee (Derby, 1905; Lake Tahoe, 1913).

New London, city (pop. 30,551), SE Conn., on harbor at Thames R. mouth on Long Isl. Sound; laid out 1646 by John Winthrop. Mfg. of metal goods and machinery. Maritime center, with U.S. coast guard academy (1932). U.S. submarine base is across river at Groton. Privateering port in Revolution, it was partly burned by Benedict Arnold in 1781. Blockaded in War of 1812. Flourished as shipbuilding and whaling port in 19th cent. Has New London Lighthouse (1760). Seat of Connecticut Col. for women (nonsectarian; chartered 1911, opened 1915). Annual Yale-Harvard boat races here.

New Madrid, city (pop. 2,726), SE Mo., on the Mississippi and SW of Cairo, Ill.; laid out 1789 by George Morgan. In Civil War, Federals captured it before taking ISLAND No. 10 (1862).

Newman, John Henry, 1801–90, English cardinal, one of the leaders in the OXFORD MOVEMENT, an eminent writer. Deeply religious from early youth, he was ordained in the Church of England (1824) and became tutor at Oriel Col. (1826) and vicar of St. Mary's, Oxford (1827). In 1832 he resigned his tutorship and went on a Mediterranean tour. While on this journey he wrote many hymns, including *Lead, Kindly Light.* On his return he threw himself into the religious discussion begun by KEBLE, began (1833) his influential series of *Tracts for the Times,* and offered guidance to the Oxford movement. Reading an article by WISEMAN turned his thoughts to Roman Catholicism, and his

Tract 90 (1841) outraged Anglicans by attempting to demonstrate that the Thirty-nine Articles were consistent with Catholicism. His conversion continued and he was received in the Roman Catholic Church in 1845, went to Rome and joined the Oratorians, and returned to England (1847), where he finally founded an Oratory at Edgbaston (near Birmingham). He was one of the most influential English Catholics of all time, both through his personal activities and his writing. His *Idea of a University Defined* (1873) grew out of a much earlier abortive attempt to found a Catholic university, stressing moral training. His *Apologia pro Vita Sua,* begun in 1864 to answer Charles Kingsley's slurs at the Roman Catholic clergy, is a masterpiece of religious autobiography. His many essays are models of lucid prose. He and another English Catholic leader, Henry Edward MANNING, disagreed on many matters, especially education, and their quarrel reached a height when Newman opposed enunciation of the dogma of papal infallibility (but not the dogma itself). The dust later settled, and Newman, made a cardinal in 1879, was universally revered at the time of his death.

Newmarket, town (pop. 5,356), S Ont., Canada, on Holland R. and N of Toronto. Here are tanneries, dairies, and furniture factories.

Newmarket, urban district (pop. 10,184), Suffolk West, England; racing center since early 17th cent.

New Market, town, N Va., in Shenandoah Valley, NE of Staunton. In Civil War battle here Union forces were defeated (May 15, 1864). Near by are limestone caverns.

New Mexico, state (121,511 sq. mi.; pop. 681,187), SW U.S.; admitted 1912 as 47th state; cap. SANTA FE. ALBUQUERQUE largest city. Main rivers are RIO GRANDE, SAN JUAN, PECOS. Grazing lands broken by mountain ranges, canyons, deserts, mesas. Cattle, sheep raising; agr. (grains, beans, potatoes, apples); mining (potash, copper, petroleum, natural gas, coal, lead, zinc). Spanish settlements destroyed by Apache revolt (1676) and by Pueblo uprising (1680). Diego de Vargas reestab. Spanish dominance in 1692. Became Mexican province 1821. Opening of SANTA FE TRAIL brought U.S. settlement. Went to U.S. after MEXICAN WAR. Occupied by Confederate troops, then by Union forces in Civil War. Indian warfare largely ended with surrender of Geronimo in 1886. Cattlemen opposed farmers and sheepherders. Atomic research laboratory at Los ALAMOS, testing ground at ALAMOGORDO. Climate, natural and historic sights make N.Mex. a resort and health center.

New Mexico, University of: see ALBUQUERQUE.

New Mexico College of Agriculture and Mechanic Arts: see LAS CRUCES.

New Milford. 1 Town (pop. 5,799), W Conn., on Housatonic R. and N of Danbury. Has Canterbury School for boys. Mgf. of metal products and textiles. **2** Residential borough (pop. 6,006), NE N.J., N of Hackensack.

Newnan, city (pop. 8,218), W Ga., SW of Atlanta. Livestock market. Has textile and lumber mills.

New Netherland, territory included in indefinite commercial grant by Holland to Dutch West India Co. in 1621. Principal settlement after 1625 was at New Amsterdam (later New York city), purchased from Indians. Territory taken by English in 1664.

Newnham College (nū'nŭm), affiliated with Cambridge Univ.; for women. Organized 1873, it has been a college since 1875. In 1881 some privileges of the university were open to women; degrees have been given only since 1921.

New Orleans (ôr'lēŭnz), city (pop. 570,445), SE La., on great bend of the Mississippi (Huey P. Long Bridge here), 107 mi. from its mouth by water; on subtropical lowlands protected by levees; near L. Pontchartrain. Largest city of the South, it is a major U.S. port of entry. Imports include coffee, sugar, bananas; exports include lumber, petroleum products, machinery. Has coastwise traffic (esp. on Intracoastal Waterway) and heavy rail and air traffic. Mfg. of twine, furniture, construction materials, and foodstuffs; sugar refining. Platted 1718 by sieur de Bienville. Ceded to Spain 1762 and back to France briefly before Louisiana Purchase 1803. French-Creole influence still felt. Andrew Jackson defeated British here, Jan. 8, 1815, in War of 1812. City became wealthy through cotton and slave trade and entered lavish period. Then as now, Negroes comprise large segment, contributing to exotic flavor. Golden era ended with fall of city (1862) to Adm. D. G. FARRAGUT in Civil War and subsequent occupation by B. F. BUTLER. Colorful past, old buildings of French Quarter (Vieux Carré), superb food, and famous Mardi Gras festival draw visitors, artists, and writers. Has parks, museums (esp. Isaac Delgado Mus. of Art), symphony, opera. Seat of TULANE UNIVERSITY; Loyola Univ. (R.C., Jesuit, partly coed.; opened 1911, chartered 1912, successor to Loyola Col., 1904, and Col. of Immaculate Conception, 1849); Dillard Univ., for Negroes (coed., chartered 1930, opened 1935; named for J. H. Dillard); and Xavier Univ. (R.C.; coed.; 1915).

New Philadelphia, city (pop. 12,948), E central Ohio, on Tuscarawas R. and S of Canton; founded 1804. Mfg. of machinery, clay products, and enamelware.

Newport, Christopher, 1565?–1617, English mariner. Commanded several early expeditions to Virginia, bringing colonists to Jamestown 1607–8.

Newport. 1 Municipal borough (pop. 20,426), cap. of Isle of Wight, England. **2** County borough (pop. 105,285), Monmouthshire, England, on Usk R. Has extensive docks and is one of Great Britain's chief coal and iron exporting points.

Newport. 1 City (pop. 6,254), NE Ark., on White R. Rail and trade center for agr. (notably pecans) area. Mfg. of button blanks. **2** City (pop. 31,044), N Ky., on Ohio R. opposite Cincinnati and at mouth of Licking R. opposite Covington; laid out 1791, annexed Clifton 1935. Mfg. of metal products. Fort Thomas near by. **3** Town (pop. 2,190), S central Maine, on Sebasticook L. W of Bangor. Fishing resort. **4** Town (pop. 5,131), SW N.H., E of Claremont. Mfg. of shoes and woolens. **5** Resort city (pop. 37,564), on SW RHODE ISLAND, SE R.I.; settled 1639 by William CODDINGTON. Newport and Portsmouth (united 1640) joined Providence and Warwick 1654. Newport was joint cap. of R.I. with Providence until 1900. Shipbuilding (after 1646) and "triangular trade" in rum, Negro slaves, molasses brought colonial prosperity. British occupation temporarily ruined town's economy (1776–79). Haven for refugees—Friends, Jews, Seventh-Day Baptists—in 17th cent. Since 19th cent. it has been fashionable resort of the very rich. Holds polo, tennis, boating meets. Has Trinity Church (1726; Episcopal), Touro Synagogue (1763; oldest in U.S.; national historic site since 1946), Redwood Library (1747), brick market house or city hall (1760), old colony house or statehouse (1739). Old Stone Mill is thought to be either Benedict Arnold's gristmill or a Norse relic. Near by are U.S. Fort Adams, naval training station, naval war college, torpedo and coast guard stations. **6** Town (pop. 3,892), E Tenn., on Pigeon R. and E of Knoxville. Near John Sevier Preserve and Great Smoky Mountains Natl. Park. **7** Resort city (pop. 5,217), N Vt., on L. Memphremagog; settled 1793. Important gateway between Canada and U.S.

Newport Beach, resort city (pop. 12,120), S Calif., SE of Long Beach and on landlocked Newport Bay.

Newport News, city (pop. 42,358), SE Va., a port of HAMPTON ROADS with harbor at mouth of James R.; settled 1611. A shipping center, with dry docks and shipbuilding plants, it has railroad shops and mfg. of paper, machinery, and foundry products. Terminus of Chesapeake and Ohio RR since 1880.

New Richmond, village (pop. 1,960), SW Ohio, on Ohio R. and SE of Cincinnati. Just S at Point Pleasant is birthplace of U. S. Grant.

New River, rising in W N.C. and flowing c.320 mi. NE, N through SW Va. into W.Va. to form the Kanawha with Gauley R. Impounded by Bluestone Dam near Hinton, W.Va.

New Rochelle (rōshĕl'), city (pop. 59,725), SE N.Y., on Long Isl. Sound and E of Mt. Vernon; settled 1688 by Huguenots. Yachting, fishing center; mfg. of plumbing and heating equipment, surgical dressings. Here is Thomas Paine's house and memorial. Seat of Col. of New Rochelle (R.C.; for women; 1904).

news agency, local, national, international, or technical agency which gathers and distributes news. Major U.S. agencies are Associated Press (AP); United Press Associations (UP), the Scripps-Howard agency; and Internatl. News Service (INS), the Hearst agency. They employ reporters and have exchange agreements. Foreign agencies include Reuters (London), Agence Havas (Paris), Wolff Agency (Berlin), Tass (USSR). Most European agencies are government controlled or subsidized.

New Salem, restored historic village, central Ill., NW of Springfield and on Sangamon R. Lincoln's home was here 1831–37. Site now state park. Settled 1828, declined rapidly after 1839. Small museum has pioneer relics.

New Sarum, Wiltshire, England: see SALISBURY.

New School for Social Research, in Manhattan borough of New York city; nonsectarian, coed.; opened 1919 for adult education. Founders included C. A. Beard, John Dewey, J. H. Robinson, Thorstein Veblen, Alvin Johnson. Its divisions include graduate faculty of political and social science (formerly called Univ. in Exile).

New Shoreham, R.I.: see BLOCK ISLAND.

New Siberian Islands, archipelago, 11,000 sq. mi., between Laptev and East Siberian seas of Arctic Ocean, belonging to Yakut Autonomous SSR, RSFSR. Includes Anjou, Lyakhov and DeLong groups. Sparsely settled, ice and snow covered, with scanty tundra.

New Smyrna Beach (smûr'nů), resort city (pop. 5,775), NE Fla., S of Daytona Beach and on coastal lagoon. Fishing, shrimping, citrus-fruit-packing, and rail center. Has ruins of Spanish Franciscan mission (1696). Recolonized 1767, abandoned 1776, and resettled c.1803.

New South Wales, state (309,433 sq. mi.; pop. 2,985,464), SE Australia; cap. SYDNEY. The Pacific is on E, Tasman Sea on SE, Victoria on S, South Australia on W, and Queensland on N. Area was visited 1770 by Capt. James Cook, who proclaimed British sovereignty over E coast of Australia. Original colony of New South Wales included Tasmania, South Australia, Victoria, Queensland, Northern Territory, and New Zealand. These territories were made separate colonies 1825–63. State has temperate climate. Murray R. waters much of S area. Rich mineral resources include coal, gold, iron, copper, silver, and lead. Exports of wool, meat, wheat, and coal are important. Within the state is AUSTRALIAN CAPITAL TERRITORY.

New Spain, Spanish viceroyalty in North America, created 1535 under Antonio de MENDOZA. Included present republic of Mexico, but indefinite N boundaries varied with decline of Spanish influence.

newspaper, publication issued periodically, usually daily or weekly, to convey news. Modern newspaper arose in 17th cent. with widespread use of printing. First English newspaper was Nathaniel Butter's *Weekly Newes* (1622–41). First French newspaper was the *Gazette* (founded 1631). In 18th cent. many journals of high literary merit were published; in 19th cent. newspapers began to reach the masses. Today newspapers range from the sober *Times* of London and the New York *Times* to tabloid newspapers of a sensational nature.

Newstead Abbey (nū'stĭd, -stĕd), Nottinghamshire, England, by Sherwood Forest. Founded (1170) by Henry II to atone for the murder of Thomas à Becket. Byron inherited the estate (1798); later sold it.

New Stone Age: see NEOLITHIC PERIOD.

New Sweden, Swedish colony (1638–55) on Delaware R., including parts of present Pa., N.J., and Del. Tinicum Isl. became cap. in 1643. Colony captured by Peter STUYVESANT for Dutch (1655).

newt, name for certain tailed amphibians

smaller than related salamander. Common spotted newt (pond newt or red eft) is found in U.S., parts of W U.S., and Canada. Gill-breathing larva emerges as land animal that matures in two to three years, then lives in water, rising to surface for air.

New Territories: see HONG KONG.

New Testament, the distinctively Christian portion of the Bible, consisting of 27 books dating from earliest Christian times. There are four biographies of Jesus called Gospels: MATTHEW, MARK, LUKE, and JOHN; a history of missionary activity, the ACTS OF THE APOSTLES; 21 letters or epistles named either for their addressee or for their author: ROMANS, 1 and 2 CORINTHIANS, GALATIANS, EPHESIANS, PHILIPPIANS, COLOSSIANS, 1 and 2 THESSALONIANS, 1 and 2 TIMOTHY, TITUS, PHILEMON, HEBREWS, JAMES, 1 and 2 PETER, 1, 2, and 3 JOHN, and JUDE; and finally a prophecy, the REVELATION or Apocalypse. All these are now accepted as canon by all major Christian churches. Other books considered canonical by many but finally rejected were the epistles of St. Ignatius and St. Clement and the Shepherd of Hermas. For other gospels, epistles, and prophecies, see PSEUDEPIGRAPHA.

New Thought, philosophico-religious movement based on "creative power of constructive thinking." Originating in healing practices of P. P. Quimby and mental science of W. F. Evans, Swedenborgian minister, it has evolved into optimistic philosophy of life. Name was adopted in 1890s, first annual convention held 1894. Internatl. New Thought Alliance was formed 1914. Unlike Christian Science, New Thought accepts existence of matter, but only as expression of mind. Central idea is that man is spirit or mind and by thought can so mold body and circumstances as to achieve his desires.

Newton, Sir Charles Thomas, 1816–94, English archaeologist. Discovered site of Halicarnassus. Keeper of Greek and Roman antiquities, British Mus. (1861–85).

Newton, Sir Isaac, 1642–1727, English physicist, philosopher. In his experiments on light he used the prism to break white light into colors of spectrum and recombined the colors to form white light; invented a reflecting telescope. He formulated the law of GRAVITATION and laws of MOTION.

Newton, John, 1725–1807, English clergyman and hymn writer. Curate of Olney, Buckinghamshire (from 1764). With William Cowper he published *Olney Hymns* (1779).

Newton. 1 City (pop. 11,723), central Iowa, ENE of Des Moines; settled 1846. Washing machines. **2** City (pop. 11,590), S central Kansas, N of Wichita; founded 1871. Boomed as cattle town (1871–73), when it was railhead for Chisholm Trail. In early 1870s German Mennonites from Russia brought seed for what became first hard winter wheat in Kansas. Now railway division point in grain area. Bethel Col. is near. **3** City (pop. 81,994), E Mass., on Charles R. and W of Boston; settled before 1640. City is aggregate of chiefly residential villages, but has mfg. of radio supplies, textiles, paper and rubber goods, and machinery. **4** Town (pop. 5,781), NW N.J., NW of Morristown. Dairy center. Near by is Little Flower Monastery (Benedictine). **5** Town (pop. 6,039), W central N.C., NW of Charlotte. Mfg. of furniture and textiles.

New Toronto, W suburb of Toronto (pop. 11,194), S Ont., Canada, on L. Ontario. Rubber and tire mfg.

Newtown, town (pop. 7,448), SW Conn., N of Bridgeport. Mfg. of rubber, plastic, paper, and wire products.

New Ulm (ŭlm), city (pop. 9,348), S Minn., on Minnesota R. and NW of Mankato. Farm trade center with dairy products. Harbored refugees, defended by C. E. Flandrau, in 1862 Sioux uprising.

New Waterford, town (pop. 10,423), NE N.S., Canada, on NE Cape Breton Isl., NE of Sydney. Coal-mining center and fishing port.

New Westminster, city (pop. 28,639), SW B.C., Canada, on Fraser R. and ESE of Vancouver; founded 1859 as Queensborough. Major year-round port and base of Fraser R. fishing fleet. Varied industries include oil refining, processing of food and lumber, and distilling. Seat of Columbia and St. Louis colleges. Was cap. of B.C. until union of B.C. with the former crown colony of Vancouver Isl.

New Windsor, Berkshire, England: see WINDSOR.

New York, state (47,576 sq. mi.; pop. 14,830,192), E U.S.; one of Thirteen Colonies; cap. ALBANY. NEW YORK city, BUFFALO, ROCHESTER, SYRACUSE, YONKERS, UTICA, SCHENECTADY are other chief cities. Bounded NE by L. Champlain; SE by LONG ISLAND SOUND, Atlantic Ocean; W by L. Erie, NIAGARA R. (with NIAGARA FALLS), L. Ontario; N by St. Lawrence R. Main waterways are HUDSON R., MOHAWK R., NEW YORK STATE BARGE CANAL. CATSKILL MOUNTAINS are in SE, ADIRONDACK MOUNTAINS in N. FINGER LAKES are in W hill country. Mfg. of clothing, machinery, metal products, textiles, chemicals, paper, electrical and scientific equipment; printing and publishing; food processing. Farming (dairying, fruits, truck, grains); mining (natural gas, oil, lead, zinc, salt, talc, limestone); fishing; tourism. IROQUOIS CONFEDERACY dominated area before white man. Dutch West India Co. (on claims of Henry HUDSON) founded NEW NETHERLAND; English (on claims of John CABOT) seized area from Peter STUYVESANT in 1664, renaming region New York. Scene of much fighting in American Revolution (see CROWN POINT; LONG ISLAND, BATTLE OF; SARATOGA CAMPAIGN). New Yorkers such as Alexander HAMILTON, John JAY, and Gouverneur MORRIS were important political figures after Revolution. Old landed families, such as LIVINGSTON family, retained much power, but the ERIE CANAL (1825) gave impetus to early industrialization. New York city grew to be nation's metropolis, and conflict in "Empire State" between city and rural "upstate" appeared. Albany regency controlled politics 1820s to 1840s. Great industrial growth after Civil War brought political corruption (e.g., activities of W. M. TWEED, Roscoe CONKLING, and T. C. PLATT). Reform movements and social improvement measures were carried out in late 19th and early 20th cent.

Election of Thomas E. Dewey in 1942 brought Republican party back to power after Democratic governorships of Alfred E. Smith, F. D. Roosevelt, and Herbert H. Lehman.

New York, city (area with water surface c.365 sq. mi.; land only, 299; pop. 7,891,957), SE N.Y., largest city in U.S., on NEW YORK BAY at mouth of HUDSON R. Comprised of five boroughs, each coextensive with a county: MANHATTAN, the BRONX, QUEENS, BROOKLYN, Richmond (see STATEN ISLAND). The metropolitan area (1952 census, preliminary total pop. 12,831,914) includes industrial and residential parts of SE N.Y. and NE N.J. Many bridges and tunnels link the boroughs. With a magnificent natural harbor and over 500 mi. of water front, New York is largest port in the world. Extensive industries, chiefly consumer goods, are led by mfg. of clothing, textiles; printing and publishing; food and metal processing. Leading U.S. commercial (since 1840) and financial (stock exchange founded 1792) metropolis, it is a world center of banking (Bank of New York founded 1784 under Alexander Hamilton) and trade. With its vast array of cultural and educational resources, famous shops and restaurants, places of entertainment, striking architecture, colorful national neighborhoods, and rich historic background, New York is almost unparalleled. Began with settlement (NEW AMSTERDAM) made by Dutch on Manhattan isl. in 1625. British seized control 1664. City divided in its loyalties, but Washington's troops defended it until after battle of LONG ISLAND in Revolution. State cap. until 1797, first U.S. cap. under the Constitution (1789–90); Pres. Washington was inaugurated here. Until 1874, when portions of Westchester co. were annexed, city's boundaries were confined to present-day Manhattan. Charter of 1898 set up five boroughts of Greater New York. Flatiron Bldg., first skyscraper, completed 1902; first subway, 1904. Many planning and administrative bodies (e.g., PORT OF NEW YORK AUTHORITY, 1921; Municipal Housing Authority, 1934) have been set up to cope with problems of the vast metropolis. Seat of permanent UN hq.

New York, College of the City of, system organized 1929, including Brooklyn Col., at Flatbush, Brooklyn (coed.; opened 1930 by merging branches of City Col. and Hunter Col.); City Col., in Manhattan (mainly for men; chartered 1847; opened 1849, through Townsend Harris's efforts, as Free Acad.; granted degrees after 1854), with Lewisohn Stadium (summer musical performances); Hunter Col., in Manhattan and the Bronx (first free college for women; opened 1870 as Normal Col., chartered 1888, renamed 1914); and Queens Col. at Flushing, Queens (coed.; opened 1937).

New York, State University of, founded by N.Y. state legislature in 1948. Consists of colleges, technical institutes, and professional schools in different parts of the state, administered by single board of 15 trustees.

New York, University of the State of, unique organization which oversees all educational activities in state; chartered 1784. Board of regents (1894) heads state education department and determines policy subject to N.Y. legislature.

New York Bay, Atlantic arm, at junction of Hudson and East rivers, opening SE to the Atlantic between Sandy Hook, N.J., and Rockaway Point, N.Y. Its Upper and Lower bays are connected by the Narrows (a strait c.3 mi. long, 1 mi. wide), which separates Staten Isl. from Brooklyn. Upper Bay, c.6 mi. in diameter, is joined to Newark Bay by Kill Van Kull (bridged 1931 between Staten Isl. and Bayonne, N.J.) and to Long Isl. Sound by East R. Extensive port facilities on N.J., Manhattan, Brooklyn shores (see PORT OF NEW YORK AUTHORITY). Islands include Ellis, Governors, Bedloes. Lower Bay joined to Newark Bay by Arthur Kill. Ambrose Channel (called Anchorage in Upper Bay) leads to piers of New York harbor; Buttermilk Channel leads into East R.

New York Central Railroad. In 1853 many small N.Y. state railroads were consolidated into New York Central Railroad Co. to connect Albany with Buffalo. A series of mergers by Cornelius VANDERBILT after 1866 connected New York and Buffalo. Many subsequent mergers extended line. By 1930 New York Central was one of leading railroads connecting Eastern seaboard cities with those of Midwest.

New York International Airport: see QUEENS.

New York, New Haven, and Hartford Railroad, incorporated 1872 as a consolidation of New York and New Haven RR (opened 1849) with Hartford and New Haven RR (completed 1839). Railroad's holdings were vastly expanded after 1903. Line went bankrupt in 1934, but later under new management recovered and prospered after 1940.

New York Philharmonic-Symphony Orchestra, formed 1928 when the New York Philharmonic Society (founded 1842) merged with the New York Symphony (founded 1878). Arturo Toscanini, who had been a conductor of the Philharmonic Society since 1926, continued as conductor of the Philharmonic-Symphony until 1936. Among the many conductors who have contributed to the orchestra's development are Toscanini, Leopold and Walter Damrosch, Willem Mengelberg, Bruno Walter, and Dimitri Mitropoulos, its present conductor.

New York Public Library, free library supported by private endowments and gifts and by New York city, chartered 1895. John Jacob Astor endowed (1848) a reference library opened 1854. J. G. COGSWELL was first superintendent (1848–61). James Lenox endowed the Lenox Library (chartered 1870; opened 1876). The will of S. J. Tilden estab. (1886) the Tilden Trust (chartered 1887) for maintenance of a free reading room. These three were combined in 1895. J. S. BILLINGS was appointed first director. In 1897 New York city agreed to build and equip a central building on Fifth Ave. at 42d St. and to provide for its maintenance and repair. It was designed by Thomas Hastings and J. M. Carrère and completed in 1911. A circulation department was formed by the absorption (1901) of the 11 branches of the New York Free Circulating Library founded 1878. In 1901 Andrew Carnegie gave more than $5,000,000 for buildings for circulation branches provided the city would give land and maintenance. The circulating department also absorbed several independently endowed circulating libraries including the Harlem Library, the Washington Heights Library, the Aguilar Free Library (Jewish; four branches), and the Cathedral Library (Roman Catholic; five branches). The department in 1952 had 70 branches in the boroughs of Manhattan, the Bronx, and Richmond; Queens and Brooklyn have independent systems. The central library also has an art gallery and a library for the blind. The library has especially fine collections on Americana, art, economics, folklore, music, Negro history and literature, New York city, and Semitic languages.

New York School of Social Work: see COLUMBIA UNIVERSITY.

New York State Barge Canal, 525 mi. long, traversing N.Y. and connecting Great Lakes with Hudson R. and L. Champlain. Begun 1905, completed 1918. Modification and improvement of Erie Canal. The 12-foot deep Barge Canal has 310-foot electrically operated locks, accommodates 2,000-ton vessels.

New York State College of Forestry: see SYRACUSE UNIVERSITY.

New York University, at University Heights in the Bronx and Washington Square in Manhattan, New York city; private, nonsectarian, mainly coed.; opened 1832 as Univ. of the City of New York; renamed 1896. Much expanded under Chancellor H. M. MacCracken 1891–1910. Has large evening and graduate classes. Its medical school absorbed Bellevue Hospital Medical Col. 1898. HALL OF FAME is in Bronx.

New Zealand, British dominion (103,416 sq. mi.; pop. 1,702,298), in the S Pacific; cap. WELLINGTON. Comprises NORTH ISLAND (site of Auckland, largest city and chief port), SOUTH ISLAND, STEWART ISLAND, and Chatham Isls. Cook Isls. are most important of the dependencies; Western Samoa is under New Zealand trusteeship. Islands are known for variety and beauty of scenery. Flora includes kauri pine and giant tree ferns. Among fauna are the kiwi and tuatara (survivor of a prehistoric order of reptiles); there are no land snakes. Over 90% of Maoris, the Polynesian natives, live on North Isl. Maori art (esp. wood carvings) is famous. Chief exports are dairy products, meat, wool, and kauri gum. Islands were discovered 1642 by A. J. Tasman and visited 1769 by Capt. James Cook. First missionary arrived 1814. Colony became a dependency of New South Wales in 1840, a separate British colony 1841, and a dominion 1907. Treaty of Waitangi (1840) guaranteed natives full possession of their land in exchange for admission of British settlers, but their hostility brought bloody conflict, 1854–64. Extensive social welfare program is notable—New Zealand was first to adopt noncontributory old-age pensions (1898). Began program of socialized medicine 1941. A governor general represents the British crown. Parliament is bicameral.

Nexo, Martin Andersen: see ANDERSEN NEXO

Ney, Elisabeth or **Elisabet** (nī), 1833–1907 German-American sculptor, b. Germany Made busts of Garibaldi, Bismarck, S. F Austin, Samuel Houston.

Ney, Michel (mēshĕl′ nā′), 1769–1815, marsha of France, b. Saarlouis; called by Napoleo I "the bravest of the brave." Covered retrea from Moscow (1812); was created duke o Elchingen and prince of the Moskowa b Napoleon and raised to peerage by Loui XVIII, whom he supported after Napoleon' abdication. On Napoleon's return from Elb he promised the king that he would brin Napoleon to Paris in a cage, but he change his mind and joined forces with the emperor After Waterloo, where he commanded th Old Guard, he was tried for treason and sho on orders of the house of peers.

Nez Percé Indians (nā″ pûrsā′, nĕz″ pûrs′ [Fr.,= pierced nose], North American tribe also called Sahaptin, of Shahaptin linguisti stock, occupying in the early 19th cent. region in W Idaho, NE Oregon, and SE Wash. After introduction of the hors (c.1700) they added some Plains custom (notably buffalo hunting) to their origina fishing and root-gathering culture. Gol rushes in the 1860s and '70s caused the up rising led by Chief Joseph (1877). A fev Nez Percé are on Colville reservation i Wash., most on an Idaho reservation.

Ni, chemical symbol of the element NICKEL.

niacin: see VITAMINS.

Niagara, Ont.: see NIAGARA-ON-THE-LAKE.

Niagara, river, c.34 mi. long, issuing from L Erie between Buffalo, N.Y., and Fort Erie Ont. It flows N, forming international line around Grand Isl. and over Niagara Falls t L. Ontario. Navigable c.20 mi. above fall and again 7 mi. before entering L. Ontario N.Y. State Barge Canal enters river a Tonawanda, N.Y. In Ont., Welland Canal i lake-freighter route around falls. Man bridges cross the Niagara.

Niagara, Fort, post on E side of Niagara R Strategic spot in fur trade. Captured by Brit ish from French in 1759. Surrendered to U.S in 1796, but held by British in War of 1812

Niagara Falls, city (pop. 22,874), S Ont., Can ada, on Niagara R. (bridged) opposite Ni agara Falls, N.Y. and overlooking Niagar Falls. Port of entry, hydroelectric and indus trial center. Queen Victoria Park extends be tween city and river.

Niagara Falls, city (pop. 90,872), W N.Y., o Niagara R. (bridged to Niagara Falls city Ont.) and NW of Buffalo; settled after 1800 Power from falls here is widely distributed Mfg. of chemicals, paper, abrasives, cereals and metal products. Tourist trade long a important industry. Has Niagara Falls Mus (historical, natural-history collections). Ni agara Univ. (R.C.; partly coed.; 1856) i near.

Niagara Falls, in Niagara R., W N.Y. and Ont., famous natural wonder of North Amer ica and important source of hydroelectri power. Falls are on international line, be tween Niagara Falls, N.Y., and Niagar Falls, Ont. Goat Isl. splits cataract int American Falls (c.165 ft. high, c.1,000 ft wide) and Canadian or Horseshoe Fall (c.155 ft. high, c.2,500 ft. wide). Behind American Falls is Cave of the Winds, natural chamber made by water action. Recession of the crest (now lessening) has formed narrow gorge, with Whirlpool Rapids, below the falls. Here is Rainbow Bridge (1941) between U.S. and Canada. The two governments control appearance of the area, largely in parks. Colored lights illuminate falls at night. Diversion of water for power is internationally controlled; weirs divert some flow above Canadian Falls to supplement shallower American Falls. Regional collections are in Niagara Falls Mus., Niagara Falls, N.Y.

Niagara-on-the-Lake or **Niagara,** town (pop. 2,108), S Ont., Canada, on L. Ontario at mouth of Niagara R.; settled 1780 by Loyalists. As Newark was cap. of Upper Canada 1792–96. Fort George built here in 1790s. Taken by Americans in 1813 but retaken by British in same year.

Nibelungen, Niebelungen (both: nē'bŭlo͝ong"-ŭn), or **Nibelungs,** in Germanic myth and literature, an evil family possessing an accursed magic hoard of gold. The **Nibelungenlied** (–lēt") [Ger.,= song of the Nibelungen] is a long Middle High German epic composed by an Austrian or S German poet c.1160. Siegfried obtains the Nibelung hoard, marries Kriemhild, and procures for King Gunther, her brother, the Icelandic maiden Brunhild, who contrives Siegfried's death at the hands of Hagen. Hagen buries the treasure in the Rhine. Kriemhild marries Etzel (Attila the Hun) and contrives to avenge Siegfried's death; out of the final slaughter only Etzel and a few others survive. **Der Ring des Nibelungen** (dĕr rĭng dĕs) [Ger.,= the ring of the Nibelung] is an operatic tetralogy by Richard Wagner (*Das Rheingold, Die Walküre, Siegfried,* and *Die Götterdämmerung*). Elements from the *Nibelungenlied* are used, although most of the legends are Icelandic, mainly from the VOLSUNGASAGA.

Nicaea (nīsē'ŭ), anc. city of Asia Minor; founded 4th cent. B.C. A flourishing trade center under Roman rule, it was the seat of two church councils (325, 787) and remained prominent through the Middle Ages. It was captured by the Crusaders in 1097. It became in 1204 the center of the **empire of Nicaea,** one of the Greek states founded after the Fourth Crusade had broken up the Byzantine Empire. Its rulers defeated the Seljuk Turks in the S, warred successfully against the Latin Empire, and in 1261 Emperor MICHAEL VIII recaptured Constantinople and restored the Byzantine Empire.

Nicaea, Councils of. 1 325, first ecumenical council, convened by Constantine I to deal with the problems raised by ARIANISM. The chief figures were Arius himself and his opponent, St. ATHANASIUS. The council adopted a simple baptismal creed presented by Eusebius of Caesarea, in which the word *homoousion* [consubstantial] was used of the Son and the Father, thus ruling out the Arian doctrine of the Trinity. It was adopted by all the bishops except two. It was not, however, the misnamed Nicene Creed (see CREED). **2** 787, seventh ecumenical council, convened by Empress Irene. Opposing ICONOCLASM, it decreed that images ought to be venerated (not worshiped) and restored them to the churches.

Nicanor (nīkā'–), one of the seven deacons. Acts 6.5.

Nicaragua (nĭkûrä'gwä), republic (57,145 sq. mi.; pop. 1,053,189), Central America; cap. MANAGUA. To the N and NW lies Honduras; to the E, the Caribbean; to the S, Costa Rica; to the SW, the Pacific. The highlands of the NW produce cattle and gold; the Caribbean coast (see MOSQUITO COAST) produces hardwoods and bananas. The real productive wealth of the country, however, lies between the Pacific and the lakes—L. Managua and L. Nicaragua—in a narrow volcanic belt, where most of the mestizo population is concentrated. From Corinto are shipped coffee, cotton, and sugar. The Spanish under Gil González de Ávila defeated the Indian cacique, Nicarao, in 1522, and Fernández de Córdoba founded LEÓN and GRANADA in 1524. León became the political and intellectual capital, and Granada the stronghold of aristocracy. Because of constant strife between the two, Managua was founded as compromise capital in 1855. After gaining independence from Spain in 1821, Nicaragua was briefly part of Iturbide's empire, and from 1823 to 1838 it was a member of the CENTRAL AMERICAN FEDERATION. Since then, the nation's history has been one of almost continual internal strife and foreign controversy—with Great Britain over control of Mosquito Coast and Bay Isls., and with the U.S. over rights to transisthmian route and financial matters. The vigorous government of José Santos Zelaya (1894–1909) was met with U.S. hostility. Later, U.S. marines were stationed in Nicaragua from 1912 to 1925 and again from 1926 to 1933. Anastacio Somoza emerged as the strong man of Nicaragua in 1936 and dominated the political scene after that time, although opposed by the head of the Conservative party, Emiliano Chamorro, and bitterly criticized by liberals the world over. Prolonged political strife has slowed down Nicaragua's development, but the Inter-American Highway has opened up parts of the NW highlands, and the W section has railroads and roads.

Nicaragua, Lake, area 3,100 sq. mi., SW Nicaragua, largest between Great Lakes and Peru. It forms a vital part of long-proposed Nicaragua Canal.

Nicaragua Canal, proposed waterway between the Atlantic and the Pacific, which would use the San Juan R. and L. Nicaragua and would shorten water route between New York and San Francisco by 500 mi. Plans for it from early 19th cent. were abandoned when the Panama route was chosen but were later revived and led to Bryan-Chamorro Treaty (1916) by which Nicaragua gave U.S. a canal option and naval bases. The Central American Court of Justice upheld protests that rights of Costa Rica and Honduras were infringed, and when U.S. and Nicaragua ignored the ruling, ill feeling resulted and the court was eventually dissolved.

Niccoli, Niccolò de' (nēk-kōlô' dā nēk'kōlē), 1363–1437, Italian humanist. The Laurentian Library of Florence began with his collection of manuscripts.

Nice (nēs), Ital. *Nizza,* city (pop. 181,984), Alpes-Maritimes dept., SE France. The most famous resort on the French Riviera, it also is a center of the perfumery industry. It probably originated with the Greek colony of Nicaea (estab. 5th cent. B.C.). Ceded to France by Sardinia in 1796, it was restored to Sardinia in 1814, and ceded again to France in 1860, after a plebiscite.

Nicene Creed: see CREED.

Nicephorus, Saint (nīsĕ'fŭrŭs), 758?–829?, patriarch of Constantinople (806–15), Byzantine historian, theologian, opponent of ICONOCLASM.

Nicephorus, Byzantine emperors. **Nicephorus I,** d. 811, deposed and succeeded Empress IRENE (802). His assertion of imperial authority over the Church was opposed by THEODORE OF STUDIUM. **Nicephorus II** (Nicephorus Phocas), c.913–969, usurped the throne in 963, after marrying Theophano, widow of Romanus II. Oppressive taxation and anticlerical legislation made him unpopular. He was murdered by his wife's lover, who became John I.

Nicholas, Saint, 4th cent., bishop of Myra, Asia Minor; patron of boys, of sailors, of Greece and Sicily; also called St. Nicholas of Bari (Italy) because his relics, when stolen, were taken there. In the Netherlands and elsewhere, his feast (Dec. 6) is a children's holiday. The English in New York accepted him from the Dutch, made him Santa Claus.

Nicholas I, Saint, c.825–867, pope (858–67). He set many precedents (e.g., right of a bishop to appeal to the pope over his superior's head) and forced Lothair of Lotharingia to reinstate his wife. Nicholas also challenged the right of PHOTIUS to occupy the see of Constantinople and tried to have St. Ignatius restored.

Nicholas III, d. 1280, pope (1277–80), a Roman named Giovanni Gaetano Orsini. As cardinal he was notable as diplomatic agent for earlier popes. He set out to free the papacy from civil interference, got Rudolf I to give up control over the Romagna, and thwarted the ambitions of Charles I, king of Naples, to dominate central Italy. Called the founder of the Vatican. Dante denounced Nicholas as a nepotist.

Nicholas V, antipope (1328–30): see RAINALDUCCI.

Nicholas V, 1397–1455, pope (1447–55), an Italian named Tommaso Parentucelli. He consolidated the close of the Great Schism by concluding with Frederick III the Concordat of Vienna (1448), which undid much of the work of the Council of BASEL. He made the repentant antipope, Felix V (Amadeus VIII), a cardinal. Nicholas was a learned man and a patron of learning.

Nicholas, emperors and tsars of Russia. **Nicholas I,** 1796–1855, succeeded his brother Alexander I in 1825. The confused circumstances of his accession (his elder brother Constantine had secretly renounced the succession in 1823) made possible the DECEMBRIST CONSPIRACY, which he crushed. He ruled despotically according to his motto, "Orthodoxy, autocracy, national unity," and strove to control national life through censorship and secret police. He suppressed the Polish uprising (1830–31) and abrogated the Polish constitution; aided Austria in suppressing the Hungarian republic (1849); and through his aggressive militarism invited the CRIMEAN WAR, which ended disastrously soon after his death. His great-grandson **Nicholas II,** 1868–1918, son and successor of Alexander III, was last of the Russian emperors (reigned 1894–1917). Against growing revolutionary and terroristic agitation and liberal opposition he stoutly upheld the autocratic principle. His efforts for international peace (see HAGUE CONFERENCES) did not keep Russia from becoming embroiled in the RUSSO-JAPANESE WAR (1904–5). Its humiliating outcome resulted in the violent outbreaks known as the Revolution of 1905. In Jan., 1905, a crowd of workers who had come to petition the tsar peacefully were fired upon before the Winter Palace; this "Bloody Sunday" proved fateful. After the general strike of Oct., 1905, Count WITTE induced Nicholas to sign a manifesto promising civil liberties and representative government. Nicholas, however, soon replaced Witte with STOLYPIN and curtailed the DUMA. In World War I, he personally took the field in 1915, leaving Empress ALEXANDRA FEODOROVNA in charge. The influence of RASPUTIN over the imperial household became intolerable and undermined Nicholas's authority; after Rasputin's murder (1916) he ceased in effect to reign. Forced to abdicate in March, 1917, by the RUSSIAN REVOLUTION, he was imprisoned first at Tsarskoye Selo palace, then at Tobolsk, and was shot with his family by the soviets in a cellar at Ekaterinburg (now Sverdlovsk) on July 16, 1918.

Nicholas I, 1841–1921, king of Montenegro. Acceded as prince in 1860; changed his title to king in 1910; was deposed 1918 because of his opposition to union of Montenegro with Serbia. King "Nikita" married his five beautiful daughters to Peter I of Serbia, Victor Emmanuel III of Italy, Grand Dukes Nicholas and Peter of Russia, and a prince of Battenberg.

Nicholas of Cusa (kū'zŭ), 1401?–1464, German churchman, humanist, and mystic. Made a cardinal (1448), he tried to reform monasteries all over the Holy Roman Empire (1451–52). A Renaissance man, he wrote much on classics. He was first to expose the False Decretals.

Nicholls, Francis Redding Tillou, 1834–1912, governor of La. (1877–80, 1888–92). Involved in disputed state and presidential election returns of 1876. Destroyed La. state lottery.

Nicholson, Francis, 1655–1728, British colonial administrator. Lieutenant governor of New York, he fled (1689) during revolt of Jacob Leisler. Commanded (1709–10) expedition against Port Royal, N.S. Governor of Maryland (1694–98), Virginia (1698–1705), Nova Scotia (1713), and South Carolina (1720–25).

Nicias (nĭ'shēŭs), d. 413 B.C., Athenian statesman. In the Peloponnesian War he arranged the truce called the Peace of Nicias (421 B.C.). Opposed the scheme of Alcibiades for an expedition to Syracuse but was chosen as one of its commanders. By his indecision and his superstition (he refused to retreat in time because of an eclipse of the moon) he brought the expedition to ruin. He was killed in the retreat.

nickel, lustrous, silver-white metallic element (symbol = Ni; see also ELEMENT, table). It is malleable, ductile, hard; takes high polish. Resembles iron in magnetic properties and chemical activity. Forms nickelous (valence = 2) and nickelic (valence = 3) compounds. Compounds are used in nickel plating; element is used in alloys to add strength, ductility, resistance to corrosion and heat. Occurs in a number of minerals and in meteorites.

nickel silver: see GERMAN SILVER.

Nicobar Islands: see ANDAMAN AND NICOBAR ISLANDS.

Nicodemus (nĭ″kůdē′-), a prominent Pharisee who visited Jesus at night and later helped to bury Jesus. John 3.1–21; 7.50,51; 19.39–42. Among the PSEUDEPIGRAPHA is a Gospel of Nicodemus.

Nicolai, Otto (nē′kōlī), 1810–49, German composer and conductor. His masterpiece was the comic opera *The Merry Wives of Windsor.*

Nicola Pisano: see PISANO, NICOLA.

Nicolas (nĭ′-), one of the seven deacons. Acts 6.5.

Nicolay, John George (nĭ′kůlā), 1832–1901, American biographer. He and John Hay, who had both been secretaries to Lincoln, brought out in 1890 authorized biography, *Abraham Lincoln: a History* (10 vols.).

Nicolet, Jean (zhã′ nēkôlā′), 1598?–1642, French explorer in Old Northwest. Explored L. Michigan, Green Bay, and Fox R. in 1634.

Nicolle, Charles (shärl′ nēkôl′), 1866–1936, French physician and microbiologist. Won 1928 Nobel Prize in Physiology and Medicine for work on transmission of typhus.

Nicollet, Joseph Nicolas (zhôzĕf′ nēkôlä′ nēkôlā′), 1786–1843, French mathematician and astronomer, explorer in America. Led expedition seeking source of the Mississippi (1836–37); went on government surveying expedition up the Missouri (1838–39).

Nicolls, Richard, 1624–72, first English governor of New York (1664–68). Seized colony from Dutch.

Nicol prism (nĭ′kůl), optical device, consisting of crystal of calcite or Iceland spar cut at angle into two pieces and joined together again. Beam of light entering prism undergoes double refraction; one part undergoes total reflection, other passes on through crystal. Used in POLARIZATION OF LIGHT.

Nicolson, Harold, 1886–, English biographer and historian, a diplomat and a member of Parliament. Wrote skillful, sympathetic biographies of Verlaine (1921), Tennyson (1923), Byron (1924), Swinburne (1926), and others; *Peacemaking, 1919* (1933) and *The Congress of Vienna* (1946).

Nicomedia (nĭkōmē′dēů), anc. city of NW Asia Minor, on the site of modern Izmit, Turkey; cap. of Bithynia. Goths sacked it in A.D. 258. Diocletian chose it as E capital, but it was soon superseded by Constantinople.

Nicosia (nĭkůsē′ů), Gr. *Levkosia,* city (pop. 34,485), cap. of Cyprus. Also called Lefkosha (Turkish). Agr. trade center, it also has mfg. of brandy, cigarettes, and leather. Was residence (after 1192) of Lusignan kings of Cyprus.

nicotiana (nĭkō″shēā′nů), annual or perennial plant of genus *Nicotiana,* chiefly native to tropical America. The fragrant, tubular flowers (often white, yellow, or purple) usually open at night. Commercial TOBACCO is obtained from the leaves of *Nicotiana tabacum.*

nicotine, colorless oily liquid alkaloid with pungent odor and biting taste. Occurs in leaves of tobacco. Very poisonous; used as insecticide.

nicotinic acid: see VITAMINS.

Nicoya, Gulf of (nēkō′yä), Pacific inlet, Central America, between Nicoya Peninsula and NW mainland of Costa Rica.

Nidaros, Norway: see TRONDHEIM.

Nidwalden, Switzerland: see UNTERWALDEN.

Niebelungen: see NIBELUNGEN.

Niebuhr, Barthold Georg (bär′tôlt gā′ôrk nē′-bŏŏr), 1776–1831, German historian. His history of Rome (3 vols., 1811–32; Eng. tr., 1828–42) inaugurated modern scientific historical method.

Niebuhr, Reinhold (rīn′hōld nē′bŏŏr), 1892–, American theologian; teacher at Union Theological Seminary after 1928. A liberal in politics, theologically he has stressed sinful man's dependence upon the goodness of God. His works include *The Nature and Destiny of Man* (Vol. I, 1941; Vol. II, 1943), *Faith and History* (1949), *The Irony of American History* (1952).

Niel, Adolphe (ädôlf′ nyĕl′), 1802–69, marshal of France; minister of war 1867–69. His program of far-seeing military reforms was halted by his death.

Niemcewicz, Julian Ursyn (yŏŏl′yän ŏŏr′sĭn nyĕmtsĕ′vēch), 1757–1841, Polish writer and patriot. Served in 1794 insurrection under Kosciusko (whom he later accompanied to U.S.); held high posts under duchy of Warsaw (1807–13); took part in 1831 insurrection; died in exile. His works include historical and political plays, novels, and epics.

Niemen (nē′mun, Pol. nyĕ′mĕn), Ger. *Memel,* Lithuanian *Nemunas,* Rus. *Neman,* river, 597 mi. long, rising in Belorussia and flowing W through Lithuania and along former East Prussian border, past Kaunas and Tilsit, into the Baltic Sea at Memel. It is partly navigable.

Niemeyer, John Henry (nē′mīůr), 1839–1932, American painter and teacher, b. Germany. Taught at the Yale school of fine arts, 1871–1908.

Niemoeller or **Niemöller, Martin** (both: mär′-tēn nē′mûlůr), 1892–, German Protestant churchman. Originally a National Socialist, he fought neopaganism of Hitler regime and "German Christian Church." Imprisoned 1938; liberated by Allies 1945.

Nietzsche, Friedrich Wilhelm (nē′chů), 1844–1900, German philosopher. His brilliance was early apparent and he was made professor of philology at Basel in 1869, but increasing ill health and nervous afflictions made him give up the post in 1879 and in 1889 he became hopelessly insane. His works have a poetic and passionate grandeur and show a morbid sensitivity; they have attracted many readers and are capable of widely varying interpretation. The best-known is *Thus Spake Zarathustra* (1883, 1891), which condemns traditional Christian morality as the code of the slavish masses and preaches the superiority of the morality of the masters (the natural aristocrats), which arises from the will to power. The will of man must create the superman, who would be beyond good and evil and would by his own power destroy decadent democracy. Essentially poetic and symbolic, the book is obscure. Other well-known works are *The Birth of Tragedy* (1872) and *Beyond Good and Evil* (1886).

Nièvre (nyĕ'vrů), department (2,659 sq. mi.; pop. 248,559), central France, in Nivernais; cap. Nevers.

Niger (nī'jůr), overseas territory (449,400 sq. mi.; pop. c.1,873,000), French West Africa; cap. Niamey. Mainly desert in N; in SW are fertile areas along Nigeria border and Niger R. Stock raising.

Niger, river, c.2,600 mi. long, in French West Africa and Nigeria. Empties into Gulf of Guinea through 200-mi. delta in Nigeria. Has little economic value. First explored by Mungo Park.

Nigeria (nījēr'ēů), British colony and protectorate (372,674 sq. mi.; est. pop. 24,000,000), W Africa, on Gulf of Guinea; cap. Lagos. Includes British CAMEROONS. Named for Niger R., which crosses it. Has desert in N, savannas in central highlands, and rain forests in S. Main ports are Lagos and Port Harcourt. Exports include goatskins, palm oil, tin, peanuts, and cacao. British rule began 1861 with annexation of Lagos, then a notorious slave depot, and was extended 1885–1906 to include entire territory. Appointed governor is assisted by legislative council with native majority.

night-blooming cereus (sēr'ēůs), name for various plants (chiefly of genera *Hylocereus* and *Selenicereus*) of the cactus family, which bloom at night. They are mostly climbing or sprawling plants with large flowers, usually lasting one night.

nighthawk or **bull bat,** North American bird of goatsucker family, related to whippoorwill. Eastern nighthawk has mottled brown, gray, black plumage, with white wing, throat, and (in male) tail bands.

Nightingale, Florence, 1820–1910, English hospital administrator and reformer of nurses' training. In 1844 she began visiting hospitals and studying methods of training. In Crimean War she organized (1854) hospital unit of 38 nurses, estab. hospitals at Scutari and Balaklava, and operated them against bitter opposition. Founded (1860) Nightingale School and Home for training nurses, at St. Thomas's Hospital, London. Known as the "Lady of the Lamp."

nightingale, migratory bird of thrush family. Common nightingale of England and W Europe is c.6½ in. long, reddish brown above, grayish white underneath. It is noted for song during breeding season. Winters in Africa. For nightingale in mythology see PHILOMELA.

nightshade, any plant of the widely distributed genus *Solanum,* with star-shaped flowers and showy berries. Many have poisonous qualities, e.g., juice from wilted leaves of the deadly nightshade (*Solanum nigrum*). The orange-fruited Jerusalem cherry (*S. pseudocapsicum*) is grown in pots. Potato and eggplant are also of the genus *Solanum.*

nihilism (nī'ůlĭzům), a theory, held mainly by Russian revolutionists under the tsarist regime, that existing economic and social institutions had to be destroyed, whatever the succeeding situation might prove to be. Direct action, such as assassination and arson, was characteristic. Nihilists' constructive programs, which were relatively moderate, included establishment of a parliamentary government.

Niigata (nē'gätä), industrial city (pop. 204,477), NW Honshu, Japan, on Sea of Japan. Main port for W Honshu; ships oil, machinery, textiles.

Niihau (nē'hou), island (72 sq. mi.; pop. 222), Hawaiian Isls.; privately owned. Cattle grazing.

Nijinsky, Vaslav (vŭsläf' nyĭzhĕn'skē), 1890–1950, Russian ballet dancer. Won fame (e.g., in *Petrouchka, The Afternoon of a Faun, The Spectre of the Rose*) as one of the world's greatest dancers. His career was cut short (1919) by insanity.

Nijmegen (nī'mā"khůn), Ger. *Nimwegen,* Fr. *Nimègue,* municipality (pop. 106,523), Gelderland prov., E Netherlands, on Waal R. and near German border; chartered 1184. It is a railroad junction and inland shipping center, with mfg. of electrical equipment, machinery, and clothing. Treaty of Nijmegen was signed here, 1678–79 (see DUTCH WARS). Allied air-borne troops wrested Nijmegen from Germans in Sept., 1944. Landmarks include remains of palace built by Charlemagne, 13th-cent. church, 16th-cent. city hall, and 17th-cent. weighhouse. Formerly also spelled Nimeguen, Nymegen, and Nymwegen.

Nike (nī'kē), in Greek mythology, daughter of Pallas and Styx. She presided over all contests, including war, and so was goddess of victory; identified with Roman Victoria. Of many portrayals in art, most famous is *Victory* (or *Nike*) *of Samothrace* (Louvre).

Nikko (nēk'kō), town (pop. 27,931), central Honshu, Japan; tourist resort and religious center. Splendid 17th-cent. shrine houses tomb of Ieyasu.

Nikolayev (nyĭkůlī'ůf), city (pop. 167,108), SW Ukraine, on the Southern Bug. Major Black Sea port with shipyards, flour mills. Founded 1784.

Nikolayevsk or **Nikolayevsk-on-Amur** (nyĭkůlī'ůfsk), city (pop. over 50,000), Khabarovsk Territory, RSFSR, in Far Eastern Siberia; port on the Amur. Center of fishing, gold-mining, fur-hunting area.

Nikolsburg (nē'kôlsbŏŏrk), Czech *Mikulov,* town (pop. 5,220), Moravia, Czechoslovakia, near Austrian border. Three important treaties were signed here: 1621, between Gabriel Bethlen, who renounced Hungarian crown, and Emperor Ferdinand II; 1805, armistice between France and Austria, followed by Treaty of PRESSBURG; 1866, armistice between Prussia and Austria (see AUSTRO-PRUSSIAN WAR).

Nikon (nē'kōn), 1605–81, Russian churchman,

patriarch of the Russian Orthodox Church (1652–66). His sweeping reforms, accomplished without state interference, rejuvenated the Church but awakened much opposition. The Raskolniki (Old Believers) became an opposition sect and were reinforced by such heterodox groups as the Dukhobors. Nikon was deposed by Tsar Alexis, but his reforms lasted.

Nikopol (nēkô′pôl), town (pop. 5,409), N Bulgaria, on the Danube opposite Rumania. Scene of major Turkish victory, under Bajazet I, over a Christian army led by Sigismund of Hungary (later Emperor Sigismund) in 1396. It laid the Balkans open to Turkish conquest.

Nikopol (nyĭkô′pŭl), city (pop. 57,841), S central Ukraine, on the Dnieper. Industrial center of large manganese-mining area.

Nile, great river of Africa. One of the world's longest rivers, it flows c.4,150 mi. from its ultimate headstream (the Kagera, which rises near border between Tanganyika and Ruanda-Urundi) to the Mediterranean. Drains c.1,100,000 sq. mi. The Nile proper, formed by junction of the BLUE NILE and the WHITE NILE at Khartoum (in Anglo-Egyptian Sudan) is c.1,875 mi. long. Below Cairo in Egypt, it enters its delta, which it crosses chiefly through Damietta and Rosetta channels. Between Khartoum and Aswan, the Nile drops 935 ft. in a series of six rapids (called cataracts). The river's periodic floods are due to abundant waters of the Blue Nile, fed by heavy rains of monsoon season in Ethiopia. The source of the Blue Nile, L. Tana, was discovered c.1770 by James Bruce; that of the While Nile, L. Victoria, by John Speke in 1858. Attempts to harness the flood-waters date back to 4000 B.C. Today, Nile waters are stored in several reservoirs (e.g., ASWAN), and agr. is no longer dependent on annual floods alone.

Nile, battle of the: see ABOUKIR.

Niles, Hezekiah, 1777–1839, American journalist, founder (1811) of *Niles' Weekly Register*.

Niles. 1 City (pop. 13,145), SW Mich., on St. Joseph R. and N of South Bend, Ind. Permanently settled 1827 on site of Jesuit mission (1690) and French Fort St. Joseph (1697; successively occupied by French, British, Indians, Spanish). Center of agr. area with mfg. of metal, wood, and leather products. **2** City (pop. 16,773), NE Ohio, on Mahoning R., near Warren; settled 1806. Iron and steel mills. Birthplace of William McKinley (memorial).

Niles Center, Ill.: see SKOKIE.

Nimègue or **Nimeguen,** Netherlands: see NIJMEGEN.

Nîmes (nēm), city (pop. 75,398), cap. of Gard dept., S France. Trades in wines and fruits. Its Roman remains include the great arena (still used), Maison Carrée (a perfectly preserved temple of 1st or 2d cent. A.D.), and temple of Diana (2d cent.). Near by is Pont du Gard, a Roman aqueduct.

Nimitz, Chester W(illiam) (nĭ′mĭts), 1885–, American admiral. Commanded Pacific Fleet throughout World War II. Made admiral of fleet ("five-star admiral") 1944. Chief of naval operations (1945–47).

Nimrod, mighty hunter. Gen. 10.8; 1 Chron. 1.10.

Nimwegen, Netherlands: see NIJMEGEN.

ninebark, hardy, ornamental, deciduous shrub (*Physocarpus*), chiefly native to North America. The shrubs have shreddy bark and clusters of small white or pinkish flowers in the spring.

Nine-Power Treaty: see NAVAL CONFERENCES.

Nineveh (nĭ′nŭvŭ), capital of anc. ASSYRIA, on the Tigris, opposite modern Mosul, Iraq. Reached its full glory under SENNACHERIB and ASSUR-BANI-PAL. Fell in 612 B.C. to the Medes and Chaldaean Babylonians, and the Assyrian Empire came to an end.

Ning-hsia, China: see NINGSIA.

Ninghsien, China: see NINGPO.

Ningpo (nĭng′bŭ′), commercial city (pop. 210,-377), NE Chekiang prov., China, on Yung R. Became a treaty port in 1842. Formerly called Ninghsien.

Ningsia or **Ning-hsia** (both: nĭng′shyä′), province (100,000 sq. mi.; pop. 750,000), NW China, largely in Inner Mongolia; cap. Yinchwan. Region divided into fertile Yellow R. valley and Alashan Desert. Wool weaving, fur processing.

Niobe (nī′ōbē), in Greek legend, queen of Thebes. Because she boasted of her children (accounts vary from 12 to 20) to LETO, Apollo and Artemis killed them all. Niobe became a stone image of sorrow.

niobium (nīō′bēŭm), steel-gray lustrous metallic element (symbol = Nb; see also ELEMENT, table). It is malleable and ductile and can be welded; reacts with nonmetals at high temperatures. Used in vacuum tubes and to make stainless steel and cutting tools. Columbium (Cb) was formerly an alternate name.

Niobrara (nīŭbrâ′rŭ), river rising in E Wyo. and flowing 431 mi. across N Nebr. to Missouri R. on NE line. Box Butte Dam, SW of Rushville, Nebr., is in Mirage Flats project.

Niort (nyôr), town (pop. 29,068), cap. of Deux-Sèvres dept., W France. Glove mfg. Two towers of the old fortress (12th–13th cent.) and several Renaissance buildings are preserved.

Nipigon Lake (nĭ′pĭgŏn), 66 mi. long, 46 mi. wide, W central Ont., Canada, NE of Port Arthur. Has many islands. Drains S into L. Superior via Nipigon R.

Nipissing, Lake (nĭ′pĭsĭng), S Ont., Canada, between Ottawa R. and L. Huron, extending W from North Bay city. It drains WSW to Georgian Bay via the French R.

Nippur (nĭpŏŏr′), city of anc. Mesopotamia, on the Euphrates; a Sumerian city-state of great antiquity, seat of the worship of the god En-lil.

nirvana: see BUDDHISM.

Nis or **Nish** (nēsh), Serbo-Croatian *Niš*, city (pop. 50,962), S Serbia, Yugoslavia. Railroad center; iron and tobacco mfg. Birthplace of Constantine the Great. The city was held by the Turks from c.1386 to 1878, but with several interludes when Christians captured it. It has a medieval fortress.

Nishapur (nēshäpŏŏr′), town (pop. 24,270), NE Iran, on site of anc. city built by the Sassanidae. Omar Khayyam was born and buried here. Near by are valuable turquoise mines.

Nishinomiya (nē″shēnō′mēä), manufacturing city (pop. 108,893), S Honshu, Japan, on Osaka Bay. Seat of Kobe Women's Col.

niter: see SALTPETER.

Niterói (nētŭroi′), city (pop. 174,535), cap. of Rio de Janeiro state, SE Brazil, on Guanabara Bay; primarily a residential suburb of near-by Rio de Janeiro.

niton: see RADON.

nitrate (nī′trāt), either a salt or an ester of nitric acid, a compound with the nitrate radical (NO_3). Nearly all metallic nitrates are water soluble and therefore are widely used—to make explosives, as fertilizers, in fireworks, and in medicine. Nitrates in soil are source of nitrogen needed by plants for growth.

nitric acid (nī′trĭk), corrosive, colorless liquid which gives off choking fumes in air. It is a good conductor of electricity, ionizes readily, is a strong oxidizing agent, and reacts with metals, oxides, and hydroxides to form nitrates. Used to make explosives, dyes, some organic compounds. Aqua regia is mixture of one part nitric acid, three parts sulphuric; it dissolves gold and platinum.

nitrifying bacteria: see NITROGEN-FIXING BACTERIA.

nitrobenzene (nī″trōbĕn″zēn′), poisonous, yellow, oily liquid. It is used in making some soaps, perfumes, and aniline.

nitrogen (nī′trŭjŭn), colorless, odorless, tasteless gaseous element (symbol = N; see also ELEMENT, table). Does not burn or support combustion; is relatively inactive; combines with some active metals and oxygen. It is a constituent of ammonia, nitric acid, many explosives, proteins. It forms c.⅘ of earth's atmosphere and is present in all living matter and its compounds are therefore essential to life. It is used in electric-light bulbs, thermometers, certain industrial processes, and fertilizers. **Nitrogen cycle,** the continuous course of nitrogen in nature. Nitrogen compounds are stored in plants which animals use for food. Nitrogen enters into other compounds in body of animal; animal waste matter with high nitrogen content passes into soil or sea. Certain bacteria convert these new compounds into forms which can be utilized by plants and then transformed into form usable by animals. Cycle is thus completed. **Nitrogen fixation** refers to extraction of nitrogen from the atmosphere and its combination with other elements to form compounds. Commercially it is accomplished by various processes, e.g., the arc process for preparing nitric acid, cyanamide process used in producing ammonia, and Haber process in which ammonia is synthesized by direct combination of nitrogen and hydrogen. In nature, nitrogen-fixing bacteria accomplish nitrogen fixation.

nitrogen-fixing bacteria and nitrifying bacteria (nī′trŭfī″ĭng), bacteria which convert nitrogen into forms usable by higher plants. Nitrogen, essential to all protoplasm formation, is constantly depleted in soil by plants, making restoration vital. Nitrogen-fixing bacteria live in soil or in nodules on roots of leguminous plants (e.g., alfalfa, peas, beans, clover, lupine, soybeans); they convert nitrogen in atmosphere or from other sources into forms usable by plants. Nitrifying bacteria convert nitrogen compounds from decayed organic material of soil into forms that plants can use.

nitroglycerin (nī″trōglĭ′sŭrĭn), very explosive, heavy, colorless, oily liquid. It is an ester of glycerin and nitric acid and is more accurately called glyceryl trinitrate. Very sensitive to slight shocks, it is usually mixed with glycerin to form blasting gelatin or used as DYNAMITE. It is used also to make smokeless powder, and in medicine.

nitrous oxide: see LAUGHING GAS.

Nitti, Francesco Saverio (fränchā′skō sävā′rēō nĕt′tē), 1868–1953, Italian premier (1919–20). A liberal, he was exiled during Fascist period.

Nivernais, French province: see NEVERS.

Nixon, Richard M(ilhous), 1913–, Vice President of the United States (1953–). U.S. Senator from Calif. (1951–53); known for investigation of Communists.

Niza, Marcos de: see MARCOS DE NIZA.

Nizhni Novgorod, RSFSR: see GORKI.

Nizhni Tagil (nyēzh′nyē tŭgēl′), city (pop. c.250,000), RSFSR, in central Urals. Metallurgical center.

Nizza, Italian name of NICE, France.

NKVD: see SECRET POLICE.

no: see JAPANESE DRAMA.

Noah (nō′ŭ) [Heb.,= rest] or **Noe** (nō′ē), builder of the ARK that saved human and animal life from the DELUGE. Noah's sons, Shem, Ham, and Japheth, are ancestors of the races of mankind as divided in Bible. Gen. 6–10; 1 Chron. 1.4; Ezek. 14.14,20; Mat. 24.37; Luke 3.36; 17.26; Heb. 11.7.

Noailles, Maurice, duc de (mōrēs′ dük′ dŭ nōī′yŭ), 1678–1766, marshal of France. Commanded in War of the Austrian Succession.

Nobel, Alfred Bernhard (äl′frĕd bĕrn′härd nōbĕl′), 1833–96, Swedish chemist and inventor. In 1863 patented mixture of nitroglycerine and gunpowder, in 1866 dynamite. Bequeathed fund for annual awards in physics, chemistry, physiology and medicine, and literature, and for promotion of international peace. Nobel Prizes are awarded on international basis by board named by Nobel, with hq. in Stockholm. See NOBEL PRIZES (table).

Nobile, Umberto (nô′bēlā), 1885–, Italian aeronautical engineer and arctic explorer. Designed and piloted dirigible, *Norge,* in Amundsen-Ellsworth flight over North Pole (1926). Commanded another polar dirigible flight in 1928; ship crashed on return. Technical adviser for airship construction in USSR (1931–36).

Noblesville, city (pop. 6,567), central Ind., NNE of Indianapolis. Mfg. of wood and rubber products. Breeds draft horses.

Nobunaga (Nobunaga Oda) (nōbōōnä′gä), 1534–82, Japanese military commander. Became virtual dictator in 1568 despite continued existence of Ashikaga shogunate. Crushed rival feudal barons and laid basis for country's unification, later completed by former lieutenants, Hideyoshi and Ieyasu.

Year	*Peace*	*Chemistry*	*Physics*	*Physiology and Medicine*	*Literature*
1901	J. H. Dunant Frédéric Passy	J. H. van't Hoff	W. C. Roentgen	E. A. von Behring	R. F. A. Sully-Prudhomme
1902	Élie Ducommun C. A. Gobat	Emil Fischer	H. A. Lorentz Pieter Zeeman	Sir Ronald Ross	Theodor Mommsen
1903	Sir William R. Cremer	S. A. Arrhenius	A. H. Becquerel Pierre Curie Marie S. Curie	N. R. Finsen	Bjornstjerne Bjornson
1904	Institute of International Law	Sir William Ramsey	J. W. S. Rayleigh	Ivan P. Pavlov	Frédéric Mistral José Echegaray
1905	Baroness Bertha von Suttner	Adolf von Baeyer	Philipp Lenard	Robert Koch	Henryk Sienkiewicz
1906	Theodore Roosevelt	Henri Moissan	Sir Joseph Thomson	Camillo Golgi S. Ramón y Cajal	Giosuè Carducci
1907	E. T. Moneta Louis Renault	Eduard Buchner	A. A. Michelson	C. L. A. Laveran	Rudyard Kipling
1908	K. P. Arnoldson Fredrik Bajer	Sir Ernest Rutherford	Gabriel Lippman	Paul Ehrlich Élie Metchnikoff	R. C. Eucken
1909	Auguste Beernaert P. H. B. Estournelles de Constant	Wilhelm Ostwald	Guglielmo Marconi C. F. Braun	Emil T. Kocher	Selma Lagerlof
1910	International Peace Bureau	Otto Wallach	J. D. van der Waals	Albrecht Kossel	P. J. L. Heyse
1911	T. M. C. Asser A. H. Fried	Marie S. Curie	Wilhelm Wien	Allvar Gullstrand	Maurice Maeterlinck
1912	Elihu Root	Victor Grignard Paul Sabatier	N. G. Dalen	Alexis Carrel	Gerhart Hauptmann
1913	Henri La Fontaine	Alfred Werner	Heike Kamerlingh Onnes	C. R. Richet	Sir Rabindranath Tagore
1914		T. W. Richards	Max von Laue	Robert Barany	
1915		Richard Willstätter	Sir William H. Bragg Sir William L. Bragg		Romain Rolland
1916					Verner von Heidenstam
1917	International Red Cross		C. G. Barkla		K. A. Gjellerup Henrik Pontoppidan
1918		Fritz Haber	Max Planck		
1919	Woodrow Wilson		Johannes Stark	Jules Bordet	C. F. G. Spitteler
1920	Léon Bourgeois	Walther Nernst	C. E. Guillaume	August Krogh	Knut Hamsun
1921	Hjalmar Branting C. L. Lange	Frederick Soddy	Albert Einstein		Anatole France
1922	Fridtjof Nansen	F. W. Aston	N. H. D. Bohr	A. V. Hill Otto Meyerhof	Jacinto Benavente y Martínez
1923		Fritz Pregl	Robert A. Millikan	Sir Frederick G. Banting J. J. R. Macleod	W. B. Yeats
1924			K. M. G. Siegbahn	Willem Einthoven	L. S. Reymont
1925	Sir Joseph Austen Chamberlain Charles G. Dawes	Richard Zsigmondy	James Franck Gustav Hertz		G. B. Shaw
1926	Aristide Briand Gustav Stresemann	Theodor Svedberg	J. B. Perrin	Johannes Fibiger	Grazia Deledda
1927	F. É. Buisson Ludwig Quidde	Heinrich Wieland	A. H. Compton C. T. R. Wilson	Julius Wagner Jauregg	Henri Bergson
1928		Adolf Windaus	Sir Owen W. Richardson	C. J. H. Nicolle	Sigrid Undset
1929	Frank B. Kellogg	Sir Arthur Harden Hans von Euler-Chelpin	L. V. Broglie	Christian Eijkman Sir Frederick G. Hopkins	Thomas Mann
1930	Nathan Soderblom	Hans Fischer	Sir Chandrasekhara V. Raman	Karl Landsteiner	Sinclair Lewis
1931	Jane Addams Nicholas Murray Butler	Carl Bosch Friedrich Bergius		Otto H. Warburg	E. A. Karlfeldt
1932		Irving Langmuir	Werner Heisenberg	E. D. Adrian Sir Charles Sherrington	John Galsworthy

NOBEL PRIZES (continued)

Year	Peace	Chemistry	Physics	Physiology and Medicine	Literature
1933	Sir Norman Angell		P. A. M. Dirac Erwin Schrödinger	Thomas H. Morgan	I. A. Bunin
1934	Arthur Henderson	Harold C. Urey		G. H. Whipple G. R. Minot W. P. Murphy	Luigi Pirandello
1935	Carl von Ossietzky	Frédéric Joliot-Curie Irène Joliot-Curie	Sir James Chadwick	Hans Spemann	
1936	Carlos Saavedra Lamas	P. J. W. Debye	C. D. Anderson V. F. Hess	Sir Henry H. Dale Otto Loewi	Eugene O'Neill
1937	E. A. R. Cecil, Viscount	Sir Walter N. Haworth Paul Karrer	C. J. Davisson Sir George P. Thomson	Albert von Szent-Gyorgyi	Roger Martin du Gard
1938	Nansen International Office for Refugees		Enrico Fermi		Pearl S. Buck
1939		Adolf Butenandt Leopold Ruzicka	E. O. Lawrence	Gerhard Domagk	F. E. Sillanpää
1940					
1941					
1942					
1943		Georg von Hevesy	Otto Stern	E. A. Doisy Henrik Dam	
1944	International Red Cross	Otto Hahn	I. I. Rabi	Joseph Erlanger H. S. Gasser	J. V. Jensen
1945	Cordell Hull	A. I. Virtanen	Wolfgang Pauli	Sir Alexander Fleming E. B. Chain Sir Howard W. Florey	Gabriela Mistral
1946	J. R. Mott Emily G. Balch	J. B. Sumner J. H. Northrop W. M. Stanley	P. W. Bridgman	H. J. Muller	Hermann Hesse
1947	American Friends Service Committee and Friends Service Council	Sir Robert Robinson	Sir Edward V. Appleton	C. F. Cori Gerty T. Cori B. A. Houssay	André Gide
1948		Arne Tiselius	P. M. S. Blackett	Paul H. Mueller	T. S. Eliot
1949	John Boyd Orr, Baron	W. F. Giauque	Hideki Yukawa	W. R. Hess Egas Moniz	William Faulkner
1950	R. J. Bunche	Otto Diels Kurt Alder	C. F. Powell	P. S. Hench E. C. Kendall Tadeus Reichstein	Bertrand Russell
1951	Leon Jouhaux	G. T. Seaborg E. M. McMillan	J. D. Cockcroft E. T. S. Walton	Max Theiler	P. F. Lagerkvist
1952		Archer Martin Richard Synge	Felix Bloch E. M. Purcell	S. A. Waksman	François Mauriac

Nod, Land of, in Bible, refuge of Cain. Gen. 4.16.

Noe (nō'ē), variant of NOAH.

Noé, Amédée, comte de: see CHAM.

Nogales (nōgä'lās), town (pop. 13,866), Sonora, NW Mexico, contiguous to Nogales, Ariz. Derives its importance chiefly from international trade.

Nogales (nōgă'lĭs), city (pop. 6,153), S Ariz., adjoining Nogales, Mexico. Port of entry in rich mining and ranching area. To N are Tumacacori (1696; now a national monument) and Guevavi (1692; in ruins), missions founded by Father Kino, and the ruins of Tubac (1752), pioneer Spanish settlement.

Nogi, Maresuke, Count (märĕs'kā nō'gē), 1849–1912, Japanese general and hero of Russo-Japanese War.

Noguchi, Hideyo (hēdā'ō nōgōō'chē), 1876–1928, Japanese bacteriologist, on staff of Rockefeller Inst. from 1904. Worked on yellow fever, smallpox, snake venoms, and diagnosis of syphilis.

Noguchi, Isamu, 1904–, American sculptor, known for stylized portraits and abstractions. Studied in New York and Paris (under Brancusi). His father, **Yone Noguchi,** 1875–1947, was a Japanese poet, who also wrote critical essays in English.

Nola (nō'lä), town (pop. 10,733), Campania, S Italy. It was a flourishing Roman colony influenced by Greek culture. Augustus died here A.D. 14.

Nolde, Emil (ā'mĕl nŏl'dŭ), 1867–, German expressionist painter. Draws subject matter from nature (seascapes, flower gardens) and the supernatural.

Nolichucky (nŏ"lĭchŭ'kē), river rising in Blue Ridge in W N.C. and flowing c.150 mi. NW into Tenn. and W to French Broad R. (Douglas Reservoir) near Newport. Power dam near Greeneville.

Nome (nōm), city (pop. 1,876), W Alaska, on Norton Sound on S side of Seward Peninsula; estab. 1899 with discovery of gold. Had c.30,000 population by summer of 1900, but many died or left because of arctic hardships. Dredge mining introduced later. Trade, supply, and tourist center for NW Alaska and center of Eskimo handicrafts; fur farming and fishing. Annual fair and dog race. Airport; steamer to Seattle (May–Nov.). Cape Nome is SE.

nominative: see CASE.

Nomura, Kichisaburo (kēchēsäbo͝orō' nō'mo͝o"rä), 1877–, Japanese admiral and diplomat. Commanded fighting at Shanghai in 1932. Sent to U.S. in 1940 as ambassador. He conducted Washington negotiations (1941) cut short by Japanese attack on Pearl Harbor.

nonconformists, those who refuse to comply with rules of discipline or doctrine of an estab. church. Term applied especially to Protestant dissenters from the Church of England, a group arising soon after the Reformation. The Act of Uniformity (1662), making episcopal ordination compulsory, made a split inevitable. Term *dissenter* came into use with Toleration Act (1689).

nonjurors [from Latin,= not swearing], the English and Scottish clergymen who refused to break allegiance to James II and take oath to William III in 1689. Five bishops were deprived of their sees in 1690. James II in exile appointed bishops. Nonjuring episcopal succession lasted until 1805 although the Scots actually submitted in 1788.

nonmetal, chemical ELEMENT distinguished from METAL in appearing as negative ion or in negative radical and in that its oxide yields an acid. Nonmetal may be solid, liquid, or gas. Some nonmetals form crystals. All lack metallic luster. They vary in hardness and are poor conductors of heat and electricity. Most do not occur free, but exist in numerous relatively abundant compounds.

Nonpartisan League, organization of business farmers formed by A. C. Townley in N.Dak. in 1915. Subsequently expanded into Wis. and other Western states. Set out to improve farm business conditions by legislation; endorsed, sometimes nominated candidates. Though strongly opposed, it had permanent effects on legislation in some states.

Nootka Indians (no͞ot'kû), North American tribe, of Wakashan linguistic stock, living on W coast of Vancouver Isl. Name is also given generally to the Aht Confederacy, including more than 20 tribes. They fish for salmon and live in long wooden houses.

Nootka Sound, harbor on W coast of Vancouver Isl., B.C., Canada, lying between it and Nootka Isl. First visited by Juan Pérez 1774. Fort built here by John Meares 1788. Its seizure by the Spanish 1789 led to controversy with Great Britain. Agreement in Nootka Convention (1790) opened N Pacific coast to British settlement.

Noranda, city (pop. 9,672), W Que., Canada, N of Rouyn. Gold, copper, and zinc mining center.

Nord (nôr), department (2,229 sq. mi.; pop. 1,917,452), N France, bordering on North Sea and Belgium; cap. Lille, chief port Dunkirk. Occupying French Flanders and Hainaut, it is a traditional battleground and a vital industrial region (coal mines).

Nordenskjold, Nils Adolf Erik, Baron (no͞or'dûnshûld), 1832–1901, Swedish geologist and arctic explorer, first to navigate Northeast Passage (1878–79), b. Finland. Commanded series of mapping and scientific expeditions to Spitsbergen and Greenland.

Norderney (nôrdûrnī'), island (9 sq. mi.; pop. 6,452), off N Germany, in North Sea, one of East Frisian Isls.; a popular bathing resort.

Nord Fjord (nôr' fyôr"), inlet, 70 mi. long, Sogn og Fjordane co., W Norway; Norway's third largest fjord. The JOSTEDALSBREEN is just S.

Nordhoff, Charles, 1830–1901, American journalist and author of books on the sea and on politics, b. Germany. Some of his works were edited by his grandson, **Charles Nordhoff,** 1887–1947, who also wrote with James Norman Hall *Mutiny on the Bounty* (1932) and other works.

Nordkyn, Cape: see NORTH CAPE.

Nördlingen (nûrt'lĭngûn), town (pop. 13,268), W Bavaria. Free imperial city 1217–1803. In the Thirty Years War, the imperialist victory here (1634) was a major cause for direct French intervention in 1635. In 1645 Nördlingen was the scene of a French victory. The town has kept much architecture of the 14th–15th cent.

Nore (nôr), river of Ireland, flowing 70 mi. from Co. Tipperary to the Barrow N of New Ross.

Nore, the, sandbank in the Thames estuary, England. Name also given to anchorage in the estuary, scene of a famous mutiny in the British fleet in 1797.

Norfolk, dukes of (Howard line): see HOWARD, family.

Norfolk, Hugh Bigod, 1st **earl of** (bĭ'gŏd, nôr'fûk), d. 1177, English nobleman. Supported Stephen (1135) and later (1153) Henry II. When he unsuccessfully rebelled against Henry (1173), his lands were seized.

Norfolk, Thomas Mowbray, 1st **duke of,** c.1366–1399, English statesman. With the Lords Appellants, he drove out the king's favorites (1387) and virtually ruled until Richard II regained control (1389) but retained king's favor. Banished for life after a dispute with earl of Hereford (later Henry IV).

Norfolk (nôr'fûk), maritime county (2,053 sq. mi.; pop. 546,550), E England; co. town Norwich. Region of flat, fertile farmlands. Cereals, root crops, cattle and poultry breeding, and fishing are important. Has many prehistoric remains.

Norfolk (nôr'fôk), **1** Resort town (pop. 1,572), NW Conn., in Litchfield Hills. Annual Litchfield county choral concerts began here 1899. **2** (nôr'fûk) City (pop. 11,335), NE Nebr., on Elkhorn R. and NW of Omaha; settled 1866. Rail and trade center in grain and livestock area. **3** City (pop. 213,513), SE Va., on Elizabeth R. and HAMPTON ROADS; founded 1682. Port with superior natural harbor, it is a major E coast naval installation (hq. of Atlantic fleet). Shipping of food products, seafood, lumber. Mfg. of textiles, fertilizers, and metal products. Town burned in Revolution; commerce ruined by embargo of 1807. Notable are St. Paul's Church (1739), Fort Norfolk (1794), and Myers House (1791). Near by are resort areas and historic sites.

Norfolk Island (nôr'fûk), island (13 sq. mi.;

pop. 1,231), S Pacific, belonging to Australia. Discovered 1774 by Capt. James Cook. In 1856 some descendants of *Bounty* mutineers were moved here from Pitcairn Isl. Known for pine trees, scenic island thrives as a resort.

Noricum (nŏ'rĭkŭm), province of the Roman Empire, occupying modern Austria S of the Danube and W of Vienna. Conquered 16 B.C.–A.D. 14, it was Roman until the 6th cent.

Normal, town (pop. 9,772), central Ill., adjacent to Bloomington. Has canneries. Illinois State Normal Univ. is here.

Norman, city (pop. 27,006), central Okla., SE of Oklahoma City; settled 1889. Center of agr. area. Seat of Univ. of OKLAHOMA.

Norman architecture, name applied to the buildings erected by the Normans in all lands under their rule. Norman buildings in England and France (built 1066–1154) were Romanesque, with massive proportions, sparsely adorned masonry, and use of round arch. Dormitory and refectory of Westminster Abbey are earliest extant Norman work in England. Of the many English cathedrals commenced by the Normans, Durham (begun 1093) is considered the finest. In both England and Normandy church plans were cruciform, with square tower over crossing of nave and transepts. In Sicily, the large Norman cathedrals of Cefalù, Palermo, and Monreale were commenced after 1130. They are in composite style incorporating domes and pointed arches of Saracens, wood roofs and geometric ornament of Normans, and interior mosaic decorations of Byzantine-Greek artisans.

Norman Conquest, conquest of England after defeat in 1066 of Harold by William, duke of Normandy (WILLIAM I). Intercourse with Europe in politics and trade grew and sped England's rise as major European power. Life and property became more secure, and ecclesiastical jurisdiction increased. To English judicial system was added jury system. General survey of the country was compiled in DOMESDAY BOOK. Cause of learning was enhanced (e.g., by Lanfranc and Anselm). ENGLISH LANGUAGE was superseded by French as language of culture and was much influenced by French. Norman architecture and new methods of warfare were also introduced.

Normandy (nôr'mŭndē), Fr. *Normandie,* former province, N France, on English Channel, in Seine-Inférieure, Eure, Calvados, Manche, and Orne depts.; historic cap. Rouen. Rich agr. region; dairying, cattle raising, apple orchards. Important fisheries; shipping (at Le Havre and Cherbourg). Many seaside resorts (e.g., Dieppe, Deauville). The region is named for its conquerors, the NORSEMEN or Normans, to whose leader ROLLO it was given as a duchy in 911 by Charles III (the Simple) of France. The Normans accepted Christianity and soon adopted French speech and customs but kept their taste for adventure and conquest. In 1066 Duke William II conquered England, where he became king as WILLIAM I. About the same time Norman adventurers conquered S Italy and Sicily (see ROBERT GUISCARD; ROGER I). Normandy itself was wrested from Duke ROBERT II by his brother, HENRY I of England, in 1106; in 1144, it was conquered by GEOFFREY of Anjou. Geoffrey's son, Henry Plantagenet, became duke of Normandy 1151 and king of England 1154 (see HENRY II); thus the ANGEVIN dynasty was estab. in England. Recovered for France by Philip II (1204), Normandy was devastated in the Hundred Years War, when England conquered it once again (1415). It was definitively restored to France in 1450. In World War II Normandy was the scene of the Allied invasion of the Continent (operation "Overlord," June 6, 1944), directed by Gen. Eisenhower. In the subsequent Normandy campaign the Cotentin peninsula (U.S. sector) and the Caen area (British sector) were devastated in heavy fighting. Capture of Saint-Lô (July 18) by U.S. forces cut off the German force under Rommel. The British, after taking Caen (July 19), were stalled but resumed their offensive in Aug. and captured Falaise Aug. 16. Nearly an entire German army was caught in the "Falaise pocket" between U.S. and British forces, and the rest of France was liberated in the following weeks.

Norman Isles: see CHANNEL ISLANDS.

Normans: see NORMANDY; NORSEMEN.

Norns, in Germanic mythology, the FATES, who spun and wove web of life. There were three —URTH (past), Verthandi (present), and Skuld (future).

Norrbotten (nôr'bôtŭn), Swed. *Norrbottens län,* northernmost and largest county (40,-750 sq. mi.; pop. 241,602) of Sweden, bordering on Gulf of Bothnia, Finland, and Norway; cap. Lulea. It comprises historic Norrbotten prov. and larger part of Lappland prov. Its economy is based on cattle, sheep, and reindeer herds; hay; and iron ore (see KIRUNA). The KEBNEKAISE peak is here.

Norris, (Benjamin) Frank(lin), 1870–1902, American novelist, known for his powerful *Epic of Wheat,* a planned trilogy, including *The Octopus* (1901), *The Pit* (1903), and *The Wolf* (unfinished). A brother, **Charles G(ilman) Norris,** 1881–1945, wrote analytical novels of American life such as *Brass* (1921). His wife, Kathleen Norris (1880–), is known for her many romantic novels.

Norris, George William, 1861–1944, U.S. Representative (1903–13) and Senator (1913–43) from Nebr. Fearless, liberal Republican; secured reform of House rules (1910). Became an independent (1936). Author of Twentieth Amendment to Constitution, father of bills creating TVA.

Norris Dam: see TENNESSEE VALLEY AUTHORITY.

Norristown, borough (pop. 38,126), SE Pa., NW of Philadelphia and on Schuylkill R., near E end of Pa. Turnpike; settled 1784. Agr. shipping center with mfg. of machinery, metal products, and asbestos. Most populous independent borough in U.S.

Norrkoping, Swed. *Norrköping* (nôr'chû"-pĭng), city (pop. 84,939), Ostergotland co., SE Sweden, a Baltic port. Sweden's chief textile center, it also produces paper, lumber, and ships. Burned 1719 by Russians, but its 16th-cent. castle remains.

Norrland: see SWEDEN.

Norse language, language of Norway or of Iceland at any period, a branch of Germanic subfamily of Indo-European languages. Sagas are written in Old Norse. See LANGUAGE (table).

Norse literature: see OLD NORSE LITERATURE.

Norsemen, Northmen, or **Normans,** Scandinavian VIKINGS who raided the coasts of continental Europe, particularly of France, in the 9th–10th cent. They were known as Danes in England, as Varangians in Russia. Their sudden appearance was caused partly by overpopulation in Scandinavia, partly by the measures taken by HAROLD I of Norway against the independent nobles. Norse raiders began to sail up French rivers c.843, repeatedly sacked Paris and Rouen, and threatened, with rapacious destructiveness, to plunge France back into barbarism. They estab. settlements at the river mouths and in 911 received the duchy of NORMANDY.

Norse religion: see GERMANIC RELIGION.

North, Christopher, pseud. of **John Wilson,** 1785–1854, Scottish author of critical articles in *Blackwood's Magazine* and (with J. G. Lockhart and others) of *Noctes Ambrosianae,* a potpourri of humorous sketches and verse.

North, Frederick, 2d **earl of Guilford** and 8th **Baron North,** 1732–92, English statesman, known as Lord North. Prime minister (1770–82) during the American Revolution, he supported George III's policies.

North, Sir Thomas, 1535?–1601?, English translator of Plutarch's *Lives.*

North Adams, city (pop. 21,567), NW Mass., in the Berkshires, on Hoosic R. near W termini of Hoosac Tunnel and Mohawk Trail; settled c.1737. Electrical goods, textiles, paper. Mt. Greylock in SW.

North Africa, campaigns in. Italy's entrance into World War II (June 10, 1940) made North Africa an active theater in which the ultimate prize was control of the Mediterranean. Fighting began in Sept., 1940, after the swift Italian conquest of British Somaliland. The great desert war took place (except in final phases) along Libya-Egypt coast, where the level terrain provided poor defensive positions; success or failure hinged on speed in amassing armored and air strength. In Sept., 1940, Italian forces (under Graziani) from Libya penetrated c.60 mi. into Egypt, but a British surprise attack led by Wavell (Dec. 9, 1940) all but destroyed Italian army in a 500-mi. pursuit back into Libya. But the Italians were quickly reinforced by Rommel's Afrika Korps, and in March, 1941, they drove the British back to the Egyptian border, by-passing the strong Australian garrison at TOBRUK. Rommel was forced back into Libya in Nov., 1941, by a British counterattack led by Auchinleck. When Rommel struck back, May 26, 1942, the British suffered a crushing defeat and were driven c.250 mi. into Egypt, where they dug in along a 35-mi. line from ALAMEIN to Qattara Depression, only c.70 mi. W of Alexandria. Commanded by Montgomery, they withstood German attacks while reinforcements (esp. tanks and planes from U.S.) poured in. Montgomery's decisive thrust of Oct. 23, 1942, sent Axis troops through Libya into Tunisia on one of the longest sustained retreats in history. Allied troops under Eisenhower landed in Morocco and Algeria in Nov., 1942, and pushed toward Tunisia. Axis troops were compressed in a diminishing pocket in Tunisia between Eisenhower's forces on W, British 8th Army on E, Free French forces on S, and Allied planes and ships in the Mediterranean. After bitter fighting (notably at KASSERINE PASS) Axis forces in North Africa capitulated on May 12, 1943. Meanwhile, the Allies had won E Africa—British and Italian Somaliland had fallen by Feb., 1941, Eritrea and Ethiopia had been conquered by Nov., 1942.

Northallerton, urban district (pop. 6,087), cap. of North Riding of Yorkshire, England; a trade center. Battle of the Standard, between English and Scots, fought near here in 1138.

North America, N continent of Western Hemisphere; including ALASKA, CANADA, UNITED STATES, MEXICO; area c.8,000,000 sq. mi.; pop. c.200,000,000. Central America, generally considered S part of North America, is separated from South America by Isthmus of Panama. Continent is roughly triangular in shape, narrowest toward S. Offshore are Greenland (northernmost region of Western Hemisphere) and the West Indies. Highest point is Mt. MCKINLEY (Alaska); lowest, DEATH VALLEY (Calif.). Vast central plain, c.1,500 mi. wide, separates E coastal plain and mountain systems (LAURENTIAN MOUNTAINS, ADIRONDACK MOUNTAINS, APPALACHIAN MOUNTAINS) from extensive, high, rugged mountains of W (COAST RANGES and ROCKY MOUNTAINS, with GREAT BASIN between). Central plain drained by great river systems: the MISSISSIPPI, MISSOURI, SASKATCHEWAN, MACKENZIE and SAINT LAWRENCE (with GREAT LAKES). Other great rivers are the YUKON, COLUMBIA, COLORADO, and RIO GRANDE. Continental temperatures reach great extremes. Rainfall abundant along parts of coast, deficient in parts of interior. Mountainous E and W have heavily forested areas; N are the BARREN GROUNDS; central part is main agr. region; and large desert areas are SW. Generally fertile soil provides some of world's largest wheat, cotton, and grazing areas. Continent has extensive mineral resources. Present population consists chiefly of descendants of Europeans, together with Negroes, Asiatics, and remnants of aboriginal INDIANS.

Northampton, Henry Howard, earl of: see HOWARD, family.

Northampton, England: see NORTHAMPTONSHIRE.

Northampton. 1 City (pop. 29,063), W Mass., on Connecticut R. above Springfield. Mfg. of hosiery, brushes, and cutlery. Seat of SMITH COLLEGE. The Northampton Association of Education and Industry, communistic settlement, was here 1842–46. **2** Borough (pop. 9,332), E Pa., N of Allentown. Mfg. of cement and textiles.

Northamptonshire (nôrthămp'tŭnshĭr) or **North Hants** (hănts), inland county (914 sq. mi.; pop. 359,550), central England. Soke of PETERBOROUGH, separate administrative county, is in NE. Agr. county devoted to sheep and cattle pasturage, it has long been a center of boot and shoe mfg. The county town is **Northampton,** county borough (pop. 104,429), on the Nene. Was important settlement of Angles and Danes. Has one of four round churches in England. An Eleanor Cross (ELEANOR OF CASTILE) is near by. Shoemaking is the chief industry.

North Andover, town (pop. 8,485), NE Mass., on Merrimack R. and just E of Lawrence. Textiles.

North Arlington, borough (pop. 15,970), NE N.J., NE of Newark. Metal, plastic, and rubber products.

North Atlantic Drift, warm ocean current in northern Atlantic Ocean, a continuation of the GULF STREAM. It tempers climate of Western and N Europe.

North Atlantic Treaty, defensive alliance signed in 1949 by the U.S., Canada, Great Britain, France, the Netherlands, Belgium, Luxembourg, Italy, Norway, Denmark, Iceland, and Portugal. Greece and Turkey were admitted in 1951. North Atlantic Treaty Organization (NATO) consists of a supreme council, a staff headed by a secretary general (Lord Hastings Ismay, appointed 1952), and military hq. under a supreme commander (Gen. Dwight Eisenhower, 1950–52; Gen. Matthew Ridgway, 1952–). Treaty, set up as a regional alliance under the Charter of the United Nations, is to be renewed in 10 years.

North Attleboro, town (pop. 12,146), SE Mass., at R.I. line; settled 1669. Mfg. of jewelry (since 18th cent.), silverware, and foundry products.

North Australia: see NORTHERN TERRITORY.

North Battleford, city (pop. 7,473), W Sask., Canada, on North Saskatchewan R. at mouth of Battle R., NW of Saskatoon and opposite Battleford. Trade center for W Sask.

North Bay, city (pop. 17,944), S Ont., Canada, on L. Nipissing and N of Toronto. Rail center in lumber and mining area and outfitting point for hunting and fishing region.

North Bend, city (pop. 6,099), SW Oregon, on Coos Bay. Lumber mills and fisheries.

North Bergen, suburban township (pop. 41,560), NE N.J., NE of Jersey City. Mfg. of ink, electrical equipment, radio parts, clothing, and metal goods.

North Borneo or **British North Borneo,** British colony (29,307 sq. mi.; est. pop. 330,000), NE BORNEO; cap. Jesselton. Was protectorate until 1946. Here is Mt. Kinabalu, highest peak of Borneo. Products include rubber and timber.

North Brabant (brŭbănt'), Dutch *Noordbrabant,* province (1,894 sq. mi.; pop. 1,180,133), S Netherlands; cap. 's Hertogenbosch. Agr. in N; heathland in S. Textile mfg.; electrical appliances (notably at Eindhoven). Shared history of BRABANT until 1648, when Spain ceded it to the United Provs.

North Braddock, borough (pop. 14,724), SW Pa., ESE suburb of Pittsburgh. Mfg. of steel.

Northbridge, town (pop. 10,476), S Mass., SE of Worcester; settled 1704. Includes Whitinsville village (pop. 5,662), with mfg. of textiles.

North Canadian, river rising in NE N.Mex. and flowing E into Okla. Panhandle, SE through Oklahoma City, to South Canadian R. near junction with Arkansas R. in E Okla. With Wolf Creek tributary, it is in Arkansas R. basin project.

North Cape, N Norway, near N end of Mageroy isl., Finnmark co., NE of Hammerfest. At lat. 71°10'N, it is northernmost important point of Europe. Tourist steamers call here. Cape Nordkyn (nôr'chün) or Kinnarodden (chĭ'närô"dûn), at lat. 71°8'N, on Barents Sea, is northernmost point on mainland.

North Carolina, state (52,712 sq. mi.; pop. 4,061,929), SE U.S.; one of Thirteen Colonies; cap. RALEIGH. Other cities include CHARLOTTE, WINSTON-SALEM, GREENSBORO, DURHAM, ASHVILLE, WILMINGTON. Bordered E by the Atlantic (tidewater region), with capes HATTERAS, FEAR, LOOKOUT. Coastal plains rise to fall line and piedmont area. W are the BLUE RIDGE and GREAT SMOKY MOUNTAINS. Mt. MITCHELL (6,684 ft.) highest point E of Mississippi R. Rivers include Catawba (WATEREE), Yadkin (PEE DEE), TAR, ROANOKE, NEUSE, CAPE FEAR RIVER. Farming (tobacco, cotton, peanuts, corn, dairying); minerals (granite, mica, feldspar); fishing. Mfg. of tobacco products, textiles, clothing, paper, fertilizer, aluminum. Ralegh's colonies at ROANOKE ISLAND (1580s) failed; Va. colonists estab. settlements beginning 1653. Made royal colony (1729) after dissatisfaction with proprietors. Farmers organized REGULATOR MOVEMENT (1768); it was suppressed in 1771. MECKLENBURG DECLARATION OF INDEPENDENCE allegedly proclaimed in May, 1775. Invaded in Revolution in CAROLINA CAMPAIGN (1780–81). Tidewater planter aristocracy dominated government until 1830s. Seceded from Union after Lincoln called for troops. Tobacco mfg. grew with introduction of cigarette-making machinery in 1880s. Farm tenancy system dominated agr. Since World War I state government has followed policy of consolidation and centralization.

North Carolina, Agricultural and Technical College of: see GREENSBORO.

North Carolina, University of, at Chapel Hill; state supported; partly coed.; chartered 1789, first to open as state university 1795. Consolidated Univ. of North Carolina includes State Col. of Agriculture and Engineering (Raleigh; coed., 1887), Woman's Col. (Greensboro, 1891). Has planetarium, art gallery, folk theater, folklore council, and press.

North Channel, strait between Northern Ireland and Scotland, connecting Irish Sea with the Atlantic.

North Chicago, city (pop. 8,628), NE Ill., N of Chicago on L. Michigan, adjoining Waukegan. Mfg. of metal products. Steel strike (1937) here led to Supreme Court ruling (1939) that made sit-down strikes illegal. Great Lakes Naval Training Station near by.

Northcliffe, Alfred Charles William Harmsworth, Viscount, 1865–1922, British journalist. With his brother Harold, later Viscount Rothermere, he formed the world's largest newspaper combine, the Amalgamated Press. In 1896 he founded the *Daily Mail,* and in 1903 the *Daily Mirror.* In 1908 he bought *The Times* and gave it new life. His activities revolutionized journalism and in-

CAPITAL CITIES are designated by CAPITAL AND SMALL CAPITAL type

fluenced war policies as well as political affairs. He was made viscount in 1917.

North Conway, N.H.: see CONWAY.

North Dakota, state (70,665 sq. mi.; pop. 619,636), N central U.S.; admitted 1889 as 39th state; cap. BISMARCK. Other cities are FARGO and GRAND FORKS. Bounded E by RED RIVER OF THE NORTH. Crossed by MISSOURI R. Central lowlands in E, hills and Badlands in W. Farming grains (esp. wheat), livestock, dairying. Processing of these products. Deposits of lignite, clay, bentonite. Explorations began 1738 with VÉRENDRYE. U.S. got NW N.Dak. in Louisiana Purchase (1803), SE half from Great Britain (1818). Fur trade dominated region for over half a century. Dakota Territory organized 1861. Indian warfare disturbed region in 1860s and 1870s. Wheat fields, homesteading, railroad building brought settlers. Struggle between farmers and corporate interests dominated politics in late 19th cent. Drought of 1930s brought about irrigation, power developments. Additional improvement is proposed in MISSOURI RIVER BASIN PROJECT.

North Dakota, University of: see GRAND FORKS.

North Dakota Agricultural College: see FARGO.

North Downs, England: see DOWNS, THE, chalk hills.

Northeast Boundary Dispute, controversy between U.S. and Great Britain concerning Maine-New Brunswick boundary. Treaty of 1783 had described NE U.S. boundary as a line drawn due N from source of St. Croix R. to highlands dividing the Atlantic and St. Lawrence tributaries and along those highlands to NW head of Connecticut R. Disputes over that definition lasted almost 60 years. In 1839 dispute led to so-called AROOSTOOK WAR. WEBSTER-ASHBURTON TREATY ended controversy.

Northeast Harbor, Maine: see MOUNT DESERT ISLAND.

North East Land, island: see SPITSBERGEN.

Northeast Passage, passage from North Sea to the Pacific. Sought notably by William Barentz (16th cent.), Henry Hudson (17th cent.), Vitus Bering (18th cent.). First successful navigation by N. A. E. Nordenskjold of Sweden (1878–79). Passage has become regular shipping route for Siberian ports, navigable from June to Sept.

Northern Dvina, RSFSR: see DVINA.

Northern Ireland, administrative unit (5,238 sq. mi.; pop. 1,370,709) of United Kingdom; cap. Belfast. Estab. by Government of Ireland Act of 1920, Ireland (often called ULSTER) comprises six counties of Armagh, Down, Antrim, Londonderry, Tyrone, and Fermanagh, with county boroughs of Belfast and Londonderry. Republic of IRELAND refuses to recognize division as valid. N Ireland, represented in British Parliament by 12 members, has large degree of self-government. History began in early 17th cent. when British confiscated much of land and "planted" it with Scotch and English settlers. Rift between two parts came with Gladstone's proposed first HOME RULE Bill (1886). Protestant North feared domination by southern Catholic majority. By World War I civil war was a danger. Bill of 1920 set up separate parliaments for N and S Ireland. Growing Catholic minority now threatens Protestant hegemony. Land is mountainous; farming is the main industry. Area is famous for its fine linens. Heavier industry is concentrated in and around Belfast, one of chief ports of British Isles.

Northern Land, RSFSR: see SEVERNAYA ZEMLYA.

northern lights: see AURORA BOREALIS.

Northern Pacific Railway, American railway system, chartered 1864. Construction began in 1870. Jay COOKE first managed enterprise. After financial contest with E. H. Harriman, group under J. J. Hill and J. P. Morgan secured control. Line extends from Duluth and St. Paul, Minn., to Seattle, Wash., and Portland, Oregon; operating several branch systems, it controls nearly 6,900 mi. of trackage. Numerous traffic connections give it access to L. Superior, Gulf of Mexico, Pacific Ocean.

Northern Rhodesia (rōdē'zhu̇), British protectorate (292,323 sq. mi.; est. pop. 1,565,-547), S central Africa; cap. Lusaka. On high plateau with generally healthful climate. Chief crops are corn, tobacco, and coffee. Copper is leading export. Livingstone first came on missionary journeys in 1851; traveled through Barotseland (in W part) and in 1855 discovered Victoria Falls. In 1891 the British made Barotseland a protectorate. British control over area was estab. 1891–94 by ousting Arab slave traders. Governed as part of RHODESIA until 1911. Controlled by British South Africa Co. until 1924, when direct British rule was estab. with appointed governor aided by executive and legislative councils.

Northern Territories, British protectorate (30,-600 sq. mi.; pop. 1,077,138), N Gold Coast, W Africa; cap. Tamale. Stock raising and cotton growing.

Northern Territory (523,620 sq. mi.; pop. 10,-866), N Australia, on Timor and Arafura seas; cap. Darwin. Originally a part of New South Wales, it later belonged to South Australia. In 1911 it came under direct control of federal government; divided 1926 into North Australia and Central Australia, reunited 1931. First explored by Leichhardt (1844–45). Climate is tropical, with monsoon season. Sparse population is composed mainly of aborigines, who occupy 15 reservations. Discovery of uranium ore has boosted area's economic development.

Northern War, 1700–1721, conflict arising from the desire of Sweden's neighbors to break Swedish supremacy in N Europe. In 1699 PETER I of Russia, FREDERICK IV of Denmark, and AUGUSTUS II of Poland and Saxony allied themselves against CHARLES XII of Sweden. Hostilities opened in 1700. Against immense odds, the young Swedish king quickly forced Denmark out of the war and routed Peter at Narva (1700); took Warsaw and Cracow (1702); had STANISLAUS I elected king of Poland (1704); and forced Augustus to renounce Poland and his alliance with Russia (Treaty of Altranstädt, 1706). In 1707 Charles invaded the Ukraine with the help of MAZEPPA. Utterly defeated by Peter at Poltava (1709), he found asylum in Turkey and induced the sultan to declare war on Russia (1710). When Peter bought off Turkey in the Peace of the Pruth (1711), Charles's position became untenable. Nevertheless, he stubbornly stayed on in Turkey until 1714. Meanwhile Augustus reconquered Poland; Peter completed the conquest of Swedish Livonia, Ingermanland, and Karelia; and Denmark resumed warfare in alliance with Hanover and Prussia. Undaunted, Charles invaded Norway but was fatally shot in 1718. By the treaties of Stockholm and Frederiksborg (1719–20) Sweden made peace with all the allies but Russia, ceding the duchies of Verden and Bremen to Hanover and part of W Pomerania to Prussia. By the Treaty of Nystad (1721), Sweden ceded Livonia, Ingermanland, and part of Karelia to Russia. Russia became a major European power.

Northfield. **1** Town (pop. 2,246), N Mass., on Connecticut R. and NE of Greenfield. Birthplace of D. L. Moody, founder of Northfield Seminary (now Northfield School) for girls and Mt. Hermon School for boys; he started summer religious conferences. First youth hostel in U.S. opened here 1934. **2** City (pop. 7,487), SE Minn., S of St. Paul, in farm area. Seat of Carleton Col. (coed.; 1866) and Saint Olaf Col. (Lutheran; coed.; opened by Norwegians as school 1875, became college 1886, chartered 1889). Jesse James gang tried to rob bank here, Sept. 7, 1876. **3** Town (pop. 4,314), central Vt., SW of Montpelier. Includes Northfield village (pop. 2,262). Town is seat of Norwich Univ. (state military college, but privately controlled, for men; founded 1819, opened 1820 at Norwich, became university 1834, moved to Northfield 1866).

North German Confederation, alliance of 22 German states N of Main R., under Prussian leadership, which replaced the GERMAN CONFEDERATION, destroyed by the Austro-Prussian War (1866). The S German states, though excluded, were closely bound to it through membership in the ZOLLVEREIN. Constitution, prepared by Bismarck, provided for federal council and diet (Reichstag); king of Prussia was the president. In 1871 this constitution, with some modification, was adopted by the German Empire.

North Hants, England: see NORTHAMPTONSHIRE.

North Haven, town (pop. 9,444), S Conn., N of New Haven. Mfg. of bricks and hardware.

North Holland, Dutch *Noordholland,* province (1,017 sq. mi.; pop. 1,774,273), NW Netherlands; cap. Haarlem; largest city Amsterdam. A peninsula between the North Sea and the Ijsselmeer, it is a lowland drained by numerous small rivers and canals and protected by dikes. Agr., cattle raising, dairying, flower growing, fishing. Famed for its many windmills, drawbridges, tulip fields. For history, see HOLLAND.

North Island (44,281 sq. mi.; pop. 1,146,292), New Zealand, separated from South Isl. by Cook Strait. Chief towns are Wellington (cap. of New Zealand) and Auckland. Irregularly shaped with long NW peninsula. Has volcanic peaks and many hot springs. Drained mainly by Waikato R., which rises in L. Taupo.

North Kingstown (kĭng'stŭn), town (pop. 14,810), S R.I., on Narragansett Bay S of Providence; settled 1641. Birthplace of Gilbert Stuart. Mfg. of woolens and elastic braid. Includes old Wickford resort (pop. 2,437) and Quonset Point (kwŏn'sĭt), site of Northeastern Naval Air Station (1941).

North Little Rock, city (pop. 44,097), central Ark., on Arkansas R. opposite LITTLE ROCK; settled c.1856, annexed Levy 1946. It has railroad shops, stockyards, and processing plants for timber-creosoting and cottonseed oil.

Northmen: see NORSEMEN.

North Miami, town (pop. 10,734), SE Fla., near Miami; renamed 1931 from Miami Shores.

North Minch, Scotland: see MINCH.

North Olmsted, city (pop. 6,604), NE Ohio, W suburb of Cleveland. Makes machine tools.

North Ossetia, RSFSR: see OSSETIA.

North Platte (plăt), city (pop. 15,433), central Nebr., at junction of North Platte and South Platte rivers; laid out 1866. In irrigated grain and livestock area, it is a Great Plains shipping point on transcontinental rail and air lines.

North Platte, river rising in N Colo. and flowing 680 mi. in great bend through Wyo. and across W Nebr. to join the South Platte and form the Platte. Has 27 major reservoirs. Dams include Kingsley Dam at OGALLALA, Nebr., those of Kendrick project at CASPER, Wyo., and of North Platte project.

North Platte project, developed by U.S. in North Platte valley in W Nebr. and E Wyo. Irrigates 237,000 acres and supplies some 175,000 privately developed acres. Guernsey Reservoir is created by Guernsey Dam (105 ft. high) in North Platte R. and is fed by Pathfinder Reservoir, made by Pathfinder Dam (214 ft. high), and by three small reservoirs near Scottsbluff. On project are Glendo Reservoir, Whalen Diversion Dam, and Guernsey Dam and Lingle power plants. Main activities in area are agr. and livestock raising. Serves Bridgeport, Bayard, Minatare, Scottsbluff, Mitchell, and Gering, Nebr., and Torrington, Wyo.

North Pole, northern end of earth's axis, lat. 90° and long. 0°. It is distinguished from the north magnetic pole. R. E. Peary reached the North Pole (1909). See also ARCTIC REGIONS.

North Providence, textile town (pop. 13,927), NE R.I., NW of Providence.

North Rhine–Westphalia (–wĕstfāl'yŭ), Ger. *Nordrhein-Westfalen,* German state (13,157 sq. mi.; pop. 13,147,066), NW Germany; cap. DÜSSELDORF. Formed 1947 in British zone of occupation, it includes the former Prussian WESTPHALIA prov. and RHINE PROVINCE and the former state of Lippe. With the RUHR and the Rhenish industrial dists., it is one of the world's greatest centers of heavy industries. Joined Federal Republic of [West] Germany 1949.

North Riding: see YORKSHIRE, England.

North River, N.Y.: see HUDSON, river.

Northrop, John Howard, 1891–, American biochemist. He shared 1946 Nobel Prize in Chemistry for work on enzymes and viruses.

North Saskatchewan: see SASKATCHEWAN, river.

North Schleswig, Denmark: see SCHLESWIG.

North Sea, part of the Atlantic (c.600 mi. long) between British Isles and NW Central Europe. 400 mi. at widest, it narrows to Strait of Dover. Has many shallows. Largest is Dogger Bank, between England and Denmark, a center of the North Sea fisheries.

North Smithfield, textile town (pop. 5,726), N R.I., at Mass. line and NW of Providence.

North Star: see POLESTAR.

North Sydney, town (pop. 7,354), NE Cape Breton Isl., N.S., Canada, on Sydney Harbour, NW of Sydney. Coal-shipping port and winter fishing base.

North Tarrytown, residential village (pop. 8,740), SE N.Y., on E bank of Hudson R. near Tarrytown. Has Castle Philipse (see PHILIPSE MANOR) and Dutch Reformed Church (c.1697), where Washington Irving is buried, in Sleepy Hollow, the setting for his story, "Legend of Sleepy Hollow." John André's capture here revealed Benedict Arnold's treachery. Near by are Rockefeller estates.

North Tonawanda (tŏnůwŭn′dů), city (pop. 24,731), W N.Y., on Niagara R., at W end of the Barge Canal; settled 1808. Lumber port; mfg. of iron, steel, wood products, boats, paper, and musical instruments.

Northumberland, earls of: see PERCY, family.

Northumberland, John Dudley, duke of, c.1502–1553, English statesman. Helped estab. Edward SEYMOUR as protector of EDWARD VI, later deposed (1549) and executed him. Posed as a Protestant and persuaded dying Edward to name Lady Jane Grey as successor. Deserted by his army, he was executed for treason.

Northumberland, border county (2,019 sq mi.; pop. 798,175), N England; co. town Newcastle-on-Tyne. Has rugged coastline, with high moorlands and fertile valleys in the interior. Oats, barley, and turnips are grown; sheep grazing is important. There are great coal deposits in SE. Newcastle is major coal-shipping port and a shipbuilding and industrial center.

Northumbria, kingdom of (nôrthŭm′brēů), one of the Anglo-Saxon heptarchy, England. Originally it comprised kingdoms of Bernicia and Deira, settled by invading Angles c.500. United by Aethelfrith. Edwin estab. Northumbrian supremacy, which declined as that of MERCIA increased. 8th and early 9th cent. saw golden age of Church and culture. Invading Danes occupied S Northumbria and Angles had to acknowledge (920) Edward the Elder of Wessex as overking.

North Vancouver, city (pop. 15,687), SE B.C., Canada, on Burrard Inlet of Strait of Georgia, opposite Vancouver (bridge, ferry). Port and fishing base with shipbuilding, lumbering, and woodworking.

Northwest Boundary Dispute: see SAN JUAN BOUNDARY DISPUTE.

North West Company, organized 1787 by Montreal merchants and fur traders as rival of HUDSON'S BAY COMPANY. Extended fur trade W. Explorers such as Sir Alexander MACKENZIE and David THOMPSON were North West Co. men. Company pushed business into territory of U.S. American post, Astoria, was purchased by company in 1813. Rivalry with Hudson's Bay Co. reached peak in quarrel over RED RIVER SETTLEMENT; two companies were forced to unite in 1821.

Northwestern University, at Evanston and Chicago, Ill., coed.; chartered 1851, opened 1855 by Methodists. In 1873 absorbed Evanston Col. for Ladies (opened 1871), headed by Frances Willard, with which Northwestern Female Col. (opened 1855) had merged.

North-West Frontier Province (41,057 sq. mi.; pop. 5,699,000), W Pakistan; cap. Peshawar. Mostly mountainous, with caravan trade via Khyber Pass. Main occupations are agr. and livestock raising. In ancient times area belonged to Persian empire; today most inhabitants speak Pushtu, an Iranian language. Islam was introduced in 11th cent. by Afghan invaders. Under Sikh control from 1818 to 1849, when area was taken by the British. Areas bordering on Afghanistan are inhabited by Moslem tribes, which have long resisted outside authority.

Northwest Mounted Police: see ROYAL CANADIAN MOUNTED POLICE.

Northwest Ordinance: see ORDINANCE OF 1787.

Northwest Passage, route sought through American continent to South Sea for commercial purposes. Spurred exploration in the 16th and 17th cent. Later scientific expeditions estab. existence of a passage though icy seas N of the continent; this was traversed 1903–6.

Northwest Territories, region (1,304,903 sq. mi.; pop. 16,004), NW Canada, W of Hudson Bay, E of Yukon, N of lat. 60°N. Includes islands of Hudson Bay, Hudson Strait, and James Bay. Area is divided into three provisional districts: Keewatin, W of Hudson Bay; Mackenzie, E of Yukon; and Franklin, N and including the Arctic Archipelago. Most development has been in Mackenzie dist. Fur trading is extensive. Although vast mineral resources remain untapped, oil is produced at Fort Norman, gold at Yellowknife, copper from Coppermine R. area, and pitchblende and uranium on Great Bear L. Here are two of world's largest lakes, GREAT BEAR and GREAT SLAVE, which drain into Arctic Ocean via Mackenzie R. Much of Keewatin dist. is part of the BARREN GROUNDS and here, as in Franklin dist., fur trapping is the major occupation. Franklin dist. is a game preserve. Region's transport and travel is largely by air. Henry Hudson opened the gateway to the area 1610. After that Hudson's Bay Co. sponsored many explorations and opened trading posts. Area was known as RUPERT'S LAND until it was ceded to Canada by HUDSON'S BAY Co. 1870, then including Man., Sask., Alta., and parts of B.C. and Que. The S border of 60°N was estab. 1912. Government of the territories, enforced by the Royal Canadian Mounted Police, is under a commissioner and council.

Northwest Territory, first national territory of U.S., comprising geographical region generally known as Old Northwest. This area about the Great Lakes and between the Ohio and the Mississippi included present states of Ohio, Ind., Ill., Mich., Wis., and part of Minn. French control here began with exploring and trading in early 17th cent. By the

Treaty of Paris (1763), which ended French and Indian Wars, British obtained Canada and Old Northwest. G. R. Clark led expedition against British in American Revolution. Treaty of Paris (1783), ending Revolution, declared Old Northwest within U.S. boundaries. Cession of all lands to U.S. government by 1786 ended strife among states over rival claims. Ordinance of 1787 set up machinery for organization of territories and admission of states. Ohio Company of Associates was most active force in early colonization. Jay's Treaty and subsequent negotiations smoothed out some British-American difficulties, but British influence remained strong among the Indians. Quarrel over Northwest was a chief cause of War of 1812. Treaty of Ghent (1814) irrevocably settled region upon U.S.

Northwich, urban district (pop. 17,480), Cheshire, England; center of England's salt industry.

Norton, Caroline (Elizabeth Sarah Sheridan), 1808–77, English author; granddaughter of R. B. Sheridan. She became the subject of notoriety when her husband, suing for divorce, accused her of an affair with Lord Melbourne. She wrote vigorously to improve the status of women and to better working conditions, especially for children.

Norton, Charles Eliot, 1827–1908, American scholar; an influential professor of history of art at Harvard (1875–98); an editor of the *North American Review* and a founder of the *Nation*. Translated Dante and edited poems of John Donne, as well as letters of Carlyle, Emerson, Lowell, and Ruskin.

Norton, town (pop. 4,401), SE Mass., NW of Taunton. Seat of Wheaton Col. (nonsectarian; for women; opened 1835, chartered as pioneer female seminary 1837, organized by Mary Lyon, became college 1912).

Norton Sound, 130 mi. long, inlet of Bering Sea, on W coast of Alaska, S of Seward Peninsula. Nome is on N shore; Yukon R. enters sea on S side. Explored by Capt. James Cook 1778.

Norumbega (nôrŭmbĕ'gŭ), region or city on E coast of North America, possibly mythical, used on 16th–17th cent. maps. Location and identity uncertain.

Norwalk. 1 City (pop. 49,460), SW Conn., on harbor on Long Isl. Sound SW of Bridgeport; settled 1649. Mfg. of hats, textiles, hardware, and machinery. Includes South Norwalk (annexed 1913; rail junction), Silvermine (artists' colony), other villages, and offshore islands. **2** City (pop. 9,775), N Ohio, SSE of Sandusky. Mfg. of wood and rubber goods.

Norway, Nor. *Norge,* kingdom (119,240 sq. mi.; with water surface 125,182 sq. mi.; pop. 3,156,950), N Europe, occupying the mountainous W part of the Scandinavian peninsula. Largest cities: Oslo (cap.), Bergen, Trondheim, Stavanger. Overseas possessions: Spitsbergen and Jan Mayen (Arctic Ocean); Bouvet and Peter I isls. (S Atlantic). Extending from the Skagerrak NE to North Cape, Norway has a W coastline c.2,100 mi. long, fringed with islands (incl. Lofoten) and deeply indented by fjords. Its land borders are with Sweden (W) and Finland and USSR (N). Land rises precipitously from coast to high plateaus (e.g., Dovrefjell); culminates at 8,098 ft. in Jotunheim range. Only 4% of land is under cultivation. Climate is mild because of North Atlantic Drift. Chief natural resources are timber (covers c.25% of Norway), minerals (pyrites, copper, iron), hydroelectric power. Fishing (cod, herring, mackerel) and whaling provide chief exports. Other important industries: pulp and paper milling, electrochemistry, electrometallurgy. Merchant fleet ranks third in world. The population, predominantly Lutheran, is concentrated in S. Lapps and Finns predominate in N. Norway is a constitutional monarchy, with legislative powers vested in the Storting. Reigning king: Haakon VII. The several petty kingdoms of Norway were united (872) by Harold I in the age of the Vikings. (See also Norsemen; Iceland.) Olaf II (reigned 1015–28) estab. Christianity. He was driven out by Canute, but his son Magnus I was restored on the Norwegian throne 1035. After a period of anarchy, King Sverre defeated the nobles (1201) and centralized royal power. Medieval Norway reached its flowering under Magnus VI and Haakon IV (13th cent.) but soon declined when the Hanseatic League monopolized its trade. It ceased to exist as a separate kingdom in the 14th cent. Under Queen Margaret its crown was permanently united with that of Denmark (1397); Danish governors ruled Norway until 1814, when Denmark ceded the kingdom to Sweden. Norway attempted to set itself up as a separate kingdom but was forced to accept union with Sweden in 1815. It did, however, retain its separate constitution of 1814. Late in 19th cent. the Liberal leader, Johan Sverdrup, obtained concessions from Sweden, but Sweden refused to grant Norway a separate consular service and flag. This, among other issues, led the Storting to declare the union dissolved. Sweden acquiesced; Haakon VII was chosen king of Norway. The late 19th and early 20th cent. saw a large-scale emigration of Norwegians to the U.S. Norway was neutral in World War I. In World War II Germany invaded Norway without warning (April, 1940). Norwegian troops briefly resisted, but French and British aid was inadequate. The government continued the war from abroad, bringing the Norwegian merchant fleet to the Allies. The attempts of Quisling to enlist the people in his collaboration with the German authorities failed utterly. Russian troops entered N Norway late in 1944; the rest of the country remained under German occupation until May, 1945. A charter member of the UN, Norway also joined the European Recovery Program (1947) and North Atlantic Treaty (1949).

Norway, resort town (pop. 3,811), SW Maine, NW of Auburn. Mfg. of wooden articles, shoes, moccasins, and equipment for winter sports.

Norwegian language, either of two slightly different North Germanic standard languages. Dano-Norwegian or Rigsmaal is Oslo dialect of standard Danish, which was official until 20th cent. Landsmaal is a standardization of

Norwegian dialects, introduced by Ivar AASEN. See LANGUAGE (table).

Norwegian Sea, name of that part of the Atlantic NW of Norway between Greenland Sea and North Sea.

Norwich (nŏ'rĭj, –rĭch), county borough (pop. 121,226), co. seat of Norfolk, England. In 11th cent. it ranked with London, York, and Bristol in ecclesiastical and commercial importance. Has many ancient churches and buildings, including 11th-cent. cathedral. Saw much early fighting, and twice suffered Black Death. A grain market, it has varied mfg.

Norwich. 1 (nŏr'wĭch, nŏ'rĭch), Industrial city (pop. 23,429) in Norwich town (pop. 37,-633), SE Conn., at head of Thames R. estuary. Mfg. of metal and leather goods, textiles, and chemicals. Pewter making began here 1730. Has art gallery, with art school. **2** (nôr'wĭch), City (pop. 8,816), S central N.Y., on Chenango R. and NE of Binghamton. Mfg. of pharmaceuticals, dairy goods, and machinery.

Norwich University: see NORTHFIELD, Vt.

Norwood. 1 Town (pop. 16,636), E Mass., SW of Boston; settled 1678. Printing and tanning. **2** City (pop. 35,001), SW Ohio, suburb of Cincinnati; settled as Sharpsburg in early 19th cent. Mfg. of automobiles, electrical and metal goods. **3** Borough (pop. 5,246), SE Pa., SW suburb of Philadelphia.

Noske, Gustav (gōōs'tăf nôs'kủ), 1868–1946, German politician, a Social Democrat. As minister of defense (1919–20), he ruthlessly suppressed SPARTACUS PARTY and other radical uprisings.

Nostradamus (nŏs"trủdā'mủs), Fr. *Michel de Nostredame,* 1503–66, French astrologer and physician. His obscure rhymed prophecies (*Centuries,* 1555) have enjoyed popularity for centuries.

Notker Labeo (lā'bēō), c.950–1022, German monk, teacher at St. Gall, a founder of German literature. He translated Boethius, Aristotle, Capella, and Gregory I into Old High German.

Notre Dame, University of (nō"tủr dām'), at Notre Dame, Ind., N of South Bend; Holy Cross Fathers, mainly for men; chartered and opened 1844. Knute ROCKNE was a famous football coach here.

Notre Dame de Paris (nô'trủ däm' dủ pärē'), cathedral church on Île de la Cité, Paris. Site was originally occupied by Roman temple and later by two Christian churches, which were demolished by Maurice de Sully in order to erect the cathedral. Construction began 1163, finished c.1230. Spires of original design were never added to the twin towers. In French Revolution rioters destroyed sculptures of W façade. Under Viollet-le-Duc restorations were begun 1845. In Notre Dame, Gothic forms are clearly dominant, with few traces of Romanesque design.

Notre Dame Mountains, continuation of Green Mts. of Vt., c.3,500 ft. high, SE and E Que., Canada, extending NE to St. Lawrence R. below Quebec and E into the Gaspé Peninsula where they are continued by Shickshock Mts.

Nott, Eliphalet (ĭlĭ'fủlĭt nŏt'), 1773–1866, American educator, clergyman, and inventor. He was president of Union Col., 1804–66. Among his inventions was first anthracite coal base-burner stove.

Nottaway (nŏ'tủwā), river of W Que., Canada, rising in Mattagami L. Flows c.400 mi. NW to James Bay.

Nottingham, Charles Howard, 1st **earl of:** see HOWARD, family.

Nottinghamshire (nŏ'tĭng-ủmshĭr) or **Nottingham,** inland county (844 sq. mi.; pop. 841,-083), central England. In S are upland moors, the Wolds, bordering low-lying fertile land. Sherwood Forest, scene of Robin Hood legends, includes the Dukeries, area noted for fine estates. Dairying and cereal crops are important. Coal fields are along W border. Textiles, bicycles, and motors are manufactured. The county town is **Nottingham** (nŏ'tĭng-ủm), county borough (pop. 306,-008), on the Trent. Was an important Danish borough in 9th cent. In 1642 standard of Charles I was raised here, marking start of civil war. Site of a Catholic cathedral and Univ. Col. Manufactures include cotton and silk goods. Traditional birthplace of Robin Hood.

Notus (nō'tủs), in Greek mythology, personification of the south wind, bringer of fog and sickness.

Nouméa (nōōmē'ủ, nōōmāä'), port town (pop. 11,108), New Caledonia; cap. of French colony of New Caledonia. Airline base on Calif.–New Zealand route. Exports nickel, chrome, and copra. Had U.S. air base in World War II. Name is sometimes spelled Numea.

nova: see VARIABLE STAR.

Novalis (nōvä'lĭs), pseud. of **Friedrich von Hardenberg** (frē'drĭkh fŭn här'dủnbĕrk), 1772–1801, German poet, one of the most extreme and most gifted romanticists. His works include the unfinished novel *Heinrich von Ofterdingen,* the deeply religious *Hymnen an die Nacht* [hymns to the night] (1800; Eng. tr., 1948), and *Christendom or Europe* (1826; Eng. tr., 1844), an exposition of his Catholicism.

Novara (nōvä'rä), city (pop. 52,269), Piedmont, N Italy. Chemical plants; rice, flour, and textile mills. Produces Gorgonzola cheese. The Swiss defeated the French here in 1513, and in 1849 the Austrians defeated the Sardinians.

Nova Scotia (nō'vủ skō'shủ), province (20,743 sq. mi.; with water surface 21,068 sq. mi.; pop. 642,584), E Canada; cap. HALIFAX. Other large cities are SYDNEY, GLACE BAY, DARTMOUTH, TRURO, and NEW WATERFORD. Fisheries operate out of numerous bays and inlets on Atlantic Ocean (E, S, W) and Gulf of St. Lawrence and Northumberland Strait (NE, N). Hills, lakes, and streams nourish lumber and woodworking industry, and river valleys and reclaimed lowlands provide grain, fruit, and dairy products. Fine railroad and highway system serves province and encourages tourism, while sailing, fishing, and hunting attract sportsmen. Province settled by French as ACADIA, with Port Royal estab. 1605. British bitterly contested French claims and were awarded the area now in provinces of N.S. (excluding Cape Breton Isl.) and N.B. by Treaty of Utrecht (1713–14). Hostilities continued to 1763, during which time the British expelled many Acadians. Prince Edward Isl. was annexed 1763, but made separate colony 1769. Cape Breton Isl. was united with N.S. 1763–84 and reunited 1820. Became first colony to achieve responsible government 1848 and accepted Canadian confederation 1867.

Novatian (nōvā'shŭn), fl. 250, Roman priest, antipope (after 251) in opposition to St. Cornelius. He espoused MONTANISM and won some following, but later the Church generally, led by St. Cyprian of Carthage, recognized Cornelius. Novatian's successors continued to have their own hierarchy until in the 4th cent. they were merged with DONATISM. Novatian wrote *On the Trinity* and other works.

Novaya Zemlya (nô"vīŭ zĭmlyä') [Rus.,= new land], archipelago (c.35,000 sq. mi.; pop. c.400), N European RSFSR, in Arctic Ocean between Barents and Kara seas. Ice-covered in N; mountainous in central section; tundra lowlands in S. Inhabitants, the Nentsy (formerly SAMOYEDES), subsist on hunting and fishing. Mineral deposits include copper, lead, zinc, pyrite.

Novels: see CORPUS JURIS CIVILIS.

November: see MONTH.

Novgorod (nôv'gŭrŭt), city (1926 pop. 32,764), W European RSFSR, on Volkhov R. near L. Ilmen. One of oldest Russian cities, it was a major commercial center of medieval Europe. Here RURIK is said to have founded the Russian state (862). A dependency of Kiev, Novgorod became the cap. of an independent republic in the 12th cent. It was governed by a popular assembly, which elected the dukes. Situated on the great trade route to the Volga valley, it became one of the four chief foreign centers of the HANSEATIC LEAGUE, extended its rule over all N Russia and several colonies, and reached its peak in the 14th cent., with a population of c.400,000. Its colorful splendor in that period had inspired much of Russian art and folklore. Novgorod fell to Moscow in 1478; in 1570 Ivan the Terrible laid it waste to punish it for suspected treachery and abolished its last remaining liberties. It was called the "museum city" for its magnificent architectural monuments until World War II, when it suffered heavily during German occupation (1941–44). Chief among its losses was the 12th-cent. KREMLIN, which included the Cathedral of St. Sophia (founded 1045).

Novibazar, Yugoslavia: see NOVI PAZAR.

Novikov, Nikolai Ivanovich (nyĭkŭlī' ēvä'nŭvĭch nô'vĕkŭf), 1744–1818, Russian publicist, an advocate of Enlightenment. Catherine II suspended his satirical journal *The Drone* in 1774 for attacking serfdom. Later his press, which published books for popular education, was closed down, and he was imprisoned for several years.

Novi Pazar (nô"vē päzär'), town (pop. 12,196), W Serbia, Yugoslavia. The Turkish sanjak (district) of Novibazar (an older spelling) was occupied by Austrian troops 1889–1908; passed to Serbia 1913.

Novi Sad (säd), Ger. *Neusatz,* Hung. *Újvidék,* city (pop. 77,127), N Serbia, Yugoslavia, on the Danube; cap. of Vojvodina. Flour-milling center. Orthodox metropolitan see. Though it belonged to Hungary until 1920, it was the center of Serbian cultural revival in 18th and early 19th cent.

Novocherkassk (nô"vŭchŭrkäsk'), city (pop. 81,286), S European RSFSR, near Don R. Mfg. of locomotives, machinery, explosives; lumber mills, distilleries. Founded 1865 as headquarters of Don Cossacks, it has former hetman's palace.

Novorossisk or **Novorossiisk** (nô"vŭrŭsēsk'), city (pop. 95,280), W Krasnodar Territory, S European RSFSR; a major Black Sea port. It has petroleum refineries, machinery plants, shipyards. Founded 1838. Was occupied by Germans 1942–43.

Novosibirsk (nŭvŭsēbērsk'), city (pop. c.750,000), RSFSR, in S central Siberia, on upper Ob R. and on Trans-Siberian RR. Founded 1893 as Novonikolayevsk (renamed 1925), it grew rapidly (partly because of proximity of KUZNETSK BASIN) into cultural, transportation, and industrial center of Asiatic Russia. Produces heavy machinery, steel, textiles.

Noyes, Alfred, 1880–, English poet. His poems, chiefly narrative and traditional in form, include *Drake* (1908; an epic); *Tales of the Mermaid Tavern* (1912); and *The Torch Bearers* (1922–30; a trilogy on science). Familiar short poems are "The Barrel-Organ" and "The Highwayman." Works also include criticism, biography, novels, and an account of his conversion to Roman Catholicism.

Noyes, John Humphrey, 1811–86, American reformer, founder of the ONEIDA COMMUNITY. He taught "perfectionism," doctrine that man's innate sinlessness could be regained through communion with Christ.

Noyon (nwäyō'), city (pop. 5,900), Oise dept., N France. Here in 768 Charlemagne was crowned king of the Franks. Cathedral of Notre Dame (12th–13th cent.) and the birthplace of John Calvin are preserved here.

Np, chemical symbol of element NEPTUNIUM.

Nubia (nū'bēŭ), anc. country, NE Africa. Extended from First Cataract of the Nile (near Aswan, Egypt) to Khartoum in Anglo-Egyptian Sudan. In 8th cent. B.C. the Nubians estab. the short-lived XXV dynasty in Egypt. A Negro tribe, the Nobatae, settled in Nubia in 3d cent. and formed a powerful kingdom. Converted to Christianity in 6th cent., the kingdom long resisted Moslem encroachment but finally collapsed in 1366. The area was conquered in 19th cent. by Mohammed Ali of Egypt.

Nuevo Laredo (nwā'vō lärā'dhō), city (pop. 28,872), Tamaulipas, NE Mexico, across Rio Grande from Laredo, Texas. The N terminus of the Inter-American Highway, it is a center of international trade in an agr. and stock-raising region.

Nuevo León (nwā'vō lāōn'), state (25,136 sq. mi.; pop. 743,297), NE Mexico; cap. MONTERREY. S and W parts of state are traversed by Sierra Madre Oriental and extreme W portion lies in semiarid basin lands of N Mexico, which are cultivable under irrigation. Mining is chief industry, and refining ores has helped make Monterrey a booming industrial city.

nullification, in U.S. history, doctrine expounded by advocates of extreme STATES' RIGHTS. Held states have right to declare null and void and to set aside in practice any Federal law which violates their voluntary compact embodied in U.S. Constitution. KENTUCKY AND VIRGINIA RESOLUTIONS gave first notable expression to doctrine. After tariff act of 1832 John C. CALHOUN brought about ordinance of nullification passed by S.C. legislature. U.S. FORCE BILL was a result. Following passage of compromise tariff (1833), S.C. rescinded ordinance nullifying tariff acts, but passed new ordinance nullifying force bill. Issue not pressed further until doctrine of SECESSION was brought to fore.

Numantia (no͞omăn'shů), anc. settlement, Spain, near the Duero. After repeated attacks it was finally captured (133 B.C.) by Scipio Aemilianus after an eight-month siege.

Numa Pompilius (nū'–, –pĭl'–), legendary king of Rome, successor to Romulus. To him was ascribed origin of Roman ceremonial law and religious rites.

number, in arithmetic, indicates count (or sum) of group of objects or their positions in an ordered list. Count is indicated by cardinal numbers, position by ordinal numbers. System of cardinal numbers consisting only of natural numbers (positive whole numbers) has been extended from time to time to include new types of numbers as concept of quantity became more complicated. Negative numbers and zero were added, forming with natural numbers the group called integers, which, with fractions added, comprise rational numbers. Rational plus irrational numbers (such as $\sqrt{2}$, $\sqrt[3]{4}$) form real number system. Imaginary or complex numbers (i.e., numbers involving $\sqrt{-1}$) set a precedent for many further modern extensions. See also DECIMAL SYSTEM.

number, in grammar, class (see GENDER) referring to distinctions of number. In English, nouns are said to be singular or plural. Some languages (e.g., anc. Greek and Arabic) have singular, dual, and plural numbers. *Individual* vs. *collective* is the number distinction in still other languages.

Numbers, book of Old Testament, 4th of five books of Law (the Pentateuch or Torah), ascribed by tradition to Moses. It continues the history (begun in Exodus) of the Hebrews' journey from Egypt to Canaan, the Promised Land; contains two censuses, whence the title; and tells of the rise of Joshua as leader.

numbers, theory of, branch of mathematics concerned with higher arithmetic in which properties of integers only are studied. A prime number has no factors other than itself and 1. One of the important theorems states that every composite integer can be expressed as the product of primes and only one combination of primes (disregarding order). Divisibility, another topic in theory of numbers, is related to concept of prime numbers. Also important is theory of congruences, a generalization of idea of classification of numbers into odd and even.

Numea, New Caledonia: see NOUMÉA.

Numidia (nūmĭ'dēů), anc. country, NW Africa, very roughly the modern Algeria. Part of Carthaginian empire until in the Punic Wars, MASINISSA sided with Rome and gained independence (201 B.C.). Numidia flourished until JUGURTHA engaged in a fatal war with Rome. Juba II was restored as prince subject to Rome (1st cent. A.D.), and Numidia survived Vandal invasion (5th cent.) but declined after Arabs came (8th cent.).

nun: see MONASTICISM.

Nun'Álvares Pereira: see PEREIRA, NUN'ÁLVARES.

Nuneaton (nŭnē'tůn), municipal borough (pop. 54,408), Warwickshire, England. George Eliot, born here, used town in several of her novels. Has varied mfg. There are coal mines in the vicinity.

Núñez Cabeza de Vaca, Álvar: see CABEZA DE VACA.

Núñez Vela, Blasco (blä'skō no͞o'nyās vä'lä), d. 1546, first viceroy of Peru (1544–46). Sent by Charles V to enforce the New Laws, he met tremendous opposition which ended when he was arrested by *audiencia.* Put aboard ship for return to Spain, he escaped, returned to Peru but was defeated by Gonzalo Pizarro, and was put to death.

Nunivak (no͞o'nĭvăk), island, 56 mi. long, off W Alaska, in Bering Sea; discovered 1821. Treeless and fogbound with primitive native culture. Reindeer and musk ox recently introduced.

Nureddin (no͞o'rĕdēn'), 1118–74, ruler of Syria (1145–74). Fought with BALDWIN III of Jerusalem. Gained control of Egypt through his lieutenants Shirkuh (predecessor of Saladin), who defeated Amalric I.

Nuremberg (nyo͞o'rŭmbûrg), Ger. *Nürnberg,* city (pop. 360,017), Middle Franconia, N Bavaria, on Pegnitz R. Mfg. center (machinery, precision instruments, chemicals; breweries; toys, gingerbread). A free imperial city 1219–1803, it was independent from the burgraviate of Nuremberg, which comprised a large part of Franconia and was ruled by the Hohenzollern family from 1192. A major trade center, the city reached its flower in the 15th and 16th cent., when it was the center of the German Renaissance (birthplace of Albrecht Dürer, Hans Sachs, Peter Vischer, Veit Stoss, Michael Wolgemut; center of MEISTERSINGER; early printing center). First pocket watches ("Nuremberg eggs") were made here. Nuremberg early accepted the Reformation. By the religious Peace of Nuremberg (1532) the Protestants won important concessions. City declined after Thirty Years War; passed to Bavaria 1806; became industrial center. First German railroad (Nuremberg-Fürth) was opened 1835. Under Hitler, Nuremberg was the scene of the National Socialist party congresses. The Nuremberg Laws (1935) deprived German Jews of civic rights, forbade intermarriage between Jews and "Aryans." In World War II Nuremberg, as a major production center for airplane, submarine, and tank engines, was heavily bombed by the Allies. Its old section, once a marvel of Gothic and Renaissance architecture, was gutted, though many famous landmarks escaped total destruction—e.g., Church of St. Sebaldus, burgraves' castle, city hall, Dürer's house. In 1945–46 Nuremberg was the scene of the first international WAR-CRIMES trial.

Nurmi, Paavo (pä'vō nŏŏr'mē), 1897–, Finnish track star. Between 1920 and 1932 he set 20 world running records, won six Olympic titles at distances from 1,500 meters to 10,000 meters.

Nürnberg, Bavaria: see NUREMBERG.

nursery school, educational institution for children from two to four years old, designed to promote their social adjustment. The first nursery schools were opened in London in 1907. Pioneers in nursery school work in U.S. were State Univ. of Iowa; Teachers Col., Columbia Univ.; and Smith and Vassar. Most such schools in U.S. are privately owned.

nursing, care of sick. Practiced by women outside of own homes since early Christian era. Training was encouraged by St. Vincent de Paul in 17th cent. First hospital training school estab. 1836 at Kaiserswerth, Germany. Here Florence Nightingale studied. School she established at St. Thomas's Hospital, London, was pattern for other schools of nursing. Legislation regulating practice of nursing was initiated in 20th cent. and nursing education began to be improved and expanded in scope to meet modern needs.

nut, a dry one-seeded fruit which does not open in maturity, e.g., acorn, chestnut, filbert, and hazelnut. Commonly the word is used also for any seed or fruit with an edible kernel surrounded by a hard or brittle covering, including the ALMOND, BRAZIL NUT, CASHEW, COCONUT, LITCHI, PEANUT, PECAN, and WALNUT.

nuthatch (nŭt'hăch), name for various Old and New World small birds related to titmouse and creeper.

Nutley, town (pop. 26,992), NE N.J., N of Newark. Mfg. of chemicals, metal products, drugs, paper.

nutmeg, the seed, a valuable spice, of an evergreen tree (*Myristica fragrans*), also called nutmeg, and native to the Moluccas. The seeds are sold whole or ground. Mace, also a spice, is derived from the seed covering. Both seed and covering yield an oil used in medicine and cosmetics.

nutria (nōō'trēu, nū'–), large aquatic South American rodent (*Myocastor*) introduced into S U.S. Valued for beaverlike fur.

nutrition (nūtrĭ'shŭn), term generally used to include various processes concerned with the securing, digestion, and utilization of food substances. Plants containing green pigment chlorophyll can synthesize their food in process called PHOTOSYNTHESIS. Parasitic nutrition (see PARASITE) is characteristic of some plants and animals. Scientific research in nutrition has made great strides in recent years. Human nutrition is subject of vital importance to individual and to communities and nations. Importance of the daily DIET in helping to maintain good physical as well as mental health is recognized. Discoveries of value of VITAMINS in preventing deficiency diseases and in contributing to optimum health are significant. Good nutritional status depends on normal functioning of digestive, circulatory, excretory, and other systems and demands that food intake be chosen to include essential nutrients (vitamins, proteins, carbohydrates, fats, and minerals) and that calorie value be considered in relation to energy output. Food intake of too high calorie value results in overweight and sometimes in obesity, which, like underweight, indicates faulty nutrition. Ratio of height to weight is not an adequate indication of whether a child or an adult is well nourished; other factors include condition of skin, eyes, hair, subcutaneous fat, muscles, skeletal structures, and the posture.

Nuttall, Thomas, 1786–1859, American naturalist, b. England; pioneer paleontologist; curator of Harvard botanical garden (1822–32); author of *Travels into the Arkansa Territory* (1821).

Nutting, Mary Adelaide, 1858–1948, American teacher of nursing, authority on history of nursing.

Nuuanu Pali: see KOOLAU RANGE.

Nyack (nī'ăk), residential village (pop. 5,889), SE N.Y., on W bank of Hudson R. opposite Tarrytown. Leather goods, organs, sewing machines. Hook Mt. section of Palisades Interstate Park is just N.

Nyasa, Lake (nīă'sŭ), 360 mi. long, 15–50 mi. wide, E Africa, between Nyasaland on W and Tanganyika and Mozambique on E; southernmost of Africa's great lakes. Discovered c.1616 by Portuguese explorers, rediscovered 1859 by Livingstone.

Nyasaland, British protectorate (37,374 sq. mi.; pop. 2,314,000), E Africa; cap. Zomba. Bordered on E by L. Nyasa and on W by Northern Rhodesia. Lies in Great Rift Valley, flanked by high plateaus. Chief exports are tobacco, tea, cotton, and sisal. Visited 17th–18th cent. by Portuguese explorers. Rediscovered 1859 by Livingstone, it became British protectorate in 1891. Ruled by appointed governor aided by executive and legislative councils.

Nyborg (nü'bôr), town (pop. 10,775), Fyn isl., Denmark, on Great Belt. Has shipyards and textile mills. It was important medieval fort and trade center.

Nye, Edgar Wilson (nī), known as **Bill Nye,** 1850–96, American humorist. His comments and yarns are collected in a number of volumes.

Nykobing, Dan. *Nykøbing* (nü'kû"bĭng), name of several places in Denmark, especially a city (pop. 17,192) on Falster isl. It is a Baltic port, with sugar refineries, shipyards, and fishing fleet. Ruins of 12th-cent. castle and a Gothic church remain. Lutheran espiscopal see.

Nykoping, Swed. *Nyköping* (nü'chû"pĭng), Baltic port (pop. 20,447), co. seat of Sodermanland co., SE Sweden. It has mfg. of furniture, textiles, and autos. There remain 13th-cent. castle ruins and 17th-cent. town hall, though city burned 1665 and 1719.

nylon, synthetic material derived from coal, air, and water. Strong, elastic, resistant to abrasion and chemicals, and low in moisture absorbency, it can be permanently set by heat. It is manufactured as filaments (for hosiery and textiles), and in sheets and molded shapes. Introduced after 10 years of research by E. I. du Pont de Nemours & Co. in 1938.

Nymegen, Netherlands: see NIJMEGEN.

Nymphenburg (nüm′fŏŏnbo͝ork), suburb of Munich, Bavaria. Has magnificent royal château and park (begun 1664); famous china manufacture (founded 1761).

Nymwegen, Netherlands: see NIJMEGEN.

Nyssa (nĭ′sù), town (pop. 2,525), E Oregon, on the Snake near OWYHEE R. mouth and NW of Boise, Idaho. Market for Owyhee, Vale, and Boise projects.

Nystad, Treaty of, 1721: see NORTHERN WAR.

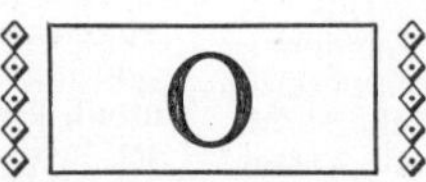

O, chemical symbol of the element OXYGEN.

Oahu (ōä′hōō), island (589 sq. mi.; pop. 353,020), third largest but most important of Hawaiian Isls. On SE shore is HONOLULU (territorial cap.), near which is famous beach of Waikiki. A vital defense area, with PEARL HARBOR naval base and military posts. Landscape is dominated by Waianae and KOOLAU ranges. Manoa Valley is site of Univ. of Hawaii. Rural areas produce pineapples, sugar cane.

oak, deciduous or evergreen tree and shrub of the genus *Quercus* including about 300 species widely distributed in the north temperate zone. Oaks have long been valued for their durable wood. The bark of some is used in tanning and medicine; that of the cork oak (*Quercus suber*) supplies the cork of commerce. Group known as black or red oaks (e.g., scarlet, black or yellow, pin, and laurel oaks) have leaves or leaf lobes usually bristle-tipped and acorns mature in two years. White oaks (e.g., the white, bur, post, holly, cork, and live oaks) have leaves or leaf lobes not bristle-tipped and mostly rounded, and acorns mature in one year.

Oak Bluffs, resort town (pop. 1,521), on NE Martha's Vineyard, SE Mass. Has summer theater.

Oakdale, city (pop. 5,598), SW La., near Calcasieu R. and SW of Alexandria, in timber and agr. area.

Oak Island, S N.S., Canada, in Mahone Bay. Reputed hiding place of Captain Kidd's treasure.

Oakland. 1 City (pop. 384,575), W Calif., on E side of San Francisco Bay; founded 1850. Port and industrial center. Has oil refineries, shipyards, railroad shops, and lumber mills. Processes fruits and produces automobiles, glass, beer, wine, chemicals, and building materials. City rises inland to 1,550 ft. in Berkeley Hills (residential section). Connected by San Francisco–Oakland Bay Bridge (1936) and several tunnels with near-by cities. Seat of Mills Col. (nonsectarian, mainly for women; opened 1852 as a seminary; chartered 1885 as a college, it was first woman's college in Far West). St. Mary's Col. (R.C.; for men; 1863) is near. **2** Town (pop. 1,640), NW Md., SW of Cumberland. Resort hq. near Backbone Mt.

Oak Lawn, residential village (pop. 8,751), NE Ill., near Chicago. Nurseries, truck farms.

Oakley, Annie, 1860–1926, American markswoman, performer with Buffalo Bill's Wild West Show.

Oakmont, borough (pop. 7,264), SW Pa., on Allegheny R., NE suburb of Pittsburgh. National tournaments have been held on golf links here.

Oak Park. 1 Residential village (pop. 63,259), NE Ill., adjoining Chicago; settled 1833. One of largest communities with village form of government. Mfg. of food and metal products. Has many houses designed by F. L. Wright, who lived here. **2** City (pop. 5,267), SE Mich., NW suburb of Detroit.

Oak Ridge, area (pop. 30,229), E Tenn., on Black Oak Ridge and Clinch R. near Clinton. Chosen 1942 as site for "Manhattan District" atom bomb project (called Clinton Engineer Works before). Existence and purpose secret until July, 1945. Transferred from U.S. Corps of Engineers to Atomic Energy Commission, Dec. 31, 1946. Has Oak Ridge Natl. Laboratory (formerly Clinton Natl. Laboratory) for nuclear research. Plants make radioactive isotopes for medical, industrial use and U-235 (may be used in atomic bombs). Has Oak Ridge Inst. of Nuclear Studies (1948; 14 member univs.).

Oakville, town (pop. 6,910), S Ont., Canada, on L. Ontario and SW of Toronto. Port with boatbuilding, woodworking, and mfg. of automobiles.

oasis (ōā′sĭs, ō′ùsĭs), fertile area in deserts, found where moisture is enough for growth of vegetation. Water comes to surface in springs or is collected and retained in mountain hollows. Irrigation is used to create oases, e.g., S Israel (Negev). Oases range from ponds with date palms to important centers of caravan trade with extensive agr.

Oates, Titus, 1649–1705, English conspirator. Invented (1678) the story of the Popish plot, a Jesuit-guided plan to assassinate Charles II. In ensuing frenzy many Catholics were persecuted and killed.

oats, hardy grasses, mostly annual, of genus

Avena, grown for grain, forage, and hay. In North America and the British Isles, oatmeal is a popular breakfast cereal. Oats are much used for horse feed. Common species is *Avena sativa.*

Oaxaca (wähä'kä), state (36,375 sq. mi.; pop. 1,444,929), S Mexico, on the Pacific and its inlet, Gulf of Tehuantepec. Benito Juárez and Porfirio Díaz were born here. Mountainous with deep tortuous valleys in S, it has broad, semiarid valleys and plateaus in N. Agr. and stock raising are important. Mixtec and Zapotec Indians predominate in the population. Has two famous archaeological sites: Mitla and Monte Alban. The capital, **Oaxaca** (pop. 29,306), is most important city in S Mexico. It lies in a long, broad valley. Noted for handwrought gold and silver filigree, pottery, and serapes.

Ob (Rus. ôp), river, 2,113 mi. long, RSFSR, in W Siberia, formed by junction of Biya and Katun rivers in Altai region and flowing generally N past Novosibirsk into Ob Bay, an estuary (c.500 mi. long, 35–50 mi. wide) of the Kara Sea. The Irtysh is its main tributary. The Ob is an important trade route, though frozen for six months of the year.

Obadiah (ō"bůdī'ů) or **Abdias** (ăbdī'ůs), book of Old Testament. The prophet, otherwise unknown, calls down doom on Edom and predicts triumph for Israel.

Obaidallah: see FATIMITE.

Oban (ō'bůn), burgh (pop. 6,227), Argyllshire, Scotland, on Firth of Lorne; port and seaside resort. Scene of annual Argyllshire Highland Gathering.

obbligato (ŏblēgä'tō) [Ital.,= obliged], in music, originally a term by which a composer indicated that a certain part was indispensable to the music. Misunderstanding of the term, however, resulted in a reversal of its meaning; when a violin part, for example, is added to a song it is called a violin obbligato, meaning that it is a superfluous ornament and unnecessary to the music.

Obed (ō'–), son of Ruth and grandfather of David. Ruth 4.21,22; 1 Chron. 2.12; Mat. 1.5; Luke 3.32.

obelisk (ŏ'bůlĭsk), a slender four-sided tapering monument, usually hewn of single piece of stone, with pointed or pyramidal top. Among ancient Egyptians these monoliths, commonly of red granite, were dedicated to the sun god. On each of four sides were hieroglyphs, giving names and titles of the Pharaoh. Some obelisks date as far back as IV dynasty (c.2900–c.2750 B.C.). Of those still standing in Egypt, one is at Heliopolis and two at Karnak. Many have been taken to other countries, notably one depicting reign of Ramses II, now in Place de la Concorde, Paris, and CLEOPATRA'S NEEDLES in London and New York.

Oberammergau (ō"bůrä'můrgou), village (pop. 5,101), Upper Bavaria, in Bavarian Alps near Garmisch-Partenkirchen. PASSION PLAY here attracts tourists.

Oberhausen (ō'bůrhou"zůn), city (pop. 202,343), North Rhine–Westphalia, NW Germany; an industrial center of RUHR dist.

Oberholtzer, Ellis Paxson (ō'bůrhōlt"sůr), 1868–1936, American historian, author of *A History of the United States since the Civil War* (5 vols., 1917–37).

Oberland, Bernese: see BERN.

Oberlin (ō'bůrlĭn), village (pop. 7,062), N Ohio, S of Lorain. Most of **Oberlin College** (nonsectarian; coed.; opened 1833) is here. Pioneered in coeducation; was abolitionist center in Civil War and one of first colleges to admit Negroes. Alumni and students sponsor Oberlin-in-China. **Oberlin theology,** a modified form of Calvinism, was developed by early theological faculty members of the college.

Oberon (ō'bůrŏn), in literature of Western Europe, fairy king, husband of Titania. He appears in Middle French *Huon de Bordeaux,* probable source for Chaucer, Spencer, and Shakspere.

obesity (ōbē'sĭtē, ōbĕ'–), excessive accumulation of fat in body. Usually it results from excess food intake. Certain obese persons have low rate of metabolism associated with glandular disturbances.

oboe: see WIND INSTRUMENTS.

Obregón, Álvaro (äl'värō ōbrāgōn'), 1880–1928, Mexican general and president (1920–24). He supported Madero in the revolution against Porfirio Díaz (1911) and by a coup was made president in 1920. His administration saw the educational reforms of Vasconcelos. Obregón was reelected president in 1928 but was assassinated before taking office.

Obrenovich (ōbrĕ'nůvĭch), family name of princes MILOSH and MICHAEL and kings MILAN and ALEXANDER of Serbia. The dynasty, in constant feud with the KARAGEORGEVICH family, ruled 1817–42, 1858–1903.

O'Brien, William, 1852–1928, Irish journalist and political leader. His paper *United Ireland* championed agrarian cause. Helped shape Wyndham Land Act (1903) to solve Irish Land Question.

O'Brien, William Smith, 1803–64, Irish revolutionary. Follower of Daniel O'Connell in nationalist struggle, he seceded from him and helped to organize abortive revolt of 1848.

observatory, building or institution for observation and recording of astronomical, meteorological, magnetic, or seismological phenomena. Term is chiefly applied to astronomical observatories. The earliest on record estab. c.300 B.C. at Alexandria. Early notable observatory in Europe estab. by Tycho Brahe (1584) on island of Ven. Application of telescope to astronomical use by Galileo stimulated founding of observatories by rulers, individuals, and institutions. National observatories include Royal Observatory (1675), Greenwich, England; Paris Observatory (1667–71); UNITED STATES NAVAL OBSERVATORY. Observatories with important refracting telescopes include Yerkes Observatory (40 in.), Univ. of Chicago, at Williams Bay, Wis.; Lick Observatory (36 in.), Univ. of California, on Mt. Hamilton; Allegheny Observatory (30 in.), Univ. of Pittsburgh; Leander McCormick Observatory (26 in.), Univ. of Virginia; Lowell Observatory (24 in.), Flagstaff, Ariz. Noted for great reflecting telescopes are Mt. Palomar Observatory (200 in.), California Inst. of Technology, near Pasadena; Mt. Wilson Observatory (100 in.), Carnegie Inst., at Mt. Wilson, Calif.; McDonald Observatory (82 in.), Univ. of Texas, at Mt. Locke, Texas; David Dunlap Observatory (74 in.), Univ. of Toronto; Dominion Astrophysical Observatory (73 in.), Victoria, British Columbia.

obsidian (ŏbsĭ'dēŭn), a lava resembling black glass. The fine texture results from very rapid cooling. Primitive people used it for stone tools and weapons.

obstetrics (ŏbstĕ'trĭks), branch of medicine dealing with pregnancy and labor. Care during labor was originally known as midwifery and was in hands of women. Began to pass to physicians in 16th cent. Use of forceps was introduced in 17th cent. Anesthesia during labor was first used by Sir J. Y. Simpson. Incidence of puerperal fever was reduced by methods of Semmelweis and Lister.

Obwalden, Switzerland: see UNTERWALDEN.

Ocala (ōkă'lŭ), city (pop. 11,741), N central Fla., W of L. George. Processes and ships fruit, limestone, phosphate, and lumber. Grew around Fort King (protection against the Seminoles 1827–43), near site of Indian village visited by De Soto, 1639. SILVER SPRINGS is near.

O'Casey, Sean (shôn' ōkā'sē), 1884–, Irish dramatist, noted playwright of Abbey Theatre. Well-known plays are *Juno and the Paycock* (1924), *The Plough and the Stars* (1926), and *Within the Gates* (1934). His autobiographical works, including *Inishfallen, Fare Thee Well* (1949) and *Rose and Crown* (1952), depict his early life, with anticapitalist slant and impeccable prose.

Occam, William of: see WILLIAM OF OCCAM.

Occidental College: see LOS ANGELES, Calif.

occultism, belief in supernatural sciences or powers, such as magic, astrology, alchemy, theosophy, and spiritism—for purpose of enlarging man's powers, protecting him from evil forces, or predicting future. All the so-called natural sciences were partly occult in origin, and scientists were suspect because of secrecy.

occupational diseases, illnesses contracted through working conditions. They result from extrahazardous conditions; work under abnormal air pressures (see CAISSON DISEASE); handling or breathing fumes of poisonous substances including lead, phosphorus, mercury compounds, and silica dust (see SILICOSIS); exposure to radioactive substances and release of atomic energy. Preventive legislation dates from Factory Act of 1802 in England. In U.S., workmen's compensation acts cover many occupational illnesses.

occupational therapy, any form of activity devised to aid recovery from disease and adjustment to living. It is essential in treating mental disorders or paralysis. Was used in ancient Greece and Egypt. Natl. Association of Occupational Therapists formed in U.S. 1917.

ocean, connected mass of water which covers c.71% of earth's surface. Arbitrarily delimited into the Pacific, Atlantic, and Indian oceans; popular usage also distinguishes the Arctic and the Antarctic. Oceans retain heat; currents and winds distribute it. Air temperatures over oceans vary little from that of the water. Ocean waters shift constantly. Currents move masses of water; in waves particles of water oscillate, hardly change position except when carried forward by crest of breakers. Friction of water and wind probably causes surface waves. Average ocean depth is c.12,500 ft. Pressure increases by one atmosphere (15 lb. per sq. ft.) for 33 ft. of depth. Greatest known depth (35,400 ft.) is in the Pacific off Mindanao. Sea-water density increases with coldness and salinity (average salinity is c.3%). Sea water is believed to have in solution all chemical elements; chlorine, sodium, sulphur, magnesium are most common. Distribution of marine life varies with temperature, salinity, pressure, light.

Ocean City. 1 Resort town (pop. 1,234), SE Md., on Atlantic Ocean. Game-fishing port. **2** Atlantic resort city (pop. 6,040), SE N.J., SW of Atlantic City. Fishing, boatbuilding.

ocean currents, progressive movements of ocean waters. Density currents are chief circulators of ocean waters. Hot equatorial waters expand; higher sea level causes surface flow poleward, but trade winds force water masses westward. Waters flow along the western shores of the Atlantic and the Pacific—clockwise in N Hemisphere, counterclockwise in S Hemisphere, due to earth's rotation (e.g., GULF STREAM and JAPAN CURRENT). The currents cool gradually; their higher salinity (from evaporation in hot latitudes) makes them denser than adjacent waters of equal temperature, causes them to sink and displaced waters to rise. Masses of poleward-flowing water result in compensating surface currents of less saline water (partly from melting ice) that flow from subpolar to temperate regions (e.g., Labrador Current). Pressure from added mass of equatorial waters causes an equatorward drift of bottom water that completes circulatory cycle by welling up in equatorial zones to replace water carried poleward. Wind affects rate and direction of density currents, also causes wind currents. By friction on sea's surface, wind causes surface drift, each moving layer affecting next underlying layer. Currents are classed as streams (well defined, relatively fast, 2–4 mi. per hr.), drifts (slow), or creeps (barely perceptible). Flow of ocean currents effects a transfer of heat globally that modifies climate of lands receiving sea winds and influences distribution of marine life. For tidal currents, see TIDE.

Ocean Grove, Atlantic resort village (pop. 3,806) in Neptune township (pop. 13,613), E N.J., S of Asbury Park; founded 1869, owned and controlled by Methodist camp meeting association. Has tent city and auditorium for summer camp meetings.

Oceania (ōshēă'nēŭ, –ā'nēŭ) or **Oceanica** (ōshēă'nĭkŭ), collective name for Pacific islands, sometimes including Australasia and Malaysia. Usually considered as synonymous with South Sea Isls.

Ocean Island, phosphate island (2.2 sq. mi.; pop. 2,060), central Pacific. Formerly the cap. of British colony of Gilbert and Ellice Isls. Discovered 1804 by British, annexed 1915. Occupied by Japanese 1942–45. Formerly called Banaba.

Ocean Island, T.H.: see KURE ISLAND.

oceanography (ō″shŭnŏ′grŭfē), study of the sea. It integrates marine applications of geography, geology, physics, chemistry, and biology and draws upon astronomy and meteorology. Sometimes term is restricted to study of topography and sediments of ocean basins and shores and characteristics and dynamics of ocean waters, but MARINE BIOLOGY is also usually included. Term *oceanography* dates from CHALLENGER EXPEDITION (1872–76) and became current through expedition reports. The science is important to shipping, fisheries, laying of telegraph cables, climatological studies. Many ocean phenomena (e.g., waves, currents) are not fully explained.

Oceanport, borough (pop. 7,588), E N.J., NW of Long Branch. Near by is U.S. Fort Monmouth.

Oceanside, city (pop. 18,377), S Calif., N of San Diego. Beach resort and agr. trade center. San Luis Rey Mission (1798) is near.

Ocean Springs, Miss.: see BILOXI, Miss.

Oceanus (ōcē′ŭnŭs), in Greek mythology. **1** Circular stream flowing round edge of earth, source of rivers. **2** Personification of this stream; a Titan, son of Uranus and Gaea.

ocelot (ŏ′sŭlŭt), New World cat (*Felis*) ranging from S Texas to South America. Fur is tawny to gray with variable pattern of black spots, streaks, rings.

Ochakov (ŭchä′kŭf), city (pop. over 10,000), SW Ukraine; a Black Sea port. Its fall (1788) as a Turkish fortress was a decisive Russian victory.

ocher (ō′kŭr), mixture of hydrated iron oxide and clay used as pigment, the colors ranging from yellow to red. It is produced in U.S., France, Italy.

Ochil Hills (ō′khĭl), range, c.25 mi. long, in Perth, Clackmannan, Kinross, and Fife Counties, Scotland. They have valuable mineral deposits.

Ochino, Bernardino (bārnärdē′nō ōkē′nō), 1487–1564, Italian religious reformer. A Capuchin friar, he accepted belief in justification by faith alone and gave his life to forwarding of Protestantism.

Ochrida or **Okhrida** (both: ŏ′krĭdŭ), Serbo-Croatian *Ohrid,* town (pop. 11,419), Macedonia, SW Yugoslavia, on rock above L. Ochrida. An important trading town under Roman rule, it flourished as cultural and political cap. of Bulgaria in 10th cent. A.D. Among its many ancient churches are cathedrals of St. Sophia (founded 9th cent.) and of St. Clement (1299). **Lake Ochrida,** area 134 sq. mi., forms part of Yugoslav-Albanian border.

Ochs, Adolph S. (ŏks), 1858–1935, American newspaper publisher. He became publisher of the Chattanooga *Times* in 1878. In 1896 he acquired the New York *Times* and brought it to national eminence.

Ockham, William of: see WILLIAM OF OCCAM.

Ocmulgee (ōkmŭl′gē), river formed in NW Ga., SE of Atlanta. Flows c.255 mi. SSE to join Oconee R. and form Altamaha R.

Ocmulgee National Monument: see NATIONAL PARKS AND MONUMENTS (table).

O Come, All Ye Faithful: see ADESTE FIDELES.

Oconee (ōkō′nē), river rising in N Ga., NE of Atlanta and flowing 282 mi. SSE to join Ocmulgee R. and form Altamaha A.

O'Connell, Daniel, 1775–1847, Irish political leader. Founded (1823) the powerful Catholic Association whose pressure led to Catholic Emancipation Act of 1829. Urged repeal of union with Great Britain and worked to solve Irish Land Question.

O'Connor, Rory or **Roderick,** 1116?–1198, last high king of Ireland. King of Connaught after 1156, he seized (1166) the high kingship. Dermot McMurrough brought in the English against O'Connor, who was forced to submit (1175) as a vassal to Henry II.

O'Connor, T(homas) P(ower), 1848–1929, Irish journalist and nationalist, known as Tay Pay O'Connor. Member of Parliament after 1880, he supported Parnell until 1891. Founded many newspapers (e.g., *T.P.'s Weekly*) in London. Worked for Home Rule.

Oconomowoc (ōkŏn′ŭmōwôk″), city (pop. 5,345), SE Wis., W of Milwaukee. Resort in lake and mineral-spring area with processing of foodstuffs.

Oconto (ōkŏn′tō), city (pop. 5,055), NE Wis., on W shore of Green Bay and at mouth of Oconto R. Lumber products. First church erected specifically for Christian Science worship was built here 1886.

Octavia (ŏktā′vēŭ). **1** Died 11 B.C., sister of AUGUSTUS and wife of Marc ANTONY. Helped keep peace between them until Antony deserted her for Cleopatra. **2** A.D. 42–A.D. 62, daughter of Claudius I. She was the wife of NERO, who deserted her for Poppaea; later on false charges he had Octavia put to death.

Octavian and **Octavius:** see AUGUSTUS.

October: see MONTH.

octopus (ŏk′tŭpŭs), cephalopod mollusk, also called devilfish, found in temperate and tropical waters. It has a pouch-shaped body, eight arms, each bearing two rows of suction disks, and no shell. Ink sac darkens water in case of danger. Span of arms from tip to tip ranges from few feet to more than 20 ft. Poisonous saliva paralyzes prey.

Oda Nobunaga: see NOBUNAGA.

ode, originally, in Greek, a poem sung to musical accompaniment. Odes of Sappho, Alcaeus, and Anacreon are for a single voice. Pindar's choral odes are formal, elaborate, passionate; Horace's Latin odes are personal, simple, controlled. Odes were revived in France most successfully by Ronsard (16th cent.). Horace's odes influenced 17th-cent. English poets, although Milton shows Pindaric influence, and Cowley and Dryden tried to imitate Pindar in poems for public occasions. Odes of romantic and later poets tend to be more free in form and subject matter.

Odenathus, Septimius (sĕptĭ′mēŭs ŏdĭnā′thŭs), d. 267, king of PALMYRA. He cooperated with Rome and made his state powerful. He and his eldest son were murdered, possibly through machination of his second wife, ZENOBIA, who brought Palmyra to ruin.

Ödenburg, Hungary: see SOPRON.

Odense (ō′dhŭnsŭ), city (pop. 100,940), port on N Fyn isl., Denmark. Lutheran episcopal see. Many industries (shipyards, canneries; machinery, rubber, tobacco, textiles, sugar, and glass factories). Has 14th-cent. cathedral. Birthplace of Hans Christian Andersen.

Oder (ō'dûr), Czech and Pol. *Odra,* river, 563 mi. long, rising in Moravia, Czechoslovakia, and flowing N through Silesia, Brandenburg, and Pomerania into the Baltic at Stettin. Breslau and Frankfurt-an-der-Oder lie on its course. From its junction with the Lausitzer Neisse it forms the boundary line between Russian-occupied Germany and the former German territory placed under Polish administration in 1945. Navigable from Ratibor, it is linked by canals with the Spree, Elbe, and Vistula.

Odessa (ōdě'sů, Rus. ŭdyě'sŭ), city (pop. 604,-223), SW Ukraine, on Black Sea. It is one of the chief ports of the USSR, an industrial center (machinery, chemicals, petroleum, flour), and a cultural center (university, technical schools, famous opera house and conservatory). Founded in late 18th cent. on site of an ancient Greek colony (Odessos or Ordyssos), it soon became the chief Russian grain-exporting center. Severe pogroms, following the mutiny on the battleship *Potemkin* at Odessa (1905), caused large-scale emigration of the Jews (then c.35% of pop.). Between 1918 and its final fall to the Red Army in 1920, Odessa was successively occupied by the Central Powers, the French, the Ukrainians, the Reds, and the Whites. In World War II it was occupied by the Rumanians (1941–43) and suffered much destruction; 280,000 civilians, mostly Jews, are said to have been massacred or deported.

Odessa (ōdě'sů), city (pop. 29,495), W Texas, WNW of San Angelo; founded 1881. Oil center with refineries, carbon-black plant, and oiling supplies. Meteor crater near. Region has potash.

Odets, Clifford (ōděts'), 1906–, American dramatist. Among his plays (mostly concerned with social problems) are *Waiting for Lefty, Awake and Sing* (both 1935), and *Golden Boy* (1937).

Odin, Norse name for chief Germanic god, WODEN.

Odo, French king: see EUDES.

Odoacer (ōdōā'sůr) or **Odovacar** (ōdōvā'kůr), c.435–493, German conqueror of the West Roman Empire; chieftain of the Heruli, a people allied to the Goths. He and his soldiers were mercenaries in Roman service, but in 476 the Heruli rebelled and proclaimed him king. Odoacer defeated the general ORESTES, took Ravenna, deposed ROMULUS AUGUSTULUS (last Roman Emperor of the West until Charlemagne), and was recognized in authority over Italy by the Eastern emperor Zeno. The year 476 is the conventional date of the fall of West Rome; in fact, chaos had prevailed for some time before, and Roman administration continued to function under Odoacer. In 488 ZENO sent THEODORIC THE GREAT, king of the Ostrogoths, into Italy to expel Odoacer. After several defeats, Odoacer in 493 agreed to share his authority with Theodoric, who then invited him to a banquet and had him murdered.

O'Donnell, Leopoldo (lāōpōl'dō ōdhō'něl), 1809–67, Spanish general and statesman, of Irish descent. As premier (1856–57, 1858–63, 1865–66) he followed a relatively liberal policy; restored the old constitution (1856); and commanded in the Spanish campaign in Morocco (1859–60), for which he was created duque de Tetuán.

Odovacar: see ODOACER.

O'Dwyer, William (ōdwī'ůr), 1890–, American public official, b. Ireland. Mayor of New York city (1946–50), U.S. ambassador to Mexico (1950–52).

Odysseus (ōdĭs'ūs, ōdĭ'sēůs), Latin *Ulysses* (ūlĭ'sēz), in Greek mythology, king of Ithaca. He was husband of Penelope and father of Telemachus. A Greek leader in Trojan War, he was famed for cunning strategy and wisdom. Afterward he wandered for 10 years before returning home. The story of his wanderings and regaining of his kingdom is told in the **Odyssey** (ŏ'dĭsē), Homeric Greek epic in 24 books.

Oecolampadius, Johannes (jōhă'nēz ē″kůlămpā'dēůs), 1482–1531, German reformer, associate of ZWINGLI in Reformation of Switzerland.

Oedipus (ĕ'dĭpůs, ē'–), hero in Greek mythology. When it was foretold that he would kill his father, Laius, king of Thebes, and marry his mother, Jocasta, baby Oedipus was exposed on Mt. Cithaeron, but he was saved and raised by king of Corinth. On learning of the prophecy when grown, and ignorant of his real parentage, he fled from Corinth to Thebes. En route, he met and quarreled with Laius and killed him. He won Jocasta by answering riddle of the Sphinx. When, after many years, he learned the truth, he blinded himself, and Jocasta committed suicide. CREON, Jocasta's brother, became king. Oedipus died in peace at Colonus, but his unwitting sin still cursed Thebes and his children (see SEVEN AGAINST THEBES). Legend has been used often in literature, music, and art and gives name to the **Oedipus complex** (ĕ'dĭpůs), psychological condition, especially evident between ages of four and five, in which boys love mothers intensely, hate fathers; girls, the reverse (Electra complex). Freudians hold that if complex is not worked out in childhood or by PSYCHOANALYSIS, adult relationships are determined by feelings in the original situation.

Oehlenschläger, Adam Gottlob (û'lůnshlāgůr), 1779–1850, Danish author of poems and dramas dealing with Scandinavian history.

Oelwein (ōl'wīn), city (pop. 7,858), NE Iowa, NE of Waterloo, in farm and livestock area.

Oenone (ēnō'nē), in Greek legend, nymph loved by Paris, who deserted her for Helen. When he was later wounded, she refused to use her healing powers to heal him, but on hearing of his death she killed herself.

Oersted, Hans Christian (häns' krĭs'tyän ûr'-stĭdh), 1777–1851, Danish physicist and chemist. His work estab. a relationship between magnetism and electricity; he was first to isolate aluminum.

O'Faoláin Seán (shôn' ōfā'län), 1900–, Irish writer, interpreter of Ireland through biographies, travel books, historical writing, short stories, and novels.

Offa (ŏ'fů), d. 796, king of Mercia (757–96). Gradually asserted his overlordship in Kent and Sussex, also ruled East Anglia. Signed (796) with Charlemagne the first recorded

English commercial treaty. Built OFFA's DYKE in late 8th cent.

Offaly (ŏ'fùlē), formerly **King's,** county (771 sq. mi.; pop. 53,686), central Ireland, in Leinster; co. town Tullamore. Mostly flat, covered largely by Bog of Allen, it has Slieve Bloom mts. in S. Agr. and livestock breeding are main occupations. Clonmacnoise has ruins of an early religious center.

Offa's Dyke, entrenchment along England-Wales border. Built in 8th cent. by Offa, king of Mercia, as a barrier against the Welsh. Paralleled at a distance of c.2 mi. by Watt's Dyke.

Offenbach, Jacques (ô'fùnbŏk), 1819–80, French composer, b. Cologne. Creator of the French operetta and composer of over 100, e.g., *Orphée aux enfers, La Vie parisienne, La Belle Hélène.* His one serious opera, *The Tales of Hoffmann,* was his masterpiece.

Office of Price Administration (OPA), estab. April, 1941, by executive order as Office of Price Administration and Civilian Supply and renamed Aug., 1941. Fixed consumer prices, rent ceilings; rationed scarce consumer goods. After World War II rationing ended, and price controls were gradually abolished. Rent-control functions were transferred to Office of the Housing Expediter in May, 1947. In 1950 the Office of Price Stabilization was created under Economic Stabilization Agency; discontinued 1953.

Office of Strategic Services (OSS), secret agency of U.S., created 1942 for purpose of obtaining information about enemy nations and of sabotaging their war potential and morale. Headed by W. H. Donovan. In 1945 Pres. Truman transferred the research and analysis branch to Dept. of State and the rest to War Dept.

offset: see PRINTING.

O'Flaherty, Liam (lē'ùm ōflă'hùrtē), 1896–, Irish novelist. One of his realistic, psychological works, *The Informer* (1925), gained awards both as fiction and as a film. He has also written notable short stories and autobiographical works.

Og (ŏg), giant king of Bashan conquered by the Israelites. Deut. 3.1–13.

Ogaden (ōgä'dān), arid region, SE Ethiopia, bordering British Somaliland and Italian Somaliland. A clash between Italian and Ethiopian troops at village of Walwal in 1934 helped to precipitate Italo-Ethiopian War.

Ogallala (ōgùlă'lù), city (pop. 3,456), W central Nebr., on South Platte R. and W of North Platte city. Kingsley Dam (162 ft. high, 10,700 ft. long; earthen; completed 1941) in North Platte R. is near.

Ogata, Korin: see KORIN.

Ogden, city (pop. 57,112), N Utah, at junction of Ogden and Weber rivers and N of Salt Lake City; founded on trading-post site by Mormons after 1847. Important intermountain rail junction. Processes and ships fruit, grain, livestock of irrigated area. Seat of Weber Col. Mt. Ogden (9,592 ft.), ski center, and Ogden Canyon, recreational area, are near.

Ogden, river rising in N Utah in Wasatch Range and flowing c.35 mi. S to Weber R. at Ogden. Used for c.100 years for irrigation.

Ogdensburg, city (pop. 16,166), N N.Y., on St. Lawrence R. and NE of Watertown; settled 1749. Ships grain and lumber; mfg. of paper, wood, and metal products. Here is Remington Art Memorial.

ogham (ŏ'gùm, ō'ùm), anc. alphabet of the British Isles (esp. Ireland), used in early Christian era for gravestone inscriptions. Language is local Celtic. Key is given in Irish manuscripts.

Ogier the Dane (ō'jēùr, ōzhyā'), in the chansons de geste, a paladin who rebelled against Charlemagne. William Morris uses story in *The Earthly Paradise.*

Oglethorpe, James Edward (ō'gùlthôrp), 1696–1785, English general, founder of Ga. Estab. colony (1733) as refuge for imprisoned debtors. His defeat of Spanish in 1742 assured English control of area.

Oglethorpe University: see ATLANTA, Ga.

OGPU: see SECRET POLICE.

Ogunquit, Maine: see WELLS.

O'Higgins, Bernardo (bĕrnär'dhō ōē'gēns), 1776–1842, Chilean revolutionist and dictator, b. Chillán; natural son of Ambrosio O'Higgins, an Irish-born Spanish colonial administrator. Bernardo took part in early uprisings in Chile, was forced to flee to Argentina, returned with San Martín's victorious army, and became supreme director of Chile (1818). His reform movements were opposed, and he was exiled to Peru (1823).

Ohio, state (41,288 sq. mi.; pop. 7,946,627), NE central U.S.; admitted 1803 as 17th state (free); cap. COLUMBUS. Other cities are CLEVELAND, CINCINNATI, TOLEDO, DAYTON, AKRON, YOUNGSTOWN, CANTON. Bordered S and SE by OHIO R., partly N by L. Erie. Generally level. Iron and steel mills; mfg. of machinery, motor vehicles and parts, rubber products, metal goods, paper, foodstuffs, clothing, chemicals, cement, glass. Mining coal, clay products, lime, rock salt, natural gas, oil. Agr. of grains, fruit, truck; dairying, livestock. Activities of OHIO COMPANY helped pave way for last of French and Indian Wars, in which English won land from French. QUEBEC ACT (1774) sought to make territory a dependency of Canada. Passed to U.S. after Revolution. Trouble over claims to land by old states ended with dropping of all (see WESTERN RESERVE) and adoption of ORDINANCE OF 1787. OHIO COMPANY OF ASSOCIATES promoted development. Anthony WAYNE defeated Indians at Fallen Timbers (1794). Became territory in 1799. Supported Union in Civil War despite activity of COPPERHEADS. Mfg. expanded after war. Big business and politics became entwined as in relations of Mark HANNA and McKinley. Labor strife marked 1930s. World War II brought great industrial prosperity. Flood-control measures increased in 20th cent.

Ohio, river, 981 mi. long, E central U.S., formed by confluence of Allegheny R. and Monongahela R. at Pittsburgh, Pa. Flows NW then generally SW as state line between Ohio–W.Va., Ohio–Ky., Ind.–Ky., and Ill.–Ky., entering the Mississippi at Cairo, Ill., as its chief E tributary. Drains a highly populated and productive area, receiving as its major tributaries the Muskingum, Scioto, Great Miami, and Wabash from the N, and the Kanawha, Big Sandy, Licking, Kentucky,

Green, Cumberland, and Tennessee from the S. Important cities on its route include Pittsburgh, Cincinnati, Wheeling, W.Va., Evansville, Ind., and Louisville and Paducah, Ky. Water control system reduces the danger of floods, provides hydroelectric power, and extends navigation. Used by Indians, then French, was a focus of conflict in the French and Indian Wars. After the Revolution it became a route of westward migration. A temporary set-back after the Erie Canal opening was compensated for by the success of steamboats. The Ohio remains an important channel of freight transport despite the inroads of railroads.

Ohio Company, organization formed in 1748 to extend Va. settlements W into Ohio valley. Rivalry with French claims helped cause final French and Indian War. This and the Revolution blocked company plans.

Ohio Company of Associates, organization for purchase and settlement of lands on Ohio R., founded at Boston, Mass., in 1786. Negotiations by Manasseh Cutler with Congress in 1787 resulted in company's gaining right to purchase 1,500,000 acres at junction of the Ohio and Muskingum rivers. Settlement of company's grant began in April, 1788, at town of Marietta.

Ohio State University, at Columbus; land-grant supported, coed.; chartered 1870, opened 1873 as Ohio Agricultural and Mechanical Col., renamed 1878. There are various research bureaus, experiment stations, and clinics. The university also has the Ohio Biological Survey and a radio station and owns large telescope with Ohio Wesleyan Univ.

Ohio University: see ATHENS.

Ohio Wesleyan University: see DELAWARE, Ohio.

Ohm, Georg Simon (gā'ôrk zē'môn ōm'), 1787–1854, German physicist. Formulated **Ohm's law:** V (volts) = A (amperes) × R (resistance in ohms), or E (electromotive force or volts) = I (current) × R. The **ohm,** unit of electrical resistance, was named in his honor. International ohm is resistance offered to flow of unwavering electric current by column of mercury at 0°C., 106.3 cm. long, constant in cross section, with mass of 14.4521 g.

Ohrid, Yugoslavia: see OCHRIDA.

Oil City, city (pop. 19,581), NW Pa., on Allegheny R. and NNE of Pittsburgh; laid out c.1860. Oil center since discovery of oil at near-by Titusville 1859, it has mfg. of oil equipment.

Oildale, village (pop. 16,615), S central Calif., oil-field center N of Bakersfield, across Kern R.

oil of vitriol: see SULPHURIC ACID.

oils, term commonly used for greasy, fluid substances, generally viscous liquids, insoluble in water, soluble in ether and alcohol and inflammable. Petroleum and its products are classified as mineral oils. **Fatty oils** or **fixed oils** are obtained from animals and plants and are carbon-hydrogen-oxygen compounds. There is no real difference between them and fats (see FATS AND OILS). Depending on ability to absorb oxygen when exposed to atmosphere and form skinlike layer over surface, they are classed as drying and non-drying oils. **Essential oils** or **volatile oils** occur in plants and to them certain plants owe their characteristic odor, flavor, or other properties. They are used in perfumes, flavorings, medicine. In general they are complex mixtures of various chemicals, differing from fixed oils in being volatile.

Oise (wäz), department (2,273 sq. mi.; pop. 396,724), N France, in Ile-de-France and Picardy; cap. Beauvais. It is drained by the **Oise** river, 186 mi. long, rising in the Ardennes mts., Belgium, and flowing SW into N France to the Seine NW of Paris.

Oisin: see OSSIAN.

Ojibwa Indians (ōjĭb'wŭ), North American tribes of Algonquian linguistic stock, commonly also called Chippewa, occupying the shores of L. Superior in the 17th cent. With French firearms they drove the Fox from N Wis., drove the Sioux to the W, penetrating to N.Dak., and conquered the peninsula between L. Huron and L. Erie from the Iroquois. By the mid-18th cent. they were very powerful. Except for the most westerly (Plains Ojibwa) they had an Eastern woodlands culture, with agr. supporting fishing and hunting and with their usual dwelling the wigwam. They had picture writing connected with religious rites of their Midewin society. They fought on the side of the French in the French and Indian Wars and on the side of the British in the War of 1812. Later they were settled on reservations in Mich., Wis., Minn., and N.Dak. Also Chippeway, Ojibway.

Oka (ŭkä'), rivers of RSFSR. **1** In central European RSFSR. Rises S of Orel and flows 918 mi., N, E, and NE to the Volga at Gorki. Navigable for 550 mi. **2** In S central Siberia. Rises in Sayan Mts. and flows 500 mi. N to the Angara.

Okanagan Lake (ōkŭnä'gŭn), 69 mi. long and 2–4 mi. wide, S B.C., Canada. Drained S by Okanogan R. to Osoyoos L.

Okanogan (ōkŭnä'gŭn), town (pop. 2,013), N central Wash., on Okanogan R. and near site of first American settlement in Wash. Territory.

Okayama (ōkä'yämŭ), city (pop. 140,631), SW Honshu, Japan. Railroad and mfg. center (porcelain ware, cotton textiles). Medical university.

Okeechobee, Lake (ō"kēchō'bē), S central Fla., N of the EVERGLADES; second largest fresh-water lake wholly in U.S. It is c.35 mi. long, 30 mi. wide, and 15 ft. deep and covers c.750 sq. mi. Most important canals of Everglades reclamation project are those of Okeechobee Waterway. Drained lands around lake yield winter vegetables and sugar cane. Grasslands W of lake support cattle raising. Levees built after hurricane of 1926. Resort and commercial fisheries.

O'Keeffe, Georgia, 1887–, American painter, known for her enlarged and stylized flower studies.

Okefenokee Swamp (ō"kŭfŭnōk', –nō'kē), c.45 mi. long, 30 mi. wide, NE Ga. and N Fla. Main part of Okefenokee Wildlife Refuge. One of most primitive swamps in U.S., has varied wildlife; drained by Suwanee and St. Marys rivers. Abundant timber is too expensive to bring out.

Okhotsk, Sea of (ōkŏtsk′), NW arm of the Pacific, W of Kamchatka Peninsula and Kurile Isls. Connected with Sea of Japan on SW by Tatar and La Pérouse straits. N part is icebound during much of the year.

Okhrida, Yugoslavia: see OCHRIDA.

Okinawa (ō″kĭnä′wä), volcanic island (467 sq. mi.; pop. 517,634), SW Pacific; largest of Okinawa Isls. in Ryukyu chain. Mountainous with dense vegetation. Produces sugar cane. NAHA is chief city and port. Scene of last great U.S. amphibious campaign (April 1–June 25, 1945) in World War II. Ie-jima (islet off W coast) was also a battleground.

Oklahoma, state (69,283 sq. mi.; pop. 2,233,-351), SW U.S.; admitted 1907 as 46th state; cap. OKLAHOMA CITY. TULSA other large city. Bounded S by RED RIVER. Great Plains in W, broken by Black Mesa in Panhandle and by Wichita Mts. in SW. Mostly prairie in E, with Ozark Mts. in NE, Ouachita Mts. in SE. Great oil state, also natural gas, lead, zinc, gypsum. Farming (wheat, corn, cotton, grain, sorghums, oats, livestock). Petroleum refining, mfg. of flour, grain products, cotton goods, packed meat. Scene of several Indian cultures before early Spanish exploration. Set aside for FIVE CIVILIZED TRIBES after Louisiana Purchase in what became INDIAN TERRITORY. These groups sided with Confederacy in Civil War; as punishment they lost W part of territory. Advent of railroads and desire for grazing land for cattle brought white settlers. April 22, 1889, saw first land run for legal settlement. Oklahoma Territory organized in 1890. DAWES COMMISSION divided tribal lands of Indian Territory; two territories combined into state. Suffered seriously from drought in 1930s; irrigation and conservation measures brought back degree of prosperity.

Oklahoma, University of, mainly at Norman; state supported, coed.; chartered 1890, opened 1892. Law and medical schools are in Oklahoma City. Has radio station and university press.

Oklahoma Agricultural and Mechanical College, at Stillwater; land-grant and state supported, coed.; chartered 1890, opened 1891.

Oklahoma City, city (pop. 243,504), state cap., central Okla., on North Canadian R.; settled 1889, made cap. 1910. Industrial, commercial, and distribution center for oil and agr. area. Mfg. of oil equipment, flour, and metal and wood products. Has civic center, capitol, historical society building, and air base.

Oklawaha (ŏklůwô′hô), river, c.140 mi. long, rising in central Fla. lake system. Flows N, receiving waters of SILVER SPRINGS, then E to St. Johns R. S of Palatka.

Okmulgee (ōk″mŭl′gē), city (pop. 18,317), E central Okla., SE of Tulsa; settled c.1899 on site of Creek town. Trade center of oil and agr. area. Oil, glass, cotton, and food processing. Old Creek council house and L. Okmulgee near by.

okra or **gumbo,** African plant (*Hibiscus esculentus*) grown for its mucilaginous seed pods, eaten as a vegetable and used to thicken gumbo soups.

Okubo, Toshimichi (tō″shēmē′chē ō′kōōbō), 1832?–1878, Japanese statesman. After Meiji restoration he became chief figure in new government and influenced Westernization of Japan. Opposed fellow clansmen in Satsuma rebellion (1877) against imperial government.

Okuma, Shigenobu, Marquis (shēgā′nōbōō ō′kōōmä), 1838–1922, Japanese statesman. Founder of a reform party (Kaishinto), forerunner of Minseito; agitated for parliamentary government. Favored working with zaibatsu to strengthen Japan's industry. In second premiership (1914–16), Japan entered World War I, seized Kiaochow, and presented China with Twenty-one Demands.

Olaf (ō′läf), kings of Norway. **Olaf I** (Olaf Tryggvason), c.963–1000, reigned 995–1000. He undertook conversion of Norway to Christianity—by force and by persuasion. **Olaf II** (Saint Olaf), c.995–1030, also a convert, reigned 1015–28. He completed the Christianization of Norway but failed in attempt to unify his kingdom. An insurrection in favor of CANUTE of England and Denmark forced him to flee abroad (1028). He returned in 1030 to seek his throne but was defeated and slain at Stiklestad. Patron saint of Norway. Feast: July 29.

Olaf, 1903–, crown prince of Norway; son of Haakon VII. Supreme commander of Norwegian forces (1944–45) in World War II.

Oland (û′länd), Swed. *Öland,* Baltic island, area 520 sq. mi., SE Sweden, separated from mainland by Kalmar Sound; chief town Borgholm. Agr., cattle raising; quarrying. Has summer resorts and Stone Age monuments.

Olathe (ōlā′thē), city (pop. 5,593), E Kansas, SW of Kansas City. Agr. trade center on Old Santa Fe Trail and near Oregon Trail.

Olcott, Chauncey, 1860–1932, American actor and singer. Developed (after 1893) a type of drama featuring his own ballads (e.g., *My Wild Irish Rose*).

old-age pension: see PENSION; SOCIAL SECURITY.

Old Castile, Spain: see CASTILE.

Oldcastle, Sir John, d. 1417, English leader of LOLLARDS and martyr. Performed military service for Henry IV and was a friend of Henry V. Condemned (1413) for heresy, he escaped and was active in plots until his capture and execution. He was known as "the good Lord Cobham" (he had married into the Cobham family). See also FALSTAFF.

Old Catholics, Christian church estab. (1874) by Germans who rejected the decrees of the Vatican Council (notably papal infallibility). Leader of the movement, Döllinger, had not intended to found a new church, but the break with the Roman Catholics was complete. A Dutch Jansenist bishop consecrated the first Old Catholic bishop. The Roman ritual is retained in German, priests are allowed to marry, confession is optional.

Old Dominion, name for state of Va., probably derived from phrase (found in old documents) "the colony and dominion of Virginia."

Oldenbarneveldt, Jan van (yän′ vän′ ôl″dŭnbär′nůvĕlt), 1547–1619, Dutch statesman. Aided William the Silent; later helped concentrate military power in hands of MAURICE OF NASSAU. As permanent advocate of Holland from 1586, he controlled civil affairs of United Provs.; expanded Dutch commercial empire; sided with States-General against nobles and house of Orange. His adherence to the Remonstrants gave his enemies a pretext for securing his death sentence as a traitor, without a shred of evidence.

Oldenburg (ôl'dŭnbŏŏrk), former German state, now a district (2,085 sq. mi.; pop. 812,371) of Lower Saxony, NW Germany, on the North Sea. Largely a marshy lowland, it has fertile agr. districts; cattle and horse breeding; peat bogs. Counts of Oldenburg came into prominence in 12th cent. The accession of Count Christian as king of Denmark (see CHRISTIAN I) in 1448 gave the house of Oldenburg international importance. The main line ruled Denmark until 1863 and was succeeded by its offshoot, the line of Schleswig-Holstein-Sonderburg-Glücksburg; another offshoot, the ducal line of Holstein-Gottorp, ruled Sweden 1751–1818 and merged with the Russian Romanov dynasty in the person of Peter III. Oldenburg itself was ruled by a younger line 1448–1667, then passed to the main (i.e., Danish) line. In 1773 Christian VII ceded Oldenburg to Grand Duke (later Emperor) Paul of Russia, in exchange for Paul's claim to part of Schleswig. Paul, in turn, ceded Oldenburg to his great-uncle, Frederick Augustus of Holstein-Gottorp, bishop of Lübeck. Oldenburg was annexed to France 1806–13, was made a grand duchy in 1815 under Frederick Augustus' nephew, and continued a grand duchy to 1918. It joined the German Empire (1871) and the Weimar Republic (1919) and was incorporated into Lower Saxony 1946. Two distant districts—Birkenfeld and the former bishopric of LÜBECK—were ruled by Oldenburg from 1815. Annexed by Prussia in 1937, they passed after World War II to, respectively, Rhineland-Palatinate and Schleswig-Holstein. The cap., **Oldenburg** (pop. 121,643), is a commercial center with varied mfg. Has Renaissance castle.

Old English: see TYPE; ENGLISH LANGUAGE; ANGLO-SAXON LITERATURE.

old English sheep dog: see SHEEP DOGS.

Old Forge, borough (pop. 9,749), NE Pa., SW of Scranton and on Lackawanna R. Anthracite mining.

Oldham, county borough (pop. 121,212), Lancashire, England; chief cotton-spinning center of county.

Old Hickory, industrial village (1940 pop. 5,993), N central Tenn., on Cumberland R. and NNE of Nashville. Owned by E. I. du Pont de Nemours and Co., town produces rayon, cellophane, and chemicals.

Old Hundred: see DOXOLOGY.

Old Ironsides: see CONSTITUTION, ship.

Old Kasaan National Monument: see NATIONAL PARKS AND MONUMENTS (table).

Old Man of the Mountain: see ASSASSIN.

Old Man of the Mountain: see FRANCONIA MOUNTAINS.

Old Norse literature, the literature of the Northmen, almost entirely medieval ICELANDIC LITERATURE. Its best-known form, the saga, was, however, borrowed from the Celts and was probably first used by Vikings in the British Isles. The golden period of Old Norse was in the 11th, 12th, and early 13th cent. The poets, called scalds, composed for recitation, not reading; metrical rules were strictly observed; phrases were ingenious. As time went on strict form and ingenuity deadened scaldic verse, and a new type of rhymed verse appeared (used chiefly to translate foreign romances). Norse prose developed in remarkably limpid, forceful style as in the works of the historian Ari Thorgilsson and the celebrated SNORRI STURLUSON. See also EDDA.

Old Northwest: see NORTHWEST TERRITORY.

Old Orchard Beach, resort town (pop. 4,707), SW Maine, on the coast SSW of Portland.

Old Point Comfort, resort, SE Va., on Chesapeake Bay at entrance to Hampton Roads. Here is U.S. Fort MONROE.

Old Red Sandstone, series of sandstones and shales deposited in parts of Wales, Scotland, and England in the Devonian period. It is largely a fresh-water formation, with many well-preserved fossils.

Old Sarum (sâr'ŭm), site of ancient city, Wiltshire, England, N of New Sarum or Salisbury. Excavations have shown remains of ancient British, Roman and Saxon settlements. Parts of the cathedral were used in building Salisbury cathedral. Declined after removal of the see to New Sarum in 1220.

Old Saybrook, resort town (pop. 2,499), S Conn., at Connecticut R. mouth on Long Isl. Sound.

Old Stone Age: see PALEOLITHIC PERIOD.

Old Testament, the older portion of the Bible, of Jewish authorship. It consists of a varying number of books given in varying order. Traditional Jewish grouping is as follows: (1) the Torah or Law, consisting of the five books of the Pentateuch, i.e., Genesis, Exodus, Leviticus, Numbers, and Deuteronomy; (2) the Prophets—Joshua, Judges, 1 and 2 Samuel, 1 and 2 Kings, Isaiah, Jeremiah, Ezekiel, and the minor prophets; (3) the Writings (Hagiographa)—Psalms, Proverbs, Job, Song of Solomon, Ruth, Lamentations, Ecclesiastes, Esther, Daniel, Ezra and Nehemiah together, and Chronicles. This order and canon dates back to Hebrew source called the Masoretic text (see MASORA). The Old Testament first used in the Christian church was not derived from Masoretic text, but from a Greek translation of c.3d cent. B.C. called the Septuagint. The number and order of books in the Septuagint differs from that of the Masoretic. The Latin Bible which found its official form in the Vulgate of St. Jerome largely agreed with the list of books of the Septuagint. The Vulgate was the form accepted by the Western Church; its order is called Western canon. At the Reformation, English Protestants denied canonical standing to those books of the Old Testament which appeared in Western canon but not in the Masoretic text. These are called deuterocanonical books and are described as suitable for instruction but not divinely inspired. To set them clearly apart from works considered inspired, the AV (Authorized Version or King James Version) translators put them together in an appendix to the Old Testament which they called the APOCRYPHA. Thus, AV canon became like the Masoretic, but retained the Western order. Difference between Western canon and AV can be seen by comparing King James Version with the Douay version (representing Western canon). The following are the books of the Old Testament according to AV; the names in parentheses are the usual names in Douay when it differs from that used in AV, names in italics are those appearing in Douay and not in AV: Genesis, Exodus, Leviticus, Numbers, Deuteronomy, Joshua (Josue), Judges, Ruth, 1 and 2 Samuel (1 and 2 Kings), 1 and 2 Kings (3 and 4 Kings), 1 and 2 Chronicles (1 and 2 Paralipomenon), Ezra (1 Esdras), Nehemiah (2 Esdras), *Tobias, Judith,* Esther, Job, Psalms, Proverbs, Ecclesiastes, Song of Solomon (Canticle of Canticles), *Wisdom, Ecclesiasticus,* Isaiah (Isaias), Jeremiah (Jeremias), Lamentations, *Baruch,* Ezekiel (Ezechiel), Daniel, Hosea (Osee), Joel, Amos, Obadiah (Abdias), Jonah (Jonas), Micah (Micaeus), Nahum, Habakkuk (Habacuc), Zephaniah (Sophonias), Haggai (Aggeus), Zechariah (Zecharias), Malachi (Malachias), *1 and 2 Maccabees.*

Old Town, city (pop. 8,261), S central Maine, on Penobscot R. above Bangor; settled 1774. Mfg. of canoes, shoes, paper, and woolens. Penobscot Indian reservation is on island. Maine's first railroad connected Old Town with Bangor (1836).

Olean (ō'lēăn''), city (pop. 22,884), W N.Y., SE of Buffalo and on Allegheny R. near Pa. line; settled 1804. Oil-storage center. Mfg. of carbon black, clothing, chemicals, and metal goods.

oleander (ōlēăn'dŭr), Old World evergreen shrub of genus *Nerium* with white, pink, or red flowers. Used as a hedge in warm regions; elsewhere a pot plant.

Oleg (ō'lĕg), d. 912, semilegendary Varangian ruler of Russia, possibly b. Norway. Succeeded his father, Rurik, 879; took KIEV from Khazars 882.

Olenek (ŭlyĭnyôk'), river, 1,345 mi. long, rising in central Siberia, RSFSR, and flowing E and N into Laptev Sea. Navigable for c.500 mi.

oleomargarine: see MARGARINE.

Oléron (ōlārō'), island (68 sq. mi.; pop. 12,-820), W France, in Bay of Biscay; chief town Saint-Pierre. Oyster beds. Law of Oléron, a maritime code, was promulgated by Louis IX.

Olga, Saint, d. 969?, duchess of Kiev, widow of Igor (d. 945), regent (945–57) for her son, Svyatoslav. She promoted Christianity in Russia.

Oligocene epoch (ŏ'lĭgosēn''), third epoch of the Cenozoic period of geologic time (second if Paleocene and Eocene are classed as one). More of North America was dry land than in the preceding Eocene. Archaic mammals of the Paleocene had vanished and were replaced by true carnivores (dogs, cats, sabertooth cats), beavers, mice, rabbits, squirrels. The horse was developing. Giant hogs and camels were other new arrivals.

Oliva, Peace of (ōlē'vŭ), 1660, treaty signed at Oliva (now a suburb of Danzig) by Poland and Sweden. John II of Poland renounced claim to Swedish crown and confirmed Sweden in possession of N Livonia. Frederick William, elector of Brandenburg, was recognized in full sovereignty over Prussia but in turn confirmed West Prussia as Polish.

Olivares, Gaspur de Guzmán, conde de (gäspär' dā gōōthmän' kōn'dā dā ōlēvä'rās), 1587–1645, chief minister of Philip IV of Spain from 1621 to 1643. Hardworking and honest, he cleaned up corruption at court but involved Spain in Thirty Years War, levied oppressive taxation to finance campaigns, and pursued a centralizing policy which caused several insurrections and led to secession of Portugal (1640). He was a patron of Rubens, Velázquez, Murillo, and Lope de Vega.

olive, small evergreen tree (*Olea europaea*), native to Mediterranean region and cultivated from prehistoric times for its fruit (the olive), which is eaten pickled green or ripe and is the source of OLIVE OIL. In Calif. the olive has been of commercial importance since c.1890. The olive branch has been the symbol of peace since before Christian times.

Olive Hill, town (pop. 1,351), E Ky., WSW of Ashland. Near are Carter and Cascade caves and several natural bridges.

olive oil, clear, bland, usually yellowish oil expressed from the olive. Best grade (virgin oil) comes from slightly unripe fruit, peeled and gently pressed; this pulp, repeatedly pressed, then yields oil of inferior quality, as do fully ripe or imperfect olives. Technical oil, for industrial uses, is yielded after extraction of edible grades. Countries in Mediterranean region are chief exporters.

Olives, Mount of, or **Olivet,** ridge E of Jerusalem, frequently visited by Jesus. Garden of Gethsemane is on W slope. 2 Sam. 15.30; Mat. 21.1; Acts 1.12.

Olivet College (ŏ'lĭvĕt), at Olivet, Mich.; coeducational, founded 1844.

Olivier, Sir Laurence (Kerr) (ōlĭ'vēŭr), 1907–, English actor and director. His notable films include *Henry V* and *Hamlet.* A director (after 1944) of the Old Vic company, he won acclaim for such productions as *Oedipus* and *Uncle Vanya.*

Ollivier, Émile (āmēl' ôlēvyā'), 1825–1913, French statesman. A leader of liberal opposition to Napoleon III; after 1863 a supporter of Napoleon's "Liberal Empire." Made premier in 1869, he was dismissed after outbreak of Franco-Prussian War (1870).

Olmedo, José Joaquín (hōsā' hwäkēn' ōlmā'-dhō), 1780?–1847, Ecuadorian poet. He and Bello and Heredia are considered the three outstanding poets of revolutionary period in Spanish America.

Olmsted, Frederick Law, 1822–1903, American landscape architect, noted as planner of city parks, notably Central Park, New York city, and Jackson Park, Chicago. Also wrote books about the South. His son, **Frederick Law Olmsted,** 1870–, is also a landscape architect and city planner.

Olmütz (ôl'müts), Czech *Olomouc,* city (pop. 58,617), Moravia, Czechoslovakia, on the Morava. Varied mfg.; breweries. Archiepiscopal see. The Treaty of Olmütz (1850), between Austria and Prussia, dissolved the German Union (under Prussian presidency) and restored the German Confederation (under Austrian leadership). Prussia smarted under the "humiliation of Olmütz" until its victory over Austria in 1866. Olmütz has a 12th-cent. cathedral and a 13th-cent. city hall.

Olney, Jesse (ŏl'nē), 1798–1872, American geographer. His *Practical System of Modern Geography* (1828) was standard text with wide influence.

Olney, Richard, 1835–1917, American statesman. U.S. Attorney General (1893–95); U.S. Secretary of State (1895–97). Took part in negotiations over Venezuela Boundary Dispute.

Olney (ōl'nē, ō'nē), village, Buckinghamshire, England. Home (1767–86) of William Cowper, who with John Newton wrote *Olney Hymns,* is now a museum.

Olney (ŏl'nē), city (pop. 8,612), SE Ill., W of Vincennes, Ind. Center of farm and timber area. Mfg. of shoes and flour.

Olomouc, Czechoslovakia: see OLMÜTZ.

Olsztyn, East Prussia: see ALLENSTEIN.

Oltenia, Rumania: see WALACHIA.

Olustee (ōlŭ'stē), village, N Fla., on Ocean Pond E of Lake City. Site of most important Civil War battle (Feb. 20, 1864) fought in Fla. Federal defeat saved supplies of interior Fla. for the Confederacy.

Olympia (ōlĭm'pēů), city (pop. 15,819), state cap., W Wash., at S end of Puget Sound; founded 1850. Made territorial cap. 1853. Ships and processes lumber, fish, food products. Farm machinery and canning equipment. Was end of a branch of Oregon Trail.

Olympia, small plain of Elis, anc. Greece, near Alpheus R. From earliest times it was a center of worship of Zeus and scene of the Olympic games. Excavation here revealed the great temple which contained celebrated statue of Zeus by Phidias—one of the Seven Wonders of the World.

Olympiad, four-year chronological unit of anc. Greece, each beginning with OLYMPIC GAMES. First Olympiad was reckoned from 776 B.C.

Olympian, in Greek religion, one of 12 major gods, who lived on Mt. Olympus. Zeus, father, ruled over Hera, his sister and wife; Athena, Hebe, Artemis, and Aphrodite, his daughters; Hermes, Ares, Apollo, and Hephaestus, his sons; Hestia, his elder sister; and Poseidon, his brother. Their sanctuary was Olympia, in Elis, where Olympic games were held in their honor.

Olympias, d. 316 B.C., wife of Philip II of Macedon and mother of Alexander the Great. After Alexander's death tried to seize Macedon, but was defeated and killed by Cassander.

Olympic games, principal athletic meeting of ancient Greece, held in summer once every four years at Olympia in honor of Olympian Zeus. According to tradition, games began 776 B.C., were discontinued by Emperor Theodosius I of Rome at end of 4th cent. A.D. Games were first confined to running. Later, pentathlon, boxing, chariot racing, other sports were introduced. Modern revival of Olympic games began (1896) at Athens.

Olympic Mountains, part of Coast Ranges, NW Wash., S of Juan de Fuca Strait and W of Puget Sound. Rise to 7,954 ft. in Mt. Olympus, center of **Olympic National Park** (see NATIONAL PARKS AND MONUMENTS, table).

Olympus (ōlĭm'půs), mountain range, 25 mi. long, N Greece, between Thessaly and Macedonia and near Aegean coast. Its summit (9,570 ft.), highest point in Greece, was in Greek religion the home of the OLYMPIAN gods. Later the name Olympus was applied to heavenly palace of the gods.

Olympus, Mount: see CYPRUS; OLYMPIC MOUNTAINS; OLYMPUS (Greece).

Olynthus (ōlĭn'thůs), city of anc. Greece, on Chalcidice peninsula. Headed Chalcidian League and opposed Athens and Sparta. Olynthus at first was allied with Philip II against Athens, then asked Athenian aid against Philip. Demosthenes in the Olynthiac orations pleaded for Athenians to send the aid. Philip razed the city (348 B.C.).

Olyphant (ŏ'lĭfůnt), borough (pop. 7,047), NE Pa., on Lackawanna R. and NE of Scranton. Coal mines, silk mill, and iron foundries.

Omaha (ō'můhä), city (pop. 251,117), E Nebr., largest city in state, on the Missouri opposite Council Bluffs, Iowa. Founded 1854 with opening of Nebr. Territory. Grew as river port and supply point for pioneers, but great expansion came after arrival of Union Pacific RR (1865). Territorial cap. 1855–67. Transportation, shipping, and industrial center, it is served by railroads, transcontinental air lines, bus lines, and highways. Has oil refineries, lead smelters, grain elevators, and meat-packing plants; mfg. of farm implements, flour, and dairy products. Seat of Creighton Univ. (Jesuit; for men; opened 1878; includes Univ. Col. for women), Univ. of Nebraska medical school, Municipal Univ. of Omaha, and Joslyn Memorial (1931). Fort Omaha (1868) and Boys Town are near.

Omaha Indians, North American tribe of Siouan linguistic stock. Probably emigrated with the Ponca from the Ohio valley to Iowa, then to the Niobrara R. Separated from the Ponca and went up the Missouri, but after a smallpox epidemic (1802) they moved to NE Nebr. Sold lands W of the Missouri in 1854 and settled in Dakota co., Nebr. Sold part of their reservation to the U.S. in 1865 and in 1882 got right to own land individually. They had a typical Plains culture.

Oman, Sir Charles William Chadwick (ō'mŭn), 1860–1946, British historian, authority on military history. His many works include exhaustive *History of the Peninsular War* (7 vols., 1902–30).

Oman (ōmän', ō'măn), sultanate (c.82,000 sq. mi.; est. pop. 550,000), SE Arabia; cap. Muscat. Officially called Oman and Muscat. Mainly a narrow coastal plain (along Gulf of Oman and Arabian Sea), backed by hills and sandy interior plateau. Dates are main export. Occupied 1508 by the Portuguese, who controlled much of coastal area until mid-17th cent. Present royal line was founded 1741 by Ahmed ibn Said of Yemen. In early 19th cent. Oman was most powerful state of Arabia, controlling ZANZIBAR and coastal areas of Persia and Baluchistan. Today its only possession outside Arabia is Gwadar in Baluchistan. Bound to Britain by treaty.

Omar, c.581–644, 2d caliph. Converted to Islam by 618, he succeeded ABU BAKR (634). In his reign Islam became imperial power by many conquests. Omar created the administrative system.

Omar Khayyam (kīäm'), fl. 11th cent., Persian poet and mathematician. His fame as mathematician and astronomer has been eclipsed by popularity of his *Rubáiyát,* epigrammatic verse quatrains, which became widely known after 1859 through Edward FITZGERALD'S paraphrased translation. Other translations in English and other languages have been made.

Omayyad (ömä'yäd), Arabian dynasty of caliphs, founded in 7th cent. by MUAWIYA. Islam was united by the 5th caliph, ABDU-L-MALIK. The Omayyad cap. was usually Damascus until 750, when Marwan II (14th caliph) was defeated in battle by the ABBASID clan, who then massacred the Omayyad family. One member escaped to Spain, where he estab. himself over the Moors as ABDU-R-RAHMAN I, emir of Córdoba, in 756. In the 10th cent. the emirate became a caliphate. The brilliant civilization created by the dynasty reached its peak under Abdu-r-Rahman III, and in late 10th cent. Al MANSUR put almost all Spain under Omayyad rule. The caliphate survived until 1031; it included most of Moslem Spain.

Omdurman (ŏmdůrmän'), city (pop. 125,300), central Anglo-Egyptian Sudan, on the Nile near Khartoum; largest city of the Sudan. Became headquarters of the Mahdi in 1884. Captured 1898 by Kitchener. City trades in cotton, grain, and livestock.

Omei (ō'mā'), peak, 9,957 ft. high, SW Szechwan prov., China, near Loshan. On its slopes are many temples and monasteries.

Omphale (ŏm'fůlē), in Greek legend, queen of Lydia. To expiate for murder of his son, Hercules had to serve her for three years. She made him wear women's clothes and spin, while she wore his lion's skin and carried his club.

Omri (ŏm'rī), d. c.874 B.C., king of Israel (c.885–c.874 B.C.). When ZIMRI murdered King Elah, Omri, a general in Elah's army, seized the throne for himself. He moved the capital to Samaria, making it Israel's chief city. Name mentioned on Moabite stone. Succeeded by his son Ahab. I Kings 16.16–28; 20.34.

Omsk (ômsk), city (pop. c.450,000), RSFSR, in W Siberia, on confluence of Om and Irtysh and on Trans-Siberian RR. Transportation and industrial center (machinery, locomotives, rolling stock, cars, lumber). Has several scientific institutes. Became administrative center of Siberia 1824; industrialization began under Soviet regime.

Omuta (ō'mōōtä), industrial city (pop. 166,438), W Kyushu, Japan; coal-shipping port on Amakusa Sea.

Onan (ō'nůn), Judah's son whose wickedness was punished by sudden death. Gen. 38.

Oñate, Juan de (hwän' dā ōnyä'tā), d. c.1624?, Spanish explorer in Southwest. Conquered and settled New Mexico in 1598. Led search for Quivira (1601). Explored Colorado R.

Oncken, Hermann (hĕr'män ông'kůn), 1869–1946, German historian. Works on poiltical and diplomatic history include *Napoleon III and the Rhine* (1926; Eng. tr., 1928) and *Nation und Geschichte* (1935).

Oncken, Wilhelm (vĭl'hĕlm), 1838–1905, German historian. Edited cooperative history, *Allgemeine Geschichte in Einzeldarstellungen* (45 vols., 1879–93), to which he contributed three major studies.

Onega (ōnē'gů, ōnä'gů), river, N European RSFSR, rising in L Lacha and flowing 252 mi. N into Onega Gulf of White Sea. **Lake Onega,** area c.3,800 sq. mi., S Karelo-Finnish SSR and NW European RSFSR, is Europe's second largest lake (140 mi. long, 50 mi. wide, max. depth 400 ft.). Receives Vytegra R. in S and drains through Svir R. in SW to L. Ladoga. Baltic–White Sea Canal has its S terminus at Povenets. Petrozavodsk is chief city and port on the lake (frozen Nov.–May). **Onega Canal,** 45 mi. long, part of MARIINSK SYSTEM, runs parallel to S shore of the lake and joins Svir and Vytegra rivers.

Oneida (ōnī'dů), city (pop. 11,325), central N.Y., E of Syracuse and SE of Oneida L. Several industries, notably silverware, introduced by **Oneida Community,** religious communistic society estab. here 1848 by J. H. NOYES and reorganized 1881 as stock company.

Oneida Indians: see IROQUOIS CONFEDERACY.

Oneida Lake, 20 mi. long and 1–5 mi. wide, central N.Y., NE of Syracuse. Resorts. The Barge Canal links E end with Mohawk R. and from W end follows Oneida R., which joins Seneca R. to form Oswego R.

O'Neill, Eugene (Gladstone), 1888–, American dramatist. Son of a well-known actor, James O'Neill, he knew the stage before he became a seaman, a prospector, and a newspaperman. He studied briefly under George Pierce Baker, and his career began with association with the Provincetown Players in 1916. A number of short plays came before *Beyond the Horizon* (1920), first in a succession of plays generally viewed as the best written in the U.S. Among them are *The Emperor Jones* (1920), *Anna Christie* (1921), *The Hairy Ape* (1922), *Desire under the Elms* (1924), *The Great God Brown* (1926), *Strange Interlude* (1928), *Mourning Becomes Electra* (1931; a trilogy expressing the Electra story in modern terms; generally considered his masterpiece), *Ah, Wilderness!* (1933; his only comedy), and *The Iceman Cometh* (1946). His plays are notable for symbol in stage effects and words (e.g., the beating of tom-toms in *The Emperor Jones* and masks in *The Great God Brown*) and for their brooding philosophical and psychological studies of modern man.

O'Neill, Hugh: see TYRONE, HUGH O'NEILL, 2D EARL OF.

O'Neill, Margaret, c.1796–1879, wife of J. H. EATON. Peggy O'Neill was snubbed socially because of her alleged intimacy with Maj. Eaton before their marriage and because of her humble birth. Attempt of Pres. Jackson to insure her place in society almost disrupted cabinet and worsened his relations with Vice Pres. J. C. Calhoun, whose wife was a social leader.

O'Neill, Owen Roe, 1590?–1649, Irish rebel. Nephew of earl of Tyrone, he left Ireland after "flight of the earls" in 1607. Spent 30 years in Spanish army. Returned to Ireland (1642); became leader of his clan; led Catholic faction against the English.

O'Neill, Shane, c.1530–67, Irish chieftain. Fought with his father over his succession. Refused to acknowledge Elizabeth, but submitted in 1564. Carried on tribal warfare and was murdered.

Oneonta (ōnēŏn'tŭ), city (pop. 13,564), E central N.Y., on Susquehanna R. and NE of Binghamton; settled c.1780. Railroad shops; clothing, gloves, and flour.

onion, biennial bulbous plant (*Allium cepa*) of lily family, native to W Asia but widely grown elsewhere for its edible bulbs. Plants are grown from seeds, "sets" (seedlings arrested in development by being ripened off early in the season), bulb division (as in multiplier onions), and "tops" (small bulbs which form in place of seed on some varieties). There are red, yellow, and white varieties; the Spanish and Bermuda types are large and mild. See *ill.*, p. 999.

Onkelos (ŏng'kŭlōs), reputed author (c.100–130) of the Targum Onkelos, standard Aramaic translation of the Pentateuch according to the Talmud.

Onnes, Heike Kamerlingh: see KAMERLINGH ONNES, HEIKE.

Onondaga Indians: see IROQUOIS CONFEDERACY.

Onondaga Lake (ŏnŭndä'gŭ), 5 mi. long and 1 mi. wide, central N.Y., extending NW from Syracuse. Bought by state from Indians for salt resources 1795.

Ontario (ŏntâ'rēō), province (363,282 sq. mi., with water surface 412,582 sq. mi.; pop. 4,597,542), central Canada; cap. TORONTO. Other large cities are OTTAWA (cap. of Canada), HAMILTON, WINDSOR and LONDON. Bounded N and NE by Hudson and James Bays, S by the Great Lakes. NW Ont. is part of the LAURENTIAN PLATEAU, a mineral-rich forested region threaded by lakes and rivers where trapping is main activity. Mining (nickel, gold, silver, copper) is important in central Ont., which also attracts sportsmen and vacationists. Old Ontario (the S peninsula hemmed in by the Great Lakes) is the center of population and economic development. Access to raw materials and hydroelectric power encourages mfg. of machinery and other iron and steel products and varied consumer goods. Diverse agr. is intensive. Its geographical position makes Ont. the focus of E–W trade and distribution is facilitated by fine ports, railroads, and highways. Area first visited by Champlain 1615, and French posts were soon estab. England gained control 1763 and in 1774 the region became part of Quebec province. An influx of UNITED EMPIRE LOYALISTS 1784 led to the formation of Upper Canada (W of Ottawa R.). York (now Toronto), the cap., was burned in War of 1812. Internal dissension between the FAMILY COMPACT and reformers under W. L. MACKENZIE led to the rebellion of 1837. The insurgents were quickly repulsed but the movement for responsible government, under the more moderate leadership of ROBERT BALDWIN, gained strength. The Act of Union (1840) uniting Upper and Lower Canada proved unsuccessful and in 1867 confederation was achieved and Ont. became a province of the new dominion. In 1912 the province was enlarged by part of the Keewatin dist. of Northwest Territories. Politically Ont. fluctuates between the Liberal and Conservative parties, with considerable strength in the CO-OPERATIVE COMMONWEALTH FEDERATION. Because of its population and economic importance, Ontario's politics are a major factor in Canadian government.

Ontario. 1 City (pop. 22,872), S Calif., E of Los Angeles; founded 1882. Processes citrus fruits, olives, and wine. Mfg. of electrical equipment and aircraft parts. **2** City (pop. 4,465), E Oregon, on Snake R. at mouth of Malheur R. A center in OWYHEE project. Gateway to Oregon cattle country.

Ontario, Lake, 193 mi. long and 53 mi. wide, smallest and most easterly of the Great Lakes, lying between province of Ontario and N.Y. Connected with L. Erie, L. Huron, Hudson R., and Ottawa by various canals. Fed chiefly by Niagara R. and drained NE by St. Lawrence R. Major ports are Hamilton, Toronto, Cobourg, and Kingston, Canada; Rochester and Oswego, N.Y. Étienne Brulé was first white man to see lake 1615, and Champlain visited (also 1615).

onyx (ŏ'nĭks), variety of quartz showing parallel and regular color bands. The black and white specimens are used for cameos.

OPA: see OFFICE OF PRICE ADMINISTRATION.

opal (ō'pŭl), gem characterized by remarkable play of colors (opalescence). Opals have wide color range, including orange-red (fire opal). Main sources: Czechoslovakia, Australia, Honduras, Nevada, Mexico.

Opava, Czechoslovakia: see TROPPAU.

Opelika (ōpŭlī'kŭ), city (pop. 12,295), E Ala., ENE of Montgomery near Chattahoochee R., in farm area; settled 1836. Has textile plants.

Opelousas (ŏpŭlōō'sŭs), city (pop. 11,659), S central La., W of Baton Rouge; founded 1765. Temporary state cap. during Civil War. Processes and ships cotton, rice, sugar cane and truck.

Open Door, maintenance in area of equal commercial and industrial rights for all nations. Notable example was policy in treaties with China after OPIUM WAR (1839–42). Policy was made effective for China through efforts of John Hay in 1899 and was confirmed after the BOXER REBELLION (1900). Japan in 1915 flouted it by presenting the TWENTY-ONE DEMANDS, but the Nine-Power Treaty after the Washington Conference (1921–22) guaranteed China's integrity and reaffirmed principle of Open Door, which lasted until World War II. Then recognition of China's absolute sovereignty ended Open Door policy.

open shop: see CLOSED SHOP AND OPEN SHOP.

Opéra (ôpärä'), chief opera house of Paris on Place de l'Opéra on right bank of the Seine. Designed by Garnier and built 1863–75. Its ornate grand staircase is famous.

opera, drama set to music. Although its antecedents date from the lyric theater of ancient Greece, true opera was a creation of the baroque in Italy. First opera on record (although the music is lost) is *Dafne* (1597) by Jacopo Peri; opera's first real master was Monteverdi; first public opera house was opened in Venice in 1637. A definite opera style emerged wherein the aria and virtuoso soloist became more important than the recitative and chorus. Early operas took their plots from mythology; later comedy and parody became popular. In the late 17th cent., the dramatically unified, three-act *opera seria* was created in an effort to purge opera of irrelevant episodes, bombast, and mechanical contrivances then so prevalent. Distinguished from *opera seria* were *opéra comique,* which meant any opera—regardless of subject matter—that had spoken dialogue, and *opera buffa,* which did not have spoken dialogue. After the French Revolution, spectacular and melodramatic operas became popular, evolving into 19th-cent. grand opera with its emphasis on historical subjects, religious elements, and violent passions (as in operas of Meyerbeer). Outstanding among opera composers are Gluck, Mozart, Verdi, Wagner, and Puccini.

operetta, type of theatrical presentation with a frivolous, sentimental story (often employing satire) and both spoken dialogue and much light, pleasant music. It developed from *opéra comique.* Noted operetta composers have been Offenbach, Johann Strauss the younger, Gilbert and Sullivan, Victor Herbert, and Sigmund Romberg.

Ophion (ōfī'ŭn), in Greek legend, Titan who ruled the world before Cronus. His wife was Eurynome.

Ophir (ō'fŭr), in Bible, seaport or region from which ships of Solomon brought gold and also gems, ivory, apes, and peacocks. Variously identified with India, Ceylon, Malay Peninsula, Africa, and Arabia.

Opitz, Martin (mär'tēn ō'pĭts), 1597–1639, German poet, critic, metrical reformer. Known for his translations and writings on poetry, especially the *Buch von der deutschen Poeterey* [book on German poetry] (1624).

opium (ō'pēŭm), bitter dried juice from unripe capsules of opium poppy. Contains alkaloids including morphine (of which heroin is a derivative) and codeine, valuable drugs but, like opium, habit-forming NARCOTICS. Laudanum is a tincture of opium. Opium addiction is a serious problem especially in Orient.

Opium War, 1839–42, struggle between Great Britain and China. The British had long wanted China to end restrictions on foreign trade; they found pretext for war (which they easily won) when China banned import of opium in 1839 and destroyed British-owned opium stored at Canton. Treaty of Nanking (1842) opened ports of Canton, Shanghai, Amoy, Foochow, and Ningpo to British trade and ceded Hong Kong to Britain.

Oporto (ŭpôr'tō, ō–), Port. *Pôrto,* city (pop. 279,738), Douro Litoral prov., NW Portugal, on Douro R. Second city of Portugal and an important port, with its harbor at near-by Leixões on the Atlantic, it exports its famous port wine (since 17th cent.). Textile mfg. Traditionally founded c.138 B.C. by Romans as Cale (later Portus Cale). Henry of Burgundy secured the title duke of Portucalense in 11th cent., and thus Oporto gave its name to the future kingdom. It was ruled by its bishops until after the Cortes of Leiria (1254), when kings estab. control. First city to revolt in the Peninsular War, it was retaken by the French but liberated 1809 by Wellington. Suffered siege in 1832 in Miguelist Wars.

opossum (pŏ'sŭm, ŭpŏ'sŭm), MARSUPIAL of South America and U.S. Virginia opossum (*Didelphis*) of U.S. somewhat resembles a large rat, has a white face, disordered grayish fur, a nearly naked prehensile tail (the opossum can sleep while hanging head down), and is nocturnal and largely arboreal. Practice of lying absolutely still when frightened gives rise to term "playing 'possum."

Opp, city (pop. 5,240), E Ala., near Fla. line, in pine and farm area.

Oppeln (ô'pŭln), Pol. *Opole,* city (1939 pop. 52,977; 1946 pop. 27,666), Upper Silesia, on Oder R.; since 1945 under Polish administration. Seat of dukes of Oppeln, of PIAST dynasty, 1163–1532. Duchy passed 1532 to the Hapsburgs and 1742 to Prussia.

Oppenheimer, J. Robert (ŏ'pŭnhī"mŭr), 1904–, American physicist. He was director of atomic-energy research project at Los Alamos, N.Mex. (1942–45). He later became chairman of general advisory committee of U.S. Atomic Energy Commission and director of the Inst. for Advanced Study, Princeton, N.J.

Opper, Frederick Burr, 1857–1937, American cartoonist and illustrator of books.

Ops (ŏps), in Roman religion, goddess of fertility; wife of Saturn and mother of Jupiter. As goddess of sowing and reaping she was known as Consiva. Identified with Greek Rhea.

Optic, Oliver, pseud. of William Taylor Adams, 1822–97, American juvenile writer. His 116 books combine exciting tales with wholesome instruction.

optics, a branch of physics, the study of LIGHT. Physical optics is concerned with the nature and properties of light; physiological, with role of light in VISION; geometrical, with geometry of REFLECTION and REFRACTION of light as encountered in study of the MIRROR and the LENS.

optometry (ŏptŏm'ŭtrē), science of detecting and correcting, usually with spectacles, certain nonpathological ocular defects. Word came into use 1903, with establishment of American Optometric Association. Legislation regulating practice of optometry was enacted in 20th cent.

oracle, in Greek religion, response given by a god to a human question; term also used commonly to refer to institution itself. Oracles were fixed in a locality, and each represented a god (e.g., Zeus at Dodona and Apollo at Delphi). Some oracles were uttered by persons entranced, some were heard in rustling of leaves, and some came in dreams. Priests or priestesses, who were greatly respected, interpreted oracles. The Delphic oracle, the most influential, was chiefly interested in preserving piety and in extending Greek colonies.

Oradea (orä'dyä) or **Oradea-Mare** (–mä'rĕ), Ger. *Grosswardein,* Hung. *Nagyvárad,* city (pop. 82,282), W. Rumania, on Rapid Koros R. Commercial center of grape-growing area. Episcopal see. Ceded by Hungary to Rumania after World War I, though population is about half Magyar.

Oraefajokull, Icelandic *Öræfajökull* (û'rīvä-yû"kütůl), highest mountain (6,952 ft.) of Iceland, rising from VATNAJOKULL ice field near SE coast.

Oraibi (ōrī'bē), Indian pueblo on a mesa c.100 mi. N of Winslow, Ariz.; built c.1150. A mission estab. here (1629) was destroyed in the revolt of 1680. Long the most important pueblo of the Hopi, it declined because of economic troubles and internal quarrels.

Oran (ōrăn', ōrän'), city (pop. 244,594), NW Algeria; port on the Mediterranean, chief French naval base in N Africa. Founded in 10th cent. by Moorish Andalusian traders. Alternately under Spanish and Turkish rule, 16th–18th cent. Occupied 1831 by the French. Old quarter has casbah and 18th-cent. mosque. City's rise dates from late 19th cent., when port facilities (here and in adjacent Mers-el-Kebir) were improved. In Nov., 1942, Oran was a key landing area of Allied invasion forces.

Orange (Fr. ô'rãzh'), city (pop. 8,145), Vaucluse dept., SE France, near Avignon. Its fine Roman amphitheater is still in use. In 11th cent. it became the cap. of a county, later the principality of Orange, which in 1544 passed to William the Silent of the house of NASSAU. Orange was conquered for France by Louis XIV, but the title remained with the Dutch princes of Orange. House of Orange is the reigning dynasty of the Netherlands.

Orange. 1 City (pop. 10,027), S Calif., SE of Los Angeles; founded 1868. Processes citrus fruits. **2** Town (pop. 5,894), N Mass., E of Greenfield. Mfg. of metal goods, shoes, and clothing. **3** Industrial city (pop. 38,037), NE N.J., W suburb of Newark and New York city; settled c.1675. Mfg. of clothing, chemicals, metal products. Orange, East Orange, South Orange, West Orange, and Maplewood known as "The Oranges," a suburban unit. **4** City (pop. 21,174), SE Texas, on Sabine R. and E of Beaumont; founded 1836. Deepwater port (channel to Gulf) shipping oil, lumber, and food. Has paper mills, nylon and salt plants, shipyards, and rail shops. **5** Town (pop. 2,571), central Va., NE of Charlottesville. MONTPELIER is near by.

orange, citrus fruit, the most important fresh fruit of international commerce, native to tropical Asia. Trees bearing the sweet orange (*Citrus sinensis*) were estab. in Fla. by 1600 and in Calif. about 175 years later; its varieties are now the most important commercially. The sour or Seville orange (*C. aurantium*) is grown in U.S. chiefly for understock; the fruits are used, mostly in Europe, for marmalade. The trifoliate orange (*Poncirus trifoliata*), a hardier species, is also used as an understock. Orange trees begin to bear when three years old and flowers and fruits may appear throughout the year. The tangerine is a variety of the high-quality king orange (*C. nobilis*). Hybrids include the citrange (result of crossing trifoliate orange and a sweet orange variety) and tangelo (obtained by crossing tangerine and grapefruit).

Orangeburg, city (pop. 15,322), central S.C., SSE of Columbia on North Fork of Edisto R.; settled c.1735. Mfg. of cotton, timber and food products. Seat of South Carolina State Agricultural and Mechanical Col. (Negro; land grant; coed.; 1896).

Orange Free State, province (49,647 sq. mi.; pop. 879,071), E central South Africa; cap. Bloemfontein. Bounded by Orange R. (S) and Vaal R. (N). Mainly a plateau. Major crops are wheat and corn. Diamonds, gold, and coal are mined. Settled 1835–48 by Boers, who created free republic, 1854. Annexed 1902 by the British. Joined Union of South Africa 1910.

Orangemen, members of the Loyal Orange Institution, an Irish society in province of Ulster. Estab. 1795 to maintain Protestant ascendancy. Name taken from family of William III of England.

Orange Mountains: see WATCHUNG MOUNTAINS.

Orange River, c.1,300 mi. long, South Africa. Near its mouth are extensive diamond deposits.

orangutan (ōrăng'ŏŏtăn) or **orangoutang** (–tăng), anthropoid ape (genus *Pongo* or *Simia*) of swampy coastal forests of Borneo and Sumatra. It is intelligent and teachable. Walks on all fours or swings through trees. It has shaggy, reddish hair, and the adult male is c.5 ft. high and weighs c.250 lb.

Oranienbaum, RSFSR: see LOMONOSOV.

Oranienburg (ōrä'nyůnbŏŏrk), town (pop. 18,-633), Brandenburg, N Germany, on the Havel. Site of one of the first concentration camps of Nazi regime.

oratorio, musical form employing chorus, orchestra (or organ), and soloists, usually having a sacred libretto and always performed without stage action or scenery. It developed in the late 16th and early 17th cent. and reached its peak in works of Bach, Handel, Haydn, and Mendelssohn.

oratory, the art of eloquent speech. In ancient Greece and Rome oratory was part of rhetoric (composition and delivery of speeches) and was important in public and private life. Aristotle and Quintilian discussed theory of rhetoric; subject, with definite rules and models, was emphasized in education of Middle Ages and Renaissance, though generally confined to the Church. With development of parliaments in 18th cent., great political orators appeared. Recently, especially with advent of radio, oratory has become less grandiloquent, more conversational, as in "fireside chats" of Pres. F. D. Roosevelt. Term *oratory* has given way to *public speaking*.

Oratory, Congregation of the, Roman Catholic secular priests organized locally according to the rule of St. PHILIP NERI. J. H. NEWMAN introduced the order in England.

orbit, in astronomy, path described by one heavenly body in its revolution about another whose attracting force controls the orbit. Position of a planet at a given time can be computed by using KEPLER'S LAWS and allowing for deviations from elliptic orbit if certain numerical elements of orbit are known. These include the major axis; eccentricity; inclination (angle of plane of planet's orbit to ECLIPTIC); longitudes of perihelion and of ascending node (one of two points of intersection of planes of planet and earth); and date when planet passes a determinate part of orbit, e.g., perihelion. Orbits of most comets are nearly parabolic, those of satellites, nearly circular. See *ill.*, p. 1187.

Orcagna (ōrkä'nyä) or **Arcagnolo** (ärkä'nyōlō), c.1308–1368, Florentine artist, whose real name was Andrea di Cione. Studied sculpture with Andrea Pisano. His marble tabernacle at Or San Michele, Florence, is an Italian Gothic masterpiece. In fresco painting he was a follower of Giotto.

orchestra. As composers began to develop an instrumental style as distinct from a vocal style and as orchestral music became valued for its own sake and was freed from subservience to vocal music, the orchestra began its long, slow period of development. The baroque period was the beginning. Until then, instruments that played in ensemble were members of one family rather than a blend of the different sonorities of the orchestra. The center of the baroque orchestra was a keyboard instrument (usually the harpsichord). Artistic need and the development of instruments themselves are interweaving factors influencing the make-up of the orchestra. First of modern instruments to be fully developed and assume dominance of the orchestra was the violin and its family. As the various wind and percussion instruments were introduced and more strings were added to balance them, the keyboard instrument (though often still present) was no longer needed to fill in the harmony. The 19th century saw the completion of the modern symphony orchestra—often augmented to extremes by composers such as Richard Strauss and Mahler. Instruments most often found in the modern orchestra are strings (violin, viola, cello, bass, harp); winds (piccolo, flute, oboe, clarinet, bassoon, contrabassoon, English horn, French horn, trumpet, trombone, tuba); and tympani and percussion instruments. See *ill.*, p. 857.

orchid (ôr'kĭd), flowering plant of orchid family, containing c.500 genera, most abundant in the tropics. Many have curiously shaped and beautifully colored flowers. An orchid may be an air plant or a terrestrial form, e.g., the hardy North American species, including LADY'S-SLIPPER and orchis.

Orcus: see HELL.

ordeal, anc. legal custom allied to divination. By it appeal was made to divine authority to decide guilt or innocence of one accused, or to choose between disputants. It persisted in W Europe until trial by JURY became common. Forms varied from ordeal by fire or by water to drawing lots. Trial by battle or by combat was recognized form in Middle Ages. DUEL has also been recognized form based on idea that God would favor cause of righteous.

Order of American Knights: see KNIGHTS OF THE GOLDEN CIRCLE.

orders, holy. In the Roman Catholic and Eastern churches the clergy are empowered to undertake their sacred duties by receiving holy orders in a sacrament called order (the ceremony is called ordination or in the case of bishops, consecration). There are three orders—bishop, priest, and deacon. Priests and bishops have double functions, liturgical and administrative; a deacon is only an assistant. The bishop may confer all sacraments, the priest all except confirmation and holy orders. A priest may head a parish, a bishop heads a diocese made up of a number of parishes. An archbishop is the bishop of an important center; he may have a province (made up of several dioceses) assigned to him, but his authority over other bishops is not strong. A patriarch is an archbishop with several provinces. In the Roman Catholic Church all bishops are ruled by the pope because he is the bishop of Rome. There are priests who are in monastic orders and do not usually head parishes; these are the regular clergy. Those who do not belong to orders are called secular clergy.

orders in council, in British government. **1** An order given by the king on advice of all or some of members of his privy council, without prior consent of parliament. First so named in 18th cent. Most commonly used in emergencies. Most notable use was blockade of Europe and system of embargoes after 1806 as an answer to Napoleon's Continental System. **2** Administrative orders, issued on authority of a parliamentary act, to carry out the act's provisions. Corresponds to "executive order" in U.S.

orders of architecture: see DORIC ORDER; IONIC ORDER; CORINTHIAN ORDER.

Ordinance of 1787, adopted by Congress of Confederation for government of Western territories ceded to U.S. by the states. Frequently called Northwest Ordinance; it created Northwest Territory in region N of the Ohio. Provided for admission of states from the territory; prohibited slavery there. Ordinance was most significant achievement of Congress under Articles of Confederation.

Ordovician period (ôrdùvĭ'shùn), second period of the Paleozoic era of geologic time. Shallow seas flooded much of N Eurasia and North America. Low elevation of solid land restricted erosion, so that limestone formations are more characteristic than sandstone and shale. The seas were rich in invertebrate life, trilobites being very numerous. A few fishlike vertebrates made their appearance.

ore, mineral carrying enough metal to make its extraction profitable. Ores usually occur in concentrated deposits, classed as primary and secondary. Primary ores may be formed at the same time as the enclosing rock or later by filling of fissures. Chief types are sulphides and oxides. Secondary ores result chiefly from weathering of primary deposits.

Orebro (ûrùbrōō'), Swed. *Örebro,* city (pop. 66,548), co. seat of Orebro co., central Sweden, on Hjalmaren L. Shoe mfg. The national diet meeting at Orebro in 1810 elected Bernadotte king of Sweden as Charles XIV. Has 13th-cent. church and castle.

Oregon, state (96,981 sq. mi.; pop. 1,521,341), NW U.S.; admitted 1859 as 33d state (free); cap. SALEM. PORTLAND largest city. Bordered partly N by COLUMBIA R., partly E by Snake R., W by Pacific Ocean. Varies from coast-mountain-valley region (W) to upland plateau (E). GREAT BASIN wastelands in SE. CASCADE RANGE runs N–S. Agr. of fruits, grains, nuts, truck; livestock, dairying, poultry; lumbering, fishing. Processing of agr. and forest resources; mfg. of lumbering and agr. equipment, chemicals; publishing. Some mining of gold, silver, copper, manganese. U.S. claim to region estab. by Robert GRAY (1792). J. J. Astor estab. fur-trading post at ASTORIA in 1811. U.S.–Great Britain ruled jointly 1818–46, when 49th parallel was made international boundary. Oregon Territory created 1848 (N part made Washington Territory 1853). Settlers arrived over OREGON TRAIL. Indians subdued by 1880. Lumbering and agr. prospered with completion of railroads; population increased. Columbia Valley Authority project brought much development of industries and farming lands, but its merits have been disputed.

Oregon, city (pop. 3,205), N Ill., on Rock R. and below Rockford. Near by is Eagle's Nest Art Colony, founded 1898 by Lorado Taft and others; has Taft's *Black Hawk* statue.

Oregon, name sometimes applied to COLUMBIA R. in early days of American settlement in its valley.

Oregon, University of: see EUGENE.

Oregon Caves National Monument: see NATIONAL PARKS AND MONUMENTS (table).

Oregon City, city (pop. 7,682), NW Oregon, at falls of Willamette R. and S of Portland, in fruit and dairy area; platted 1842 by John McLoughlin of Hudson's Bay Co., who later lost his claims to American immigrants. Territorial cap. until 1851. Had first newspaper (*Oregon Spectator,* 1846) W of Missouri R. Has paper, pulp, and wool mills.

Oregon grape, evergreen shrub (*Mahonia aquifolium*) of NW North America. Formerly considered a barberry, it has hollylike leaflets, yellow flowers, and showy grapelike clusters of edible blue berries.

Oregon State College: see CORVALLIS.

Oregon Trail, overland emigrant trail in U.S. from Missouri R. to Columbia R. country. Pioneers by wagon train did not, however, follow any single narrow route. Independence and Westport (now in Kansas City) were favorite starting points. Pioneers starting from Independence followed same route as SANTA FE TRAIL for some 40 mi. Trail's "end" shifted as settlement spread. Mountain men were chiefly responsible for making route known. First genuine emigrant train was that led by John Bidwell in 1841, which turned off on what was to be California Trail. First emigrant train to reach Oregon was led by Elijah White in 1842. Trail was used for many years. See also OVERLAND TRAIL.

Orel (ōrĕl'), city (pop. 110,567), central European RSFSR, on Oka R. Important industrial transportation center of a fertile agr. region. During World War II it was held by the Germans 1941–43 and was the scene of heavy fighting.

Orellana, Francisco de (fränthē'skō dā ōrĕlyä'nä), d. c.1546, Spanish explorer of Amazon R. Took part in conquest of Peru and was with Gonzalo Pizarro on expedition into interior of South America (begun 1538). At Napo R. his detachment was separated from expedition and he went down Amazon, arriving at the mouth 1541. His tales of female warriors gave the river its name. A later attempt to return up river took him to his death.

Orem (ô'rŭm), town (pop. 8,351), N central Utah, near Utah L. and N of Provo. Served by Provo R. project. Vegetable canning. Steel plant near.

Ore Mountains: see ERZGEBIRGE.

Orenburg, RSFSR: see CHKALOV.

Orestes (ōrĕ'stēz), in Greek mythology, prince of Mycenae; only son of Agamemnon and Clytemnestra. When his mother and Aegisthus murdered Agamemnon, she sent boy away for fear of his vengeance. He later returned and joined his sister Electra in killing his mother and her lover. The Erinyes then persecuted him until he reached Athens, where he was tried and acquitted by the Areopagus. To complete his purification, he brought sacred image of Artemis from Tauris. There he found his sister Iphigenia.

Orestes, d. 476, Roman general. Raised his son ROMULUS AUGUSTULUS to the throne (475); was defeated and slain by ODOACER at Piacenza.

Oresund (ûrŭsŭnd') or **the Sound,** Scandinavian *Öresund* and *Øresund,* sound, 87 mi. long, between Sweden and Denmark, connecting Kattegat with Baltic Sea. Narrowest place (2½ mi.) is between Halsinborg and Elsinore.

Orford, Robert Walpole, 1st earl of: see WALPOLE, ROBERT, 1ST EARL OF ORFORD.

organ, musical wind instrument in which sound is produced by one or more ranks (or rows) of pipes and which has a mechanically produced wind supply. Modern organ pipes vary in size from 64 ft. to less than an inch. The several keyboards of the organ which are played with the hands are called manuals. The projecting knobs (called stops), usually both to the left and to the right of the keyboard, operate wooden sliders which pass under the mouths of a rank of pipes and can keep a particular rank out of action or "stopped." The pedals of the organ do not have the same function as those of a piano but are rather like another keyboard, played with the feet. The entire assembly of keyboards and stops is called the console. The organ has existed, if in crude form, since ancient times. Organs of the Middle Ages already had several rows or ranks of pipes; these were all diapasons, those pipes whose timbre is characteristic of the organ alone. The keyboard was a creation of the 13th cent.; reed pipes and stops with timbres imitative of other instruments (e.g., the flute) were added in the late 15th and early 16th cent. Organ building reached its peak during the baroque era, and then declined. In the 19th cent., the increased use of stops imitative of orchestral tone and the overuse of the swell and crescendo led to the obscuring of the diapason pipes. The early 20th cent. saw the electrifying of mechanical parts, thus continuing the trend toward monstrous size and overwhelming power. Under the leadership of Albert Schweitzer and others, however, interest in the organ of the baroque era has revived.

Organization of American States, international organ created at Bogotá, Colombia (1948), by agreement of the 21 American republics. Treaty ratified 1951.

Organ Pipe Cactus National Monument: see NATIONAL PARKS AND MONUMENTS (table).

Orgetorix (ôrgĕ'tùrĭks), d. 60? B.C., Helvetian leader. Planned a migration of the Helvetii across Gaul, but plan was discovered. He died soon after, but his people undertook the migration, bringing on the GALLIC WARS.

Oriel College: see OXFORD UNIVERSITY.

Origen (ô'rijin), 185?–254?), Christian philosopher, b. Egypt. He taught with great acclaim in Alexandria and then in Caesarea. Edited the Bible in six parallel Hebrew and Greek versions (the *Hexapla*) and wrote many works. Among them was his theological *De principiis* and his polemical *Contra Celsum.*

Orillia (ōrĭ'lēù), town (pop. 12,110), S Ont., Canada, on L. Couchiching and N of Toronto. Resort with boatbuilding, woodworking, and flour milling. Was home of Stephen Leacock.

Orinoco (ôrùnō'kō), river rising in Guiana Highlands and flowing NW to Colombia, then N to Apure and E to Atlantic. Most of course is in Venezuela. One of largest South American rivers, its estimated length is from 1,200 to 1,700 mi. Navigable for most of length, it is joined to Amazon system by natural channel of Casiquiare and the Rio Negro. Chief port is CIUDAD BOLÍVAR. Probably discovered by Columbus (1498), explored by Lope de Aguirre (1560), and centuries later by Alexander von Humboldt. The origin of river in mountain wilderness, sought by several expeditions, was finally determined in 1951.

oriole (ôr'ēōl), name for various Old and New World perching birds. European orioles are allied to crows; golden oriole, orange-yellow with black wings and tail, ranges from England to Siberia and winters in Africa. Related species include mango bird of India. American orioles, called hangnests, are of blackbird and meadowlark family. Best known is Baltimore oriole; plumage of male is black and orange. See *ill.*, p. 135.

Orion (ōrī'ùn), in Greek mythology, gigantic Boeotian hunter. He loved Merope but violated her and was blinded by her father. His eyes were healed by the sun's rays. At death he became a constellation, of which Orion's belt is a part.

Orissa (ùrĭ'sù), state (59,869 sq. mi.; pop. 14,-644,293), W India, cap. Bhubaneswar. Mainly hilly with fertile coastal strip. Major iron-ore deposits are mined in N. Except for Munda-speaking aborigines in interior, inhabitants speak Oriya language. Conquered 1803 by the British. Absorbed 24 former princely states in reorganization of 1948–49.

Orizaba (ōrēsä'bä), city (pop. 47,910), Veracruz, E Mexico, in a fertile valley surrounded by wooded hills; a popular resort and agr. center. Development of water power has made it an important mfg. city.

Orizaba, peak, 18,700 ft. high, E Mexico, on Veracruz-Puebla border. A snow-capped inactive volcano, it is the highest point in Mexico.

Orkhon (ôr'kŏn), river, c.700 mi. long, rising in Khangai mts., NW Mongolian People's Republic, and flowing NE to Selenga R. just S of boundary with USSR. **Orkhon Inscriptions,** dating from 8th cent., were found near river's lower course. They comprise minor Chinese texts and oldest known material in a Turkic language.

Orkney, county (376 sq. mi.; pop. 21,258), NE Scotland, consisting of **Orkney Islands** or **Orkneys,** archipelago c.50 mi. long, made up of 90 islands. Less than a third are inhabited. Largest, Pomona or Mainland, has county town, Kirkwall. Except for Hoy, they are mostly low, rocky, and treeless. Fishing and farming are main occupations. Belonged to Norway 865–1468. Scapa Flow is naval base.

Orland, town (pop. 2,067), N Calif., NNW of Sacramento. Hq. of an irrigation project (1910). Three dams supply water from a Sacramento R. tributary.

Orlando: see ROLAND.

Orlando, Vittorio Emmanuele (vēt-tō'rēō āmänwā'lā ōrlän'dō), 1860–1952, Italian premier (1917–19). One of "Big Four" at Paris Peace Conference of 1919, he failed to secure, largely because of Wilson's opposition, the territorial gains promised Italy in the Secret Treaty of London (1915). In protest, he left the conference (April–May) and resigned soon afterward. He opposed Fascism; after its fall in 1943 he served as elder statesman.

Orlando (ôrlăn'dō), city (pop. 52,367), central Fla., SE of L. Apopka; settled near Fort Gatlin (1837–48). Largest inland city in Fla. Trade, processing, and shipping center for citrus fruits, lumber, and naval stores. Mfg. of machinery.

Orléans (ôrlāā'), name of two branches of the French royal line; derived their name from the duchy of Orléans, held in appanage by various princes of the blood.

Valois-Orléans. This branch was founded by **Louis, duc d'Orléans,** 1372–1407, brother of King Charles VI. His murder by John the Fearless of Burgundy caused the civil war between ARMAGNACS AND BURGUNDIANS. His son **Charles, duc d'Orléans,** 1391–1465, was captured by the English at Agincourt (1415) and remained captive until 1440. He was a fine poet; his court at Blois was a center of literary life. His son became king as LOUIS XII (last of the line).

Bourbon-Orléans. **Gaston, duc d'Orléans,** 1608–60, younger brother of Louis XIII, was the first Bourbon duke of Orléans. He conspired against Richelieu but won his pardon by betraying his associates (e.g., CINQ MARS), and he played a leading part in the FRONDE (as did his daughter, Mlle de MONTPENSIER). He had no male issue. The present house of Bourbon-Orléans began with **Philippe I, duc d'Orléans,** 1640–1701, brother of Louis XIV. His first wife was HENRIETTA OF ENGLAND; his second wife, Elizabeth Charlotte of Bavaria. A notorious libertine, he was excluded from state affairs. His son **Philippe II, duc d'Orléans,** 1674–1723, was regent for Louis XV. Cynical, debauched, and dictatorial, he set the tone for the licentiousness of the regency period. He was responsible for the rise of John LAW. The ambitions of the regent and his descendants brought them in conflict with the ruling house. His great-grandson, **Louis Philippe Joseph, duc d'Orléans,** 1747–93, supported the French Revolution, helped the Jacobins into power, and changed his name to Philippe Égalité. A member of the Convention, he voted for the execution of Louis XVI but was guillotined soon afterward on the charge of aspiring to the crown. His son was King LOUIS PHILIPPE (reigned 1830–48). Louis Philippe's grandson, **Louis Philippe Albert d'Orléans, comte de Paris,** 1838–94, went to the U.S. after 1848 and fought in the Civil War under McClellan. Back in France in 1871, he renounced his claim to the throne in favor of the legitimist pretender, Henri de CHAMBORD (1873). After Chambord's death (1883), he became head of the entire house of Bourbon. He wrote *Workingmen's Associations in England* (1869) and *History of the Civil War in America* (Eng. tr., 4 vols. 1875–88), a standard work of military history. He was succeeded as pretender by his son, **Louis Philippe Robert, duc d'Orléans,** 1869–1926, who spent his life in England and in the Indian army; by his nephew, **Jean d'Orléans, duc de Guise,** 1874–1940; and by the duc de Guise's son **Henri Robert Ferdinand d'Orléans, comte de Paris,** 1908–.

Orléans (ôr'lēünz, Fr. ôrlāā'), city (pop. 64,755), cap. of Loiret dept., N central France, on the Loire. Clothes mfg.; food processing. Dating from Roman times, it became (6th cent.) the cap. of a Frankish kingdom which in 7th cent. was united with Neustria. With surrounding Orléanais prov., Orléans was part of the original royal domain of the Capetians and was given at times in appanage to members of the royal family (dukes of Orléans). The siege by the English in 1428–29 threatened to bring all France under English rule until the appearance of JOAN OF ARC. After Joan had taken several of the English forts, the English lifted the siege, and the tide of the Hundred Years War was turned. The city, including Sainte-Croix cathedral and Joan of Arc museum, suffered severe damage in World War II.

Orléans, Île d' (ēl" dôrlāā'), or **Orléans Island** (20 mi. long, 5 mi. wide), S Que., Canada, in St. Lawrence R. and NE of Quebec; settled 1651 by French. Site of one of Wolfe's camps 1759. Highway bridge built to mainland 1935.

Orlon, trade name for synthetic fiber developed by E. I. du Pont de Nemours & Co. It is made from natural gas, oxygen, and atmospheric nitrogen and is resistant to sunlight, moisture, alkalis, acids, and to attacks by fungus diseases and insects.

Orlov, Aleksey Grigoryevich, Count (ŭlyĭksyā' grĭgôr'yůvĭch ŭrlôf'), 1737–1808, Russian nobleman. He took part in the conspiracy which placed Catherine II on the throne and probably murdered PETER III. Leader of the conspiracy was his brother, **Count Grigori Grigoryevich Orlov** (grĭgô'rē), 1734–83, a favorite of Catherine II. He later held high posts but had little political influence.

Ormandy, Eugene (ôr'můndē), 1899–, American conductor, b. Budapest. Conductor of the Minneapolis Symphony Orchestra, 1931–36. In 1936 he became conductor of the Philadelphia Symphony Orchestra.

Ormond, city (pop. 3,418), NE Fla., N of Daytona Beach. Ormond Beach, across Halifax R. (lagoon), has part of Daytona Beach speedway and former winter home of J. D. Rockefeller.

Ormonde, dukes and **earls of:** see BUTLER, family.

Ormuz, Iran: see HORMUZ.

Orne (ôrn), department (2,372 sq. mi.; pop. 273,181), N France, in Normandy; cap. Alençon.

Orono (ô'růnō), town (pop. 7,504), S Maine, on Penobscot R. above Bangor; settled c.1775. Mfg. of wood products. Seat of Univ. of Maine (land-grant, state supported; coed.); chartered 1865 as Maine State Col. of Agriculture and the Mechanic Arts, opened 1868, and renamed 1897.

Orontes (ōrŏn'tēs), river, c.240 mi. long, SW Asia. Rises in Lebanon and flows through Syria and Turkey to the Mediterranean near Antioch. On its banks are Antioch, Homs, Hama, and other centers dating from ancient times.

Orosius, Paulus (ōrō'shēůs), c.385–420, Iberian historian and theologian, a priest; friend and disciple of St. Augustine. In Africa he completed *Seven Books of History against the Pagans,* a work of universal history, demonstrating how events proved the truth of Biblical prophecies.

Oroville (ô'rōvĭl), city (pop. 5,387), N Calif., N of Sacramento and on Feather R.; settled 1849 as gold camp. Center of an olive and orchard region. Feather River Canyon and Feather Falls are near.

Orozco, José Clemente (hōsā' klāmān'tā ōrō'skō), 1883–1949, Mexican mural and genre painter. With Rivera he led the Mexican renaissance. Deals mainly with social themes in starkly simple style.

Orpah (ôr'pů), sister-in-law of Ruth. Ruth 1.4,14.

Orpen, Sir William, 1878–1931, British portrait and genre painter, b. Ireland.

Orpheus (ôr'fēůs, ôr'fūs), in Greek mythology, celebrated Thracian bard, the beautiful music of whose lyre charmed even trees and rocks. He was son of Calliope by Apollo or Oeagrus. After Argonaut expedition, he married the nymph Eurydice. When she was killed by a snake, he sought her in Hades, where the gods, charmed by his music, freed her on condition that he not look at her before they reached earth. He disobeyed and she vanished. This myth has been popular as an operatic libretto. Orpheus is considered founder of Orphism.

Orphic Mysteries (ôr'fĭk), secret religious rites in worship of Dionysus. These were based on myth of Dionysus Zagreus. Zagreus, son of Zeus and Persephone, was devoured by Titans to please the jealous Hera. Zeus destroyed Titans by lightning, and from their ashes sprang the race of men, who were now part evil (Titan) and part divine (Zagreus). Zeus swallowed Zagreus' heart and from it was born the new Dionysus Zagreus. Thus initiate to cult had to eat raw flesh to achieve union with god. Poems purported to have been written by Orpheus in 6th cent. B.C. were basis of Greek mystery religion **Orphism.** This explained good and evil in men by myth of Dionysus Zagreus, and it taught importance of pure moral and ritual life for immortality.

Orr, John Boyd Orr, 1st **Baron,** 1880–, British nutritionist and agr. scientist. Won 1949 Nobel Peace Prize. Contributed to science of nutrition and solution of world food problems.

Orrefors (ôrûfôrs′, –fôsh′), village, SE Sweden; famous for its fine glassware, which is known over the world.

Orrery, Roger Boyle, 1st **earl of:** see BOYLE.

orrisroot: see IRIS.

Orrville, city (pop. 5,153), NE Ohio, NE of Wooster, in agr. area. Mfg. of food and dairy products.

Orsini (ōrsē′nē), Roman family which included Popes Celestine III, Nicholas III, Benedict XIII. Rose in 13th cent. Rivalry between Guelph Orsini and Ghibelline Colonna families often plunged Rome into anarchy. Members were made princes of Holy Roman Empire in 17th cent.

Orsk (ôrsk), city (pop. c.100,000), E European RSFSR, on Ural R. Metallurgical plants, oil refineries.

Ortegal, Cape (ôrtägäl′), NW Spain, in Galicia, on Atlantic coast; SW limit of Bay of Biscay.

Ortega y Gasset, José (hōsā′ ôrtā′gä ē gäsĕt′), 1883–, Spanish essayist and philosopher; long a professor of metaphysics at Madrid. Wrote much on Spanish and other national cultures and held (notably in *The Revolt of the Masses,* 1930) that an intellectual minority should direct the masses to prevent chaos.

Ortelius, Abraham (ôrtē′lyůs), 1527–98, Flemish geographer, of German origin. Noted for his atlas, *Theatrum orbis terrarum* (1570).

Orthez (ôrtĕz′), town (pop. 4,609), Basses-Pyrénées dept., SW France; former cap. of Béarn. Here Wellington defeated the French under Soult (1814).

Orthodox Eastern Church, community of Christian churches, independent but mutually recognized; originating in E Europe and SW Asia through a split with the Western Church. They agree in accepting the decrees of the first seven ecumenical councils and in rejecting the authority of the bishop of Rome (the pope). Orthodox and Roman Catholics view each other as schismatic, but consider the Nestorian, Coptic, Jacobite, and Armenian church as heretical. There were differences within the whole church in early days, but the split between the E and W began only in the 5th cent. and became definite only with the challenge to papal authority by Photius (9th cent.) and the condemnation of the patriarch of Constantinople by Pope Leo IX (1054). The Crusades embittered feelings, and many attempts at reunion since that time have been unsuccessful. There is considerable variation of practice between the two. Thus in the Eastern Church the liturgy is always sung and is not usually celebrated daily as in the West, and communion is given with a spoon. Parish priests are usually married; monks and bishops are not. The relationship with the various churches of the E community is complex and even terms vary greatly. Thus the term *Greek Church* may be used very loosely, though it is best confined to the patriarchate of Constantinople, the Church of Greece (dating from the Greek War of Independence), and churches using the Byzantine rite (liturgy in Greek). There are six other national churches, the most ancient being the Church of Cyprus and for centuries by far the most important being the Russian Orthodox Church. This was headed at first by the metropolitan of Kiev, under Constantinople; the see was moved to Moscow and a patriarchate was set up in 1589. The rite is in Old Slavonic. Peter I abolished this (1721) and set up a synod. In general the relations of church and state were very close and influence was mutual. Perhaps the greatest single early event in the Church was the reform movement under Nikon. In the Russian Revolution the Church suffered greatly and went into an eclipse. The patriarchate (just revived in 1917) lapsed in 1925, but a new patriarch was appointed in 1943. Relation of the Church to the Communist state appeared to be highly intimate. As Communist influence spread after World War II it greatly weakened the Orthodox Churches of Bulgaria, Yugoslavia, Rumania, Finland, and Poland (these last two founded only after World War I).

Ortles (ôrt′lās), Ger. *Ortler,* Alpine group, Trentino–Alto Adige, N Italy, rising to 12,792 ft.

Orton, Edward, 1829–99, American geologist and educator. He served as professor and president at Antioch and at Ohio Agricultural and Mechanical Col. (later Ohio State Univ.). From 1869 he was affiliated with Ohio geological survey; he made important studies of natural gas and petroleum.

Oruro (ōrōō′rō), city (pop. 52,600), W Bolivia; founded 1595 to exploit near-by silver deposits. Declined in importance as silver production declined in 19th cent., but with exploitation of other minerals (notably tin), it grew again and is third largest city in Bolivia.

Orvieto (ôrvyā′tō), town (pop. 8,883), Umbria, central Italy, on a rocky hill; probable site of the Etruscan VOLSINII. Near by are remains of an Etruscan necropolis. Cathedral, begun 1290 to commemorate miracle of BOLSENA and completed in 16th cent., has black and white marble façade. Its chapel was frescoed by Fra Angelico and Luca Signorelli.

Orwell, George, pseud. of Eric Blair, 1903–50, English satirist. His hatred of authoritarianism and fears for loss of individual liberty are shown in his novels *Animal Farm* (1946) and *Nineteen Eighty-Four* (1949).

Os, chemical symbol of the element OSMIUM.

Osage, river formed in W Mo. by Marais des Cygnes and Little Osage rivers. Winds c.250 mi. NE to the Missouri below Jefferson City. Impounded by BAGNELL DAM, it forms L. of the OZARKS.

Osage Indians (ō′sāj, ōsāj′), North American tribe of Siouan linguistic stock, once living in the Ohio valley, but removed by 1673 to the Osage R. in Mo. They were a typical Plains tribe. Early they allied themselves with the French. They were moved to a reservation in N central Okla., which turned out to be rich oil land.

Osage orange, deciduous spiny tree (*Maclura pomifera*) native to Ark. and Texas, useful as a hedge. It has inedible orangelike fruits. The flexible, durable wood was a favorite bow wood of the Osage Indians.

Osaka (ō'säkä), city (pop. 1,559,310), S Honshu, Japan; port on Osaka Bay. Second largest city and chief commercial center of Japan; focal point of industrial belt. Seat of Osaka Imperial Univ. and Kansai Univ. Has Buddhist temple founded in 6th cent. Noted for puppet theater. As Naniwa, city was 4th-cent. cap. of Japan. Seat of Hideyoshi in 16th cent.

O Salutaris Hostia (săl″ūtā'rĭs, sä'lōōtä'rĭs) [Latin,= O saving victim], hymn to the Host, one of two hymns regularly sung at the exposition in Benediction of the Blessed Sacrament in the Roman Catholic Church. The other hymn is *Tantum ergo. O Salutaris* is the last two stanzas of a Corpus Christi hymn, probably written by St. Thomas Aquinas.

Osawatomie (ō″sůwŏ'tůmē), city (pop. 4,347), E Kansas, SSW of Kansas City. Once a station on the Underground Railroad, it has cabin where John Brown lived in 1856. Monument commemorates raid in which five of Brown's men were killed.

Osborn, Henry Fairfield, 1857–1935, American geologist. He was distinguished as teacher at Princeton and Columbia, as member of the U.S. Geological Survey, and for his long association with the American Mus. of Natural History (president 1908–33). His son, **Fairfield Osborn,** 1887–, became a naturalist and a conservationist.

Osborne, Dorothy, later **Lady Temple** (ŏz'bůrn), 1627–95, English letter writer. Letters to Sir William Temple (pub. 1888) clearly portray her period.

Osborne, Thomas Mott, 1859–1926, American prison reformer. Became a voluntary prisoner in Auburn, N.Y., penitentiary to investigate conditions and wrote *Within Prison Walls* (1914). As warden of Sing Sing (1914–15) instituted a system of self-government. Argued that prisons should educate, not punish.

Osborne House, a residence of Queen Victoria (who died here in 1901) near East Cowes, Isle of Wight.

Oscan, language of the Italic subfamily of the Indo-European languages. See LANGUAGE (table).

Oscar, Swedish kings. **Oscar I,** 1799–1859, king of Sweden and Norway (1844–59); son of Charles XIV (Bernadotte). **Oscar II,** 1829–1907, succeeded his father Charles XV as king of Sweden and Norway in 1872 but lost Norway when it severed its union with Sweden (1905).

Osceola (ŏsēō'lů, ō–), c.1800–1838, leader of SEMINOLE INDIANS. Also called Powell, surname of his supposed white father. Led fight against U.S. troops (1835–37).

oscillator (ŏ'sĭlātůr), in electronics, circuit producing alternating audio-frequency or radio-frequency voltage. In transmitters, it generates carrier wave; in receivers, is used in SUPERHETERODYNE and superregenerative circuits and in heterodyne method of receiving unmodulated code transmission.

Osee (ōsē'), variant of HOSEA.

Ösel, Estonia: see SAARE.

Osgood, Herbert Levi, 1855–1918, American historian. Author *The American Colonies in the Seventeenth Century* (3 vols.. 1904–7) and *The American Colonies in the Eighteenth Century* (4 vols., 1924).

Osh (ôsh), city (pop. 33,315), Kirghiz SSR, in Fergana Valley. A major silk production center for the last thousand years, it is one of the oldest cities of central Asia. Has Oriental and Russian sections.

Oshawa (ŏ'shůwů), city (pop. 41,545), S Ont., Canada, on L. Ontario and ENE of Toronto. Has mfg. of automobiles, steel products, and woolen goods.

Oshkosh (ŏsh'kŏsh″), city (pop. 41,084), E Wis., on L. Winnebago where Upper Fox R. enters; settled 1836. Father Allouez visited site 1670; French fur-trading post estab. early 19th cent. Resort center with mfg. of woodwork, machinery, and clothing.

osier: see WILLOW.

Osijek (ō'sēyĕk), Ger. *Esseg,* Hung. *Eszék,* city (pop. 50,398), NE Croatia, Yugoslavia; a port on Drava R. and chief city of Slavonia. Varied mfg.

Osiris (ōsī'rĭs), in Egyptian religion, god of the underworld. In a famous myth he was son of Keb (Earth) and Nut (Sky), husband of ISIS, and father of HORUS. He was slain by his evil brother Set (Night). Osiris was identified with forces of fertility, e.g., the sun and the Nile. He was also the creative force giving life to seeds and thus was linked with doctrine of immortality, a potent force in Egyptian life. The trio of Osiris, Isis, and Horus were long important in Egypt, and were later worshiped in Greece and Rome.

Oskaloosa (ŏskůlōō'sů), city (pop. 11,124), SE Iowa, ESE of Des Moines; settled 1843 by Quakers. Center of livestock, farm, and coal area with mfg. of food, clay, and metal products, and music publishing. Annual Quaker meeting.

Osler, Sir William (ō'slůr), 1849–1919, Canadian physician, renowned also as teacher and medical historian. Associated with Johns Hopkins Univ. (1889–1904) and Oxford (from 1905). Author of *The Principles and Practice of Medicine* (1892; 16th ed., 1947).

Oslo (ŏs'lō, ŏz'lō, Nor. ōōs'lōō), cap. and largest city of Norway, coterminous with Oslo co. (175 sq. mi.; pop. 417,238), SE Norway, at head of Oslo Fjord, a large inlet of the Skagerrak. Norway's commercial, industrial, and intellectual center; seat of a university (founded 1811), of a Lutheran bishop, and of Nobel Inst. Its busy harbor is kept ice free. Metalworking; mfg. of chemicals, clothing, paper and food products; brewing. Founded 1050 by Harold III, Oslo came under Hanseatic dominance in 14th cent. Rebuilt by Christian IV after destructive fire of 1624, it was called Christiania (or Kristiania) from then until 1925. It was under German occupation 1940–45. Built on modern lines, Oslo has fostered contemporary art in public projects, e.g., sculptures of VIGELAND in Frogner Park and new city hall (1950). Planned residential sections have eliminated slums. Points of interest include royal palace, the Storting (parliament), Folk

Mus., ruins of Oslo's first cathedral (St. Hallvard), Akerskirke (12th-cent. church), and Akershus fortress (13th cent.).

Osman, caliph: see OTHMAN.

Osman I (ŏz'mŭn, ŏsmän') or **Othman I** (ŏth'mŭn, ŏthmän'), 1259–1326, leader of the Osmanli or Ottoman TURKS, who were named for him. Founded Ottoman dynasty (see OTTOMAN EMPIRE).

Osmeña, Sergio (sĕr'hēō ōsmā'nyä), 1878–, Filipino statesman. President 1944–46. Returned to Philippines with U.S. invasion forces in Oct., 1944.

osmium (ŏz'mēŭm), metallic element (symbol = Os; see also ELEMENT, table). It has highest specific gravity of the elements, is hard to fuse, not affected by ordinary acids. Member of group of platinum metals.

osmosis (ŏsmō'sĭs), selective passage of fluids through semipermeable substance or membrane. Makes possible the absorption of water by plant roots and, in animals, passage of digested foods through walls of digestive tract into blood stream. Tendency is for less dense material to pass through membrane toward more dense material; water generally moves from place where its molecules are more numerous to where they are less so. Osmotic pressure develops as result of differences in concentrations of substance on opposite sides of membrane; it increases with heat.

Osnabrück (ŏz'nŭbrŏŏk, Ger. ôs"näbrük'), city (pop. 108,900), Lower Saxony, NW Germany, on Hase R., linked by canal with Ems-Weser Canal. Inland port; industrial center (iron, steel, machinery, textiles, paper). Became episcopal see 8th cent.; later joined Hanseatic League; accepted Reformation 1543. For the treaty signed here 1648, see WESTPHALIA, PEACE OF. Under treaty of 1648, bishopric alternated between Catholics and Lutherans. It was secularized 1803, but Catholic diocese was restored 1858. Osnabrück passed to Hanover 1815 and shared its subsequent history. Much of its fine Gothic architecture was destroyed in World War II.

Osorno (ōsôr'nō), city (pop. 22,772), S central Chile, in the heart of the lake district. Founded 1558, it was destroyed by Araucanian Indians and was reestab. in 1776. It had large German immigration in latter half of 19th cent. and is a modern progressive city.

osprey (ŏs'prĕ), bird of prey found in most parts of world. American osprey or fish hawk is usually seen near large bodies of fresh or salt water. It has long, angular wings and white under parts.

Ossa, mountain, Greece: see PELION.

Ossetia (ŏsē'shŭ), region, RSFSR and Georgian SSR, in central Greater Caucasus. On N slope is North Ossetian ASSR (3,550 sq. mi.; pop. c.450,000), RSFSR; cap. Dzhaudzhikau (formerly Vladikavkaz). On S slope is South Ossetian Autonomous Oblast [region] (1,500 sq. mi.; pop. c.116,000), Georgian SSR; cap. Stalinir. Ossetia produces fruit, wine, grain, cotton, lumber, and livestock. Silver, lead, and zinc are mined in N Ossetia. The Ossetians are an ancient people speaking an Iranian language. They are Moslem in N and Eastern Orthodox in S.

Ossian (ŏsh'ŭn) or **Oisin** (ŭshēn'), legendary Gaelic poet, supposed author of poems and tales about the exploits of his father, FINN MAC CUMHAIL, hero of the 3d cent. In 18th cent. James MACPHERSON produced forged "Ossianic" poems.

Ossietzky, Carl von (fŭn ôsyĕt'skē), 1898–1938, German pacifist. Coeditor of antimilitaristic weekly *Weltbühne,* he led German peace movement after World War I, was imprisoned 1931–32, and held in a concentration camp 1933–36. The award to Ossietzky of the 1935 Nobel Peace Prize was sharply protested by the Nazi regime.

Ossining (ŏ'sŭnĭng), village (pop. 16,098), SE N.Y., on Hudson R. and near Tarrytown; settled c.1750, named Sing Sing 1813–1901. Mfg. of machinery, clothing, wire, and paper goods. Seat of Sing Sing state prison, where T. M. OSBORNE and L. E. LAWES introduced notable reforms.

Ossipee (ŏ'sĭpē), resort town (pop. 1,412), E N.H., on Ossipee L. and E of L. Winnipesaukee. Whittier summered here.

Ossory, Thomas Butler, earl of: see BUTLER, family.

Ossory, anc. kingdom of Ireland, including Co. Kilkenny and parts of Co. Offaly and Co. Laoighise.

Ostade, Adriaen van (ä'drēän vän ô'städŭ), 1610–85, Dutch painter of everyday scenes of village life. Studied with Frans Hals. His brother **Isaac van Ostade,** 1621–49, was a landscape painter.

Ostend (ŏstĕnd'), Flemish *Oostende,* Fr. *Ostende,* city (pop. 50,225), West Flanders prov., N Belgium; a port and resort on North Sea. Has large fishing fleet. Fortified 1583, it heroically resisted a Spanish siege (1601–4) but eventually surrendered. It was a German submarine base in World War I; in 1918 the British, in a daring raid, partially sealed off the harbors of Ostend and Zeebrugge by sinking ships at their entrances. Again used by the Germans in World War II, Ostend suffered some damage.

Ostend Manifesto, document drawn up in Oct., 1854, at Ostend, Belgium, by James Buchanan, American minister to Great Britain, J. Y. Mason, minister to France, and Pierre Soulé, minister to Spain. Outlined value of Cuba to U.S.; implied that if Spain refused to sell, U.S. might consider taking island by force. Widely denounced, manifesto was immediately repudiated by Secretary of State W. L. Marcy for U.S. government.

osteopathy (ŏstēŏ'pŭthē), system of therapy emphasizing manipulation, founded 1874 by A. T. Still. Based on principle that most ailments result from "structural derangement" of body. Osteopaths may usually prescribe drugs and perform surgery.

Ostergotland (û'stŭryût"länd), Swed. *Östergötlands län,* county and historic province (4,266 sq. mi.; pop. 347,996), SE Sweden, E of Vattern L.; cap. Linkoping. Agr., stock raising, lumbering, mining (iron, zinc).

Ostia (ŏ'stēŭ), anc. city, Italy, at the mouth of the Tiber. Founded (4th cent. B.C.) as protection for Rome, it became Rome's port. Declined after 3d cent. A.D.

Ostrava, Czechoslovakia: see MORAVSKA OSTRAVA.

ostrich (ŏ'strĭch), flightless bird of Africa and parts of SW Asia, allied to rhea, emu, moa. Largest of living birds. Head, neck, and thighs are scantily feathered; long, white plumes from wings and tail of male were formerly in great demand for trimming millinery, etc.

Ostrogoths (ŏ'strŭgŏths") or **East Goths,** division of the Goths, one of chief groups of anc. German peoples. Descended, according to unproved tradition, from the Gotar of S SWEDEN, the Goths by the 3d cent. A.D. were settled in region N of the Black Sea. They split into two divisions in the 4th cent. The VISIGOTHS, under pressure of the HUNS, moved W; the Ostrogoths were subjected by the Huns and served in their army. On Attila's death (453), they settled in Pannonia (modern Hungary) as allies of East Rome. In 493 their king THEODORIC THE GREAT, after conquering Italy from ODOACER, set up the Ostrogothic kingdom of Italy. The murder of his daughter AMALASUNTHA (535) gave Emperor Justinian I the pretext for reconquering Italy through his generals BELISARIUS and NARSES. Narses' victory over TOTILA (552) ended the kingdom of the Ostrogoths, who soon lost their ethnic identity. Although they had largely preserved Roman law and institutions, the Ostrogoths had clung to their Arian religion.

Ostroleka (ôstrôwĕ'kä), Pol. *Ostrołeka,* Rus. *Ostrolenka,* town (pop. 9,279), Poland, on Narew R. Russians defeated Polish insurgents here in 1831.

Ostrovsky, Aleksandr Nikolayevich (ŭlyĭksän'dŭr nyĭkŭlī'ŭvĭch ŭstrôf'skē), 1823–86, Russian dramatist. Most of his plays deal critically with the merchant and petty-official class. His chief plays, among which *The Storm* (1860) is best known, have been translated into English.

Ostrovsky, Nikolai Alekseyevich (nyĭkŭlī' ŭlĭksyā'ĭvĭch), 1904–37, Russian novelist. *How the Steel Was Tempered* (1936; Eng. tr., *The Making of a Hero*), an autobiographical tale of the civil war, was one of the most popular of all the novels of Soviet literature.

Ostwald, Wilhelm (vĭl'hĕlm ôst'vält), 1853–1932, German chemist. Won 1909 Nobel Prize for work on catalysis and research on fundamental principles of equilibrium and rates of reaction. Invented **Ostwald process** for making nitric acid by oxidation of ammonia. Did outstanding research on color.

Oswego (ŏswē'gō), city (pop. 22,647), N N.Y., on L. Ontario at Oswego R. mouth and NW of Syracuse, at N end of the Barge Canal; founded 1722 by English. Important lake port with mfg. of machinery, textiles, and matches. Early fur-trading post. Present Fort Ontario (1755) held alternately by French and British in colonial wars.

Oswego, river formed in central N.Y. by confluence of Oneida and Seneca rivers. Flows c.23 mi. NW to L. Ontario at Oswego. Part of the Barge Canal.

Oswego tea or **bee balm,** aromatic perennial plant (*Monarda didyma*) of the mint family with showy heads of scarlet or salmon flowers. Indians and colonists made tea from the leaves.

Oswiecim (ôshfyĕ'chēm), Ger. *Auschwitz,* town (pop. 6,708), S Poland, E of Cracow. Here in World War II the Germans maintained a concentration camp where c.4,000,000 inmates, mostly Jews, were exterminated by gas, phenol injections, shooting, hanging, hunger, and disease.

Oswy or **Oswiu** (both: ŏz'wē), d. 671, king of Northumbria. Continued conversion of England to Christianity and called Synod of WHITBY.

Otaru (ōtä'rōō), city (pop. 164,934), SW Hokkaido, Japan; chief coal-shipping port of island.

Othman (ŏth'mŭn, ōth'män) or **Osman** (ŏz'mŭn), c.574–656, 3d caliph (644–56); son-in-law of Mohammed; of OMAYYAD family.

Othman I, Turkish leader: see OSMAN I.

Otho, Marcus Salvius (ō'thō), A.D. 32–A.D. 69, Roman emperor (A.D. 69). His wife, Poppaea Sabina, became NERO's mistress. He joined Galba against Nero, killed Galba, and was briefly emperor until defeated by Vitellius.

Otis, Elisha Graves, 1811–61, American inventor. From his invention (1854) of a device to prevent fall of hoisting machinery, he developed first passenger elevator (1857). Invention made feasible the building of skyscrapers and Otis's company became great industrial enterprise.

Otis, James, 1725–83, American colonial orator and patriot. Led radical wing of colonial opposition to British measures. Proposed Stamp Act Congress.

Oto Indians (ō'tō), North American tribe of Siouan linguistic stock, once a part of the Winnebago nation N of the Great Lakes, later in S Minn., then on the Platte R. In 1880–82 they migrated to Okla. They had a typical Plains culture. Also Otto.

Otranto (ōtrăn'tō, Ital. ô'träntō), town (pop. 2,507), Apulia, S Italy. Until its destruction by the Turks in 1480 it was a flourishing port on the Strait of Otranto, which connects the Adriatic with the Ionian Sea between Italy and Albania.

Otsego Lake (ŏtsē'gō), 8 mi. long, E central N.Y., SE of Utica, in resort area. Susquehanna R. issues from S end at Cooperstown.

ottava rima: see PENTAMETER.

Ottawa (ŏ'tŭwŭ), city (pop. 202,045), cap. of Canada, SE Ont., Canada, on Ottawa R. (bridge) opposite Hull, Que., WSW of Montreal. Industries include paper milling, woodworking, and watchmaking. Rideau Canal separates city into upper and lower sections. Parks and drives line canal and river banks. Founded 1827 and called Bytown until 1854. Became cap. of Canada in 1858 and cap. of the dominion in 1867. Places of interest include Parliament buildings, Natl. Victoria Mus., Natl. Art Gall., Royal Mint, Anglican and R.C. cathedrals, dominion observatory, and Rideau Hall (residence of governor general). Seat of Univ. of Ottawa (bilingual; R.C., pontifical; coed.; estab. 1848).

Ottawa. 1 City (pop. 16,957), N Ill., at junction of Illinois and Fox rivers; laid out 1830, settled 1832 after Black Hawk War. Coal mines, clay and sand pits in area. Mfg. of food, glass, and clay products and farm machinery. Scene of first Lincoln-Douglas debate 1858. Near by is Starved Rock. **2** City (pop. 10,081), E Kansas, SE of Topeka. Settled 1832 by Ottawa Indians, who moved to Okla. 1867. Baptist mission estab. 1837. Trade center for grain and poultry area.

Ottawa, river of Ont. and Que., Canada, 696 mi. long, largest tributary of the St. Lawrence. Rises in W Que. NE of North Bay and flows W, then SE to the St. Lawrence above Montreal forming the Ont.-Que. line for much of its length. Lower course has several expansions. Numerous rapids furnish hydroelectric power. Connects with L. Ontario by Rideau Canal system. Valley explored by Champlain 1613–15. As Grand R. it was important highway for fur traders, explorers, and missionaries.

Ottawa Indians, North American tribe of Algonquian linguistic stock, in the 17th cent. on Manitoulin Isl. in L. Huron and on the shores of Georgian Bay. Allied themselves with French and were forced by the Iroquois to move to the W Great Lakes region. Under French protection they returned to Manitoulin (1670), later joined the Huron. Pontiac was an Ottawa Indian.

otter (ŏ'tûr), aquatic carnivorous mammal of weasel family, found on all continents except Australia. North American otter has slender body, c.3½–4½ ft. long including heavy tail, a flat head, and webbed hind feet. The fur is valuable. **Sea otter** (*Enhydra*) of N Pacific is larger, heavier; swims on back. Hunted for fur, it is now protected in Alaskan waters.

Otter, Peaks of, two peaks, western Va., in Blue Ridge Mts., W of Lynchburg; 4,001 and 3,875 ft. high.

Otterbein, Philip William, 1726–1813, German-American clergyman, a founder of United Brethren in Christ. Missionary in America for German Reformed Church in 1752. With Martin Boehm he carried on evangelistic work in Pa. and Md. and helped lay foundation (1789) for new church. He was bishop in 1800.

Otterbein College: see WESTERVILLE, Ohio.

Otto, emperors and German kings. **Otto I** or **Otto the Great,** 912–73, succeeded his father Henry I as German king in 936. He defeated the rebellious nobles, led by Duke Eberhard of Franconia, at Andernach (939); interfered in French affairs (940–50); and invaded Italy (951). His pretext for that last move was the appeal addressed to him by Adelaide or Adelheid, widow of King Hugh of Italy, who was about to be forced into marriage with the son of BERENGAR II. Otto forced Berengar to become his vassal, took the title king of the Lombards, married Adelaide, and returned to Germany. Another rebellion, led by CONRAD THE RED of Lorraine, broke up under the threat of invasion by the Magyars, whom Otto routed at the Lechfeld (955). Meanwhile Berengar II had resumed his aggressions. Pope JOHN XII appealed to Otto, who entered Rome and was crowned emperor by the pope (962). This union of Germany and Italy under the imperial crown created the HOLY ROMAN EMPIRE; it also began the long struggle between emperors and popes, as Otto's subsequent struggle with John XII and the Romans shows. Otto's reign saw the expansion and growing commercial prosperity of the German towns. He was succeeded as German king by his son **Otto II,** 955–83. He married the Byzantine princess Theophano (972) and in 980 was crowned emperor at Rome. Successful in putting down internal rebellions and in checking Danish and Bohemian inroads (974–77), he was disastrously defeated by the Arabs in Calabria (982). His son **Otto III,** 980–1002, was elected German king just before Otto II's death. The regency was held by his mother Theophano and later by his grandmother Adelaide. In 996 he estab. his cousin Bruno as Pope Gregory V; in 999 he made his tutor Gerbert pope as SYLVESTER II. Crowned emperor in 996, he keenly felt his high position as scion of both the Eastern and Western imperial houses. He resided at Rome after 998 and seriously set about acting like an ancient Roman emperor, which made him unpopular both in Germany and in Italy. In 1001 a Roman mob forced him to flee to Sicily, where he died. **Otto IV,** 1182?–1218, second son of HENRY THE LION of Saxony, was chosen antiking to PHILIP OF SWABIA in 1198, was reelected king after Philip's death in 1208, and was crowned emperor at Rome in 1209. Though he had acknowledged the papacy's rights to the Papal States and Sicily in 1208, he later disregarded his commitments, seized the lands of MATILDA of Tuscany (1210), and invaded Apulia. Pope INNOCENT III excommunicated him, and part of the German nobles rebelled and elected Frederick of Hohenstaufen (later Emperor FREDERICK II) as king. In the ensuing war Otto was supported by his uncle, King John of England, but was defeated at Bouvines by Philip II of France (1214). He was deposed in 1215 and retired to Saxony.

Otto I, 1848–1916, king of Bavaria (1886–1913); brother of Louis II. Incurably insane from 1872. His uncle Luitpold was regent 1886–1912; Luitpold's son, regent from 1912, deposed Otto and became king as Louis III.

Otto I, 1815–67, first king of the Hellenes (1832–62); second son of Louis I of Bavaria. Was placed on Greek throne by Great Powers. An uprising forced him to adopt a constitution (1843). Was deposed 1862.

Otto, 1912–, Austrian archduke and pretender to the Austro-Hungarian throne; son of Emperor Charles I and Empress Zita.

Otto, Nikolaus August (nē'kōlous ou'gŏŏst ō'tō), 1832–91, German engineer. He was coinventor (1867) of an internal-combustion engine and devised (1876) four-stroke Otto cycle widely adopted for motors.

Ottocar, kings of Bohemia, of the PREMYSL dynasty. **Ottocar I,** d. 1230, became duke of Bohemia in 1197 and in 1198 was given the title king by Philip of Swabia. His grandson **Ottocar II,** d. 1278, reigned 1253–78. By marriage, conquest, and diplomacy he acquired Austria (1251), Styria (1260), and Carinthia, Carniola, and Istria (1269). In Bohemia, he encouraged the growth of the towns and sought to reduce the power of the nobles. His ambition was to act as arbiter of the Holy Roman Empire, but the election in 1273 of Rudolf of Hapsburg (see RUDOLF I) as German king proved Ottocar's undoing. Having contested Rudolf's election, he was declared forfeit of his dominions (1274), and in 1276 he was forced to surrender all but Bohemia and Moravia to Rudolf. A new war with Rudolf ended with Ottocar's defeat and death on the MARCHFELD, scene of Ottocar's earlier victory over Bela IV of Hungary.

Otto Indians: see OTO INDIANS.

Ottoman Empire (ŏ'tŭmŭn), greatest of Moslem states, formed (14th–16th cent.) in Near East by the Ottoman or Osmanli TURKS after the breakdown of the Seljuk empire. It was also called Turkey, but modern Turkey formed only a part of it. The Ottoman state emerged and expanded under OSMAN I (founder of the empire's dynasty), MURAD I, and BAJAZET I at the expense of the Byzantine Empire, Bulgaria, and Serbia. After their victories at BURSA (1326), Kossovo (1389), and NIKOPOL (1396), the Turks were only temporarily checked by TAMERLANE (1402). In 1453 MOHAMMED II conquered CONSTANTINOPLE and became heir to the Byzantine Empire. The Ottoman Empire reached its height in the 16th cent. under SELIM I, who assumed the CALIPHATE after his victories in Syria and Egypt (1516–17), and under SULEIMAN I (the Magnificent). Algiers, most of Greece and Hungary, and much of Persia and Arabia had come under Turkish rule; Transylvania, Walachia, and Moldavia had become tributary principalities. However, in every respect Turkey remained a medieval state, with its Byzantine-Asiatic despotic system mitigated only by observance of Moslem law. Decline began with Suleiman's death. Militarily, the first setback was the naval defeat at LEPANTO (1571), but the decisive blow was the repulse of the Turkish siege of Vienna (1683), followed 1699 by the Treaty of KARLOWITZ. Political decay set in—e.g., the JANIZARIES made and unmade sultans; corruption and bribery were raised to a system of administration. The breakup of the state was accelerated by the RUSSO-TURKISH WARS of the 18th cent. After the Greek War of Independence the fate of the "Sick Man of Europe" became a major European concern; the Western Powers feared Russian expansion (see EASTERN QUESTION) and loss of their investments in Turkey, which in a series of treaties, called capitulations, had virtually surrendered its economic independence to them. Civil reforms were attempted. MIDHAT PASHA framed a constitution (1876), but ABDU-L-HAMID II soon abolished it. In 1908 the Young Turks, a reformist and nationalist movement, forced the restoration of the constitution, but the dissolution of the empire was beyond remedy. With much of its territory already lost, most of remaining European Turkey went in the BALKAN WARS (1912–13). ENVER PASHA, leader of the Young Turks, assumed dictatorial powers in 1913. In World War I Turkey was allied with Germany. Turkish troops were successful in the GALLIPOLI CAMPAIGN (1915), but in 1918 all resistance collapsed, and the Treaty of SÈVRES confirmed the dissolution of the empire. With the overthrow of the last sultan by Ataturk (1922) the history of modern TURKEY began.

Otto of Freising (frī'zĭng), d. 1158, German chronicler, bishop of Freising. Wrote world history to 1146, *The Two Cities,* a most valuable source book.

Otto the Great: see OTTO I, emperor.

Ottumwa (ŏtŭm'wŭ), city (pop. 33,631), SE Iowa, on Des Moines R. and SE of Des Moines; settled 1843. Rail and industrial center of farm and coal area with mfg. of food and metal products.

Otway, Thomas, 1652–85, English dramatist. His plays *The Orphan* (1680) and *Venice Preserved* (1682) reach highest point of pathetic tragedy in Restoration drama. His genius lay in portraying heights of passion and love and depths of misery and despair.

Otztal Alps (ûts'täl), mountain group, Tyrol, W Austria, S of the Inn. Wildspitze (12,379 ft.) is highest peak in Tyrol.

Ouachita (wŏ'shĭtô"), river rising in W Ark. in Ouachita Mts. and flowing c.605 mi. SE into NE La., becoming part of Red R. system. Partially navigable. Lakes Hamilton and Catherine were created by Carpenter (1931) and Remmel (1924) dams.

Ouachita Mountains, range S of Arkansas R., extending from central Ark. into SE Okla., and rising to 2,800 ft. in Mt. Magazine. Several public parks and forest reservations in region.

Ouchy, Switzerland: see LAUSANNE.

Oud, J(acobus) J(ohannes) P(ieter) (out'), 1890–, Dutch architect, who influenced growth of modern architecture. Associated with Mondrian.

Oude Maas, Dutch name of Old MEUSE, river.

Oudenarde (ōō'dŭnärd, ou'–), Fr. *Audenarde,* town (pop. 6,567), East Flanders prov., NW Belgium, on the Scheldt. Here Marlborough and Eugene of Savoy defeated the French under Vendôme (1708).

Oudh, province, India, see UTTAR PRADESH.

Oudjda, French Morocco: see OUJDA.

Oudry, Jean Baptiste (zhã' bätēst' ōōdrē'), 1686–1755, French animal painter, who served Louis XV. Illustrated La Fontaine's *Fables.*

Ouessant, French island: see USHANT.

Ouida (wē'dŭ), pseud. of Louise de la Ramée (dŭ lä rŭmā'), 1839–1908, English writer of sentimental romantic novels (e.g., *Under Two Flags,* 1867; *A Dog of Flanders,* 1872).

Oujda or **Oudjda** (both: ōōjdä'), city (pop. 88,658), NE French Morocco, near Algerian border; founded 10th cent. Under French rule since 1907. Important rail junction and trade center.

Oulu (ō'lōō), Swed. *Uleåborg,* city (pop. 38,-703), NW Finland; a Baltic seaport on Gulf of Bothnia and at mouth of Oulu R. Shipyards; lumber and cellulose mfg. City grew around castle which was founded by Swedes in 1375.

Ouray (ōōrā', yōōrā'), city (pop. 1,089; alt. c.7,800 ft.), SW Colo., on Uncompahgre R. Health resort.

Ourcq (ōōrk), river, 50 mi. long, N France, a tributary of the Marne. Crosses CHÂTEAU-THIERRY battlefield of World War I.

Our Father: see LORD'S PRAYER.

Ourique (ôrēk'), town (pop. 1,378), SE Portugal, in Alentejo, S of Beja. According to tradition, it was the scene of the great victory of Alfonso I of Portugal over the Moors

(1139); actually, battle took place elsewhere, probably near Santarém.

Ouro Prêto (ō'rōō prā'tōō) [Port.,= black gold], city (pop. 8,819), in Minas Gerais state, E Brazil, in mountains SE of Belo Horizonte. An important gold-mining center in 18th cent., is now almost a ghost city; with its former grandeur it is kept as a national museum.

Ouse (ōōz), rivers in England. **1** Also called **Great Ouse.** Flows 156 mi., through six counties, from Oxfordshire to the Wash. **2** Sussex, flows 30 mi. to English Channel at Newhaven. **3** Yorkshire, formed by confluence of Ure and Swale rivers NW of York; flows 45 mi. to join Trent R. and form the Humber.

Outardes (ōō"tärd'), river of E central Que., Canada, rising in Otish Mts. and flowing 300 mi. S to St. Lawrence R. SW of Baie Comeau.

Outer Hebrides, Scotland: see HEBRIDES.

Outer Mongolia: see MONGOLIA.

Outremont (ōōtrůmō'), city (pop. 30,057), S Que., Canada, on Montreal Isl., NW suburb of Montreal.

ovary (ō'vůrē), female reproductive gland in which eggs (ova) are formed. In humans and higher vertebrates there are two ovaries, one on each side of uterus. These secrete hormones which function in control of menstruation and mammary gland development. From puberty successive eggs mature; one is released about every 28 days.

ovenbird, name in North America for a bird of wood warbler family, whose nests resemble Dutch ovens. In South America, it is name for several species of thrushlike birds.

Overbeck, Johann Friedrich (yō'hän frē'drĭkh ō'vůrbĕk), 1789–1869, German religious painter, a member of the NAZARENES.

Overbury, Sir Thomas, 1581–1613, English author of verse and informal essays. Among his works are a poem, *A Wife* (1614), and sketches called "characters," describing types and individuals. He was murdered in prison; his former friend, Robert Carr, earl of Somerset, and Carr's wife were convicted of the crime but pardoned by the king's favor.

Overijssel (ō'vůrī'sůl), province (1,254.6 sq. mi.; pop. 638,797), NE Netherlands, between the Ijsselmeer (W) and Germany (E); cap. Zwolle. Drained by Ijssel R. and several canals. Stock raising, dairying, textiles, machinery. Under bishops of Utrecht in Middle Ages, it was sold to Emperor Charles V in 1527. Joined Union of Utrecht 1579. It is also spelled Overyssel.

Overland Trail, name given to several trails of westward migration in U.S. Sometimes used to mean all trails W from the Missouri to the Pacific and sometimes for central trails only. Particularly, term is applied to southern alternate route of Oregon Trail. Term also particularly applied to a route to Calif. going W from Fort Bridger.

overture, instrumental music written as an introduction to a stage work or oratorio. The early opera overture was simply a piece of symphonic music; in Gluck's time, it began to foreshadow what was to come in the opera. By the 19th cent. it was often just a potpourri of the opera's tunes. The concert overture is a separate work. Those of Mendelssohn, Beethoven, and Brahms are especially popular.

Overyssel, Netherlands: see OVERIJSSEL.

Ovid (Publius Ovidius Naso) (ŏ'vĭd), 43 B.C.–A.D. 18, Latin poet, always popular for his imaginative and facile verse. His poems, which reflect his ideal of poetry as the ministry of pleasure, fall into three groups—erotic poems (notably the *Art of Love,* in masterful elegiacs), mythological poems (notably *Metamorphoses,* his greatest work, in hexameters), and poems of exile (he was mysteriously exiled in A.D. 8 to a Black Sea outpost, where he died).

Oviedo (ōvyā'dhō), city (pop. 51,410), cap. of Asturias, N Spain, near iron-mining dist. of Cantabrian Mts. Armaments factories, chemical plants; distilleries. Flourished in 9th cent. as cap. of Asturian kings. Has famous cathedral (begun 1388) and Cámara Santa (9th and 11th cent.), containing cathedral's relics and treasures. University was founded 1604.

Ovoca: see AVOCA, river.

ovum, in biology, female sexual cell produced in ovary. In higher animals it is larger than male sexual cell (sperm) because of stored food and it is nonmotile. Before fertilization ovum undergoes maturation divisions; these include reduction division (meiosis; see MITOSIS) by which chromosomes are reduced to one half number normally present in cells. Union of mature ovum and sperm (fertilization) results in single cell with full number of chromosomes. Successive cell divisions result in development of new individual. Reproductive cells undergo similar processes in plants. Term *egg* commonly is used also for complex structure such as bird's egg, in which yolk is ovum swollen by stored food and rest of egg is secreted in oviduct. Development from unfertilized ovum is called PARTHENOGENESIS.

Owasco Lake: see FINGER LAKES.

Owatonna (ōwůtŏ'nů), city (pop. 10,191), SE Minn., S of St. Paul; settled in early 1850s. Center for farm region with mineral springs. Produces dairy products and farm equipment.

Owego (ōwē'gō), village (pop. 5,350), S N.Y., on Susquehanna R. and W of Binghamton. Shoes, furniture.

Owen, John, 1616–83, English Puritan divine and theologian. At Oxford he became Presbyterian, but later was Congregationalist. In civil war he supported Parliament. Later made dean of Christ Church, Oxford (1651) and vice chancellor of university (1652).

Owen, Robert, 1771–1858, British social reformer and socialist, pioneer in the cooperative movement. A successful cotton manufacturer of New Lanark, Scotland, he reconstructed the community into a model industrial town, with nonprofitmaking stores and, for the time, excellent working conditions. The Factory Act of 1819 was instigated by him. He estab. (1825) the ill-fated community of NEW HARMONY, Ind., promoted the Natl. Equitable Labor Exchange and other cooperative societies trading goods for labor, and assisted the trade-union movement His son, **Robert Dale Owen,** 1801–77, became a social reformer in the U.S. At NEW HARMONY he met Frances WRIGHT, with whom he estab. (1829) the New York *Free Enquirer*. In 1830 he advocated birth control publicly for the first time in America. He was a member of Congress, favored emancipation of slaves, helped found the Smithsonian Inst., and served as minister to Naples.

Owen, Ruth Bryan, 1885–, U.S. minister to Denmark (1933–36); daughter of W. J. Bryan. First woman minister of U.S. Married Reginald Owen in 1910; later married Boerge Rohde of Danish army.

Owen Glendower (glĕn'dou"ûr, glĕndou'ûr), 1359?–1416?, Welsh leader. Allied with the Percy family, he led revolt against Henry IV. Recognized as prince of Wales by Scotland and France. Weakened by military failures, he disappeared into the mountains.

Owens, Jesse, 1915–, American Negro track star. At 1936 Olympic games at Berlin he equaled world record (10.3 sec.) in 100-meter race, set new records in 200-meter race (20.7 sec.), broad jump (26 ft. 5 21/64 in.).

Owens, river, E Calif., rising in the Sierra Nevada SE of Yosemite Natl. Park and flowing c.120 mi. SSE, nominally to enter Owens L. (now nearly dry), near Mt. Whitney. At point above lake, aqueduct diverts most of river's water to Los Angeles.

Owensboro, city (pop. 33,651), W Ky., on Ohio R. and SW of Louisville; settled c.1800. Center of agr., oil, coal, and tobacco area with mfg. of electrical equipment, foodstuffs, and whisky.

Owen Sound, city (pop. 16,423), S Ont., Canada, on Owen Sound of Georgian Bay and NW of Toronto. Port and railroad terminal in farm region.

Owen Stanley Range, on SE New Guinea, containing Mt. Victoria (13,240 ft.), highest peak of Territory of Papua. Japanese attempt in 1942 to reach Port Moresby through mountain pass was checked by Allies.

owl, chiefly nocturnal bird of prey found in most parts of world; related to nighthawk and whippoorwill. Order of owls is divided into barn owl family (those with heart-shaped faces) and family including all other species.

Owl and the Nightingale, The, Middle English poem written c.1200, probably by a Nicholas de Guildford of Dorsetshire. It is a humorous debate between the birds as to their respective merits.

Owosso (ōwŏ'sō), city (pop. 15,948), S Mich., on Shiwassee R. and NE of Lansing; settled c.1835. Mfg. of machinery. Here are Indian relics and birthplace of T. E. Dewey.

Owyhee (ōwī'ē), river rising in SW Idaho, N Nev., SE Oregon, and flowing 170 mi. NE across SE Oregon to Snake R. near Nyssa. Owyhee power and irrigation project (estab. 1928), W of the Snake, improves 82,000 acres in Oregon near Owyhee R. mouth, and 30,500 acres in SW Idaho near Homedale; is contiguous with BOISE PROJECT and project at Vale. Owyhee Dam, SW of Nyssa, is 417 ft. high, 833 ft. long, forms reservoir 48 mi. long.

oxalic acid (ŏksă'lĭk), strong, poisonous, organic acid, a colorless crystalline solid with a sour taste. It is present (usually in harmless quantities) in many plants either as the acid or in the form of some of its many salts. It is used in bleaching, in printing cloth, and removing stains.

oxalis (ŏk'sùlĭs) or **wood sorrel,** low-growing plant of genus *Oxalis,* widely distributed. Most species have cloverlike leaves, dainty flowers, and tuberous roots, sometimes used for food in South America. The European wood sorrel (*Oxalis acetosella*) is one of the plants identified as the SHAMROCK.

oxbow lake, stagnant lake formed in old bed when river cuts through the neck of a meander or loop.

Oxenstierna, Count Axel Gustavsson (ŏk'-sùnstûr"nù, Swed. äk'sùl gŭs'täfsôn ōōk'-sùnshĕr"nä), 1583–1654, chancellor of Sweden (1612–54), a leading figure in the THIRTY YEARS WAR. During the reign of GUSTAVUS II he controlled the administration, organized the territories conquered by his king, and proved a successful diplomat. Though originally opposed to Sweden's entry into the Thirty Years War, he directed the war in Germany after Gustavus's death (1632) and secured open French intervention (1636). He virtually ruled Sweden during the minority of CHRISTINA (1632–44); instituted far-reaching reforms; and centralized the administration. He often clashed with the queen but opposed her abdication (1654).

Oxford, Edward de Vere, 17th **earl of,** 1550–1604, English poet, supposed by a few to have written Shakspere's plays.

Oxford, Robert Harley, 1st earl of: see HARLEY.

Oxford, county, England: see OXFORDSHIRE.

Oxford, Latin *Oxonia,* city (pop. 98,675), co. seat of Oxfordshire, England, on the Thames or Isis R. Site of OXFORD UNIVERSITY. Was royalist capital in civil wars. Historic buildings (other than colleges) include Radcliffe Observatory, Sheldonian Theatre (Wren), and old churches and inns. Has important automobile mfg. at suburb Cowley and Iffley.

Oxford. 1 Town (pop. 5,851), S Mass., SSW of Worcester. Mfg. of wooden boxes and woolens. **2** City (pop. 3,956), N central Miss., SE of Memphis, Tenn. Seat of Univ. of Mississippi (state supported; coed.; 1844; liberal arts college). Home of William Faulkner. **3** Town (pop. 6,685), N N.C., N of Raleigh. Markets tobacco and has mfg. of yarn and furniture. **4** City (pop. 6,944), SW Ohio, NW of Hamilton. Seat of Miami Univ. (state supported; coed.; chartered 1809, opened 1824; W. H. McGuffey taught here), and Western Col. (for women; 1853).

Oxford, Provisions of: see PROVISIONS OF OXFORD.

Oxford and Asquith, Herbert Henry Asquith, 1st **earl of,** 1852–1928. British statesman. Prime minister 1908–16, he saw triumphs of LIBERAL PARTY. Social-insurance program was started after power of House of Lords was broken. Attempts were made to establish Irish Home Rule. World War I brought his downfall in favor of David Lloyd George. His second wife, **Margot (Tennant) Asquith, countess of Oxford and Asquith,** 1864–1945, was noted for her wit. Author of a frank autobiography, a novel, and several volumes of personal reminiscences.

Oxford Group: see BUCHMAN, FRANK N. D.

Oxford movement, known first as Tractarian movement, an attempt to revitalize Established Church. It began in Oriel Col., Oxford, among spiritual leaders, notably J. H. NEWMAN, John KEBLE, and R. H. Froude. Keble, whose *Christian Year* had appeared in 1827, preached in July, 1833, a sermon *On the National Apostasy,* which Newman considered the start of the movement. Newman, with Keble and E. B. PUSEY, launched a series of pamphlets, *Tracts for the Times,* which preached Anglicanism as *via media* between Catholicism and evangelicalism. Newman was chief defending advocate. Pusey stressed observance of ritual, earning for the movement the name of "Puseyism." Newman's *Tract 90* on Thirty-nine Articles was counted "perilous to the peace of the Church" and brought series to an end (1841). The movement lost valuable supporters, among them Newman, in secession to the Church of Rome in 1842. This trend was checked by Pusey, whose leadership effected firm organization. Movement eventually spread into Scotland and Wales and overseas. Clergy made changes such as intoning sermons, wearing vestments in chancel, and facing east while praying. Hence group became known as "ritualists," and also as Anglo-Catholics.

Oxfordshire or **Oxford,** inland county (748 sq. mi.; pop. 275,765), S central England. County town is Oxford, seat of the university and an automobile mfg. center. Mostly flat terrain, drained by the Thames (or Isis, the local name). Farming is chief occupation. Blenheim Palace is at Woodstock.

Oxford University, Oxford, England, one of the two ancient English universities. Began in early 12th cent. Residential college system (see CAMBRIDGE UNIVERSITY) began in 1264 with Merton Col. A center of learning throughout Middle Ages, the medieval college maintained (and still does) almost complete autonomy within the university. The colleges are University (1249), Balliol (1263), Merton (1264), St. Edmund Hall (1269), Exeter (1314), Oriel (1326), Queen's (1340), New (1379), Lincoln (1427), All Souls (1437), Magdalen (1458; pronounced môd'lĭn), Brasenose (1509; pronounced brāz'nōz), Corpus Christi (1516), Christ Church (1546), Trinity (1554), St. John's (1555), Jesus (1571), Wadham (1610, charter received 1612), Pembroke (1624), Worcester (1714), Keble (1871) and Hertford (1874). Women's colleges are Lady Margaret Hall (1878), Somerville (1879), St. Hugh's (1886), and St. Hilda's (1893). Oxford has eleven faculties and has led in the classics, theology, and political science. Oxford Union is world's most famous debating club. Ashmolean Mus. and BODLEIAN LIBRARY are notable. Instruction is by lectures and tutorial system. Cecil J. RHODES left large sum for scholarships.

oxidation and reduction. Originally oxidation indicated reaction in which oxygen and some other substance combined; reduction, the removal of oxygen from substance. Rapid oxidation is COMBUSTION. Terms were later redefined on basis of electron theory: when substance loses electrons and increases positive valence, this is termed oxidation and substance causing it is an oxidizing agent. Also, when substance gains electrons and increases its negative valence, it is said to be reduced and the substance causing this change is a reducing agent. Oxygen need not be involved in either reaction. When oxidation of a substance occurs, it is accompanied by reduction of another substance.

oxide (ŏk'sīd), compound of oxygen and some other elemental substance. Oxygen combines directly with many other elements; these binary compounds (composed of two substances) occur abundantly and widely distributed in nature. Monoxides, dioxides, and trioxides are named according to number of oxygen atoms in molecule. Oxides may be acidic or basic oxides or anhydrides. Oxides of metals may be acidic, basic, neutral, or amphoteric (i.e., react with both acids and bases). Inert gases do not form oxides; halogens and inactive metals do not combine directly with oxygen, but oxides can be formed by indirect methods.

Oxnam, G(arfield) Bromley, 1891–, American Methodist bishop; president (1928–36) of DePauw Univ. Bishop of Omaha (1936–39), of Boston (1939–44), of New York (1944); a president of the World Council of Churches.

Oxnard, city (pop. 26,353), S Calif., near coast and WNW of Los Angeles; founded 1898. Processes beet sugar, fruit, and oil. Mfg. of implements.

Oxonia, Latin name of OXFORD, England.

Oxus: see AMU DARYA.

oxyacetylene flame (ŏk"sēŭsĕt'ŭlēn). Acetylene flame is hot and luminous, combines with oxygen to liberate enormous amount of heat. **Oxyacetylene torch** is designed to supply proper amount of oxygen to acetylene flame. It is used in cutting steel and in welding various metals.

oxygen, colorless, odorless, tasteless gaseous element (symbol = O; see also ELEMENT, table). It is heavier than air, slightly soluble in water, and a poor conductor; it supports combustion but does not burn. Active and important chemically, it is involved in OXIDATION, COMBUSTION, RESPIRATION, rusting, and corrosion. It is the most abundant element, forms many compounds, and is present in all living things (since it is a constituent of protoplasm) and in the atmosphere. OZONE is an allotropic form. **Heavy oxygen** is name for two isotopes of oxygen of mass 17 and 18.

Oxyrhynchus (ŏk"sĭrĭng'kŭs), place, Upper Egypt, near the Fayum where in 1896–97, 1906–7 a great number of papyri were found, mostly Roman and Byzantine.

oyster, edible mollusk (*Ostrea*) found in beds in coastal waters of most temperate regions. Shell consists of two unequal valves with rough outer surface. Sexes in some species are separate, in others united in one individual. Each female lays 5–50 million eggs, larva swims about before attaching itself to rough surface. Pearl oyster is of another family.

Oyster Bay, town (pop. 66,930), SE N.Y. on arm of Long Island Sound and W of Huntington. Includes resort and residential villages, e.g., Oyster Bay (pop. 5,215). Oyster industry is important. Park and bird sanctuary are memorials to Theodore Roosevelt, whose home was "Sagamore Hill."

Ozaki, Yukio (yo͞o'kyō ōzä'kē), 1859–, Japanese statesman, the outstanding liberal of modern Japan. Helped form the Kaishinto (reform party); joined Seiyukai party in 1900. Fought for universal manhood suffrage. After 1931 he was almost alone in protest against Japanese militarism in China.

Ozanam, Antoine Frédéric (ãtwän' frādārēk' ōzänäm'), 1813–53, French Catholic scholar. A leader of 19th-cent. Catholic social thought, and a founder of the St. Vincent de Paul Society (1833), he also wrote notable works on early medieval history and on medieval literature and thought.

Ozark (ō'zärk), city (pop. 5,238), SE Ala., NW of Dothan, in diversified farm area.

Ozark Mountains, dissected plateau, c.50,000 sq. mi., chiefly in Mo., but partly in Ark., Okla., and Kansas, lying between Arkansas and Missouri rivers. Averaging 2,000 ft. in altitude, plateau slopes gently into the plains: BOSTON MOUNTAINS are highest, most rugged sector. Minerals (lead, zinc) are present; there is some fruit growing. Scenery, forests, and mineral springs make region a resort.

Ozarks, Lake of the, central Mo. Created by BAGNELL DAM in Osage R., it is c.130 mi. long and of irregular shape. The lake offers numerous recreation facilities.

ozocerite (ōzō'kůrīt, –sůrīt), waxy solid mixture of hydrocarbons, a mineral wax occurring in rock deposits. Used as substitute for beeswax; adulterant; in making candles, hard-rubber substitutes, and polishes; and in electrotyping.

ozone (ō'zōn), allotropic form of oxygen with molecule consisting of three oxygen atoms. It is an unstable, bluish gas with a fresh penetrating odor, more active than oxygen and one and one-half times as heavy. It is formed when an electrical discharge passes through oxygen and is present in air after electrical storms. It is used as a bleach and in purifying water and air.

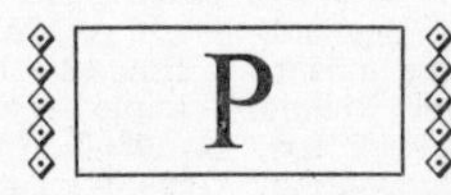

P, chemical symbol of the element PHOSPHORUS.

Pa, chemical symbol of the element PROTACTINIUM.

Pacher, Michael (mĭkh'äĕl pä'khůr), c.1435–1498, German religious painter and wood carver; native of the Tyrol. Famous for grand altarpiece at Sankt Wolfgang, Austria.

Pachuca (pächo͞o'kä), city (pop. 53,345), cap. of Hidalgo, central Mexico; founded (1534) on site of anc. Toltec city. Region has richest silver deposits in Mexico, mined since Aztec days.

Pacific, College of the: see STOCKTON, Calif.

Pacific, War of the, 1879–84, war between Chile and allied nations, Peru and Bolivia. Trouble began when in 1879 the president of Bolivia rescinded the contract that had given a Chilean company the right to exploit nitrate deposits in Atacama prov. Chile took port of Antofagasta, and war was declared. Peru, bound by a defensive alliance to Bolivia, became involved. Chile was victorious, and separate treaties were signed—Treaty of Ancón (1883) between Peru and Chile and a truce (1884) and final treaty (1904) between Chile and Bolivia. Chile acquired from Bolivia, prov. of Atacama (now Antofagasta) and from Peru, control of provs. of Tacna and Arica (See TACNA-ARICA CONTROVERSY).

Pacific Grove, residential and resort city (pop. 9,623), W Calif., on Monterey Bay. Has Hopkins Marine Laboratory of Stanford Univ.

Pacific Islands, Trust Territory of the (685 sq. mi.; pop. 53,900), consisting of CAROLINE ISLANDS, MARSHALL ISLANDS, MARIANAS ISLANDS, held by U.S. under UN trusteeship (since 1947).

Pacific Ocean, largest ocean, c.70,000,000 sq. mi.; max. length, c.7,000 mi.; greatest width, c.11,000 mi. Named by Magellan (1520). Its numerous islands are concentrated in S and W. The deepest ocean, its average depth is c.14,000 ft.; greatest known ocean depth (35,400 ft.) is off Mindanao. Chief Pacific currents are N and S equatorial, East Australian, Humboldt (or Peru), Japan and California currents; West Wind and North Pacific drifts. Recognition of the Pacific as distinct from the Atlantic dates from Balboa's discovery of its eastern shore (1513). In 16th cent. supremacy in Pacific area was shared by Spain and Portugal; English, Dutch foothold was estab. in 17th cent.; French, Russian in 18th; German, Japanese, and U.S. in 19th cent. Desire to exploit Pacific commerce was a factor in U.S. westward expansion. Area has great strategic importance.

Pacific scandal, 1873, a major event in Canadian political history. Charges were made that Conservative administration of Sir J. A. Macdonald had accepted campaign funds from Sir Hugh Allan in return for promise to award his syndicate contract to build Canadian Pacific Railway. Government was forced to resign, and Conservative party was badly defeated in ensuing elections.

pacifism (pă'sĭfĭzům), advocacy of suppression of war by individual or collective obstruction of militarism. Although complete, enduring peace is goal of all pacifists, methods differ.

Some oppose international war, but advocate revolution for suppressed nationalities; others countenance defensive but not offensive war; still others oppose all war, but accept police force; a few believe in no coercive, disciplinary force at all. Line is often drawn between advocates of absolute peace, pacifists, and those who would prevent war by international cooperation, internationalists (see PEACE CONGRESSES). In all peace movements religion has been potent force, on basis that willful taking of human life is evil. Strong pacifistic elements exist in Eastern religions and in Christianity, later sects of which like Quakers, Moravians, and Dukhobors advocate nonresistance. Humanitarian and economic motives have also played a part. Peace associations and movements have been numerous in 19th and 20th cent. Award of Nobel Peace Prize has encouraged pacifist thought, as have life and teachings of Mohandas K. GANDHI in India. Among many groups working for peace are Carnegie Endowment for Internatl. Peace, Women's Internatl. League for Peace and Freedom, World Peace Foundation, Natl. Council for Prevention of War, and Natl. Peace Foundation (London).

packing industry: see MEAT PACKING.

Pactolus (păktō'lŭs), small river of anc. Lydia, W central Asia Minor (now Turkey). Famous for gold washed from its sands.

paddlefish, scaleless, fresh-water fish of Mississippi valley. It is also called duckbill because of long paddle-shaped snout. Sometimes is 6 ft. long and over 150 lb.

Paderborn (pä″dŭrbôrn'), city (pop. 40,440), North Rhine–Westphalia, NW Germany, in Westphalia. Archiepiscopal see (since 1930). Became episcopal see c.800. Under Holy Roman Empire prince-bishops ruled large area until secularization (1803). City, once famed for medieval and baroque architecture, was largely destroyed in World War II.

Paderewski, Ignace Jan (pädŭrĕf'skē), 1860–1941, Polish pianist and statesman. His worldwide popularity exceeded that of any pianist since Liszt; he made his American debut in 1891. He represented Poland at the Versailles peace table (1919) and was for 10 months premier of a coalition ministry. In addition to his famous Minuet in G, he composed two symphonies, a piano concerto, and an opera, *Manru.*

Padilla, Juan de (hwän' dā pädhē'lyä), c.1490–1521, Spanish revolutionary leader in the war of the *communidades* [municipalities] against Emperor Charles V (1520–21). Rising against Charles's oppressive taxation, Toledo, Segovia, and other Castilian cities demanded severe limitations on the royal power, and together formed a provisional government under the Santa Junta, but the movement soon degenerated into class warfare. Padilla's army was defeated at Villalar (1521), and he was executed.

Padua (pă'dūŭ), Ital. *Padova,* city (pop. 90,325), Venetia, NE Italy. Commercial and transportation center. The ancient Patavium, it has flourished since Roman times and won its greatest fame through its university (founded 1222), which had the first anatomy hall in Europe and where Galileo taught. It was a free city (12th–14th cent., except during rule of EZZELINO DA ROMANO); passed to the Carrara family in 1318; became Venetian in 1405. Among its art treasures are the Capella degli Scrovegni, with frescoes by Giotto; the 13th-cent. basilica, with the tomb of St. Anthony of Padua; the 13th-cent. Eremitani church, with frescoes by Mantegna; and the equestrian statue of Gattamelatta, by Donatello.

Paducah (pŭdū'kŭ, –dōō'kŭ), city (pop. 32,828), SW Ky., on Ohio R. (bridged) at mouth of Tennessee R.; settled 1821 as Pekin, laid out and renamed 1827. Taken (1861) by Grant in Civil War, and raided unsuccessfully by Forrest in 1864. Important tobacco market and shipping center for agr. and mining area, it has mfg. of shoes, machinery, and chemicals. Irvin S. Cobb was born and lived here. Atomic Energy Commission plant to W.

Paean (pē'ŭn), in Greek mythology, divine physician of Olympic gods. Later an epithet for Apollo as healer, it came to be a hymn of praise or a prayer for safety or deliverance.

Paeonius (pēō'nēŭs), fl. 5th cent. B.C., Greek sculptor of Thrace. His statue of Nike (Victory) is at Olympia.

Páez, José Antonio (hōsā' äntō'nyō pä'ās), 1790–1873, Venezuelan revolutionist, president (1831–35, 1839–43), supreme dictator (1861–63). A powerful *caudillo,* he assisted Bolívar in gaining Venezuelan independence from Spain but later disrupted Bolívar's dream of a large republic and made Venezuela a separate nation. Died in exile.

Pagan (pŭgän'), ruined city, Upper Burma, on Irrawaddy R. Was cap. of a Burmese dynasty from 11th cent. to 1287. Has imposing temple ruins.

Paganini, Niccolo (nēkōlō' pägänē'nē), 1782–1840, Italian violinist, whose virtuosity became a legend. Among his compositions are the 24 caprices for solo violin (Brahms and Rachmaninov wrote variations on one of them), his Concerto in D, and the often-performed *Perpetual Motion.*

Page, Thomas Nelson, 1853–1922, American novelist and diplomat, author of romantic stories and novels of the Old South, such as *In Ole Virginia* (1887) and *Red Rock* (1898). He was ambassador to Italy from 1913 to 1919.

Page, Walter Hines, 1855–1918, American journalist, editor of periodicals, and diplomat; U.S. ambassador to Great Britain (1913–18).

pageant, semidramatic spectacle, generally held outdoors and performed by local talent. Usually elaborates an event in the history of a locality, e.g., the Coventry pageant depicting Lady Godiva's story. Processional spectacles (e.g., New Orleans Mardi Gras) are also termed pageants.

Paget, Sir James (pă'jĭt), 1814–99, British surgeon and pathologist, authority on bone diseases.

pagoda, name given in the East to tower-like buildings which are generally part of a temple or monastery group and serve as shrines. Those of India are chiefly pyramidal structures of masonry, tapering to a point and adorned with carving and sculptures. In China the pagoda, derived from India, is usually octagonal in plan and built (usually of brick) in superimposed stories, decreasing in size toward the top. In Japan the pagodas were introduced from China with Buddhism. Built of wood, they are usually square in plan and five stories high, each with its projecting roof.

Pagopago (päng'ōpäng'ō), village (pop. 1,610), SE Tutuila, American Samoa; ceded to U.S. 1872 as naval and coaling station. Only port of call in American Samoa; landlocked harbor. Wireless station, naval hospital. Also Pangopango.

Pagosa Springs (pùgō'sù), resort town (pop. 1,379; alt. 7,077 ft.), SW Colo., on San Juan R. Hot Springs. Chimney Rock ruins (cliff dwellings) to W.

Pahang: see MALAYA.

Pahlavi language (pä'lùvē") or **Pehlevi language** (pā'lùvē"), a Middle Iranian language of Indo-Iranian subfamily of Indo-European languages. It was used in Middle Ages. See LANGUAGE (table).

Pahlevi: see REZA SHAH PAHLEVI; MOHAMMED REZA SHAH PAHLEVI.

Pahlevi (pälùvē'), city (pop. 37,511), N Iran; chief Iranian port on Caspian Sea. Naval base. Formerly called Enzeli.

pain, sensation arising usually from excessive stimulation of nerve endings. Stimulus is carried by nerve fibers to centers of consciousness in brain.

Paine, Albert Bigelow, 1861–1937, American biographer and writer of juvenile stories; an editor of *St. Nicholas* (1899–1909). Friend and literary executor of Mark Twain, he wrote authorized biography (3 vols., 1912) and edited author's letters (1917), autobiography (1924), and notebook (1935).

Paine, Thomas, 1737–1809, American political theorist and writer, b. England; came to America 1774. His *Common Sense* (Jan., 1776) hastened Declaration of Independence, and his pamphlet series *The American Crisis* heartened patriots in the Revolution. In London after 1787, he defended French Revolution in *The Rights of Man* (2 parts, 1791, 1792). Prosecuted for attacks on English institutions, he fled (1792) to Paris, where he was a member of the Convention, was imprisoned (1793) for anti-Jacobinism. His deistic *Age of Reason* (2 parts, 1794, 1795) and his venomous *Letter to Washington* (1796) alienated many, and led to ostracism in U.S. on his return in 1802.

Paine College: see AUGUSTA, Ga.

Painesville, city (pop. 14,432), NE Ohio, on Grand R. and NE of Cleveland; laid out c.1805. Trade center for agr. area. Seat of Lake Erie Col.

Painlevé, Paul (pôl' pĕlùvā'), 1863–1933, French statesman and mathematician. Briefly premier in 1917, he emerged in 1924 as leader, with Herriot, of the "left cartel" (a moderate group); was premier again in 1925; later held various cabinet posts. His chief importance was as a mathematician (he made valuable contributions in field of differential equations) and as a scientist.

painted cup: see INDIAN PAINTBRUSH.

Painted Desert, vividly colored badlands on E bank of Little Colorado R., N Ariz., extending SE from Grand Canyon to Petrified Forest.

Paisley (pāz'lē), burgh (pop. 93,704), Renfrewshire, Scotland. Has cotton thread, textile, and varied mfg. Famous Paisley shawl is no longer made.

Paiute Indians (pī'o͞ot'), North American tribes of Uto-Aztecan linguistic stock, in SW Utah, NW Ariz., SE Calif., and S Nev. Two groups are distinguished: N Paiute (which some say are properly Paviotso), warlike people who opposed white miners and settlers in the 1860s and joined the Bannock in the war of 1878 (often called Snake Indians); S Paiute (often called the Digger Indians, from their digging for roots to supplement a sparse diet from hunting and fishing). Wovoka, leader of the ghost dance religion, was a Paiute.

Pakistan (pă'kĭstăn"), dominion (365,907 sq. mi.; pop. 75,687,000) of British Commonwealth of Nations, S Asia; cap. Karachi. Consists of two parts separated by c.900 mi of territory belonging to INDIA. W part is on Arabian Sea and borders Iran and Afghanistan on W; includes Baluchistan, North-West Frontier Prov., and Punjab. Region is partly desert with broad alluvial plains watered by Indus R. E Pakistan (coextensive with East Bengal prov.) is on Bay of Bengal and borders Burma on SE. Lies in fertile Ganges-Brahmaputra delta. Dominion's principal cities are Karachi and Lahore; main ports Karachi (W) and Chittagong (E), shipping jute, tea, and cotton. Pakistan was formed 1947 out of predominantly Moslem areas of India, mainly through efforts of Mohamed Ali JINNAH and MOSLEM LEAGUE. Foreign affairs were dominated by KASHMIR dispute with India and by trouble with rebellious Pathan tribes in regions about the border of Afghanistan.

Palacio Valdés, Armando (ärmän'dō pälä'thyō väldās'), 1853–1938, Spanish novelist and critic, author of realistic novels (e.g., *Marta y María,* 1883; *José,* 1885).

Palacky, Frantisek (frän'tyĭshĕk pä'lätskē), 1798–1876, Czech national leader and historian. His *Geschichte Böhmens* (Ger., 5 vols., 1836–67; Czech, 5 vols., 1848–67) influenced national consciousness.

Palaemon (pùlē'mŏn), Greek sea-god, protector of ships. Isthmian games were celebrated in his honor.

palaeo–, for words beginning thus: see also PALEO–.

Palaeologus (pālēŏ'lùgùs), Greek dynasty ruling Byzantine Empire 1261–1453. Included Michael VIII, Andronicus III, John V, John VI, Andronicus IV, Manuel II, John VII, John VIII, Constantine XI. Were humane, erudite; helped revive Hellenism.

Palafox, José de (hōsā' dā pälāfōkh'), 1776?–1847, Spanish general in Peninsular War. Celebrated for his heroic defense of SARAGOSSA (1808–9) with an improvised garrison of citizens and peasants. Was created duke of Saragossa 1834.

Palafox y Mendoza, Juan de (hwän' dā pälāfōkh' ē mändō'thä), 1600–1659, Spanish churchman, administrator in Mexico. Was made bishop of Puebla and visitor general of New Spain (1640). Named viceroy ad interim (1642). Ruled vigorously, corrected financial abuses, but quarrels with Jesuits forced him to flee to Spain (1649).

Palamas, Kostes (kôstēs′ pälämäs′), 1859–1943, Greek poet; secretary of Univ. of Athens (1897–1943). Except for his early work, he wrote in vernacular Greek. His works include *Life Unshakable* (1904) and *The Twelve Speeches of the Gypsy* (1907).

Palamedes (pălůmē′dēz), in Greek mythology, crafty Greek hero in Trojan War. He was credited with invention of measures, scales, dice, discus, alphabet, and lighthouses.

Palatinate (půlă′tĭnĭt), Ger. *Pfalz,* two regions of Germany, historically but not geographically related. The **Rhenish** or **Lower Palatinate** (Ger. *Rheinpfalz* or *Niederpfalz*), often called simply the Palatinate, extends W from the Rhine to France and the Saar Territory; cap. Neustadt an der Haardt. Other cities: Ludwigshafen, Speyer. Agr.; famous vineyards. Bavarian until 1945, it became a district (2,111 sq. mi.; pop. 1,047,844) of RHINELAND-PALATINATE in 1946. The **Upper Palatinate** (Ger. *Oberpfalz*), a province (3,724 sq. mi.; pop. 896,520) of Bavaria, is separated in E from Czechoslovakia by the Bohemian Forest; cap. REGENSBURG. Agr. *History.* The name Palatinate is derived from the office of count palatine, a title of Roman origin. In 1214 the Rhenish Palatinate (then comprising parts of Baden and Hesse, but not the bishopric of SPEYER) passed to the Bavarian WITTELSBACH dynasty, which also acquired the present Upper Palatinate. After the 14th cent., the senior Wittelsbach line held the two palatinates, the junior line ruled Bavaria. The rank of ELECTORS was permanently assigned to senior line 1356; Rhenish Palatinate hence was known as Electoral Palatinate (Ger. *Kurpfalz*). After extinction of direct line, it passed to successive junior branches—the Protestant branch of Simmern (1559) and the Catholic branches of Neuburg (1685), Sulzbach (1742), and Birkenfeld-Zweibrücken (1799). Mannheim replaced Heidelberg as cap. 1720. The election (1619) and defeat (1620) of Elector Frederick V as king of Bohemia (see FREDERICK THE WINTER KING) led to transfer of Upper Palatinate and of electoral vote to Bavaria, but in 1648 a new vote was created for Frederick's successor. Ravaged in the Thirty Years War, the Palatinate was systematically devastated by the French in the War of the Grand Alliance (1688–89). Extinction of Bavarian Wittelsbach line (1777) and accession of Duke Maximilian of Zweibrücken (1799) reunited all Wittelsbach lands under single ruler—but France had annexed all lands W of the Rhine, and in 1803 Maximilian ceded the palatine lands E of the Rhine to Baden, Hesse, and Nassau. In 1815 Maximilian (king of a much-enlarged Bavaria since 1806) received the territory forming present Rhenish Palatinate, which remained Bavarian until 1945.

Palatka (půlăt′ků), city (pop. 9,176), NE Fla., port on St. Johns R. and S of Jacksonville. Founded 1821 as trading post, it was site of military post in Seminole War. Processes wood, sea food, and citrus fruits. Noted for azalea gardens.

Palau (pälou′), island group (188 sq. mi.; pop. 5,900), W Pacific, in W Caroline Isls. Includes four volcanic islands and many coral islets. Phosphate and bauxite are produced. Was major Japanese naval base in World War II. Name is sometimes spelled Pelew.

Palawan (pälä′wän), island (4,550 sq. mi.; pop. 43,813), Philippine Isls., N of Borneo and between Sulu and South China seas. Rice, corn, tobacco, copra. Populated by Moros. Has U.S. naval air base. Puerto Princesa is on E coast.

Pale, in Irish history, area around Dublin under English rule. Term first used 14th cent. An English Pale centered around Calais until 1558, another in Scotland in 16th cent. In Russia, Pale was region where Jews might live, estab. in first partition of Poland and existing until Revolution of 1917.

Palembang (pälĕmbäng′), city (pop. 108,145), on SE Sumatra, Indonesia; port on Musi R. and largest city on island. Trade center for area producing rubber and oil. Cap. of Hindu-Indonesian kingdom in 8th cent.

Palenque (pälĕng′kā), anc. city of the Maya in Chiapas, S Mexico. Its architectural elegance shows the high degree of skill the Maya attained.

Paleocene epoch: see EOCENE EPOCH.

paleography (pālēŏ′grůfē) [Gr.,= early writing], term sometimes meaning all study and interpretation of old ways of recording language, but in a narrower sense excluding epigraphy (study of inscriptions). Letters made with a stylus, brush, or pen favor curved lines and tend to become cursive. In Western European ways of writing, letters of all kinds are derived from capital letters of Roman inscriptions. From these "square" capitals developed less severe "rustic" capitals and uncial letters (with more curves). Capitals and uncials are called majuscules, lower-case letters minuscules. Lower-case letters became estab. in Alcuin's school at Tours in Charlemagne's time. The black letter, sometimes called Gothic, is no longer in common use except for German language; it developed from efforts at ornateness. In type, italic letters were introduced by Aldus Manutius. Experts in handwriting can often assign a place and a date to a document of earlier times (for a simple example, Spencerian script denotes 19th cent.), and they can sometimes even identify a particular writer and distinguish forgeries from authentic documents.

paleolith (pā′lēůlĭth), crude implement of flint or other hard stone shaped by chipping, found in caves which served primitive man as shelters and in old gravel beds. Their great antiquity is proved by association with the remains of extinct animals.

Paleolithic period (pā″lēůlĭ′thĭk, -lēō, pă″-) or **Old Stone Age,** earliest and longest period of human history, approximately coextensive with Pleistocene geologic epoch. It is usually divided into lower Paleolithic—generally subdivided into Pre-Chellean, Abbevillain (or Chellean), Acheulian, and Mousterian (sometimes considered middle Paleolithic); and upper Paleolithic—embracing Aurignacian, Solutrean, and Magdalenian phases. Early Paleolithic humans probably were nomadic hunters and food gatherers who sought shelter in caves and had knowledge of fire. Characteristic tool of lower Paleolithic was *coup de poing* or hand axe, shaped on a central core or rock mass. Flake implements were fashioned from struck-off fragments. Neanderthal man, a cave dweller of Mousterian times, made carefully shaped flake tools. Sculpture and painting probably had their beginning in the caves and rock shelters of these times. Throughout upper Paleolithic lived Cro-Magnon man generally considered a race of modern man (*Homo sapiens*). Caves and rock shelters housed man in Aurignacian and Magdalenian times; CAVE ART reached its height in Magdalenian period. Bone devices including needles appeared in upper Paleolithic. Long, slender flint blades struck from a core were feature of the period. Magdalenian blade industries derived from upper Aurignacian. Relatively brief appearance of Solutrean culture, with its fine lance points and blades, was perhaps an invasion from Iran. By close of the Paleolithic, agriculture and domesticated animals, both features of Neolithic, were about to appear.

paleontology (pā″lēŭntŏ′lŭjē, pā″lēŏn–), science of the life of past geologic time as studied through the FOSSIL, which serves as the most important means of correlating the ages of rock strata.

Paleozoic era (pā″lēŭzō′ĭk), third grand division of geologic time. In North America two great geosynclines (downfolds) were main physical features—the Appalachian and the Cordilleran geosynclines. The rhythm of Cambrian, Ordovician, and Silurian periods of the era was alternating submergence and uplift. In the Carboniferous began major disturbances which continued in Permian and brought Paleozoic to a close. Early Paleozoic was rich in marine invertebrate life. Amphibians appeared in the Devonian period, and reptiles in the Carboniferous; in this period plant life reached its climax. See also GEOLOGY, table.

Palermo (pŭlûr′mō, Ital. pälĕr′mō), city (pop. 339,497; with suburbs 411,879), cap. and largest city and port of Sicily, at the edge of the Conca d'Oro, a fertile plain on the NW coast. Exports citrus fruit and wine. Founded (probably by Phoenicians) between 8th and 6th cent. B.C., it later was a Carthaginian military base until its conquest by Rome (254–253 B.C.). It was under Byzantine rule A.D. 535–831, then fell to the Arabs, and was conquered 1072 by the Normans, who made it the cap. of Sicily. Its cultural and economic flowering began under the Arabs and reached its peak under Emperor Frederick II (13th cent.). The SICILIAN VESPERS began at Palermo (1282). The city is rich in architecture; Byzantine, Arabic, and Norman influences are blended in many of its churches and palaces. There was much damage in World War II. University was founded 1805.

Palermo stone, diorite stone engraved probably in 28th cent. B.C. with earliest extant annals, a list of kings of anc. Egypt. Part of it is in Palermo, Italy, part in Cairo, Egypt.

Palestine [ultimately from Philistine], country on E shore of the Mediterranean. This article covers the region's history up to the formation of ISRAEL in 1948. In the Bible, Palestine is called Canaan before the invasion of Joshua. It is the Holy Land, of the Jews as having been promised them by God, of Christians because it was the home of Christ, and of Moslems as heirs of Jews and Christians. Places of pilgrimage include Jerusalem, Bethlehem, Nazareth, and Hebron. Its boundaries, never long constant, have always included the region between the Mediterranean and Jordan R., bordering SW on Egypt. Comprises three zones (E-W): the depression (part of Great Rift Valley) in which lie Jordan R. and Dead Sea; a steep ridge (running from GALILEE through SAMARIA) and the mountains of JUDAEA; and a narrow coastal plain. Detailed history begins with the Hebrews (see JEWS). By 1000 B.C. the Hebrew kingdom, consolidated by Saul and David, was well estab. at Jerusalem. After the reign of Solomon the kingdom fell into two states, Israel and Judah, which were destroyed by Assyria and Babylonia. The Persian-sponsored autonomous Jewish community, subsequently estab. at Jerusalem, was perhaps the foundation of the modern Jewish people. Palestine was conquered in 4th cent. B.C. by Alexander the Great, but eventually the Jews revolted under the MACCABEES, who set up a new state in 141 B.C.; this yielded to Rome after 70 years. Palestine of the time of Christ had puppet kings in the Herods (see HEROD) who never succeeded in reconciling Jews and Romans. To quell a revolt the Romans destroyed the Temple in A.D. 70 and expelled the Jews from Judaea. With Constantine I, Palestine became a center of Christian pilgrimage; under Justinian, the country flourished. But after 640 when it came under Moslem rule, the country declined, its land wasting into barrenness. In 9th cent., when Palestine passed to Egypt, the Fatimite rulers provoked the CRUSADES by destroying the Church of the Holy Sepulcher and molesting pilgrims. The Latin Kingdom of Jerusalem, estab. 1099 by the Crusaders, lasted less than 100 years. The next rulers of Palestine were the Mamelukes, who ruled until 1516, when Ottoman Turks took over. Jewish colonization from Europe began c.1870, but ZIONISM entered the field only in early 20th cent. In 1920 the British, who had won the area in World War I, acquired Palestine and Trans-Jordan (now JORDAN) as mandates; they designated Palestine for the establishment of a Jewish national home, but with due regard for rights of non-Jewish Palestinians. There followed (esp. in '30s) Jewish-Arab clashes resulting from Arab resentment of Jewish immigration and land purchases. The British White Paper of 1939 revealed plans for an independent, predominantly Arab state, which would be closed to Jewish immigration after 1944. Political tensions were eased by World War II, in which all parties cooperated with the British, but at war's end enmity flared into open conflict, out of which the state of Israel was forged.

Palestine (pă′lŭstēn), city (pop. 12,503), E Texas, N of Houston; settled 1846. Center of oil and agr. area, has railroad shops and large salt dome.

Palestrina, Giovanni Pierluigi da (jōvän′nē

pyĕrlo͞oē'jē pä'lāstrē'nä), c.1525–1594, Italian composer. Conducted choirs of the Sistine Chapel, St. John Lateran, and Julian Chapel at the Vatican. Composer mostly of religious choral music—motets and Masses, of which the *Missa Papae Marcelli* is best known. He is often called "the first Catholic Church musician."

Paley, William, 1743–1805, English theologian. Wrote *Principles of Moral and Political Philosophy* (1785), an 18th-cent. statement of utilitarianism, and *A View of the Evidences of Christianity* (1794).

Palgrave, Francis Turner, 1824–97, English poet and anthologist. Edited *The Golden Treasury of the Best Songs and Lyrical Poems in the English Language* (1861; a notable anthology).

Pali (pä'lē), dead language of Indic group of Indo-Iranian subfamily of Indo-European languages; a dialect of Sanskrit. Pali literature was the sacred literature of Buddhism, written 5th cent.–3d cent. B.C. The canon is the *Tipitaka* [threefold basket], consisting of *Vinayapitaka* [basket of discipline], *Suttapitaka* [basket of teaching] and *Abhidhammapitaka* [basket of metaphysics]. Commentaries in Pali still written in Ceylon, Burma, and Siam.

Palikao, Charles Guillaume Cousin-Montauban, comte de (shärl' gēyōm' ko͞ozē'-mōtōbā' kōt' dù pälēkäō'), 1796–1878, French general. Commanded French forces in China (1860); created count after victory at Palichiao, near Peking. His premiership (1870) ended with fall of Second Empire after battle of Sedan.

Pali literature (pä'lē), sacred literature of Buddhism. Written 483–250 B.C., the canon is called the *Tipitaka* [threefold basket]. Divided into three parts: monastic rules; statement of tenets, plus a miscellany of speeches and dialogues of Buddha and his disciples, lives of the saints, poems, and fables; and an analytical elaboration of doctrine. Pali (a dialect of Sanskrit) died out in India but was brought 2d cent. B.C. to Ceylon, where it has been studied up to present day. Also used to some extent in Burma and Siam as language of literature and religion.

Palisades, bluffs along W bank of the Hudson, NE N.J. and SE N.Y., from N of Jersey City, N.J., to vicinity of Piermont, N.Y.; general alt. 350–550 ft. The Palisades, rising vertically from near the river's edge, are a margin of a sill of diabase, slowly cooled; probably uplift and faulting occurred at close of Triassic period. Much of the most scenic section, between Fort Lee, N.J., and Newburgh, N.Y., is in **Palisades Interstate Park,** with summer and winter sports facilities. Notable points are BEAR MOUNTAIN and STORM KING.

Palisades Park, residential borough (pop. 9,635), NE N.J., adjoining Fort Lee. Amusement park.

Palissy, Bernard (bĕrnär' pälēsē'), c.1510–c.1589, French potter. Created pottery with smooth glazes in richly colored enamels. Noted for pieces decorated with reptiles, insects, and plants.

Palladio, Andrea (ändrā'ä päl-lä'dēō), 1518–80, Italian architect of the Renaissance, b. Vicenza. Known for formal, grandiose designs based on Roman style. Designed San Giorgio Maggiore in Venice. Palladian style imported into England in 17th cent. by Inigo Jones was closely followed by architects of Georgian period. Palladio's famous treatise, which appeared 1713 as *The Four Books of Architecture,* was widely influential. Much imitated "Palladian motive" consists of arches supported on minor columns and framed between larger columns.

Palladium (pùlā'dēùm) [Gr.,= belonging to Pallas], in Greek and Roman religion, anc. sacred image of Pallas Athena. It was guardian of the safety of a city. Palladium of Troy protected the city until Diomed and Odysseus stole it. Only then did Troy fall.

palladium (pùlā'dēùm), rare, silver-white, lustrous metallic element (symbol = Pd; see also ELEMENT, table), strongly resistant to corrosion. A member of the platinum group of metals, it occurs in ores of this metal. It can absorb great quantities of hydrogen. It is used for plating and in alloys with gold and platinum.

pallah: see IMPALA.

Pallas (pă'lùs), in Greek mythology. **1** Name given to Athena. **2** Giant killed by Athena. **3** Titan; son of Creus, husband of Styx, and father of Nike.

Pall Mall (pĕl mĕl', păl măl'), street in W London. Originally constructed by Charles II for playing the game pall-mall. Here are St. James's Palace, Marlborough House, and a number of clubs.

palm, evergreen treelike, bushy, or climbing plant of the family Palmaceae, native mostly to tropics but with some representatives in warm temperate regions. Most palms have a tall, woody, unbranched stem with a crown of compound leaves. The COCONUT, the DATE, and the SAGO palm are important commercially. Carnauba wax is obtained from the leaves of a South American palm (*Copernicia cerifera*). Other palms include the royal palm (*Roystonea*) and PALMETTO palm. **Palm oil** is yellowish orange to brownish red fat pressed from fibrous flesh of fruit of the African oil palm (*Elaeis guineensis*). Palm-kernel oil is a white oil obtained from the endosperm.

Palma, Jacopo (yä'kōpō päl'mä), c.1480–1528, Venetian painter, called Palma Vecchio. Known for idyllic landscape backgrounds and female portraits.

Palma, Ricardo (rēkär'dhō päl'mä), 1833–1919, Peruvian writer, known chiefly for sketches of colonial days of Peru (*Tradiciones peruanes*).

Palma or **Palma de Mallorca** (päl'mä dā mälyôr'kä), seaport (pop. 97,009), cap. of Majorca isl., chief city of Balearic Islands, Spain. Has Gothic cathedral (founded 1229), remains of Moorish castle, 15th-cent. Lonja (exchange). Near by is former royal castle of Bellver (14th cent.).

Palm Beach, town (pop. 3,886), SE Fla., on an island between the Atlantic and L. Worth (lagoon bridged to West Palm Beach). With H. M. Flagler's arriving 1893, it began development as wealthy, exclusive resort.

Palmer, A(lexander) Mitchell, 1872–1936, U.S. Attorney General (1919–21). Ardently prosecuted those suspected of disloyalty to U.S.

Palmer, Nathaniel Brown, 1799–1877, American sea captain. First sighted PALMER PENINSULA on whaling voyage (1820–21).

Palmer, Samuel, 1805–81, English etcher and landscape painter, a follower of William Blake.

Palmer, town (pop. 9,533), S Mass., ENE of Springfield; settled 1716. Metal goods.

Palmer Archipelago, Antarctic island group off NW Palmer Peninsula. Discovered 1898 by Adrien de Gerlache. Sometimes called Antarctic Archipelago.

Palmer Peninsula, Antarctica, c.800 mi. long; tip is 650 mi. from Cape Horn. Mostly mountainous, covered with shelf ice; W coast washed by Weddell Sea. Discovered 1820 by N. B. Palmer. Claimed by British as Graham Land (or Graham Coast) a Falkland Island dependency, and by Chile and Argentina as O'Higgins Land.

Palmerston, Henry John Temple, 3d **Viscount,** 1784–1865, English statesman. As foreign minister (1830–41) he pursued a liberal policy (e.g., aided Belgian independence). Twice prime minister (1855–58, 1859–65), he prosecuted Crimean War, aided Italian independence, and dealt with Sepoy Rebellion. His reckless diplomacy advanced British prestige.

Palmerton, borough (pop. 6,646), E Pa., on Lehigh R. and NNW of Allentown. Zinc refining.

palmetto palm or **palmetto** (pălmĕ'tō), palm tree of genus *Sabal,* native to the W Hemisphere. The young head of leaves of the cabbage palmetto (*Sabal palmetto*), native to the SE U.S., is edible. The wood is used for piles, and the leaves for thatch.

palmitin (păl'mŭtĭn), name for any fat that is ester of palmitic acid and glycerin but generally refers to the tripalmitate. Occurs in most FATS AND OILS.

palm oil: see PALM.

Palms, Isle of, resort island, SE S.C., E of Charleston.

Palm Springs, desert resort city (pop. 7,660), S Calif., in Coachella Valley near San Jacinto Peak and E of Los Angeles.

Palmyra (pălmī'rŭ), anc. city of central Syria, NE of Damascus, traditionally founded by Solomon and called in the Bible Tadmor. A trade center, it grew to political importance after the Romans had established control and a local family the Septimii ruled. The greatest of these, Septimius ODENATHUS, defeated the Persians for Emperor Gallienus and made Palmyra an enormous autonomous state (including Syria, Mesopotamia, and E Armenia). His widow, ZENOBIA, conquered Egypt and most of Asia Minor, but her ambition brought a Roman expedition (A.D. 272), which humbled and partly ruined Palmyra. It declined and after a sack by Tamerlane disappeared.

Palmyra. 1 Borough (pop. 5,802), SW N.J., on Delaware R. (bridged 1929), above Camden. Metal products. **2** Village (pop. 3,034), W central N.Y., SE of Rochester. Joseph Smith lived here and published Book of Mormon here. **3** Borough (pop. 5,910), SE Pa., E of Harrisburg. Limestone quarrying and mfg. of textiles.

Palmyra, atoll (pop. 32), comprising 55 islets, c.1,105 mi. SSW of Honolulu, central Pacific. Included in city and county of Honolulu. Discovered 1802 by Americans and annexed 1912; naval base authorized 1939. Privately owned.

Palo Alto (pă"lō ăl'tō), residential city (pop. 25,475), W Calif., SSE of San Francisco; founded 1891. Seat of STANFORD UNIVERSITY.

Palo Alto (pă"lō ăl'tō), locality not far from Brownsville, Texas, where first battle of Mexican War was fought, May 8, 1846. U.S. troops under Gen. Zachary Taylor won victory.

Palomar, Mount (pă'lōmär), 6,126 ft. high, S Calif., NE of San Diego. Site of Mt. Palomar Observatory, with 200-in. reflecting telescope, operated by California Inst. of Technology and Carnegie Inst.

Palomino de Castro y Velasco, Acislo Antonio (pälōmē'nō dā käs'trō ē välä'skō), 1653–1726, Spanish painter and writer on art, called the Spanish Vasari.

palsy: see PARALYSIS.

Pamir (pŭmēr', pä–) or **Pamirs,** mountainous region, central Asia. Mainly in Tadzhik SSR and Mountain Badakhshan; extends also into China and Afghanistan. Mt. Stalin (24,590 ft.) is highest in USSR.

Pamlico Sound (păm'lĭkō), 80 mi. long, E N.C., separated from Atlantic Ocean by islands and sand bars ending to E in Cape Hatteras. Receives Pamlico (see TAR) and Neuse rivers.

Pampa (păm'pŭ), city (pop. 16,583), N Texas, ENE of Amarillo. Shipping center in cattle and wheat area, it has oil refineries and carbon-black plants.

pampas (păm'pŭz), wide, treeless grassy plains in S South America, particularly in Argentina, Uruguay, and Paraguay. In central and N Argentina, the **Pampa** (c.250,000 sq. mi.) has given Argentina wealth from cattle raising, agr., and dairying; industries based on them—meat packing, milling, and processing of dairy products; and traditional character from early gauchos and later S European immigrants.

pampas grass, tall South American grass (*Cortaderia*). Common pampas grass (*Cortaderia selloana*) is a perennial with clusters of long narrow leaf blades. Plants bearing female flowers are most ornamental.

Pampeluna, Spain: see PAMPLONA.

Pamplona (pämplō'nä), city (pop. 45,885), cap. of Spanish Navarre, N Spain, at foot of Pyrenees. Communications center; iron and lead works; linen mfg. The Basque kingdom of Pamplona, founded 824, was the nucleus of NAVARRE. Made a stronghold by Philip II, Pamplona is still surrounded by old walls. An older spelling is Pampeluna.

Pan, in Greek religion, pastoral god of fertility. Worshiped chiefly in Arcadia. He was portrayed as merry, ugly man with horns, beard, tail, and goat's feet. All his myths deal with amorous affairs: e.g., his unsuccessful pursuit of the nymph Syrinx, who became a reed, which Pan plays in memory of her. He was later identified with Greek Dionysus and Roman Faunus, both gods of fertility.

Pana (pā'nŭ), city (pop. 6,178), S central Ill., SE of Springfield. Shipping center in farm and coal area. Rose-growing industry.

Panama (pă'nŭmä"), Span. *Panamá* (pänämä'),

republic (29,128 sq. mi., including PANAMA CANAL ZONE; pop. 801,290), Latin America, occupying the Isthmus of Panama which forms connecting link between Central and South America; cap. PANAMA city. Panama has an extreme length of c.385 mi. and varies from c.32 to 113 mi. in width. In the W there is a range of mountains of volcanic orgin; the middle of the country about the Panama Canal is lower; and in the E it rises again. Soil is of volcanic origin and fertile; vast forest reserves are unexploited. Subsistence crops are grown on upland savannas. Main exports are bananas, abaca, cacao, rubber, and mahogany. Population is divided into whites, mestizos (about two thirds of population), Indians, and Negroes. Panama city and COLÓN have grown because of their strategic world position rather than their relation with the hinterland. Roman Catholicism is prevailing religion, and Spanish the official language. Rodrigo de Bastidas discovered the coast (1501) and Columbus anchored there (1502), but not until 1513 when BALBOA took control of region and made his famous trip across isthmus to discover Pacific did the area become important—then mainly as a channel of trade. The immense wealth carried through the port of Portobelo attracted raids of British buccaneers 16th through 18th cent. Panama was a part of viceroyalty of Peru until 1740 when it was transferred to New Granada. After independence from Spain it became a part of Colombia. When the goldfields in California were discovered, interest in the long-discussed canal across the isthmus was revived in the U.S. The project ultimately led in 1903 to a Panamanian revolt against Colombia and—with assistance from the U.S.—independence was gained and the Panama Canal built. The U.S. was generally criticized throughout the world and in 1921 agreed to pay to Colombia $25,000,000 as redress for the loss of Panama. One immediate benefit to Panama of the revolution was eradication of yellow fever and improved sanitation in the country. Panama has taken an active part in Pan-Americanism and is a member of UN. Internal politics have been stormy with frequent changes in administration; Arnulfo Árias became a dominant figure in 1931.

Panama, city (pop. 127,874), central Panama, cap. and largest city of Panama, on the Gulf of Panama. Founded 1519 by Pedro Arias de Ávila, it flourished during colonial times as Pacific port for transshipment of Andean riches to Spain. Construction of the Panama Canal brought prosperity, and American sanitary measures have made it a healthful city. Univ. of Panama is here.

Panama Canal, waterway across Isthmus of Panama, connecting the Atlantic and Pacific oceans, built by U.S. (1904–14) on territory leased in perpetuity from republic of Panama. Canal, running S and SE from Limón Bay at Colón on the Atlantic to the Bay of Panama at Balboa on the Pacific, is 40.27 mi. long from shore to shore, 50.72 mi. long between channel entrances. Min. depth is 41 ft. Passage, aided by several sets of locks, takes 7 to 8 hr. There was rivalry with Great Britain over proposed canal (see CLAYTON-BULWER TREATY and HAY-PAUNCEFOTE TREATY). Interest also developed in alternate route, NICARAGUA CANAL. Negotiations with Colombia led to abortive HAY-HERRÁN TREATY (1903). By Hay-Bunau-Varilla Treaty of 1903, the new republic of Panama granted U.S., in return for an initial cash payment of $10,000,000 and a stipulated annuity, exclusive control of a canal zone in perpetuity, other sites necessary for defense, and sanitary control of Panama city and Colón. Actual construction, headed by G. W. Goethals, took seven years; eradication of malaria and yellow fever was a notable achievement. In 1921 U.S. paid Colombia $25,000,000 in damages.

Panama Canal Zone, administrative area (552.8 sq. mi.) of U.S., extending 5 mi. on either side of Panama Canal, bounded by the Caribbean on N, the Pacific on S, and Panama on E and W. Administered by a governor appointed by U.S. CRISTOBAL, BALBOA, ANCON are chief towns.

Panama City, city (pop. 25,814), NW Fla., on St. Andrews Bay and E of Pensacola. Gulf resort. Processes lumber and paper. Fishing.

Pan American Highway, projected system of roads, 15,714 mi. long, to link nations of W Hemisphere.

Pan-Americanism, movement towards commercial, social, economic, military, and political cooperation among the 21 republics of North, Central, and South America. The struggle for independence from Spain after 1810 evoked a sense of unity among the Latin American nations and the U.S. was looked on as a model. In 1820 Henry Clay set forth principles for Pan-Americanism, but soon afterwards the Monroe Doctrine was declared and became a source of irritation to the Latin American countries as they believed it to be only a mask for U.S. imperialistic ambition. An early limited attempt at union (see CENTRAL AMERICAN FEDERATION) failed, and national rivalries and wars split the Latin American republics. An attempt by Simón Bolívar to assemble a Pan-American conference in 1826 failed, and it was not until 1889–90 that the first of the Pan-American Conferences (or Congresses) was held at Washington. Subsequent meetings were at Mexico city (1901–2), Rio de Janeiro (1906), Buenos Aires (1910), Santiago (1923), Havana (1928), Montevideo (1933), Lima (1938), and Bogotá (1948). Their achievements include treaties for arbitration of disputes and adjustment of tariffs, establishment of Pan American Union, codification of international law, acceptance of peace machinery, and creation of scientific and social agencies. F. D. Roosevelt was responsible for the "Good Neighbor" policy which bettered relations between U.S. and Latin America. Most of the republics supported or actively participated in World War II on the side of the Allies. Further evidence of cooperation, friendliness, and interdependence are the Inter-American Conferences—Buenos Aires, 1936; Mexico city, 1945; Rio de Janeiro, 1947—and the formation of the ORGANIZATION OF AMERICAN STATES, 1948.

Pan American Union, international agency founded April 14, 1890, at first Pan-American

Conference; name adopted 1910. The day of its founding is Pan-American Day.

Panamint Range (pă'nŭmĭnt), SE Calif., near Nev. line. Rugged mountains between Death (E) and Panamint valleys. Altitudes range from c.6,000 ft. to 11,145 ft. in Telescope Peak.

Panay (pänī'), island (4,446 sq. mi.; pop. 1,291,548), one of Visayan Isls., in Philippine Isls.; NW of Negros. Rice, coconuts, citrus fruit, copper, manganese. Horses are bred in mountainous interior. Chief town is Iloilo.

Panchatantra (pän"chŭtän'trŭ), chief Sanskrit collection of animal fables, probably compiled before A.D. 500. Bidpai is the supposed author. The Buddhistic prose fables are interspersed with wise sayings in verse.

pancreas (păn'krēŭs, păng'–), gland found in most vertebrates and lying in abdominal cavity. In man it secretes fluid (containing digestive enzymes) which flows via bile duct into small intestine. Scattered cell groups (islands of Langerhans) in the pancreas produce hormone INSULIN. See *ill.*, p. 763.

panda (păn'dŭ). Lesser panda or cat bear (*Ailurus*) resembles raccoon, but has longer body and tail, more rounded head. Its fur is rust to deep chestnut, black on under parts, legs, and ears, with dark eye patches on white face. Found in Himalayas; a Chinese subspecies is in Yunnan, Szechwan, N Burma. Giant panda (*Ailuropoda*) lives in Szechwan, Kansu, at 6,000–14,000 ft. altitudes. Its bear-like body is chiefly white, with dark limbs and shoulders, and black ears and eye patches. Feeds on bamboo shoots.

Pandarus (păn'dŭrŭs), in Greek mythology, the Trojan who broke the truce by wounding Menelaus. He was killed by Diomed. Another Pandarus was the go-between in the story of Troilus and Cressida.

Pandects: see CORPUS JURIS CIVILIS.

Pandit, Vijaya Lakshmi (vĭjī'ŭ läk'shmē pŭn'dĭt), 1900–, Indian diplomat; sister of Jawaharlal Nehru. Active in Indian Natl. Congress since 1920s, she was first woman in India to hold ministerial office (1937). Madame Pandit was ambassador to USSR 1947–49 and to U.S. 1949–51. Headed Indian delegation to UN for first time in 1946; reappointed 1952.

Pandora (păn"dô'rŭ) [Gr.,= all gifts], in Greek mythology, first woman on earth. Zeus ordered her creation as vengeance on man and sent her as wife to Prometheus' brother, Epimetheus, with box that he forbade her to open. She disobeyed and loosed all evils attending man. Only Hope stayed inside.

Pange lingua (pän'jā lĭng'gwä) [Latin,= sing, O tongue], Corpus Christi hymn of the Roman Catholic Church, written by St. Thomas Aquinas; used in honor of the Sacrament. The last two stanzas, called, as a separate hymn, *Tantum ergo* (tän'tŏŏm âr'gō), are sung at Benediction of the Blessed Sacrament.

Pangim, Portuguese India: see GOA.

Pangnirtung (păng"nûrtŭng'), trading post, E Baffin Isl., Northwest Territories, Canada, on N side of Cumberland Sound; estab. 1921. Here are radio and meteorological station, mounted police post, and medical center for Baffin Bay with hospital.

pangolin (păng-gō'lĭn), toothless insectivorous mammal (*Manis*) of Asia and Africa, probably related to South American anteater. It has heavy scales on head, upper part and sides of body, and on tail; hairs are on under parts and scattered among scales.

Pangopango: see PAGOPAGO.

panic, sudden and widespread loss of confidence in the soundness of financial institutions. There is a general rush to convert assets into money, resulting in numerous bank failures and bankruptcies. A panic often occurs at the end of a period of prosperity, thereby coinciding with a "crash" or economic crisis. Among severe U.S. panics were that of 1837, the panic on "Black Friday," Sept. 19, 1873, and the stock-market crash of Oct., 1929.

Panipat (pä'nēpŭt"), town (pop. 37,837), E Punjab, India. Here in 1526 Baber won decisive victory over Delhi Sultanate.

Panizzi, Sir Anthony (pänēt'sē), 1797–1879, British librarian, b. Italy. He was chief librarian (1856–67) at British Mus. library. His 91 rules (1839) became basis of the museum's catalogue. Enforced act requiring deposition at the museum of copies of books copyrighted in Great Britain.

Panjabi (pŭnjä'bē), language of Indic group of Indo-Iranian subfamily of Indo-European languages. See LANGUAGE (table).

Pankhurst, Emmeline (Goulden) (păngk'hûrst), 1857–1928, English woman-suffragist, leader of militant movement. Organized (1905) Women's Social and Political Union; its methods invited arrest and imprisonment. In 1928, after voting rights were granted to women, she stood for Parliament as a Conservative. Her daughters, **Christabel Pankhurst,** 1880–, educated for law but barred by her sex, and **Sylvia Pankhurst,** 1882–, shared her activities in promoting woman suffrage.

Panmunjom (păn"mōōnjŏm, pän–), village, central Korea, S of 38th parallel, 6 mi. SE of Kaesong. Scene of truce talks, Oct., 1951–Oct., 1952, and of prisoner exchange, April, 1953.

Pannonia (pănō'nēŭ), anc. Roman province, S and W of the Danube. The natives, identified by Romans with the Illyrians, were subjugated by A.D. 9, and the territory was held by Rome until after 395.

pansy, garden flower (*Viola tricolor hortensis*), closely related to the violet, also called heartsease. Probably one of the plants longest cultivated.

Pantaloon (păntŭlōōn'), stock *commedia dell' arte* character, a mean miserly old man in pantaloons.

Pantelleria (pän"tāl-lārē'ä), volcanic island (32 sq. mi.; pop. 9,306), in the Mediterranean between Sicily and Africa. Was a strategic Italian military and air base; capitulated to Allies after severe bombing (1943).

pantheism (păn'thēĭzŭm), belief that God is in all things and all things are in God: God and the universe are identical. There are wide variations in the belief, depending largely on whether it is based principally on religious mysticism (e.g., in Hinduism), poetic appreciation of nature, or philosophical logic (e.g., in teachings of Spinoza). Varieties of pantheism have been known from early times and persistently crop up in the history of thought.

pantheon (păn'thēŏn", –thēůn) [Gr.,= of all gods], term applied originally to a temple to all the gods and now to a building dedicated to a nation's illustrious dead. The **Pantheon** at Rome was built by Agrippa in 27 B.C. and rebuilt in 2d cent. by Hadrian. Converted in 609 into a Christian church. The **Panthéon** (pãtãõ') in Paris was designed by J. G. Soufflot and built 1764–81; now a mausoleum for illustrious Frenchmen.

panther, name applied to LEOPARD and less correctly to PUMA and other large cats.

pantomime (păn'tůmīm) [Gr.,= all in mimic], silent drama using movement, gesture, and facial expression. Dates from ancient times and is seen in primitive cultures. Traditional pantomime characters (e.g., Harlequin, Columbine) originated in 16th cent. COMMEDIA DELL' ARTE. English pantomime is pageant rather than pantomime. Charles Chaplin was a great pantomime actor in silent films in America.

Pánuco (pä'nōōkō), river rising in San Luis Potosí, N central Mexico, flowing generally E to Gulf of Mexico near Tampico. Drains much of central plateau and, by artificial means, Valley of Mexico.

Panza, Sancho: see DON QUIXOTE DE LA MANCHA.

Paoli, Pasquale (päskwä'lā pä'ōlē), 1725–1807, Corsican patriot. Headed Corsican insurrection against Genoa (1755); president of Corsica 1755–69. In 1768 Genoa sold its rights to Corsica to France. Defeated by the French (1769), Paoli fled to England, but in 1791 Louis XVI appointed him governor of Corsica. Opposed to the radical turn of the French Revolution, Paoli proclaimed Corsica independent and called on British aid. With help of Admiral Hood, he defeated the French (1794), but instead of declaring independence, the Corsican assembly made the island a British protectorate. Paoli was recalled to England in 1795. In 1796 the Corsicans drove out the English with French help.

papacy (pā'půsē), office of the pope, head of the ROMAN CATHOLIC CHURCH. According to the belief of that Church he is, as bishop of Rome, successor to St. Peter, the first bishop of Rome and the chief of the Apostles and the representative (vicar or vicegerent) of Christ; hence, the pope is the head of Christendom. This is the theory of Petrine supremacy. It is not held by other churches; some interpret early assertions of papal dignity as expressing a position of honor only, others deny all papal claims whatever. This question of papal supremacy was the chief cause of division between the Roman Catholic Church and the ORTHODOX EASTERN CHURCH, and Protestant churches since the Reformation reject all papal claims of any sort. In the Roman Catholic Church, however, the belief, held from earlier times, that the pope is infallible when speaking *ex cathedra* (i.e., as solemn official head of the Church) on matters of faith and morals was made into dogma at the Vatican Council in 1870. Early popes (e.g., Clement I) asserted rights to guide the Church, and with the decline of the Roman Empire in the W the pope became an important political leader. Such men as Julius I, Innocent I, Leo I, Gregory I, and Martin I enhanced the position of the pope not only by leadership but also by promoting missionary efforts, thus tying the expanding Church more closely to the Holy See (the papal seat at Rome). Conflict with lay rulers ensued, and the popes struggled with some, allied themselves with others. PEPIN THE SHORT by his Donation made the pope the lord of a large area, and down to modern times the pope was secular ruler of the Papal States as well as religious ruler. This fact caused many difficulties, but more came from the contest between lay rulers (notably the emperor, head of the Holy Roman Empire, and the kings of France and England, and, later, of Spain) and the pope over their relative spheres of influence. The more ambitious emperors and kings tried to control all affairs of the Church in their dominions, the more extreme of the popes claimed overlordship over all princes. The 10th cent. was the low point for the papacy; the office was bought and sold in a game of corrupt Roman politics. After the reforms of Gregory VII in the 11th cent., however, the popes had great prestige, and by the end of the 12th cent. Innocent III was trying with some success to assert his claims as arbiter of all lay affairs. By the 14th cent. a new period began when Philip IV of France defied Boniface VIII, and France secured control of the Church. The papal see was moved by Clement V to Avignon, and it remained there from 1309 to 1378; this is the "Babylonian captivity" of the pope. His return to Rome brought on the Great SCHISM (1378–1417), in which there were two or three rival popes, a contest ended by the Council of Constance. Since that time there has been no schism in the papacy, though there was a brief and unsuccessful effort to make the general Church council superior to the pope. In the 15th cent. the popes generally devoted themselves to worldly rule in Italy, to patronizing Renaissance art, and to forwarding their family fortunes. Upon this spiritual apathy fell the REFORMATION, but it was some time before the popes realized that the Protestant leaders had really broken Christendom. Reform within the Church followed election of Paul III (see REFORM, CATHOLIC). Spiritual leadership of the papacy was reasserted, but unfortunately the contest with the Catholic rulers of the empire, Spain, and France grew more pronounced. In the 18th cent. the papacy seemed doomed to be subordinated to lay rulers, but with the overthrow of the absolutist states in the late 18th and early 19th cent. the pope was enabled to reassert his rule within the Church. Even the loss of the Papal States (1870) proved in the end to be a boon (see LATERAN TREATY) since it made the pope perforce a purely ecclesiastic ruler. He governs the tiny Vatican state (see VATICAN), where he has his court, the Curia Romana, under the direction of his officers (see CARDINAL). The following is a list of the popes. The date of election is given rather than that of consecration. Before St. Victor I dates may err by one year. Official lists no longer number the popes in sequence. St. Peter, d. 67?; St. Linus, 67?–76?; St. Cletus or Anacletus, 76?–88?; St. Clement I, 88?–97?; St. Evaristus, 97?–105?; St. Alexander I, 105?–115?; St. Sixtus I, 115?–125?; St. Telesphorus, 125?–136?; St. Hyginus, 136?–140?; St. Pius I, 140?–155?; St. Anicetus, 155?–166?; St. Soter, 166?–175?; St. Eleutherius, 175?–189?; St. Victor I, 189–99; St. Zephyrinus, 199–217; St. Calixtus I, 217–222 (antipope, St. Hippolytus, 217–35); St. Urban I, 222–30; St. Pontian, 230–35; St. Anterus, 235–36; St. Fabian, 236–50; St. Cornelius, 251–53 (antipope, Novatian, 251); St. Lucius I, 253–54; St. Stephen I, 254–57; St. Sixtus II, 257–58; St. Dionysius, 259–68; St. Felix I, 269–74; St. Eutychian, 275–83; St. Caius, 283–96; St. Marcellinus, 296–304; St. Marcellus I, 308–9; St. Eusebius, 309 or 310; St. Miltiades or Melchiades, 311–14; St. Sylvester I, 314–35; St. Marcus, 336; St. Julius I, 337–52; Liberius, 352–66 (antipope, Felix II, 355–65); St. Damasus I, 366–84 (antipope, Ursinus, 366–67); St. Siricius, 384–99; St. Anastasius I, 399–401; St. Innocent I, 401–17; St. Zosimus, 417–18; St. Boniface I, 418–22 (antipope, Eulalius, 418–19); St. Celestine I, 422–32; St. Sixtus III, 432–40; St. Leo I, 440–61; St. Hilary, 461–68; St. Simplicius, 468–83; St. Felix III (II), 483–92; St. Gelasius I, 492–96; Anatasius II, 496–98; St. Symmachus, 498–514 (antipope, Lawrence, 498, 501–5); St. Hormisdas, 514–23; St. John I, 523–26; St. Felix IV (III), 526–30; Boniface II, 530–32 (pope or antipope, Dioscurus, 530); John II, 533–35; St. Agapetus I, 535–36; St. Silverius, 536–37; Vigilius, 537–55; Pelagius I, 556–61; John III, 561–74; Benedict I, 575–79; Pelagius II, 579–90; St. Gregory I, 590–604; Sabinianus, 604–6; Boniface III, 607; St. Boniface IV, 608–15; St. Deusdedit or Adeodatus I, 615–18; Boniface V, 619–25; Honorius I, 625–38; Severinus, 640; John IV, 640–42; Theodore I, 642–49; St. Martin I, 649–55; St. Eugene I, 654–57; St. Vitalian, 657–72; Adeodatus II, 672–76; Donus, 676–78; St. Agathon, 678–81; St. Leo II, 682–83; St. Benedict II, 684–85; John V, 685–86; Conon, 686–87 (antipopes: Theodore, 687; Paschal, 687); St. Sergius I, 687–701; John VI, 701–5; John VII, 705–7; Sisinnius, 708; Constantine, 708–15; St. Gregory II, 715–31; St. Gregory III, 731–41; St. Zacharias, 741–52; Stephen II, 752 (never consecrated); Stephen III (II), 752–57; St. Paul I, 757–67 (antipopes: Constantine, 767–69; Philip, 768); Stephen IV (III), 768–72; Adrian I, 772–95; St. Leo III, 795–816; Stephen V (IV), 816–17; St. Paschal I, 817–24; Eugene II, 824–27; Valentine, 827; Gregory IV, 827–44 (antipope, John, 844); Sergius II, 844–47; St. Leo IV, 847–55; Benedict III, 855–58 (antipope, Anastasius, 855); St. Nicholas I, 858–67; Adrian II, 867–72; John VIII, 872–82; Marinus I, 882–84; St. Adrian III, 884–85; Stephen VI (V), 885–91; Formosus, 891–96; Boniface VI, 896; Stephen VII (VI), 896–97; Romanus, 897; Theodore II, 897; John IX, 898–900; Benedict IV, 900–903; Leo V, 903 (antipope, Christopher, 903–4); Sergius III, 904–11; Anastasius III, 911–13; Lando, 913–14; John X, 914–28; Leo VI, 928; Stephen VIII (VII), 928–31; John XI, 931–35; Leo VII, 936–39; Stephen IX (VIII), 939–42; Marinus II, 942–46; Agapetus II, 946–55; John XII, 955–64; Leo VIII, 963–65, or Benedict V, 964–66 (one of these was an antipope); John XIII, 965–72; Benedict VI, 973–74 (antipope, Boniface VII, 974, 984–85); Benedict VII, 974–83; John XIV, 983–84; John XV, 985–96; Gregory V, 996–99 (antipope, John XVI, 997–98); Sylvester II, 999–1003; John XVII, 1003; John XVIII, 1004–9; Sergius IV, 1009–12; Benedict VIII, 1012–24 (antipope, Gregory, 1012); John XIX, 1024–32; Benedict IX, 1032–44, 1045, 1047–48 (popes or antipopes: Sylvester III, 1045; Gregory VI, 1045–46; Clement II, 1046–47); Damasus II, 1048; St. Leo IX, 1049–54; Victor II, 1055–57; Stephen X (IX), 1057–58 (antipope, Benedict X, 1058–59); Nicholas II, 1059–61; Alexander II, 1061–73 (antipope, Honorius II, 1061–72); St. Gregory VII, 1073–85 (antipope, Clement III, 1080–1100); Victor III, 1086–87; Urban II, 1088–99; Paschal II, 1099–1118 (antipopes: Theodoric, 1100; Albert, 1102; Sylvester IV, 1105–11); Gelasius II, 1118–19 (antipope, Gregory VIII, 1118–21); Calixtus II, 1119–24; Honorius II, 1124–30 (antipope, Celestine II, 1124); Innocent II, 1130–43 (antipopes: Anacletus II, 1130–38; Victor IV, 1138); Celestine II, 1143–44; Lucius II, 1144–45; Eugene III, 1145–53; Anastasius IV, 1153–54; Adrian IV; 1154–59; Alexander III, 1159–81 (antipopes: Victor IV, 1159–64; Paschal III, 1164–68; Calixtus III, 1168–78; Innocent III, 1179–80); Lucius III, 1181–85; Urban III, 1185–87; Gregory VIII, 1187; Clement III, 1187–91; Celestine III, 1191–98; Innocent III, 1198–1216; Honorius III, 1216–27; Gregory IX, 1227–41; Celestine IV, 1241; Innocent IV, 1243–54; Alexander IV, 1254–61; Urban IV, 1261–64; Clement IV, 1265–68; Gregory X, 1271–76; Innocent V, 1276; Adrian V, 1276; John XXI, 1276–77; Nicholas III, 1277–80; Martin IV, 1281–85; Honorius IV, 1285–87; Nicholas IV, 1288–92; St. Celestine V, 1294; Boniface VIII, 1294–1303; Benedict XI, 1303–4; Clement V, 1305–14; John XXII, 1316–34 (antipope, Nicholas V, 1328–30); Benedict XII, 1334–42; Clement VI, 1342–52; Innocent VI, 1352–62; Urban V, 1362–70; Gregory XI, 1370–78; Urban VI, 1378–89; Boniface IX, 1389–1404; Innocent VII, 1404–6; Gregory XII, 1406–15 (Avignon succession of antipopes: Clement VII, 1378–94; Benedict XIII, 1394–1423; Clement VIII, 1423–29; Benedict XIV, 1425–30; Pisan succession of antipopes: Alexander V, 1409–10; John XXIII, 1410–15); Martin V, 1417–31; Eugene IV, 1431–47 (antipope, Felix V, 1439–49); Nicholas V, 1447–55; Calixtus III, 1455–58; Pius II, 1458–64; Paul II, 1464–71; Sixtus IV, 1471–84; Innocent VIII, 1484–92; Alexander VI, 1492–1503; Pius III, 1503; Julius II, 1503–13; Leo X, 1513–21; Adrian VI, 1522–23; Clement VII, 1523–34; Paul III, 1534–49; Julius III, 1550–55; Marcellus II, 1555; Paul IV, 1555–59; Pius IV, 1559–65; St. Pius V, 1566–72; Gregory XIII, 1572–85; Sixtus V, 1585–90; Urban VII, 1590; Gregory XIV, 1590–91; Innocent IX, 1591; Clement VIII, 1592–1605; Leo XI, 1605; Paul V, 1605–21; Gregory XV, 1621–23;

Urban VIII, 1623–44; Innocent X, 1644–55; Alexander VII, 1655–67; Clement IX, 1667–69; Clement X, 1670–76; Innocent XI, 1676–89; Alexander VIII, 1689–91; Innocent XII, 1691–1700; Clement XI, 1700–1721; Innocent XIII, 1721–24; Benedict XIII, 1724–30; Clement XII, 1730–40; Benedict XIV, 1740–58; Clement XIII, 1758–69; Clement XIV, 1769–74; Pius VI, 1775–99; Pius VII, 1800–1823; Leo XII, 1823–29; Pius VIII, 1829–30; Gregory XVI, 1831–46; Pius IX, 1846–78; Leo XIII, 1878–1903; Pius X, 1903–14; Benedict XV, 1914–22; Pius XI, 1922–39; Pius XII, 1939–.

Papal States, former independent territory under temporal rule of the popes; cap. Rome. Also called States of the Church and Pontifical States, they extended across the Italian peninsula from the Adriatic Sea and the lower Po (N) to the Tyrrhenian Sea (S) and included Latium, Umbria, the Marches, Emilia, and Romagna. The states had their origin in land endowments given to the popes in the 4th cent.—the "Patrimony of St. Peter"—in Italy, Sicily, and Sardinia. The popes gradually lost their more distant lands, but in the duchy of Rome their power grew and made Rome independent of the Eastern emperors. Pepin the Short's donation of RAVENNA and the PENTAPOLIS to the papacy (754; confirmed by Charlemagne 774) and the forged Donation of CONSTANTINE gave the popes claims of overlordship over central and S Italy, Sicily, and Sardinia, but they did not give them effective control. The bequest of Countess MATILDA of Tuscany (1115) resulted in a long struggle between emperors and popes over Matilda's lands; in the 14th cent. the emperors renounced their claims to the duchy of Spoleto, the ROMAGNA, and the March of Ancona. However, the free communes and petty tyrants of these regions long resisted papal domination, while the "Babylonian Captivity" of the popes in Avignon and the Great Schism (1309–1420) threw the Papal States into chaos. Actual control by the papacy of its states began in the 16th cent. under JULIUS II. After the French invasion of 1796 the Papal States were curtailed, occupied, and twice abolished, but they were fully restored and placed under Austrian protection by the Congress of Vienna (1814–15). PIUS IX granted a constitution but revoked it after the Revolution of 1848–49. During the RISORGIMENTO, the Papal States lost Bologna, the Romagna, the Marches, and Umbria to Sardinia (1860), but French intervention prevented their total absorption until the fall of Napoleon III (1870), when Victor Emmanuel II annexed Rome. The popes refused to recognize their loss of temporal power, and in 1929 they received full sovereignty over VATICAN CITY by the Lateran Treaty.

papaw tree or **pawpaw,** deciduous tree (*Asimina triloba*), native E of Mississippi. It has purple flowers and fleshy fruits with custardlike edible pulp.

papaya (pŭpī'ŭ), palmlike tropical American tree (*Carica papaya*). It bears edible yellow fruits which yield a juice containing the enzyme papain.

Papeete (päpā-ā'tā), port town (pop. 12,428), on Tahiti, S Pacific; cap. of French Establishments in Oceania and of Tahiti.

Papen, Franz von (fränts' fŭn pä'pŭn), 1879–, German politician. His implication in sabotage plots as military attaché in Washington caused U.S. to request his recall (1915). In 1932 he succeeded Brüning as chancellor of Germany, heading a conservative cabinet. His actions soon afterward led to his expulsion from his party (the Catholic Center). He resigned when he could not secure a working majority in the Reichstag; Schleicher succeeded him. Early in 1933 his behind-the-scenes maneuvers were instrumental in bringing about Hitler's appointment as chancellor. Under Hitler, he served as ambassador to Austria and to Turkey. At the war-crimes trial he was acquitted (1946).

paper, thin sheet or layer made from vegetable fiber (commonly wood pulp) and used in some 14,000 products. Papermaking is said to have originated c.105 in China and spread via Samarkand and N Africa to Spain (c.1150), thence through Europe, and in 1690 to American colonies. Fiber, mixed with water, is reduced mechanically or chemically to pulp introduced into mesh mold, then pressed and dried. Watermark is made by design attached to mold. Dipping molds were superseded by machine forming continuous web invented 1798 in France by Nicolas Robert and improved in England by Henry and Sealy Fourdrinier. In modern Fourdrinier machine, pulp is poured on endless wire-mesh belt edged with deckle strips, then pressed between revolving rolls and carried over series of drying rolls. Paper is modified for various purposes by sizing or other materials added to pulp or used as coating.

Paphlagonia (păʺflŭgō'nēŭ), anc. region, N Asia Minor, on the Black Sea, famous for timber, horses, and mules. Greeks colonized the coast.

Paphos (pā'fŏs), two anc. cities, SW Cyprus. The first, founded by Phoenicians, was center of the worship of Astarte or Aphrodite. The second was cap. of Cyprus in Roman times.

Papineau, Louis Joseph (päpēnō'), 1786–1871, French Canadian political leader and insurgent. Speaker of legislative assembly of Lower Canada (1815–37). Leader of Reform party. Believing British government in Canada unfair to French Canadians, he inflamed some of his followers, the *Patriotes,* to open rebellion in 1837. Took no part in uprising but fled to U.S. Returned to Canada c.1845.

Papini, Giovanni (jōvän'nē päpē'nē), 1881–, Italian writer. *Un uomo finito* (1912) was his first success. After embracing Catholicism, he wrote the famous *Life of Christ* (1921) and *Dante vivo* (1933).

Papinian (pŭpĭ'nēŭn), d. 212, Roman jurist, one of the greatest figures of Roman law. He was a friend of Septimius Severus, but was put to death by Caracalla, son of Septimius Severus.

Pappus (pă'pŭs), fl. c.300, Greek mathematician of Alexandria whose works (which recorded and enlarged those of his predecessors) stimulated 17th-cent. revival of geometry. Descartes expounded several of his theorems.

Papua: see NEW GUINEA.

Papua, Territory of (pă′pūŭ), area (90,540 sq. mi.; pop. 373,000), belonging to Australia and including SE NEW GUINEA and near-by islands; cap. Port Moresby. Became British protectorate 1884. Annexed to Great Britain as British New Guinea. Governed by Australia since 1906.

papyrus (pŭpī′rŭs), sedge (*Cyperus papyrus*). Ancient Egyptians used roots as fuel, pith as food, and stem for boats, cloth, twine, and sheets of writing material. This writing material, also called papyrus, was made from slices of the sedge laid side by side in two layers at right angles, pressed together with adhesive, glued end to end, and rolled on rods to form manuscripts.

Pará (pŭrä′), state (469,778 sq. mi.; pop. 1,142,846), N Brazil, in lower Amazon basin, S of the Guianas; cap., BELÉM. A hot, humid region, not extensively developed. Chief products: rubber, hardwoods, Brazil nuts, medicinal plants.

Pará, river, c.200 mi. long, E Brazil. Actually is SE arm of Amazon, divided from rest of river by Marajó isl. Great port of Belém is on right bank.

parable, in Bible. Term used in the Gospels for a short narrative illustrating a moral or for a figurative statement. There are a few parables in the Old Testament, e.g., the ewe lamb (2 Sam. 12.1–4). Among the many parables told by Jesus were: the Good Samaritan (Luke 10.29–37); the prodigal son (Luke 15.11–32); the sower (Mat. 13.3–9,18–23; Mark 4.3–9; 14–20; Luke 8.4–15); the Pharisee and the publican (Luke 18.9–14); the lost sheep (Mat. 18.11–14); the rich man (Dives) and Lazarus (Luke 16.19–31).

parabola (pŭră′bŭlŭ), plane curve such that distances from any point on it to fixed point (focus) and fixed line (directrix) are equal; also a conic section cut by plane parallel to one element of cone. Axis of parabola is line through focus perpendicular to directrix; vertex is point in which axis intersects curve; latus rectum is chord through focus perpendicular to axis.

Paracelsus, Philippus Aureolus (fĭlĭ′pŭs ôrēō′lŭs părŭsĕl′sŭs), 1493?–1541, Swiss physician, alchemist, and chemist. He promoted use of specific remedies and was author of many medical and occult works. Real name was Theophrastus Bombastus von Hohenheim.

parachute (pă′rŭshōōt), umbrellalike device designed to slow descent of body falling through air and permit safe landing on surface. Jean Pierre Blanchard claimed invention (1785). Jacques Garnerin made first successful descent (from balloon, 1797). Modern designs for carrying aviators and cargo.

Paraclete (pă′rŭklēt) [Gr.,= advocate], title of the Holy Ghost, often translated as "Comforter" or "Advocate." John 14.16,26; 15.26; 16.7; 1 John 2.1.

Paradise, name sometimes used for Garden of Eden or synonymously with HEAVEN. It originally was a Persian word meaning park or garden. Many ancient peoples had myths about a place where man lived in a state of bliss until he lost it through sinning. With the beginning of the Messianic concept in late Jewish thought came the hope of regaining this earthly bliss, and Paradise became identified with the promised Messianic kingdom. In some Christian thought, Paradise is regarded as a state of bliss secondary to heaven itself; the souls of certain righteous dwell free from pain and punishment in this place but are denied seeing God face to face.

paraffin or **paraffine** (both: pă′rŭfĭn), colorless, odorless, tasteless mineral wax, a mixture of hydrocarbons, chiefly of methane series. It is used in making candles, tapers, and paper matches, in sizing and waterproofing, and in sealing jams and jellies.

Paragould (pă′rŭgōōld), city (pop. 9,668), NE Ark., near St. Francis R. Railroad shops. Processes wood, cotton, and food.

Paraguay (pă′rŭgwā, Span. pärägwī′), republic (157,047 sq. mi.; pop. 1,259,826), SE South America; cap. ASUNCIÓN. Paraguay has no seacoast and is surrounded by Bolivia, Brazil, and Argentina. The E part, where most of population lives, lies between the Paraguay and Paraná rivers. To the W of the Paraguay R. lies the Chaco, largely uninhabited and unexploited, although there is some cattle raising, quebracho is found in the forests, and petroleum has been discovered. Agr. products in the E are cotton, tobacco, citrus fruits, and *mate* (Paraguayan tea). Industries include meat packing, the extraction of petitgrain from wild oranges (Paraguay furnishes most of world's supply) and manufacture of rum, molasses, and alcohol. Chief cities besides Asunción are Villarica, Concepción, and Encarnación. Population is largely a homogeneous mixture of Spanish and Guarani strains, and the Paraguayans are almost all bilingual. German, Italian, and French immigration have added new elements to the distinctive civilization of Paraguay, which has arts and crafts showing the varied strains. In music, the *guarania* is a notable form of modern music and the handmade lace, called *nanduti,* is exquisite. The established religion is Roman Catholic, but other faiths are tolerated and Mennonite settlements were founded before and during World War II. Asunción was founded in 1536 or 1537, and it was from here that Buenos Aires was re-established and many of the Argentine cities were founded. It was through the forceful rule of Hernando Árias de Saavedra (called Hernandárias) that Paraguay's virtual independence from the Spanish administrators in Buenos Aires and Peru was established. Also in his regime the Jesuit missions, which played such an important part in Paraguayan culture from the late 16th cent. to the 18th, were founded. Independence from Spain came with Argentina's successful revolution (1810); the next year Paraguay quietly overthrew the colonial officials, and in 1814, the first of the three great dictators who were to mold Paraguay came into power (José Gaspar Rodríguez FRANCIA, Carlos Antonio López, and Francisco Solano LÓPEZ). During the rule of F. S. López a war was fought against the combined forces of Brazil, Argentina, and Uruguay (1865–70; see TRIPLE ALLIANCE, WAR OF THE). The disastrous effects of that war were slow to disappear, and political confusion was added to economic depression. Decades later, as the country was slowly recovering, it was plunged again into war with Bolivia over the boundary in the Chaco (1932–35). This time Paraguay emerged victorious but exhausted. A rapid succession of governments ensued, with Higinio Morínigo's regime lasting the longest (1940–48).

Paraguay, river, c.1,300 mi. long, rising in Mato Grosso state, W Brazil, with headstreams in E Bolivia. Flows S, making border between Brazil and Paraguay, divides Paraguayan Chaco from E Paraguay, and forms boundary between Argentina and Paraguay; is important in Río de la Plata system.

Paraguay tea: see MATE.

Paraíba or **Parahiba** (both: pärůē'bů), state (21,730 sq. mi.; pop. 1,730,784), NE Brazil; cap. Joâo Pessoa, on the Atlantic. Primarily cotton growing area with some copper and tin mining. Settled by Portuguese (1584).

Paraíba or **Paraíba do Sul** (do͞o so͞ol), river, c.600 mi. long, rising W of Rio de Janiero, SE Brazil. Flows SW to a point near São Paulo, then NE to the Atlantic. Valley produces rice, sugar cane, livestock.

parakeet or **parrakeet** (pă'růkēt), any of various small parrots of Australia, Polynesia, Asia, Africa. Carolina parakeet of E and S U.S. believed extinct. Shell (or zebra) parakeet is a green cage bird with yellow head, grayish green wings with black markings, and a long narrow blue and black tail. It is sometimes called love bird but true love birds are African and have short wide tails and short bodies.

Paralipomenon: see CHRONICLES.

paralysis or **palsy** (pôl'zē), loss of motion or sensation resulting from lesion in brain, spinal cord, nerves, or muscles and caused by injury, poison, or disease. Types include general; hemiplegia (on one side); paraplegia (on both sides at one level); *paralysis agitans* or Parkinson's disease, accompanied by tremor; cerebral palsy, usually caused by lesion in brain motor tissue resulting from birth injury.

Paramaribo (pă"růmă'rĭbō), city (pop. 76,-466), cap. of Dutch Guiana, port on Surinam R. Founded 1650 as cap. of a new English colony. Leading exports today are rum, coffee, timber, and bauxite.

Paramus (půră'můs), residential borough (pop. 6,268), NE N.J., NE of Paterson. Truck farming.

Paran (pā'răn), wilderness, probably S of Beersheba. Ishmael settled here.

Paraná (pärůnä'), state (77,717 sq. mi.; pop. 2,149,509), S Brazil, between Paraná R. and Atlantic; cap., CURITIBA. Grows coffee, cotton, fruit. Population includes Italians, Germans, and Slavs.

Paraná, city (pop. 84,153), cap. of Entre Rios prov., NE Argentina, port on Paraná R. Center of grain and cattle district. Founded 1730, it was cap. of Argentine confederation (1853–61).

Paraná, river, c.2,050 mi. long, formed in S Brazil by junction of Paranaíba and Rio Grande. Flows S and W to confluence with Paraguay and then S and E through N section of Argentina to join Uruguay R. at head of Río de la Plata. Principal ports are: Posadas, Corrientes, Santa Fe, Paraná, Rosario.

Paranaíba (pä"růnäē'bů), river, c.500 mi. long, rising in W Minas Gerais state, E central Brazil, and flowing W to join Rio Grande in forming Paraná.

paranoia (pă"růnoi'ů), type of psychosis characterized by persistent, logically reasoned delusions, especially of persecution or grandeur. True paranoia is rare; often paranoid reactions are caused by schizophrenia. Recovery is considered unlikely.

parapsychology: see PSYCHICAL RESEARCH.

Para rubber tree (půrä'), large tree (*Hevea brasiliensis*), native to South America and a member of the spurge family. The most important source of natural RUBBER, it is widely grown in tropical regions. Latex, the milky juice from which rubber is made, is obtained by tapping the tree's trunk at regular intervals, beginning after the fifth to seventh year.

parasite (pă'růsīt), plant or animal which, at some stage of existence, obtains nourishment from another living organism, called its host. Includes many disease-causing bacteria, protozoans, and worms; fungi, e.g., rust, smut; and insects, e.g., flea, louse. A saprophyte obtains nourishment from organic matter, not from a living host; mushrooms and Indian pipe are examples of saprophytes.

Paray-le-Monial (pärā'-lů-mônyäl'), town (pop. 6,240), Saône-et-Loire dept., E central France. It is a major place of pilgrimage, where St. Margaret Mary founded the cult of the Sacred Heart (17th cent.).

Parca (pär'ků), Roman goddess of childbirth. Her name pluralized (Parcae) was applied to FATES.

parcel post, system of package delivery, established on an international basis in 1878. The U.S. delayed organizing domestic parcel post service until 1913; rural parcel-post routes were established in 1919. Packages are limited to 70 lb. and to 100 in. for girth and length combined.

parchment, untanned animal skins, dehaired, stretched, and rubbed with chalk and pumice. Name is a corruption of Pergamum where it was prepared c.2d cent. B.C. It slowly superseded papyrus and was used for the handwritten copies of books until the advent of printing. Superseded by paper.

Pardo Bazán, Emilia, condesa de (āmē'lyä kōndā'sä dā pär'dhō bäthän'), 1852–1921, Spanish novelist and critic. She wrote *La cuestión palpitante* (1883; in defense of Zola's naturalism), regional novels of Galicia, and other works.

Paré, Ambroise (ãbrwäz' pärā'), c.1510–1590, French army surgeon, known for advancing humane methods of treating wounds.

parent education, movement to help parents' understanding of child life. Carried on through adult education and parent-teacher associations. Child Study Association (1888) and Natl. Congress of Parents and Teachers (1897) are active in field.

Pareto, Vilfredo (vēlfrā'dō pärā'tō), 1848–1923, Italian economist and sociologist. He applied mathematics to economic theory and sought to differentiate rational and nonrational factors in social action and the cyclical rise and fall of governing elite groups. Italian Fascist ideology utilized some of his theories. His chief work (1916) was translated (1935) as *Mind and Society*.

Paria, Gulf of (pär′yä), between mainland of Venezuela and island of Trinidad.

Parian marble: see Paros.

Paricutín (pärēkōōtēn′), volcano, c.8,200 ft. high, Michoacán, W central Mexico. Erupting from a level field in 1943, it grew c.800 ft. before it became quiescent in 1952.

Parini, Giuseppe (jōōzĕp′pā pärē′nē), 1729–99, Italian poet, a priest; author of the satiric masterpiece, *Il giorno* [the day] (1763–1801), a mock-didactic poem about a young nobleman's daily life.

Paris or **Alexander,** in Greek legend, Trojan prince; son of Priam and Hecuba. Because of a prophecy that he would destroy Troy, his parents exposed him, but he was saved and grew up as a shepherd. His elopement with Helen caused the Trojan War.

Paris, Matthew: see Matthew of Paris.

Paris (pă′rĭs), town (pop. 5,249), S Ont., Canada, on Grand R. and W of Hamilton. Woolen mill center.

Paris (pă′rĭs, Fr. pärē), city (pop. 2,691,473), cap. of France, on the Seine; Greater Paris, with industrial and residential suburbs, virtually covers all Seine dept. (pop. 4,775,711). Largest city and industrial center of France; transport and communications center of W Europe (large river port, seven major railroad stations, two airports); world center of fashions and luxury goods; probably world's greatest tourist center. Archiepiscopal see. Intellectually and artistically, Paris led the W world in the 17th–19th cent. and in some respects retains a unique position ("city of light"). Among its many cultural institutions are the university (see Sorbonne), French Academy, Pasteur Institute, École des Beaux Arts, Conservatoire, Comédie Française, Opéra, and Louvre. Divided into 20 *arrondissements* [boroughs], Paris is governed by a municipal council. N of the Seine extends the right bank, center of fashions and business. Here are the great boulevards and some of the world's most celebrated thoroughfares (the Champs Élysées, from the Arc de Triomphe to the Place de la Concorde; Rue de la Paix; Place Vendôme); here also are the Bois de Boulogne and Montmartre, topped by the Church of Sacré-Cœur. On the left bank are the Old Latin Quarter, for centuries the preserve of the university; Montparnasse; the Luxembourg Palace; many governmental buildings; the Hôtel des Invalides and its domed church (tomb of Napoleon I); and the Eiffel Tower. The historic core of Paris is the Île de la Cité, a small island occupied in part by the Palais de Justice (incl. Sainte Chapelle), the city hall, and the Cathedral of Notre Dame de Paris. A fishing hamlet at the time of Caesar's conquest, ancient Lutetia Parisiorum soon grew into an important Roman town. It became (5th cent. A.D.) a cap. of the Merovingian kings but was devastated by Norse raids in 9th cent. With the accession (987) of Hugh Capet, count of Paris, as king of France, Paris became the national cap. It flowered as a medieval commercial center and as the fountainhead of scholasticism but suffered severely during the Hundred Years War (English occupation 1420–36). Throughout its history, Paris displayed a rebellious and independent spirit—as in the civil troubles under Étienne Marcel (1358), its resistance to Henry IV (1589–93), the first Fronde (1648–49), the revolutions of 1789, 1830, and 1848, the German siege of 1870–71, and the Commune of Paris of 1871. Most of modern Paris was planned in the 19th cent. by Haussmann. Occupied by the Germans in 1940, Paris was liberated Aug. 25, 1944, by U.S., French, and Parisian resistance forces. Its industrial districts suffered considerable bomb damage.

Paris (pă′rĭs). **1** City (pop. 9,460), E Ill., NW of Terre Haute, Ind. Rail center in farm and coal area. Mfg. of brooms, shoes, and metal products. **2** City (pop. 6,912), N Ky., NE of Lexington, on South Fork of Licking R. in bluegrass country. Tobacco and bluegrass-seed market. One of first distilleries in state (1790) here; whisky from region called bourbon after county. **3** City (pop. 8,826), W Tenn., near Ky. line, in farm, clay, and timber area. Railroad shops, cotton gins; mfg. of cosmetics and pottery. **4** City (pop. 21,643), E Texas, NE of Dallas. Processing and shipping center for agr. area, it has woodworking, flour and cottonseed oil milling, and meat packing.

Paris, Commune of: see Commune of Paris.

Paris, Congress of, 1856, conference held by representatives of France, Great Britain, Turkey, Sardinia, Russia, Austria, and Prussia to negotiate the peace after the Crimean War. In the Treaty of Paris (March 30, 1856) Russia agreed to neutralization of Black Sea; the Danubian principalities (Moldavia and Walachia, after 1859 called Rumania) became semi-independent states under nominal Turkish suzerainty; Russian-Turkish boundary in Asia was restored to pre-war status. Turkey became a member of the European concert. Provisions were altered (1878) by Treaty of San Stefano and Congress of Berlin. The Congress also issued the **Declaration of Paris,** an agreement concerning the rules of maritime warfare. Its four principles were: privateering was no longer legal; a neutral flag would protect the goods of an enemy, except for contraband of war; neutral goods, except for such contraband would not be liable to capture when under the enemy's flag; a blockade would be binding only if it prevented access to the coast of the enemy. The U.S. refused to accept the declaration, but later followed its principles.

Paris, Pact of: see Kellogg-Briand Pact.

Paris, Treaty of, name given to several important treaties signed in or near Paris. **1763** treaty signed by England, France, and Spain ending (with Peace of Hubertusburg) the Seven Years War. France lost Canada and possessions E of Mississippi R. to England and ceded W Louisiana to its ally, Spain, in compensation for Florida, which Spain lost to England. In India, France recovered its posts but was forbidden to maintain troops or build forts in Bengal. Treaty laid foundation of British colonial supremacy. **1783** treaties ending war of American Revolution. (1) U.S. treaty with England (negotiated, for U.S., by John Adams, Benjamin Franklin, and John Jay) fixed boundaries of U.S. and settled other problems arising ou of severance of U.S. from Britain. (2) Anglo-French treaty generally restored mutual status quo as of 1763. (3) Anglo-Spanish treaty restored Floridas and Minorca to Spain; England kept Gibraltar. (4) Anglo-Dutch treaty (ratified 1784) awarded several Dutch colonies to Britain. **1814,** treaty between France and the principal allies (England, Russia, Austria, Prussia) after Napoleon's first abdication. Reduced France to boundaries of 1792. France paid no indemnities. England returned most French colonies to France but kept Malta. A general conference was called to settle all other territorial questions (see VIENNA, CONGRESS OF). Leniency of treaty was due chiefly to skill of TALLEYRAND. **1815,** between France and the allies after Napoleon's return and defeat at Waterloo. Reduced France to 1790 boundaries; exacted heavy indemnity; provided for five-year occupation of NE France; ratified Final Act of Congress of Vienna. Simultaneously, QUADRUPLE ALLIANCE was renewed. **1856:** see PARIS, CONGRESS OF. **1898:** see SPANISH-AMERICAN WAR. **1919–20:** see Treaties of VERSAILLES, SAINT-GERMAIN, NEUILLY, TRIANON, and SÈVRES. **1947:** see ITALY; RUMANIA; HUNGARY; BULGARIA; FINLAND.

Paris green, highly poisonous compound containing arsenic and copper. Used as insecticide and fungicide.

Paris Peace Conference, 1919: see VERSAILLES, TREATY OF.

Park, Mungo, 1771–1806, Scottish explorer in Africa. Explored course of Niger R. Drowned when natives attacked party.

Park, William Hallock, 1863–1939, American bacteriologist, known for work in public health and preventive medicine. Author of standard works in field.

Park College, at Parkville, Mo., NW of Kansas City; coed.; opened 1875, chartered 1879 by Presbyterians. School industries operated by students.

Parker, Alton B(rooks), 1852–1926, American jurist, U.S. Democratic presidential candidate (1904). Noted for liberal decisions in labor cases.

Parker, Dorothy, 1893–, American short-story and verse writer, best known for sardonic, humorous light verse and stories of social satire.

Parker, Francis Wayland, 1837–1902, American educator. He was superintendent of schools in Quincy, Mass., 1875–80, and there originated "Quincy movement," emphasizing learning by doing, socialized activities, teaching of science, and informal instruction. He was founder and principal (1899–1901) of part of Univ. of Chicago's school of education.

Parker, Sir Gilbert, 1862–1932, Canadian novelist. Many of his novels and collections of tales deal with material from Canadian history.

Parker, Sir Hyde, 1739–1807, British admiral. In American Revolution he broke North River defenses at New York city in 1776. Horatio Nelson's refusal to obey his cease-fire signal at Copenhagen victory (1801) is famous incident in naval history.

Parker, Lottie Blair, 1858?–1937, American playwright, author of melodrama *Way Down East* (1898).

Parker, Matthew, 1504–75, English prelate. Archbishop of Canterbury after 1559, he revised (1562) Thirty-nine Articles and supervised (1563–68) preparation of Bishops' Bible.

Parker, Theodore, 1810–60, American theologian and social reformer. As Unitarian pastor in Boston, he set forth views in *Discourse of Matters Pertaining to Religion* (1842) then thought radical but later accepted. He was a transcendentalist and contributor to the *Dial,* a lyceum lecturer, and a leader in antislavery and prison-reform activities.

Parker Dam, 320 ft. high, 856 ft. long, at Ariz.-Calif. line, in Colorado R.; completed 1938. Used for water supply, power, irrigation.

Parkersburg, city (pop. 29,684), NW W.Va., SSW of Wheeling and at junction of Little Kanawha and Ohio rivers; settled 1785. Shipping center for oil, gas, and coal region with mfg. of rayon, implements, oil-well equipment. Near by in the Ohio is Blennerhasset Isl.

Parkhurst, Charles Henry, 1842–1933, American clergyman and reformer, pastor (1880–1918) of Madison Square Presbyterian Church, New York city. As president after 1891 of Society for Prevention of Crime, he instigated investigation of Tammany by Lexow committee.

Parkman, Francis, 1823–93, American historian. On basis of travel and study in W U.S. (1846) he wrote famous work, *The Oregon Trail* (1849). Also wrote studies of early Northwest and Canada, notably *Pioneers of France in the New World* (1865), *The Discovery of the Great West* (1869), *The Old Régime in Canada* (1874), *A Half-Century of Conflict* (1892).

Park Range, part of Rocky Mts., central Colo. and S Wyo., N from Colorado R. Gore Range is SE part, Sierra Madre (Wyo.) is NW extension. Mt. Lincoln (14,284 ft.) is highest point.

Park Ridge, residential city (pop. 16,602), NE Ill., NW suburb of Chicago.

parlement (Fr. pärlůmã'), in French history, the chief judiciary body until 1789. There were (as of 1789) 14 provincial parlements and the Parlement of Paris, which had superior authority. Growing out of the feudal Curia Regis, the Parlement of Paris began its separate existence under Louis IX (13th cent.) and grew into an extremely elaborate organization. Its political power rested on the fact that it registered royal edicts, which thereby became law, and it repeatedly challenged royal authority, notably in the first FRONDE. It was abolished (1771–74) by Chancellor MAUPEOU, whose attempted judicial reform failed largely for lack of new magistrates to replace the old ones. The defiance of the parlements when Loménie de Brienne proposed fiscal reforms (1787–88) led to the calling of the States-General (1789) and the beginning of the French Revolution.

Parley, Peter: see GOODRICH, SAMUEL GRISWOLD.

Parliament, legislative assembly of Great Britain and British Empire. Has come to be the actual sovereign rather than the king, whose authority is nominal. Consists technically of the king, House of Commons, and House of Lords. Membership in Lords is hereditary (except for the Anglican bishops) for peers of England, Ireland, and Scotland; since 1911 its powers have been slight. The power of Commons lies in its control of finances. An elective body of 625 members (506 for England, Wales and Monmouth 36, Scotland 71, N. Ireland 12), it is presided over by the speaker, elected from party in power. The two-party system is feature of English parliamentary government. The majority party chooses executive head (the prime minister) and must call general election if unable to get support on major issues. Unlike the U.S. system the government executive branch is in effect a committee of the legislature. Parliament drew from many ancient institutions. Its first modern developments were in 13th cent. King's feudal court of Curia Regis produced the House of Lords (so-named in Henry VIII's reign). Irregular assemblies of other social elements of the state grew into the House of Commons. Until early 14th cent. judicial issues prevailed over financial. Attempts of the barons to win support led to the Mad Parliament at Oxford (1258) and Parliament of Simon de MONTFORT (1265). Edward I's Model Parliament (1295) set a precedent for future development. Familiar parliamentary features did not appear until transfer of taxation control from king to Parliament (1340) and soon to Commons. Power to withhold financial grants enabled Parliament to force the king's acceptance of national petitions, which were gradually supplanted by bills enacted by Commons, Lords, and king. Under the Tudors the king used Parliament as his instrument. Its claim to actual sovereignty became the issue of the PURITAN REVOLUTION. Petition of Right presented (1628) to Charles I demanded recognition of sole authority to levy taxes. The Long Parliament (1640–49) opposed the king in the civil war. After control by Oliver Cromwell, the Restoration returned Parliament to power. The Glorious Revolution affirmed its permanent sovereignty (1688). The appearance of parties led to parliamentary control of the ministries. Representation was limited to the propertied upper classes until democratic agitation and Chartism led to REFORM BILLS (1832, 1867) and finally to universal suffrage (1918). House of Lords was stripped of power by Parliament Act of 1911. Parliament is housed in Westminster Palace.

parliamentary law, rules under which deliberative bodies conduct their proceedings. Based on the practice of the English Parliament (largely conventional, rather than statutory) and including practices from the U.S. congressional bodies, they have been codified in H. M. Robert's *Rules of Order* (1876), the usually accepted authority, though the presiding officers of the British and U.S. legislative bodies are the respective interpreters of parliamentary law.

Parma (pär'mä), city (pop. 65,126), Emilia-Romagna, N central Italy, on Aemilian way. Agr. market; silk mfg. A Roman colony after 183 B.C., it became a free commune in 12th cent.; annexed to Papal States 16th cent. In 1545 Pope Paul III created the duchy of Parma and Piacenza for his son Pierluigi Farnese. The duchy continued under the FARNESE family till 1731, when it passed to the Spanish Bourbons. The cadet line of BOURBON-PARMA began 1748. The duchy was annexed to France 1802; awarded to MARIE LOUISE 1815; restored to Bourbons 1847; annexed to Sardinia 1860. Parma is rich in works of Correggio (frescoes in Convent of St. Paul and in Romanesque cathedral). Among notable buildings are the baptistery (13th cent.) and the wooden Farnese Theater (built 1618; damaged in World War II). University dates from 1502. Region is noted for Parmesan cheese.

Parma, city (pop. 28,897), NE Ohio, S suburb of Cleveland; inc. 1925.

Parmenas (pär'–), one of the seven deacons. Acts 6.5.

Parmenides (pärmĕn'ĭdēz), b. c.514 B.C., Greek philosopher of the ELEATIC SCHOOL. He believed in the unity of existence and held that "being" is eternal reality, change an illusion.

Parmenion (pärmē'nēŭn), d. 330 B.C., Macedonian general under Philip II and Alexander the Great, prominent in Alexander's Persian battles. A plot against Alexander in 330 B.C. seemed to implicate Parmenion's son Philotas, who under torture accused his father. Alexander had both killed.

Parmigiano (pärmējä'nō) or **Parmigianino** (–jänē'nō), 1503–40, Italian painter, whose real name was Francesco Mazzola, b. Parma. Influenced by Correggio and Raphael. Best-known picture is *Cupid Making a Bow* (Vienna). Credited with introducing etching into Italy.

Parnaíba (pärnäē'bŭ), river, c.750 mi. long, rising in NE Brazil. Flows N to Atlantic near town of Parnaíba (pop. 30,900), which is shipping point for river valley.

Parnassians (pärnă'shŭnz), group of 19th-cent. French poets, named for their journal *Parnasse contemporain* (1866–76) and including Leconte de Lisle, Banville, Sully-Prudhomme, and Heredia. In reaction against romanticism, they stood for rigid forms and careful workmanship.

Parnassus (pärnă'sŭs), mountain, more than 8,000 ft. high, SW Phocis, Greece, sacred to Apollo, Dionysus, and the Muses; therefore a symbol of the apex of literature, art, and culture. The Castalian fountain was on its slopes. Here the Pythian games were held. At the foot lay Delphi.

Parnell, Charles Stewart, 1846–91, Irish nationalist leader. United diverse elements of Irish patriots. Elected to British parliament in 1875, he used filibusters to stress gravity of Irish problem. His agitation on the IRISH LAND QUESTION led to increased crime against landlords and he was arrested. Released after issuing popular no-rent manifesto from jail. Formed an alliance with Gladstone who introduced (1886) first HOME RULE Bill. Named co-respondent in divorce suit (1889), he lost his political influence, and died a broken man.

Parnell, Thomas, 1679–1718, British poet. He was a friend of Pope and Swift, and his verse (e.g., "The Hermit") was praised by Johnson and Goldsmith.

Paros (pâ'rŏs, Gr. pä'rôs), Aegean island (77 sq. mi.; pop. 8,993), Greece; one of the Cyclades. Famed for quarries of Parian marble, used by sculptors from 6th cent. B.C. After Persian Wars, Paros was taken into Athenian confederacy. The Parian Chronicle, found here, consists of two marble fragments of a great inscription relating events 1581 B.C.–263 B.C. The larger is at Oxford, the other at Paros.

Parowan (pă'rŭwăn″), city (pop. 1,455), SW Utah, NE of Cedar City. Nominal territorial cap. 1858–59.

Parr, Catherine, 1512–48, queen consort; sixth wife of Henry VIII of England. Served as queen regent in 1544. After Henry's death in 1547 she married Baron Seymour of Sudeley.

parrakeet: see PARAKEET.

Parran, Thomas (pä'rŭn), 1892–, American surgeon general (1936–48). Launched campaign against venereal diseases (1937). Wrote *Shadow on the Land* (1937).

Parrhasius (pûrā'shēŭs), fl. c.400 B.C., Greek painter. Reputedly the first painter to create figures with correct proportions and a sense of contour.

Parrington, Vernon L(ouis), 1871–1929, American educator and literary critic, author of *Main Currents in American Thought* (3 vols., 1927–30).

Parrish, Maxfield, 1870–, American illustrator and mural decorator. His brilliant colors (esp. blue) are characteristic.

Parris Island: see SEA ISLANDS.

parrot, name for certain members of order of birds (Psittaciformes) which includes PARAKEET, COCKATOO, and MACAW, occurring chiefly in tropics and subtropics of both hemispheres. In parrots the bill is strong and hooked; the feet have four toes. Many species learn to speak by imitation. See *ill.*, p. 135.

parrot fever: see PSITTACOSIS.

Parry, Sir William Edward, 1790–1855, British arctic explorer and rear admiral. Served in and commanded several expeditions seeking Northwest Passage. All were unsuccessful but informative.

Parry Islands, archipelago off N Canada, in Arctic Ocean; part of Franklin dist., Northwest Territories. Discovered by Sir W. E. Parry 1819–20.

Parry Sound, town (pop. 5,183), S Ont., Canada, on Parry Sound (inlet of Georgian Bay), NNW of Toronto. Resort with railroad shops, lumbering and woodworking.

Parsees: see PARSIS.

Parsifal (pär'sĭfäl), figure of ARTHURIAN LEGEND, also known as Sir Percivale, who is in turn a later form of a hero (also identified as Gawain) of Celtic myth. CHRESTIEN DE TROYES first wrote the story of the hero's quest for the HOLY GRAIL; WOLFRAM VON ESCHENBACH's *Parzival,* considered one of the greatest medieval poems, became the basis for Wagner's music drama *Parsifal.*

Parsis or **Parsees** (both: pär'sēz), religious community of India (esp. Bombay) practicing Zoroastrianism. They say they reverence, but do not worship, fire. The dead are exposed in "towers of silence," where vultures devour them. Parsis are important in cotton and steel industries. They stress education.

parsley, Old World aromatic herb (*Petroselinum crispum*). Its curly leaves are used as a garnish and in salads.

Parsnip, river rising in central B.C., Canada, and flowing 150 mi. NW to join Finlay R. and form Peace R. Became important fur-trade route after discovery by Sir Alexander Mackenzie in 1793.

parsnip, Old World vegetable plant (*Pastinaca sativa*), with edible fleshy roots.

Parsons, William: see ROSSE, WILLIAM PARSONS, 3d EARL OF.

Parsons, city (pop. 14,750), SE Kansas, W of Pittsburg; laid out 1870. Ships grain and dairy products.

parthenogenesis (pär″thŭnōjĕn'ŭsĭs), in biology, form of reproduction in which egg (female sexual cell) develops without fertilization (i.e., without union with sperm cell). It is considered sexual reproduction because the cell is an ovum, undergoing maturation as do other ova; in some cases it may develop whether fertilized or unfertilized. Eggs of several invertebrates yield to artificial parthenogenesis by mechanical or chemical stimulation.

Parthenon (pär'thŭnŏn) [Gr.,= the virgin's place], temple to Athena, built 447–432 B.C. on the ACROPOLIS at Athens; a masterpiece of Greek architecture. Its architects were Ictinus and Callicrates; Phidias supervised the sculpture. Has 8 Doric columns at front and rear and 17 along the two sides. Within the building, at W end of nave, stood the 40-ft. high *Athena Parthenos.* Friezes representing procession regularly held in homage to Athena formed a continuous band of sculpture around the building; of the 525 ft. of the frieze 335 ft. still exist (see ELGIN MARBLES). In 6th cent. the temple became a Christian church and later a mosque (with addition of a minaret). Used for storing gunpowder by the Turks in 1687, center section was destroyed by an explosion. Recognition of its beauty began 18th cent.; reconstruction work has continued up to the present.

Parthenopean Republic (pär″thŭnōpē'ŭn) [from Parthenope, anc. name of Naples], Jan.–June, 1799, set up in Naples by liberal leaders, under French auspices, after flight of Bourbon king. After military reverses in N Italy forced the French to evacuate, Naples fell to Cardinal RUFFO and Admiral Nelson.

Parthia (pär'thēŭ), anc. country of Asia, SE of the Caspian Sea, with heart of the region in modern Khurasan. The Parthians, of Scythian origin, were famous horsemen and archers in the Assyrian and Persian empires. Under Arsaces in 250 B.C. they shook off the rule of the Seleucids and estab. their own empire, which in the 1st cent. B.C. extended into India. They defeated the Romans under Crassus in 53 B.C., but they suffered defeat by the Romans 39–38 B.C. and began to decline. In A.D. 226 Ardashir I overthrew the Parthians finally and estab. the Sassanian empire. The expression "a Parthian shot" came from the Parthian ruse of pretending to flee in order to shoot arrows more successfully.

partridge, name used for various henlike birds

including ruffed grouse and bobwhite. True partridges are native to Old World; common European partridge has been introduced in parts of North America.

partridgeberry, small evergreen plant (*Mitchella repens*) of North American woods. Also known as squawberry and twinberry, it has white flowers borne in pairs and red berries which last all winter.

Parzifal: see PARSIFAL.

Pasadena (pă″sŭdē′nŭ). **1** Residential and resort city, (pop. 104,577), S Calif., NE of Los Angeles between San Gabriel Mts. and San Rafael Hills; founded 1874. Scene of annual Tournament of Roses and of post-season football game (Jan. 1) in Rose Bowl. Here are California Inst. of Technology (nonsectarian; for men; opened 1891), a technical school of university grade, which cooperates in Mt. Palomar and Mt. Wilson observatories; Pasadena Col. (Nazarene; coed.; 1901); playhouse; and Busch Gardens. **2** Town (pop. 22,483), S Texas, SE of Houston. Has oil refining and paper milling.

Pasargadae (pŭsär′gŭdē), anc. Persian city, NE of Persepolis, cap. under Cyrus the Great.

Pascagoula (păskŭgōō′lŭ), city (pop. 10,805), SE Miss., port on Mississippi Sound at mouth of Pascagoula R.; grew around "Old Spanish Fort" 1718. Resort; pecan, fishing, and boatbuilding center. Has U.S. dry docks and coast guard base.

Pascal, Blaise (blĕz′ päskäl′), 1623–62, French scientist and religious philosopher. His family embraced Jansenism, and Pascal himself lived for a time at Port-Royal and wrote the ironic *Provincial Letters* (1656) in defense of Jansenism. His religious writings, collected in *Pensées* (1670), are profoundly mystical and extremely pure in literary style. His scientific work was wide: he laid the foundation for the modern theory of probabilities, invented the mathematical triangle (Pascal's triangle), discovered the properties of the cycloid, advanced differential calculus, and formulated Pascal's law.

Pascal's law [for Blaise Pascal] states that pressure applied to confined fluid at any point is transmitted undiminished through fluid in all directions and acts upon every part of confining vessel at right angles to its interior surfaces and equally on equal areas.

Paschal II (pă′skŭl), d. 1118, pope (1099–1118), a Cluniac monk and member of the reform group of Gregory VII. In his reign Philip I of France was reconciled with the Church, St. Anselm triumphed in England, and Emperor Henry IV was deposed, but Henry V invaded Italy (1110), seized the pope and made him surrender the papal position on investiture. Paschal later repudiated this surrender to force. Succeeded by Gelasius II. Also Pascal.

Pasco (păs′kō), city (pop. 10,228), SE Wash., near junction of Columbia and Snake rivers. Farm trade center and rail junction. Boomed in World War II by atomic project near Richland.

Pascoli, Giovanni (jōvän′nē pä′skōlē), 1855–1912, Italian poet. He wrote thoughtful idyllic verse.

Pas-de-Calais (pä-dŭ-kälā′), department (2,607 sq. mi.; pop. 1,168,545), N France, on Strait of Dover (Fr. *Pas de Calais*); cap. Arras.

Pashitch, Nikola (nē′kôlä pä′shĭch), Serbo-Croatian *Pašić*, 1846–1926, Serbian statesman. He controlled Serbia from 1903 to his death and was repeatedly premier. His pro-Russian, anti-Austrian policy was a factor leading to World War I. In 1917 he negotiated the union of Serbia, Croatia, and Slovenia (see YUGOSLAVIA).

Pasiphaë (pŭsĭ′fäē), in Greek legend, wife of Minos and mother of Ariadne and Phaedra. When Poseidon gave Minos a bull for sacrifice, Minos kept it for himself. Poseidon aroused a passion for the bull in Pasiphaë, who bore the monstrous Minotaur.

Paso Robles (pă′sō rō′bŭlz, pä′sō rō′blĕs), resort city (pop. 4,835), S Calif., on Salinas R. and N of San Luis Obispo. Has hot springs.

pasqueflower (păsk–), wild flower (*Anemone patens*) of North American prairie regions, with open bluish flowers followed by silvery heads of feathery seeds. Its European counterpart (*A. pulsatilla*) is a spring garden flower.

Passaic (pŭsā′ĭk, pŭsăk′), city (pop. 57,702), NE N.J., on Passaic R. and N of Newark; settled 1678 by Dutch traders as Acquackanonk. Developed industrially in late 19th cent.; textile and metal-products center. Famous strike here (1926), against wage cut, involved right of free assembly.

Passaic, river, c.80 mi. long, rising SW of Morristown, N.J., and winding S, then N to Paterson (c.70-ft. falls), then S again to Newark Bay. Power aided industrial growth of many towns in NE N.J.

Passamaquoddy Bay (păsŭmŭkwŏ′dē), inlet of Bay of Fundy, between Maine and N.B., at mouth of St. Croix R. Most of it (including Campobello island) is in Canada. Towns on the bay are St. Andrews and St. George (N.B.), Lubec (at entrance) and Eastport (Maine). Hydroelectric project (also called Quoddy project), begun 1935 with PWA funds to harness heavy tides (18-ft. average range) in U.S. sector, was suspended after Congress refused funds (1936).

Passarowitz, Treaty of (päsä′rōvĭts), 1718, signed at Pozarevac (Ger. *Passarowitz*), Yugoslavia, between Turkey and Holy Roman Empire and Venice. In war of 1714–18 the Turks had defeated the Venetians in Greece and Crete and the imperials had defeated the Turks in the Balkans. In the treaty, Turkey lost the Banat of Temesvar and N Serbia (incl. Belgrade) to Emperor Charles VI but gained all Venetian possessions in the Peloponnesus and on Crete.

Passau (pä′sou), city (pop. 34,338), Lower Bavaria, on Austrian border; a port on confluence of Danube and Inn rivers. Textile and machinery mfg. Seat of prince-bishopric till 1803. Has fine Gothic and baroque architecture. By Treaty of Passau (1552) King Ferdinand I (representing Emperor Charles V) secured agreement of the Protestant princes to submit the religious question to a diet; the Peace of AUGSBURG resulted (1555).

Passchendale, formerly **Passchendaele** (both pä′sŭndä″lŭ), small town near Ypres, Belgium. In World War I it was carried by the

British after heavy losses (1917); retaken by the Germans (1918).

Pass Christian (păs″ krĭs″chēăn′), resort city (pop. 3,383), SE Miss., on Mississippi Sound.

passenger pigeon, extinct E North American wild pigeon, abundant until late 19th cent. In form and color it resembled the smaller mourning dove.

passionflower, chiefly tropical American vine of genus *Passiflora.* The most common North American species, *Passiflora incarnata,* native from Va. to Texas, has purple and white flowers and edible fruits called maypops. Others are grown in the tropics and in greenhouses in northern regions.

Passion play, genre of miracle play about Jesus' suffering and death—surviving from Middle Ages into modern times. First given in Latin, by 15th cent. they were entirely in German. Chief surviving Passion play is that at Oberammergau, Bavaria.

passive: see VOICE.

Passover, Jewish festival celebrating the deliverance of the Israelites from bondage in Egypt. The observance begins on the evening of the 14th of Nisan (first month of the religious calendar, corresponding to March-April) and lasts seven days. The narrative of the Exodus is recited at the ceremonial evening meals (called Seders) which are served during the first and second nights of the festival. Only unleavened bread (matzoth) may be eaten during the seven days of Passover, in memory of the fact that the Jews, hastening from Egypt, had no time to leaven their bread. The Christian feast of Easter is calculated from the Pasch or Passover.

Passy, Frédéric (päsē′), 1822–1912, French internationalist. Abandoned law for journalism and study of economics and the problems of peace. He founded (1867) a French society to promote international arbitration and (with Sir William R. Cremer) the Interparliamentary Union of Arbitration. Wrote much on peace. Awarded, with J. H. Dunant, the first (1901) Nobel Peace Prize.

Pasternak, Boris Leonidovich (bŭrēs′ lyä″ūnyē′-dŭvĭch pŭstyĭrnäk′), 1890–, Russian poet. Began as futurist, but his talent transcends classification. His work includes two narrative poems (*Spektorsky,* 1926; *The Year 1905,* 1927). See his *Collected Prose Works* (Eng. tr., 1945); *Selected Poems* (Eng. tr., 1947).

Pasteur, Louis (păstŭr′), 1822–95, French chemist. Through his experiments with bacteria he exploded the myth of spontaneous generation. His work on wine, vinegar, and beer led to PASTEURIZATION. He solved the problems of control of silkworm disease and chicken cholera. He developed the technique of vaccination against anthrax and extended it to hydrophobia. **Pasteur Institute,** opened in Paris in 1888, includes clinic for treatment of hydrophobia and teaching and research center for work on virulent and contagious diseases. Pasteur Institutes have been estab. in other countries.

pasteurization (păs″chōōrĭzā′shŭn), method of treating foods, especially milk, to make them free from disease-causing bacteria. Milk is heated to c.145° F. for 30 min., then cooled rapidly.

Pasto (pä′stō), city (pop. 27,564), SW Colombia; founded 1539. It was a royalist city in revolution against Spain. Volcano El Pasto is near by.

Paston Letters, collection of personal and business correspondence of Paston family of Norfolk and others, 1422–1509; indispensable source for history and customs of England at close of Middle Ages.

Pastor, Tony, c.1837–1908, American theater manager. Opened his first theater in 1861. Introduced many performers who became famous; made vaudeville suitable for a mixed audience.

pastoral (pă′stŭrŭl), literary work in which shepherd life is presented in conventionalized manner. Contrasts pure simplicity of shepherd life to corrupt artificiality of court and city. Many subjects have been presented in pastoral setting. Theocritus, 3d cent. B.C., wrote first pastoral poetry recorded, and delineated the Daphnis, Lycidas, Corydon, and Amaryllis of pastoral convention. Vergil's *Bucolics* (37 B.C.) present unrealistic characters and landscape (Arcadia); allegorical scenes celebrate Roman greatness, prophesy a golden age. Renaissance saw great revival of pastoral eclogue. Milton's "Lycidas" (1637) is most famous pastoral elegy in English. Except for Shelley's *Adonais* (1821) and Matthew Arnold's *Thyrsis* (1866), 19th and 20th cent. poets rarely use conventions of Vergil and Theocritus.

pastry, general name for foods made wholly or partly of paste, which is composed of flour, liquid (milk, water, or beaten egg), and shortening; best-known form is pie crust. Name is also given to small fancy sweets ("French pastry") and bunlike Danish pastry.

Patagonia (pătŭgō′nēŭ), region primarily in S Argentina, S of Río Colorado and E of Andes, but including extreme SE Chile and N TIERRA DEL FUEGO. Patagonia, except for S plains, subandean region, and Andes, is vast semiarid grassy plateau, terminating in cliffs along Atlantic. In W are large lakes fed by Andean glaciers. (Nahuel Huapí National Park, estab. 1934, is resort area here.) Sheep raising is principal industry in Patagonia, although oil production around Comodoro Rivadavia is of great importance. The coast, probably first visited by Vespucci (1501), was explored by Magellan (1520). Area not permanently settled until late in 19th cent. Has more than half Argentina's territory but sparse population.

Patan (pä′tŭn), city (pop. 104,928), Nepal, near Katmandu. Has ancient Buddhist temples.

Patapsco (pŭtăp′skō), river rising in N Md. Flows c.65 mi. SE to Chesapeake Bay SE of Baltimore.

Patay (pätā′), village (pop. 1,313), Loiret dept., N central France, NW of Orléans. Here Joan of Arc defeated the English in 1429.

Patchogue (pă′chäg″), resort and fishing village (pop. 7,361), SE N.Y., on S shore (Great South Bay) of Long Isl.

patchouli (păch′ōōlē), fragrant shrubby plant (*Pogostemon heyneanus*) of India. It yields an essential oil, used in the perfume patchouli.

Patel, Vallabhbhai (vŭ'lŭbī pŭtĕl'), 1876–1950, Indian statesman. As deputy prime minister of India (1947), he directed the integration of the numerous princely states into the new political structure.

Patenier, Joachim de: see PATINIR, JOACHIM DE.

Pater, Walter (Horatio) (pā'tŭr), 1839–94, English essayist and critic, long at Brasenose Col., Oxford. He was the leader of a movement stressing the moral importance of artistic perfection, urging that literature should "burn with a hard, gemlike flame." His own writing is superb in precision and clarity. Among his works are *Studies in the History of the Renaissance* (1873), *Marius the Epicurean* (1885; his masterpiece), *Imaginary Portraits* (1887), and *Plato and Platonism* (1893).

Pater Noster: see LORD'S PRAYER.

Paterson, William, 1658–1719, British financier, adviser to William III, and projector (1691) of the Bank of England. He also promoted (1695) the ill-fated DARIEN SCHEME. Advocated union of Scotland and England.

Paterson, William, 1745–1806, American statesman, b. Ireland. Set forth the New Jersey or small-state plan in Federal Constitutional Convention. U.S. Senator (1789–90).

Paterson, city (pop. 139,336), NE N.J., at Passaic R. falls and N of Newark; founded 1791 by Alexander Hamilton. Water power used for cotton spinning after 1794. Important silk industry started 1839; first loom for silk fabric built here 1842. Industry characterized by many small "family" shops; has had numerous strikes, notably in 1912–13, 1933, 1936. City devastated by fire, flood, and tornado, 1902. In World War II nylon, rubber, aircraft, and metal industries employed many former silk workers. Public library designed by Henry Bacon.

Patiala and East Punjab States Union (pŭtēä'lŭ, pŭnjäb'), state (10,099 sq. mi.; pop. 3,468,631), NW India; cap. Patiala. A center of Sikh population. Formed 1948 by merging eight former princely states. Name often abbreviated as Pepsu.

Patinir, Patenier, or **Patiner, Joachim de** (all: yō'äkhĭm dŭ pätĭnēr'), c.1485–1524, first Flemish painter to subordinate figures to landscape.

Patiño, Simón Iturí (sēmōn' ētōō'rē pätē'nyō), 1886–1947, Bolivian capitalist, owner of tin mines and other enterprises in Bolivia. His fortune was considered one of largest in world.

Patmore, Coventry (Kersey Dighton), 1823–96, English poet, associated with the Pre-Raphaelites. *The Angel in the House* (1854–63) is on married love, *The Unknown Eros* (1877) is a series of odes on his conversion to Catholicism.

Patmos (păt'môs), Aegean island (13 sq. mi.; pop. 2,428), Greece, off SW Asia Minor, in the Dodecanese. St. John the Divine wrote the Revelation here.

Patna (păt'nŭ), city (pop. 196,415), cap. of Bihar, India, on the Ganges. As Pataliputra, it was cap. of Maghada kingdom in 6th cent. B.C. Univ. of Patna opened 1917. Cotton mills.

Patras (pŭträs', pă'trŭs), Gr. *Patrai,* city (pop. 88,414), Greece, in N Peloponnesus; a port near head of Gulf of Patras, which connects Gulf of Corinth with the Ionian Sea. Commercial and industrial center (exports currants, olive oil, wine, citrus fruit). In antiquity, Patras was a member of both Achaean Leagues. Was held by Venice in 15th cent.; later passed to Turkey, but was again held by Venice 1687–1715. Destroyed 1821 in Greek War of Independence, it was rebuilt.

patriarch (pā'trēärk) [Gr.,= head of a family], revered male head of a kinship group; in the Bible, one of the antediluvian progenitors of the race or one of the ancestors of the Jews (Abraham, Isaac, Jacob, the sons of Jacob). The name, therefore, came to be used as a high title in Christian churches, especially E churches. Original patriarchates were those of Alexandria, Antioch, and Rome (the bishop—not patriarch—of Rome; the pope). To these were added Constantinople (chief prelate of the Byzantine Empire) and Jerusalem. The triumph of heresies created new churches, many headed by patriarchs. In the Russian Church a patriarch of Moscow was set up (1589), abolished by Peter I (1721), reestab. 1917 (see ORTHODOX EASTERN CHURCH).

patriarchy (pā'trēär"kē), term, meaning "father right," used to designate certain features of family or kinship group ruled by father or eldest male. In patriarchal family, succession is in male line, the patriarch's name, property, and authority passing to sons. Patriarchal family is strongly developed among nomads of Asia and in Africa, China, and Japan, and in ancient times was firmly estab. in Palestine, Greece, and Rome.

Patrick, Saint, c.385–461, Christian missionary, called the Apostle of Ireland. His life is shrouded in legend, and even the dates of birth and death are obscure. He is said to have been born in Britain and enslaved by the Irish until, in response to a voice, he escaped and went to Gaul. Later he studied at Auxerre and went as missionary to Ireland, where he converted many. In 441 he went to Rome and received the pallium from the pope. Later he was archbishop of Armagh. When he retired (457) Ireland was Christian. He wrote much, including his *Confessions* and probably *The Lorica of St. Patrick* (called also *The Cry of the Deer*). Buried at Downpatrick. Feast: March 17.

Patrimony of Saint Peter: see PAPAL STATES.

patristic literature, writings of the Christian Church Fathers in the first few centuries of the Christian era. They are in Greek and in Latin. Early writings are principally apologetics, addressed to pagans or to Christians in disagreement with the author. Later they were more devoted to larger theological works, sermons, and exegesis of Scripture. Among the many authors are St. Clement I, St. Ignatius of Antioch, St. Justin Martyr, Origen, Tertullian, St. Cyprian, Eusebius of Caesarea, St. Gregory Nazianzen, St. Basil the Great, St. John Chrysostom, St. Ambrose, St. Jerome, St. Gregory I, St. John of Damascus. The 3d-cent. writers are called the ante-Nicene Fathers, the later ones post-Nicene

Patroclus (pŭtrō'klŭs), in Greek legend (esp

in the *Iliad*), hero of the Trojan War, intimate friend of Achilles. When Patroclus was slain fighting in his place, Achilles returned to battle and slew Hector. Thus Patroclus' excursion is crux of the epic.

Patrons of Husbandry: see GRANGER MOVEMENT.

Patterson, family of American journalists. **Robert Wilson Patterson,** 1850–1910, was editor-in-chief of the Chicago *Tribune* (1899–1910). He married daughter of the owner, Joseph MEDILL. His son, **Joseph Medill Patterson,** 1879–1946, was coeditor of the *Tribune* (1914–25) with his cousin, R. R. MCCORMICK. Founded New York *Daily News,* first successful tabloid in country, in 1919. His sister, **Eleanor Medill Patterson,** 1884–1948, merged Washington newspapers to form *Times-Herald* (1939). "Cissy" Patterson became well known for her spectacular news presentation.

Patterson, Elizabeth, 1785–1879, American wife of Jérôme Bonaparte, and celebrated beauty. Marriage performed in 1803 was annulled by Napoleon in 1806.

Patterson, Robert Porter, 1891–1952, U.S. Secretary of War (1945–47). Designed unification of armed forces under single establishment.

Patti, Adelina (pă'tē), 1843–1919, coloratura soprano, b. Madrid of Italian parents. She made her debut in New York in 1859 and eventually became the most popular and most highly paid singer of her day.

Patton, George S(mith), Jr., 1885–1945, American general. As commander of 3d Army he spearheaded the spectacular final thrusts of U.S. forces in Europe in World War II.

Pátzcuaro (pät'skwärō), lake, Michoacán, W. Mexico; popular resort area. Town of Pátzcuaro (pop. 9,557) is primarily Tarascan fishing settlement.

Patzinaks: see PETCHENEGS.

Pau (po), city (pop. 40,604), cap. of Basses-Pyrénées dept., SW France; a tourist center at foot of the Pyrenees. It was the cap. of Béarn and the residence of the kings of Navarre. Birthplace of Henry IV.

Paul, Saint, d. A.D. 67?, the apostle to the Gentiles, one of the greatest figures in the history of the Christian church, b. Tarsus. He was a Jew, originally named Saul, a tentmaker by trade, and a Roman citizen. Educated in Jerusalem, he was a zealous Jewish nationalist. To trace the course of his life minutely is difficult. The chief sources are the Acts of the Apostles and the EPISTLES attributed to Paul himself. These Epistles are recognized as masterpieces of world literature as well as fountainheads of Christian doctrine. Of them several are undoubtedly by him (Romans, 1 and 2 Corinthians, 1 Thessalonians, Philemon), two are accepted by all but a few as his (Ephesians, 2 Thessalonians), three are considered by many to be in their present form later (1 and 2 Timothy, Titus), and one is usually said not to have been written by Paul, though possibly at his request (Hebrews). Paul's first contact with the Christians was his approving presence at the martyrdom of St. Stephen. Soon afterward (A.D. 35?) he was on his way to Damascus to help suppress Christianity there, when he was halted by a blinding light and a Voice asking, "Why persecutest thou me?" Thus was he converted to Christianity. Saul turned Paul was the greatest of all early Christian missionaries. With different companions he went about the Near East and the Greek world, making conversions, setting up churches, and ever moving on to spread the Gospel. In Jerusalem (A.D. 57) he was arrested for provoking a riot and imprisoned two years before being sent to Rome, where he was again imprisoned (A.D. 60–62) before being cleared of all charges. He was apparently martyred in the persecution under Nero, traditionally by beheading and traditionally on the same day that Peter was killed. They are commemorated together on June 29; the conversion of St. Paul is celebrated on Jan. 25.

Paul III, 1468–1549, pope (1534–49), a Roman named Alessandro Farnese. His election ushered in the Catholic REFORM. After long preparation the Council of TRENT began in 1545. He favored the reform party and encouraged the new Society of Jesus. Paul created the modern Congregation of the Holy Office (see INQUISITION **3**). He also was an art patron, founded the Farnese Palace, and had Michelangelo decorate the Sistine Chapel.

Paul IV, 1476–1559, pope (1555–59), a Neapolitan named Gian Pietro Carafa. A strict ascetic monk and a rigid reformer, he did much to purify the clergy and to do away with papal wordliness and nepotism. His rigidity brought him into conflict with all the Catholic monarchs, even Mary Tudor.

Paul V, 1552–1621, pope (1605–21), a Roman named Camillo Borghese, an expert in canon law. He tried to reassert all the lay powers the pope had ever enjoyed, but he was defeated in a quarrel with Venice that ended in 1607 and did not fare well in arguments with the French and English kings. He built the Villa Borghese and was responsible for a lovely chapel in the Church of Santa Maria Maggiore.

Paul I, 1754–1801, emperor and tsar of Russia (1796–1801); son and successor of Catherine II. He joined in the Second Coalition against France but withdrew in the same year (1799; see FRENCH REVOLUTIONARY WARS) and concluded the Northern Convention with Sweden, Denmark and Prussia, aimed against British rules on neutral shipping (1800). His insanity, which often was violent, became apparent, and a conspiracy was formed to force his abdication. When Paul refused, the conspirators, crazed by fear, strangled him. His son and successor, Alexander I, was a party to the plot but was blameless in the murder.

Paul, 1901–, king of the Hellenes (1947–); brother and successor of George II.

Paul, Jean: see RICHTER, JOHANN PAUL FRIEDRICH.

Paulding, James Kirke, 1779–1860, American author, Secretary of the Navy under Van Buren. He collaborated with Washington Irving in producing *Salmagundi,* wrote the satirical *John Bull in America* (1825), tales, novels (e.g., *Koningsmarke,* 1823; *The*

Dutchman's Fireside, 1831), and a life of Washington.

Pauli, Wolfgang (vŏlf′gäng pou′lē), 1900–, Austrian physicist. Won 1945 Nobel Prize for discovery of exclusion principle, according to which no two electrons in atom may be in same quantum state.

Paulicians (pôlĭ′shůnz), Christian heretical sect holding obscure tenets. Almost certainly they were dualists and they may have taken doctrines from Manichaeism. They rejected sacraments, images, and much of the Bible. They had arisen by the 4th cent., and some believe them to have been a survival of primitive Christianity. They were strong in the Byzantine Empire by the 7th cent. and though put down in the time of Michael III they persisted in Thrace. In Bulgaria they joined the Bogomils.

Paulist Fathers, order of Roman Catholic priests (in full, Society of Missionary Priests of St. Paul the Apostle); founded 1858 by Isaac HECKER primarily for the purpose of converting Americans.

Paul Knutson (nōōt′sůn, kůnōōt′sůn), fl. 1354–64, Norse leader, alleged to have explored America.

Paullus, Aemilius, c.229–169 B.C., Roman general, consul (182 B.C., 168 B.C.). He defeated Perseus of Macedon at Pydna (168 B.C.) and made Macedon a Roman province. Also Paulus.

Paul of Aegina (ējī′nů), 7th cent.?, Greek physician, author of influential treatise on surgery. Known also as Paulus Aegineta.

Paul of Samosata (sůmŏ′sůtů), fl. 260–72, Syrian theologian, who enjoyed the favor of Zenobia of Palmyra. He denied the doctrine of the Trinity. His teachings influenced Arius, Nestorius, and, possibly, the Paulicians.

Paulsboro, borough (pop. 7,842), SW N.J., near Delaware R. and SW of Camden. Fortified in the Revolution. Oil refineries, chemical plants.

Pauls Valley, city (pop. 6,896), S central Okla., on Washita R. and SW of Ada, in rich agr. area. Oil industries.

Paul the Deacon, c.725–799?, Lombard historian, also called Paulus Diaconus. Chief work is history of Lombards in 6th, 7th, and 8th cent.

Paulus (pô′lůs), fl. c.200, Roman jurist.

Paulus, Aemilius: see PAULLUS, AEMILIUS.

Paulus Diaconus: see PAUL THE DEACON.

Paulus Hook, N.J.: see JERSEY CITY.

Paumotu: see TUAMOTU ISLANDS.

Pausanias (pôsā′nēůs), d. c.470 B.C., Spartan general, victor at the battle of Plataea in the Persian Wars. Twice he was accused of treason to Sparta, the second time taking refuge in a temple, where he starved to death.

Pausanias, fl. A.D. 174, traveler and geographer, probably b. Lydia. His *Description of Greece* is valuable source on ancient Greek topography, monuments, and legends.

Pausias (pô′shēůs), fl. 1st half of 4th cent. B.C., Greek painter, famous for decorative works. *A Sacrifice* is preserved in Pompey's temple, Rome.

pavement, wearing surface of road, street, or sidewalk. Paving surfaces include concrete, penetration macadam, bituminous-mixed macadam, sheet asphalt, bituminous concrete, and brick, wood, or stone-block pavements. Subgrade must be shaped and rolled; concrete road slab is commonly used as foundation. Both foundation and surface should be crowned or sloped for shedding of water and, if concrete, provided with expansion joints. Concrete is often reinforced with steel mesh or bars. ROMAN ROADS were noted for durable paving; cobblestones were common from Middle Ages to 19th cent.; MACADAM ROAD was popular in 19th cent.

Pavia (pävē′ä), city (pop. 40,208), Lombardy, N Italy, on Ticino R. near its confluence with the Po. It was the cap. of the Lombard and Carolingian kingdoms of Italy; became a free commune 12th cent.; fell to VISCONTI family 1359; shared later history of Lombardy. In 1525 Emperor Charles V defeated and captured Francis I of France near Pavia. Its celebrated law school, founded 11th cent., became a university 1361. The most notable building is the celebrated CERTOSA DI PAVIA.

Pavlov, Ivan Petrovich (ēvän′ pētrô′vĭch päv′lůf), 1849–1936, Russian physiologist, pioneer in study of conditioned reflexes. Won 1904 Nobel Prize in Physiology and Medicine for work on digestive glands.

Pavlova, Anna Matveyevna (pävlō′vů), 1882–1931, Russian ballet dancer, famed for classic technique and ethereal quality. After European tours she made U.S. debut in 1910. Excelled in *Giselle* and in *The Dying Swan* (composed for her by Fokine).

Pavlovsk (päv′lůfsk), city (pop. over 10,000), RSFSR, near Leningrad. Formerly a summer residence of St. Petersburg nobility.

Pawcatuck, Conn.: see STONINGTON.

Pawhuska (pôhŭ′sků), city (pop. 5,331), NE Okla., NW of Tulsa, in oil, agr., and stock area. Osage Indian cap.; has tribal museum.

Pawling, village (pop. 1,430), E N.Y., SE of Poughkeepsie, in hilly country; settled c.1740 by Quakers. Trinity-Pawling School for boys is here.

Pawnee Indians (pônē′), North American tribe of Caddoan linguistic stock, possibly once living in Texas, but by the time of Coronado's visit (1541) apparently in the Platte R. valley. Later they extended their territory to the Republican R. and the Niobrara R. Though fierce fighters against the Cheyenne they were friendly to the U.S. and helped protect the builders of the Union Pacific. Put on a reservation in present Okla. in 1876. Also spelled Pani.

pawpaw: see PAPAW TREE.

Pawtucket (půtŭ′kĕt), industrial city (pop. 81,436), NE R.I., on Blackstone R. at Pawtucket Falls. Area deeded to Roger Williams 1638; city was in Mass. until 1862. Mfg. of textiles, electrical equipment, machinery metal, paper, wood products. Samuel Slater built first successful water-power cotton mill in U.S. here 1790; Slater mill (1793) now museum. Narragansett race track is in Pawtucket and East Providence.

Pax, in Roman religion, goddess of Peace.

Payette (păĕt′), city (pop. 4,032), W Idaho near junction of Payette R. and Snake R. Serves BOISE PROJECT and Vale project Oregon.

Payette, river rising in mountains of W Idaho

and flowing c.70 mi. S and W to Snake R. near Payette; used in BOISE PROJECT.

Payne, John Howard, 1791–1852, American actor and playwright, famous for song *Home, Sweet Home,* in his opera, *Clari, the Maid of Milan* (London, 1823).

Payne-Aldrich Tariff Act, 1909, passed by U.S. Congress. Sponsored by Rep. Sereno E. Payne and Sen. Nelson W. Aldrich. Less aggressively protectionist than McKinley Tariff Act of 1890 and Dingley Act of 1897. Adopted principle of max. and min. tariffs for compelling concessions from other countries.

Paysandú (pīsändōō'), city (pop. 46,000), cap. of Paysandú dept., W Uruguay, port on Uruguay R., founded 1772. In rich stock raising and farming region, it is at head of ocean navigation.

Payson, city (pop. 3,998), N central Utah, near Utah L.; served by STRAWBERRY VALLEY PROJECT.

Pazmany, Peter, Hung. *Pázmány* (päz'mänyů), 1570–1637, Hungarian cardinal. A convert from Calvinism, he entered the Society of Jesus, became primate of Hungary, and, without coercion, won a large part of his people back to Catholicism. He founded a university at Trnava (later transferred to Budapest) and wrote many literary works.

Pazzi conspiracy (pät'tsē), 1478, against Lorenzo and Giuliano de' MEDICI to end family's hegemony in Florence. Largely carried out by the Pazzi family, it had the support of Pope SIXTUS IV. During Mass in cathedral, Giuliano was stabbed to death while Lorenzo escaped. Conspirators were killed; the Medici remained in power.

Pb, chemical symbol of the element LEAD.

Pd, chemical symbol of the element PALLADIUM.

pea, annual climbing leguminous plant (*Pisum sativum*), with edible pod-borne seeds high in protein, grown in home gardens and commercially for canning. The plants are used for forage. Split peas are obtained from the field pea (*P. arvense*). The CHICK-PEA and SWEET PEA belong to other genera.

Peabody, Elizabeth Palmer, 1804–94, American educator, lecturer, and reformer. With her sister Mary (wife of Horace Mann) she estab. school near Boston. After its failure she turned to writing history textbooks and lecturing. Her path crossed those of most of great New Englanders of her day, and her bookshop in Boston (1840–49) was a literary center. She also did some publishing: notably the *Dial,* pamphlets of Anti-Slavery Society, and some of Hawthorne's early works. In 1861 she opened one of first kindergartens in U.S., and she later estab. first kindergarten training school in U.S.

Peabody, Endicott, 1857–1944, American educator, founder of Groton School, Groton, Mass., in 1884.

Peabody, Francis Greenwood, 1847–1936, American Unitarian theologian; pastor (1874–80) of First Parish Church, Cambridge; teacher (1881–1913) at Harvard.

Peabody, George, 1795–1869, American financier and philanthropist. Became prosperous broker in London. Numerous philanthropies include Peabody Education Fund, given to promote education in the South.

Peabody, city (pop. 22,645), NE Mass., adjoining W Salem. Tanning (since early 18th cent.).

Peace, river of N B.C., Canada, formed by union of Parsnip and Finlay rivers. Flows E into Alta., then N and ENE to Great Slave R. near L. Athabaska. Was fur-trade route. Settlement in fertile valley dates from early 20th cent. Length 1,054 mi. to head of Finlay R.

peace congresses. Although PACIFISM is almost as old as war, organized efforts to outlaw war began in middle of 19th cent. Term "peace congress" applies to meetings of diplomats to end specific wars by acceptable treaties, and to convenings of internationalists to prevent future wars. International peace efforts have in general followed five lines: international arbitration; a league of nations or international authority; codification of international law by tribunal such as WORLD COURT or INTERNATIONAL COURT OF JUSTICE; sanctions or international coercion of state adjudged in wrong; and disarmament. First international peace congress met in London 1843, followed by series of conferences and Universal Peace Congress in London 1851. Agitation for peace was stopped for many years by Crimean War, then by American Civil War, but after Franco-Prussian War (1870–71) efforts were renewed. Important Paris Congress met in 1878, first Pan-American Conference in 1889. The First Hague Conference estab. the Permanent Court of Arbitration (1899). Again all peace efforts were interrupted by World War I, but from Versailles Treaty were born LEAGUE OF NATIONS and World Court. Between two world wars NAVAL CONFERENCES were held at Washington and at London; with DISARMAMENT CONFERENCE and other meetings, they led to KELLOGG-BRIAND PACT and LOCARNO PACT. Horrors of World War II intensified world-wide peace movements, with much hope and determination that UNITED NATIONS would succeed where the League had failed.

peach, fruit tree (*Prunus persica*) with decorative pink blossoms and a juicy, fine-flavored stone fruit. Native to China, it is an important fruit of temperate climates. The Elberta is the chief commercial variety. Purple-leaved and double-flowering forms are grown for ornament. The nectarine is a smooth-skinned variety of peach (*P. persica nectarina*) cultivated from early times.

Peacock, Thomas Love, 1785–1866, English novelist and poet. His rather eccentric novels blend satire and extravagant romance, with lyrics interspersed. They include *Headlong Hall* (1816), *Melincourt* (1817), *Nightmare Abbey* (1818), *Crotchet Castle* (1831), and *Gryll Grange* (1860).

peacock, large forest bird of pheasant family. Male is the peacock; female is peahen. Common peacock is found in India and Ceylon, the Burmese or Javan peacock in Indo-China. Male displays during courtship the green and gold erectile tail marked by eye-like spots.

Peacock Throne: see DELHI.

Peak, the, tableland c.30 mi. long and 22 mi. wide, Derbyshire, England, forming S extremity of Pennine Chain. Highest point is Kinderscout (2,088 ft.).

Peaks of Otter: see OTTER, PEAKS OF.

Peale, Charles Willson, 1741–1827, American portrait painter. Studied under J. S. Copley and Benjamin West. Painted earliest known portrait of Washington (1772; Washington and Lee Univ.). Succeeded Copley as most popular portrait painter in U.S. His brother, **James Peale,** 1749–1831, painted landscapes and miniature portraits. Of his 11 children, three became painters—**Raphaelle Peale,** 1774–1825, who painted still lifes; **Titian Peale,** 1799–1885, who did portraits; and **Rembrandt Peale,** 1778–1860, who was a portrait and historical painter.

peanut, annual leguminous plant (*Arachis hypogaea*), and its edible seeds, usually two to a pod. Native to South America, it is an important crop in S U.S. The seeds are eaten fresh or roasted, used in confectionery, and yield an oil, peanut butter, and other products. The plants are used for forage. Goober and groundnut are other names.

pear, fruit tree of genus *Pyrus* (closely related to the apple), and its fruit, grown for canning as well as for eating fresh. Most varieties come from two species, the common European pear (*Pyrus communis*) and the Oriental pear (*P. pyrifolia*). Leading varieties in the U.S. include Bartlett, Kieffer, Seckel, Anjou, Bosc, and Comice.

Pea Ridge, chain of hills, NW Ark., where Civil War battle of Pea Ridge (or Elkhorn Tavern) was fought March 6–8, 1862. Strongly entrenched Union army defeated Confederate attack.

Pearl, river, China: see CANTON, river.

Pearl, river, rising in E central Miss. and flowing 485 mi. SW and S to L. Borgne, Gulf of Mexico inlet. Forms Miss.–La. boundary for 116 mi.

Pearl, The, one of four anonymous alliterative poems composed c.1370–90 in West Midland dialect by a gifted Middle English poet. *The Pearl* is usually explained as an allegorical elegy for the poet's little daughter. *Patience* and *Cleanness* or *Purity* teach those virtues. *Sir Gawain and the Green Knight,* one of greatest medieval romances, recounts the adventures of Gawain, one of King Arthur's knights.

pearl, secretion of certain mollusks used as a gem. It is formed of the same organic material as the mollusk shell, usually with a grain of sand or a parasite as nucleus. Pearls occur in various shapes and colors. Main sources are pearl oyster and the fresh-water mussel. Cultured pearls are produced by inserting a bead in the mantle of pearl oyster.

Pearl Harbor, U.S. naval base, S Oahu, T.H. A key naval base with installations and anchorages around 10 sq. mi. of navigable water. Air bases at Fords Isl. and Barbers Point. In area are also army, air force, and marine bases (e.g., Hickham Field, Ewa). U.S. gained coaling and repair station here 1887; it became naval station 1900. The base was strengthened, especially after signing of Axis Pact (1940). Japanese attack on Pearl Harbor, Dec. 7, 1941, severely damaged installations and plunged U.S. into World War II. Charges of negligence on part of those responsible for base's defense resulted in a commission accusing (1942) Gen. W. C. Short and Adm. H. E. Kimmel of dereliction of duty. Army and navy announced (1944) that no grounds existed for court-martial. A congressional committee report (1946) found Pres. Roosevelt blameless, absolved Kimmel and Short, but censured War Dept. and Dept. of the Navy.

pearl millet, annual grass (*Pennisetum glaucum*) of the E Hemisphere, grown from anc. times for food. It has spikes of white grains. Indian millet is another name.

Pearse, Patrick Henry, 1879–1916, Irish educator and patriot. Active in Gaelic League. Leader of Irish forces in Easter Rebellion (1916), he was shot.

Pearson, Sir Cyril Arthur, 1866–1921, English publisher. He founded and directed the London *Daily Express* (1900), as well as several periodicals. His own sight failed, and he founded St. Dunstan's for soldiers blinded in World War I.

Pearson, Karl, 1857–1936, English scientist. He applied statistical methods to biological problems, a science he called biometry.

Peary, Robert E(dwin) (pēr'ē), 1856–1920, American arctic explorer, discoverer of North Pole. Led several expeditions to Greenland. Made various attempts to reach North Pole before success on April 6, 1909. Although challenged by prior claim of F. A. COOK, Peary's achievement was recognized and later verified scientifically. In 1891–92 and later he explored **Peary Land,** peninsula, N Greenland, in Arctic Ocean. Mountainous, fertile area, free of inland icecap, it terminates in Cape Morris Jessup, northernmost arctic land point yet discovered.

Peasants' War, 1524–26, general rising of the peasants in central and S Germany against increased exploitation by the nobles, introduction of Roman law (which interpreted peasant status as servile), and progressive encroachments on their rights. Peasants' demands were listed in 12 Articles of Memmingen (1525). The revolt was partly religious in spirit. Zwingli encouraged it, and the Anabaptist Thomas MÜNZER led it in Thuringia, but Luther's savage condemnation of the rebels was a major factor in their defeat. Despite their able leadership by Florian Geyer, Götz von BERLICHINGEN, and other discontented nobles, the peasants were routed by the princes and the SWABIAN LEAGUE (1525). The peasants' few acts of atrocity were far surpassed by the victors. In Tyrol, the peasants won some concessions in 1526, but in general the peasants' defeat prolonged serfdom in Germany for nearly three centuries and stunted democratic development.

peat, carbonized, decayed vegetation, found in bogs of the temperate zone. Formed by slow decay of plants, e.g., sedges, reeds, rushes, and mosses, it is an early stage in the formation of coal. Two types of commercial peat are peat moss, derived from SPHAGNUM, and fuel peat.

peat moss: see SPHAGNUM.

pecan (pĭkăn', pĭkän', pē'kăn), tree (*Carya illinoensis* or *C. pecan*), a species of hickory, native from S Ill. to Texas and Mexico. The most important North American nut-bearing tree, it yields nuts used as table delicacies, in ice creams, and in confectionery.

peccary (pĕ'kûrē), piglike mammal (*Tayassu*). Collared peccary or javelina is found in parts of Ariz., N.Mex., Texas, and S to Patagonia; white-lipped peccary found from central Mexico to Paraguay. Peccaries fight viciously with their tusks.

Pechenga (pyĕ'chĭn-gŭ), Finnish *Petsamo*, town (pop. over 2,000), N European RSFSR, on inlet of Barents Sea and near Norwegian border. Nickel mines near by. Ceded by Russia to Finland 1920; retroceded to USSR 1944 (confirmed 1947).

Pechora (pyĭchô'rŭ), river, N European RSFSR, rising in N Urals and flowing 1,110 mi. N into Pechora Bay (inlet of Barents Sea). Navigable for 470 mi. in summer, for 1,040 mi. in freshets of spring and autumn. Pechora coal basin extends E from river's middle course.

Peck, Annie Smith, 1850–1935, American mountain climber. First American to reach (1908) summit (22,205 ft.) of Huascarán in Peru.

Pecos (pā'kŭs), city (pop. 8,054), W Texas, on Pecos R. (irrigation). Trade and shipping center of cattle, agr., and oil region.

Pecos, river rising in N N.Mex. near the Truchas peaks and flowing 926 mi. S and SE across N.Mex. and Texas to the Rio Grande above Del Rio. Dams in N.Mex. serve Carlsbad project. Federal bill (1949) settled interstate disputes over water use. Pecos State Monument, near Pecos, N.Mex., encloses ruins of Pecos pueblo, mighty in Coronado's time.

Pecs, Hung. *Pécs* (pāch), Ger. *Fünfkirchen*, city (pop. 73,000), SW Hungary, in a coal-mining region. Produces tobacco, leather goods, vegetable oil. Seat of first Hungarian university (1367).

pectin, any of a group of amorphous, complex carbohydrates occurring in ripe fruits and some vegetables. Pectin content causes jellying when fruit of proper acidity and sugar are cooked together for jelly or jam. Commercial preparations may be used if fruit is low in pectin. Pectin also has medical uses (e.g., in treating sores and in slowing the rate of absorbing certain drugs).

Peculiar People, small Protestant sect founded in London, 1838, also known as Plumstead peculiars. Relying on prayer, they refused medical aid.

Pedrarias: see ARIAS DE ÁVILA, PEDRO.

Pedro I (pā'drō), 1798–1834, first emperor of Brazil (1822–31), son of John VI of Portugal. Growing up in Brazil after royal family fled Portugal before Napoleon's conquering French, he remained as regent of Brazil when King John returned to Portugal (1821). Heeding Brazilian advisers, Dom Pedro issued, Sept. 7, 1822, the *grito de Ipiranga*, making Brazil a separate empire. Abdicated 1831. Succeeded to Portuguese throne (1826), abdicated in favor of his daughter, Maria, and after 1831 assisted in securing rule for her. In Brazil he was succeeded by his son, **Pedro II,** 1825–91, emperor (1831–89). His long reign was period of internal peace and material progress. He was personally popular, but events worked against him, and in 1889 while he was in Europe, a revolution established a republic. Pedro did not return.

Pedro. For Spanish and Portuguese rulers thus named, see PETER.

Peeblesshire (pē'bŭlz-shĭr), **Peebles,** or **Tweeddale,** county (347 sq. mi.; pop. 15,226), S central Scotland, co. town Peebles. Mainly a hilly pastoral region, it has little arable land.

Pee Dee, river rising in W N.C. in Blue Ridge and flowing 435 mi. SE to Winyah Bay, S.C. Called the Yadkin in central N.C.

Peekskill, city (pop. 17,731), SE N.Y., on E bank of Hudson R. (bridged NW to Bear Mt.) and N of Ossining, in farm and resort area. Mfg. of food products, alcohol, jewelry, and textiles.

Peel, Sir Robert, 1788–1850, English statesman. As home secretary he secured passage (1829) of a Catholic Emancipation bill (which he had earlier opposed) and estab. (1829) London police force. Sought to form a conservative party favorable to general reforms. Abandonment of custom duties and repeal of the corn laws during his second premiership (1841–46) split the party.

peewee: see PEWEE.

Pegasus (pĕ'gŭsŭs), in Greek legend, immortal winged horse; offspring of Poseidon and Medusa. He was faithful companion of Bellerophon. His hoof print made the spring of Hippocrene (sacred to the Muses), which gave gift of song to those who drank of it. His name is given to a constellation.

Pegram, George Braxton (pē'grŭm), 1876–, American physicist, educator. Demonstrated transmutation of elements by splitting atom with slow neutrons; in 1939 announced successful splitting of uranium atom. He was associated with Columbia Univ. from 1900.

Pegu (pĕgōō'), city (pop. 21,712), Lower Burma, on Pegu R. and on Rangoon-Mandalay railroad. Was cap. of Burma in 16th cent.

Péguy, Charles (shärl' pāgē'), 1873–1914, French author. A Socialist, he later became imbued with Catholic mysticism and (though usually at odds with the Church) became one of the foremost modern Catholic writers. He took a part in the Dreyfus Affair (on Dreyfus's side) and continued his fiery polemics against social injustice. His poetry gains power from his original, chantlike verse, as in *Le Mystère de la charité de Jeanne d'Arc* (1910; Eng. tr. by Julian Green, 1950). He fell in World War I.

Peham, artists: see BEHAM.

Pehlevi language: see PAHLAVI LANGUAGE.

Peiping, China: see PEKING.

Peipus, Lake (pī'pŭs), Estonian *Peipsi Järv*, Rus. *Chudskoye Ozero*, lake, area c.1,400 sq. mi., NE Europe, between Estonia and RSFSR. It empties through Narva R. into Gulf of Finland. Connected by 15-mi.-long strait with L. PSKOV.

Peirce, Charles Sanders, 1839–1914, American philosopher. He considered the meaning of an idea to lie in an examination of consequences to which idea would lead. From him William James adopted term PRAGMATISM. Works of Josiah Royce and John Dewey reflect Peirce's influence.

Peirce, Waldo, 1884–, American painter. Worked in France, Spain, Tunis, and Algiers, 1919–30.

Peisistratus, tyrant of Athens: see PISISTRATUS.

Pekah (pē′kŭ), d. c.730 B.C., king of Israel (c.736–c.730 B.C.). Murdered Pekahiah for the throne. Lost part of his kingdom to Assyria. 2 Kings 15.26–16.9.

Pekahiah (pē″kŭhī′ŭ), d. c.736 B.C., king of Israel (c.737–c.736 B.C.) Murdered by Pekah, one of his generals, who seized the throne. 2 Kings 15.26–16.9.

Pekalongan (pĕ″kälông′gän), town (pop. 65,982), on N Java, Indonesia; port on Java Sea. Exports sugar, rubber, and tea.

Pekin (pē′kĭn), city (pop. 21,858), central Ill., on Illinois R. and S of Peoria; settled 1829. Shipping and industrial center in farm and coal area. Mfg. of food and leather products.

Peking (pē′kĭng′) or **Peiping** (pā′pĭng′), city (pop. 1,603,324), Hopeh prov., cap. of People's Republic of China. Cultural center; seat of several universities and national library. Consists of Outer or Chinese City (walled 15th cent.) and Inner or Tartar City (walled 16th cent.). Latter contains Forbidden City (formerly emperor's residence), Imperial City, and Legation Quarter (which contained foreign concessions 1860–1946). At near-by Chowkowtien were discovered the bones of Peking man (*Sinanthropus pekinensis*). First known city to have existed on Peking's site was Chi of Chou dynasty. In 13th cent. Kublai Khan's cap., called Cambuluc, was built here. As Peking, the city was cap. of China from 15th cent. to 1928 with one brief break in early Ming period. City was renamed Peiping in 1928 when Nationalists moved cap. to Nanking. Occupied 1937–45 by the Japanese. In 1949 it became cap. of Chinese Communists, who restored historical name of Peking.

Pekingese or **Pekinese:** see TOY DOGS.

Peking man: see MAN, PRIMITIVE.

Pelagianism (pŭlā′jŭnĭzŭm), 5th-cent. Christian heretical sect, deriving its name from a monk and theologian, Pelagius (c.355–c.425). He rejected the teaching of St. Augustine on predestination and grace, calling them pessimistic. In his preaching in N Africa and Palestine Pelagius maintained that a child is born innocent (without original sin) and therefore need not be baptized. He argued that grace consists of the natural attributes in man that lead him to God—reason, free will, understanding of the gospel. Anyone could thus enter Heaven, even the pagans. This challenged the whole function of the Church and the sacraments. St. Augustine and St. Jerome fought Pelagianism vigorously, and it was condemned at the Council of Ephesus (431). A modified doctrine, Semi-Pelagianism, continued popular in France and the British Isles into the 6th cent.; this accepted all of Augustine's views except those of predestination. This was condemned at the Council of Orange (529).

Pelasgians (pĭlăz′jēŭnz), name meaning aboriginal, non-Greek inhabitants of Greece; possibly the builders of Mycenaean civilization.

Pele (pā′lā), Hawaiian goddess of the volcano. Her traditional home is Halemaumau, fire pit of Kilauea crater on Hawaii isl.

Pelée (pŭlā′), volcano, 4,429 ft. high, on N Martinique, French West Indies; erupted 1792, 1851, 1902. Last eruption killed c.40,000 people, and a thick deposit of volcanic ash left area a wasteland.

Peleus (pē′lūs, pē′lēŭs), in Greek mythology, king of the Myrmidons; father of Achilles by the nymph Thetis. He took part in Calydonian hunt and Argonaut expedition. All the gods were invited to his wedding except Eris. In revenge she sent the APPLE OF DISCORD.

Pelew, Caroline Isls.: see PALAU.

Pelias, uncle of JASON.

pelican (pĕ′lĭkŭn), large, gregarious bird of warm regions, allied to cormorant and gannet. Upper mandible is hooked, lower one has pouch to hold fish; feet are webbed. Great white, eastern brown, and California brown pelicans are found in U.S. See *ill.*, p. 135.

Pelican Rapids, village (pop. 1,676), W Minn., N of Fergus Falls and on Pelican R. "Minnesota man," human skeleton believed prehistoric, was found near by, 1932.

Pelion (pē′lēŭn), mountain, 5,252 ft. high, N Greece, in E Thessaly, near Aegean coast. In ancient legend, giants known as the Aloadae tried to storm heaven and overthrow the gods by piling Mt. Ossa on Olympus and Pelion on Ossa. They were killed by Apollo.

pellagra (pŭlă′grŭ, pŭlā′grŭ), disease resulting from diet deficient in vitamin B complex constituents, especially niacin. The disease is attended by reddening of parts of body and by gastrointestinal and nervous disturbances.

Pelletier, Pierre Joseph (pyĕr′ zhôzĕf′ pĕlütyā′), 1788–1842, French chemist; codiscoverer of quinine, strychnine, brucine, and other alkaloids.

Pellico, Silvio (sēl′vyō pĕl′lēkō), 1789–1854, Italian author of dramatic poetry (e.g., *Francesca da Rimini,* 1815) and of *Le mie prigioni* (1832), a moving account of his life as a political prisoner.

Pelly, river of S central Yukon, rising W of Mackenzie Mts. and flowing 330 mi. WNW to join Lewes R. and form Yukon R. at Fort Selkirk. Receives Ross and Macmillan rivers.

Pelopidas (pĭlŏ′pĭdŭs), d. 364 B.C., Theban general. Recovered Thebes from Spartans (379 B.C.) and later won victories over Sparta (e.g., at Leuctra, 371 B.C.). With Epaminondas he successfully invaded the Peloponnesus (370–369 B.C.). Captured on expedition to Macedonia (368 B.C.), he was rescued by Epaminondas.

Peloponnesian League: see SPARTA.

Peloponnesian War (pĕ″lŭpŭnē′zhŭn), 431–404 B.C., struggle in anc. Greece between Athens and Sparta, long-standing rivals. The war began with a contest between Athens and Corinth (Sparta's ally) over dependencies. In 431 a Spartan army first invaded Attica, but Athens and its port, Piraeus, were walled and resisted. The Athenian fleet raided Spartan allies and was victorious off Naupactus. Though plague wiped out a quarter of the Athenians and Pericles died, Athens was still able to maintain itself and refused a Spartan bid for peace. The tide began to turn when the Spartan Brasidas led a brilliant campaign that ended with a decisive victory at Amphipolis (424). The Athenian leader, Nicias, arranged a peace that was little more than a truce, and soon the brilliant Athenian general Alcibiades was aiding a revolt of Spartan allies. He also forwarded the plan for an Athenian expedition against Syracuse but was charged with sacrilege; the expedition was led by Nicias to disastrous loss (413). Alcibiades going over to Sparta helped create a Spartan fleet. Though he returned to Athenian service and won victories over the Spartans (notably at Cyzicus, 410), the rise of Lysander as Spartan leader prepared the end of the war. With a new fleet he won at Notium (407?) and, despite an Athenian victory at Arginusae, sealed the fate of Athens by crushing the Athenian navy under Conon at Aegospotamos (405) and taking the proud city itself by land and sea attack. After its surrender in 404 Athens was never to regain its old glory. Sparta was briefly mistress of Greece.

Peloponnesus (pĕ″lủpủnē′sủs) or **Morea** (mōrē′ủ), southernmost region of continental Greece. Morea, its medieval name, was used until recently, when its classic name was restored. A mountainous peninsula between the Ionian and Aegean seas, it extends c.140 mi. S from the Isthmus of Corinth to Cape Matapan. Patras, Corinth, Kalamata, and Nauplia are its chief cities and ports. It produces currants, grapes, tobacco, and olives but lacks grain crops. Sheep and goat raising; silk-culture; fishing. Industries are little developed. In ancient times, the chief political divisions were Elis, Achaea, Argolis, Corinth, Arcadia, and Lacedaemonia (comprising Messenia and Laconia). Sparta, Corinth, Argos, and Megalopolis were among chief cities. SPARTA long had hegemony over peninsula (except over Achaea and Argos). Its power was broken by Thebes and Macedon in 4th cent. B.C. Conquered by Rome (146 B.C.), the Peloponnesus became a Roman, later a Byzantine, province. After A.D. 1204 the VILLEHARDOUIN family (followed by other foreign rulers) held the whole peninsula except several ports, which went to Venice. Byzantine control, restored by 1432, was replaced by Turkish rule in 1460. Venice held parts of Morea at various times between 15th cent. and 1718.

Pelops (pē′lŏps), in Greek myth, son of Tantalus. He won Hippodamia by defeating her father in a race, in which he bribed charioteer. Later, rather than pay him, he drowned the charioteer, who cursed Pelops' seed. Peloponnesus was named for him.

pelota (pālō′tä), name for several Spanish ball games, generally played with rackets. Originated in the Basque provinces. Best known in U.S. is the game of jai alai (hī′ älī). Jai alai, one of fastest of sports, is scored on same general principles as handball.

Pelotas (pĕlō′täsh), city (pop. 79,649), S Rio Grande do Sul state, SE Brazil, port on lagoon SSW of Pôrto Alegre; leading meat-packing and exporting center.

Pemaquid, peninsula: see BRISTOL, Maine.

Pemba (pĕm′bủ), island (380 sq. mi.; pop. c.100,000), off E Africa, in Indian Ocean; part of Zanzibar protectorate. Formerly a slave market, it now has a large trade in cloves.

Pembina (pĕm′bēnủ), city (pop. 640), extreme NE N.Dak., at junction of Pembina and Red rivers. Trading post here in 1797; first settlers came 1812. Became state's first permanent settlement 1819. Base for early buffalo hunts.

Pembroke, Mary Herbert, countess of, 1561–1621, sister of Sir Philip Sidney and patroness of poets (including Spenser and Jonson). Her son, **William Herbert,** 3d **earl of Pembroke,** 1580–1630, was a patron of letters. He is one of those suggested as "Mr. W. H." of dedication of Shakspere's sonnets. Pembroke Col., Oxford, is named for him.

Pembroke, Richard de Clare, 2d **earl of,** d. 1176, English nobleman, known as Richard Strongbow. Went to Ireland (1170) to aid Dermot McMurrough and recoup his fortune. Subdued much of E Ireland.

Pembroke, William Marshal, 1st **earl of,** d. 1219, English nobleman. As regent for Henry III he repelled invasion of Louis VIII of France.

Pembroke, county, Wales: see PEMBROKESHIRE.

Pembroke, town (pop. 12,704), S Ont., Canada, WNW of Ottawa and on Ottawa R. Has pulp, paper, wool, lumber, flour mills. Gateway to Algonquin Prov. Park.

Pembroke College: see BROWN UNIVERSITY; OXFORD UNIVERSITY; CAMBRIDGE UNIVERSITY.

Pembrokeshire (pĕm′bro͝ok-shĭr) or **Pembroke,** maritime county (614 sq. mi.; pop. 90,896), SW Wales; co. town Pembroke. Largely agr. region of rolling hills and fertile valleys, it has metal deposits. SAINT DAVID's has noted cathedral.

pemmican, a travel food of North American Indians. Lean meat, sun dried, was pulverized and packed with melted fat, and sometimes dried berries, into rawhide bags. Fish was also used in the Northwest.

pen, pointed writing implement for applying ink or similar material. Reeds frayed at end were used in antiquity; quills were introduced in Middle Ages. Metal slip-in nib came into common use after 1828; fountain pen, in 1880s. Ball-point pen, introduced c.1944, is tipped by ball bearing which rolls gelatinous ink onto paper.

Penal Laws (pē′nủl), general term for oppressive legislation against Catholics of England and Ireland. Begun under Henry VIII, they were inspired as much by political and economic fear as by religious hatred. Plots against Elizabeth and the Gunpowder Plot inflamed anti-Catholic feeling. Stuart attempts to soften the laws were a factor in the Puritan Revolution, and the laws became connected with efforts to limit power of the crown. TEST ACT (1673) kept Catholics from holding office. Act of SETTLEMENT (1701) excluded Catholics from the throne. Small number of Catholics in England and Scotland made laws unimportant after failure of Jacobite rebellions (1745). In Ireland, however, most of the population was Catholic. Laws there made harsher in 1695 for purpose of strengthening English possession of land. Made so strict that many left country and Protestants aided in evasion. The laws were repealed and conditions remedied by long process of CATHOLIC EMANCIPATION.

penance, SACRAMENT of the Roman Catholic Church. By it the penitent is absolved of his sins by his confessor, to whom he recites verbally the serious sins he has committed since his last confession or since his baptism. The confessor must be a priest or bishop, the person receiving the sacrament must be truly sorry and determined to amend his life. The confessor inflicts a penance as punishment for guilt (usually recital of stipulated prayers), and the penitent must, of course, make restitution for any injuries done to others. The confessor acts only as instrument of God, not with any powers of his own right, and he may not reveal what is told him in confession. Every Roman Catholic must receive the sacrament of penance once a year.

Penang (pŏnăng'), settlement (400 sq. mi.; pop. 473,227), NW MALAYA, on Straits of Malacca; cap. George Town. Consists of Penang isl. (110 sq. mi.) and Province Wellesley (290 sq. mi.), a strip on Malay Peninsula facing the island. Chief products are rubber and tin. Chinese greatly outnumber Malays and Indians. Britain has held Penang isl. since 1786 and Province Wellesley since 1791. Penang was one of STRAITS SETTLEMENTS, 1826–1946.

penates, household gods: see LARES AND PENATES.

Penck, Albrecht (äl'brĕkht pĕngk'), 1858–1945, German geographer and geologist. Noted for glaciation study, pioneer classification of land forms, development of modern regional geography.

Penda, d. 655, king of Mercia (632–55). A great fighter, he extended his power over Wessex and East Anglia. Killed fighting Oswy of Northumbria.

Pend d'Oreille Indians (pŏn"dŏrā'), North American tribe of Salishan linguistic stock. Togther with the Kalispel (from whom they cannot well be distinguished), they occupied NW Mont., N Idaho, and NE Wash. in early 19th cent. Today on reservations in Mont. and Wash.

Pendergast, Thomas Joseph, 1873–1945, American political boss. Kansas City, Mo., and Mo. state Democratic leader. Convicted in 1939 of income-tax evasions.

Pendleton, Edmund (pĕn'dŏltŏn), 1721–1803, American Revolutionary patriot and Va. jurist. His great-grandnephew, **George Hunt Pendleton,** 1825–89, was U.S. Representative from Ohio (1857–65) and U.S. Senator (1879–85). Secured legislation introducing competitive examinations in CIVIL SERVICE.

Pendleton, city (pop. 11,774), NE Oregon, on Umatilla R. and SW of Walla Walla, Wash.; founded 1869 on old Oregon Trail. Ships wheat, sheep, and cattle. Flour and woolen mills; leather goods. Indians from near-by reservation take part in annual Pendleton Roundup.

Pend Oreille (pŏn"dŏrā') [Fr.,= ear ornament], river, 119 mi. long, N Idaho, rising in Pend Oreille L. and flowing W, NW into Wash., joining Columbia R. in Canada near border (see CLARK FORK). **Pend Oreille Lake,** c.40 mi. long, N Idaho; state's largest lake. Fed by Clark Fork. Noted for beauty.

Pendragon, Uther: see ARTHURIAN LEGEND.

pendulum, a weight suspended from fixed point so that it can vibrate in arc determined by its momentum and the force of gravity. Galileo found each swing of a pendulum to be of equal duration. Christiaan Huygens determined relation between length of pendulum and vibration time and in 1673 applied pendulum control to clocks. Pendulum is used to control other mechanisms, measure intensity of gravity, register direction of earthquakes, demonstrate rotation of earth (1851 by J. B. L. Foucault in Paris).

Penelope (pŏnĕ'lŏpē), in Greek legend, queen of Ithaca; faithful wife of Odysseus. In the *Odyssey,* while Odysseus was away, she was beset by suitors. To evade them she said she would decide after weaving Laertes' shroud, then unraveled each night each day's work. Her plan was discovered and she agreed to marry the one who could bend Odysseus' bow, but none could. Odysseus, returning disguised as a beggar, bent the bow, was reunited with Penelope, and slew the suitors.

Peneus (pĭnē'ŭs), river, 135 mi. long, N Greece, in Thessaly, rising in Pindus mts. and flowing E past Larissa, through valley of Tempe to Aegean Sea.

Penfield, Edward, 1866–1925, American illustrator, originator of the colored poster in America.

penguin (pĕng'gwĭn, pĕn'–), flightless, webfooted, swimming and diving bird of S Hemisphere from Galapagos Isls. to antarctic regions. It has a white breast and gray or gray-blue back. On land it usually walks upright.

penicillin (pĕ"nĭsĭ'lĭn), antibiotic secreted by certain strains of the mold *Penicillium notatum.* Discovered by Sir Alexander Fleming; its antibacterial powers and nontoxicity to humans estab. 1941 by Florey, Chain, and others.

Penikese Island: see ELIZABETH ISLANDS.

Peninsular campaign, April-July, 1862, of Civil War. Attempt of G. B. McClellan to take Richmond, Va., via peninsula between York and James rivers. J. E. Johnston withdrew Confederate forces from Yorktown (May 3), fighting rear-guard action. Norfolk also abandoned (May 10). Two retreats opened both rivers to Union gunboats, which were repulsed, however, at Drewrys Bluff (9 mi. S of Richmond). Union army spread across Chickahominy R., but Stonewall Jackson's brilliant campaign in Shenandoah Valley diverted Irvin McDowell's Army of the Rappahannock, and heavy rains menaced Union communications. On May 31–June 1 Johnston and James Longstreet attacked at Fair Oaks or Seven Pines; Federals held ground. R. E. Lee took command and withdrew to Richmond. His offensive in SEVEN DAYS BATTLES closed campaign with Southern victory.

Peninsular War, 1808–14, fought by France in Iberian Peninsula against the British (with Spanish and Portuguese volunteer forces). Background: Spain, having become dependent on Napoleon I, agreed to French occupation of Portugal (1807). In March, 1808, a palace revolution deposed the pro-French CHARLES IV and put his son FERDINAND VII on Spanish throne, thus giving Napoleon a pretext for occupying Madrid and other Spanish cities. An uprising in Madrid was bloodily suppressed by the French (May 2); Charles IV and Ferdinand VII were both lured into France and forced to abdicate; Napoleon's brother Joseph Bonaparte was proclaimed king of Spain (June 15). The Spanish and Portuguese rose in revolt. Military operations: Spanish insurrectionists forced French to abandon Madrid and the siege of SARAGOSSA, while a British expeditionary force under Arthur Wellesley (later duke of WELLINGTON) landed in Portugal and defeated Junot's French forces at Vimeiro (Aug. 21, 1808). By the Convention of Cintra, Junot surrendered Lisbon and agreed to evacuation of his troops. The British under Sir John MOORE now invaded Spain, where Napoleon personally took the field with 200,000 troops. The conflict thus grew into a major war. Napoleon stormed Madrid; Lannes took Saragossa; Soult pursued Moore's forces into Galicia and forced them to evacuate (Dec., 1808–Jan., 1809). These French successes were offset by Wellington after April, 1809. He drove the French out of Portugal and defeated them at Talavera (1809); repulsed them at Bussaco (1810); prevented the junction of Soult's and Masséna's forces (battles of Fuentes de Oñoro and Albuera, 1811); and, by then in supeme command, routed King Joseph and Jourdan at Vitoria (1813) and invaded France. He had reached Toulouse (1814), when Napoleon's abdication ended the war.

Penitentes (pĕnĭtĕn'tēz), secret lay order in SW U.S. (esp. N.Mex.), arising originally from the third order of the Franciscans. They are notorious for practicing flagellation in Holy Week (ending with a crucifixion). Though condemned (1889) by the Roman Catholic Church, the rites persist somewhat.

penitentiary: see PRISON.

Penitent Thief: see Good Thief.

Penn, Sir William, 1621–70, British admiral. Fought in the Dutch Wars and captured Jamaica. Father of **William Penn,** 1644–1718, English Quaker, founder of Pennsylvania. Laid out Philadelphia in 1682. Estab. liberal government in colony.

Pennamite Wars, conflicts between Pa. and Conn. settlers over claims to WYOMING VALLEY.

Pennell, Joseph (pĕ'nul), 1860–1926, American illustrator, etcher, lithographer; one of the foremost American graphic artists. Treated mainly landscapes and architectural views. Influenced by Whistler.

Pennine Chain (pĕ'nīn), long hill range ("backbone of England"), extending from the Cheviot Hills to the Peak in NW Derbyshire. Consists of a series of upland blocks separated by transverse river valleys. Cross Fell (2,930 ft.) is highest peak.

Pennsauken (pĕnsô'kĭn), township (pop. 22,767), SW N.J., near Camden. Bricks, terra cotta, beer.

Penns Grove, residential borough (pop. 6,669), SW N.J., on the Delaware R. opposite Wilmington, Del.

Pennsylvania, state (45,333 sq. mi.; pop. 10,498,012), NE U.S.; one of Thirteen Colonies; cap. HARRISBURG. Main cities are PHILADELPHIA, PITTSBURGH, ERIE, ALLENTOWN, SCRANTON, READING. Bounded E by Delaware R. (Atlantic Ocean outlet). Country of mountains, hills, valleys but for L. Erie coastal plains (NW). Drained by Delaware, Susquehanna, Allegheny, Monongahela rivers (last two form the Ohio at Pittsburgh). Mines coal, oil, natural gas, limestone, slate; mfg. of steel, iron, textiles, petroleum products, machinery, electrical goods, metal and food products. Farming (dairying, poultry, grains, tobacco, fruits, vegetables), fishing. William PENN secured proprietary rights in 1681 (few settlements before by Swedes and Dutch), added Lower Counties (Del.) in 1682. Colony designed around liberal principles. Penn signed good-will treaty with Indians. Active in American Revolution (see BRANDYWINE, GERMANTOWN, VALLEY FORGE). Benjamin FRANKLIN one of leaders in revolutionary movement. Philadelphia was important center of activities—scene of First and Second Continental Congresses, signing of Declaration of Independence, drafting of Federal Constitution. Surged forward after war; national capital 1790–1800. Boundary disputes settled (see WYOMING VALLEY). Economic dislocation expressed in WHISKY REBELLION (1794), Fries Rebellion of 1798 (see FRIES, JOHN). Active for Union in Civil War (see GETTYSBURG CAMPAIGN, CHAMBERSBURG). Post-war industry boomed. Labor troubles appeared in activities of MOLLY MAGUIRES, HOMESTEAD strike of 1892. Simon CAMERON built powerful political machine for Republicans. High degree of regional individuality has been retained by some groups, e.g., PENNSYLVANIA DUTCH.

Pennsylvania, University of, in Philadelphia; nonsectarian, private, for men and women; planned 1740 as charity school, opened 1751 as academy with Benjamin Franklin as chief founder, chartered 1755 as college, reorganized 1779 as university. Pioneer in secular education in the colonies; had first university medical and business schools in U.S. Pennsylvania School of Social Work is affiliated.

Pennsylvania Academy of the Fine Arts, at Philadelphia, estab. 1805, inc. 1806. An outgrowth of the Columbianum, which held first art exhibition in U.S. (1794). Present building was erected 1876 to house academy's art collection, notable for early and modern American paintings and 19th-cent. European paintings. Privately supported. Connected with oldest art school in U.S.

Pennsylania Dutch, name popularly but erroneously applied to the descendants of Germans who settled in Pa. (esp. in Northampton, Berks, Lancaster, Lehigh, Lebanon, and York counties). Most of the original settlers belonged to religious sects persecuted in Europe—Mennonites, Dunkards, Moravians, Amish. Germantown was founded in 1683, but the large immigration came from the Palatinate after 1710. Most of the Germans became prosperous farmers, and over the decades they preserved their religious customs, dress, and language (a blend of several dialects, with some High German and English; see LANGUAGE, table) to a remarkable degree. A considerable body of Pennsylvanian German literature was written. Pennsylvania German folk art (e.g., in pottery, barns, illuminated writing) has attracted much attention in recent years.

Pennsylvania Museum of Art: see PHILADELPHIA MUSEUM OF ART.

Pennsylvanian period: see CARBONIFEROUS PERIOD.

Pennsylvania Railroad. Incorporated in 1846 by act of Pa. legislature. Company completed in 1854 a single-track line between Philadelphia and Pittsburgh. In 1857 company purchased many railroads owned and operated by state of Pa. Railroad rapidly extended operations between Atlantic seaboard and Mississippi R. and between Great Lakes and Ohio R.

Pennsylvania State College: see STATE COLLEGE.

Penn Yan (pĕn″ yăn′), village (pop. 5,481), W central N.Y., in FINGER LAKES region, on Keuka L. Mfg. of wines, fruit juices, machinery, baskets. Near by is Keuka Col. (Baptist; for women; 1888). Jemima WILKINSON lived near by.

pennyroyal, name for two similar plants of the mint family, true or European pennyroyal (*Mentha pulegium*) and American or mock pennyroyal (*Hedeoma pulegioides*). Both have small bluish flowers in the leaf axils and both yield a pungent oil.

Penobscot (půnŏb′skůt), river, 350 mi. long (from head of longest branch), formed in central Maine. Its headstreams are the outlets of many lakes. Flows S, past Old Town and Bangor (head of navigation), to Penobscot Bay. Furnishes power for pulp and paper mills. Upper course is favorite canoe route. Chief freight is lumber.

Penobscot Bay, islanded inlet of the Atlantic, S Maine, at Penobscot R. mouth. Shores lined with summer resorts. Bay entered by Martin Pring, 1603; Champlain ascended the river, 1604. Long Anglo-French dispute over area. Chief French port was Castine.

Penobscot Indians, North American tribe of Algonquian linguistic stock, occupying the region around the Penobscot R. in 17th cent. They were the largest tribe of the Abnaki Confederacy. They were friendly with the French until they changed allegiance to the British in 1749.

Penrhyn (pĕn′rĭn) or **Tongareva** (tŏng″gůrē′vů), atoll in S Pacific belonging to New Zealand. Discovered 1788 by the British. Exports copra and pearl shells.

Penrose, Boies (boiz′), 1860–1921, U.S. Senator from Pa. (1897–1921) and Republican state boss.

Penry, John, 1559–93, British Puritan author, an instigator of MARPRELATE CONTROVERSY. With others he issued (1588–89), under name Martin Marprelate, seven pamphlets attacking Church of England.

Pensacola (pĕnsůkō′lů), city (pop. 43,479), extreme NW Fla., on fine natural harbor on Pensacola Bay. Shipping, fishing, and wood-processing center, it also has shipyards and seafood canneries. Nylon plant near by. Site of a major U.S. naval air station (estab. 1914). Spanish settlement, 1559–61; recolonized by Spanish in 1698, and Fort San Carlos erected on Santa Rosa Isl., across the bay. Shuttled between Spain and France, 1719–63. British held it until 1783, when it was formally returned to Spain (Bernardo de Gálvez had captured it, 1781). British base (though city still Spanish) in War of 1812. Captured by Andrew Jackson in 1814 and 1818. U.S. took formal possession 1821. Held alternately by Federals and Confederates in Civil War, though Fort PICKENS remained Federal throughout. Fort Barrancas is only garrisoned fort here now. Has ruins of forts Barrancas (old), San Carlos (1780s), Pickens, and McRae (1830s).

Pensacola Bay, inlet of Gulf of Mexico, c.13 mi. long and 2½ mi. wide, NW Fla. Pensacola city is c.7 mi. from the entrance (protected by peninsula and Santa Rosa Isl.). Receives Escambia R.

Pensacola Dam: see GRAND RIVER DAM.

pension, originally a gratuity to persons favored by the sovereign, to soldiers, and, later, to superannuated public servants. The idea of extending old-age protection to all persons appeared in 19th-cent. Germany and was developed in the U.S. in 1935 as a form of SOCIAL SECURITY. Many corporations and groups give supplementary pensions to their workers. The usual method is through group insurance, to which the employee contributes as well as employer or government.

penstemon: see BEARDTONGUE.

pentameter (pĕntă′můtůr), in prosody, a line scanning in five feet. Iambic pentameter is great English meter. Chaucer used seven iambic pentameters rhyming *ababbcc;* as he pronounced a final short *e,* his pentameters often ended in an 11th unstressed syllable. When final *e* disappeared from speech, the pentameter became strict; as heroic couplet it was prominent in poetry of 17th and 18th cent., notably that of Dryden and Pope. Blank verse—unrhymed iambic pentameters—has been used in great dramatic and epic verse from Shakspere and Milton to the present. Renaissance England borrowed the ottava rima (eight iambic pentameters rhyming *abababcc* of Ariosto and Tasso; Spenser added to it an alexandrine (a line of six iambic feet) rhyming with the last pentameter. The sonnet is a notable use of iambic pentameter.

Pentapolis (pentă′půlĭs) [Gr.,= five cities], any group of five cities. One such was the combination of the cities of Cyrenaica (Apollonia, Arsinoë, Berenice, Cyrene, Ptolemais), so called from the 4th cent. B.C. to 7th cent. A.D. Another was that of five cities on the Adriatic coast of Italy (Rimini, Ancona, Fano, Pesaro, Senigallia), important as a group 5th–11th cent. A.D., largely as outposts of Byzantine culture.

Pentateuch (pĕn′tůtůk) [Gr.,= five books], the first five books of Old Testament, the books of the Law.

Pentecost (pĕn′tůkôst) [Gr.,= fiftieth], important Jewish and Christian feasts. In Jewish calendar it comes 50 days after Passover and marks the closing of the Palestinian harvest, a period of 49 days or seven weeks. Called in Bible the Feast of Weeks, Feast of Harvest, or Feast of Firstfruits; 50th day is Feast of Pentecost, in Hebrew *Shabuot.* Also known as anniversary of the giving of the Law; this aspect stressed in modern Judaism. See Ex.

23.16; 34.18–26; Lev. 23.15–22; Num. 28.26; Deut. 16.9–12; 2 Chron. 8.13. In Christian calendar Pentecost falls on seventh Sunday after Easter. On the Pentecost after the resurrection of Jesus (i.e., 50 days from the Passover in which He was crucified), the spirit of the Holy Ghost descended upon his followers (Acts 2). The Christian feast commemorates this event and has always been solemnly observed by the Church as her birthday and as the feast of the Holy Ghost. Anciently converts were baptized at this time; from white garments worn by them comes Whitsunday, an English name for Pentecost. The great Latin hymns *Veni Creator Spiritus* and *Veni Sancte Spiritus* were composed for Pentecost.

Penthesilea (pĕn″thĕsúlē′ù), in Greek mythology, queen of the Amazons. She joined the Trojans in the Trojan War and was killed by Achilles.

Penticton, city (pop. 10,548), S B.C., Canada, on Okanagan R. at S end of Okanagan L. Fruit-growing center with canning and packing plants. Resort.

Pentland Firth (pĕnt′lùnd fûrth′), channel 6½–8 mi. wide and c.14 mi. long, separating the Orkneys from mainland of Scotland.

Penuel (pēnū′ùl) [Heb.,= face of God], place by Jabbok R. where Jacob wrestled with the angel.

Penza (pyĕn′zù), city (pop. 157,145), E central RSFSR, on Sura R., in a fertile black-earth district. Machinery mfg. and food processing.

Penzance (pĕnzăns′), municipal borough (pop. 20,648), Cornwall, England, NE of Lands End. Fishing center and resort, it is a port for the Scilly Isls.

peony, hardy perennial plant of genus *Paeonia,* prized for the large handsome flowers in spring. Herbaceous peonies have single or double, often fragrant, flowers in white, red, or pink. Tree peonies, with woody stems, are less commonly grown. Both kinds, chiefly native to Asia and Europe, have been venerated in China and Japan.

People's Charter: see CHARTISM.

People's party: see POPULIST PARTY.

Peoria (pēō′rēù), city (pop. 111,856), central Ill., on Illinois R. where it widens into L. Peoria. Second largest city in Ill. Trade and shipping center in agr. (esp. grain) and coal area. Mfg. of agr. equipment and food products. Oil refining. Distilling center. La Salle estab. Fort Creve Coeur in area 1680; it became trading post 1691 and was abandoned in Revolution. Fort Clark (1813) was nucleus of American settlement, 1818. Lincoln made speech on slavery here 1854. Seat of Bradley Univ. (coed.; 1896).

Pepi (pā′pē), name of two kings of anc. Egypt, of the VI dynasty. **Pepi I** ruled c.2595–c.2571 B.C. His son, **Pepi II** ruled supposedly for more than 90 years (c.2567–c.2473) in an area of prosperity. He took expeditions into Nubia.

Pepin (pĕ′pĭn) or **Pippin** (pĭ–), Frankish mayors of the palace and kings. **Pepin of Landen,** d. 639?, helped CLOTAIRE II of Neustria in conquest of Austrasia (613), which he later governed for Dagobert I as mayor of the palace. Out of the marriage of his daughter with the son of Arnulf, bishop of Metz, arose the Carolingian dynasty. His grandson, **Pepin of Héristal,** d. c.714, ruled Austrasia and Neustria as mayor of the palace, the Merovingian dynasty retaining nominal kingship. He was father of CHARLES MARTEL and grandfather of **Pepin the Short,** c.714–768, who became mayor in 741. In 751, with the consent of Pope Zacharias, he forced the last Merovingian king, Childeric III, into a monastery and had himself proclaimed king of the Franks. He defended Rome against the Lombards (754, 756), from whom he wrested Ravenna and other cities. These he ceded to the pope, laying the foundation for the Papal States. He was the father of Charlemagne. His great-grandson **Pepin I,** d. 838, son of Emperor LOUIS I, was king of Aquitaine (817–38). He joined in the rebellions of 830 and 833 against his father but each time helped restore him.

Pepin, Lake (pĕ′pĭn), widening of the Mississippi, 21 mi. long, 3 mi. wide, SE Minn., SE of Red Wing.

pepper, name for pungent fruit of several plants, used as condiments and in medicine. True or black pepper (*Piper nigrum*) is a perennial shrub native to East Indies; black and white pepper are prepared from its dried berries. Red peppers, eaten green or ripe as a vegetable or pickled, used as condiments, and in medicine, are various species of the genus *Capsicum,* either annuals or biennials. Well-known kinds are the pimento and the sweet or bell pepper. Cayenne pepper, very sharp, is made from a species perennial in the tropics. Paprika is prepared from a milder kind. Pungent "chili" pepper is used in Mexican food and in pepper sauces.

peppergrass, widely distributed herbs of genus *Lepidium,* especially garden cress (*Lepidium sativum*), sometimes used in salads.

pepperidge: see BLACK GUM.

peppermint, aromatic European perennial herb (*Mentha piperita*), naturalized in the U.S. It is a typical MINT, grown commercially for the oil and its derivative menthol.

Pepperrell, Sir William, 1696–1759, American colonial military commander. Led land forces at capture of Louisburg (1745) in French and Indian Wars. First native American to be created baronet.

pepper tree, ornamental resinous evergreen tree (*Schinus*) native to Peru but widely grown in mild climates. The California pepper tree (*Schinus molle*) has panicles of greenish flowers followed by rose berrylike fruits, sometimes used as a substitute for pepper.

pepsin: see STOMACH.

Pepusch, John Christopher (pā′po͝osh), 1667–1752, German musician; lived in London after 1700. Composed the overture and arranged the rest of the music for John Gay's *The Beggar's Opera* (1728).

Pepys, Samuel (pēps), 1633–1703, English diarist. A diligent naval official, he rose to be secretary to the admiralty (1672–79, 1684–89). In 1684 he also became president of the Royal Society. In retirement after the accession of William III, he wrote his *Memoirs . . . of the Royal Navy* (1690). His famous diary, in cipher, left with his books to Magdalene Col., Cambridge, was deciphered and was first published in 1825. It is an intimate record of his daily domestic, social, and political life from 1660 to 1669 and furnishes a graphic picture of social life and manners and court morals of the Restoration period.

Pequot Indians (pē'kwŏt), North American tribe of Algonquian linguistic stock. They had a culture typical of the E Woodlands area. Originally united with the Mohegan, they moved S to the Conn. coast in 17th cent. There by murdering John Oldham they brought on the Pequot War (1637), which ended with dispersal of the tribe.

Pera, Turkey: see ISTANBUL.

Peraea (pērē'ů), in Roman times, region E of Jordan R. It is the Gilead of the Old Testament.

Perak: see MALAYA.

Percé Rock (pĕrsā'), E Que., Canada, in the Atlantic off E Gaspé Peninsula opposite Percé village. A bird sanctuary and tourist attraction, it is 1,420 ft. long, 300 ft. wide, 290 ft. high.

perch, small, beautifully colored, fresh-water game fish of Europe, Asia, North America. It is typical of large family of spiny-finned fishes. Maximum weight is c.5 lb. It is an excellent food fish.

Percier, Charles (shärl' pĕrsyā'), 1764–1838, French architect. He and Pierre FONTAINE were official architects under Napoleon. They worked as partners on Louvre and Tuileries palaces. Their influence on interior decoration of Empire period was enormous. They also collaborated on books on architecture.

Percivale, Sir, knight of King Arthur's court: see ARTHURIAN LEGEND; PARSIFAL.

percussion instruments, in music, those instruments whose sound is usually produced by a blow from a mallet or stick. There are many varieties of percussion instruments, but those discussed in this article are most often found today in a symphony orchestra. Scientifically, percussion instruments are classified as idiophones (those made of a substance, such as wood or metal, which vibrates when struck) and membranophones (those whose sound producing agent is a stretched skin); musically, they are considered as to whether or not they can be tuned to produce a sound of definite pitch. The only drums which can be tuned are kettledrums (also called timpani), kettle-shaped metal vessels over which a membrane (the drumhead) is stretched; they are tuned by adjusting tension of the head. The celesta (sĭlĕ'stů), a keyboard instrument whose set of steel bars are struck by hammers operated from the keyboard, has a range of 4 octaves upward from middle C. The glockenspiel, a set of steel plates played by hand with two little hammers, and the XYLOPHONE also produce tones of definite pitch. The snare drum has two drumheads; across one of them are stretched several strings (called snares) that cause a rattling sound of indefinite pitch when the opposite head is struck. The bass drum, the largest drum used; the cymbals, a pair of metal discs which are sounded by being struck together; the gong; the tambourine, a single drumhead stretched over a wooden frame with metal plates or jingles in the frame; and the triangle, made of steel and struck with a small steel stick, are all of indefinite pitch.

Percy, English noble family. **Henry Percy,** 1st **earl of Northumberland,** 1342–1408, received earldom from Richard II. Banished by Richard in 1398, he was instrumental in securing crown for Henry IV. Took part in family rebellion of 1403, but submitted. Later fled to France, made attempt to invade England (1408), and was killed at Branham Moor. His son, **Sir Henry Percy,** 1366–1403, called Hotspur, was active against the Scots. Fought battles of Otterburn (1388) and Humbledon Hill (1402). Quarreled with Henry IV and plotted to crown Edmund Mortimer, 5th earl of March. Plot is treated in Shakspere's *Henry IV*. Killed at battle of Shrewsbury. His uncle, **Thomas Percy, earl of Worcester,** c.1344–1403, fought against France and Spain and served as a diplomat under Richard II. Later supported Henry IV. Joining his brother and nephew in 1403 revolt, he was captured at Shrewsbury and executed. **Henry Percy,** 4th **earl of Northumberland,** 1446–89, served Yorkish king Edward IV after imprisonment following death of his Lancastrian father, the 3d earl. Withheld aid from Richard III in favor of Henry VII. **Thomas Percy,** 7th **earl of Northumberland,** 1528–72, defended Scottish border for Mary I. Under Elizabeth, he plotted (1569) to release Mary Queen of Scots and restore Catholicism. Led unsuccessful revolt and was beheaded. **Algernon Percy,** 10th **earl of Northumberland,** 1602–68, was lord high admiral of England. Commanded Charles I's expedition against Scotland. Disagreement with king's policy led him to support Parliament, giving it control of fleet.

Percy, Thomas, 1729–1811, English antiquary, a churchman. His collection of English and Scottish ballads, *Reliques of Ancient English Poetry* (3 vols., 1765), aroused interest in earlier literary forms.

Perdiccas (pûrdĭ'kůs), d. 321 B.C., Macedonian general under Philip II and Alexander the Great. Regent after the death of Alexander (323 B.C.), he failed to hold the empire together and was defeated in the wars of the Diadochi by Ptolemy I.

Pereda, José María de (hōsā' märē'ä dā pārā'-dhä), 1833–1906, Spanish novelist. Wrote stories of his native Santander.

Pereira, Nun'Álvares (nōōn'äl'vůrĭsh pĕrā'rů), 1360–1431, Portuguese hero, called the Great Constable. He was the friend, counselor, and general of JOHN I, who largely owed him the victory at Aljubarrota (1385) and his throne. From the union of his daughter with a natural son of John I the house of Braganza is descended.

Perekop, Isthmus of (pĕrĭkôp'), c.20 mi. long and 4–15 mi. wide, USSR, connecting Crimea with mainland and separating Gulf of Perekop (an arm of Black Sea) from Sivash Sea (an inlet of Sea of Azov).

perennial, a plant that lives for more than two years in contrast to an ANNUAL and BIENNIAL. Perennials are either herbaceous (surviving winter chiefly by rootstocks), e.g., iris and chrysanthemum, or woody (surviving by roots, stems, and sometimes leaves), e.g., most trees and shrubs. Some perennials act as annuals outside their natural habitat.

Peretz, Isaac Loeb (lōb′ pĕ′rĕts), 1851–1915, Yiddish-Hebrew playwright and poet, b. Poland. His work is imbued with the spirit of his people and an understanding of Jewish life.

Pérez, Antonio (äntō′nyō pä′räth), b. between 1534 and 1540, d. 1611, Spanish nobleman, confidential adviser of Philip II and lover of the princess of ÉBOLI. His ruin was brought about by his arrest (1579) for the murder of John of Austria's secretary. He was prosecuted on various charges until in 1590 he escaped to Saragossa, where he placed himself in the hands of the authorities of his native Aragon and openly accused the king of having procured the murder. The people of Aragon, jealous of their privileges, sided with Pérez; an uprising was crushed in 1591, and Pérez fled abroad.

Pérez de Ayala, Ramón (rämōn′ pä′räth dā äyä′lä), 1881–, Spanish poet, novelist, and essayist. His poetry's chief theme is nature (e.g., in *La paz del sendero* and *El sendero innumerable*). One of his novels is *The Fox's Paw* (1912), the story of his courtship of his American wife.

Pérez Galdós, Benito (bānē′tō pä′räth gäldōs′), 1843–1920, Spanish novelist and dramatist. Wrote *Episodios nacionales,* 46 novels on 19th-cent. Spain; other novels, including *Doña Perfecta* (1876), *Gloria* (1877), and *Marianela* (1878).

Perez-uzza or **Perez-uzzah** (both: pē′rĕz-ŭz′ù) [Heb.,= breach of Uzzah], name given to threshing floor where Uzzah touched the ark and died. 2 Sam. 6.6–8; 1 Chron. 13.9–11. Previously called Chidon or Nachon.

perfume, aroma produced by essential oils of plants and synthetic aromatics. Used from antiquity. Modern perfumes are commonly blends of natural and synthetic scents and fixatives which add pungency and equalize vaporization of ingredients. Ingredients are combined with alcohol for liquid scents, with fatty base for many cosmetics.

Pergamum (pûr′gùmŭm), anc. city of Asia Minor (now Turkey) on the Caicus R. An independent kingdom, it flourished as a brilliant center of Hellenistic culture 3d–2d cent. B.C., particularly notable for sculpture and for a large library (with books on parchment, which takes its name from the city). Attalus III (d. 133 B.C.) bequeathed Pergamum to Rome. Also Pergamos, Pergamus, Pergamon.

Pergolesi, Giovanni (Battista) (jōvän′nē pĕrgōlā′zē), 1710–36, Italian composer. His *La serva padrona* (1733) became the model for *opera buffa*. He is also known for his *Stabat Mater*.

Peri, Jacopo (yä′kōpō pā′rē), 1561–c.1633, Italian composer. With Caccini, he wrote *Dafne* (c.1597), the earliest opera on record, and *Euridice* (1600), the earliest opera whose music is extant.

Periander (pĕ′rēăn″dùr), d. 585 B.C., tyrant of Corinth, one of the Seven Wise Men of Greece.

Peribonca, river of central Que., Canada, rising in Otish Mts. and flowing 300 mi. S to L. St. John.

Pericles (pĕ′rĭklēz), c.495–429 B.C., Athenian statesman, of the distinguished family of the Alcmaeonidae. Well educated and interested in the arts, he was determined to make Athens a center of culture as well as a political power. Under his leadership Athens reached her zenith: the Delian League was powerful, Athens was beautiful, rich, and increasingly democratic. Peace was made with Persia in 448 B.C. after the death of Pericles' rival, Cimon, and the Peloponnesian War did not begin until 431 B.C. The new war and a disastrous plague brought Pericles' deposition. He was later reinstated, but died soon afterward. Aspasia was his mistress, Alcibiades his ward.

Périer, Casimir Pierre (käzēmēr′ pyĕr′ pĕryā′), 1777–1832, French banker and statesman. He played a large part in the overthrow of Charles X and served as premier (1831–32) under Louis Philippe. Conservative, he sought to repress republicanism, failed to send aid to the Polish revolutionists, but helped Belgium gain its independence. His descendants took the name Casimir-Perier.

Périgord (pārēgôr′), region and former county, SW France; historic cap. Périgueux. Consists of arid limestone plateaus cut by fertile valleys. Truffles and goose liver pâté are major exports. County, estab. 9th cent., was wrested from English rule c.1370, passed to house of Bourbon, and was inc. into royal domain after 1589.

Perigueux (pārēgû′), city (pop. 37,287), cap. of Dordogne dept., SW France; historic cap. of Périgord. Has 12th-cent. cathedral and basilica.

Perim (pārēm′), island (5 sq. mi.; pop. 360), belonging to British colony of Aden; off SW coast of Arabia. Formerly a coaling station.

periodical, publication issued at regular intervals usually distinguished from the newspaper in purporting to express authors' and editors' points of view instead of recounting current news, also by the frequency of its publication. The term *periodical* applies to journals, literary reviews, and fiction magazines; term *magazine* is usually limited to periodicals designed primarily for entertainment. A list of contemporary periodicals may be found in the annual *N. W. Ayer & Son's Directory*.

periodic law. J. W. Döbereiner (1829) arranged a number of elements in groups of three (triads) on basis of physical and chemical properties; element lying between the other two had properties that were intermediate, and ATOMIC WEIGHT that was average of other two. J. A. R. Newlands discovered (1863–65) that when elements are listed in order of increasing atomic wt., starting with the second, the 8th and 16th elements following a given element are similar in properties. Because of counting by groups of eight, this is known as law of octaves. About the same time, A. E. B. de Chancourtois arranged elements in one continuous order by atomic wts. In 1869 Mendelejeff stated periodic law: properties of chemical elements are periodic functions of their atomic wt., i.e., a definite relationship is seen in periodic occurrence of similar properties in certain elements when all are arranged according to increasing atomic wt. Lothar Meyer drew same conclusion independently; pointed out relation between atomic volume of elements (ratio of atomic wt. to specific gravity). Arrangement of elements showed a number of spaces into which no known element would fit; Mendelejeff said these indicated undiscovered elements and predicted the atomic wts. and properties of these elements with great accuracy. Not all elements fall in positions corresponding correctly to properties. This was corrected by work of Henry Gwyn Jeffreys Moseley which led to statement of new periodic law. In this system the elements are arranged in order of decreasing wave length of X-ray spectra. Order is almost the same as that by atomic wt. Elements are numbered according to position they occupy; this number, the atomic number, indicates the number of positive charges on nucleus and the number of extranuclear electrons, number and arrangement of which are believed to determine the properties of the element. New periodic law states that properties of elements are a function of their atomic numbers. Tabulation consists of nine vertical columns (groups) and a number of horizontal columns (periods).

Peripatetics (pĕ″rŭpŭtĕ′tĭks) [from Gr.,= walking about; from Aristotle's method of teaching], followers of Aristotle. Theophrastus and Strato of Lampsacus were later leaders of the school, which concerned itself with interpreting Aristotle.

periscope (pĕ′rĭskōp), device for viewing objects out of line of vision or concealed by intervening body. Essential parts are prisms, mirrors, tube, lenses, and eyepiece. Image received in one mirror is reflected through tube with its lenses to a mirror visible to the viewer.

peritonitis (pĕ″rĭtŭnī′tĭs), inflammation of peritoneum, the membranous tissue lining abdominal cavity and enclosing many organs. Causes include perforation of gastrointestinal tract, ruptured appendix, abdominal surgery, abortion, primary infection. Causative agents are usually bacteria.

periwinkle (pe′rŭwĭng″kŭl), small mollusk with conical, spiral shell, found in temperate and cold waters.

periwinkle, plant of Old World genus *Vinca,* especially the common periwinkle or myrtle (*Vinca minor*), a trailing ground cover for shade. It has evergreen leaves and blue flowers.

Perkins, Charles Callahan, 1823–86, American art critic, whose writings had great influence on development of American art. Illustrated his *Italian Sculptors* (1868) with his own etchings.

Perkins, Frances, 1882–, U.S. Secretary of Labor (1933–45), first U.S. woman cabinet member.

Perkins Institution and Massachusetts School for the Blind, at Watertown, Mass., chartered 1829, opened 1832 in South Boston, as New England Asylum for the Blind, given present name 1877, moved 1912. S. G. HOWE was first director. Laura BRIDGMAN and Anne Sullivan MACY were pupils.

Perkin Warbeck: see WARBECK, PERKIN.

Perlis: see MALAYA.

Perm, RSFSR: see MOLOTOV.

Permanent Court of Arbitration: see HAGUE TRIBUNAL.

Permanent Court of International Justice: see WORLD COURT.

Permian period (pûr′mēŭn), sixth and last period of the Paleozoic era of geologic time. It saw climax of the changes in the earth's surface begun in Carboniferous, which together with extremes of cold and aridity resulted in extinction of some marine animals and some plants; aridity is proved by extensive salt and gypsum deposits. A long marine submergence occurred during early Permian in SW U.S., with deposits of sandstones and limestones up to 6,000 ft. thick. Also submerged was the Cordilleran area, where red sediments were laid down. In Upper Permian practically all of North America was above sea level and Appalachian Mts. were thrust up. Plant and animal life in general transitional between that of Paleozoic and Mesozoic. See also GEOLOGY, table.

Pernambuco (pĕr″nŭmbōō′kō), state (37,458 sq. mi.; pop. 3,430,630), NE Brazil, extending inland from the Atlantic; cap., RECIFE. First European settlement made here in 1530s; occupied by Dutch, 1630–54; scene of several revolts in early 19th cent. Stock-raising and agr. region.

Perón, Juan (Domingo) (hwän′ dōmĕng′gō pārōn′), 1895–, president of Argentina (1946–). Rose to prominence as one of the officers in the "colonels' group" that overthrew government of Ramón Castillo in 1943, and he thereafter dominated Argentine politics. Perón developed a large following among the working class while he was secretary of labor and social welfare. His dictatorship, supported by a combination of labor and conservatives, has sought to maintain a highly nationalistic economy. He married (1945) Eva Duarte de Perón (d. 1952), who was largely responsible for his release from prison when in 1945 he was temporarily divested of his offices, and she thereafter played a spectacular part in his government.

Péronne (pārôn′), town (pop. 3,669), Somme dept., N France, on Somme R. Here in 1468 took place the "interview" between LOUIS XI of France and Charles the Bold of Burgundy.

Pérouse, Jean François de Galaup, comte de la: see LA PÉROUSE.

Perov, Vasily Grigoryevich (vŭsē′lyē grĭgôr′yŭvĭch pyĭrôf′), 1833–82, Russian painter, leader of Russian realists. Best known for scenes of peasant life.

peroxide of hydrogen: see HYDROGEN PEROXIDE.

Perpignan (pĕrpēnyã′), city (pop. 64,358), cap. of Pyrénées-Orientales dept., S France, near Spanish border and the Mediterranean. Trades in fruit and wine. Was cap. of Spanish kingdom of Majorca and, after 1642, of Roussillon prov. (France). Has 14th-cent. Loge (merchants' exchange), Gothic cathedral (14th–16th cent.), and royal castle (13th–15th cent.).

Perrault, Charles (shärl′ pĕrō′), 1628–1703, French poet. Author of *Histoires ou contes du temps passé* (1697), which gave classic form to the stories of Bluebeard, Sleeping Beauty, Cinderella, and other fairy tales. He opposed Boileau and the ancients in the "quarrel of the ancients and the moderns."

His brother **Claude Perrault** (klōd), 1613–88, French architect and scientist, designed famous east façade (Colonnade) of the Louvre.

Perrers, Alice (pĕr'ŭrz), d. 1400, mistress of EDWARD III of England, over whom she had great power.

Perrin, Jean Baptiste (zhã bätēst' pĕrē'), 1870–1942, French physicist. Won 1926 Nobel Prize for work on discontinuous structure of matter and discovery of equilibrium of sedimentation.

Perry, Bliss, 1860–, American educator, author, and editor; professor of English at Williams, Princeton, and Harvard; editor of *Atlantic Monthly* (1899–1909). Works include biographies of Whitman, Whittier, and R. H. Dana; critical works and selections; and his autobiography, *And Gladly Teach* (1935).

Perry, Frederick John, 1909–, English tennis player. Won U.S. singles title (1933–34, 1936), British singles crown (1934–36), many other amateur championships. Professional singles champion, 1938 and 1941.

Perry, Matthew Calbraith, 1794–1858, American naval officer. In 1853–54 he visited Japan with a fleet; concluded treaty guaranteeing protection for shipwrecked U.S. seamen, right to buy coal, opening of ports of Shimoda and Hakodate to U.S. trade. His brother, **Oliver Hazard Perry,** 1785–1819, was also an American naval officer. During War of 1812 he secured British surrender in battle of L. Erie (Sept. 10, 1813). His report—"We have met the enemy and they are ours"—has become familiar to Americans.

Perry, Ralph Barton, 1876–, American philosopher, long a professor at Harvard. Edited the works of William James and wrote *The Thought and Character of William James* (1935), *The New Realism* (1912).

Perry. 1 City (pop. 6,174), central Iowa, near Raccoon R. and NW of Des Moines. Center of farm area. **2** City (pop. 5,137), N central Okla., NE of Oklahoma City, in farm area.

Perrysburg, village (pop. 4,006), NW Ohio, on Maumee R., S suburb of Toledo. Monument near by marks site of Fort MEIGS.

Perry's Victory and International Peace Memorial National Monument: see NATIONAL PARKS AND MONUMENTS (table).

Perryton, city (pop. 4,417), N Texas, NE of Amarillo near Okla. line. Shipping, mfg. center for wheat area.

Perryville, town (pop. 660), central Ky., W of Danville, SW of Lexington. Near by is site of battle (Oct. 8, 1862) between Bragg's Confederates and Buell's Federals which, though called indecisive, ended Bragg's invasion of Ky. Natl. cemetery in area.

Perse, Saint-Jean: see LÉGER, ALEXIS SAINT-LÉGER.

Persephone (pŭrsĕ'fŭnē), Latin *Proserpine* (prŏ'sŭrpīn), or *Proserpina* (prōsûr'pĭnŭ), in Greek religion, goddess of fertility; daughter of Zeus and Demeter and wife of Hades, ruler of the underworld. He stole her, but Demeter induced gods to let her return to earth for eight months of each year. She had to remain in the underworld four months because Hades had tricked her into eating four pomegranate seeds. On her return to earth plants blossomed anew. She personified birth and decay of vegetation. As queen of the underworld she was a stern woman, but as daughter of Demeter, a lovely young maiden with horn of plenty as her symbol.

Persepolis (pŭrsĕ'pŭlĭs) [Gr.,= city of Persia], anc. city of Persia, NE of present Shiraz; ceremonial (but not administrative) cap. of the Persian empire under Darius and successors. It has been excavated. The area was inhabited as early as 4000 B.C.

Perseus (pûr'sūs, -sēŭs), in Greek mythology, hero; son of Zeus and Danaë and grandson of Acrisius. Told by an oracle that Perseus would kill him, Acrisius set him and Danaë afloat in a chest, but King Polydectes rescued them. Later, because Perseus was an obstacle to his love for Danaë, the king sent him to get Medusa's head, expecting him to die. However, aided by the gods he slew MEDUSA. When Atlas refused him help in his flight from the Gorgons, Perseus used Medusa's head to turn him into a stone mountain. He killed Polydectes and, with his mother and wife (ANDROMEDA), went to ARGOS. Here in a discus contest he killed his grandfather, thus fulfilling the prophecy. The statue *Perseus* by Benvenuto Cellini is in Florence. A N constellation is named for him.

Perseus, c.212–166 B.C., last king of Macedon (179–168 B.C.), son and successor of Philip V. His vigorous and anti-Roman policy brought on the Third Macedonian War (171–168), and the Roman general L. Aemilius Paullus thoroughly defeated Perseus at Pydna (168).

Pershing, John J(oseph) (pûr'shĭng), 1860–1948, American general, commander in chief of American Expeditionary Force in World War I.

Persia, old alternate name for the Asiatic country IRAN, in which anc. Persian Empire had its core. Early Persians were presumably a nomadic tribe who filtered down at an unknown time through the Caucasus to Iranian plateau. By 7th cent. B.C. they were estab. in present region of Fars, which then belonged to Assyrian Empire. Persian rulers were early associated with the Medes, who created a strong state in 7th cent. B.C. CYRUS THE GREAT (first of the Achaemenidae) made himself ruler of MEDIA in mid-6th cent. B.C. and by rapid conquest estab. the great Persian Empire. From the beginning the Persians built on foundations of earlier states, borrowing political structure of Assyria and arts of Babylonia and Egypt. Country was beset by dynastic troubles, concerning first the claims of CAMBYSES and later those of DARIUS I. Under Darius a highly efficient centralized system of administration was organized and Persian rule was extended E into modern Afghanistan and NW India and as far N as the Danube. Although the Greeks revolted successfully in PERSIAN WARS, Persian influence continued strong in Greece. After mid-5th cent., however, signs of decay began to appear. The state was weakened by dynastic troubles (notably the rebellion of CYRUS THE YOUNGER against ARTAXERXES II), increasing power of the satraps (regional governors), and successful revolt of Egypt. Finally, ALEXANDER THE GREAT routed the Persians on the Granicus in 334 B.C., and in

331 the battle of Gaugamela destroyed the Achaemenid empire. After Alexander's death most of Persia fell to the Seleucids, who, though they introduced a fruitful Hellenistic culture, were unable to maintain control. Parthia, which broke away in mid-3d cent. B.C., became a kind of successor to the old Persian Empire, and came to rival Rome. Its decline was followed by establishment of new empire in A.D. c.226 under the SASSANIDAE. This magnificent state flourished until 641 or 642, when invading Arabs took the cap., Ctesiphon. Islam replaced Zoroastrianism, and the caliphate made Persia part of a larger pattern, from which modern Iran later emerged.

Persian art and architecture. Ancient pottery, cult figurines, and bronzes already embody Persian feeling for decorative motifs. Artistic culture, to which Zoroastrian cult contributed bases for symbolism, arose in Achaemenidae period (c.550–330 B.C.). The great columned palaces set on high terraces at Pasargadae and Persepolis reveal distinctive sense of space and scale. Persepolitan columns were slenderer and more closely fluted than those of Greece, and their bases were often bell shaped. In sculpture, stylization is subtly combined with realism; typical is the *Frieze of Archers* (Louvre), done in molded and enameled brick. Outstanding among minor arts is exquisite metalwork (esp. gold and silver ornaments). For 500 years after the conquest by Alexander the Great, Persian art was strongly influenced by Hellenistic and Roman motifs. Under the Sassanidae (c.226–c.640) there was a revival of native aesthetic feeling. Enormous palaces were built, richly decorated in stucco. Painting was encouraged, especially by Mani, founder of Manichaeism and himself a painter. A favorite motif was the *simurgh,* a beast with head of an animal and body of a bird. In 7th cent. there was gradual merging of Persian and Islamic cultures (see MOSQUE). Great Mosque at Isfahan, one of world's great architectural monuments, was built during high period of Persian art (11th–12th cent.). With the invasion (1220) of Jenghiz Khan, Chinese influence became important. The arts of book illumination, mosaic faience, and tile marquetry developed throughout 14th cent. Dynasty estab. by Tamerlane (14th–15th cent.) saw another flowering of Persian culture. Miniature painting emerged, stressing intense colors and economy of line, harmonized in a deliberately flat decorative pattern. Earliest extant carpets, unsurpassed in beauty of design and material, date from early 16th cent., when native Persian dynasty was restored. European influences, which began operating in 17th cent., have tended to debase rather than invigorate native art.

Persian Gulf, arm of Arabian Sea, between Iran and Arabia. Connected with Gulf of Oman by Strait of Ormuz. Major oil-shipping lane.

Persian language, Iranian language of Indo-Iranian subfamily of Indo-European languages. See LANGUAGE (table).

Persian literature. Among its most ancient examples is the literature of ZOROASTRIANISM. After overthrow of the Sassanidae by the Arabs (7th cent. A.D.), new religion of Islam became dominant theme and many notable works in Arabic were written by Persian authors. In 9th cent., Persian re-emerged as literary language and was given new luster by the great poet FIRDAUSI and OMAR KHAYYAM. The period 13th–15th cent. saw flowering of mystic poetry of SUFISM (see FERID ED-DIN ATTAR, RUMI, SADI, and HAFIZ). The mass of Persian writings after 15th cent. is almost entirely untranslated.

Persian lynx: see CARACAL.

Persian Wars, 500–449 B.C., contest of Greek city-states and the Persian Empire. The war started with the revolt of Ionian Greek cities on the coast of Asia Minor against the rule of Darius I. Athens and Eretria aided them, but the Persians crushed the revolt (494 B.C.). Darius then set out to punish Athens and Eretria and annex all Greece. The first Persian expedition (492 B.C.) ended when a storm crippled the Persian fleet. A second (490 B.C.) destroyed Eretria and set out for Athens but was defeated at Marathon by a smaller Athenian force (aided by some men from Plataea) under the brilliant Miltiades. The Spartans, sent to aid, arrived the day after the battle. Darius was planning a gigantic third expedition when he died, and his son, Xerxes I, undertook it (480 B.C.). His vast army was held back by a small group headed by Leonidas of Sparta at Thermopylae, where the Greeks died to a man. Athens under Themistocles made no attempt to defend the city but crushed the Persian fleet off Salamis. Xerxes returned to Persia, leaving in Greece an army under Mardonius, who was decisively defeated at Plataea (479 B.C.) by Greeks under the Spartan Pausanias, with Athenian troops led by Aristides. The Athenian fleet also won a victory at Mycale. Though the wars dragged on for many years, the Greek cities were then free, and the great period of Greek history was begun.

persimmon, name for several trees of genus *Diospyros* and their fleshy orange fruits. The common native persimmon of the U.S. (*Diospyros virginiana*) bears fruit of good flavor but too soft to market. The Japanese persimmon (*D. kaki*) is grown commercially in S U.S. and Calif. for its large red fruits.

Persius (Aulus Persius Flaccus) (pûr'shēŭs), A.D. 34–A.D. 62, Roman satirical poet. His six satires preach Stoic morality, censure vice of Rome.

personnel management: see INDUSTRIAL MANAGEMENT.

Perth, county, Scotland: see PERTHSHIRE.

Perth, city (pop. 98,890; metropolitan pop. 272,528), cap. of Western Australia, on estuary of Swan R.; founded 1829. Commercial and cultural center of the state. Its port is Fremantle. Univ. of Western Australia is at near-by Crawley.

Perth, town (pop. 5,034), S Ont., Canada, SW of Ottawa. Textile mills and woodworking.

Perth, burgh (pop. 40,466), co. seat of Perthshire, Scotland, on the Tay. Cap. of Scotland until murder here of James I in 1437. Battle of two clans here (1396) is told in Scott's *Fair Maid of Perth.* Has General Prison for

Scotland (estab. 1812). Has mfg. of carpets, textiles, and farm machinery.

Perth Amboy, city (pop. 41,330), NE N.J., on harbor at Raritan R. mouth on Arthur Kill (Outerbridge Crossing to Staten Isl., 1928); settled 1683. Cap. of East Jersey 1686–1702; then, until 1790, alternate cap. with Burlington of united Jerseys. Grew as coal-shipping center after becoming tidewater terminal of Lehigh Valley RR 1876. Shipyards, drydocks, oil refineries; mfg. of metal and clay (from local deposits) products, plastics, and chemicals. Here are mansion of Gov. William Franklin, used as a British hq. in Revolution; St. Peter's Church (1722); and Parker Castle (1723).

Perthshire or **Perth,** inland county (2,493 sq. mi.; pop. 128,072), central Scotland; co. town Perth. Mountainous region with many lochs, wild forests, and moors. Agr. and grazing are main industries. Scottish kings were long crowned at Scone.

Pertz, Georg Heinrich (pĕrts), 1795–1876, German historian, first editor (1823–74) of *Monumenta Germaniae historica.*

Peru (pûrōō'), Span. *Perú,* republic (514,059 sq. mi.; pop. 8,277,031). W South America; cap. LIMA. The chief port is CALLAO. Stretching from the Pacific on the W across the Andes and down to the rain forests of the W Amazon basin on the E, Peru has a wide variety of climate and topography. The E country is well-watered by the Ucayali and Marañón; great resources largely unexploited. Its population is largely Indian. The Andes in Peru fan out in E and W ranges, the W range including the lofty volcanoes, Huascarán and El Misti. Between these two cordilleras lie the upland basins of the altiplano (more than 10,000 ft. above sea level) —cold, windy, and generally barren, though around L. Titicaca (which Peru shares with Bolivia) some foodstuff is raised and there is grazing land for llamas, sheep. The Inca capital, CUZCO, is on the altiplano. Chief industry in the mountains is mining (gold, silver, copper, lead, zinc, bismuth). Along the Pacific for 1,400 mi. stretches desert land, where agr. (mostly cotton and sugarcane) depends on irrigation from streams from the mountains. Off the coast lie the Peruvian Lobos and Chincha islands which yield GUANO, rich in nitrate and an excellent fertilizer. Petroleum resources in the NW are proving an important source of income. Industrial activities include ore reduction, oil refining, and cotton and woolen textile mills. Transportation is one of Peru's chief problems, as few railroads or highways have been built over the mountains. Air transport now supplements the railroads and roads that were built with much difficulty. Indians account for about half the population; the remainder is largely mestizo, with some Orientals and Europeans. The prevailing religion is Roman Catholic. Education is free, but illiteracy rate is high. The Univ. of San Marcos at Lima is one of oldest institutions of higher learning in America. The Spanish Conquest began in 1532 when Francisco Pizarro with a small band of adventurers landed on coast and with bold audacity and the use of firearms (which the Indians had never seen) undertook the overthrow of the INCA empire; he captured the ruler, ATAHUALPA, and treacherously executed him. Expeditions of conquest went out from the conquered Inca capital into present Ecuador and Chile and although the conquistadors fought against each other for power and spoils, they stood together in their mistreatment of the Indians. The New Laws, which were intended to do away with many of the wrongs done to the Indians, were never enforced in Peru, which early became a viceroyalty. Francisco de Toledo arrived in 1569, and through his superior administration a pattern was set for a functioning government throughout the colonial period. There was an abortive uprising in Cuzco against the Spanish regime in 1813, but independence did not come to Peru until after SAN MARTÍN, and, later, BOLÍVAR arrived to assist. At the battles of Junín and Ayacucho, Spanish forces were defeated (1826). Efforts to form Bolivia and Peru into one state failed, and after 1839 they went their separate ways. Dictatorships and revolts came in succession, and a disastrous war in 1879 (see PACIFIC, WAR OF THE) slowed the material advancement of Peru (see also TACNA-ARICA CONTROVERSY). Foreign influence and holdings have been detrimental to the economy. After World War I, APRA, a political party under the leadership of Víctor Raúl Haya de la Torre, was organized with a program of radical reform in the government and betterment of conditions among the Indians. Though it has never been in power, it has continued to play an important role in Peruvian political life.

Peru (pûrōō'). **1** City (pop. 8,653), N Ill., on Illinois R. (bridged) adjoining La Salle. Processes zinc in agr. and coal area. **2** City (pop. 13,308), N Ind., on Wabash R. and E of Logansport in farm area; laid out 1825. Electrical equipment. Has winter quarters for circuses and historical museum.

Perugia (pārōō'jä), city (pop. 31,839), cap. of Umbria, central Italy, on hill overlooking Tiber valley. Agr. center; chocolate mfg. Inhabited by Umbrians and Etruscans before it fell to Rome 3d cent. B.C. Became free commune in 12th cent. A.D., with hegemony over other Umbrian cities. Was annexed to Papal States 1540. Seat of Umbrian school of painting (13th–16th cent.), which reached its zenith with Perugino and Pinturicchio. Perugino's frescoes decorate the Cambio [exchange]. Other noted buildings include cathedral (14th–15th cent.), town hall (13th cent.), and Church of Sant' Angelo (5th or 6th cent.). There are medieval quarters; the city walls are Etruscan, Roman, and medieval. University may be traced to 13th cent.; it now holds special courses for foreign students.

Perugino (pārōōjē'nō), c.1445–1523?, Umbrian painter, b. near Perugia. Real name was Pietro di Cristoforo Vannucci. Was a fellow pupil of Leonardo da Vinci in Verrocchio's studio in Florence. Called to Rome in 1480 by Pope Sixtus IV to paint in Sistine Chapel; of his four frescoes for the chapel only one remains. Spent productive last period mainly in Perugia, where he had many pupils, notably Raphael. His many religious paintings, which include *The Annunciation* (Natl. Gall. of Art, Washington, D.C.), are noted for their grace and tenderness.

Peruzzi, Baldassare (bäldäs-sä'rā pārōōt'tsē), 1481–1536, Italian architect of the Renaissance. Designed Massimo Palace in Rome and assisted Bramante in plan for St. Peter's.

Pesaro (pā'zärō), city (pop. 24,163), the Marches, central Italy; a Mediterranean port. A city of the PENTAPOLIS, it was ruled 13th–17th cent. by the Malatesta, Sforza, and Della Rovere families and passed to Papal States in 1631. Has rich collection of ceramics, manufactured here since 15th cent. Birthplace of Rossini.

Pescadores (pĕskůdô'rûz), Chinese *P'eng-hu,* island group (49 sq. mi.; pop. 66,843) between Formosa and mainland of China. Comprises 64 islands. Named in 16th cent. by the Portuguese. Ceded 1895 to Japan, restored 1945 to China. Held in early 1953 by Nationalists.

Pesellino, Il (ēl pāzĕl-lē'nō), 1422–57, Florentine painter, whose real name was Francesco di Stefano; grandson and pupil of Giuliano Giuochi, called Pesello. Famous for animal paintings and for *cassone* pictures (decorative panels for chests). Assisted Fra Lippo Lippi in painting of altarpieces.

Peshawar (pŭshä'wŭr), city (pop. 114,000), cap. of North-West Frontier Prov., W Pakistan, near Khyber Pass; trade center. Ancient Buddhist center. The British captured it (1848) in Afghan Wars.

Pest, Hungary: see BUDAPEST.

Pestalozzi, Johann Heinrich (yō'hän hīn'rĭkh pĕ"stälôt'sē), 1746–1827, Swiss educational reformer. He conducted school for poor children, 1769–98. From 1805 to 1825 he was director of an experimental institute at Yverdon. Pestalozzi's theory stresses a pedagogical method corresponding to natural order of individual development and of concrete experiences. His theory and methods laid foundation for modern elementary education.

Pestszenterzsebet (pĕsht'sĕntĕr"zhābĕt), industrial city (pop. 76,876), N central Hungary, near Budapest. Petroleum refineries; iron and steel plants. Former name is Erzsebetfalva.

Pétain, Henri Philippe (ãrē' fēlēp' pātē), 1856–1951, marshal of France. Halted Germans at VERDUN in World War I; brought joint French-Spanish campaign against ABD-EL-KRIM to victorious end (1926); ambassador to Spain 1939–40. In World War II, France being on the brink of collapse, he succeeded Reynaud as premier and concluded armistice with Germany (June, 1940). A rump parliament suspended the republican constitution (July), and Pétain took office as "chief of state" at Vichy (see VICHY GOVERNMENT). After 1942, when LAVAL took power, Pétain became a mere figurehead. He was tried for treason after the war and sentenced to death (1945), but Gen. de Gaulle commuted the sentence to life imprisonment. The impartiality of the court has been widely questioned, and the extent of his collaboration with Germany is still under debate.

Petaluma (pĕtůlōō'mů), city (pop. 10,315), W Calif., N of San Francisco; founded 1852. Center of large poultry and egg industry.

Petchenegs (pĕchůnĕgz') or **Patzinaks** (pätsĭnäks'), nomadic people of Turkic family. Advanced from Ural region into lower Danube area in A.D. c.880, ousting the Magyars. Besieged Kiev in 968 and killed the Kievan duke Sviatoslav. Twice threatened Constantinople (934, c.1075). Defeated 1091 by Emperor Alexius I.

Petén (pātān'), region (c.15,000 sq. mi.), mostly in N Guatemala. Sparsely populated today, it was once center of the Old Empire of the Maya and has many ruins (e.g., Tikal, Uaxactún). A region of heavy rains and many lakes, it has largely undeveloped resources.

Peter, Saint [Gr. *Petros* as tr. of Aramaic *Cephas* = rock, nickname given him by Jesus], d. A.D. 67?, disciple of Jesus, listed first in the Gospels, called Prince of the Apostles. His original name was Simon; he was a native of Bethsaida; and he and his brother, St. Andrew, were fishermen when called to follow Jesus. He was generally considered as leader and spokesman of the Twelve Apostles. He was, with James and John, at the transfiguration. When Judas came to betray Jesus, Peter drew his sword in defense. Later the same night Peter denied being of Jesus' following. After the Resurrection Jesus appeared and charged Peter to "feed my sheep." The first part of the Acts of the Apostles tells of Peter acting as leader. Sources of the 2d cent. say he left Antioch for Rome and headed the local church there. He is said to have been martyred at the time of Nero, traditionally on the same day as St. Paul and traditionally by being crucified head downward. The Vatican hill has been since early times considered the place of his martyrdom, and St. Peter's Church houses his tomb, one of the great shrines of the Roman Catholic Church. Recent archaeological discoveries seem to show that from earliest Christian times Christians believed this to be the tomb of Peter. There is an old tradition that Peter helped write the Gospel of Mark. Many critics hold that the epistles of Peter are falsely attributed to him. Roman Catholics believe that the bishop of Rome (the pope) is supreme in the Church as successor to Peter. This is the doctrine of the Petrine supremacy, based principally on Mat. 16.13–20 and John 21.15–25 (see PAPACY). Probably because he is represented with keys, he is popularly considered the gatekeeper of Heaven. Besides the feast of St. Peter and St. Paul (June 29), there are three feasts of St. Peter in the West: St. Peter's Chains (Lammas Day), Aug. 1; St. Peter's Chair, Jan. 18; St. Peter's Chair at Antioch, Feb. 22.

Peter, emperors and tsars of Russia. **Peter I** or **Peter the Great,** 1672–1725, founder of the modern Russian state; son of Tsar Alexis by his second wife. He became tsar in 1682 jointly with his half-brother IVAN V under the regency of their sister SOPHIA ALEKSEYEVNA. He was brought up in virtual exile and utter neglect, but in 1689 he overthrew Sophia with the help of some loyal troops and began his personal rule. Ivan died 1696. "Westernization" and expansion toward the Baltic and the Black Sea were the fixed objects of Peter's policies. After taking Azov from the Turks (1696), he toured W Europe (1697–98), studying European industrial techniques and even working, for a time, as ship's carpenter in Holland. Recalled to Russia by the news of a military revolt, he punished his enemies with characteristic sadism. In the NORTHERN WAR (1700–1721) he won access to the Baltic; in 1713 he shifted his cap. from Moscow to this "window of Europe," where he built St. Petersburg (see LENINGRAD). His conquests in the S, from Turkey and Persia, were less permanent. Peter's internal reforms were thorough. He introduced universal taxation; created a new nobility of civil and military officers and a new administration; reformed the calendar and the alphabet; founded hospitals, medical schools, and fire departments; encouraged private industries, trade expansion, and exploration (notably Vitus Bering); emancipated women from servile status; estab. government control over monastic estates; abolished the patriarchate of Moscow and replaced it by a holy synod, headed by the tsar himself; and even ordered his subjects to shave their beards and wear Western garments. On the other hand, he made the serfs virtual slaves of the landowners. In 1721 Peter took the title emperor; in 1722 he declared the choice of a successor dependent on the sovereign's will; in 1724 he made his second wife, CATHERINE I, joint empress. The conservative opposition and clergy saw Peter as the Antichrist. His own son Alexis joined the opposition, was tortured, and died in prison (1718). Of bearlike constitution, Peter was capable of stupendous orgies as well as utmost self-discipline and devotion to work. Ruthless in his demands on others, he did not spare himself. His genius was undoubtedly tinged with madness. He has been regarded by posterity with horror and with adulation. **Peter II,** 1715–30, grandson of Peter I, succeeded Catherine I in 1727 under a regency. During his reign MENSHIKOV fell from power and the reactionary nobility took over. Empress Anna succeeded him. **Peter III,** 1728–62, son of Peter I's daughter Anna and of Charles Frederick, dispossessed duke of Holstein-Gottorp, succeeded his aunt Elizabeth in 1762. An admirer of Frederick II of Prussia, he took Russia out of the SEVEN YEARS WAR. In 1744 he had married Sophia of Anhalt-Zerbst, better known as CATHERINE II. Debauched and half insane, he was unfit to rule. A conspiracy headed by the ORLOV brothers forced Peter to abdicate and proclaimed Catherine sole ruler. A few days later Peter died in mysterious circumstances, presumably assassinated.

Peter, kings of Aragon and counts of Barcelona. **Peter II,** 1174–1213, reigned 1196–1213. Helped Alfonso VIII of Castile defeat the Moors at Navas de Tolosa (1212). When Simon de Montfort, leader of the Albigensian Crusade, refused Pope Innocent III's command to do homage to Peter for his conquests, Peter joined Raymond VI of Toulouse against the crusaders. His defeat and death at Muret ended Catalan influence in S France. **Peter III,** 1239?–1285, succeeded his father James I in 1276. From his marriage to Constance, daughter of MANFRED of Sicily, the house of Aragon derived its claims to SICILY and Naples. After the SICILIAN VESPERS he was offered the crown of Sicily, and he took possession of the island in 1282. Pope Martin IV thereupon excommunicated him and, jointly with the French, organized a crusade against him, but the invaders were repulsed by Peter and defeated at sea by ROGER OF LORIA. Peter IV (the Ceremonious), 1319?–1387, reigned 1336–87. Recovered Majorca (1343–44); won overlordship over Athens (1381).

Peter, kings of Portugal. **Peter I,** 1320–67, reigned 1357–67. Before his accession he married a Castilian noblewoman but fell violently in love with her lady in waiting, Inés de CASTRO. In 1355 Inés was murdered, with the complicity of his father, Alfonso IV. Peter, after a brief rebellion, was forced to pardon the murderers, but when he became king he had two of them hunted down and had their hearts drawn out. He was known as Peter the Severe, the Justiciar, and the Cruel. **Peter II,** 1648–1706, forced his brother ALFONSO VI to abdicate in 1667, and married Alfonso's queen after having her marriage annulled. He ruled as regent 1667–83 and as king 1683–1706. Chief event of his reign was signing of Methuen Treaty with England (1703). **Peter III,** 1717–86, married his niece, MARIA I, and ruled jointly with her.

Peter, kings of Serbia and Yugoslavia. **Peter I,** 1844–1921, son of Prince ALEXANDER Karageorgevich. Spent his youth in exile. Called to throne in 1903, after assassination of King ALEXANDER (Alexander Obrenovich), he ruled ably, with PASHITCH the dominating figure of his reign. In 1918 he was chosen to rule the kingdom of the Serbs, Croats, and Slovenes (later known as Yugoslavia). His son and successor Alexander was regent for the ailing king from 1914. **Peter II,** 1923–, became king of Yugoslavia on the murder of his father, Alexander (1934). The regent, his cousin Prince Paul, was overthrown early in 1941 after signing an agreement with the Axis Powers. Peter's personal rule began with the German invasion of Yugoslavia. He fled to England, where he headed the government in exile. In 1945 the Yugoslav assembly, dominated by Marshal Tito, proclaimed a republic and deposed Peter, who remained in exile.

Peter I (Peter Mauclerc), d. 1250, duke of Brittany (1213–37), count of Dreux. A grandson of Louis VI of France, he became duke by marrying Constance, sister and heiress of Arthur I of Brittany. His quarrels with the clergy earned him his excommunication (1217) and his nickname Mauclerc. He took part in several rebellions of nobles, but later did penance by going on crusade (1248–50).

Peter, epistles of New Testament, called 1 and 2 Peter, traditionally ascribed to St. Peter. 1 Peter, early to be accepted as canonical, discusses the duties of Christians, encourages those facing persecution. 2 Peter, one of the last of New Testament books to be considered canonical, warns of heresies, ends with a reminder of the Second Coming.

Peter, Apocalypse of: see PSEUDEPIGRAPHA.

Peterborough, city (pop. 38,272), S Ont., Canada, NE of Toronto and at falls on Otonabee

R. Connected via Trent Canal with L. Ontario and L. Huron. Rail center with mfg. of textiles and machinery.

Peterborough, municipal borough (pop. 53,412), Northamptonshire, England, co. seat of administrative co. of Soke of Peterborough. Rail, engineering, and farm trade center, it has varied mfg. Has an impressive cathedral, a bishop's palace, and ruins of a great Benedictine abbey (founded 655).

Peterborough or **Peterboro,** town (pop. 2,556), S N.H., between Keene and Nashua. Seat of an artists' colony, planned by Edward MacDowell and founded (1907) and sustained by his widow. Has first free tax-supported library in U.S. (1833).

Peter Damian, Saint (dā'mēůn), 1007?–1072, Italian reformer, Doctor of the Church. He was a member of the reform party of Hildebrand (Gregory VII) and was violent in attacking simony, concubinage, and other abuses among the clergy. His *Gomorrhianus* is a violent denunciation of such wrong-doing. Feast: Feb. 23.

Peter des Roches (dā rōsh'), d. 1238, English churchman and statesman. Bishop of Winchester, he was guardian of young Henry III (1216). Waged prolonged struggle for power with Hubert de Burgh.

Peter Gonzalez, Saint (gŏnzā'lĭs), 1190–1246, Spanish Dominican priest. Worked among mariners and became confused as patron of sailors with St. Elmo, a 4th-cent. martyr, who was also a patron of sailors (recalled in the name of St. Elmo's fire). Peter has not been canonized.

Peterhead (pētůrhĕd'), burgh (pop. 12,765), Aberdeenshire, Scotland; herring fishing center. James Edward Stuart landed here secretly in 1715.

Peterhof (pē'tůrhŏf), city (pop. 28,000), RSFSR, on Gulf of Finland, SW of Leningrad. Founded 1711 by Peter I; became summer residence of the tsars. Includes Great Palace (built 1715) and vast parks, famous for their fountains and cascades. Sacked by the Germans in World War II, it was afterwards restored. Name was Russianized to Petrodvorets 1944.

Peterhouse College: see CAMBRIDGE UNIVERSITY.

Peter Lombard, Latin *Petrus Lombardus,* c.1100–c.1160, Italian theologian, archbishop of Paris. Studied at Bologna, Rheims, and Paris. His *Sentences,* largely a compilation of the opinions of theologians (sometimes conflicting), has been widely used. His doctrine on the sacraments was made official by the Council of Trent.

Peterloo massacre, public disturbance in St. Peter's field, Manchester, England, Aug. 16, 1819. Crowd of 60,000 men, women, and children, petitioning for corn laws repeal and reform of Parliament, were charged by cavalry. Caused great indignation.

Peter Martyr: see ANGHIERA, PIETRO MARTIRE D'; VERMIGLI, PIETRO MARTIRE.

Petersburg, town (pop. 1,619), on Mitkof Isl., in Alexander Archipelago, SE Alaska. Population largely Scandinavian. Fishing and lumbering. Univ. of Alaska has experimental fur farm here.

Petersburg. 1 City (pop. 2,325), central Ill., on Sangamon R. and NNW of Springfield. Has grave of Ann Rutledge. Near by is New Salem. **2** City (pop. 35,054), SE Va., port on Appomattox R., S of Richmond. Important shipping point in agr. (peanuts, tobacco) area, it has mfg. of luggage and clothing. Fort Henry built here 1646. In Revolution city taken by British (1781); from here Cornwallis initiated campaign which ended at Yorktown. In Civil War Petersburg withstood assault by Grant's forces (June, 1864), but was under partial siege until city fell in April, 1865. Petersburg Natl. Military Park commemorates battle. Seat of Virginia State Col. Points of interest include Blandford Church (1735) and Cemetery (with Confederate dead), Golden Ball Tavern (c.1750), Center Hill Mansion (1825), "Battersea" (18th cent.), Wallace-Seward House (Grant and Lincoln conferred here after Lee's retreat).

Peter the Cruel, 1334–69, king of Castile and Leon (1350–69). He punished a rebellion fomented by his half-brothers by having two of them murdered in 1358. His surviving half-brother, Henry of Trastamara, obtained the help of Aragon and of DU GUESCLIN, defeated Peter, who fled, and was crowned as HENRY II (1366). In 1367 Peter, aided by EDWARD THE BLACK PRINCE, defeated Henry and Du Guesclin at Nájera, but in 1369 he was defeated and slain at Montiel. His daughter Constance married John of Gaunt; his daughter Isabella married Edmund, duke of York.

Peter the Great: see PETER I, emperor and tsar.

Peter the Hermit, c.1050–1115, French preacher. He promoted the First Crusade and led one of the bands of Crusaders, arriving at Constantinople in 1096. Returned to Europe after taking of Jerusalem. His importance has been much exaggerated.

Petition of Right, 1628, sent by English Parliament to Charles I. Secured recognition of four principles—no taxes without consent of Parliament; no imprisonment without cause; no quartering of soldiers on citizenry; no martial law in peacetime.

Petit Nord Peninsula: see GREAT NORTHERN PENINSULA.

Petitot, Jean (pŭtētō'), 1607–91, French painter of portraits in enamel, b. Switzerland. Patronized by Charles I of England and Louis XIV. His son and successor, **Jean Louis Petitot,** 1652–c.1730, served Charles II.

Petofi, Alexander (pĕ'tûfē), Hung. *Petőfi,* 1822–49, Hungarian poet and patriot, killed in the Hungarian revolutionary war. Author of exquisite lyrics, several epics, and the national poem "Up, Magyar."

Petoskey (pētŏ'skē), resort city (pop. 6,468), N Mich., on Little Traverse Bay, in agr. area. Limestone quarrying and mfg. of Portland cement.

Petra (pē'trů), anc. city of Jordan, near the foot of Mt. Hor, on the Wadi Musa; cap. of Edomites and Nabataeans. It declined in late Roman times, was conquered by the Moslems (7th cent.), and had a Crusaders' citadel (12th cent.). Called by J. W. Burgon, poetically, "A rose-bed city half as old as time."

Petrarch (pē'trärk) or **Francesco Petrarca** (fränchā'skō pāträr'kä), 1304–74, Italian poet, surpassed in Italian literature by Dante alone. First and greatest of all humanists, he hunted manuscripts, refined his Latin style, even Latinized his name, in an effort to revive the spirit of antiquity. In Rome (1341) he was crowned with the poet's laurel. Proud of his Latin epic *Africa,* he is honored instead for his Italian *Trionfi* and for the great songs and sonnets of his *Canzoniere* [song book], telling of his love for Laura, in life and death.

petrel (pĕ'trŭl), sea bird belonging to order of tube-nosed swimmers, which includes albatross and shearwater. Diving petrels are unlike birds of S Hemisphere.

Petrie, Sir (William Matthew) Flinders (pē'trē), 1853–1942, English archaeologist, noted Egyptologist. Made many outstanding discoveries in excavating ancient remains in Egypt and Palestine.

petrifaction: see FOSSIL.

Petrified Forest National Monument: see NATIONAL PARKS AND MONUMENTS (table).

Petrillo, James Caesar (pētrĭ'lō, pĭ–), 1892–, American labor leader, president of the American Federation of Musicians (1940–).

Petrodvorets, RSFSR: see PETERHOF.

Petrograd, RSFSR: see LENINGRAD.

petrolatum (pĕtrŭlā'tŭm), colorless to yellow-white hydrocarbon from petroleum. Semi-solid form is used in ointments and for lubrication; refined liquid is mineral oil—a laxative.

petroleum, name applied to an oily, inflammable liquid, usually dark brown or greenish in hue, but sometimes black or even colorless. It is rather widely found in the upper strata of the earth and is generally believed to be of organic origin. Known throughout historic times, petroleum was early used for coating walls and the hulls of ships, as a fire weapon, and sometimes in lamps. The real age of petroleum began with the development of the gasoline engine, and modern civilization is heavily dependent on petroleum for motive power, lubrication, fuel, dyes, drugs, and many synthetics. Crude petroleum is refined by a process known as fractional distillation. It is based upon the fact that the different components of petroleum have different boiling points and can, therefore, be separated from one another by heating the crude oil to successively higher temperatures and collecting the portions that boil off within certain temperature ranges. These portions are known as fractions. Gasoline, benzine, naphtha, and kerosene are important fractions. To meet the great demand for gasoline another process, called cracking, is used; in this the heavier molecules are broken down by heat, pressure, and the use of catalysts into the lighter ones that make up gasoline. Leading producers of petroleum are the U.S. (chiefly Texas, Calif., La., Okla., and Kansas), the USSR, Venezuela, and Iran.

petrology (pētrŏ'lŭjē), branch of geology concerned with origin, structure, and properties of rock.

Petronius (pĭtrō'nēŭs), d. c.66, Roman satirist, called Petronius Arbiter, known for his profligate love of luxury. When he lost Nero's favor, he opened his veins and made even dying leisurely, playing host at a feast. The fragments (notably *Trimalchio's Dinner*) of his *Satyricon* that remain are vivid studies in colloquial language of life and manners.

Petropavlovsk or **Petropavlovsk-Kamchatski** (pyĕtrŭpäv'lŭfsk-kŭmchăt'skē), city (pop. over 20,000), Khabarovsk Territory, RSFSR, on SE coast of Kamchatka peninsula and on Avacha Bay of Pacific Ocean. Naval base and port (ice-free nine months a year).

Petrópolis (pŭtrô'pŭlĭsh), city (pop. 61,843), Rio de Janeiro state, SE Brazil, situated in hills just N of Rio de Janeiro. Colonized by German immigrants (1845). Fashionable resort and industrial city.

Petrov, Yevgeny Petrovich (yĭvgā'nyē pētrô'vĭch pētrôf'), pseud. of Y. P. Katayev, 1903–43, Russian author, collaborator of I. A. ILF.

Petsamo, RSFSR: see PECHENGA.

Pettit, Edison, 1890–, American astronomer, noted for research in physics of the sun.

petunia, South American flowering plant of genus *Petunia.* Petunias are grown as annuals and are prized for their funnel-shaped flowers, often fragrant, and of various colors.

Peutinger, Konrad (kôn'rät poi'tĭng-ŭr), 1465–1547, German humanist and antiquarian. He owned the *Peutinger Table,* ancient chart showing plan of military roads of Roman Empire radiating from Rome. It is probably a 13th-cent. copy of a 3d-cent. original.

Pevensey (pĕv'ŭnzē), village, Sussex East, England, near Hastings. Landing place of William I, it was a "member" of the CINQUE PORTS.

pewee or **peewee** (pē'wē), small American woodland bird of flycatcher family, related to phoebe.

pewter, name applied to various silver-white alloys consisting chiefly of tin. Pewters vary with the percentage of tin used and with the nature of the added material. Lead imparts a bluish tinge and increases malleability; antimony adds whiteness and hardness; other metals often added include copper, bismuth, and zinc. Pewter is shaped by casting, hammering, or lathe spinning on a mold, and may be variously decorated. It was early used in the Far East. In the West it was the chief tableware until superseded by china. Pewter making was an important activity in colonial America.

peyote (pāō'tē), Aztec *peyotl,* a spineless cactus (*Lophophora williamsi*) producing a drug used by Indians in N Mexico and the SW U.S. The mushroom-shaped plant tops are eaten or made into a beverage; the drug causes nausea and hallucinations but the general effect is a feeling of well-being.

Pflüger, Eduard (ā'dōōärt pflü'gŭr), 1829–1910, German experimental physiologist. Showed that respiration occurs in tissues, not in lungs or blood.

pH, symbol of hydrogen-ion concentration: see ION.

Phaeacia (fēā'shŭ), in Greek mythology, island of Scheria (location unknown). In Books VI–XIII of the *Odyssey,* a place where Odysseus was shipwrecked.

Phaedra (fē'drŭ), in Greek legend, daughter of Minos and Pasiphaë, wife of Theseus. Her advances were rejected by her stepson, Hippolytus, and she brought about his death.

Phaëthon (fā'ŭthŭn, –tŭn) or **Phaëton,** in Greek mythology, son of HELIOS and the nymph

Clymene. He once tried to drive his father's chariot but could not control the horses. Falling, it dried the earth of Libyan Desert.

phagocyte: see WHITE CORPUSCLE.

phalanx, anc. Greek formation of infantry. The soldiers formed a solid block of 8 or 16 rows that could sweep through the more dispersed ranks of the enemy. Originally used by Spartans, developed by Epaminondas, and brought to its height by Alexander. The phalanx became obsolete after its weaknesses (poor maneuverability and lack of protection of the right because shields were carried on the left arms) were demonstrated in battle with the Romans, notably at Pydna (168 B.C.).

Phaleron (fûlēr'ŭn) or **Phalerum** (-ŭm), port of ancient Athens, Greece, on Bay of Phaleron, an inlet of the Saronic Gulf of Aegean Sea. Was superseded in 5th cent. B.C. by Piraeus.

phallicism, worship of reproductive powers of nature as symbolized by male generative organ. Its aim was to increase tribe, flocks, and crops, and it was part of fertility rites of many peoples, often incorporated into existing religions.

Phanariots or **Fanariots** (both: fûnă'rēŭts), in the Ottoman Empire, the Greeks of Constantinople; so called for their quarter, Phanar. In the 18th and 19th cent., Phanariots held high positions in the Greek Orthodox Church, as Turkish governors of Moldavia and Walachia, and as chief dragomans [interpreters] of the Porte. Their rule was often corrupt. Many Phanariots joined the fight for Greek independence in the 1820s and played a vital role in later Greek politics and cultural life.

Pharaoh (fâ'rō, -rēō, fā'-) [Heb., from Egyptian,= the great house], biblical title of kings of Egypt.

Pharisees (fă'rĭsēz), one of two great Jewish religious parties that arose within the synagogue (the opponents were the Sadducees) after the Maccabees had freed their people from Syrian oppression. The Hasidim aimed to keep all that was Jewish set apart and thus undefiled; the extremists among them were known as Pharisees. Basing all upon the Law, the Pharisees insisted upon the strictest observance of the ordinances of Judaism, in all aspects of life. The active period of Pharisaism, which was influential in the development of orthodox Judaism, extended to A.D. c.135.

pharmacopoeia (fär"mŭkŭpē'ŭ), authoritative list of drugs, describing their properties, use, dosage, and tests of purity. First U.S. national pharmacopoeia issued 1820; periodically revised. Became legal standard 1906.

pharmacy (fär'mŭsē), practice of preparing and dispensing medicines and also a place used for these purposes. Practice separated from that of medicine in 18th cent. First U.S. pharmacy school founded in Philadelphia 1821. Study of pharmacy became a four-year course in U.S. in 1932.

Pharos (fâ'rŏs), peninsula at Alexandria, Egypt. Originally an offshore island, it was joined to mainland by a mole built by order of Alexander the Great. Here was the lighthouse completed c.280 B.C. by Ptolemy II which was one of Seven Wonders of the World; destroyed 14th cent. by earthquake.

Pharpar (fär'pŭr), river of Damascus. 2 Kings 5.12. The other river of Damascus was the ABANA.

Pharr (fär), city (pop. 8,690), S Texas, WNW of Brownsville. Packs and ships fruit and vegetables.

Pharsala (fär'sälä), anc. city, Thessaly, Greece. Near here in 48 B.C. Caesar routed Pompey.

pheasant (fĕ'zŭnt), Old World game bird. It has a wattled head and long tail, and the male has brilliant plumage. Many hybrids of English, Chinese ring-necked, and Japanese pheasants exist. Hybrid ring-necked pheasant is common in E U.S.

Pheidias: see PHIDIAS.

Pheidippides (fīdĭ'pĭdēz), fl. 490 B.C., Athenian courier said to have run 150 mi. in two days to ask Spartan help against the Persians.

Phenicia: see PHOENICIA.

Phenix City, city (pop. 23,305), E. Ala., on Chattahoochee R. opposite Columbus, Ga. Cotton, bricks.

phenol: see CARBOLIC ACID.

phenolphthalein (fē"nôlthă'lēn), white, crystalline compound of carbon, hydrogen, and oxygen. Used as indicator because it turns red when added to solution of alkali; used also as a laxative.

Phi Beta Kappa, oldest Greek-letter society in U.S., founded 1776 at Col. of William and Mary, Williamsburg, Va. It became a scholarship honor society.

Phidias or **Pheidias** (both: fĭ'dēŭs), c.500–c.432 B.C., Greek sculptor, considered the greatest artist of anc. Greece. No extant original can be definitely ascribed to him; his fame rests mainly on estimates and descriptions of ancient writers and on his influence on all later sculpture. His greatest works were ATHENA PARTHENOS at Athens and *Zeus* (one of Seven Wonders of the World) at Olympia. According to tradition he supervised the sculpture for the great works on the Acropolis.

Philadelphia, city (pop. 2,071,605), SE Pa., on Delaware R. at mouth of Schuylkill R. Largest city in Pa. and third largest in nation, it is one of chief U.S. ports and a great commercial, industrial, and cultural center. Important industries are oil refining, metalworking, printing and publishing, and shipbuilding. Mfg. of petroleum-derived chemicals, railroad cars, and textiles. Has large navy yard, U.S. mint, and U.S. arsenals. Swedes settled here in 17th cent. In 1682 William PENN founded the "City of Brotherly Love" as a Quaker colony. It quickly became a major colonial center. Had first magazine (1741) and first daily newspaper (1784) in America. In Revolution Philadelphia was American cap. except during British occupation, Oct., 1777 to July, 1778; and was cap. of U.S. 1790–1800 and state cap. to 1799. Well-known residential sections are Chestnut Hill and Germantown. "Main Line," on Pennsylvania RR, is a wealthy outlying area. City has Pennsylvania Acad. of Fine Arts (1805). PHILADELPHIA MUSEUM OF ART, PHILADELPHIA ORCHESTRA, American Philosophical Society (organized by Benjamin Franklin), FRANKLIN INSTITUTE, Univ. of

PENNSYLVANIA, TEMPLE UNIVERSITY, Drexel Inst. of Technology (nonsectarian; coed.; opened 1892), Girard Col. (see GIRARD, STEPHEN), Curtis Inst. of Music (coed.; founded 1924; on scholarship basis), HAHNEMANN MEDICAL COLLEGE, and Woman's Medical Col. of Pennsylvania (1850). Historic shrines include INDEPENDENCE HALL (houses LIBERTY BELL), Congress Hall, Carpenters Hall (where first Continental Congress met), Betsy Ross House, and Gloria Dei (Old Swedes') Church. Fairmount Park, one of world's largest, includes Rodin Mus. and Robin Hood Dell.

Philadelphia Museum of Art, estab. 1875, chartered 1876; called Pennsylvania Mus. of Art until 1938. Occupied its present building (city owned) in 1928. Most notable of its many fine collections is that of European old masters. Museum is connected with School of Industrial Art (estab. 1877) and Textile Inst. (estab. 1883).

Philadelphia Orchestra, founded 1900. Under the leadership of Leopold Stokowski 1912–36, and of Eugene Ormandy from 1936, it became world famous.

Philae (fī'lē), island, S Egypt, in the Nile above Aswan Dam. Submerged during most of the year. Site of temple to Isis, built by early Ptolemies.

Philaret or **Filaret, Vasily Drosdov** (vŭsē'lyē drŭsdôf' fēlŭrĕt'), 1782–1867, Russian prelate, metropolitan of Moscow. Wrote the standard catechism and supposedly drafted the Edict of Emancipation for Alexander II (1861).

Philemon (fīlē'–) [Gr.,= loving], epistle of New Testament, written by St. Paul to Philemon, a Christian, whose runaway slave had joined Paul. Paul sent the slave home, carrying this letter urging Philemon to show Christian mercy to the fugitive.

Philemon and Baucis (bô'sĭs), in Greek legend. Zeus and Hermes were refused food and shelter by all except this couple, who survived flood sent to destroy their unkind neighbors. They later died together and became trees.

Philip, Saint [Gr.,= lover of horses], one of the Twelve Apostles. Mat. 10.3; John 1.43–51; 6.5,7; 12.21,22; Acts 1.3. Feast: May 1.

Philip, Saint, one of the seven deacons. He converted the eunuch of Queen Candace of Ethiopia. Also called St. Philip the Evangelist and St. Philip the Deacon. Acts 6.5; 8.25–40; 21.8–10. Feast: June 6.

Philip (the Arabian), 204?–249, Roman emperor (244–49). He brought about the murder of Gordian III. Made peace with Persia, celebrated the millennium of Rome with splendor (248). Decius with rebel troops killed Philip in battle.

Philip, kings of France. **Philip I,** 1052–1108, reigned 1060–1108. **Philip II** or **Philip Augustus,** 1165–1223, reigned 1180–1223. One of greatest French medieval kings, he doubled size of royal domain; consolidated royal power at expense of feudalism; created advisory council (to replace hereditary offices) and a royal court of justice with wide powers. Repeatedly at war with England, he supported ARTHUR I of Brittany against King John, whom he forced to surrender Normandy, Brittany, Anjou, Maine, and Touraine (1204). His victory at BOUVINES (1214) estab. France as leading power; his campaigns against the ALBIGENSES (1215, 1219) prepared annexation of S France. Philip joined in the Third Crusade in 1190 but after a quarrel with RICHARD I of England returned to France (1191). His reign saw the virtual disappearance of serfdom, the growing prosperity of the cities and the merchant class, and the building of the great cathedrals. **Philip III** (the Bold), 1245–85, son of St. Louis, reigned 1270–85. Annexed county of Toulouse to royal domain (1271). Died while campaigning in Spain and was succeeded by his son **Philip IV** (the Fair), 1268–1314. His first quarrel with Pope BONIFACE VIII grew out of his attempt to perpetuate an emergency tax of the clergy. When Philip forbade the export of precious metals, thus depriving the pope of revenues, Boniface capitulated (1297). In 1301 the quarrel was revived by the arrest of Bishop SAISSET. While Philip called the first STATES-GENERAL to justify his course, Boniface issued the bull *Unam sanctam* (1302). Philip countered by having his troops seize the pope at Anagni (1303) and later estab. French control over the papacy through the election of CLEMENT V, who transferred his see to Avignon. He replenished his treasury by persecuting the KNIGHTS TEMPLARS, the Jews, and the Lombard bankers, whose wealth he confiscated, and by debasing the coinage. His war with Edward I of England over possession of Guienne (1294–97) ended with Philip conceding Guienne to Edward. His attempt to control Flanders ended with the French rout at Courtrai (BATTLE OF THE SPURS, 1302). He was the father of Louis X and of **Philip V** (the Tall), c.1294–1322. On Louis X's death (1316), Philip became regent for his nephew John I, who died in infancy (1317); declaring the SALIC LAW to govern the French succession, he proclaimed himself king. His reign was notable for his administrative reforms. Although he suppressed fanatical anti-Jewish outbreaks (1321), he confiscated the Jews' property. **Philip VI,** 1293–1350, son of CHARLES OF VALOIS, was the first Valois king of France. He succeeded his cousin Charles IV in 1328, invoking the SALIC LAW to set aside Charles's daughter and Charles's nephew, EDWARD III of England. In the same year, by his victory at Cassel, he reinstated the count of Flanders, whom the rebellious Flemings had deposed. The HUNDRED YEARS WAR began in 1337. Defeated at Crécy (1346), Philip made a truce (1347) which lasted till after his death. His son John II succeeded him.

Philip, kings of anc. Macedon. **Philip II,** 382–336 B.C., reigned 359–336 B.C. after seizing the throne. He reorganized and trained the army and set out to expand his kingdom by conquest and diplomacy. Took over the gold mines of Thrace and the Chalcidice by 348. Despite the thunderings of Demosthenes, Philip continued to build his power. He crushed Athens and Thebes at Chaeronea (338) and was master of Greece. He was planning an expedition against Persia when he was killed (possibly by his wife Olympias). His son, Alexander the Great, carried conquest further. **Philip V,** 238–179 B.C., reigned 221–179 B.C.; son of Demetrius II, successor of Antigonus III. He interfered successfully in Greece and tried to take Illyria from Rome. In the First Macedonian War with Rome (215–205 B.C.) he managed to hold his own, but in the Second (200–197 B.C.) he was decisively defeated by Flaminius at Cynoscephalae (197 B.C.). His son was Perseus.

Philip, Spanish kings. **Philip I** (the Handsome), 1478–1506, king of Castile (1506); son of Emperor Maximilian I and of MARY OF BURGUNDY, whose possessions in the Low Countries he inherited in 1482. Was kept a virtual prisoner of city of Ghent until 1493, when he became nominal governor of the Netherlands under his father's guardianship. He married Queen JOANNA of Castile and became joint king in 1506. He was the first Hapsburg ruler in Spain and the father of Emperor CHARLES V. **Philip II,** 1527–98, became king of Spain, Naples, and Sicily on the abdication of his father Charles V (1556). Previously, he had received the Low Countries, Franche-Comté, and Milan. After the death of his first wife, Mary of Portugal, he married MARY I of England, but he left England in 1555 after failing to obtain his coronation there. He continued his father's war against France and at the Treaty of CATEAU-CAMBRÉSIS (1559) made Spain the chief power of Europe. Though repeatedly at odds with the papacy, he was a fanatic Catholic. To secure absolute power and to stamp out heresy became his immutable aims. The Spanish INQUISITION reached its height during his reign, and its attempted introduction into the Low Countries led to the rebellion of the NETHERLANDS and the loss of the Dutch provinces. In 1580, when Henry I of Portugal died without issue, Philip claimed the succession, seized Portugal, and was recognized as king by the Portuguese Cortes. The aid given by England to the Dutch rebels and the raid by Sir Francis Drake on the port of Cádiz (1587) determined Philip to fit out the Invincible ARMADA for an invasion of England (1588). The destruction of the Armada made British seapower supreme. Philip also aided the Catholic LEAGUE in the French Wars of Religion, ultimately without success. His chief colonial conquest was that of the PHILIPPINE ISLANDS. Despite the tremendous influx of American gold, Philip's wars necessitated increasing tax burdens. His reign, however, saw a short-lived economic prosperity. His coldness, cruel fanaticism, and tyrannical attention to detail are well-known. His third wife, Elizabeth of Valois, and his unfortunate son Don CARLOS died in 1568. His fourth wife, Anne of Austria (daughter of Emperor Maximilian II) gave birth to his successor, **Philip III,** 1578–1621, king of Spain, Sicily, Naples, and Portugal (1598–1621). He left the actual government to Francisco de LERMA. Peace was made with England (1604), and a truce with the United Provs. (1609), but in 1620 Spain entered the Thirty Years War. Philip's bigotry was a factor in the expulsion of the MORISCOS (1609). His reign was a glorious period of Spanish civilization—the age of Cervantes, Lope de Vega, and El Greco. He was succeeded by his son, **Philip IV,** 1605–65, who lost PORTUGAL in 1640. His reign was a period of decline and was dominated until 1643 by OLIVARES. The Peace of the PYRENEES with France (1659) was humiliating for Spain. His son Charles II succeeded him. **Philip V,** 1683–1746, first Bourbon king of Spain (1700–1746), was a grandson of Louis XIV. CHARLES II of Spain designated him as his successor. Louis XIV, by accepting the Spanish throne for his grandson, set off the War of the SPANISH SUCCESSION (1701–14), which greatly reduced Spanish power (see UTRECHT, PEACE OF). Weak and mentally unbalanced, he was dominated by women—first by the princesse des URSINS, who made French influence paramount, then by his queen, ELIZABETH FARNESE, who in turn was dominated by Cardinal ALBERONI. Alberoni's attempt to regain the Spanish possessions in Italy led to the QUADRUPLE ALLIANCE of 1718, to which Spain had to submit (1720). The dynastic interests of the Bourbon family involved Spain in the Wars of the POLISH SUCCESSION and the AUSTRIAN SUCCESSION. His son Ferdinand VI succeeded him.

Philip, duke of Edinburgh: see EDINBURGH.

Philip (King Philip), d. 1676, Indian leader in most important Indian war of New England, chief of Wampanoag Indians; son of Massasoit. Hostility of Indians over forced land cessions, aided by execution of three Indians for murder by English, led to **King Philip's War,** 1675–76. Attacks on border settlements involved New England colonies and several Indian tribes. War, costly to colonists, brought end of fur trade and virtual end of tribal Indian life in S New England.

Philip Augustus: see PHILIP II, king of France.

Philip Neri, Saint (nā'rē), 1515–95, Italian priest. As a layman and later as a priest (after 1551) he worked among the poor of Rome, especially among men and boys. He founded a community of secular priests, which became the Oratory, and his oratories at San Girolamo in Rome and San Giovanni were very influential. Besides revivifying the faith of many, he also extended the use of the vernacular in services. Feast: May 26.

Philip of Hesse (Philip the Magnanimous), 1504–67, landgrave of Hesse (1509–67), champion of the Reformation. After vainly trying to reconcile Zwingli and Luther, he signed the Lutheran Augsburg Confession. He formed the SCHMALKALDIC LEAGUE (1531) and after its defeat at Mühlberg was held prisoner by Emperor Charles V (1547–52).

Philip of Swabia, c.1177–1208, German king (1198–1208); brother of Henry VI. On Henry's death (1197) he sought to secure the succession of his infant nephew, the later Emperor FREDERICK II, but he finally agreed to his own election. A minority of princes chose OTTO IV as antiking. The resulting warfare between the Ghibelline and the Guelphic rivals ended 1206 in Philip's favor, but Philip's murder by a private enemy eventually placed Otto on the throne. It is widely held that Philip was instrumental in diverting the Fourth Crusade in order to restore his father-in-law, ISAAC II of Byzantium.

Philippe Égalité: see ORLÉANS, LOUIS PHILIPPE JOSEPH, DUC D' (under ORLÉANS, family).

Philippeville (fēlēpvēl'), city (pop. 40,647), NE Algeria; port on the Mediterranean and outlet for Constantine. Founded 1838 by the French on site of Carthaginian colony.

Philippi (fĭlĭ'pī), anc. city of Macedonia founded (358? B.C.) by Philip II. Near here Octavian (Augustus) and Antony defeated Brutus and Cassius (42 B.C.). Paul addressed his epistle to the Philippians to the church recently estab. here.

Philippians, epistle of New Testament, written by St. Paul to Christians of Philippi (Macedonia). Letter contains eloquent lines on humility, on Christian joy and fear, and on renunciation for Christ.

Philippics (fĭlĭ'pĭks), three denunciatory orations against Philip II of Macedon by DEMOSTHENES. Cicero's polemics against Marc Antony are also called Philippics.

Philippine Islands (fĭ'lĭpēn), group of some 7,000 islands and rocks off SE Asia, in Malay Archipelago, constituting republic of the Philippines (total land area 114,830 sq. mi.; 1948 pop. 19,234,182). QUEZON CITY, near metropolis of MANILA, on LUZON, is cap.; there are 51 provinces. Largest island is Luzon (40,420 sq. mi.). Most of the islands are of volcanic origin; only c.400 are permanently inhabited. Mountain ranges traverse larger islands; Mt. Apo (9,690 ft.) on MINDANAO is highest peak. Of the many navigable rivers, CAGAYAN on Luzon is largest. The Philippines are entirely within the tropical zone; monsoons bring heavy rainfalls. Economy is predominantly agr.; rice and corn cover largest areas; sugar and copra are among principal exports. Islands have one of world's great stands of commercial timber, abound in mineral resources. Vast majority of inhabitants belong to Malay group, are known as Filipinos. Tagalog is basis of new national language; many Filipinos speak English. Ferdinand MAGELLAN led first Europeans to visit here (1521). Spanish conquest began in 1564, with arrival of Miguel LÓPEZ DE LEGASPI. Religious orders became increasingly powerful as Spanish Empire waned. Opposition to this power furthered sentiment for independence in 19th cent. in movement led by José RIZAL. Following SPANISH-AMERICAN WAR islands were transferred to U.S. control; Emilio AQUINALDO led insurrection. With inauguration of M. L. QUEZON as president (Nov. 15, 1935), Commonwealth of the Philippines was formally estab. After a ten-year transition period complete independence was to be estab. on July 4, 1946. War came in 1941 with Japanese attack; after fall of CORREGIDOR, Japanese occupied islands. U.S. forces, under Gen. Douglas MacArthur, liberated islands in 1944–45. Independence came as scheduled in 1946, but long-term U.S. trading rights and provisions for U.S. bases were granted.

Philippines, University of the, mainly at Manila; coed., state controlled; founded 1908. There are an agr. college at Laguna and junior colleges at Vigan and Cebu.

Philips, Ambrose, 1675?–1749, English author. His pastoral poems provoked Pope's ridicule and a famous quarrel. Wrote play *The Distrest Mother* (1712), from Racine, and estab. periodical *Freethinker* (1718).

Philips, John, 1676–1709, English poet, known for use of blank verse, as in *The Splendid Shilling* (1705), and for his turn to interest in nature, as in *Cyder* (1708).

Philipse Manor or **Philipsburgh Manor,** SE N.Y., colonial estate of Frederick Philipse, confirmed by royal charter in 1693, between Hudson (W) and Bronx rivers and between what are now North Tarrytown (N) and Yonkers. Manor hall (c.1682) at Yonkers, now state-owned, has historical collections. Castle Philipse (c.1683) at North Tarrytown has been restored as a museum of colonial Dutch life.

Philip the Bold, king of France: see PHILIP III.

Philip the Bold, 1342–1404, duke of Burgundy (1363–1404) and count of Flanders (1384–1404); younger son of John II of France. His father invested him with Burgundy; his marriage with Margaret, heiress of Flanders, brought him the succession to Flanders after his victory over Philip van ARTEVELDE (1382). He virtually ruled France as regent during the minority of Charles VI (1380–88). After the outbreak of the king's madness began Philip's struggle for power with the king's brother, Louis, duc d'ORLÉANS. His son, JOHN THE FEARLESS, inherited the quarrel.

Philip the Fair, king of France: see PHILIP IV.

Philip the Good, 1396–1467, duke of Burgundy and count of Flanders (1419–67); son of JOHN THE FEARLESS. Through marriage, treaty, conquest, and purchase, he acquired Hainaut, Holland, Zeeland, Friesland, Brabant, Limburg, Namur, Luxembourg, and Liége—i.e., the entire Low Countries. Supporting England in the Hundred Years War, he sponsored the Treaty of TROYES (1420) and helped estab. English rule in France; in 1435, however, he changed sides by concluding the Treaty of Arras with Charles VII of France. He later supported the PRAGUERIE rebellion against Charles and gave asylum to the dauphin (later LOUIS XI). His court was the most splendid in W Europe. His son Charles the Bold succeeded him.

Philip the Handsome, king of Castile: see PHILIP I, Spanish king.

Philip the Tall, king of France: see PHILIP V.

Philistia (fĭlĭs'tyŭ), anc. region of SW Palestine reaching to the Mediterranean. The five chief cities, Gaza, Ashkelon, Ashdod, Ekron, and Gath, formed a confederacy. In Bible the great Hebrew antagonists of the Philistines are Samson, Saul, and David. Philistines later paid tribute to Assyria; were assimilated by various Semitic races.

Phillips, Stephen, 1868–1915, English poet and dramatist. His works include the poetic dramas *Paolo and Francesca* (1900) and *Herod* (1901).

Phillips, Wendell, 1811–84, American reformer and orator. Fought for many unpopular causes. Prominent as an abolitionist. His oratorical style was easy, colloquial.

Phillips Academy: see ANDOVER, Mass.

Phillipsburg, industrial town (pop. 18,919), NW N.J., on Delaware R. (bridged) opposite Easton, Pa.; settled 1739. Peter Cooper introduced Bessemer process here 1856. Mfg.

of metal products, chemicals, cement, and textiles.

Phillips Exeter Academy: see EXETER, N.H.

Philo (fī'lō) or **Philo Judaeus** (jōōdē'ůs), c.20 B.C.–A.D. c.50, Alexandrian Jewish philosopher. He took the Mosaic law as the foundation of philosophy, but he held that God had created the world indirectly through his potencies and attributes. All beings between the perfection of God and imperfect, finite matter have their unity in, and proceed from, the divine Logos. These teachings had a profound influence on Jewish and Christian writers.

Philoctetes (fĭlŏktē'tēz), in Greek mythology, king of Malians. He inherited bow and poisonous arrows of his friend Hercules. Oracle said that Troy could not be taken without these weapons. Though ill, Philoctetes was taken to Troy, where he was healed and where he then killed Paris.

philology [Gr.,= love of the word], study of texts (esp. to establish correct ones). In 19th cent. term was extended to include comparative study of languages. Later the word LINGUISTICS was applied to scientific study of language (including comparative linguistics), and philology fell back into its old restricted use.

Philomela (fĭlōmē'lů), in Greek myth, sister of Procne. Tereus, Thracian king, married Procne, then hid her and married Philomela, whose tongue he cut out to silence her. The gods changed them all into birds. Philomela became the nightingale, and her name is used in poetic references to that bird (as in Milton and Keats).

philosopher's stone: see ALCHEMY.

Philostratus (Flavius Philostratus) (fĭlŏ'strůtůs), fl. c.217, Greek Sophist, called the Athenian, author of *Lives of the Sophists.*

Phinehas or **Phinees** (both: fĭ'nēůs). **1** Grandson of Aaron. His swift punishment of two sinners made his name a symbol of holy indignation. Ex. 6.25; Num. 25; 31.6; Joshua 22.13; 24.33; Judges 20.28; 1 Chron. 6.4,50; 9.20; Ezra 7.5; Ps. 106.30; 1 Mac. 2.26,54. **2** Son of Eli who, with his brother Hophni, met death because of sacrileges. 1 Sam. 1–4.

Phippsburg, town (pop. 1,134), including Popham Beach resort, SW Maine, at Kennebec R. mouth and S of Bath. Site of Fort St. George (1607), a Plymouth Co. colony led by George Popham, destroyed by Indians, and resettled c.1737.

Phips, Sir William, 1651–95, American colonial governor. Became first royal governor of Mass. in 1692 through support of Increase MATHER.

Phiz: see BROWNE, HABLOT KNIGHT.

phlogiston theory (flōjĭ'stŏn) of combustion; propounded by J. J. Becher and G. E. Stahl. It stated that phlogiston is present in all materials that burn and is given off during burning. It was widely supported until Lavoisier showed true nature of combustion.

phlox (flŏks), annual or perennial plant of genus *Phlox,* native to North America and widely cultivated. They range in size from the tall, showy border types with masses of fragrant flowers, to the creeping moss pink (*Phlox subulata*). The annuals are mostly derived from a Texan native, *P. drummondi.*

Phocis (fō'sĭs), anc. state, central Greece, N of the Gulf of Corinth. Included Mt. Parnassus and particularly Delphi, which after the Sacred War of c.596 B.C. was put in control of a council of states. With Athenian help Phocis regained it in 457 B.C. Later Phocis was under Theban control; an attempt to regain independence led to the Sacred War of 356–346 B.C., in which Philip II of Macedon triumphed.

Phocylides (fůsĭ'lĭdēz), fl. early 6th cent. B.C., Greek gnomic poet. His moral epigrams exist in fragments.

Phoebe (fē'bē), in Greek mythology. **1** Daughter of Gaea, mother of Leto, and grandmother of Artemis. **2** Name of Artemis as goddess of the moon.

phoebe, small migratory bird of flycatcher family of North America. Eastern phoebe or water pewee is brownish gray above, gray and yellow below.

Phoebus: see APOLLO.

Phoenicia (fĭnē'shů, fĭnĭ'shů), territory of Phoenician civilization. Area of Tyre and Sidon, coast of present Lebanon. Also spelled Phenice, Phenicia.

Phoenician civilization. Early in history in Middle East, people speaking Semitic language moved westward and occupied coast of E Mediterranean. By 1250 B.C. Phoenicians were well estab. as navigators and traders. Organized politically into city-states, they later estab. outposts, notably Utica and Carthage. They sailed and traded all over Mediterranean and even into Atlantic. They made glass and metal articles, and were skilled weavers, dyers, and architects. Greatest contribution was alphabet, an idea adopted by Greeks. Rise of Persians and Greeks destroyed their maritime power, and Hellenistic culture finally eliminated last traces of Phoenician civilization.

Phoenix (fē'nĭks), city (pop. 106,818), state cap., S central Ariz., on Salt R.; founded 1867. Largest city in state. Sunny winter and health resort, it has opulent hotels and homes. Commercial and processing center for rich SALT RIVER VALLEY (irrigated farming), it also serves surrounding desert and mountains (mining, ranching). Succeeded Prescott as territorial cap., 1889. Has Heard (prehistoric relics) and Arizona museums, La Ciudad (Indian pueblo ruins), U.S. Indian school. Near by are South Mt. Park, with active gold mine, and Frank Lloyd Wright's "Taliesin West." Annual rodeo in Feb.

phoenix (fē'nĭks), fabulous bird of Egyptian legend. When it became 500 years old, it burned itself on a pyre. From its ashes another phoenix arose. As symbol of death and resurrection it has been favorite metaphor in pagan and Christian literature.

Phoenix Islands, group of eight coral islands (11 sq. mi.; pop. 984), central Pacific. CANTON ISLAND and Enderbury Isl. are under Anglo-American control; other islands belong to British colony of Gilbert and Ellice Islands. Group produces copra. Formerly worked for guano.

Phoenixville, borough (pop. 12,932), SE Pa., on Schuylkill R. and NW of Philadelphia; settled 1720. Near by is Valley Forge. Most western point of British advance in Pa. in

Revolution (1777). Ironworks, meat packing plants, and textile mills.

phonetics and **phonemics,** system of sounds of language, studied from two basic points of view. Phonetics is study of sounds of language according to their production in the vocal organs (articulatory phonetics) or their effect on the ear (acoustic phonetics). All phonetics is interrelated because human articulatory and auditory mechanisms are uniform. Systems of phonetic writing are aimed at transcribing accurately any sequence of speech sounds; most famous is International Phonetic Alphabet. Phonemics of a language is study of its phonemes and their arrangement. A phoneme is a group of variants of a speech sound, where the phonetic differences (including features of accent, pitch, intonation) are nonsignificant to the hearer-speaker. The sounds grouped in one phoneme of a particular language may in other languages be so distinct (significant) as to form separate phonemes.

phonograph, a device for reproducing sound waves already recorded in a spiral groove on a cylinder or disk. In 1877 Thomas A. Edison built the first such machine, with tin-foil cylinder. Disks were introduced by Emil Berliner in 1887. Capabilities of the machine were limited until electrical recording devices were developed (1925). A late innovation (1948) was the long playing record, made to revolve at a slower speed. This improved the quality of the sound and increased the amount of material that could be put on one disk. The "juke box," a coin-operated phonograph capable of playing by automatic selection up to 100 records, has a history which dates from the early part of the century and the coin-operated machines of the penny arcade.

phosphate, salt of phosphoric acid. Calcium phosphate is the most abundant and important. Acid calcium phosphate for fertilizers is prepared from it. Trisodium phosphate is used as a cleaner and in water softening, disodium salt in medicine. Acid phosphate of sodium is used in some baking powders.

phosphorescence (fŏsfûrĕ'sŭns) or **luminescence** (lo͞omĭnĕ'sŭns), in general sense, property of emitting light without perceptible heat. It is believed to result from motion of electrons and is classified according to nature of motion. Chemiluminescence is produced by chemical reactions, electroluminescence by electrical discharges, triboluminescence by rubbing or crushing crystals. It is also caused by absorption of radiant energy by certain substances; if it ceases when radiation stops it is called fluorescence; it is phosphorescence if it continues. Bioluminescence is luminescence emitted by living organism, e.g., luminous bacteria, glowworms, fireflies, and many deep-sea fish.

phosphoric acid (fŏsfô'rĭk). Three phosphoric acids are known, all derived from phosphorus pentoxide by addition of water. Metaphosphoric acid results from addition of one water molecule to one of pentoxide; pyro- of two; ortho- of three. Orthophosphoric acid is the common form; it appears as a crystalline solid and thick liquid. It is used in the laboratory and in medicine in form of salts.

phosphorus (fŏs'fûrŭs), nonmetallic chemical element (symbol = P; see also ELEMENT, table). Shows ALLOTROPY, appears in three forms. White phosphorus is a poisonous waxy solid, which ignites spontaneously in air and glows in dark at low temperatures. Red phosphorus is a dull, reddish brown crystalline powder, less active than the white form, and nonpoisonous. Black phosphorus is also known. Phosphorus does not occur free but is found abundantly in some compounds, e.g., calcium phosphate. The element is a constituent of protoplasm and therefore essential to life. It is used in fertilizers, in making matches, in smoke screens, in rodent poisons, and in certain alloys. White (or yellow) phosphorus melts at 44°C., boils at c.280°C.; red sublimes when heated under atmospheric pressure and under excess pressure melts at 550°–600°C.

Photius (fō'shŭs), c.820–892?, Greek churchman and theologian. He was a learned professor at the Univ. of Constantinople and president of the imperial chancellery under Michael III. Photius was in favor of treating the iconoclasts leniently, and when St. Ignatius of Constantinople was forced from the office of patriarch of Constantinople (858) Photius was rushed through ordination and made patriarch. Pope Nicholas I refused to recognize him. Photius called a synod that questioned some Latin customs, including the right of the pope to pass on election of patriarch. Under Basil I, Ignatius was patriarch again, and Photius was condemned at the Fourth Council of Constantinople; but Photius was restored on the death of Ignatius (877) and recognized by Pope John VIII. On the accession of Leo VI (886) Photius was forced to resign. He died in exile. The split of East and West is conventionally reckoned from this schism, though the significance can be easily exaggerated.

photoelectric cell or **phototube,** electron tube in which one of two electrodes emits electrons as a result of irradiation by visible light, ultraviolet, or infrared rays. Main types are highly evacuated or vacuum tube and gas tube, containing inert gas; form varies with purpose. Current is slight so battery is connected with tube so that anode is made positive and attracts electrons. Cell is integral part of "electric eye" devices which can act as switches to operate electrical devices when light reaches cell and to stop operation when light disappears. As phototube, the cell is used in sound-reproducing and television apparatus. See *ill.*, p. 377.

photoengraving, photomechanical process used in printing (notably for illustrations). A photograph of the subject to be reproduced is recorded on a sensitized metal plate which is then etched in an acid bath. For line cuts (solid black and white subjects) photoengravings are done on zinc. Half-tone cuts are photographed through a screen; the copper plate used is thus sensitized in a dotted pattern, larger dots creating darker areas, smaller dots, high lights.

photogrammetry: see AERIAL PHOTOGRAPHY.

photography, science and art concerned with forming and fixing an image on a film or a plate made sensitive to light. Earliest known form is camera obscura (see CAMERA) described by Leonardo da Vinci but generally credited to Giambattista della Porta. Development of light-sensitive surface which would retain an image stemmed from discovery (1727) that light causes darkening of silver salts. Thomas Wedgwood, Sir Humphry Davy, and others contributed to extending knowledge of silver salts. Sir John Herschel discovered hyposulphites (1819) and pointed out value of sodium hyposulphite as fixative for silver chloride when daguerreotypy became known (1839). Joseph Nicephore Niepce is generally credited with making first photograph (probably in 1822) by exposure of a light-sensitive surface within a camera. Niepce and later his son Isidore worked with Louis J. M. Daguerre on improving methods. Daguerre discovered (1837) principle of making daguerreotypes, which won popularity. Coloring of daguerreotypes was probably practiced by 1840. Tintypes also became popular in 19th cent. W. H. F. Talbot introduced practical method of photography in which negative image was formed within camera on light-sensitive paper from which positive images or prints could be made; he called his later modifications calotype and afterward talbotype process. Although others, too, claim the discovery, F. S. Archer is usually credited with making practicable the wet collodion process (1851) which replaced earlier photographic methods. Mathew B. Brady made notable photographs of Civil War scenes by wet collodion process. Eadweard Muybridge made early action photographs. Stereoscopic photography (see STEREOSCOPE) was popular in second half of 19th cent. Twin-lens cameras were developed for taking the pictures. Their use has been revived recently. By 1850s photography had begun to develop into an art. Among those who contributed to its development are H. P. Robinson, O. G. Rejlander, P. H. Emerson, Alfred Stieglitz, E. J. Steichen, Charles Sheeler, Paul Strand, Edward Weston, and C. H. White. Jacob Riis made early photographs of slum areas; later Dorothea Lange and Margaret Bourke-White depicted the lot of itinerant agricultural workers. Berenice Abbott became known especially for her scenes of life in New York city and her portraits. Photography became important, also, as a means of preserving a record of events; for illustrating books, periodicals, newspapers, and advertising matter; for documentary material; for teaching, e.g., in medical education and certain manual skills; for decorative purposes, e.g., photomurals. This growth was in part made possible by improvement in photographic equipment. The introduction of roll film by George Eastman in 1884 freed the photographer from the difficulties of coping with the fragile plates and bulky equipment used in both wet and dry collodion plate methods. Daylight-loading roll-film camera came into use in 1891. Film made with varying degrees of sensitivity and for special purposes was developed for use in the box, folding, miniature, and other styles of cameras. Color film that required only one exposure and could be used in ordinary cameras (commonly the 35-millimeter size) was introduced in 1935; the processed film forms transparencies which can be projected in color on a screen and from which enlarged color prints can be made. Another type of color film became available (1942) in most ordinary camera sizes; this forms negatives that show a reversal of color and of light and shade, and color prints can be made from them. The cost of a camera depends to a great extent upon the quality of the lens. Modern lenses are designed to prevent astigmatism and the better ones to avoid chromatic and spherical aberration and other defects. One system for indicating diaphragm opening (size of which determines amount of light permitted to pass through lens) is F number system, in which F number represents ratio of focal length to effective diameter of lens. Methods of using cameras and of developing and printing and principles of composition are given in many books on photography.

photometry (fōtŏ'mụtrē), branch of physics dealing with measurement of intensity of a light source, such as a lamp. Measuring instruments (photometers) make possible the comparison of unknown light intensity with known intensity. Experiments show that as light source moves away from surface it illuminates, illumination decreases in inverse proportion to square of distance. Commonly, electric-light intensity is given in candle power, intensity of illumination in foot-candles.

photosphere (fō'tụsfēr″), layer of gases beneath sun's chromosphere. Its incandescent gases, reaching temperature of c.6000° C., are so bright as to be seen as the sun's apparent surface.

photosynthesis (fō″tōsĭn'thụsĭs), process in which green plants utilize energy of sunlight to make carbohydrates from carbon dioxide and water. All animal and plant life are ultimately dependent upon it for food and oxygen. All plant forms containing the essential green pigment (see CHLOROPHYLL) are capable of photosynthesis; this process occurs only where chlorophyll is present. Oxygen is liberated in the process.

phototube: see PHOTOELECTRIC CELL.

Phrixus (frĭk'sụs), in Greek mythology. He was carried over the Hellespont to Colchis by the ram with the GOLDEN FLEECE.

Phrygia (frĭ'jēụ), anc. region of central Asia Minor, now in central Turkey. The Phrygians apparently came here from Europe c.1200 B.C. Little is known of their history. After 700 Lydia dominated the area. Later invaded by Gauls, then ruled by Pergamum and by Rome.

Phrynichus (frĭ'nĭkụs), fl. c.512–476 B.C., Athenian tragedian, by some ancients considered the founder of tragedy. The painful theme of his *The Taking of Miletus* so moved the audience that he was fined.

Phuket (po͝o'kĭt), island, area c.200 sq. mi., off W coast of Malay Peninsula, belonging to Thailand. Chief town (pop. 18,759) is also called Phuket; chief tin-mining center of Thailand. Malay name, Ujong Salang, was corrupted by early European voyagers to Junkceylon.

Phumiphon (po͞om'ĭpōn″), 1927–, king of

Thailand (1950–). Succeeded Ananda, his elder brother, who died mysteriously in 1946. A regency exercised the royal power until Phumiphon ascended the throne.

Phyfe, Duncan (fīf), c.1768–1854, American cabinetmaker, b. Scotland. During most productive period (until 1820) he was influenced by the Adam brothers, Hepplewhite, Sheraton, and French Directoire and Consulate styles. Designs of early period are marked by simple ornament and decorative motifs such as the lyre and the acanthus; those of last period tended to be heavy and overornamented. Used mainly solid mahogany but also satinwood, maple, and rosewood. See *ill.*, p. 456.

phylacteries (fĭlăk'tŭrēz) [Gr.,= safeguard], two small leather boxes worn during prayers by orthodox Jews after the age of 13 years. Each box contains strips of parchment inscribed with verses from the Scriptures: Ex. 13.1–10; 13.11–16; Deut. 6.4–9; 11.13–21. One box is fastened to the forehead and the other to the left arm. They are intended to serve as a reminder of the constant presence of God. They are not worn on the Sabbath or holy days.

phylloxera (fĭlŏk'sŭrŭ, fĭlŭksēr'ŭ), small greenish insect, classed with aphids or with closely related group. Many phylloxeras produce galls on deciduous trees. Best-known is grape phylloxera, *Phylloxera vitifoliae,* harmful pest of W U.S. and Europe.

physical geography: see GEOGRAPHY.

physical therapy (thĕ'rŭpē) or **physiotherapy** (fĭ"zēō–), treatment of disease with the aid of physical agents including radiation, light, heat, water, massage, and exercise.

Physick, Philip Syng, 1768–1837, pioneer American surgeon, first professor of surgery at Univ. of Pennsylvania (1805–19).

physics, science dealing with matter and energy and the relations between them. In addition to its major objective, the rational explanation of natural phenomena, it seeks quantitative definition of these phenomena. Its various branches include HEAT, MECHANICS, SOUND, MAGNETISM, ELECTRICITY. With discovery that matter is fundamentally electrical, higher physics and chemistry have become closely interrelated. Biophysics is concerned with the physical analysis of biological behavior, determination of effects of physical agents on biological material, and application of physical techniques to biological measurements.

physiocrats (fĭ'zēŭkrăts"), 18th-cent. French thinkers who evolved the first complete system of economics. Founder of the group was François QUESNAY; his most ardent disciple was Victor de Mirabeau. Quesnay held that all wealth originated with the land and that agriculture alone would multiply wealth. Laissez faire was necessary if the total economic process, based on agriculture, were to follow its natural course. Taxation was to be on land alone—an argument not without charm for industrialists. Physiocracy influenced Turgot and Joseph II, and, even more profoundly, Adam SMITH and Henry GEORGE, but today is it a dead doctrine.

physiology (fĭzēŏ'lŭjē), study of normal functioning of plants and animals and of activities by which life is maintained and transmitted. Includes vital activities of cells, tissues, organs, and systems (e.g., circulatory, nervous) and, in plants, also photosynthesis and transpiration.

physiotherapy: see PHYSICAL THERAPY.

pi, in mathematics, ratio of circumference of circle to its diameter (symbol is π). Ratio is same for all circles (c.3.1416). It is important in such advanced mathematics as continued fractions, periodic functions, and logarithms of imaginary numbers.

Piacenza (pyächĕn'tsä), city (pop. 49,527), Emilia-Romagna, N central Italy, on Po R. Agr. center. Formed part of duchy of PARMA and Piacenza 1545–1860. Has several fine churches.

piano or **pianoforte,** keyboard musical instrument, historically the youngest member of its family which includes the DULCIMER, the clavichord, the harpsichord, the spinet, and the virginal. The basic difference between the clavichord and harpsichord is that the strings of the clavichord are struck with hammers (called tangents), whereas the strings of the harpsichord are plucked by quills. Both instruments reached the height of their popularity between the 16th and 18th cent. The clavichord consists of a small, rectangular wooden box containing a sounding board and strings running parallel to the keyboard. The tone, which can be modified by the touch of the performer, is expressive but faint. The harpsichord of the 15th cent. was wing-shaped (similar to today's grand piano), but the square harpsichord, with strings at right angles to the keyboard, was more common in the 16th cent. Varying the touch in harpsichord playing does not alter the quality or volume of tone. The spinet and virginal are similar to the harpsichord in that their strings are plucked. The terms *spinet* and *virginal,* interchangeable until the 17th cent., were sometimes used indiscriminately to designate any harpsichord. The spinet is generally distinguished by its wing-shaped case and strings at a 45° angle to the keyboard in contrast to the virginal's rectangular case and strings parallel to the keyboard. A keyboard instrument was needed that would combine the brilliance of the harpsichord with the expressiveness of the clavichord. Bartolomeo Cristofori, a Florentine harpsichord maker, is given credit for making the first piano in 1709. He called his instrument *gravicembalo col piano e forte.* In the piano, like the clavichord, the strings are struck with a hammer. The design of the piano's case and the arrangement of strings was taken from the harpsichord. Because of its great capabilities (further increased by technical developments of the 19th cent.), the piano displaced the clavichord and harpsichord and steadily evolved into the concert grand of today. In the 19th cent. appeared the upright piano and the small oblong piano called the spinet. Mozart and Haydn were the first major composers to write for the piano; with the works of Beethoven, Chopin, Schumann, and Liszt, the piano became the outstanding solo instrument.

Piast (pyäst), first dynasty of Polish dukes and kings. Duke Mieszko I (962–92) introduced

Christianity and began unification of Poland. BOLESLAUS I, his son, was crowned king 1025. The law of succession introduced by Boleslaus III (1102–38), which provided for the rotation of the crown among four branches of the family, destroyed Polish unity until CASIMIR II and LADISLAUS I restored the royal authority. The dynasty died out in Poland proper with Casimir III (1370) and was succeeded by the JAGIELLO dynasty. In SILESIA, members of the Piast dynasty ruled several principalities (after 1335 under Bohemian overlordship)—the duchy of Oppeln until 1532 and the principalities of Brieg and Liegnitz until 1675.

Piatigorsky, Gregor (pyätĭgôr'skē), 1903–, Russian-American cellist and teacher. First cellist with the Berlin Philharmonic in 1923, he became a solo cellist in 1928 and came to the U.S. in 1929.

Piauí (pyouē'), state (97,261 sq. mi.; pop. 1,064,438), NE Brazil, on E bank of Parnaíba R.; cap. TERESINA. Extensive livestock grazing. Exports include oilseeds, babassu nuts, cotton, tobacco, rubber.

Piave (pyä'vā), river, 137 mi. long, flowing through Venetia, N Italy, to the Adriatic. In World War I Italians entrenched here withstood Austrian attacks from 1917 until Austrian rout by Allies in 1918.

Piazzi, Giuseppe (jōōzĕp'pā pyät'tsē), 1746–1826, Italian astronomer, a Theatine priest. Discovered first asteroid (Ceres; 1801). Made star catalogue.

Picard, Jean (zhã' pēkär'), 1620–82, French astronomer, first to measure accurately the length of one-degree arc of earth's surface.

Picardy (pĭ'kûrdē), Fr. *Picardie,* region and former province, N France, in Somme, Aisne, Oise, and Pas-de-Calais depts. and bordering on English Channel and Belgium; historic cap. Amiens. Other cities: Abbeville, Calais, Boulogne-sur-Mer. Agr.; textile mfg. Name was first used in 13th cent. to designate fiefs added to royal domain by Philip II.

Picasso, Pablo (Ruiz y) (pä'blō pēkä'sō), 1881–, Spanish painter, b. Malaga. Studied in Barcelona and in Paris (after 1900), where he remained and associated with Derain, Bracque, and Matisse. His "blue" and "rose" periods (1901–6), named for dominant colors of the paintings, tended to be conventional. Influenced by Iberian sculpture, Negro masks, and the art of Cézanne, he began c.1906 to create compositions in angular planes, painting such works as *Les Demoiselles d'Avignon* and the portrait of Gertrude Stein (Metropolitan Mus.). By 1909 his dissection of forms developed into the style known as CUBISM. There followed a neoclassical period in '20s. A new period of powerful expression was climaxed (1937) by the mural *Guernica,* a dramatic response to agonies of Spanish civil war. He continued to produce paintings and sculptures, working as always in many styles simultaneously. Much of his later output has been in pottery. The dove he drew for Communist-sponsored Congress of Partisans of Peace (1949) became famous as a political symbol.

Picayune (pĭkûyōōn'), city (pop. 6,707), S Miss., near Pearl R. and NE of New Orleans. Processing and shipping tung products and naval stores.

Piccadilly (pĭk"ùdĭl'ē), famous street of shops, hotels, and clubs in W London, extending from Piccadilly Circus to Hyde Park Corner.

Piccard, Auguste (ōgüst' pēkär'), 1884–, Belgian physicist. Ascended into stratosphere in balloons to study cosmic rays; in 1932 ascended to c.55,500 ft. After 1938 made undersea dives with bathysphere. His twin brother, **Jean Piccard** (zhã), 1884–, American citizen from 1931, chemist and aeronautical engineer on Univ. of Minnesota faculty, also made stratosphere balloon ascents.

Piccinni or **Piccini, Niccolò** (both: pēchē'nē), 1728–1800, Italian composer of over 100 operas, of which *La buona figliuola* was most successful. Opponents to opera reforms of GLUCK made Piccinni their unwilling champion.

Piccirilli (pēt-chērē'lē), family of Italian-American marble cutters and sculptors. Workshop in Bronx, New York, is widely known. Came to U.S. in 1888.

piccolo: see WIND INSTRUMENTS.

Piccolomini, Enea Silvio de': see PIUS II.

Piccolomini, Octavio (ōktä'vyō pēk-kōlô'mēnē), 1599–1656, Italian general in imperial service during Thirty Years War. Supported conspiracy against WALLENSTEIN.

Pic du Midi (pēk' dü mēdē'), two peaks of Pyrenees, S France—**Pic du Midi de Bigorre** (dù bēgôr'), 9,439 ft. high, in central Pyrenees; **Pic du Midi d'Ossau** (dôsō'), 9,465 ft. high, in W Pyrenees.

Pickens, Andrew, 1739–1817, American Revolutionary partisan leader. Formed armed band to harass British in S.C. His grandson, **Francis Wilkinson Pickens,** 1805–69, was governor of S.C. (1860–62) when that state seceded.

Pickens, Fort, fortification on W end of Santa Rosa Isl. at entrance to Pensacola Bay, Fla. Occupied and held by Union throughout Civil War.

pickerel (pĭ'krùl, pĭ'kùrùl), name for various small fish of pike family. Eastern or common and barred pickerel are in fresh waters of E U.S.

Pickering, Edward Charles (pĭ'kûrĭng), 1846–1919, American astronomer and physicist, pioneer in photographic photometry and spectroscopy. His brother **William Henry Pickering,** 1858–1938, also a noted astronomer, predicted discovery and location of Pluto, discovered ninth satellite of Saturn, added to knowledge of Mars, other planets, and moon.

Pickering, Timothy, 1745–1829, American Revolutionary general and statesman. Quartermaster general (1780–85). U.S. Secretary of State (1795–1800); dismissed by Pres. John Adams. U.S. Senator (1803–11). A strong Federalist.

picketing, act of guarding a place of work affected by a strike in order to discourage patronage and often to prevent strikebreakers (scabs) from taking over the strikers' jobs. Has also been used by political movements to influence legislation.

Pickett, George Edward, 1825–75, Confederate general. Best known for "Pickett's charge" in Gettysburg campaign (July 3, 1863), a

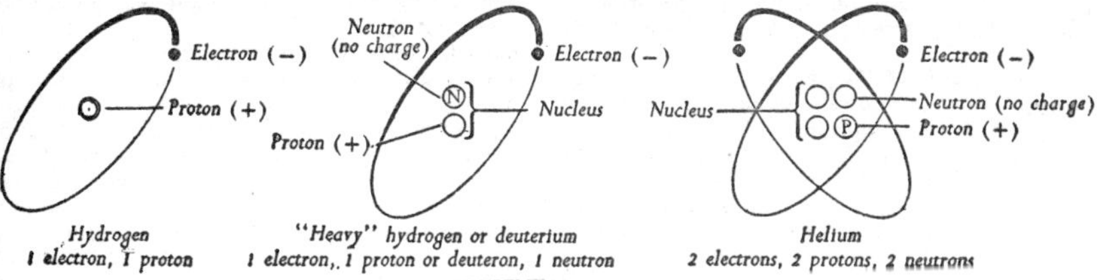

DIAGRAMMATIC REPRESENTATION OF SIMPLE NUCLEI
(These are conventional diagrams; actually the electron orbits are not precisely determined geometric curves.)

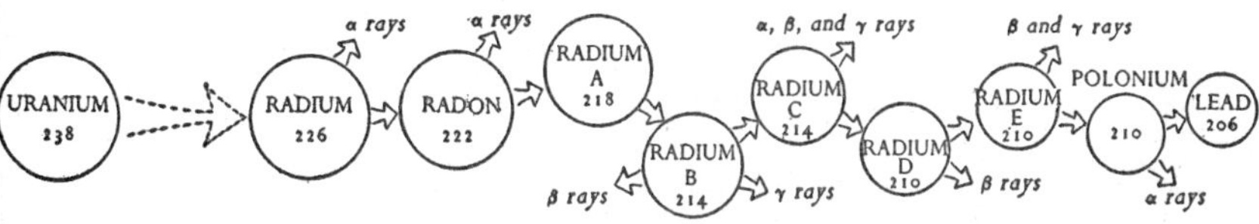

SPONTANEOUS DISINTEGRATION OF RADIOACTIVE ELEMENTS
Energy is released in the form of α rays (helium ion), β rays (electrons), and γ rays (X rays)

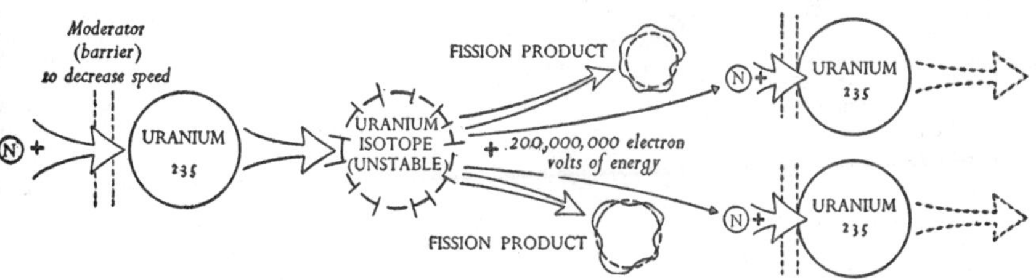

NUCLEAR FISSION RESULTING FROM HITTING URANIUM-235 WITH NEUTRON BULLETS
The released neutrons at the right contribute to a "chain reaction" with other uranium atoms. U-235 is a scarce isotope; uranium ore contains U-235 and U-238 in proportion ca. 1:140.

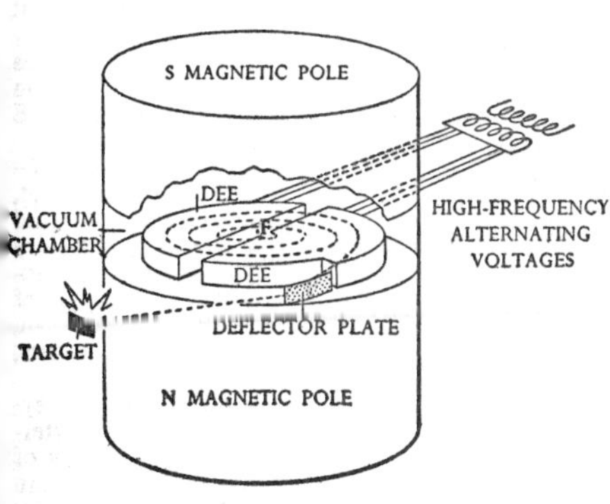

DIAGRAM OF A CYCLOTRON USED IN NUCLEAR RESEARCH

Protons or deuterons produced at a source F rotate within the dee spaces, between the poles of a heavy magnet. They are accelerated by the alternating current every time they cross the gap. When their velocity is great enough they pass out of the dee, rebound from the deflector plate, and bombard the target.

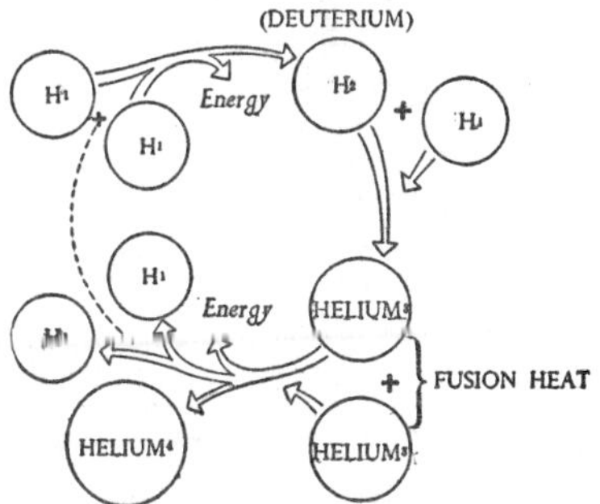

PROTON-PROTON CYCLE TAKING PLACE IN THE SUN

During this continuous cycle vast amounts of energy (heat, light, ultraviolet rays) are given off. The H-bomb employs a similar principle. Whereas the energy of the A-bomb is derived from *fission* of a heavy atom, here energy is released when light hydrogen nuclei *fuse* to form a helium nucleus. The reaction is thermonuclear, since it takes place only at temperatures of some 15-20 million degrees C. In the H-bomb this temperature is provided by a preceding A-type explosion.

heroic effort ending in virtual annihilation of his division. Defeated at Five Forks (April 1, 1865).

Pickford, Mary, 1893–, American film actress, whose real name is Gladys Smith. Known as "America's Sweetheart" for simple, sentimental roles (e.g., in *Poor Little Rich Girl, Daddy Long Legs*).

pickle, name for fruits and vegetables preserved in vinegar, often with spices or sugar or both. Many materials and combinations have been used in many lands; perhaps best known in U.S. is the cucumber pickle, either sweet or flavored with dill. In a wider sense, a pickle is a preservative liquid, such as brine for meat, brandy for fruit.

Pico della Mirandola, Giovanni, Conte (jōvän'nē kōn'tā pē'kō dĕl'lä mērän'dōlä), 1463–94, Italian humanist, renowned for youthful brilliance and learning. He was interested in science and magic.

Picquart, Georges (zhôrzh' pēkär'), 1854–1914, French officer. As chief of intelligence in 1895 he discovered the evidence which eventually exonerated Capt. Dreyfus (see DREYFUS AFFAIR). In reprisal for disclosing the evidence he was dismissed, but he was later reinstated and served as war minister.

picric acid (pĭ'krĭk), explosive, pale yellow, bitter tasting crystalline solid compound of carbon, hydrogen, oxygen, and nitrogen; also called trinitrophenol. It reacts with metals to form explosive salts; explodes on detonation; is basic substance in high explosive lyddite (British). Used also as dye and as antiseptic.

Picts, anc. inhabitants of central and N Scotland and N Ireland. Those in Scotland came from Continent in pre-Celtic times (possibly c.1000 B.C.) and probably emigrated to Ireland in 2d cent. A.D.

pidgin English or **pigeon English** [*pidgin,* supposedly from *business*], auxiliary language, a LINGUA FRANCA, of Far Eastern ports, used principally for trading between Europeans and Chinese. Basic English vocabulary has Malay, Chinese, and Portuguese words.

pie, meat, fish, fowl, fruit, or vegetables baked in a crust of pastry. Pies were known to Romans, and were common in England by 14th cent.; mince pie early became a festive Christmas dish. Early Americans evolved new kinds, including pumpkin pie.

Piedmont (pēd'mŏnt), Ital. *Piemonte,* region (9,817 sq. mi.; pop. 3,418,300), NW Italy, bounded along Alpine crests by France and Switzerland; cap. TURIN. Mountain pastures slope down to upper Po valley (cereals, fruits). Has automobile and textile mfg.; hydroelectric plants. Marquisates of Turin and Ivrea passed in 11th cent. to SAVOY dynasty, which emerged by 15th cent. as chief power in Piedmont and which ruled the kingdom of Sardinia from 1720. Annexed to France 1798, Piedmont was restored to Sardinia 1814.

Piedmont, residential city (pop. 10,132), W Calif., surrounded by Oakland.

Pied Piper of Hamelin, legendary figure of Hameln, Germany. He rid the town of rats and mice by charming them away with his flute playing. Refused the price agreed upon by the townspeople, he charmed away their children in revenge.

Piedras Negras (pyā'dhräs nā'gräs), city (pop. 15,663), Coahuila, N Mexico, on the Rio Grande opposite Eagle Pass, Texas.

Pierce, Franklin, 1804–69, 14th President of the United States (1853–57). U.S. Representative from N.H. (1833–37) and U.S. Senator (1837–42). Gained Democratic presidential nomination in 1852 as a candidate unobjectionable to the South. A well-meaning mediocrity, he worked in difficult times; his administration fared poorly. A vigorous foreign policy failed of most of its objectives. Domestically, GADSDEN PURCHASE was made, but plans for transcontinental railroad fell through: KANSAS-NEBRASKA BILL brought on explosive sectional difficulties.

Pieria (pīēr'ēŭ), region of anc. Macedonia, including Mt. Olympus and Mt. Pierus (sacred to Orpheus and the Muses), with the Pierian Spring (bubbling with the water of learning and the arts).

Piermont, village (pop. 1,897), SE N.Y., on Hudson R. near N.J. line. Pier, built by Erie RR, was debarkation point for troops in World War II.

Pierné, (Henri Constant) Gabriel (gäbrēĕl' pyĕrnā'), 1863–1937, French organist, conductor, and composer. Organist at Ste Clotilde, Paris, 1890–98 (succeeding his former teacher, César Franck). His oratorio *La Croisade des Enfants* is perhaps best known of his serious music; of his shorter works, the *March of the Little Lead Soldiers* and the *Entrance of the Little Fauns* are highly popular.

Piero della Francesca (pyā'rō dĕl'lä fränchā'skä), c.1420–1492, Umbrian painter, known also as Piero de' Franceschi. Renowned for innovations in perspective and for mastery of light and atmosphere. Among notable works are *Flagellation* (Urbino) and *Nativity* and *Baptism of Christ* (Natl. Gall., London). Wrote a remarkable treatise on geometry.

Piero di Cosimo (dē kô'zēmō), 1462–1521, Florentine painter, whose real name was Piero di Lorenzo. Adopted the name of his master, Cosimo Rosseli, whom he assisted in decorating Sistine Chapel. Famed for landscape backgrounds of his mythological and religious pictures. Influenced in later years by Leonardo da Vinci.

Pierpont, Francis Harrison, 1814–99, Civil War leader of Union government in Va., "father of West Virginia." Aided creation of new state of W.Va (admitted 1863) after secession of Va.

Pierpont Morgan Library, originally the private library of J. Pierpont Morgan, in 1924 made a public institution as a memorial by his son. The library is rich in illuminated manuscripts and in authors' manuscripts (including some of Dickens, of Scott, and of Balzac).

Pierre (pēr), city (pop. 5,715), state cap. (since 1889), central S.Dak., on the Missouri opposite Fort Pierre; founded 1880. Ships livestock from ranches in W part of state and produce from farms in E part. Has memorial hall with historical collection.

Pierrot (pē'ŭrō) [Fr.,= little Peter], French pantomime character, a buffoon in a large tunic, whose face is painted white.

Piers Plowman (pērz). *The Vision Concerning Piers Plowman* is a 14th-cent. allegorical

English poem in unrhymed alliterative verse, written in three stages (1362, 1376–77, 1393–99), probably by William LANGLAND. Recounts vivid dreams in which poet attacks venality in clergy and people and exalts dedicated Christianity.

Pietermaritzburg (pē″tûrmă′rĭtsbûrg), city (pop. 60,609), cap. of Natal, South Africa; founded 1838 by the Boers. Seat of Univ. of Natal Col. Popularly called Maritzburg.

Pietism, movement in Lutheran Church in 17th and 18th cent. to combat settled, intellectual attitude. P. J. Spener began in 1670 to hold devotional meetings, stressing Bible study and practice of Christian belief. Aim was not Puritanism, but placing of spirit of living above letter of doctrine, implying a justification by works contrary to Luther's views.

Pietro d'Abano: see ABANO, PIETRO D'.

pig: see SWINE.

Pigeon, short river flowing E into L. Superior and forming part of boundary between NE Minn. and W Ont. Once terminus of the GRAND PORTAGE.

pigeon, bird of family (Columbidae) related to plover; also called DOVE. Found in most temperate and tropical regions. Common pigeon, seen on city streets, is descended from rock dove of European coasts. Favorite domesticated varieties include Jacobin, fantail, tumbler, pouter, carrier, homing pigeon. Young are fed on "pigeon's milk" from parents' crops.

pigeon English: see PIDGIN ENGLISH.

pig iron: see IRON.

pigment, in paint, powdered substance which is mixed in the liquid medium to add color. Most pigments are metallic compounds, but most black pigments are organic. Some metallic pigments occur naturally in rock and soil and in plant and animal bodies. A LAKE is prepared artificially.

pigmentation, coloring matter found in certain plant and animal cells. Common plant pigment is CHLOROPHYLL. In higher animals, the black pigment melanin is present in dermis of skin, in hair, and in retina of eye; degree of melanin determines dominant skin color; skin has several other pigments.

Pigmy: see PYGMY.

pignut, a species of HICKORY.

Pike, Zebulon M(ontgomery), 1779–1813, American explorer, an army officer. Led expedition (1806–7) through the Southwest into Colo.; sighted peak called after him Pikes Peak. Wrote valuable narrative of his travels.

pike, fresh-water game fish of N Hemisphere. It has long jaws, strong teeth, and elongated body.

pike, in U.S. history: see TURNPIKE.

Pikes Peak, 14,110 ft. high, central Colo., in S part of Front Range; discovered 1806 by Z. M. PIKE. Best known and most conspicuous peak in the Rockies, it stands on edge of Great Plains. Colorado Springs is at E base. Railroad, highway to snow-covered top.

Pikeville, town (pop. 5,154), E Ky., in Cumberlands on Levisa Fork, in coal and timber region.

Pilate: see PONTIUS PILATE.

Pilcomayo (pēlkōmä′yō), river rising in the Bolivian Andes E of L. Poopó and flowing 700 mi. SE across Chaco to Paraguay R. near Asunción. In Chaco it is boundary between Argentina and Paraguay.

pile, post of timber, steel, or concrete for supporting a structure. Vertical piles or bearing piles (most common form) generally are needed for foundations of bridges, docks, piers, and buildings. Wooden piles are usually shaped for driving, sometimes tipped with iron. Concrete piles are of two types, precast and cast in place.

piles, in medicine: see HEMORRHOIDS.

pilgrim, one who travels to a shrine out of religious motives. Pilgrimages are a feature of many cultures. Jews made annual pilgrimage to Jerusalem at Passover. Moslems make pilgrimage to Mecca. Protection of Holy Places in Palestine was the aim of the Crusades. Since 1300 the popes have set aside Holy Years for special pilgrimages to Rome. Modern Western shrines of the Roman Catholic Church include Loreto, Santiago de Compostela, Lourdes, and Fátima. Canterbury was an important shrine in the Middle Ages. In the New World well-known shrines are Ste Anne de Beaupré and Guadalupe Hidalgo.

Pilgrimage of Grace, 1536, rising of Roman Catholics in N England to protest against the abolition of papal supremacy and the confiscation of the monarchy. The significant part of the movement was led by Robert Aske in Yorkshire; he and his many followers reopened monasteries at York and moved on to Doncaster. But met by representatives of Henry VIII who offered them general pardon and a Parliament to be held in a year, they dispersed. Aske went to London and was received well. In 1537 Francis Bigod led a new rising at Beverly. Although Aske and other leaders of the Pilgrimage had tried to prevent this new move, they were arrested, tried, and executed with Bigod.

Pilgrims, in American history, founders of PLYMOUTH COLONY in Mass. Nucleus of group was English separatists who had moved to Holland in 1607–8. Obtained charter from London Co. and, with help of London merchants, sailed in MAYFLOWER in 1620.

Pillars of Hercules (hûr′kyo͝olēz), promontories at Gibraltar in Europe and at Ceuta in Africa, at E end of Strait of Gibraltar.

Pillnitz, Declaration of, 1791, statement issued at Castle of Pillnitz, Saxony, by Emperor Leopold II and Frederick William II of Prussia. Its call on the European powers to restore Louis XVI to his full authority as king of France helped to bring on the FRENCH REVOLUTIONARY WARS.

Pillow, Gideon Johnson, 1806–78, American general. Commanded in Mexican War. Confederate general in Civil War; suspended from command because of his conduct in escaping from Fort Donelson before Confederate surrender (1862).

Pillow, Fort, Civil War fortification on Mississippi R., c.40 mi. N of Memphis, built by G. J. Pillow in 1862. Taken by Union in 1862, it was captured by N. B. Forrest in 1864.

Pilnyak, Boris (bûrēs′ pēlnyäk′), pseud. of Boris Andreyevich Vogau, 1894–, Russian author. Among his works are *The Naked Year* (1922; Eng. tr., 1928), *Mahogany*

(1927), and *The Volga Falls into the Caspian Sea* (1930; Eng. tr., 1931)—novels on revolutionary and postrevolutionary Russia—and *OK* (1932), an unflattering report on a trip to the U.S. His antiurbanism and his criticism of mechanized society brought him into suspicion with Communist critics.

Piloty, Karl von (kärl' fŭn pēlō'tē), 1826–86, German historical painter, an influential teacher.

Pilsen (pĭl'sŭn), Czech *Plzeň,* city (pop. 103,767), NW Bohemia, Czechoslovakia. Famous for its beer. Has huge Skoda works, producing locomotives, cars, armaments. City was a center of Catholicism in Hussite Wars and withstood many sieges (15th cent.).

Pilsudski, Joseph (pĭlsŏŏd'skē), 1867–1935, Polish marshal and statesman. Originally a Socialist, he was repeatedly exiled and imprisoned by Russian authorities. In World War I he commanded Polish forces under Austrian sponsorship, but toward the war's end he quarrelled with the Central Powers and was interned. Released in Nov., 1918, he proclaimed an independent Polish republic, with himself as chief of state. His campaigr against Russia (aimed at restoring E frontier of 1772) ended victoriously with the Treaty of RIGA (1921). He retired to private life in 1922 but in 1926 overthrew the government by a coup d'état and from then to his death governed as virtual dictator.

Pima Indians (pē'mŭ), North American tribe of Uto-Aztecan linguistic stock, in S Ariz. Visited early by Spanish missionaries, they were friendly to the whites. They were hostile to the Apache. They farm with use of irrigation and are noted for basketry.

pimento, name for tree which bears ALLSPICE berry and also for a large sweet Spanish PEPPER.

Pimlico (pĭm'lĭkō), district of W London, England.

pimpernel (pĭm'pŭrnĕl), Old World flowering plant of genus *Anagallis.* Scarlet pimpernel (*Anagallis arvensis*) has red (sometimes white or blue) starlike flowers which remain open only in sunshine.

Pinchot, Gifford (gĭ'fŭrd pĭn'chō), 1865–1946, American forester and public official. Served in division of forestry, U.S. Dept. of Agriculture (1898–1910). Member of many conservation commissions. Governor of Pa. (1923–27, 1931–35).

Pinckney, Charles, 1757–1824, American statesman, governor of S.C. (1789–92, 1796–98, 1806–8). As minister to Spain (1801–5) he failed to gain cession of Fla. to U.S. His cousin, **Charles Cotesworth Pinckney,** 1746–1825, participated in mission which led to XYZ AFFAIR. C. C. Pinckney's brother, **Thomas Pinckney,** 1750–1828, served as envoy extraordinary to Spain (1794–95). Negotiated treaty with Spain (1795).

pincushion flower: see SCABIOSA.

Pindar (pĭn'dŭr), 518?–c.438 B.C., generally regarded as greatest Greek lyric poet. Wrote chiefly choral lyrics; developed triumphal ode or epinicion, celebrating athletic victories but usually invoking a myth. Extant are 44 complete odes and numerous fragments. His style is marked by high-flown diction, intricate word order, and religious tone. The **Pindaric ode** (pĭndă'rĭk) is a verse form used especially in England in 17th and early 18th cent., based on incorrect understanding of Pindar's metrics. Form, originated (1656) by COWLEY, and used by Dryden, Pope, and Swift, was irregular and of grandiose diction.

Pindus (pĭn'dŭs), Gr. *Pindos,* mountain range, 100 mi. long, NW and W central Greece, along border of Thessaly and Epirus. Rises to 8,650 ft.

pine, coniferous pyramidal tree of genus *Pinus,* represented by c.80 species in the N Hemisphere. The needlelike leaves (1–12 in. long) are produced singly or in clusters up to five; they remain on the branch from two to ten years. Staminate and pistillate cones are borne on the same tree. Pine nuts are the edible seeds of various species, e.g., the Colorado pine nut or piñon tree (*Pinus cembroides edulis*). The white pine (*P. strobus*) of E North America is a valuable timber tree. Species with similar straight-grained, soft wood containing little resin include the western white pine (*P. monticola*), the lodgepole pine (*P. contorta latifolia*), and the sugar pine (*P. lambertiana*). Yellow or pitch pines have harder, more resinous wood. These include the longleaf pine (*P. palustris*), a source of turpentine and other naval stores; the red or Norway pine (*P. resinosa*); and the shortleaf pine (*P. echinata*). In European forests the Scotch pine (*P. sylvestris*) is one of the chief coniferous trees.

pineal gland (pĭ'nēŭl), small cone-shaped body on roof of brain. In man, its glandular tissue begins to become fibrous at age of about seven. Function not definitely known. Gland is rudimentary in vertebrates from fish to mammals.

pineapple, herbaceous perennial (*Ananas comosus*) of tropical America, and its spiny delicious fruit. Cuba, Puerto Rico, and Hawaii lead in commercial production of the fruit, the juice and flesh of which are canned in large quantities. A fiber from the spiny leaves is made into piña or pineapple cloth in the Philippines.

Pine Barrens, coastal plain region (area c.3,000 sq. mi.) of S and SE N.J. Region of sandy soils and swamp-edged streams; supports pine stands and tracts of cranberries and blueberries.

Pine Bluff, city (pop. 37,162), SE central Ark., on Arkansas R. and SE of Little Rock; settled 1819. Rail and market center for agr. area. Cotton and lumber processing; chemical mfg.; stockyards. Seat of Arkansas Agricultural, Mechanical, and Normal Col. (Negro; coed.; chartered 1873).

Pinehurst, winter resort (pop. 1,016), central N.C., SW of Raleigh. Golf courses and horse-training facilities.

Pinel, Philippe (fēlēp' pēnĕl'), 1745–1826, French physician. He advocated humane treatment of the insane, empirical study of mental disease. He stressed the role of the passions in mental disease, kept well-documented case histories for research.

Pinero, Sir Arthur Wing (pĭnēr'ō), 1855–1934, English dramatist. Wrote realistic "problem" plays such as *The Second Mrs. Tanqueray* (1893), *The Notorious Mrs. Ebbsmith*

(1895), and *Mid-Channel* (1909) and the farce *Trelawny of the Wells* (1898).

Pines, Isle of, Span. *Isla de Pinos,* island (1,182 sq. mi.; pop. 9,812), off SW Cuba. Discovered by Columbus (1494), it was used as penal colony and rendezvous for buccaneers. Claimed by U.S. citizens but confirmed as belonging to Cuba (1925). Popular tourist resort. Chief products are tobacco, fruits, vegetables.

Pineville. 1 Town (pop. 3,890), S Ky., on Cumberland R. near Cumberland Gap. Resort, holds annual laurel festival. **2** Town (pop. 6,423), central La., on Red R. opposite Alexandria. Mfg. of stone monuments and wood products. U.S. Camp Beauregard and U.S. veterans' hospital near. **3** Town (pop. 1,373), S N.C., at S.C. line, S of Charlotte. J. K. Polk born near by.

ping pong: see TABLE TENNIS.

Pingyuan (pĭng'yüăn'), province (18,000 sq. mi.; pop. 13,000,000), N central China; cap. Sinsiang. Formed 1949 from sections of Honan, Hopeh, and Shantung provs. Lies on level plain drained by Yellow, Tsin, and Wei rivers. Wheat, millet, and kaoliang are grown. Coal mines.

pink or **dianthus,** Old World annual and perennial plant (*Dianthus*) with spicily fragrant flowers. The grass pink (*Dianthus plumarius*) and maiden pink (*D. deltoides*) are popular species. See also CARNATION and SWEET WILLIAM.

Pinkerton, Allan, 1819–84, American detective, founder of the Pinkerton National Detective Agency, which solved train robberies, acted as a Union spy service in the Civil War, broke up the MOLLY MAGUIRES, and was active in the 1892 Homestead strike; its methods (particularly its use of labor spies) have been bitterly attacked by unions.

pinkeye: see CONJUNCTIVITIS.

Pinkie, battlefield E of Edinburgh, Scotland. Scene of a victory (1547) by English over larger Scottish force. The Scots, fearing that Princess Mary (later Mary Queen of Scots) would be forced to marry Edward VI, then sent her to France.

Pinnacles National Monument: see NATIONAL PARKS AND MONUMENTS (table).

Pinocchio: see COLLODI, CARLO.

pinochle (pē'nŭ"kŭl), card game played by two, three, or four players, with a deck of 48 cards. Types include auction (most popular), two-handed, and partnership pinochle. Probably originated in Europe in 19th cent.; later became very popular in the U.S.

piñon: see PINE.

Pinsk (pĭnsk, Rus. pēnsk), city (1931 pop. 31,913), W Belorussia, in Pripet Marshes. Varied mfg. Ceded to USSR by Poland 1945. Until World War II majority of inhabitants were Jews; they were virtually exterminated during German occupation.

Pinski, David (pĭn'skē), 1872–, Yiddish novelist and playwright. Among his successful plays are *The Treasure,* and *King David and His Wives.*

Pinturicchio (pēntōōrēk'kyō) or **Pintoricchio** (pēntō–) [Ital.,= little painter], c.1454–1513, Umbrian painter, influenced by Perugino. Real name was Bernardino di Betto. Known for frescoes depicting life of Pius II in cathedral library at Siena.

Pinza, Ezio (āts'yō pēn'tsä), 1892– or 1895–, Italian-American basso; with the Metropolitan Opera, New York, 1926–48. He has been especially successful in *Don Giovanni* and *Boris Godunov.* In 1949 he appeared in the musical comedy *South Pacific.*

Pinzón, Martín Alonso (märtēn' älōn'sō pēnthōn'), d. 1493, Spanish navigator. Commander of *Pinta* on Columbus's first voyage to New World (1492). Died soon after return to Spain. His younger brother, **Francisco Martín Pinzón** (fränthē'skō), fl. 1492, was master of *Pinta.* Youngest brother, **Vicente Yáñez Pinzón** (vēthān'tā yä'nyāth), fl. 1492–1509, commanded *Niña* on Columbus's expedition. Returning to New World (1500), he discovered mouth of Amazon R.; was made governor of Puerto Rico (1505); explored the coasts of Yucatan, Honduras, and Venezuela with Solís (1508–9).

Piombo, Sebastiano del: see SEBASTIANO DEL PIOMBO.

Piozzi, Madame: see THRALE, HESTER LYNCH.

pipal: see BO TREE.

pipe, tubular structure used to carry liquids or gases, as structural material, and for electrical wiring conduits. Pipe materials include metal, the most commonly used; fireclay, for drains; fiber, chiefly for chemicals; cement and concrete, for large water pipes. Cast iron is extensively used for gas and water mains. **Pipe lines** convey water, petroleum products, and natural gas over long distances from source to refinery or point of consumption. U.S. government financed construction (completed 1943) of "Big Inch" pipe line for carrying crude oil and "Little Big Inch" for carrying petroleum products from Texas to New York and Philadelphia areas.

pipe rolls, old records of crown revenue and expenditures of England. Dating from 1131, they are invaluable source of social history. Not completely replaced by modern accounting methods until 1833.

Pipe Spring National Monument: see NATIONAL PARKS AND MONUMENTS (table).

Pipestone, city (pop. 5,269), SW Minn., near S.Dak. line, in agr. area. Near by are pipestone quarries used by Indians, seen by Catlin 1836; made part of Pipestone Natl. Monument (115.6 acres) 1937.

pipestone, dull red clay stone, used by Indians in making ceremonial pipes, and found in Canada, the Dakotas, and Minn. Also called catlinite, after George Catlin, who lived many years among Indians.

Pippin, Frankish rulers: see PEPIN.

Piqua (pĭ'kwā), city (pop. 17,447), W Ohio, on Great Miami R. and N of Dayton; settled 1797 as Washington. Mfg. of fabrics and machinery.

piracy, robbery committed on high seas by force of arms, comparable to brigandage on land. Distinguished from PRIVATEERING in that pirate holds no commission, is not under national flag, and attacks vessels of all nations; he is highwayman of seas. Piracy flourished in Mediterranean until Great Britain, Netherlands, and U.S. wiped out Barbary pirates in 1815–16. English buccaneers of SPANISH MAIN pillaged Spanish American coast settlements and returned to England to share spoils and receive pardon. Piracy was destroyed in West Indies by David Porter in 1825. In long history of piracy are many famous names, such as Sir Francis Drake, Sir John Hawkins, and Henry Morgan. Other well-known pirates were Jean Laffite, Edward Teach (Blackbeard), and semi-mythical Capt. Kidd.

Piraeus (pīrē'ůs), Gr. *Peiraieus* or *Piraieus,* city (pop. 184,802), E central Greece, on the Saronic Gulf; port of Athens and largest port of Greece. Built c.450 B.C., it was linked with Athens by the Long Walls, two parallel walls c.5 mi. long (built 461–456 B.C.; destroyed by Spartans 404 B.C., rebuilt 393 B.C.). After Sulla destroyed the arsenal and fortifications in 86 B.C., Piraeus sank into insignificance until the 19th cent. It was heavily bombed in World War II.

Pirandello, Luigi (lwē'jē pērändĕl'lō), 1867–1936, Italian dramatist. He wrote many short stories and novels, but is famous for his plays, among them *Six Characters in Search of an Author* (1921), *Right You Are if You Think So* (1917), and *As You Desire Me* (1930). Awarded the 1934 Nobel Prize in Literature.

Piranesi, Giovanni Battista (jōvän'nē bät-tē'-stä pē"rānā'zē), or **Giambattista Piranesi** (jäm"–), 1720–78, Italian engraver. Made numerous copperplates of buildings in Rome.

Pirate Coast, Arabia: see TRUCIAL OMAN.

Pirenne, Henri (ārē' pērĕn'), 1862–1935, Belgian historian. Chief works are *History of Belgium* (Eng. tr., 7 vols., 1899–1932), *Belgian Democracy* (Eng. tr., 1915), and *Medieval Cities* (Eng. tr., 1925).

Pisa (pē'sä), city (pop. 49,471), Tuscany, central Italy, on Arno R. and near Tyrrhenian Sea. By late 11th cent. Pisa was a powerful maritime republic, but its naval power was crushed by Genoa in 1284. Ghibelline Pisa defended its independence against Guelphic Florence until 1406. It was the seat of a school of sculpture (13th–14th cent.), founded by Nicola Pisano. Galileo, born here, was a student and teacher at the university (founded 14th cent.). Many of Pisa's architectural treasures suffered in World War II, but the old cathedral, the baptistery, and the famous leaning tower (180 ft. high; 14 ft. out of perpendicular) were only slightly damaged.

Pisa, Council of, 1409, council of the Roman Catholic Church, summoned to end the Great SCHISM. Supporters of both GREGORY XII and Benedict XIII (Pedro de LUNA) agreed to depose both men as heretical and schismatic. They chose a new pope with the result that there were three claimants, not two. At Pisa the theory that councils are superior to the pope in the Church was put forward. This was to appear again at the Councils of Constance and Basel.

Pisan, Christine de (krēstēn' dů pēzã'), b. 1364, d. between 1429 and 1431, French poet, b. Italy. One of the first professional woman writers, she is esteemed for her lyric poems, concerned mostly with love and chivalry.

Pisanello (pēzänĕl'lō), c.1395–1455?, Italian artist of the early Renaissance. Also called Vittore Pisano, but real name was Antonio Pisano. His medals are valued as historic memorials of the period. Famed also for animal drawings. Most of his paintings have perished.

Pisano, Andrea (ändrā'ä pēzä'nō), c.1270–c.1348, Italian sculptor, also called Andrea da Pontedera. Considered the founder of Florentine school of sculpture. Strongly influenced by Giotto, whom he succeeded as director of the work on Florence cathedral; made first bronze doors (depicting life of John the Baptist) for the baptistery (1336). Also directed work on façade of Orvieto cathedral.

Pisano, Nicola (nēkō'lä), b. c.1220, d. between 1278 and 1287, Italian sculptor and architect, founder of new school of sculpture which combined Gothic and classic elements. Made marble pulpit for Pisa baptistery c.1260. In creating pulpit for Siena cathedral and great fountain for Perugia he was assisted by his son, **Giovanni Pisano,** b. 1245, d. after 1314. Giovanni also carved a pulpit for Sant' Andrea, Pistoia, his masterpiece, and designed cloisters of the Pisa *camposanto* and façade of Siena cathedral.

Pisano, Vittore: see PISANELLO.

Piscataqua, river: see SALMON FALLS RIVER.

Pisces (pī'sēz) [Latin,= fishes], 12th sign of ZODIAC.

Pisgah (pĭz'gů), mountain ridge, N central Jordan, E of N end of Dead Sea. Its summit identified with biblical Mt. NEBO.

Pisistratus (pīsĭs'trůtůs), c.605–527 B.C., tyrant of Athens. Apparently gained popularity by liberal laws. He pushed the hegemony of Athens over Ionian cities. Twice exiled by his rivals, the Alcmaeonidae and the aristocracy, he nevertheless left a strong state to his sons, Hippias and Hipparchus. Also Peisistratus.

Piso (pī'sō), name of a Roman family. **Lucius Calpurnius Piso Caesoninus,** d. after 43 B.C., as consul helped banish Cicero (58 B.C.). Cicero attacked him bitterly. His daughter married Julius Caesar. **Caius Calpurnius Piso,** d. A.D. 65, a patron of literature, was discovered in a plot against Nero and killed himself.

Pissarro, Camille (kämē'yů pēsärō'), 1830–1903, French impressionist painter. The Barbizon school influenced his early work; later he allied himself with the impressionists, painting chiefly street scenes of Paris and London. Achieved light effects by use of broken color.

pistachio (pĭstă'shēō), tree (*Pistacia vera*), native to the Orient and Mediterranean region, and its greenish seeds. The seeds, known as pistachio nuts, are eaten salted or used in confections. Other species include the TEREBINTH; the Chinese pistachio (*P. chinensis*), grown in Fla. and Calif. for ornament; and *P. lentiscus,* a source of mastic and an oil.

Pistoia (pēstô'yä), city (pop. 29,532), Tuscany, central Italy, at foot of the Apennines. A free commune in 12th and 13th cent., it came under Florentine rule in 14th cent. The Ospedale del Ceppo has a frieze by Giovanni della Robbia. There are several fine churches. Pistols, first made here (16th cent.), were named after Pistoia.

pistol, small firearm designed for use with one

hand. First manufactured in the 16th cent. in Pistoia, Italy (hence the name pistol). The early pistol (short-barreled and with heavy butts) was superseded by the revolver (carrying ammunition in a revolving drum) and the automatic pistol (with ammunition in a clip inside the stock).

Piston, Walter, 1894–, American composer; pupil of Nadia Boulanger. Among his works are three symphonies, concertos, chamber music, the *Suite for Orchestra,* and the ballet, *The Incredible Flutist.*

Pitcairn, borough (pop. 5,857), SW Pa., E suburb of Pittsburgh. Railroad shops and brickworks.

Pitcairn Island, volcanic island (2 sq. mi.; pop. 126), S Pacific, belonging to Great Britain. Discovered 1767 by Adm. Philip Carteret. Natives are descendants of mutineers of the BOUNTY and their Tahitian wives who settled here 1790. Colony was discovered 1808 by Americans. Overpopulation caused removal of part of colony to NORFOLK ISLAND.

pitch, in music, the position of a TONE in the musical scale, determined by the number of vibrations per second of the sound and today designated by a letter name. Present-day standard of pitch is an A (the A above middle C) of 440 vibrations per second (in the U.S.) or of 435 vibrations per second (in Europe). Other tones vibrate less frequently if below A, more frequently if above. The upper note of an octave has twice as many vibrations per second as the lower note.

pitch: see TAR AND PITCH.

pitchblende (pĭch'blĕnd"), dark, lustrous, amorphous mineral, a source of radium, uranium, polonium, and plutonium. Uranium yield is 50–80%. Occurs in small quantities throughout the world; Canadian Great Lakes, Belgian Congo, and Czechoslovakia are major sources.

Pitcher, Molly, c.1754–1832, American Revolutionary heroine; real name was Mary Ludwig Hays or Heis. Carried water for soldiers at battle of Monmouth (1778), thus earning sobriquet.

pitcher plant, insectivorous flowering plant with leaves adapted for trapping insects. Each leaf forms a "pitcher" that usually holds liquid. The common pitcher plant of North America is *Sarracenia purpurea,* native to bogs from Labrador to Fla. and Iowa. The California pitcher plant (*Darlingtonia californica*) resembles *Sarracenia.* Oriental pitcher plants (*Nepenthes*) are sometimes cultivated. See *ill.,* p. 999.

Pitch Lake: see TRINIDAD AND TOBAGO.

pith, plant tissue, chiefly a region of food storage, composed of relatively large cells loosely fitted together. Present in the center of the stem of certain herbaceous and woody plants (becoming much reduced in trees as woody tissue grows). In Orient rice paper has been made from pith of certain shrubs.

Pithecanthropus: see MAN, PRIMITIVE.

Pitman, Sir Isaac, 1813–97, English deviser of a shorthand system based on phonetic rather than orthographic principles (in *Stenographic Soundhand,* 1837); this became one of most-used systems in the world. His brother, **Benn Pitman,** 1822–1910, and Stephen P. Andrews introduced Pitman system to U.S.

Pitman, borough (pop. 6,960), SW N.J., S of Camden; settled 1871 as site of Methodist camp meetings.

Pitt, William, 1st **earl of Chatham** (chă'tŭm), 1708–78, English statesman. His criticism of War of the Austrian Succession led to downfall (1742) of Robert Walpole. By denouncing goverment policy in Seven Years War he became head of coalition government in 1757. Shrewd policy led to defeat of French in India and Canada. Broke with Whigs over American colonies. Urged conciliation, then any settlement short of independence. Forced to retire by mental disorder (1768). Known as the Great Commoner for his insistence on constitutional rights. His second son, **William Pitt,** 1759–1806, was prime minister (1783–1801) under George III. Estab. the custom of general elections. A liberal Tory, his policies included new taxes to cut national debt, reforms in India and Canada, and parliamentary reform. French Revolutionary and Napoleonic Wars doomed these policies. Financial support of allies led to monetary crisis. Military coalitions against France failed on land. Using bribery to achieve union with Ireland, he resigned on king's veto of CATHOLIC EMANCIPATION. Recalled 1804, but defeat at Austerlitz was the death blow to his political career.

Pitt, Fort: see DUQUESNE, FORT.

Pittsburg. 1 Industrial city (pop. 12,763), W Calif., at junction of Sacramento and San Joaquin rivers. Steelworks and canneries (fish, fruit). **2** City (pop. 19,341), SE Kansas, near Mo. line; founded 1872 in mining area. Mfg. of coal by-products and food products.

Pittsburgh, city (pop. 676,806), SW Pa., at point where Allegheny and Monongahela rivers join to form the Ohio. One of main U.S. industrial centers, city is in rich coal, gas, and oil region. Large part of nation's iron and steel produced here. Fine port and rail facilities ship diverse goods, including coke, aluminum, and petroleum products, tin plate, and electrical equipment. A 17th-cent. fur-trading post supplanted an Indian village here, and itself gave way to French Fort DUQUESNE in 1754. Taken by British and renamed Fort Pitt. Village around fort settled 1755. City grew with development of coal and iron resources and because of its position on E–W transportation arteries. Here are Carnegie Mus.; Carnegie Library; Buhl Planetarium; Duquesne Univ. (R.C.; coed.; 1878); an atomic-energy research laboratory; CARNEGIE INSTITUTE OF TECHNOLOGY. The **University of Pittsburgh** (nonsectarian, private, coed.; opened 1787) includes Mellon Inst. of Industrial Research.

Pittsburgh Landing: see SHILOH, BATTLE OF.

Pittsfield, city (pop. 53,348), W Mass., on branches of Housatonic R.; settled 1752. Metropolis of the Berkshires. Mfg. of electrical machinery, woolen goods, paper, metal products. "Arrowhead" was Herman Melville's home, 1850–63.

Pittston, city (pop. 15,012), NE Pa., on Susquehanna R. and NE of Wilkes-Barre; settled 1770. Mfg. of textile and metal products; coal mining.

pituitary gland (pĭtū'ĭtē"rē), small, round three-lobed organ attached to base of brain; it is a ductless, or endocrine, gland. Anterior lobe produces hormones regulating growth, development of sexual characteristics, and lactation. Posterior lobe hormones affect blood pressure, kidney function, and certain muscles.

Pius II (pī'ŭs), 1405–64, pope (1458–64), a Sienese named Enea Silvio de' Piccolomini. At the Council of Basel he supported the theory that the council should be superior to the pope in the Church and was later at the court of Antipope Felix V (Amadeus VIII of Savoy). Piccolomini was a humanist and court poet and an official under Emperor Frederick III before he was converted to a holy life (1445), became a priest (1446), bishop of Trieste (1447), bishop of Siena (1450) and a cardinal (1456). As pope he tried in vain to unite Europe against the Turks, struggled with Louis XI of France, and continued opposition to George of Podebrad. Wrote many works, one autobiographical.

Pius IV, 1499–1565, pope (1559–65), a Milanese named Giovan Angelo de' Medici. He convened the last session of the Council of TRENT. His chief aid was his nephew, St. Charles Borromeo.

Pius V, Saint, 1504–72, pope (1566–72), an Italian named Michele Ghislieri, a Dominican. He put the decrees of the Council of Trent into vigorous effect, took a firm tone in declaring Elizabeth I of England deposed, and by uniting with Spain and Venice against the Turks helped bring about Don John of Austria's victory at Lepanto. Pius was a leading figure of the Catholic Reform. Feast: May 5.

Pius VI, 1717–99, pope (1775–99), an Italian named G. Angelo Braschi. Early in his reign he tried in vain to stop the efforts of Emperor Joseph II to "reform" the Church by suppressing monasteries and taking over control. Later even more serious trouble came with the French Revolution. Pius forbade the French clergy (1791) to take oath under the new Civil Constitution of the clergy. Later he sided with the anti-French coalition, and Napoleon attacked the Papal States. Pius was forced (1797) to cede Avignon, Venaissin, Ferrara, Bologna, and the Romagna to the French and pay them a large indemnity. After a French general was murdered in Rome, the French set up a republic (1798) and took Pius to Siena, then to Turin. He died at Valence.

Pius VII, 1740–1823, pope (1800–1823), an Italian named Barnaba Chiaramonti. Succeeded Pius VI in the midst of trouble with the French. He and Napoleon signed the CONCORDAT OF 1801, but when Napoleon's Organic Articles virtually rescinded much of it Pius would not accept them. Napoleon made Pius come to Paris to consecrate him as emperor; the French took Rome (1808) and the Papal States (1809); when Pius excommunicated the enemies of the Holy See, he was taken prisoner, moved to Fontainebleau, and forced to sign a new concordat. This humiliation Pius bore with stolid dignity. As Napoleon's star fell, Pius disavowed the enforced contract, recovered the Papal States, and set about restoring the Church. He reconstituted the Society of Jesus. His secretary was the able Ercole Consalvi, who regained the Papal States at the Congress of Vienna.

Pius IX, 1792–1878, pope (1846–78), an Italian named Giovanni M. Mastai Ferretti. In 1848 revolutionary rioting drove him from Rome to Gaeta and from a liberal policy in the Papal States to ruling, after his return to Rome, with the support of Napoleon III's soldiers. He opposed the Italian nationalists. In 1870, when the Italians entered Rome, Pius retired to the Vatican and refused to treat with the new kingdom, thus creating the Roman Question (not settled until the Lateran Treaty). He also had difficulties in Germany in the KULTURKAMPF. His encyclical *Quanta Cura* (1864) denounced errors of modernism. He declared the dogma of the Immaculate Conception of the Virgin an article of faith (1854) and summoned the Vatican Council, which enunciated the doctrine of papal infallibility. Sometimes called in English by Italian form, *Pio Nono.*

Pius X, 1835–1914, pope (1903–14), an Italian named Giuseppe Sarto. He had an invigorating effect upon the Church, and his firm resistance to the anticlerical laws on church property and education in France (1904) was supported by all French Catholics. In the decree *Lamentabili* and the encyclical *Pasccendi* (1907) he opposed modernism in the Church. He was notable for his love of the common people.

Pius XI, 1857–1939, pope (1922–39), an Italian named Achille Ratti. Before becoming pope he was legate and then nuncio to Poland and archbishop of Milan. As pope he sought friendly relations with all powers. The Lateran Treaty (1929) ended the quarrel between Church and state in Italy, but Pius expressed his strong disapproval of Fascist methods in a letter *Non abbiamo bisogno* (1931). A concordat with Germany (1933) was flouted by the Nazis; the pope in a powerful encyclical (*Mit brennender Sorge,* 1937) denounced the tenets of National Socialism. He also issued the statement *On Atheistic Communism.* Pius opposed nationalism, racism, and anti-Semitism. His criticism of laissez-faire capitalism in the encyclical *Quadragesimo anno* (1931; forty years after Leo XIII's plea on the subject) urged social reform. He also stressed the part to be played by lay people in all things religious and the recognition of the rights of Eastern Catholics and of native cultures. His chief assistants were the cardinals Pietro Gasparri and Eugenio Pacelli (Pius XII).

Pius XII, 1876–, pope (1939–), an Italian named Eugenio Pacelli. As a cardinal under Pius XI, he had much experience in diplomatic affairs, and international questions occupied much of his pontificate. Before, during, and after World War II he preached the blessings of peace and tried to alleviate the sufferings of prisoners and, later, of displaced persons. He early opposed the use of atomic energy in warfare and urged international accord. He continued Pius XI's opposition to laissez-faire capitalism. The contest between Catholicism and atheistic Communism became a burning issue in Italian politics, and the pope asked Catholics to oppose Communism but refused to approve a "crusade." In 1946 the pope created some 32 new cardinals from 22 nations; in Jan., 1953, he elevated 24 more cardinals, bringing the college to its maximum of 70. He proclaimed 1950 a Holy Year, and in that year enunciated the doctrine of the Assumption of the Virgin Mary as a Catholic dogma.

Piute Indians: see PAIUTE INDIANS.

Pi y Margall, Francisco (fränthē'skō pē' ē märgäl'), 1824–1901, Spanish liberal statesman, journalist, and author. Was president of first Spanish republic (1873). As deputy in the Cortes after Bourbon restoration he advocated federalism.

Pizarro, Francisco (fränthē'skō pēthä'rō), c.1476–1541, Spanish conquistador, conqueror of Peru, b. Trujillo, Spain. Accompanied Ojeda to Colombia (1510) and Balboa in discovery of Pacific. Hearing of wealth of the Inca, Pizarro formed partnership with Almagro and Fernando de Luque (a priest who secured funds) and made several expeditions S. In 1532 he landed at Tumbes and ascended Andes to Cajamarca where he met the Inca, ATAHUALPA, and professing friendship at first, seized and killed him. With conquest of Peru assured, he founded new settlements (among them, Lima) and allotted lands and Indians to his followers. He sent Almagro, whom he had cheated several times, to conquer Chile. When Almagro returned empty-handed, Pizarro had him put to death. By alienating Almagro's followers, he paved way for his own assassination (1541). His brother, **Gonzalo Pizarro** (gônthä'lō), c.1506–1548, assisted in conquest of Peru. Commanded disastrous expedition down Napo. On his return, he learned of Francisco's assassination and offered to help the crown's representative but was refused. Led revolt against viceroy when New Laws to protect Indians were enforced. When the laws were revoked, his followers disbanded and he was beheaded. Another brother, **Juan Pizarro** (hwän), d. 1536, aided in conquest of Peru. Killed leading attack on Indian fortress, Sacsahuaman. A half brother, **Hernando Pizarro** (ĕrnän'dō), fl. 1530–60, also took part in conquest. He returned to Spain to advance fortunes of family at court (at expense of Almagro). Back in Peru, he fought against and defeated Almagro. In 1539, he returned to Spain to argue case of Pizarros but was imprisoned for 20 years.

Place, Francis, 1771–1854, English radical reformer. Active in the trade-union movement, he secured repeal (1824) of Combination Acts of 1799–1800. An early Chartist leader, he helped draft "People's Charter," the primary document of the Chartist movement.

placenta (plŭsĕn'tŭ) or **afterbirth,** thick, disk-shaped mass connected with fetus by umbilical cord. Made up of tissue from mother and embryo. Permits mutual passage of components of blood, but blood itself does not mingle. Expelled after BIRTH.

Placentia Bay, Atlantic inlet, SE N.F., Canada, between Burin and Avalon peninsulas. Has been a naval base since 1622. In World War II U.S. estab. naval and air base at Argentia, on E shore.

placer mining: see MINING.

Placerville, city (pop. 3,749), N central Calif., ENE of Sacramento. Boomed with 1848 discovery of gold at near-by Coloma. Gateway to sierra resorts.

Placid, Lake, N.Y.: see LAKE PLACID village.

Placidia, Roman empress: see GALLA PLACIDIA.

plague (plāg), infectious epidemic disease carried by fleas infected through biting diseased animals, especially rats. Types include bubonic, marked by swellings (buboes) of lymph nodes; pneumonic, affecting lungs; and septicemic, infecting blood. Probably only pneumonic plague spreads from person to person; other types are eradicated by destroying infected animals. Causative agent of plague, a rod-shaped bacterium, discovered independently by Kitasato and Yersin during 1894 epidemic in China. Catastrophic European epidemic (Black Death) began in Constantinople 1347. Great London plague 1665.

plagues of Egypt, in Bible, 10 disasters brought upon Egypt by God through Moses because Pharaoh refused to free the Hebrews. Story told in Exodus 7.19–12.36. Among plagues: Egyptian waters turning into blood, swarms of insects, an epidemic of boils. Finally when death struck the firstborn of all of Egypt—both man and beast—from Pharaoh's palace to the rudest hut—the terrified ruler allowed the children of Israel to leave Egypt. The first Passover was observed on the night of the last plague.

plaice (plās), edible flatfish of N European seas.

plaid (plăd), long shawl or wrap of woolen cloth, usually with checks or tartan figures; part of the Highland costume. Tartan plaids have designs of colored crossbars; each Scottish clan has its distinctive pattern. Today, term sometimes signifies merely a pattern, as a plaid gingham.

Plain, the, in French history, the independent members of the National Convention during the French Revolution; occupied lower benches of the chamber. Though forming a majority, the Plain was a leaderless mass, easily dominated by the radical MOUNTAIN.

plain, large area of level or nearly level land. Plains have different names in different countries and climates, including tundra, steppe, prairie, pampas, savanna, llanos. Causes of formation include erosive action of water, glaciation, draining of a lake, deposition of sediment, and uplift of continental shelf or part of ocean floor.

plain chant: see PLAIN SONG.

Plainfield. 1 Town (pop. 8,071), E Conn., E of Willimantic; settled c.1690. Textiles and wood products. **2** City (pop. 42,366), NE N.J., near Watchung Mts., SW of Newark; settled 1684 by Friends. Mfg. of trucks, printing machinery, and concrete products. Has Martine house (1717), Drake house (1746), and Friends' Meetinghouse (1788).

Plains of Abraham: see ABRAHAM, PLAINS OF.

plain song or **plain chant,** unison vocal music of the church, particularly the Roman Catholic Church. Texts of plain song are taken from the Mass, the Bible, and hymns. Term often used synonymously with Gregorian chant although, in a broad sense, the chant of the Orthodox Eastern Church, as well as that of the four main Western rites—Ambrosian, Roman, Mozarabic, and Gallican—is considered plain song. Gregorian chant underwent its greatest development and codification in the 7th cent. after the reign of Gregory I. In the Middle Ages polyphony largely supplanted plain song, and distortions crept into its performance in succeeding centuries. In the 19th cent. the Benedictine monks of Solesmes undertook years of research to restore Gregorian chant to its original form and to establish its proper rhythm. The tonality of Gregorian chant derives from eight modes (see MODE). Its rhythm stems from that inherent in the text, whether prose or verse.

Plainview, city (pop. 14,044), NW Texas, SW of Amarillo on Llano Estacado; founded 1886. Processes and ships grains, cotton, truck, and dairy products.

Plainville, town (pop. 9,994), central Conn., SW of Hartford. Metal goods.

Planck, Max (mäks plängk), 1858–1947, German physicist. Won 1918 Nobel Prize for evolving QUANTUM THEORY in thermodynamics.

plane, in geometry, flat surface of infinite extent but no thickness. It is defined as surface containing all of any straight line with two of its points on the surface. Any three points, a point and line, or two parallel lines determine a plane.

planet (plă'nĭt), opaque, spherical body, revolving counterclockwise about sun and shining by reflected sunlight. Term [Gr.,= wanderer] was given by Greeks to heavenly bodies that changed position relative to constellations; believing earth to be central heavenly body, they included moon and sun as well as planets visible to unaided eye. Copernicus showed sun to be center of SOLAR SYSTEM and moon a satellite of earth. KEPLER'S LAWS of planetary motion state that orbit of a planet is ellipse. Order of orbits of large planets outward from sun is MERCURY, VENUS, EARTH, MARS, JUPITER, SATURN, URANUS, NEPTUNE, PLUTO. Orbits of minor planets (see ASTEROID) lie between orbits of Mars and Jupiter. See *ill.*, p. 1187.

planetarium (plănútâ'rēùm), name used both for projecting device or model portraying heavenly bodies and for theaterlike chamber with hemispherical ceiling upon which celestial phenomena are reproduced by optical projection. Juxtaposition and movements of lights reproduce panorama of sky. Notable chamber planetaria include Hayden Planetarium, New York city; Adler Planetarium, Chicago; Fels Planetarium (of Franklin Inst.), Philadelphia; Planetarium Theatre of Griffith Observatory, Los Angeles; Buhl Planetarium, Pittsburgh; Morehead Planetarium, Chapel Hill, N.C.; Montevideo has planetarium made in U.S.

planetesimal hypothesis (plănútĕ'sùmùl), theory of origin of planets developed after 1900 by T. C. Chamberlin and F. R. Moulton. Assumes that in distant past attractive force of star passing close to sun raised tidal bulges on sun's fluid mass. Materials ejected from bulges by sun's eruptions, affected by cross-pull of moving star, were set to moving in elliptical orbits. Small masses solidified into planetesimals; the larger of these swept in the smaller, forming planets. Theory accepted with modifications (e.g., TIDAL THEORY) by many scientists.

planetoid: see ASTEROID.

plane tree, deciduous tree of genus *Platanus* of temperate regions. The loose bark scales off causing a mottled appearance. The American plane (*Platanus occidentalis*), also known as sycamore and buttonwood (from the hard brown seed balls), has hard wood used for furniture. The London plane (*P. acerifolia*) is common in cities of E U.S.

plankton: see MARINE BIOLOGY.

plant, organism of vegetable kingdom as contrasted with one of animal kingdom. It may be as small and simple as one of the algae or complex as a tree. Plants perform PHOTOSYNTHESIS and are therefore ultimate source of food, and probably of most of oxygen, for all animals. For growth, plants need light, water, oxygen, carbon dioxide, varying amounts of nitrogen, phosphorus, potassium, sulphur, magnesium, calcium, and iron, and small amounts of other elements. Organic matter from plants of past ages is found in coal and probably in petroleum. Plants are divided into four large groups or phyla: spermatophytes or seed plants (conifers and flowering plants); the pteridophytes (ferns, club mosses, and horsetails); the bryophytes (mosses and liverworts); and the thallophytes (algae, fungi, lichens, and bacteria). Each group is further divided into classes, orders, families, genera, species, and varieties. BOTANY is scientific study of plants; ECOLOGY, study of their relation to environment; HORTICULTURE, their cultivation for food and decoration. See *ill.*, p. 999.

Plantagenet, English royal house: see ANGEVIN.

plantain (plăn'tĭn), name for plants of genus *Plantago,* chiefly annual or perennial weeds. The mucilaginous seeds of an Old World species (*Plantago psyllium*) are imported as psyllium seed for use as a laxative. Tropical plantain is a BANANA.

Plant City, city (pop. 9,230), W central Fla., E of Tampa. Processes and ships fruit (esp. strawberries) and vegetables. Produces phosphates.

Plantin, Christophe (plãtē'), 1514–89, leading printer of his time. He began (1555) printing in Antwerp, and his shop continued until 1867.

plant louse: see APHID.

Planudes Maximus (plùnū'dēz), c.1260–c.1330, Greek scholar, also known as Maximus Planudes, a learned monk. His edition of the *Greek Anthology* was long standard.

Plaquemine (plă'kùmĭn), town (pop. 5,747), SE La., near the Mississippi and S of Baton Rouge. Government locks connect Bayou Plaquemine and Intracoastal Waterway with the Mississippi. U.S. waterfowl refuge (1936) is near.

Plassey (plă'cē), village, S West Bengal, India. Clive's defeat of Nawab of Bengal here in 1757 helped establish British rule in NE India.

plaster of Paris: see GYPSUM.

plastics, name for organic derivatives of resin, cellulose, and protein that can be shaped by applying heat, pressure, or both. Celluloid

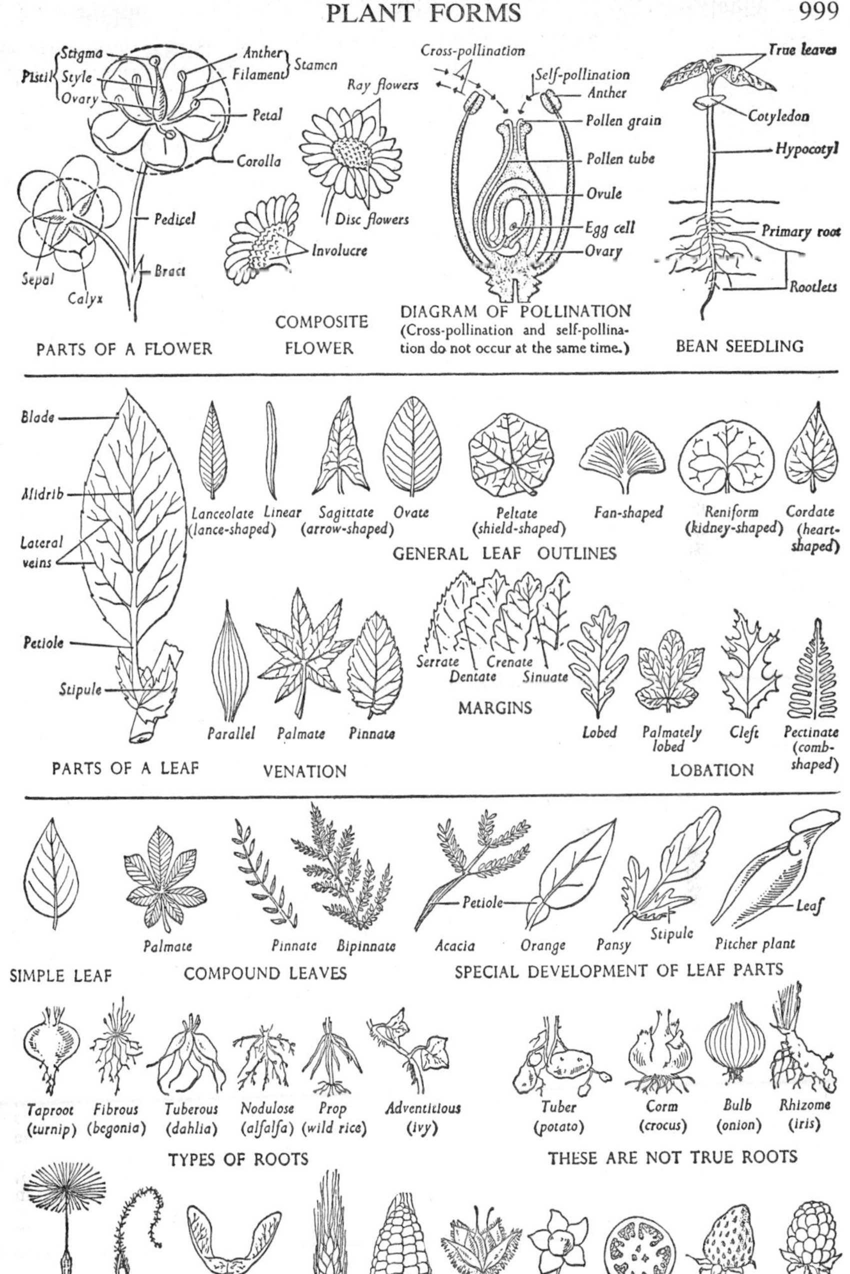
Pistil
Stigma
Style
Ovary
Anther
Filament
Stamen
Petal
Corolla
Pedicel
Bract
Sepal
Calyx
PARTS OF A FLOWER
Ray flowers
Disc flowers
Involucre
COMPOSITE FLOWER
Cross-pollination
Self-pollination
Anther
Pollen grain
Pollen tube
Ovule
Egg cell
Ovary
DIAGRAM OF POLLINATION
(Cross-pollination and self-pollination do not occur at the same time.)
True leaves
Cotyledon
Hypocotyl
Primary root
Rootlets
BEAN SEEDLING
Blade
Midrib
Lateral veins
Petiole
Stipule
PARTS OF A LEAF
Lanceolate (lance-shaped)
Linear
Sagittate (arrow-shaped)
Ovate
Peltate (shield-shaped)
Fan-shaped
Reniform (kidney-shaped)
Cordate (heart-shaped)
GENERAL LEAF OUTLINES
Parallel
Palmate
Pinnate
VENATION
Serrate
Dentate
Crenate
Sinuate
MARGINS
Lobed
Palmately lobed
Cleft
Pectinate (comb-shaped)
LOBATION
SIMPLE LEAF
Palmate
Pinnate
Bipinnate
COMPOUND LEAVES
Petiole
Acacia
Orange
Pansy
Stipule
Leaf
Pitcher plant
SPECIAL DEVELOPMENT OF LEAF PARTS
Taproot (turnip)
Fibrous (begonia)
Tuberous (dahlia)
Nodulose (alfalfa)
Prop (wild rice)
Adventitious (ivy)
TYPES OF ROOTS
Tuber (potato)
Corm (crocus)
Bulb (onion)
Rhizome (iris)
THESE ARE NOT TRUE ROOTS
Dandelion
Anemone
Maple
Wheat
Corn
Chestnut
DRY FRUITS
Belladonna
Tomato
FLESHY FRUITS
Strawberry
Raspberry
AGGREGATE FRUITS
TYPES OF FRUITS

was discovered c.1869, but plastics did not come into industrial use until after Bakelite was produced c.1907. Plastics are either thermoplastic, i.e., they soften again and again at high temperatures, or thermosetting, i.e., they become infusible, insoluble mass at high temperatures. According to substance from which they are derived plastics are further grouped as phenolic, urea, cellulose, acrylic, polystyrene, or vinyl. Almost any color or shape, and many combinations of hardness, durability, elasticity, and resistance to heat, cold, and acid can be obtained. Endless variety of plastic products has become available.

Plata, Río de la (rē'ō dā lä plä'tä), estuary, SE South America, formed by Paraná R. and Uruguay R. It is c.120 mi. wide at mouth on Atlantic, decreasing to c.20 mi. near head. Focal point of one of great river systems; its ports are Buenos Aires and Montevideo. Discovered by Juan Díaz de Solís (1516), explored by Magellan (1520) and by Sebastian Cabot (1526–29). First settlement on its banks was made at Buenos Aires by Pedro de Mendoza (1536).

Plataea (plůtē'ů), anc. city, S Boeotia, Greece. For aid to Athens at Marathon (490 B.C.), it was destroyed by Xerxes I of Persia (480). In 479 B.C. the Greeks under Pausanias defeated the Persians here. In the Peloponnesian War it was besieged (429–427), taken, and sacked by Spartans.

plateau (plă"tō'), level elevated portion of the earth's surface, with lower land on at least one side. Causes of formation include earth movements, great lava flows, erosion of adjacent lands.

plate mark: see HALLMARK.

Platen, August, Graf von (ou'gŏŏst gräf' fŭn plä'tůn), 1796–1835, German poet. His sonnets and odes express his tormented inner life in forms of classical perfection.

plating, application of coat of metal to metallic or other object for decoration, protection against corrosion, or increased wearing qualities. Art of gilding was practiced in early Egypt, Greece, and Rome; was much used during Renaissance and in Orient in all periods. Production of Sheffield plate and GALVANIZING of iron started in 18th cent. Plating by dipping, fusing, and soldering has been largely replaced by electrolysis methods. Term *electroplating* refers to electrolytic deposition of decorative or protective coats, and *electroforming* to formation of metallic objects by deposition of metal on temporary cores and to coating of electrically negative casts or molds called electrotypes, used for reproducing printers' type, engravings, medals.

platinite: see GUILLAUME, CHARLES ÉDOUARD.

platinum, grayish white metallic element (symbol = Pt; see also ELEMENT, table), malleable, ductile, and chemically inactive. Because of its resistance to corrosion, it is used in alloys for making laboratory utensils, electric wires and contact points, standard weights, and foils. It acts as a strong catalytic agent. It is used in dentistry, in photography, and in making jewelry. Most important alloys are those with iridium. In nature it is found chiefly alloyed with other metals.

Plato (plā'tō), 427?–347? B.C., Greek philosopher, one of the most influential thinkers of all time. Born of a good Athenian family, he studied under Socrates, who appears as chief speaker in all Plato's early writings. Plato traveled, stayed for a time in Syracuse, and on returning to Athens founded the ACADEMY, where he taught for the rest of his life (with two more brief visits to Syracuse). His philosophy is expressed in his dialogues. These, because of their beauty of style as well as their depth and range of thought, are outstanding masterpieces of world literature. Among them, besides the early defense of Socrates in the *Apology,* are *Charmides, Crito, Protagoras, Ion, Phaedrus, Gorgias, Meno, Theaetetus, Sophist, Parmenides, Symposium, Phaedo, Philebus, Republic* (perhaps the most celebrated; a demonstration of justice by picturing the ideal state), *Timaeus, Critias,* and *Laws.* They cover many subjects with richness and complexity. Primarily, however, Platonism, based on his teachings, stressed the importance of the idea, the general form, as the basis of true reality, permanent and sure behind all appearances. Knowledge is, when true, eternal and unchangeable. By the logical process of dialectic general ideas may be obtained through induction and may be classified. The supreme Idea is the Idea of the Good. He also suggested that there is a world soul and postulated a Demiurge, creator of the physical universe. He believed the rational soul to be immortal. Virtue consists in the harmony of the soul with the universe of Ideas, attained by man when reason governs his conduct. The cardinal virtues are justice, temperance, courage, and wisdom. The world of Platonism is a world of order, and all disorder is evil. Hence the best state is one ruled by a man who is a philosopher as well as a ruler; in it each class and each person has his assigned place. In the Platonic views of literature and art, the love of ideal beauty leads to the Idea of the Good, hence, anything that merely pictures the physical world is generally rejected. The Platonic teachings and the doctrines of Plato's pupil, Aristotle, are still much alive in the world of today.

Platt, Charles Adams, 1861–1933, American architect, inspired by Italian and Georgian traditions. Designed Freer Gall. of Art, Washington, D.C.

Platt, Orville Hitchcock, 1827–1905, U.S. Senator from Conn. (1879–1905). Framed **Platt Amendment.** A rider attached to Army Appropriations Bill of 1901, it stipulated conditions for American intervention in Cuban affairs. Incorporated in permanent treaty between U.S. and Cuba; revoked in 1934.

Platt, Thomas Collier, 1833–1910, American politician. U.S. Representative from N.Y. (1873–77); U.S. Senator (1881, 1897–1909). Powerful Republican politician; largely responsible for election of Theodore Roosevelt as governor of N.Y. (1898).

Platt Amendment: see PLATT, ORVILLE HITCHCOCK.

Plattdeutsch, Low German. See LANGUAGE (table).

Platte (plăt), river formed in S central Nebr.

by junction of North Platte and South Platte rivers. Flows 310 mi. E to Missouri R. S of Omaha. Used for power and irrigation.

Plattensee, Hungary: see BALATON.

Platteville (plăt'vĭl), city (pop. 5,751), SW Wis., SW of Madison and on Little Platte R. Lead- and zinc-mining and dairying center. In near-by state park is restored Wis. territorial capitol (1836).

Platt National Park: see NATIONAL PARKS AND MONUMENTS (table).

Plattsburg, city (pop. 17,738), NE N.Y., on L. Champlain at mouth of Saranac R.; laid out 1784. Agr. and Adirondack-resort trade center, with paper mills. Military training camps, estab. in World War I, were closed in 1946 and the barracks converted for use by Champlain Col., a state emergency college for veterans and now part of State Univ. of New York. British invasion from Canada repulsed near by (Sept., 1814) by Thomas MACDONOUGH and Alexander Macomb.

platypus (plă'tŭpŭs), semiaquatic Australian egg-laying mammal (*Ornithorhynchus*), of order Monotremata (most primitive living mammals); also called duckbill. Considered a link between mammals and reptiles. It has thick, brown fur and the head, trunk, and tail are broad and flattened. The muzzle is shaped like a duck's bill, the feet are webbed, and the heel bears a spur connected with a poison gland. Adult male is c.2 ft. long.

Plauen (plou'ŭn), city (pop. 84,778), Saxony, E Germany, at NW foot of the Erzgebirge. Textile-mfg. center since 15th cent.; machinery, electrical appliances, leather. Ancient buildings include former castle of Teutonic Knights (1224).

Plautus (Titus Maccius Plautus) (plô'tŭs), c.254–184 B.C., Roman comic poet. His 21 surviving plays (adapted from Greek New Comedy), vigorous portrayals of middle- and lower-class life, are governed by a genius for situation and coarse humor and have characteristic stock figures. His influence on later European literature was enormous.

playing cards. There is evidence that playing cards were used in the ancient world, but they were probably first known to Europeans in 14th cent. Present-day variety of hearts, diamonds, clubs, and spades adopted in France in 16th cent. Modern deck consists of 52 cards.

Pleasantville. 1 Residential city (pop. 11,938), SE N.J., near Atlantic City. Farm products. **2** Residential village (pop. 4,861), SE N.Y., N of White Plains. Publishing.

plebiscite (plĕ'bĭsīt) [Latin,= popular decree], vote of the people on a question submitted to them, as in a referendum. Plebiscites may be taken on ordinary legislation, on national constitutions, and to decide the national allegiance of a population.

Plehve, Vyacheslav Konstantinovich (vyĕ"-chĭsläf' kŭnstŭntyē'nŭvĭch plyĕ'vyĭ), 1864–1904, Russian statesman. An ultrareactionary, he controlled police from 1881; was minister of interior 1902–4. Sought to divert popular discontent by Jewish pogroms, Russo-Japanese War. Assassinated.

Pleiad (plē'ăd) [from Pleiades], group of seven tragic poets of Alexandria under Ptolemy II, c.280 B.C. It gave its name to the **Pléiade** (plāyäd'), a group of French poets formed c.1553 for the purpose of purifying and enriching the French language and of creating a modern French literature equal to any other. The group cultivated classical forms and the sonnet. Led by RONSARD and DU BELLAY, it also included Remy Belleau, Antoine de Baïf, Estienne Jodelle, Pontus de Tyard, and Jean Daurat.

Pleiades (plē'ŭdēz, plī'–), in Greek mythology, seven daughters of Atlas and the nymph Pleione, attendants of Artemis. They became stars.

Pleistocene epoch (plī'stŭsēn), last epoch of the Cenozoic period of geologic time, notable as the great ice age and for being coextensive with human evolution. The ice came south at least four times, alternating with warmer periods of retreat. At their maximum, ice sheets covered Antarctica, large portions of Europe, North and South America, and parts of Asia. In America ice radiated from two main centers, the Keewatin, W and NW of Hudson Bay, and the Labrador, E of James Bay. Characteristic Pleistocene mammals included four types of elephants, true horses, sabertooth cats, giant wolves, sloths, armadillos, bisons, camels, pigs, and man. See also NEOLITHIC PERIOD; PALEOLITHIC PERIOD; GEOLOGY, table.

Plekhanov, Georgi Valentinovich (gēôr'gē vŭlyĭntyē'nŭvĭch plyĭkhä'nŭf), 1857–1918, Russian revolutionist and Marxist social philosopher. Lived abroad 1882–1917; collaborated with Lenin until 1903. His view that Russia was not ripe for socialism before capitalism and industrialization had sufficiently progressed was adopted by the Mensheviks (see BOLSHEVISM AND MENSHEVISM). Also wrote on relationship between art and economics.

plesiosaurus (plē"sēŭsô'rŭs), marine reptile which existed in the Mesozoic era. It had a small head, long neck, broad body, and paddlelike legs, and in total length ranged from c.10–60 ft.

Plessisville (plĕ'sēvĭl), village (pop. 5,094), S Que., Canada, on Becancour R. and SW of Quebec.

pleurisy (plo͞o'rĭsē), inflammation of pleurae (serous membranes), causing friction between pleurae covering lungs and those lining chest wall.

pleurisy root: see BUTTERFLY WEED.

Plevna (plĕv'nŭ), Bulgarian *Pleven,* city (pop. 38,997), N Bulgaria. Agr. center; mfg. of textiles, foodstuffs, machinery. Famous for its stubborn defense by Turks in Russo-Turkish War of 1877–78; its fall (1877) caused Turks to demand armistice.

Plimsoll, Samuel (plĭm'sŭl), 1824–98, English reformer. Because he secured legislation to limit loading of ships, the compulsory load line is called Plimsoll line.

Pliny the Elder (Caius Plinius Secundus) (plĭ'nē), A.D. 23–79, Roman naturalist. His one remaining work is the encyclopedic *Natural History,* in 37 books, a prodigious collection of secondhand information. His nephew and ward was **Pliny the Younger** (Caius Plinius Caecilius Secundus), A.D. 62?–c.113, orator and statesman, who became consul in 100. His letters mirror Roman life.

Pliocene epoch (plī'ūsēn), fifth epoch of the Cenozoic period of geologic time (fourth if Paleocene is not considered a separate epoch). Continental outlines of North America were much as at present. Close of the epoch was marked by uplift of Cascades, Rockies, Colorado plateau, and Appalachians; there was volcanic activity in W North America. Pliocene sea covered parts of NW Europe; Vesuvius, Etna, and other volcanoes were active; mountain building included folding and thrusting of Alps. Cool climate foreshadowed the ice age. See also GEOLOGY, table.

Plock (plôtsk), Pol. *Płock,* city (pop. 28,508), central Poland, on the Vistula. Agr. market center; metal and electrical industries. Was residence of medieval dukes of Masovia. Passed to Prussia 1793, to Russia 1815, to Poland 1921.

Ploesti (plôyĕsht'), city (pop. 95,632), S central Rumania, in Walachia. Chief center of Rumanian petroleum industry and of the important Ploesti oil region.

Plombières (plõbyĕr'), spa in Vosges dept., E France. Scene of agreement (1858) between Napoleon III and Cavour calling for French military aid to kingdom of Sardinia in exchange for Nice and Savoy.

Plotinus (plōtī'nŭs), c.205–270, Egyptian philosopher, for a time at Alexandria, later at Rome; chief philosopher of NEOPLATONISM. His pupil Porphyry preserved his works.

plough: see PLOW.

Plovdiv (plôv'dĭf), city (pop. 125,440), central Bulgaria, on the Maritsa. Commercial center with varied mfg. Was founded as Philippopolis by Philip II of Macedon (341 B.C.); became cap. of Thrace under Roman rule and of Eastern RUMELIA in 19th cent.

plover (plŭ'vûr), small shore bird of Old and New Worlds, related to gulls. It has a plump body, short neck and tail, rather long legs, and long, pointed wings. Nonstop flights of over 2,000 mi. are often made by eastern American golden plover (on autumn migration from arctic and Canadian breeding grounds to Nova Scotia, thence over the Atlantic to South America) and by Pacific golden plover, which breeds in Alaska and Siberia and winters in Hawaiian Isls.

plow or **plough,** implement to turn or break up soil. Probably originated in Bronze Age as single piece of wood drawn by man. Later was drawn by draught animals and in 20th cent. often by tractor. The share or point was early made of iron or steel and moldboard was often faced with metal. John Deere and Leonard Andrus led in introducing steel moldboard (c.1837).

Plücker, Julius (yōō'lyōōs plü'kûr), 1801–68, German mathematician, physicist. Known for work in analytical geometry, magnetic properties, spectroscopy (first to suggest lines in spectrum of element were peculiar to that element); originated line geometry.

plum, low wide-spreading tree and its edible fruit, classed as a drupe, comprising many species of *Prunus,* widely grown in temperate zones. The plum has been grown from ancient times, perhaps longer than any fruit except the apple. Many plums, including the greengage and Damson types, as well as prune varieties, are derived from the common plum (*Prunus domestica*), probably of Asiatic origin but long cultivated in Europe and the U.S. Of more than 100 species, about 30 are native to North America, including the beach plum (*P. maritima*) found along the E coast. Double-flowered varieties, often with red or purple foliage, are used in landscaping, especially in Japan.

plumbing, portion of water supply and sewage inside buildings. Modern water-supply piping, usually of brass, is concealed within walls or partitions; exposed piping under fixtures usually is chromium-plated brass or nickel. Waste and soil piping must be impervious to gas and water and there should be no corners where filth may collect. Water-sealed trap usually separates fixture and piping.

Plumptre, Edward Hayes (plŭmp'trē), 1821–91, English clergyman and classical scholar; chaplain (1847–68) and professor (1853–81) at King's Col., London. A reviser (1869–74) of Old Testament, an author, and translator of Sophocles, Aeschylus, and Dante.

Plutarch (plōō'tärk), A.D. 46?–c.120, Greek biographer and essayist. His great work is the *Parallel Lives,* 46 paired Greek and Roman biographies and 4 single biographies. Using anecdotes, he vividly portrays character and its moral implications. His dignity, narrative charm, and ethical insight have made him widely read and loved. His *Moralia,* dialogues and essays on ethical, literary, and historical subjects, also have great charm.

Pluto [Gr.,= rich], in Greek religion, god of the underworld. Also called Hades and, by the Romans, Dis. He ruled HELL with his wife, PERSEPHONE.

Pluto, in astronomy, ninth major PLANET in order of distance from sun. Revolves about sun at mean distance of 3,670,000,000 mi. in c.248 years. Discovered 1930 by C. W. Tombaugh while working from reckonings made in 1914 by Percival Lowell.

plutonium (plōōtō'nēŭm), metallic element (symbol = Pu; see also ELEMENT, table) exhibiting RADIOACTIVITY. Produced in cyclotron in 1940 by fission of uranium. One of three atomic bombs in World War II was made of plutonium.

Plymouth (plĭ'mûth), county borough (pop. 208,985), Devonshire, England, on Plymouth Sound. Seaport and naval base, it comprises Plymouth, Stonehouse, and Devonport. Has important trade in minerals, granite, marble, and fish. Was rendezvous of anti-armada fleet. Drake, Hawkins, and Ralegh set out from here. Last English port touched by *Mayflower*. Noteworthy are marine biological laboratories, aquarium, municipal museum and Athenaeum, several old churches, and Catholic cathedral. Sections of city were destroyed in 1941 bombing.

Plymouth. 1 Town (pop. 6,771), W Conn., N of Waterbury; settled 1728. Metal goods. **2** City (pop. 6,704), N Ind., S of South Bend. Shipping, trading center with mfg. of metal products. Near by are resort lakes. **3** Town (pop. 13,608), including Plymouth village (pop. 10,540), SE Mass., on Plymouth Bay and SE of Boston. Site of 1st permanent European settlement in New England (see PILGRIMS and PLYMOUTH COLONY). Plymouth Rock, on which legend says Pilgrims disembarked from *Mayflower* in 1620, is shrine (since 1880 on original site). Leyden St. was the 1st laid out. Pilgrim Hall has relics. *Natl. Monument to the Forefathers* erected 1889. **4** City (pop. 6,637), SE Mich., on branch of the River Rouge and W of Detroit. Mfg. of metal and rubber products. **5** Winter-resort town (pop. 3,039), central N.H., S of Franconia Notch. Daniel Webster pleaded his first case here. Nathaniel Hawthorne died here. **6** Borough (pop. 13,021), NE Pa., on Susquehanna R. and SW of Wilkes-Barre. Coal mining. **7** Town (pop. 348), S central Vt., SE of Rutland. Birthplace of Calvin Coolidge, who took oath of office near by and whose grave is here. **8** City (pop. 4,543), E Wis., W of Sheboygan. Cheese center, it is seat of Wisconsin Cheesemakers' Association and its cheese exchange.

Plymouth Brethren, evangelical sect originating in early 19th cent. in Ireland under J. N. Darby, and spreading to Continent, British dominions, and U.S. Name derived from association formed c.1830 at Plymouth, England. Sect was reaction against formality of church practices; it has no set organization or ordained ministers.

Plymouth Colony, settlement made by PILGRIMS on coast of Mass. (1620), after sailing in MAYFLOWER. Compact drawn up aboard ship remained basis of colony's government. Colony slowly expanded after first harsh winter, especially under governorship of William BRADFORD. Developed into quasi-theocracy. Joined NEW ENGLAND CONFEDERATION in 1643. United with Mass. Bay colony in 1691.

Plymouth Sound, deep inlet of English Channel, between Devonshire and Cornwall, England. Famous roadstead, it forms bay c.3 mi. broad. Receives Tamar and Plym rivers.

Plzen, Czechoslovakia: see PILSEN.

Pm, chemical symbol of element PROMETHIUM.

pneumatic appliances and tools (no͞omă'tĭk, nū–) use compressed air as source of power. Pneumatic tools include percussion tools, which employ a piston striking successive blows, e.g., pneumatic hammers, rock drills; and reciprocating-motor-driven tools, in which tool is held by spindle revolved by gearing actuated by reciprocating piston, e.g., drills, grinders, buffers, hoists. Other pneumatic devices are air lifts, chucks for holding work or tool, blowguns, air brushes, and air guns.

pneumonia (nūmō'nyu̇), lung inflammation caused by bacterial or virus infection and attended by fever, chills, pain, cough. In primary or lobar form, first critical days are followed by sudden improvement (crisis). Secondary form (bronchopneumonia) is often sequel of other disease. Atypical pneumonia (probably caused by virus) relatively mild. Fatalities are reduced by use of sulfa drugs and antibiotics.

Pnom Penh (nŏm"pĕn', pu̇no͞om"–), city (pop. 110,639), cap. of Cambodia; port on Tonle Sap R. at confluence with the Mekong. Founded 14th cent., it succeeded Angkor as Khmer cap. in 15th cent. Permanent cap. of Cambodia since 1867.

Po, longest river of Italy, 405 mi. long, rising in Cottian Alps, flowing E past Turin, and emptying into the Adriatic through a delta. Forms widest and most fertile valley in Italy. Its chief tributaries are from the Alps. Navigable to Casale.

Po, chemical symbol of the element POLONIUM.

Pobyedonostzev, Konstantin Petrovich (kŭnstŭntyēn' pētrô'vĭch pŭbyĕdŭnôs'tsyĭf), 1827–1907, Russian statesman and jurist. Procurator of holy synod (1880–1905). Promoted Russification of minorities, persecution of nonconformists; sought to raise spiritual level of clergy; opposed Western liberalism.

Pocahontas (pōku̇hŏn'tu̇s), c.1595–1617, daughter of American Indian chief Powhatan. Authenticity of story of her saving John Smith is disputed. Marriage to John ROLFE estab. peace with English.

Pocahontas, town (pop. 2,410), SW Va., near W.Va. line. Has only exhibition coal mine in world.

Pocatello (pōku̇tĕ'lō), city (pop. 26,131), SE Idaho, on Portneuf R., near American Falls Reservoir. Begun as rail junction in 1882, settled in 1887–88. Second largest city in Idaho. Shipping point and rail center for irrigated agr. area. Seat of Idaho State Col.

Po Chü-i (bô' jo͞o-ē'), 772–846, Chinese poet of T'ang dynasty. A government official, he wrote c.3,000 poems, mostly topical and quite short.

pocket gopher: see GOPHER.

Pocono Mountains (pō'ku̇nō), range of Appalachian system, E Pa., NW of Stroudsburg; c.2,000 ft. high. Summer and winter resort area.

Podgorica, Yugoslavia: see TITOGRAD.

Podolia (pŏdō'lyu̇), agr. region, W central Ukraine, between Dniester and Southern Bug rivers. Part of Kievan Russia from 10th to 13th cent., it was later ruled, successively, by Tatars, Lithuanians, Poles, Turks, and Poles again, until it passed to Russia in 1793. Large Jewish minority, here since Middle Ages, has suffered much persecution.

Poe, Edgar Allan, 1809–49, American author and critic. Orphaned in 1812, he was given a home and educated by John Allan, of Richmond, Va. After a quarrel with Allan, Poe went to Boston, where he published *Tamerlane and Other Poems* (1827). He was appointed to West Point, but was dismissed for breaking rules. After *Poems* appeared (New York, 1831), he went to Baltimore to live with his aunt, Mrs. Clemm, and her daughter Virginia, whom he married in 1836. In 1835 he became an editor of *Southern Literary Messenger,* but lost position through excessive drinking. In 1838 he published *The Narrative of Arthur Gordon Pym.* In Philadelphia (1838–44), he edited Burton's *Gentleman's Magazine* (1839–40) and *Graham's Magazine* (1841–42), winning fame as a caustic but just critic. In 1840 he collected his stories in *Tales of the Grotesque and Arabesque.* In New York after 1844, he edited *Broadway Journal* and lived, after 1846, with his wife and Mrs. Clemm in a cottage at Fordham. After Mrs. Poe died in

1847, Poe returned to Richmond. He died of excessive drinking in Baltimore, ending a career brilliant but tragic. In 1845 *The Raven and Other Poems* won him fame at home and abroad. His poetry is noted for its haunting melody and rhythm, as in "To Helen," "The Raven," "The Bells," "Israfel," and "Annabel Lee." His stories are characterized by skillful plotting and unity of tone. Poe is recognized abroad, and belatedly at home, as one of America's greatest literary geniuses.

poet laureate (lô′rēĭt), title conferred in England by the king on a poet, whose duty it becomes to write commemorative odes and verse. Ben Jonson held an analogous position in 1617, but Dryden first had the actual title in 1670. His successors have included Southey, Wordsworth, Tennyson, Bridges, and Masefield.

Poggio Bracciolini, Gian Francesco (jän′ fränchā′skō pŏd′jō brät″chōlē′nē), 1380–1459, Italian humanist. Best known for his tales *Facetiae* (1474) and for scholarly quarrels.

pogrom (pō′grŭm, pōgrŏm′), Russian word, originally connoting a riot, but later meaning attacks on Jews in Russia. The tsarist regime sought to divert upon the Jews the revolutionary anger of the masses. Pogroms were especially serious in 1881–82 and 1903–21.

Pohai, China: see CHIHLI, GULF OF.

poi, fermented, sticky food paste of the Pacific islands, made by pounding the roasted roots of the taro.

Poincaré, Jules Henri (zhül ãrē′ pwẽkärā′), 1854–1912, French mathematician, physicist. One of greatest mathematicians of his age, he enlarged field of mathematical physics by research on theory of functions (esp. automorphic, Fuchsian, Abelian functions) and did notable work on differential equations and astronomical theory of orbits.

Poincaré, Raymond (rāmõ′), 1860–1934, French statesman; cousin of Jules Poincaré. He was president of the republic 1913–20; premier 1912, 1922–24, 1926–29. A conservative and ardent nationalist, he called for harsh punishment of Germany after World War I; ordered occupation of the RUHR in 1923; secured stabilization of currency in 1928.

poinciana, royal (poinsēā′nŭ, –ă′nŭ), name for a tropical leguminous tree (*Delonix regia*) native to Madagascar, and known also as peacock flower. It is widely grown in many warm regions for its vivid clusters of scarlet flowers. The fruits are long pods (6 in.–c.2 ft.). There is also a genus *Poinciana,* chiefly of tropical America, a shrub or small tree with bright orange or yellow flowers.

poinsettia (poinsĕt′ŭ, –sĕt′ēŭ), ornamental shrub (*Euphorbia pulcherrima*), native to tropical America. It has small true flowers in the center of a rosette of red bracts. It is much used as a pot plant especially for Chrismas decoration.

Point Barrow, northernmost point of Alaska, on Arctic Ocean. Discovered 1826 by F. W. Beechey. Prominent in arctic exploration and aviation. Naval station estab. 1944; navigation open 2–3 months a year. Barrow village in SW, with weather station, airfield, school, hospital, and monument to Will Rogers and Wiley Post, killed in airplane crash here (1935).

Pointe aux Trembles (pwẽtōtrã′blŭ), residential town (pop. 8,241), S Que., Canada, on St. Lawrence R. and NNE of Montreal.

Pointe Claire (point klâr′, Fr., pwẽt klĕr′), residential town (pop. 8,753), S Que., Canada, on S shore of Montreal Isl., SW suburb of Montreal.

pointer: see HUNTING DOGS.

Point Grey, W suburb of Vancouver, SW B.C., Canada. Site of the Univ. of British Columbia.

Point Judith, R.I.: see NARRAGANSETT.

Point Pleasant. 1 Atlantic resort borough (pop. 4,009), E N.J., S of Asbury Park; settled 1850. **2** City (pop. 4,596), W W.Va., on Ohio R. at mouth of Kanawha R. In battle of Point Pleasant (1774) frontiersmen defeated Indians.

Point Roberts, summer resort, NW Wash., on Strait of Georgia, at tip of peninsula extending S from British Columbia and separated from Wash. mainland by Boundary Bay. Salmon fishing. Reachable by land only from Canada.

Poiré, Emmanuel: see CARAN D'ACHE.

poison, agent which may produce chemically an injurious or deadly effect when introduced into organism in sufficient quantity. Poisons are classed as irritant, corrosive, or systemic. Call doctor when poisoning is suspected. If poison has been swallowed, several glasses of water should usually be given immediately to dilute poison. Avoid use of emetics for corrosive poisons. Treat patient for shock if necessary. Give artificial respiration if breathing fails and for gas poisoning. See also CARBON MONOXIDE; FOOD POISONING; LEAD POISONING; POISON IVY; SNAKE BITE.

Poison Affair, scandal involving various prominent persons at the court of Louis XIV, beginning with the trial and execution (1676) of the Marquise de Brinvilliers, who had confessed to poisoning her father and brother. Her trial attracted attention to other "mysterious" deaths. Parisian society had been indulging in a fad for séances, fortunetelling, and love potions. When the quack practitioners (some may also have sold poisons) were arrested, they revealed the names of high-ranking clients. A celebrated case was that of La Voisin (or Catherine Monvoisin), midwife and fortuneteller, whose clientèle included Mme de Montespan, two nieces of Cardinal Mazarin, Marshal Luxembourg, and Racine. No formal charges were made nor was any evidence found against any of these, but La Voisin, after a sensational trial, was burned as a sorceress (1680). A special court, the *chambre ardente* [burning court] was estab. to judge poison and witchcraft cases; the poison epidemic subsided. Although indulging in less hysteria and judicial irregularities, the Affair was symptomatic of witchcraft trials then prevalent in Europe and New England.

poison gas, name for substances used in warfare because of poisonous or corrosive nature. Some are gases at ordinary temperatures but commonly they are liquids or solids that vaporize. CHLORINE was first used by

Germans; difficulties of use led to development of others. Phosgene was used in shells; like chlorine, it affects lungs. MUSTARD GAS and lewisite attack skin; TEAR GAS affects eyes. See also CHEMICAL WARFARE.

poison ivy, native woody vine or shrub (*Rhus radicans, R. toxicodendron,* or *Toxicodendron radicans*) and the skin irritation it causes. The flowers are small, greenish clusters and the fruits are berrylike. The leaves, composed of three leaflets, may have entire or lobed margins. Plants with wavy-margined leaves are often called poison oak. The poison toxicodendrol, which causes itching and blistering, is present in all plant parts, and the irritation may result from touching the plant itself or from contact with clothes, tools, animals, smoke, etc., contaminated by the poison. Washing with an alkaline, non-oily soap after exposure may help prevent the skin irritation.

Poisson, Siméon Denis (sēmäõ' dünē' pwäsõ'), 1781–1840, French mathematician and physicist. Known for work in many fields, especially definite integrals, but his chief interest was in applications of mathematics to physics (esp. electrostatics and magnetism).

Poitiers, Diane de: see DIANE DE POITIERS.

Poitiers (pwätyā'), city (pop. 41,279) cap. of Vienne dept., W France; historic cap. of POITOU. Dating from pre-Roman times, it was an early episcopal see and a residence of the Visigothic kings (until its capture by Clovis I, 507). In 732 Charles Martel routed the Saracens between Poitiers and Tours; in 1356 John II was defeated and captured at Poitiers by Edward the Black Prince. The scene of many other historic events, Poitiers has retained a Roman amphitheater and many magnificent churches and residences dating from the 4th cent. to the Renaissance. University was founded 1432.

Poitou (pwätōō'), region and former province, W France, on Atlantic coast, in Vendée, Deux-Sèvres, and Vienne depts.; historic cap. Poitiers. The Vendée is largely pasture land; Upper Poitou is a rich agr. region. Counts of Poitou took the title dukes of AQUITAINE in 9th cent. With Aquitaine, Poitou passed to England 1152; was recovered by Philip II of France 1204; ceded to England 1360; and recovered for France by Du Guesclin c.1370.

poker, card game, believed to have been first played in U.S. on Mississippi river steamboats. Two basic forms are draw and stud poker, many variations include high-low poker, seven-card stud poker, "spit in the ocean."

pokeweed, tall perennial herb (*Phytolacca americana*) native to North America and naturalized in Europe. It has dark, flattened berries containing a red juice. Young shoots of the plant are eaten but the roots are poisonous.

Pola (pō'lä), Serbo-Croatian *Pula,* city (pop. 22,714), Croatia, NW Yugoslavia: an Adriatic seaport near S tip of Istria. A Venetian possession from 1148, it passed to Austria 1797 and became a major naval base. Was transferred to Italy 1919; to Yugoslavia 1947. Has well-preserved Roman amphitheater, triumphal arch, and temple.

Poland, Pol. *Polska,* republic (120,359 sq. mi.; pop. 24,976,926, incl. former German territories placed under Polish administration in 1945), E central Europe, between the Baltic Sea (N) and the Carpathian mts. (S); cap. Warsaw. It is mostly a lowland but rises to 8,210 ft. in the Tatra group of the Carpathians. Chief rivers: Vistula, Oder, Warta, Western Bug. Largest cities: Warsaw, Lodz, Cracow, Poznan (Poland proper); Breslau, Danzig (formerly German). Largely agr. and forested, Poland also has important coal and ore mines (esp. in KATOWICE area); large salt deposits; some petroleum. Chief industries: metallurgy, textiles. Majority religion: Roman Catholicism. The Slavic Poles were united (10th cent.) by the PIAST dynasty. The early Piasts vastly increased their domains, but the kingdom split in 1138 and was fully reunited only in 1320. The TEUTONIC KNIGHTS, defeated at Tannenberg (1410), accepted Polish overlordship in 1466. In 1370 the crown passed to Louis I of Hungary. His daughter Jadwiga married the grand duke of LITHUANIA, who as LADISLAUS II of Poland founded the JAGIELLO dynasty (1386–1572). The Polish-Lithuanian state, mightiest of E Europe, was fully merged in 1569 (Union of Lublin). Under the Jagiellos, Poland reached its political and cultural zenith. At the same time, under pressure of the gentry, the kings conceded extraordinary powers to the diet; any single deputy to the *sejm* (lower house) could dissolve the diet. This practice (*liberum veto*) was recklessly applied after 1572, when Poland became a "royal republic," with the entire nobility taking part in the royal elections. STEPHEN BATHORY and the VASA kings (1587–1668) were involved in bitter struggles with Russia and Sweden. Poland, though preserved by the miracle of CZESTOCHOWA, lost much territory in the treaties of OLIVA and ANDRUSOV. JOHN III briefly restored Polish prestige, but with the accession (1697) of the electors of Saxony as kings of Poland, national independence was virtually lost (see AUGUSTUS II; AUGUSTUS III; NORTHERN WAR; POLISH SUCCESSION, WAR OF THE). STANISLAUS II, elected 1764, maintained himself only through Russian aid and in 1772 had to cede vast areas to Russia, Austria, and Prussia (first Partition of Poland). He attempted a constitutional reform (1791), but the second partition (1793, between Russia and Prussia) and, after Kosciusko's unsuccessful uprising, the third partition (1795, among Russia, Prussia, and Austria) took Poland off the map of Europe. Napoleon I sponsored the duchy of Warsaw (1807–13), a buffer state under the king of Saxony. The Congress of Vienna (1814–15) gave WEST PRUSSIA and POZNAN prov. to Prussia and GALICIA to Austria; made CRACOW a separate republic (annexed by Austria, 1846); and created a kingdom of Poland (cap. Warsaw), in personal union with Russia but with its own constitution ("Congress-Poland"). The defeat of a general insurrection in Congress-Poland (1830–31) led to suspension of its constitution; another insurrection (1863) was followed by intense Russification, paralleled in German Poland by Bismarck's Germanization program. Austrian Poland kept considerable autonomy. Polish dreams of national rebirth materialized in World War I. A Polish republic was proclaimed by PILSUDSKI (1918). Its W and S boundaries were fixed at, approximately, those of 1772 (see POLISH CORRIDOR; SILESIA). Polish insistence on restoration of its 1772 border in the E led to war with Russia (1920–21). The Treaty of RIGA gave Poland most of its claims; moreover, Poland seized VILNA from Lithuania. A third of Poland's population consisted of minorities—Germans, Ukrainians, Belorussians, Jews—whose treatment was not always equitable. In 1926 Pilsudski assumed virtual dictatorship, continued after his death (1935) by the "colonels' clique," a military junta. On Sept. 1, 1939, Poland having rejected German demands for DANZIG, Hitler attacked Poland and began WORLD WAR II. On Sept. 17, Soviet troops invaded from the E. Polish resistance, though gallant, was soon crushed. Germany annexed W Poland, Russia the E; the central portion ("Government General") was placed under German occupation. When Germany attacked the USSR (1941) all Poland came under German occupation. Though all Poles suffered cruelly, none fared worse than the Jews, nearly all of whom (c.3,000,000) were exterminated. Polish forces under a government in exile continued to fight alongside the Allies. In Poland itself there arose an effective underground army. Polish charges regarding the KATYN massacre, Russian demands for cession of E Poland, and the creation of a Russian-sponsored provisional Polish government at LUBLIN created a tense situation. Early in 1945 all Poland was in Russian hands, and the YALTA CONFERENCE prepared Allied recognition of a somewhat broadened Lublin government. The Polish-Russian border was shifted considerably W, while the POTSDAM CONFERENCE transferred large parts of E Germany to Polish administration, pending a general peace treaty. Most of the German population was expelled. By 1947 Communists and left-wing Socialists had gained full control of the government. Poland became a "people's democracy" within the Soviet orbit.

Poland, town (pop. 1,503), including Poland Spring resort (mineral water), SW Maine, W of Auburn. Mansion House inn dates from 1797.

polar bear, large white or cream-colored bear (*Thalarctos*) of arctic regions. It has a relatively small head and neck. It is a strong swimmer and the hairy soles facilitate walking on ice. Fish, seal, and other animals form its food. Probably does not hibernate. Cubs are born in burrows in ice and drifted snow.

polar exploration: see ARCTIC REGIONS and ANTARCTICA.

polar front, in meteorology, surface separating cold polar air masses of north and warmer air masses of lower latitudes.

polarimeter: see POLARIZATION OF LIGHT.

Polaris: see POLESTAR.

polariscope: see POLARIZATION OF LIGHT.

polarization of light. Certain crystals cause double REFRACTION, i.e., separate an entering light ray into two parts, one passing through with ordinary refraction, the other (extraordinary ray) bent farther from original direction; each emerging part is said to be polarized. Ordinary light vibrates in all planes perpendicular to line of travel; polarized light vibrates in one plane or circularly or elliptically. A single polarized ray can be produced by a crystal that absorbs the ordinary ray or by a NICOL PRISM. Certain organic substances (called optically active) rotate polarized light either to right or left. Rotation direction can be determined by polariscope; amount, by polarimeter.

polar regions: see ARCTIC REGIONS and ANTARCTICA.

Polasek, Albin (pôlä'shĕk), 1879–, American sculptor of busts and memorials, b. Czechoslovakia.

Pole, English noble family. **Michael de la Pole,** 1st **earl of Suffolk,** d. 1389, was trusted adviser and chancellor of Richard II. His grandson, **William de la Pole,** 4th **earl** and 1st **duke of Suffolk,** 1396–1450, had great power under Henry VI (whose marriage he arranged). Accused of treason for his efforts to secure peace in France, he was exiled and murdered. His son, **John de la Pole,** 2d **duke of Suffolk,** 1442–91, married Edward IV's sister. His son, **John de la Pole, earl of Lincoln,** c.1464–1487, had claim to throne by Richard III. Joined Lambert Simnel's revolt and was killed. His brother, **Edmund de la Pole, earl of Suffolk,** c.1472–1513, aspired to the throne. Captured and long imprisoned, he was executed by Henry VIII.

Pole, Reginald, 1500–1558, English churchman, archbishop of Canterbury (1556–58), a cardinal. He remained Catholic when Henry VIII broke with the papacy and spent much time in Rome. After Mary was made queen Cardinal Pole was sent as papal legate to England, but plans to restore Catholicism there failed. Died the same day as Mary.

polecat (pōl'kăt″), mammal (*Mustela*) of Europe and Asia, allied to ferret, weasel, marten (not closely to skunk). Destroys poultry. Scent gland emits fetid odor. Fur of European polecat is called fitch.

poles, magnetic: see MAGNETIC POLES; MAGNETISM.

polestar, conspicuous star nearest north celestial pole; also called North Star. Star holding position at present is Polaris (Alpha of constellation Ursa Minor or Little Dipper) which lies c.1°9′ from pole; its light power is c.47 times that of sun. Alpha Draconis was polestar c.2300 B.C.; Vega will hold position in c.12,000 years.

police, agents concerned with enforcement of law, order, and public protection. In many countries they have a political function (see SECRET POLICE). European police forces are centralized; U.S. ones are mostly under local control. SCOTLAND YARD was reorganized (1829) under the police system laid out by Sir Robert Peel. In the U.S. regular police forces followed the establishment (1844) of the New York city organization. There is no regular Federal force except the FBI for detection.

police dog: see SHEEP DOGS.

police power, in law, right of a government to make laws necessary for health, morals, and welfare of the populace. In the U.S. it has been defined by Supreme Court as power of the states to enact such laws even if they contravene literal terms of the Constitution. Doctrine first stated by John Marshall; broadened by Roger B. Taney. Concept became of great importance after passage of Fourteenth Amendment. Supreme Court gradually evolved an attitude tolerant toward economic regulation by the states.

Polignac, Jules Armand, prince de (zhül' ärmä' prēs' dü pôlēnyäk'), 1780–1847, French premier (1829–30), an ultraroyalist and reactionary. In March, 1830, the chamber of deputies demanded his dismissal. Instead, Charles X dissolved the chamber. When the new elections again produced a liberal majority, Polignac issued the July ordinances, which dissolved the new chamber even before it met, estab. a new electoral law, and ended freedom of the press. This precipitated the JULY REVOLUTION. Arrested in 1830, Polignac was amnestied in 1836 and withdrew to England.

Poling, Daniel A(lfred), 1884–, American clergyman, editor, and author. Pastor of Marble Collegiate Church, New York city (1923–30) and of Baptist Temple, Philadelphia (1936–48), he became (1948) chaplain of Chapel of Four Chaplains, Philadelphia. Editor of *Christian Herald* and *Christian Endeavor World.*

poliomyelitis (pō"lēōmī"ŭlī'tĭs, pŏ–) or **infantile paralysis,** inflammation of gray matter of spinal cord, caused by virus. In a minority of cases, motor nerve paralysis causes atrophy of groups of muscles. Physical therapy is preferred treatment. Chilling and overfatigue increase susceptibility.

Polish Corridor, strip of territory along the lower Vistula, separating East Prussia from rest of Germany, which was given to Poland by the Treaty of Versailles (1919) to provide it with an outlet to the Baltic Sea. Once part of Polish POMERANIA, Polish Corridor had a large German minority and was cause of chronic Polish-German friction. Failure of negotiations over return of Free City of DANZIG and creation of extraterritorial German corridor across Polish Corridor produced the immediate cause of the German invasion of Poland and World War II.

Polish language, one of the Slavonic subfamily of Indo-European languages. See LANGUAGE (table).

Polish Succession, War of the, 1733–35, European war which broke out of the death of Augustus II of Poland. STANISLAUS I, who sought to regain his throne, was elected by a majority of Polish nobles and was backed by France (later also by Spain and Sardinia). Augustus's son, elected by a minority as AUGUSTUS III, was backed by Emperor Charles VI and by Russia. Stanislaus was defeated in 1734, but fighting continued along the Rhine and in Italy, for reasons which had nothing to do with Poland. By the Treaty of Vienna (1735; ratified 1738) a general settlement was reached: Augustus kept Poland; Stanislaus received LORRAINE; Francis of Lorraine was promised succession of TUSCANY; Austria ceded Naples and Sicily to Spain; Spain ceded to Austria its claim to Parma; Sardinia received nothing, lost nothing, exchanged nothing.

Politian (pōlĭ'shŭn), Ital. *Poliziano,* surname of **Angelo Ambrogini,** 1454–94, Italian poet and humanist. His *Orfeo* (1471) marks the transition from sacred to profane drama, and *Stanze per la giostra* (1475–76) are descriptive lyric masterpieces hardly surpassed by Ariosto or Tasso.

political science, the science of the nature of the state and of government. Its considerations include such subjects as the nature of sovereignty, international law, colonial government, and constitutions.

Polk, James K(nox) (pōk), 1795–1849, 11th President of the United States (1845–49). U.S. Representative from Tenn. (1825–39), speaker of the House (1835–39). A leading Jacksonian Democrat. As President he ably managed MEXICAN WAR. Achieved reduction of tariff, reestablishment of INDEPENDENT TREASURY SYSTEM, settlement of dispute over Oregon, acquisition of Calif. Few Presidents have equaled his record of attaining specific, stated aims; few have worked harder.

Polk, Leonidas, 1806–64, Protestant Episcopal bishop and Confederate general. Bishop of La. (1841–61). A founder of Univ. of the South, Sewanee, Tenn. (1857). Fought at Shiloh, Murfreesboro, in Chattanooga campaign. Killed at Pine Mountain, Ga.

Pollaiuolo (pōl-läyōō-ō'lō), family of Florentine artists. **Jacopo Pollaiuolo** (yä'kōpō) was a noted 15th-cent. goldsmith. His son and pupil, **Antonio Pollaiuolo,** 1429?–1498, is said to have been first artist to study anatomy by dissection. Famous for drawings and paintings with active, muscular figures, as in *Labors of Hercules* (Uffizi). Executed bronze tomb of Sixtus IV in Rome (1484) and monument to Innocent VIII in St. Peter's, aided by his brother **Piero Pollaiuolo** (pyā'rō), 1443–96, who also collaborated with him on many paintings. Their nephew, **Simone del Pollaiuolo** (sēmō'nā dĕl), 1457–1508, was an architect. Worked mainly in Florence, where he finished the Strozzi Palace. Nicknamed Il Cronaca.

polled shorthorn cattle: see CATTLE.

pollination, the transfer of pollen from the stamen to the pistil of the same or another flower. Pollen grains, microscopic grains invisible to the naked eye except in quantity, are borne, usually as a yellow powder, on the stamens within the corolla of a flower. Insects, wind, and hummingbirds serve to transfer pollen. Self-pollination is usually prevented in flowers by adaptations to insure cross-pollination, believed to make for stronger offspring. After pollination, the pollen grain germinates and produces a tube which grows down through the pistil of the flower to the embryo sac; one of the sperm nuclei formed from living matter within the pollen grain fuses, in the act of fertilization, with the ovum or egg lying in the embryo sac. See *ill.,* p. 999.

Pollock, Sir Frederick (pŏ'lŭk), 1845–1937, English jurist, professor of jurisprudence (1887–1903), judge of the admiralty court of the Cinque Ports. Wrote much on law, including *The History of English Law* (1895; with F. W. Maitland). His correspondence with Justice O. W. Holmes has been published (1941).

Pollonarrua or **Polonnaruwa** (both: pŏ"lŭnŭ-rōō'ŭ), ruined anc. city, E central Ceylon. Was cap. of Ceylon in 8th cent. Has impressive ruins of Buddhist temples.

poll tax, in U.S. history, a tax levied by a state on its voters, usually ranging from $1 to $5. Many otherwise eligible voters, particularly in the South, have thus been disfranchised. Though some southern states have passed legislation forbidding poll taxes (North Carolina in 1920, Louisiana in 1934, Florida in 1937, and Georgia in 1945), efforts to enact a Federal anti-poll-tax law have failed.

Pollux, Greek hero: see CASTOR AND POLLUX.

Polo, Marco, 1254?–1324?, Venetian traveler in China. Accompanied father and uncle on Eastern expedition (1271). Reached Cambuluc (Peiping) in 1275; Marco became Kublai Khan's favorite and his agent. Traveled widely. Returned to Venice in 1295. Later dictated account of his experiences—chief Renaissance source of information on East.

polo, game played on horseback by teams of four on field 200 by 300 yd. Said to have originated in Persia. Revived in India in 19th cent., it became popular with British officers stationed there, spread to other countries. Introduced in England 1869, in U.S. 1876.

polonium (pŭlō'nēŭm), element similar to radium (symbol = Po; see also ELEMENT, table) exhibiting RADIOACTIVITY. See *ill.*, p. 989.

Polonnaruwa, Ceylon: see POLLONARRUA.

Polovtsi, Russian name of the CUMANS.

Polson (pōl'sŭn), resort city (pop. 2,280), NW Mont., on Flathead L.

Poltava (pŭltä'vŭ), city (pop. 130,305), E central Ukraine; agr. center. Near here Peter I routed Charles XII of Sweden in 1709.

polyandry: see MARRIAGE.

Polybius (pōlĭ'bēŭs), 203? B.C.–c.120 B.C., Greek historian. In Rome, under patronage of the Scipios, he wrote great universal history, covering Mediterranean world of 220–146 B.C. Of 40 books, first five are intact, with large fragments of others.

Polycarp, Saint (pŏ'lĭkärp), A.D. c.70–156?, Greek bishop of Smyrna, Father of the Church; author of an *Epistle to the Philippians* (said by some to be two letters). Said to have died a martyr in Rome. Feast: Jan. 26.

Polycletus (pŏlĭklē'tŭs) or **Polyclitus** (–klī'tŭs), two Greek sculptors of school of Argos. **Polycletus,** the elder, fl. c.450–c.420 B.C., was a contemporary of Phidias. Famous for his *Doryphorus* or *Spear-Bearer* (a copy is in Naples), which embodied his ideal of physical perfection. None of his originals exists today. **Polycletus,** the younger, worked in 4th cent. B.C. and was also a sculptor of athletes.

Polydorus: see LAOCOÖN.

Polyglot Bible (pŏ'lēglŏt), a Bible in which different versions, often in different languages, are given in parallel columns. Origen's HEXAPLA is most famous anc. example. Most elaborate of modern Polyglot Bibles is the London, or Walton's, Polyglot (1657), containing Hebrew, Greek, Syriac, Ethiopic, Arabic, and Persian texts.

Polyhymnia: see MUSES.

polymerization (pŏ"lĭmŭrĭzā'shŭn), joining of a number of molecules of same kind to form one larger molecule. Two compounds having molecules so related are called polymers.

Polynesia (pŏlĭnē'zhŭ) [Gr.,= many islands], one of three main divisions of Pacific isls., in central and S Pacific. Includes Hawaiian Isls., Samoa, Tonga, islands of French Establishments in Oceania, and, ethnologically, New Zealand. Languages are Malayo-Polynesian (see LANGUAGE, table).

Polynesian languages or **Malayo-Polynesian languages:** see LANGUAGE (table).

Polynices (–nī'sēz), in Greek legend, leader of the SEVEN AGAINST THEBES; son of Oedipus, brother of Eteocles and Antigone, and nephew of CREON. Polynices and Eteocles killed each other in battle.

polyp (pŏ'lĭp), elongated or hybrid form of various coelenterates (jellyfish and relatives). Alternation of generations between polyp and jellyfish or medusa stage is common. Coral animal and sea anemone are polyp forms.

Polyphemus (pŏlĭfē'mŭs), in Greek mythology, a Cyclops or one-eyed giant; son of Poseidon. In the *Odyssey,* Odysseus was captured by him but escaped by blinding him.

polyphony (pŭlĭ'fŭnĭ), music whose texture is formed by the interweaving of several more or less independent melodic lines. Term practically synonymous with COUNTERPOINT. Contrasting terms are homophony (one part dominates while others serve only a harmonic function) and monody (a single melodic line, for example, plain song). The 16th cent. was the great age of polyphony. With the gradual acceptance of tonality, polyphonic music adopted a style more dependent on harmony, evolving into the homophonic music of the 19th cent. Some 20th-cent. music recalls medieval and Renaissance polyphony.

Pombal, Sebastião José de Carvalho e Melo, marquês de (sĕbästyā'ō zhōōzā' dŭ kärvä'lyō ē mĕ'lō märkās' dŭ pômbäl'), 1699–1782, Portuguese statesman. As secretary of state for foreign affairs and war he ruled Portugal under King Joseph for 26 years (1750–77). Absolutist and anticlerical, he crushed all opposition, expelled the Jesuits, curbed the Inquisition, reformed the schools and the army, fostered agr. and industry, built up Brazil, and reconstructed Lisbon after earthquake of 1755. Maria I dismissed and exiled him.

pomegranate (pŭm'gră"nĭt, pŏm'–), handsome, thorny shrub or small tree (*Punica granatum*) native to S Asia and its fruit, about the size of an apple with hard yellowish to purple rind. It has shining leaves and showy red-orange flowers. Grenadine syrup is made from the red pulp of the fruits. Commercial orchards are found in Ariz. and Calif. Pomegranate connected with legend of PERSEPHONE.

pomelo: see GRAPEFRUIT.

Pomerania (pŏmŭrā'nēŭ), Ger. *Pommern,* former Prussian province (14,830 sq. mi.; 1939 pop. 2,393,844; cap. Stettin), N Germany, on the Baltic Sea. Agr. lowland; forests, lakes; fishing. Inhabited by Slavic tribes by the 10th cent., Pomerania became a duchy 11th cent.; was Christianized and passed under Polish overlordship 12th cent. By 1181 it had split into two principalities. (1) The E part, including DANZIG, continued separately as Pomerelia (Ger. *Pommerellen,* Pol. *Pomorze*). Annexed by Poland 1295, it was ceded to the TEUTONIC KNIGHTS 1308; reverted to Poland 1466; was ceded to Prussia in the partitions of Poland (1772, 1793). Part of WEST PRUSSIA prov. till 1919, Pomerelia was partitioned by the Treaty of Versailles: the larger part became Polish; Danzig became a free city; the rest remained Prussian (2) The W part, or Pomerania proper, became a duchy of the Holy Roman Empire. It was occupied (1628), with the consent of its last native duke, Bogislav XIV, by Wallenstein in the Thirty Years War. The resistance of STRALSUND precipitated Swedish intervention. The Peace of Westphalia (1648) gave W or Hither Pomerania (incl. Stettin and Stralsund) to Sweden; E or Farther Pomerania went to Brandenburg-Prussia, which in 1720 also acquired the E half, and in 1815 the whole, of Swedish Pomerania. While Pomerelia was largely Polish-speaking and Catholic, Pomerania had long been thoroughly Germanized and Protestant. The Potsdam Conference of 1945 assigned Pomerania E of the Oder (incl. Stettin) to Polish administration, pending a peace treaty with Germany. Danzig and the rest of Pomerelia, after German annexation in World War II, reverted to Poland. Pomerania W of the Oder became part of Mecklenburg.

Pomeranian dog: see TOY DOG.

Pomerelia: see POMERANIA.

Pommerellen and **Pommern:** see POMERANIA.

Pomona (pŭmō'nŭ), Roman goddess, protectress of fruit trees.

Pomona (pŭmō'nŭ), city (pop. 35,405), S Calif., E of Los Angeles; laid out 1875. Packs and ships citrus fruit, refines oil, produces metal and paper products.

Pomona (pŭmō'nŭ, pō–) or **Mainland,** island (c.189 sq. mi.; pop. 13,352), off N Scotland, largest of Orkney Isls. Kirkwall (cap.) is here. Irregular coastline is indented by Kirkwall Bay and Scapa Flow. Interior has hills, lakes, and fertile valleys.

Pomona College: see CLAREMONT, Calif.

Pomorze: see POMERANIA.

Pompadour, Antoinette Poisson, marquise de (pŏm'pŭdôr, Fr. ātwänĕt' pwäsō' märkēz' dŭ pōpädōōr'), 1721–64, mistress of Louis XV of France from 1745 to her death. Of humble origin, she rose through her beauty, intelligence, and ambition to become virtual ruler of France. Her foreign policy was responsible for the French alliance with Austria, which involved France in the Seven Years War. She was a lavish patron to artists and writers.

Pompano (pŏm'pŭnō), city (pop. 5,682), SE Fla., on Atlantic coast N of Fort Lauderdale. Packs vegetables.

Pompeii (pŏmpā'), ruined Roman city, S Italy, at the foot of Mt. Vesuvius, near Naples. A Samnite city long before it became Roman (1st cent. B.C.), it was a flourishing port and wealthy resort when it was injured (A.D. 63) by earthquake and buried (A.D. 79) by an eruption of Vesuvius. Volcanic ashes and cinders preserved the ruins, which were rediscovered in 1748 and have been since much excavated.

Pompeius, Sextus (sĕk'stŭs pŏmpā'ŭs), d. 35 B.C., Roman commander; son of Pompey the Great. After his father's defeat, he warred against Caesar from Spain until 44 B.C. Later outlawed, he seized Sicily and stopped grain ships from reaching Rome—a practice he resumed against Octavian (Augustus). He won two battles with the aid of storms, but was later defeated, captured, and killed.

Pompey (Cneius Pompeius Magnus; Pompey the Great) (pŏm'pē), 106 B.C.–48 B.C., Roman general. Fought for Sulla successfully, then (76 B.C.) forwarded Roman conquest in Spain and with great severity broke up the last of the revolt of Spartacus (72 B.C.). He served as consul before undertaking successfully to rid the Mediterranean of pirates and to defeat Mithridates VI of Pontus (65 B.C.). Back in Rome, he met opposition from extremists in the senate and was driven into combination with his rival and the senate's enemy, Julius CAESAR. He, Caesar, and Crassus formed the First Triumvirate (60 B.C.). The rivalry would not down, and though peace was kept while Pompey's wife, Julia, who was Caesar's daughter, lived, the two men became open enemies later. Pompey took measures against Clodius, supporting MILO, and went over to the senate and became consul (52 B.C.). Later senate measures against Caesar and for Pompey caused Caesar to cross the Rubicon and begin the civil war (49 B.C.). Pompey was defeated at Pharsala (48 B.C.) and fled to Egypt, where he was assassinated by one of his soldiers.

Pomponazzi, Pietro (pōmpōnät'tsē), 1462–1525, Italian philosopher, a humanist who attacked scholasticism, argued that the soul was mortal (*De immortalitate,* 1516).

Ponape (pō'näpā), volcanic island (129 sq. mi.; pop. 5,735), W Pacific, E Caroline Isls. Has deposits of bauxite and iron. Produces copra and dried bonito. Site of Japanese air base in World War II.

Ponca City, city (pop. 20,180), N Okla., near Arkansas R.; founded 1893. Trade and mfg. center for agr. and oil area with grain elevators, refineries, and food processing plants.

Ponce (pōn'sā), city (pop. 99,429), S Puerto Rico. Second largest city on island, it is thriving port and center of agr. area.

Ponce de León, Juan (Span. hwän' pōn'thā dā lāōn'), c.1460–1521, Spanish explorer. Made fortune as governor of Puerto Rico (1509–12). Discovered Fla. in 1513, explored coast. Legend of fountain of youth he supposedly sought has been discredited. Mortally wounded by Indians in later colonization expedition to Fla.

Poncelet, Jean Victor (zhā' vēktôr' pōslā'), 1788–1867, French mathematician, army engineer. He evolved basis of modern form of projective geometry.

Ponchielli, Amilcare (ämēlkä'rā pōngkyĕl'lē), 1834–86, Italian composer of the opera *La*

Gioconda, containing the popular ballet, *The Dance of the Hours.*

Pond, Peter, 1740–1807, American fur trader, explorer of Old Northwest. Best known for his maps of country covered in voyages.

Pondichéry (pōdēshärē′) or **Pondicherry** (pŏndĭchĕ′rē), French settlement (112 sq. mi.; pop. 222,572), on Bay of Bengal, adjacent to Madras state, India. Territorial limits were estab. 1815. The town **Pondichéry** (pop. 59,835) is cap. of French India. Acquired 1674, it fell three times to the British in 18th cent.

pond lily, coarse aquatic plant of genus *Nuphar* of north temperate zone; also called cow lily and spatterdock. It has yellow cup-shaped flowers and erect or floating leaves.

pondweed, weedy aquatic plant (*Potamogeton*), with both narrow, grasslike, submerged leaves and stouter floating ones.

Poniatowski (pônyätôf′skē), Polish noble family. Stanislaus Augustus Poniatowski was king of Poland (see STANISLAUS II). His nephew, **Prince Jozef Anton Poniatowski,** 1763–1813, Polish general, fought the Russians under Kosciusko (1794); commanded Polish forces under Napoleon in campaigns of 1809 and 1812. He committed suicide after battle of Leipzig.

Pons, Lily, 1904–, French-American coloratura soprano. First appeared at the Metropolitan Opera, New York, 1930. Her many successes include *Lakmé, La Fille du regiment,* and *Lucia di Lammermoor.*

Ponselle, Rosa (pŏnzĕl′), 1894–, American soprano. With the Metropolitan Opera, New York, 1918–37; she made her debut singing opposite Caruso in Verdi's *La forza del destino.*

Ponsonby, Sir Henry (Frederick) (pŭn′sŭnbē), 1825–95, English administrator, private secretary to Queen Victoria (1870–95). His son **Sir Frederick Ponsonby,** 1867–1935, served in the households of Victoria, Edward VII, and George V. Author of *Recollections of Three Reigns* (1951). Created Baron Sysonby 1935.

Pontchartrain, Lake (pŏn′chŭrtrān), shallow lake, 41 mi. long, 25 mi. wide, SE La., N of New Orleans. Connected with L. Maurepas, the Mississippi, and Gulf of Mexico (through L. Borgne). Crossed by bridge (10 mi. long) at narrow eastern end. Has many small resorts.

Pont du Gard (pō′ dü gär′), perfectly preserved Roman aqueduct (c.900 ft. long, c.160 ft. high), built 19 B.C. across Gard R. near Remoulins, S France, to supply Nîmes with water. Has three tiers of arches (lowest in use as road bridge).

Pontefract (pŏn′tĭfrăct, pŭm′frĭt), municipal borough (pop. 23,173), West Riding of Yorkshire, England. Had 11th-cent. castle where Richard II died (1400); dismantled in 1649.

Pontiac, Indian chief: see PONTIAC'S REBELLION.

Pontiac (pŏn′tēăk″). **1** City (pop. 8,990), NE central Ill., on Vermilion R. and NE of Bloomington. Trade, rail, industrial center in agr. and coal area. **2** City (pop. 73,681), SE Mich., on Clinton R. and NW of Detroit, in agr., lake, and resort area; founded 1818. Carriage making, important in 1880s, gave way to automobile industry. Also has mfg. of rubber, metalwork, and other products contributing to the automobile industry.

Pontiac's Rebellion or **Pontiac's Conspiracy,** 1763–66, Indian uprising against British after close of French and Indian Wars, so called after one of its leaders, Pontiac (d. 1769), Ottawa Indian chief. Resistance was aroused by English assumption of ownership to Indian lands. Pontiac led siege of Detroit. Many outposts were destroyed before an offensive campaign by the English brought treaties of peace.

Ponticus, Aquila: see AQUILA PONTICUS.

Pontine Marshes (pŏn′tĭn, –tīn), low-lying region, S Latium, central Italy, between Tyrrhenian Sea and Apennine foothills. Populated and fertile in antiquity; later abandoned because of malaria. Though repeatedly begun, drainage of marshlands was completed only under Mussolini.

Pontius Pilate (pŏn′shŭs pī′–), fl. A.D. 26, Roman procurator of Judaea (A.D. c.26–A.D. c.36?). To satisfy the people, he condemned Jesus to death. Mat. 27; John 18.28–19.42. According to tradition, Pilate committed suicide. The Acts of Pilate, one of the PSEUDEPIGRAPHA, is part of Gospel of Nicodemus.

pontoon (pŏn′tŭn, pŏntōōn′), flat-bottomed boat or other floating unit for building bridges, raising sunken ships, and the like. Barrels or casks, open boats, and enclosed watertight compartments of wood, metal, concrete, canvas, or rubber have been used in pontoon bridges. Floating foundation units are joined and anchored, and roadway is laid across them. Most frequent use is in warfare. Darius I built pontoon bridges across Bosporus and Danube in war against Scythians; his son Xerxes I built bridge of boats across Hellespont in war against Greece. U.S. army experimented with rubber pontoons from 1846 on. In 1941 collapsible rubber fabric floats were adopted and steel treadways made roadway; navy introduced light welded steel box pontoons for making ship-to-shore bridges, docks, or causeways and, with addition of motor, for use as self-propelled barges. For raising sunken ships, watertight cylinders filled with water are made fast to vessel and then emptied by compressed air. Hydroplane landing floats are a form of pontoon. See *ill.,* p. 167.

Pontoppidan, Henrik (pôntô′pĭdän), 1857–1943, Danish novelist, who in books such as *The Kingdom of the Dead* (1912–16) and *Man's Heaven* (1927) attacked materialism. Shared 1917 Nobel Prize in Literature with Gjellerup.

Pontormo, Jacopo da (yä′kōpō dä pōntōr′mō), 1494–1557?, Florentine painter, whose real name was Jacopo Carucci or Carrucci. Imitated Michelangelo in later period.

Pontus, anc. country, NE Asia Minor, on Black Sea coast. It grew important in the 4th cent. B.C. as an independent kingdom and continued to wax until King MITHRIDATES VI controlled Asia Minor and the Crimea and threatened Roman power in Greece. He was defeated by the Romans under Pompey (65

B.C.). An attempt by a later king, Pharnaces II, to increase the greatness of Pontus was ended by Julius Caesar at Zela (47 B.C.).

poodle, medium-sized and small dog of superior intelligence. Depending upon their size poodles are classed as standard, miniature, or toy poodles. The standard poodle measures c.15 in. or more at the shoulder; the miniature, well under 15 in.; and the toy poodle weighs less than 12 lb. The curly coat of poodles grows profusely and is clipped in several rather fantastic styles; it is solid in color, often black or silver, but sometimes white, blue, cream, apricot, or red.

pool: see BILLIARDS.

Poole, Ernest, 1880–1950, American writer. His novels include *The Harbor* (1915) and *His Family* (1917).

Poole, William Frederick, 1821–94, American librarian and bibliographer. He compiled the first general index to periodicals in the U.S., *Poole's Index to Periodical Literature* (1848; later to become *Reader's Guide to Periodical Literature*).

Poole, municipal borough (pop. 82,958), Dorsetshire, England, on N side of Poole Harbour, an inlet of English Channel. A naval supply station and seaplane base, it has a considerable coastal trade.

Poona (po͞o'nů), commercial city (pop. 298,-001), central Bombay, India. Was center of Mahratta empire in 18th cent. Has pleasant climate; formerly a favorite residential area of British officials.

Poopó (pō"ōpō'), salt lake, area 970 sq. mi., c.8 ft. deep, alt. 12,106 ft., on plateau of E Bolivia. No outlet except in time of flood.

Poor, Henry Varnum, 1888–, American painter of still lifes, portraits, and landscapes.

poor law, legislation relating to public assistance for the poor. In 1601 England passed a poor relief act that recognized the state's obligation to the needy; poorhouses, supported by local levies, grouped the aged, sick, and insane together; work relief for the able-bodied was emphasized. From c.1700 workhouses were established. In late 18th cent. home relief became customary. Laws in 1834 placed relief under national supervision; a liberalized poor law was passed in 1927. In U.S., where poor-relief statutes of the different states were based on English poor law, uniform relief on a national scale was introduced in 20th cent. See also SOCIAL SECURITY.

poor-man's-orchid: see BUTTERFLY FLOWER

Pope, Alexander, 1688–1744, English poet. Son of a prosperous linen draper, he early began study of poetry and literary criticism. In 1711 appeared his *Essay on Criticism,* a poem outlining contemporary critical tastes and standards. In 1713 he published *Windsor Forest,* and in 1714 *The Rape of the Lock,* a mock-heroic satire based on an incident in high society. In 1717 he issued a volume of poetry, including "Elegy to the Memory of an Unfortunate Lady" and "Eloisa to Abelard." In 1720 appeared his translation of the *Iliad,* and in 1725–26 the *Odyssey,* both tremendous literary and financial successes. At famous estate at Twickenham he edited Shakspere (1725). This work was adversely criticized by Lewis Theobald, who drew down on his head Pope's *Dunciad* (1728), a comprehensive satire on literary dullness of the time. Between 1732 and 1734 Pope composed *An Essay on Man,* a poetical defense of deism. He also wrote a series of epistles in verse, *Moral Essays* (1731–35), and ethical satires (1733–38), including the celebrated "Epistle to Dr. Arbuthnot." Pope's important poetry is in the heroic couplet, and only Dryden rivals him in the use of it.

Pope, John, 1822–92, Union general in Civil War. Captured ISLAND No. 10. Removed from command after defeat at second battle of BULL RUN (1862).

Pope, John Russell, 1874–1937, American architect, whose work was inspired by classic styles. Designed National Gall. of Art, Washington, D.C.

pope: see PAPACY.

Popham, George (pŏ'pům), c.1550–1608, early American colonist, b. England. Estab. short-lived colony (1607–8) at mouth of Kennebec R., Maine.

Popham Beach, Maine: see PHIPPSBURG.

Popish Plot: see OATES, TITUS.

Poplar, city (pop. 1,169), NE Mont., on Missouri R. at mouth of Poplar R. Has Indian agency. Chief GALL surrendered here.

poplar, deciduous fast-growing tree of genus *Populus.* The Lombardy poplar is a variety of the Eurasian black poplar (*Populus nigra*). Some poplars, especially those with cottony seed coverings, are called cottonwoods, e.g., the eastern cottonwood (*P. deltoides*); others include ASPEN and BALM OF GILEAD.

Poplar Bluff, city (pop. 15,064), SE Mo., in Ozark foothills, on Black R. near Ark. line; founded 1850. Center of a farm and resort area, it has railroad shops and mfg. of shoes and wood products. Wappapello Dam is near.

Popocatepetl (pōpůkă'tůpětůl, pōpō"kätā'-půtůl) [Aztec,= smoking mountain], volcano, 17,887 ft. high, central Mexico, on border between Puebla and Mexico states. Perpetually snow-capped, it has large crater with practically pure sulphur deposits, partially exploited. Dormant since 1702.

Popol Vuh (pōpōl' vo͞o') [Quiché,= collection of the council], sacred book of Quiché Indians, containing their cosmogony, religion, mythology, migratory traditions, and history. Original was destroyed by Pedro de Alvarado, but it was rewritten soon after. Content and style reveal high level of learning.

Poppaea Sabina (pŏpē'ů sůbī'nů), d. A.D. 65, mistress and later wife of NERO (her third husband). She is said to have influenced him to evil. He finally had her killed, but the legend that he kicked her to death is probably false.

poppy, annual, biennial, or perennial plant of genus *Papaver,* mostly native to the Old World, cultivated for the brilliant but short-lived flowers. Well known are the Oriental poppy, Iceland poppy, and Shirley poppy. OPIUM, and poppy or maw seed (not narcotic) used to flavor rolls, are obtained from the opium poppy (*Papaver somniferum*). The poppy of "Flanders Field" is the European red corn poppy (*P. rhoeas*).

population. The world contains roughly 2,000,-000,000 people, over half of whom are in

Asia, a fourth in Europe, and an eighth in the Americas. From the time of the Industrial Revolution, European population has quadrupled, but is now becoming stabilized, due to such factors as BIRTH CONTROL. Overpopulation is still a serious threat to many countries, particularly in Asia. See MALTHUS, EUGENICS.

Populist party. After Panic of 1873 farmers of Middle West and South grew poorer, while financial-industrial group in the East grew wealthier. Farmers blamed management of currency. GREENBACK PARTY accomplished little. Advocating government ownership of railways and free coinage of silver, Populist party was formed in 1891. Party convention of 1892 adopted platform calling for these and other reforms (e.g., graduated income tax); J. B. Weaver, Populist presidential candidate, polled over 1,041,000 votes. Helped by the eloquence of W. J. BRYAN, Democratic party captured bulk of Populist votes in 1896. Period of rising farm prices thereafter brought about dissolution of party.

porcelain: see POTTERY.

Porcupine, gold-mining district: see TIMMINS, Ont.

Porcupine, river, N Yukon and NE Alaska, rising N of Dawson and flowing 525 mi. NE then W to enter Yukon R. at Fort Yukon in NE Alaska. Discovered 1842 by John Bell.

porcupine (pôr'kyŏŏpīn), heavy, short-legged, slow-moving rodent, with erectile barbed quills. Old World forms are chiefly terrestrial. New World porcupines, of a different family, are partly arboreal. North American porcupine belongs to genus *Erethizon.*

Porcupine Mountains, NW Upper Peninsula, N Mich., near L. Superior, with highest point (2,023 ft.) in state.

porgy (pôr'gē), name for several fishes of Sparidae family found in warm coastal seas of the Americas and Europe.

Porjus (pôr'yŭs), cataract, c.170 ft. high, in Stora Lule R., N Sweden. Supplies power to Sweden's second largest hydroelectric plant, which operates Lapland RR, iron mines at Kiruna and Gallivare, and iron smelters and electrochemical plants.

pork, the flesh of swine prepared as food, either fresh, cured (as ham, bacon), or in other products. Lard, the refined fat, is used as shortening. Pork must be thoroughly cooked to prevent TRICHINOSIS.

Porkkala (pôrk'kälä), small peninsula in Gulf of Finland. Leased (1947) by Finland to Russia for 50 years as naval base.

Porphyry (pôr'fĭrē), 233–c.304, Greek Neoplatonic philosopher, disciple and editor of Plotinus.

porphyry (pôr'fĭrē), igneous rock composed of large crystals embedded in matrix or ground mass. This texture indicates its two states of solidification.

porpoise (pôr'pŭs), blunt-nosed sea mammal (*Phocaena*), order Cetacea, allied to whale. Travels in schools, appearing chiefly in N Atlantic and N Pacific.

Porpora, Niccolò Antonio (pôr'pōrä), b. 1686, d. 1766 or 1767, Italian composer and outstanding voice teacher. His best compositions were cantatas for harpsichord and voice. He taught all the greatest singers of the 18th cent., including Farinelli.

Porrentruy (pôrãtrüē'), town (pop. 6,121), Bern canton, NW Switzerland, in Bernese Jura. Watch mfg. Was a residence of prince-bishops of Basel 1528–1792; their territory passed to Bern 1815.

Porsena, Lars: see LARS PORSENA.

Porson, Richard, 1759–1808, English classical scholar. He created a sensation by supporting Edward Gibbon in declaring that John 1.7 was spurious. Noted for his textual criticism of Greek drama and for his grasp of metrical principles of Greek poetry. Translated Euripides.

port, fortified wine made in Portugal from grapes grown in the Douro valley. Blending and the length and manner of storage determine whether vintage, ruby, tawny, crusted, or white port is produced.

Porta, Giacomo della (jä'kōmō dĕl'lä pōr'tä), c.1540–1602. Italian architect. Completed some works by Vignola and Michelangelo, such as dome of St. Peter's and Farnese Palace.

Port Adelaide, city (pop. 33,382), South Australia, on inlet of Gulf St. Vincent; the state's chief port and wool-trading center.

Portage (pôr'tĭj), city (pop. 7,334), central Wis., on Wisconsin R. Portage here (now ship canal) between Wisconsin and Fox rivers first used by Jolliet and Father Marquette 1673. Town is farm trade center. Has site of Fort Winnebago (1828) and restored Indian Agency House (1832). Birthplace of Zona Gale and F. J. Turner.

Portage Lake, inlet of Keweenaw Bay, c.20 mi. long and 2 mi. wide, N Mich. Once connected to L. Superior by portage across Keweenaw peninsula; passage now made by a ship canal.

Portage la Prairie (pôr"tĭj lŭ prâ'rē), city (pop. 8,511), S Man., Canada, near Assiniboine R. and W of Winnipeg. Center of wheat-growing region. Near site of Fort La Reine, built 1738 by Vérendrye.

Port Alberni, city (pop. 7,845), on S central Vancouver Isl., SW B.C., Canada, NW of Victoria. Inland port and lumbering and fishing center at head of Alberni Canal.

Portales (pôrtă'lĭs), city (pop. 8,112), E N.Mex., near Texas line. Trade center of irrigated truck-farm and grazing area.

Port Angeles (ăn'jŭlŭs), port city (pop. 11,233), NW Wash., on Juan de Fuca Strait opposite Victoria, British Columbia. Fish, lumber, cellulose, dairy, and paper products. Hq. for Olympic Natl. Park.

Port Apra, Guam: see APRA HARBOR.

Port Arthur, city (pop. 31,161), W Ont., Canada, on NW shore of L. Superior and NE of Duluth, Minn. With its twin city, Fort William, is major grain and iron shipping center with grain elevators, shipyards, and paper, pulp, and lumber mills. Tourist center for hunting and fishing area.

Port Arthur, Chinese *Lüshun,* city (pop. 27,241), S Manchuria, on LIAOTUNG peninsula; naval base on Yellow Sea. Included in Kwantung leased territory 1898–1945. Became joint Sino-Soviet naval base and headquarters of Port Arthur–Dairen administrative district in 1945.

Port Arthur, city (pop. 57,530), SE Texas, on Sabine L. and SE of Beaumont; founded 1895. Oil discovered 1901 at near-by Spindletop. Oil port and rail focus on Sabine-Neches Canal and Intracoastal Waterway. Has refineries, foundries, shipyards, chemical plants and railroad shops.

Port-au-Prince (pôrt-ů-prĭns'), city (commune pop. 195,672), S Haiti, cap. of republic, at head of the Gulf of Gonaïves. Founded in 1749 by French sugar planters moving southward; replaced Cap-Haïtien as capital in 1770. Ships half of Haiti's exports.

Port Chester, residential village (pop. 23,970), SE N.Y., at Conn. line and on Long Isl. Sound. Electric razors, food products, hardware, machinery.

Port Clinton, city (pop. 5,541), N Ohio, on L. Erie W of Sandusky and at mouth of Portage R. Mfg. of auto parts and boats. Near by is Camp Perry.

Port Colborne, town (pop. 8,275), S Ont., Canada, on L. Erie, S of St. Catharines; port at S end of Welland Ship Canal. Nickel-refining center with iron smelters, cereal mills, and grain elevators.

Port Elizabeth, city (pop. 133,400), S Cape Prov., South Africa, on Algoa Bay of Indian Ocean. Developed after 1873, when railroad to Kimberley was completed. Exports wool, mohair, and diamonds.

Porter, Cole, 1893–, American composer of musical comedies. His lyrics, which he writes himself, are known for their wit and sophistication. Among his many successes are *Night and Day* (his most famous song) from *The Gay Divorce* (1932); *You're the Top,* from *Anything Goes* (1934); *My Heart Belongs to Daddy,* from *Leave It to Me* (1938); *Begin the Beguine,* from *Jubilee* (1935); *In the Still of the Night,* from *Rosalie* (1937).

Porter, David, 1780–1843, American naval officer. Achieved greatest success as commander of *Essex* in War of 1812. His son, **David Dixon Porter,** 1813–91, was also a naval officer. Next to D. G. Farragut, he was outstanding Union naval commander in Civil War. Appointed full admiral in 1870.

Porter, Horace, 1837–1921, American soldier and diplomat. Aide-de-camp to Gen. Grant (1864–65). Amended DRAGO DOCTRINE to provide arbitration for collection of contract debts (1907).

Porter, Katherine Anne, 1894–, American author. Short stories, notable for purity of style, are collected in *Flowering Judas* (1930), *Pale Horse, Pale Rider* (1939), and *The Leaning Tower* (1944). Essays are in *The Days Before* (1952).

Porter, Noah, 1811–92, American educator and philosopher. At Yale he became professor of philosophy (1846) and was president 1871–86. He edited revised editions of Webster's dictionary (1864, 1890).

Porter, William Sydney: see HENRY, O.

Porterville, city (pop. 6,904), S central Calif., SE of Fresno. Fruit-packing center.

Port Gibson, town (pop. 2,920), SW Miss., near Mississippi R. and S of Vicksburg. Civil War battle fought here in Vicksburg campaign. Near by is Alcorn Agricultural and Mechanical Col. (Negro; land-grant; coed.; 1871).

Port Glasgow, burgh (pop. 21,612), Renfrewshire, Scotland, on S shore of Firth of Clyde. Founded as port for Glasgow before that city was accessible to large ships. Has a large graving dock.

Port Hope, town (pop. 6,548), S Ont., Canada, on L. Ontario and E of Toronto. Summer resort and radium-refining center.

Port Hudson, village, SE La., on E bank of the Mississippi, 20 mi. N of Baton Rouge. Fortified 1862 by Confederates, it was surrendered to N. P. Banks in July, 1863.

Port Huron (hyŏŏ'rŭn), city (pop. 35,725), E Mich., at junction of St. Clair R. with Black R. and at foot of L. Huron; settled 1686 as French fort. Grew in 1800s with lumbering. Rail and water shipping center, it has shipyards, railroad shops, grain elevators, and mfg. of metal products, cement, and paper. Connected by bridge and tunnel with Ontario.

Portinari, Cândido (kän'dēdō pōrtēnä'rē), 1903–, Brazilian painter, known for his frescoes.

Port Isabel, fishing resort (pop. 2,372), S Texas, on Intracoastal Waterway and NE of Brownsville. Was American supply base in Mexican War.

Port Jefferson, resort and residential village (pop. 3,296), SE N.Y., on Long Island Sound (ferry) opposite Bridgeport, Conn.

Port Jervis, city (pop. 9,372), SE N.Y., on Delaware R. and near point where N.Y., N.J., and Pa. meet. Rail center. Mfg. of textiles, glass, concrete, silverware.

Portland, William Bentinck, 1st **earl of,** 1649–1709, Dutch statesman in England; William III's most trusted adviser. Negotiated treaty of Ryswick with France and the unpopular Partition Treaties.

Portland, urban district (pop. 11,324), Dorsetshire, England. On Isle of Portland, a rocky peninsula composed of limestone which has long been used for building. Scene of some of Hardy's works.

Portland. 1 Town (pop. 5,186), central Conn., on Connecticut R. (bridged to Middletown); settled c.1690. Sandstone is quarried. Mfg. of metal products. **2** City (pop. 7,064), E Ind., NE of Muncie. Mfg. of vehicle parts. **3** City (pop. 77,634), SW Maine, on harbor on Casco Bay; settled 1632, set off from Falmouth town 1786. Almost destroyed by British in 1775 and by great fire, 1866. State cap. 1820–31. Largest city and commercial center of Maine, it serves large farm, lumber, paper-milling, fishing, and resort region. Mfg. of paper, cellulose, shoes, wood products, steel, and explosives. Maine's first newspaper, Falmouth *Gazette,* was published here 1785. Has birthplace and home of Longfellow. Was important U.S. naval base and shipping center in World War II. **4** City (pop. 373,628), NW Oregon, on Willamette R. near its mouth in Columbia R.; laid out 1845. Grew fast after 1850 as supply point for Calif. gold fields, after 1883, when railroad came, 1897–1900 during Alaska gold rush. Largest city in state and its major freshwater port served by oceangoing vessels, with shipyards and mfg. of furniture, paper, and food, wool, and lumber products. Partly flooded by Columbia R., May, 1948. Seat of

Univ. of Portland (R.C.; for men; 1901); Reed Col. (nonsectarian; coed.; 1911), which pioneered in progressive and individualized education; Univ. of Oregon medical and dental schools. Holds Pacific International Livestock Exposition and a rose festival annually.

Portland vase, a funerary urn, probably of 1st cent. B.C., known also as the Barberini vase. Made of violet-blue glass overlaid with opaque white glass with cameo relief. Found in ancient tomb near Rome in 17th cent., it was placed in library of Barberini Palace. Bought by duchess of Portland in late 18th cent. and by British Mus. in 1945.

Port Lavaca (lůvă'ků), city (pop. 5,599), S Texas, on Lavaca Bay and SE of San Antonio; founded 1815, destroyed 1840 by Comanches. Deepwater port with refineries, cotton gins, and fish-processing plants. Near by is an aluminum plant. Connected with Intracoastal Waterway.

Port Moresby (môrz'bē), town (pop. 1,300), on SE New Guinea, cap. of Territory of Papua; port on Fairfax Harbor. In World War II chief Allied base on island was here.

Port Neches (nĕ'chĭz), city (pop. 5,448), SE Texas, on Neches R. below Beaumont. Port on Sabine-Neches Canal, it processes and ships oil, synthetic rubber, and chemicals.

Porto, Portugal: see OPORTO.

Pôrto Alegre (pôr'tō ůlā'grů), city (pop. 381,-964), cap. of Rio Grande do Sul state, SE Brazil; port at N end of Lagoa dos Patos; founded in 1742 by immigrants from Azores. Population increased since 19th cent. by Germans and Italians. Shipping center for agr. and pastoral hinterland.

Portobelo (pôr"tōbĕ'lō), town (pop. 573), Panama; port on Caribbean coast. Visited by Columbus; founded 1597; became an important colonial port often attacked by British buccaneers. Also Porto Bello, Puerto Bello.

Portoferraio (pôr'tōfĕr-rä'yō), seaport (pop. 7,682), Elba isl., Italy. Ships iron. While sovereign of Elba, Napoleon I lived here (1814–15).

Port of New York Authority, self-sustaining public corporation, estab. 1921 by N.Y. and N.J. to administer and develop terminal and transportation facilities of the New York city port area (771-mi. water front). Manages George Washington Bridge; Holland and Lincoln tunnels; LaGuardia, New York Internatl., Teterboro, and Newark airports.

Port of Spain, town (pop. 92,793), on Trinidad, cap. of Trinidad and Tobago, on fine harbor of Gulf of Paria opposite Venezuela. Transference of bauxite from British and Dutch Guiana and iron ore from Venezuela is made here from coastal and river steamers to ocean-going vessels.

Portolá, Gaspar de (gäspär' dā pôrtōlä'), fl. 1734–84, Spanish explorer in Far West. Extended Spanish control up Pacific coast to Monterey (1769–70).

Port Phillip Bay, large inlet of Bass Strait, S Victoria, Australia. Its N arm, Hobson's Bay, is site of Port Melbourne.

Port Pirie (pĭ'rē), city (pop. 12,019), South Australia; port at base of Yorke Peninsula, on inlet of Spencer Gulf. Smelting works for silver-lead mines at Broken Hill, ENE of Port Pirie.

Port Radium or **Eldorado Mines,** arctic village, Mackenzie dist., Northwest Territories, Canada, on Great Bear L. Pitchblende and uranium mining center. Site of government radio and meteorological station and Royal Canadian Mounted Police post. Mines taken over by Canadian government 1944.

Port Republic, village, NW Va., at junction of North and South rivers, which form the South Fork of Shenandoah R. Scene of battle in Stonewall Jackson's Shenandoah Valley campaign (1862), a Confederate victory.

Port Royal, N.S.: see ANNAPOLIS ROYAL.

Port-Royal (pôr'-rwäyäl'), former abbey for women, c.17 mi. W of Paris, founded 1204 as Benedictine, later Cistercian. Its importance came after its abbess, Angélique ARNAULD, began a reform in 1608. In 1626 the abbey was moved to Paris, becoming Port-Royal-de-Paris and the prime center of JANSENISM. The old buildings, Port-Royal-des-Champs, were used as a retreat for men and after 1638 for successful classes for boys. When the Church repudiated Jansenism, Port-Royal-des-Champs was suppressed (1704) and the buildings razed (1710). The nuns were expelled from Port-Royal-de-Paris.

Port Royal Island, c.13 mi. long, 7 mi. wide, S S.C., at head of Port Royal Sound, one of SEA ISLANDS. Resort with fishing and farming.

Port Said (sīd, sād, säēd'), city (pop. 178,432), NE Egypt, on the Mediterranean at entrance to Suez Canal. Founded 1859 by builders of canal and named for Said Pasha, then khedive of Egypt. Important coaling station. On its outer pier is a massive statue of Ferdinand de Lesseps.

Portsmouth, Louise Renée de Kéroualle, duchess of (kārōōäl', pôrts'můth), 1649–1734, French mistress of Charles II of England. Exerted great influence in favor of France after 1671. Hated in England, she lived mainly in France after Charles's death.

Portsmouth, county borough (pop. 233,464), on Portsea Isl., Hampshire, England, at entrance to Portsmouth Harbour; chief naval base of Great Britain. Includes Portsea (over 300 acres of dockyards), Southsea (resort), and Portsmouth (garrison town). Cathedral of Thomas à Becket dates from 12th cent. H.M.S. *Victory,* Nelson's flagship at Trafalgar, is a museum. City and harbor were bombed 1940–41.

Portsmouth. 1 City (pop. 18,830), SE N.H., on harbor at Piscataqua R. mouth (bridged) opposite Kittery, Maine. A lumbering and fishing base was estab. at near-by Odiorne's Point 1623. Portsmouth was made a town by Mass. 1653. Provincial cap. of N.H. until Revolution. Shipbuilding began early. U.S. Naval Base (estab. 1800), located on islands linked together and to Kittery by bridges, was ceded to U.S. government by Kittery. Treaty of Portsmouth signed here 1905. City is commercial center for agr. and resort area and only N.H. seaport. It is rich in 18th- and early 19th-cent. homes (many preserved by historical societies). Richard Jackson House (1664) is restored. First N.H. newspaper, *New Hampshire Gazette,* was published here. Daniel Webster was a resident. **2** City (pop. 36,798), S Ohio, on Ohio R. at mouth of Scioto R. and S of Columbus; laid out 1803. Industrial and railroad center with mfg. of steel and iron products and shoes. **3** Resort and residential town (pop. 6,578), on N RHODE ISLAND, SE R.I., connected with Bristol by Mt. Hope Bridge; includes Prudence Isl.; founded 1638. Colony's first general assembly met here, 1647. Colonial fishing and shipping center. Scene of battle of R.I., 1778. **4** City (pop. 30,039), SE Va., on Elizabeth R. opposite Norfolk; laid out 1750. A port of HAMPTON ROADS, seat of Norfolk Navy Yard. Rail and shipping center with food processing and mfg. of paving materials, fertilizer, and knit goods. Landing base for British in American Revolution. In Civil War navy yard was burned and evacuated by Federals (1861) and occupied by Confederates; retaken by Union forces 1862. Places of interest are Trinity Church (1762), U.S. naval hospital (1827–30), and late-18th-cent. houses.

Portsmouth, Treaty of, 1905, ending Russo-Japanese War, signed at Portsmouth Naval Base, N.H. Achieved through good offices of Theodore Roosevelt. Japan secured Russian evacuation of S Manchuria; cession of S section of Manchurian RR; "paramount" interests in Korea; S half of Sakhalin; and ownership of Russian lease of Liaotung peninsula.

Port Sudan (so͞odăn'), city (pop. 47,450), NE Anglo-Egyptian Sudan; port on Red Sea; founded 1906. Chief port of entry into the Sudan.

Port Talbot (tôl'bŭt), municipal borough (pop. 44,024), Glamorganshire, Wales. Export point for coal and mineral industries of the Avon valley.

Port Tobacco, village, SW Md., on inlet of Potomac R. Was important port until harbor silted up. Near by are old manor houses. Jesuit missionaries bought land here in 1649 which order still maintains. Indian name was Potopaco.

Port Townsend, city (pop. 6,888), NW Wash., at entrance to Puget Sound. Ships lumber, coal, fish.

Portugal (pôr'chŭgŭl), republic (35,409 sq. mi.; pop. 8,490,455, incl. MADEIRA ISLANDS and AZORES), W Europe; cap. LISBON. Continental Portugal, in W part of Iberian Peninsula, borders on the Atlantic (W and S) and on Spain (E and N). Largely mountainous, it is crossed by the Tagus, Douro, and Minho rivers. Their fertile valleys and the coastal plains support agr. and vineyards (port wine is a major export). Mountains have cork oak forests, pastures, (sheep, cattle, horses); olive groves on lower slopes. Fishing and canning (sardines, tuna) are major industries. Large transit and tourist trade. Continental Portugal's six historic provinces (now redistributed into 11 provinces) are ALENTEJO (cap. ÉVORA), ALGARVE (cap. FARO), BEIRA (cap. COIMBRA), Entre Douro e MINHO (cap. BRAGA; chief port OPORTO), ESTREMADURA (cap. Lisbon), and TRÁS-OS-MONTES (cap. BRAGANÇA). For Portuguese colonies, see ANGOLA; CAPE VERDE ISLANDS; MACAO; MOZAMBIQUE; PORTUGUESE GUINEA; PORTUGUESE INDIA; SÃO TOMÉ AND PRINCIPE; TIMOR. Roman Catholicism is predominant religion. Constitution of 1933 made Portugal a CORPORATIVE STATE, with a corporative chamber (representing industries and professions) alongside national assembly. The state is nominally headed by a president, but as of 1953 Premier Antonio de Oliveira SALAZAR held virtual dictatorial power. Part of modern Portugal coincides with ancient LUSITANIA; its conquest by Rome became final only under Augustus. The region was thoroughly Romanized but fell to the Germanic Suebi and VISIGOTHS (5th cent. A.D.) and to the Moors (711). Portugal as a state was born (11th cent.) as a result of the Christian reconquest. Ferdinand I of Castile took Coimbra (1064); his son Alfonso VI made HENRY OF BURGUNDY count of Coimbra (1095?), a title later changed to count of Portucalense (so called for the land port—i.e., toll station—at the old city of Cale). Henry's son styled himself king as ALFONSO I (1139) and conquered Lisbon with aid of foreign crusaders (1147). The next 250 years saw Portuguese expansion at expense of the Moors (completed by conquest of Algarve, 1249); the development of the towns, of agr., and Portuguese culture, particularly under kings ALFONSO III and DINIZ; the chronic struggle of the crown against nobles and Church; and unceasing dynastic wars with the Spanish kingdoms, notably with Castile in the reign (1367–83) of FERDINAND I. Ferdinand's succession would have passed to Castile but for the leadership of Nun'Álvares PEREIRA, who defeated the Castilians at Aljubarrota (1385) and estab. JOHN I, founder of the AVIZ dynasty, on the throne. John's son, Prince HENRY THE NAVIGATOR, laid the foundation of the Portuguese empire. Explorers and naval commanders such as Da GAMA, CABRAL, Francisco de ALMEIDA, and ALBUQUERQUE made Portugal the world's leading commercial nation, dominating the East Indian and the African slave trade and owning colonies in Africa, South America (see BRAZIL), and Asia. The zenith was reached under MANUEL I and JOHN III (15th–16th cent.), but depopulation (through colonization and expulsion of the Jews) and neglect of agr. brought rapid decline. The reign of SEBASTIAN ended in the disaster of his African campaign (1578). In 1580 the house of Aviz died out, and Philip II of Spain, nephew of John III, made good his claim to Portugal by force of arms. Under Spanish rule, Portugal lost most of its empire to the Dutch. In 1640 the Portuguese threw off the Spanish yoke; JOHN IV, first king of the BRAGANZA dynasty, cemented Portugal's traditional alliance with England in 1654. Royal absolutism reached its height in the 18th cent. under John V and Joseph. The reforms of POMBAL, Joseph's minister, revitalized Portuguese economy. On the losing side in the French Revolutionary Wars, Portugal made peace in 1801 but was occupied by the French in 1807. Portuguese patriots fought heroically in the PENINSULAR WAR while the royal family was safely in Brazil. In 1822 Brazil became a separate empire under PEDRO I. JOHN

VI continued as king of Portugal, but his death (1826) opened the vexed question of his succession. In the Miguelist Wars, MARIA II, backed by the liberals, eventually won out over her uncle MIGUEL (1834). Her and her successors' reigns (see FERDINAND II; CHARLES I; MANUEL II) were a chaotic era of coups and dictatorships, ending with Manuel's abdication and the establishment of a republic (1910). Political troubles continued under the republic until in 1926 Gen. CARMONA estab. his dictatorship. After 1928 Salazar held power. His financial efficiency considerably improved Portugal's economy, though at the expense of democratic rights. Portugal sided with the Allies in World War I; was neutral in World War II; joined the North Atlantic Treaty 1949.

Portuguese East Africa: see MOZAMBIQUE.

Portuguese Guinea (gĭ'nē), colony (13,948 sq. mi.; pop. 351,089), W Africa, on the Atlantic; cap. Bissau. An enclave in French West Africa, it includes Bijagós Isls., off Geba R. estuary. Exports rice, palm oil, and copra. Discovered by the Portuguese in mid-15th cent. Boundaries were estab. 1886.

Portuguese India, colony (1,538 sq. mi.; pop. 624,177), comprising DAMAO, GOA, and DIU.

Portuguese language, Romance language of Italic subfamily of Indo-European languages. See LANGUAGE (table).

Portuguese West Africa: see ANGOLA.

portulaca (pôr"tūlăk'ů), fleshy annual plant (*Portulaca grandiflora*), native to Brazil. It is widely grown for its bright flowers. Also called rose moss or purslane.

Port Washington, resort and residential village (1940 pop. 10,509), on N shore of Long Isl., SE N.Y., NNW of Mineola. Shellfishing; mfg. of machinery, and concrete products.

Posada, José Guadalupe (pōsä'dhä), 1852–1913, Mexican artist, who strongly influenced the generation of Orozco and Rivera. Produced thousands of prints which were sold cheaply to the masses.

Posadas (pōsä'dhäs), city (pop. 37,588), NE Argentina, port on upper Paraná R. Center of mate industry; tobacco, grains, fruit also grown.

Poseidon (pōsī'důn), in Greek religion, sea-god, protector of all waters; son of Cronus and Rhea, husband of Amphitrite, and father of Pegasus, Orion, Polyphemus, and other giants and monsters. Horse was his gift to man. He bore the TRIDENT, with which he caused storms. Identified with Roman Neptune.

Posen, Poland: see POZNAN.

positive, in photography: see NEGATIVE.

positivism (pŏ'zĭtĭvĭzm), any philosophical system which rejects metaphysics and maintains that knowledge is founded exclusively on sense experience and the positive sciences. The term is applied specifically to the thought of Auguste COMTE.

positron (pŏ'zĭtrŏn"), positively charged, short-lived particle with same mass as electron.

Post, Emily (Price), 1873–, American authority on etiquette. Her famous book *Etiquette* (1922) has had a number of editions. In the field of interior decoration she is known for *The Personality of a House* (1930).

Post, Wiley, 1900–1935, American aviator. Made round-the-world flights (in 1931, with Harold Gatty; in 1933, alone). Killed in crash near Point Barrow, Alaska, on flight with Will Rogers.

postage stamp, government stamp affixed to mail to indicate payment of postage. Adopted in England in 1839, custom spread throughout the world by 1850. First U.S. official issue was in 1847. Special stamps include air-mail, special-delivery, and postage-due stamps.

postal savings bank, government savings bank operated through local post offices. First established in England in 1861, in U.S. in 1910.

postal service, arrangement for delivering letters, packages, and periodicals. Courier systems for government use existed under the Persian Empire. Britain's postal service, an outgrowth of royal courier routes, was estab. finally in 1657 and penny postage (see POSTAGE STAMP) was begun in 1839. The U.S. system was derived from the colonial service established by England. In the U.S. postage stamps were first used 1847, registered mail 1855, city delivery 1863, money orders 1864, penny post cards 1873, special delivery 1885, rural delivery 1896, postal savings 1910, parcel post 1913. The pony express operated across the continent, 1860–61, rail service was instituted in 1862, AIR MAIL in 1918. The Universal Postal Union was established after the International Postal Convention of 1874.

postimpressionism, term applied to the work of various French painters of the late 19th cent. who wished to apply certain features of IMPRESSIONISM to a more subjective art. Group included Cézanne, Van Gogh, and Gauguin.

Postojna (pô'stoinä), Ger. *Adelsberg,* Ital. *Postumia,* resort town (pop. 3,651), Slovenia, N Yugoslavia, in the KARST. Famous for its stalactite caves (largest in Europe). Was ceded by Italy 1947.

Postumia, Yugoslavia: see POSTOJNA.

potash, name for certain potassium compounds, particularly potassium carbonate, a white crystalline substance when pure. Originally obtained from wood ashes or from residue left in pots after burning plants in them, it is now usually prepared from potassium chloride. It is used to make other potassium compounds, hard glass, and soap, and as a fertilizer. Caustic potash is potassium hydroxide, a strong alkali.

potassium (pŭtă'sēům), active, silver-white, soft metallic element (symbol = K; see also ELEMENT, table). It is so active that it must be kept submerged in oil, out of contact with air. The metal has no commercial value but its compounds are used widely. It reacts violently with water to form potassium hydroxide; combines directly with many nonmetallic elements. It is not found free but occurs in many compounds.

potato, perennial plant (*Solanum tuberosum*) and its swollen underground stem, a tuber, a widely used staple food in temperate climates. The plant belongs to the nightshade family and is probably native to the Andes; it is believed that it was introduced into Spain from Peru in the 16th cent. By the mid-18th cent. it had reached even remote parts of Europe. It became the major food in Ireland (it is often called the Irish potato); a crop failure from blight in 1846 caused famine resulting in death, disease, and emigration. Potatoes contain c.78% water and are a source of carbohydrates (c.18%, mostly starch), iron, and vitamins (esp. vitamin C, much of which is lost by long boiling of peeled potatoes). A potato plant, which needs rich soil high in potash, may produce five tubers. Propagation is by planting pieces of tubers bearing two or three eyes. Plants sometimes produce yellow-green fruits containing seeds. The Colorado potato beetle is the worst pest. See *ill.*, p. 999.

potato bug: see COLORADO POTATO BEETLE.

Potawatami Indians (pŏ″tŭwŏ′tŭmē), North American tribe of Algonquian linguistic stock, closely related to the Ojibwa and Ottawa. In the early 17th cent. they were at Green Bay but later moved to the S end of L. Michigan and expanded E. They supported the French against the British, supported Pontiac, opposed the expansion of the U.S., and sided with the British in the War of 1812. They later retreated W to Iowa and Kansas, and a large group was moved (1868) to Okla. where they took lands individually. Others are on reservations in Kansas, Mich., Wis., and Okla. and in Canada. Also Pottawatomi, Pottawatami.

Potchefstroom (pŏ′chŭfstrōm, –strŏŏm), town (pop. 27,205), SW Transvaal, South Africa; founded 1838. Was first cap. of Transvaal (1838–60). Has college connected with Univ. of South Africa.

Potemkin, Grigori Aleksandrovich (grĭgô′rē ŭlyĭksän′drŭvĭch pŭtyôm′kĭn), 1739–91, Russian field marshal, favorite and adviser of Catherine II, to whom he was perhaps secretly married. Played important part in annexation of Crimea (1783); was created prince and governor of new province, which he administered ably despite his personal eccentricities. The allegation that he had sham villages built to impress Catherine is probably false.

Potenza (pōtĕn′tsä), city (pop. 18,872), cap. of Basilicata, S Italy, in the Apennines.

pothole, deep round hole in bedrock along a stream, usually near falls or rapids, formed by erosive action of whirling water which carries rock debris.

Potidaea (pōtĭdē′ŭ), anc. city, NE Greece, in Chalcidice. With Corinthian help it attempted to defy Athens and leave the Delian League in 432 B.C., thus providing one immediate cause of the Peloponnesian War. Philip II is said to have destroyed it. Later Cassander rebuilt it as Cassandreia.

Potiphar (pŏ′tĭfŭr), Joseph's high-ranking Egyptian master whose wife falsely accused Joseph. Gen. 39.

Poti-pherah (pōtĭ′fŭrŭ), priest of On and father of Joseph's wife Asenath. Gen. 41.45,-50; 46.20.

pot marigold: see CALENDULA.

Potomac (pŭtō′mŭk), river formed SE of Cumberland, Md., and flowing generally SE 285 mi. to Chesapeake Bay. Part of boundary between Md.-W.Va., Md.-Va., and Va.-D.C. Tidal and navigable for large ships to Washington (there bridged); just upstream are Great Falls of the Potomac. Receives the Shenandoah at Harpers Ferry, W.Va. Noted for its beauty and historical associations. Mt. Vernon is on Va. shore below Washington.

Potosí (pōtōsē′), city (pop. 43,700), S Bolivia; founded c.1545 at foot of one of world's richest ore mountains. In Andes at height of 13,780 ft., it is one of highest cities in world. For first 50 years Potosí produced vast amounts of silver, but because of rigorous living conditions, population declined until recent technological developments have revived commerce. Tin, wolfram, and copper also mined.

Potosi (pŭtō′sē), city (pop. 2,359), E Mo., SW of St. Louis. Center of a barite-mining area, with zinc, iron, and limestone deposits. Grew with development of lead mines by Moses Austin in 1790s.

Potsdam (pôts′däm), city (pop. 113,568), cap. of Brandenburg, E Germany, on the Havel, near Berlin. Primarily residential. Has moving picture industry (at suburb of Babelsberg); observatory of Univ. of Berlin; astrophysical observatory. Chartered 14th cent.; became electoral residence in 17th cent., later royal residence. Frederick II of Prussia rebuilt the Town Palace and built SANS SOUCI and the New Palace. The Garrison Church (built 1731–35) was destroyed in World War II. Potsdam was the scene of the POTSDAM CONFERENCE of 1945.

Potsdam, village (pop. 7,491), N N.Y., E of Ogdensburg. Mfg. of paper and cheese. Seat of Clarkson Col. of Technology (for men; 1896).

Potsdam Conference, meeting (July 17–Aug. 2, 1945) of principal Allies in World War II (U.S., USSR, and Great Britain) to supplement, clarify, and implement agreements reached at YALTA CONFERENCE. Present were Pres. Truman, Premier Stalin, and Prime Minister Churchill (later replaced by C. R. Attlee), and their foreign ministers. So-called Potsdam Agreement gave chief authority in Germany to American, Russian, British, and French military commanders in respective zones of occupation (see GERMANY) and to four-power Allied Control Council. It abolished former military and political power in Germany and called for punishment of war criminals, controlled education to foster democratic ideals, restored local self-government with close supervision, and controlled German economy and production. Allies further agreed to transfer former German territory E of Neisse and Oder rivers to Polish and Russian administration pending peace treaty. Rift between USSR and Western powers caused agreement to fail.

Pott, Percivall, 1714–88, English surgeon. He wrote classic descriptions of an ankle fracture and a spine deformity (both known by his name), of hernia, and other conditions.

Pottawatami Indians or **Pottawatomi Indians:** see POTAWATAMI INDIANS.

Potter, Alonzo, 1800–1865, American Episcopal bishop. As bishop of Pa. (1845–65), he founded in Philadelphia an Episcopal hospital and a divinity school. His son, **Henry Codman Potter,** 1835–1908, was bishop coadjutor of New York (after 1883), bishop after 1887. Initiated first stages of Cathedral of St. John the Divine.

Potter, Beatrix (Mrs. William Heelis), 1866–1943, English author and illustrator of over 25 children's books, such as *The Tale of Peter Rabbit* (1902).

Potter, Edward Clark, 1857–1923, American sculptor of animals. Produced equestrian statuary in collaboration with Daniel Chester French.

Potter, Henry Codman: see POTTER, ALONZO.

Potter, Paul or **Paulus,** 1625–54, Dutch animal painter, noted for simplicity and naturalism of his works. Worked mainly in Delft and The Hague.

Potteries, the, district, c.9 mi. long and 3 mi. wide, Staffordshire, England, in the Trent valley. Densely populated, it has been a center of pottery making since the 16th cent. Includes STOKE-ON-TRENT. Region is "Five Towns" of Arnold Bennett's works.

potter's field: see ACELDAMA.

pottery embraces all the baked clay wares of the ceramics field, from coarse, unglazed, and crudely painted earthenware, through the glazed but heavy faïence and stoneware, to the crowning achievements of the art—porcelain and lusterware. The process for all these is essentially the same: the clay is shaped by building (piece by piece) or is thrown upon a potter's wheel which spins the clay as the hands give it form; it is then slowly dried; and finally it is fired in a kiln which brings it to a permanent hardness. Temperatures of firing vary, reaching as much as 2500° F. for hard porcelain. To give the pottery finish, a vitreous coating called a glaze is often fired on the clay. Glazes may be transparent, white, or colored and of many kinds (e.g., alkaline, lead, felspar) to suit the nature of the pottery. Variations in these techniques produce the many different kinds of pottery. Earthenware is fired at a relatively low temperature so that the clay does not vitrify; stoneware is fired at a high temperature, but unlike porcelain, it is heavy and opaque. On stoneware a salt glaze is produced by putting salt in the fires at the proper time. Porcelain is known for its delicate translucence. After the first firing, body and glaze are fired together at a very high temperature. Lusterware has an overglaze finish containing copper or silver which gives it an iridescence as well as luster. The film producing this effect is applied over the glaze, and the ware receives a third firing. Majolica (or maiolica) is an enameled and decorated faïence of Spain and Italy. The clay object is first fired, given a coating of tin enamel, refired, then decorated in brilliant colors and fired again. Pottery is one of the most enduring materials known to man and is in most places the oldest art. Archaic and later examples are of value as historical and literary records; Assyrian and Babylonian writings have been inscribed upon clay tablets and perpetuated as pottery, many ancient wares are decorated with human and animal figures and portray dress, customs, and events of the times. The Egyptians, Persians, and Greeks all had highly developed forms of pottery. Porcelain probably originated in 14th-cent. China. European wares of the Middle Ages were crudely fashioned and coarsely glazed; Chinese porcelain was a luxury of the wealthy. European imitation of the Chinese art began in the 17th and 18th cent. Since then many places throughout the world have lent their names to potteries which have become famous—Sèvres and Limoges china in France, Cologne and Dresden ware in Germany, delftware in Holland, and the English potteries of Staffordshire, Lambeth (Doulton ware), Bow, Chelsea, Lowestoft, Worcester, Derby, Wedgwood, Minton, and Spode.

Pottstown, borough (pop. 22,589), SE Pa., on Schuylkill R. and NW of Philadelphia; settled 1775. Mfg. of steel and rubber products. First ironworks in state estab. here 1716.

Pottsville, city (pop. 23,640), E Pa., on Schuylkill R. and NW of Reading; settled c.1780. Anthracite mining center with mfg. of clothing, aluminum and steel products. Rallying place for Molly Maguires, who were tried here 1877. Seat of branch of Pennsylvania State Col.

Poughkeepsie (pŭkĭp'sē), city (pop. 41,023), E N.Y., on E bank of Hudson R. (Mid-Hudson Bridge to Highland); settled 1687 by Dutch. Agr. trade center; mfg. of ball bearings, cream separators, business machines, hardware. VASSAR COLLEGE is at adjacent Arlington village (pop. 5,374). Intercollegiate Rowing Regatta held here 1895–1950. Has Van Kleeck Homestead (1702). Federal Constitution ratified here 1788.

Poulenc, Francis (pōōlăk'), 1899–, French composer and pianist. Among his numerous works are concertos and short pieces for piano, chamber music, ballets, and songs.

Poulsen, Valdemar (väl'dŭmär poul'sŭn), 1869–1942, Danish electrical engineer. Invented telegraphone (electromagnetic telephone-conversation recorder) and high-frequency Poulsen arc used in radio.

poultry, domestic birds raised for food (eggs or meat). The chief poultry bird is the chicken, once a jungle fowl in SW Asia, and domesticated over 3,000 years ago. There are over 100 varieties, including egg, meat, and dual-purpose breeds, classed according to their place of origin. Popular American breeds include Plymouth Rocks, Rhode Island Reds, and New Hampshires—all dual-purpose breeds. An outstanding European breed raised in the U.S. for egg production is the Leghorn. Among chickens raised for ornament and other uses are the small Bantam and the Game (formerly bred for cockfighting). Commercial poultry raising is a large-scale enterprise which often includes raising chickens in mechanized indoor batteries with each bird in a separate compartment, and artificial hatching of eggs in an incubator. See also DUCK; GOOSE; GUINEA FOWL; PHEASANT; PIGEON; TURKEY.

Pound, Ezra (Loomis), 1885–, American poet. Led poetic movement of IMAGISTS, later turned to VORTICISM. Works include *Cathay* (1915; from Chinese) and *Umbra* (1920; from Latin). His later work was in series of *Cantos* (1925–48; including *Pisan Cantos*), brilliant, erudite, allusive poems woven of scraps from many literatures. His controversial work has had much influence. Much criticized for his Fascist activity in Italy in World War II. Later put in mental hospital.

Pound, Roscoe, 1870–, American jurist, professor (1910–17) and dean (1916–36) of Harvard Law School; author of influential works on jurisprudence.

Poussin, Nicolas (nĕkôlä′ po͞osē′), 1594–1665, French classical painter, b. Normandy. Spent most of his life in Rome, where he first won recognition. During brief stay in Paris (1640–43) he served Louis XIII and Richelieu. Famous for discipline and intellectuality of his compositions (e.g., *Shepherds in Arcadia* in Louvre). Influenced many French painters, notably Claude Lorrain and Cézanne.

Powder, river rising in N Wyo. and flowing 486 mi. NE into Mont. to join Yellowstone R. near Terry.

powder, substance composed of finely granulated particles. In special sense word is applied to powdered propellent explosives, e.g., GUNPOWDER, and to powders that produce bright light when ignited. In 19th cent. various smokeless powders began to supersede gunpowder. In 1864 Edward Schultze, Prussian artillery captain, invented a smokeless powder (probably first successful kind) known after 1870 as Schultze powder and made chiefly of nitrocellulose; used in shotguns, blank cartridges, hand grenades, and in igniting propellent powder used in artillery. Paul Vieille invented (1885) *poudre* B (nitrocotton and ether-alcohol) for rifles. Ballistite (nitrocotton gelatinized by nitroglycerine) was later added to the growing list of powders by Alfred Nobel. Cordite, another smokeless powder, invented (1889) by Sir F. A. Abel and Sir James Dewar, contained highly nitrated guncotton and nitroglycerine blended by means of acetone. Indurite, invented (1891) by C. E. Monroe, is made from guncotton colloided with nitrobenzene.

Powderly, Terence Vincent, 1849–1924, American labor leader. Joined (1874) KNIGHTS OF LABOR, which he led (1879–93) during its greatest strength.

Powell, Cecil Frank, 1903–, English physicist. Won 1950 Nobel Prize for developing photographic method for studying atomic nucleus and for discoveries regarding the nuclear particles called mesons.

Powell, John Wesley, 1834–1902, American geologist and ethnologist, noted for his explorations of W U.S. While making a survey of the Colorado R. he led a party by boat through the Grand Canyon. He was instrumental in founding U.S. Geological Survey; served as director (1881–94).

Powell, town (pop. 3,804), NW Wyo. Hq. of SHOSHONE PROJECT. Fossil beds in area.

power, defined as energy made capable of doing work. In mechanics, capacity is measured by units of accomplishment correlated with time. Commonly used is the horsepower unit (550 foot-pounds per second; a foot-pound is ability to lift a pound one foot). In engineering, power is energy of all kinds taking the form of mechanical or electrical energy. The simple water wheel, rotated by falling or swiftly flowing water, has given way to the modern turbine linked to electric generators, for the production of hydroelectric power. Hydroelectric plants in U.S. include those at Boulder Dam, Grand Coulee Dam, and Hoover Dam in the Central Valley Project. Energy of fuel is converted to mechanical energy in INTERNAL-COMBUSTION ENGINE and STEAM ENGINE. In various devices power is transmitted by means of belt, rope, and chain drives, by gears or shafts, by pipes (steam and compressed air), and wires (electrical currents). Potential source is atomic, or nuclear, energy. See *ills.*, pp. 389, 793.

Powers, Hiram, 1805–73, American sculptor, who was extremely popular in his day. His *Greek Slave* (1843) was renowned in Europe and America. Worked mainly in Florence.

Powhatan (pou″ŭtăn′), d. 1618, American Indian chief of Powhatan tribe in Va.; father of POCAHONTAS. He extended dominion of **Powhatan Confederacy,** group of tribes extending along coast and up rivers of tidewater Va. Indian attacks after Powhatan's death led to bloody reprisals by English. Confederacy yielded much territory in 1646 and disappeared after 1722.

Pownal, town (pop. 1,453), SW Vt., S of Bennington. J. A. Garfield and C. A. Arthur taught here. Scene of land-grant strife between N.Y. and N.H.

Pownall, Thomas (pou′nŭl), 1722–1805, English statesman and colonial governor of Mass. (1757–59). Urged stronger union of colonies with mother country. Member of Parliament (1767–1780).

Powys, John Cowper (pō′ĭs), 1872–, English author and lecturer. His works include novels (e.g., *Wolf Solent,* 1929), poetry, essays and criticism (e.g., *The Enjoyment of Literature,* 1938), and autobiography. His brother, **Theodore Francis Powys,** 1875–, wrote novels (e.g., *Black Bryony,* 1923) and short stories. Another brother, **Llewelyn Powys,** 1884–1939, was also an author. His works include novels (e.g., *Love and Death,* 1939), essays and sketches (e.g., *Earth Memories,* 1938), and autobiography.

Poyang (pō′yäng), shallow lake, area 1,070 sq. mi., N Kiangsi prov., China. Connected with Yangtze R. by Hukow Canal.

Poynings, Sir Edward, 1459–1521, English statesman. Lord deputy of Ireland 1494–96, he had enacted (1494) **Poynings's Law,** providing that English privy council must assent to calling of Irish Parliament and to any of its legislation. Henry Grattan procured its repeal in 1782.

Poznan, Pol. *Poznań* (pôz′nänyů), Ger. *Posen,* city (pop. 267,978), W Poland, on Warta R. Commercial center. See of Catholic primate of Poland since 1821 (when it was transferred from Gniezno). It became (10th cent.) the first Polish episcopal see and was a nucleus of the Polish state. Passed to Prussia in second Polish partition (1793); was included in duchy of Warsaw 1807; reverted to Prussia 1815; to Poland 1919. Was heavily bombed in World War II. University was founded 1919. Poznan prov. includes sections of Brandenburg, Pomerania, and Lower Silesia, placed under Polish administration in 1945.

Pozsony, Czechoslovakia: see BRATISLAVA.

Pozzo di Borgo, Carlo Andrea (kär′lō ändrā′ä pôt′tsō dē bōr′gō), 1764–1842, Russian diplomat, b. Corsica. Supported British occupation of Corsica (1794); superseded Paoli in authority. An exile after French reconquest, he entered Russian service (1804), promoted Russian opposition to Napoleon I, and served as ambassador to France after 1814.

Pr, chemical symbol of the element PRASEODYMIUM.

Prado (prä'dō), national Spanish museum of painting and sculpture, on Paseo del Prado, Madrid. Begun by Juan Villanueva under Charles III and finished 1830 under Ferdinand VII. Has priceless masterpieces of Spanish, Flemish, and Venetian schools.

Praetorians (prētô'rēůnz), bodyguard of the Roman emperors, formally organized in the time of Augustus from the troop that had guarded the general commanding in Rome. They attended the emperor everywhere, had special privileges, and, in times of trouble, chose many of the emperors. Constantine I disbanded them (312).

Praetorius, Michael (prētô'rēůs), 1571–1621, German composer and musicologist, whose name originally was Schultheiss. Chiefly known today for his *Syntagma musicum* (3 vols.), which minutely describes the musical practices and instruments of his day.

pragmatic sanction (prăgmă'tĭk), decision of state dealing with a matter of great importance and having force of fundamental law. The **Pragmatic Sanction of Bourges,** issued by Charles VII of France in 1438, limited papal authority over Church in France and estab. liberty of Gallican Church (see GALLICANISM). It was revoked by Louis XI (1461). The **Pragmatic Sanction** of 1713, issued by Emperor Charles VI, altered the HAPSBURG family law. In absence of a male heir, it reserved succession to all Hapsburg lands (but not to the elective imperial dignity) to MARIA THERESA. Charles obtained, after much labor, the adherence to the Pragmatic Sanction of most European powers and of the local diets of the various Hapsburg lands. However, at his death several monarchs challenged Maria Theresa's rights to succession—notably Augustus III of Poland and Saxony and Elector Charles Albert of Bavaria (later Emperor Charles VII), both of whom had married nieces of Charles VI. The War of the AUSTRIAN SUCCESSION resulted.

pragmatism (prăg'mŭtĭzŭm), any system of philosophy in which it is held that the truth of a proposition must be measured by its correspondence with experimental results and by its practical outcome. Thus in pragmatism any metaphysical significance of thought is discarded, and all methods supposedly leading to truth through deduction from a priori grounds are rejected. Pragmatists hold that truth is modified as discoveries are made and that truth evolves, being relative to time, place, and purpose. Most pragmatists hold that in ethics knowledge which contributes to human values is real and that values inhere in the means as much as in the end. These principles are generally said to have been first developed formally by C. S. PEIRCE. William JAMES advanced them greatly, and they have had great force in philosophy since (as in the instrumentalism of John DEWEY).

Prague (präg, prāg), Czech *Praha,* Ger. *Prag,* city (pop. 922,284), cap. of Czechoslovakia and of Bohemia, on the Moldau. Commercial and industrial center (machinery, foodstuffs); archiepiscopal see. A castle from the 9th cent., it was chartered 1232 and settled by German colonists. Under Emperor Charles IV it became one of the most splendid cities of Europe. The reforms preached by John HUSS led to civil troubles; in 1419 the first Defenestration of Prague (see WENCESLAUS, emperor) touched off the Hussite Wars. The second Defenestration of Prague took place in 1618, when the Protestant Czech nobles threw two royal councilors and the secretary of the royal council of Bohemia out of the windows of Hradcany Castle. Nobody was hurt, but the event marked the outbreak of the THIRTY YEARS WAR, which resulted in the total subjection of Bohemia to Austrian rule. Until 1860 German was the sole official language. The cap. of Czechoslovakia from 1918, Prague was occupied by the Germans 1939–45 but suffered very little war damage. On the W bank of the Moldau are the imposing Hradcany Castle, formerly the royal, now the presidential residence (14th–18th cent.); the Gothic Cathedral of St. Vitus, with the tombs of St. Wenceslaus and of several kings and emperors; the 18th-cent. archiepiscopal palace; the baroque Church of Our Lady of Victory, with the miraculous statuette of the Infant Jesus of Prague; several magnificent baroque palaces (Waldstein, Schwarzenberg, Czernin); and the quaint Alchemists' or Golden Lane. Among the 12 bridges the most famous is Charles Bridge (14th cent.). On the E bank are the university and the Gothic Old Town Hall and Tyn Cathedral; the business district, with Wenceslaus Square; and the ancient Visehrad quarter. The **University of Prague** (Charles Univ.) was founded 1348 by Charles IV. Its faculty was organized in four "nations"—Czech, Saxon, Bavarian, Polish. In 1409, by the Decree of Kutna Hora, Emperor Wenceslaus gave the Czech "nation" preponderance in the voting procedure, thus making possible the election of Huss as rector; the Germans left and founded the Univ. of Leipzig. In the Hussite Wars, Charles Univ. was the stronghold of the Utraquists. It was Germanized after 1620, but in 1882 two branches were organized—Charles Univ. (Czech) and Ferdinand Univ. (German). In 1939–45 the Czech university was suppressed; in 1945 the German university was abolished.

Prague, Peace of, 1635: see THIRTY YEARS WAR.

Prague, Treaty of, 1866: see AUSTRO-PRUSSIAN WAR.

Praguerie (prägůrē'), 1440, revolt of great feudal lords against Charles VII of France; so called by allusion to Hussite uprising in Prague. The dauphin (later Louis XI) was among rebels, who received support from Philip the Good of Burgundy. Charles suppressed the revolt, but treated the rebels leniently.

Praha, Czechoslovakia: see PRAGUE.

prairie chicken, American game bird of GROUSE family. Found in parts of Canada; on Great Plains; in Texas and La.

prairie dog, North American rodent (*Cynomys*)

of squirrel family. The short fur is brownish or buff, whitish on the under parts; plump body is 12–15 in. long. Prairie dogs live in burrows grouped in colonies.

Prairie du Chien (prâ'rē dù shēn'), city (pop. 5,392), SE Wis., on the Mississippi just above mouth of Wisconsin R. Fox-Wisconsin river route from Great Lakes reached the Mississippi here, and here Nicolas Perrot built Fort St. Nicolas 1686. War of 1812 fort here changed hands, burned. Town grew around American Fur Co. post; later was important river port. Fort Crawford built here 1816. Dr. William Beaumont conducted his experiments there. Site of fort now has museum.

Prairie Grove, town (pop. 939), NW Ark., SW of Fayetteville. Civil War battle here (Dec. 7, 1862) resulted in Confederate defeat, thus strengthening Union hold in NW Ark.

Prairie Provinces, see: MANITOBA; SASKATCHEWAN; ALBERTA.

prairies, generally level, originally grass-covered and treeless plains of U.S., stretching from W Ohio through Ind., Ill., and Iowa to Great Plains region. Prairie belt also extends into N Mo., S Mich., Wis., and Minn., E N.Dak. and S.Dak., and S Canada. With rich prairie soil, area is one of most productive regions of U.S.

prairie schooner, wagon covered with white canvas, almost universally used in migration across plains of W U.S. Commonly it was a farm wagon with top drawn in at ends and drawn by two or four horses or by oxen. Often traveled in wagon train.

prairie wolf: see COYOTE.

Praise, Ky.: see ELKHORN CITY.

Prajadhipok (prùchä'tĭpôk), 1893–1941, king of THAILAND (1925–35). Constitutional limits placed on the royal power led to his abdication.

Prakrit (prä'krĭt) [Sanskrit,= common], any of several languages of Indic group of Indo-Iranian subfamily of Indo-European languages. See LANGUAGE (table).

Prakrit literature is mostly devoted to JAINISM, but it also includes secular literature and lyric poetry. The sacred texts (*Siddhanta* or *Agama*) of the two main sects of the Jains are written in three types of Prakrit: Ardha-Magadhi, Maharastri, and Savraseni. In Sanskrit drama, Prakrit was often used as the speech of the common people.

Prasad, Rajendra (rùjĕn'drù prùsäd'), 1884–, first president of India (1950–); educated at Univ. of Allahabad. Admitted to the bar, 1911. Headed Indian Natl. Congress four times. Presided 1948–49 over drafting of Indian constitution. Reelected 1952.

praseodymium (prā"zēōdĭ'mēùm), rare metallic element of rare earths (symbol = Pr; see also ELEMENT, table). Its salts are used to color glass.

Pratt, Charles, 1st **Earl Camden,** 1714–94, English jurist, lord Chancellor (1766–70). Declared the prosecution of John Wilkes illegal. Denounced British policy toward American colonists.

Pratt, Edwin John, 1883–, Canadian poet. With *Titans* (1926) he broke away from romantic tradition of Canadian poetry. *Dunkirk* (1941) is considered one of the best poems of World War II.

Pratt, Orson, 1811–81, Mormon apostle. Appointed (1835) missionary abroad. In Utah, he was after 1847 influential member of assembly. His brother, **Parley Parker Pratt,** 1807–57, was also apostle (1835) and missionary in England. He helped frame constitution of state of Deseret and devised a Mormon alphabet.

Pratt, city (pop. 7,523), S Kansas, W of Wichita. Shipping center for wheat area.

Pratt Institute, at Brooklyn, New York city; nonsectarian, coed; chartered and opened 1887. Has schools of architecture, art, engineering, home economics, and library science.

prawn, decapod crustacean closely allied to shrimp, found in temperate and tropical, salt and fresh waters.

Praxiteles (prăksĭ'tùlēz), fl. c.370–c.330 B.C., most famous of the Attic sculptors. His *Hermes with the Infant Dionysius* is the only undisputed extant original by an ancient master. A copy of his *Aphrodite of Cnidus* is in the Vatican. He was unsurpassed as a worker in marble.

Prayer, Book of Common: see BOOK OF COMMON PRAYER.

praying mantis: see MANTIS.

Preble, Edward (prĕ'bùl), 1761–1807, American naval officer. Commanded a squadron in war against Barbary States (see TRIPOLITAN WAR).

Pre-Cambrian: see ARCHEOZOIC ERA; PROTEROZOIC ERA.

precession of the equinoxes (prēsĕ'shùn), progression of equinoctial points (see EQUINOX) whereby each point reaches a given meridian progressively sooner than a given star in successive passages. The motion results in completion of a cone figure by earth's axis in c.25,800 years and in westward movement of vernal equinox along ZODIAC.

precipitation, in chemistry, reaction in which an insoluble substance is formed when some specific reagent is added to a solution. Colloids can be precipitated by addition of strong electrolyte. Precipitation is believed to result from neutralizing effect of ions with charge opposite to that of suspended particles.

predestination, Christian theological doctrine regarding question of free will. Fundamental dilemma is whether man is free to take responsibility for actions or whether his choice is controlled. Christian predestination is based on two assumptions—that God's plan is absolute and that God elects or condemns men to salvation or damnation. John Calvin formulated doctrine of absolute predestination, expressed later in Westminster Confession and in Westminster Larger Catechism. Less extreme forms exist in many Christian systems, such as Luther's.

Preemption Act, passed in 1841 by U.S. Congress in response to demands of Western states that squatters be allowed to preempt lands. Permitted settlers to locate a claim of 160 acres and after six months of residence to purchase it from the government for as low as $1.25 an acre. After passage of HOMESTEAD ACT (1862), value of preemption declined. Preemption act repealed in 1891.

Pregl, Fritz (frĭts' prā'gŭl), 1869–1930, Austrian physiologist and chemist. Won 1923 Nobel Prize in Chemistry for work on quantitative organic microanalysis.

pregnancy or **gestation** (jĕstā'shŭn), period between fertilization of ovum and birth. Duration in humans is c.280 days. Chief early symptom is cessation of menstruation. Tests for pregnancy are based on changes in certain animals injected with urine from pregnant woman. Fetal heart beat and movements are detectable by end of fifth month. Disorders include ABORTION and toxemia. See also PRENATAL CARE.

prehistoric man: see MAN, PRIMITIVE.

premier: see PRIME MINISTER.

Premysl, Czech *Přemysl* (pshĕ'mĭsŭl), earliest dynasty of Bohemia, founded 8th cent. by the semilegendary peasant Premysl, whom the Bohemian princess Libussa chose as husband. Best-known among early Premysl dukes of Bohemia is St. WENCESLAUS ("Good King Wenceslaus"). The title king became hereditary with OTTOCAR I (1198). His successors were WENCESLAUS I, OTTOCAR II, WENCESLAUS II, and WENCESLAUS III, on whose death in 1306 John of Luxemburg succeeded.

prenatal care (prē"nā'tŭl), medical attention given expectant mother during PREGNANCY. Comprises thorough examination, blood and urine tests, and periodic checks of mother and of growth of embryo. Suitable regimen is set up; pregnancy diet, usually high in protein, calcium, iron, and vitamins, may be enriched to counteract anemia and vitamin deficiencies.

Prendergast, Maurice (Brazil), 1859–1924, American painter, a member of The Eight. Used small dots of colors to create landscapes with tapestry effect.

Pre-Raphaelites (prē"-ră'fēŭlīts"), brotherhood of British painters and poets formed 1848 in protest against prevailing standards of British art. Chief founders were ROSSETTI, Holman Hunt, and John Millais. So called because they found inspiration in work of Italian painters prior to Raphael. Also influenced by Ford Madox Brown and by the NAZARENES. Defended by Ruskin and attracted such followers as Burne-Jones, G. F. Watts, and William Morris. Movement died out before end of 19th cent.

Presbyterianism, system of church polity based on government by series of courts composed of clerical and lay presbyters. It stands between episcopacy and Congregationalism. Presbyters or elders manage spiritual conduct of church; deacons and trustees, temporal affairs. Court of congregation is session; next higher is synod; highest is general assembly, with supervisory power over denomination. Presiding officer is moderator. Presbyterian churches are direct heirs of CALVINISM in doctrine and polity. They believe in Bible as sole rule of faith and in sacraments of baptism and Lord's Supper. Presbyterianism organized in British Isles uses Westminster Confession of Faith and Luther's Catechisms. By mid-16th cent. system was strong in England and esp. in Scotland under John KNOX. Divisions of Church of Scotland were Cameronians or Covenanters, Associate Synod, "Burghers," and Free Church of Scotland. Irish Presbyterianism is largely confined to Northern Ireland. Welsh Presbyterianism is represented by Calvinistic Methodist Church. In America Francis Makemie, Irish missionary, set up first presbytery at Philadelphia 1706; synod was formed 1716. Main body today is Presbyterian Church in U.S.A. Other bodies include Presbyterian Church in the U.S., Cumberland Presbyterian Church, Orthodox Presbyterian Church, and United Presbyterian Church of North America.

Prescott, William Hickling, 1796–1859, American historian. Known especially for *History of the Conquest of Mexico* (1843) and *The Conquest of Peru* (1847). He wrote in style that made history live.

Prescott, town (pop. 3,518), SE Ont., Canada, on St. Lawrence R. and S of Ottawa, opposite Ogdensburg, N.Y. Fort Wellington, now a museum, was built in War of 1812. At near-by Windmill Point, British repulsed large American force 1814.

Prescott, city (pop. 6,764), central Ariz., in mountains NNW of Phoenix. Built near Fort Whipple (now a VA hospital) in 1864, was territorial cap. 1865–67 and 1877–89. Center for mining (e.g., copper), ranching; health and summer resort. Has annual Frontier Days rodeo and reenactment of Indian ceremonials.

president, in modern republics, the chief executive and therefore highest officer in a government. Powers vary greatly in different countries; status ranges from largely honorific (e.g., in France) to dictatorial (as sporadically occurs in many Latin American countries). In U.S., President has been delegated substantial powers by Constitution, amplified by statutes. He serves a four-year term, taking office on Jan. 20 (according to Twentieth Amendment); must be 35 years old, a native of U.S., 14 years a resident within U.S. F. D. Roosevelt in 1940 broke the precedent of no third term estab. by Washington. See ELECTORAL COLLEGE. For a list of U.S. Presidents, see UNITED STATES.

Presidential Range, group of the White Mts., N N.H. Includes mounts WASHINGTON (6,288 ft.), Adams (5,798 ft.), Jefferson (5,715 ft.), Clay (5,532 ft.), Monroe (5,385 ft.), and Madison (5,363 ft.).

Prespa, Lake (prĕ'spä), area 112 sq. mi., in SW Yugoslavia, NW Greece, and E Albania. Underground channels connect it with L. Ochrida.

Presque Isle (prĕskīl'), city (pop. 9,954), NE Maine, N of Houlton. Trade and shipping center of Aroostook valley (potatoes). Site of U.S. air base (1941).

press, freedom of the. Pervasive censorship was estab. by Church and state in Europe soon after the advent of printing. In post-Reformation England, monopolies were granted to a few printers by the crown, licensing of all publications before printing was required (1534–1695), criticism of government was made a felony, and until the 1770s publishing of parliamentary debates was closely restricted. Compulsory stamp duties on newspapers were rescinded by 1855; truth became admissible as defense in libel cases in 1868. The First Amendment to U.S. Constitution forbade Congress to make laws abridging freedom of the press; this was made binding on the states by judicial interpretation of Fourteenth Amendment (1868). ALIEN AND SEDITION ACTS (1798) were first serious threat to this guarantee. During World War I government censorship was widely enforced for the first time. After 1919 the Supreme Court used a "clear and present danger" test—to determine whether the words would induce acts that Congress had a right to prevent. During World War II an effective Office of Censorship operated (1941–45). In dictatorships, governments control the press; in a free-enterprise system, freedom of the press may be eclipsed by consolidation and monopolization of press by limited private interests.

Pressburg, German name of BRATISLAVA, Czechoslovakia. The **Treaty of Pressburg,** 1805, restored peace between France and Austria after Napoleon's victory at Austerlitz. Austria ceded Venetia to Napoleon (in his quality as king of Italy); Tyrol and Vorarlberg to Bavaria; and its Swabian holdings to Württemberg and Baden. Salzburg was annexed to Austria.

pressure, in mechanics, FORCE acting upon unit area of surface of a body, distinct from total force applied to the body. Atmospheric pressure is c.15 lb. per square inch at sea level. It is measured by a BAROMETER. Term "pressure gauge" is commonly used for other pressure-measuring instruments. Pressure variations are accompanied by observable changes in boiling point and melting point of materials.

Prester John (prĕ'stûr) [Mid. Eng., *prester* = priest], legendary Christian monarch of a vast, wealthy empire in Asia or Africa. The legend appeared in the 12th cent. and may have been based on Ethiopia or some Nestorian kingdom.

Preston, town (pop. 7,619), S Ont., Canada, on Grand R. and ESE of Kitchener. Resort with sulphur springs and flour and woolen mills.

Preston, county borough (pop. 119,243), Lancashire, England. A center of cotton mfg., it has harbor with extensive docks. A guild-merchant festival is held every 20 years. Scene of a Cromwell victory (1648) and Jacobite surrender (1715).

Prestonpans, burgh (pop. 2,907), East Lothian, Scotland. Scene of a famous rout (1745) of forces under Sir John Cope by the Jacobites.

Prestwick, burgh (pop. 11,386), Ayrshire, Scotland; a resort. A large airport, built in World War II, is now a civil airport.

Pretoria (prĭtô'rēù), city (pop. 168,058), S central Transvaal; administrative cap. of South Africa and cap. of Transvaal prov. Founded 1855 and named for Andries Pretorius. Seat of Univ. of Pretoria. Has steel mills and railroad workshops.

Pretorius, Andries Wilhemus Jacobus (prĭtô'rēùs), 1799–1853, Boer leader. Helped create the nucleus of South African Republic estab. 1853 in the Transvaal. City of Pretoria was named for him. His son **Martinus Wessel Pretorius,** 1818?–1901, was first president of South African Republic in the Transvaal (1857–71) and concurrently president of Orange Free State (1859–63).

Prevost, Sir George (prĕ'vō), 1767–1816, English general, governor in chief of Canada (1811–15). Commanded British forces in Canada in War of 1812; blamed for retreat at Sackets Harbor (1813) and defeat at Plattsburg (1814).

Prévost, Marcel (märsĕl' prāvō'), 1862–1941, French novelist. His best-known novel is *Les Demi-Vierges* (1894; Eng. tr., 1895).

Prévost d'Exiles, Antoine François (ãtwän' frãswä' prāvō' dāgzēl'), known as **Abbé Prévost** (äbā'), 1697–1763, French author. He entered the Benedictine order in 1720; fled in 1727; led an adventurous life as a journalist in England, Holland, and Germany; later was readmitted into the order and died as a prior. Of his innumerable writings, only the novel *Manon Lescaut* (1732), his masterpiece, is still widely read. It served as basis for the operas *Manon,* by Massenet, and *Manon Lescaut,* by Puccini.

Priam (prī'ùm), in Greek legend, Trojan king; husband of Hecuba and father of Hector, Paris, Troilus, Cassandra, and others. Killed in Trojan War.

Priapus (prīā'pùs), in Greek religion, god of the countryside, associated with phallicism. Represented as very ugly. Priapic rites were orgiastic.

Pribilof Islands (prĭ'bĭlŏf"), group of four islands off SW Alaska, in Bering Sea and N of Aleutian Isls. Visited and named 1786 by Russian navigator, Gerasim Pribilof. Residents are Aleuts and few U.S. government representatives. Important seal breeding ground. To prevent extinction of seals, U.S., Great Britain, Japan, and Russia in 1911 settled BERING SEA FUR-SEAL CONTROVERSY by giving U.S. right to enforce its provisions. Japan withdrew 1941. Under protection, seal herd has greatly increased. Aleuts make living by processing seal and fox furs.

Price, Sterling, 1809–67, Confederate general. Helped defeat Union forces at Wilson Creek, Mo. (1861), but his campaign in Miss. (Oct., 1862) was unsuccessful. His defeat at Westport, Mo. (1864), marked last Confederate thrust in Far West.

Price, city (pop. 6,010), E central Utah, on Price R. Coal-mining center in irrigated agr. area.

Prichard, industrial city (pop. 19,014), SW Ala., N suburb of Mobile. Meat packing; canning.

prickly ash, deciduous shrub or tree (*Zanthoxylum americanum*) of E North America with prickly twigs, foliage similar to that of the ash, small flower clusters, and red pods with black seeds.

prickly pear, jointed flat-stemmed cactus plant of genus *Opuntia,* often spiny, and with colorful edible fruits. Some are grown as hedge plants in Mexico and Calif. and as pot plants farther north. Prickly pears known as Indian fig (*Opuntia ficus-indica*) and tuna (*O. tuna*) are grown in warm regions; the fruits, stems, and seeds yield various food products.

Pride, Thomas, d. 1658, English soldier in Puritan Revolution. Carried out (1648)

Pride's Purge, excluding Presbyterians from Parliament as royalists. Remaining Rump Parliament tried Charles I.

Priestley, J(ohn) B(oynton), 1894–, English author, best known for novels (e.g., *The Good Companions,* 1929; *Angel Pavement,* 1930) and plays (e.g., *Laburnum Grove,* 1933).

Priestley, Joseph, 1733–1804, English theologian and scientist. He prepared for Presbyterian ministry, but gradually adopted Unitarian views. He founded the *Theological Repository*. He opposed orthodox doctrines and some government policies. Because of his sympathy with the French Revolution his home and scientific materials were destroyed and he emigrated to the U.S. 1794. In his *History of Electricity* (1767) he explained the rings (Priestley's rings) formed by discharge on metallic surface. He produced oxygen, but did not realize importance of discovery.

Prim, Juan (hwän' prēm'), 1814–70, Spanish general and politician. Supported Isabella II against Carlists; fought in Morocco (1859–60) and Mexico (1861–62). Held high offices under Isabella but was repeatedly exiled by his rivals; took a major part in Isabella's overthrow (1868). Was assassinated.

primary, in U.S., a preliminary election in which a party candidate is nominated directly by the voters. Resulted from demand to eliminate evils of nomination by party conventions. Primary was first used in local elections in 1868; in 1903 Gov. R. M. La Follette secured in Wis. a direct primary law for nomination of state-wide candidates. By 1917 all but four states had enacted primary laws. Some states extend primary principle to national party conventions by electing state delegates who reflect popular preference for presidential candidates. U.S. Congress has power to regulate primaries for Federal candidates.

primate (prī'māt, –mĭt), animal of highest order of mammals, the Primates (as order pronounced prīmā'tēz). Includes APE, LEMUR, MONKEY, MAN. Subdivisions are controversial.

Primaticcio, Francesco (fränchā'skō prēmätēt'-chō), 1504–70, Italian artist. Influenced by Giulio Romano and Corregio. Helped extend influence of Italian art in France mainly through his frescoes and stucco work at Fontainebleau.

prime minister or **premier** (prē'mēûr, prŭmēr', prĕm'yûr), the chief member of a responsible cabinet, as in England. He is in effect the leader of his party, he appoints the ministry, and makes government policy.

primitive man: see MAN, PRIMITIVE.

Primitive Methodist Church, group which seceded from Wesleyan Methodist Church in England under William Clowes and Hugh Bourne. Merged (1932) with Wesleyan and United Methodists. Branch estab. in U.S. c.1830.

Primo de Rivera, Miguel (mēgĕl' prē'mō dā rēvä'rä), 1870–1930, Spanish general and dictator (1923–30). His reactionary rule was supported by Alfonso XIII but was overthrown when part of the army joined the Socialist, liberal, and Catalan separatist opposition. His son José Antonio, founder of the FALANGE, was executed by the Loyalists in the civil war (1936).

primogeniture (prī"mōjĕn'ĭchûr), in law, rule of inheritance whereby land descends to oldest son. Under feudal system, primogeniture governed land held in military tenure; disinherited younger sons in knight service. When payment of a tax supplanted military service, need for primogeniture lessened, but the custom continued in England.

Primrose, William, 1904–, Scottish-American violist, generally regarded as the world's outstanding solo violist.

primrose, low herbaceous perennial of genus *Primula,* of north temperate zone, with spring-blooming flowers of various colors borne in heads or umbels. Primroses are grown in rock gardens, borders, or indoors in pots. In England a yellow species (*Primula veris*) is called cowslip.

Prince, Thomas, 1687–1758, American clergyman and historian; copastor from 1718 of Old South Church, Boston. Best known for *Chronological History of New England* (2 vols., 1736, 1755), covering years 1602–33.

Prince Albert, city (pop. 17,149), central Sask., Canada, on North Saskatchewan R. and NNE of Saskatoon; founded 1866. Trade center in fur-trapping, lumbering, and ranch area. Gateway to Prince Albert Natl. Park (NW). Hq. of Royal Canadian Mounted Police for central and N Sask.

Prince Albert National Park, 1,496 sq. mi., central Sask., Canada, NW of Prince Albert; estab. 1927. Largely wooded parklands with many lakes. Animal sanctuary. Hq. at Waskesiu, on L. Waskesiu.

Prince Edward Island, province and island (2,184 sq. mi.; 145 mi. long, 5–35 mi. wide; pop. 98,429), E Canada, in Gulf of St. Lawrence, off Nova Scotia and New Brunswick; cap. CHARLOTTETOWN. One of the Maritime Provs. Although the most densely populated Canadian province, SUMMERSIDE is the only other city. Along N shore is Prince Edward Natl. Park (estab. 1936). Farming and stock raising provide more than half of the island's income. Fisheries and fox-fur farms are important. Mfg. is limited to food processing. Discovered by Cartier 1534 and first settled by Acadians, it was annexed to Nova Scotia 1763, and became a separate colony 1769. Lord Selkirk settled impoverished Scottish colonists here 1803 and the population is largely descended from this group. Responsible government was estab. 1851 and confederation with Canada accepted 1873.

Prince George, city (pop. 4,703), central B.C., Canada, on Fraser R. at mouth of the Nechako and N of Vancouver. Railroad division point; center of lumbering, mining, and ranching region. Fort George, fur-trading post, estab. here 1807.

Prince of Wales, Cape, westernmost point of North America, NW Alaska, on Bering Strait, opposite East Cape (Cape Dezhnev) in Siberia.

Prince of Wales Island, area 2,231 sq. mi., off SE Alaska. Largest island of Alexander Archipelago; 135 mi. long, 45 mi. wide.

Densely wooded. On E coast is Old Kasaan Natl. Monument.

Prince of Wales Island, area 13,736 sq. mi., Franklin dist., Northwest Territories, in the Arctic Ocean. Magnetic pole located here in 1948.

Prince Rupert, city (pop. 8,546), W B.C., Canada, on Kaien Isl. in Chatham Sound, near mouth of Skeena R. Highway and railroad terminus with fish-processing plants and cellulose factory; year-round port serves wide area. A major supply base for U.S. forces in Alaska during World War II.

Princess Anne, town (pop. 1,407), Eastern Shore, Md., SW of Salisbury. Seat of Maryland State Col., formerly Princess Anne Col. (coed.; for Negroes), a branch of Univ. of Maryland.

Princeton. 1 City (pop. 5,765), N Ill., N of Peoria, in coal, nursery, and farm area. Mfg. of clay products, vinegar, and sealing wax. **2** City (pop. 7,673), SW Ind., N of Evansville. Trade and rail center with oil refining and mfg. of paint brushes and clocks. **3** City (pop. 5,388), W Ky., between Cumberland and Tradewater rivers and E of Paducah. Rail point shipping tobacco, livestock, farm goods, clothing, and fluorspar. **4** Borough (pop. 12,230), W N.J., NE of Trenton; settled 1696 by Friends. Residential and education center; mfg. prohibited within borough limits. Washington defeated British here on Jan. 3, 1777, but Gen. Hugh Mercer was mortally wounded. Nassau Hall (of Princeton Univ.) served as barracks for British and colonial troops, and meeting place of Continental Congress, June–Nov., 1783. Seat of PRINCETON UNIVERSITY, INSTITUTE FOR ADVANCED STUDY, Princeton Theological Seminary (Presbyterian; for men; founded 1812), Rockefeller Inst. for Medical Research. Includes Palmer Square (civic center on Nassau St., with Colonial-style buildings), Bainbridge birthplace (now public library), battle monument (by F. W. MacMonnies), and "Morven" (1701; Richard Stockton's home and Cornwallis's hq.). **5** City (pop. 8,279), S W.Va., NE of Bluefield. Trade center of agr. and coal area.

Princeton University, at Princeton, N.J.; nonsectarian, for men; chartered 1746 and 1748 as Col. of New Jersey by Presbyterians, renamed 1896. Opened at Elizabethtown (now Elizabeth) (see DICKINSON, JONATHAN) and moved to Newark 1747, to Princeton 1756. An administrative feature which led trend toward more individualized college instruction was the preceptorial system introduced by Woodrow Wilson as president. Other distinguished presidents have been Jonathan Edwards, Witherspoon, McCosh, Hibben. Princeton's special schools include: public and international affairs, architecture, and engineering; has various research bureaus and museums and a university press (1905). Shares many of the resources of the Inst. for Advanced Study. Notable buildings include Nassau Hall (1756), Cleveland Tower, Fine Hall, Frick Laboratory, and Harvey S. Firestone Memorial Library.

Prince William Sound, large, irregular, islanded inlet of Gulf of Alaska, S. Alaska, S of Chugach Mts. Good harbors; access to interior by highway, railroad. Fishing and some mining. Valdez (NE) and Cordova (E) are ports.

Principe, Africa: see SÃO TOMÉ AND PRINCIPE.

Principia, The: see ALTON, Ill.

printing. For the early history of printing and its introduction to Europe, see TYPE. After Johann Gutenberg's first work at Mainz, the art spread rapidly over the Continent. By 1476 it had been brought to England by William Caxton; by 1539 a press had been set up in New Spain (Mexico). In the region now the U.S., printing first appeared with the work of Stephen and Matthew DAYE. The mechanical processes of printing changed little between the 15th and 19th centuries. In 1810 Friedrich König applied steam power to printing; in 1846–47 Richard March Hoe designed a rotary press in which the types were arranged on a cylinder; in 1866 a press using curved stereotype plates was patented in England; late in the 19th cent. typesetting machines were invented. In recent years photographic processes have been much used to produce books from typewritten (or drawn) copy, and very recently the application of electronics to typesetting has been proved practical. Printing in relief (with type projecting above the surface of the plate) continues to be the most widely used process, but two other kinds of printing have been developed. For intaglio printing—as in etchings and engravings—the design to be printed is cut into the surface of the plate, and the paper receives an impression from the incised design filled with ink. Gravure processes are of the intaglio kind; in photogravure the plates are made photographically. Planographic printing is done from a flat surface. The original process of this sort was lithography, in which a drawing is made with greasy crayon on a specially prepared flat stone. The stone is rolled with water, then with greasy ink. The ink adheres only to the crayon drawing, and is then transferred to the paper. The basic process has been much refined and altered. In offset printing, the inked plate transfers the impression to a rubber roller, which in turn carries the ink to the paper. Collotype plates employ a gelatin surface on which the printing image has been obtained by exposure to light. PHOTOENGRAVING is widely used, especially for illustrations. See also Ben DAY.

Prior, Matthew, 1664–1721, English poet and diplomat. Noted as a wit, he wrote, with Charles Montagu, *The City Mouse and the Country Mouse* (1687), a parody of Dryden's *The Hind and the Panther*. He also wrote pleasant "society verse" and two satiric poems and served as envoy to draw up the Peace of Utrecht.

Pripet (prĭ'pĕt), Pol. *Prypeć*, Rus. *Pripyat*, river, c.500 mi. long, Belorussia, flowing E into the Dnieper. The **Pripet Marshes** are a forested, swampy area (c.33,500 sq. mi.) extending S from the Pripet and its affluents. A natural defense barrier, the marshes were a battlefield in World War I, but they were bypassed by the Germans in 1941.

Priscian (Priscianus Caesariensis) (prĭ'shŭn), fl. 500, Latin grammarian. Among his extant works is *Commentarii grammatici*, long a standard grammar and basis of the work of Rabanus Maurus.

Priscilla or **Prisca,** wife of Aquila, a Jew living in Rome. They were friendly to Paul.

prism: see SPECTRUM.

prison, place of detention for the punishment and reform of convicts. At the end of the 18th cent., when it had become the chief mode of punishment, a reform movement (led by BECCARIA in Italy and John Howard in England) improved some of the unspeakable prison conditions. Reform in the U.S. began in Philadelphia (1790) and Auburn, N.Y. In the 19th cent. reform was led by Elizabeth Fry and Dorothea L. Dix. British (especially Irish) influences led to the practice of parole. There is a growing tendency to regard the aim of imprisonment as regeneration, with constructive labor policies and social readjustment, but such notoriously brutal forms as chain gangs still exist. There are now usually separate institutions for the insane, sick, minor offenders, and the young.

prisoners of war. The first international convention on prisoners of war was signed at the Hague Peace Conference of 1899 and broadened in 1907. The rules proved to be insufficient in World War I, and the Internatl. Red Cross proposed a new code which was signed at Geneva, Switzerland, in 1929. This Geneva Convention is still in effect. Provides that prisoner need divulge only name and rank, is entitled to food and medical care, has right to exchange correspondence and receive parcels, must obey military discipline, and may attempt escape at his own risk. Detention camps should be open to inspection by a neutral power. Nations which do not adhere to (and hence are not bound by) the Geneva Convention include USSR and Communist China.

Pritchett, Henry Smith (prĭ'chĭt), 1857–1939, American astronomer and educator. Among his posts after 1878 were superintendent of U.S. Coast and Geodetic Survey and president of Massachusetts Inst. of Technology. He was president of Carnegie Foundation for the Advancement of Teaching, 1906–30.

privateering, former usage of war permitting privately owned war vessels (privateers) under government commission to capture enemy shipping. Great era was 1692–1814. After defeat of French fleet in 1692, France commissioned privateers to prey on English shipping. In American Revolution and in War of 1812 American privateersmen (notably Stephen Decatur) took hundreds of prizes. The system was subject to much abuse later as a mask for piracy, and it was abolished by Declaration of Paris (1856).

privet (prĭv'ĭt), Old World evergreen or deciduous shrub or small tree (*Ligustrum*). The common privet (*Ligustrum vulgare*) and California privet (*L. ovalifolium*) are hedge plants.

Prix de Rome, Grand (grã' prē' dü rōm'), prize awarded by French government, through competitive examination, to students of fine arts (including music). Instituted 1666 by Louis XIV. Award involves four years' study in Rome and exemption from military service. Open to those between ages of 15 and 20 who have done required work at École des Beaux-Arts and elsewhere.

prize fighting: see BOXING.

probability, in mathematics, a precisely defined value indicating chance of (or odds for) occurrence of a given event. Sometimes it is defined as ratio of number of ways event can happen to total ways in which it can or cannot happen. Where this is undeterminable, it is then defined as limiting value of a sequence of ratios of number of successes (occurrences of event) to number of trials, as number of trials is increased indefinitely. Blaise Pascal developed theory of probability c.1654.

Probus, d. 282, Roman emperor (276–82), a commander under Valerian and successor to M. Claudius Tacitus. He did much to restore order in the empire before his troops mutinied and killed him.

procedure, in law, body of formal rules that must be observed to obtain legal redress and satisfaction of claims through the courts. It does not include evidence but does embrace all other matters concerning legal actions and is the means for enforcing the rights determined by the substantive law. Criminal procedure concerns the forms of enforcing criminal law by public prosecution. Civil procedure concerns the enforcement of a civil claim by private action before the court, begun by the plaintiff's having a process (e.g., a summons) served upon the defendant, which gives a court jurisdiction over the case. In early common law an action could be brought only if it conformed closely to a writ ("no writ, no right"). This situation stimluated the growth of equity. In the 19th cent., however, technical intricacy of law procedure caused too many cases to hinge on technicalities of procedural detail. In New York the civil code in 1848 abolished the distinction of law and equity and made the cause of the action the procedural cornerstone. A similar reform was accomplished in Great Britain by the Judicature Acts of 1875. Today procedure in most American states is based on codes, as that in civil-law countries has been since early times. The guarantee of proper procedure ("due process") is included in the Constitution of the U.S.

Prochorus (prŏ'kûrùs), one of the seven deacons. Acts 6.5. Traditionally bishop of Nicodemia.

Procida, John of: see JOHN OF PROCIDA.

Procne, wife of Tereus and sister of PHILOMELA.

Procopius (prōkō'pēùs), d. 562?, Byzantine historian. Chief works are *Procopius' History of His Own Time* and *Secret History of Procopius.* His authorship of the latter has been questioned.

Procopius the Great, d. 1434, Czech Hussite leader, called Prokop; a married priest. Becoming chief of the radical TABORITES (c.1425), he defeated the Saxons at Usti-nad-Labem (1426); invaded Hungary, Silesia, Saxony, Thuringia (1426–30); and as chief commander of Czech forces routed an anti-Hussite crusade at Domazlice (1431). He continued hostilities even after peace negotiations were under way at Council of Basel, and rejected the Compactata, to which the

UTRAQUISTS (moderate wing of Hussites) had agreed. Utraquist and Catholic Bohemian forces now united against the Taborites, whom they crushed at Lipany (1434). Procopius fell in the battle, as did his ally **Procopuis the Little** (Prokupek), leader of the Orphans, a radical group close to the Taborites.

Procrustes (prōkrŭ'stēz) [Gr.,= stretcher], in Greek legend. He forced guests to lie on either a very long or a very short bed and fitted them to beds either by stretching them or by cutting off their legs.

Procter, Bryan Waller: see CORNWALL, BARRY.

Proctor, town (pop. 1,917), W Vt., NW of Rutland. Vermont Marble Co. was developed here.

prodigal son, parable of Jesus illustrating heaven's welcome of the repentant sinner. Luke 15.11–32.

producer gas, fuel gas consisting chiefly of carbon monoxide and nitrogen (60%). It has low heating value but it can be made with cheap fuel.

progressive education, modern movement, based on idea of learning by doing. Developed in Europe by Froebel, Pestalozzi, and Montessori and in U.S. by F. W. Parker and John Dewey. Postulates are that child learns best in situations involving self-interest, and that modes of behavior are learned most easily by actual performance; hence education must be reconstruction of life experiences directed by child without authoritarian control. Notable experiments in U.S. have been Dewey's project method, used at his Laboratory School in Chicago (1896–1904); Dalton (Mass.) plan (1919), which subdivides traditional curriculum into contract units for individual pupils; and Winnetka (Ill.) plan (1919), which follows Dalton plan but uses cooperative methods and socialized activities. Many conventional schools now add an activities program to supply values of progressive education.

Progressive party, in U.S. history, name of three different political organizations. In 1912 the Republican national convention renominated W. H. TAFT, whereupon supporters of Theodore ROOSEVELT organized Progressive party (Bull Moose party), nominated Roosevelt for President. Progressive platform called for lower tariff, political and social reforms. In the election Roosevelt received 88 electoral and 4,000,000 popular votes, faring better than Taft. Party maintained its organization until 1916, when most Progressives supported Republican ticket. In 1924 another Progressive party nominated R. M. LA FOLLETTE for President. Program, supported by most non-Communist left-wing groups, called for social and economic reforms. La Follette won only 13 electoral votes of Wis., polled nearly 5,000,000 popular votes. Party continued strong in Wis. until 1938, dissolved in 1946. Third Progressive party, organized as challenge to Democratic party, nominated H. A. WALLACE for President in 1948. It was endorsed to some degree by Communist party, which was said by many to control it. Its candidates won no electoral votes, only slightly more than 1,000,000 popular votes.

prohibition, legal method of controlling the manufacture and sale of alcoholic beverages, the extreme of regulatory LIQUOR LAWS. TEMPERANCE MOVEMENTS, especially the ANTI-SALOON LEAGUE and the PROHIBITION PARTY, became increasingly militant in the U.S. during the 19th cent. After World War I, national prohibition became law by the Eighteenth Amendment to the Constitution. In spite of the strict VOLSTEAD ACT, law enforcement proved impossible. It was a period of bootlegging and unparalleled drinking. In 1933, prohibition was repealed by the Twenty-first Amendment. A number of states, counties, and divisions maintain full or partial prohibition under local option.

Prohibition party, in U.S. history, minor political party formed in 1869 primarily for legislative prohibition of the manufacture, transportation, and sale of alcoholic beverages. Since 1872 party has offered candidates in every presidential election. Other reform planks were adopted over the years. Peak of popular support came in 1892 with 271,000 votes. Party split in 1896 over currency issue. Institution of PROHIBITION by Eighteenth Amendment and its later repeal greatly weakened party.

projection or **map projection.** Only a globe can represent earth's surface features correctly with reference to area, shape, scale, and directions. Projection from a globe to flat map causes distortion of some of these characteristics. A grid or net of two intersecting systems of lines corresponding to parallels and meridians must be drawn on plane surface. Some projections (equidistant) aim to keep correct distances in all directions from center of map; other projections show areas (equal-area) or shapes (conformal) equal to those on globe of the same scale. Projections are cylindrical, conical, or azimuthal in geometric origin. Mercator's projection, first published in 1569 and widely used, has parallels and meridians as straight lines, intersecting at right angles, with all parallels as long as the equator; high latitudes are badly distorted. It is of great value in navigation.

Prokofiev, Sergei (Sergeyevich) (syĭrgā'prōkôf'-ēĕf), 1891–1953, Russian composer. His music is often witty and satirical, ranging from the harsh and energetic to the lyrical. Among his compositions are symphonies (including the popular Classical Symphony); concertos for piano and for violin; operas (e.g., *Love for Three Oranges*); orchestral suites (e.g., *Lieutenant Kije*); an orchestral fairy tale, *Peter and the Wolf;* chamber music; and ballets. He toured the U.S. and Europe several times, both as a pianist and as a conductor, but in later years remained in the USSR.

proletariat (prōlůtâ'rēůt), in socialist theory, the class of exploited wage earners who depend on their labor for their existence. In ancient Rome, a proletarian was a citizen without property or assured income. Marxist theory holds that the proletariat must take power from the capitalist class in order to create a classless society.

Prometheus (prōmē'thēůs) [Gr.,= forethought], in Greek religion, a Titan. He gave fire and arts to mankind. Zeus punished him for this by chaining him to a mountain where a vulture devoured his liver. He was freed by Hercules. This is the theme of Aeschylus' *Prometheus Bound*. Shelly wrote *Prometheus Unbound* on theme of mankind's deliverance.

promethium (prōmē'thēŭm), rare metallic element of rare earths (symbol = Pm; see also ELEMENT, table). Its existence was predicted in early 20th cent.; discovery reported in 1926, but definite identification not made until 1945. Illinium was a former name.

prominences: see CHROMOSPHERE.

pronghorn or **prongbuck,** North American hoofed mammal of SW U.S., Mexico. Called antelope but is only living member of different family (Antilocapridae). Usually the back is reddish brown; the under parts, neck bands, and rump patch are white. The horns have a bony core with a horny covering, shed annually.

propaganda (prŏpŭgăn'dŭ) [from Latin *de propaganda fide* = for the propagation of the faith], method of creating an attitude toward some person, organization, or ideal by the influencing of opinion. It may be religious, social, cultural, or political. It may be effected by all media of communication and by the arts. The Congregation of the Propaganda (see CARDINAL) and Protestant missionary boards (see MISSIONS) are disseminators of religious propaganda. All the warring countries found it necessary to estab. departments of propaganda, often called information services. Nazi Germany's was particularly effective. Dissemination of propaganda is one of the chief activities of COMMUNISM.

propagation of plants is commonly effected by seeds and spores. Such vegetative means as CUTTING, layering, root or tuber division, and GRAFTING are also used, especially with plants not breeding true from seed.

Propertius, Sextus (sĕk'stŭs prōpûr'shŭs), c.50 B.C.–c.16 B.C., Roman elegiac poet of the circle of Maecenas. His poems are mostly love lyrics to his mistress, Cynthia.

property, things of economic value to which ownership rights are applicable. Realty (or real estate or real property) is distinguished from personalty (or personal property). Realty is chiefly land and improvements built thereupon. Personal property is chiefly movable objects, whose distribution the owner may determine by WILL, gift, or sale. Realty in medieval society was the basis of wealth and was controlled in many ways to protect society, while ownership of personalty, considered unimportant, was almost unfettered. Gradually, personalty grew to be the economic mainstay of a large class, and the law of realty tended to be assimilated to that of personalty. See PUBLIC OWNERSHIP.

prophet [Gr.,= foreteller], in Bible, religious leader of Israel. The Major Prophets are Isaiah, Jeremiah, Ezekiel, and Daniel. The Minor Prophets are Hosea, Joel, Amos, Obadiah, Jonah, Micah, Nahum, Habbakuk, Zephaniah, Haggai, Zechariah, and Malachi. All have Old Testament books ascribed to them. Title also given to other biblical persons, e.g., Moses, Elijah, Elisha, and Nathan. In the writings of the prophets monotheism receives its most eloquent support. From earliest times they were studied for revelations of the future, especially of the Messiah to come. It is part of traditional Christian belief that the Holy Ghost "spoke through the prophets" (Nicene Creed), who foretold the life and passion of Christ. In New Testament, the term *prophecy* is used of enthusiastic, and presumably inspired, utterance. At times this sort of prophecy has played a dubious role in the history of Christianity, but there have been orthodox Christian preachers and mystics who have spoken and acted like prophets, e.g., St. Vincent Ferrer and St. Catherine of Siena. In some forms of Protestantism prophecy is essential, e.g., Quakerism. Emanuel Swedenborg and Joseph Smith are examples of prophets with a Protestant background. Outside Christianity, Islam recognizes Mohammed as the last and greatest of prophets. Men and women who interpret for a divine power have existed in the religions and cults of the world since ancient times.

proportion, in mathematics, the equality of two ratios. Two pairs of quantities a,b and c,d, are in proportion if their ratios a/b and c/d are equal (i.e., if equation $a/b = c/d$ is true). Product of means (b,c) equals product of extremes (a,d); this rule is result of algebraic operation.

propylaeum (prŏpĭlē'ŭm), in Greek architecture, a monumental roofed entrance to a sacred enclosure or group of buildings. An outstanding example is the **Propylaea,** built (477–432 B.C.) on the Acropolis at Athens by Mnesicles.

Proserpina or **Proserpine:** see PERSEPHONE.

prospecting, the search for mineral deposits suitable for mining. Modern prospecting employs sampling and analysis of deposits; geophysical methods, using the dipping needle (to measure variations in earth's magnetic attraction), torsion balance (to measure variations in gravitational pull), and seismograph; electrical methods, using instruments (galvanometer, potentiometer) to indicate relative conductivity between points on earth; and, in searching for radioactive materials, the Geiger counter. In spotting outcrops of metals airplanes are used.

prostate gland (prŏ'stāt), small muscular and glandular organ in male situated at beginning of urethra and neck of bladder. Its alkaline secretion aids motility of sperm.

prostitution, act of offering oneself for sexual intercourse for mercenary purpose. In ancient times prostitution had religious connotations—intercourse with temple maidens was an act of worship of the temple deity. In the Middle Ages prostitution flourished, but serious efforts were made to control it after an epidemic of venereal disease in the 16th cent. Paris began to register prostitutes in 1785. Cooperation on an international scale to stamp out the white-slave traffic began with a London congress in 1899. The League of Nations set up (1919) a fact-gathering body, and in 1921 a Geneva conference set up a committee whose work was assumed (1946) by the UN. By 1930, 30 countries had no system of licensing houses of prostitution. Until 1945 France registered prostitutes, but in 1946 passed a bill suppressing prostitution. In the U.S. no serious efforts were made to curtail prostitution until the passage (1910) of the Mann Act (forbidding interstate transportation of women for immoral purposes). The May Act (July, 1941) makes it a Federal offense to practice prostitution in designated military neighborhoods. In all states except Ariz. and Nev. it is a crime to keep a house of prostitution.

protactinium (prō″tăktĭ′nēŭm), rare radioactive element (symbol = Pa; see also ELEMENT, table), precursor of actinium. Formerly called protoactinium.

Protagoras (prōtă′gûrŭs), c.480–c.410 B.C., Greek Sophist of Abdera. He taught at Athens but was compelled to flee when charged with agnosticism. He originated the saying, "Man is the measure of all things." One of Plato's dialogues uses his name.

protection, regulation of imports and exports in order to shield domestic industries from foreign competition. The usual method is to impose duties on imports (see CUSTOMS). England abandoned protection for FREE TRADE c.1860, but returned to it between World Wars I and II. The U.S. has always followed a protectionist policy.

protective coloration, color or color pattern of animal affording it protection. Resemblance to features of native habitat is achieved by color similarity supplemented by various effects, e.g., pattern of deepened and softened shades to counteract light and shadow contrasts, irregular color contrasts to distract predatory eye from mass beneath, and dappled and barred patterns to blend with leaves, water, or other features of habitat. Protective coloration includes resemblance and MIMICRY.

Protectorate, in English history, the name given to the English government 1653–59. After civil war (see PURITAN REVOLUTION) the Rump Parliament was ended by OLIVER CROMWELL. The army made him lord protector of commonwealth of England, Ireland, and Scotland, to rule with Parliament of one house. Was virtual dictator. Laws were puritanical, and the army collected taxes. Peace was made in first of Dutch Wars; English sea power used against Spain. Cromwell became hereditary protector after refusing crown in 1657. Resignation of his successor, Richard Cromwell, led to restoration of the monarchy.

proteins (prō′tēĭnz, –tēnz), class of complex substances forming essential part of protoplasm. Their presence in cells and tissue is essential to life—they serve as nitrogen source, aid in tissue building, are source of energy. Most are insoluble in water; those that are soluble form colloidal solutions. Carbon, hydrogen, oxygen, nitrogen are always present; other elements sometimes occur. Molecules are very large and are made up of amino acids; nature of protein depends on nature and number of amino acids in molecule. Simple proteins yield only amino acids or derivatives on hydrolysis; examples are albumins, glutelins, globulins, etc. Conjugated proteins are composed of proteins combined with one or more other compounds; e.g., nucleoproteins, glycoproteins, chromo-proteins, etc. Derived proteins (peptones, proteoses, peptides) are intermediate products of protein decomposition.

Proterozoic era (prŏ″tûrŭzō′ĭk, prō″–), second grand division of geologic time, the Archeozoic being first. The two eras are often called Pre-Cambrian time. Following the Archeozoic there was prolonged erosion, when sediments of the Huronian system were deposited. The Mesabi iron ores (in Minn.) are late Huronian. The Keweenawan was a period of great volcanic activity and was followed by upthrusting of mountains, and later by long erosion. Though many forms of primitive life probably existed, the Proterozoic is poorly represented by fossils. The Pre-Cambrian eras are believed to have lasted c.500 million years each. See also GEOLOGY, table.

Protestant Episcopal Church: see EPISCOPAL CHURCH, PROTESTANT.

Protestantism, religious movement originating with REFORMATION, and principles underlying it. Name Protestant, used in many senses, broadly applies to Christians not belonging to Roman Catholic Church or to an Eastern church. Protestantism embodies conceptions of liberty in secular as well as religious matters, of private judgment and religious toleration, as against tradition and authority. Essence is responsibility of individual to God alone and not to Church. For some major tendencies of Protestantism see ADVENTISTS; ANABAPTISTS; BAPTISTS; CALVINISM; CONGREGATIONALISM; FUNDAMENTALISM; LUTHERANISM; METHODISM; MODERNISM; PRESBYTERIANISM; PURITANISM; UNITARIANISM.

Protestant Union. 1 In German history, defensive alliance of German Protestant states, founded 1608 by Elector Palatine Frederick IV; also known as Evangelical League. It opposed the attempt of the imperial government to impose an exact fulfillment of the Peace of Augsburg of 1555, which provided for restoration of all former church lands appropriated by Protestant princes after 1552. Weak from the start, the Protestant Union never really became operative and went out of existence in 1621. **2** In French history, the alliance (1573–74) of Huguenot cities, districts, and nobles in the Wars of Religion.

Proteus (prō′tēŭs, –tūs), in Greek legend, old man of the sea. Could change into any shape, but if seized and held, he would foretell the future.

Protevangelium of James: see PSEUDEPIGRAPHA.

protoactinium: see PROTACTINIUM.

protocol (prō′tûkŏl), diplomatic term referring usually to a more or less informal written document. Examples are the minutes of international conferences, preliminary agreements which lead to a treaty, and agreements which do not need ratification. Diplomatic protocol is the code of courtesy governing conduct of diplomatic service. Term is sometimes applied to agreement similar to a treaty. Thus, the Geneva Protocol of 1924, adopted by the League of Nations, made aggressive warfare an international crime. British refusal to adhere to it kept the protocol from coming into force.

Protogenes (prōtŏ'jůnēz), fl. c.300 B.C., Greek painter, considered second only to Apelles by the ancients. His works included decorations for the Propylaea, Athens.

proton, term for single positive (+) unit charge of electricity believed to form nucleus of hydrogen ATOM. Hydrogen ion or proton is believed to be fundamental positively charged unit of the atom. See *ill.*, p. 989.

protoplasm (prō'tůplăzům), fundamental material of which all living things are composed. It exists in all living plants and animals in units called cells, and is enclosed by thin surface (called plasma membrane) which controls passage of materials in and out of cell. Protoplasm is composed of water (70–90% by weight), protein (c.15%), fatty substances (c.3%), carbohydrates (less than 1%), and inorganic salts (c.1%). The elements carbon, oxygen, hydrogen, and nitrogen make up c.99% of protoplasm; sulphur, phosphorus, potassium, iron, and magnesium are also present. In both plant and animal cells the protoplasm consists of a more dense portion forming the nucleus (rounded or ovoid) and a less dense portion, the cytoplasm (this forms bulk of cell in animal cells and in plant cells is usually found in rather thin layers or strands). Since it is living material, protoplasm exhibits the properties associated with life, i.e., capacity to respond to environmental influences and ability to perform physiological functions. See *ill.*, p. 813.

Protopopov, Aleksandr Dmitreyevich (ŭlyĭksän'důr důmē'trēůvĭch prŭtůpô'půf), 1866–1918, Russian landowner and statesman. A trusted friend of Nicholas II and of Rasputin and an extreme reactionary, he was minister of the interior from 1916 until his fall in February Revolution of 1917. He was executed.

protozoa (prōtůzō'ů), phylum of microscopic one-celled animals. Most are solitary, a few are colonial. Majority are aquatic species of salt and fresh water, found on surface and at great depths, at sea level and high altitudes; some live in damp sand and moss. Many are parasitic. Phylum is usually divided into four classes: Sarcodina, Mastigophora, Infusoria, and Sporozoa. Reproduction in various forms is by fission, conjugation, budding, and spore formation. See also AMOEBA and FORAMINIFERA. See *ill.*, p. 813.

Proudhon, Pierre Joseph (pyĕr' zhôzĕf' prōōdō'), 1809–65, French social theorist. He achieved prominence through his pamphlet, *What Is Property?* (1840; Eng. tr., 1876), a condemnation of the abuses of private property. He sought a society of loosely federated groups, in which the government might become unnecessary. He believed in the moral responsibility of the individual rather than in any system authoritatively imposed.

Proust, Joseph Louis (zhôzĕf' lwē' prōōst'), 1754–1826, French chemist. He discovered grape sugar. Was establisher of law of definite proportions (Proust's law) which states that in any compound the elements are present in a fixed proportion by weight.

Proust, Marcel (märsĕl' prōōst'), 1871–1922, French novelist. As a youth he sought the company of fashionable and intellectual society, but after 1905 he retired almost completely and began work on his semi-autobiographical cyclic novel *À la recherche du temps perdu* (16 vols., 1913–27; Eng. tr., *Remembrance of Things Past*, 1922–32). His complicated style seeks by total recall to recapture the minutest psychological and sensory detail, and his work succeeds in recreating a past society with the illusion of complete objectiveness. His influence on later novelists is incalculable.

Prout, William, 1785–1850, English chemist and physician. He demonstrated presence of free hydrochloric acid in gastric juice. Prout's hypothesis: atomic weights of elements are multiples of that of hydrogen and elements are formed by condensation or grouping of hydrogen atoms.

Prouts Neck, Maine: see SCARBORO.

Provençal (prôvăsäl'), *langue d'oc* dialect of SE France. A Romance language (see LANGUAGE, table) developed by troubadours of Provence, it became the standard literary idiom of S France in the Middle Ages. It enjoyed a literary revival commencing in mid-19th cent., and a group of seven poets, including Frédéric Mistral, formed the Felibrige to introduce standard Provençal, but French remains the standard language.

Provence (prôvăs'), former province, SE France, in Var, Bouches-du-Rhône, Vaucluse, Basses-Alpes, and Alpes-Maritimes depts. Chief cities: MARSEILLES, NICE, TOULON, AVIGNON, AIX-EN-PROVENCE, ARLES. Region borders on Mediterranean in S (see RIVIERA), on Rhone R. (W), and on Italy (E). Rhone valley and S slopes of Maritime Alps produce wine, silk, fruits, olives, flowers, vegetables. Cattle raising (esp. on CAMARGUE). Interior is rugged and largely unproductive. Large tourist trade. Coast was settled after 600 B.C. by Greeks and Phoenicians. Romans estab. colonies 2d cent. B.C. and made the region their first transalpine province (hence its name). Provence fell to the Visigoths (5th cent. A.D.), the Franks (6th cent.), and, briefly, to the Arabs (8th cent.). In 879 Count Boso of Arles estab. the kingdom of Provence, which in 933 was joined with Transjurane Burgundy to form the kingdom of ARLES. The county of Provence, which later emerged as a nominal fief of the Holy Roman Empire, passed by marriage from the house of Aragon to the ANGEVIN dynasty of Naples (1246). After the Angevins' extinction it fell to the French crown (1486). ORANGE was added 1672; Avignon and the Comtat VENAISSIN 1791; Nice and Menton 1860.

Proverbs, book of Old Testament. It is a collection of sayings, many of them moral maxims, mostly ascribed by tradition to Solomon. Book is an early example of wisdom literature popular among Jews of post-exilic times (see WISDOM).

Providence, city (pop. 248,674), state cap., NE R.I., on harbor receiving Seekonk and other rivers at head of Providence R., arm of Narragansett Bay. Largest city in R.I. Port and industrial center noted for silverware (since 1831) and jewelry; mfg. also of textiles, machine tools, hardware, watches, oil products, chemicals, plastics. Roger WIL-

LIAMS secured title to site from Narragansett chiefs after his exile from Mass. 1636; named it in gratitude for "God's merciful providence." Prosperity came with 18th-cent. foreign trade. After Revolution the Brown brothers played leading role in town's growth and industrial development. Became sole state cap. in 1900 (Newport had been joint cap.). Has many historic structures—e.g., old colony house or statehouse (1762), old market house (1773)—and Roger Williams Park (over 450 acres). Seat of BROWN UNIVERSITY, Providence Col. (R.C., Dominican; for men; 1919), R.I. School of Design (1877).

Provincetown, town (pop. 3,795), SE Mass., on N Cape Cod, on harbor on Cape Cod Bay; Pilgrims landed here 1620; permanently settled c.1700. Has Pilgrim Memorial (1910). Whaling, saltmaking, rumrunning, smuggling were once important. Fishing is still staple industry, but town gained fame as resort (esp. for artists) in 20th cent. Provincetown Players pioneered in Little Theater movement.

Province Wellesley, Malaya: see PENANG.

Provisions of Oxford, 1258, a scheme of governmental reform forced upon Henry III of England by his barons. Drawn up by Simon de Montfort, it provided for an advisory council and tried to limit taxing power. Repudiation (1261) of the agreement by King Henry III led to Barons' War (1263–67).

Provo (prō'vō), city (pop. 28,937), N central Utah, on Provo R. near Utah L., at base of Wasatch Range and SSE of Salt Lake City; settled 1849 by Mormons. Grew as shipping center of mining (silver, lead, copper, gold) and agr. area. Now a rail, trade, industrial hub. Water supply supplemented by Provo R. project. Large steel plant at near-by Geneva. Seat of BRIGHAM YOUNG UNIVERSITY. Provo Peak (11,054 ft.) and Mt. Timpanogos (12,008 ft.) are near.

Provo, river rising in NE Utah in Uinta Mts. and flowing c.70 mi. SW, past Provo, to Utah L. Project begun in 1930s to rehabilitate and expand early irrigation facilities. Water from the Weber (via canal) and the Duchesne (via mountain tunnel) feeds into Provo R. to irrigate Utah Valley and supply local towns and Salt Lake City (via 41-mi. Salt Lake Aqueduct).

Provoost, Samuel (prō'vōst), 1742–1815, first Episcopal bishop of N.Y. after 1786; chaplain to Continental Congress (1785) and U.S. Senate (1789).

Prud'hon, Pierre Paul (prüdō'), 1758–1823, French painter. Noted for subtle use of light and shade. Portrait of Empress Josephine is in the Louvre.

prune, a dried PLUM, especially varieties of *Prunus domestica*. After falling from tree, plums are dipped in lye solution to prevent fermentation and are then dried in the sun or in kilns.

pruning, removing parts of plants, especially woody ones, to increase flower or fruit production or to control shape or dimensions. It is also practiced to prolong a plant's survival by cutting off diseased portions or to induce vigorous branching growth. Pruning roots and top parts proportionately is done when trees and shrubs are transplanted. There is no set rule for the best time of year to prune plants.

Prussia (prŭ'shŭ), Ger. *Preussen,* former German state (113,410 sq. mi.; 1933 pop. 39,934,011); cap. Berlin. It occupied, roughly, the N half of GERMANY, with nearly two thirds of the total German population, and led Germany politically and economically. Its historic roots were the electorate of BRANDENBURG and the duchy of Prussia, united as a kingdom in 1701 under the HOHENZOLLERN dynasty. Originally, Prussia was the region along the Baltic Sea between the Niemen and Vistula rivers—i.e., the later EAST PRUSSIA. Its pagan population (of the Baltic language group) was largely exterminated in the 13th cent. by the TEUTONIC KNIGHTS, who made Prussia their domain. In 1525 their grand master ALBERT OF BRANDENBURG embraced Protestantism and transformed the domain into a hereditary duchy under Polish overlordship. The duchy passed, by inheritance, to the electors of Brandenburg (1618), who shook off Polish overlordship in 1660. In 1701 Elector Frederick III had himself crowned king of Prussia as Frederick I. Under his successors FREDERICK WILLIAM I and FREDERICK II (the Great), Prussia rose to a European power and threatened Austrian leadership in Germany. In the War of the AUSTRIAN SUCCESSION (1740–48) Prussia won most of SILESIA; in the SEVEN YEARS WAR (1756–63) it defeated a formidable coalition; in the Polish partitions (1772, 1793, 1795) it gained WEST PRUSSIA prov. and W Poland. The reigns (1786–1840) of Frederick William II and Frederick William III saw the French Revolutionary and Napoleonic Wars. Defeated, Prussia withdrew from the First Coalition against France in 1795 but joined the Third Coalition in 1806, was routed at Jena, and accepted the harsh Treaty of TILSIT (1807). Yet, at the same time, under the leadership of Freiherr vom STEIN, K. A. von HARDENBERG, Wilhelm von HUMBOLDT, and SCHARNHORST, a series of drastic social, cultural, and military reforms prepared the rebirth of Prussian greatness. Joining the allies in 1813, Prussian forces under BLÜCHER were decisive in Napoleon's defeat. The Congress of Vienna (1814–15) gave Prussia the RHINE PROVINCE, WESTPHALIA, half of SAXONY, Swedish POMERANIA, West Prussia, and W Poland (incl. Poznan). In the GERMAN CONFEDERATION Prussia was overshadowed by Metternich's Austria, but it led in forming the ZOLLVEREIN. FREDERICK WILLIAM IV put down the Revolution of 1848 and yielded to Austria in the Treaty of OLMÜTZ (1850). WILLIAM I, his successor, entrusted the government to BISMARCK, who brought Prussia to its ultimate triumph. The war on Denmark (1864; see SCHLESWIG-HOLSTEIN) served as prelude to the AUSTRO-PRUSSIAN WAR of 1866, which excluded Austria from German affairs, brought Schleswig-Holstein, HANOVER, Electoral HESSE, NASSAU, and FRANKFURT to Prussia, and resulted in creation of the NORTH GERMAN CONFEDERATION. The FRANKO-PRUSSIAN WAR led to the formation of a German Empire, with the king of Prussia as emperor (1871). The history of Prussia became essentially that of Germany. Prussia retained its constitution of 1850, which reserved the vote to the propertied classes, until the overthrow of the monarchy in 1918; it joined the Weimar Republic in 1919. As a result of World War I it lost most of West Prussia, Prussian Poland, and parts of Silesia to Poland (temporarily reannexed 1939–45). After World War II, Prussia was redivided into several new states (see GERMANY). It was formally dissolved by the Allied Control Council in 1947.

Prussian blue, pigment used for laundry bluing, dyeing, making inks and paints.

prussic acid: see HYDROCYANIC ACID.

Pruth or **Prut** (pro͞ot), river 530 mi. long, USSR and Rumania, rising in Carpathians and flowing generally SE (forming border between Moldavian SSR and Rumania) into the Danube at Galati. By the Peace of the Pruth (1711) Peter I of Russia restored Azov to the Turks.

Prynne, William (prĭn), 1600–1669, English political figure and pamphleteer, an extreme Puritan. Imprisoned (1634), he was released (1640) by Long Parliament. Opposed Presbyterians, Independents; disputed with John Milton. Expelled from Parliament in Pride's Purge, he attacked the Commonwealth and was imprisoned (1650–53). Worked for Stuart cause.

Przhevalsky, Nikolai Mikhailovich (pûrzhĭväl'skē), 1839–88, Russian explorer in Asia. First Westerner to explore systematically mountainous region of W China and E Tibet. Credited with discovering Lob Nor and Altyn Tagh range.

Przhevalsky's horse: see TARPAN.

Przybyszewski, Stanislaus (pshĭbĭshĕf'skē), 1868–1927, Polish author. Wrote in Polish and German. His philosophy repudiates reason, exalts intuition. His works include the drama *For Happiness* (1912; Eng. tr., 1912) and the novel *Homo Sapiens* (1898; Eng. tr., 1915).

Psalmanazar, George (săl"mûnā'zûr), 1679?–1763, English literary impostor, whose real name is unknown. He posed as Formosan Christian convert and wrote fraudulent books on Formosa. Exposed and disgraced in 1706.

Psalms (sämz) or **Psalter** (sôl'tûr), book of Old Testament, a collection of 150 poetic pieces, the hymnal par excellence of Judaism and Christendom. Many of the poems traditionally ascribed to David. Different versions vary in dividing individual psalms, thus making citation of number and verse confusing. Hebrew, AV, and RV texts use one numbering; other versions, such as Douay, use another, as follows: AV Pss. 1–8 = Douay 1–8; AV 9–10 = Douay 9; AV 11–113 = Douay 10–112; AV 114–115 = Douay 113; AV 116 = Douay 114–115; AV 117–146 = Douay 116–145; AV 147 = Douay 146–147; AV 148–150 = Douay 148–150. The poems vary in tone and subject. Some are called penitential psalms, e.g., 51 (called, from opening word in Latin, Miserere), 130 (De profundis). Others express the poet's awareness of the presence of God, e.g., 23. (Numbers cited above are those of AV.) The Psalms have been translated into more languages and into greater varieties of form than any other part of the Old Testament.

Psalms of Solomon: see PSEUDEPIGRAPHA.

Psalter: see PSALMS.

Psaltery: see STRINGED INSTRUMENTS.

Psamtik (säm'tĭk, săm'–), d. 609 B.C., king of anc. Egypt (663–609 B.C.), founder of the XXVI dynasty; son of Necho, lord of Saïs. Viceroy of Lower Egypt under Assur-banipal, he shook off the Assyrian yoke and became master of the whole country. His son was the Pharaoh Necho.

pseudepigrapha (sū"dĭpĭ'grûfû) [Gr.,= things falsely ascribed], uncanonical writings of a biblical type, usually of spurious date and authorship. Pseudepigrapha of Jewish origin were composed 200 B.C.–A.D. 200. They are usually named after some great Hebrew leader or seer to give them an air of authenticity and are generally apocalyptic in nature, describing the Day of Judgment and foretelling the coming of the Messiah. Other books are romantic embroideries of biblical stories and religious histories of the world. Among Jewish pseudepigrapha are: the Ethiopic Book of Enoch; the Secrets of Enoch; the Testaments of the Twelve Patriarchs (i. e., the sons of Jacob); the Assumption of Moses; the Sibylline Oracles; the Apocalypse of Baruch; Books of Adam and Eve, Joseph and Asenath, Jannes and Jambres; the Psalms of Solomon; the Book of Jubilees or Little Genesis; the Book of Biblical Antiquities; and 3, 4, and 5 Maccabees. Three pseudepigrapha are placed in the APOCRYPHA of AV: 3 and 4 Esdras and the Prayer of Manasses. Christian pseudepigrapha were composed A.D. 50–A.D. 400. Many of them were written to support various heresies, or, in sincere but misguided piety, to surround the life story of Jesus with glamorous legend. Nearly all the apostles have apocalypses, gospels, and acts ascribed to them. Some roughly follow canonical writings; others contain accounts of alleged miracles of a sensational and even violent nature and attribute fantastic words and deeds to Jesus, Mary, and others. Among these many books are: the Apocalypse of Peter; the Shepherd of Hermas; the Ascension of Isaiah; the Gospel of Nicodemus (containing the Acts of Pilate and the Harrowing of Hell); Gospels according to the Hebrews, the Egyptians, Thomas, Judas Iscariot, and the Twelve; the Protevangelium of James; the Arabic Gospel of the Infancy of Jesus; and spurious epistles ascribed to Jesus (Epistles of Abgar), Barnabas, Paul, Clement, Ignatius, and others. Certain other epistles of Ignatius, Clement, and Polycarp are considered genuine (actually written by these men) but not canonical (of divine inspiration). Probably genuine are the DIDACHE and Apostolic CONSTITUTIONS. For canonical writings, see OLD TESTAMENT; NEW TESTAMENT.

Pseudo-Dionysius: see DIONYSIUS THE AREOPAGITE, SAINT.

psittacosis (sĭtûkō'sĭs) or **parrot fever,** contagious disease of certain birds (esp. parrot family) probably caused by virus. Transmissible to man.

Pskov (pu̇skôf′), city (pop. 59,898), W European RSFSR, near S end of L. Pskov (sometimes considered S part of L. PEIPUS). Machinery and linen mfg. One of oldest Russian cities, it became (14th cent.) a democratic city-state and flourishing commercial center. Annexed by Moscow 1510. Scene of Nicholas II's abdication (1917). Damaged in World War II. Inner walled city contains famous kremlin (12th–16th cent.).

Psyche (sī′kē), [Gr.,= breath, soul, spirit], in Greek literature, personification of human soul. Legend says Cupid (or Eros) loved her but forbade her to look at him. When she disobeyed, he left her, but she became immortal and was united with him forever.

psychiatry (su̇kī′u̇trē, sī–), branch of medicine dealing with diagnosis and treatment of mental disorders. Organized attempt to study or treat mental ills, to improve institutional conditions, began with Philippe PINEL. Humanitarian reformers of 19th cent. fought for legislation (see MENTAL HYGIENE) while scientists sought underlying causes of mental and nervous disorders. Emil Kraepelin was first to delineate PSYCHOSIS; FREUD turned attention to patient's behavior and emotional history, initiated PSYCHOANALYSIS. SHOCK THERAPY, PSYCHOTHERAPY, new methods of psychosurgery, PSYCHOSOMATIC MEDICINE, are used to treat mental and some apparently physical ills.

psychical research or **parapsychology,** study of mental phenomena not explainable by accepted principles of science. Society for Psychical Research, founded 1882 in London, first used the scientific method for this study, dissociating psychical phenomena from spiritualism and superstition and making careful investigations of mediums. Best known work done by American Society for Psychical Research is that of J. B. Rhine of Duke Univ. in extrasensory perception and in psychokinesis (mental influence over matter). Increasing interest in psychical research is shown by fellowships at Cambridge and Harvard and laboratory at Univ. of Gröningen.

psychoanalysis (sī′kōu̇nă′lu̇sĭs), name given by Freud to a system of psychopathology and therapeutic procedure for treating NEUROSIS. FREUD saw the UNCONSCIOUS as dynamic, an area of great psychic activity affecting all action but operating from repressed material that resists recall. Therefore he made conscious recognition of forgotten scenes, especially by free association, the basis of therapy; dreams were also a key to the unconscious. Therapy also depended on transference. Freud and his followers introduced a vast body of theory, with emphasis on two oppositional instincts—the destructive (aggressive or hostile) death instinct and the constructive sexual instinct. An idea adjustment neutralizes the overt primitive expression of each, but damming up of instinctual energies is a factor in causing neurosis. Freud believed that in the emotionally mature person much of the libidinal energy could be deflected by sublimation from its unconscious sexual aim to nonsexual, socially useful goals. Psychoanalysts believe that the ego has available, besides repression and sublimation, other means (see DEFENSE MECHANISM) of protecting itself against the demands of the id (the reservoir, deep in the mind, of instinctual drives). After 1906 Freud was joined by others, among them JUNG and Alfred ADLER, both of whom later parted from him. In the 1920s Freudian psychoanalysis was challenged by Otto RANK, Sandor Ferenczi, Wilhelm Reich; in the 1930s by Karen HORNEY, Erich Fromm, and H. S. SULLIVAN, a group emphasizing social and cultural factors in neurosis and, in therapy, stressing the interpersonal aspect of the analyst-patient relationship.

psychology, the science of the mind. Psychologists do not agree upon any one definition of mind, some considering it almost synonymous with soul and therefore a thing apart from the body, others tying mind closely with brain, making each a function of the other. Generally modern psychology is defined as the science that studies all interactions between living organisms and environment, thus avoiding the mechanistic approach of strict behaviorism as well as the extreme idealism of philosophy. Although psychology is close to the biological, physical, and social sciences, it remains a specific science since no complete explanation of individual behavior can be given solely in the terms of any other one science. Its important concepts (i.e., of emotions, instincts, consciousness, and the intelligence) are therefore described in terms of their relationship to the behavior of the individual as a whole. Aristotle's *De anima* is considered the first great psychological work. Modern psychology grew from work of Hobbes (17th cent.). Emphasis in the 19th cent. on experimental methods led to the work of J. M. Charcot and Pierre Janet; the theory of evolution led to dynamic psychology, as of William James. Sigmund Freud laid the basis of PSYCHOANALYSIS and widened the scope of psychology. GESTALT psychology and BEHAVIORISM greatly influenced 20th-cent. thought. Applied psychology is adapted to industry and commerce.

psychoneurosis: see NEUROSIS.

psychosis (sīkō′sĭs), mental disease involving emotional disturbances that prevent realistic adjustment to environment. Symptoms may include hallucinations, delusions, severe deviation of mood, lack or inappropriateness of apparent emotional response, severe distortion of judgment. The term INSANITY is applied to those psychoses where moral judgment is considered impaired. Organic psychoses are caused by structural damage of brain; functional psychoses show no observable organic damage. Psychoanalysts emphasize the role of emotional conflicts. New techniques of psychosurgery and SHOCK THERAPY are useful in treating certain psychoses.

psychosomatic medicine (sī″kōsōmă′tĭk) treats emotional disturbances, often unconscious, manifested as physical disorders. Treatment usually involves a medical regimen and some PSYCHOTHERAPY. Freud's theories, Adolf Meyer's psychobiology, W. B. Cannon's research on physiological effects of acute emotion, were reinforced psychosomatics. Stomach ulcer, heart diseases, rheumatics, asthma, endocrine disorders, are sometimes treated by psychosomatics.

psychotherapy, treatment of mental disorders by psychological methods. Freudian psychoanalysis was the first systematized form. When this seems inadvisable or unwarranted, direction, support, suggestion, and often occupational therapy, are used to help patients function more efficiently without awareness of unconscious motives of behavior.

psyllium seed: see PLANTAIN.

Pt, chemical symbol of the element PLATINUM.

ptarmigan (tär'mĭgůn), northen game bird of grouse family. The legs are almost completely feathered. Seasonal changes in plumage result in protective coloration all year.

pterodactyl (tĕrůdăk'tĭl), extinct flying reptile of the Mesozoic, not related to birds or mammals. Pterodactyls ranged in size from very small up to a flying dragon with wingspread of more than 20 ft.

Ptolemy (tŏ'lůmē), kings of the Macedonian, Lagid, or XXXI dynasty of anc. Egypt. **Ptolemy I** (Soter), d. 283 B.C., was a general of Alexander the Great and in the wars of the DIADOCHI estab. himself as king of Egypt (304 B.C.), the defeat of Antigonus making his position firm. Founded the library at Alexandria. His son, **Ptolemy II** (Philadelphus), c.308–246? B.C., reigned 283?–246? B.C. Warred against Antiochus II of Syria until he married his daughter Berenice to Antiochus. Helped Rome in the First Punic War. His son, **Potolemy III** (Euergetes), d. 222? B.C., reigned 246?–222? B.C. Plunged into war with Syria to aid his sister Berenice, but she and her son were murdered before he arrived. Controlled coasts of Asia Minor and E Greece. His son, **Ptolemy IV** (Philopator), d. 204? B.C., reigned 222?–204? B.C. Defeated Antiochus III at Raphia (217) but saw Egyptian administration decline. It declined even more under his son, **Ptolemy V** (Epiphanes), d. 181? B.C., who reigned 204?–181? B.C. Civil wars and invasions weakened Egypt. His son, **Ptolemy VI** (Philometor), d. 145 B.C., reigned 181?–145 B.C., but was first under the regency of his mother, Cleopatra, then was forced after defeat by Antiochus IV of Syria (170 B.C.) to share the reign with his wife, Cleopatra (also his sister), and his brother **Ptolemy VII** (Physcon), d. 117? B.C., who reigned alone after 145. He had his nephew put to death and married his sister-in-law (also his sister), Cleopatra, whom he repudiated to marry her daughter, also Cleopatra. The elder Cleopatra briefly drove him from the throne. His son, **Ptolemy VIII** (Lathyrus), d. 81 B.C., reigned 117?–107, 89–81 B.C. His mother, the younger Cleopatra, made him accept as coruler his brother, **Ptolemy IX** (Alexander), d. 89? B.C., who drove his brother from the throne in 107. He was defeated by a revolt in Alexandria (89 B.C.). His son, **Ptolemy X** (Alexander), d. 80 B.C., under Roman pressure married his stepmother Cleopatra Berenice (daughter of Ptolemy VIII). He ruled jointly with her, then murdered her and was in turn killed by the angry Alexandrians. **Ptolemy XI** (Auletes), d. 51 B.C., was the illegitimate son of Ptolemy VIII. He succeeded Ptolemy X, was ousted by the Alexandrians (58 B.C.), but got Roman aid of Pompey and Aulus Gabinius (to whom he paid vast sums) and was restored in 55 B.C. He made the Roman senate executor of his will and Pompey guardian of his elder son, **Ptolemy XII,** 61?–47 B.C., who was overshadowed by his wife and sister, the famous Cleopatra. Trouble arose, and Ptolemy was defeated. After he drowned in the Nile, Cleopatra married her younger brother, **Ptolemy XIII,** d. 44 B.C. He was joint ruler with her until she had him murdered. **Ptolemy XIV** (Caesarion), 47–30 B.C., was the son of Cleopatra and (almost certainly) Julius Caesar. He was joint ruler with his mother. After she and Antony met defeat, Octavian (Augustus) had Caesarion put to death.

Ptolemy (Claudius Ptolemaeus), fl. 127 to 141 or 151, Greco-Egyptian astronomer, mathematician, and geographer. He systematized, recorded, and added to data and doctrines known to Alexandrian scientists. His *Almagest,* widely translated and influential in Europe until superseded by findings of Copernicus, presented Ptolemaic system of astronomy, based chiefly on concepts of Hipparchus, which represented spherical earth as stationary center of universe, with sun and other heavenly bodies revolving about it.

ptomaine poisoning: see FOOD POISONING.

public health, field of medicine and hygiene dealing with disease prevention and health promotion. Activities are carried on chiefly by federal, state, and local public health and education services and by private agencies. Public health work includes regulation of sanitation and communicable diseases (see SOCIAL HYGIENE); collection of vital statistics; promotion of health education, school and industrial hygiene, and maternal and child health.

public land, in U.S. history, land owned by Federal government but not reserved for any special purpose, e.g., for a park. Settlement was encouraged by selling tracts of 160 acres or more (see HOMESTEAD ACT). Vast tracts were given railroads and land-grant colleges. To insure CONSERVATION OF NATURAL RESOURCES public lands were withdrawn from sale in late 19th cent. In New Deal period public domain was increased by purchase of barren lands. Public land sometimes called land in public domain, term also applied to products or operations on which copyright or patent protection has lapsed or was not taken out.

public ownership, government ownership of lands, streets, utilities, and other enterprises. The theory that all land and resources belong to the people and therefore to the government is very ancient and from it comes the doctrine of eminent domain. Until the policy of laissez faire in the 18th cent. emphasized capitalistic activity, public ownership was unquestioned. Public ownership is to be distinguished from government control of private enterprises. Examples of U.S. public ownership are the Panama Canal, the atomic energy development, and TVA.

Public Works Administration (PWA), government organ estab. 1933 by U.S. Congress as Federal Administration of Public Works.

Administered construction of various public works, made loans to states and municipalities for similar projects. H. L. Ickes headed it 1933–39. Virtually liquidated by Jan. 1, 1947.

publishing, in the broadest sense, making some information publicly known; generally as the term is used today, the issuing of printed materials (books, pamphlets, periodicals, and the like). Publishing is not easily distinguished from the allied occupations of printing and bookselling, since these all may overlap. Properly, publishing may be said to be primarily the service of preparing the work of an author in the most suitable form and presenting it in the most efficient manner to the widest possible audience for that particular work (through dealers or directly). The dissemination of books in manuscript form and for sale was known in ancient Greece and was an organized business in the Roman Empire. In the Middle Ages manuscript reproduction was wholly in the hands of the monks, and publication as such ceased. It was revived somewhat in the Renaissance, but it was only with the introduction into Europe of movable TYPE in the middle of the 15th cent. that large-scale reproduction of written material was possible. Printing spread rapidly, its growth encouraged somewhat by the religious quarrels following the Reformation, when polemical works were numerous. The beginning of separation of publishing from printing appeared early. It is commonly said that the first great publishing house was that of the Elzevir family, which began publishing books in 1583. The true distinction between printer, publisher, and seller of printed materials did not, however, become sharp until the 19th cent., and in many cases the lines between them are still blurred.

Puccini, Giacomo (jä'kōmō po͞ot-chē'nē), 1858–1924, Italian operatic composer. His outstanding operas are *Manon Lescaut* (1893); *La Bohème* (1896); *La Tosca* (1900); *Madame Butterfly* (1904); *Turandot* (completed by Franco Alfano); and *The Girl of the Golden West* (1910), based on Belasco's play.

Puck (pŭk), in Germanic folklore, generic name for a minor order of devils, sprites, goblins, or demons. In *Piers Plowman* the name (spelled *pouke*) signifies the devil. Shakspere was first to identify Puck as a merry attractive elf.

Puebla (pwā'blä), state (13,126 sq. mi.; pop. 1,595,920), E central Mexico. Extremely mountainous with Sierra Madre Oriental in N and volcanic belt across center, with three highest peaks of Mexico—Orizaba, Popocatepetl, and Ixtacihuatl—on its borders. NE section is on humid coastal plain of Gulf of Mexico. Agr., stock raising, and mining are important. **Puebla,** the capital (pop. 138,491), is commercial center of state. Founded 1535, it is today noted for cotton mills, onyx quarries, pottery, fine tiles. Cathedral, constructed between 1552 and 1649, is one of finest in Mexico.

Pueblo (pwĕ'blō, pūĕ'blō), city (pop. 63,685), S central Colo., on Arkansas R. (levee-controlled) in foothills of the Rockies. Z. M. Pike visited area in 1806. Here were a trading post (1842) and a Mormon settlement (1846–47). Pueblo City laid out 1860. Second largest city in Colo., it is a shipping and industrial center for livestock and irrigated farm area. Mfg. of many metal products and building materials, oil refining, and meat packing.

Pueblo Indians, North American people, in SW U.S., living in stone or adobe community houses, comprising villages called pueblos. Their ancestors came into this area, succeeding the BASKET MAKERS, who had already developed agr. The newcomers advanced in civilization but later had to retreat from predatory tribes and became CLIFF DWELLERS. This period ended A.D. c.1300 after a severe drought and invasions of the Navaho and the Apache. The Pueblos had by the time of the Spanish conquest of Mexico developed the highest Indian civilization N of Mexico, and the Zuni pueblos were apparently the originals of the mythical Seven Cities of Cibola that attracted Spanish interest. Coronado's party in 1540 began Spanish penetration; missions were founded by 1580 and Spanish colonies in 1598. The Pueblos were hostile and finally in 1680 rose and drove the Spanish out. In 1692 the Spanish reconquered the territory, and since that time the Pueblos have generally lived in peace. They are noted for rich, polychrome pottery, for baskets, and for textiles. Their public religious ceremonies attract tourists annually. They are divided into four linguistic families—Tanoan (11 pueblos, incl. Taos, Isleta, Jemez, San Juan, San Ildefonso, and the Hopi pueblo of Hano), Western Keresan (Acoma and Laguna), Eastern Keresan (San Felipe, Santa Ana, Sia, Cochiti, and Santo Domingo), and Hopi.

puerperal fever (pūûr'pûrŭl), acute disease of genital tract caused by septic infection contracted during childbirth, usually from failure to use aseptic methods. Early advocates of prevention by cleanliness include Semmelweis and Oliver Wendell Holmes.

Puerto Montt (pwĕr'tō mōnt'), city (pop. 18,688), S central Chile, port on the Pacific; founded 1853. S terminus of railroad and starting point for navigation through inland waterways. Near-by hills, lakes, and fjords make city a popular resort. Sheep raising and fishing are major commercial activities.

Puerto Rico (pwĕr'tō rē'kō), formerly Porto Rico, island (3,425 sq. mi.; pop. 2,210,703), smallest and most easterly of Greater Antilles, in West Indies. It is coextensive with the Commonwealth of Puerto Rico; cap. and largest city, SAN JUAN. Other important cities are Ponce and Mayagüez. The island is crossed by mountain ranges and has short rivers, unnavigable but useful for irrigation and hydroelectric power. The climate is mildly tropical; the fertile soil supports one of the densest populations of a purely agr. area in the world. Sugar is its major product, but the Puerto Rican government is working out a program of diversification (coffee, tobacco, tropical fruits, winter vegetables) in order to help solve the economic problems caused by a one-crop economy. Processing of sugar (mills, refineries, distilleries) is the main industry. Puerto Rican needlework is distinctive and popular in U.S. The people are descended from Spanish colonists, with an admixture of Indian and African strains. The language is Spanish, the religion predominantly Roman Catholic. The island, called by the natives Boriquén or Borinquén, was visited by Columbus in 1493. It was first settled by Ponce de León in 1508. Caparra, the first settlement, was replaced by San Juan, 4 mi. away, in 1521. The Indians—of Arawak stock—were soon wiped out, and Negro slaves were imported to work on plantations (slavery was abolished in 1873). In 1898, during the Spanish-American War, U.S. troops landed; with little difficulty, military occupation was accomplished. In the Treaty of Paris, Puerto Rico was ceded outright to U.S. There has been a progressive development toward self-rule in the island; now the governor is elected by the people (Luis Muñoz Marín was the first, 1948), there is an elected commissioner in U.S. Congress, and the Puerto Ricans have U.S. citizenship. In 1952, it ceased to be a colonial possession and became a "Free Commonwealth" and the way lay open for statehood in the U.S. Health and sanitary conditions and educational facilities have improved with U.S. occupation, but a one-crop economy, absentee ownership, and overpopulation still plague the island. Emigration to continental U.S. became very heavy after World War II.

Puerto Rico, University of, mainly at Río Piedras, near San Juan; coed.; founded 1903. Agr. and mechanical college at Mayagüez, school of tropical medicine at San Juan.

Pueyrredón, Juan Martín de (hwän' märtēn' dā pwāīrādōn'), 1776–1850, Argentine general, supreme director of United Provs. of La Plata (1816–19). With Liniers resisted invasion of Buenos Aires by British (1806). Took important part in revolutionary government (1810–18). When unitarian constitution was rejected, Pueyrredón resigned.

Pufendorf, Samuel, Freiherr von (po͞o'fůndôrf), 1632–94, German jurist and historian, writer on international law. He considered the law of nations a part of natural rights. Wrote *Elementa jurisprudentiae universalis* (1661) and *De jure naturae et gentium* (1672). Also wrote a historical work on the Holy Roman Empire.

puffball or **smokeball,** fungus with a globular spore-bearing body, usually stalkless, common in meadows and woods. None are poisonous and most are edible when young. When mature, they emit their dustlike spores like puffs of smoke.

puffin, swimming and diving bird of N Atlantic, N Pacific, and arctic regions, related to auk. It has short legs, a dumpy body, and large bill.

Pugachev, Yemelyan Ivanovich (yĭmĭlyän' ēvä'nůvĭch po͞ogŭchôf'), d. 1775, Russian rebel leader. An illiterate Don Cossack, he claimed to be PETER III. Became figurehead of formidable peasant revolt (1773–75), seized large parts of E Russia, proclaimed abolition of serfdom. He was betrayed, captured, and beheaded.

Puget, Pierre (püzhā'), 1622–94, French sculptor and painter. Spent most of his life in S France and Italy. His famous statue of St. Sebastian is in Genoa. Well represented in the Louvre.

Puget Sound (pū'jĭt), NW Wash., connected with the Pacific by Juan de Fuca Strait and extending c.100 mi. S from the strait to Olympia. Navigable, it serves rich industrial and agr. region. Seattle, Tacoma, and Everett are on E shore, Port Townsend at entrance. Explored by George Vancouver 1792.

Puget Sound, College of: see TACOMA, Wash.

Pugin, Augustus Charles (pū'jĭn), English writer on medieval architecture, b. France. He and his son, **Augustus Welby Northmore Pugin,** 1812–52, who was an eminent architect, were important for their prominent role in the Gothic revival.

Pula, Yugoslavia: see POLA.

Pulaski, Casimir (kă'sĭmēr půlă'skē), c.1748–1779, Polish military commander in American Revolution. Organized cavalry unit in 1778. Mortally wounded in attack on Savannah.

Pulaski (půlă'skē). **1** Town (pop. 5,762), S Tenn., SSW of Nashville. Trade, processing, and shipping for farm area. Ku Klux Klan organized here 1865. **2** Town (pop. 9,202), SW Va., SW of Roanoke. Trade and processing center of agr., lumber, mining area.

Pulaski, Fort (půlă'skē), fortification on Cockspur Isl., SE Ga., at mouth of Savannah R. Constructed 1829–47. Seized Jan., 1861, by Confederates, retaken by Union force under Q. A. Gillmore, April 11, 1862. Fort Pulaski Natl. Monument (estab. 1924) now includes all Cockspur Isl.

Pulci, Luigi (lwē'jē po͞ol'chē), 1432–84, Italian poet; protégé of Lorenzo de' Medici and author of *Morgante maggiore* (1460–70), a mock-heroic poem.

Pulitzer, Joseph (po͞o'lĭtsůr, pū'–), 1847–1911, American newspaper owner, b. Hungary; in U.S. after 1864. He was a journalist under Carl Schurz in St. Louis and in 1878 became successful owner-publisher of the *Post-Dispatch*. In 1883 he bought the New York *World* and built it up aggressively, adding in 1887 the *Evening World*. Outstripped in popular appeal by Hearst's *Journal,* his papers became more conservative after 1900. In 1931 the *Evening World* was merged with the New York *Telegram*. Pulitzer left funds to found the School of Journalism at Columbia Univ. Since 1917 **Pulitzer Prizes** have been awarded annually for achievements in American journalism and letters. There are seven awards in specific fields of journalism; in letters, for fiction, drama, history, biography, poetry, and musical composition. In addition, there are four traveling scholarships given each year.

pulley, simple machine consisting of sheave (wheel with grooved rim in which rope can run) and block (frame in which wheel turns freely on axle). Fixed pulley has frame attached to rigid support; movable pulley frame is free to move. One block may contain several wheels. No mechanical advantage is obtained by single fixed pulley; single movable pulley has mechanical advantage of 2 (i.e., given weight, or resistance, can be balanced by a force, or effort, of one half that amount). By combinations of fixed and movable pulleys, a small effort can overcome a large resistance; amount of work done is not increased, since the effort applied moves through a greater distance than the load. See *ill.*, p. 793.

Pullman, George Mortimer (pŏŏl'mŭn), 1831–97, American industrialist. Founded Pullman Palace Car Co. in 1867.

Pullman. 1 Former city, part (since 1889) of Chicago, Ill. Founded 1880 by G. M. Pullman as model community for workers of his sleeping-car company. Strike over wage cuts (May–July, 1894) here resulted in jail for E. V. DEBS, president of American Railway Union, and a complaint from Ill. governor J. P. ALTGELD because Pres. Cleveland quelled strike with U.S. troops. **2** City (pop. 12,022), SE Wash., near Idaho line, in grain, livestock, poultry area; founded 1884. Seat of State Col. of Washington (land-grant, state supported; coed.; opened 1892).

pulque (pŏŏl'kā), Mexican spirituous liquor made by fermenting sap of maguey (see AGAVE).

pulse, alternate expansion and contraction of artery walls as heart action causes changes in arterial blood volume. Normal rate at rest is about 70–80 pulsations a minute in adults.

puma (pū'mŭ), New World predatory cat (*Felis*), variously called cougar, mountain lion, catamount, panther. Ranges from Canada to Patagonia. Northerly puma reddish to grayish brown above; adult male is 7–8 ft. long. Tropical races are smaller and redder.

pumice (pŭ'mĭs), volcanic glass permeated with bubbles. Used as abrasive, included in many scouring materials. Lipari Isls. off Italy are chief source.

pump, device for lifting fluid or varying fluid pressure. Atmospheric pressure limits lift of suction pump to c.34 ft. Variation of pressure inside cylinder and attached pipe of pump is basic to its operation. Other types include reciprocating pumps, centrifugal and force pumps, and air lift. Rotary pump employs the screw principle.

pumpkin, vinelike tender annual (*Cucurbita pepo*), of unknown origin, and its large yellow edible fruit. The name pumpkin is often used interchangeably with squash. It was among the fruits of the first Thanksgiving and has been a favorite pie filling of autumn festivities ever since. Its shell is the Jack-o'-lantern of Halloween.

puna (pōō'nä) [South American], high plateau region between ridges of Andes in Peru and Bolivia. Icy wind sweeping plateaus also called *puna.*

Punch and Judy, English puppet play, popular with children. Probably originated in *commedia dell' arte.* Punch is cruel and boastful, his wife Judy faithless and obstreperous.

Punchbowl, hill, 498 ft. high, Honolulu, T.H. In bowl-like extinct crater at summit is Natl. Cemetery of the Pacific for World War II dead.

punctuation, device of using special arbitrary marks other than letters in written material. These marks supplement the spelling by giving some indication of tone, accent, pauses, and relationships that are significant in the use of a language but are not shown by letters alone. In English, punctuation particularly represents the intonations. Marks commonly used are the comma, the semicolon, the period, full stop, or point, the exclamation point, the interrogation point or question mark, the colon, quotation marks, and the dash. With the increase of silent as opposed to vocal reading other marks have come into use, such as the apostrophe (marking an omission or a possessive case), square brackets (secondary parentheses), and the hyphen (to indicate a more or less intimate joining of two words). Today punctuation is properly used only when it makes the meaning clear to the eye; arbitrary rules that reached an elaborate point in the 19th cent. have lost some of their force. In other Western languages the same signs and a few others are used, but each language has its own system of punctuation, since marks are actually arbitrary and conventional symbols gaining their meaning only from use.

Punic language, language of Carthage, belonging to Canaanite group of Semitic languages. See LANGUAGE (table).

Punic Wars, series of three contests between Rome and Carthage for dominance of the Mediterranean. When they began Carthage was a great power dominating NW Africa and the islands and commerce of the W Mediterranean. When they ended Carthage was a ruin and Rome the greatest power W of China. The **First Punic War,** 264–241 B.C., began when Messana called on both Rome and Carthage for help in a quarrel with Syracuse. The Carthaginians arrived first and arranged a peace, but the Romans ejected them and took E Sicily. The Roman fleet won at Mylae (260) and off Cape Economus (256), but a Roman expedition to Africa failed. Hamilcar Barca kept the Romans from taking Lilybaeum, but a new Roman victory at sea off the Aegadian Isles (241) caused Carthage to ask for peace. Rome now had Sicily and (contrary to the treaty) set out to conquer Sardinia and Corsica. When the Carthaginians under HANNIBAL took Saguntum (Sagunto) in Spain (219), Rome declared war. The **Second Punic** (or Hannibalic) **War,** 218–201 B.C., was the most celebrated of the three. It was marked by Hannibal's invasion of Italy and success there (against Fabius and others) until the failure of supplies and the defeat of his brother Hasdrubal on the Metaurus (207) made his attempt hopeless. He returned to Africa to defend Carthage against SCIPIO AFRICANUS MAJOR, but failed in the battle of Zama (202). Carthage surrendered its Spanish province and its war fleet and did not recover. Nevertheless CATO THE ELDER long agitated for complete destruction of Carthage and the **Third Punic War,** 149–146 B.C., originated when Rome charged Carthage with technical breach of the treaty by resisting the aggression of Rome's ally Masinissa. Carthage was blockaded but did not surrender. SCIPIO AFRICANUS MINOR conquered it and razed it.

punishment: see CAPITAL PUNISHMENT; CORPORAL PUNISHMENT; CRIMINAL LAW; PRISON.

Punjab (pŭn″jäb′) [Sanskrit,= five rivers], region of NW India and W Pakistan, lying between Indus and Jumna rivers. Mainly a level plain irrigated by Jhelum, Chenab, Ravi, Sutlej, and Beas rivers. Region was probably seat of earliest Aryan settlements in India. Occupied 326 B.C. by Alexander the Great and later by Maurya empire. Moslems occupied W Punjab by 8th cent. and implanted Islam but failed to dislodge Hinduism as dominant religion in E Punjab, which they conquered (12th cent.). Sikhs rose to power in late 18th cent. as Mogul empire declined. Twice defeated in battle, they lost the area to the British in 1849. Punjab was divided 1947 between Pakistan and India on basis of concentrations of Moslem and Hindu population. Indian state of Punjab (37,428 sq. mi.; pop. 12,638,111) was originally called East Punjab; cap. Simla. First known as West Punjab, Pakistan's province (62,987 sq. mi.; pop. 18,814,000) is also called Punjab; cap. Lahore.

Punta Arenas (pōōn′tä ärā′näs) [Span.,= sandy point], city (pop. 24,706), cap. of Magallanes prov., S Chile. Only city on Strait of Magellan and world's southernmost city. Founded 1847 to maintain Chile's claim to strait. Exports Patagonian wool and mutton.

Punxsutawney (pŭngksŭtô′nē), industrial borough (pop. 8,969), W Pa., NE of Pittsburgh. Coal mining.

pupa (pū′pù), third stage in life of insect undergoing complete metamorphosis (egg, larva, pupa, adult). Complete metamorphosis is characteristic of members of orders Coleoptera (beetles), Diptera (flies, mosquitoes, gnats, etc.), Lepidoptera (moths, butterflies). Some pupae are active, but most are enclosed in a hard covering and are quiescent. Butterfly pupa case is called chrysalis. Most moth pupae are covered by cocoon, often silk secreted by larva. See *ill.*, p 601.

Pupin, Michael (Idvorsky) (pūpēn′) 1858–1935, American physicist and inventor, b. in the present Yugoslavia. He came to U.S. in 1874 and from 1889 was associated with Columbia Univ. Known for researches in X ray, for invention of many electrical devices used in telegraphy and telephony, and for Pulitzer Prize-winning autobiography (1923).

puppet, small figure of man or animal performing on miniature stage, manipulated by unseen operator who also speaks the dialogue. Distinction is made between marionettes (moved by strings or wire from above) and puppets (in which operator's hand is concealed in doll's costume). Puppet show is so ancient that it is impossible to tell where it first appeared. In Europe (16th–18th cent.) great writers and composers created works for puppets.

Purbeck, Isle of, peninsular district, c.12 mi. long and 8 mi. wide, Dorsetshire, England. Noted for production of Purbeck marble and china clay.

Purcell, Edward Mills, 1912–, American physicist. Shared 1952 Nobel Prize for development of a new method of measuring magnetic fields in atomic nuclei. Associated with Harvard from 1938.

Purcell, Henry (pûr′sùl), 1659–95, English composer; organist at Westminster Abbey, 1679–95. Among his many stage works are *The Fairy Queen* (based on Shakspere's *Midsummer Night's Dream*) and his music for Dryden's *King Arthur. Dido and Aeneas* (1689) is his only opera in the modern sense. He also wrote anthems, instrumental music, and secular songs.

Purchas, Samuel (pûr′chùs, -kùs), 1577–1626, English clergyman and compiler of travel books. Wrote *Purchas His Pilgrimage* (1613) and compiled famous *Hakluytus Posthumus; or, Purchas His Pilgrims* (1625).

Purdue University (pûrdū′), at Lafayette, Ind.; land-grant, state supported; coed.; chartered 1865, opened 1874. Known for large engineering schools. Has public safety institute.

pure-food laws: see FOOD ADULTERATION.

purgatory, in the teaching of the Roman Catholic Church, the state after death in which the soul destined for heaven is purged of all taint of unpunished or unrepented minor sins. Souls in purgatory may be aided by the prayers of the living (one form of prayer is the requiem Mass).

Puri (pōō′rē), town (pop. 41,055), E Orissa, India, on Bay of Bengal. A center of cult of Juggernaut (or Jagannath), a form of Krishna avatar (incarnation) of Vishnu. In annual festival, god's image is mounted on huge cart and dragged by pilgrims through main street. Contrary to common belief, festival rite does not require pilgrims to hurl themselves under the cart wheels.

Purim (pyōō′rĭm, pōō′-) [Heb.,= lots], Jewish festival which commemorates the deliverance of the Persian Jews from a massacre (Esther 3.7; 9.24,26). It is celebrated on the 14th and 15th of Adar, the sixth month in the Jewish calendar, and is a day of joy.

Puritanism, a composite of social, political, ethical, and theological ideas in English and American Protestantism. It originated in reign of Elizabeth I as a movement for reform in state church, intended to do away with ritual, vestments, and hierarchical organization. At first there was no quarrel over doctrine and no plan for secession. But by 1567 a group in London was worshiping after the pattern of Geneva. Gradually, congregation by congregation, they tended to become separatists, Presbyterians, and Independents (later Congregationalists), joined in Calvinistic opposition to the Church of England. But when their cause triumphed in the PURITAN REVOLUTION they fell to quarreling among themselves. The Restoration ended the brief Puritan dominance, and by the end of the 17th cent. Puritanism ceased as an organized movement. The early settlements in New England were Puritan in origin, and the spirit of Puritanism long persisted there. The Puritan ideal of society was a theocracy, with powerful ministers and absolute control of individual conduct. The family was the fortress of godliness, and life was to be lived in strict obedience to detailed laws of God as read in the Bible. The term today is used generally to refer only to repressive aspects.

Puritan Revolution, usual name for the conflict between English kings JAMES I (1603–25) and CHARLES I (1625–49) and the large middle-class parliamentary party. To the religious issue of Puritanism and episcopacy was added the conflict between king's divine-right claims and Parliament's desire to govern, with legal rights instead of favors from the king. James I's need for money made him temporize with Parliament. Sir Edward Coke upheld its rights; was dismissed by the king. Sir Francis Bacon upheld royal prerogative; was impeached by Parliament. James's last Parliament directed him how to use its financial grant. Charles I proved more intractable. Parliament tried by every means to limit his powers; withheld grant till he signed PETITION OF RIGHT. Charles still levied forced taxes and dissolved Parliament for its further opposition. He governed alone for 11 years; recalled Parliament for financial needs of Bishops' Wars. In the Grand Remonstrance, Parliament recited the evils of Charles's reign. By a militia bill it tried to gather an army. King also organized an army and refused Parliament's final 19 demands. His attempt to seize five members of Commons made civil war inevitable. Both sides bid for popular support. Charles was aided by the nobles, Anglicans, and Catholics; Parliament by the trading and artisan classes and by the Scotch Covenanters (after it accepted the Solemn League and Covenant). After first indecisive campaign, victories of Oliver CROMWELL at Marston Moor and Naseby led to king's surrender (1645) and end of first civil war. His escape caused second civil war (1647); it failed quickly. PRIDE'S PURGE expelled from Parliament all those opposed to the army. The remainder sentenced and beheaded Charles for treason (1649). A quasi-democratic Commonwealth was followed by Cromwell's domination in the PROTECTORATE. The Puritan Revolution assured emergence of the middle class, aided religious toleration, and settled contest between king and Parliament. Results confirmed by the glorious Revolution of 1688.

Purkinje, Johannes Evangelista (yōhä'nůs ā"väng-gālĭs'tä pŏŏr'kĭnyā), 1787–1869, Czech physiologist. He contributed to microscope technique, study of tissues, and embryology.

purslane, weedy, fleshy annual (*Portulaca oleracea*), also known as pussley. In the Old World it has been used as a potherb.

Purus (pŏŏrōōs'), river, c.2,100 mi. long, rising in E Peru. Flows generally NE across Brazil into Amazon well above Manaus.

Purvey, John, c.1354–c.1421, English scholar. In support of LOLLARDRY he completed the first thorough translation of the Bible into English (c.1395).

Purvits, Vilhelms (vĭl'hĕlms pŏŏr'vĭts), 1872–, Latvian landscape painter. As director of Latvian museums he was among the first to introduce modern Western art into E Europe.

Pusan (pōō'sän), city (pop. 473,619), S Korea, on Korea Strait; largest port of Korea. In 1950 it became chief UN supply port in Korean war.

Pusey, Edward Bouverie, 1800–1882, English clergyman, leader in OXFORD MOVEMENT, known also as Puseyism. He was regius professor of Hebrew at Oxford, with canonry of Christ Church. His sermon "The Rule of Faith" (1851) checked secessions to Roman Church, caused in part by controversy over church government.

Pushkin, Aleksandr Sergeyevich (ŭlyĭksän'důr sĭrgā'ůvĭch pōōsh'kĭn), 1799–1837, greatest of Russian poets. He came of an old Russian family, but a great-grandfather was Hannibal, the Negro general of Peter I. His best-known works include the drama *Boris Godunov* (1831) and *Eugene Onegin* (1831), a novel of manners in verse, his masterpiece. Other works are the fairy romance *Russlan and Ludmilla* (1820), the poems *The Prisoner of the Caucasus* (1821), *The Fountains of Bakchiserai* (1822), and *The Gypsies* (1823–24), written under Byron's influence; the historical poems *Poltava* (1828) and *The Bronze Horseman* (1833); *The Golden Cockerel* (1833), a folk-tale; and *The Queen of Spades* (1834), a short story. He died in a duel.

Pushkin, city (pop. over 50,000), RSFSR, S of Leningrad. Founded under Peter I as Tsarskoye Selo; renamed Detskoye Selo in 1920s and Pushkin 1937. Amid large parks are baroque summer palace of Catherine II and classic summer palace of Alexander I, which were partially destroyed in World War II.

Pushtu (pŭsh'tōō), language of Afghanistan, belonging to Iranian group of Indo-Iranian subfamily of Indo-European languages. Also called Afghan. See LANGUAGE (table).

pussy willow: see WILLOW.

Puszta (pōō'stä), grazing lands which once covered a large part of Hungarian plain and were used for extensive cattle raising. Irrigation and drainage have caused disappearance of the Puszta except in a small district near Debrecen.

Puteoli (pūtē'ůlī), anc. city of Campania, Italy; founded c.520 B.C. by Greeks. A wealthy port in Roman times, it was destroyed by Germans in 5th cent. A.D. Modern Pozzuoli is near.

Put in Bay, harbor of South Bass Isl., N Ohio, in L. Erie NW of Sandusky. At Put in Bay village, resort on bay, is Perry's Victory and Internatl. Peace Memorial Natl. Monument.

Putnam, Amelia Earhart: see EARHART, AMELIA.

Putnam, George Palmer, 1814–72, American publisher; grandnephew of Israel Putnam. Founder (1848) of G. P. Putnam's Sons; owner of *Putnam's Magazine* (estab. 1853). A founder and honorary superintendent of Metropolitan Mus. of Art. A son, **George Haven Putnam,** 1844–1930, succeeded his father in 1872 as head of the firm. He served in the Civil War, was active in civil and social causes, and wrote many books. Another son, **Herbert Putnam,** 1861–, was Librarian of Congress (1899–1938). **George Palmer Putnam,** 1887–1950, a grandson of the founder, served the firm as treasurer (1919–30). He was also an explorer, and author of a biography of his wife, Amelia Earhart (1939).

Putnam, Israel, 1718–90, American Revolutionary general. A farmer, he left plow in furrow to join patriot forces. Commanded at Long Island (1776).

Putnam, Rufus, 1738–1824, American Revolutionary general, a founder of Ohio Company of Associates. Laid out Marietta, Ohio (1788).

Putnam, textile city (pop. 8,181) in Putnam town (pop. 9,304), NE Conn., NE of Willimantic; settled 1693.

Putney, district of SW London, England, on the S side of the Thames. Swinburne and William Pitt lived here. Putney Heath was the scene of duels.

Putney, town (pop. 1,019), SE Vt., N of Brattleboro, on Connecticut R. Has Putney School (progressive; coed; 1935). J. H. NOYES formed first of his three Perfectionist societies here, 1839.

Putrid Sea, RSFSR: see SIVASH SEA.

Putumayo (po͞oto͞omä'yō), river, c.1,000 mi. long, formed by tributaries rising in Colombian Andes, flowing SE to Amazon. Marks part of boundary of Colombia with Ecuador and Peru. Called Içá in Brazil. In wild-rubber boom an investigation showed shocking working conditions in area.

Puvis de Chavannes, Pierre (pyĕr' püvēs' dů shävän'), 1824–98, French mural painter. Studied with the romanticists (notably Delacroix), but his work is classical in inspiration.

Puy, Le (lů püē'), city (pop. 18,347), cap. of Haute-Loire dept., S central France. Has old lace industry. An episcopal see from 6th cent., it became the cap. of the medieval county of Velay (part of Aquitaine; inc. into Languedoc 15th cent.). Its shrine to the Virgin has been a major goal of pilgrimage since the 10th cent. The old part of the city lies at the foot of a bare rock nearly 500 ft. high, capped by the 50-ft. bronze statue of the Virgin (erected 1860). It has a daringly constructed cathedral (12th cent.) and many Gothic buildings. Atop a lesser, needle-shaped rock is the Romanesque Church of St. Michel d'Aiguilhe.

Puyallup (pūă'lůp), city (pop. 10,010), W Wash., on Puyallup R. and E of Tacoma; settled 1877. Berries, bulbs, truck, and wood products. Canneries.

Puy-de-Dôme (püē'-dů-dōm'), department (3,095 sq. mi.; pop. 478,876), S central France, in Auvergne; cap. Clermont-Ferrand. Named for the **Puy de Dôme,** an extinct volcano near Clermont, 4,806 ft. high. Here in 1648 Florence Périer, following instructions of his brother-in-law Blaise Pascal, conducted historic experiment which confirmed Torricelli's theory on air pressure.

Puy de Sancy, France: see MONT-DORE.

Pu Yi, Henry (po͞o'ē), 1905–, last emperor (1908–12) of China, who ruled as Hsüan T'ung. Abdication in 1912 ended Ch'ing dynasty. In 1934 he became emperor of Japanese puppet state of MANCHUKUO. Testified in 1946 at war-crimes trial that he had been the unwilling tool of Japanese militarists.

Pyatigorsk (pyĭtyēgôrsk'), city (pop. 62,875), S Stavropol Territory, RSFSR, in N Caucasus. Health resort, with hot sulphur springs and mud baths.

Pydna (pĭd'nů), anc. town, S Macedonia, near the Gulf of Salonica. Here Romans under Aemilius Paullus defeated Perseus, king of Macedon (168 B.C.).

Pye, John, 1782–1874, English engraver, founder of modern landscape engraving.

Pygmalion (pĭgmāl'yůn), in Greek mythology, king of Cyprus and sculptor of GALATEA.

Pygmy or **Pigmy,** any of various populations of short stature scattered from Africa to New Guinea. African Pygmies, often called Negrillos, average less than 5 ft. in height; are lighter in color than Negroids among whom they live and whose languages they speak. Far Eastern Pygmies, sometimes called Negritos, include Aetas of Philippines, Semangs of Malay Peninsula, and several other small groups from Andaman Isls. eastward; there is pygmy admixture in populations of Malaya and Melanesia. In this area the Pygmies average c.5 ft. tall, have thick lips, very dark skin, scant body hair and woolly head hair.

Pyle, Howard, 1853–1911, American illustrator and writer of tales of chivalry and adventure, such as *The Merry Adventures of Robin Hood of Great Renown* (1883).

Pylos (pī'lŏs), harbor of anc. Messenia, Greece; a center of Mycenaean civilization (13th cent. B.C.). A town, formerly known as Navarino, now as Pylos, is on the S shore of the Bay of Pylos. In the bay Athenians beat Spartans in 425 B.C., and British, French, and Russian ships defeated Egyptians in battle of Navarino (1827) in Greek War for independence.

Pym, John (pĭm), 1583?–1643, English Puritan leader in Parliament. Leader in both Short and Long Parliaments, he opposed the royalist party of Charles I's reign. One of five members of Commons that Charles tried to arrest. Arranged alliance with Scots after signing (1642) the Covenant.

Pynchon, William (pĭn'chůn), c.1590–1662, American colonist and theologian, b. England. Settled Springfield, Mass., in 1636. Denounced as heretic.

Pynson, Richard (pĭn'sůn), d. 1530, English printer, b. Normandy, supposedly the most skillful printer in England at his time.

Pyongyang (pyŭng'yäng'), industrial city (pop. 342,551), N Korea; cap. of People's Republic of Korea. According to legend it was founded 1122 B.C. by the Chinese sage Ki-tze. Invaded by the Japanese in 1592, 1894, and 1904. After World War II it was hq. of Russian occupation zone.

pyorrhea (pīůrē'ů), a discharge of pus. Term is used commonly for alveolar pyorrhea, or Riggs's disease, a disease of bony supporting structure of teeth, described by an American dentist, John M. Riggs.

pyramid. The pyramids in Egypt are square in plan with triangular sides meeting at a point. The pyramid was evolved in period of IV dynasty (2900 B.C.). Each monarch built his own pyramid to preserve his mummified body for eternity; its building required measureless time and labor. Sepulchral chamber, excavated from rock on which pyramid is built, lies deep beneath structure. Great Pyramid of Khufu or Cheops at Gizeh, one of Seven Wonders of the World, is largest pyramid ever built; covering 13 acres, it was originally 768 ft. square and 482 ft. high. Though the pyramids were usually built of rough limestone blocks, many were of mud bricks with stone casing. Pyramidal structures were also built by Assyrians and by the Maya of Central America and Mexico. Assyrian ziggurat was square in plan and built up in receding terraces formed by ramp winding around sides and leading to temple chamber at top. Maya pyramids were also topped by ritual chambers. The **battle of the Pyramids** was a notable victory won by Napoleon over the Mamelukes in Egypt (July, 1798) which gave him brief control over Egypt until Nelson destroyed his fleet at Aboukir, Aug., 1798.

Pyramid Lake, c.30 mi. long and c.10 mi. wide, W Nev., NNE of Reno in Pyramid Lake Indian Reservation. Remnant of ancient L. Lahontan. Discovered 1844 by J. C. Frémont. Receives Truckee R.

Pyramus and Thisbe (pĭ'rŭmŭs, thĭz'bē), in classic legend, youth and maiden of Babylon. At their trysting place Thisbe fled from a lion, dropping her mantle. Pyramus found the bloodied mantle and, thinking her dead, killed himself. Thisbe, on returning, killed herself with his sword. White fruit of the mulberry tree, stained by Pyramus' blood, was red ever after.

Pyrenees (pĭ'rŭnēz), mountain chain, SW Europe, separating Iberian Peninsula from European mainland and France from Spain. Extending c.270 mi. from Bay of Biscay (W) to the Mediterranean (E), it rises to 11,168 ft. in the Pico de Aneto (Spain). The French slopes, much steeper than the Spanish, have many resorts (e.g., Pau, Tarbes) and celebrated sights (e.g., the Cirque de GAVARNIE). The Pyrenees are rich in timber, pastures, hydroelectric power. Stock raising and agr. are chief occupations. In the W, the population is largely of Basque stock. Among the passes, which are high and difficult, the Col de Perthus and Roncesvalles are the best known. The chief rail lines skirt the mountains in the W and E. Wedged between France and Spain, in the E Pyrenees, is the republic of Andorra.

Pyrénées, Hautes and **Basses,** France: see HAUTES-PYRÉNÉES; BASSES-PYRÉNÉES.

Pyrenees, Peace of the, 1659, peace treaty between France and Spain, which had remained at war after Peace of Westphalia (1648). Franco-Spanish border was fixed at Pyrenees; Spain ceded Roussillon and parts of Flanders to France; Louis XIV was to marry Marie Thérèse, daughter of Philip IV of Spain.

Pyrénées-Orientales (pērānā'-zôryătāl'), department (1,600 sq. mi.; pop. 228,776), S France, virtually identical with ROUSSILLON; cap. Perpignan.

pyrethrum (pīrē'thrŭm), hardy perennial (*Chrysanthemum coccineum*), also called painted daisy, with lacy foliage and red, pink, or white daisies in late spring. It is one of the species from which the insecticide pyrethrum is derived.

pyridine (pĭ'rĭdēn), colorless liquid with putrid odor. It is chemically stable and somewhat like benzene in structure. Used as solvent, denaturant, antiseptic.

pyrite (pī'rīt), widely distributed pale brass-yellow mineral, iron bisulphide. Sometimes called "fool's gold," it often does contain gold. Used as source of sulphur in manufacture of sulphuric acid.

Pyrmont (pĭrmônt') or **Bad Pyrmont** (bät'), town (pop. 16,534), Lower Saxony, W Germany. Noted spa. Former small principality of Pyrmont was united with WALDECK.

pyrogallol (pī"rōgă'lōl) or **pyrogallic acid** (–lĭk), colorless, crystalline phenol with biting taste. It is used as developing agent in photography and in ointments.

pyroligneous acid (pī"rōlĭg'nēŭs), dark liquid mixture of acetic acid and wood alcohol obtained by destructive distillation of wood. It is a source of acetic acid.

pyrotechnics (pī"rōtĕk'nĭks), science and art of making and using fireworks. Gunpowder was used in fireworks in 9th cent. by Chinese, who brought the art to high stage of development. Many combustibles, explosives, and combinations are used for displays. Fireworks are also used as signal devices.

pyroxene (pī'rŏksēn), name given to a group of widely distributed rock minerals, metasilicates of magnesium, iron, and calcium, often with aluminum, sodium, lithium, manganese, or zinc.

pyroxylin (pīrŏk'sĭlĭn), highly inflammable, cottonlike mixture of lower cellulose nitrates made by treating cellulose with nitric acid. It is used to make celluloid, collodion, and paints.

Pyrrha: see DEUCALION.

Pyrrho (pĭ'rō), c.360–270 B.C., Greek philosopher, much respected at Elis and Athens; called the father of skepticism.

Pyrrhus (pĭ'rŭs), c.318–272 B.C., king of Epirus (295–272 B.C.). He gained the throne with the aid of Ptolemy I and invaded Macedon but was driven out by Lysimachus (283 B.C.). Leading an expedition to Italy to aid the Tarentines, he had a large force and some elephants and defeated the Romans at Heraclea (280 B.C.). He beat them again at Asculum (279 B.C.) but with such heavy casualties that he said, "One more such victory and I am lost"—this was the "Pyrrhic victory." He was defeated at Beneventum (275 B.C.), but regained prestige by defeating Antigonus II of Macedon (273 B.C.). He was killed in Argos by a falling roof tile.

Pythagoras (pĭthă'gŭrŭs), c.582–c.507 B.C., Greek philosopher, b. Samos. At Crotona he founded a religious brotherhood, which borrowed the idea of transmigration of souls from Orphism and practiced purification rites to get release from reincarnations. The Pythagoreans believed that the essence of all things was number and that all relationships could be expressed numerically. This view led them to discover the numerical relationship of tones in music and to some knowledge of later Euclidean geometry. They considered the earth as a planet revolving about a fixed point ("the hearth of the universe"). They took part in politics, and their opposition to accepted religion caused them to be persecuted from existence in Magna Graecia. See NEO-PYTHAGOREANISM.

Pythagoras of Rhegium (rē'jŭm), 5th cent. B.C., Greek sculptor. His works formed part of transition from archaic style to that of the masters.

Pythia (pĭ'thēŭ), in Greek religion, priestess

of the oracle at DELPHI. Pythian games, held every four years at Delphi, included musical, literary, and athletic contests. Twelve of Pindar's odes honoring winners of games are called Pythian odes.

Pythias: see DAMON AND PYTHIAS.

python (pī'thŏn", pī'thůn), nonvenomous snake, found chiefly in tropical Africa, Asia, East Indies, Australia. It climbs and swims expertly. Most pythons are egg layers. They kill prey by constrictor force of body muscles.

pyxie, low evergreen plant (*Pyxidanthera barbulata*) of pine barrens of E U.S. It has pink or white flowers in the spring. Other names are flowering moss and pine barren beauty.

"Q": see QUILLER-COUCH, SIR ARTHUR THOMAS.

Qatar (kä'tär), sheikdom (4,000 sq. mi.; pop. 20,000), Arabia, on peninsula projecting into Persian Gulf; cap. Doha. Largely barren. Oil fields, fisheries. Closely bound to Britain by treaty.

Qazvin, Iran: see KAZVIN.

Qom, Iran: see KUM.

Quabbin Reservoir (kwŏ'bĭn), covers 39.4 sq. mi. in Swift R. valley, central Mass., NE of Springfield; completed 1937. Water flows to WACHUSETT RESERVOIR through Quabbin Aqueduct (24.6 mi. long).

quack grass, Old World perennial grass (*Agropyron repens*), widely distributed and a troublesome weed in the U.S. It has creeping, yellowish rootstalks.

quadrant (kwŏ'drůnt). **1** Instrument for measuring angular altitudes, generally consisting of graduated arc of 90° or more, an index arm, and a sighting arrangement with plumb line or spirit level. Superseded by sextant. **2** Heavy casting for turning ship's rudder. **3** Fourth part of a circle, i.e., area bounded by an arc and two radii drawn at right angles to each other.

quadrivium: see LIBERAL ARTS.

Quadruple Alliance, several European alliances. That of **1718** (England, France, Austria, Netherlands) forced Spain, by military intervention, to give up in 1720 Sicily and Sardinia, which it had seized in violation of the Peace of Utrecht. The Quadruple Alliance of **1814** (England, Austria, Russia, Prussia) was formed at Chaumont, France, to strengthen the coalition against Napoleon I. Renewed at Paris in 1815, it aimed at cooperation among the Great Powers for peace and the preservation of the status quo, but it came to be dominated by the spirit of the HOLY ALLIANCE. It was joined in 1818 by France. The congresses at Aachen (1818), Troppau (1820), Laibach (1821), and Verona (1822) were held under its provisions. The withdrawal of England (1822) effectively ended the alliance.

quagga (kwă'gů), extinct African mammal of genus *Equus,* which includes horse, ass, zebra. Hunted for its skin, it was exterminated in 19th cent.

Quai d'Orsay (kā dôrsā'), quay on left bank of the Seine, in Paris, France. The French foreign ministry, which is situated on it, is often referred to as the Quai d'Orsay.

quail, name for various small game birds of Old and New Worlds. Originally the name referred to common Old World quail. New World birds sometimes called quail include bobwhite, mountain or plumed quail (or partridge), Gambel's quail, California and valley quails. Quails eat insects and weed seeds.

quaker-ladies: see BLUET.

Quakers: see FRIENDS, SOCIETY OF.

Quakertown, borough (pop. 5,673), SE Pa., N of Philadelphia. Mfg. of clothing and luggage. Has a Quaker meetinghouse (1802).

quaking grass, name for annual or perennial grasses of genus *Briza,* with graceful seed panicles which vibrate in a breeze.

Quanah (kwä'nů), city (pop. 4,589), N Texas, WNW of Wichita Falls. Center of agr. (wheat) area; has mfg. of gypsum products. Annual Texas-Okla. Wolf Hunt held near by.

Quantico (kwŏn'tĭkō), town (pop. 1,240), N. Va., on Potomac R. below Washington, D.C. Here is an important U.S. Marine Corps base.

Quantrill, William (Clarke) (kwŏn'trĭl), 1837–65, Confederate guerrilla leader. Known for Civil War raids in Mo. and Kansas; notably brutal one at Lawrence, Kansas, in 1863.

quantum theory, theory concerning emission and absorption, by atomic and subatomic particles, of light and energy. In 1900 Max Planck hypothesized that energy transfer is discontinuous and involves unit of energy (quantum), which is a function ($q = h\nu$) of Planck's constant (*h;* value c.6.6 $\times 10^{-27}$ erg-second) and of radiation frequency of particle (ν). Einstein postulated (1905) comparable light quanta (photons). Quantum theory as extended by Niels Bohr and others to atomic structure held inconsistencies. Reorganization initiated c.1923 by Louis de Broglie's suggestion that matter has dual aspects and that electrons be regarded not only as individual particles but also as associated in wave systems. Mathematical formulations (wave mechanics) of theory were developed independently by Schrödinger and Heisenberg and were amalgamated 1927 by P. A. M. Dirac. This new form became basis of modern quantum mechanics which has revolutionized methods of dealing with atomic phenomena and undermined concept of causality in physics because theory cannot as yet predict behavior of individual particles but considers statistically large numbers of particles.

Quapaw Indians (kwô'pô), North American tribe of Siouan linguistic stock, living when visited by Hernando De Soto (1540) on the W bank of the Mississippi N of the Arkansas R.; called also the Arkansas. They are now in Okla.

quarantine (kwŏ'rŭntēn), limitation of movement imposed upon humans and animals for time just beyond incubation period of disease to which they may have been exposed. Public health regulations require physician's report of cases of certain diseases; posting of warning notices; disinfection. Quarantine originated in 12th cent. in Venice, where 40-day offshore wait was required of ships.

Quarnero, Gulf of (kwärnä'rō), arm of Adriatic Sea, between Istria and Dalmatia.

quarrying (kwŏ'rēĭng), removing rock from a natural deposit. Methods employed depend on nature and location of stone and uses intended. Nonshattering rock can be blasted. Soft varieties are channeled by power drills; in some cases by wire saws.

quartz (kwôrts), one of the commonest and most important rock-forming minerals, silicon dioxide or silica. It may be transparent, translucent, or opaque; it varies widely in color and often forms hexagonal crystals (if colorless these are called rock crystal). Among the varieties of quartz are amethyst, cat's-eye, flint, and chalcedony, including such colored varieties as carnelian, agate, jasper, onyx, and sardonyx.

quartzite, tough rock composed of firmly cemented quartz grains. Usually a metamorphosed sandstone.

Quaternary period, name originally given to the second period of the Cenozoic era of geologic time, the Tertiary being the first. Many geologists tend to abandon these divisions as unjustified, and use the term Cenozoic both for era and period.

Quay, Matthew Stanley (kwā), 1833–1904, American political leader. Boss of state Republican machine in Pa. U.S. Senator (1887–99, 1901–4).

Quebec (kwēbĕk'), Fr. *Québec* (kābĕk'), province (523,860 sq. mi.; with water surface 594,860 sq. mi.; pop. 4,055,681), E Canada; cap. QUEBEC. Other cities are MONTREAL, VERDUN, SHERBROOKE, TROIS RIVIÈRES, and HULL. Bounded N by Hudson Strait and Ungava Bay, W by James and Hudson bays, SE by Gulf of St. Lawrence. The N LAURENTIAN PLATEAU, well-forested and rich in minerals (iron, gold, silver, copper, zinc), is largely uninhabited and undeveloped. The St. Lawrence R. cuts NW–SE through S part of the province. Industrial, commercial, and agr. life is centered in St. Lawrence Valley (S). Lumbering is extensive and feeds pulpwood and paper mfg. Other industries include metal smelting, textile milling, and mfg. of shoes, industrial equipment, and consumer goods. ARVIDA leads world aluminum production. Quebec is first in Canada in water power and second in total value of production. Served by many lakes and rivers. SE the GASPÉ PENINSULA, a region of small coastal fishing and farming villages, extends into the Gulf of St. Lawrence. Tourist trade is important. Province early became center of French colonization in America. Cartier landed on the Gaspé 1634. Champlain founded trading post on the site of Quebec 1608, and soon exploring, trading and missionary expeditions radiated from this center. In 1663 chartered fur trade ended and royal government of New France was estab. Struggle for control between France and England in FRENCH AND INDIAN WARS ended with establishment of British control (1763) after Wolfe's defeat of Montcalm on the Plains of ABRAHAM. England sought to pacify French Canadians in the QUEBEC ACT of 1774 which guaranteed civil liberties and the retention of customs and institutions. The Constitutional Act of 1791 introduced representative government and Quebec became Lower Canada. Resentment against arbitrary rule resulted in the revolution of 1837 under Louis PAPINEAU. In 1840 Lower and Upper (Ontario) Canada were joined under the Act of Union and in 1849 responsible government was instituted. With the BRITISH NORTH AMERICA ACT (1867) Canadian federation was achieved and Quebec again became a province. A dual school system was set up to meet the needs of a pop. three quarters French-Canadian and predominantly Catholic. The conflict between French and British cultures continues to hamper Canadian unity.

Quebec, city (pop. 164,016), provincial cap., S Que., Canada, on St. Lawrence R. at mouth of St. Charles R. and NE of Montreal. Cultural and tourist center of French Canada, divided into Lower Town (on river front) and Upper Town (on Cape Diamond, bluff 300 ft. above river). Dufferin Terrace, a promenade, extends 1,400 ft. along bluff. Seaport trading extensively in wheat and fur. Tanning, brewing, and mfg. of paper, metal products, shoes, clothing, and bricks. Visited 1535 by Cartier; Champlain estab. colony in Lower Town 1608. Held by the British 1629–32. Made cap. of New France 1663. Unsuccessfully attacked by the British 1690 and 1711, it finally fell when Wolfe defeated Montcalm on the Plains of ABRAHAM 1759. Became cap. of Lower Canada 1791; after the Union of Upper and Lower Canada was cap. 1851–55, 1859–65. Population largely French-speaking. Points of interest include the Citadel, Basilica, Chapel of Notre-Dame-des-Victoires, Quebec seminary, Kent House, Parliament buildings, and remains of early fortifications. Seat of Laval Univ. (R.C.; partly coed.; chartered 1852, outgrowth of seminary estab. 1663 by Bishop Laval).

Quebec Act, 1774, passed by British Parliament to institute permanent administration in Canada. Allowed political and legal concessions and gave French Canadians religious freedom. Considered one of INTOLERABLE ACTS because it nullified many Western claims of coast colonies.

Quebec campaign, 1775–76, of American Revolution. Expedition sent to Canada to protect frontier from Indians and to persuade Canada to join revolt against England. Richard Montgomery captured Montreal, Nov., 1775, and aided Benedict Arnold in unsuccessful assault on Quebec, Dec., 1775. Americans were pushed back to Crown Point in spring.

Quebec Conference, two meetings held in World War II. First (Aug., 1943), attended by Pres. F. D. Roosevelt, Prime Ministers Churchill and Mackenzie King, and Foreign Minister Soong. Created China-Burma-India theater of operations, approved plans for landing in France. Second meeting (Sept., 1944), attended by Roosevelt and Churchill and military aides, dealt with broad strategy of war.

quebracho (kābrä'chō), name for South American hardwood trees of various genera and their wood. Wood of both the red quebracho (*Schinopsis*) and the white quebracho (*Aspidosperma*) is used in construction. The red quebracho also yields tannin. Both are sources of medicinal substances.

Quedlinburg (kvād'lēnbŏŏrk), city (pop. 35,142), Saxony-Anhalt, E central Germany, at foot of lower Harz. Walled 922 by Henry I. He and his wife, St. Mathilda (who with Otto I founded famous convent here in 936), are buried in castle church. Castle, church, and convent (secularized 1803) were built 10th–14th cent.

Queen Anne's lace: see WILD CARROT.

Queen Anne's War: see FRENCH AND INDIAN WARS.

Queen Charlotte Islands, archipelago of c.150 islands off coast of W B.C., Canada. Main islands are Graham and Moresby. Haida Indians form bulk of population. Valuable timber and fishing resources. First visited 1774 by Juan Pérez.

Queens, borough (land area 108 sq. mi.; pop. 1,550,849) of NEW YORK city, SE N.Y., at W end of Long Isl. adjoining Brooklyn borough. Separated from Manhattan and the Bronx by East R. (many bridges, e.g., Queensboro Bridge, built 1909, which stimulated borough's greatest growth; and tunnel connections); on S is Jamaica Bay, separated from the Atlantic by Rockaway peninsula (c.12 mi. long; resorts and commuters' communities). First settled by Dutch 1635; old Queens co. estab. 1683; divided in 1898 into Queens and Nassau counties, when Queens also became a New York city borough (largest in area). Mainly residential as in communities of Flushing, with Flushing Meadows park (site of New York World's Fair in 1939–40, later site of General Assembly meetings of the UN) and Queens Col. (see NEW YORK, COLLEGE OF THE CITY OF); and Forest Hills (has West Side Tennis Club where national and international matches are held). Heavily industrialized in area of Long Island City (shipping facilities on East R.; rail yards; consumer commodities); also at Astoria and Jamaica (important railroad transfer point, with extensive business and residential sections). Has two municipal airports, both administered by Port of New York Authority—LaGuardia (lŭgwär'dēŭ) (558 acres; opened 1939) and New York Internatl. Airport (4,900 acres; opened 1948; sometimes called Idlewild). Here are Jamaica and Aqueduct race tracks.

Queensberry, James Douglas, 2d duke of, 1662–1711, Scottish statesman. One of the first Scots to favor William III. Worked for Scottish-English union.

Queensberry, John Sholto Douglas, 8th marquess of, 1844–1900, English nobleman, originator of rules which govern modern boxing. Drafted (1865), with aid of Arthur Chambers, Queensberry rules, superseding London prize-ring rules introduced (1743) by Jack Broughton.

Queens' College: see CAMBRIDGE UNIVERSITY.

Queen's College: see OXFORD UNIVERSITY.

Queens College: see CHARLOTTE, N.C.; QUEENS, New York city borough.

Queensland, state (670,500 sq. mi.; pop. 1,106,269), NE Australia; cap. Brisbane. Bounded on E by Coral Sea and the Pacific, on S by New South Wales, and on W by Northern Territory. Most of its coast line is sheltered by Great Barrier Reef. Moreton Bay area (where Capt. James Cook landed 1770) was used for penal settlement, 1824–43. Queensland became a British colony in 1859 and a state of Commonwealth of Australia in 1901. Roughly half of state is tropical, with rainfall ranging from 5 in. in SW desert to 160 in. in NE jungle area. Great Dividing Range separates fertile coast from interior plains. Great Artesian Basin (376,000 sq. mi.) in interior provides water for large stock-raising area. Main products are sugar cane, cotton, wheat, and fruits.

Queensland, University of: see BRISBANE, Australia.

Queenston Heights, S Ont., Canada, on Niagara peninsula and N of Niagara Falls. Battle of Queenston Heights fought here in War of 1812.

Queenstown, Co. Cork, Ireland: see CÓBH.

Queen's University: see KINGSTON, Ont.

Quellinus or **Quellin, Artus** (är'tŭs kvĕlē'nŭs, kvĕ'lĭn), 1609–68, Flemish sculptor, follower of Rubens tradition in sculpture. Notable for his decorations of royal palace of Amsterdam.

Quemoy (kĭmoi'), island (pop. 49,485), in Formosa Strait, off the coast of Fukien prov., China, 15 mi. E of Amoy. Held by Nationalists after Communist conquest of China (1949).

Quental, Antero de (äntĕ'rō dŭ kēntäl'), 1842–91, Portuguese poet, notable for restrained, finely fashioned *Odas modernas* (1865) and *Sonetos* (1881).

Quercia, Jacopo della (yä'kōpō dĕl'lä kwĕr'chä), c.1374–1438, Italian sculptor. Called Jacopo della Fonte for his Gaia Fountain (Siena). Masterpiece is central doorway of San Petronio (Bologna).

Quercy (kĕrsē'), region and former county, S Central France in Lot and Tarn-et-Garonne depts; historic cap. Cahors. Consists of arid limestone plateaus (*causses*) and fertile river valleys. Sheep raising.

Querétaro (kārā'tärō), state (4,432 sq. mi.; pop. 282,608), central Mexico, on central plateau; cap. Querétaro (pop. 33,629). Mountainous in N with valleys and plains in S. Famous for opals, it also produces silver, iron, tin, mercury. Agr. products include sugar cane, cotton, tobacco, grains. Indians were conquered 1531, but territory was not colonized until 1550; became state 1824.

Quesnay, François (frãswä′ kĕnā′), 1694–1774, French economist, founder of the physiocratic school (see PHYSIOCRATS). He wrote *Tableau économique* [economic table] (1758).

Quesnel, Pasquier (päskyā′ kĕnĕl′), 1634–1719, French priest. His editions of the works of Leo I and of the New Testament were condemned for JANSENISM.

Quetta (kwĕ′tů), town (pop. 82,000), cap. of Baluchistan, W Pakistan, on trade route (via Bolan Pass) between Afghanistan and Indus valley.

quetzal (kĕtsäl′) or **quezal** (kĕsäl′), bird of high-altitude rain forests of Central America and Mexico. It is iridescent green above, crimson below, and has streamerlike tail coverts and crested head. Revered by Maya and Aztec. It is national emblem of Guatemala.

Quetzalcoatl (kĕt″sälkōä′tůl) [Nahuatl,= feathered serpent], anc. god and legendary ruler of Toltec in Mexico. As god, represented goodness and light in combat with darkness and evil. As culture hero and ruler, he was credited with discovery of maize, the arts, science, and the calendar. When culture hero disappeared on E coast of Mexico A.D. c.1000, he left promise to return. Some Aztec viewed later Spanish invaders as returning hosts of Quetzalcoatl. In poetic sense, plumed serpent is symbol of Mexico.

Quevedo y Villegas, Francisco Gómez de (frãnthē′skō gō′māth dā kāvā′dhō ē vēlyā′gäs), 1580–1645, Spanish satirist, novelist, and poet, one of the greatest writers of the Golden Age.

quezal: see QUETZAL.

Quezaltenango (kāsältānäng′gō), city (pop. 27,782), SW Guatemala; metropolis of W highlands; second city of Guatemala. Center of fertile area producing coffee, sugar cane, cacao, grains, and tropical fruits. Mfg. has increased with development of hydroelectric power.

Quezon, Manuel Luis (mänwĕl′ lwēs′ kā′sōn), 1878–1944, Filipino statesman. As president of Philippine senate (1916–35) he ardently crusaded for independence. First president of Commonwealth of the Philippines (1935–44); loyal friend of U.S.

Quezon City (kā′sōn), city (1948 pop. 107,977), central Luzon, P.I., near Manila. Replaced Manila as cap. of republic, July, 1948.

Quiberon (kēbrõ′), peninsula of Brittany, Morbihan dept., NW France, in Bay of Biscay. Here in 1795 c.3,000 Royalists were landed by British ships in hope of reviving Vendée uprising. Failure resulted in capitulation of the invaders, of whom c.800 were shot. **Quiberon Bay** was scene of British naval victory over France 1759.

Quichua (kēch′wä), linguistic family of W South America whose member languages are spoken in the plateaus of Peru, Ecuador, much of Bolivia, and NW Argentina. Official language of Inca empire was of this family. See LANGUAGE (table).

quicklime: see LIME.

quicksilver: see MERCURY.

Quidde, Ludwig (lo͞ot′vĭkh kvĭ′dů), 1858–1941, German pacifist and historian. Imprisoned for *Caligula* (1894), portrait of Emperor William II. Supported League of Nations; shared 1927 Nobel Peace Prize.

quietism, extreme form of mysticism proposed by Miguel de Molinos and more moderately by Fénelon and Madame Guyon. Its essence is passivity of soul before God for sake of achieving unity with Him. This involves abandonment of effort, reason, emotion, sacraments, even of prayer. Fundamental principle is common in Oriental religions.

Quill, Michael J(oseph), 1905–, American labor leader, president of Transport Workers Union of America, affiliated (1937) with the CIO, of which he is a leading figure.

Quiller-Couch, Sir Arthur Thomas (kwĭl′ůr-ko͞och″), pseud. **Q,** 1863–1944, English man of letters; professor of English at Cambridge after 1912. Wrote novels of Cornwall and essays; edited many anthologies, including *Oxford Book of English Verse* (1900) and *Oxford Book of English Prose* (1923).

Quilmes (kēl′mās), city (pop. 115,113), E Argentina, 11 mi. S of Buenos Aires and on Río de la Plata. Summer resort and industrial city.

quilting, antique form of needlework in which two layers of fabric are sewn together over an interlining. Quilting has been long used for adding warmth to clothing in N Asia and Europe. It has been a distinctive type of American needlework, used since colonial days chiefly for bed coverings.

Quimby, Phineas Parkhurst, 1802–66, American mental healer and mesmerist. He had many followers. The extent of his influence on Mary Baker Eddy and on Christian Science is a subject of much controversy.

Quimper (kēpĕr′), town (pop. 17,722), cap. of Finistère dept., NW France; a fishing port on an inlet of the Atlantic. It is famous for its pottery.

Quinault, Philippe (fēlēp′ kēnō′), 1635–88, French dramatist. Best known for his opera librettos, for which Lully wrote the music. *Armide* (1686) is considered his masterpiece.

quince, shrub or small tree (*Cydonia oblonga*) of rose family, native to Asia but widely grown elsewhere, and its stemless, fuzzy yellow fruits. The fruits, which follow white or pink flowers, are fragrant but astringent and chiefly used in jelly. For ornamental quinces, see FLOWERING QUINCE.

Quincy, Josiah (kwĭn′zē), 1744–75, American Revolutionary patriot. Opposed British colonial policies through writings. His son, **Josiah Quincy,** 1772–1864, was a Federalist leader in U.S. Congress (1805–13) and president of Harvard (1829–45).

Quincy. 1 City (pop. 6,505), NW Fla., near Ga. line NW of Tallahassee. Fuller's earth and tobacco. **2** City (pop. 41,450), W Ill., on the Mississippi and W of Springfield; settled 1822. Has good harbor, was important mid-19th cent. river port. Industrial and distributing center for agr. area. Mfg. of machinery, flour, and furniture. Scene of several pro-slavery-abolitionist struggles. **3** Industrial city (pop. 83,835), E Mass., on Boston Bay SE of Boston. T. MORTON ran trading post here 1625–27; town settled 1634. Granite quarrying (since 1750); shipbuilding; mfg. of metal and rubber products, chemicals. John and John Quincy Adams are buried in Old Stone Temple; their home is a national historic site (since 1946). For Quincy movement in education, see PARKER, F. W.

quinine (kwī′nīn″, kwĭnēn′), bitter alkaloid derived chiefly from cinchona bark. Used in treating malaria and allaying fever and pain. Isolated 1820; synthesized 1944. Excess dosage or continuous use may result in poisoning (cinchonism).

Quintana Roo (kēntä′nä rō′ō), territory (19,630 sq. mi.; pop. 26,996), SE Mexico, on Caribbean; cap. Chetumal (pop. 4,672). Occupies most of E half of Yucatan peninsula, population mostly Maya. Has been little explored; climate is hot, rainfall heavy.

Quintanilla, Luis (lwēs′ kēntänē′lyä), 1895–, Spanish painter. Known for scenes of popular life in mildly satirical vein. Settled in U.S. in 1942.

Quintero, Serafín Álvarez, and **Joaquín Álvarez Quintero:** see ÁLVAREZ QUINTERO.

Quintilian (Marcus Fabius Quintilianus) (kwĭntĭ′lyŭn), A.D. c.35–A.D. c.95, Roman rhetorician, known for his beautiful Latin style. His *Institutio oratoria,* a 12-book survey of rhetoric, also has acute comments on the great writers.

Quirino, Elpidio (ĕlpē′dhyō kērē′nō), 1890–, Filipino statesman. Long an aide to Manuel Quezon, he was elected first vice president of independent Philippine republic in 1946, president in 1949.

Quirinus (kwĭr′ĭnŭs), in Roman religion, name of ROMULUS as a god. The Quirinalia honored him.

Quiroga, Juan Facundo (hwän′ fäkōōn′dhō kērō′gä), 1790–1835, Argentine *caudillo.* A zealous advocate of federalism, he rejected unitarian constitution of 1826 and participated in civil strife that followed. Was assassinated. Sarmiento's *Facundo* is study of him and his era.

Quisling, Vidkun (kwĭz′lĭng, Nor. vĭd′kōōn kvĭs′lĭng), 1887–1945, Norwegian fascist leader. Founded Nasjonal Samling [national unity] party (1933); assisted German invasion of Norway (1940); was premier (1940, 1942–45) under German occupation. After the war convicted of high treason and shot. His name became a common noun meaning traitor.

Quitman, John Anthony, 1798–1858, American general in Mexican War and statesman. Fought at Monterrey, Veracruz, and Chapultepec. U.S. Representative from Miss. (1855–58).

Quito (kē′tō), city (pop. 212,873), cap. of Ecuador and second largest city. Educational, cultural, and political center. A Quito Indian settlement, it was captured by the Inca shortly before conquest by Benalcázar (1534). In 1563 it became seat of *audiencia.* Presidency of Quito was shifted between viceroyalty of Peru and New Granada. Freed from Spain by Sucre (1822).

Quivira (kēvē′rä), fabulous land sought by CORONADO and others. Site uncertain but probably in Kansas. Name finally (and quite erroneously) settled on Gran Quivira Natl. Monument, N.Mex.

Quixote, Don: see DON QUIXOTE DE LA MANCHA.

Qum, Iran: see KUM.

Quonset Point, R.I.: see NORTH KINGSTOWN.

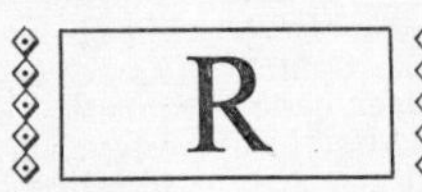

R

Ra (rä), Egyptian sun-god. His worship centered at Heliopolis but later became widespread. The obelisk was his chief symbol. His worship was later joined with that of Amon. Also Re (rā).

Ra, chemical symbol of the element RADIUM.

Raabe, Wilhelm (vĭl′hĕlm rä′bŭ), pseud. Jakob Corvinus, 1831–1910, German novelist. His novels include *Die Chronik der Sperlingsgasse* (1857) and *Der Hungerpastor* (1864; Eng. tr. 1885).

Raasay (rä′zā), island, off NW Scotland, in Inverness-shire, one of the Inner Hebrides.

Rabat (räbät′), city (pop. 161,416), French Morocco; port on the Atlantic at mouth of Bon Regreg. Seat of French resident general and sultan's residence. Old walled town was founded 12th cent. by Abdu-l-Mumin. Was stronghold of corsairs, 17th–18th cent. Exports agr. products. Textile mfg.

Rebaul: see NEW BRITAIN, Bismarck Archipelago.

rabbi (răb′bī) [Heb.,= my master or my teacher], in the U.S., the title of a Jewish minister. He is called *rav* [great] among certain Jews in Eastern Europe, where the word *rabbi* is used only for a scholar or teacher. The title originated among the Palestinian Jews. The modern rabbi serves to expound Judaism and act as a leader of Israel.

Rabbi Ben Ezra: see IBN EZRA, ABRAHAM BEN MEIR.

rabbit, herbivorous mammal of hare family (Leporidae). Some species mature at six months and bear four litters a year. Species of genus *Sylvilagus* (e.g., cottontail, marsh, and swamp rabbits) are found from U.S. to N South America. Domesticated breeds are varieties of European rabbit (*Oryctolagus*). Fur is known as cony or coney. Some fur is used in making felt.

rabbit fever: see TULAREMIA.

Rabboni (răbō'nī) [Heb.,= my great master], title of respect addressed to Jesus. John 20.16.

Rabelais, François (ră'bůlā', Fr. frãswä' räblā'), c.1490–1553, French author of the satirical romances *Gargantua* and *Pantagruel.* A Benedictine monk, he took a medical degree at Montpellier (1530), where he later also taught (1537–39). It was during his stay at Lyons (1532–34) that Rabelais wrote the first two books of his history of the giant Gargantua and his son Pantagruel. The third and fourth books followed in 1546–52; the fifth book (of doubtful authorship) was published 1562. Under its burlesque humor, sometimes ribald, this masterpiece conceals serious discussions of education, politics, and philosophy. The breadth of Rabelais's learning, his zest for living, and his humanistic outlook are evident. Primarily, the work is a satire against the vulgarity and abuses of society. Its verbal virtuosity has been approximated in the classic 17th-cent. translation by Sir Thomas Urquhart (Books I–III) and Pierre Motteux (Books IV–V). After the death of his patron, King Francis I, Rabelais spent his last years as curate at Meudon.

Rabi, Isidor Isaac (rŏ'bē), 1898–, American physicist, b. Austria. Known for work in magnetism, molecular beams, and quantum mechanics. Discovered and measured radiations of atoms. Won 1944 Nobel Prize.

rabies: see HYDROPHOBIA.

Rabinowitz, Solomon or **Shalom:** see ALEICHEM, SHOLOM.

raccoon (răkōōn'), New World mammal (*Procyon*) related to kinkajou and panda. It is c.2½–3 ft. long, has brown and black hair, a black-masked, pointed face, and a black-ringed bushy tail. It often nests in trees.

race, obsolete division of humanity based on such physical criteria as skin color and hair texture. Concept of race had great vogue in 19th cent., when such divisions as Alpine, Aryan, Caucasian, Nordic, etc., were freely referred to. Although lack of scientific foundation of concept has been demonstrated, notion of race continues potent in 20th cent. Chief arguments against race concept are that multiple origins of man have not been proven; that population movement, and hence interbreeding, has been constant since man's beginning; and that no pure stocks exist, populations grading into each other with respect to the physical criteria that are supposed to distinguish one alleged race from another. Long isolation, rather than original purity, is held to account for relative distinctiveness of such stocks as the Eskimo and Japanese.

Race, Cape, SE tip of Avalon Peninsula, SE N.F., Canada. Has lighthouse and radio direction-finding station.

Raceland, city (pop. 1,001), E Ky., on Ohio R. and near Ashland. Has noted race track.

Rachel [Heb.,= ewe], Jacob's favorite wife, mother of Joseph and Benjamin, daughter of Laban. Although Jacob had been promised Rachel in marriage if he worked seven years for Laban, at the end of that time he was tricked into marrying Leah, her older sister. Jacob then had to serve Laban another seven years for Rachel. Gen. 29–33; 35; Mat. 2.18.

Rachel (räshĕl'), 1821–58, stage name of Elisa or Elizabeth Félix, French actress. Queen of the French stage in tragic roles, she was notable in works of Racine (esp. *Phèdre*) and Corneille.

Rachmaninov, Sergei (Vasilyevich) (syĭrgā' räkhmä'nĕnôf), 1873–1943, Russian pianist, composer, and conductor. The romanticism and lyricism of his music owes much to his friend Tchaikovsky. Outstanding are his Second Piano Concerto, his Second Symphony; *Rhapsody on a Theme of Paganini,* for piano and orchestra; a tone poem, *The Isle of the Dead;* and his piano preludes in C sharp minor and G minor.

Racine, Jean (zhã' räsēn'), 1639–99, French dramatist, foremost representative of modern classic tragedy. His third play, *Andromaque* (1667), gave him Corneille's place as leading dramatist and won him the protection of Louis XIV. His next six tragedies were all masterpieces: *Britannicus* (1669), *Bérénice* (1670), *Bajazet* (1672), *Mithridate* (1673), *Iphigénie en Aulide* (1674), and *Phèdre* (1677). Representing French classicism at its perfection, they are unsurpassed in nobility and simplicity of diction, musicality of verse, psychological insight, and dramatic construction. His only comedy, *Les Plaideurs* (1668), wittily satirizes the law courts. After a concerted attack on *Phèdre,* Racine gave up the theater, but Mme de Maintenon persuaded him to write two more plays for performance at her school at Saint-Cyr—*Esther* (1689) and *Athalie* (1691). Based on biblical themes, these two tragedies contain notable innovations, particularly the use of choruses, and rank among his best. Racine is generally considered the greatest of French dramatists.

Racine (růsēn'), industrial city (pop. 71,193), SE Wis., on L. Michigan at mouth of Root R. and S of Milwaukee; settled 1834. Site known to French explorers and fur traders. Industrial growth came with harbor improvement and railroad. Mfg. of farm machinery, waxes and polishes, and paints and varnishes.

racing. Earliest Olympic Games consisted of foot races only. In Roman era chariot racing was favorite pastime. Organized horse racing under saddle dates from 12th cent. in England. After 1830, introduction of racing sulky led to harness racing. Automobile racing, boat racing, bicycle racing, dog racing also popular in U.S.

Rackham, Arthur (ră'kům), 1867–1939, English artist, known for illustrations for children's books.

Racovian Catechism: see SOCINIANISM.

racquets (ră'kĭts), game played by two or four persons on court 60 ft. by 30 ft., surrounded by three walls 30 ft. high and backwall 15 ft. high. Originated in 18th-cent. England, probably in debtors' prison, but was soon taken up by wealthy classes.

radar (rā'där), radio detecting and ranging device used to locate planes and ships and to bomb precisely. Consists of short-wave radio transmitter; wave-concentrating, beam-directing antenna, which receives beam reflected back upon hitting an object; receiver; and indicator (usually cathode-ray tubes that act as radar screen). Target found by revolving antenna to direction of strongest echo or by synchronizing cathode beam to revolve on screen in conjunction with antenna so as to show target bearing. Reception time lag of two antennae varying in height gives target altitude.

Radburn, N.J.: see FAIR LAWN.

Radcliffe, Ann (Ward), 1764–1823, English novelist, author of stories of mystery and intrigue, such as *The Mysteries of Udolpho* (1794).

Radcliffe College: see HARVARD UNIVERSITY.

Radetzky, Joseph, Graf (yō'zĕf gräf rädĕt'skē), 1766–1858, Austrian field marshal. Routed Sardinians at Custozza (1848) and Novara (1849).

Radford, city (pop. 9,026), SW Va., WSW of Roanoke. Mfg. of foundry products and textiles; railroad shops. Near by are Claytor L. and hydroelectric dam.

radiation, emission of energy by matter and its transfer through space; sunlight is best-known form. Invisible radiation also occurs; ultraviolet rays range in wave length from 0.10–0.4 microns; X rays are still shorter, as are gamma rays of RADIOACTIVITY. Radio waves and infrared are longer than light. All these waves travel through space at c.186,000 mi. per second. Radiometer detects radiant energy. See *ill.*, p. 989.

radiator (rā'dēā"tŭr). Radiators of hot-water heating systems in buildings are usually constructed in sections which can be joined for required radiating surface, and are made of cast iron, steel, brass, or copper. Heating efficiency is reduced by covering radiator with screens, shelves, and even certain paints. Coil radiators set in walls or ceilings are essentially long steam pipes. Automobile radiator is part of cooling system.

radical, in chemistry, elements which are grouped together in same proportion by weight in different compounds and act as units in many reactions. Common radicals are hydroxyl, sulphate, ammonium, carbonate, chlorate, nitrate, phosphate. Carboxyl group (COOH) is characteristic of organic acids.

radio. Growing from studies of electromagnetic waves, radiotelegraphy demonstrated by Marconi in 1895. Radiotelephony (transmission of speech and music) began with invention of diode rectifier tube, 1904, and triode amplifier tube, 1906. FACSIMILE, TELEVISION, RADAR developed later. Transmitter, through antenna, emits magnetic field inducing voltage in any receiver within radiation area; voltage (carrier wave) generated by oscillator is amplified and combined, by amplitude modulation or FREQUENCY MODULATION, with amplified audio-frequency microphone signal. Receiver selects, amplifies desired carrier (see SUPERHETERODYNE); detects or demodulates; LOUDSPEAKER transforms signal into sound. See *ill.*, p. 377.

radioactivity, property shown by certain elements, e.g., actinium, polonium, plutonium, radium, thorium, and uranium that involves emission of special types of RADIATION. It is a property of the atom of the element. Radiation is of three kinds: alpha, beta, and gamma rays. Alpha rays are positive particles, helium nuclei, hurled from atom; have lower velocity, smaller penetrating power than other radiations; direction is slightly changed by magnetic field. Beta rays are electrons (negative charges); faster than alpha rays; their direction is changed markedly by magnetic field. Gamma rays have greatest penetrating power; velocity almost that of light; direction not changed by magnetic field. Atoms of radioactive elements are not stable; disintegration proceeds at definite rate (each element has a definite "life"). Disintegration cannot be changed by known means. Elements of lower atomic weights are produced from those with higher one; final result is nonradioactive element; series is called disintegration series. For example, disintegration of uranium yields ionium and this yields radium which also disintegrates; lead is end product of uranium series. See also ISOTOPE. See *ill.*, p. 989.

radio beacon, radio transmitting station to aid plane and ship navigation. Airport radio-range signals, known as A (.–) and N (–.), transmitted in alternate quadrants produce overlap zones or beams in which only a steady hum can be received; zones coincide with standard flight approaches to field. Pilot follows beam in to cone of silence over beacon. Very high frequency (VHF) beacon is omnidirectional; distance-measuring equipment (DME) used. Fan and Z markers give vertical, horizontal orientation.

Radio City: see ROCKEFELLER CENTER.

radio frequency. Electromagnetic waves with periods or cycles suitable for use in wireless communication have radio frequency. They carry the lower frequency audio waves from the microphone.

radiometer (rā"dēŏ'mŭtŭr), instrument for detecting radiant energy and measuring its intensity. Within vacuum bulb are two delicate crossed bars free to rotate about the top of vertical support; each bar end has upright metal vane with one polished side, one blackened (energy-absorbent) side. Radiant energy absorbed by blackened side heats vane, increases activity of air molecules left within bulb, and sets all vanes moving. Speed of rotating vanes indicates intensity of radiant energy.

radiotherapy (rā"dēōthĕ'rŭpē), treatment by means of radiation. Chief agents are X RAY; penetrating gamma rays given off by radium salts and radon and used to treat growths; and beta rays from radium salts, used for superficial conditions.

radish, annual or biennial vegetable (*Raphanus sativus*) of mustard family with tuberlike root used in spring salads and as a garnish. In one variety, the rat-tailed radish, the long seed pods are eaten raw or pickled.

Radisson, Pierre Esprit (pyĕr' ĕprē' rädēsō'), c.1632–1710, French explorer and fur trader in North America. In 1659–60 he went as far W as present Minn. with his brother-in-law, Médard Chouart, sieur des Groseilliers. Largely responsible for formation of Hudson's Bay Co.

radium, lustrous, white, radioactive element (symbol = Ra; see also ELEMENT, table). Corrodes on exposure to air; resembles calcium in chemical activity. Bromide is usual commercial form. RADIOACTIVITY high for salts and metal. Element is derived indirectly from disintegration of URANIUM. Disintegrates to yield RADON; this disintegrates, producing in order radium A, B, C, D, E, F (polonium), and G (uranium lead). Present in ores in minute amounts; difficult to extract. Used in treating cancer, in making luminous paints and varnishes. Mme Curie isolated it from pitchblende (1910). See *ill.*, p. 989.

radium emanation: see RADON.

Radnorshire (răd'nŭr-shĭr) or **Radnor,** border county (471 sq. mi.; pop. 19,998), E central Wales; co. town New Radnor. Terrain, mostly hilly, includes Forest of Radnor (moorland 2,000 ft. high). Sheep and cattle raising is chief occupation. Sparsely populated region, it has no large towns and no mfg.

Radom (rä'dôm), city (pop. 69,455), central Poland, S of Warsaw. Mfg. of clothes, metal products. One of oldest Polish towns, it was seat of Polish diets (14th–16th cent.). Passed to Austria 1795; to Russia 1815; reverted to Poland 1919.

radon (rā'dŏn), **radium emanation,** or **niton** (nī'tŏn), gaseous, radioactive element (symbol = Rn; see also ELEMENT, table). It is an inert gas derived from disintegration of RADIUM; yields radium A. See *ill.*, p. 989.

Raeburn, Sir Henry (rā'bûrn), 1756–1823, Scottish portrait painter. Rose from humble beginnings as son of a miller. Worked in Edinburgh, where he enjoyed much popularity. His frank likenesses of Scottish celebrities have a quality of intimacy.

Rafa or **Rafah** (both: rä'fä), anc. *Raphia,* village, on border of Egypt and Palestine. Here in 217 B.C. Ptolemy IV defeated Antiochus III. Under Egyptian control since 1948.

raffia, fiber obtained from large leaves of the raffia palm (*Raphia*) of Madagascar. The tan-colored fiber is easily dyed and is exported for such uses as weaving baskets, hats, and mats, and tying up plants which need support.

Raffles, Sir Thomas Stamford Bingley, 1781–1826, English East Indian administrator. Lieutenant governor of Java 1811–15, he reduced power of native princes and made reforms in taxation and land tenure. Secured Singapore for East India Company 1819.

Rages (rā'jēz) or **Rhagae** (rā'jē), city of Persia prominent in anc. and medieval days. It was on an important trade route. Religious dissension damaged the city in 1186 and the Mongols destroyed more of it in 1220. Also Ray, Rei, and Rey.

ragged robin, perennial plant (*Lychnis flosculi*) native to Europe and Asia but naturalized in E North America. It has clusters of pink or red flowers with deeply cleft petals.

Ragnarok (räg'närûk") [Norse,= history of the gods], in the *Elder Edda,* a conception of the end of heaven, earth, and hell.

Ragusa, Yugoslavia; see DUBROVNIK.

ragweed, weedy American annual plant of genus *Ambrosia* with soft, lobed leaves and inconspicuous flowers. Pollen of the common ragweed (*Ambrosia artemisifolia*) is a chief cause of hay fever.

Rahab (rā'hăb), woman of Jericho who aided Joshua's spies, thus saving herself and family from destruction. Joshua 2. May be same as Rachab of Mat. 1.5.

Rahway (rô'wā), city (pop. 21,290), NE N.J., SW of Newark; settled c.1720 from Elizabeth. Mfg. of pharmaceuticals, lubricating oil, chemicals, cereals, metal and rubber goods.

Raiatea: see SOCIETY ISLANDS.

Raikes, Robert (rāks), 1735–1811, English philanthropist. His school held on Sunday for poor children (after 1780) was basis for Sunday-school system.

railroad or **railway.** The first railroads were horse-drawn wagons on wooden rails used in England to haul coal and ore in 17th and 18th cent. Iron rails replaced wooden ones in 18th cent. when inventors in England, France, and the U.S. experimented with steam locomotives. Among these inventors were Oliver EVANS, James WATT, and Richard Trevithick, who in 1801 perfected a steam locomotive capable of pulling a heavy load. Famous early locomotives were the *Stourbridge Lion,* imported from England, the first locomotive to run on any American railway; the *Rocket,* invented in 1829 by George STEPHENSON; and the *Tom Thumb,* built by Peter COOPER, which made a successful run in 1830. Major cities on the Atlantic coast became nerve centers for many short railroads, while inland points were readily connected with one another. Soon railroads were undermining the commercial value of the turnpike and canal. The Civil War gave great impetus to railroads which aided in the transportation of troops and supplies. The first transcontinental railroad was the Union Pacific, completed 1869. The great railway financiers, among them Cornelius Vanderbilt (who consolidated the New York Central Railroad) Jay Gould, Daniel Drew, James Fisk, and others were accused of acting with complete disregard for the American public. One of the greatest financial battles was fought by James J. HILL and Edward H. Harriman. The GRANGER MOVEMENT protested the rebate and other abuses. The 1880s saw the creation of the INTERSTATE COMMERCE COMMISSION, which sought to fix adequate controls upon railroads, and the adoption of a standard gauge (4 ft. 8½ in. between rails). Labor became a potent force with the organization of the four independent brotherhoods in the late 19th cent. After World War I, railroads in part met the increasing competition of bus, automobile, and airplane by measures for increasing safety and comfort. Outstanding railroads in the U.S. not previously mentioned include the Pennsylvania, the Baltimore and Ohio, the Erie, the Northern Pacific, the Southern Pacific, and the Santa Fe. Among other well-integrated systems are those of England, the

European continent, India, and Japan. Of world importance are the Baghdad, Chinese Eastern, and Transandine railways, and the Trans-Caspian and Trans-Siberian railroads, all serving large areas.

Raimondi, Marcantonio (märkäntō'nyō rīmōn'dē), b. c.1480, d. before c.1534, Italian copperplate engraver of works by Dürer and Raphael.

rain, precipitation formed by further condensing of cloud moisture. Drops grow by coalescing on impact and by condensation on their surface of moisture in air as they fall. Evaporation begins as drops leave cloud, rate depending on lower-air warmth, dryness. Rain a primary climatic element; great factor in distribution of plant and animal life. Annual rainfall varies from less than 2 in. in arid DESERT to 400 in. in Khasi hills, Assam, and on windward slopes of Hawaiian mountains. Controlling factors in earth's rain distribution: converging-ascending air-flow belts (e.g., the doldrums), air temperature, moisture-bearing winds, ocean currents, distance inland from coast, mountain ranges. Ascending air cools, forms cloud, and causes rain. Descending air belts (horse latitudes) mark great deserts.

Rainalducci, Pietro (pyā'trō rīnäldōōt'chē), d. 1333, Italian churchman, antipope as Nicholas V, a Franciscan. When Emperor Louis IV declared Pope John XXII (at Avignon) deposed for heresy, he set up Pietro instead (at Rome) in 1328. Finding his position untenable, Pietro gave up the office in 1330 and was held in honorable captivity at Avignon.

rainbow, arc with colors of SPECTRUM that appears in sky, opposite sun, when sun shines through water droplets. The sun, observer's eye, and center of arc must be in line. Bow is caused by reflection and refraction of sun's rays. Sometimes two bows are seen, one paler than and outside of the primary bow. Symbolizes God's promise of mercy to man after the flood (Gen. 9.13).

Rainbow Bridge National Monument: see NATIONAL PARKS AND MONUMENTS (table).

Rainbow Division, nickname of 42nd Division of U.S. army in World War I. First American combat division to arrive in France, it fought through several campaigns, suffered heavy losses.

Rainier, Mount (rūnēr', rā'–), 14,408 ft. high, SW central Wash., in Mt. Rainier Natl. Park (see NATIONAL PARKS AND MONUMENTS, table). Snow-crowned volcanic peak with 26 glaciers and heavily forested lower slopes. Highest point in Wash. and in CASCADE RANGE.

Rain-in-the-Face, d. 1905, North American Indian chief, leader of the Sioux. A commander at annihilation of G. A. Custer's force on Little Bighorn R. in Mont., June 25, 1876.

Rainy Lake, c.60 mi. long, W Ont., lying partly on Minn.-Ont. boundary, in wooded area with many islands. Outlet, **Rainy River,** flows W 85 mi. along international line to L. of the Woods.

Rais, Gilles de: see RETZ, GILLES DE LAVAL, SEIGNEUR DE.

Raisin, river rising in S Mich. and flowing c.115 mi. E to L. Erie at Monroe. Scene of defeat in War of 1812 of U.S. troops by British and Indians and subsequent massacre (Jan. 22, 1813) of remaining Americans by Indians.

raisin, dried fruit of certain varieties of grapevines of the European type (*Vitis vinifera*). Production is limited to regions with a long, hot growing season, since grapes must stay on vines until fully mature and are then dried, usually in the sun. Most seedless raisins, especially in Calif., are produced from the Sultanina or Thompson seedless grape, known in international trade as the Sultana; a different kind, produced in Calif., is known there as the Sultana. The Muscat is a flavorful variety, commonly sold in clusters for table use. Raisins of sharp flavor and firm texture are often called currants. Raisins are valuable nutritionally because of their sugar, mineral (esp. iron), and vitamin A and B content.

Rajagopalachari, Chakravarti (chŭkrŭvär'tē rä"jŭgōpä"lŭchä'rē), 1879–, Indian nationalist. Joined Indian Natl. Congress in 1919. In World War II he broke with the Congress because he favored support of British war effort, but rejoined it after the war. Was last governor general of India (1948–50). Became minister of home affairs, 1951.

Rajasthan (rä'jŭstän), state (128,424 sq. mi.; pop. 15,297,979), NW India; cap. Jaipur. Formed 1948–50 largely by merging princely states (notably Bikaner and Jaipur) formerly making up region of Rajputana. Partly desert. Agr. area in E part produces grains and cotton. Region was settled 7th cent. by the Rajputs, who resisted Moslem invasion until 16th cent., when Mogul rule was estab. In 19th cent. the British ousted Mahratta invaders and assumed protection of the princely states.

Rajasthani (rä'jŭstä'nē), a language of Indic group of Indo-Iranian subfamily of Indo-European languages. See LANGUAGE (table).

Rajputana, India: see RAJASTHAN.

Rajputs (räj'pōōts), a people, numbering c.650,000, mostly in Rajasthan, India. They are of the warrior caste and claim divine origin. Dominant in Rajputana since 7th cent.

Rakoczy, Hung. *Rákóczy* (rä'kôtsĭ), noble Hungarian family, princes of TRANSYLVANIA. **Sigismund Rakoczy,** 1544–1608, succeeded Stephen Bocskay as prince 1607. His son **George I Rakoczy,** 1591–1648 (reigned 1630–48), made war on Emperor Ferdinand III and forced him to grant religious freedom to Hungary (Peace of Linz, 1645). His son **George II Rakoczy,** 1621–60, succeeded his father as prince but was deposed 1657 after unsuccessfully invading Poland. His son **Francis I Rakoczy,** 1645–76, claimed succession but never was recognized as prince. Conspired with his father-in-law, Peter ZRINYI, against Emperor Leopold I. His son **Francis II Rakoczy,** 1675–1735, led Hungarian uprising against Hapsburgs in 1703; was elected "ruling prince" of Hungary 1704; secured aid of Louis XIV. Defeated in 1708 and 1710, the Hungarians made peace with the emperor 1711, but Rakoczy refused to accept treaty, fled abroad, and died an exile in Turkey. He is a national hero of Hungary. The Rakoczy March, named for him, was composed 1809 by John Bihari but may be based on an older tune; Berlioz and Liszt made use of it.

Ralegh or **Raleigh, Sir Walter** (both: rô'lē, ră'–), 1552?–1618, English statesman and man of letters. A favorite of Queen Elizabeth, he was involved in rivalry with the earl of Essex. Originated colonizing expeditions to America (see ROANOKE ISLAND); introduced potatoes and tobacco to England. Associated with poetic group called "school of night" which gained a reputation for atheism. In 1595 Ralegh made first expedition up Orinoco R. His fortunes fell with James I's accession. He was convicted of treason on slim evidence and imprisoned in Tower. Released (1616) to make another voyage to the Orinoco. On his return he was executed under the original sentence for treason. His writings include poetry and political and philosophical works.

Raleigh (rô'lē), city (pop. 65,679), state cap., central N.C. Selected as state cap. 1788, laid out 1792. Taken by Sherman in Civil War, April 14, 1865. Cottonseed-oil and lumber mills; printing, publishing; tobacco market. Birthplace of Andrew Johnson. Seat of Meredith Col. (Baptist; women; 1891), State Col. of Agriculture and Engineering of Univ. of NORTH CAROLINA, Shaw Univ. (Negro; Baptist; coed.; 1865), and St. Augustine's Col. (Negro; Episcopal; coed.; 1867).

Raleigh, Fort: see ROANOKE ISLAND.

Rama, hero: see RAMAYANA.

Ramadan (rämädän', ră"mŭdăn'), in ISLAM, ninth month of the year, when Moslems fast strictly during daylight. It commemorates the first revelation of the Koran. Because the Islamic calendar is lunar, Ramadan falls in different seasons.

Ramah (rā'mŭ), traditional burial place of Rachel, an important outpost N of Jerusalem.

Ramakrishna (rä"mŭkrĭsh'nŭ), 1836–86, Hindu mystic. Advocating active benevolence rather than quietism, he believed all religions equally valid forms needed (except by mystics) to approach the Eternal. He won many followers, even in the West.

Raman, Sir Chandrasekhara Venkata (chŭn'drŭsĕkä'rŭ vĕng'kŭtŭ rä'mŭn), 1888–, Indian physicist. Won 1930 Nobel Prize for research on diffusion of light and discovery of **Raman effect:** produced when part of beam of monochromatic light is scattered in passing through transparent medium; light is changed in wave length (mainly increased) and in frequency (mainly decreased).

Ramapo Mountains (răm'ŭpō"), forested range of the Appalachians, NE N.J. and SE N.Y. Hiking trails.

Ramayana (rämä'yŭnŭ) [story of Rama], great Sanskrit epic of India, perhaps written in 2d cent. B.C. In c.43,000 couplets of 16-syllable lines, it tells the adventures of Rama, heir to kingdom of Ajodhya, who, with his half brothers, collectively made up an avatar (incarnation) of the god Vishnu.

Rambam: see MAIMONIDES.

Rambaud, Alfred Nicolas (älfrĕd' nēkôlä' rābō'), 1842–1905, French historian and politician. Minister of public instruction (1896–98). Author of Byzantine history, notably *L'Empire grec au dixième siècle* (1870) and *Études sur l'histoire Byzantine* (1912).

Rambouillet, Catherine de Vivonne, marquise de (kätrēn' dŭ vēvôn' märkēz' dŭ rābŏŏyā'), 1588–1665, famous Frenchwoman, whose salon exercised deep influence on French literature. Her circle included Mme de Sévigné, Mme de La Fayette, Corneille, Balzac, Richelieu, Malherbe, Bossuet, Scarron, La Rochefoucauld. The preciosity made fashionable by her salon later degenerated into extravagance and was much ridiculed by Molière.

Rambouillet (rābŏŏyā'), town (pop. 6,531), Seine-et-Oise dept., N France, S of Paris. Château is summer residence of French presidents. Vast Forest of Rambouillet is used for official hunting parties.

Rameau, Jean Philippe (rämō'), 1683–1764, French composer and theorist. His compositions include harpsichord suites and operas (e.g., *Castor et Pollux*). His treatises on harmony, in which he introduced the doctrine of inversions of chords (i.e., E-G-C and G-C-E are the same chord as C-E-G), are the basis of musical theory today.

Ramée, Pierre de la: see RAMUS, PETRUS.

Rameses or **Ramesses:** see RAMSES.

ramie (răm'ē), tall perennial plant (*Boehmeria nivea*), also called China grass, long grown in the Far East for its fiber, obtained from the bast. It has been made into underwear, paper, and in the Orient, grass cloth and other fabrics.

Ramillies (ră'mĭlēz, Fr. rämēyē'), village near Namur, Belgium. Scene of brilliant victory of allies under Marlborough over French under Villeroi (1706).

Ramiro I (rämē'rō), d. 1063, first king of Aragon (1035–63), natural son of Sancho III of Navarre. Annexed Sobrarbe and Ribagorza and fought the Moors.

Ramón y Cajal, Santiago (säntyä'gō rämōn' ē kähäl'), 1852–1934, Spanish histologist. Shared 1906 Nobel Prize in Physiology and Medicine for work on structure of nervous system.

Ramos, João de Deus (zhwã'ō dŭ dā'ŏŏsh rä'mŏŏsh), 1830–96, Portuguese poet; author of *Campo de flores* (1893; a collection of lyrics in the popular idiom).

Ramoth-Gilead (rā'mŏth-gĭ'lēăd) or **Ramoth in Gilead,** anc. town, E of Jordan R., named by Joshua as city of refuge. Site of Ahab's last battle.

Ramsay, Allan, 1686–1758, Scottish poet, major figure in revival of vernacular poetry; best known for his pastoral comedy *The Gentle Shepherd* (1725).

Ramsay, Sir William, 1852–1916, Scottish chemist. Discovered helium; was codiscoverer of argon, krypton, neon, xenon; worked on radium emanation. Won 1904 Nobel Prize for his work.

Ramsden, Jesse, 1735–1800, English optician and mechanician, noted for mathematical instruments.

Ramses (răm'sēz), **Rameses** (răm'ŭsēz", rŭmē'sēs), or **Ramesses** (răm'ŭsēz"), kings of anc. Egypt of XIX and XX dynasties. **Ramses I,** d. 1314 B.C., was successor to Harmhab. He began the hypostyle at Karnak. His grandson, **Ramses II,** d. 1225 B.C., was the son of SETI I but not the heir. He usurped the throne and in his long reign (1292–1225 B.C.) brought Egypt to unprecedented splendor. The empire stretched from S Syria to the fourth cataract of the Nile, and social life was very luxurious for the upper classes. Ramses left many monuments, completing the temple at Karnak and building a mortuary temple at Thebes and the great rock temple at Abu-Simbel. He long warred on the Hittites. He was succeeded by Merneptah. Anarchy later was ended by **Ramses III,** d. 1167 B.C., who reigned c.1198–1167 B.C., second king of the XX dynasty. He warred successfully in Libya and Syria. The great luxury of his reign, particularly the riches of the temples and nobles, presaged the decay that followed. Toward the end of his reign his wife Tiy conspired unsuccessfully against him.

Ramsey (răm'zē), market town (pop. 5,772), Huntingdonshire, England. Ramsey Abbey was founded in 10th cent. Property later held by Cromwell family.

Ramsgate (rămz'gĭt), municipal borough (pop. 35,748) on Isle of Thanet, Kent, England; a resort and seaport. Victoria lived here as a princess. Near-by Ebbsfleet was landing place of St. Augustine and, traditionally, of Hengist and Horsa. Site of a Jewish college founded by Montefiore.

Ramus, Petrus (pē'trŭs rā'mŭs), Fr. *Pierre de la Ramée,* 1515–72, French humanist. After 1551 taught rhetoric and philosophy at the Collège de France, but having become Protestant had to flee to Germany. Returned and was killed in the massacre of St. Bartholomew's Day. He tried to develop a logic to supersede Aristotle's and encouraged skeptical thought.

Ramusio, Giambattista (jäm"bät-tē'stä rämōō'zyō), 1485–1557, Italian editor and compiler. Known for his *Delle navigationi e viaggi,* collection of geographical accounts of explorations.

Ramuz, Charles Ferdinand (shärl' fĕrdēnä' rämü'), 1878–1947, Swiss novelist, who wrote in French. His novels, dealing with simple people faced with elemental nature, include *The Reign of the Evil One* (1917; Eng. tr., 1922) and *Derborence* (1935; Eng. tr., *When the Mountain Fell,* 1947).

Rancagua (rängkä'gwä), city (pop. 29,442), central Chile, S of Santiago; founded 1743 in fertile valley of Andean foothills. Although one of Chile's largest copper mines is near by, city has developed primarily as agr. center. Here in 1814 revolutionary forces resisted a siege and escaped.

Rand, the, South Africa: see WITWATERSRAND.

Randers (rä'nŭrs), city (pop. 40,098), E Jutland, Denmark; a port on Randers Fjord (inlet of the Kattegat) and at mouth of Guden R. Varied mfg. Important trade center in Middle Ages.

Randolph, Edmund (răn'dŏlf), 1753–1813, American statesman. At Federal Constitutional Convention (1787) he presented Virginia or Randolph Plan, favoring large states. U.S. Attorney General (1789–94); U.S. Secretary of State (1794–95). His uncle, **Peyton Randolph,** c.1721–1775, was first president of Continental Congress (1774) and was active in patriot cause in Va. before American Revolution.

Randolph, Edward, c.1632–1703, British colonial agent. Attacked legality of Mass. Bay charter.

Randolph, John, 1773–1833, American statesman, known as John Randolph of Roanoke. U.S. Representative (1799–1813, 1815–17, 1819–25, 1827–29) and U.S. Senator (1825–27) from Va. Known for sharp, biting tongue; opposed Madison and Northern Democrats, War of 1812, Missouri Compromise.

Randolph, Peyton: see RANDOLPH, EDMUND.

Randolph, town (pop. 9,982), E Mass., S of Boston; settled c.1710. Food products.

Randolph-Macon College, at Ashland, Va.; Methodist, for men; chartered 1830, opened 1832 at Boydton, moved 1868, named for John Randolph and Nathaniel Macon. Same board controls **Randolph-Macon Woman's College** (1893) at Lynchburg.

Rand School of Social Science, in New York City; opened 1906; a socialist institution but not officially connected with the Socialist party. Classes scheduled to suit needs of working people.

Randwick, municipality (pop. 100,931), New South Wales, Australia, just SE of Sydney, in metropolitan area. Large race track is here.

Ranelagh (ră'nĭlŭ), former amusement resort in Chelsea, London. Founded (1742) on the estate of the earl of Ranelagh, it was closed in 1803 or 1804.

Rangabe (rāgäbā') or **Rhangavis, Alexandros Rizos** (älĕk'sändhrôs rē'zôs räng"gävēs'), 1810–92, Greek scholar, author, and diplomat. Was prominent in Greek classicist revival. Particularly notable as dramatist, he wrote in classic Greek.

range, grazing land of large area in W U.S. and Canada, formerly unfenced public land, now chiefly privately owned. Rights to the grazing on unfenced land in the national forests are purchased.

Rangeley, town (pop. 1,228), W Maine, NNW of Rumford and on Rangeley L. (7 mi. long), one of a group of lakes in Maine and N.H. Hq. of famous fishing and hunting region.

Rangoon (răng"gōōn'), city (pop. 500,800), cap. and chief port of Burma, on Rangoon R., near its mouth on Gulf of Martaban. Modernized after 1852, when British rule was estab. Exports rice, oil, and teak. Site of the famous Shwe Dagon Pagoda and a university (founded 1920). In World War II it was occupied 1942–45 by the Japanese and was severely damaged by bombing.

Ranjit Singh (rŭn'jĭt sĭng'), 1780–1839, Sikh ruler, who conquered the Punjab and Kashmir. After Second Sikh War (1848–49) his domain fell to the British.

Rank, Otto (ô'tō rängk), 1884–1939, Austrian psychoanalyst, an early pupil of Freud. He used Freudian techniques to interpret myths, but differed from Freud in that he regarded the birth trauma (rather than Oedipus complex) as chief cause of neurosis.

Ranke, Leopold von (lā'ōpôlt fŭn räng'kŭ), 1795–1886, German historian. Known as father of modern objective historical school, through teaching and writing he influenced generation of historians. In writings he ranged over all European nations; collected works fill 54 volumes (1867–90). Culminating work was *Weltgeschichte* (9 vols., 1881–88).

Rankin, borough (pop. 6,941), SW Pa., ESE of Pittsburgh. Mfg. of steel.

Rannoch, Loch (lŏkh ră'nŭkh), lake, c.9½ mi. long and 1 mi. wide, Perthshire, Scotland.

Ransom, John Crowe, 1888–, American poet and critic. His verse includes *Selected Poems* (1945).

Ranters, adherents of antinomian movement in England during Commonwealth. Teaching was pantheistic. Individuals were given freedom of thought. In 19th cent. Primitive Methodists were called Ranters.

Rantoul (răn"tōōl'), village (pop. 6,387), E Ill., N of Champaign, in farm area. Chanute Air Force Base is here.

Raoul (räōōl'), d. 936, French king (923–36), duke of Burgundy. Was elected king to succeed his father-in-law, Robert I. Established his authority over claims of Charles III (the Simple).

Raoult's law (räōōlz') states that lowering of vapor pressure of a solvent is proportional to concentration (molar) of substance dissolved. Formulated by François Marie Raoult (1830–1901), French chemist.

Rapallo (räpäl'-lō), resort town (pop. 6,766), Liguria, NW Italy, on the Riviera. For the **Treaty of Rapallo** of 1920, see FIUME. The **Treaty of Rapallo** of 1922 was an agreement signed by Germany and the USSR during but independently of the Conference of GENOA. Germany accorded the Soviet government its first *de jure* recognition; both signatories mutually canceled all pre-war debts and war claims; extensive trade agreements were made.

rape, annual or biennial plant (*Brassica napus*) related to the cabbage and grown chiefly for forage in North America. The seed yields an oil and is used in birdseed mixtures.

rape, in law, crime of sexual intercourse with a woman (other than one's wife) without her consent. A woman is deemed legally incapable of consent if insane, feebleminded, or below the age set by statute as the age of consent. Failure on the part of the woman to resist—unless resistance would be obviously useless—usually is considered to imply consent.

Raphael (ră'fēŭl, rä'–) [Heb.,=God heals], archangel. Prominent in book of TOBIT as companion of Tobias, healer of Tobit, and rescuer of Sara. Feast: Oct. 24. Appears in Milton's *Paradise Lost.*

Raphael, Ital. *Raffaello Santi* or *Raffaello Sanzio,* 1483–1520, Italian painter, one of the greatest artists of the Renaissance, b. Urbino. His father, Giovanni Santi, was court painter and poet to duke of Urbino. In c.1500 Raphael entered the workshop of Perugino, whose influence is seen in coloring and graceful composition of such early works as *The Three Graces* (Chantilly) and the *Sposalizio* (Brera, Milan). In Florence (1504–8) he painted *The Entombment* (Rome) and the many famous Madonnas, whose landscape backgrounds reflect influence of Leonardo and Massaccio. From 1508 until his death he worked in Rome, where he succeeded Bramante as chief architect of St. Peter's (1514). Here his mature style benefited from Michelangelo's influence. For his patron, Leo X, he made a survey of ancient Rome showing the chief monuments. His many works for the Vatican include 10 tapestries with themes from Acts of the Apostles for the Sistine Chapel and the great mural *School of Athens* for the Stanza della Segnatura. Also of the Roman period are the *Sistine Madonna* (perhaps his best-known work), named after the Church of San Sisto, Piacenza, and the superb portraits of Baldassare Castiglione (Louvre) and Pope Leo X (Pitti Palace, Florence).

Raphia: see RAFA, Egypt.

Rapidan, river rising in N Va., in Blue Ridge mts., and flowing SW then NE to the Rappahannock.

Rapid City, city (pop. 25,310), SW S.Dak., near Black Hills, SE of Lead; founded 1876 after gold discovered. Trade center for gold and silver mines, farms, and dairies. Seat of South Dakota School of Mines and Technology (state supported; mainly for men; opened 1887), with collection of prehistoric fossils in Dinosaur Park. Near-by Deerfield Dam (1947) is in Rapid valley project.

Rapido (rä'pēdō), short river, S central Italy. Joins Liri below Cassino. In World War II, Allied attempt to outflank Cassino by crossing the Rapido resulted in heavy losses, particularly to U.S. troops (Jan., 1944).

Rappahannock, river rising in N Va., on E slope of Blue Ridge E of Front Royal, and flowing SW 212 mi. to Chesapeake Bay. Navigable to Fredericksburg. Much Civil War fighting took place along river.

rare earths, group of rare, vari-colored, earthy, mineral substances (oxides of certain metals). Originally were thought to be elements, but later metals were obtained from them. These **metals of the rare earths** have a valence of 3; atomic nos. range from 57 to 71; are obtained only in small amounts.

Raritan (ră'rĭtŭn), town (pop. 5,131), N central N.J., on Raritan R. and near Somerville.

Raritan, river, N central N.J., formed by branches W of Raritan and flowing c.35 mi. generally SE, past New Brunswick, to Raritan Bay (arm of Lower New York Bay) between Perth Amboy and South Amboy. Connected with Delaware R. by old Delaware and Raritan Canal.

Rarotonga: see COOK ISLANDS.

Rashi (rä'shē), 1040–1105, Jewish scholar, b. France; author of important commentaries on the Talmud and the Pentateuch. Real name Rabbi Solomon bar Isaac.

Rasis, Persian physician: see RHAZES.

Rask, Rasmus Christian (räs'mōōs krĭs'tyän räsk), 1787–1832, Danish philologist. He published perhaps the first usable Anglo-Saxon and Icelandic grammars (translated into English), and did valuable work on relationship of the Indo-European languages.

Rasmussen, Knud Johan Victor (räs'mōōsŭn), 1879–1933, Danish arctic explorer and ethnologist, authority on Greenland Eskimo. Sought confirmation of theory that Eskimo and North American Indian are of same

Asian stock. First to traverse Northwest Passage by dog sled.

raspberry, prickly deciduous shrub of genus *Rubus* which includes other brambles, and the red, purple, or black fruits. In North America most cultivated red raspberries are derived from *Rubus idaeus strigosus.* Blackcap raspberries are varieties of *R. occidentalis,* also native to North America. Purple varieties are hybrids of these and European species.

Rasputin, Grigori Yefimovich (grĭgô'rē yĭfē'-mŭvĭch rŭspŏŏ'tyĭn), 1872–1916, Russian monk, notorious figure at court of Nicholas II. An illiterate peasant and debauchee, he gained complete control over imperial couple through his miraculous "cure" of the hemophilic tsarevich, exerted sinister influence over politics and appointments, and was suspected of pro-German sympathies in World War I. Assassinated by group of noblemen headed by Prince Yussupov.

Rassam, Hormuzd (hôrmŏŏzd' räsäm'), 1826–1910, Turkish archaeologist. In Assyria and Babylonia he discovered the palace of Assurbani-pal and the site of Sippar.

Rastatt (rä'shtät), town (pop. 16,551), S Baden, SW Germany. For Treaty of Rastatt (1714), see UTRECHT, PEACE OF.

Rastrelli, Bartolomeo Francesco, Conte (rästrĕl'lē), 1700–1771, Italian architect, important in development of St. Petersburg (now Leningrad). Designed Winter Palace and Stroganov Palace.

rat, rodent of global distribution. Brown house rat (*Rattus norvegicus*) and black house rat (*R. rattus*) of Asia spread to Europe and New World. Rats cause huge property losses, spread typhus, bubonic plague, rat-bite fever, tularemia, and rabies.

ratchet and pawl, mechanical device generally used to permit motion in one direction only. Ratchet (toothed wheel) is arranged with pawl (lever with catch) so that pawl moves smoothly over teeth in one direction but catches teeth if reversed.

rath (rä, räth), hill fort protected by earthworks, used by anc. Irish as retreat in time of danger. Many remain throughout Ireland (esp. at Tara).

Rathenau, Walter (väl'tûr rä'tŭnou), 1867–1922, German industrialist and statesman. As minister of reconstruction (1921) and foreign minister (1922) he made sincere attempts to meet German reparations obligations. A Jew, he was assassinated by nationalist fanatics. His idealistic social philosophy found expression in several writings.

Rathlin (răth'lĭn), island (3,564 acres; pop. 245), off N. Ireland, in Co. Antrim. St. Columba founded a church here in 6th cent.

Ratibor (rä'tēbôr), Pol. *Racibórz,* city (1939 pop. 50,004; 1946 pop. 19,605), Upper Silesia, on Oder R.; transferred to Polish administration 1945. Mfg. of precision instruments, textiles, chemicals. Cap. of principality founded in 13th cent., it passed to Austria 1526, to Prussia 1745. Raised to a titular duchy 1840.

ratio. Ratio of two quantities (in terms of same unit) is fraction with first quantity as numerator and second as denominator.

rationalism (ră'shŭnŭlĭzŭm) [Latin,= belonging to reason], any philosophic theory assigning first place to reason in attainment of knowledge, from that of Plato to idealists of today. The term is most commonly applied to the 18th-cent. philosophers who attacked religion by rejecting all claims based on faith or revelation. Rationalism may also be opposed to EMPIRICISM, if the rationalist argues that truth may be obtained by reasoning from "self-evident" premises; empiricism rejects such premises.

Ratisbon, Bavaria: see REGENSBURG.

Rat Islands: see ALEUTIAN ISLANDS.

Raton (ră"tōōn'), city (pop. 8,241; alt. 6,400 ft.), NE N.Mex., near Colo. line; settled in 1870s on Santa Fe Trail. Resort and trade center in coal and livestock area. Capulin Mt. Natl. Monument, Folsom (see FOLSOM CULTURE), and Raton Pass (7,834 ft.) are near by.

rattan (rătăn'), name for certain climbing palms of genera *Calamus* and *Daemonorops* of tropical Asia from which the rattan cane of commerce is obtained. The cane, flexible and strong, is split for use in wickerwork, baskets, and chair seats.

rattlesnake, poisonous New World snake of pit viper family. Head is widened at base; "rattle" (series of dried, hollow segments making whirring sound if shaken) is at end of tail. Well known are timber, diamondback (largest), western diamondback, and prairie rattlesnakes.

Ratzel, Friedrich (frē'drĭkh rät'sŭl), 1844–1904, German geographer. Pioneered in development of anthropogeography and emphasized effects of physical environment on human activity.

Rauschenbusch, Walter, 1861–1918, American Baptist clergyman; professor of church history (after 1902) at Rochester Theological Seminary. Wrote influential books on social interpretation of Christianity.

Ravaillac, François (frãswä' räväyäk'), 1578–1610, assassin of Henry IV of France; a religious fanatic. Was drawn and quartered.

Ravel, Maurice (rävĕl'), 1875–1937, French composer. His music, subtle and lucid, often combines exotic materials with classic form. His works for piano include the suite *Le Tombeau de Couperin, Pavane pour une infante défunte, Ma Mère l'Oye, Valse nobles et sentimentales,* and two concertos; for orchestra, *Daphnis et Chloé, La Valse, Rhapsodie Espagnole,* and the popular *Bolero.*

raven, large glossy black bird of crow family, native to N Eurasia and North America. It can be tamed and learns to imitate words. Is primarily a scavenger.

Ravenna (rävĕn'nä), city (pop. 31,251), Emilia-Romagna, N central Italy, near the Po delta and Adriatic Sea. Augustus made its port, Classis, a major Roman naval station. Cap. of West Roman Empire from 402, Ravenna was after 476 the seat of Odoacer and Theodoric the Great; after 540 the seat of the Byzantine exarchs (governors) of Italy. The Lombards seized it in 751 but lost it to Pepin the Short, who deeded it to the pope (754; see PAPAL STATES). Ruled by the Da Polenta family 13th–15th cent., then briefly by Venice, it passed under the effective control of the popes only in 1509. Ravenna is famous for its Roman and Byzantine buildings—mausoleums of Galla Placidia and Theodoric; octagonal baptistery (earlier a Roman bath); churches of San Vitale, Sant' Apollinare Nuovo, and Sant' Apollinare in Classe. These contain unique mosaics of the 5th and 6th cent. Dante's tomb is at Ravenna.

Ravenna, city (pop. 9,857), NE Ohio, NE of Akron. Mfg. of rubber goods, yarn, and textiles.

Ravensberg (rä'vůnsběrk), former county, NW Germany, in Westphalia, NW of Lippe. Passed to count of Berg 1346, to duke of Jülich 1348, to duke of Cleves 1524, to Brandenburg 1614.

Rawalpindi (räwůlpĭn'dē), city (pop. 243,000), Punjab prov., W Pakistan; mfg. and trade center. Formerly British military hq. in the Punjab. Liaquat Ali Khan was assassinated here in 1952.

Rawlings, Marjorie Kinnan, 1896–, American author, writing usually of Florida backwoods. Novel *The Yearling* (1938) very popular.

Rawlins, city (pop. 7,415; alt. 6,755 ft.), S Wyo., WNW of Laramie. Oil, coal, and livestock center.

Rawlinson, Sir Henry Creswicke, 1810–95, English Orientalist and administrator. He investigated the inscription, in Persian CUNEIFORM, of Darius I at BEHISTUN. From 1865 to 1868 he sat in Parliament, and after that was a member of the India council.

ray, marine fish related to shark. It has a flat, disklike body and wide, fleshy, pectoral fins. Sting rays can inflict wound with saw-toothed tail spine. Devilfish or manta is a gigantic warm-water ray.

ray, in physics, narrow pencil of light or other radiation that proceeds through space in straight line from source. See also COSMIC RAYS; INFRARED RAYS; ULTRAVIOLET RAY; X RAY.

Rayburn, Sam(uel Taliaferro), 1882–, U.S. Congressman (1913–) from Texas. Democratic speaker of the House (1940–46, 1949–53), he had the longest record in that office.

Rayleigh, John William Strutt, 3d Baron (rā'lē), 1842–1919, English physicist. Won 1904 Nobel Prize. Known for research in sound, light, codiscovery of argon, determinations of electrical units, application of Boyle's law to gases at low pressures.

Raymond, counts of TOULOUSE. **Raymond IV,** d. 1105?, a leader in the First Crusade. Refused oath of fealty to Alexius I; quarreled with BOHEMOND over possession of Antioch; laid siege to Tripoli, later made into a county by his descendants. **Raymond VI,** d. 1222, was repeatedly excommunicated for support he gave to the ALBIGENSES. Attacked by Simon de MONTFORT, he received aid of PETER II of Aragon but was defeated at Muret (1213). His attempts to regain his lands from Montfort were continued by his son and successor, **Raymond VII,** 1197–1249. In 1229 Raymond VII was forced to sign a treaty which transferred most of S France to the French crown—partly through immediate cession, partly through the marriage of his daughter to Alphonse of Poitiers (a brother of Louis IX of France), who eventually inherited Toulouse. Raymond permitted establishment of the INQUISITION (1233).

Raymond, c.1140–1187, count of Tripoli (1152–87); great-great-grandson of Raymond IV of Toulouse. Regent for BALDWIN IV and Baldwin V during the last years of the Latin Kingdom of Jerusalem, he allied himself with SALADIN when Guy of LUSIGNAN succeeded Baldwin V. After a reconciliation, he fought on Christian side at Hattin (1187), where Jerusalem fell to the Moslems.

Raymond Berengar IV (bě'rûngär), d. 1162, count of Barcelona (1131–62). By his marriage to Petronella, daughter and heir of Ramiro II of Aragon, Catalonia and Aragon were united.

Raymondville, city (pop. 9,136), S Texas, NNW of Brownsville. Trade and shipping center for agr. area with some oil. Tourist trade.

Rayne, town (pop. 6,485), SW La., SW of Baton Rouge. Mills rice and ships frogs.

rayon (rā'ŏn"), synthetic fibers made from CELLULOSE and the fabrics woven from them. Rayon is produced by dissolving cellulose (from wood pulp or cotton linters) in chemicals, then forcing it through minute holes so that filaments, hardened either in liquid or warm air, are formed. Filaments are then either twisted into thread or cut into lengths and spun. Spun rayon can be made to simulate wool, linen, or cotton. Methods of manufacturing rayon include the nitrocellulose process, developed in 1880s and no longer important; the VISCOSE PROCESS, discovered in 1892; the cuprammonium process, yielding very fine, strong yarn; and the acetate process, originated in England in 1918, which produces an acetate derivative of cellulose rather than the regenerated cellulose of the other types. Rayon yarns with new properties are constantly being developed, as are such substances as cellulose substitutes for sponge rubber, acetate fillers for nonshatterable glass, and flexible grease-proof and moistureproof sheets such as CELLOPHANE.

Razin, Stenka (stěng'kä rä'zēn), d. 1671, ataman (leader) of Don Cossacks, celebrated in song and legend. Aided by peasants and local tribes, he rebelled against tsar (1670), took lower and middle Volga region, but was ultimately defeated and beheaded.

Rb, chemical symbol of the element RUBIDIUM.

Ré (rā), island (33 sq. mi.; pop. 7,908), off La Rochelle, W France, in Bay of Biscay; formerly also spelled Rhé. Citadel, built by Vauban (1681), is now a penitentiary.

Re, chemical symbol of the element RHENIUM.

reaction, chemical: see CHEMICAL REACTION.

Read, Opie (Percival), 1852–1939, American author, editor of the humorous *Arkansas Traveler,* author of robust novels (e.g., *A Kentucky Colonel,* 1889).

Read, Thomas Buchanan, 1822–72, American poet and artist, author of the poem, "Sheridan's Ride."

Reade, Charles, 1814–84, English novelist. Wrote propagandist novels in favor of various causes, but is remembered for his great medieval romance, *The Cloister and the Hearth* (1861).

Reading, Rufus Daniel Isaacs, 1st marquess of (rĕ′dĭng), 1860–1935, British statesman. A successful lawyer, he became (1910) attorney general. Accused of buying American Marconi Corp. stock while government was negotiating with the firm, he was cleared. Was lord chief justice (1913–21), viceroy of India (1921–26), and foreign secretary (1931).

Reading (rĕ′dĭng), county borough (pop. 114,-176), co. town of Berkshire, England. History dates from 871. Univ. of Reading (1926) has noted departments of agr. and dairying. Oscar Wilde wrote *Ballad of Reading Gaol* while in prison here. Town was Aldbrickham of Hardy's *Jude the Obscure.*

Reading (rĕ′dĭng). **1** Town (pop. 14,006), NE Mass., N of Boston; settled 1639. Photographic supplies, stoves. **2** City (pop. 7,836), SW Ohio, N of Cincinnati. Lithographing, mfg. of chemicals. **3** City (pop. 109,320), SE Pa., on Schuylkill R. and NW of Philadelphia; laid out 1748. Important commercial and industrial center of Pennsylvania Dutch region with railroad shops and mfg. of aluminum, steel, and brass products. Provided cannon for Revolution. Seat of Albright Col.

real estate: see PROPERTY.

realism, in literature, the attempt to describe life without idealization. In 19th-cent. France it became a conscious literary movement opposing romanticism; novelists (e.g., Flaubert, in *Madame Bovary*) presented the sordid and trivial as well as the noble and dramatic. Flaubert also insisted that stories exclude the writer's reactions. Naturalism, as exemplified by Émile Zola, advocated a thorough, dispassionate inquiry into all aspects of society. Some recent novelists, reacting to an overemphasis on facts as such, tried to reach the underlying meaning of the facts. With diverse 20th-cent. interpretations, term *realism* has lost much of its meaning although it is still a major literary force.

real property: see PROPERTY.

reaper, machine for reaping grain. A practical reaper for field work was introduced 1831 by C. H. MCCORMICK. Marsh harvester, patented 1858, carried driver and two men to bind grain. Reaper improvements include self-binder and combine which also threshes grain.

Réaumur, René Antoine Ferchault de (rā′ü-myŏŏr, Fr. rünā′ ätwän′ fĕrshō′ dü rāōmür′), 1683–1757, French physicist and naturalist. Invented a thermometer (1731), studied expansion, improved iron manufacture, isolated gastric juice of birds, studied and wrote six-volume study of insects.

rebate, in U.S. history, a return of part of the transportation charges formerly given by railroads to favored shippers. Railroad rebates are now prohibited by laws (e.g., Elkins Act of 1903) and penalized by the Interstate Commerce Commission.

rebec or **rebeck** (rē′bĕk), medieval stringed musical instrument, played with a bow. It usually had three strings. Although popular with amateurs, it was never considered of concert caliber. See *ill.*, p. 857.

Rebecca or **Rebekah** (both: rēbĕ′kù) [Heb.,= noose], wife of Isaac, mother of Jacob and Esau. Helped Jacob to secure the birthright that should have been Esau's. Gen. 24–27; 49.31; Rom. 9.10.

Récamier, Juliette (zhülyĕt′ rākämyā′), 1777–1849, French beauty and social figure. From Consulate through July Monarchy, Mme Récamier's salon was meeting place of political and literary figures, among them Mme de Staël, Sainte-Beuve, Constant, and Chateaubriand, to whom she devoted her later years.

Recared (rĕ′kùrĕd), d. 601, Visigothic king in Spain (586–601). His conversion to Catholicism brought about conversion of Arian Visigoths.

Receswinth (rĕ′kùswĭnth), d. 672, Visigothic king in Spain (653–72). Either he or his father Chindaswinth revoked the Breviary of Alaric, and he completed a new code, called *Forum Judicum,* which combined German and Roman law and was the basis of Spanish medieval law.

Rechabites (rē′kùbīts), in Bible, a clan given to asceticism, similar to the NAZARITES. Jer. 35.

Recife (rùsē′fù) [Port.,= reef], city (pop. 522,-466), cap. of Pernambuco state, NE Brazil; port on the Atlantic. City lies partly on mainland, partly on island. Exports great quantities of hinterland's products—sugar, rum, fruits, hides, cotton, lumber. Founded in 1530s by Portuguese.

reciprocity, commercial agreement whereby nations grant each other mutual privileges. In Germany, the ZOLLVEREIN was based on reciprocity, and reciprocity has been part of the U.S. tariff policy since 1880. In European countries, reciprocity usually involves the MOST-FAVORED-NATION CLAUSE, but American treaties ordinarily do not make reference to a third state.

recitative (rĕ″sĭtùtēv′), musical declamation for solo voice, used in opera and oratorio for dialogue and narration. Its development at end of the 16th cent. contributed to the rise of opera, since it enabled words to be clearly understood and the rhythms of natural speech to be followed. Musical accompaniment to recitative ranges from a few occasional chords to the complete molding of music and text used by Wagner.

Reclamation, United States Bureau of, agency set up in Dept. of the Interior under Reclamation Act of 1902. Its purpose is to encourage and promote irrigation of lands in arid and semiarid regions of the West by examination, survey, and construction of irrigation works. CAREY LAND ACT (1894) rendered governmental help to reclamation schemes. Attention focused sharply on conservation of natural resources in time of Theodore Roosevelt. Interest in reclamation quickened after drought of late '20s and early '30s; program was linked with flood control and development of power.

reclamation of land, practice of making unproductive land productive, by IRRIGATION, drainage, flood control, improvement of physical condition of soil, and by checking EROSION. U.S. Bureau of Reclamation relies mostly on irrigation and flood control.

Reclus, Jean Jacques Élisée (ālēzā′ rùklü′), 1830–1905, French geographer. Chief among his many valuable works was *Nouvelle Géographie universelle* (20 vols., 1876–94).

recognition, political action acknowledging that a new state is qualified to assume its responsibilities under international law. Three varieties exist: recognition of the formation of a new state; recognition of the establishment of a new political regime; and recognition of belligerency. When a nation recognizes belligerency, it offends the state against which the rebellion is directed.

Reconstruction. During Civil War, Pres. Lincoln launched a moderate restoration program in areas of Confederacy occupied by Union armies. Congressional radicals opposed his plan. His successor, Andrew JOHNSON, adopted a plan much like Lincoln's. By end of 1865 every ex-Confederate state except Texas had fulfilled President's requirements for restoration of civil government. Control of white over Negro, however, seemed to have been resumed. Whites refused to enfranchise the blacks; black codes (laws defining new status of emancipated Negroes) were generally severe. Republican party ascendancy depended on Negro suffrage. Rep. Thaddeus STEVENS and Sen. Charles SUMNER led Congressional movement to make Reconstruction dependent on civil rights for Negro. Radicals won 1866 election; on March 2, 1867, Congress enacted Reconstruction Act, which, supplemented by later acts, divided the South (except Tenn.) into five military districts, in which authority of army commander was supreme. House impeached Johnson for defiance of TENURE OF OFFICE ACT, scuttled his program. South was reduced to degradation, with state governments falling to CARPETBAGGERS and scalawags. Aided by FREEDMEN'S BUREAU and UNION LEAGUE CLUBS, they shamelessly manipulated Negro votes, terrorized communities with Negro troops. In some districts anarchy and crime ruled; KU KLUX KLAN appeared. Its own corruption broke down the carpetbagger governmental structure. By 1876 only Fla., S.C., La. remained under Republican domination. Following disputed national election of that year, all Federal troops were withdrawn from the South; home rule was restored. Social and economic rehabilitation began years later.

Reconstruction Finance Corporation (RFC), U.S. government organ, created 1932. Originally designed to facilitate economic activity in the depression by making loans, it later helped finance World War II. Removed from Dept. of Commerce control in 1945. In 1948 its life was extended to 1956, but its lending powers were sharply curtailed.

recorder: see WIND INSTRUMENTS.

Red Bank, borough (pop. 12,743), E N.J., on Navesink estuary and NE of Long Branch. Resort and distributing center; mfg. of clothing, machinery, boats. Albert Brisbane helped estab. Fourierist community near here 1843. U.S. Fort Monmouth is S.

redbird: see CARDINAL.

redbreast: see ROBIN.

redbud or **Judas tree,** names for handsome leguminous trees and shrubs of genus *Cercis*, with rose or white flowers in spring. The common redbud (*Cercis canadensis*) is native to E North America.

red bug, name for various red insects. Apple red bug is reddish black hemipterous insect; in nymph stage, it attacks leaves and fruits of certain trees. Cotton red bug discolors fiber in cotton seeds. See also CHIGGER.

Red Cloud, 1822–1909, North American Indian chief, leader of the Oglala Sioux. Led massacre of party under William J. FETTERMAN (1866).

Red Cloud, city (pop. 1,744), S Nebr., on Republican R. Childhood home of Willa Cather.

Red Cross, international organization for the alleviation of human suffering and the promotion of public health; estab. at Geneva convention of 1864, largely through the efforts of J. H. Dunant, a Swiss. A red cross on a white background—the Swiss flag with its colors reversed—is its symbol. There are self-governing Red Cross societies in 68 countries, and two international groups. The American Natl. Red Cross was organized (1881) by Clara BARTON. It is supported entirely by voluntary contributions.

Red Deer, city (pop. 7,575), S central Alta., Canada, on Red Deer R. and S of Edmonton. Trade center in agr. area. Oil refineries, grain elevators.

Red Deer, river of S Alta., Canada, rising in Banff Natl. Park and flowing 385 mi. NE, S, SE, and S across Alta. to South Saskatchewan R.

Redding. **1** City (pop. 10,256), N Calif., on Sacramento R. near Shasta Dam. Trade and processing center for lumbering, gold and copper mining, and fruitgrowing region. Gateway to mountain hunting and fishing regions. Lassen Volcanic Natl. Park is near. **2** Town (pop. 2,037), SW Conn., NW of Bridgeport. Mark Twain summered here. Israel Putnam Memorial Campground commemorates winter of 1778–79.

Redfield, William C., 1789–1857, American scientist. Developed theory of rotary motion of hurricanes. An organizer (1848) and first president of American Association for the Advancement of Science.

Redfield, resort city (pop. 2,655), NE S.Dak., S of Aberdeen. Game-bird hunting.

Redi, Francesco (fränchä'skō rā'dē), 1626?–1698?, Italian naturalist, poet, and court physician to dukes of Tuscany. He helped to disprove theory of spontaneous generation through controlled experiments which showed that certain living organisms, notably maggots in rotting meat, arose only by reproduction of like living things. His chief poetical work was a dithyrambic ode, *Bacchus in Tuscany* (1685; Eng. tr., 1825).

Redlands, city (pop. 18,429), S Calif., in San Bernardino Valley E of Los Angeles. Ships oranges. Seat of Univ. of Redlands (Baptist; coed.; 1907).

red lead, red powdery lead tetroxide (also called minium). Used in making storage batteries, glass, red pigments, and red paint.

Red Lion, borough (pop. 5,119), SE Pa., near York. German customs preserved here.

Redmond, John Edward, 1856–1918, Irish political leader. Head (after 1890) of Parnellite faction in Parliament, he became (1900) chairman of combined Irish party. Supported Home Rule bills; opposed exclusion of Ulster. Rebellion of 1916 was a blow to him; his influence waned with rise of the revolutionary Sinn Fein.

Red Oak, city (pop. 6,526), SW Iowa, on East Nishnabotna R. and SE of Council Bluffs, in farm area. Printing of art calendars.

Redon, Odilon (ôdĕlō' rủdō'), 1840–1916, French painter. Depicted mystical subjects and flowers.

Redondo Beach (rĭdŏn'dō), resort and residential city (pop. 25,226), S Calif., SSW of Los Angeles.

Red River, chief river of Tonkin, c.730 mi. long, rising in Yunan prov., China, and flowing SE through Tonkin to South China Sea. Near head of delta is Hanoi.

Red River. 1 River, 1,300 mi. long, southernmost of large Mississippi R. tributaries. Rises near Amarillo in Texas Panhandle and flows ESE between Texas and Okla., and Texas and Ark., then S and SE through La. to ATCHAFALAYA R. and Mississippi R. Has DENISON DAM and reclamation project on North Fork near Altus, Okla. Shipping important for a time; still navigable for small ships to above Shreveport. Many lakes and bayous along lower course; reservoirs planned as flood control measures. Expedition under Gen. N. P. Banks and Adm. Porter went up river (1864) in Civil War to open way to Texas, but was defeated at Sabine Crossroads. **2** Or **Red River of the North,** river formed in N.Dak. N of L. Traverse by junction of Bois de Sioux and Otter Tail rivers and flowing 533 mi. N between Minn. and N.Dak. and through Manitoba to L. Winnipeg. Drains principal spring-wheat area of U.S. Chief tributary is Assiniboine R.

Red River Rebellion: see RIEL, LOUIS.

Red River Settlement, agr. colony in present Man., N.Dak., and Minn., promoted by Thomas Douglas, 5th earl of SELKIRK. He desired to assist dispossessed and impoverished of Scotland and N Ireland. He secured sufficient financial interest in Hudson's Bay Co. to obtain grant of land called Assiniboia. Settlement was strongly opposed by fur traders, mainly from North West Co. A small group of Scotch and Irish attempted to start a colony (1812), but North West Co. men persuaded settlers to desert. In 1816, when colony was restored, settlers were attacked and some 22 killed in massacre of Seven Oaks. Selkirk seized Fort William, a North West Co. post. In court action that ensued Selkirk was impoverished and union between North West Co. and Hudson's Bay Co. furthered.

Red Sea, anc. *Sinus Arabicus,* narrow sea, c.1,500 mi. long, between Africa and Arabia, in Great Rift Valley; important shipping lane linking Europe and Asia. Connected with the Mediterranean by Suez Canal and with Gulf of Aden by the strait Bab el Mandeb. Its N arms, Gulf of Aqaba and Gulf of Suez, enclose Sinai peninsula. The Bible in telling of Red Sea crossing by the Israelites probably intended the Gulf of Suez.

Red Springs, town (pop. 2,245), S N.C., SW of Fayetteville. Flora Macdonald Col. (Presbyterian; women; 1896) is here.

reduction: see OXIDATION AND REDUCTION.

Red Wing, city (pop. 10,645), SE Minn., at head of L. Pepin; settled 1852. Farm trade center with mfg. of pottery and dairy products. Swiss mission to Indians here 1836–40.

redwood: see SEQUOIA.

Redwood City, city (pop. 25,544), W Calif., SSE of San Francisco. Grows and ships chrysanthemums. Has tanning, food canning, and mfg. of rubber goods.

Reed, John, 1887–1920, American journalist and radical. Attached to radical magazine the *Masses* after 1913. *Ten Days That Shook the World* is his eyewitness account of the Russian Revolution. Buried at the Kremlin.

Reed, Thomas Brackett, 1839–1902, American legislator. U.S. Representative from Maine (1877–99). As speaker of House (1889–91, 1895–99) he used his power to aid orthodox Republican legislation.

Reed, Walter, 1851–1902, American army surgeon, head of Havana commission for study of YELLOW FEVER (1900). Washington, D.C., medical center and army hospital were named for him.

reed, name for several grasses. The common reed (*Phragmites communis*) is a tall grass which has been used for thatching and, in SW U.S., for adobe huts. The giant reed (*Arundo donax*) is sometimes used in reed musical instruments.

Reed College: see PORTLAND, Oregon.

reed instruments: see WIND INSTRUMENTS.

reed mace: see CATTAIL.

Reelfoot Lake, c.20 mi. long, W Tenn., near Mississippi R. and Ky. line. Formed 1811–12 by earthquakes; filled with river water. In Reelfoot L. Fish and Game Preserve.

Reese, Lizette Woodworth, 1856–1935, American poet, noted for lyric treatment of nature. *A Wayside Lute* (1909) includes her best-known poem, "Tears."

Reeve, Tapping, 1744–1823, American lawyer and jurist. Had famous law school at Litchfield, Conn.

referendum: see INITIATIVE AND REFERENDUM.

refining includes processes of metallurgy, separation of petroleum into its products, purification of sugars and other substances. Nature of process varies according to material involved, value of end product, degree of purity required, etc. Electrolysis is much used for metals: BLAST FURNACE and REVERBERATORY FURNACE for copper and iron particularly; and amalgamation process and CYANIDE PROCESS for chemical refining of metals. Sugar refining involves adding lime in some form, filtration, evaporation, and crystallization.

reflection occurs when light ray or sound wave strikes surface and is thrown back into medium through which it has come. Principles are similar for light and sound since both travel in straight lines and are wave phenomena. Objects are visible because of light reflected from their surfaces; their color depends on ability to reflect light of certain wave length. Smooth surfaces give regular reflection; rough or uneven surfaces give diffuse reflection. Total reflection is seen when light passing from one medium to less dense one reaches one of surfaces and is thrown back into denser medium again; this occurs when light strikes at an oblique angle greater than a certain degree up to which refraction (not reflection) takes place. Internal reflection accounts in part for rainbow and mirage. Reflection of sound waves causes ECHO. Heat and other forms of radiant energy also are reflected.

reflex action: see NERVOUS SYSTEM.

Reform, Catholic, 16th-cent. reformation within the Roman Catholic Church. Frequently called the Counter Reformation by Protestants, but Catholics object to the term on the grounds that reform had begun within the Church before the first rumblings of the Reformation and that Protestantism, with its aim of destroying the old Church organization, is entirely different from the Counter Reform with its aim of removing abuses within the organization. Those abuses were mainly simony (buying and selling of church offices and favors and even sometimes of purely spiritual things, such as indulgences), worldliness and corruption of the higher clergy, ignorance on the part of the lower clergy, and general apathy toward doctrinal matters and care of the faithful. Some, such as St. Catherine of Siena, had cried out against such abuses in the 14th cent., but quarrels within the Church (notably the Great SCHISM), the heavy hand of kings and princes, and the entrenched position of rich, worldly, and powerful prelates prevented reform; thus Nicholas of Cusa had in 1451 been unable to reform the German church against the opposition of the bishops. The tide of the Renaissance had washed worldly corruption as well as artistic sensibility into the papal court. The reform began with a small group at Rome, with Cardinal Carafa (later Paul IV) and Cardinal CAJETAN at its center, in the late 15th cent. They were supported from abroad by such humanists as Erasmus, St. Thomas More, and Cardinal Jiménez. The first major effort failed with the failure of the Fifth Lateran Council, but reformers were growing in number and forming new orders (Theatines, 1524; Capuchins, 1525) to carry the gospel to the common people just as the storm of the Reformation was breaking. Emperor Charles V helped the reform not only by encouragment but by the sack of Rome by his soldiers (1527), an event that stirred even the most complacent cardinals. In 1534 PAUL III became pope. St. IGNATIUS OF LOYOLA and the Society of JESUS began their work. In 1545 after long delay and preparation the Council of TRENT was convened. This council was the central feature of the Reform under Paul III, Julius III and Pius IV. PAUL IV reformed the papacy itself and instituted the quasi-monastic air that has prevailed at the Vatican since. The council ended in 1563, but its gains were consolidated under St. Pius V, Gregory XIII, and Sixtus V. Simony was uprooted, worship was standardized, the administration of the Church was reorganized, educational requirements for priests were set, the moral life of all the clergy came under scrutiny. The new spirit breathing in the Church was shown by St. Charles Borromeo, St. Philip Neri, St. Theresa of Ávila and St. John of the Cross in Spain, St. Francis of Sales and St. Vincent de Paul in France, the Jesuit missionaries in England (e.g., Edmund Campion, Robert Parsons).

Reformation, religious revolution in Western Europe in 16th cent. beginning as reform movement in Catholic Church, but evolving into doctrines of Protestantism. There had long been outcries against abuses in Church. In 14th cent. John Wyclif had led dissident movement; this was followed by larger reform group of John Huss in Bohemia. Movement was stimulated by growth of Renaissance humanism with its questioning of authority. It was also hastened by invention of printing. In secular affairs conflict between the Church and state (and more particularly in Germany, conflict of princes and emperors), rise of commerce and the middle class were factors. The Reformation itself began when Martin Luther, stirred by Johann Tetzel's campaign for dispensing indulgences, on Oct. 31, 1517, posted his 95 theses on the church door in Wittenberg. Open attack upon doctrines and authority of Church came soon. His defiance of pope led in 1520 to open breach with Church, which Diet of Worms failed to heal. Luther's doctrince of justification by faith alone instead of by sacraments, good works, and mediation of Church, and his insistence on reading Bible gave individual a greater responsibility for his own salvation. The new faith met widespread acceptance, and revolt spread rapidly in Germany and beyond. Quarrel with Church and the emperor was long and bitter, unresolved by Diets of Speyer (1526, 1529) and Diet of Augsburg (1530). A temporary and ineffective settlement, the Augsburg Interim (1548) was followed by the more stable Peace of Augsburg (1555) but conflict went on later. Within Protestant movement many differences arose, as in doctrinal arguments on the Lord's Supper, debated inconclusively at Colloquy of Marburg (1529) by Luther and Melanchthon with Oecolampadius and Zwingli. Radical social and religious ideas were spread by the Anabaptists, and such leaders as Carlstadt, Thomas Münzer, and John of Leiden. Most important of all, in 1536 Geneva became the center for teachings of John Calvin, greatest theologian of Reformation. His influence was enormous. In France, Huguenots, fired by his doctrine, resisted Catholic majority until Henry IV issued Edict of Nantes in 1598. Calvinism superseded Lutheranism in Netherlands. It conquered Scotland through victory of John Knox over Mary Queen of Scots. Both Calvanism and Lutheranism came into conflict with Evangelicalism. In England, Henry VIII signed the Act of Supremacy (1534), rejecting papal control and creating Church of England. But Calvinistic and Evangelical thought were strong in England and influenced course of Reformation there, notably in Puritanism. On the Continent, divisions in Protestant churches served to forward counterrevolution within Catholic Church with some recovery of lost ground. The Peace of Westphalia (1648) brought stabilization after the exhaustion of war. This marks the end of the period of the

Reformation, but Protestantism, born of it, has been a basic force in the Western world to the present day.

Reform Bills, in English history, name given to five measures liberalizing representation in House of Commons. System had not changed after time of Elizabeth despite population shifts and rise of new social classes in Industrial Revolution. Corruption and sale of seats flourished. **Reform Bill of 1832,** passed by Earl Grey's Whig ministry, redistributed seats in interest of larger communities; gave franchise to middle-class men. **Reform Bill of 1867,** enacted by Benjamin Disraeli, gave franchise to workingmen in the towns; more than doubled electorate. **Reform Bill of 1884,** passed by William Gladstone, reduced rural qualifications; added 2,000,000 voters. Last two bills (1918, 1928) are usually called REPRESENTATION OF THE PEOPLE ACTS.

Reformed churches, in general sense, all Protestant churches stemming from Reformation; in particular, those having origin in Calvinism, as distinct from those that are Lutheran or Evangelical.

Reformed Church in America, better known as Dutch Reformed Church, founded in colonial times by Dutch Protestant settlers. Reformed Church in Holland grew in 16th cent. from Calvinistic Reformation. In 1571 the synod at Emden adopted presbyterian polity and formulated liturgical worship, with Belgic Confession of Faith (1561) and Heidelberg Catechism (1563). In America, congregation was formed in New Amsterdam in 1628. In 1754 assembly declared itself independent of Classis of Amsterdam. In 1766 charter was secured for Queens Col. (now Rutgers Univ.). In 1792 constitution was adopted; name became official 1867.

Reformed Church in the United States: see EVANGELICAL AND REFORMED CHURCH.

Reformed Episcopal Church, formed 1873 by group who withdrew from Protestant Episcopal Church because of ritualistic dissensions.

Reformed Presbyterianism: see CAMERON, RICHARD.

refraction, in physics, bending of light ray, sound wave, or heat ray away from original direction when passing from medium of one density into that of another. No bending occurs if the ray enters surface at right angles. Light travels with greater velocity in some media than in others; front of wave is flat and at right angles to direction it is following; e.g., when light traveling through air strikes glass at oblique angle, under part of ray entering glass first is slowed first and turns from original direction; upper part follows same direction as lower part. When passing from less to more dense medium, ray is bent toward normal (perpendicular to surface). A constant ratio exists between the velocities of light in two given media. This ratio is called index of refraction or refractive index for the two media.

refrigeration, the act of drawing heat away from solids or liquids to lower their temperatures, generally for purposes of preservation. Most systems of refrigeration are based on the principle that heat is absorbed from the surrounding area when a solid is liquefied (ice melting), or a liquid changed into gas, or when compressed air is permitted to expand. Ammonia, carbon dioxide, and sulphur dioxide are widely used as refrigerants. These become, in a constantly alternating evaporation and condensation process, part of a sealed system kept in motion through electricity or gas apparatus. For example, an electric motor is used to exert pressure on ammonia before it moves into the coils of the refrigeration compartment. As the ammonia changes to its gaseous form heat is drawn to the coils. The motor then acts to compress the gas issuing from the coils, rendering it liquid for its passage back into the coils. A development of the preservation of foods by refrigeration is preparation of frozen foods.

Refugio (rĭfū'ēō), town (pop. 4,666), S Texas, on Mission R. and NNE of Corpus Christi; settled 1829. Previously estab. Spanish mission moved here 1795. Taken by Mexicans in Texas Revolution, 1836, and again briefly in invasion of 1842. Bells of present R.C. church, from original mission, were taken and returned by Mexicans.

regatta (rĭgă'tů), series of rowing or other boating races. Royal Henley Regatta, most famous race for eight-oared boats, is held annually on the Thames. First was held 1839. In U.S., Poughkeepsie Regatta was held annually 1895–1949; since 1950 it has been held at other sites.

Regence style (rē'jùns), in French architecture and decoration, was prevalent during regency (1715–23) of Philippe II, duc d'Orléans. Retaining the restraint and symmetry of Louis XIV style, it introduced curved lines and intricate motifs (e.g., shells) that were to be developed later in rococo design. Leaders in creating the style were Boulle, Cressent, J. A. Meissonier, Boucher, and Watteau.

Regency, in British history, the last nine years (1811–20) of reign of George III when, due to his periodic insanity, government was conducted in name of Prince of Wales (later George IV). The rise of Tories like Lord Castlereagh accompanied reform agitation of such men as Jeremy Bentham and William Cobbett. Social color was given by gay and dissolute group around the prince regent. There was a flowering of arts, letters, and architecture.

Regency style, in English architecture, flourished during regency and reign of George IV (1811–30) and was represented mainly by John NASH. Stucco was widely used. Effect of simplicity was achieved by flat painted surfaces, elegant Greek ornament, glazed casement doors, and flat, partitioned bay windows. Balconies (popular for first time in England) were usually supported by slender columns or brackets. Characteristic buildings are town houses on Regent's Park terraces.

Regensburg (rā'gùnzbûrg, rā'gùnsbŏŏrk), city (pop. 116,997), cap. of Upper Palatinate, E Bavaria, on the Danube; in English, also known as Ratisbon. River port; mfg. center (precision instruments; printing; brewing). Was important Roman frontier station (Regina Castra); became episcopal see 739; free imperial city 1245–1803; permanent seat of diet of Holy Roman Empire 1663–1803. Flourished as medieval trade center; accepted Reformation 16th cent.; passed to Bavaria 1810. Last diet (1801–3) prepared liquidation of Holy Roman Empire. Its final resolution (tersely named *Reichsdeputationshauptschluss*) secularized the ecclesiastic principalities and "mediatized" most of the petty princes—gave their lands to the larger states but left them their titles. Though severely bombed in World War II, city retains its fine medieval cathedral, churches, and city hall.

Reger, Max (rā'gŭr), 1873–1916, German composer, pianist, and conductor. His complicated technique has kept his music from becoming generally popular. His best-known works are for organ. He also wrote a symphony, sonatas, concertos, and chamber music.

Reggio di Calabria (rĕd'jō dē kälä'brēä), city (pop. 60,342), cap. of Calabria, S Italy, on Strait of Messina.

Reggio nell' Emilia (nĕl' lāmē'lyä), city (pop. 49,069), Emilia-Romagna, N central Italy, on Aemilian Way. Agr. trade center. Passed to Este family 1289 and became part of duchy of Modena. Birthplace of Ariosto.

regicides (rĕ'jĭsīdz) [Latin,= king-killers], name given to judges and court officers responsible for trial and execution of Charles I of England. After Restoration (1660) 10 regicides were condemned to death and 25 to life imprisonment. Some escaped.

Regina (rĭjī'nŭ), city (pop. 71,319), provincial cap., S Sask., Canada, SE of Saskatoon; founded 1882. Principal trade and rail center of province with stockyards, oil refineries, and auto-assembly, meat-packing, woodworking, and printing plants. Western hq. of Royal Canadian Mounted Police. Cap. of Northwest Territories 1883–1905.

Regiomontanus (rē"jēōmŏn"tā'nŭs), 1436–76, German astronomer and mathematician; original name Johannes Müller. Improved instruments and methods of observation and calculation.

Régnier, Henri de (ārē' dŭ rānyā'), 1864–1936, French poet, a leader of the young SYMBOLISTS.

Regulator movement, organized (1768) by small farmers of W N.C. to protest oppressive local government. Unjust taxation and extortion by officials were chief grievances. Unable to secure legal relief, they resorted to violence. Routed in battle by militia, May 16, 1771; leaders were executed and movement collapsed.

Regulus, Marcus Atilius (rĕ'gyŏŏlŭs), d. c.250 B.C., Roman general. After some successes in the First Punic War he led an expedition to Africa that ended in his defeat and capture. It is said that he was sent with Carthaginian envoys to seek peace but instead bravely urged the senate to go on with the war and to refuse exchange of prisoners. He honored his parole, returned to Carthage, and was tortured to death.

rehabilitation, in therapy, restoration of maximum physical, mental, and vocational capacities to handicapped persons. It sometimes requires services of physician, surgeon, psychologist, physiotherapist, and social worker; vocational guidance; training for new work or to restore skills. Rehabilitation achieved notable success in the course of World War II.

Rehan, Ada (rē'ŭn), 1860–1916, American actress, whose real name was Crehan, b. Ireland. In Daly's company 1879–99, she co-starred with John Drew in French, German, and Shaksperian comedies.

Rehnskiold or **Rehnskjold, Karl Gustaf,** Swed. *Rehnskiöld* (rān'shûld"), 1651–1722, Swedish field marshal under Charles XII. Won important victories in Poland during Northern War but was outnumbered, defeated, and captured at Poltava (1709), where the wounded king had delegated the command to him.

Rehoboam (rē'ŭbō'ŭm), d. c.914 B.C., Hebrew king (c.932–c.914 B.C.), son of Solomon. Under him the northern tribes revolted and formed a new kingdom under Jeroboam I, retaining the name Israel. Only Judah and part of Benjamin remained loyal to Rehoboam; these formed a kingdom in the S called Judah. 1 Kings 11.43–12.24; 14.21–31; 2 Chron. 9.31–12.16.

Rehoboth Beach (rĭhō'bŭth), Atlantic resort town (pop. 1,794), SE Del., SE of Lewes.

Reichenbach Falls (rī'khŭnbäkh), cataract, Bern canton, Switzerland, where the Reichenbach joins Aar R. Name is familiar to readers of A. Conan Doyle. Has hydroelectric project.

Reichenberg, Czechoslovakia: see LIBEREC.

Reichstadt, Napoleon, duke of: see NAPOLEON II.

Reichstag (rīkhs'täk). **1** The DIET of the Holy Roman Empire (until 1806). **2** The lower chamber of the federal parliament of Germany, 1871–1945. The upper chamber, called Bundesrat in imperial Germany (1871–1918) and Reichsrat under the Weimar Republic (1919–34), represented the member states, whereas the Reichstag was elected by direct suffrage and represented the country at large. When Hitler became chancellor (Jan., 1933), he lacked an absolute majority in the Reichstag. As a result, Pres. Hindenburg ordered new elections (as was his constitutional right). On Feb. 27 a carefully planned fire broke out in the Reichstag building in Berlin. Hitler immediately accused the Communists of setting the fire; yet, despite his terrorist measures, the elections of March 5 still gave him no absolute majority. Only after he had expelled the 81 Communist deputies from the Reichstag could he muster a majority to vote him dictatorial powers (March 23). The sensational Reichstag fire trial ended with the conviction and beheading of Marinus van der Lubbe (1933). The other defendants, all Communists (incl. Georgi Dimitrov and Ernst Torgler), were acquitted. It is almost certain that the fire was actually instigated by the Nazis, notably Goering, who used Van der Lubbe as their tool. Under the Hitler regime, only the National Socialist Party was represented in the Reichstag, which was summoned merely to ratify major government decisions. The Reichsrat was abolished 1934. After 1949 the Reichstag was replaced in W Germany by a federal diet or Bundestag, in E Germany by a "people's chamber" (1949).

Reichstein, Tadeus, 1897–, Swiss chemist. Shared 1950 Nobel Prize in Physiology and Medicine for work on the chemistry of the hormone cortisone and other secretions of the adrenal glands.

Reid, (Thomas) Mayne, 1818–83, British novelist. Came to the U.S. in 1840 and had adventures reflected in his stories for boys.

Reid, Robert, 1862–1929, American figure and mural painter, a noted teacher.

Reid, Thomas, 1710–96, Scottish philosopher, teacher at King's College, Aberdeen, and Univ. of Glasgow. The leader of the common-sense school, he held that we know the objects of the external world directly and in their true sense because such knowledge is self-evident. He based morality on conscience, the intuitive moral sense.

Reid, Whitelaw, 1837–1912, American journalist and diplomat. Distinguished himself as Civil War correspondent of Cincinnati *Gazette.* Made managing editor of New York *Tribune* (1868), he later gained full control. Was minister to France (1889–92), ambassador to England (1905–12).

Reidsville, city (pop. 11,708), N N.C., NNE of Greensboro; settled c.1815. Cigarette mfg. center.

Reigate (rī'gĭt), municipal borough (pop. 42,-234), Surrey, England; residential suburb of London. Has vestiges of an old castle with caves beneath it.

Reign of Terror, 1793–94, culminating phase of the FRENCH REVOLUTION, when France was under the dictatorship of the Committee of Public Safety (incl. ROBESPIERRE, COUTHON, SAINT-JUST, Lazare CARNOT). Its measures were aimed at routing out counterrevolutionary elements (Law of Suspects, carried out by Committee of General Security and by Revolutionary Tribunal, brought c.2,500 persons to the guillotine); at raising new armies by universal conscription; and at preventing run-away inflation through maximum price and wage laws. After ousting the GIRONDISTS, the JACOBINS held the sole power; Robespierre's purges of his own party (e.g., of DANTON and HÉBERT) eventually goaded the Convention into overthrowing his dictatorship (9 THERMIDOR).

Reims, France: see RHEIMS.

Reinach, Salomon (sälômō' rĕnäk'), 1858–1932, French archaeologist, one of first to relate archaeology and anthropology. Wrote history of religion, *Orpheus* (1909; rev. Eng. ed., 1933), and history of art, *Apollo* (1904; rev. Eng. ed., 1935).

reindeer, gregarious, migratory mammal (*Rangifer*) of deer family, found in arctic and subarctic regions. Both sexes have antlers. Reindeer was early domesticated from CARIBOU and provides meat, milk, clothing, and transportation.

Reindeer Lake, 2,444 sq. mi., NE Sask. and NW Man., Canada. Many islands. Outlet is Reindeer R.

reindeer moss, low-growing LICHEN (*Cladonia rangiferina*) of arctic regions, a chief food of reindeer and caribou.

Reinhardt, Max (mäks' rīn'härt), 1873–1943, Austrian theatrical director, whose real name was Goldmann. A great innovator, he was a master of spectacle. Made Salzburg Festivals a world theatrical center after World War I. Forced to flee Germany (1933), he became a U.S. citizen in 1940.

Réjane (rāzhän'), 1857–1920, stage name of Gabrielle Réju, French actress. Versatile and vivacious, she appeared notably in Sardou's *Mme Sans-Gêne.*

relativity, theory in physics, introduced by Einstein, which discards the concept of time and space as absolute entities and views them as relative to moving frames of reference. Einstein enunciated (1905) the special relativity theory. Included among its assertions and consequences are the propositions that the maximum velocity attainable is that of light; that mass appears to increase with velocity; that mass and energy are equivalent and interchangeable; that events which appear simultaneous to observer in one system may not seem so to observer in another system and that both may be correct since absolute time cannot be measured and must therefore be excluded from physical reasoning. Physical realities cannot be visualized, but may be represented mathematically in a four-dimensional geometry of space time. Einstein extended the theory into a general theory (completed c.1916) applicable also to systems in nonuniform motion. This recognizes the equivalence of gravitation and inertia and asserts that material bodies produce curvatures in space that form a gravitational field. In 1950 Einstein presented a unified field theory, as yet unevaluated, which applies also to subatomic and electromagnetic phenomena.

Religion, Wars of, 1562–98, series of civil wars in France. Ostensibly a struggle between Protestants (see HUGUENOTS) and Catholics, the wars were also a contest for power between the crown and the great nobles and among the nobles themselves for control of the king. The Catholics were led by the GUISE family; foremost Protestant leaders were, successively, Louis I de CONDÉ, Gaspard de COLIGNY, and Henry of Navarre (after 1589 HENRY IV of France). A third party, the *Politiques* (moderate Catholics) sided with the Protestants, while CATHERINE DE' MEDICI and her sons CHARLES IX and HENRY III vainly sought to estab. a balance of power. The wars were marked by fanatic cruelty on both sides. The first three wars (1562–63, 1567–68, 1568–70) ended favorably for the Protestants. The massacre of SAINT BARTHOLOMEW'S DAY started off the fourth war (1572–73). The fifth war (1574–76) ended with the Edict of Beaulieu, granting freedom of worship throughout France except in Paris. The Catholics now formed the LEAGUE. After a sixth war (1577), the Edict of Beaulieu was confirmed, but Henry failed to carry it out. The seventh war (1580) was inconsequential, but in 1585 Henry of Navarre's nomination as heir presumptive to Henry III precipitated the War of the Three Henrys (see HENRY III; HENRY IV; Henri, 3d duc de GUISE). After Henry IV's accession (1589), the League invoked Spanish aid. Henry defeated the League and entered Paris in 1594. The Treaty of VERVINS with Spain and the Edict of NANTES restored peace in 1598.

relocation center, in U.S. history. War Relocation Authority, created March, 1942, enabled army to move all persons of Japanese ancestry from defined area on West Coast to ten relocation centers in Western states. After July, 1943, loyal persons were released to live anywhere except in proscribed area. Many young men left centers to serve in the army. In Dec., 1944, mass exclusion orders were revoked. War Relocation Authority was terminated 1946.

Remarque, Erich Maria (ā'rĭkh märē'ä rŭmärk'), 1897–, German novelist. His fame rests mainly on his first novel, *All Quiet on the Western Front* (1929), a bitter antiwar story. He fled the Nazis and became an American citizen in 1947.

Rembrandt (Harmenszoon van Rijn or **Ryn)** (rĕm'brănt, –bränt), 1606–69, celebrated Dutch painter and etcher, b. Leiden. In 1631 he moved to Amsterdam, where he became the most popular painter of his day. In 1634 he married the wealthy Saskia van Uylenburgh, who bore him four children, only one of whom, Titus, survived. To this period belong such canvases as *Portrait of an Old Woman* (Natl. Gall., London), which show the golden tone and bold brushwork of his most characteristic work. After Saskia's death in 1642, he painted the *Sortie of the Banning Cocq Company* (Rijks Mus.), which brought his downfall as a popular portraitist. It was derisively called *The Night Watch* because of its departure from convention in focusing strong light only on a few central figures, leaving the others in shadow. Declared bankrupt in 1657, he was supported in his last years by Titus and his housekeeper, Hendrickje Stoffles. Many fine self-portraits were done in his last period of poverty and retirement. The famous *Lesson in Anatomy* (the Hague) was painted in his early period. In addition to c.700 paintings, he produced a vast number of superb etchings.

Remington, Eliphalet (ĭlĭ'fŭlĭt), 1793–1861, American inventor and gunsmith. His firearms factory, estab. c.1828, at Ilion, N.Y., was expanded 1856 to make agr. implements. Directed after 1861 by his son **Philo Remington,** 1816–89. He became a pioneer typewriter manufacturer after 1873.

Remington, Frederic, 1861–1909, American sculptor and painter of subjects drawn from life in the West.

Remonstrants, Dutch Protestants, adherents to ideas of Jacobus Arminius, known later as Arminianism. Under Simon Episcopius they practiced modified Calvinism as set forth in the "Remonstrance." Synod of Dort (1618–19) condemned the Remonstrants, but ban was lifted in 1625. Group was recognized 1795 as independent church.

Remscheid (rĕm'shī), industrial city (pop. 102,-929), North Rhine-Westphalia, W Germany, on the Wupper, adjoining Solingen and Wuppertal. Tool and tool-machines; steel; textiles. Heavily damaged in World War II.

Remus, in Roman legend, twin of ROMULUS.

Renaissance (rĕnŭsäns', –zäns') [Fr.,= rebirth], period of transition from medieval to modern times. Though term may denote chronological period (14th–16th cent.), it more often designates cultural and intellectual currents that began in 14th cent. in Italy, where it reached highest flower in 15th and 16th cent. From Italy Renaissance spread to France, Spain, Germany, Low Countries, England, and rest of Europe. Italian Renaissance culminated under patronage of MEDICI at Florence, of SFORZA at Milan, of Renaissance popes at Rome, of ESTE at Ferrara, and of GONZAGA at Mantua. Important figures of Italian Renaissance were LEONARDO DA VINCI, MICHELANGELO, GUICCIARDINI, and MACHIAVELLI. Other great figures of period were ERASMUS, RABELAIS, and MONTAIGNE. Period had far-reaching influence in art and architecture and in formation of modern mind.

Renaissance architecture. The 15th-cent. rebirth of classic architecture in Italy ended the supremacy of the Gothic style. Façades and interiors, rather than structure, became the important elements. Three periods of the Italian Renaissance can be seen: early (c.1420–c.1500), with its chief centers at Florence (its birthplace), Milan, and Venice; high, or classic (c.1500–c.1580), with Rome as the center; and late, or BAROQUE and ROCOCO (c.1580–c.1780). The great designers of the early period were Brunelleschi, Alberti, and Bramante. The second period began roughly with Bramante's later works, notably SAINT PETER'S CHURCH, which made full use of the classical orders of architecture and show a deeper understanding of the monumental Roman works of the classic period. To bigness of scale the baroque architects (notably BERNINI) of the last period added a theatrical character, giving the classic details a bold sense of movement. Introduced into France, the style passed through three general phases: early (c.1490–c.1547), in which Renaissance details were mingled with Gothic elements; classical (c.1547–c.1610), in which the LOUVRE was begun; and the LOUIS PERIOD STYLES (c.1610–1793). In the 16th cent. the style was adopted in Germany, Spain, and England (where Inigo JONES became its chief exponent).

Renaissance art was the natural outgrowth of the new humanism which replaced medieval thought. Based on classic forms, it developed first and most fully in Italy. The period saw the important development of perspective and of modeling in light and shadow, which replaced the medieval over-all brightness. Italian Renaissance developed three periods (see RENAISSANCE ARCHITECTURE). Florence was the great center of many Renaissance masters, including Giotto, Fra Angelico, Leonardo da Vinci, Botticelli, and Michelangelo. Siena, Venice, Rome (where Raphael did much of his work), and other Italian cities also developed important schools. With Charles VIII's expedition to Naples, Renaissance influences penetrated into France. Francis I imported Italian artists, and Henry II's marriage to Catherine de' Medici strengthened Italian prestige. Renaissance France was most active in the minor arts (esp. glass and miniature painting). Filtering into Spain in late 15th cent. the style assumed a definitely native character in the early 16th cent. Under Renaissance influences the Low Countries produced such masters as the Van Eyck brothers, Roger van der Weyden, and Rubens. The Renaissance spirit had relatively little effect on the contemporary art of England and Germany.

Renan, Ernest (ĕrnĕst′ rünā′), 1823–92, French historian and critic, apostle of the scientific approach to history, religion, and literature. Among his best-known works are *L'Avenir de la science* (1890) and *Life of Jesus* (Vol. I of *The History of the Origins of Christianity*, 8 vols., 1863–83).

Renault, Louis (lwē′ rünō′), 1843–1918, French jurist, professor of international law at Univ. of Paris. Sat on Hague Tribunal, helped advance international arbitration. Shared 1907 Nobel Peace Prize with E. T. Moneta.

René (rünā′), 1409–80, titular king of Naples, of the ANGEVIN dynasty; younger son of Louis II. By marriage, he became count of Bar and duke of Lorraine. In 1434 he inherited Anjou and Provence from his brother, LOUIS III of Naples, and was adopted as heir by Queen JOANNA II of Naples (d. 1435). He was defeated (1438) by his rival claimant, Alfonso V of Aragon, and retired to Angers, later to Tarascon, where he devoted himself to poetry, painting, and pastoral games, bringing medieval Provençal culture to a last flowering. He made Lorraine and Bar over to his son John in 1452 and left Anjou to Louis XI of France. Provence and his claim to Naples passed first to his nephew Charles, duke of Maine (d. 1486), then to the French crown. His daughter, Margaret of Anjou, married Henry VI of England.

Renewed Church of the Brethren: see MORAVIAN CHURCH.

Renfrew (rĕn′frōō), town (pop. 7,360), S Ont., Canada, on Bonnechere R. and W of Ottawa. Woolen mills, wood works, mfg. of metal products.

Renfrewshire or **Renfrew,** county (227 sq. mi.; pop. 324,652), SW Scotland, on the Clyde estuary. One of smallest but most populous Scottish counties, it is a hilly region with rich mineral deposits. Important industrial area, it has mfg. (sugar, chemicals, textiles, and whisky), coal mining, shipbuilding, and shale quarrying. County town is **Renfrew,** burgh (pop. 17,093), one of oldest Clyde R. ports and site of Glasgow's airport.

Reni, Guido: see GUIDO RENI.

Rennes (rĕn), city (pop. 102,617), cap. of Ille-et-Vilaine dept., NW France, on Ille and Vilaine rivers; historic cap. of Brittany. Varied mfg.; archiepiscopal see; university (founded 1735). Seat of a powerful provincial parlement before French Revolution. Damaged in World War II. Notable buildings include 17th-cent. palace of justice, 18th-cent. cathedral.

rennet (rĕ′nĭt), substance containing rennin, an enzyme that curdles milk. It is obtained from stomachs of young milk-feeding mammals and is made and sold commercially. It is used in making cheese. Heat interferes with its action.

Reno, city (pop. 32,497), W Nev., on Truckee R. near L. Tahoe. Site was camping place on Donner Pass route to Calif. in pioneer days. Town laid out as Reno in 1868 when railroad came. Largest city in Nev., it is shipping center for cattle, minerals, and farm produce. Crisp climate, resort facilities, legalized gambling, and quick and easy divorces keep Reno prosperous. Has annual rodeo. Seat of Univ. of Nevada (land-grant, state supported; coed.; opened 1874), which includes Mackay School of Mines.

Renoir, Pierre Auguste (rünwär′), 1841–1919, French painter, an outstanding master of the French school. Began working at age of 13 as decorator of porcelain in a Paris factory. In 1862 he entered Gleyre's art school, where he met Cézanne, Monet, and Sisley. Lived in extreme poverty until 1870, when portrait commissions brought him some prosperity. After 1890 he lived in Provence. Especially famous for pictures of women and children and for nude figure compositions, all characterized by lyrical quality, lovely color, and rhythmic line. He is often grouped with the postimpressionists.

Renouvier, Charles Bernard (rünōōvyā′), 1815–1903, French philosopher. He tried to meld some of the ideas of Comte's positivism and Kant's idealism (though he rejected Kant's doctrines of the unknowable and the infinite).

Rensselaer (rĕnsülēr′, rĕn′sülür), city (pop. 10,856), E N.Y., on E bank of Hudson R. (bridged) opposite Albany; settled by Dutch in 17th cent. Mfg. of textile products and chemicals. *Yankee Doodle* was supposedly written at Fort Crailo.

Rensselaer Polytechnic Institute, at Troy, N.Y.; nonsectarian, for men; founded 1824 by Stephen Van Rensselaer, opened 1825, chartered 1826 to give degrees. University courses in architecture, business administration, engineering, science. Pioneer technical school. Granted first U.S. engineering degrees (1835).

rent, in law, the amount that a tenant is required to pay for use of another's property. In economics, however, it has a broader, more complex meaning—any income or yield from an object capable of producing wealth (e.g., land, tools, machinery). Early English writers on economics (16th–18th cent.) used the word also to mean interest on a loan. Modern rent doctrine began with the physiocrats and Adam Smith. There have been many and contradictory theories.

Renton, city (pop. 16,039), W Wash., near L. Washington, SE of Seattle. Produces aircraft, coal, clay products, timber, poultry, and truck.

Renwick, James, 1818–95, American architect, who designed St. Patrick's Cathedral, New York.

reparations, payments imposed by victorious on defeated nations as indemnity for material losses in war. After World War I, a reparations commission fixed the sum to be paid by Germany to the Allies (excluding the U.S., which waived its claims) at 132,000,000,000 gold marks, partly payable in kind. When Germany fell behind in its payments, the Allies took the stand that they could not honor their WAR DEBTS to the U.S.—a view not shared by the U.S. Attempted solutions to the problem were the Dawes Plan (1924), by which Germany received a foreign loan and undertook to pay 1,000,000,000 gold marks yearly in reparations; and the Young Plan (1929), which eased the annuities, sought to secure their payment by mortgaging the German state railways, and estab. Bank for Internatl. Settlements at Basel. The economic world crisis led in 1931 to a one-year moratorium on all intergovernmental debts, proposed by Pres. Hoover; reparations payments were never resumed. In World War II the principles of reparation payments by Germany were worked out in the Yalta and Potsdam conferences (1945). The USSR was to receive 50%, of which 15% was to go to Poland; Great Britain and the U.S. were to distribute the rest among the other claimants. Payments were to be effected through removal of assets and equipment. Soviet authorities dismantled German industries on a large scale (as they also did with Austrian and Manchurian plants); in W Germany, Allied measures to collect reparations were fitful. Disagreement over the settlement of reparations was a factor in the split between the USSR and the Western Powers. Reparations varying from $125,000,000 to $360,000,000 were also imposed on Bulgaria, Finland, Hungary, Italy, and Rumania; the U.S., France, and Britain claimed no part of these.

repartimiento (rāpärtēmyĕn'tō), a Spanish system of distribution of lands, goods, and services of conquered peoples to conquerors. Introduced in Spanish America at beginning of conquest, system became core of peonage in New Spain and *mita* in Peru. See also ENCOMIENDA.

replacement series: see METAL.

Repplier, Agnes (rĕ'plēr), 1855–1950, American essayist, noted for scholarly, keen, and witty social criticism. Also wrote biographies, historical studies.

Representation of the People Acts, enacted by British Parliament to extend the franchise reform begun by REFORM BILLS. **Representation of the People Act of 1918** gave vote to most men of 21 or over; to women over 30. **Representation of the People Act of 1928** gave vote to all women on same terms as men. Later acts of 1948 and 1949 made minor changes.

Representatives, House of: see CONGRESS OF THE UNITED STATES.

reproduction, a fundamental function of all living things, the production of new individuals by other individuals. Varies widely in method and complexity; two main types are asexual (production of offspring by one individual) and sexual (involving two individuals). Asexual reproduction is common in plants, but in animals is found only in some lower organisms. Simplest form of process is division (fission) of single cell, followed by reorganization of material in each part. Sexual type involves union of two cells to form a third cell capable of developing into new organism; if two cells are of like nature, it is called conjugation; if unlike, it is FERTILIZATION. Sexual cells in higher animals and plants are distinguished as OVUM and SPERM.

reptile (rĕp'tůl, –tīl), member of the class of cold-blooded and lung-breathing vertebrate animals called Reptilia, ranking higher than amphibians and lower than birds and mammals. Reptiles are covered by scales, bony plates, or horny shells. Probably appeared in Carboniferous era.

Repton, town and parish (pop. 1,518), Derbyshire, England; site of Repton School (1557) for boys.

republic, a sovereign state ruled by representatives of a widely inclusive electorate. The U.S. exemplifies a federal republic whose central government is restricted in power. In the French republic, power is centralized, and constituent regions are permitted to perform only limited functions.

Republican, river, 422 mi. long, formed in S Nebr. and flowing E across Nebr. and SE across Kansas to join Smoky Hill R. and form the Kansas at Junction City. Included in several units of the Missouri river basin project.

Republican party, in U.S. history, name first used by Thomas Jefferson's party, later called Democratic Republican party or, simply, Democratic party. Name reappeared when the Republican party of today was founded in 1854. Party opposed extension of slavery. Election of Abraham Lincoln, Republican candidate, in 1860, brought about secession of Southern states. Republican radicals (e.g., Thaddeus STEVENS) opposed Andrew Johnson's moderate RECONSTRUCTION program. Their excesses under Pres. Grant and the open scandals of his administration created a new schism (see LIBERAL REPUBLICAN PARTY). In disputed election of 1876 Republican candidate R. B. Hayes was successful, but Republican domination of the South and radical rule of party ended with that election. The MUGWUMPS illustrated the lack of real issues between Republicans and Democrats in period after 1876. Party became champion of gold standard and conservative economic doctrines in late 19th cent. Many party INSURGENTS supported Theodore ROOSEVELT and the new PROGRESSIVE PARTY in 1912. Republican opposition was a large factor in defeating peace program of Democrat Woodrow Wilson. Republicans were blamed for disastrous economic depression that began in the administration of Herbert HOOVER. Led by Sen. A. H. Vandenberg, party joined Democratic administration in a bipartisan foreign policy after World War II. Victory in 1952 of party candidate, Dwight D. Eisenhower, returned presidency to Republican hands after 20 years of Democratic rule.

requiem (rĕ'kwēŭm) [Latin,= rest; from the first words of the introit, "Eternal rest grant unto them"], proper MASS for the souls of the dead, performed on All Souls' Day, at funerals, and in other Masses for the dead. The sequence is the DIES IRAE. Vestments are black. Among modern musical settings for the Mass are those of Mozart and Verdi.

Resaca de la Palma (rāsä'kä dā lä päl'mä), valley, an abandoned bed of the Rio Grande, N of Brownsville, Texas, where second battle of Mexican War was fought, May 9, 1846. U.S. forces under Gen. Zachary Taylor won victory.

reservoir (rĕ'zůrvôr, –vwär), storage tank for

water or a wholly or partly artificial lake for water supply. Use of dam to preserve water for irrigation arose in ancient times. In building reservoirs for water supply, factors to be considered include all aspects of CATCHMENT AREA. Some reservoirs are built to insure water supply for hydroelectric plants, to aid flood control, or to maintain water level for navigation (esp. on canals).

residence: see DOMICILE.

resin (rĕ'zĭn), any of a class of amorphous solids, yellowish to brown in color, tasteless and odorless or slightly aromatic, translucent and sometimes transparent, brittle, and inflammable. Chemical composition varies but all contain carbon, hydrogen, oxygen. There are many kinds, classified by source or qualities. Natural resins are found as exudations from trees or from insects or as fossils. Among the natural resins are copaiba, turpentine, benzoin, Canada balsam, dragon's blood, frankincense, mastic. Resins are used mostly in varnish, shellac, lacquer; medicines; material for molded articles; electric insulators; phonograph records; radio parts. Synthetic resins (see PLASTICS) are used in varnishes and for great variety of molded articles.

resorcinol (rĭzôr'sĭnōl) or **resorcin** (–sĭn), colorless, sweetish, crystalline substance made from benzene. Used to make dyes and medicines.

Respighi, Ottorino (ôt"tōrē'nō rāspē'gē), 1879–1936, Italian composer. His outstanding works are the romantic tone poems *The Fountains of Rome, The Pines of Rome,* and *Roman Festivals.* He also wrote operas, suites, songs, and chamber music.

respiration, process by which air enters plant or animal body, oxygen is absorbed by cells in which oxidation occurs, and carbon dioxide and water are expelled. In man, combined action of inspiration and expiration occurs about 18 times per minute when body is at rest. Blood absorbs oxygen in lungs and distributes it through body.

respiratory tract, air passages consisting of nasal passages, pharynx, larynx, windpipe, two bronchi with terminal branches (bronchioles) connecting with air sacs in lungs. See *ill.,* p. 763.

restaurant, an establishment serving food to the public. In inns of 16th-cent. England, a common table served all comers; such dining rooms, early called "ordinaries," became popular gathering places, particularly in London. The name restaurant was first used c.1765 for a Paris place serving light ("restoring") dishes. Delmonico's, opened c.1834, was New York city's first modern restaurant, as distinct from inns. Peculiar to U.S. is the self-service cafeteria.

Restif de la Bretonne, Nicolas Edme (nēkôlä' ĕd'mů rĕstēf' dů lä brůtôn'), 1734–1806, French author of some 250 novels, mostly based on incidents of his own rather libertine life and characterized by detailed realism. *Le Paysan perverti* (1775) is among the best-known.

Restigouche (rĕstĭgōōsh'), river, E Canada, rising in NW N.B. and flowing 130 mi. NE, ENE to Chaleur Bay at Dalhousie. Lower course is Que.–N.B. line.

Restoration, in English history, the reestab. of monarchy on accession (1660) of CHARLES II. Period extends to fall of JAMES II in 1688. Death of Oliver Cromwell was followed by reaction against Puritan and military control in favor of recall of exiled king. After his return power went first to earl of Clarendon, then to the Cabal. All remaining military republicans and Quakers were persecuted; militant Anglicanism was restored. Unwillingness of both kings to accept financial dependence on Parliament was one cause of James II's deposition in Glorious Revolution. Period was marked by advance in colonization and trade, by Dutch Wars, by birth of Whig and Tory parties, by opposition to Catholics, and by the revival of drama and poetry.

Restoration, in French history, the period from abdication of Napoleon I (1814) to July Revolution (1830). Includes reigns of LOUIS XVIII (interrupted by HUNDRED DAYS) and of CHARLES X.

resurrection [from Latin,= arising again], arising again from death to life. In Christian theology, the resurrection of Jesus from the tomb (celebrated at Easter) to dwell on earth 40 days before ascending to heaven is a cornerstone of Christian experience. It guaranteed His mission and promised the resurrection of all men. The doctrine of the resurrection of the body has been variously interpreted. Most Christians hold that on Judgment Day the souls of men will be rejoined with their risen (but glorified and incorruptible) bodies. Myths of resurrection of gods and heroes are common in pagan mythologies and are often associated with the change of seasons (see FERTILITY RITES).

resurrectionists: see BODY SNATCHING.

Reszke, Jean de (jän dů rĕ'skē), 1850–1925, Polish operatic tenor and teacher; known for both lyric and Wagnerian roles. He was leading tenor of the Metropolitan Opera, New York, 1891–1901. His brother, **Edouard de Reszke,** 1855–1917, was a leading bass at the Metropolitan Opera, 1891–1903.

Rethel (růtĕl'), town (pop. 4,482), Ardennes dept., N France, on Aisne R. Scene of heavy fighting in both world wars. The county of Rethel, held by the house of Burgundy from 1384 and by the cadet branch of Burgundy-Nevers from 1477, was raised to a duchy in 1581 and passed, by marriage, to the Nevers branch of the Gonzaga family. The Mazarin family bought the ducal title in 1663 from the Gonzagas.

retriever: see HUNTING DOGS.

Retz or **Rais, Gilles de Laval, seigneur de** (zhēl' dů läväl' sānyûr' dů rĕts', rĕs'), 1404–40, marshal of France in Hundred Years War. Rumors of satanic doings at his castle led to trial. He confessed to kidnaping, torturing, and killing over 100 children and was executed. Giles de Retz is supposed by some to be the original of Bluebeard.

Retz, Paul de Gondi, Cardinal de (pôl' dů gōdē', dů rĕts'), 1613–79, French cardinal and politician. Was prominent in the FRONDE. His memoirs (1717; Eng. tr., 4 vols., 1723) are among classics of French literature.

Reuben (rōō'bůn) [Heb.,= behold a son!], Jacob's eldest son, ancestor of one of the

12 tribes of Israel. Tribe settled E of Jordan R. and near the Dead Sea. Gen. 29.32; 35.22; 37; 42.22,37; 46.8; 49.3,4; Num. 1.20,21; 2.10; 26.5–10; 32.37; Joshua 22; 1 Chron. 5.26.

Reuchlin, Johann (yō'hän roikh'lůn), 1455–1522, German humanist, a scholar of Greek and Hebrew. His *Rudimenta Hebraica* (1506) was first Hebrew grammar written by a Christian. When a converted Jew, Johann Pfefferkorn, advocated destruction of all Hebrew books, Reuchlin suggested in return that only those Hebrew books which calumniated Christianity should be suppressed, and that the Jews should be required to furnish books for universities, with two chairs of Hebrew learning to be set up in every university in Germany. In struggle that developed between humanists supporting Reuchlin and clericals supporting Pfefferkorn, Reuchlin was victorious.

Réunion (räünyō'), island (970 sq. mi.; pop. 242,067), of Mascarene group, in Indian Ocean, an overseas department of France; cap. Saint-Denis. Settled c.1646 by the French and held by the British in Napoleonic Wars. Volcanic and mountainous. Exports sugar and rum. Formerly called Bourbon.

Reuss (rois), two former principalities in E Thuringia, central Germany. House of Reuss dates from 12th cent. Two branches emerged —Reuss Older Line, which held princely rank from 1778 and which had cap. at Greiz, and Reuss Younger Line, which held princely rank from 1806 and had cap. at Gera. Rule was abdicated 1918, and both territories became part of Thuringia 1920.

Reuss (rois), river, 99 mi. long, central Switzland. Flows N from St. Gotthard Pass, through L. of Lucerne, then joins Aar R.

Reuter, Paul Julius (roi'tůr), 1816–99, founder of Reuter's Telegraph Co., b. Germany.

Reuther, Walter (Philip) (rōō'thůr), 1907–, American labor leader, president of United Automobile Workers of America (1946–), president of C.I.O. (1952–). Important anti-Communist liberal spokesman.

Reval, Estonia: see TALLINN.

Revelation or **Apocalypse** (ůpŏ'kůlĭps), last book of New Testament, traditionally ascribed to St. John the Disciple. Book is a mysterious prophetic work full of visions of God and the New Jerusalem and dramatic portrayals of the triumph of good over evil. One immediate purpose of Revelation was to encourage Christians faced with martyrdom. Whether the author intended a deeper and more esoteric meaning is greatly debated. The veiled symbolism (e.g., the beast with the number 666, recurrence of the number seven) has been subject to cabalistic explanations in every period of Christian history.

Revelstoke, city (pop. 2,917), SE B.C., Canada, on Columbia R. at mouth of Illecillewaet R. and E of Kamloops. Center of mining and lumbering area, outfitting point for sportsmen and tourists, and gateway to Mt. Revelstoke Natl. Park.

reverberatory furnace, furnace used for separating metal from ore and in refining some metals. Differs from blast furnace chiefly in having separate compartments for burning fuel and for treating material. Used in producing wrought iron from pig and lead from its sulphide ores, and in refining copper.

Revere, Paul, 1735–1818, American Revolutionary patriot. He was a silversmith, designer, and printer. Took part in Boston Tea Party. Remembered for ride, April 18, 1775, to warn Mass. countryside of advance of British soldiers.

Revere, suburban city (pop. 36,763), E Mass., on the coast NE of Boston; settled c.1630; named for Paul Revere. Optical goods, processed foods. Includes Revere Beach, popular resort.

Revillagigedo Island (růvĭ'lůgůgē'dō), area, 1,120 sq. mi., off SE Alaska, in Alexander Archipelago, E of Prince of Wales Isl. Ketchikan is chief town.

Revillagigedo Islands (rāvē'yä-hēhä'dō), archipelago (320 sq. mi.), belonging to Colima, Mexico, in the Pacific, c.400 mi. W of mainland. A new volcano erupted here in 1952.

revival, religious, renewal of religious faith and service in church, community, or district. It is often marked by intense fervor in spiritual expression. Christian revivals began c.1737 in England and Europe with the evangelistic preaching of John and Charles Wesley and George Whitefield. In America simultaneously Great Awakening occurred. Revivals were common on frontier, often in form of a CAMP MEETING. Preeminent figure in modern revivalism was Dwight L. Moody, who with singing evangelist Ira D. Sankey moved audiences for 25 years. Other notable revivalists were Billy Sunday, Gipsy Smith, Aimee Semple McPherson.

revolver, a pistol with a revolving cylinder capable of firing several shots without reloading. An early type appeared in the 16th cent., but usable revolvers were introduced only early in the 19th cent. The first to become a standard weapon was that made by Samuel COLT. The "six-shooter" is said to have civilized the "Wild West."

revue (rĭvū'), stage presentation, originally a light, satirical commentary on current events. Developed, especially in England and U.S., as musical shows (e.g., Ziegfeld's *Follies*) notable for extravagant staging and the display of feminine beauty.

Reyes, Alfonso (älfōn'sō rā'äs), 1889–, Mexican writer, notable especially for his superb poetical prose style.

Reykjavik (rā'kyůvĭk), Icelandic *Reykjavík,* city (pop. 54,707), cap. of Iceland, on Faxa Fjord, SW Iceland; founded 874, chartered 1786. It is Iceland's chief port and fishing and fish-processing center; a Lutheran episcopal see; and seat of a university (founded 1911). At Keflavik (to W) is international airfield, built by U.S. Army in World War II. Hot-water supply system (completed 1945) uses natural hot springs.

Reymont, Ladislaus (Stanislaus) (rā'mônt), Pol. *Władisław Stanisław Reymont,* 1867–1925, Polish novelist. His best-known work is *The Peasants* (4 vols., 1902–9; Eng. tr., 1924–25). Was awarded 1924 Nobel Prize in Literature.

Reynard the Fox (rĕ'nůrd, rā'närd), hero of medieval beast epics, fables that satirize the upper classes and the clergy. The type of story probably originated in Alsace and Lorraine, but versions of Reynard stories occur in Low German, Dutch and Flemish, High German, Latin, French, and English. There is much dispute as to priority of the versions. Caxton's *Historie of Reynart the Foxe* (1481) was translated from Flemish.

Reynaud, Paul (pôl' rānō'), 1878–, French minister of finance (1938–40) and premier (1940); a conservative. When Marshal Pétain insisted on concluding armistice, Reynaud resigned. One of defendants at RIOM trial, he was imprisoned by Germans until 1945.

Reynolds, Sir Joshua, 1723–92, celebrated English portrait painter. His career was advanced by his social gifts no less than his artistic talent; the wide circle he entertained included the great literary figures of the day, and he was known for his eloquence as first president of the Royal Acad. Employing assistants, he painted c.2,000 portraits and historical paintings. His works are notable for richness of color; in design he surpassed his rivals Gainsborough and Romney. One of his masterpieces, *Mrs. Siddons as the Tragic Muse,* is in the Huntington Gall., San Marino, Calif.

Reza Shah Pahlevi (rē'zä shä' pälävē'), 1877–1944, shah of Iran (1925–41). Headed a coup d'état in 1921 and assumed full dictatorial power in 1925 as first of Pahlevi dynasty. Deposed and succeeded by his son, Mohammed Reza Shah. Name is also written Riza Shah Pahlavi.

Rh, chemical symbol of the element RHODIUM.

Rhaetia (rē'shů), anc. Roman province including parts of S Bavaria, Tyrol, and E Switzerland; annexed by the Romans c.15 B.C.; cap. Augusta Vindelicorum (Augsburg).

Rhaeto-Romanic (rē'tō-rōmă'nĭk), generic name for several Romance dialects spoken in Switzerland and small bordering areas. They include Romansh, an official Swiss language, Ladin, and Fruili or Friouli. See LANGUAGE (table).

Rhagae: see RAGES.

Rhangavis, Alexandros Rizos: see RANGABE.

Rhazes (rā'zēz) or **Rasis** (rā'sĭs, –zĭs), c.860–c.925, Persian physician. Author of influential works including medical text, *Almansor,* and encyclopedia, *Liber continens.*

Rhé, island, France: see RÉ.

Rhea (rē'ů), in Greek religion, Titaness, Great Mother of the Gods; daughter of Uranus and Gaea, sister and wife of Cronus, and mother of Zeus, Poseidon, Demeter, Hera, Pluto, and Hestia. Her worship was associated with fertility rites. Identified with Cybele in Crete, with Ops in Rome.

Rhea Silvia, mother of ROMULUS and Remus.

Rhee, Syngman (sĭng'män rē), 1875–, president of Republic of Korea in S Korea (1948–). Reelected 1952.

Rhegium (rē'jēům), anc. city, S Italy, on the Strait of Messina, today Reggio di Calabria. Founded in the 8th cent. B.C. by Greeks, it was powerful until destroyed by Dionysius the Elder of Syracuse (386 B.C.). It was also important under the Romans as Rhegium Julium.

Rheims (rēmz), Fr. *Reims* (rēs), city (pop. 106,081), Marne dept., NE France. Archiepiscopal see from 8th cent.; seat of university (founded 1547). Center of French champagne industry since 18th cent. Clovis I was crowned here king of the Franks (496), and Rheims was the traditional place of coronation of the kings of France. Most famous coronation, in present cathedral, was that of Charles VII, with Joan of Arc standing by his side (1429). The cathedral, a treasure of Gothic architecture, was begun by Robert de Coucy in 1211. Partly destroyed in World War I by German shells, it was restored (except for its irreplaceable stained-glass windows) and reopened in 1938. On May 7, 1945, German emissaries signed Germany's unconditional surrender at Allied hq. in Rheims.

Rhenish Palatinate: see PALATINATE.

rhenium (rē'nēům) or **dvi-manganese** (dvī"-măng'gůnēs), heavy, silvery, metallic element (symbol = Re; see also ELEMENT, table).

rheostat (rē'ůstăt), device using varying resistance to control electrical equipment. Metallic type is wire-wound insulated cylinder in contact with an arm movable one way to decrease windings and lessen resistance, other way to increase windings and resistance. Other types are carbon and electrolytic rheostats.

rhetoric: see ORATORY.

Rhett, Robert Barnwell, 1800–1876, American secessionist. A leading "fire-eater" at Nashville Convention of 1850; member of S.C. secession convention of 1860.

rheumatic fever: see RHEUMATISM.

rheumatism (ro͞o'můtĭzům), term applied to painful conditions of muscle, bone, joint, or nerve. Associated diseases include arthritis, bursitis, neuritis, lumbago, sciatica, gout. Some forms are relieved by Cortisone, derived from adrenal gland cortex. Rheumatic fever is an acute disease marked by migratory arthritis and often affecting heart.

Rh factor, factor in blood of c.85% of population. Discovered 1940 in blood of rhesus monkey by Landsteiner and A. S. Wiener. Introduction of Rh positive blood by blood transfusion induces forming of antibodies in Rh negative recipient; these may cause fatal reaction if Rh factor is introduced by second transfusion. Factor passing from blood of Rh positive fetus to blood of negative mother may cause antibody formation in maternal blood. If such antibodies enter fetal blood the child may have a critical disease.

Rhine (rīn), Dutch *Rijn,* Fr. *Rhin,* Ger. *Rhein,* river of Europe, c.820 mi. long, formed in E Switzerland by the junction of two headstreams (Vorder-Rhein, Hinter-Rhein). After traversing the L. of Constance it turns W, passes Schaffhausen, where it falls in a cataract, and forms Swiss-German border to Basel (head of steamship navigation). At Basel it turns N. forming French-German border, passes Strasbourg, and fully enters German territory below Karlsruhe. Continuing N (past Speyer, Mannheim, Ludwigshafen, Worms, Mainz, Wiesbaden, Coblenz, Bonn, Cologne, and Duisburg), it enters the Netherlands and divides into two branches—the WAAL and the Lower Rhine. The latter in turn fans out into the IJSSEL, the LEK, and the Old Rhine, which enters the North Sea below Leiden. The Waal and Lek link the Rhine with the Meuse estuary and the port of Rotterdam; the Rhine-Herne and Dortmund-Ems canals, with the Ruhr dist. and the German port of Emden. Other canals: Rhine-Marne Canal, Rhine-Rhone Canal (long but unimportant), Rhine-Main-Danube Canal (incomplete). Among tributaries are the Aar, Neckar, Main, Moselle, Ruhr, and Wupper. Section between Mainz and Bonn is particularly famous for its idyllic landscape, noble vineyards, ruined castles, and legendary landmarks (e.g., LORELEI; DRACHENFELS). The Rhenish Slate Mts., through which it winds here, include the Taunus and EIFEL. The industrial RUHR, WUPPER, and DÜSSELDORF dists. make the Rhine the chief commercial river of Europe (coal, iron, grain). An international navigation commission, estab. 1919, resumed functioning after World War II (hq. Strasbourg).

Rhine, Confederation of the: see CONFEDERATION OF THE RHINE.

Rhineland (rīn′lănd), Ger. *Rheinland.* **1** Alternate name of the former RHINE PROVINCE of Prussia. **2** Region of W Germany, along the Rhine, comprising Rhine Prov., Rhenish Palatinate, and parts of Hesse and Baden. Under the Treaty of Versailles (1919) the Allies were to occupy parts of the region for 5–15 years, and Germany was forbidden to build fortifications or maintain troop concentrations W of a line running 50 km. E of the Rhine. U.S. troops, first of the occupation forces to withdraw, were replaced by the French. The entire RUHR dist. was occupied by French and Belgian troops in 1923–25. Last French troops left Rhineland in 1930, five years ahead of time. Although Germany had reaffirmed the demilitarization of the Rhineland in the Locarno Pact (1925), Hitler in 1936 began its remilitarization. The Siegfried Line, a formidable defense system, was penetrated by the Allies in World War II after heavy fighting (1944–45).

Rhinelander, city (pop. 8,774), N Wis., on Wisconsin R. and NW of Green Bay, in lake and dairy region. Trade center for resort area with mfg. of wood products.

Rhineland-Palatinate (pùlă′tĭnĭt″), Ger. *Rheinland-Pfalz,* German state (7,666 sq. mi.; pop. 2,993,652), W Germany, W of the Rhine; cap. Mainz. Formed 1946 in French zone of occupation, it includes S part of former RHINE PROVINCE (with Trier and Coblenz), the Rhenish PALATINATE, and Rhenish HESSE. Produces Rhine wines. Has many spas (e.g., Bad Ems). Joined Federal Republic of [West] Germany 1949.

Rhine Province, Ger. *Rheinprovinz,* former Prussian province (9,451 sq. mi.; 1939 pop. 7,915,830), W Germany, bordering on the Netherlands, Belgium, and Luxembourg; also known as Rhenish Prussia and as Rhineland. Contained historic cities of AACHEN and COLOGNE; part of the industrial RUHR dist.; the industrial centers of DÜSSELDORF, WUPPERTAL, and SOLINGEN; and the MOSELLE wine dist., with Coblenz (former provincial cap.). Earliest acquisition by the house of Brandenburg-Prussia in this part of Germany was the duchy of CLEVES (1614). The remainder (incl. former bishoprics of Cologne and TRIER and former duchies of JÜLICH and BERG) was awarded to Prussia by the Congress of Vienna (1814–15). The Rhine Prov. was vital in the industrialization of Germany. Strongly Roman Catholic, it played a major part in the Kulturkampf. The Treaty of Versailles (1919) deprived it of the Saar Territory and of Eupen and Malmédy. After World War II the province was partitioned among British occupied NORTH RHINE-WESTPHALIA and French-occupied RHINELAND-PALATINATE. See also RHINELAND.

rhinoceros (rīnŏ′sùrùs), massive herbivorous ungulate mammal, of Africa, India, SE Asia, with thick skin, often deeply folded. African black rhinoceros (*Diceros*) and white rhinoceros (*Ceratotherium* or *Diceros*) have two nasal horns. Indian and Javan rhinoceroses (*Rhinoceros*) have one nasal horn.

rhizome (rī′zōm), fleshy, creeping rootstock, actually an underground stem. Among plants that can be propagated by dividing or cutting up their rhizomes are iris, ginger, and trillium. See *ill.*, p. 999.

Rhode Island, state (1,058 sq. mi.; pop. 791,-896), NE U.S.; one of Thirteen Colonies; cap. PROVIDENCE. Smallest, most densely inhabited state. Bordered on S by Atlantic Ocean. Takes name from largest island in NARRAGANSETT BAY. Rolling land cut by short, swift streams. Mfg. of textiles, machine tools, jewelry, silverware, rubber goods; some mining; some farming, especially poultry. Roger WILLIAMS estab. Providence (1636). Anne HUTCHINSON and other Puritan exiles founded PORTSMOUTH (1638). Royal charter of 1663 reaffirmed religious freedom. NEWPORT occupied by British forces (1776–79) in American Revolution. Textile mfg. advanced by Samuel SLATER and Moses BROWN in late 18th cent. Suffrage extended after rebellion of Thomas W. DORR (1842). Mill owners dominated political and economic life until well into 20th cent. Recently new, diversified industries have been introduced.

Rhode Island, island, c.15 mi. long and 3½ mi. wide, S R.I., at entrance to Narragansett Bay. Largest island in state. Site of NEWPORT, Middletown, PORTSMOUTH. Known to Indians and early colonials as Aquidneck, named Rhode Isl. 1644.

Rhode Island, University of, and **Rhode Island State College:** see SOUTH KINGSTOWN.

Rhoden, Ausser and **Inner,** Switzerland: see APPENZELL.

Rhodes, Cecil (John), 1853–1902, British statesman and capitalist. Made fortune in South Africa by monopoly of Kimberley diamond production. Persuaded Britain to annex Bechuanaland in 1881. Formed British South Africa Co. to exploit mining concessions. Prime minister and virtual dictator of Cape Colony 1890–96, he conspired to seize Transvaal; forced to resign after raid of Sir Leander Jameson. Developed Rhodesia. Left fortune to public service, including Rhodes Scholarships (32 for U.S.; others for Germany and British colonies).

Rhodes, James Ford, 1848–1927, American historian. Major work was *History of the*

United States from the Compromise of 1850 (7 vols., 1893–1906). His *History of the Civil War, 1861–1865* (1917) won him 1918 Pulitzer Prize in history.

Rhodes (rōdz), Gr. *Rhodos,* Aegean island (542 sq. mi.; pop. 55,181), Greece, off SW Asia Minor, largest of the Dodecanese; cap. Rhodes (pop. 21,694), on NE coast. Mountainous in the interior, the island has a fertile coastal strip. Fishing; sponge diving. Population is 11% Italian. Settled by Dorians before 1000 B.C., Rhodes reached its height as a commercial power and a center of culture in the 4th–3d cent. B.C. The COLOSSUS OF RHODES was one of the wonders of the world. After its decline, Rhodes became an ally of Rome. Involved in the civil wars, it was seized and sacked by Cassius 43 B.C. At that period, Rhodes had a famous school of rhetoric, where Caesar studied. Captured from the Byzantines in the Fourth Crusade (1204), Rhodes passed to various lords. In 1309 the KNIGHTS HOSPITALERS took it from the Seljuk Turks; after defending the island for 50 years against the Ottoman sultans, the knights capitulated to Suleiman I on Jan. 1, 1523. It was taken from Turkey by Italy 1912; ceded to Greece 1947.

Rhodes, Knights of: see KNIGHTS HOSPITALERS.

Rhodesia (rōdē′zhů), region of Africa, comprising NORTHERN RHODESIA and SOUTHERN RHODESIA. Named 1894 for Cecil RHODES, who took it for British South Africa Co. in 1888. Divided in 1923.

rhodium (rō′dēům), hard, gray-white, metallic element (symbol = Rh; see also ELEMENT, table). Alloyed with platinum it is used to make thermocouples for measuring high temperatures; alone it is used to plate reflecting surfaces and to prevent tarnish of metals.

rhododendron (rō″důdĕn′drůn), evergreen or deciduous flowering shrub of genus *Rhododendron,* widely distributed, especially in mountainous regions. Azaleas, once considered a separate genus, are rhododendrons with largely deciduous foliage and funnel-shaped flowers, in contrast to the mostly evergreen leaves and bell-shaped flowers of rhododendrons. Both types are much used as ornamentals; many tender azaleas are grown as house plants. All require an acid, woodsy soil. American species include the rose bay (*Rhododendron maximum*), the Carolina rhododendron (*R. catawbiense*), the flame azalea (*R. calendulceum*), the fragrant swamp honeysuckle (*R. viscosum*), and the pinxter flower (*R. nudiflorum*).

Rhodope (rŏ′důpē), mountain range of Balkan Peninsula, in S Bulgaria and NE Greece. Extends E from Struma R. to the Maritsa, rising to 9,596 ft. in the Musala (Bulgaria).

Rhoecus (rē′kůs), 6th cent. B.C., Greek sculptor. Helped improve methods of casting bronze statues.

Rhondda (rŏn′dů), urban district (pop. 111,357), Glamorganshire, Wales, on Rhondda R. Lower Rhondda valley is the great coal-mining region of S Wales.

Rhône (rōn), department (1,104 sq. mi.; pop. 918,866), E central France; cap. Lyons.

Rhone, Fr. *Rhône* (both: rōn), river, 505 mi. long, Switzerland and SE France. Springing from Rhone glacier in the upper Valais (Switzerland), it flows W and passes through L. of Geneva, then enters France and receives the Saône at Lyons, where it becomes navigable. Flowing S, it separates at Arles into two branches which enclose Camargue isl. and enter the Mediterranean W of Marseilles. These branches are silted up, but the Rove Tunnel, a 4.4-mi. underground channel, connects the Rhone with Marseilles (opened 1927). The fertile Rhone valley, cradle of Provençal culture, is covered with fine vineyards, orchards, olive groves, and vegetable gardens. In the S silkworms are raised. A large project for making the Rhone navigable up to Geneva and for exploiting its huge power potential is under way. The Génissiat Dam and hydroelectric plant, one of the world's largest, c.20 mi. S of Geneva, was inaugurated in 1948. A related Swiss project would link the L. of Geneva with the Rhine.

Rhône, Bouches du, France: see BOUCHES-DU-RHÔNE.

rhubarb, hardy large-leaved perennial plant (*Rheum rhaponticum*), also called pieplant. Its fleshy leafstalks are used in pies and sauces, especially in spring. Leaf blades are poisonous.

rhyme or **rime,** a literary artifice used in versification. Used in oldest extant Oriental poetry, but rare among ancient Greeks and Romans; began to develop when classical quantitative meters gave way to accentual meters. Alliteration and assonance used to be called rhyme; now, however, words are said to rhyme only when their final accented syllables sound alike. For proper rhyme, vowels and succeeding consonants must agree, but preceding consonants must differ. Words rhyme only when accented on the same syllable. Single or masculine rhyme is of one syllable or ends in a consonant with no mute *e* following; when rhymes are of two syllables or when they are not accented on last syllable or end in final mute *e,* they are called double or feminine rhymes.

rhythm, the element of music concerned with the relative duration of tones and with the stress or accent placed on certain tones. The practice of using a recurrent rhythm pattern throughout a composition began in the late 12th cent. and led to dividing a work into units of equal time value called measures. One 20th-cent. trend is to use several different rhythm patterns at the same time.

Riad, Riyad, or **Riyadh** (all: rēäd′), city (pop. 80,000), cap. (with Mecca) of Saudi Arabia and cap. of the Nejd; in an oasis. Center of Wahabi movement in Islam since early 19th cent.

Rialto (rēäl′tō), originally island and oldest quarter of Venice, Italy. Name is now applied to Rialto bridge, built 1588–91, a single marble arch with shop-lined arcades.

Ribalta, Francisco (fränthē′skō rēbäl′tä), c.1555–1628, Spanish religious painter, a pioneer in Spain in the use of dramatic light and shade. Taught Ribera.

Ribaut or **Ribault, Jean** (both: zhã′ rēbō′), c.1520–1565, French mariner and colonizer in Fla. Estab. unsuccessful colony on present Parris Isl., S.C. (1562). Killed in massacre by Pedro MENÉNDEZ DE AVILÉS on coast S of St. Augustine.

Ribbentrop, Joachim von (yō'äkhĭm fŭn rĭ'bŭntrôp), 1893–1946, German foreign minister under Hitler (1938–45), influential in forming German-Soviet pact of 1939. Was hanged as war criminal.

Ribble, river of England. Flows 75 mi. SW from the Pennines in Yorkshire to the Irish Sea.

Ribera, Jusepe, José or **Giuseppe** (hōōsā'pā rēbā'rä, hōsā', jōōzĕp'pā), c.1590–c.1652, Spanish painter. Studied in Valencia with Ribalta. Lived mainly in Naples where he enjoyed great prestige and influence as court painter to the Spanish viceroy. Famous for austere, realistic figures in strong light and shade against a dark background. His style reflects influence of Caravaggio.

Rib Mountain, 1,940 ft. high, central Wis., quartzite outcrop near Wausau. Summit is state park. Winter sports.

riboflavin: see VITAMINS.

Ricardo, David (rĭkär'dō), 1772–1823, British economist. He held that wages cannot rise above the lowest level necessary for subsistence, and that the value (not the price) of goods is measured by the amount of labor involved in their production. Greatly influenced radical economists. His chief work was *Principles of Economics and Taxation* (1817).

Ricci, Matteo (mät-tā'ō rēt'chē), 1552–1610, Italian Jesuit missionary. In China after 1582 he won much Chinese respect for Christianity and sent back to Europe valuable reports on Chinese life.

Rice, Elmer, 1892–, American dramatist. Plays include *On Trial* (1914), *The Adding Machine* (1923), *Street Scene* (1929), *Counsellor-at-Law* (1931), and *Dream Girl* (1945).

rice, cereal (*Oryza sativa*), native to deltas of great Asiatic rivers (Ganges, Tigris, Yangtze, and Euphrates), and cultivated mainly in tropical and subtropical areas. The plant is an annual grass, 2–4 ft. tall, with round, jointed stem, long, pointed leaves, and seeds borne in a dense head on separate stalks. Much rice is grown on lowlands which can be flooded when desirable; terraced hillsides irrigated by means of pumps are also used in both Orient and Occident. Primitive methods are still used in much of the Orient but in W countries cutting and threshing are usually done by machines. The threshed rice is known as paddy (rice fields are also called paddy fields or rice paddies) and is covered by a brown hull or coating which is removed before marketing. This is done in the Orient mainly by flailing, treading, or working in a mortar, though machinery is being introduced; in the U.S. a special mill is used. After husking, grains are usually polished and become white and glistening. Brown rice (without the bran layer removed) has much greater food value since brown coating and germ are rich in B-complex vitamins and minerals. Rice is rich in starch but low in protein and fat; combined with meat, oil, cheese, or soybean sauces it is a valuable food. In the Orient the fine, soft straw is plaited for hats and shoes. Broken grain is used in making laundry starch and also by distillers. Arrack is a distilled liquor sometimes prepared from a rice infusion; in Japan the beverage sake is brewed from rice. Important rice-producing countries are China, India, Japan, Indo-China, Java, Egypt, Brazil, U.S. (esp. La., Texas, Ark., Calif., S.C.).

Rice Institute, at Houston, Texas; non-sectarian, coed.; chartered 1891, endowed by W. M. Rice, opened 1912. University courses with no tuition fees.

Rice Lake, city (pop. 6,898), NW Wis., NW of Eau Claire and on Rice L. and Red Cedar R. Farm and resort center.

Rich, Edmund: see EDMUND, SAINT.

Rich, John, 1692–1761, English pantomime actor and originator of pantomime in England. Unexcelled as Harlequin, he imported pantomime in annual productions 1717–60. Built Covent Garden theater (1732).

Richard, kings of England. **Richard I, Richard Cœur de Lion** (kŭr" dŭ lē'ŭn), or **Richard Lion-Heart,** 1157–99, was king of England (1188–99), duke of Aquitaine and Normandy, and count of Anjou. Warred against his father, Henry II, as ally of his mother, Eleanor of Aquitaine. Went (1190) on Third Crusade with PHILIP II of France, who afterwards plotted with Richard's brother JOHN to divide England. Richard, on his way home, was imprisoned by Leopold II, who surrendered him to Emperor Henry VI. Was released by huge ransom and surrender of England, which was returned as a fief. Fought Philip in France, was killed in minor engagement. Although seldom in England, his personal qualities have made him an English symbol of chivalry. **Richard II,** 1367–1400, king of England 1377–99, was son of Edward the Black Prince. In peasant uprising under Wat Tyler in 1381 young king met insurgents and won their allegiance. Asserted his independence as ruler 1383. In struggle for power party of barons led by Thomas of Woodstock, earl of Gloucester, dismissed (1388) Richard's favorites. Richard had Gloucester murdered 1397. Richard's cousin, Henry of Bolingbroke, returned to England in his absence, forced him to abdicate, and was crowned HENRY IV (1399). Richard was imprisoned and died in Pontefract Castle. His reign was outstanding in literary and ecclesiastical history of England. Subject of Shakspere's *Richard II*. **Richard III,** 1452–85, king 1483–85, was brother of Edward IV. Gained control of his nephew, young EDWARD V, and had himself named king. Murder of Edward in Tower (1483) led to unsuccessful rebellion of Henry Stafford. Earl of Richmond landed in England (1485), Richard was killed at Bosworth Field, and Richmond became HENRY VII. Death of Richard, last Yorkish king, ended Wars of the Roses. Subject of Shakspere's *Richard III*.

Richard, earl of Cornwall, 1209–72, titular king of the Romans (see HOLY ROMAN EMPIRE). Brother of Henry III of England, he became Henry's adviser and acted as regent in king's absence. Wanted to be emperor and was elected king of the Germans (1257) but never ruled all of the country.

Richard Cœur de Lion: see RICHARD I, of England.

Richard de Bury (bĕr'ē), 1287–1345, English bibliophile, and bishop of Durham. *Philobiblon* describes his experiences as book collector.

Richard Lion-Heart: see RICHARD I, of England.

Richards, Laura E(lizabeth Howe), 1850–1943, American writer of children's books, notably *Captain January* (1890).

Richards, Theodore William, 1868–1928, American chemist. Won 1914 Nobel Prize for determining atomic weights of many elements.

Richardson, Dorothy M., 1882–, English novelist, author of *Pilgrimage* (12 vols., 1915–38). She introduced as a narrative method "interior monologue"—akin to "stream of consciousness."

Richardson, Henry Handel, pseud. of Henrietta Richardson Robertson, 1870–1946, Australian novelist. Abandoned music for writing. Her major work is the trilogy *The Fortunes of Richard Mahony* (1930).

Richardson, Henry Hobson, 1838–86, American architect, noted exponent of Romanesque design. Finest work is Trinity Church in Boston (1872–77).

Richardson, John, 1796–1852, first Canadian novelist to write in English. Wrote frontier romances.

Richardson, Sir Owen Willans, 1879–, English physicist. Won 1928 Nobel Prize for researches on electrons and establishment of Richardson's law of motions of electrons emanating from hot bodies.

Richardson, Samuel, 1689–1761, English novelist. At 50 a prosperous printer, he conceived idea of a moral novel in letter form, and wrote *Pamela; or, Virtue Rewarded* (4 vols., 1740–41). Similar works followed: *Clarissa; or, The History of a Young Lady* (7 vols., 1747–48) and *The History of Sir Charles Grandison* (7 vols., 1753–54). These realistic, sentimental stories were immensely popular. Richardson ranks as one of the great inventors of the novel.

Richelieu, Armand Jean du Plessis, duc de (ärmā' zhā' dü plĕsē' dük' dŭ rēshŭlyû'), 1585–1642, French prelate and statesman; commonly known as Cardinal Richelieu. Became bishop of Luçon 1607; secretary of state 1616; cardinal 1622; chief minister to Louis XIII 1624. Though he owed his rise to the regent, MARIE DE' MEDICI, he turned against her, reversed her pro-Hapsburg policy, had her exiled in 1630, and governed as virtual dictator until his death. The founder of French absolutism, he broke the power of the HUGUENOTS (capture of La Rochelle, 1628; Peace of Alais, 1629) and kept the recalcitrant great nobles under control, rigorously suppressing their ceaseless conspiracies. He intervened in the THIRTY YEARS WAR—indirectly at first, by subsidizing Sweden (1631), then by active participation on the Protestant side (from 1635). He encouraged trade with India and Canada, but his reckless expenditures and taxation depleted the treasury and made him highly unpopular. Founder of the French Academy, he also wrote literary works.

Richelieu (rĭ'shŭlōō), river, issuing from N end of L. Champlain and flowing c.75 mi. N across S Quebec to St. Lawrence R. at Sorel. Link in waterway between Hudson R. and St. Lawrence R. Discovered 1609 by Champlain; was route of early explorers.

Richet, Charles Robert (shärl' rōbĕr' rēshā'), 1850–1935, French physiologist. Won 1913 Nobel Prize in Physiology and Medicine for work on body sensitivity to alien proteins (anaphylaxis).

Richland, village (pop. 21,809), SE central Wash., on Columbia R. and E of Yakima. Built 1943–45 to house workers of Hanford Works, U.S. atomic-energy research and production plant.

Richmond, municipal borough (pop. 41,945), Surrey, England, on Thames R. Site of Palace of Sheen (where many sovereigns lived), a large deer park, and Kew Observatory. Inn of the Star and Garter, which figures in Scott's works, was torn down in 1919.

Richmond. 1 City (pop. 99,545), W Calif., across the bay from San Francisco. Settled on Spanish ranch site when railroad came, 1899. Deep-water port with oil refining, railroad shops, foundries, metal-products and chemical plants, and canneries. Its shipyards were active in World War II. **2** City (pop. 39,539), E Ind., near Ohio line E of Indianapolis; settled 1806. Trade center of farm area. Mfg. of machinery. Earlham College is at adjacent Earlham. **3** City (pop. 10,268), central Ky., SSE of Lexington; settled 1784. Confederates won first Ky. victory near by (Aug. 30, 1862). Tobacco, livestock, corn, clothing, and concrete products. **4** New York city borough: see STATEN ISLAND. **5** City (pop. 230,310), state cap., E Va., port on James R. at head of navigation. State's largest city, it is a cultural, financial, commercial, and industrial center of the South. A great tobacco marketing and processing center, it has mfg. of synthetic textiles, paper, fertilizer, and metal goods. Settled 1637 as trading post, town was projected 1733 by Col. William Byrd and made state cap. 1779. Pillaged by British 1781. As cap. of CONFEDERACY in Civil War, it was constant objective of Union forces. Seriously threatened in PENINSULA CAMPAIGN of 1862 (saved in SEVEN DAYS BATTLES) and again in Wilderness campaign (1864), the city fell and was burned, April 3, 1865, at end of Grant's campaign (see PETERSBURG). Richmond Battlefield Natl. Park includes battlefields in and near city. Seat of Richmond Professional Inst. of the Col. of WILLIAM AND MARY, Medical Col. of Virginia, and Univ. of Richmond (Baptist; coed.; 1832). Points of interest include capitol (begun 1785), Washington Monument, White House of the Confederacy, St. John's Church (1741), Poe Foundation (city's oldest building, c.1686), John Marshall's house (1793), and Virginia Mus. of Fine Arts.

Richmond and Derby, Margaret Beaufort, countess of: see BEAUFORT, MARGARET.

Richter, Johann Paul Friedrich (yō'hän poul' frē'drĭkh rĭkh'tŭr), pseud. **Jean Paul** (zhā pôl'), 1763–1825, German author. His fantasies *Quintus Fixlein* (1796; Eng. tr. by Carlyle, 1827) and *Siebenkäs* (1796–97; Eng. tr., 1845), influenced by Laurence Sterne, won him a wide vogue.

Richwood, city (pop. 5,321), S W.Va., on

Cherry R. Lumber mills, limestone quarries, coal mines.

Ricimer (rĭ'sĭmůr), d. 472, Roman general of German birth. Won naval victory over Vandals and deposed Emperor Avitus (456). Thereafter was real ruler of Italy, making and deposing several puppet emperors, among them MAJORIAN.

Rickenbacker, Edward Vernon (rĭ'kůnbă"kůr), 1890–, American aviator. Awarded Congressional Medal of Honor and Croix de Guerre in World War I. Eddie Rickenbacker became (1938) Eastern Airlines president. Adrift 27 days on Pacific after World War II plane crash.

rickets (rĭ'kĭts) (rachitis), deficiency disease of infancy and childhood affecting calcium metabolism and resulting in softening of bone structure and consequent bone deformities. Prevented and treated by adequate intake of vitamin D, calcium, and phosphorus.

Ricketts, Charles, 1866–1931, British artist, b. Geneva. As designer-manager of Vale Press (1896–1904), he contributed greatly to fine bookmaking.

Rickman, Thomas, 1776–1841, English architect, important in the Gothic revival. Wrote first systematic treatise on English medieval period (1817).

Rideau Canal (rēdō', rē'dō), SE Ont., Canada, extends 126 mi. between Ottawa R. (at Ottawa) and L. Ontario (at Kingston). Built 1826–32 to connect St. Lawrence R. to L. Ontario without exposure to American attack. Now popular recreation area.

Ridgefield. 1 Residential town (pop. 4,356), SW Conn., at N.Y. line. Has fine homes. Scene of Revolutionary battle on April 27, 1777. **2** Borough (pop. 8,312), NE N.J., E of Rutherford.

Ridgefield Park, residential village (pop. 11,-993), NE N.J., NW of Ridgefield. N end of N.J. Turnpike.

Ridgewood, residential village (pop. 17,481), NE N.J., NNE of Paterson.

Ridgway, Matthew B(unker), 1895–, American general. Commanded 82d Airborne Div. in World War II (1942–44). UN and U.S. commander in Japan, Korea, and Far East (1951–52). Replaced Dwight D. Eisenhower as supreme commander of Allied powers in Europe in 1952.

Ridgway, borough (pop. 6,244), NW Pa., S of Bradford. Mfg. of electrical products.

Riding, East, North, West: see YORKSHIRE, England.

Riding Mountain National Park, 1,148 sq. mi., SW Man., Canada, S of Dauphin, W of L. Manitoba; estab. 1929. Recreation area and big game preserve.

Ridley, Nicholas, 1500?–1555, English prelate and Protestant martyr; bishop of Rochester (after 1547), of London (from 1550). Under Mary Tudor, excommunicated (1553) as heretic. Convicted at second trial (1555) and, with Latimer, burned at stake at Oxford.

Riel, Louis (rēĕl'), 1844–85, Canadian insurgent. In 1869–70 he led rebels of Red R. settlements and headed provisional government of their founding. His followers felt that transfer of Hudson's Bay Co. territory to Canada threatened their land rights. Rebellion collapsed without bloodshed. In 1884 **Riel's Rebellion** occurred when he led a group in Saskatchewan bent on securing land titles. Riel was captured, tried for treason, and hanged.

Riemann, Georg Friedrich Bernhard (gā'ôrk frē'drĭkh bĕrn'härt rē'män), 1826–66, German mathematician. Contributions include work on theory of functions of complex variables and method of representing them on coincident planes or sheets (Riemann's surfaces). He laid foundations of Riemannian geometry (non-Euclidian geometry system representing elliptic space).

Rienzi or **Rienzo, Cola di** (kō'lä dē rēĕn'tsē, rēĕn'tsō), 1313?–1354, Roman popular leader and humanist. Made papal notary by Clement VI at Avignon, he returned to Rome and in 1347 assumed, with popular support, wide dictatorial powers, styling himself tribune of the sacred Roman republic. His dream was to create a popular Italian state, unified under Roman leadership. Rienzi quickly lost Clement's support and was forced to leave Rome after a tumult (1347), but Clement's successor, Innocent VI, restored him to favor and sent him to Italy with ALBORNOZ. Made senator of Rome, Rienzi entered the city in triumph (1353), but his violent and arbitrary rule soon ended with his murder. Subject of an early opera by Richard Wagner.

Riesener, Jean Henri (rē'zůnůr), 1734–1806, French cabinetmaker, b. Germany; one of artists who helped form Louis XVI style.

Riesengebirge (rē'zŭngůbĭr'gů) or **Giant Mountains,** Czech. *Krkonše,* Pol. *Karkonosze,* range along border of Bohemia (Czechoslovakia) and Silesia; a part of the Sudetes. Highest peak, Schneekoppe, rises 5,258 ft. on Czech-Silesian border. There are many spas and resorts.

Rievaulx (rē'vōz, rĭv'ůz), village, North Riding of Yorkshire, England. Has ruins of Rievaulx Abbey.

Rif or **Riff,** mountainous region on Mediterranean coast of Spanish Morocco. Berber tribes here were unsubdued until 1926, when joint French-Spanish campaign defeated their leader, Abd-el-Krim.

rifle, firearm with the bore spirally grooved to impart a spinning motion to the bullet. The rifle's history goes back to the 15th cent. but its widespread use dates from the settling of the woodland regions of the present E U.S. in the 18th cent. Early muzzle-loading weapons were succeeded by breech-loading rifles (used in the Civil War). The model 1903 Springfield armory rifle was long standard. The semi-automatic Garand rifle, a self-loading, clip-fed, gas-operated shoulder weapon, was much used in World War II. The principle of grooving or "rifling" the inner surface of the barrel is used also in artillery and pistols.

Riga (rē'gů), city (pop. 392,926), cap. of Latvia, on the mouth of the Western Dvina and on the Gulf of Riga (an E inlet of the Baltic Sea). A major seaport (though frozen Dec.-Jan.); mfg. center (machinery, precision instruments, food products, paper, textiles); cultural center (university, founded 1919; academy of fine arts; conservatory of music).

Founded 1201, Riga was the base from which the LIVONIAN KNIGHTS conquered the Baltic coast. It joined the Hanseatic League 1282 and accepted the Reformation; its culture was German. Riga passed to Poland 1582; to Sweden 1621; to Russia 1710 (officially ceded 1721). Became cap. of independent Latvia 1919; of Latvian SSR 1940. Was occupied by the Germans in both world wars (1917–19; 1941–44). Its old section, or Hansa town, was damaged in World War II. It contains many fine medieval buildings—castle, Lutheran cathedral, Church of St. Peter. Across the Dvina is industrial Jelgava. The **Treaty of Riga of 1920,** between the USSR and Latvia, confirmed Latvian independence. The **Treaty of Riga of 1921,** between the USSR and Poland, fixed the Russo-Polish frontier. It awarded Poland large parts of Belorussia and the Ukraine. Was superseded by Polish-Russian treaty of 1945.

Rigaud, Hyacinthe (rēgō′), 1659–1743, French portrait painter, b. Perpignan, of Spanish ancestry. Sitters included most of the notables of the day.

rigging, wire, rope, and chain supporting and operating the masts, yards, booms, and sails of a ship. The shrouds are mast supports, crossing ropes ratlines. Footropes hung from stirrups to help the crew furl the sails. Running rigging includes the ropes, blocks, and other apparatus needed to operate the yards, booms, gaffs, and sails, to raise and lower boats, and to handle cargo. For the chief simple types of rigging, see *ill.,* p. 1109.

Riggs, Lynn, 1899–, American dramatist, known especially for *Green Grow the Lilacs* (produced 1931; basis for musical comedy, *Oklahoma!*).

Rights, Bill of: see BILL OF RIGHTS.

Rights of Man: see DECLARATION OF THE RIGHTS OF MAN.

Rigsdag (rĭks′dä), national parliament of Denmark. Consists of an upper house (Landsting) and a lower house (Folketing).

Rigsmaal: see NORWEGIAN LANGUAGE.

Riis, Jacob August (rēs), 1849–1914, Danish-American journalist and philanthropist. He wrote and lectured in behalf of slum clearance in New York. His first book, *How the Other Half Lives* (1890), began lifelong association with Theodore Roosevelt in civic betterment. *The Making of an American* (1901) is autobiographical.

Rijeka-Susak, Yugoslavia: see FIUME.

Rijks Museum or **Ryks Museum** (both: rīks′), at Amsterdam, opened 1885. Has the outstanding collection of Dutch master paintings, notably those of Rembrandt.

Rijswijk, Netherlands: see RYSWICK, TREATY OF.

Riksdag (rēks′däg, rēks′tä), national parliament of Sweden. Upper house is elected by county and city councils, lower house by direct universal suffrage. Except in matter of taxation, king has right (rarely used) to absolute veto on legislation.

Riley, James Whitcomb, 1849–1916, American poet, b. Indiana. As the "Hoosier poet" he wrote homely, appealing poems such as "Little Orphant Annie" and "The Raggedy Man." Collections include *Rhymes of Childhood* (1890) and *An Old Sweetheart of Mine* (1902).

Riley, Fort, U.S. military post, estab. in 1852 on Kansas R. near Junction City, Kansas, to protect travelers on Santa Fe Trail from Indian attacks. Today it maintains permanent garrison for training field artillery, cavalry, and other units.

Rilke, Rainer Maria (rī′nůr märē′ä rĭl′ků), 1875–1926, German lyric poet, b. Prague. His peculiar blending of impressionism and mysticism was first recognized with *Das Buch der Bilder* (1902; enlarged ed., 1906). Though his poetry collections became more popular and he won wide popularity with the prose ballad *The Tale of the Love and Death of Cornet Christopher Rilke* (1906; Eng. tr., 1932), his stature as a major poet of his time developed only after his death. His later poetry—*Duinese Elegies* (1923; Eng. tr., 1930, 1939) and *Sonnets to Orpheus* (1923; Eng. tr., 1936)—was profound and austere.

Rimbaud, Arthur (ärtür′ rēbō′), 1854–91, French poet, precursor of the SYMBOLISTS and usually classed with the DECADENTS. He stopped writing at 19. His poems, noted for a hallucinatory, dreamworld quality, include "Le Bateau ivre." *Une Saison en enfer* (1873) is his adolescent memoirs. A close, tempestuous relationship with VERLAINE was followed by a life of adventure in Ethiopia.

rime: see RHYME.

Rimini (rē′mēnē), anc. *Ariminium,* city (pop. 31,505), Emilia-Romagna, N central Italy; an Adriatic port and bathing resort. At junction of Flaminian and Aemilian Ways, it had strategic importance in Roman days; was a member of the Pentapolis under Byzantine rule. It was included in Pepin's donation to the pope (754). MALATESTA family seized power in 1295 and later conquered neighboring cities. Papal possession became effective in 1509. City was heavily damaged in World War II; the famous Malatesta temple (a 13th-cent. church rebuilt by Sigismondo Malatesta, c.1450), one of the finest Renaissance buildings, was partly destroyed.

Rimmer, William, 1816–79, American sculptor. His knowledge of anatomy (gained from his medical studies) is apparent in his few surviving works (e.g., *The Dying Centaur,* Metropolitan Mus.).

Rimmon (rĭ′mŭn), Syrian god. 2 Kings 5.18.

Rimouski (rĭmōō′skē), town (pop. 11,565), E Que., Canada, on St. Lawrence R. at mouth of Rimouski R. and NE of Quebec. Lumbering, woodworking.

Rimsky-Korsakov, Nicolai (Andreyevich) (nyĭkŭlī rĭm′skē-kôr′sůkôf), 1844–1908, Russian composer; one of the Five (see BALAKIREV). The subjects of his operas are chiefly drawn from Russian history or legend—*Le Coq d'Or, The Snow Maiden, The Maid of Pskov* (also known as *Ivan the Terrible*). He also wrote the orchestral suite *Scheherezade;* three symphonies; the *Russian Easter* overture, and the well-known *Flight of the Bumblebee.* He was a master of orchestral color and often arranged works of other composers (e.g., Moussorgsky's *Boris Godunov* and parts of Borodin's *Prince Igor*).

rinderpest (rĭn′dûrpĕst″), communicable virus

disease of cattle, endemic to Russia, central Asia, and Africa; also called cattle plague. It is unknown in U.S. and Canada. High fever, chills, mouth and udder eruptions, and labored breathing are characteristic; disease is usually fatal. A preventive vaccine was discovered during World War II.

Rinehart, Mary Roberts, 1876–, American novelist and dramatist. Known especially for mystery novels, such as *The Circular Staircase* (1908; dramatized by her and Avery Hopwood, 1920, as *The Bat*) and *The Man in Lower Ten* (1909), and for her humorous "Tish" stories.

Rinehart, William Henry, 1825–74, American sculptor. His masterpiece, *Clytie,* is in Peabody Inst., Baltimore, along with casts of many of his works.

Ringwood, borough (pop. 1,752), N N.J., in Ramapo Mts. near N.Y. line. Iron mines developed after 1764; munitions made in Revolution. Ringwood Manor State Park has historic manor house, now a museum.

ringworm (tinea), fungus infection of skin marked by reddish, disk-shaped areas. Interdigital ringworm is often called athlete's foot.

Río and **Rio,** respectively Spanish and Portuguese terms for river. For those not listed here, see under second element of name—e.g., for Rio Amazonas, see AMAZON.

Rio de Janeiro (rē'ō dŭ jŭnâ'rō), state (16,443 sq. mi.; pop. 2,326,201), SE Brazil, on the Atlantic; cap. Niterói. Encloses but does not include Federal District (with city of Rio de Janeiro). Escarpment divides area into coastal lowland, central hill section, and fertile Paraíba R. valley in west. Is leading industrial region.

Rio de Janeiro, city (pop. 2,335,931), colloquially Rio; cap. of Brazil on Guanabara Bay of Atlantic, in Federal District. Beautiful harbor is surrounded by landmarks—Sugar Loaf Mt.; Corcovado peak, on which stands huge statue of Christ; crescent-shaped beaches—notably, Copacabana. City handles much of Brazil's trade, exporting coffee, iron ore, manganese, meat, cotton, hides. Varied manufactures include glass, textiles, household appliances, chemicals, trucks. Has botanical garden (founded 1808), and many fine public buildings and educational institutions. Area was visited by Portuguese explorers, Jan., 1502 (whence name meaning January River). French Huguenots estab. colony here (1555) but were driven out (1567) by Mem de Sá. Replaced Bahia as capital of Brazil (1763).

Río de Oro: see SPANISH SAHARA.

Rio Grande (rē'ō grănd', rē'ō grän'dē), river, c.1,800 mi. long, rising in San Juan Mts. of SW Colo. Flows S through middle of N.Mex., then SE as Texas-Mexico line, empties into Gulf of Mexico at Brownsville, Texas, and Matamoros, Mexico. Coronado saw its Indian pueblos and irrigation 1540. Elephant Butte Dam, near Hot Springs, N.Mex., serves large area. Irrigation continues downstream, aids citrus-truck region near mouth (Rio Grande Valley). U.S.-Mexico pact of 1945 provided new projects. In Mexico: Río Bravo del Norte.

Rio Grande de Cagayan, P.I.: see CAGAYAN.

Rio Grande do Norte (rē'ō grän'dŭ dōō nôr'tŭ), state (20,482 sq. mi.; pop. 983,572), NE Brazil, on the Atlantic; cap. NATAL. Has valuable mineral resources. Sugar cane is widely grown. First European settlement 1599. Dutch occupied area briefly in 17th cent.

Rio Grande do Sul (rē'ō grän'dŭ dōō sōōl'), state (109,066 sq. mi.; pop. 4,213,316), S Brazil; cap. PÔRTO ALEGRE. Southernmost state of Brazil, it is leading stock-raising and meat-processing state and most important producer of wheat and wine. First European settlement made by Jesuits in 17th cent. Many German and Italian farmers immigrated to area. **Rio Grande do Sul,** city (pop. 64,241), is in S part of state, on Lagoa dos Patos; an important port.

Riom (rēõ'), town (pop. 10,420), Puy-de-Dôme dept., S central France. Here in 1942 the VICHY GOVERNMENT tried several French political and military leaders (incl. Léon Blum and Édouard Daladier) for having plunged France into World War II unprepared. The trial was indefinitely postponed when the defendants produced evidence detrimental to their accusers.

Río Muni: see SPANISH GUINEA.

Rion (rēôn'), anc. *Phasis,* river, 180 mi. long, rising in the Caucasus in W Georgian SSR and flowing S and W past Kutais into Black Sea at Poti. Upper course used for hydroelectric power.

Río Piedras (pyā'dhräs), town (pop. 132,438), NE Puerto Rico. Seat of Univ. of Puerto Rico.

Río Tinto, Ríotinto (rē'ōtēn'tō) or **Minas de Ríotinto** (mē'näs dā), town (pop. 2,727), SW Spain, in Andalusia. Center of rich copper-mining region.

Riouw Archipelago (rē'ou, rē'ō), island group (2,279 sq. mi.; pop. 77,149), Indonesia, at entrance to Strait of Malacca. Important bauxite and tin mines on Bintan isl.

Ripley, George, 1802–80, American literary critic and author. A Unitarian minister, he was a noted transcendentalist and wrote for *Dial.* Left ministry (1841) to found BROOK FARM. Later he became an influential literary critic on New York *Tribune.*

Ripley, village (pop. 1,792), SW Ohio, SE of Cincinnati. Here is Rankin Home, said to be original of Underground Railroad station where Eliza of *Uncle Tom's Cabin* found refuge.

Ripon (rĭ'pŭn), municipal borough (pop. 9,464), West Riding of Yorkshire, England. St. Cuthbert founded monastery here c.660. Present minster dates from 12th–15th cent. Treaty signed here (1640) ended second of Bishops' Wars.

Ripon (rĭ'pŭn), city (pop. 5,619), central Wis., NW of Fond du Lac; settled 1844 as Ceresco, a Fourierist community. Birthplace of Carrie C. Catt. Seat of Ripon Col. (coed.; 1851).

Rip Van Winkle, name of character and story by Washington IRVING, in *The Sketch Book of Geoffrey Crayon, Gent.* (first pub. serially, 1819–20). It tells of a man who slept 20 years.

Risorgimento (rēsôr"jēmĕn'tō) [Ital.,= resurgence], in Italian history, the period of national unification (c.1815–1870). After the French Revolution and Napoleon had disappointed Italian hopes of unity and independence, the Congress of Vienna in 1814–15 again divided ITALY into several states, of which only SARDINIA was free of Austrian influence or domination. Uprisings of secret patriotic societies (e.g., the CARBONARI) were suppressed by the Italian rulers with the sanction of the HOLY ALLIANCE, but the movement toward unity could not be stopped. There were three main parties—a republican, anticlerical group, led by MAZZINI; a conservative group, advocating a confederation under the presidency of the pope; and a middle-of-the-road group, which favored unification under the house of Savoy (i.e., the kings of Sardinia). This last group, led by CAVOUR, eventually won out. Revolutions flared up throughout Italy in 1848–49 but were suppressed by Austria. Sardinian forces, who twice came to the rebels' aid, were defeated at Custozza (1848) and Novara (1849). In Rome, French troops restored PIUS IX. Cavour's diplomacy secured the alliance of France (see PLOMBIÈRES) for Sardinia's war of 1859 against Austria. The French and Sardinians won costly victories at Magenta and Solferino, but the preliminary peace of VILLAFRANCA DI VERONA disappointed Sardinia's ambitions by giving it only Lombardy. In 1860 Sardinia annexed Tuscany, Parma, Modena, and Romagna, then joined in the campaign of GARIBALDI, annexing Umbria and the Marches while Garibaldi's volunteers were conquering the Two Sicilies. In 1861 VICTOR EMMANUEL II was proclaimed king of united Italy. Venetia came to Italy after the Austro-Prussian War (1866). The remnant of the Papal States—Rome and Latium—remained under French protection until 1870, when it was annexed by Italy.

Ristori, Adelaide (rēstō'rē), 1822–1906, Italian actress. A tragedienne, she won fame in Europe and U.S. in familiar Italian roles, classical French drama, and as Lady Macbeth and Medea.

Ritter, Karl, 1779–1859, German geographer, a founder of modern human geography. His major work was *Die Erdkunde* (2d ed., 19 vols., 1822–59).

river, stream of running fresh water larger than a brook or creek. Runoff after precipitation flows downward by the shortest and steepest course in depressions formed by intersecting slopes. Runoff may join in a stream that deepens its bed by erosion; it becomes permanent when it cuts deeply enough to be fed by subsurface water. Sea level is the ultimate base level, but floor of lake or basin into which stream flows may become local and temporary base level. A river's discharge depends on the cross-section area of its channel and on its velocity (governed by water volume, bed slope, and channel shape). Rivers modify topography by erosion and by deposition. Young streams have steep-sided valleys, steep gradients, and irregularities in the bed; mature streams have valleys with wide floors and flaring sides, advanced headward erosion by tributaries, and a more smoothly graded bed; the old stream has graded its course to base level and runs through a peneplain.

Rivera, Diego (dēā'gō rēvā'ä), 1886–, Mexican painter. Worked in Europe 1907–9, 1912–21; became friendly with Cézanne and Picasso and with Russian communists. Believing that art should express "new order of things" through mass medium of murals in public buildings, he became a sort of prophet to peasants and workers. Visited Moscow 1927–28. Through his influence Trotzky was allowed to enter Mexico. Several of his murals depict the life, history, and problems of Mexico. A mural for Rockefeller Center, New York, was rejected because it contained a portrait of Lenin.

Rivera, Primo de: see PRIMO DE RIVERA, MIGUEL.

River Brethren, Christian group originating 1770 in E Pa. among Swiss Mennonites settled along Susquehanna R. Sect probably took name from practice of baptism in river. In 1843 conservative group in York co. withdrew as Old Order or Yorker Brethren. Main body became Brethren in Christ. They are like Dunkards in church practices, dress, and customs.

Riverdale. 1 Village (pop. 5,840), NE Ill., just S of Chicago. Rail center with steel plant. **2** Town (pop. 5,530), W central Md., suburb of Washington, D.C.

River Edge, borough (pop. 9,204), NE N.J., on Hackensack R. and E of Paterson.

River Forest, residential village (pop. 10,283), NE Ill., W suburb of Chicago; settled 1836.

Riverhead, town (pop. 9,973), on E Long Isl., SE N.Y., on Peconic Bay. Fishing center in farm area (potatoes, truck).

Riverina (rĭ"vürē'nü), rural administrative district (26,560 sq. mi.; pop. 83,000), S New South Wales, Australia, between Lachlan and Murray rivers.

River Junction: see CHATTAHOOCHEE, Fla.

River Oaks, city (pop. 7,097), N Texas, NW suburb of Fort Worth. Formerly Castleberry.

River Rouge (rōōzh'), city (pop. 20,549), SE Mich., on Detroit R. at mouth of the River Rouge, next to S Detroit. Grew in 1920s with expansion of Ford Motor Co. in area.

Riverside, town (pop. 9,214), S Ont., Canada, on Detroit R., E suburb of Windsor.

Riverside. 1 Residential and resort city (pop. 46,764), S Calif., E of Los Angeles. Citrus center where navel orange was introduced in 1873. Annual Easter sunrise services are held on Mt. Rubidoux, site of huge cross to Father Junípero Serra. March Field (U.S.) is near. **2** Residential village (pop. 9,153), NE Ill., W suburb of Chicago. Designed as model suburb by F. L. Olmsted and Calvert Vaux. **3** Village (pop. 7,199), SW N.J., on Delaware R. above Camden. Mfg. of watch cases, clothing, roller skates, metal products, textiles.

Riverton, town (pop. 4,142), W central Wyo., where Wind and Popo Agie rivers form Bighorn R. Served by Riverton project.

Riviera (rĭvēâ'rü), coastal strip between Alps and N Apennines and the Mediterranean, extending from La Spezia (Italy) to Hyères (France). French Riviera is also called Côte d'Azur. Celebrated for scenery, mild climate, vegetation; dotted with resorts: Rapallo, San Remo (Italy); Nice, Monte Carlo, Cannes (Côte d'Azur).

Rivière du Loup (rēvyĕr' dü lōō'), city (pop. 9,425), E Que., Canada, on St. Lawrence R. at mouth of Rivière du Loup and NE of Quebec. Resort, tourist, and trade center with railroad shops, lumbering, and woodworking.

Rivoli (rē'vōlē), village, Venetia, NE Italy, on Adige R., near Verona. Scene of decisive victory of French under Bonaparte over Austrians (1797).

Riyad or **Riyadh,** Arabia: see RIAD.

Rizal, José (hōsā' rēsäl'), 1861–96, Philippine patriot and author, a physician. His first novel, *Noli me tangere* (1886), attacking Spanish administration and the religious orders in Philippines, brought about his exile in 1887. Arrested and returned to Manila in 1896, he was executed as instigator of insurrection.

Riza Shah Pahlavi: see REZA SHAH PAHLEVI.

Rizzio, David (rĭt'sēō), 1535?–1566, favorite of MARY QUEEN OF SCOTS. A Piedmontese musician, he became Mary's secretary. Jealous nobles persuaded Lord Darnley that Rizzio was Mary's lover and, with Darnley's aid, murdered him in Mary's presence.

Rjukan (rēōō'kän), village (pop. 5,460), S Norway, on the Rjukanfoss, a waterfall (983 ft. high) of Mane R. Its hydroelectric and nitrogen-fixation plants were destroyed by Allied bombings 1943. Has heavy-water plant.

Rn, chemical symbol of the element RADON.

road. History of roads is related to centralizing of populations in powerful cities, which they served for military purposes and for collection of supplies and tribute. In Persia between 500 and 400 B.C., the capital, Susa, had roads leading to every province. Greeks, opposed to centralization, built few roads. Famous ROMAN ROADS were surfaced with large stone slabs; parts of them are still serviceable. From fall of Rome to 19th cent., European roads were generally neglected, although in France there were some good military roads. Development of MACADAM ROAD was important to Industrial Revolution. Inca empire had fine roads. North American Indians used chiefly footpaths and waterways. With stagecoaches came TURNPIKE and the NATIONAL ROAD but canal and railroad took precedence until automobile again made road paramount and U.S. highways became complex system. Road-building is now a major branch of engineering.

road runner, cuckoo found in cactus country of W U.S. and parts of Mexico. It flies with ease but more often runs over ground, with head down.

Roanoke. 1 City (pop. 5,392), E Ala., near Ga. line SE of Anniston, in farm area. **2** City (pop. 91,921), SW Va., on Roanoke R., between Blue Ridge and Allegheny Mts., S gateway to Shenandoah Valley; founded 1834. Center of agr., coal, and lumber area. Mfg. of iron and steel products, textiles, and chemicals. Near by is Hollins Col. (nonsectarian; for women; 1842).

Roanoke, river rising in SW Va. and flowing 410 mi. SE to Albemarle Sound, N.C. Flood-control and power projects under way.

Roanoke Island, NE N.C., off coast in Croatan Sound between Albemarle and Pamlico sounds. Manteo (pop. 635) is chief town. Island is 12 mi. long, averages 3 mi. in width; fishing main industry. Site of unsuccessful colonies organized by Sir Walter Ralegh in 1585 and 1587. Discovery of stone tablets in 1930s, supposedly recording history of "lost colony," would seem to dispel CROATAN theory of second colony's disappearance. Fort Raleigh Natl. Historic Site estab. 1941.

Roanoke Rapids, city (pop. 8,156), N N.C., on Roanoke R. and NNE of Rocky Mount. Textile and paper mills.

Robber Synod: see EUTYCHES.

robbery, felonious taking of property from a person against his will by threatening or committing force or violence. The threat may be against his property or against someone else rather than his own person. If there is no use of force or fear, the crime is not robbery but larceny; if force or fear is used to get the consent of the victim the crime is extortion.

Robbia, Italian sculptors: see DELLA ROBBIA.

Robbins, village (pop. 4,766), NE Ill., near Chicago; an all-Negro community.

Robbinsdale, city (pop. 11,289), E Minn., NW suburb of Minneapolis.

Robert, kings of France. **Robert I,** c.865–923, younger brother of Eudes, led rebellion against Charles III (the Simple) and was crowned 922 but was soon killed in battle. His son-in-law Raoul succeeded him. **Robert II** (the Pious), c.970–1031, son of Hugh Capet, reigned 996–1031. Sought to strengthen royal power, with moderate success. Henry I succeeded him.

Robert, kings of Scotland. **Robert I** or **Robert the Bruce,** 1274–1329, king 1306–29, led in the struggle for national independence. Defeated at Methven after defying Edward I by being crowned (1306) at Scone. Legend says Bruce learned courage and hope while in hiding from watching a spider spinning its web. Defeated Edward II at Bannockburn in 1314. Bruce's title to throne was recognized by Treaty of Northampton in 1328. By his skill and courage he delivered Scotland from English control. **Robert II,** 1316–90, king 1371–90, was founder of STUART dynasty. Various of his sons acted as guardian during most of his reign. Scots fought off English invasions and won great victory at Otterburn in 1388. His eldest son, **Robert III,** c.1340–1406, king 1390–1406, was an invalid. Real power held by his brother Robert Stuart, duke of Albany.

Robert, dukes of Normandy. **Robert I** (the Magnificent), d. 1035, reigned 1027–35; often identified with ROBERT THE DEVIL. Designated his natural son, William the Conqueror, as successor. **Robert II** or **Robert Curthose,** c.1054–1134, succeeded his father, William I of England, as duke of Normandy in 1087. Warred against WILLIAM II and HENRY I of England, whose throne he claimed. Henry defeated him at Tinchebrai (1106) and imprisoned him in England.

Robert, Henry Martyn, 1837–1923, American military engineer. During Civil War he worked as engineer on defenses of Washington, Philadelphia, and New England coast. From 1867 to 1895 he was in charge of river, harbor, and coast improvements of Pacific and Gulf coasts, Great Lakes, and Long Isl. Sound. He is more widely known for his

Pocket Manual of Rules of Order for Deliberative Assemblies (1876).

Robert Bruce: see ROBERT I, king of Scotland.

Robert College, at Istanbul, opened 1863 with funds contributed by Christopher R. Robert and other Americans for education of Turkish men.

Robert Curthose: see ROBERT II, duke of Normandy.

Robert Grosseteste: see GROSSETESTE, ROBERT.

Robert Guiscard (gēskär′), c.1015–1085, Norman conqueror of S Italy; son of Tancred de Hauteville, a Norman nobleman. His brothers William Iron Arm, Drogo, and Humphrey preceded him to Italy. Humphrey in 1053 forced the pope to invest him with Apulia and all other S Italian lands the Normans had acquired or were to acquire from the Byzantines and the Arabs. Robert, succeeding Humphrey in 1057, completed the conquest of S Italy while his brother ROGER I took Sicily from the Arabs. In 1081, Robert began his expedition against the Byzantine Empire. He took Corfu and defeated Alexius I but returned in 1083 to aid Pope GREGORY VII against Emperor Henry IV. He briefly held and sacked Rome (1084). Expelled again by Henry's forces, he resumed his campaign in the E and died of fever on Cephalonia. His possessions in S Italy, after passing to his son and grandson, were annexed by Roger II of Sicily.

Robert of Courtenay (kôrt′nē, kŏŏrtünā′), d. 1228, Latin emperor of Constantinople (1221–28). His empire was reduced to city of Constantinople.

Robert of Geneva, d. 1394, Genevan churchman, antipope as Clement VII. After the death of Gregory XI, who had returned the papacy from Avignon to Rome, the cardinals elected URBAN VI (1378) but shortly reconsidered and elected Robert instead. He fled to Avignon, and the Great SCHISM was begun. Robert was succeeded as antipope by Pedro de Luna.

Roberts, Sir Charles George Douglas, 1860–1943, Canadian author. He influenced other Canadian poets of "Confederation school" with his nature lyrics and idyls. Wrote tales of wildlife, a popular *History of Canada* (1897).

Roberts, Elizabeth Madox, 1885–1941, American poet and novelist, known for stories of her native Kentucky (e.g., *The Time of Man,* 1926; *The Great Meadow,* 1930), with faithful lyric renditions of regional speech. Her lyrics and ballads (in *Song in the Meadow,* 1940) have been much admired.

Roberts, Frederick Sleigh, 1st **Earl Roberts of Kandahar** (kăndühär′), 1832–1914, British field marshal. Forced Afghans to accept British demands in 1879. Commanded all Indian forces 1885–93. Was commander in chief in SOUTH AFRICAN WAR 1899–1900.

Roberts, Kenneth L(ewis), 1885–, American author of historical novels, including the series *Chronicles of Arundel.* Also well known are *Northwest Passage* (1937), *Oliver Wiswell* (1940), and *Lydia Bailey* (1946).

Roberts, Owen J(osephus), 1875–, American jurist, Associate Justice of U.S. Supreme Court (1930–45).

Robertson, James, 1742–1814, American frontiersman, a founder of Tenn. Founded Nashville (1780); primarily responsible for its survival.

Robertson, Thomas William, 1829–71, English author of superficial realistic comedies (e.g., *Caste,* 1867).

Robert the Bruce: see ROBERT I, king of Scotland.

Robert the Devil, hero of medieval legend, who was sold to the devil by his mother, did penance, and purified himself. Often identified with Robert I of Normandy.

Robeson, Paul (rōb′sün), 1898–, American Negro actor and singer. Roles in O'Neill's *Emperor Jones* and *All God's Chillun Got Wings* preceded his wide fame as a singer. Appeared later in *Showboat, Othello, Hairy Ape,* and films. A controversial figure because of leftist political affiliations.

Robespierre, Maximilien (rōbz′pēēr, –pĕr, Fr. mäksēmēlyē′ rôbĕspyĕr′), 1758–94, French revolutionist. Practiced law at Arras; was elected to States-General of 1789 and to Convention (1792); slowly rose to leadership of JACOBINS and took part in destruction of GIRONDISTS. It was his entry into the Committee of Public Safety (July, 1793) that raised him to the first rank. The REIGN OF TERROR enabled him to remove his chief rivals (notably HÉBERT, DANTON, and DESMOULINS) and to attempt the realization of his dogmatic version of J. J. Rousseau's theories. With his lieutenants SAINT-JUST and COUTHON he initiated the horrors of the Great Terror. The Law of 22 Prairial (June 10, 1784) made the Revolutionary Tribunal supreme. By establishing the worship of the Supreme Being, Robespierre even sought to impose his deism as state religion. On 9 THERMIDOR (July 27), when Saint-Just was about to demand the heads of another installment of "traitors," the Convention at last rallied in self-defense. In face of the Convention's dramatic uprising, Robespierre was surprisingly timid and undecided. He was summarily tried and guillotined with several followers (July 28). Robespierre's fanatic devotion to virtue, which earned him the epithet "The Incorruptible," has never been questioned, but in other respects he has been variously appraised as a maniac, a self-seeking dictator, and an idealistic champion of social revolution.

robin or **robin redbreast,** Old World name for small bird of warbler family. In New World it is name for migratory bird of thrush family; eastern American robin is c.10 in. long, with brownish-olive head, back, and tail, black-barred white throat, and chestnut-red breast.

Robin Hood, legendary outlaw of medieval England. With Little John (his chief archer), Friar Tuck, Maid Marian, and his band, he lived in Sherwood Forest and robbed the rich to help the poor.

Robinson, Boardman, 1876–1952, American painter, b. Canada. Cartoonist for newspapers and periodicals, 1907–24. Murals in Rockefeller Center, N.Y.

Robinson, Charles, 1818–94, first governor of state of Kansas (1861–63), b. Mass. EMIGRANT AID COMPANY agent, thrice elected territorial governor; opposed by proslavery forces.

Robinson, E(dwin) A(rlington), 1869–1935, American poet, b. Maine. Early work appeared in *The Torrent and the Night Before* (1896) and *The Children of the Night* (1897). After a courageous struggle he won long-delayed fame with *The Man against the Sky* (1916). Longer poems include *Avon's Harvest* (1921), *Cavender's House* (1929), and Arthurian romances. His somber, ironic analysis of character is shown in such poems as "Flammonde," "Miniver Cheevy," and "Ben Jonson Entertains a Man from Stratford." Robinson wrote in traditional metrical forms, often in colloquial language, and always with strong emotional power.

Robinson, Jackie (Jack Roosevelt Robinson), 1919–, American baseball infielder, first Negro to play in major leagues. Won (1949) National League batting title, named most valuable player in league.

Robinson, James Harvey, 1863–1936, American historian. Through writings and teaching he stressed "new history," i.e., social and scientific rather than purely political, and influenced study and teaching of history. Works include *The New History* (1912) and *The Mind in the Making* (1921).

Robinson, John, 1576?–1625, English nonconformist pastor of Pilgrim Fathers in Holland. He led separatist group from Scrooby, England, to Amsterdam (1608), and to Leiden (1609). He encouraged but did not join emigration (1620) to America.

Robinson, Lennox, 1886–, Irish dramatist, connected with Abbey Theatre. His dramas of Irish life include *The Dreamers* (1915), *The Lost Leader* (1918), *The Whiteheaded Boy* (1920), and *The Far-off Hills* (1928).

Robinson, Ray, 1921–, American boxer, whose real name is Walker Smith. Considered one of the greatest boxers of his time, "Sugar Ray" was welterweight champion 1946–51, middleweight champion 1951–52. Retired (1952) after unsuccessful try for light heavyweight title.

Robinson, Sir Robert, 1886–, English biochemist. Worked on structures of vegetable substances, synthesis of hormones, plant pigments; won 1947 Nobel Prize in Chemistry.

Robinson, city (pop. 6,407), E Ill., NNW of Vincennes, Ind., in oil and farm area. Mfg. of china, pottery, and glycerin.

Robinson Crusoe, character created by Daniel DEFOE in his story (1719) of a castaway on a desert island, suggested in part by adventures of Alexander Selkirk, a Scottish sailor.

Robinson-Patman Act, 1936, passed by U.S. Congress to supplement CLAYTON ANTI-TRUST ACT. Designed to protect independent retailer from chain-store competition.

robot (rō'bŭt, rŏ'bŭt), mechanical device designed to perform actions or work generally performed by humans. Karel Capek, Czech dramatist, used the expression in his play *R. U. R.* (*Rossum's Universal Robots*), to describe artificial workers with human form and intelligence, but devoid of feelings. Terms *automaton* and *robot* are both commonly used for devices supplanting a human in given task of some complexity. Examples include many electronic devices for industrial functions, automatic pilot which keeps plane on course, electronic calculators, and robot bombs or "buzz-bombs" used against England by Germany in World War II.

Rob Roy [Scottish Gaelic,= red Rob], 1671–1734, Scottish freebooter, whose real name was Robert MacGregor. Known by Sir Walter Scott's novel *Rob Roy*. An outlaw, he pillaged and burned (with aid of his clan). Pardoned (1727) after voluntary submission. Also used his maternal name of Campbell.

Robsart, Amy (rŏb'särt), 1532?–1560, maiden name of wife of Robert Dudley, earl of Leicester. She was found dead and it was rumored that Dudley had arranged her death. Mystery has never been cleared up. Story figures in Scott's *Kenilworth.*

Robson, Mount: see MOUNT ROBSON PROVINCIAL PARK.

Robstown, city (pop. 8,278), S Texas, W of Corpus Christi. Processing and shipping center for oil and agr. area.

Roca, Julio Argentino (hōō'lyō ärhäntē'nō rô'kä), 1843–1914, Argentine general and statesman, president of republic (1880–86, 1898–1904). Drove Patagonian Indians beyond Río Negro (1878–79), thus opening vast territory for colonization. Accomplishments during his administrations include federalization of Buenos Aires, great material expansion, settlement of boundary dispute between Chile and Argentina (see CHRIST OF THE ANDES), and formulation of DRAGO DOCTRINE.

Roca, Cape (rô'kŭ), W Portugal, near Lisbon, on the Atlantic; western extremity of Europe.

Rochambeau, Jean Baptiste Donatien de Vimeur, comte de (zhā' bätēst' dônäsyē' dŭ vēmûr', kōt' dŭ rôshābō'), 1725–1807, marshal of France. Landed in 1780 at Newport, R.I., with 6,000 regulars to aid American Revolution. Joined Washington on the Hudson 1781. Planned YORKTOWN CAMPAIGN with Washington. In 1792 he resigned command of Northern Army in French Revolutionary Wars; was imprisoned during Reign of Terror. His son **Donatien Marie Joseph de Vimeur, viscomte de Rochambeau** (märē' zhôzĕf', vēkōt'), 1750–1813, fought in American Revolution; quelled Negro revolt on the island of Haiti (1793); fell at Leipzig.

Rochdale (rŏch'dāl), county borough (pop. 87,734), Lancashire, England. Has mfg. of cotton and woolen goods. Birthplace of John Bright.

Rochdale Society of Equitable Pioneers, one of the first consumers' cooperatives, founded 1844 in Rochdale, England. Laid down basic tenets of the COOPERATIVE.

Rochefort (rôshfôr') or **Rochefort-sur-Mer** (–sür-mĕr'), fishing port (pop. 22,930), Charente-Maritime dept., W France, on Charente R. near Bay of Biscay. Was founded 1666 and fortified by Vauban. Its important arsenal and shipyards were severely damaged in World War II.

Rochelle (rōshĕl'), city (pop. 5,449), N Ill., S of Rockford. Center of farm area.

Rochelle, La (lä rôshĕl'), city (pop. 45,864), cap. of Charente-Maritime dept., W France; an Atlantic port. Fishing; canning; shipbuilding. Chartered 12th cent., it became a major port of medieval France. The last stronghold of the HUGUENOTS, it fell to Richelieu's forces after a 14-month siege (1627–28). La Rochelle prospered again as chief trade center with Canada (17th–18th cent.). La Palisse, its chief port (c.3 mi. from city) was a German submarine base in World War II. The picturesque old city escaped war damage.

Rochelle salt, sodium potassium tartrate, first made in Rochelle, France (1672). Used in Seidlitz powders and FEHLING'S SOLUTION.

Rochester, John Wilmot, 2d earl of (rŏ'chĭstůr), 1647?–1680, English poet and courtier, remembered for his witty satires and occasional lyrics.

Rochester (rŏ'chĭstůr), municipal borough (pop. 43,899), Kent, England. Norman wall (12 ft. thick) surrounds ruins of 12th-cent. castle. Dickens's home, "Gadshill Place," is near by.

Rochester (rŏ'chĕ"stůr, rŏ'chĭstůr). **1** City (pop. 29,885), SE Minn., SSE of St. Paul; settled 1854. Farm trade center. Seat of Mayo Clinic, founded 1889 by Dr. W. W. Mayo, with sons C. H. MAYO, and W. J. Mayo. Large transient population because of medical center. **2** City (pop. 13,776), SE N.H., on Salmon Falls R. and NW of Dover; settled 1728. Mfg. of woolens, shoes, and wood products. **3** City (pop. 332,488), W N.Y., at Genesee R. mouth on L. Ontario and E of Buffalo; permanent settlement began 1812. State's third-largest city and a major lake port. Mfg. of photographic and optical goods, clothing, precision instruments, business machines, chemicals; extensive nurseries. Has Philharmonic, civic, and Eastman orchestras; Mus. of Arts and Sciences, Memorial Art Gall., Rundel Memorial Building; Highland Park (lilacs). Seat of Nazareth Col. (R.C.; for women; 1924); Univ. of Rochester (nonsectarian; private; coed.; chartered and opened 1850 by Baptists), which is especially known for Eastman School of Music (1918; Howard Hanson became director 1924), school of medicine and dentistry, courses in engineering, optics, physics. Susan B. Anthony and Frederick Douglass lived here. George EASTMAN was prominent in city's modern growth. **4** Borough (pop. 7,197), W Pa., at union of Ohio and Beaver rivers and NW of Pittsburgh. Mfg. of abrasives and food products.

rock, solid matter composed of one or more minerals forming the earth's crust. Rocks are divided into three major classes: igneous rocks are formed by cooling of molten material from earth's interior (e.g., granite, obsidian, basalt, pumice); sedimentary rocks, often called stratified rock (see STRATIFICATION), are consolidated fragments of older rocks (forming shale, sandstone, conglomerate), or lime rocks made of cemented shells or calcium carbonate precipitated out of solution (e.g., limestone); metamorphic rocks have been changed by heat and pressure (slate, schist, gneiss, marble, quartzite).

Rockaway peninsula: see QUEENS.

Rockefeller, John D(avison), 1839–1937, American industrialist and philanthropist. By strict economy, mergers with competitors, and ruthless crushing of opponents his Standard Oil Co. dominated U.S. oil-refining industry. Founded Univ. of Chicago (1892). Other philanthropies, amounting to some $500,000,000, included Rockefeller Foundation, estab. in 1913 to promote public health and to further science. His son, **John D(avison) Rockefeller, Jr.,** 1874–, took over active management of his father's interests in 1911, engaged in numerous philanthropies, founded ROCKEFELLER CENTER. His son, **Nelson Aldrich Rockefeller,** 1908–, served as Coordinator of Inter-American Affairs in U.S. Dept. of State (1940–45). J. D. Rockefeller's brother, **William Rockefeller,** 1841–1922, was associated with Standard Oil Co. His vast resources built up Natl. City Bank of New York.

Rockefeller Center, in central Manhattan, New York city, between 48th and 51st streets and Fifth Ave. and the Ave. of the Americas; built 1931–39. Comprises 14 buildings, including a 70-story skyscraper and a radio and entertainment section (Radio City).

Rockefeller Foundation, founded 1913 by John D. Rockefeller with an endowment of $150,000,000. Its expressed purpose is to promote the well-being of mankind throughout the world.

Rockefeller Institute for Medical Research, philanthropic organization (founded 1901) for study of nature, cause, and treatment of diseases of humans, animals, and plants. Maintains laboratories and hospital in New York city.

rocket, name for several plants of mustard family. Sweet or dame's rocket (*Hesperis matronalis*) is an Old World biennial, naturalized in North America, with fragrant white to purple flowers. Rocket salad (*Eruca sativa*), the roquette of Europe, is a coarse plant, with creamy flowers; it is used in salads.

rocket, projectile propelled by force within itself. It is set in motion by reaction of rapid stream of gas escaping through vents. Rockets were used in Asia before discovery of gunpowder and have been widely used in festive and military activities; in World War II they became basis of various explosive projectiles (e.g., "buzz-bombs" or German V-2 weapons). Rockets provide motive force for skyrockets, airplane rockets, "bazookas," plane catapults, and the like. See *ill.*, p. 23.

Rock Falls, city (pop. 7,983), NW Ill., on Rock R. opposite Sterling, in farm area. Mfg. of farm machinery.

Rockford, city (pop. 92,927), N Ill., on both banks of Rock R. (power dam) near Wis. line; founded 1834. Industrial, shipping, trade center in grain, dairy, and livestock area. Mfg. of knit goods, furniture, and metal products. Seat of Rockford Col. Near by is U.S. Camp Grant.

rock garden, garden among natural rock formations or rocks artificially arranged, with deep soil pockets to accommodate the long roots of plants. Alpine plants, low herbaceous plants, and dwarf shrubs are suitable.

Rockhampton (rŏkhămp'tůn), city (pop. 34,988), Queensland, Australia, on Fitzroy R. near its mouth on the Pacific; founded 1858. Chief port for pastoral and mining regions of central Queensland.

Rock Hill, city (pop. 24,502), N S.C., SSW of Charlotte, N.C. Textile mills. Seat of Winthrop Col. (state supported; for women; 1886).

Rockingham, Charles Watson-Wentworth, 2d **marquess of,** 1730–82, English Whig statesman. His coalition government (1765–66) saw repeal of Stamp Act and attempted conciliation with America. His second ministry (1782) saw repeal of Poynings's Law.

Rockingham, town (pop. 5,499), SE Vt., on Connecticut R. N. of Brattleboro. Includes industrial village of Bellows Falls (pop. 3,881); mfg. of paper since 1802. Navigation canal, said to have been first to be undertaken in U.S., was built around falls here (1792–1802), and rebuilt as part of hydroelectric power project (1926–28).

Rock Island, city (pop. 48,710), NW Ill., on the Mississippi. Forms, with MOLINE, EAST MOLINE (Ill.), and DAVENPORT (Iowa), an economic unit called Quad Cities. Rail, industrial, trade, and insurance center. Mfg. of metal products, electrical and heating equipment, and clothing. George DAVENPORT built house (1833) on fortified island, which had been important in Black Hawk War. Now site of U.S. arsenal. Seat of Augustana Col. and Theological Seminary (see SIOUX FALLS, S. Dak.), noted choir.

Rockland. 1 City (pop. 9,234), S Maine, on harbor on Penobscot Bay. Fishing, trading, and resort center. Ships lime from its quarries. **2** Town (pop. 8,960), SE Mass., SE of Boston; settled 1673. Shoes.

Rockne, Knute (Kenneth) (rŏk'nē), 1888–1931, American football coach. From 1918 through 1930 his Notre Dame teams won 105, lost 12, tied 5, were undefeated, untied five seasons (1919–20, 1924, 1929–30).

Rockport. 1 City (pop. 2,493), SW Ind., on Ohio R. and E of Evansville. Has Lincoln Pioneer Village, memorial with reconstructed homes. **2** Town (pop. 4,231), NE Mass., on Cape Ann; resort and artists' colony. **3** City (pop. 2,266), S Texas, on Aransas Bay and NE of Corpus Christi. Resort with fisheries.

Rock River, c.285 mi. long, rising in S Wis. and flowing S and SW through NW Ill. to the Mississippi near Rock Island. Irrigates fertile farm area.

rock salt: see SALT.

Rock Springs, city (pop. 10,857; alt. c.6,270 ft.), SW Wyo., on Bitter Creek; estab. in 1860s. Trade center in livestock and coal area with hunting and fishing supplies. Polyglot population holds annual Internat. Night.

Rockville. 1 City (pop. 8,016) in agr. Vernon town (pop. 10,115; settled c.1726), N Conn., NE of Hartford; chartered 1889. Textiles. **2** Town (pop. 6,934), W central Md., NNW of Washington, D.C. Near by are Clara Barton's house and testing laboratory of Navy Dept.

Rockville Centre, residential village (22,362), on SW Long Isl., SE N.Y., S of Hempstead. Machinery, lighting fixtures, metal and rubber products.

Rockwall, city (pop. 1,501), N Texas, near East Fork of Trinity R. and NE of Dallas. Named for geological formation that looks man-made.

Rockwell, Norman, 1894–, American illustrator, best known for magazine covers.

Rocky Hill, town (pop. 5,108), central Conn., on Connecticut R. below Hartford. Rayon yarn.

Rocky Mount, city (pop. 27,697), E N.C., on Tar R. and ENE of Raleigh. Processes and markets tobacco and cotton.

Rocky Mountain College: see BILLINGS, Mont.

Rocky Mountain goat, goatlike mammal (*Oreamnos*) of Rocky Mts. of Alaska, Canada, NW U.S. Not a true goat, it is related to the antelope and chamois. It has a white coat and the male stands c.3 ft. high at the humped shoulder.

Rocky Mountain House, town (pop. 1,147), S central Alta., Canada, at foot of Rocky Mts., on North Saskatchewan R. Founded 1799 as fur-trading post.

Rocky Mountain National Park: see NATIONAL PARKS AND MONUMENTS (table).

Rocky Mountains, longest and highest mountain system of North America, composed of many complex systems, extending S from N Alaska through W Canada and into SW U.S. Alaska has the BROOKS RANGE; Canadian portion includes CARIBOO MOUNTAINS, SELKIRK MOUNTAINS. Section at boundary between British Columbia and Alberta is called Canadian Rockies. In U.S. the Rocky Mts. cross portions of Wash., Idaho, Mont., Utah, Wyo., and Colo. and end in N N.Mex. Include WIND RIVER RANGE, TETON RANGE, FRONT RANGE. E the system rises from the GREAT PLAINS; W the GREAT BASIN and other depressions separate it from the Coast Ranges. Continental Divide follows crests of the Rockies, source of great river systems (e.g., the Yukon, the Missouri). The Rockies, geologically young, are chiefly a granite and gneiss mass with occasional evidence of volcanic action. System has some glaciers, many peaks over 14,000 ft. (e.g., Pikes Peak, Colo.). Gold, silver, copper, lead, and coal are found; extensive farming and grazing regions. Many national parks in Canada and U.S. For early travelers' routes, see OREGON TRAIL and OVERLAND TRAIL. Early explorations included LEWIS AND CLARK EXPEDITION and those of Z. M. PIKE, J. C. FRÉMONT, and the MOUNTAIN MEN.

Rocky Mountain sheep: see BIGHORN.

Rocky Mountain spotted fever, acute infectious disease transmitted by bite of certain ticks. Caused by rickettsia (forms intermediate between viruses and bacteria). Fatalities among livestock and humans are reduced by use of serum and preventive vaccine.

Rocky River, city (pop. 11,237), NE Ohio, on L. Erie at mouth of Rocky R., W suburb of Cleveland.

rococo (růkō'kō, rō–), style in architecture, especially in interiors and the decorative arts, which originated in France under Louis XV in early 18th cent. A more delicate offshoot of the BAROQUE, it made use of such forms as shells, scrolls, and flowers in room decorations and furniture. The craze for Chinese art added bizarre motives to the style and produced decorative work known as *chinoiserie*. The style spread to other countries (esp. Germany and Austria); in England it had a marked influence on the furniture of Chippendale.

rococo, in music, an offshoot of the baroque, less formal and more graceful in style; began in France. Its chief medium was keyboard music, its greatest composer François Couperin (1668–1733).

Rocroi (rôkrōōä'), village, Ardennes dept., N France, where French under Louis II de Condé decisively defeated the Spanish (1643).

rodent, member of largest order of mammals, Rodentia, with teeth fitted for gnawing and chewing. The enlarged upper and lower incisor teeth grow throughout life. In size, rodents range from harvest mouse (4½–7 in. long, including tail) to CAPYBARA (c.4 ft. long). Among the rodents are chipmunk, squirrel, rat, beaver, porcupine, guinea pig, chinchilla. Hare and rabbit are now usually placed in another family.

Roderick (rŏ'dûrĭk), d. 713?, last Visigothic king in Spain (710–713?). Was defeated by the Moslems under TARIK (711). Subject of many legends.

Rodez (rôdĕz'), city (pop. 16,366), cap of Aveyron dept., S France; historic cap. of Rouergue.

Rodgers, John, 1773–1838, American naval officer. Served in Tripolitan War. His defeat of British vessel, the *Little Belt,* was an incident leading to War of 1812. Saw distinguished service in war.

Rodgers, Richard, 1902–, American composer of musical comedies. He collaborated with lyricist Lorenz Hart (1895–1943) in many successes, e.g., *The Girl Friend* (1926); *A Connecticut Yankee* (1927), containing the song *My Heart Stood Still; Babes in Arms* (1937); and *The Boys from Syracuse* (1938), containing *Falling in Love with Love.* Rodgers's collaboration with Oscar Hammerstein 2d began with *Oklahoma!* (1943) and was continued in *Carousel* (1945), *South Pacific* (1949), and *The King and I* (1951).

Rodin, Auguste (ōgüst' rōdẽ'), 1840–1917, French sculptor. Began art studies at age of 14, while working for an ornament maker; later worked for architectural sculptors. In Salon of 1877 he exhibited a nude male figure for which he was praised by some, while others accused him of having cast from life. Upshot was that he gained official support; the government gave him a studio in Paris, where he worked the rest of his life. Considered the most important sculptor of his time, he produced works that are both realistic and poetic. Most famous works include *The Thinker* (Paris) and *Adam and Eve* (Metropolitan Mus.). Rodin museums in Paris and Philadelphia.

Rodney, George Brydges Rodney, 1st Baron, 1719–92, British admiral. His defeat (1782) of French fleet under De Grasse in West Indies led to better peace terms with French after American Revolution.

Rodó, José Enrique (hōsā' ānrē'kā rôdō'), 1872–1917, Uruguayan essayist, literary and social critic, and moralist. His *Ariel* (1900) calls on Latin America to resist materialism of U.S.

Rodriguez (rōdrē'gůs), island (40 sq. mi.; pop. 11,885), of Mascarene group, in Indian Ocean. Belongs to British colony of Mauritius. Discovered 1645 by the Portuguese, taken 1810 by the British.

Roe, E(dward) P(ayson), 1838–88, American clergyman, author of moralistic novels, e.g., *Barriers Burned Away* (1872) and *The Opening of a Chestnut Burr* (1874).

Roebling, John Augustus (rō'blĭng) 1806–69, German-American engineer, b. Mulhouse. In 1831 he came to U.S. He was a pioneer in the use and manufacture of steel cable and in building steel suspension bridges. His ambitious Brooklyn Bridge project was scarcely begun when injuries suffered in an accident while directing the work caused his death. Thereafter the construction was in charge of his son, **Washington Augustus Roebling,** 1837–1926, who had aided his father in earlier work. Because he worked underground so much he was stricken (1872) with caisson disease, but despite invalidism he directed the project until the bridge was opened to traffic (1883).

Roemer, Olaus: see RÖMER, OLAUS.

Roentgen or **Röntgen, Wilhelm Conrad** (rĕnt'gĭn, Ger. vĭl'hĕlm kôn'rät rûnt'gůn), 1845–1923, German physicist. Won 1901 Nobel Prize for discovery of X ray.

Roentgen ray: see X RAY.

Roerich, Nicholas (Konstantin) (rûr'ĭkh), 1874–1947, Russian painter and archaeologist. Associated with Moscow Art Theater and Diaghilev ballet. Spent five years exploring the Himalayas. Roerich Mus. (N.Y.) founded 1921 in his honor.

Rogation Days, in the Roman Catholic Church, four days set apart for solemn processions to invoke God's mercy: April 25 (the Major Rogation), three days before Ascension Day (Minor Rogations). Processions are a Christian adaptation of Roman pagan custom.

Roger, Norman rulers of Sicily. **Roger I,** c.1031–1101, joined with his brother ROBERT GUISCARD in the conquest of Apulia and Calabria from Byzantium and of Sicily from the Arabs (1057–91). Robert made him count of Sicily and Calabria (1072). His son and successor, **Roger II,** c.1097–1154, conquered Apulia and Salerno (1127), despite opposition of Pope Innocent II, and was crowned king of Sicily by Antipope Anacletus II (1130). Innocent eventually yielded and invested Roger with the lands he already possessed. Roger estab. a strong central administration. His brilliant court at Palermo was a center of arts, letters, and sciences.

Roger de Coverley (dů kŭ'vûrlē) or **Roger of Coverley,** old English country dance and tune, resembling Virginia reel. Sir Roger de Coverley, literary figure in *Spectator* (1711), is introduced as a descendant of the originator of the dance.

Roger of Loria or **Lauria,** c.1245–1304, Sicilian admiral in service of Peter III and James II, kings of Aragon and Sicily. As commander of the Aragonese fleet during the struggle between the house of Aragon and the Angevin dynasty for possession of Sicily, he repeatedly defeated the Angevins.

Rogers, Bruce, 1870–, American book designer. As printing adviser to Cambridge Univ. Press, Harvard Univ. Press, and special commercial houses, he did much to advance fine book design.

Rogers, John, 1500?–1555, English Protestant martyr. First a Catholic priest, he became Protestant 1535. Using name of Thomas Matthew, he helped prepare second Coverdale Bible. Under Queen Mary he was imprisoned in 1554, tried, and burned as heretic at Smithfield.

Rogers, John, 1829–1904, American sculptor. An early clay group, *The Slave Auction*, was publicized by the abolitionists. Many "Rogers groups" were reproduced in quantity by machine.

Rogers, Lindsay, 1891–, American political scientist; teacher at Columbia Univ. after 1920.

Rogers, Robert, 1731–95, American frontiersman. Headed famous company of frontier rangers in last of French and Indian Wars. Commanded post at Mackinac (1765–68), sent out expedition of Jonathan CARVER, and was arrested on charges of conspiracy. Joined Loyalists in American Revolution. Often reviled for drunkenness and dishonesty.

Rogers, Will(iam Penn Adair), 1879–1935, American humorist. The "cowboy philosopher" was known for his salty comments, on the stage, in motion pictures, and in newspapers, on the passing show.

Rogers, Mount, peak, 5,720 ft. high, SW Va., near Tenn.–N.C. line; highest point in state.

Roger van der Weyden: see WEYDEN, ROGER VAN DER.

Roget, Peter Mark (rō′zhā, rōzhā′), 1779–1869, English lexicographer, a physician. Successive editions of his *Thesaurus of English Words and Phrases* (1852) remain standard reference books.

Rogue, river, SW Oregon, rising in Cascade Range N of Crater L. and flowing c.200 mi. SW and W, through fruitgrowing area, to the Pacific near Calif. line.

Rohan, Édouard, prince de (ādwär′ prēs′ dů rôā′), 1734–1803, French cardinal, archbishop of Strasbourg, grand almoner of Louis XVI. His anti-Austrian attitude earned him the hatred of Marie Antoinette. In his eagerness to gain the queen's favor he fell victim to a confidence game—the inglorious Affair of the DIAMOND NECKLACE. Though acquitted (1780), he was disgraced.

Rohan, Henri, duc de (ãrē′ dük′), 1579–1638, French Protestant general. Led Huguenot resistance against Richelieu, notably in 1627–29, but was chosen in 1635 by Richelieu to command French forces in the Grisons. Treachery forced his retreat in 1637. He joined the Protestant forces in Germany and fell at Rheinfelden.

Rohde, Ruth Bryan: see OWEN, RUTH BRYAN.

Rojas, Fernando de (fĕrnän′dō dā rō′häs), 1465?–1526?, Spanish novelist. See CELESTINA, LA.

Rojas Zorrilla, Francisco de (fränthē′skō dā rō′häs thōrē′lyä), 1607–48, Spanish dramatist, author of farces exaggerating peculiarities of characters.

Rokitansky, Karl (kärl rōkĭtän′skē), 1804–78, Austrian pathologist. He wrote valuable descriptions of diseases based on post-mortem examinations.

Roland, d. 778, French hero of medieval legend and of the 11th-cent. epic, *La Chanson de Roland*. The historic Roland, prefect of the Breton march, was among the slain when the rear guard of Charlemagne's army, returning from Spain, was ambushed by the Basques in the Pyrenees. Legend changes the Basques into Saracens, locates the action at Roncesvalles, and vastly exaggerates the importance of both the event and its hero. The skillful characterization of its main protagonists and its simple, moving poetry make the epic one of the best-loved masterpieces of medieval literature. Roland also appears in other chansons of the Charlemagne cycle. As Orlando, he is transformed beyond recognition in the epics of BOIARDO and ARIOSTO.

Roland de la Platière, Jean Marie (zhã′ märē′ rôlã′ dů lä plätyĕr′), 1734–93, and **Manon (Phlipon) Roland de la Platière** (Mme Roland) (mänõ′ flēpõ′), 1754–93, French revolutionists; husband and wife. Mme Roland, imbued with classical ideals and with Rousseau's philosophy, made her house the intellectual center of the GIRONDISTS. Her husband, an inspector general of commerce before the Revolution, was strongly influenced by her and became minister of the interior in the Girondist ministry of 1792. When the Girondists fell, Mme Roland was arrested; she walked to the guillotine crying out, "O Liberty, what crimes are committed in your name!" Her husband, who had fled Paris, committed suicide upon hearing her fate.

Rolfe, John (rŏlf), 1585–1622, English colonist in Va. Introduced regular cultivation of tobacco (1612). Married POCAHONTAS.

Rolla (rŏ′lů). **1** City (pop. 9,354), S central Mo., SE of Jefferson City, in a farm, timber, clay, and pyrite area of the Ozarks. Seat of Univ. of Missouri school of mines and metallurgy. **2** City (pop. 1,176), N N.Dak., near Canadian border and NNW of Devils Lake. Hq. for International Peace Garden.

Rolland, Romain (rômẽ′ rôlã′), 1866–1944, French author. He wrote biographies of Beethoven (1903), Michelangelo (1905), Tolstoy (1911), and Gandhi (1924). His magnum opus is the 10-vol. novel *Jean-Christophe* (1904–12; Eng. tr., 1910–13). *The Wolves* (1898) is his best-known play. He received the 1915 Nobel Prize in Literature. His pacifism, reflected in *Above the Battle* (1915) led to self-imposed exile in Switzerland until 1938. His chief works have been translated into English.

roller skating: see SKATING.

Rollins College, at Winter Park, Fla.; nonsectarian, coed.; founded 1884 by Congregationalists, chartered 1885. Stresses conference plan and individualized curriculum. Has Inter-American Center.

Rollo (rŏ′lō), c.860–c.932, leader of Norman pirates. By Treaty of Saint-Clair-sur-Epte (911) Charles III of France gave him in fief the territory which became the duchy of Normandy. In return, he accepted Christianity. Was direct ancestor of William the Conqueror.

Rolvaag, Ole (Edvart) (ō′lů ĕd′värt rōl′väg), 1876–1931, Norwegian-American novelist, known for his *Giants in the Earth* (1927) and other powerful realistic novels of Norwegian pioneers in Northwest.

Romagna (rōmä'nyä), historic region, N central Italy, on the Adriatic, now part of EMILIA-ROMAGNA. Contains RAVENNA, RIMINI, and independent republic of SAN MARINO. Under Byzantine rule 540–751, region was donated to papacy by Pepin the Short (754) and Charlemagne (774) but was claimed by later emperors. The rise of free communes and of petty tyrants prevented effective control by either emperors or popes. Cesare BORGIA, created duke of Romagna by Pope Alexander VI (1501), made himself master of the region. His downfall resulted in the effective incorporation of Romagna with the PAPAL STATES.

Romains, Jules (jhül' rômē'), 1885–, French novelist, whose real name is Louis Farigoule. Principal work is the cycle *Men of Good Will* (27 vols., 1932–46; Eng. tr., 13 vols., 1933–46). His plays include *Cromedeyre-le-Vieil* (1920) and the farce *Doctor Knock* (1923; Eng. tr. 1925). Elected to the French Academy 1946.

roman: see TYPE.

Roman architecture. First inspired by Greek buildings of S Italy and Sicily, it later borrowed from Greece itself and the Hellenistic East. From the Etruscans came the true arch, vault, and dome. Introducing the use of concrete after 2d cent. B.C. the Romans developed revolutionary structural forms, in which the arch eventually came to be the chief structural element, with the columns serving merely as buttresses or for decoration. Of early Rome and of the republic (c.500 B.C.–27 B.C.) the aqueducts outside Rome are the most impressive remains. The main examples of Roman architecture belong to the period between 100 B.C. and A.D. 300. Though unfired brick was used in all periods, under the empire baked bricks became popular as a facing for concrete walls. From early times stucco was used as a finish for important buildings. Vaults were highly developed; types included the barrel vault, cross or groined vault, and dome and semi-dome (see *ill.*, p. 61). Roman architecture reached its climax under Trajan (A.D. 98–A.D. 117). In all periods splendor and utility were the Roman ideals, as opposed to the subtle refinements of the Greeks. Civic planning resulted in the series of great fora created to extend the area of the Old Roman Forum (see FORUM). Most important among the buildings developed by the Romans were basilicas, baths, amphitheaters, and triumphal arches. A type of Roman dwelling was the luxurious country home or villa.

Roman art. Early Etruscan art, though strongly influenced by that of archaic Greece, reveals a native feeling for bold decorative color effects and exuberance of spirit. From c.400 B.C. the vitality of the earlier art gave way to imitation of Greek classical models. Romano-Etruscan art between 300 B.C. and 100 B.C. with its imitation of early Etruscan as well as Greek forms throws light on the eclecticism of Roman taste. In the Augustan period (30 B.C.–A.D. 14) there was an attempt to combine realism with the Greek feeling for idealization and abstract harmony of forms; subsequent decades produced magnificent portrait busts, notable for psychological penetration. From the time of Trajan (A.D. 98–A.D. 117) the influence of the Egyptian or Near Eastern illustrative tradition became important and is reflected in such works as the spiral band of narrative reliefs on Trajan's Column (Rome). Under Hadrian (117–38) there was a reversion to idealization, but the later assimilation of Oriental influence (211–337) encouraged a tendency toward abstraction. Roman painting, like sculpture, was strongly influenced by the art of Greece. The few extant paintings (e.g., murals at Pompeii) suggest that the art was mainly one of interior decoration. In general the Roman minor arts (esp. cameos, metalwork, pottery, glassware) tended to emphasize richness of materials and ornamentation.

Roman Catholic Church, Christian church headed by the pope, the bishop of Rome, whose primacy is based on his claim as successor to St. Peter (the "Petrine supremacy"; see PAPACY). The term "Roman Catholic Church" dates only from the 19th cent., but is now in common use among English-speaking people; the use of the term "Roman Church" for the whole Church is, however, unfortunate, since it means when used officially the archdiocese of Rome. There are at least some adherents in most of the countries of the world, and the claim that there are, in all, hundreds of millions of Catholics is probably true, though no actual census has been made. The vast majority belong to the Roman rite, i.e., have a liturgy said in Latin and follow the usages of the church at Rome. Even in the West, however, there are variant rites with somewhat different usages (e.g., the Ambrosian rite, the Dominican rite, the Mozarabic rite). In the East there are groups in communion with the pope that have other rites—Byzantine, W Syrian or Antiochene, E Syrian or Chaldean, Alexandrian, and Armenian. Some of the adherents to these have left other churches to accept communion with the pope. (For information on some of these Eastern groups, see ARMENIAN CHURCH; JACOBITE CHURCH; MARONITES; NESTORIAN CHURCH.) All members of the Church accept the gospel of Christ as handed down, uncontaminated, by the Church. They accept the teachings of the Bible together with the interpretations placed upon those teachings by the Church. Central to Catholic belief is the doctrine that God conveys His grace direct to man through the sacraments (see SACRAMENT). The EUCHARIST is the center of Catholic worship, which may have much pomp and color (see MASS). Emphasis is laid on oneness and wholeness of the whole Christian body, which includes the dead as well as the living, the Virgin Mary and other saints in heaven, the souls in PURGATORY, and struggling mortals on earth. Many traits of Catholic life are more conspicuous to non-Catholics than essential to the Catholic faith (e.g., many ceremonies, the use of incense, eating fish on Friday). The sense of solidarity and the grace given by the sacraments rather heightens than lessens the burden put upon the individual, who must act according to the dictates of his conscience and be judged (as he believes) by God according to his motives in acting. The integrated structure of the Church from the parish priests through the bishops to the pope is impressive (see ORDERS, HOLY). The heart of the Church is in the papal court at VATICAN City in Rome, where matters of central administration are handled by papal officials, Offices, and commissions (see CARDINAL). The Church strives for spiritual universality. Outside the secular organization of the Church are the orders of regular priests, brothers, and nuns, who are part of the body of the Church (see MONASTICISM). In early centuries of the Christian era the Christian body was one, though split by numerous heresies, which withered away as they were opposed by the organized strength of ecumenical councils and by the popes, who gained increasing power in the West despite some faltering (see PAPACY). The contest between the pope on the one hand and lay rulers on the other over ecclesiastic and lay power was a dominant theme of the Middle Ages. Mingled with this were recurrent reforms within the Church, notably the Cluniac reform (10th–11th cent.) and the reform led by Gregory VII (11th cent.). The 12th cent. saw the great effort of the CRUSADES, the purging influence of Bernard of Clairvaux, and the codification of CANON LAW by Gratian. The 13th cent. was marked by the development of SCHOLASTICISM and the flowering of the Church. The new orders of friars, DOMINICANS and FRANCISCANS, had much to do with this. The pope was in eclipse in the "Babylonian captivity" of the papacy (1309–78), and the Church was rocked later by the Great SCHISM. Reform stagnated, and most churchmen were involved in politics and worldliness—a tendency increased by the Renaissance. Some moves had been made for internal reform, before the REFORMATION in the 16th cent. brought revolt and the break-up of the Church. The Catholic REFORM, especially through the Council of TRENT, purified the Church of many abuses, but the papacy was still beset by the demands of "Catholic princes" until the late 18th cent. The overthrow of despotism released the Church soon afterward, and in the 19th cent. the reign of Pius IX saw the loss of the PAPAL STATES (a blessing in disguise) and also enunciation of the doctrine of papal infallibility in matters of faith and doctrine. The Church in the 19th and 20th cent. has had as one of its great problems adjustment to modern political and social conditions, under the leadership of such men as Leo XIII, Pius XI, and Pius XII. The Church in America was founded first by Spanish and French missionaries, but in the English-speaking colonies may fairly be said to have begun with John Carroll, first bishop (1790).

romance [O.Fr.,= something written in popular languages, i.e., Romance language]. The *roman* of Middle Ages in Europe was a chivalric and romantic narrative. It was lengthened into *roman d'adventure*, or romance of love and adventure, from which the modern romance derives.

Romance languages or **Romanic languages,** group of Italic languages of Indo-European family. See LANGUAGE (table).

Roman de la Rose, Le (lü rōmã' dü lä rōz'), French poem of 22,000 lines in two parts. The first, written c.1237 by Guillaume de Lorris, is an allegory on the psychology of love, often subtle and charming. The second, written in 1275–80 by Jean de Meun, is wholly different in its satirical tone and seems to typify the medieval bourgeois spirit as against Guillaume's courtly ideals. Chaucer translated the first 1,700 lines of the *Roman* (or *Romaunt*).

Roman Empire: see ROME; BYZANTINE EMPIRE; HOLY ROMAN EMPIRE.

Romanesque architecture (rōmùnĕsk'), style which prevailed throughout Europe, 11th–13th cent.; influenced chiefly by buildings of the Roman Empire. In early Middle Ages the artistic revival fostered by monasteries resulted in the building of many churches and abbeys. From about 11th cent. to middle of 15th, the great evolution progressed from the Romanesque with its round arch to the pointed arch of the Gothic. Notable in Romanesque style was the return to masonry vaulting which after the decline of Roman building had been ignored. Unlike the Roman type, however, the Romanesque vault was built of blocks of cut stone, and not of brick and concrete. The attempt to create a vaulted style forced a steady progression in technique; the vital problem of interrelating vaults, supports, and abutments (for receiving the pressure of arches and vaults), was ultimately solved by the creation of the stone skeleton (exemplified by the abbey church of St. Denis, France). An adequate framework for carrying the weight of the vault surface was provided by the groined vault (see *ill.*, p. 61), supported by upright shafts. Early Romanesque churches followed the general plan of the Christian basilica, but those after c.1050 show the advance toward the more complex Gothic plan. NORMAN ARCHITECTURE was based on the Romanesque style.

Romanesque art developed roughly from 500 to 1200, the period of transition from Roman to Gothic. Roman and Byzantine elements remained more or less dominant though blended with Eastern influences (esp. Persian and Mesopotamian). Barbaric vigor was lent by Celtic and Lombard elements. Sculpture was developed as decoration for Romanesque buildings, such dramatic scenes as the *Last Judgment* being used to enrich the portals of churches. Silverwork, bronze casting, mosaic work, needlework (notably BAYEUX TAPESTRY), and other crafts flourished during the period. In painting there was no marked deveolpment, but Romanesque artists excelled in the decoration of manuscripts, the most brilliant school being produced in 7th-cent. Ireland.

Romania: see RUMANIA.

Romanic languages: see ROMANCE LANGUAGES.

Roman law, system of law developed in the republic of Rome, the Roman Empire, and the Byzantine Empire. Highly formalistic in the beginning, it developed from the Law of the Twelve Tables (450 B.C.?) to the THEODOSIAN CODE (A.D. 438), and in the time of Justinian I was compiled by Tribonian and others in the CORPUS JURIS CIVILIS, probably the most influential code of law ever made. The clarity, completeness, and systematic construction of Roman law made it admirably adaptable. It was continued in the GERMANIC LAWS and CANON LAW and persisted as well itself. In the 12th and 13th cent. there was a return to the study of original Roman law, spreading from the center of the law school of Bologna (with such masters as Irnerius and Accursius). It is the base of the legal systems of continental Europe (see CIVIL LAW). In English-speaking countries COMMON LAW has been dominant, but Roman law entered through EQUITY and has greatly affected all statute law.

Romano, Giulio: see GIULIO ROMANO.

Romanov (rō'mŭnôf), ruling dynasty of Russia, 1613–1917. Ivan IV's first wife was Anastasia Romanov. Her grandnephew MICHAEL was chosen tsar in 1613. In the following list of Michael's successors, the names of rulers not descended from Michael are placed within brackets.

Descendants through males (1645–1730): ALEXIS, FEODOR III, IVAN V, PETER I, [CATHERINE I], PETER II.

Descendants through females (1730–1917): ANNA, IVAN VI (deposed, later murdered), ELIZABETH, PETER III (deposed, probably murdered), [CATHERINE II], PAUL I (murdered), ALEXANDER I, NICHOLAS I, ALEXANDER II (assassinated), ALEXANDER III, NICHOLAS II (executed). Members of the Romanov family who escaped execution by the Bolsheviks fled abroad. Grand Duke Cyril (1876–1938), a grandson of Alexander II, was succeeded as pretender by his son Vladimir (b. 1917).

Roman religion. The indigenous Italic religion, nucleus of Roman religion, was animistic. The spirits in natural objects were thought to control human destiny and were placated to secure peace between men and gods. In early period, when Italy was dotted with small agr. groups, family and household were basic religious units. To perpetuate the family, for household safety, for an abundant harvest, and for protection from spirits of the dead the Romans made offerings, prayed, and took part in festivals. In performing these religious functions head of the family acted as the priest. Presumably as families coalesced into tribes and then into a state, family cult and ritual became the basis of state cult and ritual. Early Rome honored the gods of war and justice—Jupiter, Mars, and Quirinus. The Romans adopted many foreign gods—e.g., in 7th cent. B.C., Minerva from Etruscans and in 3d to 1st cent., Greek gods and Oriental cults (e.g., Isis). At end of the republic there were in general three religions in Rome—the old religion of the countryside, the Greco-Roman religion of upper classes, and Oriental cult-worship. Emperor Augustus tried to revive old religious ways because public morality was at a low ebb when he came to the throne, but Roman religion finally degenerated into Oriental emperor-worship. With loss of family and tribal worship the individual Roman sought a more dramatic, emotional, and optimistic religion that would satisfy his yearnings. This was religious soil in which Christianity took root.

Roman roads, network of hard-surfaced roads built to connect the city of Rome with the outposts of Roman control. They were built usually in four layers, the top one of hard stones, concrete, or pebbles set in mortar. They were remarkably durable, and many are in part still used today. The first great highway was the APPIAN WAY. Other famous roads included: the Praenestine Way (short, SE from Rome to present Palestrina); the Latin Way (S from Rome to Capua, to join Appian Way); three routes to the N and the Alps—the Flaminian Way, the Aurelian Way, and the Aemilian Way (an extension of the Flaminian); two routes across the Appenines—Salanian Way and Valerian Way. In Britain, Romans used old routes and built new ones for military purposes; notable were Icknield Street (pre-Roman), Watling Street, Ermine Street, Fosse Way.

Romans, epistle of New Testament, written by St. Paul to Christians at Rome. Subject treated is central in Paul's teaching, justification by faith (i.e., that salvation must be achieved through faith). The love and mercy of God extend to all mankind. It is for the individual to claim this love and mercy by accepting the gospel of Jesus Christ and His sacrifice on the Cross. Romans is claimed as an authority by various theologians; thus, Lutheran and Roman Catholic interpretations of justification, diametrically opposed, both depend on this epistle.

Romansh: see RHAETO-ROMANIC.

romanticism, a movement in the arts variously defined as a return to nature, exaltation of emotion and the senses over the intellect, and revolt against 18th-cent. rationalism. J. J. Rousseau had proposed that man is good by nature but corrupted by society; early romanticists idealized the "noble savage," peasants, children, and emphasized the individual. The romantic movement influenced 19th-cent. writers in every country and found expression in historical novels, tales of fantasy and horror, romances of love and adventure, as well as in poetry; although no longer a literary movement, it remains influential and controversial. In painting, romanticism was the chief 19th-cent. movement. Classic forms and rules were avoided; the emotional and spiritual were emphasized; themes were drawn from simpler or less civilized ways of living. Its major, and international, phase was landscape painting, which emphasized intimate and spiritual in nature. Musical romanticism emphasized feeling and dealt freely with form. Romanticism as the spirit of a work of art may be present in any age and can be found notably in Middle Ages and early baroque. See CLASSICISM.

Romanus (rōmā'nŭs), Byzantine emperors. **Romanus I,** d. 948, usurped throne of Constantine VII (919–44). Issued laws to protect peasant and military holdings from absorption into great landed states. **Romanus II,** 939–63, reigned 959–63. With his wife Theophano, a former courtesan, he probably poisoned his father, Constantine VII. On his death Theophano married his successor, Nicephorus II. **Romanus III,** d. 1034, became emperor by marrying ZOË. His generous aid to victims of plague and earthquake and his building mania depleted the treasury. Took Edessa from Saracens (1031). Michael IV, who probably murdered him, succeeded him as emperor and husband. **Romanus IV,** d. 1071, reigned 1067–71. Was routed by the Seljuks at MANZIKERT (1071).

Romany (rŏ'mùnē, rō'–), the GYPSY language, member of Indic group of Indo-Iranian subfamily of Indo-European languages. See LANGUAGE (table).

Romberg, Sigmund, 1887–1951, Hungarian-American composer of operettas; came to U.S. in 1910. Among his successes were *Maytime* (1917), *The Student Prince* (1924), *The Desert Song* (1926), *Blossom Time* (1926), and *The New Moon* (1927).

Rome, Ital. *Roma,* city (1948 est. pop. 1,613,-660), central Italy near the W coast, on both sides of the Tiber R.; cap. of Rome prov., Latium, and Italy; see of the pope, who resides in VATICAN City. The "Eternal City," it has long been a cultural, artistic, and religious center (called also the Holy City).

Rome before Augustus. Founded on the E bank of the Tiber, Rome was originally a trading place and meeting ground of Latins, Sabines, and Etruscans. City-states were merged and grew to cover seven hills (Palatine, Capitoline, Quirinal, Viminal, Esquiline, Caelian, Aventine) as well as other hills and plains (e.g., the Martian Fields or *Campus Martius*). Tradition says it was founded by ROMULUS in 753 B.C. Tradition also tells of kings of the TARQUIN family. Probably the young city was under Etruscan rule until c.500 B.C. Then began the rule of the Roman republic, which was not a democracy, but a state governed by the patrician class (with increasing concessions to the lower-class plebs) and later by the senate. The ruling magistrates were the consuls. Gradually the city asserted hegemony over the neighboring Latin states, then over surrounding peoples (e.g., the Samnites). Though sacked by the Gauls in 390 B.C., Rome continued its climb to greatness and was by the 3d cent. A.D. a land power strong enough to challenge CARTHAGE in the PUNIC WARS. Success crowned Roman ambitions, and Rome became undisputed mistress of the W Mediterranean by 201 B.C. Then came the spread of power to the E, the defeat of Philip V of Macedon and Antiochus III of Syria and the humbling of Egypt by 168 B.C. The spread of Roman influence, however, benefited only the senatorial class and the *equites* (knights). Class dissension grew, and agrarian laws were adopted to pacify the masses while slave revolts were ruthlessly put down (as in Sicily, c.136–c.131, 104–c.101 B.C.). The attempted reforms of the GRACCHI came to nothing. Yet despite discontent, Rome continued its march. The Social War (90 B.C.–88 B.C.) forced Rome to widen the privileges of citizenship to other Italians. The contest between the people and the conservative rulers came to a head in the bloody struggle between MARIUS and SULLA in civil war. The result was only to make division between the senatorial and popular parties more pronounced. POMPEY secured the Roman power in the E and Julius CAESAR spread it in the W by his GALLIC WARS. The two had been temporarily joined with the rich CRASSUS in the First Triumvirate (60 B.C.), but rivalry brought out Pompey as leader of the senatorial party, Caesar as leader of the popular party. Civil war between them ended with the victory of Caesar at Pharsala (48 B.C.). Caesar then governed until he was assassinated (44 B.C.) and introduced the golden age of Roman culture and the beginnings of the empire.

The Roman Empire. Out of the anarchy following Caesar's murder came his adopted son, AUGUSTUS, who aided ANTONY in destroying the murderers of Caesar, then defeated Antony at Actium (31 B.C.). He actually estab. the Roman Empire and created the atmosphere for the golden age of Latin literature and Roman art and architecture, notable for spacious nobility and sound engineering skill (seen also in aqueducts, roads, and other projects). The Romans also were notable for developing administrative techniques to control the vast empire, which expanded under TIBERIUS, CALIGULA, and CLAUDIUS I to stretch from Britain to the Orient, the largest unified state the West has known. In the reign of NERO (A.D. 54–A.D. 68) occurred the great fire of Rome; rebuilding made the city more beautiful. At this time Christianity first began to assume importance, which was to grow through the centuries of the empire. After Nero's death there was a brief struggle (see GALBA; OTHO; VITELLIUS) before VESPASIAN (A.D. 69–A.D. 79) estab. the Flavian line. TITUS, DOMITIAN, and NERVA preceded TRAJAN, an able administrator. Under HADRIAN the Romans drew back the frontiers of empire slightly, but within the borders were peace and prosperity. The empire was thriving and continued to do so under ANTONINUS PIUS and MARCUS AURELIUS. It is conventional to date the beginning of the wavering decline with COMMODUS (180–92), but, the process was slow and such emperors as Septimius SEVERUS and CARACALLA were able to assert themselves, as did CLAUDIUS II and AURELIAN. The reign of DIOCLETIAN (283–305) marked the division of the empire into East and West, a split deepened when CONSTANTINE I moved the capital to Constantinople. He granted tolerance (313) to the Christians, and the church grew, despite such setbacks as the revival of paganism under Julian the Apostate. German invaders were pounding at the borders and gaining some successes before THEODOSIUS strengthened Roman power. The West was now weakened as the BYZANTINE EMPIRE emerged. Rome was sacked by the Ostrogoths under ALARIC I (410), taken by GAISERIC (455), and saved from ATTILA only by the efforts of Pope Leo I. The state disintegrated, and it is customary to say that the Roman Empire in the West ended when ODOACER deposed the last emperor, Romulus Augustulus, in 476.

Medieval Rome. With the disappearance of the Roman Empire the city lost importance, suffering severely in wars of Germans and Byzantines. Yet it cradled a new institution, the PAPACY, and held the memory of the Roman commune. Popes such as GREGORY I (reigned 590–604) made Rome once more a notable city and helped shake off the burdensome but ineffective rule of Byzantine exarchs of Ravenna. Rome reasserted itself as capital of the PAPAL STATES and as center of Christianity. Even sack by the Arabs (846) and the unhappy days of the 10th cent., when great families (such as the Orsini and Colonna) controlled city and papacy, did not extinguish the light of Rome. German kings came there to be crowned emperor. Reforms in the Church by GREGORY VII had little effect on the city; he died in exile after Emperor Henry IV had taken Rome (1083), and the expedition of Normans under Robert Guiscard to aid him led only to the sack of Rome (1084). Later the commune was revived, and Arnold of Brescia set up communal government (1144–45). This was put down. A republic followed, under papal patronage, but civil strife was vigorous between GUELPHS AND GHIBELLINES. In the "Babylonian captivity" of the papacy (1309–78) Rome was desolate and disturbed. Cola di RIENZI attempted (1347) to revive the old Roman institutions, but failed. Only after the Great SCHISM was ended and Pope MARTIN V estab. himself in Rome (1420) did Rome reach stability.

Renaissance and Modern Rome. The popes who ruled Rome in the Renaissance were paradoxically responsible for moral decay in the clergy and the beautification of the city by such artists as Bramante, Michelangelo, Raphael, and Domenico Fontana. The political activities of the pope led to the sack of Rome by the soldiers of Emperor Charles V (1527). The Catholic REFORM cleansed the papal court and made the city prosperous as well as rather strictly noble in mien. Artistically the baroque style flowered in the creations of Bernini, and Rome has post-Renaissance as well as Renaissance monuments. The city became more than ever a center of world civilization. In 1796, Pope Pius VI bought a truce with the soldiers of Napoleon Bonaparte and surrendered Roman art treasures to the French. In 1798 the French occupied Rome and declared it a republic. Trouble between the pope and the French emperor continued until 1814 when papal rule was restored. Pope Pius IX (reigned 1846–78) granted a liberal constitution, but was nevertheless driven from Rome, which became a republic under Mazzini. French troops restored the pope and kept him in power until the fall of Napoleon III. In 1871 the troops of a uniting Italy took the city and made it the capital. The pope refused to recognize his loss of temporal sovereignty, and it was only with the LATERAN TREATY of 1929 that the Roman Question was solved; at that time the pope relinquished sovereignty over all but Vatican City. Rome of today has expanded greatly but retains its great monuments of the past. Among them are the Forum and the Colosseum, the Lateran, St. Peter's Church and other great churches (St. Mary Major, St. Lawrence without the Walls, St. Paul's without the Walls, St. Peter in Chains), and graceful palaces and villas (e.g., Farnese Palace, Farnesina, Villa Borghese). The immense riches of art and its religious importance make Rome one of the most-visited cities of the world. It is also an immense center of commerce and has varied and flourishing industries (e.g., printing, publishing, mfg. of machinery, and motion pictures).

Rome. 1 City (pop. 29,615), NW Ga., at confluence of Etowah and Oostanaula rivers and NW of Atlanta; founded 1834 on a Cherokee village site. Mfg. of textile goods, machinery, and furniture; meat packing. Sherman destroyed city's industrial facilities in Nov., 1864. Shorter Col. (Baptist; for women; 1873) is here. Mountain schools, founded by Martha M. BERRY, are near. **2** Industrial city (pop. 41,682), central N.Y., on Mohawk R. and the Barge Canal and NW of Utica; laid out c.1786. Copper and brass-working center; mfg. of wire products, machinery, heating and cooling equipment, textiles. Building of Erie Canal (begun here 1817) stimulated city's growth.

Römer, Olaus or **Ole** (ōlä'ōōs, ō'lů rû'mûr), 1644–1710, Danish astronomer. Noted for discovery that light travels, not instantaneously, but at definite speed. Name also appears as Roemer.

Romford (rŭm'–), municipal borough (pop. 87,991), Essex, England; a market town. Was cap. of Saxon royal lands called "Liberty of Havering-atte-Bower."

Romilly, Sir Samuel (rŏ'mĭlē), 1757–1818, English law reformer. He heartily approved the French Revolution in *Letters Containing an Account of the Late Revolution in France* (1792). His *Thoughts on Executive Justice* (1786) developed the humane views of Beccaria on punishment of criminals.

Rommel, Erwin (ĕr'vēn rô'mŭl), 1891–1944, German field marshal. Commanded in North African desert warfare 1941–43. His initial successes were turned into defeat after ALAMEIN (1942). He commanded German forces in N France in 1944. It is said that he was ordered to take poison for his alleged part in the plot on Hitler's life. Known as the "desert fox," Rommel is considered one of the most brilliant generals of World War II.

Romney, George (rŏm'nē), 1734–1802, English portrait painter, b. Lancashire. In 1762 he went to London, where he estab. a fashionable practice and soon rivaled Reynolds. His best portraits (esp. those of women) rank among finest of English school. A notable portrait of Lady Hamilton as a bacchante is in National Gall., London.

Romsdal (rōōms'däl"), valley of Rauma R., central Norway. Piercing Dovrefjell mts., it leads through the Kringen pass to central and SE Norway. Weird outlines of peaks have inspired many legends.

Romulo, Carlos P(ena) (rō'mūlō, Span. kär'lōs pä'nä rō'ōōlō), 1900–, Filipino statesman. Became a delegate to UN in 1945; president of UN General Assembly in 1949. Appointed ambassador to U.S. in 1951.

Romulus (rŏm′ūlŭs), in Roman legend, founder of Rome. He and his twin, Remus, were sons of Mars and Rhea Silvia, daughter of Numitor, king of Alba Longa. Amulius, usurper of Numitor's throne, cast them adrift on the Tiber but they were suckled by a she-wolf and reared by a shepherd. When grown, they slew Amulius and restored throne to Numitor. Then they founded a new city (traditionally c.753 B.C.), but quarreled, and Remus was slain. To get wives, Romulus led rape of Sabine women. He estab. a constitution. After disappearing he was worshiped as Quirinus.

Romulus Augustulus (ôgŭs′tūlŭs), d. after 476, last West Roman emperor (475–76); son of Orestes. Was captured, deposed, and pensioned off by Odoacer.

Roncesvalles (rōn″thäsvä′lyäs), Fr. *Roncevaux* (rõsůvō′), pass in W Pyrenees between Spain and France; traditionally the scene of death of Roland.

Ronkonkoma, Lake (rŏngkŏng′kůmů), central Long Isl., SE N.Y., SE of Smithtown; resort.

Ronsard, Pierre de (pyĕr′ dů rõsär′), 1525–1585, French poet and courtier; leader of the Pléïade. A prolific writer in all forms, he excelled in love poetry (e.g., *Sonnets pour Hélène,* 1578). Among his patriotic poems are the epic fragment, *La Franciade* (1572) and two powerful appeals to the French people in which he deplores the Wars of Religion—*Discours des misères de ce temps* and *Remontrances au peuple de France* (both 1582).

Röntgen, Wilhelm Conrad: see Roentgen.

Röntgen ray: see X ray.

rook (ro͝ok), common European bird of crow family, slightly smaller than American crow. Rooks nest in large colonies.

Rookwood pottery, American artware made in Cincinnati. Known for superior glazes and wide range of rich colors.

Roon, Albrecht, Graf von (äl′brĕkht gräf fŭn rōn′), 1803–79, Prussian field marshal. As minister of war (1859–73) he reorganized the Prussian army, making possible the success of Prussia in the Danish, Austro-Prussian, and Franco-Prussian wars.

Roosebeke (rō′zůbā″ků), modern Flemish *Rozebeke,* village, East Flanders, Belgium. French victory here over Philip van Artevelde (1382) restored Flanders to its count, Louis de Maële, and prepared succession of Louis's son-in-law, Philip the Bold.

Roosevelt, Franklin Delano (dĕ′lůnō rō′zůvĕlt), 1882–1945, 31st President of the United States, b. Hyde Park, N.Y. U.S. Assistant Secretary of the Navy (1913–20). Democratic vice presidential candidate in 1920. Stricken with poliomyelitis in 1921, he recovered partial use of his legs by unremitting effort. Later he estab. a foundation at Warm Springs, Ga., for poliomyelitis victims. Governor of N.Y. (1929–33). Inaugurated President at height of crisis (1933), he promptly declared a general bank holiday. New Deal was born. Government agencies were set up to revive economy by vast expenditures of public money, by developing natural resources, by offering work to unemployed. Following reelection in 1936, Roosevelt encountered increasing opposition. Supreme Court declared several New Deal measures invalid. Attempted reorganization of Supreme Court in 1937 failed. Attempt to "purge" New Deal opponents in Congress also failed. In foreign affairs, Roosevelt furthered "good neighbor" policy toward Latin America. Reelected to unprecedented third term in 1940, he helped align U.S. more and more with Britain, while first peacetime selective service act came into being. Following U.S. entry into World War II, his diplomatic duties were heavy. During his fourth administration he engaged in international conferences (see Casablanca Conference; Quebec Conference; Teheran Conference; Yalta Conference); labored for perpetual peace through United Nations. Died suddenly; buried at Hyde Park. His character and achievements are still hotly argued. His wife, **(Anna) Eleanor Roosevelt,** 1884–, a niece of Theodore Roosevelt and a distant cousin of F. D. Roosevelt, has worked for social betterment as lecturer, newspaper columnist, world-wide traveler. A U.S. delegate to UN (1945–52), she was made chairman of Commission on Human Rights in 1946.

Roosevelt, Theodore, 1858–1919, 25th President of the United States (1901–9), b. New York city. His health was delicate in childhood; his determination to rebuild his strength later had a marked effect on his character. U.S. Assistant Secretary of the Navy (1897–98), he resigned to organize the Rough Riders. He was a popular hero when he returned from Cuba. Governor of N.Y. (1899–1900). U.S. Vice President (1901), succeeding to presidency on death of McKinley. Vigorously championed rights of "little man," denounced "malefactors of great wealth." Engaged in "trust busting" under terms of Sherman Anti-Trust Act; brought about progressive reforms not so much directed at abolition of "big business" as at its regulation. Followed policy of conservation of natural resources. Claimed that U.S. had direct interest and some police power in foreign affairs of Latin American countries; this "big stick" policy awoke great indignation in Latin America. Promoted "dollar diplomacy" in the Caribbean area; sought to keep Open Door in China; mediated to end Russo-Japanese War. His hand-picked successor was W. H. Taft, but, as candidate of Progressive party, Roosevelt ran against Taft in 1912. Engaged in hunting and exploring expeditions throughout his career; also wrote many books dealing with history, hunting, wildlife, politics.

Roosevelt, river, c.400 mi. long, W Brazil, rising in E Guaporé territory and flowing N across NW Mato Grosso and SE Amazonas. Called River of Doubt until explored by Theodore Roosevelt.

Roosevelt Dam: see Salt River Valley.

Roosevelt Lake: see Grand Coulee Dam.

Root, Elihu, 1845–1937, American statesman. U.S. Secretary of War (1899–1904); U.S. Secretary of State (1905–9); U.S. Senator from N.Y. (1909–15). One of the greatest of internationalists. Awarded 1912 Nobel Peace Prize.

Root, John Wellborn, 1850–91, American architect. Worked with James Renwick and D. H. Burnham. Developed a Romanesque type of ornament.

root, in botany, the descending axis of a plant, usually underground. Its function is to absorb water and food from the soil and to provide support. Bulbs, corms, rhizomes, and some tubers, although found underground, are actually stem structures. Taproot (long main root) is edible in carrot, parsnip, radish, and other root crops. An epiphyte is a plant without soil roots. See *ill.*, p. 999.

root, in mathematics. If a quantity is multiplied by itself a given number of times, the product is a power of that quantity, and that quantity is a root. Second root is called square root; third root is cube root.

Rops, Félicien (fālēsyē′ rôps′), 1833–98, Belgian artist, of Hungarian descent. Worked mainly in Paris, where he became known as an illustrator. Also produced many etchings and lithographs.

Rorschach Test: see MENTAL TESTS.

Rosa, Salvator (sälvätōr′ rō′zä), 1615–73, Neapolitan painter, famous for vigorous landscapes and spirited battlepieces. Worked in Rome and Florence (under patronage of the Medici). Known also as a satiric poet.

Rosa, Monte (mōn″tā rō′zä), mountain group on Swiss-Italian border. Highest peak, Dufourspitze, 15,203 ft., is also highest point in Switzerland.

Rosalie, Fort: see NATCHEZ.

Rosamond, fl. c.570, Lombard queen. She supposedly had her husband, King Alboin, murdered after he had forced her to drink from a cup made from the skull of her father, whom Alboin had slain. She married her accomplice Helmechis, but later regretted it and offered him a poisoned drink. Helmechis drank half and forced her to swallow the rest. The pretty story was used by Swinburne and by Alfieri in two tragedies.

Rosamond, d. 1176?, mistress of Henry II of England, known as the "fair Rosamond." There is much legendary material by medieval chroniclers concerning her supposed murder by Eleanor of Aquitaine.

Rosario, city (pop. 467,937), Santa Fe prov., E central Argentina, port on Paraná R., on E margin of Pampa. Second largest city in Argentina, it is primarily an export-import center for central and N provinces.

Rosas, Juan Manuel de (hwän′ mänwĕl′ dā rô′säs), 1793–1877, Argentine dictator, governor of Buenos Aires prov. (1829–32, 1835–52). In 1820 he began his political career by leading his well-trained gaucho troops in support of conservatives and federalism. Soon became governor of Buenos Aires and temporarily but with sanguinary thoroughness destroyed unitarian cause. Surrendered office (1832) but maintained prestige by successful expedition against Indians. Returning to office (1835) he soon assumed dictatorship over most of Argentina. Instituted régime of terror. Finally, because of foreign difficulties and economic crisis, a revolt, led by Urquiza and backed by Brazil and Uruguay, succeeded, and he fled to England, where he lived until his death.

Roscius, Quintus (kwĭn′tŭs rŏ′shŭs), c.126 B.C.–62 B.C., greatest Roman actor of his day.

Roscommon (rŏskŏ′mŭn), inland county (951 sq. mi.; pop. 72,510), N central Ireland, in Connaught; co. town Roscommon. Low-lying region with many lakes and bogs, it is an agr. county.

rose, wild and cultivated plant and its flower, a favorite all over the world since prehistoric times. There are many hundreds of species and varieties, ranging from tiny rock garden forms to large shrub or climbing types, with single or double flowers often fragrant, in white, yellow, and shades of red and pink. Among the old species are the damask rose and the cabbage or hundred-leaved rose, cultivated in Europe for attar of roses. Famous roses of England include the white rose, emblem of the house of York, the red rose of the house of Lancaster in the Wars of the Roses, and the variegated red and white rose, now called the York and Lancaster. Hybridization, resulting in the rambler, tea, and hybrid tea, began when the East India Company's ships brought new everblooming roses from the Orient.

Rosebery, Archibald Philip Primrose, 5th **earl of** (rōz′bŭrē), 1847–1929, English statesman. Prime minister 1894–95, he split Liberal party by advocating a form of imperial federation. Was leader of Liberal imperialist division of party 1895–1905.

Rosebud, river of SE Mont., tributary of the Yellowstone. Also called Rosebud Creek. On its banks Indians under Crazy Horse defeated U.S. troops under Gen. George Crook in June, 1876.

Roseburg, city (pop. 8,390), SW Oregon, S of Eugene and on Umpqua R.; settled c.1851. Rail and trade center with fruit canneries and lumber mills.

Rosecrans, William Starke, 1818–98, Union general in Civil War. Victor at Iuka and Corinth (1862). Commanded Army of the Cumberland, victor at Murfreesboro. In CHATTANOOGA CAMPAIGN, defeated at Chickamauga, relieved of command.

Roselle (rōzĕl′), borough (pop. 17,681), NE N.J., near Elizabeth. Mfg. of machinery, metal products.

Roselle Park, borough (pop. 11,537), NE N.J., near Roselle. Mfg. of rugs, machinery, oil burners.

rosemary, evergreen shrub (*Rosmarinus officinalis*) of Mediterranean region, widely grown for its aromatic leaves used for seasoning and perfume.

Rosemont, village, SE Pa., seat of Rosemont Col. (R.C.; for women; 1921).

Rosenberg, Alfred (äl′frät rō′zŭnbĕrk), 1893–1946, German National Socialist leader, b. Estonia. His book *Der Mythus des 20 Jahrhunderts* [the myth of the 20th cent.] (1930) supplied Hitler with the spurious philosophical and scientific basis for his racist doctrine. As minister for the occupied Eastern territories after 1941 he was responsible for German atrocities in the Baltic states and Russia. He was hanged after conviction at Nuremberg war crimes trial.

Rosenberg, city (pop. 6,210), S Texas, near Brazos R. and SW of Houston. Market and shipping center for agr. area with cotton ginning and some oil.

Rosenthal, Moriz (mō'rĭts rō'zùntäl), 1862–1946, Polish pianist; pupil of Liszt. His American debut was in 1888 with Fritz Kreisler. He was considered one of the greatest pianists of his time.

Rosenwald, Julius (rō'zùnwôld), 1862–1932, American merchant and philanthropist. In 1917 he estab. Julius Rosenwald Fund, used mainly to found rural schools for Negroes. He also gave to Jewish relief in the Near East and to Y.M.C.A. and Y.W.C.A.

rose of Jericho, name for certain desert plants (esp. *Anastatica hierochuntica*), of Asia Minor, sometimes called resurrection plants. Their branches curl up when dry and unfold when moist.

Rose of Lima, Saint, 1586–1617, Peruvian Dominican nun, noted for austerities; first saint of the New World to be canonized (1671). Feast: Aug. 30.

rose of Sharon, ornamental Asiatic shrub (*Hibiscus syriacus*), also called shrubby althea. It has white, rose, or purple, single or double flowers resembling those of the hollyhock.

Roses, Wars of the, name given to struggle for the throne of England 1455–84 between houses of LANCASTER (whose badge was a red rose) and YORK (whose badge was a white rose). Lancastrians had held the throne since the deposition of Richard II (1399). HENRY VI was controlled by his queen, MARGARET OF ANJOU, and by William de la Pole, duke of Suffolk, and Edmund Beaufort, duke of Somerset. They were opposed by Richard, duke of York, who gained support from popular unrest over losses in France and corruption at court. Suffolk was banished and murdered in 1450. York was made protector during insanity of king 1453–54. Yorkists won first battle of St. Albans (1455). After a period of comparative quiet, Yorkists captured Henry at battle of Northampton (1460) and arranged compromise whereby Richard would succeed Henry. Queen (whose son would be disinherited) raised an army and slew York at battle of Wakefield (1460). Richard NEVILLE, earl of Warwick, became real leader of Yorkist party. Margaret defeated Warwick and rescued Henry (1461) but Richard's son meanwhile had entered London and been crowned as EDWARD IV. Lancastrians were repeatedly defeated, Margaret fled to France, and Henry was imprisoned (1465). Warwick and Edward quarreled over king's marriage (1464) and Warwick intrigued with George, duke of Clarence. They fled to France (1470). Warwick and Margaret were reconciled, and he returned to England and restored Henry. Edward secured aid and regained the throne (1471). Warwick was killed and Henry soon died. Edward was succeeded (1483) by his 12-year-old son, EDWARD V. The boy's uncle gained control, had himself made king as RICHARD III, and had young Edward murdered. Henry Stafford, duke of Buckingham, unsuccessfully revolted in 1483. Lancastrian claimant, Henry Tudor, landed in England and defeated Richard at Bosworth Field (1485). Became king as HENRY VII and united the two houses by marrying Edward IV's daughter. Wars ended feudalism in England because they so weakened the nobles that they could not contest rise of the monarchy under the Tudors.

Rosetsu (Nagasawa) (rō'sĕtsōō), 1755–99, Japanese painter of landscapes with amusing animals.

Rosetta (rōzĕ'tù), Arabic *Rashid,* city (pop. 24,094), Egypt, near Rosetta mouth of the Nile. **Rosetta stone,** a basalt slab inscribed by priests of Ptolemy V in hieroglyphic, demotic, and Greek, was found near here by troops of Napoleon in 1799. Captured 1801 by British, it is now in British Mus. It gave Champollion and others key to Egyptian HIEROGLYPHIC.

Roseville. 1 City (pop. 8,723), N central Calif., NE of Sacramento. Fruit-shipping center. **2** Residential village (pop. 15,816), SE Mich., NE suburb of Detroit. Sheet metal plant.

rosewood, name for ornamental heartwood of several tropical trees of Brazil. Brazilian rosewood or jacaranda, from *Dalbergia nigra,* fragrant and purple-black, has long been used whole or in veneers for piano castings, cabinetwork, and tools. Other rosewoods include East Indian and Honduras rosewood.

Rosh ha-Shanah (hù-shä'nù) [Heb.,= head of the year], the Jewish New Year, observed on the first two days of the seventh month, Tishri, occurring usually in Sept. Considered days of judgment, they are spent in prayer. A trumpet (shofar—a ram's horn) is sounded during the religious ceremonies. Various other spellings, e.g., Rosh-ha-Shonah.

Rosicrucians, esoteric groups, all claiming origin in ancient Egypt. Secret learning deals with occult symbols—rosy cross, swastika, pyramid—and cabalistic writings. American Rosicrucians follow theosophical doctrines. Rosicrucian Order has hq. in San Jose, Calif.; Rosicrucian Brotherhood, in Quakertown, Pa.; Society of Rosicrucians, in New York city.

rosin (rŏ'zĭn), solid residue from crude turpentine after oil of turpentine is distilled off; also called colophony. It is hard, brittle, translucent, tasteless, pale yellow or amber; color and appearance depend on crude turpentine used and method of preparation. Used to make soaps, varnishes, paints, sealing wax; for treating violin bows; in pharmacy.

Roskilde (rôs'kĭlù), city (pop. 26,355), E Zealand, Denmark, W of Copenhagen; a port on Roskilde Fjord (inlet of the Kattegat). Fishing; varied mfg. It was the cap. of Denmark until 1443; ecclesiastical cap. until 1536. Many Danish kings are buried in magnificent cathedral (11th–12th cent.). By Treaty of Roskilde (1658) Denmark ceded lands in Sweden to CHARLES X of Sweden.

Roslyn (rŏz'lĭn), village (pop. 1,612), on NW Long Isl., SE N.Y., N of Mineola. William Cullen Bryant's home ("Cedarmere") and grave are here.

Ross, Betsy (Elizabeth Griscom Ross), 1752–1836, American flagmaker. Story that she designed and made first American national flag now generally discredited.

Ross, Sir John, 1777–1856, British arctic explorer and rear admiral. Sought Northwest Passage. Discovered Boothia Peninsula, Gulf of Boothia, and King William Isl. Accompanied on voyages by his nephew, **Sir James Clark Ross,** 1800–1862, also a rear admiral. Discovered Ross Isl. in command of expedition to Antarctica (1839–43); also discovered Victoria Land.

Ross, John, called in Cherokee *Kooweskoowe* (kōō″wĭs″kōōwē′), 1790–1866, Indian chief, of mixed Scottish and Cherokee (one eighth) blood. Led Cherokee journey to present Okla. (1838–39). Chief, united Cherokee nation (1839–66).

Ross, Sir Ronald, 1857–1932, English physician, authority on tropical medicine. Won 1912 Nobel Prize in Physiology and Medicine for work on transmission of malaria.

Rossa, O'Donovan, 1831–1915, Irish rebel, whose original name was Jeremiah O'Donovan. Edited a Fenian newspaper. Convicted of treason, he was released (1871) and emigrated to New York.

Ross and Cromarty (krŏ′mûrtē), maritime county (3,089 sq. mi.; pop. 60,503), N Scotland; co. town Dingwall. Includes Lewis and other islands. Mainly a mountainous region with fertile strip along E coast, grazing and fishing are main occupations.

Rossbach (rôs′bäkh), village, Saxony-Anhalt, E central Germany, near Weimar. Here in 1757 Frederick II of Prussia defeated the imperials and French under Soubise in one of his most brilliant victories.

Rosse, William Parsons, 3d earl of (rôs), 1800–1867, British astronomer. Noted for construction of telescope reflectors and for observations of nebulae.

Rosselli, Cosimo (kô′zēmō rōs-sĕl′lē), 1439–1507, Florentine painter. Painted *The Last Supper* for Sistine Chapel, Vatican.

Rossellino, Bernardo (bĕrnär′dō rōs-sĕl-lē′nō), 1409–64, Florentine architect, whose real name was Bernardo di Matteo di Domenico Gambarelli. Built Rucellai Palace in Florence. His most famous sculpture is tomb of Leonardo Bruni in Santa Croce, Florence. His brother, **Antonio Rossellino,** 1427–c.1478, was also a celebrated sculptor.

Rossetti, Gabriele (gäbrēā′lā rōs-sĕt′tē), 1783–1854, Italian author of patriotic verse, a political exile in England after 1824. His son, **Dante Gabriel Rossetti** (dăn′tē gā′brēŭl), 1828–82, was an English Pre-Raphaelite painter and poet. With W. Holman Hunt, Millais, and others he formed brotherhood of PRE-RAPHAELITES (1848). In their journal, the *Germ,* edited by his brother William Michael Rossetti (1829–1919), appeared his poem "The Blessed Damozel." In 1860 he married his model, Elizabeth Siddal, who died in 1862. In his grief Rossetti buried with her the manuscript of his poems, later recovered. His *Poems* (1870) and *Ballads and Sonnets* (1881) contain the great sonnet sequence "The House of Life" and the ballad "Sister Helen." Among his best-known paintings are *Beata Beatrix, The Blessed Damozel,* and a triptych, *Francesca and Paolo.* His sister **Christina (Georgina) Rossetti,** 1830–94, was also a poet, with a true lyric gift. Some of her poems appeared in the *Germ.* Very religious, she spent last years as a recluse, and her poetry is usually religious, often melancholy. Her works include *Goblin Market and Other Poems* (1862), *The Prince's Progress* (1866), and *Sing-Song* (1872).

Rossini, Gioacchino (Antonio) (jōäk-kē′nō rôs-ē′nē), 1792–1868, Italian operatic composer. His *Barber of Seville* is a masterpiece of comic opera. Selections from *La gazza ladra* [the thieving magpie], *L'italiana in Algeri, Semiramide,* and *William Tell* are popular.

Ross Sea, large Antarctic inlet of Pacific Ocean, E of Victoria Land. Its southern extension is Ross Shelf Ice or Barrier, between Marie Byrd Land and Victoria Land. Indented by Bay of Whales, site of Little America. Discovered by Sir James Clark Ross 1839–43.

Rostand, Edmond (ĕdmõ′ rôstã′), 1868–1918, French poet and dramatist. Best-known for the dramas *Cyrano de Bergerac* (1897) and *L'Aiglon* (1900) and the barnyard fable *Chantecler* (1910).

Rostock (rŏs′tŏk), city (pop. 114,869), Mecklenburg, NE Germany, on Baltic Sea. Port with petroleum tank installations and shipyards. Mfg. of machinery and chemicals. University was founded 1419. City was important in Hanseatic League. Heavily damaged by World War II air raids.

Rostov (rŏ′stŏv). **1** Or **Rostov-on-Don,** Rus. *Rostov-na-Donu,* city (pop. 510,253), S European RSFSR; a major port and rail hub on the Don c.25 mi. above its mouth on Sea of Azov. Produces machinery, sheet metal, autos, rolling stock, ships, textiles, and leather goods. Founded 1761 as fortress, it became a major grain-export center in 19th cent. Twice held (1941, 1942–43) by Germans in their drive on the Caucasus in World War II, and heavily damaged. **2** City (1926 pop. 20,864), N Central European RSFSR, NE of Moscow. One of oldest Russian cities (founded 864), it was cap. (from 10th cent.) of a principality which passed to Moscow in 1474. Its old kremlin contains Uspenski Cathedral (1214).

Rostovtzeff, Michael Ivanovich (rŏstŏv′tsĕf), 1870–, American historian, b. Kiev; an authority on the history of the ancient world.

Roswell, city (pop. 25,738), SE N.Mex., on Rio Hondo in Pecos valley; settled 1869. Resort; trade center in livestock and irrigated farm area, with oil wells and potash mines. Ships wool, processes food, refines oil, distills cottonseed oil. Carlsbad Caverns Natl. Park is c.100 mi. S.

Roswitha: see HROSWITHA.

Rotary International, organization of business and professional men, founded 1905. Supports charities and encourages international friendship.

rotation of crops, agr. practice of varying crops in a planned series to conserve and enrich soil and to eradicate weeds, insects, plant diseases.

rotenone: see INSECTICIDE.

Rothenburg ob der Tauber (rō′tŭnbōōrk ôp dĕr tou′bûr), town (pop. 11,223), Middle Franconia, W Bavaria, on Tauber R. Founded in 11th cent., it almost completely preserves its medieval appearance; encircling walls date from 14th–15th cent.

Rothenstein, Sir William (rō′thŭnstīn), 1872–1945, English portrait painter and writer.

Rothermere, Harold Sidney Harmsworth, 1st **Viscount** (rŏ′dhûrmēr), 1868–1940, English publisher; financial wizard of publishing firm headed by his brother, Viscount NORTHCLIFFE. Founded (1915) *Sunday Pictorial;* gained control of newspaper empire after his brother's death. Though earlier friendly to fascism, he supported British cause valiantly in World War II.

Rothesay (rŏth′sē, –sā), burgh (pop. 10,145), county town of Buteshire, Scotland, on Bute Isl.; a resort. Has hq. of Royal Northern Yacht Club.

Rothschild (rŏth′chīld, Ger. rōt′shĭlt), prominent international family of bankers. **Mayer Amschel Rothschild** (mī′ûr äm′shûl), 1743–1812, son of a small Jewish money-changer in Frankfurt, Germany, rendered great services as financial agent of the landgraves of Hesse-Kassel and laid the foundation of the family fortune. Of his five sons, the oldest continued the business in Frankfurt. The other four estab. branches in Vienna, London, Naples, and Paris. All five were created barons by Francis I of Austria (1822), a title which continues in the family. Ablest of the brothers was **Nathan Meyer Rothschild,** 1777–1836, who opened the London branch in 1805. As agent of the British government in the Napoleonic Wars, he was of vital help in Napoleon's ultimate defeat. Under his guidance and that of his son, **Baron Lionel Nathan de Rothschild,** 1808–79, the family gained immense power by floating loans to various countries, but the family's virtual monopoly on these transactions was soon broken, and its wealth also declined. Members of the family were prominent as philanthropists, patrons of the arts, sportsmen, writers, physicians.

rotogravure: see PRINTING.

Rotorua (rōtûroo′ŭ), borough (pop. 7,512), on N North Isl., New Zealand; health resort in Hot Springs Dist.

Rotten Row, track in Hyde Park, London, for horseback riders. The origin of the name is unknown.

Rotterdam (rŏ′tûrdăm″, Dutch rôtûrdäm′), municipality (pop. 646,248), South Holland prov., W Netherlands, on the Nieuwe Maas near its mouth on the North Sea. Largest port and second largest city of Netherlands; accessible to ocean-going vessels through New Waterway (constructed 1866–90). Connected by waterways with the Rhineland-Ruhr industrial area of Germany, it has a huge volume of transit trade, with Antwerp its only rival on continental Europe. It has large shipyards, petroleum refineries, and mfg. of chemicals, machinery, and food products. Chartered 1328, it grew to major importance only in the 19th cent. In World War II, Rotterdam suffered a most destructive aerial bombardment, even though it had capitulated to the Germans several hours earlier (May 14, 1940). The old city center (incl. house where Erasmus was born) was obliterated.

Roty, Louis Oscar (lwē′ ôskär′ rôtē′), 1846–1911, eminent French medalist.

Rouault, Georges (zhôrzh′ roo-ō′), 1871–, French painter. Studied under Gustave Moreau and was a fauvist in his early period. His characteristic works have rough conventionalized forms and movingly portray injustice and human suffering. Recurrent subjects are clowns, corrupt judges, passion of Christ, and misery of war.

Roubaix (roobā′), city (pop. 98,834), Nord dept., N France. Center of French wool industry.

Rouen (rooã′), city (pop. 101,187), cap. of Seine-Inférieure dept., N France, on the Seine near its mouth; historic cap. of Normandy. Major port. Cotton mfg. Archiepiscopal see since 5th cent. Held by English 1419–49 during Hundred Years War; scene of burning of Joan of Arc (1431). Seat of a provincial parlement (1499–1789) and proverbial breeding place of lawyers. Though heavily damaged in World War II, Rouen remains famous for its magnificent Gothic architecture—Cathedral of Notre Dame (13th–15th cent., with two strikingly different towers; damaged); churches of St. Maclou (15th–16th cent.; damaged) and St. Ouen (begun 14th cent.; intact); palace of justice (15th–16th cent.; damaged). Birthplace of Corneille and Flaubert.

Rouergue (rooĕrg′), region and former county, S France, in Aveyron dept.; historic cap. Rodez. Part of Massif Central, it has eroded limestone plateaus (*causses*), used for sheep raising (Roquefort cheese). Agr. in valleys. A Bourbon family possession, it was inc. into Guyenne prov. 1589.

Rouge (roozh′), river rising in S Mich. and winding c.30 mi. S and SE to Detroit R. at River Rouge city.

Rouget de Lisle, Claude Joseph (roozhā′ dû lēl′), 1760–1836, French poet, musician, and army officer. He wrote the words and music of the MARSEILLAISE as a marching song for his soldiers. Although the song later was associated with the Revolution, he himself was a royalist and barely escaped the guillotine.

Rough Riders, name popularly given to 1st Regiment of U.S. Cavalry Volunteers in Spanish-American War. Recruited largely by Theodore Roosevelt, lieutenant colonel in regiment. Exploits, especially at San Juan Hill, were highly publicized.

roulette (roolĕt′), game of chance popular at Monte Carlo and other gambling resorts. Dates from late 18th cent.

Roumelia: see RUMELIA.

Round Table: see ARTHURIAN LEGEND.

Round Tops: see GETTYSBURG CAMPAIGN.

roup (roop), infectious disease of poultry, causing inflammation of mucous membranes of air passages and of eyes. Argyrol is used in treatment.

Rourke, Constance, 1885–1941, American writer of works on social history (e.g., *American Humor,* 1931) and biographies of American figures.

Rouses Point (rou′sĭz), village (pop. 2,001), extreme NE N.Y., on L. Champlain. On the Que. line, it is a port of entry.

Rousseau, Henri (ãrē′ roosō′), 1844–1910, French painter, self-taught. Called Le Douanier from his profession as customs official. Known for jungle scenes painted in exotic colors.

Rousseau, Jean Jacques (zhã′ zhäk′), 1712–78,

French philosopher, b. Geneva. His wandering and troubled life was made tolerable by patrons and friends—notably Mme de Warens (his mistress as well as protector), Mme d'Épinay, the duc de Luxembourg, Diderot, and other Encyclopedists. His daring statements got him into trouble with authorities at Paris and Geneva and he had to seek asylum in the 1760s in Bern canton and then (1765) with David Hume in England. With Hume as with Diderot and other friends he quarreled bitterly, for his mind darkened with paranoiac ideas as he grew older, and he thought all were in a gigantic plot against him—including his common-law wife, Thérèse Le Vasseur (who may or may not have borne him five children, put into foundling homes, according to his account). Rousseau probably had more influence in shaping romanticism and later thought than any other man of the 18th cent. His important works include an essay contending that man is good by nature and corrupted by civilization; another essay, *Discours sur l'origine de l'inégalité des hommes* (1754); a didactic novel, *La Nouvelle Héloïse* (1761); *Le Contrat social* (1762); a novel on education, *Émile* (1762); and draft constitutions for Corsica and Poland—neither put in effect. His ideas were too complex for a brief summary, but some of them that had great effect were these. "Natural man" was a pure animal, neither good nor bad. Equality between men disappeared with the introduction of property, agriculture, and industries. Laws were instituted to preserve the inequality of oppressor and oppressed. Men may, however, enter into a social contract among themselves to set up a government (monarchic, aristocratic, or democratic), but holding the sovereignty inalienably among the people as a whole. The aim of government and education is to offset the corrupting influence of institutions. The child should be allowed to develop without interference. These ideas are also reflected in Rousseau's *Confessions,* one of the most celebrated autobiographical works ever written. This shows also in full the romantic sensibility and love of nature that was to dominate literature in the 19th cent. Rousseau was also a self-taught authority on musical theory and a composer.

Rousseau, Théodore (tāōdôr'), 1812–67, French landscape painter of the Barbizon school.

Roussel, Albert (rōōsĕl'), 1869–1937, French composer. His music is romantic and impressionistic; later works show the influence of polytonality. His compositions include the orchestral-choral *Evocations; Padmavati* (which adapts Hindu scales and story to 18th-cent. opera-ballet technique); symphonies; piano pieces; and chamber music.

Roussillon (rōōsēyō'), region and former province, S France, on Spanish border, in Pyrénées-Orientales dept.; historic cap. Perpignan. Conquered by the Franks from the Arabs in the 8th cent., it later was held by the house of Aragon and by Spain. It was ceded by Spain to France in 1659.

Rouvray, battle of: see HERRINGS, BATTLE OF THE.

Roux, (Pierre Paul) Émile (āmēl' rōō'), 1853–1933, French bacteriologist and physician. Contributed to study of diphtheria and syphilis. Director of Pasteur Institute (1904–18).

Roux, Wilhelm (vĭl'hĕlm), 1850–1924, German anatomist, a founder of experimental embryology.

Rouyn (rōō'ĭn, Fr. rōōē'), city (pop. 14,633), W Que., Canada, on Osisko L. and S of Noranda. Gold, copper, and zinc mining center.

Rowe, Nicholas (rō), 1674–1718, English dramatist, author of tragedies (e.g., *Jane Shore,* 1714). Also edited Shakspere (1709). Made poet laureate in 1715.

rowing. Boats propelled by oars were used in ancient times for both war and commerce. Rowing is now mainly a sport. Most famous annual crew race, between Oxford and Cambridge, was first held at Henley, in 1839.

Rowlandson, Thomas, 1756–1827, English caricaturist, known for humorous commentary on social life. Notable work is series of drawings *Tour of Dr. Syntax* (3 vols., 1812–21).

Rowley, William (rou'lē), 1585?–1642?, English playwright and actor, best known for plays written with Thomas Middleton (e.g., *The Changeling,* presented 1623).

Rowson, Susanna Haswell (rou'sûn), 1762–1824, American author, actress, and teacher; author of the novel *Charlotte Temple* (1791).

Roxana (rŏksă'nů) or **Roxane** (rŏksă'nē), d. 311 B.C., Bactrian (Persian) princess, wife of Alexander the Great. After his death, she and Alexander's posthumous son, Alexander Aegeus, were imprisoned by Cassander and finally killed.

Roxas, Manuel (mänwĕl' rô'häs), 1892–1948, Filipino statesman. Supporting Japanese-sponsored government during World War II, he is said to have aided Filipino underground at same time. First president of Philippine republic (1946–48).

Roxburghshire (rŏks'bûrûshĭr) or **Roxburgh,** border county (666 sq. mi.; pop. 45,562), S Scotland; co. town Jedburgh. Has Cheviot Hills in S. Drained by the Teviot and the Tweed, county is often called Teviotdale. Main occupation is sheep grazing.

Roxelana: see SULEIMAN I.

Royal Academy of Arts, London, in Burlington House; founded 1769 by George III at suggestion of Sir William Chambers and Benjamin West. Sir Joshua Reynolds was first president. Has two yearly exhibitions, one of old masters and one of contemporary art. Membership is fixed at 40.

Royal Canadian Mounted Police, constabulary organized (1873) as Northwest Mounted Police to bring law and order to Canadian Far West and especially to prevent Indian disorders. Present name acquired 1920. Enforces dominion law throughout Canada.

Royal Gorge: see ARKANSAS, river.

Royal Highlanders: see BLACK WATCH.

Royal Leamington Spa, England: see LEAMINGTON.

Royal Oak, residential city (pop. 46,898), SE Mich., NW suburb of Detroit; settled c.1820. Mfg. of tools, abrasives, paint, and mattresses.

royal poinciana: see POINCIANA, ROYAL.

Royal Society, first incorporated in 1662, in 1663 and again in 1669 chartered as Royal Society of London for Improving Natural Knowledge. Founded by learned men who met for scientific discussion, especially in physical sciences. Government-subsidized, it stimulates research and advises government. Publishes its *Proceedings* and *The Philosophical Transactions.*

Royce, Josiah (rois), 1855–1916, American philosopher, a teacher at Univ. of Calif. (1878–82) and later at Harvard. The foremost American idealist, he held that the world exists only in so far as beings with minds know it and that the finite self knows truth only because the individual mind is part of the world-mind. Among his works are *The Spirit of Modern Philosophy* (1892), *The World and the Individual* (1900–1901), and *The Philosophy of Loyalty* (1908).

Rozebeke, Belgium: see ROOSEBEKE.

RSFSR: see RUSSIAN SOVIET FEDERATED SOCIALIST REPUBLIC.

Ru, chemical symbol of the element RUTHENIUM.

Ruanda-Urundi (ro͞oän'dä-o͝oro͞on'dē), UN trust territory (20,575 sq. mi.; pop. 3,889,-058), E Africa, under Belgian administration; cap. Usumbura. Bordered on N by Uganda, on E by Tanganyika, and on W by Belgian Congo and L. Tanganyika. Lies on a plateau. Cotton, coffee, tobacco, and sisal are grown; tin and gold are mined. Belonged to German East Africa 1899–1917. After World War I it became a mandate under Belgium; status was changed to that of UN trust territory in 1946.

Ruapehu (ro͞oo͝upä'ho͞o), extinct volcanic peak, 9,175 ft. high, on central North Isl., New Zealand; island's highest mountain. Skiing center.

Rub al Khali (ro͞ob' äl khä'lē), great desert, 250,000 sq. mi., S Arabia. Relatively unexplored.

rubber, hydrocarbon obtained from milky secretion (latex) of various plants. Its elasticity, toughness, impermeability, adhesiveness, and electrical resistance make it useful as adhesive, coating, fiber, molding compound, and electrical insulator. Over 95% is obtained from PARA RUBBER TREE. Some latex (treated to prevent coagulation) is shipped to manufacturing centers but more is exported as crude rubber rolled into sheets from slabs of coagulated latex. For use in most products rubber is ground; dissolved; compounded with fillers, pigments, plasticizers, and other ingredients; sheeted, extruded in various shapes, molded, or applied as coating; then vulcanized. Uncoagulated latex may be extruded as thread, coated on other materials, or beaten to a foam (sponge rubber). Over one half of world supply is used by U.S., chiefly for tires and inner tubes; U.S. manufacturing center is Akron, Ohio. Early use of rubber by Indians of South and Central America was recorded by Spanish in 16th cent. First factory estab. 1811 in Vienna. In 1823 Charles Macintosh developed practical waterproofing process; in 1839 Charles Goodyear invented VULCANIZATION process which revolutionized rubber industry. See also RUBBER, SYNTHETIC.

rubber, synthetic. Various rubberlike commercial products are generally known as synthetic rubber, but no synthetic substance completely identical with natural rubber in chemical and elastic properties has yet been produced. Basic materials from which most synthetic rubbers are derived are the hydrocarbon substances (e.g., petroleum, alcohol, coal tar, natural gas, and acetylene). Rubberlike qualities are obtained by polymerization (i.e., linking molecules of the basic substances into long chains) or sometimes by a process of condensation. Natural rubber is superior to synthetic rubber in that it is easier to process, usually has greater elasticity (and keeps it even at low temperatures), and resists tearing; synthetic rubbers, however, are less affected by oils, solvents, sunlight, heat, and acids, and are less permeable to gases and liquids. In the U.S., butadiene (a hydrocarbon derived from ethyl alcohol or petroleum) is the basis of many leading synthetic rubber materials; among these are GR-S (general-purpose rubber, styrene; the type produced in largest quantities during World War II), Perbunan (formerly Buna N), Hycar (Ameripol), and Chemigum. Other commercially important synthetics include Butyl rubber and neoprene (successfully produced in U.S. from c.1931). The term *elastics* is sometimes used in preference to "synthetic rubber" and the term *elastomer* has been accepted by many for synthetic rubber material.

rubber plant or **India rubber tree,** a large tree (*Ficus elastica*) in its native Asia, but elsewhere grown as a pot plant. It has long, leathery, evergreen leaves.

Rubens, Peter Paul (ro͞o'bŭnz), 1577–1640, foremost painter of the Flemish school. After spending eight years in the service of the duke of Mantua, he returned to Antwerp in 1608 and won immediate success. Besieged with commissions, he organized a workshop of skilled apprentices, who did much of the work on the larger works (esp. allegorical paintings and altarpieces), although he himself made the designs and added the finishing touches. He did many paintings for the Spanish and French courts, notably a series of 24 paintings of the life of Marie de' Medici (Louvre). Entering diplomatic service in 1626, after the death of his wife, Isabella Brant, he went on a mission to Spain in 1628; here he met Velázquez and painted the royal family. In London, where he was knighted, he painted the ceiling at Whitehall. Returning to Antwerp in 1630 he married the young beauty Helen Fourment, who became the subject of some of his masterpieces. Equally skillful in all fields of painting, Rubens was one of the most popular and prolific artists of all time. Over 2,000 paintings are attributed to his studio. The works of his mature period are lustily painted in bright, clear colors with a pervading luminosity. Among his masterpieces are the *Descent from the Cross* (cathedral, Antwerp) and *Venus and Adonis* (Metropolitan Mus.).

Rubicon (ro͞o'bĭkŏn), stream that in days of early Rome divided Gaul from Italy; not certainly identified. In 49 B.C. Caesar led his army across it, defying the Roman senate and commencing civil war. He is reported to have said, "The die is cast." Hence to cross the Rubicon is to take an irrevocable step.

rubidium (ro͞obĭ'dēŭm), rare, silver-white, soft metallic element (symbol = Rb; see also ELEMENT, table). It is an alkali metal and very active; resembles potassium in activity; not found free.

Rubinstein, Anton (Grigoryevich) (ro͞o'bĭnstīn), 1829–94, Russian virtuoso pianist and composer, founder (1862) of the St. Petersburg Conservatory. His concertos, symphonies, and operas were successful in his lifetime, but his *Kamennoi-Ostrov* is his best-known work today. His brother, **Nicholas (Grigoryevich) Rubinstein,** 1835–81, a pianist and teacher, founded (1864) the Moscow Conservatory.

Rubinstein, Artur, 1886–, Polish-American piano virtuoso. First appeared in the U.S. in 1906, but it was after his third appearance here, in 1937, that he achieved his greatest acclaim.

ruby, precious stone, variety of red corundum, classed among the most valuable of gems. Found in Burma, Siam, and Ceylon.

Rückert, Friedrich (frē'drĭkh rü'kûrt), 1788–1866, German Orientalist and lyric poet.

Ruckstull, Frederick Wellington (rŭk'stŭl″), 1853–1942, American sculptor, b. Alsace. Principal founder of the Natl. Sculpture Society (1893).

rudbeckia: see BLACK-EYED SUSAN; GOLDEN GLOW.

Rude, François (frãswä' rüd'), 1784–1855, French sculptor. Works include the patriotic group, *Le Départ,* on Arc de Triomphe, Paris.

Rüdesheim (rü'dùs-hīm), town (pop. 5,736), Hesse, W Germany, on the Rhine, in famous wine district.

Rudolf (ro͞o'dŏlf), emperors and German kings. **Rudolf I** (Rudolf of Hapsburg), 1218–91, count of Hapsburg, was elected king in 1273 after a lawless interregnum of 20 years. He sought friendly relations with the papacy and tried, with moderate success, to stamp out feudal warfare and the robber barons. His victories over OTTOCAR II of Bohemia (1276, 1278) enabled him to confiscate Austria, Styria, and Carniola, which he bestowed in 1282 on his sons. It was thus that the Hapsburg family began its rise to world empire. **Rudolf II,** 1552–1612, son of Emperor Maximilian II, was crowned king of Hungary (1572) and Bohemia (1575) before succeeding his father as emperor (1576). Mentally unbalanced, he had to delegate his imperial power to his brother MATTHIAS (1606), to whom he also ceded Hungary, Moravia, and Austria (1608) and, finally, Bohemia (1611). Remembered for his passionate—if misguided—interest in science, he called Kepler and Tycho Brahe to his court at Prague and locked up alchemists, under orders to make gold, in the little houses of Golden Lane.

Rudolf, 1858–89, Austrian archduke, crown prince of Austria and Hungary; only son of Emperor Francis Joseph and Empress Elizabeth. Was found shot dead, with his mistress, Baroness Maria Vetsera, at Mayerling. Supposedly a double suicide, their deaths remain a mystery.

Rudolf, Lake, 180 mi. long, 10–30 mi. wide, NW Kenya, in Great Rift Valley. Has no outlet.

rue (ro͞o), aromatic woody herb of genus *Ruta.* Common rue, *Ruta graveolans,* has green-yellow flowers and blue-green, bitter leaves. In medieval times it was used as a drug.

Rueda, Lope de: see LOPE DE RUEDA.

Ruef, Abraham (Abe Ruef) (ro͞of'), 1865–1936, American political boss in San Francisco. Sentenced to 14-year prison term (1909) after sensational trial for bribery and extortion.

Ruffin, Edmund (rŭ'fĭn), 1794–1865, American agriculturist, a Southern "FIRE-EATER." He was a pioneer in soil chemistry. An ardent supporter of states' rights and secession, on April 12, 1861, he was allowed to fire first shot against Fort Sumter. After Lee surrendered, he committed suicide.

Ruffo, Fabrizio (fäbrē'tsēō ro͞of'fō), 1744–1827, Italian cardinal. Led royal Neapolitan army against PARTHENOPEAN REPUBLIC and obtained capitulation of Naples by promising full pardon (June, 1799). Admiral Nelson peremptorily revoked Ruffo's terms, had CARACCIOLO executed on his flagship, and permitted a general massacre of the rebels.

Rufinus (ro͞ofī'nùs), d. 395, Roman statesman. As minister to Theodosius I he made himself hated for his rapacity. After the accession of Arcadius he virtually ruled the Eastern Empire, but his ambitions led to his murder by Gothic mercenaries, perhaps on the instigation of Stilicho.

rug: see CARPET AND RUGS.

Rugby, urban district (pop. 45,418), Warwickshire, England. Important railroad junction and engineering center. Chiefly known as seat of great public school, Rugby School (1567). Became famous in 19th cent. under headmastership of Thomas Arnold. *Tom Brown's School Days* by Thomas Hughes deals with Rugby life. Rugby football originated here 1823.

rugby, game which originated (1823) on playing fields of Rugby in England. Has many characteristics of soccer and American football. Field about 160 yd. long, 75 yd. wide. Team consists of 15 men. No substitutions permitted.

Rügen (rü'gùn), Baltic island (358 sq. mi.; pop. 89,306), Pomerania, NE Germany; connected by a dam with Stralsund, on mainland. Agr., fishing; seaside resorts. Conquered by Denmark 1168; passed to Pomerania 1325, to Prussia 1815. Was incorporated with Russian-occupied Mecklenburg 1945.

Ruhr (ro͝or), river, 145 mi. long, NW Germany, a right (E) tributary of the Rhine, which it joins at Duisburg. Its lower course is the S limit of the **Ruhr** district (c.2,000 sq. mi.; pop. c.4,000,000) of North Rhine-Westphalia, one of the world's densest and most important industrial concentrations. Its huge anthracite basin provides coal for its own heavy industries (steel, machinery, chemicals) and for the industries of other countries. An almost continuous urbanized district, it comprises such cities as Essen, Dortmund, Gelsenkirchen, Bochum, and Duisburg and is linked by waterways with the ports of Rotterdam and Emden. After World War I the Ruhr dist. was occupied by French and Belgian troops (1923–25), on the ground that Germany had defaulted on reparations payment. Germany in turn stopped all payments; a passive resistance movement in the Ruhr led to severe reprisals by the occupation authorities. After Stresemann became chancellor (Aug., 1923), passive resistance ceased and Germany sought to fulfill its treaty obligations punctiliously. German acceptance of the Dawes Plan prepared the evacuation of the occupation forces. In World War II the Ruhr dist., being the chief arsenal of the Axis forces, was devastated by Allied air raids. Postwar reconstruction was spectacularly speedy. In 1949 an international authority for the Ruhr was set up, with hq. at Düsseldorf (members: Belgium, Federal Republic of [West] Germany, France, Great Britain, Luxembourg, Netherlands, U.S.). The economic interdependence of the Ruhr and the industries of neighboring countries—notably of Ruhr coal and Lorraine iron ore—was a basic factor in the establishment in 1952 of the European Coal and Steel Community (see Schuman Plan).

Ruisdael or **Ruysdael, Jacob van** (both: yä′kōp vän rois′däl), c.1628–1682, Dutch painter, most celebrated of the Dutch landscapists. His somber landscapes (usually with overcast skies) were painted from memory and imagination. Rembrandt's influence is seen in the impressive light effects of his mature work.

Ruiz, Juan (hwän′ ro͞oēth′), 1283?–1350?, Spanish poet, archpriest of Hita. Wrote *Libro de buen amor,* satire of medieval life.

rum, spirituous liquor distilled from molasses dissolved in the lees of a previous distillation, then fermented. Inferior rum is made in other ways. Deep brown color of some rums comes from long storage and addition of caramel.

Rumania (ro͞omā′nēŭ) or **Romania** (rōmā′nēŭ), republic (91,700 sq. mi.; pop. 15,872,624), SE Europe; cap. Bucharest. Bounded by the USSR, the Black Sea, Bulgaria, Yugoslavia, and Hungary, it is crossed by the Carpathians and the lower Danube. Its chief regions are low-lying Walachia, Moldavia, and N Dobruja; mountainous Transylvania and S Bukovina; and, geographically part of the Hungarian Plain, Crisana-Maramures (with Arad and Oradea) and the Banat of Timisoara. Chief cities: Bucharest, Cluj, Jassy, Timisoara. Ports: Galati, Constanta. Primarily agr., Rumania is a major producer of wheat and corn. Other products are timber, wine, fruit, processed foods. Sheep and cattle raising. Important petroleum industry in Ploesti area. Majority of population belongs to Orthodox Eastern Church. There are large Magyar and German minorities; also Jews, Roman Catholics, Protestants, Moslems. Corresponding, roughly, to the Roman province of Dacia, Rumania has retained its Latin tongue despite centuries of invasions and foreign rule. The history of Rumania before 1856 is that of the principalities of Moldavia and Walachia. The Congress of Paris (1856) gave these virtual independence under nominal Turkish overlordship. In 1861 they were united as the principality of Rumania under Alexander John Cuza (deposed 1866). Cuza's successor was Carol I. Rumania joined Russia in its war on Turkey (1877); obtained full independence at the Congress of Berlin (1878); and was proclaimed a kingdom in 1881. It won S Dobruja from Bulgaria in the second Balkan War (1913) and joined (1916) the Allies in World War I. The treaties of Saint-Germain (1919) and Trianon (1920) awarded it Transylvania, the E Banat, Crisana-Maramures, and Bukovina. Rumania's annexation of Bessarabia from Russia (1918) was never recognized by the USSR. To safeguard its acquisitions, Rumania entered the Little Entente (1921). Internal history is one of chronic violence, turmoil, and corruption. The wretched lot of the peasantry was somewhat improved by agrarian reforms after 1917, but inequality of wealth remained extreme. After World War I, electoral laws were constantly revised in favor of the party in power; in 1927 the death of King Ferdinand threw the succession in confusion (see Michael; Carol II). Violence increased in the 1930s with the rise of the Iron Guard. In 1938 Carol II assumed dictatorial powers, and in 1940 he joined the Axis as a neutral partner. Russian and German pressure forced Rumania to cede N Bukovina and Bessarabia to the USSR; S Dobruja to Bulgaria; and part of Transylvania and other border lands to Hungary (1940). Soon afterward, Ion Antonescu seized power, exiled Carol, restored Michael as king, and began his dictatorship (1940–44). Rumania declared war on the USSR (1941). By the Treaty of Paris of 1947 Rumania recovered its lost territories except N Bukovina, Bessarabia, and S Dobruja. A Communist-led government came into power in 1945, forced Michael to abdicate in 1947, and made Rumania a "people's republic" in 1948. Suppressing all opposition, it nationalized industries and resources (giving the USSR virtual control over its production).

Rumanian language, Romance language, belonging to Italic subfamily of Indo-European languages. See language (table).

Rumelia or **Roumelia** (both: ro͞omē′lēŭ), former administrative region of the Ottoman Empire, comprising most of S Balkan Peninsula; cap. Sofia (until 1878). The Congress of Berlin (1878) made N Bulgaria a principality under nominal Turkish overlordship; S Bulgaria, or **Eastern Rumelia,** became an autonomous province. In 1885 Bulgaria annexed Eastern Rumelia. Serbia, which also claimed the area, made war but was defeated (1886). Turkey tacitly consented to the annexation.

Rumford, Benjamin Thompson, Count, 1753–1814, American-British scientist and administrator. He was born in Mass. and went to England in 1776. Later he served the elector of Bavaria as administrator and in 1791 was created count of Holy Roman Empire.

His title was from town Rumford (later Concord), N.H., where his wife was born. He reorganized the army in Bavaria and introduced sociological reforms there and in England and Ireland. He made contributions to methods of heating, lighting, and cooking and introduced a scientific theory of heat.

Rumford, town (pop. 9,954), including Rumford village (pop. 7,888), W Maine, at Androscoggin R. falls and NW of Augusta. Paper mills. Winter sports.

Rumi, Jalal ed-Din (jŏŏläl′ ŏŏdēn′ rōō′mē), 1207–73, Persian poet. A major Sufist poet; his lyrics express mystic thought in finely wrought symbols.

rummy, card game played by two to six players with an ordinary deck. Variations include knock rummy, gin rummy (very popular in U.S. in early 1940s), contract rummy, continental rummy, and five-hundred rummy. Canasta (kŏŏnă′stŏŏ)[fr. Span.,= basket], another variation, is played with two decks of cards plus four jokers.

Rump Parliament: see PRIDE'S PURGE.

Rumsey, James (rŭm′zē), 1743–92, American inventor of a steamship tried out on the Potomac in 1787.

Rumson, resort borough (pop. 4,044), E N.J., near the Atlantic, S of Sandy Hook; estate and boating center.

Runcorn, urban district (pop. 23,933), Cheshire, England, on the Mersey, at terminus of Manchester Ship Canal and Bridgewater Canal. It is a tanning and mfg. subport of Manchester.

Rundstedt, Gerd von (gĕrt′ fŭn rōōnt′shtĕt), 1875–1953, German field marshal in World War II. Commanded German forces in West (1944–45). Defeated in Normandy campaign and in BATTLE OF THE BULGE, he was replaced by Kesselring.

Runeberg, Johan Ludvig (yōō′hän lŭd′vĭg rü′nŏŏbĕryŏŏ), 1804–77, Finnish national poet. His works include an epic, *The Elkhunters* (1832), and long romances based on Scandinavian legend and history, such as *King Ejalar* (1844) and *The Tales of Ensign Stal* (1848; from it the Finnish national anthem is taken). He wrote in Swedish.

runes (rōōnz), anc. Germanic alphabet, adapted to carving inscriptions on wood. Probably first used by East Goths (c.300) and suggested by a Greek cursive script. There were two alphabets, one of 16 signs, the other of 24 (the 16, plus 8). In historical times runes were used in England and Scandinavia, in parts of Sweden after the Middle Ages.

Runnymede or **Runnimede** (rŭ′nĭmēd), meadow near London, England. Either here or on near-by Charter Isl., King John accepted the Magna Carta in 1215.

Rupert, 1352–1410, German king and emperor-elect (1400–1410), elector palatine. Chosen to succeed the deposed Emperor WENCESLAUS, he never was able to impose his authority.

Rupert, Prince, 1619–82, son of Frederick the Winter King and Elizabeth of Bohemia; grandson of James I of England. After fighting for the Dutch in the Thirty Years War, he went to England (1641) to assist Charles I in the civil wars. He was successful until his defeat at Marston Moor (1644). Returning to England after the Restoration, he served Charles II as admiral in the Dutch Wars and took part in colonial schemes, notably in ventures of the Hudson's Bay Co.

Rupert, city (pop. 3,098), S Idaho, NE of Burley near Snake R., in Minidoka project.

Rupert, river of W Que., Canada, issuing from L. Mistassini and flowing 380 mi. W to James Bay.

Rupert House, village and oldest Hudson's Bay Co. fur-trading post, W Que., Canada, on Rupert R., E of its mouth on James Bay; founded 1668 as Fort Charles. Captured 1686 by French and alternately held by French and English to 1713.

Rupert's Land, Canadian territory held 1670–1869 by Hudson's Bay Co., named for Prince Rupert, company's first governor. Region comprised drainage basin of Hudson Bay. Land was transferred to Canada in 1869 for £300,000, but certain blocks of land were retained.

rupture: see HERNIA.

Rural Electrification Administration (REA), created in 1935 as independent U.S. bureau, reorganized 1939 as a division of Dept. of Agriculture. Its loan system provides farms with cheap electricity.

Rurik (rōō′rĭk), d. 879, reputed founder of Russia. Supposedly led a band of VARANGIANS who settled in Novgorod 862. His heirs ruled RUSSIA till 1598.

Ruse (rōō′sĕ), city (pop. 53,420), NE Bulgaria, on the Danube. Communications center. Mfg. of machinery, textiles, tobacco. It is noted for its mosques and ruins of medieval fortress.

Rush, Benjamin, 1745?–1813, American physician, signer of Declaration of Independence. Estab. first free dispensary in U.S. at Philadelphia (1786). Taught medical theory and practice at Univ. of Pennsylvania; made notable contributions to psychiatry. His son, **Richard Rush,** 1780–1859, was temporarily U.S. Secretary of State (1817), minister to Great Britain (1817–25). Helped negotiate RUSH-BAGOT CONVENTION. Obtained Smithson bequest for establishment of the Smithsonian Inst.

Rush, William, 1756–1833, American sculptor, whose wood carvings and clay models were famous in his day. His wooden statue of Washington is in Independence Hall, Philadelphia.

rush, name for various tall grasslike plants with hollow stems. The common or bog rush (*Juncus effusus*) grows in moist places and has been used for basketwork and mats. Others include the BULRUSH, wood rush (*Luzula*), Dutch or scouring rush (*Equisetum hyemale*), and sweet rush or flag (*Acorus calamus*).

Rush-Bagot Convention (băg′ŭt), 1817, agreement between U.S. and Great Britain concerning Canadian border. Consisted of exchange of notes by U.S. Acting Secretary of State Richard Rush and Charles Bagot, British minister in Washington. Provided for practical disarmament of U.S.-Canadian frontier. Set precedent for pacific settlement of all Anglo-American difficulties and inaugurated policy of strict peace between U.S. and Canada.

Rush Medical College: see ILLINOIS, UNIVERSITY OF.

Rushmore, Mount, SW S.Dak., in Mt. Rushmore Natl. Memorial (1,220.32 acres; estab. 1929, completed 1941) and in Black Hills. On it are carved Gutzon Borglum's huge busts of presidents Washington, Jefferson, Lincoln, and Theodore Roosevelt.

Rushville, city (pop. 6,761), E Ind., ESE of Indianapolis. Farm trade center with wood products.

Rusk, town (pop. 6,598), E Texas, E of Palestine. Center for truck, dairy, lumber, and oil area. Near by is a steel plant.

Ruskin, John, 1819–1900, English author and critic. Spurred by wealthy evangelical parents, he ardently studied painting and continued education at Oxford. His first work, *Modern Painters* (5 vols., 1843–60), begun as a defense of the painter J. M. W. Turner, developed the principle that art is based on national and individual integrity and morality. *The Seven Lamps of Architecture* (1849) and *The Stones of Venice* (1851–53) applied the same principle to architecture. After 1860 Ruskin turned increasingly to attacking economic and social evils and proposing reforms, in *Munera Pulveris* (1862–63), *Sesame and Lilies* (1865), *The Crown of Wild Olive* (1866), *Time and Tide* (1867), and *Fors Clavigera* (1871–84). Last work was autobiographical *Praeterita* (1885–89).

Russell, English noble family. First appeared prominently in reign of Henry VIII with rise of **John Russell,** 1st **earl of Bedford,** 1486?–1555, who helped to arrange marriage of Mary I to Philip II of Spain. He gained great wealth and lands that are still in the family. His son, **Francis Russell,** 2d **earl of Bedford,** c.1527–1585, was influential under Elizabeth. **Francis Russell,** 4th **earl of Bedford,** 1593–1641, was the most important opponent of Charles I in House of Lords. His son, **William Russell,** 5th **earl and** 1st **duke of Bedford,** 1613–1700, fought on alternate sides in civil war. His son, **Lord William Russell,** 1639–83, joined the opposition under Charles II. Was executed for supposed complicity in the RYE HOUSE PLOT. **John Russell,** 4th **duke of Bedford,** 1710–71, attacked Robert Walpole and succeeded him in government. His grandson, **Francis Russell,** 5th **duke of Bedford,** 1765–1802, by his criticism of Edmund Burke's pension, elicited Burke's *Letter to a Noble Lord* (1796). His nephew was **John Russell,** 1st **Earl Russell,** 1792–1878, a statesman. Gave name to the newly formed Liberal party. Supported Catholic Emancipation; helped introduce the Reform Bill of 1832. Twice prime minister (1846–52, 1865–66), he forced the resignation (1851) of Palmerston, his foreign secretary, for recognizing Louis Napoleon's coup d'état in France without authorization. As foreign secretary (1860–65) he advocated English neutrality during American Civil War and worked for liberation of Italy. His grandson, **Bertrand (Arthur William) Russell,** 3d **Earl Russell,** 1872–, is a philosopher and mathematician. With A. N. Whitehead he wrote *Principia Mathematica* (1910–13), a pioneer work in symbolic logic. A realist, his object has been to give philosophy a scientific basis. As social thinker he stresses creative activity of man, which he calls the principle of growth. Won Nobel Prize in Literature for 1950. The Bedford title is now held by **Hastings William Sackville Russell,** 12th **duke of Bedford,** 1888–.

Russell, Bertrand: see RUSSELL, family.

Russell, George William, pseud. **A. E.,** 1867–1935, Irish poet. An active nationalist, a famous conversationalist, and a convincing lecturer, he worked for agricultural cooperatives. He was a mystic and theosophist, and his poetry (as in *The Candle of Vision,* 1918; *Selected Poems,* 1935) is noted for religious tone and melody. Also known as a landscape painter.

Russell, Hastings William Sackville, 12th **duke of Bedford:** see RUSSELL, family.

Russell, Henry Norris, 1877–, American astronomer, propounder of theory of stellar evolution based on spectroscopic studies.

Russell, James Earl, 1864–1945, American educator. As professor of education and dean at Teachers Col., Columbia Univ. after 1897, he developed it into a leading professional college. He became dean emeritus in 1927, but taught until 1931. His son, **William Fletcher Russell,** 1890–, succeeded him as dean in 1927, becoming president in 1949.

Russell, John, dukes and earls of Bedford; Earl Russell: see RUSSELL, family.

Russell, Lillian, 1861–1922, American actress and singer, whose real name was Helen Louise Leonard. Famous for her beauty and talent in light opera.

Russell, William, 5th **earl and** 1st **duke of Bedford,** and **Lord William Russell:** see RUSSELL, family.

Russell, city (pop. 6,483), central Kansas, W of Salina near Smoky Hill R., in oil region.

Russell Sage College: see TROY, N.Y.

Russellville. 1 City (pop. 6,012), NW Ala., S of Florence, in cotton, grain, and iron area. **2** City (pop. 8,166), NW central Ark., near Arkansas R., in area yielding coal, natural gas, lumber, and farm products.

Russia, Rus. *Rossiya,* name commonly applied to the UNION OF SOVIET SOCIALIST REPUBLICS, of which Great Russia (see RUSSIAN SOVIET FEDERATED SOCIALIST REPUBLIC) is the chief constituent member. Historically—as used in this article—the term refers to the Russian state before the revolution of 1917.

Medieval Russia. From earliest times the steppes of S Russia and the Volga basin attracted invaders. The SCYTHIANS were replaced by the SARMATIANS (3d cent. B.C.), who in turn made way for the Goths, Huns, Avars, KHAZARS, and E BULGARS (3d cent. A.D.–8th cent. A.D.). By the 9th cent. the E SLAVS, ancestors of the Russians, were estab. in the W and were rapidly expanding. In the S, they were subject to the Khazar empire. The foundation of the Russian state is traditionally credited to RURIK, leader of a band of Scandinavian traders (see VARANGIANS), who estab. himself at NOVGOROD in 862. His successors united the E Slavs, freed them from Khazar rule, took KIEV (882).

Duke SVIATOSLAV crushed the Khazar empire and extended the borders of Kievan Russia to the Caucasus and the Balkans. VLADIMIR I estab. the Orthodox Eastern Church as state religion (c.989). The cultural tie with Byzantium and the civilizing and unifying influence of the Church kept medieval Russia alive despite its political disunity. In 1154 the Kievan empire broke up into several principalities, ruled by branches of the house of Rurik. Perpetual warfare among the princes and the raids of the CUMANS caused large-scale migration to the NE, where VLADIMIR became the new center. In 1237–40, the Mongols (commonly called TATARS) subjugated Russia, estab. the empire of the GOLDEN HORDE in the S and E, and forced the Russian princes to pay tribute. W Russia (incl. BELORUSSIA and the UKRAINE but not the merchant republics of Novgorod and Pskov) was absorbed by LITHUANIA. From the ruins of old Russia there rose in the 14th cent. a new powerful state, patterned in its autocratic organization on the Mongol model and destined to lead Russia on the road of empire. This was the grand duchy of Moscow, which under IVAN III shook off the Tatar yoke (1480) and under IVAN IV (the Terrible) controlled much of present European Russian and began to penetrate SIBERIA (1581). Ivan IV imposed his autocratic regime on all his conquests and changed his title from grand duke of Moscow to tsar of all Russia. With his son, Feodor I, the Rurik dynasty ended (1598). The reign of Boris GODUNOV (1598–1605) and the ensuing "Time of Troubles" was a turbulent period of false pretenders (see DMITRI) and of Polish invasion, but the election of Michael Romanov as tsar restored order in 1613. The march of conquest was resumed.

Growth of Empire. The Russian ambition to gain access to the sea and the weakening of Russia's principal neighbors—Poland, Sweden, Turkey, Persia—furthered the continuous expansion of Russia's frontiers, notably in the NORTHERN WAR (1700–1721); the RUSSO-TURKISH WARS of the 18th–19th cent.; the partitions of POLAND of 1772, 1793, and 1795; and the annexations of the CRIMEA (1783), FINLAND (1809), BESSARABIA (1812), and the Caucasus (Georgia, 1801; parts of Armenia and Azerbaijan, 1813, 1828; Circassia, 1829–64). Russian aggrandizement at the expense of Turkey created the EASTERN QUESTION and met the firm opposition of the Western Powers in the CRIMEAN WAR (1853–56) and at the Congress of BERLIN (1878). Russian colonists reached the Pacific Ocean by 1640 and went on to ALASKA in the 18th cent. Central Asia (i.e., the present Turkmen, Uzbek, Tadzhik, Kirghiz, and Kazakh SSRs) and the Far Eastern Territory were annexed in the mid-19th cent., but further expansion in Asia was checked by the RUSSO-JAPANESE WAR of 1904–5.

Rise and fall of autocracy. Russia in the 17th cent. was still a medieval, semi-Oriental state. In the 18th cent., particularly under PETER I and CATHERINE II, it was transformed into a European power. It was this enforced "Westernization" that brought absolutism to its peak. To make Russia a modern state, Peter had to crush the opposition of the nobles or boyars (on whom he foisted a new nobility of officers and civil servants) and of the Church, which he made subservient to the state. To compensate the nobles, he gave them increasing rights over their serfs. Serfdom began in Russia in the 15th cent. and reached its peak in 1785, when Catherine II gave the serfs the status of chattels. One third of the nation became enslaved to the landowning aristocracy. By shifting his cap. to St. Petersburg and taking the title emperor, Peter I emphasized the Western character of the new Russia. The mass of the people, however, were little touched by Westernization, whereas many of the nobles and the educated classes began to absorb European liberal ideals along with European customs. This trend became marked in the late 18th cent. The early liberalizm of ALEXANDER I and the patriotic fervor generated by the War of 1812 against NAPOLEON I offered an opportunity for reform, but after 1815 Alexander turned to a thoroughly reactionary policy, continued by NICHOLAS I. Alongside the liberal, constitutionalist opposition there rose groups of radical terrorists—nihilists, anarchists, and, ultimately, Marxists. ALEXANDER II, a liberal, abolished serfdom in 1861 (see EMANCIPATION, EDICT OF) but failed to create a landowning peasantry. His assassination (1881) by revolutionists opened a reign of terror under ALEXANDER III. Russia became a thorough police state. Under NICHOLAS II the Russo-Japanese War revealed the weakness of the régime and led to the RUSSIAN REVOLUTION of 1905. A parliamentary constitution was granted (see DUMA). The ministries of WITTE and STOLYPIN were marked by industrial expansion and land reform, but the régime as a whole quickly regained its authoritarian character. Its foreign policy, notably its support of Slavic nationalism in central Europe and the Balkans, brought Russia into conflict with Austria-Hungary and Germany, led to its alliance with France and England (see TRIPLE ALLIANCE AND TRIPLE ENTENTE), and eventually drew it into WORLD WAR I (1914). Russian reverses and economic suffering were both cause and occasion for the February Revolution of 1917, which overthrew the tsarist régime and which in turn was superseded by the Communist October Revolution (see RUSSIAN REVOLUTION). Though old Russia ceased to exist, its problems and trends were carried over into the new Soviet Russia. For a list of Russian rulers 1613–1917, see ROMANOV.

Russia Company: see MUSCOVY COMPANY.

Russian Church: see ORTHODOX EASTERN CHURCH.

Russian language, language of Slavic subfamily of Indo-European languages. See LANGUAGE (table).

Russian Revolution. For a brief sketch of conditions leading to the revolutions of 1905 and 1917, see RUSSIA. Discontent with tsarist autocracy was nearly universal—among the land-hungry peasantry, the new industrial proletariat, the lower ranks of the armed forces, the frustrated intelligentsia, the oppressed national and religious minorities, and a large segment of the bourgeoisie and aristocracy. Among opposition groups the most important were the moderate Constitutional Democrats, the Socialist Revolutionaries (mostly peasants and intelligentsia), and the Marxist Social Democrats (split into BOLSHEVISM AND MENSHEVISM). In 1905, as Russia was losing the RUSSO-JAPANESE WAR, discontent flared up in a series of strikes and mutinies, collectively known as the Revolution of 1905. Its only results were the granting of civil rights and the establishment of a parliament (see DUMA), but these concessions were soon curtailed by STOLYPIN. Russian reverses in World War I and the reactionary policy of NICHOLAS II brought the situation to a head in March, 1917 (in old-style calendar February; hence, "February Revolution"). The striking Petrograd workers seized the capital while the Duma defied Nicholas's order to dissolve and set up a provisional government under Prince Lvov. The emperor abdicated March 15. Lvov's decision to continue the war clashed with the Socialists' demand for immediate peace, propagated by workers', peasants', and soldiers' councils (see SOVIET) and particularly by the Bolsheviks under the leadership of LENIN. Though outnumbered by Socialist Revolutionaries and Mensheviks at the first all-Russian soviet congress (June, 1917), Lenin staged an unsuccessful uprising at Petrograd (July). Lvov resigned, and KERENSKY organized a moderate Socialist cabinet. Kerensky's vacillation and his unpopularity both with right and left enabled the Bolsheviks to seize power in Petrograd (Nov. 7, 1917; "October Revolution" according to old-style calendar). A council of people's commissars, headed by Lenin and approved by the second soviet congress, immediately decreed the abolition of private land ownership, set up a "dictatorship of the proletariat"—actually, of the Communist party, as the Bolsheviks came to be called—and began a reign of terror against all opposition. Peace negotiations led to the humiliating Treaty of BREST-LITOVSK (March, 1918). The Bolsheviks had extended their authority over Moscow and a large part of European Russia, but elsewhere they faced the resistance of the anti-Bolshevik parties, whose supporters ranged from Socialist Revolutionaries to tsarists. The resulting civil war lasted till 1920 and was complicated by foreign intervention. The main areas of warfare between "Reds" and "Whites" were: S Russia and the Caucasus, where KORNILOV, DENIKIN, and P. N. WRANGEL commanded, in turn, the White forces; the UKRAINE, where Germany, France, and Poland intervened; the N, where British, French, and U.S. forces held Murmansk and Archangel, 1918–19; the Baltic states, where a White army and German free corps battled the Reds; and Siberia, where KOLCHAK set up his government and where the Japanese held Vladivostok until 1922. The organizing genius of the Red Army was TROTSKY; its victory, however, was largely due to bad cooperation among the White Commanders. By the end of 1920 the last White troops evacuated the Crimea. Russia recognized the independence of Finland and the Baltic republics and made peace with Poland (see RIGA, TREATY OF) but recovered all other territories save Bessarabia. In 1922 the USSR was organized and the stringent "War Communism" was replaced by the NEW ECONOMIC POLICY, designed to put the starving, devastated country back on its feet.

Russian Soviet Federated Socialist Republic (RSFSR), chief constituent republic (6,533,600 sq. mi.; pop. c.111,000,000) of the USSR; cap. Moscow. Extending W-E from the Baltic Sea to the Pacific Ocean and N-S from the Arctic to the Black and Caspian seas and the Caucasus, Altai, and Sayan mts., it comprises 76% of the area and 58% of the population of the USSR. The Asiatic part of the RSFSR (4,922,800 sq. mi.; pop. c.19,500,000, excluding the URALS) is commonly known as Siberia. Although 74% of the population are Great Russians, there are many non-Slavic groups, 12 of which form autonomous republics—BASHKIR ASSR, BURYAT-MONGOL ASSR, CHUVASH ASSR, DAGESTAN, KABARDIAN ASSR, KOMI ASSR, MARI ASSR, MORDVINIAN ASSR, N OSSETIA, TATAR ASSR, UDMURT ASSR, YAKUT ASSR. Other large administrative divisions include ALTAI, KHABAROVSK, KRASNODAR, KRASNOYARSK, MARITIME, and STAVROPOL Territories. The RSFSR possesses the chief industrial and mining areas of the Soviet Union and exerts a dominant influence over Soviet life. For history, geography, and economy, see RUSSIA; SIBERIA; UNION OF SOVIET SOCIALIST REPUBLICS.

Russian wolfhound: see HOUND.

Russo-Japanese War, 1904–5, imperialistic conflict which grew out of rival designs of Russia and Japan on Manchuria and Korea. Russia had penetrated these areas and refused to negotiate with Japan for their division into spheres of influence. Without declaring war, Japan attacked Port Arthur and bottled up the Russian fleet. In 1905 the Japanese captured Port Arthur, defeated the Russians at Mukden, and destroyed a Russian fleet at Tsushima. Peace was made through the mediation of U.S. Pres. Theodore Roosevelt (see PORTSMOUTH, TREATY OF). The war helped bring on the Russian Revolution of 1905 and made Japan a world power.

Russo-Turkish Wars, 1696–1878, series of campaigns in which Russia expanded at the expense of the decaying Ottoman Empire. The Black Sea was Russia's original goal. Peter I took Azov in 1696 but lost it again in the Peace of the Pruth (1711; see NORTHERN WAR). In the war of 1736–39 Russia recaptured Azov and occupied Moldavia but had to give up its gains after its ally, Austria, made a separate peace. The Treaty of KUCHUK KAINARJI, which ended Catherine II's first Turkish war (1768–74), gave Russia a voice in Turkish affairs and prepared the annexation of CRIMEA and the S Ukraine (1783). This treaty and a secret plan for partitioning the Ottoman Empire between Russia and Austria alarmed the Western Powers and created the explosive EASTERN QUESTION. Catherine's second war (1787–92), ending with the Treaty of Jassy, gave Russia the SW Ukraine, with Odessa; the war of

1806–12 gave it BESSARABIA; the war of 1828–29, linked with the Greek War of Independence, brought Russian power in the Near East to a peak (see ADRIANOPLE, TREATY OF) and completed the conquest of the Caucasus. (The Persian parts of the Caucasus fell to Russia by the treaties of Gulistan, 1813, and Turkamanchai, 1828.) In the CRIMEAN WAR (1853–56) Turkey found allies in Britain and France. The Congress of PARIS (1856) was a severe setback for Russia, but another opportunity for extending Russian influence to the Balkan peninsula came with the anti-Turkish uprising in Bulgaria, Bosnia, and Hercegovina (1875). Serbia and Montenegro, on Russian instigation, joined the rebels, and in 1877 Russia and Rumania declared war on Turkey. The fall of PLEVNA was followed by the Treaty of SAN STEFANO (1878), which revised the map so drastically in favor of Russia and Bulgaria that the European powers called a conference to review its terms (see BERLIN, CONGRESS OF).

rust, name for various fungi which parasitize plants, forming brown or rusty patches of spores on the host. Some live entirely on one plant; others (e.g., cedar rust of juniper and apple and stem rust of wheat and barberry) require two or more different plants to complete their life cycles.

rusting of metals is essentially OXIDATION. Rust is formed by combination of metal with atmospheric oxygen; when iron is exposed to moist air, reddish brown substance forms on surface; this flakes off and process continues on new surface. For protection against rust, certain paints, layers of other metals, and oil are used.

Ruston, town (pop. 10,372), N La., E of Shreveport; estab. c.1884. Center of agr. and dairying area. Seat of Louisiana Polytechnic Inst.

rutabaga: see TURNIP.

Rutebeuf (rütbûf'), fl. 1254–85, French poet. Wrote an early miracle play, *Le Miracle de Théophile,* fabliaux, and satires.

Rutgers University, mainly at New Brunswick, N.J.; undenominational, with land-grant, state, and private support, for men and women. Chartered 1766 as Queens Col. by George III in response to petition of leaders of Dutch Reformed Church; opened 1771 as 8th colonial college. Name changed 1825 to honor Henry Rutgers (1745–1830), Revolutionary captain. In 1864 Rutgers Scientific School became State Col. for the Benefit of Agriculture and the Mechanic Arts; name changed to State Univ. of N.J. 1917. Entire institution became Rutgers Univ. 1924, and in 1945, State Univ. of New Jersey. A branch, New Jersey Col. for Women, estab. 1918. Univ. of Newark (chartered 1933) became Newark Colleges of Rutgers Univ. 1946.

Ruth, George Herman (Babe Ruth), 1895–1948, American baseball player. As left-handed Boston Red Sox pitcher (1914–19), he won 87, lost 44 games. Sold (1920) to N.Y. Yankees, where he became star outfielder. Set many slugging records, including most home runs in one season (60 in 1927), most home runs in major-league play (714).

Ruth, book of Old Testament. Story, one of most popular in Bible, tells of Ruth, a Moabite widow, who refused to desert her Jewish mother-in-law, Naomi. Together they returned to Naomi's home in Bethlehem. There Ruth married Boaz, a wealthy kinsman. Ruth and Boaz are ancestors of David.

Ruthenia (roothē'nēü) [Latin,= Russia], in medieval usage, Russia in general. In later usage, the term *Ruthenians* was used in the Austro-Hungarian Monarchy to designate the Ukrainian population of the NE Carpathians (i.e., in Poland, Hungary, and Bukovina). There was no difference between Ukrainians and Ruthenians except a religious distinction: the Eastern Orthodox Ruthenians outside Russia had entered into union with the Roman Church (1596 in Poland; 1649 in Hungary) and belonged to the Ruthenian Uniate Church of the Eastern Rite; in the Russian Ukraine, the Greek Orthodox Church was fully restored in the 17th cent. The Hungarian part of Ruthenia became in 1919 the easternmost province of Czechoslovakia (Carpathian Russia or Carpathian Ukraine, Czech *Podkarpatská Rus;* 4,890 sq. mi.; pop. c.900,000; cap. Uzhgorod). A thousand years of feudal exploitation had made it one of Europe's most backward areas. Annexed by Hungary 1939 and recovered by Czechoslovakia 1944, it was ceded to the USSR 1945. Along with SE Poland and N Bukovina, it was incorporated with the Ukrainian SSR. Under Soviet pressure the Uniate Church seceded from Rome and united with the Russian Orthodox Church.

ruthenium (roothē'nēüm), rare, gray-white metallic element (symbol = Ru; see also ELEMENT, table). Is in platinum group of metals and occurs chiefly in platinum ores.

Rutherford, Daniel (rŭ'dhûrfürd), 1749–1819, Scottish physician, botanist, and chemist; uncle of Sir Walter Scott. Discovered nitrogen (1772).

Rutherford, Ernest Rutherford, 1st **Baron,** 1871–1937, British physicist. Won 1908 Nobel Prize in chemistry for research in radioactivity. Contributed greatly to knowledge of structure of atom.

Rutherford, residential suburban borough (pop. 17,411), NE N.J., NE of Newark. Seat of Fairleigh Dickinson Col. (coed.; 1942). Dye works; mfg. of metal products, and asphalt.

Ruthven (rĭ'vün, rooth'vün), noble family of Scotland. **Patrick Ruthven,** 3d **lord of Ruthven,** 1520?–1566, was privy councilor to Mary Queen of Scots. Aided in murder of Rizzio, as did his son, **William Ruthven,** 4th **lord of Ruthven and** 1st **earl of Gowrie,** 1541?–1584. Beheaded for treason as head of confederated nobles who captured James VI in "raid of Ruthven" in 1582. His two sons, **John Ruthven,** 3d **earl of Gowrie and** 6th **lord of Ruthven,** 1578?–1600, and **Alexander Ruthven,** 1580?–1600, were killed for making an attempt on king's person in mysterious Gowrie conspiracy. Descended in collateral line, **Patrick Ruthven,** 1573?–1651, supported Charles I in Scotland and England. Was general in chief of royalist forces 1643–44.

rutile (roo'tēl), a mineral, one of three forms of titanium dioxide. Crystals are tetragonal.

Mineral typically brownish red, found in igneous rock.

Rutland or **Rutlandshire** (rŭt'lŭndshĭr), inland county (151 sq. mi.; pop. 20,510), central England; co. town Oakham. Smallest of English shires, it has rolling terrain devoted to agr.

Rutland, city (pop. 17,659), W Vt., N of Bennington and surrounded by separate Rutland town (pop. 1,416); settled 1770. Second-largest Vt. city, it is rail center with mfg. of metal products, tools, machinery, and scales. Marble no longer quarried here, though quarrying flourished after c.1845.

Rutlandshire, England: see RUTLAND, county.

Rutledge, Ann, 1813?–1835, American heroine of romantic story concerning Abraham Lincoln. Her sudden death grieved Lincoln deeply; from this one known fact W. H. Herndon wove story of Lincoln's alleged great love for the girl. Actually, Ann was engaged to Lincoln's friend, John McNamar.

Rutledge, John, 1739–1800, American jurist and statesman. Member of Continental Congress (1774–76, 1782–83). Associate Justice of U.S. Supreme Court (1789–91); nominated Chief Justice in 1795, but Senate refused to confirm appointment.

Rütli (rüt'lē) or **Grütli** (grüt'lē), meadow, Uri canton, Switzerland, on shore of L. of Lucerne. Here, according to legend of William TELL, representatives of Uri, Schwyz, and Unterwalden met 1307 to swear the **Rütli Oath,** on which Swiss freedom was founded. The 19th-cent. discovery of a written alliance of the cantons, dated Aug. 1, 1291, reduced historic importance of Rütli meeting.

Ruwenzori (rōō"wŭnzō'rē), mountain range, central Africa, on Uganda-Belgian Congo border. Highest peaks are Mt. Margherita (16,795 ft.) and Mt. Alexandra (16,750 ft.). The range may be the "Mountains of the Moon," supposed by the ancients to be the source of the Nile.

Ruxton, George Frederick, 1820–48, English traveler and author. His *Adventures in Mexico and the Rocky Mountains* (1847) and *Life in the Far West* (1849) are valuable works on the U.S. frontier.

Ruysbroeck, John, Dutch *Jan van Ruusbroec* (rois'brōōk), 1293–1381, Brabantine mystic, a Roman Catholic Augustinian monk. Wrote mystical treatises and also by his counsel aided such men as Tauler and Gerard Groote.

Ruysdael, Jacob van: see RUISDAEL, JACOB VAN.

Ruyter, Michiel Adriaanszoon de (mēkhēl' ä'drēänsōn" dŭ roi'tŭr), 1607–76, Dutch admiral. Served under Tromp in first of DUTCH WARS (1652–54). Captured English holdings on Gold and Guinea coasts in Second Dutch War (1664–67); saved Dutch fleet after defeat at North Foreland 1666; burned English ships in the Medway 1667. Led Dutch fleet with Tromp in Third Dutch War (1672–78), saving Dutch ports from attack 1672. Killed at Messina.

Ruzicka, Leopold (lā'ōpôlt rōō'tsĭkä), 1887–, Swiss chemist. Shared 1939 Nobel Prize for production of androsterone and testosterone from sterols.

RV, the Revised Version of the BIBLE.

Ryan, Loch (lŏkh rī'ŭn), long narrow inlet (9 mi. long; c.1½ mi. wide), Wigtownshire, Scotland, at S entrance to Firth of Clyde. Has good harbor.

Ryazan (ryŭzän'yŭ), city (pop. 95,358), central European RSFSR, on Oka R. Agr.-processing center. Became cap. of Ryazan principality when Mongols destroyed Old Ryazan (1237); was annexed by Moscow 1520. Has picturesque medieval churches and a kremlin wall (1209). In World War II German advance on Moscow was stopped just short of Ryazan.

Rybinsk, RSFSR: see SHCHERBAKOV.

Rydberg, Abraham Viktor (ä'brähäm vĭk'tôr rüd'bĕryŭ), 1828–95, Swedish philosopher, lyric poet, and novelist.

Ryder, Albert Pinkham, 1847–1917, American painter. Moonlight and the sea are predominant in his work. Was a recluse during much of his life.

Rye, municipal borough (pop. 4,511), Sussex East, England, near the Channel. One of towns added to CINQUE PORTS, it had good trade until sea receded in 19th cent. A resort of writers and artists. Henry James lived here for some years.

Rye. 1 Coast-resort town (pop. 1,982), SE N.H., S of Portsmouth; settled 1623 at Odiorne's Point. Includes Rye Beach village. **2** Residential and resort city (pop. 11,721), SE N.Y., on Long Isl. Sound SW of Port Chester.

rye, staple grain crop (*Secale cereale*), widely cultivated, especially in Central and N Europe. It can be grown profitably on soil too poor for wheat. Rye is grown for flour, for making whisky and gin, and for livestock feed. Is attacked by fungus ergot.

rye grass, short-lived perennial grass used for pasturage and temporary lawns. Italian rye grass (*Lolium multiflorum*) and English or perennial rye grass (*L. perenne*) are both grown in the U.S.

Rye House Plot, conspiracy (1683) to assassinate Charles II of England and his brother (later James II) on the London road by Rumbold's Rye House in Essex. They did not make the journey; the plot was revealed.

Ryerson, (Adolphus) Egerton, 1803–82, Canadian clergyman and educator. He attacked John Strachan on questions of clergy reserves and church control of education. A founder and first president (1841) of Victoria Col., Cobourg (later Victoria Univ.).

Rykov, Aleksey Ivanovich (ŭlyĭksyā' ēvä'nŭvĭch rē'kôf), 1881–1938, Russian revolutionist. A chief lieutenant of Lenin, after whose death he supported Stalin against Trotsky and became chairman of council of commissars (i.e., Soviet premier). Accused 1930 of "rightist deviation," he recanted (1931) but was implicated (1936) in party purge trials. Pleaded guilty and was executed.

Ryks Museum: see RIJKS MUSEUM.

Rymer, Thomas, 1641–1713, English critic and historiographer. A fanatically hostile critic of drama, he excoriated Shakspere's *Othello* in *A Short View of Tragedy* (1692). He began a compilation of many documents of England's international relations, 1101–1654, in *Foedera.*

Ryswick, Treaty of, 1697, ending War of the GRAND ALLIANCE; signed at Rijswijk (formerly Ryswick), near The Hague, Netherlands. France had to surrender most conquests made after 1679, except Strasbourg; Netherlands obtained commercial concessions; independence of Savoy was recognized; William III was acknowledged king of England.

Ryukyu Islands (rēo͝o'kyo͞o), archipelago (1,803 sq. mi.; pop. 759,683), extreme W Pacific, between Formosa and Kyushu, Japan. Chain extends 650 mi.; includes Amami Isls., Okinawa Isls., and Sakishima Isls. Sugar cane, pineapples, and bananas are grown. Group constituted ancient kingdom which became tributary to China in 14th cent. and also to Japan in 17th cent. Japan won full control 1874. Governed by U.S. since Aug., 1945.

S

S, chemical symbol of the element SULPHUR.

Sá, Mem de (mān' dů sä'), d. 1572, Portuguese colonial official, governor general of Brazil (1557?–1572). After driving French away from Guanabara Bay (1567), he estab. city of Rio de Janeiro there.

Saadi: see SADI.

Saadia ben Joseph al-Fayumi (sä'dēä, älfĭo͞o'mē), 892?–942, Jewish scholar, b. Egypt. Laid the foundation of Hebrew grammar in *Book of Language.* Wrote great philosophical work, *The Book of Beliefs and Opinions* (Eng. tr., 1948).

Saale (zä'lů), river, 265 mi. long, E central Germany, rising in NE Bavaria and flowing N through Thuringia and former Saxony-Anhalt to join the Elbe SE of Magdeburg. Also called Saxonian or Thuringian Saale, to distinguish it from the Franconian **Saale,** 84 mi. long, which flows SW from the Thuringian forest into the Main.

Saar, region: see SAAR TERRITORY.

Saar (zär), Fr. *Sarre,* river, 150 mi. long, rising in Vosges mts., E France, and flowing generally N to join the Moselle SW of Trier, Germany. Forms part of border between France and Saar Territory.

Saarbrücken (zär"brü'kůn), Fr. *Sarrebruck,* city (pop. 89,700), cap. of Saar Territory, on Saar R. Industrial center (steel, machinery). Was cap. of county of Saarbrücken (a dependency of Nassau) 1381–1793. Heavily damaged in World War II.

Saare (sä'rā), Estonian *Saaremaa,* Ger. and Swed. *Ösel,* Baltic island, 1,046 sq. mi., Estonia, across entrance to Gulf of Riga; chief town Kuressaare. Dairy farming; stock raising.

Saarinen, Eliel (ĕ'lēĕl sä'rĭnĕn), 1873–1950, Finnish architect and city planner, a noted exponent of the modern school. Settled 1923 in U.S.

Saar Territory, or **Saar,** Fr. *Sarre,* region (988 sq. mi.; pop. 904,040), W Europe, between Germany and France; cap. Saarbrücken. A hilly region, drained by the Saar R., it has important coal mines and is intensely industrialized (coal, steel). Population is German-speaking and mostly Catholic. The territory was created by the Treaty of Versailles (1919) from parts of the Rhenish Palatinate and the Prussian Rhine Prov. and was administered by France, under League of Nations supervision, pending a plebiscite to be held in 1935. France also received the right to exploit the Saar coal fields until that date. The 1935 plebiscite gave an overwhelming majority in favor of reunion with Germany, but after World War II (in which the region suffered much destruction) the territory was placed under French occupation and was again detached from Germany. It obtained an autonomous government and in 1948 entered into a customs union with France. In 1950 France obtained a 50-year lease on the Saar coal mines. German claims to the Saar are a serious factor in Franco-German relations.

Saavedra Lamas, Carlos (kär'lōs sävā'dhrä lä'mäs), 1880–, Argentine statesman. Promoted League of Nations; drew up anti-war pact (1932); helped to end war in Chaco. Received 1936 Nobel Peace Prize.

Saba: see SHEBA.

Sabaeans: see SHEBA.

Sabaoth (să'băōth, săbā'ůth) [Heb.,= armies], Hebrew term used in New Testament (Romans 9.29; James 5.4) and in Christian hymns (e.g., *Sanctus* and *Te Deum*) as a title of God. Translated in Old Testament as "Lord of Hosts" (Isa. 1.9).

Sabatier, Paul (pôl' säbätyā'), 1854–1941, French chemist. Shared 1912 Nobel Prize for method of hydrogenating organic compounds in presence of metallic catalysts.

Sabbatai Zevi (säbätī' zā'vē), 1626–76, Jewish mystic and self-proclaimed Messiah, founder of the Sabbatean sect. Embraced Islam when taken by Turks, 1666.

Sabbatarians, strict observers of Sunday as Sabbath (e.g., Lord's Day Alliance of the U.S.); also observers of Saturday as Sabbath, such as Seventh-Day Adventists and Seventh-Day Baptists.

Sabbath [Heb.,= repose], last day of the week (Saturday), observed as a holy day of rest by Jews since immemorial time. Early Christians observed the first day of the week in commemoration of the Resurrection, and Sunday became the Christian Sabbath, though some sects (e.g., Seventh-Day Baptists) have reverted to Saturday. Friday is the holy day in Islam.

Sabeans: see SHEBA.

Sabellius, fl. 215, Christian theologian. Went from N Africa to Rome where he taught a variety of MONARCHIANISM. Held the doctrine of the "economic Trinity" with God one indivisible substance appearing successively as Father, Son, and Holy Spirit. He was excommunicated (220). Term **Sabellianism** came later to be given to all sorts of speculative doctrines related to monarchianism.

Sabin, Joseph (să'bĭn), 1821–81, American bibliographer, b. England; compiler of *A Dictionary of Books Relating to America* (begun in 1868; after his death continued by others).

Sabine (să"bēn'), river rising in prairies NE of Dallas, Texas, and flowing E and SE across Texas, then turning S to form part of Texas-La. line. Broadens near mouth making Sabine L. (c.17 mi. long, 7 mi. wide), then through Sabine Pass to Gulf of Mexico. Passes Port Arthur and Orange. Sabine-Neches Canal leads to Beaumont.

Sabines (sā'bīnz), anc. people of central Italy, in Sabine Hills, NE of Rome. From the earliest days there was always a Sabine element in Rome (the legend of the womanless followers of Romulus abducting Sabine women is a fictional explanation of this). They warred with Rome, but by the 3d cent. B.C. were completely amalgamated with the Romans.

sable (sā'bul), carnivorous mammal (*Martes zibellina*) of N Eurasia. Fur is thick, usually brown or black mixed with gray or brown; is highly valued in fur trade. American sable is a marten.

Sable, Cape, S Fla., southernmost extremity of U.S. mainland.

Sable Island, 30 mi. long, 2 mi. wide, in the Atlantic off SE N.S., Canada, ESE of Halifax. Exposed part of extensive sand shoal, it is a major hazard to navigation. Has lighthouse, lifesaving station, and radio beacon.

Sacajawea (să"kújuwē'ú, sukä"–), **Sacagawea** (–gúwē'ú), or **Sakakawea** (–kúwē'ú), fl. 1804–6, Indian woman guide on LEWIS AND CLARK EXPEDITION. Generally called in English the Bird Woman.

Sac and Fox Indians, North American tribes of Algonquian linguistic stock. They were driven out of the Saginaw Bay region in the 17th cent. and settled in NE Wis. as allies. They were warlike, and the French by 1730 had practically exterminated the Fox tribe. The remnants amalgamated with the Sac and after defeating the Illinois moved into Ill. A fraudulent treaty of 1804 would have compelled them to move W of the Mississippi. They resisted but were finally induced to Iowa (1831). The next year they returned E of the river, and the BLACK HAWK WAR began. Defeated they moved W, finally settling on reservations in Iowa, Kansas, and Okla. Sac is also written Sauk.

saccharin (să'kurĭn), very sweet, white, crystalline coal-tar product prepared from toluene. Has no nutritive value, but its sodium salt used in sweetening food for those who cannot eat sugar.

Sacchetti, Franco (fräng'kō säk-kĕt'tē), c.1330–1400, Italian author of *Trecento novelle* (1388–95), an imitation of Boccaccio's *Decameron.*

Sacco-Vanzetti Case (să'kō-vănzĕ'tē), case involving trial and conviction (1921) of Nicola Sacco and Bartolomeo Vanzetti for murder and robbery at Braintree, Mass. Many believed conviction had been influenced by the men's reputation as radicals. After much evidence had been discredited but denial of a new trial upheld, public outcry forced review of case. Advisory group to governor upheld judicial procedure. Execution took place Aug. 22, 1927. The two men are widely regarded as martyrs.

Sacheverell, Henry (sushĕ'vurul), 1674?–1724, English clergyman. Tried for seditious libel for attacking the Whig government in sermons, he was convicted (1710) but given a light sentence. Case created a furore and humiliated the Whigs.

Sachs, Hans (häns' zäk'), 1494–1576, German MEISTERSINGER, leading poet of the school at Nuremberg; a shoemaker. A prodigious writer, he is best known for the poem *The Nightingale of Wittenberg,* the *Schwänke* or verse anecdotes, and his Shrovetide plays. Figures as a principal character in Wagner's opera *Die Meistersinger.*

Sac Indians: see SAC AND FOX INDIANS.

Sackets Harbor, village (pop. 1,247), N N.Y., at E end of L. Ontario W of Watertown; settled c.1801. Important naval base in War of 1812.

Sackville, Charles, 6th earl of Dorset, 1638–1706, English poet and courtier. Wrote witty epigrams, short pieces, and songs (notably *To All You Ladies Now at Land*).

Sackville, Thomas, 1st earl of Dorset, 1536–1608, English statesman and poet. Served under Elizabeth and James I. Author (with Thomas Norton) of *Gorboduc* (1562), considered earliest English tragedy.

Sackville, town (pop. 2,873), SE N.B., Canada, near head of Chignecto Bay and SE of Moncton. Surrounding Tantramar marshes were reclaimed by early French settlers. Seat of Mount Allison Univ. (United Church; coed.; 1858).

Sackville-West, V(ictoria Mary), 1892–, English poet and novelist; wife of Harold Nicolson. Poetry includes *The Land* (1926). Best-known novels are *The Edwardians* (1930) and *All Passion Spent* (1931).

Saco (sô'kō), city (pop. 10,324), SW Maine, at Saco R. falls opposite Biddeford; settled 1631. Mfg. of textiles, textile machinery, shoes. Seat of first legislative and judicial "court" in Maine (1640).

Saco, river rising in N central N.H. and flowing c.105 mi. SE, crossing SW Maine, to the Atlantic below Biddeford.

sacrament, in Christianity, one of certain ceremonial observances held to be instituted by Christ when on earth. Roman Catholics and the Orthodox have seven sacraments: the EUCHARIST, baptism, confirmation, penance (the forgiveness of sins), matrimony, order (see ORDERS, HOLY), and extreme unction (anointing of those in danger of death). They hold that these actually bestow grace. Protestants generally (though not universally) all accept the Eucharist and baptism and hold these to be merely symbols of grace.

Sacramento (săkrŭmĕn'tō), city (pop. 137,572), state cap. (since 1854), central Calif., at junction of Sacramento and American rivers; founded 1848 at settlement of New Helvetia (owned by J. A. SUTTER). Gold discovery in 1848 at near-by Sutter's Mill boomed colony to pop. of 10,000. City became terminus of first railroad in Calif. in 1856, W terminus of pony express in 1860, and terminus of first transcontinental railroad in 1869. Now a shipping and rail center for agr., lumbering, mining, and recreational area. Vegetable and fruit canneries, meat- and poultry-packing plants, sugar refineries, and metal products factories. Here are Sutter's Fort (1840; restored) and Crocker Art Gall.

Sacramento, river, 382 mi. long, rising in N Calif. near Mt. Shasta and flowing SW to Suisun Bay, a San Francisco Bay arm. Receives Pit, Feather, and American rivers. San Joaquin R. forms delta with it near its mouth. Navigable 256 mi. upstream at high water. Valley prospered with 1848 gold strike here. CENTRAL VALLEY project units in river include SHASTA DAM and Keswick Dam.

Sacré-Cœur (säkrā-kûr'), basilica in Paris, dedicated to the Sacred Heart of Jesus; famous landmark in Montmartre. Designed by Paul Labadie in Byzantine-Romanesque style, with a 267-ft. high bell tower. Built 1875–1914 by subscriptions as a votive offering after Franco-Prussian War; consecrated after World War I.

Sadducees (să'jŏŏsēz, să'dyŏŏ–), sect of Jews of the time of Jesus which accepted only the five books of the Law and rejected all it thought was not taught therein, e.g., immortality and the resurrection.

Sade, Donatien Alphonse François, comte de (dônäsyē' älfōs' frāswä kōt' dù säd'), 1740–1814, French author; known as the marquis de Sade. His scandalous conduct caused his imprisonment for many years in the Bastille. He took part in the French Revolution, later was confined in the insane asylum of Charenton. His novels, such as *Justine* (1791) and *Histoire de Juliette* (6 vols., 1797), are notorious for their obscenities but had great influence on later writers; their literary merit is still subject to controversy. Sade gave his name to the perversion known as sadism.

Sá de Miranda, Francisco de (frānsēsh'kō dù sä' dù mērän'dä), d. 1558, Portuguese writer. He introduced Italian Renaissance style in Portugal. His *Estrangeiros* and *Vilhalpandos* became models for classical drama. He also wrote in Spanish.

Sadi or **Saadi** (both: sä'dē), 1184–1291, Persian poet, a Sufi writer of great power. His masterpiece, *Gulistan* (1258), combines prose and poetry.

Sadowa (zädō'vä), Czech *Sadová* (sä'dôvä), village, E Bohemia, Czechoslovakia, near Hradec Kralove (Ger. *Königgrätz*). Austria suffered its decisive defeat here in Austro-Prussian War (1866).

Safarik, Pavel Josef, Czech *Šafařík* (pä'vĕl yô'zĕf shä'fär-zhēk), 1795–1861, Slovak antiquarian, scholar, critic, journalist. Author of *History of Slavic Language and Literature* (in German, 1826; free Eng. tr., 1850) and of *Slavonic Antiquities* (1837), a pioneering work in modern Slavonic studies.

saffron, name for the autumn-flowering white or lilac crocus (*Crocus sativus*), and for its dried stigmas also called saffron, long used for coloring, flavoring, perfume, and medicine.

Saffron Walden, municipal borough (pop. 6,825), Essex, England; agr. market. Named for saffron crocus, grown here 14th–18th cent.

saga (sä'gù), in Old Norse literature, epic in prose or verse centering about a legendary or historical figure. Composed in 11th–13th cent. Among them are the *Heimskringla* and the *Starlunga Saga* by Snorri Sturluson, the *Laxdæla,* the *Njala,* and the *Frithjof* by Esaias Tegner.

Sagan (zä'gän), Pol. *Żagán,* town (1939 pop. 22,770; 1946 pop. 4,359), Lower Silesia, on Bober R.; under Polish administration since 1945. Textile mfg. Was seat of a principality 1274–1472. Passed to Saxony 1472, to Austria 1547, to Prussia 1745. Wallenstein was created duke of Sagan 1628. Title was later held by French Talleyrand family.

Sagasta, Práxedes Mateo (präk'sādhās mätā'ō sägä'stä), 1825–1903, Spanish statesman. Founded Liberal party (1880). Was five times premier between 1871 and 1903. Unable to handle the situation in Cuba, he was generally blamed for the disastrous outcome of the Spanish-American War (1898).

Sage, Russell, 1816–1906, American financier. His wife, **Margaret Olivia Slocum Sage,** 1828–1918, undertook distribution of his fortune. Russell Sage Foundation, estab. 1907 in New York city, is concerned with improvement of social and living conditions in U.S.

sage, herb or shrub of genus *Salvia* of the mint family. Common in herb gardens is *Salvia officinalis,* with blue or white flowers and grayish aromatic foliage used as a seasoning. Clary salvia (*S. sclarea*), with pink flowers, is also planted in herb gardens. Some sages, especially the scarlet sage (*S. splendens*), are grown for ornament. Most sages are good honey plants.

sagebrush, deciduous shrub of genus *Artemisia,* abundant in W North America. Common sagebrush (*Artemisia tridentata*) has silvery gray leaves; it is important as forage on cattle ranges.

sage grouse, sage hen, sage cock, or **cock of the plains,** large grouse of W North America. Plumage is chiefly mottled brown, black and gray.

Saghalien: see SAKHALIN.

Sag Harbor, resort village (pop. 2,373), on E Long Isl., SE N.Y., on Gardiners Bay; settled 1720–30. Has Whalers' Church and Whalers' Mus. (commemorates 19th-cent. importance as whaling port), first customhouse in N.Y.

Saginaw, city (pop. 92,918), S Mich., on Saginaw R. and S of Bay City; settled c.1816. Here Lewis Cass arranged treaty with Indians (1819) which ceded much of Mich. to U.S. Lumbering followed fur trade but declined after 1890. In agr. area with coal, oil, and salt deposits. Mfg. of auto parts, machinery, graphite, and wood products.

Saginaw, river formed near Saginaw in S Mich. and flowing c.22 mi. NNE to Saginaw Bay near Bay City. With headstreams and tributaries, river drains large lower Mich. area.

Saginaw Bay, arm of L. Huron, c.60 mi. long, 15–25 mi. wide, N Mich. Bay City is at head, near mouth of Saginaw R.

Sagittarius (săjĭtâ'rēŭs) [Latin,= the archer], ninth sign of ZODIAC.

sago (sā'gō), edible starch extracted from pithlike center of several East Indian palms (chiefly of genus *Metroxylon*) or palmlike plants. It is an important item of food and is exported for use in puddings and in stiffening textiles. The wild sago or coontie yields Florida arrowroot.

Saguache (sŭwŏch'), town (pop. 1,024), S central Colo., in S foothills of Sawatch Mts.

Saguaro National Monument: see NATIONAL PARKS AND MONUMENTS (table).

Saguenay (să'gŭnā), river of S Que., Canada, issuing from L. St. John in two channels (Grande Décharge and Petite Décharge) and flowing 110 mi. ESE to St. Lawrence R. at Tadoussac. Navigable below Chicoutimi, it is major lumber-transport route. Hydroelectric developments on upper tributaries. Popular for steamer excursions and fishing.

Sagunto (sägōōn'tō), Latin *Saguntum,* city (pop. 10,352), E Spain, in Valencia, near Mediterranean. Was ally of Rome when its siege and capture by Carthaginians under Hannibal (219–218 B.C.) led to Second Punic War. Conquered by Rome 214 B.C. Has notable Roman remains (esp. theater).

Sahara (sŭhâ'rŭ) [Arabic,= desert], desert, N Africa; largest desert on earth. Generally defined as extending from the Atlantic to Red Sea and from the Mediterranean to the Sudan. ATLAS MOUNTAINS form N boundary. Area comprises high sand dunes, plateaus of denuded rock, and beds of gravel. Though mostly a low plateau, the Sahara is also marked by several volcanic masses (e.g., Ahaggar Mts. in Algeria) and by depressions (50–100 ft. below sea level), notably in N edge. Many of the date-bearing oases lie on the courses of intermittent streams. In ancient times the inhabitants of the Sahara were predominantly Sudanese Negroes. With introduction of the camel (probably in early Christian era), BERBERS and, later, Arabs became dominant in the area. Most of the Sahara was not penetrated by European explorers until 19th cent. René Caillié was one of earliest European explorers to cross the desert and return (c.1828). Today the Sahara is crossed by automobile and air routes; only a short N section of trans-Sahara railroad (contemplated since 1850s) has been completed.

Saigo, Takamori: see SATSUMA.

Saigon (sīgŏn'), city (pop. 110,577), cap. of Viet Nam, on Saigon R.; greatest port and industrial city of Indo-China. A beautiful modern city (built by the French) with parks and tree-lined avenues. Chief export is rice. Rice mills and shipyards. Merged with near-by city of Cholon in 1932.

sail, device for wind propulsion of a ship. Sails of papyrus were used c.6000 B.C. in Egypt, and sails of grass and fiber have been used in China since early days. Canvas made of flax was used for centuries, and the best sailcloth is made of long flax, but cotton has been used since the mid-19th cent. A ship may be square-rigged or fore-and-aft rigged or both. For names of sails, see *ill.*, p. 1109. Sail is designated by prefixing name of its mast (e.g., lower mizzen topsail). Reducing sail area is known as reefing; complete rolling up of sails is furling.

sailfish, marine game and food fish of tropical waters, related to swordfish. Body sometimes reaches 10 ft. in length; it has a saillike dorsal fin (blue spotted with black) and a spearlike upper jaw.

Saima (sī'mä), lake system of central Finland, comprising over 120 connecting lakes and covering c.1,700 sq. mi. It drains into L. Ladoga. Numerous canals facilitate steamship and lumber traffic to Gulf of Finland through the **Saima Canal** (c.36 mi. long, completed 1856), terminating at Vyborg, USSR.

Saint. Names of places beginning thus are written out in this book for alphabetization. Most of them in English form are commonly written with abbreviation St., those in French form with S.

Saint Albans (sŭnt ôl'bŭnz), municipal borough (pop. 44,106), Hertfordshire, England. Benedictine abbey (founded 793 to honor St. Alban and rebuilt 1077) is excellent example of Norman architecture. Scene of two battles in Wars of the Roses. Site of an Eleanor Cross (see ELEANOR OF CASTILE).

Saint Albans (sānt âl'bŭnz). **1** City (pop. 8,552), NW Vt., N of Burlington and surrounded by St. Albans town (pop. 1,908), on L. Champlain. Rail and mfg. center (metal, wood, paper products; processed foodstuffs). Smugglers' base after embargo of 1807. Scene of Confederate bank raid from Canada 1864. Fenians gathered here in 1866 to plan invasion of Canada. **2** City (pop. 9,870), W W.Va., at junction of Coal and Kanawha rivers and W of Charlestown. Mfg. of machine-shop products. Battle of Scary Creek fought near by, 1861.

Saint Andrews, town (pop. 1,458), SW N.B., Canada, on Passamaquoddy Bay; a golf and fishing resort.

Saint Andrews, burgh (pop. 9,459), Fifeshire, Scotland; summer resort. Has famous golf courses and rules for the game are estab. here. Univ. of St. Andrews (founded 1411) is oldest in Scotland.

Saint Anthony, city (pop. 2,695), E Idaho, on Henrys Fork and NE of Idaho Falls. Crystal Falls Cave and site of a fur-trading post (1810) are near.

Saint Anthony, Falls of: see MINNEAPOLIS, Minn.

Saint Augustine, city (pop. 13,555), NE Fla., on peninsula between Matanzas and San Sebastian rivers and separated from the Atlantic by Anastasia Isl. Shrimping and shipping center and resort. Oldest city in U.S., it was founded in Sept., 1565, by MENÉNDEZ DE AVILÉS on site of old Indian village near Ponce de León's landing place (1513). Burned and sacked by Sir Francis Drake in 1586 and by Capt. John Davis, 1665. Withstood attacks by South Carolinians in 1702–3 and by Oglethorpe, 1740. Passed to England in 1763, becoming a Tory refuge until 1783, when Spain reclaimed it. Ceded to U.S. 1821. Rapid growth checked by Seminole War. Held by Union troops from March, 1862, throughout Civil War. Here are Castillo de San Marcos (built 1672–1756; called Fort Marion after 1825), oldest masonry fort in U.S., and Fort Matanzas, built 1737 by Spanish near site of Menéndez's massacre of French Huguenots (for both, see NATIONAL PARKS AND MONUMENTS, table); old city gates (1804); old schoolhouse, the so-called "oldest house" in U.S. (possibly dating from late 1500s); slave market; and cathedral (1793–97; partly restored).

Saint Bartholomew's Day, massacre of, massacre of French Protestants which began in Paris, Aug. 24, 1572. The failure of an attempt (Aug. 22) on life of Adm. COLIGNY, plotted by Catherine de' Medici, led to plan for general massacre (many Protestants were in Paris for wedding of Henry of Navarre, later King HENRY IV). Coligny was the first victim. Involved with Catherine were duke of Anjou, later King Henry III; Henri, 3d duc de Guise; and King Charles IX. Massacre spread beyond Paris and resulted in resumption of Wars of RELIGION.

Saint Bernard, city (pop. 7,066), SW Ohio, suburb of Cincinnati. Mfg. of soap and fertilizer.

Saint Bernard (sānt' bûrnärd'), two Alpine passes. The **Great Saint Bernard,** 8,110 ft. high, links Val d'Aosta (Italy) with Rhone valley (Switzerland). Has famous hospice, founded c.982 by St. Bernard of Menthon. St. Bernard dogs are bred by the Augustinian friars. The **Little Saint Bernard,** 7,178 ft. high, connects Val d'Aosta with French Savoy.

Saint Bernard dog: see SHEEP DOGS.

Saint Bonaventure College and **Saint Bonaventure University:** see ALLEGANY, N.Y.

Saint Boniface (bŏ'nĭfās), city (pop. 26,342), SE Man., Canada, on Red R. opposite Winnipeg. Industrial center with oil refineries and paper, lumber and flour mills. Population largely French. Here is St. Boniface Col. (affiliated with Univ. of Manitoba). Has memorial to Vérendrye's explorations.

Saint-Brieuc (sē-brēû'), town (pop. 28,596), cap. of Côtes-du-Nord dept., NW France, on English Channel. Important in Breton history. Gothic cathedral.

Saint Catharines, city (pop. 37,984), S Ont., Canada, on Welland Ship Canal and S of Toronto; founded 1792 as Anglican mission. Resort and health center in fruit-growing region, with textile and paper milling.

Saint Catharine's College: see CAMBRIDGE UNIVERSITY.

Saint Charles. 1 City (pop. 6,709), NE Ill., W of Chicago and on Fox R. Residential and industrial center in farm area. **2** City (pop. 14,314), E Mo., on Missouri R. and NW of St. Louis. Settled 1769 by French traders, it was earliest permanent white settlement on the Missouri. Trading post and starting point westward on Boone's Lick Trail. Was state cap. to 1826. Now a farm center, with mfg. of metal products. Seat of Lindenwood Col. for Women.

Saint Christopher: see SAINT KITTS.

St. Clair, Arthur, 1734–1818, American general, b. Scotland. Fought in American Revolution; abandoned Ticonderoga to British in 1777. First governor (1787–1802) of Northwest Territory. Defeated by Indians under Little Turtle in 1791.

Saint Clair, borough (pop. 5,856), E Pa., N of Pottsville. Coal and textiles.

Saint Clair, Lake, c.27 mi. long, 24 mi. wide, between S Ontario and SE Mich. Joined to L. Erie by Detroit R. and to L. Huron by St. Clair R.

Saint Clair Shores, residential village (pop. 19,823), SE Mich., on L. St. Clair and NE of Detroit.

Saint-Cloud (sē-klōō'), town (pop. 17,101), Seine-et-Oise dept., N France, on Seine R.; W suburb of Paris. Palace (built 1572; destroyed by fire 1870) was scene of Napoleon's proclamation as emperor (1804).

Saint Cloud (sānt kloud'), city (pop. 28,410), central Minn., on the Mississippi and NW of Minneapolis, in farm area; settled 1852. Granite quarrying and finishing and mfg. of wood and metal products.

Saint Croix: see VIRGIN ISLANDS OF THE UNITED STATES.

Saint Croix (sānt kroi'). **1** River rising in the Chiputneticook Lakes on Maine-N.B. border and flowing 75 mi. S and E, past Calais, Maine, to Passamaquoddy Bay, forming international boundary. **2** River rising in N Wis. lake region and flowing 164 mi. SW, then S, through L. St. Croix to the Mississippi at Prescott, Wis. Forms part of Wis.-Minn. boundary.

Saint Croix Falls, village (pop. 1,065), NW Wis., on St. Croix R. Park has Old Man of the Dalles and other rock formations.

Saint-Cyr-l'École (sē-sēr'-lākôl'), town (pop. 4,288), Seine-et-Oise dept., France, near Versailles. Mme de Maintenon estab. here famous girls' school (1684). Building later housed Saint-Cyr military academy (estab. by Napoleon 1808; the "West Point" of France).

Saint David's, village, Pembrokeshire, Wales. Cathedral (12th cent.) is most famous one in Wales. Was for centuries one of most important places of pilgrimage in Great Britain. **St. David's Head,** NW of village, is most westerly point of Wales.

St. Denis, Ruth (sānt dĕ'nĭs), 1880–, American dancer, whose real name is Dennis. Founded Denishawn School with husband Ted Shawn. A dance pioneer, she has also trained many famous dancers.

Saint-Denis (sānt-dĕ'nĭs, Fr. sē-dŭnē'), town (pop. 68,595), Seine dept., N France; a N suburb of Paris. Metalworks; chemical plants. Town grew around a Benedictine abbey, founded 626 at tomb of St. Denis, patron saint of France, which played prominent part in French medieval history. Its basilica (12th–13th cent.) deeply influenced evolution of Gothic architecture. In it are tombs of the kings of France.

Saint-Dié (sē-dyā'), city (pop. 11,423), Vosges dept., E France, on Meurthe R. Grew around monastery founded in 7th cent. In 1944 re-

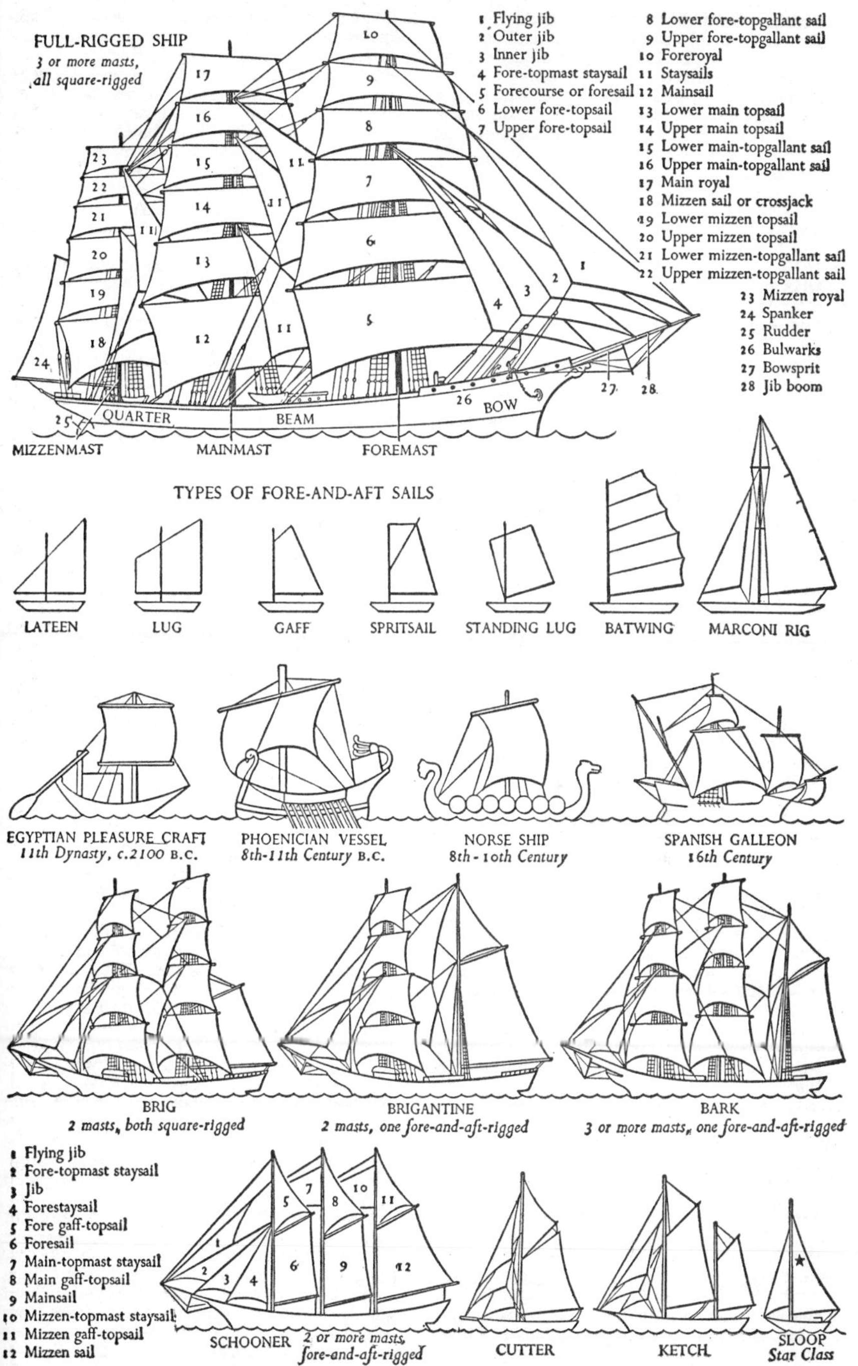
FULL-RIGGED SHIP
3 or more masts, all square-rigged
1 Flying jib
2 Outer jib
3 Inner jib
4 Fore-topmast staysail
5 Forecourse or foresail
6 Lower fore-topsail
7 Upper fore-topsail
8 Lower fore-topgallant sail
9 Upper fore-topgallant sail
10 Foreroyal
11 Staysails
12 Mainsail
13 Lower main topsail
14 Upper main topsail
15 Lower main-topgallant sail
16 Upper main-topgallant sail
17 Main royal
18 Mizzen sail or crossjack
19 Lower mizzen topsail
20 Upper mizzen topsail
21 Lower mizzen-topgallant sail
22 Upper mizzen-topgallant sail
23 Mizzen royal
24 Spanker
25 Rudder
26 Bulwarks
27 Bowsprit
28 Jib boom
QUARTER
BEAM
BOW
MIZZENMAST
MAINMAST
FOREMAST
TYPES OF FORE-AND-AFT SAILS
LATEEN
LUG
GAFF
SPRITSAIL
STANDING LUG
BATWING
MARCONI RIG
EGYPTIAN PLEASURE CRAFT
11th Dynasty, c.2100 B.C.
PHOENICIAN VESSEL
8th-11th Century B.C.
NORSE SHIP
8th - 10th Century
SPANISH GALLEON
16th Century
BRIG
2 masts, both square-rigged
BRIGANTINE
2 masts, one fore-and-aft-rigged
BARK
3 or more masts, one fore-and-aft-rigged
1 Flying jib
2 Fore-topmast staysail
3 Jib
4 Forestaysail
5 Fore gaff-topsail
6 Foresail
7 Main-topmast staysail
8 Main gaff-topsail
9 Mainsail
10 Mizzen-topmast staysail
11 Mizzen gaff-topsail
12 Mizzen sail
SCHOONER
2 or more masts, fore-and-aft-rigged
CUTTER
KETCH
SLOOP
Star Class

treating German troops destroyed most of the city, including cathedral and Gothic cloisters. Here in 1507 was printed the *Cosmographiae introductio,* first book to refer to newly discovered continent as America.

Sainte Agathe des Monts (sētägät″ dā mō′), town (pop. 5,169), S Que., Canada, on North R. and NW of Montreal. Health and ski resort.

Sainte Anne de Beaupré (sānt ăn′ dů bōprā′, Fr. sētän″), village and pilgrim resort (pop. 1,827), S Que., Canada, on St. Lawrence R. and NE of Quebec. Noted shrine here estab. 1620 by shipwrecked sailors. Chapel built 1658, church 1876; magnificently rebuilt after 1922 fire.

Sainte Anne de Bellevue (sētän″ dů bĕl′vü′), town (pop. 3,342), S Que., on Montreal isl. Has lumbering and publishing. In fur-trading days town was point of departure for canoes going west. Thomas Moore's "Canadian Boat Song" mentions it. Seat of Macdonald Col., a branch of McGill Univ.

Sainte-Beuve, Charles Augustin (shärl′ ōgüstē′ sēt-bûv′), 1804–69, French literary historian and critic. Much of his vast critical output is gathered under the title *Causeries du lundi* (1851–70; Eng. tr., *Monday Chats,* 1877). His *Port-Royal* (1840–60) places him among the greatest modern critics and cultural historians.

Sainte-Chapelle (sēt-shäpĕl′), former chapel, Paris, part of Palais de Justice. Built 1242–48 by order of Louis IX, it is one of purest jewels of medieval art. Magnificent stained glass windows, separated only by buttresses, form walls of the upper chapel (there is also a lower chapel and a spire).

Saint Edmund Hall: see OXFORD UNIVERSITY.

Sainte Genevieve (sănt jĕ′nůvēv), city (pop. 3,992), E Mo., on the Mississippi below St. Louis. Earliest permanent white settlement in Mo., it was founded before 1750 as French trading post.

Saint Elias, Mount (ĭlī′ůs), 18,008 ft. high, on Yukon-Alaska border in **St. Elias Mountains,** section of the Coast Ranges. Highest peak Mt. LOGAN.

Saint Elmo's fire, luminous electrical discharge into atmosphere from projecting or elevated object. Usually observed as brushlike, fiery jets. Occurs when atmosphere is charged and electrical potential strong enough to cause discharge is created between object and air.

Saintes (sēt), town (pop. 20,711), Charente-Maritime dept., W France, on Charente R.; historic cap. of Saintonge. Trade center for grain and spirits. Has well-preserved Roman remains.

Sainte Thérèse (sēt′ tārĕz′), town (pop. 7,038), S Que., Canada, WNW of Montreal. Mfg. of furniture.

Saint-Étienne (sētātyĕn′), industrial city (pop. 156,315), cap. of Loire dept., E central France, in a mining district (coal, iron). Produces steel, machinery, arms, textiles.

Saint-Évremond, Charles de (shärl′ dů sēt-āvrůmō′), 1616?–1703, French author and soldier. Was a political exile from France after 1659; buried in Westminster Abbey. His free-thinking skepticism is revealed in his *Comédie des académistes* and in his acute critical essays.

Saint Exupéry, Antoine de (ãtwän′ dů sēt-ĕgzüpārē′), 1900–1944, French author and aviator. *Night Flight* (1931; Eng. tr., 1932), *Wind, Sand, and Stars* (1939), and *Flight to Arras* (1942), all based on his own flying experiences, and the fantasy *The Little Prince* (1943) are works imbued with poetry, introspection, and deep thought. He was reported missing in action in 1944.

Saint Francis, river rising in SE Mo. hills and flowing c.470 mi. S through Ark. to join the Mississippi above Helena. Forms part of Ark.-Mo. line.

Saint Francis Indians, group of Abnaki Indians, attacked by Robert Rogers and his Rangers (1759).

Saint Francis Xavier University: see ANTIGONISH, N.S.

Saint Gall (sānt gôl′), Ger. *Sankt Gallen,* canton (777 sq. mi.; pop. 308,483), NE Switzerland. Largely mountainous, it borders on L. of Constance and on the Rhine and entirely surrounds Appenzell canton. Population is German-speaking. Has noted silk, cotton, and embroidery mfg., especially in its cap., **Saint Gall** (pop. 67,865). The early history of St. Gall is that of its former Benedictine abbey, which originated in a cell built c.614 by St. Gall, an Irish missionary and companion of St. Columban. An abbey from 8th cent., it became a major center of early medieval learning, where invaluable classic manuscripts were copied and preserved. Its abbots, who ruled present St. Gall and APPENZELL cantons, were made princes of Holy Roman empire in 1204. The town of St. Gall joined the Swiss Confederation in 1454, and in 1457 bought its freedom from the prince-abbot. While the territory ruled by the abbot remained Catholic, the town became Protestant—a source of civil strife until 1718. The abbey was secularized in 1798 and its domains, together with the town, became a canton in 1803. The present abbey buildings date from the 18th cent.; former abbey church became cathedral in 1846. Library has important medieval manuscripts.

Saint-Gaudens, Augustus (sānt-gô′dünz), 1848–1907, foremost American sculptor of his time, b. Dublin, Ireland. Best known for public monuments (e.g., statue of Gen. Sherman at entrance to Central Park, New York). Also created portrait plaques and low reliefs. His brother, **Louis Saint-Gaudens,** 1854–1913, was also a sculptor.

Saint George, town (pop. c.1,500), on St. George's isl., Bermuda; cap. of Bermuda until Hamilton was selected in 1815.

Saint George, city (pop. 4,562), extreme SW Utah, in Virgin R. valley. Former cotton center, now tourist center. Has Mormon temple and tabernacle.

Saint George's, town (pop. 5,772), cap. of Grenada, British West Indies; administrative hq. of Grenada and Windward Isls. colony.

Saint George's Channel, sea arm, c.100 mi. long and 50–95 mi. wide, linking the Atlantic and the Irish Sea. It separates SE Ireland from Wales.

Saint-Germain, Treaty of (sē-zhĕrmē′). Several treaties were signed at Saint-Germain-en-Laye, France. Treaty of **1570** ended first phase of Wars of RELIGION. Treaty of **1679,** between France and Brandenburg at end of Third Dutch War, forced Elector Frederick William to restore most of his conquests to Sweden. Treaty of **1919,** between Austria and Allies of World War I, dissolved Austro-Hungarian Monarchy; reduced AUSTRIA to its present size; awarded the rest of the former Austrian Empire to the new states of Poland, Czechoslovakia, and Yugoslavia (whose independence was recognized) and to Italy and Rumania; prohibited political or economic union of Austria with Germany (see ANSCHLUSS). The U.S. did not ratify the treaty because it contained the Covenant of the League of Nations.

Saint-Germain-des-Prés (sē-zhĕrmē″-dā-prā′), historic abbey and church of Paris, founded 6th cent. Present Romanesque church dates from early 11th cent. Only ruins of once powerful abbey remain (it was destroyed in French Revolution), but 16th-cent. Renaissance palace of abbots stands near by.

Saint-Germain-en-Laye (sē-zhĕrmē″nā-lā′), town (pop. 20,028), Seine-et-Oise dept., N France; a W suburb of Paris. Renaissance château (now museum) was chief royal residence from Francis I to Louis XIII; birthplace of Louis XIV.

Saint Gotthard (sānt gŏ′thůrd), Alpine group, S central Switzerland, crossed by the **Saint Gotthard Pass,** 6,929 feet high, used since 13th cent. Road was built 1820–30. The **Saint Gotthard Tunnel** (length 9.3 mi.; maximum alt. 3,786 ft.) was constructed 1872–80 and is used by St. Gotthard RR., which links N and S Switzerland.

Saint Helena (hůlē′nů), British island (47 sq. mi.; pop. 4,748), in the Atlantic, 1,200 mi. W of Africa; cap. Jamestown. A British crown colony since 1834, it now includes Ascension and Tristan da Cunha. Best known as place of Napoleon's exile 1815–21.

Saint Helena Island (sānt hĕ′lůnů), c.15 mi. long, 3–5 mi. wide, S S.C., between St. Helena and Port Royal sounds, one of largest SEA ISLANDS. Discovered early 16th cent. by Spanish. Inhabited by Negro descendants of sea-island plantation slaves. Gullah (Sea Island Negro dialect) spoken. Farming.

Saint Helens, county borough (pop. 110,276), Lancashire, England. Center of glass mfg. in England, it also has iron and copper foundries, chemical and soap factories, and potteries.

Saint Helier (sānt hĕl′yůr), town (pop. 25,-360), cap. of Jersey, Channel Isls. Resort and export point of local produce. Scene of a battle (1781) when the French tried unsuccessfully to regain Jersey. Victoria Col. was founded in 1852.

Saint Hilda's College: see OXFORD UNIVERSITY.

Saint Hugh's College: see OXFORD UNIVERSITY.

Saint Hyacinthe (sānt hī′ůsĭnth, Fr. sĕtyäsĕt′), city (pop. 20,236), S Que., Canada, on Yamaska R. and ENE of Montreal. Hosiery and textile mills.

Saint Ignace (sānt′ ĭg′nůs), resort city (pop. 2,946), E Upper Peninsula, N Mich., on Straits of Mackinac. Here are early French fort (restored 1938), and grave of Père Marquette.

Saint Ives (sůnt īvz′), municipal borough (pop. 9,037), Cornwall, England, on St. Ives Bay. Fishing town and resort, it has a noted artists' colony.

Saint James's Palace, in London, on St. James's St. and fronting on Pall Mall. Henry VIII built palace and park about it. Royal residence from 1697 until Victoria's time, it is now occasionally used. British court is still called the Court of St. James's.

Saint Jean, Que.: see SAINT JOHNS.

Saint-Jean-de-Luz (sē-zhā″-dů-lüz′), town (pop. 8,848), Basses-Pyrénées dept., SW France. Fishing port and beach resort on Bay of Biscay.

Saint Jérôme (sē zhārōm′), city (pop. 17,685), S Que., Canada, on North R. and NW of Montreal. Mfg. center with woolen and paper mills. Scene of annual passion play.

St. John, Henry, Viscount Bolingbroke (sĭn′-jůn, bŏ′lĭngbrŏŏk), 1678–1751, English statesman. As Tory secretary of state (1710–14) under Robert HARLEY he intrigued to end unpopular War of Spanish Succession and tried to weaken Whigs by laws against dissenters. Gradually supplanted Harley, who was dismissed (1714). For intriguing with the Old Pretender he was dismissed by George I and attainted by Parliament after flight to France. Helped plan Jacobite rising of 1715. After leaving Jacobite cause he was pardoned (1723). Organized opposition to Robert Walpole. A lucid writer and great orator, he reflected low moral standard of politics in his time. Friend of Pope and of Voltaire.

Saint John, city (pop. 50,779), S N.B., Canada, at mouth of St. John R. on Bay of Fundy. Major year-round port with extensive shipping connections. Provincial center with important fishing industry and mfg. of cotton goods, sugar, pulpwood and metal products. Fort estab. here 1631–35. Contested by French and British until British control estab. 1758. United Empire Loyalists built settlement (called Parr Town) here 1783; renamed 1785. Much of old city destroyed by fire 1877.

Saint John, Virgin Islands: see VIRGIN ISLANDS OF THE UNITED STATES.

Saint John, river, c.400 mi. long, rising in N Maine and flowing NE to N.B., then SE below Edmundston to Bay of Fundy at St. John. Forms Maine-N.B. line for 75 mi. At Grand Falls drops 75 ft. in great cataract, soon drops 50 ft. more in rapids through mile-long gorge. At mouth, within St. John city, are Reversing Falls Rapids, caused by Bay of Fundy tides which force river to reverse flow at high tide. River discovered by Champlain and Monts on St. John the Baptist's Day 1604. Navigable to Fredericton for vessels of 120 tons.

Saint John, Lake, area 375 sq. mi., S Que., Canada, NNW of Quebec, drained by Saguenay R.

Saint John of Jerusalem, Knights of: see KNIGHTS HOSPITALERS.

Saint John's, town (pop. 10,965), cap. of Leeward Isls. colony and Antigua presidency, British West Indies, port on Antigua isl.

Saint John's, city (pop. 52,873), provincial cap., SE N.F., Canada, on NE coast of Avalon Peninsula; estab. early 16th cent.

Center of provincial life, with shipping connections with U.S., Canada, and Great Britain and rail connections with W coast of island. Base of fishing fleet with many industries connected with fishing. Control fluctuated between French and British until British authority was estab. 1763. Naval base in Revolution and War of 1812. Here Marconi heard first transatlantic wireless message 1901, and from here first nonstop transatlantic flight was made 1919. In World War II U.S. army and naval base and Canadian air base were estab. N of city.

Saint Johns or **Saint Jean** (sē zhã'), city (pop. 19,305), S Que., Canada, on Richelieu R. and SE of Montreal. Silk, paper, and hosiery mills. Fort built here 1666, rebuilt 1749, was captured by American forces 1775, and retaken by British and used as supply base. Terminal of first railroad from Laprairie 1836.

Saint Johns, river rising in swamps of SE Fla. Flows c.300 mi. N, forming eight lakes, and turns E at Jacksonville to enter the Atlantic 28 mi. away. Receives many streams, notably the Oklawaha. Navigable for 200 mi.

St.-John's-bread: see CAROB.

Saint Johnsbury, town (pop. 9,292), including St. Johnsbury village (7,370), NE Vt., NE of Montpelier; settled 1786. Has famous maple-sugar industry. Mfg. of scales and farm implements; granite works. Platform scales invented here. Seat of St. Johnsbury Acad. (1842).

Saint John's College: see CAMBRIDGE UNIVERSITY; OXFORD UNIVERSITY.

Saint John's College: see ANNAPOLIS, Md.

Saint John's University: see BROOKLYN, N.Y.

Saint John's Wood, residential district of NW London, England. Many artists have lived here. Lord's Cricket Ground is hq. of Marylebone Cricket Club, authority for rules of the game.

Saint-John's-wort, widely distributed herbaceous or woody plant of genus *Hypericum,* usually with yellow flowers. Common European St.-John's-wort (*Hypericum perforatum*) is naturalized in North America.

Saint John the Divine, Cathedral of, New York city. Charter for building was granted 1873 to Episcopal diocese. Building began 1892, and crypt was opened for worship 1899. Entire length of cathedral was opened 1941. In 1911 plans were changed from Romanesque to Gothic, with adoption of design by Ralph Adams Cram.

Saint Joseph. 1 City (pop. 10,223), SW Mich., on L. Michigan at mouth of St. Joseph R. opposite BENTON HARBOR; settled permanently c.1830 on site of Fort Miami (built 1679 by LA SALLE). Resort and port, it is trade center for fruit growing region with metal products. **2** City (pop. 78,588), NW Mo., on bluffs above the Missouri and NNW of Kansas City; laid out c.1843 on site of trading post (1826). Was E terminus of pony express from 1860. Now a huge livestock and grain market, it has meat-packing and grain-processing plants and railroad shops. The home of Jesse James is here.

Saint Joseph, river rising near Hillsdale, Mich., and flowing c.210 mi. W, past South Bend, Ind., to L. Michigan between St. Joseph and Benton Harbor, Mich. Important route for Indians and early travelers.

Saint Joseph d'Alma (sē zhôzĕf" dälmä'), town (pop. 7,975), S Que., Canada, on Saguenay R. and WNW of Chicoutimi. Wool carding and lumbering.

Saint Jovite (sē zhôvēt'), village (pop. 1,453), S Que.; a skiing resort in the Laurentians.

Saint-Just, Louis de (lwē' dů sē-zhüst'), 1767–94, French revolutionist, known as the "archangel of the Revolution." During the REIGN OF TERROR (1793–94) he and Couthon were the chief aides of Robespierre. He believed fanatically in the possibility of a perfect state, based on Spartan virtue. He fell with Robespierre on 9 THERMIDOR and was guillotined the next day.

Saint Kitts or **Saint Christopher,** island (68 sq. mi.; pop. 28,818), British West Indies, in Leeward Isls. With Nevis and smaller islands makes up St. Kitts–Nevis presidency; cap. BASSETERRE. Discovered by Columbus (1492); long disputed by British and French; awarded to Great Britain (1713).

Saint Lambert, residential city (pop. 8,615), S Que., Canada, on St. Lawrence R. opposite Montreal.

St. Laurent, Louis Stephen (sē lôrã'), 1882–, Canadian prime minister (1948–).

Saint Laurent (sē lôrã'), town (pop. 20,426), S Que., Canada, on Montreal isl., W suburb of Montreal.

Saint Lawrence, a principal river of North America, linking Great Lakes to Gulf of St. Lawrence to form waterway c.2,350 mi. long from W end of L. Superior to the Atlantic. River proper issues from NE end of L. Ontario and flows 774 mi. NE to its mouth (c.90 mi. wide), N of Cape Gaspé. Tidal below Quebec city. Forms c.114 mi. of international boundary between N.Y. and Ont. Between Kingston and Brockville, Ont., are scenic Thousand Isls. L. St. Francis, L. St. Louis, L. St. Peter are widened sections. Montreal is head of ocean-going navigation, but canals make entire river navigable by smaller vessels. Important source of hydroelectric power. A S tributary is Richelieu R. (link to L. Champlain and Hudson R.). GREAT LAKES-SAINT LAWRENCE SEAWAY AND POWER PROJECT has long been discussed. River visited by Jacques CARTIER 1534–35. River system long used by explorers, fur traders, and missionaries. Valley taken by British from French 1763. River became international boundary 1783.

Saint Lawrence, Gulf of, large bay of the Atlantic, SE Canada, at mouth of St. Lawrence R. between N.S. (S), Newfoundland (E), Que. (N), and N.B. and Gaspé Peninsula (W). Chaleur Bay is W inlet. Strait of Belle Isle, Cabot Strait, and Strait of Canso lead to the Atlantic. Ice-free mid-April to early Dec., it has important fishing grounds, especially cod.

Saint Lawrence Island, 90 mi. long, 8–22 mi. wide, off W Alaska, in Bering Sea. Barren and snow-covered. Natives engage in whaling, fox trapping. Discovered 1728 by Vitus Bering. Primitive Eskimo culture interests anthropologists.

Saint Lawrence Islands National Park, 189.4 acres, S Ont., Canada, in the THOUSAND

ISLANDS; estab. 1914. Contains 13 Canadian islands and some adjacent mainland.

Saint Lawrence University: see CANTON, N.Y.

St. Leger, Barry (sĭl'ŭnjŭr, sānt" lĕj'ŭr), 1737–89, British officer in American Revolution. Laid siege to Fort Stanwix in SARATOGA CAMPAIGN.

Saint-Lô (sē-lō'), town (pop. 5,190), cap. of Manche dept., NW France, in Normandy. It was partially destroyed in 1944, when its capture by U.S. troops (July 18) cut off German forces under Rommel.

Saint Louis (sānt lōō'ĭs), city (pop. 856,796), E Mo., largest city in state and eighth largest in U.S., on W bank of the Mississippi below mouth of the Missouri. Post chosen and built by Pierre LACLEDE and R. A. CHOUTEAU, 1763–64. Transferred to Spain 1770 and later returned to France, it was acquired by U.S. in LOUISIANA PURCHASE. Mainly French into 19th cent., it received Germans after 1850. Gateway to the Missouri and West for fur traders and explorers. Became great river port after W migration following War of 1812. Union base in Civil War, it had industrial expansion after that war. Great traffic handler, it is a livestock, agr., fur, and lumber market, and a financial and cultural center. Has food processing, brewing, distilling, and mfg. of chemicals, apparel, transportation equipment, and metal, oil, wood, and coal products. Here are SAINT LOUIS UNIVERSITY, WASHINGTON UNIVERSITY, and Jefferson Natl. Expansion Memorial (historic buildings). Near by is Jefferson Barracks, military base.

Saint Louis Park, village (pop. 22,644), E Minn., SW suburb of Minneapolis; settled 1853. Produces ice cream and tools.

Saint Louis University, mainly at St. Louis, Mo.; R.C. (Jesuit), for men and women; opened 1818, oldest college W of the Mississippi, chartered as a university 1832. Includes University Col.; Webster Col. (at WEBSTER GROVES); Parks Col. of Aeronautical Technology (at East St. Louis, Ill.); and Inst. of Geophysical Technology.

Saint Lucia (sānt lōō'shŭ), island (233 sq. mi.; pop. 70,113), British West Indies, part of Windward Isls.; cap. CASTRIES. British attempts to settle it in early 17th cent. met with fierce resistance from Carib Indians. French and British contested ownership until 1803, when British gained control. U.S. obtained 99-year lease for naval base here (1940).

Saint-Malo (sē-mälō'), town (pop. 10,873), Ille-et-Vilaine dept., NW France, built 9th cent. on a rocky promontory in English Channel. Its prosperity as a port dates from 16th cent. Famed old ramparts, Gothic and Renaissance cathedral, and 17th-cent. houses here were damaged in World War II, particularly in 11-day siege of the citadel constructed by the Germans on a harbor island (Aug., 1944).

Saint Mark's Church, Venice. Originally a Romanesque church, built in 9th cent. and destroyed by fire in 976. Rebuilt c.1071 with help of Byzantine architects. Façade received Gothic additions in 15th cent. Its plan is a Greek cross, with a dome over the center and one over each arm of the cross; each dome is covered with mosaics on a golden background. Over the main entrance are the Four Horses of St. Mark's in gilded bronze. Originally in Rome, they were moved to Constantinople, Venice, and Paris (by Napoleon in 1797); in 1815 they were returned to Venice by Francis I of Austria.

Saint Martin, island (33 sq. mi.), West Indies, in Leeward Isls. Divided since 1648 between Dutch in S part (pop. 1,600) and French in N (pop. 6,786).

Saint Martin's-in-the-Fields, church in London, on Trafalgar Square. Built 1722–26, it has a Corinthian portico and elaborate spire. Crypt is open all night for use of homeless.

Saint Martinville, historic town (pop. 4,614), S La., on Bayou Teche; first settled c.1760 by French. Conflicting French groups came (royalists, republicans, Acadians); also Spanish. Quiet French town today. Alleged site of Evangeline romance, it has Longfellow-Evangeline state park.

Saint Marylebone, London: see MARYLEBONE, SAINT.

Saint Marys. 1 City (pop. 1,201), NE Kansas, on Kansas R. and WNW of Topeka; laid out 1866. One of oldest Kansas towns, it was site (1847–48) of Catholic mission to Potawatami Indians. **2** City (pop. 6,208), W Ohio, on St. Marys R. and SW of Lima. Trade center for Grand L. resort area. **3** Borough (pop. 7,846), NW Pa., on Elk Creek and E of Ridgway. Mfg. of carbon and clay products and electrical equipment.

Saint Marys. 1 River rising in Okefenokee Swamp, SE Ga., and flowing with south bend 175 mi. E to Cumberland Sound, arm of the Atlantic. Forms part of Ga.-Fla. line. **2** River, c.63 mi. long, flowing SE from L. Superior to L. Huron and forming part of international boundary. On river are cities of Sault Ste Marie, Mich. and Ont.; canals with five locks bypass falls here.

Saint Mary's City, first town settled (1634) in Md., on St. Mary's R., S Md. Leonard Calvert's colonists built Fort St. George on site of Indian village. Was provincial cap. 1676–94.

Saint Mary's College: see OAKLAND, Calif.; SOUTH BEND, Ind.

Saint Mary's Loch (lŏkh), lake, Selkirkshire, Scotland. Sir Walter Scott celebrates its beauty.

Saint Maurice (Fr. sē môrēs'), river, S Que., Canada, rising in Laurentian Mts. and flowing 325 mi. SE and S to St. Lawrence R. at Trois Rivières.

Saint Michaels, resort town (pop. 1,470), Eastern Shore, Md., NNW of Cambridge. Oyster-dredging center. Historic house (c.1670) still stands.

Saint Michel (sē mēshĕl') or **Cote Saint Michel** (kōt'), town (pop. 10,539), S Que., Canada, on Montreal isl., N suburb of Montreal.

Saint Michel, Mont: see MONT-SAINT-MICHEL.

Saint-Mihiel (sē-mēēl'), town (pop. 4,134), Meuse dept., NE France, on the Meuse. Captured 1914 by Germans, recovered 1918 in one of most important American actions of the war. Gothic Church of St. Étienne contains sculptures by Ligier Richier.

Saint Moritz (sānt mô'rĭts), Ger. *Sankt Moritz,* resort (resident pop. 2,418), Upper Engadine, Grisons canton, Switzerland, on L. of St. Moritz. Winter sports center; mineral springs.

Saint-Nazaire (sẽ-näzĕr′), town (1936 pop. 37,-710; 1946 pop. 4,408), Loire Inférieure dept., W France, at mouth of the Loire on the Bay of Biscay. As port of Nantes, it had, until its destruction by Allied bombing in 1943, the largest shipyards in France. Chief German submarine base in World War II. German garrison resisted Allied siege 1944–45.

Saint Olaf College: see NORTHFIELD, Minn.

Saint-Omer (sẽtômĕr′), city (pop. 15,785), Pas-de-Calais dept., N France. Gothic Basilica of Notre Dame (13th–14th cent.) is rich in works of art.

Saintonge (sẽtõzh′), region and former province, W France, in Charente-Maritime dept., on Atlantic at mouth of the Gironde; historic cap. Saintes. Cognac mfg. A subfief of Aquitaine, it passed to the French crown 1372.

Saint Patrick's Cathedral, New York city, on Fifth Av., largest Roman Catholic church in U.S. Designed in Gothic style by James Renwick. Begun 1858, dedicated 1879. Built of marble, it has 12 side chapels and a chime of 19 bells.

Saint Patrick's Purgatory, place where St. Patrick had a vision of purgatory, traditionally located on little Station Isl. in Lough Derg, SE Donegal, Ireland. Place of pilgrimage since Middle Ages though location is not accepted by modern scholars.

Saint Paul, city (pop. 311,349), state cap. (since 1858), E Minn., on the Mississippi at mouth of Minnesota R. and adjoining Minneapolis. Permanent white settlement in area began with establishment of MENDOTA fur-trading post and Fort Snelling; traders, lumbermen, settlers made homes here. Took name 1841 from St. Paul's Church. Settlers came from east after treaties with Indians opened land to settlement, lumbering; increased by immigrants, many of them Irish, and German Catholics (Bishop IRELAND long their leader). City became territorial cap. 1849. Location of St. Paul and Minneapolis at head of navigation of the Mississippi made Twin Cities metropolis of large area. St. Paul became center of railroad empire of James J. HILL. Second largest city of state, it has printing, publishing, meat packing, and automobile assembling. *Pioneer Press* (1849) is one of oldest papers in Middle West. Seat of Hamline Univ. (Methodist; coed.; 1854), Macalester Col. (coed.; 1874), Col. of St. Thomas (R.C.; for men; 1885), and Col. of St. Catherine.

Saint Paul's Cathedral, London, at the head of Ludgate Hill; masterpiece of Sir Christopher Wren. Built 1675–1710 on site of a 13th-cent. church which was badly ruined by the great fire of London (1666) and was demolished 1668. Wren's original design, in the shape of a Greek cross, was modified to provide the long nave and choir of the traditional medieval plan. The crossing is covered by a great dome, which rises impressively above a colonnaded drum. Bombed in World War II; the E end with altar and chapel behind it and roof and floor of N transept were destroyed.

Saint Paul's School, London, England, noted public school. Founded 1512 in St. Paul's churchyard. Mainly a day school with a few boarders, it is now in Kensington. Milton and Pepys were pupils.

Saint Peter, city (pop. 7,754), S Minn., on Minnesota R. and N of Mankato. Farm trade center. Seat of Gustavus Adolphus Col. (Lutheran; coed.; 1862). Traverse des Sioux, near site of St. Peter, was scene of treaty with Sioux in 1851.

Saint Peter Port, town and parish (pop. 16,-720), cap. of Guernsey, Channel Isls. Exports vegetables, fruits, and flowers. Victor Hugo lived here 1856–70. Elizabeth Col. for boys was established here in 1563.

Saint Petersburg, Russia: see LENINGRAD.

Saint Petersburg, city (pop. 96,738), W Fla., on Pinellas peninsula in Tampa Bay (Gandy Bridge to Tampa); settled in mid-19th cent., but really estab. c.1876. Ships fish, fruit, and vegetables. Has yacht basin, municipal pier, alligator farm, Indian shell mounds, and U.S. coast guard base. A veterans' hospital is near. Winter training ground of big-league baseball teams.

Saint Peter's Church, Rome, principal and largest Christian church in the world. Built on site of Nero's circus and of a 4th-cent. basilica. Original design for the present church was by Bernardo Rossellino, but little was done until c.1503, when Julius II selected Bramante's Greek-cross plan with a central dome. After Bramante's death (1514) several architects, including Raphael, directed the work but accomplished little. In 1546 Michelangelo was made chief architect; disregarding recommended changes, he returned to Bramante's original plan. He designed the great dome and finished part of it. His successor, Vignola, built the secondary domes, and Giacomo della Porta and Domenico Fontana completed the central dome after Michelangelo's drawings, 1573–90. The dome, 404 ft. high from the pavement, has an interior diameter of 137 ft. Beneath it is the high altar, covered by Bernini's bronze baldachin, 95 ft. high. At this altar only the pope may read Mass. Beneath it is the crypt containing St. Peter's tomb. Church plan was transformed 1605 into a Latin cross with addition of a long nave by Carlo Maderna. The church was dedicated 1626 by Urban VIII. The forecourt and majestic elliptical piazza bounded by colonnades were created 1629–67 by Bernini.

Saint-Pierre, Jacques Henri Bernardin de: see BERNARDIN DE SAINT-PIERRE, JACQUES HENRI.

Saint Pierre, island: see MIQUELON.

Saint-Quentin (sānt-kwĕn′tĭn, Fr. sẽ-kãtẽ′), city (pop. 46,876), Aisne dept., N France, on the Somme. Textile mfg. Its capture by Emmanuel Philibert of Savoy (1557) was a major Spanish victory. It was the center of heavy fighting in World War I and was virtually destroyed, but its fine Gothic collegiate church and city hall survived.

Saint Regis (sānt′ rē′jĭs), settlement of Catholic Iroquois, on the S bank of the St. Lawrence, partly in Que., partly in N.Y.; founded c.1755.

Saint-Saëns, (Charles) Camille (kämēy′ sẽ-sãs′), 1835–1921, French composer. He is known for his symphonies; the opera, *Samson et*

Dalila; the *Introduction and Rondo Capriccioso,* for violin and orchestra; the piano concertos in G minor and C minor; and symphonic poems, notably *Omphale's Spinning Wheel* and *Danse macabre.*

Saintsbury, George (Edward Bateman), 1845–1933, English critic, authority on French and English literature. Wrote histories, special studies, and biographies of Dryden, Scott, Arnold, and Thackeray.

Saint-Simon, Claude Henri de Rouvroy, comte de (klōd′ ārē dü ro͞ovrwä′ kōt′ dü sē-sēmō′), 1760–1825, French social philosopher. His writings foreshadow socialism, European federation, and the positivism of Comte. His pupils constructed system of **Saint-Simonianism** (sānt sīmō′nēünĭzm), calling for public control of means of production, abolition of inheritance rights, and gradual emancipation of women.

Saint-Simon, Louis de Rouvroy, duc de (lwē′, dük′), 1675–1755, French courtier, author of memoirs on the court of Louis XIV (first pub. 1788; complete ed., 41 vols., 1879–1928; abridged Eng. tr., 4 vols., 1899). A monument of French literature, the memoirs are remarkable for his psychological observations and brilliant sketches. Saint-Simon's arrogance, petulant resentments (particularly against the king), and hatred of the rising bourgeoisie give his work both a strong bias and an intensely personal flavor.

Saint Simons Island: see SEA ISLANDS.

Saint Sophia: see HAGIA SOPHIA.

Saint Stephen, town (pop. 3,769), SW N.B., Canada, on St. Croix R. and W of St. John. Opposite is Calais, Maine, connected by international bridge. Two towns cooperate in providing public services. Founded by Loyalists after Revolution.

Saint Stephens, hamlet, SW Ala., on Tombigbee R. and N of Mobile. First Ala. territorial legislature met here (1818) on site of Spanish fort (1789; became U.S. possession by demarcation line of 1798) and on site of U.S. trading post (1803).

Saint Thomas, city (pop. 18,173), S Ont., Canada, near L. Erie and S of London. Trade center in farm and orchard district with railroad shops, foundries, and lumber mills.

Saint Thomas: see VIRGIN ISLANDS.

Saint Thomas, College of: see SAINT PAUL, Minn.

Saint-Tropez (sē-trôpĕz′), town (pop. 3,171), Var dept., SE France; a resort on French Riviera.

Saint Vincent, island (133 sq. mi.; pop. 57,168), British West Indies; cap. KINGSTOWN. British and French contested ownership until 1783, when it was restored to British. Eruption of SOUFRIÈRE caused much damage in 1902.

Saint Vincent, Cape, Port. *Cabo de São Vicente,* SW extremity of Portugal. In 1797 the British under Jervis defeated a Spanish fleet near by.

Saint Vincent, Gulf, large inlet of Indian Ocean, South Australia, E of Yorke Peninsula. Port Adelaide on E shore.

Saint Vitus's dance: see CHOREA.

Saionji, Kimmochi, Prince (kēm′mō′chē sīōn′jē), 1850–1940, Japanese statesman, member of old court nobility and supporter of Meiji restoration. With Prince Ito he visited Europe in 1882 to study foreign governments. Prime minister 1906–8, 1911–12. Officially retired 1914, but as genro [elder statesman] he exerted great influence until his death.

Saipan: see MARIANAS ISLANDS.

Saisset, Bernard (bĕrnär′ sĕsā′), d. 1314, French churchman, bishop of Pamiers. His arrest in 1301 by PHILIP IV on the charge of inciting rebellion sparked the struggle between Philip and Pope BONIFACE VIII. He later was allowed to go to Rome and recovered his see in 1308.

Sakai (säkī′), industrial city (pop. 194,048), S Honshu, Japan, on Osaka Bay.

Sakakawea: see SACAJAWEA.

sake (sä′kē), chief alcoholic beverage of Japan. Yellowish and somewhat sherrylike, it is made by fermenting rice.

Sakhalin (să′kùlēn″) or **Saghalien** (să′gùlēn′), Jap. *Karafuto,* island (29,700 sq. mi.; pop. c.500,000), RSFSR, off the coast of Siberia, between Sea of Okhotsk and Sea of Japan. Mainly mountainous. Lumbering, coal mining, herring fishing; agr. is limited by severe climate. Colonized by Russia and Japan 18th–19th cent. Under joint control until 1905, when Treaty of Portsmouth gave Japan the S half of the island. After World War II Japanese territory was given to USSR in accordance with agreement at Yalta Conference.

Saki, pseud.: see MUNRO, HECTOR HUGH.

Sakonnet, R.I.: see LITTLE COMPTON.

Sakuntala: see KALIDASA.

Saladin (să′lùdĭn), 1137?–1193, Moslem warrior and sultan of Egypt, the great opponent of the Crusaders; b. Mesopotamia, of Kurdish descent. Lived for 10 years in Damascus at the court of NUREDDIN, where he became known for his knowledge of Sunnite theology. Went with his uncle, Shirkuh, a lieutenant of Nureddin, on campaigns against the Fatimite rulers of Egypt. Shirkuh became vizier there and on his death (1169) was succeeded by Saladin. After Nureddin's death Saladin made himself sultan of Egypt, thus beginning the Ayyubite dynasty. He extended his domain W into what is now Tunisia and E into Yemen, Palestine, and Syria. With a large force of Moslems of various groups (collectively called Saracens by the Christians) he defeated the Crusaders (see CRUSADES) in 1187 in the great battle of Hattin (near Tiberias), which led to his capture of Jerusalem. His celebrated encounter with Richard I of England came during the Third Crusade (1189), which failed to recover the Holy City. Saladin is said to have been respected by the Christians for his chivalry and generosity. A man of culture, he encouraged literature and learning.

Salamanca (sălùmăng′kù, Span. sälämäng′kä), city (pop. 71,725), W Spain, in Leon, on Tormez R. Conquered 1085 from the Moors, it became world-famous after foundation (c.1230) of its university, which made Arabic philosophy available to Western world. In late Middle Ages and Renaissance city was center of Spanish cultural life and fountainhead of Spanish theology. Among notable sights are the Plaza Mayor (fine colonnaded square); 12th-cent. Gothic cathedral, adjoined by new cathedral (1513–1733); university building (15th cent.); several splendid palaces (e.g., Casa de las Conchas).

Salamanca (sălůmăng'ků), city (pop. 8,861), W N.Y., on Allegheny R. and S of Buffalo, in Allegany Indian Reservation. Farm trade center; mfg. of furniture, dairy products, metal goods, textiles.

salamander (să'lůmăn'důr), tailed amphibian with small, weak legs, related to newt. Regenerates lost limbs or tail. Many are gregarious at breeding time. Larvae breathe by means of gills. Giant salamander of China and Japan is 3–5 ft. long. Salamander was portrayed in legends as unharmed by flames.

Salamis (să'lůmĭs), island, E Greece, in the Gulf of Aegina. Off its shore the Greek fleet decisively defeated the Persians in 480 B.C.

sal ammoniac (săl ůmō'nēăk), ammonium chloride, a white crystalline substance with biting taste. Used in dry cells, metals for soldering, smoke screens, ammonia, and in medicine.

Salazar, Antonio de Oliveira (äntô'nyō dů ōlēvā'rů sůläzär'), 1889–, Portuguese statesman. Taught economics at Univ. of Coimbra; was appointed finance minister in 1926 and again in 1928; premier and dictator from 1932. Through his reforms he put Portugal's chaotic finances on a stable footing, and in 1933 he devised the constitution of the *Novo Estado* [new state], a CORPORATIVE STATE influenced by the social principles expressed in the encyclicals of Pope Leo XIII. The attempt in 1945 to institute a democratic party system came to nought.

Salem (sā'lům) [Heb.,= peace], in Bible. **1** Unidentified kingdom of Melchizedek. Gen. 14.18; Heb. 7.1,2. May be Jerusalem. **2** Abbreviation for Jerusalem. Ps. 76.2.

Salem. 1 City (pop. 6,159), S central Ill., NE of Centralia, in coal, oil, timber, agr. area. Railroad shops. Mfg. of clothing. Birthplace of W. J. Bryan. **2** City (pop. 41,880), NE Mass., NE of Boston; settled 1626. Witchcraft trials of 1692 held here (SEWALL was a judge). A leading port from colonial times until mid-19th cent.; harbor is now silted up. Salem Maritime Natl. Historic Site preserves waterfront area. City rich in fine old mansions, some of them designed by McIntire. Hawthorne was surveyor of the port, 1846–49; his birthplace (17th cent.) and House of the Seven Gables are preserved. Essex Inst. and Peabody marine museum are here. Mfg. of electrical supplies, textiles, shoes, machinery. **3** City (pop. 9,050), SW N.J., near Delaware R., NW of Bridgeton; settled 1675 by Friends; first permanent English settlement in Delaware valley. Farm market center with mfg. of glass, linoleum; canneries. Has Alexander Grant House (1721; contains co. historical society collections) and Friends' meetinghouse (1772). **4** City (pop. 12,754), NE Ohio, SW of Youngstown; laid out 1806 by Friends. Early abolitionist center and station on Underground RR. Has mfg. of machinery and metal products. **5** City (pop. 43,140), state cap. (since 1859), NW Oregon, on Willamette R. and SSW of Portland; founded 1841 by Jason Lee. Territorial cap. after 1851. Processes fruit, grain, flax, hops, livestock, meat, lumber, linen, paper, and woolens. Seat of Willamette Univ. (coed.; opened 1844 as Oregon Inst.; chartered, renamed 1853), oldest institution of higher learning in Far West. **6** Town (pop. 6,823), SW Va., on Roanoke R. and W of Roanoke. Seat of Roanoke Col. Mfg. of textiles.

Salerno (sůlûr'nō, Ital. sälĕr'nō), city (pop. 41,925), Campania, S Italy; a port on inlet of Tyrrhenian Sea. Part of duchy of Benevento after 6th cent., it became (9th cent.) an independent principality, which fell to the Normans in 1076. Was scene of fierce battle (Sept., 1943) between Allied landing forces and Germans, who retreated towards Naples. Its famous medical school, founded 9th cent., reached its peak in 12th cent., and closed 1817. Cathedral has 11th-cent. bronze doors and ancient mosaics.

Salford (sŏl'fůrd, sôl'–), county borough (pop. 178,036), Lancashire, England. Textile center, it shares mfg. and commercial activities of Manchester.

Salic law (sā'lĭk), rule of succession in certain noble families of Europe, forbidding females and those descended in the female line to succeed to titles or offices in the family. It is so called on the mistaken supposition that it was part of the law of the Salian Franks. The rule has been of much importance at several crucial points in history. It was maintained by the Valois and the Bourbons in France (notably in accession of Philip V and Philip VI of France) and was taken to Spain by Philip V of Spain. There in the 19th cent. it was rescinded to allow the succession of Isabella II, and her opponents led the Carlist Wars. Another line observing this law was the Guelph; therefore Queen Victoria of England did not succeed to the rule in Hanover.

salicylic acid (sălĭsĭ'lĭk), white, crystalline, odorless, organic acid with a sweet taste. Used as food preservative since it inhibits bacterial growth. The acetate (aspirin) and salicylates are used as antipyretics, antiseptics, in treatment of rheumatism and other ailments. Methyl salicylate is used as flavoring and in liniments. Acid is used in making dyes.

Salida (sůlī'dů), city (pop. 4,553; alt. 7,050 ft.), central Colo., on Arkansas R. Resort near hot springs. Trade center for quarries, farms, mines.

Salina (sůlī'nů). **1** City (pop. 26,176), central Kansas, near junction of Saline and Smoky Hill rivers; platted 1858. Trade and distribution center for winter wheat and livestock area, it produces flour and farm implements. **2** Town (pop. 905), NE Okla., on Grand R. and ENE of Tulsa. Settled on site of first Okla. trading post, founded early 19th cent. by J. P. CHOUTEAU.

Salinas, Pedro (pā'dhrō sälē'näs), 1892–1951, Spanish lyric poet and critic; in the U.S. after 1936.

Salinas (sůlē'nůs), city (pop. 18,319), W Calif., SSE of San Francisco; settled 1856. Shipping and processing center for truck (esp. lettuce) and livestock valley. At edge is East Salinas (1933; pop. c.5,000), migratory farm camp.

Salinas, river rising in S Calif., in Santa Lucia Mts. E of San Luis Obispo, and flowing c.150

mi. NW (partly underground) past Salinas, to Monterey Bay.

Saline (sùlēn′), partly navigable river rising in Ouachita Mts., W Ark., and flowing c.300 mi. S to Ouachita R. in S Ark.

Salisbury, John of: see JOHN OF SALISBURY.

Salisbury, Robert Arthur Talbot Gascoyne-Cecil, 3d marquess of (sôlz′bûrē), 1830–1903, British Conservative statesman and diplomat. Foreign secretary under Disraeli, in his "Salisbury Circular" led to Congress of Berlin (1878). Prime minister three times (1885; 1886–92; 1895–1902), he was his own foreign minister. Maintained peaceful relations with major powers and achieved some domestic reforms.

Salisbury, Robert Cecil, 1st earl of, 1563?–1612, English statesman, son of Baron Burghley. Succeeded (1598) his father as chief minister to Elizabeth. Prepared (after fall of earl of Essex) the peaceful accession of James I to English throne. Responsible for administration until his death.

Salisbury (sôlz′–) or **New Sarum** (sâr′ùm), municipal borough (pop. 32,910), co. town of Wiltshire, England. Bishopric moved here from OLD SARUM in 1220. Great cathedral, with highest spire in England (404 ft.), was built 1220–60. Noteworthy are 13th-cent. churches and bishops' palace. Town is the Melchester of Thomas Hardy's Wessex novels.

Salisbury (sôlz′–), city (pop. 53,211), cap of Southern Rhodesia, in gold-mining area; founded 1890.

Salisbury. 1 Resort town (pop. 3,132), extreme NW Conn., in Taconic Mts.; settled c.1720. Includes Bear Mt., 2,355 ft., highest peak in state, and Lakeville, a resort center, on L. Wononskopomuc; seat of Hotchkiss School for boys. **2** City (pop. 15,141), Eastern Shore, Md., at head of Wicimico R.; settled 1732. Trade center for much of Eastern Shore, it has mfg. of clothing, tools, pumps, and boats. **3** City (pop. 20,102), W central N.C., NNE of Charlotte in piedmont; settled 1751. Textile mills and granite quarries. Here are Salisbury Natl. Cemetery and Livingstone Col. (Negro; Methodist Episcopal Zion; coed.; 1879).

Salisbury Plain, chalk plateau, 300 sq. mi., Wiltshire, England, NW of Salisbury. Site of many ancient monuments, of which STONEHENGE is most famous. Important training ground for British army.

Salishan (sā′lĭshùn, să′–), linguistic stock of North American Indians of NW U.S. and British Columbia, Canada. It includes the Flathead (also called Salish), Pend d'Oreille, Okanogan, Puyallup, Spokan, Coeur d'Alene, Bella Coola, and others. See LANGUAGE (table).

saliva (sùlī′vù), alkaline fluid containing digestive enzyme (ptyalin) that converts starch to sugar. Secreted by salivary glands and carried by ducts into mouth.

Sallust (Caius Sallustius Crispus) (să′lùst), 86 B.C.–c.34 B.C., Roman historian. Chief work *Bellum Catilinarium* or *Catilina,* on conspiracy of Catiline.

Salmasius, Claudius (klô′dēùs sălmā′shùs), 1588–1653, French humanist and philologist. Knew Hebrew, Persian and Arabic as well as Latin and Greek. Wrote many learned works. Also wrote in support of the Stuarts a book upholding divine right of monarchy, which brought a dissenting reply from John Milton. He discovered the Greek anthology of Cephalas at Heidelberg in 1606.

Salmon (să′mùn), river, c.425 mi. long, rising in central Idaho in Sawtooth and Salmon River Mts. and flowing NE (joined at Salmon by Lemhi R.), W (joined by Middle and South forks), then N to Snake R. Has large salmon run. Lower gorge is impressive.

salmon, marine game fish which breeds in fresh water. N Atlantic salmon (*Salmo*) is nearly exterminated; some remain in rivers of Maine, E Canada, Europe, and near Labrador. Pacific coast salmon (*Oncorhynchus*) is taken from Monterey, Calif., to Nome, Alaska, and near Japan and Siberia. Over half of canned salmon comes from Alaska. At spawning time salmon migrate from the ocean, each species seeking the region where it hatched. Pacific salmon, most of which make long hazardous journey against current, falls, and rapids, die soon after eggs are laid and fertilized; Atlantic salmon return to sea. The young of both groups remain in fresh water for varying periods, then travel to salt water.

Salmon Falls River, rising in lakes around Maine-N.H. line, which it forms, and flowing SSE, past Dover, N.H., below which it is called Piscataqua R. (pĭskă′tùkwù), to the Atlantic at Portsmouth Harbor.

Salome (sùlō′mē). **1** Daughter of Herodias. Usually identified with the dancer who asked Herod Antipas for John the Baptist's head. Mark 6.16–28. **2** One of the women who stood at the foot of the cross and later visited the empty tomb. Mark 15.40; 16.1.

Salomon, Haym, 1740–85, American Revolutionary patriot and financier, b. Poland.

Salona (sùlō′nù), Latin *Salonae,* port of Dalmatia, on the Adriatic. Here Diocletian built a magnificent palace, which in the 7th cent. became the core of Spalato (now Split, Yugoslavia).

Salonica, Salonika (both: sălùnē′kù), or **Saloniki** (sălùnē′kē), Gr. *Thessalonike* or *Thessaloniki,* city (pop. 216,138), cap. of Greek Macedonia, NE Greece, on Gulf of Salonica, an inlet of Aegean Sea, and at neck of Chalcidice Peninsula. Second largest Greek city, major port, mfg. center (textiles, cigarettes, leather goods, machine tools). University was opened 1926. Founded c.315 B.C.; flourished under Roman and Byzantine rules. Kingdom of Thessalonica, created 1204, comprised most of N and central Greece and was largest fief of Latin Empire of Constantinople but was recaptured by the Greeks in 1222. After changing hands several times, Salonica passed finally to Turkey in 1430, to Greece 1912. World War II inflicted much damage. Famous churches include that of Hagia Sophia (notable mosaics). Ruins include triumphal arch of Emperor Constantine. The **Salonica campaigns** of World War I began, after the fall of the VENIZELOS government, with the landing of an Allied force at Salonica for "peaceful blockade" of neutral Greece (1915). Allies estab. (1916) a rival Greek government under

Venizelos at Salonica. This body declared war on Central Powers. After Allies began to invade central Greece, King CONSTANTINE abdicated (June, 1917). On the Macedonian front, Allied operations were stalled by disunity and, especially, by malaria, but in 1918 fresh forces were landed and pushed N under Gen. Franchet d'Esperey. Bulgaria fell Sept. 30; Serbia was recovered by Nov. 1; Rumania fell Nov. 10.

Salop, county, England: see SHROPSHIRE.

salsify: see GOATSBEARD.

Salt, Sir Titus, 1803–76, English textile manufacturer and inventor. Model manufacturing village, Saltaire, near Shipley, Yorkshire, estab. by him 1851. Invented machine for making worsted and process for spinning and weaving alpaca.

salt. 1 A common and widely used substance, sodium chloride. Soluble in water; in solution it is a conductor of electricity. Constitutes large proportion of all solid matter dissolved in sea water and inland salt lakes; also occurs as large deposits of rock salt. Obtained by mining, by dissolving it in water underground and pumping to surface, and by evaporation of sea water. Salt is chief source of sodium and its compounds, and a source of chlorine. It is used in making glass, pottery, textile dyes, soap, and in preservation of foods. It is important in diet of man and animals. **2** In chemistry, a compound with metal or metallic radical as positive ion and nonmetal or nonmetallic radical as negative ion. Normal salt has neither hydrogen nor hydroxyl ion; acid salts have hydrogen with another positive ion; basic salts have hydroxyl and another negative ion. Salts are named from elements composing them and acid from which they are derived. Salt with two elements has name of nonmetallic element with ending *-ide,* e.g., sodium chloride. Salts made of more than two elements derived from acids ending in *-ic* have ending *-ate,* e.g., carbonate, sulphate. Salts from *-ous* acids have ending *-ite.*

Salta (säl'tä), city (pop. 67,403), cap. of Salta prov., NW Argentina; founded 1582. Center of rich agr. and oil area.

Salten, Felix (fā'lĭks zäl'tůn), 1869–1945, Austrian novelist. Best known for his animal stories, notably *Bambi* (1923; Eng. tr., 1928).

Saltillo (sältē'yō), city (pop. 49,430), cap. of Coahuila, N Mexico; founded 1575. Primarily an agr. and mining community, it is also a rail center. Famous for woolen serapes.

Salt Lake City, city (pop. 182,121), state cap., N central Utah, on Jordan R., SE of Great Salt L., and at foot of Wasatch Range. Founded 1847 by Brigham YOUNG as cap. of MORMONS, it was state's leading city from beginning. Huge Temple (built 1853–93) and Tabernacle (1867) at city's heart show that this is still City of the Saints. Utah's largest city; distributing and commercial center; transcontinental air and highway focus. Mfg. of steel, petroleum, iron products; food processing, saltmaking; ore smelters, stockyards. Ships farm produce of rich irrigated area. Seat of Univ. of UTAH. Outfitting point for Calif. gold rush. Fort Douglas founded here in 1862 by Gen. P. E. Connor. Center for many years of Mormon Church-U.S. government dispute.

Salto (säl'tō), city (pop. 44,000), cap. of Salto dept., NW Uruguay, on Uruguay R. across from Concordia, Argentina, its commercial rival. Extensive citrus fruit orchards and vineyards in environs.

Salton Sea, shallow saline lake, c.30 mi. long and 10 mi. wide, SE Calif., between IMPERIAL VALLEY (S) and Coachella Valley. Was salt-covered lowland called Salton Sink until flooded by Colorado R. (1905–7). Receives irrigation water to help counteract evaporation. Surface is 245 ft. below sea level.

saltpeter or **niter** (nī'tůr), naturally occurring potassium nitrate. Used to make explosives, fireworks, and matches, and as food preservative. **Chile saltpeter,** natural sodium nitrate (called *caliche* when impure) is used to make potassium nitrate, fertilizers, explosives, and nitric acid.

Salt River Valley, S central Ariz., irrigated region around lower Salt R., which flows 200 mi. WSW from near Mogollon Rim to Gila R. WSW of Phoenix. Early Indians and U.S. settlers used Salt R. for irrigation. Salt R. project (begun 1905) was first major undertaking under Federal reclamation act; chief dams are Roosevelt (c.280 ft. high; built 1906–11), Horse Mesa, Mormon Flat, Stewart Mountain, all in Salt R., Bartlett in Verde R. Valley is farm (truck, citrus, alfalfa, cotton) and winter resort area. Centers are PHOENIX, Mesa, Glendale, Tempe.

Saltus, Edgar (Evertson) (sôltůs), 1858–1921, American author. His works, combining violent plots and lavish descriptions, include novels (e.g., *The Pace That Kills,* 1889) and a history of the Roman emperors (*Imperial Purple,* 1892).

Saltville, town (pop. 2,678), SW Va., in Holston R. valley SW of Marion. Saltmaking began here 1788. Saltworks taken by Union forces and destroyed 1864; later re-established.

Saltykov, Mikhail Evgrafovich (mēkhŭyēl' yĭvgrä'fůvĭch sŭltĭkôf'), pseud. of Nikolai E. Shchedrin, 1826–89, Russian author. His satirical *Fables* (1885; Eng. tr., 1931) attacked contemporary conditions in Aesopic language. His novel *The Golovlyov Family* (1876; Eng. tr., 1917) is a study of decaying gentry.

Saluafata (sä"lo͞oufä'tů), U.S. naval station, NE Upolu isl., Western Samoa.

Saluda (sůlo͞o'dů), river rising in Blue Ridge of W S.C. and flowing c.145 mi. SE across piedmont to Broad R. (forming Congaree) at Columbia. Has Saluda (or Dreher Shoals) Dam (1930) forming L. Murray and Buzzard Roost Dam forming L. Greenwood.

Salvador (sälvädhōr") or **El Salvador,** republic, (13,176 sq. mi.; pop. 1,858,656), Central America, on the Pacific; cap. SAN SALVADOR. Homogeneity of population (about 80% ladino or mestizo, less than 20% Indian) and uniformity of terrain have contributed to agr. prosperity. From W to E, Salvador is broken by two roughly parallel volcanic ranges; between them lie warm valleys with excellent grazing land for cattle. Dominant crop is coffee; indigo is produced in W. Communication is good, with Inter-American

Highway extending the length of the country and railroads and highways leading out from the cap. to interior and coast. Throughout colonial period, Salvador was under captaincy general of Guatemala and after independence from Spain (1821) was briefly a part of Iturbide's empire and then a member of Central American Federation (1825–38). With development of coffeegrowing in second half of 19th cent. there was a phenomenal increase in population, and today Salvador is one of Latin America's most densely populated countries. Other cities of importance besides San Salvador are La Libertad, La Unión, and Acajutla on the coast and Santa Ana in highlands.

Salvador (sälvädôr'), city (pop. 395,993), cap. of Bahia state, E Brazil; a port on the Atlantic at entrance to Todos os Santos Bay. City formerly called Bahia. Founded by Tomé de Souza (1549), it was cap. of Portuguese possessions in America until 1763.

salvage, in maritime law, compensation the owner must pay for having his vessel or cargo saved from peril such as shipwreck and fire. Salvage is distributed by the court to the owner, the master, and the crew of the rescue ship according to fixed ratios.

Salvation Army, international body for religious and philanthropic work, chiefly among those not ordinarily under influence of Christian churches. It was started in London (1865) by William Booth (see BOOTH, family) as East London Revival Society or Christian Mission. It was in 1878 named Salvation Army and organized on military lines with ministers as officers and members as soldiers. By 1890 Army had spread to Continent, North America, Australia, and India. Work in U.S. began 1880 with branch in Pa. Evangeline Booth became commander of work in U.S. (1904) and general of international Army (1934). There is no formal creed, but belief is evangelical. Army operates various practical social projects throughout world.

Salvemini, Gaetano (gäätä'nō sălvāmē'nē), 1873–, Italian historian. Became U.S. citizen in 1940. Chief works deal with contemporary history, particularly the Fascist period.

Salvian (săl'vēŭn), 5th cent., Christian writer in Gaul, a renowned preacher and teacher of rhetoric. Wrote part of *De gubernatione Dei* and all of *Contra avaritiam*.

Salween (săl"wēn'), river, c.1,750 mi. long, rising in E Tibet. Flows through Yünnan prov., China, and Burma to Gulf of Martaban of Andaman Sea.

Salzburg (sôlz'bŭrg, Ger. zälts'boork), province (2,762 sq. mi.; pop. 324,117), W central Austria, in the Alps. Has large salt deposits and several small gold and copper mines. Includes part of SALZKAMMERGUT and has huge tourist trade. Its history is that of its cap., **Salzburg** (pop. 100,096), on the Salzach R. Its archbishops ruled the region as princes of the Holy Roman Empire from 1278 to 1802, when Salzburg passed to Austria. It was transferred to Bavaria 1809; reverted to Austria 1815. The city is world-famous for its Renaissance and baroque architecture—e.g., the cathedral, the archiepiscopal palace (*Residenz*), Mirabell castle and garden. The Hohensalzburg, an 11th-cent. fortress, dominates it from a hill. Of the university (founded 1623) only the theological faculty still exists. The birthplace of Mozart, Salzburg honors his memory by annual music and theatrical festivals. Its prosperity is largely due to the tourist trade.

Salzkammergut (zälts'kä"mŭrgoot"), Alpine resort area in Upper Austria, Styria, and Salzburg, Austria. Has beautiful mountain lakes (Sankt Wolfgangsee, Traunsee, Mondsee) and resorts (Ischl, Sankt Wolfgang, Hallstatt, Gmunden, Altaussee). Salt mines.

Samar (sä'mär), island (5,050 sq. mi.; pop. 470,678), one of Visayan Isls., P.I.; NE of Leyte. Lumbering, agr. (rice, hemp, corn), iron mining.

Samara, RSFSR: see KUIBYSHEV.

Samaria (sŭmâ'rēŭ), anc. city, central Palestine, NW of Nablus (Shechem); site now occupied by Sebaste village. Samaria built by King Omri as cap. of Israel in early 9th cent. B.C.; fell in 722 B.C. to Assyria. Destroyed in 120 B.C. by John Hyrcanus; rebuilt by Herod the Great. Traditional burial place of John the Baptist. City gave its name to **Samaritans,** a sect recognizing only the Pentateuch of the Bible and rigidly adhering to its law. In Jesus' time a great enmity existed between them and the Jews, since each claimed to be the only true inheritors of Abraham and Moses; hence the choice of a Samaritan for Jesus' parable. Luke 10.30–37. A small group of Samaritans still live at Nablus. The Samaritan language is a type of Aramaic.

samarium (sŭmâ'rēŭm), lustrous gray element (symbol = Sm; see also ELEMENT, table), a metal of the rare earths.

Samarkand (sămŭrkănd'), city (pop. 134,346), Uzbek SSR, on Trans-Caspian RR. Major cotton and silk center. One of oldest existing cities in the world and oldest of central Asia, it was built on site of Afrosiab (ruins extant), which dated from 3d or 4th millennium B.C., and was chief city of SOGDIANA. After conquest by Alexander the Great in 329 B.C. it became a meeting point of Western and Chinese cultures. Fell to Moslems early in 8th cent. A.D. and developed as a center of Arabic civilization. First paper mill outside China was estab. here 751. City continued to prosper as part of Khurasan (874–999) and of Khorezm. Though taken and devastated by Jenghiz Khan in 1220, Samarkand reached its greatest splendor as cap. of Tamerlane's empire in 14th cent. After breakup of Timurid empire (15th cent.), Samarkand region was ruled by Uzbeks until 1920 as part of emirate of BUKHARA, which came under Russian overlordship in 1868. Old Samarkand contains, among other remarkable monuments, Tamerlane's mausoleum and Bibi Khan mosque (now ruined).

Samarra (sämä'rä), town (pop. c.8,000), Iraq, on the Tigris. Seat of Abbasid caliphs from 836 to 876. Has a mosque sacred to Shiites.

Sambre (sã'brŭ), river, 120 mi. long, N France and SE Belgium, flowing NE to the Meuse at Namur. Scene of heavy fighting in World War I.

Samnites (săm'nīts), anc. people of central Italy, Oscan-speaking and perhaps related to the Sabines. Rome defeated them in the Samnite Wars (328 or 326–304 B.C., 298–290 B.C.), and they declined. They sided with Marius and were crushed by Sulla in 82 B.C. Their territory was called **Samnium.**

Samoa (sùmō'ù), island group, S Pacific, between Honolulu and Sydney. Has 10 principal and several uninhabited islands in 350 mi.-long chain. Formerly Navigators' Isls. Volcanic and mountainous, it has tropical trees (fern, coconut, hardwood, rubber) and tropical produce (copra, taro, fruits, cacao, yams). Discovered 1722 by Dutch. Savaii, Upolu, Apolima, Manono, and four uninhabited islands are known as **Territory of Western Samoa** (1,135 sq. mi.; pop. 68,197), under New Zealand trusteeship in UN. Rest of group is **American Samoa** (76 sq. mi.; pop. 18,602), consisting of TUTUILA, Aunuu, Manua group, Swains Isl., Rose Isl. PAGO-PAGO is on Tutuila. Almost all land owned by Polynesians.

Samos (sā'mŏs), Aegean island (194 sq. mi.; pop. 56,273), Greece, off W Asia Minor; one of the Sporades. Largely mountainous, it produces wine, tobacco, fruit. Colonized c.11th cent. B.C. by Ionian Greeks. Flourished under Polycrates (6th cent. B.C.). Anacreon and legendary Aesop lived here; birthplace of Pythagoras. Samian ware is ancient Roman pottery of a soft, deep red.

Samothrace (să'mōthrās"), Gr. *Samothrake*, Aegean island, area 71 sq. mi., Greece, between mainland of Thrace and Gallipoli Peninsula. Mountainous. In ancient times it was the center of worship of the Cabiri. Winged *Nike* (or *Victory*) *of Samothrace* (now in Louvre, Paris) was erected here 306 B.C. Island was first stop in St. Paul's Macedonian itinerary. Ceded by Turkey to Greece 1913.

Samoyedes or **Samoyeds** (both: sămoi-ĕdz'), partly nomadic, partly settled agricultural tribes of N Siberia and the Taimyr Peninsula. They are also known as Nentsy. Samoyede language perhaps related to Finno-Ugric.

Sampson, William Thomas, 1840–1902, American naval officer. Commanded N Atlantic squadron in Spanish-American War. Laid down instructions for battle of Santiago, but the credit for victory went to W. S. SCHLEY.

Sampson, N.Y.: see FINGER LAKES.

Samson [Heb.,= sun], judge and hero of Israel, proverbial for his strength. Samson, a NAZARITE, owed his strength to his vow to God that he would never cut his hair. He was betrayed to his enemies the Philistines by Delilah. His revenge came when he pulled down the Philistine temple, crushing his enemies as well as himself. Judges 13–16.

Samsun (sämsōōn'), city (pop. 43,937), N Turkey; a Black Sea port. Tobacco-mfg. center; agr. market. The ancient Amisus, it was founded 6th cent. B.C. Important in Pontic and Roman empires. Fell to Ottoman Turks 14th cent.

Samuel, books of Old Testament, called 1 and 2 Samuel in AV, 1 and 2 Kings in Western canon. They are histories of Israel, chiefly covering the careers of Samuel, Saul, and David. Samuel, last and one of the greatest of Israel's judges, was, as a boy, dedicated to the service of God and grew up in the temple at Shiloh. He led his people against their Philistine oppressors. When an old man, and at divine behest, he anointed Saul as first king of Israel and later anointed David as Saul's successor.

samurai (sä"mōōrī'), members of aristocratic warrior class of feudal Japan; retainers of the daimyo. Followed BUSHIDO as code of conduct. Abolished as a class after Meiji restoration, but former samurai were leaders in building modern Japan.

Sana or **Sanaa:** see YEMEN.

San Angelo (săn ăn'jùlō), city (pop. 52,093), W Texas, at start of Concho R.; laid out 1869 beside border fort (still extant). Processes, markets, and ships wool, cotton, livestock, farm produce, and oil. Near by is L. Nasworthy, reservoir.

San Antonio (săn ăntō'nyù, –nēō), city (pop. 408,442), S central Texas, at source of San Antonio R. Spanish knew site long before mission and presidio were founded here 1718. Other missions followed 1720–31; San Fernando, now city's heart, founded 1731. Taken by Texans in Texas Revolution, Dec., 1835, and saw fall of the ALAMO, March, 1836. Group of Comanches killed 1840 in "council house fight." City taken by Mexicans 1842. Prospered as cowtown after Civil War and with coming of railroad. Port and rail focus, it ships cattle, cotton, truck, fruits, pecans, oil, and gas and processes food, oil, and metals. Mfg. of clay products and garments. Here are Fort Sam Houston (1865) and Brooks, Kelly, and Randolph airfields. Seat of Trinity Univ. (Presbyterian; coed.; 1869). History, climate and exotic atmosphere make it a resort.

San Augustine (săn ô'gùstēn), town (pop. 2,510), E Texas, on Ayish Canyon and ESE of Nacogdoches. Spanish mission estab. 1716, abandoned 1719, and refounded 1721. Presidio estab. 1756 for guarding French-Spanish border. All abandoned before American settlement began 1818. Large Negro population.

San Benito (săn bùnē'tō), city (pop. 13,271), S Texas, NW of Brownsville. Processes citrus fruit, vegetables, and cotton. Resort trade.

San Bernardino (săn bûrnùrdē'nō), city (pop. 63,058), S Calif., E of Los Angeles; laid out 1853. Rail and citrus-fruit center. Annual national orange show. Gateway to mountain and lake resort region.

San Bernardino Mountains, S Calif., extending c.55 mi. SE from Cajon Pass at E end of San Gabriel Mts. to N end of San Jacinto Mts. and rising to 11,485 ft. in Mt. San Gorgonio.

San Blas (sän bläs'), archipelago off NE coast of Panama, comprising c.332 islands. Also called Mulatas. Islanders mostly pure-blooded aborigines of Carib origin, protected by treaty with Panama.

Sanborn, Franklin Benjamin, 1831–1917, American author and philanthropist. Founded several welfare societies. Member of Emerson's group; wrote lives of Alcott, Emerson, W. E. Channing, Hawthorne, and Thoreau, as well as one of his friend John Brown.

San Bruno, residential city (pop. 12,478), W Calif., S of San Francisco. Ships truck and poultry.

San Buenaventura: see VENTURA, Calif.

San Carlos, residential city (pop. 14,371), W

Calif., S of San Francisco. Flower shipping point.

Sánchez-Coello, Alonso: see COELLO, ALONSO SÁNCHEZ.

Sancho III or **Sancho the Great** (sän'chō), c.965–1035, king of Navarre (1000–1035). He inherited Navarre and Aragon; conquered territories from the Moors; married heiress of Castile, Vizcaya, and Álava. His kingdom thus included most of Christian Spain, but at his death it was divided among his sons García (Navarre), Ferdinand I (Castile), Ramiro I (Aragon), and Gonzalo (Sobrarbe and Ribagorza).

Sancho Panza: see DON QUIXOTE DE LA MANCHA.

sanction, inducement to follow or abstain from a course of action. Legal sanction may be positive (reward) or negative (penalty). Word *sanctions* designated coercive measures of League of Nations to stop aggression, e.g., economic sanctions (1935) against Italy for invasion of Ethiopia. Powers of UN also include infliction of sanctions.

Sanctis, Francesco de: see DE SANCTIS, FRANCESCO.

Sanctorius (săngktô'rēŭs), Ital., *Santorio,* 1561–1636, Italian physiologist. Laid foundation for metabolism study through quantitative experiments.

Sanctus (also *Tersanctus*) [Latin,= holy], choral ending of the preface in Roman MASS. Parts of the short hymn are called the *Benedictus* and the *Hosanna.*

Sand, George (sănd, Fr. zhôrzh' sã'), pseud. of Aurore Dupin, baronne Dudevant, 1804–76, French novelist. Her grandmother was a natural daughter of Maurice, comte de Saxe. Divorced in 1836, she asserted her independence through her eccentric manners and a series of open liaisons—notably with Jules SANDEAU, Musset (whom she betrayed somewhat cynically), and Chopin (with whom her relations were tempestuous). She was, however, a devoted mother, and her unconventional conduct was motivated chiefly by her belief in equal rights for women. Her novels, which rank high in French fiction, are marked by deep love for nature and the soil and by moral idealism. They include *La Mare au diable* (1846; Eng. tr., *The Haunted Pool*), *Indiana* (1832), and *La Petite Fadette* (1848; Eng. tr., *Fanchon the Cricket*). *Elle et lui* (1858) is her version of her affair with Musset; *Un Hiver à Majorque* [a winter in Majorca] tells of her life with Chopin.

sand, mineral material occurring as loose grains, formed from weathering of rocks, and usually consisting in the main of quartz. Most extensive deposits are seen in deserts and on beaches. Uses include making brick, cement, glass, pottery; as an abrasive, and in filtering water.

sandalwood, name for several fragrant tropical woods, especially that of an evergreen semiparasitic tree, *Santalum album,* of India. The wood is made into various wares; the oil has been used in perfume since early days.

sandbur, weedy sandy-soil grass of genus *Cenchrus* with burlike seeds. Bur grass is another name.

Sandburg, Carl, 1878–, American poet and biographer, b. Ill. Life as a day laborer, soldier, secretary, and newspaperman influenced his poetry. It is frank, often slangy and vernacular in style, but sometimes impressionistic. Collected verses as in *Chicago Poems* (1916) and *The People, Yes* (1936) estab. him as an artist. His biography of Lincoln (6 vols., 1926–39) won acclaim. Also wrote children's poems and stories; a novel, *Remembrance Rock* (1948); autobiographical *Always the Young Strangers* (1953).

Sandeau, Jules (zhül' sãdō'), 1811–83, French novelist. Collaborated with George SAND, who took her pen name from him.

Sanderson, village (pop. 2,047), W Texas, N of Rio Grande, on El Paso-Del Rio highway. Ships wool, mohair, and livestock.

sand fly, minute biting, bloodsucking, water-breeding fly, also called punkie and nosee-um.

Sandhurst, village, Berkshire, England; site of the Royal Military Col. (founded in 1802).

San Diego (săn dēā'gō), city (pop. 434,924), S Calif., port on fine natural harbor on E side of San Diego Bay. State's first permanent white settlement. Cabrillo entered bay 1542. Junípero Serra founded San Diego de Alcalá Mission 1769. Beach and fishing resort. Produces aircraft, and processes fish (esp. tuna), fruit, and dairy goods. Seat of important U.S. naval installations. Balboa Park contains points of scenic and historic interest. City's Old Town district has early adobe houses.

Sandomierz (sändô'myĕsh), town (pop. 8,357), S Poland, at confluence of Vistula and San rivers. Became cap. of a duchy 1139. A synod held here in 1570 united all Polish Protestants. Passed to Austria 1795; to Russia 1815; reverted to Poland 1919.

San Domingo, old form of SANTO DOMINGO.

sandpiper, small wading bird of Old and New Worlds, related to snipe and curlew. Has long bill and legs; plumage is usually streaked brown or gray above, lighter with streaks or spots below.

Sandpoint, resort city (pop. 4,265), N Idaho, on Pend Oreille L. (spanned here by 2-mi. bridge).

Sandracottus (săndrŭkŏ'tŭs), Greek name of **Chandragupta** (chăndrŭgŏŏp'tŭ), d. c.298 B.C., Indian ruler, founder of MAURYA empire. Conquered the Magadha kingdom in c.320 B.C. and expelled the garrisons of Alexander the Great from NW India.

Sandringham (săn'drĭngŭm), village, Norfolk, England. Sandringham House (7,000 acres) was bought by Edward VII in 1861. George V died here (1936).

Sand Springs, industrial suburb (pop. 6,994) of Tulsa, NE Okla., on Arkansas R. Has memorial group by Lorado Taft.

sandstone, rock formed of sand grains cemented by iron oxide, calcium carbonate, quartz. Commonly gray, red, brown. Chief use is building material.

sandstorm, dry desert wind carrying sand or dust which often reduces visibility to zero, obscures sun. Called simoom or simoon in Arabia and N Africa.

Sandusky, city (pop. 29,375), N Ohio, W of Cleveland and on Sandusky Bay of L. Erie; laid out 1817 as Portland. Port and coal-shipping point with mfg. of paper products and communications equipment. Center of resort area.

Sandusky, river, c.120 mi. long, rising in N Ohio and flowing W, then N to Sandusky Bay of L. Erie.

Sandwich, Edward Montagu, 1st earl of (mŏn'tūgū), 1625–72, English statesman and admiral. Served (1653–56) on Cromwell's council of state. Aided restoration of Charles II. Held high naval command in Dutch Wars. Killed in battle of Southwold Bay.

Sandwich, John Montagu, 4th earl of, 1718–92, English politician. Twice first lord of the admiralty, he used the navy for political ends. His mismanagement led largely to British failure in American Revolution. Sandwich (Hawaiian) Isls. were named for him, as was (supposedly) the sandwich.

Sandwich (săn'wĭch, săn'dwĭch), municipal borough (pop. 4,142), Kent, England. One of the Cinque Ports, it was chief naval and military port under Henry VII. Harbor is now silted up.

Sandwich, town (pop. 2,418), SE Mass., on W Cape Cod E of Bourne; settled 1637. Historical museum displays Sandwich glass (made here 1825–88).

Sandwich Islands: see HAWAIIAN ISLANDS.

Sandy Hook, peninsula, NE N.J., projecting c.5 mi. N toward New York city, between Sandy Hook Bay and the Atlantic. U.S. reservation with Fort Hancock at tip. Lighthouse (1763; 85 ft. high) is oldest in use in U.S. Hudson's men explored here 1609.

Sandys, Sir Edwin (săndz), 1561–1629, English statesman, leading promoter of the colony in Virginia. Won dislike of James I by speech (1614) denying doctrine of divine right. Leader of liberal faction in Virginia Co., he was responsible for many progressive features of company's rule. His brother, **George Sandys,** 1578–1644, was a traveler and poet. Wrote *Relation of a Journey* (1615) about his trip to Europe and Near East. While in Virginia (1621–31), he translated (1626) Ovid's *Metamorphoses.*

San Felipe (săn fĕ'lĭpē), town, S Texas, on Brazos R. and W of Houston. Founded 1823 as hq. of S. F. Austin's colony; Texans met here (1832, 1833, 1835), and it was burned in Texas Revolution. Declined in late 19th cent. Also called San Felipe de Austin.

San Felipe (săn" fůlē'pā), Indian pueblo village (1948 pop. 787), N central N.Mex., on Rio Grande and SW of Santa Fe; estab. in early 1700s. Semi-annual ceremonial dances. Keresan language.

San Fernando, city (pop. 12,992), S Calif., N of Los Angeles, in farm (citrus, truck) and oil region. San Fernando Valley entered by white men in 1769. Produced some gold after 1842. San Fernando Rey Mission (1797) is near.

Sanford. 1 City (pop. 11,935), E central Fla., on L. Monroe NE of Orlando. Resort and celery market. **2** Town (pop. 15,177), including Sanford village (pop. 11,094), SW Maine, SW of Portland. Mfg. of textiles (since mid-18th cent.). **3** Town (pop. 10,013), central N.C., SW of Raleigh. Tobacco, cotton, and clay products. Annexed Jonesboro 1947.

San Francisco, city (pop. 775,357), W Calif., on hilly peninsula between Pacific Ocean and SAN FRANCISCO BAY (connected by Golden Gate strait). Founded 1776 by Spanish as Yerba Buena, and taken by U.S. 1846, it became San Francisco 1847. Grew tremendously after 1848 gold rush. Ensuing period of lawlessness on BARBARY COAST saw rise of VIGILANTES. Linked with East by Pony Express (1860), then by Union Pacific RR (1869). Rebuilt rapidly after costly earthquake and fire of 1906. Panama Canal opening (celebrated with exposition, 1915) brought increased trade. Inter-city communication was improved, notably by SAN FRANCISCO-OAKLAND BAY BRIDGE (1936) and GOLDEN GATE BRIDGE (1937). Golden Gate International Exposition (1939–40) saw city largely industrialized. Recent historic events occurring here were drafting of UN Charter (1945) and signing of Japanese treaty (1951). One of most important U.S. ports, it is also a transportation and cultural center, key city of a great metropolitan area, and market for huge agr. and mining area. Besides oil refining, shipbuilding, and food processing, it has milling and processing of steel and iron and mfg. of machinery, chemicals, clothing, and wood and rubber products. Scenically beautiful, it has a reputation for individual charm. Among many points of interest are Market Street, Telegraph Hill, Opera House, Embarcadero, Chinatown (largest Chinese settlement outside Orient), wharves, bridges, and Mission Dolores (1782). Seat of Univ. of San Francisco (Jesuit; for men; 1855).

San Francisco Bay, 50 mi. long and 3–12 mi. wide, W Calif., entered between two peninsulas via Golden Gate strait. This natural harbor is one of best sheltered in the world. On S peninsula is San Francisco and on E shore are Alameda, Oakland, Berkeley, and Richmond. In bay are Alcatraz, Angel, and Yerba Buena islands. San Pablo Bay (N) and Suisun Bay are subsidiary waters. Sir Francis Drake entered bay 1579. Late 1700s brought Spanish explorations. **San Francisco-Oakland Bay Bridge,** built 1933–36, crosses bay to Yerba Buena Isl. where tunnel connects with spans to Oakland. Double-decked structure, it is 8¼ mi. long.

San Francisco Peaks, N Ariz., N of Flagstaff, consisting of Humphreys, 12,655 ft. (highest in Ariz.); Agassiz, 12,340 ft.; and Fremont, 11,940 ft.

San Gabriel, residential city (pop. 20,343), S Calif., E of Los Angeles. Spanish mission (1771).

San Gabriel Mountains, S Calif., E and NE of Los Angeles, running c.60 mi. W from Cajon Pass, NNW of San Bernardino. Rises to 10,080 ft. in San Antonio Peak. Includes Mt. Wilson (5,710 ft. high), with observatory estab. 1904 and operated by Carnegie Inst. and California Inst. of Technology.

Sangallo (säng-gäl'lō), three Italian architects. **Giuliano da Sangallo** (jōōlyä'nō), 1445–1516, worked on St. Peter's at Rome with Raphael and Fra Giocondo. His brother, **Antonio da Sangallo,** the elder, 1455–1534, built the domed church at Montepulchiano. Their nephew, **Antonio da Sangallo,** the younger, 1485–1546, designed Farnese Palace and Pauline Chapel (Vatican). Collaborated with Bramante.

Sangamon (săng'gůmůn), river, c.250 mi. long, rising in E central Ill., NE of Springfield. Flows SW to Decatur (dammed, forming L. Decatur), then W and NW to Illinois R. above Beardstown. Much of Lincoln's youth spent in its environs.

Sanger, Margaret (Higgins), 1883–, American leader in the BIRTH CONTROL movement. Organized first American (1921) and international (1925) birth control conferences; estab. many clinics.

Sanger, city (pop. 6,400), S central Calif., near Fresno in San Joaquin Valley. Packs raisins.

San Gimignano (sän jēmēnyä'nō), town (pop. 3,426), Tuscany, central Italy. With its city walls, palaces, and 13 towers, it has preserved its medieval aspect more than any other Italian town. It suffered some damage in World War II.

Sangre de Cristo Mountains (săng'grē dē krĭ'stō), part of Rocky Mts., including Sierra Blanca in S central Colo. (with Blanca Peak, 14,363 ft. high) and Truchas peaks in N.Mex.

Sanhedrin (să'nĭdrĭn, săn'hĭ–), Jewish legal and religious court in anc. Jerusalem. There probably were two Sanhedrins—one political and civil, the other purely religious. Both organizations perished with the destruction of the Temple.

San Ildefonso (săn" ēl"důfōns'sō), Indian pueblo village (1948 pop. 174), N central N.Mex., on Rio Grande and NW of Santa Fe; present settlement estab. early 1700s. Tanoan language. Famous for fine pottery, paintings. Annual ceremonial dances.

San Ildefonso, Treaty of (sän ēldāfōn'sō), name of several treaties signed at village of San Ildefonso, central Spain, in the royal summer palace of La Granja. By the treaty of **1796** Spain became the ally of France in the French Revolutionary Wars. The treaty of **1800** (actually a draft, confirmed by later treaties in 1801 and 1802), restored Louisiana to France; prepared Louisiana Purchase of 1803.

sanitation: see HYGIENE; PLUMBING; PUBLIC HEALTH.

San Jacinto (săn jůsĭn'tů), river rising E central Texas and flowing c.50 mi. S to Galveston Bay arm. Lower river used with Buffalo Bayou (tributary) for Houston ship channel. Monument to Sam Houston's defeat of Mexicans in final battle of Texas Revolution on river near Houston.

San Jacinto Mountains, range extending c.30 mi. SSE from S end of San Bernardino Mts. At N end, near Palm Springs, San Jacinto Peak or Mt. San Jacinto rises to 10,805 ft.

San Joaquin (săn wäkēn'), river, 317 mi. long, rising in E Calif., in the Sierra Nevada and flowing briefly W, then N through S part of CENTRAL VALLEY (San Joaquin Valley) to form delta with Sacramento R. near Suisun Bay, a San Francisco Bay arm. Receives many streams from Sierra Nevada. Rich irrigated agr. valley (see FRIANT DAM) includes independent Kings and Kern rivers. Chief centers are Bakersfield, Modesto, Merced, Fresno, and Stockton.

San José (sän hōsā'), city (pop. 86,909), W central Costa Rica, cap. and largest city of Costa Rica; founded c.1738. Center of economic, political, and social life of republic. University located here.

San Jose (sănůsā', săn hōzā'), city (pop. 95,280), W Calif., SE of San Francisco; founded 1777. Meeting place of first state legislature (1849) and first state cap. (1849–51). Important canning and dried-fruit packing center in Santa Clara Valley. Annexed Willow Glen 1936. Mission San Jose de Guadalupe (1797) is near.

San Jose scale, scale insect introduced from China into San Jose, Calif. It spread over North American fruit-growing areas. Drains sap, attacks fruit of many trees. Covers bark with waxy scales it secretes, under which females remain for life. Some control possible with oil and lime sulphur sprays.

San Juan (sän hwän'), city (pop. 82,410), cap. of San Juan prov., W Argentina, on San Juan R.; founded 1562. Center of irrigated region, it also has mining and cattle raising.

San Juan, city (pop. 224,767), cap. and chief city of Puerto Rico, on NE coast; founded 1521. Grew in importance as West Indian port during 18th and 19th cent. and was scene of uprising (1885) against Spanish rule. Taken over by U.S. troops (Oct., 1898) in Spanish-American War. Points of interest include: El Morro castle (begun 1539), San Cristóbal castle (begun 1631), and La Fortaleza (begun 1529; now the governor's palace). Most of Univ. of Puerto Rico and School of Tropical Medicine are here.

San Juan (săn" wän'), Indian pueblo village (1948 pop. 788), N N.Mex., on Rio Grande and NW of Santa Fe. State's first Spanish settlement made here in 1598 by Juan de Oñate. Popé, medicine man of San Juan, led Pueblo revolt of 1680. Tanoan language. Annual festival honors St. John the Baptist.

San Juan (sän hwän'), river, 108 mi. long, flowing from SE corner of L. Nicaragua to Caribbean. Lower course is boundary of Nicaragua and Costa Rica. Would be vital link in projected Nicaragua Canal.

San Juan (săn" wän'), river, c.400 mi. long, rising in San Juan Mts. of SW Colo. and flowing SW into N.Mex., NW into Utah, and W to Colorado R. near Rainbow Bridge Natl. Monument.

San Juan Boundary Dispute, controversy between U.S. and Great Britain over U.S.–British Columbia boundary. Sometimes called Northwest Boundary Dispute. Difficulty arose from faulty wording of treaty settling Oregon question in 1846. Boundary line it set ran through middle of Juan de Fuca Strait. Strait, however, breaks into several channels; between two main ones lie San Juan Isls. Ownership of islands, especially San Juan itself, was disputed. Crisis loomed in 1859 when U.S. troops occupied San Juan Isl., but Gen. Winfield Scott arranged with British for joint occupation. Emperor William I of Germany arbitrated in 1872; decision gave archipelago to U.S.

San Juan Capistrano (săn" wän" kăpĭsträ'nō), town, S Calif., SE of Los Angeles. Junípero Serra estab. mission here 1776. Swallows said to return annually on March 19 and to depart on Oct. 23.

San Juan del Norte (sän hwä' dĕl nôr'tā),

town (pop. 307), E Nicaragua, a Caribbean port at N mouth of San Juan R. Occupied briefly by British after 1848 in effort to keep U.S. from building interoceanic canal. Also called Greytown.

San Juan Hill, E Cuba, near Santiago de Cuba; scene of battle in Spanish-American War (1898), in which Theodore Roosevelt and Rough Riders took part.

San Juan Islands (săn' wän"), archipelago of 172 islands, NW Wash., E of Vancouver Isl., between Haro and Rosario straits; discovered c.1790 by Spanish. Awarded to U.S. 1872 after SAN JUAN BOUNDARY DISPUTE. San Juan, Orcas, Lopez are largest.

San Juan Mountains, in Rocky Mts., SW Colo. and NW N.Mex., W of San Luis Valley, S of Gunnison R. Rises to 14,306 ft. in Uncompahgre Peak, Colo.

Sankt Moritz, Switzerland: see SAINT MORITZ.

Sankt Wolfgang (zängkt vôlf'gäng), resort (pop. 2,640) in the Salzkammergut, Upper Austria, on L. of Sankt Wolfgang. Gothic church has altar carved by Michael Pacher.

San Leandro (săn lēăn'drō), city (pop. 27,542), W Calif., adjoining Oakland, in truck and flower area. It has canneries and automotive and metal-goods plants.

San Luis (sän lwēs'), city (pop. 25,147), cap. of San Luis prov., W central Argentina; founded c.1596. Oasis in arid region, in center of irrigated area; also has mining and cattle raising.

San Luis Obispo (săn lo͞o'ĭs ōbĭ'spō), city (pop. 14,180), S Calif., near San Luis Obispo Bay and NW of Los Angeles. Farm and oil center. San Luis Obispo de Tolosa Mission (1772) is now church.

San Luis Potosí (sän lwēs' pōtōsē'), state (24,-417 sq. mi.; pop. 855,336), N central Mexico. Most of state lies on E tablelands of central plateau. Although soil is fertile, agr. is economically unimportant because rainfall is light. Stock raising and mining are principal industries. Capital, **San Luis Potosí** (pop. 77,161), was founded 1576. Of strategic importance in colonial times and revolutionary period of 1910. Has smelters and factories (matches, candles, textiles, flour).

San Marcos (săn mär'kus), city (pop. 9,980), S central Texas, on San Marcos R. and SW of Austin. Resort with mfg. of cotton products, cottonseed oil, and clothing. Here are military air field and Southwest Texas State Teachers Col.

San Marcos, University of: see LIMA, Peru.

San Marino (sän märē'nō), independent republic (23 sq. mi.; pop. c.14,000), in the Apennines SW of Rimini, Italy. Agr., stock-raising. Its independence dates from early Middle Ages. Government is exercised by two *reggenti* and a general council. Its picturesque cap., **San Marino,** stands on a rocky height and has kept part of medieval fortifications.

San Marino (săn murē'nō), residential city (pop. 11,230), S Calif., near Pasadena. Seat of Henry E. Huntington Library and Art Gall.

San Martín, José de (hōsā dā sän märtēn'), 1778–1850, South American revolutionist. Returned to Argentina from Europe in 1812 to assist in revolution against Spain. Took command of insurgent army and accomplished the difficult feat of leading them across the Andean passes into Chile. Brought revolution to successful culmination in Chile at Chacabuco (1817) and Maipú (1818) and entered Peru. At a secret meeting at Guayaquil with Bolívar, who was entering Peru from the N, San Martín agreed to leave conquest of Peru to Bolívar and retired to private life.

San Mateo (săn mutā'ō), residential city (pop. 41,782), W. Calif., S of San Francisco on San Francisco Bay, in a well-settled area; laid out 1863.

Sanmicheli, Michele (mēkā'lā sänmēkā'lē), 1484–1559, Italian architect and engineer. Built Grimani Palace, Venice, and Pompei Palace, Verona.

Sannazaro, Jacopo (yä'kōpō sän-nätsä'rō), 1458–1530, Italian author. His pastoral romance in prose and verse, *Arcadia* (1504), had great influence in Italian and European literature.

Sannikov Island (sä'nĭkôf), mythical island, N of New Siberian Islands, RSFSR. Reported by Russian explorer Sanikov 1810; existence disproved by 1937–40 expedition of Russian icebreaker *Sedov*.

San Pablo, city (pop. 14,476), W Calif., just N of Richmond near San Pablo Bay.

San Pedro (săn pē'drō) former city (est. 1940 pop. c.40,000), S Calif.; laid out 1882, consolidated 1909 with Los Angeles. Important port for Los Angeles. Has shipyards, dry docks, fish canneries, and oil refineries. Santa Catalina Isl. is across San Pedro Channel. Bay discovered by Cabrillo 1542.

San Pedro Sula (sän pā'dhrō so͞o'lä), city (pop. 22,116), NW Honduras, second largest city of country. It is, with Puerto Cortés, the chief port for banana and sugar plantations.

San Quentin, small peninsula in San Francisco Bay, W Calif. State prison here was begun 1852.

San Rafael (săn rufĕl'), residential city (pop. 13,848), W Calif., N of San Francisco. Seat of Mission San Rafael Arcángel (1817; restored).

San Remo (sän rā'mō), city (pop. 23,963), Liguria, NW Italy; a resort on the Riviera. Gambling casino.

San Salvador (sän sälvädhōr'), city (pop. 160,-380), W central Salvador, cap. and largest city of Salvador. Founded early in 16th cent., it was for a time (1831–38) capital of Central American Federation. Suffers from recurrent and severe earthquakes.

San Salvador, name given by Columbus to one of Bahama Isls., first land discovered in the New World (Oct. 12, 1492). Long thought to have been what is now Cat Island, historians presently identify it with Watling or Watlings Island.

sans-culottes (sã-külôt') [French,= without knee breeches], term applied to lowest class in France during French Revolution, who wore long trousers. Jacobins identified themselves with sans-culottes.

San Sebastián (sän sābästyän'), seaport (pop. 89,276), cap. of Guipúzcoa prov., N Spain, in Basque Provs., on Bay of Biscay. Fashionable resort; former summer residence of Spanish court.

Sanskrit (săn′skrĭt) [Sanskrit,= perfect], classical standard language of India, of Indic group of Indo-Iranian subfamily of Indo-European languages (see LANGUAGE, table). Its earliest form, Vedic, is that of the VEDA. Sanskrit was spoken c.400 B.C. as standard court language, and Sanskrit remains are among oldest Indo-European documents. It was formerly supposed to be a "parent language."

Sanskrit literature, main body of the classical literature of India. It is generally divided into two main groups—writings in Vedic (c.1500–c.200 B.C.), the parent language of Sanskrit, and writings in classical Sanskrit (c.200 B.C.–A.D. c.1100). The early Vedic period produced the VEDA, the most sacred and ancient scriptures of Hinduism. The middle Vedic period produced the *Brahmanas,* which are prose commentaries relating the meaning of the Vedas to religious rites. Parts of the *Brahmanas* are theosophical treatises called *Aranyakas* [forest books], so named because they were meant to be studied in solitude. Late *Aranyakas* are the *Upanishads* (see VEDANTA). Both the Veda and the *Brahmanas* came to be called sruti [Sanskrit,= hearing, i.e., revealed], while all later works are called smitri [Sanskrit,= memory or tradition]. The *Sutras,* dealing with ritual and law, were written toward the end of the Vedic period and are the oldest source of Hindu law. Literature of the Sanskrit period is nearly all in verse. It began with the great epics, notably the MAHABHARATA and the RAMAYANA. The *Mahabharata,* which incorporates the *Bhagavad Gita,* also inspired the *Puranas,* a group of 18 epics. Although lyric poetry was chiefly erotic, many lyric poems were ethical in tone, stressing the vanity of worldly life. Sanskrit drama was an outgrowth of those hymns of the *Rig-Veda* which contain dialogue, and it borrowed stories from popular legend. A famous Sanskrit drama is the *Sakuntala* of KALIDASA. Sanskrit stories and fables (e.g., the PANCHATANTRA) contain stories within stories and thus have many levels to the narrative. Today, Sanskrit is chiefly used for academic exercise; modern INDIAN LITERATURE is mostly written in vernacular languages.

Sansovino, Jacopo (yä′kōpō sänsōvē′nō), 1486–1570, Italian sculptor and architect, whose real name was Tatti. Worked in Rome and Venice, where he built Library of St. Mark's.

Sans Souci (sã so͞osē′) [Fr.,= without cares, content], palace built 1745–47 at Potsdam, Germany, by Frederick the Great. Executed by Knobelsdorff, but believed to have been designed by Frederick himself. The one-story palace is in a magnificent park.

San Stefano, Treaty of (săn stĕ′fŭnō), 1878, between Russia and Turkey, signed at village of San Stefano (now Yesilkoy), near Istanbul. Ending the last of the RUSSO-TURKISH WARS, it forced Turkey to cede parts of Armenia and the Dobruja to Russia; to recognize the independence of Rumania, Serbia, and Montenegro; and to make Bulgaria an autonomous principality including a large part of Macedonia. The tremendous influence the treaty gave Russia in the Balkans caused the other great powers to obtain its revision at the Congress of BERLIN.

Santa Ana (sän′tä ä′nä), city (pop. 51,676), W Salvador. In warm, fertile valley, it is center of coffee, sugar, and cattle region. Santa Ana volcano is near by.

Santa Ana, city (pop. 45,533), S Calif., SE of Los Angeles, in Santa Ana valley; founded 1869. Beet sugar, canned fruits and vegetables, walnuts.

Santa Ana, Indian pueblo village (1948 pop. 294), central N.Mex., N of Albuquerque. Keresan language. Has Santa Ana de Alamillo church (1692).

Santa Anna, Antonio López de (äntō′nyō lō′pās dā sän′tä ä′nä), 1794–1876, Mexican general and politician, president of Mexico (1833–36, 1841–44, 1846–47, 1853–55). His political career was marked by opportunistic rather than fixed principles. First fought with royalist army in Mexico's struggle for independence, then supported ITURBIDE; turned against Iturbide; then opposed Guerrero and Bustamante, whom he had helped to power. His failure in crushing the revolution in Texas (1836) temporarily halted his political career, but his success in repulsing the French (1838) again brought him popularity. Failure in the Mexican War (1846) sent him into exile from which he returned to rule briefly as "perpetual dictator." He was exiled in 1855 when Benito Júarez came into power but was allowed to return to Mexico two years before his death.

Santa Barbara, residential and resort city (pop. 44,913), S Calif., on Santa Barbara Channel. Presidio founded 1782 and mission 1786 (present structure completed 1820). City retains some old Spanish flavor and is known for subtropical luxuriance of its flowers and fruit. Has museums of art and natural history. Holds annual historical fiesta.

Santa Barbara Islands, extending c.150 mi. along coast of S Calif. and separated from coast in N by Santa Barbara Channel. Anacapa Isl. and Santa Barbara Isl. are in Channel Isls. Natl. Monument. Include Santa Catalina (săn″tŭ kă″tŭlē′nŭ) or Catalina Isl., 22 mi. long, off Long Beach. Discovered 1542 by Cabrillo. In 1919 William Wrigley bought and developed it as a pleasure resort. Avalon city (pop. 1,506) is center of this island's resort and sport activities. Has museums, aquarium, bird haven, and casino.

Santa Catalina or **Catalina Island:** see SANTA BARBARA ISLANDS.

Santa Catarina (sãn′tŭ kätŭrē′nŭ), state (36,435 sq. mi.; pop. 1,578,159), SE Brazil; cap. FLORIANÓPOLIS on Santa Catarina isl., just off coast. The mainland is between the Atlantic on E and Argentina on W. From coastal area, which has farming, state rises to tableland, where cattle and hogs are raised; in SE, coal is mined. Settled by Portuguese in 17th cent. Germans immigrated in 19th cent.

Santa Clara, city (pop. 14,178), W Calif., adjoining San Jose. Fruit and meat processing. Has Santa Clara de Asís Mission (1777; restored). Seat of Univ. of Santa Clara (R.C.; for men; 1851).

Santa Clara, Indian pueblo village (1948 pop.

579), N N.Mex., on Rio Grande and NW of Santa Fe; settled c.1700. Tanoan language. Distinctive black pottery is made. Annual St. Clare of Assisi feast. Near by are Puyé ruins of 15th-cent. pueblo.

Santa Claus: see NICHOLAS, SAINT.

Santa Cruz (sän'tä kroōs'), city (pop. 36,400), cap. of Santa Cruz dept., central Bolivia; founded 1557, reestab. at present site 1595 by settlers from Asunción, Paraguay. Center of agr. region and has potential importance; when railroad is completed, city will have access to the Pacific through Peru and to the Atlantic through Brazil.

Santa Cruz (săn'tů kroōz'), city (pop. 21,970), W Calif., on Monterey Bay, in area of fine beaches near Santa Cruz Mts. Fishing and fish canning.

Santa Cruz de Tenerife: see CANARY ISLANDS.

Santa Cruz Islands (săn'tů kroōz'), small volcanic group, S Pacific, in SOLOMON ISLANDS. In 1942 Japanese relief of Guadalcanal was prevented by U.S. victory here.

Santa Fe (sän'tä fā'), city (pop. 168,791), cap. of Santa Fe prov., E central Argentina; river port near Paraná R., with which it is connected by canal. Founded (1573) by Juan de Garay, it has been important in Argentine history. On margin of Pampa, it is transshipping point for grain and meat.

Santa Fe (săn'tů fā'), city (pop. 27,998; alt. c.7,000 ft.), state cap., N N.Mex., between Pecos R. and Rio Grande. Second largest city in N.Mex., resort center with artists' and writers' colony, and shipping point for Indian wares, minerals (lead, zinc, coal, gold, silver), and farm products (fruit, potatoes). Founded c.1609 by Spanish under Oñate, it was Spanish-Indian trade center for over 200 years. Seat of government since its founding, it is oldest cap. city in U.S. Pueblo revolt of 1680 drove Spanish out for 12 years. Commerce with U.S. developed via Santa Fe Trail after Mexican freedom from Spain (1821). Gen. S. W. KEARNY took city for U.S. 1846. Railroad reached Lamy (station for Santa Fe), 16 mi. S, 1879. See of an archbishopric since 1875, city is a Roman Catholic center. Has San Miguel Mission Church (c.1636), Cathedral of St. Francis, and Palace of the Governors (over 300 years old). Near by are many Indian pueblos and Bandelier Natl. Monument.

Santa Fe Railroad. Chartered in Kansas as Atchison and Topeka Railroad in 1859. Formal name since 1895 is Atchison, Topeka & Santa Fe Railway Co. Made connection with city of Santa Fe in 1880. By early 1890s the Santa Fe became one of longest railroad systems in the world. Today its 13,000 mi. of trackage reach L. Michigan, Gulf of Mexico, the Rio Grande, and the Pacific.

Santa Fe Trail, important caravan route of W U.S., leading from W Mo. to Santa Fe, N.Mex. In Nov., 1821, William Becknell brought news that Mexico was free and that Santa Fe now welcomed trade; he organized trading party. Franklin was first outfitting point, succeeded by Westport (now part of Kansas City) and Independence. In 1850 a monthly stage line was estab. between Independence and Santa Fe. Coming of Atchison, Topeka, and Santa Fe RR in 1880 marked death of old trail. See also OREGON TRAIL.

Santa Maria, city (pop. 10,440), S Calif., near San Luis Obispo Bay. Has oil and beet-sugar refineries. Ships vegetables and flower seeds.

Santa Marta (sän'tä mär'tä), city (pop. 25,-113), N Colombia; port on the Caribbean; founded by Bastidas (1525) on deep harbor surrounded by hills. Important in colonial times as seaport for Magdalena R., it was royalist center in revolution against Spain, but was finally liberated (1821). Today banana industry, operated by United Fruit Co., is most important on continent.

Santa Monica, resort and residential city (pop. 71,595), S Calif., W of Los Angeles and between Santa Monica Bay and Santa Monica Mts. Aircraft.

Santander, Francisco de Paula (fränsē'skō dā pou'lä säntändĕr'), 1792–1840, Colombian revolutionist. Ably assisted Bolívar in revolution against Spain and afterwards as vice president of Colombia. A believer in constitutional government, he led federalist opposition to Bolívar and was banished (1828). After Bolívar's death and breakup of Greater Colombia, Santander returned and served ably as president of New Granada (1832–36).

Santander (säntändĕr'), city (pop. 84,971), cap. of Santander prov., N Spain, in Old Castile; a port on Bay of Biscay. Bathing resort. Has ironworks and shipyards.

Santa Paula, city (pop. 11,049), S Calif., NW of Los Angeles, in fruit and oil area.

Santaquin (săntůkēn'), city (pop. 1,214), N central Utah, S of Provo, in STRAWBERRY VALLEY PROJECT.

Santarém (sântůrān'), city (pop. 11,785), W Portugal, in Estremadura, on Tagus R. Agr. trade center. Taken from the Moors by Alfonso I (1147), it played an important part in Portuguese history. Old royal palace is now in ruins.

Santa Rita, village (pop. 2,135), SW N.Mex., near Silver City. Has large open-pit copper mines.

Santa Rosa, city (pop. 17,902), W Calif., N of San Francisco. Trade center for Sonoma Valley. Processes fruits and produces wines and shoes. Has home and gardens of Luther Burbank.

Santa Sophia: see HAGIA SOPHIA.

Santayana, George (säntäyä'nä), 1863–1952, American philosopher and poet, b. Madrid. He taught for many years at Harvard, but in 1912 returned to Europe, eventually settling in Italy, where he lived secluded in a convent. He rejected organized religion, but in his later works stressed the role of faith in the life of man—faith in the unknowable in a world entirely material. His broad views and his mastery of literary style gave him a large public even for such strictly philosophical works as *The Sense of Beauty* (1896), *The Life of Reason* (1905–6) and *The Realms of Being* (4 vols., 1927–40). A novel, *The Last Puritan* (1935), and his autobiography, *Persons and Places* (3 vols., 1944–53), gained more popular notice. Of his poems, his sonnets are best known.

Santee (săntē'), river formed by confluence of Congaree and Wateree rivers, central S.C.,

SE of Columbia. Flows 143 mi. to the Atlantic, S of Georgetown. Center of hydroelectric and navigation project (1942).

Santiago (säntēä'gō), city (pop. 1,161,633), central Chile, cap. of Chile and Santiago prov.; one of the largest cities in South America. Founded 1541 by Valdivia, it has been focal point of intellectual and cultural development of Chile; also the political, commercial, and financial heart of nation. National Univ. is here.

Santiago de Compostela (säntyä'gō dā kōmpōstā'lä), city (pop. 30,127), NW Spain, in Galicia. It has been one of chief Christian shrines of pilgrimage since the 9th cent., when a sanctuary was built here over the supposed tomb of the apostle St. James. Destroyed by the Moors (10th cent.), the earlier sanctuary was replaced by a Romanesque cathedral (11th–12th cent.), later transformed by baroque and plateresque additions. Here too are the Hospital Real (1501–11), built for accommodation of poor pilgrims, and a university (estab. 1501).

Santiago de Cuba (dā kōō'bä), city (pop. 118,266), SE Cuba. Founded in 1514 by Diego de Velásquez, it was for some time capital of Cuba. Exports mineral, agr., and wood products. In 1898 it played important part in Spanish-American War. With elimination of yellow fever, Santiago has become a fine modern port.

Santiago del Estero (děl āstā'rō), city (pop. 63,491), cap. of Santiago del Estero prov., N central Argentina. Founded 1553, it is center of cattle-raising and agr. region and popular health resort.

Santiago de los Caballeros (dā lōs käbäyā'rōs), city (pop. 56,192), N central Dominican Republic; commercial and agr. distributing point for the most densely populated part of republic.

Santillana, Iñigo López de Mendoza, marqués de (ēnyē'gō lō'pāth dā měndō'thä märkās' dā säntēlyä'nä), 1398–1458, chief Spanish poet and author of his era. Wrote first Spanish sonnets.

Santo Domingo (sän'tō dōmēng'gō), former Spanish colony on HISPANIOLA. Columbus discovered island in 1492 and left settlement there, but upon his return in 1493 settlers had vanished. He administered new colony until complaints of harsh rule caused his replacement by Bobadilla (1500), who in turn was replaced by Diego Columbus (1509). Finding no mineral wealth in quantity, settlers turned to farming with work done by Indians under *encomienda* system. No colonization of W part of island (present Haiti) being undertaken by Spanish, French planters began to settle there. Sugar cane was introduced in late 18th cent. and became dominant product. Spain ceded part of island to France 1697 and gave up whole island 1795. Spanish colonists resisted French rule and—after Haiti gained independence—Haitian rule. (For later history of island, see HAITI; DOMINICAN REPUBLIC.) Seat of colonial administration was city of **Santo Domingo,** founded 1496, which is oldest continuously inhabited settlement in W Hemisphere. After hurricane of 1930, city was rebuilt and renamed TRUJILLO.

Santo Domingo, Indian pueblo (pop. 1,169), central N.Mex., on Rio Grande and SW of Santa Fe; present village founded c.1700. Eastern Keresan language. Farming, pottery making. Annual Green Corn dance.

santonin (săn'tùnĭn), colorless, odorless, crystalline solid obtained from certain plants. It is used in medicines to expel worms and is poisonous in large doses.

Santos (sän'tōōsh), city (pop. 201,739), São Paulo state, SE Brazil, on small island in Atlantic, just off mainland, port for São Paulo (35 mi. inland); founded c.1545. World's greatest coffee port, also exports cotton, sugar, fruit, and meat.

Santos-Dumont, Alberto (săn'tōs-dōō'mōnt), 1873–1932, Brazilian aeronaut. Pioneered in constructing and flying gasoline-motored airship (1898).

Santo Tomás, University of, at Manila, P.I.; R.C., coed.; founded 1611 by Dominicans.

São Francisco (sã'õ fränsēsh'kō), river, c.1,800 mi. long, rising in SW Minas Gerais state, E Brazil, and flowing generally NE to Atlantic. Vast irrigation and hydroelectric project in its basin begun 1949.

São Luís (sã'õ lōōēsh'), city (pop. 81,432), cap. of Maranhão state, N Brazil, on São Luís isl., at mouth of Itapecuru R. Founded (1612) by French, captured (1615) by Portuguese. Exports cotton, babassu oil, sugar, balsam, and hides.

Saône (sōn), river, 267 mi. long, E France, rising in Vosges mts. and flowing S through Franche-Comté and Burgundy into the Rhone at Lyons.

Saône, Haute: see HAUTE-SAÔNE.

Saône-et-Loire (sōn"-ā-lwär'), department (3,331 sq. mi.; pop. 506,749), E central France, in Burgundy; cap. Mâcon.

São Paulo (sã'õ pou'lō), state (95,453 sq. mi.; pop. 9,242,610), SE Brazil; cap. São Paulo. State extends inland from the Atlantic to Paraná R. and is most populous and most important agr. and industrial state in Brazil. Coffee is dominant crop; vast quantities are exported from Santos. Development of coffee production and progressive agr. methods aided by immigration in 19th and 20th cent. Cattle are raised in many sections, and textile milling and processing and shipping agr. products important. Its cap., **São Paulo,** is a plateau city (pop. 2,227,512; alt. 2,700 ft.); commercial and industrial center of Brazil and one of most important Latin American cities. Transportation and shipping point for rich agr. hinterland, it has numerous factories (machinery, textiles, chemicals, automobiles, shoes, household appliances, cement, and processed foods). Educational institutions include Univ. of São Paulo, McKenzie Inst., police training school, and technical and professional schools. Founded 1554 by Jesuits, it became capital of area in 1681. Its residents are called *paulistas.*

São Tiago: see CAPE VERDE ISLANDS.

São Tomé and Principe (sãõ tōōmā', prēn'sēpā), islands in Gulf of Guinea, off coast of Africa, comprising a province (372 sq. mi.; pop. 60,159) of Portugal. Export cacao, coffee, and palm oil.

São Vicente, Cabo de: see SAINT VINCENT, CAPE.

sap, fluid of plants consisting of water, dissolved plant foods (esp. sugars, salts, and organic acids), and pigments. Sap water enters through root hairs by osmosis and is carried by vascular tissues (xylem or wood) to parts containing chlorophyll, usually the leaves. It is believed that sap ascent is caused by osmotic pull from higher sap concentrations in leaves after loss of water by transpiration and to some extent from osmotic pressure arising in the roots (esp. great in the spring). Maple sugar is made from the sap of the sugar maple. Other specialized plant fluids such as the milky juice latex are sometimes called sap.

Sapir, Edward (sůpēr′), 1884–1939, American linguist and anthropologist, b. Germany. Contributed greatly to development of descriptive linguistics.

Sapor, Persian kings: see SHAPUR.

Sapphira (sůfī′rů), wife of ANANIAS **1.**

sapphire (să′fīůr), variety of transparent blue corundum, among the most valuable of gems. Found in Ceylon, Siam, Burma, India, Australia, Montana.

Sappho (să′fō), fl. early 6th cent. B.C., greatest early Greek lyric poet, b. Lesbos, an aristocrat. Her life is obscured by legend. Her verse, of which fragments survive, is the classic example of the "pure" love lyric, characterized by vehement expression of passion and perfect control of meter.

Sapporo (säp-pō′rō), city (pop. 259,602), SW Hokkaido, Japan; cap. and largest city of Hokkaido. Seat of Hokkaido Imperial Univ.

sapsucker, small North American woodpecker. Yellow-bellied sapsucker damages or kills trees because it girdles them with holes, eats inner tissue, drinks sap.

Sapulpa (sůpŭl′pů), city (pop. 13,031), NE central Okla., SW of Tulsa. Trade center of agr. and oil region with mfg. of glass, clay products, and gasoline. Has U.S. Indian school.

Saracens, term used in the Middle Ages to mean Arabs and more generally Moslems. Strictly the term should have been applied only to the people of NW Arabia, but instead it finally came to be applied more particularly to the Seljuk Turks.

Saragossa (să″růgŏ′sů), Span. *Zaragoza,* city (pop. 205,833), cap. of Saragossa prov. and of Aragon, NE Spain, on the Ebro. Communications and commercial center. Archiepiscopal see; seat of a university (founded 1474). The ancient Caesarea Augusta, it later was the cap. of a Moorish emirate (1017–1118). In the Peninsula War, Saragossa under the leadership of PALAFOX heroically repulsed the first French siege (1808) but surrendered after c.50,000 defenders had died in the second siege (1808–9). Many of the city's rich works of art show Moorish influence. There are two cathedrals—La Seo (12th–16th cent.), a former mosque, and El Pilar, with frescoes by Velázquez and Goya. Other monuments include Aljafería castle (Moorish; later royal residence).

Sarah or **Sara** [Heb.,= princess], wife of Abraham, mother of Isaac. Her original name of Sarai was changed to Sarah when Abram became Abraham. Her jealousy drove HAGAR into the desert. Gen. 11.31–23.20; Rom. 4.19; 9.9; Heb. 11.11; 1 Peter 3.6.

Sarah Lawrence College: see EASTCHESTER, N.Y.

Sarajevo (sä″rä′yĕvô), city (pop. 118,158), cap. of Bosnia and Hercegovina, central Yugoslavia, in Bosnia. Trade and railroad center; tobacco, carpet, and other mfg. See of Orthodox Eastern Metropolitan, Roman Catholic archbishop, and chief ulema of Yugoslavia Moslems. Fell to Turkey 1429. Shared history of BOSNIA AND HERZEGOVINA after 1878. Assassination of Archduke FRANCIS FERDINAND here (June 28, 1914) was immediate cause of World War I. City has largely Moslem population.

Saranac Lake (să′růnăk), village (pop. 6,913), N N.Y., SW of Plattsburg, in the Adirondacks on Flower L. and near Saranac Lakes. Health and year-round resort. Has tuberculosis sanatorium (1884) and research laboratory (1894) founded by E. L. Trudeau; Will Rogers Memorial Sanatorium (1930).

Saranac Lakes, N N.Y., three resort lakes in the Adirondacks. Upper (c.8 mi. long), Middle (c.2 mi. long), Lower (c.5 mi. long) lakes linked by Saranac R., which flows c.50 mi. NE to L. Champlain.

Sarasate, Pablo de (pä′blō dā säräsä′tā), 1844–1908, Spanish violin virtuoso. He wrote many brilliant violin pieces in a Spanish idiom (e.g., *Jota Aragonesa* and *Zigeunerweisen*).

Sarasota (să″růsō′tů), city (pop. 18,896), SW Fla., on Sarasota Bay S of Tampa; settled c.1884 by Scotch. Winter resort. Packs and ships citrus fruit and vegetables (esp. celery). Fishing. The John and Mable Ringling Mus. of Art and winter hq. of Ringling Brothers–Barnum and Bailey Circus are here. Holds annual Sara de Sota pageant.

Saratoga campaign (să″rŭtō′gů), June–Oct., 1777, of American Revolution. British planned three-fold advance—S from Canada, N from New York city, and E along the Mohawk—to split colonies along the Hudson by meeting at Albany. Force advancing N never arrived at Albany. Barry St. Leger, coming E, besieged Fort Stanwix but retreated to Canada before Benedict Arnold's advance. John Burgoyne, coming from N, captured Ticonderoga, was beaten at Bennington, and halted near present Saratoga Springs. American forces, commanded by Horatio Gates, prevented break-through of British at Freeman's Farm and Bemis Heights; Burgoyne surrendered Oct. 17, 1777. Battle was first great American victory of war. Battlefield included in Saratoga Natl. Historical Park (estab. 1948).

Saratoga Springs, city (pop. 15,473), E N.Y., near Saratoga L., N of Albany. Health and pleasure resort with mineral springs; state-owned spa (1935) contains curative baths, Simon Baruch Research Inst. Bottles and ships springs' waters. Mfg. of chemicals, textiles, wallpaper. Horse racing after 1850. Seat of Skidmore Col. (nonsectarian; chiefly for women; men admitted 1946; chartered and opened 1911; chartered as a college 1922). Last battles of SARATOGA CAMPAIGN fought near by.

Saratov (sŭrä′tůf), city (pop. c.450,000), SE European RSFSR; a port on high right bank of the Volga. Major industrial center (machinery, chemicals, and textile plants; oil refineries; lumber mills; shipyards). Its important natural gas wells, discovered in World War II, were linked 1946 by pipe line with Moscow. Founded 1590 on left river bank; moved to present site 1674. University founded 1919.

Sarawak (sûrä'wŭk), British crown colony (47,071 sq. mi.; pop. 546,385), NW Borneo; cap. Kuching. Produces oil, rubber, rice, sago, and pepper. In 1841 sultan of Brunan ceded area to James Brooke, an Englishman, who became raja of independent state. As British protectorate (1888–1946) Sarawak was ruled by Brooke family. Occupied 1941–45 by Japanese. Became a colony in 1946.

Sarazen, Gene (sä'rŭzŭn), 1901–, American golfer. Won U.S. Open (1922, 1932), British Open (1932), Professional Golfers Association (1922–23, 1933) and many other championships.

sarcoma (särkō'mŭ), malignant tumor composed of connective-type cells. Grows very large and spreads through tissues and along blood vessels and nerves.

Sardanapalus (särdŭnă'pŭlŭs), Assyrian monarch, who, after being besieged in Nineveh by the Medes for two years, burned his palace and himself. Some identify him with Assur-bani-pal.

sardine (särdēn'), name for various small fish canned with oil or sauce. True sardine is usually young pilchard (*Sardinia pilchardus*) of Mediterranean and warm Atlantic coastal waters. Young sprat and herring are also packed as sardines.

Sardinia (särdĭ'nēŭ), Ital. *Sardegna,* island and autonomous region (9,302 sq. mi.; pop. 1,034,206), Italy, in the W Mediterranean; cap. Cagliari. The Strait of Bonifacio separates it from Corsica (N). Mostly mountainous (max. alt. 6,016 ft.), Sardinia has large pasture lands (horses, sheep, goats), minerals (zinc, lead, lignite), some agr., and important fisheries. Malaria and feudalism (abolished 1835) hampered its development until recent times, when reclamation projects were undertaken. Sardinia was settled by Carthaginians before its conquest by Rome (238 B.C.). It fell to the Vandals 5th cent. A.D.; was recovered by Byzantium 6th cent. The popes, however, claimed it as their patrimony (see PAPAL STATES) and acted as overlords. With their help, Sardinia repulsed Arab attacks (8th–11th cent.). Pisa and Genoa fought through the 11th–14th cent. for supremacy over the island, but in the 14th cent. the pope bestowed it on the house of Aragon. Sardinia remained Spanish until 1713, when it passed to Austria by the Peace of Utrecht. Spain forcibly recovered it in 1717 but was obliged by the QUADRUPLE ALLIANCE to give it up (1720). It was then awarded to the duke of Savoy, who took the title king of Sardinia. The **kingdom of Sardinia** comprised SAVOY, PIEDMONT, NICE, Sardinia, and (after 1815) LIGURIA (incl. Genoa). Its cap. was Turin. Sardinia's defeat in the French Revolutionary Wars led to the annexation (1798–1814) of all its mainland possessions to France. Sardinia, especially under VICTOR EMMANUEL II, played the leading part in the Italian RISORGIMENTO. After annexing Lombardy (1859), Parma, Modena, and the N part of the Papal States (1860), and the Two Sicilies (1861), it became the kingdom of Italy. See also SAVOY, HOUSE OF.

Sardis (sär'dĭs), cap. of anc. Lydia, W Asia Minor. It was captured by the Persians with the conquest of Lydia. The city was finally destroyed by Tamerlane. Hittite inscriptions have been found here. Also Sardes.

Sardou, Victorien (vēktôryē' särdōō'), 1831–1908, French dramatist, author of some 70 popular plays ranging from light comedy to elaborate historical pieces. Best-known are *La Tosca* (1887; Eng. tr., 1925) and *Madame Sans-Gêne* (1893; Eng. tr., 1901).

Sargasso Sea (särgă'sō), part of N Atlantic Ocean, extending between West Indies and the Azores, from about lat. 20° N to lat. 35° N. Relatively still, it is the center of a swirl of ocean currents and is a rich field for marine biologists.

Sargent, John Singer, 1856–1925, American painter, b. Florence, Italy, of American parents. Educated in Europe. Spent early period in Paris, where first exhibit (1878) brought him recognition as a portraitist. In 1884 he moved to London, where he painted the portraits of American and English celebrities for which he is famous. Also produced many impressionistic landscapes in water color.

Sargon (sär'gŏn), fl. c.2800? B.C., king of Akkad or Agade in Mesopotamia. Conquered much territory and created a loose-knit empire. His dynasty seems to have spread Semitic and Sumerian civilization. Also Sharrukin.

Sargon, d. 705 B.C., king of Assyria (722–705 B.C.). He is supposed to have completed Shalmaneser's conquest of Samaria, and he certainly pushed conquests, taking Carchemish, subduing Babylon, and going E into Kurdistan. Won a great victory at Raphia (720). His palace of Dur Sharrukin (Khorsabad) was notably magnificent.

Sark, Fr. *Sercq* (sĕrk), island (2 sq. mi.; pop. 560), in English Channel, one of CHANNEL ISLANDS.

Sarmatia (särmā'shŭ), district about the lower Don R., occupied by the Sarmatians 3d cent. B.C.–2d cent. A.D. The area to which they were driven by the Germans, along the Danube and across the Carpathians, is also called Sarmatia. The **Sarmatians** were pastoral nomads related to the Scythians, whom they displaced in the Don region. Main divisions were Rhoxolani, Iazyges, and Alani. They spoke an Indo-Iranian language. They long warred against the Romans, then sought Roman help against the Germans, who forced them out.

Sarmiento, Domingo Faustino (dōmēng'gō foustē'nō särmyän'tō), 1811–88, Argentine statesman, educator, and author, president of republic (1868–74). Exiled as an opponent of Rosas, he was impressed in his travels with the educational system of the U.S. and after the downfall of Rosas (1852), he returned to Argentina and upon becoming president, effected educational reforms in Argentina patterned after U.S. school system. Best-known literary work is *Facundo,* a study of the *caudillo* as a type.

Sarnath (särnät′), archaeological site, SE Uttar Pradesh, India, near Benares. The deer park, traditional site where Buddha first preached, is located here.

Sarnia, city (pop. 34,697), S Ont., Canada, on St. Clair R., at S end of L. Huron opposite Port Huron, Mich. (connected by bridge, tunnel, and ferries); settled 1833 as The Rapids. Port and oil-refining center with steel, lumber, and flour mills.

Saronic Gulf (sůrŏ′nĭk), inlet of Aegean Sea, W central Greece, bounded by Attica (NE), Isthmus of Corinth (N), Argolis peninsula (SW). Isthmian Canal connects it with Gulf of Corinth. Piraeus is among cities on Saronic Gulf, which also contains many islands (e.g., Aegina and Salamis). Also known as Gulf of Aegina.

Saroyan, William (sůroi′ůn), 1908–, American short-story writer and dramatist. Best known for short stories (e.g., those in *The Daring Young Man on the Flying Trapeze,* 1934) and semiautobiographical *My Name is Aram* (1940). *The Time of Your Life* (1939) is his best-known play.

Sarre: see SAAR, river; SAAR TERRITORY.

Sarrebruck, Saar Territory: see SAARBRÜCKEN.

Sars, Michael (mēkäl′ särs′), 1805–69, Norwegian biologist and pioneer in marine research.

sarsaparilla (särs″půrĭl′ů), name for various plants and the extract from their roots, used in medicine and beverages. True sarsaparilla is obtained from tropical species of *Smilax,* and a substitute from wild sarsaparilla (*Aralia nudicaulis*) of North America.

Sartain, John (särtān′), 1808–97, American engraver, b. London. In 1830 he came to U.S., where he pioneered in mezzotint engraving. His pupils included his daughter, **Emily Sartain,** 1841–1927, and two sons, **Samuel Sartain,** 1830–1906, and **William Sartain,** 1843–1924.

Sarthe (särt), department (2,411 sq. mi.; pop. 412,214), NW France, in Maine; cap. Le Mans. It is crossed by the **Sarthe** R., 175 mi. long, which joins with the Mayenne R., above Angers, to form the Maine R.

Sarto, Andrea del (ändrā′ä dĕl sär′tō), 1486–1531, Florentine painter, equally famous for his frescoes and his oils. His work is marked by sumptuous color and monumental composition. Notable paintings include *Madonna of the Harpies* (Uffizi) and *Holy Family* (Metropolitan Mus.).

Sartre, Jean Paul (zhã′ pôl′ sär′trů), 1905–, French philosopher and writer. Noted as originator of EXISTENTIALISM, expounded in *L'Être et le néant* (1943) and *Existentialism* (1946). Has written novels (e.g., *Nausea,* 1938; *Age of Reason,* 1945), and dramas (e.g., *The Flies,* 1943; *No Exit,* 1944; *The Respectful Prostitute,* 1946).

Sarum, England: see OLD SARUM; SALISBURY.

Sasanidae or Sasanians: see SASSANIDAE.

Sasebo (säsā′bō), city (pop. 175,233), W Kyushu, Japan; naval base on East China Sea.

Saskatchewan (sůskă′chůwůn), province (237,-975 sq. mi.; with water surface 251,700 sq. mi.; pop. 831,728), W Canada; cap. REGINA. Largest other cities are SASKATOON, MOOSE JAW, and PRINCE ALBERT. Abundant mineral resources, including pitchblende-yielding ore of high uranium content, are encouraging development in the far NW region of Sask. around L. ATHABASKA. Parklands of central Sask. have large timber resources, much of it in PRINCE ALBERT NATIONAL PARK. Most settlement is S on prairies well-suited to large-scale mechanized farming (wheat, ranching, dairying). First explored by white men in late 17th cent. French fur-trading posts estab. in mid-18th cent. Later North West and Hudson's Bay companies operated here. Dominion bought territorial rights from Hudson's Bay Co. 1869, when area became part of Northwest Territories. Saw rebellion of Louis RIEL 1884–85. Farm settlement, aided by free land grants, followed arrival of Canadian Pacific RR 1882. Political experimentation under CO-OPERATIVE COMMONWEALTH FEDERATION has promoted farm and labor legislation.

Saskatchewan, river of W Canada, formed E of Prince Albert, Sask., by confluence of North Saskatchewan and South Saskatchewan rivers. Flows 340 mi. E to L. Winnipeg, Man. The North Saskatchewan rises at foot of Mt. Saskatchewan, SW Alta. flows E 760 mi. South Saskatchewan R. forms in S Alta. by confluence of Bow and Oldman rivers, flows 550 mi. (with the Bow 865 mi.) E then NE to junction with North Saskatchewan R. Was chief transportation route of old Northwest Territories before railroad.

Saskatchewan, University of: see SASKATOON.

Saskatoon, city (pop. 53,268), S central Sask., Canada, on South Saskatchewan R. and NW of Regina; laid out 1883. Mfg. and trade center for central and N Sask. with grain elevators, stockyards, breweries, and meat-packing, wood, and metal-working plants. Seat of Univ. of Saskatchewan (provincially supported; coed.; 1909).

sassafras (să′sůfrăs″), tree or shrub (*Sassafras albidum*) of E North America with entire, two- or three-lobed leaves. Bark from the roots is used to make sassafras tea and root beers.

Sassafras Mountain, peak, 3,560 ft. high, NW S.C., in the Blue Ridge. State's highest point.

Sassanidae (săsā′nĭdē), **Sassanids** (să′sůnĭdz), or **Sassanians** (săsā′nyůnz), last dynasty of native rulers to reign in Persia (A.D. c.226–c.640). Ctesiphon was its capital. The name (also spelled Sasanidae or Sasanian) derives from Sassan, an ancestor of dynasty's founder, ARDASHIR I. Sassanids were much occupied with wars, especially with Rome and Byzantium. Overthrown by the Arabs. Notable rulers were SHAPUR I, SHAPUR II, and KHOSRU II.

Sassoon, Siegfried (sůsōōn′), 1886–, English poet and novelist. After World War I he wrote powerful anti-war novels collected in *The Memories of George Sherston* (1937) and vigorous lyrics (in *Collected Poems,* 1949).

Satalia or Satalieh: see ANTALYA, Turkey.

Satan (sā′tůn) [Heb.,= adversary], in Judaism, Christianity, and Islam, the principle of evil conceived as a person. Also called the devil [from Gr.,= accuser]. Originally an angel, he rebelled against God and fell from heaven to eternal damnation. He presides over hell and is served by minor angels (called devils) who fell with him. To Satan is ascribed the origin of evil; he is the destroyer of souls and tempter of man to sin. He is the subject of much popular legend. Among literary representations of him are the Mephistopheles of Goethe's *Faust* and the Lucifer of Milton's *Paradise Lost*. Names and nicknames of Satan are legion, e.g., Abaddon, Apollyon, Dragon, Serpent, Lucifer, Asmodeus (see TOBIT), Beelzebub or Baalzebub, and Belial. Antichrist is not a proper name of Satan. There are many references in Bible to Satan: 1 Chron. 21.1; Job 1; 2; Zech. 3.2; Isa. 14.12; Mat. 4.1; 9.34; 10.25; 12.22–30; 13.13,39; 25.41; Mark 3.22–30; Luke 10.18; 11.14–26; John 8.44; 12.31; 14.30; 16.11; Acts 26.18; 2 Cor. 2.11; 4.4; 11.14; Eph. 2.2; 1 Thess. 3.5; Jude 6; and the book of REVELATION.

satellite (săʹtŭlīt), in astronomy, smaller celestial body revolving about a planet or star and shining only by reflected light. All planets except Mercury, Venus, and Pluto have one or more known satellites, most of them moving eastward in almost circular orbits, but a few having retrograde motion. Earth's only satellite, the moon, is largest in relation to its planet.

Satie, Erik (sätēʹ), 1866–1925, French composer. He rebelled against romanticism and impressionism in music and urged a return to simplicity in style. He gathered around himself a group of young composers—Poulenc, Honegger, Georges Auric (1899–), Louis Durey (1888–), Germaine Tailleferre (1892–), and Milhaud—who were to become known as *Les Six*. Satie himself wrote ballet and film music and piano pieces, including the popular *Gymnopédies*.

satin, lustrous fabric, usually silk, with the filling arranged so that practically nothing shows but warp. First made in China, it was made in Europe after secrets of silk making were carried westward in the Middle Ages.

satinwood, hard, durable wood with satinlike sheen, used in cabinetmaking, especially in marquetry. East Indian or Ceylon satinwood, the heartwood of *Chloroxylon swietenia*, is used for furniture and veneers. West Indian satinwood, also called yellowwood, the wood of *Zanthoxylum* (or *Xanthoxylum*) *flavum*, is superior.

satire, term applied to any literary form, in prose or poetry, which ridicules situations, individuals, or ideas. Its purpose is to correct manners and morals through mockery, broad humor, sophisticated wit, harsh invective, parody, or gentle irony. It may be humorous or serious, but object is generally made to seem ridiculous rather than evil.

Satsuma (sätsōōʹmä), peninsula, SW Kyushu, Japan. Was domain of powerful Satsuma clan and scene of Takamori Saigo's unsuccessful revolt (1877) against imperial government. Famous porcelain, Satsuma ware, made here.

Satterlee, Henry Yates, 1843–1908, American Episcopal bishop; first bishop of diocese of Washington D.C. (1896). Planned and began National or Washington Cathedral.

Satu-Mare (säʹtōō-mäʹrĕ), Hung. *Szatmárnémeti* or *Szatmár*, city (pop. 46,519), NW Rumania, near Hungarian border. Commercial center; textile and machinery mfg. Population is c.60% Hungarian.

Saturday: see SABBATH; WEEK.

Saturn, in Roman religion, god of harvest; husband of Ops and father of Ceres. His festival was **Saturnalia;** work ceased, gifts were exchanged, and slaves could do as they pleased.

Saturn, in astronomy, planet sixth in order of distance from sun. Revolves about sun at mean distance of 886,120,000 mi. in c.30 years. Equatorial diameter is c.75,000 mi. Vaporous surface is indicated by latitudinal variations in rotation period (shortest at equator, c.10 hr. 14 min.). Has atmosphere and nine known satellites. Unique feature is system of rings composed of swarms of particles moving in individual orbits and encircling the planet in its equatorial plane. System comprises inner and outer bright rings separated by dark rift (Cassini's division) and a faint inner area (crape ring). Extreme diameter of ring system is c.172,000 mi.; thickness, 10–50 mi. See *ill.*, p. 1187.

Saturnalia: see SATURN, in Roman religion.

satyr, in Greek mythology, one of a tribe of creatures inhabiting forests and mountains. A lesser deity of fertility and a follower of Dionysus, he was fond of revelry and mischief. He is pictured as a hairy little man, with tail and goatlike ears.

Saud, Ibn: see IBN SAUD.

Saudi Arabia (säōōʹdē ŭrāʹbēŭ), kingdom (600,000 sq. mi.; pop. c.6,000,000), SW Asia, occupying most of Arabian peninsula. Its two capitals are RIAD and MECCA. Bounded on N by Jordan, Iraq, and Kuwait, on E by Persian Gulf, on W by Red Sea, and on S by the desert Rub al Khali. In the HEJAZ are the holy cities of Mecca and MEDINA. Basic economy is agr. and pastoral, but country's wealth lies in its oil industry, having perhaps the world's largest oil reserves. Arabian American Oil Co. (organized in Delaware) has held the oil concession since 1933. Saudi Arabia had its beginnings in 1925, when IBN SAUD, then king of the NEJD, formally annexed the Hejaz. His rule was recognized by Great Britain in 1927, and the name Saudi Arabia was adopted in 1932. Belongs to the UN and the Arab League.

Sauer, Christopher: see SOWER, CHRISTOPHER.

Saugus (sôʹgŭs), town (pop. 17,162), NE Mass., N of Boston; settled before 1637. Saugus ironworks (1645) were first successful ones in the colonies.

Sauk Centre (sôk), city (pop. 3,140), central Minn., WNW of St. Cloud. Birthplace of Sinclair Lewis, who used it as model for town in *Main Street*.

Sauk Indians: see SAC AND FOX INDIANS.

Saul [Heb.,= asked for], fl. 1025 B.C., first king of the Hebrews. Saul was heroic in battle but proved himself unworthy of kingship by willful and foolish actions. He tried to destroy the rising star of David, his former protégé, who usurped his place, first in the hearts of the people and then on the throne itself. Adding to Saul's bitterness was the great friendship between his son Jonathan and David. Saul fell in battle on Mt. Gilboa. 1 Sam. 10–31.

Sault Sainte Marie (so͞o′ sānt mŭrē′), city (pop. 32,452), S Ont., Canada, on St. Mary's R. opposite Sault Ste Marie, Mich. (connected by railroad bridge and ferry). Government canal and lock completed here 1895. Port with ore docks and steel, pulp, paper, and lumber mills. Tourist center and gateway to hunting and fishing region.

Sault Sainte Marie, city (pop. 17,912), E Upper Peninsula, N Mich., on St. Mary's R. opposite Sault Ste Marie, Ontario. Region named 1641 by French missionaries. Père Marquette estab. mission here 1668; this was followed by fur-trading posts. Fort Brady, built here after Lewis Cass negotiated treaty with Indians (1820), served until end of World War II. Present canals and locks link lakes Superior and Huron on Mich. side. City connected to Ont. by railroad bridge and ferry. Resort and shipping center with hydroelectric plants and mfg. of carbide, leather, and foundry products. Has U.S. Coast Guard station.

Saumur (sōmür′), town (pop. 14,885), Maine-et-Loire dept., W France, on Loire R. Noted for sparkling wine and for its cavalry school (estab. 18th cent.). Huguenot center in 16th–17th cent. Has early 12th-cent. church, 16th-cent. town hall. City was damaged in World War II.

Saurashtra (sourăsh′trŭ), state (21,062 sq. mi.; pop. 4,136,005), W India; cap. Rajkot. Comprises major portion of Kathiawar peninsula.

sausage, food made of chopped meat, seasonings, and often other ingredients, usually packed into casings made of cleaned intestines or of cellulose, and sometimes pickled, smoked, or boiled. Over a hundred kinds are known; some, such as English black pudding, are of great antiquity. Popular in U.S. are frankfurters and wienerwursts, pork sausage, salami, and Bologna sausage.

Sausalito (sô″sŭlē′tŭ), residential city (pop. 4,828), W Calif., N of San Francisco across the Golden Gate. Shipyards built here in World War II.

Saussure, Horace Bénédict de (ôrăs′ bānādēkt′ dŭ sōsür′), 1740–99, Swiss physicist and geologist. He made studies of the geology, meteorology, and botany of European mountain regions, particularly the Alps, which he described in his *Voyages dans les Alpes* (4 vols., 1779–96). His son, **Nicolas Théodore de Saussure** (nēkôlä′ tāōdôr′), 1767–1845, was a chemist and plant physiologist, known especially for work on plant respiration and on fermentation.

Sava (sä′vä) or **Save** (säv), river, 583 mi. long, N Yugoslavia, rising in Julian Alps and flowing SE past Ljubljana and Zagreb into the Danube at Belgrade. Sava basin is fertile agr. region.

Savage, Richard, 1697?–1743, English poet. Now discredited story of his illegitimate noble descent and persecutions, set forth in a biography by Dr. Johnson, won him reputation his works did not merit.

Savage's Station: see SEVEN DAYS BATTLES.

Savaii (sävī′ē), volcanic island (703 sq. mi.; pop. 18,654), Western SAMOA, under New Zealand mandate; largest and most westerly of Samoan isls. Tuasivi is seat of resident commissioner.

Savanna (sŭvă′nŭ), city (pop. 5,058), NW Ill., on the Mississippi (bridged) above Clinton, Iowa. Trade and shipping center in rich agr. area.

Savannah. 1 City (pop. 119,638), SE Ga., port on Savannah R. near its mouth on the Atlantic. A major market for naval stores, it also has mfg. of pulp and paper, chemicals, and metal products; a sugar refinery; shipyards; seafood and truck canneries. Winter resort. Oldest and second largest city of Ga., founded 1733 by OGLETHORPE, it was colonial seat of government and later state cap. (1782–85). British captured and held it until Dec. 29, 1778, in the American Revolution. Trade grew after Revolution and War of 1812. The *Savannah,* first steamship to cross the Atlantic, sailed from here to Liverpool in 1819. Fort PULASKI, now a national monument, captured by Federals 1862, but city did not fall until Dec. 21, 1864, when Sherman ended his march to the sea here. Has Christ Episcopal Church (1838) and co-cathedral of St. John the Baptist (R.C.; 1876). **2** Town (pop. 1,698), S Tenn., on Tennessee R. and SE of Jackson. Nearby are Shiloh Natl. Military Park, Shiloh Natl. Cemetery (see SHILOH, BATTLE OF), and Pickwick Dam.

Savannah, river formed by confluence of Tugaloo and Seneca rivers, and forming part of Ga.-S.C. line. Flows 314 mi. SE to Tybee Sound, arm of the Atlantic. Has Clark Hill Dam.

Save, river, Yugoslavia: see SAVA.

Savigny, Friedrich Karl von (frē′drĭkh kärl′ fŭn sä′vĭnyē), 1779–1861, German jurist, teacher of Roman law at the Univ. of Berlin (1810–42). His works on Roman law are models of historical research.

Savile, Sir Henry (să′vĭl), 1549–1622, English classical scholar and mathematician. He translated four books of Tacitus' history (1591), edited St. John Chrysostom (8 vols., 1610–13), and was a translator of the Bible under King James. At Oxford he founded chairs of geometry and astronomy.

Saville, Marshall Howard (sŭvĭl′), 1867–1935, American archaeologist, an authority on Mayan ruins.

Savoie (sävwä′), department (2,389 sq. mi.; pop. 235,939), E France, in SAVOY; cap. Chambéry.

Savoie, Haute: see HAUTE-SAVOIE.

Savo Island: see SOLOMON ISLANDS.

Savona (sävō′nä), city (pop. 57,354), Liguria, NW Italy; a Mediterranean port. Heavy industries.

Savonarola, Girolamo (jērō′lämō sävōnärō′lä), 1452–98, Italian religious reformer. A Dominican, he was sent to Florence, where his burning eloquence and direct attack on all sorts of moral laxity made him a popular preacher. He also foretold events, sometimes with success. When the Medici were exiled (1494), he became the virtual ruler of Florence, where he imposed a rigidly Puritan regime. Horrified at the immorality at the court of Pope Alexander VI, he allied Florence with Alexander's opponent, Charles

VIII of France. Alexander silenced him, but he resumed preaching, and was excommunicated (1497). He then denounced Alexander. Matters reached a point of great tension, with rioting in Florence. City officials arrested him and put him to the torture. He was said to have confessed being a false prophet and was hanged.

Savoy, Prince Eugene of: see EUGENE OF SAVOY.

Savoy (sŭvoi'), Fr. *Savoie,* Alpine region, E France, bordering on Italy and Switzerland; historic cap. Chambéry. It is divided into Haute-Savoie dept. (cap. Annecy), with MONT BLANC and the S shore of L. of Geneva; and Savoie dept., with Chambéry and Aix-les-Bains. Dairying, agr., tourist trade. Conquered for Rome by Julius Caesar, Savoy later was part of the successive kingdoms of BURGUNDY and ARLES. It was split into many fiefs when the first counts of Savoy appeared in the 11th cent. Its history became that of the **house of Savoy,** which through conquest, exchange, and marriage acquired most of PIEDMONT (now Italy); the lower VALAIS, GENEVA, and VAUD (now Switzerland); BRESSE, Bugey, Gex, and NICE (now France). AMADEUS VIII took the title duke in 1416. By 1536 Savoy had lost its Swiss holdings. In that year Francis I of France occupied the rest of the duchy, which, however, was restored to EMMANUEL PHILIBERT in 1559. Turin replaced Chambéry as cap., but French remained the official language. Later dukes took part in the major wars of the 17th–18th cent., repeatedly changing sides. The Peace of Utrecht (1713–14) gave them Sicily, which they exchanged for Sardinia in 1720. Thus the kingdom of SARDINIA came into existence. In 1831 the cadet line of Savoy-Carignano succeeded the senior line on the throne. The family had by now shifted its orientation from France to Italy. Under CHARLES ALBERT it identified itself with the Italian RISORGIMENTO, which led to the unification of Italy under his son VICTOR EMMANUEL II. Savoy itself, which is French-speaking, was annexed to France 1792, restored to Sardinia 1815, and again ceded to France 1860 (in return for French aid against Austria). Later kings of Italy of Savoy line were HUMBERT I, VICTOR EMMANUEL III, HUMBERT II (abdicated 1946).

Savoy, the, chapel in London, between the Strand and the Thames. Completed 1511, it is sole remaining part of palace built c.1245 by Peter of Savoy. Near by is the **Savoy Theatre,** built (1881) by D'Oyly Carte for Gilbert and Sullivan operas.

saw, cutting tool, usually with flat, toothed blade. Stone saws were used in Neolithic period. Types include circular saw; band saw, running like belt over two wheels; and cylinder or drum saw for making circular cut. Teeth usually are bent outward alternately in opposite directions to make cut wider than blade to eliminate binding.

Sawatch Mountains (sŭwŏch'), high range of Rocky Mts., W central Colo., extending c.110 mi. S from Eagle R. to near Saguache. Arkansas R. is on E, Elk Mts. on W. Includes three highest peaks of U.S. Rockies: Mt. Elbert, 14,431 ft.; Mt. Massive, 14,418 ft.; in Collegiate Range, Mt. Harvard, 14,399 ft.

sawfish, sharklike ray fish of most warm seas. It enters the Mississippi and rivers of Africa, India. Upper jaw has flat extension (up to 6 ft. long, 1 ft. wide) with row of strong, toothlike structures.

sawfly, insect of order Hymenoptera resembling wasp. Female saws with ovipositor into plant tissues to deposit eggs. Some species produce galls.

Sawtooth Mountains, central Idaho, NE of Boise. Castle Peak is 11,820 ft. high. Mt. Hyndman (12,078 ft.) and Ryan Peak (11,900 ft.) are in Pioneer Mts., sometimes considered part of Sawtooth Mts.

Sax, Charles Joseph (săks'), 1791–1865, Belgian maker of musical instruments. His son, **Adolphe (Antoine Joseph) Sax,** 1814–94, designed the saxhorn, the saxophone, and the saxotromba.

Saxe, Maurice, comte de (mōrēs' kōt' dŭ săks'), 1696–1750, marshal of France; natural son of Augustus II of Poland and Saxony by Countess Königsmark. Entered French service 1720. A brilliant commander, he won the great victory at FONTENOY (1745). He wrote *Mes Rêveries* (1757), a remarkable work on the art of war.

Saxe-Altenburg (săks'-ăl'tŭnbûrg), Ger. *Sachsen-Altenburg,* former duchy, central Germany; cap. Altenburg. A possession of WETTIN dynasty (Ernestine line), it passed to SAXE-GOTHA 1672; was separate duchy 1826–1918; was incorporated into Thuringia 1920.

Saxe-Coburg (-kō'bûrg), Ger. *Sachsen-Coburg,* former duchy, central Germany; cap. Coburg. A possession of WETTIN dynasty (Ernestine line), it was detached from SAXE-GOTHA 1679; passed to collateral branch of dukes of Saxe-Saalfeld 1699. In 1826 Ernest III of Saxe-Coburg gave Saalfeld to SAXE-MEININGEN, received Saxe-Gotha, and became Grand Duke ERNEST I of **Saxe-Coburg-Gotha** (-gō'thŭ). His brother was Leopold I, king of the Belgians; his younger son, Prince Albert, married Queen Victoria of England. The family was deposed 1918; Gotha was incorporated into Thuringia, Coburg into Bavaria.

Saxe-Eisenach: see SAXE-WEIMAR.

Saxe-Gotha (-gō'thŭ), Ger. *Sachsen-Gotha,* former duchy, Thuringia, central Germany; cap. Gotha. A possession of WETTIN dynasty (Ernestine line), it was united with Saxe-Altenburg 1672. In 1679, on the death of Duke Ernest the Pious, Gotha and Altenburg passed to Ernest's oldest son; Saxe-Coburg went to a younger son. The Saxe-Gotha line died out in 1825; Gotha passed to Saxe-Coburg in 1826, while Altenburg continued under a collateral branch.

Saxe-Meiningen (-mī'nĭng-ŭn), Ger. *Sachsen-Meiningen,* former duchy, central Germany; cap. MEININGEN. A possession of WETTIN dynasty (Ernestine line) it became a separate duchy in 17th cent. and in 1826 also received Saalfeld (see SAXE-COBURG). Last duke abdicated 1918. Joined state of Thuringia 1920.

Saxe-Saalfeld: see SAXE-COBURG.

Saxe-Weimar (-vī'mär), Ger. *Sachsen-Weimar,*

former duchy, Thuringia, central Germany; cap. WEIMAR. When Saxony was redivided in 1547, the Ernestine line of WETTIN dynasty retained only its Thuringian possessions. These were divided among the sons of John Frederick, former elector of Saxony, into several duchies, of which Saxe-Weimar was the most important. The duchies were repeatedly redivided among the several collateral lines. In 1741 the duchy of Saxe-Eisenach (incl. Jena) was united with Saxe-Weimar, which thus became the duchy (after 1815, grand duchy) of **Saxe-Weimar-Eisenach** (–ī′zůnäkh). Duke CHARLES AUGUSTUS, patron and friend of Goethe, had considerable political influence in the Napoleonic era. The last grand duke abdicated 1918; the grand duchy was incorporated into Thuringia 1920.

saxifrage (săk′sĭfrĭj), low, rock-loving perennial of genus *Saxifraga* with tufts or rosettes of leaves and clusters of small flowers in spring. Most species are prized for gardens, especially rock gardens, but the strawberry geranium (*Saxifraga sarmentosa*), also called mother-of-thousands, is commonly grown as a house plant.

Saxo Grammaticus (săk′sō grůmă′tĭkůs), fl. 1188–1201, Danish historian. Wrote *Gesta Danorum* in 16 books (Eng. tr., Books I–IX, 1894).

Saxons, Germanic people, first known to history in 2d cent. as living in area of Schleswig. In 3d and 4th cent. they spread into Roman territory, and in 5th cent. settled in N Gaul. They made many raids in SE Britain, finally settling there in 6th cent., and with Angles estab. Anglo-Saxon kingdoms such as Wessex. In Germany "Old Saxons" occupied NW area, and after Treaty of Verdun (843) formed core of section that was beginning of modern Germany.

Saxony (săk′sůnē), Ger. *Sachsen,* name originally applied to the land inhabited in ancient and early medieval times by the SAXONS—i.e., roughly, present LOWER SAXONY, in NW Germany—and later given to several other political units. Late in the 9th cent. the first **duchy of Saxony,** comprising nearly all territory between the Elbe and the Rhine, emerged from the ruins of the Carolingian empire. In 919 Duke Henry I of Saxony was elected German king. His son, Emperor Otto I, founder of the Holy Roman Empire, bestowed Saxony on Hermann Billung (960). From the Billung dynasty the duchy passed (1137) to HENRY THE PROUD of Bavaria. His son, HENRY THE LION, was deprived of his duchies by Emperor Frederick I, who broke them up into smaller fiefs (1180). Henry's Guelphic descendants retained only BRUNSWICK (incl. the later kingdom of HANOVER). The ducal title of Saxony went to Bernard of Anhalt, a son of Albert the Bear of Brandenburg and founder of the Ascanian line of Saxon dukes. His dominions included ANHALT, LAUENBURG, and the country around WITTENBERG, which after 1260 were ruled by separate branches of the family. In 1356 the dukes of Saxe-Wittenberg received permanent rank of ELECTORS. Their territory, **Electoral Saxony,** along the middle Elbe, lay outside the original duchy, being part of the E march conquered from the Slavs. S of Electoral Saxony extended the margraviate of Meissen, ruled by the increasingly powerful house of WETTIN. The margraves acquired (13th–14th cent.) most of THURINGIA and Lower LUSATIA, and in 1423 Margrave Frederick the Warlike also received Electoral Saxony. The Wettin lands were partitioned (1485) between two brothers—Ernest, founder of the Ernestine line of Wettin, received Electoral Saxony and most of Thuringia; Albert, founder of the Albertine line, received ducal rank and the Meissen territories (incl. Dresden and Leipzig). Electors FREDERICK III and JOHN FREDERICK I were Protestant leaders. After his defeat at Mühlberg (1547), John Frederick lost the electorate to Duke MAURICE of Saxony, of the Albertine line; the Ernestine line kept only Thuringia. Electoral Saxony changed sides several times in the Thirty Years War and was thoroughly devastated but received advantageous terms at the peace (1648). From 1697 to 1763 the electors of Saxony were also kings of Poland as AUGUSTUS II and AUGUSTUS III. Under them, Saxony reached its cultural flowering, but it declined politically, being caught between its powerful neighbors, Prussia and Austria (see AUSTRIAN SUCCESSION, WAR OF THE; SEVEN YEARS WAR). Saxony sided staunchly with France in the Napoleonic Wars; in 1806 it became the **kingdom of Saxony** under FREDERICK AUGUSTUS I. The king's loyalty to Napoleon cost him half his kingdom at the Congress of Vienna (1814–15). Defeated by Prussia in the AUSTRO-PRUSSIAN WAR of 1866, Saxony joined the North German Confederation and, in 1871, the German Empire. The last king of Saxony was deposed 1918, and in 1919 the country joined the Weimar Republic as the **state of Saxony** (6,561 sq. mi.; 1946 pop. 5,558,566), with DRESDEN its cap. Heavily industrialized (textiles, machinery), Saxony also has important mineral resources in the ERZGEBIRGE. LEIPZIG and CHEMNITZ are the chief commercial and mfg. centers. In 1949 the state joined the [East] German Democratic Republic. Most of the territories lost by Saxony in 1815 were merged with other Prussian possessions into the Prussian **province of Saxony** (9,853 sq. mi.; 1939 pop. 3,616,635), with Magdeburg its cap. This was united in 1946 with Anhalt to form the new state of SAXONY-ANHALT.

Saxony-Anhalt (–än′hält), Ger. *Sachsen-Anhalt,* state (9,515 sq. mi.; pop. 4,160,539), [East] German Democratic Republic; cap. Halle. Among other cities are Magdeburg, Dessau, Wittenberg, Eisleben. Formed 1946 in the Russian occupation zone from the former state of ANHALT and Prussian province of Saxony, it includes E part of HARZ mts. Its N section is largely agr. The state has important mineral resources (potash, coal, iron, copper) and industries (sugar, metallurgy, chemicals). It has no historic unity.

saxophone: see WIND INSTRUMENTS.

Say, Jean Baptiste (sā), 1767–1832, French economist. Reorganized and popularized theories of Adam Smith. Developed a theory of markets and concept of the entrepreneur.

Sayan Mountains (säyän'), central Asia, chiefly in RSFSR, in E Siberia. E Sayan Mts. rise to 11,453 ft., W Sayan Mts. to 9,180 ft. Yield gold, silver, lead, graphite, and coal.

Saybrook Platform: see CAMBRIDGE PLATFORM.

Saye and Sele, William Fiennes, 1st **Viscount** (fĭnz, sā'ùnsēl), 1582–1662, English statesman and promoter of colonization in America. A Puritan and leader in House of Lords against the king. Engaged (1630–44) in several colonization schemes (e.g., at Saybrook, Conn.). In Puritan Revolution, he pursued an independent course.

Sayers, Dorothy (Leigh) (sârz), 1893–, English writer of detective novels featuring the nobleman-detective Lord Peter Wimsey. Later devoted herself to religious poetry and prose.

Sayre, borough (pop. 1,735), NE Pa., NW of Towanda. Railroad shops. Mfg. of metal products.

Sayreville, borough (pop. 10,338), E N.J., on Raritan R., ESE of New Brunswick. Bricks, chemicals.

Sayville, resort village (pop. 4,251), on S Long Isl., SE N.Y., on Great South Bay. It is a yachting center.

Sazonov, Sergei Dmitreyevich (sĭrgā' dùmē'-trēùvĭch sŭzô'nùf), 1861–1927, Russian foreign minister (1910–16). Urged Russian mobilization (July 29, 1914) at eve of World War I.

Sb, chemical symbol of the element ANTIMONY.

Sc, chemical symbol of the element SCANDIUM.

scabies (skā'bē-ēz, skā'bēz) or **itch,** contagious disease caused by penetration of skin by a mite. Occurs on hands and wrists, in armpit and groin, around anus.

scabiosa (skābēō'sù), annual or perennial plant (*Scabiosa*) native to Old World. It has lacy, flat-topped flowers in various colors. It is also called mourning bride, pincushion flower, and scabious.

Scaevola (sĕ'vôlù), Roman family name. **Caius Mucius Scaevola,** 6th cent.? B.C., legendary Roman hero. One story says that he tried to murder Lars Porsena, who was besieging Rome. Porsena condemned him to be burned at the stake, but when Scaevola thrust his hand into the flame and held it there Porsena was so impressed that he freed him and in face of such Roman courage gave up the siege. There are other stories of Porsena's change of heart. **Quintus Mucius Scaevola,** d. 82 B.C., was consul in 95 B.C. He and Crassus took citizenship away from many allies and helped bring on the Social War. He was pontifex maximus when he was killed in the proscription of Marius.

Scafell (skô'fĕl') or **Scaw Fell,** mountain group, Cumberland, England, in Lake District. Includes Scafell (3,162 ft.), Scafell Pike (3,-210 ft.; England's highest peak), Great End, and Lingmell.

Scala, Can Francesco della (kän' fränchā'skō dĕl'lä skä'lä), or **Can Grande della Scala** (käng-grän'dā), 1291–1329, lord of Verona. As Ghibelline leader and imperial vicar, he fought the Guelphs and conquered a large part of Venetia (incl. Padua and Vicenza). He was a protector of Dante.

scalawags (skă'lùwăgz), opprobious epithet used in the South after Civil War to describe native white Southerners who joined Republican party and aided RECONSTRUCTION program.

scalds: see BURNS.

scale, in cartography, ratio between distances on a map and those on earth's surface. Expressed numerically as a ratio or fraction; graphically, by recording mileage on a graduated line.

scale, in music, any series of tones arranged in rising or falling order of pitches. Since the 17th cent., the most common scale in Western music has been the diatonic scale which divides the octave into five whole tones and two half-tones as follows: major scale—1, 1, ½, 1, 1, 1, ½; minor scale—1, ½, 1, 1, ½, 1, 1. The pattern of tones and half-tones in a major or in a minor diatonic scale is always the same. The chromatic scale, which divides the octave into 12 equal half-tones, contains all the tonal material generally found in Western music. Since the end of the 19th cent., composers have experimented with whole-tone scales (C, D, E, F sharp, G sharp, A sharp) such as used by Debussy; five-tone scales (prevalent in Oriental music); quarter-tone scales (hence 24 tones in an octave and impossible on a modern keyboard instrument); and even up to 42-tone scales (which call for special instruments). See also EQUAL TEMPERAMENT; ATONALITY; TONE; and MODE.

scale, in weights and measures: see SCALES.

scale, in zoology, an outgrowth, bony or horny, of skin of animal. Scales characteristic of fish are bony. Teeth of vetebrates (from fish to man) are thought to be evolved from scales. Horny scales are found on most reptiles, on feet of birds, and on body of armadillo and pangolin. Some mammals have scales on the tail.

Scale Force, waterfall, c.120 ft. high, Cumberland, England, one of the finest of the Lake District.

scale insect, small sap-sucking insect of family Coccidae, destructive to many trees and greenhouse plants. Armored scale insects (e.g., cottony-cushion scale) secrete protective wax covering; unarmored are protected by chitinized body wall. Ladybird beetle destroys scale insects.

scales, instrument for determining weight, generally for other than laboratory use. For the principles of operation of weighing devices see BALANCE. Platform scales, used for large objects, utilize a succession of multiplying levers which transmit weight to a beam or other registering device. Counter scales, used commercially, are largely of the beam type. Cylinder, drum, or barrel scales have their calibrations on a rotatable chart. A variety of scales are constructed for industrial uses in which continuous flow of material must be weighed.

Scaliger, Julius Caesar (skă'lĭjùr), 1484–1558, Italian philologist and physician in France. In his *De causis linguae Latinae* (1540) he analyzed Cicero's style and pointed out over 600 errors of his humanist predecessors. He wrote commentaries on medical and botanical works of Hippocrates, Theophrastus, and Aristotle and urged an improved classification of plants. His *Poetics* (1561) was important in creation of neoclassic principles.

His son, **Joseph Justus Scaliger,** 1540–1609, was renowned for learning in mathematics, philosophy, languages, and critical methods. He did much work on the chronology of history. Was professor of philosophy at Geneva (1572–74), research professor at Leiden after 1593.

scallop (skŏ'lŭp, skă'–), marine bivalve mollusk, with radially ridged shell, winged at side of hinge. Moves through water flapping shells. Adductor muscle (which closes shell) is edible.

scalping, taking the scalp of an enemy, a custom comparable to head-hunting. Formerly practiced in Europe, Asia, and Africa, as well as by some American Indians, who believed scalp bestowed on scalper some powers of the scalped enemy, dead or alive.

Scamander (skŭmăn'dŭr), anc. name of the Kucuk Menderes, a small river of NW Turkey, in Asia Minor. Flows W and NW from the Ida Mts. through the Troas into the Mediterranean.

scammony (skă'mŭnē), twining plant (*Convolvulus scammonia*) of bindweed family, native to Asia Minor. Its taproot yields a resin used medicinally.

Scanderbeg (skăn'dŭrbĕg), c.1404–1468, Albanian national hero, whose original name was George Castriota. Also known as Skanderbeg or Iskander Bey. Educated in the Moslem faith as a hostage of Sultan Murad II, he won the sultan's favor and was given a command with the title bey. In 1443 he fled home, abjured Islam, and proclaimed himself prince of Albania. He received Venetian support and was named captain general of an anti-Turkish Crusade by the pope (1457). Throughout his remaining years, he held out against the Turks—at the end virtually alone, in his fortress of Kroia. With his death, resistance collapsed.

Scandinavia, region of N Europe, comprising SWEDEN, NORWAY, and DENMARK and usually understood to include also FINLAND and ICELAND. The Scandinavian peninsula, occupied by Sweden and Norway, is washed by the Baltic Sea (E); the Kattegat, Skagerrak, and North Sea (S); the Atlantic Ocean (W); and the Arctic Ocean (N). Mountainous and indented by fjords in the W (Norway), it slopes down in the E and S (Sweden). Its N extremity is Cape Nordkyn. See articles on individual countries.

scandium (skăn'dēŭm), metallic element of rare earths (symbol = Sc; see also ELEMENT, table). Occurs in compounds in rare minerals. Separation from its compounds is difficult.

Scania, Sweden: see SKANE.

Scapa Flow (skă'pŭ), area of water, c.15 mi. long and 8 mi. wide, in Orkney Isls., Scotland. Part of interned German fleet was scuttled here in 1919.

scarab (skă'rŭb), name for certain members of a beetle family (Scarabaeidae), especially the dung beetle (*Scarabaeus sacer*), the Egyptian sacred scarab. Stone, metal, and faïence representations of beetle have long been used as symbols and seals.

Scaramouch (skă'rŭmouch, -mōōsh), stock character in *commedia dell' arte,* a cowardly, boastful parody of grandiloquent Spanish don.

Scarboro or **Scarborough,** town (pop. 4,600), SW Maine, between Saco and Portland. Birthplace of Rufus King. Scarboro Beach and Prouts Neck resorts.

Scarborough, municipal borough (pop. 43,983), North Riding of Yorkshire, England; North Sea port and resort. Castle (12th cent.) was besieged many times. Has annual music festival and sports meet.

Scarlatti, Alessandro (skärlät'tē), b. 1658 or 1659, d. 1725, Italian composer. He developed the *aria de capo* and the Italian overture and wrote 115 operas, 200 Masses, and over 700 cantatas and oratorios. His son, **(Giuseppe) Domenico Scarlatti,** 1685–1757, was a harpsichord virtuoso and composed 545 sonatas mostly for that instrument.

scarlet fever (or scarlatina), acute communicable disease probably caused by a streptococcus. Attended by high fever, sore throat, skin eruption; early symptoms include vomiting or chills. Incubation period several hours to week. Attack usually gives permanent immunity. DICK TEST determines immunity.

scarp: see ESCARPMENT.

Scarpanto: see KARPATHOS.

Scarron, Paul (pôl' skärõ'), 1610–60, French novelist, noted for his picaresque, burlesque style. His masterwork is *Le Romant comique* (1651). He was bedfast with paralysis most of his life. His wife, Françoise d'Aubigné, later became the marquise de MAINTENON.

Scarsdale, suburban village (pop. 13,156), SE N.Y., S of White Plains; settled c.1701.

Scaw Fell, mountain group, England: see SCAFELL.

Schacht, Hjalmar Horace Greeley (yäl'mär, skäkht'), 1877–, German banker and financial expert. President of the Reichsbank 1923–30, 1934–39; minister of economy 1934–37. Stabilized inflated currency (1924–25); elaborated intricate system of currency exchange controls and barter trade with foreign countries, thus helping German rearmament program under Hitler. A nationalist but not a Nazi, he took part in plot on Hitler's life (1944) and was placed in a concentration camp. He was acquitted at the Nuremberg war-crimes trial (1946).

Schadow, Johann Gottfried (yō'hän gôt'frēt shä'dō), 1764–1850, German sculptor of neoclassic school. His son **Rudolph Schadow,** 1786–1822, was also a sculptor. Another son, **Friedrich Wilhelm von Schadow-Godenhaus** (-gō'dŭnhous), 1789–1862, was a religious and historical painter and one of the Nazarenes in Rome.

Schaff, Philip (shäf), 1819–93, biblical scholar and church historian in U.S., b. Switzerland. He was professor (after 1870) at Union Theological Seminary, and edited *Schaff-Herzog Encyclopedia of Religious Knowledge* (1882–84).

Schaffhausen (shäfhou'zŭn), canton (115 sq. mi.; pop. 57,448), N Switzerland, on N bank of the Rhine. Consists of three unconnected agr. and forested areas, largely surrounded by German territory. Its cap., **Schaffhausen** (pop. 25,901), on the Rhine, was originally a Benedictine abbey (founded c.1050), whose 11th-cent. minster is preserved. Became a free imperial city c.1208 and joined Swiss Confederation 1501. Bombed by mistake in World War II by American aircraft. Hydroelectric works exploit falls near here on the Rhine for wool and metal goods mfg.

Scharnhorst, Gerhard von (gär'härt fŭn shärn'hôrst), 1755–1813, Prussian general. In charge of war ministry after Treaty of TILSIT (1807), he reorganized the army on a more democratic basis, cleverly evaded the treaty limitations on Prussia's armed strength, and created the army which in 1813–15 had a major share in Napoleon's downfall.

Schaulen, Lithuania: see SIAULIAI.

Schaumburg-Lippe (shoum'bŏŏrk-lĭ'pŭ), former state (131 sq. mi.; 1939 pop. 53,195), W Germany, W of Hanover and E of Weser R.; cap. Bückeburg. After 1945 incorporated with British-occupied Lower Saxony. County of Schauenburg (as Schaumburg was originally called) occupied much of Westphalia in 12th cent. Counts held Holstein 1111–1459. In 1640 Schaumburg was divided among Brunswick-Lüneburg, Hesse-Kassel, and county of LIPPE. Principality of Schaumburg-Lippe was created 1790. Last prince abdicated 1918, and Schaumburg-Lippe joined Weimar Republic.

Scheele, Karl Wilhelm (kärl vĭl'hĕlm shā'lŭ), 1742–86, Swedish chemist. Prepared and studied oxygen; discovered nitrogen independently of Daniel Rutherford; was influential in discovery of manganese, barium, chlorine; isolated glycerin.

Scheer, Reinhard (rīn'härt shār'), 1863–1928, German admiral. Commanded in Battle of JUTLAND (1916).

Scheffer, Ary (ärē' shĕfĕr'), 1795–1858, Dutch painter in France. Best known for his religious paintings.

Scheffler, Johannes: see ANGELUS SILESIUS.

Scheherazade: see THOUSAND AND ONE NIGHTS.

Scheidemann, Philipp (fē'lĭp shī'dŭmän), 1865–1939, first chancellor of German republic (1918–19), a Social Democrat. Resigned in protest over Treaty of Versailles.

Scheldt (skĕlt), Dutch and Flemish *Schelde,* Fr. *Escaut,* river, 270 mi. long, rising in N France and flowing NNE through Belgium, past Tournai, Ghent, and Antwerp, into the North Sea. Navigable for most of its course. The mouth forms estuary between Belgium and the Dutch islands of South Beveland and Walcheren. From 1648 until 1863 (except during Napoleonic period) the Netherlands possessed right to close the estuary, thus controlling Antwerp.

Schelling, Friedrich Wilhelm Joseph von (shĕ'lĭng), 1775–1854, German philosopher. He studied and taught at various universities (Tübingen, Leipzig, Jena, Würzburg, Erlangen) and lived at Munich before being called to the Univ. of Berlin (1841). He was early a collaborator of Fichte, and though they drew apart his philosophy started from a Fichtean base. He held that nature and mind cannot be separated, differing in force by degree, not in kind, with unity of mind and matter in the Absolute. He also argued that God takes part in the unfolding and development that is history and holds within Himself the limiting factors that define personality.

Schenectady (skŭnĕk'tŭdē), city (pop. 91,785), E N.Y., on Mohawk R. and the Barge Canal and NW of Albany; founded 1662. Center for mfg. of electrical equipment; athletic equipment; locomotive works. C. P. Steinmetz's home and laboratory are now a science museum. Seat of Union Col. (nonsectarian; for men; chartered and opened 1795), which pioneered in engineering courses; associated in Union Univ. (partly coed.; 1873) with Albany Medical Col. (1839), Albany Law School (1851), Albany Col. of Pharmacy (1881), and other schools.

scherzo (sker'tsō) [Ital.,= joke], name given to several types of music, but chiefly one of a lively or facetious nature. Often appears as one of the movements of a symphony. Composers vary in their treatment of the scherzo, and often its humor is apparent only to the man who wrote it.

Scheveningen (skhā'vŭnĭng"ŭn), bathing resort, W Netherlands, on North Sea; forms part of The Hague.

Schiaparelli, Giovanni Virginio (jōvän'nē vērjē'nyō skyäpärĕl'lē), 1835–1910, Italian astronomer. Discoveries include markings on Mars known as canals.

Schick test, skin test to determine susceptibility to diphtheria. Devised 1913 by **Bela Schick,** 1877–, Hungarian-born American pediatrician and allergist.

Schiedam (skhē"däm'), municipality (pop. 69,728), South Holland prov., W Netherlands, on the New Maas. Its gin is exported throughout the world.

Schiehallion (shĭhă'yŭn), mountain, 3,547 ft. high, Perthshire, Scotland, near Loch Rannoch.

Schiff, Jacob Henry (shĭf), 1847–1920, American banker and philanthropist, b. Germany. Head of Kuhn, Loeb and Co. in New York city after 1885. Endowed Jewish Theological Seminary.

Schiller, F(erdinand) C(anning) S(cott) (shĭ'lŭr), 1864–1937, British philosopher, professor at Oxford (1897–1926) and at the Univ. of Southern California (1929–37). Called his pragmatic philosophy humanism, holding that "man is the measure of all things."

Schiller, Friedrich von (frē'drĭkh fŭn shĭ'lŭr), 1759–1805, German poet, dramatist, historian, and philosopher, b. Marbach, Württemberg. His first play, *Die Räuber* (1781), was a major STURM UND DRANG work. His many works include "An die Freude" (1875), the hymn to joy used by Beethoven in the Ninth Symphony; the drama *Don Carlos* (1787); historical studies, including one on the Thirty Years War (1793); the dramatic trilogy (1798–99) on Wallenstein, the last two parts translated by Coleridge as *Wallenstein* (1800); *Maria Stuart* (1800); *Die Jungfrau von Orleans* (1801); and *Wilhelm Tell* (1804; Eng. tr., 1825). A favorite among his many ballads is "The Song of the Bell." Schiller's friendship with Goethe is celebrated; his fruitful last years were spent in Weimar. One of the founders of German literature, second in his time only to Goethe. Strongly influenced by Kant, his idealism and hatred of tyranny were a powerful influence in modern German literature.

Schinkel, Karl Friedrich (kärl' frē'drĭkh shĭng'kŭl), 1781–1841, German architect of the classical tradition. Built the imposing Old Mus. in Berlin.

Schipa, Tito (skē'pä), 1889–, Italian operatic tenor. He made his U.S. debut in 1919 with the Chicago Opera Co.; sang at the Metropolitan Opera, New York, 1932–35. He was a leading lyric tenor.

Schism, Great, split in the Roman Catholic Church, 1378–1417, after GREGORY XI had returned to Rome, ending the "Babylonian captivity" of the papacy. On his death (1378) the Roman mob brought pressure on the cardinals, who elected URBAN VI. He soon alienated all, and the cardinals declared his election null on the grounds of coercion and chose ROBERT OF GENEVA (Antipope Clement VII), who fled to Avignon. There he was succeeded in 1394 by Pedro de LUNA (Antipope Benedict XIII). In Rome, Urban was succeeded by Boniface IX, Innocent VII, and GREGORY XII. The two lines were completely divided. Theologians led by Pierre d'Ailly and John Gerson promoted the Council of PISA (1409), which advanced the theory of the superiority of councils to the pope but succeeded only in creating a third papal line (later represented by Baldassarre COSSA). The quarrel was ended at the Council of CONSTANCE with election of MARTIN V. One result of the schism was delay in beginning the Catholic Reform. Called also Schism of the West.

schist (shĭst), metamorphic rock having its minerals elongated and arranged in bands parallel to each other and to cleavage planes of the minerals. Common varieties are mica schist, chlorite schist, talc schist. Schists are abundant in Pre-Cambrian rocks. Schists split readily along their planes of schistosity, like slates along cleavage lines.

schizophrenia (skĭt'sŭfrē'nēŭ), functional psychosis, characterized by faulty mental processes, unrealistic behavior, absorption in an inner world, and sometimes hallucinations. In 1896 Emil Kraepelin grouped various mental diseases under the heading of dementia praecox, using four subdivisions (simple, hebephremic, catatonic, and paranoid). In 1911 Eugen Bleuler pronounced the disease curable, using the term *schizophrenia* (as emphasizing the splitting phenomena in the mind) to replace dementia praecox (which implied a hopeless outlook for cure). Patients are usually hospitalized; treatment may include psychosurgery or shock therapy as well as psychotherapy.

Schlegel, August Wilhelm von (ou'gŏost vĭl'hĕlm fŭn shlā'gŭl), 1767–1845, German author and scholar, a champion of romanticism. His excellent translations of Shakspere (1797–1810) were completed by others. He and his brother **Friedrich von Schlegel** (frēd'rĭkh), 1772–1829, founded and edited the influential periodical *Athenaeum*. Friedrich von Schlegel turned from literature to philosophy and the study of Sanskrit and of Hindu thought; in 1808 he joined the Catholic Church, in which he saw the union of Christian and romantic ideals. His wife, **Dorothea von Schlegel,** 1763–1839, daughter of Moses Mendelssohn, shared his conversion and was his literary assistant.

Schleicher, Kurt von (kŏort' fŭn shlī'khŭr), 1882–1934, German general. Appointed chancellor of Germany in Dec., 1932, he vainly requested emergency powers to stem the Nazi tide. Upon his resignation, Hitler became chancellor (Jan., 1933). Schleicher and his wife were murdered by the Nazis in the "blood purge" of 1934.

Schleiden, Matthias Jakob (mätē'äs yä'kôp shlī'dŭn), 1804–81, German botanist. A pioneer in development of cell theory, he showed plant tissues were composed of cells and emphasized importance of nucleus.

Schleiermacher, Friedrich Daniel Ernst (frē'drĭkh dä'nyĕl ĕrnst' shlī'ŭrmäkh'ŭr), 1768–1834, German philosopher and Protestant theologian. Professor at Halle (1804–10) and Berlin (after 1810), he in *The Christian Faith* (1821–22) and other works sought to reconcile modern social theories and Evangelical religious beliefs.

Schlesinger, Arthur M(eier) (shlā'zĭng-gŭr), 1888–, American historian, professor at Harvard. Special interest has been interpretation of social history, as in *The Rise of the City, 1878–1898* (1933). His son is **Arthur M(eier) Schlesinger, Jr.,** 1917–, historian, author of the Pulitzer Prize-winning *Age of Jackson* (1945), and associate professor at Harvard. He has vigorously defended liberal causes.

Schleswig (shlĕz'wĭg, Ger. shlās'vĭkh), Dan. *Slesvig,* former duchy, N Germany and S Denmark, in S Jutland. German Schleswig (part of Schleswig-Holstein), has Schleswig, Flensburg, and Husum as chief towns. Danish Schleswig or North Schleswig includes Sonderborg and Tondern. The duchy was created 1115 as a fief held directly from the kings of Denmark; it passed in 1386 to the counts of HOLSTEIN, and in 1460 to Christian I of Denmark. (For later history, see SCHLESWIG-HOLSTEIN.) The historic cap., **Schleswig** (pop. 36,668), is a port on an inlet of the Baltic Sea. Has Romanesque-Gothic cathedral (Lutheran); Gottorp or Gottorf castle (16th-17th cent.), former residence of dukes of Holstein-Gottorp.

Schleswig-Holstein (–hōl'stīn, Ger. –hôl'shtīn), German state (6,045 sq. mi.; pop. 2,593,617), N Germany, in S part and at base of the Jutland peninsula; cap. Kiel. A low-lying region between the North Sea and the Baltic (linked by Kiel Canal), it has fertile agr. land (cattle raising). In the center, heaths and moors predominate. It produces ships, machinery, processed foods. Population is Protestant. The state consists of the former duchies of SCHLESWIG (N of Eider R.), HOLSTEIN (S), and LAUENBURG (SW). Concerning the history of Schleswig-Holstein Lord Palmerston once stated that of the three men who had ever understood it, one was dead (Prince Albert), one was insane (a professor), and the third (Palmerston himself) had forgotten it. Both Schleswig and Holstein were inherited in 1460 by Christian I of Denmark. Schleswig was a fief held directly from the Danish crown; Holstein was held in fief from the Holy Roman Empire. Both duchies were connected with the Danish crown through personal union only and could not be incorporated into the Danish crownlands. In the 16th cent. the duchies underwent a complex subdivision. A "ducal portion" was conferred on a younger brother of King Christian III and on his descendants, the dukes of Holstein-Gottorp; a "royal portion" was ruled directly by the Danish kings; a "common portion" was ruled jointly by the Danish kings and the dukes of Holstein-Gottorp. Within the royal portion, the duchy of SONDERBORG was created in favor of King Frederick II's youngest brother; this Sonderborg branch in turn split into the Augustenburg line and the cadet Glücksburg line. As a result of the NORTHERN WAR (1700–1721) Duke Charles Frederick of Holstein-Gottorp, who had sided with Sweden, was dispossessed. His grandson, Grand Duke (later Emperor) Paul of Russia, renounced his claim to the ducal portion in exchange for OLDENBURG (1773). Thus both duchies were reunited under the Danish crown. The Congress of Vienna left status unchanged, except that the German Confederation replaced the Holy Roman Empire as suzerain over Holstein. The struggle between the German nationalists in the duchies and the Danish nationalists, who tried to impose the Danish constitution on them, flared into warfare in 1848. The German Confederation, particularly Prussia, gave military support to the rebellious duchies, but in 1850 peace was made on inconclusive terms. The London Conference of 1852 settled the succession of the childless Frederick VII on the Glücksburg line of the royal house; Denmark guaranteed the inseparability and autonomy of the duchies. However, in 1863 Christian IX signed a new constitution, which was to have force in Schleswig as well as in Denmark. On the ground that the London Protocol had been violated, Prussia and Austria declared war on Denmark, which was quickly defeated (1864). Austria favored the installation of the Augustenburg line in the duchies, but Prussia, under Bismarck's leadership, imposed the Treaty of Gastein (1865): Schleswig was to be administered by Prussia, Holstein by Austria. As Bismarck had anticipated, this solution led to friction with Austria, which in 1866 declared war on Prussia (see AUSTRO-PRUSSIAN WAR). Victorious Prussia annexed both duchies, which together with Lauenburg became a Prussian province. In 1920 a plebiscite restored Danish-speaking N Schleswig to Denmark. LÜBECK and the Lübeck dist. of Oldenburg were added to the province in 1937. Schleswig-Holstein became a state within the British occupation zone in 1946 and joined the Federal Republic of [West] Germany in 1949. The influx of displaced persons after World War II increased its population c.60%.

Schley, Winfield Scott (slī), 1839–1911, American naval officer. In command at battle of Santiago in Spanish-American War. Controversy over credit for victory arose between him and W. T. SAMPSON.

Schlieffen, Alfred, Graf von (äl'frāt grāf' fŭn shlē'fŭn), 1833–1913, German field marshal, chief of the general staff 1891–1906. He developed the **Schlieffen plan,** based on Hannibal's tactics at Cannae. In case of war with France, an overwhelmingly strong right wing was to strike through the Low Countries, capture the Channel ports, and bear down on Paris from the W. Meanwhile a weak left wing was to draw out the French further S, along the Franco-German border. In World War I, the German command lacked the boldness to put all its strength into the right wing and thus ruined the plan. In World War II the plan was carried out successfully.

Schliemann, Heinrich (shlē'män), 1822–90, German archaeologist. Inspired by Homeric studies, he retired from business (1863) to find Troy and other Homeric sites. In 1871 he undertook at own expense excavations at Hissarlik, uncovering four superimposed towns. Made other notable excavations.

Schlüsselburg (shlü'sŭlbŏŏrk), fortress, NW European RSFSR, E of Leningrad and on an island in L. Ladoga. Built 1323 by Novgorod, it fell to Sweden in 17th cent. but was recovered by Peter I in 1702. Used until 1917 for high-ranking and political prisoners. In World War II its recapture by Russians opened land route to besieged Leningrad (1943).

Schlüter, Andreas (ändrā'äs shlü'tŭr), 1664–1714, German baroque sculptor. Among his notable works in Berlin is the pulpit in the Marienkirche.

Schmalkalden (shmäl'käl"dŭn), town (pop. 12,663), Thuringia, central Germany. Health resort; mineral springs. In its town hall (built 1419) was formed in 1531 the alliance of German Protestant princes and cities known as the **Schmalkaldic League** (shmälkäl'dĭk). It was led by Philip of Hesse and John Frederick I of Saxony. Emperor Charles V crushed the League in the Schmalkaldic War (1546–47) through his victory at Mühlberg.

Schmeling, Max, 1905–, German boxer. Won (1930) heavyweight championship when Jack Sharkey was disqualified for fouling, lost (1932) title when Sharkey defeated him in 15 rounds. First fighter to defeat Joe Louis, knocking him out (1936) in 12th round.

Schnabel, Artur (shnä'bŭl), 1882–1951, Austrian pianist and teacher. He first toured the U.S., 1921–22. Best known for his interpretations of Beethoven's works. His own compositions, which are extremely modern, include his First Symphony and his Rhapsody for Orchestra.

Schnakenburg, Henry, 1892–, American painter, best known for naturalistic landscapes.

schnauzer: see TERRIER.

Schnitzler, Arthur (är'tŏŏr shnĭts'lŭr), 1862–1931, Austrian author. His works, distinguished by brilliance of style and acuteness of observation, mark the turn from romanticism to gloomy realism. They include the plays *Anatol* (1892), *Liebelei* (1895), and *Professor Bernhardi* (1912); several novels; and many short stories.

Schnorr von Carolsfeld, Julius (yōō'lyōōs shnôr' fŭn kä'rôlsfĕlt), 1794–1872, German religious and historical painter.

Schoenbrunn Memorial State Park (shān'brŭn, -brōōn), E central Ohio, near New Philadelphia. Site of first town in Ohio, settled 1772, abandoned 1776; now being restored.

Schofield, John McAllister (skō'fēld), 1831–

1906, Union general in Civil War. Led Army of the Ohio in Atlanta campaign. Secretary of War (1868–69). Commander of U.S. army (1888–95).

Schofield Barracks, U.S. army military post (estab. 1909), central Oahu, T.H. WHEELER FIELD is at S edge.

scholasticism (skōlăs'tĭsĭzŭm), philosophical thought of medieval Christian Europe. It does not have the unity seemingly imputed to it by contemptuous later philosophers—an attitude still reflected in the popular mind, though medieval philosophy, reassessed in recent years, is now generally recognized as rich, varied, and subtle. Chief among the early sources were the writings of St. Augustine and other Church Fathers, and as learning revived in the 9th cent. it was tinted with Platonic and Neoplatonic thought. ERIGENA was one of the first to introduce speculative thought into medieval philosophy. By the 11th cent. the "schoolmen" (scholastics) were embarked on wide-ranging discussions. One major problem was that of the nature of universal concepts (i.e., the fundamental ideas of things, the idea of "chair" as opposed to an individual example). Some teachers, the realists, held that the basic forms had reality in and of themselves; others, the nominalists, claimed that the forms were only abstractions from particular examples. Another theme of argument was that concerning the place of reason and the place of faith in man's knowledge. Prominent among the earlier scholastics were St. ANSELM, ABELARD, WILLAM OF CHAMPEAUX, HUGH OF SAINT VICTOR, and PETER LOMBARD. As knowledge of Aristotle's work reached W Europe again through acquaintance with Arabian learning, scholasticism rose to its crest in the 13th cent. with the brilliant synthesis of Aristotelian rationalism and Christian thought. Robert GROSSETESTE and St. ALBERTUS MAGNUS preceded St. THOMAS AQUINAS, whose closely wrought system was one of the greatest achievements of European thought. His rationalism was opposed by several Franciscans, notably DUNS SCOTUS, St. BONAVENTURE, and WILLIAM OF OCCAM, who stressed the necessity of faith and the weakness of reason in solving questions of theology. Both schools of thought persist in the Roman Catholic Church, though that of St. Thomas is dominant. The secular currents of the Renaissance and the growth of natural science caused scholasticism to decline and disappear.

Schomberg, Frederick Herman, 1st **duke of** (shŏm'bûrg), Ger. *Friedrich Hermann von Schönburg,* 1615–90, German soldier of fortune. Fought in Thirty Years War on Protestant side. Later commanded successfully in the service of Portugal (created conde de Mertola), France (created marshal of France and duke), and William III of Orange. He assisted William in the Glorious Revolution, was created duke in the English peerage (1688), and commanded the English forces in Ireland, where he won the battle of the Boyne, in which he was fatally wounded.

Schomburgk, Sir Robert Hermann (shŏm'bûrk) 1804–65, British explorer, b. Germany. Went on botanical and geographical expedition to British Guiana (1835). Surveyed that colony for British government (1841–43), outlining boundary important in subsequent boundary disputes with Venezuela.

Schön, Martin: see SCHONGAUER, MARTIN.

Schönbein, Christian Friedrich (krĭs'tyän frē'drĭkh shûn'bīn), 1799–1868, German chemist. Discovered ozone; developed guncotton and collodion.

Schönberg, Arnold (shûn'bĕrkh), 1874–1951, Austrian composer, in the U.S. after 1933. His early works, such as *Verklärte Nacht* (1899), are in the romantic tradition. In his first *Kammersymphonie* (1906), the use of chords built in fourths (C, F sharp, B flat) foreshadows his later use of atonality. Some of his vocal music (e.g., *Erwartung*) requires a special technique that is neither singing nor speaking. In 1914 he arrived at the 12-tone technique (see ATONALITY), which he first used explicitly in his *Serenade* (1924). Among his works are a violin concerto (1940); *Ode to Napoleon* (1944), to Byron's poem, for male reciter, piano, and string orchestra; and songs and piano pieces. Performances of his music offer great technical difficulties. Among pupils who follow his 12-tone technique are Alban Berg, Ernst Krenek, and Anton von Webern.

Schönbrunn (shûnbrōōn'), former imperial palace in Vienna, Austria, built 18th cent. Park emulates Versailles. Heavily damaged in World War II. By **Peace of Schönbrunn,** 1809, imposed by Napoleon I, Austria temporarily lost W Galicia to duchy of Warsaw and Illyria to France.

Schongauer, Martin (mär'tēn shōn'gou-ûr), c.1445–1491, German engraver, known also as Martin Schön. Worked in Colmar. Noted for engravings of religious subjects.

Schoodic Lake (skōō'dĭk), 9 mi. long, central Maine, SSW of Millinocket. Lumbering, hunting, fishing.

Schoolcraft, Henry Rowe, 1793–1864, American ethnologist, chief pioneer in study of the Indians.

schooner, fore-and-aft rigged sailing vessel, having two to seven masts. First designed by Capt. Andrew Robinson of Gloucester, Mass. (1713), it became a favorite craft in Newfoundland fisheries. See *ill.*, p. 1109.

Schopenhauer, Arthur (är'tōōr shō'pûnhou"ûr), 1788–1860, German philosopher. Studied at several German universities, traveled widely, and after 1831 lived mainly at Frankfurt-am-Main in seclusion. His philosophy of pessimism was presented with clarity and literary skill in books, of which *The World as Will and Idea* (1818) and *Will in Nature* (1836) are best known. He held that true reality is a blind impelling force, appearing in individual man as will. The constant mutual resistance of various wills causes strife, and the individual cannot satisfy the wants of his will and therefore lives in pain. The only escape is a negation of the will, but temporary escape can be found in science and art. Ethics rests only on sympathy for the pain of others.

Schouten, Willem Cornelis (vĭ'lŭm kôrnā'lĭs skhou'tŭn), 1567?–1625, Dutch navigator. Commanded expedition (1615) to evade

Dutch East India Co. trade restrictions by finding new route to Pacific. Rounded and named Cape Horn (1616). Despite new route, Schouten was arrested and his ship was confiscated.

Schreckhörner (shrĕk'hûr"nùr), two peaks of Bernese Alps, Switzerland—Gross Schreckhorn, 13,390 ft.; Klein Schreckhorn, 11,474 ft.

Schreiner, Olive (shrī'nùr), pseud. Ralph Iron, 1855–1920, South African author and feminist, known for her novel *The Story of an African Farm* (1883). Her other works include an unfinished novel, *From Man to Man* (1926).

Schröder, Friedrich Ludwig (shrû'dùr), 1744–1816, German actor and dramatist. One of most famous tragic actors of his day, he translated Shakspere and other classics into German.

Schrödinger, Erwin (ĕr'vĭn shrû'dĭng-ùr), 1887–, Austrian physicist. Shared 1933 Nobel Prize for mathematical formulation of wave mechanics.

Schubert, Franz (Peter) (shōō'bûrt), 1797–1828, Austrian composer, foremost of the romantic movement. German lieder came to their fullest flower in his songs, especially his two great cycles, *Die schöne Müllerin* and *Die Winterreise*. The Quartet in D Minor (*Death and the Maiden*) and the Quintet in A (*The Trout*) are perhaps best known of his many chamber works. Among his symphonies are the B minor (the Unfinished Symphony) and the C major symphony. He also wrote overtures, Masses, and much piano music, including the *Moments musicaux*. Two of his most popular songs are the *Erlkönig* and his *Ave Maria*.

Schultze, Max Johann Sigismund (mäks yō'hän zēgĭsmŏŏnd shōōl'tsù), 1825–74, German biologist known for work on cell theory, protoplasm, protozoa.

Schumacher, Peder: see GRIFFENFELD, PEDER SCHUMACHER, COUNT.

Schuman, Robert (rōbĕr' shōōmä'), 1886–, French premier (1947–48) and foreign minister (1948–53), a member of the Catholic Mouvement Républicain Populaire (MRP). He proposed in 1950 the so-called **Schuman Plan,** which became effective in 1952 as the European Coal and Steel Community (members: France, Federal Republic of [West] Germany, Belgium, Netherlands, Luxembourg, Italy). The first practical step toward European unification, the ECSC has eliminated all restrictions, among the six member nations, on exports, imports, and currency exchange affecting coal, scrap iron, and iron ore. In 1953 the first international tax, a levy on coal and steel production in the member countries, took effect. The ECSC, with hq. at Luxembourg, thus has pooled the chief industrial resources of one of the world's most vital industrial areas, including the Ruhr coal basin and the Lorraine iron ore basin.

Schuman, William (shōō'mùn), 1910–, American composer. His music is contrapuntal and often suggests jazz rhythms. His chief works are his Third and his Fourth Symphony (both 1941); the ballet *Undertow* (1945); several suites; and chamber music.

Schumann, Robert (Alexander) (shōō'män), 1810–56, German romantic composer. He wrote many piano works, including *Papillons, Carnaval, Kinderszenen,* and *Kreisleriana,* and nearly 150 songs. His piano concerto in A Minor (1841–45), Spring Symphony (1841), Third, or Rhenish, Symphony (1850), and Fourth Symphony in D Minor (1841–51) and later chamber works are well known. He was a great personal friend of the young Brahms and championed his music. His last years were clouded by attacks of insanity, and he died in a sanitarium. His wife, **Clara (Wieck) Schumann,** 1819–96, was an outstanding pianist.

Schumann-Heink, Ernestine (shōō'mùn-hīngk'), 1861–1936, American contralto, b. near Prague. She sang with the Metropolitan Opera, New York, 1899–1904. Her concert tours won her the lasting affection of the public.

Schuman Plan: see SCHUMAN, ROBERT.

Schumpeter, Joseph Alois (yō'zĕf ä'lōēs shŏŏm'pā"tùr), 1883–1950, Austrian-American economist. Proposed theory of entrepreneur as the dynamic factor in disturbing business equilibrium.

Schurman, Jacob Gould (shûr'mùn), 1854–1942, American educator and diplomat. He was president (1892–1920) of Cornell Univ. and founder and editor of the *Philosophical Review*. He headed first U.S. Philippines Commission (1899) and served as minister to Greece (1912–13), envoy to China (1921–25), and ambassador to Germany (1925–30).

Schurz, Carl (shŏŏrts), 1829–1906, American political leader, b. Germany. Civil War general of volunteers (1862–65). U.S. Senator from Mo. (1869–75); helped form LIBERAL REPUBLICAN PARTY. U.S. Secretary of the Interior (1877–81). Led MUGWUMPS in 1884. Edited various publications. Exercised wide influence through writings and speeches.

Schuschnigg, Kurt von (kŏŏrt' fŭn shŏŏsh'nĭk), 1897–, chancellor of Austria (1934–38). Succeeded DOLLFUSS, under whom he had served as minister of justice. After 1936 he acted as virtual dictator. He resisted Hitler's attempts, through the large Nazi party of Austria, to unite Austria with Germany, but his situation became hopeless after he lost Mussolini's support (1937). Early in 1938 Hitler's pressure forced Schuschnigg to make concessions to the Nazis. In March, Schuschnigg called for a plebiscite on Austria's continued independence. Two days later (March 11) German troops occupied Austria. Schuschnigg resigned and was kept a prisoner until 1945. He settled in U.S. 1947.

Schütz, Heinrich (hīn'rĭkh shüts'), 1585–1672, German composer. His *Dafne* (no longer extant) is considered the first German opera. His chief works are *Seven Last Words of Christ on the Cross* and settings of the Passion as narrated in each of the Gospels. These works influenced Bach and Handel.

Schuyler, Philip John (skī'lùr), 1733–1804, American Revolutionary general. Command dispute between him and Horatio Gates in 1776 ended with Gates as commander of Saratoga campaign. Schuyler was court-martialed for negligence but acquitted.

Schuylerville, village (pop. 1,314), E N.Y., on W bank of Hudson R. and E of Saratoga Springs. Scene of Burgoyne's surrender in SARATOGA CAMPAIGN.

Schuylkill (sko͞olʹkĭl″, sko͞oʹkŭl), river rising in Schuylkill co., Pa., and flowing 130 mi. SE into Delaware R. at Philadelphia. Project to take anthracite from river started 1948.

Schuylkill Haven, borough (pop. 6,597), E Pa., on Schuylkill R. and SSE of Pottsville. Mfg. of shoes and clothing.

Schwab, Charles M(ichael) (shwäb), 1862–1939, American steel magnate. Made Bethlehem Steel Co. the leading manufacturer of war materials for Allies in World War I.

Schwabach (shväʹbäkh), town (pop. 19,448), Middle Franconia, W central Bavaria. Metalworking; lead processing. **Articles of Schwabach,** drawn up 1529, were used in drafting Augsburg Confession (1530).

Schwann, Theodor (tāʹōdōr shvänʹ), 1810–82, German physiologist and histologist. Continued and amended work of Schleiden; showed cell to be basis of animal as well as of plant tissue.

Schwanthaler, Ludwig von (lo͞otʹvĭkh fŭn shvänʹtälŭr), 1802–48, German sculptor. Created sculptures for the Ruhmeshalle and other buildings in Munich. His portrait statue of Mozart is at Salzburg.

Schwarzenberg, Karl Philipp, Fürst zu (kärlʹ fēʹlĭp fürstʹ tso͞o shvärʹtsŭnbĕrk), 1771–1820, Austrian field marshal. Commanded allied armies in campaign of 1813–14 against Napoleon. His nephew **Felix, Fürst zu Schwarzenberg** (fāʹlĭks), 1800–1852, was Austrian prime minister 1848–52. He forced Emperor Ferdinand's abdication (1848), suppressed the 1848 revolution throughout the empire, and restored Austrian leadership through the Treaty of OLMÜTZ.

Schwarzwald, Germany: see BLACK FOREST.

Schwatka, Frederick (shwŏtʹkŭ), 1849–92, American explorer. On arctic expedition (1878–80) he unearthed evidence of fate of Sir John Franklin's party. Explored Alaska, Mexico, Southwest.

Schweinfurt (shvīnʹfo͝ort), city (pop. 45,901), Lower Franconia, NW Bavaria. Machine tools and dyes (Paris green is also called Schweinfurt green). Center of German ball-bearing industry in World War II. Heavily damaged in air raids of 1943–44.

Schweitzer, Albert (shvīʹtsŭr), 1875–, Alsatian philosopher, a physician and missionary in French Equatorial Africa. He is a scientist, humanitarian, theologian, and a skilled organist (also author of a biography of Bach and editor of his organ music). His works have attracted international attention.

Schwenkfeld, Kaspar von (käʹspär fŭn shvĕngkʹfĕlt), 1490–1561, German religious reformer; a follower of Zwingli. His Anabaptist leanings caused enmity of Luther, and his books were banned. His followers, called Schwenkfeldians or Schwenkfelders, were persecuted and fled, some to America, where sect still exists in E Pa.

Schwerin, Kurt Christoph, Graf von (ko͝ortʹ krĭsʹtôf gräfʹ fŭn shvārēnʹ), 1684–1757, Prussian field marshal, b. Pomerania. Served under Charles XII of Sweden; entered Prussian service 1720; defeated Austrians at Mollwitz (1740); fell at Prague. He was one of Frederick II's ablest lieutenants.

Schwerin (shvārēnʹ), city (pop. 88,164), cap. of Macklenburg, NE Germany, on L. of Schwerin. Center of agr. and dairying region. Bishopric, here since 1167, was secularized 1648 and passed to duke of Mecklenburg. City was cap. of Mecklenburg-Schwerin 1701–1934.

Schwyz (shvēts), canton (351 sq. mi.; pop. 71,-246), Switzerland, one of FOUR FOREST CANTONS. Mountainous, forested, and pastoral region; large hydroelectric plants in N. German-speaking population. In 1274 Rudolf I of Hapsburg revoked charter granted by Emperor Frederick II in 1240. In protest, Schwyz concluded with Uri and Unterwalden the pact which became the basis for Swiss liberty (1291; see SWITZERLAND, which derives name from Schwyz). Schwyz joined Catholic SONDERBUND 1845. Its cap., **Schwyz** (pop. 10,192), has 16th-cent. town hall with historic paintings. Swiss federal archives here contain original pact of 1291.

Scilla (shēlʹlä), modern name of SCYLLA strait.

Scilly Islands (sĭlʹē), archipelago of over 150 isles off SW England. Many ships were once wrecked on the rocky coasts, now marked by lighthouses. Five isles are inhabited, St. Mary's (has cap., Hugh Town), Tresco, St. Martin's, St. Agnes, and Bryher. Climate is mild and growing flowers for export is a leading occupation.

Scioto (sīōʹtŭ), river, c.245 mi. long, rising in W Ohio and flowing E, then S, passing Columbus and Chillicothe, to enter Ohio R. at Portsmouth.

Scipio (sĭʹpēō), patrician family of anc. Rome, notable for love of learning as well as taking part in Roman warfare. **Cneius Cornelius Scipio Calvus** (nēʹŭs), d. 211 B.C., was consul in 222 B.C. Sent to Spain (218 B.C.) in the Second Punic War to wreck the supply lines of Hannibal. He and his brother defeated Hasdrubal (215 B.C.) and captured Saguntum (212 B.C.), but both were killed in Spain. That brother, **Publius Cornelius Scipio,** d. c.211 B.C., had been consul in 218 B.C. He opposed Hannibal and was defeated at the Ticino and Trebia (218 B.C.) before going to Spain. His wife was the sister of Aemilius Paullus, and CORNELIA was their daughter. One of their sons was the greatest of the family, **Scipio Africanus Major** (Publius Cornelius Scipio Africanus) (ăfrĭkāʹnŭs), 234?–183 B.C., the conqueror of HANNIBAL. He was with his father at the Ticino (218 B.C.) and survived the disastrous defeat at Cannae (216 B.C.). After his father's death he was elected proconsul of Spain. There he showed his military genius; by 209 he had conquered Cartagena and in a few years had taken all of Spain. In 205 B.C. he was consul, but the senate denied him permission to take the war to Africa. He went to Sicily, where he drilled a volunteer army. In 204 B.C. he was permitted to go to Africa, where, after answering Hannibal's peace offers with impossible demands, he defeated the Carthaginians in the decisive battle of Zama (202 B.C.). Later he tried in vain to prevent the Romans from hounding Hannibal to death. His pride and position gained him jealous enemies, who brought him to trial on charges (probably false) of receiving bribes when he accompanied his brother on a campaign against Antiochus III in 190. Cato the Elder headed the party against him, and Scipio was saved only by his son-in-law, T. Sempronius Gracchus. He ordered that his body should not be buried in the ungrateful city. His eldest son adopted the son of Aemilius PAULLUS, who became **Scipio Africanus Minor** (Publius Cornelius Scipio Aemilianus Africanus Numantinus), c.185–129 B.C. He was a patron of literature and friend of Terence, Laelius, and Polybius. He had considerable military experience before he became consul (147 B.C.) in the Third Punic War. He went to Africa and destroyed Carthage utterly. Consul again in 134 B.C., he put down a rebellion in Spain, destroying Numantia. Though Tiberius Gracchus was his adoptive cousin and brother of Scipio's wife, he rejoiced openly at the murder of Gracchus and tried to destroy the Gracchan reforms. After a public denunciation of Gracchus he was himself murdered, possibly by his wife or his mother-in-law. His friendship with Laelius is celebrated in Cicero's *De amicitia,* and the *Dream of Scipio* in Cicero's *De republica* tells of an apparition of the greater Scipio to this Scipio. A kinsman, **Publius Cornelius Scipio Nasica Serapio** (nā'sĭkŭ sĭrā'pēō), d. c.132 B.C., had actually been a leader in the mob that murdered Tiberius Gracchus. He had to flee later to escape popular wrath. A descendant of his, **Quintus Caecilius Metellus Pius Scipio,** d. 46 B.C., was an ardent supporter of Pompey, who made him colleague in the consulship in 52 B.C. In the civil war he was a commander for Pompey at Pharsala, and after defeat went to Africa. Caesar defeated him at Thapsus, and he took to the sea to escape. About to be captured by Caesar's men, he committed suicide.

scissor-tailed flycatcher, bird of New World flycatcher family Tyrannidae. Male is gray with reddish patch at base of wing and shades of pinkish and orange-red in the gray; dark tail feathers are marked with white. Deeply forked tail is 7–10 in. long. Bird breeds chiefly in parts of Texas, Okla., Kansas, Nebr.; usually winters in Central America.

Scituate (sĭ'choowat, –wĭt), resort town (pop. 5,993), SE Mass., on the coast SE of Boston; settled c.1630. Irish moss found here.

Scone (skōōn), parish (pop. 2,559), Perthshire, Scotland. Was royal residence of Scottish kings 1157–1488. Stone of Scone or CORONATION STONE is now in Westminster Abbey. Last coronation here was that of Charles II in 1651.

'Sconset, Mass.: see NANTUCKET.

Scopas (skō'pŭs), Greek sculptor, fl. 4th cent. B.C., first to portray violent facial expressions.

Scopes trial, July, 1925, trial of public-school teacher John T. Scopes at Dayton, Tenn., for teaching Darwinian theory contrary to state statute. C. S. Darrow was a defense attorney, W. J. Bryan prosecuted. Convicted, Scopes was later released on a technicality.

scopolamine (skōpŏ'lŭmēn, –mĭn) or **hyoscine** (hī'ŭsēn, –sĭn), alkaloid drug obtained from plants of nightshade family. Acts as depressant of central nervous system; used as sedative.

scorbutus: see SCURVY.

Scoresby, William, 1789–1857, English arctic explorer and scientist. On yearly trips to Greenland (1803–22) he collected scientific data, giving special attention to terrestrial magnetism, a study he pursued further on visit to Australia (1856).

Scoresby Sound, inlet of E Greenland. Several of its branches extend c.150 mi. inland.

Scorpio (skôr'pēō) [Latin,= scorpion], eighth sign of ZODIAC.

scorpion (skôr'pēŭn), nocturnal arachnid, ½–8 in. long, of warm and tropical regions. With pincerlike claws attacks spiders and insects; paralyzes prey with poison injected by sharp, curved spine of post-abdomen. Sting of some is fatal to children.

Scot, Michael, c.1175–1232, medieval scholar. He supervised translations of Arabian works and of Aristotle into Latin, and in 1230 he introduced study of Aristotle at Oxford. He was also famous for occult learning and reputed miraculous powers. As a magician he figures in Dante's *Inferno.*

Scotia (skō'shŭ), Latin name for Scotland.

Scotland, northern part of Great Britain (30,405 sq. mi.; pop. 5,095,969), cap. EDINBURGH. Separated from England by Tweed and Liddell rivers, Cheviot Hills, and Solway Firth. It is 274 mi. long, 26–154 mi. wide. Irregular coastline with numerous lochs and firths (Moray, Tay, and Forth firths in E; Solway, Clyde, and Lorne firths in W) is 2,300 mi. long. In N are Orkney and Shetland isls.; W are Inner and Outer Hebrides, or Western Isles; SW are Arran and Bute isls. Scotland is divided into three physical regions: Highlands, central Lowlands, and southern uplands. Highlands (including Hebrides) are almost entirely mountainous and include highest point in Great Britain, Ben Nevis (4,406 ft.). Grampians are chief chain. Principal waterways are Dee, Don, Deveron, Spey, and Beauly rivers and Caledonian Canal. Central Lowlands, with general elevation of 500 ft., have many hill ridges and fine lakes. Here, on Clyde R., is Glasgow. In E are other mfg. towns. Coal and iron in this area have aided growth of heavy industry. Southern uplands, a slightly mountainous region of rolling moorlands, rise abruptly from Lowlands. Chief rivers are Nith, Cree, Ayr, and Tweed. Only c.25% of Scotland can be cultivated. Main crops are barley, oats, wheat, turnips, and beans. Chief occupations are mfg. of woolens, worsteds, linen, silk, whisky, beer, and paper, and sheep-raising and fisheries. Scotland, united with England since 1707, is represented in House of Commons and House of Lords. Secretary of state for Scotland is a cabinet member. Counties are Shetland, Orkney, Caithness, Sutherlandshire, Ross and Cromarty, Inverness-shire, Nairnshire, Morayshire, Banffshire, Aberdeenshire, Argyllshire, Perthshire, Angus, Buteshire, Kincardineshire, Dumbartonshire, Stirlingshire, Clackmannanshire, Kinross-shire, Fife, Renfrewshire, Ayrshire, Lanarkshire, West Lothian, Midlothian, East Lothian, Peebleshire, Wigtownshire, Kirkcudbrightshire, Berwick, Dumfriesshire, Selkirkshire, and Roxburghshire. Church of SCOTLAND, estab. 1560, is Presbyterian; was united (1929) with United Free Church (see SCOTLAND, FREE CHURCH OF). Universities are those of Edinburgh, Glasgow, Aberdeen, and St. Andrews. Scottish law is based on Roman rather than common law (as in England). For pre-Roman history of Scotland, see BRITAIN. Picts, here from beginning of historic times, with Gaels or Celts from Ireland kept Romans from penetrating far into Scotland or having much influence, despite Agricola's invasion of A.D. 80. St. Ninian introduced Christianity in 5th cent.; St. Columba extended it in 6th cent. In next century and a half, four kingdoms were estab.: Picts in N; Scots from Ireland; Britains from Strathclyde; and Northumbria, founded by Angles. Country was raided by Norsemen 8th–12th cent. Reign of MALCOLM III, who succeeded Macbeth (murderer of King Duncan), was long and peaceful. Peace with England came with marriage of King Edgar's sister Maud to Henry I of England. Under David I, Scotland achieved stature of a nation. Alexander II and Alexander III pushed Norsemen out of Scotland. Alexander III's heiress, Margaret Maid of Norway, died a child and John de Baliol became king. Scotland's long relationship with France began in 13th cent.; they were allied against Edward I of England. Robert Bruce, crowned ROBERT I in 1306, defeated Edward II at Bannockburn 1314. In 1349 Black Death killed c.30% of the people. JAMES I was one of Scotland's most learned kings and best Chaucerian poets. His murder (1437) threw country into civil war for 100 years. Reformation was brought to Scotland by John KNOX. When MARY QUEEN OF SCOTS arrived from France, Catholicism had almost disappeared from Lowlands. Her struggle against Protestantism ended in loss of the throne, imprisonment in England, and execution. Her son succeeded Elizabeth as JAMES I of England, uniting the two crowns. The CONVENANTERS resisted Charles I in BISHOPS' WARS (1639–40), and PURITAN REVOLUTION became civil war. Act of Union (1707) gave Scotland representation in Parliament of GREAT BRITAIN. JACOBITES tried unsuccessfully to destroy Union, economic results of which were favorable. As result of late 18th cent. and early 19th cent. inclosures, many Highlanders emigrated. By end of 18th cent. textile industry was preeminent. Commerce with British Empire led to growth of shipping, and Glasgow became great commercial center. By late 19th cent. coal and iron industries had taken lead in economy, and steamships were built at Clydeside. Concentration of heavy industry made Scotland important arsenal in both World Wars. Efforts to attract tourists include Edinburgh's festival of arts. There is still a nationalist movement which urges greater autonomy for Scotland.

Scotland, Church of, established church of Scotland. Under John KNOX Scottish reformers followed Calvinist teachings. After First Covenant (1557) Parliament abolished jurisdiction of Roman Church in Scotland in 1560. When it ratified *Second Book of Discipline* in 1592, it estab. Presbyterian polity and Calvinistic doctrine as recognized religion of Scotland. National Covenant was signed 1638; in 1643 the Solemn League and Covenant was signed in both England and Scotland. Westminster Confession was adopted 1647. Act of Settlement (1690) and union of England and Scotland (1707) ratified existence of Church of Scotland.

Scotland, Free Church of, formed 1843 by secession group from Church of Scotland, led by Thomas Chalmers, in dispute between church and state over patronage, and interference of the state. In 1900 main body of Free Church joined United Presbyterian Church as United Free Church of Scotland. In 1929 rejoined Church of Scotland.

Scotland Yard, short street in London which became hq. of metropolitan police in 1829. New hq. (New Scotland Yard) estab. 1890 on the Thames. The Criminal Investigation Department (CID), popularly known as "Scotland Yard," is part of it.

Scott, Cyril (Meir), 1879–, English impressionist composer of symphonies, operas, choral works, chamber music, songs, and piano pieces. He is also an author of books on musical and scientific subjects and occultism.

Scott, Sir George Gilbert, 1811–78, English architect, prominent in the Gothic revival. Designed Albert Memorial, London, and restored part of Westminster Abbey. His grandson, **Sir Giles Gilbert Scott,** 1880–, designed Liverpool Cathedral.

Scott, James Brown, 1866–1943, American authority on international law, b. Canada; dean of the law school at the Univ. of Southern California (1896–99) and the Univ. of Illinois (1899–1903) and professor at several other universities. Had many public posts concerned with international affairs.

Scott, John: see ELDON, JOHN SCOTT, 1ST EARL OF.

Scott, Robert Falcon, 1868–1912, British naval officer, antarctic explorer. Commanded expedition (1901–4) to explore Ross Sea region. Set forth in 1910 to seek South Pole. Reached it with four companions, Jan. 18, 1912, one month after Roald Amundsen. All died on return journey, but remains and records of epic journey were later recovered.

Scott, Sir Walter, 1771–1832, British novelist and poet. He studied at Univ. of Edinburgh and was called to the bar in 1792. In vacations he learned to know the Border countryside, and he collected folk songs in *Minstrelsy of the Scottish Border* (2 vols., 1802; 3 vols., 1803). This interest led to his *Lay of the Last Minstrel* (1805), *Marmion* (1808), and *The Lady of the Lake* (1810). Later narrative poems proving less popular, he turned to prose romances, among them *Waverley* (1814; beginning series called Waverley novels), *Guy Mannering* (1815), *The Heart of Midlothian* (1818), and *The Bride of Lammermoor* (1819). He was made baronet in 1820. *Ivanhoe* (1820) began the long series of romances of British history, such as *Kenilworth* (1821), *Quentin Dur-*

ward (1823), and *The Talisman* (1825). Scott now met financial reverses. He had bought Abbotsford in 1812, and he had invested heavily in the Ballantyne publishing house. When the firm failed in 1825, Scott herocially assumed its entire indebtedness. He wrote incessantly, and ruined his health, but the entire debt was paid off from the sale of his books after his death. In his ringing rhymes, such as "Lochinvar" and "Proud Maisie," and in his novels Scott re-created the heroic spirit of Scotland—and of England.

Scott, Winfield, 1786–1866, American general. A hero of War of 1812. His peacemaking talents were often useful to U.S., e.g., in Aroostook War (1839). From July, 1841, to Nov., 1861, he was supreme commander of U.S. army. In Mexican War he headed southern expedition; campaign was triumph for Scott's daring strategy and confirmed his reputation as a bold fighter. Made poor showing as Whig candidate for President in 1852. Although vain and pompous (he was called "Old Fuss and Feathers"), he was also generous and fair-minded. Greatest American general between Washington and Lee.

Scott City, city (pop. 3,204), W central Kansas, N of Garden City. To N are remains of an Indian pueblo.

Scottdale, borough (pop. 6,249), SW Pa., SE of Pittsburgh. Coal mining; mfg. of metal products.

Scotti, Antonio (skŏ'tē), 1868–1936, Italian baritone. He sang at the Metropolitan Opera, New York, 1899–1933, in such roles as Iago in *Otello,* Scarpia in *La Tosca,* and Hans Sachs in *Die Meistersinger.*

Scottish dialect, English dialect of the Lowlands, a modern form of Northumbrian Old English. Used in 11th-cent. courts, it became official language when Malcolm III abandoned Scottish Gaelic. History of Scottish grammar roughly parallels that of standard ENGLISH LANGUAGE, but in details of sound changes Scottish frequently differs from standard English, and in vocabulary it is more archaic than standard English. Oldest literary monument in Scottish dialect is *The Bruce* (14th cent.) by John Barbour. Following early great Scottish poets (Chaucerians such as James I) came a golden age in 15th and 16th cent., but thereafter Scottish declined as a literary medium (except for 18th-cent. revival by Allan Ramsay, Robert Burns, and others), and English has made continual inroads into the vernacular since early 17th cent. This fact may be explained by Stuart accession to English throne with loss of a Scottish national self-consciousness and use in Scotland of the English Bible.

Scottish Gaelic language and literature: see GAELIC; GAELIC LITERATURE.

Scottish terrier: see TERRIER.

Scottsbluff, city (pop. 12,858), W Nebr., on North Platte R., in Great Plains region near Wyo. line; settled after 1885. Trade center of irrigated agr. area, it produces beet sugar, flour, dairy products, and refined oil. Scotts Bluff National Monument (see NATIONAL PARKS AND MONUMENTS, table) is across the river.

Scottsboro, city (pop. 4,731), NE Ala., near Tennessee R. at edge of Cumberland Plateau. Gave name to **Scottsboro Case.** On March 31, 1931, nine Negro boys were indicted on charges of having raped two white girls. After several trials and two U.S. Supreme Court reversals of conviction, five were convicted and sentenced (in Jan., 1936, and July, 1937) and four were acquitted. By Sept., 1946, all had been released except Haywood Patterson, the alleged ringleader; he escaped later (d. 1952 in Mich. prison). Northern liberals and radicals, charging anti-Negro bias in Ala., made the case a *cause célèbre.* Communists used it for propaganda purposes. The Scottsboro Defense Committee, for the most part representing liberal, non-Communist organizations, was largely responsible for ultimate freeing of the boys.

Scotus: see DUNS SCOTUS and ERIGENA, JOHN SCOTUS.

scouting: see BOY SCOUTS; GIRL SCOUTS.

Scranton, city (pop. 125,536), NE Pa., on Lackawanna R. and NW of New York city; settled late in 18th cent. Commercial and industrial center of anthracite region of NE Pa. with mfg. of textiles, clothing, and metal products.

screw, simple machine consisting of cylinder around which an inclined plane winds spirally. Mechanical advantage theoretically is ratio between circumference through which the end moves and pitch (distance between threads). Although, because of friction, the efficiency is small, screw devices such as jackscrew used to lift automobiles, houses, etc., are of great value because of enormous load raised by relatively small effort. See *ill.,* p. 793.

Scriabin, Aleksandr (Nikolayevich) (ŭlyĭksän'dŭr skrēä'bĭn), 1872–1915, Russian composer. A bold innovator, he introduced chords built in fourths (C–F sharp–B flat) instead of triads (C–E–G). His orchestral music includes his *Divine Poem* and *Prometheus: a Poem of Fire,* which calls for the play of colored lights upon a screen during the performance.

Scribe, Eugène (ûzhĕn' skrĕb'), 1791–1861, French author of popular plays of every description and librettos for grand opera (notably for Auber, Meyerbeer, Boieldieu, Jacques Halévy). *Le Verre d'eau* is perhaps his best-known comedy.

scribe (skrīb), originally a Jewish scholar who knew the art of writing, later an official teacher of Jewish law. The work of the scribes developed into the Oral Law, as distinct from the Written Law of the Torah. The scribes lost their religious leadership in the 1st cent. A.D. and were followed by the Tannaim (plural of Tanna), scholars and teachers of the Oral Law who flourished between A.D. 10 and A.D. 220. The Mishna is the work of this group. They were succeeded by the Amoraim (c.200 to 350), who developed the Gemara of the Talmud. The period of the Geonim, who became the authoritative interpreters of the Old Testament and the Talmud, ended in 1038.

Scriblerus Club, English literary group formed (1713) to satirize "false tastes in learning." Members included Gay, Pope, Swift, and

Arbuthnot, chief author of club's "Memoirs of . . . Martinus Scriblerus."

Scribner, Charles, 1821–71, American publisher. In 1846 founded publishing house which in 1878 became Charles Scribner's Sons. Founded in 1870 *Scribner's Monthly* (later *Century Magazine*). His son, **Charles Scribner,** 1854–1930, became head of firm in 1879; founded in 1887 *Scribner's Magazine.*

Scripps, Edward Wyllis, 1854–1926, American newspaper publisher. With brother George and M. A. McRae founded Scripps-McRae League, a powerful liberal, pro-labor newspaper chain. In 1907 estab. United Press Association, with R. W. Howard as manager (after 1908). After 1922 his son R. P. Scripps joined with Howard to control chain, now known as Scripps-Howard papers.

Scripps College: see CLAREMONT, Calif.

Scripps Institution of Oceanography: see LA JOLLA, Calif.

scrofula: see TUBERCULOSIS.

Scrooby, village, Nottinghamshire, England. Home of William Brewster, it was center of group later known as Pilgrims.

Scudder, Henry Martyn, 1822–95, American missionary, b. Ceylon; son of a missionary. He worked in India (1844–64) under American Board and Dutch Reformed Church. Missionary in Japan (1887–90).

Scudéry, Madeleine de (mädůlĕn′ dů skűdärē′), 1607?–1701, French author of the romances *Artamène; ou, Le Grand Cyrus* (1649–53) and *Clélie* (1654–60). Despite their extreme preciosity, these foreshadowed in their analysis of sentiment and character the later French psychological novel.

scurvy (scorbutus), deficiency disease resulting from insufficient vitamin C (ascorbic acid) in diet. Attended by bleeding of gums, anemia, debility. Formerly common among sailors. May occur in babies after six months of age if diet lacks vitamin C.

scutage (skū′tĭj), feudal impost originating as a fine or cash impost in lieu of military service due by a vassal to a suzerain, especially to a king. Collected by kings for military expenses and other purposes. Impost resisted by barons, and in Magna Carta (1215) King John agreed to collect scutage only with counsel of barons. Growth of taxes after time of Edward III displaced scutage.

Scutari (skōō′tůrē), Albanian *Shkodër* or *Shkodra,* city (pop. 33,852), N Albania. Has textile, tobacco, and other mfg. An ancient Illyrian capital and a Roman colony (Scodra) from 168 B.C., it fell to the Serbs in 7th cent. A.D. Was seat of princes of Zeta (i.e., Montenegro) from 14th cent. to its fall to Turkey (1479). Though occupied by Montenegrin troops in the Balkan Wars (1913), it was assigned by the European powers to Albania. In World War I it was successively under Montenegrin, Austrian, and Allied occupation. Scutari lies on the SE end of **Lake Scutari,** part of which extends into Yugoslavia. Because of seasonal variations in depth, its area varies from 150 to 200 sq. mi. Abundant fishing.

Scutari or **Uskudar** (üskü′där), urban district (pop. 60,722) of Istanbul, Turkey, on Asiatic side. Florence Nightingale worked in British military hospital here during Crimean War.

Scylla (sĭ′lů), in Greek mythology, sea nymph. Circe, her rival in love for Glaucus, made her a monster, who lived on a rock on Italian side of Strait of Messina. Opposite, on Sicilian side, was whirlpool of Charybdis. Odysseus passed safely through strait of Scylla and Charybdis (now called Scilla), as did Argonaut heroes.

Scyllis: see DIPOENUS AND SCYLLIS.

Scyros, Greek island: see SKYROS.

Scythia (sĭ′thēů), region of S Europe inhabited by the Scythians, varying in extent as their power grew or waned, but generally with its core on the N shore of the Black Sea about the lower Don and lower Dnieper and in the Crimea. The **Scythians** were nomadic and warlike horsemen, who were in the area by the 9th cent. B.C. They spoke an Indo-Iranian language. They traded with the Greeks and acted as Greek mercenaries. In the 7th cent. they invaded the Assyrian Empire and for a time held Palestine. Darius I led an expedition (c.512 B.C.) and Alexander the Great also led an expedition against them. In the 3d cent. B.C. they were replaced by their kinsmen, the Sarmatians.

Se, chemical symbol of the element SELENIUM.

sea, law of the: see MARITIME LAW.

sea anemone (ůnĕ′můnē), marine invertebrate related to jellyfish and coral. It has a cylindrical body and stinging tentacles. Attaches to rock, shell, or seaweed in shallow water.

Seabees [from the initials of Construction Battalion], colloquial name for the U.S. Naval Construction Battalions of World War II. The first regiment was authorized in Dec., 1941. Force grew to c.250,000 men.

Seaborg, Glenn Theodore, 1912–, American chemist and physicist. Shared 1951 Nobel Prize in Chemistry for discoveries in chemistry of elements having atomic number greater than that of uranium. He is codiscoverer of plutonium (element 94), americium (element 95), curium (element 96), berkelium (element 97), and californium (element 98). Associated with Univ. of California from 1937, and with atomic bomb project (1942–46).

Sea Bright, summer-resort borough (pop. 999), NE N.J., between Shrewsbury R. and the Atlantic. In an estate area, it holds national and international tennis and polo matches.

Seabury, Samuel, 1729–96, American clergyman, first bishop of Protestant Episcopal Church. Consecrated in Scotland in 1784; became presiding bishop of Church in U.S. in 1789. His great-great-grandson, **Samuel Seabury,** 1873–, headed investigations in 1930–31 of New York city's magistrate courts and of New York city politics.

Seaford, town (pop. 3,087), SW Del., on Nanticoke R. Nylon-industry center.

sea horse, small warm-water fish (chiefly of genus *Hippocampus*). Elongated head and snout suggest appearance of horse. It swims weakly in upright position. Male has abdominal pouch in which eggs are carried until young hatch.

Sea Islands, chain of low islands along coast of S.C., Ga., and N Fla., between mouths of Santee and St. Johns rivers. Spanish, early in control, gave way to English. SAINT HELENA

ISLAND and Port Royal Isl. (S.C.) had great cotton plantations in early 19th cent. Land divided among slaves by U.S. after Civil War. Carolina islands still largely inhabited by Negroes, who retain many old customs and dialects. Farming and fishing important. BEAUFORT (Port Royal Isl.) is main city. Parris Isl. has U.S. marine base. St. Simons, Sea, and Jekyll islands are Ga. resorts. St. Simons Isl. has ruins of Fort Frederica (now national monument), built 1736–54 by James Oglethorpe during English-Spanish struggle for SE U.S. Spanish defeated near by in battle of Bloody Marsh, July 7, 1742. Jekyll Isl. is state park. Cumberland Isl., Ga., largest (c.22 mi. long, 1–5 mi. wide), still mostly private.

seal, carnivorous aquatic mammal with front and hind flippers, found chiefly in cold regions. Suborder Pinnipedia (of order Carnivora) consists of three families; true, earless, or hair seals (Phocidae); eared fur seals and sea lions (Otariidae); walruses (Odobenidae). Alaskan fur seals winter from Alaska to N coast of Calif. and in spring migrate N to breeding grounds on Pribilof Isls.

Seal Harbor, Maine: see MOUNT DESERT ISLAND.

Seal Islands: see LOBOS ISLANDS.

Sealyham terrier: see TERRIER.

sea pink or **thrift,** perennial garden plant (*Armeria*), with papery, globe-shaped flower clusters and grasslike evergreen foliage. The sea lavenders (*Limonium*), also called sea pink, have panicles of dainty flowers. Plants of both genera are often called statice.

sea power. According to A. T. MAHAN, the naval strength which enables state to control part of sea and deny its use to enemy nations or to uphold its maritime rights in peace or war. Development of sea power dates from earliest history. By it Phoenicians controlled Mediterranean, and Athens defeated Persians at Salamis. Contributed to Rome's victory over Carthage and subsequent spread of empire. Italian city-states and HANSEATIC LEAGUE derived wealth from control of seas. Battle of LEPANTO (1571) ended Turkish naval power. Portugal built empire on seas, and Spain ruled the waves until the defeat of the Armada by England. Dutch gained importance through sea power. Great Britain vanquished France in 18th and 19th cent. to become mistress of seas. Sea power of U.S. increased rapidly from War of 1812 through Civil and Spanish-American wars. Bottling-up of German navy contributed to Allied victory in World War I. Despite growth of air power, necessity of navy in Pacific and in invasion of Europe in World War II pointed to its continuing importance. Naval forces have been of great value in atom-bomb experiments.

searchlight, device using lens and reflecting surface to direct a beam of light. After 1900 acetylene came into use as an illuminant and in 1916 Edison invented portable apparatus fed from batteries. Searchlights mounted on trucks and railroad cars came into use in World War I. In 1915 E. A. Sperry, American inventor, introduced high-intensity arc lamp. Revolving searchlights as beacons spaced along air routes have yielded to radio beacons. Use of powerful lights coordinated with anti-aircraft guns developed considerably in World War II.

Searcy (sûr'sē), city (pop. 6,024), N central Ark., NE of Little Rock, in strawberry area.

Searsport, resort town (pop. 1,457), S Maine, on Penobscot Bay. Has Penobscot Marine Mus. (1936).

Seaside. 1 Village (pop. 10,226), W Calif., on S shore of Monterey Bay. **2** Resort city (pop. 3,886), NW Oregon, on the Pacific and S of Astoria. Monument marks point sometimes considered end of Oregon Trail.

seasons, divisions of year characterized by variations in amount of heat received from sun. Variations depend on inclination of equator in plane of the ecliptic and on revolution of earth around the sun. The heat at a given point depends chiefly on the angle of the sun's rays and the daily duration of exposure to them. In temperate zones there are four well-defined seasons. In low latitudes and in certain areas (e.g., India), where oceans and winds especially affect seasonal changes, there are "wet" and "dry" seasons. See *ill.*, p. 1187.

Seattle, city (pop. 467,491), W Wash., between Elliott Bay of Puget Sound and L. Washington, and between Olympic Mts. and Cascade Range; settled 1852 as lumber town. Grew after railroads came (1884) despite strikes, anti-Chinese riots, and fire of 1889. Boomed with Alaska gold rush (1897) and opening of Panama Canal (1914). Largest city in Wash., a metropolis of the Pacific Northwest. Great port and commercial center, with Alaskan and Far Eastern trade; has foreign trade zone (opened 1949). Mfg. of lumber, food products (fruit, fish, meat), aluminum, iron, steel, textiles. Important fur market. Hq. for fishing (esp. halibut) and pleasure boats. Great expansion brought by World War II (aircraft, shipbuilding) and new hydroelectric projects in region. Seat of Univ. of WASHINGTON, Seattle Univ. (Jesuit; coed.; 1898), Fort Lawton, and Sand Point Naval Air Station.

sea urchin, marine animal, like the starfish an echinoderm. Globular outer skeleton protects body. Irregular spines aid the tube feet in locomotion. In mouth region on underneath surface most forms have complex structure containing five sharp teeth. Sea urchins are scavengers.

seaweed, name for marine algae. Simple forms are of a single cell or a few cells, but higher forms have a disklike base and ribbonlike or leaflike frond of green, brown, or red. Few seaweeds grow below a depth of 150 ft. Some red seaweeds are eaten, especially in the Orient; commercial AGAR is obtained from a red alga. See also GULFWEED; IRISH MOSS; KELP.

Sebago Lake (sĭbā'gō), 12 mi. long and 1–8 mi. wide, SW Maine, NW of Portland, in resort area. Supplies Portland's water.

Sebastian, Saint, 3d cent.?, Roman martyr, said to have been beloved by Diocletian, who turned against him when he was converted to Christianity and had him killed with arrows. Feast: Jan. 20.

Sebastian, 1554–78, king of Portugal (1557-

78). Was under regency of his grandmother 1557–62; under that of his uncle and successor, Henry, 1562–68. Fanatically religious, he led a great expedition against Moslems in Morocco but was defeated and slain in the battle of Alcazarquivir. His army was wiped out. A legend prophesying his return long persisted.

Sebastiano del Piombo (säbästyä'nō dĕl pyōm'bō), c.1485–1547, Venetian painter, whose real name was Sebastiano Luciani. So called because he held the office of *piombo* (keeper of papal seals). Influenced by Michelangelo.

Sebastopol, RSFSR: see SEVASTOPOL.

Sebec Lake (sē'bĭk), 11 mi. long and ½–3 mi. wide, central Maine, SE of Moosehead L. Noted for salmon and bass fishing.

Sebring (sē'brĭng), city (pop. 5,006), S central Fla., on L. Jackson, in citrus-fruit area.

Secaucus (sēkô'kŭs), town (pop. 9,750), NE N.J., N of Jersey City. Silk and metal products.

Secchi, (Pietro) Angelo (pyā'trō än'jälō sĕk'kē), 1818–78, Italian astronomer, a Jesuit priest, pioneer in classifying stars by their spectra.

secession, formal withdrawal from association by group discontented with decisions or actions of majority. Best-known example was withdrawal in 1860–61 of 11 Southern states from U.S. to form CONFEDERACY, which fought Civil War with Northern states. Central issue was question of STATES' RIGHTS. Secessionists held Constitution was a compact between sovereign states, not paramount in power; hence they could legally secede from a voluntary union. Opponents held that Constitution created sovereign and inviolable union and that withdrawal was impossible. One course of action was NULLIFICATION movement. When Southern states felt threatened by election of Lincoln, they seceded.

Secession, War of: see CIVIL WAR.

Second Adventists: see ADVENTISTS.

Second Empire: see NAPOLEON III.

secretary bird, African bird of prey c.4 ft. high, with long legs, hooked beak, and black-feathered crest (like quill pens). Destroys reptiles and other animals.

secretion, in biology, substance formed by single cells or organ of animal or plant and performing special function or eliminated as waste. Secretions in man include external and internal secretions (see GLAND) and lubricants, e.g., synovial fluid in joints and tears. Wastes include urine and sweat.

secret police. Law enforcement has required in almost all organized societies a certain amount of secrecy, particularly in investigation of crime. Emergence of recognizable, uniformed police is probably more recent than secret bodies formed against external or internal attack. Generally secret police include all who operate without knowledge of a suspect that he is under investigation. In democracy, role of secret police usually ceases once investigation is closed. This limitation and right of offender to open trial and access to evidence against him are guarantees of individual freedom notable in countries which have adopted English and American systems. Secret police not bound by these conditions are endowed with authority superior to other law-enforcing agencies. They may investigate, apprehend, and sometimes judge a suspect and are responsible only to executive branch. A particular danger inherent in this type of secret police is that it may become a state within the state and ultimately overthrow the government, e.g., Nazi secret police under Heinrich Himmler. In 1933 the Gestapo was formed under Hermann Goering and in 1936 was combined with the SS (see NATIONAL SOCIALISM) under Himmler. He subordinated it to the *Sicherheitsdienst* or SD [security service]. This body, with its intricate ramifications and agents in all branches of government, eventually became so powerful as to make Himmler the real master of Germany. German crimes and atrocities in World War II were largely carried out by the SS and Gestapo. Secret police forces do not always have their roots in maintenance of security of the state. Such organizations as the VEHME of medieval Germany may be a spontaneous creation of a segment of the people to protect its interests. The institution has existed in most societies where a minority exercised uneasy rule over a majority. Sparta had secret police, and in Rome paid informers were employed. Venetian Inquisition saw early secret police organized along modern lines (see TEN, COUNCIL OF); also notable was the Oprichnina of Tsar IVAN IV. Russia saw organization of another secret police after Decembrist uprising of 1825. This group, like all others, worked with censorship to control not only subversive acts but even subversive thought. (This trend culminated in Japanese Thought Police in World War II.) After Russian Revolution of 1917, Soviets created own secret police, the dread Cheka. This was renamed OGPU or GPU [united department of political police] 1922, and was abolished 1934 to be absorbed by people's commissariat (later ministry) of internal affairs (NKVD, later MVD). Its responsibilities include detection of subversive elements, supervision of prison and labor camps, and "reeducation" of political offenders. Secret political police strengthened Mussolini's power in Italy.

secret society. Organization of almost universal occurrence and ancient origin. Typically, membership follows initiation rite involving pledge of secrecy, acceptance of obligations, and tests of worthiness. Candidate is then introduced to group's mysteries. Societies range from schools of tribal lore to FRATERNAL ORDERS. See also FREEMASONRY.

Securities and Exchange Commission (SEC), U.S. government agency created by Securities Exchange Act of 1934 to prevent unfair practices in the securities market. Administers government regulations on investments and supervises stock exchanges.

Security Council: see UNITED NATIONS.

Sedalia (sĭdā'lyŭ), city (pop. 20,354) W central Mo., ESE of Kansas City; laid out 1859. Center of a farm and limestone area. Has railroad shops and mfg. of disinfectants and food products.

Sedan (sĭdăn', Fr. sůdā'), garrison town (pop. 12,987), Ardennes dept., NE France, on

Meuse R. near Belgian border. Textile mfg. Until cession (1642) to France it was part of duchy of Bouillon. Served as a Protestant stronghold 16th–17th cent. It was scene in Franco-Prussian War of decisive French defeat and of capture of Napoleon III (1870); in World War II of German breakthrough starting "battle of France" (1940).

sedge, name for grasslike and rushlike marsh plants of family Cyperaceae, of temperate and tropical regions. Some (species of *Carex, Cyperus,* and *Scirpus*) yield hay and can be woven into mats and chair seats.

Sedgemoor, moorland, Somerset, England. Site of duke of Monmouth's defeat in 1685 by James II.

Sedgwick, John, 1813–64, Union general in Civil War. Served with Army of the Potomac in the Peninsular, Antietam, and Wilderness campaigns.

sedimentary rock: see ROCK.

sedum (sē'dŭm), succulent perennial plant of genus *Sedum,* also called stonecrop, often grown in rock gardens and borders. The creeping, yellow-flowered *Sedum acre* is naturalized from the Old World. The showy sedum (*S. spectabile*), white or rosy-flowered, is common in gardens.

seed, product of the fertilization of the ovum of a flower after POLLINATION. It is a many-celled structure borne within a fruit (see *ill.,* p. 999) and contains the embryo or young plant and stored food. Seeds are produced by the highest group of plants while those in lower orders (mosses and ferns) bear spores which are unicellular and contain no embryo. Seeds vary in size from the dustlike seed of some orchids to the huge seeds of a palm. Many seeds require a resting period before germination. A plant grown from seed may differ from its parent plant as a result of cross pollination or other causes.

Seeger, Alan, 1888–1916, American poet, famous for war poem "I Have a Rendezvous with Death," poignantly prophetic of his own death in action in 1916.

seeing-eye dog, trained to guide a blind person. Breeds used for this purpose include German shepherds, Doberman pinschers, and some bulldogs. At the Seeing Eye, Inc., a school in Morristown, N.J., each dog is first trained alone, and then dog and master are trained together. Many blind people have gained new independence with a seeing-eye dog.

Seekonk, river: see BLACKSTONE, river.

Seeland, Denmark: see ZEALAND.

Seeley, Sir John Robert, 1834–95, English historian. Books include *Ecce Homo* (1865), a life of Christ; *The Expansion of England* (1883); and *Growth of British Policy* (1895).

Seelye, Julius Hawley (sē'lē), 1824–95, American clergyman, president (1876–90) of Amherst. Initiated first student self-government in America. His brother **Laurenus Clark Seelye,** 1837–1924, also a clergyman, in 1873 became first president of Smith Col., retiring in 1910.

sego lily (sē'gō), ornamental tuliplike white flower (*Calochortus nuttalli*), native to the W U.S.

Segonzac, André Dunoyer de (ãdrā' dünwäyā' dü sügõzäk'), 1884–, French painter. His landscapes, still lifes, and nudes are done in highly simplified style.

Segovia, Andrés (ändrās' sāgō'vyä), 1894–, Spanish virtuoso guitarist, most notable performer of his time. In transcriptions of early contrapuntal music he made the guitar a concert instrument.

Segovia (sāgō'vyä), city (pop. 24,253), cap. of Segovia prov., central Spain, in Old Castile. Crowning the city are magnificent Gothic cathedral (1526–1616) and 14th-cent. alcazar, where Isabella I of Castile was proclaimed queen. Famous Roman aqueduct (c.900 yards long) is still in use.

Seguin (sügēn'), city (pop. 9,733), S central Texas, on Guadalupe R. and ENE of San Antonio; settled 1832 by Germans. Trade and processing center for cotton, farm, cattle, and oil area. River and near-by L. McQueeney attract visitors.

Seignobos, Charles (shärl' sānyōbō'), 1854–1942, French historian. Known for studies of French and European history and civilization, notably *The Feudal Régime* (Eng. tr., 1902; new ed., 1926).

seignorial system: see MANORIAL SYSTEM; FEUDALISM.

Seine (sān, Fr. sĕn), department (185 sq. mi.; pop. 4,775,711), N France, coextensive with Greater Paris (i.e., PARIS proper with its residential and industrial suburbs, the *banlieue*). Here is largest industrial concentration of population in France. Produces machinery, autos, airplanes, textiles, chemicals, and luxury goods.

Seine, river, 482 mi. long, N France. With its tributaries (e.g., Aube, Yonne, Marne, Oise) it drains entire Paris basin. Rising in Langres Plateau, it winds NW past Paris and Rouen to enter English Channel through a wide estuary (max. 6 mi.) at Le Havre. These three ports handle bulk of French river and ocean trade.

Seine-et-Marne (sĕn"-ā-märn'), department (2,290 sq. mi.; pop. 407,137), N France in Île-de-France; cap. Melun.

Seine-et-Oise (sĕn"-ā-wäz'), department (2,185 sq. mi.; pop, 1,414,910), N France, in Île-de-France; cap. Versailles.

Seine-Inférieure (sĕn"-ēfārēûr'), department (2,448 sq. mi.; pop. 846,131), N France, in Normandy; cap. Rouen.

Seir (sē'ŭr), mountainous region, S Palestine, identical with EDOM. Frequently called Mt. Seir.

seismology (sīzmŏ'lŭjē, sīs–), scientific study of earthquakes. Instruments used are called seismographs, and the record, traced on a rotating drum, is the seismogram. From this graph information about the earthquake can be learned. An important commercial application is use of seismology in prospecting for petroleum. Earth tremors are caused by high explosive and the resulting waves recorded by the seismograph. Formations associated with oil can thus be located.

Seiyukai (sā'yōōkī"), Japanese political party, founded 1900. Derived from the Jiyuto, founded 1881. Ito was its first president, Saionji its second. First leader to form party cabinet (1918) on parliamentary principles was Takashi Hara. Seiyukai cabinets alternated 1927–32 with MINSEITO governments, with both having basically similar programs. After 1932, rising militarist power forced decline of political parties; all finally disbanded 1940 in favor of single government-sponsored party.

Sejanus, Lucius Aelius (sĭjā'nŭs), d. A.D. 31, Roman statesman, commander of the Praetorian guards, and a favorite of Tiberius, until he was suspected of plots and was put to death.

Sekia el Hamra: see SPANISH SAHARA.

Selangor: see MALAYA.

Selborne (sĕl'bôrn), village, Hampshire, England. Home of Gilbert White, author of *The Natural History and Antiquities of Selborne.* His grave is here.

Selden, John, 1584–1654, English jurist and scholar. Active in Parliament's struggle with crown, and in trial of George Villiers. One of most erudite men of his time, an authority in legal antiquarianism, he wrote *England's Epinomis, Jani Anglorum* (1610), and *Analecton Anglo-Britannicon* (1615).

selection. In Darwinism the mechanism of natural selection is considered of major importance in process of evolution. According to Darwin, because of various environmental factors (e.g., quantity of available food and water and conditions of temperature and pressure) and overproduction in animals and plants, a struggle for existence arises and only those best adapted to environment survive (survival of the fittest) and reproduce. In plant and animal breeding man practices artificial selection, choosing individuals best suited for his purpose.

selective service, in U.S. history. Although national military conscription was begun in 1863 in Civil War, Congress authorized release from service to anyone who furnished a satisfactory substitute and, at first, to those who paid $300. General conscription took place in World War I. First peacetime conscription in U.S. was undertaken in 1940. Following U.S. entry into World War II a new selective service act was passed. Selective service act of 1948 required all men from 18 through 25 to register, made men from 19 to 25 liable for induction for 21-month service; in 1951 the draft age was lowered to 18½, service period was raised to 24 months active service, 8 years in reserve.

Selene (sŭlē'nē) [Gr.,= moon], in Greek religion, moon-goddess; identified with Artemis.

Selenga (sĕlĕng-gä'), river, c.750 mi. long, rising in Mongolian People's Republic and flowing through Buryat Mongol ASSR to L. Baikal. Orkhon is main tributary.

selenium (sŭlē'nēŭm), rare, nonmetallic element (symbol = Se; see also ELEMENT, table). It is allotropic, appearing in red powdery, red crystalline, and gray metallike forms; its conductivity increases with illumination, hence it has been used in some photoelectric tubes (see *ill.*, p. 377). It is used in rubber, red glass, enamels. Resembles sulphur in activity; rarely occurs uncombined in nature. In parts of U.S., livestock suffer from selenium poisoning caused by eating vegetation that has absorbed selenium from soil.

Seleucia (sŭlū'shŭ), anc. city of Mesopotamia on the Tigris below Baghdad. Founded by Seleucus I c.312 B.C., it replaced Babylon as chief city of region. Later the Parthians built Ctesiphon across the river. Seleucia was destroyed by Romans in A.D. 164.

Seleucus (sŭlū'kŭs), kings of anc. Syria of the Seleucid dynasty. **Seleucus I** (Nicator), d. 280 B.C., was a general of Alexander the Great and a leading figure in the wars of the DIADOCHI. He got Babylonia in the breakup of the empire and expanded his power E to the Indus. He joined the league against ANTIGONUS I and benefited from the battle of Ipsus (301 B.C.). Later gained more by defeating LYSIMACHUS (281 B.C.). **Seleucus II** (Callinicus), d. 226 B.C., was the son of ANTIOCHUS II. On his father's death he seized the throne, killing his stepmother, Berenice, and his infant half-brother before Berenice's brother, PTOLEMY III, could arrive with an army. A long war followed, as did civil wars, with loss of power. ANTIOCHUS III was his son.

Seligman, Edwin Robert Anderson (sĕ'lĭgmŭn), 1861–1939, American economist, professor at Columbia Univ. 1885–1931. Edited *Encyclopaedia of the Social Sciences* and advanced the economic interpretation of history.

Selim (sē'lĭm, sŭlēm'), Ottoman sultans. **Selim I** (the Grim), 1467–1520, became sultan 1512 by deposing his father, Bajazet II, and killing his brothers. During his reign Turkey entered the height of its power. He defeated Shah Ismail of Persia (1514) and annexed Kurdistan. After his victory over the Mamelukes of Syria and Egypt (1516–17) he assumed the CALIPHATE for himself and his successors and took control over the holy cities, Mecca and Medina. A bloodthirsty despot, he ordered the massacre of 40,000 Shiites. His son Suleiman I succeeded him. **Selim II** (the Drunkard), c.1524–1574, son of Suleiman I, reigned 1566–74. Conquered Cyprus; recovered Morocco. His fleet was defeated at LEPANTO (1571). **Selim III,** 1761–1808, reigned 1789–1807. Concluded war with Russia by accepting humiliating Treaty of Jassy (1792), then set about to reform his empire with efficient zeal. He joined the anti-French coalition of 1798. His troops yielded Jaffa to Bonaparte but forced the French to retreat from Acre (1799). War with Russia broke out again in 1806, and in 1807 Selim was deposed by the rebellious Janizaries. He was strangled in prison.

Seljuks: see TURKS.

Selkirk, Alexander, 1676–1721, Scottish sailor, whose adventures suggested story of *Robinson Crusoe* (1719) to Daniel Defoe. Put ashore on one of the Juan Fernández Isls., he remained for over four years before rescue.

Selkirk, Thomas Douglas, 5th **earl of,** 1771–1820, Scottish philanthropist, founder of RED RIVER SETTLEMENT. To aid his impoverished countrymen he promoted a successful settlement on P.E.I., Canada (1803).

Selkirk, county, Scotland: see SELKIRKSHIRE.

Selkirk, town (pop. 6,218), SE Man., Canada, on Red R., NE of Winnipeg and S of L. Winnipeg. Center of RED RIVER SETTLE-

MENT, estab. 1812 by earl of Selkirk. Transships L. Winnipeg fish.

Selkirk Mountains, range of Rocky Mts., SE B.C., Canada, near Alta. border; extends NW 200 mi. from Idaho and Mont. borders.

Selkirkshire (sĕl'kûrkshĭr) or **Selkirk,** inland county (267 sq. mi.; pop. 21,724), S Scotland; co. town Selkirk. Region of rolling hills, sheep raising is the chief occupation. Associated with Sir Walter Scott and James Hogg. Saw much border warfare between England and Scotland.

Selma. 1 City (pop. 22,840), SW central Ala., on Alabama R. and W of Montgomery; settled 1816. Rail center in livestock and cotton area; processes foodstuffs, cotton, cottonseed oil, iron, lumber. Ravaged as Confederate supply base (1865). U.S. military aviation school (1941) is near. **2** City (pop. 5,964), central Calif., SE of Fresno in San Joaquin Valley. Area produces fruit, truck, and dairy products.

seltzer water, alkaline water, rich in salts, very popular in 19th cent. as beverage and medicine.

Selwyn College: see CAMBRIDGE UNIVERSITY.

Semarang (sůmä'räng), city (pop. 217,796), on N Java, Indonesia; port on Java Sea. Exports tobacco, sugar, copra, rubber, kapok, and coffee. Textile mills.

Sembrich, Marcella (sĕm'brĭk), 1858–1935, stage name of Praxede Marcelline Kochanska, Polish coloratura soprano. She appeared regularly at the Metropolitan Opera, New York, 1898–1909, and was outstanding as Violetta in *La Traviata.*

Semele (sĕ'mĭlē), in Greek religion; mother of Dionysus by Zeus. She asked Zeus to appear in his majesty, but when he did she died of terror. Dionysus later found her in Hades and took her to Olympus.

Seminole (sĕ'mĭnōl), city (pop. 11,863), central Okla., SE of Oklahoma City; settled 1890. Trade center for farm and oil region with refineries and carbon-black plant.

Seminole Indians, North American tribe of Natchez-Muskogean linguistic stock, originating when a group of Creek Indians separated from the main body in the early 18th cent. and settled in Fla. They absorbed remnants of the Apalachee and many runaway Negro slaves. They were hostile to the U.S., and in 1817–18 Andrew Jackson led a force into Spanish territory to punish them. By a treaty of 1832 they were bound to move W of the Mississippi, but many, led by Osceola, refused. The Seminole War began in 1835 and lasted until 1842, when the heroic resistance of the Seminole was beaten down. The American troops were led for a time by Richard Keith Call. Some remained in the Everglades, but most moved to Okla.

Semipalatinsk (syĭmē"pŭlä'tyĭnsk), city (pop. 109,779), E Kazakh SSR, on Irtysh R. and Turksib RR. Founded 1718 as Russian frontier post.

Semi-Pelagianism: see PELAGIANISM.

Semiramis (sĕmĭ'rŭmĭs), in Assyrian mythology, queen of Assyria. Wife of King Ninus, she reigned 42 years after his death, and is said to have conquered Persia, Libya, and Ethiopia and to have founded Babylon and Nineveh. She was worshipped as a dove after her death. Sammuramat, who was regent of Assyria from 810 to 805 B.C., was probably historical figure behind this legend.

Semite, originally one believed to be descendant of Shem, son of Noah. Today term includes Arabs; Akkadians of ancient Babylon; Assyrians; Canaanites (Amorites, Moabites, Edomites, Ammonites, and Phoenicians); Aramaean tribes (including Hebrews); and large part of Ethiopians. These peoples are grouped as Semites chiefly because their languages were derived from common tongue, Semitic (see LANGUAGE, table). Original home probably was Arabia, whence they spread to Mesopotamia (see SUMER), E Mediterranean area (see PHOENICIAN CIVILIZATION), and Nile delta. These last formed basis of new nation and religion (see JEWS and JUDAISM).

Semitic languages (sůmĭ'tĭk), great linguistic family. See LANGUAGE (table).

Semmelweis, Ignaz Philipp (ĭg'näts fē'lĭp zĕ'mŭlvīs), 1818–65, Hungarian physician. A pioneer in use of antiseptic methods in obstetrics, he greatly reduced deaths from puerperal fever, which he recognized as infectious.

Semmering (zĕ'mŭrĭng), resort region, E Austria, on border of Styria and Lower Austria. The Alps here are crossed by the **Semmering Pass,** 3,215 ft. high. Beneath the pass runs the world's oldest mountain railroad (built 1848–54).

Semmes, Raphael (sĕmz), 1809–77, American naval officer. In Civil War he served with Confederate navy, first on *Sumter,* then on *Alabama,* whose two-year cruise made him naval hero of Confederacy.

Sempach (zĕm'päkh), town (pop. 1,229), Lucerne canton, central Switzerland. Here the Swiss won a decisive victory over Austria in 1386, which legend credits to the self-sacrifice of Arnold von WINKELRIED.

Semper, Gottfried (gôt'frēt zĕm'pŭr), 1803–79, German architect, an exponent of Italian Renaissance style.

Semple, Ellen Churchill, 1863–1932, American geographer. Helped develop study of anthropogeography.

Senancour, Étienne de (ātyĕn' dů sůnãko͞or'), 1770–1846, French author. Best known for his autobiographical epistolary novel *Obermann* (1804; Eng. tr., 1903), remarkable for its morbid melancholy.

Senate, United States: see CONGRESS OF THE UNITED STATES.

senate, Roman, governing council of the Roman republic. An outgrowth of the royal privy council, it gained immense power as Rome expanded in the 2d and 3d cent. B.C., sending out armies, making treaties, organizing the new domain. Membership in the senate was limited to ex-magistrates almost entirely from old families. Its tone tended to be reactionary. Yet there was no real challenge to its authority until the agitation of the Gracchi. This failed, but a popular party grew up to oppose the conservatives. MARIUS headed this but the popular party was thoroughly defeated by SULLA. The struggle was, however, resumed later with Julius CAESAR heading the popular group and POMPEY heading the senatorial party. Caesar triumphed (48 B.C.) and though he was assassinated the senate did not regain power. It was docile under AUGUSTUS and became a mere cipher in the later empire.

Sendai (sändī'), city (pop. 293,816), N Honshu, Japan. Mfg. of silk textiles, lacquer ware, and sake. Seat of Tohoku Imperial Univ.

Sender, Ramón José (rämōn' hōsā' sänděr'), 1902–, Spanish novelist. An active revolutionist, he has written works on social problems (e.g., *Seven Red Sundays,* 1932).

Seneca (Lucius Annaeus Seneca) (sě'nůků), c.3 B.C.–A.D. 65, Roman philosopher, dramatist, and statesman. Exiled by Claudius (A.D. 41), he was recalled to tutor Nero and became virtual ruler. Later in disfavor, he opened his veins; his death scene was considered remarkably noble by the Romans. He wrote Stoic essays on ethics and philosophy, but his nine tragedies (notably *Medea, Phaedra, Agamemnon, Oedipus,* and *Thyestes*), contrived but high-toned, were most influential in the Renaissance and in later European literature.

Seneca (sě'nůků), village (pop. c.1,500), N Ill., on Illinois R. and E of La Salle. Was World War II shipbuilding center with c.11,000 pop.

Seneca, river flowing ENE from Seneca L., W central N.Y., to Cayuga L. (this part in Barge Canal system), thence NE to join Oneida R. in forming Oswego R.

Seneca Falls, village (pop. 6,634), W central N.Y., on Seneca R. and E of Geneva. Machinery and metal goods. First woman's-rights convention in U.S., organized partly by Elizabeth Cady Stanton (who lived here), held here, 1848.

Seneca Indians: see IROQUOIS CONFEDERACY.

Seneca Lake, N.Y.: see FINGER LAKES.

Senefelder, Aloys (zā'nůfěl"důr), 1771–1834, inventor of lithography (1796), b. Prague. Worked in Munich.

Seneff or **Seneffe** (sůněf'), town (pop. 3,270), Hainaut, Belgium, NW of Charleroi. Here the French under Louis II de Condé defeated the Dutch (1674).

Senegal (sě'nĭgôl), overseas territory (c.75,750 sq. mi.; pop. c.1,895,000), French West Africa, on the Atlantic; cap. Saint-Louis, chief city Dakar. Bordered on N by Senegal R. (c.1,000 mi. long). British colony of Gambia forms narrow enclave along Gambia R. Generally a flat region. Peanuts are chief crop and export. First explored by Portuguese in 15th cent. French occupation began 1854, and in 1895 Senegal became part of French West Africa.

senega snakeroot (sěn'ĭgů), perennial wildflower (*Polygala senega*) with white blooms. Its roots, once used by Indians for snake bite, are source of drug senega.

Senigallia (sānēgäl'lyä), town (pop. 11,394), Marches, central Italy; a bathing resort on Adriatic. In 1502 Cesare Borgia had a number of his enemies treacherously slain in its castle.

Senlis (sälēs'), city (pop. 6,049), Oise dept., N France, NE of Paris. A royal residence from 6th cent. Church of Notre Dame is one of earliest Gothic structures (12th cent.). Here in 1493 Charles VIII signed treaty yielding Franche-Comté, Artois, and Charolais to Emperor Maximilian I.

senna, leguminous herb, shrub, or tree of genus *Cassia,* most common in warm regions. Dried leaves of Alexandria senna (*Cassia acutifolia*) and Indian senna (*C. angustifolia*) are used medicinally.

Sennacherib (sěnă'kůrĭb), d. 681 B.C., king of Assyria (705–681 B.C.). The son of Sargon, he spent his reign trying to maintain the empire. Defeated the Egyptians (701) and prepared to take Jerusalem, but instead exacted only tribute. It is uncertain whether the destruction of his army took place at this time or later (Byron's "Destruction of Sennacherib" is based on 2 Chron. 32). He fought successfully in Babylonia and destroyed Babylon (c.689 B.C.). Built a magnificent palace at Nineveh. He was murdered, possibly by his sons. Esar-Haddon succeeded.

Sennett, Mack (sě'nĭt), 1884–, American film director and producer, whose real name was Michael Sinnott. His films (e.g., *Tillie's Punctured Romance*) were slapstick comedies with chases, custard pie wars, and Keystone cops. Starred Charles Chaplin, "Fatty" Arbuckle, and others.

Sens (säs), city (pop. 15,936), Yonne dept., N France. An archiepiscopal see, it has a famous 12th-cent. cathedral, one of the oldest Gothic monuments (slightly damaged in World War II). Sens was the scene of several ecclesiastic councils and of a massacre of Huguenots (1562) which rekindled the Wars of Religion.

sensitive plant: see MIMOSA.

Senta (sěn'tä), Hung. *Zenta,* city (pop. 24,916), N Serbia, Yugoslavia. Here in 1697 Prince Eugene of Savoy won a decisive victory over the Turks.

sentence, in law, punishment inflicted by court order on a person convicted of crime. A sentence may consist of a fine or imprisonment (or both) or execution. The sentence imposed is often fixed by statute. If a person is convicted of more than one crime at his trial, sentences may run concurrently or consecutively. In some cases a sentence may be indeterminate, with a maximum and minimum term for imprisonment; if his behavior in prison is good, the convict may be freed on probation at any time after the end of his minimum term.

Sentinel Ridge, SW Wis., near Prairie du Chien, in Wyalusing State Park. Indian mounds.

Seoul (sā'o͞ol', sōl), Jap. *Keijo,* city (1949 pop. 1,446,019), cap. of South Korean Republic. Was cap. of Korea from 1393 until the partition of the country after World War II. Here is Univ. of Seoul. Severely damaged 1950–51 in Korean War.

sepal: see CALYX.

separation, in law, either the voluntary agreement of a husband and wife to live apart or a partial dissolution of a marriage bond by court order. Unlike divorce, separation leaves the marriage bond intact and prohibits remarriage. Separation by court decree is called a divorce *a mensa et thora* [from bed and board]. Separation is more usual in states where divorce is hard to obtain.

separatists, in religion, groups that withdrew from Established Church in England. A 16th-cent. group were called Brownists after their leader, Robert Browne. Name Independents used in 17th cent. See CONGREGATIONALISM; PURITANISM.

separator, cream, dairy machine used to separate fresh milk into cream and skim milk. Design of the machine varies, but principle is that of centrifuge. The cream separator controls the amount of fat in the milk and lessens injury by bacterial action.

Sephardim, Jews descended from the Jews of Spain and Portugal. Some of their practices, notably pronunciation of Hebrew, differ from those of other Jews; Sephardic Hebrew is now the language of Israel.

Sepik (sä'pēk), river of NE New Guinea, 700 mi. long, emptying into Bismarck Sea.

Sepoy Rebellion (sē'poi), 1857–58, rebellion of native soldiers (sepoys) in Bengal army of East India Co. Many Indian princes, fearing confiscation of land by Gen. DALHOUSIE, may have encouraged unrest. The Bengalese soldiers (all Brahmins) resented the annexation in 1856 of Oudh, their homeland, and were further angered by issuing of cartridges coated with what they believed to be beef grease, the handling of which violated Hindu law. Revolt began at Berhampore, Feb., 1857, and soon raged over N central India. Lucknow was besieged, and Cawnpore and Delhi were captured, with Nana Sahib massacring the entire British colony at Cawnpore. British reconquest was completed March, 1858. Rebellion led to many reforms, principally the transfer of rule from British East India Co. to the crown. Also called Indian Mutiny.

Seppänen, Unto Kalervo (o͞on'tō kä'lĕrvō sĕp'pănĕn), 1904–, Finnish writer of novels (e.g., *Sun and Storm,* 1931–34) and stories about Karelia.

September: see MONTH.

septicemia (sĕptĭsē'mēů), serious form of blood poisoning in which blood stream is infected by both toxins and bacteria which multiply in the blood. It is commonly caused by streptococci and staphylococci. Blood poisoning in which only the toxins are absorbed into the blood is known as toxemia.

septic tank, sedimentation tank for sewage discharge, where it remains for periods of 8–24 hr. While oxygen is present, aerobic bacteria attack organic matter in sewage; when oxygen is exhausted, anaerobic bacteria attack it, causing it to disintegrate, liquefy, and give off gases.

Septimius Severus, Roman emperor: see SEVERUS.

Septuagint (sĕp'tūůjĭnt) [Latin,= 70], translation of Old Testament into Greek, made between 250 B.C. and c.100 B.C. Supposedly done in 72 days by 72 translators, hence its name. It includes the Apocrypha and some pseudepigrapha. This version used by Greek-speaking Christians such as St. Paul and is still used in the Greek church. Its symbol: LXX.

Séquard, Charles Édouard Brown-: see BROWN-SÉQUARD.

sequoia (sĭkwoi'ů), name for two huge, coniferous, evergreen trees of genus *Sequoia.* Once widespread in temperate regions of the N Hemisphere, only two species survive in a narrow strip near the Pacific coast of the U.S. The redwood (*Sequoia sempervirens*), growing from 100 to 340 ft. high, is the world's tallest tree. The big tree or giant sequoia (*S. gigantea* or *Sequoiadendron gigantea*) grows from 150 to 325 ft.; some specimens are believed to be 3,000 to 4,000 years old. Wood of both species is valued for outdoor building uses. China's "dawn redwood" (*Metasequoia*) is related.

Sequoia National Park: see NATIONAL PARKS AND MONUMENTS (table).

Sequoyah (sĭkwoi'ů), c.1770–1843, North American Indian leader, creator of the Cherokee syllabary. His "white" name was George Guess.

seraph (sĕ'rŭf), plural **seraphim,** kind of ANGEL; with cherubim, attendant upon God. According to Bible, seraphim have six wings. Isa. 6.2–6.

Serbia (sûr'bēů), Serbo-Croatian *Srbija,* constituent republic (34,194 sq. mi.; pop. 6,523-224) of Yugoslavia, of which it occupies the E part; cap. Belgrade. Its NE section (incl. VOJVODINA prov.), acquired from Hungary in 1920, is part of the fertile Danubian plain; the rest is largely mountainous. Most of the population is agricultural. The Serbs are distinguished from the closely related Croats and Slovenes through their historic affiliation with the Eastern Orthodox Church, which also gave them the Cyrillic alphabet. They settled in the Balkan Peninsula in the 6th and 7th cent., under Byzantine overlordship; accepted Christianity 9th cent.; and formed an independent kingdom in 1217. Under STEPHEN DUSHAN medieval Serbia reached its greatest expansion (14th cent.), but it quickly declined. Its defeat at Kossovo (1389) made it tributary to Turkey, which in 1459 annexed it outright. Belgrade, then held by Hungary, fell to the Turks in 1521. Turkish rule was particularly oppressive in Serbia, but the weakening of the Ottoman Empire in the 18th cent. gave Serbia new hopes of independence. The uprising led by MILOSH Obrenovich was successful (1817); in 1828 the Sultan recognized Serbia as a vassal principality. Despite internal feuds (notably that of the OBRENOVICH and KARAGEORGEVICH factions), Serbia, largely with Russian backing, gained increasing independence and leadership of the S Slavs. The last Turkish troops left in 1867. In 1876 Serbia declared war on Turkey (see RUSSO-TURKISH WARS); in 1878 the Congress of Berlin, though disappointing its territorial claims, declared Serbia independent. In 1882 Prince MILAN proclaimed himself king. The opposition of Serbian ambitions to those of its neighbors led to war with Bulgaria over E RUMELIA in 1885 (which Bulgaria won), to the BALKAN WARS of 1912–13 (in which Serbia won), and, after the assassination of Archduke Francis Ferdinand by a Serb, to WORLD WAR I (1914). Though at first successful, Serbia was overrun by the Central Powers in 1915. Its troops and government were evacuated to Corfu, where in 1917 a S Slavic congress declared the union of Serbia, Croatia, Slovenia, and Montenegro under King PETER I of Serbia. The history of the new kingdom, which formally came into existence in 1918, is that of YUGOSLAVIA, as it was later called. In World War II a much-reduced Serbia was set up by the Axis powers in 1941 under a puppet government, but the Serbs continued guerrilla warfare. The Yugoslav constitution of 1945 made Serbia one of the federated republics of Yugoslavia and stripped it of Macedonia, Montenegro, and Bosnia and Hercegovina.

Serbo-Croat (-krō'ăt), language of S group of Slavic subfamily of Indo-European languages. See LANGUAGE (table).

serf. Serfdom was state of half freedom characteristic of peasant labor under FEUDALISM and MANORIAL SYSTEM. Distinguished from slavery by body of rights serf had and by strict group arrangement of serfdom. True serf was subject to labor service at will of his lord, but such matters came to be governed by custom and worked in set pattern. Although serfdom existed from earliest history, it developed in Middle Ages in France, Spain, and Italy, spread to Germany and in 15th cent. to Slavic lands. Developed separately in England after Norman Conquest, when most free villeins were depressed to serfdom, and disappeared before end of Middle Ages. In Hapsburg monarchy it was ended (1781) by Emperor Joseph II. In France it was swept away by French Revolution. It persisted in Russia until all serfs were freed in 1861 by Alexander II. Serfdom appeared and disappeared with feudalism in Japan, China, India, pre-Columbian Mexico, and elsewhere.

sergeanty: see SERJEANTY.

Sergiev or **Sergievski Posad,** RSFSR: see ZAGORSK.

series, in mathematics, a sum of several terms. An infinite series is a sum of infinitely many terms, the first several of which establish the pattern of formation for subsequent terms. Some infinite series converge toward a value called limit; i.e., the adding together of terms results in sums (called partial sums) that form a sequence of values approaching closer and closer the value called the limit. The series ½ + ¼ + ⅛ + 1/16 . . . converges to value 1 because partial sums form sequence ½, ¾, ⅞, 15/16, ... Series such as ½ + ⅓ + ¼ . . . do not converge.

Seringapatam (sŭrĭng"gŭpŭtăm'), town (pop. 7,678), S Mysore, India, on island in Cauvery R. Was cap. of Mysore, 17th–18th cent. Tippoo Sahib was killed here in British siege of 1799.

serjeanty or **sergeanty** (both: sär'jĕntē), type of TENURE in British FEUDALISM in which tenant held lands from king or overlord in return for service.

serpent, name applied to any crawling creature, chiefly to snake. Legends of sea serpents are unsubstantiated. In religion and art, serpent symbolizes Satan.

serpentine (sûr'pŭntēn, -tīn), a mineral, hydrous silicate of magnesium, usually some shade of green. Commercial asbestos is a fibrous variety. Massive varieties are used for interior decoration.

Serpent Mound State Park, S Ohio, NW of Portsmouth. Has prehistoric Indian mounds. Largest (c.1,330 ft. long) represents serpent swallowing egg.

Serra, Junípero (hōōnē'pārō sĕ'rä), 1713–84, Spanish Franciscan missionary in North America. Directed founding of many missions in Calif.

Sert, José María (hōsā' märē'ä sĕrt'), 1876–1945, Spanish painter, best known for his murals.

Sertorius, Quintus (sŭrtô'rēŭs), d. 72 B.C., Roman general, who became leader of the Lusitanians. He had been a supporter of Marius and fled to Africa to escape death at the hands of Sulla's party. Called to Spain by rebels in 80 B.C., he held off Roman armies sent against him until assassinated by one of his own men.

serum (sēr'ŭm), straw-colored fluid blood component which separates from corpuscles when clotting occurs. Immunity to certain communicable diseases is obtained for varying periods by introduction of serum containing specific antibodies. Human serum is sometimes used to counteract shock or loss of fluid.

Servetus, Michael (sŭrvē'tŭs), Span. *Miguel Serveto,* 1511–53, Spanish theologian and physician. He early came into contact with reformers in Germany and Switzerland, but his views on the Trinity were condemned by Catholics as well as Protestants. Fled to Lyons, where he edited Ptolemy's geography, and to Paris, where he studied medicine. He gained fame in medicine and was (1541–53) physician to the archbishop of Vienne. After he had a work on theology secretly printed (1553), the Inquisition moved against him. He escaped from prison and made for Italy but was seized on Calvin's order, tried, and burned at the stake. His doctrines are said to have anticipated Unitarianism.

Service, Robert W(illiam), 1876–, Canadian poet and novelist, b. England. He achieved considerable popularity with his works about the Yukon.

serviceberry: see SHADBUSH.

Servile Wars, in Roman history, three uprisings of slaves (134?–132? B.C., 104?–101? B.C., 73–71 B.C.). The first two took place in Sicily. The third was the famous uprising led by SPARTACUS in S Italy, eventually put down with great cruelty by Crassus and Pompey.

sesame (sĕs'ŭmē), herb (*Sesamum indicum* or *S. orientale*) native to the tropics. It has long been grown for the seeds which are added to pastries; seeds yield the valuable benne oil, used in cooking and medicine, especially in India.

Sesostris (sĭsŏ'strĭs), kings of anc. Egypt of the XII dynasty. **Sesostris I,** d. 1935 B.C., was the son of Amenemhet I and coregent with him after 1980; sole ruler 1970–1938; coruler with his son Amenemhet II 1938–1935. He campaigned in the present Sudan. **Sesostris II,** d. 1887 B.C., was the son of Amenemhet II and coregent with him 1906–1903; sole ruler 1903–1887. His son **Sesostris III,** d. 1849 B.C., reigned 1887–1849. He put down the nobles, led an expedition to Syria, and set the S boundary of Egypt near present Wadi Halfa.

Sesshu (sĕs'shōō"), 1420–1506, Japanese painter and Buddhist priest, an outstanding figure in Japanese art. Famous for his murals and screen decorations. Visited China.

Sessions, Roger, 1896–, American composer and teacher. His works include incidental music (1923) for Andreyev's *Black Maskers;*

choral preludes for organ; two symphonies (1926, 1946); a violin concerto (1931–35); a choral work, *Turn O Libertad* (1948); piano pieces; and a string quartet (1936).

Sestos (sĕ'stŏs), anc. town on the Thracian shore of the Hellespont, opposite Abydos. Xerxes crossed the Hellespont here on a bridge of boats. Scene of story of Hero and Leander.

Sète, formerly **Cette** (both: sĕt), town (pop. 29,914), Hérault dept., S France; a Mediterranean port.

Setesdal (sā'tůsdäl), narrow valley, S Norway, drained by Otra R. There are several lakes. Noted for its ancient dress, speech, customs, and handicrafts, which are still cultivated.

Seth, son of Adam and Eve, father of Enos. Gen. 4.25,26; 5.3. Sheth: 1 Chron. 1.1.

Seti (sē'tī, sā'tē), kings of anc. Egypt of XIX dynasty. **Seti I,** d. 1292 B.C., succeeded his father Ramses I (c.1313 B.C.). Invaded Palestine and Syria; defeated the Libyans. Built temples and also a magnificent tomb at Abydos. Succeeded by Ramses II. **Seti II,** d. 1205 B.C., was the last king of the dynasty. Succeeded by Ramses III.

Seton, Elizabeth Ann (Bayley) (sē'tůn), 1774–1821, American Roman Catholic leader, called Mother Seton. She was the widow of a merchant William Seton before she was converted to Catholicism (1805). In 1808 she opened a school in Baltimore, later moved to Emmitsburg, Md., where she opened the first Catholic free school. She also founded St. Joseph's College for women and formed a community that adopted the rule of the Daughters of Charity (more commonly called Sisters of Charity). Her contribution to Catholic education in the U.S. was enormous.

Seton, Ernest Thompson, 1860–1946, American writer and artist, originally named Ernest Seton Thompson. Interpreted nature for boys and girls (as in *Wild Animals I Have Known,* 1898). Founded Woodcraft Indians, precursor of Boy Scouts.

Seton Hall University: see South Orange, N.J.

Seton Hill College: see Greensburg, Pa.

setter: see hunting dogs.

Settignano, Desiderio da: see Desiderio da Settignano.

Settlement, Act of, 1701, passed by English Parliament to provide that if William III and Princess (later Queen) Anne died without heirs, the succession should pass to members of house of Hanover, if Protestants. From 1714 (George I) house of Hanover owes claim to this act. Prompted partly by fear of Jacobites, further provisions, similar to those in Bill of Rights, limited king's power.

settlement house: see social settlement.

Setúbal (sůtōō'bäl), city (pop. 37,071), W Portugal, in Estremadura; a port on the Atlantic. Exports wine, fruit, cork. Fishing base.

Seurat, Georges (zhôrzh' sûrä'), 1859–91, French postimpressionist painter. Developed a technique of painting in dots of pure color, called pointillism, a refinement on the broken color of the impressionists. His masterpiece, *Un Dimanche à la Grande Jatte,* is at Art Inst., Chicago.

Sevan (syĭvän'), mountain lake, area 546 sq. mi., central Armenian SSR. Fed by c.30 streams, but Zanga R. is only outlet. Sevan-Zanga hydroelectric project (begun 1930) has drained part of the lake. Formerly called Gokcha, its Turkish name.

Sevastopol (sĭvă'stůpōl"), city (pop. 111,946), RSFSR, in S Crimea; a major naval base and strategic stronghold on an inlet of Black Sea. Founded by Catherine II. In Crimean War, city heroically resisted besieging British, French, and Turks for 11 months. It was Wrangel's hq. during last stand of the "Whites" (1920) in Russian civil war. In World War II city was besieged for eight months by the Germans. Virtually destroyed, it fell July 3, 1942; recaptured May, 1944.

Seven against Thebes, in Greek legend, seven heroes—Polynices, Adrastus, Amphiaraüs, Hippomedon, Capaneus, Tydeus, and Parthenopaeus—who made war on Eteocles, who was king of Thebes, son of Oedipus, and brother of Polynices. Brothers killed each other, and only Adrastus survived. Ten years later the Epigoni avenged their fathers, the Seven against Thebes.

Seven Churches in Asia, in Bible, churches addressed in Revelation 1–3. They are Ephesus, Smyrna, Pergamos, Thyatira, Sardis, Philadelphia, and Laodicea.

Seven Days battles, in Civil War, week of heavy fighting near Richmond, Va. (June 26–July 2, 1862. After battle of Fair Oaks in Peninsular campaign, R. E. Lee moved to cut McClellan off from base at White House Landing. A. P. Hill attacked Union advance lines at Mechanicsville on June 26, was repulsed. Federals fell back to Gaines's Mill, where on June 27 a strong Confederate force was victor. As McClellan moved main force toward James R., Lee pursued and engaged him at Savage's Station on June 29 and at Frayser's Farm or Glendale on June 30 without stopping him. On July 1, Federals, posted on Malvern Hill, again repulsed attack, then withdrew to James R. Lee had suffered heavy losses, but he had saved Richmond.

Seven Pines: see Peninsular campaign.

Seventh-day Adventists: see Adventists.

Seventh-Day Baptists, sect of Calvinistic Baptists, observing Saturday as Sabbath. First American group (1671) in R.I. In Pa., German group led by J. C. Beissel estab. (1728–33) Ephrata.

Seven Weeks War: see Austro-Prussian War.

Seven Wise Men of Greece. Arbitrary lists of wise men have drawn from among the best intellects of ancient Greece. A usual one is: Bias, Chilon, Cleobulus, Periander, Pittacus, Solon, and Thales.

Seven Wonders of the World, in anc. classifications were Great Pyramid of Khufu or all the pyramids with or without the Sphinx; Hanging Gardens of Babylon, with or without the walls; mausoleum at Halicarnassus; Artemision at Ephesus; Colossus of Rhodes; Olympian *Zeus,* statue by Phidias; and Pharos at Alexandria, or, instead, walls of Babylon.

Seven Years War, 1756–63, world-wide conflict fought in Europe, N America, and India between, on the one side, France, Austria,

Russia, Saxony, Sweden, and (after 1762) Spain and, on the other side, Prussia, England, and Hanover. Two main issues were involved—(1) French-English colonial rivalry in America (see FRENCH AND INDIAN WARS) and in India (see CLIVE and DUPLEIX); (2) the struggle for supremacy in Germany between MARIA THERESA of Austria and FREDERICK II of Prussia. The years following the War of the AUSTRIAN SUCCESSION (ended 1748) were employed in maneuvering for alliances preparatory to a new test of strength. Hostilities were opened by Prussia invading Saxony (1756) and Bohemia (1757). Routed at Kolin, Frederick had to evacuate Bohemia but defeated the Austrians at Rossbach and Leuthen (late 1757) and the Russians at Zorndorf (1758). Nevertheless, his situation became nearly hopeless after his defeats at Kunersdorf and Maxen (1759). In 1760 the Russians briefly occupied Berlin. Frederick expelled them and defeated the Austrians at Torgau, but his final victory became assured only after the accession of Peter III of Russia, who made a separate peace with him (1762). Meanwhile England, after an inauspicious start, pushed the war vigorously under the leadership of William Pitt (1st earl of Chatham) and won victories at Krefeld, Minden, and Quiberon Bay in Europe; Louisburg and Quebec in America; and Plassey in India (1757–59). After protracted negotiations, peace was made at HUBERTUSBURG and at Paris (see PARIS, TREATY OF, 1763). The war confirmed Prussia's new rank as leading power and made England the world's chief colonial power, at the expense of France.

Severn, Joseph (sĕ'vůrn), 1793–1879, English portrait painter. Best known as a devoted friend to Keats. Was consul at Rome, 1861–72.

Severn. 1 River rising in W Ont., Canada, and flowing 420 mi. NE to Hudson Bay. At mouth is Fort Severn, Hudson's Bay Co. trading post, estab. 1689. **2** River, S Ont., Canada, issuing from N end of L. Couchiching and flowing 20 mi. WNW to Georgian Bay. Forms part of inland waterway linking Georgian Bay with L. Ontario via Trent Canal.

Severn, one of principal rivers of England. Flows c.200 mi. from Plinlimmon, Wales, through great estuary, to Bristol Channel. Following a winding course, it borders or passes through Montgomery, Shropshire, Worcester, and Gloucester counties. Connected by canal with the Thames, Mersey, Trent, and other streams, it is an important transportation route.

Severnaya Zemlya (syĕ'vĭrnĭŭ zĭmlyä') [Rus.,= northern land], archipelago, area 14,300 sq. mi., in Arctic Ocean, in Krasnoyarsk Territory, RSFSR, separating Kara and Laptev seas. Discovered 1913.

Severovostochny: Russian name of Cape CHELYUSKIN.

Severus or **Septimius Severus** (sĕptĭ'mēůs sēvē'růs), 146–211, Roman emperor (193–211), b. Africa. He took the imperial throne by force, put down opponents, and reduced the empire to peace in Mesopotamia, Gaul, and Britain. He died at York. Did much to beautify Rome. Left the empire to his sons, but Caracalla took power.

Severus (Flavius Valerius Severus), d. 307, Roman emporor (306–7). In the struggle for power after the abdication of Diocletian and Maximian, he was proclaimed emperor by Galerius, but was captured at Ravenna by Maximian and was treacherously killed.

Sevier, John (sůvēr'), 1745–1815, American frontiersman, governor of the State of Franklin (1784–88) and of Tenn. (1796–1801, 1803–9).

Sevier (sůvēr'), river formed in SW Utah and flowing N through mountain canyons, then SW through desert to Sevier L.; 325 mi. long. Used for irrigation.

Sevierville (sůvēr'vĭl), town (pop. 1,620), E Tenn., ESE of Knoxville. Near by are Great Smoky Mts. Natl. Park and Douglas Dam.

Sévigné, Marie de Rabutin-Chantal, marquise de (märē' dů räbütē'-shätäl' märkēz' dů sāvēnyā'), 1626–96, French noblewoman. Her correspondence (some 1,500 letters, mostly to her daughter, the comtesse de Grignan) are masterpieces of French prose. Their unaffected vivacity, whether she discusses personal, social, political, or literary news, makes them the most living account of the age of Louis XIV. Several English translations.

Seville (sůvĭl', sĕ'vĭl), Span. *Sevilla,* city (pop. 270,126), cap. of Seville prov. and chief city of Andalusia, SW Spain. Connected with the Atlantic by Guadalquivir R. and by canal accessible to ocean-going vessels, it is a major port and industrial center, mfg. tobacco, ammunition, perfumes, textiles, and other goods. It is an archiepiscopal see and seat of a university (founded 1502). Important in Phoenician times, it was made cap. of Baetica prov. by the Romans. Continued to flourish under the Moors (from 712), when it was the seat (1023–91) of an independent emirate under the ABBADIDES, and under the Christians (from 1248), when it reached its greatest prosperity through its monopoly (until 1718) on trade with the New World. City was seat of a great school of painting to which Velázquez and Murillo belonged. Its Gothic cathedral (1401–1519), one of world's largest, includes Giralda tower and Court of Oranges (parts of a former mosque) and contains tomb of Columbus. It is adjoined by Moorish alcazar (14th cent.). Colombina library contains manuscripts by Columbus, and there are many notable churches and palaces.

Sèvres (sĕv'rů), town (pop. 15,112), Seine-et-Oise dept., N France; a SW suburb of Paris. Hq. of Internatl. Bureau of Weights and Standards. It is famous for producing **Sèvres ware,** delicate porcelain made by the royal (now national) potteries (estab. c.1740 by Louis XV at Vincennes, moved 1756 to Sèvres). The **Treaty of Sèvres,** 1920, restored peace after World War I between Mohammed VI of Turkey and the Allies (excluding Russia and the U.S.). It liquidated the Ottoman Empire, reducing Turkey to Anatolia in Asia and Constantinople, with environs, in Europe. Armenia was made a separate republic; Smyrna was placed under Greek administration pending a plebiscite;

the Straits zone was internationalized; Allies were given virtual control over Turkish economy. The refusal of Kemal ATATURK to accept the treaty forced the Allies to negotiate another (see LAUSANNE, CONFERENCE OF).

sewage. Modern water-carriage sewerage systems for cities are conduits of iron, concrete, brick, stone, or earthenware through which sewage is discharged from plumbing fixtures to house sewer and thence to street sewer system. Sewage-treating methods include dilution, screening, tank treatment by sedimentation or precipitation, septic-tank treatment, broad irrigation, filtration, disinfection, and combinations of these methods. All rely on oxidation of organic matter and destruction of bacteria by chemicals or by burning.

Sewall, Samuel (sū'ůl), 1652–1730, American jurist, b. England. Repented part played in Salem witchcraft cases of 1692.

Sewanee: see SOUTH, UNIVERSITY OF THE.

Seward, William H(enry), 1801–72, American statesman. U.S. Senator from N.Y. (1849–61), prominent in troubled years before Civil War. As Lincoln's Secretary of State he sought to dominate policy, but President's ingenuity kept him in cabinet. In war period he was able statesman, handling adeptly such delicate matters as TRENT AFFAIR. He held his post under Andrew Johnson and supported Johnson's Reconstruction policy. Notable achievement was his far-sighted purchase of Alaska (1867), unappreciated at time and called "Seward's folly."

Seward, town (pop. 2,114), S Alaska, on E side of Kenai Peninsula, at head of Resurrection Bay. Founded 1902 as ocean terminus by surveyors for Alaska RR. Important supply center for Alaska interior. Major port of entry for U.S. troops and matériel in World War II.

Seward Peninsula, W Alaska, projecting c.200 mi. into Bering Sea, between Norton Sound and Kotzebue Sound, just below Arctic Circle. Mostly perpetually frozen tundra. Placer gold mining and trapping. Nome is on S coast.

Sewell, Anna (sū'ůl), 1820–78, English author. Her *Black Beauty* (1877), the story of a horse, is a children's classic.

Sewickley, residential borough (pop. 5,836), SW Pa., on Ohio R. and NW of Pittsburgh.

sewing machine. Devices for sewing mechanically were made in England (1790), France (1830 and later), and by Walter Hunt of New York city (1832), but the first successful machine was made by Elias HOWE in 1846. A. B. Wilson contributed improvements, as did Isaac M. SINGER, who coordinated previous attempts into the modern machine and began large-scale manufacturing. Both chain- and lock-stitch machines employ an eye-pointed needle; rising and falling rapidly, it pierces the material and casts a loop of thread to the under side of the seam. In the lock-stitch machine (the type of most domestic machines) a second loop of thread, fed from underneath, engages the loop to complete the stitch. In the chain stitch, the loop is held while the needle rises, the cloth is fed forward, and the needle descends again to engage the loop with the beginning of a second loop. Efficiency of household machines has been increased by electrification and an ever-increasing number of attachments. Power-driven specialized machines are used in industry.

sex, term used to refer both to the two groups distinguished as males and females and to anatomical and physiological characteristics associated with maleness and femaleness. Sex is associated with ability to produce special reproductive cells known as gametes (see REPRODUCTION). Among higher animals, i.e., the vertebrate animals, sexes are usually easily distinguishable by certain anatomical differences (e.g., structure of reproductive organs) and by secondary sexual characteristics (e.g., brightness of coloring of males in fish and birds, antlers of male deer, growth of beard and deepening of voice in human male). In higher plants there are male and female reproductive organs (see FLOWER). Sex is less easily distinguishable in simpler forms of plants and animals. Some animals are hermaphroditic, i.e., one individual produces both egg and sperm cells. In both plants and animals that form egg and sperm cells the union of two cells (see FERTILIZATION) results in formation of a fertilized egg or zygote from which new individual develops. Factors that determine sex of an individual vary and are not fully understood. In humans and some other forms sex is believed to be determined by chance, depending upon the nature of the chromosome combinations resulting when egg and sperm unite.

sextant, instrument for finding geographical position by measuring the altitude of the sun or the stars; invented independently by Thomas Godfrey in the U.S. and John Hadley in England in 1731. It made maritime navigation much easier.

Seychelles (sāshĕlz'), British crown colony (156 sq. mi.; pop. 34,632), comprising c.30 volcanic islands in Indian Ocean, c.1,000 mi. E of Zanzibar; cap. Victoria, on Mahé (largest island). Occupied in 18th cent. by the French, who ceded it to the British in 1814. Copra, vanilla, cinnamon, and guano are exported. The inhabitants, of African-European descent, speak a French patois.

Seydlitz, Friedrich Wilhelm, Freiherr von (frē'drĭkh vĭl'hĕlm frī'hĕr fŭn zīd'lĭts), 1721–73, Prussian general. Made cavalry a decisive weapon and took major part in all of Frederick II's chief victories.

Seyhan (sāhän'), anc. *Saurus,* river, 320 mi. long, Turkey. Flows SSW from Anti-Taurus mts. to the E Mediterranean. Also known as Sihun.

Seymour (sē'môr, sē'mûr), English noble family. **Jane Seymour,** 1509?–1537, was the third queen of Henry VIII. Her insistence on marriage was a cause of the trial of Anne Boleyn. She died after the birth of her son, Edward VI. Her brother, **Edward Seymour, duke of Somerset,** 1506?–1552, gained possession of young EDWARD VI on Henry VIII's death and was made protector of England. Wielded almost royal authority in making Protestant reforms. With Thomas Cranmer, he introduced (1549) Book of Common Prayer. He alienated Scots by laying waste SE Scotland. Ousted by duke of NORTHUMBERLAND, he was eventually beheaded. Of firm beliefs and great military ability, he was a practical leader of English Reformation. His brother, **Thomas Seymour, Baron Seymour of Sudeley** (sūd'lē), 1508?–1549, was lord high admiral of England. Tried to supplant his brother as the king's guardian. Secretly married (1547) Catherine Parr, the dowager queen. He was executed for treason.

Seymour, Horatio, 1810–86, American statesman. Governor of N.Y. (1853–55, 1863–65). Opposed Federal conscription. Democratic presidential candidate in 1868.

Seymour, Jane: see SEYMOUR, family.

Seymour. **1** Town (pop. 7,832), including Seymour village (pop. 5,342; metal products), SW Conn., on Naugatuck R. and NW of New Haven; settled c.1680. **2** City (pop. 9,629), SE Ind., S of Columbus. Mfg. of automobile parts, home appliances.

Seymour of Sudeley, Thomas Seymour, Baron: see SEYMOUR, family.

Sforza (sfōr'tsä), Italian family which ruled duchy of Milan 1450–1535. First prominent member was **Muzio Attendolo Sforza** (mōō'-tsēō ät-tĕn'dōlō), 1369–1424, a great CONDOTTIERE. His natural son, **Francesco I Sforza** (fränchā'skō), 1401–66, was one of most powerful condottieri of his time. He married Bianca Maria, daughter of Duke Filippo Maria Visconti of Milan, after whose death he seized power and was proclaimed duke (1450). His eldest son and successor, **Galeazzo Maria Sforza** (gäläät'-tsō märē'ä), 1444–76, a patron of the arts but a dissolute and cruel ruler, was murdered in a republican plot. The anticipated popular uprising did not materialize. His daughter Bianca Maria married Emperor Maximilian I; a natural daughter, **Caterina Sforza,** 1463?–1509, married Gerolamo Riario, lord of Imola and Forlì, after whose murder in 1488 she ruled both cities until she lost them to Cesare Borgia (1499). Her second husband was Giovanni de' Medici; to him she bore the famous condottiere Giovanni delle Bande Nere (see MEDICI). Galeazzo Maria's son **Gian Galeazzo Sforza** (jän'), 1468–94, succeeded him as duke in 1476 under the regency of his mother, Bona of Savoy. He was the father of Bona Sforza, queen of SIGISMUND I of Poland. His rule was usurped after 1480 by his paternal uncle, **Ludovico** or **Lodovico Sforza** (lōōdōvē'kō, lōdōvē'kō), 1451–1508, called Ludovico il Moro (the Moor) because of his swarthy complexion. On Gian Galeazzo's death, Ludovico became duke. His alliance with Charles VIII of France was a factor in starting the ITALIAN WARS (1494). Ludovico turned against his French ally in 1495. In 1499 he lost his duchy to Louis XII of France, who claimed it as a great-grandson of Gian Galeazzo Visconti. He died a prisoner in France. With his wife, Beatrice d'Este, he is chiefly remembered as one of the most lavish princes of the Renaissance and as the patron of LEONARDO DA VINCI and Bramante. His son **Massimiliano Sforza** (mäs"sēmēlyä'nō), 1491–1530, recovered Milan with Swiss help (1512) but had to surrender it to Francis I of France in 1515. He relinquished his title to the duchy to his brother **Francesco II Sforza,** 1495–1535, who entered in possession of Milan in 1522 with the help of Emperor Charles V. He died without issue; Milan, after a long contest between France and Spain, passed to Spain in 1559.

Sforza, Carlo, Conte (kär'lō, kōn'tā), 1872–1952, Italian foreign minister (1920–21; 1947–51). Led liberal opposition against Mussolini in the senate until 1927, when he went into exile. After Mussolini's fall (1943) he returned to Italy and played a major role in the overthrow of the monarchy.

's Gravenhage, Netherlands: see HAGUE, THE.

Shackleton, Sir Ernest Henry, 1874–1922, British antarctic explorer, b. Ireland. Member of Scott expedition (1901–4). Commanded south polar expedition (1907–9); located south magnetic pole; achieved important scientific results. Led perilous transantarctic expedition (1914–17). Died on expedition to study Enderby Land.

shad, N Atlantic fish of herring family. Flesh and roe of American shad are valued as food.

shadbush, Juneberry, or **serviceberry,** tree or shrub of genus *Amelanchier,* chiefly native to North America. The showy white flowers appear in early spring and are followed by edible, berrylike fruits.

shadow, relative darkness caused by interception of light waves by opaque mass. Factors involved are size and intensity of light source, proximity to opaque body, bulk of body, angle and distance of surface on which shadow appears. Complete shadow, where light is wholly interfered with, is called umbra. Penumbra is partial shadow.

Shadrach (shā'drăk), one of THREE HOLY CHILDREN.

Shadwell, Thomas, 1642?–1692, English poet and playwright, poet laureate 1688–92. Attacked Dryden in *The Medal of John Bayes* (1682) and was lampooned in Dryden's *Absalom and Achitophel* and *MacFlecknoe.*

Shafter, William Rufus, 1835–1906, American general. Commanded army invading Cuba in Spanish-American War. Received little credit for victories.

Shafter, Fort, military hq. of Hawaiian Dept., Oahu, T.H., NW of Honolulu. First post occupied (1907) after annexation by U.S.

Shaftesbury, Anthony Ashley Cooper, 1st **earl of,** 1621–83, English statesman. Distrust of autocratic rule caused his support to fluctuate between Stuarts and parliamentarians. Helped restore Charles II, but urged leniency for the Regicides. Was member of the CABAL and opposed 1st earl of Clarendon. Anti-Catholic lord chancellor 1672–73, he supported TEST ACT and was dismissed. Promoted opposition to Danby, and on his fall became president of the council. Arrested (1681) for supporting claim to throne of duke of Monmouth, he fled to Holland 1682. His grandson, **Anthony Ashley Cooper,** 3d **earl of Shaftesbury,** 1671–1713, was a philosopher. Educated by John Locke. Held true morality to be a balance between egoism and altruism. Balance is made possible by a harmony between individual and society;

man has innate instincts ("moral sense") to promote harmony. Most of his essays were collected in *Characteristics of Men, Manners, Opinions, Times* (1711). **Anthony Ashley Cooper, 7th earl of Shaftesbury,** 1801–85, was a social reformer. In Parliament after 1826, he introduced leigslation prohibiting employment of women and children in coal mines (1842), providing care for the insane (1845), and estab. 10-hour day for factory workers. Promoted building of model tenements.

Shah Jehan or **Shah Jahan** (both: shä′ jŭhän′), d. 1666, Mogul emperor (1628–58), who conquered much of S India. Built extensively in Delhi and Agra (noted for TAJ MAHAL). Deposed and imprisoned in 1658 by his son Aurangzeb.

Shaker Heights, residential city (pop. 28,222), NE Ohio, SE suburb of Cleveland; founded 1905.

Shakers, religious group self-styled "The United Society of Believers in Christ's Second Coming." Originated in 18th cent. in England as group called "Shaking Quakers" because of their tremblings during worship. Ann LEE, with eight followers, came (1774) to N.Y., settling (1776) at present Watervliet. Later communities were in N.Y., New England, Ky., Ohio, and Ind. After 1860 Shakerism declined. Shakers believed in strict separation of sexes and practiced communal ownership.

Shakespeare, William: see SHAKSPERE, WILLIAM.

Shakhty (shäkh′tē), city (pop. 155,081), S European RSFSR, NE of Rostov; major anthracite-mining center of Donets Basin.

Shakspere, Shakespeare, or **Shakspeare, William,** 1564–1616, greatest of English poets and dramatists, b. Stratford-on-Avon. Comparatively little is known of his life, and many theories concerning it have been advanced. He was fairly well educated and may have been a schoolmaster. In 1582 he married Anne Hathaway, and the couple may have had three children. As early as 1588 he had moved to London and linked his life with the stage, probably as an apprentice. About 1589 his first drama was produced—either *The Comedy of Errors* or the first part of *Henry VI*. He continued to produce plays in a steady stream until after his retirement to Stratford-on-Avon (c.1610) with a modest fortune. By 1593 he had Henry Wriothesley, earl of Southampton, as his patron. He was a member (1594–95) of the Lord Chamberlain's Men, later the King's Men of James I, and he seems to have been writer and actor for the group until his retirement. He was (1599) a partner in the Globe Theatre and (1609) in the Blackfriars Theatre. Most scholars accept some 38 plays as being by him, partially or totally. The chronology is very shaky, and indeed his authorship has been challenged—in earlier days by the proponents of Francis Bacon, in later days by proponents of the earl of Oxford as writer of all of them. Regardless of the name, Shakspere's plays show forth one of the towering geniuses of all time. They are sometimes divided, for the sake of convenience, into four groups. The first includes *The Comedy of Errors,* the three parts of *Henry VI, Titus Andronicus, The Two Gentlemen of Verona, Richard III, Love's Labour's Lost, The Taming of the Shrew,* and *King John.* Several of these are only dubiously of his authorship. The second period includes plays that are much surer, including most of his best comedies and chronicle plays—*Richard II, A Midsummer Night's Dream, The Merchant of Venice, Romeo and Juliet,* the two parts of *Henry IV, The Merry Wives of Windsor* (supposedly written at the behest of Queen Elizabeth I), *Much Ado about Nothing, Henry V, Julius Caesar, As You Like It,* and *Twelfth Night.* The third period saw the greatest of his tragedies and some of his light comedies—*Hamlet, Troilus and Cressida, All's Well That Ends Well, Measure for Measure, Othello, King Lear, Macbeth, Antony and Cleopatra, Timon of Athens, Coriolanus,* and *Pericles, Prince of Tyre.* The fourth period includes *Cymbeline, The Winter's Tale, The Tempest, Henry VIII,* and *The Two Noble Kinsmen.* Shakspere apparently was not the sole author of the first part of *Henry VI,* of *Timon of Athens,* and of *Pericles.* John FLETCHER was almost certainly the collaborator on *Henry VIII* and *The Two Noble Kinsmen.* The plays contain the richness of Shakspere's contribution to the world. Their poetry, at times majestic, at times lyric, at times surpassingly witty, has a beauty beyond comparison. Yet without the plays he would have been remembered for his sonnets (1593?–1596?) dedicated to a mysterious W. H. whose identity is much disputed. Other poems include *Venus and Adonis* (1593), *The Rape of Lucrece* (1594), *The Phoenix and the Turtle* (1601), and *The Passionate Pilgrim* (1599). It is doubtful whether he wrote *A Lover's Complaint* (1609), attributed to him. His genius transcends any specific accomplishments, but in many techniques he had a mastery that affected all followers, such as his perfection of the blank-verse line and his superlative development of the Renaissance tragedy.

shale (shāl), sedimentary rock formed by consolidation of mud or clay, having the property of splitting into thin layers parallel to bedding planes. Some shales are a potential source of petroleum.

shallot (shŭlŏt′), perennial plant (*Allium ascalonicum*), closely related to the onion. Its leaves and bulbs are similar to but milder than garlic.

Shallum (shă′lŭm). **1** Died c.749 B.C., king of Israel for a month. He killed Zachariah for the throne and was himself killed by Menahem. 2 Kings 15.13–15. **2** King of Judah: see JEHOAHAZ.

Shalmaneser (shălmŭnē′zŭr), kings of anc. Assyria. **Shalmaneser I,** d. 1290 B.C., removed the capital from Assur to Calah and estab. a royal residence at Nineveh. **Shalmaneser III,** d. 825 B.C., had black obelisk inscribed with claims of victories in Syria and Palestine (including one over Ahab of Israel). Built a huge tower in Calah. **Shalmaneser V,** d. 722 B.C., attacked Hosea of Israel and captured Samaria.

shaman, a healer, priest, or magician, especially

one capable of controlling or gaining aid of supernatural agencies. Term originally referred to this functionary in Siberian tribes and now extends to practitioners among all primitives. The American Indian medicine man performed same functions as the shaman and was usually a person of superior intellect and ability whose advice was sought by chiefs and elders. Shamans employ hypnotism, ventriloquism, sleight of hand, trancelike states, and other devices.

Shamokin (shùmō'kĭn), borough (pop. 16,879), E Pa., ESE of Sunbury. Center in anthracite region; mfg. of textiles, clothing, and machinery.

Shamrock, city (pop. 3,322), N Texas, E of Amarillo in Panhandle. Has oil and gas refining.

shamrock, a plant with leaves of three leaflets which, according to legend, was used by St. Patrick to explain the doctrine of the Trinity. It is now the emblem of Ireland. In U.S., plants most often used as substitutes for shamrock are the white and hop clovers, black medic, and wood sorrel.

Shamyl (shä'mĭl), c.1798–1871, religious and political leader (imam) of Moslem mountaineers of E Caucasus in their Holy War against Russia (1834–59). Was captured 1859. Died in Mecca, where he was allowed to go 1870.

Shang (shäng) or **Yin,** dynasty of China. Varying dates given are c.1766–c.1122 B.C. and c.1523–c.1027 B.C. Empire comprised N China and part of Korea. Succeeded by Chou dynasty.

Shanghai (shăng'hī'), city (pop. 4,300,630), in, but independent of, Kiangsu prov., China; a great port on Whangpoo R. Largest city of China, it grew after 1842 when Treaty of Nanking opened it to foreign trade and ceded sections of it to foreign powers. Modern section of city is area formerly comprising Internatl. Settlement (estab. by Great Britain and U.S.) and French concession. Chief mfg. center of China; textile mills and food-processing plants. Seat of several universities, it ranks second to Peking as educational center. Invaded 1932 by the Japanese; under Japanese occupation 1937–45. At end of World War II the entire city (including foreign holdings) was restored to Nationalists. Fell 1949 to Chinese Communists.

Shanhaikwan (shän'hī'gwän'), city (pop. 70,000), NE Hopeh prov., China, on Tientsin-Mukden RR. Strategic gateway to Manchuria, at easternmost end of Great Wall. Formerly called Linyü.

Shannon, principal river of Ireland. Rising in Co. Cavan, it flows mostly S c.220 mi. through several loughs to Limerick, where it turns W in broad estuary (c.70 mi. long) to the Atlantic. Between Limerick and Lough Derg is an important hydroelectric plant. River has valuable fisheries.

Shannontown, village (pop. 5,828), central S.C., S of Sumter. Woodworking plants.

Shansi (shän'shē'), province (50,000 sq. mi.; pop. 10,000,000), N China; cap. Taiyüan. Bounded S by Yellow R. Mainly a plateau containing large deposits of coal. Crops include millet and wheat.

Shan State (shän'), constituent unit (61,090 sq. mi.; pop. 1,699,585) of Union of Burma; cap. Lashio. Essentially a hilly plateau. The Shans, who are related to the Siamese, dominated N Burma 13th–16th cent. Came under British rule in 1885. In late 19th cent. area was split into c.30 petty states; most of these were merged 1922 to form Federated Shan States. Integrated 1948 as a single state within Union of Burma.

Shantung (shăn'tŭng', shän'dōōng'), province (55,000 sq. mi.; pop. 36,000,000), E China, on peninsula in Yellow Sea; cap. Tsinan. Partly mountainous, partly on Yellow R. delta. Produces much coal. Chief crops are millet, wheat, kaoliang, peanuts, and cotton. Parts of province, WEIHAIWEI and KIAOCHOW, were formerly leased by Great Britain and Germany. Occupied by the Japanese 1937–45; fell to Chinese Communists 1948. A variety of silk is called shantung.

Shapiro, Karl (shùpēr'ō), 1913–, American poet. Works include *V-Mail* (1944) and critical poem *Essay on Rime* (1945).

Shapley, Harlow (shăp'lē), 1885–, American astronomer. Noted for photometric and spectroscopic research and investigations of structure of universe.

Shapur I (shäpōōr') or **Sapor I** (sā'pôr), d. 272, king of Persia (241–72), son and successor of Ardashir I, of Sassanid dynasty. His defeat of Valerian at Edessa (260) was a landmark in decline of Rome.

Shapur II or **Sapor II,** 309–79, king of Persia (309–79), of Sassanid dynasty, called Shapur the Great. Defeated the Romans under Constantius II and later under Julian. His reign saw great prosperity.

Sharaku (shä'räkōō), fl. 1794, Japanese color-print artist, known for portraits of *kabuki* actors.

share, in finance: see STOCK.

share cropping, system of farm tenancy common in the U.S. The system, which arose at the end of the Civil War, perpetuated system of having workers constantly devoted to cotton cultivation under rigid supervision. The cropper brings to the farm only his own and his family's labor while land, animals, and equipment are provided by the landowner, who also advances credit for living expenses. In return the cropper gets a share of the money realized; from this his debt to the landlord is deducted. Mechanization and reduction in cotton acreage have tended to reduce share cropping.

shark, member of fish group more primitive than bony fish, most abundant in warm seas. It has a cartilaginous skeleton; lacks scales and air bladder; dermal denticles roughen the body surface; toothed mouth is on ventral surface. Eats almost any animal food, including carrion and refuse. Length 2–50 ft.; larger species usually bear their young like mammals. See also DOGFISH.

Shark Island: see DRY TORTUGAS.

Sharon (shā'rùn, shă'–), fertile plain of W Israel, between Samarian hills and the Mediterranean.

Sharon. 1 Town (pop. 1,889), NW Conn., in Taconic Mts. Noah Webster wrote his *Spelling Book* here. **2** City (pop. 26,454), NW Pa., on Shenango R. near Ohio line; settled c.1800. Mfg. of steel, metal, and electrical products. **3** Town (pop. 470), E Vt., NE of Rutland. Birthplace of Joseph Smith, founder of Mormonism.

Sharon Springs, resort village, E central N.Y., NW of Albany. Sulphur springs used in hydrotherapy.

Sharp, James, 1618?–1679, Scottish divine. A Presbyterian minister, he supported conciliation with royalists. After Restoration he was made (1661) archbishop of St. Andrews and opposed Covenanters, a band of whom murdered him.

Sharp, William, pseud. **Fiona Macleod** (fē'nů mŭkloud'), 1855–1905, Scottish poet and literary biographer. Wrote poems, biographies, and novels under his own name, but verse, prose, and plays written under his pseudonym are better known because of their nebulous Celtic charm.

Sharpsburg. 1 Town (pop. 866), NW Md.: see ANTIETAM CAMPAIGN. **2** Borough (pop. 7,296), SW Pa., on Allegheny R. and near Pittsburgh. Mfg. of hardware and chemicals.

Sharpsville, borough (pop. 5,414), NW Pa., on Shenango R. and near Sharon. Mfg. of metal products.

Shasta, Mount: see CASCADE RANGE.

Shasta Dam, N Calif., in Sacramento R. and near Redding; built 1938–45 for power, flood control, and navigation. It is huge unit (602 ft. high, 3,500 ft. long) in CENTRAL VALLEY project.

Shatt el Arab (shăt' ĕl ä'räb), river, c.120 mi. long, formed by confluence of Tigris and Euphrates rivers. Flows through Iraq to Persian Gulf. Forms part of Iraq-Iran border.

Shaw, Anna Howard, 1847–1919, American woman-suffrage leader, b. England. Holder of a medical degree and a minister of the Methodist Protestant Church, she devoted herself after 1888 to woman-suffrage movement.

Shaw, George Bernard, 1856–1950, British dramatist, b. Dublin. He went to London, where he wrote five little-known novels. He became music critic (1888) for the *Star* and (1890) for the *World,* his lively music reviews showing his enthusiasm for Wagner. In 1895 he became dramatic critic for the *Saturday Review.* Long interested in economics and socialism, he was an early member of the FABIAN SOCIETY. Through Sidney and Beatrice Webb he met Charlotte Payne-Townshend, whom he married in 1898. His first collection of plays appeared in 1898 as *Plays Pleasant and Unpleasant,* and included "pleasant" *Candida* and *Arms and the Man* and "unpleasant" *Widowers' Houses* and *Mrs. Warren's Profession.* His major plays include *The Devil's Disciple* (written 1896); *Caesar and Cleopatra* (1899); *Captain Brassbound's Conversion* (written 1899), played in 1906 by Ellen Terry, with whom Shaw corresponded for years; *Man and Superman* (pub. 1903); *Major Barbara* (produced 1905); *The Doctor's Dilemma* (produced 1906); *Androcles and the Lion* (1911); *Pygmalion* (1912); *Heartbreak House* (produced 1920); *Back to Methuselah* (1924); and his masterpiece, *Saint Joan* (produced 1924). He was awarded the 1925 Nobel Prize in Literature. He also wrote essays on widely varying subjects, including *The Quintessence of Ibsenism* (1891) and *The Intelligent Woman's Guide to Socialism and Capitalism* (1928). His complete works were published in 1930–32 in 30 volumes. In his 60 years of literary and dramatic activity Shaw always expressed himself on all subjects with great frankness, sometimes with wisdom, but always with wit.

Shawangunk Mountain (shŏng'gŭm, –gŭngk), ridge of Appalachian system, SE N.Y., extending NE from junction with Kittatinny Mt. near N.J. border.

Shawano (shô'nō, shô'wůnō), city (pop. 5,894), NE Wis., on Wolf R. and NW of Green Bay. Farm trade center with wood products. Menominee Indian reservation is to the N.

Shawinigan Falls (shůwĭ'nĭgůn), city (pop. 26,903), S Que., Canada, on St. Maurice R. and NW of Trois Rivières. Falls (N) supply power for paper mills and other industries.

Shawnee (shô"nē'), city (pop. 22,948), central Okla., on North Canadian R. and SE of Oklahoma City. Trade, mfg., and rail center of agr. and oil area. Has U.S. Indian tuberculosis sanatorium.

Shawnee Indians, North American tribe of Algonquian linguistic stock. In mid-18th cent. they settled in Ohio and there took part in battles against the whites. The Treaty of Greenville forced them W, and they founded a village on the Tippecanoe in Ind. under command of the Shawnee Prophet and Tecumseh. This was the village destroyed by William Henry Harrison in the battle of Tippecanoe (1811). The Shawnee are living on reservations in Okla. Also Shawano.

Shawnee Prophet, 1768–1837, North American Indian of Shawnee tribe; twin brother of TECUMSEH. His Indian name was Tenskwatawa. Urged renunciation of white man's ways and return to Indian modes.

Shawneetown, city (pop. 1,917), SE Ill., on Ohio R. One of state's oldest towns, settled after 1800, laid out 1808. Important river port and commercial center in early 19th cent. First bank chartered in state preserved. After 1937 flood city moved few miles W to higher ground.

Shaw University: see RALEIGH, N.C.

Shays, Daniel (shāz) c.1747–1825, American soldier. Fought in Revolution. Led **Shays's Rebellion,** 1786–87, an armed insurrection in W Mass. Farmers showed economic discontent by rising against the merchants and the lawyers of the seaboard towns. Rebellion prevented sitting of courts. State troops routed rebels. Shays escaped, was later pardoned.

Shchedrin, Nikolai Evgrafovich: see SALTYKOV.

Shcherbakov (shchĕrbŭkôf'), city (pop. 139,011), central European RSFSR. A major inland port and lumber center. Site of dam and hydroelectric station of Rybinsk Reservoir (area 1,800 sq. mi.), formed 1941 between the upper Volga and its left affluents (Mologa and Sheksna) as part of Mariinsk System. City was called Rybinsk until 1946.

Sheba (shē'bů), biblical name of region of S Arabia, including Yemen and the Hadramaut; also called Saba. Its inhabitants, Sabaeans or Sabeans, estab. an ancient culture there, as shown by inscriptions in a Semitic language. Legend said it was very wealthy. Its queen (called, in Moslem tradition, Balkis) visited Solomon (1 Kings 10). Sheba colonized Ethiopia, was later (6th cent. A.D.) under Ethiopian control.

Sheboygan (shĭboi'gŭn), city (pop. 42,365), E Wis., on L. Michigan at mouth of Sheboygan R.; formed 1836 in site of North West Co. post (1795). Center of important dairy and cheese-making area. Liberal German refugees arrived in mid-19th cent.

Shechem (shē'kŭm), one of the cities of refuge, central Palestine, N of Jerusalem; in modern Arabic NABLUS. Traditionally it is the site of Jacob's well and Joseph's tomb. Also Sichem and Sychem.

Sheeler, Charles, 1883–, American painter and photographer. Exhibited in Armory Show (1913).

Sheen, Fulton J(ohn), 1895–, American Roman Catholic clergyman, known for his radio broadcasts and his inspirational books (e.g., *Peace of Soul,* 1949). Made auxiliary bishop 1951.

sheep, wild and domesticated ruminant mammal of genus *Ovis,* of cattle family. The male is a ram (if castrated a wether), the female, a ewe, and their young are lambs. The wild BIGHORN has never been domesticated. Sheep are valued for wool, meat (mutton), and their skins. Cheese is made from the milk. Among leading breeds are the Karakul, prized for pelts used for coats and trimmings; the long-wool Cotswold; the Hampshire, hornless and black-faced, a leading breed in U.S. for market lambs; Merino, esteemed for fine wool; Shropshire and Southdown, producers of both mutton and wool. Colorado and Nebraska are important sheep-raising areas. The sheep was the literal and symbolic sacrifice in Judaism; hence in Christianity Jesus is called the Lamb of God.

sheep dogs. Various breeds of dogs which may be used in guarding or herding sheep or cattle. The name *sheep dog* forms part of the breed name of only certain dogs. These include the old English sheep dog, probably developed in 18th-cent. England for driving sheep and cattle to market and known by its long shaggy coat that covers the face as well as the body, and the Shetland sheep dog or "Sheltie" which greatly resembles the collie, but is 12–15 in. at the shoulder in contrast to the collie's 22–24 in. The collie, originally bred as a shepherd dog and recognized by its tapering nose, usually long hair, and abundant ruff, has become more of a show dog and a pet since the late 19th cent. The German shepherd dog, commonly called the police dog because of its extensive use in police work, has a long, straight back, plumed tail, and, when at attention, erect ears. Its stamina, intelligence, alertness, and loyalty make it an excellent war dog, watch dog, and seeing-eye dog. Two of the largest of all dogs (sometimes over 27 in. at the shoulder) are the St. Bernard (named after St. Bernard de Menthon, founder, c.982, of the well-known hospice in the Swiss Alps) and the Newfoundland. Although both may be used in guarding sheep, the St. Bernard is more famous for its Alpine rescue work, while the aquatic skill of the Newfoundland makes it an able saver of drowning persons. Both dogs have thick coats. The Newfoundland is usually black (sometimes with white markings) and has a domed forehead. The St. Bernard is red or brindle, with white; its wrinkled forehead gives it a morose expression.

Sheerness, urban district (pop. 15,727), on Isle of Sheppey, Kent, England. Seaport with government dockyards; much of town's industry depends upon the garrison. Another section is a resort.

Sheffield, county borough (pop. 512,834), West Riding of Yorkshire, England, on Don R.; a leading industrial center of England. Seat of cutlery mfg. since 14th cent.; silver and electroplate goods, tools, and heavy steel goods are also made. Mary Queen of Scots was imprisoned here 1569–84. Univ. of Sheffield (1905) has medical school and technical college. Mappin Art Galleries are noted. City was heavily bombed in 1940.

Sheffield, city (pop. 10,767), NW Ala., on Pickwick L. of Tennessee R. opposite Florence. Mfg. of aluminum products, ferroalloys, stoves, castings.

Sheherazade: see THOUSAND AND ONE NIGHTS.

Shelburne, William Petty Fitzmaurice, 2d **earl of,** 1737–1805, British statesman. Supported John Wilkes. Secretary of state under both William Pitts. Concluded Treaty of Paris (1783) giving independence to new U.S., but was driven from office by Tory-Whig coalition. Liberal but unpopular.

Shelby. 1 City (pop. 15,508), W N.C., W of Charlotte in the piedmont. Textile milling center. **2** City (pop. 7,971), N central Ohio, NW of Mansfield. Mfg. of steel tubing.

Shelbyville. 1 City (pop. 11,734), SE Ind., SE of Indianapolis; platted 1832. Farm trade center in Corn Belt. Mfg. of furniture. **2** Town (pop. 9,456), central Tenn., on Duck R. and SSE of Nashville. Mfg. of rubber goods and pencils. The Tennessee "walking horse" is bred in the area.

Sheldon, Charles Monroe, 1857–1946, American Congregational clergyman, author of the widely read religious novel, *In His Steps* (1896).

Shelekhov, Grigori Ivanovich (grĭgô'rē ēvä'nŭvĭch shĕ'lyĭkhŭf), 1747–95, Russian fur merchant. In 1784 he founded first permanent settlement in Alaska on Kodiak Isl.

shell, in zoology, hard outer covering secreted by animal. Usually refers to calcareous shells of many MOLLUSK species, but is also applied to the exoskeleton (outer skeleton) of crab and other crustaceans, and to the bony covering of turtle.

shellac (shŭlăk'), name for solution of LAC in alcohol or for the resin itself. It is orange to light yellow in color. Used as surface coating, spirit varnish, for stiffening and in electrical insulation.

Shelley, Percy Bysshe, 1792–1822, English poet. Educated at Eton and Oxford, he was expelled from Oxford in 1811 because of his pamphlet *The Necessity of Atheism.* He then eloped to Scotland with his sister's schoolmate Harriet Westbrook. Three years later he eloped with Mary Wollstonecraft Godwin. The summer of 1816 was spent in Switzerland, where he began his friendship with

Byron. Soon afterward, Harriet committed suicide, and Shelley married Mary Godwin. In 1818 they went to Italy, where he composed the greater part of his poetry. He was drowned on July 8, 1822, when sailing in the Bay of Lerici. His chief works include *Queen Mab* (1813); *Alastor* (1816); *The Revolt of Islam* (1817); *The Cenci* and *Prometheus Unbound* (both 1820), closet dramas; *Epipsychidion* (1821), praise of ideal love; and *Adonais* (1821), a threnody on the death of Keats. Shelley's political philosophy long inspired radical thinkers, but his reputation is based most firmly upon the fresh imagery and subtle melody of his inspired lyrics, such as "Ode to the West Wind," "To a Skylark," "The Indian Serenade," and "When the Lamp Is Shattered." His wife, **Mary (Wollstonecraft Godwin) Shelley,** 1797–1851, daughter of William Godwin and Mary Wollstonecraft, is remembered as a writer chiefly for her novel of terror, *Frankenstein* (1818).

shellfish, popular name for certain edible aquatic animals, including mollusks (e.g., oyster and clam) and crustaceans (e.g., crab, lobster, and shrimp).

Shelter Island, c.7 mi. long, between N and S peninsulas of Long Isl., SE N.Y. Summer resort.

Shelton. 1 City (pop. 12,694), SW Conn., on Housatonic R. and W of New Haven; settled 1697. Mfg. of textiles and metal products. **2** Lumber city (pop. 5,045), NW Wash., on a Puget Sound arm NW of Olympia. Oysters, lumber.

Shem, eldest son of Noah, ancestor of the Semites. Gen. 5.32; 7.13; 9.25–27; 11.10. Sem: Luke 3.36.

Shemya (shĕm'yŭ), island, 4 mi. long, off W Alaska, one of Aleutian Islands. U.S. air base estab. here in World War II.

Shenandoah (shĕnŭndō'ŭ). **1** City (pop. 6,938), SW Iowa, SE of Council Bluffs and on East Nishnabotna R. (power). Industrial center of agr. area. **2** Borough (pop. 15,704), E Pa., in Schuylkill anthracite region near Pottsville; settled 1835. Coal mining; mfg. of textiles.

Shenandoah, river formed in western Va. and flowing c.170 mi. N to the Potomac at Harpers Ferry, W.Va. Shenandoah Valley, site of much Civil War activity, figured in 1862 diversion of T. J. JACKSON, in GETTYSBURG CAMPAIGN (1863), in raid of J. A. Early (1864), and as retreat for Lee after Antietam campaign. Main Confederate supply source. Taken and ravaged by P. H. SHERIDAN 1864–65.

Shenandoah, ship: see CONFEDERATE CRUISERS.

Shenandoah National Park: see NATIONAL PARKS AND MONUMENTS (table).

Shenandoah Valley: see SHENANDOAH, river.

Shensi (shĕn'sē'), province (75,000 sq. mi.; pop. 10,000,000), N central China; cap. Sian. Bounded on E by Yellow R. Economic center of province is Wei R. valley. Major producer of oil, but rich coal deposits are largely untouched. Chief crops are wheat, millet, and kaoliang. Yenan (pop. 29,856) in N Shensi was center of Chinese Communists 1937–47.

Shenstone, William, 1714–63, English poet and landscape gardener, author of *The Schoolmistress* (1742).

Shenyang, Manchuria: see MUKDEN.

Sheol: see HELL.

shepherd dog: see SHEEP DOGS.

Shepherdstown, town (pop. 1,173), in E Panhandle of W.Va., on Potomac R. and SE of Martinsburg; settled 1762, one of oldest towns in state.

Sheppard, Jack, 1702–24, English criminal. Had short, spectacular career as thief, robber, and escape artist before he was hanged. His exploits became subject of many narratives and plays.

Sheppey, Isle of, Kent, England, in the Thames estuary. Largely flat with fertile soil. Vegetables, grain, and sheep are raised.

Sheraton, Thomas (shĕ'rŭtŭn), 1751–1806, English designer of furniture. Wrote influential manuals of cabinetwork. His style is marked by simplicity, emphasis on straight lines, and preference for inlay decoration and classical motifs. See *ill.*, p. 456.

Sherborne (shûr'bŭrn), urban district (pop. 5,987), Dorsetshire, England. Site of Sherborne School (founded 1550), noted public school which has a library rich in musical scores.

Sherbrooke, city (pop. 50,543), SE Que., Canada, on St. Francis R. at mouth of Magog R. and E of Montreal. Trade center in agr. area with textile and knitting mills, foundries, and railroad shops.

Shere Ali (shēr' ä'lē, shâr'), 1825–79, emir of Afghanistan (1863–79), son of Dost Mohammed. His friendly relations with Russia led to second Afghan War (1878–80) with the British. Died in exile.

Sheridan, Philip Henry, 1831–88, Union general in Civil War. An outstanding cavalry leader, he gave brilliant support in many campaigns. Distinguished himself at Perryville (1862). In Chattanooga campaign (1863) he aided G. H. Thomas. Commander in Army of the Potomac (1864). Defeated J. E. B. Stuart at Yellow Tavern, J. A. Early at Winchester. Laid waste to Shenandoah Valley (1864). After victory at Five Forks (April 1, 1865) he cut off Lee's retreat at Appomattox Courthouse, forcing Lee's surrender.

Sheridan, Richard Brinsley, 1751–1816, British dramatist and politician. Director and part owner (1776) of the Drury Lane Theatre, he wrote many pieces (most enduring the comedies of manners, *The Rivals,* 1775, and *The School for Scandal,* 1777). In Parliament after 1780, he was among the most brilliant orators of his day, prominent in impeachment of Warren Hastings and defense of French Revolution.

Sheridan, city (pop. 11,500), N Wyo., E of Bighorn Mts., near Mont. line, in coal, cattle, farm, and dude-ranch area; settled 1878. Railroad division point; food processing (beet sugar, cereals). Annual rodeo. Near by are site of Fetterman massacre and replica of Fort Phil Kearny (1860s).

Sheriffmuir (shĕ'rĭfmyo͝or"), battlefield in Perthshire, Scotland; scene of indecisive battle (1715) between Jacobites and forces of George I.

Sherman, John: see SHERMAN, WILLIAM TECUMSEH.

Sherman, Stuart P(ratt), 1881–1926, American critic and educator; professor of English at Univ. of Illinois (1907–24). An editor of *The Cambridge History of American Literature,* he wrote conservative critical works such as *Americans* (1922) and *The Main Stream* (1927).

Sherman, William Tecumseh, 1820–91, Union general in Civil War. Fought in Vicksburg and Chattanooga campaigns. Commander in the West, he launched ATLANTA CAMPAIGN (1864). City fell on Sept. 2, evacuation was ordered Sept. 9, and city was burned Nov. 15. Then with 60,000 men he marched through Ga., devastating country as he went. In Feb., 1865, he turned N through S.C., repeating destruction of country. He justified his actions on ground that in war it is necessary to break spirit of whole people to win victory. His brother, **John Sherman,** 1823–1900, was U.S. Representative from Ohio (1855–61) and U.S. Senator (1861–77, 1881–97). Gave his name to Sherman Anti-Trust Act and Sherman Silver Purchase Act. He was U.S. Secretary of the Treasury (1877–81), U.S. Secretary of State (1897–98).

Sherman, city (pop. 20,150), N Texas, near Red R. and NNE of Dallas; settled 1849. Highway and rail junction, it processes farm produce, grains, and cotton. Mfg. of textiles and machinery.

Sherman Anti-Trust Act, 1890, passed by U.S. Congress. Based on constitutional power of Congress to regulate interstate commerce, act declared illegal every contract, combination, or conspiracy in restraint of interstate and foreign trade. Supreme Court decisions reduced force of act for a decade. Pres. Theodore ROOSEVELT invoked it with some success. Pres. W. H. Taft employed act in 1911 to dissolve Standard Oil trust and American Tobacco Co. CLAYTON ANTI-TRUST ACT (1914) supplemented it. Antitrust action was resumed under Pres. F. D. Roosevelt; further supplementing acts (e.g., ROBINSON-PATMAN ACT) were passed.

Sherman Siver Purchase Act, 1890, passed by U.S. Congress to supplant BLAND-ALLISON ACT. Required U.S. government to purchase nearly twice as much silver as before; added substantially to amount of money already in circulation. In operation it threatened to undermine U.S. Treasury's gold reserves. Act repealed in 1893.

Sherrington, Sir Charles Scott, 1857–1952, English physiologist, authority on nervous system. Shared 1932 Nobel Prize in Physiology and Medicine for research on function of neuron.

sherry, naturally dry, fortified wine (15 to 23 percent alcohol), originally made only from grapes grown in region of Jerez de la Frontera, Spain, but now also produced in the U.S. and Latin America. After long maturing, sherries are classed as *palma,* very dry; *raya,* full and rich; or *palo cortado,* intermediate. Blending and, in some cases, sweetening produce many varieties, ranging from dry cocktail wines to dessert types.

's Hertogenbosch (sĕr'tōkhŭnbôs'), Fr. *Bois-le-Duc,* municipality (pop. 53,208), cap. of North Brabant prov., S central Netherlands; chartered 1184. Mfg. center (electrical appliances, bicycles, food, tobacco). Heavily damaged in World War II.

Sherwood, Robert E(mmet), 1896–, American playwright. Among his many plays are *The Road to Rome* (1927), *The Petrified Forest* (1935), *Idiot's Delight* (1936), *Abe Lincoln in Illinois* (1938), and *There Shall Be No Night* (1940). Was director of overseas operations of Office of War Information and wrote speeches for F. D. Roosevelt. His memoir *Roosevelt and Hopkins* (1948) won popular notice.

Sherwood Forest, once a large royal forest, Nottinghamshire, England; famous as home of Robin Hood.

Sheshonk I (shē'shŏngk), d. c.924 B.C., king of anc. Egypt (c.945–c.924 B.C.). A commander of mercenaries, he took the throne when the line of Tanis died out and estab. Libyan (XXII) dynasty. Captured Gaza and presented it to Solomon. Later overran Palestine. Enlarged the Karnak temple. He is the biblical Shishak.

Shetland (shĕt'lŭnd) or **Zetland** (zĕt'–), county (550 sq. mi.; pop. 19,343) of Scotland, consisting of **Shetland Islands** or **Shetlands,** archipelago c.70 mi. long. Of some 100 islands, c.25% are inhabited. Mainland, longest island, has Lerwick, county seat and chief port. Surface is mostly low and rocky, with little good farm land. Oats and barley are chief crops, but fishing and cattle and sheep raising are more important. Knitted woolen goods are famous. The Shetland pony is bred here.

Shetland sheep dog: see SHEEP DOGS.

Shibboleth (shĭ'bōlĕth) [Heb.,= stream or ear of corn], password used by Gileadites to detect fugitive Ephraimites because Ephraimites, unable to pronounce *sh,* said "Sibboleth." Judges 12. Hence, *shibboleth* came to mean watchword, cant phrase of a particular party, meaningless standard of conformity.

Shickshock Mountains, E Que., Canada, range of Appalachian Mts. extending from Notre Dame Mts. c.100 mi. E-W near coast of Gaspé Peninsula. Rise to 4,160 ft. in Tabletop Mt. or Mt. Jacques Cartier.

Shidehara, Kijuro, Baron (shēdā'härä), 1872–1951, Japanese statesman, a career diplomat. Foreign minister 1929–31, premier Oct., 1945–May, 1946.

Shiel, Loch (lŏkh shēl'), lake, c.17 mi. long and 1 mi. wide, Inverness-shire, Scotland.

Shields, James, 1806–79, American soldier and statesman, b. Ireland. U.S. Senator from Ill. (1849–55), from Minn. (1858–59). In Civil War he fought in Shenandoah Valley (1862), was defeated at Port Republic. Resigned commission in 1863.

Shields, England: see SOUTH SHIELDS; TYNEMOUTH.

Shigatse (shēgät'sĕ), town (pop. c.14,000), SE Tibet, on tributary of Brahmaputra R. Near by is monastery of Tashilunpo (founded 1446), whose abbot is the powerful Panchen Lama.

Shiites (shē'ītz) [Arabic,= sectarian], the group of Moslems who split from the rest of ISLAM (see SUNNITES) by holding that Ali and his successors are divinely ordained caliphs (see CALIPHATE). Husein is considered by them a martyr. The nationalism of Persia helped build the sect, which accepts the idea of the hidden IMAM and of the MAHDI. These beliefs bred fanaticism, expressed in such sects as the FATIMITE believers and the ASSASSIN zealots. Shiism is the religion of Iran.

Shikoku (shĭkō'kōō), island (c.6,860 sq. mi.; pop. 4,074,708), Japan, S of Honshu, E of Kyushu, between Inland Sea and Philippine Sea. Smallest of major Japanese islands. Interior is mountainous and sparsely settled. Exports salt, copper, tobacco, lumber, fruit.

Shillelagh (shĭlā'lŭ), town, Co. Wicklow, Ireland. Ancient forest of Shillelagh gave name to the Irishman's oak or blackthorn cudgel, the shillelagh.

Shillington, borough (pop. 5,059), SE Pa., near Reading. Mfg. of building blocks and textiles.

Shiloh (shī'lō), in Bible, sanctuary where Ark of the Covenant rested after conquest of Canaan until it was captured by Philistines. Home of Eli and young Samuel.

Shiloh, battle of, April 6–7, 1862, also called battle of Pittsburg Landing, one of great battles of Civil War. Took name from Shiloh Church, meetinghouse c.3 mi. SSW of Pittsburg Landing, community in Tenn., 9 mi. S of Savannah, on W bank of Tennessee R. After victory at Fort Donelson, Grant moved up river for attack on Corinth, Miss. On April 6, A. S. Johnston and P. G. T. Beauregard made surprise attack, routing Federals; Johnston was killed. On next day Grant, with aid of D. C. Buell's Army of the Ohio, counterattacked. Outnumbered, Beauregard withdrew to Corinth; city was later abandoned to Federals. Shiloh, one of bloodiest and most controversial battles of war, was Union victory in that it led to later successful campaigns in West.

Shiloh National Military Park: see NATIONAL PARKS AND MONUMENTS (table).

Shimoda (shĭmō'dä), resort town (pop. 8,973), central Honshu, Japan, on Izu peninsula. First U.S. consulate, under Townsend Harris, opened here in 1856.

Shimonoseki (shē'mōnōsākē), industrial city (pop. 176,666), extreme SW Honshu, Japan; port on Shimonoseki Strait. Connected by tunnel with Moji, Kyushu. Engineering works, shipyards, chemical plants, and fish canneries. Treaty of Shimonoseki ending First Chino-Japanese War signed here 1895.

Shimonoseki, Treaty of: see CHINO-JAPANESE WAR, FIRST.

Shinano (shĭnä'nō), river, 229 mi. long, central and N Honshu, Japan; longest in Japan.

Shinar (shī'när), in Bible, name for whole or part of Babylonia. Gen. 10.10; 11.2; 14.1; Isa. 11.11; Dan. 1.2; Zech. 5.11.

Shinn, Everett, 1876–, American muralist and magazine illustrator, a member of The EIGHT.

Shinto (shĭn'tō), religion of Japan, based on old animistic beliefs, modified by Buddhism and Confucianism, unsystematized, more a set of rituals and customs than an organized church. There are three compilations of beliefs and customs—the *Kojiki* (completed A.D. 712), the *Nihongi* (completed 720), the *Yengishiki* (10th cent.). The Kami in Shinto are supernatural beings, mostly beneficent. The sun-goddess gradually became much exalted and was held to be ancestress of the Japanese emperors (divine ancestry disavowed by Hirohito, 1946). Shinto worship consists primarily in prayer and food offerings.

ship, large craft for water transport. Homer's *Odyssey* and the legendary quest of Jason for the Golden Fleece hint that long voyages were common near the dawn of history. Ancient ships used oars, sails, or both, and the slow, heavier ships carried grain, while the oar-propelled Graeco-Roman trireme (later developed to the quinquireme) was the favored warship. Early medieval seafaring was marked by the appearance of the Nordic Vikings, whose fleet ships enabled them to forage French and English coasts; Alfred the Great's defense of England centered in the founding of a navy. Oar-and-sail driven Viking ships could make long voyages (e.g., Leif Ericsson's crossing to America). The Crusades, the tale of Marco Polo, the consequent desire for Eastern trade, and the activities of Prince Henry the Navigator introduced the great exploratory activity of the Renaissance, which was in a way capped by Columbus's discovery of the New World (1492). Sturdier, more refined vessels (bark, brig, clipper, and schooner) appeared later. The needs of warfare led to the men-of-war. Shipbuilding became a vital industry in Britain and America. The successful run of Fulton's *Clermont* on the Hudson R. (1807) began the era of the steamship, and in mid-19th cent. the first steel ships were built. Finally, the turbine and Diesel engine brought new speed and power to shipping. See *ill.*, p. 1109.

Shipka (shĭp'kä), pass through Balkans, central Bulgaria, 4,166 ft. high.

Shippen, Margaret, 1760–1804, wife of Benedict Arnold, daughter of a prominent Philadelphia Tory. Her influence on her husband is much debated.

Shippensburg, borough (pop. 5,722), S Pa., SW of Carlisle. Mfg. of clothing and furniture.

Shipton, Mother, traditional English prophetess. Supposedly predicted great fire of London (1666).

shipworm, wormlike marine bivalve mollusk (*Teredo*). Makes cavities in wood damaging to ships and piers.

Shiraz (shēräz'), city (pop. 129,023), S central Iran; chief city of Fars region. Founded 7th cent., it was cap. of Persia 1750–94. Tombs of the great Persian poets Hafiz and Sadi are here. Founder of Babism was also a native of Shiraz.

Shirley, James, 1596–1666, English dramatist. He wrote some 40 plays, such as *The Lady of Pleasure* (1635) and *The Contention of Ajax and Ulysses* (1659; containing the dirge, "The glories of our blood and state").

Shirpurla: see LAGASH.

Shishak: see SHESHONK I.

Shittim, last camping place of the Hebrews before they entered Canaan. Num. 25; Joshua 2; 3.

shittim wood, of shittah tree, probably an acacia, used, according to Bible, to make Ark of the Covenant and furniture of the Tabernacle (Ex. 25.5).

Shiva: see HINDUISM.

Shizuoka (shĭzōō'ôkä), city (pop. 205,737), central Honshu, Japan; port on Suruga Bay. Known for tea and lacquer ware. Site of castle of last Tokugawa Shogun and Hodai-in, important Buddhist temple.

Shkodër or **Shkodra,** Albania: see SCUTARI.

shock, sudden depression of vital centers of nervous system. Causes include injury, surgery, certain drugs. Marked by pallor, rapid pulse and breathing, low temperature and blood pressure. Injury should be treated; patient must be kept warm and lying down.

shock therapy, in psychiatry, a treatment by chemical agents or electricity to improve or cure mental diseases, or to make the patient rational enough for psychotherapy. Its overall value is disputed although electric shock has had notable success with depressive disorders, and metrazol and insulin have effected a few remissions of schizophrenia.

shoe, foot covering, commonly of leather and consisting of a sole and an upper. Sandal was probably earliest form. Probably the forerunner (15th cent.) of heeled shoe was the patten, raised on blocks and later attached to the upper. Early shoemakers worked at home or as itinerants. Industry was revolutionized by machine for stitching together soles and uppers, invented c.1858 by Lyman Blake and developed by Gordon McKay. Over 180 different machines are used in modern shoemaking.

shogun (shō'gōōn), title of military dictators who ruled Japan, 12th–19th cent. Title itself dates back to 794 and originally meant commander of imperial armies. Shogunate as system of government was estab. by Yoritomo and known as *bakufu* [literally, army hq.]. Emperor ruled only theoretically, with real power wielded by hereditary shogun. Minamoto family held shogunate 1192–1333; Ashikaga, 1338–1597; Tokugawa, 1603–1867. Overthrow of shogun brought Meiji restoration (1868) and birth of modern Japan.

Sholapur (shō'lŏopōōr), city (pop. 203,691), E Bombay, India; major cotton-milling center.

Sholokhov, Mikhail Aleksandrovich (mēkhŭyĕl' ŭlyĭksän'drŏovĭch shô'lŏokhŏof), 1905–, Russian author, best known for his epic novel of the Don Cossacks, *The Silent Don* (1928–40; Eng. tr., *And Quiet Flows the Don,* 1934, and *The Don Flows Home to Sea,* 1940).

Sholom Aleichem: see ALEICHEM, SHOLOM.

shooting star, North American perennial wild flower (*Dodecatheon meadia*) of primrose family. Also called American primrose or cowslip, it bears a cluster of nodding flowers with white or lilac petals which flare backwards.

shooting star: see METEOR.

Shore, Jane, d.1527?, mistress of Edward IV of England, over whom she exerted great influence. Accused (1483) of sorcery by Richard III, placed in Tower, forced to do public penance as harlot.

Shoreditch, metropolitan borough (pop. 44,885), E London, England; center of furniture-making industry. London's first theater was built here c.1576. Suffered much bomb damage in World War II.

Shorewood, residential suburban village (pop. 16,199), SE Wis., on L. Michigan and Milwaukee R., adjoining N Milwaukee; settled c.1834.

short circuit occurs when current is deflected to path of less resistance. Term is often used for a broken electric circuit as when a fuse blows out or when connection wire in circuit is broken.

shorthand, any brief, rapid system of writing that may be used in transcribing or in recording the spoken word. Such systems, their characters based on letters of the alphabet, were used even in ancient times. Modern systems, frequently based on sound, date from 1558, when Timothy Bright published his symbols for words. Dozens of systems followed before 1837, when shorthand of Isaac Pitman appeared. Using geometric outlines, with shading and differences in slope and position on a given line, it is difficult to master but makes possible very great speed. J. R. Gregg published (1888) a popular system of business shorthand. Its outlines, curved and natural, with variations in length of line, call for a cursive motion, which promotes speed. Pitman and Gregg systems are widely used today.

Short Hills, N.J.: see MILLBURN.

shorthorn cattle: see CATTLE.

Shoshone (shōshō'nē), village (pop. 1,420), S Idaho, in MINIDOKA PROJECT and N of Twin Falls. Magic Dam (1907) in Big Wood R. is near. Gateway to Sun Valley and Sawtooth Mts.

Shoshone Cavern National Monument: see NATIONAL PARKS AND MONUMENTS (table).

Shoshone Falls, S Idaho, in Snake R., near Twin Falls. Shoshone Falls, once c.200 ft. high, are now reduced by irrigation projects upstream.

Shoshone Indians, North American tribe of Uto-Aztecan linguistic stock, living in the early 19th cent. in SW Mont., W Wyo., S Idaho, and NE Nev. The E Shoshone were buffalo hunters, the W Shoshone did not have horses and hunted no buffalo; they lived on nuts and wild plants. They were sometimes called Snake Indians.

Shoshone project, NW Wyo., near Shoshone R. in Bighorn R. basin. Provides power and irrigation for 161,654 acres. Has small dams, canals; Buffalo Bill Dam (largest) forms Shoshone Reservoir. Serves Cody and Powell.

Shostakovich, Dmitri (dyĭmē'trē shŏstŏkô'vĭch), 1906–, Russian composer. Notable among his nine symyhonies are the First (1925), the Fifth (1937), and the Seventh (1942, composed during the siege of Leningrad). Other works include a satirical ballet, *The Golden Age* (1930); Twenty-four Preludes (1933) for piano; a piano concerto (1933); a piano quintet (1940); and other chamber works. The Soviet government has repudiated much of his music, including the opera *Lady Macbeth of Mzensk.*

shotgun, smooth-bore firearm designed for firing a number of small shot at short range. When the gun is fired, the shot spreads in a widening circle.

Shottery, village, Warwickshire, England, 1 mi.

W of Stratford-on-Avon. Has cottage in which Shakspere's wife, Anne Hathaway, lived.

Shotwell, James T(homson), 1874–, American historian. Active in national and international labor, peace, and historical conferences. Works include *War as an Instrument of National Policy* (1929) and *The Great Decision* (1944). An editor (1904–5) *Encyclopaedia Britannica.* Editor *Economic and Social History of the World War* (150 vols., 1919–29).

Shrapnel, Henry, 1761–1842, British general, inventor of the shrapnel shell, which is fired by a time fuse in mid-air and scatters shot and shell fragments over a wide area.

Shreve, Henry Miller, 1785–1851, American inventor of steamboats. His *Washington* opened the Mississippi and the Ohio to steam navigation.

Shreveport (shrēv′pôrt), city (pop. 127,206), NW La., on Red R. near Texas and Ark. borders; founded c.1834. Confederate cap. of La. 1863. Oil center processing cotton, glass, and lumber. Centenary Col. of Louisiana (Methodist; coed.; 1825) is here.

shrew (shrōō), insectivorous mammal, of family Soricidae, of North America and extreme N South America, Europe, and Asia. Related to mole. It has a musky odor. Common species of both hemispheres are of genus *Sorex.* Range in body length (including tail) is c.2½–6¼ in. Shrews are prodigious eaters and vicious fighters.

Shrewsbury, Charles Talbot, duke of, 1660–1718, English statesman. One of seven signers of invitation to William III to take throne in 1688. Regarded by king as his chief Whig minister, he was won to Tory cause by Robert Harley in 1706.

Shrewsbury (shrōz′bûrē, shrōōz′–), municipal borough (pop. 44,926), co. seat of Shropshire, England. Ancient Saxon and Norman stronghold, it has much medieval atmosphere. Henry IV defeated (1403) Hotspur near by. Shrewsbury School founded 1551.

Shrewsbury, town (pop. 10,594), central Mass., NE of Worcester; settled 1722. Leather products.

shrike (shrīk) or **butcher bird,** bird of prey, chiefly of Old World but with two New World species (the northern and loggerhead shrikes). Certain shrikes impale prey on thorn or twig while tearing it apart.

shrimp, small marine crustacean, usually 1½–3 in. long, found along most coasts. Has 10 jointed legs and a translucent, flexible outer skeleton.

Shropshire (shrŏp′shĭr, –shûr), border county (1,346 sq. mi.; pop. 289,844), W England; co. town Shrewsbury. Chiefly pastoral and agr., county has some coal mining. On the edge of Welsh Marches, it was scene of much strife and has ruins of medieval castles. County is sometimes called Salop.

Shropshire sheep: see SHEEP.

Shubun (shōō′bōōn′), fl. early 15th cent., Chinese painter of Ming period. Naturalized c.1420 in Japan, where he founded Soga school of Ashikaga.

Shulamite (shōō′lùmīt), character addressed in the Song of Solomon. Cant. 6.13.

Shumen (shōō′mĕn), city (pop. 31,169), NE Bulgaria. Trade and railroad center. Founded 927; strategic fortress during Turkish rule. Noted for Moslem architecture.

Shuster, George N(auman), 1894–, American educator and author. Dean and acting president of Hunter Col. 1939–40, he has been president since 1940. He was on editorial board of *Commonweal,* 1925–37. He became state commissioner for Bavaria (1950).

Si, chemical symbol of the element SILICON.

Sialkot (sēäl′kōt″), city (pop. 152,000), E Punjab prov., W Pakistan. Has 12th-cent. fortress. Mfg. of surgical instruments and sports goods.

Siam: see THAILAND.

Siam, Gulf of, arm of South China Sea, separating Malay Peninsula on W from Indo-China on E.

Siamese language, standard accepted speech of Thailand. Name sometimes includes all of Tai group of Indo-Chinese languages. The standard speech is also called Tai or Thai. See LANGUAGE (table).

Siamese twins, twins united by tissue. Term derived from male twins born in Siam (1811) and long exhibited in P. T. Barnum's circus.

Sian (sē′än′, shē′än′), city (pop. 502,988), cap. Shensi prov., NW China; trade center. Was cap. of Han dynasty (206 B.C.–A.D. 220) and western cap. of Tang dynasty (618–906). Ancient center of foreign religious colonies; 8th-cent. Nestorian stone tablet is preserved. In 1936 Chang Hsueh-liang kidnaped Chiang Kai-shek here.

Siang (shyäng), river, c.715 mi. long, in Kwangsi and Hunan provs., China.

Siangtan (shyäng′tän′), city (pop. 82,589), NE Hunan prov., China; port on Siang R.

Siasconset, Mass.: see NANTUCKET.

Siauliai (shēou′lyī), Ger. *Schaulen,* Rus. *Shavli,* city (pop. 31,641), N Lithuania. Mfg. (shoes, textiles). Here Lithuanians defeated LIVONIAN KNIGHTS in 1236 and a German free corps in 1919.

Sibboleth: see SHIBBOLETH.

Sibelius, Jean (Julius Christian) (zhän′ sĭbā′lyŭs), 1865–, Finnish composer. His orchestral works include tone poems on national subjects, such as *En Saga* (1892) and *Finlandia* (1900); *The Swan of Tuonela* (1893); *Valse triste;* a violin concerto (1903); and seven symphonies (1899–1924).

Sibenik, Serbo-Croatian *Šibenik* (shēbĕ′nĭk), town (pop. 16,015), Croatia, NW Yugoslavia; an Adriatic seaport. Chemical mfg. Its noted architecture (esp. its 15th-cent. cathedral) dates from its period under Venetian rule (1412–1797).

Siberia (sībē′rēû), Rus. *Sibir,* name commonly applied to the Asiatic part (c.5,000,000 sq. mi.; pop. c.20,000,000) of the RSFSR. Occupying the N third of Asia, it stretches from the Urals to the Pacific, from the Arctic Ocean to Mongolia and Manchuria. Its four great vegetation belts are, from N to S: tundras; taiga; mixed forest belt; steppe. W Siberia, between Ural Mts. and Yenisei R., is a plain drained by the Ob and the Irtysh; it is agr. in the S and contains the KUZNETSK BASIN (coal) at the foot of the ALTAI. Largest cities: Novosibirsk, Omsk, Stalinsk. E Siberia, drained by the Lena, extends from the Yenisei to a huge mountain chain (Yablonovy, Stanovoi, Verkhoyansk, Kolyma, Anadir ranges) and contains L. Baikal. Largest cities (all in S): Krasnoyarsk, Irkutsk, Yakutsk, Ulan-Ude, Chita. The Far East comprises CHUKCHI PENINSULA, KAMCHATKA, and the MARITIME TERRITORY. Chief cities: Vladivostok, Khabarovsk, Komsomolsk. Nearly entire population (90% Russian) lives in S, mainly along the TRANS-SIBERIAN RAILROAD. Non-Russian groups include Turkic and Mongol peoples (S); Finno-Ugric peoples and Samoyedes (NW and N); Chukchis and Kamchatkans (NE); Jews (in Birobidzhan); Tungus (center). Lumbering, fur-trapping, hunting, fishing, reindeer raising are the chief occupations in the thinly populated wilderness. Climate is extreme, ranging at Verkhoyansk from —92°F. to above 90°F. S central Siberia was the point of departure of the Huns, Mongols, and Manchus in their great conquests. Russian conquest of Siberia began 1581, when the Cossack YERMAK conquered the Tatar khanate of SIBIR. By 1640 the Cossacks reached the Pacific. By the Treaty of Nerchinsk (1689) Russia abandoned to China the FAR EASTERN TERRITORY (acquired by Russia 1858 and 1860). S Sakhalin Isl. and Kurile Isls. were annexed from Japan after World War II. Siberia was used as penal colony and place of exile from early 17th cent. Large-scale colonization began only with construction of Trans-Siberian RR; population was doubled between 1914 and 1946. During civil war of 1918–20 Siberia was held by the "Whites" under KOLCHAK; Vladivostok was occupied by Japanese till 1922. The tremendous industrial growth of Siberia dates from the first Five-Year Plan and was speeded during World War II. Siberian grain became a vital factor in Soviet economy; the Urals and W Siberia became the new center of Soviet heavy industries. These changes were carried out in part through forced resettlements and forced labor, particularly in the case of road and railroad construction projects and in the exploitation of the rich gold mines of the Aldan and Kolyma ranges.

Sibir (sĭbēr′), former city, SE of present Tobolsk, RSFSR; cap. of Tatar khanate of Sibir or Siberia. Was conquered by Ivan IV 1582.

Sibiu (sēbyōō′), Ger. *Hermannstadt,* Hung. *Nagyszeben,* city (pop. 60,602), central Rumania, in S Transylvania. Orthodox metropolitan see. Mfg. of machinery, textiles, foodstuffs. Founded 12th cent. by German colonists, it has preserved much of its German medieval character and has long been a cultural center of Transylvania.

sibyl, in Greek mythology, one of a group of prophetic old women. Most famous was Cumaean Sibyl, who sold to Tarquin the Sibylline Books, prophecies about Rome's destiny. Whatever their origin, they were kept at Rome until destroyed by fire in 83 B.C.

Sibylline Oracles: see PSEUDEPIGRAPHA.

Sicilian Vespers, 1282, rebellion of Sicily against King CHARLES I (Charles of Anjou), who had transferred his seat from Palermo to Naples and left Sicily to be governed by arrogant French officials. The general massacre of the French began at Palermo on Easter Monday and spread quickly through the island. It was probably prepared by John of Procida, agent of PETER III of Aragon, who also had negotiated for the support of Emperor Michael VIII against Charles. Peter was proclaimed King of Sicily by a federal assembly.

Sicily (sĭ′cĭlē), Ital. *Sicilia,* island and autonomous region (9,928 sq. mi.; pop. 4,000,078), Italy, separated from mainland by Strait of Messina; cap. Palermo. Largest and most populous Mediterranean island, it lies between the Ionian and Tyrrhenian seas, c.100 mi. N of Africa, and is roughly triangular in shape (hence its ancient name, Trinacria). Except for the fertile plain of Catania, it is mostly mountainous, culminating in Mt. ETNA. Agr., its main resource, is hampered by absentee ownership, primitive methods, lack of irrigation. Chief exports: grapes, olives, oranges; sulphur; fish. The ancient cities of Sicily were founded by Phoenicians (PALERMO), Carthaginians (LILYBAEUM, TRAPANI), and Greeks (SYRACUSE; CATANIA; MESSINA; GELA; AGRIGENTO; HIMERA). Among the Greek city-states, Syracuse took the lead. Roman-Carthaginian rivalry in Sicily led to the PUNIC WARS and resulted (241 B.C.) in Sicily's becoming a Roman colony. Rome thoroughly exploited the island. Large estates and plantation slavery were introduced; slave revolts were cruelly suppressed (3d cent. B.C.). Sicily passed under Byzantine rule (6th cent A.D.), then fell to the Arabs (9th cent.). Agr., commerce, and sciences flourished under the Arabs, who, however, were driven out by the Normans under ROGER I (11th cent.). ROGER II became the first king of Sicily (1130), under nominal overlordship of the pope. The marriage of Queen CONSTANCE to Emperor Henry VI brought the kingdom (incl. S Italy, with Naples) to the Hohenstaufen dynasty, which reached its apex with Emperor FREDERICK II (reigned 1197–1250). Frederick's successors (see CONRAD IV; MANFRED; CONRADIN) fought unsuccessfully against the popes; in 1266 Clement IV crowned Charles of Anjou (see CHARLES I of Naples) king of Sicily. Charles's unpopular rule was ended in Sicily by the SICILIAN VESPERS (1282). The island passed to the house of ARAGON; S Italy continued separately as the kingdom of NAPLES, which in 1442 also passed to Aragon. Ruled first by a branch of the Aragon dynasty, after 1409 by viceroys, Sicily deteriorated under its Spanish masters. The Peace of Utrecht gave Sicily to Savoy (1713), which in 1720 exchanged it with Austria for Sardinia. The War of the Polish Succession resulted in the transfer of Sicily and Naples to the Spanish Bourbons (1735). After 1759 the two kingdoms were ruled from Naples by a separate dynasty (see BOURBON-SICILY) and in 1816 they were united, despite Sicilian protests, into the kingdom of the Two SICILIES. Rebellions against the Bourbon kings were ruthlessly suppressed (1820, 1848–49). After Sicily's conquest by GARIBALDI (1860), the island voted its union with Italy. In World

War II it fell to the Allies after heavy fighting (July–Aug., 1943). It received self-rule in 1947.

Sickingen, Franz von (fränts' fŭn zĭ'kĭng-ŭn), 1481–1523, German knight. Influenced by Ulrich von HUTTEN, he gave refuge to persecuted reformers at his castles and, with a private army, waged war against the ecclesiastic princes, aiming at secularization of their lands. He laid siege to Trier (1522), was placed under the ban of the empire, and after a long siege of his castle of Landstuhl was forced to capitulate and died of his wounds. His defeat symbolized the end of the power of German knighthood.

Sickles, Daniel Edgar, 1819–1914, American politician, Union general in Civil War. U.S. Congressman (1857–61, 1893–95). Fought in Peninsular, Antietam, and Gettysburg campaigns. Reconstruction commander in Carolinas (1865–67). Minister to Spain (1869–73).

Sicyon (sĭ'shēŏn), anc. city of Greece, in the Peloponnesus, just S of the Gulf of Corinth. Notable for its bronze work, it also had famous schools of painting and sculpture. It also was of some political importance, and briefly after the destruction of Corinth by the Romans (146 B.C.) was dominant in the region.

Siddons, Sarah Kemble, 1755–1831, English actress, most distinguished of the KEMBLE family. By her warm voice and majestic presence Mrs. Siddons won fame in such roles as Desdemona and Ophelia; she was unequaled as Lady Macbeth. Reynolds painted her portrait, *The Tragic Muse*.

Sidlaw Hills (sĭd'lô), range, E Scotland, extending NE from near Perth into Angus county.

Sidmouth, Henry Addington, Viscount, 1757–1844, English statesman. His ministry (1801–4) after William Pitt's resignation saw Treaty of Amiens with Napoleon 1802. As home secretary (1812–21) he incurred odium for repressive policy in face of hunger.

Sidney or **Sydney, Sir Philip,** 1554–86, English soldier, statesman, author, outstanding figure in Queen Elizabeth's brilliant court. His writings include unfinished *Arcadia* (1590), prose romance; *The Defense of Poesie* and *An Apology for Poetry* (both 1595), slightly different expositions of his critical tenets; *Astrophel and Stella* (1591), one of greatest English sonnet sequences, inspired by love for Penelope Devereux. He was a diplomat and an English foreign agent.

Sidney. 1 City (pop. 3,987), E Mont., in Yellowstone valley near N.Dak. line. Chief city of Lower Yellowstone project (estab. 1906). Beet sugar refining. **2** City (pop. 11,491), W Ohio, on Great Miami R. and N of Dayton; settled 1820. Machinery.

Sidney Sussex College: see CAMBRIDGE UNIVERSITY.

Sidon (sĭ'dŭn), anc. Phoenician city, seaport on the Mediterranean, modern Saida, Lebanon. It was famed for purple dyes and glassware. Continued important through Roman times.

Sidra, Gulf of (sĭ'drŭ), arm of the Mediterranean, indenting coast of Libya.

Siegbahn, Karl Manne Georg (kärl' mä'nŭ yā'ôryŭ sēg'bän), 1886–, Swedish physicist. Won 1924 Nobel Prize for method for precise measurement of X-ray wave lengths.

Siegen, Ludwig von (fŭn zē'gŭn), c.1609–1680, German engraver, b. Holland, inventor of mezzotint process of engraving.

Siegfried (sēg'frēd, Ger. zēk'frēt) or **Sigurd** (sĭ'gŭrd), great ideal hero of Germanic mythology. In the NIBELUNGENLIED, he is conqueror of Brunhild. His role is similar when he appears as Sigurd (Icelandic form) in the VOLSUNGASAGA. In Wagner's opera **Siegfried**, he kills the dragon Fafnir, gains the ring, and wins Brünnehilde.

Siena (sēĕ'nŭ, Ital. syā'nä), city (pop. 36,064), Tuscany, central Italy, one of richest art cities in Italy. Produces wine and marble. Its university was estab. 13th cent. A free commune by 12th cent., it developed into a wealthy republic, but in 1555 it fell to Emperor Charles V and passed to the Medici of Florence. Sienese art reached its zenith 13th–15th cent. The Sienese school of painting included Duccio di Buoninsegna, Simone Martini, and Pietro and Ambrogio Lorenzetti. The main square of Siena (the Piazza del Campo) is one of the marvels of medieval architecture. Here the Palio festival, a horse race of medieval origin, is still held. The cathedral, one of finest examples of Italian Gothic, has elaborate marble façade. The adjoining Piccolomini Library is adorned with Pinturicchio's frescoes. Siena was birthplace of St. Catherine of Siena.

Sienkiewicz, Henryk (hĕn'rĭk shēnkyĕ'vĭch), 1846–1916, Polish author. His novel of early Christianity, *Quo Vadis?* (1895; Eng. tr., 1896), had immense popular success. Among other novels is the trilogy *With Fire and Sword, The Deluge,* and *Pan Michael* (1883–88; Eng. tr., 1890–93), on 17th-cent. Poland's struggle for national existence. Won 1905 Nobel Prize in Literature.

Sierra, Justo (hōō'stō syĕ'rä), 1848–1912, Mexican educator and historian, largely responsible for intellectual renaissance in Mexico in early 20th cent.

Sierra Blanca (sēĕ'rŭ blăng'kŭ), village, W Texas. Rail junction in ranch region.

Sierra Blanca: see SANGRE DE CRISTO MOUNTAINS.

Sierra Leone (sēĕ'rŭ lēō'nē, lēōn'), British colony and protectorate (27,968 sq. mi.; pop. 1,858,275), W Africa, on the Atlantic; cap. Freetown. Colony consists mainly of small peninsula; area comprising protectorate has swamps, high savannas, and an arid plateau. Chief export crops are palm oil, cacao, and ginger. Iron, diamonds, and chromite are mined. Visited c.1462 by the Portuguese, who were followed by English slave traders. Settled in late 18th cent. by liberated slaves. Colony was created in 1808, protectorate in 1896.

Sierra Madre (sēĕ'rŭ mä'drā), city (pop. 7,273), S Calif., at foot of Mt. Wilson. Orange groves.

Sierra Madre (syĕ'rä mä'dhrā), chief mountain system of Mexico and greatest single geographic force in Mexican life. The **Sierra Madre Oriental** (ōryĕntäl') begins S of Rio Grande and runs 1,000 mi. roughly parallel to coast of Gulf of Mexico, ranging from 10 to 200 mi. inland. Reaches its highest elevation in ORIZABA peak (18,700 ft.), which belongs also to volcanic belt. This belt, which divides Mexico (E-W), also includes POPOCATEPETL and IXTACIHUATL. The **Sierra Madre Occidental** (ōk″sēdĕntäl′), parallels Pacific coast, extending SE from Ariz. The **Sierra Madre del Sur** (dĕl so͝or′) spreads over S Mexico between volcanic belt and Isthmus of Tehuantepec.

Sierra Madre, Rocky Mts.: see PARK RANGE.

Sierra Maestra (syĕ′rä mää′strä), mountain range, SE Cuba, rising abruptly from coast; rich in minerals. Turquino (alt. 6,560 ft.) is highest peak.

Sierra Morena (syĕ′rä mōrā′nä), mountain range, SW Spain. Highest peak is at 4,340 ft.

Sierra Nevada (syĕ′rä nāvä′dhä), chief mountain range of S Spain; c.60 mi. long. Highest peak of range and of Spain is Mulhacen (11,411 ft.).

Sierra Nevada (sēĕ′rů nůvä′dů), mountain range, E Calif., extending c.430 mi. NW from Tehachapi Pass, SE of Bakersfield, to gap S of LASSEN PEAK. E front has steep walls and rugged peaks; W face slopes into Sacramento and San Joaquin valleys. Mt. WHITNEY (14,495 ft.) is highest peak in U.S. (outside Alaska). Truckee Pass, N of Lake Tahoe, is best-known pass through the range. Snow-covered peaks feed W streams used for water power and irrigation in Calif. Range contains Yosemite, Sequoia, and Kings Canyon national parks.

Sierra Nevada de Mérida (syĕ′rä nāvä′dhä dā mā′rēdhä), mountain range, NW Venezuela, spur of Andes, beginning at Colombian border and extending 200 mi. NE to the Caribbean. From 30 to 50 mi. wide, it has snow-capped peaks over 15,000 ft. high.

Sieyès, Emmanuel Joseph (ĕmänüĕl′ zhôzĕf′ syāĕs′), 1748–1836, French revolutionary pamphleteer and statesman; originally a priest. Played a leading part in States-General of 1789; edited DECLARATION OF RIGHTS OF MAN and constitution of 1791; led in Thermidorian reaction after Robespierre's fall (1794); entered the Directory in 1799 and conspired with Bonaparte in coup d'état of 18 BRUMAIRE. Lived in exile at Brussels after 1815.

Sigebert (sĭ′gůbûrt), d. 575, Frankish king of Austrasia (561–75); husband of BRUNHILDA. When his brother, CHILPERIC I of Neustria, attacked Austrasia (573), Sigebert overran Neustria and was about to be proclaimed its king but was murdered by order of Chilperic's second wife, FREDEGUNDE.

Sigel, Franz (fränts′ sē′gůl), 1824–1902, Union general in Civil War, b. Germany. Fought in Mo. and at second battle of Bull Run. Briefly commanded Dept. of West Virginia (1864).

sight: see VISION.

Sigismund (sĭ′jĭsmůnd, sĭ′gĭs–), 1368–1437, emperor (crowned 1433) and German king. His marriage to Mary, daughter of Louis I of Hungary, brought him the Hungarian crown in 1387. He was elected German king in 1410, though his brother WENCESLAUS acknowledged his election only in 1411. Sigismund led a crusade against Bajazet I of Turkey, who routed him at Nikopol (1396). To heal the Great SCHISM, he joined with John XXIII in summoning the Council of CONSTANCE, where he also secured the condemnation and burning of John HUSS (although he had granted Huss a safe-conduct). When Wenceslaus died (1419) the Hussites bitterly opposed Sigismund's succession to the Bohemian crown. The HUSSITE WARS resulted. Sigismund had himself crowned at Prague (1420) but was repeatedly defeated and gained control over Bohemia only in 1436 through the aid of the UTRAQUISTS. His failure to keep his promises to the Czechs led to further disorders. The last emperor of the Luxemburg dynasty, he was succeeded by his son-in-law Albert II, a Hapsburg.

Sigismund, kings of Poland. **Sigismund I,** 1467–1548, reigned 1506–48. Estab. regular army and a fiscal system to maintain it; consented to double marriage contract arranged by his brother, ULADISLAUS II of Bohemia and Hungary (1515); accepted homage of ALBERT OF BRADENBURG for duchy of Prussia (1525). He and his queen, Bona Sforza, fostered the Polish Renaissance culture, which began to flower during his reign. Was succeeded by his son **Sigismund II** or **Sigismund Augustus,** 1520–72. His greatest accomplishment was the Union of Lublin (1569), which fused LITHUANIA and Poland into a single state. The dissolution of the Livonian Knights (1561) enabled him to acquire Courland and parts of Livonia, but he was drawn into war with Ivan IV of Russia, to whom he lost Polotsk (1563). He halted the growth of Protestantism by peaceful, tolerant means, introducing the Jesuits (1565) and favoring the Catholic Reform. Sigismund himself was an accomplished humanist and theologian. With his death the Jagiello dynasty was extinct in Poland. **Sigismund III,** 1566–1632, was the son of John III of Sweden and of Catherine, sister of Sigismund II of Poland. He was elected king of Poland in 1587, largely through the aid of Jan ZAMOJSKI; in 1592 he succeeded his father on the Swedish throne, but his staunch Catholicism brought him into conflict with his uncle (later CHARLES IX of Sweden), who defeated him at Stangebro (1598) and formally deposed him (1599). In 1621–29 he made war on his nephew, Gustavus II of Sweden, to whom he lost most of Livonia. He intervened in the Russian troubles which followed the appearance of the pretender DMITRI, but his army was expelled from Moscow and from Russia in 1612. His son Ladislaus IV succeeded him as king of Poland.

Siglufjord (sĭ′glo͞ofyôrd″), town (pop. 3,069), NE Iceland. Herring center.

Sigmaringen (zēk′märĭng″ůn), town (pop. 6,158), Württemberg-Hohenzollern, S Germany, on the Danube; cap. of HOHENZOLLERN until 1945. Has 16th-cent. castle (rebuilt 19th cent.).

Signac, Paul (pôl′ sēnyäk′), 1863–1935, French postimpressionist painter, known for Parisian scenes.

Signal Hill: see LONG BEACH, Calif.

sign language, substitute for normal language, not including letter-for-letter signaling. Celebrated sign languages by use of the hands have been developed by deaf-mutes, by Trappist monks, who have a rule of silence, and by Plains Indians, where speakers of mutually unintelligible languages communicated freely. Many languages have conventionalized body gestures (e.g., nodding), and some of these are highly elaborated to accompany or supplement speech.

Signorelli, Luca (lo͞o'kä sēnyōrĕl'lē), 1441?–1523, Italian painter of Umbrian school. Worked with his master, Piero della Francesca, on frescoes in San Francesco, Arezzo. Introduced powerful treatment of anatomy, as in *End of the World* (Orvieto), which influenced Michelangelo. His paintings in the Vatican were later sacrificed to make way for some of Raphael's work.

Sigourney, Lydia (Huntley) (sĭ'gûrnē), 1791–1865, American sentimental poet ("the sweet singer of Hartford") and author of edifying children's books.

Sigurd, Icelandic form of SIEGFRIED.

Sigurdsson, Jon (yōn' sĭ'khûrdhsōn), 1811–79, Icelandic statesman and historian. Leader in Copenhagen of Icelandic writers, scholars, and diplomats. Instrumental in securing constitution of Iceland (1874), and many reforms and institutions. President Icelandic Literary Society, he directed monumental studies in Icelandic history and literature, including *Diplomatarium Islandicum.*

Sikang (sē'kăng'), province (90,000 sq. mi.; pop. 2,000,000), SW China; cap. Yaan. Bounded on W by Tibet. Consists mainly of high mountains, cut by gorges of Yangtze, Yalung, and other rivers. Stock raising and hunting. In 1950 part of W Sikang became the Tibetan Autonomous Dist. (60,000 sq. mi.; pop. 700,000), with cap. at Kangting.

Sikeston, city (pop. 11,640), SE Mo., in the Mississippi plain WSW of Cairo, Ill.; laid out 1860. Processes and ships cotton.

Sikhs (sēks), religious community of India and Pakistan, numbering c.5,500,000 persons, mainly in the Punjab. Religion was founded by Nanak (b. 1469), first guru [Hindustani, = teacher], who taught a monotheistic creed and opposed maintenance of a priesthood and the caste system. The 10th and last guru, Govind Singh (b. 1666), welded the Sikhs into a military community which adopted the caste practices and polytheistic beliefs typical of Hinduism. He introduced the customs of wearing turbans and never cutting the hair. Each Sikh in the warrior caste took the name Singh [lion]. Greatest leader in early 19th cent. was RANJIT SINGH. See SIKH WARS.

Sikh Wars. By a treaty with the British in 1809, the Sikhs had accepted the Sutlej R. as S boundary of their domain. Fearing British conquest, they crossed the river in 1845 to attack the enemy. Defeated in 1846, they were forced to accept a protectorate and to cede Kashmir. Resentment caused an uprising in 1848; this was quelled in 1849 and resulted in British annexation of all Sikh territory.

Si-kiang, China: see WEST RIVER.

Sikkim (sĭ'kĭm), protectorate (2,745 sq. mi.; pop. 135,646) of India; cap. Gangtok. In Himalayas between India and Tibet. Inhabitants are pastoral nomads who speak Tibeto-Burman languages. Hinduism has the most numerous adherents, although Buddhism is the state religion. Ruled since 17th cent. by rajas of Tibetan descent. Under British protection 1890–1947. India assumed control 1949.

silage: see ENSILAGE.

Silas, early Christian, companion of Paul. Acts 15.22–18.5. Probably same as Silvanus of 2 Cor. 1.19; 1 Thess. 1.1; 2 Thess. 1.1.; 1 Peter 5.12.

Silenus (sīlē'nŭs), in Greek mythology, god of wine and fertility; son of Hermes. A jolly old man, he was friend and teacher of Dionysus.

Silesia (sīlē'zhŭ, sī–), Czech *Slezsko,* Ger. *Schlesien,* Pol. *Śląsk,* historic region, SE Germany, SW Poland, and N Czechoslovakia. Drained by the Oder, it is largely an agr. and forested lowland, except in the S, where it is occupied by the SUDETES. The S mountainous part is heavily industrialized, with coal, lignite, zinc, lead, and iron mines, steel mills, and textile mfg. Of its three political subdivisions, Czech Silesia, with Troppau as chief city, is much the smallest; it was part of Moravia and Silesia prov. until 1949, when the province was merged with Bohemia to form the Czech Lands. Polish Silesia consists of the KATOWICE industrial area and other former Prussian districts ceded to Poland in 1921 and of part of the former Austrian principality of TESCHEN. German Silesia (by far the largest part) was placed under Polish administration in 1945. It consists of the former Prussian provinces of Upper Silesia (cap. OPPELN) and Lower Silesia (cap. BRESLAU). Together, Polish and Polish-administered Silesia have an area of c.15,400 sq. mi. and a population of 4,764,500. Settled by Slavic tribes A.D. c.500, Silesia was part of Poland by the 11th cent. After 1200 it fell into several minor principalities, ruled by branches of the Polish PIAST dynasty who in 1335 accepted the kings of Bohemia as overlords. Most of Silesia became thoroughly Germanized. With the accession of the Hapsburgs on the Bohemian throne (1526), Silesia tended to become an Austrian province. The ducal title, along with the principalities of Brieg and Liegnitz, remained with the Piasts until their extinction in 1675, when they passed to the house of Austria. In 1740, on very shaky grounds, Frederick II of Prussia claimed parts of Silesia from Maria Theresa. The resulting Silesian Wars of 1740–42 and 1744–45 were part of the War of the AUSTRIAN SUCCESSION and ended in the cession of all but present Czech Silesia and Teschen to Prussia (treaties of Berlin and Dresden, 1742, 1745). Under the Treaty of Versailles, a plebiscite was held in 1921 which gave the predominantly Polish-speaking parts of Upper Silesia to Poland. After World War II the POTSDAM CONFERENCE allowed the transfer of German Silesia to Polish administration and the expulsion of the German population (in an "orderly and humane" manner) from all Silesia, pending a general peace with Germany. A small section W of the Neisse was incorporated with Saxony.

Silesian Wars: see AUSTRIAN SUCCESSION, WAR OF THE; SEVEN YEARS WAR.

Silesius, Angelus: see ANGELUS SILESIUS.

silica (sĭ'lĭkŭ), common name for silicon dioxide, widely and abundantly distributed. Occurs in many forms, e.g., in the different varieties of quartz, in sand, as a constituent of rocks, in the skeletal parts of certain animals and plants. It has many important uses, e.g., as an abrasive, in glass making, ceramics, and in preparation of Carborundum (silicon carbide).

silicate (sĭ'lĭkāt, –kĭt), compound containing silicon and oxygen combined with such metals as aluminum, barium, calcium, iron, magnesium, sodium, potassium. Silicates are widely distributed and include many familiar substances, e.g., asbestos, feldspar, talc, clay, emerald, garnet, beryl.

silicon (sĭ'lĭkŭn), nonmetallic element (symbol = Si; see also ELEMENT, table). Has two allotropic forms. Resembles carbon chemically. Very abundant, makes up large part of earth's crust; occurs in silica and silicates, but not uncombined. Used in making low-carbon steel, in alloys to add hardness and resistance to corrosion. Silicones, alternating chains of silicon and oxygen, are used to make silicone rubber, liquids used in hydraulic systems of airplanes, and varnishes.

silicon carbide, hard crystalline compound of silicon and carbon, used as an abrasive. Trade names include Carborundum and Crystolon.

silicosis (sĭlĭkō'sĭs), occupational disease caused by excessive inhalation of rock dust or sand particles high in silica. Silica causes inflammation of lungs and growth of fibrous tissue; victims are susceptible to tuberculosis. National publicity resulted when workers constructing tunnel (begun 1929) at Gauley Bridge, W.Va., died from disease.

silk, fine, horny, translucent, yellowish fiber produced by the SILKWORM in making its cocoon. The silkworm of commerce is the larva of *Bombyx mori,* the mulberry silkworm; wild silk, woven into Shantung or pongee, is produced by the tussah worm of India and China, a feeder on oaks. Silkworm culture and silk weaving began in remote ages in China and spread A.D. c.550 to Byzantium and thence over Europe and North Africa. In silk manufacture, the cocoon, after steaming or soaking to soften the gum that covers the fiber, is unwound, several strands of filament being reeled together to make a thread. A cocoon may yield 2,000–3,000 ft. of filament. Other steps in preparation include doubling and twisting the thread to form yarn, removing the remaining gum, bleaching when needed, dyeing (in yarn or the piece), and sometimes weighting fabric by loading with metallic salts, as of tin. Silk is woven into innumerable fabrics, from airy gauzes to heavy plushes and velvets.

Silkeborg (sĭl'kŭbôr"), city (pop. 23,372), E central Jutland, Denmark, on Guden R. Health resort among woods and lakes.

silkworm, larva of various moth species of Asia and Africa. Now raised for silk in most of temperate zone. Matures 32–38 days after hatching from tiny egg, then attaches self to twig to spin cocoon from secretion emitted from lip. See also SILK. See *ill.*, p. 601.

Sill, Edward Rowland, 1841–87, American poet, best known for two didactic lyrics—"The Fool's Prayer" and "Opportunity."

Sill, Fort, U.S. military reservation, estab. 1869 near Lawton, Okla. Reservation also used for Indians, and formerly fort was stronghold against Indian uprisings. Tribes trained in agr.; Geronimo, Satanta, and others imprisoned here. Lessened in importance until made field artillery school 1911. Two world wars made it important.

Sillanpää, Frans Eemil (fräns' ā'mĭl sĭl'-lämpă"), 1888–, Finnish author of novels that are masterpieces of lyrical impressionism (e.g., *Meek Heritage,* 1919; *The Maid Silja,* 1931). Awarded 1939 Nobel Prize in Literature.

Sillery (Fr. sēyürē'), city (pop. 10,376), S Que., Canada, on St. Lawrence R., SW suburb of Quebec.

silo (sī'lō), watertight, airtight storage tank for ensilage, either pitlike or cylindrical in shape.

Siloam (sīlō'ŭm), pool, SE of Jerusalem, in Kidron valley. Connected with Virgin's Pool by 1,700-ft. tunnel; undated inscription (found 1880) describes digging of tunnel. Jesus put clay on a blind man's eye and told him to wash it off at Siloam, thus curing him. John 9.7. Also Shiloah and Siloah.

Siloam Springs (sī'lōm), city (pop. 3,270), NW Ark., in the Ozarks near Okla. line. Resort, with mineral springs. Baptist campgrounds here.

Silone, Ignazio (ēnyä'tsyō sēlō'nā), 1900–, Italian author, whose real name is Secondo Tranquilli. An anti-Fascist, he fled Italy in 1931 and returned in 1944. Well known are his novels *Fontamara* (1933) and *Pane e vino* (1937; Eng. tr., *Bread and Wine,* 1936).

silt, earth particles finer than sand but coarser than clay, produced by weathering. When consolidated into rock, silt becomes shale.

Silurian period (sĭlōō'rēŭn), third period of the PALEOZOIC ERA of geologic time. Continents were about the same as in Ordovician period. In North America the main event was flooding of interior basin from north and deposition of Niagaran limestone, best seen at the falls. Desert conditions seem to have followed, with extensive salt deposits. Economic resources of Silurian strata include salt, iron ore, quartz sandstone. Primitive fish increased in the sea; on land, scorpions appeared, possibly the first animals to take oxygen from the air. See also GEOLOGY, table.

Silva, Antonio José da (äntô'nyō zhōōzā' dä sēl'vŭ), 1705–39, Brazilian-Portuguese playwright; known as *o Judeo* [the Jew].

Silva, José Asunción (hōsā' äsōōnsyōn' sēl'vä), 1865–96, Colombian poet, one of creators of *modernismo.* Well-known poem is "Nocturno III." Morbidly sensitive and pessimistic, he committed suicide at 31.

silver, metallic element (symbol = Ag; see also ELEMENT, table). It is nearly white, lustrous, soft, ductile, malleable, and a good conductor of heat and electricity. Chemically it is not active. At ordinary temperatures it unites with sulphur (tarnishes) to form the sulphide. Its halogen compounds are used in photography because of their light sensitivity. Silver nitrate is used in medicine either in solution or in fused sticklike form (lunar caustic); in indelible inks; for silvering mirrors; as a reagent. Occurs uncombined in ores; greatest amount is obtained in refining of lead and copper. Much silver is used in making coins and silver plate, utensils, jewelry, and other products.

Silver City, town (pop. 7,022) SW N.Mex., near Ariz. line. Trade and shipping point for mines (esp. copper), stock ranches, and irrigated farms. Health resort. Flourished as silver- and gold-mining camp in late 1800s. Near by is Gila Cliff Dwellings Natl. Monument.

silver nitrate: see SILVER.

Silver Purchase Act: see SHERMAN SILVER PURCHASE ACT.

Silver Springs, spring, N central Fla., E of Ocala, with outlet to Oklawaha R. Basin is 80 ft. deep; flow is c.25,000,000 gal. per hour.

Silvester: see SYLVESTER.

Silvretta (sĭlvrĕ'tů, Ger. zĭlvrĕ'tä), Alpine group at Swiss-Austrian border. Highest peak is Piz Linard (11,200 ft.), in Grisons canton, Switzerland.

Simbirsk, RSFSR: see ULYANOVSK.

Simcoe, John Graves (sĭm'kō), 1752–1806, British army officer, first governor of Upper Canada.

Simcoe, town (pop. 7,269), S Ont., Canada, on Lynn R. and SW of Hamilton. Center in agr. area with canneries and woolen and lumber mills.

Simcoe, Lake, 28 mi. long, 26 mi. wide, S Ont., Canada, N of Toronto. Drains N through L. Couchiching and Severn R. to Georgian Bay, forming part of TRENT CANAL system. Resort area.

Simeon, tsars of Bulgaria. **Simeon I,** d. 927, reigned 893–927. An extremely warlike ruler, he twice threatened Constantinople (913, 924), conquered most of Serbia, and, with papal consent, took the title tsar. Under his rule the first Bulgarian empire reached its greatest power. Simeon also was an able scholar and fostered Old Slavonic literature. **Simeon II,** 1937–, succeeded his father Boris III in 1943, under a regency. He went into exile in 1946, when the monarchy was abolished.

Simeon. 1 Son of Jacob and ancestor of one of the 12 tribes of Israel. Tribe settled in S Palestine. Gen. 29.33; 34; 49.5–7; Joshua 19. **2** Devout man who blessed the infant Jesus at the Temple. Luke 2.21–34. In Acts 15.14 Simeon appears for Simon, referring to St. Peter.

Simeon Stylites, Saint (stīlī'tēz) [Gr.,= of a pillar], d. 459?, Syrian hermit, who lived many years on a platform atop a pillar. Feast: Jan. 5.

Simferopol (sēmfyĭrô'půl), city (pop. 142,678), cap. of Crimea, RSFSR, on Salgir R., in orchard, vineyard, and tobacco region. Food processing. It occupies site of an ancient Scythian cap. and of Greek colony Neapolis. Old part of city retains Oriental aspect.

simile: see METAPHOR.

Simla (sĭm'lů), town (pop. 18,348; alt. 7,100 ft.) cap. of Himachal Pradesh, India; resort in Himalayas. Formerly summer cap. of India (1867–1947).

Simmons College: see BOSTON, Mass.

Simms, William Gilmore, 1806–70, American novelist; a prolific writer, best remembered for historical romances of S.C., such as *Guy Rivers* (1834), *The Yemassee,* and *The Partisan* (both 1835).

Simnel, Lambert (sĭm'nůl), fl. 1486–1525, English impostor. Impersonating Edward, earl of Warwick (then confined in tower by Henry VII), he was, with Yorkist support, crowned at Dublin (1486) as Edward VI. Returning to England, he and supporters were defeated by royal forces. Simnel was pardoned.

Simoïs (sĭ'mōĭs), small river, NW Turkey; a tributary of the SCAMANDER. Scene of legendary events in siege of Troy.

Simon, in Bible. **1** One of the MACCABEES. **2** Or **Simon Peter:** see PETER, SAINT. **3** or **Saint Simon,** one of the Twelve Apostles. Called the Canaanite or Cananaean or Zelotes, terms which may mean he was a member of the ZEALOTS. Mat. 10.4; Mark 3.18; Luke 6.15; Acts 1.13. Feast: Oct. 28. **4** Leper in whose home a woman anointed Jesus' feet. He may have been father of Lazarus. **5** See SIMON OF CYRENE. **6** See SIMON MAGUS.

Simonides of Ceos (sĭmŏ'nĭdēz, sē'ŏs), c.556–468? B.C., Greek lyric poet; rival of Pindar at Syracuse. Among the ancients a classic example of moderation in all things, he wrote masterful verse in an epigrammatic manner; two of his finest epitaphs are on Marathon and Thermopylae.

Simon Magus (mā'gůs), Samaritan sorcerer who tried to buy spiritual power from the apostles, hence the term *simony.* Acts 8.9–24.

Simon of Cyrene (sīrē'nē), bystander forced to carry Jesus' cross. Mat. 27.32; Mark 15.21; Luke 23.26.

Simonov, Konstantin (kŭnstůntyĕn' sē'můnůf), 1915–, Russian author. Wrote *Days and Nights* (1945; Eng. tr., 1945), a novel on the defense of Stalingrad in World War II. His anti-American play *The Russian Question* (1947) won the Stalin Prize.

Simon Peter: see PETER, SAINT.

Simons, Walter (väl'tůr zē'môns), 1861–1937, German foreign minister (1920–21) and president of supreme court (1922–29). Outstanding authority on international law.

Simonson, Lee, 1888–, American scenic artist. Associated with Washington Square Players, 1915–17, and with Theatre Guild as director, 1919–40.

Simonstown (sī'můnz–), town (pop. 7,315), SW Cape Prov., South Africa, on the Atlantic; major British naval base (estab. 1814).

simoom or **simoon:** see SANDSTORM.

Simplon (sĭm'plŏn"; sēplō'), pass, 6,589 ft. high, over Pennine Alps. Crossed by **Simplon Road,** built by Napoleon 1800–1806. Simplon RR passes through **Simplon Tunnel** (alt. 2,313 ft.), longest in world (12¼ mi.). Opened 1906, tunnel crosses Swiss-Italian border.

Simpson, Sir George, 1792–1860, governor of Hudson's Bay Co. in Canada and traveler, b. Scotland. Made famous "overland" trip around world (1841–42).

Simpson, Sir James Young, 1811–70, Scottish obstetrician, first to use general anesthetic in childbirth (1847).

Simpson College: see INDIANOLA, Iowa.

Sims, James Marion, 1813–83, American surgeon, specialist in diseases of women.

Founded Woman's Hospital in New York city (1855).

Sims, William S(owden), 1858–1936, American admiral. In World War I he commanded American operations in European waters (1917–18).

Simsbury, town (pop. 4,822), Conn., NW of Hartford; settled 1660. Westminster School for boys and Ethel Walker School for girls are here.

Sin, wilderness through which the Israelites wandered after leaving Egypt. Ex. 16.1.

sin, in religion, unethical act in disobedience to a personal God. Among the ancient Jews there was besides personal sin the concept of national sin (usually idolatry). Except for original sin (which in Christian thought is the evil universally inherent in man since the fall of Adam, to be removed by baptism), Christians and Moslems have no idea of collective sin. Some Christians hold that all acts are good, indifferent, or sinful, others that there are no indifferent acts, only good or sinful. In Roman Catholic doctrine, a mortal sin is one committed with full knowledge and deliberate intent in a serious matter; others are venial. The seven deadly or capital sins are pride, covetousness, lust, anger, gluttony, envy, and sloth. The sins that cry out to heaven for vengeance are willful murder, the sin of Sodom, oppression of the poor, and defrauding a laborer of his wages. The "sin of angels" is pride.

Sinai (sī'nī, sī'nēī), triangular peninsula, E Egypt, extending from its broad base on the Mediterranean to Red Sea, whose two arms bound it on W (Gulf of Suez) and on E (Gulf of Aqaba). In S is Jebel Musa [Arabic,= mount of Moses] or Mt. Sinai. On its slope is the famed Greek Orthodox monastery of St. Catherine, founded c.250. Here in 19th cent. was found the Codex Sinaiticus, one of the oldest manuscripts of the New Testament. Produces manganese, iron, and oil.

Sinaja (sēnī'ä), town (pop. 6,531), S central Rumania, in Walachia. Health and winter sports resort in Transylvanian Alps. Former summer residence of Rumanian kings. One of two former royal palaces contains noted art collection.

Sinaloa (sēnälō'ä), state (22,582 sq. mi.; pop. 618,439), NW Mexico, on Gulf of California and the Pacific; cap. CULIACÁN. Various crops are produced on its fertile land, but mining of gold, silver, and copper is most important occupation. Has only one port of importance, MAZATLÁN. Culiacán was important in colonial period. Sinaloa and Sonora were made separate states in 1830.

Sinan (sĭnän'), 1489?–1578?, outstanding Moslem architect. Masterpieces are mosque of Selim I at Adrianople and mosque of Suleiman I at Istanbul.

Sinclair, May, 1865?–1946, English novelist. Wrote *The Divine Fire* (1904). *Mary Olivier* (1919) is among first examples of stream-of-consciousness technique.

Sinclair, Upton, 1878–, American novelist and socialist. His many novels voice social protest, as in *The Jungle* (1906) and *Boston* (1928). His social studies such as *The Brass Check* (1919) are impressive. Political adventure novels in "Lanny Budd" series, begun in 1940, have attracted wide audiences.

Sind (sĭnd) province (50,443 sq. mi.; pop. 4,619,000), W Pakistan, on Arabian Sea; cap. Hyderabad. Grain and fruit are grown in areas irrigated by the Indus. At MOHENJO-DARO in NW are remains of an ancient civilization. Sind was converted to Islam after its conquest by Arabs in 8th cent. Taken 1843 by the British, until 1937 administered as part of Bombay.

Sindhi (sĭn'dē), modern language of Indic group of Indo-Iranian subfamily of Indo-European languages. See LANGUAGE (table).

Sinding, Christian (sĭn'dĭng), 1856–1941, Norwegian composer of the opera *Der heilige Berg* [the holy mountain]; orchestral and chamber music; and piano pieces, including the popular *Rustle of Spring.*

Singapore (sĭng'gŏpôr), city (pop. 679,659), on Singapore island (217 sq. mi.; pop. 938,-144), off S tip of Malay Peninsula. A great commercial center and major British naval base in Far East. Island was ceded 1824 to the British by sultan of Johore. A principal founder of modern city was T. Stamford RAFFLES. Development of Malaya under British rule made Singapore a leading port for export of tin and rubber. Inhabited mainly by Chinese. Although considered the key point in defense of SE Asia, island was quickly taken in final phase of Japan's Malaya campaign, Feb., 1945, in World War II. Part of the STRAITS SETTLEMENTS colony until 1946, it is now a crown colony, which includes Christmas Isl. in Indian Ocean.

Singer, Isaac Merrit, 1811–75, American inventor. In 1851 he patented a practical sewing machine and subsequently became a leading manufacturer. He later patented many improvements.

Singhalese (sĭng'gŭlēz) or **Sinhalese** (sĭn'-hŭlēz), language of Ceylon, belonging to Indic group of Indo-Iranian subfamily of Indo-European languages. See LANGUAGE (table).

single tax, tax derived from economic rent. It is based on the doctrine that land is the source of all wealth. See PHYSIOCRATS and Henry GEORGE.

Sing Sing: see OSSINING, N.Y.

Sinhalese: see SINGHALESE.

Sinkiang (shĭn'jyäng'), province (700,000 sq. mi.; pop. 4,000,000) NW China; cap. Urumchi. Largest province of China. Bounded on S by Tibet and Kashmir, on W and NW by USSR. Roughly coextensive with Chinese Turkistan; consists of Dzungaria tableland and Taklamakan Desert. Dominant element in population is Turkic Uigurs. Products include cotton, silk, and grain. Region was ruled successively by Uigurs and Mongols before its annexation by China in 18th cent.

Sinn Fein (shĭn'fān') [Irish,= we, ourselves], Irish nationalistic movement which triumphed in establishment of Irish Free State (see IRELAND). Founded 1899 by Arthur GRIFFITH, advocate of an economically and politically self-sufficient Ireland. Started with passive resistance to British. After Home Rule Bill (1912) and tension between Ulster and S Ireland, it aided Patrick PEARSE in Easter Rebellion (1916). Suppression of rebellion and Ireland's military occupation aided Sinn Fein, under leadership of DE VALERA. It set up Irish assembly called DÁIL ÉIREANN which declared independence. The resulting disorders (extremists led by Michael Collins) were suppressed violently by British military irregulars known as Black and Tans. Continued resistance led to negotiations for Irish Free State. After period of civil war, De Valera became president 1932. With outlaw of Irish Republican army, Sinn Fein virtually ended.

Sinnott, Edmund W(are) (sĭ'nŭt), 1888–, American botanist, known especially for research in plant morphology, morphogenesis, and genetics. After serving as professor of botany at Barnard, Columbia, and Yale he became director of the Sheffield Scientific School (1945) and dean of the graduate school (1950) at Yale.

Sino-Japanese War: see CHINO-JAPANESE WAR.

Sinope (sĭnō'pē), anc. city of Asia Minor, on the Black Sea. Rose to commercial and political importance after 7th cent. B.C. One of its exports, cinnabar, is named for Sinope. Sinope fell to kings of Pontus in 2d cent. B.C. and became their cap.; was taken by Romans under Lucullus in Third Mithridatic War (74–63 B.C.); reached a great prosperity under Roman and later under Byzantine rule; declined after its capture by Seljuk Turks (13th cent.). Modern Turkish town of Sinop (pop. 5,780) has excellent harbor but poor land communications.

Sintra, Portugal: see CINTRA.

Sinuiju (sēn'ōō'ē'jōō), city (1944 pop. 118,414), N Korea, on Yalu R., opposite Antung, China.

Sion (sī'ŭn), in Bible: see ZION; HERMON, MOUNT.

Sion (syõ), Ger. *Sitten,* town (pop. 11,031), cap. of VALAIS canton, Switzerland, on the Rhone. Episcopal see since 6th cent. Hydroelectric station.

Siouan (sōō'ŭn), linguistic family of North America. One of most widely distributed of American Indian stocks, Siouan stock includes languages spoken from Gulf of Mexico to Saskatchewan, mainly on Great Plains and W prairies. See LANGUAGE (table).

Sioux City, city (pop. 83,991), NW Iowa, at junction of Big Sioux and Floyd rivers with the Missouri; settled 1848. Second largest city of state, it is shipping, trade, and industrial center for agr. and livestock area. Has railroad shops and mfg. of food and clay products and machinery. Seat of Morningside Col.

Sioux Falls, city (pop. 52,696), SE S.Dak., on Big Sioux R. and N of Sioux City, Iowa; founded 1857, abandoned 1862, resettled 1865 when Fort Dakota was estab. Largest city in state, it is trade, industrial, and shipping center for agr. area; processes foodstuffs. Seat of Augustana Col. (Lutheran; coed.; opened 1860 as seminary in Chicago, chartered 1865; had various names and sites as it followed Norwegian pioneers W); a Swedish section split off and founded Augustana Col. and Theological Seminary (1869), at Rock Island, Ill.

Sioux Indians (sōō) or **Dakota Indians** (dŭkō'tŭ), seven North American tribes of Siouan linguistic stock, the largest and most important being the Teton. They were driven (17th cent.) by the Ojibwa from the Great Lakes region to the N Great Plains and the prairies. They had a typical Plains culture, mainly dependent on the horse and the buffalo hunt. Their hostility to Americans grew as settlers came into their lands, and Little Crow led a band of Sioux in a massacre of whites in Minn. in 1862. The Sioux agreed (1867) to retire to a reservation. This was invaded by Black Hills gold prospectors, and in 1874 began the Sioux wars that were notably marked by the defeat of Custer (1876). The troubles did not fully end until the expedition under Nelson A. Miles (1890–91).

Siqueiros, David Alfaro (dävēdh' älfä'rō sēkā'rōs), 1898–, Mexican painter. Figured in revolutionary political movements. Best known for murals and frescoes, he uses his art as a means of social protest. Uses swirling brushwork and striking contrasts of light and dark.

Sirach (sī'rŭk), father of the author of Ecclesiasticus, which is sometimes called Sirach.

Siren, in Greek mythology, one of three sea nymphs, whose sweet song lured men to shipwreck on rocky coast where they lived. Argonaut heroes were saved by music of Orpheus. Odysseus escaped by tying himself to the mast and stopping ears of his men.

Sir Roger de Coverley: see ROGER DE COVERLEY.

sisal hemp (sī'sŭl), cordage fiber obtained from the leaves of the sisal hemp plant, a tropical agave (*Agave sisalana*). It is second only to Manila hemp in strength and value. Henequen, a fiber from *A. fourcroydes,* is also called sisal hemp, and is used to make binder twine, chiefly in Yucatan.

Sisera (sĭ'sŭrŭ), Canaanite captain, defeated by Deborah and Barak, murdered by Jael. Judges 4.5.

Sisley, Alfred (älfrĕd' sēslā'), 1839–99, French impressionist painter, b. Paris, of English parents. Known for sunny landscapes, e.g., *The Banks of the Loing.*

Sismondi, Jean Charles Léonard Simonde de (zhã' shärl' lāônär' sēmõd' dŭ sēsmõdē'), 1773–1842, Swiss historian. Major work *History of the Italian Republics in the Middle Ages* (16 vols., 1809–18).

Sisters of Charity, name given several communities of Roman Catholic nuns devoted to work in schools, hospitals, and charitable institutions. Most of them stem from the work of the institute founded (1633) by St. VINCENT DE PAUL.

Sistine Chapel (sĭs'tēn), private chapel of the popes in Rome, one of the glories of the Vatican. Built 1473 for Pope Sixtus IV. Famous for its decorations, notably Michelangelo's frescoes of Old Testament scenes on vaulted ceiling and his *Last Judgment* on end wall. On side walls are frescoes by Perugino, Pinturicchio, Botticelli, and Ghirlandaio. Collection of illuminated music manuscripts is in archives of the choir.

Sisyphus (sĭ'sĭfŭs), in Greek mythology, king of Corinth. Zeus, angered by his disrespect, condemned him to push a heavy rock up a steep hill forever.

Sitka (sĭt'kŭ), town (pop. 1,985), SE Alaska, on Baranof Isl., in Alexander Archipelago.

Founded 1799 as New Archangel by Aleksandr Baranov. Destroyed by Indians 1802, rebuilt, renamed, and made Baranov's hq. 1804. U.S. officially took possession of Alaska from Russia here, 1867. Remained cap. of Alaska until 1900. Harbor dominated by Mt. Edgecumbe. Fishing, canning, and lumbering. Naval station since 1940. Has Sitka Natl. Monument and Russian Orthodox Cathedral of St. Michael (1844).

Sitka National Monument: see NATIONAL PARKS AND MONUMENTS (table).

Sitten, Switzerland: see SION.

Sitter, Willem de (vĭ'lŭm dŭ sĭ'tŭr), 1872–1934, Dutch astronomer and mathematician. Proposed theory of expanding universe.

Sitting Bull, d. 1890, Indian chief, Sioux leader in battle of the Little Bighorn, in which G. A. CUSTER and his force were killed.

Sitwell, Edith (sĭt'wŭl), 1887–, English poet and critic. Her poetry is collected in *The Canticle of the Rose, 1917–1949* (1949). Her criticism includes *Aspects of Modern Poetry* (1934) and *A Poet's Notebook* (1943). She wrote *Twentieth Century Harlequinade* (1916) with her brother **Sir Osbert Sitwell,** 1892–, poet and novelist. Among his works are *Selected Poems* (1943); *Before the Bombardment* (1926), a novel; and his remarkable autobiographical family history in several volumes. Another brother, **Sacheverell Sitwell** (sŭshĕ'vŭrŭl), 1900–, is also a poet and an art critic. His verse includes *Dr. Donne and Gargantua* (1930). He has also written histories of art, e.g., *The Gothick North* (1929), *British Architects and Craftsmen* (1945), and biographies.

Siva: see HINDUISM.

Sivas (sĭväs'), city (pop. 52,269), central Turkey, on the Kizil Irmak. Trade center. Cement and rug mfg. Copper mines near by. Known as Sebaste, Sebastia, or Cabira in ancient times. Here in 1919 Kemal Ataturk began nationalist revolution. Has many fine relics of medieval Moslem art.

Sivash Sea (sēväsh') or **Putrid Sea,** salt lagoon, area c.1,000 sq. mi., RSFSR, along NE coast of Crimea. Separated—except at Genichesk Strait—from Sea of Azov by Arabat land tongue, from Black Sea by Perekop Isthmus.

Siward (sū'ŭrd), d. 1055, earl of Northumberland in England. Danish warrior, he probably came with Canute. Supported Edward the Confessor against Earl Godwin (1051); defeated (1054) Macbeth, Scottish king, for his nephew (later Malcolm III).

Sixtus IV, 1414–84, pope (1471–84), an Italian named Francesco della Rovere, a Franciscan. He struggled with Louis XI over control of the Church in France and Louis's attempts to interfere in Naples. A quarrel with Lorenzo de' Medici was embittered when a nephew of Sixtus led the PAZZI CONSPIRACY (1478), and Sixtus waged war on Florence. He consented to the establishment of the Spanish Inquisition. Although he was a politician and a nepotist, he was a good administrator. Founded the Sistine Chapel.

Sixtus V, 1521–90, pope (1585–90), an Italian named Felice Peretti, a Franciscan and a zealous preacher. He was sent to Spain to look into accusations against the archbishop of Toledo (1565) and there fell out with his companion, later Gregory XIII. Cardinal Peretti lived in retirement for a time, editing the works of St. Ambrose. He then succeeded Gregory, administered the Papal States and the Church well, and beautified Rome. He set the maximum number of cardinals at 70.

Sixtus of Bourbon-Parma, Prince, 1886–1934, son of Robert, last duke of Parma. Served in Belgian army in World War I. Served as intermediary for his brother-in-law, Charles I of Austria-Hungary, in Charles's secret quest for a separate peace (1917).

Sjaelland, Denmark: see ZEALAND.

Skagen (skä'gŭn), town (pop. 6,446), N Jutland, Denmark; a port on the Kattegat. Fisheries. Also known in English as the Skaw.

Skagerrak (skă'gŭrăk), strait, 80–90 mi. wide, between Norway and Denmark, stretching NE from North Sea and continued SE by the KATTEGAT. For battle of the Skagerrak, see JUTLAND, BATTLE OF.

Skagit (skă'jĭt), river, rising in Cascade Range, B.C., Canada, and flowing 163 mi. SW through Wash. to Puget Sound. Seattle owns three power dams (Diablo, Ross, Gorge) on upper Skagit.

Skagway (skăg'wā"), city (pop. 758), SE Alaska, at head of Lynn Canal and NNW of Juneau. At foot of White Pass, it was gateway to the Klondike in 1897–98 gold rush. Trade and tourist center and coastal terminus of White Pass and Yukon Railway.

Skanderbeg: see SCANDERBEG.

Skane, Swed. *Skåne* (skō'nŭ), historic province of extreme S Sweden; chief city Malmo. Was held by Denmark until conquest by Charles X of Sweden (1658). Has prehistoric remains, medieval castles, manors.

Skaneateles, N.Y.: see FINGER LAKES.

skating, gliding on ice surface on skates. Earliest skates were made of bone. Iron skates introduced in 17th cent., steel skates first produced in 1850s. English books contain references to skating as early as 12th cent. **Roller skating,** gliding on smooth surface on skates with rollers or wheels, dates from 1860s. Ballbearing skate wheel invented in 1880s.

Skaw, the, Denmark: see SKAGEN.

Skeat, W(alter) W(illiam), 1835–1912, English philologist. A scholar of Old English and Anglo-Saxon, he founded English Dialect Society in 1873. He edited many early English works.

Skeena (skē'nŭ), river of W B.C., Canada, rising in Stikine Mts. and flowing 360 mi. S and SW to Hecate Strait of the Pacific, SE of Prince Rupert.

skeleton, supporting or protective structure in animals. In invertebrate animals it is chiefly outside of body and is called an exoskeleton e.g., shell of a clam); in vertebrates it is within the body and called an endoskeleton. In adult human, skeleton is a bony and cartilaginous framework of c.200 bones (plus 6 ear bones). Axial skeleton includes skull, SPINAL COLUMN, ribs (12 pairs), breast bone. Bones of arms and legs called appendicular skeleton. See *ill.*, p. 763.

Skelton, John, 1460?–1529, English poet and

clergyman, best known for satires largely against clergy, such as *The Bowge of Court* (1499), *Colin Clout* (1522), and *Why Come Ye Not to Court?* (c.1522). His short-lined, alliterative verses with insistent rhymes are called Skeltonics.

Skiddaw (skĭd'ô), mountain, 3,054 ft. high, Cumberland, England, in the Lake District near Keswick.

Skidmore College: see SARATOGA SPRINGS, N.Y.

skin, body covering composed of epidermis made up of layers of similar cells from which dried cells are shed, and underlayer or dermis containing blood capillaries, nerve endings, sweat glands, hair follicles, and sebaceous glands. Functions include protection, heat regulation, secretion, excretion, and sensation.

Skinner, Otis, 1858–1942, American actor. Was extremely popular in such plays as *Kismet* (1911) and *Blood and Sand* (1921) and in Shakspere. His daughter, **Cornelia Otis Skinner,** 1901–, is an actress and author, particularly noted for her monologues.

Skobelev, Mikhail Dmitreyevich (mēkhŭyēl' dŭmē'trēŭvĭch skô'bĭlyĭf), 1843–82, Russian general. Led expedition to Kokand (1875–76) and march to Geok-Tepe (1881), which completed conquest of Turkistan.

Skokie (skō'kē), village (pop. 14,832), NE Ill., N suburb of Chicago; called Niles Center until 1940.

Skoplje (skôp'ŭlyŭ), Macedonian *Skopje,* city (pop. 91, 557), cap. of Yugoslav Macedonia, S Yugoslavia, on Vardar R. Orthodox metropolitan see. University. Was scene of Stephen Dushan's coronation as tsar of Serbia (1346). Has medieval bridge, cathedral, mosques, and citadel; Oriental bazaar. Its Turkish name was Üsküb.

Skowhegan (skouhē'gĭn), town (pop. 7,422), including Skowhegan village (pop. 6,183), central Maine, on Kennebec R. above Waterville. Mfg. of textiles, shoes, and boats. Vacationists' supply point. Lakewood resort, with summer theater (1901), is near.

skull, bony framework of head, consisting of cranial bones and facial bones. In man, bones of cranium are occipital, parietal, temporal, frontal, ethmoid, sphenoid. Those of face are lachrymal, nasal, palatine, inferior turbinates, maxillary (upper jaw), malar (zygoma or cheek bones), vomer, and mandible (lower jaw). Brain is encased in bones of cranium and communicates with spinal cord through an opening (*foramen magnum*) at base of skull. Certain areas of cranial bones are not completely ossified at birth; these soft areas, called fontanels, close at different ages, but all are normally completely ossified by second year. See *ill.,* p. 763.

skunk, carnivorous, nocturnal mammal of weasel family. Common or striped skunk (*Mephitis*) of U.S., N Mexico, and Canada has thick black fur and two white stripes on the back, and is c.2 ft. long including the bushy tail. It destroys insect pests. Protected by ability to spray offensive-smelling oily liquid from vents under tail.

skunk cabbage, early spring-blooming, rank-odored perennial (*Symplocarpus foetidus*) found in wet places in North America. Flower is enclosed in a low cowl-shaped dark red spathe. Yellow skunk cabbage of W U.S. (*Lysichitum americanum*) is similar.

Skutari, Turkey: see SCUTARI.

sky, apparent dome over earth, background of celestial bodies and atmospheric phenomena. Blue color results from selective scattering of light waves by minute particles of dust and vapor in atmosphere. Since shorter rays (blues) are scattered most readily, sky appears bluest when dust particles are few and small.

Skye (skī), island (with surrounding islets 428,998 acres; pop. 9,908), off NW Scotland, in Inverness-shire, one of Inner Hebrides. Has hilly terrain with many lochs. Sheep and cattle raising and fishing are main occupations. Cap. Portree.

Skye terrier: see TERRIER.

skylark, Old World bird famous for spirited song as it soars into air. Upper parts are brown streaked with black, and under parts are light with black streaks on breast. It is the subject of Shelley's "To a Skylark."

Skyros (skē'rŏs, skī'rŭs) or **Scyros** (sī'rŭs), Aegean island (81 sq. mi.; pop. 3,395), Greece, E of Euboea; largest of N Cyclades. Marble quarries; fishing; sponge diving. In ancient legend, Thetis concealed her son Achilles here in woman's attire and Theseus was killed here. Rupert Brooke is buried on Skyros.

skyscraper, building of great height, constructed on a steel skeleton, a purely modern and almost exclusively American type of structure. The birthplace of early skyscrapers was Chicago, where William Le Baron Jenney built the 10-story Home Insurance Bldg. (1883), generally considered to be the first skyscraper. In New York, the Flatiron Bldg. was built 1902, Metropolitan Life Insurance Tower 1909, and Woolworth Bldg. 1913. Tallest skyscraper in the world is EMPIRE STATE BUILDING.

skywriting, controlled emission of thick smoke by aircraft aloft to form message visible below. Engine heat turns light paraffin oil into white smoke exhausted under pressure, with added patented oil compound causing smoke particles to adhere. Invented by J. C. Savage of England (1922).

slaked lime: see LIME.

slander: see LIBEL AND SLANDER.

slang, novel, ostensibly careless, more or less humorous language. In colloquial standard English, slang has been a feature for more than a century, mainly consisting of faddish tricks of vocabulary. Yet some of the expressions have passed into ordinary vocabulary (e.g., "O.K.").

Slankamen (släng-kä'mĕn), village, N Serbia, Yugoslavia, where the imperials under Margrave Louis of Baden routed the Turks in 1691. Also known as Salem Kemen, Szalankemen.

slate, fine-grained gray-blue rock formed by metamorphism of shale. Splits into very thin layers presumably at right angles to metamorphic pressure; this slaty cleavage is parallel to longer axis of mineral particles. Better grades are used for roofing.

Slater, Samuel (slā'tŭr), 1768–1835, American pioneer in cotton textile industry, b. England. At Providence, R.I., he reproduced from memory the machinery of Richard Arkwright (1790). Estab. mills in R.I. and elsewhere in New England.

Slaton (slā'tŭn), city (pop. 5,036), NE Texas, SE of Lubbock on Llano Estacado. Rail division point processing grain and cotton.

Slaughterhouse Cases. In 1869 the La. legislature, chiefly to protect health of New Orleans residents, granted a 25-year monopoly to a slaughterhouse concern in that city. Other slaughterhouse operators brought suit, claiming they had been deprived of their property without due process of law in violation of Fourteenth Amendment. Justice S. F. Miller rendered U.S. Supreme Court majority decision against slaughterhouse operators in 1873. A conservative decision, it declared old police power of states intact and did not seize opportunity to extend Federal power.

Slave, river: see GREAT SLAVE LAKE.

Slave Coast, coast bordering Bight of Benin of Gulf of Guinea, W Africa. Main source of slaves from W Africa, 16th–18th cent.

Slave dynasty: see DELHI SULTANATE.

slavery. The institution of slavery has been known among peoples in all quarters of the world, not only among agriculturists but in other cultures (e.g., among American Indians and Asiatic nomads). Generally the ownership of human beings has been a form of private property, but there were examples of public slavery (e.g., temple slaves). Slavery was already well estab. before the first recorded days of history in Mesopotamia and Egypt. A large part of the population of the Greek city-states was servile. In Roman times arose a new type of slavery, what might be called the "plantation type," though there continued to be many house slaves and personal slaves. In the Middle Ages slavery continued in Europe but in diminishing form, since the manorial system largely replaced it with the semifreedom of serfdom. The discovery and conquest of the New World, however, created a slave trade on a world-wide scale after it was found that Negroes from Africa could be used on plantations in the warmer climates. The first ones were introduced into what is now the U.S. in 1619, and over the years slavery became "the peculiar institution" at the base of the plantation system in the South; it did not take lasting root in the North. The doctrines of the American and French revolutions implied the end of slavery, and the slaves in Haiti arose, ousted their masters, and were recognized as an independent nation by 1804. Many newly born Latin American nations banned slavery from their start. Humanitarianism played a part in abolition of the English slave trade (1807) and of slavery in the British West Indies (1833). In the U.S. antislavery sentiment rose in the North and was made a burning issue by the abolitionists. Most of the serious clashes in the period 1820–60 were between South and North and hinged on the question of extension of slavery to new territories. The matter did not end until Abraham Lincoln's EMANCIPATION PROCLAMATION (1863) and the North's victory in the Civil War freed the slaves. Emancipation in Brazil in 1888 virtually ended the institution in the New World. The Berlin Conference of 1885, the Brussels Act of 1890, and the activities of the League of Nations (particularly the convention of 1926) largely succeeded in banishing slavery from Asia and Africa.

Slavic (slă'vĭk, slä'–), subfamily of Indo-European languages. See LANGUAGE (table).

Slavonia (slůvō'nēů), region, E Croatia, N Yugoslavia, between Drava and Sava rivers; cap. Osijek. Fertile agr. and forested lowland. Was ceded by Turkey to Hungary 1699; became Austrian crownland 1848; was restored to Hungarian crown and united with CROATIA 1868; part of Yugoslavia since 1918.

Slavonic (slůvŏ'nĭk), subfamily of Indo-European languages. See LANGUAGE (table).

Slavs, large ethnic and linguistic group of peoples belonging to Indo-European linguistic family (see LANGUAGE, table). Classified usually in three main divisions. West Slavs include Poles, Czechs, Slovaks, and WENDS and other small groups in E Germany. East Slavs include Great Russians, Ukrainians (Little Russians), and White Russians (Belorussians). South Slavs include Serbs, Croats, Slovenes, Macedonians, and Bulgarians. Culturally all Slavs fall into two groups—those traditionally associated with Orthodox Eastern Church and those historically affiliated with Roman Catholic Church. Prominent in Slavic history is story of Russia's rise from separate states. Pan-Slavism has been powerful instrument of Russian expansion.

sleeping sickness, either of two diseases marked by somnolence or lethargy. One, *encephalitis lethargica* (ĕnsĕ"fůlī'tĭs lĕthär'jĭků), is infectious and believed to be caused by a virus. The other, trypanosomiasis (trĭ"půnōsōmī'ůsĭs, trī"–), is a disease of tropical Africa caused by a protozoan transmitted by tsetse fly.

Sleepy Hollow, N.Y.: see NORTH TARRYTOWN.

sleet, name for several forms of winter precipitation: small, hard, globular ice grains, differing in form and occurrence from hail; ice coating formed by freezing rain; rain and snow mingled.

Slesvig, Danish name of SCHLESWIG.

Slick, Sam: see HALIBURTON, THOMAS CHANDLER.

Slidell, John (slīdĕl', slī'důl), 1793–1871, American politician and diplomat. U.S. Senator from La. (1853–61). Joined Confederacy, made commissioner to France. With J. M. Mason, figured in TRENT AFFAIR.

Slide Mountain: see CATSKILL MOUNTAINS.

slide rule, instrument for making numerical computations and readings by simple manipulations. Based on principle of logarithm, and on creation of logarithmic scale (1620), modern slide rule appeared in 1850. Three parts are stock, slide, and cursor (indicator). In one form of rule, stock consists of two parallel rules, each with scale on inner edge; slide is single rule, moving between them, with scales on outer edge. Cursor is glass square with hair line, movable along length of rule to aid in reading. On reverse side of slide rule are tables usable, in conjunction with scales, for determining sines, tangents, and logarithms. Calculating circle and calculating cylinder, for more complex calculations, are based on same principle.

Slieve Bloom (slēv), mountain range, 15 mi. long, central Ireland. Rises to 1,733 ft. at Arderin.

Sligo (slī'gō), maritime county (694 sq. mi.; pop. 62,375), NW Ireland, in Connaught. Has irregular coastline and mountainous interior. Cattle raising and farming are chief occupations. County town is **Sligo,** urban district (pop. 12,920), seaport, fishing center.

Slipher, Vesto Melvin (slī'fûr), 1875–, American astronomer, noted for spectroscopic research revealing rapid rotation and high velocities of nebulae.

Sloan, John, 1871–1952, American painter, a member of The EIGHT. Long a popular teacher at Art Students League. Painted realistic scenes of city life.

Sloane, Sir Hans (slōn), 1660–1753, British physician, naturalist. He was president of Royal College of Physicians (1719–35) and of Royal Society (1724–40). His collections of botanical specimens (some gathered in West Indies) and of books and manuscripts formed beginning of British Mus.

sloop, fore-and-aft rigged sailing vessel similar to the cutter, but with broader beam, center board and fixed bowsprit and a jibstay. The fast sloop-of-war, carrying 12 to 18 guns, used by the British navy in the mid-19th cent., resembled the later schooner. See *ill.*, p. 1109.

sloth (slōth, slôth), arboreal mammal of tropical America. Eats, sleeps, and travels upside down clinging to branches. Three-toed (*Bradypus*) feeds on cecropia leaves, buds, and stems; two-toed sloth (*Choloepus*) has less restricted vegetarian diet.

Slovakia (slōvä'kēŭ), Slovak *Slovensko,* constituent state (18,902 sq. mi.; pop. 3,434,369) of Czechoslovakia, occupying E part of Czechoslovak republic; cap. Bratislava. Except for S section, which is part of the Hungarian Plain, it is traversed by the Carpathian mts., culminating in the TATRA. Agr., forests, pastures. Iron, copper, mercury, lead, gold, silver, lignite mines. Slovakia was part of Hungary from the early 10th cent. until 1918. Hungarian nobles owned most of land. Germans and Jews formed large part of urban population. Slovak national consciousness began to stir in 19th cent. Independence movement was backed by many Slovak emigrants in U.S. In World War I, Czech and Slovak leaders agreed on union of the two nations; CZECHOSLOVAKIA was proclaimed 1918; Treaty of Trianon (1920) estab. present boundary with Hungary, leaving a minority of over 1,000,000 Magyars in Slovakia. The minority problem was complicated by Slovak nationalist agitation for home rule and by friction between the intensely Catholic Slovaks and the anticlerical Prague government. After the MUNICH PACT of 1938 Slovakia ceded some territory to Hungary and became an autonomous state. The German seizure of Bohemia and Moravia (March, 1939) left Slovakia nominally independent under the dictatorship of the nationalist leader, Father Joseph Tiso. Actually a puppet of Germany, it entered World War II as an Axis partner but was occupied by Russian troops in 1944. Reunited to Czechoslovakia, it recovered its lost territories. The constitution of 1948 gave it its own legislature and cabinet, but in fact the Communist party seized all power. Exchange of the Magyar minority for Slovak minorities in Hungary began in 1945.

Slovenia (slōvē'nēŭ), autonomous republic (7,796 sq. mi.; pop. 1,389,084), NW Yugoslavia, bordering on Austria (N) and Italy (W); cap. Ljubljana. It includes most of the Julian Alps (highest point, TRIGLAV) and the KARST and is drained by the Drava and Sava. The Slovenes are Roman Catholics. Most of Slovenia was comprised in the Austrian crownlands of Carniola, Styria, and Carinthia until 1918, when the kingdom of the Serbs, Croats and Slovenes—later called Yugoslavia—was formed. After World War II, Slovenia received autonomous status and was awarded part of formerly Italian VENEZIA GIULIA.

Slowacki, Julius, Pol. *Juliusz Słowacki* (yōōl'-yōōsh swôväts'kē), 1809–49, Polish romantic poet. Wrote historic dramas—e.g., *Mazeppa* (1834; Eng. tr., 1929); *Mary Stuart* (1830; Eng. tr. 1937)—and the allegorical prose epic *Anhelli* (1838; Eng. tr., 1930).

slug, name for a terrestrial mollusk similar to land snail and also for a marine sea slug of another mollusk order. Shell lacking or rudimentary. Terrestrial slug (*Limax*) is garden pest.

Sluis (slois) Fr. *L'Écluse,* town (pop. 1,615), Zeeland prov., SW Netherlands, on Scheldt estuary. Founded 13th cent. as subsidiary port of Bruges. Scene of English naval victory over French (1340) in Hundred Years War. Conquered by Dutch from Spanish in 1604. Formerly spelled Sluys.

Sluter, Claus (klous' slü'tûr), d. c.1406, Flemish sculptor, chief master of early Burgundian school. Famous for realistic and powerful works at Dijon.

Sluys, Netherlands: see SLUIS.

Sm, chemical symbol of the element SAMARIUM.

Smaland, Swed. *Småland* (smō'länd), historic province of S central Sweden; chief cities are Jonkoping and Kalmar.

small holding, term used in England for tract of agr. land larger than a cottage holding (three acres or less), but not too large to be cultivated by owner or tenant and his family. Maximum size was fixed by law at 50 acres. Unlike cottage holding, small holding is meant to provide a business capable of supporting family which farms it.

smallpox, infectious, contagious disease caused by a virus. Marked by red spots that form blisters and may leave scars (pocks). Attack usually gives permanent immunity. Disease can be wiped out by universal vaccination. Edward Jenner introduced vaccination with cowpox virus.

smaltite (smôl'tīt), opaque, white to gray mineral of pyrite group, a compound of cobalt and arsenic.

Smart, Christopher, 1722–71, English poet, author of cryptic poetry, such as *A Song to David* (1763, in biblical language; written in an asylum).

smartweed, annual species of genus *Polygonum*

containing an acrid juice and bearing catkin-like pink flowers. Prince's-feather (*Polygonum orientale*) is often cultivated.

smell, sense by which odors are perceived. In man, organs of smell, olfactory cells in nasal cavity, receive at one end stimuli transmitted to brain by nerve fibers at other end. Smell long believed to be chemical; some evidence that infrared radiation is involved. Sense highly developed in certain animals in food getting and attracting mate.

smelt, small slender fish of north temperate waters, related to salmon. It is chiefly marine but many spawn in fresh waters; some are found in landlocked lakes. Adults average c.8 in. in length. Delicate flesh. Common American smelt of Atlantic coast is *Osmerus mordax.*

smelting, in metallurgy, any heat process for preparing a metal from its ores. Processes vary according to metal involved but are typified in use of BLAST FURNACE and REVERBERATORY FURNACE.

Smet, Pierre Jean de: see DE SMET, PIERRE JEAN.

Smetana, Friedrich, Czech *Bedřich Smetana* (smĕt'änä), 1824–84, Czech composer. Drawing on Czech folk music he created a national style. Of his eight operas only *The Bartered Bride* was successful outside his own country. He also wrote a symphonic cycle, *My Fatherland,* which contains the popular *Vltava* (*The Moldau*); and two string quartets, *From My Life.* He died both deaf and insane.

Smibert or **Smybert, John** (both: smī'bûrt), 1688–1751, American portrait painter, b. Scotland. Among his subjects were George Berkeley and Jonathan Edwards. Practiced in Boston.

smilax (smī'lăks), South African twining vine (*Asparagus asparagoides*), commonly grown for greenery for florist trade. Greenbriers, prickly vines often weedy in parts of North America, belong to genus *Smilax.*

Smirke, Sir Robert, 1781–1867, English architect, a noted exponent of the classic revival. Designed main façade of British Mus. His brother, **Sydney Smirke,** 1793–1877, worked in the same style.

Smith, Adam, 1723–90, Scottish economist, author of *An Inquiry into the Nature and Causes of the Wealth of Nations* (1776). He postulated theory of division of labor, of laissez faire, and of value as a result of labor expended in the process of production. An opponent of mercantilism, he admitted that certain restrictions to free trade might be necessary. As an analyst of institutions and an influence on later economists he has perhaps never been surpassed.

Smith, Alfred E(manuel), 1873–1944, American political leader. Governor of N.Y. (1919–20, 1923–28); one of the most forceful in the history of the state. Accomplished many reforms. Democratic candidate for President in 1928.

Smith, Donald Alexander: see STRATHCONA AND MOUNT ROYAL, DONALD ALEXANDER SMITH, 1ST BARON.

Smith, Edmund Kirby, or **Edmund Kirby-Smith,** 1824–93, Confederate general. Commanded Trans-Mississippi Dept. (1863–65). Last general to surrender (May 26, 1865).

Smith, Gerrit, 1797–1874, American philanthropist and reformer. Aided various reforms (esp. temperance and abolition). Devoted friend of John Brown. Urged moderation toward South after Civil War.

Smith, Gipsy (Rodney), 1860–1947, British evangelist; son of a gypsy. He worked in Gen. Booth's Christian Mission, but later preached independently. From 1883 his evangelistic labors spanned England, Scotland, U.S., and Australia.

Smith, Henry John Stephen, 1826–83, British mathematician, known especially for work on theory of numbers and elliptic functions.

Smith, Horatio or **Horace,** 1779–1849, and **James Smith,** 1775–1839, English parodists, brothers. Wrote famous *Rejected Addresses* (1812), parodies of Wordsworth, Scott, Coleridge, and Byron.

Smith, Jedediah Strong, 1799–1831, American explorer, one of the greatest of the mountain men. He more than any other was breaker of trails to Calif. and Pacific Northwest.

Smith, John, 1580–1631, English colonist in America. Guided Jamestown settlement through periods of hardship. Supposedly saved from death by POCAHONTAS. Urged settlement of New England.

Smith, Joseph, 1805–44, American founder of Church of Jesus Christ of the Latter-Day Saints. In Palmyra, N.Y., in 1823, a vision revealed existence of secret records. When in 1827 their hiding place was made known to him, he unearthed golden tablets with sacred writing, which he translated as Book of Mormon. As prophet and seer he founded first church in 1830. Hostility of neighbors led him to move to Kirtland, Ohio, to Mo., and to Nauvoo, Ill. Disaffection grew, and trouble with non-Mormons led to arrest of Joseph and his brother Hyrum on charges of treason. On June 27, 1844, they were murdered by a mob at Carthage, Ill. His revelations, including one on plural marriage, were accepted as doctrine by the Mormons.

Smith, Kirby: see SMITH, EDMUND KIRBY.

Smith, Logan Pearsall, 1865–1946, Anglo-American author, b. N.J., in England after 1888. Wrote exquisite essays in *Trivia* (1902; with sequels), criticism in *On Reading Shakespeare* (1933) and *Milton and His Modern Critics* (1940).

Smith, Seba, 1792–1868, American editor and humorist. Editor of Portland (Maine) *Courier,* famous for humorous political letters signed "Major Jack Downing," later collected.

Smith, Sydney, 1771–1845, English clergyman, writer, and wit. With others he founded (1802) the *Edinburgh Review.* His "Peter Plymley" letters in defense of Catholic Emancipation promoted religious toleration —an example of his defense of the oppressed.

Smith, Theobald, 1859–1934, American pathologist. Discovered cause of Texas cattle fever. Contributed much to preventive medicine.

Smith, Walter Bedell, 1895–, American general. Chief of staff (1942–45) to Dwight Eisenhower in World War II, he became ambassador to USSR (1946–49) and director of

Central Intelligence Agency (1950–53). Appointed Undersecretary of State in 1953.

Smith, William Robertson, 1846–94, Scottish biblical scholar and encyclopedist. Ejected (1881) from professorship at Free Church college, Aberdeen, because of biblical articles written for *The Encyclopaedia Britannica,* he became an editor of that work, later (1887) editor in chief.

Smith College, at Northampton, Mass.; nonsectarian, for women; chartered 1871, opened 1875 through bequest of Sophia Smith. Pres. L. C. Seelye estab. high ideals of scholarship. Col. has school of architecture and landscape architecture at Cambridge, school for social work. Had pioneer music courses. Honors work is stressed. Conducted school for women naval officers in World War II.

Smithfield, district of central London, England. Site of the Central Meat Market. Formerly used for markets, fairs, jousts, and executions.

Smithfield. 1 Town (pop. 5,574), E central N.C., SE of Raleigh and on Neuse R. Cotton, tobacco. **2** Town (pop. 6,690), N R.I., NW of Providence, in agr. area. Textiles. **3** City (pop. 2,383), N Utah, in Cache Valley N of Logan. Near by is Newton Dam, started 1871 by Mormons, replaced 1946 by U.S. **4** Town (pop. 1,180), SE Va., NW of Portsmouth. Noted for its hams. Near by are St. Luke's Church (1632 or 1682; one of oldest Protestant churches in America), and Bacon's Castle (1655; house fortified during Bacon's Rebellion).

Smiths Falls, town (pop. 8,441), SE Ont., Canada, SW of Ottawa, on Rideau R. Rail and mfg. center.

Smithson, James, 1765?–1829, English founder of Smithsonian Inst., b. France. He was the illegitimate son of Sir Hugh Smithson and Elizabeth Macie. He wrote valuable scientific papers for Royal Society publications and *Annals of Philosophy*. His fortune was willed to the U.S. for establishment of Smithsonian Inst. for the "increase and diffusion of knowledge among men."

Smithsonian Institution (smĭthsō′nēŭn), estab. at Washington, D.C., by congressional act in 1846. Governing board of regents consists of Vice President of U.S., Chief Justice, three Senators, three Representatives, and six nonofficials. Secretary to the board is the executive officer of the Smithsonian and keeper of the U.S. National Mus. The Institution's activities embrace all branches of science relating to U.S., with special emphasis on scientific research. Under Smithsonian auspices are Bureau of American Ethnology, National Zoological Park, Astrophysical Observatory, Canal Zone Biological Area, National Air Mus., and U.S. National Mus. (including National Coll. of Fine Arts and Freer Gall. of Art).

smoke, visible gaseous product of incomplete combustion. Usually consists of carbon particles and tarry substances, or soot. Soft coal produces greatest amount; proper firing and equipment can eliminate much smoke. Smoke has caused much contamination in cities, and various means are used to reduce amount escaping into air, e.g., precipitation by electricity, sound waves, or chemicals. Among evils of smoke are interference with sunlight, disfiguring deposits on buildings, destructive chemical effects of acids in deposits, cost of cleaning off deposits, damaging effect on plant life and on animal respiratory systems. Smoke has been used as concealment in warfare (as smoke screens) at least since the late 17th cent. It is also used for a variety of sign language; particularly among the Indians of the W U.S.

Smoky, river of W Alta., Canada, rising in Jasper Natl. Park and flowing 245 mi. NNE to Peace R.

Smoky Hill River, rising in E Colo. and flowing c.560 mi. E across Kansas to join Republican R. and form Kansas R. at Junction City. Basin is in MISSOURI RIVER BASIN PROJECT. Kanopolis Dam, for flood control, completed 1948.

Smoky Mountains: see GREAT SMOKY MOUNTAINS.

Smolensk (smōlĕnsk′, smô–), city (pop. 156,677), W European RSFSR, on the Dnieper. Rail junction and industrial center (textiles, machinery, flour, lumber, spirits). Founded 882, it became a great medieval commercial center and the cap. of a principality which fell to Lithuania in 14th cent.; ceded to Russia 1667. Captured by Napoleon I in Aug., 1812. German-held (1941–43) in World War II and virtually razed by heavy fighting.

Smollett, Tobias (George), 1721–71, Scottish novelist. A naval surgeon, he turned to writing. His picaresque novels, realistic and vigorous in style, include *The Adventures of Roderick Random* (1748), *The Adventures of Peregrine Pickle* (1751), and *The Expedition of Humphry Clinker* (1771).

Smoot, Reed (smo͞ot), 1862–1941, U.S. Senator from Utah (1903–33). First Mormon elected to Senate. Co-author of HAWLEY-SMOOT TARIFF ACT (1930).

smut, fungus disease of cereal plants which produces sootlike masses of spores on the host. Smuts lower vitality and may cause deformity. Among crops attacked are corn, oats, and wheat; stinking smut or bunt causes annual losses by spoiling wheat grain.

Smuts, Jan Christiaan, 1870–1950, South African statesman, soldier. Of Dutch stock, he gave up British citizenship after Jameson raid. Believed cooperation of Boers and British essential; was instrumental (with Louis Botha) in creation (1910) of Union of South Africa. Continuously held office in Botha's cabinet. Signed Treaty of Versailles (1918) protesting that its terms outraged Germany. Advocated League of Nations. Prime minister of South Africa 1919–24. In World War II he was again prime minister and held high place in British war councils; was active in organizing U.N.

Smybert, John: see SMIBERT, JOHN.

Smyrna (smûr′nŭ), Turkish *Izmir,* city (pop. 230,508), W Turkey; a port on the Bay of Smyrna of the Aegean Sea. Varied mfg. An early Ionian colony, it was rebuilt by Antigonus I (4th cent. B.C.) and became one of the largest and richest cities of Asia Minor under Roman and Byzantine rule. An early Christian center, it was one of the Seven Churches of Asia (Rev. 2–8). It was sacked by Tamerlane (1402) and fell in 1424 to the

Ottoman Turks, who kept it until 1919, when it was occupied by Greek forces. The Treaty of SÈVRES (1920) placed the Smyrna region under Greek administration; it was nullified by the Treaty of Lausanne (1923), after the Turkish nationalists under Kemal Ataturk had driven the Greeks from Asia Minor in the campaign of 1920–22. The large Greek population of Smyrna was exchanged for Turkish minorities in Greece. With the loss of this prosperous, cultured element, Smyrna declined somewhat. It is one of the cities claiming to have given birth to Homer.

Smythe, Francis Sydney, 1901–49, English mountain climber. Climbed (1931) Kamet (25,447 ft.) in Garwhal Himalayas.

Sn, chemical symbol of the element TIN.

snail, gastropod mollusk with spiral shell. Thousands of species include land, fresh-water, and marine forms. Used for food, especially in Europe. Both sexes are represented in each individual.

Snake, river, c.1,000 mi. long, NW U.S., chief tributary (formerly, Lewis R. or Lewis Fork) of the Columbia. Rises in Yellowstone Natl. Park, NW Wyo., and flows S through Jackson L., S and W into Idaho, NW to be joined by Henrys Fork, then runs SW and NW across Idaho, bends into Oregon, turns N as Idaho-Oregon and Idaho-Wash. line (receiving Boise, Salmon, other rivers), and flows W into Columbia R. near Pasco, Wash. Grand Canyon of the Snake (between Wallowa Mts., Oregon, and Seven Devils Mts., Idaho) is one of world's deepest; reaches maximum depth of 7,900 ft. Discovered 1805 by Lewis and Clark, the Snake aided expansion of NW U.S. Much used for irrigation privately (see TWIN FALLS), by U.S. in MINIDOKA PROJECT, BOISE PROJECT, and others. Major Idaho cities are in valley.

snake, reptile with elongated scaly body, limbless or with only traces of hind limbs, with forked retractile tongue, and recurved teeth. The eyes are covered by clear scales (instead of movable eyelids); there are no ears, and only one lung is developed. The skin is shed, usually several times a year. A snake moves by means of body muscles aided by elongated scales on abdomen and by ends of ribs. About 80% of the c.2,500 species are non-venomous. Venom, produced by modified salivary glands, passes through a groove or bore in fangs into victim.

snake bite. Venom of poisonous snakes introduced by fangs. May injure nerves, blood vessels, or blood cells or cause hemorrhage. Treatment usually involves application of tourniquet between wound and heart; injection of antitoxin; cutting of wound to cause bleeding.

Snake Indians, popular name given to several tribes, notably the Shoshone and N Paiute.

snakeroot, name for several plants, including SENEGA SNAKEROOT and WHITE SNAKEROOT.

snapdragon, Old World perennial (*Antirrhinum majus*) grown as an annual in greenhouses and gardens. The handsome flower spikes come in various colors.

snare drum: see PERCUSSION INSTRUMENTS.

Snead, Sam(uel Jackson) (snēd), 1912–, American golfer. Won Professional Golfers Association (1942, 1949), British Open (1946) championships.

Snell or **Snellius, Willebrord** (vĭ'lůbrôrt snĕl', snĕ'lēůs), 1591–1626, Dutch mathematician. Generally credited with discovery of law of refraction of light (1621).

Snelling, Fort, estab. 1819 on a bluff above the Mississippi at confluence of the Minnesota. Minneapolis later grew on fort reservation.

Snellius, Willebrord: see SNELL, WILLEBRORD.

snipe, wading bird of Old and New Worlds, related to woodcock. Plumage is usually brown, chestnut, and buff. Its long bill probes earth for insects and worms.

Snorri Sturluson (snô'rē stür'lüsôn), 1179–1241, Icelandic historian. His prose EDDA is a treatise on writing poetry and a compendium of Norse mythology. The *Heimskringla* is a series of biographies of Norse kings. Powerful in politics, he lost favor and was murdered.

snow, form of precipitation, hexagonal ice crystals, produced by condensation of vapor about a dust particle at below-freezing temperatures. Snowflakes usually consist of more than one crystal. Snowfall usually part of rainfall statistics (10 in. averages 1 in. rain).

snowball: see VIBURNUM.

snowberry, ornamental white-fruited shrub (*Symphoricarpos*), chiefly native to North America. The common snowberry (*Symphoricarpos albus*) has pink flowers and waxy berries.

Snowden, Philip Snowden, 1st **Viscount,** 1864–1937, British socialist statesman. Chancellor of exchequer in ministries of Ramsay MacDonald 1924, 1929. Advocate of free trade. Demanded increased German war reparations at Hague Convention 1929.

Snowdon, Welsh *Eryri,* mountain, 3,560 ft. high, Caernarvonshire, Wales; highest in Wales. Has five peaks, separated by passes. Railway to the summit. District (Snowdonia) has beautiful scenery.

snowdrop, hardy, low bulbous plant (*Galanthus nivalis*) of Old World. It has a single, nodding bell-shaped white flower in early spring.

snow-on-the-mountain: see SPURGE.

Snyder, town (pop. 12,010), NW Texas, NW of Sweetwater; settled 1876. Shipping and processing center for agr., oil, dairying, and livestock region.

Snyders, Frans (fräns' snī'důrs), 1579–1657, Flemish painter of luminous still lifes and spirited animal compositions. Often collaborated with Rubens and Jordaens. Influenced mainly by Rubens.

Soane, Sir John (sōn), 1753–1837, English architect, a leader of the classic revival in England. Noted for his work on Bank of England.

soap, agent that cleanses by lowering surface tension of water, emulsifying grease, and adsorbing dirt into the foam. Results from reaction (saponification) of alkali and fat, forming metallic acid (soap) and glycerin. Made essentially by stirring alkali into heated fats or oils and adding salt to cause soap to form curds; these are usually churned and poured into frames, or, for hard-milled soaps, run over chilled rollers, scraped off, and shaped. Properties vary according to alkalis, fats, and fillers employed. Used in industry as paint driers, lubricating greases, and in other forms. Substitutes include certain plants (see SOAP PLANT) and soapless detergents (commonly sulfonated alcohols).

soap plant, any of various plants containing cleansing properties. The soapbark tree (*Quillaja saponaria*), the tropical American soapberry (*Sapindus*), the California soap plant (*Chlorogalum pomeridianum*), SOAPWORT (*Saponaria*), and species of agave, are among plants containing the lather-producing substance, saponin. The poisonous quality of saponin was used by Indians who caught fish by first stupefying them with plant bits thrown into pools.

soapstone or **steatite** (stē'ùtīt), massive gray to green rock usually composed chiefly of talc. It is very soft, has soapy feel, is highly resistant to heat and acids. Used for laboratory equipment, sinks, laundry tubs, electrical apparatus.

soapwort, perennial plant (*Saponaria officinalis*), grown in gardens in colonial America and now escaped along roads and railroads. It is also called bouncing Bet. It has pink or white flower clusters, and its leaves produce a cleansing lather.

Sobieski, John: see JOHN III, king of Poland.

soccer (sŏ'kûr), game played by teams of 11 men on grassy field preferably measuring 120 yd. by 75 yd. Name derived by usage from abbreviation of word *association*.

Sochi (sô'chē), city (pop. c.50,000), S Krasnodar Territory, SE European RSFSR; a port and health resort on the Black Sea.

social contract, agreement with which men are said to have abandoned the "state of nature" to form the society in which they now live. Theory of such a covenant, formulated by Hobbes and Locke, and expanded by Rousseau, had a strong effect on development of government responsibilities and the citizen's "natural rights" in a democracy.

Social Credit, economic plan, based on theories of Clifford H. Douglas. Central idea is that economic depressions are caused by maldistribution due to insufficient purchasing power. It was proposed to redistribute purchasing power by issuing dividends to every citizen. Scheme was adopted by a political party in Alta., Canada, led by William Aberhart, which won 1935 elections. Confederation government and courts disallowed attempts to tax banks and promote currency schemes. However, the party continued to win elections and after World War II it sponsored much social welfare legislation.

social hygiene deals with sex behavior relative to individual and social aspects of health. Stresses relation of VENEREAL DISEASE and poor sexual adjustment. Strives to improve sex education and to correct social ills resulting in such problems as sex crimes, prostitution, unmarried mothers.

socialism, general term for any economic doctrine that challenges sanctity of private property and favors its use for public welfare. In this sense it embraces great variety of economic theories, from those holding that only certain public utilities and natural resources should be owned by state, to thoroughgoing Marxian socialism, and, further, to edges of ANARCHISM. Industrial Revolution, first in British Isles in 18th cent. and later on Continent, created social and economic conditions that led intellectuals to plan reorganization. *Socialism* and *communism* emerged as terms, often used interchangeably, and movements were utopian. Thus in France, Étienne CABET and Charles FOURIER planned COMMUNISTIC SETTLEMENTS. In England, Robert OWEN and Thomas SPENCE were influential. American leaders were Albert BRISBANE and Bronson ALCOTT. A more practical leader in France was Louis BLANC. Marxian socialism appeared with *The Communist Manifesto* (1848) of Karl MARX and Friedrich ENGELS. CHRISTIAN SOCIALISM appeared in England under F. D. Maurice and Charles KINGSLEY. In Germany, Ferdinand LASSALLE, Wilhelm LIEBKNECHT, and August BEBEL prepared way for rise of Social Democratic parties under guidance of INTERNATIONAL. In Russia, PLEKHANOV founded Social Democratic party, which split between BOLSHEVISM AND MENSHEVISM. Similar parties gained strength on Continent between two world wars and after World War II. In England, FABIAN SOCIETY (leaders included G. B. SHAW and Sidney and Beatrice WEBB) led to establishment of Labour party. U.S. Socialist groups have had as leaders Daniel DE LEON, E. V. DEBS, Morris HILLQUIT, and Norman THOMAS.

Socialist Labor party, in U.S. history, formed in 1870s. In 1880 it temporarily allied itself with Greenback party. Under Daniel DE LEON in 1890s, it advocated a syndicalist type of socialism. Party sharply declined after De Leon's opponents withdrew in 1899 to join Social Democratic party (see SOCIALIST PARTY).

Socialist party, in U.S. history, formed 1898 as Social Democratic party, redesignated Socialist party 1901. E. V. Debs was its candidate for President five times between 1900 and 1920; Morris HILLQUIT dominant figure of early period. After 1928 party was led by Norman THOMAS. Party's objectives are reformist, calling for evolutionary socialism.

socialization of medicine: see HEALTH INSURANCE.

social psychology, study of human relationships; the science in which experimental psychology, sociology, anthropology, and psychiatry meet. It is concerned with the influence of family, school, church, and economic and political background on the individual; the study of behavior patterns; the nature and forming of attitudes and ways of measuring and changing them; and the effects of interracial and international relations on the individual. Attempts have been made to adapt techniques of the physical and biological laboratory to the measuring and describing of human behavior.

social security, program of social insurance, brought about by government legislation, to protect wage earners and their dependents against major economic hazards. First adopted in Germany in the 1880s to forestall the program of the Socialists. Britain's Natl. Insurance Act of 1914 included sickness, unemployment, and old-age insurance (see

PENSION). Social security did not reach the U.S. until 1935, when it became part of Roosevelt's New Deal program. It now covers approximately 46,000,000 people, but certain types of workers are still not covered, and HEALTH INSURANCE has not yet been added.

social settlement, institution in a poor and overcrowded area where resident workers improve conditions by promoting community cooperation and services. Among the famous settlement houses are Toynbee Hall (founded 1884 in London), Hull House (Chicago), and the Henry Street Settlement and Greenwich House (New York).

Social War, 90 B.C.–88 B.C., struggle of the Italian allies of Rome (the *socii*) to secure Roman citizenship promised them by the laws of M. Livius Drusus, but denied by the senate. A people called the Marsians were first to rise, and this is sometimes called the Marsic War. It ended only when L. Julius Caesar got a law passed giving citizenship to allies who had not joined the war or who laid down arms immediately.

social work, organized effort to aid needy or maladjusted individuals. Originally, churches and philanthropic groups sought to relieve poverty and distress of those "worthy of charity." In 1874 the Natl. Conference of Charities and Correction (later renamed Natl. Conference of Social Work) was organized in U.S. After 1930 the Federal government entered the field of social work, although private welfare funds are still raised (see COMMUNITY CHEST).

Society for the Prevention of Cruelty to Animals (S.P.C.A.). The English organization was founded 1824, the American 1866.

Society Islands (c.650 sq. mi.; pop. 42,129), S Pacific, part of FRENCH ESTABLISHMENTS IN OCEANIA. The 450-mi. chain comprises Windward Isls. (including TAHITI, site of the cap. Papeete) and Leeward Isls. (including Raiatea). Larger islands are mountainous and volcanic and produce copra, sugar, rum, mother-of-pearl, and phosphate. Natives are Polynesians. Discovered 1767 by the British; visited 1769 by Capt. James Cook and members of Royal Society, in whose honor the group was named. The French came in late 18th cent. and set up a protectorate in 1844. Group became a French colony in 1880.

Socinianism (sōsĭ'nēŭnĭzŭm), anti-Trinitarian religious system in 16th cent. Based on ideas of Laelius and Faustus Socinus. It accepted rationalist doctrines and rejected belief in the Trinity; sometimes called Old Unitarianism. Basic ideas are in Racovian Catechism of 1605.

Socinus, Laelius (lē'lēŭs sōsī'nŭs), originally **Lelio Sozzini,** 1525–62, Italian religious reformer. Lived in Switzerland from 1544. Never actually voiced anti-Trinitarian views, but from his writings his nephew, **Faustus Socinus** (fô'stŭs), originally **Fausto Sozzini,** 1539–1604, formulated doctrinal basis of Socinianism. In Poland (after 1579) he organized anti-Trinitarian groups into Polish Brethren.

sociology, the science of human groups or societies; the study of man in his collective aspect. An ancient philosophical study, it was first treated (1838) systematically by Auguste Comte. Herbert Spencer was also important in the founding of its principles.

Socorro (sōkô'rō), city (pop. 4,334), W central N.Mex., on Rio Grande and S of Albuquerque. On site of Piro pueblo, visited 1598 by Oñate. Part of Church of San Miguel dates from this period.

Socrates (sŏ'krŭtēz), 469–399 B.C., Greek philosopher of Athens, generally regarded as one of the wisest men of all time. At about 30 he dedicated himself to combat skepticism and arouse love of truth and virtue. He gathered about him a group of young men and instilled into them a love of inquiry that would lead to knowledge and justice. The Socratic method was to question someone, then show skillfully the inadequacy of the answer by further questions, all guiding toward a sounder answer. He said that his wisdom consisted in knowing that he knew nothing finally (the Socratic irony). Athenian conservatives, fearing new ideas, had him brought to trial for corrupting youth and introducing strange divinities. Condemned to die, he drank poison hemlock with noble calm and courage. He wrote nothing, and is known to us through the writings of his greatest pupil, Plato, and of Xenophon. His wife was XANTHIPPE.

soda, sodium carbonate, originally called soda ash. Forms alkaline solution on hydrolysis; obtained by LEBLANC PROCESS and SOLVAY PROCESS. Used in making glass, soap, caustic soda, enamel; as cleaning agent; as water softener. Baking soda is sodium bicarbonate; it is used in BAKING POWDER and in medicine and in the laboratory for neutralizing acids. Caustic soda is sodium hydroxide, also called lye.

Soda Springs, village (pop. 1,329), SE Idaho, near Bear R.; founded 1863. Its mineral springs (esp. Steamboat Spring) have drawn travelers since days of Oregon Trail. Area has phosphate deposits.

Soddy, Frederick (sŏ'dē), 1877–, English chemist. Won 1921 Nobel Prize for discovery (with others) of relationship between radioactive elements and parent compound that led to his theory of isotopes.

Soderberg, Hjalmar, Swed. *Söderberg* (yäl'mär sû'dŭrbĕr"yŭ), 1869–1941, Swedish author of dramas, novels, and short stories depicting Stockholm life.

Soderblom, Nathan, Swed. *Söderblom* (nä'tän sû'dŭrblōōm), 1866–1931, archbishop of Uppsala, Sweden. Awarded 1930 Nobel Peace Prize.

Sodermanland, Swed. *Södermanland* (sû'dŭr-mänländ"), historic province of E central Sweden, on the Baltic coast. It includes S part of Stockholm co. and Sodermanland co. Stockholm and Nykoping are the chief cities. Truck farming and dairying. Iron and steel industry at Eskilstuna.

sodium (sō'dēŭm), soft, silver-white, lustrous metallic element (symbol = Na; see also ELEMENT, table), a very active alkali metal. Oxidizes rapidly in air; must be kept under oil. Metallic sodium is of little commercial value. Sodium compounds are numerous and widely distributed and are used in chemical processes and in commercial preparation of other substances. Sodium hydroxide is used wherever cheap alkali is needed, e.g., in making soap. Compounds also occur in animal and plant cells.

sodium benzoate (bĕn'zōāt) or **benzoate of soda,** salt of benzoic acid, used as a preservative, but harmful except in small quantities.

Sodom (sŏ'dům), one of the Cities of the Plain destroyed by fire from heaven because of unnatural carnal wickedness. Others were Gomorrah, Admah, and Zeboiim; Zoar was spared. Gen. 10.19; 13; 14; 18; 19; Deut. 29.23; Amos 4.11; Mat. 10.15; Mark 6.11; 2 Peter 2.6; Jude 7. Sodoma: Rom. 9.29.

Sodoma, Il (ēl sô'dōmä), c.1477–1549, Italian painter, b. Lombardy. Real name was Giovanni Antonio Bazzi. His many frescoes in Siena and vicinity show influence of Leonardo da Vinci.

Soekarno: see SUKARNO.

Soerabaja, Indonesia: see SURABAYA.

Soerakarta, Indonesia: see SURAKARTA.

Soest (zōst), town (pop. 28,914), North Rhine-Westphalia, W Germany. The leading town of Westphalia in the later Middle Ages, it was comprised in the archbishopric of Cologne and later in the county of Mark (under dukes of Cleves) but enjoyed virtual independence. Passed to Brandenburg 1613. Heavy destruction in World War II included damage to many of its architectural treasures, notably the Romanesque cathedral (Patroklikirche, 10th cent.).

Sofia (sōfē'ů), city (pop. 366,925), cap. of Bulgaria, at the foot of the Balkans. Mfg. of machinery, chemicals, rubber, textiles, tobacco. Orthodox and Roman Catholic episcopal sees. University (founded 1889). The ancient Sardica, it was destroyed by the Huns (447) and restored by Justinian I (6th cent.). It was part of the first Bulgarian empire (9th–11th cent.), reverted to Byzantium, became part of the second Bulgarian empire in the 13th cent., passed to the Ottoman Empire 1386, and was the cap. of Turkish Rumelia until 1878, when it became the cap. of Bulgaria. It is largely a modern city.

Sogdiana (sŏgdēā'nů), part of anc. Persian Empire in central Asia between Oxus and Jaxartes rivers. Chief city was Samarkand.

Sogne Fjord (sông'nů fyôr"), inlet of Norwegian Sea, on W coast of Norway; longest (112 mi.) and deepest (4,081 ft.) fjord of Norway. Branches cut into the JOTUNHEIM and JOSTEDALSBREEN. The region is rich in Viking traditions and celebrated for its wild beauty.

Soho (sōhō', sů–), district of W London, England, noted for its French and Italian restaurants. Earlier a fashionable quarter, it was popular in the 19th cent. with writers and artists.

soil, substance in which most plants grow. It is made up of disintegrated rock, in the form of sand or clay, and organic matter (decaying vegetation), both in various stages of decomposition. Soils are acid, neutral, or alkaline (see ALKALI SOILS). Fertility may depend on texture, chemical composition, water supply, temperature and nature of subsoil. FERTILIZER may add to a soil's fertility, but unless the humus content is maintained, productivity will eventually decrease.

soilless gardening or **hydroponics,** growing of plants without soil in a medium (e.g., water, sand, gravel, or sawdust) to which nutrients have been added. Nutrient solutions must supply in correct balance nitrogen, phosphorus, potassium, and other essentials to plant growth normally found in soil. Light requirements of the crops must be satisfied. Though soilless gardening is still in an experimental stage, good results have been obtained commercially in producing tomatoes, carnations, roses, and gardenias.

Soissons (swäsō'), city (pop. 17,136), Aisne dept., N France, on Aisne R. Scene of decisive victory of CLOVIS I (486). Cap. of several Merovingian kings. Suffered severely in both world wars. Its cathedral (13th cent.) and its ancient abbey, where Thomas à Becket lived, were damaged.

Sojourner Truth: see TRUTH, SOJOURNER.

solan goose: see GANNET.

solar system, SUN and celestial bodies held in their orbits by its power of gravitation. Includes planets (see PLANET; ASTEROID), satellites, some comets and meteors. Theories of origin include NEBULAR HYPOTHESIS, PLANETESIMAL HYPOTHESIS, TIDAL THEORY.

solder (sŏ'důr), metal alloy used as a metallic cement. Type used depends on metals to be united. Soft solders are basically lead and tin and have low melting points; hard solders have high melting points and are of metal compounds suited for amalgamation with metals to be joined. When brass is used in the solder or when brass surfaces are to be joined, process is known as brazing, a name sometimes applied also to other hard soldering.

sole, name for several food fish of flatfish order. Most accurately refers to European sole (*Solea vulgaris*); American soles are small and bony. In U.S. flounder, cod, and haddock fillets are often sold as sole.

Solemn League and Covenant: see COVENANTERS.

Solent, the (sō'lůnt), western part of channel between Isle of Wight and Hampshire, England.

Solesmes (sôlĕm'), famous Benedictine abbey, in Solesmes village, Sarthe dept., W France, on Sarthe R. Founded 1010 and enlarged in 19th cent. Led in revival of pure Gregorian chant.

Soleure, Switzerland: see SOLOTHURN.

solfège (sôlfĕzh') [Fr.] or **solfeggio** (sōlfĕd'jō) [Ital.], systems of musical training in vocalization and sight reading using the solmization syllables (do, re, mi, etc.) of Guido d'Arezzo. Term also used to mean training in various fundamentals of music.

Solferino (sōlfārē'nō), village NW of Mantua, N Italy. Scene (1859) of bloody battle between Austrians and allied French and Sardinians (combined casualties, c.30,000). No clear decision was won, but peace was made soon afterward at VILLAFRANCA DI VERONA. J. H. Dunant was present at battle, which inspired him to promote the Red Cross.

solid, one of three states of matter, a substance having both definite shape and volume. Some solids are crystalline, others noncrystalline. Molecules in solids are relatively closer together than in liquid or gas, cohesion between them is greater, and they move more slowly. Solid changes to liquid when temperature is raised to melting point; heat needed is heat of fusion. When substance passes from solid to gas without liquid stage it is sublimation; most substances pass through liquid phase.

Soliman, Ottoman sultans: see SULEIMAN.

Solingen (zō'lĭng-ùn), city (pop. 147,782), North Rhine-Westphalia, W Germany, on the Wupper and adjoining Wuppertal and Remscheid. Its cutlery mfg. has been famous for centuries. City shared history of duchy of Berg.

Solís, Juan Díaz de (hwän dē'äth dā sōlēs'), d. 1516, Spanish navigator, discoverer of the Río de la Plata. After numerous voyages to New World, he was commissioned (1514) to seek passage between Atlantic and Pacific oceans. He entered estuary of the Río de la Plata (1516) and, landing on coast of present Uruguay, was killed by Indians.

Solnhofen (zō'lùnhō"fùn), village of Middle Franconia, W central Bavaria. Large quarries of lithographic stone near by have yielded fossils of the ARCHAEOPTERIX.

Solomon [Heb.,= peaceful], d. c.932 B.C., king of the Hebrews (c.972–c.932 B.C.), son of David. The bright side of his reign was characterized by peace, commercial expansion, and intensive building (e.g., the Temple at Jerusalem); the dark side by extravagance, heavy taxes, and rising discontent among the northern tribes. Several books of the Bible are traditionally ascribed to him: Proverbs, Ecclesiastes, Wisdom, and Song of Solomon. Among the PSEUDEPIGRAPHA is the Psalms of Solomon. Solomon is in popular legend the figure of the wise man and also the husband of many wives.

Solomon Islands, volcanic groups (16,000 sq. mi.; pop. 160,000), SW Pacific. Includes BOUGAINVILLE, GUADALCANAL, SANTA CRUZ ISLANDS, New Georgia, Choiseul, and Santa Isabela. Natives are Melanesians and Polynesians. Discovered 1567 by Spaniards. S and E Solomons were placed 1893–98 under British protectorate; N Solomons were transferred by treaty from Germany to Great Britain, 1900. Buka and Bougainville are governed separately by Australia as part of Territory of New Guinea. In World War II larger islands were occupied by the Japanese from early 1942 until 1943, when they were taken by Allied forces. Battle of Savo Isl. was only naval action lost by Allies.

Solomons, town, on Solomons Isl., S Md., in Patuxent R. Has fishing and yachting and is seat of Chesapeake Biological Laboratory.

Solomon's-seal, perennial spring-blooming plant of genus *Polygonatum.* Well-known wild flowers of North America, they have small, tubular greenish flowers attached along an arching stalk. False Solomon's-seal (*Smilacina*), a similar plant, has small white flowers in a terminal cluster.

Solon (sō'lùn), c.639–c.559 B.C., Athenian lawgiver. As archon in 594 B.C. he moved to protect the peasants of Attica from losing their farms to capitalists; threw open the assembly to all freemen; gave the Areopagus new powers; created a new Council of Four Hundred. His goal was a moderate democracy. Also a poet.

Solothurn (zō'lōto͞orn), Fr. *Soleure,* canton (306 sq. mi.; pop. 170,325), W Switzerland, mostly in the Jura mts. Agr. Population is mainly German-speaking and Catholic. History is that of its cap., **Solothurn** (pop. 16,745), on Aar R. Mfg. of electrical apparatus and watches. A free imperial city from 1218, it joined the Swiss Confederation in 1481. The French ambassadors who resided here until the French Revolution held very great power. Has a cathedral (see of bishop of Basel and Lugano) and has some charming medieval architecture.

Solovetski Islands (sŭlùvyĕt'skē), archipelago, area c.150 sq. mi., N European RSFSR, in White Sea. On largest island is a 15th-cent. monastery, which became a dreaded place of exile for political prisoners under tsarist and Communist regimes.

Soloviev, Sergei Mikhailovich (sĭrgā' mēkhī'lùvĭch sŭlùvyôf'), 1820–79, Russian historian, author of the monumental *History of Russia* (29 vols., 1851–79, in Russian). His son, **Vladimir Sergeyevich Soloviev** (vlŭdyē'mĕr sĭrgā'ùvĭch), 1853–1900, Russian religious philosopher and poet, urged synthesis of Eastern and Western churches into a Church of the Universe. His best-known work is *War, Progress, and the End of History* (1899; Eng. tr., 1915). His poetry influenced the symbolists, notably Bely and Blok.

solstice (sŏl'stĭs), astronomical term for each of two points in ecliptic at which sun reaches its position farthest from equator, i.e., its greatest declination, north or south. Each solstice is 90° from equinoxes, lying halfway between them. In this position sun seems to "stand still" for several days, i.e., its noontime elevation appears not to change in that time. In N Hemisphere summer and winter solstices are about June 22 and about Dec. 22 respectively. See *ill.*, p. 1187.

soluble glass: see WATER GLASS.

solution. True solution is homogeneous mixture of substance doing dissolving, the solvent, and substance being dissolved, the solute. Particles are held to be of molecular fineness, smaller than those in COLLOID or SUSPENSION, invisible even under ultramicroscope, and they do not "settle out." Solvent and solute cannot be separated by filtration. Composition of true solution can be varied within limits. Substances differ in solubility in specific solvents; solubility of solid in a liquid usually increases with temperature. In saturated solution, solvent has dissolved all solute it can at given temperature. Boiling point of solvent is usually raised by solute, melting point lowered. Electrolytes undergo dissociation in solution. Molar solution is one in which gram-molecular weight or mol of solute is present in 1,000 c.c. of solution. Normal solution has one gram of replaceable hydrogen or its equivalent in 1,000 c.c. of solution.

Solutré (sôlütrā'), village, E central France, near Mâcon. Site of a burial place of prehistoric man (discovered 1867); gives name to Solutrean phase of Paleolithic period.

Solvay (sŏl'vā), village (pop. 7,868), central N.Y., near Syracuse. Mfg. of soda ash, salt, chinaware.

Solvay process (sŏl'vā), commercial process

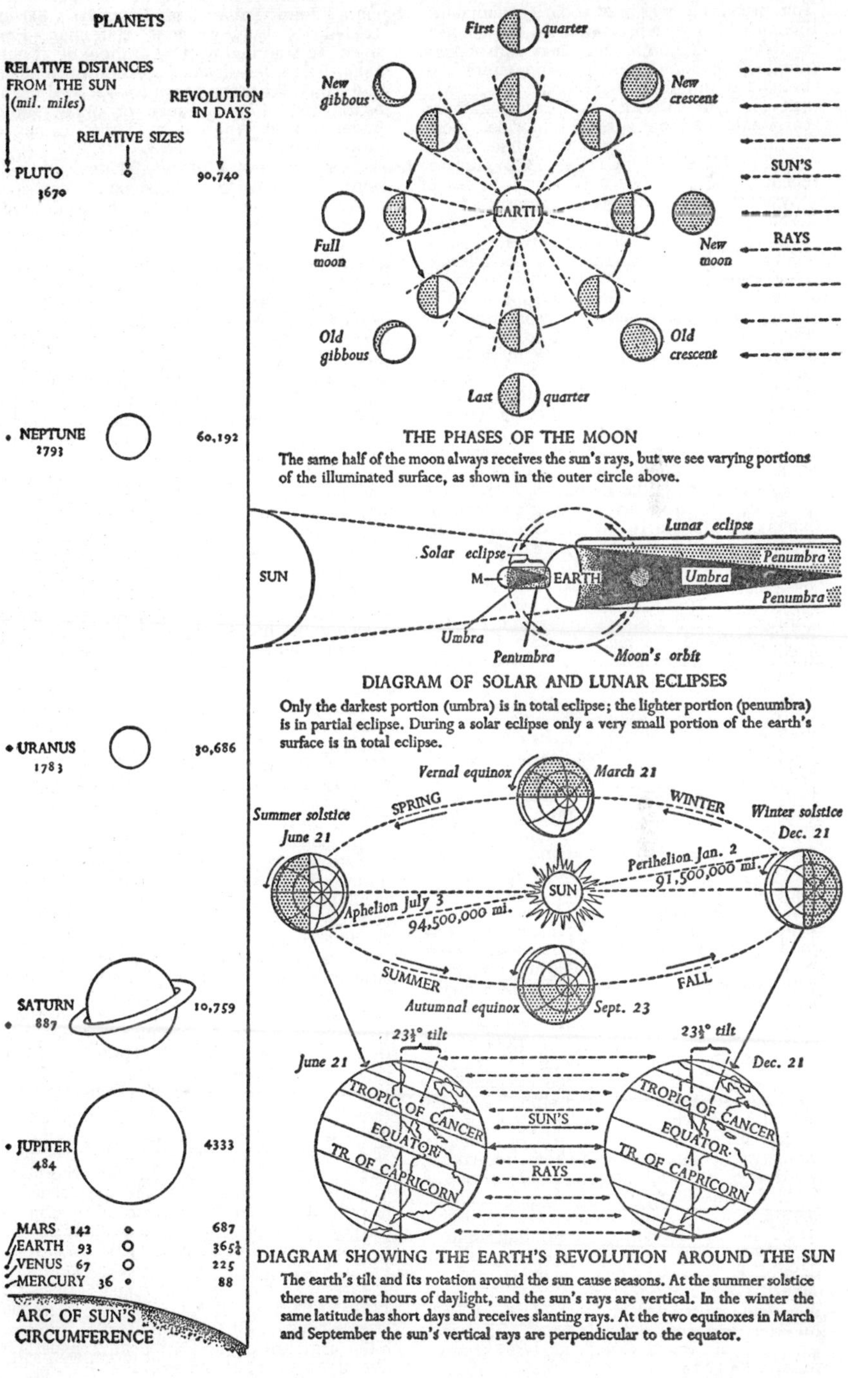

THE PHASES OF THE MOON

The same half of the moon always receives the sun's rays, but we see varying portions of the illuminated surface, as shown in the outer circle above.

DIAGRAM OF SOLAR AND LUNAR ECLIPSES

Only the darkest portion (umbra) is in total eclipse; the lighter portion (penumbra) is in partial eclipse. During a solar eclipse only a very small portion of the earth's surface is in total eclipse.

DIAGRAM SHOWING THE EARTH'S REVOLUTION AROUND THE SUN

The earth's tilt and its rotation around the sun cause seasons. At the summer solstice there are more hours of daylight, and the sun's rays are vertical. In the winter the same latitude has short days and receives slanting rays. At the two equinoxes in March and September the sun's vertical rays are perpendicular to the equator.

for preparing washing soda (sodium carbonate). Three steps: saturated salt solution is treated with ammonia, then with carbon dioxide, reaction yielding ammonium carbonate; ammonium bicarbonate reacts with salt (sodium chloride) forming sodium bicarbonate and ammonium chloride; bicarbonate is heated to give carbonate. Originated by Ernest Solvay (1838–1922), Belgian chemist and founder of Solvay institutes of physiology and sociology at Brussels.

solvent (sŏl'vŭnt), liquid substance in which another substance is dissolved. Water is most common solvent; others include alcohol, benzene, ether.

Solway Firth (sŏl'wā), inlet (c.40 mi. long) of Irish Sea at Esk R. estuary, separating NW England from SW Scotland. Receives several rivers. Firth figures in Scott's *Guy Mannering* and *Redgauntlet*.

Solyman, Ottoman sultans: see SULEIMAN.

Somaliland (sōmä'lēlănd"), **Somalia** (sōmä'lēü), or **Somali Coast,** coastal region of easternmost section of Africa, between Gulf of Aden and Indian Ocean. Name is derived from the Somali, the dominant native people, who are Moslems and speak a Hamitic language. Climate is hot and dry. Generally a great plateau fringed by barren coastal strip. Exports include salt, hides, cotton, pearls, and mother-of-pearl. Politically divided into four parts, one belonging to Ethiopia, and the others to Britain, France, and Italy (who now has only temporary control over her former colony). In World War II, British Somaliland was captured Aug., 1940, by Italian forces. In early 1941 the British conquered Italian Somaliland before regaining their own territory. **British Somaliland** or **Somaliland Protectorate** (c.68,000 sq. mi.; pop. c.500,000) is on Gulf of Aden; cap. Hargeisa. Most of the area was occupied by Egyptian forces until 1884, when British troops moved in and established the protectorate. **French Somaliland** is an overseas territory (c.8,500 sq. mi.; pop. 45,867) on Gulf of Aden and Bab el Mandeb (entrance to Red Sea); cap. Djibouti. France won a foothold here in 1862, and area was made a colony in 1896. **Italian Somaliland** is a former colony (c.194,000 sq. mi.; pop. 970,000), comprising the section of Somaliland on Indian Ocean; cap. Mogadishu. Nucleus of colony was a small protectorate created in central region in 1889; later other protectorates were estab. in N, and much territory in S was ceded by Zanzibar. In 1925 Jubaland or Trans-Juba was detached from Kenya to become part of the Italian possession. In 1936 Italian Somaliland was combined with Somali-speaking districts of Ethiopia into a province of newly formed Italian East Africa. Area was under British military rule from 1941 to 1950, when the UN returned it to Italian control to be exercised until 1959, the provisional date of the former colony's independence.

Sombart, Werner (zôm'bärt), 1863–1941, German economist; professor at Univ. of Berlin after 1917. Influenced by Marx's historical approach, he wrote several analyses of capitalism. Later turned to German romanticism and accepted National Socialism.

Somers, John Somers or **Sommers, Baron,** 1651–1716, English jurist, statesman. Presided at framing of Declaration of Rights 1688. Estab. legality of accession of William and Mary. Attorney general 1692; lord chancellor 1697–1700. Leader of Whig Junto under Queen Anne until Tories came to power 1710.

Somerset, Edmund Beaufort, 2d duke of (sŭ'mûrsĕt"), d. 1455, English statesman and general. Replaced (1447) Richard, duke of York, in France in the Hundred Years War and (by 1453) lost all England's French territories except Calais. Leader of the Lancastrian faction, he was protected by Henry VI. Killed in first battle of Wars of the Roses.

Somerset, Edward Seymour, duke of: see SEYMOUR, family.

Somerset, Robert Carr, earl of, c.1589–1645, lord chamberlain of England. A favorite of James I, he later alienated the king by his arrogance. He and his wife were found guilty (1616) of murder of Sir Thomas OVERBURY, but were released in 1622.

Somerset, county (1,616 sq. mi.; pop. 551,188), SW England; co. town Taunton. Terrain includes Mendip, Exmoor, and Quantock Hills and fertile agr. valleys. Dairying and fruitgrowing are important. Bath, fashionable 18th-cent. watering place, has important Roman remains. County is associated with King Alfred and with King Arthur legend. Glastonbury has religious legend and history. Famous churches include cathedral of Bath and Wells.

Somerset. 1 City (pop. 7,097), S Ky., S of Lexington in Cumberland foothills. Rail and industrial city in farm, coal, and timber area. Near by are national cemetery and Zollicoffer Memorial Park. **2** Residential town (pop. 8,566), SE Mass., on Taunton R. above Fall River; settled 1677. **3** Borough (pop. 5,936), SW Pa., ESE of Pittsburgh. Products include maple sugar, lumber, and coal.

Somersworth, city (pop. 6,927), SE N.H., on Salmon Falls R. and N of Dover. Electrical machinery.

Somerville. 1 City (pop. 102,351), E Mass., residential and industrial suburb just N of Boston; settled 1630. Food, paper, metal products; auto assembling. **2** Residential borough (pop. 11,571), N central N.J., on Raritan R. and SW of Plainfield; settled 1683. Farm trade center. Has Wallace House (residence of the Washingtons, 1778–79). Duke estate is near.

Somerville College: see OXFORD UNIVERSITY.

Somme (sôm), department (2,424 sq. mi.; pop. 441,368), N France, in Picardy; cap. Amiens. The **Somme** river, 152 mi. long, flows past Saint-Quentin, Amiens, and Abbeville into the English Channel. It was the scene of heavy fighting between British and Germans throughout World War I, especially in the so-called battles of Somme (1916, 1917).

Somoza, Anastacio (änästä'syō sōmō'sä), 1896–, president of Nicaragua (1937–47; 1951–). Became virtual ruler of Nicaragua after a coup (1936). His dictatorial rule met bitter criticism of the Caribbean League and liberals throughout the world.

sonar (sō'när), naval device using sound waves

for navigation and ranging. First used in World War II to detect enemy submarines, torpedoes, and mines. Usually the device operates by emitting its own sound waves which are reflected back by any object in their path; the sonar device receives the echo of the reflected waves and the echo is converted into an electric current and interpreted for range, speed, bearing, and nature of the target.

sonata (sùnä'tù), a form of instrumental composition which arose in the baroque period in Italy. The music of baroque sonatas was usually contrapuntal in texture; the rococo sonata had one outstanding melodic line and accompanying harmonic background. The classical sonata was developed by Haydn and Mozart; the first movement (and sometimes others) is in what is called **sonata form.** This form consists of an exposition of two (or more) contrasting themes, their development, and recapitulation. It is used in the string quartet, the symphony, and to some extent the concerto.

Sonderborg, Dan. *Sønderborg* (sû'nùrbôr), town (pop. 16,204), SE Jutland, Denmark; also known by its German name, Sonderburg. A port on the Als Sound, it also has textile and other mfg. It was part of SCHLESWIG until the 16th cent., when Christian III of Denmark created the duchy of Sonderburg for his younger son John, from whom the branch of Schleswig-Holstein-Sonderburg-Glücksburg (the present Danish royal line) is descended. Annexed to Prussia 1866; restored to Denmark by a plebiscite 1920.

Sonderbund (zôn'dùrbo͝ont) [Ger.,= separate league], 1845–47, defensive alliance of the Catholic cantons of Switzerland—Uri, Schwyz, Unterwalden, Lucerne, Valais, Fribourg, Zug—against the Radical party's anticlerical measures and program for closer federal union. The Radical majority in the federal diet declared the Sonderbund dissolved (1847) and dispatched a federal army under Gen. Dufour against the separatist forces. The Sonderbund's defeat in an almost bloodless campaign led to the adoption of a federal constitution (1848) and the expulsion of the Jesuits from Switzerland.

song, one of the most natural forms of musical expression, found in all cultures. In Western music, song is broadly classified as art song or folk song. Early art songs were those of the troubadour and meistersinger. The refined, lyrical *air de cour* of late 16th-cent. France provided inspiration for the *ayre* of early 17th-cent. English lutanists such as Thomas Campion and Thomas Morley. Outstanding among art songs is the German romantic lied of the 19th cent., in which the vocal line and piano accompaniment have equal musical significance. The style reached its peak in works of Schubert, Schumann, Brahms, and Hugo Wolf. All nations have contributed much to art-song literature, with perhaps the exception of Italy, where attention centered on the opera and the aria.

song, bird. Songs, call notes, and certain mechanical sounds constitute bird communication. Song, usually confined to male, is at its height in breeding season. It serves to announce selection of nesting place, warns away other males, and attracts females. Song is produced in syrinx at base of windpipe, is modified by larynx and tongue.

Song of Solomon, Song of Songs, or **Canticles,** book of Old Testament, written in form of a love poem, traditionally ascribed to Solomon. Accepted in Jewish and Christian canon as an allegory or parable of God's love for Israel, for the Church, and for the soul that loves Him.

sonnet, poem of 14 lines, usually in iambic pentameter, in definite rhyme scheme. The main types are the Italian (Petrarchan) sonnet, an octave and sestet rhyming *abbaabba cdecde,* and the Elizabethan (Shaksperian) sonnet, three quatrains and couplet rhyming *abab cdcd efef gg.* Essence of sonnet is unity of thought or idea.

Sonnino, Sidney, Barone (bärō'nā sōn-nē'nō), 1847–1922, Italian statesman and economist. Minister of finance 1893–96; premier (1906, 1909–10). As foreign minister in World War I he negotiated secret Treaty of London (1915), by which Italy joined Allies in return for promises of vast territorial gains. He and ORLANDO represented Italy at Paris Peace Conference (1919).

Sonoma (sùnō'mù), city (pop. 2,015), W Calif., N of San Francisco; founded 1835. J. C. FRÉMONT raised Bear Flag of Calif. republic here in 1846.

Sonora (sōnō'rä), state (70,484 sq. mi.; pop. 503,095), NW Mexico; cap. Hermosillo. On Gulf of California, S of Ariz., it is mountainous with vast desert stretches. Agr. by irrigation, cattle raising, and mining are chief occupations. Hermosillo, Guaymas, and Nogales (on Ariz. border) are principal cities. Spanish exploration of area was intensive after Coronado's expedition (1540). Originally part of Nueva Viscaya, it was later joined to Sinaloa. They were made separate states in 1830.

Sonora (sùnô'rù). **1** City (pop. 2,448), central Calif., E of Stockton, in famed Mother Lode gold-mining area. Site of Big Bonanza mine. **2** Ranch town (pop. 2,633), W Texas, S of San Angelo and on Dry Fork of Devils R.

Sons of Liberty, secret societies in American colonies, organized in protest against Stamp Act. In Civil War, name was adopted by KNIGHTS OF THE GOLDEN CIRCLE in 1864.

Sons of the American Revolution, national patriotic organization, founded in N.Y. in 1889 by union of Sons of Revolutionary Sires and certain members of the Society of the Sons of the Revolution. Membership is open to those whose ancestors saw active service in Revolutionary forces.

Soochow (so͞o'jō), city (pop. 381,288), S Kiangsu prov., China, on Grand Canal, in scenic lake district. Textile mills. Dates from c.1000 B.C. Became treaty port 1896. Held 1937–45 by the Japanese. Formerly called Wuhsien.

Soong (so͝ong), Chinese family prominent in public affairs. **Soong Yao-ju** or **Charles Jones Soong,** d. 1924, was a Methodist missionary and merchant in Shanghai. His son, **T. V. Soong,** 1894–, was educated at Harvard Univ. Ranked second to Chiang Kai-shek in Nationalist government, 1945–49. Left China 1949, resigned from Kuomintang to remain abroad (1950). Soong Yao-ju's three daughters all graduated from colleges in U.S. **Soong Ai-ling** (ī-lĭng'), 1888–, is wife of H. H. Kung. **Soong Ching-ling** (chĭng'-lĭng'), 1890–, married Sun Yat-sen, 1915. After his death (1925) she held high posts in Nationalist government; left it twice (1927, 1945) in protest against anti-Communist policy. In 1949 she became non-Communist member of central executive committee of Chinese People's Republic. **Soong Mei-ling** (mā'-lĭng'), 1896–, married Chiang Kai-shek, 1927. Addressed U.S. Congress 1943; again visited U.S. 1948 to seek aid for Nationalists. Joined husband on Formosa, 1950.

soot, black or brown deposit resulting from imperfect combustion of high-carbon fuel and consisting of amorphous carbon and tarry substances. Lampblack is fine soot used in making printer's and India ink.

Sophia (sōfī'ů, Ger. zōfē'ä), 1630–1714, electress of Hanover, consort of Elector Ernest Augustus; daughter of Frederick the Winter King and Elizabeth of Bohemia; granddaughter of James I of England. Through Act of SETTLEMENT (1701) her son succeeded to English throne as George I (1714).

Sophia, Santa: see HAGIA SOPHIA.

Sophia Alekseyevna (sô'fyů ŭlyĭksyā'ĭvnŭ), 1657–1704, regent of Russia (1682–89). Ruled autocratically during minority of her brother IVAN V and her half-brother PETER I. Peter overthrew her after accusing her of plotting against his life and confined her to a convent (1689). In 1698, charging her with instigating a revolt of the Strelitsi (Moscow garrison), he forced her to take the veil.

Sophia Dorothea, 1666–1726, electress of Hanover, wife of Elector George Louis (later George I of England). Divorced (1694) for an alleged love affair, she was thereafter imprisoned.

sophist (sŏ'fĭst), in present usage, one who employs seemingly sound but fallacious arguments. Somewhat unfairly derived from the Greek Sophists, teachers who denied the possibility of reaching objective truth. Their chief function was to instill worldly wisdom in rich pupils. Socrates attacked them violently.

Sophocles (sŏ'fůklēz), c.496–c.406 B.C., Greek tragic poet. Gained first dramatic triumph (over Aeschylus) in 468 B.C. and thereafter won first place about 20 times. He added a third actor, introduced scene painting, and abandoned the trilogy for the self-contained tragedy. His characters, on a more human level than those of Aeschylus, are governed in their fate more by their own faults than by the gods. Seven complete plays survive: *Ajax, Antigone, Oedipus Rex* or *Oedipus Tyrannus* (in which Greek dramatic irony reaches an apex; cited by Aristotle as a perfect example of tragedy), *Electra,* the *Trachiniae, Philoctetes,* and *Oedipus at Colonus.*

Sophonias (sō"fůnī'ůs), Greek form of ZEPHANIAH.

Sophonisba (sōfůnĭz'bů), 3d cent. B.C., Carthaginian lady, daughter of Hasdrubal, the brother of Hannibal. Legend (partly true) says she was betrothed to Masinissa before her father married her to Syphax of Numidia, who became an ally of Carthage. When he was defeated and slain by Masinissa (203 B.C.), the victor, to keep her from gracing a Roman triumph, sent her a bowl of poison to drink.

Sopron (shô'prôn), Ger. *Ödenburg,* city (pop. 42,255), W Hungary, in Hungarian section of BURGENLAND. An old cultural center, it has three 13th-cent. churches, a 15th-cent. palace, and a university.

Soracte (sōrăk'tē), isolated mountain, 2,267 ft. high, central Italy, N of Rome. Celebrated by Vergil and Horace.

Soranus (sůrā'nůs), fl. 1st–2d cent., Greek physician. His treatise on obstetrics, diseases of women, and pediatrics influential until 16th cent.

Sorbonne (sôrbôn'), traditional name of the Univ. of Paris, France; more properly, the name of its first endowed college, founded by Robert de Sorbon (1201–74), chaplain of Louis IX, and opened c.1257. Because of its academic and theological reputation it gained precedence over earlier colleges at Paris; its doctors were often called upon to render decisions on important ecclesiastical and theological issues; its name was extended to the entire faculty of theology. The Univ. of Paris was thoroughly reorganized in the 19th cent., and the name Sorbonne is not official.

Sorbs: see WENDS.

Sordello (sōrdĕl'lō), 13th cent., Italian poet, author of Provençal verse; immortalized by a reference in Dante, subject of a poem by Browning.

Sorel, Agnès (änyĕs' sôrĕl'), c.1422–1450, mistress of Charles VII of France after 1444. Famed for her beauty and intelligence; had beneficial influence on king's policies. Unfounded rumor that she was poisoned was spread by enemies of Jacques CŒUR.

Sorel, Georges (zhôrzh'), 1847–1922, French social philosopher, author of *Reflections on Violence* (1908). Finding in democracy the triumph of mediocrity, he espoused syndicalism and the creation of a revolutionary elite. His views influenced Fascism.

Sorel, city (pop. 14,961), S Que., Canada, on St. Lawrence R. at mouth of Richelieu R. and NNE of Montreal. Grain shipping center with shipbuilding and iron and steel foundries. Fort Richelieu built here 1665.

sorghum, cornlike annual grass (*Sorghum vulgare*), widely cultivated in many varieties, and bearing grain in panicles. Sorghums are cultivated for forage and fodder and the grain is used for livestock feed. A molasses is obtained from sweet sorghum. Other varieties include milo, kaffir corn, broomcorn, Sudan grass, feterita, durra.

Sorokin, Pitirim Alexandrovitch (sōrō'kĭn), 1889–, Russian-American historian and sociologist. Banished by Bolsheviks, he came to U.S. 1923; naturalized 1930. Works include *Sociology of Revolution* (1925), *Social and Cultural Dynamics* (4 vols., 1937–41), and *Russia and the United States* (1944).

Sorolla y Bastida, Joaquín (hwäkēn' sōrō'lyä ē bästē'dhä), 1863–1923, Spanish painter of large figure compositions in full, glowing sunlight.

sorrel, name for several plants, especially DOCK and OXALIS.

Sorrento (sůrěn'tō, Ital. sōr-rěn'tō), town (pop. 7,031), Campania, S Italy; a famous resort on the Bay of Naples. Birthplace of Tasso.

Sosen (sōsän'), 1747–1821, Japanese painter, noted for animal paintings (esp. monkeys). His name literally means "monkey saint."

Sothern, Edward A(skew) (sŭ'dhûrn), 1826–81, English actor; in U.S. after 1852. Acted in such dramas as *Camille* and *Our American Cousin.* His son, **E(dward) H(ugh) Sothern,** 1859–1933, acted with Frohman's Lyceum company (1886–99) in such plays as *The Prisoner of Zenda* and *If I Were King.* Acted Shakspere almost exclusively after 1900, co-starring with Julia MARLOWE (whom he married in 1911).

Soto, Hernando de: see DE SOTO, HERNANDO.

Soufrière, volcano, 4,048 ft. high, on St. Vincent, British West Indies. Eruption in 1902 laid waste a third of island, killing more than 1,000 people.

soul, vital principle of a body, conceived as existing with it. Materialist philosophies deny its existence, pantheism denies that the soul can be individual. The concept on various levels (e.g., the idea of a world soul) is known in various religions and philosophies. Among many Christians it is considered the thinking life of man opposed to the material body. The scholastics distinguished among the rational soul of man, the animal soul of beasts, and the vegetative soul of plants, considering only the rational soul immortal. The question of the soul's immortality has been debated from Plato's time to ours. Some Eastern religions do not distinguish the soul of man from that of animals.

Soulé, Pierre (pyĕr' sōōlā'), 1801–70, American political leader and diplomat, b. France. U.S. Senator from La. (1847, 1849–53). Minister to Spain (1853–54); helped draft OSTEND MANIFESTO. Served in government of Confederacy (1863–64).

Soulouque, Faustin Élie (fōstē' ālē' sōōlōōk'), c.1785–1867, Negro emperor of Haiti (1849–59). An illiterate ex-slave, he became president (1847) and then declared himself emperor as Faustin I. Reign was corrupt and bloody.

Soult, Nicolas (nēkôlä' sōōlt'), 1769–1851, marshal of France; created duke of Dalmatia by Napoleon I (1808). Commanded in PENINSULAR WAR 1808–13. Minister of war under Louis XVIII (1814), but joined Napoleon in Hundred Days. Under Louis Philippe he again was minister of war (1830–34) and prime minister (1840–44).

Sound, the: see ORESUND.

sound, waves of vibratory motion radiating from a body moving to and fro so as to cause alternately in a given space a condensation and a rarefaction of molecules. Sound wave is longitudinal since vibration is along direction of wave. WAVE length depends on velocity in a given medium at a given temperature and on frequency of vibration of body causing sound. Sounds of frequencies of c.20–20,000 vibrations per second are considered audible to human ear. Sound is conducted best through dense media; will not pass through vacuum. Pitch is higher as frequency increases; sound is louder as vibration amplitude is greater; intensity decreases as distance from source increases. Sound waves can be reflected (see ECHO), refracted, or absorbed. See also INTERFERENCE; DOPPLER'S PRINCIPLE.

sound recording, process of converting acoustic energy of sound waves into electromechanical energy for inscription on various substances. In disk recording, sound-wave frequencies are converted into electrical voltages which vibrate a stylus, causing the stylus to cut into a soft disk revolving beneath it; the cuts (groovings) vary with the amplitude and frequency of the voltage. The soft disk serves as a mold for making a metal stamp from which more durable disks are pressed. In reproduction, as the disk revolves, a needle traverses the grooves and transmits the vibrations to a diaphragm; the vibrations of the diaphragm produce a voltage which is reconverted into sound waves and passed on to a loudspeaker. One device for reproducing recorded sound is the PHONOGRAPH. In wire or tape recording, disturbances in a magnetic field cause varying realignments of magnetic particles in the wire or tape passing through the field; when the wire is played back, the realignments redisturb the field and produce a voltage. Sound recordings for use with motion pictures are commonly made on film and interpret the acoustic characteristics of sound into photo or light characteristics.

sour gum: see BLACK GUM.

Souris (sōō'rĭs), river, c.435 mi. long, rising in S Saskatchewan, looping into N.Dak., and entering Assiniboine R. in SW Manitoba.

Sousa, John Philip (sōō'zů), 1854–1932, American bandmaster and composer. He was leader of the U.S. Marine Band from 1880 to 1892, when he formed his own band. In 1910–11 he and his band toured the world. He wrote c.100 marches, including *Semper fidelis, The Washington Post March, The Stars and Stripes Forever,* and comic operas, such as *El Capitan.*

Sousa, Martim Afonso de (märtēn' äfō'zō dů sō'zů), 1500?–1571?, Portuguese colonial administrator. Commissioned (1530) to drive French from Brazilian coast and to estab. colonies, he did both. He was true founder of Brazil.

South, the, region of U.S. embracing all of the southeast and part of the southwest. It includes, at the most, 14 states—Md., Va., N.C., S.C., Ga., Fla., Ky., Tenn., Ala., Miss., Ark., La., Okla., Texas. To many the region is restricted to 11 states below the Potomac which comprised the CONFEDERACY. The South has many distinctive areas. Whole region has greater humidity, more sunshine, less wind than other sections. Predominantly agr. economy led to introduction of NEGRO as source of cheap labor under institutions of plantation and SLAVERY. The MISSOURI COMPROMISE marked rise of Southern sectionalism, rooted in doctrine of STATES' RIGHTS. The Old South died in RECONSTRUCTION period after CIVIL WAR; increased industrialization came later. Agrarian revolt of late 19th cent. turned conservative Democrats out of power. Various Southern demagogues have achieved national attention (e.g., Huey LONG); so, too, has latter-day KU KLUX KLAN. The South has always had a strong regional literature.

South, University of the, called **Sewanee,** Sewanee, Tenn., on Cumberland Plateau and E of Winchester; Episcopal; for men, chartered 1858, opened 1868. Arts and sciences, theology, military academy. Publishes *Sewanee Review.*

South Africa, Union of, dominion (472,494 sq. mi.; pop. 11,418,349) of British Commonwealth of Nations; cap. Pretoria. Bounded on W by the Atlantic and on E by Indian Ocean. Comprises four provinces, CAPE OF GOOD HOPE, NATAL, ORANGE FREE STATE, and TRANSVAAL; administers SOUTH-WEST AFRICA. Basutoland is an enclave. Drakensburg mts. are in E, but country is mostly a plateau (2,000–6,000 ft. high). Climate is mild and dry. Crops include cereals, tobacco, cotton, peanuts, fruits, and sugar. Mineral wealth is enormous. Gold (mined mainly in WITWATERSRAND) makes up half of export volume. Other important minerals are diamonds (at Kimberley), coal, copper, iron, and manganese. Commerce, largely developed by Cecil RHODES, centers on JOHANNESBURG; major ports are CAPETOWN and DURBAN. First European to visit South Africa was the Portuguese Bartholomew Diaz (1488). Dutch East India Co. estab. first white settlement on the cape in 1652. In 1841 the British assumed control over the area. Boer settlers migrated N in 1830s to found republics of Transvaal, Orange Free State, and Natal. In latter half of 19th cent. the discovery of diamonds in Orange Free State and of gold in Transvaal brought numerous prospectors, mainly British, against whom the Boer governments took repressive measures. Mutual hostility exploded in SOUTH AFRICAN WAR (1899–1902). British victory was followed 1910 by establishment of Union of South Africa, but Boer population was recognized by retention of Roman-Dutch law and by making Afrikaans an official language along with English. Two main political parties developed: the Unionist, headed by J. C. SMUTS, who advocated cooperation between the Boer and British elements; and the Nationalist, which espoused Boer superiority and even opposed the country's entry into World War II. After the war, race relations became increasingly strained as the Nationalists, led by Daniel MALAN, sought to ensure white supremacy at all costs. The repressive Nationalist policy was violently opposed by the nonwhites, who comprise 8,000,000 Negroes, 300,000 immigrants from India, and 700,000 "Coloreds" or part-white persons (the only nonwhite group with the right to vote). In 1952 Malan clashed with the South African supreme court when he resorted to unconstitutional means in trying to disfranchise the "Coloreds."

South African War or **Boer War,** 1899–1902, war of the South African Republic (Transvaal) and Orange Free State against Great Britain. The Boers had long resented the British advance into S African territories, and the hostility was inflamed after the discovery of gold (1886) brought an influx of British prospectors. The Boer government denied these newcomers citizenship and taxed them heavily, despite British protests. The situation was aggravated in 1895 by the Jameson raid (see JAMESON, SIR LEANDER STARR), which was interpreted by S. J. P. KRUGER as a British plot to seize Transvaal and which led to the military alliance of Transvaal and Orange Free State (1896). The British brought in troops to defend what they considered their commercial rights. When they refused to withdraw, the Boer states declared war (Oct. 12, 1899). The large and well-equipped Boer forces won great victories, capturing Mafeking and besieging Kimberley and Ladysmith. But the tide turned in 1900, with the landing of heavy British reinforcements. Under the leadership of F. S. Roberts and Lord Kitchener the British occupied all the major cities and formally annexed the Boer states. The war was thought to be over, and Kitchener remained only for the mopping-up. The Boers, however, began guerrilla attacks, led by such men as Botha and Smuts. Kitchener struck back by interning Boer women and children and building chains of blockhouses to cut off large areas, while his troops combed the guerrilla country, section by section. Boer submission was formalized in the Treaty of Vereeniging (May 31, 1902). The bitterness caused by the war continues to affect political life in South Africa.

South Amboy, city (pop. 8,422), E N.J., on harbor at Raritan R. mouth (bridged) opposite Perth Amboy. Transships coal; makes clay products. Terminal (1832) of Camden and Amboy RR, state's first.

South America, continent (c.6,850,000 sq. mi.; pop. c.110,000,000), S continent of the W Hemisphere. Divided politically into 10 republics (ARGENTINA, BOLIVIA, BRAZIL, CHILE, COLOMBIA, ECUADOR, PARAGUAY, PERU, URUGUAY, and VENEZUELA) and three colonies (British, Dutch, and French GUIANA). Geographical features include: the ANDES, range of mountains paralleling Pacific coast; great river systems emptying into Atlantic (N to S —MAGDALENA, ORINOCO, AMAZON, RÍO DE LA PLATA); GUIANA HIGHLANDS in Guiana and Venezuela; the PAMPA and frigid PATAGONIA; desert of ATACAMA in Chile; Lake TITICACA in Andes. See *map,* p. 1193.

Southampton, Thomas Wriothesley, 1st **earl of** (rŏt'slē; rĭs'lē), 1505–50, lord chancellor of England. Noted for severity, he was dismissed by Edward Seymour. Later helped overthrow Seymour as protector. His grandson, **Henry Wriothesley,** 3d **earl of Southampton,** 1573–1624, was a patron of letters. He is best known as patron of William Shakspere. Sometimes thought to be man to whom sonnets are dedicated and by some thought to be author of Shakspere. Deeply involved in rebellion (1601) of Robert Devereux, earl of Essex, he was imprisoned by Elizabeth I. Restored to favor by James I. His son, **Thomas Wriothesley,** 4th **earl of Southampton,** 1607–67, was an adviser of Charles I. Opposed extreme policies of Strafford. Negotiated for king with Parliament (1643, 1645).

Southampton, county borough (pop. 178,326),

Capital Cities are designated by Capital and Small Capital type

Hampshire, England, at head of Southampton Water. Has large dockyards and is a major port. Was one of chief British military transport stations in both world wars. There are many ancient churches and buildings. Crusaders and Pilgrim Fathers embarked here. City has shipbuilding and varied mfg. Center of city was almost entirely destroyed by bombing in 1940. Administrative county of Southampton is mainland part of HAMPSHIRE.

Southampton, village (pop. 4,042), on SE Long Isl., SE N.Y. Summer resort with many fine estates. Here is Parrish Memorial Art Mus.

Southampton Insurrection, 1831, slave uprising in Va., led by Nat TURNER.

South Australia, state (380,070 sq. mi.; pop. 646,216), S Australia; cap. Adelaide. Bounded on N by Northern Territory, on S by Indian Ocean, on W by Western Australia, and on E by New South Wales and Victoria. Coastal area was visited 1627 by the Dutch. In 1836 South Australia became a British colony and in 1901 a state of the commonwealth. Included Northern Territory from 1863 to 1911, when it was transferred to federal government. Much of the state is wasteland, and population is largely concentrated in fertile SE area. Chief exports are pig lead, silver, wheat, wool, wine, and meat.

South Bakersfield, village (pop. 12,120), S central Calif., near Bakersfield.

South Bass Island: see PUT IN BAY.

South Bend, city (pop. 115,911), N Ind., on great bend of St. Joseph R. and ESE of Chicago; settled 1820 on site of French mission, trading post. Center for farming, dairying area. Mfg. of metal products, paint, paper, clothing. Univ. of NOTRE DAME and St. Mary's Col. (R.C.; for women; opened 1844, chartered 1851 at Bertrand, Mich., chartered 1853 by Indiana, moved 1855, became col. 1903) are near by.

South Boston, town (pop. 6,057), S. Va., on Ran R. and ENE of Danville. Has important tobacco market.

South Bound Brook, industrial borough (pop. 2,905), N central N.J., on Raritan R. opposite Bound Brook. Von Steuben had hq. here 1778–79.

Southbridge, town (pop. 17,519), including Southbridge village (pop. 16,748), S Mass., SW of Worcester; settled 1730. Optical, textile, metal products.

South Carolina, state (31,055 sq. mi.; pop. 2,117,027), SE U.S.; one of Thirteen Colonies; cap. COLUMBIA. CHARLESTON, GREENVILLE, SPARTANBURG largest cities. Bounded on W and S by Savannah R., E by the Atlantic. Fall line separates coastal plain from piedmont. Blue Ridge in NW. Other rivers are PEE DEE, SANTEE, EDISTO. Cotton, tobacco, corn main agr. products; also grains, truck, fruit. Mining (clay, granite, gravel, limestone). Mfg. of cotton textiles main industry; also lumbering, fishing. Short-lived Spanish and French settlements before English founded colony at Albemarle Point 1670 (moved to Charleston 1680). Indian and Spanish threats eventually removed. Became royal colony 1729. Rice and indigo were then main crops. In American Revolution British took Charleston in second attempt (1780). Ensuing CAROLINA CAMPAIGN forced British to retreat. First state to secede (Dec. 20, 1860) from Union; firing on Fort Sumter (see SUMTER, FORT) opened war. W. T. SHERMAN destroyed much of state in 1865. Suffered under Reconstruction. Soil erosion, high illiteracy rate, and discrimination are problems recently confronting state.

South Carolina, University of: see COLUMBIA.

South Carolina State Agricultural and Mechanical College: see ORANGEBURG.

South Charleston, town (pop. 16,686), W W.Va., on Kanawha R. and near Charleston; settled c.1900. Mfg. of chemicals; U.S. naval ordnance plant.

South China Sea, arm of the Pacific Ocean, between SE Asian mainland and Malay Archipelago.

Southcott, Joanna, 1750–1814, English religious visionary. Uneducated, she claimed (c.1792) the gift of prophecy and gained many followers.

South Dakota, state (77,047 sq. mi.; pop. 652,740), N central U.S.; admitted 1889 as 40th state; cap. PIERRE. Missouri R. bisects state. BLACK HILLS and BADLANDS are in SW. Agr. of grains (esp. corn, rye, wheat); dairying, livestock. Mining (gold, silver, feldspar, tantalum, lithium, limestone). Processes farm products; mfg. of farm implements and wood products. Land of SIOUX INDIANS. Dakota Territory estab. 1861. Immigrants came with railroad. Gold rush occurred in 1870s, continued despite trouble with Indians. DEADWOOD and LEAD had brief heyday. Boom stimulated settlement and cattle ranching. Hurt by recurrent droughts and depression of 1930s. Irrigation and power projects, erosion measures brought relief; proposed MISSOURI RIVER BASIN PROJECT would aid area.

South Dakota, University of: see VERMILLION.

South Dakota School of Mines and Technology: see RAPID CITY.

South Dakota State College of Agriculture and Mechanic Arts: see BROOKINGS.

Southdown sheep: see SHEEP.

South Downs: see DOWNS, THE, chalk hills.

Southend-on-Sea, county borough (pop. 151,830), Essex, England; popular seaside resort.

Southern Alps, mountain range, on South Isl., New Zealand, paralleling W coast and containing Mt. Cook (12,349 ft.), dominion's highest peak.

Southern California, University of, at Los Angeles; nonsectarian, private, coed.; chartered and opened 1880 by Methodists. Affiliates are Los Angeles Univ. of International Relations and dental college.

Southern Methodist University, at University Park, Texas (suburb of Dallas); coed.; chartered 1911, opened 1915. Has theater and history museums.

Southern Pacific Company, transportation system chartered in 1865 in Calif., reincorporated in Ky. in 1884 and in Del. in 1947. Built in S Calif. to provide Central Pacific RR with feeder lines and eventually to connect San Francisco and New Orleans. In 1884 the Southern Pacific and the Central Pacific were combined under Leland STANFORD and C. P. HUNTINGTON as a unit of interdependent systems. E. H. HARRIMAN expanded the railroads. In 1923 the Southern Pacific leased the Central Pacific RR's facilities. Also controls bus lines in Far West and a trucking service.

Southern Pines, winter resort (pop. 4,272), central N.C., SW of Raleigh. Mild climate; sports.

Southern Rhodesia (rōdē'zhů), British colony (150,333 sq. mi.; pop. 2,021,900), SE Africa; cap. Salisbury. Bordered on NW by Northern Rhodesia and on N and E by Mozambique. Mainly a high plateau. Gold, asbestos, coal, and chromite are mined; cotton, tobacco, peanuts, and wheat are grown. Stock raising and lumbering are also important. Originally inhabited by the Mashona tribe, who were supplanted by the MATABELE. Occupied 1888 by the British. When RHODESIA was divided (1923), S Rhodesia became a colony ruled by an appointed governor. A legislative council is elected by white British subjects.

Southern University and Agricultural and Mechanical College: see BATON ROUGE, La.

South Euclid (ū'klĭd), city (pop. 15,432), NE Ohio, NE suburb of Cleveland. Seat of Notre Dame Col.

Southey, Robert (sou'dhē, sŭ'–), 1774–1843, English poet and historian. In 1803 he settled in the Lake District with Coleridge and Wordsworth. In 1813 he became poet laureate. His ambitious epics are little read; he is remembered rather for shorter poems (e.g., "The Battle of Blenheim" and "Inchcape Rock"). His prose includes a history of Brazil, a history of the Peninsular War (1823–32), and a masterly life of Nelson (1813).

South Gastonia (găstō'nēů), village (pop. 6,465), S N.C., S of Gastonia. Post office name, Pinkney.

South Gate, city (pop. 51,116), S Calif., S of Los Angeles. Mfg. of furniture, building materials, tires, and chemicals.

South Georgia, island (c.1,450 sq. mi.; pop. c.700 during whaling season, c.250 at other times), S Atlantic, c.1,200 mi. E of Cape Horn. Capt. James Cook took possession for British in 1775. Included as dependency in British colony of Falkland Isls. Also claimed by Argentina.

South Hadley, town (pop. 10,145), W Mass., on Connecticut R above Springfield; settled c.1660. Mfg. of paper. Seat of Mt. Holyoke Col. (hōl'yōk) (nonsectarian; for women; provides graduate work); chartered 1836, opened 1837 as Mt. Holyoke Female Seminary by Mary LYON, rechartered and renamed 1888 and 1893; model for many early women's schools.

South Haven, resort city (pop. 5,629), SW Mich., on L. Michigan at mouth of Black R. and N of Benton Harbor. Center of fruit-growing area with fisheries and mfg. of pianos and organs.

South Holland, Dutch *Zuidholland,* province (1,085 sq. mi.; pop. 2,284,080), W Netherlands, on the North Sea; cap. The Hague. Other chief cities include Rotterdam and Leiden. Similar in character to NORTH HOLLAND, with which it was united until 1840 as HOLLAND.

Southington, village (pop. 5,955) in Southington town (pop. 13,061), central Conn., SW of Hartford; settled 1696. Mfg. of metal and wood products.

South Island (58,093 sq. mi.; pop. 556,006), New Zealand, larger of the dominion's two principal islands. SOUTHERN ALPS are dominant physical feature, with certain sections included in national parks. Wild SW area is mainly in Fiordland Natl. Park. Grain, timber, and sheep are chief products. Some coal and gold are mined in W. Christchurch and Dunedin are principal centers.

South Kingstown (kĭng'stůn), town (pop. 10,148), S R.I., between Narragansett and Charlestown; settled 1641. Textiles. Narragansett Indians made final stand 1675 W of Kingston village in the town. Seat of Univ. of Rhode Island (land-grant; coed.); chartered 1888, opened as school 1890, became college of agriculture and mechanic arts 1892, named R.I. State Col. 1909, renamed 1950.

South Manchurian Railroad, trunk line between Changchun and Dairen. Originally part of Russian-built Chinese Eastern RR (with main section in N Manchuria), it was part of Japan's indemnity after Russo-Japanese War (1904–5). After World War II entire Manchurian rail system (renamed Chinese Changchun RR) passed to joint Soviet-Chinese control. The **South Manchurian Railroad Company** was main agency of Japanese penetration of Manchuria. It controlled all major economic activities (e.g., coal and iron mining, harbor improvements, and construction of towns).

South Milwaukee (mĭlwô'kē), city (pop. 12,855), SE Wis., on L. Michigan near Milwaukee; settled 1835. Mfg. of electrical equipment and machinery.

South Norfolk, city (pop. 10,434), SE Va., suburb of Norfolk. Has lumber milling.

South Norwalk, Conn.: see NORWALK.

Southold (south'hōld), town (pop. 11,632), on NE Long Isl., SE N.Y., on Long Isl. Sound; settled 1640. Includes resort village of Southold (pop. 1,027).

South Orange, residential suburban village (pop. 15,230), NE N.J., W of Newark. Seat of Seton Hall Univ. (R.C.; men and women; 1856; became university on merging with John Marshall Col., 1950–51).

South Orkney Islands, group, S Atlantic, c.850 mi. ESE of Cape Horn. Claimed by British (1821) and included as dependencies of Falkland Isls. colony. Also claimed by Argentina.

South Ossetia, Georgian SSR: see OSSETIA.

South Pasadena (pă"sůdē'nů), residential city (pop. 16,935), S Calif., between Pasadena and Los Angeles. Has citrus orchards and animal farms.

South Pass, valley (alt. c.7,550 ft.), SW Wyo., in Wind River Range of the Rockies. Used by pioneers crossing Continental Divide on Oregon Trail.

South Platte (plăt), river, c.450 mi. long, rising in Rocky Mts. in many branches which join in central Colo. Flows E and NE to Denver, then NE across Colo. to join North Platte R. in S central Nebr. and form the Platte. Basin has many private irrigation dams. Colo.

section in COLORADO–BIG THOMPSON PROJECT, similar Blue–South Platte project.

South Pole, southern end of earth's axis, lat. 90° S and long. 0°. It is distinguished from the south magnetic pole. The South Pole was reached (1911) by Roald Amundsen. See also ANTARCTICA.

Southport, county borough (pop. 84,057), Lancashire, England; seaside resort. Has an observatory, art and technical schools, and a fine boulevard.

South Portland, city (pop. 21,866), SW Maine, across Fore R. from Portland. Has shipyards, foundries, and marine hardware plants. U.S. Fort Preble is here. Just S are U.S. Fort Williams and Portland Head Light, oldest lighthouse (1791) on Maine coast.

South River, borough (pop. 11,308), E N.J., SE of New Brunswick. Embroideries, clay products.

South Saint Paul, city (pop. 15,709), SE Minn., near St. Paul on the Mississippi. Stockyards, packing plants, tanneries, and foundries.

South San Francisco, city (pop. 19,351), W Calif., S of San Francisco. Has metalworking and meat-packing plants.

South Saskatchewan: see SASKATCHEWAN, river.

South Sea Bubble, popular name in England for speculation in the South Sea Co. formed (1711) by Robert Harley. Company assumed the national debt in return for annual payment by government plus a monopoly of British trade with islands of South Seas and South America. Fraudulent schemes resulted and the bubble burst (1720). Robert Walpole was made chancellor of the exchequer to restore company's credit.

South Shetland Islands, Antarctic archipelago off N Palmer Peninsula, in S Atlantic. Barren, snow-covered islands. Figured 1906–31 in whaling activity and later antarctic exploration. Discovered 1819 by an English mariner. Claimed by Great Britain, Argentina, and Chile.

South Shields, county borough (pop. 106,605), Durham, England, at mouth of the Tyne. North Shields, part of TYNEMOUTH, is opposite. Docks cover 50 acres. There is fishing and varied mfg.

South Victoria Land: see VICTORIA LAND.

Southwark (sŭdh'ŭrk, south'wûrk), metropolitan borough (pop. 97,171), of S London, England. Also called "the Borough." Famous inns (including Tabard Inn) and Globe Theatre were here.

Southwell, Robert, 1561?–1595, English Jesuit poet and martyr. After ministering to oppressed English Catholics (1586–92), he was convicted and executed for treason. Wrote deeply religious poems (e.g., *St. Peter's Complaint* and *The Burning Babe*).

South-West Africa, territory (318,099 sq. mi.; pop. 384,627), SW Africa, on the Atlantic; cap. Windhoek. Bordered on N by Angola, on E by Bechuanaland, and on S and SE by South Africa. Mainly an arid plateau. Minerals worked include copper, tin, and gold. Chief export is karakul felt. Native population comprises several Bantu tribes. Area was visited 1486 by Bartholomew Diaz. Annexed 1892 by Germany; occupied in World War I by South African forces. Governed under a mandate from League of Nations by South Africa, which refused to make it a UN trust territory because of its intention of annexing it.

Southwestern at Memphis: see MEMPHIS, Tenn.

Southwestern College: see WINFIELD, Kansas.

Southwestern Louisiana Institute: see LAFAYETTE.

Southwestern University: see GEORGETOWN, Texas.

South Williamsport, borough (pop. 6,364), N central Pa., on West Branch of Susquehanna R. opposite Williamsport. Mfg. of furniture and hardware.

Southwold (south'wōld), municipal borough (pop. 2,473), Suffolk East, England; a resort. Battle of Southwold Bay or Sole Bay was fought (1672) by Dutch under De Ruyter and English and French under duke of York (later James II).

Southworth, E(mma) D(orothy) E(liza) N(evitte), 1819–99, American author of popular, romantic, melodramatic novels such as *The Hidden Hand* (1859).

sovereignty. A sovereign state is a free and independent state. In external relations it can send and receive ambassadors, make international agreements, and declare war and make peace. In internal relations it makes and enforces law of land, controls money and military power. Internal power may be exercised by individual (monarchy), class (oligarchy), or entire people (democracy). Tendency in modern practice has been to curb external powers of nation, especially in making of war, through League of Nations and through UN.

soviet (sōvēĕt') [Rus.,= council], primary unit in political organization of USSR. First revolutionary soviets were committees organized by the Socialists in 1905 among striking factory workers. Workers', peasants', and soldiers' soviets sprang up during RUSSIAN REVOLUTION of 1917. Bolshevik-dominated soviets overthrew the Kerensky government. Under constitution of the USSR, soviets form a hierarchy from rural councils to congress of soviets of Soviet Union (all elected by universal suffrage). In practice, they are subservient to the Communist party.

Sower or **Sauer, Christopher** (both: sō'ŭr, sou'ŭr), 1693–1758, American printer, b. Germany. His German Bible (1743) was the second Bible printed in America. His son, Christopher Sower, estab. the first type foundry in America (1772).

Soya Strait: see LA PÉROUSE STRAIT.

soybean, leguminous annual plant (*Glycine soja*), native to the Orient, where it has been grown for over 5,000 years. The beans are made into meal, oil, cheese, curds, or cake. Soybeans are now grown in the Occident, to some extent for food, but chiefly for soil improvement and forage; the oil has been used in manufacture of various products.

Sozzini, Lelio, and **Fausto Sozzini:** see SOCINUS.

Spa (spä), town (pop. 8,929), Liége prov., SE Belgium, in the Ardennes and near German border. Mineral springs and baths, frequented from 16th cent., have made it one of world's most fashionable watering places. Name now designates all similar health resorts. Spa Conference (1920) dealt with German reparations problem.

Spaak, Paul Henri (pôl′ ãrē′ späk′), 1899–, Belgian foreign minister (1938–49) and twice premier (1938–39, 1947–49); a moderate Socialist. Presided over first UN Assembly (1946), Council for European Recovery (1948–49), and first consultative assembly of Council of Europe (1949).

Spaatz, Carl Andrew (spŏts), 1891–, American general, chief of staff of U.S. Air Force (1947–48).

space time, concept in physics which holds that time and space are indissolubly united. It was suggested by H. A. Lorentz. Einstein's special theory of relativity is partly based on this concept; the universe is described as a four-dimensional continuum in which events are located by three space coordinates and a time coordinate (fourth dimension).

spaghetti: see MACARONI.

Spain, Span. *España,* sovereign state (194,232 sq. mi.; pop. 27,909,009, incl. BALEARIC ISLANDS and CANARY ISLANDS), SW Europe; cap. MADRID. In Africa, Spain has Spanish West Africa, Spanish Guinea, and a protectorate over Spanish Morocco. Continental Spain occupies all the Iberian peninsula except Portugal and tiny Andorra. It stretches from the Pyrenees (boundary with France) and the Bay of Biscay in the N to the Strait of Gibraltar in the S. It has a long Mediterranean coast in the E and SE, Atlantic shores in the NW and the SW. Central Spain is a vast plateau, the *Meseta Central,* between the Cantabrian Mts. in the N and the Sierra Morena in the S. It is cut by mountains (notably the Sierra de Guadarrama) and river valleys (Duero, Tagus, Guadiana). N of the *Meseta* the Ebro flows to the Mediterranean. In the S the climate is subtropical; the great river is the Guadalquivir. Spanish products are mostly agr.—citrus fruit, olives, grapes (such wines as sherry and Malaga are well known), vegetables, cork, and cereals. Much of the soil of the *Meseta,* however, has been exhausted by sheep grazing and poor care. From the mountains come various minerals (e.g., copper, iron), and fishing is a major industry on the coasts. Industry has been developed particularly around Madrid, around Barcelona, and in the NW (Basque Provs.). Though there are strong elements of unity in Spain (e.g., Roman Catholicism is at least nominally almost universal), there are great regional variations. The standard language is Castilian Spanish, but there are dialects. In two regions (CATALONIA and the BASQUE PROVINCES) non-Spanish languages are spoken, and there have been many moves to autonomy or independence. Other regional divisions are more or less related to medieval kingdoms and historical provinces, among them: Andalusia, Aragon, Asturias, Old and New Castile, Estremadura, Galicia, Leon, Murcia, Navarre, Valencia (see articles on these for information on industries, cities, and history).

Spain before the Conquest of America. The Basques were in Spain in the Stone Age before the coming of the Iberians (who later amalgamated with invading Celts to become the Celt-Iberians). Phoenicians estab. trading posts in the S by the 11th cent. B.C., and later came Greek settlers and then the Carthaginians, who conquered most of Spain (3d cent. B.C.). Rome took it from them in the second of the PUNIC WARS (218–201 B.C.), completed conquest of most of the peninsula by 133 B.C. Spain was Romanized and integrated into the empire. Its Roman heritage was not lost even after the Germanic invasions, which began in A.D. 409. The Visigothic kings, who created a large state in the N and pushed to the S, kept Roman law (see ALARIC II) and much of Roman civilization. Christianity had been introduced early and survived. The Visigothic state was, however, weak, and collapsed when a Moslem army from N Africa defeated King Roderick (711). Thus began the rule of the Moslems, called in Spain the Moors. The emirate (later the Western caliphate) was estab. at Córdoba, and a rich civilization grew up, with prosperous cities, well-regulated agr. and industries, and flowering of architecture (as in the Alhambra at Granada) and learning (much knowledge of classic learning passed to W Europe through Spain). The Moors were, however, divided among themselves, not only with successive dynasties (ABBADIDES, ALMORAVIDES, ALMOHADES) but with local rivalry. They never controlled the N, where the kingdom of Asturias survived as the seed of the Christian conquest. Leon, Castile, and Aragon grew more powerful, and despite constant wars among themselves, dotted with temporary alliances with various Moorish rulers, the Spanish Christian states gradually conquered the Moors. A landmark was the Spanish victory at Navas de Tolosa (1212), but the last Moorish stronghold did not fall until 1492. By that time most of Spain had been united by the marriage of the rulers of Castile and Aragon, FERDINAND V and ISABELLA I. Their reign saw also the expulsion of the Jews from Spain (1492) and they later forced the Moors to accept Christianity (they were finally expelled). But the most important event of 1492 was the discovery of the New World by Christopher Columbus. This was the foundation of the Spanish Empire on which by the accession of Charles I (Emperor Charles V) in 1516 "the sun never set."

Golden Age and Decline. The reign of Charles's son, PHILIP II, saw Spain finally centralized (even Portugal was annexed in 1580, to become free again in 1640), the Spanish INQUISITION reached its height of terrible power, and wealth flowed in from Spanish lands in North and South America and the Philippines. Spanish literature and art flourished in the late 16th and the 17th cent. (the Golden Age). Economic and military decline, however, had set in, marked by the defeat of the Spanish Armada sent to conquer England (1588). Spanish warfare over Europe and connection with the Holy Roman Empire ultimately also worked to the ill of Spain. The Thirty Years War (1618–48) cost Spain territory and prestige. When the Hapsburg line disappeared, the War of the SPANISH SUCCESSION occurred (1701–14), costing Spain dearly and putting PHILIP V on the throne. Despite efforts at revival Spain stagnated, gradually sinking through numerous wars and treaties until humiliation by Napoleon, who forced the abdications of CHARLES IV and FERDINAND VII and in 1808 put his brother Joseph BONAPARTE (1808) on the throne. This caused a nationalist upsurge, and Spanish patriots played a part in the PENINSULAR WAR. In 1812 Ferdinand was restored to the throne. *Monarchists and Republicans.* The Napoleonic invasion helped bring on the wars of independence in Latin America which had by 1825 stripped Spain of most of its empire (with Cuba, Puerto Rico, and the Philippines to be lost later in the SPANISH-AMERICAN WAR). In Spain itself conservatives and liberals struggled endlessly. Ferdinand's changing of the law of succession in favor of his daughter, ISABELLA II, brought on the first uprising of the Carlists (1836–39). Reactionary monarchists, constitutional monarchists, and republicans vied for power. Isabella had to abdicate (1868), as did her successor, Amadeus (1873). A brief republic (1873–74) was torn by new war. In 1876 Alfonso XII was put on the throne; he was succeeded by Alfonso XIII, who reigned until 1931. Spain was neutral in World War I. In 1923 a dictatorship was set up under PRIMO DE RIVERA, but republican opposition ended this (1930) and deposed the king (1931). A republic was set up. In 1936 a combination of radical parties won a majority, and there was an immediate military uprising. The bloody civil war was finally won by the Insurgents in 1939, and Francisco FRANCO set up a state on corporative lines. Fascistic Spain sympathized with the Axis in World War II but kept legal neutrality. The UN refused Spain membership. Long-drawn negotiations between the Franco government and Western powers had come to nothing by 1953. In 1947 Franco declared the country a monarchy, but no steps were taken to restore the Bourbons.

Spalato, Yugoslavia: see SPLIT.

Spalding, Albert, 1888–, American violinist. He made his New York debut 1908 and toured extensively. Wrote his autobiography, *Rise to Follow,* and a historical novel, *A Fiddle, a Sword, and a Lady.*

Spalding, Lyman, 1775–1821, American physician, founder of U.S. Pharmacopoeia (1820), a descriptive catalogue of approved therapeutic agents.

Spandau (shpän'dou), former town, since 1920 a W district (pop. 159,599) of Berlin, Germany, on Spree and Havel rivers. Mfg. of steel and electrical equipment. Its fortress became a political prison in 19th cent.

Spangenberg, August Gottlieb (ou'gōost gôt'lĕp shpăng'ŭnbĕrk), 1704–92, a founder and bishop of Moravian Church in America, b. Prussia. After 1735 he founded settlements, churches, and schools in Ga., Pa., and N.C. He became bishop in 1744. One of his works was adopted as official Moravian doctrine.

spaniel, name of a large group of dogs, believed to have originated in Spain; records of existence date from 14th cent. In general, spaniels have silky coats (sometimes wavy or curled), relatively short legs, and long ears. Colors in land spaniels are greatly varied—solid colors include black, red, liver, gold, or cream; mixed colors include orange, lemon, liver, red, black, or mahogany, with white. Spaniels are all excellent in flushing game. Varieties include the clumber spaniel (weighing 50–60 lb.), the field and the springer spaniel (weighing 30–45 lb.), and the small cocker spaniel (weighing 18–24 lb.), widely popular as a pet. There are two breeds of water spaniel, the American and the Irish. The American breed, weighing from 28 to 45 lb., is a good swimmer and is useful as a retriever on land and in the water. It has a tightly curled coat of dark chocolate or liver color. The Irish water spaniel, the tallest member of the spaniel family (22–24 in. at shoulder), has a tightly curled coat of a solid liver color and a curly topknot.

Spanish Africa, name for Spanish possessions in Africa, i.e., Ifni, Spanish Guinea, Spanish Morocco, and Spanish Sahara.

Spanish America, Spanish-speaking countries of LATIN AMERICA (also called Hispanic America). Included are: Mexico, Central America (except British Honduras), South America (except Brazil and Guiana), Cuba, Dominican Republic, and Puerto Rico.

Spanish-American War, 1898, struggle of U.S. and Cuban revolutionists against Spain with chief object of liberating CUBA from Spanish control. Revolution broke out in Cuba in 1895, with heavy losses to American investments. U.S. government recognized strategic importance of Cuba to projected canal in Central America. War sentiment in U.S. rose with publication of a letter written by Spanish minister at Washington disparaging U.S. Pres. McKinley and with sinking of U.S. battleship MAINE. U.S. demanded Spain's withdrawal from Cuba; on April 24 Spain declared war. On May 1 a U.S. squadron under George DEWEY thoroughly defeated Spanish fleet at Manila, Philippine Isls. Spanish fleet at Santiago de Cuba was destroyed on July 3. U.S. troops secured surrender of Santiago. Armistice was signed on Aug. 12. Treaty of Paris, signed Dec. 10, 1898, freed Cuba (but under U.S. tutelage by Platt Amendment); ceded Puerto Rico and Guam to U.S.; surrendered the Philippines to U.S. for $20,000,000. Spanish Empire was practically dissolved. U.S. was entangled in Latin America in a new fashion and was tied more closely to course of Far Eastern events.

Spanish Armada: see ARMADA, SPANISH.

Spanish bayonet and **Spanish dagger:** see YUCCA.

Spanish colonial architecture flourished from 16th to late 18th cent. Though basically Spanish in style, it developed original features (esp. in Mexico and Peru). Intricate ornamentation was often used, as in the richly decorated portal of W façade of Santo Domingo cathedral (1521–41), earliest cathedral in America. But the chief characteristic of colonial building was simple, solid construction, as shown in Spanish missions of Calif. and Jesuit missions of Paraguay. In 16th-cent. Mexico the great builders were the Augustinian, Franciscan, and Dominican orders; they invented the open chapel, built with only three walls to speed construction. During most of 17th and 18th cent. the baroque style predominated, but simpler elements of early period were retained. A more conservative trend in Colombia kept the style severely simple. The baroque combined with native inventiveness to produce the ultra-baroque cathedral of Mexico city, with its strong light-and-shade patterns, richly carved columns, and violent contrasts of curves and angles. Central American buildings were generally provincial versions of the Mexican, but in Peru a rich architecture, more massive than the Mexican, was evolved, with wall surfaces divided into large compartments rather than covered with shallow carving as in Mexico. In S Peru and in Bolivia, Indian influence in ornament pervaded the basic European architectural forms. An invasion of neoclassicism ended the great days of Spanish colonial architecture.

Spanish Fork, city (pop. 5,230), N central Utah, S of Provo near Utah L.; processing center in irrigated region served by STRAWBERRY VALLEY PROJECT.

Spanish Guinea (gĭ'nē), colony (10,800 sq. mi.; pop. 170,582), W Africa, on Gulf of Guinea; cap. Santa Isabel on Fernando Po isl. Consists of mainland section, Río Muni (between French Cameroons and French Equatorial Africa) and several islands, of which Fernando Po is most important. Exports are cacao, palm oil, bananas, and coffee. Fernando Po was ceded by Portugal to Spain, 1778. Boundaries of Río Muni estab. 1885 by Treaty of Berlin.

Spanish language, language of Romance group of Italic subfamily of Indo-European languages. See LANGUAGE (table).

Spanish Main, mainland of Spanish America, particularly coast of South America from Isthmus of Panama to mouth of the Orinoco. From coast English buccaneers would attack Spanish treasure fleets sailing home from New World. Term now used to describe entire Caribbean area associated with piracy.

Spanish Morocco: see MOROCCO.

Spanish moss, fibrous gray air plant (*Tillandsia usneoides*) that hangs on trees of tropical America and the U.S. It belongs to the pineapple family.

Spanish Sahara, division (103,600 sq. mi.; pop. 37,000), Spanish West Africa, on the Atlantic; cap. Aiun. Comprises colony of Río de Oro (70,000 sq. mi.; pop. 24,000) and territory of Sekia el Hamra (32,000 sq. mi.; pop. 13,000).

Spanish Succession, War of the, 1701–14, general European war, fought for the sucession to the Spanish empire after the death of Charles II, last Hapsburg king of Spain. Complicated negotiations regarding the succession of the childless king had been going on for years. By 1699 the chief claimants to the succession were Louis XIV of France, on behalf of his grandson Philip, a great-grandson of Philip IV of Spain; and Emperor Leopold I, as head of the Austrian house of Hapsburg, on behalf of his son Charles (later Emperor CHARLES VI). The reunion of the Austrian and Spanish Hapsburg dominions was unacceptable to England, France, and the United Provs. of the Netherlands; the union of France and Spain under the Bourbon dynasty was equally unacceptable to England, Austria, and the United Provs. In 1700 the dying Charles II named Philip his sole heir; Louis XIV accepted on behalf of his grandson, who became PHILIP V of Spain. England, the United Provs., and Austria allied themselves against France and were joined by most of the German states. Bavaria sided with France. Portugal and Savoy sided with France till 1703, then joined the allies. Military operations began in the Low Countries and Italy (1701) and became general in 1702. Of the French commanders, only VILLARS and L. J. de VENDÔME were a match to the great allied leaders—MARLBOROUGH and EUGENE OF SAVOY. However, despite such major allied victories as Blenheim and Gibraltar (1704), Oudenarde (1708), and Malplaquet (1709), the campaigns in Spain, Italy, and the Low Countries were indecisive, and England withdrew from the fighting in 1711. The war ended with the treaties of Utrecht, Rastatt, and Baden (1713–14; see UTRECHT, PEACE OF), with England and the United Provs. the real winners. France had to compromise with Austria and was economically exhausted. In America, the conflict was known as Queen Anne's War (see FRENCH AND INDIAN WARS).

Spanish Town, city (pop. 12,007), S Jamaica, British West Indies. Was leading city of Jamaica until Kingston rose to prominence.

Sparks, Jared, 1789–1866, American historian, editor, and educator. Editor *North American Review* (1817–18, 1824–30). President Harvard (1849–53). Works include *The Writings of George Washington* (12 vols., 1834–37) and *Library of American Biography* (25 vols., 1834–48).

Sparks, city (pop. 8,203), W Nev., on Truckee R. just E of Reno. Rail hub in irrigated agr. area.

sparrow, name for various small Old and New World birds of finch family. Plumage is usually streaked brown and gray. Sparrows destroy weed seeds. English or house sparrow is not a true sparrow, but of weaver bird family.

Spars [from the motto "Semper Paratus"], Women's Reserve of U.S. Coast Guard Reserve, created Nov., 1942. In World War II Spars took over shore duty to release men for sea duty. Demobilized by June, 1946.

Sparta, city of anc. Greece, cap. of Laconia, chief city of the Peloponnesus, on the Eurotas R. The city-state was founded by Dorian conquerors of Laconia and Messenia and grew strong. In the 7th cent. B.C. it was a center of literature, but after 600 B.C. military arts were dominant, sons of the ruling class, Spartiates, were trained as soldiers, and the city was an armed camp. Below the warrior class were the perioeci (artisans and tradesmen) and helots (slaves attached to the land). Only Spartiates had legal and civil rights. The government was headed by two kings, but the board of five ephors held more governing power. Sparta took part in the PERSIAN WARS, and Spartans conducted themselves heroically at THERMOPYLAE (490) and also fought at Salamis

(480) and, more gallantly, at Plataea under Pausanias (479). Sparta built the loose Peloponnesian League before 500 B.C. but made no effort to turn it into an empire. Sparta was the rival of Athens and was in the end involved in a ruinous war, the PELOPONNESIAN WAR (431–404 B.C.). Sparta emerged triumphant, but shortly was defeated by Thebans at Leuctra (371 B.C.). Sparta declined after conquest by Philip II of Macedon and disappeared altogether under Roman sway. Modern Sparta (pop. 9,700) was founded in the 19th cent. near ruins of the old city.

Sparta, city (pop. 5,893), W central Wis., NE of La Crosse and on La Crosse R., in agr. area. Creameries and tobacco warehouses.

Spartacus (spär'tůkůs), d. 71 B.C., Roman gladiator, leader of a slave revolt that was last and most important of the Servile Wars, b. Thrace. Escaped from gladiators' school at Capua, gathered many runaway slaves about him and in 72 B.C. dominated much of S Italy. Crassus and Pompey put down revolt and crucified some 6,000 captured slaves.

Spartacus party or **Spartacists,** radical group of German Socialists, founded c.1916 and led by Karl LIEBKNECHT and Rosa LUXEMBURG. In December, 1918, it was officially transformed into the German Communist party. An outbreak and demonstration in Berlin (Jan., 1920) was suppressed by Gustav NOSKE.

Spartanburg, city (pop. 36,795), NW S.C., NW of Columbia, in piedmont; selected as co. seat 1785. Center of mill village area and important textile-milling center with railroad shops and mfg. of metal and lumber products and fertilizer. Supply point in Civil War. Seat of Converse Col. (nonsectarian; mainly women; 1889) and Textile Inst. Annual music festival.

spastic paralysis (spă'stĭk), condition characterized by muscle rigidity and exaggerated reflexes, generally resulting from injury to brain motor center. Causes include birth injuries and multiple sclerosis.

spatterdock: see POND LILY.

spavin (spă'vĭn), permanent deformity from bony enlargement on bones of hock joint in the horse. Probable cause is structural deformity aggravated by overweight and injury; lameness results.

Speaker, Tris(tram E.), 1888–, American baseball outfielder. Had lifetime major-league batting average of .344, was regarded as one of the best defensive outfielders in the American League.

spearmint, aromatic perennial mint (*Mentha spicata*), native to Old World but naturalized in U.S. It is a flavoring for chewing gum, medicine, candy.

species, in biology, a unit or category of classification lower than a genus and higher than a subspecies or variety. It is used for a plant or animal group in a genus possessing in common certain characters that distinguish the members as a group from other similar groups of the same genus. The species name is the second of the scientific names by which plants and animals are identified. In the case of the white oak, *Quercus alba,* the genus name is *Quercus* (oak) and the species is *alba* (white). Species names are usually descriptive of a characteristic, or are derived from the discoverer, the geographic area, or geologic period of the plant or animal.

specific gravity, pure number representing ratio of the mass or weight of a given volume of a substance and the given weight of an equal volume of another substance chosen as arbitrary standard. In metric system it is the same as DENSITY if water is taken as standard; but unlike density it is an abstract number. In English system density and specific gravity are not numerically the same. Methods of determining specific gravity vary as solid is more or less dense than water. It is calculated by dividing weight in air by loss of weight in water. HYDROMETER gives direct specific-gravity reading. Specific gravity of a gas is determined by comparing weight of one liter of gas with weight of equal volume of air or hydrogen as unity.

spectacles, device to protect eyes or improve vision. Convex lenses suggested 13th cent. by Roger Bacon; concave, used in 14th cent. Bifocals, with upper part for viewing distant objects and lower for near objects, invented by Benjamin Franklin. Trifocals later developed. Contact lenses, shaped to fit eye and worn under eyelid, first used 1887; popularity increased after 1930s because of improved grinding and fitting techniques.

Spectator, London daily journal (March, 1711–Dec., 1712) conducted by Richard Steele and Joseph Addison; successor to their *Tatler* (April, 1709–Jan., 1711). Written supposedly by members of a club, e.g., the famous Sir Roger de Coverley, but really by Addison and Steele. Consisted mainly of news, literary and theatrical essays, and criticisms of current follies and vices. Both papers greatly influenced public opinion and English journalism.

spectroscope (spĕk'trůskōp), instrument used to produce spectra in SPECTRUM analysis. Usually consists of three hollow tubes mounted horizontally on disk supported by vertical shaft. One tube has slit at outer end and lens at inner end, which transforms light entering through slit into parallel rays. Another tube is telescope for observing spectrum formed. Third tube contains scale by which direct measurement of spectrum is made. Prism in center of disk disperses light entering tube through the slit and bends it into telescope for observation.

spectrum. When narrow beam of white light passes through prism, rays of colors of which it is composed are bent at different angles; they emerge as narrow band of color shading from red at one end to violet at other. This is a spectrum; process of breaking up the white light is DISPERSION. Spectrum also is produced by reflection from a grating ruled with fine lines. When such a band is unbroken it is a continuous spectrum; these are produced by incandescent solids. Characteristics displayed by spectra depend on nature of source. Presence of an element in a substance can be detected by examining with spectroscope the spectrum (called a line spectrum) produced by its incandescent vapor; each element can be identified by the appearance of one or more bright lines of characteristic color and in characteristic position in its spectrum. No two elements have the same spectral lines. An absorption spectrum is produced when light from one source passes through an incandescent gaseous substance; it has dark lines corresponding in position to bright lines which appear in spectrum of light source. Spectrum of sunlight shows dark lines called Fraunhofer lines. Kirchhoff explained these as caused by presence in sun's atmosphere of incandescent elements which absorb from sunlight passing through them those rays of light producing their characteristic spectra. Rays having photochemical effects, chiefly green, blue, and ultraviolent rays of sun's spectrum, are sometimes called actinic rays.

Spee, Maximilian, Graf von (gräf′ fŭn shpā′), 1861–1914, German admiral in World War I. Defeated English off Coronel but was defeated near Falkland Isls. and went down with his ship.

speech, freedom of, the right of citizens to voice opinions without interference, subject only to the laws against slander, profanity, and incitement to unlawful acts. Historically, the right has frequently been denied and it is usually curtailed somewhat even by democracies in wartime. Freedom of speech in the U.S. is guaranteed by the Bill of Rights and, as interpreted by the Supreme Court, by the Fourteenth Amendment, though the Supreme Court has justified restriction of free speech at the point where the spoken word creates "a clear and present danger."

speech defect, faulty speech such as stuttering, lisping, nasality, monopitch, mumbling, excessive sibilance, may result from improper training, psychological or neurological factors, or organic faults. Methods for eliminating or reducing defects include surgery, orthodontia, rhythmical and relaxing exercises, psychological aid, and clinical instruction in breathing, phrasing, and enunciation.

speedometer for automobiles utilizes flexible cable which, driven by drive gear, rotates permanent magnet and induces magnetic drag on drum held back by hairspring. As speed increases the magnetic force and drum movement increase. Numbers on drum rim indicate speed. Other speedometers use centrifugal force. Airplanes have air-speed indicators.

Speedway, town (pop. 5,498), central Ind., near Indianapolis. Has Indianapolis motor speedway.

speedwell or **veronica,** perennial flowering plant of genus *Veronica.* Veronicas vary from creeping types suitable for rock gardens to tall, bushy plants—all with showy flower spikes, usually blue. Closely related shrubby kinds are of genus *Hebe.*

Speer, Albert (äl′bĕrt shpār′), 1905–, German architect and National Socialist leader. For a time he was official architect of Nazi regime. In 1942 he succeeded the engineer Fritz Todt as minister for armaments, inheriting *Organisation Todt* (for building roads and defenses), important in German war machine. Indicted at Nuremberg Trial as a war criminal because of wide use of slave labor; sentenced 1946 to 20-year imprisonment.

Speicher, Eugene Edward (spī′kûr), 1883–, American portrait and landscape painter.

Speier, Germany: see SPEYER.

Speke, John Hanning (spēk), 1827–64, English explorer in Africa. Discovered L. Tanganyika in 1858 with Sir Richard Burton. Discovered Victoria Nyanza, later proved it was source of Victoria Nile.

Spellman, Francis J(oseph), 1889–, American Roman Catholic clergyman, made archbishop of New York (1939) and cardinal (1946).

Spemann, Hans (häns′ shpā′män), 1869–1941, German embryologist. Won 1935 Nobel Prize in Physiology and Medicine for research on cells.

Spence, Thomas (spĕns), 1750–1814, English agrarian socialist. Devised scheme of land tenure by parish, in which rent would be the only tax. Founded a society of Spenceans. Author of *The Real Rights of Man* (1775) and other pamphlets.

Spencer, Herbert, 1820–1903, English philosopher. He applied wide study of the natural sciences and psychology to philosophy, finding in the doctrine of evolution the unifying principle of knowledge and applying it to all phenomena. He did not deal with the "unknowable" (metaphysics and such scientific ideas as matter, space, time, motion, and force) but instead dealt only with those things which could be compared with and related to other things. Among his works are *First Principles* (1862), *The Principles of Biology* (1864–67), *The Principles of Psychology* (1855), *The Principles of Sociology* (1876–96), and *The Principles of Ethics* (1891).

Spencer, Platt Rogers, 1800–1864, American penman, originator of the style of handwriting known as Spencerian script.

Spencer. 1 City (pop. 7,446), NW Iowa, on Little Sioux R. and S of Spirit L., in agr. area. Has annual county fair. **2** Town (pop. 7,027), including Spencer village (pop. 5,259), central Mass., W of Worcester.

Spencer Gulf, inlet of Indian Ocean, indenting South Australia, between Eyre and Yorke peninsulas.

Spender, Stephen, 1909–, English poet and critic, educ. at Oxford. His poems (as in *Poems,* 1933) voiced social protest. Also wrote stories, a novel, works of criticism (e.g., *The Destructive Element,* 1935; *Life and the Poet,* 1942), a book on Germany (*European Witness,* 1946), and the autobiographical *World within World* (1951).

Spener, Philipp Jakob (fē′lĭp yä′kôp shpā′nûr), 1635–1705, German theologian, founder of PIETISM. By organizing groups and by his writings he revivified religion through stress on Bible study, spiritual exercises, and good works. Made Halle (where he helped found the university) a center of his beliefs.

Spengler, Oswald (ôs′vält shpĕng′glûr), 1880-1936, German philosopher. His theory that every culture passes through a life cycle similar to that of human life is set forth in *The Decline of the West* (1918).

Spenser, Edmund, c.1552–1599, English poet. *The Shepheardes Calender* (1579) early marked him as gifted. He held a succession of minor civil offices in Ireland and after 1580 made his home there. Disappointment in getting court preferment was voiced in *Complaints* (1591) and *Colin Clouts Come Home Again* (1595). *Astrophel* is an elegy for Sir Philip Sidney; *Amoretti*, a sonnet sequence commemorating Spencer's courtship of Elizabeth Boyle; and *Epithalamion*, finest wedding poem in English, written for their marriage. All these appeared in 1595, followed by *Fowre Hymnes* (1596). His masterpiece, *The Faerie Queene* (Books I–III, 1590; I–VI, 1596), though unfinished, is one of the greatest English poems. A richly intricate allegory set in the kingdom of Gloriana (or Elizabeth), it expresses Spenser's moral, political, and religious beliefs. Spenser was a consummate artist in language, melody, and verse technique.

Speranski, Mikhail Mikhailovich (mēkhŭyēl' mēkhī'lŭvĭch spyĭrän'skē), 1772–1839, Russian minister of justice under Alexander I (1809–11). Drafted program of liberal reform, providing for emancipation of serfs and limited constitution, but fell from favor in 1812. Codified Russian law under Nicholas I.

sperm or **spermatozoon** (spûr"mŭtŭzō'ŭn, –zō'ŏn), sexual cell formed in testis of male of humans and other higher animals. Smaller than ovum; whiplike process permits movement through fluid. As in OVUM, reduction division (reduction of number of chromosomes by one half) precedes process of FERTILIZATION as a result of which normal number is restored.

spermaceti (spûrmŭsē'tē), white, odorless, tasteless wax obtained chiefly from sperm whale. Used in ointments, cosmetics, candles, waterproofing.

sperm oil, liquid wax from blubber and oil cavity in head of sperm whale. It is clear pale yellow to brownish yellow. Formerly principally used for lamps, it today has several uses—as a machine lubricant, as a dressing for leather, and as a fat for soap.

Sperry, Elmer Ambrose, 1860–1930, American inventor of gyroscope, automatic ship steersman, gyrocompass, and numerous other electrical devices.

Spey (spā), river of Scotland. Flows 110 mi. NE from Inverness-shire highlands to Moray Firth. Rapid and unnavigable; valuable salmon fisheries.

Speyer (shpī'ŭr), city (pop. 31,706), Rhineland-Palatinate, W Germany, on left bank of the Rhine; also called Spires in English; occasionally spelled Speier in German. Of pre-Roman origin, it became an episcopal see in 7th cent. and a free imperial city in 1111. Several imperial diets were held here, notably that of 1529, which granted toleration to Catholics in Lutheran states but not to Lutherans in Catholic states nor to Zwinglians and Anabaptists anywhere. The Protest of Speyer, signed by Elector John of Saxony, Landgrave Philip of Hesse, and other delegates who opposed this decision, gave the Protestants their name. Speyer was the seat of the imperial chamber of justice from 1527 until 1689, when the French devastated the city. Distinct from the city was the bishopric of Speyer, consisting of considerable territories held by the bishops as princes of the Holy Roman Empire. Both the city and the bishopric W of the Rhine were ceded to France in 1797 and were given to Bavaria in 1815. They were part of Rhenish Palatinate 1815–1945, Speyer being the cap. The episcopal lands E of the Rhine passed to Baden in 1803. Speyer has kept parts of its medieval walls. Its fine Romanesque cathedral (10th cent., several times restored) contains the tombs of eight emperors. An early printing center, the city was the home of John of Speyer.

Spezia, La (lä spā'tsyä), city (pop. 80,399), Liguria, NW Italy; a Mediterranean port on the Gulf of Spezia. Chief Italian naval station. Has arsenal, navigation school, shipyards, steel mills, oil refineries. Was heavily bombed in World War II.

sphagnum (sfăg'nŭm) or **peat moss,** pale green, weak-stemmed bog plant of genus *Sphagnum*, economically the most valuable of any MOSS. Sphagnum mosses are the principal constituent of peat. In horticulture sphagnum is used as a mulch and as a packing material for plants being shipped.

sphalerite (sfă'lŭrīt, sfā'–), mineral, zinc sulphide, usually with iron, manganese, cadmium, mercury. It is white when pure, but often is colored by slight impurities. It is the most important source of zinc. Found in Bohemia, Saxony, Cornwall, Japan, and U.S.

sphere, in geometry, three-dimensional analogue of circle (i.e., a solid with circle as its basic form). Term is applied to spherical surface, every point of which is same distance (radius) from fixed point (center) and also to volume enclosed by surface.

Sphinx (sfĭngks), in Greek mythology, a monster taken from Egyptian religion. She was a winged lion with a woman's head, who lived on a rock near Thebes. She asked of all a riddle and killed all who failed to answer. Oedipus solved it, and she leaped from the rock. Oedipus became king of Thebes. Egyptian sphinxes were recumbent figures, usually with men's heads. Most famous of all is the Great Sphinx of Gizeh (Egypt), a colossal figure carved from natural rock, guardian of the Nile valley.

spice, aromatic vegetable product used as a flavoring or condiment. Today, the term tends to be restricted to flavorings for food or drinks, although many spices have other commercial uses, e.g., in medicines, perfumes, incense, soap. Types include stimulating condiments (e.g., pepper), aromatics (cloves, cinnamon), and such sweet herbs as mint and marjoram. Spices are taken from part of plant richest in flavor (bark, stem, flower bud, fruit, seed, or leaf). They are commonly prepared as powder, but some are used as tinctures made from essential oils and others are used whole, as are many herbs. From ancient times, spices from the Far East were in great demand; after a lapse in trade in the early Middle Ages, the traffic grew greatly, especially after the Crusades. Later, the European demand was responsible for important explorations in search of new trade routes.

spicebush, ornamental and spicily fragrant shrub (*Lindera benzoin*) native to E North

America. It bears small densely clustered yellow flowers in early spring followed by red berries which are sometimes used as a substitute for allspice.

Spice Islands, Indonesia: see MOLUCCAS.

spider, air-breathing arachnid, with body divided into two parts, four pairs of legs, usually four pairs of eyes, and without true jaws. Spinnerets under abdomen produce silk thread used for making webs and lines, encasing eggs, and lining retreats. Venom of black-widow spider is sometimes fatal.

spikenard (spĭk'närd), name for several plants. The spikenard in the Bible was an aromatic ointment believed to be derived from *Nardostachys jatamansi,* of the valerian family. The American spikenard, or Indian root, is *Aralia racemosa,* with aromatic roots used medicinally.

Spillville, town (pop. 363), NE Iowa, on Turkey R. and SW of Decorah. Anton Dvorak composed (1893) part of symphony *From the New World* in this Czech community; his house became a clock museum.

spinach, annual vegetable plant (*Spinacia oleracea*) of Persian origin, long grown as a potherb. Its leaves are a dietary source of vitamins and iron.

spinal column, backbone, spine, or **vertebral column,** portion of vertebrate skeleton consisting of segments (vertebrae) united by cartilaginous disks and ligaments. Segments form a column supporting body and enclosing spinal cord. Human adult has 26 segments: 7 in neck; 12 in chest region; 5 in lumbar area; sacrum consisting of 5 fused vertebrae; coccyx, usually 4 fused bones. See *ill.,* p. 763.

spinal cord, whitish cord incased in spinal column and serving as pathway for impulses to and from brain and as system of reflex centers controlling activities of glands, organs, and muscles. Consists of central canal, layers of gray matter and of white matter, and three membranes. Along the spinal cord are 31 pairs of nerves. See *ill.,* p. 763.

Spinario (spĭnä'rēō), celebrated statue, probably of 1st cent. B.C., representing a boy pulling a thorn from his foot. Copies in Rome and London are possibly based on a work by Boethus.

Spinden, Herbert Joseph, 1879–, American anthropologist, authority on primitive cultures and Mayan calendar and chronology.

spine: see SPINAL COLUMN.

Spinello di Luca Spinelli (spēnĕl'lō dē lōō'kä spēnĕl'lē), c.1333–1410, Italian painter of the late Giotto school. Usually called Spinello Aretino.

spinet: see PIANO.

spinning, the drawing out, twisting, and winding of fibers into a continuous thread. Spinning was first done by holding fiber in one hand, twisting with the other; the earliest tools were the distaff, a stick on which fiber was wrapped, and the spindle, a shorter, weighted stick which was twirled to twist the thread. After the 14th cent., the spinning wheel, employing a spindle revolved by a belt passing over a wheel, came into use in Europe. Principal types were the great, or wool, wheel, with an intermittent action, and the flax, or Saxony wheel, a more elaborate mechanism operated by a treadle. In 18th-cent. England, improved looms stimulated spinning inventions. Notable were James Hargreaves's spinning jenny (c.1765), capable of spinning 8 to 11 threads at once, and Richard Arkwright's frame (1769), which eventually forced spinning into the factory. In 1779 Samuel Crompton combined the best features of these two devices into the mule spinning frame, the forerunner of the self-acting mule used today for fine yarns. Coarser yarns are made on the ring frame, an elaboration of Arkwright's invention.

Spinoza, Baruch or **Benedict** (spĭnō'zů), 1632–77, Dutch philosopher. Because of independence of thought he was excommunicated (1656) from the Jewish group in which he was reared, but he continued to follow his own bent, earned his living as a lens grinder, and lived very quietly even when other philosophers broke his retirement by visiting him. He applied great learning to the building of his philosophic system. He unswervingly insisted that all existence is embraced in one substance—God (or Nature). Mind and matter, time, everything that appears is only a manifestation of the One. Evil exists only for finite minds and dissolves when seen as part of the whole. Man should try to adjust to the infinite plan, surrendering passion and accepting order, seeing events under the aspect of eternity. Spinoza favored democratic government.

spiraea or **spirea** (both: spīrē'ů), deciduous flowering shrub of genus *Spiraea* native to the N Hemisphere. Single or double small white or rose flowers are in rounded or spire-like clusters. Most common are the bridal wreath (*Spiraea prunifolia*) and the similar hybrid *S. vanhouttei.* Native to North America is the pink- or white-flowered *S. latifolia,* often called meadowsweet.

Spires, Germany: see SPEYER.

Spirit Lake, town (pop. 2,467), NW Iowa, near Minn. line. Tourist center between West Okoboji L. and Spirit L., largest glaciated lake in Iowa.

spirit level, instrument for determining direction of gravity. Position of a bubble in tube of alcohol, ether, or mixture of both indicates whether instrument is horizontal.

spiritual, in music, religious folk music. American Negro spirituals, long regarded as the spontaneous creation of the Negro, have been shown to be either adapted from, or inspired by, the spirituals of white Americans used in Southern camp and revival meetings throughout the 19th cent. Despite this, the distinctive quality and beauty of the Negro spiritual make it a major contribution to American music.

Spithead (spĭt'hĕd), eastern part of channel between Hampshire, England, and Isle of Wight. English defeated the French in battle here (1595). Scene of a famous fleet mutiny (1797).

Spitsbergen (spĭts'bûrgůn), archipelago, in Arctic Ocean, c.400 mi. N of Norwegian mainland, between lat. 76° and 81° N. With Bear Isl., farther S, it constitutes the Norwegian possession of Svalbard (23,979 sq. mi.; pop. 1,034, incl. 505 citizens of USSR).

Chief island is West Spitsbergen (c.15,000 sq. mi.), which also has principal settlements (New Alesund, Longyear City). Other islands include North East Land, Hope Isl., King Charles Land, and Barents Isl. Chief wealth is coal. Islands were discovered by Vikings 12th cent., named Svalbard by them; rediscovered by Willem Barentz 1596. Henry Hudson reported good whaling here 1607; in 1618 Dutch limited own whaling operations to N Spitsbergen, leaving the rest to competitors. Russian fur traders began operations 18th cent.; Scandinavians followed. Islands were mapped late 19th cent. Conflicting claims to Spitsbergen were settled 1920 by international treaty (later ratified by Sweden, USSR, and others) which awarded archipelago to Norway, forbade military installations, and insured recognition of claims by other countries to parts of the coal fields. In 1941 the Allies of World War II set fire to the mines. German garrison was expelled by Norwegians in 1942, but in 1943 a German raid completed devastation of the mines. Demand by USSR for share in administration and defense of islands was rejected (1944).

Spitteler, Carl (kärl′ shpĭ′tůlůr), 1845–1924, Swiss poet, author of the epics *Prometheus und Epimetheus* (1881; Eng. tr., 1931) and *Olympischer Frühling* [Olympian spring] (1900–1910). Was awarded 1919 Nobel Prize in Literature.

spitz dog: see CHOW.

Spitzka, Edward Charles (spĭts′ků), 1852–1914, American physician and psychiatrist. He pioneered in anatomical studies of the brain and in classification of mental disorders. His son, **Edward Anthony Spitzka,** 1876–1922, also a physician, made important studies of the human brain (esp. in criminals).

spleen, soft, purplish-red organ in upper part of abdominal cavity to left of stomach and close to diaphragm. Functions are not fully understood. It holds a reserve supply of blood which enters the circulation when need arises. Like other lymphoid tissue it produces lymphocytes; also it helps to destroy worn-out red corpuscles. Sometimes removal of the organ is necessary. See *ill.,* p. 763.

Split (splēt), Ital. *Spalato,* city (pop. 49,885), S Croatia, Yugoslavia; largest city of Dalmatia and a major Adriatic port. Tourist resort. Among its many Roman remains is the huge palace of Diocletian (who died here), begun in A.D. 295. Split became a city after the people of near-by Salona took refuge from the Avars in the palace (7th cent.). It became a Roman Catholic archiepiscopal see (episcopal see after 1820) and a flourishing medieval port. Contested between Hungary and Venice 13th–15th cent., it was under Venetian rule 1420–1797, then under Austrian rule until 1918. Cathedral and baptistery were originally Roman buildings; old walls and city hall date from Venetian period.

Splügen (shplü′gůn), Ital. *Spluga,* Alpine pass, 6,945 ft. high, on Swiss-Italian border, N of L. Como.

Spode, Josiah (spōd), 1754–1827, English potter at Stoke-on-Trent. Created the porcelain known as spode ware, a fine bone china similar to the French soft Sèvres ware.

spoils system, in U.S. history, practice of giving appointive offices to loyal members of party in power. First adopted on large scale by Andrew Jackson. Name supposedly derives from speech by W. L. MARCY. Corruption and inefficiency bred in system reached a peak in administration of U. S. Grant. Reaction helped bring about civil service reform; Civil Service Commission created in 1871. System has, however, continued for many Federal offices.

Spokane (spōkăn′), city (pop. 161,721), E Wash., at falls of Spokane R.; founded c.1872. Recovered rapidly from great fire of 1889. Trade and rail hub for "Inland Empire," a rich region yielding lumber, minerals, wheat, livestock, and fruit. Processes flour, meat, milk, oil, and lumber. Here are aluminum mills, machine and rail shops. Cultural center for the region. Seat of Gonzaga Univ. (Jesuit; mainly for men; 1887). Resorts in area.

Spokane, river, rising in Coeur d'Alene L., N Idaho, and flowing c.100 mi. W and NW through Wash. to Columbia R.

Spoleto (spōlā′tō), city (pop. 10,579), Umbria, central Italy. Of great antiquity, it was the cap. of a large duchy (founded by the Lombards about A.D. 570; under papal rule from 13th cent.). Has cathedral with fresco by Filippo Lippi; several churches with early mosaics and paintings; Roman remains.

sponge, animal of phylum Porifera (world-wide distribution; c.2,500 species). All but one family are marine forms. Live at all depths, usually in colonies attached to rocks or other surface. Usually classified by type of skeleton secreted by simple, jellylike body; some have skeleton with calcium carbonate crystals or glassy spicules, others have skeleton of spongin (chemically related to silk with no hard crystals) used as commercial bath sponge.

spontaneous combustion: see COMBUSTION.

spoonbill, large wading bird of Old and New Worlds related to ibis. With its long bill, like flattened spoon at end, it captures small aquatic animals. Roseate spoonbill has rosy pink plumage accentuated by the carmine of lesser wing coverts; range S North America to Argentina and Chile. See *ill.,* p. 135.

Sporades (spô′růdēz), scattered islands in Aegean Sea, belonging to Greece. Grouped variously at different periods. N Sporades are generally understood to include Skyros and lesser islands off the coasts of Magnesia and Euboea, sometimes also Lemnos and Lesbos, off NW Asia Minor. S Sporades include Icaria, Samos, the Dodecanese, and Chios.

spore, term applied to a reproductive cell of certain plants (e.g., mosses, ferns) and protozoa (unicellular animals) and also to a resistant resting cell stage found especially among bacteria. Some spores develop into new organisms independently; others (called gametes) first unite with similar or dissimilar (male or female) cells. Organisms that form spores often reproduce also by fission or by budding. See *ill.,* p. 813.

spots and stains: see STAIN REMOVAL.

Spotswood, Alexander, 1676–1740, colonial

governor of Va. (1710–22), b. Morocco. Encouraged settlement of frontier.

Spotsylvania, rural county, NE Va., between Rappahannock and North Anna rivers, formerly part of estate of Alexander Spotswood. In Civil War, scene of battles of Fredericksburg and Chancellorsville and of Spotsylvania Courthouse in WILDERNESS CAMPAIGN.

Spottiswoode, John, 1565–1639, Scottish prelate and church historian. Wrote *History of the Church of Scotland* (1655); advocated episcopacy in Church. For opposing King Charles I's attempt to impose Anglican liturgy he was excommunicated (1638). Also Spottiswood, Spotswood.

Spottiswoode, William, 1825–83, English mathematician and physicist. His elementary treatise on determinants (1851) was probably the first published.

sprat, European fish (*Clupea*) of herring family. Canned in Norway as sardines or anchovies.

Spray (sprā), village (pop. 5,542), N N.C., NNW of Reidsville, near Va. line. Mfg. of textiles.

Spree (shprā), river, c.250 mi. long, E Germany, rising in Lusatian Mts. of Saxony and flowing N and NW through Brandenburg and Berlin into the Havel. The picturesque **Spree Forest** (Ger. *Spreewald*), in Lower Lusatia, is a marshy region crisscrossed by small waterways which are the only traffic lanes connecting its villages. WENDS here have kept colorful traditions, local costumes.

Sprengel pump, device to produce partial vacuum by fall through tubes of liquid, usually mercury. It was important in early experiments for which production of vacuum was necessary and especially in development of X-ray tubes. Invented by Hermann J. P. Sprengel (1834–1906), German chemist and physicist who became naturalized British subject.

spring, natural flow of water from ground or rock. Hot springs occur when the water issues from great depths or is heated by volcanic force. Mineral springs have a high content of dissolved substances. See also ARTESIAN WELL; GEYSER; MINERAL WATER.

Springdale, city (pop. 5,835), NW Ark., in the Ozarks. Ships fruit; produces grape juice and wine.

springer spaniel: see SPANIEL.

Springfield. 1 City (pop. 81,628), state cap. (since 1839), central Ill., on Sangamon R. and SW of Chicago; settled 1818. Trade, industrial, and distribution center in agr. (Corn Belt) and coal area. Mfg. of farm machinery and food products. Abraham Lincoln lived and practiced here 1837–61; helped make city cap. He is buried here; his home is shrine. State historical society rich in Lincolniana. Birthplace of Vachel Lindsay. Near by are NEW SALEM, Camp Butler Natl. Cemetery. **2** Town (pop. 2,032), central Ky., SE of Louisville. Marriage certificate of Thomas Lincoln and Nancy Hanks in courthouse. Lincoln Homestead Park near by. **3** Industrial city (pop. 162,399), SW Mass., on Connecticut R. near Conn. line; settled 1636 by W. PYNCHON. Mfg. of electrical and other machinery, firearms, motorcycles, plastics. Was in Shays's Rebellion (1786–87); station on Underground Railroad. U.S. armory here was founded by Washington. It has first American-made planetarium (1937). Saint-Gaudens's *Puritan* is in Merrick Park. Seat of Springfield and American Internatl. colleges. Near by Eastern States Fair is held at Storrowton, reconstructed colonial village. **4** City (pop. 66,731), SW Mo., in resort area of the Ozarks; laid out c.1835. Agr. and industrial center, it has railroad shops, stockyards, metal-working plants, and mfg. of clothing and food products. Seat of Drury Col. (Congregationalist; coed.; 1873). Battlefield (1861) of Wilson Creek is near by. **5** City (pop. 78,508), W central Ohio, on Mad R. and NE of Dayton; settled 1799. Mfg. of machinery, foundry and machine-shop products. Here is Wittenberg Col. (Lutheran; coed.; 1844). **6** City (pop. 10,807), W Oregon, on Willamette R. just E of Eugene, in lumber, grain area. **7** City (pop. 6,506), N Tenn., N of Nashville. Tobacco market; mfg. of blankets. **8** Town (pop. 9,190), including industrial Springfield village (pop. 4,940), SE Vt., on Connecticut R. and SE of Rutland. Machinery and machine-tool factories have flourished since before 1900. Crown Point military road crossed this area.

Springhill, town (pop. 7,138), N N.S.. SE of Amherst. Important coal-mining center.

Spring Hill College: see MOBILE, Ala.

Spring Valley, residential village (pop. 4,500), SE N.Y., W of Nyack. Summer resort.

Springville, city (pop. 6,475), N central Utah, S of Provo. Served by STRAWBERRY VALLEY PROJECT.

spruce, coniferous evergreen tree of the genus *Picea,* widely distributed in the N Hemisphere. Many species are grown as ornamentals; the wood, usually light, soft, and straight-grained, is important commercially. Best-known species of spruce include the Norway (*Picea abies*), white (*P. glauca* and *P. engelmanni*), Sitka (*P. sitchensis*), Colorado (*P. pungens*) and its variety, Colorado blue spruce.

Spruce Knob, mountain peak (4,860 ft.) of the Alleghenies, E W.Va.; highest point in state.

Spur, city (pop. 2,183), NW Texas, ESE of Lubbock on plain below Cap Rock escarpment. Processes and markets for cattle and agr. area.

spurge, name for any plant of genus *Euphorbia* and some related plants. Many are cactuslike succulents, with milky juice, often poisonous. Spurges have been used medicinally, others yield gums, oils, or dyes. Such spurges, as the green and white snow-on-the-mountain and poinsettia, are grown as ornamentals.

Spurgeon, Charles Haddon, 1834–92, English Baptist preacher. His popularity led to erection of Metropolitan Tabernacle, London, in 1861. His sermons (finally collected in 50 volumes) were widely read.

spurry, weedy annual plant with small white flowers. Field spurry (*Spergula sativa*) naturalized in U.S., is native to Europe where it is used for forage and binding sandy soils. Its seeds are edible and yield oil.

Spurs, Battle of the: see BATTLE OF THE SPURS.

Spuyten Duyvil Creek: see HARLEM RIVER.

Spyril, Johanna (yōhä'nä shpē'rē), 1827–1901,

Swiss author of children's books, notably of *Heidi* (1880).

Squanto or **Tisquantum,** d. 1622, North American Indian of Pawtuxet tribe. Aided Plymouth colonists as interpreter and in their planting.

square, in geometry, figure bounded by four equal straight lines (sides) meeting at four points (vertices) to form four right angles. Opposite sides are parallel. Perimeter of a square is sum of its sides. Area is product of one side multiplied by itself or by any other side. In arithmetic, when a number is multiplied by itself product is called the square of that number. In algebra, an expression such as x^2 indicates that a quantity is multiplied by itself, the product being the square of that quantity.

squash, edible fruit of a vine of the same genus, *Cucurbita,* as the PUMPKIN. Summer squashes are of either the pattypan or long type and are used when young; winter squashes, chiefly varieties of *Cucurbita maxima,* including the Hubbard and turban, called pumpkins in Europe, are hard-shelled, more flavorful, and may be kept over winter; third group contains varieties of *C. moschata,* including those called crookneck pumpkin and cheese pumpkin.

squash racquets, game played on four-walled court 16 ft. high by 18½ ft. wide by 32 ft. deep. Back wall usually measures 9 ft. In match play, usually 15 pts. win game, 2 of 3 games win match. Squash racquets probably originated in late 19th cent. from older game of RACQUETS.

squash tennis, game played on four-walled court similar to SQUASH RACQUETS court. Rule differences between squash tennis and squash racquets grew out of equipment differences. Livelier ball and heavier racquet in squash tennis emphasize hitting ball on carom.

squatter sovereignty, in U.S. history, doctrine under which slavery was permitted in territories, final question of its legal status being left to territorial settlers when they applied for statehood. First proposed in 1847, it was incorporated in COMPROMISE OF 1850 and KANSAS-NEBRASKA BILL. Its chief exponent, S. A. DOUGLAS, called it "popular sovereignty," but antislavery men contemptuously called it "squatter sovereignty."

squid, carnivorous marine mollusk with 10 arms bearing suction disks. It has a thickened mantle, and the shell is reduced to an internal horny plate; eyes highly developed. In danger, emits inky fluid.

Squier, Ephraim George (skwī'ůr), 1821–88, American archaeologist and journalist. He worked on newspapers in New York and Ohio. His lifelong interest in archaeology and his many contributions to the field began with his study of prehistoric remains in Ohio and Mississippi valleys. Served as U.S. chargé d'affaires to republics of Central America (1849) and later as American commissioner to Peru.

squill, spring-blooming, low bulbous plant (*Scilla*) with dainty bell-shaped blooms, usually deep blue. The Siberian squill (*Scilla sibirica*) is a rock-garden favorite; the wood hyacinth (*S. nonscripta*) is the common bluebell of England. Bulbs of the sea squill or sea onion (*Urginea maritima*) are sold as white squill, a drug, and red squill, a rat poison.

squirrel, small rodent (chiefly of genus *Sciurus*) of North and South America, Europe, Asia, Africa. It has soft, thick fur and a bushy tail. Usually is diurnal and partly arboreal. Conceals winter food in ground or stumps. See also FLYING SQUIRREL and GROUND SQUIRREL.

Sr, chemical symbol of the element STRONTIUM.

Srinagar (srēnŭ'gůr), city (pop. 209,595; alt. 5,227 ft.), summer cap. of Kashmir, on Jhelum R.; famed resort. Has many canals, and transportation is chiefly by boat. Textile mfg.

St. For placenames beginning thus, see SAINT and SANKT. Personal names beginning thus are filed as if spelled Saint. Persons recognized by the church as saints are under proper names (e.g., PAUL, SAINT).

Stabat Mater (stä'bät mä'tĕr), hymn of the Roman Catholic Church, a prayer meditating on the sorrows of the Virgin by the Cross; probably by Jacopone da Todi. It begins *Stabat mater dolorosa juxta crucem* [the sorrowful mother stood at the foot of the Cross]. It is the sequence for the Seven Sorrows of the Virgin and is much sung at Lenten services. Notable musical settings were composed by Josquin des Prés, Palestrina, Pergolesi, Haydn, Schubert, and Verdi.

Stabiae, Italy: see CASTELLAMMARE DI STABIA.

Staël, Germaine de (zhĕrmĕn' dů stäl'), 1766–1817, French woman of letters; daughter of Jacques Necker. Her opposition to Napoleon caused her exile, first to her estate at Coppet, on the L. of Geneva, later to Russia and England. She wrote two successful novels—*Delphine* (1802) and *Corinne* (1807)—but her chief work is *De l'Allemagne* (1811), which tremendously influenced French literature through its enthusiasm for German romanticism. Mme de Staël was the center of a brilliant circle which included Chateaubriand and Benjamin Constant.

Stafford, English noble family. **Humphrey Stafford,** 1st **duke of Buckingham,** 1402–60, fought in France in the Hundred Years War. Supported the Lancastrians in Wars of the Roses and was killed in battle. His grandson, **Henry Stafford,** 2d **duke of Buckingham,** 1454?–1483, was instrumental in having Richard III made king. Staged an unsuccessful revolt against Richard and was executed. His son, **Edward Stafford,** 3d **duke of Buckingham,** 1478–1521, was given high honors by Henry VIII. Henry actually was suspicious of Stafford and had him tried (1521) and executed for treason.

Stafford, William Howard, 1st **Viscount:** see HOWARD, family.

Stafford, county, England: see STAFFORDSHIRE.

Stafford, textile town (pop. 6,471), NE Conn., at Mass. line; settled 1719. Includes Stafford Springs borough (pop. 3,396), health resort (mineral springs).

Staffordshire (stă'fůrdshĭr) or **Stafford,** inland county (1,154 sq. mi.; pop. 1,621,013), central England. Mainly industrial, it has POTTERIES district (china, glass, bricks, and pottery) in N and the BLACK COUNTRY (coal fields, foundries, and iron and steel mills) in S. County town is **Stafford,** municipal borough (pop. 40,275), a shoe-mfg. center. Birthplace of Izaak Walton.

Stafford Springs, Conn.: see STAFFORD.

stagecoach, public road conveyance carrying passengers. Operated from early 18th cent. Early coaches usually were drawn by four or six horses changed at stages along route; the coach traveled from 12 to 18 hr. a day, covering c.25 to 40 mi. Carried eight to fourteen passengers, baggage, and mail. Schedules and comfort were improved in England by competition from mail coaches. Heyday of stagecoach was early 19th cent.

stage design. Although painted scenery was used as early at 461 B.C., both Greek and Roman theaters required little or no scenery. Medieval mystery plays often had a single setting but used machinery for hoisting clouds and heavenly bodies. Traveling *commedia dell' arte* players introduced painted backdrops. These became generally used. In 20th cent., much experimental work has been done (e.g., by Gordon Craig). Such devices as improved lighting, revolving stages, raised platforms, and gauze curtains have been used effectively. Theater-in-the-round (i.e., stage in the center with audience on all four sides) has been adopted to some extent.

Stagg, Amos Alonzo, 1862–, American football coach, known as "grand old man of football." Coached at Univ. of Chicago (1892–1933), College of the Pacific (1933–46), Susquehanna Univ. (1947–).

Stagira (stůjī'rů), anc. city on peninsula of Chalcidice, Macedonia, birthplace of Aristotle.

stained glass, in general, windows made of colored glass. Actually, staining is only one of the coloring methods used and the best medieval glass made little use of it. The true art of making stained glass reached its height in the 13th and 14th cent. Gothic glaziers used colored pot metal, i.e., glass colored with metallic oxides while in the melting pot, thus obtaining clear, transparent colors. Also used were white glass and flashed glass (glass to which a thin film of colored glass had been fused). For defining outlines and details, a brownish paint grisaille, made of powdered glass and iron oxide, was applied and then fired so as to fuse with the glass surface. A red-hot iron was used for cutting the glass to the required pieces and shapes. The pieces were then fitted into channeled lead strips, the strips soldered together at junction points, and the whole installed in a bracing framework of iron. In the 16th cent. the designs were painted on the glass with enamel paints and then fired. Thus the real art of stained glass was lost. Romanticism and the Gothic revival of the 19th cent. reawakened interest in the study of glass as well as other medieval arts. William Morris and Burne-Jones designed windows of true medieval technique and spirit (e.g., at Birmingham Cathedral and at Christ Church, Oxford). John LA FARGE contributed to American stained glass. Famous stained glass windows of medieval days can still be seen in the cathedrals of Chartres, Le Mans, and elsewhere in France, and in York, Salisbury, and Lincoln, England.

Stainer, Sir John, 1840–1901, English composer, organist at St. Paul's Cathedral, London, and professor at the Royal Col. of Music; knighted 1888. He wrote much church music, including the cantatas *The Daughter of Jairus* and *The Crucifixion.* With W. A. Barrett he wrote *A Dictionary of Musical Terms* (1876).

stain removal, from fabrics. Prompt treatment may often prevent stains from penetrating fibers and may make the use of strong chemicals unnecessary. Certain fresh stains, especially grease spots, can be removed by applying an adsorbent, e.g., chalk, whiting, or corn meal. Many spots can be removed from fabrics which water does not injure by placing the fabric on a blotter or absorbent cloth, then sponging it with a damp cloth. Certain stains are removed only by the application of chemicals, which should be first tested on an inconspicuous part of the fabric. (*Caution.* Chemical cleaning fluids should not be used in a room where there is any open flame.) In rubbing spots, use a clean cloth and work toward the center of the spot using a circular motion. Solvents used for removing spots include alcohol, benzene, carbon tetrachloride, gasoline, naphtha, and turpentine. Bleaches include hydrogen peroxide (a mild agent that may be used on many colored fabrics), commercial chlorine bleaches (not advisable for silk or wool), Javelle water, oxalic acid, and potassium permanganate (this sometimes leaves a brownish spot removable with lemon juice, oxalic acid, or hydrogen peroxide; it is not safe for use on rayon). Bleaches are often applied with a medicine dropper to fabric stretched over a bowl of steaming water.

Note. Common causes of stains and methods of removing them from washable fabrics are listed below; certain of the methods suggested may be applied with care to nonwashable fabrics.

Blood. Rinse in cold water; for stubborn stains add soap or ammonia to water and soak.

Chocolate and *cocoa.* Wash with soap or with borax and cold water.

Coffee (clear). Launder with soap or borax; remove remaining stain with potassium permanganate.

Coffee with cream. Wash with soap and cold water, then treat as for clear coffee.

Cream and *milk.* Rinse in cold water, adding a little ammonia if needed; then launder in hot, soapy water.

Egg. Scrape off excess, then use cold water, followed by hot soapy water.

Fruit juice. Pour boiling water over stain immediately; then use lemon juice and expose to sunlight.

Grass and *green foliage.* If not removed by laundering, use alcohol or a bleach, then rinse.

Gravy. Rinse in cold water; for stubborn stains add soap or ammonia to water and soak. If oily, follow with method for grease.

Grease, oil, and *wax.* Scrape off excess, then use one or more of the following methods: cover spot with chalk or other adsorbent; place blotting paper on both sides and apply hot iron; rinse in a grease solvent, e.g., gasoline or carbon tetrachloride; wash in hot, soapy water.

Gum. Remove excess with dull knife, soak in gasoline, kerosene, or carbon tetrachloride, then launder.
Ice Cream. Rinse in cool water, then follow with methods for removing chocolate, coffee, grease, fruit, or other stains.
Ink. Use commercial ink remover (consult directions on label); certain inks can be removed by soaking in cold water or milk, then laundering; bleaches are often effective.
Iodine. Soak in cold water or in very dilute ammonia solution, then launder.
Iron rust. See rust.
Lipstick. Rub lard into stain, scrape off excess, launder, then use bleach on remaining stain; or pour carbon tetrachloride on stain and blot.
Mildew. Launder, expose to sunlight; soak stubborn stains in milk or use bleach.
Milk. See cream.
Nail polish. Sponge with banana oil, then launder.
Oil. See grease.
Paint and *varnish.* Scrape off excess; many paint and varnish spots can be softened with turpentine or with lard, then laundered; alcohol is effective for certain paints.
Perspiration. Launder, then bleach and rinse or expose to sunlight.
Pitch, soot, and *tar.* Rub with lard, then launder; use gasoline, turpentine, or other solvent, if necessary.
Rust. Sprinkle with salt and lemon juice, expose to sunlight; or apply oxalic acid or very dilute hydrochloric acid with a dropper, rinse in hot water, using ammonia or borax to neutralize acid; or use commercial iron rust soap.
Scorch. Dampen and expose to sunlight.
Shoe polish. If polish contains turpentine, soak spot in turpentine, then launder; certain black liquid polishes can be removed with a bleach.
Soot. See pitch.
Stove polish. Rinse in gasoline or other solvent; launder.
Tar. See pitch.
Tea (clear). Rinse in boiling water; if stain remains, soak in borax, or apply potassium permanganate or oxalic acid, or use lemon juice and expose to sunlight.
Tea with milk. Wash with soap and cold water, then treat as for clear tea.
Varnish. See paint.
Vaseline. Remove with turpentine, then launder.
Water spots. Moisten evenly, then press while damp; or steam.
Wax. See grease.
Wine. Rinse in boiling water, then use bleach.

Stair, James Dalrymple, 1st **Viscount,** 1619–95, Scottish jurist. Prominent after the Restoration, he lost office in 1681, because of sympathy with Covenanters. Became lord advocate under William III. His son, **John Dalrymple,** 1st **earl of Stair,** 1648–1707, was joint secretary of state under William III. Dominated Scottish Parliament and promoted union with England. His son, **John Dalrymple,** 2d **earl of Stair,** 1673–1747, Scottish general and diplomat, fought under William III and was prominent in War of the Spanish Succession. Secured overthrow of Walpole in 1741.

Staked Plain: see LLANO ESTACADO.

Stakhanovism (stəkä'nŭvĭzm), movement begun in the USSR in 1935 to speed up industrial production by efficient working methods; named for Aleksey Stakhanov, a Donets Basin coal miner of fabulous efficiency. Stakhanovite workers receive higher pay and other privileges. Stakhanovism proved a successful incentive but is criticized outside the USSR as another form of the speed-up system.

stalactite (stŭlăk'tīt) and **stalagmite** (stŭlăg'mīt). A stalactite is an icicle-shaped mass of calcium carbonate hanging from the roof of a limestone cave, deposited by dripping ground water. A stalagmite forms under the stalactite, growing upward from cavern floor. If the two meet, a pillar is formed. Impurities cause color variations.

Stalin, Joseph Vissarionovich (stä'lĭn, Rus. vĭsŭryô'nŭvĭch stä'lyĭn), 1879–1953, Russian Communist dictator, b. Gori, Georgian SSR. His real name was Dzhugashvili; he called himself Stalin ["made of steel"] after joining the revolutionary movement. The son of a shoemaker, he became a Marxist while studying for the priesthood at Tiflis. He was expelled from the seminary 1899; joined the Bolshevik wing of the Social Democratic party; was arrested for the sixth time in 1913 and exiled for life to Siberia. Amnestied in 1917, he became people's commissar for nationalities in Lenin's cabinet after the October Revolution. His importance in the prerevolutionary underground and in the civil war of 1918–20 has been subject to much debate. In 1922 he was elected general secretary of the Communist party. After Lenin's death (1924) he assumed Lenin's succession jointly with KAMENEV and ZINOVIEV, but he secured in 1927 the expulsion of his two chief rivals—TROTSKY and Zinoviev—from the party, thus gaining sole leadership. Although he held no formal government office before 1941, he dictated Soviet policy as head of the Politburo of the Communist party. In 1928 he ended Lenin's NEW ECONOMIC POLICY and inaugurated the first FIVE-YEAR PLAN. Industrialization and collectivization were carried through at a tremendous cost in human life and liberty. Stalin emphasized the need for consolidating "Socialism in one country" rather than promoting world revolution, as Trotsky advocated. He made his dictatorship absolute by liquidating all opposition within the party in the "purge" trials of the 1930s—touched off by the murder of S. M. KIROV (1934). By 1938, "monolithic unity" was achieved. In 1941 Stalin took over the premiership from Molotov. Shortly after Hitler's attack on Russia, he also assumed military leadership (1941) and took the titles marshal (1943) and generalissimo (1945). At the TEHERAN CONFERENCE, YALTA CONFERENCE, and POTSDAM CONFERENCE he proved himself an astute diplomat. He continued to rule Russia with an iron fist until his death in March, 1953. He was succeeded as premier by MALENKOV. Usually hidden in the Kremlin, Stalin was both a remote figure and a subject of nearly unprecedented official adulation. His least utterances were accepted as party dogmas. Claiming to be the true interpreter of Leninism, Stalin in both his words and deeds created a version of Communism known as Stalinism and embraced by the majority of Communists the world over. To non-Stalinists, Stalinism represents the substitution of nationalism, despotism, and imperialist militarism for the internationalist, equalitarian, and pacifist ideals of earlier Communists. See also UNION OF SOVIET SOCIALIST REPUBLICS.

Stalin, formerly **Varna** (vär'nä), city (pop. 77,-792), E Bulgaria; a major Black Sea port. Shipbuilding; textile and tobacco mfg. Seaside resort. University (founded 1920). Founded as Odessus by Greek colonists (6th cent. B.C.), it became a commercial center under Thracian, later under Roman and Byzantine, rule. In 1444 the Turks decisively defeated at Varna an army of Crusaders under Ladislaus III of Poland and Hungary. City was renamed 1949 to honor Joseph Stalin's 70th birthday.

Stalinabad (stä"lyĭnŭbät'), city (pop. c.110,000), cap. of Tadzhik SSR. Agr. and transportation center. Has textile mills, tanneries, machinery and tobacco plants, distilleries.

Stalingrad (stälyĭngrät'), city (pop. 445,476), SE European RSFSR; a port on the lower Volga. Leading industrial and commercial city in Volga region; important transshipment point and rail hub; a center of heavy industry (esp. steel mills, machinery works, oil refineries). Founded 1589 as a Russian stronghold (called Tsaritsyn until 1925). During Russian civil war it was defended against the Whites by Stalin and Voroshilov. City was virtually destroyed in one of the decisive battles of World War II. German army (including Italian, Hungarian, and Rumanian forces) attacked in Sept., 1942, with superior numbers, but was unable to overcome the desperate Russian stand. Soviet reinforcements, which arrived in Nov., finally forced surrender (Feb. 2, 1943) of the Axis forces, which had lost c.330,000 men. Russians then began a mighty drive W and remained generally on offensive till end of war. Rebuilding of city started immediately after liberation.

Stalino (stä'lyĭnŭ), industrial city (pop. 462,-395), SE Ukraine, in the Donets Basin. Iron and steel mills; machinery works; nitrate and food-processing plants.

Stalin Peak, Czechoslovakia: see TATRA.

Stalin Peak, 24,590 ft., Tadzhik SSR, in the Pamir; highest in USSR. Formerly called Garmo Peak.

Stalinsk (stä'lyĭnsk), industrial city (pop. c.223,000), RSFSR, in S central Siberia, on Tom R. (head of navigation). It is the chief metallurgical center of Kuznetsk Basin.

Stallings, Laurence (stô'lĭngz), 1894–, American dramatist, best known for *What Price Glory* (1924), a successful war play written with Maxwell Anderson.

Stambul, Turkey: see ISTANBUL.

Stambuliski, Alexander, Bulgarian *Stamboliski* (stämbōlē'skē), 1879–1923, Bulgarian premier (1919–23), founder of the Radical Peasant party (1908). As virtual dictator after 1920, he carried out agrarian reforms and followed a conciliatory foreign policy. Was murdered in a nationalist coup d'état.

Stambulov, Stefan (stĕ'fän stämbōō'lôf), 1854–95, Bulgarian statesman, leader of National Liberal party. Organized revolution which put Ferdinand on throne (1887); was premier with dictatorial powers until 1894. Was assassinated.

Stamford, municipal borough (pop. 10,899), in Parts of Kesteven, Lincolnshire, England. Supposed site of defeat (449) of Picts and Scots by Saxons. Was one of Five Boroughs of the Danes.

Stamford. 1 City (pop. 74,293), SW Conn., on Long Isl. Sound SW of Norwalk; settled 1641. Many residents commute to New York city. Mfg. of metal goods, chemicals, and plastics. **2** City (pop. 5,819), W central Texas, NNW of Abilene. Trade and processing center for cotton and cattle area with oil and gas wells. Annual Texas Cowboy Reunion.

Stamford Bridge, village, East Riding of Yorkshire, England. King Harold here defeated Harold Hardrada (Harold III) and Tostig in 1066.

stammering: see STUTTERING.

Stamp Act, 1765, revenue law passed by English Parliament requiring publications and legal documents in the American colonies to bear a stamp. Act was strongly denounced. At **Stamp Act Congress,** which met Oct. 7, 1765, colonial delegates attacked law as unconstitutional because colonists were not represented in Parliament. Act repealed in 1766.

Standards, National Bureau of, in U.S. Dept. of Commerce, estab. 1901 for research in physics, mathematics, chemistry, and engineering. Determines national standards of weights and measures and advises government agencies about specifications for purchase of government supplies.

Standish, Miles or **Myles,** c.1584–1656, American colonist, b. England. Military leader of Plymouth Colony. A founder of Duxbury, Mass. Familiar as the disappointed suitor in Longfellow's poem.

standpatters, in U.S. history, term widely used early in 20th cent. to designate conservatives in Republican party as against INSURGENTS or progressive Republicans. Term derives from poker parlance.

Stanford, Leland (lē'lŭnd stăn'fŭrd), 1824–93, American railroad builder, politician, and philanthropist. A founder and president (1863–93) of Central Pacific RR; also president of Southern Pacific Co. (1885–90). U.S. Senator from Calif. (1885–93). Founded Stanford University. His wife, **Jane Lathrop Stanford,** 1825–1905, continued to aid the university after his death.

Stanford University, mainly at Palo Alto, Calif.; nonsectarian, coed.; chartered 1885, opened 1891 by Leland and Jane L. STANFORD as Leland Stanford Jr. Univ. (still its legal name). Noted for research and graduate work, leadership in curriculum plans for major subjects, and independent study. Includes Hoover Library on War, Revolution, and Peace and Hopkins Marine Laboratory at Pacific Grove, Calif.

Stanhope (stă'nŭp), English noble family.

James Stanhope, 1st Earl Stanhope, 1673–1721, won victories as commander in chief of British forces in Spain (1708) in War of Spanish Succession. Was twice (1714–17, 1718–21) secretary of state under George I. His grandson, **Charles Stanhope, 3d Earl Stanhope,** 1753–1816, supported the younger William Pitt (whose sister he married) and opposed war with American colonies. Broke with Pitt over the French Revolution. His inventions include lenses and printing machines. His daughter, **Lady Hester (Lucy) Stanhope,** 1776–1839, was hostess and secretary for William Pitt. Traveled in Levant, adopting Eastern male dress. Settled as prophetess among the Druses of the Lebanon mts. The 3d Earl's grandson, **Philip Henry Stanhope, 5th Earl Stanhope,** 1805–75, was the author of several standard histories.

Stanhope, Philip Dormer: see CHESTERFIELD, PHILIP DORMER STANHOPE, 4TH EARL OF.

Stanhope, Philip Henry Stanhope, 5th Earl: see STANHOPE, family.

Stanislaus, kings of Poland. **Stanislaus I** (Stanislaus Leszczynski), 1677–1766, was elected king in 1704 through intervention of Charles XII of Sweden (see NORTHERN WAR). After Charles's defeat at Poltava (1709), he had to yield Poland to his rival, AUGUSTUS II, and retired to France. His daughter Marie Leszczynska married Louis XV, with whose help Stanislaus again sought the Polish throne in 1733 (see POLISH SUCCESSION, WAR OF THE). Defeated by AUGUSTUS III, he retained the title king and was given the duchy of LORRAINE. A man of culture and taste, he embellished Nancy and held a distinguished court at Lunéville. **Stanislaus II** (Stanislaus Augustus Poniatowski), 1732–98, was elected (1764) to succeed Augustus III. He was backed by Frederick II of Prussia and by Catherine II of Russia, whose lover he had been. Russian influence became paramount in Poland. An anti-Russian rebellion was crushed and was followed by the first partition of POLAND (1772). Stanislaus' subsequent attempts to revitalize the Polish state and his introduction of an efficient constitution (1791) brought about joint Russian and Prussian military intervention and the second partition (1793). Stanislaus took no firm stand in the KOSCIUSKO uprising of 1794, after the failure of which he lost his remaining lands in the third partition (1795). He went to live in Russia.

Stanislav (stŭnyĭsläf′), Pol. *Stanisławów,* city (1931 pop. 61,256), W Ukraine. Rail center; oil refineries; carpet mfg. Was Polish until 1772; Austrian 1772–1918; Polish 1919–39; formally ceded to USSR 1945.

Stanislavsky, Constantin (kŭnstŭntyĕn′ stŭnyĭsläf′skē), 1863–1938, stage name of Constantin Sergeyevich Alekseyev, Russian actor, director, and theatrical producer. Cofounder of Moscow ART THEATRE (1898). As its director he eliminated mechanical theatrical techniques, training actors to strive for inner interpretations of roles.

Stanislawow, Ukraine: see STANISLAV.

Stanley, Edward George Geoffrey Smith: see DERBY, EDWARD GEORGE GEOFFREY SMITH, 14TH EARL OF.

Stanley, Sir Henry Morton, 1841–1904, British explorer, a journalist. Sent to Africa by New York *Herald* (1871) to find David LIVINGSTONE. On expedition of 1879–84 he obtained territorial concessions which led to Belgian acquisition of Congo Free State. African expedition of 1887–89 led to land concessions for British.

Stanley, Wendell Meredith, 1904–, American biochemist. Shared 1946 Nobel Prize for isolation of crystalline forms of viruses.

Stanley, William, 1858–1916, American electrical engineer. Invented multiple system of alternating-current transmission; out of this grew modern system of light and power transmission.

Stanley Falls, cataracts of Lualaba R., NE Belgian Congo, extending 60 mi. between Stanleyville and Ponthierville. Total fall, c.200 ft.

Stanley Pool, lakelike expansion, area 320 sq. mi., of Congo R. along border between Belgian Congo and French Equatorial Africa. Discovered 1877 by Stanley. On it are Leopoldville and Brazzaville.

Stanleyville, town (pop. 25,278), NE Belgian Congo; port on the Congo R. On short rail line skirting Stanley Falls. Tourist center.

Stanovoi Range (stŭnŭvoi′), mountain chain, RSFSR, in SE Siberia, extending c.450 mi. E from Olekma R. and rising to 8,143 ft. Forms watershed between Lena and Amur river basins.

Stans (stäns), town (pop. 3,449), cap. of Nidwalden half-canton, Unterwalden, Switzerland.

Stanton, Edwin McMasters, 1814–69, American cabinet officer. Became Pres. Lincoln's Secretary of War in Jan., 1862. Administered office with economy and efficiency. A radical Republican, opposed to many of Lincoln's policies, he continued under Andrew JOHNSON. Resisted Johnson's attempts to remove him; resigned 1868.

Stanton, Elizabeth Cady, 1815–1902, American reformer, a leader of woman-suffrage movement. With Lucretia Mott she organized (1848) first woman's rights convention. Also closely associated with Susan B. ANTHONY. President (1869–92) of woman-suffrage associations, she helped to compile a history of the movement.

Stanwix, Fort, colonial outpost in N.Y., near site of present city of Rome. Controlled principal route from the Hudson to L. Ontario as trading center. Besieged by British in American Revolution. Treaty between Iroquois and U.S. signed here in 1784.

Stapleton, N.Y.: see STATEN ISLAND.

star, in astronomy, luminous globular mass of intensely hot gases. Man distinguished in early times between "fixed" stars and planets and identified groups of stars (see CONSTELLATION) with mythological figures. Actually stars are in rapid motion detectable only by exacting observations over many years. Stars of our Galaxy comprise MILKY WAY SYSTEM and include our sun. Although similar in chemical composition, stars vary in luminosity (see MAGNITUDE), temperature, color, volume, density. Correlation between temperature and color is shown by classification into color series (bluish white, white, yellowish white, yellow and red stars) with temperatures decreasing from that of the hottest bluish white stars (c.20,000°C. to 50,-000°C.). Our sun is medium-sized yellow star, temperature c.6,000°C. Density ranges from over a ton per cubic inch in certain dwarf white stars to density less than one millionth that of sun in certain huge red stars known as supergiants. LIGHT-YEAR is commonly used to indicate vast stellar distances. Nearest stars, other than sun, are c.4.3 light-years distant from earth. Many apparently single stars have been discovered to consist of two or more stars. Binary stars are double stars revolving about same center of gravity. See also CLUSTER; VARIABLE STAR.

starch, white, odorless, tasteless CARBOHYDRATE, important in functions of plants and animals. Produced by PHOTOSYNTHESIS in green plants and stored. Animals obtain starch from plants; in animal body starch is stored as GLYCOGEN. Digestion converts it to sucrose, a source of energy. Test for presence of starch is blue-black color produced on addition of iodine. Starch is used for sizing paper and textiles, for stiffening, in making dextrin. Cornstarch is used to make corn syrup and glucose.

Star Chamber, anc. meeting place of king's councilors in Westminster Palace, London, named for stars painted on ceiling. Originally used to curb powers of nobles, it became criminal court under Tudors. Abuses of its power under James I and Charles I led to its abolition in 1641. "Star Chamber proceedings" now signifies acts of an arbitrary tribunal.

starfish, common marine echinoderm typically star-shaped (five or more arms or rays radiate from a disk). It has a spiny surface with calcareous plates embedded in skin; moves by tube feet; c.1,000 known species.

Starhemberg, Ernst Rüdiger, Graf von (ĕrnst′ rü′dĭgŭr gräf′ fŭn shtä′rŭmbĕrk″), 1638–1701, Austrian field marshal. Held Vienna with a small garrison in Turkish siege of 1683 until its relief by John III of Poland. His descendant, **Ernst Rüdiger von Starhemberg,** 1899–, Austrian politician, led the *Heimwehr,* a fascistic militia, supported Chancellor Dollfuss, and was vice chancellor and security minister under Schuschnigg until 1936. In World War II he served in British and Free French air forces.

Stark, Johannes (stärk, Ger. yōhä′nŭs shtärk′), 1874–, German physicist. Won 1919 Nobel Prize for discovery of Doppler effect in canal rays (positive particles produced in vacuum tube which pass through perforations in cathode) and broadening of spectrum lines in electric field (Stark effect) which confirmed quantum theory.

Stark, John, 1728–1822, American Revolutionary commander. Repulsed attack by Gen. Burgoyne at Bennington in Saratoga campaign.

Starkville, city (pop. 7,107), E Miss., W of Columbus in livestock and farm area. Near by is Mississippi State Col. (land-grant; coed.; 1878).

Starling, Ernest Henry, 1866–1927, English physiologist, authority on nervous regulation of heart and circulation. He evolved (with Bayliss) hormone concept.

starling, European bird introduced into U.S. in 1890, now common in parts of E U.S. Has iridescent black plumage and long bill (yellow in spring and summer). Destroys insects.

Star of Bethlehem, name for celestial body, probably not a single star, in east which is related in the Gospel led the Wise Men to Bethlehem (Mat. 2.1–10).

star-of-Bethlehem, low, spring-blooming bulbous plant of the Mediterranean region. The common star-of-Bethlehem (*Ornithogalum umbellatum*) has grasslike leaves and clustered white starry flowers. Other species and some other flowers are also called star-of-Bethlehem.

Starr, Belle, 1848–89, American outlaw, consort of notorious bandits of SW U.S. Original name was Myra Belle Shirley.

star route, in U.S. postal service, surface route to post offices not accessible by railroad or steamboat. U.S. Postal Guide and maps once designated such an office by an asterisk, hence the name. Private contracts to carry mail over these routes are made with bonded bidders. In April, 1881, Pres. Garfield dismissed Second Assistant Postmaster General T W. Brady, suspected of having fraudulently increased compensation of numerous star-route contractors, among them former Sen. S. W. Dorsey of Ark. Both narrowly escaped conviction in Pres. Arthur's administration. Frauds, amounting to nearly $500,-000, hastened civil service reform.

Star-spangled Banner, The, American national anthem, beginning, "Oh, say can you see." The words were written by Francis Scott Key, an American lawyer who, on a mission to recover a prisoner, was detained by the British and forced to watch the bombardment of Fort McHenry (Sept., 1814). The sight of the flag still floating over the fort at dawn inspired Key's verses. The tune, composed by John Stafford Smith (1750–1836), was taken from an English song, *To Anacreon in Heaven.* Song officially became national anthem by a presidential order in 1916, confirmed by Congress, 1931.

Starved Rock, cliff, 140 ft. high, N Ill., overlooking Illinois R. between La Salle and Ottawa. Visited by Jolliet and Père Marquette 1673, and by La Salle and de Tonti 1679 (they completed fort here, 1682–83). Legendary scene of starvation of Illinois band driven here by Ottawa Indians in 18th cent. Vicinity was hideout of brigands and outlaws in early 19th cent. Now state park.

Stassen, Harold E(dward) (stă′sŭn), 1907–, American statesman, president of Univ. of Pennsylvania (1948–53). Governor of Minn. (1939–43). Delegate to conference creating UN (1945). Became Mutual Security Director in 1953.

Stassfurt (shtäs′fo͝ort), city (pop. 29,762), Saxony-Anhalt, E central Germany. Center of one of world's chief potash-mining areas. Produces chemicals and machinery.

State, United States Department of, executive department of Federal government responsible for determination and execution, under the President's direction, of American foreign policy. Estab. Sept., 1789, to replace Dept. of Foreign Affairs; oldest Federal department. Secretary of State is first ranking cabinet officer. Successive reorganizations of department culminated in 1909 reorganization, which gave department essentials of its present-day structure. At that time foreign policy and relations were reorganized along new geographical divisions—Western European, Near Eastern, Far Eastern, and Latin American. During Cordell Hull's administration (1933–44) changes were effected to meet rising tide of World War II. At close of the war the department's machinery was geared to dispense information to foreign nations, to estab. strict secrecy concerning its operation, to integrate foreign policy with the economic-aid programs, and to bring about effective liaison between U.S. and the U.N.

State College, residential borough (pop. 17,227), central Pa., NW of Harrisburg. Seat of Pennsylvania State Col. (land-grant and state supported, coed.; opened 1859). Has forest school at Mont Alto, institute of animal nutrition, Ellen H. Richards Inst. for textile research, and five jr. branches.

state flowers. Each state of the U.S. has designated a floral emblem; the U.S. as a whole has none. The emblem of the Dist. of Columbia is the American Beauty rose; those of the states are: Ala., goldenrod; Ariz., saguaro; Ark., apple blossom; Calif., California poppy; Colo., blue-and-white columbine; Conn., mountain laurel; Del., peach blossom; Fla., orange blossom; Ga., Cherokee rose; Idaho, mock orange; Ill., violet; Ind., zinnia; Iowa, wild rose; Kansas, sunflower; Ky., goldenrod; La., magnolia; Maine, pine cone and tassel; Md., black-eyed Susan; Mass., trailing arbutus; Mich., apple blossom; Minn., lady's slipper; Miss., magnolia; Mo., hawthorn; Mont., bitterroot; Nebr., goldenrod; Nev., sagebrush; N.H., lilac; N.J., violet; N.Mex., yucca; N.Y., rose; N.C., daisy; N.Dak., wild rose; Ohio, red carnation; Okla., mistletoe; Oregon, Oregon grape; Pa., mountain laurel; R.I., violet; S.C., Carolina jasmine; S.Dak., pasqueflower; Tenn., iris; Texas, bluebonnet; Utah, sego lily; Vt., red clover; Va., dogwood; Wash., rhododendron; W.Va., rhododendron; Wis., violet; Wyo., Indian paintbrush.

Staten Island (57 sq. mi.; pop. 191,555), SE N.Y., in NEW YORK BAY, forming (with small adjacent islands) Richmond borough (since 1898) of NEW YORK city and Richmond co. of N.Y. state. N and W, bridges cross to N.J. over Kill Van Kull and Arthur Kill; ferries connect with Manhattan (NE) and Brooklyn. Generally residential, with some semirural sections and resort beaches (SE shore). Industries (shipbuilding and repairing, oil refining, lumber milling) mainly in N. Trade centers are St. George, Stapleton (site of first U.S. free port), Port Richmond. Staten Isl. visited by Henry Hudson 1609; permanent community estab. by 1661. Early buildings include Billopp (or Conference) House (built before 1688), where Lord Howe negotiated with Continentals in 1776; Church of St. Andrew (founded 1708); Garibaldi House (Italian liberator lived here in 1850s).

Statesboro, city (pop. 6,097), E Ga., NW of Savannah. Tobacco and livestock market; food processing.

States-General or **Estates-General. 1** In French history, national assembly in which the chief estates—clergy, nobility, and commons—were represented as separate bodies. It was comparable to the DIET of the Holy Roman Empire, to the old Spanish CORTES, and, in some respects, to the English PARLIAMENT, but it never developed the power and organization of these bodies. Originating in the king's council, or Curia Regis, the French States-General was first summoned in 1302 by Philip IV. Its powers were never clearly defined; its main function was to approve royal legislation. Its attempt, promoted by Étienne MARCEL, to secure wider authority collapsed in 1358. After the States-General of 1614, which accomplished nothing, no further meeting was called till 1789. There were, however, provincial estates in a number of provinces. The States-General of 1789 was called by Louis XVI as a last resort to solve the government's financial crisis (see FRENCH REVOLUTION). It first met on May 5, at Versailles, and it became immediately evident that the third estate (commons) and the liberals among the clergy and nobles intended to transform it from a consultative into a legislative assembly. The third estate (with 50% of total delegates) rejected the customary voting procedure (by estates) and insisted that balloting should proceed by head. In June, it and its sympathizers forced the issue by openly defying the king and declaring themselves the National Assembly. Louis XVI accepted the accomplished fact; the States-General ceased to exist; the Revolution began. **2** The name States-General also designates the two houses of parliament in the Netherlands, in which the upper house represents the provincial estates, the lower house the nation at large.

States of the Church: see PAPAL STATES.

states' rights, in U.S. history, an issue which has existed since the beginnings of national government. Tenth Amendment to U.S. Constitution says: "The powers not delegated to the United States by the Constitution, nor prohibited by it to the States, are reserved to the States respectively, or to the people." Controversy arose over interpretation of enumerated powers granted Federal government, which are not at all specific. Alexander Hamilton and Federalist party favored broad interpretation; Thomas Jefferson and his followers insisted that all powers not specifically granted Federal government be reserved to the states. KENTUCKY AND VIRGINIA RESOLUTIONS represent first formulation of states' rights school. Second important manifestation of states' rights occurred among Federalists of HARTFORD CONVENTION (1814). Opposition of S.C. to tariff acts of 1828 and 1832 caused state, guided by John C. CALHOUN, to pass its ordinance of NULLIFICATION. Proslavery forces soon backed a strong doctrine which ultimately led to SECESSION. Although today states' rights doctrine is usually associated with Southern wing of Democratic party, actually doctrine is not exclusive with any particular section or political party.

Statesville, city (pop. 16,901), W central N.C., SW of Winston-Salem, in piedmont; founded 1789. Mfg. of textiles, flour, and furniture.

static, radio reception noises unrelated to signal, usually from electrical discharges. Caused by atmospheric disturbances, electrical or motor-driven devices. Reduced by FREQUENCY MODULATION.

statice: see SEA PINK.

statistics, science of determining certain values representing tendencies indicated in large collection of observations or measurements. Statistical measures include: arithmetic MEAN; MEDIAN; MODE; standard deviation (measure of extent individual observations are scattered about mean). Important in statistical theory is sampling, an effort to determine for what larger group of individuals or characteristics the statistics of a smaller (sample) group would be representative and how representative it would be. This makes possible the applications of statistics to scientific and social research, insurance, finance, and various other fields.

Statius, Publius Papinious (stā'shŭs), A.D., c.40–c.96, Latin epic poet. Surviving are 2 epics—the *Thebaid* and the *Achilleid* (incomplete)—and some minor poems.

Statuary Hall, National, in the Capitol, Washington, D.C. Formerly the chamber of U.S. Representatives (1807–57). In 1864 it was made a gallery for statues of distinguished Americans, each state being allowed two. Many have since been removed.

Statue of Liberty: see LIBERTY, STATUE OF.

statute, formal, written enactment by a legislature. Statute law is to be distinguished from COMMON LAW, which is derived from judicial decisions and custom. Statutes have been much used in common-law countries to meet new needs of changing society and economy, and therefore statute law has grown much. In nearly all European countries the law is statutory and covered by code.

Statute of Frauds: see CONTRACT.

Staunton (stăn'tŭn), city (pop. 19,927), western Va., in Shenandoah Valley WNW of Charlottesville; settled c.1738. Trade center in agr. area, it has mfg. of clothing, textiles, and furniture. Cap. of Northwest Territory 1738–70. Birthplace of Woodrow Wilson. Seat of Mary Baldwin Col. (for women; 1842).

Stavanger (stäväng'ŭr), city (pop. 50,320), SW Norway; a seaport on Stavanger Fjord. Shipbuilding; fish-canning. Gothic Cathedral of St. Swithin dates from 11th cent. Stavanger was one of first places taken by Germans in invasion of Norway (April 9, 1940).

Stavropol Territory (stä'vrŭpŭl), administrative division (2,950 sq. mi.; pop. c.1,500,000), S European RSFSR, extending N from main Caucasus range. Comprises MANYCH DEPRESSION (N), hilly Stavropol Plateau (center), and Pyatigorsk region, a major resort area. Irrigated since c.1945, territory now produces cereals, cotton, wine, fruit, vegetables. Population is Russian and Ukrainian, with seminomadic Turkmen and Nogai Tatar minorities. Cap. is **Stavropol** (pop. 85,100), agr. city on the plateau. It was an important base in Russian conquest of the Caucasus in 1830s.

Stead, W(illiam) T(homas) (stĕd), 1849–1912, English journalist, editor of *Pall Mall Gazette* (1883–89), founder of *Review of Reviews* (1890). Pioneered in modern journalistic methods and championed naval reform and social welfare. Lost life on *Titanic.*

Steamboat Springs, resort town (pop. 1,913; alt. 6,762 ft.), NW Colo., W of Park Range.

steam engine, machine to convert heat energy into mechanical energy. Expanding steam from boiler moves piston forward within cylinder. As expansive force ceases, piston is pressed back. Crank and flywheel convert total action into rotational motion which does work. Heron of Alexandria probably first harnassed steam, and many minds contributed to development of the steam engine; first practical solution came when James Watt patented his engine (1769). His separate condenser reduced fuel 75% and moved piston back as well as forward (reciprocal motion). Improvements he later introduced —governor, mercury steam gauge, and crank-flywheel mechanism—helped make steam engine the catalyst of the Industrial Revolution. Large-scale electrical generation has replaced steam engine as chief industrial power source. Steam TURBINE now provides most electrical power. See *ill.*, p. 389.

steamship, watercraft propelled by a steam engine or a steam turbine. In 1787 a steamboat built by James RUMSEY was demonstrated successfully. At the same time John FITCH was experimenting with building steamboats. Other Americans had worked with the problem (notably John Stevens) and the *Charlotte Dundas* was launched on the Forth and Clyde Canal (1803) before Robert FULTON successfully demonstrated his famous *Clermont* on the Hudson (1807). The first steamship to cross the Atlantic in 15 days was I. K. Brunel's *Great Western* (1838). The *Great Britain* was the first large iron steamship to use a screw propeller in Atlantic passage (1845). In the 1850s and 1860s the steamship began to supplant the sailing ship —a triumph complete by 1900. The *Turbinia* was the first powered by a turbine (1897).

stearin (stē'ŭrĭn), white, crystalline fat, an ester of stearic acid. Used in making soap, candles, and polishes, and in tanning.

steatite: see SOAPSTONE.

Stedman, Edmund Clarence, 1833–1908, American poet and critic, a Wall Street broker; a popular poet of his day and compiler of excellent anthologies.

steel, compound of iron and carbon with varying small amounts of other minerals. Steelmaking processes include cementation process—heating two iron bars with charcoal to give them high carbon content, then fusing them; crucible process—receptacle of fire clay or graphite is charged with iron and charcoal and fired (various grades of fine steel are obtained by adding other components in small quantities); BESSEMER PROCESS; and open-hearth process. Openhearth uses a regenerative furnace (type of reverberatory furnace) developed by Sir William Siemens c.1866. Pierre Martin with Siemens developed variation of process. Rolling mills shape steel for commercial use. Tensile strength of metal varies directly with carbon content. Alloy steels, now most widely used, contain one or more other minerals to give them special qualities; these include nickel (most widely used; nonmagnetic, has tensile strength but is not brittle), chromium (hard, strong, elastic), nickel-chromium (shock-resistant), and stainless (noncorrosive) steels. Most high-grade alloy steels are manufactured in electric furnace. U.S., USSR, and Great Britain lead in steel production.

Steele, Joel Dorman (stēl), 1836–86, American educator and textbook writer. Author of series of science texts which helped to popularize the subject.

Steele, Sir Richard, 1672–1729, English essayist and playwright. In 1709 he began famous journal *Tatler* and was soon joined by Joseph Addison. It was followed by the *Spectator* (1711–12), the *Guardian* (1713), and lesser papers. Perhaps the best known of many plays is *The Conscious Lovers* (1722). He became manager of Drury Lane Theatre in 1714, and that same year entered Parliament as a stalwart Whig. He was knighted in 1715. Plagued by financial troubles, he retired to Wales in 1724. Although impulsive and improvident, Steele was a man of engaging personality and charm, qualities reflected in his spontaneous and witty prose.

Steelton, borough (pop. 12,574), SE Pa., on Susquehanna R. below Harrisburg; settled 1865. Produces steel and limestone. First practical production of Bessemer steel in U.S. here 1867.

Steelyard, Merchants of the, German hanse or guild merchants (see HANSEATIC LEAGUE), residing at the Steelyard or German House, a separate walled community inside London, England. First Hanseatic merchants in England were licensed in 1157. Steelyard Merchants of Lübeck and Hamburg were chartered 1266 and gained wide privileges which made them highly unpopular. Queen Elizabeth I expelled the merchants and closed Steelyard 1597.

Steen, Jan (yän′ stān′), 1626–79, Dutch genre painter, b. Leiden. Studied in Utrecht and Haarlem. Largely humorous or moralistic, his works depict social life of his day. Favorite themes were scenes of revelry.

Steenkerke (stān′kĕr″kŭ), village near Mons, Belgium. Here in 1692 William III of England defeated the French under Marshal Luxembourg.

Stefansson, Vilhjalmur (vĭl′hyoulmŭr stĕ′fŭnsŭn), 1879–, arctic explorer, b. Canada, of Icelandic parents. Led several expeditions of exploration and of ethnological and archaeological investigation, successfully using Eskimo techniques of survival.

Steffens, (Joseph) Lincoln, 1866–1936, American editor and author. A magazine editor in muckraking era, he wrote exposés, collected in such works as *The Shame of the Cities* (1904) and *Upbuilders* (1909). Also wrote an illuminating autobiography (1931).

Stegosaurus (stĕgŭsô′rŭs), quadruped vegetarian dinosaur. It was c.20 ft. long, weighed c.10 tons, had short forelegs, two rows of upright bony plates on the back, and spines on the tail. Brain weighed c.2½ oz. Complete skeletons were found in the Jurassic of Colo. and Wyo.

Steichen, Edward (stī′kŭn), 1879–, American photographer and painter, b. Luxembourg. His early paintings are in various museums including the Metropolitan, and his work in photography has been widely exhibited. He was chief photographer for Condé Nast Publications (1923–38); in World War II he commanded U.S. navy photographic department.

Steilacoom (stĭ′lŭkŭm″), town (pop. 1,233), W Wash., on Puget Sound, S of Tacoma, State's oldest inc. town (1854), it has historic landmarks.

Stein, Charlotte von (shärlô′tŭ fŭn shtīn′), 1742–1827, German noblewoman, noted for her friendship with Goethe. After a separation from him, she wrote a tragedy, *Dido* (1794).

Stein, Gertrude (stīn), 1874–1946, American author, b. Pa. Through her salon and patronage of arts in Paris after 1903, she influenced many writers and artists. Her own writing is notable for repetitious, colloquially impressionistic style. She wrote stories, poems, a novel, art criticism, operas (notably *Four Saints in Three Acts* with music by Virgil Thomson, 1934), and several autobiographical works (esp. *The Autobiography of Alice B. Toklas,* 1933).

Stein, Karl, Freiherr vom und zum (kärl′ frī′hĕr fŭm″ ŏŏnt tsŏŏm″ shtīn′), 1757–1831, Prussian statesman and reformer. He was minister of commerce (1804–7) and premier (1807–8); was dismissed on pressure of Napoleon I; went to Russia and helped form Russo-Prussian alliance of 1813. Stein in 1807–8 abolished serfdom and all feudal class privileges or restrictions, began emancipation of Jews, abolished internal customs barriers, instituted local self-government. His reforms were continued by Hardenberg, Scharnhorst, and Humboldt and transformed Prussia into a modern state.

Steinach, Eugen (oigān′ stī′näkh), 1861–1944, Austrian physiologist. Studied influence of sex glands and hormones in retarding senility.

Steinbeck, John (Ernst) (stīn′bĕk), 1902–, American author, known especially for realistic, compassionate novels of lowly people —*Tortilla Flat* (1935), *Of Mice and Men* (1937), *The Grapes of Wrath* (1939). Also wrote anti-Nazi fiction (both novel and play), *The Moon Is Down* (1942), a novel of Calif., *East of Eden* (1952), and several works of nonfiction.

Steiner, Jakob (yä′kôp shtī′nŭr), 1796–1863, Swiss mathematician, a pioneer in synthetic geometry.

Steinmetz, Charles Proteus (stīn′mĕts), 1865–1923, American electrical engineer. Discovered law of hysteresis, making it possible to reduce loss of efficiency in electrical apparatus resulting from alternating magnetism; developed practical calculation method for alternating current; did valuable research on lightning and built generator for producing it artificially.

Stella, poetical name used by several writers for loved ones. Stella of the sonnets of Sir Philip SIDNEY was Penelope Devereaux. Stella who was the friend of Jonathan SWIFT was Esther Johnson.

Stellarton, town (pop. 5,575), N N.S., Canada,

S of New Glasgow. Coal-mining center with railroad shops and mfg. of metal products.

Steller, Georg Wilhelm (gā'ôrk vĭl'hĕhlm shtĕ'lŭr), 1709–46, German naturalist, whose name was originally Stöhler. Made extensive observations and collections as member of scientific staff of Vitus Bering's second expedition.

Stelvio Pass (stĕl'vyō), Alpine pass, 9,048 ft. high, N Italy, near Swiss border. It is crossed by the highest road in the Alps, connecting Valtellina and Engadine with Adige valley.

stem, part of a plant to which the leaves, roots, or floral parts are attached. The region at which a leaf is attached is called a node; the space between adjacent nodes is the internode. Stem transports food downward from leaves to roots and carries water and minerals upward to branches and leaves. Some plants have underground stems differentiated as bulbs, corms, tubers, or rhizomes. See *ill.*, p. 999.

Stenbock, Count Magnus (măng'nŭs stān'bôk), 1665–1717, Swedish field marshal; one of the ablest lieutenants of Charles XII.

Stendhal (stĕdäl'), pseud. of **Henri Beyle** (ãrē' bāl'), 1783–1842, French author. He was an officer in Napoleon's army, later served as consul at Civitavecchia. Practically ignored in his lifetime, he produced such masterpieces as *The Red and the Black* (1830) and *The Charterhouse of Parma* (1839), which rank with the greatest novels of all times. His deep psychological insight, his dislike for lush romantic prose, and his sharp wit all combined to antagonize his contemporaries (except Balzac), but his greatness was recognized after his death. Most of his many other works and fragments were published posthumously.

Stentor (stĕn'tôr), Greek herald in the Trojan War. His voice was as loud as the voices of 50 men.

Stephan, Heinrich von (hīn'rĭkh fŭn stĕ'fän), 1831–97, German statesman, chief founder of Universal Postal Union.

Stephanus, family of printers: see ESTIENNE.

Stephen, Saint (stē'vŭn) [Gr.,= garland], first Christian martyr, stoned to death. One of the seven deacons. Acts 6; 7. Feasts: Dec. 26; Aug. 3.

Stephen, Saint, or **Stephen I,** 969–1038, duke (997–1001) and first king (1001–38) of Hungary, national hero of the Magyars, called the Apostle of Hungary. He continued the Christianization begun by his father, put down revolts of pagan nobles, and modeled his administration on that of German kings. The Hungarian state may be said to date from his time. The crown given him by Pope Sylvester II became the sacred symbol of Hungarian national existence. Feast: Sept. 2, but Hungarians celebrate Aug. 20 in his honor.

Stephen, 1097–1154, king of England (1135–54). He swore fealty to Henry I's daughter, MATILDA, but on Henry's death was proclaimed king. His long reign was constant struggle to maintain throne. He alienated clergy by threatening bishops who opposed him. Matilda, aided by her half-brother Robert, earl of GLOUCESTER, captured Stephen in 1141 and reigned briefly before Stephen regained throne. When his son Eustace died, Stephen was forced to name (1153) Matilda's son Henry (Henry II) as heir.

Stephen I, king of Hungary: see STEPHEN, SAINT (969–1038).

Stephen, George: see MOUNT STEPHEN, GEORGE STEPHEN, 1ST BARON.

Stephen, Sir Leslie, 1832–1904, English man of letters and philosopher; editor (1871–82) of the *Cornhill Magazine* and first editor (1882–91) of the *Dictionary of National Biography*. Works include *History of English Thought in the Eighteenth Century* (1876); biographies of Johnson, Pope, Swift, George Eliot; essays on mountain climbing. He was the father of Virginia Woolf.

Stephen Bathory (bä'tôrĭ), Hung. *Báthory István*, Pol. *Stefan Batory*, 1533–86, king of Poland (1575–86), prince of Transylvania (1571–75); married Anna, daughter of Sigismund II of Poland. He fought successfully against Ivan IV of Russia over Livonia, retaking Polotsk in 1582. His plan for subjugation of Russia and a Christian crusade against Turkey miscarried. Fostered Catholic Reform. His chancellor, Jan ZAMOJSKI, was a dominant figure of his reign.

Stephen Dushan (dōō'shän), Serbo-Croatian *Stefan Dušan*, c.1308–1355, king (1331–46) and tsar (1346–55) of Serbia. Ruthless and of unlimited ambitions, he conquered Bulgaria, Macedonia, Thessaly, Epirus; died while marching on Constantinople. Under him Serbia attained its greatest glory, but his empire disintegrated after his death.

Stephen Harding, Saint, d. 1134, English monastic reformer, founder of an abbey at Cîteaux (1098; see CISTERCIANS). Feasts: April 17, July 16.

Stephens, Alexander Hamilton, 1812–83, American statesman, vice president of Confederacy (1861–65). U.S. Congressman from Ga. (1843–59, 1873–82). Consistently opposed policies of Jefferson DAVIS. Early advocate of peace, commissioner to Hampton Roads Peace Conference.

Stephens, James, 1882–1950, Irish poet and novelist. Wrote many fanciful lyrics, but is perhaps best remembered for tales using Irish fairy lore or Irish legend, as in *The Crock of Gold* (1912).

Stephens, John Lloyd, 1805–52, American author of travel books (notably *Incidents of Travel in Central America, Chiapas, and Yucatan,* 1841; *Incidents of Travel in Yucatan,* 1843), an amateur archaeologist. Helped lay out Panama RR.

Stephens College: see COLUMBIA, Mo.

Stephenson, George (stē'vŭnsŭn), 1781–1848, English engineer, a noted locomotive builder. He constructed (1814) a traveling engine or locomotive to haul coal from mines and in 1815 built first locomotive to use steam blast. His locomotive the *Rocket* bested the others in a contest in 1829 and was used on the Liverpool-Manchester Railway. He devised c.1815 a miner's safety lamp considered by some to have antedated the similar one invented by Sir Humphry Davy. His son **Robert Stephenson,** 1803–59, and a nephew, **George Robert Stephenson,** 1819–1905, were also railroad engineers.

Stephenville, city (pop. 7,155), N central

Texas, on Bosque R. and SW of Fort Worth. Processing center in farm and dairy area.

Stepney (stĕp'nē), metropolitan borough (pop. 95,581), of E London. Industrial district, it was severely bombed in 1940–41. Includes Whitechapel, Limehouse, Wapping, and the Tower of London.

Stepniak, S. (styĭpnyäk'), pseud. of Sergei Mikhailovich Kravchinski, 1852–95, Russian revolutionist and author. He wrote *Underground Russia* (in Italian), *The Career of a Nihilist* (in English), and propaganda stories in disguise of fairy tales. He spent many years abroad, in exile.

steppe (stĕp), level, treeless plain of S and SE European RSFSR and of SW Asiatic USSR. Originally grassland; now largely under cultivation. Though the word is usually restricted to Russia, actually many of the world's most productive agr. districts are in steppe country—(e.g., U.S. prairies and Argentine Pampa).

stereopticon (stĕrēŏp'tĭkun), improved form of magic lantern for throwing on screen a magnified image of a photograph, a drawing, a page of a book, or a microscopic slide. Moving pictures utilize principles applied in the stereopticon.

stereoscope (stĕ'rēuskōp"), optical instrument that unites two similar pictures to give illusion of depth. In humans a mental image is composite of what the two eyes see separately from slightly different positions, thus giving the impression of depth. Stereoscope combines two photographs (taken from positions related approximately as positions of a person's two eyes) into a composite that has depth. Principle of stereoscope is applied in binocular field glasses and microscope.

sterility, inability to reproduce resulting from any of a number of causes, including impotence, glandular imbalance, production of defective sex cells, disease (e.g., gonorrhea), and emotional disturbances. In the female it sometimes is caused also by failure of the ovum (egg) to remain implanted on the uterine wall.

Sterling. 1 City (pop. 7,534), NE Colo., on South Platte R. Trade and shipping center for sugar-beet, grain, livestock region. A buffalo ranch is near. **2** City (pop. 12,817), NW Ill., on Rock R. (bridged) opposite Rock Falls, in farm and dairy area. Steel and oil products.

Stern, Daniel: see AGOULT, COMTESSE D'.

Stern, G(ladys) B(ronwyn), 1890–, English novelist, author of a series about a Jewish family —*The Rakonitz Chronicles* (1932; later called *The Matriarch Chronicles,* 1936).

Stern, Otto, 1888–, American physicist, b. Germany. Won 1943 Nobel Prize for contributions to atomic-ray method and discovery of magnetic moment (force) of proton.

Sterne, Laurence, 1713–68, British author, b. Ireland. An Anglican clergyman, he published some sermons, but is remembered for his worldly writing, notably *The Life and Opinions of Tristram Shandy* (1759–67), a deliberately rambling, whimsical novel that ranks as one of the great works of English literature. Only a little less important is *A Sentimental Journey through France and Italy* (1768). Sterne started the great vogue of the sentimental novel, but none of his imitators approached his level of writing, his somewhat perverse wit, and his charm rising above his exaggerated and mock emotions.

Sterne, Maurice, 1877–, American painter and sculptor, b. Latvia. Still lifes, landscapes, figures.

Stesichorus (stĕsĭ'kurus), fl. c.600 B.C., Greek lyric poet. Legend says he invented the choral "heroic hymn" and the triad structure—strophe, antistrophe, epode—thenceforth much used.

stethoscope (stĕ'thuskōp"), medical instrument used by physicians to auscultate (listen to) sounds in body. Especially valuable in diagnosing heart and lung conditions. Earliest form, invented by Laënnec, was a slender tube terminating in flanged opening placed against patient's body. Modern binaural type is composed of hollow cone connected by tubing to two earpieces.

Stetson, John Batterson, 1830–1906, American hat manufacturer.

Stettin (shtĕtēn'), Pol. *Szczecin,* city (1939 pop. 374,017; 1946 pop. 72,948), cap. of Pomerania; a major Baltic seaport at mouth of Oder R. and terminus of Berlin–Stettin Canal. Industrial center (shipyards; iron and coke works). Was seat of dukes of Pomerania until its transfer to Sweden (1648); passed to Prussia 1720; under French occupation 1806–13; heavily bombed in World War II. Although most of Stettin lies on W bank of the Oder, the Potsdam agreement of 1945 was interpreted by Poland as including Stettin in the German territory E of the Oder which was transferred to Polish administration. German population was expelled and replaced by Poles; Stettin was made cap. of a Polish province.

Stettinius, Edward R(eilly), Jr. (stutĭ'nēus), 1900–1949, American industrialist and statesman. Executive of General Motors (1926–34), chairman of board of U.S. Steel Corp. (1938–40). U.S. Secretary of State (1944–45). Resigned to serve as U.S. representative to UN (1945–46).

Steuben, Friedrich Wilhelm, Baron von (stū'bun), 1730–94, Prussian officer, general in American Revolution. Helped train Continental army.

Steubenville (stōō'bunvĭl), city (pop. 25,872), E Ohio, on Ohio R. and near Wheeling, W.Va.; laid out c.1797. Steel center in coal and clay region.

Stevens, John, 1749–1838, American inventor. He served in the American Revolution as treasurer of New Jersey, was later (1782–83) state surveyor, and played a major role in the establishment of the first U.S. patent laws. His interest in steamboat transportation led to his building (1806–8), with Nicholas J. Roosevelt, the *Phoenix,* a seagoing steamboat which later shuttled between Philadelphia and Trenton. After 1810 Stevens devoted himself to railroad activities; he received the first railroad charter in the U.S. and built a pioneer locomotive. His elder son, **Robert Livingston Stevens,** 1787–1856, was a mechanical engineer and inventor. He improved the construction of steamboats and also designed a rail (the American or Stevens rail) widely used in railroad track construction.

Another son, **Edwin Augustus Stevens,** 1795–1868, invented the Stevens plow and was a pioneer builder of ironclad warships. He founded the STEVENS INSTITUTE OF TECHNOLOGY.

Stevens, Thaddeus, 1792–1868, U.S. Representative from Pa. (1849–53, 1859–68). A leader of radical Republican RECONSTRUCTION program; viewed Southern states as "conquered provinces." Proposed Fourteenth Amendment. He was both sincere in his devotion to Negro betterment and anxious to keep Republican party in power. He was a prime mover in impeaching Pres. Johnson.

Stevens, Wallace, 1879–, American poet, a successful insurance executive. His elegant, philosophic poems are collected in volumes such as *Harmonium* (1923), *Ideas of Order* (1935), *Owl's Clover* (1936), *The Man with the Blue Guitar and Other Poems* (1937), and *Transport to Summer* (1947).

Stevens Institute of Technology, at Hoboken, N.J.; nonsectarian, mainly for men; chartered 1870, opened 1871, engineering college of university grade. Gave first U.S. mechanical engineering degrees.

Stevenson, Adlai E(wing), 1835–1914, Vice President of the United States (1893–97). His grandson **Adlai E(wing) Stevenson,** 1900–, was governor of Ill. (1948–53) and Democratic candidate for President in 1952.

Stevenson, Robert Louis, 1850–94, British novelist, poet, and essayist. A lifelong victim of tuberculosis, he traveled much in search of health. In 1876 he began writing essays (collected in such volumes as *Virginibus Puerisque,* 1881). He wrote many short stories and travel books such as *Travels with a Donkey in the Cévennes* (1879). On a trip to California in 1879 he married, returning to Europe in 1880. His books, still avidly read, include such diverse works as *Treasure Island* (1883), *A Child's Garden of Verses* (1885), *Kidnapped* and *The Strange Case of Dr. Jekyll and Mr. Hyde* (both 1886). In 1887 he went to Saranac Lake, N.Y., where he began *The Master of Ballantrae* (1889). In 1889 he made an extensive tour of the South Seas and then settled down to write on his estate (Vailima) in Samoa. *Weir of Hermiston* (1896) and *St. Ives* (1897) were unfinished at his death.

Stevens Point, city (pop. 16,564), central Wis., on Wisconsin R. and S of Wausau; founded 1839. Wood products and fishing equipment.

Stewart, alternate form of the name STUART.

Stewart, William Morris, 1827–1909, American politician, a lawyer. U.S. Senator from Nev. (1864–75, 1887–1905). Sided with free-silver forces, but later returned to Republican party. Wrote Fifteenth Amendment to Constitution.

Stewart, river of central Yukon, rising in Mackenzie Mts. and flowing 320 mi. W to the Yukon S of Dawson. Used as transportation route for lead ore.

Stewart Island, volcanic island (c.660 sq. mi.; pop. 343), New Zealand, 20 mi. S of South Isl. Discovered 1808 by the British, who bought it from Maori natives in 1864. Summer resort.

Steyr (shtī'ůr), city (pop. 36,727), Upper Austria, on Enns and Steyr rivers. Automobile-mfg. center.

stibnite (stĭb'nīt), antimony trisulfide, gray with metallic luster. Important source of antimony.

stickleback, small fresh-water and marine fish of temperate and subarctic waters of N Hemisphere. Lacks true scales but often has plates along the sides; has spines on back. Male builds and guards nest in which a number of females lay eggs.

Stiegel, Henry William (stē'gůl), 1729–85, American glass manufacturer, b. Germany. Produced ironwork before he turned to glassmaking, bringing European glassworkers to his plant at Manheim, Pa. Stiegel glass (in a variety of colors, such as light green, wine, amethyst, and blue) has become a collector's item.

Stieglitz, Alfred (stēg'lĭts), 1864–1946, American photographer and art exhibitor. Promoted photography as a fine art; edited photography magazines, 1892–1917. In 1905 he opened the famous gallery "291" at 291 Fifth Ave., New York, for exhibition of photographic art and introduced to America the works of Cézanne, Picasso, and other modern French masters.

Stifter, Adalbert (ä'dälbĕrt shtĭf'tůr), 1805–68, Austrian author, b. Bohemia. An outstanding stylist, he is best known for his tales and short novels, many of which appear in *Studien* (6 vols., 1840–45). One of these has been translated as *Rock Crystal* (1945).

Stikine (stĭkēn'), river rising in NW B.C., Canada, in Stikine Mts., and flowing 335 mi. in arc W and SW across SE Alaska to the Pacific N of Wrangell Isl. Navigable 130 mi. above mouth. Chief route to Cassiar mining region. Noted salmon stream.

Stikine Mountains, range of the Rocky Mts., NW B.C., Canada, extending 250 mi. NW-SE.

Stiklestad (stĭ'klůstä"), site of battle (1030), on Trondheim Fjord, W Norway, where OLAF II was slain.

Stiles, Ezra, 1727–95, American theologian and educator. He was ordained in 1749 and tutored at Yale until 1855. After studying law, he returned to the ministry for 22 years. He was president and professor of ecclesiastical history at Yale after 1778.

Stilicho, Flavius (flā'vēůs stĭ'lĭkō), d. 408, Roman general and statesman, of Vandal birth. Was chief general of Theodosius I; guardian of HONORIUS and regent of the West (395–408). He fought against Alaric I and other barbarian invaders. Arrested by Honorius on false accusations, he was executed.

Still, Andrew Taylor, 1828–1917, founder of OSTEOPATHY and school of osteopathy (1892) and author of works in field.

Stillwater. 1 City (pop. 7,674), E Minn., on St. Croix R. and NE of St. Paul. Former lumber center with mfg. of agr. equipment. In 1848 convention here drew up petition for territorial organization of Minn. **2** City (pop. 20,238), N central Okla., NNE of Oklahoma City; settled 1889. Industrial center of agr., livestock, and poultry area. Seat of OKLAHOMA AGRICULTURAL AND MECHANICAL COLLEGE.

Stilwell, Joseph W(arren), 1883–1946, American general, commander of Chinese troops, then of U.S. forces in China-Burma-India area (1942–44). His retreat and counterattack in Burma were masterly. His friction with Chiang Kai-shek caused his recall in 1944. Later commanded 10th Army on Okinawa (1945). Nicknamed "Vinegar Joe."

Stimson, Henry L(ewis), 1867–1950, American statesman. Secretary of War (1911–13) and Secretary of State (1929–33). Denounced Japanese invasion of Manchuria. Again Secretary of War (1940–45). Urged unification of U.S. armed forces (1944).

sting, organ of insects of order Hymenoptera (bees, many wasps, some ants) and of scorpions, used chiefly to paralyze or kill prey or enemy. In insects, it is found only in females and workers; venom secreted by glands is injected into victim.

Stirling, William Alexander, earl of, 1567?–1640, British poet, b. Scotland. Works include *Aurora* (1604), love poems; *Doomsday* (1614), 11,000-line epic; and *Four Monarchicke Tragedies* (1664–67), on Croesus, Darius, Alexander, and Julius Caesar.

Stirlingshire (stûr'lĭngshĭr) or **Stirling,** inland country (451 sq. mi.; pop. 187,432), central Scotland. Has a varied terrain of farm lands, bogs, pasture, and moorland. Falkirk (industrial center of county) produces iron, steel, textiles, and wool. Many decisive battles of Scottish history were fought in the county. County town is **Stirling,** burgh (pop. 26,960), which has varied industries. Castle long rivaled Edinburgh as royal residence. Mary Queen of Scots and James VI were crowned here. There are many ancient buildings and monuments.

stoat, European weasel (*Mustela erminea*). In north, male turns white (except for black-tipped tail) in winter; it is then known as ERMINE.

stock, in horticulture, annual, perennial, or biennial plant of Old World genus *Mathiola,* grown for spikes of fragrant, single or double blooms of various colors. Commonly cultivated are Brampton stock or gillyflower (*Mathiola incanis*) and night-blooming evening stock (*M. bicornis*). Virginia stock, without fragrance, belongs to genus *Malcomia.*

stock, in finance, an instrument certifying to shares in the ownership of a corporation. Preferred stock is entitled to fixed dividends, while common stock shares in the remainder of the profits. Holders of common stock may vote in the corporation's management.

Stockbridge, resort town (pop. 2,311), SW Mass., on Housatonic R., in the Berkshires S of Pittsfield. Has Berkshire Playhouse, a leading summer theater, and large art colony. Tanglewood estate is largely in Stockbridge, though near LENOX center. Birthplace of C. W. Field. Jonathan Edwards taught here.

stock exchange, organized market for stocks and bonds, in Europe called bourse. It is important to corporate capitalism because it facilitates financing of business. Certain of its practices are regulated by SECURITIES AND EXCHANGE COMMISSION.

Stockholm (stôk'hôlm"), city (pop. 745,936), cap. of Sweden, beautifully situated on L. Malaren and its outlet to the Baltic. Has large port, shipbuilding, mfg. of machinery, textiles, chemicals, rubber. Seat of a university (founded 1877) and cultural and artistic center. Founded 1255, it was an important Hanseatic trade center. In 1520 Christian II of Denmark proclaimed himself king of Sweden at Stockholm and ordered massacre of anti-Danish nobles. The massacre led to the successful uprising of Sweden under Gustavus Vasa, who became king as Gustavus I. Called the Venice of the North, Stockholm is built on several peninsulas and islands and is a model of modern urban planning. Its city hall, built 1923, is an impressive modern interpretation of the Scandinavian Renaissance style. A slumless city, Stockholm has many fine parks and cooperative residential districts. Staden isl. has retained much of its medieval and Renaissance architecture.

Stockmar, Christian Friedrich, Baron (krĭs'tyän frē'drĭkh bärōn' shtôk'mär), 1787–1863, Anglo-Belgian diplomat and courtier, b. Coburg, Germany, of Swedish parents. Unofficial adviser to Leopold I of the Belgians, Queen Victoria of England, and Prince Albert.

Stockport, county borough (pop. 141,660), partly in Cheshire, partly in Lancashire, England. Cotton-mfg. center, it also has varied mfg.

Stockton, Frank R(ichard), 1834–1902, American humorist, author of novels *Rudder Grange* (1879) and *The Casting Away of Mrs. Lecks and Mrs. Aleshine* (1886) and of many short stories (best known, "The Lady or the Tiger?").

Stockton, Robert Field, 1795–1866, American naval officer. Commanded Pacific squadron in Mexican War, aided in taking of Calif.

Stockton, city (pop. 70,853), central Calif., SE of San Francisco and on deepwater channel to San Joaquin R.; founded 1847. Supply point in gold-rush. Now an inland seaport and rail center, it ships farm produce of San Joaquin Valley. Produces lumber, farm machinery, flour, feeds, and canned goods. Seat of College of the Pacific (coed.; 1851).

Stockton-on-Tees (–tēz), municipal borough (pop. 74,024), Durham, England. First important railroad in United Kingdom opened here in 1825. Has large shipbuilding industry.

Stoicism (stō'ĭsĭzům) [from the Stoa Poecile, in Athens], school of philosophy founded (c.200 B.C.) by Zeno of Citium and developed by his followers. Introduced into Rome in the 2d cent B.C., it there attracted such notable followers as Seneca, Epictetus, and Marcus Aurelius. The Stoics held that all reality is material and that a universal working force (God) pervades everything. They sought "to live consistently with nature" and stressed putting aside passion, unjust thoughts, and indulgence in order to perform duty and gain true freedom.

Stoke-on-Trent, county borough (pop. 275,-095), Staffordshire, England. Formed in 1910 of Hanley, Burslem, Tunstall, Longton, Fenton, and Stoke-upon-Trent and made a city in 1925. Center of Staffordshire pottery making, district is known as the Potteries or the "Five Towns."

Stoke Poges (pō'jĭs), village, Buckinghamshire,

England, near Slough. Churchyard of St. Giles is generally held to be the scene of Gray's "Elegy."

Stoker, Bram, 1847–1912, British novelist, whose real first name was Abraham; author of *Dracula* (1897).

Stokes, Sir George Gabriel, 1819–1903, British mathematician and physicist. His researches developed modern theory of viscous fluids, revealed nature of fluorescence, made studies of chlorophyll.

Stokes, Isaac Newton Phelps, 1867–1944, American architect, housing expert, and historian.

Stokes, Whitley, 1830–1909, Irish scholar. A member of viceroy's council (1877–82) in India, he drafted Anglo-Indian civil and criminal codes. He is known for his translations of Celtic works.

Stokowski, Leopold (stůkŏf'skē), 1882–, American conductor, b. London, of Polish-Irish parentage. Was organist at St. Bartholomew's Church, New York, 1905–8; conductor of the Cincinnati Symphony, 1909–12. As the highly dramatic and vigorous conductor of the Philadelphia Orchestra (1912–36), he introduced much unfamiliar music. He conducted in several films.

Stolypin, Piotr Arkadevich (pyô'tůr ŭrkä'dyĭvĭch stŭlĭ'pĭn), 1863–1911, Russian premier (1906–11). He fought the revolutionary movement by a régime of courts-martial; thousands were executed and exiled. His agrarian legislation facilitated the purchase of land by the peasants but was opposed by the leftist majority of the first DUMA, who favored expropriation of the large landowners. Stolypin dissolved the first two Dumas and secured a conservative majority in the third Duma by altering the election laws (1907). His Russification program for Finland was widely opposed. He was assassinated.

stomach, saclike portion of alimentary canal serving as temporary storage place for food. In humans, it is a pear-shaped organ lying below diaphragm and continuous in its upper portion with esophagus and in lower region with small intestine. Food is converted into semiliquid chyme by action of muscular walls and by gastric juice secreted by glands in stomach lining. Juice contains hydrochloric acid and enzymes rennin, which curdles milk, and pepsin, which acts on proteins in acid medium. Chyme is gradually sent by muscular action into the small intestine. See *ill.*, p. 763.

Stone, Harlan F(iske), 1872–1946, Chief Justice of U.S. Supreme Court (1942–46). Estab. reputation as Justice (from 1925) for vigorous minority opinions.

Stone, Lucy, 1818–93, American reformer, leader in woman suffrage and eloquent lecturer for Anti-Slavery Society. Married (1855) H. B. Blackwell, but kept own name (hence, Lucy Stone Leaguers, married women who keep their maiden names).

stone, in medicine: see CALCULUS.

Stone Age: see NEOLITHIC PERIOD; PALEOLITHIC PERIOD.

Stoneham (stō'nům), residential town (pop. 13,229), NE Mass., N of Boston; settled 1645.

Stonehenge (stōn'hĕnj"), group of standing stones on Salisbury Plain, Wiltshire, England, preeminent among MEGALITHIC MONUMENTS of British Isles. Enclosed by a circular ditch 300 ft. in diameter, stones are arranged in four series. Two outermost form circles; third is horseshoe shape; innermost is ovoid form. Outer circle is c.100 ft. in diameter. Some original uprights (up to 22 ft. high) remain. Within ovoid lies the "Altar Stone." Many explanations as to structure's purpose have been given. Excavations since 1920 indicate that it probably was a Bronze Age burying ground.

Stone Mountain, city (pop. 1,899), NW Ga., near Atlanta. Near by is partly completed **Stone Mountain Memorial** to Confederacy, carved into side of Stone Mt., an exposed granite dome.

Stones River National Military Park: see NATIONAL PARKS AND MONUMENTS (table).

stoneware: see POTTERY.

Stonington, town (pop. 11,801), extreme SE Conn., on Long Isl. Sound; settled 1649. Mfg. of textiles, machinery, tools. Includes Mystic village (pop. 2,266), former whaling port, now artists' resort; Pawcatuck village (pop. 5,269); and shore resorts.

Stony Brook, resort village (1940 pop. 768), on N shore of Long Isl., SE N.Y., near Port Jefferson. Restored (1941) to resemble 18th-cent. village.

Stony Point, village (pop. 1,438), SE N.Y., on Hudson R. and N of Nyack. Museum near by commemorates storming of Stony Point under Anthony Wayne in Revolution.

Stopes, Marie C(armichael) (stōps), 1880–, English eugenist, founder of first birth-control clinic in British Empire. She was author of books on eugenics, birth control, and paleobotany.

storage battery: see BATTERY, ELECTRIC.

Stor Fjord (stôr' fyôr"), inlet of Norwegian Sea, on coast of SW Norway. Extends 70 mi. inland from Alesund. Wild and imposing in aspect. Most famous branch in Geiranger Fjord.

stork, large migratory wading bird related to heron. White and black wood ibis is only U.S. species. Many superstitions are connected with the stork, which is allowed to nest on house roofs in Europe (particularly the Low Countries). Said in some tales for children to bring babies from heaven. See *ill.*, p. 133.

Storm, Theodor (tā'ōdōr shtôrm'), 1817–88, German poet and writer of *Novellen*. Best known for *Immensee* (1851; Eng. tr., 1858) and *Aquis Submersus* (1876; Eng. tr., 1910). His work is imbued with melancholy and poetic realism.

Storm and Stress: see STURM UND DRANG.

Storm King, mountain, 1,355 ft. high, SE N.Y., in Palisades Interstate Park, overlooking Hudson R. near West Point.

Storm Lake, city (pop. 6,954), NW Iowa, on Storm L. W of Fort Dodge. Has meat and poultry packing.

Storrowton, Mass.: see SPRINGFIELD.

Storrs, Conn.: see MANSFIELD.

Storting (stôr'tĭng), parliament of Norway, elected by direct universal suffrage. It elects one fourth of its members to form the

Lagting or upper house, the remainder constituting the lower house, or Odelsting.

Story, Joseph, 1779–1845, American jurist; Associate Justice of U.S. Supreme Court (1811–45). Story's decision in *Martin* vs. *Hunter's Lessee* (1816) estab. court's power to review issues of constitutional law raised in state cases. His legal texts have been important formative influences on American jurisprudence and legal education. His son, **William Wetmore Story,** 1819–95, was a sculptor, whose brilliant social gifts made his studio in Rome a social and artistic center. His classic figures were among the most admired sculptures of his day. Lived in Italy after 1856.

Stoss, Veit (fīt' shtōs'), c.1445–1533, German wood carver. Worked in Cracow and in Nuremberg, where he did his best-known carving, the *Annunciation* for Church of St. Lorenz. Also worked in stone.

Stotsenburg, Fort, central Luzon, P.I. Main U.S. military base in Philippines. Clark Field is near.

Stoughton (stō'tůn), town (pop. 11,146), E Mass., S of Boston; settled c.1713. Shoes, rubber products.

stove, heating and cooking device. Heating stoves of clay, tile, earthenware were used in Europe from Roman times. From late 15th cent. dates cast-iron stove, composed of iron plates; typical early form was wall-jamb five-plate box fueled from adjoining room. Five-plate stove was introduced in American colonies by settlers, but was superseded in the late 18th cent. by English 10-plate stove, standing free of wall and used also for cooking. Coal-burning ranges with removable lids were used for cooking from about middle of 19th cent. until displaced by modern appliances. Popular for heating was Franklin stove, invented 1743, essentially a portable iron fireplace set into chimney.

Stow, John, 1525?–1605, English chronicler and antiquarian. Known for *Chronicles of England* (1580), better known as *Annales of England* (1592); and for immensely valuable *Survay of London* (1598).

Stowe, Harriet Beecher, 1811–96, American novelist; daughter of Lyman Beecher. Her interest in religious problems and social reforms was encouraged by her husband, Calvin E. Stowe, and she is remembered chiefly for *Uncle Tom's Cabin; or, Life among the Lowly* (serially 1851–52), an antislavery novel that was enormously popular. Dramatized, it was a stage success for many years. She also wrote another novel of slavery, *Dred* (1856), and novels of New England life (e.g., *The Pearl of Orr's Island,* 1862). She was also interested in other causes such as temperance and woman suffrage.

Stowe, town (pop. 1,720), N central Vt., NW of Montpelier and SE of Mt. Mansfield. Includes Stowe village (pop. 556), resort and winter sports center.

Strabo (strā'bō), b. c.63 B.C., d. after A.D. 21, Greek geographer and historian. His only extant work, a geography in 17 books, is a rich source of ancient knowledge of the world.

Strachan, John (strôn), 1778–1867, Canadian prelate, first Anglican bishop of Toronto (1839–67). An influential Conservative leader.

Strachey, (Giles) Lytton (strā'chē), 1880–1932, English biographer, known for keen, witty miniatures, in such works as *Eminent Victorians* (1918) and *Portraits in Miniature* (1931), and for longer biographies (e.g., *Queen Victoria,* 1921; *Elizabeth and Essex,* 1928).

Stradella, Alessandro (strädĕl'lä), c.1645–1682, Italian composer of oratorios, operas, cantatas, and *concerti grossi.* Many legends surround his life; one, that he was murdered at the behest of a Venetian nobleman, inspired an opera by Flotow.

Stradivari, Antonio (strädēvä'rē) or **Antonius Stradivarius,** 1644–1737, Italian violinmaker of Cremona; pupil of Niccolò Amati. His earliest extant label is dated 1666, and his last 1737; his finest work was done after 1700. He produced at least 1,116 instruments, including violas, cellos, viols, guitars, and mandolins. His artistry brought the violin to perfection; later craftsmen have tried to imitate his work. His son Francesco and Omobono Stradivari continued the craft after his death.

Strafford, Thomas Wentworth, 1st **earl of,** 1593–1641, English statesman. Lord deputy of Ireland 1632–39, he enforced rule of Charles I. To aid king in Bishops' Wars he advised severity against Scots. With Archbishop Laud he was king's chief adviser in 1639. Beheaded for alleged intention to use Irish soldiers against the British.

Straits: see DARDANELLES; BOSPORUS.

Straits Settlements, former British crown colony in Malaya. PENANG, MALACCA, and SINGAPORE were controlled as a unit by British East India Co., 1826–58, and briefly by the India Office. Colony was estab. 1867, dissolved 1946.

Stralsund (shträl'zŏŏnt"), city (pop. 50,389), Mecklenburg, NE Germany; a seaport on an inlet of the Baltic Sea opposite Rügen isl. Shipyards; machinery plants; sugar refineries. Founded 1209, it became a leading member of the Hanseatic League but remained under the overlordship of the dukes of POMERANIA. By the Treaty of Stralsund (1370) with Waldemar IV of Denmark, the league won supremacy in the Baltic. Aided by Danish and later by Swedish troops, Stralsund withstood Wallenstein's siege (1628) in the Thirty Years War. It passed to Sweden (1648), to Prussia (1815), and to Mecklenburg (after World War II). Its rich medieval architecture suffered heavy war damage.

Strand, street of hotels, theaters, and office buildings in central London, running parallel with the Thames from Trafalgar Square to the Temple.

Strang, James Jesse (străng), 1813–56, American Mormon leader. Claimed succession to Joseph Smith. Excommunicated, he organized colony in Wis., later (1847) estab. colony on Beaver Isl. in L. Michigan. Crowned King James in 1850, he ruled despotically. Died by assassination.

Strasbourg (străs'bûrg, Fr. sträzbŏŏr'), Ger. *Strassburg,* city (pop. 167,149), cap. of Bas-Rhin dept., E France, on the Ill near its junction with the Rhine; cultural and commercial cap. of Alsace. Has a port on the Rhine, varied industries (leather, beer, goose liver *pâté*), and is the seat of a university (founded 1538) and of the Council of Europe. Its importance dates from Roman times. Its bishops ruled a considerable territory as princes of the Holy Roman Empire, but Strasbourg itself became a free imperial city (13th cent.), ruled by its guild corporations. Here medieval German literature reached its flower in Gottfried von Strassburg, and here Gutenberg may have invented the printing press. Strasbourg accepted the Reformation, in which it played an important part. Seized by Louis XIV in 1681, it shared the subsequent history of ALSACE and largely embraced French customs and speech. It was damaged in World War II, but its magnificent Catholic cathedral (built 1015–1439) was preserved.

Strasbourg, Oath of, 842, sworn by Charles the Bald and Louis the German in alliance against their brother Lothair I. The French version is the oldest known specimen of French.

Strasburg (strôz'bûrg), town (pop. 2,022), N Va., in Shenandoah Valley SSW of Winchester. Near by are Crystal Caverns, Hupp's Fort (c.1755), and Harmony Hall or Fort Bowman (c.1753).

Strassburg, France: see STRASBOURG.

Stratford, city (pop. 18,785), S Ont., Canada, on Avon R. and WSW of Toronto. Railroad shops and textile mills.

Stratford, town (pop. 33,428), SW Conn., at mouth of Housatonic R. on Long Isl. Sound near Bridgeport; settled 1639. Mfg. of asbestos and metal products.

Stratford, estate of the Lee family, SE Va., overlooking the Potomac, ESE of Fredericksburg. Stratford Hall, built 1716 by Thomas Lee, was birthplace of R. H. Lee, F. L. Lee, R. E. Lee; home of Henry Lee. Dedicated as national shrine 1935.

Stratford de Redcliffe, Stratford Canning, Viscount, 1786–1880, British diplomat. Aided internal reform in Turkey. Helped to bring on Crimean War by advising Turkish resistance to Russian demands.

Stratford-on-Avon or **Stratford-upon-Avon,** municipal borough (pop. 14,980), Warwickshire, England, on Upper Avon R. Market town, its fame is connected with Shakspere. He is buried in 14th-cent. Church of the Holy Trinity. Chief memorial is theater, scene of annual Shakspere festivals. Most buildings connected with him now belong to the nation.

Strathclyde (străth"klīd') **and Cumbria** (kŭm'-brēŭ), early medieval kingdom of Great Britain in what is now S Scotland and N England. One of four great British units after Anglo-Saxon invasion, it remained independent until 9th cent.

Strathcona and Mount Royal, Donald Alexander Smith, 1st **Baron** (străthkō'nŭ), 1820–1914, Canadian fur trader, financier, and railroad builder, b. Scotland. Governor of Hudson's Bay Co. (1889–1914). With others he acquired control of Great Northern lines (1878), and later was a leading member of company that completed Canadian Pacific (1885). Served as Canadian high commissioner in England (1896–1914).

Strathcona Provincial Park, 828 sq. mi., on central Vancouver Isl., SW B.C., Canada. Game sanctuary and recreation area.

Strathmore (străthmôr'), the "great valley" of Scotland, a plain c.100 mi. long and 5–10 mi. wide, largely in Perthshire and Angus.

stratification (stră"tĭfĭkā'shŭn), division of sediments into parallel layers. Water tends to sort rock debris, depositing it according to weight, so coarser particles are dropped first. Sediments are thus graded horizontally and each distinct layer is called a stratum. Stratified rocks are classed as series if laid down during epochs of geologic time; as systems if deposited during periods.

stratosphere: see ATMOSPHERE.

Straus (strous), family of American merchants, public officials, and philanthropists. **Isidor Straus,** 1845–1912, b. Rhenish Bavaria, acquired ownership of R. H. Macy & Co. in New York city by 1896. Later he devoted his attention to philanthropy and reform. His brother, **Nathan Straus,** 1848–1931, b. Rhenish Bavaria, joined his brother in business and was also outstanding for philanthropy. Another brother, **Oscar S(olomon) Straus,** 1850–1926, b. Rhenish Bavaria, was a diplomat and author. Minister to Turkey (1887–89, 1898–1900). U.S. Secretary of Commerce and Labor (1906–9). His books include *Roger Williams* (1894). A son of Isidor Straus, **Jesse Isidor Straus,** 1872–1936, became president of R. H. Macy & Co. in 1919 and served as ambassador to France (1933–36). **Nathan Straus,** 1889–, son of Nathan Straus (1848–1931), headed U.S. Housing Authority (1937–42).

Straus, Oscar (strous), 1870–, Austrian composer. His best-known works are operettas, including *A Waltz Dream* (1907) and *The Chocolate Soldier* (1908; based on G. B. Shaw's *Arms and the Man*).

Strauss, family of Viennese musicians. **Johann Strauss,** 1804–49, composer and conductor, won fame during his lifetime with his waltzes but was surpassed by his son, **Johann Strauss,** 1825–99, composer and conductor, whose popularity reached fantastic heights. He wrote more than 400 waltzes, including *The Blue Danube* and *Tales from the Vienna Woods;* and operettas, including *Die Fledermaus* [the bat]. His brothers, **Josef Strauss,** 1827–70, and **Eduard Strauss,** 1835–1916, were also successful composers and conductors. Neither Oscar Straus nor Richard Strauss are related to this family.

Strauss, David Friedrich (dä'vĕt frē'drĭkh shtrous), 1808–74, German theologian and philosopher. His *Das Leben Jesu* (2 vols., 1835–36; Eng. tr. by George Eliot, 1846) treated Gospel story as history.

Strauss, Eduard, Johann Strauss, Josef Strauss: see STRAUSS, family.

Strauss, Richard (Georg) (rĭkh'ärt shtrous), 1864–1949, German composer and conductor. His music is characterized by rich harmonic and orchestral effects. His tone poems include *Don Juan* (1888), *Death and Transfiguration* (1889), *Till Eulenspiegel* (1894), *Thus Spake Zarathustra* (1895), *Don Quixote* (1897), and *Ein Heldenleben*

(1898). His operas include *Salomé* (1905), *Elektra* (1909), and *Der Rosenkavalier* (1911); Hugo von Hofmannsthal was his librettist. Strauss also wrote lieder.

Stravinsky, Igor (Feodorovich) (strŭvĭn′skē), 1882–, Russian composer; became U.S. citizen 1945. His rhythms are often bold, his harmonies harshly dissonant. His most popular works are the ballets written during his association with Sergei Diaghilev—*The Fire Bird* (1910), *Petrouchka* (1911), and *Le Sacre du printemps* (1913). He has also written the opera-ballet *Histoire du soldat* (1918); the ballet *Le Baiser de la fée* (1928); the opera-oratorio *Oedipus Rex* (1926–27); *Symphonie de psaumes* (1930), for chorus and orchestra; and the opera *The Rake's Progress* (1951).

strawberry, low, white-flowered, herbaceous perennial of genus *Fragaria* and its fleshy, fragrant red fruit, an important commercial crop in U.S.

strawberry geranium: see SAXIFRAGE.

Strawberry Hill, western suburb of London, England, named for Horace Walpole's estate.

Strawberry valley project, N central Utah, developed 1906–13 by U.S. to irrigate lands S of Utah L. Strawberry R. water is diverted through Wasatch Range to Spanish Fork R. for use around Spanish Fork, Springville, Payson, and Santaquin.

strawflower, garden annual (*Helichrysum bracteatum*), an EVERLASTING, with papery blooms of various colors.

Streator (strē′tŭr), city (pop. 16,469), N central Ill., on Vermilion R. and NE of Peoria; laid out 1863. Railroad shops. Mfg. of glass, clay, and metal products.

street cries, the imaginative, musical cries of itinerant vendors and workers of various sorts. The London cry "Who'll buy my sweet lavender?" provided a theme for Vaughan Williams's London Symphony. Few cries survive in cities such as London and New York, an exception being the ragpicker's "I cash clo'." Many picturesque cries exist among Negroes in the Southern U.S. (e.g., the cries of fish vendors and flower sellers used by Gershwin in *Porgy and Bess*).

Streicher, Julius (yo͞o′lyo͞os shtrī′khŭr), 1885–1946, German National Socialist leader. A sadistic pervert, he edited the pornographic and anti-Semitic periodical *Der Stürmer,* became *Gauleiter* of Franconia in 1933, and was hanged after conviction of crimes against humanity at Nuremberg war crimes trial.

strength of materials, measurement in engineering of capacity of steel, wood, concrete, and other materials to withstand stress and strain. Stress is internal force exerted by one part of a body upon adjoining part, while strain is deformation or change in dimension occasioned by stress. Materials are considered elastic in relation to applied stress if strain disappears after force is removed; elastic limit is stretch point beyond which material will not return to original form. In calculating dimensions of materials required for given functions, engineer uses working stresses that are ultimate strengths, or elastic limits, divided by a quantity called factor of safety. In laboratories static tests are run to determine a material's elastic limit, ductility, hardness, reaction to temperature change, and other qualities. Dynamic tests are those in which material is exposed to impact, vibration, fluctuating loads, fatigue, and other expected operating conditions. Polarized light, X rays, and microscopic examination are some means of testing materials.

streptococcus (strĕp″to͝okŏ′kŭs), genus of bacteria, spherical in shape and dividing by fission to form beadlike chains. Two major types are green-colony or viridans streptococci and hemolytic streptococci (producing substance which dissolves red blood cells). They include many disease-causing forms. See *ill.*, p. 813.

streptomycin: see ANTIBIOTIC SUBSTANCES.

Stresa (strā′zä), resort, Piedmont, N Italy, on Lago Maggiore. Here in 1935 England, France, and Italy held an inconclusive conference after Hitler announced the rearmament of Germany.

Stresemann, Gustav (go͞os′täf shtrā′zŭmän), 1878–1929, German chancellor (1923) and foreign minister (1923–29). Originally a spokesman for industrial interests, he devoted himself after 1923 to securing a respected place for Germany by conscientious fulfillment of its treaty obligations and by conciliation of its former enemies. He obtained the evacuation of the RUHR (1924) and later of the Rhineland; accepted the Dawes Plan (1924) and the Young Plan (1929) for reparations; was one of the architects of the LOCARNO PACT (1925); had Germany admitted into the League of Nations as a great power (1926); and signed the KELLOGG-BRIAND PACT (1928). Shared 1929 Nobel Peace Prize with Briand.

Streuvels, Stijn (stīn strû′vŭls), pseud. of **Frank Lateur** (lätûr′), 1871–, Flemish novelist and short-story writer; one of the chief artists in his language. His works (e.g., *Old Jan,* 1902) are realistic portrayals of everyday life.

Streymoy, Faeroe Islands: see STROMO.

Strickland, William, 1787–1854, American architect of the classic revival. Worked in Philadelphia.

strike, concerted stoppage of work by a group of employees, the chief weapon of labor in industrial disputes. A suspension of work on the employer's part is called a lockout. Issues usually involved are employees' demands for higher wages, shorter hours, better working conditions, and union recognition. See PICKETING; GENERAL STRIKE; TAFT-HARTLEY LABOR ACT.

Strindberg, (Johan) August (strĭnd′bûrg, Swed. strĭnd′bĕr″yŭ), 1849–1912, Swedish dramatist, novelist, and short-story writer. Notable for its masterly use of language and for its innovations, his writing varies from naturalistic to mystical but is always individual. Wrote some 70 plays, *The Father* (1887) and *Julie* (or *Miss Julia* or *Countess Julia,* 1888) being particularly well known abroad. Much of his fiction concerns his unhappy life and three disastrous marriages (e.g., *Married,* 1884–85; *The Son of a Servant,* 1886–87, 1909; *The Inferno,* 1897).

stringed instruments, musical instruments whose tone is produced by vibrating strings. For those played with a bow, see VIOL and VIOLIN family. Those whose strings are plucked with the fingers or a plectrum include the HARP, the lute and mandolin, the guitar and members of its family, the psaltery and zither, and the lyre. Both the lute and mandolin have a pear-shaped body, a rounded back, a fretted neck (the lute's neck being sometimes longer than its body, sometimes shorter), and a variable number of strings. Both are of concert caliber—the lute being the chief European instrument of the Middle Ages and Renaissance. The guitar has a fretted neck, a flat back, sides which curve inward, and from four to seven strings or pairs of strings. It appeared in 12th-cent. Spain, and concert music has been written for it. Resembling the guitar in shape, but smaller and with very limited capabilities, is the ukulele, which has four strings. Another member of the guitar family, the banjo, has from five to nine strings. Its body consists of a hoop over which parchment is stretched, resembling a tambourine. The balalaika (associated with Russia) has a triangular body, a long fretted neck, and usually three strings. Various sizes of balalaikas are often used in ensemble. Two instruments related to the DULCIMER (except that their strings are plucked instead of struck) are the psaltery and the zither. Both have a sounding board over which strings are stretched (a variable number in the psaltery; from 30 to 45 in the zither). The zither has four or five melody strings, which are fretted; remaining strings furnish the accompaniment. The last of the plucked-stringed instruments is the lyre, usually shaped somewhat like a U, with a sound box at the base and a crossbar connecting the two arms. Strings (varying in number) are stretched between the crossbar and sound box. Instruments whose strings are struck include the dulcimer and some keyboard instruments such as the PIANO and clavichord. See *ill.*, p. 857.

Stritch, Samuel Alphonsus, 1887–, American Roman Catholic clergyman; bishop of Toledo (1921–30), archbishop of Milwaukee (1930–40), archbishop of Chicago (1940–); made cardinal 1946.

stroke: see APOPLEXY.

Stromboli, island, Italy: see LIPARI ISLANDS.

Stromo, Dan. *Strømø* (strû'mû"), Faeroese *Streymoy,* largest island (144 sq. mi.; pop. 7,865) of Faeroe Isls., Denmark. Thorshavn, cap. of the Faeroes, is here.

Strong, George Templeton, 1820–75, American diarist, a lawyer. His diary (4 vols., 1952) is a valuable record of New York life.

Strong, Theodore, 1790–1869, American mathematician, known for solving Cardan's irreducible case of cubic equation and for mathematical treatises.

Strongbow, Richard: see PEMBROKE, RICHARD DE CLARE, 2D EARL OF.

strontium (strŏn'shŭm), soft, white, metallic element (symbol = Sr; see also ELEMENT, table), a metal of alkaline earths. The metal is prepared by electrolysis of the fused chloride. Compounds are used to add crimson color to fireworks; hydroxide is used to purify beet sugar. Isolated in 1808 by Sir Humphry Davy.

Stroudsburg, resort borough (pop. 6,361), E Pa., near Delaware Water Gap in Pocono Mts. region.

Strozzi (strôt'tsē), noble Florentine family which produced eminent soldiers, scholars, and men of letters. They usually opposed the Medici rule in Florence. The celebrated Strozzi Palace, Florence, was begun by Filippo Strozzi (1426–91).

Struensee, Johann Friedrich (yō'hän frē'drĭkh shtrōō'ŭnzā, strōō'–), 1737–72, Danish statesman, b. Germany. As physician to Christian VII he gained complete mastery over the insane king and became the favorite of the young queen, Caroline Matilda. Made minister of state and a count (1771) he governed dictatorially and accomplished many reforms in favor of the lower classes (esp. the peasants). His enemies among the nobles terrorized the king into arresting him on the charge of adultery with the queen. He was executed.

Struma (strōō'mä), Gr. *Strymon,* river, 215 mi. long, rising S of Sofia, Bulgaria. Flows S into Greece and to the Aegean Sea.

Struthers, city (pop. 11,941), NE Ohio, on Mahoning R. and SE of Youngstown. Iron and steel mills.

Struve, Friedrich Georg Wilhelm von (frē'drĭkh gāôrk vĭl'hĕlm fŭn shtrōō'vü), 1793–1864, German-Russian astronomer. Discovered many double stars, pioneered in measuring star parallax; developed noted Pulkovo Observatory. His son **Otto Wilhelm von Struve** (ô'tō), 1819–1905, succeeded him as director and made many discoveries, especially of double stars. **Otto Struve** (ŏ'tō strōō'vē), 1897–, grandson of Otto W., came to U.S. 1921. Distinguished as professor of astrophysics (Univ. of Chicago) and director of Yerkes and McDonald observatories.

strychnine (strĭk'nĭn), alkaloid derived from seeds of a tree (*Strychnos nux vomica*) native to India. It has long been used to poison rats. In small doses it is sometimes used medicinally; it stimulates the central nervous system (esp. the spinal cord), the respiratory center, and the circulatory system.

Stuart or **Stewart,** royal family which ruled Scotland and England. Began as family of hereditary stewards of Scotland c.1160. Royal power remained in family after accession of ROBERT II in 1371. Marriage of JAMES IV of Scotland to Margaret Tudor, daughter of Henry VII of England, eventually made MARY QUEEN OF SCOTS claimant to English throne. This claim was recognized when her son, James VI of Scotland, became JAMES I of England in 1603. After PURITAN REVOLUTION and execution of Charles I, his son CHARLES II was restored to throne. After deposition of James II, crown passed to Mary II and William III. Anne, last Stuart to rule England, saw crowns of Scotland and England united by Act of Union of 1707. On Anne's death crown passed to George I of house of Hanover by Act of Settlement. Hanoverian claim was through a granddaughter of James I. Parliamentary rule of succession was adopted because claim to throne by James Edward STUART and his descendants was upheld by JACOBITES. After

1807 this claim ceased to be politically important.

Stuart or **Stewart, Alexander, duke of Albany,** 1454?–1485, son of James II of Scotland. Imprisoned by his brother, James III, who suspected him of plotting against throne, he escaped to England. Agreed with Edward IV to rule Scotland as England's vassal and returned to Scotland with English army. Later was reconciled with the nobles who controlled the government. His son, **John Stuart** or **Stewart,** 4th **duke of Albany,** 1481–1536, was regent (1515–24) for James V. Worked for the French interest in Scotland against English party and Margaret Tudor. After military failures, his regency was annulled.

Stuart or **Stewart, Arabella,** 1575–1615, cousin of James I of England. Secretly married William Seymour, heir to throne by will of Henry VIII. They were imprisoned and escaped. Recaptured (1611), she died insane in the Tower.

Stuart or **Stewart, Charles Edward:** see STUART OR STEWART, JAMES FRANCIS EDWARD.

Stuart or **Stewart, Esmé,** 1st **duke of Lennox,** 1542?–1583, cousin of James VI of Scotland (later James I of England). Reared in France, he was sent (1579) to Scotland to weaken Protestantism. Quickly became powerful, but was forced to return to France after the "raid of Ruthven" (1582) placed the king in control of Protestant lords. His son, **Ludovick Stuart** or **Stewart,** 2d **duke of Lennox** and **duke of Richmond,** 1574–1624, was recalled by James and remained influential.

Stuart or **Stewart, Frances Teresa, duchess of Richmond and Lennox,** 1648–1702, mistress of Charles II of England. King planned to divorce queen and marry "La Belle Stuart," but she eloped (1667) with duke of Richmond and Lennox. Later returned to court.

Stuart, Gilbert, 1775–1828, American portrait painter, the most eminent of his day, b. North Kingstown, R.I. Studied under Benjamin West. Though highly successful in London, he was kept in debt by his lavish mode of living. Returned c.1792 to America with plans of achieving solvency by painting the portrait of Washington and making replicas of it. Settled 1794 in Philadelphia, but moved 1805 to Boston. Painted three portraits of Washington from life. The so-called Vaughan Type (1795) shows head and shoulders; the original has vanished, but at least 15 replicas exist. The Lansdowne Type (1796), painted for marquess of Lansdowne, shows Washington standing (original in Pennsylvania Acad. of Fine Arts). The unfinished Athenaeum Head was acquired first by Boston Athenaeum and later by Mus. of Fine Arts, Boston; of this there are 75 replicas. Other famous sitters included Jefferson, Madison, Benjamin West, and Sir Joshua Reynolds.

Stuart or **Stewart, Henry:** see DARNLEY, HENRY STUART OR STEWART, LORD.

Stuart or **Stewart, Henry Benedict Maria:** see STUART OR STEWART, JAMES FRANCIS EDWARD.

Stuart or **Stewart, James, earl of Arran** (ăr'ŭn), d. 1596, Scottish nobleman. Became powerful (after 1579) at court of James VI (later James I of England). Imprisoned at "raid of Ruthven" (1582) that put king in hands of nobles, he later set out to crush his opponents. Was banished in 1586.

Stuart or **Stewart, James:** see MURRAY, JAMES STUART OR STEWART, 1ST EARL OF.

Stuart, James, 1713–88, English architect, archaeologist, and painter. Visited Athens in 1751 with Nicholas Revett. Their joint work, *Classical Antiquities of Athens* (first volume published 1762), vitally influenced the CLASSIC REVIVAL.

Stuart, J(ames) E(well) B(rown) (Jeb Stuart), 1833–64, Confederate cavalry commander. Noted for brilliant raids and ability to get information. His first raid greatly aided Lee in Seven Days battles. He covered Stonewall Jackson at second battle of Bull Run (Aug., 1862). Aided victory at battle of CHANCELLORSVILLE (1863). Fought his greatest cavalry battle at Brandy Station (June, 1863). Mortally wounded at Yellow Tavern (May 11, 1864).

Stuart or **Stewart, James Francis Edward,** 1688–1766, claimant to the English throne, son of JAMES II and Mary of Modena. Called the Old Pretender. Glorious Revolution (1688) was followed by Act of Settlement, excluding male STUART line from succession. Recognition of James as king by Louis XIV was minor cause of English involvement in War of the Spanish Succession. His hopes of succeeding Queen Anne were dashed by succession of George I in 1714. After rising of earl of Mar (1715), he was hailed as James VIII of Scotland and as James III of England by the JACOBITES. Their many abortive plots (1708–45) to restore him as king included rising of 1745, led by his son, **Charles Edward Stuart** or **Stewart,** 1720–88, known as Bonnie Prince Charlie and the Young Pretender. After defeat at Culloden Moor he escaped abroad. Expelled from France after Treaty of Aix-la-Chapelle, he died in Rome. He married Louise of Stoberg Gedern. Subject of much English and Scottish poetry. His brother, **Henry Benedict Maria Stuart** or **Stewart,** known as **Cardinal York,** 1725–1807, was the last of the direct male Stuart line to claim the throne (as Henry IX). He was made a cardinal of the Catholic Church in 1747.

Stuart or **Stewart, John,** 4th **duke of Albany:** see STUART OR STEWART, ALEXANDER, DUKE OF ALBANY.

Stuart, John: see BUTE, JOHN STUART, 3D EARL OF.

Stuart or **Stewart, John,** 4th **earl of Atholl** (ăth'ŭl), d. 1579, Scottish nobleman. Leader of Catholic nobles, he supported Mary Queen of Scots until the rise of Bothwell. After Mary's capture (1567), he was again friendly to her. Ousted Morton as regent in 1578.

Stuart, John McDouall, 1815–66, Scottish explorer in Australia. First to reach center of Australia (1860).

Stuart or **Stewart, Ludovick,** 2d **duke of Lennox** and **duke of Richmond:** see STUART OR STEWART, ESMÉ, 1ST DUKE OF LENNOX.

Stuart or **Stewart, Mary:** see MARY QUEEN OF SCOTS.

Stuart or **Stewart, Matthew:** see LENNOX, MATTHEW STUART OR STEWART, 4TH EARL OF.

Stuart or **Stewart, Robert,** 1st **duke of Albany,** d. 1420, regent of Scotand. Given control (1388) because of old age of his father, Robert II, he kept it during reign of his brother, Robert III. Ousted (1399) by David Stewart, he returned to power in 1402. James I, successor of Robert III, was a prisoner in England, and Albany ruled until his death.

Stuart, Australia: see ALICE SPRINGS.

Stubbs, William, 1825–1901, English historian. Major work *Constitutional History of England* (3 vols., 1874–78). Bishop of Chester (1884).

Stuhlweissenburg, Hungary: see SZEKESFEHERVAR.

Sture (stü'rů), noble Swedish family which played a leading role in the 15th–16th cent. **Sten Sture** (stān'), c.1440–1503, regent after 1470, defeated the Danes at Brunkeberg (1471) but recognized Sweden's personal union with Denmark in 1497. Founded Univ. of Uppsala. **Svante Sture** (svän'tů"), d. 1512, succeeded him as regent. His rule was one of continual warfare. His son and successor as regent, **Sten Sture,** c.1492–1520, asserted the superiority of state over Church by causing the deposition of his rival, Archbishop Gustav Trolle (1517), and refused his recognition to Christian II of Denmark as king of Sweden. War resulted, but Sture died in battle before Christian took Stockholm and had himself crowned.

sturgeon, large fish of fresh and salt water in Eurasia and North America. It is a primitive fish with cartilaginous skeleton. Largest (up to c.2,000 lb.) is beluga of Caspian and Black seas and Sea of Azov. Sturgeon roe is source of CAVIAR.

Sturgeon Bay, city (pop. 7,054), NE Wis., at head of Sturgeon Bay, inlet of Green Bay. Ship canal here cuts across DOOR PENINSULA to L. Michigan. Summer resort, shipping, and shipbuilding center.

Sturgis, Russell (stûr'jĭs), 1836–1909, American architect and writer, an authority on history of architecture and art.

Sturgis, city (pop. 7,786), S Mich., SE of Kalamazoo. Trade center with mfg. of wood products.

Stürgkh, Karl, Graf von (kärl' gräf' fŭn shtürk'), 1859–1916, premier of Austria (1911–16). Suspended parliament in World War I. Was assassinated by Friedrich ADLER.

Sturluson, Snorri: see SNORRI STURLUSON.

Sturm, Jacques Charles François (zhäk' shärl' frãswä' stürm'), 1803–55, French mathematician. Originated Sturm's theorem for determination of the number of real roots of an equation (algebraic or numerical) within given limits. Wrote on optics, mechanics, mathematical analysis.

Sturm und Drang (shtoo͝rm' oo͝nt dräng') or **Storm and Stress,** term applied to the period (roughly 1767–87) of German literature in which youthful genius revolted against accepted standards. Influenced by Rousseau and Lessing, the period takes its name from Klinger's *Die Wirrwarr; oder, Sturm und Drang* (1776). Goethe's *Götz von Berlichingen* and *The Sorrows of Werther* and Schiller's *Robbers* are major expressions of the movement.

Sturt, Charles (stûrt), 1795–1869, English explorer and administrator in Australia. Explored river system of S Australia; discovered Darling R. in 1828. Colonial secretary (1849–51).

stuttering or **stammering** (dysphemia), inability to enunciate consonants without spasmodic repetition, generally attributed to psychological disorders. Stuttering is usually precipitated in childhood by sudden emotional shock or by the cumulative impact of a neurotic environment. It tends to cause feelings of inadequacy and morbid anxiety, thus intensifying the condition. Before a child realizes that he stutters, removal of stress plus a regime of relaxation and counseling may correct the condition. If personality deviations have already developed because of self-consciousness, intensive and prolonged psychiatric treatment may be needed.

Stuttgart (stŭt'gärt, Ger. shtoo͝t'gärt), city (pop. 481,845), cap. of Württemberg-Baden, SW Germany, on the Neckar; until 1945 cap. of all Württemberg. Lutheran episcopal see. Important communications point. Publishing center. Produces vehicles, machinery, precision instruments, chemicals, textiles. Chartered 13th cent. Expanded rapidly 19th–20th cent. Became famous after 1918 for its pioneering housing developments. Old central part of city was largely destroyed in World War II.

Stuttgart (stŭt'gärt), city (pop. 7,276), E Ark., NE of Pine Bluff. Trade center for farm area (esp. rice).

Stuyvesant, Peter (stī'vůsůnt), 1592–1672, Dutch director general of New Netherland (1647–64). Ruled autocratically. Conquered NEW SWEDEN in 1655. Surrendered New Netherland to English in 1664.

Stymphalian birds (stĭmfā'lēůn), in Greek mythology, man-eating birds. HERCULES killed them as one of his 12 labors.

Styria (stĭ'rēů), Ger. *Steiermark,* province (6,326 sq. mi.; pop. 1,106,581), SE and central Austria; cap. Graz. Predominantly mountainous. Chief Austrian mining district (iron, lignite, magnesite), with metal industry. Has many mountain resorts. Originally part of Carinthia, Styria became a separate duchy 1180. It passed to dukes of Austria 1192; to Ottocar II of Bohemia 1260; to Rudolf I of Hapsburg 1276. S portion passed to Yugoslavia 1919.

Styx (stĭks), in Greek religion, river in the underworld (see HELL), which souls of the dead must cross on their trip from earth. There is a real Styx R. in N Peloponnesus.

Suárez, Francisco (soo͞ä'rĕz), 1548–1617, Spanish Jesuit theologian, last of the old scholastics. His political doctrine that the power of kings is properly derived from the body of men and not by divine right was significant, as was his distinction between natural law and international law (anticipating Grotius).

subconscious: see UNCONSCIOUS.

Subiaco (soo͞byä'kō), village, Latium, central Italy, in the Apennines. Out of community of St. Benedict of Nursia, who lived here c.497–529, grew a Benedictine abbey which rose to great wealth and power in the Middle

Ages. St. Scholastica estab. here first monastic community for women.

sublimation, in chemistry, process in which solid changes directly to vapor without passing through liquid stage, then reverts to solid on sudden cooling. When iodine is heated it changes from a dark solid to a purplish vapor, then condenses to a solid on striking a cool surface.

sublimation, in psychology: see DEFENSE MECHANISM.

submarine, naval craft capable of operating under water, used in warfare to attack surface vessels, mainly with torpedoes. First practical one was a leather-covered rowboat built (c.1620) in England by C. J. Drebbel. In the American Revolution, David Bushnell tried to sink a warship with an underwater vessel (1776). Several used in the Civil War. The work of J. P. Holland and Simon LAKE did much to advance the modern submarine, first used on a large scale by Germany in World War I. Germans and Japanese used them extensively in World War II. Antisubmarine tactics rely on spotting from the air or the surface, and radio devices for spotting were developed. Experiments with use of atomic energy in submarines seemed in 1953 to promise a new era.

Subotica (sōō″bô′tĭtsä), Ger. *Maria Theresiopel,* Hung. *Szabadka,* city (pop. 112,551), N Serbia, Yugoslavia; chief city of Vojvodina. Has meat-packing plants, flour mills, chemical and electrotechnical industries. Was part of Hungary until 1920.

subsidy, financial assistance granted by a government for the furtherance of an enterprise considered in the public good. For example, subsidies are granted to private business concerns under certain circumstances (e.g., to encourage shipping) and to farmers (to encourage growing of certain crops).

subtraction, one of four fundamental operations of arithmetic. Symbol for the operation is the minus sign (−). Result of subtracting one number from another is the difference; number subtracted is subtrahend; minuend is number from which subtrahend is subtracted. The inverse of addition, subtraction is process of finding what number added to subtrahend gives minuend. Only like quantities can be subtracted. Operation does not have properties of associativity and commutivity but does have distributivity, i.e., result of multiplying difference of two numbers by a third is same as result of multiplying each of first two numbers by third and subtracting these products.

subtreasury. Subtreasury system was finally estab. in 1846 with creation of INDEPENDENT TREASURY SYSTEM. Public funds were not to be deposited in any bank, but must be kept in coin in the Treasury or in subtreasuries or retained by public officers receiving them until paid out on proper authority, and no banknotes were to be received in payments to the government. After passage of General Appropriations Act, May 29, 1920, transfer was made of subtreasury functions to the Treasury, the mints and assay offices, and Federal reserve banks.

Succession Act: see SETTLEMENT, ACT OF.

succory: see CHICORY.

sucker, sluggish fresh-water fish related to carp, found in most of North America. Flesh is palatable but the fish is bony.

Suckert, Curzio: see MALAPARTE, CURZIO.

Suckling, Sir John, 1609–1642?, one of the CAVALIER POETS. Handsome, talented, he was a model courtier and royalist. Best known for "Ballad upon a Wedding" and for his lyrics, including "Constancy" and the song "Why so pale and wan, fond lover" from his play *Aglaura* (presented 1637).

Sucre, Antonio José de (äntō′nyō hōsā′ dā sōō′krā), 1795–1830, South American revolutionist, b. Venezuela. Was Bolivar's chief lieutenant in fight against Spain and victor at Ayacucho (1824), completing liberation of N South America. Later reluctant president of Bolivia and a chief figure at the Quito Conference for maintaining unity in the N independent countries, he was ambushed and killed by local patriots. A military genius but ineffective administrator.

Sucre (sōō′krā′), city (pop. 32,500), S central Bolivia, legal capital of Bolivia (*de facto* capital is La Paz). Founded as La Plata (1538), it has also been called Chuquisaca and Charcas: cap. of captaincy general of Charcas in colonial period. First revolt in wars of independence in South America broke out here (1809). Today it is a commercial and agr. center.

sucrose (sōō′krōs), commonest sugar, a white, crystalline solid. Yields caramel when heated above melting point. It is a carbohydrate with 12 carbon atoms, 22 hydrogen, 11 oxygen. Yields glucose and fructose on HYDROLYSIS; process called inversion and mixture is called invert sugar because it rotates plane of polarized light to left, while sucrose rotates it to right. It is obtained from sugar cane, sugar beet, sugar maple.

Sudan (sōōdăn′), vaguely defined region, E Africa, S of the Sahara. Generally considered to include parts of French West Africa (including FRENCH SUDAN), N French Equatorial Africa, and N and central ANGLO-EGYPTIAN SUDAN. Comprises mainly desert and grassy plains.

Sudbury, city (pop. 42,410), S Ont., Canada, E of Sault Ste Marie. Center of important mining region.

Sudbury, town (pop. 2,596), E Mass., W of Boston. Howe or Red Horse tavern (built 1686; restored) was scene of Longfellow's *Tales of a Wayside Inn.*

Sudermann, Hermann (hĕr′män zōō′dûrmän), 1857–1928, German dramatist and novelist. His most popular works include the play *Honor* (1889; Eng. trs., 1906, 1915); the novel *Dame Care* (1887; Eng. tr., 1891); the play *Heimat* (1893; Eng. tr., *Magda,* 1896); and the short stories *The Excursion to Tilsit* (1917; Eng. tr., 1930). Influenced by Ibsen and Nietzsche.

Sudetes (sōōdē′tēz), Czech *Sudety,* Ger. *Sudeten,* mountain system, extending c.170 mi. along N border of Czechoslovakia between Elbe and Oder rivers and rising to 5,259 ft. in the RIESENGEBIRGE range. Rich mineral deposits (e.g., coal, iron); mineral springs; resorts. Lumbering; glass, porcelain, and textile mfg. The term "Sudete Germans" designated all Germans in the regions of

Czechoslovakia bordering on Germany. The Sudete German party (founded 1934), an offshoot of the German National Socialist party, was instrumental in the annexation of the Sudetenland to Germany after the MUNICH PACT (1938). District reverted to Czechoslovakia 1945; majority of Germans were expelled.

Sue, Eugène (ûzhĕn′ sü′), 1804–57, French novelist, author of *The Mysteries of Paris* (1842–43) and *The Wandering Jew* (1844–45), both widely translated.

Suetonius (Caius Suetonius Tranquillus) (swētō′nēùs), fl. c.120, Roman biographer. His *De vita Caesarum* survives almost in full.

Suez (sōōēz′), city (pop. 108,250), NE Egypt; port at S end of Suez Canal. In near-by oasis, the Springs of Moses, is a spring which Moses is supposed to have miraculously made sweet.

Suez Canal, waterway of Egypt extending from Port Said to Port Tewfik (near Suez) and connecting the Mediterranean with Gulf of Suez and thus with Red Sea. Canal is 107 mi. long, 42.5 ft. deep, and 197 ft. wide. These are no locks. As early as 20th or 19th cent. B.C. a canal was built to L. Timsah, then the N end of Red Sea. When Red Sea receded, the canal was extended by Xerxes I, but in 8th cent. A.D. it was closed and fell into disrepair. The modern canal was built 1859–69 by Ferdinand de Lesseps. Owned by Suez Canal Co., with an important part of its stock held (since 1875) by Great Britain. Concession terminates 1968, when the canal reverts to the Egyptian government.

Suffolk, dukes and earls of: see also POLE, family.

Suffolk, Charles Brandon, 1st **duke of** (sŭ′fùk), d. 1545. Married Mary of England, widow of Louis XII and sister of Henry VIII. Led troops in two invasions of France (1523, 1544) and in Pilgrimage of Grace (1536). He supported all of Henry's policies and achieved great power.

Suffolk, Henry Grey, duke of, d. 1554. Father of Lady Jane Grey, whom he tried to place on throne on death of Edward VI. Joined rebellion of Sir Thomas Wyatt, was convicted of treason, and executed.

Suffolk, Thomas Howard, 1st **earl of:** see HOWARD, family.

Suffolk (sŭ′fùk), maritime county, E England, divided administratively into Suffolk East (871 sq. mi.; pop. 321,849) and Suffolk West (611 sq. mi.; pop. 120,590). Low, undulating, mainly agr. region, it is one of England's chief grain producers. Ipswich and Bury St. Edmonds are chief towns.

Suffolk, city (pop. 12,339), SE Va., on Nansemond R. and near Dismal Swamp; settled 1720. Peanut market and processing center with mfg. of machinery and boxes. Burned by British 1779; occupied by Union troops 1862; besieged by Confederates 1863.

Sufism (sōō′fĭzùm), mystical philosophy in Islam, arising in late 10th and early 11th cent. and gaining great strength particularly in Persia. Members of a semimonastic order (Sufis) emphasized personal union of the soul with God. The great philosopher of the movement was Al-Gazel. Its chief importance was, however, its expression in symbolic Persian poetry (e.g., poets Ferid ed-Din Attar, Hafiz, Jami, Omar Khayyam).

sugar, compound of carbon, hydrogen, oxygen, a carbohydrate. There are several types of sugars—monosaccharides, the simplest, include glucose and fructose; disaccharides, as the name implies, are formed by two monosaccharides with loss of one molecule of water and include lactose, maltose, and sucrose; and trisaccharides, of which little is known. Letters d- and l- before name of sugar indicate position of certain hydroxyl group in molecule. The transformation and use of various sugars in body chemistry are essential to human life, and intravenous injection of sugar is much used to keep persons alive when they are unable to take nourishment.

sugar cane, tall perennial grass (*Saccharum officinarum*), somewhat like corn in appearance, widely cultivated in tropics and subtropics. Sugar (sucrose) is obtained from its stalks; by-products include molasses, rum, alcohol, livestock food, and wallboard. One planting may yield several harvests.

sugar of lead, lead acetate, a white, very poisonous, crystalline substance with sweet taste. Used as mordant in textile dyeing and as drier in paints.

Sui (swē), dynasty of China, which ruled from A.D. 581 to 618. Succeeded by T'ang dynasty.

Suidas (sū′ĭdùs), name of a Greek lexicon-encyclopedia, also applied to its compiler, who seems to have lived in the 10th cent. A.D.

suite, in music, a succession of short pieces, an instrumental form which developed from the 16th-cent. practice of playing in sequence dances of contrasting meter. Usually the dances were linked together by a common key. The best-known suites of the baroque period are those of J. S. Bach. Suites of the 19th cent. were often collections of pieces drawn from incidental music to a play or from ballet (e.g., Grieg's *Peer Gynt Suite;* Tchaikovsky's *Nutcracker Suite*).

Suiyuan (swā′yüän′), province (135,000 sq. mi.; pop. 2,000,000), N China, partly in Inner Mongolia; cap. Kweisui. Mainly an arid plateau crossed by Yellow R. Livestock raising and limited agr. (grains, ramie). Held 1937–45 by Japan.

Sukarno or **Soekarno** (both: sōōkär′nō), 1902–, first president of Indonesia. Headed the original Indonesian republic (founded Aug., 1945), which comprised only a part of Indonesia. Became president of sovereign state of United States of Indonesia, created Dec., 1949, and of Republic of Indonesia, which replaced the federation, Aug., 1950.

Sukhum (sōōkhōōm′) or **Sukhumi** (sōōkhōō′mē), city (pop. 44,350), cap. of Abkhaz ASSR, Georgian SSR; a Black Sea port and subtropical resort with sulphur baths (since Roman times).

Sukkertoppen (sōō′kùrtô″pùn), district (pop. 1,831), SW Greenland. The chief settlement, Sukkertoppen (pop. 821), is a harbor N of Godthaab.

Sukkoth: see TABERNACLES, FEAST OF.

Suleiman (sōō′lĭmän″, –lā–, sōō″lāmän′), Ottoman sultans; also spelled Soliman or Solyman. **Suleiman I,** 1494–1566, called the Magnificent in the West and the Lawgiver by

Moslems, succeeded his father Selim I in 1520. He is also known (erroneously) as Suleiman II. Under his rule the Ottoman Empire reached the height of its glory. He conquered Belgrade (1521) and Rhodes (1522); crushed Hungary at MOHACS (1526); annexed most of Hungary 1541; undertook several successful campaigns against Persia; conquered the Arabian coast lands. His vassal, BARBAROSSA, made the Turkish fleet the terror of the Mediterranean. His failures were hardly less important than his victories. His siege of Vienna (1529) and his attack on Malta (1565) were repulsed; he lost Tunis to Emperor Charles V (1535); his naval warfare against Spain and Venice was generally unsuccessful. Suleiman's alliance with France against Austria (1536) set the pattern for later Turkish foreign policy. His grand vizier Ibrahim had a large share in Suleiman's rule, but in 1536, for obscure reasons, he had Ibrahim strangled. A still blacker spot in his career was the murder (1553) of his own son Mustafa, instigated by his favorite wife, Roxelana, who thus secured the succession for her own son, Selim II. His government was, however, generally mild. He introduced important reforms and was a lavish patron of the arts and of literature. **Suleiman II,** 1642–91, reigned 1687–91. His whole reign was taken up with war on Austria.

sulfa drugs (sŭl'fù), name for sulfanilamide, a synthetic, organic drug, and certain of its compounds and derivatives. They are believed to check growth and reproduction of many bacteria; used to treat variety of bacterial infections. Bactericidal properties of prontosil discovered 1932 by Domagk; active agent found to be sulfanilamide, whose therapeutic value was confirmed 1936.

Sulgrave Manor, Tudor house, Sulgrave village, Northamptonshire, England; home of George Washington's ancestors. Now a museum and shrine.

Sulitelma or **Sulitjelma** (both: sōōlētyĕl'mä), mountain, 6,279 ft. high, N Norway, on Swedish border. Copper mines operated by a Swedish company.

Sulla, Lucius Cornelius (sŭ'lù), 138 B.C.–78 B.C., Roman general, leader of the conservative senatorial party. He and MARIUS both wanted the appointment as commander against Mithridates VI; Sulla got it by marching against Rome (88 B.C.). He conquered Mithridates, sacked Athens (86 B.C.), defeated Fimbria (a Roman general sent to Greece originally by Marius' party), and returned triumphantly to Rome. In the civil war that followed he defeated the Marians. He captured and massacred 8,000 prisoners, declared himself dictator (82 B.C.), and butchered all who had opposed him. Retired 79 B.C.

Sullivan, Anne, maiden name of MACY, ANNE S.

Sullivan, Sir Arthur (Seymour), 1842–1900, English composer. Although he wrote oratorios and serious operas, and although his songs (e.g., *The Lost Chord*) and hymns (e.g., *Onward, Christian Soldiers*) became very popular, he is best known for writing the music for the Gilbert and Sullivan operas (see GILBERT, SIR W(ILLIAM) S(CHWENK).

Sullivan, Harry Stack, 1892–1949, American psychiatrist. He believed psychoanalysis should be supplemented by a thorough study of the impact of cultural forces on the personality. As head of the William Alanson White Foundation (1934–43) and the Washington School of Psychiatry (1936–47), he brought this view to public and professional attention.

Sullivan, John, 1740–95, American Revolutionary general. Led punitive expedition against Iroquois in Chemung valley, N.Y. (1778); defeated John and Walter Butler.

Sullivan, John L(awrence), 1858–1918, American boxer. Won (1882) bare-knuckles heavyweight championship. Fighting with gloves under Queensberry rules for boxing, Sullivan was defeated (1892) by James J. Corbett. Sullivan retired (1896) from ring, still in possession of bare-knuckles crown.

Sullivan, Louis H(enry), 1856–1924, American architect, important in evolution of modern architecture in U.S. Associated with William Le Baron Jenney and Dankmar Adler. His designs, mainly in Chicago, expressed a new functional approach, exemplified by his famous Transportation Bldg. at World's Columbian Exposition (1893).

Sullivan, city (pop. 5,423), SW Ind., near Wabash R. and S of Terre Haute. Coal mining.

Sullivans Island: see MOULTRIE, FORT.

Sully, Maximilien de Béthune, duc de (mäksēmēlyē' dù bātün' dük' dù sülē'), 1560–1641, French statesman, chief adviser to Henry IV. He was a Protestant. As superintendent of finances (1598–1611) he restored French prosperity by encouraging agr. and industry; built network of roads and canals; left a surplus in the treasury. He was the author of the Great Design, a plan for a confederation of all Christian nations, which he attributed to Henry IV.

Sully, Thomas (sŭ'lē), 1783–1872, American portrait painter, b. England. Influenced by Sir Thomas Lawrence. Flourished in Philadelphia, where he painted many eminent contemporaries.

Sully-Prudhomme, Armand (ärmā' sülē'-prüdôm'), 1839–1907, French poet; one of the PARNASSIANS. Won 1901 Nobel Prize in Literature. His works include *Les Solitudes* (1869), *Les Vaines Tendresses* (1875), *La Justice* (1878), and *Le Bonheur* (1888).

sulphate, salt or ester of SULPHURIC ACID. Consists in general of a metal or radical united with sulphate radical (one sulphur, four oxygen atoms). Acid sulphates have hydrogen atom in addition. Generally metallic sulphates are water soluble; test for sulphate ion involves precipitation of insoluble barium sulphate. Lead sulphate is used in pigments; potassium sulphate in fertilizers and in medicine; sodium sulphate used to make sulphide and window glass.

sulphide, compound of sulphur and one other element or radical. Sulphides are salts of hydrosulphuric acid, a water solution of hydrogen sulphide. Hydrogen sulphide is colorless gas that smells like rotten eggs; used as test for metals. Tarnishing of silver results from formation of silver sulphide. Sulphides are important ores of metals. Carbon disulphide is an important organic solvent.

Sulphur. 1 Town (pop. 5,996), SW La., near Lake Charles. Oil discovered near by, 1924. 2 Resort city (pop. 4,389), S Okla., near Washita R. and Arbuckle Mts. Near by is Platte Natl. Park.

sulphur, nonmetallic element (symbol = S; see also ELEMENT, table). It shows ALLOTROPY, having two crystalline yellow forms and one amorphous, dark form. It is chemically active; widely and abundantly distributed in nature. As one of the elements in protoplasm it is a constituent of organic matter. FRASCH PROCESS is used to extract uncombined sulphur from deposits. It is used in making gunpowder, sulphur dioxide, sulphuric acid, pulp paper, rubber, matches, insecticides. Was known to the ancients and is the brimstone of the Bible.

sulphuric acid, colorless, heavy, oily, inorganic, strong acid. It is a compound of hydrogen, sulphur, and oxygen. Ionizes readily. Concentrated acid is sometimes called oil of vitriol; it is used as dehydrating agent and oxidizing agent. Sulphuric acid has two replaceable hydrogen atoms (is dibasic); forms normal and acid salts. It is a stable acid and one of most important chemicals in industry. For commercial use it is prepared chiefly by the contact process and the lead-chamber process. It is used in making dyes, drugs, explosives, fertilizers, lead storage batteries, and in metallurgical processes, petroleum refining. Its salts (see SULPHATE) are widely used.

Sulphur Springs, city (pop. 8,991), E Texas, WSW of Texarkana, in dairying and agr. region.

Sulu Archipelago (sōō'lōō), island group (1,086 sq. mi.; pop. 240,826), P.I., W of Mindanao, between Celebes and Sulu seas. Basilan is largest of several hundred volcanic islands and coral islets. Pearl fishing, cattle, agr. Populated mainly by Moros. Under Spanish control in 19th cent.; under U.S. control 1899–1940. Ceded to Philippines 1940.

sumac (sōō'măk), name for shrubs and trees of a widely distributed genus *Rhus*. The large pinnate leaves turn bright red in fall; conical fruit clusters are usually deep red. Most botanists now place the poisonous forms in a separate genus, *Toxicodendron*. From Asiatic *Toxicodendron vernicifluum* (or *Rhus verniciflua*) is produced lacquer. Poison sumac *Toxicodendron vernix* (or *Rhus vernix*) grows in swamps and bears white fruits.

Sumatra (sōōmä'trŭ), island (163,557 sq. mi.; pop. c.12,000,000), Indonesia, in Indian Ocean, S and W of Malay Peninsula and NW of Java. Volcanic Barisan Mts. form central ridge of long, narrow island, and much of interior is jungle. Has large oil and coal fields. Forest and agr. products include camphor, ebony, rattan, tea, coffee, rubber, and pepper. PALEMBANG is chief center. Sumatra was nucleus of Hindu kingdom of Sri Vijaya, which flourished in 8th cent. and controlled much of Indonesia and Malay Peninsula. By 14th cent. Sumatran supremacy had waned, and center of power shifted to Java. First European traders were the Portuguese. After 1596 the Dutch slowly gained control of all the native states including Achin (subjugated 1904).

Sumava: see BOHEMIAN FOREST.

Sumer (sōō'mûr) and **Sumerian civilization** (sōōmĕr'ēŭn). A notable culture appeared in S Mesopotamia (Sumer) at least as early as the 5th millennium B.C. Sumerian city-states (e.g., Erech, Kish, Lagash, Ur) developed considerable power, based on flourishing agr. (with irrigation). Pottery and metalwork were made into fine arts, and the Sumerians began cuneiform writing. They rivaled the Semitic cities and ultimately were conquered by them (e.g., Akkad under Sargon). A Sumerian revival at Ur (c.2300) fell before the rise of Elam, and growth of Babylonia ended Sumerians as a nation.

Sumer Is Icumen In (sōō'mûr ĭs ēkōō'mŭn ĭn) [Mid. Eng.,= summer has (literally: is) come in], English round, dating from the 13th or 14th cent. It is a CANON for four voices supported by a short, two-voice ground bass.

Summerfield, Arthur E(llsworth), 1899–, U.S. Postmaster General (1953–). President of automobile agency in Flint, Mich., since 1929. Republican national chairman in 1952.

Summerside, town (pop. 6,547), SW Prince Edward Isl., Canada, WNW of Charlottetown and on Bedeque Bay. Port and resort with fox farms.

Summit. 1 Village (pop. 8,957), NE Ill., near Chicago. Corn products. Limestone quarried near by. 2 Residential suburban city (pop. 17,929), NE N.J., in Watchung Mts. and W of Newark.

Summit Hill, resort borough (pop. 4,924), E Pa., SW of Mauch Chunk. Burning Mine here has been smoldering since 1859.

Sumner, Charles, 1811–74, U.S. Senator from Mass. (1851–74). Victim of assault by Rep. P. S. Brooks after notable antislavery speech on May 19–20, 1856. Sumner was a leader of radical RECONSTRUCTION program. Opposed Pres. Grant on annexation of Santo Domingo.

Sumner, James Batcheller, 1887–, American biochemist. Shared 1946 Nobel Prize for work on enzymes.

Sumner, William Graham, 1840–1910, American sociologist and economist, professor at Yale. In economics he advocated an extreme laissez-faire policy. As a sociologist he concluded that human folkways and customs were so entrenched as to make reform useless. He wrote *Folkways* (1907); his monumental 4-volume study *Science of Society*, with A. G. Keller, appeared in 1927.

Sumter, Thomas, 1734–1832, American partisan leader in revolution. Harassed British in S.C. as leader of guerrilla band; called the Gamecock. Fort Sumter named for him.

Sumter, city (pop. 20,185), central S.C., ESE of Columbia; laid out 1800. Trade, processing, and shipping center of lumber, livestock and farm area with mfg. of furniture.

Sumter, Fort, fortification at mouth of harbor of Charleston, S.C., scene of first clash of Civil War. When S.C. seceded (Dec. 20, 1860) it demanded all Federal property within the state, particularly Forts Moultrie and Sumter. Major Robert Anderson moved his U.S. army command from Fort Moultrie to stronger site of Fort Sumter. After refusals to surrender, Confederates opened fire (April 12, 1861) and bombarded fort for 34 hours. Anderson finally accepted terms. Civil War had begun. Fort Sumter was made a national monument in 1948.

Sun, river rising in NW Mont. near Great Divide and flowing c.130 mi. SE and E to Missouri R. at Great Falls. Sun R. project waters c.100,000 acres.

sun, STAR whose gravitational attraction maintains the bodies of the SOLAR SYSTEM in their orbits. Appears larger than other stars because of relative nearness to earth (mean distance is c.93,004,000 mi.). Life as we know it could not exist without heat and light from sun. Its light is ultimate source of energy stored in food and coal; its heat sets up air currents and is related to water cycle. Sun's diameter c.865,400 mi.; its mass c.332,000 times mass of earth; its volume c.1,300,000 times that of earth. Gaseous nature causes latitudinal variation in speed of rotation; period c.25 days at equator, c.35 days at poles. At least ⅔ of elements known on earth have been identified in sun's atmosphere. Above surface (PHOTOSPHERE) lie CHROMOSPHERE and CORONA. Vast and continual production of energy has been attributed chiefly to release of energy in a "carbon cycle" involving atomic disintegrations and transmutations and more recently to a reaction of proton upon proton (i.e., hydrogen nuclei interact to produce double-weight hydrogen atoms with release of energy). See also ECLIPSE; SUNSPOTS. See *ills.*, pp. 989, 1187.

Sunapee (sŭ'nŭpē), town (pop. 1,108), SW N.H., NW of Concord and on L. Sunapee (9 mi. long, 3 mi. wide), a fishing and boating resort.

Sunbury, city, (pop. 15,570), E Pa., on Susquehanna R. and N of Harrisburg; laid out 1772. Rail center with mfg. of textiles and clothing. Site of Indian village in early 18th cent.; mission estab. 1742; Fort Augusta built 1756.

Sunda Islands (sŭn'dŭ, sōōn'dŭ), Indonesia, between South China Sea and Indian Ocean, comprising part of Malay Archipelago. Largest islands (Borneo, Sumatra, Java, and Celebes) are sometimes called the Greater Sundas. Between Java and Timor are the Lesser Sundas, including Bali, Lombok, and Flores.

Sunday, William Ashley (Billy Sunday), 1863–1935, American evangelist (after 1896), a baseball player who was converted to religious work.

Sunday: see SABBATH; WEEK.

Sunday school, institution for instruction in religion and morals, usually part of church organization. Idea developed by Robert Raikes in Gloucester, England, 1780. Plan was widely copied; by 1795 Sunday School Society (1785) had helped found over 1,000 schools. Sunday School Union (1803) provided lesson plans, spellers, catechisms, and other aids. The effect of the movement in spreading popular education in England is almost incalculable. In 1786 Francis Asbury estab. in Hanover co., Va. first Sunday school in present U.S. after Raikes's plan. American Sunday-School Union was founded 1824. Plan of uniform lessons was adopted (1872) in cooperation with British Sunday School Union. World Council of Christian Education (1947) has units in 55 countries.

Sunderland, county borough (pop. 181,515), Durham, England, at mouth of the Wear. Includes Bishopwearmouth and Monkwearmouth. Bede studied here at monastery founded in 674 and destroyed by the Danes. Shipbuilding and rail center and coal-shipping port, it also has varied industry.

sundial, instrument that indicates time of day by shadow of an object. Forerunners include poles, upright stones; pyramids and obelisks were used in ancient Egypt. Development of trigonometry permitted precise calculations for marking dials. Difference between solar time indicated by sundials and clock (mean) time is correlated by use of standard tables. Correction is made also for difference between local standard meridian and longitude of sundial.

sunfish, name for certain small perchlike fishes of family Centrarchidae, abundant in North American fresh waters, and also for a saltwater fish of family Molidae.

sunflower, annual or perennial plant of genus *Helianthus,* native to the New World. The composite flowers, usually with yellow rays, are up to a foot across. The common sunflower (*Helianthus annuus*) is grown throughout the world for its edible seeds, also used as poultry food and as source of oil. Tuber of the Jerusalem artichoke (*H. tuberosus*) is eaten as a vegetable.

Sung (sōōng), dynasty of China, which ruled A.D. 960–1279. Empire at its height extended from Great Wall to Hainan. Its early period saw improvements in transport facilities and increased trade with India and Persia. Notable achievements in literature (novel, drama) and landscape painting. Overthrown by Mongols who estab. Yüan dynasty.

Sungari (sōōng"gŭrē'), Chinese *Sunghwa Kiang,* largest river of Manchuria, c.1,150 mi. long, converges with Amur R. Important trade artery.

Sungkiang: see MANCHURIA.

Sunnites (sōō'nīts) [from Arabic *Sunna* = tradition], majority group of Moslems, predominant in Arabia, Turkey, and Africa. See ISLAM.

Sunnyvale, residential city (pop. 9,829), W Calif., E of San Francisco. Ironworks, fruit canneries.

Sunset Crater National Monument: see NATIONAL PARKS AND MONUMENTS (table).

sunspots, dark spots visible on sun's surface and believed to be tornadolike solar storms. Average duration about two weeks. Periods of sunspot activity occur in 11-year cycles; correlated with disturbances on earth including magnetic storms and increased rainfall.

sunstroke or **heatstroke,** illness caused by exposure to excessive heat. Believed to result from disturbance of heat-regulating mechanism of body and to be aggravated by loss of sodium chloride through perspiration. Commonly attended by unconsciousness, labored breathing, rapid pulse, high temperature. Requires prompt treatment by a physician.

Sun Valley, resort, S central Idaho, N of Hailey

and SW of Mt. Hyndman; built 1936. Winter sports.

Sun Yat-sen (so͝on' yät'-sĕn'), 1866–1925, Chinese revolutionary hero, b. near Canton, of Christian family. Received medical diploma in 1892. Thereafter he devoted himself to revolutionary work against Ch'ing dynasty. Developed political theory embodied in Three People's Principles (San Min Chu I), namely, nationalism, democracy, and guaranteed livelihood. After the revolution (1911) he was elected first president of Chinese republic (Dec., 1911) but resigned four months later in favor of Yüan Shih-kai. Withdrew from northern government and estab. power in S, organizing the KUOMINTANG. Elected president of unofficial government at Canton, 1921; agreed 1924 to work with Chinese Communists and accept Russian help. His tomb at Nanking is a national shrine. His widow is SOONG Chingling.

Suomenlinna (so͞o'ômĕnlĭn'nä), Swed. *Sveaborg,* fortress, S Finland, at entrance to Helsinki harbor. Built 1749, it now covers seven small islands. Was known as Gibraltar of the North.

superheterodyne (syo͞o"pûrhĕ'tûrůdīn), in radio receivers, commonest and most efficient circuit for selecting and amplifying radio frequency. Incoming signals mix with oscillator voltage, producing intermediate-voltage frequency equal to arithmetical difference between the two voltages.

Superior, city (pop. 35,325), NW Wis., on Superior Bay of W L. Superior, where St. Louis and Nemadji rivers enter; platted 1852. Radisson explored region 1661, sieur Duluth visited site 1679. Grew after 1880s discovery of iron ore in Gogebic range. Shares harbor with Duluth, Minn. Ships iron ore and grain; mfg. of coal briquettes. A major consumer cooperative center.

Superior, Lake, largest of Great Lakes and largest fresh-water lake in world; 350 mi. long, 160 mi. wide, covers 31,820 sq. mi. Bounded by Minn., Ont., Wis., and Mich., it lies c.602 ft. above sea level with maximum depth of 1,290 ft. Connects with L. Huron by St. Marys R. Receives many rivers, e.g., Kaministikwia and Pigeon. Islands include Grand Isl. and Apostle group. Iron, copper, silver, and nickel in region. Cities on shores ship ore, grain, fish. Étienne Brulé possibly first white man to see lake; sieur Duluth visited it 1678–79.

Suppé, Franz von (fŭn zo͞o'pā), 1819–95, Austrian composer of operettas. His *Poet and Peasant* and *Light Cavalry* overtures are still popular.

suprarenal gland: see ADRENAL GLAND.

Supreme Court, United States, highest court of U.S., estab. by Article 3 of U.S. Constitution. Judicial power extends to all cases arising under the Constitution, laws, and treaties of U.S.; to cases concerning foreign diplomats and admiralty practice; to diversity cases (those between citizens of different states) and cases in which U.S. or a state is a party (Eleventh Amendment forbids Federal cognizance of cases brought against a state by a private party). Cases in which another court need not first consider the controversy are those in which diplomats or a state is a party; even here, it has been held, inferior courts may enjoy concomitant jurisdiction. In all other Federal cases Supreme Court exercises appellate jurisdiction, but subject to all limitations and regulations made by Congress. Members of court are appointed by the President with advice and consent of Senate. Size of Supreme Court is not prescribed by the Constitution and is set by statute. It began in 1789 with six members; since 1869 there have been nine members. Under Judiciary Law as amended in 1934 cases are usually brought to the court by appeal or by writ of certiorari. Court has basically a dual function. It must interpret and expand all congressional enactments brought before it in proper cases; it has power (superseding that of all other courts) to examine Federal and state statutes and executive actions to determine whether they conform to U.S. Constitution. Although in U.S. governmental system the Supreme Court potentially wields the highest power, the court has found many constitutional limitations on its powers and has voluntarily adopted others. History of the court reflects development of U.S. economy, alteration of political views, evolution of the Federal structure. John MARSHALL increased power of court. R. B. TANEY increased power of states by advancing concept of POLICE POWER. Most recent instance of hostility between court and various Presidents occurred under F. D. ROOSEVELT.

Surabaya or **Soerabaja** (both: so͞oräbä'yä), city (pop. 341,675), on NE Java, Indonesia; industrial center. Its port is Tanjungperak (on Madura Strait), which ships sugar, tobacco, coffee, tea, rubber, and spices. Near by is Ujung, site of Indonesia's chief naval base.

Surakarta or **Soerakarta** (both: so͞oräkär'tä), town (pop. 165,484), on central Java, Indonesia, on Solo R. Here is vast walled palace of sultan of Surakarta. European section has Dutch fort built 1779.

Surat (so͞o'rŭt), city (pop. 171,443), NW Bombay, India; port on Gulf of Cambay. Main center of European trade in 17th cent. Ships cotton goods.

surface, in geometry, boundary (curved or flat) between two volumes. It has no thickness but separates two regions in space. May be closed or finite, like a sphere, or of infinite extent, like a plane.

surface tension, property of liquids in which surface exposed tends to be reduced to smallest possible area. Attributed to cohesion between molecules of liquid; molecules at surface tend to be drawn toward center by other molecules; surface then appears to act like very thin membrane.

surgery, branch of MEDICINE concerned with diagnosis and treatment of conditions requiring operations. From prehistoric times date trephining (removal of circular pieces of skull), opening abscesses, and performing amputations. Greek physicians skilled in surgery include Hippocrates, Erasistratus, Herophilus. During the Middle Ages arose belief that surgery was demeaning and its practice fell into hands of barber-surgeons, often unskilled itinerants. However, before surgery began to achieve professional status in the 18th cent., there were a few notable surgeons, among them Guy de CHAULIAC and Ambrose PARÉ. Infections resulted in mortality rate so high that surgery was practiced chiefly in desperate cases until introduction of antiseptic methods by LISTER. The development of ANESTHESIA facilitated complex surgical feats. Surgery has benefited by evolution of instruments, X-ray techniques, fluoroscope, blood transfusion, and drugs including anticlotting agents, and sulfa drugs and antibiotic substances valuable in conquering infection.

Surinam (so͞orĭnäm'), name for Dutch GUIANA.

Surratt, Mary Eugenia (sůrăt'), 1820–65, alleged conspirator in assassination of Abraham Lincoln, hanged on July 7, 1865. Kept boardinghouse where J. W. BOOTH hatched unsuccessful plot to abduct Lincoln. It now seems certain she was not a party to assassination plans. Her hanging is generally considered a gross miscarriage of justice.

surrealism (sůrē'ůlĭzům), literary and art movement, influenced by Freudianism and aiming to express the imagination as revealed in dreams. Founded 1924 in Paris by André Breton, with his *Manifeste du surréalisme,* but its ancestry is traceable to Baudelaire and Rimbaud. In literature it was confined almost exclusively to France, where Breton and Paul Eluard were its main exponents. In art it became internationally important in '20s and '30s and dominated the works of many artists using varying techniques; these included Salvador Dali, Yves Tanguy, Max Ernst, Marc Chagall, Giorgio de Chirico, Joan Miró, and Marcel Duchamp. Surrealism has also been used in films, notably by Jean Cocteau.

Surrey, Henry Howard, earl of, c.1517–1547, English poet, son of the duke of Norfolk. Beheaded for treason. A friend of Wyatt, he introduced blank verse into English.

Surrey, inland county (722 sq. mi.; pop. 1,601,555), S England; co. town Guildford. One of "Home Counties" around London, it is chiefly agr. with dairying and sheep raising. Towns include Croyden (airport), Wimbledon (tennis matches), Epsom (horse racing), and Kew (botanical gardens). King John signed Magna Carta at Runnymede in 1215.

Surtees, Robert Smith (sûr'tēz), 1803–64, English novelist, known for his stories of hunting life (e.g., *Jorrocks' Jaunts and Jollities,* 1838).

surveying, the science of finding the relative position of points on or near the earth's surface. Boundaries, areas, elevations, construction lines, geographical or artificial features are determined by measuring horizontal and vertical distances and angles and by computations based partly on geometry and trigonometry. Field work consists in obtaining data for delineation on maps, charts, and profiles or in fixing points from predetermined data. Methods of surveying include transit, plane-table, or photogrammetic surveying. The height of points in relation to a datum line (usually mean sea level) is measured by a leveling instrument consisting of a telescope fitted with a spirit level, usually on a tripod, and used with a leveling rod.

Susa (sū'zů), city, cap. of anc. Elam, SW of present Dizful, Iran. Destroyed by Assurbani-pal, it was revived by ancient Persian kings, who built winter palaces there.

Susak, Yugoslavia: see FIUME.

Susanna [Gr. from Heb.,= lily], heroine of story told in Dan. 13, a chapter placed in the Apocrypha of AV, included in Western canon. Two elders try to seduce Susanna and are repulsed; they accuse her of misconduct, but she is exonerated by Daniel.

Susanville, city (pop. 5,338), NE Calif., in timber, dairy, and grain area. Lassen Volcanic Natl. Park and Honey L. are near.

suspension, in chemistry, mixture of finely divided solid and liquid or gas in which solid remains dispersed and suspended before settling out. Particles are larger than those of colloid. Mixture is not homogeneous like solution. Emulsions are mixtures of liquids, one suspended in another.

Susquehanna (sŭskwĭhă'nů), river, 450 mi. long, crossing N.Y. and Pa. coal region. Flows from Otsego L., N.Y., SE and SW to point near Pittston, Pa., where Lackawanna R. enters, thence SW joining West Branch. Juniata R. enters united stream above Harrisburg; river then flows S and SE into Md. and enters Chesapeake Bay at Havre de Grace. Commonly called North Branch above juncture with West Branch. U.S. flood control plan approved 1936.

Susquehanna Company or **Susquehannah Company,** land company formed in Conn. (1753) to develop Wyoming Valley in Pa.

Sussex, maritime county, S England, divided administratively into Sussex East (829 sq. mi.; pop. 618,083) and Sussex West (628 sq. mi.; pop. 318,661); co. town Lewes. South Downs cross county from E to W. It is almost entirely an agr. and pastoral region. William the Conqueror defeated Saxons at Hastings in 1066. Chichester is famous for its cathedral. Brighton and Eastbourne are noted as resorts.

Sussex, kingdom of, in England. Settled, according to tradition, in 477 by Saxons who defeated Celts. After 5th cent. it became subkingdom and later included modern Sussex, E Hampshire, and Isle of Wight. St. Wilfrid of York led (681–86) conversion of people. Conquered by Caedwalla of Wessex (685–88) and later by Offa of Mercia. Remained under Mercia from 771 until it submitted to Egbert of Wessex in 825. Thereafter it existed as an earldom.

Sutherlandshire (sŭ'dhůrlůndshĭr) or **Sutherland,** maritime county (2,028 sq. mi.; pop. 13,664), N Scotland; co. town Dornoch. Mountainous region with moors and forests, its poor soil and heavy rainfall make farming difficult. Sheep raising is important. Deer, grouse, fishing attract sportsmen.

Sutlej (sŭt'lĕj), river, flowing c.900 mi. from SW Tibet through India and Pakistan to Indus R.

suttee, funeral practice of Hindus according to which the widow sacrificed herself on husband's pyre. Aim was to help her soul and his in world to come.

Sutter, John Augustus, 1803–80, American

frontiersman, b. Baden, of Swiss parents. Original name was Johann August Suter. Built Sutter's Fort (see SACRAMENTO). After discovery of gold at Sutter's Mill, activities of gold-seekers ruined Sutter.

Sutter Creek, city (pop. 1,151), central Calif., ESE of Sacramento, in gold-mining area. Leland Stanford made his fortune here.

Suttner, Bertha (Kinsky), Baroness von (bĕr'tä, fŭn zōōt'nůr), 1843–1914, Austrian novelist and pacifist. Her novel *Lay Down Your Arms* (1889; Eng. tr., 1906) had immense influence on the pacifist movement. Was awarded 1905 Nobel Peace Prize.

Suva (sōō'vä), town (pop. 11,398; Greater Suva pop. 23,513), on Viti Levu; cap. and chief port of British colony of Fiji. Exports sugar and gold.

Suvarov, Aleksandr Vasilyevich (ŭlyĭksän'důr vŭsē'lyůvĭch sōōvô'růf), 1729–1800, Russian field marshal. He fought in the Russo-Turkish Wars and put down the Pugachev rebellion (1775) and the Kosciusko rebellion (1794). In the FRENCH REVOLUTIONARY WARS he defeated the French in N Italy (1798), crossed the St. Gotthard and, after the defeat of his colleague Korsakov at Zurich, led his ragged troops across the Alps to Lindau (late 1799). The Russian defeat in Switzerland was due largely to poor Austrian cooperation. Suvarov was idolized by his soldiers.

Suwanee (swô'nē), river rising in Okefenokee Swamp, SE Ga., and winding 250 mi. S through N Fla. to Gulf of Mexico. Name used in Stephen Foster's song *Old Folks at Home* or *Swanee River*.

Suzdal (sōōz'dŭl), city (1926 pop. 6,904), central European RSFSR, ENE of Moscow. An important city of VLADIMIR-Suzdal in 12th cent. and a religious center of NE Russia, it was destroyed by Tatars 1238 and annexed by Moscow 1451. Has kremlin with 13th-cent. monastery and cathedral.

Svalbard: see SPITSBERGEN.

Sveaborg, Finland: see SUOMENLINNA.

Svealand or **Svearike:** see SWEDEN.

Svedberg, Theodor (tā'ōdôr svād'bĕryů), 1884–, Swedish chemist. Won 1926 Nobel Prize for fundamental research on colloid chemistry. Made studies of protein molecules and developed a centrifuge.

Svein, king of Denmark: see SWEYN.

Sverdlovsk (svyĭrdlôfsk'), city (pop. c.600,000), RSFSR, in E foothills of the central Urals. Leading industrial city of the Urals and a major machine-mfg. center of the USSR; W terminus of Trans-Siberian RR. It was founded 1722 as a fortress and originally named Ekaterinburg (until 1924). Its earliest ironworks were built 1725. Here in 1918 Emperor Nicholas II and his family were shot by the Bolsheviks.

Sverdrup, Johan (yōhän' svĕr'drōōp), 1816–92, Norwegian statesman. He founded the party of the Left (1869) and fought for parliamentary government. In 1880 he submitted a resolution in the Storting which would have waived a royal veto. The struggle over the veto question continued till 1884, when the Conservative cabinet was impeached and Sverdrup became premier. He failed to satisfy the extremists in his party and resigned 1889.

Sverre (svĕ'rů), d. 1202, king of Norway (1177–1202); possibly a natural son of King Sigurd. His cause was adopted by the popular Birkebeiner party, who fought the Baglar (aristocratic and clerical party) until 1201. The Birkebeiner's victory led to the destruction of the nobles' power. Sverre prepared the way for absolute monarchy.

Sviatoslav (svyä'tůslŭf), 920–72, duke of Kiev (964–72); son of Igor and St. Olga. He overthrew the empire of the KHAZARS and brought Kievan Russia to the height of its power. His defeat by John I of Byzantium (971) forced him to evacuate Bulgaria.

Svir (svēr), river, NW European RSFSR, issuing from L. Onega and flowing 140 mi. W into L. Ladoga. Wholly navigable, it is part of MARIINSK SYSTEM.

Swabia (swā'bēů), Ger. *Schwaben,* region, SW Germany, comprising SW Bavaria, S Württemberg, Hohenzollern, and S Baden. It includes the BLACK FOREST, Swabian Jura range, and upper waters of the Danube and Neckar. Mainly agr. and forested, it is famous for its loveliness. Settled by Germanic Suevi and Alemanni during the great migrations, it was also known as Alamannia. Swabia, which then also comprised Alsace and E Switzerland, became a stem duchy of Germany in the 9th cent. and passed to the HOHENSTAUFEN dynasty 1079. After 1268 it broke up into smaller temporal and ecclesiastic lordships and free imperial cities, such as AUGSBURG and ULM. While the cities accepted the Reformation, the country remained largely Catholic. In 1801–3 Swabia was apportioned among Bavaria, Württemberg, and Baden. The **Swabian League** of 1488–1534 was an association of 26 cities and several ecclesiastical and temporal lords which sought to oppose the large territorial princes and supported the cause of imperial reform. It had a powerful army, a court, and a formal constitution, and it played a major role in the defeat of Franz von SICKINGEN and of the peasants in the PEASANTS' WAR. Its dissolution resulted from the split caused by the Reformation. There had been other Swabian leagues of somewhat lesser importance in earlier centuries.

Swahili (swähē'lē) [Arabic,= coast people], generic name for native population of coast of Kenya, Tanganyika, and Zanzibar, who are descendants of Bantu Negroes and Arab traders. **Swahili language,** a Bantu tongue, with large Arabic admixtures, is lingua franca of much of E Africa.

swallow, small migratory bird of both hemispheres. Including the martin there are c.100 species. Plumage is usually iridescent black or blue. Swallows are graceful in flight; they have long, narrow wings, forked or notched tails, and weak feet. Have short bills and wide mouths; they catch insects on the wing.

Swammerdam, Jan (yän' svä'můrdäm), 1637–80, Dutch naturalist. Pioneered in use of microscope and was probably first to detect red corpuscles and valves of lymphatics.

swamp, area where the soil, saturated with water, is spongy and in places inundated.

Moisture accumulates where normal drainage is prevented by flatness of land, impervious subsoil, or luxuriant vegetation. Types of swamp include the BOG; the fen, inundated lowland; the marsh, covered with water and treeless; the moorland, overlaid with peat and in N Europe characterized by heather.

Swampscott (swŏmp′skŭt), coast-resort town (pop. 11,580), E Mass., NE of Boston; settled 1629.

swan, large aquatic bird of both hemispheres, related to duck and goose. It has a long, graceful neck; its convoluted trachea makes possible its loud trumpeting call. Much used in poetry as a symbol of remote unworldly beauty, the swan is the subject of many legends, the most familiar being that the swan sings once in his life and then when he is dying (hence, "swan song"). In Germanic legend used by Wagner, the Swan Knight is the mysterious deliverer (Lohengrin). The swan was a chief symbol in Spanish *modernismo* poetry.

Swanee, river: see SUWANEE, river.

Swansea (swŏn′sē, –zē), village (pop. 8,072), S Ont., Canada, W residential suburb of Toronto.

Swansea (swŏn′zē), town (pop. 6,121), SE Mass., NW of Fall River. Textiles.

Swansea (swŏn′zē, –sē) or **Abertawe** (ăbûrtou′ē), county borough (pop. 160,832), Glamorganshire, Wales. Metallurgical center with sheet-metal mills and foundries. Has Royal Inst. of South Wales and Univ. Col. of Swansea. Heavily bombed 1941.

Swarthmore, residential borough (pop. 4,825), SE Pa., near Philadelphia. Seat of **Swarthmore College** (nonsectarian; coed.; opened 1869 by Friends). Pioneer in plan by which exceptional upperclassmen replace usual schedule by reading for honor, with comprehensive examinations. On campus is birthplace of Benjamin West.

Swat (svät), state (4,000 sq. mi.; pop. 569,000), North-West Frontier Prov., W Pakistan. Ruler is called the wali.

Swatow (swä′tou′), Mandarin *Shan-t'ou,* city (pop. 214,990), Kwangtung prov., China; port in Han R. delta on South China Sea. Opened 1860 to foreign trade. Sugar is chief export.

Swaziland (swä′zēlănd), British protectorate (6,704 sq. mi.; pop. 186,880), SE Africa; cap. Mbabane. Bordered on S, W, and N by South Africa. Mainly a high plateau. Chief export is cattle. Asbestos, tin, and gold are mined.

Sweden, Swed. *Sverige,* kingdom (173,423 sq. mi., incl. 14,937 sq. mi. covered by lakes; pop. 7,046,920), N Europe, in E part of Scandinavian peninsula; cap. Stockholm. Its W border, with Norway, is mountainous, rising to 6,965 ft. in the Kebnekaise. In the NE Sweden borders on Finland; in the E and S, on the Baltic Sea. The three main subdivisions are Gotaland or Gotarike (S), Svealand or Svearike (S center), and Norrland (occupying N two thirds, incl. LAPLAND). The chief Baltic islands are GOTLAND and OLAND. The largest cities (all coastal), such as Stockholm, Goteborg, and Malmo, are in the S half, as are the largest lakes—Vanern, Vattern, and Malaren. Less than 10% of Sweden is under cultivation, but the agr. districts are very prosperous (wheat growing, dairying). The chief resources are timber (covering more than half of Sweden), high-grade iron ore (esp. at Kiruna), and hydroelectric power, which has been used on a large scale in the absence of coal. Chief industries: lumber and lumber products (furniture, paper, matches); electrometallurgy (quality steels, machinery, cutlery, armaments); fishing; shipbuilding; glass mfg. (Orrefors ware). In practice, Sweden is a parliamentary democracy, with a bicameral RIKSDAG. The king enjoys wide powers but rarely uses them. Reigning king: Gustavus VI. Population is predominantly Lutheran. Sweden has an advanced social legislation and has pioneered in the cooperative movement. Its prosperity and harmonious solution of social economic problems have made it a widely admired, little imitated model. Except for Lapps and Finns in the N, most Swedes are descendants of Germanic tribes that were propably settled in Scandinavia by the neolithic period. By the 6th cent. A.D. the Svear, from whom the Swedes derive their name, had conquered their S neighbors, the Gotar (traditionally identified with the Goths). The early Swedes shared in the Viking raids and were known in Russia as VARANGIANS. Christianity, introduced c.829 by St. Ansgar, became fully estab. only in the 12th cent. by ERIC IX, who also conquered Finland. Sweden and Norway were united 1319 by MAGNUS VII; in 1397 Queen MARGARET estab. the KALMAR UNION of Denmark, Norway, and Sweden. The actual power, however, was held by regents (esp. those of the STURE family) in the 15th cent. After Christian II's STOCKHOLM massacre (1520), the Swedes rose against the Danes and chose as their king GUSTAVUS I, founder of the VASA dynasty. Under him and his successors ERIC XIV, CHARLES IX, GUSTAVUS II, CHRISTINA, CHARLES X, and CHARLES XI Sweden became a major European power, conquering LIVONIA, INGERMANLAND, KARELIA, the S provinces of Sweden (Danish till 1658), and POMERANIA. Its intervention in the THIRTY YEARS WAR was decisive, and its numerous wars against Poland and Denmark all proved its military superiority. Lutheranism was estab. by Gustavus I; Charles XI made the monarchy absolute. In the NORTHERN WAR (1700–21), which broke out on the accession of CHARLES XII, Sweden at first won its greatest victories, then was crushed by an overpowering coalition, headed by Russia. In the 18th cent. Sweden was torn in the factional strife between the "Hats" (anti-Russian nobles) and the "Caps" (who favored peaceful relations with Russia). GUSTAVUS III restored absolutism (1772) but was murdered. His despotic successor, GUSTAVUS IV, joined the coalition against Napoleon I (1803), lost Finland to Russia (1808), and was deposed by a liberal revolution. His successor, Charles XIII, adopted Marshal Bernadotte (later CHARLES XIV) as heir. Sweden again made war on Napoleon in 1813–14 and was rewarded at the Congress of Vienna, which estab. a personal union of

Sweden and NORWAY (dissolved 1905). Since 1815 Sweden has remained neutral in all wars. The 19th cent. was marked by industrial progress, liberalization of the government, and large-scale emigration (c.1,500,000) to the U.S. The 20th cent. saw the rise of the Social Democratic party and the introduction of cooperatives and social legislation. Sweden entered the UN 1946.

Swedenborg, Emanuel (swē'dŭnbôrg, Swed., āmä'nüĕl" svā'dŭnbôry"), 1688–1772, Swedish scientist, philosopher, and theologian, whose original name was Swedberg. Appointed (1716) assessor of Royal Col. of Mines, but in 1747 he resigned position, abandoned science, and turned wholly to religious study. He believed that Scriptures reveal law of correspondence—that every natural object is expression of a spiritual cause. There is one God; in Him is divine Trinity, not of persons but of essence. Several experiences of divine revelation convinced Swedenborg that he was direct instrument of God. He had no intention of founding a new sect, but after his death his followers organized Church of the NEW JERUSALEM.

Swedesboro, borough (pop. 2,459), SW N.J., SW of Camden. Swedes bought area from Indians 1641, built fort, planted settlement c.1670. Partly burned by British 1778. Trinity Church built 1784.

Swedish language, North Germanic language of Indo-European family. See LANGUAGE (table).

Sweet, Henry, 1845–1912, English philologist and phonetician. An authority on Anglo-Saxon and the history of the English language, he was also a pioneer in modern scientific phonetics.

sweet alyssum: see ALYSSUM.

sweet bay: see LAUREL; MAGNOLIA.

sweetbread, term given to certain parts of calf and lamb when prepared as food. They are principally the thymus gland (throat sweetbread) and the pancreas (stomach sweetbread). They are highly regarded in some regions and are believed to be rich in minerals and vitamins.

Sweet Briar College: see LYNCHBURG, Va.

sweetbrier, wild pink rose of Europe (*Rosa eglanteria* or *R. rubiginosa*), naturalized in U.S. Often called eglantine, a name also used for other roses and for a honeysuckle (*Lonicera periclymenum*).

sweet cicely (sĭs'ŭlē), European perennial herb (*Myrrhis odorata*), also called myrrh. It has fragrant foliage, white flowers, and licorice-flavored roots.

sweet clover, leguminous plant (*Melilotus*) with three leaflets and white or yellow flower clusters. It is valued for forage, cover crops, and hay.

sweet fern, small North American shrub (*Comptonia peregrina*), related to bayberry, with fragrant, fernlike foliage. It is also a name for a true fern.

sweet flag, perennial bog plant (*Acorus calamus*) of N Hemisphere, with leaves resembling those of the iris and a club-shaped yellow inflorescence. The rootstalk is used as a confection, a flavoring, and in perfumery.

sweet gum, deciduous tree (*Liquidambar styraciflua*) native from S New England to Mexico and Guatemala. The star-shaped leaves display vivid yellow to crimson autumn colors; the round fruits have hornlike projections. Its hard wood is valuable commercially. In southern part of range, it produces a fragrant balsam called American storax or copalm.

sweet marjoram (mär'jŭrŭm), Old World aromatic downy herb (*Majorana hortensis*), grown for flavoring.

sweet pea, annual climbing legume (*Lathyrus odoratus*), cultivated as a cut flower. Its fragrant blooms range from white to deep red and purple.

sweet potato, tropical vinelike plant (*Ipomoea batatas*) widely grown for its edible tuberous roots. It is an important crop in the S U.S. The sweet potato is often, though incorrectly, called YAM.

Sweetwater, city (pop. 13,619), W Texas, W of Abilene; founded c.1876, moved to railroad 1881. Ships wool, mohair, livestock, and grains and processes dairy products and cotton. Has gypsum plant, oil refinery, and railroad shops. Near by are L. Trammel and L. Sweetwater reservoirs.

sweet William, biennial species (*Dianthus barbatus*) of pink. It has dense clusters of fragrant flowers usually white and shades of red. Wild sweet William is a kind of phlox.

Sweyn (swān), c.960–1014, king of Denmark (986–1014), son of Harold Bluetooth; also spelled Svein. He apostatized from Christianity and rebelled against his father, who was slain in battle. In alliance with Sweden, he defeated Olaf I of Norway at Svolder (1000) and partitioned Norway. Having exacted Danegeld from King ÆTHELRED on a previous occasion, he again invaded England in 1003–4 and in 1013, when the English accepted him as king. His son Canute succeeded him.

Swift, Jonathan, 1667–1745, English author, b. Dublin; greatest satirist in the English language; a clergyman, dean of St. Patrick's, Dublin, after 1713. As a young man he was secretary to Sir William Temple, wrote for him *The Battle of the Books* (1704; with *A Tale of a Tub*), and tutored Esther Johnson (the "Stella" of his *Journal to Stella*). Spent much time in London after 1708, taking part in literary and political life (as Tory propagandist). His friendship for Esther Vanhomrigh ("Vanessa") led to his poem *Cadenus and Vanessa*. Later works included two on the Irish question: *Drapier Letters* (1724) and the savage *A Modest Proposal* (1729). His most familiar and greatest work is *Gulliver's Travels* (1726), a brilliantly imaginative and bitter attack an humankind. Swift's last years were lost in insanity. He is generally considered one of the masters of English prose.

swift, bird related to hummingbird and superficially resembling swallow. It has long wings and flies rapidly, catching its insect food on the wing. Inhabits most of world, particularly the tropics. See *ill.*, p. 135.

Swift Current, city (pop. 7,458), SW Sask., Canada, on Swift Current Creek and W of Moose Jaw. Trade center for SW Sask. with grain elevators, lumber and coal yards, and oil refinery.

Swinburne, Algernon (Charles), 1837–1909, English poet, whose work represents a blending of classical theme with flamboyant romanticism. His life was disorderly. In 1878–79 he became very ill, but was restored to health and thereafter supervised by Theodore Watts-Dunton. He wrote more than 25 volumes of poetry, which showed almost too great technical ability in alliteration, assonance, internal rhyme, and intricate metrical pattern. This fault does not appear in such masterly poems as the choruses in *Atalanta in Calydon* (1865; a poetic drama; best-known chorus, "When the hounds of spring") and shorter pieces such as "The Garden of Proserpine," "The Triumph of Time," and "A Forsaken Garden." Two volumes, *A Song of Italy* (1867) and *Songs before Sunrise* (1871), show his enthusiasm for Mazzini's Italian nationalism. Three poetic dramas deal with Mary Queen of Scots —*Chastelard* (1865), *Bothwell* (1874), and *Mary Stuart* (1881); *Tristram of Lyonesse* (1882) is a rich retelling of a medieval legend. His literary criticism, though extravagant, helped to popularize older English dramatists.

swine, cloven-hoofed mammal of genus *Sus* and family Suidae, with a long snout, thick bristly hide, and heavy short-legged body. Domestic breeds are also known as hogs or pigs, although pigs is more correctly a term for the young animals. Wild hogs, found in Tenn., N.C., and elsewhere, are descendants of the European wild boar (*Sus scrofa*), introduced for hunting. Modern hog breeds are descended from this boar and a smaller Asiatic species. Swine are valued for meat (ham, bacon, pork), fat (lard), leather, and bristles. The Corn Belt of the Middle West is the chief hog-raising region in U.S.

swing music, a type of American popular music. An offshoot of jazz, it uses highly stylized arrangements rather than improvisation. Important names in swing music have been Benny Goodman, Artie Shaw, Glen Miller, and the brothers Tommy and Jimmy Dorsey.

Swiss Confederation: see SWITZERLAND.

Swiss Family Robinson: see WYSS, JOHANN DAVID.

Swiss Guards. Swiss mercenaries served in various European armies from the 15th cent. to 1874, when the Swiss constitution forbade service under foreign flags. Usually, Swiss contingents were furnished to the hiring powers under special treaties (called capitulations) with the Swiss diet or individual cantons. Swiss troops played a conspicuous role in France, where they furnished the royal palace guard, called "Hundred Swiss," and several regiments, including the regiment of Swiss Guards, which was part of the king's military household. On Aug. 10, 1792, when a mob invaded the Tuileries palace in Paris, the Swiss Guards resisted until Louis XVI sent orders to cease fighting; some 500 Swiss were massacred in the resulting confusion. The Lion of Lucerne, a monument by Thorvaldsen at Lucerne, commemorates the event. Swiss troops, abolished in 1792, were again used after the Bourbon restoration; many were massacred in the July Revolution of 1830, after which they were permanently abolished. The Swiss Guards of the Vatican, founded 1505 by Julius II, are not a military body but the pope's personal guard. Famed for their colorful Renaissance costumes, they are recruited from the Catholic cantons of Switzerland.

Swissvale, borough (pop. 16,488), SW Pa., on Monongahela R. and near Pittsburgh; settled c.1760. Mfg. of railroad equipment and glass products.

Swithin, Saint (swĭ'dhŭn), fl. 860, English bishop of Winchester. Folklore says that weather of his day (July 15) foretells weather for 40 days.

Switzerland (swĭ'tsŭrlŭnd), Fr. *Suisse,* Ger. *Schweiz,* Ital. *Svizzera,* more properly **Swiss Confederation,** republic (15,944 sq. mi.; pop. 4,700,297), central Europe, between France, Germany, Austria, and Italy; cap. Bern. Largest cities: Zurich, Basel, Geneva, Bern. Between the ALPS, which cover more than half the country, and the JURA mts. (W), there is an agr. plateau, drained by the Aar R. and containing the L. of Zurich and the L. of Neuchâtel. Other large lakes are those of Geneva, Constance, Lucerne, and Lugano. The Rhine and Rhone have their sources in Switzerland. Numerous passes and tunnels (notably the SIMPLON and SAINT GOTTHARD) assure trans-Alpine communications. With few natural resources and a largely barren soil, Switzerland has achieved prosperity through technological skill and export mfg. —textiles, machinery, watch movements, processed foods (esp. cheese and chocolate), chemicals. Its beauty attracts a huge tourist trade. Politically, Switzerland consists of 22 cantons. Admitted into confederation 1291–1513: URI; SCHWYZ; UNTERWALDEN; LUCERNE; ZURICH; ZUG; GLARUS; BERN; FRIBOURG; SOLOTHURN; BASEL; SCHAFFHAUSEN; APPENZELL. Admitted as cantons 1803–15: AARGAU; THURGAU; SAINT GALL; TICINO; GRISONS; VALAIS; VAUD; GENEVA; NEUCHÂTEL. Three of these—Unterwalden, Basel, Appenzell—are divided into half-cantons. Constitution of 1874 assigns foreign relations and tariffs to federal government, leaving cantons sovereign in most other respects. The chief executive is the federal council, chosen by the federal assembly; its seven members rotate as presidents. Popular initiative and referendum have much reduced the importance of the assembly's two legislative chambers. German dialects are spoken by c.72% of population; French, by 20% (mostly in SW); Italian and Romansh by the rest (Ticino and Grisons). German, French, and Italian are the official languages of the confederation. Protestantism prevails in 11½ cantons and is the faith of 57% of the people. Conquered by Rome 58 B.C. (see HELVETIA; RHAETIA), the region fell to the Germanic Alemanni and Burgundii (5th cent. A.D.) and to the Franks (6th cent.). Split between SWABIA and Transjurane BURGUNDY (9th cent.), it was held for the most part by feudal families after the 11th cent. By the 13th cent. the counts of HAPSBURG and SAVOY had emerged as the chief lords. Hapsburg encroachments on local rights caused Uri, Schwyz, and Unterwalden to enter into a defensive alliance (1291), basis of the rapidly growing confederation. Victorious over the Austrians at Morgarten (1315), Sempach (1386), and Näfels (1388), the Swiss expelled the Hapsburgs; won virtual independence from Holy Roman Empire 1499; full independence 1648. Swiss Confederation until 1798 consisted of 13 cantons, which ruled their conquests (e.g., Vaud, Aargau, Ticino) as subject territories, and of several allies (e.g., Grisons, Valais, Geneva). Its military prestige reached its climax through victories over CHARLES THE BOLD of Burgundy and in the ITALIAN WARS, but the Swiss defeat at Marignano (1515) resulted in a policy of neutrality. Swiss mercenaries continued to fight in foreign armies (see SWISS GUARDS). The Reformation split the loose confederation into two hostile halves and led to several civil wars. In the 17th–18th cent. the cantons were governed largely by patrician oligarchies. Democracy disappeared, but prosperity grew. Revolutionary outbreaks led to French occupation and the creation of the Helvetic Republic (1798), but in 1803 Napoleon's Act of Mediation somewhat restored the old confederation. In 1815 the old regime was substantially restored; Treaty of Paris guaranteed Switzerland's perpetual neutrality. In the 1830s the Radical party estab. democratic governments in most cantons, but Catholic opposition led to the SONDERBUND war (1847) and the transformation of Switzerland from a federation into a federal state (constitution of 1848). Switzerland joined the League of Nations, but its strict neutrality policy prevents its membership in the UN.

Swope, Herbert Bayard, 1882–, American journalist and public official. Executive editor of New York *World* (1920–29); consultant to U.S. Secretary of War (1942–46).

swordfish, food fish of warmer parts of Atlantic and Pacific oceans. It has an elongated, blade-shaped upper jaw; weighs up to 250–400 lb.

Swoyersville (swoi'ûrzvĭl), borough (pop. 7,795), NE Pa., N of Wilkes-Barre. Anthracite mining; mfg. of textiles and metal products.

Sybaris (sĭ'bûrĭs), anc. Greek city in S Italy, on the Gulf of Taranto; founded 720 B.C. The voluptuousness of its people gave rise to the term *sybaritic*. Destroyed 510 B.C.

Sybel, Heinrich von (hīn'rĭkh fŭn zē'bûl), 1817–95, German historian. Chief works *Founding of the German Empire by William I* (Eng. tr., 7 vols., 1890–98) and *Geschichte des ersten Kruezzugs* (1841).

Sycamore, city (pop. 5,912), N Ill., W of Chicago; center of farm area. Metal products.

sycamore: see PLANE TREE.

Sydenham, Thomas (sĭ'dûnûm), 1624–89, English physician, a founder of modern clinical medicine and of epidemiology.

Sydney, Sir Philip: see SIDNEY, SIR PHILIP.

Sydney, city (pop. 95,925); metropolitan pop. 1,484,004), cap. of New South Wales, Australia, on S shore of Port JACKSON. Seat of Univ. of Sydney (1852), Natl. Art Gall. (1904), and Australian Mus. (1830). Produces textiles, automobiles, and chemicals. Founded 1788 as Australia's first penal settlement, Sydney became cap. of early colony of New South Wales. In World War II an Allied naval and air base was here.

Sydney, city (pop. 31,317) on NE coast of Cape Breton Isl., NE N.S., Canada, NE of Halifax. Center of coal-mining and agr. area with steel mills, shipyards, and mfg. of wood, food, and metal products. Founded 1783. Cap. of Cape Breton prov. 1784–1820.

Sydney Harbour, Australia: see JACKSON, PORT.

Sydney Mines, town (pop. 8,410), on NE coast of Cape Breton Isl., N.S., Canada, NNW of Sydney. Coal-mining center.

Sylacauga (sĭlûkŏ'gû), city (pop. 9,606), central Ala., SE of Birmingham. Processes cotton, lumber, marble (quarries near), dairy products.

Sylt (zĭlt), island (36 sq. mi.; pop. 26,346), N Germany, in North Sea off Schleswig-Holstein; one of North Frisian Isls. Seaside resort.

Sylva, Carmen: see ELIZABETH, queen of Rumania.

Sylvester II (sĭlvĕ'stûr), d. 1003, pope (999–1003), a Frenchman. Under his original name, Gerbert, he was widely known for his learning and for ability shown in the school at Rheims. He taught Emperor Otto III, who brought about his election as pope. He proved able and energetic. Also Silvester.

symbiosis (sĭmbēō'sĭs), habitual living together of organisms of different species. Usually it refers to a relationship benefiting at least one participant and harming none. One example is relationship between NITROGEN-FIXING BACTERIA and leguminous plants.

symbol, sign representing something having an independent existence (i.e., standing for something else). Writing and use of numbers are both symbolic processes. Science employs many symbols for conciseness (e.g., chemical symbols). In art a symbol is generally distinguished from a likeness of a person or an object. Symbols have been used in religion from most ancient days and are now used in complex combinations (e.g., candle, incense, the figures of iconography). Patriotism also uses such symbols as the flag, and business uses symbols in trade-marks. Freud's studies in psychology make much of the use of symbols.

symbolists, in literature, school originating in France, late 19th cent. Designed to convey impressions by suggestion instead of direct statement, symbolism first appeared in poetry, later in drama (Maeterlinck), criticism (Remy de Gourmont), music (Debussy). Early symbolists (e.g., Verlaine, Mallarmé, Rimbaud) were accused of decadent morbidity, partly for using imagination as a reality; their experiments led to free verse. Symbolist influence was very wide; it appears in development of the imagists and decadents, in work of T. S. Eliot, Proust, James Joyce, Gertrude Stein.

Symonds, John Addington (sĭm'ûnz), 1840–93, English author of *The Renaissance in Italy* (7 vols., 1875–86), a classic of cultural history.

Symons, Arthur (sĭm'ûnz), 1865–1945, English lyric poet and literary critic; leader of symbolists in England and interpreter of French poets.

sympathetic nervous system: see NERVOUS SYSTEM.

symphonic poem: see TONE POEM.

symphony, a SONATA for orchestra, developed from the 17th-cent. Italian operatic overture (called the *sinfonia,* of three sections in contrasting tempi). It is in the works of Haydn and Mozart that the classical symphony reached maturity. As further developed by Beethoven, Schubert, and later, Brahms, the symphony emerges as one of the highest forms of musical expression. The romantic symphony of the late 19th cent. (usually in four sections) emphasized emotional appeal before classical form. Some 20th-cent. composers have adhered to the classic form but use modern harmonic techniques, others apply the term *symphony* freely to compositions of all types.

Symplegades (sĭmplĕ'gúdēz) [Gr.,= dashing together], in Greek mythology, two floating cliffs. After the ARGO passed between them without being crushed, they remained still, forming Black Sea entrance.

synagogue (sĭ'núgŏg) [from Gr.,= assembly], building where Jews gather for worship. As early as the days of Moses, the term was used to denote a gathering of Jews, usually for religious purposes. The synagogue assumed importance after the destruction of the first Temple; in the Middle Ages, it was the intellectual and social center of Jewish life. The services were simple; there was no officially appointed priest. Its use is now restricted almost purely to religious purposes. The oldest U.S. synagogue is at Newport, R.I. (1763).

syndicalism includes both a strategy of revolution and a plan for social reorganization. Syndicalists believe that the state, an instrument of oppression, should be abolished, and that the trade union is the essential unit of production and of government. Their doctrines were inspired by P. J. Proudhon and Georges SOREL. In the U.S., they formed the INDUSTRIAL WORKERS OF THE WORLD.

Synge, J(ohn) M(illington) (sĭng), 1871–1909, Irish poet and dramatist, notable for plays of Irish peasant life in rhythmic, expressive language of the people of W Ireland. A friend of W. B. Yeats and Lady Gregory, he helped to found the Abbey Theatre. Best known of his works are one-act plays, *In the Shadow of the Glen* (1903) and *Riders to the Sea* (1904); full-length comedies, *The Well of the Saints* (1905) and *The Playboy of the Western World* (1907); and unfinished tragedy, *Deirdre of the Sorrows.*

Synge, Richard Laurence Millington, 1914–, British biochemist. Shared 1952 Nobel Prize in Chemistry for discovery of partition chromatography, a new method for separating compounds in chemical analysis.

Synoptic Gospels (sĭnŏp'tĭk) [Gr. *synopsis* = view together], name given to the first three Gospels (Matthew, Mark, and Luke) as contrasted to John. They are similar to each other in that they are chiefly straight biographical narratives whereas John is primarily a philosophical essay on the mission of Jesus. The question of relationship between the three is called the Synoptic problem, the heart of the problem being why Matthew and Luke contain material that does not appear in Mark. Critics have proposed numerous answers.

synthesis, chemical reaction in which two or more substances combine to form another substance. In synthesis of a compound, definite quantities of each constituent are needed to form given quantity of compound.

syphilis (sĭ'fúlĭs), contagious VENEREAL DISEASE caused by infection with a spirochete. Usually is acquired through sexual intercourse or through infection before birth. Initial sore (chancre) precedes second stage in which spirochetes spread through body and a Wassermann test is positive. In third stage, lesions (gummata) occur in various sites; if nervous system is affected, victim may have LOCOMOTOR ATAXIA or paresis (a brain disease). Syphilis is treated by use of penicillin or derivatives of arsenic, mercury, and bismuth. See *ill.,* p. 813.

Syracuse (sĭ'rúkūs, –kūz), Italian *Siracusa,* city (pop. 43,639), cap. of Syracuse prov., SE Sicily, Italy; port on the Ionian Sea. Founded by Greeks in 743 B.C., it became the leading city of ancient Sicily under the tyrant GELON, who defeated the Carthaginians (480 B.C.). Later it was a center of Greek culture under several celebrated tyrants (with periods of democratic government); among them were Hiero I, Dionysius the Elder, Dionysius the Younger, Dion of Syracuse, and Hiero II. Syracuse in 413 B.C. defeated a great Athenian force sent against it. Taking the side of Carthage in the Second Punic War, it was sacked by the Romans (212 B.C.) and declined.

Syracuse (sĭ'rúkūs), city (pop. 220,583), central N.Y., at S end of Onondaga L., on the Barge Canal and SE of Rochester; settled 1805. Rail center; mfg. of typewriters, farm machinery, cooling equipment; metal, paper, wood, food, soap products. Saltmaking declined after Civil War, but Erie Canal (opened here 1819) and railroads stimulated industrial growth. Has Mus. of Fine Arts and Mills Rose Garden. Seat of **Syracuse University** (coed.; chartered as Genesee Col., at Lima, N.Y., 1849, moved to Syracuse 1869, rechartered 1870); has Goudy typographical laboratory and a natural science museum.

Syr Darya (sēr" där'yä), anc. *Jaxartes* or *Yaxartes,* river, c.1,300 mi. long, USSR. Formed in FERGANA VALLEY (Uzbek SSR) by junction of Naryn and Kara Darya rivers, flows through Tadzhik SSR and Kazakh SSR to Aral Sea. Unfit for navigation but used for irrigation. Trans-Caspian RR parallels the river's lower course.

Syria (sĭ'rēú), Arabic *Esh Sham,* republic (66,063 sq. mi.; pop. 3,006,028), SW Asia; cap. DAMASCUS. Bounded on W by the Mediterranean and Lebanon, S by Jordan, E by Iraq, and N by Turkey. Most of Syria is occupied by Syrian Desert, crossed by Euphrates R. In W are the Anti-Lebanon mts. and in SW the fertile HAURAN plain. Syria is mainly a pastoral and agr. country. Most of the people are of Arab origin and are Moslems; the DRUSES inhabit the S. Historically, the name Syria has comprised those lands of the Levant corresponding to modern Syria and Lebanon, most of Israel and Jordan, and parts of N Arabia. The area was probably under the HITTITES, 19th–13th cent. B.C. First great indigenous culture was PHOENICIAN CIVILIZATION, which flourished after 1250 B.C. Before it became part of Persian Empire, Syria suffered under invasions by Assyrians, Babylonians, and Egyptians. After its conquest by Alexander the Great (332–331 B.C.) Syria came under the rule of Seleucus I and his successors, the Seleucidae. Romans under Pompey conquered the region by 63 B.C. After division of Roman Empire, Syria was under Byzantine rule until it came under Arab influence in 7th cent. Syria was largely converted to Islam, but there still remained groups of Christians, who later gave aid to Crusaders. By end of 12th cent. the conqueror SALADIN was dominant. His rule was followed by that of the Mamelukes and by Mongol invasions. In early 16th cent. Ottoman Turks took over the area, which in early 19th cent. was held by Egyptians under IBRAHIM PASHA. After World War I France was given a mandate in 1920 over the Levant States (roughly present Syria and Lebanon). In 1926 Lebanon was made a separate state, but Syria remained a region split into separate territories until 1941, when republic of Syria was proclaimed. In World War II British and Free French forces invaded and occupied Syria in June, 1941. In 1944 France declared Syria completely independent. A member of Arab League, Syria joined in war against Israel (1948). A military regime was estab. 1949.

Syriac language, Aramaic language of Semitic family. See LANGUAGE (table).

syringa: see MOCK ORANGE. For the genus *Syringa,* see LILAC.

Syros (sī'rōs), Aegean island (33 sq. mi.; pop. 25,918), one of the Cyclades; cap. Hermopolis.

Syzran (sĭzrän'yů), city (pop. c.150,000), E European RSFSR; a port on the Volga. It is a rapidly expanding industrial and mining center (oil shale, asphalt, phosphorite).

Szatmarnemeti or **Szatmar:** see SATU-MARE.

Szechwan (sĕ'chwän, sŭ'chwän), province (120,000 sq. mi.; pop. 45,000,000), SW China; cap. Chengtu. Surrounded by mountains and crossed by Yangtze R. Extensive agr. (rice, sugar cane, tobacco); gold and iron mining. Tung oil and salt industries.

Szeged (sĕ'gĕd), formerly **Szegedin** (–ēn), city (pop. 136,752), S Hungary, on the Tisza. Agr. processing center. University was founded 1921.

Szekely (sā'kā), one of the three historic "nations" of TRANSYLVANIA.

Szekesfehervar (sā'kĕshfĕ"hârvär), Ger. *Stuhlweissenburg,* city (pop. 47,968), W central Hungary. Dates from Roman times. Hungarian kings were crowned here 1027–1527.

Szent-Gyorgyi, Albert von (äl'bĕrt fŭn sĕnt"-dyûr'dyĭ), 1893–, Hungarian biochemist. Won 1937 Nobel Prize in Physiology and Medicine for work on biological oxidation and on ascorbic acid.

Szigeti, Joseph (sēgĕ'tē), 1892–, Hungarian violinist. Made his American debut in 1925. He is known for playing unfamiliar works.

Szold, Henrietta (zōld), 1860–1945, American Jewish leader. Founder of the American women's organization Hadassah, president from 1912 to 1926. Translated many works from French, German, and Hebrew.

Szondi Test: see MENTAL TESTS.

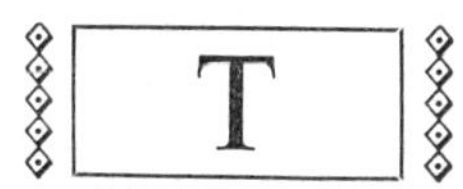

Ta, chemical symbol of the element TANTALUM.

Taaffe, Eduard, Graf von (ā'dōōärt gräf' fŭn tä'fů), 1833–95, Austrian statesman of Irish descent. Premier 1868–69, 1879–93.

Taal, Lake (tä-äl'), 94 sq. mi., SW Luzon, P.I., S of Manila. Contains Volcano Isl. with Mt. Taal (active; 984 ft. high).

Tabard Inn (tă'bûrd), Southwark, London; traditional starting place of Canterbury pilgrims. Described in Prologue of Chaucer's *Canterbury Tales.*

Tabasco (täbä'skō), state (9,783 sq. mi.; pop. 351,106), SE Mexico, on Gulf of Campeche; cap. VILLAHERMOSA. State is predominantly a jungle plain broken by swamps, lagoons, and rivers, which provide practically the only means of communication. Cortés crossed region on march to Honduras (1524), and Montejo conquered it (1530). Tropical agr. is main occupation.

Tabernacle [Latin,= tent, hut], in Bible, the portable holy place of the Hebrews during their wanderings in the wilderness. It was considered in a peculiar sense the dwelling of God Himself, and the Ark of the Covenant was kept here. For description see Ex. 25–27; 30–31; 35–40. Term is applied also to a small receptacle, used in the Roman Catholic Church, in which the Host is reserved on the altar.

Tabernacles, Feast of, often called by its Hebrew name, Sukkoth (sōōkōth') [Heb.,= booth], in anc. Palestine a harvest festival, now observed by the taking of meals in lattice huts which commemorate the wanderings of the Jews. It begins on the 15th day of Tishri, the 7th month of the Jewish calendar, and lasts for 9 days.

Tabitha (tă′bĭthů), same as DORCAS.

tablature (tă′blůchŏŏr), in music, name for various systems of MUSICAL NOTATION used from the 15th to 17 cent. for keyboard and lute music. These systems used letters, numbers, or symbols to indicate the pitch and duration of a tone. Lute tablatures have lines representing the strings of the lute, with numbers or letters to indicate the position for stopping the strings. In general, tablatures tell the player what to do rather than what music to play. They are used today to notate music for guitar and ukulele. These have vertical lines representing the strings of the instrument, horizontal lines for the frets, and dots to show the position of the fingers.

Table Mountain, 3,549 ft. high, W Cape Prov., South Africa, overlooking Capetown and Table Bay (inlet of the Atlantic).

table tennis. Also called ping-pong, trade name of kind of table tennis. Played on table which should measure 9 ft. by 5 ft. and which should stand 2½ ft. above floor. Table tennis probably originated in 19th cent., first became popular in England.

taboo or tabu (both: tăbōō′), prohibition of an action under pain of supernatural punishment. Name originated in Polynesia but its use is common among all primitive peoples.

Tabor, Horace Austin Warner (tā′bûr), 1830–99, American prospector, known as Silver Dollar Tabor. Made fortune mining silver from Matchless Mine at Leadville, Colo. Spent money lavishly and lost his fortune. His second wife **Elizabeth McCourt ("Baby Doe") Tabor,** 1862–1935, refused to give up faith in the mine, lived beside it in poverty, and died of exposure there.

Tabor, in Bible: see TABOR, MOUNT.

Tabor (tä′bôr), town (pop. 17,596), S Bohemia, Czechoslovakia. Founded (1420) by John ZIZKA and named after Mt. Tabor in Palestine, it became the stronghold of the TABORITES. Town hall (16th cent.) has collection of Hussite relics.

Tabor (tā′bůr), town (pop. 373), SE S.Dak., near Nebr. line SW of Yankton. HUTTERISCHE COMMUNITY settled here 1874.

Tabor, Mount, mountain of N Palestine. Here Barak assembled the army which defeated Sisera.

Taborites (tā′bůrīts), HUSSITES, called after their stronghold in Bohemia, Tabor. More radical than UTRAQUISTS, they rejected belief in the real presence of Christ in the Eucharist and swept away rites and forms. Under the leadership of John Zizka and Procopius the Great, they were for years triumphant in the Hussite Wars but, after refusing to accept the settlement of the Compactata (1434), were defeated by Catholics and Utraquists at Lipany. The Moravian Church is supposed to have continued Taborite movement.

Tabriz (täbrēz′), anc. *Tauris,* city (pop. 213,-542), NW Iran, in Azerbaijan; second largest city of Iran. Has manufactures and handicrafts, notably rugmaking. Despite severe earthquakes, several old buildings (including the 15th-cent. Blue Mosque) survive. In c.1500 Iranians took the city from Turks, who subsequently recaptured it several times. Occupied by Russians 1827–28 and in World War I and World War II. In 1946 it was hq. of a short-lived regime set up by leftist Tudeh party and supported by Russians.

tabu: see TABOO.

Taché, Sir Étienne Paschal (ātyĕn′ päskäl′ tächā′), 1795–1865, Canadian statesman. Premier with J. A. Macdonald (1856–57, 1864–65).

Tacitus (tă′sĭtůs), A.D. c.55–c.117, Roman historian. His high moral tone and severe criticism of Rome are present in all three of his most notable surviving works—the *Germania* (an accurate account of the Germanic tribes), the *Histories* (of which 4 books and a fragment, covering Galba's reign and the beginning of Vespasian's, survive), and the *Annals* (of which 12 books, covering the reign of Tiberius and parts of the reigns of Claudius and Nero, survive). The style of these works is clean, polished, highly individualistic.

Tacloban (täklō′bän), town (pop. 45,421), NE Leyte, P.I. Port; ships rice and sugar. Captured by Japanese (1942) in World War II; retaken, Oct., 1944, and made temporary cap. of Philippines.

Tacna-Arica Controversy, 1883–1929, dispute between Chile and Peru which arose from provisions of the treaty ending war of Pacific (see PACIFIC, WAR OF THE). Victorious Chile was ceded S provinces of Peru (Tacna and Arica), with understanding that plebiscite would be held at end of 10 years to determine ownership. Plebiscite was not held, and Chile began to colonize area (1909). In 1922 the two countries agreed to arbitration by president of U.S. and accepted decision (1929) that Tacna be returned to Peru; that Chile retain Arica, construct free port for Peru with port and rail installations, transfer all state-owned real estate and buildings in Tacna to Peru, and pay indemnity of $6,000,-000.

Tacoma (tůkō′mů), city (pop. 143,673), W Wash., on Commencement Bay of Puget Sound, near Mt. Rainier; settled 1852. Important port, rail terminus, and industrial center. Produces lumber, flour, food and foundry products, and electrochemicals. Fur Market. Seat of College of Puget Sound (Methodist; coed.; 1888). In Point Defiance Park is reconstructed Fort Nisqually, historic trading post. Near by are an air force base and Fort Lewis.

Taconic Mountains (tůkŏ′nĭk), range of Appalachian Mts., extending c.150 mi. S from point in Vt. In Vt. range is W of Green Mts. and in N.Y. is E of Hudson R. Mt. Equinox (3,816 ft.), near Manchester, Vt., is highest point. Includes BERKSHIRE HILLS.

Tadoussac (tă′dōōsăk, Fr. tädōōsäk′), village (pop. 1,064), S Que., at the mouth of the Saguenay on the St. Lawrence; visited by Cartier 1535. An unsuccessful French colony was founded here (1600–1601), and a later fur-trading post was successful.

tadpole, larval, aquatic form of any amphibian animal from time of hatching to growth of adult organs.

Tadzhik Soviet Socialist Republic (täjĭk′) or **Tadzhikistan** (tůjĭ′kĭstän″), constituent republic (c.55,000 sq. mi.; pop. c.1,455,000) of the USSR, in central Asia; cap. Stalinabad. Contains part of Pamir mts. (incl. STALIN PEAK); a high, arid plateau (SE); and FERGANA VALLEY (N). Amu Darya and Syr Darya rivers are used for irrigation. Chief products: cotton, rice, wheat, fruit, silk. Livestock raising. Mining (lead, zinc, silver, uranium, gold, coal). Tadzhiks (c.78% of pop.) are an Iranian people of Moslem faith. Most of Tadzhikistan was part of emirate of BUKHARA until the Russian Revolution of 1917. Became constituent republic 1929.

Tafilelt or **Tafilalet** (both: täfē'lĕlt), largest Saharan oasis, area c.530 sq. mi., of S French Morocco. Town of Sijilmassa (now in ruins) was Berber stronghold, 8th–9th cent. A.D. Ruling dynasty of Morocco, estab. 1649, originated here.

Taft, Lorado (lürā'dō), 1860–1936, American sculptor, writer, and lecturer on art. Exerted a wide influence on young sculptors of the West.

Taft, William Howard, 1857–1930, 26th President of the United States (1909–13), Chief Justice of the Supreme Court (1921–30). First civil governor of Philippine Isls. (1901–4). As U.S. Secretary of War (1904–8) Taft was prominent in Latin American affairs. As President he continued Theodore Roosevelt's trust-busting policy; promoted "dollar diplomacy" in Latin America. However, his emphasis was more conservative than Roosevelt's. Critics quarreled with what they regarded as undue favoritism toward individual enterprises; there was great dissatisfaction over Payne-Aldrich Tariff Act. Opposition to Taft led to disaffection of Republican progressives and to Taft's defeat in 1912 election. His son, **Robert A(lphonso) Taft,** 1889–, is U.S. Senator (1939–) from Ohio. Expert in financial affairs. Helped write TAFT-HARTLEY LABOR ACT. Several times candidate for Republican presidential nomination.

Taft-Hartley Labor Act, 1947, passed by U.S. Congress, also known as Labor-Management Relations Act. Sponsored by Sen. R. A. Taft and Rep. F. A. Hartley. Estab. control of labor disputes on a new basis. Enlarged the NATIONAL LABOR RELATIONS BOARD; empowered government to obtain 80-day injunction against any strike endangering national health or safety; prohibited jurisdictional strikes; retained most collective-bargaining provisions, adding provision for signing of affidavit that union officers are not Communists. Passed over Pres. Truman's veto, act has been target of much criticism.

Tagalog (tügä'lüg, tägä'lŏg) or **Tagal** (tägäl'), dominant people of Luzon, Philippine Isls., second in population of the Philippine peoples. Tagalog is a Malayo-Polynesian language, made official in 1940.

Taganrog (tŭgŭnrôk'), city (pop. 188,808), E European RSFSR; a port on a gulf of the Sea of Azov. Metallurgy; mfg. of machinery; fish canning. Founded 1698 as a fortress, it was later captured by the Turks but definitively passed to Russia 1774. Was Denikin's hq. in civil war (1919); twice occupied by Germans in World War II (1941, 1942–43). Birthplace of Anton Chekhov.

Taglioni, Filippo (tälyō'nē), 1777–1871, Italian ballet master and composer of ballets. Trained his daughter, **Maria Taglioni,** 1804–84, considered greatest dancer of her day. Was the idol of Paris when she appeared (1832) in his ballet, *La Sylphide.*

Tagore, Sir Rabindranath (rübĭn'drünät tü-gōr'), 1861–1941, Indian author, b. Calcutta. Briefly studied law in England (1877) and for a time managed his father's vast estates in Bengal. Joining the Indian nationalists, he wrote many propaganda poems and songs. Gradually he evolved his characteristic later manner, combining delicate descriptions of nature with religious and philosophical speculation. He wrote c.50 dramas, c.100 books of verse, and c.40 volumes of fiction and philosophical writings. His wide range of material and style made his appeal in India nearly universal. He wrote in Bengali but translated much of his work into English. In 1913 he won the Nobel Prize in Literature. The school he founded in 1901 at Santiniketan, Bengal, was expanded in 1922 into Visva-Bahrati Univ.

tagua (tä'gwä), fruit of the ivory-nut palm (*Phytelephas macrocarpa*), commercially produced chiefly in Ecuador, Panama, Colombia, and N Peru. Fruit is a burr or pod containing up to 40 or more very hard nuts c.2 in. in diameter whose content is used as a substitute for ivory (known as vegetable ivory). It is shipped to the U.S. and Europe for making buttons and other small articles. When tested with a concentrated solution of sulphuric acid, tagua becomes reddish; true ivory is unaffected. Tagua is also known as coroza.

Tagus (tā'güs), Span. *Tajo,* Port. *Tejo,* river, 565–625 mi. long, rising in E Spain and flowing W and SW, along part of Spanish-Portuguese border and through Portugal, into the Atlantic at Lisbon. Usually considered longest river of Iberian Peninsula.

Taharka, Egyptian king: see TIRHAKAH.

Tahiti (tähē'tē), island (402 sq. mi.; pop. 24,-820), S Pacific, in Windward group of SOCIETY ISLANDS; cap. PAPEETE, which is also cap. of French Oceania. Mountainous and scenic. Discovered 1767 by British, visited 1788 by the *Bounty.* French and English missionaries arrived in late 18th cent. Became French protectorate 1843, ceded to France 1880. GAUGUIN did his most famous paintings here.

Tahlequah (tă'lükwô), city (pop. 4,750), NE Okla., SE of Tulsa. Settled by Cherokees 1839 and made their cap., it has museum with Indian relics.

Tahoe, Lake (tä'hō, tā'–), 21.6 mi. long, 12 mi. wide, on Calif.-Nev. line, between Sierra Nevada (W) and Carson Range, in beautiful summer-resort area.

Tahquamenon (tükwä'münün), river rising in E Upper Peninsula, N Mich., and flowing E and NE to Whitefish Bay of L. Superior. Noted for waterfalls, it was celebrated in Longfellow's *Hiawatha.*

Tai (tī), Chinese *Tai Shan,* sacred peak, 5,069 ft. high, W central Shantung prov., China.

Tai, lake, c.40 mi. long, 35 mi. wide, China, on Kiangsu-Chekiang border.

taille: see TALLAGE.

Taimyr Peninsula (tīmĭr'), northernmost projection of Siberia, RSFSR, on the Kara and Laptev seas, terminating in Cape Chelyuskin; also spelled Taymyr. Tundra region. Inhabited by nomadic Nentsy (formerly called Samoyedes) and Dolgans, who subsist on reindeer raising, hunting, and fishing.

Tainan (tī'nän'), city (pop. 229,452), Formosa; port on Formosa Strait. Cap. of Formosa 1662–1885.

Taine, Hippolyte (tān, Fr. ēpôlēt' tĕn'), 1828–93, French critic and historian. His deterministic theories, regarding man as the product of heredity and environment, formed the basis of the naturalistic school. Wrote *History of English Literature* (1864), *The Origins of Contemporary France* (6 vols., 1876–93).

Taipei or **Taipeh** (both: tī'pā), Jap. *Taihoku*, industrial city (pop. 326,407), cap. of Formosa, China. In 1949 it became seat of Nationalist government.

Taiping Rebellion (tī'pĭng'), 1850–65, revolt against Ch'ing dynasty of China. Led by Hung Hsiu-ch'üan, a visionary scholar, who tried to set up a new dynasty, the Taiping [great peace]. Nanking, captured 1853, became his capital. Serious threat to Ch'ing dynasty brought aid of Western powers; revolt was crushed by army led by Charles George Gordon.

Tait, Archibald Campbell, 1811–82, Anglican prelate. Succeeded Thomas Arnold as headmaster of Rugby (1842). He became dean of Carlisle (1849), bishop of London (1856), and archbishop of Canterbury (1869). Stoutly supported the Low Church cause.

Taiwan: see FORMOSA.

Taiyüan (tī'yüän'), city (pop. 251,566), cap. of Shansi prov., China; agr. and industrial center. Formerly called Yangkü.

Taj Mahal (täj' mŏhŭl'), mausoleum, Agra, Uttar Pradesh, India. Considered to be greatest example of late style of Indian Moslem architecture. Built (1630–1648?) by Shah Jehan for his favorite wife, Mumtaz Mahal, and himself. The building, reflected in an oblong pool, is of white marble inlaid with semiprecious stones. Its bulbous dome tapers to a spire topped by a crescent, and a minaret rises from each corner of the platform on which the building stands. The royal couple lie in a vault beneath the illuminated tomb chamber.

Tajo, river: see TAGUS.

Taklamakan (tä"klämäkän'), sandy desert, c.125,000 sq. mi., Sinkiang prov., China. Rimmed by oases.

Takoma Park, town (pop. 13,341), W central Md., NE suburb of Washington, D.C.

Talbot, Richard: see TYRCONNEL, RICHARD TALBOT, DUKE AND EARL OF.

talc, very soft mineral with a greasy, soapy feel. It is a hydrous silicate of magnesium, usually with small amounts of nickel, iron, aluminum; ranges in color from white through shades of gray and green to red and brown. Of wide distribution, commonly associated with metamorphic rocks. Used in making paper, paints, cosmetics, soap, lubricants, linoleum, electrical insulation, and pottery.

Talca (täl'cä), city (pop. 42,994), S central Chile; founded 1692; today one of most important cities in central valley of Chile, in a wheat- and wine-producing area. Rebuilt after earthquake of 1928. Here Bernardo O'Higgins proclaimed Chile's independence (1818).

Talcahuano (tälkäwä'nō), city (pop. 38,605), S central Chile, port just N of Concepción. Has fishing industries, dry-dock facilities, metallurgical plants.

Talien, China: see DAIREN.

Taliesin or **Taliessin** (both: tălē'sĭn), 6th cent.?, Welsh bard, whose *Book of Taliesin* is one of great works of Welsh poetry.

Talitha cumi (tă'lĭthŭ kū'mī) [Aramaic,= maiden, arise], words spoken by Jesus to the daughter of the ruler of the synagogue as he raised her from the dead. Mark 5.41. Aramaic words left and translation given in all Continental vernacular versions of this Gospel.

Talladega (tălŭdē'gŭ), city (pop. 13,134), NE central Ala., E of Birmingham and in Blue Ridge foothills. Cotton and metal goods. Andrew Jackson defeated Creek Indians here, Nov., 1813. Seat of Talladega Col. (Negro; coed.; opened 1867).

tallage (tă'lĭj), feudal impost in medieval England. Important chiefly because king collected it from demesne lands, with which chartered towns were included. Instituted by Henry I to replace DANEGELD, it was imposed, usually over protest, until reign of Edward III. French *taille*, originally similar to tallage, was later part personal, part land tax.

Tallahassee (tălŭhă'sē), city (pop. 27,237), state cap., NW Fla., in hilly agr. area. Processes wood. De Soto arrived here 1539, and region was subsequently settled by Spanish. City founded 1824 as cap. of Fla. Territory. Ordinance of secession adopted here, 1861. Union capture resisted in Civil War. Seat of FLORIDA STATE UNIVERSITY and FLORIDA AGRICULTURAL AND MECHANICAL COLLEGE.

Tallapoosa (tălŭpōō'sŭ), river rising in Ga. and flowing 268 mi. S and W through Ala. to Coosa R., forming Alabama R. near Montgomery. Martin Dam forms Martin L.

Talleyrand or **Talleyrand-Périgord, Charles Maurice de** (tă'lērănd", Fr. shärl' mōrēs' dŭ tälārã', -pārēgôr'), 1754–1838, French statesman, of an anc. noble family. A childhood accident left him lame, and he was intended for the Church. Made bishop of Autun (1788) despite his notorious immorality, he was a deputy of the clergy in the States-General of 1789; sided with the revolutionists; was excommunicated by the pope (1791); fled to England, then to the U.S., after the fall of the monarchy; returned to France 1795; became foreign minister under the Directory (1797–99) and under Napoleon (1799–1807). Napoleon ignored his cautious advice, and although Talleyrand served on diplomatic missions after his resignation, he secretly worked in Austria's rather than Napoleon's interest. When the allies entered Paris (1814), Talleyrand persuaded them to restore the Bourbons and won mild peace terms (see PARIS, TREATY OF, 1814). As foreign minister of Louis XVIII, he scored his greatest diplomatic triumph at the Congress of VIENNA (1814–15), which his intervention saved from collapse. He resigned his ministry after the Treaty of Paris of 1815. Under Louis Philippe, he served as ambassador to London (1830–34). His excommunication was lifted 1802. Corrupt, cynical, witty, dissolute, Talleyrand was nevertheless above all a good European. In his seeming deviousness he pursued the steadfast aim of European peace and stability. He wrote memoirs (Eng. tr., 5 vols., 1891–92).

Tallien, Jean Lambert (zhã' lãběr' tälyẽ'), 1767–1820, French revolutionist. As secretary of Commune of Paris and member of the Convention he took active part in September massacres of 1792 and in Reign of Terror. In 1794 he led in overthrow of Robespierre and in subsequent Thermidorian reaction. His wife, **Thérésa (Cabarrus) Tallien,** 1773–1835, of Spanish parentage, strongly influenced his policies; was nicknamed Notre Dame de Septembre and Notre Dame de Thermidor. A leading social figure, she originated neo-Greek fashions of Directoire period. She divorced Tallien 1805 and married the banker Caraman, later created prince de Chimay.

Tallinn (tä'lĭn), Ger. *Reval,* city (pop. c.168,-000), cap. of Estonia; a major Baltic port on S coast of Gulf of Finland. Produces textiles, machinery, plastics, plywood, furniture. Founded 1219 by Waldemar II of Denmark; joined Hanseatic League 1285; was sold 1346 by Denmark to Livonian Knights; passed to Sweden 1561; was captured by Peter I of Russia 1710. Suffered heavy damage during German occupation (1941–44) in World War II. The picturesque lower town, dating from Hanseatic times, is surrounded by medieval walls.

Tallis or **Tallys, Thomas,** c.1510–1585, English organist and composer. He wrote madrigals, motets, and instrumental music, but is best known for his hymn tunes, services, and anthems.

tallow, solid fat extracted from tissues and fat deposits of animals. Pure form is white, odorless, tasteless. Used to make soap, candles, and butter substitutes; formerly was used as a lubricant.

tallow tree, popular name for trees of spurge family that yield vegetable tallow. Seed coverings of the Chinese tallow tree (*Sapium sebiferum*) yield a substance used to make candles and soap. Nuts of the tropical candlenut tree (*Aleurites moluccana*) produce a valuable oil and have been used as candles.

Tallulah (tŭlōō'lŭ), village (pop. 7,758), NE La., W of Vicksburg, Miss. Cotton raising, commercial fishing, and frog raising.

Tallys, Thomas: see TALLIS, THOMAS.

Talma, François Joseph (tälmä'), 1763–1826, French actor; greatest tragedian of his time. Made important reforms in costuming and technique.

Talmadge, Eugene, 1884–1946, governor of Ga. (1933–37, 1941–43). A leader of a "white supremacy" group largely made up of small farmers, he triumphed over the "liberal" group in Ga. and instituted reactionary, anti-intellectual measures. His mantle fell upon his son, **Herman Talmadge,** 1913–, who became governor in 1947.

Talmage, (Thomas) De Witt, 1832–1902, American Presbyterian clergyman. His dramatic preaching drew great audiences to the Brooklyn (N.Y.) Tabernacle.

Talmud (tăl'mŭd) [Aramaic from Heb.,= learning], compilation of the Oral Law of the Jews, with rabbinical commentaries, in contradistinction to the Scriptures or Written Laws; the accepted authority for orthodox Jews everywhere. Its two divisions are the Mishna or text of the Oral Law (in Hebrew) and the Gemara (in Aramaic), a sort of commentary upon the Mishna, which it supplements. The Mishna is divided into six orders (Sedarim) and comprises 63 tractates, only 36½ of which have a Gemara. The compilation of the present Mishna is practically the work of Judah I (ha-Nassi). Although the mission of the Gemara was to expound the text of the Mishna, it became a mass of information on a variety of subjects. The legal sections of the Gemara are known as the halakah; the poetical digressions, the haggada. Talmuds were produced in Palestine and in Babylon in the 5th and 6th cent. The Babylonian Talmud became the authoritative work. The term *Talmud* is sometimes used with reference to the Gemara alone.

talus (tā'lŭs), fragmentary mantle rock detached from cliffs by weathering (chiefly by frost action) and piled up at bases of mountain slopes.

tamale (tŭmä'lē), Mexican dish in which a thick dough of corn meal surrounds filling of meat, chilies, and seasonings; the whole, wrapped in cornhusks, is then steamed.

Tamalpais, Mount (tă'mŭlpīs"), 2,604 ft. high, W Calif., across the Golden Gate from San Francisco. Game preserve and resort.

Tamaqua (tŭmô'kwŭ), borough (pop. 11,508), E Pa., NE of Pottsville; settled 1799. Coal mining.

Tamar (tā'mär). **1** Daughter-in-law of Judah; widow of his eldest sons in succession. When Judah failed to keep his promise to give her in marriage to his third son, she tricked Judah himself into marriage. Gen. 38; Ruth 4.12; 1 Chron. 2.4 Thamar: Mat. 1.3. **2** Daughter of David, sister of Absalom. Victim of Amnon's passion. 2 Sam. 13.

tamarack: see LARCH.

tamarind (tă'mŭrĭnd), tropical, ornamental, leguminous tree (*Tamarindus indica*). Its fruit, a brown pod, contains a juicy acid pulp used in chutneys and curries, in medicine, and for preserving fish.

tamarisk (tă'mŭrĭsk), small ornamental tree or shrub of genus *Tamarix,* native to S Europe and Asia and cultivated in U.S. The slender branches are covered with small leaves and bear inconspicuous white or pink blossoms in spring or summer. Tamarisks thrive on seacoasts, even in salt-water spray.

Tamaulipas (tämoulē'päs), state (30,734 sq. mi.; pop. 716,029), NE Mexico, on Gulf of Mexico; cap. VICTORIA. Chief cities: MATAMOROS and TAMPICO. Central and W sections are mountainous; S and N have arable plains. Chief products: agr. produce, cattle and hides, asphalt and petroleum. In colonial days called Pánuco, then Nuevo Santander.

tambourine: see PERCUSSION INSTRUMENTS.

Tamerlane (tă'mŭrlān) or **Timur** (tĭmōōr'), c.1336–1405, Mongol conqueror, first of the

TIMURIDS; also called Timur Leng [Timur the lame]. Claimed descent from Jenghiz Khan. From SAMARKAND, his capital, in what is now Russian Turkistan he invaded Persia, S Russia, India (where to took Delhi), and the Levant. In Asia Minor he defeated the Ottoman Turks at Angora (1402) and captured their sultan, Bajazet I. Though notorious for his deeds of cruelty, he was also capable of constructive action; he encouraged the arts and sciences and built vast public works. Christopher Marlowe's play *Tamburlaine* luridly recounts his conquests.

Tamil (tă'mĭl), language of Dravidian family. Grouped with Malayalam. See LANGUAGE (table).

Tammany (tă'mŭnē). The Tammany Society or Columbian Order of New York city, formed c.1786, is only survivor of several Tammany societies founded in various American cities after American Revolution; name was taken from an Indian chief. Its activities at first mostly social, ceremonial, and patriotic, the society became a leading political force, furthering reforms in behalf of the common man, though increasingly controlled by men of privileged classes. Tammany domination of New York city politics began in 1854, and Tammany bosses (e.g., W. M. TWEED, Richard CROKER) were a source of corrupt city politics for many years. Election of 1932 gave Tammany a telling defeat, and it did not regain its former strength in succeeding elections.

Tammerfors, Finland: see TAMPERE.

Tammuz (tă'mŭz''), in Babylonian religion, young god loved by Ishtar. She killed him, but restored him to life. His festival symbolized yearly death and rebirth of vegetation.

Tampa (tăm'pŭ), city (pop. 124,681), W Fla., on fine harbor on Tampa Bay (bridged to Pinellas peninsula), at mouth of Hillsboro R. Chief cigar-mfg. center and phosphate-shipping port in U.S., it is also a major citrus-fruit (esp. grapefruit) canner and shipper. Has mfg. of wood products and shipyards and rail shops. Resort. Probably visited by Narváez in 1528 and by De Soto in 1539. Grew around U.S. Fort Brooke (1823). Taken by Federals in Civil War. City was military base during Spanish-American War; Theodore Roosevelt's Rough Riders trained here. Ybor City in Tampa is hq. of cigar industry and home of its Spanish and Cuban workers. David Isls. (artificial) here are residential.

Tampa Bay, inlet of Gulf of Mexico, c.25 mi. long and 7–12 mi. wide, W Fla. The double-necked bay is sheltered on extreme W by Pinellas peninsula, where is St. Petersburg. E neck dredged to Tampa.

Tampere (täm'pĕrā), Swed. *Tammerfors,* city (pop. 102,910), SW Finland. Its industries (textiles, footwear, iron and pulp mills) receive power from near-by rapids.

Tampico (tämpē'kō), city (pop. 82,475), Tamaulipas, NE Mexico, rivaling Veracruz as Mexico's most important seaport; founded c.1554 on Pánuco R. a few miles inland from Gulf of Mexico. With discovery of oil (c.1900) rapid expansion began. Until Mexico expropriated foreign-owned property (1938), about a third of landowners were American. Besides oil, other exports include cattle and hides, rubber, vanilla, fruits, coconuts, coffee.

Tamworth (tăm'wûrth), municipal borough (pop. 12,889), Staffordshire, England. Burned (9th cent.) by Danes, town was rebuilt (10th cent.) by Æthelflæd. Church of St. Editha was built 8th cent.; rebuilt 1345. Tamworth hogs originally raised here.

Tamworth, resort town (pop. 1,025), E central N.H., NW of Ossipee, in lake and mountain region.

Tana (tä'nä) or **Tsana** (tsä'nä), lake, area c.1,400 sq. mi., NE Ethiopia; largest in Ethiopia. Its outlet is the Blue Nile.

tanager (tă'nŭjŭr), New World migratory perching bird, chiefly tropical. North American species include scarlet tanager; male is scarlet with black wings, tail, beak; female, olive green and yellow.

Tanagra (tă'nŭgrŭ), anc. town, E Boeotia, Greece. Spartans defeated Athenians here 457 B.C. Town is best known for **Tanagra figurines,** delicate statuettes made here in the Hellenistic period.

Tanaka, Giichi, Baron (gē-ē'chē tä'näkä), 1863–1929, Japanese general. Best known as alleged author of so-called Tanaka Memorial (1927) mapping Japan's plans for foreign conquest. Premier 1927–29.

Tananarive (tänänärēv'), city (pop. 171,000), cap. of Madagascar; mfg. and commercial center.

Tancred (Tancred of Lecce) (tăng'krĭd; lĕ'chā), d. 1194, king of Sicily (1190–94); natural son of Roger of Apulia, grandson of Roger II of Sicily. Usurped Sicilian throne from his aunt, Empress CONSTANCE.

Tancred, d. 1112, Crusader; a relative of BOHEMOND I. Took part in capture of Antioch and Jerusalem. Regent of Antioch for Bohemond 1100–1103 and after 1108. Although Bohemond in 1108 submitted to Alexius I, Tancred refused to do the emperor homage.

Taney, Roger Brooke (tô'nē), 1777–1864, Chief Justice of U.S. Supreme Court (1836–64). As U.S. Attorney General (1831–33) and Secretary of State (1833–34), Taney aided Pres. Jackson in struggle with Bank of the United States. As Chief Justice, Taney outraged conservatives by his opinion in Charles River Bridge Case (1837). He felt that state's POLICE POWER entitled it to make reasonable regulatory laws even if they appeared to override provisions of U.S. Constitution. His support of slavery laws was most clearly expressed in DRED SCOTT CASE (1857).

Taneycomo, Lake (tā''nēkō'mō), c.25 mi. long, SW Mo., S of Springfield and near Ark. line. Formed by Forsyth Dam in White R. Resort in the Ozarks.

T'ang (täng), dynasty of China, which ruled 618–906, succeeding the Sui. Empire at its height included Korea and Turkistan. Its highest artistic achievements were in sculpture and poetry. Confucianism provided basis for reforming civil-service examinations. Dynasty's decline began 9th cent.; succeeded by the Sung after chaotic period of Five Dynasties.

Tanganyika (tăng''gŭnyē'kŭ), UN trust territory (343,000 sq. mi.; pop. 7,412,327), E Africa, on Indian Ocean; cap. Dar-es-

Salaam. Under British administration. Borders are formed partly by Victoria Nyanza, L. Tanganyika, and L. Nyasa. Comprises coastal lowlands and high central plateau rising to Mt. Kilimanjaro (19,565 ft.). Diamonds, gold, and tin are mined. Crops include sisal, cotton, tobacco, coffee, and peanuts. Most of the natives are Bantu. The coast, which had previously been ruled from Zanzibar, was explored in 16th cent. by the Portuguese. In 17th cent., when area came under Arab sultans of Muscat, there was much trade in ivory and slaves. Brought under German protection in 1885, the area was called German East Africa until 1920 when it became a British mandate under League of Nations. Became a UN trust territory in 1945.

Tanganyika, Lake, area 12,700 sq. mi., E central Africa, in Great Rift Valley, forming boundary between Belgian Congo and Tanganyika. It is c.450 mi. long and 15–50 mi. wide. About 4,700 ft. deep, it is the world's deepest fresh-water lake except for L. Baikal. Discovered 1858 by John Speke and Sir Richard Burton. Explored in 1870s by David Livingstone and Henry Stanley.

tangerine, small, thin-skinned variety of mandarin orange (*Citrus reticulata*) with a sweet, dry pulp. It is easily peeled. The tangelo is a hybrid, the result of crossing the tangerine and grapefruit.

Tangier (tănjēr'), international zone (147 sq. mi.; pop. c.151,000), NW Africa, on Strait of Gibraltar and bordered by Spanish Morocco. Zone is named for port city of Tangier, where most of the population lives. City consists of a walled Moorish town and modern garden suburb. Probably founded by the Phoenicians, Tangier was successively under the Romans, Portuguese, Arabs, Spaniards, English, and Moors. In 19th cent. it became a focus of the dispute among the European powers over MOROCCO. In accordance with convention of 1925 the area is governed by the consuls of major European powers and by a legislative assembly headed by a representative of sultan of Morocco.

Tangier (tănjēr'), town (pop. 915) on Tangier Isl., E Va., in Chesapeake Bay near Eastern Shore of Md.; island discovered by John Smith 1608, town settled in late 17th cent.

Tanglewood: see LENOX, Mass.

Tanis (tā'nĭs), anc. city, NE Egypt, cap. of XXI dynasty. Important in strategy and commerce until it was abandoned. The biblical Zoan.

Tanjore (tănjôr'), town (pop. 68,702), S Madras, India. Has noted 11th-cent. Dravidian temple. Long known for silks, carpets, and jewelry.

tank, military, armored vehicle with caterpillar traction, armed with weapons for offense in warfare, first used by the British on the Somme (1916) in World War I. Tanks were highly important in World War II, notably in the campaigns in N Africa.

Tannenberg (tä'nŭnbĕrk"), Pol. *Sztymbark,* village near Allenstein, former East Prussia; after 1945 in Polish-administered territory. In 1410 the Poles and Lithuanians under Ladislaus II defeated the Teutonic Knights between Tannenberg and near-by Grünwald, thus halting the order's eastward expansion. In World War I the Germans under Hindenburg and Ludendorff routed the Russian army under Samsonov at Tannenberg, taking over 100,000 prisoners (Aug. 26-30, 1914). Samsonov committed suicide. A second Russian army, under Rennenkampf (whose failure to come to Samsonov's aid has been much criticized), was defeated soon afterward in the battle of the MASURIAN LAKES.

Tannhäuser (tän'hoizŭr), 13th cent., German minnesinger at the court of the duke of Austria. According to a legend, he escaped from the Venusberg but was refused papal absolution until the miraculous budding of his staff indicated divine grace. The legend is used in Wagner's opera *Tannhäuser.*

tannin and **tannic acid,** astringent, water-soluble compounds found associated in many plants; terms are commonly used as synonyms. Used as tanning agent, in inks, as mordant in dyeing, and to clarify solutions. Syntans are synthesized tannins.

tanning, process of converting skins and hides into leather. Methods include vegetable tanning with tannin, used for heavy leathers; mineral tanning with chrome (commonly used for light leathers) or alum; methods employing artificial agents (syntans).

Tannu-Tuva, RSFSR: see TUVA AUTONOMOUS OBLAST.

tansy, strong-scented European perennial herb (*Tanacetum vulgare*), with fine-cut foliage and clustered yellow, buttonlike flowers. Naturalized in America, it was long used in cookery and for medicinal tea.

tantalum (tăn'tŭlŭm), rare, lustrous, silver-white metallic element (symbol = Ta; see also ELEMENT, table). Has great ductility and malleability, high resistance to acids and corrosion. Used in making laboratory apparatus and surgical instruments.

Tantalus (tăn'tŭlŭs), in Greek legend, a king. His father, Zeus, angered by his insolence, condemned him to Tartarus. There he suffered thirst and hunger in presence of water and fruit he could not reach.

Tantum ergo, hymn: see PANGE LINGUA.

Taoism (dou'ĭzŭm, tou'–), philosophical system of China, chiefly derived from the book *Tao-teh-king,* ascribed to LAO-TZE, elucidated by Chuang-Tze. Broadly the *Tao* is the path natural events take, with spontaneous creativity and regular alternation (e.g., day and night). Man to follow the *Tao* gives up all striving; his highest goal is to escape from the illusion of desire through mystical contemplation. Taoism, a fully developed religious system by the 5th cent. A.D., adopted many gods and developed monastic orders. Taoists later tended to stress alchemy and the search for the elixir of immortality. It offered more emotional outlet than the rival system, Confucianism.

Taormina (täōrmē'nä), town (pop. 4,293), E Sicily, Italy; a winter resort near Ionian Sea at foot of Mt. Etna. Has remains of large Greek theater.

Taos (tous), resort village (pop. 1,815; alt. c.7,000 ft.), N N.Mex., between Sangre de Cristo Mts. and Rio Grande. Founded in early 1600s by Spanish; long-time center of Spanish-Indian trade; hub of Pueblo revolt of 1680 and anti-American Indian revolt of 1847. In scenic region, Taos developed after 1898 as a colony for painters and writers, notably D. H. Lawrence. Has art groups, galleries, Harwood Foundation of Univ. of New Mexico, and Kit Carson's house. Near are adobe farm village with old mission and **Taos,** Indian pueblo village (1948 pop. 921). Seat in early 1600s of San Gerónimo mission, destroyed in Pueblo revolt of 1680. Scene of 1847 revolt, in which Indians killed Gov. Charles Bent. Tanoan language. Grain, livestock raised. Corn and sundown ceremonial dances.

tapa cloth: see BARK CLOTH.

Tapajós (täpäzhôsh'), river formed at border of Mato Grosso, Pará, and Amazonas states, N Brazil, and flowing c.500 mi. NNE into Amazon R. at Santarém.

tapestry, heavy hand-woven fabric of plain weave, made by threading the design of weft threads into the warp with the fingers or a bobbin. The warp (linen or wool), entirely covered by the weft (wool, silk, or metal), is evident only as ribs. Each color is worked in separately, in blocks or patches; the slits between blocks are later sewn up. The name tapestry is sometimes given to materials woven on Jacquard looms and to types of carpets and upholstery stuffs. The so-called BAYEUX TAPESTRY is actually an embroidery. History of tapestry is continuous; true tapestries were woven in ancient Egypt, China, Greece, and pre-Columbian Peru. European wool tapestries from the 10th or 11th cent. are preserved, and beautiful examples from 14th to 17th cent. are treasured by museums and cathedrals. The first great French weaving was done, in wool, at Arras in the 14th cent. (hence the name, Arras, given to tapestry in use in England long before any was made there); other notable centers were Brussels, Paris (particularly after rise in 17th cent. of Gobelins works, still in operation), Beauvais, and Aubusson. France leads in weaving modern tapestries.

tapeworm, parasitic cestode flat worm. Some species spend one stage of life cycle in muscle tissue of certain mammals and fish; if tissue is eaten improperly cooked, worm may enter host from whose intestinal walls it absorbs food. Some grow many feet long.

tapioca (tăpēō'ků), starchy food obtained by heating the root of the bitter CASSAVA. Sold as flour, flakes, or pellets, it is used to thicken puddings and soups.

tapir (tā'půr), nocturnal, herbivorous ungulate mammal (genus *Tapirus*) of Central and South America and SE Asia.

Tappan, Arthur (tă'půn), 1786–1865, American abolitionist. First president of American Anti-Slavery Society; split with W. L. Garrison. His brother, **Lewis Tappan,** 1788–1873, was also an abolitionist.

Tappan (tăpăn'), village (1940 pop. 1,249), SE N.Y., SW of Nyack. De Wint mansion was Washington's hq. 1780, 1783. John André was tried and hanged here.

Tappan Zee: see HUDSON, river.

Tar, river rising in N N.C. and flowing 217 mi. SE to Pamlico Sound. Called the Pamlico below Washington, N.C.

Tara (tă'rů), village, Co. Meath, Ireland. Hill of Tara was until 6th cent. seat of Irish kings. Supposedly the Coronation Stone of the ancient high kings was here. There are ruins.

tar and pitch, viscous, black substances obtained from destructive distillation of coal, wood, petroleum, etc. Tar is more fluid than pitch. Most tar produced now is fractionated to give naphtha, creosote, and other crude products; pine wood tar is used in soap and medications. Pitch is used to make roofing paper, as lubricant, in varnishes.

Taranto (tä'räntō), Latin *Tarentum,* city (pop. 103,306), Apulia, S Italy, on Gulf of Taranto, an arm of the Ionian Sea. Major naval base; agr., commercial, and fishing center. A flourishing town of Magna Graecia, it resisted Rome until 272 B.C. Was strongly fortified under kingdom of Naples. Restored cathedral dates from 11th cent.; Byzantine castle was restored 1480.

tarantula (tůrăn'chůlů, –tůlů), wolf spider (*Lycosa tarantula*) of Italy. Name is also applied to some Asiatic spiders and various species of large, dark, hairy spiders (family Aviculariidae) of W Hemisphere. *Tarantula* is genus name of certain tailless whip scorpions.

Tarascan (tärä'skän), Indian people of Michoacán, Mexico. Stubbornly resisted Aztec and Spanish domination. Depend on agr. and fishing (in L. Pátzcuaro) for livelihood. Former cap. Tzintzuntzan.

Tarascon (täräskõ'), town (pop. 4,919), Bouches-du-Rhône dept., SE France, on the Rhone. Was immortalized by Alphonse Daudet in his *Tartarin de Tarascon.* Its medieval castle was the residence of RENÉ of Anjou.

Tarawa: see GILBERT ISLANDS.

Tarbell, Ida M(inerva), 1857–1944, American author. One of the "muckrakers," who attacked evils in American business, she wrote a much-read *History of the Standard Oil Company* (2 vols., 1904). Also wrote books on Lincoln.

Tarbes (tärb), city (pop. 42,778), cap. of Hautes-Pyrénées dept., SW France, on Adour R. Has Romanesque cathedral (11th–13th cent.). Tourist center.

Tarboro (tär'bŭrů), town (pop. 8,120), E N.C., E of Rocky Mount and on Tar R. Farm center (tobacco, peanuts, corn) with cotton mills.

Tarde, Gabriel de (gäbrēĕl' dů tärd'), 1843–1904, French sociologist and criminologist, known for his general social theory, distinguishing between inventive and imitative persons.

Tardieu, André (ãdrā' tärdyû'), 1876–1945, French statesman, a conservative and nationalist. Helped write Treaty of Versailles. Was premier in 1929–30 and in 1932. His insistence on safeguard of French security wrecked Disarmament Conference of 1932.

tare (târ), a VETCH. The tare of the Bible was probably darnel rye grass (*Lolium temulentum*).

Tarentum (tůrĕn'tům), borough (pop. 9,540), SW Pa., on Allegheny R. and NE of Pittsburgh. Mfg. of metal, wood, and paper products; coal mining.

Targoviste (tŭr"gôvēsh'tě), town (pop. 26,-

038), S central Rumania, in Walachia. Commercial center. Cap. of Walachia 1383–1698. Has remarkable 16th-cent. cathedral.

Targul-Mures (tûr'gōōl-mōō'rĕsh) or **Targu-Mures** (tûr'gōō–), Hung. *Maros Vásárhely,* city (pop. 47,043), central Rumania, in Transylvania, on Mures R. Agr. processing; oil refinery. Old cultural center dating from 12th cent. Has Telekiana library (13th cent.), repository of valuable manuscripts; modern "cultural" palace, containing art gallery, ethnographic museum, library, and conservatory of music. Under Hungary 1940–45.

Targum (tär'gŭm) [Aramaic,= translation], Aramaic paraphrase of the Old Testament written when Aramaic replaced Hebrew among Jews of Palestine and Babylon.

Tarifa (tärē'fä), city (pop. 6,362), S Spain, in Andalusia, a fortified seaport on Strait of Gibraltar. Southernmost city of European mainland.

tariff: see CUSTOMS; FREE TRADE; PROTECTION.

Tariff Commission, United States, created (1916) by act of U.S. Congress. Consists of six members, who advise on tariff legislation. Since 1949 the commission has had further functions in administration of reciprocal trade agreements.

Tarik (tä'rĭk), fl. 711, Berber conqueror of Spain. Crossed 711 from Africa to Gibraltar (named for him, in Arabic, Jebel-al-Tarik, i.e., Tarik's mountain); defeated King RODERICK.

Tarim (därēm'), river, c.1,300 mi. long, Sinkiang prov., China. Terminates in marshes near Lob Nor.

Tarkington, (Newton) Booth, 1869–1946, American author and dramatist, b. Indianapolis. Realistic novels on Indiana include *The Gentleman from Indiana* (1899); *The Turmoil* (1915); *The Magnificent Ambersons* (1918); *The Midlander* (1923); *Alice Adams* (1921). His highly popular stories of boyhood include *Penrod* (1914) and *Seventeen* (1916). He dramatized his romance, *Monsieur Beaucaire* (1900), which was also a successful movie, as were other novels.

Tarn (tärn), department (2,232 sq. mi.; pop. 298,117), S France, in Languedoc; cap. Albi. The **Tarn** river, 233 mi. long, rises in the Cévennes and flows SW past Albi and Montauban into the Garonne.

Tarn-et-Garonne (–ā-gärôn'), department (1,440 sq. mi.; pop. 167,664), SW France, in Guienne and Languedoc, cap. Montauban.

Tarnopol (tärnô'pôl), Rus. *Ternopol,* city (1931 pop. 35,831), W Ukraine, on the Seret. Agr. center. Once an important fortress, it passed from Poland to Austria 1772; reverted to Poland 1919; was ceded to USSR 1945. Here in 1915 Russians resisted Austrians.

Tarnow, Pol. *Tarnów* (tär'nōōf), city (pop. 33,108), S Poland. Trade center. Noted for medieval architecture, particularly cathedral (c.1400). Was under Austrian rule 1772–1918.

taro (tä'rō, tâ'rō), name for several coarse, perennial herbs (genus *Colocasia*). The starchy rootstocks (baked, boiled, or made into poi) form a major food in many tropical and subtropical regions. The common taro (*Colocasia antiquorum*), probably native to SE Asia, has been introduced in tropical Africa and America. Dasheen (*C. esculenta*) has mealy flesh rich in carbohydrates and proteins; it is sometimes considered a variant of taro rather than a separate species. Because of their large ornamental leaves some taro plants are called elephant's-ear.

tarpan (tär'păn) or **Przhevalsky's horse** (pûrzhĭväl'skēz), wild horse of central Asia, the only extant wild horse not descended from tame horses. Smaller than domestic horse, it is dun color with brown mane (short, erect) and tail, large head, bulging forehead. Breeds in captivity; seen in some zoological gardens. Name *Przhevalsky's horse* is in honor of Russian explorer.

Tarpeia (tärpē'yŭ), in Roman legend, woman who betrayed her city to Sabines for their gold bracelets. They killed her. **Tarpeian Rock** at Rome, from which criminals were thrown, bears her name.

tarpon (tär'pŏn), large herringlike marine game fish (genus *Tarpon*). Ranges from Long Island to Brazil and Africa; sometimes enters rivers. It has silvery scales and is 6–8 ft. long.

Tarpon Springs, city (pop. 4,323), W Fla., on Gulf coast NW of Tampa. Major sponge-fishing center. Greek religious festivals draw visitors.

Tarquin (tär'kwĭn), Latin *Tarquinius,* legendary Etruscan family ruling in early Rome. **Lucius Tarquinius Priscus** is said to have come to Rome on the advice of his prophetess wife, Tanaquil. There he was made king (616 B.C.). His son, **Lucius Tarquinius Superbus** (Tarquin the Proud), murdered his father-in-law, Servius Tullius, to get the throne. He ruled with despotism and cruelty. His son, **Sextus Tarquinius,** ravaged LUCRECE, wife of his kinsman, **Tarquinius Collatinus.** The Romans drove Tarquin the Proud from the throne (510 B.C.). Lars Porsena restored the family but only briefly (c.500? B.C.).

tarragon, tender perennial Old World herb (*Artemisia dracunculus*), related to wormwood. It is a flavoring for vinegars, salads, sauces, and soups.

Tarragona (tärägō'nä), city (pop. 33,708), cap. of Tarragona prov., NE Spain, in Catalonia; a Mediterranean port. Archiepiscopal see. Wine. Captured by Romans 218 B.C.; became cap. of **Tarraconensis** prov. Recovered from Moors 1089. Ruins include Roman and pre-Roman walls. There is a well-preserved Roman aqueduct. Romanesque-Gothic cathedral has one of finest cloisters (13th cent.) in Spain.

Tarrant (tă'rŭnt) or **Tarrant City,** city (pop. 7,571), N central Ala., near Birmingham. Foundry products.

Tarrytown, residential village (pop. 8,851), SE N.Y., on Hudson R. and N of New York city; settled 17th cent. by Dutch. Auto assembling. Near by is Marymount Col. (R.C.; for women; 1918).

Tarsus (tär'sŭs), city (pop. 33,822), S Turkey, on the Tarsus (anc. Cydnus); agr. center. Ancient Tarsus was cap. of Cilicia and a major city in Asia Minor. Birthplace of St. Paul.

tartan: see PLAID.

tartar (tär'tůr) or **argol** (är'gůl), impure acid potassium tartrate deposited as crust in vessels with fermented wine. CREAM OF TARTAR is purified form.

tartar emetic, white, crystalline, water-soluble salt. Used as emetic, expectorant, diaphoretic, and in dyeing and calico printing as a mordant.

Tartars: see TATARS.

Tartarus: see HELL.

Tartini, Giuseppe (tärtē'nē), 1692–1770, Italian violinist, the greatest master of his day. He altered the shape of the bow and revised bowing technique. He composed much violin music, including the G major sonata and the famous *Devil's Trill,* supposedly played to him by the devil in a dream.

Tartu (tär'tōō), Ger. and Swed. *Dorpat,* city (pop. c.71,000), E Estonia. Its noted university (founded 1632 by Gustavus II of Sweden) makes it the cultural center of Estonia. Tartu was founded 1030 by a Kievan prince; fell to Livonian Knights 1224; joined Hanseatic League 14th cent.; was contested after 1561 among Russia, Sweden, and Poland; fell to Peter I of Russia 1704. It has an old castle and a 13th-cent. cathedral.

Tashkent (tăshkĕnt', täsh–), city (pop. 585,-005), cap. of Uzbek SSR, in Tashkent oasis, on Trans-Caspian RR. Largest and one of oldest cities of central Asia. Has large cotton-textile industry. Seat of Central Asian State Univ. and of other scientific and cultural institutions. Founded 7th cent, it passed from Arabic rule to shahs of Khorezm in 12th cent. A center on Samarkand-Peking trade route, it was conquered 13th cent. by Jenghiz Khan and 1361 by Tamerlane. As part of khanate of KOKAND it fell to Russia in 1865 and became cap. of Russian Turkistan. Has few historic relics. Tashkent oasis produces fruit, vegetables, cotton, silk.

Tasman, Abel Janszoon (tăz'mŭn), 1603?–1659, Dutch navigator. Made trading and exploring voyages (c.1632–1653) in Pacific and Indian oceans. Discovered Tasmania, New Zealand; sailed around Australia.

Tasmania (tăzmā'nēŭ), island, area c.24,450 sq. mi., S of SE Australia, between Indian Ocean and Tasman Sea and separated from Victoria by Bass Strait. Geologically a continuation of Australian continent. Mountainous and partly forested. Exports wool, canned fruit, and metals (copper, zinc, tin, lead, gold, and silver). Fauna includes the marsupials popularly known as the Tasmanian tiger and Tasmanian devil. The island was discovered 1642 by Tasman, who named it Van Diemen's Land. Visited 1777 by Capt. James Cook and brought under British control in 1803, when a penal colony was estab. here. **Tasmania** state (26,215 sq. mi.; pop. 257,117), with cap. at Hobart, is part of the Commonwealth of Australia. Attached to New South Wales until 1825, it joined the commonwealth as a state in 1901.

Tasman Sea, arm of the S Pacific, with SE Australia and Tasmania on W and New Zealand on E.

Tasso, Torquato (tōrkwä'tō täs'sō), 1544–95, Italian epic poet, b. Sorrento. Wrote *Jerusalem Delivered* (1575; Ital., *Gerusalemme liberata*), an epic rivaling Ariosto's *Orlando Furioso* in popularity. Tasso also wrote the pastoral drama *Aminta.*

taste, sense produced by stimulation of taste buds, which occur chiefly on tongue. Four fundamental tastes are—bitter, salt, sweet, acid.

Tatar Autonomous Soviet Socialist Republic (tä'tůr), administrative division (26,100 sq. mi.; pop. 2,919,423), E central European RSFSR, in middle Volga and lower Kama valleys; cap. KAZAN. Predominantly agr. Rich in timber. Population is 49% Turco-Tatar (Moslems) and 43% Russian.

Tatars (tä'tůrz) or **Tartars** (tär'tůrz), collective name applied to peoples that overran parts of Asia and Europe under Mongol leadership in 13th cent. The original Tatars probably came from E central Asia or central Siberia. After the wave of invasion receded eastward, the Tatars continued to dominate nearly all of Russia and Siberia. The Empire of the GOLDEN HORDE lasted until the late 15th cent., when it broke up into several independent khanates, which fell to the Ottoman Turks and Tsar Ivan IV. Nevertheless Siberia long continued to be known as Tartary and CRIMEA as Little Tartary. By the late 16th cent. the majority of the Tatars in Russia had reached a high degree of civilization, and only minorities (e.g., the Nogais) remained nomadic. The whole course of Russian history shows great Tatar influence. In 1939 there were c.4,300,000 Tatars in the USSR. They speak a Turkic language and are mainly Moslems. They predominate in Tatar ASSR, but the majority live dispersed in E European RSFSR and in W Siberia.

Tate, Allen, 1899–, American poet and critic. Helped found the magazine *Fugitive* to express Southern agrarian views. Taught at Princeton and other universities, held chair of poetry at Library of Congress (1943–44). Works include *Poems, 1922–1947* (1948) and essay *On the Limits of Poetry* (1948).

Tate, Nahum (nā'hům), 1652–1715, British poet, poet laureate after 1692. Collaborated with Dryden on second part of *Absalom and Achitophel* (1682).

Tate Gallery, Millbank, London, originally the National Gall. of British Art; opened 1897. Building and original collection were given by the sugar merchant and philanthropist Sir Henry Tate. Notable features are the Turner wing (gift of Sir Joseph Duveen), a gallery of works of John Singer Sargent, and four galleries of modern foreign art.

Tatler, journal: see SPECTATOR.

Tatra (tä'trů) or **Tatras,** Pol. and Slovak *Tatry,* highest mountain group of Carpathians, extending along Polish-Czechoslovak border. Stalin Peak (formerly Franz Joseph Spitze and Gerlachovka) rises to 8,737 ft. Has many mountaineering and winter sports resorts, notably Zakopane (Poland).

Tauber, Richard (tou'bůr), 1892–1948, Austrian tenor. Although he was noted as an opera and lieder singer, he was best known for his work in operettas, particularly those of Lehar.

Tauler, Johannes (tou'lůr), c.1300–1361, German mystic, a Dominican, disciple of Meister Eckhart. Associated with the popular mystical movement, the Friends of God, he was a notable preacher.

Taunton (tôn'tŭn), municipal borough (pop. 33,613), co. seat of Somerset, England; trade center. Lord Jeffreys held "Bloody Assizes" here in 1685.

Taunton (tăn'tŭn, tôn–), city (pop. 40,109), SE Mass., on Taunton R.; area settled 1638. Textiles, silverware, stoves, machinery, and plastics.

Taupo, Lake (tou'pō), largest lake of New Zealand, area 238 sq. mi., on central North Isl.

Tauroggen or **Taurage, Convention of:** see YORCK VON WARTENBURG.

Taurus (tô'rŭs), mountain chain, S Turkey, extending parallel to Mediterranean coast of S Asia Minor. Its NE extension is called the Anti-Taurus. Rises to 12,251 ft. at Ala Dag. Chain is crossed, N of Tarsus, by CILICIAN GATES. Mineral deposits include chromium, copper, silver, and lignite.

Taurus (tô'rŭs) [Latin,= the bull], sign of ZODIAC.

tavern: see INN.

Tawas City (tô'wŭs), city (pop. 1,441), N Mich., on Tawas Bay, inlet of Saginaw Bay. Resort and commercial fishing center.

Tawney, R(ichard) H(enry) (tô'nē), 1880–, English economist, author of *Religion and the Rise of Capitalism* (1926).

taxation, regular levy to provide revenue for a government. Emergency levies and special fees (such as postage) are not taxes. Ease of collection is accounted a merit in a tax, and ability to pay is one test of the amount that an individual should contribute. See INCOME TAX; SINGLE TAX; POLL TAX.

Taxco (tä'skō), city (pop. 4,963), Guerrero, SW Mexico. Founded as silver-mining community (1529), it was also important stop between Mexico City and Acapulco in Spanish colonial trade with Philippines. Kept as an example of colonial town, it is a tourist center.

Tay (tā), largest river of Scotland, 118 mi. long. Rising in Argyllshire, it is called Fillan as far as Loch Dochart and then called Dochart as far as Loch Tay (14½ mi. long and 1 mi. wide). It enters North Sea through tidal Firth of Tay (25 mi. long). River has valuable salmon fisheries.

Taylor, Bayard, 1825–78, American journalist and author. Correspondent for New York *Tribune,* he traveled widely and wrote travel books, such as *Views Afoot* (1846). Verse in such volumes as *Poems of the Orient* (1854) is highly rhymed, singable, and exotic in content (as in "Bedouin Love Song"). His verse translation of Goethe's *Faust* is still read.

Taylor, Brook, 1685–1731, English mathematician. Known for Taylor's theorem (complex mathematical formula concerning functions), which forms basis of differential calculus; first exposition of principle of vanishing points; solution of problem of center of oscillation which led to mathematical expression of principles governing vibration of string.

Taylor, (Joseph) Deems, 1885–, American composer and music critic. His compositions include the orchestral suite *Through the Looking Glass* and the operas *The King's Henchman* (libretto by Edna St. Vincent Millay) and *Peter Ibbetson* (based on George Du Maurier's novel). Also a newspaper music critic and music consultant and commentator for radio.

Taylor, Edward, c.1645–1729, American poet and clergyman, long a Congregational minister at Westfield, Mass.

Taylor, Edward Thompson, 1793–1871, American Methodist missionary preacher, called Father Taylor. A sailor in youth, he began in 1830 his successful work as missionary in Seamen's Bethel, Boston. He appears as Father Mapple in Melville's *Moby Dick.*

Taylor, Francis Henry, 1903–, American museum director. Director of Worcester (Mass.) Art Mus. (1931–40) and of Metropolitan Mus., New York (1940–).

Taylor, Henry Osborn, 1856–1941, American scholar, author of the much-admired *The Medieval Mind* (1911).

Taylor, Jeremy, 1613–67, English bishop, theological and devotional writer. Chaplain to Archbishop Laud and chaplain in ordinary to Charles I, he received on the Restoration (1660) bishopric of Down and Connor in Ireland. In sermons he was master of fine metaphor and poetic imagination. Author of *Holy Living* (1650) and *Holy Dying* (1651).

Taylor, John, 1753–1824, American political philosopher. Known as "John Taylor of Caroline." Early formulator of STATES' RIGHTS doctrine. His greatest work is *An Inquiry into the Principles and Policy of the Government of the United States* (1814).

Taylor, John, 1808–87, American Mormon leader, b. England. In the U.S. he was made (1838) apostle and missionary. He succeeded Brigham Young as president of Mormon church.

Taylor, Tom, 1817–80, English dramatist, editor of *Punch* (1874–80). Wrote over 100 plays, notably *Our American Cousin* (1858) and *The Ticket of Leave Man* (1863).

Taylor, Zachary (ză'kŭrē), 1784–1850, 12th President of the United States. Won nickname of "Old Rough and Ready" in army campaigns against Indians. Commanding U.S. troops in MEXICAN WAR, he won victories at Palo Alto, Resaca de la Palma, and Buena Vista. Elected President on Whig party ticket, he took office in 1849. On his death Millard Fillmore became president. Taylor's son, **Richard (Dick) Taylor,** 1826–79, was a Confederate general. Fought in Shenandoah Valley and Seven Days battles. Commander in W La. (1862), later commander of Lower South.

Taylor. 1 Industrial borough (pop. 7,176), NE Pa., on Lackawanna R. and near Scranton. **2** City (pop. 9,071), central Texas, NNE of Austin. Center of agr. area with mattress factory; meat and poultry packing.

Taylorville, city (pop. 9,188), central Ill., SE of Springfield. Center of farm and coal area with mfg. of paper, feed, and tools.

Tb, chemical symbol of the element TERBIUM.

Tbilisi, Georgian SSR: see TIFLIS.

Tc, chemical symbol of the element TECHNETIUM.

Tch–. For Russian names not listed thus, see CH–; e.g., Tchekhoff, see CHEKHOV.

Tchaikovsky, Piotr Ilich (pyô'tŭr ĭlyēch' chĭkôf'skē), 1840–93, Russian composer. He taught at the Moscow Conservatory until an annuity from a wealthy patroness, Mme von Meck (whom he knew only through letters), allowed him to devote himself to composition. His music, melodious and emotional, is perhaps today the most popular and most often played of all notable composers. Most successful are his orchestral works—his last three symphonies, including the Fifth Symphony and the Sixth, or Pathetique, Symphony; the fantasies *Romeo and Juliet* and *Francesca da Rimini;* the ballets *Swan Lake, The Sleeping Beauty,* and the *Nutcracker;* the Piano Concerto in B Flat Minor; the Violin Concerto in D; and the popular "1812" Overture. His operas include *Eugene Onegin* and *Pique Dame* (*The Queen of Spades*), both based on stories by Pushkin; of his many songs, perhaps *None But the Lonely Heart* is best known. He conducted at the opening concert in Carnegie Hall in 1891. Tschaikowsky is another spelling of the name.

Tchelitchew, Pavel (chĕlĭ'chĕf, Rus. pä'vĭl chĭlyĕ'chĭf), 1898–, Russian-American painter. His technique involves the juxtaposition of many objects in such a way that most of them are not apparent at first glance. Best-known work is *Hide and Seek* (Mus. of Modern Art, New York).

Te, chemical symbol of the element TELLURIUM.

tea, a tree or bush, its leaves, and the beverage made from them. The common tea plant (*Camellia sinensis* or *Thea sinensis*), an evergreen native to E Asia, grows to c.30 ft., but is usually pruned in cultivation to 3–5 ft. Leading producers are India, China, Ceylon, Indonesia, Japan, Formosa. Shrubs, propagated from seed, can be picked in three years and may yield for 50 years. Leaves are picked by hand during active growth periods and are then withered, rolled, and fired (or heated). For green tea, firing follows close upon picking; for black, leaves are fermented for c.24 hours; for oolong, intermediate in flavor and color, they are partly fermented. Most teas are classed under either the Chinese or the English system of nomenclature; some are named for the growing district. Flavor of tea is produced by volatile oils, the stimulating properties by caffeine, and the astringency by tannin. Tea is world's most widely used beverage other than water.

Teach, Edward: see BLACKBEARD.

teak (tēk), tall, deciduous tree (*Tectona grandis*), native to India, Burma, and Siam, with 10- to 20-inch rough-surfaced leaves. Teakwood, which darkens on exposure, is hard but easily worked; it is used for shipbuilding, agricultural implements, flooring.

Teaneck (tē'nĕk"), residential suburban township (pop. 33,772), NE N.J., E of Hackensack.

Teapot Dome, area near Casper, Wyo., set aside by Pres. Wilson in 1915 as naval oil reserve, transferred to Dept. of the Interior in 1921. In 1922 A. B. FALL, Secretary of the Interior, leased, without competitive bidding, the Teapot Dome fields and another field in Calif. Senate investigation under Sen. T. J. Walsh led to criminal prosecutions, bringing notoriety upon a number of prominent officials.

tear gas, gas (usually a compound of bromine), causing temporary blindness through excessive flow of tears. Used in warfare and mob dispersal.

Teasdale, Sara, 1884–1933, American lyric poet. Her *Collected Poems* appeared in 1937.

teasel (tē'zŭl), Old World thistlelike biennial plant with small lilac flower heads. The common teasel (*Dipsacus sylvestris*) is naturalized in North America. Fuller's teasel (*D. fullonum*) was long used to raise the nap on wool. Both species are grown for use in EVERLASTING bouquets.

Teche, Bayou (bī'ō tĕsh', bī'ōō), S La., flows from E of Lafayette SE between Atchafalaya basin and Gulf of Mexico to Atchafalaya R. Navigable for over 100 mi. Setting for Longfellow's *Evangeline*.

tecnetium (tĕknē'shŭm), silvery metallic element (symbol = Tc; atomic no. = 43), similar to rhenium in properties. Existence reported in 1925 (then called masurium); radioactive isotopes produced 1937.

Tecumseh (tĭkŭm'sē), 1768?–1813, chief of the SHAWNEE INDIANS. Sought to unite Indian tribes against U.S. Plan failed with defeat of his brother Tenskwatawa, the SHAWNEE PROPHET, at Tippecanoe (1811). Aided British in War of 1812; killed at battle of the THAMES.

Tedder, Arthur William Tedder, 1st **Baron,** 1890–, British air chief marshal. Helped sweep Germans from Libya (1941–43). Deputy supreme commander and chief of allied air operations in W Europe (1944). Air chief of staff 1946–50.

Teddington, former urban district, now part of Twickenham, Middlesex, England, on the Thames. Port of London officially begins here.

Te Deum laudamus (tā dē'ōōm loudä'mōōs [Latin,= we praise Thee, O God], anc. hymn of the Western Church, dating from the 4th or 5th cent. It is sung at morning prayer in Anglican churches and is the chief hymn of rejoicing of the Roman Catholic Church.

Tees, river rising in Cumberland, England, and flowing c.70 mi. E to the North Sea.

teeth, structures embedded in jaws of many vertebrates and serving chiefly to masticate food. In man a set of 20 deciduous teeth (also called milk teeth) begins to erupt at c.6 months; these are replaced by 32 permanent teeth erupting after sixth year. Each tooth is composed of dentine surrounding core of nerves and blood vessels; visible portion (crown) is coated with enamel; cement-coated roots are attached to jaw by membrane.

Tegucigalpa (tāgōō"sēgäl'pä), city (pop. 55,-755 including Comayagüela, its twin city across river), S central Honduras, cap. and largest city of republic, in mountain valley. Founded late 16th cent., it was colonial mining center.

Teheran (tē"hŭrän'), or **Tehran** (tĕrän'), city (pop. 989,871), cap. of Iran, in N Iran, at foot of Elburz mts. and c.70 mi. S of Caspian Sea; commercial center. Trans-Iranian RR connects it with Persian Gulf and with Caspian Sea. University here was founded 1934. City is near ancient Rages and was itself a medieval town. Its rise dates from 1788, when Aga Mohamad Khan made it the capital. Modernized by Reza Shah Pahlevi, it has grown steadily in recent years. An important war conference was held here in 1943.

Teheran Conference, Nov. 28–Dec. 1, 1943, meeting of Pres. F. D. Roosevelt, Prime Minister Churchill, and Premier Stalin in World War II. Agreed on scope and timing of war against Germany and cooperation of UN for problems for peace. Protocol pledged respect for sovereignty and integrity of Iran.

Tehuantepec (tāwäntāpĕk′), town (pop. 6,731), Oaxaca, S Mexico, on wide bend of river not far from Gulf of Tehuantepec, an arm of Pacific. Town is on S end of Isthmus of Tehuantepec, a narrow strip of land between Gulf of Campeche and Gulf of Tehuantepec. Climate is hot and tropical; the population is largely Zapotec.

Teixeira, Pedro (pä′drō tä′shärü), d. 1640, Portuguese explorer, one of the early voyagers on the Amazon (1637–38).

Tejo, river: see TAGUS.

Tekoa or **Tekoah** (both: tēkō′ŭ), anc. town, S of Bethlehem, at the extreme edge of cultivated lands and at the beginning of the wilderness of Tekoa. This wilderness was the home of Amos.

Tel-Aviv (tĕl″ŭvēv′), city (pop. c.250,000), central Israel, on the Mediterranean; founded 1909. Largest city and financial center of Israel; a joint municipality with adjoining Jaffa (since 1949). Has textile mills and clothing factories. Cultural institutions include Herzliah Hebrew Col. and famed Habima theater. After World War II there was sporadic fighting between this all-Jewish city and Jaffa, then predominantly Arab. State of Israel was proclaimed here, May 14, 1948.

telegraph. Name now generally restricted to electric telegraph but used earlier for methods of signaling, by sound or sight, beyond the range of human voice. Method of electric signaling that has come into general use over most of world is based on invention by S. F. B. Morse; electric circuit is set up generally with only a single overhead wire and using earth as other conductor to complete the circuit. Signals are sent by making and breaking current in this circuit. Receiving instrument is actuated by an electromagnet; reception by sound, in which Morse code signals are received as audible clicks, has proved swift and reliable method. First permanently successful telegraphic cable crossing Atlantic Ocean was laid in 1866. J. B. Stearns introduced (1872) method of sending two messages over same wire at same time and Thomas A. Edison invented (1874) "quadruplex" method for sending four messages over same wire at same time. Later instruments include those for receiving messages in printed form (e.g., by teletypewriter), for transmitting messages in handwriting of sender (telautograph), for transmitting photographs and other pictures. For wireless telegraphy, see RADIO.

Teleki, Count Paul, Hung. *Teleki Pál* (tĕ′lĕkĭ päl′), 1879–1941, Hungarian statesman and scholar; a geographer and political writer. Premier 1920–21 and 1939–41. Signed Berlin Pact (1940; see AXIS) but committed suicide on eve of attack on Yugoslavia.

Tel-el-Amarna (tĕl″-ĕl-ämär′nä), locality, near the Nile, N of Asyut, Egypt. Here was Ikhnaton's capital, and here were found (1887–88) tablets with inscriptions of Amenhotep III and Ikhnaton. Also Tell-el-Amarna.

Telemachus (tĭlĕ′mŭkŭs), in Greek legend, son of PENELOPE and Odysseus. After Odysseus' return from Trojan War, Telemachus helped his father kill his mother's unwelcome suitors.

Telemark (tĕ′lŭmärk), county of S Norway, between Hardanger plateau and the Skagerrak; cap. Skien. Famous for lake and mountain scenery, handicrafts (e.g., wood carving, silversmith work, weaving). Birthplace of skiing as a sport (late 19th cent.).

telepathy, word invented 1862 by F. W. H. Myers to indicate the communication of impressions from one living mind to another without recourse to physical (sensory) channels. Also known as thought or mind reading. See also PSYCHICAL RESEARCH.

telephone. Telephones now in general use developed from a device invented by Alexander Graham Bell (patented 1876 and 1877). It used an electric current of fluctuating intensity and frequency generated by mirroring the acoustic characteristics of sound waves. A diaphragm (thin iron plate) vibrated to sound waves just as does the human eardrum. These vibrations disturbed the magnetic field of a near-by bar magnet inducing an electric current in a thin copper wire wound about the magnet. The current, upon reaching a distant instrument, caused its diaphragm to vibrate by similarly fluctuating the near-by magnetic field. Bell's instrument was both transmitter and receiver; first major improvement made transmitter and receiver separate. Telephone lines used include open wire lines, lead-sheathed cables consisting of many lines, and coaxial cables (underground). Radio telephony accomplishes wireless transmission of sound over long distances and bodies of water.

telescope, optical instrument for viewing distant objects. Invention (1608) is attributed to Hans Lippershey; development for astronomical use to Galileo (1609). In refracting telescope, light is collected by lens set at far end of tube; image magnified by smaller lens (eyepiece). In reflecting telescope, light is gathered by mirror; image magnified by eyepiece. Refractors are preferred for detailed observation of nearer celestial bodies; reflectors, for viewing of more distant bodies. Practicable limit of refractors probably attained in 40-in. instrument at Yerkes Observatory. Reflectors larger than 200-in. Mt. Palomar telescope theoretically achievable. Visual telescopes have been adjusted for use with camera and spectroscope.

teletypewriter: see TYPEWRITER.

television, transmission of pictures and sound simultaneously by electrical impulses. Development of television followed discovery in 1873 of variation in electrical conductivity of selenium when exposed to light; selenium cells were used in early devices but really satisfactory results were obtained only after invention of electron tube (phototube). Progress toward television can be traced through demonstration of nature of electron by Sir J. J. Thomson in 1897, development of Einstein's theory of photoelectric effect (1905), Lee de Forest's three-element vacuum tube (1906), and E. H. Armstrong's regenerative circuit (1912). Decade of 1930–40 saw laboratory perfection of television equipment which began to be marketed at end of World War II. Integral part of television device is some method of "scanning" picture to be transmitted. In 1926 television using mechanical scanning disk was demonstrated in U.S. and England. Mechanical method was soon superseded by electronic scanning methods. Basic types of camera tubes include the Iconoscope invented by V. K. Zworykin and the Orthicon, a later development. The main steps in effecting television can be merely touched upon in a brief description of the process. The scene before the camera is focused by a lens on the plate or mosaic (the specially treated surface) of the electronic pickup tube; differing light intensities of the scene cause photosensitive particles of mosaic to develop a charge (greatest where light is brightest). A beam of electrons sweeps over mosaic in a 525-line zigzag, 30 times each second; beam causes formation of current which passes through external circuit of camera tube and thence through various stages of amplification to be sent out on carrier wave. Minute parts of picture are transmitted in orderly sequence. In receiving set dissected images are reconstructed by changing electrical impulses back into light values; this is done in a cathode-ray tube where an electronic beam scans inner surface of tube at synchronized rate of 525 lines every 1/30 of a second. Several systems of color television have been developed but none had been adopted commercially by early 1953.

Tell, William, legendary Swiss hero. In best-known version of his story, Tell, a native of Bürglen in Uri, refused obeisance to Gessler, the Austrian bailiff, was forced in punishment to shoot an apple off his son's head, and shot Gessler in revenge from an ambush at Kussnacht, thus setting off the revolt which ousted the bailiffs on Jan. 1, 1308. Connected with the legend is the story of the RÜTLI OATH. Tell probably never existed, and the account is a distortion of the historic events of 1291 (see SWITZERLAND). Its best-known treatments are Schiller's drama (1804) and Rossini's opera (1829).

Tell (tĕl), Mediterranean coastal region, 50–120 mi. wide, of French North Africa. In E Algeria it includes the coastal Atlas ranges. Exports include cereals, wine, and olive oil.

Tell City, city (pop. 5,735), S Ind., on Ohio R. and W of Evansville; settled 1857 by Swiss. Wood products.

Tell-el-Amarna, Egypt: see TEL-EL-AMARNA.

Téllez, Gabriel: see TIRSO DE MOLINA.

tellurium (tĕlo͝o'rēum), element with some metallic properties (symbol = Te; see also ELEMENT, table). Appears in white crystalline form and as black powder. Resembles sulphur in properties.

Telugu (tĕ'lŭgo͞o), language of Dravidian family. See LANGUAGE (table).

Temesvar, Banat of: see BANAT.

Tempe (tĕm'pē'), city (pop. 7,684), S central Ariz., in SALT RIVER VALLEY, on the river; founded 1872.

Tempe (tĕm'pē), valley, NE Thessaly, Greece, between Mt. Olympus and Mt. Ossa. Crossed by Peneus R. Vale of Tempe was sacred to Apollo; ancient poets celebrated its beauty.

Tempelhof (tĕm'pŭlhōf), district (pop. 119,-825), S central Berlin, Germany, after 1945 in U.S. occupation sector. Workers' residential quarter. Has chief airfield of Berlin (terminal of American "air lift" 1948–49).

temperature movements, organized efforts to induce people to abstain from alcoholic beverages. Among the most powerful of the movements in U.S. were the Woman's Christian Temperance Union (founded 1874) and the Anti-Saloon League (1893). They influenced passage of many liquor laws, and secured Federal PROHIBITION (1919–33).

temperature, measurement of relative "hotness" or "coldness" of body, not a measurement of heat contained in that body. Water is used as basis for comparison; comparison is made by scale so designed that temperature can be given in degrees. There are several different scales; all have two fixed points—the melting point of ice and the boiling point of water. THERMOMETER is named for scale with which it is marked. On centigrade scale or Celsius scale freezing point of water is 0°C., boiling point, 100°C.; there are 100 equal degrees between these two. On Fahrenheit scale, the corresponding figures ar 32°F. and 212°F., respectively, with 180 degrees between. One Fahrenheit degree is 5/9 of a centigrade degree. On the Kelvin (absolute) scale, the freezing point of water is 273°K., boiling point, 373°K.; this is used in formulae derived from gas laws. Zero point is absolute zero, point at which molecules have no heat energy. On Réaumur scale, freezing point of water is 0°R., boiling point 80°R. For changes between centigrade, Fahrenheit, and Réaumur scales, values can be found by working out the formula $\frac{F-32}{9}=\frac{C}{5}=\frac{R}{4}$. To convert from Kelvin scale, the formula is $C + 273° = K$ or $C = K - 273°$.

Templars: see KNIGHTS TEMPLARS.

Temple, Frederick, 1821–1902, Anglican prelate. Appointed (1858) headmaster of Rugby, he became bishop of Exeter (1869), of London (1885), and archbishop of Canterbury (1896). His son, **William Temple,** 1881–1944, was bishop of Manchester (1921–29), archbishop of York (after 1929), and archbishop of Canterbury (after 1942). He was first president (1908–24) of the Workers' Educational Association, and a leader in the movement to form a world council of churches.

Temple, Richard Grenville-Temple, Earl, 1711–79, English statesman. Opposed his brother, George Grenville, and supported his brother-in-law, William Pitt. Backed Pitt's war policy (1761), but later broke with him and was reconciled with Grenville.

Temple, Sir William, 1628–99, English statesman and author. Married Dorothy OSBORNE. Negotiated (1668) triple alliance with Netherlands and Sweden against France. As ambassador to The Hague arranged (1677) marriage of William of Orange to Princess Mary. Retired (1681) and wrote essays.

Temple, William: see TEMPLE, FREDERICK.

Temple, city (pop. 25,467), central Texas, SSW of Waco; founded 1881 by Santa Fe RR. Center of agr. area with railroad shops, it has textile, flour, and cottonseed oil mills and mfg. of mattresses, rock wool, and tools. Stonecutting. Has VA hospital. Near by is cooperative conservation project.

Temple, the, district of central London, England. Here are Inner and Middle Temple, belonging to INNS OF COURT. World War II bombing destroyed Temple Church and part of Inner Temple. Temple Bar was gate built c.1672 by Wren on the site of one of City of London's entrances.

Temple, Knights of the: see KNIGHTS TEMPLARS.

Temple University, at Philadelphia; nonsectarian, coed.; opened 1884 by R. H. Conwell, chartered 1888, became university 1907.

tempo, in music, the speed of a composition. A composer usually indicates tempo by a set of Italian terms, such as *presto* (very fast), *allegro* (fast), *andante* (moderate; literally "walking"), *adagio* (slow), and *largo* (very slow); *accelerando* and *ritardando* are used to indicate a momentary increase or decrease of tempo. Despite such indications, tempo remains a matter of the individual interpretation of the performer.

Temuco (tāmōō'kō), city (pop. 37,375), S central Chile; founded 1881 at N limit of lake district. On near-by hill a treaty was signed (1881) ending last serious uprising of Araucanian Indians. German immigrants began colonization of S Chile here.

Ten, Council of, secret tribunal set up in Venice in 1310 to safeguard internal security. It soon became the supreme organ of the republic, dealing with foreign affairs and finances, but also remained a dreaded secret court from which there was no appeal. It actually was made up of the doge and 16 members, 10 of whom were elected, and was assisted by three inquisitors of state and by an efficient secret police.

Tenafly (tĕn'ŭflī), residential borough (pop. 9,651), NE N.J., near the Hudson and N of Englewood.

Tenasserim (tĕnă'sŭrĭm), division (31,588 sq. mi.; pop. 1,635,562), Lower Burma. Long disputed by Burma and Thailand, area came under British control after first Anglo-Burmese War (1824–26). Contains principal tin and tungsten mines of Burma.

Ten Commandments or **Decalogue** [Gr.,= ten words], in Bible, the cardinal summary of divine law, given by God to Moses on Mt. Sinai. Ex. 20.2–17; 31.18; 32.15–19; 34; Deut. 5.6–21; 9–10. They are of primary importance in the ethical systems of Judaism, Christianity, and Islam. There are two traditions concerning the division of the commandments; one survives in Roman Catholic and Lutheran churches, the other in Orthodox and most Protestant churches. Roman Catholics and Lutherans combine injunction to worship only one God and not to adore graven images in first commandment; others make them first two. Numbering continues different through commands: not to profane the name of the Lord; to keep the Sabbath holy; to honor one's parents; not to kill; not to give way to lust; not to steal; not to bear false witness. Catholics and Lutherans make prohibition on coveting a neighbor's wife (ninth commandment) separate from prohibition on coveting a neighbor's goods (tenth); others combine as the tenth.

Tenda or **Tende:** see BRIGUE AND TENDE.

Tenedos (tĕ'nŭdŏs), Aegean island (15 sq. mi.; pop. 1,765), Turkey, off NW Asia Minor. Modern name Bozca. Was station of Greek fleet in Trojan Wars and of Xerxes in 5th cent. B.C.

Tenerife: see CANARY ISLANDS.

Teniers, David (tŭnērz', tĕn'yŭrz, Flemish tĕnērs'), the elder, 1582–1649, Flemish painter. His little scenes of peasant life are sometimes confused with the brownish early work of his famous son, **David Teniers,** the younger, 1610–90, who in his mature period used silver tones and subtle color.

Tennent, Gilbert, 1703–64, American Presbyterian clergyman, a leader in GREAT AWAKENING, b. Ireland. As pastor (after 1726) at New Brunswick, N.J., and friend of Whitefield, he became evangelistic leader in E U.S. His father, **William Tennent,** 1673–1745, Presbyterian clergyman and educator, founded c.1726 at Neshaminy, Pa., the famous Log College, predecessor of many schools along frontier. Here many revivalists were trained.

Tennessee, state (41,961 sq. mi.; pop. 3,291,-718), S central U.S.; admitted 1796 as 16th state (slaveholding); cap. NASHVILLE. Other cities are MEMPHIS, CHATTANOOGA, KNOXVILLE. Bounded W by Mississippi R. E are GREAT SMOKY MOUNTAINS, CUMBERLAND PLATEAU; W Tenn. is broad rolling plain. Mfg. of textiles, chemicals, food products, wool and metal products, cement. Farming (cotton, corn, tobacco, livestock). Mining (pyrites, phosphate, zinc, barite, coal, clay, marble, limestone); lumbering. French claim to area lost by British victory in French and Indian Wars. First permanent settlement in Watauga valley 1769; WATAUGA ASSOCIATION formed 1772. JONESBORO, oldest town, founded 1779. Settlers in E Tenn. formed short-lived government (1784–88) under John Sevier (see FRANKLIN, STATE OF). Andrew Jackson was a state and national leader. State seceded 1861. Biggest Civil War battleground, next to Va. (see SHILOH, BATTLE OF; MURFREESBORO; CHATTANOOGA CAMPAIGN). KU KLUX KLAN estab. here 1865. Recently state has profited much from benefits of TENNESSEE VALLEY AUTHORITY. Atomic energy plant at OAK RIDGE.

Tennessee, river, main Ohio R. tributary, formed by junction of Holston and French Broad rivers near Knoxville, Tenn. Flows 650 mi. SW, W, and N through E Tenn., N Ala., W Tenn., and SW Ky. to the Ohio at Paducah. Receives Clinch, Little Tennessee, Hiwassee, Elk, and Duck rivers; has drainage basin of c.41,000 sq. mi. Much benefited by TENNESSEE VALLEY AUTHORITY. Important during Civil War.

Tennessee, University of, mainly at Knoxville; land-grant, state supported, coed.; chartered 1794, opened 1795, became Univ. of Tennessee 1879. Branches at Memphis and Martin.

Tennessee Valley Authority (TVA), independent corporate agency, created May 18, 1933, by U.S. Congress. Agency empowered to take over and operate installations at MUSCLE SHOALS, Ala., and to integrate development of entire Tennessee R. basin. Main offices in the region. TVA's most noteworthy feature is system of multipurpose dams and reservoirs which dominate the valley's economic life. Hydroelectric plants provide cheap power. A navigation channel from the Tennessee's mouth to Knoxville, Tenn., has greatly increased river traffic, chiefly in petroleum, grain, automobiles, and steel. Other TVA activities include conservation and development of natural resources, social and educational programs. In World War II, TVA supplied power to the atomic energy plant at Oak Ridge, Tenn. Although it has been bitterly criticized as being "socialistic," TVA has been declared constitutional, and its remarkable success has made it a model for similar river projects.

Tenniel, Sir John (tĕn'yŭl), 1820–1914, English caricaturist and illustrator. Perhaps best known for illustrations of Lewis Carroll's *Alice in Wonderland*. Did political cartoons for *Punch*, 1851–1901.

tennis, game played indoors or outdoors by two or four players on level, hard court. In singles play court measures 78 ft. by 27 ft.; in doubles 78 ft. by 36 ft. Probably descendant of court tennis, it was introduced (1873) as a new game by Walter C. Wingfield in Wales. First championship match was held (1887) at Wimbledon, England. In 1881 U.S. Lawn Tennis Association was formed.

Tennyson, Alfred Tennyson, 1st Baron, 1809–92, English poet; poet laureate after 1850. While at Cambridge he wrote *Poems, Chiefly Lyrical* (1830) and began his friendship with Arthur Henry Hallam. *Poems* (1832) was scathingly attacked, and Hallam's sudden death in 1833 overwhelmed him. But *Poems* (2 vols., 1842)—including revisions of earlier work and powerful new poems such as "Locksley Hall," "Ulysses," and "Break, Break, Break"—won him wide acclaim. *The Princess* (1847) was reissued with beautiful interspersed songs in 1850. *In Memoriam* (1850) is a series of elegies written after Hallam's death, some of Tennyson's best poetry. As laureate he wrote occasional poems such as *The Charge of the Light Brigade* (1855). Other works include the "monodrama" *Maud* (1855); *Idylls of the King* (1859; enlarged 1869, 1872); *Enoch Arden* (1864); and *Demeter and Other Poems* (1889), containing "Crossing the Bar." Master of lyric perfection, Tennyson is the representative poet of the Victorian period.

Tenochtitlán (tānōchtētlän'), anc. city, central Mexico, in valley of Mexico; cap. of the Aztec, founded on a marshy island c.1325. Spanish came to city in 1519, retreated in 1520, and Cortés took it after three-month siege (1521). Mexico city was built on its ruins.

Tenos or **Tinos** (both: tē'nôs), Aegean island (74 sq. mi.; pop. 11,380), Greece; one of the Cyclades. Wine, figs, wheat, silk, marble. Venetian colony after 1390; fell to Turks 1715.

tense [O.Fr., from Latin,= time], category of verb forms referring to the time of an action. Inflection of Latin and other languages has sets of personal verb forms that are themselves members of moods. English tenses are simple (*look, looked*) or compound (*have looked, am looking*). Some languages (e.g., Russian, Hebrew) in verb forms include aspect—the completeness or incompleteness of the action. English borrows from Greek some aspectlike terms (imperfect, perfect, pluperfect).

tent caterpillar, destructive larva of native American moth. Apple-tree tent caterpillar larvae live in broods of 150 or more in white silk tent woven in tree fork; they feed on leaves.

Ten Thousand Smokes, Valley of: see VALLEY OF TEN THOUSAND SMOKES.

Tenure of Office Act, in U.S. history, measure passed on March 2, 1867, by Congress over veto of Pres. Andrew JOHNSON which forbade the President to remove any Federal officeholder "appointed by and with the advice and consent of the Senate" without further Senate approval. It also provided for tenure of cabinet members throughout full term of President who had appointed them and for one month thereafter, subject to removal by Senate. With this measure radical Republicans hoped to assure tenure of Secretary of War E. M. STANTON and thus prevent any interference with military occupation of South in their RECONSTRUCTION plan. Johnson's alleged violation of act in dismissing Stanton was principal charge in impeachment proceedings against him. Act was in large part repealed in 1887; in 1926 Supreme Court declared it unconstitutional.

Ten Years War, 1868–78, struggle for Cuban independence from Spain. Cuban discontent with excessive taxation, trade restrictions, and virtual exclusion of Cubans from government grew until revolt started in 1868. A rebel republic was set up, and guerrilla warfare was bloody and costly. Seemingly without result, it actually foreshadowed Cuban war of independence (1895) and the Spanish-American War (1898). Spain deeply resented U.S. sympathy for Cuba in the Ten Years War, shown notably in trouble over the ship *Virginius*.

teosinte (tēŭsĭn'tē), tall, cornlike, broad-leaved, annual grass (*Euchlaena mexicana*), native to Central America and Mexico. It is grown for forage in S U.S. Perennial species is *E. perennis*.

Teotihuacán (tāōtēwäkän'), ruins of Toltec religious center (c.6th–11th cent. A.D.), central Mexico, c.30 mi. NE of Mexico city. Pyramids to the Sun, to the Moon, numerous smaller pyramids, and the Temple of QUETZALCOATL still stand.

Tepic (tāpēk'), city (pop. 17,547), cap. of Nayarit, W Mexico, on Tepic R. in rich agr.

region that produces grains, coffee, rice, and sugar.

teraphim (tĕ'rŭfĭm) [Heb.,= idols], anc. household idols of the Jews, used for divination. Probably similar to the LARES AND PENATES of Rome.

terbium (tûr'bēŭm), rare metallic element (symbol = Tb; see also ELEMENT, table).

Ter Borch or **Terburg, Gerard** (gā'rärt tŭr bôrkh', tŭrbûrkh'), 1617–81. one of Dutch Little Masters. Portrayed life and customs of wealthy burgher class. His celebrated group *The Peace of Münster* is in National Gall., London.

terebinth (tĕ'rŭbĭnth) or **turpentine tree,** small deciduous tree (*Pictacia terebinthus*), native to Mediterranean region. It yielded the earliest known form of turpentine.

Terek (tyĕ'rĭk), river, 367 mi. long, USSR, rising in glaciers of Caucasus near Mt. Kazbek and flowing through DARYAL gorge and past Dzaudzhikau into Caspian Sea. Its swampy delta is 60 mi. wide. Lower course is used for irrigation. Cossacks of Terek valley formed autonomous community under tsars.

Terence (Publius Terentius Afer) (tĕ'rŭns), b. c.185 or c.195 B.C., d. c.159 B.C., Roman writer of comedies. Six comedies survive—*Andria, Heautontimorumenos, Eunuchus, Phormio, Adelphi,* and *Hecyra.* All are adapted from the Greek plays of Menander and others. The writing is skillful, the humor broad, the characters realistic.

Teresa, Saint: see THERESA, SAINT.

Teresina (tĕrŭzē'nŭ), city (pop. 53,425), cap. of Piauí state, NE Brazil, on Parnaíba R. Name formerly spelled Therezina. Has cotton and sugar mills and trades in cattle, hides, and rice.

Tereus, Thracian king: see PHILOMELA.

Terman, Lewis Madison, 1877–, American psychologist, known for his application of intelligence tests to school children. His chief work is the Stanford Revision of the Binet-Simon Intelligence Tests.

Terminus [Latin,= boundary], in Roman religion, aspect of Jupiter as god of boundaries. Immobility of feast of boundaries forced peculiar system of counting days in extra years interpolated in the calendar.

termite (tûr'mīt), social insect of order Isoptera. Often called white ant but is not an ant (has no constriction at waist as ants have) and is more closely related to roaches. Termites are divided into soil dwellers and wood dwellers. Subterranean soil dwellers do most damage in U.S.; they attack only wood in contact with ground or close to it. See *ill.,* p. 601.

tern, bird of Old and New Worlds, smaller than the related gull. Some terns are called sea swallows because of long, pointed wings and graceful flight. Arctic tern migrates from arctic to antarctic.

Ternate (tĕrnä'tā), volcanic island (41 sq. mi.; pop. 130,022), E Indonesia, in Molucca Sea W of Halmahera. Became important Moslem center in 15th cent. Forts were built here in 1522 by the Portuguese and by the Dutch in 1607.

Terni (tĕr'nē), city (pop. 37,295), Umbria, central Italy. Mfg. center (arms, machinery, chemicals; iron and steel plants). Uses hydroelectric power.

Ternopol, Ukraine: see TARNOPOL.

Terpsichore: see MUSES.

terrapin (tĕ'rŭpĭn), edible fresh-water TURTLE.

Terre Haute (tĕ'rŭ hōt'), city (pop. 64,214), W Ind., on Wabash R. and WSW of Indianapolis; settled 1811. Commercial, banking center for farming, mining area. Mfg. of paint, coke by-products, metal products, brick, and tile. Birthplace of E. V. Debs, Theodore Dreiser. Seat of Rose Polytechnic Inst.

Terrell (tĕ'rŭl), city (pop. 11,544), N Texas, E of Dallas; settled c.1860, laid out 1872. Processes cotton, lumber, wheat, and milk.

terrier, any of a number of alert, lively dogs once bred chiefly for hunting foxes, badgers, rabbits, and rats, but now raised mostly for pets. Terriers are known for their intelligence and their courage which is all out of proportion to their rather small size. One of the best-known terriers is the Airedale, whose tan, wiry coat is marked with a black or dark grizzled saddle. It stands c.22 in. high at the shoulder and weighs 35–40 lb. Resembling the Airedale but smaller (18 in. high; weighing c.27 lb.) are the Irish terrier, whose wiry coat is of solid color, usually red, red wheaten, or golden red; and the Welsh terrier (15 in. high; weighing c.20 lb.), a black and tan dog, sometimes marked with a saddle like the Airedale's. Fox terriers are of two kinds, the smooth and the wire-haired. Both stand at c.15½ in. at the shoulder, weigh c.18 lb., and are predominantly white marked with black and tan. There are three distinct breeds of schnauzers, the miniature (averaging 12 in. shoulder height), the standard (c.18 in. at shoulder), and the giant (c.24 in. at shoulder). All have wiry coats of pepper-and-salt mixture, solid black, or black and tan. The Scottish terrier or "Scottie" is easily known by its low-slung silhouette, short, strong legs, and rather broad muzzle. Its rough coat is usually black, gray, brindle, or wheaten. Resembling the Scottie in size and shape is the West Highland white terrier whose rather long coat is always white. The Sealyham is low-slung like the Scottie, its body length equal to its shoulder height (c.10½ in.). It weighs c.20 lb. and its wiry topcoat is white or white marked with lemon, tan, or liver. One of the smallest of this general type of dog is the Skye terrier, c.9 in. high at shoulder and weighing c.18 lb. Its body, including head and tail, is c.40 in. long. It is generally blue, gray, or fawn in color with black-tipped hairs c.5½ in. long which almost brush the floor and hang over the eyes. The Bedlington terrier is easily recognized because its head is shaped somewhat like that of a sheep. It is c.15 in. high, weighs c.24 lb., and is usually dark blue, liver, or sandy in color. The Manchester terrier, also known as the black-and-tan terrier, stands c.18 in. high at shoulder and weighs 16–20 lb. With its glossy black and tan coat, it resembles the much larger DOBERMAN PINSCHER. The bull terrier was originally bred for dog fighting in a pit. It is a strong, tenacious dog with a long even muzzle and heavy jaw muscles. The majority of bull terriers weigh over 35 lb. The coat is glossy and pure white, and the nose is black.

territory, in U.S. history, portion of national domain which is given limited self-government, usually in preparation for statehood. ORDINANCE OF 1787 furnished basis for organization of territorial governments. Following Louisiana Purchase U.S. Supreme Court decision gave Congress right to establish territorial governments and to admit territories to the Union. A territory may be admitted as a state after its officers petition Congress for an enabling act, establish a constitution, meet certain requirements set by Congress. Present territories of Hawaii, Puerto Rico, Alaska are supervised by Dept. of the Interior. Each has a nonvoting Congressional delegate.

Terror, Reign of: see REIGN OF TERROR.

Terry, Dame Ellen (Alicia), 1848–1928, English actress, of a prominent theatrical family. With Sir Henry Irving she formed (1878) an acting partnership which lasted over 20 years. Charming and graceful, she was unrivaled in Shaksperian roles.

Tertiary period (tûr'shēē"rē), name given in mid-18th cent. to first and main portion of Cenozoic era. Portion following Tertiary was called Quaternary. Geologists now tend to drop these divisions and to consider the Cenozoic era of one period only, called also Cenozoic. North American outlines were similar to the present, with marine submergence along both coasts and Mississippi valley. There was extensive mountain making in North America with reelevation of existing ranges; in Europe the formation of Alps, Pyrenees, Carpathians, and others; and in Asia, the Himalayas. Volcanic activity was almost continuous. At the beginning mammals replaced reptiles as dominant animals, and modern forms of life soon became numerous—these included modern types of birds, reptiles, amphibians, and invertebrates.

Tertullian (tûrtŭl'yùn), c.150–c.230, Roman theologian, b. Carthage. He wrote many theological works. Some of his opinions departed from the main course of Christian thought, and the Montanists are sometimes called Tertullianists.

Teruel (tĕrwĕl'), city (pop. 14,377), cap. of Teruel prov., E central Spain, in Aragon, on Guadalaviar R. Agr. trade center. Was almost totally destroyed in civil war of 1936–39, during which it changed hands three times; later rebuilt.

Teschen (tĕ'shùn), city and former principality (c.850 sq. mi.), now divided between Czechoslovakia and Poland. As part of Silesia, principality was held by Austria 1526–1918. Has important coal basin. The Conference of Ambassadors (1922) divided disputed territory and city: W section (with coal basin) and W suburb (*Český Těšín;* pop. 9,986) went to Czechoslovakia; Poland received E section and main part of city (*Cieszyn;* pop. 16,536). Poland seized W section Oct., 1938, but status quo as of 1920 was restored in 1945.

Tesla, Nikola (tĕ'slù), 1856–1943, American electrician and inventor, b. Croatia (then in Austria-Hungary). Came to U.S. in 1884. Pioneer in field of high-tension electricity, he made many inventions of great value to development of radio transmission, wireless communication, alternating-current transmission. He designed power system at Niagara.

Test Act, 1673, passed by British Parliament to exclude from office all who refused to take oaths of allegiance and supremacy, to receive communion according to Church of England, and to renounce belief in transubstantiation. Directed mainly against Catholics. Extended to members of Parliament (1678). Repealed at time of Catholic Emancipation.

testament: see NEW TESTAMENT; OLD TESTAMENT; WILL.

testis (tĕ'stĭs) or **testicle** (tĕ'stĭkùl), one of two glands in male functioning in production of sperm and secretion of male hormone testosterone.

Tesuque (tĕsōō'kā), Indian pueblo village (1948 pop. 162), N central N.Mex., in Sangre de Cristo Mts., N of Santa Fe; present village settled c.1700. Tanoan language. Painting and pottery making. Annual San Diego feast.

tetanus (tĕ'tùnùs) or **lockjaw,** infectious disease caused by bacillus and marked by muscular spasms and difficulty in opening mouth. Fatalities resulting from effect of toxin on heart and breathing muscles are reduced by injection of antitoxin after a wound. Toxoid injections give immunity. See *ill.,* p. 813.

Teterboro (tē'tùr–), borough (pop. 28), NE N.J., E of Passaic. Freight airport here administered by Port of New York Authority. Called Bendix 1937–43.

Teton (tētŏn'), river, 60 mi. long, rising in W Wyo., in forks which join in SE Idaho. Flows N and W to Henrys Fork R. Early course is through Teton Basin (as Pierre's Hole a haunt of trappers).

Teton Range, branch of Rocky Mts., NW Wyo. and SE Idaho, just S of Yellowstone Natl. Park and W of Jackson L. and Snake R. Largely in Grand Teton Natl. Park (see NATIONAL PARKS AND MONUMENTS, table), and partly in Targhee Natl. Forest. Frequented by mountain men in first half of 19th cent. Topped by Grand Teton (13,766 ft.).

Tetrazzini, Luisa (tĕtrùzē'nē), 1871–1940, Italian coloratura soprano. She sang with the Manhattan Opera Co., 1908–10; with the Metropolitan Opera, New York, 1911–12. Was especially notable for her brilliant high tones and her range.

Tetuán (tātwän'), city (pop. 93,658), cap. of Spanish Morocco, near the Mediterranean; industrial center of protectorate. Its port is Río Martín. Founded in 14th cent., it was an early Corsair stronghold. Rebuilt 1492 by Jewish refugees from Portugal. Fell 1860 to Spaniards led by Leopoldo O'Donnell; permanently occupied by Spain 1915.

Tetzel, Johann (yō'hän tĕt'sĕl), 1465–1519, German Dominican preacher. He promoted (1516) in Germany a campaign of indulgences and was plunged into a dispute with Martin Luther.

Teutoburg Forest, Ger. *Teutoburger Wald* (toi'tōbōōr"gùr vält'), hilly, forested range, Westphalia, NW Germany, largely in former state of Lippe. Monument near Detmold commemorates victory of ARMINIUS over

VARUS (A.D. 9), when the Germans annihilated three Roman legions.

Teutones or **Teutons:** see GERMANS.

Teutonic Knights (to͞otŏ'nĭk, tū–) or **German Order,** German military religious order, founded 1090–91 in Holy Land and modeled on those of the Templars and Hospitalers. It rose into prominence when it undertook the conquest of pagan PRUSSIA (1226). Its domains on the Baltic were at first under nominal papal overlordship but in 1466 the knights lost territories to Poland and accepted Polish suzerainty. They were united with the LIVONIAN KNIGHTS 1237–1525. After virtually exterminating the native population, they resettled Prussia with German colonists. Their first seat was MARIENBURG, replaced after 1466 by KÖNIGSBERG. In 1525 Grand Master ALBERT OF BRANDENBURG accepted Protestantism and changed the order's domain into the hereditary duchy of Prussia. The order continued in Catholic Germany till 1805; was later revived in Austria as an honorary body. Habit: white robe with black cross embroidered in gold.

Teutonic religion: see GERMANIC RELIGION.

Teviot (tē'vēŭt, tĕ'–), river, mainly in Roxburghshire, Scotland. Flows 40 mi. NE to the Tweed.

Tewfik Pasha (tū'fĭk), 1852–92, khedive of Egypt (1879–92). Succeeded his father, Ismail Pasha. Under British military pressure he gave up Egypt's claim to full sovereignty over the Sudan, which later came under joint Anglo-Egyptian control.

Tewkesbury (tūks'bŭrē), municipal borough (pop. 5,292), Gloucestershire, England. Site of one of richest and most renowned 12th-cent. Benedictine abbeys. Dramatic festivals are held, a survival of festival plays which began in the 17th cent.

Tewksbury, residential town (pop. 7,505), NE Mass., ESE of Lowell.

Texarkana (tĕx"särkă'nŭ), city (pop. in Texas, 24,753; in Ark., 15,875), on Texas-Ark. line, settled 1873. Rail center, it ships cotton, livestock, and dairy products. Mfg. of cotton, wood, and clay products, fertilizer, and feeds.

Texas, state (267,339 sq. mi.; pop. 7,711,194), SW U.S.; admitted 1845 as 28th state (slaveholding); cap. AUSTIN. Other cities are HOUSTON, DALLAS, SAN ANTONIO, FORT WORTH, EL PASO, CORPUS CHRISTI, GALVESTON. Bordered S by Gulf of Mexico, SW by the RIO GRANDE. Central Texas has rolling prairies; W are plains, hills; S is Rio Grande Valley; SE are Gulf plains. The Panhandle projects N. Cotton main crop; also livestock, winter wheat, oats, corn, rice, truck, pecans, grain sorghums. Mines petroleum, natural gas, sulphur, salt, clay products, limestone, magnesium, other minerals. Processing of minerals, metals, food, lumber; mfg. of paper, textiles, cement, leather goods, airplanes, ships. Spanish estab. first white settlement at YSLETA in 1681 or 1682. Several American filibustering expeditions were undertaken in early 19th cent. S. F. AUSTIN brought settlers in 1821. In the revolution for independence from Mexico fall of the ALAMO was redeemed by victory of Sam HOUSTON in battle of SAN JACINTO (1836). Texas was independent republic until its annexation to the U.S. (1845), which led to MEXICAN WAR. Joined Confederacy in 1861. Railroads expanded stockraising, increased settlement. Discovery of oil (esp. after 1901) hastened industrialization. Industrial output greatly increased by World War II.

Texas, Agricultural and Mechanical College of, at College Station; land-grant, state supported; for men; chartered 1871, opened 1876. Military plan. Has firemen's training school and radio station. Prairie View Agricultural and Mechanical Col. of Texas (Negro; land-grant; coed.; 1876) is branch.

Texas, University of, mainly at Austin; state supported, coed.; chartered 1881, opened 1883. Research bureaus include anthropology, bio-chemistry, zoology, and economic geology. Has several museums, institute of Latin American studies, observatory, and notable library. Owns rich oil lands. Texas Western Col. (formerly Texas Col. of Mines and Metallurgy; coed.; 1913) is El Paso branch.

Texas Christian University, at Fort Worth; coed.; opened 1873, chartered 1874 by Disciples of Christ. Called Add-Ran Col. or Add-Ran Christian Univ. until 1902; moved to Fort Worth 1910. Has Brite Col. of the Bible.

Texas City, city (pop. 16,620), S Texas, on Galveston Bay NW of Galveston. World War II brought expansion. It has tin smelter, chemical plants, and refineries. Recovered from disastrous fires, blasts from exploding ship (April 16, 1947).

Texas Rangers, mounted fighting force organized (1835) during Texas Revolution. In time of the republic they became estab. as guardians of Texas frontier, particularly against marauding Indians. Served in Mexican War, Civil War. Organized for first time on permanent basis in 1874, their heyday was the period of great cattle business, with its feuds, its outlaws and "rustlers." By act of Texas legislature in 1935, rangers were merged with state highway patrol.

Texas State College for Women: see DENTON.

Texas Technological College: see LUBBOCK.

Texas Western College: see TEXAS, UNIVERSITY OF.

Texcoco, Lake: see MEXICO, city; TENOCHTITLÁN.

Texel (tĕk'sŭl), island (64 sq. mi.; pop. 9,401), North Holland prov., NW Netherlands, in North Sea. Largest and southernmost of West Frisian Isls.

Texoma, Lake: see DENISON DAM.

textiles, all fabrics made by weaving, felting, knitting, braiding, or netting. They can be classified according to their component fibers as SILK, WOOL, LINEN, and COTTON, synthetics such as RAYON and NYLON, and some inorganic substances, such as cloth of gold, and glass and asbestos cloth. Fabrics are also classed as to structure according to the manner in which warp and weft cross each other in the loom (see WEAVING). Modern textile manufacture is mostly carried on in factories with power machinery, but many fine fabrics are still made by hand. Textile tools have been found among the earliest relics of human habitation. Exquisite fabrics have been made in many lands since antiquity;

basic processes have not changed since about the 14th cent., though equipment and methods have altered.

Th, chemical symbol of the element THORIUM.

Thackeray, William Makepeace, 1811–63, English novelist, b. India. Went to England in 1817. Traveled on Continent in 1830 and then studied law. In 1836 he married and, having lost his patrimony, was forced to do literary hack work. Tragedy struck in 1841 when his wife became hopelessly insane. During the 1830s and '40s he did miscellaneous magazine writing, such as the satiric "Yellowplush Correspondence" in *Frazer's Magazine* in 1837–38, and wrote novels which appeared serially. In 1848 his satirical *Book of Snobs* and the novel *Vanity Fair,* his masterpiece, won him fame. This grew with the novels *Pendennis* (1850), *Henry Esmond* (1852), *The Newcomes* (1853–55), and *The Virginians* (1857–59). In 1851 and 1852–53 he lectured in England and in the U.S. on *English Humorists of the Eighteenth Century*. A satirical and disillusioned man, Thackeray wrote parodies of and satires against romantic sentiment, expressing the futility and vanity of human life.

Thaddaeus, apostle: see JUDE, SAINT.

Thailand (tī'lănd) or **Siam** (sīăm'), kingdom (197,242 sq. mi.; pop. 17,324,291), SE Asia, between Burma and Indo-China, and extending S into Malay Peninsula; cap. Bangkok. The heart of the country is the central plain, where much rice is grown. The mountainous NW area has teak forests, while the peninsular section is mostly jungle, with tin, tungsten, and rubber production. Fisheries are important along the coast. The population, mostly Buddhist, includes Chinese, Malays, Annamese, Cambodians, Mons, and Negritos, as well as the dominant Thai or Siamese. In 11th cent., part of the country fell to the KHMER EMPIRE. History of modern Siam began when the Khmers were expelled in 13th cent. and a rising Thai dynasty made its capital at Ayuthia. Arrival of Portuguese traders and missionaries in 16th cent. marked the beginning of Siam's relations with the West. Her independence was threatened in 19th cent. by the British and the French, but the Siamese managed to remain free by bringing in Western advisers and by playing off British against French interests. Even so, Siam lost its claims to Cambodia, Laos, and other territories. The Chakkri dynasty (founded 1782 and still in power today) produced some able monarchs, including Mongkut (reigned 1851–68) and Chulalongkorn (reigned 1868–1910), who introduced economic and social reforms. Politically, however, Siam continued as an absolute monarchy until 1932, when a coup d'état forced Prajadhipok (reigned 1925–35) to grant a constitution. But the trend toward democratization was checked in 1938 by the rise of the militarist Gen. Luang Pibul Songgram (later known as Phibun Songgram) in the reign of Ananda (1935–46). He was ousted in 1944 but returned to power in 1947. Occupied by Japanese troops in Dec., 1941, Thailand was allied with Japan in World War II. Phumiphon succeeded to the throne in 1950.

Thaïs (thā'ĭs, tä'ēs), 4th cent. B.C., legendary Athenian courtesan, said to have been mistress of Alexander the Great and Ptolemy I.

Thaïs, 4th cent. A.D., legendary Alexandrian courtesan, supposed to have been converted to Christianity by St. Paphnutius or by Bessarion.

Thales (thā'lēz) c.636–c.546 B.C., Greek philosopher, called the first Greek philosopher. Thought water the origin of all things.

Thalia, one of the MUSES: also one of the GRACES.

thallium (thă'lēŭm), rare, soft, malleable, metallic element (symbol = Tl; see also ELEMENT, table). Salts are poisons. Metal is used in alloys with lead and other metals and in making optical glass.

Thames (tĕmz), principal river of England. Rising in Gloucestershire in four headstreams (the Thames or Isis, the Churn, the Coln, and the Leach), it bounds part of nine counties and flows through London to enter the North Sea at the Nore. Joined by canals (including Oxford, Thames, Severn, and Grand Junction), it is navigable by barges to Lechlade, Gloucestershire. Part near London Bridge is called the Pool. Port of London extends from London Bridge to Blackwall. Docks and tidal area are administered by Port of London Authority. River's total length is 210 mi.; its width at Gravesend is 2,700 ft. Up to London the Thames valley is mainly agr. and, in parts, very beautiful; much used for boating.

Thames (thāmz, tĕmz), tidal estuary, E Conn. Extends 15 mi. S from Norwich to Long Isl. Sound at New London, whose harbor it forms. Scene of annual Yale–Harvard rowing contests since 1878.

Thames, battle of the, Oct. 5, 1813, in War of 1812, fought near Chatham on Thames R. in S Ont., Canada, which rises NNW of Woodstock and flows 163 mi. SW to L. St. Clair, WSW of Chatham. American forces under Gen. W. H. Harrison defeated British army, reinforced by Indians under Tecumseh. Victory restored U.S. control in Northwest.

Thanet, Isle of (thă'nĭt), island forming NE part of Kent, England. There are many seaside resorts.

Thanksgiving Day, national holiday in U.S. commemorating harvest of Plymouth Colony in 1621, following a winter of great hardship. Colonists and neighboring Indians shared the first feast. A national day of thanks was proclaimed by George Washington for Nov. 26, 1789. Lincoln revived the custom in 1863. Since 1941, according to a joint resolution of Congress, holiday falls on fourth Thursday in Nov. Customary turkey is reminder of four wild turkeys served at Pilgrims' first Thanksgiving.

Thasos (thā'sŏs), Aegean island (170 sq. mi.; pop. 13,829), Greece, off Macedonia. Olive oil, wine, timber, lead-zinc ores. In legend Thasus, son of Poseidon, led earliest colonists here. The ancient Phoenicians exploited island's famous gold mines. Parians colonized it 708 B.C. Later came under Persia and Athens. Held by Genoese and Venetians 14th–15th cent.

Thaxter, Celia (Laighton), 1835–94, American poet, known especially for *Drift-Weed*

(1879). This and her prose *Among the Isles of Shoals* (1873) mirror life along her native N.H. coast.

Thayer, Abbott Handerson, 1849–1921, American painter, known for idealized figures of women.

Théâtre Français: see COMÉDIE FRANÇAISE.

Theatre Guild, organization formed in 1919 by members of the Washington Square Players, New York city. Financed largely by subscription. Has successfully presented works of such dramatists as Shaw, O'Neill, Molnar, and S. N. Behrman.

Thebes (thēbz), city of anc. Egypt, on the site occupied later by Karnak and Luxor. Magnificent ruins recall the rise of the XI dynasty, which made Thebes, the center of Amon worship, important (c.2160 B.C.). Thebes remained important for many centuries. It was sacked by Assyrians (661 B.C.) and Romans (29 B.C.). It is biblical No.

Thebes, anc. city of Boeotia, Greece. Prominent in Greek legends (see CADMUS, OEDIPUS, SEVEN AGAINST THEBES, EPIGONI). Jealous of Athens, Thebes favored the Persians in the Persian Wars, the Spartans in the Peloponnesian War. Afraid of Sparta later, Thebes joined the confederacy against Sparta, and, under Pelopidas, Thebans won independence (379 B.C.), guaranteed by the victory of Epaminondas at Leuctra (371 B.C.). Thebes joined Athens against Philip II of Macedon and shared in the defeat at Chaeronea (338 B.C.). A revolt against Alexander the Great brought destruction of the city (336 B.C.). The modern Thevai or Thivai occupies part of the site.

The Dalles (dălz), inland port city (pop. 7,-676), N Oregon, on Columbia R. and E of Portland. Grew c.1852 around fort on mission (1838–47) site. Canal with locks (1908–15) by-passes river's rapids. Downstream, ships also use locks (1937) at Bonneville Dam. Processes and ships grain, fruit, wool, livestock, salmon, and lumber.

The Dells: see DELLS OF THE WISCONSIN.

Theiler, Max, 1899–, American research physician, b. South Africa. Won 1951 Nobel Prize in Physiology and Medicine for his work in developing the first effective vaccine (called 17-D) against yellow fever. Associated with Harvard (1922–29) and with Rockefeller Inst. for Medical Research (1930–).

theine: see CAFFEINE.

Theiss (tīs), Hung. *Tisza*, river, c.800 mi. long, rising in the Carpathians and flowing S across Hungary to join the Danube above Belgrade, Yugoslavia. Navigable in part.

Thematic Apperception Test: see MENTAL TESTS.

Themis (thē'mĭs), in Greek religion, a Titaness, goddess of law and order; daughter of Uranus and Gaea and mother by Zeus of the Horae and Fates.

Themistocles (thůmy'stůklēz), c.525–c.460 B.C., Athenian statesman. In the PERSIAN WARS he persuaded the Athenians to build a navy. Though he could not prevent the Persians from taking Athens, it was his strategy that triumphed in the naval victory at Salamis (480 B.C.) and his foresight that built the strength of Athens. Died in exile in Persia.

Theocritus (thēŏ'krĭtůs), fl. c.270 B.C., Alexandrian Greek poet. The pastoral begins with him. His poetic form is finished, his characters realistic. His idyls—much imitated—show his sensitivity to nature.

Theodora (thēůdô'rů) d. 548, Byzantine empress, wife of JUSTINIAN I. She suppressed the *Nika* sedition (532; see BLUES AND GREENS) and determined many of her husband's religious policies. The account of her origins and early career as a circus and dancing girl in the *Secret History* of Procopius is probably spitefully colored.

Theodore, Russian rulers: see FEODOR.

Theodore of Mopsuestia (mŏp"sūĕs'chů), c.350–428, Syrian theologian; friend of St. John Chrysostom. Wrote historical, rationalistic commentaries on the Bible. Some of his writings were influenced by monarchianism. Nestorius was his pupil.

Theodore of Studium, Saint, 759–826, Byzantine monastic reformer. His reforms at the monastery of Studium had a lasting effect on the Basilian monks. He opposed iconoclasm and was thrice exiled for stiff-necked opposition by three emperors, Constantine VI, Nicephorus I, and Leo V. Feast: Nov. 12.

Theodore Roosevelt National Memorial Park: see NATIONAL PARKS AND MONUMENTS (table).

Theodoric I (thēŏd'ůrĭk) or **Thierry I** (tērē', tēĕr'ē), d. 534, Frankish king of Austrasia (511–34); son of Clovis I. Divided his brother Clodomer's kingdom of Orléans with his brothers Childebert I and Clotaire I. Subjugated Thuringians with Clotaire.

Theodoric the Great, c.454–526, king of the OSTROGOTHS (c.474–526). Under Emperor ZENO, he was made imperial master of soldiers (483) and consul (484) and was sent to Italy to fight ODOACER (488). He repeatedly defeated Odoacer, took Ravenna (493), had Odoacer murdered after accepting his surrender, and took the title "governor of the Romans." His rule in Italy was beneficent, and he respected Roman institutions. His last years were clouded by a quarrel with the pope over his Arianism and by his hasty execution of BOETHIUS and Symmachas. His tomb is one of Ravenna's finest monuments.

Theodosia, RSFSR: see FEODOSIYA.

Theodosian Code (thē"ůdō'shůn), Roman legal code issued by Theodosius II, emperor of the East (A.D. 438). Based on Gregorian and Hermogenian codes; used in making the *Corpus Juris Civilis*.

Theodosius, Roman emperors. **Theodosius I** (the Great), 346?–395, son of the general Theodosius, was chosen by Emperor Gratian to rule the East as co-Augustus (379). He made an advantageous peace with the Visigoths. When Gratian's legal successor in the West, Valentinian II, was deposed in 387 by Maximus (Gratian's assassin), Theodosius invaded Italy, slew the usurper, and restored Valentinian (388). He again entered Italy when Valentinian was strangled, presumably by order of ARBOGAST, who installed the puppet emperor Eugenius (392). Claiming the succession of the West, Theodosius defeated the pagan army of Eugenius and Arbogast in a two-day battle (394). His death, however, left the Roman Empire permanently divided. His sons, Arcadius and Honorius succeeded him, respectively, in the East and West. Theodosius rooted out ARIANISM and called the First Council of CONSTANTINOPLE. When St. AMBROSE excommunicated him for the massacre of the rebellious citizens of Salonica (390), the emperor humbly did penance in Milan Cathedral. **Theodosius II,** 401–50, emperor of the East (408–50), summoned the Council of EPHESUS (431), upheld the Robber Synod (449; see EUTYCHES), and published the THEODOSIAN CODE (438). During his reign ATTILA invaded the empire and obtained heavy tribute.

Theognis (thēŏg'nĭs), fl. late 6th cent. B.C., Greek didactic poet of Megara. His elegies, often passionate in hate and love, counsel moderation and faithfulness.

Theophilus (thēŏ'fĭlůs), person addressed at beginning of Gospel according to St. Luke and the Acts of the Apostles. Luke 1.3; Acts 1.1.

Theophrastus (thē"ōfră'stůs), c.372–c.287 B.C., Greek philosopher, successor to Aristotle as head of the Peripatetic school. His *Characters,* sketches of various types, was imitated by later writers (e.g., La Bruyère).

theosophy (thēŏ'sůfē), any philosophical system starting with mystical belief in the pervading force of infinite divinity (God) in the universe, with evil the result of man's devotion to finite goals. The Neoplatonists and the Cabalists had theosophical systems, as did Jacob Boehme. More specifically, theosophy is the movement fostered by Helena Petrovna BLAVATSKY in the late 19th cent., based largely on Indian philosophy and stressing the latent spiritual power of man, refined by various transmigrations of the soul and enlightened by occult knowledge. Annie BESANT wrote much on theosophy.

The Pas (thů päz'), town (pop. 3,376), W Man., Canada, on the Saskatchewan and SSE of Flin Flon. Trade center for mining and fur-trapping region.

Thera (thēr'ů), volcanic island (31 sq. mi.; pop. 9,704), Greece, in Aegean Sea; one of the Cyclades. Wine, pumice stone. Prehistoric and classical remains have been excavated.

Theresa, Saint (Theresa of Jesus), Span. *Teresa de Ávila,* 1515–82, Spanish Carmelite nun, one of the chief women saints; originally named Teresa de Cepeda y Ahumada; of a well-to-do family. She founded (1562) a convent of Discalced Carmelites in Ávila and later many other convents. A friend of St. John of the Cross, she combined her talents with his to advance the Catholic Reform, bringing about a remarkable awakening of religious fervor—a movement that finally spread far beyond Spain. Her writings, in simple, earth-born language, are some of the greatest in mystical literature. Among them are her spiritual autobiography (written 1562–65), supplementary *Relations, The Way of Perfection, The Interior Castle, Foundations* (1573–82), *Exclamations of the Soul to God* (1569), and *Constitutions* (for the Discalced Carmelites). Also Teresa.

Theresa, Saint (Theresa of the Child Jesus), Fr. *Thérèse de Lisieux,* 1873–97, French Carmelite nun, one of the most beloved of Roman Catholic saints, called the Little Flower of Jesus; originally named Thérèse Martin. Her complete and shining goodness is reflected in her much-read spiritual autobiography. She taught the Little Way—sanctity through humble tasks. Her cryptic promise, "After my death I will let fall a shower of roses," is recalled by statues showing her with an armful of roses. Also Teresa.

Thermidor (Fr. tĕrmēdôr'), 11th month of French Revolutionary calendar. The coup d'état of 9 Thermidor (July 27, 1794) marked the downfall of ROBESPIERRE and the end of the Great Terror. The Thermidorian leaders (Barras, Cambacérès, Sieyès, Tallian) took reprisals against the Terrorists (though some had themselves taken part in the Terror); repealed the maximum-price laws; made a truce with the counterrevolutionists in the Vendée. The period of "Thermidorian reaction" ended with the establishment of the DIRECTORY (1795).

thermometer, instrument for measuring TEMPERATURE. Fahrenheit thermometer (developed by G. D. Fahrenheit) initiated mercury as heat-measuring medium; Réaumur thermometer (invented by R. A. F. de Réaumur) used alcohol. Centigrade or Celsius thermometer (invented by Anders Celsius) is most commonly used in laboratories. Clinical thermometer is small, uses mercury, and is marked with Fahrenheit or Centigrade scales. Maximum and minimum thermometers indicate highest and lowest temperatures during period of exposure. For low temperatures alcohol, ether, and toluol are used; for very high, there are special devices that work on principle of measureable change varying with temperature (e.g., electrical resistance).

Thermopolis (thůrmŏ'půlĭs), town (pop. 2,870), N central Wyo., on Bighorn R. Resort with hot springs. Near by is Wind River Canyon.

Thermopylae (thůrmŏ'pĭlē), pass between Mt. Oeta and the swamps of the shore of the Malic Gulf, Greece. Here in 480 B.C. Leonidas and his Spartans and their allies fought against the Persians to the last man (see PERSIAN WARS). The Greeks long held back the Gauls under Brennus at this pass in 279 B.C., and the Romans defeated Antiochus III of Syria in 191 B.C.

thermostat, device for automatically regulating temperature. Is commonly connected to heating systems which it turns on or off, according to need, to maintain predetermined temperature. Principle of operation is based on expansion of metals, liquids, and gases when heated; movement of component substance as it takes expanded or contracted position actuates a control on a furnace, cooling system, or piece of machinery.

Thersander (thůrsăn'důr), in Greek legend, son of POLYNICES. The Epigoni made him king of Thebes.

Theseus (thē'sūs, -sēůs), in Greek mythology, hero of Athens; son of AEGEUS, king of Athens. He had many adventures, e.g., slaying of the bull of Marathon and the Minotaur of Crete (with Ariadne's help). He succeeded his father as king of Athens. After participating in expedition against the Ama-

zons and in Calydonian hunt he married Phaedra, who caused death of his son, HIPPOLYTUS.

Thespis (thĕ'spĭs), fl. 534 B.C., in Greek tradition, the inventor of tragedy. He modified the dithyramb so as to introduce a second actor.

Thessalonians (thĕ"sůlō'nēůnz), epistles of New Testament, called 1 and 2 Thessalonians, written by St. Paul to church at Thessalonica. In 1 Thessalonians, Paul praises the church for the strength of its faith but corrects certain misconceptions that had arisen regarding the Second Coming of Christ. In 2 Thessalonians, Paul strongly condemns these false notions. Authenticity of apocalyptic passages (1.6–10 and 2.1–12) questioned by some critics.

Thessalonica, Thessalonike, or **Thessaloniki,** Greece: see SALONICA.

Thessaly (thĕ'sůlē), region of N Greece. In ancient times the mountain-girt plains yielded grain, horses, and cattle. Jason, tyrant of Pherae, briefly united it with other cities, Larissa and Crannon (374 B.C.), but Thessaly fell to Philip II of Macedon in 344 B.C. A province in the late Roman Empire, it passed to the Venetians (1204), the Turks (1355), and modern Greece (1881).

Thetford, municipal borough (pop. 4,445), Norfolk, England. Here is Castle Hill, one of Great Britain's largest earthworks.

Thetford Mines, city (pop. 15,095), SE Que., Canada, S of Quebec. Asbestos-mining center.

Thetis (thē'tĭs), in Greek legend, a nereid; mother of Achilles. Because of a prophecy that her son would be greater than his father, Zeus and Poseidon, who loved her, gave her to a mortal, PELEUS.

thiamine: see VITAMINS.

Thiaucourt (tyōkōōr'), village (1946 pop. 995), NE France, in Lorraine, NW of Nancy. Captured by American troops (Sept., 1918) in World War I; now site of Saint-Mihiel American cemetery.

Thibault, Jacques Anatole: see FRANCE, ANATOLE.

Thibodaux (tĭ'bůdō), town (pop. 7,730) SE La., on Bayou Lafourche and SW of New Orleans, in oil and sugar area. Chief Justice White born near by.

Thief River Falls, city (pop. 6,926), NW Minn., at junction of Thief and Red Lake rivers. Farm trade center. Near-by tracts were used in Federal resettlement project for farm families.

Thierry I, Frankish king: see THEODORIC I.

Thierry, Augustin (ōgüstē' tyĕrē'), 1795–1856, French historian. Chief work is *Récits des temps mérovingiens* (1870).

Thiers, Adolphe (ädôlf' tyĕr'), 1797–1877, French statesman, journalist, and historian. In the opposition against Charles X he represented the middle-of-the-road *Doctrinaires* or bourgeois liberals. His journal *Le National* helped to bring about the JULY REVOLUTION of 1830. Under Louis Philippe he was minister of the interior (1832–34) and twice premier (1836, 1840), then passed to the opposition. He was a leader of the right-wing liberals in the Second Republic and Second Empire; voted against declaring war on Prussia (1870); was chosen, during the FRANCO-PRUSSIAN WAR, chief executive of the provisional government. After negotiating the preliminary Peace of Versailles with Bismarck, he suppressed the COMMUNE OF PARIS of 1871 with ferocious severity and was named president of the republic. Though an Orleanist at heart, he sought to conciliate the republican minority in the national assembly and was forced to resign by the monarchists. MacMahon succeeded him. Thiers' historic works—*History of the French Revolution* (10 vols., 1823–27; Eng. tr., 5 vols., 1895); *History of the Consulate and the Empire* (20 vols., 1840–55; Eng. tr., 1845–62)—hail the French Revolution and Napoleon and reflect his somewhat shallow liberalism.

Thionville (tyōvēl'), Ger. *Diedenhofen,* town (pop. 15,195), Moselle dept., NE France, in a rich iron-mining district. Scene of a Prussian victory over Bazaine (1870).

Third Republic: see FRANCE.

Thirteen Colonies, the, term used for colonies of British North America that joined in American Revolution and became the United States. They were New Hampshire, Massachusetts, Rhode Island, Connecticut, New York, New Jersey, Pennsylvania, Delaware, Maryland, Virginia, North Carolina, South Carolina, and Georgia.

Thirty-nine Articles: see CREED.

Thirty Tyrants, oligarchy organized at Athens after Sparta had won the Peloponnesian War (404 B.C.). Lysander was its leader. They were overthrown by Thrasybulus (403 B.C.).

Thirty Years War, 1618–48, general European war, fought mainly in Germany. There were many issues—territorial, dynastic, religious—and throughout the war there were shifting alliances and local peace treaties. The whole conflict can be understood only as the struggle of a number of German princes, backed by foreign powers such as France, Sweden, Denmark, and England, against the unity of the Holy Roman Empire and the house of Hapsburg, which then ruled Spain, the empire, Austria, Bohemia, Hungary, most of Italy, and the S Netherlands. The war began when the Protestant Bohemian nobles deposed King Ferdinand (later Emperor Ferdinand II) and elected FREDERICK THE WINTER KING in his stead. The imperialist forces under TILLY and the Catholic League under Duke MAXIMILIAN I of Bavaria defeated the Bohemians at the White Mt. (1620) and were victorious in the Palatinate over Mansfeld and Christian of Brunswick (1622–23), but the intervention of CHRISTIAN IV of Denmark on the "Protestant" side opened a new phase. Defeated by Tilly and WALLENSTEIN, the Danes by the Treaty of Lübeck withdrew from the war (1629). A new issue was brought up in 1629, when Ferdinand II attempted to enforce the Peace of AUGSBURG of 1555 and to confiscate lands that had been secularized after 1552. GUSTAVUS II of Sweden, backed by France, marched into Germany, defeated the imperials at Breitenfeld (1631), on the Lech (1632), and at Lützen (1632); though he was killed in his last victory, the Swedes continued in the war. The tide seemed to turn in 1634, when the imperials won the great victory of Nördlingen. A compromise peace was concluded among the German states at Prague (1635). To prevent an imperial victory and the expulsion of the Swedes, France now openly joined Sweden, and the war entered its last and bloodiest phase, spreading to the Low Countries, Italy, the Iberian Peninsula, and Scandinavia. BERNHARD OF SAXE-WEIMAR, the Swedes BANÉR, TORSTENSSON, and WRANGEL, and the French under Louis II de CONDÉ and TURENNE were, despite temporary setbacks, victorious. Peace negotiations began 1640 but the fighting continued until the Peace of WESTPHALIA (1648) and—in the case of France and Spain—until the Peace of the PYRENEES (1659). Germany was in ruins, depopulated and starving. The Holy Roman Empire became a hollow shell. The house of Austria began its decline. France emerged as the chief power of Europe.

Thisbe: see PYRAMUS AND THISBE.

thistle, spiny, usually weedy plant with showy flower heads (purple, rose, yellow, or white), and thistledown seeds. The Scotch thistle (*Onopordum acanthium*) is the emblem of Scotland. The blessed thistle or St.-Benedict's-thistle (*Cnicus benedictus*), an ancient heal-all, is sometimes grown in gardens. Other thistles are the bull thistle (*Cirsium lanceolatum*) and a pernicious weed, Canada thistle (*C. arvense*).

Thistlewood, Arthur, 1770–1820, English conspirator. Plotted to assassinate cabinet members. Government (warned of plan) discovered arsenal in Cato Street. He was executed. Plot is known as Cato Street Conspiracy.

Thokoly or **Tokoly, Emeric** (both: tû'kûē), Hung. *Thököly Imre,* 1665–1705, Hungarian nobleman. Commanded Hungarian uprising against Austrian rule; received French subsidies; persuaded Sultan Mohammed IV to undertake siege of VIENNA (1683). He later was interned near Constantinople.

Thomas, Saint, one of the Twelve Apostles, called Didymus [Gr.,= twin]. He doubted the Resurrection until he saw Jesus and touched His side. John 11.16; 14.5; 20.24–29; 21.2. Feast: Dec. 21. Among the pseudepigrapha are a Gospel and an Acts of Thomas.

Thomas, Albert (älbĕr' tômä'), 1878–1932, French Socialist. Held cabinet positions in World War I; directed International Labor Office (1919–32).

Thomas, Ambroise (tōmä'), 1811–96, French composer of numerous ballets and 20 operas, of which *Mignon, Le Caïd,* and *Hamlet* were the most successful.

Thomas, Augustus (tŏ'mûs), 1857–1934, American dramatist. Highly popular plays include *Alabama* (1891), *The Witching Hour* (1907), *The Copperhead* (1918).

Thomas, Dylan (Marlais) (dĭ'lûn), 1914–, British poet, b. Wales. His fresh, exuberant poems have caused him to be considered one of the most important of living poets. His *Collected Poems* appeared in 1952.

Thomas, George Henry, 1816–70, Union general in Civil War. In CHATTANOOGA CAMPAIGN his stand on Sept. 20, 1863, won him sobriquet Rock of Chickamauga. He commanded Army of the Cumberland, fought under Sherman in Atlanta campaign.

Thomas, M(artha) Carey, 1857–1935, American educator and feminist. In 1884 she organized Bryn Mawr, serving as dean until 1894 and then as president until 1922. She was president (1906–13) of Natl. Collegiate Equal Suffrage League.

Thomas, Norman M(attoon), 1884–, American Socialist leader. Often Socialist party candidate for President since 1928.

Thomas, Seth, 1785–1859, American clock manufacturer. Estab. 1812 at Plymouth Hollow (later Thomaston), Conn., factory enlarged by son **Seth Thomas,** 1816–88.

Thomas, Theodore, 1835–1905, American conductor, b. Germany; came to the U.S. 1845. He conducted his own orchestra (founded 1862) with which he toured the country; the New York Philharmonic, 1877–78 and after 1880; and the Chicago Orchestra, 1891–1905. He introduced major works of Brahms, Wagner, and Richard Strauss to American audiences and did much to create an interest in music.

Thomas à Becket, Saint, 1117–70, English martyr, archbishop of Canterbury. Of good family and well educated, he attracted the attention of Henry II, who made him chancellor (1155). Then, contrary to Thomas's wishes, he was made archbishop, after being ordained and consecrated (1162). King and archbishop were then opposed, particularly over the king's effort to gain jurisdiction over "criminous clerks" (i.e., clergymen accused of crime). Thomas refused to accept the Constitutions of Clarendon (1164) and opposed the growing royal power. He fled to the Continent (1164). In 1170 a sort of peace was patched up, and Thomas returned to England. Meanwhile, Henry had had his son crowned by the archbishop of York. The bishops who took part in the ceremony were suspended by the pope. Feeling between king and archbishop grew high. Thomas was on Dec. 29, 1170, murdered in the cathedral by partisans of Henry, who may or may not have known of the plot to kill Thomas. In 1174 the king was forced to do penance at the tomb of St. Thomas in Canterbury, which became the greatest of English shrines. Feast: Dec. 29. Also Thomas Becket.

Thomas à Kempis, b. 1379 or 1380, d. 1471, German monk, b. Kempen, author or copyist of the devotional work, *The Following* (or *Imitation*) *of Christ,* possibly an adaptation of a work by Gerard GROOTE.

Thomas Aquinas, Saint (ûkwī'nûs), 1225–74, Italian philosopher, known as the Angelic Doctor; of the ruling family of Aquino, S Italy. A Dominican, he became the favorite pupil of Albertus Magnus at Paris and in 1248 went to Cologne with Albertus. He returned to Paris, where he was professor of theology. He opposed the Averroistic philosophy of Siger de Brabant successfully. He spent his last years at Naples. Called the Dumb Ox because he was slow and heavy, he was nevertheless the most brilliant of scholastic philosophers. His major work is the *Summa theologica* (1267–73), an incomplete but systematic exposition of theology on rational principles. Thomas, holding that theology and science cannot contradict each other since truth is indivisible, set out to reconcile Aristotelian philosophy and Christian belief. His synthesis of these is one of the greatest achievements of philosophy and the highest point of SCHOLASTICISM. He held to the distinction between form and matter—erased only in God himself. He argued that a thing that needs completion by another is in a state of potency. Everything is arranged in ascending order to God, who combines potency and act. To Thomas, evil is only the absence of good. Long misunderstood in the Church, he was finally accepted and his philosophy, Thomism, was declared official by Leo XIII (1879). This does not mean that all Catholics must subscribe to Thomistic doctrines, but they are held in respect by all Catholic believers. Neo-Thomism is a 20th-cent. school of thought both within and outside the Church, applying the principles of St. Thomas Aquinas to modern economic, social, and political problems. Prominent in the movement have been Jacques Maritain, Étienne Gilson, and Mortimer Adler. Feast: March 7.

Thomas Jefferson Memorial, monument, Washington, D.C., in East Potomac Park and on Tidal Basin; dedicated 1943. Building is of white marble in modified Pantheon form. Inside is a statue of Jefferson by Rudulph Evans.

Thomas More, Saint: see MORE, SIR THOMAS.

Thomaston (tŏ'mŭstŭn), city (pop. 6,580), W central Ga., W of Macon near Flint R. Textile center in agr. (cotton, peaches) and livestock area.

Thomasville. 1 City (pop. 14,424), SW Ga., near Fla. line and Ochlockonee R.; founded 1826. Processing center for agr. (cotton, fruit, vegetables, peanuts), livestock, and timber area. Winter resort in section of large estates and gardens. **2** City (pop. 11,154), central N.C., SE of Winston-Salem. Mfg. of furniture and textiles.

Thompson, Benjamin: see RUMFORD, BENJAMIN THOMPSON, COUNT.

Thompson, David, 1770–1857, Canadian geographer, fur trader, and explorer, b. England. Made important map of W Canada. Explored Columbia R. region.

Thompson, Denman, 1833–1911, American actor, author of rural drama *The Old Homestead* (1886).

Thompson, Ernest Seton: see SETON.

Thompson, Francis, 1859–1907, English Roman Catholic poet. Abandoning medicine, he lived in poverty, ill and an opium addict, until in 1888 Wilfrid and Alice Meynell took care of him. His poetry, in three slender volumes—*Poems* (1893), including "The Hound of Heaven"; *Sister Songs* (1895); and *New Poems* (1897)—reveals a deep religious sense, expressed in brilliant imagery and sonorous language.

Thompson, town (pop. 5,585), extreme NE Conn., at R.I. and Mass. lines. Has mfg. of textiles.

Thompson, river of S B.C., Canada, formed by junction of the North Thompson and South Thompson at Kamloops and flowing W and S to the Fraser at Lytton. Discovered 1808 by Simon Fraser.

Thompsonville, Conn.: see ENFIELD.

Thomsen, Vilhelm (vĭl'hĕlm tŏm'sĕn), 1842–1927, Danish philologist. Deciphered bilingual Turkish-Chinese inscription found on Orkhon R. in Mongolia.

Thomson, Sir George Paget: see THOMSON, SIR JOSEPH JOHN.

Thomson, James, 1700–1748, British poet, b. Scotland. Most notable work is blank-verse poem, *The Seasons* ("Winter," 1726; "Summer," 1727; "Spring," 1728; collected, with "Autumn," 1730). Also wrote plays, e.g., *Coriolanus* (produced 1749), and, with David Mallet, masque *Alfred* (1840), containing the famous ode, "Rule Britannia." His poetry, first to challenge 18th-cent. classicism, influenced later poets such as Gray and Cowper.

Thomson, James, 1834–82, British poet and essayist, who used the pseudonym B. V. (Bysshe Vanolis). Noted for darkly pessimistic poem *The City of Dreadful Night* (1880) and lyrics such as "Sunday up the River." Also wrote essays and much criticism.

Thomson, Joseph, 1858–95, Scottish explorer in Africa. Explored Great Rift Valley lakes (1879). Explored Sudan (1885), forestalling German designs on area by concluding treaties with natives for British. In 1890 he explored Zambezi R.

Thomson, Sir Joseph John, 1856–1940. English physicist. Won 1906 Nobel Prize for study of electrical conduction through gases; known also for discovery of electron, study of its mass and charge, development of mathematical theory of electricity and magnetism, and work in radioactivity. His son, **Sir George Paget Thomson,** 1892–, also a physicist, shared the 1937 Nobel Prize for discovery of diffraction phenomena in the electron.

Thomson, Virgil, 1896–, American music critic and composer. Among his works are the opera *Four Saints in Three Acts* (1928; libretto by Gertrude Stein) and film music, including *The Plough That Broke the Plains* (1936), *The River* (1937), and *Louisiana Story* (1948). Music critic for the New York *Herald Tribune* after 1940.

Thomson, William: see KELVIN, WILLIAM THOMSON, 1st BARON.

Thor (thôr), in Germanic religion, Norse god of thunder, hence of might and war, son of Odin. Armed with magical hammer that returned to him, belt of strength, and iron gloves, he warred on giants. His chariot wheels made the thunder. He was kind to humanity and protected marriage. His was chief cult among Norsemen. Identification with Jupiter resulted in translation of *Jove's Day* into *Thursday.*

Thoreau, Henry David (thô'rō, thûrō'), 1817–62, American poet, naturalist, and essayist. A native of Concord, Mass., he was a transcendentalist and an intimate friend of Emerson. Wrote for the *Dial.* A strong individualist, he lived for two years in a cabin at Walden Pond; from this experience came his best-known and classic work, *Walden* (1854). Other works are *A Week on the Concord and Merrimack Rivers* (1849), *The*

Maine Woods (1863), and *Cape Cod* (1865). He was a powerful social critic, and his essay "Civil Disobedience" inspired such men as Gandhi. More famous now than in his own time, he and his ideas have been widely influential.

Thorfinn Karlsefni (thôr'fĭn kärl'sĕvnē), fl. 1002–10, Icelandic leader of attempt to colonize North America. Sought VINLAND; returned to Greenland after three winters. There is disagreement on the dates of his expedition and sites visited.

thorium (thô'rēŭm), gray, metallic, radioactive element (symbol = Th; see also ELEMENT, table). Undergoes disintegration, final product is an isotope of lead. Present in number of minerals. Is a source of atomic energy; some salts are used in medicine.

Thorn, Poland: see TORUN.

Thorndike, Ashley H(orace), 1871–1933, American educator and scholar, professor of English at Columbia Univ. from 1906. Wrote distinguished studies on the drama (e.g., *Tragedy,* 1908; *Shakespeare's Theater,* 1916). A brother, **Edward L(ee) Thorndike,** 1874–1949, was an educator and psychologist at Teachers Col., Columbia (1899–1940). Made important contributions to educational psychology in methods to test and measure intelligence. Another brother, **Lynn Thorndike,** 1882–, became a historian, professor at Columbia after 1924. Known especially for studies on magic and early science.

Thorndike, Dame Sybil, 1882–, English actress. Won acclaim for her Shaksperian portrayals and in such plays as *Medea, Candida,* and *Saint Joan.*

Thornton, William, 1759–1828, American architect, b. Tortola, British Virgin Isls. Received his medical degree in Scotland and came to U.S. in 1787. Though untrained as an architect he submitted a plan for the Capitol at Washington which was accepted in 1793. E. S. Hallet and James Hoban were the original supervisors, but Thornton himself was in charge 1794–1802. Served as commissioner of patents from 1802 until his death.

Thorold, town (pop. 6,397), S Ont., Canada, on Welland Ship Canal and SE of St. Catharines. Paper, pulp, and lumber mills and abrasive works.

thorough bass: see FIGURED BASS.

Thorpe, James, 1888–1953, U.S. athlete. All-American left-halfback at Carlisle Indian School; led team to upset wins (1911–12) over Harvard, Army, and Univ. of Pennsylvania. Won (1912) Olympic pentathlon and decathlon, but was forced to surrender awards because he had played semi-professional baseball. Thorpe later played professional baseball, football.

Thorvaldsen or **Thorwaldsen, Albert Bertel** (tôr'välsŭn), 1770–1844, Danish sculptor, a leader of the neoclassicists. Worked mainly in Rome and Copenhagen. Designed the *Lion of Lucerne,* carved from the native rock at Lucerne by his pupils. Thorvaldsen Mus. in Copenhagen has a large collection of his work (originals and models).

Thoth (thŏth, tōt), moon-god and secretary god of anc. Egyptian religion. He supposedly possessed all secret wisdom. Equated with the Greek Hermes, he is intended by the name HERMES TRISMEGISTUS.

Thothmes, Egyptian kings: see THUTMOSE.

Thousand and One Nights or **Arabian Nights,** a series of stories in Arabic, strung together by the story of Scheherazade or Sheherazade, who kept her husband (a sultan) from killing her by telling these tales over 1,001 nights. Includes stories of Ali Baba and Aladdin. Many of the stories were derived from India, but the collection in its present form is probably native to Persia. First European translation was that by Antoine Galland into French (1704–17). English translations include E. W. Lane's expurgated edition (1840) and Richard Burton's unexpurgated edition (1885–88).

Thousand Islands, N N.Y. and S Ont., Canada, group of over 1,500 islands in the St. Lawrence at outlet of L. Ontario. Some belong to the U.S. and some to Canada. Many are privately owned. Popular summer resort. N.Y. and Ont. mainlands connected by international bridge and viaducts.

Thrace (thrās), region, SE Europe, occupying SE tip of the Balkan Peninsula and comprising NE Greece, S Bulgaria, and Turkey in Europe. Chief cities are Istanbul (considered a separate entity), Adrianople, and Gallipoli. Region is largely agr. Early Thracians inhabited area extending W to the Adriatic; they were pushed E by the Illyrians (c.1300 B.C.) and by the Macedonians (5th cent. B.C.). Although Greek colonies were founded (e.g., at Byzantium), Thrace did not absorb Greek culture. Philip II of Macedon subdued (342 B.C.) S Thrace; Lysimachus ruled (after 323 B.C.) most of the region. Roman rule (after 1st cent. B.C.) greatly benefited Thrace. Since the barbarian invasions (3d cent.) it has remained a battleground. N Thrace passed (7th cent.) to Bulgarians. Ottoman Turks ruled the entire region after the fall of Constantinople (1453). After Bulgaria annexed (1885) Eastern Rumelia, term Thrace referred only to S part of region. After the BALKAN WARS (1912–13), Turkey held E Thrace and Bulgaria held W Thrace. In World War I Greece gained part of Bulgarian Thrace and most of E Thrace, but was later required (1923) to restore E Thrace to Turkey. In World War II, Bulgaria occupied (1941–44) Greek Thrace, but previous boundaries were restored.

Thrale, Hester Lynch, later **Madame Piozzi** (pēŏz'ē, pēōt'sē), 1741–1821, English friend of Dr. Johnson.

thrasher, bird of mockingbird and catbird family. Name probably refers to its habit of tail twitching. Brown thrasher of E U.S. (often miscalled brown thrush) is larger than a robin and reddish brown above with pale under parts streaked with brown. Other species found in W and SW U.S.

Thrasybulus (thră"sĭbū'lŭs), d. c.389 B.C., Athenian leader. After Athens lost the Peloponnesian War, he got Theban help and came back from Phyle with other exiles to overthrow the Thirty Tyrants installed in Athens by Sparta (403 B.C.).

Three Emperors' League, informal alliance among Austria-Hungary, Germany, and Russia, announced officially 1872. Its aim was to insure peace among the three powers in case any of them became involved in war. Shaken by Russo-Turkish War (1877–78), it was eclipsed by German-Austrian alliance (1879), which later became the Triple Alliance.

Three Holy Children, the three Jews who were cast into the fiery furnace by Nebuchadnezzar and delivered by an angel. Their names are Shadrach, Meshach, and Abed-nego, in Babylonian; Azariah, Hananiah, and Mishael, in Hebrew; and Azarias, Ananias, and Misael, in Greek. Dan. 1.7; 3. The Song of the Three Holy Children, consisting of their prayers while in the furnace, is included in Western canon but is placed in the Apocrypha in AV.

Three Kingdoms, period of Chinese history from 220 to 265, following collapse of Han dynasty. So called because of division of China into three states: Wei, Shu, and Wu. The Wei became dominant and estab. TSIN dynasty.

Three Kings: see WISE MEN OF THE EAST.

Three Rivers, Que.: see TROIS RIVIÈRES.

Three Rivers, city (pop. 6,785), SW Mich., S of Kalamazoo, on St. Joseph R. at junction of Portage and Rocky rivers. Farm trade center with mfg. of metal products. Has Indian remains.

threshing, separation of seed or grain from plant stalks. The first known method, flail threshing, was striking the ear with a stick. The essential operation in Andrew Meikle's drum threshing machine, invented in 1784, is implicit in the thresher of today. The machines feed in the grain, which is threshed from the head, separated from the straw, and delivered, after cleaning, to a weigher. A combine is a machine that first reaps and then threshes. Tractors powered by gasoline or kerosene are commonly used to operate threshing equipment.

thrift: see SEA PINK.

thrips, minute, agile, black, yellowish, or reddish-brown sapsucking insect found on plants. Species include onion, pear, greenhouse, and grass thrips.

thrombosis (thrŏmbō'sĭs), formation of blood clot (thrombus) in heart or blood vessels. If circulation is blocked, instant death may follow. In coronary thrombosis, clot forms in a coronary artery supplying blood to the heart.

Throop, borough (pop. 5,861), NE Pa., on Lackawanna R. and NE of Scranton. Coal mining.

thrush (thrŭsh), bird of family (Turdidae) of c.700 species and subspecies of almost worldwide distribution and noted for their beautiful songs. Includes North American ROBIN and BLUEBIRD and the solitaire, hermit, and wood thrushes.

Thucydides (thūsĭ'dĭdēz), c.460–400 B.C., Greek historian of Athens, one of greatest ancient historians. His one work, history of Peloponnesian War to 411 B.C., is military record devoid of social and political references apart from war, noted for famous speeches, e.g., Pericles' funeral oration.

Thugs (thŭgz), former religious fraternity of robbers and murderers in India, also called Phansigars [stranglers]. Disguised as merchants or holy men, they waylaid wealthy travelers whom they killed as sacrifices to Hindu goddess Kali. Repressed 1829–36 by British, who executed some 300 of them.

Thule (thū'lē, thōō'lē), name the ancients gave to most northerly land of Europe, an island discovered c.310 B.C. by Pytheas and variously identified with modern lands. Phrase "Ultima Thule" figuratively denotes the most distant goal of human endeavor.

Thule (thōō'lē), settlement and colony district (pop. 322), NW Greenland. Founded 1910 by Knud Rasmussen. In 1952 an air base was being built here.

thulium (thū'lēŭm), metallic element of rare earths (symbol = Tm; see also ELEMENT, table).

Thun (tōōn), resort town (pop. 24,135), Bern canton, Switzerland, on Aar R. and L. of Thun, at foot of Bernese Alps.

thunderstorm, violent local atmospheric disturbance with lightning, thunder, heavy rain, often strong wind gusts, sometimes HAIL. Caused by instability; may result from sun's heating of moist air mass near surface on summer afternoon. Expansion-cooled rising air condenses, forming cumulus (turning to cumulonimbus) cloud, turbulent within. Amidst turbulence raindrops continually break up and reunite, building up electrical charges that produce lightning. (Discharge of lightning may take place within cloud, between two clouds, or between cloud and earth.) Storms are also caused by cooling of upper layers of air at night and by advance of wedge-shaped cold air mass against warm air, forcing it to rise.

Thurber, James, 1894–, American humorist. Many of his drawings and sketches appeared in *The New Yorker;* they are collected in such books as *The Seal in the Bedroom* (1932) and *The Thurber Album* (1952). With E. B. White he wrote the satire *Is Sex Necessary?* (1929); and with Elliott Nugent the comedy *The Male Animal* (1940).

Thurgau (tōōr'gou), canton (388 sq. mi.; pop. 149,360), NE Switzerland, on L. of Constance; cap. Frauenfeld. Fertile cultivated region, watered by Thur R. Was conquered in 1460 from the Hapsburgs by the Swiss cantons, which ruled it jointly until 1798. Became canton 1803. Population is mainly Protestant and German-speaking.

Thuringia (thyōōrĭn'jŭ), Ger. *Thüringen,* state (6,022 sq. mi.; pop. 2,927,497), central Germany; cap. Erfurt. It is crossed by the Thuringian Forest, a wooded range rising to 3,222 ft., and extends to the foot of the Harz mts. in the N. Fertile agr. land. Industries (textiles, optical and precision instruments, machinery, glass) are centered at Jena, Gotha, Gera Erfurt, Mühlhausen. Ancient Germanic tribe of Thuringians were conquered by the Franks in 6th–8th cent. and converted to Christianity by St. Boniface. Landgraves of Thuringia, whose seat was the Wartburg, became immediate princes of Holy Roman Empire in 11th cent., but after 1247 the succession was long contested; the major share eventually fell to the WETTIN dynasty of Saxony. The division of Wettin lands (1485) left most of Thuringia to the Ernestine branch, which split up into several duchies (see SAXE-ALTENBURG; SAXE-COBURG; SAXE-COBURG-GOTHA; SAXE-GOTHA;

SAXE-MEININGEN; SAXE-WEIMER; SAXE-WEIMAR-EISENACH). The Reformation was introduced in the 16th cent. The duchies joined the German Confederation (1815), the German Empire (1871), and, after the expulsion of the dukes in 1918, were united as the state of Thuringia under the Weimar Republic (1920). After World War II its territory was considerably increased by the addition of Prussian enclaves and the state came under Russian occupation. It joined the [East] German Democratic Republic in 1949.

Thursday: see WEEK.

Thurso (thûr'sō), burgh (pop. 3,203), Caithness, Scotland, most northerly burgh on Scottish mainland.

Thutmose (thŭt'mōz, tŭt'–), kings of anc. Egypt. Name also Thothmes. **Thutmose I,** fl. 1540 B.C., successor of Amenhotep I in XVIII dynasty. Subjugated peoples of the upper Nile and Syria. Had two sons, **Thutmose II** and **Thutmose III,** and a daughter, Hatshepsut (also wife of Thutmose III). Thutmose III seized the throne from his father (1501 B.C.), and Thutmose II ruled briefly, but it was Hatshepsut who triumphantly ruled long as "king." After her death (c.1481 B.C.), Thutmose III defeated the Syrians and their allies at Megiddo (1479? B.C.) and made all Asia Minor tributary to Egypt. **Thutmose IV** was son and successor of Amenhotep II and reigned c.1420–c.1411 B.C.

Thyestes (thīĕ'stēz), in Greek legend, son of PELOPS, brother of ATREUS, and father of AEGISTHUS.

thyme (tīm), aromatic herb or shrubby plant (*Thymus*) of the mint family. The common Old World thyme (*Thymus vulgaris*) is used for seasoning and yields an essential oil containing THYMOL. Creeping thyme or mother-of-thyme (*T. serpyllum*), a ground cover and rock garden plant, has small purple flowers.

thymol (thī'mōl), colorless, crystalline organic compound with thymelike odor. Used as antiseptic and in treatment of hookworm disease and trichinosis.

thymus gland (thī'mus), mass of lymphoid tissue found in many vertebrates. In man, it lies in chest cavity. Enlarges until puberty, then grows smaller. Function is uncertain; there is some evidence that its secretion helps to control growth.

thyroid gland (thī'roid), ductless gland in neck functioning in control of metabolism rate. Secretes thyroxin, an iodine compound, directly into blood. Enlargement of gland is known as goiter. Simple (endemic) goiter results from iodine deficiency; prevented or cured by adding iodine to diet. Exophthalmic goiter (Graves's disease) is caused by oversecretion of thyroxin. Thyroid insufficiency may result in myxedema in adult or in CRETINISM.

Ti, chemical symbol of the element TITANIUM.

Tia Juana, Mexico: see TIJUANA.

Tibbett, Lawrence, 1896–, American baritone. Made his debut at the Metropolitan Opera, New York, in 1923. Also appeared in several moving pictures.

Tiber (tī'bur), Ital. *Tevere,* Latin *Tiberis,* river, 251 mi. long, central Italy, rising in Tuscan Apennines and flowing S and SW through Rome into the Tyrrhenian.

Tiberias (tībēr'ēus), town (est. pop. 7,700), NE Israel, on Sea of Galilee. Built by Herod Antipas, it was named for Emperor Tiberius. Became a center for Jews after destruction of Jerusalem. Health resort with hot springs.

Tiberius (tībēr'ēus), 42 B.C.–A.D. 37, Roman emperor (A.D. 14–37); son of Tiberius Claudius Nero and Livia Drusilla. He was governor of Transalpine Gaul, aided his brother Drusus in Germany, and later campaigned in Germany and in Illyricum himself. He succeeded his stepfather Augustus and regularized state finances. For years Sejanus was his chief aid, but Tiberius in later years grew suspicious of everyone and even had Sejanus killed.

Tibet (tībĕt'), country (560,000 sq. mi.; pop. 3,000,000), central Asia; cap. Lhasa; autonomous province (since 1951) of China. Bordered on N and E by China proper and on S by India. One of highest regions of the world (average elevation c.15,000 ft.), it is mainly a vast plateau between Kunlun mts. (N) and Himalayas (S). Farming is possible only in valleys of Tsangpo (Brahmaputra), Indus, and Sutlej rivers. Chief mineral deposits are gold, iron pyrites, salt, soda, and borax. Tibet's religion is LAMAISM, derived from a form of Buddhism. Titular head of Tibetan government is the Dalai Lama, with the Panchen (or Tashi) Lama second in importance. After adopting Buddhism from India in 8th cent. Tibet practically isolated itself from the rest of the world. China conquered the area in 1720 and thereafter claimed suzerainty, but Tibet, encouraged by Britain, declared its independence in 1913. Chinese Communists invaded Tibet in 1950 and reduced it to its present status. Though supposedly still ruled by the Dalai Lama and the Panchen Lama (installed by the Chinese), Tibet is actually under a Chinese military commission.

Tibetan art shows the influence of India, China, and Persia. The Bon (pre-Buddhist) statues are Chinese in feeling. After the introduction of Buddhism from India (8th cent.), Tibetan artists copied the sculptures and paintings illustrating Buddhist teachings, giving a native interpretation to their work but failing to create a truly original art. In architecture the Chinese roof and the bulbous dome of India are much used. Tibetan painting, usually in tempera, appears most often in temple banners (tankas) made of cotton or silk and is characterized by crude colors (e.g., vermilion, vivid green, and blue). The rendering of the restricted subject matter (controlled by the lamas) has been so unvarying that examples of ancient art have sometimes been confused with those of the modern period. Tibetan craftsmen excel in all kinds of metalwork, ranging from the huge bronze statues, with their many heads and arms, to jewelry and intricate silver and gold receptacles for religious objects.

Tibetan language, Tibeto-Burman language of Indo-Chinese family. See LANGUAGE (table).

Tibullus (Albius Tibullus) (tĭbŭ'lus), c.55 B.C.–19 B.C., Roman poet. Master of the Latin love elegy.

Ticino (tēchē′nō), canton (1,086 sq. mi.; pop. 175,520), S Switzerland, on S slope of central Alps, bordering on Italy; cap. Bellinzona. Has pastures, vineyards; some agr. There are many resorts on Lake MAGGIORE and L. LUGANO. Population is largely Catholic and Italian-speaking. Region shared history of Lombardy until its conquest by the Swiss from Milan in 15th–16th cent. It was ruled as subject territory by Schwyz and Uri cantons until 1798; became a canton 1803. The **Ticino** river, 154 mi. long, rises in the Saint Gotthard and flows S through L. Maggiore into Italy, joining the Po below Padua. The river was the scene of Hannibal's victory over Scipio (218 B.C.).

tick, an arachnid, nearly identical with mite but larger than most species. It is parasitic, living on mammal or bird blood. Certain ticks spread diseases including tularemia and Rocky Mountain spotted fever, relapsing fever, and cattle fever.

Ticknor, George, 1791–1871, American author and teacher of languages. At Harvard after study abroad, he introduced thorough German methods. His *History of Spanish Literature* (1849) was notable.

tickseed: see COREOPSIS.

Ticonderoga (tī″kŏndûrō′gů), resort village (pop. 3,517), NE N.Y., between Lakes George and Champlain; settled in 17th cent. Graphite mines supply local pencil industry. Site of battles in French and Indian Wars and American Revolution.

tidal theory, hypothesis of origin of solar system, formulated 1918 by James Jeans and later modified by Harold Jeffreys. Differs from PLANETESIMAL HYPOTHESIS chiefly in assuming tidal-wave crest was detached from sun by attraction of visiting star and separated into masses which then condensed to form planets.

tide, alternate rise and fall of waters in large bodies of water, caused by the gravitational effect of moon, sun, and, slightly, of other planets and stars. The moon's effective force is about 2¼ times that of the sun. Two high tides come at once: direct, on the side of the globe facing the moon; indirect, on the opposite side. The average interval between them is 12 hr. and 25 min. Irregularities from other factors cause (1) two high and two low water tides per lunar day, (2) one tidal cycle per lunar day, (3) two tidal cycles with marked disparities in height and duration. Tidal range is difference in level of successive high and low waters. Max. range (spring tide) occurs when earth, moon, and sun are in line; min. range (neap tide) occurs when sun and moon are at right angles. Tidal range also varies with coastal configuration and barometric pressure. Tidal ebb and flow cause tidal currents.

tidewater, in U.S. history, that part of the Atlantic coastal plain extending inland to the area reached by oceanic tides or to the fall line. Settled first, it became in the Southern colonies the region of large plantations and of important commercial towns. Tidewater aristocracy, allied with colonial officialdom, so completely dominated local government that frontier people were several times driven to insurrection. Eventually other areas triumphed.

Tieck, Ludwig (lo͞ot′vĭkh tēk′), 1773–1853, German romantic poet, dramatist, and novelist. Made notable translation of *Don Quixote* and with others completed Schlegel's translation of Shakspere. His works include the satirical comedy *Puss in Boots* (1797; Eng. tr., 1913) and *Tales from the Phantasus* (1812–16; Eng. tr., 1845).

Tien Shan (tyĕn′ shän′), mountain system of central Asia, in Russian Turkestan and Sinkiang prov., China. Highest peaks are Pobeda Peak (24,406 ft.) and Khan Tengri (22,949 ft.).

Tienstin (tĭn″tsĭn′, tĭn″sĭn′), city (pop. 1,686,543), Hopeh prov., China, at junction of Pai R. and Grand Canal; leading port of N China plain. It produces textiles, glass, leather goods, and processed foods. Seat of two universities. Occupied by British and French in mid-19th cent. After 1861 when it became a treaty port, concessions were made for foreign settlements. Occupied by foreign troops in Boxer Rebellion (1900). Held 1937–45 by the Japanese. Fell to Communists in 1949.

Tiepolo, (Giovanni Battista) (tyā′pōlō), 1696–1770, Venetian painter. Revived the grand manner of Venetian baroque. Won fame by his early frescoes in Labia Palace and the doge's palace in Venice. Worked in Würzburg and Madrid (after 1763), where he created frescoes for palaces. Also produced many oils. His style is marked by superb draughtsmanship and scintillating brushwork.

Tierra del Fuego (tyĕ′rä dĕl fwā′gō), archipelago, area c.18,500 sq. mi., off S South America, comprising one large and several small islands separated from mainland by Strait of Magellan. E part, an extension of Patagonia, belongs to Argentina (cap. Ushuaia); W part, a continuation of Andes, belongs to Chile (cap. PUNTA ARENAS). Sheep are raised, timber is exported, and there is some mining. Aborigines are called Fuegians.

Tiffany, Charles Lewis (tĭ′fůnē), 1812–1902, American merchant, founder of Tiffany and Co., New York city. Introduced English standard of sterling silver, 1851. An art patron in later life. His son, **Louis Comfort Tiffany,** 1848–1943, was an artist and manufacturer of stained glass. In 1919 he endowed a foundation providing for study of art at his summer home at Oyster Bay, N.Y. Foundation was reorganized 1946 to provide for study and travel grants to art students.

Tiffin, city (pop. 18,952), N Ohio, on Sandusky R. and SE of Toledo; founded c.1820. Mfg. of glass and electrical products. Seat of Heidelberg Col. (Evangelical-Reformed; coed.; 1850).

Tiflis (tĭ′flĭs), Georgian *Tbilisi,* city (pop. 519,175), cap. of Georgian SSR, on Kura R., hemmed in by spurs of Greater and Lesser Caucasus. Economic and cultural metropolis of Transcaucasia. Produces machinery, silk, cotton, tobacco, and wine. Has a university (founded 1918), polytechnic and medical schools, opera, and other cultural institutions. First mentioned 4th cent. A.D., it reached its greatest flowering in the 12th–13th cent. Its old section, with picturesque streets and bazaars, has hot sulphur springs. Most of city, however, is modern. Among many churches are Zion Cathedral (first built 7th cent.), St. David's (6th cent.), and Metskh Church (13th cent.; now a museum). Mt. David, a favorite excursion point, dominates the city.

Tifton, city (pop. 6,831), S central Ga., ESE of Albany. Tobacco market. Yarns, cottonseed oil.

tiger, Asiatic carnivorous mammal (*Panthera tigris* or *Felis tigris*) of cat family. It has no mane; coat is usually orange-yellow striped with black. Males are 8–10 ft. in total length and some weigh over 500 lb. Hunt mostly at night.

Tiglath-pileser (tĭ'glăth-pĭlē'zûr), kings of anc. Assyria. **Tiglath-pileser I,** d. c.1102 B.C. He conquered much of Asia Minor. **Tiglath-pileser III,** d. 728 B.C., made himself master of rebellious Babylonia, of Syria, and of Media. He aided Ahaz, king of Judah.

Tigris (tī'grĭs), biblical *Hiddekil,* river, SW Asia, rising in E Turkey and flowing c.1,150 mi., mostly in Iraq, to join the EUPHRATES, with which it forms the SHATT EL ARAB. Ancient cities of Nineveh and Ctesiphon were on its banks. Navigable by small steamers upstream to Baghdad. Lower course is connected with the Euphrates by canals.

Tihwa, China: see URUMCHI.

Tijuana (tēhwä'nä), city (pop. 16,486), Lower California, NW Mexico; formerly Tia Juana. Popular resort with famous race tracks and gambling casinos at Agua Caliente.

Tilburg (tĭl'bûrg), municipality (pop. 114,-312), North Brabant prov., S Netherlands. Mfg. center (textiles, dyes).

Tilbury (tĭl'bûrē), former urban district (1931 pop. 16,825), now part of Thurrock, Essex, England, on Thames R. Tilbury Docks (part of Port of London) are terminus of passenger steamship lines.

Tilden, Samuel J(ones), 1814–86, American presidential candidate of the Democratic party in 1876. Governor of N.Y. (1875–76). It seems clear now that Tilden actually won 1876 election, but division of electoral commission along partisan lines gave victory to Republican R. B. Hayes.

Tilden, William Tatem, Jr. (Bill), 1893–, American tennis player. Won U.S. singles (1920–26, 1929), British singles (1920–21, 1930) championships, many other amateur titles. Won (1931, 1935) professional singles crown.

Tillamook (tĭ'lûmŏŏk), city (pop. 3,685), NW Oregon, at head of Tillamook Bay and W of Portland. Noted for cheese.

Till Eulenspiegel: see EULENSPIEGEL, TILL.

Tillman, Benjamin Ryan, 1847–1918, U.S. Senator from S.C. (1895–1918). Governor of S.C. (1890–94); helped to restrict Negro suffrage. As Senator he opposed Cleveland, generally supported Wilson.

Tillsonburg, town (pop. 5,330), E Ont., Canada, ENE of St. Thomas, in tobacco and fruit region.

Tilly, Johannes Tserklaes, count of (yōhä'nûs tsĕrkläs' tĭ'lē), 1559–1632, imperialist general in Thirty Years War, b. Brabant. Commanded army of the Catholic League in victories at WHITE MOUNTAIN (1620), Wimpfen and Höchst (1622), and LUTTER AM BARENBERGE (1626). Took over Wallenstein's command 1630. Stormed MAGDEBURG 1631 (but was not responsible for ensuing massacre). Was defeated by Gustavus II of Sweden at Breitenfeld (1631) and on the Lech, where he was mortally wounded.

Tilsit (tĭl'zĭt), city (1939 pop., 58,468), former East Prussia, a port on the Niemen; transferred to Russian administration 1945 and renamed Sovetsk. Produces leather, a well-known cheese, and lumber. By the Treaty of Tilsit of July 7, 1807, Napoleon I and Alexander I restored peace between France and Russia. Russia recognized the duchy of Warsaw and secretly promised its alliance against England. Two days later, in a second treaty, Napoleon forced Frederick William III of Prussia to cede all Prussian territory W of the Elbe to France and Prussian Poland to the duchy of Warsaw; to reduce his army to 42,000 men; to surrender his chief fortresses to French garrisons; and to join the Continental system.

Tilton, Theodore, 1835–1907, American journalist. He and his wife were parishioners of H. W. BEECHER, whom Tilton sued in 1874 for alleged adultery with Mrs. Tilton. Jury disagreed.

Timanthes (tĭmăn'thēz), c.400 B.C., Greek painter. His masterpiece was the *Sacrifice of Iphigenia.*

timber line, line beyond which trees do not grow. It depends on conditions affecting temperature—altitude, latitude, winds, exposure. Probably limited by an isotherm of 50°F. for warmest month.

Timbuktu (tĭm"bŭktōō'), town (pop. c.7,000), French Sudan, near the Niger; center of caravan trade on trans-Saharan road to Algeria and Morocco. Settled 1087, it flourished as a center of Moslem culture until late 16th cent. and was famous for its gold and slave market.

time, concept variously defined from philosophical, psychological, physical, and biological aspects. Distinction is usually made between experienced duration and time measured by movements of bodies through space. Methods of measuring time are based on some recurring phenomenon, usually on rotation of earth either in relation to sun (solar time) or star (sidereal time). Since solar days are unequal in length, modern time reckoning is based on mean solar day. Because sun's apparent course is westward, local time is 4 min. later for each degree of longitude westward. Standard time (estab. 1884) is based on mean solar day reckoned by Royal Observatory, Greenwich, England, whose longitude is accepted as 0°. Earth's circumference is divided into 24 time belts of 15° each. See also CALENDAR; CLOCK; DAYLIGHT-SAVING TIME; SPACE TIME; SUNDIAL.

time, in music: see TEMPO; RHYTHM; MUSICAL NOTATION.

Timgad (tĭm'găd), ruined city, Algeria, S of Constantine. Called the Pompeii of N Africa because of extensive ruins of a Roman city founded here by Trajan in A.D. 100.

Timiskaming, Lake (tĭmĭ'skŭmĭng), SW Que.

and E Ont., Canada, an expansion of Ottawa R., 62 mi. long. Haileybury is on NW shore.

Timisoara (tēmĕshwä'rä), Hung. *Temesvár,* city (pop. 111,987), W Rumania; chief city of the Banat (former BANAT OF TEMESVAR). Commercial and industrial center. Roman Catholic and Orthodox episcopal see. University (founded 1945). A Roman settlement, Timisoara was annexed to Hungary 1010; fell to the Turks 1552; was recaptured by Eugene of Savoy 1716; was transferred to Rumania 1920. Castle of John of Hunyadi is now a barracks.

Timmins, town (pop. 27,743), E Ont., Canada, on Mattagami R. and NNW of Sudbury. Trade center in rich Porcupine gold-mining district.

Timon (tī'mŭn), one of the seven deacons. Acts 6.5.

Timon of Athens, fl. after 450 B.C., Greek misanthrope, who supported Alcibiades, who, he thought, would ruin Athens. A play about him is attributed to Shakspere.

Timor (tē'môr), island, area 13,071 sq. mi., Indonesia, largest and easternmost of the Lesser Sundas. Long, narrow, and mountainous. Natives are of Malay and Papuan stock. Products include copra and sandalwood. The Portuguese settled here c.1520, the Dutch in 1613. Border between their territories was settled 1859 by treaty and made effective 1914. With creation of state of Indonesia (1949), Dutch Timor (5,765 sq. mi.; pop. 350,064), comprising W half of island, became Indonesian territory. Colony of Portuguese Timor (7,383 sq. mi.; pop. 438,350) comprises E half of island and territory of Oe-Cusse in Indonesian section; cap. Dili.

Timothy, Saint, d. c.100, early Christian, companion of St. Paul. Also called Timotheus. Two epistles bear his name. Acts 16.1–3; Rom. 16.21; 1 Cor. 4.17; 2 Cor. 1.1; Philip 2.19; 1 Thess. 3.2; 2 Thess. 1.1; Philemon 1; Heb. 13.23. Feast: Jan. 24.

Timothy, epistles of New Testament, called 1 and 2 Timothy, traditionally written by St. Paul to Timothy. In 1 Timothy Paul discusses public prayer and qualifications of the clergy. 2 Timothy is more a personal letter. Paul emphasizes courage and fidelity and speaks of his own impending death.

timothy, widely planted North American perennial hay grass (*Phleum pratense*), introduced from Europe. It is not suitable for permanent pasture since it will not survive continuous grazing.

timpani: see PERCUSSION INSTRUMENTS.

Timpanogos Cave National Monument: see NATIONAL PARKS AND MONUMENTS (table).

Timrod, Henry, 1828–67, American poet of the Old South and Civil War, b. S.C. Among his poems are "The Cotton Boll," "Carolina," and "Ethnogenesis," an ode.

Timurids (tĭmōō'rĭdz), dynasty founded by TAMERLANE (or Timur). At his death (1405) his empire extended from Euphrates R. to Jaxartes and Indus rivers. The western empire was quickly brought to an end by capture of Baghdad by the Turkoman horde (1410). But the eastern empire (E of Amu Darya R.) continued to flourish, with Samarkand and Herat as its great cultural centers. In mid-15th cent. the Timurid empire fell into anarchy; the Turkoman horde took much territory, while Uzbeks looted Samarkand. The last of the Timurids, BABER, was one of the petty princes who took over the rule.

tin, lustrous, silver-white, crystalline, metallic element (symbol = Sn; see also ELEMENT, table). Below 18°C. tends to turn to gray powder; very soft, malleable, barely affected by moisture. Used to protect other metals, in alloys. Relatively active, forms stannous (valence = 2) and stannic (valence = 4) compounds. Compounds are used in dyeing, enamels, weighting silk, fireproofing, and medicine. Tin plate for tin cans is iron or steel with thin coating of tin. Tin rarely occurs uncombined in nature; ores are found in Bolivia, Indonesia, Malay Peninsula, Belgian Congo, Nigeria, Cornwall (England).

tinamou (tĭ'nŭmōō), South American game bird resembling partridge but more closely related to ostrich. Plumage is dark, usually barred; bill is slender, wings short.

Tinchebrai or **Tinchebray** (tēshbrā'), small town in Normandy, NW France, where Henry I of England defeated his brother Robert II of Normandy (1106).

Tindal or **Tindale, William:** see TYNDALE, WILLIAM.

Tinian: see MARIANAS ISLANDS.

Tinicum Island (tĭn'ĭkŭm), SE Pa., in Delaware R., SW of Philadelphia; separated from mainland by marshes. Cap. of New Sweden 1643–55.

Tinos: see TENOS.

Tintagel Head (tĭntăj'ŭl), cape, Cornwall, England. Ruined Tintagel Castle (Norman) is the reputed birthplace of King Arthur.

Tintern Abbey, ruins of an abbey, Monmouthshire, England. Subject of a poem by Wordsworth.

Tinto, Río: see RÍO TINTO.

Tintoretto (tĭntŭrĕ'tō, Ital. tēntōrĕt'tō), 1518–94, Venetian painter, one of the great masters of the Renaissance. Real name was Jacopo Robusti; called Il Tintoretto [little dyer] from his father's trade. His impressive paintings (esp. those of late period) are marked by dramatic lighting and broad impressionistic brushwork. Worked c.1564–c.1587 on the great cycle of paintings in Scuola di San Rocco (Venice), which includes the enormous *Crucifixion.* Reputedly the largest oil canvas in the world is his *Paradiso* in the ducal palace at Venice.

Tippecanoe (tĭ"pŭkŭnōō'), river rising in the lake district of NE Ind. and flowing 200 mi. SW to Wabash R. above Lafayette. Gen W. H. Harrison broke power of the Indians in battle of Tippecanoe, Nov. 7, 1811, on site of present village of Battle Ground.

Tipperary (tĭ"pŭrâ'rē), inland county (1,643 sq. mi.; pop. 136,014), S Ireland, in Munster; co. town Tipperary. Administratively divided into North Riding and South Riding. Mountains include Knockmealdowns and Galtees. Golden Vale is richest agr. land in Ireland; dairying is chief occupation. Some lead mining and slate quarrying.

Tippoo Sahib (tĭ'pōō sä'hĭb), 1753–99, maharajah of Mysore, India (1782–99), son of HYDER ALI. Generally allied with French against British, whom he defeated 1782. His invasion of British-held Travancore resulted in his defeat by Cornwallis. Rejecting British demand to disarm, he was besieged and killed at Seringapatam.

Tipton, city (pop. 5,633), central Ind., W of Elwood, in agr. area. Mfg. of machinery.

Tiptonville, town (pop. 1,953), W Tenn., center of recreation area on Reelfoot L.

Tirana or **Tiranë** (tērä'nä, –nů), city (pop. 59,887), cap. of Albania, in central Albania. Was founded early 17th cent. by Turks; modern city was built after 1920, when it became the cap. Has fine mosques of the 17th and 18th cent.

tire. Rubber or synthetic rubber tires include solid tires used on some heavy trucks and pneumatic tires, first manufactured commercially for bicycles c.1889 by John Dunlop in Ireland. One form in common use has inner tube and outer casing built up of alternate plies of diagonal cords and sheets of rubber, topped with rubber padding, breaker strips, and tough thread added after side walls; molds for vulcanizing form tread pattern. Pneumatic tire requiring no inner tube has been developed.

Tiresias (tīrē'shůs, –sēůs), in Greek mythology, blind prophet of Thebes. Blinded either by Athena or by Hera, he was given in compensation prophetic powers. He is said to have foretold most of the great events of Greek mythology.

Tirhakah (tēr'ůků, tērhä'ků) or **Taharka** (tůhär'ků), d. 663 B.C., king of anc. Egypt (688–663 B.C.), last of XXV dynasty, ruling from Tanis. He lost Lower Egypt to Esar-Haddon and later to Assur-bani-pal.

Tirol, Austria: see TYROL.

Tirpitz, Alfred von (äl'frāt fŭn tĭr'pĭts), 1849–1930, German admiral; secretary of state for naval affairs 1897–1916. In World War I he began construction of submarines and advocated unrestricted warfare.

Tirso de Molina (tēr'sō dā mōlē'nä), pseud. of **Gabriel Téllez** (gäbrēēl' tĕl'yāth), 1571–1648, Spanish dramatist, an outstanding figure of the Golden Age, author of 300 to 400 plays.

Tisbury, Mass.: see VINEYARD HAVEN.

Tiselius, Arne (är'nů tēsā'lyŭs), 1902–, Swedish biochemist. Won 1948 Nobel Prize for developing new methods of separating and detecting colloids.

Tishomingo (tĭshůmĭn'gō), city (pop. 2,325), S Okla., NW of Durant and on L. Texoma. Long chief city of Chickasaw Indians.

Tisquantum: see SQUANTO.

Tissaphernes (tĭ"sůfûr'nēz), d. 395 B.C., Persian satrap (governor) in Asia Minor. Aided Artaxerxes II to defeat Cyrus the Younger at Cunaxa (401 B.C.) and pursued the Greeks who had supported Cyrus.

Tisza, Count Stephen, Hung. *Tisza István* (tĭ'sŏ ĭst'vän), 1861–1918, premier of Hungary (1903–5, 1913–17). A nationalist, he sought to make Hungary the dominant partner in Austro-Hungarian Monarchy; took repressive measure against Serbian and Rumanian minorities. In 1914 he at first opposed declaration of war against Serbia, but reversed himself when assured that no Serbian territory would be annexed. Was murdered by soldiers who believed him chief instigator of war.

Tisza, river: see THEISS.

Titan, in Greek mythology, one of 12 male and female giants; children of Uranus and Gaea. They were Cronus, Iapetus, Hyperion, Oceanus, Coeus, Creus, Theia, Rhea, Mnemosyne, Phoebe, Tethys, and Themis. Led by Cronus, they deposed Uranus, and were themselves overthrown by their descendants, the Olympians, in the battle called TITANOMACHY.

Titanic, White Star liner sunk on night of April 14–15, 1912, after hitting iceberg in N Atlantic, with loss of 1,517 lives among some 2,000 passengers. Causes included excessive speed and insufficient, inefficiently manned lifeboats. Resulted in iceberg patrol and in stringent safety rules.

titanium (tītā'nēům), silver-white, lustrous, metallic element (symbol = Ti; see also ELEMENT, table). Adds hardness and tensile strength to steel alloys. It is active chemically; forms a number of compounds. Titanium tetrachloride is used in making smoke screens; titanium dioxide, as white pigment; other compounds are used as yellow pigments, mordants, electric-arc electrodes.

Titanomachy (tī"tůnō'můkē), in Greek mythology, battle between Titans under Cronus and Olympian gods under Zeus, in Thessaly. After 10 years of battle Titans were overthrown when the Cyclopes forged thunderbolt for Zeus. Cronus then went to rule Isles of the Blessed. Atlas had to hold up the sky, and all the other Titans, except Prometheus and Oceanus, who had aided Zeus, were condemned to Tartarus.

Tithonus (tĭthō'nůs), mythical handsome prince of Troy; father of Memnon by the goddess Eos. She won for him immortality but not eternal youth. When he was old, she changed him into a grasshopper.

Titian (tĭ'shůn), 1477–1576, celebrated Venetian painter, whose real name was Tiziano Vecellio, b. Pieve di Cadore in the Dolomites. Influenced by Giovanni Bellini and Giorgione, he developed a sumptuous, coloristic style in the grand manner typical of the High Renaissance. Throughout his long career he was showered with honors. On his visit to Rome (1545–46) he did the famous portrait of Pope Paul III with his nephews (Naples); at this time he met Michelangelo. He was twice invited to Augsburg by Charles V, for whom he painted the *Trinity,* "La Gloria" (Prado). For Philip II Titian painted many religious works and a cycle of mythological paintings which included the *Rape of Europa* (Gardner Mus., Boston). Typifying the heightened emotional content of his final phase is his last work, the magnificent *Pietà* (Academy, Venice).

Titicaca, Lake (tētēkä'kä), area 3,205 sq. mi., divided between Bolivia and Peru. Largest fresh-water lake in South America and highest in world (c.12,500 ft. above sea level; max. depth c.900 ft.). From pre-Incan times it has been center of Indian life. In middle of lake is an island, the legendary birthplace of first Inca. Lake is drained by Desaguadero R.

titles of sovereignty, nobility, and honor. Highest-ranking title, emperor, was originally military. Assumed by Augustus Caesar and sovereigns of later Roman and Byzantine empires; conferred on Charlemagne 800; and assumed by Napoleon 1804. Queen Victoria proclaimed Empress of India 1877. Under Holy Roman Empire titles in descending order below emperor or king were *Herzog* (feminine *Herzogin*); *Pfalzgraf* (*Pfalzgräfin*), *Markgraf* (*Markgräfin*), and *Landgraf* (*Landgräfin*); *Graf* (*Gräfin*); *Baron* (*Baronin*) and *Freiherr* (*Freiherrin*); and *Ritter*. Prefix *Reichs–* before these indicated holding direct from emperor. French titles in descending order are *duc* (*duchesse*); *prince* (*princesse*); *marquis* (*marquise*); *comte* (*comtesse*); *vicomte* (*vicomtesse*); *baron* (*baronne*); *seigneur* or *sire;* and *chevalier*. English titles are *prince* (*princess*); *duke* (*duchess*); *marquess* (*marchioness*); *earl* (*countess*); *viscount* (*viscountess*); *baron* (*baroness*); *baronet;* and *knight* (*dame*). In Italy titles of nobility are *duca* (*duchessa*); *principe* (*principessa*); *marchese* (*marchesa*); *conte* (*contessa*); *visconte* (*viscontessa*); *barone* (*baronessa*). Spanish titles are *duque* (*duquesa*); *príncipe* (*princípesa*); *marqués* (*marquesa*); *conde* (*condesa*); *visconde* (*viscondesa*); and *barón* (*baronesa*).

Tito, Josip Broz (yô'sēp brôz' tē'tô), 1892–, Yugoslav Communist leader, b. Croatia, whose original name was Josip Broz. A blacksmith's son, he turned to Communism in his poverty-stricken youth; was imprisoned by Yugoslav authorities; emerged in 1941 as a partisan leader against the Axis occupation forces in World War II. His successful raids immobilized large Axis forces in Yugoslavia, and by 1943 Tito controlled vast areas with an army of more than 200,000. His rival, Gen. MIKHAILOVICH, soon clashed with Tito, who by 1944 had the full support of the USSR, England, and the U.S. and who was in full control of Yugoslavia at the war's end. After the electoral victory of his Communist-led National Liberation Front (the opposition abstained from voting), Marshal Tito had King Peter II deposed and became premier of the People's Republic of YUGOSLAVIA (1945). He ruled dictatorially. In 1948 the COMINFORM accused him of deviationism, but Tito held his own against Russian pressure. Yugoslav relations with the USSR and other Communist countries grew tense. Tito, while continuing with his Communist program at home, had to turn to the West in his foreign policy.

Titograd (tē'tōgräd), formerly **Podgorica** (pôd'gô"rĭtsä), town (pop. 12,206), cap. of Montenegro, Yugoslavia. Trade center.

Titus (tī'tŭs), A.D. c.40–81, Roman emperor (79–81), son of Vespasian and coruler after 71. It was Titus who destroyed Jerusalem. In Rome he was notable as a builder, completing the Colosseum and building a large bath. Succeeded by Domitian, who erected the **Arch of Titus.**

Titus, early Christian, a missionary and friend of St. Paul. An epistle bears his name. 2 Cor. 2.13; 7.6,7; 8.16–24; Gal. 2.3. Feast: Jan. 4.

Titus, epistle of New Testament, traditionally written by St. Paul to Titus. Like 1 Timothy, it gives points of regulation for governing the church.

Titusville, city (pop. 8,923), NW Pa., N of Oil City. Mfg. of machinery and tools. Near-by state park marks site of first successful oil well (1859) in U.S.

Tiumen, RSFSR: see TYUMEN.

Tiverton (tĭ'vûrtŭn), town (pop. 5,659), SE R.I., SE of Providence. Farming, fishing, mfg. of textiles; resorts.

Tivoli (tē'vōlē), town (pop. 16,886), Latium, central Italy, NE of Rome. Famed for its beautiful site, villas, gardens (notably the VILLA D'ESTE) and for the falls of the Aniene R. Has ruins of Roman villas. Roman Temple of Vesta is now a church.

Tiw (tē'ōō), in Germanic religion, god of battle. Called Tyr by the Norse. He was a wrestler. Tiw's identification with Mars caused Latin *Mars' day* to be translated into *Tiw's Day*, now *Tuesday*.

Tiy (tē), queens of anc. Egypt. **Tiy,** fl. 1400 B.C., was influential in the reigns of her husband, Amenhotep III, and her son, Ikhnaton. Another **Tiy,** fl. 1167 B.C., led an unsuccessful conspiracy against her husband, Ramses III.

Tl, chemical symbol of the element THALLIUM.

Tlaxcala (tläskä'lä), state (1,555 sq. mi.; pop. 282,495), E central Mexico; cap. Tlaxcala (pop. 3,261). Smallest of Mexican states, it is almost surrounded by Puebla. Tlaxcaltec Indians fiercely resisted Cortés but, when defeated, were his valuable allies against Aztec.

Tlemcen (tlĕmsĕn'), city (pop. 50,272), NW Algeria, in the Tell. Flourished 13th–15th cent. as cap. of Moslem Berber dynasty. Known for its numerous splendid mosques and handicraft industries.

Tm, chemical symbol of the element THULIUM.

T.N.T. or **TNT:** see TRINITROTOLUENE.

toad, amphibian animal, more terrestrial than the related frog. It has dry, warty skin and often is dull reddish or yellowish brown with gray median stripe and dark markings. Lives usually in moist, cool place. Horned toad is a LIZARD.

toadflax: see BUTTER-AND-EGGS.

toadstool: see MUSHROOM.

tobacco, plant (genus *Nicotiana*) and product manufactured from leaf. Use originated in W Hemisphere in pre-Columbian times, reached Spain and Portugal in mid-16th cent. and spread into Europe, Asia, Africa. Chief commercial species *Nicotiana tabacum*, native to America, is best grown from seed as annual in regions with mean temperature of c.40°F. Leaves are cured, fermented, and aged. U.S. produces annually c.1,400,000,000 lb. of which c.60% is grown in N.C. and Ky. See also CIGAR AND CIGARETTE.

Tobago: see TRINIDAD AND TOBAGO.

Tobit (tō'–) or **Tobias** (–bī'–), book of Old Testament, placed in Apocrypha in AV, included in Western canon. It tells of Tobit (Vulgate Tobias), a devout Jew in exile, and of his son Tobias. Sent on business to a distant city, the young Tobias and his dog are guided by the archangel Raphael in the form of a young man. They come to the house of a Jew whose daughter, Sara, is afflicted by a demon (Asmodeus). Tobias under the guidance of Raphael exorcises the demon and marries Sara. They return home where Tobias, with Raphael's help, cures his father's blindness. Tobias and his dog with the angel have been a favorite subject of Christian art.

Tobol (tŭbôl′), river, 1,042 mi. long, W Siberia, rising in Mugodzhar Hills, Kazakh SSR, and flowing NNE into RSFSR to join the Irtysh at Tobolsk.

Tobolsk (tŭbôlsk′), city (pop. 32,200), RSFSR, in W Siberia, on Irtysh and Tobol rivers. Market center for furs and fish. Shipyards, sawmills. Founded 1587 near former Tatar cap. of Sibir, it was administrative center of W Siberia until replaced by Omsk in 1824. Nicholas II and family were exiled here 1917–18. Birthplace of Mendelejeff.

Tobruk (tōbrŏŏk′), town (pop. 4,130), Cyrenaica, Libya, on the Mediterranean. A major supply port in World War II, it was taken Jan., 1941, by Australians. Later besieged by Rommel's forces for more than eight months until relieved Dec., 1941. In Rommel's second great offensive it fell June, 1942. Recaptured by the British late in 1942. See NORTH AFRICA, CAMPAIGNS IN.

Tocantins (tōkāntēnsh′), river, c.1,560 mi. long, rising in S central Goiás state, Brazil, and flowing N to Pará R., southern arm of the Amazon.

Toccoa (tŏ′kōu), city (pop. 6,781), NE Ga., in Appalachian foothills near Tugaloo R. Industrial center producing textile goods and machinery.

Tocqueville, Alexis de (ălĕksēs′ dŭ tôkvēl′), 1805–59, French liberal politician and writer. His *Democracy in America* (2 vols., 1835; Eng. tr., 4 vols., 1835–40, revised ed., 2 vols., 1945) is a classic.

Todhunter, Isaac, 1820–84, English mathematician, known for mathematics textbooks, work on equations and calculus, and research and writings on history of mathematics.

Todos os Santos Bay (tō′dŏŏs ŏŏs sān′tŏŏsh), inlet of the Atlantic, 25 mi. long and 20 mi. wide, Bahia, E Brazil. Discovered by Vespucci (1501).

toga (tō′gŭ), Roman garment worn in earliest days by both men and women of all classes, later by men alone. It ultimately became a roughly semicircular garment, c.7 ft. wide and three times the wearer's height in length, and was elaborately draped over the tunic. Status was indicated by color of the toga itself, or by a colored border or embroidery. It expressed the dignity of citizenship and was forbidden to foreigners, subjects, and exiles. It was the ceremonial state dress of patricians until the TUNIC came to be preferred.

Toggenburg (tô′gŭnbŏŏrk), district in St. Gall canton, E Switzerland. Cotton textiles; dairying (Toggenburg goats were developed here). Territory was purchased by abbot of St. Gall 1468. In 1712 quarrels between abbot and Protestant communities of Toggenburg led to **War of the Toggenburg,** between Catholic and Protestant cantons of Swiss Confederation. Protestants won; religious equality was estab.

Togliatti, Palmiro (pälmē′rō tōlyät′tē), 1893–, leader of Italian Communist party.

Togo, Heihachiro, Count (hā′hächĭrō′ tō′gō), 1847–1934, Japanese admiral, hero of Russo-Japanese War.

Togoland (tō′gōlănd″) or **Togo** (tō′gō), former German protectorate (c.35,000 sq. mi.), W Africa, on Gulf of Guinea. Under German control from 1886 to 1914, when it was occupied by French and British troops. In 1922 the League of Nations divided it into two mandates—French Togoland (c.21,500 sq. mi.; pop. c.944,500) in E on the coast, with cap. at Lomé, and British Togoland (13,040 sq. mi.; pop. 378,666), in W and inland, and governed as part of Gold Coast. These became UN trust territories in 1946. Products include cattle, cacao, and cotton.

Tojo, Hideki (hēdā′kē tō′jō), 1884–1948, Japanese general. Rise to premiership in Oct., 1941 marked final triumph of military party which favored war with the Allies. Resigned July, 1944, after loss of Marianas. Executed as war criminal after the war.

Tokay (tōkā′), Hung. *Tokaj,* town (pop. 5,903), NE Hungary, on the Tisza. Famed for its wine, of which there are three types (dry, sweet, and Tokay Essence, made from unpressed grapes).

Tokelau (tōkŭlou′) or **Union Islands,** group of three atolls in S Pacific, c.300 mi. N of Western Samoa. Discovered 1765 by the British. Governed by New Zealand since 1926.

Tokio, Japan: see TOKYO.

Tokoly, Emeric: see THOKOLY, EMERIC.

Tokugawa (tō″kŏŏgä′wä), family that held the shogunate (see SHOGUN) and controlled Japan, 1603–1867. Founded by IEYASU. Under its system of centralized feudalism the family itself held only a quarter of the land but kept close watch on the daimyo, who ruled over separate domains. Its collapse was caused by a complex of internal and external pressures. Its overthrow restored power to the emperor.

Tokyo or **Tokio** (both: tō′kēō), city (pop. 6,275,190) cap. of Japan, in central Honshu; port on Tokyo Bay. Crossed by small Sumida R. Financial, industrial and cultural center; focal point of urban belt (including Yokohama). Founded 12th cent. as Yedo (or Edo), it rose after 1603 when it became the seat of Ieyasu, first Tokugawa shogun. After Meiji restoration (1868) city was renamed Tokyo and succeeded Kyoto as imperial cap. Earthquake of 1923 ruined nearly half the city. In World War II it was first raided by U.S. bombers under Gen. James Doolittle, April, 1942. Later raids destroyed half the city, including most of its industrial plant. Chief academic institutions are Keio-Gijuku Univ. (1867), Tokyo Univ. (1869; formerly Tokyo Imperial Univ.), Waseda Univ. (1882), and Rikkyo or St. Paul's Univ. (1883).

Tolbukhin (tôlbŏŏ′khĭn), formerly **Dobrich** (dô′brĭch), city (pop. 31,049), NE Bulgaria, in S Dobruja. Agr. trade center. Under Rumanian rule 1913–40 (Rumanian name was Bazargic). Renamed in 1949 in honor of Marshal Tolbukhin of USSR.

Toledo, Francisco de (fränthē′skō dā tōlā′dhō), d. 1584, Spanish viceroy of Peru (1569–81). Of one of noblest families in Spain, he had served with distinction there before going to Peru. His able administration marked the end of tumultuous period after Spanish Conquest. One blot on his career was the unjust execution of last Inca, Tupac Amaru.

Toledo (tůlē'dō, Span. tōlā'dhō), city (pop. 27,427), cap. of Toledo prov., central Spain, in New Castile, on a granite hill surrounded on three sides by a gorge of the Tagus. Played important role in Spanish history and culture. It fell to Rome 193 B.C.; became an early archiepiscopal see, scene of several Church councils (see TOLEDO, COUNCILS OF), and cap. of Visigothic Spain. Under Moorish rule (A.D. 712–1085) it was the cap. of an emirate (after 1031 an independent kingdom) and a center of Moorish, Spanish, and Jewish cultures. Its great prosperity was due to its steel industry (Toledan sword blades were famous throughout the world) and to its silk and wool mfg. After its conquest by Castile, Toledo became the chief royal residence but was superseded by Valladolid in the 15th cent. Its general aspect has changed little since El GRECO painted his famous *View of Toledo,* but the alcazar (originally a Moorish structure) was heavily damaged (1936) in the Spanish civil war, when the Insurgents heroically resisted a two-month siege of the fortress. Among other landmarks are the Gothic cathedral (begun 1227), with paintings by El Greco, and the Church of Santo Tomé, with El Greco's *Burial of the Conde de Orgaz.*

Toledo (tůlē'dō), city (pop. 303,616), NW Ohio on Maumee R. near its mouth on L. Erie; settled 1817 as Port Lawrence on site of Fort Industry (1794). A major Great Lakes' shipping point with shipbuilding, oil refining, and mfg. of automobiles, glass, and electrical equipment. Toledo War (1835–36) was Ohio-Mich. boundary dispute, settled by Congress awarding Toledo strip to Ohio. Growth stimulated by completion of canals and railroads, and by development of gas, oil, and coal resources. Toledo plan of labor conciliation (1946) has been adopted by other cities. Seat of Univ. of Toledo (coed.; 1875). City has art museum, zoological park, Catholic cathedral, and, near by, memorials on sites of Fort Meigs and battle of Fallen Timbers.

Toledo, Councils of, assemblies of the nation and Church of Spain from the 4th to the 16th cent. At one of them in 589 Visigothic king Recared abjured Arianism. The council of 1565–66 saw enunciation of many regulations later embodied in canon law.

Toller, Ernst (ĕrnst' tô'lůr), 1893–1939, German dramatist. His plays, strong in social protest, include *Man and the Masses* (1920; Eng. tr., 1924) and *Hinkeman* (1924; Eng. tr., *Brokenbrow,* 1926). Died in New York by suicide.

Tolosa (tōlō'sä), town (pop. 10,114), N Spain, in Basque Provs.; former cap. of Guipúzcoa. Mfg. of paper, textiles, machinery. Old section has preserved medieval aspect.

Tolstoy, Leo (tŏl'stoi), Rus. *Lev Nikolayevich Tolstoi,* 1828–1910, Russian writer and religious philosopher, b. Yasnaya Polyana, the estate of his noble family. His youth was spent like that of other Russian nobles, in army service (campaigns in the Caucasus and the Crimean War) and in dissipated pleasure, but his soul-searching and desire for social reform were early expressed by his attempt to create a school for serfs in 1849 (he made another attempt in 1859). Early autobiographical works (*Childhood,* 1852; *Boyhood,* 1854; *Youth,* 1857) strengthened his position as a literary figure. Trips (1857, 1860) to the West led him to question the basis of modern civilization. After marriage (1862), he retired to Yasnaya Polyana, where he wrote *The Cossacks* (1863); *War and Peace* (1865–69), a prose epic of the Napoleonic Wars, considered by many the greatest novel ever written; *Anna Karenina* (1875–77), a moral tragedy against the background of St. Petersburg society; and lesser works. He underwent about 1876 a "conversion" to belief in Christian love, nonresistance to evil, and the simple faith of the peasants. He gathered many followers, and his cult of nonviolence and the simple life has many admirers in the world today. He attempted to give up all his property, broke with his wife, and died at the railroad station of Astapovo, where he was accompanied only by his daughter Alexandra. His later works in fiction include *The Death of Ivan Ilyich* (1884), *The Kreutzer Sonata* (1889), *Hadji Murad* (1896–1904), *Resurrection* (1889–1900), and the dramas *The Power of Darkness* (1886) and *The Living Corpse* (1911). Other works deal with religion, ethics, and moral aesthetics.

Toltec (tŏl'tĕk), anc. civilization of Mexico estab. sometime between the 6th and 8th cent. A.D. Toltec language was related to that of later Aztec civilization. Cap. was Tollán (modern Tule, Hidalgo); other centers at Teotihuacán and Cholula. Had fundamentals of earlier Olmec culture, advanced features such as metallurgy, massive pyramid construction, and astronomical knowledge. Civilization fell after the destruction of Tollán (c.1116?).

Toluca (tōlōō'kä), city (pop. 43,429), cap. of Mexico state, central Mexico. On SW border of central plateau, Toluca is high and cold. Settlement established by Hernán Cortés (1530). Agr. and cattle raising are important. Noted for its basket weaving. Volcano, Nevado de Toluca, is near by.

toluene (tŏl'ūēn), **methylbenzene** (mĕ"thĭlbĕn'zēn), or **toluol** (tŏl'ūōl), colorless, liquid hydrocarbon of BENZENE SERIES. Used as solvent and to make dyes and explosives (e.g., T.N.T.).

Tomar (tōōmär'), city (pop. 6,246), central Portugal, in Estremadura. Noted as center of the Knights Templars and, after their suppression in 14th cent., of the wealthy Military Order of Christ, whose great convent-castle overlooks the city from a hill.

tomato, tender perennial plant (*Lycopersicon esculentum*) of nightshade family, native to W South America and widely grown for its juicy, globular red or yellow fruits. In early days the tomato was known as the love apple. The vitamin-rich fruit is used in salads, soups, sauces, and as juice. There are many varieties, including small-fruited types. The currant tomato (*L. pimpinellifolium*) has red fruits of c.½ in. diameter. See *ill.,* p. 999.

Tombaugh, Clyde William (tŏm'bô), 1906–, American astronomer, discoverer (1930) of planet Pluto.

Tombigbee (tŏmbĭg'bē), river, 409 mi. long, rising in NE Miss. and flowing SSE into W Ala., then S to Alabama R. near Mobile, forming Mobile R.

Tombstone, city (pop. 910), SE Ariz., NNW of Bisbee. Laid out 1879 by Ed Schieffelin, who found silver here, 1877. Was large, rich, tough mining town till c.1900; lead, gold, silver still mined. Now a health resort; tourism is main industry.

Tomlinson, H(enry) M(ajor), 1873–, English novelist, author of sea stories (e.g., *Gallions Reach,* 1927). Other works include *The Sea and the Jungle* (1912).

Tomsk (tômsk), city (pop. 141,215), RSFSR, in W central Siberia, on Tom R. and on a spur of Trans-Siberian RR. Cultural center (university, founded 1888). Light mfg.; agr. processing. Founded 1604. Was the leading Siberian city in 19th cent.

Toms River, village (pop. 2,517), E N.J., on Toms R. near Barnegat Bay. Fishing center. Privateering port in Revolution, when burned by British.

Tom Thumb, 1838–83, American dwarf and entertainer, whose real name was Charles Sherwood Stratton. Named and made famous (after 1842) by P. T. Barnum. Appearing with his wife (also a Barnum dwarf) he was enormously popular until his retirement in 1882.

tonality, in music, the quality by which all tones of a composition are heard in relation to a central tone called the keynote or tonic. In music which has harmony, tonality is practically synonomous with *key,* a term used to indicate the SCALE from which the tonal material of a composition is derived. A composition in C major uses as its basic tonal material the tones from the C major scale; its harmony employs chords built on tones of that scale; and C is the keynote. Deliberate avoidance of a feeling of key is called ATONALITY.

Tonawanda (tŏnůwŏn'dů), city (pop. 14,617), W N.Y., N of Buffalo and on Niagara R. at end of the Barge Canal; organized 1836. Canal-shipping and rail center. Chemicals and paper, metal, wood products.

Tone, (Theobald) Wolfe, 1763–98, Irish revolutionary. Intrigued for French aid in an Irish rebellion and fostered several abortive expeditions to Ireland. In 1798 rebellion he was defeated and captured by the English. Committed suicide.

tone, in music, a sound of definite pitch caused by the regularity of vibrations which produce it. Through EQUAL TEMPERAMENT, the octave is divided into 12 tones of equal intervals, an interval being the difference in PITCH between two tones. In a SCALE, a tone whose interval from the tone preceding it is approximately one-sixth that of the octave is called a whole tone or whole step (e.g., C-D, F sharp-G sharp, A-B); a tone whose interval from the tone preceding it is approximately one-twelfth that of the octave is called a half tone, half step, or semi-tone (e.g., C-C sharp, A sharp to B, or E-F).

tone poem or **symphonic poem,** type of orchestral composition created by Liszt. It discards classical form and favors poetic or other literary inspiration. Tone poems can "tell a story," as in those of Richard Strauss; state feelings of nationalism, as in those of Sibelius; or reflect impressions, as in those of Debussy.

Tonga (tŏng'gů), island group (250 sq. mi.; pop. 34,130), S Pacific. Most of the islands are coral; a few are volcanic. Discovered 1616–43 by the Dutch. Visited 1773 by Capt. James Cook, the group received English missionaries in 1797. Constitutional monarchy was estab. 1862; group became British protectorate, 1900. Its present ruler, Queen Salote, is last hereditary monarch of Polynesia.

Tongareva, island: see PENRHYN.

tonka bean (tŏng'ků), seed of the pod of a leguminous tree (*Dipteryx odorata*) of tropical South America. Used as a vanilla substitute and in perfume.

Tonkin (tŏn'kĭn), state (44,670 sq. mi.; pop. 9,851,200), N Indo-China, constituting part of VIET NAM; cap. Hanoi. Bounded on N by China, SW by Laos, S by Annam, and SE by Gulf of Tonkin. Consists mainly of highlands enclosing the Red R. delta. Crops include rice, corn, coffee, and tea. Tonkin has the only important coal fields of Indo-China. Population is mainly Annamese, with a large minority of Chinese. Area surrounding Tonkin was the original state of ANNAM (10th–16th cent.). The French first came in 1866 to open the Red R. to trade. After war with China (1882–85), which claimed sovereignty over Tonkin, the French established a protectorate over the area 1884–85, and Tonkin joined Union of Indo-China in 1887. After World War II it was the seat of the Vietminh revolt.

Tonle Sap (tŏn'lā säp'), lake, central Cambodia. At low water, it covers c.1,000 sq. mi.; in flood periods the area is more than tripled. Its outlet joins Mekong R. near Pnom Penh.

Tonsberg, Nor. *Tønsberg* (tûns'bĕr), city (pop. 11,883), SE Norway; a seaport on the Skagerrak near mouth of Oslo Fjord. Norway's oldest city. Major whaling base since 18th cent.

tonsils, lymphoid masses of tissue. Palatine tonsils lie in throat on either side of soft palate. Pharyngeal tonsils are commonly called adenoids.

Tonti or **Tonty, Henri de,** c.1650–1704, French explorer in present Canada and U.S., b. Italy. Lieutenant of LA SALLE.

Tonto National Monument: see NATIONAL PARKS AND MONUMENTS (table).

Tonty, Henri de: see TONTI, HENRI DE.

Tooele (tōōĭ'lů), city (pop. 7,269), N central Utah, S of Great Salt L. Smelting and reduction of ores (silver, lead, copper). Elton Tunnel (built 1937–42) extends E to Bingham Canyon mines.

Toombs, Robert, 1810–85, American statesman, Confederate leader. U.S. Senator from Ga. (1853–61). Active in Ga. secession and organization of Confederacy. Commanded Ga. troops in Civil War. Active in post-war Ga. politics.

tooth: see TEETH.

topaz, widely distributed aluminum silicate mineral used as gem. Color varies, but is usually pale yellow. Occurs in certain igneous and metamorphic rocks. Sources include

Russia, Czechoslovakia, Norway, Sweden, Brazil, Mexico, and parts of U.S.

Topeka (tůpē'ků), city (pop. 78,791), state cap., NE Kansas, on Kansas R. and W of Kansas City. Laid out 1854 by Free State settlers as rail center on old Oregon Trail ferry site (1842). Short-lived Free State constitution was framed here 1855. Became state cap. when Kansas entered the Union in 1861. Trade and industrial center for rich agr. area, it has railway shops and offices, wholesale houses, and food-processing plants. Seat of Menninger Clinic for psychiatric research and Washburn Municipal Univ. of Topeka (coed.; 1865).

Tophet (tō'fĭt), place in vale of HINNOM. Associated with evil cults, hence became a name for hell. 2 Kings 23.10; Isa. 30.33; Jer. 7.31–33.

Toppenish (tŏ'půnĭsh), farm trade city (pop. 5,265), S Wash., S of Yakima. Processes food.

Torah (tō'rů), Hebrew name for the first five books of the Bible, the Law of Moses or the Pentateuch, supposed in Judaism to have been given to Moses on Mt. Sinai.

Tordesillas (tōr"dhāsē'lyäs), town (pop. 3,700), N central Spain, in Leon. Here in 1494 Spain and Portugal signed treaty dividing non-Christian world into two zones of influence. The treaty followed the papal bull of 1493 which had given the New World to Spain and Africa and India to Portugal, but it shifted the line of demarcation to the W, giving Portugal a claim to Brazil. Castle of Tordesillas was residence of Joanna of Castile 1516–55.

Torgau (tôr'gou), town (pop. 18,455), Saxony-Anhalt, E Germany, on the Elbe. Chemicals, glass, pottery, machinery. Torgau League of Protestant princes was founded here 1526. Frederick II of Prussia defeated Austrians near here 1760. U.S. and USSR troops made their first contact here April 27, 1945.

Torino, Italy: see TURIN.

tornado (tôrnā'dō), rotating storm, more violent and of shorter duration than hurricane and with lower barometric pressure at center. Dark funnel-shaped cloud, around axis of which winds blow spirally upward, extends toward earth, twists, rises, and falls, causing destruction. Diameter of tornado ranges from few feet to a mile; winds estimated at 200–300 mi. per hour. Occur chiefly in central U.S.

Torne (tōr'nů), Finnish *Tornio,* Swed. *Torne älv,* river, 250 mi. long, rising in N Sweden and flowing SW into Gulf of Bothnia at Tornio, Finland. Forms Swedish–Finnish frontier below its junction with the Muonio.

Torngat Mountains, N Labrador, northernmost range of Laurentian Plateau, extending 120 mi. N–S between Atlantic coast and Que. border.

Toronto (tůrŏn'tō), city (pop. 675,754), provincial cap., S Ont., Canada, on N shore of L. Ontario at mouth of Humber R. and NNW of Buffalo, N.Y. Second largest city in Canada, port of entry, and important commercial, financial, and industrial center with railroad shops, food processing, printing, and mfg. of machinery and other metal products. Here are Royal Ontario Mus., Ontario Mus. of Archaeology, Osgoode Hale Law School, Anglican and Roman Catholic cathedrals. Seat of Univ. of Toronto (nonsectarian; coed.; opened 1843 by Anglicans as King's Col.) with many affiliated colleges. French built Fort Rouillé here (1749); post destroyed (1759) and site occupied by British as Fort Toronto. After American Revolution it received many United Empire Loyalists. As York, it became cap. of Upper Canada in 1796. Twice taken by Americans in War of 1812. Renamed Toronto 1834, it became center of insurrection led by W. L. Mackenzie (1837). By the Act of Union (1840) cap. was moved to Kingston, but returned 1849.

Toronto, city (pop. 7,253), E Ohio, on Ohio R. and near Steubenville. Mfg. of steel and clay products and glass.

Toronto, University of: see TORONTO, Ont.

torpedo, in naval warfare, a self-propelled submarine projectile. The first effective torpedo, built in 1866 by an Englishman, Robert Whitehead, operated with compressed air. A typical modern torpedo is 21 in. in diameter and from 20 ft. to 24 ft. long. It may be driven by a steam or electric engine, or it may be jet-propelled.

Torquay (tôrkē'), municipal borough (pop. 53,216), Devonshire, England; seaside resort and yachting center. South Devon Technical Col. is here.

Torquemada, Juan de (hwän' dā tôrkāmä'dhä), 1388–1468, Spanish cardinal; a Dominican monk. Upheld papal authority against conciliar theory at councils of Constance and Basel. His nephew, **Tomás de Torquemada** (tōmäs'), 1420–98, also a Dominican, was confessor to Ferdinand and Isabella, and in 1483 became inquisitor general of Castile and Aragon. The founder of the Spanish INQUISITION, he devised extremely harsh rules of procedure and enforced them rigorously. He also played a major part in the expulsion of the Jews (1492). His name became a byword for cruelty.

Torrance, residential city (pop. 31,834), S Calif., S of Los Angeles; planned 1911. Oil wells and rail shops. Produces steel and metal products.

Torrence, (Frederic) Ridgely, 1875–1950, American poet and dramatist. Works include *Plays for a Negro Theater* (1917); *Hesperides* (1925) and *Poems* (1941).

Torrens, Lake, shallow salt lake, 120 mi. long, 40 mi. wide, S central South Australia.

Torreón (tōrāōn'), city (pop. 75,796), Coahuila, N Mexico; metropolis of LAGUNA DISTRICT; estab. 1893. Grew rapidly. Has rubber factory, cotton and flour mills, brewery, foundries, and smelter.

Tôrres Vedras (tô'rĭsh vā'drůsh), town (pop. 4,762), W Portugal, in Estremadura. Important fortress and royal residence in Middle Ages. In the Peninsular War it was the key point of Wellington's line of defense.

Torrey, John, 1796–1873, American botanist and chemist. He was founder of the New York Academy of Sciences and of the Torrey Botanical Club and author of works on North American plants.

Torricelli, Evangelista (tôrĭchě'lē, Ital. āvänjālē'stä tōr-rēchěl'lē), 1608–47, Italian physicist and mathematician. Invented mercurial

BAROMETER and a microscope and improved the telescope.

torrid zone: see TROPICS.

Torrington, George Byng, Viscount, 1663–1733, British admiral. Was a commander in War of Spanish Succession. Drove off (1708) the fleet with which James Edward Stuart hoped to invade Great Britain.

Torrington, city (pop. 27,820), NW Conn., on Naugatuck R. and W of Hartford; settled c.1735. Metal (esp. brass) products center. Site of John Brown's birthplace is marked.

torsion (tôr'shŭn). Force can be applied to solid body—e.g., metal rod, wire, or thread—in such a way as to turn or twist one part of it in plane parallel to adjoining part. Such stress is torsion. Since metal shafts used as rotating parts in machines must resist twisting of this kind, materials used in making them are tested to determine capacity to resist without breaking or becoming permanently deformed. **Torsion balance** is instrument one type of which is used for measuring small electric or magnetic forces and another type for measuring small weights, like the ordinary balance. Is based on fact that a wire or thread resists twisting with force proportional to stress. Torsion balance has wire or thread attached at one end so that force applied at free end tends to twist it out of shape; extent of twisting is a measure of the force.

Torstensson, Lennart (lĕ'närt tōr'stŭnsōn), 1603–51, Swedish general in Thirty Years War. A brilliant artillery commander, he succeeded Baner as commander in chief (1641). Fought victoriously in Saxony, Bohemia, Moravia, and Silesia; overran Denmark (1643–44). His victory at Jankau (1645) laid Prague and Vienna open to Swedish attack.

tortoise (tôr'tŭs), reptile of order Chelonia (or Testudinata), often called TURTLE. In U.S., tortoise usually is applied only to terrestrial forms.

Tortosa (tōrtō'sä), city (pop. 11,951), NE Spain, in Catalonia, on Ebro R. Founded as Roman colony. Held by Moors 8th cent.–1148. Has Gothic cathedral.

Tortugas: see DRY TORTUGAS.

Torun (tô'rōōnyŭ), Ger. *Thorn,* city (pop. 68,-085), NW Poland, on the Vistula. Trade center. Founded 1231 as castle by Teutonic Knights. First Peace of Torun (1411) was short-lived settlement of struggle between Poland and Teutonic Knights; Second Peace of Torun (1466) gave Poland access to Baltic Sea and overlordship over domain of the knights. City passed to Prussia 1793, reverted to Poland 1919. Birthplace of Copernicus.

Tory, Geofroy (tôrē'), c.1480–1533, Parisian printer, artist, engraver, bookbinder. His *Book of Hours* (1525) introduced type design independent of the influence of handwriting. Also wrote *Champfleury* (1529).

Tory, English political party. Name first used for supporters of duke of York (later James II). After 1688 the Tories favored landed aristocracy and opposed rights of non-Anglicans and foreign entanglements. Reaching zenith under Queen Anne, with Robert HARLEY and Henry ST. JOHN as leaders, the party was discredited for Jacobite leanings under George I. WHIG party ruled for 50 years. Revived by younger William Pitt, Tories promoted idea of popular rule. Made reactionary again by French Revolution, Tories lost power after Reform Bill of 1832 and evolved into the CONSERVATIVE PARTY.

Toscana, Italy: see TUSCANY.

Toscanelli, Paolo dal Pozzo (päō'lō däl pôt'tsō tōskänĕl'lē), 1397–1482, Italian cosmographer and mathematician, a physician. It is said that his map of the world was used by Columbus on the 1492 voyage to America.

Toscanini, Arturo (tŏ"skŭnē'nē), 1867–, Italian conductor. He began his career as a cellist, until, substituting as conductor in Rio de Janeiro (1886), he was so successful that he was engaged for the rest of the season. In Italy he conducted the world première of Puccini's *La Bohème* (1896) and Italian premières of Wagner's *Götterdämmerung, Die Meistersinger,* and *Siegfried.* He later conducted at La Scala, Milan (where he was musical director) and at the Bayreuth and Salzburg Festivals. In the U.S. he conducted at the Metropolitan Opera, New York, 1908–14, and the New York Philharmonic, 1926–36. In 1937 the NBC Symphony was especially formed for him.

Tosti, Sir Francesco (Paolo) (fränchā'skō tô'stē), 1846–1916, Italian composer and teacher. Went to London 1875; knighted 1908. His *Serenade* and *Goodbye* are the best known of his many songs.

Tostig (tŏ'stĭg), d. 1066, earl of Northumbria. Northumbrians revolted (1055) against his severe rule and chose Morcar as their earl. Tostig and his ally, Harold III of Norway, were killed by Tostig's brother, Harold, at battle of Stamford Bridge.

totem (tō'tŭm), in animistic religion, an object, usually animal, which a man regards with unusual respect, and to which he considers himself intimately related, as by kinship or descent. Clan totem, to which all members of clan consider themselves related in same way, is most common form. Member of clan totem bears totem name; must marry outside totem group (exogamy); believes himself to be descended from totem; and must not kill, eat, or touch totem animal, or call it by its true name. Totemism exists largely in Australia, Melanesia, and North America. No generally acceptable theory for origin of totemism exists.

Totila (tŏ'tĭlŭ) or **Baduila** (bădūĭ'lŭ), d. 552, last king of the Ostrogoths (541–52). Took Naples (543) and Rome (546) from the Byzantines, making himself master of central and S Italy. In 552 Justinian I sent an army under NARSES against him. Totila's defeat and death in battle restored temporary control over Italy to Byzantium.

Tottenham (tŏt'ŭnŭm), urban district (pop. 126,921), Middlesex, England; residential suburb of London.

toucan (tōō'kăn'), perching bird of tropical America. It has an enormous bill, usually brightly colored. See *ill.*, p. 135.

touch, sense by which pressure against body is perceived. Stimulus is received in specialized nerve cells or end organs in skin or membranes.

touch-me-not: see IMPATIENS.

Toul (to͝ol), city (pop. 8,971), Meurthe-et-Moselle dept., NE France, on the Moselle. Episcopal see 5th cent.–1801; free imperial city until annexation to France (1552). Was fortified by Vauban. Damaged in World War II.

Toulon (to͞olō′), city (pop. 116,141), Var dept., SE France; a Mediterranean port and chief French naval station. After its surrender to English by royalists (1793), Bonaparte won his first fame in its recapture. French fleet was scuttled here in Nov., 1942, to avoid capture by Germans. Toulon was heavily bombed as German submarine base (1944).

Toulouse (to͞olo͞oz′), city (pop. 225,854), cap. of Haute-Garonne dept., S France, on the Garonne; historic cap. of Languedoc. Commercial and cultural center. Archiepiscopal see. Has university (founded 1230). Dating from pre-Roman times, it was the cap. of the Visigoths A.D. 419–507; later became a county which, by the 12th cent., held overlordship over most of Languedoc. The court of the counts was the center of S French medieval culture. The crusades against the ALBIGENSES (13th cent.) laid the county waste. On the death of Count Raymond VII (1249) Toulouse passed to Alphonse, brother of King Louis IX, and in 1271 it was added to the royal domain. The famous annual poetic contests—Académie des Jeux Floraux—began c.1223 and are still held. Toulouse is rich in historic monuments (e.g., Romanesque basilica, with tomb of St. Thomas Aquinas; Gothic cathedral; 18th-cent. "old quarter").

Toulouse-Lautrec (Monfa), Henri de (to͞olo͞oz′ lōtrĕk′), 1864–1901, French artist, son of a wealthy nobleman. Prolific as a painter, poster artist, and illustrator, he is noted for his satiric studies of music halls, circuses, and low-life types of Paris. Grotesquely deformed since childhood, he led a life of debauchery in Paris.

Toungoo, (toung′go͞o′), town (pop. 23,223), SE Burma, on Rangoon-Mandalay railroad. Preceded Pegu as cap. of unified Burmese kingdom in 16th cent.

Touraine (to͞orān′, Fr. to͞orĕn′), region and former province, W central France, in Indre-et-Loire dept., drained by Loire R.; cap. Tours. The "garden of France," it is a fertile region of orchards and vineyards, famed for its many historic castles (e.g., Chinon and Amboise). Originally the county of Tours, it passed to the counts of Blois (10th cent.), then to Anjou (11th cent.) and to England (1152). It was retaken by Philip II in 1204 and incorporated into the royal domain.

Tourcoing (to͞orkwē′), city (pop. 73,772), Nord dept., N France. Textile center.

tourmaline (to͞or′mŭlĭn, –lēn), complex borosilicate mineral used as gem. Occurs in three-, six-, and nine-sided crystals. Color varies with impurities—red and pink, blue, green, yellow, violet-red. Sources include Burma, Siberia, Brazil, U.S.

Tournai (to͞ornā′), Flemish *Doornik,* city (pop. 32,507), Hainaut prov., W Belgium, on the Scheldt. Textile center (wool, linen, carpets). Dates from Roman times. Has 11th-cent. cathedral; 17th-cent. cloth hall. Also spelled Tournay and Doornijk.

Tournefort, Joseph Pitton de (zhôzĕf′ pētõ′ dü to͞ornfôr′), 1656–1708, French botanist. His system of classification, in vogue until superseded by that of Linnaeus, based plant genera on similarities in flower and fruit and classed plants as herbs, bushes, and trees.

Tours (to͞or, to͞orz), city (pop. 76,207), cap. of Indre-et-Loire dept., W central France, on the Loire; historic cap. of Touraine. Has wine, silk, and other industries. An old Gallo-Roman town, it grew after death (397?) of St. MARTIN, bishop of Tours (buried in Basilica of St. Martin, built 1887–1924). Charles Martel defeated Saracens in great battle between Tours and Poitiers (732). Gregory of Tours (6th cent.) and Alcuin (9th cent.) made city a center of medieval learning. Louis XI died in near-by château of Plessis-lès-Tours. Tours was temporary French cap. 1870–71 and 1940. Despite damage suffered in World War II, it remains a handsome city and important tourist center. Birthplace of Balzac.

Toussaint L'Ouverture, François Dominique (fräswä′ dômēnēk′ to͞osē′ lo͞ovĕrtür′), c.1744–1803, Haitian Negro patriot and martyr. A self-educated slave, he led Negro rebellion, and because of his fast-moving campaigns became known as L'Ouverture [opening]. In 1793 when the British occupied Haiti's coastal cities and allied themselves with Spanish in E part of island, Toussaint forced their withdrawal. In 1801 he conquered Santo Domingo and governed whole island until Napoleon sent Gen. Leclerc in 1802. Haitian resistance was stubborn, and a peace treaty was drawn up, but Toussaint was treacherously seized and taken to France, where he died in prison.

Tower of London, anc. fortress and royal residence in London, on N bank of the Thames, covering c.13 acres. Now mainly an arsenal, it was for centuries the jail of illustrious prisoners. Enclosed by a dry moat, in center is White Tower (built c.1078). Other towers include Wakefield Tower, housing the crown jewels. Traitors' Gate and Bloody Tower have many historical associations. Many persons were beheaded here. Yeomen of the Guard ("Beefeaters"), in Tudor garb, still guard the Tower. N bastion was destroyed in World War II bombing.

towhee (tō′hē), North American bird of finch family. Red-eyed towhee (also called chewink and ground robin) is found E of Great Plains in U.S. and in parts of Canada; male has glossy back upper parts, chestnut brown sides, white breast and abdomen.

Townsend, Francis Everett (toun′zŭnd), 1867–, American reformer, author of popular Townsend plan (1933). Plan proposed an old-age pension, to be financed by a 2% Federal sales tax.

Townshend, Charles Townshend, 2d **Viscount** (toun′zĕnd), 1674–1738, English statesman. Concluded Barrier Treaty (1709) guaranteeing Hanoverian Succession. As Whig secretary of state (1714–16) under George I he crushed Jacobite rising of 1715. Shared power with his brother-in-law, Robert WAL-

POLE, but opposed his foreign policy and retired (1730).

Townshend, Charles, 1725–67, English statesman. Chancellor of exchequer (1766–67), he undertook the hated levies known as the **Townshend Acts** (1767). Passed by English Parliament after repeal of Stamp Act, they imposed customs duties on imports of glass, lead, paints, paper, and tea. Resulting colonial unrest led to BOSTON MASSACRE and BOSTON TEA PARTY.

Townsville, town (pop. 34,109), Queensland, Australia; state's second port on inlet of Pacific Ocean; founded 1868. Exports include wool and sugar.

Towson (tou'sŭn), town (1940 pop. 10,606), N Md., N of Baltimore; settled c.1750. Near by is new campus of Goucher Col. (nonsectarian; for women; opened 1888 by Methodists). Mfg. of tools and aircraft precision equipment.

Towton Field (tou'tŭn), West Riding of Yorkshire, England. Forces of Edward IV defeated the Lancastrians here in 1461.

toxin (tŏk'sĭn), poison produced by certain organisms, especially bacteria. Presence of toxins in blood stream stimulates production of antitoxins tending to counteract poison. Use of toxin or toxin-antitoxin mixture to produce immunity to toxin-caused disease (e.g., diphtheria) has been largely replaced by injections of toxoids (toxins treated to destroy poisonous property but retain capacity to stimulate antitoxin formation).

toy. Over 100,000 different kinds are made; some known since prehistoric times. Toy industry was initiated during Middle Ages by distributors, chiefly of Sonneberg and Nuremberg in Germany, who obtained toys from home craftsmen. Large-scale manufacture dates from c.1850; leaders are U.S., Germany, Japan, and Czechoslovakia.

toy dogs. Many small dogs have been developed from the larger breeds for the sole purpose of being pets. One of the smallest of these is the Chihuahua, which weighs from 1 to 6 lb. It has a round skull, wide-set eyes, and large, erect ears, and varies in color from white, through shades of tan, to black. The Mexican hairless is about the size of a fox terrier. Its body is hairless except for fuzz on the top of its head, and its smooth skin may be any of several colors and is often mottled. Easily recognized by its flat nose and round, protruding eyes is the Pekingese (or Pekinese). Its coat is straight and silky and may be black, tan, fawn, brown, or white. The Pomeranian, resembling a miniature spitz dog, has a long-haired tail curling over its back. Its coat is especially abundant around the head and neck and may be black, brown, red, cream, blue, or white. The dog usually weighs less than 8 lb. The pug is distinguished by its short blunt muzzle and tightly curled tail. Its smooth short coat may be silver, fawn, or black. One variety of POODLE is a toy dog.

Toynbee, Arnold, 1852–83, English economic historian and reformer. His *Lectures on the Industrial Revolution of the 18th Century in England* (1884) is a pioneer work in economic history. Toynbee Hall, first social settlement, was named for him. His nephew, **Arnold J(oseph) Toynbee,** 1889– is an English historian. His *Study of History* (6 vols., 1934–39; incomplete) rejects deterministic philosophy and holds that course of history is ruled by psychic, not materialistic, forces. He maintains that the well-being of a civilization lies in its ability to respond successfully to human and environmental challenges. He was working on final volume in 1952.

Toyokuni (tōyō'kōōnē), 1769–1825, Japanese color-print artist, famous for portrayals of stage favorites in dramatic situations.

toyon: see CHRISTMASBERRY.

Trabzon, Turkey: see TREBIZOND.

trachea: see WINDPIPE.

trachoma (trŭkō'mŭ), chronic, contagious granular inflammation of lining of eyelid and eyeball, a form of conjunctivitis. Probably caused by a virus. Incidence is high in Egypt and Palestine and in parts of U.S. Unless healed in early stages, may result in blindness.

track and field athletics, athletic events, principally running, jumping, and throwing (as of a javelin). These events dominated early Olympic Games, were popular in Rome, but lapsed in early Middle Ages. Revived in England in 12th cent. In modern Olympic games track events include 100-, 200-, 400-, 800-, 1,500-, 5,000-, and 10,000-meter runs; the MARATHON RACE; 110- and 400-meter hurdle races; 400- and 1,600-meter relay; 3,000-meter steeplechase; 50,000-meter walk. Field events include broad jump, high jump, pole vault, shot-put, discus throw, javelin throw, hammer throw, and running hop-step-and-jump.

Tractarian movement: see OXFORD MOVEMENT.

tractor, machine, usually powered by gasoline, used primarily to draw agricultural implements, e.g., plow and harvester, and to furnish power for spraying, sawing, and other purposes. Main types are wheel type and crawler or caterpillar type, from which military tank is adapted.

Tracy, city (pop. 8,410), central Calif., SW of Stockton. Agr. shipping and processing center. Has a pumping plant of Central Valley project.

trade union: see UNION, LABOR.

Trafalgar, Cape (trŭfăl'gŭr), on SW coast of Spain, near NW shore of Strait of Gibraltar. In the **battle of Trafalgar,** Oct. 21, 1805, the British under Nelson defeated the French and Spanish fleets under Villeneuve, capturing 20 ships and losing none. Nelson's maneuvers were among the most brilliant in naval history. At the beginning of the battle his flagship, the *Victory,* signaled the famous words: "England expects that every man will do his duty." Nelson was fatally wounded in the battle.

Trafalgar Square, in London, named for Nelson's victory; site of the Nelson column.

tragacanth (tră'gŭkănth), gummy exudation from shrub *Astragalus gummifer* and related plants of E Europe and Asia. It is used as an emulsifying agent, in pills, hand lotions, medicinal lubricating jellies, and for sizing.

tragedy. Aristotle defined tragedy as imitation of a painful action (usually resulting in death) by a person of stature which by pity and fear purges these emotions. Modern tragedy may contain comic elements or subplots for contrast or relief of emotional intensity. Tragedy evolved from ancient Greek religious rites, but the tragedies of Aeschylus, Sophocles, and Euripides were literary rather than ritual. Tragedy in 17th-cent. France (esp. in plays of Racine and Corneille) held to the classical unities of time, place, action; this unity contrasts with such English tragedy as the plays of Shakspere. In recent times tragedy in traditional sense has declined. In Ibsen's work the tragedy is often in political and social problems. Some modern writers of tragedy are Chekhov, Strindberg, Synge, Eugene O'Neill, Maxwell Anderson.

Traherne, Thomas (trůhûrn′), b. 1637 or 1639, d. 1674, English author, one of the metaphysical poets.

Trail, city (pop. 11,430), SE B.C., Canada, on Columbia R., just N of Wash. border. Metal-smelting center in mining region.

trailing arbutus or **Mayflower,** one of the best loved of American wild flowers, a creeping plant (*Epigaea repens*) with hairy evergreen leaves which often hide the sweetly fragrant, flesh-tinted flowers in early spring. Wild plants are difficult to establish in the garden, but nursery-grown plants (from cuttings or seeds) can be cultivated in acid soil and shade. In England, a hawthorn is called Mayflower; the strawberry tree and madroña of genus *Arbutus* are not related to trailing arbutus.

Trajan (trā′jůn), A.D. c.53–117, Roman emperor (A.D. 98–117), b. Spain; the adopted son and successor of Nerva. Brought Dacia under Roman control and conquered much of Parthia. Built much in Rome (including the Forum of Trajan). Succeeded by Hadrian.

Tralee (trůlē′, trā–), urban district (pop. 9,990), county town of Co. Kerry, Ireland; seaport.

Trani (trä′nē), city (pop. 29,962), Apulia, S Italy; an Adriatic port. Famous for its wine. Flourished at times of Crusades. Its *ordinamenta maris* of 1063 were probably the first medieval maritime code. Has noted Romanesque cathedral.

Trans-Alai (trăns″-älī′), mountain range, central Asia; part of Pamir system. Extends c.125 mi. W from USSR-China border into USSR. Rises to Lenin Peak (23,382 ft. high).

Transandine Railway, between Mendoza, Argentina, and Los Andes, Chile (distance 156 mi.), traversing Uspallata Pass. Completed in 1910, road rises to c.10,500 ft. at tunnel on international boundary. Another Transandine Railway extending from Antofagasta (Chile) to Salta (Argentina) was completed in 1948.

Trans-Caspian Railroad, important rail link of Soviet central Asia; also known as Central Asiatic RR. Built 1880–1905, it begins at Krasnovodsk on Caspian Sea, passes Bukhara, Samarkand, and Tashkent, and ends at Chkalov. Connected with Turkistan-Siberia RR N of Tashkent.

transcendentalism, in philosophy, any system holding that there are modes of being beyond the reach of mundane experience. The term is generally associated with Kant, who felt that space, time, and categories of judgment were transcendent—above the evidence of the senses. In American literature, a movement in New England from 1836 to 1860 is called transcendentalism. The transcendentalists (Emerson, Thoreau, Margaret Fuller, Bronson Alcott, and others) were high-minded and idealistic, laying stress on individualism, self-reliance, and social reform. Their journal was the *Dial* (1840–44), and BROOK FARM stemmed from transcendentalism.

Transcona, town (pop. 6,752), SE Man., Canada, E of Winnipeg. Railroad and industrial center.

transference: see PSYCHOANALYSIS.

Transfiguration, the "shining" appearance of Jesus before Peter, James, and John. Mat. 17; Mark 9.

transformer, in electricity, device commonly used for increasing or decreasing voltage of an alternating current. Two separate insulated coils wound around iron core are used. Alternating current led through first (primary) coil induces similar current in other (secondary) coil of different voltage. If secondary coil has more turns than primary, voltage is "stepped up"; if secondary has less turns than primary the voltage is "stepped down." Since alternating current of high voltage is cheaper to transmit than low voltage, transformers are used first to step up voltage for transmission and then to step it down when lower voltage and higher amperage are required for ordinary needs.

transit, in astronomy, passage of one heavenly body across disk of another. Transit obscuring a disk is called an eclipse. Transits of MERCURY and VENUS occur if either of these planets passes between earth and sun when earth crosses intersection of ecliptic and the planet's orbit.

Trans-Jordan or **Transjordania:** see JORDAN.

Transkeian Territories (trănskī′ůn, –kā′ůn), division (16,554 sq. mi.; pop. 1,279,922), E Cape Prov., South Africa. Largely a native reservation.

transmutation of elements, conversion of one element into another. One of the quests of the alchemists was to turn other metals into gold by the philosopher's stone. Transmutation occurs during RADIOACTIVITY and bombardment of elements in the cyclotron. See *ill.*, p. 989.

Transpadane Republic: see CISALPINE REPUBLIC.

transpiration, in botany, the normal loss of water by evaporation through the pores (stomata) of a plant's leaves. Transpiration is usually correlated with the dryness of the air although closing of the stomata retards excessive loss of water to some extent. Wilting of a plant results when more water is lost than is absorbed by the roots. Many plants (e.g., cacti) have structural modifications to reduce transpiration.

Trans-Siberian Railroad, c.4,350 mi. long, linking European Russia with Pacific coast. Vladivostok is the terminus. A S branch crosses Manchuria and is known as Chinese Eastern Railway. Construction of railroad (1892–1905) opened up Siberia for colonization and economic exploitation.

transubstantiation: see EUCHARIST.

Transvaal (trănzväl'), province (110,450 sq. mi.; pop. 4,283,038), South Africa; cap. Pretoria. Bordered on S by Vaal R., the boundary with Orange Free State. Mainly in the veld, it has good ranching land and a relatively large European population. Wool, hides, and skins are exported, and grain and citrus fruit are grown. The area's wealth, however, lies in its vast mineral resources (esp. of the WITWATERSRAND), including gold, diamonds, coal, and platinum. Settled by the Boers (see TREK), who by 1837 had driven out the Matabele tribe and set up a strong Boer state under A. W. Pretorius. The new state was recognized by the British in 1852 and was named the South African Republic; its chief leader was S. J. P. KRUGER. Britain annexed it in 1877 but restored its independence in 1881. The discovery of gold (1886) led to an influx of British prospectors, whose difficulties with the Boer government were a major cause of the SOUTH AFRICAN WAR. With the Boer defeat, Transvaal was made a British crown colony (1902). It became self-governing in 1907 and joined the Union in 1910.

Transylvania (trăn"sĭlvā'nyů), Ger. *Siebenbürgen,* Hung. *Erdély,* Rumanian *Transilvania* or *Ardeal,* historic province (24,009 sq. mi.; pop. 3,420,829), central Rumania. Chief cities: Cluj, Brasov, Sibiu. A high plateau (1,000–1,600 ft.), it rises in the E and S to the Carpathians. S part of Carpathians, known as Transylvanian Alps, reach 8,361 ft. in Negoiul. The region has agr., vineyards, pastures, orchards and is rich in natural resources (timber, lignite, methane, iron, manganese, lead, sulphur). It has metallurgical, chemical, and textile industries. The large Magyar and German-speaking minorities are mostly urban and largely Protestant. Part of ancient Dacia, Transylvania came, after many invasions, into possession of Hungary (11th cent.). With the Szekely (originally a Turkic tribe which arrived with or before the Magyars and adopted the Magyar language) and the "Saxons" (German colonists who settled in 12th cent.), the Magyars formed the three privileged "nations" of Transylvania. The Rumanians (called Vlachs or Walachs) began to arrive in the 13th cent. and formed the bulk of the peasant serfs. A voivode (royal governor) governed the seven counties of Transylvania for the Hungarian crown. After 1526 the voivode John Zapolya claimed the Hungarian throne as JOHN I against the later emperor FERDINAND I. In the subsequent tripartite partition of HUNGARY, Transylvania became a semi-independent principality, frequently changing allegiance between the emperors and the sultans. Notable among the princes of the 16th–17th cent. were the BATHORY family, Stephen BOCSKAY (who obtained recognition of freedom of worship from the emperor), Gabriel BETHLEN, Emeric THOKOLY, and the RAKOCZY family. In 1711 the princes' efforts to maintain independence from Austrian interference collapsed; Transylvania passed under direct Hapsburg rule. Under the Austro-Hungarian Monarchy (estab. 1867), full Hungarian control was restored, much to the detriment of the Rumanian peasants. Transylvania was seized by Rumania after World War I and was formally ceded by Hungary 1920. The Magyar magnates were expropriated, their vast estates redistributed among the peasants. In World War II many Transylvanian Germans fled to Germany before the arrival of the Russian armies.

Transylvania College: see LEXINGTON, Ky.

Transylvania Company, organized under leadership of Richard Henderson to exploit and colonize territory embraced by Ohio, Kentucky, and Cumberland rivers. Charter claims by Va. and N.C. voided company's land titles.

Trapani (trä'pänē), anc. *Drepanum,* city (pop. 52,661), W Sicily, Italy. A Carthaginian naval base, it fell to Rome after battle of Aegates (241 B.C.).

Trappists, Roman Catholic monks (Reformed CISTERCIANS or Cistercians of the Stricter Observance), whose name comes from La Trappe, France, where a monastic reform was begun c.1660. Trappists lead lives of strict seclusion, giving their hours to worship, labor, and study. There is no recreation, no meat is eaten, and silence is observed (except under unusual circumstances).

Trasimeno (träzēmā'nō), lake, area 50 sq. mi., Umbria, central Italy. Scene of Hannibal's great victory over Romans under Flaminius (217 B.C.).

Tras-os-Montes (trä'zo͝ozhmō"tĭsh), former province, NE Portugal, N of Douro R.; historic cap. Braganza. Sheep raising. Vineyards in Douro valley. Region now is part of Trás-os-Montes-e-Alto-Douro prov. (4,569 sq. mi.; pop. 592,079; cap. Vila Real).

Travancore (trăvůnkôr'), former princely state, SW India, on Arabian Sea. Unified in 18th cent. by descendant of ancient Chera kings. Allied with the British in wars with Hyder Ali and Tippoo Sahib. Was known for progressive government and comparatively high rate of literacy. Merged 1949 with Cochin to form state of **Travancore-Cochin** (9,155 sq. mi.; pop. 9,265,157), with cap. at Trivandrum. Cardamom, tea, and coffee plantations. Deposits of ilmenite and monazite.

Traverse, Lake (tră'vůrs), c.30 mi. long, on Minn.-S.Dak. line, source of Bois de Sioux R. and a headstream of Red R.

Traverse City, city (pop. 16,974), N Mich., N. of Cadillac and at head of West Arm of Grand Traverse Bay; settled 1847. In cherry-growing area, has annual national cherry festival. Lakes attract tourists. Mfg. of metal and wood products.

Travis, William Barrett (trăv'ĭs), 1811–36, hero of Texas Revolution. Commanded forces at the Alamo.

treason, crime of endangering the security of the state by acts threatening the existence of the legal government (in monarchies attempts on the life of the monarch or heir) or the security of the armed forces (e.g., by aiding the enemy). Such acts were called high treason in the English Statute of Treasons (1350), petit treason being the murder of one's lawful superior. In the 19th cent. petit treason was abolished. Treason is defined in Article 3 of the U.S. Constitution as levying war against the U.S. or giving aid and comfort to its enemies.

Treasury, United States Department of the, executive department of Federal government, estab. by act of Congress in 1789 to collect taxes, take charge of Federal funds, and keep accounts. Functions of department have been considerably broadened, including affairs indirectly related to finance. See also BANK OF THE UNITED STATES; FEDERAL RESERVE SYSTEM; INDEPENDENT TREASURY SYSTEM; SUBTREASURY.

Treat, Robert, 1622?–1710, British governor of colony of Conn. (1683–87, 1689–98). Helped found Newark, N.J., in 1666.

treaty port, port opened to foreign trade by treaty, especially in China and Japan in 19th cent. After OPIUM WAR, treaty of Nanking (1842) opened five Chinese treaty ports, later increased to 69. In all, foreigners enjoyed EXTERRITORIALITY. Similar system in Japan followed 1854 expedition of Matthew Perry. End of exterritoriality saw disappearance of treaty ports—in Japan 1899, in China 1946.

Trebbia (trĕb'byä), river, 70 mi. long, N Italy, rising in Liguria and flowing NE into the Po. In 218 B.C. Hannibal won a major victory on the Trebbia near Piacenza.

Trebizond (trĕ'bĭzŏnd"), Turkish *Trabzon,* city (pop. 33,969), NE Turkey, in Turkish Armenia; a Black Sea port. Exports food products, tobacco. The ancient Trapezus, city was founded 8th cent. B.C. Conquered by Mithridates VI 1st cent. B.C.; incorporated into Roman Empire 1st cent. A.D. Again a prosperous port under Byzantine Empire, but reached zenith after establishment of empire of Trebizond. Under rule of Alexius III (1349–90), city was one of world's great trade centers, renowned for wealth and beauty. Declined under Turkish rule. Included 1920 in ephemeral independent state of Armenia. Large Greek population was deported 1923. The **empire of Trebizond,** 1204–1461, was one of the Greek successor states formed after the overthrow (1204) of the Byzantine Empire by the Crusaders. Founded by Alexius I (Comnesus), it remained separate when the Byzantine Empire was restored 1261. Despite periods of vassalage to the Turks and Mongols, the empire prospered economically because of its position on trade route to Middle East and Russia. In 1461, Trebizond, last refuge of Hellenistic civilization, was taken by Mohammed II.

Tree, Ellen: see KEAN, EDMUND.

Tree, Sir Herbert Beerbohm, 1853–1917, English actor-manager, originally named Beerbohm; half brother of Max Beerbohm. At Haymarket theater (1887–97) and at Her Majesty's Theatre (which he built in 1897) he produced and acted in Shakspere, Ibsen, Wilde, and Maeterlinck dramas.

tree, perennial plant with single trunk or stem branching some distance from the ground. Differences between trees and shrubs are often slight; there are some trees with more than one trunk and some shrubs with a single treelike stem. Generally trees are taller and have larger stems. Leaves of deciduous trees and shrubs are shed regularly at the end of the growing season. Leaves of both coniferous and broad-leaved evergreens are shed gradually, often over a period of several years. See also BARK; CAMBIUM; FOREST; LEAF; WOOD.

tree fern, any fern with a treelike trunk, chiefly native to tropics. They often resemble palms.

tree frog, small arboreal frog with adhesive disk on each digit. Common tree frog is also called tree toad. Spring peeper is a tree frog which inflates its throat sac to deliver its loud "peeping."

tree of heaven: see AILANTHUS.

tree surgery, practice of repairing cut or injured trees to preserve their appearance or prevent disease. Cavities are filled with cement or rubber; fresh wounds are often treated with shellac. Extensive repairs should be done by a qualified tree surgeon.

trefoil, name for several plants, chiefly legumes, with trifoliate leaves, e.g., clover, tick trefoil (*Desmodium*), bird's-foot trefoil (*Lotus corniculatus*), a forage plant and weed, and shrubby trefoil.

Treitschke, Heinrich von (hīn'rĭkh fŭn trīch'-kü), 1834–96, German historian. Known for stirring and graphic works, notably *History of Germany in the Nineteenth Century* (Eng. tr., 7 vols., 1915–19).

trek (trĕk) [Dutch,= draft], South African term applied to an organized migration. In the Great Trek (1835–36), Boer farmers moved N from Cape of Good Hope to escape British domination.

Trelease, William (trĭlēs'), 1857–1945, American botanist. Director of the Missouri Botanical Garden from 1889 to 1912, he made a special study of genus *Agave.* His son, **Sam Farlow Trelease,** 1892–, a plant physiologist, became head of department of botany, Columbia Univ., in 1930. He has contributed especially to knowledge of photosynthesis, plant respiration, and selenium poisoning of grazing animals.

trench mouth (Vicent's stomatitis), inflammation of soft tissues of mouth. Causative agents believed to be two associated organisms, a bacillus and a spirochete, normally found in mouth. Predisposing factors include certain diseases, effects of certain drugs, vitamin deficiencies, allergies.

Trengganu: see MALAYA.

Trent, Ital. *Trento,* Latin *Tridentum,* city (pop. 37,290), cap. of Trentino-Alto Adige, N Italy, on Adige R. Was cap. of prince-bishopric of Trent from 12th cent. until its secularization and annexation to TYROL (1802). Italian in language and culture, it was awarded to Italy 1919. Was scene of Council of Trent (16th cent.). Landmarks include former episcopal residence, Romanesque cathedral, and statue of Dante.

Trent, third longest river of England. Flows 170 mi. from Staffordshire to join the Ouse W of Hull and form the Humber. Navigable for barges to Nottingham; connects with other streams by canal.

Trent, Council of, 1545–47, 1551–52, 1562–63, 19th ecumenical council of the Roman Catholic Church, chief instrument of the Catholic REFORM; called by PAUL III, after long delays; continued by Julius III and PIUS IV. It clarified Catholic doctrines and issued lucid definitions. The reform measure of the council touched all aspects of religious life and set the pattern for modern Catholicism. The work of the council was confirmed by a bull of Pius IV (*Benedictus Deus,* 1564) and issuance of the official *Cathechism of the Council of Trent* (1566).

Trent Affair, incident in diplomatic relations of U.S. and Great Britain in Civil War. On Nov. 8, 1861, Capt. Charles Wilkes halted British ship *Trent,* removed Confederate commissioners J. M. MASON and John SLIDELL, and had them interned at Boston. Britain's sharp protest led U.S. Secretary of State W. H. Seward to send note disavowing action and to release men, thus averting trouble.

Trent Canal, waterways system, 240 mi. long, S Ont., Canada, connecting L. Ontario (from Trenton on Bay of Quinte) with L. Huron (at Georgian Bay). Comprises Trent R., Rice L., Otonabee R., Kawartha Lakes, artificial channels to L. Simcoe, L. Couchiching, and Severn R. Primarily for water power.

Trentino-Alto Adige (trāntē'nō-äl'tō-ä'dējā), autonomous region (5,252 sq. mi.; pop. 669,029), N Italy, bordering on Switzerland and Austria; cap. Trent. Includes Tyrolean Alps S of Brenner Pass, part of DOLOMITES. Has forests, pastures, vineyards, orchards. Many resorts. Hydroelectric plants. Trento prov. (i.e., the Trentino) is predominantly Italian-speaking. BOLZANO prov. (i.e., the Alto Adige or Upper Adige valley) is largely German-speaking. History up to 1801 is that of bishoprics of TRENT and Bressanone; after 1801, that of S TYROL. Passing to Italy in 1919, it was called Venezia Tridentina until it was granted autonomy (1947), with special rights for German population.

Trento, Italy: see TRENT.

Trenton, town (pop. 10,085), S Ont., Canada, on Bay of Quinte at mouth of Trent R. and at S end of Trent Canal. Wool, paper, and flour mills, and mfg. of machinery and clothing.

Trenton. 1 Village (pop. 6,222), SE Mich., port on Detroit R. Farm trade center producing chemicals. **2** City (pop. 6,157), N Mo., N of Chillicothe. Farm shipping center with railroad shops and food-processing plants. Socialist experiment here 1897–1905. **3** City (pop. 128,009), state cap. (since 1790), W N.J., on Delaware R. (head of navigation) above Camden; settled by Friends 1679. Mfg. of wire rope, structural steel, pottery, rubber goods, airplane and auto equipment, steam turbines, and hardware. Monument (1893) commemorates Revolutionary battle of Dec. 20, 1776, when Washington crossed the Delaware to surprise and capture c.900 Hessians. Notable buildings include the capitol (1792); capitol annex (1931), with state library and museum; World War I memorial (1932); barracks (1758), now restored as museum; Bloomsbury Court (c.1719); Friends' meetinghouse (1739).

Tresca, Carlo (kär'lō trĕ'skä), c.1877–1943, Italian-American anti-Fascist leader and syndicalist, b. Italy, assassinated in New York city.

Tres Marías, Las (läs trās' märē'äs), archipelago, N Mexico, in the Pacific off coast of Nayarit. Islands produce maguey, salt, lumber. One island is used as federal penal colony.

Trevelyan, Sir George Otto, 1838–1928, English historian and politician. *Early History of Charles James Fox* (1880), *American Revolution* (4 vols., 1899–1907), and *George the Third and Charles Fox* (2 vols., 1912) were widely popular in U.S. He also wrote a biography of Lord Macaulay (1876). His son **George Macaulay Trevelyan,** 1876–, a "literary" rather than a "scientific" historian, is best known for *History of England* (1926).

Treves or **Trèves,** Germany: see TRIER.

Trevithick, Richard (trĕ'vĭthĭk), 1771–1833, English engineer. Inventor of a high-pressure steam engine (1800), a locomotive (1801); builder and developer of a steam-operated carriage (1803), steam engines for use in mines, and a steam threshing machine.

triangle, in mathematics, a plane figure bounded by three straight lines. Their points of intersection are called vertices; lines between vertices are called sides; altitude is perpendicular distance from base (any side) to opposite vertex. Area of triangle equals one half product of base and corresponding altitude. Median is line joining midpoint of side to opposite vertex. Triangles usually are classified according to size of angles as equilateral (all three angles equal), isosceles (two angles equal), scalene (all angles different), and right (having one right angle).

triangle, in music: see PERCUSSION INSTRUMENTS.

Trianon (trēänō'), two small châteaux in the park of Versailles, France. The Grand Trianon was built by J. H. Mansart in 1687; the Petit Trianon, favorite residence of Marie Antoinette, was finished by J. A. Gabriel in 1768. The **Treaty of Trianon,** 1920, was signed in the Grand Trianon after World War I by Hungary and the Allies (excluding U.S. and USSR). Reducing Hungary by one third and depriving it of access to the sea, it gave Transylvania, the E Banat, and other districts to Rumania; Slovakia and Ruthenia to Czechoslovakia; Croatia, Slavonia, and the W Banat to Yugoslavia; the BURGENLAND to Austria. Subsequent Hungarian efforts to secure revision of the treaty were supported by the 3,000,000 Magyars living in the ceded territories.

Triassic period (trīă'sĭk), first period of the Mesozoic ero of geologic time. Throughout Triassic, E North America was elevated; there was prolonged erosion; at the end extensive faulting (Palisade disturbance). In the West were submergences (with emergence at end of period) and much volcanic activity. Reptiles were dominant in the sea and on land; numerous types of dinosaurs had developed. Conifers were the principal plant life. A new group, cycads (intermediate between tree ferns and palms), arose. See also GEOLOGY, table.

tribe, an aggregate of peoples sharing common descent, dialect, territory, culture. Intermarriage permitted except within proscribed relationships.

Tribonian (trībō'nēùn), d. 545?, Roman jurist, who at command of Justinian I directed the compilation of the CORPUS JURIS CIVILIS.

Trichinopoly (trĭchĭnŏ'pùlē), city (pop. 159,566), S Madras, India, on Cauvery R. Here is an enormous rock topped by a Dravidian temple. Was cap. of Chola kingdom, 15th–16th cent. Cotton mills.

trichinosis (trĭ″kĭnō′sĭs) or **trichiniasis** (trĭ″-kinī′ùsis), serious disease caused by *Trichinella spiralis,* a round worm. Parasite reproduces in intestine; young migrate to muscle and encyst. Caused in man by eating insufficiently cooked infected pork.

trident, in Greek legend, three-pronged fork borne by Poseidon. It probably represented a fishing spear, goad, and forked lightning, because he was god of the sea, of horses, and of forked lightning.

Tridentum: see TRENT, Italy.

Trier (trēr), city (pop. 74,709), Rhineland-Palatinate, W Germany, on the Moselle; also called Treves (trēvz), in English. Center of Moselle wine dist. Textile mfg.; steel industry. Founded by Augustus as Augusta Treverorum, it was a flourishing Roman city (pop. c.50,000) and a residence of the Western emperors from c.295 until its capture by the Franks (early 5th cent.). The archbishops of Trier later ruled considerable territory on both sides of the Rhine as princes and electors of the Holy Roman Empire. Under them Trier prospered and was the seat (1473–1797) of a university. Trier passed to France 1797; the archbishopric was secularized. In 1815 the Congress of Vienna gave the former archiepiscopal lands W of the Rhine (incl. Trier) to Prussia; the rest went to Nassau. Catholic episcopal see was estab. 1821. Trier suffered much destruction in World War II. Its Roman monuments (Porta Nigra, a well-preserved fortified gate; amphitheater; imperial baths) were preserved, but the Gothic Liebfrauenkirche (13th-cent. church), the Romanesque cathedral (partly dating from 4th cent.), and the baroque electoral palace all were heavily damaged. The cathedral contains the Holy Coat, supposedly the seamless coat of Jesus.

Trieste (trēĕst′, Ital. trēĕ′stā), Serbo-Croatian *Trst,* city (pop. 248,379); major seaport at head of the Adriatic. Has shipyards, ironworks, and oil refineries. A free commune from the 12th cent., it placed itself (1382) under the dukes of Austria, but kept its administrative autonomy until 18th cent. Became a free port in 1719, flourishing as outlet of Central Europe and the only Austrian port. Having retained Italian language and culture, it was a center of Italian irredentism until annexed to Italy in 1919. Landmarks include Cathedral of San Giusto (partly 6th cent.) and Miramar castle (built for Archduke Maximilian of Austria). Trieste is now cap. of **Free Territory of Trieste,** free state (285 sq. mi.; pop. c.380,000) under protection of UN Security Council. It comprises the city and a coastal strip of NW ISTRIA, with Slovenian population. The Free Territory was created in 1947 by annexes to Italian peace treaty as a compromise between conflicting claims of Italy and Yugoslavia.

trifoliate orange, small ornamental spiny tree (*Poncirus trifoliata*) of China, with white flowers and aromatic orangelike fruits. Used as an understock for the orange to increase its hardiness.

Triglav (trē′gläv), highest peak (c.9,395 ft.) of Yugoslavia, in Julian Alps.

trigonometry, literally, the science of measuring a TRIANGLE, i.e., measuring its sides, angles, and particularly the ratios of certain pairs of sides. For all right angles having a given acute angle, ratio of a certain pair of sides (side opposite the given angle divided by hypotenuse) is same; hence value of this ratio is function solely of the given acute angle. Using various pairs of sides, six such ratios are obtainable and are called trigonometric functions of a given angle; they are the sine, cosine, tangent, cotangent, secant, and cosecant. Values of these have been tabulated for acute angles of all sizes. Thus, generally, if any three (independent) parts of a triangle are known, its altitude, area, length of all sides, and sizes of all angles, are computable. If all six functions are defined for angles of all sizes, they have certain properties which are periodic (values repeat previous value sequence of preceding interval of angle sizes) and thus indispensable in mathematical applications to study of physical phenomena such as light, sound, color, etc.

Trillium or **wake-robin,** spring wild flower of genus *Trillium,* chiefly native to North America. Leaves, petals, and sepals are in threes, the single flower (white, pink, or purplish) is borne erect or nodding from the center of the whorl of leaves.

trilobite (trī′lùbīt), primitive arthropod having body divided into three sections (head, thorax, abdomen). Trilobites were the most numerous inhabitants of the Cambrian seas; they became extinct in Permian period.

Trincomalee (trĭng″kùmùlē′), town (pop. 29,-146), NE Ceylon; port on Indian Ocean. In World War II it was chief British naval base in Far East after fall of Singapore.

Trinidad, city (pop. 12,204; alt. c.6,000 ft.), S Colo., E of Sangre de Cristo Mts. near N.Mex. line; settled 1859 on Santa Fe Trail. Shipping center for coal-mining, dairying, and livestock region.

Trinidad and Tobago (trĭ′nĭdäd, tōbä′gō), crown colony (pop. 557,970), British West Indies; cap. PORT OF SPAIN. Trinidad (1,864 sq. mi.), lying just N of mouths of Orinoco R. in Venezuela, has natural asphalt lake (Pitch Lake). City of San Fernando is market center for petroleum. Discovered by Columbus in 1498, island did not attract Spanish colonists because of its lack of gold. Subsequently raided by Dutch, French, and English buccaneers. Spain finally ceded island to England (1802). Tobago (116 sq. mi.), just N of Trinidad, is a mountain ridge, densely forested with hardwoods.

trinitrotoluene (T.N.T., TNT) (trī′nī″trōtŏl′-ūēn), explosive, yellow crystalline compound of carbon, hydrogen, and oxygen, prepared from toluene. It is stable and can be exploded only with a detonator. It is used alone and in mixtures.

Trinity, in Christianity, God considered as existing in three persons (Father, Son, and Holy Ghost). Definition of the doctrine came early and many of the first Church councils were concerned mainly with the problem (see CREED; NICAEA, COUNCIL OF; ARIANISM).

Trinity, river rising in N Texas through confluence of three forks and flowing c.510 mi.

SSE to Trinity Bay, Galveston Bay arm. Several reservoirs upstream (esp. for Fort Worth and Dallas). Soil conservation and flood control projects include Benbrook, Lavon, Grapevine, and Garza–Little Dam reservoirs.

Trinity Bay, Atlantic inlet, 80 mi. long, SE N.F., Canada, between Avalon Peninsula and mainland. At Trinity, port on W shore, first permanent transatlantic cable was laid 1866.

Trinity College: see CAMBRIDGE UNIVERSITY; OXFORD UNIVERSITY.

Trinity College: see DUBLIN, Ireland.

Trinity College: see HARTFORD, Conn.; WASHINGTON, D.C.

Trinity Hall: see CAMBRIDGE UNIVERSITY.

Trinity Sunday, first Sunday after PENTECOST, observed as feast of the Trinity.

Trinity University: see SAN ANTONIO, Texas.

Triple Alliance, name of several European coalitions. That of **1668** was formed by England, Sweden, and Netherlands against Louis XIV of France and forced him to end the War of DEVOLUTION. That of **1717** (among England, France, and Netherlands) became in 1718 the QUADRUPLE ALLIANCE. For alliances of **1872,** see THREE EMPERORS' LEAGUE. For alliance of **1882,** see TRIPLE ALLIANCE AND TRIPLE ENTENTE.

Triple Alliance, War of the, 1865–70, fought by Paraguay under the dictator Francisco Solano López against alliance of Argentina, Brazil, and Uruguay. Defense of Paraguay against powerful odds was heroic, but end of war found Paraguay defeated, with land devastated and population reduced by half.

Triple Alliance and Triple Entente, two international combinations of states that dominated Europe's diplomatic history after 1882 until they came into armed conflict in WORLD WAR I. The secret Dual Alliance of Germany and Austria-Hungary, formed 1879, was joined in 1882 by Italy (incensed by the French occupation of Tunis) and thus became the Triple Alliance. Rumania joined the group 1883, but actually both Italian and Rumanian interests were opposed to Austria-Hungary's, and both states eventually entered World War I on the Allied side. A rapprochement between Russia and France began after 1890, when Germany declined to renew its reinsurance treaty with Russia. The Franco-Russian Dual Entente came into existence by gradual stages and was openly acknowledged in 1895. German commercial and colonial imperialism disquieted Great Britain, which composed its difference with France after 1898 and arrived at the Franco-British Entente Cordiale—an informal understanding. Russia's defeat in the Russo-Japanese War removed some of Britain's fears of Russian expansionism in Asia and made possible a Russo-British understanding (1907). The Triple Entente of France, England, and Russia, though not a formal alliance, proved effective at the outbreak of World War I.

Tripoli (trĭ'pùlē), anc. *Tripolis,* city (pop. 59,001), N Lebanon; port on the Mediterranean. Probably founded after 700 B.C., it was the cap. of a Phoenician federation. Flourished under Seleucids and Romans. Captured by Arabs in A.D. 638. Taken 1109 by Crusaders, sacked 1289 by sultan of Egypt. Terminus of an oil pipe line from Iraq, it has an oil refinery. Exports oil, silk, and citrus fruit.

Tripoli (trĭ'pùlē), anc. *Oea,* city (pop. 144,616), winter cap. of Libya, in Tripolitania; port on the Mediterranean. Exports include hides, dates, salt, sponges, and carpets. It was the site of a Tyrian colony (7th cent.? B.C.). Passed to Italy in 1911 and became cap. of Libya. It was a base of the Barbary corsairs, whom the U.S. fought in TRIPOLITAN WAR. An Axis base in World War II, it fell to the British in 1943.

Tripolitania (trĭ"pùlĭtā'nēù), region, W Libya, along the Mediterranean coast. Colonized 7th cent. B.C. by the Phoenicians. Under Turkish rule from 1553 to 1912, when it was acquired by Italy. In World War II it fell to the British in 1943.

Tripolitan War, 1801–5, U.S. campaigns against the BARBARY STATES, after demands for more tribute than stipulated in treaties (1786–99) to halt piracy. Expeditions were sent by the U.S. against Tripoli in 1801, 1802, 1804, and a land expedition under William Eaton. A notable incident was the firing of the PHILADELPHIA (1804) by Stephen DECATUR, who later commanded a successful expedition against Algiers (1815; the Algerine War).

Triptolemus (trĭptŏ'lĭmùs), in Greek religion, one of chief figures of Eleusinian Mysteries. He was said to be inventor of the plow and of agriculture.

Trist, Nicholas Philip, 1800–1874, American diplomat. Conducted negotiations to end Mexican War. Ignoring recall, he negotiated Treaty of GUADALUPE HIDALGO.

Tristan: see TRISTRAM AND ISOLDE.

Tristan da Cunha (trĭ'stăn dä kōōn'yù), chief island (pop. 230) of an isolated volcanic group in the S Atlantic. Has an important meteorological and radio station. Discovered (1506) by Portuguese, it was annexed (1816) by Great Britain and became a dependency of St. Helena in 1938.

Tristan l'Hermite, Louis (lwē' trēstā' lĕrmēt'), d. c.1477, provost of France under Charles VII and Louis XI. Reformed army; notorious for cruelty.

Tristram and Isolde (trĭ'strùm, ĭsōl'dù), medieval romance, mainly Irish in origin. In it Tristram, sent to Ireland to bring Isolde back as the bride of King Mark of Cornwall, drinks a love potion with her. Their irresistible passion leads to the death of both. Thomas of Britain wrote an Anglo-Norman verse account (c.1185), and Gottfried von Strassburg wrote a German version (c.1210). Sir Thomas Malory combined the story with the Arthurian legend. Also Tristan, Tristran; Isolt, Iseult, Yseult.

Triton (trī'tùn), in Greek myth, merman son of Poseidon. Later literature speaks of many Tritons. They rode over the sea on horses and blew conch shells.

Triumirate (trīŭm'vĭrĭt), in anc. Rome, governing board of three men. Most important were the First Triumvirate (Julius CAESAR, POMPEY, and CRASSUS), formed in 60 B.C., and the Second Triumvirate (AUGUSTUS, ANTONY, and LEPIDUS), formed in 43 B.C.

Trivandrum (trĭvăn'drùm), city (pop. 128,365), cap. of Tranvancore-Cochin, India. Textile mfg.

trivium: see LIBERAL ARTS.

Trnava (tŭr'nävä), Hung. *Nagyszombat,* town (pop. 24,226), SW Slovakia, Czechoslovakia. Agr. center. Religious center of medieval Slovakia; called the Slovak Rome for its many churches (incl. a notable Gothic cathedral). University founded here by Peter Pazmany (1635) was moved to Budapest 1777.

Trnovo (tûr'nōvō), town (pop. 16,182), N central Bulgaria. Was cap. of old Bulgaria under Ivan II (13th cent.). Fell to Turks 1393.

Troas (trō'ăs) or **the Troad** (trō'ăd), region about anc. Troy on NW coast of Asia Minor.

Trobriand Islands (trō'brēănd"), small volcanic group, off SE New Guinea and part of Territory of Papua. Site of Allied base in 1943.

Trogir (trō'gēr), small port and resort, Croatia, W Yugoslavia, on an Adriatic island W of Split. Contested between Hungary and Venice in Middle Ages; eventually kept by Venice until 1797. Has splendid 13th-cent. cathedral and several medieval and Renaissance castles.

Troilus and Cressida (trō'ĭlŭs, troi'lŭs, krĕ'sĭdŭ), medieval romance distantly related to a Greek legend. Troilus, a Trojan prince, loved Cressida, but she was faithless to him. Story first used by Benoît de Sainte-More, from whom Boccaccio drew. Chaucer and Shakspere followed in same tradition.

Trois Rivières (trōōä" rēvyĕr') or **Three Rivers,** city (pop. 46,074), S Que., Canada, on St. Lawrence R. at mouth of St. Maurice R. and NE of Montreal; founded 1634 by Champlain. Pulp, paper, and cotton mills, grain elevators, and foundries. Was a major trading post and fortified port. First iron forges in Que. built here 1737.

Trojan War, in Greek mythology, war between Greeks and Trojans. It is the setting for the *Iliad* and background for the *Odyssey.* Strife began when PARIS eloped with HELEN, wife of Menelaus. Greeks under Agamemnon besieged Troy for 10 years. City was well fortified, and Greeks finally won only by a deceit. Pretending to depart, they left a wooden horse, which the Trojans, deaf to warnings of Cassandra and Laocoön, took into city as an offering to Athena. Warriors hidden in the horse opened the city gates to the Greek army, which sacked Troy. Among Greek heroes were Achilles, Patroclus, Odysseus, and Nestor. Trojan heroes, led by Hector, included Paris, Aeneas, Memnon, and Penthesilea. Some of the gods took sides in the war. Trojan War in reality (c.1200 B.C.) was probably over control of trade in the Dardanelles.

Trollhattan (trôl'hĕ"tän), Swed. *Trollhättan,* city (pop. 24,264), SW Sweden, on Gota R. and near Vanern L. River here falls 108 ft. in six falls and rapids; water power is used by Sweden's largest hydroelectric plant.

Trollope (trŏ'lŭp), English family of authors. **Frances (Milton) Trollope,** 1780–1863, wrote travel books and novels. A stay in the U.S. prompted her *Domestic Manners of the Americans* (1832). Wrote many novels. Her eldest son, **Thomas Adolphus Trollope,** 1810–92, was also a prolific writer of novels and historical works. Her youngest and most famous son, **Anthony Trollope,** 1815–82, was a novelist of note, remarkable for his ability to build up character by using commonplace scenes. Travel through S England gave him background for his imaginary county of Barset, in which are set the most popular of his novels, the *Barsetshire Chronicles,* including *The Warden* (1855), *Barchester Towers* (1857), *Framley Parsonage* (1861), and *The Last Chronicle of Barset* (1867). A later group of stories, including *The Eustace Diamonds* (1873), share a common reference to parliamentary background. Besides more than 50 novels, he wrote travel books and biographies and an autobiography (pub. posthumously).

trombone: see WIND INSTRUMENTS.

Tromp, Maarten Harpertszoon (märtŭn här'pŭrtsōn trômp'), 1597–1653, Dutch admiral. His victory (1639) over the Spanish fleet in the lee of the Downs marked the passing of Spanish sea power. In the first Dutch War he defeated the English off Dungeness (1652). Though he later had to withdraw from the Channel, he eventually broke the blockade of the Dutch coast. His son **Cornelis Tromp** (kôrnā'lĭs), 1629–91, served as admiral in second and third Dutch Wars.

Tromso (trŏm'zō), Nor. *Tromsø,* city (pop. 10,990), N Norway; a port and chief city of Arctic Norway. Exports fish, fish products, furs.

Trondheim (trôn'hām), city (pop. 57,128), central Norway; a fortified seaport on Trondheim Fjord; variant spellings are Drontheim, Trondhjem. Has hydroelectric plant and shipyards; exports fish, lumber, copper ore, wood pulp. Lutheran episcopal see. Founded 997 as Nidaros, it became political and religious cap. of medieval Norway, and was an archiepiscopal see from 1152 until forcible introduction of the Reformation (1537), when city was renamed Trondheim. Its historic role was reaffirmed when Haakon VII was crowned (1906) in its splendid Gothic cathedral (12th–13th cent.; ravaged by repeated fires but restored after 1869). As a major German naval base in World War II, city was severely bombed. **Trondheim Fjord** is an inlet of Norwegian Sea. Extending c.80 mi. inland, it is considered natural boundary between N and S Norway.

tropical medicine, branch of medicine concerned with diseases occurring most frequently in warmer climates. Causative organisms of certain diseases including malaria, yellow fever, amoebic dysentery, hookworm, dengue fever, and filariasis breed best in the warmth, humidity, and conditions of life in the tropics. Pioneer work accomplished in field by Latin-American scientists, notably at Univ. of Puerto Rico, and by several U.S. universities.

tropics. The Tropics of Cancer (23½°N) Capricorn (23½°S) delimit the tropical or torrid zone. Since this zone receives more of the direct rays of the sun than areas in other latitudes and since the angle at which the rays strike varies little, the average annual temperature is high and seasonal change of temperature is less than in other zones. Tropical climate types (determined by latitude, distance from oceans, elevation, prevailing winds) include tropical rain forest, savanna, steppe, desert, and highland.

tropism (trō'pĭzŭm), involuntary response of whole or part of organism involving orientation toward (positive tropism) or away from (negative tropism) external stimulus. Tropistic stimuli include heat, light, moisture, gravity, electricity, and chemical agents. Response to sun is heliotropism; to gravity, geotropism; to light, phototropism.

troposphere: see ATMOSPHERE.

Troppau (trôp'ou), Czech *Opava,* city (pop. 20,441), N Czechoslovakia; former cap. of Austrian Silesia. Textile mfg. The **Congress of Troppau,** 1820, was held under the provisions of the QUADRUPLE ALLIANCE to consider action against the liberal uprisings in the Two Sicilies and Spain. These problems were merely referred to later meetings (see LAIBACH, CONGRESS OF; VERONA, CONGRESS OF). However, at the behest of Alexander I (who personally represented Russia) a protocol was signed by Russia, Austria, and Prussia, asserting that any state where a revolutionary change of government took place was to be brought back, by force of arms if necessary, into the bosom of the HOLY ALLIANCE. England rejected the protocol; France adhered with reservations.

Trossachs (trŏ'săks, -sŭks), wooded valley, Perthshire, Scotland. Associated with Scott's works.

Trotsky, Leon (trŏt'skē), 1879–1940, Russian revolutionist. His original name was Lev Davidovich Bronstein. An early convert to Marxism, he was repeatedly exiled to Siberia; spent much of the years 1902–17 abroad as propagandist, agitator, and journalist; took a major part in Bolshevik October Revolution of 1917; became commissar for foreign affairs under Lenin. He negotiated the Treaty of BREST-LITOVSK (1918) and organized the victorious Red Army in the civil war of 1918–20. After Lenin's death (1924), Trotsky led the leftist opposition against STALIN but was expelled from the party (1927), exiled to Alma-Ata, and orderd to leave the USSR (1929). He found asylum in Turkey (until 1933), then in France (until 1935) and in Norway (until 1937). The Soviet government obtained his expulsion from Norway after Trotsky's name had been linked, perhaps somewhat fantastically, with vast plots against Stalin in the Moscow treason trials of the 1930s. Trotsky denied these charges and hurled countercharges at Stalin. He settled near Mexico City in 1937, founded the Fourth International, a minor but highly articulate group of intellectuals dedicated to the establishment of pure communism. In 1940, Trotsky was killed with an axe by Jacques van den Dreschd (an *alias;* his real identity remains mysterious), who previously had wormed himself into Trotsky's confidence. Trotsky wrote numerous political and polemical works, most of them available in English.

troubadour (trōō'bŏōdôr), medieval poet of S France whose songs were composed in *langue d'oc.* His counterpart in the *langue d'oïl* of N France was the TROUVÈRE. Troubadour poetry, essentially aristocratic, was characterized by metrical and poetic skill; its main theme was romantic love. Among troubadours were Peire Vidal, Bertrand de Born, Gaucelm Faidit, Peire Cardinal. Decline began in 13th cent.

Troubetzkoy, Paul, Prince (trōōbĕtskoi', trōōbĕts'koi, Rus. trōōbyĭtskoi'), 1866–1938, Russian sculptor, b. Italy. Best known for portrait busts of famous contemporaries.

trout, game fish of salmon family, commercially valuable as food, found chiefly in clear, cold, fresh waters. Genera include *Salmo* (e.g., European sea trout), *Salvelinus* (e.g., brook trout and other chars), *Cristivomer* (e.g., lake trout).

trouvère (trōōvâr'), medieval poet of N France whose songs were composed in *langue d'oïl* (see also TROUBADOUR). Their poetry, which flourished in the 12th–13th cent., includes the CHANSONS DE GESTE. Well-known trouvères were Le Châtelain de Coucy and ADAM DE LA HALLE.

Trowbridge, John Townsend, 1827–1916, American writer, best remembered for his poem "Darius Green and His Flying Machine" and for many stories for boys (e.g., *Cudjo's Cave,* 1864).

Troy, anc. city of Asia Minor, almost universally believed to have been on the mound, Hissarlik, in Asiatic Turkey (as identified by Heinrich Schliemann). The seventh of nine settlements excavated here is said to have been that of the TROJAN WAR. Called also Ilion and Ilium.

Troy. 1 City (pop. 8,555), SE Ala., on Conecuh R. and SE of Montgomery, in cotton, peanut, corn area. **2** City (pop. 72,311), E N.Y., on E bank of Hudson R. and NE of Albany; laid out 1786. Site included in Kiliaen Van Rensselaer's patroonship. Port and industrial center, known for shirts, collars; mfg. also of machinery, valves, brushes. Seat of RENSSELAER POLYTECHNIC INSTITUTE; Russell Sage Col. (nonsectarian; for women; opened 1916; stresses preparation for group living); Emma Willard School (nonsectarian; for girls; opened 1814 at Middlebury, Vt., moved to Troy 1821; renamed 1892 for its founder, Emma WILLARD; preceded first women's colleges as experiment in higher education). **3** City (pop. 10,661), W Ohio, on Great Miami R. and N of Dayton; settled c.1807. Mfg. of machinery, airplanes, and furniture.

Troyes (trōōä'), city (pop. 53,521), cap. of Aube dept., NE France, on the Seine; historic cap. of Champagne. Textile mfg. Its two annual fairs were the most important medieval fairs of W Europe until the 14th cent.; troy weight became an international standard. Has Gothic cathedral (13th–16th cent.) and Church of St. Urban (13th cent.); fine museum. The Champenoise school of sculpture flourished at Troyes in the Renaissance. In the **Treaty of Troyes,** 1420, among HENRY V of England, CHARLES VI of France, and PHILIP THE GOOD of Burgundy, France reached its lowest point in the Hundred Years War. The dauphin (later CHARLES VII) was disinherited; Henry was made regent of France, received Catherine of Valois in marriage, and was declared heir to Charles VI (who merely retained his royal title).

troy weight: see WEIGHTS AND MEASURES.

Truchas, peaks: see SANGRE DE CRISTO MOUNTAINS.

Trucial Oman (tro͞o'shůl ōmän'), region (6,000 sq. mi.; pop. c.40,000), E Arabia, occupying Persian Gulf coast from Qatar to Oman. Comprises seven constituent states bound to Great Britain by truce (1820) and agreement (1892). Formerly notorious for piracy, the area was called the Pirate Coast. Pearl-diving and fishing are chief activities.

Truckee (trŭ'kē), mountain resort (pop. 1,025), E Calif., on Truckee R. and SW of Reno, Nev. L. Tahoe is to S and Donner L. is just W.

Truckee, river rising in NE Calif. in L. Tahoe and flowing c.100 mi. N and E into W Nev. to Pyramid L. Has L. Tahoe Dam of NEWLANDS PROJECT.

truck farming, practice of growing one or a few kinds of crops of vegetables or certain fruits on a large scale at some distance from the market. Market gardening, though similar, is more intensive and diversified.

Trudeau, Edward Livingston (tro͞o'dō), 1848–1915, American physician, a pioneer in open-air treatment of tuberculosis at Saranac Lake, N.Y.

truffle (trŭ'fůl), subterranean edible fungus, fleshy and globular (1–4 in. in diameter). Truffles are found in groups, often a foot below the ground's surface, close to roots of trees. They have not been successfully cultivated but are found in a number of European countries; they are usually hunted with dogs or hogs. In Périgord, France, their collection is an important industry.

Trujillo (Ciudad Trujillo) (tro͞ohē'yō; syo͞odhädh'), city (pop. 181,533), S Dominican Republic; cap., largest city, and chief port of republic. Founded as SANTO DOMINGO (1496), it was rebuilt after disastrous hurricane of 1930 and renamed for Trujillo Molina. Among surviving colonial edifices is oldest cathedral of the New World.

Trujillo, city (pop. 38,961), NW Peru; founded by Diego de Almagro (1534). An oasis in coastal desert of Peru, it is a thriving commercial center for irrigated area with growing of sugar cane. Near by are pre-Incan ruins of Chanchan.

Trujillo Molina, Rafael Leonidas (räfäěl' lāōnē'dhäs tro͞ohē'yō mōlē'nä), 1891–, president of Dominican Republic (1930–38, 1942–50). By a military coup he ousted President Horacio Vásquez in 1930 and later was dictator even when not president. Became constantly embroiled with other Caribbean countries. Internally, his efficient, though corrupt, rule brought material progress to country. He was appointed ambassador-at-large to UN in 1952.

Truk (trŭk, tro͝ok), island group (39 sq. mi.; pop. 9,510), W Pacific, in E Caroline Isls. Consists of c.55 volcanic islands surrounded by an atoll reef. Japanese naval base in World War II.

Truman, Harry S., 1884–, 32d President of the United States, b. Lamar, Mo. U.S. Senator from Mo. (1935–45); headed committee to investigate government expenditures in World War II. Served as Democratic Vice President of U.S. (1945); succeeded to presidency at death of F. D. Roosevelt. Attended POTSDAM CONFERENCE (July, 1945). Growing U.S.-USSR tension created problems. The "Truman Doctrine" of March, 1947, aimed at aiding Communist-threatened nations to curb spread of Soviet influence. EUROPEAN RECOVERY PROGRAM was brought forth. Fair Deal domestic program, including civil rights and price controls, was largely thwarted by Republican majority in 80th Congress. Handicapped in 1948 by a Southern bolt and disaffection under H. A. Wallace, Truman won reelection in a victory that was surprising to many. In 1949 he promoted NORTH ATLANTIC TREATY; failed to get TAFT-HARTLEY LABOR ACT repealed. Escaped assassination attempt in 1950. Embroiled in dispute with Gen. Douglas MACARTHUR (1951). Succeeded as President by Dwight D. Eisenhower in 1953.

Trumbull, John, 1750–1831, American poet and judge in Conn., a leader of Connecticut Wits. Wrote satires, *Progress of Dulness* (1772–73), *M'Fingal* (1775–82).

Trumbull, Jonathan (trŭm'bůl), 1710–85, colonial governor of Conn. (1769–84). Aided patriot cause in American Revolution. His son, **Jonathan Trumbull,** 1740–1809, was also governor of Conn. (1797–1809). Another son, **John Trumbull,** 1756–1843, was a noted historical painter, who studied under Benjamin West in London. Much of his work is in Trumbull Gall. which he founded at Yale Univ. 1831. Several large paintings (e.g., *Signing of the Declaration of Independence*) are at the Capitol, Washington, D.C. He served for a time as secretary to John Jay.

Trumbull, town (pop. 8,641), SW Conn., adjoining N Bridgeport; settled c.1690.

trumpet: see WIND INSTRUMENTS.

trumpet creeper or **trumpet vine,** woody, climbing or shrubby plant of genus *Campsis,* with clusters of large trumpet-shaped scarlet or orange-red flowers.

Truro (tro͞o'rō), town (pop. 10,756), N N.S., Canada, near head of Cobequid Bay of Bay of Fundy. Railroad center with mfg. of clothing and machinery. First settled by Acadians as Cobequid.

Truro, resort town (pop. 661), SE Mass., on N Cape Cod. Site of Highland Light, one of most powerful on Atlantic Coast.

truss, in architecture and engineering, a supporting structure commonly composed of steel or wood beams, girders, or rods, used especially in roofs and bridges. It is usually in the form of a triangle or series of triangles to insure greatest rigidity.

trust, in finance, business combination which controls the policy of a number of organizations; defined in antitrust legislation as being in restraint of trade. Term derives from use of legal trust form by many such organizations. Horizontal trust is combination of corporations which ordinarily would be in direct competition; vertical trust controls operations from procuring of materials to retailing of product. Trust is similar to cartel, but smaller in scope. Trusts grew rapidly in U.S. 1880–1905, although attacked as monopolies. Series of laws were passed to curb trusts (notably, Sherman Anti-Trust Act, 1890, and Clayton Anti-Trust Act, 1914).

trusteeship, territorial, system for control of territories not self-governing, administered by UN. Replacing MANDATES of League of Nations, and regulated by chapters 12 and 13 of UN Charter, it promotes welfare of people and prepares them for self government. Supervision is by Trusteeship Council, made up of UN members holding trust territories plus equal number of other members, and each territory is governed by a trusteeship agreement.

Truth, Sojourner, c.1797–1883, American abolitionist, a freed slave, originally named Isabella. Traveled throughout North preaching emancipation and woman's rights.

Truth or Consequences, health resort (pop. 4,563), SW N.Mex., on Rio Grande near Elephant Butte Dam. Formerly Hot Springs.

Tryon, Dwight William (trī'ŭn), 1849–1925, American landscape painter, influenced by Daubigny.

Tryon, William, 1725–88, British colonial governor of N.C. (1765–71). Rigorously suppressed REGULATOR MOVEMENT. Governor of N.Y. (1771–78). Led Tory raids in Conn.

Tsana, lake in Ethiopia; see TANA.

Tsaritsyn, RSFSR: see STALINGRAD.

Tsarskoye Selo, RSFSR: see PUSHKIN.

Tschaikowsky, Piotr Ilich: see TCHAIKOVSKY.

Tschermak-Seysenegg, Erich (ā'rĭkh chĕr'mäk-sī'zŭnĕk), 1871–, Austrian botanist, one of several scientists who simultaneously in 1900 confirmed Mendel's laws of heredity.

Tschudi, Aegidius or **Gilg** (ējĭ'dēŭs chōō'dē, gĭlk'), 1505–72, Swiss historian, author of *Chronicon Helveticum,* which immortalized the William Tell legend.

tsetse fly (tsĕt'sē), African insect (*Glossina*) slightly larger than housefly. Sucks blood; certain species transmit African sleeping sickness.

Tsin (dzĭn) or **Chin** (chĭn), dynasty of China, which ruled 265–420, after period of Three Kingdoms. Saw continued growth of Buddhism. Chaos reigned in period between its fall and founding of Sui dynasty.

Tsinan (jē'nän'), city (pop. 574,781), cap. of Shantung prov., E China; textile mfg. Cheloo Univ.

Tsinghai or **Chinghai** (both: chĭng'hī'), province (250,000 sq. mi.; pop. 1,200,000), NW China; cap. Sining. Bounded on SW by Tibet. Mainly a high plateau, it contains the lake KOKO NOR. Wool and hides are chief exports. The area came under Chinese domination, c.1724. Also called Koko Nor.

Tsingtao (chĭng'dou'), city (pop. 787,722), E Shantung prov., China; port and naval base on Yellow Sea. Under German rule 1898–1914 as part of Kiaochow lease, it was held by Japanese 1914–22. After World War II it was U.S. naval base until 1949.

Tsugaru Strait (tsōōgä'rōō), channel between Honshu and Hokkaido, Japan.

Tsu Hsi: see TZ'U HSI.

Tsunetaka (tsōō'nātä'kä), fl. 13th cent., Japanese landscape painter. Changed his name to Tosa Tsunetaka, giving the name Tosa to a school of art.

Tsushima (tsōō'shēmä), Japanese island (271 sq. mi.; pop. 57,482), in Korea Strait. In Russo-Japanese War, Japan won decisive naval battle (May, 1905) fought near the island.

Tuamotu Islands (tōōämō'tōō) or **Low Archipelago,** coral group, area c.330 sq. mi., S Pacific; part of French Oceania. Comprises 80 atolls in 1,300-mi. chain. Includes the phosphate island Makatea. Discovered 1606 by the Spanish, annexed 1881 by France. Formerly called Paumotu.

Tuareg (twä'rĕg), Moslem Berber people, nomads of the Sahara. Among most highly civilized peoples of Africa. Tuareg men go veiled, while the women are unveiled. Descent and inheritance are through female line. Long resisted European domination.

tuba: see WIND INSTRUMENTS.

Tubal-cain (tū'bŭl-kān), in Bible, son of Lamech. The first worker of brass and iron. Gen. 4.22.

tube, vacuum, or **electron tube,** electronic device used as rectifier, amplifier, mixer, and detector of audio and radio frequencies and for electrical measurements. Also called thermionic valve, it is essentially a glass vacuum tube containing a negative electrode (cathode), which when heated releases electrons that flow to positive electrode (anode). When rays emitted by cathode are focused on metal plate in tube, X rays result. See also PHOTOELECTRIC CELL; *ill.,* p. 377.

tuber, enlarged underground plant stem, such as the edible part of the potato plant. Tubers contain stored food, usually starch. See *ill.,* p. 999.

tuberculosis, contagious, infectious disease of vertebrates caused by bacterium known as tubercle bacillus. Similar forms of the germ cause the disease in humans and cattle; cows are generally tested to prevent spread of infection through milk. As bacteria attack body tissues, small nodules (tubercles) form; from unhealed tubercles in lungs of victim of pulmonary form (also called consumption and phthisis), germs enter sputum, which may spread infection. Other forms of tuberculosis attack bones, intestines, skin, lymph nodes (a form early known as scrofula and King's evil). Mortality and spread are reduced by early detection by X-ray photographs and skin tests, use of vaccines, and of sulfa drugs and antibiotics. Treatment of pulmonary type includes also rest, fresh air, and proper diet. Many sanatoriums use regime introduced in U.S. at Saranac Lake, N.Y. by TRUDEAU.

tuberose, a tuberous-rooted tender plant (*Polianthes tuberosa*), native to Mexico but grown in gardens elsewhere. It has waxy white, fragrant flowers.

Tübingen (tü'bĭng-ŭn), city (pop. 37,278), S Württemberg, SW Germany, on the Neckar; cap. (after 1945) of Württemberg-Hohenzollern. Mfg. of textiles, machinery, precision instruments. Has famous university (founded 1477), where Melanchthon taught; theological faculty was famous in 19th cent. City center, which has retained medieval character, contains late-Gothic Church of St. George.

Tubman, Harriet, c.1820–1913, American abolitionist, an escaped slave. Freed over 300 slaves through Underground Railroad. In

Civil War she was Union nurse, laundress, and spy.

Tubuai Islands (tōōbōōī') or **Austral Islands,** volcanic group, S Pacific, S of Society Isls.; part of French Oceania. Tubuai, largest of the five islands, was discovered 1777 by Capt. James Cook and annexed 1880 by France. Coffee, arrowroot, and copra are produced.

Tuckahoe, N.Y.: see EASTCHESTER.

tuckahoe, name for two Indian foods known also as Indian bread. One is the rootstock (edible when cooked) of certain plants of the arum family. The other is a fungus (*Poria cocos*) found on roots of trees in the S U.S.

Tucson (tōō'sŏn"), city (pop. 45,454), SE Ariz., SE of Phoenix; settled by Spaniards in late 17th cent. In 1776 presidio was moved here; served as border post of New Spain, of Mexico, and, after Gadsden Purchase, of U.S. Was territorial cap. 1867–77. Long-time trade center for mines, ranches, irrigated farms and (since 1880) important rail center. Sunny winter and health resort, it has annual fiesta and rodeo in Feb. To S is Mission San Xavier del Bac (founded 1700 by Father Kino). Near-by desert (Saguaro Natl. Monument) contrasts with cool Santa Catalina Mts. Davis-Monthan Air Force Base is near. Seat of Univ. of Arizona (land-grant, state supported; coed.; chartered 1885, opened 1891); pueblo remains in vicinity have stimulated study of Indian archaeology here; has U.S. experiment stations (mining, botanical, agr.).

Tucumán (tōōkōōmän'), city (pop. 194,166), cap. of Tucumán prov., NW Argentina; founded 1565, moved to present site 1685; metropolis of large irrigated area. Lumbering also important. Seat of university and popular shrine of Our Lady of Mercy.

Tucumcari (tōō'kŭmkâ"rē), city (pop. 8,419), E N.Mex., E of Albuquerque, near Texas line. Railroad division point and trade center in grain, stock area. Conchas Dam and resort area are near.

Tudor, royal family that ruled England 1485–1603. Founder was Owen Tudor, d. 1461, of an old Welsh family. Married (1429?) Catherine of Valois, widow of Henry V. Lancastrian, he was killed in the Wars of the Roses. His grandson became HENRY VII after defeating (1485) Richard III at Bosworth Field, ending Wars of the Roses. Henry's marriage to daughter of Edward IV united Lancastrian and Yorkist claims to throne. His children were MARGARET TUDOR, MARY OF ENGLAND, and HENRY VIII. Henry VIII's children ruled as EDWARD VI, MARY I, and ELIZABETH. Attempt to place Lady Jane GREY on throne ended with her execution. House of Stuart succeeded Tudor dynasty on the death of Elizabeth in 1603.

Tudor style, English architecture and decoration of first half of 16th cent., during the reigns (1485–1558) of Henry VII, Henry VIII, Edward VI, and Mary I. The manor house, a characteristic building of the period, showed greater emphasis on privacy with the introduction of many small rooms, which decreased the former importance of the great hall. Rooms frequently were fitted with oak paneling, walls and ceilings had rich plaster relief ornament, and articles of furniture (see *ill.*, p. 456) came into greater use. Typical exteriors showed use of brickwork combined with half-timber, high gables, bay windows, and numerous decorative chimneys.

Tuesday: see WEEK.

Tufts College: see MEDFORD, Mass.

Tu Fu (dōō' fōō', tōō'), 713?–770, Chinese poet of T'ang dynasty. His work reveals his sympathy with the common people and a delight in nature.

Tug Fork, river rising in S W.Va. and flowing 154 mi. NW along Ky.–W.Va. line, joining Levisa Fork to form Big Sandy R.

Tuileries (twē'lŭrēz, Fr. tüēlrē'), former palace in Paris. Planned by Catherine de' Medici and begun in 1564, it occupied part of present Tuileries gardens (laid out by Lenôtre) between Louvre and Place de la Concorde. Rarely a royal residence until French Revolution, when Louis XVI was forced to move (1789) his court here from Versailles, it served as chief residence of Napoleon I and his successors. During Commune of Paris of 1871 a mob burned it down.

Tula (tōō'lŭ), city (pop. 272,404), central European RSFSR, S of Moscow. Rail and mfg. center (machinery, arms). Flour mills, tanneries, sugar refineries. Founded 12th cent. Became a key fortress of grand duchy of Moscow in 16th cent. Withstood German siege (1941) in World War II. Its turreted, 16th-cent. kremlin occupies city center.

Tulane University of Louisiana (tōōlān'), at New Orleans; nonsectarian, private, for men and women; opened 1834, chartered 1835; received present name 1884. Famous medical school. Women's division is Newcomb Col. Tulane has Middle American Research Inst. (with Mayan library collection and museum).

Tulare (tŭlâr'), city (pop. 12,445), S central Calif., SE of Fresno. Processes and ships dairy products, cotton, and fruit.

Tulare Lake, virtually dry lake, S central Calif., S of Hanford. Fed by Kings, Kaweah, and Kern rivers only in very wet seasons. Connected by slough to Buena Vista L. Before it was used for irrigation, it was c.50 mi. long and c.35 mi. wide.

tularemia (tōōlŭrē'mēŭ) or **rabbit fever,** infectious disease of small mammals (e.g., rabbits) and birds, caused by an aerobic bacillus and transmitted to man in handling, skinning, or eating diseased animals or by bites of ticks, fleas, and lice. Symptoms include ulcer at site of inoculation, regional inflammation of lymph nodes, headache, chills, fever, and vomiting. Streptomycin is often effective in treatment.

tulip, hardy, bulbous-rooted, spring-flowering Old World plant (*Tulipa*), long popular for the cup-shaped blossoms of various rich colors. Tulips were probably introduced into Europe from Turkey in 1554. In the 17th cent. the wild speculation in tulip bulbs in Holland was known as tulipomania. Holland is still an important center for their culture, although bulbs are grown commercially in other countries.

tulip tree, yellow poplar, or **whitewood,** handsome, deciduous tree (*Liriodendron tulipifera*) of magnolia family, native E of the

Mississippi. It has yellow and orange tulip-like flowers. The wood is valued for interiors, cabinetmaking, etc.

Tull, Jethro, 1674–1741, English agriculturist and inventor. He influenced British agriculture through his writings and invented (c.1701) a machine drill.

Tullahoma (tŭlŭhō'mŭ), town (pop. 7,562), central Tenn., SE of Nashville. Industrial center in farm and timber area. Fell to Federals (July, 1863) before Chattanooga campaign.

Tully, Roman consul and philosopher: see CICERO.

Tulsa, city (pop. 182,740), NE Okla., on Arkansas R. E of junction with Cimarron R.; settled c.1860 by Indian exiles, founded as rail depot 1880. With its refineries and company hq., it is known as "oil cap. of world." Mfg. of metal products, aircraft, glass, furniture, and chemicals; commercial center of farm and mineral area. Seat of Univ. of Tulsa (coed.; 1894).

Tumacacori National Monument: see NATIONAL PARKS AND MONUMENTS (table).

tumblebug, name for dark, bronzed, or brightly colored beetles of various genera, e.g., *Scarabaeus, Canthon, Copris, Phanaeus.* They make balls of dung in each of which an egg is laid. See also SCARAB.

tumbleweed, any of several plants, especially abundant in prairie regions, that break from their roots, and, forming a dry tangle, roll before the wind scattering seeds. Common ones are the Russian thistle (*Salsola*), amaranth, and witch grass.

Tumwater, town (pop. 2,725), W Wash., S of Olympia. Sometimes considered end of Oregon Trail. First American settlement in Puget Sound area (1845).

tuna (tōō'nŭ) or **tunny** (tŭ'nē), largest game fish of mackerel family, swift and powerful. Warm-water tuna (*Thunnus*), also called bluefin and horse mackerel, travels in schools; average weight 60–200 lb. Tuna fisheries are important in Mediterranean, Atlantic, and Pacific waters; large quantities are canned, chiefly in U.S.

Tunbridge Wells, municipal borough (pop. 38,397), Kent, England. Also called Royal Tunbridge Wells. Became fashionable inland resort after chalybeate springs were discovered in 1606.

tung oil, China wood oil or nut oil, a product of the tropical tung tree. It is expressed from poisonous seeds in heart of fruit. It is widely used in paints and varnishes, in insulating compounds, in making linoleum and oilcloth. China is chief source but tung trees are grown also in S U.S.

tungsten: see WOLFRAM.

Tungting (dōōng'tĭng'), lake, N Hunan prov., China. In summer it receives overflow from the Yangtze and attains max. area of c.4,000 sq. mi.

tung tree: see TUNG OIL.

Tungus (tōōn-gōōz'), Siberian ethnic group, numbering c.40,000, called also Evenki. Closely related to the Manchus. Certain cultural traits indicate that some Japanese may be descended from the Tungus. Tungusic languages, family including Manchu literary language, may be related to Mongolic and Turkic families. Sometimes classified as Ural-Altaic.

Tunguska (tōōn-gōōs'kŭ), three E tributaries of the Yenisei R., RSFSR, in E central Siberia. They are, from N to S: the **Lower Tunguska,** 1,587 mi. long; the **Stony** or **Middle Tunguska,** 975 mi. long; and the **Upper Tunguska,** as the lower course of the Angara R. is called. The Angara, which drains L. Baikal, flows 1,075 mi. from the lake into the Yenisei and receives the Ilim and Oka. The Tunguskas flow through a large unexploited coal basin.

tunic (tū'nĭk), probably the earliest shaped garment, at first merely two skins laced together. Later it was of cloth, seamed, and usually worn with sleeves and girded. The Roman tunic, first worn under the toga, eventually became a long outer garment.

Tunis (tū'nĭs), city (pop. 364,593), cap. of Tunisia; a port on Lake of Tunis. Access to the Mediterranean is by canal. Exports iron ore, phosphates, dates, olive oil, and carpets. A tourist center with a casbah, notable mosques, a Moslem university, and a museum. Near by are ruins of CARTHAGE. Tunis is of Phoenician origin. It became cap. of Tunis under the powerful Hafsid dynasty (13th–16th cent.) and a leading center for trade with Europe. Turkish and Spanish rule alternated in 16th cent. Turkey prevailed, but her governors in Tunis were virtually independent. Until the French occupation (1881) it flourished as a center of piracy and trade. Held by Axis troops from Nov., 1942, to May 7, 1943.

Tunisia (tūnē'zhŭ), protectorate (48,362 sq. mi.; pop. 3,230,952), N Africa; since 1946 an associated state of the French Union; cap. Tunis. Bounded on N and E by the Mediterranean, on W by Algeria, and on SE by Libya. Ports include Tunis and Bizerta. Atlas Mts. are in N; in S, below a great salt lake, stretches the Sahara. Typical oasis crops are raised, including dates, cereals, olives, and grapes. Phosphates are the leading export product. The coast, early settled by Phoenicians, passed to Carthage in 6th cent. B.C. As a Roman province (from 2d cent. B.C.) it became a rich wheat-growing region. Held by Vandals and Byzantines before it fell to Arabs in 7th cent. and was converted to Islam. Tunisia reached its greatest power under the Berber Hafsid dynasty (1228–1574). Held by Turkey after 1579, it became virtually independent under the Turkish governors (beys), and as one of the BARBARY STATES it became a pirate base. Heavy debts contracted by the beys led to French, British, and Italian economic intervention in 1869. France occupied the country in 1881 and despite Italy's opposition established a protectorate under a French resident general with the bey as titular ruler. After fall of France (1940) Tunisia remained loyal to Vichy regime and became the focus of the war in N Africa (see NORTH AFRICA, CAMPAIGNS IN). After the war a growing nationalist movement led to riots in 1952. France began instituting reforms (e.g., rural elections, first held in 1953) which would give greater autonomy to Tunisia.

Tunkers, another name for DUNKARDS.

Tunney, James Joseph (Gene), 1898–, American boxer. Won (1926) heavyweight championship from Jack Dempsey. Defeated Dempsey in return bout (1927) marked by the "long count" when Tunney was knocked down in seventh round. Retired undefeated (1928).

tunny: see TUNA.

Tupac Amaru (to͞o'päk ämä'ro͞o), 1742?–1781, Indian leader in Peru, baptized José Gabriel Condorcanqui. Led rebellion in 1780; it was crushed; he was captured and brutally executed. Yet many reforms for which he fought were granted.

Tupelo (to͞o'pĭlō), city (pop. 11,527), NE Miss., NNW of Columbus; founded 1859. Processes and ships cotton, dairy, and fertilizer products. Near by are Tupelo Natl. Battlefield Site marking fight between Gen. N. B. Forrest's Confederates and Union troops, July 14, 1864; and Ackia Battleground Natl. Monument, scene of victory of Chickasaw and English over Choctaw and French, May 26, 1736.

tupelo: see BLACK GUM.

Tupí Indians: see GUARANÍ INDIANS.

Tupper Lake, resort village (pop. 5,441), N N.Y., in the Adirondacks near Big Tupper L.

Tura, Cosmé or **Cosimo** (kōzmā' to͞o'rä, kō'zēmō), c.1430–1495, Italian painter of Ferrarese school. His work is usually realistic but often symbolic.

turbine (tûr'bĭn, tûr'bīn), engine which converts force of moving air, steam, or water into mechanical energy capable of doing work. Water turbines are of the impulse type (actuated by force of water falling into buckets) or reaction type (impact of expanding pressure and kinetic energy of flow turn wheel). Steam turbines employ jets of steam, directed into and through a series of curved vanes on a rotating wheel and through similar ones on a stationary wheel. Principle of the turbine is ancient; first practical use was c.1880. See *ill.*, p. 389.

turbot (tûr'bŭt), large European flatfish, valued for food. In U.S. some flounders are inaccurately called turbots.

Turcoman: see TURKMEN, SSR.

Turenne, Henri de la Tour d'Auvergne, vicomte de (ãrē' dŭ lä to͝or' dōvĕr'nyŭ vēkōt' dŭ türĕn'), 1611–75, marshal of France; son of the duc de Bouillon. Brought up a Protestant, he became a Catholic late in life. In the last years of the Thirty Years War he led the French from victory to victory. He at first sided with the princes in the FRONDE but soon took command of the government forces and roundly defeated Condé at the Faubourg Saint-Antoine (1652) and in the battle of the Dunes (1658). He was killed in the third Dutch War after his victory at Sinzheim (1674). One of France's greatest military leaders, he is also celebrated for his courage, integrity, and serious disposition.

Turfan (to͝or'fän), depression, area c.5,000 sq. mi., N central Sinkiang prov., China; 300 ft. below sea level at its lowest point.

Turgenev, Ivan Sergeyevich (ēvän' sĭrgā'ŭvĭch to͝orgā'nyĭf), 1818–83, Russian author. His novels deal mostly with social problems. *A Sportsman's Sketches* (1852), a collection of stories on peasant life, dealt a telling blow to serfdom. In 1850–61 appeared his great novels—*A Nest of Gentlefolk, Rudin,* and *Fathers and Sons.* This last, his masterpiece, alienated his more radical followers because of its merciless portrait of Bazarov, the young nihilist. He spent most of his later life abroad. His last long works were *Smoke* (1867) and *Virgin Soil* (1876).

Turgot, Anne Robert Jacques (än' rōbĕr' zhäk' türgō'), 1727–81, French economist and statesman. As intendant of Limoges (1761–74) and as controller general of finances (1774–76) he sought to put into practice his theories—strongly influenced by the PHYSIOCRATS—of free trade, scientific agr. methods, and tax reforms. He made himself numerous enemies, and his downfall (abetted by Marie Antoinette) prevented his carrying out drastic reforms. Turgot's writings (incl. articles in the *Encyclopédie*) reveal him as a major economic thinker of his century.

Turgutlu, Turkey: see KASSABA.

Turin (to͝o'rĭn, tyo͝o'–, tyo͝orĭn'), Ital. *Torino,* city (pop. 608,211), cap. of Piedmont, NW Italy, on the Po. Leads Italy in mfg. of autos, clothing, leather goods, vermouth. A Roman city, later a Lombard duchy, a Frankish march, and a free commune, it passed to Savoy c.1280; became cap. of Savoy after 1562; cap. of kingdom of Sardinia 1720–98, 1814–61; cap. of Italy, 1861–64. Suffered severe air raids in World War II. A fine example of city planning, most of modern Turin dates from 17th–19th cent. Notable buildings include royal palace and Renaissance cathedral (with shroud in which body of Jesus is said to have been wrapped). University was founded 1404.

Turkestan: see TURKISTAN.

Turkey, republic (296,185 sq. mi.; pop. 18,790,174), Asia Minor and SE Europe; cap. Ankara. Asiatic Turkey (97% of the whole) occupies Anatolian Peninsula (W tip of Asia), washed on N by the Black Sea, on W and S by the Mediterranean. Turkey in Europe, separated from Asiatic Turkey by the DARDANELLES, Sea of Marmara, and Bosporus, comprises E Thrace and is a rolling plain. Asiatic Turkey, a semi-arid plateau, is fringed by mountains, with fertile coastal strips. Half the total area consists of pastures; only 20% is arable. Istanbul, Smyrna, Trebizond, Sinope, and Mersin are chief ports; other important cities are Adrianople, Ankara, Bursa, Adana, Konya, Kayseri, Antioch. Mining (coal, copper, lignite, chrome) is chief industry. Country is one of world's leading exporters of chrome and meerschaum. Massacres and emigration of Armenians, Greeks, and Bulgarians (19th–20th cent.) have left Turkey with a largely Turkish-speaking population. For early history of Turkey, see OTTOMAN EMPIRE and EASTERN QUESTION. History of Turkey as a national state began after World War I. Treaty of SÈVRES (1920), reducing Ottoman Empire to insignificance, was accepted by Sultan Mohammed VI. Nationalist elements, led by Kemal ATATURK, defied sultan's authority. Kemal made a treaty with Russia, routed attacking Greeks and captured Smyrna, and deposed the sultan. Conference of LAUSANNE (1923) estab. present Turkish boundaries (except for

Sanjak of Alexandretta, acquired 1939). Turkey was declared a republic (1923). Ataturk became president and, as virtual dictator, effected complete cultural transformation and Westernization—Islam ceased to be the state religion; Latin alphabet replaced Arabic script; women were emancipated. Kemal's economic policy, aimed at freedom from foreign capital, led to wide government controls and ownership of industry. Ismet Inonu, who succeeded Ataturk (1938), kept Turkey neutral in World War II until Jan., 1945, when Turkey joined the Allied side. Turkey joined the UN; received U.S. aid under the Truman Doctrine (1947); and entered North Atlantic Treaty (1951). Celal Bayar, opposition leader, succeeded Inonu in 1950 elections.

turkey, large game and poultry bird, allied to pheasant, native to North America. Plumage is chiefly greenish bronze and copper. Explorers in 16th cent. found turkeys domesticated in Central America and Mexico. American colonists ate wild turkey.

turkey buzzard: see VULTURE.

Turki (to͝or'kē) or **Turkic,** family of languages, to which Turkish belongs. See LANGUAGE (table).

Turkish, name given to several languages of Turkic family. See LANGUAGE (table).

Turkistan or **Turkestan** (both: tûrkĭstăn', –stän'), region, USSR, comprising Turkmen SSR, Uzbek SSR, Tadhzik SSR, Kirghiz SSR, and S Kazakh SSR. This region is sometimes called Western Turkistan or Russian Turkistan in distinction to Eastern Turkistan or Chinese Turkistan (now in Sinkiang prov., China). Nearly all the inhabitants speak Turkic languages. Historically Turkistan has been the bridge connecting the East and West and the route taken by many great conquerors and migrating peoples.

Turkistan-Siberia Railroad, abbreviated **Turk-Sib,** SW Asiatic USSR, links Trans-Siberian RR (junction Novosibirsk) with Trans-Caspian RR at Tashkent. Built 1926–30. Has great economic importance.

Turkmen Soviet Socialist Republic or **Turkmenistan** (tûrk"mĕnĭstăn'), constituent republic (187,200 sq. mi.; pop. c.1,170,000) of the USSR, in central Asia, bordering in S on Afghanistan, Iran, and Caspian Sea; cap. Ashkabad. KARA KUM desert occupies 90% of area (camel and caracul sheep raising). Irrigated oases and Amu Darya and Murgab river valleys yield cotton, silk, wine, fruit. Fisheries in Caspian Sea. Mineral resources include petroleum, ozocerite, iodine, bromine, salts. The population is 72% Turkmen (also called Turcomans, Turkomans), a Turkic-speaking Moslem people. Inhabited part of Turkmenistan formed part of Margiana prov. of ancient Persia (see MERV). Under Arab rule 8th–9th cent. A.D., it then passed to KHOREZM; fell to the Mongols (13th cent.), the Uzbeks (15th cent.), and the Khans of KHIVA (c.1800); and was conquered by Russia 1869–95. Became constituent republic 1924. Many Turkmen live in Iran and Afghanistan.

Turkoman: see TURKMEN SSR.

Turks, term applied in its wider meaning to the Turkic-speaking peoples of Turkey, USSR, Chinese Turkistan, and E Iran (see LANGUAGE, table). Totaling c.25,000,000 and distributed from E Siberia to the Dardanelles, their only ties are religious (Islam is religion of almost all Turks) and linguistic. Original Turks probably lived in S Siberia and in Turkistan. They expanded S and W; estab. several empires in Asia. Seljuks and Osmanli or Ottoman Turks have been two groups prominent in W Asia and Europe. Seljuks appeared (10th cent.) in Iran. By victory (1071) over Byzantine emperor at Manzikert, they estab. empire and helped cause the Crusades. Seljuk empire fell apart in 12th cent.; successor states were overrun by Tatars. Osmanli Turks under Osman I estab. (14th cent.) huge Ottoman Empire. People of modern Turkey are called Osmanli Turks.

Turks and Caicos Islands (kī'kōs), islands (c.201 sq. mi.; pop. 8,929), British West Indies. Geographically SE continuation of Bahamas, but administered by Jamaica. Produce salt, sponges, fibers.

Turk-Sib: see TURKISTAN-SIBERIA RAILROAD.

Turku (to͝or'ko͞o), Swedish *Åbo,* city (103,899), SW Finland; an ice-free Baltic port. Commercial and industrial center (shipyards, sawmills, textile mfg.). Was cap. of Finland until 1812; seat of Finnish national university (founded 1640) until its transfer to Helsinki (1828). Its present Swedish university was founded 1918, its Finnish university 1922. Called the "cradle of Finnish culture." Has 13th-cent. cathedral.

Turlock, city (pop. 6,235), central Calif., SE of Stockton. Center of an irrigation project using Tuolumne R. and producing truck, fruit, grain, dairy products.

turmeric (tûr'mŭrĭk), perennial herb (*Curcuma longa*), cultivated in the tropics for its rootstalk, which in the form of a powder is used as a condiment and dye. The plant has a spike of yellow flowers.

Turner, Frederick Jackson, 1861–1932, American historian. Known for brilliant studies of American frontier and of sectionalism. An address, "The Significance of the Frontier in American History," delivered 1893 before American Historical Association and reprinted in *The Frontier in American History* (1920), was pioneer work that opened new and important fields for historical study.

Turner, J(oseph) M(allord) W(illiam), 1775–1851, English landscape painter, a celebrated water-colorist. Received almost no general education but at 14 was a student at the Royal Acad. of Arts. Despite his early and continued success he lived the life of a recluse with his father, a London barber. In his early work he successfully imitated the classical landscape painters, notably Claude Lorrain. His later paintings (e.g., *Snow Storm*) became increasingly abstract and poetic. Turner's will left over 19,000 water colors, drawings, and oils to the nation. Most of these are in Natl. Gall. and Tate Gall., London.

Turner, Nat, 1800–1831, American Negro, leader of Southampton Insurrection of slaves in Va. (Aug., 1831). Uprising led to more stringent slave laws in South, end of manumission societies there.

Turners Falls, Mass.: see MONTAGUE.

turnip, hardy garden vegetable related to the cabbage and having edible tubers. Chief kinds are *Brassica rapa* with white tubers and rutabaga or Swedish turnip (*B. napobrassica*) with yellow tubers. Both are used also for stock feed. See *ill.*, p. 999.

turnpike, road paid for partly or wholly by fees collected at tollgates. Hinged bar preventing passage through gate until toll was paid was original turnpike from which road took its name. First American turnpike road was a state enterprise (Va., 1785). Lancaster Turnpike in Pa. (1792) inaugurated era of turnpikes as private enterprises. Great period of American turnpikes was c.1800–c.1840.

Turnu-Severin (to͝or'no͞o-sĕvĕrēn'), city (pop. 31,296), SW Rumania, in Walachia, on the Danube below the Iron Gate. River port.

Turnverein (to͝orn'fûrīn), society emphasizing gymnastic exercises as well as social and patriotic functions. Originated by F. L. Jahn, it was used to organize German resistance to Napoleon. The German government later disapproved of it as a possible source of liberal ideas.

turpentine (tûr'pŭntīn), resinous, semifluid substance from sapwood of conifers. Chemically it is a mixture of oil of turpentine and ROSIN. Used as solvent and drying agent in paints and varnishes; purest grade is used in medicine.

turpentine tree: see TEREBINTH.

Turpin, Richard, 1706–39, English robber, known as Dick Turpin. Achieved notoriety from short and brutal career of horse stealing and general crime.

turquoise (tûr'kwoiz, -koiz), hydrous phosphate of aluminum and copper used as gem. Rarely occurs in crystal form. Color varies from greenish gray to sky blue. Sources include Persia and SW U.S.

turtle, reptile of order Chelonia (or Testudinata). The name *tortoise* is often reserved for land forms, terrapin for edible fresh-water species. Turtles have strong, sharp, toothless jaws; body is encased in shell consisting usually of bony plates fused with ribs and vertebrae and overlaid with horny shields. Largest is marine leatherback turtle (c.1,000 lb.). Chief food form is marine green turtle. Tortoise shell is obtained from marine hawksbill turtle.

Turtle Creek, borough (pop. 12,363); SW Pa., ESE of Pittsburgh; settled c.1765. Coal mining; mfg. of cement blocks and electrical equipment.

turtledove, wild dove native to Europe and Asia. It has a plaintive song and affectionate ways.

Tuscaloosa (tŭskùlo͞o'sù), city (pop. 46,396), W central Ala., on Black Warrior R. and SW of Birmingham; settled after Creek revolt of 1813. State cap. 1826–46. Farm trade center; mfg. of paper, cotton goods, bricks, rubber tires; woodworking; oil refining. Coal mines. Univ. of ALABAMA near.

Tuscan order: see DORIC ORDER.

Tuscany (tŭ'skùnē), Ital. *Toscana,* region (8,876 sq. mi., incl. ELBA; pop. 2,978,013), central Italy, along Tyrrhenian Sea; cap. FLORENCE. Other cities: Leghorn, Arrezzo, Lucca, Massa, Carrara, Pisa, Pistoia, Siena. Mostly hilly, fertile region, it produces wines, olive oil, cereals. Chief river is the Arno. The Apennines (E) and the Alpi Apuane (W) yield marble, iron, magnesium, quicksilver. Mfg. of machinery, textiles, glass. Site of ancient Etruria, region has many relics of ETRUSCAN CIVILIZATION. Conquered (3d cent. B.C.) by Romans, area later became a powerful Frankish march. Most cities became free communes in 11th–12th cent. Despite Guelph-Ghibelline strife, some (i.e., PISA, LUCCA, SIENA, Florence) developed into strong republics. Florence gained hegemony (14th–15th cent.). The MEDICI created (1569) grand duchy of Tuscany, which later passed (1737) to house of Hapsburg-Lorraine who remained in control (except for Napoleonic period) until union was voted (1860) with Sardinia. Tuscany was a center of art and learning during Renaissance; Tuscan language became literary language of Italy.

Tuscumbia (tŭskŭm'bēù), city (pop. 6,734), NW Ala., on Tennessee R. near Muscle Shoals. Cotton, rubber products; fertilizer. Birthplace of Helen Keller.

Tuskegee (tŭskē'gē), city (pop. 6,712), SE Ala., E of Montgomery, in cotton, corn, potato area. U.S. Negro veterans' hospital here. Seat of **Tuskegee Institute** (Negro; nonsectarian; coed.); chartered and opened 1881 as normal school, assumed present name 1937. College dept. added 1927. Has schools of agr. (with research dept. and extension service), education, home economics and commercial dietetics, mechanical industries, nurse training (with hospital). Until his death (1915), B. T. WASHINGTON was principal; succeeded by R. R. MOTON. G. W. CARVER taught here.

Tussaud, Marie (to͞osō'), 1760–1850, Swiss modeler in wax. While imprisoned during French Reign of Terror, Mme Tussaud modeled heads of famous persons, which were brought to her. Emigrated to London in 1802 and estab. her still-famous wax museum.

Tut-ankh-amen (to͞ot"-ängk-ä'mùn), fl. c.1355 B.C., king of anc. Egypt of the XVIII dynasty; son-in-law of Ikhnaton. Revised Ikhnaton's policy, returned to worship of Amon, and restored the capital to Thebes. His chief officer was Harmhab. Tut-ankh-amen's tomb, opened (1922) by Howard Carter and the earl of Carnarvon, yielded many treasures.

Tuticorin (to͞o"tĭkôrĭn'), city (75,614), S Madras, India; port on Bay of Bengal. Founded 1540 by the Portuguese, occupied 1658 by the Dutch, ceded to the British 1825. Exports cotton, coffee, and tea.

Tutuila (to͞oto͞oē'lä), island (40 sq. mi.; pop. 15,556), largest in American SAMOA. Harbor at PAGOPAGO. Rugged E area; fertile plain in SW. Ceded to U.S. 1900 and made naval station under Dept. of Navy. Land privately owned. Copra chief product.

Tuva or **Tuvinian Autonomous Oblast** (to͞o'vù, ō'blăst; Rus. to͞ovä', ô'blŭstyù), region (66,100 sq. mi.; pop. c.150,000), Asiatic RSFSR, between Mongolia (S) and Sayan Mts. (N); cap. Kizil. Agr., livestock raising. Natural resources include timber, gold, coal, salt, asbestos, copper. Tuvinians (c.75% of pop.) are a Turkic-speaking group. Formerly part of Chinese Empire (Uriankhai Territory), region became Russian protectorate 1912; was declared independent 1921 as Tannu-Tuva (after 1934, simply Tuva), People's Republic; incorporated into USSR 1944.

Tuxedo Park, residential village (1940 pop. 1,651), SE N.Y., in the Ramapos near N.J. line. After 1886, Pierre Lorillard developed it as exclusive, wealthy colony, noted for sports and social functions. Plans made in 1941 to introduce inexpensive homes. The tuxedo or "tux" (tailless dress coat) may have originated here.

Tuxtla (to͞os'tlä) or **Tuxtla Gutiérrez** (go͞otyĕ'rās), city (pop. 15,883), cap. of Chiapas state, S Mexico, in fertile Grijalva R. valley at foot of Chiapas highlands. Chief industry is a cigar factory.

Tuzigoot National Monument: see NATIONAL PARKS AND MONUMENTS (table).

TVA: see TENNESSEE VALLEY AUTHORITY.

Tver, RSFSR: see KALININ.

Twachtman, John Henry (twäkt'mŭn), 1853–1902, American landscape painter, influenced by the impressionists.

Twain, Mark, pseud. of **Samuel Langhorne Clemens,** 1835–1910, American humorist. After youth in Hannibal, Mo., he was a pilot on the Mississippi from 1857 until the Civil War and took his pen name from the leadsman's call ("mark twain" = two fathoms sounded). In Nev. in 1862, he wrote for Virginia City *Enterprise.* He first won fame in 1865 with his story "The Celebrated Jumping Frog of Calaveras County." A trip to the Holy Land led to his very popular *Innocents Abroad* (1869). After marriage in 1870 he settled in N.Y. and then Conn. Here he wrote his masterly re-creations of his boyhood, *The Adventures of Tom Sawyer* (1876) and *The Adventures of Huckleberry Finn* (1884); also other popular works including the travel book *A Tramp Abroad* (1879), *Life on the Mississippi* (1883), and two novels, *The Prince and the Pauper* (1880) and *A Connecticut Yankee in King Arthur's Court* (1889). Plunged into debt in 1893 by unfortunate investments, he lectured his way around the world. Saddened by the deaths of two daughters and his wife, he wrote bitter pessimism into later work, such as *The Man That Corrupted Hadleyburg* (1899). Besides hearty reflections of his childhood and youth, humorous travel books, and mordant satire, he wrote the curious *Personal Recollections of Joan of Arc* (1896).

Tweed, William Marcy, 1823–78, American politician and Tammany leader. Controlled Democratic party nominations and patronage in New York city. Made great fortune chiefly from graft in city expenditures. **Tweed Ring,** consisting of Tweed and his henchmen, defrauded city at least to extent of $30,000,000 through padded and fictitious charges and through tax favors. Downfall came with publication in New York *Times* of evidence of wholesale graft; cartoons of Thomas NAST aroused public indignation. Tweed died in prison.

Tweed, river, 90 mi. long, mainly in SE Scotland, but also in England. Rises in Peeblesshire (often called Tweeddale) and enters North Sea at Berwick.

tweed, generally rough woolen fabric of a soft, flexible texture and with an unfinished surface. Genuine tweeds, such as Harris and Donegal, are especially durable and moisture resistant.

Tweeddale, county, Scotland: see PEEBLESSHIRE.

Tweed Ring: see TWEED, WILLIAM MARCY.

Tweedsmuir, John Buchan, 1st **Baron:** see BUCHAN.

Tweedsmuir Park (twēdz'myo͝or), provincial reserve, 5,400 sq. mi., W central B.C., Canada, W of Prince George; estab. 1936.

Twelfth Night, Jan. 5, vigil or eve of EPIPHANY, so called because it is 12th night from Christmas, counting Christmas as the first.

Twelve Apostles or **Twelve Dsciples:** see APOSTLE.

Twelve Tables, early code of Roman law, drawn up according to tradition c.450 B.C.

Twenty-one Demands, ultimatum secretly presented in 1915 to China by Japan. Demands provided for Japanese control over German leasehold of Kiaochow, control over Manchuria and Mongolia, exploitation of China's main coal deposits, exclusion of other powers from further territorial concessions, and guidance of China's military and domestic affairs. Treaties signed 1915 extended Japan's lease of Liaotung and of Manchurian railroads and gave Kiaochow to Japan.

Twickenham (twĭk'ŭnŭm), municipal borough (pop. 105,645), Middlesex, England, on the Thames; residential suburb of London. Scene of Oxford-Cambridge Rugby football matches. Has varied mfg. Alexander Pope lived here and Horace Walpole had famous residence (Strawberry Hill) near by.

Twin Falls, city (pop. 17,600), S Idaho, in Snake R. valley; laid out 1903. Begun as center of private irrigation project, which now serves c.360,000 acres N and S of the Snake. Flow of S falls diverted for water power; N falls are c.125 ft. high. Processing and shipping center for agr., dairying, stock-raising area.

twins, two infants born of one pregnancy. Identical twins, always of same sex and counterparts in appearance, result from division of single fertilized egg. Fraternal twins, of two-egg origin (each egg separately fertilized), resemble each other no more than do any two offspring of same parents. In U.S. twins occur once in c.86 births; one fourth of sets are identical twins.

Two Harbors, city (pop. 4,400), NE Minn., on L. Superior and NE of Duluth. Resort with U.S. coast guard base.

Two Rivers, city (pop. 10,243), E Wis., at base of Door Peninsula on L. Michigan. Commercial fishing and mfg. of aluminum ware.

Two Sicilies, kingdom of the, the kingdoms of SICILY and of NAPLES, officially merged into a single kingdom under house of BOURBON-SICILY in 1816. United with Italy 1861. Kings of the Two Sicilies: FERDINAND I; FRANCIS I; FERDINAND II; and FRANCIS II.

Tyburn (tī'bûrn), underground river of London, England. It gave its name to famous gallows. After 1783 executions were held at Newgate prison.

Tyche (tī'kē) [Gr.,= chance], in Greek religion, personification of luck, corresponding to Roman Fortuna.

Tycho Brahe: see BRAHE, TYCHO.

Tydeus (tī'dēūs), Greek legendary hero, brother of Meleager and one of the Seven against Thebes.

Tyler, John, 1790–1862, 10th President of the United States. Governor of Va. (1825–27) and U.S. Senator (1827–36); a moderate states' rights Democrat who resigned from Senate and joined WHIG PARTY out of dislike of FORCE BILL and Pres. Jackson's fiscal policies. On April 4, 1841, following death of W. H. Harrison, he became first Vice President to succeed to presidency. After he had vetoed Whig bank measures and his cabinet had resigned, Tyler became a President without a party. Nevertheless, his plan of annexation was accepted by Texas before he left office in 1845. Died before taking his seat in "permanent" Confederate Congress.

Tyler, Moses Coit, 1835–1900, American writer on intellectual history, teacher of both English (at Univ. of Mich.) and history (at Cornell). His fame rests chiefly upon *A History of American Literature, 1607–1765* (1878) and *The Literary History of the American Revolution* (1897).

Tyler, Royall, 1757–1826), American dramatist, remembered for Yankee comedy *The Contrast* (1787).

Tyler, Wat, d. 1381, English rebel. After Black Death of 1348–49 killed much of England's population, the Statute of Laborers (1351) was adopted, fixing rates of pay to prevent rises. These restrictions and the desire of the commoners of city for liberty finally flamed into rebellion when capital tax was increased. Of this movement in 1381 Tyler became leader. He seized Canterbury, then marched to London, burning prisons and public buildings. Richard II came to meet him and promised to abolish serfdom, feudal service, and market monopolies. At second meeting with the king, Tyler was killed by mayor of London. The promises were forgotten, the revolt put down with force.

Tyler, city (pop. 38,968), E Texas, ESE of Dallas; founded 1846. Center of agr. area with oil refineries and offices and railroad shops. Noted for roses.

Tylor, Sir Edward Burnett, 1832–1917, English anthropologist. His early contributions helped establish scope of anthropology. Author of *Primitive Culture* (1871; rev. ed., 1924) and other works.

Tyl Ulenspiegel: see EULENSPIEGEL, TILL.

Tyndale, Tindal, or Tindale, William (all: tĭn'dŭl), d. 1536, English reformer. A humanist, he determined to translate the New Testament, and, meeting opposition in England, he went to the Continent, where he met Luther and completed his New Testament, promptly banned by Cardinal Wolsey and the English bishops. Hunted, living in concealment, Tyndale went on translating the Scriptures and writing tracts (one against Henry VIII's divorce). He was seized at Antwerp in 1535, was condemned for heresy, and was put to death, still defending his own beliefs.

Tyndareus, king of Sparta and husband of LEDA.

Tyne (tīn), river of Northumberland, England. North Tyne (which rises 80 mi. from its mouth) joins South Tyne at Hexham and flows thence c.30 mi. to North Sea. Lower course is lined with docks, shipbuilding yards, and coal-mining and ironworking towns.

Tynemouth (tīn'mŭth, tĭn'–), county borough (pop. 66,544), Northumberland, England, on the Tyne. Includes Tynemouth, Cullercoats, Chirton, North Shields, and Preston. It is a shipbuilding center and a coal and fishing port.

type, for printing, was invented in China; movable type (made from molds of individual characters) was used in Korea before its independent invention in Europe, attributed to Johann GUTENBERG. The MAZARIN BIBLE, probably his work, is believed to have been first book printed in Europe from movable types (c.1456; at Mainz). Forms of letters were derived from handwriting of the time and place; originally "black letter" or "gothic" (now represented by "Old English" and "German" types), later "roman" and "italic." Nicholas JENSON developed roman type to the point where it became standard; italic was introduced by ALDUS MANUTIUS. "Modern" roman type faces emphasize contrast in weight of lines and have strong, level serifs; "old style" roman has less contrast and smaller, often sloping, serifs. The clean modern "sans-serif" faces (i.e., without serifs) are now much favored. Other famous type designers are GARAMOND, GRANJON, CASLON, BASKERVILLE, BODONI, DIDOT, GOUDY. For type set by machine, see LINOTYPE; MONOTYPE. See also TYPOGRAPHY.

type metal, alloy of lead with antimony, tin, and sometimes copper, extensively used for making various kinds of type. Since the alloy expands upon solidification, it takes a fine, clear impression of the mold in which it is hardening. Also used for metal parts of musical instruments and for ornaments.

typewriter. Early models were chiefly for the blind. Commercial machine with capitals only was invented 1867 by C. L. Sholes and associates and manufactured by firm of E. Remington. Shift-key model appeared 1878; electric typewriter c.1935. Teletypewriter, invented 1904, transmits typing over telephone or other electric circuit (in some cases this typing may be electrically transmuted into type). The use of typewritten copy for books through the offset process has led to the development of new typewriters that produce script closely resembling type and of many different typewriter letter faces. See *ill.*, p. 793.

typhoid fever, infectious disease caused by bacillus taken into body in food or water which has been contaminated by feces of a person having disease or of disease carrier. Attended by fever, prostration, rash. Bacteria lodge chiefly in small intestine. Recovery slow, relapse common. Vaccination gives immunity for two to three years, See *ill.*, p. 813.

typhus (tī'fŭs), infectious disease carried by body louse infected from biting diseased person. Causative organism believed to be a rickettsia. Mild type is known as Brill's disease.

typography (tīpŏ'grŭfē), in the graphic arts, is

the selection and arrangement for PRINTING of type faces, sizes, spacing, and decorative material (e.g., rules, type ornaments). The first principle is legibility. Aim is to enhance the presentation of ideas by attractive appearance, wise use of emphasis and variety, and creation of appropriate atmosphere. Books, periodicals, and advertising have special requirements related to their particular purposes. Today's styles show historic influences, such as that of inscriptions on classical monuments, medieval calligraphy, the elegant books of the ESTIENNE family and of BASKERVILLE and BODONI, as well as the blatant circus poster and the modern German (BAUHAUS) influence. A notable contemporary typographer is Bruce ROGERS.

Tyr, Norse name of TIW.

Tyrannosaurus (tĭră″nōsô′rŭs, tī–), giant biped carnivorous dinosaur, c.45 ft. in length and 19 ft. tall. Probably the greatest land-dwelling flesh eater. Existed during late Cretaceous period; parts of skeletons have been found in Mont. and S.Dak.

tyrant, in anc. history, ruler exercising absolute authority without legal warrant. In Greek city-states they generally rose to power in the struggle between popular and noble (or wealthy) classes. Some of the better-known Greek tyrants were Periander of Corinth; Pisistratus, Hipparchus, and Hippias of Athens; Gelon, Hiero I and Hiero II, Dionysius the Elder and Dionysius the Younger of Syracuse. Their reigns were frequently beneficial for the cities, but growth of democratic sentiment in Greece made the name tyrant unpleasant.

Tyrconnel, Richard Talbot, duke and earl of (tûrkŏ′nŭl), 1630–91, Irish royalist. Supporter of James II, he was (1687–88) commander in chief of forces in Ireland and lord deputy. Supplanted Protestants with Catholics in many key positions.

Tyrconnel, Rory O'Donnell, earl of, 1575–1608, Irish chieftain. Conspired with Spain to start a general uprising and was discovered. His flight marked end of political power of the tribal chieftains.

Tyrconnell, anc. kingdom (5th cent.–11th cent.) in NW Ireland in what is now Co. Donegal.

Tyre (tīr), Phoenician port, one of the great cities of the anc. world; modern Sur in Lebanon, S of Beirut. Built on an island perhaps as early as 2800 B.C., it was a great mercantile city with wide-flung colonies by 1100 B.C. Tyrians founded Carthage (9th cent. B.C.). Tyre was famous for its commerce and its purple Tyrian dye. Taken by Assyrians, Babylonians, and Persians, it survived. It recovered even from the siege and sack by Alexander the Great (333–332 B.C.), who built a mole that has since made the island a peninsula. Under the Romans after 64 B.C., it throve. Until it was destroyed by Moslems in A.D. 1291 it continued important.

Tyrol (tĭ′rŭl, tĭrōl′), Ger. *Tirol,* province (4,884 sq. mi.; pop. 426,499), W Austria, in the Alps; cap. Innsbruck. Economy is typically Alpine. Tourist trade yields large revenues. Conquered by Rome 15 B.C., later part of Frankish empire, Tyrol was divided into several fiefs under the Holy Roman Empire—the prince-bishoprics of TRENT and Bressanone (which passed to Austria in 1801, to Italy in 1919; see TRENTINO-ALTO ADIGE) and the county of Tyrol (to Austria 1363). Napoleon awarded Tyrol to Bavaria (1805–15) and suppressed the insurrection led by Andreas HOFER (1809).

Tyrone, Hugh O'Neill, 2d earl of (tĭrōn′), 1547?–1616, Irish chieftain. Siding first with English, he later joined Irish chiefs and sought aid from Spain. After defeat (1601) he surrendered tribal authority. His final flight (1607) to Flanders with other nobles marked end of tribalism in Ireland.

Tyrone (tĭrōn′), inland county (1,218 sq. mi.; pop. 132,049), N Ireland, in Ulster; cap. Omagh. This large, hilly county is pastoral and agr. Has mfg. of linens, woolen goods, and whisky.

Tyrone (tīrōn′), borough (pop. 8,214), central Pa., NE of Altoona; center of bituminous coal area.

Tyrrell, Joseph Burr (tĭ′rŭl), 1858–, Canadian explorer and geologist. A member of Canadian Geological Survey, he explored in N and W Canada. His best-known feat was crossing BARREN GROUNDS in 1893 from L. Athabaska to Chesterfield Inlet.

Tyrrhenian Sea (tĭrē′nēŭn), part of W Mediterranean, between W coast of Italy, N coast of Sicily, and E coast of Sardinia and Corsica.

Tyumen or **Tiumen** (both: tyŏŏmân′yŭ), city (pop. 75,537), RSFSR, in W Siberia, on Tura R. and on Trans-Siberian RR. Sawmilling. Oldest Russian town in Siberia (founded 1586).

Tz'u Hsi or **Tsu Hsi** (both: tsŭ′ shē′), 1834–1908, dowager empress of Ch'ing dynasty of China. As consort of Emperor Hsien Feng (d. 1861) she bore his successor T'ung Chih, after whose death (1875) she made her nephew KWANG HSÜ emperor. Forced his abdication in 1898. As direct ruler she remained hostile toward the West and encouraged BOXER REBELLION.

U, chemical symbol of the element URANIUM.

Ubangi (o͞obăng'gē), river, c.660 mi. long, major tributary of the Congo in N and W central Africa. Name was used by press agent Roland Butler, for "show" Africans, not from this area.

Ucayali (o͞okäyä'lē), river, c.1,000 mi. long, E Peru, headwater of the Amazon, formed by confluence of Apurimac and Urubamba, flowing generally N to the Marañón.

Uccello, Paolo (pä'ōlō o͞ot-chĕl'lō), c.1396–1475, Florentine painter, a pioneer in linear perspective. Famous for series called *Battle of San Romano.*

Udaipur (o͞odīpo͝or') or **Mewar** (māwär'), former princely state, NW India; part of Rajasthan since 1948.

Udine (o͞o'dēnā), city (pop. 54,638), cap. of Friuli-Venezia Giulia, NE Italy. Held by patriarchs of Aquileia from 10th cent., it passed to Venice in 1420, to Austria in 1797 and 1814, and to Italy in 1866. It was hq. of Italian army in World War I until occupied by Austria, 1917–18.

Udmurt Autonomous Soviet Socialist Republic (o͞odmo͞ort'), administrative division (16,300 sq. mi.; pop. 1,220,007), E central European RSFSR, in highlands between Kama and Vyatka rivers; cap. Izhevsk. Predominantly agr. Udmurts, formerly called Votyaks, belong to Finno-Permian language group and form 52% of population; the rest are mainly Russians. Region was ruled by Golden Horde 13th–15th cent.

Ufa (o͞ofä'), city (pop. 245,863), cap. of Bashkir ASSR, E European RSFSR; a port on Ufa and Belaya rivers. Mfg. of airplanes, mining machinery, textiles. Founded 1586, it has old cathedral and several educational and scientific institutions.

Uffizi (o͞ofē'tsē), palace in Florence, Italy, built in 16th cent. by Vasari for Cosimo I de' Medici. Houses Italian National Library and **Uffizi Gallery,** one of world's richest art collections.

Uganda (ūgăn'dů), British protectorate (93,981 sq. mi.; pop. 4,937,712), E central Africa, S of Anglo-Egyptian Sudan; cap. Entebbe. Largely a fertile plateau with well-forested hills, but also contains swampy lowlands and a desert region. Inhabited by the Bantu, who produce such export crops as cotton, coffee, and sugar. Arabs from Zanzibar tried to control the area in 19th cent. Among first Europeans to explore Uganda were John Speke (1862) and Henry Stanley (1875). In 1888 the native kingdom of Buganda was held by Arab traders and native Moslems, but in 1890 it was brought under the control of British East Africa Co. Britain estab. a protectorate over Buganda in 1894 and later added to it several adjacent regions.

Ugarit (o͞ogůrēt'), anc. city, cap. of Ugarit kingdom, W Syria. On its site is the small Arab village of Ras Shamra near modern Latakia. Remains of ancient city (dating from 5th millennium B.C.) were discovered in 1931. Among the important finds are tablets from 14th cent. B.C. written in Ugaritic, which has been identified as a Semitic language, related to classical Hebrew.

Ugolino della Gherardesca (o͞ogōlē'nō dĕl'lä gärärdā'skä), d. 1289, Italian nobleman, podestà [lord] of Pisa. Accused of treason, he was locked into a tower and left to starve to death with his sons and grandsons. Dante relates story in *Inferno.*

Ugrian (ū'grēůn, o͞o'–) or **Ugric** (ū'grĭk, o͞o'–), group of Finno-Ugric languages. See LANGUAGE (table).

Uhde, Fritz von (frĭts' fŭn o͞o'dů), 1848–1911, German genre painter, best known for his popular pictures of scriptural subjects in modern costume and setting.

Uhland, Ludwig (lo͞ot'vĭkh o͞o'länt), 1787–1862, German romantic poet. Among his ballads are *The Minstrel's Curse, The Good Comrade,* and *Taillefer.*

Uhrichsville (ū'rĭksvĭl), city (pop. 6,614), E Ohio, S of Canton. Mfg. of clay products.

Uigurs or **Uighurs** (wē'go͞orz), people of Asia, of Turkic stock. Settled along Orkhon R. in 7th cent.; founded several cities, notably Karakorum. Estab. an empire in Mongolia which lasted 745–856. Migrated to E Turkistan and estab. another empire which was conquered by the Mongols in 13th cent. Many present-day inhabitants of Sinkiang prov., China, speak the Uigur language.

Uinta Mountains (ūĭn'tů), range of Rocky Mts. in NE Utah and SW Wyo., rising to 13,498 ft. in Kings Peak. Includes High Uintas Primitive Area (243,957 acres; 1931).

Uist, North (ū'ĭst, o͞o'ĭst), and **South Uist,** islands (total pop. 7,063) of the Outer Hebrides, off NW Scotland, in Inverness-shire. Benbecula and other islands lie between the two. Most of the inhabitants are crofters.

Ujiji (o͞ojē'jē), town (pop. c.10,000), Tanganyika; port on L. Tanganyika. Henry Stanley found David Livingstone here on Nov. 10, 1871.

Uji-yamada (o͞o'jē-yä'mädä), city (pop. 65,970), S Honshu, Japan, on Ise Bay. Important Shinto center; site of shrines of Ise.

Ujjain (o͞ojīn'), city (pop. 81,272), Madhya Bharat, India; Hindu pilgrimage center. On site of cap. of ancient Aryan kingdom of Avanti.

Ujpest, Hung. *Újpest* (o͞o'ēpĕsht), city (pop. 76,001), N central Hungary. Industrial suburb of Budapest.

Ukiah (ūkī'ů), city (pop. 6,120), W Calif., NNW of San Francisco, in a fruit and hops area. Hot springs. Seat of an international latitude observatory.

Ukraine (ūkrān', ū'krān) or **Ukrainian Soviet Socialist Republic,** Rus. *Ukraina,* constituent republic (222,600 sq. mi.; pop. c.40,800,000), of the USSR, in E Europe; cap. Kiev. It is also called Little Russia. Drained by the Southern Bug, DNIEPER, and DONETS rivers, it consists largely of fertile steppes, particularly in the S Ukraine, one of Europe's chief wheat-growing regions. In the NW are the PRIPET MARSHES; in the W rise the Carpathians. Odessa, Kherson, and Zhdanov are the main Black Sea ports. The central and E Ukraine has mighty industrial concentrations, based on iron from KRIVOI ROG, coal from DONETS BASIN. Chief industrial centers: KHARKOV; DNEPROPETROVSK; ZAPOROZHE. W Ukraine, with Lvov as chief center, has petroleum. Population is c.80% Ukrainian, an E Slavic group closely akin to the Great Russians. There are Polish, Russian, and Jewish minorities. For history before Mongol invasion (13th cent.), see RUSSIA and KIEV. Most of the Ukraine fell to LITHUANIA after the Mongol invasion of Russia and became part of the Polish-Lithuanian state; the Black Sea shore fell to the Tatars of CRIMEA. Polish oppression of the Ukrainian peasants and the union of the Ukrainian Church with Rome (1596; see RUTHENIA) led to rebellion of the virtually independent ZAPOROZHE COSSACKS under CHMIELNICKI (1648). In 1667, after long Polish-Russian warfare, the NE Ukraine (incl. Kiev) was ceded by Poland to Russia. Cossack autonomy was abolished by Peter I after the rebellion of MAZEPPA. Russian annexation of Crimean khanate (1783) and the Polish partitions of 1772, 1793, and 1795 gave all Ukraine to Russia except GALICIA (Austrian) and Ruthenia (Hungarian). Ukrainian nationalists proclaimed their independence in 1918. The years 1918–20 saw a bloody four-cornered struggle among Ukrainian nationalists, Red Army, White Army of DENIKIN, and Poles—a struggle complicated by German, later by French intervention. The Soviets gained control over most of the Ukraine, which became one of the original constituent republics of the UNION OF SOVIET SOCIALIST REPUBLICS. E Galicia, N Bukovina, S Bessarabia, and Ruthenia were added 1939–45 as a result of World War II. In 1945 the Ukraine was admitted into the UN.

ukulele: see STRINGED INSTRUMENTS.

Uladislaus (ōō"lä'dĭslous), Hung. *Ulászló,* Hungarian kings. **Uladislaus I:** see LADISLAUS III, king of Poland. **Uladislaus II,** c.1456–1516, son of Casimir IV of Poland, was chosen king of Bohemia 1471, of Hungary 1490. He lost Moravia, Silesia, and Lusatia to MATTHIAS CORVINUS of Hungary in 1478. Both in Bohemia and Hungary his weakness was exploited by the great nobles for their own aggrandizement. In 1515 he made an important treaty with Emperor Maximilian I: his daughter Anna was betrothed to Maximilian's son Ferdinand (later Emperor Ferdinand I); his son Louis (later LOUIS II) was betrothed to Ferdinand's sister Mary. If Louis died childless (as he did) Hungary and Bohemia were to pass to the Hapsburgs.

Ulan Bator (ōōlän' bä'tôr), city (pop. 70,000), cap. of Mongolian People's Republic; chief center of Outer Mongolia. Formerly called Urga.

Ulan-Ude (ōōlän"-ōōdĕ'), city (pop. c.150,000), cap. of Buryat-Mongol ASSR, Asiatic RSFSR, on Selenga R. and Trans-Siberian R.R. It is a rapidly expanding transportation and mfg. center (locomotives, lumber, textiles, glass, agr. products). Founded 1666, it was first named Udinsk, later Verkhneudinsk (until c.1935). Population is 80% Russian, 20% Mongol.

ulcer (ŭl'sůr), open sore tending not to heal and usually occurring on skin or mucous membranes. Predisposing factors include injury, varicose veins, certain diseases, e.g., syphilis, leprosy, tuberculosis. Some ulcers develop into cancer.

Uleaborg, Finland: see OULU.

Ulenspiegel, Tyl: see EULENSPIEGEL, TILL.

Ulfilas (ŭl'fĭlůs), c.311–383, Gothic bishop, educated at Constantinople. An Arian, he converted many to Arianism. Translated Bible into Gothic.

Ulithi: see CAROLINE ISLANDS.

Ullswater, lake, 7½ mi. long and ¼ to ¾ mi. wide, on Cumberland-Westmorland co. border, England; second largest in the country. Beautiful Lake District scenery has inspired many writers.

Ulm (ōōlm), city (pop. 69,941), Württemberg-Baden, SW Germany; a port on the Danube, which becomes navigable here. Mfg. of metal products, beer, textiles. Politically and commercially it reached its zenith in 15th cent., but declined in religious wars and commercial revolution. Accepted Reformation c.1530. Free imperial city (incl. considerable territory N of the Danube) after 14th cent.; passed to Bavaria 1802, to Württemberg 1810. Over half the city was destroyed in World War II, but the Gothic minster (begun 1377) was spared. Birthplace of Albert Einstein.

Ulpian (ŭl'pēůn), d. 228, Roman jurist. Much of the *Corpus Juris Civilis* is based on his writings.

Ulster, northernmost of historic four provinces of Ireland. Consists of nine counties. Antrim, Armagh, Down, Fermanagh, Londonderry, and Tyrone make up NORTHERN IRELAND (or Ulster). Cavan, Donegal, and Monaghan are in the Irish republic.

Ultima Thule: see THULE.

ultraviolet ray, invisible component of sun's radiation. It can be produced artificially by electrode arc lamps, including mercury arc lamps. Much of sun's ultraviolet radiation is lost before it reaches earth; it is unable to penetrate thick clothing, window glass, or air heavy with impurities. Wave lengths range from 4,000 to 400 angstrom units, lying between visible violet light and X rays. Vitamin D is produced when rays act on ergosterol in human skin. Ultraviolet radiation can be used to enrich certain foods with vitamin D and to destroy germs in air and tissues.

Ulyanov, Vladimir Ilyich: see LENIN.

Ulyanovsk (ōōlyä'nůfsk), city (pop. 102,106),

RSFSR, on right bank of the middle Volga. River port; mfg. center (trucks, lathes, precision instruments, agr. processing). Founded 1648 as Simbirsk, it was renamed 1924 for Lenin, who was born here and whose real name was V. I. Ulyanov.

Ulysses, Latin name for ODYSSEUS.

Umanak (ōō'mŭnăk), settlement (pop. 394) and colony district (pop. 1,477), W Greenland, on an inlet of Baffin Bay. Hunting and fishing base.

Umatilla (ūmŭtĭl'lŭ), river, NE Oregon, rising in Blue Mts. and flowing c.85 mi. W and NW to Columbia R. at Umatilla town. Used for irrigation.

Umbria (ŭm'brēŭ, ōōm'brēä), region (3,270 sq. mi.; pop. 722,544), central Italy; cap. Perugia. Mainly agr., but there are hydroelectric plants around Terni, which has mfg. Little is known of the ancient Umbrians, who were conquered by Rome in the 3d cent. B.C. In the Middle Ages Umbria was noted as the home of St. Francis of Assisi. The Umbrian school of painting (15th–16th cent.) included Pinturicchio and Perugino.

Umbrian (ŭm'brēŭn), language of Italic subfamily of Indo-European languages. See LANGUAGE (table).

umlaut (ōōm'lout) in linguistics, variation of vowels in inflection (e.g., man, men; mouse, mice). It is also called mutation. See also ABLAUT.

Umnak (ōōm'năk), island, 83 mi. long, off W Alaska, one of ALEUTIAN ISLANDS. Sheep herds, introduced 1923, were destroyed when U.S. base was estab. here in World War II; island restocked in 1944.

UN: see UNITED NATIONS.

Unaka Mountains (ū'nŭkŭ), Appalachian range, forming part of N.C.–Tenn. line, NE of Great Smoky Mts.

Unalaska (ŭ"nŭlă'skŭ), island, 30 mi. long, off W Alaska, one of ALEUTIAN ISLANDS. Discovered by Vitus Bering 1741. Russian fur center until Kodiak rose. Dutch Harbor on Amaknak island in bay.

Unamuno, Miguel de (mēgĕl' dā oonamōō'nō), 1864–1936, Spanish philosopher, scholar, poet, novelist, of Basque descent. Notable is *The Tragic Sense of Life in Men and in Peoples* (1913), expressing his individualistic philosophy of faith only in faith itself.

Uncas (ŭng'kŭs), c.1588–c.1683, chief of Mohegan Indians. Sought British support, expanded tribe. Constantly at war with Miantonomo, Narragansett chief; captured him in 1643, murdered him.

uncial: see PALEOGRAPHY.

Uncle Remus: see HARRIS, JOEL CHANDLER.

Uncle Sam, name used to designate U.S. government. Uncertain origin is sometimes credited to Samuel Wilson of Troy, N.Y., known as "Uncle Sam." Wilson inspected army supplies in War of 1812; U.S. stamped on supplies was jokingly referred to as "Uncle Sam" by workmen.

Uncompahgre (ŭn-kŭmpä'grē), river rising in SW Colo. in San Juan Mts., S of Ouray, and flowing c.75 mi. NNW to Gunnison R., from which water is diverted by Gunnison Tunnel to Uncompahgre R.

Uncompahgre Peak: see SAN JUAN MOUNTAINS.

unconscious, in psychology, term generally used to mean that aspect of mental life which is apart from immediate consciousness and which is not subject to recall at will; also called the subconscious. With the work of Freud in PSYCHOANALYSIS, the concept became vital in explaining mental activity and neurosis. Freud saw the unconscious as a vast submerged part of the mind containing the motivating force of human behavior. To this concept Jung added an inherited unconscious, the collective experience of man in his total existence as a race. The concept of the unconscious is rejected or disregarded by some schools of psychology.

Underground Railroad, in U.S. history, secret system of helping fugitive slaves from South reach free states and Canada. Slaves were guided, mostly at night, over fixed routes by "conductors" from one "station" to another, often homes of abolitionists. "U.G." existed in every free state and by Civil War had delivered about 75,000 slaves to freedom.

Undset, Sigrid, 1882–1949, Norwegian novelist. Her great trilogy of medieval Norway, *Kristin Lavransdatter* (1920–22) was followed by the tetralogy *The Master of Hestviken* (1925–27). Her writing deepened in religious intensity after her conversion to Roman Catholicism in 1924. She was awarded the 1928 Nobel Prize in Literature.

undulant fever: see BRUCELLOSIS.

unemployment insurance, method of maintaining unemployed workers until they are reabsorbed into industry. Insurance may be compulsory or voluntary. First devised in late-19th-cent. Europe, such insurance schemes were gradually adopted by most countries, and in 1935 by the U.S. See SOCIAL SECURITY.

UNESCO: see UNITED NATIONS EDUCATIONAL, SCIENTIFIC, AND CULTURAL ORGANIZATION.

Ungava Bay (ŭng-gä'vŭ, –gā'vŭ), inlet, 200 mi. long, 160 mi. wide, extending S from Hudson Strait, N Que., Canada. **Ungava** region (239,780 sq. mi.), S of the bay, is a high plateau forming watershed between St. Lawrence R. and Hudson Bay. Formerly owned by Hudson's Bay Co., was made part of Northwest Territories 1869, became separate district 1895, added to Que. 1912. Boundary with Lab. estab. 1927. Rich in minerals and iron.

Ungvar, Ukraine: see UZHGOROD.

unicorn [Latin,= one horned], in fable, an equine beast of India, with long horn jutting from middle of forehead. Usually pure white, animal has been used as a symbol of virginity. Hunting of the unicorn was a favorite tapestry subject in Middle Ages and Renaissance. Unicorn, representing Scottish arms, appears in royal arms of Great Britain. Biblical unicorn is probably a wild ox.

uniformism or **unformitarianism,** in geology, the doctrine that past changes in the earth's crust were brought about by same causes as changes now taking place. Advanced in 1785 by James Hutton, it made little progress at first, because it was overshadowed by doctrine of CATASTROPHISM, and because it seemed contrary to religion and roused religious opposition. In 19th cent. it gained support largely through efforts of Sir Charles

Lyell. More recent tendency is to try to synthesize the two theories.

Unimak (o͞o′nĭmăk), volcanic island, 70 mi. long, off W Alaska, one of ALEUTIAN ISLANDS, nearest of chain to Alaska Peninsula.

Union. 1 Township (pop. 38,004), NE N.J., SW of Newark; settled from Conn. 1749. Mfg. of machinery, paint, metal and concrete products, chemicals. **2.** City (pop. 9,730), N S.C., near Broad R. and NNW of Columbus; textile center in farm area.

Unión, La (lä′o͞onyōn′), city (pop. 6,757), SE Salvador, principal port of republic, on Gulf of Fonseca. Chief exports are coffee, hides, henequen, and Peruvian balsam.

Union, Act of. For the union of England and Scotland, see GREAT BRITAIN; for the union of Ireland with Great Britain, see IRELAND. For both, see UNITED KINGDOM OF GREAT BRITAIN AND IRELAND.

Union, Fort, important trading post of American Fur Co. Erected (1828) near confluence of Yellowstone and Missouri rivers. For almost 40 years it was most important post in U.S. fur country.

union, labor, organization of workers for the purpose of improving their economic status, particularly through COLLECTIVE BARGAINING with employers. Two main types are craft and INDUSTRIAL UNIONS; company unions are employer-controlled. Unions began to organize in the 19th cent. but have often been bitterly fought by employers. See CLOSED SHOP AND OPEN SHOP; LABOR; STRIKE; AMERICAN FEDERATION OF LABOR; CONGRESS OF INDUSTRIAL ORGANIZATIONS.

Union City. 1 City (pop. 3,572), E Ind., E of Muncie. Farm produce and automobile parts. Adjoins Union City, village (pop. 1,622), Ohio. **2** City (pop. 55,537), NE N.J., N of Hoboken. Mfg. of embroideries, silk, soap, lamps, and clothing. Holy Family Church has sponsored passion play, *Veronica's Veil,* each Lent since 1914. **3** City (pop. 7,665), W Tenn., near Ky. line. Farm trade center with mfg. of shoes, shirts, and dairy products.

Union College: see BARBOURVILLE, Ky.; LINCOLN, Nebr.; SCHENECTADY, N.Y.

Union Islands: see TOKELAU.

Union League Clubs, formed in North in Civil War (1863) to further soldier relief and recruit volunteers. In South after the war, the league developed into strong Republican political organization, controlled Negro vote. Clubs of New York, Philadelphia, and Washington survive as social organizations.

Union of South Africa: see SOUTH AFRICA, UNION OF.

Union of Soviet Socialist Republics (USSR), federal state (c.8,570,600 sq. mi.; pop. c.201,300,000), E Europe and N Asia; cap. Moscow. It is also known as Soviet Union or Soviet Russia. The world's largest state, it stretches from the Baltic Sea to the Pacific; from the Arctic Ocean to the Black and Caspian seas, the CAUCASUS, and the great mountain ranges of Central Asia (PAMIR, TIEN SHAN, and ALTAI). As of 1953, the USSR consists of 16 constituent republics, of which the RUSSIAN SOVIET FEDERATED SOCIALIST REPUBLIC (RSFSR) is the largest. The 15 others are: in W USSR—KARELO-FINNISH SSR, ESTONIA, LATVIA, LITHUANIA, BELORUSSIA, UKRAINE, MOLDAVIAN SSR; in Transcaucasia—GEORGIAN SSR, ARMENIAN SSR, AZERBAIJAN SSR; in Central Asia—KAZAKH SSR, TURKMEN SSR, UZBEK SSR, TADZHIK SSR, KIRGHIZ SSR. The European USSR (incl. Transcaucasia and Ural region, c.2,100,000 sq. mi.; pop. c.162,900,000) forms the major part of the East European Plain and is drained by the Dnieper, Don, Volga, and other mighty rivers. E of the URALS extend the Asiatic RSFSR (see SIBERIA) and the steppes, deserts, and peaks of Central Asia. Mt. ELBRUS is the highest peak of Europe; STALIN PEAK, of the USSR. Vegetation zones are the arctic tundra, the dense central forest belt, the fertile S steppes, and the subtropical Black Sea and Caspian littorals. The climate is generally continental and extreme. Aside from its immense forests and rich agr. areas, the USSR possesses in abundance virtually all of the natural resources necessary for its economy. Among them are the huge coal fields of the DONETS BASIN and KUZNETSK BASIN; iron, copper, and other ores in the Urals; and petroleum (esp. at BAKU). Only tin and rubber are scarce. Main exports: timber, furs, manganese, chromium. Among largest cities are Moscow, Leningrad, Kiev, Kharkov, Baku, Gorki. Chief ports: Odessa, Leningrad, Murmansk, Vladivostok. The first country to adopt the Communist system, the USSR was formed in 1922. (For earlier history, see RUSSIA; RUSSIAN REVOLUTION. See also COMMUNISM.) Under the 1936 constitution, the constituent republics and most of the Union's 140 ethnic groups are represented in the council of nationalities—i.e., one of the chambers of the supreme SOVIET or council of the USSR. (Russians, c.50% of total pop., predominate.) The other chamber, or council of the Union, represents the USSR at large. Below these two chambers, there is a complicated hierarchy of regional, municipal, and local soviets as well as of autonomous ethnic subdivisions. The two chambers elect a presidium (the chairman of which—as of 1953, Marshal Voroshilov—acts as president of the USSR) and the council of ministers. Since the Communist party is the sole legal party and holds all power, elections and legislative deliberations are largely academic. The "dictatorship of the proletariat" (with which the Communist party identifies itself) was introduced by V. I. LENIN. In order to revive the economy of war-torn Russia, Lenin in 1921 inaugurated the mildly capitalistic NEW ECONOMIC POLICY. After his death (1924), Joseph STALIN bested his rivals for power and soon consolidated his absolute dictatorship by "purging" other Bolshevik leaders such as TROTSKY, KAMENEV, ZINOVIEV, and RYKOV. The first FIVE-YEAR PLAN (begun 1928) and its successors transformed Russia into one of the world's most powerful industrial nations; "liquidated" the independent farmers (*kulaks*); made virtually all farmland into collective farms (*kolkhoz*) or state-owned farms (*sovkhoz*); developed the Urals, Siberia, and Central Asia; and extended education and social services to backward areas. These results were achieved at the price of all political freedom and with the help of mass deportations and forced labor. At the same time, there was an evident trend toward revived nationalism and a new conservatism. Persecution of religion relented in the 1940s, but the state took virtual control over the churches. The original liberal policy toward national minorities was replaced by increasing Russification. In its foreign policy, the USSR was faced from the beginning by a hostile and apprehensive world. Russia entered the League of Nations in 1934 and its diplomatic position improved. Whatever the motives of the Russo-German nonaggression pact of Aug., 1939, it permitted Germany to begin WORLD WAR II and allowed Russia to annex E Poland, the Baltic republics, N Bukovina, and Bessarabia (1939–40) and to attack FINLAND. In 1941 Germany attacked Russia without warning, and by 1943 Axis armies had reached STALINGRAD and the Caucasus. Russia fought back heroically, but its eventual victory was achieved only after staggering material and human losses. In the postwar years, the expansion of Soviet influence in Europe and Asia created mounting world tension and intensive rearmament both in the Soviet and the Western camps. Stalin's death (March, 1953) and the accession of Malenkov as premier were interpreted by optimists as marking the beginning of a more conciliatory policy abroad and an easing of totalitarianism inside the USSR.

Union Pacific Railroad, chartered 1862 as Union Pacific Railway Co. Construction began from Omaha W in 1865. On May 10, 1869, Union Pacific joined Central Pacific W of Ogden, Utah, thus connecting Missouri R. and Pacific Ocean by rail. Joining of roads was marked by driving of a golden spike. Construction involved tremendous profiteering (see CRÉDIT MOBILIER OF AMERICA). Reincorporated 1897 as Union Pacific Railroad Co., railroad expanded under E. H. Harriman. Later, Union Pacific acquired large holdings in Eastern railroads, gained control of Western motor-coach lines.

Union Theological Seminary, in Manhattan borough of New York City; interdenominational, coed.; opened 1836, chartered 1839 by Presbyterians. Reciprocal educational relationship with Columbia Univ. since 1928. Includes school of sacred music (1928).

Uniontown, city (pop. 20,471), SW Pa., SSE of Pittsburgh; settled c.1767. Coal, coke, and metal products. Birthplace of Gen. G. C. Marshall. Near by is Fort Necessity Natl. Battlefield Site (see NECESSITY, FORT).

Union University: see SCHENECTADY, N.Y.

Unionville, Conn.: see FARMINGTON.

Unitarianism, religious belief based on conception of God in one person, in contrast to that of one God in three persons (Trinitarianism). It began in Reformation under such leaders as SERVETUS and SOCINUS. John Biddle estab. English Unitarianism, which was gradually welded into separate body. In America, it had its birth as early as 1785 when liberals withdrew from Congregational churches of New England and formed separate congregations. Its doctrines were stated in the ordination sermon (1819) of William Ellery Channing. American Unitarian Association was formed 1825; a national conference was organized 1865. Congregational polity prevails. No particular profession of faith is required of ministers or members, and no creed has been adopted.

United Brethren in Christ: see EVANGELICAL UNITED BRETHREN CHURCH.

United Church of Canada, Protestant denomination formed (1925) by union of Methodist, Congregationalist, and most Presbyterian churches in Canada.

United Empire Loyalists, name applied to Canadian settlers who, loyal to British cause in American Revolution, migrated to Canada from the Thirteen Colonies. The greatest number left the colonies in 1783–84. Most went to Nova Scotia and Quebec, resulting in establishment of New Brunswick in 1784 and creation of Upper Canada in 1791.

United Fruit Company, incorporated in N.J. in 1899 by Andrew Preston and M. C. KEITH. Soon outstripped all competition in growing, transporting, and merchandising bananas; later handled other produce. Company has often played a deciding role in Caribbean politics.

United Irishmen or **United Irish Society,** Irish political organization. Founded in 1791 by Wolfe Tone, it spread rapidly. Suppressed (1794), it became secret revolutionary body and sought aid from France. After failure of 1798 rebellion, its leaders were executed or imprisoned.

United Kingdom of Great Britain and Ireland, political body composed of ENGLAND, SCOTLAND, and IRELAND. Created by Act of Union (1800), uniting politically GREAT BRITAIN and Ireland. After formation of Irish Free State (1922) the name **United Kingdom of Great Britain and Northern Ireland** was adopted by act of Parliament 1927. Abbreviation is U.K.

United Methodist Church or **United Methodists,** nonconformist community in England, a union (1907) of Methodist New Connection, United Methodist Free Churches, and Bible Christians. Merged (1932) with Wesleyan Methodists and Primitive Methodists.

United Mine Workers of America (U.M.W.), labor union formed 1890. John L. LEWIS became president of the union in 1920. Many goals have been won, including a health and welfare fund. It was expelled (1937) from the A.F. of L., withdrew (1942) from the C.I.O., was readmitted (1946) to the A.F. of L., and was again disaffiliated (1947).

United Nations, international organization estab. after World War II to replace LEAGUE OF NATIONS. Name first officially used on Jan. 1, 1942, when 26 states joined in declaration pledging to continue joint war effort and not to make peace separately. Moscow Declaration of Oct. 30, 1943, issued by U.S., Great Britain, China, and USSR, stated need for international body to replace League. At Dumbarton Oaks Conference (Sept.–Oct., 1944) same countries drafted proposals for UN charter. At Yalta Conference (Feb. 4–11, 1945) USSR, U.S., and Great Britain agreed on "veto" system of voting in Security Council and (joined later by China and

France) decided to call a founding conference of all states that had declared war on Germany or Japan by March 1, 1945. This conference was held in San Francisco, April 25–June 26, 1945, with 51 members: Argentina, Australia, Belgium, Belorussia, Bolivia, Brazil, Canada, Chile, China, Colombia, Costa Rica, Cuba, Czechoslovakia, Denmark, Dominican Republic, Ecuador, Egypt, Ethiopia, France, Greece, Guatemala, Haiti, Honduras, India, Iran, Iraq, Lebanon, Liberia, Luxembourg, Mexico, Netherlands, New Zealand, Nicaragua, Norway, Panama, Paraguay, Peru, Philippine Isls., Poland, El Savador, Saudi Arabia, Syria, Turkey, Ukraine, Union of South Africa, USSR, United Kingdom (Great Britain), U.S., Uruguay, Venezuela, and Yugoslavia. Other nations admitted (to Dec., 1952) were Afghanistan, Burma, Iceland, Indonesia, Israel, Pakistan, Sweden, Thailand, and Yemen. San Francisco Conference drafted a governing treaty, the UN Charter, signed on June 26 and ratified by required number of states by Oct 24 (UN Day). General Assembly first met in London, Jan. 10, 1946; Security Council two days later. It was decided to place UN hq. in E U.S. UN occupied its permanent hq. in New York city in summer of 1952, with first General Assembly in Sept., 1952.

Organization and Principles. The UN Charter comprises preamble and 19 chapters with 111 articles. Principal organs of UN, as specified in Charter, are General Assembly, Security Council, Economic and Social Council, Trusteeship Council, Internatl. Court of Justice, and Secretariat. Other agencies are Food and Agriculture Organization, Internatl. Bank for Reconstruction and Development, Internatl. Civil Aviation Organization, Internatl. Labor Organization, Internatl. Monetary Fund, Internatl. Refugee Organization, Internatl. Telecommunication Union, UN Educational, Scientific, and Cultural Organization, Universal Postal Union, and World Health Organization. A temporary agency was UN Relief and Rehabilitation Administration. Charter sets forth purposes of UN as maintenance of international peace and security, development of friendly relations between states, and achievement of cooperation in the solving of international economic, social, cultural, and humanitarian problems. All UN administrative functions are handled by Secretariat, with a secretary general as its head, and a staff recruited on a wide geographical basis. The only UN body in which all members are represented is General Assembly; it meets in regular annual session beginning third Monday in Sept., with special sessions if necessary. It is primarily a deliberative body dealing to a large degree with political, social, or economic questions. Security Council is an organ with power to enforce measures to preserve peace, and it functions continuously. It has 11 members. Five—China, France, Great Britain, U.S., and USSR—are permanent; six nonpermanent members are elected for two-year terms to represent W Europe, E Europe, Arab states, Far East, and Latin America. In voting, unanimity is required among "Big Five"; hence the veto. As guardian of world peace Security Council acts for entire UN. Under Charter it can deal with all dangers to world peace. Security Council makes its own evaluation of matters brought before it, and it may either make recommendations or itself take enforcement measures.

Disagreements among the "Big Five." The Security Council has never been able, because of the veto, to come to agreement, through its Military Staff Committee, on a military force to represent UN and to enforce its decisions. Nor has it been able to agree, through its Atomic Energy Commission, to control atomic weapons, or through its Commission on Conventional Armaments, to reduce armaments. Likewise admission of new members to UN has been blocked, and Chinese representation has been a source of contention. The Interim Committee (or "Little Assembly," estab. 1947) was born as an attempt to bypass Russian misuse of the veto, and is boycotted by USSR. But on the other hand, such regional security agreements as NORTH ATLANTIC TREATY, Act of Chapultepec, and Rio Treaty have been advances toward world peace. International problems settled include complaint (1946) of Syria and Lebanon that France and Great Britain were illegally occupying their territory; acute situation in Palestine in 1947–48; end of hostilities in Indonesia between Dutch and native governments; and checking of the fighting in Kashmir between India and Pakistan. In 1950, when N Korea attacked S Korea, the Security Council on June 25, with USSR absent, voted to give military assistance to S Korea, and by the end of the year 52 nations had given moral support to UN. Communist China later joined N Korea. From Dec., 1950, UN has made efforts to secure a cease-fire, but at end of 1952 there was little progress.

United Nations Atomic Energy Commission: see ATOMIC ENERGY.

United Nations Commission for the Investigation of War Crimes: see WAR CRIMES.

United Nations Commission on Conventional Armaments: see UNITED NATIONS.

United Nations Economic and Social Council: see ECONOMIC AND SOCIAL COUNCIL.

United Nations Educational, Scientific, and Cultural Organization (UNESCO), agency of UN, hq. in Paris, estab. 1945. Furthers world peace by removing social, religious, and racial tensions, encouraging interchange of ideas and achievements, and improving and expanding education.

United Nations General Assembly: see UNITED NATIONS.

United Nations Relief and Rehabilitation Administration (UNRRA), estab. 1943 to aid in areas freed from Axis. Spent some $4,000,-000,000; repatriated 7,000,000 persons and cared for 1,000,000 others. Discontinued in Europe, June 30, 1947; in China, March 31, 1949. Work continued by FAO and IRO.

United Nations Security Council: see UNITED NATIONS.

United Nations Trusteeship Council: see TRUSTEESHIP, TERRITORIAL.

United Presbyterian Church, in Scotland, a

union (1847) of United Secession Church with part of Relief Church; in 1900 United Church merged with Free Church to form United Free Church of Scotland; in 1929 this group merged with Church of Scotland. In the U.S., United Presbyterian Church of North America represents union (1858) of Associate Presbyterian Church with Associate Reformed Presbyterian Church.

United Provinces, India: see UTTAR PRADESH.

United Provinces, Low Countries: see NETHERLANDS.

United Service Organizations (USO), organization which supplied social, recreational, welfare, and spiritual facilities for armed services and, to a limited extent, for war production workers in World War II and for a a few years thereafter. Organized 1941; had volunteer support. A new organization with same name came into existence in 1951.

United States, republic (3,022,387 sq. mi.; pop. 150,697,361), North America; cap. Washington, D.C. Continental U.S. consists of 48 states: Alabama, Arizona, Arkansas, California, Colorado, Connecticut, Delaware, Florida, Georgia, Idaho, Illinois, Indiana, Iowa, Kansas, Kentucky, Louisiana, Maine, Maryland, Massachusetts, Michigan, Minnesota, Mississippi, Missouri, Montana, Nebraska, Nevada, New Hampshire, New Jersey, New Mexico, New York, North Carolina, North Dakota, Ohio, Oklahoma, Oregon, Pennsylvania, Rhode Island, South Carolina, South Dakota, Tennessee, Texas, Utah, Vermont, Virginia, Washington, West Virginia, Wisconsin, and Wyoming, plus District of Columbia. U.S. territories and possessions: Alaska, Puerto Rico, Virgin Isls. of the United States, Hawaiian Isls., Guam, American Samoa, Wake Isl., Midway, Canton Isl., Enderbury Isl., several other islands. Trusteeship under UN of Caroline, Marshall, Marianas (except Guam) island chains. Panama Canal Zone held under perpetual lease from Panama. U.S. bounded by Atlantic Ocean (E), Pacific Ocean (W), Canada (N), Mexico and Gulf of Mexico (S). Atlantic lowlands rise to Appalachian Mts.; S drainage area of Great Lakes is in N central U.S.; heart of the country drained by great Mississippi and Missouri river systems. Prairies rise to Great Plains (W) which are sheltered by Rocky Mts. Further W, beyond Great Basin (sinking to 280 ft. below sea level in Death Valley), are the Sierra Nevada (rising to 14,495 ft. in Mt. Whitney) and Coast Ranges rising from narrow Pacific lowlands. Pacific Northwest is drainage area of Columbia R. Colorado R. drains large area and is stream of the Grand Canyon. Natural resources, man power, highly developed transportation and communication facilities make U.S. world's leading industrial nation. Agr. products include all those of temperate zone as well as subtropical produce. Has practically all resources needed for self-sufficiency.

Government. The U.S. government is that of a Federal republic set up by CONSTITUTION OF THE UNITED STATES. Division of power is between Federal and state governments. Federal government has threefold division of powers into executive (President, Vice President, cabinet); legislative (Congress); judicial (Supreme Court, lesser courts).

From Colonies to World Power. Spain, England, and France were the chief nations to establish colonies in present U.S. St. Augustine, Fla., founded 1565 by Spanish, was first permanent settlement. French influence spread through Great Lakes and down Mississippi R. to colony of Louisiana. First permanent British settlement was at Jamestown, Va., in 1607. Plymouth Colony, in New England, was estab. in 1620 by Pilgrims. British position strengthened after victory in FRENCH AND INDIAN WARS. Increasing conflict between colonies and mother country led to AMERICAN REVOLUTION, resulting in independence of Thirteen Colonies. These colonies, become states, united under Articles of Confederation, which were soon discarded for the Constitution. George WASHINGTON was first President. Controversy over division of power between states and Federal government introduced perennial problem of STATES' RIGHTS and gave rise to first political parties (see FEDERALIST PARTY; DEMOCRATIC PARTY). The frontier became a great molding force in American life. Expansion W accelerated: LOUISIANA PURCHASE (1803) added much new territory. WAR OF 1812 quickened growth of nationalism. Radical doctrines of frontier democracy focused on figure of Andrew JACKSON. Texas was annexed 1845; Calif. and vast areas of W were acquired through MEXICAN WAR. Brewing dispute over sectionalism and the slavery question erupted into CIVIL WAR (1861–65) after Abraham LINCOLN became President. War and RECONSTRUCTION period that followed left the South broken and impoverished. Industrial development became driving force in U.S. after 1865; excesses of new capitalism aroused much opposition. Through SPANISH-AMERICAN WAR, U.S. emerged as first-rate power. Imperialism expanded as a vigorous foreign policy was pursued. General progress marked period up to World War I. Despite efforts of Woodrow WILSON for peace, U.S. entered war in 1917 on side of the Allies. Boom afterwards ended in depression which began in 1929 and which was countered by measures taken under presidency of F. D. ROOSEVELT. World War II brought greatly expanded economy and underscored position of U.S. in world affairs. Today, through participation in UN and aid to other nations, U.S. has generally realized its role as a leader in world community. Action in Europe and Asia shows change from isolationism of past to responsible world position.

List of Presidents. This list uses one of two methods of numbering Presidents. The other method counts Grover Cleveland's terms separately, thus changing numbers 24 through 33 to read 25 through 34. **1** George Washington, 1789–97; **2** John Adams, 1797–1801; **3** Thomas Jefferson, 1801–9; **4** James Madison, 1809–17; **5** James Monroe, 1817–25; **6** John Quincy Adams, 1825–29; **7** Andrew Jackson, 1829–37; **8** Martin Van Buren, 1837–41; **9** William Henry Harrison (died in office), 1841; **10** John Tyler, 1841–

45; **11** James K. Polk, 1845–49; **12** Zachary Taylor (died in office), 1849–50; **13** Millard Fillmore, 1850–53; **14** Franklin Pierce, 1853–57; **15** James Buchanan, 1857–61; **16** Abraham Lincoln (assassinated), 1861–65; **17** Andrew Johnson, 1865–69; **18** Ulysses S. Grant, 1869–77; **19** Rutherford B. Hayes, 1877–81; **20** James A. Garfield (assassinated), 1881; **21** Chester A. Arthur, 1881–85; **22** Grover Cleveland, 1885–89, 1893–97; **23** Benjamin Harrison, 1889–93; **24** William McKinley (assassinated), 1897–1901; **25** Theodore Roosevelt, 1901–9; **26** William Howard Taft, 1909–13; **27** Woodrow Wilson, 1913–21; **28** Warren G. Harding (died in office), 1921–23; **29** Calvin Coolidge, 1923–29; **30** Herbert C. Hoover, 1929–33; **31** Franklin D. Roosevelt (died in office), 1933–45; **32** Harry S. Truman, 1945–53; **33** Dwight D. Eisenhower, 1953–. For further information, see articles on the states, towns and cities, physical features, major Americans, significant events in American history.

United States Government Printing Office: see GOVERNMENT PRINTING OFFICE, UNITED STATES.

United States Military Academy, institution founded (1802) at WEST POINT, N.Y., to prepare young men to be officers of U.S. army. Popularly known as West Point or Army. Act of 1812 laid basis for broader establishment of academy, and Sylvanus Thayer, superintendent 1817–33, shaped the curriculum and organization anew. War Dept. took control in 1866. Course of instruction takes four years for the students (cadets; called plebes as freshmen), who then normally become second lieutenants. The students are chosen according to Congressional dist. (with eight from states at large) except for a number from actual service.

United States National Museum: see SMITHSONIAN INSTITUTION.

United States Naval Academy, institution at Annapolis, Md., for training officers of U.S. navy. In 1845 George BANCROFT founded Naval School at Annapolis. School was reorganized 1850–51 under present name. Moved during Civil War to Newport, R.I.; returned in 1865. Four-year course for students (midshipmen) includes practical work on cruises and normally leads to commission as ensign. Many students are drawn from the Navy and the Marine Corps, others by the President, Vice President, and members of both houses of Congress.

United States Naval Observatory, government astronomical observatory in Washington, D.C. It evolved from chart and instrument depot estab. 1830; naval observatory completed 1844; moved to present site 1893. Supervised by chief of naval operations. Functions include making astronomical observations, sending time signals, publishing (from 1894) *American Ephemeris and Nautical Guide*.

United States Supreme Court: see SUPREME COURT, UNITED STATES.

Unity, religious movement inc. as Unity School of Christianity, with hq. at Lee's Summit, Mo. Founded by Charles and Myrtle Fillmore as faith-healing cult, with affinities to both Christian Science and New Thought, it has acquired character of denomination with "centers" or churches, ordained ministry, and statement of faith (1921). In 1922 it withdrew from Internatl. New Thought Alliance.

Universalist Church of America, Protestant denomination based on belief in salvation for every soul through divine grace of Jesus Christ. In Gloucester, Mass., John MURRAY became pastor of first Universalist church in U.S. Convention in Philadelphia (1790) agreed on Congregational polity and articles of faith. Movement changed (c.1796–1852) from Calvinism to Unitarianism. Winchester Profession (1803) accepts universal fatherhood of God, spiritual authority of Christ, and final harmony with God.

universal language, invented language intended for auxiliary purposes. Expanding 19th-cent. horizons brought several such creations, but Esperanto (a simplified, regular language with Latin-type grammar and European vocabulary), devised by L. L. Zamenhof, is the only one even moderately successful.

Universal Military Training (UMT). Although U.S. has used SELECTIVE SERVICE to conscript men in times of war, it has never had a system of military training for all male citizens, unlike some countries. However, such a system was urged as part of preparedness program instituted after World War II as a means of insuring enough trained men if the need for them should suddenly arise. Question of UMT has aroused much controversy. Although Pres. Truman urged passage of a bill authorizing UMT, Congress compromised by passing a draft bill in 1948 which was extended in 1951.

Universal Postal Union, agency of UN, hq. Bern, Switzerland. Originally estab. 1875, under UN 1947. Members constitute unified postal territory with easy international exchange of mail. Nearly all nations and territories in world belong.

universe, in astronomy, whole cosmic system, consisting of our Milky Way system and the many extragalactic nebulae scattered through space at average distance apart of 2,000,000 light-years. Einstein's relativity theories postulated four-dimensional space-time background; his work on cosmology (1917), stimulus for studies by De Sitter and others, defined space as curved and unlimited but finite. From spectroscopic studies revealing displacement toward red end of certain lines of spectra of extragalactic nebulae (red shift), it appears that external galaxies are moving away from our galaxy at velocities roughly proportional to their distance from us. Although controversy exists, many scientists agree that universe is expanding and finite.

University City, suburban city (pop. 39,892), E Mo., W of St. Louis.

University College: see OXFORD UNIVERSITY.

University Heights, city (pop. 11,566), NE Ohio, E suburb of Cleveland. Here is John Carroll Univ. (Jesuit; for men; 1886).

University Park, city (pop. 22,275), N Texas, adjoining Dallas; settled 1914. Seat of SOUTHERN METHODIST UNIVERSITY.

UNRRA: see UNITED NATIONS RELIEF AND REHABILITATION ADMINISTRATION.

Unruh, Fritz von (frĭts' fŭn o͝on'ro͞o), 1885–, German author. His prose epic, *The Way of Sacrifice* (1916–18; Eng. tr., 1928), is a passionate denunciation of war. The novel *The End Is Not Yet* (Eng. tr., 1947) deals with the Nazi period, during which Unruh lived in exile in the U.S.

Untermeyer, Louis, 1885–, American poet and anthologist, known for *Modern American Poetry* (1919 and later eds.) and *Modern British Poetry* (1920 and later eds.). His own works include *Selected Poems and Parodies* (1935), prose works, and criticism.

Unterwalden (o͝on'tŭrvăldŭn), canton, central Switzerland. Mountainous, forested, chiefly pastoral. Divided into half-cantons of Obwalden (190 sq. mi.; pop. 22,075; cap. Sarnen) and Nidwalden (106 sq. mi.; pop. 19,-459; cap. Stans). In 1291 Unterwalden formed with Uri and Schwyz a league which became the Swiss Confederation (see SWITZERLAND). Population is German-speaking and Catholic.

untouchables: see CASTE.

Upanishads (o͞o'păn'ĭshădz), dialogues on metaphysics, written after the Vedas and in part a commentary on them; important in development of Vedanta.

upas tree (ū'pŭs), East Indian tree (*Antiaris toxicaria*) of the mulberry family. The poisonous milky juice has been used for tipping arrows.

Updike, D(aniel) B(erkeley), 1860–1941, American printer, founder of the Merrymount Press at Boston; author of *Printing Types: Their History, Forms, and Use* (1922).

Upernivik (o͞opĕr'nŭvēk), settlement (pop. 321) and colony district (pop. 1,443), W Greenland, on small island in Baffin Bay. Sealing and whaling base.

Upjohn, Richard, 1802–78, American architect, b. England, important in the Gothic revival. Rebuilt Trinity Church, New York city.

Upland, city (pop. 9,203), S Calif., E of Los Angeles near San Antonio Peak. Packs citrus fruit.

Upolu (o͞opō'lo͞o), volcanic island (430 sq. mi.; pop. 42,764), Western SAMOA, under New Zealand mandate. Apia is seat of government; Saluafata, on N coast, is U.S. naval station. Vailima, home of Robert Louis Stevenson, is near Mt. Vaea.

Upper Austria, Ger. *Oberösterreich,* province (4,625 sq. mi.; pop. 1,107,562), N Austria, bordering on Czechoslovakia and Germany; cap. Linz. Agr. region, drained by the Danube. Includes much of the SALZKAMMERGUT. Was created a duchy 1156 and given to dukes of Austria.

Upper Palatinate: see PALATINATE.

Upper Volta (vŏl'tŭ), overseas territory (c.113,-100 sq. mi.; pop. c.3,037,000), central French West Africa; cap. Ouagadougou. Mainly a wooded savanna land used for stock raising. Export crops include peanuts and sesame. Under French control since 1897.

Uppland (ŭp'lănd), historic province of central Sweden; chief city Uppsala.

Uppsala (ŭp'sä"lä), city (pop. 63,072), E central Sweden. Archiepiscopal see since 1270 (now Lutheran). Seat of oldest Swedish university (founded 1477), one of the world's great centers of learning. University library has many invaluable manuscripts, e.g., the Codex argenteus of Ulfilas. The 13th-cent. cathedral contains the tombs of Gustavus I, Linnaeus, and Swedenborg.

Upsala College: see EAST ORANGE, N.J.

Upshur, Abel Parker (ŭp'shŭr), 1790–1844, U.S. Secretary of State (1843–44). Aided annexation of Texas. Upshur was killed in the explosion on the USS *Princeton,* and his death high-lighted the possibility of many high officials being killed at once and stressed the need for a law setting presidential succession.

Ur, anc. Sumerian city of Mesopotamia, on the Euphrates; of unknown antiquity (it was flourishing by 3500 B.C.); identified in the Bible as the home of Abraham. It was captured (c.2800 B.C.) by Sargon, but later was again independent. Ur declined after the 6th cent. B.C. C. Leonard Woolley led in excavations of the city in the late 19th cent. Called Ur of the Chaldees.

Ural (yo͞o'rŭl, Rus. o͞oräl'), river, 1,574 mi. long, RSFSR and Kazakh SSR, part of conventional geographic border between Europe and Asia. Rising in S Urals, it flows S, then W, then S again, past Magnitogorsk, to Caspian Sea. Partly navigable.

Ural-Altaic (yo͞o'rŭl-ăltā'ĭk), designation of a hypothetical grouping of certain language families of Europe and Asia. Finno-Ugric and Samoyede form Uralian stock. While Turkic, Tungusic, and Mongolian, the so-called Altaic languages, resemble one another, there is no clear evidence of relationship among them or between them and Uralian.

Urals or **Ural Mountains,** USSR, extending c.1,300 mi. N–S between Europe and Asia. Highest peak is Naroda (6,184 ft.). Densely forested (except in rocky N part), they also are rich in mineral resources (iron, manganese, nickel, chrome, copper, precious stones and metals, bauxite, asbestos, coal, oil). Huge industrial centers were created in 1930s at SVERDLOVSK, MAGNITOGORSK, Nizhni Tagil, Molotov, Chelyabinsk. During World War II entire industries were transferred to the Urals from the W USSR.

Urania (ūrā'nēŭ) [Gr.,= celestial], in Greek religion. **1** Muse of astronomy. See MUSES. **2** Aphrodite as goddess of heavens, patroness of heavenly love.

uranium (ūrā'nēŭm), hard, silver-white, radioactive metallic element (symbol = U; see also ELEMENT, table). Isotypes include those with atomic weights of 235, 238, and 239. Uranium 238 is parent substance of disintegration series, in which radium occurs; final product is lead of atomic wt. 206. Uranium occurs in ores, especially in PITCHBLENDE and carnotite. See also ATOMIC ENERGY. See *ill.,* p. 989.

Uranus (ūrā'nŭs, yo͞o'rŭnŭs) [Gr.,= sky, heaven], in Greek religion, sky-god, first ruler of universe; son of Gaea and father of Titans and Cyclopes. He was wounded and dethroned by Cronus. From his blood which fell on earth sprang the Erinyes and giants, from that which fell into the sea arose Aphrodite.

Uranus, in astronomy, PLANET seventh in distance from sun. Revolves about sun at mean distance of 1,782,700,000 mi. in period of c.84 years. Diameter c.30,878 mi. Rotation period c.10 hr. 45 min. Attended by five satellites (fifth reported 1948). Recognized as planet by Herschel 1781. See *ill.*, p. 1187.

Urban II, c.1042–1099, pope (1088–99), a Frenchman. He furthered the reforms of Gregory VII and preached at Clermont the sermon launching the First Crusade.

Urban IV, d. 1264, pope (1261–64), a Frenchman. Opposed the Hohenstaufen by offering Sicilian throne to Charles of Anjou.

Urban V, 1310–70, pope (1362–70), b. Provence; a Benedictine learned in canon law. Tried with the help of Cardinal Albornoz to move the papacy to Rome (1367), but had to return to Avignon (1370).

Urban VI, 1318?–1389, pope (1378–89), a Neapolitan. Chosen as successor to Gregory XI, he proved violently unruly. The cardinals, claiming intimidation by the Roman mob, went to Anagni and elected ROBERT OF GENEVA, thus beginning the Great SCHISM. Urban is thought by many to have been insane.

Urbana (ûrbă'nŭ). **1** City (pop. 22,834), E central Ill., adjoining CHAMPAIGN, with which it is allied economically. Trade center in farm area. Seat of Univ. of ILLINOIS. Tablet in courthouse commemorates Lincoln speech against Kansas-Nebraska bill 1854. **2** City (pop. 9,335), W central Ohio, N of Springfield, in agr area. Mfg. of paper, metal products, and tools. Simon Kenton buried here.

Urbino (o͞orbē'nō), town (pop. 5,459), the Marches, central Italy. Flourished under Montefeltro family from 12th cent. and under dukes Della Rovere (1508–1626). Had noted school of painting (15th–17th cent.). Early Renaissance ducal palace is rich in works of art. Birthplace of Raphael.

Urdu (o͞or'do͞o), language of Indic group of Indo-Iranian subfamily of Indo-European languages. See LANGUAGE (table).

Urey, Harold Clayton (yo͞o'rē), 1893–, American chemist. Won 1934 Nobel Prize for isolation of heavy hydrogen. Known also for work on atomic bomb, including methods of separating uranium isotypes and production of heavy water.

Urfa (o͞or'fä), anc. *Edessa,* city (pop. 37,456), S Turkey. An ancient center of Christianity, it fell 1144 to Moslems. Many Armenian Christians were massacred here in 19th cent.

Urfé, Honoré d' (ōnōrā' dürfā'), 1567–1625, French author of *L'Astrée* (5 vols., 1607–10), the principal French pastoral novel.

Urga, Mongolia: see ULAN BATOR.

Urgench (o͞orgyĕnch'). **1** Ancient city of central Asia, on site of present Kunya-Urgench (pop. over 2,000), Turkmen SSR, in Khiva oasis. Once the cap. of KHOREZM, it was abandoned in 16th cent. when the Amu Darya, on which it was situated, changed its course. **2** City (pop. over 10,000), Uzbek SSR, in Khiva oasis. Cotton mfg. Known as Novy [new] Urgench till 1937.

Uri (o͞o'rē), canton (415 sq. mi.; pop. 28,569), Switzerland; cap. Altdorf. Alpine region of glaciers and pastures; forests and meadows in Reuss R. valley. The scene of the TELL legend, Uri in 1291 formed with Schwyz and Unterwalden the league which became the nucleus of SWITZERLAND.

Uriah (ūrī'ŭ) [Heb.,= light of God], husband of Bathsheba. 2 Sam. 11. Urias: Mat. 1.6.

uric acid (yo͞o'rĭk), white, odorless, tasteless, weak crystalline organic acid, formed as a result of protein metabolism in humans and some other vertebrates. Occurs in small amount in human urine and blood. Pure acid is obtained from GUANO. Yields urea on decomposition.

Uriel (ū'rēŭl) [Heb.,= flame of God], name of an angel in the pseudepigrapha. He is introduced in Milton's *Paradise Lost* as the angel of the sun.

urine, in human and some other vertebrates, a fluid secreted by KIDNEYS, stored in BLADDER, and eliminated through urethra. Contains excretory products collected from tissues by circulating blood; consists of water (95%) and salts, urea, uric acid, pigments, and mucus.

Urmia (o͞or'mēŭ, o͞ormēä'), shallow salt lake, 90 mi. long, 30 mi. wide, NW Iran, in Azerbaijan; largest lake in Iran. Has no outlet.

Urquhart, Sir Thomas (û'kûrt), 1611–60, Scottish author, noted for his translation of three books of the *Gargantua* of Rabelais.

Urquiza, Justo José de (ho͞o'stō hōsā' dā o͞orkē'zä), 1801–70, Argentine political leader. In control of Entre Ríos prov., he supported Rosas until 1851, when he led the revolt, successful at the battle of Monte Caseros (1853). He was then the ruler of Argentina, but was opposed by Buenos Aires prov. The battle at Pavón (1861) was indecisive, but Urquiza surrendered power to Mitre. He was assassinated.

Urraca (o͞orä'kä), d. 1126, Spanish queen of Castile and Leon (1109–26); daughter of Alfonso VI. Her second husband, Alfonso I of Aragon, seized her lands and repudiated her in 1114. Her son and successor, Alfonso VII, helped her to recover her kingdoms from his stepfather.

Ursins, Marie Anne de la Trémoille, princesse des (märē' än' dü lä trāmwä'yü prēsĕs' dāz ürsē'), 1642–1722. French noblewoman. Arranged marriage of Philip V of Spain with María Luisa of Savoy. Held almost dictatorial powers at the Spanish court till the queen's death (1714).

Ursúa, Pedro de (pā'dhrō dā o͞orso͞o'ä), c.1526–1561, Spanish conquistador and explorer in South America. A restless adventurer, he came to New Granada in 1545, was temporary governor of Bogotá, subjugated neighboring Indians, sought El Dorado, founded towns; joined viceroy of Peru in Panama and subdued *cimarrones* (escaped Negro slaves). He was murdered on expedition to Marañón when again seeking El Dorado.

Ursula, Saint, 4th cent.?, virgin martyr of Cologne. Legend says 11,000 virgins were her companions. Feast: Oct. 21.

Uruapan (o͞orwä'pän), city (pop. 20,583), Michoacán, W Mexico; founded 1540. In semitropical, mountainous agr. region, city has mfg. of gourd lacquerware by Tarascan Indians. Near by is volcano Paricutín.

Uruguaiana (o͞o″ro͞ogwīä'nŭ), city (pop. 33,-272), W Rio Grande do Sul state, S Brazil, on Uruguay R.; rail junction and cattle-raising center, with meat-processing plants.

Uruguay (o͝oro͝ogwī'), republic (72,152 sq. mi.; pop. 2,202,936), SE South America; cap. MONTEVIDEO. The Río de la Plata and the Uruguay R. separate Uruguay from Argentina, and Brazil lies to the N; the Atlantic is to E. The BANDA ORIENTAL, a rich alluvial plain, where most of Uruguay's population lives, produces wheat, wine, tobacco, and olives, but sheep and cattle raising on the grasslands in N is most important activity. The owners and the *gauchos* of the large *estancias* there played a major role in Uruguayan economy and political life. The Spanish and Portuguese contended for ownership of the region in the 17th and 18th cent. The Spanish were in control when the movement for independence began and Uruguay declared for independence with Argentina in 1810. In 1814, however, ARTIGAS broke with the military junta of Buenos Aires and the struggle for Uruguay's separate existence began. In 1820, the Brazilians occupied Montevideo. A group of patriots known as the Thirty-three Immortals declared Uruguay independent in 1825, and at the battle of Ituzaingo in 1827 Brazil was defeated. Immediately thereafter a fratricidal struggle ensued (1828–51) between two political parties known as Colorados [reds] and Blancos [whites]; this was mixed with the rising against Rosas in Argentina and resulted in a long siege of Montevideo. In 1864, Uruguay again became involved with her neighbors, Brazil and Paraguay (see TRIPLE ALLIANCE, WAR OF THE). Not until the 20th cent. was Uruguay free from revolutions and counterrevolutions and able to launch a program of social and material progress that has characterized its subsequent development. In 1952 a nine-man council was substituted for the presidency of Uruguay's democratic government.

Uruguay, river, c.1,000 mi. long, rising in S Brazil near Atlantic and flowing in arc W to Argentina, then SW and S to Río de la Plata. Principal cities on river are Salto and Paysandú (Uruguay) and Concepción del Uruguay (Argentina).

Urumchi (o͝oro͝omchē'), Chinese *Tihwa,* commercial city (pop. 69,991), cap. of Sinkiang prov., NW China, in the Dzungaria.

Ushant (ŭ'shŭnt), Fr. *Ouessant,* island, 5 mi. long, NW France, in the Atlantic off tip of Brittany. Lord Howe defeated a French fleet here (1794).

Usher, James: see USSHER, JAMES.

Usk, river of Wales and England. Flows c.60 mi. from Caermarthenshire to the Severn estuary. Noted for its beauty and associations with King Arthur.

Uskudar, Turkey: see SCUTARI.

Uspallata Pass (o͞ospäyä'tä), c.12,500 ft. high, over Andes between Mendoza, Argentina, and Santiago, Chile. Used by San Martín for conquest of Chile 1817; Christ of the Andes was built here 1904; Transandine Railway completed through Pass 1910; Mt. Aconcagua towers N and Tupungato S of Pass.

Ussher or **Usher, James,** 1581–1656, Irish churchman, chancellor of St. Patrick's Cathedral, Dublin, bishop of Meath (1621–25), archbishop of Armagh (after 1625). He was notable for his great learning. His chronology of biblical events was long accepted as authoritative.

USSR: see UNION OF SOVIET SOCIALIST REPUBLICS.

Usti nad Labem (o͞os'tyē näd lä'bĕm), Ger. *Aussig,* city (pop. 34,410), N Bohemia, Czechoslovakia, on the Elbe. Industrial center (chemicals, machinery, foodstuffs). Founded 13th cent., city has fine Gothic and Renaissance architecture.

Ust Urt (o͝ost" o͝ort'), desert plateau, area c.62,000 sq. mi., Asiatic USSR, between Caspian and Aral seas. Sheep, goat, and camel raising.

usury: see INTEREST.

Utah, state (84,916 sq. mi.; pop. 688,862), W U.S.; admitted 1896 as 45th state; cap. SALT LAKE CITY. Other cities are PROVO, OGDEN. Has varied topography of mountains, plateaus, basins, valleys. Main rivers are the Colorado and the Green. Mining (copper, silver, gold, lead, coal, zinc). Sheep, cattle raising; agr. of wheat, grains, potatoes. Processes minerals, agr. products. MORMONS arrived 1847, led by Brigham YOUNG. Region passed to U.S. (1848) after Mexican War. Opposition between Mormons and U.S. government produced much trouble. Following repeated petitions, statehood was finally granted after Morman church renounced polygamy. Present economic problems arise from Mormon distrust of industry, high freight rates, distance from markets.

Utah, University of, at Salt Lake City; state supported, coed.; opened 1850, chartered 1851 as Univ. of Deseret, closed 1851–67, renamed 1892.

Utah Lake, N central Utah. Fresh-water lake (23 mi. long, 8 mi. wide), which was part of prehistoric L. Bonneville. Drains via Jordan R. to Great Salt L. Much used for irrigation, its low waters in 1930s caused construction of Provo R. project.

Utah State Agricultural College, at Logan; land-grant support, coed.; opened 1890.

Utamaro (o͞otä'märō), 1753–1806, one of first Japanese color-print artists to be known in Europe. Noted for landscapes, pictures of insects, and portraits of women.

Ute Indians (ūt), North American tribe of Uto-Aztecan linguistic stock, occupying W Colo. and E Utah in the early 19th cent. They were then fierce nomadic horsemen, who sometimes raided the villages of the Pueblo Indians in Ariz. and N.Mex. There was some trouble with the whites, especially in 1879, but no full-fledged war. They live on reservations in Colo. and Utah. Also called Utah Indians.

uterus (ū'tŭrŭs), hollow muscular organ in which fetus develops. In human it is normally in pelvis; supported on neck (cervix) opening into vagina. Ova pass from ovaries into openings of near-by paired oviducts leading into uterus. Ovum fertilized in oviduct is implanted in uterine wall; unfertilized ovum is eliminated during MENSTRUATION.

Uther Pendragon: see ARTHURIAN LEGEND.

Utica (ū'tĭkŭ), anc. city, N of Carthage, supposedly founded by Phoenicians from Tyre (c.1100 B.C.). Joined Rome against Carthage in the Third Punic War. Was later capital of the Roman province of Africa. Finally destroyed by Arabs (A.D. c.700).

Utica, city (pop. 101,531), central N.Y., on Mohawk R. and the Barge Canal and NW of Albany, in rich dairying region. Permanent settlement began after Revolution. Opening of Erie Canal and railroads spurred industrial growth. Has large textile industry (sheets, pillowcases, knit goods), begun 1840s; mfg. also of firearms, machinery. Park system has facilities for summer, winter sports. Large Welsh pop. holds annual eisteddfod.

utilitarianism, philosophical movement centered upon the ethical idea that the criterion of morality is attaining the greatest happiness for the greatest number. Jeremy Bentham was its founder, and John Stuart Mill and Herbert Spencer developed the doctrines.

Uto-Aztecan (ū″tō-ăztĕ′kŭn), linguistic family of North America. See LANGUAGE (table).

Utopia [Gr.,= no place], title of book by Sir Thomas MORE (in Latin, 1516). Work pictures ideal state where all is ordered for best for mankind as whole, and evils such as poverty and misery do not exist. Book's popularity has given generic name to all concepts of ideal states created by social philosophers and visionaries. Among great early utopian works are Plato's *Republic* and St. Augustine's *City of God.* Among other famous utopias before 19th cent., besides More's, were Campanella's *The City of the Sun* (1623), Francis Bacon's *The New Atlantis* (1627), and James Harrington's *Oceana* (1656). French writers on utopian themes include SAINT-SIMON, Étienne CABET, Charles FOURIER, and P. J. PROUDHON; in England Robert OWEN was typical. Famous novels on utopian theme are Edward Bellamy's *Looking Backward* (1888), Samuel Butler's *Erewhon* (1872), and William Morris's *A Dream of John Ball* (1888) and *News from Nowhere* (1891). Satiric utopias are in Aristophanes' *The Birds,* Mandeville's *The Fable of the Bees,* and parts of Swift's *Gulliver's Travels.* Legends of actual ideal states have persisted in tales of ATLANTIS, FORTUNATE ISLES, and EL DORADO.

Utraquists (ū′trŭkwĭsts), moderate HUSSITES, opposed to the radical Taborites (led by Procopius the Great). Insisted on communion in both kinds (*sub utraque specie*) but did not vary much from Roman Catholic doctrines and were reunited with the Church by signing the Compactata. Later New Utraquists joined the Lutherans. They supported George of Podebrad. Called also Calixtines.

Utrecht (ū′trĕkt, Dutch ü′trĕkht), province (502 sq. mi.; pop. 549,566), central Netherlands, bounded by the Ijsselmeer in N. Agr. lowland. It shares the history of its cap., the municipality of **Utrecht** (pop. 183,251), on a branch of the Lower Rhine. Roman Catholic archiepiscopal see. University (founded 1636). Mfg. of machinery, textiles, food. St. Willibrord was first bishop of Utrecht. Later bishops ruled Utrecht and Overijssel as princes of Holy Roman Empire until 1527, when the bishop sold his territorial rights to Emperor Charles V. Utrecht joined in the rebellion against Spain. By the Union of Utrecht (1577) the seven provinces of the N NETHERLANDS drew together for their common defense. A picturesque old city, Utrecht has retained its 14th-cent. cathedral.

Utrecht, Peace of, ending War of the SPANISH SUCCESSION, consisted of several treaties signed at Utrecht (1713) and was complemented by Franco-Austrian treaties of Rastatt and Baden (1714). Chief clauses: PHILIP V was recognized as king of Spain. Spanish Netherlands, Milan, Naples, and Sardinia were transferred to Austria; Gibraltar and Minorca, to Britain; Sicily, to Savoy. France recognized house of Hanover on English throne. Philip V renounced right of succession to French throne. England and Netherlands won advantageous commercial clauses.

Utrillo, Maurice (mōrēs′ ütrēlō′), 1883–, French painter; son of the painter Suzanne Valadon. Best known for vivid paintings of streets and suburbs of Paris.

Uttar Pradesh (ŏŏtŭr prŭdāsh′), state (112,523 sq. mi.; pop. 63,254,118), N India; cap. Allahabad. Extends S from Himalayas into plains of Ganges and Jumna rivers. Chief crops are grains and sugar cane. Has five universities and many Hindu pilgrimage centers (notably Allahabad and Benares). Dominated 13th–18th cent. by Moslems. Under the Moguls the area roughly comprised Agra prov., which was annexed by the British in late 18th cent. and joined 1877 with historic region of Oudh to form what was later called United Provinces. Enlarged 1949 by inclusion of former princely states, renamed Uttar Pradesh 1950.

Uvalde (ūvăl′dē), city (pop. 8,674), SW Texas, WSW of San Antonio. Center of ranching area, it ships cattle, mohair, pecans, honey, and asphalt. Home of J. N. Garner.

Uxbridge, town (pop. 7,007), S Mass., SE of Worcester; settled 1662. Woolens and worsteds.

Uxmal (ŏŏshmäl′), ruined city, Yucatan, E Mexico, center of Maya New Empire; founded 987, abandoned 1441. Finest expression of Mayan architectural renaissance.

Uzbek Soviet Socialist Republic (ŏŏz′bĕk, ŏŏzbĕk′) or **Uzbekistan** (ŏŏz″bĕkĭstăn′), constituent republic (157,300 sq. mi.; pop. c.6,000,000) of the USSR, in central Asia; cap. Tashkent. Drained by Amu Darya and Syr Darya rivers, it consists of the Kizil Kum desert (W) and fertile irrigated lands (E), notably the FERGANA VALLEY and the oases of KHIVA, TASHKENT, SAMARKAND, and BUKHARA. Chief products: cotton, rice, silk. Uzbeks (c.75% of pop.) are a Moslem, Turkic-speaking group of Persian culture. Ancient SOGDIANA, the region fell to the Arabs (8th cent. A.D.), to KHOREZM (12th cent.), and to the Mongols (13th cent.); was the center of Tamerlane's empire (14th cent.); fell to the Uzbeks, a remnant of the Golden Horde (16th cent.); and broke up into separate principalities (Khiva, KOKAND, Bukhara). Conquered by Russia 1875–76, Uzbekistan became a constituent republic 1924.

Uzhgorod (ŏŏzh′gŭrŭt), Czech *Užhorod,* Hung. *Ungvár,* city (pop. 35,250), W

Ukraine; former cap. of RUTHENIA. Agr. center. Founded 13th cent. Ceded by Hungary to Czechoslovakia 1920; by Czechoslovakia to USSR 1945.

Uzza or **Uzzah** (ŭ'zů), man who met sudden death after touching the ark. 2 Sam. 6.3–8; 1 Chron. 13.7–11.

Uzziah (ŭzī'ů), d. c.735 B.C., king of Judah (c.775–c.735 B.C.). He was a strong leader, but his pride made him try to usurp the duties of the high priest. For this sacrilege he was smitten with leprosy. 2 Chron. 26. Called Azariah in 2 Kings 15. Ozias: Mat. 1.8,9.

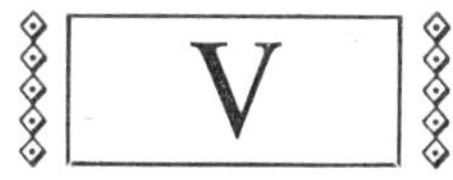

V, chemical symbol of the element VANADIUM.

Vaasa or **vasa** (both: vä'sä), city (pop. 36,178), W Finland; a Baltic port on Gulf of Bothnia. Shipping center for timber. Mfg. of textiles, motors.

Vaca, Cabeza de: see CABEZA DE VACA, ÁLVAR NÚÑEZ.

Vaca de Castro, Cristóbal (krēstō'väl vä'kä dā kä'strō), fl.1540–45, Spanish colonial administrator in Peru. Attempted to settle the Pizarro-Almagro feud, but was arrested by Núñez Vela and sent back to Spain, where he spent 12 years in prison before being cleared of charges.

vaccination, inoculation with vaccine to produce active IMMUNITY to disease. Introduced by Edward JENNER to immunize against smallpox. Vaccines usually are prepared from killed or weakened organisms causing specific disease or from their toxins.

vacuum, theoretically, space without matter in it. Perfect vacuum not yet obtained. Torricelli obtained nearly perfect one in mercury BAROMETER. Apparent "suction" caused by vacuum is measure of pressure of atmosphere tending to rush in and fill space; perfect vacuum exerts no pressure, for it contains no matter. There are a number of methods of producing vacuums and number of pumps for removing air from confined space; difficulty arises because matter is apparently composed of molecules in rapid motion and for perfect vacuum all molecules must be removed. Vacuum is used in vacuum cleaner, vacuum tube, vacuum bottle, and barometer.

vacuum tube: see TUBE, VACUUM OR ELECTRON.

Vaduz (vädōōts'), town (pop. 2,041), cap. of principality of LIECHTENSTEIN.

Vagarshapat, Armenian SSR: see ECHMIADZIN.

Vailima (vīlē'mů), estate, home of R. L. Stevenson for five years, Upolu, Western Samoa. His tomb is atop near-by Mt. Vaea.

Valais (välā'), Ger. *Wallis,* canton (2,021 sq. mi.; pop. 158,227), S Switzerland, crossed by the upper Rhone valley, with the Bernese Alps to the N and the Valais Alps (part of Pennine Alps) to the S; cap. Sion. Has many peaks (e.g., Dufourspitze, Matterhorn) and famous resorts. Stock raising, agr., vineyards. Population is Catholic, French-speaking in Lower Valais (W), mostly German-speaking in Upper Valais (E). The bishop of Sion and the communes of Upper Valais, allies of the Swiss Confederation from the 15th cent., conquered Lower Valais from Savoy 1475 and ruled it as subject territory till 1797. Valais joined Helvetic Republic 1798; became independent republic 1802; was annexed to France 1810; became Swiss canton 1815.

Valcour Island (vălkōōr'), c.2 mi. long, NE N.Y., in L. Champlain, near Plattsburg. On Oct. 11, 1776, American vessels under Benedict Arnold were routed by British.

Valdai Hills (vŭldī'), moraine region, NW European RSFSR. Extending in parallel ridges for c.300 mi. NE–SW, it rises to 1,053 ft. in Mt. Kammenik.

Valdemar. For Danish rulers, see WALDEMAR.

Valdés, Armando Palacio: see PALACIO VALDÉS.

Valdés-Leal, Juan de (hwän' dā väldās-lāäl'), 1622?–1690?, Spanish painter of Seville school. Excelled in painting gruesome subjects, such as *Two Cadavers in Their Worms.*

Valdez (văldēz'), town (pop. 554), S Alaska, on Prince William Sound. Ice-free harbor explored and named by Spanish, 1790. Created 1898 as debarkation point for Yukon gold fields. Center of gold-mining and fur-producing area. Seaplane base and coastal terminus of Richardson Highway to Fairbanks.

Valdivia, Pedro de (pā'dhrō dā väldē'vyä), c.1500–1554, Spanish conquistador, conqueror of Chile. One of Pizarro's best officers in conquest of Peru, he was commissioned by Pizarro to subdue Chile (1540). Santiago was founded (1541) and other settlements made but colony did not prosper because of scarcity of gold and ferocity of Araucanian Indians. Made governor of Chile by viceroy of Peru (1549), Valdivia continued S, founding Concepción (1550) and Valdivia (1522). In revolt of Indians (1553), led by Lautaro, Valdivia and his men were massacred.

Valdivia, city (pop. 31,674), S central Chile, on the Pacific; founded 1552 by Valdivia, on Valdivia R. 11 mi. from its port, Corral. An active industrial city, it has tanneries, sugar refineries, shipyards, breweries, flour, lumber, and steel mills.

Val d'Or (väl dôr'), town (pop. 8,685), W Que., Canada, ESE of Rouyn. Mining center producing gold, copper, zinc, lead, and molybdenum.

Valdosta (văldŏ'stů), city (pop. 20,046), S Ga., near Fla. line, in lake region; founded 1860. Processes and ships cotton, pecans, vegetables, tobacco, and lumber. Has railroad shops. Seat of Valdosta State College (coed.; 1906), formerly Georgia State Womans Col.

Vale (vāl), town (pop. 1,518), E Oregon, on Malheur R. near Idaho line. Has hot springs. Chief town in Vale irrigation project, estab. 1928 to supply c.32,000 acres (sugar beets, livestock, potatoes).

Valence (välãs'), city (pop. 34,249), cap. of Drôme dept., SE France, on Rhone R. Silk mfg. Romanesque cathedral escaped damage in World War II.

valence (vā'lůns), in chemistry, a number representing relative ability of one element to combine with another. Unit of comparison is ability of hydrogen to combine; i.e., number of hydrogen atoms an element combines with or displaces (in the case of those that do not combine with hydrogen) from a compound is valence of the element. Some elements have more than one valence but more have only one. Valence is explained by number and arrangement of electrons outside nucleus of atom. See *ill.*, p. 989.

Valencia, Guillermo (gēyĕr'mō välān'syä), 1873–1943, Colombian poet, author of austere, subtle lyrics, some of the best of the *modernismo* movement.

Valencia (vůlĕn'shů, Sp. välān'thēä), region (8,998 sq. mi.; pop. 2,176,670), E Spain, on the Mediterranean. Its fertile, irrigated coastal plain, the "garden of Spain," produces oranges, grapes, rice, olives, and vegetables. It was an independent Moorish emirate (11th cent.); later passed to the Almoravides and Almohades; was conquered by Aragon 1238–52. Its status as one of the Spanish kingdoms was abolished in 18th cent. Its cap., **Valencia** (pop. 409,670), is a commercial and industrial center and has a busy port (Villanueva del Grao). Mfg. of silk, tobacco, colored tiles. Exports oranges, wine. University was founded c.1500. A Roman colony, it later flourished under the Moors; was ruled by the CID 1094–99; rivaled Barcelona after its conquest by Aragon (1238). A picturesque city, it has a cathedral (13th–15th cent.), a 16th-cent. citadel, Renaissance palace of justice, and Gothic silk exchange (*La Lonja*).

Valencia (välĕn'syä), city (pop. 85,243), N Venezuela; founded 1555 on L. Valencia (c.120 sq. mi., second largest lake in Venezuela). City has many industries to process products from surrounding agr. and cattle-raising region.

Valenciennes (vůlĕn"sēĕnz', Fr. välãsyĕn'), town (pop. 37,716), Nord dept., N France, on Escaut R. Famous since 15th cent. for lace industry. Part of Hainaut, it passed to France 1678. Heavily damaged in World War II.

Valens (vā'lůnz), c.328–78, East Roman emperor (364–78); brother of Valentinian I. Embraced Arianism; was defeated by Visigoths in great battle of Adrianople, in which he was slain. Theodosius I (the Great) succeeded him.

Valentine, Saint, d. c.270, Roman martyr priest. Possibly by association with a pagan festival, his feast, Feb. 14, is the day of lovers.

Valentinian (vă"lůntĭ'nēůn), West Roman emperors. **Valentinian I,** 321–75, reigned 364–75. His son **Valentinian II,** 371–92, reigned 375–92 (jointly with his brother Gratian until 383). Made THEODOSIUS I emperor of the East (378). Was expelled from Italy by MAXIMUS (387), restored by Theodosius (388). Died strangled, probably by order of ARBOGAST. **Valentinian III,** 419–55, reigned 425–55, first under the regency of his mother, Galla Placidia. His general AETIUS held the actual power from 433 to 454, when Valentinian murdered him. His reign saw the invasions of VANDALS and HUNS. He was murdered.

Valentino, Rudolph (välůntē'nō), 1895–1926, American film actor, whose real name was Rodolpho d'Antonguolla, b. Italy. In U.S. after 1913, he won fame in such films as *The Sheik* and *Blood and Sand.*

Valentinus, Basilius: see BASILIUS VALENTINUS.

Valera, Eamon de: see DE VALERA, EAMON.

Valerian (vůlēr'ēůn), d. after 260, Roman emperor (253–60). Made his son Gallienus coregent and undertook a campaign against Shapur I of Persia, who defeated and captured him (260).

Valerius Maximus (vůlēr'ēůs măk'sĭmůs), 1st cent. B.C.–1st cent. A.D., Roman compiler of anecdotes.

Valéry, Paul (pôl' välārē'), 1871–1945, French poet, critic, and intellectual leader. His poems *La Jeune Parque* (1917) and *Le Cimetière marin* (1920; Eng. tr., *The Graveyard by the Sea,* 1932), considered his masterpiece, are as difficult as they are profound and had great influence on contemporary poetry. Valéry's keen intellect is revealed in his prose works—*An Evening with Mr. Teste* (1896; Eng. tr., 1925) and collections of essays, *Variétés* (5 vols., 1924–44; partial Eng. tr., 1927, 1928).

Valhalla or **Walhalla** (both: välhäl'ů) [Norse, = hall of the slain], in Norse mythology, Odin's home for slain heroes, brought there by Valkyries.

Valkyries (vălkēr'ēz) [Norse,= choosers of the slain], Ger. *Walküre,* in Germanic myth, Odin's daughters or attendants. They came to the battlefield, chose those who were to die, and bore them back to Valhalla. Chief among them was Brynhild.

Valla, Lorenzo (lōrān'tsō väl'lä), c.1407–1457, Italian humanist. Demonstration that the Donation of Constantine was a forgery was a pioneer work in textual criticism.

Valladolid (välyä-dhōlēdh'), city (pop. 111,-253), cap. of Valladolid prov., N central Spain, in Leon. Grain market; mfg. of chemicals, textiles. Conquered from Moors in 10th cent.; replaced Toledo as chief residence of kings of Castile in 15th cent.; declined after Philip II made Madrid his cap. (1561). Landmarks include the late Renaissance cathedral, completed by Churriguera; the plateresque Colegio de San José; the 15th-cent. Colegio de San Gregorio; the homes of Cervantes and Columbus; the royal palace; and the baroque building housing the university (founded 1346).

Vallandigham, Clement Laird (vŭlăn'dĭghăm", -găm"), 1820–71, American politician. U.S. Congressman from Ohio (1858–63). Court-martialed for speech sympathetic to South (1863). Most prominent of COPPERHEADS; commanded Sons of Liberty (see KNIGHTS OF THE GOLDEN CIRCLE).

Valle Inclán, Ramón del (väl'yā ēnklän'), 1866?–1936, Spanish novelist, author of four linked novels called "sonatas" (1902–5), in exquisite style.

Vallejo (vălā'hō), city (pop. 34,913), W Calif., port on San Pablo Bay at mouth of Napa R. Founded on property of Gen. M. G. Vallejo, it was nominal state cap. 1851–54. Flour and lumber milling, meat packing, and dairying. On Mare Isl. is U.S. navy yard, estab. 1854 by D. G. Farragut.

Valletta (vŭlĕ'tŭ), seaport (pop. 18,666), cap. of British colony of Malta. An old town with many relics of Knights Hospitalers or Knights of Malta, it has a 16th-cent. cathedral and a museum of antiquities. Severely bombed in World War II.

valley, the drainage basin of a river system or any elongated depression between elevations, usually formed by stream erosion. Shape of a river valley depends on age of stream and rate of erosion of river bed and valley sides. "Young" valleys have steep sides, and floor has narrow flood plain or no flood plain. Great river valleys have long been natural travel routes. The Tigris-Euphrates and Nile valleys were cradles of early civilization.

Valley City, city (pop. 6,851), SE N.Dak., on Sheyenne R. and W of Fargo. Processes flour, dairy products.

Valleyfield, city (pop. 22,414), Que., Canada, on L. St. Francis and SW of Montreal. Textile mills, distilling, and dairying.

Valley Forge, locality, SE Pa., on the Schuylkill NW of Philadelphia. Main camp of Continental army estab. here (Dec., 1777–June, 1778); troops suffered through severe winter. Site now state park.

Valley Junction, Iowa: see WEST DES MOINES.

Valley of Ten Thousand Smokes, area 72 sq. mi. in Katmai Natl. Monument, S Alaska. Punctured by thousands of small volcanoes created by eruption of Katmai volcano 1912.

Valley Stream, suburban village (pop. 26,854), SE N.Y., on SW Long Isl., SE of Jamaica.

Vallombrosa (väl-lōmbrō'zä), resort village, Tuscany, central Italy, SE of Florence, in Apennine forests. Has 11th-cent. Benedictine abbey.

Valmy (välmē'), village in the Argonne, NE France. On Sept. 20, 1792, the Prussians were stopped by French artillery at Valmy and, without further battle, began their retreat across the Rhine. The action gave France the initiative in the French Revolutionary Wars and thus was decisive.

Valois (välwä'), French dynasty, descended from CHARLES OF VALOIS, third son of Philip III. Succeeding the direct Capetians 1328, it ruled in direct line till 1498 (see PHILIP VI; JOHN II; CHARLES V; CHARLES VI; CHARLES VII; LOUIS XI; CHARLES VIII). LOUIS XII, of the collateral line of Valois-Orléans, reigned 1498–1515. He was succeeded by another collateral line—Valois-Angoulême (see FRANCES I; HENRY II; FRANCIS II; CHARLES IX; HENRY III). The line failed 1589 and was succeeded by the BOURBON dynasty.

Valona (vŭlō'nŭ), Albanian *Vlonë, Vlona, Vlorë,* or *Vlora,* anc. *Aulon,* city (pop. 14,-640), SW Albania; an Adriatic port on Bay of Valona. Trades in olive oil, bitumen, petroleum. Was important in Middle Ages. Albanian independence proclaimed here 1912.

Valparaiso (välpäräē'sō), city (pop. 182,689), central Chile, chief port of W South America and second largest city of Chile. Founded in 1536 by order of Almagro, it was not permanently established until 1544 by Valdivia. Today it is a flourishing industrial city and tourist resort, with near-by Viña del Mar.

Valparaiso (vălpŭrā'zō), city (pop. 12,028), NW Ind., SE of Gary; settled 1834. Mfg. of metal products and paints. Seat of Valparaiso Univ.

Van. For names not listed thus, see second element; e.g., for Van Gogh, see GOGH, VINCENT VAN.

Van (vän), town (pop. 13,471), SE Turkey, near E shore of L. Van. Trade center of wheat-growing region. Was cap. of ancient Vannic kingdom of Ararat. Many of the so-called Vannic inscriptions relating to early Armenian history have been found here. **Lake Van,** area 1,453 sq. mi., is largest in Turkey. It is salty.

vanadium (vŭnā'dēŭm), silver-gray, lustrous metallic element (symbol = V; see also ELEMENT, table). Its oxides are used in dyeing and ceramics, in making ink, and as catalysts; the element is used in alloys. Occurs in various minerals but not uncombined.

Vanbrugh, Sir John (văn'brŭ, vănbrōō'), 1664–1726, English dramatist and architect. Wrote coarse, witty comedies (e.g., *The Provoked Wife,* 1697). Designed Castle Howard (near York) and the palace at Blenheim Park.

Van Buren, Martin, 1782–1862, 8th President of the United States (1837–41). A principal figure in ALBANY REGENCY. As U.S. Secretary of State (1829–31) he was Pres. Jackson's close adviser. U.S. Vice President (1833–37); choice of Jackson as his successor. Panic of 1837 and subsequent hard times brought Van Buren much unpopularity. Wary of the existing banking system, he backed INDEPENDENT TREASURY SYSTEM. In 1840 campaign the Whigs unfairly painted Van Buren as man of great wealth who was out of sympathy with common man. FREE-SOIL PARTY presidential candidate in 1848.

Van Buren. 1 City (pop. 6,413), NW Ark., on Arkansas R. and near Fort Smith. Ships farm produce (chiefly strawberries). Mfg. of metal products. **2** Town (pop. 5,094), NE Maine, on St. John R. and N of Caribou. Trade center in lumbering and potato-growing area.

Vancouver, George (văn"kōō'vŭr), 1758?–1798, English navigator and explorer. Commanded expedition (1791–94) to take over Nootka Sound territory assigned to England and to explore and survey NW coast of America.

Vancouver, city (pop. 344,833), SW B.C., Canada, on Burrard Inlet of the Strait of Georgia, opposite Vancouver Isl., just N of the Wash. line; settled before 1875. Largest city in W Canada and its chief Pacific port and major rail and air terminus, it has shipbuilding, fish canning, lumbering, and mfg. of steel products and furniture. Seat of Univ. of British Columbia (provincially supported; coed.; opened 1915). Stanley Park, one of many, has zoo and noted gardens.

Vancouver, city (pop. 41,664), SW Wash., on Columbia R. (bridged) opposite Portland, Oregon, and near Bonneville Dam. Founded 1825–26 by Hudson's Bay Co. as a fort. Oldest settlement in state; became an American possession 1846. Important port; ships grain and lumber. Mfg. of paper, textiles, aluminum products, and aircraft.

Vancouver Island, 13,049 sq. mi., SW B.C., Canada, largest island off W coast of North America. Separated from mainland by Queen Charlotte Sound and Strait of Georgia (E) and from NW Wash. by Juan de Fuca Strait (S). Heavily forested and mountainous with mining, lumbering, fishing, fruitgrowing, and canning. Largest cities are VICTORIA, NANAIMO, and PORT ALBERNI. Esquimalt is naval base. Visited by English and Spanish explorers in 16th and 17th cent. John Meares built fort on NOOTKA SOUND 1778. Circumnavigated 1792 by Capt. George Vancouver. Became crown colony 1846; united with mainland colony 1866.

Vandalia (văndā'lyů), city (pop. 5,471), S central Ill., on Kaskaskia R. and SSE of Springfield, in farm and oil area. Was second state cap. 1820–39 (Lincoln and Douglas served in legislature here). Old capitol (1836) now state memorial. Was on National Road.

Vandals (văn'důlz), anc. Germanic tribe. They invaded Gaul (406), then moved into Spain and, under GAISERIC, invaded Africa and captured (439) Carthage. They gained control over the Mediterranean but declined after Gaiseric's death (477). Carthage was captured (533) by Belisarius; Vandals soon ceased to exist as a nation. Arian Christians, they severely persecuted Orthodox Christianity. Their destructive reputation may be due to their sack of Rome (455).

Vandenberg, Arthur H(endrick), 1884–1951, U.S. Senator from Mich. (1928–51). Influential Republican leader; joined Democratic administration in bipartisan foreign policy. His nephew, **Hoyt S(anford) Vandenberg,** 1899–, is a general, chief of staff of U.S. Air Force after 1948.

Van der. For names beginning thus and not listed here, see following element; e.g., for Van der Goes, see GOES, HUGO VAN DER.

Vanderbilt, Cornelius, 1794–1877, American railroad magnate. Expanded shipping interests; known as Commodore Vanderbilt. In Civil War entered railroad field and by 1867 controlled New York Central RR. He extended railroad empire and amassed large fortune. Gave money to found Vanderbilt Univ. A son, **William Henry Vanderbilt,** 1821–85, succeeded his father as president of New York Central RR. His son, **Cornelius Vanderbilt,** 1843–99, helped found Cathedral of St. John the Divine in New York city. Another son of W. H. Vanderbilt, **George Washington Vanderbilt,** 1862–1914, donated land for Teachers Col., Columbia Univ.

Vanderbilt University, at Nashville, Tenn.; nonsectarian; coed.; chartered 1872 by Methodists, rechartered 1873, opened 1875 with grant from Cornelius Vanderbilt. Here are geology museum, social science research and training institute, and joint library with George Peabody and Scarritt colleges.

Van der Goes, Hugo: see GOES, HUGO VAN DER.

Vandergrift, borough (pop. 9,524), SW Pa., NE of Pittsburgh. Iron and steel works.

Vanderlyn, John (–lĭn), 1775?–1852, American portrait and historical painter, b. Kingston, N.Y. Studied in Paris under patronage of Aaron Burr. *Landing of Columbus* is in the Capitol, Washington, D.C.

Van der Waals, Johannes Diderik: see WAALS.

Van der Weyden, Roger: see WEYDEN.

Van de Velde or **Vandevelde** (vän"důvĕl'dů), Dutch family of artists. **Jan Van de Velde** (yän), 1593?–c.1641, was a wood engraver. His brother, the marine painter **Willem Van de Velde** (vĭ'lům), c.1611–1693, was the father of **Willem Van de Velde,** 1633–1707, who is famous for his marine paintings, and **Adrian Van de Velde** (ä'drēän), 1636?–1672, the celebrated etcher and animal painter.

Van Doren, Carl (Clinton), 1885–1950, American editor and author. An editor of *The Cambridge History of American Literature* (1917–21), the *Nation* (1919–22), the *Century Magazine* (1922–25), and the *Literary Guild* (1926–34). Works include criticism (e.g., *The American Novel, 1789–1939,* 1940), history (e.g., *The Great Rehearsal,* 1948), and biography (e.g., of Swift, 1930, and of Benjamin Franklin, 1938). His brother, **Mark Van Doren,** 1894–, won a name as a poet and critic; long at Columbia. Works include critical studies (e.g., Dryden, 1920, and of Hawthorne, 1949), anthologies, novels, and several volumes of poetry (e.g., *Collected Poems, 1922–1938,* 1939).

Van Dorn, Earl, 1820–63, Confederate general. In 1862 he commanded in trans-Mississippi district; defeated at Pea Ridge, Ark. Commanded Army of the Mississippi until defeat at Corinth, Miss.; transferred to command of cavalry.

Van Dyck or **Vandyke, Sir Anthony** (both: văn dīk'), 1599–1641, Flemish portrait and religious painter, b. Antwerp. Studied under Rubens. In 1620 he was summoned to England by James I, whose portrait he painted. During his five years in Italy he studied the works of the great Venetians and painted the portraits of the Genoese nobility. Returning in 1627 to Antwerp, he soon rivaled Rubens in popularity. There he painted a series of religious pictures, including the *Crucifixion* (cathedral, Mechlin). After 1632 he lived mainly in England as court painter to Charles I and painted over 350 portraits (partly executed by assistants). His masterly *Deposition* was done on a visit to Antwerp. He also produced a fine series of etched portraits called the *Iconography*.

van Dyke, Henry, 1852–1933, American clergyman, educator, and author, best known for his Christmas story *The Other Wise Man* (1896).

Vane, Sir Henry, 1589–1655, English courtier.

Influential under James I and Charles I, he lost power after he had testified against Strafford. His son, **Sir Henry Vane,** 1613–62, was perhaps the ablest administrator of the Puritan Revolution. While he was governor of Massachusetts (1636), Harvard Col. was founded. Sat in Short and Long Parliaments. Negotiated Solemn League and Covenant with Scotland. Held office under Oliver Cromwell. Executed for treason by Restoration government.

Vanern, Swed. *Vänern* (vĕ'nûrn), lake, area 2,141 sq. mi., SW Sweden, fed by Klar R. and drained by the Gota into the Kattegat. Largest lake in Sweden.

Van Fleet, James A(lward), 1892–, American general, commander of UN forces in Korea (1951–53). Led 8th Infantry Regt., commanded 90th Div. in World War II. Led military mission to Greece (1948–50).

Van Gogh, Vincent: see GOGH, VINCENT VAN.

vanilla, tropical American climbing orchid (genus *Vanilla*) cultivated for the fruits which yield the flavoring vanilla. The fruit is a seed pod called a "bean." Vanilla is also produced synthetically.

van Loon, Hendrik Willem (văn lōn'), 1882–1944, American author and journalist, b. Netherlands; in the U.S. after 1903. Later a newspaper correspondent in Russia and in Belgium. Popular works include histories such as *The Story of Mankind* (1921); *Van Loon's Geography* (1932); and *Simón Bolívar* (1943).

Vannes (vän), city (pop. 23,510), cap. of Morbihan dept., NW France, in Brittany. Surrounding region is rich in megalithic monuments. Inner city has 13th-cent. ramparts.

Vanport, former town, NW Oregon, just N of Portland and on Columbia R. opposite Vancouver, Wash. Built 1942–43 to house World War II shipyard workers (pop. 42,000). Low-cost housing project (pop. c.18,500) after 1945. Destroyed May 30, 1948, by flood.

Van Rensselaer, Stephen, 1764–1839, American statesman and soldier, called the Patroon. Lieutenant governor of N.Y. (1795–1801). Led state militia in War of 1812. Founded school at Troy, N.Y., in 1824, which became Rensselaer Polytechnic Inst.

van't Hoff, Jacobus Hendricus (yäkō'bŭs hĕndrē'kŭs vänt hôf'), 1852–1911, Dutch physical chemist. Won 1901 Nobel Prize for work in chemical dynamics and osmotic electrical conductivity. His studies in molecular structure laid foundation of steriochemistry.

Vanua Levu: see FIJI.

Van Vechten, Carl (văn vĕk'tŭn), 1880–, American critic, novelist, and photographer. His works include criticism, sophisticated novels (e.g., *Nigger Heaven,* 1926), and an autobiography (1932).

Van Wert, city (pop. 10,364), NW Ohio, NW of Lima; settled 1835. Trade and mfg. center in farm area.

Van Zeeland, Paul (pōl' vän zā'länt), 1893–, Belgian economist and statesman; a leader of the Catholic party. As premier (1935–37) he instituted legislation similar to the American New Deal, suppressed the fascist Rexists, adopted neutrality policy. He later championed international economic cooperation; became foreign minister 1949.

vaporization, change of liquid or solid to gas or vapor. Term *gas* is commonly used to describe substance that appears in that form under standard conditions; and *vapor* for substance that is ordinarily liquid or solid. When change is from solid to vapor, it is SUBLIMATION. Vaporization is explained by kinetic molecular theory of matter; when heat is applied to substance at boiling point, molecules move faster and become farther apart until vaporization is complete. Quantity of heat needed to cause vaporization varies for each substance. Heat needed to change one gram water to steam at its boiling point, i.e., heat of vaporization, is c.540 calories. Liquids change to vapors by EVAPORATION at any temperature when surface is exposed in unconfined space.

Var (vär), department (2,325 sq. mi.; pop. 370,688), SE France, in Provence; cap. Draguignan.

Varanger Fjord (väräng'ür fyōr"), inlet of Arctic Ocean, 60 mi. long, NE Norway, near Russian border. S shore has iron mines.

Varangians (vŭrăn'jēŭnz), Scandinavian merchant-warriors who penetrated RUSSIA in 9th cent. Their leader Rurik, according to tradition, estab. himself at Novgorod 862, thus founding Russian state. They gradually merged with the Slavs. From Russia, they raided Volga region and Byzantine Empire. Varangians also served as mercenaries under Byzantine emperors.

Vardar (vär'där), river, c.230 mi. long, rising in S Yugoslavia and flowing W and S through Yugoslav and Greek Macedonia into Aegean Sea near Salonica.

Vardon, Harry, 1870–1939, British golfer. Won British Open (1896, 1898–99, 1903, 1911, 1914), U.S. Open (1900) championships, total of more than 60 important golf tournaments.

Varenius, Bernardus (vŭrē'nēŭs), or **Bernhard Varen** (vä'rŭn), 1622–50, Dutch geographer. Attempted to define geography as a science. His *Geographia generalis* (1650) was standard for a century.

Varennes (värĕn'), village, Meuse dept., NE France. Here Louis XVI and his family were arrested on their attempted flight (1791).

Varèse, Edgard (värĕs'), 1885–, French-American composer. Often uses extreme registers of orchestral instruments or new instruments of electrically produced tone to produce a harshly dissonant effect. Among his works are *Hyperprism* (1923) for wind instruments and percussion; *Ionisation* (1931), for percussion; and *Espace* (1937), a symphony with chorus.

Vargas, Getulio (Dornelles) (zhŭtōō'lyō dôrnĕ'lĭsh vär'gŭsh), 1883–, president of Brazil (1930–45; 1951–). Governor of his native state, Rio Grande do Sul (1928–30), he ran for president and, when defeated, led a successful revolt, becoming provisional president and later president. His social and industrial programs for improvement in Brazil were offset by his autocratic rule by decree. Several revolts (most serious that in São Paulo, 1932) were put down, but he was deposed in

1945 by Eurico Dutra and group of army officers. Re-elected to presidency 1951.

Vargas Zapata y Luján Ponce de León, Diego de (dyā'gō dā vär'gäs thäpä'tä ē lo͞ohän' pōn'thā dā lāōn'), c.1643–1704, Spanish governor and captain general of N.Mex. (1691–97, 1703–4). Resettled N.Mex. for Spanish after Pueblo revolt of 1680.

variable star, star that changes in brightness and often in other characteristics (e.g., color, temperature, atmosphere, apparent diameter). Classifications differ but variable stars are often grouped as temporary stars (novae and supernovae), or Cepheid, long-period, eclipsing, or irregular variables. Novae change from faintness to spectacular brightness; then fade; some recur. Usually reach absolute magnitude of —5 or —6; those reaching greater magnitudes of —14 to —15 called supernovae. Cepheid variables, believed to be pulsating stars, alternately expanding and contracting, are giant yellow stars with periods up to c.50 days. Cycles of long-period variables (red giant and supergiant stars), range from 50 days to two years. Eclipsing variables are double stars that eclipse each other as they revolve around common center. Irregular variables include other variable stars.

varicose vein, chronically enlarged vein. Congestion results from weakness of valves in veins. Commonest in legs and thighs and about rectum (see HEMORRHOIDS).

Varmland, Swed. *Värmland* (věrm'länt), historic province, W central Sweden, N of Vanern lake; cap. Karlstad. Agr.; iron mining and processing; wood products.

Varna, Bulgaria: see STALIN, Bulgaria.

varnish, solution of gum or resin in oil (oil varnish) or in volatile solvent (spirit varnish) or in volatile solvent (spirit varnish) which, on drying, forms hard, usually glossy, film. Shellac is solution of lac in alcohol; enamel is varnish with added pigments; lacquer is either cellulose derivative dissolved in volatile solvent or a natural varnish made in Orient from juice of trees.

Varro, Marcus Terentius, 116 B.C.–27? B.C., Roman man of letters. Most erudite man of his times, he wrote c.120 volumes in all fields of learning. Of his many works only one—*De re rustica libri III* (three books on farming)—remains intact. Six books out of 25 remain of *De lingua latina* (on the Latin language).

Varus, Publius Quintilius (vâ'růs), d. A.D. 9, Roman general defeated by the Germans under Arminius in the Teutoburg Forest. He committed suicide. It is said that later Augustus would cry in his sleep, "Varus, Varus, bring me back my legions!"

Vasa (vä'zů), royal dynasty of Sweden (1523–1654) and of Poland (1587–1668), founded by GUSTAVUS I. Senior line turned Catholic with SIGISMUND III, who was deposed in Sweden, and continued in Poland with Ladislaus IV and JOHN II. It was chronically at war with the Protestant Swedish line (CHARLES IX; GUSTAVUS II; CHRISTINA). Swedish Vasas were succeeded by ZWEIBRÜCKEN dynasty (1654), OLDENBURG dynasty (1751), and Bernadotte dynasty (1818).

Vasa, Finland: see VAASA.

Vasari, Giorgio (jōr'jō väzä'rē), 1511–74, Italian artist. Best known for his *Lives of the Painters,* a series of entertaining if frequently inaccurate biographies of Italian artists. His most famous architectural work is the Uffizi. Also did murals in the Vatican and in Florence cathedral.

Vasco da Gama: see GAMA, VASCO DA.

Vasconcelos, José (hōsā' våskōnsā'lōs), 1882–, Mexican educator and writer. Headed National Univ. of Mexico (1920–24); minister of education (1920–25); forced into exile by his successful opponent for the presidency, Plutarco E. Calles. Worked vigorously to raise literacy rate in Mexico.

Vashti (văsh'tī), queen whom Ahasuerus deposed for disobedience. Esther 1.

Vasily III (vŭsē'lyē), 1479–1533, grand duke of Moscow (1503–33). He rounded out the conquests of his father, Ivan III, annexing Pskov, Ryazan, and Smolensk. Father of Ivan the Terrible.

Vassar, Matthew (vă'sůr), 1792–1868, American philanthropist. He built his fortune with a brewery at Poughkeepsie, N.Y., and founded (1861) what is now VASSAR COLLEGE, giving it more than $800,000.

Vassar College, at Arlington, adjoining Poughkeepsie, N.Y.; nonsectarian, for women; chartered 1861 by Matthew Vassar, opened 1865 as Vassar Female Col., renamed 1867. Pioneered in music, physical education; had first department of euthenics; conducts summer institute of euthenics. Known for work in experimental drama. Its first woman president, Sarah G. Blanding, took office in 1946.

Vasteras, Swed. *Västerås* (věs"tůrōs'), city (pop. 59,990), E central Sweden, on Malaren L. Electrical industry. Important diets convened here, notably the Vasteras Recess (1527), when the church was taken over by the state and Lutheranized.

Vastergotland, Swed. *Västergötland* (vě'-stůryût"länd), historic province of S central Sweden, now divided between Skaraborg and Alvsborg counties.

Vatican (vă'tĭkůn), at Rome, residence of the pope, who is according to the LATERAN TREATY (1929) ruler of **Vatican City** (108.7 acres, pop. c.1,000). It has SAINT PETER'S CHURCH, the Vatican proper (pontifical palaces), basilicas and churches, the BELVEDERE. CASTEL GANDOLFO belongs to the Vatican. It is the heart of the Roman Catholic Church and is entirely churchly. The Papal Court (Curia Romana), administered by cardinals (see CARDINAL), has an austere splendor, defended by the SWISS GUARDS. There are museums of some importance and beautiful chapels, including the SISTINE CHAPEL. The **Vatican Library** (founded 15th cent.) is the oldest public library in the world. Has c.50,000 manuscripts and some 400,000 printed books (many very rare). See also PAPACY; ROMAN CATHOLIC CHURCH.

Vatican Council, 1869–70, 20th ecumenical council of the Roman Catholic Church. Convened when the seizure of the Papal States by Italy was imminent, it had to be prorogued by Pius IX when Italian soldiers took Rome. It was primarily important for the enunciation of the doctrine that the pope when speaking *ex cathedra* on matters of faith and morals cannot be wrong (papal infallibility).

Vatnajökull (vät′näyû′ko͞ol), large ice field, area 3,200 sq. mi., SE Iceland. Rises to a peak 6,952 ft. high, which is surrounded by Oraefajökull glacier.

Vattel, Emerich de (dů vätĕl′), 1714–67, Swiss philosopher and jurist. Set forth principle of a natural law superior to artificial legislation.

Vattern, Swed. *Vättern* (vĕ′tůrn), lake, area 733 sq. mi., S Sweden, draining to Baltic Sea through Motala R. Crossed by Gota Canal. Jonkoping is on its shores.

Vauban, Sébastien le Prestre, marquis de (vōbã), 1633–1707, French military engineer, famous for fortifications of French cities and treatise on fortification; marshal of France.

Vaucluse (vōklüz′), department (1,381 sq. mi.; pop. 249,838), SE France; cap. Avignon. Includes former Comtat Venaissin and principality of Orange. Named for the village of **Vaucluse** (officially, Fontaine-de-Vaucluse), made famous by Petrarch, who lived here.

Vaucouleurs (vōko͞olûr′), town (pop. 2,452), Meuse dept., NE France, on Meuse R. Here Joan of Arc persuaded Robert de Baudricourt, governor of the town, of her mission (winter 1428–29).

Vaud (vō), Ger. *Waadt,* canton (1,239 sq. mi.; pop. 376,707), SW Switzerland, between L. of Geneva, Jura mts., and Bernese Alps; cap. Lausanne. Agr., vineyards. Many resorts. Population is largely French-speaking and Protestant. Vaud was conquered by Bern from Savoy in 1536. Its rebellion (1798) against Bernese rule led to French intervention in Switzerland and creation of Helvetic Republic. Became a canton of Swiss Confederation 1803.

vaudeville (vô′důvĭl, vōd′vĭl), originally a light song, derived from *Vau,* or *Vaux, de Vire,* songs attributed to Olivier Basselin. American vaudeville was a stage entertainment consisting of unrelated sketches, humorous skits, songs, dances, and acrobatic and magic acts. Popular c.1880–c.1932. Attempts have been made to revive it (as in New York in the '50s), and many moving picture houses have "stage shows."

Vaudois, French name of WALDENSES.

Vaudreuil de Cavagnal, Pierre François de Rigaud, marquis de (vōdrû′yů dů kävänyäl′), 1698–1765, last French governor of Canada. After his surrender of Canada to British (1760), he was charged with maladministration, tried in France, and acquitted.

Vaugelas, Claude Favre de (klōd′ fä′vrů dů vōzhůlä′), 1585–1650, French grammarian. He set up, in *Remarques sur la langue française* (1647), usage of cultured people as standard for correct French.

Vaughan, Henry (vôn), 1621–95, British metaphysical poet, b. Wales. Poems (as in *Poems,* 1646; *Olor Iscanus,* 1651; *Silex Scintillans,* 1650; *Thalia Rediviva,* 1678) include secular as well as religious verse (e.g., "I saw Eternity the other night").

Vaughan, Herbert, 1832–1903, English Roman Catholic clergyman, an Oblate Father; archbishop of Westminster (1892–1903); made cardinal 1893.

Vaughan Williams, Ralph, 1872–, English composer, notable for use of English folk elements in music. Among his compositions are six symphonies, including the well-known *London Symphony* (1914; revised 1920), the *Fantasia on a Theme by Thomas Tallis* (1910), operas, choral music, concertos, and songs. Of his many stage works, his ballet *Job* (1930) is perhaps best known.

Vauxhall (vŏks′hôl′), district of Lambeth metropolitan borough, London, England. Named for former Vauxhall Gardens or New Spring Gardens, a fashionable pleasure resort c.1660–1859.

Vavilov, Nikolai Ivanovich (nyĭkůlī′ ēvä′nůvĭch vŭvē′lůf), 1887–?, Russian botanist. Said to have died in a Soviet concentration camp c.1943. His wheat studies indicated Ethiopia and Afghanistan to be birthplaces of agriculture and civilization. He opposed Lysenko's theory of heredity.

Veblen, Thorstein (thôr′stīn vĕ′blůn), 1857–1929, American social scientist. In analyzing the psychological bases of social institutions, he helped found institutional economics. His analyses of the price system, the business cycle, and the role of the technician have had great influence. His works include *The Theory of the Leisure Class* (1899) and *The Theory of Business Enterprise* (1904).

Vecchietta, Il: see LORENZO DI PIETRO.

Veda (vā′dů, vē′–), scriptures of Hinduism, including the oldest, the *Rig-Veda,* containing some 1,000 hymns; the *Sama-Veda,* a rearrangement of hymns from the *Rig-Veda;* the *Yajur-Veda,* including prose formulas. The much later *Atharva-Veda* includes spells and incantations. Immediate inspiration of the Vedas may have been the Aryan conquest of India. Indra was the warlike national god of the Vedas, which are classics of Sanskrit literature. The *Brahmanas* and *Upanishads* later augmented the Vedas.

Vedanta (vĭdän′tů), certain of the UPANISHADS, written after Vedas; also group name for six related philosophic systems interpreting them. The aim of all these philosophies is the extinction of suffering through YOGA. The three stages leading to ultimate knowledge are faith, understanding, and realization. The systems, one builded upon another (from 550 B.C.), include Nyaya, Vaisesika, Samkhya, the Mimamsa, and the Vedanta. Vedanta as a system was founded by Badarayana (fl. sometime between 500 B.C. and A.D. 200) and has a pantheistic doctrine of Brahma (the all-one), known only by intuition; there are varying schools.

Vedder, Elihu (ĕ′lĭhū), 1836–1923, American painter and illustrator, perhaps best known for illustrations for *The Rubáiyát.* Murals in Library of Congress.

veery or **Wilson's thrush,** American woodland thrush. It is reddish brown above with lightly spotted buff and white under parts. Has a delicate song.

Vega, Garcilaso de la: see GARCILASO DE LA VEGA.

Vega Carpio, Lope de: see LOPE DE VEGA CARPIO.

vegetable ivory: see TAGUA.

vegetable marrow, long, slender pumpkin variety, with yellow or green skin, especially popular in Europe.

Veglia, Yugoslavia: see KRK.

Vehmgericht (fām'gürĭkht), **Vehme** (fā'mù), or **vehmic court** (fā'mĭk), unofficial secret criminal tribunal in Middle Ages. Such courts (first estab. in Westphalia to curb lawlessness in era of weak governments), worked through secrecy and terrorism, doing much good but finally becoming menace. As central powers grew stronger in 16th cent., organizations ceased. Also Fehmgericht, Femgericht.

vein, vessel carrying blood from tissues to heart in CIRCULATION OF THE BLOOD. Most veins have valves preventing backward flow of blood. See *ill.*, p. 763.

Veit, Philipp (fĕ'lĭp fīt'), 1793–1877, German historical painter, one of the Nazarenes in Rome.

Velasco, José María (hōsā' märē'ä välä'skō), 1840–1912, Mexican landscape painter; teacher of Diego Rivera. His study of anatomy, botany, and geology enabled him to paint with scientific detail.

Velasco, Luis de (lwēs' dā välä'skō), d. 1564, Spanish administrator, second viceroy of New Spain (1550–64). An energetic, honest humanitarian, he did much to improve lot of Indians; sent out numerous exploring expeditions. Univ. of Mexico was founded (1553) during his administration. His son, **Luis de Velasco,** 1534–1617, was viceroy of New Spain (1590–95; 1607–11) and of Peru (1595–1604). Continued work of his father in Mexico by aiding Indians and extending conquests. Similar achievements marked his administration in Peru. Was later president of Council of the Indies and was granted title marqués de Salinas.

Velasco (vùlă'skō), town (pop. 2,260), S Texas, on Brazos R. opposite Freeport. Texans defeated Mexican garrison here 1832; treaty ending Texas Revolution signed here 1836. Revived by Freeport Boom.

Velázquez, Diego de (dēā'gō dā väläth'kāth), c.1460–1524?, Spanish conquistador, first governor of Cuba. Sailed with Christopher Columbus on second voyage to Hispaniola (1493) and was sent out by Diego Columbus to command expedition to conquer Cuba (1511). Completing conquest by 1514, he continued colonization and established himself as governor of island (he was later named *adelantado* by king of Spain). It was he who commissioned Hernán Cortés to conquer Mexico (1519). Later he sent Pánfilo de Narváez in an unsuccessful attempt to bring Cortés to obedience.

Velázquez, Diego Rodríguez de Silva y, 1599–1660, celebrated painter of the Spanish school, b. Seville; son of a lawyer of Portuguese descent. Studied with Francisco de Herrera and Francisco Pacheco. Moving to Madrid (1622) he became court painter to Philip IV, a post he held for the rest of his life. The famous *Borrachos* [the topers] (Prado) was done in his early period at court. On his first visit to Italy (1629–31) he painted the *Forge of Vulcan* and two landscapes of the Villa Medici gardens. To his second period (1631–49) belong the famous equestrian portraits of the king and the condé de Olivares, the *Surrender of Breda* (all: Prado), and the portrait of Philip IV (Frick Coll., New York). His superb portrait of Pope Innocent X was done on his second visit to Italy (1649–51). Outstanding works of his last period include the series of dwarfs and buffoons of the court, the portrait of the Infanta Margarita, and *Maids of Honor*.

veld or **veldt** (both: vĕlt) [Dutch,= field], term applied to grassy, undulating plateaus of South Africa and Southern Rhodesia. Elevation ranges from 500 to 6,000 ft. Used mainly for stockraising.

Velde, Van de: see VAN DE VELDE.

Vélez de Guevara, Luis (vā'lāth dā gävä'rä), 1579?–1644, Spanish author of picaresque novel, *El diablo cojuelo* (1641), many plays.

Vellore (vùlôr'), city (pop. 71,502), E central Madras, India, on Palar R. Was strategic military base during 18th-cent. struggle between French and English for dominance in India.

Velsen (vĕl'sùn), municipality (pop. 41,329), North Holland prov., W Netherlands, near mouth of North Sea Canal. Center of steel industry.

velvetweed, tall annual plant of genus *Abutilon*, also called Indian mallow. It has velvety leaves and yellow flowers. A weed in the U.S., it is grown in its native Asia as "Chinese jute" for fiber.

Venaissin (vŭnĕsē') or **Comtat Venaissin** (kōtä'), district in Vaucluse dept., SE France, in Provence, around Avignon; cap. Carpentras. Was acquired by popes 1274; annexed to France 1791.

Venantius Fortunatus, Latin poet: see FORTUNATUS.

Vendée (vãdā'), department (2,709 sq. mi.; pop. 393,787), W France, on Atlantic coast, in Poitou; cap. La Roche-sur-Yon. In 1793 the devoutly Catholic peasants of the Vendeé united with the local nobility in a formidable insurrection against the French revolutionary government. Under such leaders as Cathelineau, Charrette de la Contrie, and La Rochejaquelein, the Vendeans fought ably and heroically and soon controlled most of NW France save Nantes, but they suffered severe defeats in 1794. After Robespierre's overthrow, they concluded an advantageous peace with the central government (1795), but warfare recommenced in 1796. The royalist émigrés and the English, who had instigated the new revolt, abandoned the Vendeans to their fate after Gen. Hoche's victory over an émigré landing party at Quiberon. Hoche's moderation helped to pacify the region in 1796.

Vendémiaire (vãdāmyĕr'), first month of French Revolutionary Calendar. On 13 Vendémiaire, Year IV (Oct. 5, 1795), Napoleon Bonaparte leaped into fame by putting down an insurrection, at Paris, against the establishment of the Directory. His use of artillery he described as a "whiff of grapeshot."

Vendôme, César, duc de (sāzär' dük' dù vãdōm'), 1594–1665, French general; natural son of Henry IV and Gabrielle d'Estrées. Was imprisoned (1626–30) for conspiring against Richelieu. Fought on government side in the Fronde, taking Bordeaux (1653) and defeating Spanish fleet at Barcelona

EGYPTIAN CHARIOT
ASSYRIAN CHARIOT
GREEK CHARIOT
CAMBODIAN CHARIOT
NORSE SLEDGE
HORSE LITTER
CHAISE OR SHAY
SEDAN CHAIR
GEORGE WASHINGTON'S COACH
BAROUCHE
SPRING VICTORIA
BROUGHAM
SURREY
FULL-TOP CABRIOLET
LANDAU
HANSOM CAB
GIG
JINRIKISHA

(1655). His grandson, **Louis Joseph, duc de Vendôme** (lwē' zhôzĕf'), 1654–1712, marshal of France, fought in War of Spanish Succession. He defeated his cousin, Eugene of Savoy, at Cassano (1705); was sent to Flanders (1706), where he was successful against Eugene and Marlborough until defeated at Oudenarde (1708); expelled allies from Spain (1710).

Vendôme (vãdōm'), town (pop. 7,907), Loir-et-Cher dept., N central France. Was cap. of a county (duchy from 1515), which as part of the Bourbon lands was united with royal domain in 1589.

venereal disease (vůnēr'ēůl), infectious disease acquired usually through sexual relationships. Includes SYPHILIS and GONORRHEA. Creates problem of institutional care of victims and support of dependents. Publicity campaign (1937) resulted in legislation requiring syphilis test before marriage and during pregnancy and in spreading knowledge of how to obtain treatment. See also SOCIAL HYGIENE.

Venetia (vůnē'shů), Ital. *Veneto,* region (7,098 sq. mi.; pop. 3,566,136), NE Italy, between the Alps (N) and the Po R. and Adriatic Sea (S); cap. VENICE. Other cities include PADUA, VERONA, Vicenza. Fertile Venetian plain and Alpine foothills produce grain, grapes, fruit. Sericulture. Named for the ancient Veneti, who came under Roman rule 2d cent. B.C., Venetia suffered heavily in the barbarian invasions. After the 10th cent. the mainland towns developed into free communes, but by the 15th cent. most of present Venetia had been absorbed by the powerful republic of Venice, whose subsequent history it shared. Venetia passed to Austria 1797; to the Napoleonic kingdom of Italy 1805; to Austria 1814 (as part of Lombardo-Venetian kingdom); to Italy 1866. After World War II, Udine prov. was detached to become part of FRIULI-VENEZIA GIULIA.

Venezia, Italy: see VENICE.

Venezia Giulia (vānā'tsyä jōō'lyä), former administrative region, NE Italy, on the Adriatic, formed after World War I from territories ceded by Austria (E FRIULI, Trieste, ISTRIA, part of CARNIOLA). FIUME was added 1921. Inland population is mostly Slovenian. After World War II most of region was ceded to Yugoslavia and the Free Territory of TRIESTE. The rest was merged with Udine prov. to form new Italian region of FRIULI-VENEZIA GIULIA.

Veneziano, Domenico: see DOMENICO VENEZIANO.

Venezia Tridentina: see TRENTINO-ALTO ADIGE.

Venezuela (vĕnŭzwā'lů), republic (352,141 sq. mi.; pop. 4,985,716, not counting some 100,000 Indians not included in the census), N South America; cap. CARACAS. Faces on the Caribbean in the N and has four geographic areas. The coastal lowlands are rich with petroleum around L. Maracaibo, and oil is the chief export of the country. Off the coast lie the islands of Trinidad (British) and Margarita (Venezuelan). The ORINOCO basin has vast plains, the *llanos,* which support the cattle industry of Venezuela. The GUIANA HIGHLANDS are mostly unknown and unexplored. The mountains in the W (a continuation of the Andes) have most of the population. Coffee is grown on the cool slopes, cacao in the foothills. Chief cities of the country besides Caracas are MARACAIBO, Coro, Puerto Cabello, Cumaná, BARQUISIMETO, and VALENCIA. Columbus discovered the mouth of the Orinoco in 1498, and settlements were estab. on the coast in the early 16th cent., but conquest of the interior was accomplished by German adventurers (notably Nicolás Federmann). Associated with New Granada, Venezuela was much raided by buccaneers. Francisco de MIRANDA began (1810) the war for independence from Spain, which was successful only under the leadership of Bolívar, who made it part of Greater Colombia. In 1830 José Antonio Páez led a successful separatist movement, and Venezuela became a republic largely dominated since by *caudillos* (José T. Monagas, 1847–68; Antonio Guzmán Blanco, 1870–88; Cipriano Castro, 1901–8; Juan Vicente Gómez, 1908–35). The Spanish Conquest left a heritage of conflict between great landholders (often absentee) and propertyless workers which still goes on. A new constitution in 1947 provided for election of the president, but disorders continue.

Venezuela Boundary Dispute, diplomatic controversy arising over the limits of territory Venezuela inherited from Spain and Great Britain acquired in Guiana from the Dutch. Discovery of gold in the disputed region sharpened the issue. Great Britain refused to arbitrate the matter, and Venezuela in 1887 broke off diplomatic relations. The U.S., intervening under the Monroe Doctrine, was rebuffed by Britain, and Pres. Cleveland sent a message to Congress (1895), denouncing the British refusal to arbitrate. Difficulties in S Africa made the British conciliatory. An American Commission was appointed and in 1899 made an award generally favorable to Britain.

Venezuela Claims. In 1902, because of the internal chaotic conditions and longstanding public and private debts, Great Britain, Germany, and Italy sent a joint naval expedition against Venezuela to secure redress for their nationals. Theodore Roosevelt took no action, and refused to act as arbiter. The resentment of Spanish-American nations over the violation of sovereignty resulted in the DRAGO DOCTRINE. The claims were adjusted by mixed commissions in 1903.

Venice (vĕ'nĭs), Ital. *Venezia,* city (pop. 170,830; with suburbs, 264,027), cap. of Venetia, NE Italy, built on 118 islets within a lagoon in the Gulf of Venice (N end of Adriatic Sea). It is linked with the mainland by rail and highway bridges. On near-by islands are Murano (glass mfg.), the Lido (beach resort); Porto Marghera, the new port, is on the mainland. Famed for its splendid palaces and churches, its hundreds of canals and bridges, it is a major tourist resort and has a unique wealth of art treasures. Its narrow lanes and arched bridges allow only pedestrian traffic; all other traffic is by water. Settled by refugees from barbarian invaders (5th cent.), Venice became in 697 a republican city-state headed by an elected doge [duke]. Rising to a major maritime power, it conquered (10th–15th cent.) most of DAL-

MATIA, all VENETIA, CYPRUS, CRETE, and other Greek islands and ruled the Mediterranean as "queen of the seas." Its government early passed to a patrician oligarchy; after 1310 the Council of TEN controlled the state. Decline set in in the late 15th cent. By 1715 Venice had lost most of its Greek possessions to Turkey. In 1797 the republic fell without a blow to Bonaparte, who gave it to Austria. An anti-Austrian insurrection (1848–49) was put down, but in 1866 Venice and Venetia were united with Italy. Much of Venetian architecture shows Byzantine influences; later architecture is a graceful baroque (e.g., churches of San Giorgio Maggiore and Santa Maria della Salute). At the city's center are St. Mark's Square and the Piazzetta, with SAINT MARK'S CHURCH (see of the patriarch of Venice) and the Gothic doges' palace, joined by the BRIDGE OF SIGHS to the former prisons. The Grand Canal, chief traffic artery, is spanned by the RIALTO bridge. The churches and palaces of Venice contain treasures of Venetian painting, which reached its zenith with TITIAN, TINTORETTO, and Paolo VERONESE.

Venice (vĕ′nĭs), city (pop. 6,226), SW Ill., on the Mississippi opposite St. Louis. Steel mills.

Venizelos, Eleutherios (ĕlĕfthâ′rēôs vĕnēzĕ′lôs), 1864–1936, Greek statesman, b. Crete, leader of republican liberals. Six times premier (1910–15, 1915, 1917–20, 1924, 1928–32, 1933), he secured union of Crete with Greece (1913); led Greece victoriously through Balkan Wars (1912–13); set up a provisional pro-Allied government at Salonica (1915); led Greece into World War I after King Constantine's abdication (1917); secured establishment of Greek republic (1924); organized armed uprisings in Crete and elsewhere in unsuccessful attempt to prevent restoration of monarchy (1935). Died in exile.

Venlo (vĕn′lō), municipality (pop. 26,822), Limburg prov., SE Netherlands, on Maas (Meuse) R. and near German border. Industrial center (lumber, chemicals, electric bulbs, optical instruments).

ventilation, process of supplying fresh air to an enclosed space and removing undesirable odors, gases, and smoke. Proper ventilation requires circulation of air within the space, and maintenance of temperature and humidity that allows adequate evaporation of perspiration from skin. Injurious effects in badly ventilated room are largely the result of interference with heat-regulating mechanism of body; formerly it was thought that ill effects were caused solely by increase in carbon dioxide and decrease in oxygen. Creation of currents depends upon fact that warm air, being lighter than cold air, tends to rise, thus creating an area of low pressure into which cooler air flows. When heating systems are in use care must be taken to avoid overheating and extreme lowering of humidity. If a fuel-burning device is used in an enclosed space a supply of fresh air must be provided since the burning fuel exhausts the oxygen and forms poisonous carbon monoxide. Mechanical devices are used where simple ventilating methods are inadequate. Air conditioning systems are independent of outdoor atmospheric conditions and can therefore maintain indoor air at most healthful temperature and humidity.

Ventnor (vĕnt′nŭr) health resort, on Isle of Wight, England. Has tuberculosis sanatoriums.

Ventnor or **Ventnor City,** resort city (pop. 8,158), SE N.J., on Absecon Beach SW of Atlantic City.

Ventspils (vĕnts′pēls), Ger. *Windau,* city (pop. 15,671), NW Latvia; an icefree port on Baltic Sea. City grew around 13th-cent. castle of Livonian Knights.

Ventura (vĕntōō′rŭ), city (pop. 16,534), S Calif., on Pacific coast and NW of Los Angeles, in farm and oil area. Here is restored mission of San Buenaventura (city's official name) founded 1782.

Venus, in Roman religion, goddess of vegetation, later identified with Greek APHRODITE. In imperial times she was worshiped as Venus Genetrix, mother of Aeneas; Venus Felix, bringer of good fortune; Venus Victrix, bringer of victory; and Venus Verticordia, protector of feminine chastity. Famous statues of her are *Venus of Milo* or *Melos* (Louvre) and *Venus of Medici* or *Medicean Aphrodite* (Uffizi).

Venus, in astronomy, PLANET second in distance from sun. Revolves about sun at mean distance of 67,200,000 mi. in c.225 days. Diameter c.7,575 mi. Rotation period not known because planet is masked by layers of clouds or vapor. Appears as brilliant star in evening or morning sky. Displays phases similar to moon's. Transits across sun's disk occur in June or December. Has no known satellite. See *ill.*, p. 1187.

Venus's-flytrap, insectivorous perennial plant (*Dionaea muscipula*), native to moist, acid places in the Carolinas. Its leaves, hinged at the midrib, close when touched. Insects trapped between the halves of the leaves are digested.

Veracruz (väräkrōōs′), state (27,759 sq. mi.; pop. 2,057,175), E Mexico; cap. JALAPA. Stretching c.430 mi. along Gulf of Mexico, it rises from tropical coastal plain to temperate valleys and highlands of Sierra Madre Oriental. From tropical forests come dyewoods and hardwoods, chicle, rubber; from semitropical and temperate zones, cattle, sugar cane, cacao, coffee, vanilla, tobacco, cotton, fruits. Minerals are largely unexploited. Coast discovered by Grijalva (1518); became state 1824. Important cities are VERACRUZ, ORIZABA, CÓRDOBA.

Veracruz, city (pop. 71,720), Veracruz, E Mexico, on Gulf of Mexico E of Mexico city, rivaling Tampico as republic's chief port. Cortés landed 1519 near site later chosen for present city (1599). Has played an important part throughout Mexico's history and is today center of important oil region. Was last stronghold of Spanish in the revolution; was attacked by French in 1838, and Santa Anna won reputation for defense; taken by Winfield Scott in 1847, by Spanish, French, and British in 1861. Landing of U.S. forces in 1914 caused an international incident.

verbena, tender perennial, often shrubby, plant of genus *Verbena,* chiefly native to America. The variously colored showy flowers in broad clusters are grown as annuals in northern gardens. Verbenas are often called vervain. The fragrant lemon verbena (*Lippia citriodora*) is unrelated.

Verboeckhoven, Eugène Joseph (vůrbŏŏk-hō'-vůn), 1798–1881, Belgian animal painter.

Vercingetorix (vûr"sĭnjĕ'tůrĭks), d. 46 B.C., leader of the Gauls in a revolt against Rome put down by Julius Caesar, who besieged and took the fort of Alesia (52 B.C.). After gracing Caesar's triumph, Vercingetorix was put to death.

Verde (vĕr'dē), river, central Ariz., rising N of Prescott, flowing c.190 mi. S to Salt R. above Phoenix. Contains Bartlett Dam (see SALT RIVER VALLEY).

Verde, Cape (vûrd), westernmost extremity of Africa, on coast of Senegal.

Verdi, Guiseppe (jŏŏzĕp'pē vār'dē), 1813–1901, Italian composer. A master of dramatic composition, he is known for his operas, including *Rigoletto* (1851), *Il Trovatore* and *La Traviata* (both 1853), *Un ballo in maschera* (1859); *La forza del destino* (1862), and *Aïda* (1871). Three of his operas are based on plays of Shakspere—*Macbeth* (1847), and the two masterpieces of his old age, *Otello* (1887) and *Falstaff* (1893). His *Requiem* and *Stabat Mater* are also well known. Verdi is the outstanding figure of 19th-cent. Italian opera.

verdict, official decision of a JURY on questions of fact laid before it by a judge. A general verdict is one of "guilty" or "not guilty." A special verdict answers specific question or questions and leaves decision to judge. The judge in no criminal case may modify the verdict of "not guilty."

verdigris (vûr'důgrēs), greenish basic acetate of copper or mixture of copper acetates, formed on surface of copper plates which have been treated with acid. Poisonous; sometimes used as green pigment, mordant in dyeing, in medicine.

Verdun, city (pop. 77,391), S Que., Canada, on S shore of Montreal Isl., S suburb of Montreal.

Verdun (vĕrdŭn', Fr. vĕrdũ'), town (pop. 12,-948), Meuse dept., NE France, on the Meuse. Annexed to France 1552, it became after 1871 a key fortress and was in 1916 the scene of the longest and bloodiest battle of World War I. Of 2,000,000 men engaged, 1,000,000 were killed. Douaumont and Vaux, two outer fortresses, were taken by the Germans, but Verdun itself, under Marshal Pétain and Gen. Nivelle, repulsed all assaults. "They shall not pass" was the rallying phrase of the French. The city and battlefields, with huge military cemeteries, are a national sanctuary.

Verdun, Treaty of, 843, partition of Frankish empire among three sons of Emperor Louis I. Louis the German received E portion (Germany); Charles II, the W (France); Emperor Lothair I, the center (LOTHARINGIA, Burgundy, Provence, Italy).

Vereeniging (vůrā'nĭgĭng), city (pop. 40,490), S Transvaal, South Africa, on Vaal R. Treaty ending South African War was signed here (1902). Steel center in largest coal-mining region of South Africa.

Vérendrye, Pierre Gaultier de Varennes, sieur de la (pyĕr' gōtyā' dů vārĕn' syûr dů lä vārādrē'), 1685–1749, explorer in N Great Plains of W Canada and U.S. Estab. fur-trading posts.

Verendrye National Monument: see NATIONAL PARKS AND MONUMENTS (table).

Verga, Giovanni (jōvä'nē vĕr'gä), 1840–1922, Italian realistic novelist, b. Sicily. Outstanding works include *Cavalleria rusticana* (1880), *The House by the Medlar Tree* (1881), *Mastro-don Gesualdo* (1889).

Vergennes, Charles Gravier, comte de (shärl' grävyā' kōt' dů vĕrzhĕn'), 1717–87, French foreign minister under Louis XVI. Supported American Revolution—secretly at first, officially after signing alliance of 1778 with Benjamin Franklin.

Vergennes (vůrjĕnz'), city (pop. 1,736), W Vt., S of Burlington, near L. Champlain. Trade center of dairy region. Macdonough's fleet built here in War of 1812.

Vergil or **Virgil** (Publius Vergilius Maro) (both: vûr'jĭl), 70 B.C.–19 B.C., Roman poet, b. near Mantua. The son of a farmer, he received a good education and finally went (after 41 B.C.) to Rome and joined the circle patronized by Maecenas and Augustus. His *Eclogues,* or *Bucolics* (37 B.C.), after the Greek Theocritus, idealize rural life, while his *Georgics* (30 B.C.), also in praise of rural life, were more didactic and realistic. He devoted his remaining years to the AENEID, a national epic and a literary masterpiece, which owes much to Homer. Illness prevented its revision, and he would have burned the manuscript but for Augustus. Vergil is the dominant figure in Latin literature.

Verhaeren, Émile (āmēl' vārärĕn', vůrhä'růn), 1855–1916, Belgian poet. His feverishly imaginative style has affinities with symbolism. His themes are primarily social and humanitarian, as in *Les Villes tentaculaires* [grasping cities] (1895) and his great war poems, *Les Ailes rouges de la guerre* [red wings of war] (1917).

Veria, Macedonia, Greece: see VEROIA.

Verkhoyansk (vyĕrkhŭyänsk'), town (pop. over 500), N Yakut ASSR, RSFSR, in N Siberia. Fur-trading post. Lies in coldest part of the earth (lowest temperature recorded, −92°F.). The **Verkhoyansk Range,** a mountain chain between the Lena and Aldan rivers, rises to 8,000 ft. It has coal, silver, lead, and zinc deposits.

Verlaine, Paul (pôl' vĕrlĕn'), 1844–96, French poet, first of the SYMBOLISTS. His attempt at killing his friend RIMBAUD earned him two years' imprisonment. Though this sobering experience led Verlaine back to the Catholic faith and good resolutions (evidenced in *Sagesse,* 1881), his later years were spent in abject drunkenness. Aside from *Sagesse* his best-known collections of verse include *Romances sans paroles* (1874), *Jadis et Naguère* (1884), and *Parallèlement* (1889). At its best, his musical verse is extremely evocative and moving.

Vermeer, Jan or **Johannes** (vůrmēr', Du. yän' vůr-mār', yōhä'nůs), 1632–75, one of the great Dutch painters, b. Delft. Also known as Vermeer of Delft and as Jan or Johannes van der Meer. Excelled in painting subtle gradations of light. His intimate interiors, often with the solitary figure of a woman, are painted with almost mirror-like naturalism. A slow worker, he produced less than 40 paintings. Among most famous works is *Young Woman with a Water Jug* (Metropolitan Mus.).

Vermigli, Pietro Martire (pyā'trō märtē'rā vĕrmē'lyē), 1500–1562, Italian Protestant reformer, known as Peter Martyr. An honored Augustinian scholar and preacher, he became a Protestant and fled from persecution to Switzerland and, at the invitation of Archbishop Cranmer, to England, where he taught at Oxford (1547–53), later at Strasbourg and Zurich.

Vermilion, iron range in Minnesota: see MESABI.

vermilion, vivid red pigment, lasting and durable. It is red sulphide of mercury. Used in paints to protect iron and steel. Imitation vermilion is prepared from red lead or basic red chromate.

Vermillion, city (pop. 5,337), extreme SE S.Dak., E of Yankton and on Vermillion R. Farm trade center. Seat of Univ. of South Dakota (state supported; coed; chartered 1862, opened 1882).

Vermont, state (9,609 sq. mi.; pop. 377,747), NE U.S.; admitted 1791 as 14th state (free); cap. MONTPELIER. Other cities are BURLINGTON, RUTLAND, BARRE, BRATTLEBORO. Bordered E by Connecticut R., partly W by L. Champlain. Mountain ranges run N–S, most prominent being GREEN MOUNTAINS (center of state), TACONIC MOUNTAINS (SW). Dairy farming is chief occupation; corn, oats, potatoes, apples, maple syrup, other agr. products. Mining (granite, lime, talc, slate, asbestos). Mfg. of machinery, cut stone, wood products, paper, textiles. A summer and winter resort area. Champlain was first white man to enter area (1609). Region was object of conflicting N.H. and N.Y. claims after 1740. GREEN MOUNTAIN BOYS, under Ethan ALLEN, resisted N.Y. authority. Vt. declared its independence 1777. Settlement was rapid. SAINT ALBANS was scene of Confederate raid in Civil War (1864). State has been dominated by Republican party since party's rise in 19th cent.

Vermont, University of, and State Agricultural College: see BURLINGTON.

vermouth (vûrmo͞oth'), blended, fortified white wine, flavored with aromatic substances. It is used as an appetizer and in cocktails. Italian vermouth is sweeter and darker than French.

Vernadsky, Vladimir Ivanovich (vlŭdyē'mĭr ēvä'nŭvĭch vĕrnät'skē), 1863–1945, Russian scientist. He introduced method of determining age of rocks and minerals based on measurable rate of radioactivity. Contributed to knowledge of mineralogy, geochemistry, and isomorphism of chemical elements.

Vernal (vûr'nŭl), city (pop. 2,845), NE Utah, near Dinosaur Natl. Monument.

Verne, Jules (vûrn; zhül' vĕrn'), 1828–1905, French novelist, father of modern science fiction. Author of *From the Earth to the Moon* (1865), *Twenty Thousand Leagues under the Sea* (1870), and *The Tour of the World in Eighty Days* (1873).

Vernet (vĕrnā'), French family of artists. **Claude Joseph Vernet,** 1714–89, marine painter, studied with his father, Antoine Vernet, a decorative artist. His son **Antoine Charles Horace Vernet,** 1758–1835, called Carle Vernet, was a popular lithographer and painter of hunt scenes. Antoine's son **Émile Jean Horace Vernet,** 1789–1863, was one of most popular military painters of 19th cent.

Vernon, city (pop. 7,822), S B.C., Canada, SE of Kamloops. Fruitgrowing center with processing plants, woodworking, and mfg. of cement.

Vernon. 1 See ROCKVILLE, Conn. **2** City (pop. 12,651), N Texas, near Pease R. and NW of Wichita Falls; founded 1880 on Dodge City cattle trail. Highway and processing center for agr. and oil area, it has meat packing and cotton and cottonseed processing.

Vero Beach (vē'rō), resort city (pop. 4,746), E Fla., on Indian R. and NE of L. Okeechobee. McKee Jungle Gardens (opened 1931) are near.

Veroia or **Veria** (both: vĕ'rēä), town, Macedonia, Greece, W of Salonica. Anciently called Berea or Beroea. Paul preached here. Acts 17.10.

Verona (vûrō'nŭ, Ital. vārō'nä), city (pop. 84,862), Venetia, N Italy, on Adige R. and Brenner road. A commercial and strategic center since Roman times, it became a free commune in the 11th cent. Verona led a league of towns which merged with the LOMBARD LEAGUE in its struggle against the Hohenstaufen emperors, but in 1226 the Ghibelline EZZELINO DA ROMANO took control, and the Ghibelline Della Scala family became lords of Verona in 1277. The story of Romeo and Juliet recalls the Guelph-Ghibelline strife of the time. Verona reached its greatest power under Can Francesco della SCALA, but it fell to Milan 1387 and to Venice 1405. Under Austrian rule (1797–1805, 1814–66) Verona was the chief fortress of N Italy. At the end of World War II the Germans blew up Verona's early Roman stone bridge and the famous pinnacled Ponte Scaligero (built 1354). The Romanesque cathedral suffered bomb damage, but many other monuments survive—the huge Roman amphitheater, the 12th-cent. city hall; the Gothic Scaligeri tombs, the 14th-cent. castle; and the Renaissance Loggia del Consiglio. Birthplace of Paolo Veronese. The **Congress of Verona,** 1822, last meeting held under the provisions of the QUADRUPLE ALLIANCE of 1814, gave France a mandate for suppressing the revolution against Ferdinand VII of Spain. England protested the decision.

Verona, borough (pop. 10,921), NE N.J., near Montclair. Metal products.

Veronese, Paolo (pä'ōlō vārōnā'zä), 1528–88, celebrated Italian painter of the Venetian school, b. Verona. Real name was Paolo Caliari. In Venice after 1553, he executed many important works for the ducal palace and the Church of San Sebastiano. His decorative genius is revealed in all his works, including the many religious feast scenes (e.g., *Supper at Emmaus,* Louvre). The well-known *Rape of Europa* is now in the ducal palace. His use of cool, clear color harmonies anticipated the 18th-cent. style (esp. of Tiepolo).

veronica, plant: see SPEEDWELL.

Verrazano, Giovanni da (vĕr″rätsä′nō), c.1480–1527?, Italian navigator and explorer, in service of France. Explored North American coast (1524).

Verrocchio, Andrea del (ändrā′ä dĕl vĕr-rôk′-kyō), 1435–88, Florentine sculptor and painter of the early Renaissance. Studied under Donatello and later taught Leonardo da Vinci. Did the famous equestrian statue of Bartolomeo Colleoni in Venice.

Versailles (vûrsālz′, vûrsī′, Fr. vĕrsī′), city (pop. 63,114), cap. of Seine-et-Oise dept., N France, SW of Paris. It grew around the palace built for Louis XIV by Louis Le Vau and J. H. Mansart. Charles Le Brun was the chief decorator; Lenôtre laid out the park and gardens, with their magnificent fountains, reservoirs, and sculptures. Construction began 1661; Louis XIV moved his court to Versailles 1682, but many later additions were made, notably the Grand and Petit TRIANON palaces. The cost and labor involved were staggering, but Versailles became the world's most famous palace and remains the crowning glory of the classic age of France. The French Revolution forced Louis XVI to move to the Tuileries in Paris (1790). Louis Philippe made Versailles a national monument and museum.

Versailles, Treaty of, name of several treaties signed at palace of Versailles. For treaty of **1783,** see PARIS, TREATY OF, 1783. In preliminary treaty of **1871,** ending FRANCO-PRUSSIAN WAR and ratified by Treaty of Frankfurt, France ceded most of Alsace and part of Lorraine to Germany and agreed to pay $1,000,000,000 as indemnity. Treaty of **1919,** between Allies of World War I (except Russia) and Germany, embodied the result of the Paris Peace Conference of 1918–19. The "Big Four" in the negotiations were Pres. Wilson (U.S.), Clemenceau (France), Lloyd George (Britain), and Orlando (Italy). Wilson had to sacrifice his FOURTEEN POINTS but obtained inclusion of covenant of LEAGUE OF NATIONS in treaty. Germany, not represented in negotiations, accepted treaty after futile protests. It accepted burden of REPARATIONS payments; restored Alsace and Lorraine to France; ceded Prussian Poland and most of West Prussia to Poland. Treaty provided for plebiscites in Upper SILESIA, N SCHLESWIG, EUPEN, and Malmédy; placed SAAR TERRITORY under French administration; placed German colonies under League of Nations MANDATES; made Danzig a free city; limited German army and armaments; provided for Allied occupation and subsequent demilitarization of RHINELAND. The U.S. Senate refused to ratify the treaty. Hitler unilaterally abrogated most of its terms after 1935.

vers libre: see FREE VERSE.

vertebral column: see SPINAL COLUMN.

vertebrate (vûr′tûbrāt″), any animal having a spinal column. Subphylum Vertebrata (Craniata) is divided into classes including fish, amphibians, reptiles, birds, mammals. Vertebrates have internal skeleton of bone and cartilage or cartilage alone, spinal cord, brain enclosed in cranium, heart with two, three, or four chambers, and a maximum of four limbs (variously modified). Phylum Chordata comprises Vertebrata and three subphyla of primitive marine forms having gelatinous rod or notochord but no true spinal column.

vervain: see VERBENA.

Verviers (vĕrvyā′), town (pop. 40,422), Liége prov., E Belgium. Metal goods, textiles.

Vervins, Treaty of (vĕrvē′), 1598, between France and Spain; signed at Vervins, Aisne dept., N France. Spain withdrew support from Catholic League; Wars of Religion thus ended with victory of Henry IV.

Very, Jones, 1813–80, American poet; friend of Thoreau and of Emerson, who helped him edit his mystical *Essays and Poems* (1839).

Vesalius, Andreas (vĭsā′lēûs), 1514–64, Flemish anatomist whose discoveries overthrew many doctrines of Galen. While professor at Univ. of Padua he produced *De humani corporis fabrica* (1543), illustrated work on human anatomy based on dissections.

Vespasian (vĕspā′zhûn), A.D. 9–A.D. 79, Roman emperor (A.D. 69–A.D. 79), founder of the Flavian dynasty; proclaimed emperor by the soldiers. The warfare he waged against Jewish rebels was completed by his son TITUS. Vespasian built the Colosseum.

Vespucci, Amerigo (ämārē′gō vāspōōt′chē), 1454–1512, Italian navigator. Discovered and explored mouths of the Amazon (1499), sailed along N shore of South America. Evolved system for computing nearly exact longitude. His acceptance of South America as a new continent greatly altered cosmography. Name America was used to honor him.

Vesta, in Roman religion, goddess of hearth and home, identified with Greek HESTIA. Her temple in Rome had undying fire tended by VESTAL virgins.

vestal, in Roman religion, priestess of Vesta. The six vestals in temple at Rome were daughters of best families, dedicated to Vesta in childhood and trained in obedience and chastity, though they could marry after 30 years. Their duties included preparation of sacrifices and tending of sacred fire. Their influence was great. Penalty for breaking of vows was burial alive after public funeral.

Vesteralen Islands, Norway: see LOFOTEN.

Vestmannaeyjar, Iceland: see WESTMAN ISLANDS.

Vestris, Lucia Elizabeth (Bartolozzi) (vĕ′strĭs), 1797–1856, English actress and manager; first woman lessee of a theater. Produced (after 1831) extravaganzas and Shaksperian comedies.

Vesuvius (vûsōō′vēûs), Ital. *Vesuvio,* only active volcano on European mainland, S Italy, near E shore of Bay of Naples. Height of main cone varies (now 3,891 ft.). Fertile lower slopes have famous Lachryma Christi vineyards. Funicular railway reaches almost to crater rim. Seismological observatory at 1,995 ft. Most famous eruption was that of A.D. 79, which destroyed Pompeii and Herculaneum.

vetch, weak-stemmed leguminous plant of genus *Vicia,* chiefly annual. Common or spring vetch or tare (*Vicia sativa*) is a purple-flowered climber grown in Europe and U.S. for fodder and green manure. Blue-flowered hairy or winter vetch (*V. villosa*) is also widely grown. Certain vetches sometimes become pests in grainfields.

Veterans of Foreign Wars, organization created in 1899 at Columbus, Ohio, by veterans of Spanish-American War. Later admitted veterans who saw action in subsequent wars and U.S. military expeditions. Organization has large membership; takes firm stand on various political issues.

veterinary medicine, diagnosis and treatment of diseases and injuries of animals. The importance of the horse early led to special care; horseshoers (farriers) were sought when medical care was needed. A pioneer school of veterinary medicine was established in Lyon, France, in 1761; in the U.S. the first schools opened about the time of the Civil War. Veterinary experiments with animals, e.g., with vaccination, have contributed to medical science.

veto (Latin,= I forbid), action of a chief executive in some governments in withholding approval of laws passed by the legislature. In the U.S., the President's veto power is given in Article 1, Section 7, of the Constitution; it can be overridden by a two-thirds vote of Congress. Also, the casting of a negative vote by one of the five permanent members of the Security Council of the UN is called, unofficially, veto.

Vevey (vůvā'), resort (pop. 14,182), Vaud canton, Switzerland, on L. of Geneva.

viaduct, series of bridges or arches over a valley or low ground to carry a highway or railroad. Constructed of wood, iron, steel, stone, or concrete (usually reinforced with steel bars). A concrete and steel elevated viaduct is the Pulaski Skyway, 3 mi. long, between Jersey City and Newark, N.J.

Viardot-Garcia, Pauline (vyärdō'-gärsēä'), 1821–1910, mezzo-soprano, b. Paris; pupil of her father, Manuel GARCÍA. Her range was three and one-half octaves.

Viareggio (vēärĕd'jō), city (pop. 30,384), Tuscany, central Italy; a bathing resort and fishing port on Tyrrhenian Sea.

Viborg (vē'bôr), city (pop. 21,522), N central Jutland, Denmark. Mfg. of tobacco, beer, textiles, machinery. Religious center in pagan times. Restored cathedral was founded 1130.

Viborg, RSFSR: see VYBORG.

vibration, in physics, oscillatory motion, e.g., motion of swinging pendulum or of prongs of a struck tuning fork. SOUND is transmitted in waves and vibration is longitudinal. Light waves have transverse vibration. Heat may be defined as energy of continuous vibratory movement of molecules. See also BROWNIAN MOVEMENT.

viburnum, ornamental shrub or small tree of genus *Viburnum* of wide distribution. Viburnums have showy flat-topped clusters of white flowers (the snowballs have sterile flowers in rounded clusters) in spring followed by berrylike fruits, often edible. Well known species are the HOBBLEBUSH, HIGHBUSH CRANBERRY.

Vicente, Gil (Port. zhēl' vēsĕnt'; Span. hēl' vēcĕn'tā), 1470?–1536?, Portuguese dramatist, who wrote both in Spanish and Portuguese, one of the chief figures of the Renaissance and shaper of the drama in both countries.

Vicenza (vēchĕn'tsä), city (pop. 48,279), Venetia, NE Italy. Birthplace of Andrea PALLADIO. Basilica, Loggia del Capitano, Teatro Olimpico, Rotonda, and Chiericati Palace, all built by Palladio, inspired Georgian style in England and Colonial style in U.S.

Vichy (vĭ'shē, Fr. vēshē'), town (pop. 29,128), Allier dept., central France, on Allier R. Its hot mineral springs make it world's best-known spa for liver and stomach disorders. Bottled Vichy water is exported. Vichy was the seat (1940–44) of the **Vichy government** of France during World War II. Estab. by Marshal PÉTAIN, it effectively controlled only the part of France not occupied by the Germans and the parts of the French overseas empire not held by the "Free French" forces of Gen. de GAULLE. Operating as a CORPORATIVE STATE under its constitution of 1940, the Vichy government became a German tool in the hands of Pierre LAVAL and Jean François DARLAN. After the Allied invasion of N Africa (Nov., 1942), Hitler occupied all France. The Vichy government continued a shadow existence, fled to Germany in 1944, and broke up in 1945.

Vicksburg, city (pop. 27,948), W Miss., on Mississippi R. at mouth of Yazoo R. and W of Jackson. Important river port; commercial, processing, and shipping center for cotton, timber, and livestock area. Laid out 1819 on site of early 18th cent. French fort and Spanish Fort Nogales (1791). U.S. took possession 1798. In Civil War it was objective of Grant's VICKSBURG CAMPAIGN. River traffic aided by U.S. Mississippi River Commission (hq. here). Has U.S. Waterways Experiment Station, Vicksburg Natl. Military Park, and national cemetery.

Vicksburg campaign, Nov., 1862–July, 1863, of Civil War. Undertaken by U. S. Grant to control all of Mississippi R. and so split Confederacy. South still held Vicksburg and 200 mi. of river. In late 1862 Grant and W. T. Sherman converged on city from N and E, but were repulsed. After several attempts from N, Grant reached city from S in May, 1863; failing to storm it, he laid siege. After six weeks of resistance Vicksburg fell on July 4. Consequent fall of Port Hudson put entire river in Union hands.

Vico, Giovanni Battista (vē'kō), 1668–1744, Italian philosopher and jurist. Attempted to apply scientific method to study of history. Developed cyclical theory of civilization—three periods of society (theocracy, aristocracy, democracy), each containing seeds of its own dissolution. Long unappreciated, Vico has had great influence on such historians as Michelet, such writers as James Joyce.

Vicq-d'Azyr, Félix (fālĕks' vēk"-däzēr'), 1748–94, French comparative anatomist and physician. Noted for research on nervous system and muscles.

Victor Emmanuel, Italian kings. **Victor Emmanuel I,** 1759–1824, king of Sardinia (1802–21), was forced to abdicate by uprising against his reactionary rule. **Victor**

Emmanuel II, 1820–78, succeeded his father Charles Albert as king of Sardinia 1849; led in wars of RISORGIMENTO, aided by CAVOUR; became king of united Italy 1861; ruled as a liberal constitutional monarch. **Victor Emmanuel III,** 1869–1947, son of Humbert I, succeeded as king of Italy 1900; appointed MUSSOLINI 1922; assumed titles emperor of Ethiopia 1936 and king of Albania 1939 (both titles renounced 1943); dismissed Mussolini and made armistice with Allies of World War II (1943); abdicated 1946.

Victoria, 1819–1901, queen of England (1837–1901) and empress of India (1876–1901). Her accession ended connection between English and Hanoverian thrones. Lord Melbourne, her first prime minister, became her friend and adviser. She was married to her cousin, Prince ALBERT of Saxe-Coburg, whom she loved very deeply. Marriages of their nine children led to alliances of English royal house with Russia, Germany, Greece, Denmark, and Rumania. Their interests in foreign affairs led to friction with Lord Palmerston. Supported Crimean War. Her emergence from seclusion after three years of grief for Albert's death was due to Benjamin DISRAELI, who, with William GLADSTONE, dominated latter part of her reign. Disraeli secured title of empress of India for her 1876. Diamond jubilee (1897) proved her great popularity. Her last years saw the South African War 1899–1902. Her reign, the longest in English history, saw rise of industrial civilization, accompanied by humanitarianism at home and aggressive imperialism abroad. The term "Victorian era" attests the queen's personification of her times.

Victoria, Guadalupe: see GUADALUPE VICTORIA.

Victoria, Tomás Luis de (tōmäs' lwēs' dā vēktō'ryä), c.1540–1611, Spanish composer of sacred music. He wrote motets (e.g., *O quam gloriosum* and *O vos omnes*), Masses, settings of hymns, and Passion music. His greatest work was the *Officium defunctorum*.

Victoria, state (87,884 sq. mi.; pop. 2,055,252), SE Australia; cap. Melbourne. Most densely populated and smallest state (except Tasmania) of Australia. Climate is temperate; Australian Alps are snow-covered, May–Nov. Produces wool, wheat, and dairy products. Settlements were estab. at Portland Bay in 1834 and on site of Melbourne in 1835. Originally a part of the colony of New South Wales, it became a separate colony in 1851. Joined the commonwealth as a state in 1901.

Victoria, Brazil: see VITÓRIA.

Victoria, city (pop. 51,331), provincial cap., SW B.C., Canada, on SE tip of Vancouver Isl. Largest city, major port, and commercial center of island. Industries include fish canning, lumbering, and paper milling. Deep-sea fishing fleet. Residential and tourist city with fine scenery, mild climate, and beautiful parks. Founded 1843 as Fort Camosun (later Fort Victoria); laid out 1851–52 as Victoria. Became cap. of crown colony 1859. Here are Dominion Astrophysical Observatory and Victoria Col. (affiliated with Univ. of British Columbia).

Victoria (vēktō'ryä), city (pop. 19,513), cap. of Tamaulipas, NE Mexico; founded (1750) at foot of Sierra Madre Oriental. Principal products: sugar cane and citrus fruits. Also called Ciudad Victoria.

Victoria, city (pop. 16,126), S Texas, near Guadalupe R. and SE of San Antonio; founded 1824. Early Mexican town attracted U.S. settlers and German immigrants. Remains German in architecture and spirit. Center of oil and agr. area, it processes oil, chemicals, cotton, and food; railroad shops. Air fields estab. near by in World War II.

Victoria, Lake: see VICTORIA NYANZA.

Victoria and Albert Museum, in South Kensington, London, opened 1857 as South Kensington Mus. Housed in present building since 1901 and controlled by Board of Education. Has fine examples of decorative and applied arts as well as a noted collection of paintings and sculptures and the collections of the India Mus., which it absorbed.

Victoria Falls, in upper Zambezi R., on border of Southern Rhodesia and Northern Rhodesia; 1 mi. wide, 420 ft. high. Discovered 1855 by David Livingstone, who named them for Queen Victoria.

Victoria Island, 320 mi. long, 170–370 mi. wide, SW Franklin dist., Northwest Territories, Canada, in Arctic Ocean, one of largest islands in ARCTIC ARCHIPELAGO. On SE coast is Cambridge Bay, U.S.-Canadian weather station and trading post. Discovered by Thomas Simpson 1836–39.

Victoria Land, Antarctic region, S of New Zealand. Series of snow-covered mountains with high interior plateau; bounded E by Ross Sea, W by Wilkes Land. Discovered 1841 by Sir J. C. Ross; formerly called South Victoria Land.

Victorian style, in architecture, an eclectic fashion based on revivals of older styles. Private dwellings were supposedly based on Gothic style and public buildings on Greco-Roman models, but the basic design was lost in the mass of cluttered detail and overuse of turrets, bays, towers, and other excrescences.

Victoria Nyanza (nēän'zů, nī–), lake, area 26,-828 sq. mi., E central Africa, bordered by Uganda, Tanganyika, and Kenya. Of the fresh-water lakes of the world, only L. Superior is larger. It is 250 mi. long, 150 mi. wide, with an altitude of c.3,725 ft. Usually considered the chief source of the Nile, which (as the Victoria Nile) issues from it over Ripon Falls. Steamer service links the lakeshore towns. Discovered 1858 by John Speke and explored 1875 by Henry Stanley.

Victoriaville, town (pop. 13,124), SE Que., Canada, on Nicolet R. and N of Sherbrooke, in farm region. Mfg. of furniture and clothing.

Victory of Samothrace: see NIKE.

vicuña (vĭkū'nů), South American wild mammal (*Lama*) of camel family. Wool is woven into fine cloth.

Vidal, Peire (pĕr' vädäl'), fl. 1180–1206, Provençal troubadour. Among his patrons was Richard I of England. His love poems are notable for strong personal feeling and simple style.

Vidalia (vĭdāl'yů), city (pop. 5,819), SE Ga., W of Savannah, in farm area.

Vidocq, Eugène François (ûzhĕn' frāswä'

vēdôk′), 1775–1857, noted French detective, who, after a career of crime, joined (1809) the Paris *Sûreté*.

Vienna (vēĕ′nù), Ger. *Wien*, city (469 sq. mi.; pop. 1,760,784), cap. of Austria and of Lower Austria, on the Danube. It is coextensive with Vienna prov. Archiepiscopal see; seat of a university (founded 1365); cultural and commercial center. Varied mfg. The Roman Vindobona, it became the seat of the dukes of Austria (12th cent.) and imperial residence (15th cent.). It repulsed a Turkish siege in 1529. In the Turkish siege of 1683, the city heroically defended itself under the leadership of Starhemberg but was on the verge of starvation when it was saved by John III of Poland. In the 18th, 19th, and early 20th cent. Vienna reached its height as a center of art and science, notably of music (Mozart, Haydn, Beethoven, Schubert, Brahms, and others) and of medicine and psychiatry (Wagner-Jauregg, Freud). Its importance declined after World War I. Among the chief landmarks of Vienna are St. Stephen's cathedral (12th cent.); the Hofburg (imperial residence), Karlskirche, Schönbrunn palace, and Belvedere palace (all 18th cent., by Fischer von Erlach); the Prater (a park); the classic parliament building; and the opera and Burgtheater (in Renaissance style). Vienna was heavily damaged in World War II; its former Jewish population (c.115,-000) was virtually wiped out by the Nazis. Captured by the Russian army in April, 1945, it was jointly occupied by Russian, U.S., British, and French troops. The WIENER WALD is near by.

Vienna (vēĕ′nù), city (pop. 6,020), NW W.Va., near Parkersburg. Mfg. of glass, silk, vitrolite.

Vienna, Congress of, Sept., 1814–June, 1815, general political conference called to complement TREATY OF PARIS of 1814 in a general settlement of European affairs after the first abdication of NAPOLEON I. Among chief figures were the host, Emperor Francis I of Austria, and Metternich, chief Austrian negotiator; Alexander I of Russia; Frederick William III and K. A. von Hardenberg (Prussia); Castlereagh (Britain); and Talleyrand (France). There were hundreds of secondary representatives and agents, but no plenary session ever took place. The main work was carried on in committees and was dominated by the Big Three (Big Four, after Talleyrand secured equal status for France). The congress was the occasion for brilliant social activities, but despite the famous saying of the prince de LIGNE, work as well as dancing was done. Among the many thorny problems were those of Poland and Saxony, where Russian and Prussian interests clashed with those of Austria, France, and England. War seemed imminent when these last three powers concluded a defensive alliance (Jan., 1815), but Talleyrand's brilliant intervention, aided by Castlereagh, made the principle of legitimacy paramount and secured a compromise on which the European balance of power was based. The Final Act of the congress (June 9, 1815) was hurriedly drawn up after Napoleon's landing in France. The GERMAN CONFEDERATION was estab. For other territorial changes, see articles on countries, notably PRUSSIA; POLAND; SAXONY; NORWAY; NETHERLANDS; ITALY.

Vienne (vyĕn), department (2,720 sq. mi.; pop. 313,932), W central France, in Poitou; cap. Poitiers. It is crossed by the Vienne R., 230 mi. long, a tributary of the Loire.

Vienne, city (pop. 19,958), Isère dept., SE France, on the Rhone. Textile mfg. Was a major city of Roman Gaul; an early archiepiscopal see (suppressed 1790); seat of several kings of Burgundy (5th–9th cent.) and of counts of Vienne (see DAUPHINÉ); scene of an ecumenical council of the Roman Catholic Church (1311–12; resulted in suppression of Knights Templars by Pope Clement V). Has well-preserved Roman remains.

Vierge, Daniel (Urrabieta) (dänyĕl′ vyĕr′hā), 1851–1904, Spanish illustrator, a master of pen-and-ink drawing. Worked mainly in Paris.

Vierwaldstättersee, Switzerland: see LUCERNE.

Viète or **Vieta, François** (frãswä′ vyĕt′, vyātä′), 1540–1603, French mathematician. A founder of modern algebra, he introduced letters as algebraic symbols and correlated algebra, geometry, and trigonometry.

Viet Nam (vēĕt′ näm′), state (c.127,300 sq. mi.; pop. 22,600,000), E Indo-China; formed by the union of TONKIN, ANNAM, and COCHIN CHINA; cap. Saigon. At end of World War II, the Viet Minh party (a coalition of nationalist and Communist groups) resisted the return of French rule and set up a republic, headed by Ho CHI-MINH, with the capital at Hanoi. French objection to the inclusion of Cochin China in the new state and denial of full sovereignty led to a guerrilla war, which began Dec., 1946. In 1949 the French set up a rival Viet Nam regime, installing Bao Dai (former emperor of Annam) as ruler. A treaty granting Viet Nam independence within the French Union was ratified in 1950, and Bao Dai's government was promptly recognized by the U.S. and Great Britain, but not by the USSR and its allies, which recognized the Ho regime. The war between Viet Minh troops and French Union forces, which for seven years had been restricted to Viet Nam, spread into the neighboring state of Laos in 1953.

Vieuxtemps, Henri (vyûtã′), 1820–81, Belgian composer and violinist. A famous concert violinist, he wrote six concertos and other works, many of which are part of the standard violin repertoire.

Vigée-Lebrun, Élisabeth (ālēzäbĕt′ vēzhā′-lùbrũ′), 1755–1842, French painter, noted for her portraits of Marie Antoinette and of Mme de Staël.

Vigeland, Adolf Gustav (vē′gùlän), 1869–1943, Norwegian sculptor. Executed c.100 figures for decorating Frogner Park, Oslo.

vigilantes (vĭjĭlăn′tēz), members of a vigilance committee. Such committees were formed in U.S. frontier communities to suppress lawlessness and disorder before a regularly constituted government could be created or have real force. Most famous were those formed in San Francisco in 1851 and 1856 to bring order to the Barbary Coast. Extreme penalty imposed by vigilantes was LYNCHING. Measures taken by them were at best extralegal.

The name has sometimes been used by later groups illegally imposing force on others.

Vignemale (vēnyůmäl′), mountain, 10,821 ft. high, S France; highest in French Pyrenees.

Vignola, Giacomo da (jä′kōmō dä vēnyō′lä), 1507–73, Italian architect, one of initiators of baroque design. Real name was Giacomo Barozzi or Barocchio. Succeeded Michelangelo as architect of St. Peter's, for which he designed the lateral domes. In 1568 he designed sumptuous interior of Church of the Gesù (Rome). Universally known for treatise (based on Vitruvius) on five orders of architecture.

Vigny, Alfred, comte de (älfrĕd kōt′ dů vēnyē′), 1797–1863, French author. Primarily a poet-philosopher, he expressed his noble stoicism in *Poèmes antiques et modernes* (1826) and *Destinées* (1864) and the semiautobiographical prose sketches, *Servitude et grandeur militaires* (1835). His best-known novel is *Cinq-Mars* (1826); his best-known play, *Chatterton* (1835).

Vigo (vē′gō), city (pop. 44,188), NW Spain, in Galicia. An active Atlantic port, it has a large fishing fleet. Canning industry.

Viipuri, Finnish name of VYBORG, RSFSR.

Vikings (vī′kĭngz), Scandinavian warriors whose raids of coasts of Europe and British Isles gave period 8th–10th cent. name of the Viking Age. Causes of raids are obscure, but overpopulation was one of them. Scandinavians at that time were best shipbuilders and sailors in the world. Viking religion, Germanic paganism whose legends form Old Norse Literature, was replaced by Christianity at end of age. Vikings were known as VARANGIANS in Russia; as NORSEMEN or Danes elsewhere.

Villa, Francisco (fränsē′skō vē′yä), 1877?–1923, Mexican revolutionist, whose vigorous fighting in revolution of 1910 was largely responsible for triumph of Madero. When in 1913 Huerta overthrew Madero, Villa opposed him and later opposed Carranza; he gained control of N Mexico and with Zapata briefly occupied Mexico city (Dec. 1915). Piqued after Pres. Wilson recognized Carranza, Villa turned his wrath on U.S. citizens in Mexico and on U.S. border towns. A U.S. expedition under Pershing went then into Chihuahua (March, 1916–Feb., 1917) but was fruitless. Villa was assassinated in 1923.

Villa d'Este (vēl′lä dĕ′stā), famous villa near Tivoli, Italy, built 1550 for Cardinal Ippolito II d'Este. Its beautiful Renaissance garden has a Bernini fountain. Another Villa d'Este was built 16th cent. on W shore of L. Como; now a hotel.

Villa Doria Pamphili (vēl′lä dô′ryä päm′fēlē), Roman villa, built in 17th cent. for Camillo Pamphili, nephew of Pope Innocent X. Designed by Algardi.

Villafranca di Verona (vēl″läfräng′kä dē vārō′nä), town (pop. 4,986), Venetia, NE Italy. Here in 1859 France and Austria concluded a preliminary peace after the battle of Solferino (see RISORGIMENTO). Austria ceded Lombardy, which was added to Sardinia. Tuscany, Parma, and Modena, where revolutions had broken out, were to be restored to their rulers. Sardinia, which was not represented at the negotiations, repudiated some of the clauses and in 1860 annexed the central Italian states.

Villahermosa (vē″yäĕrmō′sä), city (pop. 25,114), cap. of Tabasco, SE Mexico; founded in late 16th cent., well inland on Grijalva R. Makes rum, hats, soap, candles, cigars, bricks and tile, and is distributing center.

Villa-Lobos, Heitor (ē′tôr vē′lä-lō′bôs), 1884?–, Brazilian composer. Inspired by Brazilian folk and popular music, he wrote a series of pieces which he called *Chôros*. Other compositions include symphonies, operas, concertos, chamber music, and many songs.

Villani, Giovanni (jōvän′nē vēl-lä′nē), c.1275–1348, Italian historian of Florence. His history in 12 books is an early monument of Italian prose, and helped fix Tuscan language as standard of Italy.

Villanova, village, SE Pa., near Philadelphia. Seat of Villanova Col. (R.C., for men; 1843).

Villard, Henry (vĭlärd′), 1835–1900, American journalist and financier, b. Germany. Original name Hilgard Villard. In the U.S. after 1853, he was a distinguished reporter through the Civil War, became interested in promoting railroads, gained controlling interest in Northern Pacific RR (1881), was forced into bankruptcy by difficulties of building (1883), regained control (1889). Also founded predecessor of General Electric Co. He bought control of the New York *Evening Post* (1881). He married a daughter of William Lloyd Garrison. Their son, **Oswald Garrison Villard,** 1872–1949, inherited and edited (until 1918) the *Evening Post* and made its weekly, the *Nation,* an outstanding liberal journal (which he owned until 1932). A militant pacifist and a friend of Germany.

Villari, Pasquale (päskwä′lā vēl′lärē), 1827–1917, Italian historian, author of notable biographies of Savonarola (1859–61) and Machiavelli (1877–82).

Villarrica (vē″yärē′kä), city (pop. 27,687), SE Paraguay; commercial center and shipping point for cattle, fruits, tobacco, and mate.

Villars, Claude, duc de (klōd′ dük dů vēlär′), 1653–1734, marshal of France. In War of the Spanish Succession he won victories at Friedlingen (1702), Höchstädt (1703), and Denain (1714); was defeated at Malplaquet (1709); negotiated Treaty of Rastatt (1714). Wrote memoirs.

Villehardouin (vēlärdwē′), French noble family that ruled Peloponnesus 1210–78. **Geoffroi de Villehardouin** (zhôfrōōä′), c.1160–c.1212, marshal of Champagne, was a leader in Fourth Crusade, which he related in his *De la conqueste de Constantinople* (first pub. 1585), an early masterpiece of French historical writing. He received a rich fief in Thrace. His nephew **Geoffroi I de Villehardouin,** d. 1218, conquered the Peloponnesus in 1205; ruled (1210–18) principality of Achaia as fief under Latin Empire. It prospered under his son **Geoffroi II de Villehardouin,** d. 1246, an excellent administrator. Another son, **Guillaume** or **William de Villehardouin** (gēyōm′), d. 1278, prince of Achaia (1246–78), waged war against Emperor Michael VIII (who had restored the Byzantine

Empire in 1261) in alliance with his son-in-law, Charles I of Naples.

villein (vĭ'lŭn) [O. Fr.,= village dweller], under MANORIAL SYSTEM, one who was personally free, though holding land that was not. He was distinguished from freeholder by services and duties owed to a lord. Term **villeinage** thus denoted half-free status. It began to disappear in England in 14th cent., due partly to substitution of money payments for work service, partly to growth of towns, which broke down local systems. See also SERF.

Ville Lasalle, Que.: see LASALLE.

Villèle, Jean Baptiste Séraphin Joseph, comte de (zhã' bätēst' säräfē' zhôzĕf' kōt' dŭ vēlĕl'), 1773–1854, French premier (1822–28); an ultraroyalist. Among other extreme reactionary measures, he enacted a plan to indemnify the émigrés out of public savings. Dissolved chamber of deputies 1827. Defeated in new elections, he resigned.

Villeneuve, Pierre de (pyĕr' dŭ vēlnûv'), 1763–1806, French admiral. Defeated at TRAFALGAR (1805), he committed suicide.

Ville Platte (vēl' plăt'), town (pop. 6,633), S central La., WNW of Baton Rouge. Trade and processing center for cotton, rice, lumber, and oil area.

Villeroi, François, duc de (frãswä' dük' dŭ vēlrwä'), 1644–1730, marshal of France; a favorite of Louis XIV. Incompetent, he was repeatedly defeated, notably at Ramillies in 1706.

Villeurbanne (vēlürbän'), city (pop. 80,193), Rhône dept., E France; an industrial suburb of Lyons. Metallurgy; rayon and chemical plants.

Villiers, George: see BUCKINGHAM, GEORGE VILLIERS, DUKE OF.

Villiers, George William Frederick: see CLARENDON, GEORGE WILLIAM FREDERICK VILLIERS, 4TH EARL OF.

Villiers de l'Isle-Adam, Auguste, comte de (ōgüst' kōt' dŭ vēyā' dŭ lēl'-ädã'), 1838–89, French author, a master of the tale of fantasy and horror. Among his works are the novel *L'Ève future* (1886) and the short stories collected in *Contes cruels* (1883).

Villon, François (frãswä' vēyõ'), b. 1431, d. after 1463, French poet. He associated with criminal gangs, was several times imprisoned for homicide and robbery, and in 1463 was sentenced to hang. His appeal resulted in commutation to 10 years' exile. One of the greatest medieval poets, Villon strikes a strongly personal, modern note. His chief works are the *Lais* or *Little Testament* (written 1456) and the *Testament* (1461)—both in the form of facetious bequests to his family, friends, and, especially, enemies. Interspersed in the *Testament* are such famous poems as "Ballade des dames du temps jadis" (with the refrain, "But where are the snows of yester-year?"). Later poems include the "Ballad of the Hanged." In turn mocking, ribald, and movingly pious, Villon's work always reflects his preoccupation with death and decay. There are several more or less successful English translations.

Vilna (vĭl'nŭ), Lithuanian *Vilnius,* Pol. *Wilno,* city (1931 pop. 196,345), cap. of Lithuania. Mfg. of agr. machinery, processed foods, lumber, electric equipment. University was founded 1578. The cap. of Lithuania from 1323, it passed to Russia 1795; was occupied by German troops in World War I; was assigned to Lithuania at the Paris Peace Conference, but was seized by Polish troops in 1920 and annexed by Poland after a plebiscite of doubtful validity (1922). The USSR occupied Vilna (along with E Poland) in 1939 but soon afterward transferred it to Lithuania. The interim Lithuanian cap., 1920–39, was Kaunas. During German occupation (1941–44) in World War II, Vilna's large Jewish population was virtually exterminated.

Vilyui (vĭlyōō'ē), river, 1,512 mi. long, RSFSR, in Siberia; a western tributary of the Lena. Platinum and gold are found along its banks.

Vimeiro (vēmā'rō), village of central Portugal, NNW of Lisbon, where Wellington defeated the French under Junot (1808).

Viña del Mar (vē'nyä dĕl mär') [Span.,= vineyard by the sea], port (pop. 98,156), central Chile. Practically a suburb of Valparaiso, it is one of the most popular resorts in South America. Its industries include sugar and oil refineries, cloth and yarn mills, dyeing and printing plants.

Vincennes (vĭnsĕnz', Fr. vẽsĕn'), town (pop. 48,851), Seine dept., N France; a W suburb of Paris. Has huge castle (once a royal residence) and dungeon (state prison in 17th–18th cent.). Forest of Vincennes is near by.

Vincennes (vĭnsĕnz'), city (pop. 18,831), SW Ind., on Wabash R. (here forms Ill. line) and S of Terre Haute. French mission estab. here 1702, fortified 1730, occupied by British 1763. Captured in American Revolution by G. R. Clark 1779. Cap. of Indiana territory 1800–1813 (W. H. Harrison then lived here). River port and rail center in agr., coal, and oil area. Mfg. of glass, metal, food, and paper products. Has memorial to G. R. Clark.

Vincent, John Heyl, 1832–1920, American Methodist bishop. His work in improving teaching methods in Sunday schools had widespread results. With Lewis Miller he organized (1874) at Chautauqua, N.Y., a Sunday-school teachers' institute, out of which grew Chautauqua movement. He became bishop in 1888. His son, **George Edgar Vincent,** 1864–1941, aided his father and was president (1907–15) of the Chautauqua Inst. As head (1917–29) of Rockefeller Foundation, he greatly expanded its activities, especially in medical aid and research.

Vincent de Paul, Saint, 1576–1660, French priest. Having himself suffered enslavement by Tunisian pirates, he later worked to better the conditions of the galley slaves. He then zealously began organized charity in France, initiated the foundling hospital, and founded an order of secular priests, the Congregation of the Mission (Lazarists or Vincentians), for rural work (1629) and the SISTERS OF CHARITY for city work. St. Francis of Sales made him director of the Order of the Visitation. Feast: July 19.

Vincent Ferrer, Saint (fĕr'ŭr), 1350?–1419, Spanish Dominican preacher. Traveled over Europe, urging sinners to repent, converting many. Feast: April 5.

Vincent of Beauvais (bōvā'), c.1190–c.1264,

French Dominican friar. Wrote three of four parts of the *Speculum majus,* a Latin encyclopedia that summarized 13th-cent. knowledge.

Vinci, Leonardo da: see LEONARDO DA VINCI.

vine, any climbing or trailing plant; the grape is often called the "vine."

vinegar, sour liquid, mainly acetic acid and water, produced by action of bacteria on solutions of ethyl alcohol derived from previous yeast FERMENTATION; varieties vary in color and flavor according to the alcoholic liquor (cider, wine, solution of barley malt, etc.) from which the vinegar is made. Used as condiment, preservative, household remedy, and in cookery. Vinegar has been known since antiquity as a natural by-product of wine.

Vineland, borough (pop. 8,155), S N.J., N of Millville. Agr. market center (poultry, fruit); clothing, fireworks, machinery. Seat of state school for sub-normal children (noted for research work).

Vineyard Haven, resort village (pop. 1,864) in Tisbury town (pop. 1,930) on N Martha's Vineyard, with harbor on Vineyard Sound, SE Mass.

Vinita (vĭnē'tù), city (pop. 5,518), NE Okla., NE of Tulsa, center of agr. and livestock area. Near by is Grand River Dam.

Vinland or **Wineland,** section of North America discovered by LEIF ERICSSON in 11th cent. A.D. Later sought by THORFINN KARLSEFNI. Southern coast of New England generally accepted as disputed site.

Vinnitsa (vē'nyĭtsŭ), city (pop. 92,868), W Ukraine, on the Southern Bug; an agr. center of Podolia. Population was 40% Jewish until German occupation (1941–43) in World War II.

Vinogradoff, Sir Paul (vĭnûgrä'dûf), 1854–1925, English historian. Works include *Villainage in England* (1892), *English Society in the Eleventh Century* (1908), and *Outlines of Historical Jurisprudence* (2 vols., 1920–23).

Vinson, Fred(erick) M(oore), 1890–, Chief Justice of U.S. Supreme Court (1946–).

viol (vī'ŭl), family of stringed instruments played with a bow, developed in the 15th cent. and popular until supplanted by the VIOLIN family. Despite a general resemblance, there are many differences between the two families. Viols have a flat rather than a rounded back; deep ribs; shoulders that slope into the neck (usually fretted); from five to eight strings; and a soft, delicate tone. The sizes and range (treble, tenor, bass) of members of the viol family correspond somewhat to those of the violin family. Many viols, regardless of size, are played usually resting on the knees—hence the term *viola da gamba* [knee viol]. In a limited sense, the viola da gamba refers to the bass (not double bass) member of the family, a six-stringed instrument similar to the cello in range. Another type of viol was the viola da braccio [arm viol]. An important arm viol is the viola d'amore. Held like a violin, it has from five to seven strings and an unfretted neck; it is distinguished by its set of sympathetic strings (strings not themselves directly played upon but stretched behind the bowed strings and tuned to vibrate sympathetically with them).

viola, flower: see VIOLET.

viola, musical instrument: see VIOLIN, family.

viola da gamba and **viola d'amore:** see VIOL.

violet, low, perennial flowering plant of genus *Viola.* Many violets are spring-blooming North American wild flowers. Florists' violets are chiefly varieties of the sweet or English violet (*Viola odorata*). Garden violets, known as violas or tufted pansies, are hybrids or varieties of *V. cornuta.* The PANSY and johnny-jump-up are derived from *V. tricolor.* Many violets bear, besides their typical flowers, capsulelike flowers which never open but produce seed after self-fertilization. The African violet is not related.

violin, family of stringed musical instruments played with a bow; chief members are the violin (the terms "first" and "second" violin refer merely to the part that a violin plays in an ensemble), the viola, the violoncello (usually simply called the cello), and the double bass. These four form the string section of the usual symphony orchestra, the first three being also used in string quartets. All except the double bass are important solo instruments. Collectively these instruments have great capabilities and a wide range (the distance between the lowest note on the double bass and the highest possible note on the violin is over six octaves). A variety of effects may be produced by different bowing techniques. Members of the violin family resemble each other in having a slightly convex front and back, an unfretted neck, and four strings—with the exception of the double bass, which more closely resembles the VIOL family. Each member has its own characteristic tone, the violin ranging from the sentimental to the brilliant; the viola (resembling a large violin) more reserved, but warm; the cello (about twice the size of the violin), known for its rich color; and the double bass, deep and serious. Both the violin and viola are played held more or less horizontally with the body of the instrument supported by the shoulder and held firm by the chin; the cello and double bass are played vertically, resting on the floor. The peak of violinmaking was reached in the 16th and 17th cent. by such master craftsmen as the Amati, Guarneri, and Stradivari families of Cremona. See *ill.,* p. 857.

Viollet-le-Duc, Eugène Emmanuel (vyôlā'-lü-dük'), 1814–79, French architect, foremost exponent of Gothic revival in France. Famous for restorations of Notre Dame and the Sainte-Chapelle in Paris and cathedrals of Amiens and of Laon. Author of standard works on medieval architecture.

violoncello: see VIOLIN, family.

viper, any of several poisonous snakes including true vipers (*Vipera*) of Europe, Asia, Africa and the pit vipers of America and Asia. ADDER is a true viper; pit vipers (pit on each side of head) include RATTLESNAKE, COPPERHEAD, WATER MOCCASIN, BUSHMASTER.

Virchow, Rudolf (rōō'dôlf fĭr'khō), 1821–1902, German pathologist, a founder of cellular pathology. Eminent also as anthropologist and in politics.

vireo (vĭr'ēō), small, migratory bird of New World. Some species nest in U.S., but majority are tropical. Most vireos are greenish above with white or yellow under parts. They are chiefly insectivorous. Some are fine singers. See *ill.*, p. 135.

Virgil, Roman poet: see VERGIL.

virginal, musical instrument: see PIANO.

Virginia, in Roman legend, daughter of a centurion. Her father stabbed her to save her from lust of Appius Claudius Crassus, a decemvir, and this precipitated downfall of the decemvirs.

Virginia, state (39,899 sq. mi.; pop. 3,318,680), E U.S.; first of the Thirteen Colonies; cap. RICHMOND. Other cities are NORFOLK, ROANOKE, PORTSMOUTH. HAMPTON ROADS is major port of entry, center of shipbuilding and shipping. The TIDEWATER region extends W from the Atlantic to the piedmont. Between the BLUE RIDGE and the Appalachian plateau farther W lies Valley of Virginia (including valley of the SHENANDOAH). Major rivers are the Potomac (part of Md. line), Rappahannock, York, and James. Farming (corn, tobacco, hay, wheat, peanuts, apples, livestock, dairying); fishing. Coal mining. Mfg. of tobacco products, wood products, textiles, chemicals, food products. JAMESTOWN was first permanent English settlement in America (1607). Early hardships lessened as new settlers arrived and as agr. was estab. House of burgesses, first representative assembly in New World, convened 1619. Became royal colony in 1624. Economic dissatisfaction of small farmers expressed in Bacon's Rebellion (1676). OHIO COMPANY grant (1749) led to further development. Va. was active in colonial opposition to British before American Revolution. Of first 12 Presidents, seven were Virginians. Joined Confederacy in 1861; chief battleground of Civil War. Counties W of the Appalachians opposed secession; this section admitted to Union as W.Va. in 1863. Industrial growth was hastened afterwards; industry boomed in both World Wars. Harry F. Byrd has been most influential political figure in state's Democratic organization since mid-1920s.

Virginia, city (pop. 12,486), NE Minn., NNW of Duluth and on Mesabi iron range; settled before 1883. Resort area and trade center with mines and foundries. Rebuilt after fires 1893, 1900.

Virginia, Confederate name for ironclad *Merrimac*. See MONITOR AND MERRIMAC.

Virginia, University of, at Charlottesville; state supported, mainly for men; chartered 1819, opened 1825. Thomas Jefferson, the first rector, planned original buildings and organization and curriculum. Had first elective system in a university. Consolidated with Mary Washington Col. (at Fredericksburg; for women; 1908) in 1944.

Virginia Beach, Atlantic resort town (pop. 5,390), SE Va., E of Norfolk. Has seafood industry. Near by are Fort Story and Cape Henry.

Virginia bluebell: see VIRGINIA COWSLIP.

Virginia City. 1 Town (pop. 323), SW Mont., SE of Butte. Founded when gold was discovered (1863) in Alder Gulch. Territorial cap. 1865–74. **2** Uninc. town (1940 pop. 952), W Nev., SE of Reno. Founded 1859, when rich gold and silver deposits, notably COMSTOCK LODE, were discovered near by. In 1880 population was c.11,000. Town is now tourist center.

Virginia Company, created in 1606 by British royal charter to estab. two colonies in America between lat. 34° N and lat. 45° N.

Virginia cowslip or **Virginia bluebell,** beautiful spring wild flower (*Mertensia virginica*), native from N.Y. to Tenn. It has nodding, blue bell-shaped flowers.

Virginia creeper, native woody vine (*Parthenocissus quinquefolia*), much used as a wall covering. It has black berries and five-fingered leaves, red in autumn. It is often called woodbine.

Virginia Military Institute: see LEXINGTON.

Virginia Mountains, W Nev., W of Pyramid L. between Astor Pass and Carson R. Here are Pyramid Range (N) and Washoe Mts. or Virginia Range (S), with Mt. Davidson (7,870 ft.), site of COMSTOCK LODE.

Virginia Polytechnic Institute: see BLACKSBURG.

Virginia Resolutions: see KENTUCKY AND VIRGINIA RESOLUTIONS.

Virgin Islands, group of c.100 small islands, West Indies, E of Puerto Rico; discovered by Columbus (1493). The **Virgin Islands of the United States** (132 sq. mi.; pop. 26,665), territory, formerly part of Danish West Indies, purchased 1917 for $25,000,000; cap. CHARLOTTE AMALIE (St. Thomas). Other cities are Christiansted and Frederiksted, on St. Croix. Although 68 islands compose group, only three are important. St. Thomas (12 mi. long) is mountainous and uncultivated but has many good harbors; St. Croix (23 mi. long) has flat terrain and is dominated by agr. (sugar cane mainly); St. John (9 mi. long) is also agricultural. Real importance of these islands is their strategic location at juncture of Caribbean and Atlantic. **British Virgin Islands** (67 sq. mi.; pop. 6,505), c.30 in number, form a presidency of the Leeward Islands colony; cap. Road Town. The principal islands are Tortola (12 mi. long), Anegada (10 mi. long), Virgin Gorda (10 mi. long). Acquired by Great Britain in 1666. Crops include sea-island cotton and tobacco; there is some grazing.

Virginius, filibustering ship, fraudulently flying American flag and carrying arms to Cubans in Ten Years War. Captured by Spanish off Cuba, Oct. 31, 1873. Captain and 52 of the crew and passengers were executed. Incident almost caused war between U.S. and Spain, but Hamilton Fish negotiated settlement. Spain paid U.S. $80,000.

Virgin Mary: see MARY.

Virgo (vûr'gō) [Latin,= the virgin], sixth sign of ZODIAC.

Viriatus (vērēä'tŭs), d. 139 B.C., leader of the Lusitani (see LUSITANIA). He headed a successful rebellion against Roman rule, inflicted defeats on Roman armies, and maintained an independent state until some of his followers were bribed to kill him.

Virtanen or **Wirtanen, Artturi Ilmari** (both: ärt'to͞orē ĭl'märē vĭr'tänĕn), 1895–, Finnish biochemist. Won 1945 Nobel Prize for work on use of nitrogen by plants.

virus (vī′rŭs), name for a submicroscopic infectious agent capable of causing disease in plants and animals. Viruses are generally considered to be filtrable, i.e., they can pass through porcelain filters having pores so fine that bacteria cannot pass through them. In general, viruses can be described as parasites incapable of growth except in the presence of living cells. An attack of some virus diseases makes the victim immune to further attacks of the same disease. Virus diseases include poliomyelitis, rabies, smallpox and chickenpox, yellow fever, mumps, measles, and probably the common cold. Mosaic diseases in plants are attributed to viruses.

Visalia (vĭsā′lyů), city (pop. 11,749), S central Calif., SE of Fresno; founded 1852. Processing center for farms and dairies of San Joaquin Valley.

Visayan Islands (vĭsī′ŭn) or **Bisayas** (bēsä′yäs), island group, in Visayan Sea, central P.I., including Samar, Leyte, Negros, Panay, Bohol, Cebu, Masbate, and others.

Visby, Sweden: see WISBY.

Vischer, Peter (fĭ′shůr), the elder, c.1455–1529, German sculptor, foremost bronze founder in Germany. Assisted by his five sons in his Nuremberg workshop. Masterpiece is richly ornamented bronze canopy over the reliquary of St. Sebald at Nuremberg.

Visconti (vēskōn′tē), Italian Ghibelline family which ruled Milan from 13th cent. to 1447 (first as lords, later as imperial vicars and dukes, from 1395 as hereditary dukes). They gradually acquired all Lombardy and neighboring districts. **Gian Galeazzo Visconti** (jän′ gälāät′tsō), 1351?–1402, bought his investiture as hereditary duke from Emperor Wenceslaus (1395) and defeated Emperor Rupert, who sought to restore imperial rule over Italy (1401). Seeking to set up an Italian kingdom, Gian Galeazzo embarked on a systematic program of conquest, in which he was assisted by the best condottieri of his time and by his own diplomatic skill, but he died of the plague while preparing an attack on Florence, his stoutest enemy. He reformed and centralized the government, promoted art and industry, and allied his house with France by marrying Isabella, daughter of King John II; his daughter Valentina married Louis d'Orléans. (It was through Valentina that Louis XII of France derived his claim to Milan.) He was succeeded by his sons **Giovanni Maria Visconti** (jōvän′nē), 1389–1412, a dissolute and cruel ruler, who was assassinated, and **Filippo Maria Visconti** (fēlēp′pō), 1392–1447, who used both force and diplomacy to restore the duchy from the chaos into which it had fallen after Gian Galeazzo's death. He warred with Venice and Florence. His daughter and sole heir, Bianca Maria, married Francesco I SFORZA, who became duke after the fall of the short-lived Ambrosian Republic (1447–50), set up after Filippo Maria's death.

viscose process (vĭs′kōs), method for preparing RAYON from cellulose. Sheets of cellulose prepared either from wood pulp or cotton linters are treated with sodium hydroxide, then carbon disulphide; product is cellulose xanthate. When this is mixed with dilute sodium hydroxide, viscose is produced. Yarn is made from this by forcing the viscose through spinneret into acid solution.

Viscount Melville Sound, arm of the Arctic Ocean, 250 mi. long, 100 mi. wide, W Franklin dist., Northwest territories, Canada. Navigable only under favorable weather conditions. W part discovered by Sir Robert McClure 1850–53.

Viseu (vēzā′o͞o), city (pop. 13,499), cap. of Beira Alta prov., N central Portugal. Grain and fruit trade; textile mfg. Founded by Romans; captured from Moors 1058. Has 12th-cent. cathedral and notable museum.

Vishinsky or **Vyshinsky, Andrei Y(anuarievich)** (ŭndrā′ yŭno͞oär′yĭvĭch vĭshĕn′skē), 1883–, Russian jurist and diplomat. Chief prosecutor at Moscow treason trials of 1936–38; deputy foreign minister 1941–49; foreign minister 1949–53; deputy foreign minister and permanent representative of USSR at UN 1953–. Wrote *The Law of the Soviet State* (Eng. tr., 1948).

Vishnu: see HINDUISM.

Visigoths or **West Goths,** division of the Goths, one of the chief groups of the GERMANS. Separated from the OSTROGOTHS early in 4th cent. A.D., they began to penetrate the Danubian provinces of the East Roman Empire. ULFILAS began their conversion to Arianism. In 376, under pressure of the Hunnic invasion, the Visigoths under their chief Fritigern fled into Roman territory. Their troubles with the Roman officials led to a punitive expedition by Emperor Valens, whom they utterly routed at Adrianople (378). Rome ceded certain provinces for their occupation (382), but in 395 ALARIC I, proclaimed king of the Visigoths, began his conquests which took the Visigoths across Italy (sack of Rome, 410) and, under King ATAULF, into S Gaul and N Spain (412). They increased their Spanish possessions at the expense of the Vandals and pushed N to the Loire. Visigothic power reached its height under EURIC, but in 507 ALARIC II was defeated by the Franks and lost nearly all his lands N of the Pyrenees. The history of the Visigoths became essentially that of SPAIN. They accepted Catholicism and merged with the Hispano-Roman population. After the death of RECESWINTH (672) Visigothic Spain fell into virtual anarchy. The last king, RODERICK, was defeated in 711 by TARIK, leader of the Moors.

vision, sense by which objects and colors are perceived. Depends on sensitivity of retina of EYE to light; rays pass through cornea and lens, by which they are bent and focused on retina. Shape of lens can be changed by accommodation so that both near and far objects are brought into focus. Layer of retina closest to choroid (or chorioid) is pigment layer, in which visual purple (rhodopsin) is believed to be made. Visual purple affects ability of eye to adapt to light and dark; it is decomposed in light; vitamin A is needed for its regeneration. Next layer has nerve cells known as rods and cones; this area is light sensitive. Nerve impulses from rods and cones are transmitted to cerebrium of brain through optic nerve. Image formed on retina is inverted because light rays cross;

mental image is right side up. Retina has central depression (where only cones are present) which is area of most acute vision. Cones are believed to be concerned with vision in bright light; rods, in darkness. Color perception is considered function of cones; no completely satisfactory theory is known. Young-Helmholtz theory is based on assumption that there are three fundamental color sensations (red, green, violet) and three groups of cones in retina, each sensitive to one color. White is produced by combination of all three, black by lack of stimulation. Hering's theory suggests existence of three photochemical substances producing six primary sensations. Man has binocular vision; separate images formed by each eye are fused to give one impression. Since each eye forms its own image from a slightly different angle, depth, distance, and solidity are appreciated.

Vistula (vĭs'cho͝olü), Pol. *Wisła,* Ger. *Weichsel,* chief river of Poland, 667 mi. long, rising in the Carpathians and flowing N past Cracow, Warsaw, and Torun into the Baltic at Danzig. Navigable for nearly entire length. Connected by canals with Oder, Dnieper, and Niemen rivers.

visual education, term denoting use of nonverbal materials to enrich learning experiences. It applies particularly to pictures and other materials appealing to the eye, but sound is also used, and the term *audio-visual* applies to combined program. Use of nonverbal materials—restricted largely to schools in U.S.—now includes all the developments of photographic industries, radio, sound recordings, and television.

visual purple: see VISION.

vitamins, group of substances essential for growth and maintenance of normal body structure and function. Well-balanced diet usually provides minimum requirements. Vitamins are often grouped as those soluble in fat (vitamins A, D, E, K) and those soluble in water (B complex and C). **Vitamin A** helps keep skin and mucous membranes healthy, is needed for normal growth of young, prevents certain eye diseases. Early symptom of deficiency is night blindness. High intake postpones senility in laboratory animals. It is a derivative of carotinoid pigments of plants and can be made synthetically on a commercial scale. Rich sources are milk and its products, fish-liver oils, dark green and yellow vegetables. About 12 water-soluble factors are grouped as **vitamin B complex.** Thiamine (thiamine hydrochloride, vitamin B_1 or B) is concerned with maintenance of normal appetite, good digestion, and carbohydrate metabolism; is essential to normal growth of young. It helps to maintain health of nervous system; prevents BERIBERI. Good sources are yeast, whole grains and their products, eggs, some meats, dried legumes. Riboflavin (vitamin B_2, vitamin G, or lactoflavin) is present in respiratory enzymes and is believed to be concerned with oxidation in body cells. Lack of the vitamin in humans results in skin lesions and damage to conjunctiva and cornea of eye. Sources include green leaf vegetables, milk, eggs, liver, and whole-grain products. Niacin (nicotinic acid) prevents PELLAGRA and a diet deficient in niacin results in disturbances of digestive and nervous systems. Vitamin B_{12} discovered in liver is believed to be effective against various kinds of anemia. A number of other substances in B complex have not yet been investigated fully. These include pyridoxine, pantothenic acid, para-aminobenzoic acid, biotin, choline, folic acid, inositol. **Vitamin C** (ascorbic acid) prevents SCURVY. Symptoms of insufficiency include tenderness and bleedings of gums, loosening of teeth, soreness of joints, weakness, fatigue, and weakening of walls of capillaries. Little can be stored in body, thus daily intake is important. Good sources are citrus fruits, tomatoes, and raw cabbage. Vitamin C is easily destroyed in cooking. **Vitamin D** plays essential role in use of calcium and phosphorus by body and prevents RICKETS. Especially important during growth, pregnancy, lactation. Present in fish-liver oils and liver. Sometimes is added to milk by irradiation with ultraviolet light. Exposure to sunlight causes irradiation of cholesterol in skin and produces much of human requirement. Certain chemical compounds have **vitamin E** activity; essential to reproduction in some animals; value in humans is not known. It is especially abundant in wheat-germ oil and lettuce. **Vitamin K** is concerned with normal clotting of blood and functioning of the liver. **Vitamin P** is believed to function with vitamin C in preventing permeability of capillary walls.

Vitebsk (vē'tĕpsk, vē'tyĭpsk), city (pop. 167,424), NE Belorussia, on the W Dvina. Textile and machinery mfg. Passed to Lithuania 14th cent., to Russia 1772. Population was c.45% Jewish until German occupation (1941–44).

Vitellius, Aulus (ô'lůs vĭtĕ'lēůs), A.D. 15–A.D. 69, Roman emperor (A.D. 69). Succeeded Galba, triumphed over Otho, but was defeated and murdred by Vespasian.

Viterbo (vētĕr'bō), city (pop. 21,281), Latium, central Italy. A residence of 13th-cent. popes, it has a picturesque medieval quarter with many fine palaces, fountains, and a Romanesque cathedral. Damaged in World War II.

Viti Levu: see FIJI.

Vitim (vētyēm'), river, 1,132 mi. long, RSFSR, in SE Siberia. Rises in gold-rich Vitim Plateau and flows S, then NE, then N into the Lena.

Vitória (vētô'rēů), formerly **Victoria,** city (pop. 51,329), cap. of Espírito Santo, E Brazil, port on the Atlantic; founded in mid-16th cent. Ships quantities of coffee and iron ore.

Vitoria (vētō'rēä), city (pop. 44,341), cap. of Álava prov., N Spain, in Basque Provs. Mfg. center (machinery, sugar, paper). Has Gothic cathedral. Here in 1813 Wellington won a decisive battle against the French under Joseph Bonaparte and Jourdan.

vitriol. For oil of vitriol, see SULPHURIC ACID; for green vitriol, see COPPERAS. See also BLUE VITRIOL and WHITE VITRIOL.

Vitruvius (Marcus Vitruvius Pollio) (vĭtro͞o'vēůs), 1st cent. A.D., Roman writer on architecture. His *de architectura* was much used by Renaissance architects in the classical revival.

Vittorino da Feltre (vēt-tōrē'nō dä fĕl'trā), 1378–1446, Italian humanist and teacher. At his school in Mantua he taught the marchese's children, together with many poor children, treating them all equally. His methods and his emphasis were novel.

Vittorio Veneto (vēt-tō'ryō vänā'tō), town (pop. 12,034), Venetia, NE Italy. Scene of decisive Italian victory over Austrians, which led to surrender of Austria-Hungary (Oct.–Nov., 1918).

Vivaldi, Antonio (vēväl'dē), c.1675–1743, Italian composer, known chiefly for his instrumental music. He standardized the three-movement form of the *concerto grosso*. Bach made organ transcriptions of four of Vivaldi's concertos.

Vivarini (vēvärē'nē), Italian family of painters. **Antonio Vivarini,** b. c.1415, d. between 1476 and 1484, had a workshop in Murano. His brother, **Bartolomeo Vivarini,** c.1432–c.1499, was one of first to paint in oils in Venice. Antonio's son, **Alvise Vivarini** (älvē'zā), c.1446–c.1503, was a religious painter.

Vives, Juan Luis (hwän' lwēs' vē'vās), 1492–1540, Spanish humanist philosopher. Opposed the conventions of scholasticism; argued for inductive reasoning and experiment.

Vizagapatam (vĭ"zŭgŭpŭ'tŭm), town (pop. 70,243), NE Madras, India, port on Bay of Bengal. Shipyards.

Vizcaíno, Sebastián (sāvästyän' vēthkäē'nō), fl. 1602, Spanish explorer. Explored Calif. coast; discovered and named Monterey bay.

Vizcaya, Spain: see BASQUE PROVINCES.

Vlachs: see WALACHIA.

Vladikavkaz, RSFSR: see DZAUDZHIKAU.

Vladimir I or **Saint Vladimir** (vlă'dĭmēr, Rus. vlŭdyē'mĭr), d. 1015, first Christian duke of Kiev (980–1015); son of Sviatoslav. Was baptized 988 or 989. Fostered friendly relations with Byzantium.

Vladimir, city (pop. 66,761), central European RSFSR, ENE of Moscow. Textile, machinery, and plastics mfg. It became (c.1150) the cap. of the grand duchy of Vladimir-Suzdal, the chief Russian principality after the breakup of the Kievan state. After its destruction by the Mongols in 1238 the dukes of Moscow emerged as leading Russian princes; they acquired Vladimir in 1364, took the title grand dukes, and long continued to be crowned at Vladimir. Among its historic buildings are the Uspenski and Demetrius cathedrals (12th cent.) and the Golden Gate, a city gate erected 1164. The Vladimir-Suzdal style of Russian architecture was a fusion of the Romanesque and Byzantine styles.

Vladimir-Volynski (–vŭlĭn'skē), Pol. *Włodzimierz,* city (1931 pop. 24,581), W Ukraine. Became c.988 the cap. of duchy of Vladimir or Lodomeria, founded by Vladimir I of Kiev. Originally dependent on Kiev, it included, for some time, all of VOLHYNIA; was united with duchy of GALICH 1188; passed to Russia 1795; reverted to Poland 1921; was ceded to USSR 1945.

Vladislav, kings of Bohemia: see LADISLAUS V and ULADISLAUS II, kings of Hungary.

Vladivostok (vlă"dĭvŏ'stŏk, –vŭstŏk'), city (pop. c.300,000), cap. of Maritime Territory, RSFSR, in Far Eastern Siberia, on a peninsula in an inlet of Sea of Japan. Chief Russian Pacific port (kept ice free in winter); terminus of Trans-Siberian RR; fishing and whaling base. Has shipyards, airplane plants, canneries, lumber mills. Several scientific institutions. Settled 1860 by Russians, it grew after completion of Trans-Siberian RR (1905) and developed as a naval base after Russian loss of Port Arthur to Japan (1905). A major supply depot in World War I, Vladivostok was occupied by Allies (incl. Americans) 1918–20; Japanese occupation troops stayed on till 1922.

Vlaminck, Maurice de (vlämēk'), 1876–, French painter. Best known for landscapes of later period, but some of best work was done in early fauvist phase.

Vlissingen, Netherlands: see FLUSHING.

Vlona, Vionë, Vlora, or **Vlorë,** Albania: see VALONA.

Vltava, river of Czechoslovakia: see MOLDAU.

vocational training, designed to advance a person's general proficiency, especially in relation to his present or future occupation. Prior to Industrial Revolution APPRENTICESHIP system and home were the sources of training. Manual training developed in Scandinavia c.1866 and became popular in U.S. after 1880. While not originally vocational in aim, it evolved into industrial training. Courses in clerical work also started early. Pioneer private trade schools in U.S. were COOPER UNION (1859) and PRATT INSTITUTE (1887), and HAMPTON INSTITUTE (1868) and TUSKEGEE INSTITUTE (1881) for Negroes. The agricultural high school (1888) of Univ. of Minnesota was first regular public vocational high school. Public schools often work closely with industries and trades in establishing curriculums, in guidance programs, and in setting up cooperative training techniques. Theorists in vocational training state its aims as being both cultural and technical. This viewpoint is shown in academic requirements of public vocational schools and in work of continuation schools.

vocative: see CASE.

vodka (vŏd'kŭ), national spirituous drink of Russia, also popular elsewhere in Europe. Best vodka is distilled from rye and barley malt; maize and potatoes are also used. May be over 90% alcohol.

voice, grammatical category according to which an action is referred to as done by the subject (active) or to the subject (passive). In Latin, voice, like mood and tense, is a category of INFLECTION.

Voisin, La, French poisoner: see POISON AFFAIR.

Vojvodina or **Voivodina** (both: voi"vōdē'nä), autonomous province (8,683 sq. mi.; pop. 1,661,632), N Serbia, Yugoslavia; cap. Novi Sad. Drained by Danube, Theiss, and Sava rivers, it is an extremely fertile region (grain, fruit, grapes, vegetables, cattle). Conquered from Hungary by Turkey in 16th cent., it reverted to Hungary 1699, passed to Yugoslavia after World War I. It includes the W Banat of Temesvar. Population includes Serbs, Croats, Magyars, Rumanians, Slovaks.

volcano, term used for aperture in earth's crust

from which gas and rock (molten and solid) are discharged and also for a conical mountain built up by erupted material. Often there is a cavity, or crater, at the summit. Eruptions range from the quiet type (Hawaiian) to the violently explosive (Mont Pelée and Krakatoa). The explosive force, which may blow a whole mountain to bits, results from accumulation of superheated steam and other gases held back by a plug of hardened lava in the vent. Torrents of rain often accompany this type of eruption.

Volcano Islands, island group (11 sq. mi.; pop. 1,154), W Pacific. Iwo JIMA is chief island. Annexed 1887 by Japan. Governed by U.S. after World War II. Sulphur is mined.

Volga (vŏl'gŭ), river, 2,290 mi. long, European RSFSR; largest river of Europe. Rising in the Valdai Hills and winding E past Gorki to Kazan, then S past Kuibyshev and Stalingrad, it forms a wide delta at Astrakhan near its mouth on the Caspian Sea. Chief tributaries: Kama and Oka. Volga basin comprises one third of European USSR. Linked by the Mariinsk system with the Baltic Sea and the Baltic-White Sea Canal, by the Moscow Canal with Moscow, and by the Volga-Don Canal (completed 1952) with the Don, it carries c.30% of total river freight of USSR and is navigable late April to late Nov. from Shcherbakov and early March to mid-Dec. at Astrakhan. There are numerous dams and hydroelectric stations along the upper Volga, notably at SHCHERBAKOV; its waters are used to irrigate the vast steppes of the lower Volga region. The "Mother Volga" of Russian folklore, it has always played an immensely important part in the life of the Russian people and was the lifeline of Russian colonization in the E.

Volhynia (vŏlĭ'nyŭ), Pol. *Wolyn,* Rus. *Volyn,* historic region, NW Ukraine, one of oldest Slavic settlements. After the breakup of the duchy of Galich-Vladimir (see GALICH; VLADIMIR-VOLYNSKI) in the 14th cent., Volhynia was disputed between Poland and Lithuania. The Polish-Lithuanian Union of Lublin (1569) made Volhynia into a quasi-autonomous Polish province. It passed to Russia in the Polish partitions of 1793 and 1795. Its W section (incl. LUTSK) was again under Polish rule 1921–39; its cession to USSR was confirmed 1945.

Vollard, Ambroise (ãbrōōäz' vôlär'), 1867–1939, French art dealer and publisher. Noted for early recognition and sponsorship of such artists as Van Gogh, Cézanne, and Rouault. Published fine editions illustrated with original prints by many of the modern masters, notably Picasso.

volleyball, outdoor or indoor game played on level court. Upright net, top of which is 8 ft. high, divides court (60 ft. long and 30 ft. wide) in half. Volleyball was originated (1895) by William C. Morgan at Holyoke, Mass.

Vologda (vô'lŭgdŭ), city (pop. 95,194), N European RSFSR, on Vologda R. Rail junction; dairy center. Founded 1147. Ruled at first by Novgorod, it became the cap. of a principality (1397); fell to Moscow 1481. Old kremlin has 18th-cent. episcopal palace (now museum). Cathedral of St. Sophia dates from 16th cent.; Spasso-Priluki monastery from 1371.

Volos (vô'lôs), city (pop. 51,134), E Greece, in SE Thessaly, on Gulf of Volos or Pagasaean Gulf, an inlet of Aegean Sea. Mfg. and trading center (textiles, tobacco, agr. produce). Damaged in World War II.

Volscians (vŏl'shŭnz) or **Volsci** (vŏl'sī), people of anc. Italy, SE of the Alban Hills. With the Samnites they opposed Rome. Story of CORIOLANUS reflects fierceness of their attacks. In the 4th cent. B.C., they were conquered and Romanized.

Volsinii (vŏlsĭ'nēī), anc. Etruscan city, probably on the site of Orvieto. Sacked by Romans (280 B.C.), it was refounded near L. Bolsena.

Volstead Act, 1919, Federal prohibition act providing for enforcement of Eighteenth Amendment.

Volsungasaga (vŏl'sŏŏng-gŭsä'gŭ) [Icelandic,= saga of the Volsungs], Icelandic prose saga founded, apparently, on earlier poetic materials (kin to German NIBELUNGENLIED) and probably assembled in the 12th or 13th cent. Its heroine, Gudrun, accomplishes the ruin of the Volsungs, who are led by Sigurd. Brynhild (see BRUNHILD) is Sigurd's beloved, whom he betrays. Elements of this saga were used by Wagner in his operas based on the Nibelungenlied.

volt [for A. Volta], unit of electromotive force (emf); both emf and difference in potential are measured in volts. Instrument for measuring emf is a type of GALVANOMETER. International volt is emf that produces current of one AMPERE when acting on conductor with resistance of one OHM.

Volta, Alessandro, Conte (älĕssän'drō kōn'tā vōl'tä), 1745–1827, Italian physicist. He invented the electrophorus, a device for producing electric charge by induction and **Volta's** (or **voltaic**) pile: a stack of metal disks (of two different metals, e.g., copper and zinc, arranged alternately). Disks of cloth or paper moistened with an electrolyte are placed between disks. Each set of two disks corresponds to a voltaic cell and the whole to an electric battery. **Voltaic cell** is an electric cell consisting of two dissimilar metal plates suspended, without touching each other, in a solution of an acid or a salt. The VOLT is named for Volta.

voltaic cell: see VOLTA, ALESSANDRO.

Voltaire, François Marie Arouet de (frãswä' märē' ärwā' dŭ vôltĕr'), 1694–1778, French philosopher and author, whose original name was Arouet. He was the leading figure of 18th-cent. ENLIGHTENMENT. Two imprisonments in the Bastille (1717, 1726) and his visit to England (1726–29) taught him hatred of arbitrary absolutism and admiration of English liberalism. His tempestuous friendship with Frederick II of Prussia, to whose court he came in 1749, ended with Voltaire's flight from Berlin (1753) but was later resumed from a safe distance. Having won a large fortune through speculation, Voltaire bought himself an estate, first at Geneva, then at near-by Ferney (1758). His trip to Paris (1778) and the triumphal acclaim he received there were too much for him, and he died. Voltaire's work is immense (rev. and enl. ed., 52 vols., 1883). Among his many tragedies, in the classic style, *Zaïre* (1732) is probably the best. His *Letters concerning the English Nation* (in Eng., 1732; in Fr., 1733) exerted a profound influence. His great historical works—*Siècle de Louis XIV* (1751) and *Essai sur l'histoire générale et sur les mœurs et l'esprit des nations* (7 vols., 1756) show a new approach to history, with the chief emphasis on cultural and economic developments. Most widely read today are his short "philosophical novels," notably *Candide* (1759) an unsurpassed masterpiece of flippant satire. His philosophy was rationalist to the point of shallowness; his religious outlook was deistic ("If God did not exist, He would have to be invented") and aggressively tolerant (*Écrasez l'infâme!* —Crush the infamous one!—was his slogan against religious fanaticism). In his political and social views, he inclined toward conservatism; the French Revolution, often blamed on him, would have horrified him. Voltaire was a propagandist in several *causes célèbres* involving victims of religious and political persecution. His correspondence was tremendous and fully reveals the glitter and polish of his style.

Volta's (voltaic) pile: see VOLTA, ALESSANDRO.

Volterra, Daniele da (dänyā'lā dä vōltĕr'rä), 1509–66, Italian painter and sculptor; pupil of Michelangelo. Real name was Ricciarelli. Famous for his *Descent from the Cross* in Church of Trinità dei Monti, Rome.

Volterra, town (pop. 11,704), Tuscany, central Italy. A powerful Etruscan town in antiquity. Has well-preserved Etruscan and medieval walls; 10th-cent. cathedral; oldest town hall in Tuscany. Medieval fortress (14th–15th cent.) is now a prison.

voltmeter: see GALVANOMETER.

Volturno (vōltōōr'nō), river, 109 mi. long, S Italy, flowing from Apennines past Capua into Tyrrhenian Sea. Scene of Garibaldi's victory over Bourbon army (1860) and of a crossing by U.S. troops, after heavy fighting (Oct., 1943).

volume, measure of solid content. Units of measurement are either the cube of a linear unit (e.g., cubic inches or cubic centimeters) or units of dry and liquid measure (e.g., bushel and gallon, and in metric system, the liter). Formulas for some common solids (B = area of base; h = height; r = radius; l = length; w = width):

Solid	*Volume*	*Solid*	*Volume*
cube	l^3	right rectangular parallelepiped	lwh
prism	Bh		
pyramid	⅓ Bh	right circular cylinder	$\pi r^2 h$
sphere	$\frac{4}{3}\pi r^3$	right circular cone	⅓ $\pi r^2 h$

Volunteers of America, religious and philanthropic body founded (1896) by Gen. Ballington Booth and his wife, Maud Ballington Booth (see BOOTH, family). The volunteers aim to act as auxiliary to churches; converts are urged to join church of their preference. They also conduct services, missions, and Sunday schools, and foster many welfare activities, notably the Volunteer Prison League, founded (1896) by Mrs. Booth.

Von. For German names beginning thus, see proper name; e.g., for Von Bismarck, see BISMARCK.

Vondel, Joost van den (vôn'dŭl), 1587–1679, Dutch poet and dramatist. His many works include translations, polemical and religious poetry, and over 30 dramas. His most famous play, *Lucifer* (1654), may have been known to Milton.

voodooism, name for beliefs and practices attributed to Negroes of West Indies (esp. Haiti) and S U.S. Rites are linked with serpent worship and in extreme cases with human sacrifice and cannibalistic ceremonies. Ritual is reminiscent of magical observances practiced by many peoples.

Voragine, Jacobus de: see JACOBUS DE VORAGINE.

Vorarlberg (fōr"ärl'bĕrk), westernmost province (1,004 sq. mi.; pop. 193,715) of Austria, in the Alps; cap Bregenz (on L. of Constance). Dairying; textile and embroidery mfg. Many resorts (esp. for winter sports). Acquired piecemeal by the Hapsburgs in 14th–16th cent., it was administered as a crownland by Tyrol 1523–1918.

Voronezh (vŏrô'nĕsh), city (pop. 326,836), S central European RSFSR, on Voronezh R. near its confluence with the Don. Industrial center (synthetic rubber, locomotives, aircraft, machinery, processed foods). University; medical, agr., and engineering schools. City was largely destroyed in World War II, when a German advance was stopped here (1942–43).

Voronoff, Serge (sĕrzh' vôrônôf'), 1866–1951, French surgeon. He transplanted animal (chiefly monkey) glands in treating thyroid deficiency in children and for rejuvenation in old age.

Voroshilov, Kliment Yefremovich (vŭrŭshē'lŭf), 1881–, Russian field marshal. Won fame as Red Army commander in civil war. Commissar for defense 1925–40. Commanded defense of Leningrad in World War II. Became chairman of the presidium of the supreme council of the USSR (i.e., president of USSR) in 1953, after Stalin's death.

Voroshilov, city (pop. 70,628), S Maritime Territory, RSFSR, in Far Eastern Siberia. Junction of Trans-Siberian RR and Chinese Eastern RR.

Voroshilovgrad (–grăd"), city (pop. 213,007), SE Ukraine, in Donets Basin; named Lugansk until c.1935. Produces locomotives, steel pipes, and machinery. German-held (1941–43) in World War II.

vortex (vôr'tĕks), mass of fluid (liquid or gas) whose particles have rotary motion. In theory, vortex motion is considered in a frictionless fluid where motion would be continuous and could be neither created nor destroyed. Since no frictionless fluid exists, a continuous supply of energy is needed to maintain vortex motion.

vorticism (vôr'tĭsĭzŭm), short-lived 20th-cent. school of art related to cubism but stressing rhythmic movement. Chief exponent was Gaudier-Brzeska, but movement was strongest in England.

Vos, Cornelis de (kôrnā'lĭs dŭ vōs'), 1585–1651, Flemish painter of the school of Rubens.

Vosges (vōzh), department (2,279 sq. mi.; pop.

342,315), E France, in Lorraine; cap. Épinal. Borders in E on **Vosges** mountain range, which extends N from Belfort for c.120 mi. Pastures; pine forests; vineyards on E slope (in Alsace). Resorts (notably Plombières). Highest point: Ballon de Guebwiller (4,672 ft.).

Vouet, Simon (sēmõ vwā'), 1590–1649, French portrait and decorative painter in service of Louis XIII.

Vouvray (vōōvrā'), town (pop. 1,567), Indre-et-Loire dept., N central France, on Loire R. near Tours. Famous white and rosé wines.

Vrchlicky, Jaroslav (yä'rôsläf vŭrkh'lĭtskē), 1853–1912, Czech writer, whose real name was Emil Bohuslav Frida. By many translations and his own writings he immensely forwarded modern Czech literature.

Vries, Hugo de (hü'gō dů vrēs'), 1848–1935, Dutch botanist. His studies of evolution led to his rediscovery (reported in 1900) of Mendel's laws of heredity and to his development of the theory of mutation.

Vulcan, Roman fire-god, same as Greek HEPHAESTUS.

vulcanization (vŭl"kůnůzā'shůn), treatment of rubber to give it certain qualities, e.g., strength, elasticity, and resistance to solvents, and to render it unaffected by moderate heat and cold. It is usually accomplished by process invented by Charles Goodyear in 1839. Rubber and sulphur are mixed (as a rule with an organic accelerator) and usually placed in molds and subjected to heat and pressure. Cold vulcanization process (treating rubber with a bath or vapors of a sulphur compound) was developed by Alexander Parkes in 1846. For most ordinary purposes natural rubbers as well as many synthetics are vulcanized.

Vulgate (vŭl'gāt) [Latin *Vulgata editio* = common edition], most ancient extant version of the whole Bible; the official, Latin version of the Roman Catholic Church. Made by St. Jerome to replace the Old Latin version (the Itala). Old Testament is a translation of the Hebrew Masoretic text; New Testament is a careful revision of the Old Latin text. Jerome translated Tobias, Judith, and the additions to Daniel of the deuterocanonical books of the Old Testament; the rest are still in the Old Latin text. In 1546 the Council of Trent made the Vulgate the official version of the Church; in 1592 the official text with no variants was promulgated by Clement VIII. The order of books is accepted as Western canon. All subsequent editions published with the Church's imprimatur represent this Clementine edition. In 20th cent., the Benedictines, deputed by the Holy See, began a thorough revision of the Vulgate.

vulture (vŭl'chůr), bird of prey of temperate and tropical regions. It eats chiefly carrion. Old World vultures are similar to hawks. New World vultures are of another family which includes CONDOR, turkey buzzard, and black vulture.

Vyatka, RSFSR: see KIROV.

Vyborg (vē'bôrg), Finnish *Viipuri,* Swed. *Viborg,* city (pop. 56,687), NW European RSFSR, NW of Leningrad, near Finnish border; a baltic port on Gulf of Finland. Chartered 1403, it was ceded by Sweden to Russia 1721; inc. with Finland (then under Russian sovereignty) 1812. It remained Finnish until 1940, when it was ceded to USSR. Though recaptured by Finnish forces in World War II, it was finally awarded to USSR in 1947.

Vyshinsky, Andrei Yanuarievich: see VISHINSKY.

Vytautas, grand duke of Lithuania: see WITOWT.

W

W, chemical symbol of the element WOLFRAM.

Waadt, Switzerland: see VAUD.

Waal (väl), main arm of Rhine R., central Netherlands. Branches off the Rhine near German border and flows W to join the Meuse near Gorinchem. Joined rivers form the upper Merwede.

Waals, Johannes Diderik van der (yōhä'nůs dē'důrĭk vän důr väls'), 1837–1923, Dutch physicist. Won 1910 Nobel Prize for evolving an equation expressing equilibrium of states of matter for homogeneous substances when pressure, volume, and temperature are stated in terms of critical constants for each substance.

Wabash, (wô'băsh"), city (pop. 10,621), NE Ind., on Wabash R. and WSW of Fort Wayne; settled 1835. Trade center of agr. area with mfg. of electronic equipment and furniture.

Wabash, river rising in W central Ohio near Ind. line and flowing 475 mi. SW across Ind. to the Ohio. Forms Ind.-Ill. line below Terre Haute.

WAC (Women's Army Corps), created in 1942 in World War II to enlist women for noncombatant duty in the army. Directed by Oveta Culp Hobby until 1945. Congressional bill of 1948 estab. Women's Auxiliary Corps within regular army.

Wace (wās, wäs), c.1100–1174, Norman-French poet, author of a British chronicle, *Roman de Brut.*

Wachusett Reservoir (wôchōō'sĭt), central

Mass., near Clinton; built 1897–1905. Receives some water from QUABBIN RESERVOIR; supplies Boston area.

Waco (wā'kō), city (pop. 84,706), E central Texas, on Brazos R. below mouth of Bosque R.; laid out 1849. Market of rich cotton area and rail, air, highway trading and shipping center, it has mfg. of tires, cloth, clothing, glass, and drugs. Near by is L. Waco on Bosque R. Here are BAYLOR UNIVERSITY and a VA hospital.

Wade, Benjamin Franklin, 1800–1878, U.S. Senator from Ohio (1851–69). Advocate of radical Reconstruction; co-author of Wade-Davis Bill, vetoed by Pres. Lincoln in favor of more lenient program.

Wadham College: see OXFORD UNIVERSITY.

Wadsworth, city (pop. 7,966), N Ohio, SW of Akron. Mfg. of matches, valves, and iron products.

Wafd (wŏft), Egyptian political party, founded 1919 by ZAGHLUL PASHA. It aimed to free Egypt from British influence and to bring about social and economic reforms. Between 1924 and 1952 the Wafd dominated the parliament, which was opposed and dissolved several times by King Fuad I and his successor, Farouk I. After 1927 the party's leader was NAHAS PASHA. Opponents have accused the Wafd of being committed less to principles than to personalities and even of being implicated in assassinations. Dissolved in early 1953 by Gen. Naguib, who assumed control of the government in Sept., 1952.

wages, payment, in goods, services, or money, for work done. Wages reckoned in money are called nominal wages; real wages are revealed by the amount of goods that the money will buy. Theories of wages have been proposed by David Ricardo and Karl Marx.

Wages and Hours Act, also called the Fair Labor Standards Act, is intended to establish min. living standards for workers in interstate commerce and to abolish oppressive child labor. Passed in 1938, it was amended in 1950 so as to provide for a 40-hr. week and a min. hourly wage of 75 cents.

Wagner, Cosima: see WAGNER, RICHARD.

Wagner, Honus (wăg'nûr), 1874–, American baseball infielder. Fine fielding shortstop with Pittsburgh Pirates. Had lifetime batting average of .329, led Natl. League in batting eight times (1900, 1903–4, 1906–9, 1911), made 3,430 base hits.

Wagner, Richard (väg'nûr), 1813–1883, German composer of operas. A difficult, violent person, he made enemies easily, attracting as friends chiefly other defiers of convention such as Franz Liszt and Friedrich Nietzsche. Many consider him the greatest operatic genius of all time. He used a continuous flow of melody instead of the sharply differentiated recitative and aria and called his operas music dramas to signify their fusion of text and music. His librettos, which he wrote himself, were drawn chiefly from the vast store of Germanic legend and literature. His works include *Rienzi* (1840); *Der fliegende Holländer* (The Flying Dutchman, 1843); *Tannhäuser* (1843–45); *Lohengrin* (1846–48); his great tetralogy, *Der Ring des Nibelungen,* comprising *Das Rheingold* (1853–54), *Die Walküre* (1854–56), *Siegfried* (completed 1871), and *Die Götterdämmerung* (completed 1874); *Tristan und Isolde* (1857–59); *Die Meistersinger von Nürnberg* (1862–67), his only comic opera; and his final work, *Parsifal* (1877–82). After moving to Bayreuth in 1872, he built a theater adequate for a proper performance of his works. His second wife, **Cosima Wagner,** 1837–1930, daughter of Franz Liszt and the Comtesse d'Agoult, was wife (1857–69) of Hans von Bülow. She was married to Wagner in 1870. She continued the Bayreuth festivals after his death. Their son, **Siegfried Wagner,** 1869–1930, was known as a conductor.

Wagner, Robert F(erdinand) (wăg'nûr), 1877–1953, U.S. Senator from N.Y. (1927–49), b. Germany. A leader in directing New Deal legislation (e.g., act establishing NATIONAL LABOR RELATIONS BOARD).

Wagner-Jauregg, Julius (yōō'lyōōs väg'nûr-you'rĕk), 1857–1940, Austrian neurologist. A pioneer of fever therapy, he treated paresis by inoculation with organisms causing malaria; for this work he won 1927 Nobel Prize in Psysiology and Medicine.

Wagram (vä'gräm), town (pop. 3,917), Lower Austria, NE of Vienna, in the Marshfield; officially called Deutsch-Wagram. Here on July 5–6, 1809, Napoleon I won a brilliant victory over Austria.

Wahabi (wähä'bē), Puritanical reform movement in Islam, begun by Mohammed ibn Abd al-Wahab (1703?–1787). Rejects veneration of saints, ostentatious rites, luxurious living. The Saud tribe adopted the religion and managed to gain control of most of Arabia. Ottoman rulers were unable to stamp out the troublesome Wahabi movement, which finally triumphed in Saudi Arabia as the official religion.

Wahiawa (wä'hēûwä'), city (pop. 8,369), Oahu, T.H., NW of Honolulu, in pineapple district.

Wahlstatt, Silesia: see LIEGNITZ.

wahoo: see BURNING BUSH.

Wahpeton (wô'pĭtûn), city (pop. 5,125), SE N.Dak., on Red R. Dairy center with U.S. Indian school.

Waialeale (wī'ä"lää'lā), peak, 5,080 ft. high, central Kauai, T.H. Contains Waimea Canyon. Average yearly rainfall on summit, 476 in. Shares, with Cherrapunji, India, record of having world's heaviest rainfall.

Waianae Range (wī'ûnī'), SW Oahu, T.H. Rises to 4,030 ft. in Mt. Kaala, highest point on island.

Waikiki (wīkēkē'), bathing beach, Honolulu, T.H. Site of Fort De Russy.

Wailuku (wīlōō'kōō), city (pop. 7,424), N Maui, T.H. Island's largest town and tourist center.

Wainwright, Jonathan M(ayhew), 1883–, American general. In World War II he led fight in Philippine Isls. which ended in surrender of Bataan and Corregidor. Prisoner of war 1942–45.

Waite, Morrison Remick (wāt), 1816–88, Chief Justice of U.S. Supreme Court (1874–88).

waits, in England, band of itinerant musicians who celebrate Christmas by the nocturnal open-air singing of carols or other seasonable music. Waits were originally watchmen, who blew a horn or sang a tune to mark the hours or change of guard. The custom survives especially in rural communities.

Wakamatsu (wäkä'mätso͞o), city (pop. 78,694), N Kyushu, Japan, on Sea of Japan; chief coal-loading port of Japan.

Wakayama (wäkä'yämů), city (pop. 171,800), S Honshu, Japan, on Inland Sea. Railroad and mfg. center. Site of castle (16th cent.) of Hideyoshi.

Wakefield, Edward Gibbon, 1796–1862, British statesman. His views on colonial affairs led to establishment (1836) of South Australian colony. His New Zealand Land Co. (1839) colonized that country.

Wakefield, county borough (pop. 60,380), cap. of West Riding of Yorkshire, England. A center of cloth industry since 14th cent., it also has varied mfg. An important farm center. Richard, duke of York, was slain in battle here in 1460. Towneley miracle plays originated here.

Wakefield, town (pop. 19,633), NE Mass., N of Boston; settled 1639. Shoes, dies, and knit goods.

Wakefield, family estate of George Washington, E Va., near Potomac R. and E of Fredericksburg. John Washington settled here 1665. Original buildings burned; period buildings reconstructed. Made national monument 1930.

Wake Forest, town (pop. 3,704), E central N.C., NNE of Raleigh. Seat of Wake Forest Col. (Baptist; mainly for men; 1833).

Wake Island, atoll and three islets, central Pacific, between Hawaii and Guam. Discovered 1796 by British. Claimed 1900 by U.S. and made a U.S. naval reservation 1934. Became Pan-American air base 1935. Appropriations made 1939 for naval air base and submarine base. Attacked by Japanese on Dec. 7, 1941; fell Dec. 23, after heroic defense by small marine garrison. Japan surrendered it Sept., 1945.

wake-robin: see TRILLIUM.

Waksman, Selman Abraham (wäks'mŭn), 1888–, American microbiologist, b. Russia. Won 1952 Nobel Prize in Physiology and Medicine for his work as codiscoverer of the antibiotic substance streptomycin and for its value in treating tuberculosis.

Walachia or **Wallachia** (both: wälā'kēů, wŭ–), historic division (29,575 sq. mi.; pop. 6,707,271), S Rumania, in the lower Danubian plain; chief city Bucharest. Largely agr., it has rich oil fields at Ploesti. It consists of two historic provinces—Muntenia or Greater Walachia (E) and Oltenia or Lesser Walachia (W). Part of Roman Dacia, it was overrun by many invaders. The native Rumanians (called Vlachs or Walachs by their Slavic neighbors) estab. a principality c.1290. Its later history paralleled that of its sister principality, Moldavia, with which it was united in 1859 (see MOLDAVIA).

Walcheren (väl'khŭrŭn), island, area 80 sq. mi., Zeeland prov., SW Netherlands, in North Sea at entrance to Scheldt estuary. Chief cities: Middleburg, Flushing. Its capture by British commandos in World War II opened up port of Antwerp for Allied use (Nov. 1, 1944).

Wald, Lillian D., 1867–1940, American social worker and pioneer in public health nursing. The visiting nurse service she founded in 1893 became the nucleus of the Henry St. Settlement in New York city.

Waldeck (väl'dĕk), former principality (433 sq. mi.; 1910 pop. 61,707), W Germany; cap. Arolsen. Agr., forests. A county from c.1200, Waldeck was united with PYRMONT and raised to a principality in the 17th cent. Waldeck-Pyrmont was incorporated with Prussia in 1922, Pyrmont becoming part of Hanover prov. and Waldeck of Hesse-Nassau prov.

Waldeck-Rousseau, René (rŭnā' väldĕk'-ro͞osō'), 1846–1904, French premier (1899–1902). Secured presidential pardon for Capt. Dreyfus. Initiated anticlerical legislation but opposed extreme measures.

Waldemar (wäl'dŭmär), Dan. *Valdemar,* kings of Denmark. **Waldemar I** (the Great), 1131–82, became king 1157, after defeating two rivals. Helped Henry the Lion and Albert the Bear in subjugating the Wends; codified Danish law; gained territory in Norway. His second son, **Waldemar II,** 1170–1241, reigned 1202–41. Extended Danish control over Estonia but was forced to relinquish control over Schwerin after his defeat at Bornhöved (1227). **Waldemar IV** (Valdemar Atterdag), c.1320–1375, reigned 1340–75. At his accession, he found Denmark dismembered by foreign rulers, but by 1361 he had succeeded in reuniting his kingdom. He conquered Skane, in violation of a treaty with the Swedish king; obtained temporary possession of Gotland through his victory over Hanseatic League (1362), but was later defeated by the Hanseatic towns and forced to accept the Treaty of STRALSUND (1370). His daughter MARGARET was to unite Denmark, Norway, and Sweden.

Walden Pond: See CONCORD, Mass.

Waldenses (wôldĕn'sēz), Fr. *Vaudois,* Protestant sect, arising from the Poor Men of Lyons, organized by Peter Waldo (d. 1217), a lay preacher, who laid great stress on poverty. Adopted unorthodox views and were condemned by Pope Lucius III in 1184. Persisted in Dauphiné until the persecution of 1487 and continued in Piedmont. Met with German and Swiss Protestants in 1532. In 1655 the French and Charles Emmanuel II of Savoy campaigned against them. When the Edict of Nantes was revoked (1686) Henri Arnaud led the Waldenses to Switzerland, later led them back. Assured of toleration after the French Revolution, they were granted full rights by Charles Albert of Savoy in 1848.

Waldseemüller, Martin (vält'zāmů"lŭr), 1470?–1522?, German cosmographer. The first cartographer to call the New World *America* (1507).

Waldstein, Albrecht von: see WALLENSTEIN.

Wales, Welsh *Cymru* (ko͝om'rē), region (8,012 sq. mi.; pop. 2,956,986, with border co. of Monmouth, included administratively in Wales), W Great Britain, a peninsula W of England. Politically united with England since 1536. Counties of Wales proper are (in the N) Anglesey, Caernarvonshire, Denbighshire, Flintshire, Merionethshire, and Montgomeryshire and (in the S) Cardiganshire,

Radnorshire, Brecknockshire, Pembrokeshire, Caermarthenshire, and Glamorganshire. Peninsula (130 mi. long N–S; 37–92 mi. wide) is bounded by Irish Sea (N), St. Georges Channel (W), and Bristol Channel (S), and is deeply indented by Cardigan Bay. Wales is almost entirely occupied by Cambrian Mts., rising to 3,560 ft. in Mt. Snowdon. Rivers include Clwyd, Conway, Teifi, Dovey, Mawddoch, Dee, Severn, and Wye. Region has kept its distinctive culture. Half population speaks Welsh in addition to English, and c.100,000 speak only Welsh. Central Highlands and N counties are pastoral, agr., and thinly populated. Modern wealth of Wales is in great coalfields and industry in S, which has cities of Cardiff, Swansea, Rhondda, and Merthyr Tydfil. Roman impress upon Wales was light, and Anglo-Saxon conquest of E Britain little affected Welsh. There were fierce border wars as kingdoms of heptarchy grew; King Offa supposedly built Offa's Dyke to mark boundary between Mercia and Wales. Welsh poetry, music, and learning (see EISTEDDFOD) flourished despite continued invasion. William I recognized power of Welsh (see WELSH MARCHES) who resisted through 200 years of guerrilla warfare. Conquest of Wales was completed (1282) by Edward I, who originated English custom of making eldest son of the king prince of Wales. In 15th cent. Owen Glendower led a revolt, and Owen Tudor (whose grandson Henry VII became first Tudor monarch) was involved in Wars of the Roses. Act of Union (1536) abolished all law at variance with that of British and estab. English as legal language. Reformation came slowly to Wales. Later many turned to CALVINISTIC METHODIST CHURCH. This bolstered Welsh Nationalism, one of world's most successful nonpolitical nationalistic movements. Industrial Revolution exploited mineral wealth. Resulting shift of population promoted emigration (esp. to U.S.). In late 19th cent. S Wales became chief coal-exporting region of world. In late 1920s and '30s Wales suffered heavily from economic decline. Industrial boom of World War II and government's control of mines improved situation. The Univ. of Wales (founded 1893) has four constituent colleges—Aberystwyth (1872), Cardiff (1883), Bangor (1884), and Swansea (1920).

Walewska, Countess Maria (mārē′ä välĕf′skä), 1789–1817, Polish noblewoman. Napoleon met her at Warsaw in 1807 and made her his mistress. She bore him a son, **Comte Alexandre Walewski,** 1810–68, who served as a diplomat under Napoleon III (foreign minister, 1855–60) and played an important part in the reforms of the "Liberal Empire."

Walhalla, in Germanic mythology: see VALHALLA.

Walhalla (wŏlhă′lŭ), city (pop. 1,463), NE N.Dak., near Canadian line and on Pembina R. Resort center for Pembina Mts.

Walker, James J(ohn), 1881–1946, mayor of New York city (1925–32). Immensely popular with voters, he resigned after investigation led by Samuel Seabury disclosed extensive municipal corruption.

Walker, Robert John, 1801–69, American statesman. Name sometimes given as Robert James. U.S. Senator from Miss. (1835–45); advocate of American expansion. U.S. Secretary of the Treasury (1845–49); one of ablest in history of department. Walker Tariff of 1846 helped build up Anglo-American commerce. Governor of Kansas in 1857.

Walker, William, 1824–60, American FILIBUSTER in Nicaragua. "Colonized" Nicaragua in 1855 at request of government at León; capturing Granada, he was "elected" president of Nicaragua, July, 1856. Administration of U.S. Pres. Franklin Pierce vacillated between recognition of his government and probability of antagonizing Great Britain. Surrendered to U.S. navy in May, 1857. Shot by firing squad in Honduras after final attempt to conquer Central America.

Walker Lake, 24 mi. long, W Nev., part of anc. L. Lahontan. Fed by Walker R., but has no outlet.

walking stick or **stick insect,** name for certain leaf insects with long, slender twiglike bodies.

Walküre, German name for VALKYRIES.

Wallace, Alfred Russel, 1823–1913, English naturalist. Independently of Charles Darwin he evolved a theory of EVOLUTION. He pioneered in the modern study of animal geography and postulated an imaginary line (Wallace's line) as the dividing line between Asiatic and Australian fauna in the Malay Archipelago.

Wallace, Henry, 1836–1916, American agr. leader. With his son Henry Cantwell Wallace he founded (1895) newspaper which later was called *Wallace's Farmer;* it became leading agr. journal of country. **Henry Cantwell Wallace,** 1866–1924, was U.S. Secretary of Agriculture (1921–24). His son, **Henry A(gard) Wallace,** 1888–, was U.S. Secretary of Agriculture (1933–41), Vice President of U.S. (1941–45), and U.S. Secretary of Commerce (1945–46). PROGRESSIVE PARTY presidential candidate 1948.

Wallace, Lew(is), 1827–1905, American soldier, diplomat, and novelist, best remembered for highly popular novel *Ben-Hur: a Tale of the Christ* (1880).

Wallace, Sir Richard, 1818–90, English art collector; natural son of marquess of Hertford. His father's collection was given to the government by Lady Wallace. The **Wallace Collection,** noted for 18th-cent. art, was opened 1900 in Hertford House, London.

Wallace, Sir William, c.1272–1306, Scottish hero in struggle against Edward I. Chief source for his life is poem attributed to Blind Harry. After burning Lanark, he organized an army and routed (1297) English at Stirling. Acted briefly as guardian of realm for John de Baliol. Later captured and executed for treason.

Wallace, city (pop. 3,140), N Idaho, near Mont. line. Trade center in Coeur d'Alene Mts.

Wallaceburg, town (pop. 7,688), S Ont., Canada, on Sydenham R. and NNW of Chatham. Sugar refining, flour milling, and lumbering.

Wallace Collection: see WALLACE, SIR RICHARD.

Wallach, Otto (ô′tō vä′läkh), 1847–1931, German chemist. Won 1910 Nobel Prize for pioneer work on alicyclic compounds; worked also on azotic compounds.

Wallachia, Rumania: see WALACHIA.

Wallack, James William (wŏ'lŭk), c.1795–1864, Anglo-American actor and manager. Leading actor (1812–32) at Drury Lane. In U.S. after 1852. His son, **Lester Wallack,** 1820–88, became manager of Wallack's Theater in 1861.

Wallas, Graham, 1858–1932, English political scientist and sociologist, member of Fabian Society. Noted for psychological analyses of politics.

Walla Walla (wŏ'lŭ wŏ'lŭ), city (pop. 24,102), SE Wash., on Walla Walla R., near Oregon line; settled c.1859 on site of mission of Marcus WHITMAN. Center for rich farm and lumber area with fruit canneries and lumber mills. Seat of Whitman Col. (nonsectarian; coed.; chartered 1859, opened 1866 as Congregationalist seminary, became college 1883). Near by are Walla Walla Col., Fort Walla Walla (estab. 1857; now VA hospital), Whitman Natl. Monument.

Wallenstein or **Waldstein, Albrecht von** (Ger. äl'brĕkht fŭn vä'lŭnshtīn, vält'shtīn), 1583–1634, imperialist generalissimo in THIRTY YEARS WAR. For his victories, Emperor Ferdinand II created him duke of Friedland (1625) and of Mecklenburg (1627). After his failure to take Stralsund (1628), his enemies secured his dismissal (1630), but he was recalled in 1632. Defeated by the Swedes at Lützen (1632), he began secret peace negotiations, was accused of treason, and was murdered, probably on the emperor's instigation, by a group of conspirators including his lieutenants Piccolomini and Gallas. He is the subject of a dramatic trilogy by Schiller.

Waller, Edmund, 1606–87, English poet. Banished for plot in behalf of Charles I, he lived in France in exile for years. His first poem, "To a King on His Return," appeared in *Rex Redux* (1633). His popular *Poems* (1645 and later eds.) contained courtly lyrics such as "Go, Lovely Rose" and "On a Girdle."

wallflower, Old World biennial or perennial (*Cheiranthus cheiri*) with fragrant, stocklike flowers in shades of red, brown, and yellow; often cultivated in America. It is also called gillyflower. The orange-flowered Siberian wallflower (*Erysimum asperum*) is found wild and cultivated in North America.

Wallingford, borough (pop. 11,994) in Wallingford town (pop. 16,976), S Conn., NNE of New Haven. Mfg. of silverware (since 1835), metal goods, and plastics. Choate School for boys (1896) is here.

Wallington, borough (pop. 8,910), NE N.J., SE of Passaic. Machinery, steel tubing, and plastics.

Wallis, John (wŏ'lĭs), 1616–1703, English mathematician. He systematized use of formulas, introduced use of symbol ∞ for infinity, studied quadrature of curves.

Wallis, Switzerland: see VALAIS.

Wallis and Futuna Islands (wŏ'lĭs, fo͞oto͞o'nä), French protectorate (c.75 sq. mi.; pop. 6,770), S Pacific, 250 mi. W of Samoa. Comprises Wallis and Hoorn Isls.

Walloons (wŭlo͞onz', wŏ–), the French-speaking people of Belgium, in contrast to the Flemings of the N provinces. More specifically, Walloon is the French dialect spoken in the Liége region. The movement for reviving Walloon literature centered in Liége in the 19th cent. Rivalry between Walloons and Flemings has long been a critical political issue in Belgium. In America, the Dutch indiscriminately called all Huguenot refugees Walloons.

Wallowa Lake (wŭlou'ŭ), NE Oregon, at foot of Wallowa Mts. Resort; used for irrigation. Drained by Wallowa R. of the Snake system.

Wall Street, narrow street in lower Manhattan, New York city, extending E from Broadway to the East River. Center of one of world's great financial districts. By extension, "Wall St." designates American financial interests.

Walmer (wôl'mŭr), former urban district, now part of Deal, Kent, England. Walmer Castle is official residence of lord warden of the CINQUE PORTS.

walnut, name for several deciduous trees of genus *Juglans,* valued for wood and nuts. Nuts of the Persian or English walnut (*Juglans regia*), which thrives in Calif., are eaten both plain and in confectionery. Nuts of the black walnut (*J. nigra*), native to E U.S., are used for flavoring. The wood is highly valued for furniture. For the white walnut, see BUTTERNUT.

Walnut Canyon National Monument: see NATIONAL PARKS AND MONUMENTS (table).

Walpi (wăl'pē), picturesque Hopi Indian pueblo (pop. c.150), NE Ariz., on mesa NE of Winslow; founded c.1700. Holds Antelope rites (even years), Hopi snake dance (odd years) in Aug. Many of its people have moved to Polacca village, at foot of mesa.

Walpole, Sir Hugh (Seymour), 1884–1941, British novelist, b. New Zealand; author of many popular novels, including *The Cathedral* (1922) and the historical series begun with *Rogue Herries* (1930).

Walpole, Robert, 1st **earl of Orford,** 1676–1745, English statesman. His successful handling of financial wreckage after SOUTH SEA BUBBLE led to his dominance in political life 1721–42. His influence with Caroline of Anspach, wife of George II, led to his becoming in effect first prime minister in English history. In domestic affairs he encouraged trade while reducing land tax to mollify the Tory gentry. In foreign affairs he favored friendship with France; avoidance of war. After War of Jenkins's Ear, leading to War of the Austrian Succession, military reverses forced him to resign in 1742. His son, **Horace** or **Horatio Walpole,** 4th **earl of Orford,** 1717–97, was an author. In 1747 he settled at Twickenham and estab. his Strawberry Hill press. A friend of Thomas Gray, he printed Gray's *Odes* as his first production. His own letters and reminiscences illuminate Georgian England, and his "terror" novel, *The Castle of Otranto* (1764), spurred the Gothic cultural revival.

Walpole, town (pop. 9,109), E Mass., SW of Boston. Machinery, building supplies, and textiles.

walrus (wŏl'rŭs, wôl'–), gregarious aquatic mammal (*Odobenus*) of arctic waters, related to seal. There are two similar species, the Atlantic and the Pacific walruses. Adult males reach length of 10–12 ft. and a weight of over a ton. Tusks in male range from 14 to 16 in. long; smaller in female. Formerly walrus was commercial source of walrus ivory (from tusks), leather, and oil.

Walsall (wôl'sôl), county borough (pop. 114,-514), Staffordshire, England. Has coal and iron mining, leather-tanning, and varied mfg.

Walsenburg (wôl'sŭnbûrg), city (pop. 5,596), S Colo., S of Pueblo, in grain, livestock, coal region.

Walsh, Thomas J(ames), 1859–1933, American statesman, U.S. Senator from Mont. (1913–33). Adviser and supporter of Pres. Wilson. Led investigation of TEAPOT DOME scancal.

Walsingham, village, Norfolk, England. Site of Walsingham Abbey, great shrine of medieval England.

Walter, Bruno, 1876–, German-American conductor, whose name was originally Bruno Walter Schlesinger. He conducted in Germany and Austria until the Nazis forced him to leave. In the U.S. he has conducted the NBC Symphony and at the Metropolitan Opera, and in 1941 he became annual guest conductor of the New York Philharmonic.

Walter, Hubert, d. 1205, English archbishop and statesman. Made archbishop of Canterbury and justiciar (1193), he was virtual ruler of England during absences of Richard I. Made important administrative and tax reforms.

Walter, Thomas Ustick, 1804–87, American architect of the classic revival. As government architect (1851–65) he designed extensions for the CAPITOL at Washington. Works in Philadelphia included main building of Girard Col. and Biddle country home.

Walter of Henley or **Walter de Henley,** 13th cent. English writer on agriculture. His *Husbandry* was for 200 years the authority in England on rural economy.

Walter the Penniless, d. 1096, French Crusader. Setting out in advance of the main army of the First Crusade, his followers plundered the Belgrade area and were set upon by the Bulgarians. They joined with the forces of Peter the Hermit at Constantinople but were routed by the Seljuks in Asia Minor.

Waltham (wôl'thăm), city (pop. 47,187), E Mass., on Charles R. and W of Boston; settled 1634. Metal goods, precision instruments, machinery. Had Waltham Watch Co., 1854–1950). Seat of Brandeis Univ. (1948), first Jewish-sponsored nonsectarian institution of higher education in U.S.

Waltham Holy Cross (wôl'tŭm, wôl'thŭm) or **Waltham Abbey,** urban district (pop. 8,197), Essex, England. Abbey, built in 1030 to contain miraculous cross found in Somerset, was enlarged by King Harold (who is probably buried here). Near by are great gunpowder factories. **Waltham Cross,** 1 mi. west, is site of an Eleanor Cross.

Walthamstow (–stō), municipal borough (pop. 121,069), Essex, England; industrial suburb of London.

Walther von der Vogelweide (väl'tŭr fŭn dĕr fō'gŭlvī'dŭ), c.1170–c.1230, Austrian minnesinger. Considered the finest German lyric poet of the Middle Ages, he wrote love lyrics, religious poems, and *Sprüche* [sayings].

Walton, Ernest Thomas Sinton, 1903–, British physicist, b. Ireland. Shared 1951 Nobel Prize for pioneer work on transmutation of atomic nuclei by means of atomic particles accelerated artificially and used as projectiles.

Walton, Izaak, 1593–1683, English author of *The Compleat Angler; or, The Contemplative Man's Recreation* (1653), a masterpiece on fishing and thought.

Walton, William (Turner), 1902–, English composer. Among his compositions are his *Façade* suite, a musical setting of poems by Edith Sitwell; *Portsmouth Point* (1925) and *Belshazzar's Feast* (1931) for orchestra; a symphony (1935); a viola concerto (1929); a violin concerto (1936–39); and musical scores for the films *Henry V* (1945) and *Hamlet* (1947).

waltz, dance in moderate triple time evolved in 18th cent. from German *Landler*. Viennese waltz made famous by Johann Strauss, father and son. Came to U.S. via England in early 19th cent.

Wanamaker, John (wŏ'nŭmākŭr), 1838–1922, American merchant, founder of large department stores in Philadelphia and New York city.

Wanaque (wŏ'nŭkē), borough (pop. 4,222), NE N.J., NW of Paterson. Wanaque Reservoir is largest in N.J.

Wanchüan, China: see CHANGKIAKOW.

Wandering Jew, legendary Jew who mocked Jesus when He was carrying the Cross and so was doomed to live a wandering life until the Last Judgment.

Wang Ching-wei (wäng' jĭng'-wā'), 1885–1944, Chinese statesman. Originally leader of left wing of Kuomintang but frequently changed sides between 1927 and 1937. Broke with the Nationalists 1938. Headed Japanese puppet government at Nanking (1939–44).

Wang Wei (wäng' wā'), 699–759, Chinese poet and painter. His quatrains delicately portray quiet scenes like those in his few extant paintings.

Wapakoneta (wŏpŭkŭnĕ'tŭ), city (pop. 5,797), W Ohio, S of Lima. Mfg. of machinery and toys.

wapiti (wŏ'pĭtē), member of deer family of genus *Cervus*. It is also called elk in America, but is not closely related to elk. Once abundant, it was exterminated in E U.S., is protected in parts of the West.

Wappers, Gustave, Baron (güstäv' väpĕrs', vä'pŭrs), 1803–74, Belgian historical and genre painter.

Wapping (wŏp'ĭng), riverside district of Stepney, London, England, near the Tower; a dock section. N terminus of Thames Tunnel to Rotherhithe.

Warbeck, Perkin, 1474?–1499, pretender to English throne. Persuaded by Yorkish adherents that he was son of Edward IV, he proclaimed himself Richard IV in 1497. Captured by forces of Henry VII, he admitted the plot and was hanged.

warbler, name in New World for birds of wood warbler family, small, migratory, insectivorous birds, usually brightly colored and mediocre singers. Old World warblers belong to another family; they are generally fine songsters with dull plumage.

Warburg, Otto Heinrich (ô'tō hīn'rĭkh vär'-bŏŏrk), 1883–, German physiologist. Won

1931 Nobel Prize in Physiology and Medicine for work on respiratory enzyme.

war crimes. In World War II Allied powers determined to punish Axis war criminals. Crimes were to include aggressive warfare and atrocities in any civilian group (notably extermination of a people or genocide). UN Commission for the Investigation of War Crimes was estab. to compile and classify lists of suspects. In Aug., 1945, U.S., USSR, and Great Britain adopted statute for trying Nazi leaders. Trials held in Nuremberg, Nov., 1945. After voluminous evidence, those sentenced to death in 1946 included Goering, Ribbentrop, and Streicher; Schacht and von Papen were acquitted. Likewise 28 war criminals were tried by 11-nation tribunal in Tokyo (1946–47). Many were also tried in civil courts for crimes committed in war.

Ward, Artemas (är'tĭmůs), 1727–1800, American general in American Revolution. Head of Mass. troops; commanded at siege of Boston (1775), directed fortification of Dorchester Heights.

Ward, Artemus (är'tůmůs), pseud. of Charles Farrar Browne, 1834–67, American humorist, a reporter for the Cleveland *Plain Dealer.* His column, "Artemus Ward's Sayings," with shrewd observations, misspelled words, and quaint turns of speech, was popular.

Ward, Mrs. Humphry, 1851–1920, English novelist; granddaughter of Thomas Arnold. Wrote many sober novels (e.g., *Robert Elsmere,* 1888).

Ward, John Quincy Adams, 1830–1910, American sculptor of portrait statues and monuments. Several of his works are in Central Park, New York city.

Ward, Lester Frank, 1841–1913, American sociologist, developed theory of planned progress called telesis, whereby man through education and development of intellect could direct social evolution. Noted for his *Dynamic Sociology* (1883).

Ward, Nathaniel, 1578–1652, British clergyman, a Puritan minister in Agawam (Ipswich), Mass. (1634–36). There he helped compile Body of Liberties (1641). *The Simple Cobler of Aggawam* (1647) is a lively, crotchety book, arguing for a new theory of constitutional government for England and against women's fashions and religious toleration.

Ward, William George, 1812–82, England Roman Catholic apologist, associated with Newman in the OXFORD MOVEMENT. Ordained an Anglican clergyman, he lost his university degrees after writing *The Ideal of a Christian Church* (1844) and shortly became a Catholic.

ward: see GUARDIAN AND WARD.

war debts, obligations to U.S. incurred by foreign nations in World War I. When U.S. entered war in 1917, allies had little foreign exchange. Credits were extended to them in and after war, in 1922 set at about $3,350,-000,000. Payments made, mostly from German reparations, until 1931, when Pres. Hoover proposed moratorium. Lausanne Pact of 1932 reduced reparations in hope U.S. would release claims, but it did not. After 1932 all nations defaulted except Finland and Hungary. For international obligations of World War II, see LEND-LEASE.

War Department, United States, organized (1789) under U.S. Constitution as an executive department of Federal government to administer the military establishment. Reconstituted in 1947 as Dept. of the Army within U.S. Dept. of Defense (see DEFENSE, UNITED STATES DEPARTMENT OF).

Ware, Henry, 1764–1845, American clergyman, a founder of Unitarianism in U.S. Opposition to his appointment as Hollis professor of divinity at Harvard (1805) hastened split of the Unitarians from Congregationalists. His son, **Henry Ware,** 1794–1843, pastor and teacher, was editor (1819–22) of first Unitarian organ, *Christian Disciple,* and a leader in development of denomination.

Ware, town (pop. 7,517), with Ware village (pop. 6,217), central Mass., W of Worcester. Textiles.

Wareham (wâr'hăm", wâ'rům), resort town (pop. 7,569), SE Mass., on inlet of Buzzards Bay. Ships cranberries and shellfish.

Warfield, David, 1866–1951, American actor. Associated with David Belasco who first sponsored him (in *The Auctioneer,* 1901). His acting was memorable in such plays as *The Return of Peter Grimm* (1911).

Warming, Johannes Eugenius Bülow (yōhä'nůs ûōōgā'nēōōs bü'lou vär'mĭng), 1841–1924, Danish botanist, a founder of the science of plant ecology.

Warm Springs, historic watering place, W Ga., NE of Columbus, famous for studying and treating aftereffects of poliomyelitis. Healthful properties of water known since Indian times. In 1927 F. D. Roosevelt founded Georgia Warm Springs Foundation, to which he donated his large farm here, to help fellow-sufferers from poliomyelitis. He died here at the "Little White House" (now a national shrine), 1945. Near by is Warm Springs city (pop. 557).

Warner, Charles Dudley, 1829–1900, American editor. Contributed to Hartford *Courant* and *Harper's Magazine* travel articles. Edited the "American Men of Letters" series and the "Library of the World's Best Literature." Collaborated with Mark Twain on a novel, *The Gilded Age* (1873).

Warner, Glenn Scobey (Pop Warner), 1871–, American football coach. Three of his Univ. of Pittsburgh football teams were unbeaten (1915–17); at Stanford (1924–32), he produced three Rose Bowl teams.

Warner, Olin Levi, 1844–96, American sculptor of portrait busts and statues. His *Diana,* an ideal figure, is in Metropolitan Mus.

Warner, Seth, 1743–84, hero of American Revolution. One of leaders of Green Mountain Boys. Captured Crown Point in 1775. Shared with John Stark the victory at Bennington in 1777.

Warner Robins, town (pop. 7,986), central Ga., S of Macon. Also called Wellston.

War of 1812, name given to war between U.S. and Great Britain, 1812–15. Partly occasioned by a desire for neutral shipping rights by Americans in a period of strain in Franco-British relations. Practice of IMPRESSMENT of British sailors from American ships was added cause of trouble. EMBARGO ACT of

1807 and its successors proved ineffective against British and French measures. Actual outbreak of hostilities, however, stemmed from desire of frontiersmen for free land, which could only be obtained at expense of the Indians and the British. The "war hawks" in Congress overrode the moderates; war was declared June 18, 1812. American navy won victories in 1812 that balanced defeat of land forces; in 1813 most American ships were either captured or bottled up in harbor for duration of the war. U.S. victories in a war that brought few decisive military gains for either side were won by Oliver PERRY on L. Erie (Sept. 1813); by W. H. Harrison at Detroit and in battle of the Thames (Oct., 1813); by Thomas MACDONOUGH on L. Champlain (Sept., 1814); and in halting of the British at Fort McHenry (Sept., 1814) after they had taken Washington. Treaty of GHENT ended war on Dec. 24, 1814. Final action occurred after signing of the treaty, when Andrew Jackson decisively defeated the British at New Orleans on Jan. 8, 1815. War quickened growth of American nationalism, opened West for expansion; country embarked on a period of political isolation from Europe.

War Production Board (WPB), estab. (1942) by executive order in World War II to direct war production and the procurement of materials. WPB assigned priorities to deliveries of scarce materials, prohibited nonessential industrial activities. Abolished in 1945.

War Relocation Authority: see RELOCATION CENTER.

Warren, Earl, 1891–, American political leader, governor of Calif. (1943–). Unsuccessful Republican vice presidential nominee in 1948.

Warren, Gouverneur Kemble (gŭvŭrnēr'), 1830–82, American army engineer, Union general in Civil War. Distinguished himself in Seven Days battles; at Gettysburg, where he saved the Round Tops; and in Wilderness campaign. Removed from command by Gen. Philip H. Sheridan in 1865, he was later exonerated.

Warren, Mercy Otis, 1728–1814, American author of propaganda for the patriot cause in the American Revolution and of the first history of that war (1805), b. Mass.; sister of James Otis.

Warren, Robert Penn, 1905–, American writer. When a student at Vanderbilt he contributed to *Fugitive* magazine. Later he was a Southern literary leader. His poetry is much admired. Novels include *Night Rider* (1939), *At Heaven's Gate* (1943), *All the King's Men* (1946), and *World Enough and Time* (1950). Distinguished short stories are collected in *Circus in the Attic and Other Stories* (1948).

Warren, Whitney, 1864–1943, American architect. Joined C. D. Wetmore in a firm known for designing of Grand Central Terminal (1913) and New York hotels (e.g., Ritz-Carlton, Biltmore).

Warren. 1 City (pop. 49,856), NE Ohio, NW of Youngstown; settled 1799. Trade and industrial center in farm area with steel mills and mfg. of metal products, machinery, and electrical apparatus. **2** Borough (pop. 14,849), NW Pa., ESE of Erie; laid out c.1795. Oil refining and mfg. of furniture and metal products. **3** Town (pop. 8,513), E R.I., N of Bristol and on Narragansett Bay arm. Shellfishing; textiles.

Warrensburg, city (pop. 6,857), W Mo., ESE of Kansas City, in agr. area with coal, sandstone, and clay deposits. Clothing mfg. and meat packing.

Warrenton. 1 City (pop. 1,584), E Mo., WNW of St. Louis. Daniel Boone lived here and was at first buried near by. **2** Town (pop. 1,799), N Va., NNW of Fredericksburg; settled 18th cent. Center of horse breeding and racing and fox hunting.

Warrington, village (pop. 13,570), NW Fla., on Pensacola Bay near Pensacola.

Warroad, resort village (pop. 1,276) NW Minn., on L. of the Woods near Canadian line.

Warsaw (wôr'sô), Pol. *Warszawa,* city (1939 pop. c.1,289,000; 1950 pop. c.650,000), cap. of Poland, on the Vistula. Right-bank section of city is called Praga. Commercial and industrial center (chemicals, automobiles, textiles, food products). Archiepiscopal see; seat of a university (founded 1818) and of many cultural institutions. Became cap. of Masovia 15th cent.; replaced Cracow as cap. of Poland 1595. Passed to Prussia 1795; was cap. of duchy of Warsaw (see POLAND) 1807–13. Congress of Vienna (1814–15) created kingdom of Poland, under rule of Russian emperors, with Warsaw as cap. Warsaw led the anti-Russian insurrection of 1830, but had to capitulate 1831. In World War II, 87% of Warsaw proper was destroyed. It fell to the Germans after stubborn resistance (Sept. 27, 1939). The Jewish ghetto (1942 pop. c.500,000) was walled in by the Germans and, after it offered armed resistance, was obliterated after a heavy battle. (Only c.200 Jews were left by 1945.) In Aug.–Oct., 1944, c.250,000 Polish underground fighters lost their lives battling the Germans in Warsaw, while the Russian army, across the Vistula, stood by inactive. The Russians took Warsaw in Jan., 1945. Little was left of the lavish palaces of the great nobility, the churches, and public buildings that had made Warsaw one of Europe's finest cities.

Warsaw. 1 City (pop. 6,625), NE Ind., SE of South Bend. Resort center in lake region. Mfg. of automotive and aircraft products. **2** City (pop. 936), central Mo., on Osage R., at W end of L. of the Ozarks. Fishing and hunting resort.

Warta (vär'tä), Ger. *Warthe,* river, 492 mi. long, Poland and Polish-administered Germany, rising near Cracow and flowing NW past Czestochowa and Poznan into the Oder at Küstrin.

Wartburg (värt'bŏŏrk), castle near Eisenach, Thuringia, central Germany. Built c.1070; later enlarged; renovated 19th cent. Was seat of medieval landgraves of Thuringia. Luther, brought to Wartburg for his safety by the elector of Saxony (1521), completed translation of New Testament here.

Warton, Joseph, 1722–1800, English author of romantic nature poetry and a work on Pope (1756–82), attacking 18th-cent. classicism.

His brother, **Thomas Warton,** 1728–90, wrote competent poetry and by his *History of English Poetry* (1774–81) awakened interest in medieval culture. Made poet laureate in 1785.

Warwick, Guy de Beauchamp, earl of (bē'-chŭm, wŏ'rĭk), d. 1315, English nobleman. Foremost opponent of Piers Gaveston, whose banishment and later death he procured. His grandson, **Thomas de Beauchamp, earl of Warwick,** d. 1401, was one of lords appellant (1387) who accused courtiers of Richard II of treason and curbed king's power. Imprisoned (1397) for treason, he was released on accession of Henry IV. His son, **Richard de Beauchamp, earl of Warwick,** 1382–1439, was famed as a chivalric knight. Made pilgrimage to Holy Land 1408–10. Served Henry IV and Henry V and was (1429–37) tutor and guardian of Henry VI. His daughter married Richard Neville.

Warwick, Richard Neville, earl of: see NEVILLE, family.

Warwick, Thomas de Beauchamp, earl of: see WARWICK, GUY DE BEAUCHAMP, EARL OF.

Warwick, England: see WARWICKSHIRE.

Warwick, city (pop. 43,028), central R.I., S of Providence; settled 1642 by Samuel GORTON. Mfg. of textiles (since 1794). Has several resort villages. Birthplace of Nathanael Greene. Warwick village nearly destroyed in King Philip's War 1676. Gaspee Point was scene of burning of *Gaspée* 1772.

Warwickshire (wŏ'rĭkshĭr) or **Warwick,** inland county (983 sq. mi.; pop. 1,860,874), central England. Largely pastoral and agr., it also has great industrial centers of Birmingham and Coventry. There are deposits of coal, iron ore, limestone, and fireclay. Rugby is site of famous school. There are remains of abbeys and Kenilworth Castle. County is rich in literary associations. Stratford-on-Avon was Shakspere's birthplace. County town is **Warwick,** municipal borough (pop. 15,350), on the Upper Avon. Castle, begun by Æthelflæd, contains Warwick Vase, antiquities, and art works. St. Mary's Church (partly 12th cent.) has Beauchamp Chapel.

Wasatch Range (wô'săch), part of Rocky Mts., extending from Idaho S to central Utah, and rising to 12,008 ft. in Mt. Timpanogos. Most of Utah's important cities are just W.

Wash, the, inlet of North Sea, 20 mi. long and 15 mi. wide, between Lincolnshire and Norfolk, England. Mostly shallow with low, marshy shores; sandbanks impede navigation.

Washburne, Elihu Benjamin, 1816–87, U.S. Representative from Ill. (1853–69), minister to France (1869–77).

Washburn Municipal University: see TOPEKA, Kansas.

Washington, Booker T(aliaferro), c.1858–1915, American Negro educator. Principal of Tuskegee Inst. after 1881, he lectured widely, urged industrial training to produce real efficiency and independence for the Negro. *Up from Slavery* (1901) is his autobiography.

Washington, George, 1732–99, first President of the United States (1789–97), commander in chief of Continental Army in American Revolution, called the Father of His Country, b. Va. First gained public notice late in 1753 by carrying a message of warning from governor of Va. to the French moving into the Ohio country. Defeated at Fort Necessity (1754), he later was an aide to Edward Braddock and commanded Va. militia defending the frontier. Married, settled at Mt. Vernon, he served in Va. house of burgesses (1759–74) and in Continental Congress (1774–75). Named, on June 15, 1775, commander in chief of Continental forces. Forced British evacuation of Boston on March 17, 1776. Defeated in attempt to defend New York city (see LONG ISLAND, BATTLE OF) and at Philadelphia (see BRANDYWINE, BATTLE OF; GERMANTOWN). Victories at Trenton and Princeton followed heroic crossing of the Delaware on Christmas night, 1776. Spent desperate winter of 1777–78 at VALLEY FORGE. Subsequent patriot victories preceded surrender of Cornwallis to Washington on Oct. 19, 1781. Washington presided over Federal Constitutional Convention (1787). Unanimously chosen first President. His efforts to remain aloof from partisan struggles were unsuccessful; he approved of Alexander Hamilton's financial measures, consistently supported conservative policies. His second administration was Federalist, bitterly criticized by Jeffersonians. Weary with political life, Washington refused a third term. His *Farewell Address* (Sept. 17, 1796) contained famous warning against "entangling alliances" with foreign powers. His figure has bulked large in American literature and American legend (e.g., legend of the cherry tree made up by "Parson" WEEMS). His wife, **Martha Washington,** 1731–1802, wealthy widow of Daniel Parke Custis when she married Washington in 1759, was noted for her great common sense, her charm, and her graciousness.

Washington, state (68,192 sq. mi.; pop. 2,378,-963), NW U.S., in Pacific Northwest; admitted 1889 as 42d state; cap. OLYMPIA. Other cities are SEATTLE, TACOMA, SPOKANE. Bounded W by Pacific Ocean. Cascade Range runs N–S, divides semiarid plains of E from Puget Sound area and Olympic Peninsula in W. COLUMBIA R. drains both regions. Chief industries are agr. (esp. fruits, wheat), fishing, lumbering; also diversified mfg. Mining (coal, silver, gold, zinc). Early history centered around fur trade. Became territory in 1853. Advent of railroads boosted lumbering and fishing industries, increased population. Shipbuilding and maritime trades grew, and labor troubles, particularly violent in the days of the I.W.W., gave Wash. a reputation as a radical state. Fruit growing and various types of agr. in 20th cent. brought new wealth, and the "Inland Empire" about Spokane grew more important. Industries developed, and Seattle was one of the great industrial centers of World War II. Continuing development of power and irrigation on the Columbia (e.g., BONNEVILLE DAM; GRAND COULEE DAM) presaged much wider development.

Washington, cap. (pop. 802,178) of the U.S., coextensive (since 1895, when GEORGETOWN became part of Washington) with DISTRICT OF COLUMBIA, on Potomac R. and SW of Baltimore. Argument as to the site (whether in North or South) was settled (1790) by compromise. Land was donated by Md. and Va. George Washington selected exact spot for "Federal City." Building of WHITE HOUSE began 1792, of CAPITOL 1793. Congress first met here in 1800. Jefferson was first President inaugurated here. British captured and sacked city in 1814. Not until 20th cent. did city cease to be unkempt village and assume urban aspect. Designed by Pierre L'ENFANT, laid out by Andrew ELLICOTT, it is a gridiron arrangement of streets cut by diagonal avenues radiating from Capitol and White House. Many parks, monuments, historic sites of city and its environs are in Natl. Capital Parks system. Parks in city include Potomac (has Tidal Basin with Japanese cherry trees), Rock Creek, Anacostia, and Natl. Zoological. Important buildings include LIBRARY OF CONGRESS, Folger Shakespeare Memorial Library, National Archives Building, Supreme Court Building, NATIONAL GALLERY OF ART, and Walter Reed General Hospital. Well-known monuments are WASHINGTON MONUMENT, LINCOLN MEMORIAL, and THOMAS JEFFERSON MEMORIAL. Outside Washington across the Potomac ARLINGTON NATIONAL CEMETERY, MOUNT VERNON, and the Pentagon. Cathedral of St. Peter and St. Paul (Protestant Episcopal; known as National Cathedral or Washington Cathedral) is on Mt. St. Alban. City is seat of CATHOLIC UNIVERSITY OF AMERICA, Georgetown Univ., GEORGE WASHINGTON UNIVERSITY, HOWARD UNIVERSITY, SMITHSONIAN INSTITUTION, BROOKINGS INSTITUTION, CARNEGIE INSTITUTION OF WASHINGTON, American Univ. (coed.; chartered 1893, opened 1914), Trinity Col. (R.C.; for women; 1897), and National War Col. Many Federal agencies, bureaus, and installations are in suburban Md. and Va.

Washington. **1** Town (pop. 344), SW Ark., near Red R.; settled c.1824. One of state's oldest towns. State cap. 1863–65. **2** Town (pop. 2,227), W Conn., NE of New Milford, in hilly resort and agr. area. The green is typical of English 17th-cent. commons. **3** City (pop. 10,987), SW Ind., E of Vincennes; settled 1805. Trade center with railroad shops and wood products. **4** City (pop. 5,902), SE Iowa, SSW of Iowa City. Trade center of agr. area with mfg. of pearl buttons and calendars. **5** City (pop. 6,850), E Mo., on the Missouri and W of St. Louis. Agr. trade center, with mfg. of shoes, clothing, and pipes. **6** City (pop. 9,698), E N.C., at head of Pamlico (Tar) estuary; founded before 1776. Shipping center for farming, fishing, and timber area. **7** City (pop. 26,280), SW Pa. SW of Pittsburgh; settled 1769. Mfg. of glass, metal, and fiber products; coal mining. David Bradford House (1787) was hq. in Whisky Rebellion. Seat of Washington and Jefferson Col. (for men; Washington Col. united with Jefferson Col. 1865). **8** Village, S central Texas, on Brazos R. and NW of Houston. Saw declaration of Texas independence from Mexico, March 2, 1836.

Washington, Mount, 6,288 ft. high, N N.H., in Presidential Range of White Mts.; highest peak in New England. Bare summit has hotel and meteorological station (estab. 1932) and offers view of several states and Canada. Ascended 1642 by Darby Field. Bridle path built 1840, road 1861, cog railway 1869.

Washington, State College of: see PULLMAN, Wash.

Washington, Treaty of, May, 1871, concluded between U.S. and Great Britain in Washington, D.C. Included provisions for arbitration of ALABAMA CLAIMS, SAN JUAN BOUNDARY DISPUTE.

Washington, University of, at Seattle; state supported, coed.; opened 1861. Has forest-products and oceanographic laboratories, large wind tunnel, and the Pacific Northwest historical collection.

Washington and Jefferson College: see WASHINGTON, Pa.

Washington and Lee University, at Lexington, Va.; nonsectarian, for men; opened 1749 by Presbyterians, had several names before receiving present title in 1871. R. E. Lee was president 1865–70. His tomb is here.

Washington Conference: see NAVAL CONFERENCES.

Washington Court House, city (pop. 10,560), SW central Ohio, SW of Columbus, in agr. area; founded c.1810. Mfg. of auto and airplane parts.

Washington Island, atoll, area c.3 sq. mi., central Pacific; part of Gilbert and Ellice Isls. colony. Discovered 1798 by the American trader Edmund Fanning, annexed 1889 by British.

Washington Monument, hollow shaft, 555 ft. 5⅛ in. high, in Washington, D.C., on the Mall. Design of Robert Mills was accepted 1836. Site was granted 1848 by Congress, but no appropriations were made until 1876. Finally completed 1884 and opened to the public four years later.

Washington University, at St. Louis, Mo.; nonsectarian, coed.; chartered 1853, opened 1856. Its Henry Shaw School of Botany works with Missouri Botanical Garden. Institute of radiology has cyclotron.

Washita (wŏ'shĭtô), river, rising in Texas Panhandle, at Okla. line, and flowing c.450 mi. SE across Okla. to L. Texoma near Tishomingo. Custer defeated Cheyenne at battle of Washita on its banks 1868.

Washoe Mountains: see VIRGINIA MOUNTAINS.

wasp, insect of order Hymenoptera. There are several wasp families. Vespidae family includes both social forms (e.g., yellow jackets, hornets, and other paper wasps) and solitary forms (e.g., potter wasp). Usually there are three castes in social forms: queens, workers, and males or drones. White-faced hornet makes papery nest of many layers of cells. A dark brown to black wasp of genus *Polistes* makes open paper nest of single layer of cells.

wassail (wŏ'sŭl), anc. drinking salutation in England, meaning "be whole" or "have health." By association, it came to mean the liquor in which healths are drunk, and it also implied revelries and drinking songs as the original meaning faded.

Wassermann, Jakob (yä'kôp vä'sŭrmän), 1873–1934, Austrian novelist, b. Bavaria. Among his best-known works are *Caspar Hauser* (1908; Eng. tr., 1928); *Das Gänsemännchen* (1915; Eng. tr., *The Goose Man*); *Christian*

Wahnschaffe (1918; Eng. tr., *The World's Illusion*), usually considered his best; and *Der Fall Maurizius* (1928; Eng. tr., *The Maurizius Case*).

Wassermann test (wŏ'sûrmŭn), test of blood or spinal fluid used in diagnosis of syphilis. Devised 1906 by German bacteriologist **August von Wassermann** (ou'gōōst fŭn vä'sûrmän), 1866–1925.

Wastwater (wŏst'–), lake, 3 mi. long and ½ mi. wide, Cumberland, England, in Lake District; deepest lake in England (258 ft. max.).

Watauga (wŏtô'gŭ), river rising in W N.C. in Blue Ridge and flowing c.75 mi. NW to Holston R. NE of Jonesboro, Tenn. Has Sycamore Shoals Monument at ELIZABETHTON, Tenn., and Watauga Dam.

Watauga Association, government (1772–75) formed by settlers along Watauga R. in present E Tenn.

watch, small portable timepiece. Probably watches were first made c.1500. Stem replaced the key for winding in late 19th cent. In modern machine-made watch the hairspring controls swing of balance wheel, which in turn regulates rate of escapement of energy through train of toothed wheels that derive their motor power from mainspring. Parts are held by pivots that rest on bearings, preferably made of jewels at points subject to wear.

Watch Hill, R.I.: see WESTERLEY.

Watchung Mountains or **Orange Mountains,** two long low ridges of volcanic origin, N central N.J., curving SW from SW of Paterson to N of Somerville.

water, when pure, is odorless, tasteless, transparent liquid, colorless in small amounts, but showing bluish tinge in large quantities. At 4°C. (temperature of maximum density) one cubic centimeter of water weighs one gram. When cooled to 0°C. (32°F.), it changes to colorless crystalline solid (ice); this is less dense than liquid at 4°C. Water expands in freezing. When heated to boiling point (100°C., 212°F.), it vaporizes to steam. Evaporates at ordinary temperatures. Pure water is poor electrical conductor. It is a compound of hydrogen (two atoms) and oxygen (one atom), its chemical formula being H_2O; composition by weight is one part of hydrogen to eight of oxygen. Water reacts with some active metals and metallic oxides to form bases; forms acids with some other oxides. HYDRATE is a salt having its molecule linked with definite number of water molecules. Efflorescence is loss of this water on exposure to air at ordinary temperatures. Deliquescent substances absorb water from air. Water is one of best solvents. MINERAL WATER has great variety and quantity of minerals; salt water has minerals in addition to large amount of sodium chloride. Temporary hardness of water occurs when bicarbonates of calcium or magnesium are present; permanent, when sulphates or chlorides of these are there. Temporary hardness can be eliminated by boiling or by adding lime; permanent, by adding such substances as sodium carbonate or sodium hydroxide, which form precipitates with materials causing hardness. Water covers about 70% of earth's surface; land is constantly being worn down, carried away, and redeposited by its action. Rain and humidity, as well as presence of large bodies of water, are important factors in climate. Water is necessary for life; it forms greater part of animal and plant protoplasm, is present in plant sap and animal blood and is essential to PHOTOSYNTHESIS. Water supply must be pure. Processes of purification of a city water supply include coagulation (usually by adding an aluminum salt or ferric iron which cause clumping and settling out of high percentage of bacteria), filtration (water passes through layers of fine sand), and disinfection (usually with chlorine). Water power is of great economic importance. Heavy water (deuterium oxide) molecule consists of two atoms of heavy hydrogen and one of oxygen.

water bug, commonly refers to the giant water bug, water strider, water boatman, back swimmer, and water scorpion of order Hemiptera (see BUG). Term is also used for Croton bug and some aquatic beetles.

Waterbury, industrial city (pop. 104,477), W Conn., on Naugatuck R. and SW of Hartford. Its brass industry began in mid-18th cent. Clocks and watches and silverware are made.

water cress, hardy perennial European herb (*Rorippa nasturtium-aquaticum* or *Nasturtium officinale*) naturalized in North America, found in or around water. The pungent leaves are used as a garnish and in salads.

Wateree (wôtûrē'), river rising in W N.C. and flowing 295 mi. SE past Camden, S.C., joining Congaree R. to form Santee R. SE of Columbia. Called the Catawba in early course.

waterfall, sudden drop in a stream passing over harder rock to softer, more easily eroded, rock. In time, the waterfall (by undercutting and erosion) will move upstream, become lower, then become a series of rapids, and finally disappear. See FALL LINE.

Waterford (wô'tûrfûrd), maritime county (710 sq. mi.; pop. 76,108), S Ireland, in Munster. Largely a hilly area, Waterford has much farming land. Dairying and hog raising are important; fishing and quarrying are also carried on. County town is **Waterford,** county borough (pop. 28,269), on Suir R. at head of Waterford Harbour. An outlet for produce of S. Ireland. Famous Waterford glass was made in 18th cent. Saw much early fighting. Has Protestant and Catholic cathedrals.

Waterford, residential town (pop. 9,100), SE Conn., on Long Isl. Sound W of New London; settled c.1653.

water gas, colorless gas which burns with very hot, light bluish flame. It is a mixture of carbon monoxide and hydrogen, with small amounts of other gases; is almost completely combustible. Used in industry in preparing hydrogen, as fuel in steelmaking, and when enriched as an illuminant.

water glass or **soluble glass,** colorless, transparent substance, usually sodium silicate, ordinarily a solid but usually marketed in water solution. It is used as a cement for glass, pottery, etc.; for fireproofing and waterproofing; for fixing pigments. It serves as preservative for eggs since it fills up pores of shell and prevents entrance of air.

water hemlock: see HEMLOCK.

water hyacinth, perennial aquatic plant (*Eichhornia crassipes*). It has round floating leaves and blue-violet flowers borne on fleshy stalks. Plants hinder navigation in waterways in Fla. and Calif.

water lily, showy-flowered aquatic plant of genus *Nymphaea* with large beautiful blossoms of various colors, often fragrant, and rounded floating leaves. Tender water lilies, prized for garden pools, are tropical species, but some hardy kinds are native, e.g., *Nymphaea odorata*. There are both day- and night-blooming types.

Waterloo, Belgium: see WATERLOO CAMPAIGN.

Waterloo, town (pop. 11,991), S Ont., Canada, NW suburb of Kitchener. Distilling center with flour mills and mfg. of shoes and clothing.

Waterloo, city (pop. 65,198), NE Iowa, on Cedar R.; settled 1845. Trade and industrial center for farm and livestock area, it has railroad shops, meat packing plants, mfg. of agr. machinery. Annual Dairy Cattle Congress, National Belgian Horse Show.

Waterloo campaign, June, 1815, last action of Napoleonic Wars, fought in S Belgium. NAPOLEON I, faced with European coalition, hoped to defeat British and Prussians before dealing with Austrians and Russians. Defeated Blücher at Ligny (June 16); detached Grouchy to pursue him; went to assist Ney in fight against Wellington at Quatre Bras. Wellington withdrew to position S of Waterloo; waited attack. Napoleon attacked June 18. English resisted successfully and were joined by Blücher, who had eluded the French. French were routed. Napoleon abdicated June 22.

watermelon, tender, annual trailing vine (*Citrullus vulgaris*) and its large, juicy, round or ovoid fruit, green-skinned and pink-fleshed. Native to Africa, it now is extensively grown in the S U.S. (esp. in Texas and Ga.). The citron melon is a variety with firm white flesh used like citron for preserving.

water moccasin or **cottonmouth,** highly venomous pit viper of S U.S. swamps and bayous. It often climbs tree branches. Mothers give direct birth to the young.

water polo, swimming sport played in pool measuring not more than 20 ft. wide, not less than 19 ft. long. An event of Olympic games since 1900.

watershed, elevation or divide separating catchment area or drainage basin of one river system from another. Rocky Mts. and Andes form watershed between westward-flowing and eastward-flowing streams. Term is also used synonymously with drainage basin.

Waters of Merom (mē'–): see BAHR EL-HULEH.

Waterton-Glacier International Peace Park, S Alta. and N Mont., created 1932 by Canadian Parliament and U.S. Congress. Consists of Waterton Lakes Natl. Park in Canada and Glacier Natl. Park in U.S.

Waterton Lakes National Park, 204 sq. mi., SW Alta., Canada, SW of Lethbridge at Mont. border. It is the Canadian part of Waterton-Glacier Internatl. Peace Park, created 1932 by acts of Canadian Parliament and U.S. Congress.

Watertown. 1 (Town (pop. 10,699), W Conn., on Naugatuck R. and NW of Waterbury. Mfg. of textile and metal goods. Has Taft School for boys (1890). **2** Town (pop. 37,-329), E Mass., on Charles R. and W of Boston; settled 1630. Footwear, textiles, and electrical supplies. Has U.S. arsenal (1816). Seat of PERKINS INSTITUTION AND MASSACHUSETTS SCHOOL FOR THE BLIND. **3** City (pop. 34,350), N N.Y., on Black R. (water power) and N of Syracuse; settled c.1800. Trade center for rich dairy area and gateway to Thousand Isl. resort region. Mfg. of air brakes and paper products. **4** City (pop. 12,-699), NE S.Dak., NNW of Sioux Falls and on Big Sioux R.; laid out 1878. Shipping and trade center for resort and agr. area, it has food processing. **5** City (pop. 12,417), SE Wis., NE of Madison and at falls of Rock R., in farm and dairy area; settled c.1836. Mfg. of shoes; goose market. Was home of Carl Schurz 1855–57. Octagon House (c.1849) near by is museum.

Waterville, city (pop. 18,287), S Maine, at Kennebec R. falls above Augusta; settled 1754. Rail and agr. trade center, with textile and paper mills. Colby Col. (for men and women; 1813) is here.

Watervliet (wô"tûrvlēt'), city (pop. 15,197), E N.Y., on Hudson R. (bridged) opposite Troy. Steel castings, abrasives, chemicals. Ann Lee headed first American community of Shakers here 1776.

Waterways, village, N Alta., Canada, on Clearwater R. and near Fort McMurray. River boat service to Wood Buffalo Natl. Park.

Watkins, Franklin (Chenault), 1894–, American painter, noted as a colorist in postimpressionist style.

Watkins Glen, resort village (pop. 3,052), W central N.Y., in Finger Lakes region at S end of Seneca L. Adjoining is Watkins Glen State Park, with 2-mi. gorge, mineral springs, waterfalls.

Watling Street (wŏt'lĭng), important anc. road in England, built by the Romans. Ran over 100 mi. NW from London, through St. Albans, to Wroxeter in Shropshire. Used throughout Middle Ages, parts of road are still in perfect condition.

Watson, J(ohn) B(roadus), 1878–, American psychologist. Director of the Johns Hopkins psychological laboratory and founder of school of psychology known as BEHAVIORISM, which describes behavior solely in terms of physiological response to stimuli. He accepted only three responses as unconditioned or unlearned—fear, love, and rage.

Watson, Sir William, 1858–1935, English traditional, romantic poet. Wrote *Wordsworth's Grave* (1890) and elegy for Tennyson, *Lachrymae Musarum* (1892).

Watson-Gordon, Sir John: see GORDON, SIR JOHN WATSON-.

Watson Lake, village, SE Yukon, Canada. Here are Royal Canadian Mounted Police post, airfield, and radio and weather station.

Watsonville, city (pop. 11,572), W Calif., near Monterey Bay. Shipping and processing center (esp. for lettuce, apples). Beach and mountain resorts are near.

Watt, James, 1736–1819, Scottish inventor of new type steam engine patented 1769. Unit of power, the watt, was named after him.

watt [for James Watt], unit of electrical power, the power necessary to maintain a current of one ampere under a pressure of one volt. Electrical power (number of watts) of a circuit is number of volts multiplied by number of amperes; is measured by a wattmeter. Kilowatt equals 1,000 watts; electric power is usually sold by kilowatt hours (kilowatts × hours).

Watteau, Antoine (wătō′, wŏ′tō, Fr. ătwän′ vätō′), 1684–1721, French painter of Flemish origin, b. Valenciennes, an outstanding colorist. Celebrated for lyric quality of his gay and sensuous scenes of open-air festivities (e.g., *Embarkation for Cythera,* Louvre).

wattle: see ACACIA.

Watts, George Frederic, 1817–1904, English painter. Used glowing color and soft contours in his popular allegorical paintings. His sculptures include many monuments. Married to Ellen Terry 1864–77.

Watts, Isaac, 1674–1748, English dissenting clergyman and hymn writer. Only a few of his several hundred hymns survive today, but they are among the finest examples of English metrical hymnody. Those beginning "When I survey the wondrous cross," "Joy to the World," and "Our God, our help in ages past," appeared in his *Psalms of David Imitated in the Language of the New Testament* (1719). *Divine Songs for Children* (1715) contains the famous "How doth the little busy bee."

Watts-Dunton, (Walter) Theodore, 1832–1914, English poet, novelist, and critic. Wrote much, but is remembered best as friend of Rossetti and especially of Swinburne.

Watt's Dyke: see OFFA'S DYKE.

Waugh, Evelyn (ēv′lĭn wô′), 1903–, English novelist, author of brilliant satires (e.g., *Decline and Fall,* 1928; *Vile Bodies,* 1930; *A Handful of Dust,* 1934) as well as more serious works (e.g., *Brideshead Revisited,* 1945; *Men at Arms,* 1952).

Waukegan (wôkē′gŭn), residential and industrial city (pop. 38,946), NE Ill., on L. Michigan and N of Chicago. Settled 1835 as Little Fort near old French stockade, on site of Indian village. Air, rail, and lake shipping center. Mfg. of metal products, chemicals, and asbestos products.

Waukesha (wô′kĭshô), city (pop. 21,233), SE Wis., on Fox R. and W of Milwaukee; settled 1834. Health resort with bottled waters and metal products.

Waupun (wôpŭn′), city (pop. 6,725), central Wis., SW of Fond du Lac and on Rock R., in farm and dairy area. Machinery and shoes.

Wausau (wô′sô), city (pop. 30,414), central Wis., on Wisconsin R. and NW of Green Bay, in dairy area; settled 1839. Wood and paper products. Winter sports at near-by Rib Mt.

Wauwatosa (wôwŭtō′sŭ), industrial city (pop. 33,324), SE Wis., near Milwaukee; settled 1835. Metal, leather, and wood products.

wave, in physics, disturbance advancing through a medium that is set in vibration as wave moves along. If particles of transmitting medium move up and down, waves are called transverse, e.g., water and LIGHT waves; if particles vibrate in line with wave direction, waves are longitudinal, i.e., SOUND waves. Wave length is distance from any point on one wave to corresponding point on next. Frequency is number of crests that pass given point in a second. See also RADIATION.

Wavell, Archibald P(ercival) Wavell, 1st **Earl** (wā′vŭl), 1883–1950, British field marshal. As World War II commander in chief of Middle East (1939–41) he defeated (1940) the Italians in Cyrenaica. Viceroy and governor general of India (1943–47).

Waverley, village, Surrey, England. Has remains of 12th-cent. abbey. Swift lived at "Moor Park," estate of Sir William Temple.

Waverly. 1 City (pop. 5,124), NE Iowa, on Cedar R. above Waterloo. Processes farm and dairy produce. **2** Village (pop. 6,037), S N.Y., at Pa. line, on Chemung R. and SE of Elmira.

Waves (Women Appointed for Voluntary Emergency Service), created 1942 in World War II to release male naval personnel for sea duty. Served in clerical and other jobs. Directed by M. H. McAfee 1942–46. Women's Armed Service Integration Act of 1948 authorized enlistment of women in regular navy.

wax, name for substance secreted by glands on abdomen of bee (beeswax) and for various similar substances. Waxes are usually mixtures containing esters of fatty acids and certain alcohols (other than glycerol) and other alcohols and sometimes hydrocarbons. They are harder and less greasy than fats. Carnauba wax is obtained from a PALM; LANOLIN from wool; SPERMACETI from whales. Mineral waxes include ozocerite and paraffin.

Waxahachie (wŏk″sĭhă′chē), city (pop. 11,-204), N Texas, S of Dallas; founded 1847. Market and processing center in rich blackland agr. area with mfg. of garments and textiles.

waxwing, perching bird of N Hemisphere of Old and New Worlds. Waxwings are crested and have sleek, brownish-gray plumage with dashes of red like sealing wax on the wings. Cedar waxwing breeds throughout most of Canada and U.S.

Waycross, city (pop. 18,899), SE Ga., SW of Savannah and just N of Okefenokee Swamp; settled 1818. Tobacco market and shipping center. Has railroad shops and mfg. of wood products.

wayfaring tree: see HOBBLEBUSH.

Wayne, Anthony, 1745–96, patriot general in American Revolution. Most famous achievement was capture of Stony Point, N.Y. (1779). Decisively defeated Indians at Fallen Timbers, Ohio (1794); negotiated treaty 1795. Known as "mad Anthony."

Wayne, village (pop. 9,409), SE Mich., on River Rouge branch and SW of Dearborn. Mfg. of aircraft and auto parts.

Waynesboro. 1 Borough (pop. 10,334), S Pa., near Md. line, SW of Harrisburg; settled 1798. Resort with fruit growing and mfg. of machinery, metal goods. **2** City (pop. 12,-257), central Va., SE of Staunton, near S entrance to Skyline Drive; settled 1700. Trade and mfg. (rayon, furniture, wood products).

Near here Union forces defeated Confederates, March, 1865.

Waynesburg, borough (pop. 5,514), SW Pa., SSW of Pittsburgh, in coal, dairy, and livestock area. Seat of Waynesburg Col.

Waynesville, resort town (pop. 5,295), W N.C., WSW of Asheville. Mfg. of shoes, rubber and wood products. Near Great Smoky Mts. Natl. Park and L. Junaluska (with Methodist assembly).

Wayne University: see DETROIT, Mich.

Wayzata (wīzĕ'tů), city (pop. 1,791), E Minn., W suburb of Minneapolis. Resort on L. Minnetonka.

Waziristan (wůzēr'ĭstän"), mountainous region, North-West Frontier Prov., W Pakistan. Inhabited by warlike Pathan tribes.

Weald, the (wēld), area between North and South Downs, England, forming part of Sussex, Surrey, and Kent Counties. Now largely an agr. district.

weasel (wē'zůl), small, carnivorous animal (*Mustela*) of Europe, Asia, North America; related to stoat. The fur is various shades of brown above and white below; in winter, weasels living in regions of snow usually become all white, except for the dark tail, and are then called ermine.

weather, atmospheric state at given place and time regarding temperature, barometric pressure, WIND, HUMIDITY, CLOUD formation, and precipitation. METEOROLOGY ancient; greatly developed today with rapid communication from remote areas. In U.S. weather service (estab. 1870) later became Weather Bureau which now includes over 200 main stations. Bureau prepares daily country-wide map showing weather elements at each station by symbols and figures (ISOBARS show areas of high or low pressure, fronts demark warm-air from cold-air masses, shading reflects precipitation); prepares upper-air charts. Predictions born of experience, since factors controlling weather not fully understood.

Weatherford, city (pop. 8,093), N Texas, W of Fort Worth. Center of rich fruit and truck area, it processes cottonseed and peanut oil, and has mfg. of oil equipment and clothing.

weathering, decomposition of rock near the earth's surface by atmospheric agencies. Involves mechanical processes, e.g., expansion and contraction resulting from sudden temperature changes, impact of running water; and chemical processes, e.g., oxidation, carbonization, loss of chemical elements by solution in water. Results of weathering include formation of soil and preparation of materials for erosion.

weather map: see WEATHER.

Weaver, James Baird, 1833–1912, American political leader. U.S. Representative from Iowa (1879–81, 1885–89). A free silver advocate, he was POPULIST PARTY presidential candidate 1892.

weaver bird, member of Old World family of birds (Ploceidae) which build intricately woven nests. The birds resemble the finch family and are sometimes called weaver finches.

weaving, art of forming a fabric by interlacing at right angles two or more sets of yarn or other material. One of the most ancient of the fundamental arts, weaving grew up independently in different parts of the world. In the 18th cent., spinning and weaving inventions virtually ended the era of domestic craftsmanship and began the huge organized industry of today; some fine fabrics, however, are still woven by hand. First step in weaving is to stretch the strong warp (longitudinal) yarns. The weft, woof, or filling crosses the warp, binding it at either side to form the selvage. After warp is stretched, three essential steps are: shedding, or raising alternate warp yarns or sets of yarns to receive the weft; picking, or inserting the weft; battening, or pressing home the weft to make the fabric compact. These operations were done by the hands before development of the LOOM. Fundamental weaves, of which all others are variations, are the plain, twill, and satin. Figure weaves are made by causing warp and weft to intersect in varied groups.

Webb, Beatrice (Potter), 1858–1943, English socialist economist, wife of **Sidney (James) Webb,** 1858–1947. The Webbs worked together in the Fabian Society, helped build the British Labour party, and wrote numerous works on socialist history and theory.

Webb, James Watson, 1802–84, American journalist and diplomat. Edited *Morning Courier and New York Enquirer*. Estab. express service by horse to hasten news, sent schooners to sea for incoming news. Minister to Brazil 1861–69.

Webb, Mary (Meredith), 1881–1927, English novelist, known for somber novels of rural Shropshire (e.g., *Precious Bane,* 1924).

Webb, Philip Speakman, 1830–1915, English architect, who influenced revival of Queen Anne and Georgian styles. Was a member of William Morris's famous decorating firm.

Webb, Sidney James: see WEBB, BEATRICE POTTER.

Webb City, city (pop. 6,919), SW Mo., near Joplin, in agr. area. Apparel and dairy products.

Weber, Carl Maria (Friedrich Ernst) von (vā'bůr), 1786–1826, German composer and pianist. He composed such romantic operas as *Der Freischütz* (1821), *Euryanthe* (1823), and *Oberon* (1826). His instrumental works include the popular *Invitation to the Dance* (1819).

Weber, Ernst Reinrich, 1795–1878, German physiologist. Noted for research on touch and sensation and on inhibitory power of vagus nerve. With his brother **Wilhelm Eduard Weber** (vĭl'hĕlm ā'dōōärt), 1804–91, a physicist, he wrote a book on wave motion (1825) and made studies of acoustics. Wilhelm also contributed to knowledge of terrestrial magnetism and electrical measurements and devised an electromagnetic telegraph.

Weber, Joseph (wĕ'bůr), 1867–1942, American comedian, partner of Lew Fields. In chin whiskers, loud check clothes, and low crown derbies, they long delighted audiences (1875–1904 and after 1912) with dialect jokes, slapstick, and burlesque.

Weber, Max (mäks' vā'bůr), 1864–1920, German sociologist. Sought to develop a methodology for social science. He opposed Marxism and stressed the plurality of causes. In his *Protestant Ethic and the Spirit of Capital-*

ism (1920; Eng. tr., 1930) he developed his thesis of the intimate connection between the ascetic character of Calvinism and the rise of capitalist institutions.

Weber, Max (wĕ'bûr), 1881–, American painter, b. Russia. Painted abstractions in early period, but later works tended toward naturalism.

Weber, Wilhelm Eduard: see WEBER, ERNST HEINRICH.

Weber (wē'bûr), river rising in N central Utah in Uinta Mts. and flowing NW to join Ogden R. at Ogden. Combined stream enters Great Salt L. Dammed for irrigation. Some water diverted to Provo R. project.

Webern, Anton von (vā'bûrn), 1883–1945, Austrian composer; pupil of Arnold Schönberg and devoted adherent to his 12-tone technique (see ATONALITY). Webern's music is even less accepted by the public than Schönberg's. His compositions are characterized by unusual combinations of instruments, a broken melodic line (two successive notes are rarely played by the same instrument), and extreme brevity (often a movement of a symphony, quartet, or sonata is less than two minutes in length). Most of his works are for small orchestral groups or piano.

Webster, Daniel, 1782–1852, American statesman, lawyer, and orator. Won fame as lawyer in DARTMOUTH COLLEGE CASE and in MCCULLOCH VS. MARYLAND. Delivered eloquent public orations. U.S. Congressman (1813–17, 1823–27). A leading political figure as U.S. Senator from Mass. (1827–41); defended Union in 1830 debate with R. Y. HAYNE. WHIG PARTY leader. U.S. Secretary of State (1841–43); signed WEBSTER-ASHBURTON TREATY. Again U.S. Senator 1845–50; cherishing preservation of the Union above his own popularity, he backed COMPROMISE OF 1850 in a notable speech. Served again as U.S. Secretary of State 1850–52.

Webster, John, 1580?–1625?, English dramatist, author of two tragedies, *The White Devil* (1612) and *The Duchess of Malfi* (c.1614). Collaborated on many plays, especially with Dekker.

Webster, Noah, 1758–1843, American scholar, a lexicographer, b. Conn. Fired with the desire to standardize American grammar and spelling, he wrote *Grammatical Institute of the English Language* (1783–85), of which the first part, often revised, became the "blue-backed speller" dominant in American schooling for generations. His later *Compendious Dictionary* (1806) preceded his *American Dictionary of the English Language* (1828); this in many revised editions to the present day made the name Webster a household word meaning standard dictionary. He hoped by his work to improve morals and patriotism as well as language and he backed many causes (including his vigorous campaign for a copyright law). He argued for a centralized government at the time of the Articles of Confederation, particularly in his *Sketches of American Policy* (1785), and later as a newspaper editor supported Washington's administration. The influence of his work through a long life is incalculable.

Webster, town (pop. 13,194), including Webster village (pop. 12,160), S Mass., SSW of Worcester; settled c.1713. Woolens, shoes, optical goods.

Webster-Ashburton Treaty, concluded in 1842 by U.S., represented by Secretary of State Daniel Webster, and Great Britain, represented by Commissioner A. B. Ashburton. Settled disputed boundaries of NE U.S.; gave U.S. over 7,000 sq. mi. of disputed area, including Aroostook Valley; opened St. Johns R. to free navigation by both countries. Also fixed U.S.-Canada border in Great Lakes region. Treaty served as precedent in peaceful settlements of subsequent Anglo-American disputes.

Webster City, city (pop. 7,611), central Iowa, on Boone R. and E of Fort Dodge. Mfg. of metal goods and dairy products.

Webster Groves, city (pop. 23,390), E Mo., just W of St. Louis; settled 1854. Petroleum products. Seat of Webster Col. (corporate college of St. Louis Univ.; for women).

Webster Springs, town (pop. 1,313), central W.Va., on Elk R.; official name Addison. Health resort and sports center.

Weddell Sea, embayment of S Atlantic, Antartica, SSE of South America. Discovered 1823 by James Weddell.

Wedekind, Frank (vā'dŏŏkĭnt), 1864–1918, German dramatist. He anticipated expressionism in his dramas *The Awakening of Spring* (1891), *Earth Spirit* (1895), and *Pandora's Box* (1903). The heroine of those, Lulu, symbolizes woman as an instinctual, amoral being. Alban Berg based *Lulu* on Wedekind's dramas.

wedge, piece of wood or metal thick at one end and sloping to thin edge at other, an application of the inclined plane. Used to separate two bodies or one part of a body from an adjoining part (e.g., in splitting wood). Ax, chisel, knife, nail, and carpenter's plane are forms of wedges. See *ill.*, p. 793.

Wedgwood, Josiah, 1730–95, celebrated English potter, descendant of a family of Staffordshire potters. In 1769 he opened his works at Etruria (a village he built for his workmen) near Stoke-upon-Trent. Here he transformed pottery making into a major industry. Invented jasper ware, best known in delicate blue with white Greek figures embossed on it. Also made cream-colored earthenware ("queen's ware"), vases of black composition ("Egyptian ware"), veined ware in imitation of granite, and an unglazed semiporcelain.

Wednesday: see WEEK.

Weed, Thurlow (thûr'lō), 1797–1882, American journalist and political leader. Newspaper editor in New York state. A power in Whig party. Guided political career of W. H. Seward. Personally genial but utterly unscrupulous politically, Weed headed a formidable state machine.

weed, name for any wild plant, especially for an undesired plant growing in cultivated ground. Weeds may crowd out desired crops by appropriating space, sunlight, moisture, and soil nutrients. Methods of control include cultivation of the soil, crop rotation, and chemicals, e.g., 2,4-*D* (dichlorophenoxyacetic acid).

Weehawken (wē'hô"kûn), township (pop. 14,830), NE N.J., on Hudson R. (Lincoln Tunnel) and N of Hoboken. Scene of Burr-Hamilton duel 1804.

week, period of time shorter than month, commonly seven days. Seven-day week believed to have originated in W Asia in ancient times as planetary week based on concept of influence of planets, then erroneously believed to be sun, moon, Mars, Mercury, Jupiter, Venus, Saturn. Use of planetary names, derived from names of deities, remained even after Constantine made Christian week beginning on Sunday official. In most languages the forms are translations from Latin or corresponding names of divinities. Latin names and translations, English equivalents (largely from names of Germanic deities) and derivations follow: *dies solis* [sun's day], Sunday; *dies lunae* [moon's day], Monday [moon-day]; *dies Martis* [Mars' day], Tuesday [Tiw's day]; *dies Mercurii* [Mercury's day] Wednesday [Woden's day]; *dies Jovis* [Jove's or Jupiter's day] Thursday [Thor's day]; *dies Veneris* [Venus's day], Friday [Frigg's day]; *dies Saturni,* Saturday [both: Saturn's day].

Weeks, Sinclair, 1893–, U.S. Secretary of Commerce (1953–). A Mass. industrialist. U.S. Senator (interim appointment) 1944.

Weems, Mason L(ocke), 1759–1825, American author, an ordained Anglican minister, called Parson Weems. An enterprising book salesman, he wrote popular works but is remembered almost solely for his baseless story of the boy George Washington chopping down a cherry tree and confessing to his father, saying, "I cannot tell a lie." This appeared in the fifth edition of his biography of Washington.

weevil, name for certain snout beetles of curculio family. Some damage stored grains, others (e.g., cotton boll weevil) attack plants.

Wei, China: see TSIN, dynasty.

weigela (wījē′lů) or **weigelia** (wījē′lyů), ornamental Asiatic shrub of genus *Weigela* widely cultivated for the funnel-shaped white, pink, or red blossoms in spring or summer.

weight, molecular: see MOLECULAR WEIGHT.

weight lifting. Popular sport in Europe for many centuries. An event in Olympic games since 1896.

weights and measures. Crude measurements of length, capacity, and weight probably date from prehistoric times. Early units were based on body measurements and plant seeds. High degree of standardization achieved by Roman Empire became diversified after its fall. Chief modern systems are American and British system and METRIC SYSTEM (see WEIGHTS AND MEASURES, table, for conversion table and common units). American and British system employs two sets of weights: avoirdupois (used in general commerce); troy (for precious metals). Avoirdupois weight is based on 16-ounce pound; troy weight (basis of apothecary weight) based on 12-ounce pound. U.S. Congress has constitutional right to fix standards; most legislation, except for customs and internal revenue purposes, has been permissive. Sets of official weights and measures were sent to the states in 1856, but legislation and enforcement are largely state prerogatives. Federal government permitted use of metric system (1866) and established a conversion table based on the pound and the yard; since 1893, yard in U.S. has been derived from international prototype meter and the pound from the prototype kilogram (both kept at International Bureau of Weights and Measures near Paris; copies are deposited with participating governments). In U.S. copies are kept by government bureau established to correlate standards (see STANDARDS, NATIONAL BUREAU OF).

Weihaiwei (wā′hī′wā) or **Weihai,** commercial city (pop. 175,000), NE Shantung prov., China; port on Yellow Sea. City and surrounding area (285 sq. mi.) was leased 1898–1920 to Great Britain. Naval base was developed by the British.

Weill, Kurt (vīl), 1900–1950, German-American composer. He wrote satirical operas, such as *Der Protagonist* (1926) and *Die Dreigroschenoper* (1928; based on *The Beggar's Opera*). Upon coming to the U.S. in 1935, he began writing musical comedies. Among these are *Knickerbocker Holiday* (1938), containing *September Song; Lady in the Dark* (1941); and *One Touch of Venus* (1943), containing *Speak Low.* His last works include a musical version of *Street Scene* (1947) and *Lost in the Stars* (1949), based on Alan Paton's novel, *Cry, the Beloved Country.*

Weimar (vī′mär), city (pop. 66,659), Thuringia, central Germany, on Ilm R. Has varied mfg. but is chiefly known as cultural center. Became cap. of duchy (later grand duchy) of SAXE-WEIMAR in 16th cent.; was cap. of Thuringia 1920–47. It was the residence of Lucas Cranach the elder (16th cent.); J. S. Bach (1708–17); Wieland, Goethe, Herder, Schiller (late 18th–early 19th cent.); Liszt (1848–59). In 1920 Weimar was the scene of the German national assembly that created the Weimar Republic (see GERMANY). The Nazis estab., in 1933, a notorious concentration camp at Buchenwald, a few miles NW of Weimar. Among Weimar's landmarks are the parish church (altarpiece by Cranach); grand ducal palace and crypt (with graves of Goethe and Schiller); theater (long directed by Goethe); residences of Goethe, Schiller, and Liszt; near-by ducal castle of Tiefurt. Weimar is the seat of the Goethe, Schiller, and Nietzsche archives.

Weinberger, Jaromir (yä′rômĕr vīn′bĕrgĕr), 1896–, Czech composer. His most popular works are the polka and fugue from the opera *Schwanda, the Bagpipe Player* (1927) and his orchestral *Variations and Fugue on Under the Spreading Chestnut Tree* (1939).

Weir, Robert Walter, 1803–89, American portrait and historical painter. His son, **John Ferguson Weir,** 1841–1926, was a painter and sculptor, who was director of School of Fine Arts, Yale, 1869–1913. Another son, **J(ulian) Alden Weir,** 1852–1919, was one of earliest American impressionist painters.

Weirton, city (pop. 24,005), NW W.Va., in N Panhandle, on Ohio R. and N of Wheeling. Mfg. of steel and chemicals. Coal and clay mining. Absorbed neighboring towns, including Hollidays Cove, 1947.

Weiser (wē′zůr), city (pop. 3,961), W Idaho, N of Payette, at confluence of Weiser and

WEIGHTS AND MEASURES COMMONLY USED

American and British System	*Metric System*	*Conversion Table*
LINEAR MEASURE	**LINEAR MEASURE**	**LINEAR MEASURE**
12 inches = 1 foot 3 feet = 1 yard 5½ yards = 1 rod 220 yards = 1 furlong 5,280 feet = 1 mile 6 feet = 1 fathom 6,080 feet = 1 nautical mile	10 millimeters = 1 centimeter 10 centimeters = 1 decimeter 10 decimeters = 1 meter 10 meters = 1 dekameter 1,000 meters = 1 kilometer	1 inch = 2.54 centimeters 0.393700 inches = 1 centimeter 1 mile = 1.609344 kilometers 0.62137 miles = 1 kilometer
SQUARE MEASURE	**SQUARE MEASURE**	**SQUARE MEASURE**
144 square inches = 1 square foot 9 square feet = 1 square yard 30¼ square yards = 1 square rod 160 square rods = 1 acre 4,840 square yards = 1 acre 640 acres = 1 square mile	100 square millimeters = 1 square centimeter 100 square centimeters = 1 square decimeter 10,000 square centimeters = 1 square meter 100 square meters = 1 are 100 ares = 1 hectare 10,000 ares = 1 square kilometer	1 square inch = 6.4516 square centimeters 0.15500 square inches = 1 square centimeter 1 hectare = 2.471 acres 1 square mile = 2.58999 square kilometers 0.3861 square miles = 1 square kilometer
CUBIC MEASURE	**CUBIC MEASURE**	**CUBIC MEASURE**
1,728 cubic inches = 1 cubic foot 27 cubic feet = 1 cubic yard	1,000 cubic millimeters = 1 cubic centimeter 1,000 cubic centimeters = 1 cubic decimeter 1,000 cubic decimeters = 1 cubic meter	1 cubic inch = 16.3871 cubic centimeters 0.061024 cubic inches = 1 cubic centimeter 1 cubic yard = 0.76455 cubic meters 1.30795 cubic yards = 1 cubic meter
LIQUID MEASURE	**LIQUID MEASURE**	**LIQUID MEASURE**
16 ounces = 1 (U.S.) pint 20 ounces = 1 imperial (British) pint 2 cups = 1 pint 2 pints = 1 quart 4 quarts = 1 gallon 1.2 U.S. gallons = 1 imperial (British) gallon	10 milliliters = 1 centiliter 100 centiliters = 1 liter 1,000 liters = 1 kiloliter	1 ounce = 0.46871 centiliters 0.33815 ounces = 1 centiliter 1 (U.S.) liquid quart = 0.9463 liters 1.0567 (U.S.) liquid quarts = 1 liter 1 (U.S.) gallon = .0037853 kiloliters 264.17 (U.S.) gallons = 1 kiloliter
WEIGHTS: AVOIRDUPOIS	**WEIGHTS**	**WEIGHTS**
16 drams = 1 ounce 16 ounces = 1 pound 112 pounds = 1 long hundredweight 2,000 pounds = 1 short ton 2,240 pounds = 1 long ton	10 milligrams = 1 centigram 10 centigrams = 1 decigram 10 decigrams = 1 gram 100 centigrams = 1 gram 10 grams = 1 dekagram 10 dekagrams = 1 hectogram 10 hectograms = 1 kilogram 1,000 grams = 1 kilogram 1,000 kilograms = 1 ton	1 ounce (avoirdupois) = 28.3495 grams 0.035274 ounces (avoirdupois) = 1 gram 1 pound (avoirdupois) = 0.453592 kilograms 2.20462 pounds (avoirdupois) = 1 kilogram 1 (short) ton = 0.90718 (metric) tons 1.10231 (short) tons = 1 (metric) ton 1 pound (avoirdupois) = 1.21528 pounds (troy) 0.82286 pounds (avoirdupois) = 1 pound (troy)
WEIGHTS: TROY AND APOTHECARY		
480 grains = 1 ounce 12 ounces = 1 pound		

Snake rivers. Terminus of North and South Panoramic Highway.

Weismann, August (ou'go͝ost vīs'män), 1834–1914, German biologist. He originated the germ-plasm theory of HEREDITY; his doctrine stressed unbroken continuity of germ plasm and nonheritability of acquired characters.

Weisshorn (vīs'hôrn"), peak, 14,792 ft. high, Valais canton, Switzerland, in Pennine Alps.

Weizmann, Chaim (khīm' vītsmän), 1874–1952, scientist and Zionist leader, first president of Israel, b. Russia. Became British citizen in 1910, and in World War I created a synthetic acetone needed by Great Britain for the manufacture of explosives. He helped procure the famous declaration of Arthur James BALFOUR. After 1920 he became the leader of Zionism.

Welch, William Henry, 1850–1934, American pathologist. Noted in research and as medical historian. Associated with the Johns Hopkins Univ. from 1884.

Welch, city (pop. 6,603), S W.Va., on Tug Fork R., NW of Bluefield. Coal mining and lumber milling.

Weld, Theodore Dwight, 1803–95, American abolitionist. Recruited converts for abolitionist cause, trained agents for American Anti-Slavery Society, directed national campaign for sending antislavery petitions to Congress.

welding, the joining of separate pieces of same kind of metal. Modern methods include: use of electric arc, thermite process, OXYACETYLENE TORCH, oxyhydrogen blowpipe, and atomic hydrogen flame.

Welfs: see GUELPHS.

Welhaven, Johan Sebastian (vĕl'hävŭn), 1807–73, Norwegian poet and critic, upholder of the classic style and opposed to Wergeland.

well, cylindrical hole in the ground through which oil or water is brought to surface. Shallow wells are usually dug or driven; deep wells are drilled. Driven wells are made by pounding into the earth a casing with sharp edges at bottom and holes near casing end to admit water. Bored wells are made by percussion or rotary drills.

Welland, city (pop. 15,382), S Ont., Canada, on Welland Ship Canal and W of Buffalo, N.Y. Port and trade center in fruitgrowing region with cotton, steel, and cordage mills.

Welland Ship Canal, S Ont., Canada, between L. Ontario (at Port Weller) and L. Erie (at Port Colborne), bypassing the Niagara Falls. Built 1914–32 to replace canal opened 1833. It is 27.6 mi. long, with eight locks overcoming 326 ft. difference in level between the two lakes.

Welles, Gideon (wĕlz), 1802–78, U.S. Secretary of the Navy (1861–69). Built powerful Union navy of Civil War; stood by Lincoln and Johnson in Reconstruction struggle. His diary is of immense value to the historian.

Welles, Orson, 1915–, American stage, film, and radio actor, director, and producer. Productions include *Julius Caesar* in modern dress, film *Citizen Kane,* and an alarmingly realistic radio version (1938) of H. G. Wells's *War of the Worlds.*

Welles, Sumner, 1892–, U.S. Undersecretary of State (1937–43). An authority on Latin America.

Wellesley, Richard Colley Wellesley, Marquess (wĕlz'lē), 1760–1842, British governor general of India (1797–1805). Extended British influence there, wiped out French power, and, aided by his brother (later duke of WELLINGTON), checked power of native rulers. Was foreign secretary (1810–12) and lord lieutenant of Ireland (1821–28, 1833–34).

Wellesley, suburban town (pop. 20,549), E Mass., WSW of Boston; settled 1660. **Wellesley College** (nonsectarian; for women; chartered 1870 and 1873, opened 1875). First to have scientific laboratories in woman's college. Has noted department of hygiene and physical education (graduate). Faculty noted for constructive influence in social movements.

Wellfleet, resort town (pop. 1,123), SE Mass., on N Cape Cod, SSE of Provincetown.

Wellington, Arthur Wellesley, 1st duke of, 1769–1852, British soldier and statesman. In India (1796–1805), he assisted his brother, Richard Wellesley, by defeating Tippoo Sahib and the Mahratta chiefs. Commander (1809–13) in the PENINSULAR WAR, he drove French from Spain. In the WATERLOO CAMPAIGN he defeated Napoleon I. Prime minister 1828–30, he secured passage of Catholic Emancipation (which he had previously opposed). Was made (1842) commander in chief for life.

Wellington, city (pop. 123,771; metropolitan pop. 173,520), cap. of New Zealand, at S tip of North Isl., on Cook Strait; founded 1840. Succeeded Auckland as dominion's capital, 1865. Here are governor general's residence, Houses of Parliament, National Art Gall. (1936), and Dominion Mus. (1936) with Maori art collection.

Wellington, city (pop. 7,747), S Kansas, S of Wichita, in wheat area on Chisholm Trail. Oil fields near.

Wells, Henry, 1805–78, American pioneer expressman. Associated in business with W. G. FARGO.

Wells, H(erbert) G(eorge), 1866–1946, English novelist. Clothed scientific speculation and social reform in fiction, as in *The Time Machine* (1895), *The Invisible Man* (1897), *The War of the Worlds* (1898), *Kipps* (1905), *Tono Bungay* (1909), *The History of Mr. Polly* (1910), and *The World of William Clissold* (1926). His *Outline of History* (1920) was overwhelmingly popular.

Wells, Horace, 1815–48, American dentist, first to use laughing gas as anesthetic in dentistry (1844).

Wells, municipal borough (pop. 5,835), Somerset, England, SW of Bath. Near by is Wookey Hole, subterranean caverns where remains of prehistoric men were found. Cathedral of Bath and Wells (12th–13th cent.) is one of England's most magnificent.

Wells, town (pop. 2,321), SW Maine, on the coast SW of Portland; settled c.1640. Includes resorts of Wells Beach and Ogunquit (1940 pop. 615), which has artists' colony and summer playhouse.

Wellsburg, city (pop. 5,787), NW W.Va., in N Panhandle, on Ohio R. and NNE of Wheeling. Mfg. of paper products, glass, and cement.

Wells College: see AURORA, N.Y.

Wellston. 1 See WARNER ROBINS, Ga. **2** Town (pop. 9,396), E Mo., W suburb of St. Louis. **3** City (pop. 5,691), S Ohio, NE of Portsmouth. Mfg. of machinery and clothing.

Wellsville. 1 Village (pop. 6,402). W N.Y., on Genesee R. and SE of Buffalo. Oil-refining center. **2** City (pop. 7,854), NE Ohio, on Ohio R. and N of Steubenville. Clay products center.

Welsh language, Brythonic language of Celtic subfamily of Indo-European languages. See LANGUAGE (table).

Welsh Marches, lands in Wales along English border. After Norman Conquest, William I estab. border earldoms to protect his English kingdom. Encouraged his barons to conquer other Welsh earldoms. Abolished by Act of Union (1536).

Welsh terrier: see TERRIER.

Welty, Eudora, 1909–, American author of short stories (as in *Curtain of Green,* 1941; *Golden Apples,* 1949) and notable novel, *Delta Wedding* (1946), about Miss. life. Her delicate, involved style and approach make all her work notable.

Wembley, municipal borough (pop. 131,369), Middlesex, England. British Empire Exhibition was held here 1924–25. Olympic Games were held (1948) in stadium which accommodates 100,000. Has metal casting and mfg. of electrical goods and chemicals.

Wenatchee (wĭnăʹchē), city (pop. 13,072), central Wash., on Columbia R. below mouth of Wenatchee R.; founded 1888. Trade center of apple-growing area. Aluminum plant. Wheat, lumber, and dairy products. Wenatchee L., 5 mi. long, is NW.

Wenceslaus, Saint (wĕnʹsŭslŭs), Czech *Vaclav,* d. 936?, duke of Bohemia, reared a Christian by his grandmother. He promoted Christianity, made peace with Henry I of Germany, and was killed by his brother Boleslav. Patron saint of Bohemia. The "good King Wenceslaus" of the English Christmas carol. Feast: Sept. 28.

Wenceslaus, 1361–1419, emperor (never crowned) and German king (1378–1400); as Wenceslaus IV, king of Bohemia (1378–1419). He was elector of Brandenburg from 1373 until he succeeded his father, Emperor Charles IV, in 1378. His main interest was in Bohemia, and his clashes with the German nobles led in 1400 to his deposition as German king and the election of Emperor RUPERT. Wenceslaus never accepted his deposition but in 1411 agreed to the election of his brother SIGISMUND as emperor. In Bohemia, Wenceslaus was popular with the commons but quarreled with the nobles and clergy, notably with the archbishop of Prague, whose vicar general, St. John of Nepomuk, he had killed in one of his recurrent fits of rage. His decree of Kutna Hora (1409) gave the Czechs preponderance in the Univ. of Prague and made possible the election of John HUSS as its rector. He continued to support Huss secretly even after the interdict was laid on Prague (1412), but the rise of the TABORITES cooled his feelings toward the reformers. When several councilors appointed by him were thrown out of the window (first Defenestration of Prague, 1419), Wenceslaus had a fit and died. His vile temper and drunken habits, though much stressed by historians, were shared by many of his contemporaries.

Wenceslaus, kings of Bohemia. **Wenceslaus I,** d. 1253, son of Ottocar I, reigned 1230–53. Called German settlers into Bohemian and Moravian cities, which received liberal charters. Repulsed Mongol invasion 1241. His grandson **Wenceslaus II,** 1271–1305, son of Ottocar II, reigned 1278–83. After a turbulent regency during which he was imprisoned, he began his personal rule with the execution of his mother's lover, Zavis of Falckenstein (1290). In 1291 he accepted the offer of the duchy of Cracow; in 1300 he was crowned king of all Poland; in 1301 he accepted the crown of Hungary for his son (later Wenceslaus III); in 1304 he repulsed the invasion of Albert I of Germany, who had demanded that Wenceslaus give up Poland and Hungary. **Wenceslaus III,** c.1289–1306, who succeeded him, was unable to assert his authority in Hungary, which he renounced in 1305. He was assassinated while preparing to invade Poland, the succession to which he claimed. The last of the Premysl dynasty, he was succeeded by his brother-in-law, John of Luxemburg. **Wenceslaus IV:** see WENCESLAUS, emperor.

Wenden, Latvia: see CESIS.

Wends (wĕndz), in medieval usage, name of all Slavs in Germany E of the Elbe; in modern usage, the small group of Slavic-speaking inhabitants of LUSATIA, E Germany. Charlemagne's conquest of the Wends (8th cent.) had no lasting effect. A crusade against the pagan Wends was launched in 1147 under HENRY THE LION and ALBERT THE BEAR; it failed, but in the following years these two princes, aided by Waldemar I of Denmark. carried out a systematic campaign of conquest. By the end of the 12th cent. nearly all Germany had been Germanized and Christianized. The term *Sorbs* (cognate with Serbs) is sometimes used interchangeably with Wends; specifically, the Sorbs were one of the Wendish nations, settled between the Elbe and Saale rivers.

Wentworth, Benning, 1696–1770, colonial governor of N.H. (1741–65). Precipitated trouble with his NEW HAMPSHIRE GRANTS. His nephew, **Sir John Wentworth,** 1737–1820, succeeded him as governor of N.H., but was forced to flee on outbreak of American Revolution because of his Loyalist sympathies.

Wentworth, Thomas: see STRAFFORD, THOMAS WENTWORTH, 1ST EARL OF.

Werfel, Franz (fräntsʹ vĕrʹfŭl), 1890–1945, Austrian author, b. Prague. His philosophy of the brotherhood of man and his mysticism were expressed in verse, drama, and epic novels. He is best known in the U.S. for the novels *The Forty Days of Musa Dagh* (1933) and *The Song of Bernadette* (1941). Died in U.S.

Wergeland, Henrik (vĕrʹgŭlän), 1808–45, Norwegian poet, novelist, and patriot. An ardent, tempestuous romanticist, he worked zealously for liberty, international cooperation, social improvement, the admission of Jews to Norway. His poetry (some in verse dramas) was aimed at liberating all humanity.

Werner, Alfred (äl'frāt vĕr'nůr), 1866–1919, Swiss chemist. Won 1913 Nobel Prize for research on the linking up of atoms in the molecule, important to development of study of isomerism.

Wertenbaker, Thomas Jefferson (wûr'tůnbākůr), 1879–, American historian, authority on colonial history of Va. Author of *Virginia under the Stuarts* (1914), *Patrician and Plebeian in Virginia* (1916), and *Planters of Virginia* (1922).

Weser (vā'zůr), river, c.300 mi. long, NW Germany, formed by junction of Fulda and Werra rivers and flowing N past Bremen into North Sea. Entirely navigable; linked by canals with Rhine, Ems, and Elbe rivers.

Weslaco (wĕs'lĭkō), city (pop. 7,514), S Texas, WNW of Brownsville. Processing and shipping center of vegetable and citrus fruit area, has mfg. of fertilizer and boxes.

Wesley, John, 1703–91, English evangelical preacher, founder of METHODISM. Ordained a priest in the Church of England, at Oxford he led a group gathered round his brother Charles, derisively called Methodists for their methodical habits of study and religious duties. In 1735 the Wesleys accompanied James Oglethorpe to Ga. On May 24, 1738, at a religious meeting in London, Wesley experienced an assurance of salvation through faith in Christ alone. This conviction formed the basis of his message to the world. In his lifelong evangelistic work, he is said to have preached some 40,000 sermons and to have traveled some 250,000 mi., mostly on horseback. Persuaded by George WHITEFIELD, he did open-air or field preaching. About 1740 he repudiated Calvinism, his act causing a religious break with Whitefield. In 1784 he estab. legal status of Methodist societies, and, though he had not thought to form a separate church, he made plans for the societies to go on after his death. His brother, **Charles Wesley,** 1707–88, was also a priest of the Church of England and a Methodist evangelical preacher. He wrote some 6,500 hymns, among them *Hark! the Herald Angels Sing* and *Jesus, Lover of My Soul.*

Wesleyan College: see MACON, Ga.

Wesleyan Methodist Church, branch of Methodism founded in England by followers of John Wesley. At Conference of 1791 they engaged "to follow strictly the plan" he had left to them when he died.

Wesleyan University: see MIDDLETOWN, Conn.

Wessex (wĕ'sĭks), Anglo-Saxon kingdom in England. Possibly settled by Saxons as early as 494. Until end of 8th cent. it was overshadowed successively by Kent, Northumbria, and Mercia. With reign of Alfred (871–99?), Wessex's history becomes that of England. In Thomas Hardy's novels Wessex is used to mean mainly Dorsetshire.

West, Benjamin, 1738–1820, American historical painter in England, b. Springfield, Pa. Worked as a portrait painter in Philadelphia and New York before going to Europe in 1760. After studying in Italy he settled in London. A founder of the Royal Acad. His many oils, done on a grand scale, show skill in composition.

West, Thomas: see DE LA WARR, THOMAS WEST, BARON.

West Allis, city (pop. 42,959), SE Wis., industrial and residential suburb of Milwaukee. Mfg. of machinery and industrial gases.

West Baden Springs (bā'důn), village (pop. 1,047), S Ind., on Lost R. and SSW of Bedford. Long a noted mineral-springs resort. Here is West Baden Col., a branch of LOYOLA UNIVERSITY (Chicago).

West Bend, city (pop. 6,849), E Wis., NW of Milwaukee and on Milwaukee R. Aluminum ware.

Westboro or **Westborough,** town (pop. 7,378), E central Mass., E of Worcester. Birthplace of Eli Whitney. Abrasives and shoes.

Westbrook, city (pop. 12,284), SW Maine, W suburb of Portland. Mfg. of textiles, paper, machinery.

Westbury, village (pop. 7,112), on W Long Isl., SE N.Y., E of Mineola. Holds auto races.

West Chester, borough (pop. 15,168), SE Pa., W of Philadelphia; laid out 1786. Farm trade center with mfg. of metal products and canned goods. Battle of Brandywine fought in area 1777.

West Columbia, city (pop. 2,100), S Texas, near Brazos R. and SSW of Houston; founded 1826. Center, with East Columbia, of S. F. Austin's plantations. Briefly cap. of Texas Republic 1836.

Westcott, Edward Noyes, 1846–98, American writer, a banker, known for his one novel, *David Harum* (1898).

West Covina (kōvē'nů), city (pop. 8,361), S Calif., E of Los Angeles, in farm area.

West Des Moines (dů moin'), city (pop. 5,615), S central Iowa, suburb of Des Moines; called Valley Junction before 1938.

Westerly, town (pop. 12,380), including Westerly village (pop. 8,415), SW R.I., between Pawcatuck R. (bridged) and Block Isl. Sound. Mfg. of textiles, machinery, furniture. Includes Watch Hill resort, site of lighthouse, coast guard station.

Westermarck, Edward Alexander (vĕ'stůrmärk), 1862–1939, Finnish anthropologist, authority on history of morals and marriage. Wrote *The History of Human Marriage* (1891; 5th ed., 3 vols., 1921) and other works.

Western Australia, state (975,920 sq. mi.; pop. 502,731), Australia, comprising a third of the continent; cap. Perth. Largest Australian state, but only SW corner is fertile and substantially settled. Most of the state is occupied by state-owned gold fields and a vast central desert. Climate is tropical in NW, temperate in SW. Products include wool, wine, wheat, fruit, and hardwood. Chief port is Fremantle. First visited by the Dutch (1616). Penal colony was estab. 1826 at Albany and first free settlement in 1829 in Perth-Fremantle area. Governed by New South Wales until 1831. Became a state 1901.

Western canon consists of books of the Bible that were accepted as official by the Western Church at the time St. Jerome edited the Bible (VULGATE). See OLD TESTAMENT.

Western College: see OXFORD, Ohio.

Western Dvina, river: see DVINA.

Western Empire: see HOLY ROMAN EMPIRE; ROME.

Western Islands: see HEBRIDES.

Western Ontario, University of: see LONDON, Ont.

Western Reserve, tract of land in NE Ohio from Pa. line to W of Sandusky, on S shore of L. Erie. Reserved by Conn. for its own settlers when it ceded its western lands in 1786 (see NORTHWEST TERRITORY). Conn. gave land as "fire lands" to its citizens who were burned out in Revolution 1792. Connecticut Land Co. bought remaining land 1795; area taken into Northwest Territory 1800.

Western Reserve University, at Cleveland; nonsectarian, for men and women; chartered and opened 1826, moved to Cleveland 1882, became university 1884. Includes two coordinate colleges—Adelbert (for men; the old Western Reserve Col.) and Flora Stone Mather (for women; 1888). Cleveland Col. is downtown center.

Western Samoa, Territory of: see SAMOA.

Westerville, village (pop. 4,112), central Ohio, NE of Columbus. Seat of Otterbein Col. (United Brethren; coed.; 1847).

Westfalen, Germany: see WESTPHALIA.

Westfield. 1 City (pop. 20,962), SW Mass., on Westfield R. and W of Springfield; settled c.1660. Metal, paper products; machinery. **2** Residential town (pop. 21,243), NE N.J., SW of Newark; settled before 1700.

West Flanders, province (1,249 sq. mi.; pop. 1,002,904), NW Belgium; cap. Bruges. Agr., stock raising, dairying. Fishing on North Sea coast. Textile mfg. (notably at Courtrai, Ypres). Population is mainly Flemish-speaking. For history, see FLANDERS.

West Florida Controversy, boundary dispute between U.S. and Spain. Developed when Great Britain ceded Fla. back to Spain after American Revolution. Treaty concluded in 1795 fixed northern boundary of W Fla. at lat. 31° N. Louisiana Purchase (1803) increased dispute. Seizure in 1810 of land between Mississippi and East Pearl rivers and, in 1813, of land between East Pearl and Perdido rivers left land in American hands.

West Frankfort, city (pop. 11,384), S Ill., NNE of Cairo. Center of coal-mining area.

West Goths: see VISIGOTHS.

West Ham, county borough (pop. 170,987), Essex, England; industrial suburb of London.

Westhampton Beach, fashionable resort village (pop. 1,087), on E Long Isl., SE N.Y., on Moriches Bay.

West Hartford, town (pop. 44,402), central Conn., suburb of Hartford; settled 1679. Mfg. of metal goods. Seat of American School for the Deaf (1817).

West Haven, town (pop. 32,010), S Conn., suburb of New Haven. Mfg. of metal goods, tires, and textiles.

West Indies, archipelago, between North and South America, curving c.2,500 mi. from Florida to NE Venezuela and separating the Caribbean from the Atlantic. Sometimes called Antilles (ăntĭ'lēz), it is divided into three main sections: BAHAMA ISLANDS; Greater Antilles (CUBA, JAMAICA, HISPANIOLA, PUERTO RICO); Lesser Antilles (LEEWARD ISLANDS, WINDWARD ISLANDS, TRINIDAD AND TOBAGO, BARBADOS, Dutch and Venezuelan islands). VIRGIN ISLANDS are considered as part of both Greater and Lesser Antilles. But for Hispaniola (HAITI and DOMINICAN REPUBLIC) and Cuba, islands are dependencies. British West Indies: Bahamas, Jamaica, British Leeward Isls., British Windward Isls., Trinidad and Tobago, Barbados, and British Virgin Isls. Dutch West Indies: CURAÇAO, Aruba, St. Eustatius, part of SAINT MARTIN. French West Indies: GUADELOUPE and MARTINIQUE. American dependencies: Puerto Rico and Virgin Isls. (U.S.) MARGARITA belongs to Venezuela. Many of islands were discovered by Columbus (1492) and first permanent white settlement was made on Hispaniola (1496). See *maps,* pp. 901, 1193.

Westinghouse, George, 1846–1914, American inventor and manufacturer. Invented reversible railway frog, air brake, and signal devices; was influential in introducing alternating current in U.S.

West Lafayette (lă"fēĕt'), city (pop. 11,873), W Ind., on Wabash R. opposite Lafayette. Business and industrial center.

West Long Branch, borough (pop. 2,739), E N.J., near Long Branch. "Shadow Lawn" here was Pres. Wilson's summer White House.

West Lothian (lō'dhēūn), formerly **Linlithgow** (lĭnlĭth'gō), county (120 sq. mi.; pop. 88,-576), S Scotland, on Firth of Forth; co. town Linlithgow. There is much dairy farming, but county is more important for its mineral wealth.

Westman Islands, Icelandic *Vestmannaeyjar,* group of 14 small islands, c.8 mi. off SW Iceland. Heimaey, the largest, has chief town (Vestmannaeyjar, pop. 3,548). Abounds in waterfowl. When Iceland was first colonized, a group of Irish slaves fled to these islands. In 1627 Algerian pirates raided islands and carried c.400 people into slavery.

Westmeath (wĕstmēth', wĕst'mēdh), inland county (681 sq. mi.; pop. 54,949), central Ireland, in Leinster; co. town Mullingar. Mostly level and fertile with many lakes and bogs. Dairy farming and cattle raising are chief occupations. Some mfg. of textiles and flour milling. Athlone is largest town.

West Memphis, cotton and lumber city (pop. 9,112), NE Ark., across the Mississippi (bridged near by) from Memphis, Tenn.

West Mifflin, borough (pop. 17,985), W Pa., SE of Pittsburgh, in industrial region.

West Milwaukee (mĭlwô'kē), village (pop. 5,429), SE Wis., near Milwaukee. Steel castings.

Westminster (wĕst'mĭnstûr), city, metropolitan borough (pop. 98,895) of W London, England. Here are WESTMINSTER ABBEY, Houses of Parliament (WESTMINSTER PALACE), BUCKINGHAM PALACE, SAINT JAMES'S PALACE, and DOWNING STREET. Westminster Cathedral is senior archiepiscopal see of Catholic Church in England and Wales. Westminster School, founded in 14th cent., is a leading public school.

Westminster. 1 City (pop. 6,140), N Md., NW of Baltimore, in farm area. Mfg. of clothing and shoes. Was Union supply base during

Gettysburg campaign. 2 Town (pop. 1,400), SE Vt., on Connecticut R. and S of Bellow Falls. "Westminster Massacre" occurred March 13, 1775, when N.Y. officials tried forcibly to hold a Cumberland co. (N.Y.) court session. Here, Jan. 15, 1777, Vt. was declared an independent state (called New Conn.).

Westminster, Statute of, 1931, an act of Parliament by which the British Commonwealth of Nations was declared to be a free association of autonomous dominions and the United Kingdom, bound only by common allegiance to the crown. Gave legal force to work of IMPERIAL CONFERENCE.

Westminster, Statutes of, legislative promulgations made by Edward I of England in Parliament at Westminster. Westminster I (1275) constitutes a code of law. Westminster II (1285) is similar. Had a clause which radically altered English landholding. Westminster III (1290) dealt with land tenure.

Westminster Abbey, in London, a national shrine and one of England's finest Gothic buildings; scene of coronation of all English kings since William I. It is the burial place of many kings and of distinguished citizens; Poets' Corner in S transept contains tombs of great English poets. Cruciform in plan, it shows French influence by the height of its nave (loftiest in England) and in strongly emphasized flying buttresses. First of several churches on the site is said to have been built in 616. Name comes from fact that church of a Benedictine monastery was here. Present church was built mainly between the 13th and 15th cent. The Lady Chapel, dedicated to Henry VII and famous for its fan vaulting, was finished in early 16th cent. The two W towers were built 1722–40 by Wren and Hawksmoor.

Westminster College: see FULTON, Mo.

Westminster Conference, 1866–67, held in London to settle the plan for Canadian confederation.

Westminster Confession: see CREED.

Westminster Palace or **Houses of Parliament,** in London. Present structure was built 1840–60, following fire of 1834. Original palace buildings were built by Edward the Confessor. Served as royal abode until 16th cent. when they became assembly place for House of Commons and House of Lords. Great Hall was built at end of 11th cent. Westminster Hall, long the meeting place of highest English court of law, was scene of many historical events. Seriously damaged in World War II.

West Monroe, city (pop. 10,302), NE La., on Ouachita R. opposite Monroe, in farm and livestock area. Processes lumber and cotton.

Westmorland, Ralph Neville, 1st **earl of:** see NEVILLE, family.

Westmorland (wĕst'mŭrlŭnd), county (789 sq. mi.; pop. 67,383), N England; co. town Appleby. Largely mountainous, it is most sparsely populated county in England. Much of country is in the LAKE DISTRICT. Dairy farming and cattle raising are chief occupations. Wordsworth and other poets are associated with the Lake District.

Westmount, city (pop. 25,222), S Que., Canada, on Montreal Isl., W residential suburb of Montreal.

West New York, town (pop. 37,683), NE N.J., on Hudson R. and N of Weehawken; settled 1790. Mfg. of radio parts, embroideries, clothing, leather goods.

Weston, town (pop. 8,677), S Ont., Canada, NW of Toronto. Mfg. of motors, bicycles, and stoves.

Weston. 1 Residential town (pop. 5,026), E Mass., W of Boston. **2** Town (pop. 8,945), central W.Va., on West Fork R. and SSW of Clarksburg. Glassmaking.

West Orange, residential town (pop. 28,605), NE N.J., NW of Newark. Edison estab. laboratories and home here 1887. Mfg. of electrical equipment.

West Palm Beach, city (pop. 43,162), SE Fla., on L. Worth (lagoon) opposite Palm Beach (connected by bridges). Resort and rail center, it has mfg. of air-conditioning equipment and prefabricated buildings. Developed 1893 by H. M. Flagler. Seat of Norton Gall. and School of Art (1941). Canal to L. Okeechobee.

Westphalia (wĕstfā'lyŭ), Ger. *Westfalen,* region, NW Germany. Level in the N, hilly in the S, it has agr. districts as well as heaths and moors. In the W, it forms part of the industrial RUHR dist. and the great Westphalian coal basin. Bielefeld has important textile mfg. Westphalia was the W part of the first duchy of SAXONY, which broke up in 1180. Most of the territory passed under the rule of ecclesiastic princes (bishops of Münster, Osnabrück, Minden, Padernborn; archbishops of Cologne) and of minor temporal lords (counts of Lippe, Ravensberg, Mark). The towns prospered as members of the Hanseatic League. Brandenburg-Prussia acquired Ravensberg, Mark, and Minden in 17th cent. In 1807 Napoleon created the kingdom of Westphalia, consisting of parts of Westphalia and of adjacent territories (notably Hesse-Kassel) for his brother Jérôme Bonaparte. The Congress of Vienna gave most of Westphalia to Prussia (1815), of which it became a province (7,806 sq. mi.; 1939 pop. 5,209,401; cap. Münster). After World War II the province became part of the state of NORTH RHINE-WESTPHALIA.

Westphalia, Peace of, 1648, general European settlement ending THIRTY YEARS WAR. Negotiations had begun 1644 at two concurrent conferences, at Münster and Osnabrück, and resulted in two treaties which together formed the peace settlement. Through the French and Swedish "satisfactions," the power of the house of Hapsburg was lessened and the HOLY ROMAN EMPIRE became a mere loose confederation of sovereign states. France obtained most of Alsace and several border fortresses. Sweden received W Pomerania and the bishoprics of Bremen and Verden. Switzerland and the United Provs. of the Netherlands obtained full independence. France, which emerged as dominant power, continued warfare with Spain until the Peace of the PYRENEES (1659).

West Pittston, residential borough (pop. 7,230), NE Pa., on Susquehanna R. and near Wilkes-Barre. Fort Jenkins built near here 1772.

West Point, city (pop. 6,432), NE Miss., NW of Columbus. Processes cottonseed oil, cheese, lumber.

West Point, U.S. military reservation, SE N.Y., on W bank of the Hudson and S of Newburg. Seat of UNITED STATES MILITARY ACADEMY since 1802. Site of Revolutionary forts guarding the Hudson. Constitution Isl., E anchorage of a chain across the river to prevent ascent of British ships in Revolution, is in reservation. Benedict Arnold's plan to surrender (1780) West Point to British was disclosed by capture of Major John André.

Westport. 1 Residential town (pop. 11,667), SW Conn., on Long Isl. Sound E of Norwalk; settled 1645–50. Has writers' and artists' colony and a summer theater. **2** See KANSAS CITY, Mo.

West Prussia, Ger. *Westpreussen,* former province of Prussia; chief city Danzig. It was formed after the Congress of Vienna from previously Polish Pomerelia (see POMERANIA) and from part of the original duchy of PRUSSIA. The Treaty of Versailles (1919) gave most of West Prussia to Poland (see POLISH CORRIDOR) and made Danzig a free city. Reannexed by Germany in 1939, the whole area was placed under Polish administration in 1945.

West Quoddy Head, promontory on Atlantic coast, SE Maine, SE of Lubec; easternmost point of U.S.

West Reading, borough (pop. 5,072), SE Pa., on Schuylkill R. and near Reading. Textiles, paper.

West Riding: see YORKSHIRE, England.

West River or **Si-kiang** (shē'jyäng'), chief river of S China, 1,250 mi. long, in Yunnan, Kwangsi, and Kwantung provs.

West Roman Empire: see ROME.

West Springfield, town (pop. 20,438), SW Mass., on Westfield and Connecticut rivers opposite Springfield; settled c.1660. Machinery, paper, chemicals.

West Virginia, state (24,282 sq. mi.; pop. 2,005,552), E central U.S.; admitted 1863 as 35th state; cap. CHARLESTON. Other cities are HUNTINGTON, PARKERSBURG, WHEELING, MOUNDSVILLE. Irregularly shaped, with one panhandle in E, another in NW. Some agr. of grains and fruit, raising of livestock. Leads in production of bituminous coal. Mfg. of iron and steel products, chemicals, glass, wood products. Settlement began c.1730; defeat of the French and the Indians speeded colonization. Although a part of Va., political and economic differences created friction. W part broke away from Va. in Civil War, joined Union, was admitted as new state. Industrial expansion began in late 19th cent., was furthered by two World Wars.

West Virginia University: see MORGANTOWN.

West Warwick, town (pop. 19,096), central R.I., SSW of Providence. Has textile mfg.

Westwego (wĕstwē'gō), town (pop. 8,328), SE La., near New Orleans. Processes seafood and chemicals.

West York, borough (pop. 5,756), SE Pa., near York. Mfg. of machinery, pottery, and hosiery.

Wethersfield, residential town (pop. 12,533), central Conn., on Connecticut R., adjoining S Hartford; settled 1633–34. One of oldest Conn. towns.

Wettin (vĕ'tĕn), German dynasty, named for a castle near Halle, Germany. Margraves of Meissen from c.1100, they acquired most of SAXONY and THURINGIA; became ELECTORS 1425; split into two main lines 1485. The Ernestine (senior) line lost Saxony and electoral title to the Albertine line (1547); its Thuringian possessions split into several duchies, which were ruled by separate branches till 1918. From one of the Ernestine branches—Saxe Coburg-Gotha—are descended the ruling houses of Great Britain (through Prince ALBERT) and Belgium (through LEOPOLD I) and former rulers of Bulgaria (through Tsar FERDINAND) and Portugal (through FERDINAND II). The Albertine line ruled Saxony 1547–1918 (in personal union with POLAND, 1697–1764).

Wewoka (wēwō'kŭ), city (pop. 6,747), central Okla., SE of Oklahoma City, in oil and agr. section.

Wexford (wĕks'fûrd), maritime county (910 sq. mi.; pop. 91,855), SE Ireland, in Leinster. Low, fertile land, it rises in W to Mt. Leinster (2,610 ft.). Agr. is the chief occupation; fishing is of some importance. County town is **Wexford,** urban district (pop. 12,296), on Wexford Harbour. Site of 12th-cent. abbey, old Bull Ring, and Church of St. Patrick. English landed here 1169.

Weyburn, city (pop. 7,148), SE Sask., Canada, SE of Regina. Trade center for agr. area.

Weyden, Roger van der (văn' dûr wī'dŭn, Flemish vän dûr vī'dŭn), c.1400–1464, Flemish artist, known also as Roger de la Pasture, successor to the Van Eycks as head of Flemish school of painting. Worked mainly in Brussels. Though his work resembles that of the Eycks in clarity and luminous glazed color, it is distinctive in its severity and dramatic power. A favorite theme is *Descent from the Cross.*

Weygand, Maxine (mäksēm' vāgã'), 1867–, French general, b. Belgium. Was chief of staff to Marshal Foch in World War I; directed defense of Warsaw against Red Army (1920); replaced Gen. Gamelin as supreme Allied commander in 1940 but could not avert French rout by Germans. He served in the Vichy government as war minister, delegate general to French Africa, and governor of Algeria; was arrested by the Germans in 1942. After his liberation (1945) he was exonerated of the charge of collaboration with Germany.

Weyler y Nicolau, Valeriano (välāryä'nō wā'lĕr ē nĕkōlä'ōō), 1839–1930, Spanish general; created marquis of Tenerife. Fought in Cuba in Ten Years War and in Spain against the Carlists (1875–76). In 1896 he replaced Martínez de Campos in Cuba, but his cruel methods against the rebels led to a protest by the U.S. and his recall (1897). He later was several times minister of war.

Weymouth (wā'mŭth), town (pop. 32,690), E Mass., on the coast SE of Boston; settled 1622. Shoes, tools, machinery, and paper boxes.

Weymouth and Melcombe Regis (wā'mŭth, mĕl'kŭm rē'jĭs), municipal borough (pop.

37,097), Dorsetshire, England; a seaport and watering place.

whale, aquatic mammal of order Cetacea. Its skin is almost hairless and a layer of fat or blubber lies beneath it; the forelimbs are swimming flippers; hind limbs are absent; horizontal, fluked tail is chief means of locomotion. Most species can remain under water 5–15 min.; condensation of moist air exhaled on emerging causes "spouting." Two major groups: whalebone or baleen whales, e.g., right whale, gray whale, rorqual; toothed whales, including sperm whale (source of sperm oil and ambergris), dolphin, and porpoise.

whale oil, oil extracted from blubber and other parts of whales. Formerly used as illuminant, it is now used in soap making, as leather dressing, and as a lubricant.

Whales, Bay of: see Ross SEA.

whaling. Large-scale whaling was first organized at Spitsbergen at beginning of 17th cent., largely by the Dutch. By middle of 17th cent. whaling from land was estab. in America. Later, New Bedford, Mass., became world's greatest whaling port until decline of industry (c.1850). Modern whaling began c.1856 with invention of a harpoon containing an explosive head. International whaling commission restricts whaling to a few months of year, determines size of legal catch. See WHALE; WHALE OIL.

Whampoa (hwămpō'ŭ), town, S Kwangtung prov., China, on an island in Canton R.; outer port for Canton. Shipbuilding. Military and naval academies.

Whangpoo or **Hwangpoo** (both: hwäng'pōō'), river, c.60 mi. long, S Kiangsu prov., China; flows past Shanghai to the Yangtze. Major navigation channel.

Wharton, Edith (Jones), 1862–1937, American novelist. Her works range widely, but she is best known for studies of high society in somewhat the manner of Henry James (e.g., *The House of Mirth,* 1905; *The Age of Innocence,* 1920; connected short novels in *Old New York,* 4 vols., 1924) and for one starkly tragic short novel of New England, *Ethan Frome* (1911). Also wrote short stories, travel books, literary criticism.

wheat, plant of genus *Triticum* of grass family. A major food and commodity on the world grain market, it was probably the first grain domesticated. Wheat has long been the white man's chief source of bread. There are varieties adapted to growing as winter wheat (fall planted) or as spring wheat. Flour from hard-kernel wheat is used to make fine cakes and bread; the hardest flour, from durum wheat, is used in making macaroni, while soft-wheat varieties provide flour for piecrust and biscuits. Wheat is used as livestock feed and in making whisky and beer. Leading wheat producers are U.S., China, USSR, India, Canada, Argentina, and Australia. See *ill.,* p. 999.

wheat fly, any of several insects harmful to wheat (e.g., HESSIAN FLY, wheat gallfly, wheat midge).

Wheatley, Henry Benjamin (hwēt'lē), 1838–1917, English bibliographer and antiquarian, a founder of the Early English Text Society and of the Index Society. He edited Pepys's diary, (10 vols., 1893–99).

Wheatley, Phillis, 1753?–1784, American Negro poet. Bought as a slave by Boston merchant John Wheatley, she learned to write and produced graceful poems.

Wheaton, residential city (pop. 11,638), NE Ill., W of Chicago, in farm area; settled in 1830s. Seat of **Wheaton College** (coed.; c.1854).

Wheaton College: see NORTON, Mass.

Wheatstone, Sir Charles (hwēt'stōn), 1802–75, English physicist and inventor. He was coinventor of an electric telegraph (patented 1837), inventor of an automatic transmitter and electric recording apparatus. Is credited with invention of concertina. Known also for research on light, sound, electricity; popularized (but did not invent) the **Wheatstone bridge,** a specially devised electric circuit for accurate measurement of electrical resistance.

wheel. Came into use during Bronze Age in Old World as potter's wheel and as solid wood disks for vehicles. Spoked wheel was introduced c.1800 B.C. **Wheel and axle** classed in physics as simple machine related to lever. Relatively small effort applied to wheel overcomes resistance acting on axle; mechanical advantage is indicated by ratio of wheel radius to that of axle radius. Crank or handle may replace wheel part. Applications include windmill, doorknob, clockwork, and waterwheel. See *ill.,* p. 793.

Wheeler, Burton K(endall), 1882–, U.S. Senator from Mont. (1923–47). New Deal backer who became a leading isolationist.

Wheeler, Joseph, 1836–1906, Confederate general. Commanded cavalry in many battles. In Chattanooga campaign he destroyed Rosecrans's supplies and covered Confederate retreat. Operated against Sherman in Atlanta campaign.

Wheeler Field, U.S. army air base, Oahu, T.H., near S edge of Schofield Barracks; estab. 1922. Bombed by Japanese, Dec. 7, 1941.

Wheeler National Monument: see NATIONAL PARKS AND MONUMENTS (table).

Wheeling, city (pop. 58,891), NW W.Va., in N Panhandle, on Ohio R. and SW of Pittsburgh; settled 1769. Third largest city in state and commercial and industrial center of rich coal and gas area, it has mfg. of iron, steel, metal products, and chinaware; railroad shops. One of last skirmishes of the Revolution fought here 1782 at Fort Henry (1774; originally Fort Fincastle). Pro-Unionist center in Civil War. Site of Wheeling Conventions 1861–62. First cap. of W.Va. (1863–70, and again 1875–85).

Wheelock, Eleazar or **Eleazer** (ĕlēā'zŭr hwē'lŏk), 1711–79, American clergyman, founder of DARTMOUTH COLLEGE (1770) and its first president. His son, **John Wheelock,** 1754–1817, was also president of Dartmouth (1779–1815).

Wheelwright, John, c.1592–1679, American Puritan clergyman, b. England. Founded Exeter, N.H., 1638.

Wheelwright, William, 1798–1873, American pioneer in South American railroad building and steam navigation of the Pacific.

Whig, English political party. Name was probably derived from *whiggamor* [cattle driver], used in 17th cent. for Scottish dissenters. Party upheld power of Parliament against the crown, and was supported by landed gentry and trade as against aristocratic TORY group. The Glorious Revolution (1688) began long period of Whig control. Dominating figure until his fall (1742) was Sir Robert WALPOLE, who gave party political power and shaped modern British cabinet government. Party, mercantilist in policy, followed democratic theories of John Locke. Accession of George III (1760) brought Tory control. Whigs took on middle-class character after French Revolution and became identified with movement which culminated in Reform Bill of 1832. Thereafter the Whigs became the LIBERAL PARTY.

Whig party, one of the dominant political parties of U.S. in second quarter of 19th cent. Groups that composed it arose in 1824. NATIONAL REPUBLICAN PARTY, created by Andrew Jackson's enemies, grew stronger after his 1828 triumph. Other opposition parties sprang up; opposition was correlated by Henry Clay in 1832 election. In 1836 Daniel Webster was one of several Whig presidential candidates. Clay and Webster were party's great leaders, but neither could lead it to victory, partly because of sectionalism within the party, partly because of power held by N.Y. "bosses," Thurlow WEED and W. H. Seward. Whigs succeeded with W. H. HARRISON in 1840, but inauguration of John TYLER brought trouble. In 1848 several Whig delegates bolted and joined FREE-SOIL PARTY. Though party won 1848 election, a bitter internal struggle developed between antislavery and proslavery elements. Marked failure in 1852 election brought quick end to party; remnants went to other parties in a new alignment.

Whipple, Abraham, 1733–1819, American Revolutionary naval officer. Led raid on GASPEE in 1772. Captured eight ships of British Jamaica fleet (1779).

Whipple, George Hoyt, 1878–, American pathologist. Shared 1934 Nobel Prize in Physiology and Medicine for his independent research on use of liver in treatment of pernicious anemia.

whippoorwill (hwĭ"pûrwĭl', hwĭ'pûrwĭl"), North American noctural bird of goatsucker family. Plumage is a mixture of brown, black, and gray above; abdomen is lighter and speckled. Weird song is monotonous repetition of its name.

whisky, spirituous liquor distilled from fermented mash of grains, usually rye, barley, oats, wheat, or corn. Inferior grades are made from potatoes or beets. Scotch whisky takes its characteristic dry, rather smoky flavor from malt cured over peat fires; the somewhat similar Irish whisky is fuller and sweeter in taste; no peat is used in the curing. American whiskies (U.S. and Canada), classed as rye and Bourbon (a corn whisky), are higher in color and flavor than Scotch and Irish.

Whisky Rebellion, 1794, insurrection in Pa. counties W of the Alleghenies, caused by Alexander Hamilton's excise tax of 1791. Settlers, who made whisky extensively, considered tax discriminatory. Troops were called out to quell rioting. Federal government's power to enforce its laws had been proved, but frontiersmen's hatred of Federalists had political consequences.

Whisky Ring, in U.S. history, conspiracy which defrauded Federal government of liquor taxes. Soon after Civil War these taxes were raised very high. Large distillers bribed government officials to retain the tax proceeds. U.S. Secretary of the Treasury B. H. Bristow struck suddenly in 1875 and arrested persons and seized distilleries involved. Over $3,000,000 in taxes were recovered; 110 persons were convicted.

Whistler, James (Abbott) McNeill, 1834–1903, American painter and etcher, b. Lowell, Mass. In 1855 he went to Paris and successfully exhibited his *Little White Girl* (1863). Moved to London, where he became famous for his eccentricities and stinging wit long before he was recognized as an artist. His famous lawsuit against Ruskin was an example of his efforts to publicize his art. Deeply influenced as a painter by Velásquez and the Japanese print artists, he created a highly personal style marked by great subtlety. Excelled also as an etcher, producing c.400 superb plates. One of the best Whistler collections is in Freer Gall. of Art, Washington, D.C., which also contains the Peacock Room (originally decorated for the Leyland home in London). His famous portrait of his mother is in the Louvre. Wrote brilliant essays and aphorisms, e.g., *The Gentle Art of Making Enemies.*

Whitby, town (pop. 7,267), S Ont., Canada, ENE of Toronto and on L. Ontario. Tanning, lumbering, mfg. of leather goods and hardware.

Whitby, urban district (pop. 11,668), North Riding of Yorkshire, England. Seaport and resort. Site of abbey (founded 657) in which poet Cædmon lived. Capt. Cook's ship *Resolution* was built here. **Synod of Whitby** was called by King Oswy of Northumbria in 664 to choose between usages of Celtic and Roman churches, primarily in determining Easter. Oswy decided for Roman usages and so determined that English church would be in main stream of European Christianity.

White, Andrew Dickson, 1832–1918, American educator and diplomat. First president of Cornell Univ. (1867–85). One of first educators to use free-elective system. Minister to Germany (1879–81) and to Russia (1892–94).

White, Edward Douglass, 1845–1921, Chief Justice of U.S. Supreme Court (1910–21).

White, E(lwyn) B(rooks), 1899–, American writer, notable for pure grace of style and humor in many contributions to the *New Yorker* magazine as well as humorous books (e.g., *Is Sex Necessary?*, 1929, with James Thurber) and juveniles (e.g., *Stuart Little,* 1945; *Charlotte's Web,* 1952). Also author of pleasantly humorous verse.

White, Gilbert, 1720–93, English naturalist. While serving as curate at Selborne and near-by parishes (from 1751), he recorded observations of nature in letters, on which he based *The Natural History and Antiquities of Selborne* (1789; often reprinted).

White, Pearl, 1889–1938, American film actress. Starred in such weekly serials as *The Perils of Pauline*. Always in danger, she was always rescued.

White, Peregrine, 1620–1704, American pioneer. He was first English child born in New England.

White, Stanford, 1853–1906, American architect, a partner of C. F. McKim and W. R. Mead. His individual works, which include Washington Arch and Century club (both in New York city), show his interest in sculptured Renaissance ornament. He was murdered by Harry K. Thaw, whose trial became a national sensation.

White, Walter (Francis), 1893–, American Negro leader, secretary of National Association for the Advancement of Colored People (1931–).

White, William, 1748–1836, American Episcopal bishop of Pa. (after 1786). He helped organize Protestant Episcopal Church in the U.S., drafted constitution, and aided in American revision of Book of Common Prayer.

White, William Alanson, 1870–1937, American psychiatrist. Superintendent of St. Elizabeth's Hospital, Washington, D.C., 1903–37. An early Freudian, he experimented with new psychiatric methods. His supporters estab. the William Alanson White Foundation (1934) which fostered the influential Washington School of Psychiatry (1936).

White, William Allen, 1868–1944, American editor and author. After 1895 owner and editor of Emporia, Kansas, *Gazette,* he was the influential exponent of "grass-roots" Republican liberal views. Wrote short stories, novels, biographies of Wilson and Coolidge, and politico-historical studies.

Whiteboys, members of small, illegal bands of Irish peasants organized c.1761 to resist demands of tax collectors, landlords. On raids they wore white disguises. Suppressed within 10 years, movement hastened establishment of Irish Parliament (1782).

white corpuscle, small protoplasmic body of which large numbers exist in blood and lymph. In humans main types are lymphocytes, of uncertain function; monocytes, functioning in repair of tissues and engulfing microorganisms not attacked by leucocytes; and leucocytes (55% to 75% of total), subdivided into three types (neutrophiles, eosinophiles or acidophiles, and basophiles). Leucocytes capable of destroying microorganisms, which they engulf by amoeboid movement, are called phagocytes. See *ill.,* p. 813.

Whiteface: see ADIRONDACK MOUNTAINS.

Whitefield, George (hwĭt'fēld), 1714–70, English evangelistic preacher, leader of Calvinistic Methodists. At Oxford he joined the Methodist group led by John and Charles WESLEY. Like the Wesleys, he was ordained in the Church of England. He made seven tours in America, where he drew great throngs and was influential in the GREAT AWAKENING. He adopted (c.1741) Calvinistic views (esp. predestination) and, breaking with the Wesleys, became leader of the Calvinistic Methodists, strong in Wales.

whitefish, fresh-water food fish of N Hemisphere, related to trout and salmon. Largest U.S. species is common or lake whitefish of Great Lakes region.

Whitefish Bay, village (pop. 14,665), SE Wis., N suburb of Milwaukee.

White Hall, city (pop. 3,082), W central Ill., N of Alton. Has Lorado Taft memorial to Annie Louise Keller, heroic teacher.

Whitehall. 1 Resort city (pop. 1,819), S Mich., N of Muskegon, on White L. near L. Michigan. Holds Swedish midsummer festival. **2** Borough (pop 7,342), SW Pa., S of Pittsburgh.

Whitehall, street in London, running from Charing Cross to Parliament St. Has government offices and Cenotaph (war memorial). Was site of palace of the archbishops of York, in which Henry VIII and Cromwell died and outside which Charles I was executed.

Whitehead, Alfred North, 1861–1947, British philosopher and mathematician; grad. Trinity Col., Cambridge, long a teacher of mathematics at Univ. of London, then professor of philosophy at Harvard (1924–37). Wrote *Principia Mathematica* (with Bertrand Russell; 3 vols., 1910–13) and other mathematical works. His books on philosophy set forth an idealism (philosophy of organism), in which God is viewed as the principle of union in a universe where interrelated organisms adjust to the environment.

White Hill, battle of the: see WHITE MOUNTAIN.

White Horse, city (pop. 2,594), S Yukon, Canada, at head of navigation of Lewes R. On Alaska Highway at terminus of White Pass and Yukon RR. Steamer connection with Dawson June–Oct. Center of mining, hunting, and trapping region. Hq. of Royal Canadian Mounted Police for S Yukon. Has airport and radio and meteorological stations. Supply point in Klondike gold rush. Center of World War II Canol oil project (closed 1945).

White Horse, Vale of the, Berkshire, England. Has many associations with King Alfred, whose victory at Ashdown is commemorated by the White Horse on White Horse Hill at Uffington. Formed by cutting away turf to expose white chalk beneath, its crude outline (over 350 ft. long) is visible for miles.

White House, executive mansion of U.S. Presidents, on S side of Pennsylvania Ave., Washington, D.C., facing Lafayette Square. Made of Va. freestone, it is simple and stately in design. Main entrance is on N front. Main building (4 stories high) is c.170 ft. long by 85 ft. wide. E and W terraces, executive office (1902), E wing (1942), and air-raid shelter (1942) have been added. Complete rebuilding of interior structure was authorized 1949 and completed 1952. Colonnade at E end is public entrance. East Room (40 ft. by 82 ft.) is scene of most large receptions, elliptical Blue Room of official receptions. Has Red and Green rooms. Oldest public building in Washington (cornerstone laid 1792), it was designed by James Hoban and is on site chosen by George Washington. John Adams was first president to live here (1800). Restored after British burned it (1814) in War of 1812. Walls were then painted white, but "White House" did not become official name until Theodore Roosevelt's administration. Attractive grounds (c.18 acres) planned by A. J. Downing.

White Huns, people of obscure origin, possibly of Tibetan or Turkish stock and apparently unrelated to the Huns. Conquered Transoxania and Khurasan before A.D. 425. Subjugated Persia 483–513 but were defeated by Khosru I. Briefly held Gupta empire in India in 6th cent. Some remained in India.

white lead, heavy, white, amorphous basic lead carbonate, very poisonous (see LEAD POISONING). One of the oldest known pigments, it is widely used in paints (as a pigment and base) and in making putty and certain pottery.

white metal: see ANTIFRICTION METAL; BABBITT METAL.

White Mountain or **White Hill,** Czech *Bílá Hora,* hill near Prague, Bohemia, Czechoslovakia. Here in 1620, Czech Protestants under Frederick the Winter King were routed by imperials under Tilly. Battle ended Bohemian independence for three centuries and was first major engagement of Thirty Years War.

White Mountains, N N.H., a granitic part of Appalachian system, rising to 6,288 ft. in Mt. WASHINGTON of PRESIDENTIAL RANGE and to 5,249 ft. in Mt. Lafayette of FRANCONIA MOUNTAINS. CRAWFORD NOTCH separates these two main groups. Some 1,200 sq. mi. of this area is in White Mt. Natl. Forest. Noted for scenic beauty, White Mts. have long been a popular resort area.

White Nile, Arabic *Bahr-el-Abiad,* river, 600 mi. long, in Anglo-Egyptian Sudan. Joins the Blue Nile at Khartoum to form the NILE.

White Pass, 2,888 ft. high, in Coast Range, on Alaska-B.C., Canada, border and NE of Skagway. Summit of White Pass and Yukon RR (built 1898–1900). Pass traversed 1897 by Klondike-bound prospectors as alternate route to CHILKOOT PASS.

white-pine blister rust: see BLISTER RUST.

White Plains, residential city (pop. 43,466), SE N.Y., NE of New York city; settled late 17th cent. Plumbing and heating equipment, wire, dairy foods, textiles. Provincial congress met here, ratified Declaration of Independence 1776. Battle of White Plains (1776) followed Washington's retreat from Manhattan. Elijah Miller House (1738) was his hq.

White River. 1 Partly navigable, rising in NW Ark. and flowing 690 mi. N into Mo., then SE through Ark. to Mississippi R. above Arkansas City. North Fork has Norfolk Dam; Bull Shoals Dam is in N Ark. **2** Rising in two forks near Muncie, E central Ind., and flowing SW to unite NE of Petersburg before entering Wabash R. **3** Rising in NW Nebr. and flowing 507 mi. N and E through Badlands of S.Dak. to Missouri R. near Chamberlain.

White River Junction, Vt.: see HARTFORD.

White Russia: see BELORUSSIA.

White Sands National Monument: see NATIONAL PARKS AND MONUMENTS (table).

White Sea, inlet of Barents Sea, N European USSR; 365 mi. long, area 36,680 sq. mi., max. depth 1,115 ft. Receives Northern Dvina and Onega rivers. Chief port is Archangel. Connected by canal system with the Baltic at Leningrad. Though frozen Nov.–May (except in center), it is important for lumber exports, fisheries, and sealing.

White Settlement, residential town (pop. 10,-827), N Texas, W suburb of Fort Worth. Formerly Liberator Village or Liberator.

white slave traffic: see PROSTITUTION.

white snakeroot, North American woodland perennial (*Eupatorium rugosum*), with clusters of white flowers. Leaves contain tremetol, a cause of milk fever.

White Sulphur Springs, town (pop. 2,643), SE W.Va., E of Lewisburg near Va. border. Health resort with mineral springs. Representatives of Axis nations confined here early in World War II.

white vitriol (vĭt'rēŭl), transparent, crystalline, hydrated zinc sulphate. Used as mordant, in making varnishes, as hide preservative, as disinfectant.

whitewash, preparation for whitening walls of cellars, stables, and various outside structures. Soluble in water, the mixture may contain quicklime, flour, glue, and whiting, often with molasses or soap added.

Whitewater, city (pop. 5,101), SE Wis., SE of Madison, in dairy and farm area. Hardware.

whitewood: see TULIP TREE.

Whiting, city (pop. 9,669), NW Ind., on L. Michigan SE of Chicago. Oil refining; chemicals.

whiting, a white powdery substance, pure calcium carbonate. Used as pigment and metal polish. Mixed with linseed oil it forms putty; with water is whitewash.

Whitinsville, Mass.: see NORTHBRIDGE.

Whitlock, Brand, 1869–1934, American author of realistic novels, a book on Belgium, and a biography of Lafayette (1929), U.S. minister and ambassador to Belgium (1913–22). A lawyer, he was also reform mayor of Toledo (1905–13).

Whitman, Marcus, 1802–47, American pioneer and missionary in Oregon country. Founded mission at Waiilatpu in 1836 (now national monument, estab. 1940, near present Walla Walla, Wash.). Following return E, he accompanied "great emigration" of 1843 over Oregon Trail. Killed in Indian massacre.

Whitman, Sarah Helen (Power), 1803–78, American poet, a widow for a time engaged to Poe.

Whitman, Walt(er), 1819–92, American poet. In early life on Long Isl., he was a country schoolteacher, a compositor, and an editor. He wrote for several papers and edited (1846–47) Brooklyn *Daily Eagle.* Spent three months in New Orleans, returned to edit (1848–49) Brooklyn *Freeman.* His *Leaves of Grass* first appeared in 1855 and was praised by Emerson. A larger edition (1856)—criticized for daring content and free-verse technique—showed him a mystic, a pantheist, and a lover of all humanity. Successive enlarged editions (final, 1892) mirrored his growth as thinker and poet. He served as unofficial nurse in Civil War, of which he wrote both in prose and in poetry; some of his best poems are included in *Drum-Taps* (1865) and *Sequel to Drum-Taps* (1866)—e.g., "When Lilacs Last in the

Dooryard Bloom'd" and "O Captain! My Captain!" He worked for the government until partially paralyzed in 1873, and lived thereafter from writing and lectures, in Camden, N.J., from 1884. Chief prose works are *Democratic Vistas* (1871) and *Specimen Days and Collect* (1882–83). He was one of America's greatest poets, and profoundly influenced both poetic form and content, particularly abroad. His major themes were love, death, nationalism and democracy, and the beauty and significance of the human body. His is the chief poetic voice of American democracy. Called "the good gray poet."

Whitman, town (pop. 8,413), SE Mass., SSE of Boston. Shoes. Toll House (1709) is restored.

Whitman College: see WALLA WALLA, Wash.

Whitman National Monument: see NATIONAL PARKS AND MONUMENTS (table).

Whitney, Eli, 1765–1825, American inventor of the cotton gin (1793). Invention made others wealthy, but not Whitney. He later manufactured first muskets to have standardized, interchangeable parts.

Whitney, Mount, E Calif., highest peak (14,495 ft.) in U.S. proper, in the Sierra Nevada at E edge of Sequoia Natl. Park. Connected by scenic highway with Death Valley (SE), lowest area in U.S.

Whitney Museum of American Art, in New York city, founded and inc. 1930 by Gertrude Vanderbilt Whitney. Most of its collection (oils, water colors, sculptures) was bought from living artists.

Whitsunday: see PENTECOST.

Whittier, John Greenleaf, 1807–92, American Quaker poet and reformer, b. Mass. He was a vigorous and politically powerful abolitionist editor and writer, especially from 1833 to 1840. In his first books, *Legends of New-England* (1831) and poem *Moll Pitcher* (1832), he was a pioneer in regional writing. His poetry was first collected in 1838. Later volumes were *Songs of Labor* (1850) and a series depicting New England, including famous *Snow-bound* (1866) and *Maud Muller* (1867). His "Barbara Frietchie," "The Barefoot Boy," "Skipper Ireson's Ride," and "Laus Deo" are among the poems, chiefly of New England life, which won him tremendous popularity in his day. Of nearly 100 hymns the best known is *Dear Lord and Father of Mankind.*

Whittier, city (pop. 29,265), S Calif., ESE of Los Angeles; founded 1887. Center of citrus fruit, dairy, and oil area with mfg. of metal products. Seat of Whittier Col. (coed.; 1888).

Whittington, Richard, d. 1423, thrice mayor of London. Contrary to the legend of Dick Whittington and his cat, he was the son of a knight. He first made his fortune as a mercer and supplied large loans to Henry IV and Henry V.

Whittredge, Worthington, 1820–1910, American landscape painter, identified with Hudson River school.

whooping cough (pertussis), infectious disease caused by a bacterium and characterized by series of coughs followed by effort to draw in breath resulting in a "whoop." Common in young children; very serious in infants. Vaccine is used to lessen severity and to immunize children.

Whymper, Edward (hwĭm'pûr), 1840–1911, English mountain climber. First to climb Matterhorn (1865).

Wichita (wĭ'chĭtô), city (pop. 168,279), S Kansas, at junction of Arkansas and Little Arkansas rivers. A Wichita Indian village (1863–65) and a trading post (1864) were estab. here, and city was founded 1868 on Chisholm Trail. Grew as cow town and rail hub after 1872. State's largest city, it has flour mills, meat-packing plants, stockyards, grain elevators, oil refineries, and airplane factories. Seat of Municipal Univ. of Wichita (coed.; 1892).

Wichita Falls, city (pop. 68,042), N Texas, on Wichita R. and NW of Fort Worth; settled in 1870s. Grew with advent of railroad 1882. Boomed c.1918 with discovery of oil. Center of oil, wheat, and cattle region with refineries, foundries, and mfg. of machinery, flour, chemicals, and glass. Kemp and Diversion lakes formed by impounded Wichita R.

Wichita Mountains, low granite range in SW Okla., c.60 mi. long, 25 mi. wide, up to 2,464 ft. high.

Wick, burgh (pop. 7,161), co. town of Caithness, Scotland; a hq. of herring fishing.

Wickenburg, town (pop. 1,736), central Ariz., NW of Phoenix. Founded as mining town after gold strike of 1863. Center now for near-by dude ranches.

Wickersham, George W(oodward), 1858–1936, American government official. Head (1929–31) of Natl. Commission on Law Observance and Law Enforcement (usually called the Wickersham Commission), which concluded that the means for enforcing criminal law in U.S. were inadequate.

Wickford, R.I.: see NORTH KINGSTOWN.

Wickham, William of: see WILLIAM OF WYKEHAM.

Wickliffe, John: see WYCLIF, JOHN.

Wickliffe (wĭ'klĭf). **1** Town (pop. 1,019), SW Ky., at confluence of Ohio and Mississippi rivers and WSW of Paducah. Buried Indian city which has yielded much material is near by. **2** City (pop. 5,002), NE Ohio, near Cleveland. Oil refining.

Wicklow (wĭ'klō), maritime county (782 sq. mi.; pop. 60,451), E Ireland, in Leinster; co. town Wicklow. Wicklow Mts. and foothills occupy most of county, which is chiefly devoted to cattle grazing. Area is popular with tourists.

Wiclif, John: see WYCLIF, JOHN.

Widsith (wĭd'sĭth), 7th-cent. Anglo-Saxon poem describing repertory and travels of Germanic minstrel.

Widukind (wĭ'do͝okĭnd) or **Wittekind** (wĭ'tůkĭnd), 8th cent., leader of the Saxons against Charlemagne. After bloody warfare over their refusal to accept baptism, Saxons were subdued when Widukind accepted baptism (785).

Wieland, Christoph Martin (vē'länt), 1733–1813, German poet. Spent later part of his life at court of Weimar. His powerful, largely satirical romances exerted much influence on German literature. Among them were *Musarion* (1768), *Die Abderiten* (1774; Eng. tr.,

The Republic of Fools), and his masterpiece, *Oberon* (1780; basis of Weber's opera).

Wieland, Heinrich, 1877–, German chemist. Won 1927 Nobel Prize for study of acids in bile.

Wien, Wilhelm (vĭl'hĕlm vēn'), 1864–1928, German physicist. Won 1911 Nobel Prize for studies on laws of heat radiation; also worked on hydrodynamics, X rays, radiation of light.

Wiener Wald (vē'nûr vält") [Ger.,= Vienna forest], low forested range, Lower Austria, W of Vienna. Its loveliness has made it a popular excursion area.

Wieniawski, Henri (vyĕnyäf'skē), 1835–80, Polish virtuoso violinist and composer. He wrote two violin concertos and some salon pieces.

Wiesbaden (vēs'bä"dûn), city (pop. 218,255), cap. of Hesse, on the Rhine and at foot of the Taunus. Famous spa, with saline springs known since antiquity. Trade center for Rhine wines. Mfg. of metal goods, chemicals, plastics, textiles. Was cap. of duchy of Nassau 1816–66; belonged to Prussia 1866–1945. The fine city was half destroyed in World War II.

wig, shortened form of periwig, an arrangement of artificial hair (human or animal) worn to conceal baldness, as a disguise, or as part of a costume, either theatrical, ceremonial, or merely fashionable. Wigs were used by the ancient Egyptians, Greeks, and Romans, and by fashionable Europeans from the middle of the 16th cent. into the 18th. They survive in England as part of the official dress of certain officials, barristers, and bishops.

Wigan (wĭg'ûn), county borough (pop. 84,-546), Lancashire, England. Has cotton factories, engineering and machinery plants, and near-by coal mines.

Wiggin, Kate Douglas (Smith), 1856–1923, American author of children's books, such as *The Birds' Christmas Carol* (1887), *Rebecca of Sunnybrook Farm* (1903), and *Mother Carey's Chickens* (1911).

Wigglesworth, Michael, 1631–1705, American didactic poet, a Puritan clergyman, b. England, known for his *Day of Doom* (1662?), Calvinist theology in verse.

Wight, Isle of (wīt), island (147 sq. mi.; pop. 95,594), off Hampshire, S England. Mild climate and picturesque scenery make it a resort. Sheep raising and dairy farming are chief occupations. Conquered by Romans A.D. 43, it was hq. of Danes at end of 10th cent. Separate administrative county since 1888. Queen Victoria's seaside home, Osborne House, is near the famous yachting center, Cowes.

Wigman, Mary, 1886–, German dancer. Her theory (that dance movement must evolve from emotion) and her angular style greatly influenced modern dance.

Wigtownshire (wĭg'tûnshĭr) or **Wigtown** (wĭg'-tûn), county (487 sq. mi.; pop. 31,625), SW Scotland, part of Galloway; co. town Wigtown. Includes peninsula, Rhinns of Galloway. Agr. is almost only industry; sheep, cattle, and pigs are raised.

Wilberforce, William, 1759–1833, British statesman and humanitarian. Friend of the younger Pitt. Secured passage of bill abolishing slave trade (1807). Worked for universal abolition of slavery. His son, **Samuel Wilberforce,** 1805–73, was bishop of Oxford (after 1845), of Winchester (after 1869). Was influential in restoring ecclesiastical authority to English church conventions.

Wilberforce University, at Wilberforce, Ohio, near Xenia; Negro, partly state supported, coed.; chartered and opened 1865 by Methodists. Bought by African Methodist Episcopal Church 1863, it absorbed Union Seminary. Named for William Wilberforce.

Wilcox, Ella Wheeler, 1855–1919, American writer of popular verse (e.g., "Laugh, and the world laughs with you"), collected in *Poems of Passion* (1883) and *Poems of Pleasure* (1888).

wild carrot or **Queen Anne's lace,** annual or biennial plant (*Daucus carota*) from which the CARROT was derived. Native to Eurasia, it is widely naturalized in North America. It has feathery foliage, a lacy flower cluster, and woody roots.

Wilde, Oscar (Fingall O'Flahertie Wills), 1854–1900, British author, b. Dublin. A conspicuous exponent of "art for art's sake" aestheticism, he wrote highly melodic poems; a novel, *The Picture of Dorian Gray* (1891); witty drawing-room comedies (e.g., *Lady Windermere's Fan,* 1892; *The Importance of Being Earnest,* 1895); and fairy tales. Convicted on morals charges, he was imprisoned (1895–97). *De Profundis* (1905) was his apologia.

Wildenbruch, Ernst von (vĭl'dûnbrōōkh), 1845–1909, German author. His verse, novels, and historical dramas (e.g., *Heinrich und Heinrichs Geschlecht,* 1895) were much admired in the days of William II.

Wilder, Thornton (Niven) (wīl'dûr), 1897–, American novelist and playwright. Of his novels perhaps *The Cabala* (1926), *The Bridge of San Luis Rey* (1927), and *The Woman of Andros* (1930) won most acclaim. His plays *Our Town* (1938) and *The Skin of Our Teeth* (1942) won popular and critical success.

Wilderness campaign, May-June, 1864, of Civil War. Attempt by U. S. Grant to clear wild woodland W of Fredericksburg before trying to destroy Army of Northern Virginia under R. E. Lee. But Lee attacked first, forcing Grant to counterattack in series of bloody battles, especially at Spotsylvania Courthouse (May 8–19, 1864). Assaulting a strongly entrenched enemy at Cold Harbor, June 3, 1864, Grant was repulsed with horrible slaughter. Grant then withdrew, having lost about 60,000 men in the campaign, and moved against Petersburg.

Wilderness Road, route taken by American pioneers of Old Southwest, running down the Valley of Virginia to Fort Watauga (now in E Tenn.). From there in 1775 Daniel Boone blazed the trail further, through Cumberland Gap, into Ky. Road became a principal avenue of migration W. Impassable and deserted for much of 19th cent., it has been a section of U.S. 25, the Dixie Highway, since 1926.

wildlife refuge, animal haven or sanctuary providing suitable environment and protection from hunters. Before conservation movement, wildlife population was reduced alarmingly and some birds had become extinct. Causes of such depletion included drainage of swamps, destruction of forests, drought, and slaughter of animals for hides, feathers, food, and sport. National and state conservation commissions resulted from 1908 conference on natural resources. National Park Service (estab. 1916) prohibited hunting in parks under its administration. Protective legislation for birds included a U.S.–Canadian treaty (1918) protecting migratory birds; Norbeck-Andresen Migratory-Bird Conservation Act (1929) providing for a system of refuges; an act (1934) requiring purchase of a stamp by hunters of migratory birds, funds to be used for developing refuges; U.S.–Mexico migratory bird treaty (1937). Inter-American Convention on Nature Protection and Wildlife Preservation (1940) was evidence of progress in international conservation movements. By 1947 there were 291 Federal refuges in U.S. and territories; these are administered by Fish and Wildlife Service of Dept. of Interior; Service was estab. 1940 by consolidation of Bureau of Biological Survey and Bureau of Fisheries. National Audubon Society maintains numerous refuges. National parks and forests and lands controlled by Soil Conservation Service of Dept. of Agriculture also afford protection to wildlife.

wild rice, tall, aquatic grass (*Zizania aquatica*) of N U.S. and its grain, one of the chief foods of certain Indian tribes, especially in Great Lakes regions. The seed is now harvested for epicurean markets. The plants provide shelter and food for fish and waterfowl. Other names are Indian rice and Canada rice.

Wildwood, resort city (pop. 5,475), S N.J., on island off Cape May.

Wiley, Harvey Washington, 1844–1930, American chemist. He was largely responsible for enactment of Food and Drugs Act of 1906.

Wilhelm. For German rulers thus named, see WILLIAM.

Wilhelmina (vĭl″hĕlmē′nä), 1880–, queen of the Netherlands (1890–1948); daughter of William III. Married (1901) to Prince Henry of Mecklenburg-Schwerin (d. 1934). Fled to England after German invasion of Netherlands (1940); returned 1945; abdicated in favor of her daughter Juliana 1948. Her strength of character and wise leadership earned her much popularity.

Wilhelmina, Mount, c.15,600 ft. high, on W central New Guinea; highest peak of Orange Range.

Wilhelmshaven (vĭl″hĕlms-hä′fŭn), city (pop. 100,926), Lower Saxony, NW Germany, NW of Bremen and on an inlet of the North Sea. Founded 1869. Was chief German naval base on North Sea until 1945. Heavily damaged in World War II. Naval installations were dismantled by Allies.

Wilkes, Charles, 1798–1877, American naval officer and explorer. In command of government exploring expedition, he circled globe (1838–42) with group of scientists. They did research in S Pacific, explored Antarctic, Fiji, Pacific Northwest. In Civil War he precipitated TRENT AFFAIR.

Wilkes, John, 1727–97, English political leader. Angered George III by criticism of speech from throne. Twice imprisoned. Often elected to Parliament but denied his seat through king's influence. Organized party for parliamentary reform and protection of civil rights; championed cause of American colonists. Became a symbol of opposition to tyranny.

Wilkes-Barre (wĭlks′-bă″rē), city (pop. 76,826), E Pa., on Susquehanna R. and SW of Scranton; settled 1769. Coal mining and mfg. of textiles, clothing, and food products. Named for John Wilkes and Isaac Barré, defenders of colonies before Parliament. Burned 1778 and 1784 by British and Indians.

Wilkes Land, part of Antarctica, bordering Indian Ocean. Named for Charles Wilkes, leader of U.S. expedition 1838–42.

Wilkins, Sir (George) Hubert, 1888–. British explorer, b. Australia. Led several polar expeditions. A pioneer explorer by air. Headed arctic submarine expedition (1931).

Wilkins, Mary Eleanor: see FREEMAN, MARY E. WILKINS.

Wilkinsburg, residential borough (pop. 31,-418), SW Pa., near Pittsburgh; settled c.1800.

Wilkinson, James, 1757–1825, American general. Fought in American Revolution. A key figure in conspiracy to split off SW U.S. as a separate nation allied with Spain. Ranking army officer after 1796. Involved in plans of Aaron BURR in Southwest; testified against Burr at trial, narrowly escaped indictment himself.

Wilkinson, Jemima (jŭmī′mŭ), 1752–1819, American religious leader, founder (c.1790) of colony of "Jerusalem" near present Penn Yan, N.Y.

will, in law, document expressing the wishes of a person concerning disposition of his property after his death. Ordinarily it must be in writing, subscribed by the person (the testator) and by at least two witnesses. In very special circumstances, an oral will is recognized in law. The testator must be of sound mind and not unduly influenced by an interested party. The usual phrase of the testator is "my last will and testament."

will, in philosophy and psychology, that inner force by which a person undertakes conscious, purposeful action. Some philosophies deny the existence of the will, others define it variously—one usual view being that on intuitive grounds the will must simply be accepted as the function that is the motive power of a personality, another that the will is the net result of interacting elements. It is not commonly discussed by present-day psychologists on the ground that such discussion is unscientific.

Willamette (wĭlă′mĭt), river, c.300 mi. long, rising in several streams in Cascade Range, W Oregon, and flowing N, past Eugene, Salem, Portland, to Columbia R. NW of Portland. Navigable to Eugene. River valley (settled in 1830s; most populous part of state) supports agr. (esp. fruit growing), food processing, lumbering. U.S. flood control, navigation, power project, begun 1938, includes Fern Ridge Dam (1941) in Long Tom R. and Cottage Grove Dam (1942) in Coast Fork.

Willamette University: see SALEM, Oregon.

Willard, Emma (Hart), 1787–1870, American educator, pioneer in women's education. After submitting her *Plan for Improving Female Education,* she came in 1818 by invitation of the governor to N.Y. state to open her school. She was head (1821–38) of TROY (N.Y.) Female Seminary, later renamed in her honor.

Willard, Frances (Elizabeth), 1839–98, American temperance leader and reformer. Helped organize (1874) the Woman's Christian Temperance Union, whose second president she was, 1879–98.

Willemstad (vĭ'lŭmstät), city (pop. 40,000), cap. of Curaçao colony, Dutch West Indies, on Curaçao isl. Important as commercial center of colony and free port, it is also transshipping point for oil sent from Maracaibo, Venezuela.

William, emperors of Germany and kings of Prussia. **William I,** 1797–1888, became regent for his insane brother, Frederick William IV, in 1858 and succeeded him as king of Prussia in 1861. His reign was dominated by BISMARCK, whom he appointed chancellor in 1862. He took personal command in the Franco-Prussian War, at the conclusion of which he was proclaimed emperor of GERMANY in the Hall of Mirrors at Versailles (Jan. 18, 1871). Bismarck continued to guide the destinies of Prussia and Germany, with the emperor little more than a symbol of the reborn unity of Germany. He was succeeded by his son Frederick III (d. 1888) and his grandson **William II,** 1859–1941, who was also a grandson of Queen Victoria of England. His overbearing character soon clashed with Bismarck, whom he dismissed in 1890. His ambitious naval, colonial, and commercial program antagonized Britain and drove it into the Entente Cordiale with France. His failure to renew the reinsurance treaty with Russia (1890) and his encouragement of Austria's Balkan policy contributed to the formation of the Triple Entente (see TRIPLE ALLIANCE AND TRIPLE ENTENTE). His intensive armament and his diplomacy (or lack of diplomacy) was in part responsible for the outbreak of World War I. His abdication having been declared a prerequisite for peace negotiation by Pres. Wilson, revolts broke out in Germany late in 1918. William fled to Holland (Nov. 10) and abdicated soon afterward. He retired to Doorn; the Dutch government refused to extradite him for trial as a promoter of the war. After the death of Empress Augusta Victoria he married the widowed princess Hermine of Schönaich-Carolath (1922). He wrote memoirs.

William, king of Albania: see WILLIAM, PRINCE OF WIED.

William, kings of England. **William I** or **William the Conqueror,** 1027?–1087, king 1066–87, was illegitimate son of Robert I, duke of Normandy. While visiting England in 1051, he was probably named by his cousin Edward the Confessor as successor to the throne. In 1064 he released HAROLD, who had been shipwrecked on French coast, after extracting his promise to support duke's claims to English throne. Hearing of Harold's coronation, William invaded England, defeated (1066) and slew Harold at battle of Hastings, and was crowned king. Built castles and garrisoned them, put down rebellions, and ravaged great sections of land. Substituted foreign prelates for many English bishops and estab. separate ecclesiastical courts. After 1075 he dealt frequently with continental quarrels, fighting with his son ROBERT II. In 1085–86 he had made a survey of England (see DOMESDAY BOOK). He estab. precedent that loyalty to king is superior to loyalty to any subordinate lord. He was one of greatest English monarchs and pivotal figures in European history. See also NORMAN CONQUEST. His son, **William II** or **William Rufus,** d. 1100, king 1087–1100, extracted enormous moneys from his subjects on flimsiest pretexts and terrified clergy by his sales of churches and church lands. He occupied Normandy when his brother, Robert II, was on crusade. Gained control of Scottish throne (1097). **William III,** 1650–1702, king of England, Scotland, and Ireland 1689–1702, was son of William II of Orange. Made peace with England in DUTCH WARS. Married Mary, Protestant daughter of JAMES II. Formed coalition with Sweden, Austria, and Spain, which began (1688) War of Grand Alliance against Louis XIV. Unable to persuade James II to abandon Louis, he turned to English opposition. After secret negotiations, William came to England, allowed James to escape to France, and accepted throne of England jointly (with his wife as MARY II). This Glorious Revolution saw no bloodshed and forced William to accept BILL OF RIGHTS (1689) and Act of SETTLEMENT (1701). In Ireland he continued ruthless policy of confiscating land and giving it to English courtiers, soldiers, and adventurers. He was constantly involved in continental wars until Louis XIV recognized him as king in 1697. Wars caused unpopular taxes; Bank of England was chartered 1694; and policy of permanent national debt was begun. William of necessity chose men of Whig persuasion, and so started system of responsible ministry. His popularity diminished with death of his wife and War of Spanish Succession. **William IV,** 1765–1837, king 1830–37, was third son of George III. Agreed to passage of Reform Bill of 1832, but political leadership was left to duke of Wellington, Earl Grey, Melbourne, and Sir Robert Peel. His niece Victoria succeeded him.

William, kings of the Netherlands and grand dukes of Luxembourg. **William I,** 1772–1843, was the son of William V of Orange, last stadholder of the Netherlands. In 1815 the Congress of Vienna made him king of the Netherlands (incl. modern Belgium) and awarded him Luxembourg in exchange for his family holdings in Germany, which he ceded to Prussia. His reactionary rule and anti-Catholic measures led to rebellion in BELGIUM, which proclaimed its independence. Anglo-French intervention eventually compelled William to withdraw his troops from Belgium. He abdicated in 1840 in favor of his son **William II,** 1792–1849, who granted a constitutional reform in 1848. His son and successor, **William III,** 1817–90, ruled as a constitutional monarch. His daughter Wilhelmina succeeded him in the Netherlands.

William, king of Scotland: see WILLIAM THE LION.

William, kings of Sicily. **William I** (the Bad), 1120–66, reigned 1154–66; son of Roger II. A wise lawgiver, despite his nickname. His son **William II** (the Good), c.1153–1189, reigned 1166–89. Sided with Lombard League against Emperor Frederick I; took Durazzo and Salonica in attempt to conquer Byzantine Empire but was defeated by Isaac II. He willed Sicily to his aunt, Empress Constance, but was succeeded by his cousin, Tancred of Lecce.

William or **Frederick William,** 1882–1951, crown prince of Prussia and Germany; son of William II. In command of attack on Verdun (1916), he ruthlessly sent thousands to certain death. Fled to Netherlands 1918 but was allowed to return to Germany 1923. Later supported Hitler regime.

William, princes of Orange. **William I:** see WILLIAM THE SILENT. **William II,** 1626–50, son of Frederick Henry, was stadholder of the Netherlands 1647–50. **William III:** see WILLIAM III, king of England.

William, prince of Wied (vēt), 1876–, king of Albania (1914); of a noble family originating in the Holy Roman Empire. Elected king 1914. Unable to impose his authority, he was forced to abdicate by Essad Pasha soon after outbreak of World War II.

William, count of Holland, 1227?–1256, German king (1254–56), previously rival king (1247–54) to CONRAD IV. His rule was purely nominal.

William, Fort: see FORT WILLIAM.

William and Mary, College of, mainly at Williamsburg, Va., with departments at Richmond and Norfolk; state supported, coed.; opened 1694 as second colonial college, became university 1779. Closed when occupied by Revolutionary troops (1781), in Civil War, and 1881–88 because of lack of funds. Phi Beta Kappa founded here 1776. Elective system (1799; suggested by Jefferson), and honor system introduced here. Main building (oldest U.S. college building, 1697) has been restored.

William of Champeaux (shămpō′, shāpō′), d. 1121, French scholastic philosopher. An extreme realist, he was loser in famous dispute with Abelard.

William of Occam or **Ockham** (both: ŏ′kŭm), d. c.1349, English scholastic philosopher, a Franciscan. Embroiled in a general quarrel with Pope John XXII, he was imprisoned in Avignon but fled to the protection of Emperor Louis IV and supported him by attacking the temporal power of the papacy. Rejecting the doctrines of St. Thomas Aquinas, he argued that reality exists solely in individual things and universals are merely abstract signs. This view led him to exclude questions such as the existence of God from intellectual knowledge, referring them to faith alone.

William of Orange: see WILLIAM THE SILENT; WILLIAM II, prince of Orange; WILLIAM III, king of England.

William of Tyre, b. c.1130, d. before 1185, historian, archbishop of Tyre; author of a notable history of the Crusades.

William of Wykeham or **William of Wickham** (both: wĭ′kŭm), 1324–1404, English churchman. Made bishop of Winchester and lord chancellor in 1367. Mediocre statesman, his lasting importance is as founder of New Col., Oxford (1379), and of Winchester Col. (1394), one of greatest English public schools.

William Rufus: see WILLIAM II, king of England.

Williams, Bill: see WILLIAMS, WILLIAM SHERLEY.

Williams, Eleazer (ĕlēā′zŭr), c.1787–1858, American Protestant Episcopal missionary among Indians. Thought by a few to be the Lost Dauphin.

Williams, Frankwood Earl, 1883–1936, American psychiatrist and psychoanalyst, a leader of the international mental hygiene movement. He helped estab. World War I psychiatric work, was on the National Committee for Mental Hygiene (1917–31), and edited *Mental Hygiene* (1917–32).

Williams, Ralph Vaughan: see VAUGHAN WILLIAMS.

Williams, Robert R., 1886–, American chemist. Isolated and synthesized thiamine (vitamin B_1); worked in alipathic and rubber chemistry.

Williams, Roger, c.1603–1683, clergyman, advocate of religious freedom, founder of R.I., b. England. Banished from Mass., he founded Providence, R.I., in 1636. Trusted friend of Indians.

Williams, Tennessee, 1914–, American dramatist, b. Miss., author of *The Glass Menagerie* (1945), *A Streetcar Named Desire* (1947), *Summer and Smoke* (1949), and *The Rose Tattoo* (1951). Original name Thomas Lanier Williams.

Williams, Theodore Samuel (Ted), 1914–, American baseball player. With Boston Red Sox, he led American League in batting 1941, 1942, 1947, 1948.

Williams, William (of Pantycelin), 1717–91, Welsh poet, a clergyman. Wrote romantic lyrics and hymns (e.g., *Guide Me, O Thou Great Jehovah*).

Williams, William Carlos, 1883–, American poet, a physician. From imagist style of early poems he went to free verse notable for use of ordinary speech, fluid lines, and stark realism. His long poem on a N.J. city, *Paterson,* began to appear in 1946; the fourth book appeared in 1951. Also wrote essays, novels, stories.

Williams, William Sherley (Old Bill Williams), 1787–1849, American trader and trapper. One of the most colorful of MOUNTAIN MEN. Guided disastrous expedition of J. C. Frémont in 1848.

Williams, tourist town (pop. 2,152), N central Ariz., W of Flagstaff. A gateway to Grand Canyon.

Williamsburg, historic city (pop. 6,735), SE Va., SE of Richmond; settled 1632 as Middle Plantation, name changed 1699. Temporary cap. after burning of Jamestown in Bacon's Rebellion (1676; see BACON, NATHANIEL); made cap. 1699. Scene of important conventions in movement for colonies' independence. City declined after cap. was moved to Richmond 1779. Rearguard action fought here in PENINSULA CAMPAIGN of Civil War. Restoration of city to colonial aspect began 1927; city now included in Colonial National Historic Park. Major points of interest are old capitol, governor's palace, Raleigh Tavern, courthouse, Bruton Parish Church. Annual Garden Week. State general assembly meets in old capitol once each session. Seat of Col. of WILLIAM AND MARY.

Williams College: see WILLIAMSTOWN, Mass.

William Smith College: see GENEVA, N.Y.

Williamson, city (pop. 8,624), SW W.Va., on Tug Fork at Ky. line. Trade center for coal region.

Williamsport, city (pop. 45,047), N central Pa., on West Branch of Susquehanna R. and N of Harrisburg; settled 1772. Tourist and trade center for agr. and mining region with mfg. of machinery and metal, wire, and wood products. Scene of Indian massacres in colonial days.

Williamstown, town (pop. 6,194), including Williamstown village (pop. 5,015), extreme NW Mass., in the Berkshires, on Hoosic R. and W of North Adams. Seat of Williams Col. (nonsectarian; for men); chartered 1785, opened as free school 1791, became college 1793, named for Ephraim Williams; has oldest U.S. observatory (1838). First American mission was outgrowth of "haystack prayer meeting" here (1806).

William Tell: see TELL, WILLIAM.

William the Conqueror: see WILLIAM I, king of England.

William the Lion, 1143–1214, king of Scotland (1165–1214). Alliance he made (1168) with Louis VII started long friendship between France and Scotland. His capture by Henry II of England (whose rebelling sons he aided) forced him to sign (1174) treaty making Scotland a feudal possession of England. Later bought annulment of treaty from Richard I.

William the Silent or **William of Orange** (William I, prince of Orange), 1533–84, chief leader in the Dutch struggle for independence. Born in Germany, a prince of the house of NASSAU, he served the Spanish court, which appointed him stadholder of Holland (1555). He supported the GUEUX against Spanish encroachments (1566) and after Alba's arrival in the Netherlands openly took up arms against Spain; became a Calvinist (1573); and was the uncrowned ruler of the United Provs. after they declared Philip II of Spain deposed (1581). He was assassinated by a Catholic fanatic while the struggle against Spain was still in a critical stage.

Willimantic, city (pop. 13,586) in Windham (wĭn'dŭm) town (pop. 15,884), E Conn., ESE of Hartford. Known as the Thread City (cotton spinning since 1822), it has mfg. of yarns, textiles, and metal goods.

Willis, N(athaniel) P(arker), 1806–67, American journalist. Founded and edited several magazines. His own contributions were gathered in volumes such as *Pencillings by the Way* (1835). Also wrote plays.

Willis, Thomas, 1621–75, English physician and anatomist, authority on brain and nervous system.

Williston, city (pop. 7,378), NW N.Dak., on the Missouri. Trade center for irrigated agr. area with rail shops, stockyards, creamery, and grain elevator. Development of Williston Basin oil field was brisk in early 1950s.

Willkie, Wendell L(ewis), 1892–1944, American industrialist and political leader, Republican candidate for the presidency in 1940. President of Commonwealth and Southern Corp. (1933–40). Led fight (1942–44) to liberalize Republican party, mainly attacking isolationism.

Willmar, city (pop. 9,410), central Minn., W of Minneapolis. Resort, trade, and rail center with dairy, wood, and metal products.

will-o'-the-wisp, pale flickering light seen over marshland at night. It may result from spontaneous ignition of gases or may be a form of phosphorescence.

Willoughby, city (pop. 5,602), NE Ohio, on Chagrin R. near L. Erie and NE of Cleveland. Mfg. of auto parts and rubber products.

Willoughby, Lake, 5 mi. long, NE Vt., N of St. Johnsbury, in high wooded resort area.

willow, deciduous tree and shrub of widely distributed genus *Salix* with long narrow leaves. Male and female flowers are borne in catkins on separate plants. The pussy willow (*Salix discolor*) of NE U.S. and Canada, and the weeping willow (*S. babylonica*) native to Eurasia, are two decorative species. The wood is used for boxes and artificial limbs; twigs for basketry and wickerwork. Willow twigs and the bushes that bear them are often called osiers.

willow-pattern ware, blue-and-white chinaware which originated in Staffordshire, England, c.1780. Thomas Minton developed the design after a Chinese legend about the elopement of a rich mandarin's daughter. The scene, set in a garden with a willow tree and a bridge, tells the story of the lovers who make their escape by being changed into birds.

Willow Run, residential and industrial suburb, SE Mich., ENE of Ypsilanti. Machinery made in huge Willow Run plant which produced bombers in World War II. Univ. of Michigan has aeronautical research center at airport here.

Wills, Helen (Newington), 1906–, American tennis player. U.S. singles champion 1923–25, 1927–29, 1931. Married F. S. Moody, 1929.

Willstätter, Richard (rĭkh'ärt vĭl'shtĕtûr), 1872–1942, German chemist. Won 1915 Nobel Prize for work on chlorophyll and red, blue, and violet plant pigments.

Wilmerding (wĭl'mûrdĭng), borough (pop. 5,325), SW Pa., ESE of Pittsburgh. Railroad equipment.

Wilmette (wĭlmĕt'), residential village (pop. 18,162), NE Ill., N suburb of Chicago. Has Bahaist Temple (see BAHAISM).

Wilmington. 1 City (pop. 110,356), NE Del., on Delaware R. at influx of Brandywine Creek and Christina R. Commercial and industrial center of state; deep-water port. Has shipyards, rail shops, and mfg. of chemicals (near by), leather, and iron, steel, cork, and rubber products. Swedes built Fort Christina here, 1638; later held by Dutch, then British; William Penn took possession in 1682. Powder mill estab. here 1802 was first of many Du Pont enterprises for which

Wilmington is hq. Here are Old Swedes Church (1698), Rodney Square (civic center), Delaware Acad. of Medicine, and Wilmington Art Center. **2** Town (pop. 7,039), NE Mass., NNW of Boston. **3** City (pop. 45,043), SE N.C., port with harbor on Cape Fear R. c.30 mi. from mouth; founded 1730. Rail and mfg. (textiles, phosphates, lumber) center. Cornwallis's hq. 1781. Important port for Confederate blockade-runners until Fort FISHER fell, Jan. 15, 1865. Has national cemetery. **4** City (pop. 7,387), SW Ohio, NE of Cincinnati. Trade center for agr. area with mfg. of metal products and electrical goods.

Wilmot Proviso, 1846, amendment to a bill put before U.S. House of Representatives. Bill provided appropriation of $2,000,000 to enable Pres. Polk to negotiate a treaty with Mexico in settlement of the boundary question. Amendment stipulated that none of the territory acquired in Mexican War should be open to slavery. Amended bill passed the House but was purposely ignored by the Senate. Wilmot Proviso created great bitterness and helped crystallize North-South conflict.

Wilno, Lithuania: see VILNA.

Wilson, Charles E(dward), 1886–, American government official and industrialist. President of General Electric Co. (1940–42, 1944–50). Executive vice chairman of War Production Board (1942–44). Directed Office of Defense Mobilization (1950–52).

Wilson, Charles E(rwin), 1890–, U.S. Secretary of Defense (1953–). President of General Motors Corp. (1941–52).

Wilson, Charles Thomson Rees, 1869–, British physicist. Shared 1927 Nobel Prize. He developed a method for studying the activity of ionized particles by means of the **Wilson cloud chamber.** This device contains air or other gas cleansed and saturated with water vapor. Vapor condenses on atoms or subatomic particles made to pass through chamber, making their paths visible as water droplets.

Wilson, Edmund, 1895–, American critic. Works include literary criticism (e.g., *Axel's Castle,* 1931; *The Wound and the Bow,* 1941; *The Shores of Light,* 1952) and social criticism (e.g., *To the Finland Station,* 1940), plays, poems, a novel, and stories (as in *Memoirs of Hecate County,* 1946).

Wilson, Ernest Henry, 1876–1930, Anglo-American horticulturist, b. England. Assistant director (1919–27) and keeper (from 1927) of Arnold Arboretum, Harvard Univ. He introduced the regal lily and other oriental plants into Western gardens.

Wilson, Harry Leon, 1867–1939, American humorist, author of mild satires such as the novels *Ruggles of Red Gap* (1915) and *Merton of the Movies* (1922).

Wilson, James, 1742–98, American jurist, signer of Declaration of Independence, b. Scotland. Incorporated into U.S. Constitution the principle that sovereignty resides in the people. He was Associate Justice of U.S. Supreme Court (1789–98).

Wilson, John: see NORTH, CHRISTOPHER.

Wilson, William Lyne, 1843–1900, American legislator. U.S. Representative from W.Va. (1883–95). Tariff bill he introduced in 1894 substantially reduced many rates; altered in Senate by A. P. GORMAN, it passed over Pres. Cleveland's veto.

Wilson, (Thomas) Woodrow, 1856–1924, 27th President of the United States (1913–21). President of Princeton Univ. (1902–10). Governor of N.J. (1911–13). As President of U.S. (Democrat) he inaugurated a series of reforms called the "New Freedom." In foreign affairs relations with Mexico were particularly difficult, but outbreak of World War I overshadowed other problems. During first term, Wilson sought to maintain an impartial neutrality; following reelection, he attempted to mediate between warring nations, but without success. German submarine warfare brought about U.S. declaration of war in 1917. Wilson viewed war as necessary to make world "safe for democracy." He outlined FOURTEEN POINTS necessary for peace settlement. At Paris Peace Conference he worked for a new world society governed by "self-determination of peoples," but in resulting treaty (see VERSAILLES, TREATY OF) he secured little except covenant establishing LEAGUE OF NATIONS. H. C. Lodge led Republican opposition in Congress to the League. Wilson, while seeking popular support on a speaking tour, suffered a breakdown on Sept. 26, 1919. Never entirely recovering he detached himself from politics for remainder of his term. His addresses are considered among the finest produced by an American.

Wilson. 1 Town (pop. 23,010), E N.C., E of Raleigh. Tobacco market with textile and fertilizer plants. **2** Borough (pop. 8,159), E Pa., W of Easton. Foundries; mfg. of textiles.

Wilson, Mount. 1 See SAN GABRIEL MOUNTAINS, Calif. **2** Peak, 14,250 ft. high, SW Colo., highest point in San Miguel Mts. of the Rockies.

Wilson cloud chamber: see WILSON, CHARLES T. R.

Wilson College: see CHAMBERSBURG, Pa.

Wilson-Gorman Tariff Act: see WILSON, WILLIAM LYNE; GORMAN, ARTHUR PUE.

Wilton, municipal borough (pop. 2,857), Wiltshire, England. Ancient cap. of Wessex and scene of a battle (871) between Alfred and the Danes. Carpets have been made here for centuries.

Wiltshire (wĭlt'shĭr, –shůr) or **Wilts,** county (1,345 sq. mi.; pop. 387,379), S England; co. town Salisbury. Salisbury Plain and Marlborough Downs cover more than half of county. Stonehenge, Avebury, and Silbury Hill have monuments of early British. Salisbury has famous cathedral. Mainly pastoral and agr., there is sheep grazing and dairy farming. Has mfg. of textiles, metal products, and pottery.

Wimbledon, municipal borough (pop. 58,158), Surrey, England, suburb of London. Tennis hq. of England, international matches are held here.

Winchendon (wĭn'chůndůn), town (pop. 6,585), N Mass., NW of Fitchburg. Wood and paper products.

Winchester (wĭn'chĭstůr), municipal borough (pop. 25,710), co. town of Hampshire, England. Was cap. of Wessex and center of art and learning. Malory mistakenly identified town with Camelot. Has had great ecclesiastical influence. Cathedral, founded 1079 and reflecting many architectural periods, is largest Gothic church in Europe. **Winchester College** (1382) is one of great English public schools.

Winchester. **1** See WINSTED, Conn. **2** City (pop. 5,467), E Ind., E of Muncie. Ships grain and livestock. Mfg. of glass products. **3** City (pop. 9,226), N central Ky., E of Lexington. Tobacco and livestock center. Henry Clay made first and last Ky. speeches here. **4** Town (pop. 15,509), E Mass., N of Boston; settled 1640. Leather mfg. center. **5** City (pop. 13,841), N Va., in Shenandoah Valley, WNW of Washington, D.C.; settled 1744. Center of agr. area; holds annual Apple Blossom Festival. Mfg. of textiles, hosiery, and rubber goods. George Washington began career as surveyor here. In Civil War city changed hands many times; many engagements fought near by.

Winchester College: see WINCHESTER, England.

Winchilsea, Anne Finch, countess of, 1661–1720, English poet, noted for attention to nature.

Winckelmann, Johann Joachim (yō'hän yōä'khĭm vĭng'kŏŏlmän), 1717–68, German classical archaeologist and historian of ancient art, who greatly promoted classic revival of late 18th and early 19th cent.

Winckler, Hugo (hōō'gō vĭng'klŭr), 1863–1913, German Orientalist. He discovered cuneiform tablets in Hittite (1906–7).

Wind (wĭnd), river rising in W Wyo. in Wind River Range and flowing c.110 mi. SE to join Popo Agie R. in forming Bighorn R. at Riverton.

wind, air flow paralleling earth's surface. Wind vane points direction it blows from (or compass point that gives name to the wind). Robinson cup anemometer (with metal cups set on arms revolving about a vertical rod) electrically records wind velocity, as measured on U.S. Weather Bureau's adaptation of Beaufort scale. Winds from 0 to 75 (or more) mi. per hour on a 0 to 12 scale, categorized as calm, light air, breeze (slight, gentle, moderate, fresh, strong), gale (moderate, fresh, strong, whole), storm, or hurricane. Earth's winds either vary day to day or blow mostly from one direction throughout year or season, reflecting general atmospheric circulation of wind systems blowing from several high-pressure belts to adjacent low-pressure belts: e.g., the trade winds, prevailing westerlies, and polar easterlies. Earth's rotation deflects winds according to Ferrel's law.

Windau, Lafvia: see VENTSPILS.

Windaus, Adolf (ä'dôlf vĭn'dous), 1876–, German chemist. Won 1928 Nobel Prize for research on sterols (higher solid alcohols), especially in relation to vitamins; discovered and synthesized vitamin D_3.

Windber (wĭnd'bŭr), borough (pop. 8,010), SW Pa., SE of Johnstown. Coal mining; mfg. of bricks.

Wind Cave National Park: see NATIONAL PARKS AND MONUMENTS (table).

Windermere (wĭn'dŭrmĕr), largest lake in England, near Scafell, between Lancashire and Westmorland. It is 10½ mi. long, 210 ft. deep and c.1 mi. wide. Windermere and Ambleside are near-by towns.

windflower: see ANEMONE.

Windham, Conn.: see WILLIMANTIC.

wind instruments, any instrument whose tone is produced by a vibrating column of air. In the ORGAN the wind supply is mechanically produced. Other instruments are blown by the performer and are divided into two groups—the wood winds and the brass winds or brasses. The wood winds include the flute family (flute, piccolo, flageolet, and recorder), the oboe family (oboe, English horn, bassoon, and contrabassoon), and the clarinet family. Brasses include the French horn, the trombone, the trumpet and cornet, and the tuba. The material (metal or wood) and the shape (straight or wound) are less important than the length of the pipe (which affects the pitch) and the mouthpiece (which affects the timbre). Kinds of mouthpieces are the mouth-hole (as in the flute and piccolo); the reed, a thin strip of wood, cane, or metal which vibrates as air is forced over it—a single reed distinguishing the clarinet family and a double reed distinguishing the oboe family; the funnel-shaped mouthpiece (the French horn); and the cup-shaped mouthpiece (the trombone, trumpet, and tuba). From earliest times, fingers were used on side holes (in the piccolo, flageolet, and recorder) to shorten or lengthen the air column temporarily; in the 18th and 19th cent. various mechanical devices such as slides (in the trombone) and crooks and valves (in the French horn, trumpet, and tuba) were developed. The wind passage of an instrument is called its bore and may either be cylindrical (as in the flute, clarinet, trumpet, and trombone) or conical (as in the oboe, French horn, and tuba); the flared edge of a wind instrument is called the bell. The principal modern flute is a transverse flute; it is held horizontally, and the player blows across the mouth-hole (the same is true of the piccolo). It replaced the less expressive recorder, which, like the flageolet, is held vertically and has a whistle-shaped mouthpiece. The oboe (sometimes called hautboy), the English horn (the alto of the oboe family, known by its pear-shaped bell), the bassoon (bass of the oboe family; called *fagotto* in Italian because of its resemblance to a bundle of sticks), and the larger, deeper-toned contrabassoon are distinguished by their expressive, melancholy tone. There are many kinds of clarinets (e.g., bass clarinet, A clarinet, E flat clarinet) and horns (e.g., E, E flat, and D) used in military bands, but the B flat clarinet and F horn are the ones in standard orchestra use today. Although its single reed makes it a member of the clarinet family, the saxophone is a hybrid instrument, having a conical bore (like an oboe) and being made of metal (like the brasses). The tuba, larger than the trumpet and therefore lower pitched, is often confused with other instruments that play the low brass parts in orchestra and band, such as the helicon (sousaphone), euphonium, *Flügelhorn,* barytone, saxhorn, Wagner tuba. See *ill.,* p. 857.

Windischgrätz or **Windisch-Grätz, Alfred, Fürst zu** (fürst′ tsŏŏ vĭn′dishgrĕts′), 1787–1862, Austrian field marshal. In Revolution of 1848 he bombarded Prague and Vienna into submission and helped Schwarzenberg in installing Francis Joseph on throne.

windmill, apparatus harnessing wind power for various uses, e.g., pumping water, grinding grain, driving sawmills. Known in Europe from 12th cent. Dutch type consists of tower topped with revolving canvas sails on frames. In U.S. type, steel tower bears wheel with metal vanes.

windpipe or **trachea** (trā′kēŭ), main air passage of respiratory tract of vertebrates. It is a membranous and cartilaginous tube c.4½ in. long, lying in front of esophagus. Extends from larynx and divides into two bronchi. See *ill.*, p. 763.

Wind River Range (wĭnd), W Wyo., part of Rocky Mts. and Continental Divide, running SE c.120 mi. Includes Gannett Peak (13,785 ft.), highest point in Wyo., and several others over 13,000 ft.; several historic passes: e.g., SOUTH PASS, Washakie (11,610 ft.), Indian (12,130 ft.), Green River (12,222 ft.), and Togwotee (9,658 ft.).

Windsor (wĭn′zûr), family name of royal house of Great Britain. The name Wettin, family name of Albert of Saxe-Coburg-Gotha, consort of Queen Victoria, was changed to Windsor by George V in 1917.

Windsor, Edward, duke of: see EDWARD VIII, king of England.

Windsor, Wallis Warfield, duchess of, 1894–, American-born English duchess. She was twice divorced. Her friendship with EDWARD VIII of England led to his abdication. After her marriage to him as duke of Windsor (1937) special letters patent denied her a share in his royal rank.

Windsor. 1 Town (pop. 3,439), W central N.S., Canada, NW of Halifax and on Avon R. Trade and shipping center in quarrying region. Has mfg. of furniture, fertilizer, and clothing. Founded 1703 by French as Piziquid. Acadians were expelled after town fell to British 1750. Seat of King's Col., first Canadian university by royal charter 1802. **2** City (pop. 120,049), S Ont., Canada, on Detroit R. opposite Detroit, Mich. (connected by bridge, tunnel, ferries). Mfg. of steel, machinery, and chemicals. Suburbs of East Windsor, Sandwich, and Walkerville merged with Windsor 1935.

Windsor or **New Windsor,** municipal borough (pop. 23,181), Berkshire, England, on the Thames. Had many inns in Elizabethan times. Nell Gwyn and Jane Seymour lived here. **Windsor Castle,** chief residence of English rulers since William the Conqueror, was rebuilt by successive sovereigns. St. George's Chapel, one of England's most splendid churches, is scene of investiture of Knights of the Garter. Many English kings are buried in its vaults.

Windsor. 1 Town (pop. 11,833), N Conn., on Connecticut R. just above Hartford, in agr. (tobacco, truck) area. Settled 1633 for Plymouth Colony, it was first English settlement in Conn. Has Loomis School for boys. **2** Town (pop. 3,467), SE Vt., on Connecticut R. and N of Bellows Falls. Convention (July, 1777) that organized Vt. as a state under that name and first Vt. legislature (1778) met here.

Windsor Castle: see WINDSOR, Berkshire, England.

Windsor Locks, town (pop. 5,221), N Conn., on Connecticut R. above Windsor. Mfg. developed after canal was built (1829) around rapids here.

Windward Islands, S group of Lesser Antilles in West Indies, curving generally S from Leeward Isls. toward NE Venezuela. Consist of French MARTINIQUE and **British Windward Islands** colony (821 sq. mi.; pop. 251,771). British islands comprise colonies of DOMINICA, SAINT LUCIA, SAINT VINCENT, and GRENADA. The Grenadines, an archipelago of tiny islands strung out between St. Vincent and Grenada, are divided administratively between them. Although discovered by Columbus, Windward Isls. were not colonized by Spanish. English and French colonization in 17th cent. brought long struggle for dominance, part of worldwide Anglo-French conflict. Present ownership confirmed by Congress of Vienna 1815.

wine, alcoholic beverage made by fermentation of the juice of the grape. Wines are distinguished by color, flavor, bouquet or aroma, and alcoholic content, and classified as natural or fortified, sweet or dry, still or sparkling. Differences between wines depend on variety of grape, climate, the location and soil of vineyards, treatment of grapes before and during wine making. For red wines the entire crushed grape is used; for white, the juice only. Grape pulp or must (juice) is fermented through action of wine yeasts (*Saccharomyces ellipsoideus*) existing on skins of grapes (additional yeast is sometimes introduced); the new wine then undergoes chemical processes including oxidation, precipitation of proteids, and formation of esters, which create bouquet. After repeated clarification and maturing in casks for months or years, the wine is ready for bottling. Light wines (e.g., claret, sauterne) contain from 7% to 15% alcohol; fortified, or brandied, wines (e.g., SHERRY, PORT) contain added alcohol; their strength varies from 16% to 35%. Natural effervescent wines (CHAMPAGNE is best known) retain some carbon dioxide. France is the world's leading wine-producing area, both for quantity and quality; best known are the wines of Bordeaux and Burgundy (both red and white), the Loire and Rhone valleys, Alsace, and the Jura mts. Fine German wines, mainly light, dry white wines, come from the Rhine districts, the Moselle valley, Baden, Bavaria. Italy makes quantities of wine, much of it of ordinary quality; however, Chianti, Lachryma Christi, Capri, and Falerno varieties are esteemed, and Sicily makes Marsala, usually fortified. The U.S. produces some excellent wines; California, the leading region, makes European-type wines from grapes of the Old World species, *Vitis vinifera;* Eastern wines, mostly from New York state and Ohio, are made from such native grapes as the Concord and the Catawba. The term *wine* is also applied to beverages made from plants other than the grape (e.g., dandelion wine, elderberry wine).

Wineland: see VINLAND.

Winfield, city (pop. 10,264), S Kansas, SSE of Wichita; laid out 1870. Rail and trade center in agr., livestock, and oil area. Seat of Southwestern Col. (Methodist; coed.; opened 1886).

Wingate, Orde Charles (ôrd), 1903–44, British general. In World War II, he ousted Italians from Ethiopia (1941); led raiders into Burma (1943). Killed in an airplane accident.

wings, FLIGHT organs of BIRD, BAT, INSECT. Birds' wings are feathered and vary in size and shape, and in the number of primaries and secondaries (principal flight feathers). Among insects, a basis for classification is the number, kind, and vein-marking of wings. See *ills.,* pp. 135, 601.

Winkelried, Arnold von (är'nôlt fŭn vĭng'-kŭlrēt), d. 1386, Swiss hero. According to legend, upheld by some historians, after the Swiss had failed to break through Austrian ranks in battle of Sempach, Winkelried of Unterwalden sacrificed himself to make an opening in the enemy ranks through which his compatriots rushed to victory.

Winnebago Indians (wĭnĭbā'gō), North American tribe of Siouan linguistic stock, in E Wis. in the 17th cent. Now on reservations in Nebr. and Wis.

Winnebago, Lake, c.30 mi. long, 5–10 mi. wide, E Wis.; largest in state. Fox R. enters at Oshkosh, leaves at Menasha; Fond du Lac is at S end.

Winnetka (wĭnĕt'kŭ), residential village (pop. 12,105), NE Ill., N suburb of Chicago, on L. Michigan. Pharmaceuticals.

Winnfield, town (pop. 5,629), N central La., NNW of Alexandria. Timber region with salt mines and limestone quarries. Birthplace of Huey Long.

Winnipeg, city (pop. 235,710), provincial cap., SE Man., Canada, on Red R. at mouth of Assiniboine R., S of L. Winnipeg. Largest city and center of the Prairie Provs. One of world's largest wheat markets with railroad yards and shops, stockyards, and meat-packing plants. Seat of Univ. of Manitoba (provincially supported; coed.; 1877). Fort Rouge built here 1738 by Vérendrye. Hudson's Bay Co. and North West Co. contested area. Fort Garry (formerly Fort Gibraltar) was important in Red R. traffic and settlement grew up around it; inc. as Winnipeg 1873. Grew rapidly after arrival of railroad 1881.

Winnipeg, river, W Ont. and SE Man., Canada, issuing from N end of Lake of the Woods and flowing 200 mi. generally NW to L. Winnipeg.

Winnipeg, Lake, 9,398 sq. mi., 240 mi. long and 55 mi. wide, S central Man., Canada, N of Winnipeg. Receives the Red, Winnipeg, and Saskatchewan rivers and drains NE by the Nelson to Hudson Bay. A remnant of glacial L. Agassiz. Lake discovered 1733 by Vérendrye. Lumbering and fishing.

Winnipegosis, Lake, 2,086 sq. mi., 125 mi. long and 25 mi. wide, W Man., Canada, W of L. Winnipeg. Drains SE into L. Manitoba, thence into L. Winnipeg.

Winnipesaukee, Lake (wĭ"nĭpŭsô'kē), 25 mi. long and 12 mi. wide, E central N.H.; largest lake in state. Girded by irregular hilly wooded shores; drains into Merrimack R. through short Winnipesaukee R. Lake region is popular summer resort.

Winona (wĭnō'nŭ, wī–), city (pop. 25,031), SE Minn., on the Mississippi and SE of St. Paul; settled 1851 as trade and lumber center, grew with river traffic. Food products, bricks, and patent medicines. Limestone quarrying. Seat of Col. of St. Teresa.

Winooski (wĭnōō'skē), city (pop. 6,734), NW Vt., on Winooski R. near Burlington. Textiles, wood and metal products. Seat of St. Michael's Col.

Winooski, river, c.90 mi. long, rising in NE Vt. and swinging SW, then NW to L. Champlain between Burlington and Winooski. Because floods devastated its valley in 1927, three flood-control dams were built, 1933–37, in its tributaries.

Winslow, Edward, 1595–1655, one of founders of Plymouth Colony in New England, b. England. Held administrative offices in colony. His son, **Josiah Winslow,** c.1629–1680, was governor of Plymouth Colony (1673–80).

Winslow, city (pop. 6,518), E central Ariz., near Little Colorado R., ESE of Flagstaff, in livestock area. To W is Meteor Crater, depression c.1 mi. in diameter and 600 ft. deep.

Winstanley, Gerrard: see DIGGERS.

Winsted, city (pop. 8,781) in Winchester (wĭn'-chĕ"stŭr) town (pop. 10,535; settled c.1750), NW Conn., in Litchfield Hills and N of Torrington. Mfg. of clocks (since 1807), clothing, and precision metal goods.

Winston-Salem (wĭn'stŭn-sā'lŭm), city (pop. 87,811), central N.C., W of Greensboro, in piedmont; Salem founded 1766 by Moravians, Winston founded 1850; united 1913. Port of entry and tobacco center, it has textile, hosiery, and furniture industries. Seat of Salem Col.

winterberry, name for two shrubby deciduous species of the holly genus, *Ilex.* The Virginia winterberry or black alder (*Ilex verticillata*), found in E U.S. and the Middle West, has bright red berries (sometimes yellow) which remain on the branches into winter. The smooth winterberry (*I. laevigata*), a similar shrub, has orange-red berries.

wintergreen, creeping, evergreen plant (*Gaultheria procumbens*) of E North America woods, with glossy, oval leaves, small, waxy white flowers, and red berrylike, edible fruits. The leaves are a source of wintergreen oil. Also called checkerberry, teaberry.

Winter Haven, city (pop. 8,605), central Fla., E of Tampa. Processes and ships citrus fruit. Boating resort with c.100 lakes in a 5-mi. radius.

Winter Park, residential and resort city (pop. 8,250), central Fla., N of Orlando. Seat of ROLLINS COLLEGE.

Winterset, city (pop. 3,570), SW Iowa, SW of Des Moines. Near by is original Delicious apple tree, planted 1872.

Winterthur (vĭn'tŭrtōōr"), city (pop. 66,971), Zurich canton, N Switzerland. Industrial center (locomotives, machinery, textiles). Has an outstanding art gallery.

Winthrop, John, 1588–1649, governor of Mass. Bay colony, b. England. Helped shape theocratic policy of colony; opposed Anne Hutchinson. His son, **John Winthrop,** 1606–76, b. England, founded New London, Conn., in 1646 and was governor of Conn. (1657, 1659–76). His son, **John Winthrop,** 1638–1707, commonly called Fitz-John Winthrop, was also governor of Conn. (1698–1707).

Winthrop, residential and resort town (pop. 19,496), E Mass., on peninsula NE of Boston; settled 1635.

Winthrop College: see ROCK HILL, S.C.

Winton, borough (pop. 6,280), NE Pa., NE of Scranton. Anthracite mines and silk mills.

wire, metal thread or rod, usually flexible. Uses include conduction of electricity, manufacture of fences, mesh, springs, and parts of various scientific instruments. For sizing, wires are arranged in series of decreasing diameter and numbered; number is known as gauge. U.S. standards are American or Brown & Sharpe wire gauge and, for steel, special steel wire gauge. Wire has been used since before 2000 B.C. Manufactured since 13th cent. by drawing metal through successively smaller holes to desired size.

wireworm, larva of elater or click beetle. Most wireworms are hard and brown. They destroy the roots, stems, seeds of many grasses, grains, and vegetables.

Wirt, William (wûrt), 1772–1834, American author and lawyer. Wrote sketches in style of Joseph Addison. Won fame as Aaron Burr's prosecutor (1807). U.S. Attorney General (1817–29).

Wirtanen, Artturi Ilmari: see VIRTANEN.

Wisby (wĭz'bē), Swed. *Visby,* city (pop. 14,770), cap. of GOTLAND co. and isl., Sweden; a Baltic port. Lutheran episcopal see. Tourist resort. As an early member of the HANSEATIC LEAGUE, medieval Visby grew into a prosperous republic, commercial center of N Europe. The ruins of 10 fine churches and the restored cathedral bear witness to its former glory. Gotland was conquered by the Swedes 1280 and by the Danes 1361–62; though restored to the Hanseatic League in 1370, it declined and became a pirate stronghold. It fell to Denmark 1570, to Sweden 1645.

Wisconsin, state (56,154 sq. mi.; pop. 3,434,575), N central U.S.; admitted 1848 as 30th state (free); cap. MADISON. Other cities are MILWAUKEE, RACINE, KENOSHA. Bordered N by L. Superior, E by L. Michigan, W by Mississippi and St. Croix rivers. Surface is broken by many glacial lakes. Major industries are farming (dairying, livestock, grains, fruits, potatoes), mfg. (dairy products, motor vehicles and parts, paper, beer), and lumbering. Region was in French hands, then fell to British. Became part of Northwest Territory in 1787; effective U.S. control began after War of 1812. Lead mines brought rush of settlers in 1820s. Made separate territory in 1836. European immigration (esp. German) was extensive. GRANGER MOVEMENT was popular in period of economic stress. Trend toward liberalism gave birth to "Wisconsin idea" under R. M. LA FOLLETTE, continued afterward.

Wisconsin, river rising in NE Wis. at Mich. line and flowing c.430 mi. generally SW to the Mississippi near Prairie du Chien. At PORTAGE it is connected by short canal with Fox R. and thus with L. Michigan. Has DELLS OF THE WISCONSIN.

Wisconsin, University of, at Madison, land-grant and state supported, coed; chartered 1848, opened 1849. Includes Washburn Observatory, libraries of state historical society, and state academy of science, arts, and letters. Long noted for graduate and research work, scientific equipment, service to state. Experimental Col. (1927–32) made influential findings (see MEIKLEJOHN, ALEXANDER).

Wisconsin Dells, city (pop. 1,957), central Wis., on Wisconsin R. and NW of Portage. Gateway to unusual rock formations in The Dells along river.

Wisconsin Rapids, city (pop. 13,496), central Wis., on Wisconsin R. and SE of Eau Claire; formed 1900 by joining of Grand Rapids and Centralia, name changed 1920. Cranberries and paper products.

Wisdom, book of Old Testament, placed in the Apocrypha in AV, included in Western canon. Traditionally named the Wisdom of Solomon. Book contains exhortations to seek wisdom, passages on immortality, and a history of God's care of the Jews. It is an example of Wisdom literature, the critical term for Jewish philosophical writings of the pre-Christian era. Old Testament books also of this type are Job, Proverbs, Ecclesiastes, and Ecclesiasticus.

Wisdom of Jesus the Son of Sirach (sī'rŭk): see ECCLESIASTICUS.

Wise, Isaac Mayer, 1819–1900, American reform rabbi and scholar, notable as the founder (1875) of Hebrew Union College.

Wise, John, 1652–1725, American Congregational clergyman; pastor (after 1680) at Ipswich, Mass. Through preaching and writing he opposed plan of Increase and Cotton Mather to put individual churches under jurisdiction of associations of ministers and expounded democratic principles.

Wise, Stephen (Samuel), 1874–1949, American reform rabbi, b. Budapest; founder (1907) of the Free Synagogue in New York city; a leader of Zionism and reformed Judaism.

Wise, Thomas James, 1859–1937, English bibliographer and book collector. He also printed privately nearly 300 works of English authors (some exposed as forgeries by John Carter and Graham Pollard).

Wiseman, Nicholas Patrick Stephen, 1802–65, English Roman Catholic clergyman, b. Seville, of Irish-English parentage. Made archbishop of Westminster and cardinal in 1850. Aided by Manning and Newman. One of his many books was the novel *Fabiola* (1854).

Wise Men of the East, Magi, or **Three Kings,** men who, bringing gifts of gold, frankincense, and myrrh, came to adore the baby Jesus. Mat. 2. They had followed the STAR OF BETHLEHEM. According to Christian tradition there were three of them, they were kings, and their names were Caspar or

Gaspar, Melchior, and Balthazar. Feast of EPIPHANY commemorates them.

Wishart, George, 1513?–1546, martyred Scottish reformer. Most eventful result of his preaching was conversion of John Knox. Charged with heresy by Cardinal BEATON, he was burned at St. Andrews.

Wishaw, Scotland: see MOTHERWELL AND WISHAW.

Wismar (vĭs'mär), city (pop. 42,018), Mecklenburg, N Germany, on the Baltic Sea. Fishing port. Has shipyards, machinery mfg. Was a leading city of Hanseatic League. Passed to Sweden 1648, to Mecklenburg-Schwerin 1803. Retained some fine medieval architecture until World War II.

Wissman, Hermann von (fŭn vĭs'män), 1853–1905, German explorer in Africa. Explored Kasai R. system, Belgian Congo (1883–85). Founded Moshi on slopes of Mt. Kilimanjaro.

Wistar, Caspar (wĭ'stûr), 1761–1818, American physician, author of first American anatomy text. Genus *Wistaria* named in his honor.

wistaria or **wisteria,** leguminous, woody twining vines of genus *Wistaria,* highly esteemed for the beautiful pendent clusters of spring flowers (similar to sweet pea blossoms) in lilac, pink, or white. Wistaria is usually grown over porches or arbors.

Wistar Institute of Anatomy and Biology, in Philadelphia, estab. 1892. Research institute; museum.

Wister, Owen, 1860–1938, American author, best known for *The Virginian* (1902), a novel of Wyoming.

wisteria: see WISTARIA.

witchcraft, practice of sorcery or magic. When Christian Church came into power in the Western world, it banned pagan religion and magic, but belief in witchcraft persisted among people and clergy. By 14th cent., witchcraft had become a complex system, and religious persecution of supposed witches was common. From 1450 to 1650 thousands of so-called witches were executed. Even scientific interest was suspect. An accusation of witchcraft became an easy means to destroy an enemy. American colonies shared in fanaticism, and Salem was the center of a famous "witch hunt" in 1692. Last execution for witchcraft was in Scotland in 1722.

witch hazel, North American deciduous shrub or small tree (*Hamamelis virginiana*), bearing bright yellow flowers in late fall or winter. An astringent is obtained from the leaves and bark.

witenagemot (wĭ"tŭnŭgĭmōt') [Old Eng.,= meeting of counselors], a session of counselors (the witan) of a king in Anglo-Saxon England. Composed of aristocrats, it was dependent upon appointments of king or his immediate predecessor. Its assent was sought by king in important matters. Probably had power (esp. in Wessex) to elect king.

Wither, George (wĭ'dhûr), 1588–1667, English poet. For his satires, *Abuses Stript and Whipt* (1613), he was imprisoned. Later wrote pastorals, which included several well-known lyrics.

Witherspoon, John, 1723–94, Scottish-American Presbyterian clergyman, signer of Declaration of Independence, b. Scotland. President (1768–94) of College of New Jersey (now Princeton Univ.).

witness: see EVIDENCE.

Witowt (vĭ'tôft), Lithuanian *Vytautas,* 1350–1430, grand duke of Lithuania. His first cousin, Ladislaus II of Poland, was obliged to recognize him as grand duke in 1392 but remained Witowt's overlord. Lithuania under Witowt reached its greatest extent—from Baltic Sea to Black Sea—and its greatest cultural flowering.

Witt, Jan de (yän' dĭ wĭt', Dutch dů vĭt'), 1625–72, Dutch republican leader. In control of state affairs as grand pensionary (1653–72), he ended first Dutch War with England (1654; see DUTCH WARS); led Netherlands to victory in Second Dutch War; abolished stadholderat in order to end power of house of Orange; negotiated TRIPLE ALLIANCE of 1668 against Louis XIV. In Third Dutch War he unsuccessfully sued for peace and resigned when popular feeling suddenly turned in favor of WILLIAM III of Orange (1672). He was killed by a mob while he visited his brother, **Cornelius de Witt,** 1623–72, a naval officer who was in prison on a charge of plotting against William. Cornelius was also slain.

Witte, Count Sergei Yulyevich (sĭrgā' yōō'lyĭvĭch vĭ'tů), 1849–1915, Russian statesman. In charge of communications, finance, commerce, and industry after 1892, he built up Russian industries with foreign loans; had Trans-Siberian RR constructed. He negotiated the Treaty of PORTSMOUTH (1905); was briefly premier after 1905 revolution.

Wittekind, Saxon leader: see WIDUKIND.

Wittelsbach (vĭ'tůlsbäkh), Bavarian dynasty. Received duchy of Bavaria 1180; Rhenish Palatinate 1214. Emperor LOUIS IV, a Wittelsbach, divided family lands between two main lines (1329). For the Palatinate line and its ramifications, see PALATINATE. The Bavarian line, which ruled Bavaria proper, gained great power and an electoral vote under Duke MAXIMILIAN I, Catholic leader in the Thirty Years War. Its failure in 1777 brought the Palatinate line on the Bavarian throne. In 1799 all family lands were reunited under a single ruler, who in 1806 became king of a much-enlarged BAVARIA. The dynasty was deposed 1918.

Wittenberg (vĭ'tůnbĕrk), city (pop. 41,304), Saxony-Anhalt, E Germany, on the Elbe. Railroad and mfg. center. It was the seat (1273–1422) of the Ascanian dukes of Saxe-Wittenberg (see SAXONY); passed (1423) to margraves of Meissen (after 1425, electors of Saxony). Univ. of Wittenberg, founded 1502, became the cradle of the Lutheran Reformation. In 1517 Luther nailed his 95 theses to the door of the Schlosskirche [castle church]; in 1520 he burned the papal bull against him in the market place; in 1534 the first complete Lutheran Bible was printed here. Wittenberg fell to Emperor Charles V in 1547. By the Capitulation of Wittenberg (1547) the electoral dignity, along with the duchy of Saxony, passed from the Ernestine to the Albertine branch of the WETTIN dynasty. With the Saxon cap. thus transferred to Dresden, Wittenberg declined. Its university was absorbed by that of Halle in 1817.

Landmarks include Schlosskirche (with Luther's tomb) and Luther's house (now a museum).

Wittenberg College: see SPRINGFIELD, Ohio.

Witwatersrand (wĭtwô'tûrzrănd") [Afrikaans, = white water ridge] or **the Rand,** region, Transvaal, South Africa. Extending c.150 mi. E-W, it includes a gold-bearing reef which produces c.33% of the world's gold. Almost entirely urban, its chief center is Johannesburg. Surface gold was discovered 1884; main reef was reached 1889 at depth of 581 ft.

Wladimir I, duke of Kiev: see VLADIMIR I.

Wladislaw, Wladyslav, and **Wladislas.** For Polish kings thus named, see LADISLAUS.

Wlodzimierz, Ukraine: see VLADIMIR-VOLYNSKI.

Woburn (wō'bûrn), city (pop. 20,492), NE Mass., NNW of Boston; settled 1640. Animal extracts.

Wodehouse, P(elham) G(renville) (wŏŏd'hous), 1881–, English humorist, author of many novels and stories notable for hilarious caricature of English types.

Woden (wō'dŭn), chief Germanic god, called by the Norse Odin and by Wagner Wotan. His cult was important mainly in Germany and England. In Icelandic literature, he is all-wise head of Asgard and VALHALLA, patron of poetry, but second in rank to his son THOR. Frigg is his consort. Woden of southerly Germans was god of battle. Identified with Mercury because of his wisdom and magic; hence Latin *Mercury's Day* became *Woden's Day* or *Wednesday*.

Woffington, Margaret, 1714?–1760, English actress. Popular (1737–57) in such roles as Ophelia, Sir Harry Wildair in Farquhar's *Constant Couple,* and Cordelia in *King Lear.* Of Peg Woffington's many affairs, her most notorious was with Garrick.

Wöhler, Friedrich (frēd'rĭkh vû'lûr), 1800–1882, German chemist. His synthesis of urea (1828) was the first synthesis of an organic compound and marked a new era in organic chemistry. He devised a new method for isolating aluminum and by this method isolated also beryllium and yttrium.

Wolf, Friedrich August (frē'drĭkh ou'gŏŏst vôlf'), 1759–1824, German classical scholar and philologist. He was in a sense founder of modern philology. His *Prolegomena ad Homerum* (1795) suggested that the Homeric works were of composite authorship and by its methods pointed the way to higher criticism of the Bible in 19th cent.

Wolf, Hugo, 1860–1903, Austrian composer; one of the greatest writers of German lied. His more than 300 lieder include settings of poems by Goethe.

Wolf, Max (mäks' vôlf'), 1863–1932, German astronomer, introducer (1891) of astronomical photography which facilitated discovery of minor planets.

Wolf, river rising in NE Wis. and flowing c.220 mi. S to Fox R. above Oshkosh.

wolf, carnivorous mammal (*Canis*) of dog family, resembling German shepherd dog. Once found over much of N Hemisphere but now exterminated in most settled areas. Commonly runs in packs whose strength, speed, and numbers cause great destruction of wild and domestic animals. European gray wolf (*Canis lupus*) formerly was common in N regions; the larger North American gray wolf (also called timber wolf or lobo) is classed by some as a subspecies, by others as a separate species.

Wolfe, Humbert, 1885–1940, English poet and critic. His fragile verse appears in such volumes as *Kensington Gardens* (1924) and *Requiem* (1927). He also wrote satires, e.g., *Lampoons* (1925), and critical biographies of Tennyson and George Moore.

Wolfe, James, 1727–59, British soldier. Second in command to Jeffrey Amherst in French and Indian War. Commanded expedition against Quebec. Wolfe forced open battle with the French under MONTCALM on the Plains of Abraham, won a victory that was decisive in giving New France to England. Both he and Montcalm were mortally wounded.

Wolfe, Thomas (Clayton), 1900–1938, American novelist, b. Asheville, N.C. His minutely realistic but lyric *Look Homeward, Angel* (1929), *Of Time and the River* (1935), *The Web and the Rock* (1939), and *You Can't Go Home Again* (1940), are drawn from his own experiences.

Wolfeboro, resort town (pop. 2,581), E N.H., on SE L. Winnipesaukee. The Friends estab. American Seminar for European refugees here in 1940.

Wolfenbüttel (vôl'fŭnbü"tŭl), town (pop. 33,968), Lower Saxony, W central Germany, on Oker R. Was residence of dukes of Brunswick-Wolfenbüttel (see BRUNSWICK) till 1753. Famous ducal library, where Leibniz and G. E. Lessing were librarians, has c.3,000 incunabula, c.7,000 manuscripts. Has ducal palace (15th–18th cent.), many 17th-cent. houses.

Wolff, Caspar Friedrich (käs'pär frē'drĭkh vôlf'), 1733–94, German biologist, a founder of observational embryology.

Wolff, Elisabeth (Bekker) (vôlf), 1738–1804, Dutch novelist. Collaborated with Agatha Deken (dā'kŭn) (1741–1804) in sentimental epistolary novels.

Wolf-Ferrari, Ermanno (ārmä'nō vôlf'-fār-rä'rē), 1876–1948, German-Italian composer. Best known of his operas are *The Secret of Suzanne* (1909) and *The Jewels of the Madonna* (1911), his one serious opera.

wolfhound: see HOUND.

wolfram (wŏŏl'frŭm), white, very hard, metallic element (symbol = W; see also ELEMENT, table); also called tungsten. It is ductile and wires made of it have very high tensile strength. Because it has a high melting point and since less electricity is needed in operation (than for carbon, for example) it is used for electric-lamp filaments. Its alloys are important in industry because of their hardness and strength. Element occurs in ores (not free) in Asia, Europe, South America, and U.S.

Wolfram von Eschenbach (vôl'främ fŭn ĕ'shŭnbäkh), c.1170–c.1220, German epic poet and minnesinger. His only complete work is the epic *Parzival,* notable for its lyric passages, humor, and profundity of conception (see PARSIFAL); this ranks him among the greatest medieval poets.

Wolfville, town (pop. 2,313), N N.S., Canada, on SW shore of Minas Bay of Bay of Fundy. Site of Acadia Univ. (Baptist; coed.; 1839).

Wollstonecraft, Mary (wo͝ol'stŭnkrăft), 1759–97, English writer and feminist. Her *Vindication of the Rights of Woman* (1792) was first great feminist document. Had an affair with Gilbert Imlay. Married William Godwin (1797); their daughter was Mary Wollstonecraft Shelley.

Wolsey, Thomas (wo͝ol'zē), 1472?–1530, English statesman and prelate, lord chancellor (1515–29), archbishop of York (1514–30), cardinal of Roman Church. Rose rapidly, gaining high favor with Henry VIII. By 1514 he virtually controlled English domestic and foreign policy. By his treaty with France, England held balance of power between France and Hapsburgs. Made cardinal (1515), he twice failed to attain papacy. Wolsey built several palaces (e.g., Hampton Court) and his court rivaled the king's in pomp. His enemies used Henry's divorce from KATHARINE OF ARAGON as a means for his ruin. Presided at Katharine's trial. Lost all honors except his archbishopric. Arrested for treason, he died en route to London. Wolsey was largely responsible for England's emergence as first-rate power in 16th cent.

Wolverhampton (wo͝ol'vŭrhăm"tŭn), county borough (pop. 162,669), Staffordshire, England. One of chief centers of Black Country, it has great factories.

wolverine, carnivorous mammal (*Gulo*), largest of weasel family, found in N parts of N Hemisphere. Long, brown fur is valued for lining parkas.

Woman's Christian Temperance Union, organization founded 1874 to press for restriction of use of alcohol and harmful drugs and abolition of prostitution. Frances Willard was its second president.

Woman's Medical College of Pennsylvania: see PHILADELPHIA.

woman suffrage. Right of U.S. women to vote was first proposed at convention of 1848, Seneca Falls, N.Y. Early leaders in U.S. were Susan B. ANTHONY, Elizabeth Cady STANTON, Lucretia MOTT, Lucy STONE, and GRIMKÉ sisters; later were Anna Howard SHAW and Carrie Chapman CATT. Suffrage groups formed in 1869—united in 1890 as National American Woman Suffrage Association—worked through state and Federal agencies for vote by amendment to Constitution. Campaign finally resulted in Nineteenth Amendment (1920). Movement in England began in 1851. Early propaganda was John Stuart Mill's *Subjection of Women* (1869). Emmeline PANKHURST and a large group waged a militant campaign. In 1928 voting rights were equalized for men and women. In Europe, Finland and Norway first granted suffrage, France in 1945, Belgium in 1946. Six Latin American nations have granted suffrage since 1934, Philippines in 1937, and Japan in 1945.

Women's Army Corps: see WAC.

women's clubs, important phase of American town life in latter part of 19th cent. One of earliest was Sorosis (1868) in New York city. In 1890 General Federation of Women's Clubs was organized. Aim of early clubs was social and cultural; they have become increasingly active in social welfare, international concern; have effected many reforms.

Wood, Edward Frederick Lindley: see HALIFAX, EDWARD FREDERICK LINDLEY WOOD, 1ST EARL OF.

Wood, Grant, 1892–1942, American painter, b. Anamosa, Iowa. Known for deliberately stylized paintings of Middle Western life. Won national recognition in 1933 with his *American Gothic.*

Wood, John, 1705?–1754, English architect. Called Wood of BATH because of his extensive work in planning that city.

Wood, Leonard, 1860–1927, American general and administrator. Commanded ROUGH RIDERS in Spanish-American War. Governor general of the Philippines (1921–27); followed harsh, unpopular policy.

wood, botanically, the elements of the secondary xylem comprising the bulk of the stem in shrubs and trees and produced by the CAMBIUM. Wood or xylem consists of cells with firm thickened walls and serves both for mechanical support and conduction of SAP. Cells in the central part (heartwood) of a tree trunk become nonfunctional as growth produces a new xylem tissue. The outer sapwood still functions for conduction. Wood is comparatively resistant to decay and to many chemicals. Proper seasoning after cutting reduces weight, prevents warping, often increases strength. Although supplanted in many uses by other natural and synthetic materials, wood is extensively used for fuel, construction, furniture, and paper manufacture. Distillation yields charcoal, methyl alcohol, tar, acetate of lime, wood gas.

wood alcohol: see METHYL ALCOHOL.

Woodberry, George Edward, 1855–1930, American poet and critic; long a professor at Columbia Univ. (1891–1904). He wrote many chiseled sonnets, and biographies of Poe and Hawthorne.

woodbine: see VIRGINIA CREEPER.

Woodbridge, Frederick James Eugene, 1867–1940, American philosopher, b. Canada. Long a professor and dean at Columbia Univ., he was author of many philosophical works (e.g., *An Essay on Nature,* 1940).

Woodbridge, township (pop. 35,758), NE N.J., N of Perth Amboy; settled 1665 from Mass. Mfg. of ceramics, bricks, and chemicals.

Wood Buffalo National Park, 17,300 sq. mi., in NE Alta. and S Mackenzie Dist., Canada, W of L. Athabaska and E of Athabaska and Slave rivers. This vast, unfenced area is largest game preserve in North America.

Woodbury, Levi, 1789–1851, American cabinet officer and jurist. U.S. Secretary of the Navy (1831–34); Secretary of the Treasury (1834–41). Associate Justice of U.S. Supreme Court (1846–51).

Woodbury, city (pop. 10,391), SW N.J., S of Camden; settled 1683. Farm trade center. Here are Cooper House, where Cornwallis stopped 1777; Lawrence House (1765); and Friends' meetinghouse.

woodchuck or **ground hog,** a North American rodent of MARMOT family, chiefly herbivorous. It is c.14 in. long and has thick, brownish fur. Old superstition holds that it leaves burrow on Candlemas Day, Feb. 2, returning to it for six weeks if it sees its shadow.

woodcock, nocturnal game bird of snipe family. It has brown and black plumage, large eyes, long bill. American woodcock, called whistling, wood, and mud snipe, is larger than European woodcock.

Woodhull, Victoria (Claflin), 1838–1927, American lecturer and journalist, a noted eccentric; proprietor, with her sister Tennessee Claflin, of *Woodhull and Claflin's Weekly* (1870). People's party nominee for President (1872).

Woodlake, city (pop. 2,525), S central Calif., SE of Fresno. Sequoia Natl. Park is near.

Woodland, city (pop. 9,386), N central Calif., NW of Sacramento. Processes meat, sugar, beets, truck, and fruit. Seat of Woodland Clinic Hospital.

wood louse, name for various small isopod crustaceans. Includes terrestrial forms, e.g., *Oniscus, Porcellio, Armadillidium* (pill bug), and marine forms.

woodpecker, widely distributed climbing bird. Bird bores into trees with chisellike bill; extracts insects with sticky, barbed tongue. Spiny tail aids in climbing. Tattoo on tree trunk is characteristic call. Male usually has red or orange head patches. North American forms include the downy (c.6½ in. long), hairy (c. 9½ in. long), and pileated (c.17 in. long) woodpeckers; the redheaded and three-toed woodpeckers; and the FLICKER and SAPSUCKER. See *ill.*, p. 135.

Wood-Ridge, borough (pop. 6,283), NE N.J., E of Passaic. Mfg. of airplane motors.

Wood River, city (pop. 10,190), SW Ill., on the Mississippi above East St. Louis; founded 1907. Oil refinery, tannery, and planing mill.

Woodruff, Lorande Loss, 1879–1947, American biologist, authority on protozoa. He was known as a teacher (at Yale Univ. from 1907), author, and editor.

Woods Hole, Mass.: see FALMOUTH.

Woodstock, city (pop. 15,544), S Ont., Canada, WSW of Toronto, in stock-raising region. Mfg. of furniture, pianos, organs, and hardware.

Woodstock, municipal borough (pop. 1,713), Oxfordshire, England. Site of castle in which the Black Prince was born and Elizabeth imprisoned. Scene of Scott's novel *Woodstock.*

Woodstock. 1 City (pop. 7,192), NE Ill., NW of Chicago. Mfg. of metal products. **2** Summer-resort village (pop. 2,271), SE N.Y. in Catskills foothills. Artists' colony founded 1902. Has Art Students League summer school. **3** Town (pop. 2,613), E Vt., W of White River Junction. Winter and summer resort with noted village green and fine old houses. **4** Town (pop. 1,816), N Va., SW of Winchester in Shenandoah Valley. Courthouse dates from 1791. Observation tower on near-by Massanuten Mt. views seven horseshoe bends of Shenandoah R.

Woodsworth, James Shaver, 1874–1942, Canadian politician and reformer. Entered Canadian House of Commons in 1921. Regarded as founder of CO-OPERATIVE COMMONWEALTH FEDERATION.

Woodville, Elizabeth, c.1437–1492, queen consort of EDWARD IV of England. Her secret marriage to Edward (1464) angered Richard Neville, earl of Warwick, who drove Edward from England and restored Henry VI. Edward recaptured throne. On his death (1483) Elizabeth claimed throne for her son, Edward V. Richard, duke of Gloucester, usurped throne as Richard III, had her sons killed, and declared void Elizabeth's marriage to Edward IV. Her daughter was queen of Henry VII.

Woodward, Robert Simpson (wo͝od'wûrd), 1849–1924, American scientist and educator. Contributed to mechanics, astronomy, geodesy. President of Carnegie Institution (1905–20).

Woodward, city (pop. 5,915), NW Okla., on North Canadian R. Trade and processing center for wheat and cattle area. Mfg. of dairy products, brooms.

wood wind instruments: see WIND INSTRUMENTS.

Wool, John Ellis, 1784–1869, American general. Brevetted major general for services in Mexican War, especially at Buena Vista.

wool, fiber from the fleece of domestic sheep. Wool is warm (its fibers do not conduct heat and its crimp permits it to enmesh air), elastic, crease resistant, absorbent, strong (one fourth stronger than cotton), and especially adaptable to felting (see FELT). Unless specially treated, it will shrink when soaked. No known wild animals bear wool; the fleece of the sheep has developed under domestication. Wool is classed as to fineness, length, and crimp of staple, and according to the age of the animal. Sheep are sheared with clippers. After removal of dirt and LANOLIN by various means, wool may be bleached and dyed (as raw stock, yarn, or in the piece), may be oiled to withstand processing, and is often blended. Woolen goods are those woven from carded short-staple fibers adapted to fulling and napping; worsted fabrics (e.g., whipcord, gabardine) have a hard, smooth texture and were formerly made only from long-staple wool; spinning methods have now been developed to use short-staple wool. Industrially, such other animal fibers as those of the camel, Angora goat, and vicuña are classed as wool. In the U.S., the term *wool* may be applied only to fabrics of new wool; *reprocessed wool* is recovered from unused articles and waste, *reused wool* from used articles.

Woolf, Virginia, 1882–1941, English novelist and essayist; daughter of Sir Leslie Stephen; wife of Leonard Woolf, with whom she estab. the Hogarth Press. Early novels (e.g., *The Voyage Out,* 1915; *Night and Day,* 1919) were traditional in form; later used stream-of-consciousness method (e.g., *Mrs. Dalloway,* 1925; *To the Lighthouse,* 1927; *The Waves,* 1931), while some (e.g., *Orlando,* 1928) were highly experimental. All are notable for subtle characterization and fluid style. Her polished and distinguished essays are collected in several volumes (e.g., *The Common Reader,* 1925). *A Room of One's Own* (1929) is feminist. She drowned herself.

Woollcott, Alexander, 1887–1943, American literary and dramatic critic, noted also for his colorful personality. Exerted great influence on popular taste, especially through a radio program (1929–40). Wrote many short pieces—reviews, popular tales, essays.

Woolley, Mary Emma, 1863–1947, American educator. She was president of Mt. Holyoke Col. (1901–37).

Woolman, John, 1720–72, American Quaker leader. Recorded a minister 1743, he traveled throughout the colonies. An ardent humanitarian, he was among first to oppose slavery. Of his works the best known is his immortal *Journal* (1774).

Woolner, Thomas (wo͝ol'nûr), 1825–92, English pre-Raphaelite sculptor and poet, best known for portrait busts of famous contemporaries.

Woolson, Constance Fenimore, 1840–94, American writer; grandniece of James Fenimore Cooper. Wrote regional stories and novels of the Old Northwest and the South.

Woolwich (wo͝ol'ĭj, –ĭch), metropolitan borough (pop. 147,824) of SE London, on Thames R. Site of Royal Military Academy (1741), Royal Arsenal, and related institutions. Suffered heavy bombing 1940.

Woolworth, Frank Winfield, 1852–1919, American merchant, founder of dime-store chain.

Woonsocket (wo͞onsŏ'kĭt), city (pop. 50,211), N R.I., at Mass. line on Blackstone R.; settled before 1675. Mfg. of textiles (since c.1814), metal, paper, and rubber products.

Wooster (wo͝o'stûr), city (pop. 14,005), N central Ohio, SW of Akron; settled 1807. Oil and gas wells and mfg. of rubber products and motor vehicles. Seat of **College of Wooster** (Presbyterian; coed.; opened 1870).

Worcester, Dean Conant (wo͝o'stûr), 1866–1924, American zoologist and authority on Philippines; secretary of the interior (1901–13) of Philippines.

Worcester, Thomas Percy, earl of: see PERCY, family.

Worcester, England: see WORCESTERSHIRE.

Worcester, city (pop. 203,486), central Mass., on Blackstone R. (canalized 1828) and W of Boston; first settled 1668, permanently settled 1713. Second largest Mass. city; rail and industrial center; metal products, electrical supplies, paper, textiles, abrasives. Courthouse besieged in Shays's Rebellion 1786. Annual music festival since 1858. Seat of Worcester Polytechnic Inst. (for men; 1865); Col. of the Holy Cross (Jesuit; for men; 1843); Clark Univ. (nonsectarian; coed.; chartered 1887, opened 1889 by J. G. Clark), with a pioneer graduate school and notable school of geography.

Worcester College: see OXFORD UNIVERSITY.

Worcestershire (wo͝o'stûrshĭr, –shûr) or **Worcester,** county (700 sq. mi.; pop. 522,974), W central England. Mostly hilly, it has famous orchards and much sheep pasturage. Avon valley is called Vale of Evesham. Has rich iron and coal deposits in N part. Population has increased in recent years. County town is **Worcester,** county borough (pop. 59,700), on the Severn. In the cathedral are held, alternatively with Hereford and Gloucester, Festivals of the Three Choirs. Last city to yield to Parliament in 1646, it was scene of Cromwell's final victory 1651. Porcelain, gloves, "Worcestershire" sauce and metal goods are made.

Wordsworth, William, 1770–1850, English romantic poet; educ. at Cambridge. In France c.1791, he was influenced by Rousseau and the French Revolution. Returning to England, he published in 1793 *An Evening Walk* and *Descriptive Sketches.* With his sister Dorothy he moved to Dorsetshire, where he began friendship with Coleridge and with him wrote *Lyrical Ballads* (1798)—including "Tintern Abbey"—an effort to use in poetry "the real language of men." In 1799 Wordsworth and Dorothy moved to the Lake District, where they lived thereafter. He married Mary Hutchinson in 1802. In 1805 he completed *The Prelude* (not pub. until much later). In 1807 appeared *Poems in Two Volumes,* including his "Ode to Duty," "Ode: Intimations of Immortality," and several famous sonnets. His creative powers diminished, but some notable later poems were *The Excursion* (1814), "Laodamia" (1815), and "Yarrow Revisited" (1835). In 1843 he succeeded Southey as poet laureate. Influenced by his life in the Lake District, Wordsworth was the greatest of English poets of nature. His attempts to show the beauty of the commonplace were often ridiculed, but his work, with its exalted air, simple language, and sheer beauty is recognized as among the world's finest poetry. Some of his shorter poems, such as the "Lucy" series, "The Solitary Reaper," "Daffodils," "The Rainbow," and the sonnet "The World Is Too Much with Us" are familiar to most English-speaking readers. His sister and devoted companion, **Dorothy Wordsworth,** 1771–1855, is known chiefly for beautifully written journals. Another brother, **Christopher Wordsworth,** 1774–1846, was an English clergyman, educator, and writer, master of Trinity Col., Cambridge (1820–41). Most noted work is *Ecclesiastical Biography* (6 vols., 1810). One of his sons, **Charles Wordsworth,** 1806–92, became bishop of St. Andrews, Dunkeld, and Dunblane, Scotland. He worked for reuniting of churches of Scotland and England. Another son, **Christopher Wordsworth,** 1807–85, became (1869) bishop of Lincoln.

work, in physics, action of some force upon some object in which friction or other resistance is overcome. Work, the product of MOTION and FORCE, is expressed in terms of distance and force, e.g., when a 10-lb. object is lifted 5 ft., work done is said to be 50 foot-pounds. ENERGY is capacity to do work. POWER involves time element and is rate at which work is done. Work unit measurements include ERG, JOULE, foot-pound, gram-centimeter. Efficiency of a machine, i.e., ratio between amount of apparent work done and amount put into it, is always less than one.

Workman, Fanny (Bullock), 1850–1925, American mountain climber. With her husband, William Hunter Workman (1847–1937), she explored and mapped Himalayan glaciers, achieved several first ascents of more than 20,000 ft. Estab. world mountaineering record for women in 1906.

Work Projects Administration (WPA), 1935–43, estab. by executive order of Pres. F. D. Roosevelt as Works Progress Administration, redesignated in 1939. Undertook extensive building and improvement program to provide work for unemployed; also included Federal Art Project (noted for decorating public buildings with murals), Federal Writers Project (produced a valuable series of U.S. guidebooks), Federal Theatre Project (introduced fresh ideas), and National Youth Administration (to 1939).

Works Progress Administration: see WORK PROJECTS ADMINISTRATION.

World Bank: see INTERNATIONAL BANK FOR RECONSTRUCTION AND DEVELOPMENT.

World Council of Churches, formally constituted by representatives from 150 Protestant and Orthodox denominations of some 44 countries, assembled at Amsterdam in 1948. Constitution provides for a permanent organization representing constituent churches. Council has no legislative power, but it gives opportunity for cooperation in matters of common concern. Hq. are at Geneva, Switzerland.

World Court, popular name for the Permanent Court of International Justice at The Hague, 1921–45; organized under the League of Nations. The court rendered judgment in international disputes voluntarily submitted to it. The U.S. did not join, but there was always a U.S. judge. Superseded by International Court of Justice.

World Health Organization (WHO), agency of UN, estab. 1948, hq. Geneva. Goal is "attainment by all peoples of the highest level of health." WHO operates by regional bodies, and has done notable work in checking cholera, malaria, and tuberculosis.

world's fair: see EXPOSITION.

World War I, 1914–18. The immediate cause of conflict was the assassination (June 28, 1914) of Archduke Francis Ferdinand of Austria-Hungary at Sarajevo by a Serbian nationalist. Hostilities began slowly, but by the end of summer, 1914, the Allies (i.e., England, France, Russia, Belgium, Serbia, Montenegro, and Japan) were involved in a general conflict with the Central Powers (i.e., Germany, Austria-Hungary, and the Ottoman Empire). On the Western Front, Germany occupied Belgium and advanced on Paris. After the first battle of the Marne and the first battle of Ypres, there was a military stalemate and grueling trench warfare for three years. On the Eastern Front, the Germans under Hindenburg, Ludendorff, and Mackensen defeated (Aug.–Sept., 1914) the Russians at Tannenberg and the Masurian Lakes. Russian counterattack failed (1916) and Russian Revolution eliminated Russia as a useful ally. Bulgaria joined (Oct., 1915) the Central Powers; Serbia and Montenegro fell by end of 1915. Allied Gallipoli campaign (1915) against Turkey was a failure. Italy joined (May, 1915) the Allies, but Italian fighting was indecisive until rout at Caporetto (1917), which was not offset until the Italian victory of Vittorio Veneto in 1918. The year 1916 saw little real change in Western Front, despite huge casualties in battles of Verdun and the Somme offensive. Portugal and Rumania joined the Allies in 1916; Greece, involved by the Salonica campaigns, declared war on the Central Powers in 1917. U.S. neutrality had been imperiled (1915) by sinking of the *Lusitania.* German fleet had been bottled up since indecisive battle of Jutland. Germany had announced (1916) decision to begin unrestricted submarine warfare. U.S. broke off relations; declared war (April 6, 1917) on Germany. American Expeditionary Force under Gen. Pershing landed in France, but did not participate in any important action until Château-Thierry battle (June, 1918). T. E. Lawrence stirred Arab revolt against Turkey; Baghdad and Jerusalem fell in 1917. Unified Allied command, under Foch, was created in April, 1918. Central Powers signed (March, 1918) Treaty of Brest-Litovsk with Russia. Germans were stopped just short of Paris in second battle of the Marne; Allied counterattack was successful. Bulgaria, Turkey, and Austria-Hungary surrendered. After revolt broke out in Germany, an armistice was signed (Nov. 11, 1918) at Compiègne. War and resulting peace treaties of Versailles, Saint-Germain, Trianon, Neuilly, and Sèvres radically changed face of Europe. Warfare itself had been revolutionized. Suffering caused by war (conservative estimate of losses is 10,000,000 dead and 20,000,000 wounded) brought on a general revulsion; led many to put their trust in newly-formed League of Nations.

World War II, 1939–45. Chief political events leading to World War II were the aggressive policies of the principal AXIS powers—Germany, Italy, Japan—culminating in the German seizure of Bohemia and Moravia (March, 1939). The W powers—Britain and France—after crowning their "appeasement policy" with the MUNICH PACT (1938), began to rearm and extended guarantees to other possible victims of aggression, notably to Poland. While Hitler demanded the return of DANZIG and the POLISH CORRIDOR, the USSR concluded a nonaggression pact with Germany (Aug., 1939). Hitler thus was left free to break off negotiations and attack POLAND (Sept. 1). England (joined by nearly all members of British Commonwealth) and France declared war on Germany. German lightning tactics (*Blitzkrieg*) won a quick victory in Poland. In the W, the British and French spent an inactive winter behind the MAGINOT LINE. In April, 1940, Germany invaded and occupied Denmark and Norway; In May, it overran the Low Countries, broke into France, swept to the Channel ports, and cut off the Allies, who were evacuated from DUNKIRK. Italy entered the war June 10. On June 22 FRANCE surrendered. England, under Churchill's leadership, fought on alone and in the "battle of Britain" resisted the German attempt to bomb it into submission. Land operations continued in N Africa, where Italy attacked the British, and in the Balkans, where Italy attacked GREECE (Oct., 1940) and where Germany, Hungary, and Bulgaria invaded YUGOSLAVIA (April, 1941). The first round appeared to be won by the Axis, and on June 22, 1941, Hitler launched the invasion of the USSR. Meanwhile, the U.S. was gradually drawn closer to the war. Congress voted LEND-LEASE aid to England (1941) and, to protect its shipping, the U.S. occupied Iceland and Greenland. Japanese aggression in Indo-China and Thailand led to extreme tension. On Dec. 7, 1941, Japan attacked Pearl Harbor, the Philippine Isls., and Malaya. The U.S., followed by most of the Allies (except USSR), declared war on Japan. Germany and its allies (except Finland) declared war on the U.S. By 1942, Japan had conquered the Philippines, many other Pacific islands, and all SE Asia; in Russia the Axis forces had reached Stalingrad and the Caucasus; in Africa, Gen. Rommel seemed about to take Cairo; in naval warfare, German submarines threatened to wipe out Allied shipping. At this dark hour the Allies rallied and in a series of victories turned the tide. In N Africa, Montgomery's victory at Alamein (Oct., 1942), followed by the U.S. landing in Algeria, resulted in total victory over the Axis forces, the Allied conquest of Sicily and S Italy, and Italy's surrender (Sept., 1943). In the Pacific, the U.S. won the naval battles of Coral Sea and Midway, landed at Guadalcanal (1942), and under the leadership of Gen. Douglas MacArthur and Admirals Halsey and Nimitz began the "island-hopping" strategy which by 1945 had won back the Philippines, and brought a striking force to Japan's doorstep at Iwo Jima and Okinawa. In Russia, the victory of Stalingrad (1943) was followed by the mighty Russian drive which by 1944 brought Russian armies deep into Poland and Hungary and drove the Axis forces out of the Balkans. The "battle of the Atlantic" ended with the virtual extermination of German submarines. In central Italy, the Allies met stubborn German resistance and slow, grueling warfare set in (see CASSINO; ANZIO), but on June 6, 1944, the Allies under the command of Gen. Eisenhower landed in NORMANDY, and in Aug. a second Allied force landed in S France. By late 1944, France and Belgium were liberated; the war was carried into the Netherlands and Germany. Allied air power was annihilating Germany's industrial centers. In April, 1945, German resistance collapsed; on May 7, Germany surrendered unconditionally. In Aug., the U.S. dropped the first atomic bombs on Hiroshima and Nagasaki; Russia declared war on Japan and invaded Manchuria. Japan announced its surrender Aug. 14 (signed Sept. 2, 1945). The fighting was over. The world's material and human losses were incalculable. Bombing of cities and German attempts at GENOCIDE (esp. of Jews) had killed millions of civilians. Entire nations were close to starving. Never had war been more destructive, and yet the world was unable to reach true peace. Peace treaties were signed (1947) with Italy, Rumania, Bulgaria, Hungary, and FINLAND (whose war with the USSR was in a manner separate from the general conflict). However, mounting tension between the U.S. and the USSR—which emerged from the war as the two chief powers—prevented agreement on general peace treaties with Germany, Austria, and Japan (as of May, 1953). The chief positive result of the war was the formation of the UNITED NATIONS.

worm, name for several phyla of elongated, soft-bodied invertebrates. These include segmented worms (Annelida or Annulata), e.g., EARTHWORM; flat worms (Platyhelminthes), e.g., TAPEWORM, FLUKE, other parasites; round or thread worms (Nemathelminthes), including agricultural pests and parasites causing diseases, e.g., hookworm, filariasis, trichinosis.

Worms (wûrmz, Ger. vôrms), city (pop. 51,857), Rhineland-Palatinate, W Germany, on the Rhine. Varied mfg.; export center for Rhine wines. Fell to Romans 14 B.C.; was an early episcopal see and cap. of first kingdom of Burgundy (5th cent.). Bishops ruled some territory as princes of Holy Roman Empire till 1803; city itself became (1150) the first free imperial city. Annexed to France 1797, it passed to Hesse-Darmstadt 1815 and to Rhineland-Palatinate after World War II, in which it was more than half destroyed. Among damaged buildings are the Romanesque basilica and the Romanesque-Gothic synagogue (founded 1034; destroyed by Nazis 1938). Worms was the scene of important historic events. The Synod of Worms (1076) declared Pope Gregory VII deposed. The **Concordat of Worms,** 1122, was an agreement between Pope Calixtus II and Emperor Henry V to end the struggle over INVESTITURE. The emperor conceded to the pope the right to invest bishops and abbots but reserved the right to veto elections of prelates to whom he objected. The **Diet of Worms,** 1521, was called by Emperor Charles V and among other matters took up the doctrines spread by Martin LUTHER. Luther arrived under a safe-conduct April 16; refused to yield ground in lengthy arguments with theologians; was ordered to leave the city April 26. The diet widened the gap between Roman Church and Reformed beliefs.

wormwood, perennial herb (*Artemisia absinthium*) with silvery gray leaves and tiny yellow composite flower heads. It is native to the Old World but also grown elsewhere. Wormwood oil has been used medicinally and as an insect repellent, and is the source of the bitter principle in ABSINTHE. Other artemisia species are also called wormwood.

worsted: see WOOL.

Worth, Charles Frederick, 1825–95, Parisian dress designer, b. England. For over a generation after the 1850s he was the leading arbiter of women's styles.

Worth, William Jenkins, 1794–1849, American general. A superior battle leader who fought under Zachary Taylor in northern campaign of Mexican War and, later, received surrender of Mexico city. Fort Worth, Texas, named for him.

Worthington, city (pop. 7,923), SW Minn., near Iowa line, in lake region. Farm trade center.

Wotan, Richard Wagner's name for WODEN.

Wouwerman, Philips (fē'lĭps vou'vûrmän), 1619–68, Dutch painter of Haarlem, best known for his spirited scenes of battles and hunts.

Wovoka, Indian messianic leader. See GHOST DANCE.

WPA: see WORK PROJECTS ADMINISTRATION.

WPB: see WAR PRODUCTION BOARD.

Wrangel or **Wrangell, Baron Ferdinand Petrovich von** (both: răng'gŭl; Rus. vrän'gĭl), 1794–1870, Russian naval officer, arctic explorer, and administrator. Commanded Russian naval arctic expedition (1820–23). Governor of Russian colonies in Alaska (1829–34); opposed sale to U.S.

Wrangel, Karl Gustaf (vrän'gĕl), 1613–76, Swedish field marshal. With Turenne, he overran Bavaria at end of Thirty Years War (1646). Commanded land and naval forces in Polish wars. Invaded Denmark 1657–58. Was created a count 1651.

Wrangel, Baron Piotr Nikolayevich (răng'gŭl; Rus. vrän'gĭl), 1878–1928, Russian general. Succeeded (1920) Denikin in command of White Army. After initial successes, he was forced back into the Crimea by the Reds and had to evacuate his forces to Constantinople.

Wrangel Island or **Wrangell Island** (both: răng'gŭl), island 75 mi. long, 45 mi. wide, off Khabarovsk Territory, RSFSR (NE Siberia), in Chukchi Sea (on edge of Arctic Ocean). Has government arctic station and trading post. Although barren, is breeding ground for arctic animals. Discovered 1867 by Thomas Long, American whaling-ship captain. Russians landed 1911, claimed it 1924, and estab. colony 1926.

Wrangell, Baron Ferdinand Petrovich von: see WRANGEL, BARON FERDINAND PETROVICH VON.

Wrangell Island (răng'gŭl), 30 mi. long, 5–14 mi. wide, off SE Alaska, in Alexander Archipelago. Occupied 1834 by Russians. **Wrangell** town (pop. 1,263) on N coast, grew out of Russian fort. U.S. military post 1867–77; later became outfitting point for miners. Lumbering, fishing, fur farming now carried on. Wrangell Inst., U.S. vocational school for natives, is near.

Wrangell Mountains, S Alaska, extending c.100 mi. SE from Copper R. to Yukon border, where St. Elias Mts. begin. Have Mt. Sanford (16,208 ft.), Mt. Blackburn (16,140 ft.), Mt. Wrangell (14,005 ft.).

Wrath, Cape, northwestern extremity of Scotland.

wreck, in law, goods washed ashore as distinguished from goods lost at sea, i.e., FLOTSAM, JETSAM, AND LIGAN. In English law the goods, unless claimed by the owner within a year and a day, became the king's property. In the U.S. (where wreck includes goods lost on lakes or rivers), laws vary; if the owner does not claim wreck promptly, title may go to the finder or to the state.

Wren, Sir Christopher, 1632–1723, outstanding English architect, whose works are notable for dignity and elegance. Also known in his time as a mathematician. Drew plans, never executed, for reconstruction of London after great fire of 1666. Of the 52 London churches he built (1670–1711), the greatest is SAINT PAUL'S CATHEDRAL. Among many secular works are Chelsea Hospital, parts of Greenwich Hospital, the garden façade of Hampton Court Palace, and the buildings of the Temple, London.

wren, small singing bird of both hemispheres, especially numerous in tropical America. Plumage is usually brown or reddish above and white, gray, or buff below. Bill is long; tail usually upturned. Destroys insects.

Wrentham (rĕn'thŭm), town (pop. 5,341), SE Mass., SW of Boston. Former home of Helen Keller and Anne Sullivan Macy is now workers' rest home.

Wrexham (rĕk'sŭm), municipal borough (pop. 30,962), Denbighshire, Wales; a livestock market. Seat of Catholic bishopric of Menevia, which includes all of Wales except Glamorganshire.

Wright, Sir Almroth Edward, 1861–1947, British pathologist, pioneer in vaccine therapy and antityphoid inoculation.

Wright, Elizur (ĭlī'zŭr), 1804–85, American actuary and antislavery leader. His actuarial work and his work in furthering laws governing insurance practices earned him the title "father of life insurance."

Wright, Frances, 1795–1852, British-American reformer. Her *Views of Society and Manners in America* (1821) enthusiastically recounted her travels (1818–20) in the U.S., where, impressed by the Rappite colonies and Robert Dale Owen's colony, she later (1825) founded NASHOBA. After its failure she lectured and, with Owen, edited the *Free Enquirer*. Her marriage (1831) to W. P. Darusmont (or D'Arusmont) was dissolved 1835.

Wright, Frank Lloyd, 1869–, American architect, b. Richland Center, Wis. He developed his so-called prairie style in Oak Park, Ill., in the series of homes he built with low horizontal proportions and strongly projecting eaves. From the beginning he practiced radical innovation both in structure and aesthetics. He pioneered in the integration of machine methods and materials into a true architectural expression and was the first to produce open planning in houses, in a break from the traditional closed volume. Among his notable works are the Imperial Hotel (1916–20), Tokyo, Japan, which survived the 1923 earthquake, and his own home "Taliesin" (1911) at Spring Green, Wis. "Taliesin West" is near Phoenix, Ariz.

Wright, Henry, 1878?–1936, American architect and community planner. Wrote *Rehousing Urban America* (1935), an outstanding technical work.

Wright, Horatio Gouverneur, 1820–99, Union general in Civil War. Captured Fla. coastal towns in 1862. Commanded 6th Corps in Wilderness campaign (1864). At Petersburg (1865) his men were first to break through Confederate lines.

Wright, Orville, 1871–1948, and **Wilbur Wright,** 1867–1912, American airplane inventors, brothers. Their interest in flying aroused by Lilienthal's glider flights of 1890s, they made early aircraft in Dayton, Ohio, bicycle repair shop. Encouraged and advised by Octave Chanute, they improved the glider. Orville designed engine for it. First controlled and sustained power-driven airplane flight made at Kitty Hawk, N.C., Dec. 17, 1903.

Wright, Richard, 1908–, American Negro author, noted especially for a powerful novel, *Native Son* (1940), and for autobiographical *Black Boy* (1945).

Wright, Russel, 1905–, American industrial designer, who popularized functional forms in furniture and chinaware.

Wright, Wilbur: see WRIGHT, ORVILLE.

Wrightstown, borough (pop. 1,199), central N.J., SE of Trenton. U.S. Fort Dix is here.

Wriothesley, English noble family: see SOUTHAMPTON, THOMAS WRIOTHESLEY, 1ST EARL OF.

writ, in law, order issued in the name of the sovereign or the state in connection with a judicial or administrative proceeding, usually compelling a person to report at a fixed time with proof of compliance or reason for disobedience. The principle of "no writ, no right" was somewhat overcome in England by development of equity. Notable survivals of writs are habeas corpus and mandamus.

Wroclaw, Lower Silesia: see BRESLAU.

wrought iron: see IRON.

Wuchang (wŏŏ′chäng′), city (pop. 204,634), cap. of Hopeh prov., China; port at junction of Yangtze and Han rivers, opposite Hanyang and Hankow. Seat of two universities.

Wuhsien, China: see SOOCHOW.

Wundt, Wilhelm Max (vĭl′hĕlm mäks vŏŏnt′), 1832–1920, German physiologist and psychologist. He founded the first experimental psychology laboratory, Leipzig, 1878, and also the science of folk psychology.

Wupatki National Monument: see NATIONAL PARKS AND MONUMENTS (table).

Wu P'ei-fu (wŏŏ′ pā′-fŏŏ′), 1873–1939, Chinese general. Leader of Peking government after Yüan Shih-kai's death (1916), he fought with other war lords, notably Chang Tso-lin, for control of N China. Defeated 1927 by Chiang Kai-shek.

Wupper (vŏŏ′pŭr), river, c.65 mi. long, NW Germany, a W tributary of the Rhine. Its middle course, with WUPPERTAL, REMSCHEID, and SOLINGEN, is of major industrial importance.

Wuppertal (vŏŏ′pŭrtäl), city (pop. 362,125), North Rhine–Westphalia, NW Germany, on the Wupper, adjoining Solingen and Remscheid. Was formed 1929 by merger of Barmen, Elberfeld, and several lesser towns. Major industrial center, producing textiles, iron, steel, dyes, pharmaceuticals. City was half destroyed in World War II.

Württemberg (wûr′tŭmbûrg″, Ger. vür′tŭmbĕrk″), former German state (7,532 sq. mi.; 1939 pop. 2,896,920), SW Germany; cap. Stuttgart. Drained by the Neckar and the upper Danube, it is a hilly, agr. region, famous for its lovely landscape. It includes the Swabian Jura (S) and part of the Black Forest (W). The county of Württemberg emerged from the ruins of the old duchies of Swabia and Franconia and became a duchy in 1495. In 1801–10, Württemberg doubled its territory by acquiring the numerous small ecclesiastic and temporal fiefs of the region and the former free imperial cities of Ulm, Hall, Gmünd, Esslingen, and others. In 1806, it was made a kingdom by Napoleon I, against whom it turned in 1813. It sided with Austria in the Austro-Prussian War of 1866 but joined the German Empire 1871. The monarchy was abolished 1918, and in 1919 Württemberg joined the Weimar Republic. After World War II the state was partitioned between WÜRTTEMBERG-BADEN and WÜRTTEMBERG-HOHENZOLLERN.

Württemberg-Baden (–bä′dŭn), German state (6,062 sq. mi.; pop. 3,884,462), SW Germany; cap. Stuttgart. Formed 1945 in U.S. occupation zone from N parts of former states of BADEN and WÜRTTEMBERG (incl. Ulm, Mannheim, Karlsruhe, Heidelberg). Joined Federal Republic of [West] Germany 1949.

Württemberg-Hohenzollern (–hō″ŭntsô′lŭrn), German state (4,018 sq. mi.; pop. 1,240,999), SW Germany; cap. Tübingen. Formed 1946 in French occupation zone from S WÜRTTEMBERG, former HOHENZOLLERN prov., and LINDAU dist. (i.e., most of SWABIA). Joined Federal Republic of [West] Germany 1949.

Wurtz, Charles Adolphe (shärl′ ädôlf′ vürts′), 1817–84, French chemist. He discovered methyl and ethyl amines, glycol, and aldol condensation; developed method of synthesizing hydrocarbons by treating alkyl halides with sodium (Wurtz reaction), adapted by Rudolf Fittig to preparation of mixed aliphatic and aromatic hydrocarbons.

Würzburg (wûrts′bûrg, Ger. vürts′bŏŏrk), city (pop. 78,195), cap. of Lower Franconia, NW Bavaria, on the Main, in a region of vineyards. Mfg. of machine tools, chemicals, textiles. Became episcopal see 741. Its prince-bishops ruled a large part of FRANCONIA until 1802. They founded Würzburg univ. (1582) and made the city one of Europe's most splendid residences in the baroque and rococo periods. The episcopal residence (1720–44), Romanesque cathedral (11th–13th cent.), and numerous other famous buildings were destroyed in World War II.

Wusih (wŏŏ′shē′), city (pop. 273,346), cap. of South Kiangsu, China, on Grand Canal. Textile center.

Wyandotte (wī′ŭndŏt), industrial city (pop. 36,846), SE Mich., on Detroit R. and S of Detroit. Salt deposits here basis of large chemical industry. Also mfg. of metal and rubber products. Bessemer steel first commercially produced here 1864.

Wyandotte Cave, S Ind., just N of Ohio R. and W of New Albany. Limestone cave (one of largest in North America) with miles of passages on five levels and notable chambers.

Wyant, Alexander Helwig (wī′ŭnt), 1836–92, American landscape painter, influenced by Inness. Best known for scenes in the Adirondacks and Catskills.

Wyatt, Sir Thomas, 1503?–1542, English poet. Wrote first sonnets in English and varied lyrics, introducing genuinely personal quality into English Renaissance love poetry. His son, **Sir Thomas Wyatt,** d. 1554, was famous conspirator. Rebelled when Mary I announced plan to marry Philip II of Spain. Temporarily successful, he was checked at London. Surrendered and was hanged.

Wycherley, William (wĭ′chŭrlē), 1640?–1716, English Restoration dramatist. In such plays as *Love in a Wood* (produced 1671), *The Country Wife* (1675), and *The Plain Dealer* (produced 1676), he added a note of realism and robust, coarse satire to the witty artificiality of Restoration comedy.

Wyclif, Wycliffe, Wickliffe, or **Wiclif, John** (all: wĭ′klĭf), c.1328–1384, English religious reformer; educ. at Oxford. He boldly asserted that Christ is man's only overlord; that the clergy should own no property; that the scriptures are the supreme authority; that many

Church doctrines (notably transubstantiation) were false. His teachings were spread by his "poor priests" (see LOLLARDRY) and influenced John Huss. He brought about the first translation of the BIBLE into English. Condemned as a heretic in 1380 and 1382, he was not molested.

Wye, river of Wales and England. Flows 130 mi. from Plinlimmon mt., Wales, to the Severn estuary. Noted for its beautiful valley, especially part forming Gloucestershire-Monmouthshire border.

Wyeth, Nathaniel Jarvis, 1802–56, American explorer and trader in Far West. Founded Fort Hall 1834.

Wykeham, William of: see WILLIAM OF WYKEHAM.

Wylie, Elinor (Hoyt), 1885–1928, American poet and novelist. Although she is best known for the exquisite lyricism and subtle irony of her poems (as in *Nets to Catch the Wind,* 1921; *Trivial Breath,* 1928; *Angels and Earthly Creatures,* sonnets, 1929), her four extraordinary novels (*Jennifer Lorn,* 1923; *The Venetian Glass Nephew,* 1925; *The Orphan Angel,* 1926; *Mr. Hodge and Mr. Hazard,* 1928) have won admirers. Her third husband was William Rose Benét.

Wyoming, state (97,914 sq. mi.; pop. 290,529), W U.S.; admitted 1890 as 44th state; cap. CHEYENNE. Other cities are CASPER, LARAMIE. Vast upland crossed by mountain ranges, with river basins and rolling plains. Continental Divide traverses state from NW corner to S central border. E of Divide are Bighorn Mts. and Absaroka Range, W is Teton Range. In NW is Yellowstone Natl. Park. Mountain snows feed many rivers, including the Snake, Yellowstone, and Green. Farming (livestock, horses, grains). Deposits of coal, petroleum, natural gas. Oil refining, beet sugar processing, mfg. on small scale. Popular health resort. Early development linked with fur trade, westward migration. Fur-trading posts were estab. at Fort Laramie and Fort Bridger. Indian wars of 1860s and 1870s failed to stem tide of immigration. Open ranges attracted cattle raisers; cattle rustling and feuds between cattlemen and sheepmen marked late 19th cent. Oil boom began in 1910. Reclamation and conservation have aided state's development.

Wyoming. 1 City (pop. 5,582), SW Ohio, N suburb of Cincinnati. **2** Borough (pop. 4,511), NE Pa., on Susquehanna R. and near Wilkes-Barre. Monument commemorates massacre (1778) of Conn. settlers in Wyoming Valley during Revolution.

Wyoming, University of: see LARAMIE.

Wyoming Valley, NE Pa., on N branch of Susquehanna R.; rich anthracite region. Scene of contest between Conn. and Pa. over conflicting land claims. Conn. settlement after 1754 resulted in Pennamite Wars. Settlers were massacred by John BUTLER in 1778. Land quarrel decided in favor of Pa.; trouble was gradually solved after 1799.

Wyspianski, Stanislaus (vĭspyä'nyŏŏskē), 1869–1907, Polish dramatist. His symbolic dramas include *The Wedding* (1901), *November Night* (1904), and *Meleager* (Eng. tr., 1933).

Wyss, Johann David (yō'hän dä'vēt vēs'), 1743–1818, Swiss author of *The Swiss Family Robinson* (1813). A juvenile classic, it is the story of a shipwrecked family, in the vein of Defoe's *Robinson Crusoe.*

Wythe, George (wĭth), 1726–1806, American jurist, signer of Declaration of Independence. One of the greatest of early U.S. lawyers.

Wytheville (wĭth'vĭl), town (pop. 5,513), SW Va., SW of Roanoke. Trade and mfg. center of agr. area.

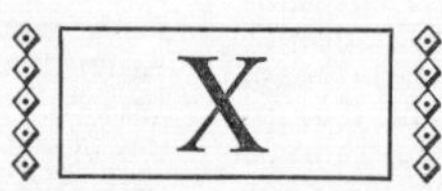

X

Xanthippe (zăntĭ'pē), 5th cent. B.C., wife of Socrates, said in legend to be a shrew. Also Xantippe.

Xauen (hou'ān), town (pop. 14,476), Spanish Morocco. Moslem holy city, founded 15th cent. by Moors expelled from Granada, and long closed to non-Moslems. Known for its crafts.

Xavier, Saint Francis: see FRANCIS XAVIER, SAINT.

Xavier University: see NEW ORLEANS, La.

Xe, chemical symbol of the element XENON.

Xenia (zē'nēŭ), city (pop. 12,877), SW Ohio, SE of Dayton; laid out 1803. Trade center for agr. area with mfg. of rope, twine, furniture, and shoes. NE is WILBERFORCE UNIVERSITY.

xenon (zē'nŏn), rare, chemically inert, gaseous element (symbol = Xe; see also ELEMENT, table). It is heavy, colorless, and odorless and is present in minute quantities in the earth's atmosphere.

Xenophon (zĕ'nŭfŭn), c.430–c.355 B.C., Greek historian, an Athenian. Well-to-do young disciple of Socrates, he joined the Greek force (the Ten Thousand) that supported CYRUS THE YOUNGER of Persia. They fought well at disastrous battle of Cunaxa (401 B.C.) and were left to fight their way back. Xenophon was chosen a leader. He tells the story of this retreat in the most celebrated of his works, the *Anabasis.* Later fought for Sparta against Athens and Thebes at Coronea (394), and the Athenians banished him. Also wrote *Hellenica* and *Memorabilia*. His memoirs on Socrates are invaluable.

Xerxes I (the Great) (zûrk'sēz), d. 465 B.C., king of Persia (485–465 B.C.), son of DARIUS I. After subduing Egypt, he invaded Greece in PERSIAN WARS by building a bridge of boats over the Hellespont. He was victorious at Thermopylae and pillaged Athens, but his fleet was destroyed at Salamis (480 B.C.). He retired to Asia, leaving army under Mardonius, who was defeated at Plataea (479). Xerxes was murdered by one of his soldiers. The Bible has his name as Ahasuerus. He was succeeded by Artaxerxes I.

Ximenes. For Spaniards thus named, see JIMÉNEZ.

Xingu (zĭng"gōō'), river, c.1,200 mi. long, rising in Mato Grosso, Brazil, and flowing N across Pará state into Amazon R. at head of Amazon delta.

Xochimilco (sōchēmēl'kō), city (pop. 14,370), central Mexico. A suburb of Mexico city, it is famous for its canals lined with poplars and flowers. Rafts which Indians had covered with soil and floated on a shallow lake became islands which continue to supply city with vegetables and flowers. Boating on canals is popular diversion.

X ray, Roentgen ray, or **Röntgen ray** (both: rĕnt'gĭn, rŭnt'gĭn, rŭnt'yĭn), invisible radiation of short wave length, discovered 1895 by Roentgen. Commonly produced in tubes called X-ray tubes (see TUBE, VACUUM) in which are sealed two electrodes (the anode and the cathode). When electric current of high voltage is applied, streams of electrons (cathode rays) flow from cathode, pass through tube, and strike plate of wolfram or platinum where X rays are given off. Penetrating ability is increased by high degree of exhaustion of gas from tube and by high voltage. Although X rays can destroy living tissue and cause severe burns, they are of inestimable value in radio-therapy, fluoroscopy, and in making pictures (radiographs) used in diagnosis. Other uses include study of crystals, examination of jewels, and paintings.

xylene (zī'lēn) or **xylol** (–lōl), colorless oily liquid mixture of three benzene hydrocarbons showing isomerism. It is widely used as a solvent.

xylophone (zī'lůfōn) [Gr.,= wood sound], musical instrument having graduated wooden (or sometimes metal) slabs which are struck by the player with small mallets. When tubular resonators are attached to the bars, instrument is called a marimba.

XYZ Affair, name usually given to an incident (1797–98) in Franco-American diplomatic relations. Three-man mission of John Marshall, Elbridge Gerry, and C. C. Pinckney, sent to France to resolve Franco-American difficulties, ran into trouble. Indirect suggestions of loans and bribes to France came through Mme de Villette, a friend of Talleyrand. Negotiations were carried on through her with X (Jean Conrad Hottinguer), Y (a Mr. Bellamy, an American banker in Hamburg), and Z (Lucien Hauteval, like Hottinguer, a Swiss). Proposal that Americans pay Talleyrand £50,000 created uproar in U.S. Mission broke up. Convention of Mortefontaine (Sept. 30, 1800) settled arguments.

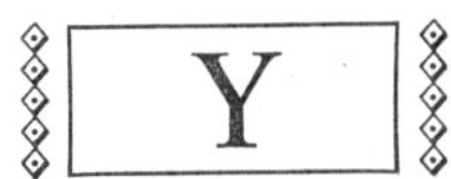

Y, chemical symbol of the element YTTRIUM.

Y–. For Dutch names beginning thus, see IJ–.

Yablonovy Range (yä'blůnůvē), mountain chain, RSFSR, in SE Siberia. Part of watershed between the Arctic and the Pacific, it extends NE from Mongolian border to Olekma R. Rises to 5,280 ft.

Yadkin, river: see PEE DEE, river.

Yahata, Japan: see YAWATA.

Yahweh: see JAHVE.

yak, mammal (genus *Bos* or *Poephagus*) of Tibet and other parts of central Asia. It is larger than most domestic cattle, has curved horns, short legs, high shoulders, and long hair hanging from flanks, legs, and tail. Domesticated yak is a source of meat and milk; it is useful also as a saddle and pack animal.

Yakima (yă'kůmô), city (pop. 38,486), S central Wash., SE of Seattle; settled near here 1861, moved here 1885. Trade center of area yielding vegetables, fruit, sugar beets, grain, and livestock. Canneries, packing plants, flour and lumber mills. City is on the **Yakima,** river rising in Cascade Range and flowing 203 mi. SE to Columbia R. near Kennewick. Supports irrigation and hydroelectric project, begun 1906.

Yakut Autonomous Soviet Socialist Republic (yŭkōōt'), (1,182,300 sq. mi.; pop. c.450,000), RSFSR, in NE Siberia, between Arctic Ocean and Stanovoi Range. Rich natural resources (forests, minerals) are little exploited because of poor transportation. Exports include furs, gold, mammoth ivory. Relatively warm in summer, climate reaches the extreme of cold at VERKHOYANSK in winter. Yakuts, of Turkic linguistic family, comprise 80% of population. The cap., **Yakutsk** (pop. 52,888), is a port on the Lena R.

Yale, Elihu, 1649–1721, English merchant, b.

Boston. Built fortune by private trade in East. Yale Univ. named for him for his financial support.

Yale University, at New Haven, Conn. Chartered 1701, opened 1702 as Collegiate School of Connecticut at Killingworth (now Clinton), moved 1707 to Saybrook (now Old Saybrook), 1716 to New Haven. Name changed 1718 to Yale Col. to honor Elihu YALE, a benefactor. School was sternly Puritan in early years, when such men as Ezra STILES and the elder Timothy DWIGHT were presidents. Special schools were estab.—medicine (1813), divinity (1822), law (1824), Sheffield Scientific School (1861), and fine arts (1869; the first in any U.S. university). Under the younger Timothy DWIGHT as president, name changed to Yale Univ. (1887). It is now nonsectarian. Core is still Yale Col., reorganized 1933 into resident-college system. Women are admitted to graduate and special schools. Yale includes allied Inst. of Human Relations (founded 1929); Peabody Mus. of Natural History; Yale Univ. Press (estab. 1908); art gallery (1832); library, with several notable collections; and observatory (1879), with a branch (Yale-Columbia Southern Station) at Univ. of Witwatersrand, Union of South Africa. Yale-in-China (Ya-li) in Changsha (1902) was much damaged by Japanese in World War II. Yale has traditional sports rivalry with Harvard (boat race since 1852, football game since 1875).

Yalta (yôl'tů, Rus. yäl'tŭ), city (pop. 78,838), S Crimea, RSFSR; a major health resort on the subtropical Black Sea coast. The former imperial palace of LIVADIYA is near by. Here was held the historic **Yalta Conference,** Feb. 4–11, 1945, attended by F. D. Roosevelt, Joseph Stalin, and Winston Churchill, at the end of World War II. Complete text of agreements was published only in 1947. Among chief decisions were: (1) Regarding Germany, renewal of policy of unconditional surrender; four-power occupation of Germany (with France as fourth power). (2) A founding conference of the UNITED NATIONS was to be held in San Francisco; "veto" system of voting was agreed upon for projected Security Council. (3) USSR secretly agreed to enter war against Japan within three months after Germany's surrender and was promised S Sakhalin, Kurile Isls., restoration of Port Arthur and Dairen to status as of 1904 (see LIAOTUNG), and joint Chinese-Soviet administration of Manchurian railroads. These last decisions were later protested by China as an infringement of its sovereignty and were much criticized in the U.S.

Yalu (yä'lo͞o'), river, on Manchuria-Korea border, rising in Changpai mts. and flowing c.500 mi. SW to Bay of Korea near Antung. Frozen Nov.–March.

yam, tropical twining plant of genus *Dioscorea* and its edible starchy, tuberous roots. The roots can be baked, boiled, ground into flour, or fed to livestock. In the S U.S. the SWEET POTATO is often called yam. The decorative cinnamon vine is *Dioscorea batatas.*

Yamagata, Aritomo, Prince (ärē'tōmō yämä'gätä), 1838–1922, Japanese soldier and statesman, chief founder of modern Japanese army. Studied military science in France and Germany. Twice prime minister, but more important as genro (elder statesman).

Yamaguchi (yämä'go͞ochē), commercial city (pop. 97,975), SW Honshu, Japan. Was great castle city from 14th to 16th cent. Site of mission estab. 1550 by St. Francis Xavier.

Yamashita, Tomoyuki (tōmō'yo͞okē yämäsh'tä), 1885–1946, Japanese general. Surrendered in Philippines to Gen. MacArthur (Sept. 2, 1945). Convicted as war criminal, he appealed in vain to U.S. Supreme Court; hanged.

Yamaska (yůmă'sků), river of S Que., Canada, rising near Vt. border and flowing 110 mi. NW and N to St. Lawrence R. at L. St. Peter.

Yancey, William Lowndes, 1814–63, American leader of SECESSION. Congressman from Ala. (1844–46). Wrote Alabama Platform (1848), demanding protection of slavery in territories by Congress. An extreme "fire-eater," he was foremost in the secession movement.

Yangchow or **Yang-chou** (both: yäng'jō'), commercial city (pop. 127,104), cap. of North Kiangsu, China, on Grand Canal. Called Yangiu when Marco Polo was its honorary governor. Formerly called Kiangtu.

Yangku, China: see TAIYÜAN.

Yangtze (yäng'dzŭ'), longest river of China, c.3,430 mi. long. Rises in SW Tsinghai prov., flows past Chungking, Hankow, and Nanking to East China Sea near Shanghai. A major trade artery of central China; navigable for 1,000 mi. by ocean liners. Disastrous floods are rare.

Yankee, term used by Americans generally to refer to native of New England and by non-Americans in reference to any American. Word is probably from Knickerbocker Dutch. Wide usage in American Revolution overcame insulting connotation. In Civil War applied generally to Northerners. Shortened form *Yank* became popular in World War I.

Yankee Doodle, song beginning, "Yankee Doodle went to town, A-riding on a pony," which was especially popular with American troops during the American Revolution and is still included in various song collections. Origin of title, tune, and words is uncertain. It seems probable that the song was first used by the British in derision of the colonial soldiers, and that it was later adopted by the Americans as their favorite marching song.

Yankton, city (pop. 7,709), SE S.Dak., on the Missouri near James R. mouth and SSW of Sioux Falls; settled 1858. Dakota territorial cap. 1861–83. Rail and shipping center in grain and livestock area. Seat of Yankton Col. (coed.; 1881).

Yannina, Greece: see IOANNINA.

Yap (yăp), island group (39 sq. mi.; pop. 2,744), W Pacific, in Caroline Isls. Consists of 14 islands surrounded by coral reef. Site of cable and radio stations. Japanese had air base here in World War II. Micronesian natives use stone money (large disks of aragonite).

Yaphank, village on E central Long Isl., SE N.Y., NE of Patchogue. Camp Upton was U.S. army induction center in both World Wars.

Yaqui Indians (yä'kē), people of Sonora, Mexico, stubbornly resistant to white conquest. Language is of Uto-Aztecan stock; engage in agr. and weaving.

Yarkand (yärkănd'), town (pop. 60,000), SW Sinkiang prov., China, on Yarkand R. and in oasis at edge of Taklamakan desert. Trade center.

Yarmouth, city (pop. 8,106), SW N.S., Canada, on the Atlantic at entrance to Bay of Fundy. Port, industrial and fishing center and summer resort. Visited by Champlain 1604. Received settlers from Yarmouth, Mass., 1759. Great shipbuilding center in days of wooden sailing ships.

Yarmouth, officially **Great Yarmouth,** county borough (pop. 51,105), Norfolk, England; resort and important fishing center. Church of St. Nicholas (12th cent.) is largest parish church in England. Borough figures in Dickens's *David Copperfield.*

Yarmouth. 1 Town (pop. 2,669), SW Maine, NNE of Portland. Includes resort and fishing village of Yarmouth (pop. 2,189) on Casco Bay. **2** Resort town (pop. 3,297), SE Mass., on Cape Cod E of Barnstable.

Yaroslavl (yŭrŭslä'vŭl), city (pop. 298,065), N central European RSFSR, on the Upper Volga. River port and mfg. center (autos, synthetic rubber, asbestos, machinery, textiles). Founded 1024; cap. of a principality after 1218; annexed by Moscow 1463. Was seat of English trading station, where first modern Russian ships were built (1564–65). Has 12th-cent. monastery; several fine 17th-cent. churches; oldest theater in Russia (founded 1747).

Yarrow or **Yarrow Water,** stream of Scotland. Rises near point where counties of Peebles, Selkirk, and Dumfries meet and flows to Ettrick Water, Selkirkshire. Valley is celebrated for its beauty.

yarrow, strong-scented Eurasian perennial. Common yarrow (*Achillea millefolium*), called also milfoil, has long been naturalized in North America. It has a flat-topped cluster of white, pink, or red composite flowers and fine, carrotlike leaves.

Yasnaya Polyana (yäs'nīŭ pŭlyä'nŭ), village near Tula, RSFSR. Here was the estate of Leo Tolstoy.

Yawata (yä"wä'tä) or **Yahata,** city (pop. 167,829), N Kyushu, Japan; island's main industrial center.

yawl, small fore-and-aft rigged sailing ship similar to the cutter, but with added mizzenmast.

Yaxartes, river: see SYR DARYA.

Yazoo (yă'zōō), river formed in W central Miss. by junction of Tallahatchie and Yalobusha rivers. Flows 189 mi. SW to Mississippi R. at Vicksburg.

Yazoo City, city (pop. 9,746), W central Miss., on Yazoo R. Trades, processes cotton.

Yazoo land claims. Ga. legislature of 1796 offered to restore purchase price of land holdings in Yazoo R. region; holdings had been secured through bribery by act of 1795 legislature. Large numbers of investors declined to accept payment and pressed their land claims. Terms of 1802 Ga.–U.S. cession agreement provided that Yazooists might receive 5,000,000 acres or the money received from their sale, an arrangement they rejected. In 1810 the U.S. Supreme Court held land claims to be valid, and speculators later received over $4,000,000 from Congress.

Yb, chemical symbol of the element YTTERBIUM.

Yeadon (yē'dŭn), borough (pop. 11,068), SE Pa., W suburb of Philadelphia.

year: see CALENDAR.

Yeardley, Sir George (yärd'lē), c.1587–1627, British colonial governor of Va. (1618–21, 1626–27). Convened first representative assembly in New World.

yeast, name given to certain microscopic fungi and to commercial preparations of yeast cells or of yeast mixed with a starchy material. True yeasts are unicellular and reproduce chiefly by budding. As chief agents in alcoholic FERMENTATION, yeasts are essential to the making of beer, wine, and industrial alcohol. In breadmaking, yeast acts upon carbohydrates to form carbon dioxide and alcohol, which are driven off in baking; escape of carbon dioxide causes the bread to rise. See *ill.*, p. 813.

Yeats, William Butler (yāts), 1865–1939, Irish poet and dramatist, b. Dublin; considered by many the greatest 20th-cent. poet to write in English. He was attracted by the occult and was concerned with Rosicrucianism and theosophy as well as old Irish legend and Irish patriotism (encouraged by his long-lasting love of Maud Gonne). Long poems in *The Wanderings of Oisin* (1889) were followed by notable poetic dramas—*The Countess Cathleen; Cathleen Ni Houlihan* (1902); *The Land of Heart's Desire* (1904); *Deirdre* (1907)—and Yeats was a towering figure in the Abbey Theatre. The rich symbolism of his lyrics and his narrative poems (e.g., in *The Green Helmet and Other Poems,* 1910; *The Wild Swans at Coole,* 1917) is partly explained by his mystical work in prose, *A Vision* (1926). Clear music unites with cloudy symbolism in his popular collected poems. Awarded 1923 Nobel Prize in Literature.

Yedo, Japan: see TOKYO.

Yehoash: see BLOOMGARDEN, SOLOMON.

Yellow Book, English illustrated quarterly periodical in book form, published in London 1894–97. Enlivened by drawings of Aubrey Beardsley, it put literary emphasis on the bizarre and "art for art's sake." Contributors included Oscar Wilde, Max Beerbohm, Richard Le Gallienne, and W. B. Yeats.

yellow fever, infectious disease caused by virus. In critical stage it is characterized by black vomit. Survivors generally are immune; immunization vaccine exists. In 1900 a commission headed by Walter Reed proved in Havana that the disease is transmitted by bite of mosquito. W. C. Gorgas demonstrated in Panama Canal zone that disease can be eradicated through mosquito control.

Yellowhead Pass, 3,711 ft. high, in Rocky Mts. on Alta.–B.C., Canada, border.

yellow jacket: see WASP.

Yellowknife, town (pop. 2,724), S Mackenzie dist., Northwest Territories, Canada, on N shore of Great Slave L. at mouth of Yellowknife R. Founded 1935 after discovery of gold and silver. Largest town in Territories, trade and transportation center with airport, radio and meteorological stations, and Royal Canadian Mounted Police post.

Yellow River, Chinese *Hwang Ho* or *Huang Ho,* river, c.2,900 mi. long, second longest in China. Rises in Tsinghai prov. and flows to Gulf of Chihli of Yellow Sea. Called "China's Sorrow" because of catastrophic floods.

Yellow Sea, Chinese *Hwang Hai,* arm of the Pacific, between China and Korea.

Yellow Springs, village (pop. 2,896), SW Ohio, S of Springfield. Here is ANTIOCH COLLEGE.

Yellowstone, river, 671 mi. long, rising in NW Wyo. in the Absaroka Range and flowing N into Yellowstone Natl. Park, where it flows through Yellowstone L. (alt. c.7,731 ft.; area 139 sq. mi.), forms great falls, and traverses deep canyon. Enters Mont. and flows NE to the Missouri near old Fort Union, just within N. Dak. Bighorn and Powder rivers among tributaries. Used for irrigation since late 1860s, it has many private developments; public projects at Miles City and Billings; and several U.S. projects in Yellowstone subbasin division of MISSOURI RIVER BASIN PROJECT.

Yellowstone National Park: see NATIONAL PARKS AND MONUMENTS (table).

yellowwood, ornamental leguminous tree (*Cladrastis* LUTEA), native to SE U.S., with panicles of fragrant white flowers. The wood yields a yellow dye.

Yemen (yĕ′mŭn), kingdom (75,000 sq. mi.; pop. c.4,500,000) SW Arabia, on Red Sea; cap. Sana (pop. 28,000). Bounded on N by Saudi Arabia, S by Aden protectorate, and E by Rub al Khali desert. Mountainous except for narrow coastal strip. Coffee, grains, and fruits are raised. Hodeida and Mocha are chief ports. Early historical records indicate an active trade between Yemen and Somali coast of Africa. Later (8th–4th cent.? B.C.) Yemen may have belonged to SHEBA. The Himyaritic dynasty, founded in 1st cent. B.C., adopted Judaism in 4th cent. A.D. Yemen fell to Ethiopians in 525 and to Persians in 570. With acceptance of Islam in A.D. 628, the history of Yemen became that of all Arabia. In 10th cent. a new power arose in Yemen, the Zeidi sect of Islam. The king of Yemen is also the IMAM of the Zeidi line. Zeidi rule was contested by Turkish occupation from 16th–17th cent. and again from 1849 until end of World War I. In 1934 Yemen was briefly conquered by Saudi Arabia, but the occupation was soon ended and the present frontier established. Yemen is a member of the Arab League and in 1947 joined the UN. In 1949–50 most of the Jewish population was evacuated to Israel.

Yenan, China: see SHENSI.

Yenisei or **Enisei** (both: yĕnĭsā′, Rus. yĕnĭsyā′), river, 2,364 mi. long, RSFSR, in central Siberia, rising in E Sayan Mts. and flowing generally N past Krasnoyarsk, Yeniseisk, and Igarka into the Kara Sea. Precipitous in its upper course, it is c.4 mi. wide in its lower section. A canal system links it with the Ob. Navigable for part of the year, it carries lumber, grain, and construction materials.

Yentai, China: see CHEFOO.

yeoman, class in English society. Generally means landowning farmers below the gentry. Under feudal system yeoman had service obligations. Agrarian and Industrial revolutions of 18th cent. took away his land. Workingman without master, he was thought to strengthen English society. Class supplied patriot armies of American Revolution. In military and naval use the term signifies rank or function.

Yeomen of the Guard, bodyguard, now ceremonial in function, of sovereign of England. When originated by Henry VII in 1485, their duties as defenders of king's person were very real. Until 1743 they accompanied king in battle. Sometimes called Beefeaters, they still wear 15th-cent. uniforms.

Yerba Buena Island (yâr′bŏŏ bwā′nŏŏ), 300 acres, W Calif., in San Francisco Bay; midpoint of SAN FRANCISCO-OAKLAND BAY BRIDGE.

yerba mate: see MATE.

Yermak or **Ermak** (yĕrmäk′), d. 1584 or 1585, Russian Cossack leader and conqueror of Siberia. With his small armed band, advancing in river boats, he conquered (1582) the Tatar khanate of SIBIR and turned it over to Tsar Ivan IV.

Yersin, Alexandre (älĕksã′drŭ yĕrsẽ), 1863–1943, French bacteriologist. Discovered PLAGUE bacillus and prepared serum to combat it. Worked on diphtheria antitoxin. Served with Pasteur Inst.

Yesenin or **Esenin, Sergei Aleksandrovich** (sĭrgā′ ŭlyĭksän′drŭvĭch yĭsyā′nĭn), 1895–1925, Russian poet. His lyrics were very popular in the early years of the revolution. Also wrote *Pugachev* (1922), a tragedy in verse. He repudiated the revolution when it turned into dictatorship. In 1922 he married Isadora Duncan but they were soon separated. Died by suicide.

Yevpatoriya, RSFSR: see EUPATORIA.

yew, handsome evergreen tree or shrub of genus *Taxus* with dark green leaves and red berrylike fruits. Since antiquity it has been associated with death and funeral rites. Ground hemlock or Canada yew of Canada and NE U.S. is *Taxus canadensis.*

Yezd (yĕzd), city (pop. 60,066), central Iran; founded c.5th cent. Has large Zoroastrian colony. Produces hand-woven carpets and textiles.

Yezo, Japan: see HOKKAIDO.

Yggdrasill (ĭg′drŭsĭl), in Norse legend, great tree of the world. At its top was an eagle, at bottom a serpent; a squirrel ran between to arouse strife.

Yiddish [Ger. *jüdisch* = Jewish], language spoken by the Jews from Eastern Europe. Descended from the German of the Middle Ages, with many Hebrew words, it has absorbed expressions from whatever country the Jews reside in. The Hebrew characters are used. Hebrew being the language of the learned Jews, Yiddish was long scorned as a medium for authors, and literature in Yiddish did not begin to flourish until the middle of the 19th cent. The father of modern Yiddish literature is MENDELE MOCHER SFORIM. He was followed by the humorist Sholom ALEICHEM and the mystic I. L. PERETZ. Yiddish journalism owes its fullest development to the immigrant Jews in the U.S., where Abraham CAHAN founded the

Jewish *Daily Forward* in 1897. Yiddish drama was born when Goldfadden, the playwright, founded a theater in Odessa in 1878. Ansky (author of *The Dybbuk*) and Singer (author of *Yoshe Kalb*) wrote notable plays in Yiddish.

Yin, dynasty of China: see SHANG.

Yoakum (yō'kŭm), city (pop. 5,231), S Texas, N of Victoria. In tomato-growing area, it processes leather, food, and wood products.

yoga (yō'gŭ) [Sanskrit,= union], mystical system developed in Hinduism, intended primarily to liberate the individual from the illusory world of sense perception. Liberation is difficult and may take several lifetimes. The yogi who believes in pantheism seeks union with the universal soul; the yogi who is atheistic seeks absolute isolation from all other souls and perfect self-knowledge. The ultimate state sought is one of perfect illumination. Yogis use physical disciplines to attain it—purgation, cleanliness, concentration, exercises.

Yoho National Park (yō'hō), 507 sq. mi., SE B.C., Canada, in Rocky Mts. at Alta. border; estab. 1886. Adjoins Banff and Kootenay national parks.

Yokohama (yō"kähä'mä), industrial city (pop. 814,379), central Honshu, Japan; major foreign-trade port on Tokyo Bay. Chief export is silk. Has steel mills, shipyards, oil refineries, and chemical and automobile plants. Visited 1854 by Commodore Perry; opened 1859 to foreign trade. Extensively rebuilt after destruction by 1923 earthquake. Heavily bombed in 1945 during World War II.

Yokosuka (yōkō'so͝okä), city (pop. 252,923), central Honshu, Japan, on Tokyo Bay; major naval base.

Yom Kippur: see ATONEMENT, DAY OF.

Yonkers, residential city (pop. 152,798), SE N.Y., on E bank of Hudson R. and N of Bronx borough of New York city. Mfg. of carpets, elevators, cables, clothing; sugar refining. Site included in land grant made 1646 by Dutch West India Co. to Adriaen Van der Donck. Frederick Philipse built a manor hall of PHILIPSE MANOR here. Seat of BOYCE THOMPSON INSTITUTE FOR PLANT RESEARCH.

Yonne (yôn), department (2,881 sq. mi.; pop. 266,014), N central France, named for a tributary of the Seine; cap. Auxerre.

Yorck von Wartenburg or York von Wartenburg, Johann David Ludwig, Graf (yō'hän dä'vĭt lo͞ot'vĭkh gräf' yôrk' fŭn vär'tŭnbo͝ork), 1759–1830, Prussian field marshal. Commanded Prussian auxiliary corps in Napoleon's campaign of 1812 against Russia. In Dec., 1812, he concluded, on his own responsibility, the Convention of Tauroggen (now Taurage, Lithuania) with the Russians, by which Prussian troops withdrew from the fighting. His action prepared Prussia's declaration of war on Napoleon (1813).

Yoritomo (Yoritomo Minamoto) (yōrē'tōmō mēnä'mōtō), 1147?–1199, Japanese warrior and dictator. Led his clan (Minamoto) to victory over rival Taira clan, 1185. Named SHOGUN 1192 by emperor and became actual ruler of Japan. Estab. system of centralized feudalism.

York, Alvin (Cullum), 1887–, American soldier. In World War I, Sgt. York was hero of an engagement in the Argonne Forest (Oct. 8, 1918).

York, Cardinal: see STUART, HENRY BENEDICT MARIA CLEMENT.

York, Edmund of Langley, duke of, 1341–1402, fifth son of Edward III. Served on various continental expeditions. Regent while Richard II was abroad, he halfheartedly opposed landing of Henry IV in 1399 and then supported him. Royal house of York dates from his creation (1385) as duke of York. His son, **Edward, duke of York,** 1373?–1415, served under Richard II, but finally supported Henry IV. Joined unsuccessful plot to kill Henry IV. Imprisoned (1405), he was later released and served the king.

York, Frederick Augustus, duke of, 1763–1827, second son of George III of England. Commanded (1793–95, 1799) unsuccessful English forces in Flanders. Influential in reforming army abuses.

York, Richard, duke of, 1411–60, English nobleman. Became heir to throne 1447. Struggled unsuccessfully against MARGARET OF ANJOU, whose son's birth (1453) displaced York as heir. Protector during insanity of Henry VI, he resorted to force after king's recovery and thus began Wars of the ROSES. Claimed throne (1460) but was slain in battle of Wakefield. His son seized throne as Edward IV in 1461.

York, Ont.: see TORONTO.

York, England: see YORKSHIRE.

York. 1 Town (pop. 3,256), SW Maine, on the coast NE of Kittery; settled 1624. Stone jail (1653) is historical museum. York is said to have been site of first sawmill (c.1624) and first pile drawbridge (pre-Revolutionary; rebuilt 1933) in U.S. Includes York Harbor and York Beach resorts. **2** City (pop. 6,178), SE Nebr., in prairie region W of Lincoln; agr. trade center. Mfg. of metal castings, bricks, and dairy products. **3** City (pop. 59,953), SE Pa., SSE of Harrisburg; laid out 1741. Farm trade center in Pa. Dutch region with mfg. of machinery, metal products, and cement. Meeting place of Continental Congress 1777–78; occupied by Confederates 1863.

York, Cape, promontory, NW Greenland, in N Baffin Bay, W of Melville Bay. In 1896–97 R. E. Peary discovered noted meteorites here.

York, house of, royal house of England, dating from creation of Edmund of Langley as duke of York in 1385. Claims of his grandson, Richard, duke of York, to the throne against Henry VI, head of the house of LANCASTER, resulted in Wars of the ROSES. Royal members were EDWARD IV, EDWARD V, and RICHARD III. Houses of York and Lancaster were united by marriage of Henry VII (first of Tudor kings) to Elizabeth, daughter of Edward IV.

Yorke Peninsula, South Australia, between Spencer Gulf and Gulf St. Vincent.

Yorker Brethren: see RIVER BRETHREN.

York Factory, fur-trading post, N Man., Canada, at mouth of Hayes R. on Hudson Bay. Fur-trading posts here (first built in late 17th cent.) fought for by England and

France. Present post (built 1788–90) is warehouse of Hudson's Bay Co.

Yorkshire (yôrk'shĭr), **York,** or **Yorks,** county (6,081 sq. mi.; pop. 4,516,362), N England. Divided into three administrative sections: East Riding, cap. Beverley; North Riding, cap. Northallerton; West Riding, cap. Wakefield. Largest English county, it borders on North Sea and extends almost to Irish Sea. Pennine Chain in W rises to 2,600 ft.; E part has fertile Yorkshire plain. West Riding, with rich coal deposits, is part of great industrial area. Hull is one of England's chief ports. There is also much stock raising and agr. Dissolution of over 100 religious institutions by Henry VIII was resisted (1536) in the Pilgrimage of Grace. There are many historic and religious remains. Has many literary associations (e.g., with Cædmon, Laurence Sterne, and the Brontë sisters). County town, **York,** county borough (pop. 105,336), is not included in any of the three ridings. As Eboracum, it was chief station of British province of Roman Empire. Constantine was proclaimed emperor here. A bishop of York is mentioned in 314, and first archbishop was consecrated in 7th cent. Ecclesiastical center of N England, it is second only to Canterbury in Church of England. Was one of most famous European centers of education in 8th cent.; St. Peter's School is one of England's oldest. Cathedral of St. Peter (York Minster) dates from Saxon and Norman period. Other noteworthy buildings include York Castle and palace of archbishops of York. There is varied mfg.

Yorkton, city (pop. 7,074), SE Sask., Canada, on Yorkton R. and NE of Regina. Rail center in E Sask.

Yorktown, historic town (pop. 384), SE Va., on York R. near Chesapeake Bay; settled 1631. Town included in Colonial Natl. Historical Park. YORKTOWN CAMPAIGN brought Revolution to a close. Town besieged and taken by Federals in PENINSULA CAMPAIGN of Civil War (April–May, 1862). Places of interest are customhouse (c.1706), Grace Church (1697), Moore House (terms of Cornwallis's surrender negotiated here), Yorktown Monument.

Yorktown campaign, 1781, closing military operations of American Revolution. After CAROLINA CAMPAIGN Cornwallis retreated into Va., fortified Yorktown, and waited for reinforcements. In August a French fleet under Adm. De Grasse blockaded Chesapeake Bay. By September Washington, aided by French troops under Rochambeau, broke through outer defenses. Cornwallis surrendered Oct. 19, 1781.

York von Wartenburg: see YORCK VON WARTENBURG.

Yosemite National Park: see NATIONAL PARKS AND MONUMENTS (table).

Yoshida, Shigeru (shēgä'rōō yō'shēdä), 1878–, Japanese statesman. Premier 1946–47, 1948–. Under his leadership conservative parties were merged into single Democratic Liberal party, 1948. Signed Japanese peace treaty at San Francisco (1951).

Yoshihito (yōshē'hētō), 1879–1926, emperor of Japan (1912–26). Under reign name of Taisho he succeeded his father, Mutsuhito. Became insane; his son Hirohito was made regent in 1921.

Youghal (yôl), urban district (pop. 4,809), Co. Cork, Ireland. Sir Walter Ralegh, mayor 1588–89, traditionally planted first potato in Ireland here.

Youghiogheny (yŏkŭgā'nē), river rising in Alleghenies near W.Va.–Md. line and flowing c.135 mi. N and NW into Pa. to Monongahela R. at McKeesport.

Young, Art(hur), 1866–1943, American cartoonist, noted for his lively satire and whimsical humor.

Young, Brigham, 1801–77, American leader of Church of Jesus Christ of Latter-Day Saints; perhaps the greatest molder of Mormonism. He led a group to Mormon community at Kirtland, Ohio, became prominent after the persecutions in Mo., and was a leader in the move to Nauvoo, Ill. After Joseph Smith's assassination (1844) he became the dominant figure, led migration West in 1846–47, and directed settlement at Salt Lake City. There he was the guiding figure in building the cooperative theocracy, which prospered greatly. Young headed the church and after creation of U.S. provisional government was territorial governor. In trouble between U.S. and Mormons that led to the military expedition of 1857–58 he avoided an open break with U.S. government. Though he is popularly best known for championing polygamy (he seems to have been married in all to 27 wives), he was actually a stern moralist as well as a brilliant leader. His grandson **Mahonri (Mackintosh) Young** (mŭhŏn'rē), 1877–, is a well-known sculptor.

Young, Denton T. (Cy), 1867–, American baseball pitcher. Won more major-league games (511) than any other pitcher; pitched three no-hitters.

Young, Edward, 1683–1765, English poet and dramatist, known best for *The Complaint; or, Night Thoughts on Life, Death and Immortality* (1742–44), a somber blank-verse poem of the "graveyard school."

Young, Mahonri Mackintosh: see YOUNG, BRIGHAM.

Young, Owen D., 1874–, American corporation official, promoter of **Young Plan,** program for settlement of German REPARATIONS debts after World War I. Adopted by Allied powers in 1930 to supersede DAWES PLAN. Defined German obligations, reduced payments. German depression and Hitler's rise to power made plan inoperative.

Young, Thomas, 1773–1829, English physicist and physician. An authority on VISION and optics he stated the Young-Helmholtz theory of color vision, studied structure of eye, and described astigmatism. He revived the wave theory of LIGHT. He established **Young's modulus,** a number representing (in pounds per square inch or dynes per square centimeter) the ratio of stress to strain for a wire or bar of a given substance.

Younger, Cole (Thomas Coleman Younger), 1844–1916, American desperado. One of band of Jesse JAMES. With two of his brothers, James and Robert, he was captured at Northfield, Minn., in 1876.

Young-Helmholtz theory: see VISION.

Younghusband, Sir Francis (Edward), 1863–

1942, British explorer. After exploring Mongolia (1887) he was sent to Tibet. Forced treaty on Dalai Lama (1904) which opened Tibet to Western trade.

Young Men's Christian Association (Y.M.C.A.), organization seeking to improve conditions and opportunities of young men, founded (1844) in London; U.S. movement begun 1851. Housing facilities, summer camps, and recreational programs are provided; Bible study is emphasized.

Young Plan: see YOUNG, OWEN D.

Young Pretender: see STUART, CHARLES EDWARD.

Young's modulus: see YOUNG, THOMAS.

Youngstown, city (pop. 168,330), NE Ohio, on Mahoning R. near Pa. line; founded 1797. Easy access to coal and iron made Youngstown one of country's largest iron and steel centers. Has mfg. of metal products, rubber tires, and furniture.

Young Turks: see OTTOMAN EMPIRE.

Young Women's Christian Association (Y.W.C.A.), organization designed to promote welfare of women and girls. Founded independently in mid-19th cent. in Britain and U.S., it is now world-wide in scope, the international organization dating from 1894. The most recent U.S. body was formed in 1906.

Ypres (ē'prů), Flemish *Ieper,* town (pop. 17,-073), West Flanders prov., NW Belgium, near French frontier. During Middle Ages, Ypres was a powerful center of the cloth industry, rivaling Ghent and Bruges. Lacking a maritime outlet, it declined in 16th cent. A battleground for centuries, it was center of one of most hotly contested theaters of World War I. In first battle of Ypres (Oct.–Nov., 1914) British and Belgians stopped German thrust toward the Channel ports. In second battle (April–May, 1915) Allied offensive was halted when Germans used poison gas. Third battle (July–Nov., 1917) saw British sacrifice c.400,000 men to push their line 5 mi. E. German assault of April, 1918, failed, and in early Oct., 1918, British began here their victorious march E. Thoroughly devastated, city was rebuilt (e.g., 13th-cent. Gothic cathedral and cloth hall). Outside city walls there are c.40 military cemeteries.

Ypsilanti (ēpsēlän'tē), prominent Greek family of PHANARIOTS. **Constantine Ypsilanti,** 1760–1816, became hospodar of Moldavia (1799) and Walachia (1802) but was deposed by the sultan in 1806 because of his pro-Russian sympathies. He entered Russian service, as did his sons, **Alexander Ypsilanti,** 1792–1828, and **Demetrios Ypsilanti,** 1793–1832. Both played important parts in the Greek War of Independence. Alexander headed the secret patriotic society, Hetairia Philike. In 1821, with Russian support, he raised a revolt at Jassy and proclaimed the independence of Greece. The Greeks in Moldavia and Walachia rallied to him, but the Rumanian population, weary of Phanariot rule, rose against the Greeks and helped the Turks defeat them. Alexander fled to Austria, where he was imprisoned till 1827. Though it failed, the uprising in Moldavia made possible the Greek insurrection in the Peloponnesus, where Demetrios Ypsilanti distinguished himself as a commander against Ibrahim Pasha.

Ypsilanti (ĭpsĭlăn'tē), city (pop. 18,302), SE Mich., on Huron R. and E of Ann Arbor; settled 1823 on sites of Indian village and French trading post (1809–c.1819). Industrial, commercial, and farm trade center with mfg. of metal products. Seat of Michigan State Normal Col. and Cleary Col.

Ysaÿe, Eugène (ēzäē'), 1858–1931, Belgian violinist, conductor, and teacher; one of the greatest violinists of his time. He made his American debut in 1894; conducted the Cincinnati Symphony, 1918–20.

Yser (ēzĕr'), river, 48 mi. long, in French and Belgian Flanders, entering North Sea at Nieuport. In World War I the German drive toward Calais was stopped here after heavy fighting (late 1914).

Yseult (ēsûlt'): see TRISTRAM AND ISOLDE.

Ysleta (ĭslĕ'tů), uninc. town. (pop. 4,782), W Texas, on Rio Grande just below El Paso. Oldest settlement in Texas, founded near mission estab. (1681–82) after Pueblo revolt.

Yssel, Netherlands: see IJSSEL.

ytterbium (ĭtûr'bēům), rare metallic element of rare earths (symbol = Yb; see also ELEMENT, table), found with other elements of the group in various minerals, especially gadolinite.

yttrium (ĭ'trēům), rare metallic element of rare earths (symbol = Y; see also ELEMENT, table), found in gadolinite and certain other minerals.

Yüan (yüän'), dynasty of China, which ruled 1260–1368; part of great empire conquered by MONGOLS. Its founder, KUBLAI KHAN, dealt final blow to Sung dynasty in 1279. Early Yüan period saw development of postal system, improvement of roads and canals, and increase in overland trade with the West. Traditional system of civil service examinations suspended until 1315. The drama (with music) notable in period. Succeeded by Ming dynasty.

Yüan Shih-kai (yüän' shē-kī'), 1859–1916, president of China (1912–16). As high official under Ch'ing dynasty he supported dowager empress Tz'u Hsi against Emperor Kwang Hsü while helping to overthrow the dynasty. Succeeded Sun Yat-sen as president of republic, 1912. Crushed opposition to his dictatorial rule by dissolving parliament, 1914. Declared himself emperor in 1915 but died before enthronement.

Yuba City (yōō'bů), town (pop. 7,861), N central Calif., N of Sacramento. Boomed in gold-rush days, like Marysville across Feather R. Processes fruits (esp. peaches), vegetables, and dairy products.

Yucatan (yōōkůtăn'), Span. *Yucatán,* peninsula, area c.70,000 sq. mi., mostly in SE Mexico, separating the Caribbean from the Gulf of Mexico. Comprises states of Yucatan and Campeche, territory of Quintana Roo, British Honduras, and part of Petén, Guatemala. For the most part, peninsula is low, limestone tableland, with tropical dry and rainy seasons, though cold winds blow from N in winter. Agricultural products include henequen (see SISAL HEMP), tobacco, maize, sugar cane, cotton, coffee. From the forests of Petén, SW Campeche, and British Honduras come logwood, mahogany, dyewood, vanilla. Peninsula had been for centuries seat of MAYA civilization when first white men arrived. Of these men, Cortés in 1519 rescued sole survivor who acted as his interpreter on the epic march across peninsula to Honduras in 1524–25. Before Cortés, Fernández de Córdoba had skirted coast (1517) and Grijalva had explored it (1518). Francisco de Montejo began conquest of the Mayas in 1527, and it was finally completed by his son of the same name (1546).

Yucatan, state (14,868 sq. mi.; pop. 515,256), SE Mexico, occupying most of N half of Yucatan peninsula; cap. MÉRIDA. Became state when Mexico won independence (1821) but seceded (1839–43). Principal product is henequen (see SISAL HEMP).

yucca (yŭk'ů), stiff-leaved stemless or treelike plant native to North and Central America and the West Indies. Yuccas produce a large stalk of white or purplish blossoms pollinated by the yucca moth. The Joshua tree (*Yucca brevifolia*) is a picturesque treelike species of desert regions, the Spanish bayonet (*Y. aloifolia*) is another treelike form, and the Spanish dagger (*Y. gloriosa*) is stemless or has a short trunk.

Yucca House National Monument: see NATIONAL PARKS AND MONUMENTS (table).

Yugoslavia (yo͞o″gōslä'vēů, –slă'vēů), Serbo-Croatian *Jugoslavija,* federal republic (99,079 sq. mi.; pop. 15,751,953), SE Europe, largely in the Balkan Peninsula; cap. Belgrade. It is mostly mountainous, with Julian Alps and KARST in NW and Dinaric Alps running parallel to Adriatic coast (see DALMATIA). TRIGLAV is highest peak. Drained by the Danube and its tributaries, the country is largely agr. There are rich mineral resources (coal, copper, iron, mercury, lead, zinc, bauxite). The Yugoslav [i.e., South Slav] people consists of four groups—Serbs (43%), Croats (34%), Slovenes (7%), Macedonians (7%)—the remainder being Magyars, Italians, and other minorities. As of 1931, 49% of Yugoslavs were Greek Orthodox, 37% Roman Catholic (Croats and Slovenes), 11% Moslem. For history before 1918 and for other geographic data, see articles on the six constituent people's republics estab. under constitution of 1946: SERBIA; CROATIA; SLOVENIA; BOSNIA AND HERCEGOVINA; MACEDONIA; MONTENEGRO. These six regions were included in the "Kingdom of the Serbs, Croats, and Slovenes," proclaimed in 1918 at the end of World War I, with King PETER I of Serbia at its head. Its name was changed to Yugoslavia 1929. Among its internal problems was the opposition between the ruling Serbian element and the Croatian nationalists, who demanded autonomy. King ALEXANDER exercised dictatorship 1929–31 and continued to rule with a firm hand under the parliamentary constitution of 1931. Violence culminated in 1934 in his assassination. Yugoslavia clashed with Italy over FIUME question (settled 1924) and had tense relations with Hungary and Bulgaria, which claimed parts of N Yugoslavia and Macedonia. Yugoslavia joined the LITTLE ENTENTE but in 1939 it drew closer to the Axis powers. The pro-Axis government was overthrown by a military coup d'état in March, 1941, but on April 6 German, Hungarian, Italian, and Bulgarian forces struck against Yugoslavia. King PETER II fled abroad; Serbia and Croatia became puppet states; the rest was partitioned among the aggressors. However, partisan troops under Gen. MIKHAILOVICH and Marshal TITO effectively battled the occupying forces. Civil war between the two rival leaders began 1943; the Communist Tito won out. In 1944 Russian and Allied forces joined with Tito in driving out the Germans. Tito became premier in 1945, deposed the king, and transformed Yugoslavia into a Communist state. The peace treaty with Italy (1947) gave Yugoslavia most of VENEZIA GIULIA. The imprisonment of Archbishop Stepinac of Zagreb led to a break with the Vatican (1946). More serious was Tito's break with the Russian-dominated COMINFORM (1948) and the resulting strain with Yugoslavia's neighbors.

Yukawa, Hideki (hē'dĕkē yo͞okä'wä), 1907–, Japanese physicist. Won 1949 Nobel Prize for predicting existence of MESON.

Yukon (yo͞o'kŏn), territory (205,346 sq. mi.; with water surface 207,076 sq. mi.; pop. 9,096), NW Canada; cap. DAWSON. WHITE HORSE is the only other city, with settlements on the river banks. The N Arctic country is generally uninhabited. The Rockies are E and the Coast Range W, with Mt. LOGAN in the SW corner. The Mackenzie R. (N and E) and the Yukon R. systems drain many snow-fed lakes. Mining (gold, silver, copper, lead, coal), fur trapping, and fishing are important. Air transport supplemented by one railroad, Alaska Highway, and summer river transport. Explored in 1840s by Robert Campbell. Posts were soon estab. The search for gold resulted in the famous KLONDIKE gold rush of 1890s, brought over 30,000 adventurers into region. Unorganized part of Northwest Territories until 1895, it was given separate administration in 1898. Rejected plan of union with B.C. 1937. Governed by a controller appointed by the dominion government, with a popularly-elected council of three members. It elects one member to the dominion Parliament. Controversial Canol oil project, started by U.S. in World War II and abandoned 1945, gained over 100 mi. of needed highway for Yukon.

Yukon, river of Yukon and Alaska, formed by Lewes R. (upper Yukon) and Pelly R. at Fort Selkirk. Flows W and N to Dawson, NW to Fort Yukon, Alaska, then SW and N to Bering Sea through several channels. With headstreams is c.2,000 mi. long, one of longest rivers in North America. White Horse on Lewes R. is head of navigation. Was major route to Klondike gold fields in 1890s. Lower reaches explored 1836–37, 1843 by Russians; upper reaches by Robert Campbell 1843.

Yule: see CHRISTMAS.

Yuma, city (pop. 9,145), extreme SW Ariz., on Colorado R. at mouth of Gila R., in warm, dry area. European settlement came after Fort Yuma was built on W bank (1850). River port and gold-boom town after 1858. Rail and trade center now of Yuma project, reclaimed desert served by ALL-AMERICAN CANAL system; cotton, alfalfa, citrus, truck are raised.

Yuman, linguistic stock of North American Indians. See LANGUAGE (table).

yungas (yōōng'gäs), region of lowland valleys in E piedmont of Andes, extending from Peru-Bolivia border SE into central Bolivia. Assumed economic importance in 20th cent. as major source of rubber and quinine before development of Far Eastern sources.

Yunnan (yün'nän'), province (160,000 sq. mi.; pop. 10,000,000), SW China; cap. Kunming. Bounded on W by Burma. Mainly a high plateau, drained by many rivers, notably the Salween, Mekong, and Yangtze. China's leading tin producer, Yunnan is rich in varied mineral resources. In Second Chino-Japanese War it was major center of Chinese resistance.

Yuste, San Jerónimo de (sän hārō'nēmō dā yōō'stā), former monastery, in Cacéres prov., W Spain, where Emperor Charles V retired (1556) and died (1558).

Yvetot (ēvtō'), town (pop. 5,789), Seine-Inférieure dept., N France, in Normandy. The lords of Yvetot held their tiny seigniory free of duties to any other lord and wore the title king 14th–16th cent., an early instance of French individualism immortalized in Béranger's song *Le Roi d'Yvetot* (Eng. tr. by Thackeray).

Z

Zaandam (zän"däm'), municipality (pop. 41,-698), North Holland prov., Netherlands. Lumber center. Famous for its many windmills. Peter I of Russia stayed at Zaandam 1697 to learn shipbuilding, which at the time flourished there.

Zabrze, Upper Silesia: see HINDENBURG.

Zacatecas (säkätä'käs), state (28,125 sq. mi.; pop. 664,394), N central Mexico; cap. Zacatecas (pop. 21,846). Semiarid plains are good grazing land, and cattle raising is a major occupation. Mining is of greatest importance, however, with copper, iron, zinc, lead, gold, silver, mercury, bismuth, antimony, and salt, all mined in the mountains of the Sierra Madre Occidental. It was important in wars and revolutions of Mexico. Zacatecas and Fresnillo are chief cities.

Zacchaeus or **Zaccheus** (both: zăkē'ůs), publican who climbed a tree to see Jesus. Luke 19.1–10.

Zachariah (ză"kůrī'ů). **1** Died c.749 B.C., king of Israel for six months. Murdered by Shallum. 2 Kings 14.29; 15.8–12. **2** See ZECHARIAH **2.**

Zacharias (zăkůrī'ůs) or **Zachary** (ză'kůrē), **Saint,** pope (741–52), a Calabrian Greek. Strengthened power of the Holy See. Opposed the Lombards and was friendly with Frankish Pepin the Short. Feast: March 22.

Zacharias or **Zachary. 1** Father of John the Baptist. Luke 1.5–80. He and Elizabeth, his wife, are saints of the Roman Catholic Church. Their feast: Nov. 5. **2** For martyred prophet, see ZECHARIAH **2. 3** For book of Old Testament, see ZECHARIAH.

Zadar, Yugoslavia: see ZARA.

Zagazig (zägäzēg'), town (pop. 82,912), N Egypt, in Nile delta; cotton-ginning center. Near by are ruins of ancient Bubastis.

Zaghlul Pasha, Saad (säd' zäglōōl'), c.1850–1927, Egyptian nationalist leader, founder of WAFD party.

Zagorsk (zŭgôrsk'), city (1926 pop. 21,563), RSFSR, NNE of Moscow. Toy mfg. Known as Sergievski Posad before 1917 and as Sergiev until c.1930, it is the site of the Troitsko-Sergievskaya Lavra, one of the most famous Russian monasteries (founded 1340; now a museum). Lavra contains Troitski Cathedral (1427); Uspenski Cathedral (16th cent.; with tomb of Boris Godunov); many treasures of liturgical art.

Zagreb (zä'grĕb), Ger. *Agram,* city (pop. 290,-417), cap. of Croatia, NW Yugoslavia, on the Sava. Has diversified mfg. See of two archbishops—Roman Catholic and Orthodox. University (founded 1669). Unlike most of Croatia, Zagreb escaped Turkish domination in the 16th–17th cent. A fine modern city, it has its historic center in the old Kaptol dist., with the Catholic cathedral (begun 1093) and archiepiscopal palace (18th cent.).

Zagros (zä'grōs), mountain range, W Iran, rising to c.15,000 ft. Its parallel ridges are separated by deep, fertile valleys. Formed boundary between Assyria and Media in ancient times.

Zaharias, Mildred Babe Didrikson: see DIDRIKSON.

Zaharoff, Sir Basil (Basileios Zacharias) (ză'hůrŏf), 1850–1936, international financier and munitions manufacturer, b. Turkey; often called Mystery Man of Europe. Generally considered greatest armament salesman of all time (notably for British firm of Vickers-Armstrong), he played an important though unofficial role in world affairs, especially in World War I. Was knighted by George V.

Zähringen (tsâ'rĭngůn), noble German family. Held extensive fiefs in Baden and W Switzerland until 1218, when main line died out with

Duke Berthold V. His domains passed largely to the related Kyburg and Hapsburg families. A younger branch continued in N Baden. It split (16th cent.) into branches of Baden-Baden and Baden-Durlach, reunited 1771, and ruled grand duchy of Baden 1806–1918.

zaibatsu (zī'bätsōō) [Jap.,= money clique], great family trusts of modern Japan. Leading zaibatsu are Mitsui, Mitsubishi, Sumitomo, and Yasuda. Dominated Japanese economy after Meiji restoration (1868), winning privileged position through financial aid to new imperial government. Vitally influenced chief political parties. Their breakup was an announced aim of Allied occupation after World War II.

Zaïmis, Alexander (zä'ēmēs), 1855–1936, Greek statesman. Six times premier between 1897 and 1928; high commissioner in Crete 1906–11; president of Greece 1929–35. In World War I he advocated "armed neutrality" but did not interfere with Allied landing at Salonica and made way for VENIZELOS on King Constantine's abdication. His presidency was marked by struggles between royalists and republicans (culminating in Venizelist uprising of 1935) and ended with restoration of King George II. Zaïmis died in exile at Vienna. He was famous for his cautious inscrutability.

Zama (zā'mů), anc. town, N coast of Africa, in present Algeria. Scipio Africanus Major defeated Hannibal at or near Zama (202 B.C.), but there were several towns named Zama.

Zambezi (zămbē'zē), river, c.1,600 mi. long, in S central and SE Africa. Rises in Northern Rhodesia, flows generally E (forming boundary between Northern Rhodesia and Southern Rhodesia), enters Mozambique, and empties into Mozambique Channel of Indian Ocean. Broken by VICTORIA FALLS.

Zamboanga (säm"bōäng'gä), city (pop. 103,317), SW Mindanao, P.I. Includes Basilan isl. Exports copra, coconuts, timber, and rubber. Japanese stronghold in World War II until taken by U.S. forces, March, 1945.

Zamojski or **Zamoyski, Jan** (yän' zämoi'skē), 1541–1605, Polish chancellor under Stephen Bathory and Sigismund III. An admirer of the constitutional principles of republican Rome, he used his tremendous influence to restrict the royal power and made POLAND into a royal republic. Held military commands under Bathory.

Zamora (thämō'rä), city (pop. 29,036), cap. of Zamora prov., NW Spain, in Leon, on Duero R. Has Romanesque cathedral, medieval fortifications.

Zamosc, Pol. *Zamość* (zä'môshch), town (pop. 20,899), SE Poland. Founded 1579 by Jan Zamojski, who also estab. a university here, it was reconstructed 1937 according to original plans.

Zampieri, Domenico: see DOMENICHINO.

Zanesville, city (pop. 40,517), E central Ohio, E of Columbus and at junction of Muskingum R. and Licking R.; platted 1799. Trade and industrial center with mfg. of glass, tile, pottery, and electrical apparatus. State cap. 1810–12. Has art institute.

Zangwill, Israel, 1864–1926, English Jewish author of *The Melting Pot* (1914); a Zionist.

Zante (zăn'tē), Gr. *Zakynthos,* island (157 sq. mi.; pop. 41,154), Greece, in Ionian Sea, one of IONIAN ISLANDS; cap. Zante (pop. 11,315). Produces fruit, wine, olive oil, wheat. Sheep and goat raising; fishing.

Zanzibar (zăn'zībär), British protectorate (1,020 sq. mi.; pop. 264,236), off the coast of Tanganyika, E Africa. Comprises two islands of coral origin, Zanzibar (640 sq. mi.; pop. 148,000) and PEMBA. Protectorate is world's leading producer of cloves. In early Moslem era, rival Arab and Persian sultanates were estab. here. In 1503 the Portuguese gained control and used Zanzibar as base for territorial gains in E Africa. In 1652 the islands fell to Oman (or Muscat) Arabs, who pushed deep into Africa in their quest for slaves, gold, and ivory. Declared independent of Oman in 1856, Zanzibar became a British protectorate in 1890. Britain satisfied Germany's claim to the islands by ceding Helgoland. Zanzibar city (pop. 45,275), cap. of protectorate, is on Zanzibar island.

Zapata, Emiliano (āmēlyä'nō säpä'tä), c.1879–1919, Mexican revolutionist, b. Morelos, of almost pure Indian blood. With army of Indians recruited from plantations and villages he led the revolution in S after 1910 and occupied Mexico city three times in 1914–15 (once with Villa). Considered a bandit by opponents, he was a savior and hero to Indians, who embraced his agrarian movement, called *zapatismo.* He was treacherously killed by emissary of Carranza.

Zapolya (zä'pôlyŏ), noble Hungarian family. **Stephen Zapolya,** d. 1499, palatine of Hungary (1492–99), successfully fought the Turks and, after conquering Austria for King Matthias Corvinus, was appointed its governor (1485). For his son, **John Zapolya,** and his grandson **John Sigismund Zapolya,** see JOHN I and JOHN II, kings of Hungary.

Zaporozhe (zäpůrô'zhē), city (pop. 289,188), S Ukraine, on the Dnieper. Industrial center (steel mills, coking and machinery plants, aluminum and magnesium works). Site of DNEPROGES dam. Suffered heavily in World War II. Khortitsa isl. in the river here was hq. of **Zaporozhe Cossacks** (16th–18th cent.; see COSSACKS). When they settled here, S Ukraine nominally belonged to Polish-Lithuanian kingdom, but they were allowed self-government in exchange for defending border. Polish encroachments and persecution of Greek Orthodox faith resulted in Cossack uprising (1648) and transfer of their allegiance to Russia (1654). Russia got left bank of the Dnieper and Kiev from Poland (1667). Cossack privileges were curtailed after MAZEPPA rebellion; abolished 1775.

Zapotec (sä'půtěk), Indian people of Mexico, primarily S Oaxaca and Isthmus of Tehuantepec. Zapotec languages are a separate linguistic family. Early Zapotec were sedentary agriculturists, city-dwellers. Highly developed civilization flourished at Monte Albán possibly more than 2,000 years ago. Their great religious center was Mitla. Had strong cultural affinity with the Maya of Old Empire and, particularly after c.1300, with the Toltec.

Zara (zä'rů), Serbo-Croatian *Zadar,* city (pop. 14,847), Croatia, NW Yugoslavia, in Dalmatia; an Adriatic port. Roman Catholic archiepiscopal see. Dating from Roman times, it fell to Venice in 1000. Zara having been seized by the Hungarians, the doge Enrico Dandolo of Venice persuaded the leaders of the Fourth Crusade to reconquer the city for Venice. The Crusaders took and sacked the city (1202), thus calling on themselves papal condemnation. Passing from Venice to Austria in 1797, Zara was the cap. of Austrian Dalmatia 1815–1918; passed to Italy 1919; to Yugoslavia 1945 (confirmed by treaty, 1947). Has several medieval churches.

Zaragoza, Spain: see SARAGOSSA.

Zarathustra: see ZOROASTER.

Zealand (zē'lůnd), Dan. *Sjælland,* Ger. *Seeland,* largest island (2,709 sq. mi.; pop. 1,482,978) of Denmark, between Kattegat and Baltic Sea, separated from Sweden by the Oresund. Chief cities: Copenhagen, Roskilde, Elsinore. Agr., dairying, fishing.

Zealots (zĕ'lůts), Jewish faction (c.37 B.C.–A.D. 70), created primarily to resist idolatrous practices. In A.D. c.6 a Roman attempt to take a census touched off a revolt of the Zealots. A period of sporadic violence ended with Roman destruction of Jerusalem (A.D. 70). The Zealots then disappeared as the Jews were dispersed from Palestine.

Zebadiah (zĕ"bůdī'ů), ally of David. 1 Chron. 12.7.

Zebedee (zĕ'bůdē), father of St. James the Greater and St. John. Mat. 4.21; 20.20; 27.56; Mark 15.40.

zebra, African animal of horse genus, *Equus.* Its form is like that of a small horse with slender legs and small hoofs. Stripes vary with species in color (black, white, brown), width, and pattern. Zebra is an example of protective coloration. It is threatened with extinction.

zebu (zē'bū), domestic cattle (*Bos indicus*) of parts of E Asia, India, Africa. It is usually fawn, gray, black, or bay and is recognizable by the large fatty lump (sometimes two lumps) over the withers. Introduced into U.S. in mid-19th cent. and again in early 20th cent., it has interbred with cattle in Gulf states.

Zebulun (zĕ'būlůn, zēbū'lůn), son of Jacob and ancestor of one of the 12 tribes of Israel. Tribe settled in N Palestine. Gen. 30.20; 46.14; Num. 26.26; Deut. 33.19,20; Joshua 19.10; Judges 5.14,18. Zabulon. Mat. 4.13,-15; Rev. 7.8.

Zechariah (zĕ'kůrī'ů). **1** Prophet and author of the book of Zechariah. **2** Prophet who was stoned to death for denouncing idolatry. 2 Chron. 24.15–22. In Mat. 23.35 and Luke 11.51 it is apparently this Zechariah (NT Zacharias) to whom Jesus referred. Zacharias, Zachariah, and Zachary are forms of Zechariah.

Zechariah or **Zacharias** (ză"kůrī'ůs), book of Old Testament. The prophet urged restoration of the Temple. Book contains: visions of a Messianic kingdom; a sermon on the observance of the Law; prophecies regarding the redemption of Jerusalem.

Zedekiah (zĕ"důkī'ů), d. after 586 B.C., last king of Judah (c.595–586 B.C.). A puppet of Nebuchadnezzar, he made an alliance with Egypt despite warnings of JEREMIAH. Nebuchadnezzar's armies came to Palestine and destroyed Judah. Zedekiah was carried into captivity with his people. 2 Kings 24.17–25.7; 1 Chron. 3.15; 2 Chron. 36.10–13; Jer. 38; 39; 52.

Zeebrugge (zā'brŭ"gů), outer port of Bruges, West Flanders prov., Belgium, on North Sea; part of Bruges commune. Was developed c.1900 to replace silted-up port of Bruges, with which it is linked by a 9-mi. canal. Was a German submarine base in World War I until April, 1918, when British blocked harbor entrance by sinking three cruisers.

Zeeland, Paul van: see VAN ZEELAND, PAUL.

Zeeland (zē'lůnd, Dutch zā'länt), province (651 sq. mi.; pop. 260,800), SW Netherlands; cap. Middelburg. Includes WALCHEREN, N and S BEVELAND, and other islands at mouth of Scheldt estuary on North Sea. Much of the land is below sea level, protected by dikes. Agr., dairying, fishing. Was part of HOLLAND from 10th cent. Later became separate county but continued to be ruled by counts of Holland. Joined Union of Utrecht 1579.

Zeeman, Pieter (pē'tůr zā'män), 1865–1943, Dutch physicist. Shared 1902 Nobel Prize. Discovered **Zeeman effect,** produced on spectrum of a beam of light as a result of its passage through magnetic field; each spectrum line is split into two or more lines.

Zeiss, Carl (zīs, Ger. kärl' tsīs'), 1816–88, German manufacturer of optical instruments. In 1846 he founded at Jena a factory that achieved world fame after Zeiss became partner (1866) of Ernst Abbe.

Zelaya, José Santos (hōsā' sän'tōs sälä'yä), 1853–1919, president of Nicaragua (1894–1909). He developed the country materially but drained its resources for his own profit. He seized MOSQUITO COAST from British (1894); attempted to reestab. CENTRAL AMERICAN FEDERATION with himself as head. Foreign opposition to his dictatorship led to Washington Conference of 1907 and establishment of Central American Court of Justice. U.S. cruisers aided rebel forces in his overthrow.

Zell am See (tsĕl' äm zā'), mountain resort (pop. 6,320), Salzburg, W central Austria, on the Zellersee.

Zelotes (zēlō'tēz) [Gr.,= zealot], name of St. Simon. See also ZEALOTS.

zemstvo (zĕmst'vō), Russia local assembly which functioned as a body of provincial self-government (1864–1917). Each county (after 1870, also each town) elected a zemstvo, which in turn elected a provincial assembly and executive council. Although the electoral system favored the landowners, the zemstvos were strongholds of liberalism and accomplished much progress in education and public health.

Zen Buddhism, Buddhist sect in Japan. Originated in India as Dhyana school founded by semilegendary Boddhidarma (fl. 516–534?). Later entered China as Chan school. Adopted in Japan in 14th cent. where its rigid discipline and utter scorn for metaphysical subtleties won special support of the samurai.

Zend: see ZOROASTRIANISM.

Zenger, John Peter (zĕng'ůr), 1697–1746,

American journalist, b. Germany. His acquittal in libel trial helped further freedom of press in America.

Zeno (zē′nō), d. 491, Roman emperor of the East (474–91). During his reign concessions were made to GAISERIC in Africa and to ODOACER in Italy. He freed the East from the raids of the Ostrogoths by encouraging THEODORIC THE GREAT to invade Italy (488).

Zenobia (zĭnō′bēů), d. after A.D. 272, queen of PALMYRA. After the murder of her husband, Septimius Odenathus, she ruled for her son, increasing the extent and power of Palmyra. Her ambition brought conflict with Rome. Aurelian took Palmyra (272) and carried the proud, beautiful queen as captive to grace his triumph in Rome. She later lived on a Roman pension.

Zeno of Citium (zē′nō, sĭ′shēům), c.336–c.264 B.C., Greek philosopher, founder of STOICISM (a name derived from Zeno's teaching in the Painted Porch at Athens [Stoa Poecile]).

Zeno of Elea (ē′lēů), c.490–c.430 B.C., Greek philosopher of the Eleatic school; follower of Parmenides.

Zenta, Yugoslavia: see SENTA.

Zephaniah (zĕ″fůnī′ů) or Sophonias (sōfōnī′ůs), book of Old Testament, named for prophet contemporary with Jeremiah. Book denounces Judah for its idolatry and wealth; ends with a prediction of salvation and the return from captivity of a remnant of Israel.

Zephyr, Greek personification of westerly winds. He had mythical role of gentle peacemaker.

Zeppelin, Ferdinand, Graf von (zĕ′půlĭn), 1838–1917, German army officer. Invented and built first rigid AIRSHIP in 1900.

Zermatt (tsĕrmät′), Alpine resort, Valais canton, Switzerland, facing the Matterhorn.

zero, digit that signifies nothing; symbol = 0. Its introduction was inestimably important in development of practical number system. Arabs probably obtained it from Hindus and passed it on to Europe in latter part of Middle Ages. Zero is used to indicate the position on a scale of integers between +1 and −1; it is used in this sense on centigrade and Fahrenheit temperature scales. Absolute zero is the theoretically lowest possible temperature; i.e., temperature at which no heat is present. Zero added to or subtracted from any number leaves the number unchanged; any number multiplied by zero gives zero; zero multiplied by or divided by any number (other than zero) is zero; there is no number which is the value of a number divided by zero.

Zeromski, Stephen (zhĕrôm′skē), 1864–1925, Polish author. Wrote *Ashes* (1904; Eng. tr., 1928), a novel of the Napoleonic period; *Faithful River* (1912), a story of the 1863 uprising.

Zerubbabel (zērůb′ůbůl), fl. 520 B.C., prince of the house of David, governor of Jerusalem. Under the encouragement of Haggai and Zechariah, he led in the rebuilding of the Temple. Ezra 2.2; 3.2,8; Hag. 1–2; Zech. 4.9,10. Zorobabel: Mat. 1.12,13; Luke 3.27.

Zetkin, Klara (klä′rä tsĕt′kēn), 1857–1933, German Communist leader; member of the Reichstag 1919–32.

Zetland, Scotland: see SHETLAND.

Zeus (zōōs), in Greek religion, supreme god; son of Cronus and Rhea and husband of his sister Hera. In the battle called Titanomachy Zeus led successful revolt against Cronus. Then he and his brothers divided up the universe, Poseidon getting the sea, Hades the underworld, and Zeus heaven and earth. Many local goddesses, mortal women, and nymphs, as well as Hera, bore him children; among his children were Aphrodite, Artemis, Hermes, Apollo, and Athena (she sprang from his brow). The name Zeus means "sky." As weather-god he had attributes of thunder and lightning, with which he exercised authority, and rain, with which he made earth fertile. He was father-god, the symbol of power and law, who enforced morals and punished those who defied him. He ruled in patriarchal majesty in his court on Mt. Olympus. Romans equated him with Jupiter or Jove.

Zeuxis (zūk′sĭs), fl. 5th cent. B.C., Greek painter. Helped develop technique of light and shadow.

Zhdanov, Andrei Aleksandrovich (ŭndrā′ ŭlyĭksän′drůvĭch zhdä′nôf), 1896–1948, Russian Communist leader; member of Politburo 1939–48. Held rank of general in World War II. Delivered important party pronouncements in post-war period (notably against cosmopolitanism in art, 1946). Organized Cominform (1947).

Zhdanov, city (pop. 222,427), SE Ukraine; a port on the Sea of Azov. Steel, machinery, and chemical mfg. Called Mariupol until 1948.

Zhitomir (zhĭtô′mēr), city (pop. 95,090), Ukraine, in Volhynia. Communications, lumber, and grain center. During German occupation (1941–43) in World War II its Jewish population (40% of total) was virtually exterminated.

Zhukov, Georgi Konstantinovich (gēôr′gē kŭnstůntyē′nůvĭch zhōō′kôf), 1896?–, Russian field marshal in World War II. Took prominent part in battle of Stalingrad, relief of Leningrad, capture of Berlin. Became deputy defense minister 1953.

Zhukovsky, Vasily Andreyevich (vůsē′lyē ŭndrä′ůvĭch zhōōkôf′skē), 1783–1852, Russian poet. Author of fine lyrics and odes. Translated English, French, and German poets.

Zia (zē′ů), Indian pueblo village (1948 pop. 269), central N.Mex. NW of Albuquerque. Keresan language. Grain and chili growing; pottery making. Mission of Nuestra Señora de la Asunción was built 1692. Annual fiesta.

Ziegfeld, Florenz (flô′rünz zēg′fēld), 1869–1932, American theatrical producer. Productions included his annual *Ziegfeld Follies* (an elaborate revue), *Sally,* and *Show Boat.*

Zieten, Hans Joachim von (häns′ yōä′khĭm fŭn tsē′tůn), 1699–1786, Prussian general of cavalry under Frederick II.

Ziklag (zĭ′klăg), place of anc. Palestine, probably S of Beersheba. David lived here while hiding from Saul.

Zillebeke (zĭ′lůbā″ků), village (pop. 1,644), West Flanders prov., NW Belgium, near Ypres. Scene of severe fighting in World War I.

Zilpah (zĭl′pŭ), Leah's maid, mother of two of Jacob's sons, Gad and Asher. Gen. 30.9–13.

Zimbabwe (zĭmbäb′wā) [Bantu,= stone houses], ruined city, Southern Rhodesia. Discovered 1871 by white explorers. Identified by some with the biblical Ophir. Ruins include a massive wall, a "temple," and a citadel.

Zimri (zĭm′rī), d. c.885 B.C., king of Israel for seven days. He murdered Elah for the throne but was deposed by Omri. Zimri set fire to the palace, destroying himself with it. I Kings 16.8–19.

Zin, wilderness through which the Hebrews wandered, probably S of the Dead Sea.

zinc, silvery, bluish-white, metallic element (symbol = Zn; see also ELEMENT, table). Brittle and crystalline at ordinary temperatures, it can be rolled into sheets when heated to 110°–150° C. It forms a number of compounds. Metal is used in alloys. Iron is galvanized by dipping it into molten zinc or coating it by electroplating. Zinc is often used for negative plates in electric cells. Zinc ores are widely and abundantly distributed.

zinc white, a white powder, zinc oxide. It is used as a paint pigment; in medicinal ointments; as filler in rubber goods, linoleum, oilcloth, etc.; in making white rubber goods and white glass.

zinnia, coarse, annual flowering plant of genus *Zinnia,* chiefly native to Mexico. Called also youth-and-old-age, it is popular in gardens and for cutting for its variety of flower forms of vivid and pastel colors.

Zinoviev, Grigori Evseyevich (grĭgô′rē yĭfsyā′ŭvĭch zēnô′vēĕf), 1883–1936, Russian Communist leader. Member of Politburo from 1918; president of the Comintern from 1919. After Lenin's death he at first cooperated with Stalin, but in 1925 he joined with TROTSKY in opposition. He was expelled from the party in 1927; though readmitted in 1928, he lost his influence. Implicated in the murder of Kirov, he was publicly tried in 1936, confessed himself guilty of all charges, and was executed. The **Zinoviev letter,** published 1924 by several English newspapers, purported to be a letter of secret instructions for a Communist uprising in England. Though later proved a forgery, it helped defeat the Labour party in 1924.

Zinsseer, Hans (zĭn′sŭr), 1878–1940, American bacteriologist, authority on typhus. Author of *Rats, Lice, and History* (1935) and medical texts.

Zinzendorf, Nikolaus Ludwig, Graf von (zĭn′zŭndôrf; Ger. tsĭn′tsŭndôrf), 1700–1760, bishop of refounded Moravian Church. He estab. (1722) Moravian colony called Herrnhut on his estate in Saxony and was forced into exile. Traveled widely in behalf of church, of which he became bishop in 1737. In America (1741–43) he was responsible for many Moravian settlements in E Pa.

Zion (zī′ŭn) or **Sion** (sī′ŭn), part of Jerusalem, defined in Bible as City of David. 2 Sam. 5.7. Tradition names SW hill of city as Zion. Name is symbolic of Jerusalem, of the Promised Land, of the Messianic hope of Israel (hence the term *Zionism*), and, among Christians, of heaven and the hoped-for realm of religion on earth.

Zion, city (pop. 8,950), extreme NE Ill., on L. Michigan and N of Chicago. Founded 1901 by J. A. DOWIE of Christian Catholic Apostolic Church; had theocratic government until 1935. Annual Passion Play. Mfg. of lace and food products.

Zionism, movement for reconstituting a Jewish nation, largely theoretical until Theodor HERZL called the first World Zionist Congress (Basel, 1897), which set up Zionist organizations in countries with large Jewish populations. Among great leaders as the movement gained strength were Max Nordau and Chaim Weizmann. The aspiration for Palestine grew promising with the 1917 Balfour Declaration (see BALFOUR, ARTHUR JAMES), which promised to help establish a home for the Jewish people there; in 1923 Great Britain was given a mandate of Palestine. Jewish colonization vastly increased (see PALESTINE for the period up to 1945), but then the British restricted immigration. After World War II, the suffering of the European Jews demanded the opening of a refuge. The majority of the Zionists reluctantly accepted the United Nations plan to partition Palestine (see ISRAEL). After the Jewish state was proclaimed (May 14, 1948), the World Zionist Congress was separated from the Israeli government.

Zionites: see CHRISTIAN CATHOLIC APOSTOLIC CHURCH IN ZION.

Zion National Park and **Zion National Monument:** see NATIONAL PARKS AND MONUMENTS (table).

Zipporah (zĭ′pŭrŭ), daughter of Jethro and wife of Moses. Ex. 2.16–22; 4.18–26; 18.1–6.

zirconium (zŭrkō′nēŭm), metallic element (symbol = Zr; see also ELEMENT, table). It appears as a black, amorphous powder or a gray crystalline solid. The oxide, resistant to extreme heat, is used for laboratory utensils. Metal is used in alloys; when added to steel it acts as a purifying agent, removing deleterious substances.

Zistersdorf (tsĭs′dŭrsdôrf″), town (pop. 3,044), Lower Austria, NNE of Vienna. Has large oil field (developed mainly in World War II). Much equipment was removed by Russian authorities after 1945.

Zita (zē′tŭ), 1892–, empress of Austria, queen of Hungary (1916–18); consort of Charles I; daughter of Duke Robert of Parma. Was blamed for Charles's secret correspondence with her brother, SIXTUS OF BOURBON-PARMA, and his later attempts to regain the Hungarian throne. Brought up her family in Belgium; lived in U.S. and Canada 1940–49. Her son, Archduke Otto, became Hapsburg pretender.

zither: see STRINGED INSTRUMENTS.

Zizka, John (zĭs′kŭ), Czech *Jan Žižka,* d. 1424, Czech soldier. Took command of Hussite forces 1420 (see HUSSITE WARS). Though totally blind after 1421, he gained brilliant victories over the Catholics. Originally belonging to the radical TABORITES, he founded (1423) the more moderate "Union" but continued to oppose the Utraquist wing of Hussites. A bold military genius, he anticipated modern tank warfare by his use of artillery on armored wagons.

Zlatoust (zlŭtŭōōst′), city (pop. 99,272), RSFSR, in S Urals. Metallurgical center.

Zlin (zlēn), city (pop. 45,737), Moravia, Czechoslovakia; renamed Gottwaldov after 1948. The center of the Czech shoe industry (now nationalized), it was developed as a model company town by the Bata family of shoe manufacturers.

Zn, chemical symbol of the element ZINC.

Zoar (zō'ůr), the one of the Cities of the Plain (see SODOM) to escape destruction. Lot and his daughters took refuge there. Also called Bela.

Zoar (zôr, zō'ůr), village (pop. c.200), E central Ohio, on the Tuscarawas river, near New Philadelphia. Formed by a group of Separatists who fled Germany in 1817, under J. M. Bimeler. A communistic system was established, and the commune flourished until after Bimeler's death. The communistic mode of life was abandoned in 1898.

zodiac (zō'dēăk), in astronomy, imaginary zone in sky, extending c.8° on each side of ECLIPTIC. Stars in zone are arranged in 12 constellations, each with a corresponding sign. In order eastward from vernal EQUINOX (point from which positions are calculated), these are:

Aries (Ram) ♈
Taurus (Bull) ♉
Gemini (Twins) ♊
Cancer (Crab) ♋
Leo (Lion) ♌
Virgo (Virgin) ♍
Libra (Balance) ♎
Scorpio (Scorpion) ♏
Sagittarius (Archer) ♐
Capricornus (Goat) ♑
Aquarius (Water-Bearer) ♒
Pisces (Fishes) ♓

First six lie north of celestial equator; others, south. Because of PRECESSION OF THE EQUINOXES, in 2,000 years each sign has moved 30° and now is in constellation W of the one to which it corresponds in theory.

Zoë (zō'ē), d. 1050, Byzantine empress, daughter of Constantine VIII. Ruled jointly with her first husband, Romanus III (murdered 1034); her second husband, Michael IV (who presumably helped her murder Romanus and who, though 30 years her junior, died 1041); Michael's nephew, Michael V (who had her briefly exiled in 1042 but whom she deposed and had blinded soon afterward); and after 1042, with her third husband, Constantine IX, and her sister, Theodora (both succeeded in surviving her). The threesome rule was remarkable for its corruption and vice even by Byzantine standards. In 1042 began the final schism between East and West (see LEO IX, pope).

Zog (zôg), 1895–, king of Albania; originally Ahmed Zogu. Premier 1922–24; dictator after 1925; proclaimed himself king 1928. In exchange for Italian loans, he gave Italy ever-increasing rights over Albania. In April, 1939, Italian troops occupied Albania and Zog fled abroad. He had married the Hungarian countess Geraldine Apponyi in 1938.

Zola, Émile (āmēl' zōlä'), 1840–1902, French novelist, leading exponent of naturalism. He wrote "scientific" novels in which characters are controlled by heredity and environment, as in his 20-vol. series *Les Rougon-Macquart* (1871–93), including *L'Assommoir* (1877; Eng. tr., *The Dram-Shop*), *Nana* (1880), and *Germinal* (1885). Anticlerical and an ardent social reformer, he took a strong stand in the DREYFUS AFFAIR with *J'accuse* (1898). Prosecuted for libel, he escaped to England.

Zollverein (tsôl'fůrīn) [Ger.,= customs union], customs union among states of 19th-cent. Germany; a major step toward German political union. Began 1818 with abolition of internal tariff barriers in Prussia; grew under Prussian leadership, absorbing other regional tariff unions; reorganized 1867 with its own constitution and parliament. Its regulations were taken over by German Empire 1871. Last to join imperial customs area were the Hanseatic cities Hamburg and Bremen (1888).

zone, in geography, an area with a certain physical unity distinguishing it from other areas. Parmenides (5th cent. B.C.) probably first divided the earth into five climatic zones —a torrid or tropical zone, two temperate zones, and two frigid or arctic zones—a classification still in use. Some modern geographers have used other bases for zoning.

zoological garden, public or private park where living animals and birds are exhibited and studied. Menageries and aviaries of China, Egypt, and Rome were famous in ancient times. Medieval rulers had private menageries, some of which later formed nucleus of public exhibits. Nearly all large cities now have zoological reserves.

zoology, branch of BIOLOGY concerned with study of animal life. Early classification systems included Aristotle's; most systems were based on external resemblances or similarity of environment. Binomial nomenclature system, commonly attributed to Linnaeus and to which John Ray earlier contributed, designates each plant or animal by two Latin names indicating genus and species. Scope of zoology was expanded by study of embryology, internal morphology and physiology, and by use of microscope and experimental method. Modern zoology has been marked by progress especially in genetics, cytology, physiology, and biochemistry.

Zorach, William (zŏr'äk), 1887–, American sculptor, b. Lithuania. His *Spirit of the Dance,* a characteristic kneeling figure (cast in aluminum), is in Radio City Music Hall, New York city.

Zorn, Anders (Leonhard) (än'důrs lā'o͞onärd sôrn'), 1860–1920, Swedish painter and etcher. Worked in London, Paris, and Mora, Sweden. Excelled in figure painting and portraits.

Zoroaster (zō"rōă'stůr), Gr. *Zarathushtra* or *Zarathustra,* 660?–583? B.C. (some say c.570?–c.500 B.C.), Persian religious leader, founder of **Zoroastrianism,** which has *Zend Avesta* as its scripture. Originally this was apparently a reformed type of Persian nature worship, but dualism was strong. Ahura Mazdah (also Ormazd) headed the gods of goodness (Amesha Spentas) and Ahriman (also Angra Mainyu) headed the gods of evil (daevas). War between these forces is the motive power of the universe, in which good will finally triumph. Much attention was given to purification rites. The religion triumphed under the Achaemenidae, but was disrupted by Alexander the Great's conquest; revived under the Sassanidae. Gave rise to Mithraism. Ghebers in Iran and Parsis in India keep Zoroastrianism alive.

Zorrilla y Moral, José (hōsā' thōrē'lyä ē mōräl'), 1817–93, Spanish romantic dramatist, author of *Don Juan Tenorio* (1844).

Zr, chemical symbol of the element ZIRCONIUM.

Zrinyi (zrĭn'yē), noble Hungarian family of Croatian origin. **Nicholas Zrinyi,** 1508–66, was appointed ban (viceroy) of Croatia by Ferdinand I (1542). Defended Szigetvar against the army of Suleiman I; was killed while attempting a sortie. His great-grandson, **Nicolas Zrinyi,** 1616–64, ban of Croatia (1647–64), campaigned successfully against the Turks. A distinguished poet, he wrote an epic on the defense of Szigetvar by his ancestor, lyric poems, and prose on political subjects. He was one of the first to use Hungarian as a literary language. His brother, **Peter Zrinyi,** 1621–71, became ban of Croatia 1665. He conspired, with French help, against Emperor Leopold I, but the plot was ill organized and he was executed. His daughter Helen (d. 1703) married Francis I Rakoczy and Emeric Thokoly.

Zsigmondy, Richard (rĭkh'ärt shĭg'mōn"dē), 1865–1929, Austrian chemist. Won 1925 Nobel Prize for work on colloids and development of ultramicroscope.

Zug (tso͝ok), canton (93 sq. mi.; pop. 42,268), central Switzerland. Has Alpine economy (meadows, forests, pastures). German-speaking. Passed to Hapsburgs 1273; joined Swiss Confederation 1352 (confirmed 1364). Member of SONDERBUND 1845–47. Its cap., **Zug** (pop. 14,601), on the L. of Zug, preserves much Gothic architecture. Machinery mfg.

Zugspitze (tso͝ok'shpĭ"tsü), mountain 9,721 ft. high, in Bavarian Alps and on Bavarian-Austrian border; highest peak of Bavaria and of Germany. A rack-and-pinion railroad reaches the summit from Garmisch-Partenkirchen.

Zuider Zee (zī'dür zē', Dutch zoi'dür zā'), former shallow inlet of North Sea, c.80 mi. long, N and central Netherlands. Once a lake, it was joined to the sea by a great flood in the 13th cent. It is now divided by the Ijsselmeer dam into the IJSSELMEER (S) and the Waddenzee (N).

Zuloaga, Ignacio (ēgnä'thyō tho͞olōä'gä), 1870–1945, Spanish painter. Lived mainly in Paris after 1889, but painted Spanish subjects (e.g., Basque peasants and bull fighters).

Zululand (zo͞o'lo͞oländ"), district (10,427 sq. mi.; pop. 398,940), NE Natal, South Africa, on Indian Ocean. Comprises mostly tribal reservations. Annexed by Great Britain in 1887, it became part of Natal in 1897. Inhabited mainly by the **Zulu,** who belong to S branch of the Bantu-speaking peoples. The MATABELE are a Zulu offshoot. Among the Zulu, marriage may be polygamous and is contracted by gifts of cattle to the bride's family. The Zulu ordinarily do not live in villages but in fenced compounds (kraals). In 1830s they waged war against the Boer settlers who came on the Great Trek. Were finally subdued in 1879 by the British.

Zumárraga, Juan de (hwän' dā tho͞omä'rägä), 1468–1584, Spanish churchman, first bishop of Mexico, a Franciscan. Going to Mexico in 1528, he did much to improve conditions in New Spain; founded College of Santa Cruz de Tlaltelolco for education of Indians; and helped bring printing to New World.

Zuni (zo͞o'nē), Indian pueblo village (pop. 2,563), W N.Mex., S of Gallup. Inhabitants are chiefly Pueblo Indians of distinct linguistic family (Zuni). Irrigated land is farmed. Noted for basketry, pottery, turquoise jewelry, weaving, and dances. Annual Shalako feast to Zuni gods. Original seven Zuni villages (usually identified with mythical Seven Cities of Cibola) attacked 1540 by Coronado. Evacuated in Pueblo revolt of 1680. Present pueblo built c.1695 on one of old sites.

Zurbarán, Francisco de (fränthē'skō dā tho͞orbärän'), 1598–1662, Spanish painter of school of Seville. Noted for vigorous realism and fine use of subdued color (esp. in his scenes of monastic life).

Zurich (zo͞o'rĭk), Ger. Zürich (tsü'rĭkh), canton (668 sq. mi.; pop. 772,617), N Switzerland, in the Alpine foothills. Has agr., meadows, forests. Population, German-speaking and largely Protestant, is mainly engaged in industry and commerce. Industrial centers include WINTERTHUR and **Zurich** city (pop. 386,485), the cantonal cap. and largest Swiss city, on the Limmat R. and the L. of Zurich. Produces textiles, machinery, radios, chemicals. Printing and publishing. Commercial, financial, and cultural center. Has university (founded as academy 1523) and world-famous Federal Inst. of Technology (1854). Became free imperial city 1218; joined Swiss Confederation 1351; acquired considerable rural districts. Its corporative guild constitution, lasting till 1798, gave its government a patrician character. ZWINGLI made Zurich the starting point of the Swiss Reformation (16th cent.). The city is a fine blend of modern and historic structures, notably the Romanesque Gross-Münster and the Romanesque-Gothic Fraumünster churches and the 17th-cent. city hall. The **Lake of Zurich,** c.25 mi. long and c.2 mi. wide, is noted for peaceful scenery. The Limmat drains it into the Aar.

Zweibrücken (tsvī"brü'kün), Fr. *Deux-Ponts,* city (pop. 25,725), Rhineland-Palatinate, W Germany, in the Rhenish PALATINATE. Metal, leather, textile mfg. Was 80% destroyed in World War II. It was the seat after 1410 of a branch of the WITTELSBACH dynasty—the counts, later dukes, palatine of Zweibrücken. Through Charles X of Sweden, nephew of Duke Palatine John II, this branch ascended the Swedish throne 1654 and held it till 1741. Zweibrücken was annexed to France 1797–1814. In 1799, however, the deprived ruler inherited all Wittelsbach lands; in 1806 he became king of Bavaria as Maximilian I.

Zweig, Arnold (är'nôlt tsvīkh'), 1887–, Austrian novelist. Best known for his great war novel *The Case of Sergeant Grischa* (1927).

Zweig, Stefan (shtĕ'fän), 1881–1942, Austrian

author. Best known for his biographies, notably of Marie Antoinette (1932) and Mary Stuart (1935). A refugee from Nazi persecution, he died by suicide in Brazil.

Zwickau (tsvĭ'kou), city (pop. 122,862), Saxony, E Germany, in an important coal-mining region. Major industrial center (textiles, machinery, automobiles, chemicals, mining equipment, pianos, paper). Free imperial city 1290–1323. Center of Anabaptist movement of Thomas Münzer 1520–23. Repeatedly plundered in Thirty Years War. Birthplace of Robert Schumann.

Zwicky, Fritz (tsvĭ'kē), 1898–, Swiss-American astrophysicist, authority on novae and supernovae. Known also for work on jet propulsion, cosmic rays, and behavior of slow electrons and ions in gases.

Zwingli, Huldreich or **Ulrich** (tsvĭng'lē), 1484–1531, Swiss Protestant reformer. A learned humanist and a priest, he became convinced that religion should be derived directly from the Bible. At Zurich he initiated Protestant practices; his *Architeles* (1522) and 67 theses (1523) set forth his doctrines. He opposed rituals, use of images and pictures in churches, clerical celibacy, the papacy, and monasticism and strongly favored individual responsibility for belief. The civil authorities of Zurich backed him, and he became a Protestant leader in S Germany as well as in much of Switzerland. His doctrine of the Lord's Supper (that it is merely a commemorative feast) differed from that of Luther, and at the Marburg Colloquy (1529) the two men (together with Oecolampadius and Melanchthon) failed to agree. Zwingli was killed at Kappel and his forces were defeated in a war between the Protestant and Catholic cantons of Switzerland. His teachings lost out to Calvinism, which is partly based on Zwinglian doctrine.

Zwolle (zwô'lŭ), municipality (pop. 47,462), cap. of Overijssel prov., N central Netherlands. Mfg. of chemicals, clothing, and metal goods. Gothic Church of St. Michael (15th cent.) is notable. Thomas à Kempis lived at 14th-cent. monastery near by.

Zworykin, Vladimir Kosma (zwô'rĭkĭn), 1889–, American physicist. Developed Iconoscope electric eye) used in television and Kinescope, cathode-ray tube of television receiver.

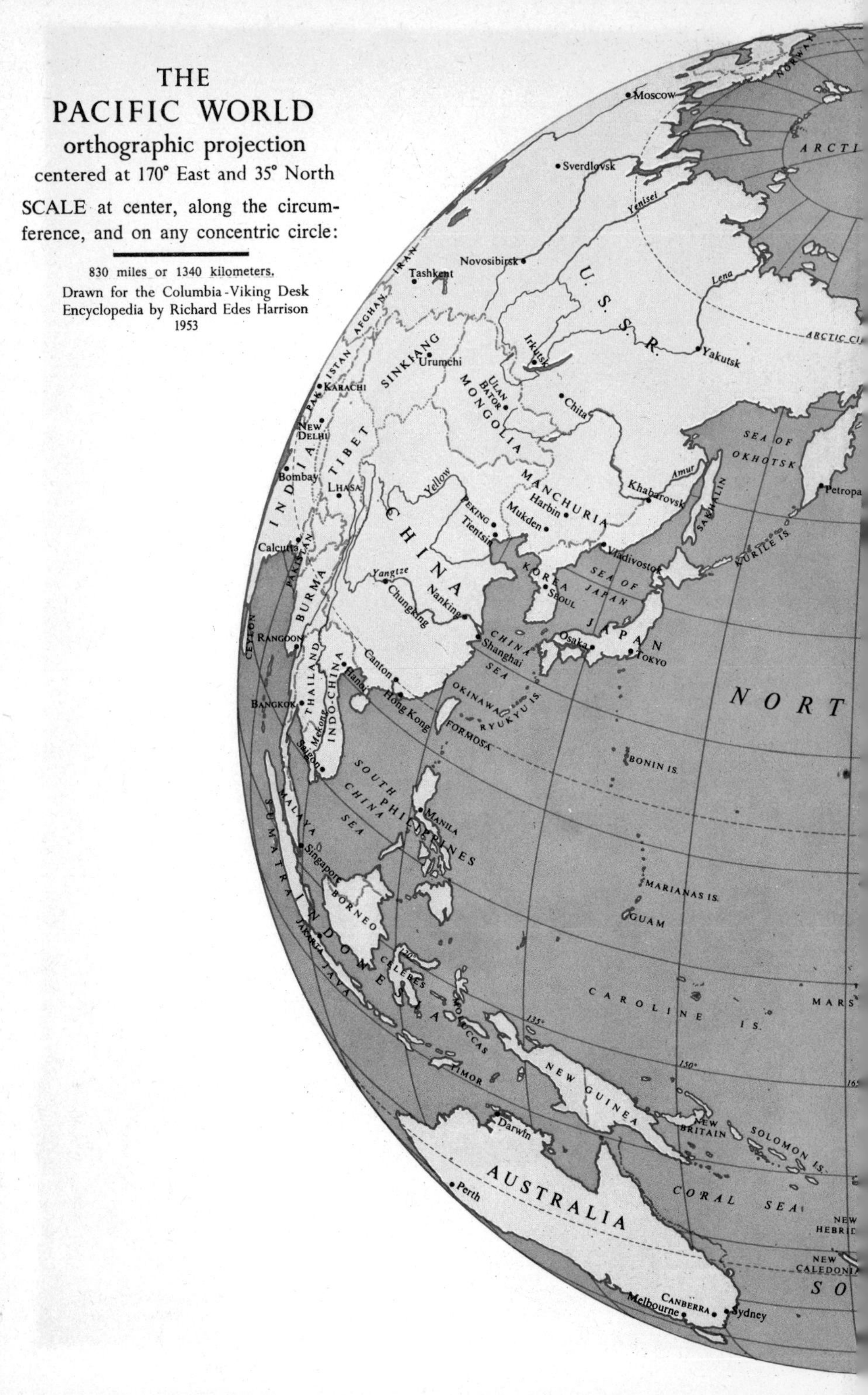
THE
PACIFIC WORLD
orthographic projection
centered at 170° East and 35° North
SCALE at center, along the circumference, and on any concentric circle:
830 miles or 1340 kilometers.
Drawn for the Columbia-Viking Desk Encyclopedia by Richard Edes Harrison
1953
Moscow
NORWAY
ARCTI
Sverdlovsk
Yenisei
IRAN
Novosibirsk
Tashkent
U. S. S. R.
Lena
AFGHAN.
ARCTIC CI
PAKISTAN
SINKIANG
Urumchi
Irkutsk
Yakutsk
KARACHI
ULAN BATOR
MONGOLIA
Chita
NEW DELHI
TIBET
SEA OF OKHOTSK
Bombay
INDIA
Yellow
MANCHURIA
Amur
Khabarovsk
Petropa
LHASA
CHINA
Harbin
SAKHALIN
PEKING
Mukden
Tientsin
KURILE IS.
Calcutta
PAKISTAN
Vladivostok
Yangtze
KOREA
SEA OF JAPAN
BURMA
Chungking
Nanking
SEOUL
JAPAN
CEYLON
RANGOON
CHINA
Shanghai
Osaka
TOKYO
THAILAND
INDO-CHINA
Canton
Hanoi
SEA
OKINAWA
RYUKYU IS.
NORT
BANGKOK
Mekong
Hong Kong
FORMOSA
Saigon
SOUTH CHINA SEA
BONIN IS.
MALAYA
MANILA
PHILIPPINES
SUMATRA
Singapore
BORNEO
MARIANAS IS.
GUAM
JAKARTA
INDONESIA
JAVA
CELEBES
MOLUCCAS
CAROLINE IS.
MARS
135°
120°
150°
TIMOR
NEW GUINEA
NEW BRITAIN
SOLOMON IS.
Darwin
AUSTRALIA
Perth
CORAL SEA
NEW HEBRID
NEW CALEDONI
SO
CANBERRA
Melbourne
Sydney